LANDSCAPE ARCHITECTURAL GRAPHIC STANDARDS

STUDENT EDITION

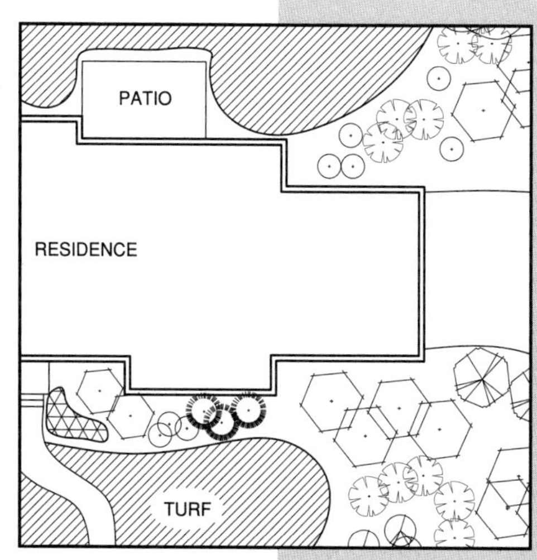

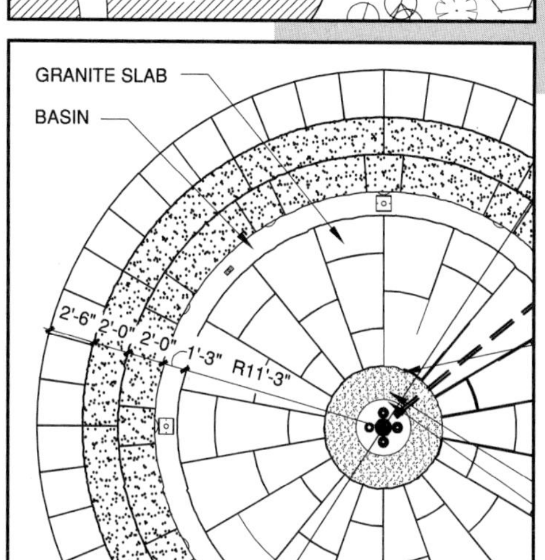

LANDSCAPE ARCHITECTURAL GRAPHIC STANDARDS

STUDENT EDITION

Leonard J. Hopper, RLA, FASLA
Editor-in-Chief

Smith Maran Architects
Graphics Editor

JOHN WILEY & SONS, INC.

This book is printed on acid-free paper. ♾

Published by John Wiley & Sons, Inc., Hoboken, New Jersey
Published simultaneously in Canada

Wiley Bicentennial Logo: Richard J. Pacifico

For general information about our other products and services, please contact our Customer Care Department within the United States at (800) 762-2974, outside the United States at (317) 572-3993 or fax (317) 572-4002.

Wiley also publishes its books in a variety of electronic formats. Some content that appears in print may not be available in electronic books. For more information about Wiley products, visit our web site at www.wiley.com.

Library of Congress Cataloging-in-Publication Data:

Landscape architectural graphic standards / Leonard Hopper, editor-in-chief. — Student ed.
p. cm.
Includes index.
ISBN 978-0-470-06797-0 (pbk.)
1. Landscape architecture. 2. Landscape design. I. Hopper, Leonard J.
SB472.L363 2007
712—dc22

2007013694

Printed in the United States of America

10 9 8 7 6 5 4 3 2 1

CONTENTS

Part 3

PROCESS, IMPLEMENTATION, AND APPLICATION 167

Part 4

PREFACE

John Wiley & Sons, Inc. is pleased to present the first *Landscape Architectural Graphic Standards Student Edition.* This edition is intended to be a valuable resource for students who are in undergraduate and graduate programs in landscape architecture and landscape design, as well as horticulture, architecture, planning, and urban design programs.

The *Student Edition* is an abridged version of *Landscape Architectural Graphic Standards.* It focuses on the practical, how-to aspect of landscape architecture, and bridges the gap between the theory of landscape architecture and the practical skill set. The broad spectrum of topics covered in the *Student Edition* makes it relevant to a number of courses throughout the typical academic career. Its content also makes it an excellent choice as a required text in professional practice, design, technology, environmental studies, and planting design, among other fields of study.

The basis for the choice of topics to include in the *Student Edition* began with a survey of accredited landscape architectural programs, as well as many related programs in other disciplines. Course syllabi were reviewed and evaluated, to help determine the most appropriate content for the publication. The evaluation process also identified material that would qualify the *Student Edition* either as a primary or strong secondary resource for a wide range of required coursework.

The process of deciding which topics to include was, understandably, a difficult one, for all the material addressed in *Landscape Architectural Graphic Standards* is important. To accomplish this task, the decision makers had to identify, first, those topics that would be most relevant for a student and, second, those courses for which the Student Edition would likely be a required text. The task was made manageable by an excellent and thoughtful Editorial Advisory Board, composed of a carefully selected cross section of highly respected members of academia: Dr. Robert D. Brown, University of Guelph; Meg Calkins, Ball State University; Bruce K. Ferguson, University of Georgia; Frederick Steiner, PhD, University of Texas at Austin; and Daniel Winterbottom, University of Washington. All were contributors to *Landscape Architectural Graphic Standards*, and each brought valued expertise to a different area of the discussion, resulting in the comprehensive coverage achieved in the *Student Edition.*

Furthermore, the creation of the complementary Web site to the *Student Edition* (www.wiley.com/go/landscapearchitecturalgraphicstandards) made it possible to provide additional material, which could not be included in this abridged volume, due to size constraints. The Web site also enabled the development of supplementary material for both students and instructors, which, together with this book, constitute a comprehensive and unique learning and teaching resource.

My thanks and appreciation go out to the Editorial Advisory Board, one of the brightest and most thoughtful group of individuals with whom I have ever had the privilege of working. I also want to thank my wife, Frances Hopper, who helped handle the administrative duties, and Patrick Weisel, one of my graduate students in the Masters of Landscape Architecture Program at City College, who performed a great deal of the preparatory work that made our task easier. My thanks also to Lauren Poplawski, Kathryn Malm Bourgoine, and Amanda Miller of John Wiley & Sons, whose support, patience, and gentle guidance shepherded this book from idea to finished project.

Leonard Hopper, RLA, FASLA
Masters in Landscape Architecture Program
School of Architecture, Urban Design and Landscape Architecture
City College of New York

ACKNOWLEDGMENTS

JOHN WILEY & SONS, INC.

Amanda Miller
Vice President and Publisher

Kathryn Malm Bourgoine
Acquisitions Editor

Roseanne Koneval
Senior Editorial Assistant

Lauren Poplawski
Editorial Assistant

Kerstin Nasdeo
Senior Production Manager

Justin Mayhew
Senior Marketing Manager

Lucinda Geist
Designer

Janice Borzendowski
Copyeditor

LGS STAFF

Leonard J. Hopper, RLA, FASLA
Editor-In-Chief

James E. Holtgreven, RLA
Assistant to the Editor-In-Chief

Frances C. Hopper
Administrative Assistant to the Editor-In-Chief

Jennifer R. Hopper
Administrative Assistant to the Editor-In-Chief

Graphics Editor

Smith Maran Architects, Montclair, NJ
Ira Smith, Principal
Erik Maran, Principal
Kimberly Murray, Graphics Manager
Maria Bucci
Katherine Cobb
Daniel D'Agostino
Michealla Lee
John Petullo
Luis Rosario

and in association with
Emina Sendich, InfoDesign

Student Edition Advisory Board

Dr. Robert D. Brown
University of Guelph, Ontario, Canada

Meg Calkins, ASLA
Ball State University, Muncie, IN

Bruce K. Ferguson, FASLA
University of Georgia, College of Environment and Design. Athens, GA

Frederick Steiner, PhD, FASLA
University of Texas at Austin, School of Architecture, Austin, TX

Daniel Winterbottom
University of Washington, Seattle, WA

Contributors

Leonardo Alvarez, ASLA, AIA
American Institute of Steel Construction
The American Society of Landscape Architects
Phillip Arnold
Randall I. Atlas, PhD, AIA, CPP

Marni Barnes, LCSW, ASLA
Michael Barnicle
Nina Bassuk, PhD
Kim A. Beasley, AIA
Michael A. Bender, ASLA
Craig Benson
Henry F. Bishop, ASLA
Wendy Bloom
Ryan Bouma
Mark E. Boyer
Don Brigham, FASLA
Dr. Robert D. Brown
Jeffrey Bruce, FASLA, ASIC, LEED

Meg Calkins, RLA, ASLA
Craig Campbell, FASLA
Dennis B. Carmichael, FASLA
Mark Cederborg
Craig Churchward, ASLA
The Cintas Foundation
Andy Clarke
Georganna Collins, RLA
Concrete Reinforcing Steel Institute
Vincente Cordero, AIA
Craig Coronato
Dr. Philip J. Craul
Timothy A. Craul

Thomas D. Davies Jr., AIA
Adam Davis
Joseph Disponzio, ASLA
Andres Duany
Kelly F. Duke

Stuart Echols

Bruce Ferguson
Carrie Fischer
Chuck Flink, FASLA
Ann Forsythe

Timothy Gilbert, ASLA
Dr. Terry J. Gillespie
Susan Goltsman, FASLA
Gary Greenan

Sarah Georgia Harrison, ASLA
Alan Harwood, AICP
Ellen Heath, AICP
Randy Hester
Todd Hill, ASLA
James E. Holtgreven, RLA
Leonard Hopper, RLA, FASLA
Thomas Hopper
MaryCarol Hunter

Nathan Imm, RLA
Industrial Fabrics Association
Industrial Perforators Association

Carol R. Johnson, FASLA
Craig Johnson
Grant R. Jones, FASLA
Stanton Jones, ASLA
Tom Jones, RLA
Eran Ben-Joseph

Greg Kamman
Niall Kirkwood
Laura L. Knott, ASLA
William B. Kuhl

Rebecca Lave
Robert T. LeBlanc
Grace S. Lee
Heather Kinkade-Levario

William T. Mahan, AIA
Doug Mann, ASLA
Clare Cooper Marcus
Marc J. Mazz, AIA, P.A.
McKey Perforating Company
Marcia McNally
Joseph P. Mensch

Isabelle Minn
Janet Lenox Moyer
Laura Musacchio

National Lands Trust
National Roofing Contractors Association
L. Robert Neville, PhD
Thomas J. Nieman, PhD, FASLA

Jeff Olson, AIA

Paralyzed Veterans of American Architecture
Charles J. Parise, FAIA, FASTM
Lawrence G. Perry, AIA
Joe Petry
Rick Phillips
Elizabeth Plater-Zyberk
Kurt T. Pronske, P.E.

D. Neil Rankins, RGA
Michelle Robinson, LEED
Paul M. Rookwood, ASLA, AICP

Ronald B. Sawhill
Janice Cervelli-Schach, FASLA
Thomas Schueler
James E. Sekela, P.E.
Iskandar Shafie

Robert W. Shuldes, P.E.
Brian Smith
Stephen W. Smith
Rob W. Sovinski, ASLA
David Spooner
Frederick Steiner, PhD, FASLA
Brodie Stephens, Esq.
James K. Stickley, ASLA, LEED
Ray Strychalski, ASLA
Sarah Sutton
Robert D. Sykes
Stephen S. Szoke, P.E.

Brian E. Trimble
Peter Trowbridge
Aaron J. Tuley

James Urban, ASLA

R. Alfred Vick

Cladie Washburn, ASLA
Susan Weiler, ASLA
Daniel Winterbottom
Patrick Wyss, FASLA

Kamal Zaharin

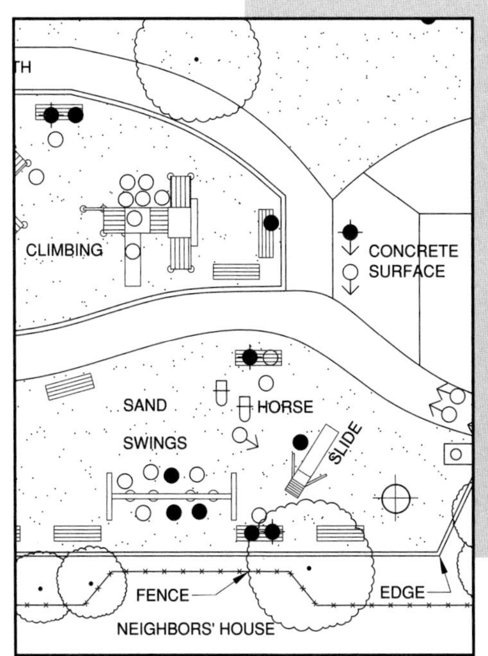

PRACTICE OF LANDSCAPE ARCHITECTURE

General

Construction Documentation

Environmental and Legal

Project Administration

Part 1

GENERAL

OVERVIEW OF THE PROFESSION

WHAT IS LANDSCAPE ARCHITECTURE?

Landscape architecture encompasses the analysis, planning, design, management, and stewardship of the natural and built environments. Types of projects include: residential, parks and recreation, monuments, urban design, streetscapes and public spaces, transportation corridors and facilities, gardens and arboreta, security design, hospitality and resorts, institutional, academic campuses, therapeutic gardens, historic preservation and restoration, reclamation, conservation, corporate and commercial, landscape art and earth sculpture, interior landscapes, and more. Landscape architects have advanced education and professional training and are licensed in 48 states (as of June 2005).

Landscape architects plan and design traditional places such as parks, residential developments, campuses, gardens, cemeteries, commercial centers, resorts, transportation facilities, corporate and institutional centers, and waterfront developments. They also design and plan the restoration of natural places disturbed by humans, such as wetlands, stream corridors, mined areas, and forested land. Having an appreciation for historic landscapes and cultural resources enables landscape architects to undertake preservation planning projects for national, regional, and local historic sites and areas.

Working with architects, city planners, civil engineers, and other professionals, landscape architects play an important role in environmental protection by designing and implementing projects that respect both the needs of people and of our environment. Professionals who can meet human needs by making wise use of our environmental resources are in demand today and will continue to be so in the future.

A wide range of opportunities are open to landscape architects today. They may work on a variety of projects, such as the development and preservation of open spaces, recreation areas, wildlife refuges, zoos, parks, golf courses, and transportation systems.

Landscape architects also may work for many types of organizations—from real estate development firms starting new projects to municipalities constructing airports or parks—and they often are involved with the development of a site from its conception. Working with architects, surveyors, and engineers, landscape architects help determine the best arrangement of roads and buildings. They also collaborate with environmental scientists, foresters, and other professionals to find the best way to conserve or restore natural resources. Once these decisions are made, landscape architects create detailed plans indicating new topography, vegetation, walkways, and other landscaping details, such as fountains and decorative features.

In planning a site, landscape architects first consider the nature and purpose of the project and the funds available. They analyze the natural elements of the site, such as the climate, soil, slope of the land, drainage, and vegetation; observe where sunlight falls on the site at different times of the day and examine the site from various angles; and assess the effect of existing buildings, roads, walkways, and utilities on the project.

After studying and analyzing the site, landscape architects prepare a preliminary design. To accommodate the needs of the client and other stakeholders in the project, as well as the conditions at the site, the design frequently evolves based on input gathered at meetings held during the design development phase. These modifications from the preliminary design lead to the approval of the final design. They also take into account any local, state, or federal regulations, such as those providing barrier-free accessibility and those protecting wetlands or historic resources.

In preparing designs, computer-aided design (CAD) has become an essential tool for most landscape architects. Many landscape architects also use video simulation to help clients envision the proposed ideas and plans. For larger-scale site planning, landscape architects also use geographic information systems (GIS) technology, a computer mapping system.

Throughout all phases of the planning and design, landscape architects consult with other professionals involved in the project. Once the design is complete, they prepare a proposal for the client. They produce detailed plans of the site, including written reports, sketches, models, photographs, land-use studies, and cost estimates, and submit them for approval by the client and by regulatory agencies. When the plans are approved, landscape architects prepare working drawings showing all existing and proposed features. They also outline in detail the methods of construction, itemize construction details, and draw up a list of necessary materials, including the written technical specifications for the project. Finally, during the construction implementation phase of the project, the landscape architect is often called upon, by the client, to monitor the installation of his or her design.

Some landscape architects work on a variety of projects, while others specialize in a particular area, such as residential development, street and highway beautification, waterfront improvement projects, parks and playgrounds, or shopping centers. Still others work in regional planning and resource management; feasibility, environmental impact, and cost studies; or site construction. Increasingly, landscape architects are becoming involved with projects in environmental remediation, such as preservation and restoration of wetlands, as well as the restoration of degraded land, such as mines or landfills. Historic landscape preservation and restoration is another important area where landscape architects are playing an increasingly important role.

The 2004 American Society for Landscape Architects (ASLA) Business Indicators Survey reveals that landscape architecture firms are growing in size, billing rates are increasing dramatically, and the client base for the profession continues to expand, most significantly in the public sector.

ASLA commissioned the first business indicators survey in 1997 and repeated it in 1999. This latest survey is based on information gathered in 2004 from more than 1,000 private sector landscape architecture firms. Indicators include market sectors; project types; client types; billing rates; contract types; design competition participation; marketing, spending and construction cost ratios; and profit margins. Of the firms and organizations responding to the survey, 80 percent are in the private sector, 16 percent are in the public sector, and 4 percent represent academic institutions. In the 2004 survey, most respondents have 21 to 25 years of experience with an average salary of $80,273. The average salary for those with 0 to 5 years of experience is $41,803. Those with 36 to 40 years of experience earn the highest average salary, at $97,564.

Demographic comparisons by gender between the 1999 and 2004 ASLA surveys indicate there has been no change in the private sector (24 percent women, 76 percent men). However, women now make up 34 percent of public practitioners and 24 percent of professionals in academia, increases of 4 percent in both sectors since 1999.

Based on projections by the Department of Labor's Bureau of Labor and Statistics, employment of landscape architects is expected to grow faster than the average for all occupations through the year 2012. New construction is increasingly dependent upon compliance with environmental regulations, land-use zoning, and water restrictions, spurring demand for landscape architects to help plan sites and integrate man-made structures with the natural environment in the least disruptive way. Landscape architects are also becoming increasingly involved in preserving and restoring wetlands and other environmentally sensitive sites. Due to growth and geographic shifts in population, the expertise of landscape architects will be highly sought after in the planning and development of new residential, commercial, and other types of construction. For the general public, their most important issues and concerns impacting their daily lives and routines have a close relationship to a landscape architect's area of practice and responsibility. Thus, the work of landscape architects will play an increasingly important role in shaping the world's future by making a positive impact on health, economic, social, and environmental issues.

Leonard Hopper, FASLA and the American Society of Landscape Architects

CONSTRUCTION DOCUMENTATION

OVERVIEW OF CONSTRUCTION DOCUMENTATION

BACKGROUND: PURPOSE

Construction documents have several purposes. They communicate technical information necessary to (1) obtain bids for construction, (2) see the project through the building permitting process, and (3) guide construction. In general, construction documents are comprised of construction drawings and specifications. The technical information communicated in the drawings indicates physical location of the improvements proposed for the project, the details of components to be built and installed, and the quantity of design elements. Specifications deal with the standards of quality expected in the construction of the improvements and the procedures to be used throughout the construction process.

LEGAL IMPLICATIONS

Construction documentation is a critical component of the construction contract process and, therefore, has legal ramification. As a matter of fact, construction documents set the scope of what is to be built, standards of quality expected and numerous parameters related to submittals, availability of materials, and timing of installation. All these matters can have far-reaching legal and financial consequences. The documents need to be meticulously and thoroughly assembled so they can prevent and/or resolve any legal disputes between the involved parties.

DESIGN INTEGRITY AND CONSISTENCY

Maintaining consistency with the original design intent is critical in the process of construction documentation. Technical issues in the design process are resolved and documented in the construction documents. During this phase, the landscape architect may lose sight of the original concept. Therefore, it is important to test details and technical solutions for their support of the original intent.

It is important to be aware that design continues through the entire construction documentation and building process. The detailing of walls, steps, planters, and structures is a critical step in the overall design process. The landscape architect needs to be vigilant to ensure that all scales and phases of the project design are internally consistent.

Design consistency also may be compromised during the construction phase of a project. For example, a program manager or subcontractor under the guise of value engineering might suggest materials that depart from the original specifications. Different building techniques or recognition of code constraints can also alter the original concept of the design. These changes need to be accepted or rejected based on how well they conform to the original design intent. The construction documents, if properly executed, will provide appropriate procedures and conditions for considering proposed substitutions.

CONSTRUCTION ADMINISTRATION VERSUS CONSTRUCTION DOCUMENTATION

To ensure design integrity, some landscape architects choose to emphasize construction administration in lieu of more thorough construction document sets. This approach has merit within certain project types and with certain clients. But in competitively bid projects, it has the potential to lead to excessive change orders, leading to excessive project cost overruns.

ROLE OF TECHNOLOGY

As in all other businesses, in landscape architecture, the World Wide Web has become integral to the rapid transfer of information, specifically construction documents. Often, the Web is used to exchange drawings and coordinate with engineers and other consultants. This is useful when design details need updating and changing. Though this is still a relatively new and different approach of interacting in the building/design process, it allows for near-instantaneous means of obtaining new information.

LEADERSHIP IN ENERGY AND ENVIRONMENTAL DESIGN (LEED) IMPLICATIONS

For projects seeking LEED certification, specific calculations and exhibits must be included in initial construction documents and follow-up documentation. For example, in order to achieve a water efficiency credit, the landscape architect has to show how captured rain or recycled site water is being used to reduce irrigation by 50 percent. With this new initiative, the landscape architect needs to document information that is not otherwise required.

CONSTRUCTION DOCUMENT ORGANIZATION

Construction documents are typically organized in two parts: the drawings (often referred to as working drawings or construction drawings) and the project manual (often referred to as just the specifications, or "specs"). The project manual has two sections, the front end documents and the technical specifications. In general, the front end documents stipulate the conditions and terms of the contract. The technical specifications complement the front end documents by establishing the quality of materials and procedures to be used in the project implementation.

ROLE OF PROJECT SCALE AND COMPLEXITY

The organization and depth of information detailed in the construction documents are dependent on the scale and complexity of the project to be built. For example, a relatively small and straightforward single-family residential landscape could be documented entirely in three drawings, without a separate specifications book. In this case, all specifications may be embedded directly in the drawings. The hardscape design could be integrated with the layout plan, and the planting plan could be combined with planting details and a plant schedule with planting notes. In contrast, a project for a major urban public park may contain a number of water features, active recreation areas, vehicle and pedestrian zones, and service areas. This would require a detailed set of drawings, which are properly indexed. In addition, a separate project manual fully detailing all aspects of the conditions of the contract, material specifications, and installation requirements would be necessary. However, regardless of project scale and complexity, the construction documents must present a complete package of the information required to bid and build the project while protecting the client's and public's interests in terms of health, safety, and welfare.

DRAWING/SPECIFICATIONS COORDINATION GUIDELINES

A primary rule to observe in coordinating drawings and specifications is to avoid duplicating information. If a material is described in the specification manual, then a notation of that same detail should not appear on the drawings. The inverse is also true: Information from drawings should not be stated in the specification manual. This is illustrated by the following example: If a project calls for 4×8 brick pavers of a particular color and manufacturer, the drawings should only state "4×8 brick paver," with no added detail. Additional information would then be referenced in the specification manual. Following this rule can avert problems during design and construction. If a change is required, the landscape architect need only alter the drawings or specifications in one place, minimizing errors and confusion. Typically, if there is a conflict in the information stated in the specifications and the drawings, the specifications will govern.

When a landscape architect works in coordination with other professionals, clarity must be maintained in the construction documents. For example, if a civil engineer is grading for drainage, the size, location, and type of drainage outlets must be consistent with the work of the landscape architect. Additionally, elements such as steepness of grades need to be carefully implemented to maintain the overall design intent of the project.

Care must also be taken within the firm or when working with other landscape architects. A typical challenge is ensuring accuracy when changing scales from working on the overall plan to the detail plan and detail section scale. Fine-tuning decisions need to be made at that point, and these can have a major impact on the final design. Therefore, the detail decisions have to be harmonious with the larger design scheme.

Leonardo Alvarez, ASLA, AIA, EDAW

QUALITY ASSURANCE

Quality assurance (QA) is a process intended to minimize errors and omissions and ensure that a project receives the highest standard of technical accuracy and thoroughness in relationship to the preparation of construction documents. This often involves a clear set of guidelines and checklists, as well as an accepted protocol for conducting the QA review. Most typically, the QA review is performed by a third party, such as an individual who is objective and has not worked on the project to be reviewed. It is highly recommended that all landscape architects institute a QA process for review of construction documents as a part of their adopted practice procedures. The preparation of a QA manual can codify these procedures and, at a minimum, should include the following:

- General protocol outline
- Timing of third-party review
- List of standards to be observed (CADD, drawings, scales, etc.)
- Contract document checklists (drawings and specifications)
- List of common problems encountered

ROLE OF SHOP DRAWINGS

Despite the thoroughness and level of detail included in a good set of construction documents, not everything can be fully detailed for implementation. Shop drawings are also usually required. Shop drawings are precisely what they imply: drawings prepared by the "shop" or manufacturer of a particular item to be installed in the project. Shop drawings are typically prepared for all manufactured items specified, such as railings, site furnishings, fountain equipment, and custom light fixtures. In preparing details in a construction document set, it is important to be aware of what should be indicated in the landscape architect's own details and what will be detailed in the shop drawings.

ROLE OF RECORD DRAWINGS

Record drawings document changes that have occurred during the construction process. These may or may not be in the scope of a typical project. The terms "record drawings" and "as-built drawings" are sometimes used interchangeably. However, the term "as-built" is being used less often in contracts due to the fact that it has been used against engineers, architects, and landscape architects in court. The legal interpretation of the term "as-built" may be taken more literally, to mean that an as-built drawing should contain absolutely everything as it was built—or exists—in the field. In contrast, a record drawing seems more likely to be interpreted as a record of all changes that occurred in the field and that are documented through change orders, addenda, or contractor/consultant drawing markups. In order to minimize exposure and liability, it is highly recommended that all landscape architects consult with an attorney on the matter of record drawings prior to executing contracts that contain either of these terms.

CONCLUSION

Construction documentation is at the core of landscape architectural practice. It is essential that construction documents be thorough and accurate, as they can determine the success or failure of a project. All changes need to be noted for future reference. And it is prudent to institute a review process for the construction document process to ensure a high-quality product.

PROJECT MANUAL

Owners, landscape architects, engineers, architects and contractors all rely on a project manual for every project to clearly convey how to bid the project, the extent of the project and the specifications related to the details for carrying out the work. The project manual includes those documents that can easily be bound into a book format, including the bidding requirements, contract forms and conditions, and technical specifications. If the landscape architect is working with a client to help prepare the project manual, it is important to take care in developing the technical specifications, including Division 1/General Requirements and Supplemental General Conditions, in a manner that is compatible with the specific public or private bidding requirements.

Most project manuals will be developed in three major sections: Division 0, Bidding and Contract Requirements; Division 1, General Requirements; followed by the Technical Specifications Divisions 2–16. Technical specifications should be organized following the Construction Specifications Institute's (CSI) 16 divisions and three-part format.

Most project manuals start off with a cover and title page that lists the project title and other pertinent information, such as the project location, project number, owner's name, designer's name and address, and, possibly, the designer's seal and signature. Next is the table of contents for the entire project manual.

Division 0 outlines the bidding and contract requirements, and may include the following:

- Public Notice—Invitation to Bid
- Instructions to Bidders
- General Conditions
- Supplementary Conditions
- Bid Bond Form
- Performance and Payment Bond
- Bid Form

The CSI 16-part format includes Division 1/General Requirements, which is used to provide greater clarification, additional requirements, or descriptions of unique project conditions. It should complement the General Conditions and Supplemental Conditions, not change them. Common examples of Division 1 material include, but are not limited to, the following:

- Summary of the work
- Work restrictions
- Alternates
- Change order procedures
- Payment application process
- Project meetings
- Submittal process
- Quality requirements
- Temporary facilities and controls
- Closeout procedures

The final portion of the project manual is the Technical Specifications, which should follow the industry-standard CSI format. Each specification section should include the general, materials, and execution CSI three-part format. In specifying products, unless the contracting agency has a specific product exemption on file, any specific product listing needs to be accompanied with "or approved equal" or similar language. In constructing these specifications, care needs to be taken to only supplement or clarify requirements listed in the General Conditions, Supplemental Conditions, and Division 1/General Requirements. Additionally, work described by each specification section should contain the acknowledgment that the requirements contained in these documents apply to the work of each and every section of the technical specifications.

Ray Strychalski, ASLA, EDAW

CONSTRUCTION DRAWING LAYOUT

INTRODUCTION

The organization and format of drawing packages is a critical element in the professional preparation of construction documents. Early on, the order drawings will appear in a set of construction documents should be determined and distributed to everyone involved in the production process. Most firms have established a standard by which to sequence the documents in a package, by discipline, and then within those disciplines as well. This organization may also be mandated by certain clients, who may have a standard process and expect to see the drawings in a particular progression. The method presented in this chapter is a frequently encountered system for construction document layout.

NAMING AND NUMBERING DRAWINGS

Before the drawings can be organized, they have to be named and numbered in a logical manner. The diagram presented here shows a typical drawing-naming standard, and explains the importance of each letter and number in that name.

DRAWING ORGANIZATION

Once the drawings are named, they can be put in order. In all cases, the package setup goes from general and nonspecific information to highly detailed and specific information. A good way to approach this is to put yourself in the contractor's shoes and imagine how you would go about understanding what the project is all about. The package should start by explaining the project location, name, owner's name, and so on—all of this information can be contained on the cover page. Next, the package should explain how the documents are organized and how to read the symbols included in the package, as well as all of the general notes that apply to the entire project. When all of this information is explained, you are ready to begin documentation of the design. Once again, the information in the package should be ordered from the general (large-scale level) down to small-scale details. Starting with overall plans and working through to the individual details, the package organization should be clear and consistent. Remember, the goal is to explain the design intent as efficiently as possible.

In addition to the preceding, the organization of the package is also loosely based on the order of construction of the project. When the contractor installs the project, the hardscape elements will generally be installed first. Thus, the package should present the hardscape plans before the landscape plans. The information is easier to understand in this order—imagine how hard it would be to understand a project if the first drawings were covered with the planting graphics necessary to explain the landscape installation, ahead of the grading, layout, and hardscape information.

The index presented here is a typical representation of the order of drawings in a package.

Sheet	Contents
G-001	Cover
L-001	Sheet Index
L-002	Notes and Legends
LS101	Site Plan
LS201	Site Elevations
LS301	Site Sections
LS401	Site Plan Enlargement
LS501	Hardscape Details
LP101	Planting Plan
LP401	Planting Plan Enlargement
LP501	Planting Details
LP601	Plant Schedule

In many cases, the package will include not only the landscape architectural drawings, but also other disciplines, such as architecture; civil engineering; structural engineering; mechanical, electrical, and plumbing engineering (MEP); and so on. The presentation of this information follows the same pattern as above, general to specific, and the drawing order follows the order of construction. For example, for a project with all of the professionals listed above, the following discipline order may most efficiently explain the information:

Civil engineering
Landscape architecture
Architecture
Structural engineering
MEP

The prime consultant is responsible for establishing and distributing this information to the entire team. This should be done as early in the construction documentation process as possible.

Drawing Layout

The individual drawings in a package should always have a few basic elements that guide their interpretation, such as the title block, a scale, a north arrow, a key map (if needed), a legend, and so on. This information should be standardized for the project.

DRAWING CHECKLIST

Many firms will have established checklists to aid in the creation of construction documents. These checklists should be referenced frequently and are a great source of valuable information.

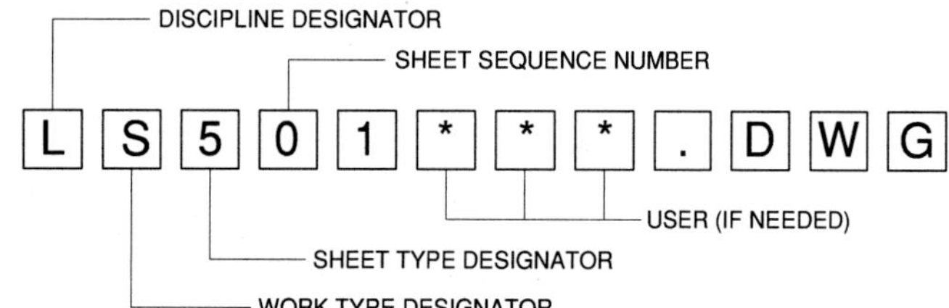

DISCIPLINE DESIGNATIONS	
G	GENERAL
H	HAZARDOUS MATERIALS
C	CIVIL
L	LANDSCAPE
S	STRUCTURAL
A	ARCHITECTURAL
I	INTERIORS
Q	EQUIPMENT
F	FIRE PROTECTION
P	PLUMBING
M	MECHANICAL
E	ELECTRICAL
T	TELECOMMUNICATIONS
R	RESOURCE
X	OTHER DISCIPLINES
Z	CONTRACT OR SHOP DRAWINGS

WORK TYPE DESIGNATIONS	
S	HARDSCAPE
I	IRRIGATION
P	PLANTING
L	LIGHTING
G	GRADING
D	DEMOLITION
R	RELOCATION

SHEET TYPE DESIGNATIONS	
0	GENERAL (SYMBOLS LEGEND, NOTES, ETC.)
1	PLANS (HORIZONTAL VIEWS)
2	ELEVATIONS (VERTICAL VIEWS)
3	SECTIONS (SECTIONAL VIEWS)
4	LARGE-SCALE VIEWS (ENLARGEMENT PLANS, ELEVATIONS OR SECTIONS THAT ARE NOT DETAILS)
5	DETAILS
6	SCHEDULES AND DIAGRAMS
7	USER-DEFINED
8	USER-DEFINED
9	3D REPRESENTATIONS (ISOMETRICS, PERSPECTIVES, PHOTOGRAPHS)

CONSTRUCTION DOCUMENT DRAWING NAMING FORMULA, FROM A TYPICAL OFFICE STANDARD

Thomas Jones, RLA, EDAW

GRAPHICS GUIDELINES

- ☐ Always draw to scale and label drawings as such.
- ☐ Use consistent scale among like details, e.g., all pavements at the same scale.
- ☐ Use common architectural scales
- ☐ Dimension on left; note on right.
- ☐ Use standard material designations; bleed judiciously.
- ☐ Use bold outlines around object in section.
- ☐ Draw object lines medium lineweight; dimension, extension, notation leaders fine lineweight.
- ☐ Align details vertically, including dimensions, object, and notes.
- ☐ Align details horizontally where possible.
- ☐ Keep details, detail enlargements, etc., of a given object or element on the same sheet when possible. This is especially important for a unique element that may be a subcontract, e.g., a garden structure.
- ☐ Always draw typical details first; when drawing unique details, refer back to typical detail note or callout. Do not redraw details.
- ☐ Use standard orthographic projection standards for three-dimensional details with plan on top, section under, elevation to the right. (A detail such as this is considered one detail—not three—in terms of callout designation.)
- ☐ For symmetrical structures, use half-plans and half-garden sections for economy and clarity. For example, on a garden structure, the left half may show the framing plan of the roof, while the right side may show the paving pattern on the floor.

TYPICAL CONSTRUCTION DOCUMENT GRAPHICS CHECKLIST

OVERALL DRAWING GUIDELINES

- ☐ Show only what you have to show to build your designs—nothing more, nothing less.
- ☐ Draw all plans at the same scale and orientation.
- ☐ Show the correct information the least number of times. Once is best.
- ☐ Don't draw any other discipline's work except to reference it.
- ☐ Use consistent terminology through the drawings and specifications.
- ☐ Don't draw at large scale what you can draw at a small scale.
- ☐ Don't draw at all what you can note, e.g., catalog items.
- ☐ Don't note what you can spec.
- ☐ Don't label what you can symbolize.
- ☐ Where possible, combine elements, e.g., layout, grading to minimize sheet count.
- ☐ Always proceed from general to specific, large to small, plan to elevation to section.
- ☐ Minimize the use of match lines.
- ☐ Maximize the use of enlargements.
- ☐ Only enlarge if enlargement is two to three times as big as original. Make sure that the enlargement area carries all the content, so that it is not repeated at the smaller scale.
- ☐ Coordinate with utility locations and actual sizes of utility appurtenances.

TYPICAL DRAWING CHECKLIST FOR CONSTRUCTION DOCUMENTS

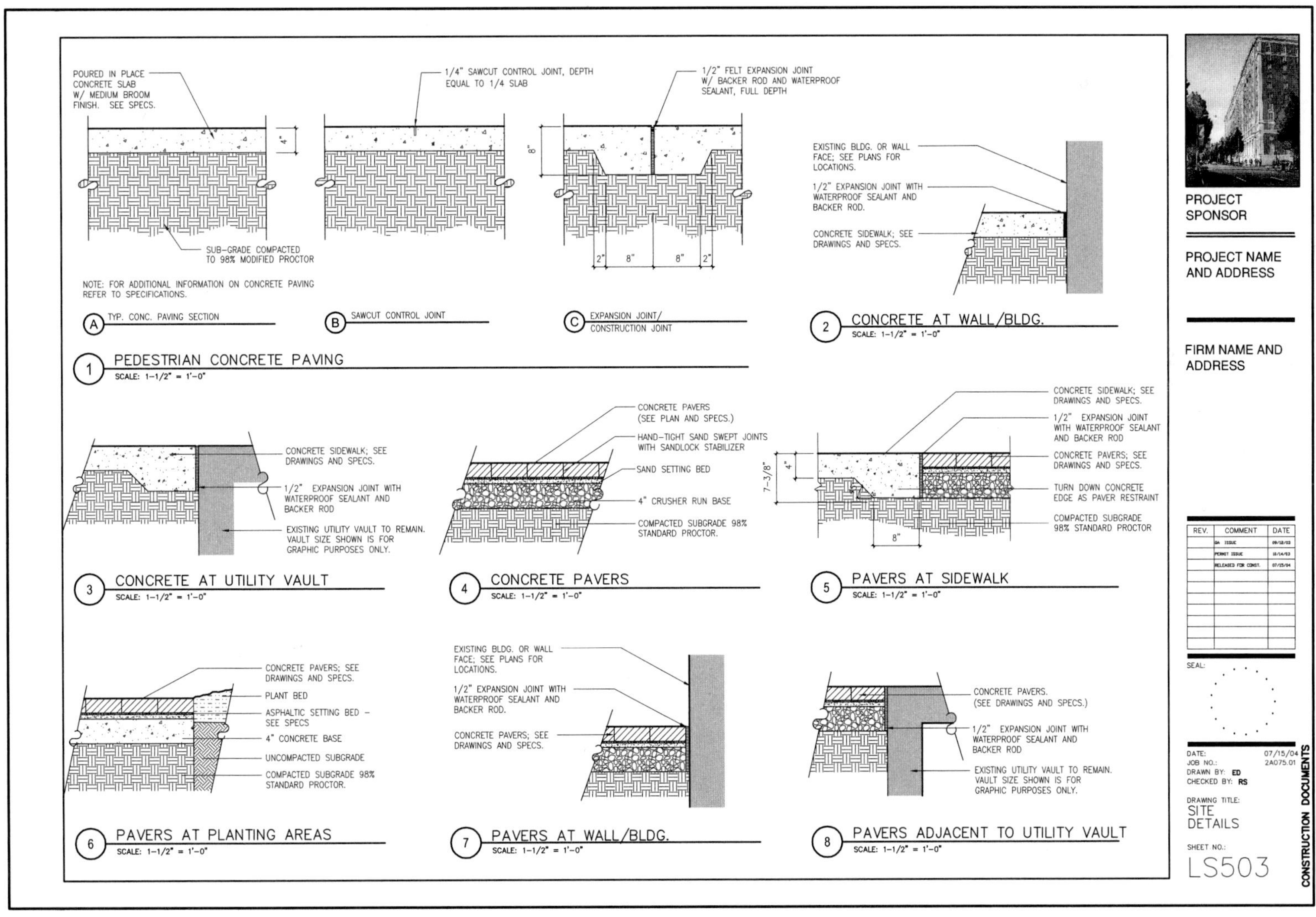

TYPICAL CONSTRUCTION DOCUMENT DETAIL SHEET

Thomas Jones, RLA, EDAW

SYMBOLS

INTRODUCTION

The goal of a set of construction documents is a successfully built project. One of the steps toward reaching this goal is the production of clear, efficient drawings that communicate the design intent and construction detailing of the various elements of the project. These drawings will always be more meaningful and more easily understood when symbols are carefully chosen and placed.

STANDARDS

Most users will follow industry standard materials symbols in the creation of their drawings, such as the stipple-and-triangle pattern that is known universally as concrete. There are also standard construction document package symbols, such as the detail reference symbol. These standard symbols form the basis for any discussion of this type and should always be kept accessible, either in the form of a drafting manual or an office graphics standard.

COMMON PROBLEMS

Some common problems and solutions to be aware of when working with symbols are presented here:

1. Always be aware of the scale of the drawing, and use this to test symbols for clarity. For example, if the drawing being produced is at a scale of 1/4″ = 1′-0″, a pattern that represents brick pavers can be drawn at their actual size, whereas at 1″ = 50′ that same pattern would be a solid, meaningless block on the drawing.
2. Always visually test symbols with each other at the scale of the drawing. For example, a tree symbol that worked on a rendered plan may be far too detailed to use alongside less detailed construction document symbols. Adjust the symbol, or use another, more appropriate one.
3. When creating plant symbols, be aware of the size and spacing of the plant. For example, a tree symbol in plan and section/elevation should be shown at two-thirds of its mature size, whereas a shrub symbol for equally spaced shrub planting should be drawn at a size that equals the installed spacing of the shrubs.
4. Remember that clarity is the key to symbol effectiveness, and the goal is to communicate the design intent, not to draft the most elaborate symbols. Include only enough detail to relay the necessary information.
5. Consider the stage of the project when choosing and/or creating symbols. For example, a symbol used in the schematic design phase may or may not be appropriate for the construction documents.

CONSTRUCTION DOCUMENT SYMBOLS

The figure "Construction Document Symbols" contains sample symbols for construction documents packages. This list is by no means exhaustive; rather, it is intended to show some possibilities and provide some guidelines for users to create their own library.

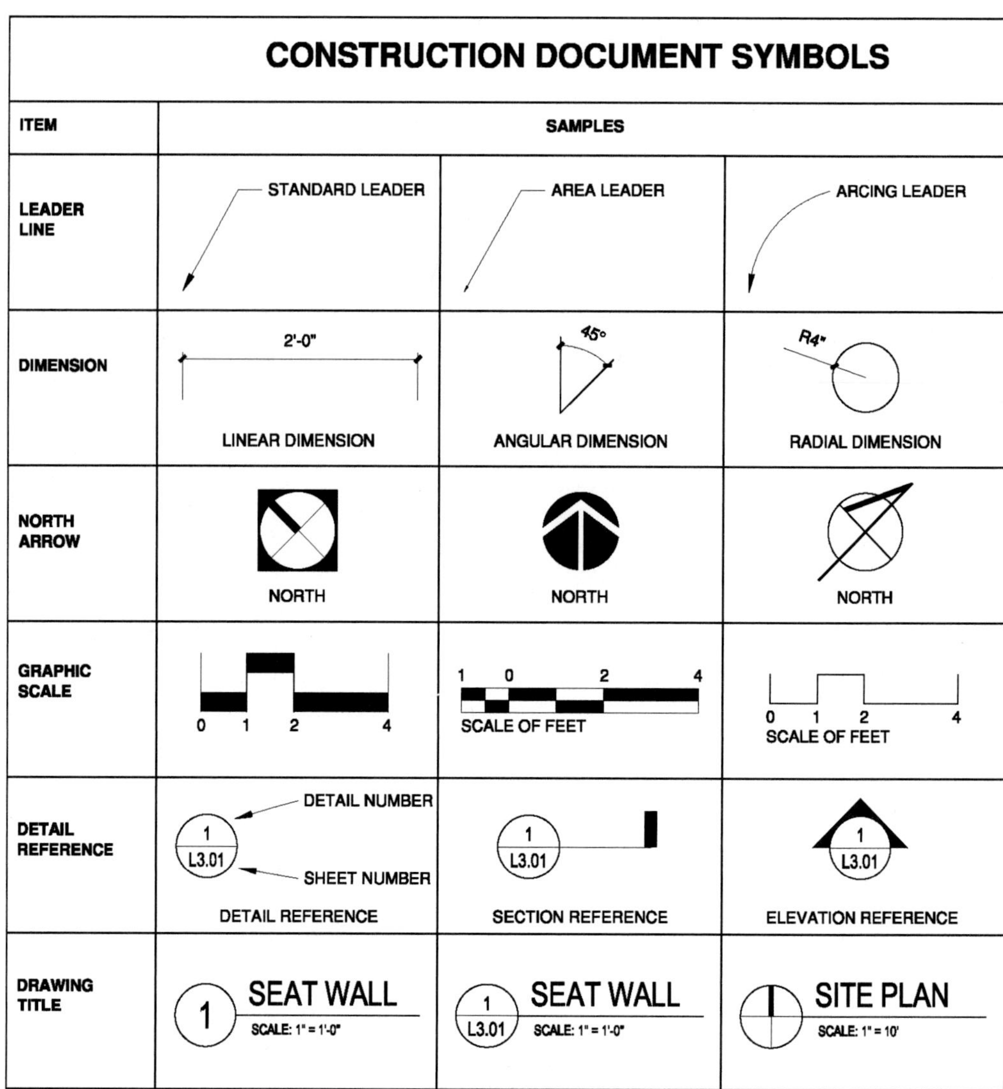

CONSTRUCTION DOCUMENT SYMBOLS

Thomas Jones, RLA, EDAW; Leonardo Alvarez, ASLA, AIA, EDAW; Cladie Washburn, ASLA, EDAW

DIMENSIONING

Plan Dimensioning

The layout/site plan is concerned with the detailed location of various objects to be built on the construction site, such as, roads, walkways, walls, plant material, and site amenities. The three basic means of locating an object on a layout plan are (a) survey lines and bearings (road centerlines and property lines); (b) coordinates for buildings; and (c) dimensioning for walk widths, location of site amenities, and paving patterns. The two types of dimensioning are (a) layout plan dimensioning and (b) construction detail dimensioning.

The layout plan must be clear, consistent, and concise.

Priority of Locating Site Elements on the Layout Plan

1. Fixed elements must be positioned exactly on the site, such as property lines, road centerlines, and structures using survey lines, bearings, and/or coordinates.
2. Semifixed elements have a direct and dependent layout relationship to a fixed element such as a building setback, road width, walkway, or street right-of way.
3. Adjustive elements require near accuracy, not exact accuracy. These floating dimensions may be adjusted to the situation as long as the overall effect is maintained. Some examples of adjustive elements are planting borders, meandering walkways, or walks that are between two fixed objects. Nondetermined elements, such as plant material, are located in an approximate location with the final location determined on-site.

Types of Plan Dimensioning Systems

Reference line: Used for locating semifixed objects; also known as a baseline.

Running system: Used for locating semifixed and adjustive objects. It should be avoided because of the high probability of layout error.

Modular system: Used for repetitive objects such as paving patterns.

Angular system: Used to locate baselines, centerlines of roads and walks; expressed in degrees.

Grid system: Used for location of adjustive objects, especially free-form lines. The smaller the grid, the greater the accuracy.

Offset system: A combination of reference lines and running systems. It is used for the location of adjustive objects such as an irregular planting border.

It is common to use a combination of dimension systems in a layout plan.

All dimensioning must start from a known reference point that is not being disturbed or removed during construction (such as structure corner or centerline, a walk intersection, etc.) or an imaginery point or line that can be easily located in the field by survey data (such as property line, property corner, a road centerline, etc.).

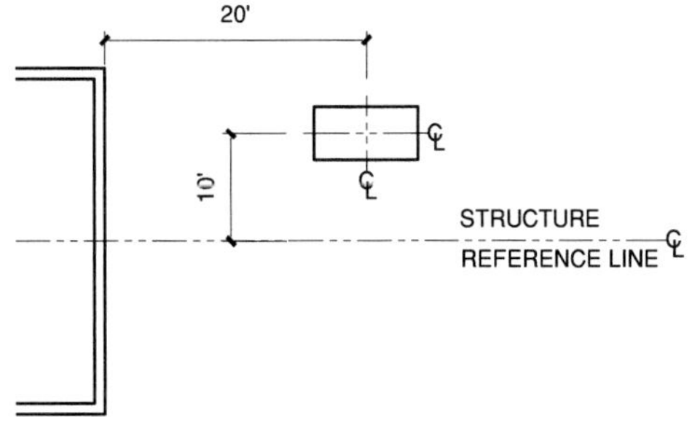

REFERENCE LINE

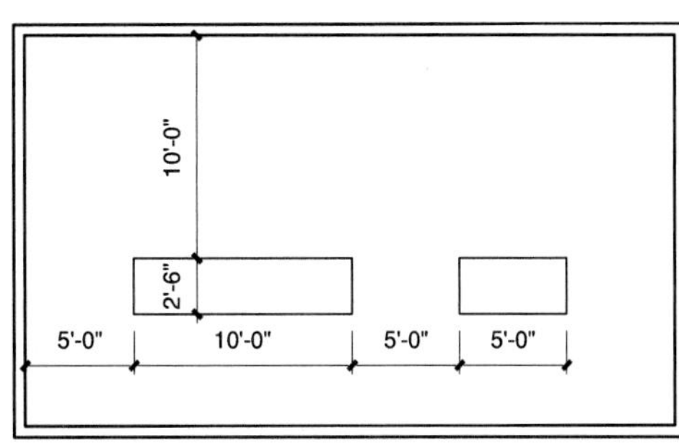

RUNNING

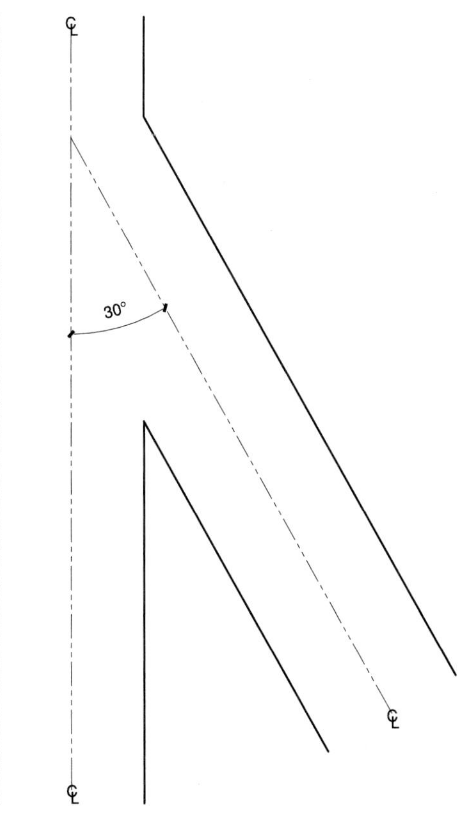

ANGULAR

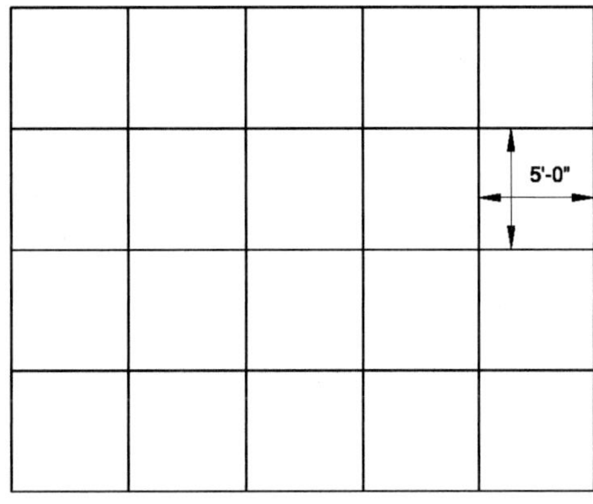

NOTE: 5'-0" SQUARE PAVING PATTERN, TYPICAL

MODULAR

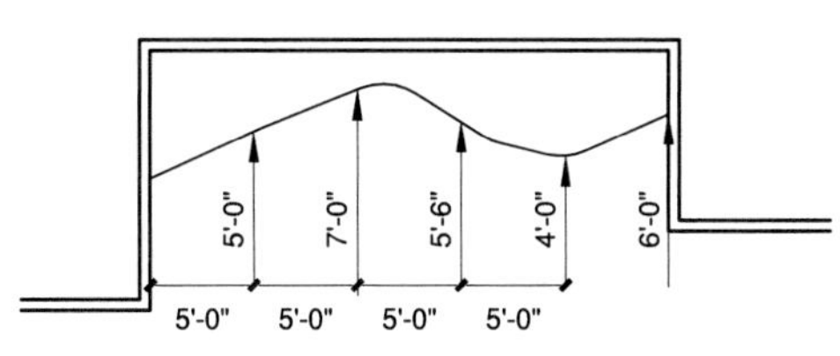

OFFSET

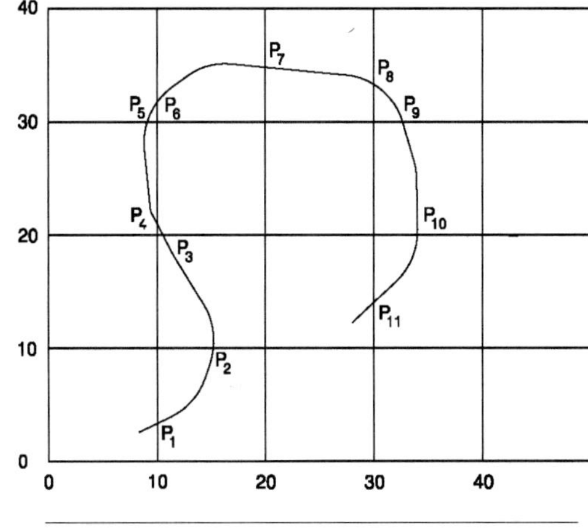

GRID

James Holtgreven, RLA

Rules of Dimensioning

There are general rules of dimensioning that need to be followed in the preparation of clear and unambiguous contract drawings. A consistency in the placement of dimension lines and figures is required. Extension lines are preferable to inside dimensioning and dimensions should never be placed in shaded or crossed hatched areas. The following are examples of other rules to adhere to while dimensioning contract drawings.

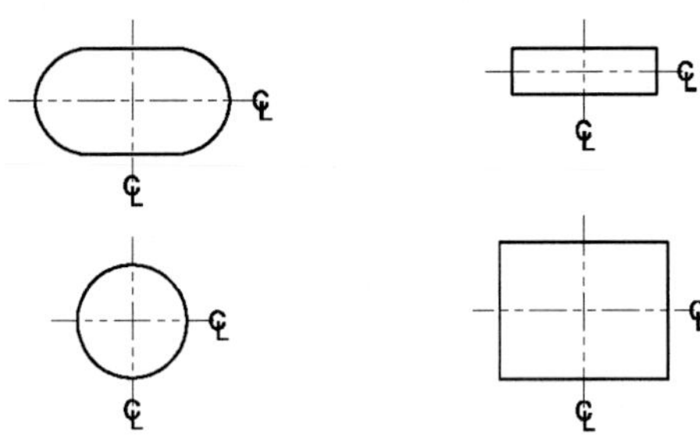

The most efficient method of locating objects is by center point or centerline, because it reduces the number of dimensions required, reduces the chance of cumulative error, allows for clearer graphic representation, and takes into account priorities of dimension lines and construction phases.

LOCATION BY CENTERLINE

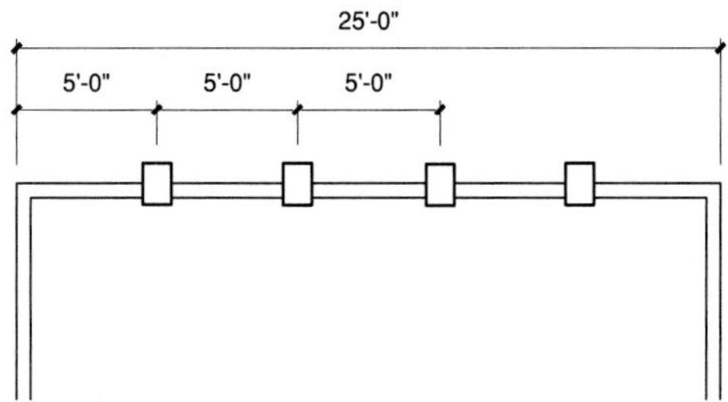

Dimensioning should be concentrated in one area rather than randomly across the plan.

CONCENTRATE DIMENSIONS

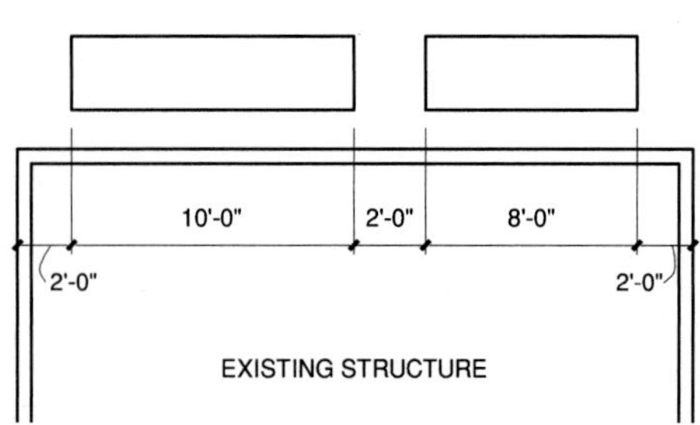

Dimensions should never be inside a structure. Never dimension an existing structure with running dimensions. This creates the potential for conflict. In this example, removing any one of the 2′–0″ dimensions would eliminate the potential of a conflict (the dimension left out shold be one that coupld vary without effecting the design intent).

WRONG

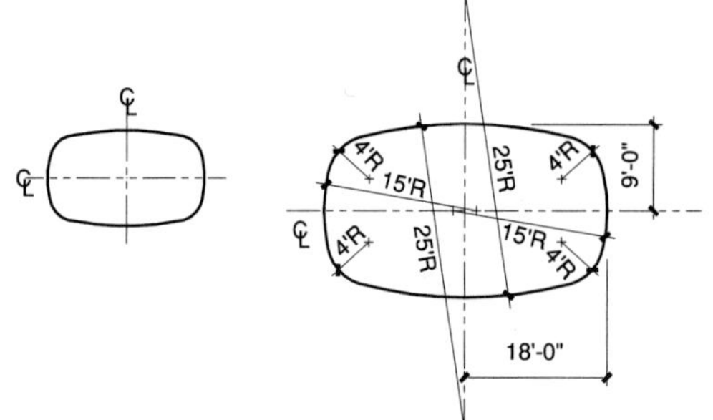

Use an enlargement when dimensioning an object that is complex and confusing.

LAYOUT PLAN ENLARGEMENT

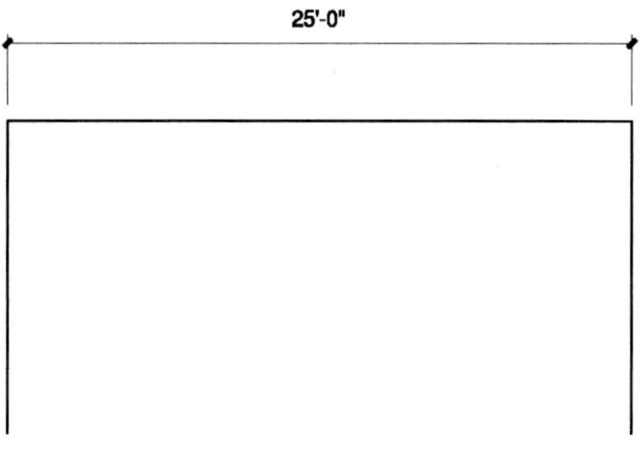

Line weights and graphics should indicate dimension priorities.

LINE WEIGHT PRIORITIES

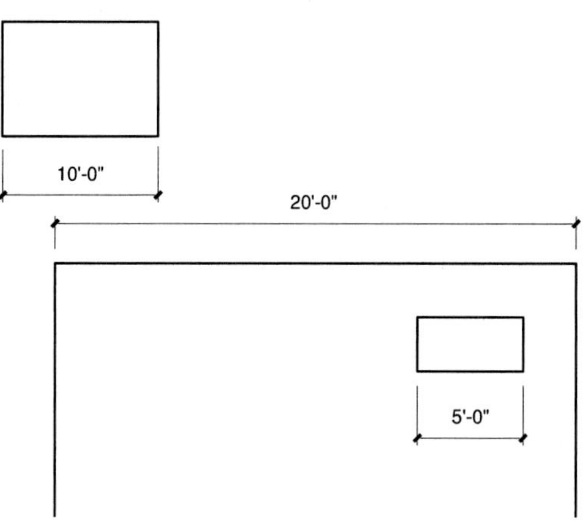

Dimension lines and extensions should never cross. When unavoidable, break the least important line.

DIMENSION LINES AND EXTENSIONS

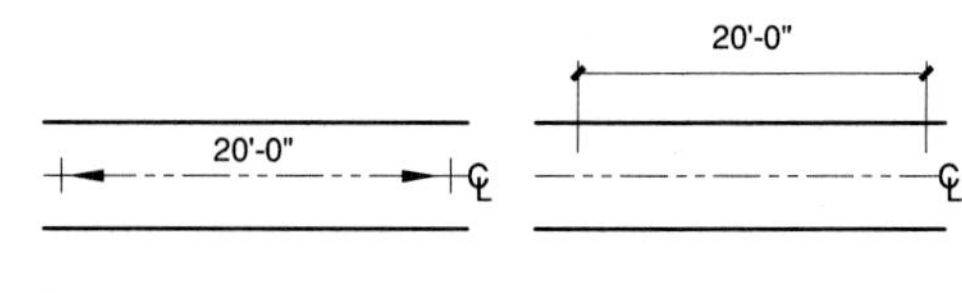

Baselines, baseline dimensions, and baseline symbols should be given graphic priority. Baseline dimensions should be placed adjacent to the baseline.

BASELINES, BASELINE DIMENSIONS, AND BASELINE SYMBOLS

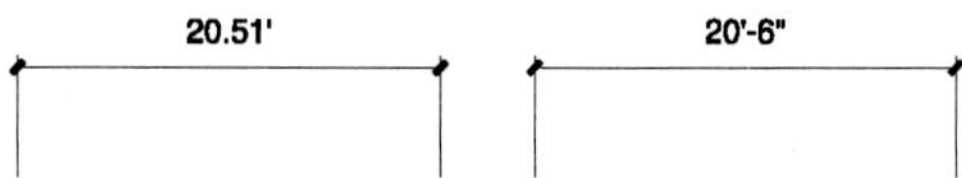

Emphasize decimal points as well as inch and foot symbols. Numbers should be small, but neat and clear.

EMPHASIZED DECIMALS AND INCH AND FOOT SYMBOLS

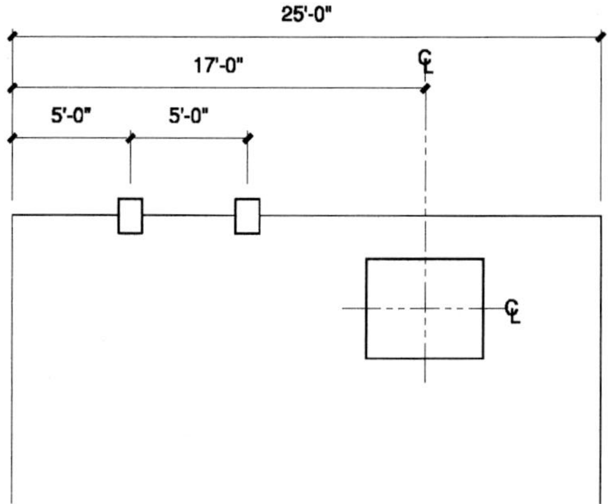

Dimensions should be in near proximity of the dimensioned object. Parallel dimensions should be spaced equally with the subdimensions nearest the object.

DIMENSIONS

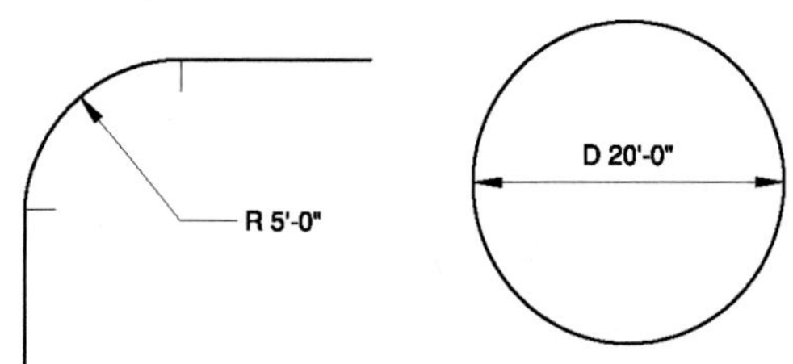

A radius is indicated with an R, and a diameter is indicated with a D, along with the dimension figure. A tick mark can be used to indicate the end of the radius.

RADIUS

James Holtgreven, RLA

LANDSCAPE PLANNING

INTRODUCTION

Planning is the use of scientific, technical, and other organized information to provide choices for decision making, as well as a process for considering and reaching consensus on a range of options. A landscape is all the natural and cultural features such as settlements, fields, hills, buildings, deserts, forests, and water bodies that distinguish one part of the surface of the earth from another part. Landscape planning, then, is the process of using natural and cultural knowledge to guide action over a relatively large area. The process results in a landscape plan, which is a written and a graphic documentation of a community or agency's goal, the strategies to achieve those goals, and the spatial consequences of the implementation strategies.

STEPS IN LANDSCAPE PLANNING

As presented in the diagram, there are 11 interacting steps in landscape planning. An issue or group of related issues is identified by an agency or by a community—that is, some collection of people—in step 1. These issues are problematic or present an opportunity to the people or the environment of an area. A goal or goals is/are then established in step 2 to address the problem(s). Next, in steps 3 and 4, inventories and analyses of biophysical and sociocultural processes are conducted, first at a larger level, such as a river drainage basin or an appropriate regional unit of government, and second at a more specific level, such as a small watershed or a local government.

In step 5, detailed studies are made to link the inventory and analysis information to the problem(s) and goal(s). Suitability analyses are one such type of detailed study. Step 6 involves the development of concepts and options. A landscape plan is then derived from these concepts in step 7. Throughout the process, a systematic educational and citizen involvement effort occurs. Such involvement is important in each step but especially so in step 8, when the plan is explained to the affected public. In step 9, detailed designs are explored that are specific at the individual land-user or site level. These designs and the plan are implemented in step 10. In step 11, the plan is administered.

The heavier arrows in the diagram indicate the flow from step 1 to step 11. The lighter arrows between each step suggest a feedback system whereby each step can modify the previous step and, in turn, change from the subsequent step. The dashed arrows also indicate other possible modifications through the process. For instance, detailed studies of a planning area (step 5) may lead to the identification of new problems or opportunities or the amendment of goals (steps 1 and 2). Design explorations (step 9) may change the landscape plan, and so on. Once the process is complete and the plan is being administered and monitored (step 11), the view of the problems and opportunities facing the region, and the goals to address these problems and opportunities may be altered, as indicated by the dashed lines in the diagram.

Step 1: Identification of Planning Problems and Opportunities

Human societies face many social, economic, political, and environmental problems and opportunities. A landscape is the interface between social and envi-

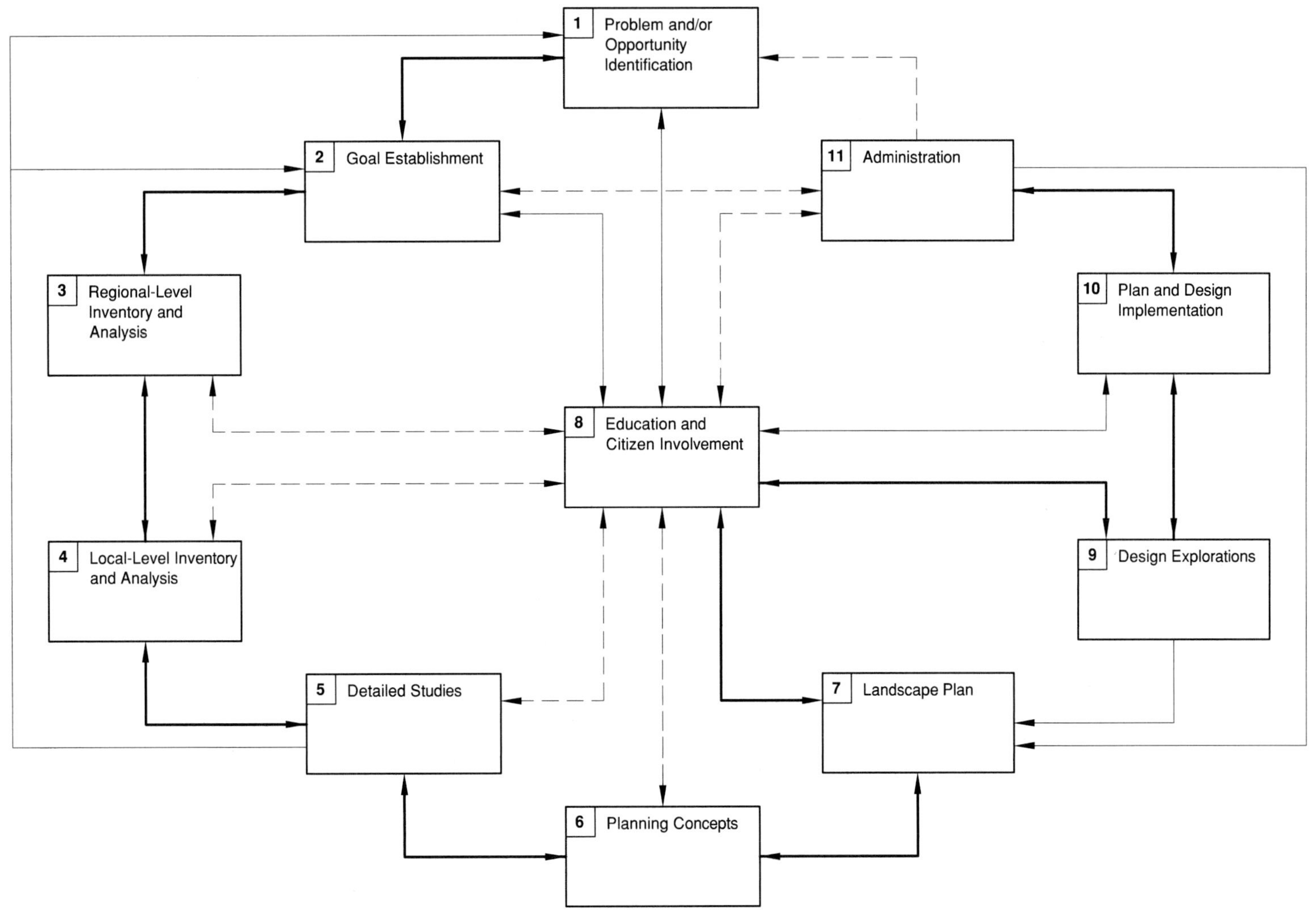

STEPS IN LANDSCAPE PLANNING

Frederick Steiner, Ph.D., FASLA, University of Texas at Austin

ronmental processes, thus landscape planning addresses those issues that concern the interrelationship between people and nature. The planet presents many opportunities for people, and there is no shortage of environmental problems.

Problems and opportunities lead to specific planning issues. For instance, suburban development often occurs on prime agricultural land, a circumstance that local officials tend to view as a problem. A number of issues arise involving land-use conflicts between the new suburban residents and the farmers—such as who will pay the costs of public services for the newly developed areas. Another example is an area, such as an ocean beach or mountain town, that presents the opportunity for new development because of its scenic beauty and recreational amenities. A key challenge would be to accommodate the new growth while protecting the natural resources that attract people to the area in the first place.

Step 2: Establishment of Planning Goals

In a democracy, the people of a region establish goals through the political process. Elected representatives will identify a particular issue affecting their region—for example, a steel plant is closing, suburban sprawl threatens agricultural land, or a new manufacturing plant is creating a housing boom. After issues have been identified, goals are established to address the problem. Such goals should provide the basis for the planning process.

Goals articulate an idealized future situation. In the context of landscape planning, it is assumed that once goals have been established, there will be a commitment by some group to address the problem or opportunity identified in step 1. Problems and opportunities can be identified at various levels. Local people may recognize a problem or opportunity and then set a goal to address it; or issues may be national, international, or global in scope. Problem solving, of which goal setting is a part, may occur at many levels or combinations of levels. Although goal setting is obviously dependent on the cultural-political system, the people affected by a goal should be involved in its establishment.

Step 3: Landscape Analysis, Regional Level

This step and the next one involve interrelated scale levels. The method addresses three scale levels: region, locality, and specific site (with an emphasis on the local). The use of different scales is consistent with the concept of levels-of-organization used by ecologists. According to this concept, each level of organization has special properties. Watersheds have been identified as one level of organization to provide boundaries for landscape and ecosystem analysis. Drainage basins and watersheds have often been advocated as useful levels of analysis for landscape planning and natural resource management.

Essentially, drainage basins and watersheds are the same thing (catchment areas), but in practical use, especially in the United States, the term "drainage basin" is generally used to refer to a larger region, and the term "watersheds" to a more specific area. Drainage basins cover a river and all of its tributaries, while watersheds generally encompass a single river or stream. The analysis at the regional drainage-basin level provides insight into how the landscape functions at the more specific local scale. Geographic information systems, called GIS, often are employed in this step and the next two.

Step 4: Landscape Analysis, Local Level

During step 4, processes taking place in the more specific planning area are studied. The major aim of local-level analysis is to obtain insight about the natural processes and human plans and activities. Such processes can be viewed as the elements of a system, with the landscape a visual expression of the system.

This step in the landscape planning process, like the previous one, involves the collection of information concerning the appropriate physical, biological, and social elements that constitute the planning area. Since cost and time are important factors in many planning processes, existing published and mapped information is the easiest and fastest to gather. If budget and time allow, the inventory and analysis step may be best accomplished by an interdisciplinary team collecting new information. In either case, this step is an interdisciplinary collection effort that involves search, accumulation, field checking, and mapping of data.

Step 5: Detailed Studies

Detailed studies link the inventory and analysis information to the problem(s) and goal(s). Suitability analyses can be used to determine the fitness of a specific place for a variety of land uses based on thorough ecological inventories and on the values of land users. The basic purpose of the detailed studies is to gain an understanding about the complex relationships between human values, environmental opportunities and constraints, and the issues being addressed. To accomplish this, it is crucial to link the studies to the local situation. As a result, a variety of scales may be used to explore linkages.

Ian McHarg popularized the "overlay technique." This technique involves maps of inventory information superimposed on one another to identify areas that provide, first, opportunities for particular land uses and, second, constraints.

Although there has been a general tendency away from hand-drawn overlays, there are still occasions when they may be useful. For instance, they may be helpful for small study sites within a larger region or for certain scales of project planning. That said, it is important to realize the limitations of hand-drawn overlays. As an example, after more than three or four overlays, they may become opaque; there are the accuracy problems that become especially acute with hand-drawn maps; and there are limitations for weighting various values represented by map units. GIS technology can help to overcome these limitations, and, frequently, these systems are used instead of hand-drawn overlays.

Step 6: Planning Area Concepts, Options, and Choices

This step involves the development of concepts and visions for the planning area. These concepts can be viewed as options for the future, based on the suitability of the use(s), which give a general conceptual model or scenario illustrating how problems may be solved. This model should be presented in such a way that the goals will be achieved. Often, more than one scenario has to be made. These concepts are based on a logical and imaginative combination of the information gathered through the inventory and analysis steps. The conceptual model shows allocations of uses and actions. The scenarios set possible directions for future management of the area and, therefore, should be viewed as a basis for discussion where choices are made by the community about its future.

Choices should be based on the goals of the planning effort. For example, if it is the goal to protect agricultural land, yet allow some low-density housing to develop, different organizations of the landscape for those two land uses should be developed. Different schemes for realizing the desired preferences also need to be explored.

Various options for implementation also need to be examined, and these must relate to the goal of the planning effort. If, for example, the planning is being conducted for a jurisdiction trying to protect its agricultural land resources, then it is necessary not only to identify lands that should be protected but also the implementation options that might be employed to achieve the farmland protection goal.

Step 7: Landscape Plan

The preferred concepts and options are brought together in a landscape plan. The plan identifies a strategy for development at the local scale. The plan also provides flexible guidelines for policymakers, land managers, and land users on how to conserve, rehabilitate, or develop an area. In such a plan, enough freedom should be left so that local officials and land users can adjust their practices to new economic demands or social changes.

This step represents a key decision-making point in the planning process. Responsible officials, such as county commissioners or city council members, are often required by law to adopt a plan. The rules for adoption and forms that the plans may take vary widely. Commonly in the United States, planning commissions recommend a plan for adoption to the legislative body after a series of public hearings. Such plans are called *comprehensive plans* in much of the United States, but are referred to as *general plans* in Arizona, California, and Utah. In some states (like Oregon), there are specific, detailed elements that local governments are required to include in such plans. Other states give local officials great flexibility as to the contents of these plans. On public lands, various federal agencies, including the U.S. Forest Service, the U.S. National Park Service, and the U.S. Bureau of Land Management, have specific statutory requirements for land management plans.

Landscape plans should incorporate natural and social considerations. A landscape plan is more than a land-use plan because it addresses the overlap and integration of land uses. A landscape plan may involve the formal recognition of previous elements in the planning process, such as the adoption of policy goals. The plan should include written statements about policies and implementation strategies, as well as a map showing the spatial organization of the landscape.

Step 8: Continued Citizen Involvement and Community Education

In step 8, the plan is explained to the affected public through education and information dissemination. Actually, such interaction occurs throughout the planning process, beginning with the identification of issues. Public involvement is especially critical as the landscape plan is developed, because it is important

Frederick Steiner, Ph.D., FASLA, University of Texas at Austin

to ensure that the goals established by the community will be achieved in the plan.

The success of a plan depends largely on how involved affected people have been in its determination. There are numerous examples of both government agencies and private businesses suddenly announcing a plan for a project that will dramatically impact people, without having consulted those individuals first. The result is predictable: The people will rise in opposition against the project. The alternative is to involve people in the planning process, soliciting their ideas and incorporating those ideas into the plan. Doing so may require a longer time to develop a plan, but local citizens will be more likely to support it than to oppose it and will often monitor its execution.

Step 9: Design Explorations

To design is to give form and to arrange elements spatially. By making specific designs based on the landscape plan, planners can help decision makers visualize the consequences of their policies. Carrying policies through to arranging the physical environment gives meaning to the process by actually conceiving change in the spatial organization of a place. Designs represent a synthesis of all the previous planning studies. During the design step, the short-term benefits for the land users or individual citizen have to be combined with the long-term economic and ecological goals for the whole area.

While some designers and planners might object to the placement of design within the planning process, in an ecological perspective, such placement helps to connect design with more comprehensive social actions and policies.

Step 10: Plan and Design Implementation

Implementation is the employment of various strategies, tactics, and procedures to realize the goals and policies adopted in the landscape plan. On the local level, several different mechanisms have been developed to control the use of land and other resources. These techniques include voluntary covenants, easements, land purchase, transfer of development rights, zoning, utility extension policies, and performance standards. The preference selected should be appropriate for the region.

One implementation technique especially well suited for landscape planning is the use of performance standards. Like many other planning implementation measures, "performance standards" is a general term that has been defined and applied in several different ways. Basically, performance standards, or criteria, are established and must be met before a certain use will be permitted. These criteria usually involve a combination of economic, environmental, and social factors. This technique lends itself to landscape ecological planning, because criteria for specific land uses can be based on suitability analysis.

Step 11: Administration

In this final step, the plan is administered. Administration involves monitoring and evaluating, on an ongoing basis, how the plan is implemented. Amendments or adjustments to the plan will no doubt be necessary because of changing conditions or new information. To achieve the goals established for the process, plan administrators should pay special attention to the design of regulation review procedures and of the management of the decision-making process.

RESOURCES

McHarg, Ian. 1969. *Design with Nature.* Garden City, NY: Natural History Press/Doubleday.

Steiner, Frederick. 2000. *The Living Landscape* (2nd edition). New York: McGraw-Hill.

Frederick Steiner, Ph.D., FASLA, University of Texas at Austin

ENVIRONMENTAL AND LEGAL

ENVIRONMENTAL REVIEW

INTRODUCTION AND BACKGROUND

The purpose of this section is to help landscape architects navigate the environmental review process as specified in the National Environmental Policy Act (NEPA). Some landscape architects may never encounter NEPA, but those firms whose work is predominately in the public sector may interact with it on a regular basis.

NEPA was established in 1969 as part of the ecological movement and in response to environmental degradation and a lack of community input in development decisions. The goals for the creation of the policy are stated in Section 2 of the act:

> *To declare a national policy which will encourage productive and enjoyable harmony between man and his environment; to promote efforts which will prevent or eliminate damage to the environment and biosphere and stimulate the health and welfare of man; to enrich the understanding of the ecological systems and natural resources important to the Nation; and to establish a Council on Environmental Quality. Sec. 2 [42 USC § 4321].*

The federal government established this act to raise environmental awareness and provide oversight of federal actions. Much like other major legislative initiatives (voting rights, equal protection under the law, etc.), the federal government set high standards to protect the national interest and set an example for local actions. The most significant benefit of environmental review is that it serves as a strong deterrent to the most inappropriate and degrading actions. For example, the original plan to drain the Everglades would not have been acceptable under NEPA and few decision-makers would consider proposing such an idea today.

NEPA is a procedural law requiring a project to undertake specific steps in order to gain approval. NEPA requires the consideration of environmental concerns and mandates opportunities for community input before final decisions can be made. Public disclosure requirements include publishing a public notice informing the public of the project and the availability of the report. This is followed by a review period, which includes a specified time for public comment.

The report produced is a comprehensive technical document covering a multidisciplinary range of manmade and natural resources. Four parts are involved:

1. Description of the project, including its justification
2. Project alternatives that must be considered
3. An assessment of existing conditions
4. An evaluation of potential impacts, with corresponding mitigation measures

Projects typically require a federal review if they are involved with federal construction, federal lands, or federal funds. Some examples include projects affecting wetlands, national parks, airports, interstate highways, federal courthouses, and federal agency headquarters. The following table contains a listing of types of projects.

Sometimes, municipal or private projects also require review. Approval of the project can be contingent on the applicant (owner/developer) completing an environmental review document for the federal agency. The contractor is required to pay for the study, but the scope of work, content, and schedule are subject to federal direction.

Some state and local governments have environmental review requirements: These are commonly referred to as "Little NEPA" laws. If the project meets federal guidelines, then a federal study typically will satisfy the local requirements as well. There are exceptions to this rule. For example, California's comparable law, California Environmental Quality Act (CEQA) has some guidelines that are more stringent than NEPA.

THE NEPA PROCESS

If a project is subject to NEPA, the first decision is to determine the level of analysis. There are primarily two types of documents that are prepared to satisfy NEPA requirements, an Environmental Assessment (EA) and an Environmental Impact Statement (EIS). An EA is a more concise product of an accelerated and streamlined process. An EIS is an extremely detailed and scientific examination of issues. The entire EA process typically takes 6 to 12 months, depending on the level of complexity. An EIS often takes from one to two years. Both types of NEPA documents follow a standard process and have a specific format, detailed below; and the following table contains a sample table of contents.

Description of the Project and Determination of Scope: The first chapter in an EA or EIS is a description of the proposed action, including the purpose and need for the project. Based on the project description, the next step is to conduct a scoping effort to determine the key issues surrounding the project with resource agencies and interested parties, even though the design has not been completed. The potential impact areas and specific issues of importance would be identified and explored. Conducting thorough scoping can avoid costly delays and problems later in the process.

Development of Project Alternatives: An important component of an EA or EIS is an analysis of alternative approaches to the project.

LISTING OF PROJECTS

TRANSPORTATION	INFRASTRUCTURE	BUILDINGS AND STRUCTURES	PARKS AND RECREATION	MILITARY	CIVIC PROJECTS	EDUCATION
Highways	Power Stations	Offices	Marinas/Docks	Military Base Plans	Memorials and Museums	Campus Master Plans
Roads	Utility Lines	Hotels	Zoos	Military Base Closure	Courthouses	Schools
Bridges	Landfills	Homes	Golf Courses	Military Housing	Prisons	Dormitories
Parking Garages	Dams and Reservoirs	Theaters	Parks/Recreation Facilities	Weapon Ranges	Hospitals	Laboratories
Airports	Water Treatment Plants	Master Plans	Trails		Stadiums	Administrative Buildings

TABLE OF CONTENTS

NATURAL RESOURCES			MANMADE RESOURCES			
Geo/Physical	**Biological**	**Air and Noise**	**Socio-Economic**	**Historic and Cultural**	**Transportation**	**Utilities**
Earth Resources	Habitat and Wildlife	Clean Air Act	Land-Use Patterns/Character	Architectural Resources	Roadways	Water Supply
Soils/Geotechnical	Vegetation/Crops	Local Noise Regulations	Demographics/Housing	Native American or Prehistoric Sites	Traffic Volume/Flow	Sewage Treatment
Water Resources	Woodlands/Timber	Ambient Noise and Air Levels	Economics/Employment	Cultural Resources	Mass Transit	Public Infrastructure
Floodplain	Wetlands		Community Facilities	Views of Significance	Pedestrian/Bicycle	Hazardous Material

Alan Harwood, AICP, EDAW

Usually two to three alternatives are considered. They need to answer two questions: "Where else could the project be located?" and "How else could the project needs be met?" The analysis of project alternatives provides critical comparisons to the preferred alternative.

Documentation of the Affected Environment: The first technical component of the document is the affected environment. This section describes the baseline conditions for the project site and surrounding context for each of the resource disciplines.

Evaluation of Environmental Consequences: The potential consequences of the project on the site and surrounding area are then identified, including short- and long-term impacts. The former refers to the ways the construction process itself alters the site and surrounding areas. The latter addresses the impacts attributable to operations once the project is complete.

The effects of a project can be viewed as having either direct or indirect affects on a site. For example, if a straightforward action occurs, such as physically removing a house, this is considered a direct impact. Less apparent are the indirect impacts, which create a situation for changes to occur off-site or later in time. For instance, a project could encourage the redevelopment of an area and ultimately result in the removal of the house, which would be considered an indirect impact.

The cumulative impacts of a proposed project and other existing and potential projects also need to be considered. This is particularly important when a new project is proposed in an area that already contains similar facilities, or may be the location of another proposed facility with adverse impacts. A single facility may not be problematic on its own; however, if additional facilities are built, the combined effect could be substantial.

Development of Mitigation Measures: The environmental review process also includes recommendations to reduce or offset the adverse impacts of the project. For example, a new amphitheater proposed in a park might raise some environmental concerns, such as greater stormwater runoff due to increased impervious surfaces, loss of open space, and additional traffic on the site. A project solution could include stormwater retention measures to minimize soil erosion and limits to vehicular access. These measures would then become conditions for project approval.

Circulation of Documents for Review: The various chapters of narrative and graphic information are compiled into a report. Once the lead federal agency and the project team approve it, the report is presented to the public for review. Typically, an EA is under review for 30 days and an EIS is given 45 days. For an EIS, a public meeting is typically required to allow everyone a chance for input. The report is also placed on the Internet, and some agencies are presented with hard copies. The public and other agencies have the opportunity to write letters in response to the report.

Completion of the Environmental Review Process: Following the public review period, all the comments are compiled and addressed, at which point the project can either be approved, change direction, or be dropped altogether. At the end of the EA process, if a project does not have significant environmental impacts, a Finding of No Significant Impact (FONSI) is prepared and signed by the appropriate federal agency, becoming the final environmental documentation for approval. If significant impacts are determined, the preparation of an EIS is required. For an EIS, the completion of the environmental review process is the Record of Decision (ROD), which documents the agency's process and findings.

RELATED STATUTES AND REQUIREMENTS

The following statutes are considered when developing an EA or EIS. The team needs to coordinate with these acts and regulations:

National Historic Preservation Act (Section 106) (NHPA)

Endangered Species Act (Sections 7 and 10) (ESA)

Clean Water Act (Section 404) (CWA)

Rivers and Harbors Act (Section 10) (COE)

Clean Air Act (Conformity Requirements) (EPA)

Other federal regulations that may apply, depending on the federal agency involved

POTENTIAL LEGAL CHALLENGES

The studies produced in accordance with NEPA are legal documents and are subject to public scrutiny. As such, there is a real potential for legal challenges. Great care must be taken in document preparation to ensure accuracy and prevent needless legal expenses. Legal challenges, if they persist, can actually derail a project due to the length and cost of legal action—even if the charges are not valid. For projects that result in judicial involvement, the judge will be most concerned with fulfillment of the procedures of the NEPA process rather than technical findings.

Alan Harwood, AICP, EDAW

LEGAL: PERMITS AND REGULATIONS

PROFESSIONAL LICENSURE OF LANDSCAPE ARCHITECTURE

Professional licensure is permissible constitutionally under the "police power" of the states. Legislation under the police power is permissible so long as the legislation is geared toward protecting the health, safety, and welfare of the citizenry. Professional licensure clearly falls within this requirement. Landscape architecture is a relatively recent newcomer to professional licensure, in comparison to its "sister" professions of architecture and civil engineering. For example, architecture was regulated in California pursuant to statute in 1901. In contrast, the amendment to the California Business and Professions Code that regulated the practice of landscape architecture was not enacted until 1953. This was the first such regulation in the United States. In the State of New York, architecture was regulated a bit later, in 1929; landscape architecture was not regulated there until 1961.

Notwithstanding its relatively recent status as a licensed profession, the history of landscape architecture is ancient and diverse. From the gardens of imperial Rome to the medieval mazes of early Christendom, landscape architecture has historic roots. The use of the professional title "landscape architect" dates from the mid-1800s, and the American Society of Landscape Architects (ASLA), the professional society for landscape architecture in the United States, was formed in 1899. It was not until a half-century later that licensure came into effect.

History of Licensure

The New York case of *Paterson v. University of the State of New York*[1] provides an interesting snapshot of the history of licensure of landscape architecture when one compares the lower court opinion (which overturned the licensure statute) with the appellate court opinion (which overturned the lower court decision and upheld the statute). The lower court expressed the concern that the definition of "landscape architecture" was unconstitutionally vague and required the exclusion of gardening, landscape contracting, horticulture, and the practice of arborists, among other services. By extension, the lower court argued that the practice of landscape architecture could not possibly imperil the health, safety, and welfare of the public if so many other quite similar (but unlicensed) services did not require licensure. As such, the lower court reasoned, it was nearly impossible to determine which services could be subject to criminal sanction and which could not. The appellate court reversed this, citing evidence that the health, safety, and welfare of the public could be imperiled by the practice of unlearned practitioners. The appellate court also referred to the then 17 degree programs providing higher degrees in landscape architecture, which demonstrated the professional nature of the practice.

Interestingly, the American Society for Landscape Architects (ASLA) continues to make many of the same arguments in its continuing efforts to pass legislation in the remaining state (Vermont) that still does not regulate the profession of landscape architecture. The efforts to promote regulation of the profession have borne significant fruit over the years, resulting in 8 that regulate only the use of the title "landscape architect," and 41 states that regulate the "practice" of landscape architecture.

"Title" Statute and "Practice" Statute

There is a fundamental difference between a "title" statute and a "practice" statute in landscape architectural practice. A jurisdiction that regulates only the use of the title "landscape architect" may have unlicensed practitioners performing services that constitute landscape architecture, but who are not in violation of the statute so long as they do not advertise themselves as landscape architects. In addition to regulating the use of the title, a jurisdiction that regulates the practice of landscape architecture defines which professional activities qualify as the practice of landscape architecture and then criminalizes the performance of those services by any unlicensed practitioner. The ASLA strongly supports the passage of "practice act" statutes in all the 50 states and continues to work toward that end. (A link to title and practice jurisdictions can be found at www.asla.org.)

About half of the states that require licensure of landscape architects individually also require licensure of any business entity that performs landscape architectural services within the state. Many such laws require that an officer or owner of the business entity be a licensed professional in the state in order for the business entity to qualify for licensure.

As noted above, landscape architectural practice overlaps with the practice of its sister design professions of architecture and civil engineering. In some jurisdictions, this overlap has been used by professional societies of civil engineers and architects as a purported justification for rejecting the licensure of landscape architects. However, overlap in professional services promotes competition and so long as the professional licensure reflects shared technical capacities, the safety of the public can be assured. In addition to overlap, of course, there are complementary skills as well. For example, surface grading and drainage may be an area where landscape architects are uniquely able to combine aesthetic and functional concerns, whereas subsurface storm drain collection and drainage may be an area where civil engineers are best able to bring their expertise to solve a site problem. Ultimately, of course, the client is probably best served by having professionally trained and licensed practitioners with diverse skills and abilities from which to choose.

CERTIFICATION BY PROFESSIONAL SOCIETIES

In addition to licensure by a state jurisdiction, certifications by professional societies or industry groups are available in related practices. Although not subject to professional licensure, these professional certifications may help to ensure quality services. However, the absence of state licensure means that the performance of services without certification is not illegal, although an action for false advertising or negligent misrepresentation may exist where providers hold themselves out as "certified" when they are not.

The International Society of Arborists offers certification in the field of arboriculture upon completion of educational requirements, practical experience, and a standardized examination. The American Society of Consulting Arborists offers additional certification as a Registered Consulting Arborist upon completion of its certification process. Certification by these professional societies establishes a level of professional knowledge and skill that the public may consider in selecting tree care services and consultants. In addition, the Pennsylvania Landscape and Nursery Association offers certification as a Pennsylvania Certified Horticulturalist, again upon fulfillment of educational, practical, and examination requirements. Other horticultural certifications also exist. Both certifications require continuing education requirements so certified individuals continue to develop skills and knowledge appropriate to the certification.

More recently, the U.S. Green Building Council, an industry group dedicated to the promotion of environmentally and ecologically sensitive building techniques and materials, has sponsored Leadership in Energy and Environmental Design (LEED) certification. LEED certification is offered to qualified individuals in the building industries or facilities management who pass a four-part examination demonstrating knowledge of building practices and design theory that furthers the expressed goals of the council.

REGULATION RELATED TO THE PRACTICE OF LANDSCAPE ARCHITECTURE

In addition to the direct regulation of the practice of landscape architecture through professional licensure, there is a whole body of regulations that affect how landscape architects render professional services. This can affect the design and planning recommendations made by landscape architects. In summary, these regulations consider the public interest in ways that include, but are not limited to:

- Land use, preservation, or development
- Protection of threatened resources and plant and animal species
- Impact on environmental change
- Preservation of historical or archeological assets
- Economic stimulation, maintenance, or restriction.

There are also other substantial bodies of related law that also apply to landscape architectural practice. For example, water law is a highly complex body of law that derives from property rights, common law, mining law, and state and local regulation.

Land-use regulation can pit the interests of individual landowners against the interests of the public, and may be limited by an analysis of whether or not regulation of private property is so extensive or comprehensive as to constitute a taking of private property without just compensation by the state. Generally the courts give the state broad discretion, and most regulations are generally upheld.

ZONING AND ENTITLEMENTS

Landscape architects must make themselves aware of any applicable zoning or entitlements, and the implications of such regulations on the professional

[1] 14 N.Y. 2nd 432 (1964).

Brodie Stephens, Esq., EDAW

practices they seek to render to private as well as public clients.

Many states have laws that specifically require the preparation of planning documents at the state and local level. These documents typically codify zoning regulations. Often, these require the consideration of factors such as noise, traffic, and pollution in assessing future land uses. As a consequence, zoning regulations can be quite complex, and address a number of factors.

Land Development and Growth Management Regulations

State and local regulations can also take the form of land development and growth management regulations. For example, a subdivision map act may regulate the division of large parcels of land into smaller units. These regulations may address the obligations imposed upon developers of land to provide for infrastructure necessary to support the intended uses of the land being developed, as well as the process by which private property or infrastructure can be "dedicated" to public use. In some cases, county or local government may place a moratorium or significant restrictions on water or sewer hookups, effectively prohibiting new development.

Some regulations require that large-scale developments perform an analysis of the Development of Regional Impacts (DRI). This is usually a stand-alone process applying specifically to projects of a certain size and scope.

Design Review

City and local regulations may include the requirement that projects be approved by a design review board, especially where either a particular architectural theme predominates or it holds historic significance. For example, the City of Santa Fe, New Mexico extensively regulates architectural design features, as well as plant selection, in its local ordinances to maintain its historic character.

Development Covenant and Restrictions

In addition to state and local regulation, many large developments contractually or by title to property bind landowners within a particular development to covenants and restrictions running with the land that restrict the ability of future landowners to develop their property. An early example of this strategy was implemented in the "Sea Ranch" development in Northern California to maintain design consistency and view corridors. Landscape architects must be aware of these "private" regulations as well.

Environment-Related Regulations

Environmental sensitivity is one of the benchmarks of good landscape architectural practice. Commonly today, training for the design professions includes study in environmental impacts and sensitivity to those impacts. This is also true for landscape architectural training. In some ways, of course, it is expected that a practice focused on living materials would be especially sensitive to environmental impacts. In practice, however, that is not always the case.

The state is also interested in environmental and ecological preservation, and numerous federal, state, and local regulations exist that are targeted toward that goal. Examples of such regulations include, but are limited to:

- *Water usage regulations mandating water conservation measures and use of xeriscape-appropriate plant species.* For example, the California Water Conservation in Landscaping Act, and municipal code sections that implement its requirements such as the City of Palm Desert Water Efficient Landscape Code, provide for maximum annual water usage as well as design review for appropriate species.
- *Invasive species regulations, including noxious weed laws, seed laws, invasive species councils and their recommendations, and aquatic plant permits and regulations.* Certain municipalities have regulations that mandate the use of native species as part of overall design guidelines, or as a specific requirement.
- *Design regulations that mandate LEED certification for projects, project elements, and/or materials.* Many municipalities, including the City of Houston, Texas, now require LEED certification of new city projects.
- *Harmful pest regulations.* These regulations require nursery practices intended to reduce or eliminate the spread of insect and other pests to noninfected areas within the state. They do not directly affect landscape architectural practice, but usually a reference is required in construction specifications, which in turn affects the nursery industry.
- *Tree preservation regulations.* This may include a prohibition against damaging or removing trees above a certain caliper diameter and are sometimes enforced by the building department or permitting authorities, as well as a planning department.

Historic Preservation

Governments have a rational basis for regulations that seek to maintain and preserve structures and sites that have historical and cultural value: They need to be preserved for future study and inspiration. Under the National Historic Preservation Act (NHPA) of 1966, and related state laws, demolition or renovation of historic structures must consider the preservation and/or documentation of the historic value of that structure. In addition, landscape-specific projects, such as the Historic American Landscapes Survey (HALS), conducted under the auspices of the National Park Service, seek to record and preserve historically significant American landscapes.

Landscape architects called upon to provide professional services related to a historic or potentially historic site should consult whether there are any applicable federal, state, or local laws that may impact the performance of those services.

REGULATION OF LANDSCAPE DESIGN AND CONSTRUCTION

The design and construction of landscape improvements, including irrigation systems, is also subject to regulation by state and local government building codes. In addition, federal law such as the Americans with Disabilities Act (ADA), and its associated design guidelines (ADAAG), may also apply.

Permitting

Most municipalities require some form of construction permitting for significant landscape construction or for construction that includes structural, electrical, or architectural improvements. Although not all landscape projects require construction permits, this is typically the hurdle (or hurdles, depending on the project) that most projects must surmount in order for a municipality in question to approve a certificate of occupancy, permitting public or private use. Regulations that are typically reviewed in conjunction with permitting include:

- Building codes, which may also include fire codes, plumbing codes, and electrical codes that apply to the proposed construction. In certain cases, specific irrigation codes that regulate the construction of irrigation systems and components must also consulted and followed.
- Federal and state regulations dealing with handicap access must frequently be followed in new construction or renovation projects. These regulations apply to path of travel, stairs, ramps, obstructions, and site amenities. In addition, small structures that are part of the landscape must also meet handicap and ADA accessibility standards.

MISCELLANEOUS MUNICIPAL REQUIREMENTS

There are a number of miscellaneous regulations that may apply to landscape design and construction projects undertaken in particular jurisdictions. Some examples may include:

- Regulation of the use of nonnative hardwoods.
- Regulation mandating the use of products made in the United States.
- Regulations mandating the use of fire-resistive plant materials in new construction or fire-resistive building components.
- Regulations mandating that new construction meet or exceed permeability requirements, or storm water drainage or discharge requirements.

Brodie Stephens, Esq., EDAW

PROJECT ADMINISTRATION

PROJECT MANAGEMENT

The project manager is essential to the success of any project. He or she is the person responsible to the client for delivering a quality project on time and within budget. The project manager is also the person responsible to his or her employer for ensuring the quality of a project, making a profit, and looking out for the company's interests. Finally, the project manager is responsible to the project team for defining roles clearly and communicating what team members need to know to be able to perform their duties well.

WHAT MAKES A GOOD PROJECT MANAGER?

The successful project manager needs to have:

- Organizational ability
- Effective communication skills
- Sense of responsibility and ownership
- Technical skills

Organization

First and foremost, the project manager must be able to organize large amounts of information for easy reference by the project team. Digital and paper files should be stored in a central place accessible to all members of the project team. Keeping records of all meetings and correspondence is essential to protecting the interests of the design firm as well as the client.

Communication

The project manager is responsible for keeping the client, principals, and project team up to date about project developments. Excellent communication skills are essential in this effort. The project manager must be able to communicate ideas effectively both verbally and in writing. Furthermore, the manager must be comfortable presenting ideas and directions in multiple settings, such as to an individual team member, to the team collectively, to the client, to the employer, and at times, to community groups or city officials.

Sense of Responsibility

The project manager must possess a strong sense of ownership of the project, fully recognizing that he or she is the person responsible for the success or failure of the project.

Technical Skills

Finally, the project manager must possess the necessary technical skills required for each specific project. Though he or she is not required to personally perform the tasks at hand—that is what specialists on the team are for—the project manager needs a general knowledge of the work required to ensure the suitability and quality of all the products of the team.

DUTIES OF A PROJECT MANAGER

The duties of a project manager include:

- Proposal writing
- Project initiation
- Scheduling and budgeting
- Work planning
- Monitoring
- Finance management
- Team/subconsultant management
- Client/owner management
- Additional services management
- Quality control
- Project closeout

Proposal Writing

Often, the project manager's first involvement in a project is the preparation of a proposal. The project manager and principal may collaborate in preparing the scope of services and fee proposal, ensuring from the outset a mutual understanding of the firm's obligations to the client. During this phase the prospective client often wants to meet the project manager, to get to know whom he or she will be working with during the life of the project.

Project Initiation

The first task of managing a project is to form the project team. Identifying the appropriate team members should be based upon the required skills, professional goals, and interests of staff members, in conjunction with project budgetary requirements. In addition, the principal and project manager must identify and secure the services of any necessary subconsultants.

It is important to have a signed contract in place before starting any work. That way project participants will understand the roles and responsibilities of all involved parties. It follows, then, that the project manager and principal are responsible for the timely preparation and execution of subcontracts that clearly spell out the tasks and responsibilities of each subconsultant. (Contract preparation is addressed at length in the Project Manual and Overview of Construction Documentation sections.)

Scheduling and Budgeting

Another of the duties of the project manager is to estimate how many hours each person on the team will need to complete each task, for the purpose of determining how most of the project budget will be spent. The most effective way to do this is to consult with each team member, the goal being to agree on an answer to the question, "How long should this task take?" This participatory approach creates a sense of ownership among the entire team for the project budget.

In addition, the project manager must determine how much money to set aside out of the budget for expenses and to pay subconsultants. Budgeting about 10 percent of the fee amount for contingency is recommended. Some tasks take longer than anticipated, so having this contingency amount in reserve can prevent a project budget overrun.

Work Planning

Once the project team is in place and all roles and responsibilities have been clearly defined, the project manager should prepare a plan for executing the project. A well-thought-out work plan and schedule helps keep the project manager and team members on track. Proper planning allows greater control over the project and helps to reduce errors, changes, and costs associated with corrections.

The work plan contains a breakdown of tasks to be performed, with clear milestones and schedules for each. It indicates the time for product delivery, as well as the effort it took to complete each task. Defining a project schedule helps keep the project within the established budget—in general, when schedules stretch out, budgets do too. Scheduling in this way from the outset communicates to the project team, as well as to the client, the expectations for timely reviews of submittals, meetings, delivery of information, and other items that can affect the timely completion of the project.

Monitoring

Once the work plan, budget, and schedule are in place, the project can get underway. Regular monitoring of these three components is essential to the success of the project, in terms of quality, client and team satisfaction, and finances. Regular team meetings with internal staff, as well as consultants, help confirm that everyone is on track and that the project is moving along according to schedule and budget. Subconsultants may be included in these meetings, or the project manager may choose to communicate with subconsultants independently.

Finance Management

Regular updates of the project budget are crucial to making sure that the project meets profitability expectations. Costly surprises later in the project can be prevented by regularly checking the hours actually expended, then correlating them to the budget. A staff member charging full-time on a project can spend between $10,000 and $15,000 in four weeks, so checking the budget on a weekly or biweekly basis can prevent expensive mistakes.

Team and Subconsultant Management

In addition to holding regular progress meetings, the project manager should meet informally with staff members and consultants on a periodic basis in order to gain a clear understanding of the personal dynamics of the project. The project manager can assess if personal goals of team members are being met and determine whether there are any problems that he or she needs to address.

Ellen Heath, AICP, EDAW

Client/Owner Management

Frequent communication with the client is essential. The project manager needs to make sure that the client is satisfied with the progress of the project. This is a preventative measure: It is always best to anticipate dissatisfaction and resolve any problems early. This reduces the chances of confrontations later, such as a client refusing to pay an invoice due to disagreements about the progress of the project or discontent with the products received.

Additional Services Management

Having a good work plan and clearly defined schedule also allows for easy tracking of any additional services. Often, clients are not intimately familiar with the provisions of the contract; and even if they are, sometimes they insist on asking for more. One of the project manager's main responsibilities is to monitor efforts and products to make sure that they are within the scope of the contract. Keeping track of additional service requests, and communicating to the client when requests constitute additional services, can help ensure the financial success of the project, as well as the goodwill of the team. To that end, the project manager should make sure that all project team members are familiar with the contracted scope of services, so that when a team member receives a request for something outside the scope, he or she can alert the project manager that there has been a request for additional services.

Quality Control

Landscape architects owe it to themselves, their firms, the profession, as well as to their clients, to ensure that all products are of the highest quality possible. Third-party review of products is often the best way to ensure that product quality is delivered; review by a professional who has not been involved in the day-to-day progress of the project can reveal inconsistencies and errors that are not obvious to the project team. Third-party review of documents, including correspondence and drawings, is advisable.

Project Closeout

Once the project has been successfully completed, all digital and paper records should be organized and stored in a secure place.

Experienced project managers reward successful teams at the completion of a project. The rewards may take several forms: celebratory drinks or meals, written thank-you notes, or commendations or announcements at office meetings.

As part of project closeout, the project manager also should meet with team members, as well as the client, to discuss where things went right and wrong, what could have done better, and what lessons were learned that can be applied to the next project.

Ellen Heath, AICP, EDAW

BUSINESS ADMINISTRATION: RECORDS, LEGAL, LIABILITY

Good business administration practices and procedures are crucial to the health of any business. They can foster a good business reputation for the company and have positive financial results. For companies that provide professional services, including landscape architecture firms, good business administration practices can also mean the difference between negligent or nonnegligent conduct. In order to understand how to do things right, it is essential to look at the converse impact of doing things wrong: The impact of bad record keeping and bad professional processes can be a significant potential liability. That said, an obsessive focus on liability can paralyze the professional. Instead, it is best to strive for a healthy attention to best practices, which free professionals to be the best they can be and potentially also have the effect of lowering the risk of liability.

PROFESSIONAL OBLIGATIONS OF LANDSCAPE ARCHITECTS

Professional Standard of Care and Negligence

First and foremost, a landscape architect is a professional. Even in those jurisdictions where there is no licensure of the practice of landscape architecture, in the event that the acts or omissions of a landscape architect result in damages, the courts entertain, and may require, testimony of other similarly situated professionals to ascertain whether the act or omission was "negligent"—that is to say, whether the act or omission fell below the standard of care practiced by similarly situated professionals in the locality. Only by comparing the typical conduct of other landscape architects to the particular conduct of the one whose acts or omissions are in question can a finder of fact assess whether the particular conduct was negligent or not negligent.

So, for example, for a jury to determine whether or not a landscape architect working in a desert environment was negligent in specifying a tree for a use that called for drought-tolerance, they would have to assess whether similarly situated landscape architects would or would not have specified the same species of tree in a similar circumstance. This "duty of care," a comparison of the practices of other similarly situated professionals in the locality, at the same time, is applicable in every circumstance where professional care and discretion are required in the rendering of professional opinion or the implementation of that opinion in action. Of course, the duty of care also applies to instances of "nonfeasance," where the professional fails to take action or render an opinion when one would have been called for. An obvious circumstance where the duty of care applies is when a landscape architect reduces a design concept to graphic representation in plan form. Less obvious circumstances include the duty to notify the client when the landscape architect receives direction that is inconsistent, or where the "client" is composed of various entities that request services or solutions that conflict with one another. In addition, the landscape architect must consider circumstances where a client must be informed that there may be unknown consequences of the use of untested materials or of tested materials used in unique ways.

The duty of professional care also requires that a landscape architect review, analyze, and conform his or her professional services to the requirements of applicable law. Just as ignorance of the law is no excuse generally, ignorance of applicable law that regulates or affects landscape architectural practice is no excuse either.

It is important to understand that even when a landscape architect is hired by a sophisticated client, blindly following the direction or decisions of that client may not insulate the landscape architect from liability if that direction or decision was wrong. Even the use of the client's "standard" specifications or details might be problematic, if they are flawed or out of date. The landscape architect is being hired to provide professional guidance and counsel; therefore it is always good practice to put in writing any professional concerns and questions raised by client direction, to communicate those to the client, and to maintain copies of those documents in the project file.

Professional liability may also be "shared" with others, including where a landscape architect may become responsible for the acts or omissions of others. The most common situation is where a landscape architect hires or otherwise engages individuals or entities to assist in the rendering of professional services generally or for a particular project. Where a landscape architect represents to the client that he or she has the capacity to oversee and coordinate the work of subconsultants or advisors, and contracts with that client for the performance of services incorporating that work, the landscape architect will be "vicariously liable" for the acts or omissions of those subconsultants and advisors. This is one of the reasons why it is always important to have a well-drafted and comprehensive written contract between a landscape architect and any subconsultant or advisor.

Another circumstance where the liability of others may be assumed by a landscape architect is where a joint venture is formed for the purpose of performing professional services and the landscape architect is a member of this joint venture. In many jurisdictions, the liability associated with joint venture participation, as well as other circumstances, may give rise to "joint and several" liability, which means that each party is fully responsible for the total damages caused. As in all instances where new entities are being formed, it is very important to consult with competent and independent counsel to ensure that you are receiving the best advice possible.

In some cases, clients will request that they be granted rights of ownership not only in the hard copy deliverables provided as part of the rendering of professional services, but also the rights of intellectual property that attach to the creation of those deliverables. This is a matter that is best discussed with competent counsel. However, a landscape architect should always consider the possible consequences of reuse of his or her work product and how to mitigate against the harm that might be associated with that reuse. Again, an attorney is a good place to start here.

Liability for professional negligence is one type of what are called "tort" liabilities (another type will be discussed later on). In general, professionals can be sued for damages that are caused by their professional negligence (subject to certain rules about who can or cannot sue in certain circumstances) and must pay the cost of restoring injured parties to the state that they would be in had the negligence not occurred. This is a very simplistic summary; again, an attorney should be consulted as to the special rules that apply to this generality.

Contractual Obligations

It is important to learn the basics of contracts as they apply to landscape architectural practice in order to have a general understanding of the liabilities associated with contracting for the performance of landscape architectural services.

Contracts are little "worlds" created by the parties that negotiate them. With limited exception, parties can enter into contracts that contain just about any provisions imaginable. This means that, in general, a party can agree to provide services of just about any type, to be performed within just about any schedule, subject to just about any terms, for just about any payment. As such, a landscape architect can contract to assume much more liability than he or she can be sued for in a court of law for negligent performance of professional services. If landscape architects don't pay attention to, or control how contracts are created, they can find themselves inhabiting a world they might regret helping to create.

In general, a contracting party can be sued for contract damages in the event that such party "breaches" (or fails to perform) the contract in some aspect and the breach causes damages. In general, nonbreaching parties can collect as damages the amount necessary to put them in the position that they would be if the contract obligations had been fulfilled.

In some cases, a contracting party may owe obligations under the contract to a third party to the contract and have liability to this third party if he or she breaches. In other cases, the contract will require that a contracting party make a representation to a third party, who then may sue on the basis of any misrepresentation. In general, anytime a contract requires a landscape architect to perform a duty to a third party, or for the benefit of a third party, or make a representation to a third party (such as a bank or lender), the landscape architect should contact an attorney to discuss the requirement.

Strict Liability

In some rare circumstances, the performance of landscape architectural services may result in the assumption of strict liability in tort, which is another type of tort liability. Generally, however, the landscape architect can and should avoid the assumption of strict liability.

The most common example of liability which a landscape architect may become involved with that is a form of strict liability is infringement of the intellectual property rights of others. A claim for infringement of copyright, trademark, or patent generally requires only that there be substantial similarity between the infringing work product and the protected intellectual property and no privilege for use of the intellectual property or other exception to liability. No "negligence" on the part of the infringing party must be shown. Infringement is most likely to come up when a landscape architect is given or comes into posses-

Brodie Stephens, Esq., EDAW

sion of the work product of another party and incorporates it into his or her own work product without permission. It is important to secure permission before using the work of others.

One type of strict liability that a landscape architect should be wary of, and not assume by contract, is that associated with the sale of goods. Work product associated with professional services is generally not a "good," but an instrument of professional services. Any contract that seeks to impose liability for sale of goods, or warranties associated with the sale of goods, such as the implied warranty of merchantability should be reviewed with an attorney.

POSSIBLE ENHANCEMENTS TO LIABILITY

There are some circumstances, relationships, or events that, on average, may tend to increase the possible liability associated with a particular project.

Certain client relationships may pose unique challenges. Again, these are general statements that do not apply to any one particular client or any specific set of circumstances; these are merely considerations for general review in appropriate circumstances.

When considering a project, a landscape architect may wish to consider the following:

- Is the client an amalgam of different groups or divisions with potentially differing interests and goals?
- Is the client sufficiently funded for the work to be performed, or is the client in part reliant upon funding that may be generated or influenced by the work to be performed?
- Is the client changing design professionals in the middle of a project; if so, why?
- Is the client embroiled in contentious or demanding negotiations with third parties that relate to the project?

None of these may be reasons *not* to take a job, but they may be reasons to ask more questions.

Some types of projects themselves may be worthy of questioning whether they represent a greater risk of liability. Landscape architectural professional liability insurers maintain lists of such project types, and it may be appropriate to consult with an insurance broker on this topic.

Some types of project delivery methods, such as fast-track projects, design/build projects where the landscape architect is taking a prime role, or design/build joint ventures, may be circumstances where additional questions need to be asked. Where the landscape architect is taking a prime consultant role, and the subconsultant team is in whole or in part dictated by the client, additional considerations regarding liability may need to be taken.

Finally, on certain projects, the services required may be beyond the particular skill set of the landscape architect, who should beware being overextended. The wise landscape architect will take on only those services he or she can perform without jeopardizing the professional quality of those services.

CONTRACTUAL LIMITATIONS ON LIABILITY

Certain contract provisions, such as indemnities and limitations of liability, can be used to partially manage the risk associated with contracting for professional services. Consulting with a competent attorney is the best way to consider whether such contractual protections may be applicable in any particular circumstance.

BEST PRACTICES AND RECORD KEEPING

This section outlines in brief terms some of the issues a landscape architect should consider, and usually document, during the successive phases of a job. This summary may be considered a rough outline for further study or solicitation of additional consultation by a competent attorney.

Precontract and Marketing

The most common issue that arises in the context of marketing the services of a landscape architect is the risk that marketing materials will make such express and definitive claims as to constitute a promise that will form the basis of either a contract or a representation that may give rise to liability. For example, saying that one's firm provides quality services using a unique "team" approach across internal disciplines is probably acceptable. In contrast, saying that one will employ only experts in their respective fields to serve as members of a team that will perform work on a project must be a true statement, or it may result in liability.

Contracting

Firstly, it's necessary to consider the law of the state under which the professional services will be contracted to determine whether there are legal requirements that dictate certain terms and conditions of the contract. Some states require that the license number of the landscape architect appear (this may also apply to marketing materials), as well as other specific requirements. In general, regardless of the applicable law, it is always good practice to have a written contract so as to fix the mutual intent and codify the expectations of the parties.

Although a letter of intent or understanding may be elected to be used to "kick off" the professional services on a temporary basis pending negotiation of a contract, a document that adequately addresses the necessary elements of a typical professional services contract should always be entered into.

Many governmental and large corporate entities use a manuscripted contract that is specific to that entity and not a standard industry contract such as one of the American Institute of Architects' or Engineers Joint Contract Documents Committee's suite of documents. These manuscripted contracts may be written to strongly favor the interests of the drafter and hence should be carefully reviewed and amended (if possible) before execution.

As discussed above, a prime landscape architect will be vicariously liable for the professional services of any subconsultant and may be able to be sued for their acts or omissions. It is therefore in the best interests of the prime landscape architect to insist upon a written contract with all of his or her subconsultants. It is also very important to ensure that every scope item contracted for in the prime agreement either is going to be performed by the prime landscape architect or appears prominently in the scope of services of one of the subconsultants. In some instances, the scope of services of the prime landscape architect is developed in conjunction with discussions held with the subconsultants, but the scope of services in their actual contract is not negotiated until later. Unless the landscape architect is careful, the later definition of scope may unintentionally omit something that is presumed by either the landscape architect or the subconsultant to be part of what the other is doing.

Services

There are a number of issues, events, or activities that should be considered and documented during the various phases of performance of services on a project. Three of these are:

- *Design.* Review, analyze, document, and respond to direction provided by, or decisions made by, the client. Document and respond to any delay in decisions and the possible impact of such delay. Confirm that the landscape architect has the right to rely upon the information provided by the client, or others at the direction of the client, as well as the implied representation that such information can be used in the landscape architect's work product without infringing upon the intellectual property rights of others. Document code changes, or differing code interpretations, and any related economic consequences. Document changes due to value engineering, and (if known) the possible implications of such changes. Document any changes to the design by others, and (if possible) the possible implications of such changes.
- *Bidding/negotiated bid.* Assist the client in ensuring that all bidders receive the same information, at the same time. Document any changes that arise out of this process and the possible implications of such changes.
- *Construction administration.* Document any change orders, field changes, substitutions, and so on. If possible, describe the possible implications of such changes. Document any changes arising out of the acts or interpretations of governmental entities or inspectors. Document and respond in a timely manner to requests for information, but ensure that the contractor is instructed to refer to the contract documents when such referral is sufficient. Act upon and respond in a timely manner to submittals by construction contractors. Deal appropriately with any submittals that are out of sequence or too early.
- Possible implications of changes made may include, but not be limited to; affects to maintenance of a project, changes to the performance of materials, equipment or design element immediately or over time, interactions with other elements or aspects of design of the project, increased risks of bodily injury or property damage, project delays, or cost implications.

Document Retention

There are three interrelated considerations that inform how long project documentation should be retained. First, consider the statute of limitations for claims that may arise out of the performance of the services being rendered. In many states, the statute of limitations for claims related to a "latent" design defect (one that is not readily observable) is approximately 10 years. This is not, in and of itself, a reason to hold onto documents for 10 years, but should be one of many considerations. Second, consider any statutory or contractual obligations to maintain records. Many professional service contracts obligate that project documentation be maintained for a certain period. Some local, state, or federal statutes may also apply and mandate periods of retention. Third, consider the business implications of losing the project documentation. Will it mean the loss of an important resource for future designs or marketing of future projects?

A demand for the production of electronic documents is a now ubiquitous feature of any claim against landscape architects. This means that email, CAD files, and document files, are typically demanded by one or more participants in a lawsuit. Given how difficult it is to "ensure" that electronic files are deleted, and the shelf-life of such documents, this has become a complex area that requires close consultation with competent counsel.

QUALITY ASSURANCE/RISK MANAGEMENT

One of the most important aspects of professional practice is good project management and project planning. Many resources are available to assist in improving the professional skill level in this area, and money invested here is almost always money well spent.

Generally, it is good practice to consider whether each particular project may benefit from a well-thought-out project work plan, driven by scope at the task level. Assignment of personnel and scheduling should follow a logical sequence that considers the impact of other projects on the project at hand, and the availability of internal and external resources. Contingencies should to be established early on, and additional services or time sought as early as possible. The landscape architect should compile an information database from documentation provided by the client and by others at the client's direction, along with any applicable codes and regulations. The landscape architect should seek to have the right to rely upon this database, as well as on the implied representation that the information contained in it can be incorporated into the work product without infringing upon the intellectual property rights of others.

Quality assurance is vital not only to the management of professional liability arising out of the services rendered by a landscape architect, but also to the business longevity and reputation of the landscape architect. A reputation for professional quality and integrity is one of the most valuable assets of any professional service provider.

A landscape architect should prepare, and then follow, a regimented process of ensuring that the work product he or she produces is reviewed for technical quality before delivery to the client. Peer review (internal and external), best practices exchanges and "lessons learned," and comprehensive checklists are all elements that could be considered and then implemented in any quality assurance program. It is, of course, important to ensure that the same level of concern for quality is met or exceeded by one's subconsultants, and a prime landscape architect may want to insist upon seeing the quality assurance plan prepared by his or her subconsultants, as well as confirmation that it is used on a particular project.

Finally, it is important to note that a quality assurance plan that is conceived but not implemented may *increase,* rather than limit, the liability of a landscape architect. Therefore, it is necessary to ensure that any program put in place is implemented, so as to avoid questions of intent should a claim arise out of the "one" project where the quality assurance process wasn't followed.

Brodie Stephens, Esq., EDAW

COST ESTIMATING

INTRODUCTION

When landscape architects know the construction costs required to implement their designs, it greatly improves their ability to control the design and documentation process. This knowledge is critical for maintaining credibility when representing proposed designs to the owner. Generally speaking, when the costs are under control, the project is under control.

Cost estimating can be a very controversial topic, and a highly scrutinized area of the overall project. In some instances, even the term, "cost estimating" is too sensitive. As a result, it is referred to as a "schedule of probable costs," to avoid warranting that the actual construction will come in as advertised. It is important that all parties acknowledge that, regardless of the term used, the effort is, at best, an educated guess of financial parameters. To limit any unforeseen financial surprises, landscape architects should always include a contingency, added to the amount of their cost estimation.

The owner often retains a professional costing consultant on the team whose job it is to examine and estimate the costs of construction. Even so, landscape architects should be aware of the construction cost of their scope elements. Landscape construction is not an exact science of measuring static building materials, so pricing can elude some cost estimation firms that are more accustomed to "sticks and bricks" in architecture projects. Sometimes, when it comes to landscape planting, they rely heavily on the landscape architect's own recommended unit costs and quantification techniques, which have been developed through extensive experience.

THE OWNER'S LANGUAGE

All owners have at least one thing in common: For them, financial considerations drive decisions. In fact, it sometimes is *the* most important factor on which to base their judgment, almost superseding the real estate program driving the project. To maintain involvement and control over the design and documents process, the landscape architect must be versed in cost analysis. It is common for the designer to hear from the owner, "It looks great, but tell me how much it costs; then I'll tell you if I like it." It is important to support the owner's comfort level early on. The more fluent the landscape architect is in relationship to project costs, the more the owner will be willing to talk about design concepts without always linking decisions back to dollars.

COST CONTROLS START EARLY

The landscape architect should begin the cost monitoring process even while proposing for the project. The fee is often developed as a function of a percentage of construction cost. Unlike some design professionals, such as interior designers, whose fees are based on commissions for elements of the design, landscape architects often work on a lump-sum fee basis. In essence, project payment does do not necessarily increase by an increase in the construction budget. However, it is commonly required that the landscape architect amend his or her design documents to bring the project within budget without an additional fee increase (if the budget amount is known to the landscape architect from the outset).

Once the project is awarded, the landscape architect should begin to track costs in association with the evolving design. It is even advisable during initial design to hold charrette workshops to quickly estimate preliminary costs and to assign relative value to plan elements.

Relative Value

Relative value is a tool used by landscape architects to speak the owner's language of cost assessment. By quickly calculating the general costs of design elements during a design work session, the landscape architect builds confidence in the process and helps the owner make decisions about the value of various parts and subparts of the project. For instance, there is a hierarchy in both the level of design and relative cost that each assigns to a project. Ranging from intensively designed, and more expensive per square foot to construct, to less complicated and cheaper, the "Hierarchy of Cost Structure Diagram" below identifies a variety of possibilities.

Each of the options has a relative value to the project and can be assigned a representational symbol, not unlike the practice of using a dollar sign scale ($$$$ vs. $) in restaurant guides to establish price level. For example, it would be expected that the primary use areas would receive the most dollar symbols ($$$$), as compared to screening and buffering, as it is the most expensive per square foot. The use of assigning relative value to the various areas of a design helps the project stay on track, and the owner understand how resources are being allocated appropriately. In turn, the process helps reduce the chances of surprises down the line.

Schedule of Probable Costs

The schedule of probable costs is a spreadsheet with quantifiable elements that calculates the estimated costs for landscape-related construction as shown in the example on the following page. The spreadsheet is constructed of columns and rows allowing for calculation of costs.

Column headings are generally:

- Item name (to be constructed, specific or general)
- Units (feet/meters, square feet/square meters, cubic yards/cubic meters, linear feet/linear meters; also could be lump sum or allowance)
- Quantity (actual or estimated count)
- Unit cost (price per each unit)
- Extension (quantity multiplied by unit cost)
- Comments (description and special notes)

Rows consist of a listing of elements in the landscape architect's scope (either specific or general):

- Earthwork
- Hardscape including paving, site structures, fountains, site furnishing, site lighting, site signs
- Landscape including trees by various sizes and categories, shrubs, groundcover, vines, turf grasses, ornamental grasses, aquatics
- Irrigation system elements (or square foot allowance)

Quantification

To estimate a cost you must consider objects by counting individual items (for example six benches) or quantify in some other way units of measurements such as linear distance, volume, or area. Landscape architects can estimate areas based on mathematical calculations; for example, area of circle or circumference. Other measurements include:

- Square foot/square meter
- Acre/hectare
- Linear foot/meter
- Cubic yard/meter
- Lump sum
- Allowance

Once these quantities have been determined they are entered into your price schedule, and the next step is to estimate unit costs. Cost estimators generally rely on a number of manufacturers specifications, numbers and quality of units, or by quantities or amounts of materials called for in the design and specifications.

Influences on Unit Pricing

Units costs and pricing estimations are influenced by a number of factors beyond strict manufacturing costs these include:

- Industry standards—cost estimates based on quality and location of installation
- Historic data—prices based on experience in the market on previous projects
- Industry trends—prices are reflecting an increase or decrease based on oversupply or intense demand
- Inflation/deflation—prices are increasing or decreasing as a result of larger economy

Factors Affecting Accuracy

- *What to estimate.* Are elements grouped or measured individually?
- *Level of detail.* More general in early design phases, more detailed toward construction documents phase.

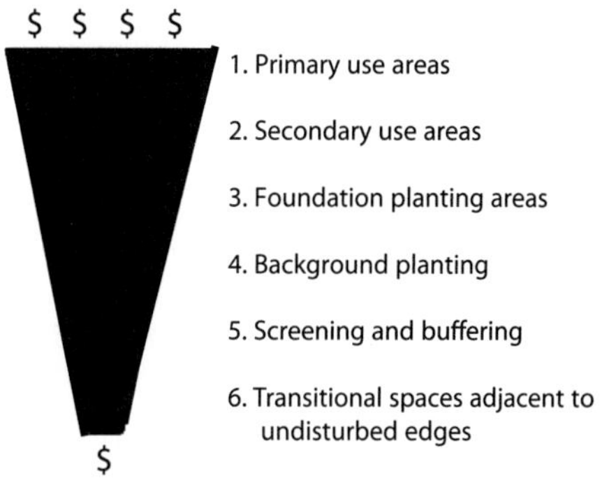

HIERARCHY OF COSTS STRUCTURE DIAGRAM

Todd Hill, ASLA, EDAW

TOWNE PARK SYSTEM, FLORIDA
PHASE ONE—SCHEMATIC COST ESTIMATE — **Prepared by: EDAW, 22 July 2003**

Urban Park

Total Park acreage:	45.54		Net park upland, SF:	106,286
Urban Plaza acreage:	2.44		Cost Per SF:	$5.53
Type:	Neighborhood			
Relative Value:	High			
ROW included:	No			

ITEM	COMMENT	UNIT	QUANTITY	UNIT COST	TOTAL
HARDSCAPE		SF			
Concrete Paving		SF	38,772	$4.50	$174,474.00
Specialty Paving	unit pavers	SF	3,448	$8.50	$29,308.00
		Total Hardscape Paving SF	**42,220**		
Street Lights	spacing 80' oc, conduit / wire NIC	ea		$7,800.00	
Pedestrian Lights	spacing 40' oc, conduit / wire NIC	ea	7	$4,800.00	$33,600.00
Landscape Uplights		lump sum	1	$2,500.00	$2,500.00
Park Signage		lump sum	1	$2,500.00	$2,500.00
Pavilion		ea		$35,000.00	
Benches		ea	13	$1,800.00	$23,400.00
Trash Cans		ea	10	$1,200.00	$12,000.00
Drinking Fountains		ea	1	$7,500.00	$7,500.00
Water Aeration		lump sum		$80,000.00	
Pedestrian Overlooks		lump sum		$110,000.00	
Entrance Monuments		lump sum		$200,000.00	
				Subtotal	$285,282.00
LANDSCAPE		SF	62,670		
Fine Grading		SF	62,670	$0.15	$9,400.50
Shrubs		SF		$2.50	
Groundcover		SF	34,559	$4.50	$155,515.50
Sod		SF	28,111	$0.40	$11,244.40
Seed		SF		$0.15	
Sod (sf)			208,168	$0.45	$93,675.60
Canopy Tree (ea)			245	$700.00	$171,500.00
Irrigation		SF	62,670	$0.45	$28,201.50
Large Canopy Tree	5-6 caliper	ea	1	$2,500.00	$2,500.00
Canopy Tree	3-3 1/2 caliper	ea	81	$700.00	$56,700.00
Flowering Ornamental Tree	2-21/2 caliper	ea	30	$350.00	$10,500.00
				Subtotal	$274,061.90
				5% contingency	$27,967.20
				Total	$587,311.10

NOTE: This estimate is based on schematic design and is approximate only.
This estimate was based on a plan drawn at 1= 40'-0 scale.
Construction details were not completed at the time of this estimate.
Items Not Included:

SCHEDULE OF PROBABLE COST SPREADSHEET EXAMPLE

- *Regional variations.* Labor and material costs vary greatly depending on location.
- *Age of unit prices.* Periodic corrections for economic fluctuations.
- *Rounding of units.* Fractions of units or extension of decimal places should be commensurate with level of detail.

Contractor Influence

- Availability of material affects price, for example sand, rock, and timber are all less expensive near where they mined or harvested.
- "Fire sales" require immediate response even if the price is significantly less expensive: Is it right for the project, even at reduced cost?
- Long lead times means reduced chance of rush charges and generally results in a lower cost.
- Competitiveness of contractor market—impacts contractor mark-ups.
- Market fluctuations in both materials manufacturing and labor availability affect contractor pricing.

Separation of Discipline

Site development estimates often cover both site landscape and civil engineering and infrastructure costs. When landscape costs estimates are included in the combined landscape and civil engineering and infrastructure budgets, it becomes difficult to get a correct price estimate, because infrastructure construction pricing can dwarf landscape construction and warp estimates. Therefore it is sometimes necessary to price landscape site development work separately from civil engineering and infrastructure work to get a more accurate estimate.

Contingency

Landscape architects must plan and budget for events which are hard to predict or unforeseen. Contingency must be built into all estimates. A greater contingency must be built into design and real estate programs with less certainty. For example those projects in the early stages of design and planning should consider upwards of 15 percent as a contingency to budget. Projects with more certainly, for example those in later phases of design and documentation where more specific quantities are known, need only budget 5 percent for contingency.

All estimates must be defensible; however, unforeseen the events must be recognized, and these events drives need for contingency in planning and budgets. Unforeseen factors include the following issues with potential examples:

- *Security issues.* A war breaks out or a security threat is uncovered.
- *Hazardous environment.* Undiscovered hazardous waste is uncovered.
- *Market influences.* The Dow Jones Industrials or Bond markets significantly rise or fall, effecting the availability of capital for building or for funding the project.
- *Location/region.* Regional issues affect project viability, weather, economies, or population shifts.
- *Commodities market.* Concrete or plywood, for example, may be in short supply when construction begins due to demand elsewhere.
- *Project funding sources.* Are the sources locked in? Will the money be available at the time construction begins?
- *Development schedule and timing.* The further out into the future, the less certain.
- *Political entitlements.* The project may requiring rezoning or other permit issues, which take time and are difficult to predict.

Qualification

The following are general qualifications that may be applied to estimates. They help explain the nature and influencing factors of an estimate:

- Describes the accuracy (or general nature) of the estimate
- Describes about the intended use of the schedule of probable costs
- Identifies sources of unit costs and measurement techniques
- Explains how calculations were derived (to re-create if necessary)
- Places a time frame limitation on accuracy of estimate

Updates

Cost estimates are typically updated at successive design/documentation phases from schematic design to design development, or design development to construction documents. As estimates are updated with the successive developments of the document, the estimates become more accurate. Estimates are also updated:

- When significant changes occur to project program
- Significant project element requantifying occurs
- Updated unit prices are received

Todd Hill, ASLA EDAW

BIDDING

In order to select a contractor or award a contract, clients or owners will often go through a bidding process. This process can vary greatly depending on whether it is a public bid or a private bid. What they do have in common is that, in most cases, qualified contractors are asked to provide their lowest responsible bid for a specific scope of work or a specific project. Below are just some of the differences between a public bid and a private bid process:

Public Bid
- A well-defined process to follow
- Predetermined time period to advertise for bid
- Specific advertising process
- Open process
- Predominately low-bid selection process
- Specific bid due date and time
- Public opening and reading of each bid
- Requirement for complete and thorough bids

Private Bid
- Not legally bound by public procurement process
- Selective, prequalified list of bidders
- Little or no advertisement
- Flexible due date and time
- Partial bids may be accepted
- Private analysis of each bid
- No requirement to select lowest bidder

The bid documents are usually made up of the drawings, specifications, and the bid manual. At a minimum, the landscape architect is responsible for providing the drawings and specifications. In some instances, the landscape architect would also develop the bid manual or might possibly coordinate with a construction manager or client representative to provide those services. To help offset the expense of printing and compiling the drawings and bid manual, the contractors are required to purchase their bid sets. This also has the advantage (depending on the cost) of deterring the not-so-serious bidders from participating.

In addition to the technical specifications, the bid manual is also made up of what is called Section One, the instructions to bidders. This section outlines the specific steps that each contractor must follow to submit an acceptable and responsive bid. This section also includes any pertinent bid forms, prequalification forms, bid bond and performance bond forms, and any other boilerplate information affecting the bid. As noted above, on a public bid there may be very specific forms and instructions that each bidder needs to follow, or risk being disqualified.

The following lists common elements found in many bids, along with their associated definitions:

Bid bond: Acceptable surety furnished by a bidder as a guaranty that he or she will enter into a contract and will furnish the contract performance bond and payment bond if a contract is awarded to him or her. The amount of the required bid bond is indicated in the bid manual.

Performance/payment bond: The approved form of security executed by the contractor and his or her surety, who guarantees complete execution of the contract and the payment of all legal debts pertaining to the construction of the project. Usually the performance bond is required in the sum equal to the full amount of the contract.

Unit prices: Some bids require that the contractor provide unit prices for the required work in the project so that if either additions or deductions are encountered, the client can negotiate these in a fair and unbiased manner.

References/prequalification: This is the process by which the prospective bidders are required to establish their responsibility and competence in advance of submission of a bid proposal. Prequalification is primarily used on either very high-dollar-amount projects or on projects that require a specific expertise or skill set.

In order for the bidding process to be successful and as fair as possible to all parties involved, it is necessary that the same project information and bidding instructions be conveyed to each and every interested party. For this reason, a prebid meeting is held by the client. The landscape architect is asked to be present at this prebid meeting to answer questions relative to the drawings, specifications, and scope of the project. It is important that the landscape architect take good notes and record every question and every answer so that this information can be distributed to all prospective bidders.

Once all of the bids have been collected, the landscape architect may be asked to help analyze the bids with the client and make recommendations for contractor selection. This process is more likely to happen with a private bid process rather than the more prescriptive public bid process. If this is requested by a client, it is important for the landscape architect to thoroughly analyze each bid before recommending the most qualified (not always the lowest) responsible bidder. This analysis would include verifying that the math is correct and that the numbers indicated on the bid actually "add up." The analysis would also include checking the contractor's list of references, calling each one and making sure that the job was completed in a satisfactory manner within a reasonable amount of time. If required, the analysis should also include making sure that each contractor supplied a valid bid bond, indicating each company's ability to carry out the work being tendered.

On many private bids, and even certain public bids, determining prequalification requirements for the contractors, if allowable, is an excellent way to make sure that the selected contractor will have the desired skills, experience, and qualifications to perform the job. Prequalification requirements help identify the contractors that don't have the proper or specific expertise required for a particular project. Prequalification can also make sure that the contractor has the labor power and resources necessary to complete a large job on time and within budget.

On most public bids, proposals will be opened and read publicly at the time and place stated in the Notice to Contractors. Bidders and their authorized agents are invited to be present, and this is the best way for contractors to see how their bids compare to the competition.

If the contract is awarded, it is usually given to the lowest responsible bidder whose proposal has met all of the prescribed requirements. From this point on, the contractor has a prescribed number of days to make sure that all of the required paperwork and forms are delivered and complete.

Ray Strychalski, ASLA, EDAW

CONSTRUCTION OBSERVATION

Construction observation, sometimes called construction administration (although this is not a legally accurate term), is a crucial function of the landscape architect to ensure that the original design intent of the documents is upheld during the construction process. Complete and well-documented construction documents will not assure a well-constructed project. Construction observation is the most important time to make sure the project meets all design intent. It is important to understand that the landscape architect is only an observer of the construction progress; he or she should not discuss means and methods with the contractor. In an observation role, the landscape architect visually compares the contract documents (drawings and specifications) with the work in place by the contractor. The landscape architect does not instruct the contractor on their methods (unless danger to personal bodily harm is imminent). The landscape architect observes and records completed work and the status of work in process and provides a written report to the owner of any discrepancies or variances from the contract documents.

Good construction observation requires knowledge of the design process from the original inception to early concepts through preparation of contract documents and on to final construction. This is crucial, as it is common for project team members to change over the course of a project on both the owner's and designer's side. Many firms are set up to transition from idea people in the early stages to technical, management, and maintenance specialists for the construction of a project. Original thoughts, ideas, and intentions may be lost in the transition, so it is the landscape architect's job to show evidence of the origin of ideas and how they are carried forward into the contract documents.

This section has been divided into subsections explaining the many roles, responsibilities, and functions associated with the landscape architect providing construction observation services.

CONSTRUCTION SITE WORK RELATIONSHIPS

The construction period of any project can be difficult. Establishing and maintaining a positive relationship with the owner, design team, general contractor, and landscape contractor can help mitigate conflicts that may arise. Having a positive attitude toward finding solutions, rather than assigning blame, also helps. Always try to couple the identification of a problem with a proposed solution, even when others may not uphold a positive outlook. By creating a calm process of observing construction, landscape architects are more likely to see successful implementation of their designs.

Today, it is not unusual for enlightened owners to conduct team-building exercises. The newly formed construction and design team conduct these exercises to break down barriers and foster strong interpersonal relationships before construction begins. The construction period can test all of the good that may come out of team building and positive relationships. Creating a strong relationship among participants will help overcome issues that arise in the field and more quickly resolve disputes.

BUSINESS CONSIDERATIONS OF CONSTRUCTION OBSERVATION

The construction observation portion of the scope begins with owner's acceptance of the 100 percent construction documents package. As a percentage of the total contract for a project, the construction observation portion may be as much as 15 percent of the fee. Often, however, the amount is reduced due to budget constraints in earlier phases of the project. Landscape architects should strive to ensure that the construction observation period is well funded so that the landscape architect can respond quickly and thoroughly to issues that inevitably arise in the construction field.

To that end, the contract agreement should include specific language regarding the construction observation scope, which outlines how to handle events related to observation of work and contractor interface. For example, revisions made to the documents to incorporate contractor-proposed changes should be performed as an hourly additional service and established in the contractual agreement. Additional site visits requested by the owner should be treated as additional service and invoiced on a time and materials basis. Preparation of as-designed and/or as-built documents may require significant hours by landscape architectural staff labor, so a provision should be considered in the scope of services.

RECORD KEEPING

It is paramount to maintain excellent records of correspondence and contractual agreements, incoming and outgoing correspondence, project information, and drawings and documents during the design and documents phase and into the construction phase.

The landscape architect will be called upon to provide backup to hearsay about conversations and "understandings" between various parties during construction. The landscape architect's job is to know the background of the design process, from the original concept design through preparation of contract documents and as construction progresses, and to rely on written documentation to support his or her recollections.

Project team members may change over the course of time, even on the owner's side. As previously stated, many organizations are set up to transition from big-idea people at the front end of a new project to technical, management, and maintenance specialists as the project progresses. Many original thoughts, ideas, and intentions could be lost in transition without careful documentation, and it is the landscape architect's job to be able to show evidence of the origin of ideas and how they are carried forward into the contract documents.

During construction, the contractor may try to "paper over" the consultant with requests for information (RFIs), submittals, memos, and so on to keep the landscape architect preoccupied. The intent is to keep consultants in a reactionary position defending their documents, when, instead, the landscape architect should be proactively observing the work in process and being mindful of the upcoming scheduled work. This is common on large complex projects where activity in the field is often accelerated or compressed due to tightening schedules and multiple contractors working in a constricted area. Careful record keeping and detailed workflow management are required to combat these potential conflicts.

A well-organized, automated document logging system should be set up at the landscape architect's office or field trailer location to record all incoming and outgoing correspondence. It is important to maintain a chronological and serial number record of when items arrived, with a date stamp, as well as when a response is sent out. To help clarify this process, provision in the project technical specifications should describe the required turnaround time for review and comment for RFIs, submittals, and shop drawings, usually measured in business days. Timeliness is paramount in the construction observation process, and the landscape architect may be called upon to defend his or her actions. It is common for designated clerical staff to log incoming and outgoing correspondence by date and type on a computerized list prior to passing it on to the landscape architect for further review. This adds professional integrity to the quality of the landscape architect's business procedures and promotes efficient access to recall needed information later in the process.

After the project is complete, the landscape architect should be the one with the best records to assist in resolving any potential disputes—the fact that they have maintained excellent records will lend credibility if mediation or other legal action becomes necessary.

SAFETY AND SECURITY

It is the responsibility of all persons on the project site to uphold safety and security practices. Even though the landscape architect is not involved in instructing the contractor in means and methods of construction, he or she should always be aware of the surroundings of an active construction site and be cognizant of his or her personal safety, as well as the safety of others. All of the persons working on the site, including the landscape architect, are responsible for reporting any dangerous situations observed on the site immediately to the site superintendent and owner.

EQUIPMENT AND CLOTHING

The landscape architect must *always* wear a hard hat, protective eyewear, boots, and long pants to access an active project construction site, per the safety standards set forth by the general contractor and owner. Additionally, the landscape architect must have the following on hand: earplugs, a mobile phone (or two-way radio), clipboard, digital level (inclinometer to check the slope of hardscape/formwork), camera, tape measure, marking spray paint (nonpermanent), rain gear, sun protection, and other appropriate clothing articles needed to walk the project site.

BIDDING ASSISTANCE

The scope of the landscape architect may include assistance during the preconstruction bidding period to represent the owner in recommending contractors, reviewing bids, and clarifying the construction docu-

Todd Hill, ASLA, EDAW

ments. This may include submitting a list of recommended vendors, suppliers, and contractors that he or she believes are qualified to bid on the project. The professional credibility of the landscape architect is considered by owners when making their decisions about contractor selections recommended by the landscape architect, so it is important to offer only qualified names.

A landscape architect versed in the preparation of the construction documents may attend or coordinate a pre-bid meeting to provide clarification and interpretation during the bid period and to represent the owner as a professional team member. At the owner's request, the landscape architect may also review and comment on the bid submissions regarding proposed bid costs, contractor-proposed changes to the design, and potential work relationships, prior to selection of a given vendor. (Also, see *Bidding* pg. 25.)

PRECONSTRUCTION CONFERENCE

Following the award of the construction contract, the landscape architect may attend a preconstruction meeting. The purpose of the meeting is to discuss the construction scheduling and sequencing, as well as address any open questions and coordination items brought up by the contractor. It is assumed that the meeting will be coordinated with the overall meeting schedule by the owner's representatives and to coincide with other design review activities. A provision should be made in the contract scope of services to limit the number of meetings and site visits so that this aspect of the landscape architect's function is not an open-ended responsibility.

OFF-SITE CONSTRUCTION OBSERVATION: SERVICES PROVIDED FROM THE LANDSCAPE ARCHITECT'S OFFICE

Before construction work begins in the field, significant up-front procurement and research are performed by the contractor to prepare the work. All of this should be logged and recorded in the files as previously described, both incoming and outgoing responses. The responsibility of the landscape architect is to compare the contractor correspondence for compliance with the construction documents and report back to the team on the findings. This is not a time to make subjective changes to the documents; once they are released for construction, they are complete and everyone on the landscape architect's team should uphold and defend the contents.

The landscape architect should be available to review and comment on contractor-proposed alternates and substitutions. Many times, the awarded contractor will try to save money by proposing an amendment or change to the documents. This may or may not directly benefit the project; for instance, the contractor may have found a less expensive unit price for a plant species not on the proposed plant list. If the team has a good working relationship, and the adjustment is minor, the change may be acceptable; but if it is not equal or an improvement, the landscape architect should recommend to the owner to not accept the substitution. Alternates and substitutions should be entertained only if they can be shown to directly benefit the owner and/or project. A written response should record the landscape architect's professional opinion, either pro or con.

PLANT PROCUREMENT

Following the award of the landscape construction contract, the landscape architect will assist the owner representative and contractor in the plant procurement process to ensure the availability and quality of the specified plant material. The contract should have a provision to establish a set number of nursery trips and duration for each trip and to determine limits of search area and region. It is possible, as a way to select plant material, to review some general plant materials (small trees, common shrubs, and ground covers) using representative photographs and information about the qualitative practices of the grower.

For specimen plants, unique species, large trees, and hard-to-find material, the landscape architect accompanies the owner representative and/or the contractor to visit qualified nurseries, collection sites, or tree farms to locate the plants.

Once trees meeting the specifications and plant list criteria are identified, a locking tree tag with firm name and serial number is secured on a branch to specifically mark each tree. The number and character comments are recorded by the landscape architect, as a record for the file, and copied to the team. Trees or plant material without these tags should not be unloaded at the construction site.

The owner may have to determine whether to make a cash or credit deposit to hold hard-to-find material, pay to have the trees "stepped up" to the next container size for later delivery as a larger caliper size, or to contract grow plant materials. The landscape architect should serve as an advisor in the discussions to represent the owner's interest.

ON-SITE CONSTRUCTION OBSERVATION

During the course of construction, members of the landscape architecture team will make visits to the project site to observe the progress of work being installed, including pedestrian hardscape, landscape, and irrigation installation. The average site visit should be of a predetermined duration, as agreed in the scope of services contract. Following each site visit, the landscape architect should prepare a field report noting the status of work in place, deficiencies, key photographs, status of stored materials, and review of mock-ups and samples.

Items for the landscape architect's observation on-site may include (depending on the specific contract):

- General overview of the work in process to observe compliance with the documents, make notes about job-site cleanliness and any apparent safety hazards, to consider upcoming work to avoid potential coordination issues and conflicts (beyond means and methods), and to note protection and maintenance of completed work prior to turnover
- Specific observation of esthetic grading for landform sculpting, and coordination with area drain location
- Formwork for hardscape paving to observe formwork prior to installation of concrete walls, curbs, and other cast-in-place (CIP) elements to ensure proper alignment, shape of edge (avoid kinks), cross slopes and primary slopes for ADA compliance, alignment, and connection with other work
- Approval of samples and mock-ups for finishes, color and texture, as well as compliance of work in place with the contract documents
- Observation of other hardscape site structures (within landscape architectural scope); carpentry, fountains, walls, fences, and so on for compliance with documents
- Irrigation mainline and lateral pipe routing, head layout, and testing
- Adherence of plant material to quality standards
- Tree and shrub placement, coordination with underground utilities, signs, and lighting to avoid conflicts
- Observation of planter bed line shape, and layout of plants at proper spacing and triangular pattern (may require the landscape architect to mark the ground with paint the preferred bed line and plant locations to illustrate to the contractor)
- Placement of site furnishings; coordination with signage and lighting locations

AMERICANS WITH DISABILITIES ACT COMPLIANCE

The Americans with Disabilities Act (ADA) is an important factor that directly affects the work of the landscape architect with regard to hardscape design. To avoid problems later on, the landscape architect should observe that the dedicated handicap route, as identified on the contract documents, does not exceed the maximum slopes and is properly laid out prior to installation of paving. A digital level (inclinometer) may be used to ensure that cross slopes of accessible routes do not exceed 2 percent, and that nonramp primary slopes are less than 5 percent.

The landscape architect may play a professional consultant support role to identify to the owner and contractor a reasonable construction tolerance for adherence and variance from the ADA guidelines.

See Section on *Accessibility* for specific guidelines and requirements.

SCHEDULING SITE VISITS

While it is generally not the responsibility of the landscape architect to control the construction schedule, it is important that the landscape architect be proactive in monitoring and contributing to upholding the schedule.

The landscape architect should avoid causing a delay in the construction schedule due to inaction or failure to provide information in an agreed time frame. By combining team coordination meetings with site visits, such as regularly scheduled monthly contractor coordination meetings, the landscape architect can streamline the construction observation process. Depending on the contract provision, the owner's representative and/or contractor should request in advance (agreed notification time) that the landscape architect arrange site visits to coincide with scheduled work so that observation of critical prior steps (formwork or plant bed layout review) be performed before permanent installation. In addition, the contract should clearly state a reasonable advance notification time (one to two weeks) before requested site visits, to avoid work disruptions in the field.

The landscape architect can assist in scheduling reviews to comment on progress, time to perform proper tree and plant procurement, and issues

Todd Hill, ASLA, EDAW

regarding plant installation and also to ensure that there is enough time for proper site reviews and punch list follow-up.

Some large and complex projects require a period of full-time on-site construction observation services, to enable the landscape architect to, essentially, be on call for site visits. This requires advance planning for efficiency.

FIELD NOTES

The more standardized the process of writing and collecting field notes, the easier it is to maintain good notes from site walks. It is common to use a formatted form for site visits, which has blanks created for various site visit data (date, time, temperature/weather); names of individuals contacted on-site; status of work being observed; and specific comments regarding work in place, potential issues coming up, as well as other significant issues. Attachments to the notes may be photographs, field sketches, or copies of contract documents to illustrate the necessary information.

The notes should be either typed or copied and distributed within an agreed time frame to the prime consultant and development team. Meeting minutes from contractor coordination meetings should also be recorded and distributed to the prime consultant and development team in a timely manner.

FIELD SKETCHES

Periodically in the course of construction a condition is encountered that does not conform to the contract documents of the landscape architect, architect, or civil engineer (or others), or it could be a combination of these packages not conforming to field conditions. Also, the existing site may be divergent from what was surveyed and represented on the documents. Whatever the cause, the landscape architect may be called upon to assist in resolving the issues in the field. The clock is running on an active construction site, with labor and equipment waiting, and it can be stressful to come up with a quick answer.

It is vital that the construction observation representative either be authorized by the owner and firm to make decisions independently or to record the conditions and solicit the assistance of others within the organization and development team to address the problem. The landscape architect should avoid being caught in a situation of directing the contractor to proceed with alternative solutions without the written authorization of the owner.

It is common to develop a field sketch or landscape sketch (LSK), which may be a single 8½ × 11 drawing, which incorporates many different drawing layers, to address one location while considering the other aspects of construction. For instance: A pipe is buried too shallow and the owner doesn't want to lower it, so the landscape architect has to essentially redesign the pedestrian pathway and grading to go over the shallow pipe—without losing the design intent. This could affect other elements, ADA, site furnishing, site lighting, planting, and irrigation. The drawings may be prepared by hand or in CAD, but the focus generally is on a specific condition. The LSK is transmitted to the owner representative, who reviews and either rejects or approves of issues to the contractor for a change order estimate.

RFIS AND CLARIFICATIONS

An RFI, or request for information, is a written question from the contractor regarding an interpretation of the construction documents. This is usually a non-cost-related question to clarify the intent of the drawings. A clarification is usually provided on a form on which the landscape architect answers the RFI to provide more information or explain the intent of the documents. A chronological record of RFIs and clarifications is logged into the landscape architect's file system.

DIRECTIVES

Directives are usually a noncost-impacting change issued by the owner to the contractor for minor adjustments in the field. The owner may request that the landscape architect provide recommendations regarding the directive. The contractor may try to negotiate a cost change associated with a directive (which would become a change order). The owner will try to prove why it is not a cost impact and may solicit the assistance of the landscape architect to support his or her argument.

CHANGE ORDERS AND CONTRACTOR-PROPOSED CHANGES

Note: A provision should be made in the contract scope of services to limit the landscape architect's open-ended responsibility.

A change order is a contract amendment issued through the owner to the contractor to alter the contract documents. It has financial impacts, either increasing or deceasing the construction contract amount. The proposed solution of an LSK or bulletin may result in a change order. It is the landscape architect's job to represent the project's interest in weighing the benefits of the proposed change to uphold the original design intent, enhancement of the overall project, or to improve efficiency or in some other way make it better.

Contractors may try to initiate a change order if they believe that the field conditions are sufficiently different from the contract documents, or if they discover errors and omissions in the documents. Often, a thorough review of contractor-proposed changes is performed by the design team to determine the benefit of the change to the final design. The role of the landscape architect is to counsel the owner as to whether the change will benefit the project as a whole and/or uphold the original design intent, and to determine if the change is driven by the contractor seeking to reduce their cash outlay.

In the event that the awarded contractor recommends to the owner specific changes to the design (beyond means and methods) that affect the documents, the landscape architect will be requested to amend the drawings. It is important to have a contract in place to address these potentially open-ended events.

The landscape architect is not authorized to approve change orders.

If it is deemed valuable by the team and owner to incorporate the recommended contractor change, the landscape architect should perform any amendments to their documents as an additional hourly service. It is potentially a volatile issue at the end of a project as to why change orders were required; and, in some instances, the owner may come back to the landscape architect in an attempt to be compensated after the fact.

BULLETINS

When a significant change to the documents is initiated once construction has commenced, and the amendment is more than can be covered in a simple landscape sketch, or affects multiple disciplines, it may trigger issuance of a bulletin document. The cause of a bulletin may be a program change driven by the owner, or discovery of a site condition that results in a redesign of a portion of the project, or an error and omission discovered after release of the documents. Beyond an error cause directly attributed to the landscape architect, the landscape architect should be prepared to negotiate an additional service to perform the redesign and document revisions for the portion of the project under study.

All changes are clouded (shaded or outlined) and numbered on the document, and the affected drawings for all disciplines are reissued for pricing to the contractor as a formal contract amendment. The prime consultant on the project, sometimes the architect, typically coordinates the team's bulletin package. This prime consultant may be the contracting entity with which the landscape architect negotiates any additional fee.

AS-DESIGNED DOCUMENTS

If the scope of services includes a provision for as-designed documents, the landscape architect will be required to provide in his or her final submittal, updated documents illustrating all actual edits and changes made during the construction phases. This typically includes updated CAD drawing files of all changes (clouded with date) and an updated specifications manual for all landscape architect-contracted scope items and subconsultants.

Preparing as-designed documents can run into hundreds of labor hours and can cost thousands of dollars. Therefore, as-designed documents should be carefully managed by updating the master files as changes occur.

AS-BUILT DOCUMENTS

If the scope of services includes a provision for as-built documents, the landscape architect may be required to provide the contractor CAD drawing files to update and edit reflecting as-installed underground elements included in the landscape architect's scope of work. (See *Overview of Construction Documentation* regarding role of record drawings.)

In some cases, the owner will request that the landscape architect perform the CAD edits based on drawing mark-ups by the contractor. In this case, the contract should be clear as to the roles and responsibility prior to commencement of work, as this may constitute an additional service.

PROJECT CLOSEOUT AND SUBSTANTIAL COMPLETION

At the point at which the general contractor believes they have reached substantial completion, they may request that landscape architect perform a final "punch"

Todd Hill, ASLA, EDAW

walk to review and identify deficient items that will need to be completed, repaired, or replaced prior to final acceptance. The landscape architect will attend a set number of site review walks for the project and prepare a formal written punchlist and associated map diagram keying the work to be completed by the contractor.

The landscape architect will attend a subsequent review walk, of set duration, to validate corrections and provide written comments to the owner's representative. The landscape architect should put limits on the number of iterations to review final work, or communicate to the owner that the project is not substantially complete.

PAYMENT APPLICATION REVIEW

The landscape architect may be requested by the owner to review the contractor invoices. To do this, the landscape architect compares the invoices with amount of work completed by the contractor to see if work has been satisfactorily completed and complies with percentage complete or if the amount is commensurate with percentage of work completed. The landscape architect then makes a written recommendation to owner regarding approval or denial of payment as requested.

The landscape architect may also be asked to review materials delivered to or stocked on site for payment. Photographs of the site-stocked materials should be attached to the payment application for verification in case the materials are stolen or removed.

OPERATION AND MAINTENANCE MANUALS (O&M MANUALS)

Projects include O&M manuals for many elements of the functioning landscape, and it is typical to provide information to the owner for ongoing maintenance of the following:

- Irrigation systems
- Fountains
- Lighting
- Plant pruning
- Plant maintenance
- Hardscape maintenance, finishes, and repair/replacement
- Site furniture, finishes, and repair/replacement

ERRORS AND OMISSIONS (E&O)

E&O generally addresses areas of the contract documents that resulted in mistakes or missing information necessary for contractors to perform their work. E&O are not caused by the intent to mislead; rather, they may be the result of documents that were not coordinated within the consultant team.

The outcome of E&O issues usually includes claims by the contractor that are initially addressed by the owner and prime consultant for resolution. In other cases, mediation may be required.

MEMORANDUM

EDAW INC.
THE BILTMORE
817 WEST PEACHTREE STREET, NW
SUITE 770
ATLANTA GEORGIA
30308

TEL 404 870 5339
FAX 404 870 6590
www.edaw.com

TO	Client Representative
FROM	Eric Bishop Ray Strychalski
DATE	May 26, 2004
CC	file
SUBJECT	Project Punchlist

Based upon an initial site punch on April 21st and a follow up visit on May 19th the following items were noted as needing correction.

1. There appear to be several issues with the finish of the colored concrete work throughout the plaza. The color is very mottled in appearance, and several pours appear to be entirely of a different color. Other issues were noted in a separate walk with Mr. Jones of Concrete Color Company. The items discussed during this meeting relating to the finish of the concrete on the plaza will be issued under separate cover as meeting minutes. (pictures attached)
2. Drainage problems were noted on the Southwest portion of the large circular (plan area C, 3.5) adjacent to the intersection with the smaller circular planter during the April site visit. Water was standing at the surface after a recent rain. During the May site visit, no problems were noted, but no substantial rain had occurred near the time of the second visit. Has this issue been corrected? Further observation is required. (photo attached)
3. Near the intersection of the small circular planter and the large circular planter, the wall has received a different finish and apparently a different colored concrete. This 'patch' needs to be of the same color and finish as the rest of the new walls on site. Other inconsistencies in the sandblast finish show within this wall section that need to be corrected. (photo attached)
4. The grading on the North side of the small circular planter has a slope that is far too steep. This area needs to be re-graded and re-sodded. (picture attached)
5. EDAW noted a possible issue with fall hazards on the small circular planter wall. This wall, although not intended to be a pathway, could pose an issue if people walk on top of it and fall. EDAW would like to review with the architect, possibly adding some railing at two strategic points on top of this wall. (pictures attached)
6. On the west side of the plaza, EDAW counted two fewer movable planters along the Client wall, than were previously counted. Were these planters removed to other parts of the plaza? In reviewing the overall planting, EDAW would also like to discuss moving four of the movable planters to the face of the national hotel on the Eastern side of the plaza. (Line up with columns)
7. The nosings for the stairs on the plaza were not installed according to detail 1/LS501.
8. The mondo grass in the small circular planter appears to be installed at 12" o.c. rather than 8" o.c. as per the plans. Contractor needs to verify that the quantity of material on the drawings was installed. EDAW will independently review in the field.
9. The large expansion joints that run through the circular planters are very roughly constructed. These need to be reviewed for possible fixes.

SAMPLE PROJECT PUNCHLIST LETTER

CONCLUSION

Observing the construction of a project is a critical step in the success of design implementation. The landscape architect responsible for this phase of a project needs to be knowledgeable about the original concept intent, have a positive attitude with regard to team relationships, represent the owner and documents favorably to the contractor, and stay informed about progress of the work being constructed in the field. The landscape architect should also be aware of potential situations that may result in contractual issues and should keep impeccable records. An adequate budget in the overall project agreement should be allocated to this key aspect of project process, as it often requires a great deal of time in order to do the job correctly.

Todd Hill, ASLA, EDAW

POSTOCCUPANCY EVALUATION

INTRODUCTION

Postoccupancy evaluation (POE), the study of the effectiveness for human users of occupied designed environments, is so named because it is done after an environment has been designed, completed, and occupied.

Unconsciously, in everyday life, humans evaluate environments all the time: which table to sit at in a restaurant, which route to take to work, and so on. And while buildings, for centuries, have been informally evaluated for structural integrity and other issues of design, it wasn't until the 1960s that researchers began to look at how well buildings and outdoor spaces satisfied the needs of users. This concern coincided with the social ferment of the times—consumer rights, civil rights, and so on—and a recognition that professional designers and planners didn't always know best.

The 1970s and 1980s saw the development of systematic methods of evaluation and analysis; the appearance of organizations that supported and disseminated this research (e.g., Environmental Design Research Association) and the publication of journals that released research results (e.g., *Environment and Behavior*, *Journal of Environmental Psychology*, *Journal of Architecture & Planning Research*, and *Landscape Journal*).

WHY CONDUCT A POE?

There are several reasons to conduct a postoccupancy evaluation:

- To generate information about how a facility is used—for example, the garden at a particular Alzheimer's facility.
- To generate a set of design guidelines—for example, a series of POEs for a particular type of outdoor space, such as downtown plazas.
- To provide information to guide the redesign of a park that no longer meets the needs of the neighborhood.
- To fine-tune a garden that isn't used as much as it might be—for example, a POE of a nursing home garden where lack of shade is the problem, prompting a redesign that adds a porch overhang, gazebo, arbor, or other problem-solving structure.

WHO SHOULD CONDUCT A POE?

Ideally, a POE should be conducted by a team that includes both social scientists and designers. And though it is desirable that designers conduct indicative POEs of their own work, to inform themselves of successes and failures, it is not recommended that designers do more detailed, published POEs of their own designs, as their evaluation may not be objective enough.

TYPES OF POE

There are three types of postoccupancy evaluations: indicative, investigative, and diagnostic.

Indicative POE

This type of POE can be accomplished in a short time span: from one to two hours to one to two days. Methods may include interviews with staff and/or designers, a walk-through evaluation, or use of an audit tool. This type of POE can provide indications of major successes and failures and is most reliable if the evaluator is familiar with the type of environment being evaluated.

Investigative POE

This type of evaluation is often prompted by issues raised in an indicative POE. It covers more issues at greater depths and reliability. The evaluation criteria are often explicitly stated—for example, the relative use by staff/patients/visitors of a therapeutic garden; or how well a neighborhood park meets the needs of nearby residents.

Diagnostic POE

This is the most comprehensive and in-depth evaluation, requiring considerable time and budget. To provide reliable findings, it is essential to use multiple methods—questionnaires, interviews, observations, physical measurements, and so on. Sometimes this level of POE is used to do comparative evaluations of several facilities of the same type. Recommendations are often aimed at improving not just one facility, but creating design guidelines for future facilities of that type—for example, outdoor spaces in assisted living facilities or therapeutic gardens for cancer centers.

POE Methods Methods for conducting postoccupancy evaluations include observation, analysis, and interviews, as detailed below.

Observation and Recording of Project Context

These activities would encompass adjacent buildings and their use, entries, and views into and from the space.

Site Analysis

A site analysis would record sun and shade patterns, prevailing winds, topography, and so on.

Interviews with Designers

Interviews with project designers makes it possible to document how client goals were translated into design. It also provides a way of understanding and interpreting goals that couldn't be met, budget problems, site issues, and other difficulties.

Interviews with Staff

Staff interviews—to include, for example, the activity director, facility manager, gardener, and others—are conducted to document views as to who uses the space and for what activities both programmed and nonprogrammed; to understand problems related to design, access, and so on; to listen to any additions and/or changes they would like to see, as well as space for activities desired by users.

Observation of Users: Behavior Traces

Observing a space for visible clues as to what users do—and don't do—which can be done even when no one is present. Clues such as, for example, cigarette butts around a bench, a short-cut path worn across a lawn, or raised gardening beds full of weeds, all tell a story. The location of these clues should be included on a site plan.

Observation of Users: Behavior Mapping

This POE method involves the systematic observation and recording of actual use at different hours of the day and different days of the week (e.g., 11 a.m. to noon, Mondays; 4 to 5 p.m., Wednesdays; noon to 1 p.m., Saturdays; 3 to 4 p.m., Sundays). Times and days might be determined in consultation with staff (at a staffed facility), or by casual observation at a more public facility, to ensure the major use periods are being covered. If the space being observed is used to a very limited degree—for example, the garden of a nursing home—the time period of each observation

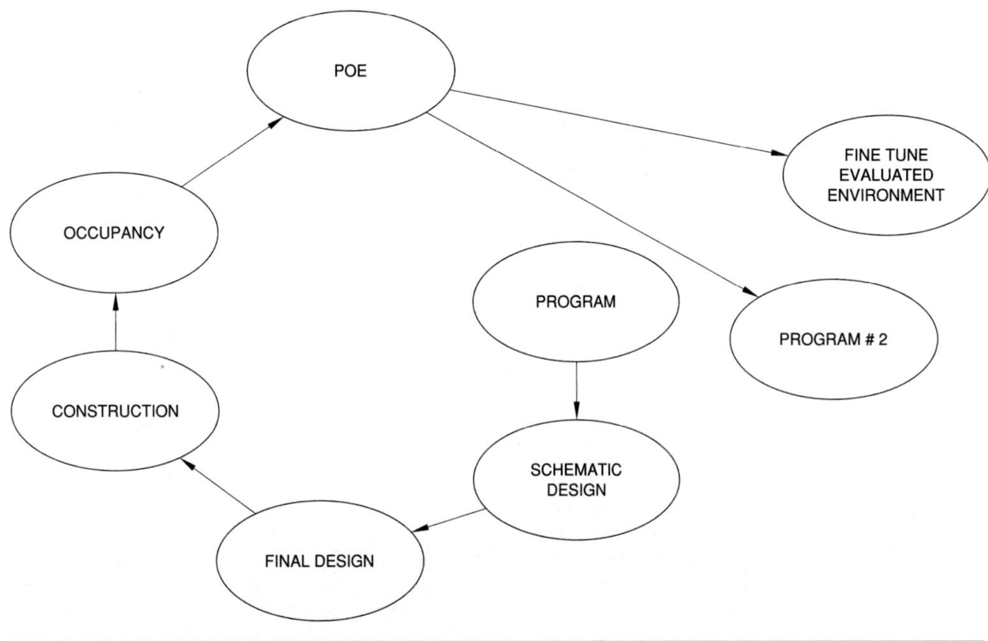

POSTOCCUPANCY EVALUATION DIAGRAM

Clare Cooper Marcus, Professor Emerita, Departments of Architecture and Landscape Architecture, University of California, Berkeley

might be one hour. If the space is heavily used—for example, a downtown plaza—15 minutes might be sufficient to record a typical pattern of use.

For each observation period, record all that is happening, as follows:

- Locate with dots on a site plan the exact location of each user.
- Number the dots.
- Record against numbers in a field notebook the age, gender, and activity of each user.
- Add arrows to indicate movement. Circle dots to indicate people in a group.

It is important to use a new copy of the site plan for each visit, as these activity maps will be used like stop frames in a movie. When all the observations are completed, the data can be aggregated onto one comprehensive site plan (typical pattern of use), aggregated by different variables (e.g., dot map of male/female use, adult/child use), displayed as bar graphs (e.g., of different activities, overall use by adults/teens/children), or displayed as a line graph (e.g., use throughout day). All the data recorded by this method is quantitative and is much more accurate than asking people. That said, this form of observation provides no information as to what people *feel*—why they come to this place. Hence, it is also necessary to conduct interviews. (See "Page of Field Notebook, Behavior Observations, Baker Beach, San Francisco, California;" and "Behavior Map, Totland, Berkeley, California.")

Interviews with Users

Interviews with users are essential to learn *why* they come to the space, *how often* they come, what they *like*, what they'd like to *change*, whether they *feel different* after being there (if yes, what it is about the place that helps them feel different). There are two basic ways of wording questions in an interview: multiple choice or open-ended. It is good to use both types.

- An example of a multiple-choice question is: "Do you come here more than once a day/once a day/once every few days/about once a week/less often." You check the appropriate box corresponding to the response on the interview form; data is quantitative.
- An open-ended question might ask, "How do you feel after spending time in the garden?" Write down all that the respondent says. This provides richer, more qualitative answers.

Later, you may categorize the answers (content analysis) and thus quantify the data. It is important to have two researchers do this independently to avoid a skewed analysis.

It is important to point out that the information will be more accurate if the researcher interviews users face to face and writes down the answers. Handing out questionnaires and collecting them later or having them mailed back is not as reliable. To be considered "scientific," researchers must interview a random sample: for example., every tenth person entering a park. Consult texts (e.g., Bechtel, Marans, and Michelson, 1987; Zeisel, 1981) regarding random sampling and interview or questionnaire design, as these important topics are beyond the scope of this discussion.

If possible, also interview nonusers. For example, a POE of the Children's Hospital in San Diego, California interviewed people using a new children's garden, as well as took a random sample inside the hospital. It was discovered that a considerable proportion of those interviewed inside the hospital didn't know the garden existed, which resulted in the hospital later adding signs.

POE REPORT

The final POE report should include data aggregated into maps, graphs, tables, and other forms; text analyzing data; quotes from interviews to "humanize" the report; a discussion of issues of use, overuse, lack of use, user benefits, nonconformities between what users want in a space and what is actually there; a discussion of nonconformities between what the designer intended/hoped would happen in this space and what is actually happening there; a discussion with management as to how space is managed/staffed/perceived; problems uncovered by the POE, clearly stated, and with proposed design and/or management changes to address each of these. The proposed design changes should then be illustrated on a revised site plan with annotations as to the reasoning behind each change. Finally, design/management guidelines should be proposed for future spaces of this type.

PROBLEM DEFINITION AND REDESIGN

As an example of problem definition and redesign, the table on page 32 lists problems associated with Boeddeker Park, in San Francisco, California, as identified through observations, data collection, and interviews with users; stated goals to mitigate the problems; and concrete solutions conforming to the goals.

An overview of these problems suggests that, primarily, adjustments in management are necessary and that the design of Boeddeker Park itself is successful in appealing to many users in both expected and unexpected ways. With changes in management, perhaps all of these subareas will be in greater demand and the users will better represent the makeup of their neighborhood.

ETHICS OF POE RESEARCH

Since 1974, the National Research Act requires approval for research involving human subjects. If the researcher works for a private design firm and has no affiliation with a university or other funding agency, he or she is not required to go through human subjects review. However, if the researcher does have an academic connection, it is likely he or she will need to have the research protocol approved by the institutional review board for human subjects.

The location of the POE is also pertinent: if it is a hospital or nursing home garden, for example, per-

PAGE OF FIELD NOTEBOOK, BEHAVIOR OBSERVATIONS, BAKER BEACH, SAN FRANCISCO, CALIFORNIA*

ZONE	BEACH	10/31/75	3:00 PM - 5:00 PM	5:00 PM	DAY OF WEEK: FRIDAY WEATHER: SUNNY, MILD						
SOCIAL				GROUP						ACTIVITY	MISC. NOTES (CONFLICTS, DISRUPTIONS, ETC.)
NUMBER	SEX	AGE	RACE	INDIVIDUAL	COUPLE	PEER	FAMILY	ORGANIZATION	NO. IN GROUP		
1	F	20	C	X						Sitting on beach against log	
2	M	20	C		X				2	Playing frisbee	
3	F	20	C		X					Playing frisbee	
4	M	30	C		X				2	Walking toward parking area	
5	F	30	C		X					Walking toward parking area	
6	F	20	C	X						Walking along beach	
7	M	40	C		X				2	Standing looking at water	
8	F	40	C		X					Standing looking at water	
9	M	20	BL	X						Jogging along beach	
10	M	40	SP			X			4	Sitting eating dinner	
11	F	40	SP			X				Sitting eating dinner	
12	M	40	C			X				Sitting eating dinner	
13	F	40	C			X				Sitting eating dinner	
14	F	5	C	X						Sitting on beach against log	
15	M	20	C	X						Walking with dog along beach	
16	F	40	C	X						Walking with dog along beach	Dog not on leash

**Adapted, original entries are handwritten onto base sheet*

Clare Cooper Marcus, Professor Emerita, Departments of Architecture and Landscape Architecture, University of California, Berkeley

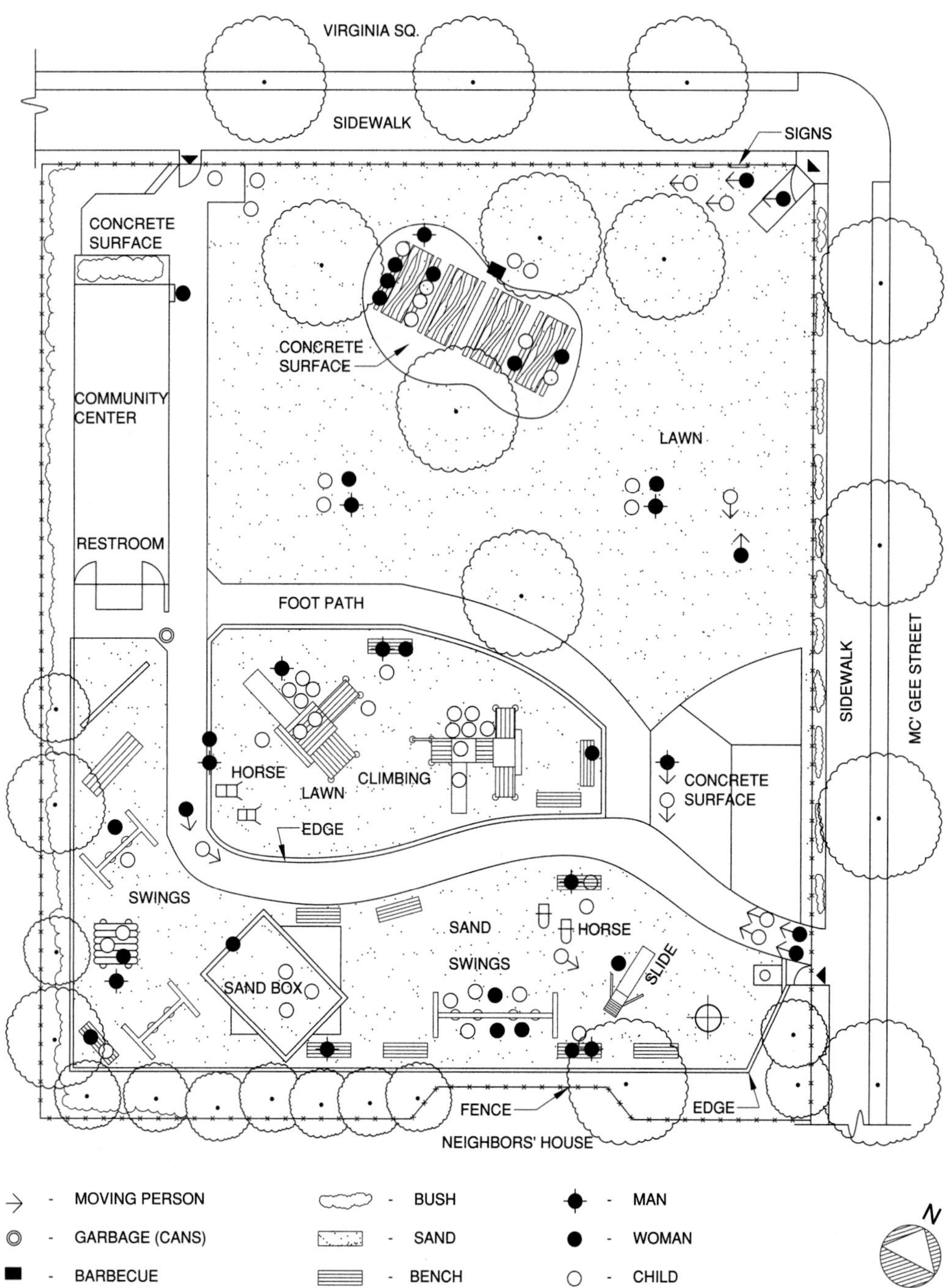

BEHAVIOR MAP, TOTLAND, BERKELEY, CALIFORNIA

SUMMARY OF PROBLEMS AND POTENTIAL SOLUTIONS AT BOEDDEKER PARK

PROBLEM (BASED ON DATA)	GOAL	SOLUTION
Children are not safely separated from "undesirable" users, e.g., prostitutes, etc.	Provide a safe environment for children to play in.	Reinstate a patrol to monitor illegal and unsafe activity.
The public bathroom is not efficiently located for the daycare group.	To accommodate the daycare group.	Placing a portable toilet would not be an ideal solution since vandalism may occur. Instead, the park director may offer to assist in monitoring the children when they need to be accompanied to the restroom.
Playgrounds can get too warm at times.	Provide shading.	Plant trees to cast shade onto the playgrounds.

mission from the institution would also be required; if it is a public park or plaza, probably not. The type of POE also matters: An indicative POE would not require approval; an investigative or diagnostic POE probably would.

REFERENCES

Research Methods

Bechtel, Robert B., Robert W. Marans, and William Michelson (eds.). 1987. *Methods in Environmental and Behavioral Research*. New York: Van Nostrand Reinhold.

Cherulnik, Paul. 1993. *Applications of Environment-Behavior Research: Case Studies and Analysis*. Cambridge, MA: Cambridge University Press.

Friedmann, Arnold, Craig Zimring, and Ervin Zube. 1978. *Environmental Design Evaluation*. New York: Plenum Press.

Marcus, Clare Cooper, and Carolyn Francis. 1998. "Post-Occupancy Evaluation," Chapter 8, in People Place: Design Guidelines for Urban Open Space (2nd ed.), Clare Cooper Marcus and Carolyn A. Francis (eds). New York: John Wiley & Sons, Inc.

Preiser, Wolfgang, Harvey Z. Rabinowitz, and Edward T. White. 1988. *Post-Occupancy Evaluation*. New York: Van Nostrand Reinhold.

Wehri, Robert. 1986. *Environmental Design Research: How to Do It and How to Apply It*. New York: John Wiley & Sons, Inc.

Zeisel, John. 1981. *Inquiry by Design: Tools for Environment-Behavior Research*. Monterey, CA: Brooks/Cole Publishing Company.

Examples of Indicative POEs

Marcus, Clare Cooper and Francis, Carolyn. October 2001. "Hospital Oasis," *Landscape Architecture*.

———. December 2001. "For Children Only," *Landscape Architecture,* Vol 95, No. 12, pp. 66–71, 85.

———. March 2005. "No Ordinary Garden," *Landscape Architecture,* Vol. 95, No. 3, pp. 26, 28–30, 32, 34–39.

Examples of Diagnostic POEs

Marcus, Clare Cooper, and Marni Barnes. 1995. *Gardens in Healthcare Facilities: Uses, Therapeutic Benefits and Design Recommendations*. Lafayette, CA: The Center for Health Design.

Project for Public Spaces, Inc. 1979. *The HUD Building, Washington D.C.: A Public Space Improvement Plan*. New York: Project for Public Spaces.

Whitehouse, Sandra, James W. Varni, Michael Seid, Clare Cooper Marcus, Mary Jane Ensberg, Jenifer R. Jacobs, and Robyn S. Mehlenbeck. 2001. "Evaluating a Children's Hospital Garden Environment: Utilization and Consumer Satisfaction," Journal of Environmental Psychology, Vol.21, 2001, pp. 301–314

Whyte, William. 1980. *The Social Life of Small Urban Spaces*. Washington, DC: Conservation Foundation.

Zeisel, John, and Mary E. Griffin. 1975. *Charlesview Housing: A Diagnostic Evaluation*. Cambridge, MA: Architecture Research Office, Harvard University.

Clare Cooper Marcus, Professor Emerita, Departments of Architecture and Landscape Architecture, University of California, Berkeley

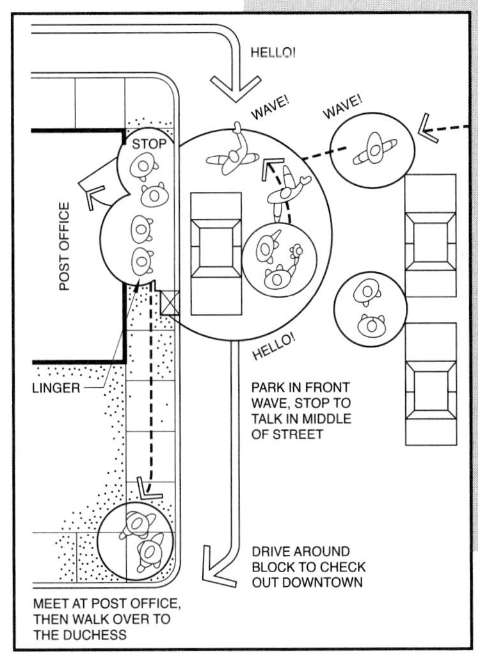

STANDARDS AND GUIDELINES

Part 2

HUMAN FACTORS

HUMAN NATURE AND SPATIAL RELATIONSHIPS

HUMAN MOTIVATION

Understanding human motivation and behavior patterns is essential to achieving socially suitable landscape design. Human factors determine acceptance or rejection of landscape technologies, green or otherwise. This section describes some basic principles of human factors, especially those related to ecologically informed landscape architecture.

BASIC PRINCIPLES

Sociopetal and Sociofugal Space

Every landscape design creates "sociopetal" or "sociofugal" space. Sociopetal space encourages face-to-face communications by inclusive form, archetypically described as an inward-oriented circle with a diameter of 6 to 12 feet. A fire circle, a semicircular bench facing the center, an enlarged path at an entryway, even a sidewalk bulge at a corner, increases informal social interaction. By the shape of the space, close eye contact and conversation are enhanced. In contrast, a straight line of benches or an outward-facing circular bench creates sociofugal spaces. This decreases interaction by reducing eye contact and conversation. Depending upon function, either or both should be emphasized.

Sociopetal space may be reinforced by concentrating people and activities, reducing distance and barriers. Social scientists suggest that, in America, more sociopetal space is needed in open space to generate a sense of face-to-face democracy and community; hence, the emphasis on using a round table as a means of small group problem solving, whereby each participant can see the faces of all other participants. Parks, too, need sociopetal space, to accommodate intimate interactions (½ to 1½ feet), personal distance (1½ to 4 feet), social distance (4 to 12 feet) and public distance (12 feet plus).

Public to Private Space Continuum

Although most open space is public, it is often sought out for privacy. For some people, open space may be the only setting that truly provides autonomy, a place for emotional release, self-evaluation, and confidential communication. Open space should provide a variety of settings, from widely shared public activity areas to those offering solitude, intimacy, anonymity, and reserve.

Motivations for Use of Open Space

Although landscape design is typically driven by a program of settings with square footages and aesthetics, people choose to use parks and open space primarily on the basis of who will or won't be there. If the people one wishes to do an activity with are likely to be present, one is likely to use that park. Conversely, if the people one wishes to avoid are present, one is unlikely to use the park.

Preoccupied with physical form, designers seldom give priority to the most important determinant of use. Every program of settings and square footages should be supplemented with projections of expected users' social patterns and their anticipated relationships. This typically leads to a better match between the potential landscape and the effective landscape. The potential is the landscape as designed; the effective is how it is used.

Social Ecology Maps

Every human activity has primary and secondary events that must be accommodated. For example, the seemingly simple event of picking up mail at the post office is much more than that. For many, the activity is more accurately described as "newsing" at the post office. Mail is exchanged in a matter of moments. More time is often spent chatting with friends and associates, catching up on local politics or gossip. This builds a sense of community and requires appropriate space for lingering comfortably near the side of entrances. Locating other public and private facilities within easy walking distance accommodates further discourse. Socially suitable design is based on understanding the nuances of anticipated activities and is best explicated for designers with social ecology maps based on careful participant observation or projection.

Territory

Individuals and groups claim territory in public open space. Seen from a positive viewpoint, their symbolic ownership leads to voluntary stewardship, personalization, and maintenance. It is important that public open space invite participation and be capable of manipulation. Seen from a negative viewpoint, territoriality may exclude others and lead to conflict. Such is sometimes the case with gangs and homeless users. Understanding the nature and extent of territories is essential. In the case of the Cambridge, Massachusetts Dana Park gang, mapping their territory explained violence between them and older park users and led to a design that accommodated the gang and multiple other groups.

NEIGHBORHOOD AND COMMUNITY

The Neighborhood Unit and Health

The neighborhood unit of 5,000 residents, living within a quarter-mile radius of a mixed-use center of stores, recreation, school, transit and jobs, is a century-old standard with new urgency. The quarter-mile distance provided everyday needs within easy walking distance of home. But today, because of land subdivision, few complete neighborhoods are being created. Most are simply low-density housing tracts without public and private facilities necessary to daily life. The lack of complete, walkable neighborhoods has been correlated to increased obesity, heart disease, and asthma, among other automobile-related health problems, as well as decreased sense of community and increased

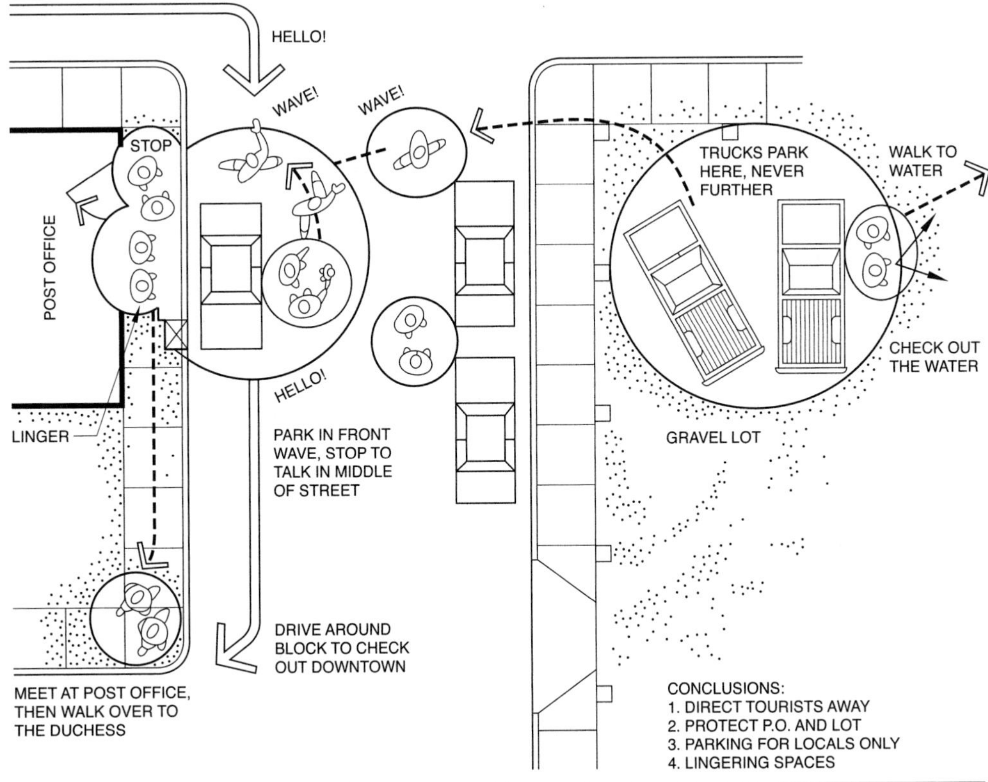

"NEWSING" AT THE POST OFFICE

Randy Hester

LAWRENCE ST.
PLAY EQUIPMENT
BASKETBALL STANDARD
BENCHES
CROSSWALK
BASKETBALL STANDARD
MAGAZINE ST.
ASPHALT PLAY AREA
CHAIN LINK FENCE
0 25 50 100
N

DANA PARK—EXISTING LAYOUT

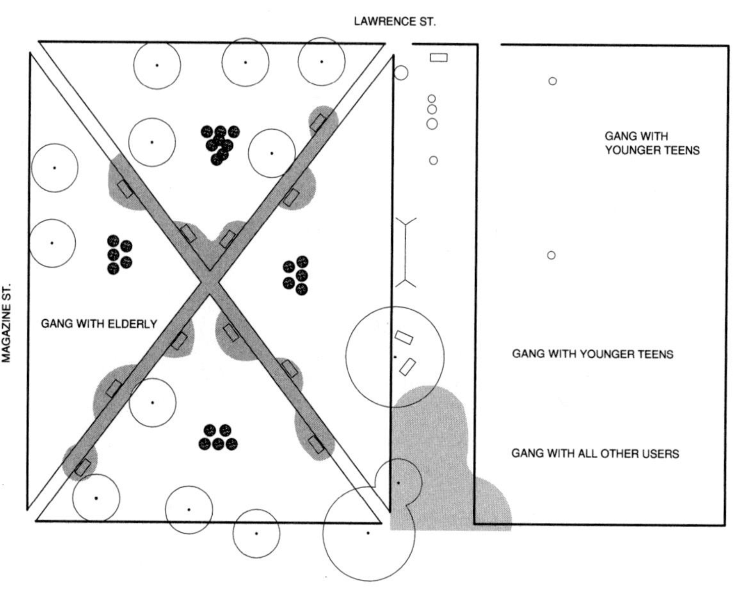

DANA PARK—USER CONFLICTS

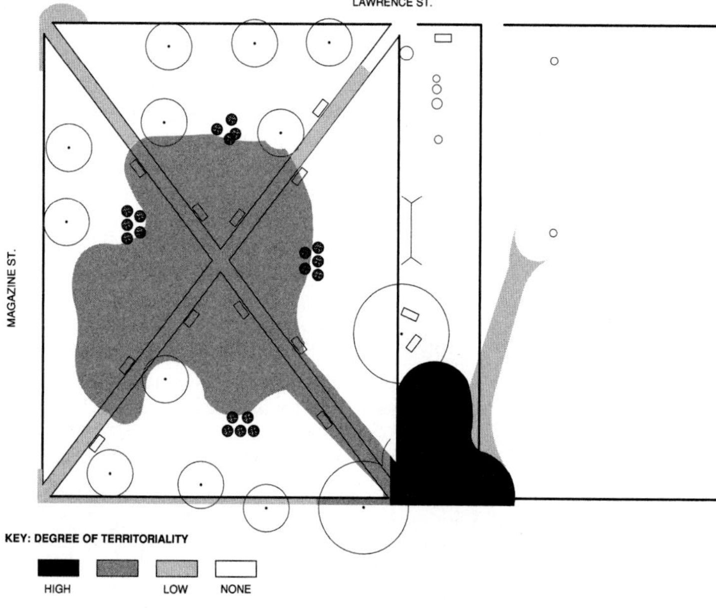

DANA PARK—DEFINITION OF TEEN GANG'S TERRITORY

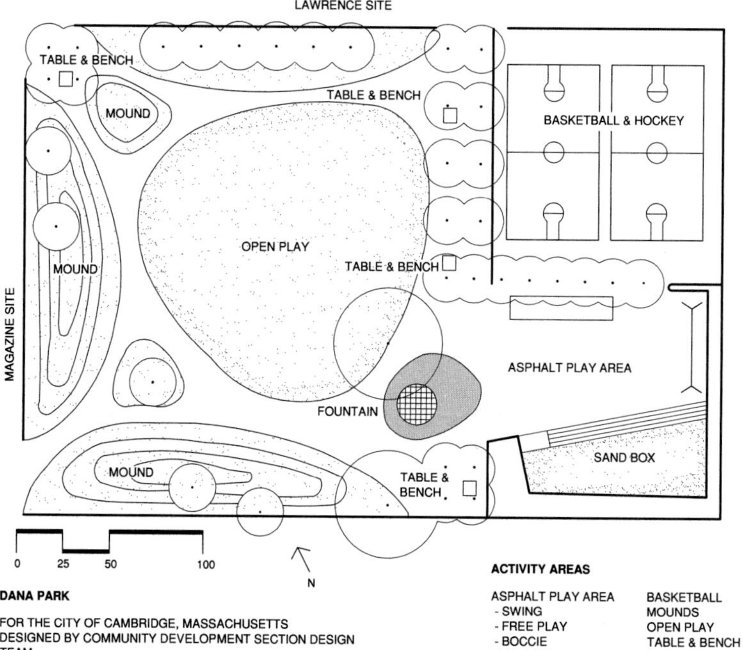

The proposed design incorporating the moving of sitting areas for the elderly to the side, relocating the play equipment, and adding a basketball court resolved many of the user conflicts while still allowing the teenagers to dominate their turf.

DANA PARK—PROPOSED DESIGN

sense of rootlessness. For these and many other reasons, the complete, walkable neighborhood unit needs to be systematically implemented.

Open Space Standards and Variations

Ten acres of open space should be provided for every 1,000 people (the professional standard), but social class and life-cycle stage of the community should direct the type and distribution of the open space. One size does not fit all in the provision of open space. As one example, due to social selectivity, upper-class residents typically recreate in backyard space more than front. In contrast, for reasons of sociability, lower-class residents usually inhabit the front yard and street for home-based recreation. In such cases, places for informal interaction close to home are critical.

Neighboring and Design

Although many social factors dominate, design also influences neighboring. As one illustration, busy streets prevent people from knowing people who live directly across from them. On less busy streets, across-the-street neighboring may be as frequent as side-to-side neighboring. For children and the elderly, the lack of safe pedestrian ways isolates them to a constricted home range. Different routes and destinations mean the neighborhood is defined differently by various residents. The neighborhood roves except where shared experiences overlap. For most people, the neighborhood is a primary political unit, the scale at which personal involvement is the greatest.

Community Welfare and Design

The most essential formal characteristics of the neighborhood are that it:

Randy Hester

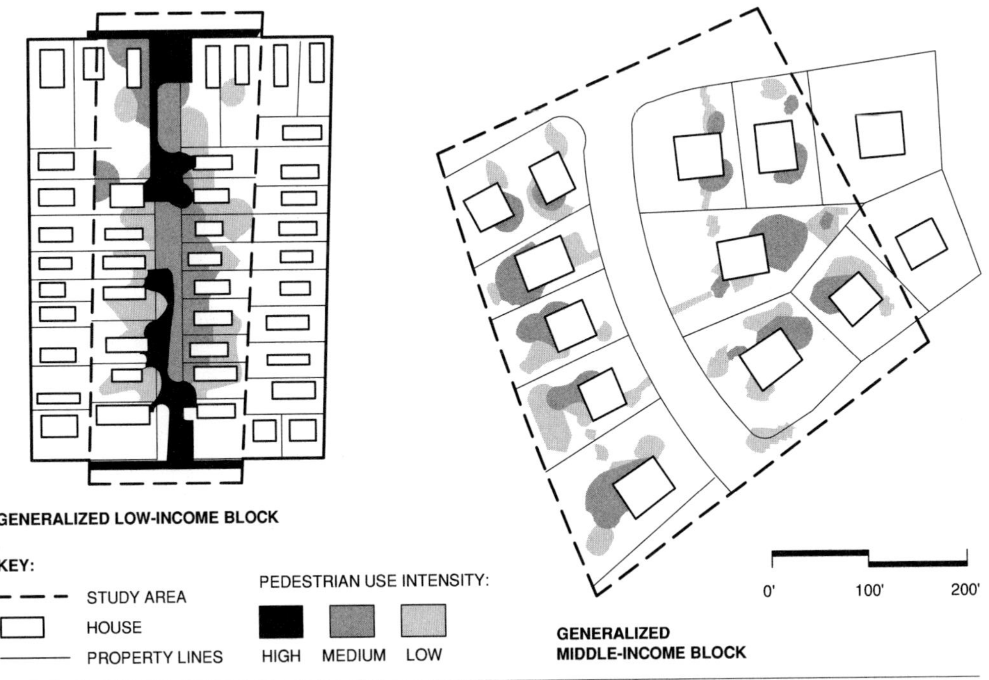

PEDESTRIAN USE INTENSITY OF VARIOUS HOME-ORIENTED SETTINGS FOR LOW-INCOME AND MIDDLE-INCOME BLOCKS

- Have a center with a great variety of activities.
- Have clear boundaries, preferably natural.
- Express its particular cultural and landscape identity.

These are fundamental to healthy human development and sense of community.

Of particular concern to landscape architects is the design of neighborhoods to reconnect people to ecological processes, such as watershed actions, and to life processes, such as food production and clean air. Providing these in the neighborhood landscape enhances ecological literacy and rootedness.

Environmental Justice

In most cities, the distribution of open space reveals a significant injustice, in that it is disproportionately available in wealthier neighborhoods. Given the impact that the design of neighborhoods has on human health and community welfare, it is essential that open space be fairly distributed, and that residents have equal access to, and not be excluded from, public places because of income, education level, race, or other social characteristics.

NATURE

Nature, Health, and City Form

People love nature and it is good for them. In fact, relating to nature is essential for healthy child development; and experiencing nature helps to keep adults healthy, strengthens concentration, and restores ill bodies and psyches. Nature even eases pain and dying. Although the idea of nature is a social construct about which there is much academic debate, it is surprisingly easy for people to define it and describe their preferences regarding it. Thus, designers need to interact with potential users to discover the forms of nature most essential to each project.

Historically, Americans defined nature as remote wilderness, something separate from urbanity and accessible only to some. What is most needed today is nearby nature, which can be experienced in everyday life. Cities need to be restructured consistent with ecological processes. Stream corridors, hillsides, and other functioning and connected landscape systems should form the boundaries of cities and neighborhoods, providing, among other things, access to urban wilderness within walking distance and public transport of every resident.

Childhood and Nature

Relationships with nature are particularly intense during childhood; hence, as noted above, nature is essential to childhood development. Nature play in youth has positive impact in adulthood in ways as diverse as reducing attention deficit and motivating environmental stewardship. Natural environments that nurture fantasy and cooperative play, role-play, construction, spontaneous creative play, wildlife observation, exploration, and mastery are important.

Plants, wildlife and other animals, water and earth, and prospect-refuges are all elements of favorite childhood settings. Natural places that children can manipulate and alter to suit their purpose, that can be perceived as adventurous, and even dangerous, are particularly formative. Therefore, designers need to create settings that are more spontaneous and less programmed. Safety concerns should not be cause for eliminating challenges and engagement with wild nature so necessary to healthy childhood development.

LANDSCAPE VALUES AND GREEN BEHAVIOR

Topophilia and Biophilia versus Placelessness

Underlying every behavior is a core value. One central value for every creature is survival of its species, which of course governs sexual activity. For homo sapiens, it also underlies sustainability and green behavior of every sort. For Americans, the core value for survival is in conflict with many other values, notably comfort, convenience, control, mobility, specialization, and status. All of these diminish "topophilia" and "biophilia," attachment to place and living systems, which are essential to sustainability.

Environmentally destructive behavior is most effectively changed through a combination of affective and intellectual processes: in short, by emotion stimulated by memory, imagination, direct experience, and by reason stimulated by new information and cognitive dissonance. Landscape architects can contribute to both the experiential (phenomenological) and informational (rational) realms. More importantly, landscape architects can create impelling alternatives that demonstrate the benefits of green lifestyles. In turn, these demonstrations serve as precedents.

Perceived Density: Phenomenological Experience in Sustainability

Increasing density is essential to creating viable centers, transit, and urban wilderness, and to preserving biological diversity, but Americans are prejudiced against housing they consider too dense. Actual residential density varies from perceived density, but only perceived density matters, because it can be lowered while actual density is increased. Reducing noise, traffic, and clutter; increasing planting in public places; providing views from residence to greenery; and providing even a small private garden space all can lower perceived density, thereby making higher density (15 to 20 units/acre) acceptable.

Wildlife Habitat: Connecting Affect with Reason in Sustainability

Americans value wildlife intensely and consistently support the preservation of critical habitats. Yet they also require freeways, to satisfy deeply held values for mobility and remote residential living. But freeways frequently cause island effects, which lead to the extinction of local cherished wildlife. By emphasizing the emotional attachment to wildlife, landscape architects can encourage public debate grounded in reasoned science, leading to well-informed and often sustainable actions regarding residential patterns, transportation, and urban form.

Status Seeking and Sustainable Precedents

Status seeking, especially the pursuit of bigness, remoteness, speed, rarity, homogeneity, and cleanliness, is destructive to the landscape and ecological function. Reasoned and joyful precedents of sustainable design can counter harmful effects. Only when people can visualize and experience alternatives will they choose healthy status-seeking options. As one example, demonstration gardens of native plants remind people of the beauty of local nature, versus the rare and remote exotic. Coupled with economic advantages of water savings and maintenance, native gardening is a relatively easy sell. Smallness and walking are more difficult to promote. But even here, delightful small houses with tiny garden views from windows and pleasantly landscaped routes to walk to work can entice some to make ecologically sound lifestyle choices.

Randy Hester

COMMUNITY PARTICIPATION

Citizen participation is an intentional engagement of the public in design, planning, and decision making. It is performed using techniques and staging activities to involve citizens on their own level while at the same time conveying the technical factors that landscape architects must consider in problem solving. The most common arena where the public is involved is in the planning of everyday environments, particularly park and recreation planning and design. Citizens also work with landscape architects on creek restoration, habitat planning, stormwater management, trail system layout, local economic development strategies, neighborhood infill projects, street design, and water quality monitoring.

BENEFITS OF COMMUNITY PARTICIPATION

Involving citizens in decision making about the landscape and its future is an essential part of the democratic process. It is also cost-effective because, more often than not, it expedites projects (as opposed to the alternative—not involving the public—which may result in lawsuits, recall elections, and so on). It usually improves the product and outcome as well.

Successful citizen participation requires a good process as well as a strong vision. Whether the landscape architect facilitates the discussion or articulates the vision is determined by local politics, in conjunction with the designer's style. Landscape architects are well positioned to do both: By virtue of the interdisciplinary nature of the profession, they are trained to visualize and to facilitate.

ORGANIZATION AND THOUGHT PROCESS

Effective community involvement requires more than showing up to a meeting with a flip chart and markers or a slick PowerPoint presentation. There are various models for leading communities in a discussion about the future. Probably the most essential ingredient is simply *to have* a process. Lawrence Halprin and Randy Hester are two landscape architects who have written extensively about the process of participation (see Halprin's *RSVP Cycles* and Hester's *Planning Neighborhood Space with People*).

An articulated process has many uses. It can be used in marketing. It can structure a proposal and contract. Timelines, budgets, and deliverables can all be tied to the process. Even Stephen Sondheim employs 10 steps when writing a song. With practice, a design team can estimate the preparation time, number of staff needed to lead a community event, the amount of meeting materials needed, and the level of follow-up required after a workshop. A clear process is also important for letting community members and other stakeholders know where you are headed, and when they are expected to participate.

There are two scales of process. One guides the overall project as discussed above. The other is the type that is applied to a particular event. The subject of how to conceive and organize a community meeting or workshop also has been written about extensively. For example, in *How to Make Meetings Work*, authors Michael Doyle and David Straus include, in addition to the nuts and bolts, great role-playing scenarios to help landscape architects anticipate sticky situations and learn how to deal with them.

Probably the three most important guidelines for meeting process are:

1. Start planning at least one month in advance.
2. Take the time to clearly define the meeting purpose.
3. Be sure that the meeting agenda ends with a "what's the next step" discussion.

SETTING A ROUND TABLE

The public is not a single entity; rather it is a collection of people with diverse backgrounds, needs, values, and interests. It can include powerful elected officials, residents of poor communities who have never participated in any kind of planning process, and everyone in between. It is usually the role of the landscape architect to negotiate these interests by ensuring that the process is fair, and open, and that all voices can be heard.

Consider this example: The landscape architect has been hired to redesign an historic park in the center of a city. It is likely that the local preservation society was instrumental in getting City Hall to appropriate funding for the project. The project has high visibility, so it is also likely that the mayor has a special interest in the outcome, as does the parks director. To be successful in this scenario, a participatory process would require reaching out beyond these obvious constituents. A logical first place to start, to determine who else should be involved, is to conduct a user analysis: Is the park being used by the homeless, teens, office workers on a lunch break, the weekly farmers' market, the annual 4th of July parade? User analysis might include person-on-the-street interviews or behavior observation (refer to *People Places*, by Clare Cooper Marcus and Carolyn Francis for behavior observation methods).

Common ways to notify the community that there is a project in the works is to post flyers, place articles in a neighborhood newsletter, or issue public service announcements on the local public TV station. But sometimes more effort and creativity is required. To engage children in the design of a neighborhood park, for example, you might have to observe, even participate in, their school and play games to learn what their park needs and preferences are. Or, to involve seniors in the design of a therapeutic garden at an assisted living housing project, you might want to share lunch with them or attend one of their weekly hobby classes. The point is, to provide everyone a "place at the table," you need to identify who should have a "place setting" and how to best make them feel comfortable and engaged in the conversation when "sitting" there.

KEY TECHNIQUES

Listening should begin every process. More than simply hearing, listening requires active engagement with a person. It most commonly takes the form of a focused interview, or it is sometimes conducted as a group session. Questions are posed to the participants to identify the issues, learn about the physical characteristics of the place and any current activity on the site, and to share ideas and dreams for the future. Listening is an opportunity to test out early ideas and encourage personal interaction with participants. By doing this, 9 times out of 10, they will be motivated to continue with the process, even when they are skeptical or hostile. Listening also guides you to fieldwork to conduct, maps to make, and data to gather.

The Nominal Group Technique, or NGT, is probably the most commonly used participatory technique, and one that has many applications. In its simplest form it is really nothing more than taking turns. To start the NGT process, the facilitator poses a question: for example, "What kinds of activities do you think should be allowed in this park?" Working independently, participants write down their answers. Then, one by one, the facilitator asks each person to say what is the first thing on his or her list. The facilitator writes it down and then asks the next person. This process is repeated until everyone has exhausted his or her list. Participants are asked not to comment on the ideas of others until it is time for discussion. During discussion the debate occurs. It is typical at the end of an NGT session to take a vote to establish the highest priorities or areas of agreement.

Goal setting provides a baseline for good planning and design, as well as criteria against which plans can be evaluated. Surveys and the NGT are often employed in needs assessments and goal setting. Taking the time to set goals ensures that actual needs will be uncovered. Subsequently, having clear goals directs proper allocation of funds.

Community workshops today often include a *design charrette* staged as a game. It also might include a *visual preference survey* where real and simulated environments are presented for community members to compare and make choices about the future. Architect Henry Sanoff, one of the early pioneers of design gaming, says that creating a good game requires being clear about the problem to be simulated, the people who will play, the rules that must govern, and the method of evaluation. He adds that testing a prototype before actually introducing a game or simulation into a community process is important. For more on design gaming, see *Community Participation Methods in Design and Planning*, by Sanoff, and *Visions for a New American Dream: Process, Principles, and an Ordinance to Plan and Design Small Communities* by Anton Nelessen.

In the early days of involving citizens in the design process, much of the work was centered on fighting the construction of freeways and the demolition of poor urban neighborhoods. Today, the application is almost ubiquitous. This means participants are more diverse, as are their needs. Likewise, the role of *community education* has increased, particularly as the design settings have become more complex. For example, restoring habitat requires a basic understanding of the principles of conservation biology. In order to weigh choices, citizens need to know, for example, enough about how many acres a mountain lion needs for species health and how many miles of wildlife corridor are required to create habitat connectivity.

Marcia McNally

A popular and satisfying way to teach citizens is on-site. *Walking tours*, much like hikes led by rangers in national parks, are an effective way to introduce participants to the nuances of a local ecology or to experience first-hand user conflicts that need to be worked out. This field-based learning has been extended to *stewardship projects*, where participants actually work on landscape restoration or long-term maintenance of a site. With the advent of computers, citizens are becoming more involved in monitoring the effects of landscape interventions. *Community sustainability indicator* projects have proliferated with Agenda 21 (the United Nations–sponsored plan of action to effect sustainable development globally, nationally, and locally), and landscape architects are often key players, whether as participants or leaders of the effort.

ACQUIRING PARTICIPATORY DESIGN SKILLS

Landscape architects who don't have experience or training in participatory design may be hesitant to join in this process, particularly if their only experience with the public has been difficult. However, today, requirements for participation are almost always mandatory, so landscape architects who don't have this training need to get it. Local universities, community colleges, and extension programs usually offer classes in public speaking. But more than classwork is necessary. One easy way to gain experience is to volunteer. There are community design centers and nonprofit organizations all over the country that are constantly holding goal-setting meetings or sponsoring visioning events, and they usually need people to help. And local chapters of the ASLA or AIA often run public charrettes to kick off a civic design project. These are low-risk ways to acquire participatory skills and overcome fear of the public and of conflict.

SOURCES AND FURTHER READING

The best facilitator in the profession is Daniel Iacofano. Fortunately, he has written a book on the subject: *Meeting of the Minds: A Guide to Successful Meeting Facilitation* (Berkeley, CA: MIG Communications, 2001).

The landmark book that lays out the art of dispute resolution, conflict mediation, and environmental negotiation is *Breaking the Impasse: Consensual Approaches to Resolving Public Disputes,* by Larry Susskind and John Cruikshank (New York, Basic Books, 1989).

Without basic "civic infrastructure" in place, visioning will not get very far. For the basics, refer to *The Civic Index: Measuring Your Community's Civic Health,* by the National Civic League (Denver: National Civic League, 1999).

Community graphics and mapping, and the technology to support them, are perhaps more familiar to landscape architects, but applying them in a participatory context may not be. For help in this regard, refer to *The Urban Design Handbook: Techniques and Working Methods,* by Urban Design Associates, for systematic application (New York: WW Norton & Co., 2003).

Knowing how to work with the media is an art, whether the project is controversial or there is simply a need to educate the public. Of the many books on the subject, *Culvert Action: How to Interest Your Local Media in Polluted Runoff Issues,* by Jennifer Kaiser, is particularly useful (Walnut Creek, CA: Lindsay Museum: 1995).

And the best source to learn about asset mapping, a proactive way to engage the public in early inventory, and goal setting is John McKnight and John Kreztmann's book *Building Communities from the Inside Out: A Path Toward Finding and Mobilizing a Community's Assets.* (Skokie, IL: ACTA Publications, 1997).

Other sources mentioned in the text include:

Cooper Marcus, Clare, and, Carolyn Francis (eds.). 1990. *People Places: Design Guidelines for Urban Open Space.* New York: Van Nostrand Reinhold.

Doyle, Michael, and David Straus. 1986. *How to Make Meetings Work.* New York: Jove.

Halprin, Lawrence. "The RSVP Cycles" (1969). In Swaffield, Simon (ed.). 2002. *Theory in Landscape Architecture: A Reader.* Philadelphia: University of Pennsylvania Press.

Hester, Jr., Randolph. 1982. *Planning Neighborhood Space with People.* Stroudsburg, PA: Hutchinson Ross,

Kaiser, Jennifer. 1995. *Culvert Action: How to Interest Your Local Media in Polluted Runoff Issues.* Walnut Creek, CA: Lindsay Museum.

Nelessen, Anton. 1994. *Visions for a New American Dream.* Chicago: American Planning Association Planners Press.

Sanoff, Henry. 2000. *Community Participation Methods in Design and Planning.* New York: John Wiley & Sons, Inc.

Marcia McNally

ENVIRONMENTAL FACTORS

MODIFYING SOLAR RADIATION

INTRODUCTION

Energy and light from the sun is called *solar radiation.* Climate stations record the amount of solar radiation received in different regions (see also *Regional Climate*). The amount of solar radiation received in a given landscape affects how comfortable people will be in outdoor areas, how much energy a building needs to maintain a comfortable indoor climate, and which plants and animals will survive and thrive in different areas. The amount of solar radiation received in different parts of a landscape can be modified through design.

The location of the sun can be readily determined for any location at any time. By knowing the location of the sun and the heights of buildings and trees, a *shadow diagram* can be generated to illustrate the areas of a site that will be sunny and shady at a given time.

STANDARDS

General Guidelines

The general guidelines for modifying the amount of solar radiation received in different parts of a landscape through design include:

- For landscapes in the northern hemisphere, orient outdoor areas toward the south to allow for maximum access to solar radiation.
- For cool season, allow unobstructed solar radiation to enter an area and be used to heat people, surfaces, and buildings.
- For warm season, provide shade to reduce the amount of solar radiation received by people, surfaces, and buildings in the landscape.

Shadow Diagrams

The sun moves through the sky in a predictable pattern. For mid to high latitudes in the northern hemisphere, the sun rises in the easterly sky and sets in the westerly sky and is in the southerly sky at midday. By determining the location of the sun at a given time on a given date, a shadow diagram can be generated to illustrate those areas of a landscape that will be sunny and those that will be shady at that time. This information can be very useful in identifying appropriate locations for various landscape features (e.g., an outdoor café to be used in a cool season should be located in full sunshine to increase the thermal comfort of patrons). The location of the sun can be determined through a variety of methods, including solar path diagrams, equations, and computer models. Many CAD and 3D computer programs have solar modeling capabilities built in.

Solar Path Diagrams

For many situations, solar path diagrams provide adequate estimates of the sun's location. Select the diagram that represents the latitude closest to the landscape to be modeled, and decide on a date and time to simulate:

- To generate the longest yearly midday shadows, select noon on December 21.
- The shortest yearly midday shadows will be on June 21.
- The equinox shadows can be generated by selecting March 21 and September 21.

It is often appropriate to select a time and date that an area will be used for a given activity (e.g., lunchtime use of an urban square).

Sun-Time versus Clock-Time

The world has been divided into *time zones* to allow synchronization of schedules. However, the time on the clock can be quite different from the actual *sun-time.* The difference between sun-time and clock-time can be determined by noting the time on the clock when the sun is due south. If the time on the clock is 12:30 when the sun is due south, then sun time can be determined by subtracting 30 minutes from the clock time.

This difference can be quite large, especially during *daylight savings time.* For example, clock time in Toronto in summer is approximately 1.5 hours ahead of sun-time. This means that when the clock says

SOLAR MODIFYING CHARACTERISTICS OF VARIOUS SPECIES OF TREES

The density of the shade varies with species. Some species (e.g., *Acer platanoides*) have a denser shade than others (e.g., *Gleditsia triacanthos* var. *inermis*). This table lists the range of densities, with and without leaves, of various tree species, as well as their approximate leaf period.

		TRANSMISSIVITY RANGE % (REPORTED IN THE LITERATURE)				
Botanical Name	**Common Name**	**Summer**	**Winter**	**Foliation**[1]	**Defoliation**[2]	**Maximum Expected Height (ft)**
Acer platanoides	Norway Maple	5–14	0–75	E	M	48–80
Acer rubrum	Red Maple	8–22	63–82	M	E	65–110
Acer saccharinum	Silver Maple	10–28	60–87	M	M	65–110
Acer saccharum	Sugar Maple	16–27	60–80	M	E	65–110
Aesculus hippocastanum	Horse Chesnut	8–27	73	M	L	70–100
Amelanchier canadensis	Serviceberry	20–25	57	L	M	20–25
Betula pendula	European Birch	14–24	48–88	M	M–L	50–100
Carya ovata	Shagbark Hickory	15–28	66	L	M	75–100
Catalpa speciosa	Western Catalpa	24–30	52–83	L	E	58–100
Fagus sylvatica	European Beech	7–15	83	L	L	58–100
Fraxinus pennsylvanica	Green Ash	10–29	70–71	M–L	M	58–80
Geldtsia triacanthos inermis	Honey Locust	25–50	50–85	M	E	65–100
Juglans nigra	Black Walnut	9	55–72	L	E–M	75–140
Liriodendron tulipifera	Tulip Tree	10	69–78	M–L	M	85–140
Picea pungens	Colorado Spruce	13–28	13–28			85–130
Pinus strobus	White Pine	25–30	25–30			75–140
Platanus acerifolia	London Plane Tree	11–17	46–64	L	M–L	100–110
Populus deltoides	Cottonwood I	0–20	68	E	M	75–100
Populus tremuloides	Trembling Aspen	20–33	*	E	M	40–48
Quercus alba	White Oak	13–38	*	M	M	75–100
Quercus rubra	Red Oak	12–23	70–81	M	M	75–100
Tilia cordata	Littleleaf Linden	7–22	46–70	L	E	58–68
Ulmus americana	American Elm	13	63–89	M	M	58–75

[1]Foliation: E = Early = Before April 30; M = Middle = May 1–15; L = Late = After May 15

[2]Defoliation: E = Early = Before November 1; M = Middle = November 1–30; L = Late = After November 30

**No data available*

Dr. Robert D. Brown, University of Guelph, Guelph, Ontario, Canada; Robert T. LeBlanc, Ekistics Planning and Design, Dartmouth, Nova Scotia, Canada

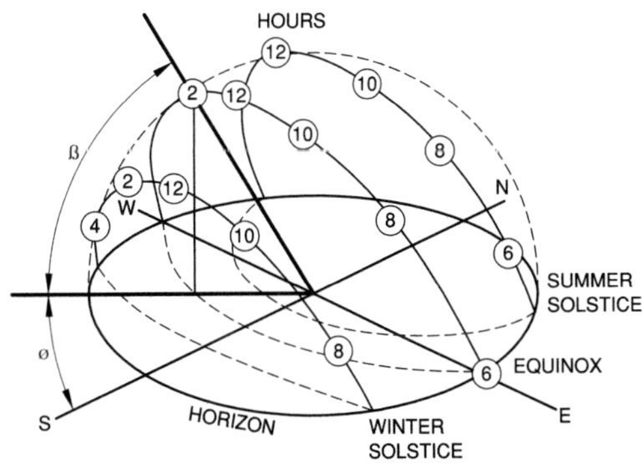

This diagram illustrates the movement of the sun through the sky at different times of the year. The winter solstice occurs on or near December 21 each year, and this is the time of year when the sun is lowest in the sky in the northern hemisphere. The sun rises in the southeast, and passes low through the southern sky, setting in the southwest. The numbers on the line represent the time of day (8 inside a circle represents 8:00 A.M.) The summer solstice occurs on or near June 21 each year, and this is the time of year when the sun is highest in the sky in the northern hemisphere. The sun rises in the northeast and sets in the northwest. At the spring and fall equinox (on or near March 21 and September 21 each year) the sun rises in the due east and sets due west everywhere in the world.

SEASONAL MOVEMENT OF THE SUN

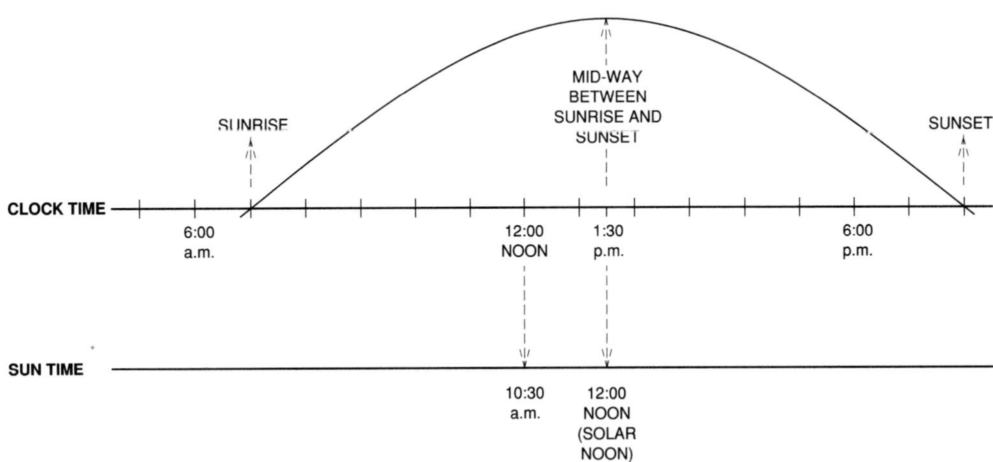

Mark the time that the sun rises and sets on the line. Sun-time noon (solar noon) will be midway between these two points.

SIMPLE METHOD FOR ESTIMATING SUN-TIME FROM CLOCK-TIME

12:00 and people are looking for a place to sit outside and have lunch, the sun is actually at 10:30 solar-time. In order to design areas that will be in the sun or in the shade during lunch, it would be necessary to consider the period of, say, 10:30 to 11:30 sun-time in order to accommodate 12:00 to 1:00 clock-time.

A simple way to determine the difference is to note the time of sunrise and sunset. This information is often provided in weather forecasts. Solar noon will be approximately halfway between these two times. So, if the sun rises at 6:30 A.M. and sets at 6:30 P.M., then solar noon would be at 12:30 P.M. To reduce confusion, a simple diagram can be used to illustrate and determine the relationship between sun-time and clock-time.

Determining the Location of the Sun

Two values are used to describe the location of the sun: the height of the sun above the horizon (called the *altitude*) and the location of the sun relative to the compass (called the *azimuth*). Consider the situation of an urban square (latitude 44°N) intended to be used as late as possible into the fall season (say, until late in October). As the weather turns cooler, a person's thermal comfort will generally be enhanced by receiving more solar radiation. By locating sitting areas in full sun during the fall and spring, those locations will be more comfortable. In this case, October 21 at noon (say, 11:00 A.M. sun-time) might be selected to generate a shadow diagram.

The steps for this process are as follows:

1. Select the 44°N solar path diagram and locate the line labeled October 21 and trace it across the diagram until you reach the line labeled 11:00. Note that this point intersects with two other sets of lines: the *concentric circles* and the *spokes* from the center of the diagram toward the edge. From the concentric circles, read the approximate *altitude* of the sun (in this case, about 32° above the horizon). From the spokes, read off the *azimuth* of the sun (in this case, about 17° east of south).
2. On the site plan, draw lines from all structures and vegetation *directly away from* the position of the sun. In this case, the lines would run 17° west of north.
3. Determine the length of each line using the relationship: length of shadow (s) = height of feature (h) / tangent of the altitude (tan alt). For a building that is 40 feet tall, the length of the shadow (s) will be 40 feet divided by tangent of 32° = 64.5 feet in length. There are two simple approaches to determining the lengths of shadows quickly once you reach this point. One is to determine the value of tan alt (in this case, it is tangent of 32°, or approximately 0.62). The height of every element in the landscape can be divided by 0.62 to give an estimate of the length of the shadow. The other approach, using multiplication, is to calculate 1/tan alt (in this case 1/0.62 = 1.61, which is approximately 1.6) and multiply the heights of all landscape elements by this value to determine shadow lengths. In this example, the length of each shadow is 1.6 times the height of the object.

Using Equations to Determine Location of the Sun

The altitude (a) of the sun can be determined using the equation:

$$\sin(\text{altitude}) = \sin(\text{latitude})\sin(\text{declination}) + \cos(\text{latitude})\cos(\text{declination})\cos 15(\text{time} - \text{solar noon})$$

Or, in shortened form:

$$\sin(a) = \sin(l)\sin(d) + \cos(l)\cos(d)\cos(15(t - n))$$

where:

l = Latitude of the test location in degrees

d = Declination angle in degrees (read off Sun Declination diagram)

t = Time of day in hours and decimals of hours using a 24-hour clock

n = Solar noon, the time that the sun is due south at the test location

For 9:30 A.M. on June 1 at latitude 42°N, the inputs would be:

l = 42; d = 22; t = 9.5 (for 9 ½ hours)
n = 12

Then sin(a)=0.797 and, therefore, e=inverse sin(a) = 52.8°. This means that the elevation of the sun would be approximately 53° above the horizon.

The azimuth (az) of the sun can be calculated using sin (az) = cos (d) sin (15(t – n))/cos(a). In the example above, the azimuth would be –69.7°, or approximately 70° east of south.

Using Computer Software to Determine Location of the Sun

There are various computer software packages, such as SketchUp and LightWave, that will calculate the position of the sun and the locations of shadows automatically.

Dates and Times for Shadow Illustrations

The date and time selected for illustrating shadows depends on the intended use. For example, for a city plaza that is intended to provide lunchtime sitting for local office workers, generate three shadow diagrams: June 21 at noon to illustrate the shortest shadows of the year; March 21 at noon to illustrate the shadows in early spring; and December 21 at noon to illustrate a late fall/early winter day when the shadows are the longest noontime shadows of the year. Alternatively, for an area to be used by children for after-school activities, it might be more appropriate to generate shadows for 4:00 or 5:00 P.M. on September 21 (same sun angle as March 21) to represent early fall (and early spring).

Important dates in the solar calendar that are useful in representing different periods are:

Dr. Robert D. Brown, University of Guelph, Guelph, Ontario, Canada; Robert T. LeBlanc, Ekistics Planning and Design, Dartmouth, Nova Scotia, Canada

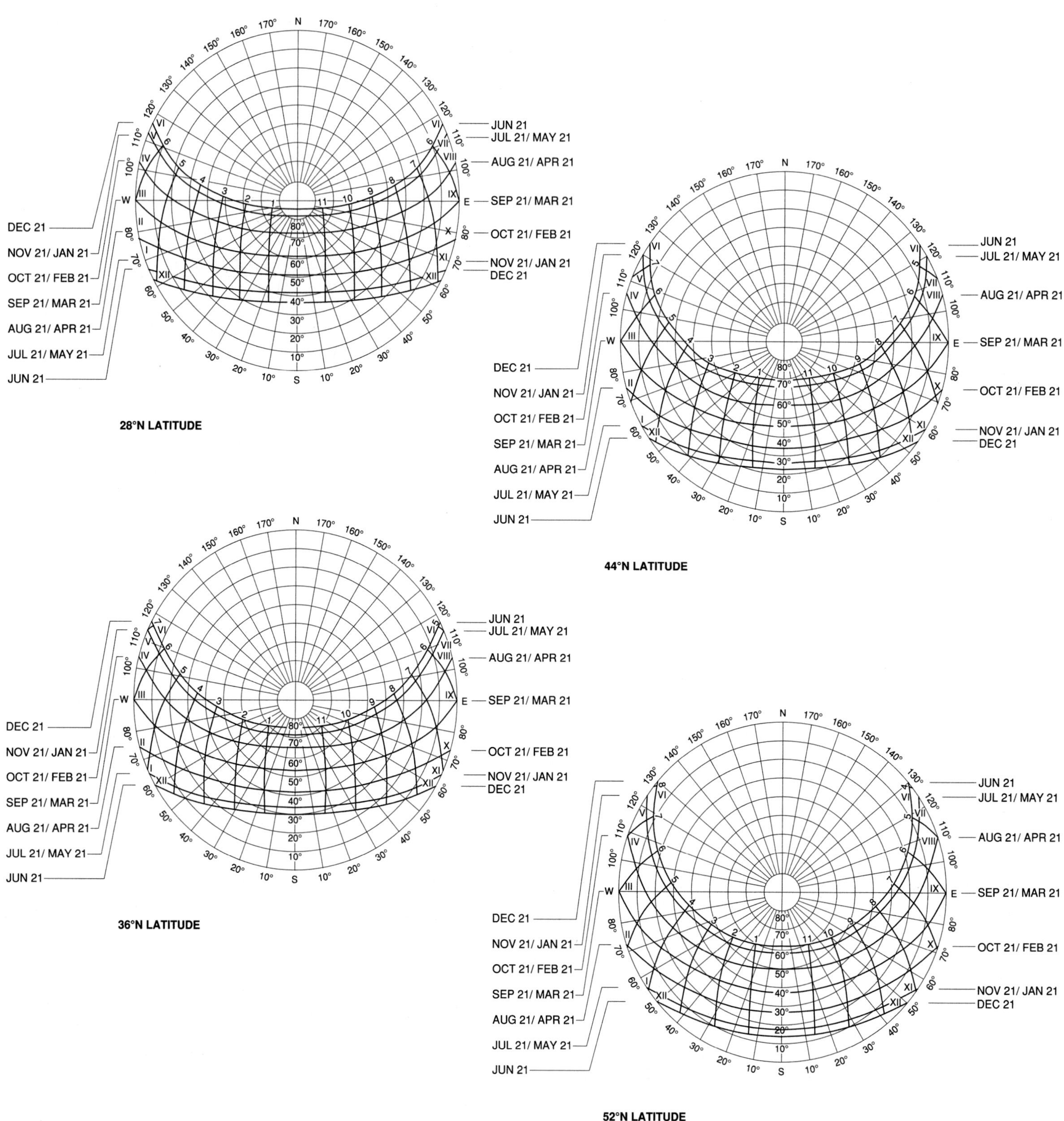

SUN PATH DIAGRAMS

Dr. Robert D. Brown, University of Guelph, Guelph, Ontario, Canada; Robert T. LeBlanc, Ekistics Planning and Design, Dartmouth, Nova Scotia, Canada

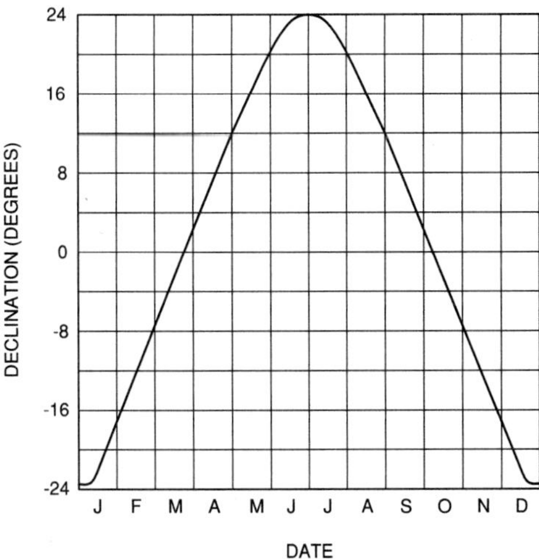

The declination of the sun can be determined from this diagram. The first letter of each month is listed across the bottom of the graph, and the declination in degrees is listed along the side. Find the date you are interested in and read the sun's declination angle off the graph.

SUN DECLINATION

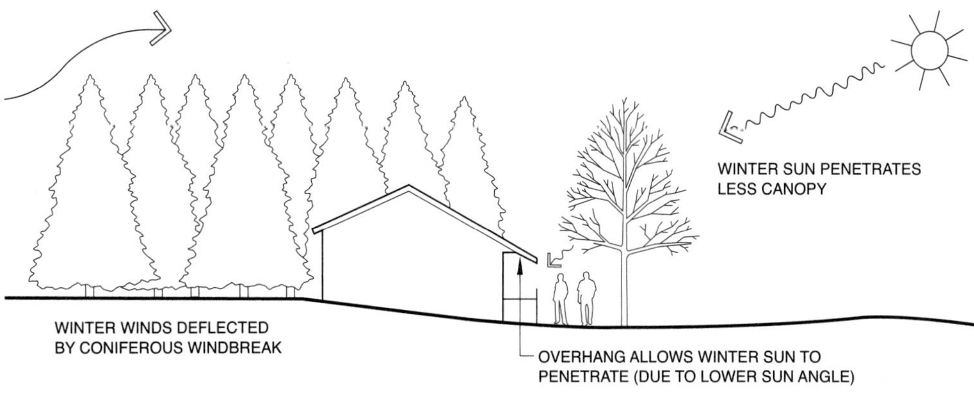

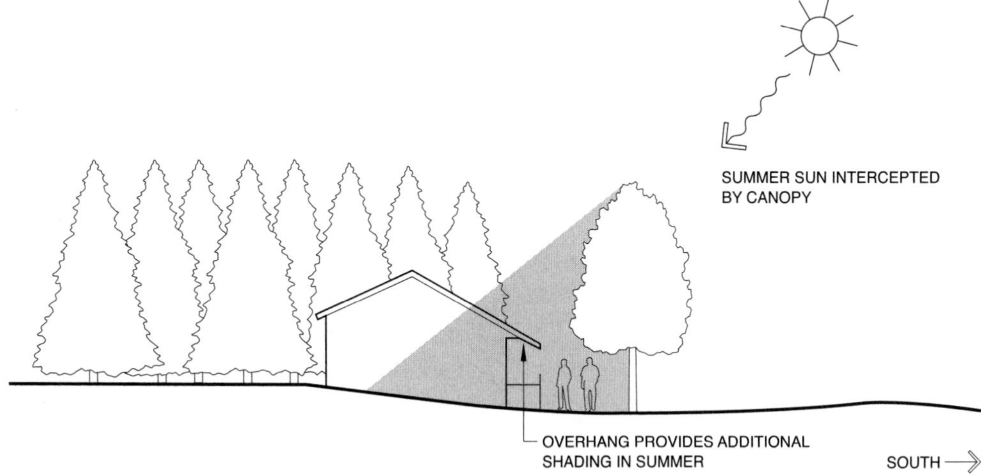

The amount of solar radiation received by people or objects in the landscape can be increased or decreased through strategic site design. During cool seasons, people will receive high levels of solar radiation in areas that are also sheltered from prevailing winter winds. During warm seasons, people will be able to sit or stand in dense shade, a more thermally comfortable microclimate.

SEASONAL MODIFICATIONS OF SOLAR RADIATION

- *June 21*. Summer solstice, when noontime shadows are the shortest of the year, and the sun rises earliest and sets latest in the year.
- *December 21*. Winter solstice, when noontime shadows are the longest of the year, and the sun rises latest and sets earliest in the year.
- *September 21 and March 21*. Fall and spring equinoxes, when there is equal amounts of day and night, and the sun rises due east and sets due west.
- *November 6 and February 6 (same sun angle)*. Mid-fall and mid-winter, which are representative of fall and winter shadows.
- *May 6 and August 6 (same sun angle)*. Mid-spring and mid-summer, which are representative of spring and summer shadows.

STANDARD APPROACHES FOR MODIFYING SOLAR RADIATION

General Guidelines

Standard approaches for modifying solar radiation include:

- Locate objects in the landscape so that their shadows fall on areas that will benefit from a reduction in solar radiation (lower levels of heat and/or light); and allow solar radiation to enter areas that will benefit from the added heat and/or light.
- Select the density of objects to provide the desired level of shade. Generally, the level of solar radiation will be lowest in the shade of buildings and solid objects; low under densely leafed trees; moderate under lightly-leafed trees, and approaching full sun levels under leafless deciduous trees.
- Increase the amount of solar radiation received by an area through reflection. Light-colored and shiny surfaces will reflect much of the solar radiation they receive, and this can be directed toward areas that would benefit from increased solar radiation.
- In designs, consider modification of both solar radiation and wind (see also *Modifying Wind*) to provide the most beneficial microclimates (see also *Modifying Microclimates*).

LIMITATIONS

Caution must be exercised in interpreting shadow diagrams, because they provide a *static view* of a *dynamic process*. The sun is moving continuously and shadows are constantly changing. Also, due to the unpredictable nature of weather, there are no guarantees that the sun will shine on any given day.

EMERGING ALTERNATIVE APPROACHES

With increases in computer speed and memory, modeling and simulation are becoming more reasonable alternatives. For complex landscapes (such as one building casting a shadow onto another building, or sloping roofs of buildings casting complex shadows), it is often worthwhile to use computer programs that both calculate the position of the sun and shadows and illustrate the resulting shadows through a time-lapse simulation. This process can be used to illustrate the solar access to an area over a period of time in a way that is very understandable.

ADDITIONAL APPLICATIONS

Strategic modification of solar radiation can also be beneficial for:

- Active and passive solar heating of buildings
- Survival of plants
- Habitat for animals

RESOURCES

Brown, G. Z., and M. DeKay. 2001. *Sun, Wind & Light: Architectural Design Strategies* (2nd ed.). New York: John Wiley & Sons, Inc.

Brown, Robert D., and Terry J. Gillespie. 1995. *Microclimatic Landscape Design: Creating Thermal Comfort and Energy Efficiency*. New York: John Wiley & Sons, Inc.

Oke, T. R. 1987. *Boundary Layer Climates*. New York: Routledge.

See also:

Modifying Air Quality
Modifying Microclimates
Modifying Wind
Regional Climate

Dr. Robert D. Brown, University of Guelph, Guelph, Ontario, Canada; Robert T. LeBlanc, Ekistics Planning and Design, Dartmouth, Nova Scotia, Canada

MODIFYING WIND

INTRODUCTION

Air moves from areas of high pressure to areas of low pressure, and in doing so creates wind. The wind varies in direction of flow and strength throughout the day and through the year. Climate stations record wind speed and direction on an hourly basis, and these values are generally available (see *Regional Climate*). The wind does not normally blow equally from all directions, but often comes predominantly from one direction. This dominant direction is known as the "prevailing wind" or "dominant wind." The amount of time that the wind blows from each direction can be illustrated by a "wind rose." Wind patterns that have been observed in the past generally provide a reasonable estimate of wind patterns that can be expected to occur in future.

As wind moves through a landscape, it is modified by objects that it encounters. Solid objects, such as buildings, affect the wind differently from porous objects, such as tree canopies. The wind will heat or cool objects it encounters (including people, buildings, plants, etc.) depending on the relative temperature. If the air is cooler than a person, for example, the air will have a cooling effect. The greater the difference in temperature between the air and the object, the greater the cooling effect. For this reason, the wind is a very effective cooling agent during winter when the temperature difference between a person and the air is at a maximum. This is often described as "windchill" in weather forecasts. In warmer weather, though, when the air is at or near the temperature of a person, the cooling effect is minimized. This means that designs for areas to be used in cool seasons should focus on reducing wind speed. However, areas to be used in hot seasons will be less substantially improved by increasing the wind. Areas to be used in hot seasons are more effectively cooled by providing shade (see *Modifying Solar Radiation*) than by increasing wind.

Other reasons to modify wind in the landscape include strategic diversion or deposition of snow or sand carried by the wind, dissipation of air pollution (see *Modifying Air Quality*), and energy conservation in buildings.

Wind in a landscape can be readily modified by design. It is quite easy to reduce, but difficult to increase, wind speed in an area. Wind diagrams can be generated to illustrate areas that are inherently appropriate for use in different seasons.

STANDARDS

General Guidelines

General guidelines for modifying wind for design purposes include:

- Orient outdoor areas away from prevailing cool season winds.
- For areas to be used in cool seasons, provide upwind barriers perpendicular to prevailing seasonal winds.
- For areas to be used in warm seasons, do not block, and if possible increase, prevailing seasonal winds.

Regional Winds

Wind data from a climate station (see *Regional Climate*) can be tabulated for different time periods. Yearly data will often yield patterns that are different from seasonal patterns.

These tabulated data can be illustrated as a wind rose by drawing the length of each line proportional to the amount of time the wind blows from that direction. These patterns often change with the season, and in general it is the wind patterns during cool to cold periods that are the most important when designing outdoor areas.

Local Winds

The wind that has been measured at a climate station provides a view of the general wind patterns of a region, but these patterns are modified at a local scale by elements of a landscape. At present, the most effective way to determine local winds in a landscape is to build a scale model and test it in a wind tunnel; however, this can be expensive and time-consuming. Computer models currently are not available for use in simulating wind in a complex landscape.

A less expensive, but also less accurate, approach to estimating local winds in a landscape is to use empirically based diagrams. Over time people have

TABLE OF CLIMATE STATION DATA

Wind data from a climate station can be tabulated in a format that is useful in design. Some standard approaches include the percentage of the time that the wind blows from each direction by season (columns 1 through 4) and throughout the year (column 5).

	PERCENTAGES				
	1	2	3	4	5
	Winter	Spring	Summer	Fall	Year
N	19.3	19.8	15.5	17.6	18.0
NE	4.7	5.6	3.5	4.5	4.6
E	4.9	5.4	3.1	4.6	4.5
SE	8.6	11.9	8.2	8.4	9.3
S	12.6	20.6	25.7	14.9	18.5
SW	11.7	13.2	20.1	15.2	15.1
W	17.6	10.8	12.1	16.8	14.3
NW	20.6	12.6	11.8	18.1	15.8

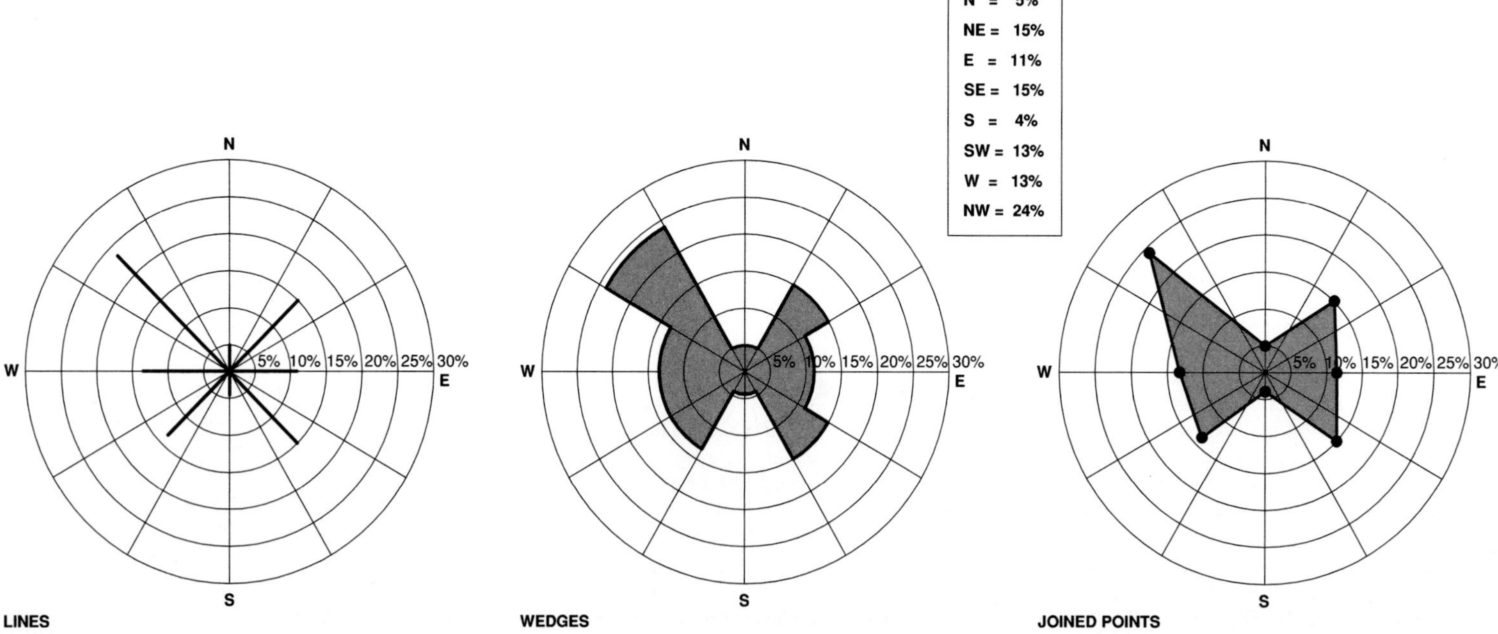

A wind rose diagram can be used to illustrate the amount of time that the wind blows from each compass direction. In this example, the prevailing wind is from the northwest.

THREE ALTERNATIVES TO SHOWING THE AMOUNT OF TIME WIND BLOWS FROM EACH COMPASS DIRECTION

Dr. Robert D. Brown, University of Guelph, Guelph, Ontario, Canada; Robert T. LeBlanc, Ekistics Planning and Design, Dartmouth, Nova Scotia, Canada

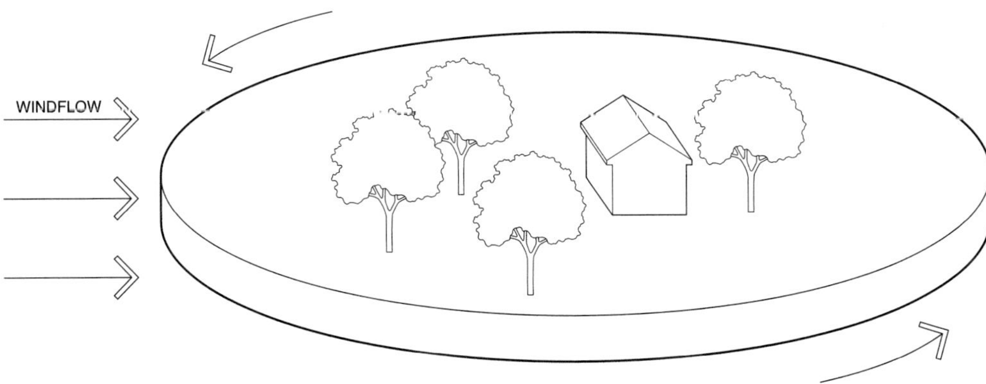

A scale model of a landscape is constructed, typically on a circular base, and set into a wind tunnel. The fan is turned on to generate wind, and sensors can be used to measure the wind speed at various locations around the model. When considering outdoor areas for use by people, the sensors measure the wind speed at about chest height in the landscape. The model is turned periodically so that each direction of wind is allowed to flow over the model. The model can be modified according to the proposed design, and the design can be tested for the effect on the wind. This approach can identify and alleviate problems before construction.

ROTATING WIND TUNNEL MODEL

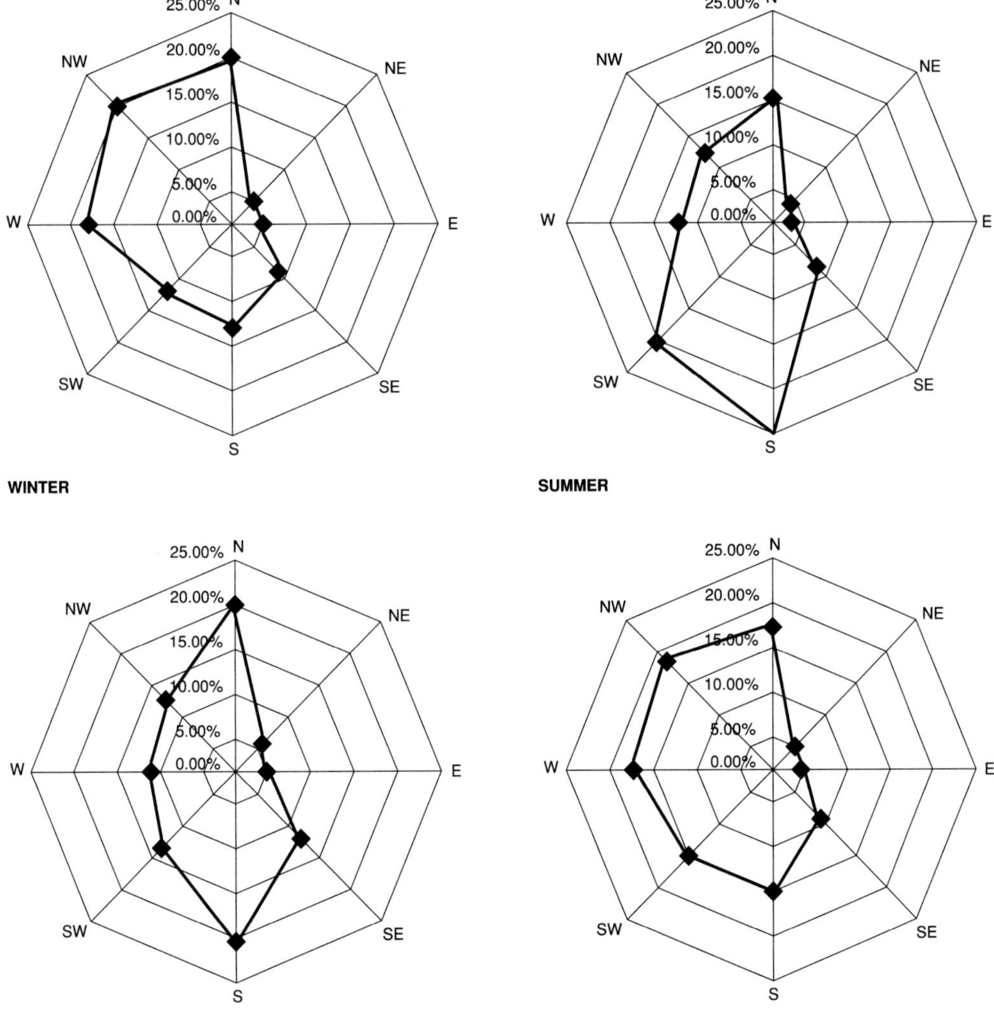

Wind data from climate stations can be illustrated through the use of wind roses. The data from "Table of Climate Station Data" has been used to generate seasonal wind roses.

WIND ROSES TO SHOW SEASONAL DIFFERENCES

observed and measured patterns of wind flow around standard elements in a landscape. These patterns can be used to illustrate both approximately how the wind will flow across a landscape and how the design of the landscape will affect future wind patterns.

STANDARD APPROACHES FOR MODIFYING WINDS

General Guidelines

Standard approaches for modifying winds can be summarized in these general guidelines:

- Locate objects in the landscape so that their "wind reduction zones" will occur in areas that will benefit from a lower wind speed (less cooling when air is cooler than an object); and allow wind to enter areas that will benefit from the increased convective cooling.
- Select the porosity of objects to provide the desired amount of wind reduction and size of wind reduction zones. Generally, the wind speed will be lowest behind buildings and solid objects, but the wind reduction zone will be very small and will probably experience turbulence; wind speed will be low behind trees with approximately 50 percent porosity and whose branches extend to the ground, and the wind reduction zone will be relatively large; and wind speed will be nearly the same as in the open when behind lightly leafed and leafless deciduous trees and coniferous trees whose branches don't extend to the ground.
- The amount of wind received in an area can be increased through deflection and/or channeling. "Conservation of mass" requires that air must go somewhere, even when it encounters a solid object. Air moving as wind over a landscape is analogous to water flowing in a channel. When the water encounters an obstruction, the water flows over and around and keeps going. Similarly, when wind meets a solid object, it has to go somewhere, so it flows over and around. The air can be deflected, through design, to flow through areas that would benefit from increased wind. Also, just as water will increase in speed when flowing through a constricted channel, air will also increase in speed if channeled between two solid objects such as buildings.
- Designs should consider modification of both wind and solar radiation (see *Modifying Solar Radiation*) to provide the most beneficial microclimates (see *Modifying Microclimates*).

LIMITATIONS

Of all the biological and physical elements in a landscape, the wind is probably the most difficult to characterize and control through design. The standard approaches and patterns described here provide only an estimate of the general conditions of wind on a site. Reality can be quite different. As noted, the complexity of wind flow in the landscape has yet to be effectively modeled by computers.

Dr. Robert D. Brown, University of Guelph, Guelph, Ontario, Canada; Robert T. LeBlanc, Ekistics Planning and Design, Dartmouth, Nova Scotia, Canada

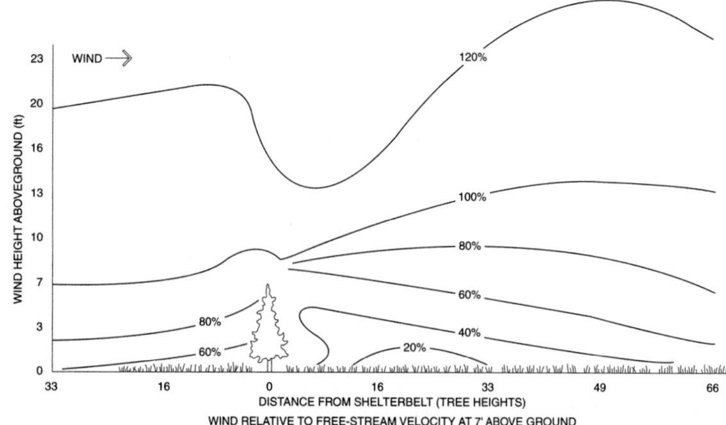

ILLUSTRATION OF WIND PATTERN AROUND A PERMEABLE WINDBREAK SUCH AS A THUJA OCCIDENTALIS HEDGE

Over time people have observed patterns of wind flow around buildings and plants in the landscape. These diagrams can be used in conjunction with the wind rose diagrams to estimate local winds on a site. They can also be used strategically to modify the wind on a site to achieve design goals. Note: the numbers across the bottom represent multiples of windbreak height. For example, if the windbreak is 5 feet tall, the value 16 represents 5 x 16 = 80 feet downwind of the windbreak.

STANDARD PATTERNS OF WIND FLOW IN THE LANDSCAPE

EMERGING ALTERNATIVE APPROACHES

Although computer modeling of wind is still not practical for complex landscapes, there are encouraging developments of programs that model and simulate wind in the landscape.

ADDITIONAL APPLICATIONS

Information about winds can be useful in many different kinds of design decisions, including:

- Human thermal comfort
- Energy use in buildings
- Effects on plants and animals
- Deposition of snow or sand

RESOURCES

Brown, G. Z., and M. DeKay. 2001. *Sun, Wind & Light: Architectural Design Strategies* (2nd ed.). New York: John Wiley & Sons, Inc.

Brown, Robert D., and Terry J. Gillespie. 1995. *Microclimatic Landscape Design: Creating Thermal Comfort and Energy Efficiency*. New York: John Wiley & Sons, Inc.

Oke, T. R. 1987. *Boundary Layer Climates*. New York: Routledge.

See also:

Modifying Air Quality
Modifying Microclimates
Modifying Solar Radiation
Regional Climate

Dr. Robert D. Brown, University of Guelph, Guelph, Ontario, Canada; Robert T. LeBlanc, Ekistics Planning and Design, Dartmouth, Nova Scotia, Canada

REGIONAL CLIMATE

INTRODUCTION

The climate at a site is an integration of daily weather events over a selected period of time. The World Meteorological Organization of the United Nations recommends that climate normals be computed for 30-year periods and updated at the beginning of each decade. The currently recommended climate data are for the 1971–2000 period.

Two main drivers of climate will be reflected in the data for a site:

- Proximity to a significant body of water
- Latitude

Regional climate must be considered in the landscape design process. Location and orientation of landscape elements will affect such things as human comfort, energy consumption by buildings, and convenient use of outdoor spaces. Consideration of climate data will improve the landscape architect's design of any site, regardless of whether he or she has lived there and is familiar with the climate or not.

The most widely available climate variables are temperature and precipitation. Fewer stations record other useful elements such as wind, solar radiation, and humidity; that said, such data can still usually be found for a location that is sufficiently close to a design site.

The weather elements most easily modified in the design process are wind and solar radiation. The table "General Climatic Categories for Different Locations" suggests the first broad overview of climate that should be considered at the outset of the landscape design process.

Modification of solar radiation is given priority over modifying the wind in a warm, dry (sunny) situation. This is because providing four times deeper shade obeys a direct proportion rule and reduces solar overheating by exactly the same factor of 4; but cooling by the wind usually obeys a square root rule, so enhancing the wind by four times only increases the cooling by a factor of 2. However, in cold, dry (sunny) situations, available solar energy is often still not sufficient to cope with heat losses due to windchill, so attention to wind is given top priority.

Four examples of locations with seasons that fit into the four categories from the table "General Climatic Categories for Different Locations" are illustrated in the table "Monthly Degree Days for Selected Regions." Summer at the Southwestern Desert station fits into the Warm-Dry box, with very little rainfall and a very high percentage of sunny days. In contrast, summer at the West Coast Mexico station is quite cloudy and fits the Warm-Wet category. Winters at the Great Plains and Great Lakes stations have similar temperatures, but the western station has significantly less winter precipitation and more sunshine (Cold-Dry) than the eastern one (Cold-Wet). There is very limited potential for utilizing solar radiation in the lee of the Great Lakes in winter.

GENERAL CLIMATIC CATEGORIES FOR DIFFERENT LOCATIONS

The climate attributes are given in the top row and left column; then, within each table cell, the elements to consider are listed in order of priority. The climate attributes may apply to a whole year or to a season when most use of a site will occur.

	DRY	WET
WARM	1. Minimize solar heating using shade (since dry climates or seasons are usually sunny) 2. Maximize cooling by wind	1. Maximize cooling by wind 2. Minimize solar heating (but wet climates or seasons are usually already cloudy)
COLD	1. Minimize cooling by wind 2. Maximize solar heating (since dry climates or seasons are usually sunny)	1. Minimize cooling by wind 2. Maximize solar heating (but wet climates or seasons may have little solar energy available)

MONTHLY DEGREE DAYS FOR SELECTED REGIONS

This table illustrates climate data for four representative North American regions. These summary statistics are useful in providing a general sense of the climate issues that should be addressed in design.

DAYS IN MONTHS	31	28	31	30	31	30	31	31	30	31	30	31
	JAN.	**FEB.**	**MAR**	**APR.**	**MAY**	**JUNE**	**JULY**	**AUG.**	**SEPT.**	**OCT.**	**NOV.**	**DEC.**
WARM-DRY: SOUTHWESTERN DESERT												
Avg. temp. (C/F)	10/50	12/53	16/61	20/68	25/77	30/86	33/91	32/90	29/84	22/72	15/59	11/52
Precip. (mm./inches)	19/.75	22/.87	17/.67	8/.31	3/.12	2/.08	20/.79	28/1.10	19/.75	12/.47	12.47	22/.87
Precip., days	2	4	2	1	1	0	3	4	3	1	2	3
Percent sunny	77	79	83	88	93	94	84	85	89	88	84	77
CDD	0	0	0	60/108	217/391	360/648	465/837	434/781	330/594	124/223	0	0
HDD	248/446	168/302	62/112	0	0	0	0	0	0	0	90/162	217/391
GDD	155/279	196/353	341/614	450/310	620/1116	750/1350	868/1562	837/1507	720/1296	527/949	300/540	186/335

	JAN.	FEB.	MAR	APR.	MAY	JUNE	JULY	AUG.	SEPT.	OCT.	NOV.	DEC.
WARM-WET: WEST COAST MEXICO												
Avg. temp. (C/F)	26/79	26/79	27/81	27/81	28/82	29/84	29/84	29/84	29/84	28/82	28/82	27/81
Precip. (mm./inches)	8/.31	1/.04	0	1/.04	36/1.41	325/12.80	230/9.06	236/9.30	353/13.90	170/6.70	30/1.18	9/.35
Precip., days	1	1	0	1	3	13	12	12	15	9	2	1
Percent sunny	69	77	73	69	58	49	40	41	41	51	60	63
CDD	248/446	224/403	279/502	270/486	310/558	330/594	341/614	341/614	330/594	310/558	300/540	279/502
HDD	0	0	0	0	0	0	0	0	0	0	0	0
GDD	651/1172	588/1058	682/1228	660/1188	713/1283	720/1296	744/1339	744/1339	720/1296	713/1283	690/1242	682/1228

	JAN.	FEB.	MAR	APR.	MAY	JUNE	JULY	AUG.	SEPT.	OCT.	NOV.	DEC.
COOL-DRY: GREAT PLAINS												
Avg. temp. (C/F)	-6/21	-5/23	0/32	6/43	12/53	17/63	22/72	21/70	15/59	9/48	1/34	-3/27
Precip. (mm./inches)	16/.63	19/.75	36/1.41	55/2.17	65/2.56	65/2.56	30/1.18	23/.91	30/1.18	29/1.14	20/.79	16/.63
Precip., days	5	5	8	8	9	8	5	3	5	5	5	4
Percent sunny	57	57	61	58	57	61	76	74	66	65	53	53
CDD	0	0	0	0	0	0	124/223	93/167	0	0	0	0
HDD	744/1339	644/1159	558/1004	360/648	186/335	30/54	0	0	90/162	279/502	510/918	651/1172
GDD	0	0	0	30/54	217/391	360/648	527/949	496/893	300/540	124/223	0	0

	JAN.	FEB.	MAR	APR.	MAY	JUNE	JULY	AUG.	SEPT.	OCT.	NOV.	DEC.
COOL-WET: GREAT LAKES												
Avg. temp. (C/F)	-6/21	-5/23	-1/30	7/45	12/53	18/64	21/70	20/68	16/61	10/50	3/37	-3/27
Precip. (mm./inches)	58/2.28	52/2.05	65/2.56	63/2.48	81/3.12	61/2.40	74/2.91	67/2.64	66/2.60	62/2.44	56/2.20	55/2.17
Precip., days	16	13	14	12	12	10	10	9	11	10	13	14
Percent sunny	27	35	38	42	48	56	61	60	53	45	29	27
CDD	0	0	0	0	0	0	93	62	0	0	0	0
HDD	744/1339	644/1159	589/1060	330/594	186/335	0	0	0	60/108	248/446	450/810	651/1172
GDD	0	0	0	60/108	217/391	390/702	496/893	465/837	330/594	155/279	0	0

STANDARDS

A standard approach to including climate in landscape design can begin by locating the site on a map that shows the basic temperature and moisture attributes, and then using the table "General Climatic

Dr. Terry J. Gillespie and Dr. Robert D. Brown, University of Guelph, Guelph, Ontario, Canada

Categories for Different Locations." A widely used climatic classification that utilizes temperature and precipitation to categorize regions was devised by Wladimir Köppen and is shown for North America in the map of climate regions.

Temperature and precipitation data such as those used to create the map are generally available from national or regional meteorological agencies. Data for sites in the United States are available through the National Oceanic and Atmospheric Administration (NOAA) (www.noaa.gov) and for sites in Canada through Environment Canada (www.weatheroffice.ec.gc.ca).

Temperature Indices

The temperature data are often worked into indices that can be more useful for landscape design than the raw information. One such index is degree-days. It is computed simply, by averaging the maximum and minimum temperatures (Tmax and Tmin, respectively) each day and adjusting this daily mean value using a base temperature (Tbase) as follows.

Growing Degree-Days (GDD)

The equation for growing degree-days is:

$$GDD = (Tmax + Tmin)/2 - Tbase$$

Subtracting Tbase from the daily average temperature recognizes that plant growth typically begins at an air temperature warmer than freezing, so temperatures below the base should not be "counted" for judging growth. The base temperature for perennial plants is usually set at 41°F. For example, a day with a Tmax of 60°F and a Tmin of 46°F would have an average temperature of 53°F, and 53 − 41 = 12 GDD.

Cooling Degree-Days (CDD)

The "recipe" for calculating CDDs is the same as for GDDs, except that the base temperature is adjusted to 65°F, so only those days with average temperatures that prompt the use of air conditioners are counted. For example, a day with a Tmax of 80°F and a Tmin of 70°F would have an average temperature of 75°F, and 75 − 65 = 10 CDD. If the average of Tmax and and Tmin is less than the base of 65°F, then the CDD = 0.

Heating Degree-Days (HDD)

In this index, the daily average temperature is subtracted from the base temperature to indicate the likely demand for space heating. The base temperature chosen is typically 65°F. For example, a day with Tmax = 50°F and Tmin = 36°F would have an average temperature of 43°F, and 65 − 43 = 22 HDD. If the average of Tmax and Tmin is greater than the base of 65°F, then the HDD = 0.

For each degree-day index, the values are accumulated day after day, and normal sums are computed for months or seasons and are generally available through meteorological agency websites (monthly values for selected regions are listed in the table Monthly Degree Days for Selected Regions).

Indices Summary

These indices are particularly useful for comparing conditions at a new site to a known site. Power authorities and heating fuel suppliers can often offer guidance in the local use of CDD and HDD to estimate cooling and heating requirements. For regions with high CDD values, consider reducing solar radiation (refer to *Modifying Solar Radiation*). In regions with high HDD values, consider reducing local winds (see *Modifying Wind*) and maximizing solar input.

GDD can help estimate whether a particular plant might be suitable at a new site, especially when combined with a map of plant hardiness zones that gives guidance about plant survival in the winter. For annual plants, it is also necessary to consider the frost-free season, particularly the dates of last spring and first fall frosts.

Precipitation and Evapotranspiration

Data on the average number of days in a month with precipitation are available for selected locations and can aid in estimating use patterns for outdoor facilities.

Data on precipitation amounts (P) may also be used to judge the need for irrigation at a site, when combined with an estimate of water use by soil and plant evapotranspiration (ET). One simple index of irrigation need is P − ET, with negative values indicating a water deficit. A general guideline is that more than 2 inches of deficit in the growing season suggests some periods of plant water stress normally occur; therefore, irrigation should be considered if optimum plant growth must be maintained. This guideline will be lower for soils with poor water-holding capacity or shallow-rooted plants and higher for deep-rooted plants or trees.

Check with the regional meteorological or agricultural office to see if average ET estimates are available. If not, then the table "Monthly Radiation Factors" can be used to provide broad estimates; but for projects where irrigation is an important component, the professional advice of an irrigation specialist or agrometeorologist should be sought to provide suitable ET estimates.

Solar Radiation

The most widely available data related to solar radiation are hours of bright sunshine. These data can be compared to the total number of daylight hours to estimate whether shade manipulation or solar power are worthwhile options. Measurements of the solar power (watts per square meter) arriving on a horizontal surface are available from some weather stations, but hours of bright sunshine are recorded at more locations. These sunny hours are often compared to the length of time between sunrise and sunset, to give percent sunny data, as shown in the table "Monthly Degree Days for Selected Regions." The examples in this table show this index ranging widely between 25 and 95 percent, depending on season and location.

Wind

Published data on wind usually indicate both the average speed and direction and are available through meteorological services. The wind speed data can point to the times of the year when wind

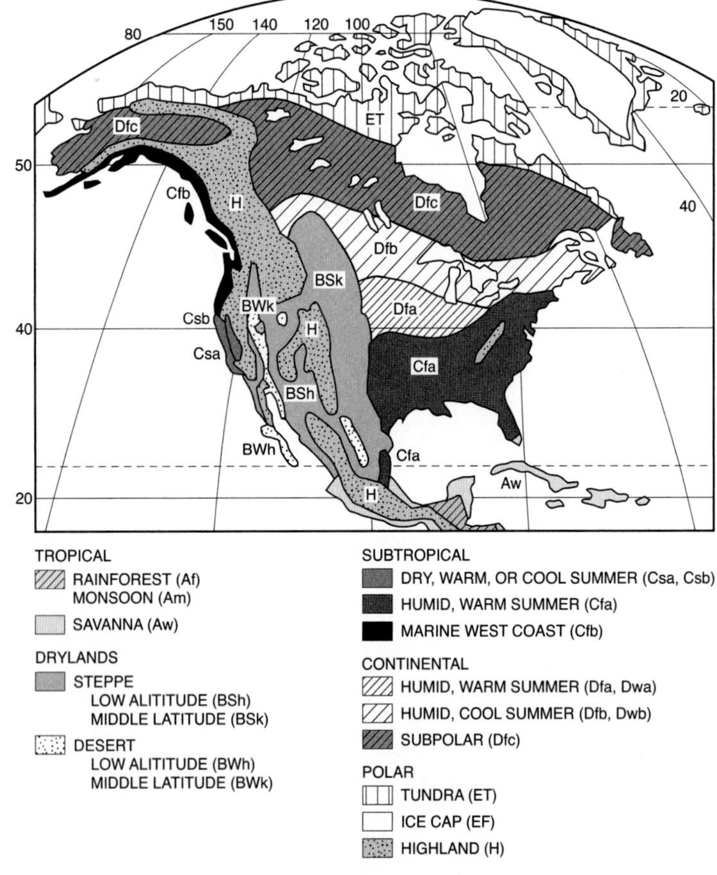

The information on this map can be useful when designing a landscape in a region that is unfamiliar.

A MAP OF THE KÖPPEN CLIMATE REGIONS OF NORTH AMERICA.

Dr. Terry J. Gillespie and Dr. Robert D. Brown, University of Guelph, Guelph, Ontario, Canada

MONTHLY RADIATION FACTORS

Use these factors in estimating potential evapotranspiration for various latitudes. To estimate the monthly water needs (in millimeters) of vigorously growing plants that are free of water stress, determine the appropriate radiation factor (R) from the table and use it in the following equation:

$$R \times (0.48 + (\text{Average Celsius Temperature}/100)) = \text{monthly water need (mm)}$$

For example, the Great Lakes station (about 40° latitude) in the table, "Monthly Degree Days for Selected Regions," normally has about 60 percent sunshine in August. Using this value in the table below suggests a radiation factor of 191. The average temperature is 20°C, giving a temperature factor of 0.48 + (20/100) = 0.68. So the water need of a vigorous vegetation cover is 0.68 × 191 = 130 mm. The difference between plant needs and the average precipitation in this month is 130 − 67 = 63 mm, so some water stress is normally expected if irrigation is not used at this location. (To convert mm to inches, divide by 25.4.)

LATITUDE	MONTHS AND SUNSHINE FRACTIONS																	
	FEB. 28			APR. 30			JUNE 30			AUG. 31			OCT. 31			DEC. 31		
	0.3	**0.6**	**0.9**	**0.3**	**0.6**	**0.9**	**0.3**	**0.6**	**0.9**	**0.3**	**0.6**	**0.9**	**0.3**	**0.6**	**0.9**	**0.3**	**0.6**	**0.9**
30	74	117	160	118	183	249	134	207	280	128	198	268	90	142	194	58	94	131
40	55	89	123	111	172	234	137	211	286	123	191	259	72	115	158	35	60	85
50	35	59	84	99	155	211	136	211	285	115	179	242	51	84	117	12	26	40

To calculate monthly PE, multiply radiation factor by 0.48 + (avg. celscius temp. /100)

	SOLAR AT TOP OF ATMOSPHERE																	
30		631			895			1002			931			687			480	
40		499			844			1020			901			569			331	
50		355			768			1017			847			434			183	

control will be most effective at a design site (see *Modifying Wind*). The wind direction data suggest the best locations for wind control features. For example, a site on the Great Plains might benefit from a line of coniferous trees planted to the west to protect it from cold winter winds.

LIMITATIONS

Design using climate data must recognize that individual weather events have been smoothed out in the averaging process, so extreme occurrences of heat, cold, wind, and precipitation are not revealed in these data. Guidance on extreme events for design of water management or strength of built features can be obtained from regional weather offices.

It may be difficult to achieve optimum design objectives for all seasons at a site. For example, summer blockage and winter utilization of solar radiation can be achieved with deciduous trees, but this scheme is not suited to wind blockage in the winter and free wind flow for outdoor comfort in the summer. In this case, a movable wind barrier that is not tall enough to block the winter sun may be an option, or the average wind direction may be different enough from winter to summer to solve this problem.

EMERGING ALTERNATIVE APPROACHES

Regional climate databases are becoming increasingly well organized and accessible directly over the Internet or by contacting the local weather office. Therefore, custom requests are becoming more and more feasible. For example, the landscape architect might wish to know the hourly course of temperature, wind, and sunshine for a typical day at various times of the year. Or some conditional climatology information might be requested, such as the usual wind directions under the condition that the wind speed exceeds some selected value (points to the best location for wind barriers) or the average hours of bright sunshine and/or wind speed under the condition that the temperature is warmer than 80°F (30°C) or colder than 20°F (−8°C), which more specifically highlights the potential for solar and wind manipulation or use. Such conditional data can sharpen the decision process by highlighting specific situations that would otherwise be buried in the usual average climatology.

ADDITIONAL CONSIDERATIONS

The focus of this article has been on North America; however, landscape architects based in North America may face design challenges working on projects in other parts of the world. The Köppen map shows that there are a wide variety of climate types represented in North America. This same classification system has been applied all over the world, and a global scale map can be found in most introductory meteorology textbooks by looking for the name Wladimir Köppen in the book's index. Therefore, considering extrapolation of successful designs that exist in appropriate climatic zones in North America to other parts of the world (or vice versa) may be a productive way to start a new project.

RESOURCES

Brown, R. D., and T. J. Gillespie. 1985. *Microclimatic Landscape Design: Creating Thermal Comfort and Energy Efficiency*. New York: John Wiley & Sons, Inc.

Lutgens, F. K., and E. J. Tarbuck. 2004. *The Atmosphere* (9th ed.). New York: Prentice-Hall.

Oke, T .R. 1987. *Boundary Layer Climates*. New York: Routledge.

See also:

Modifying Air Quality
Modifying Microclimates
Modifying Solar Radiation
Modifying Wind

Dr. Terry J. Gillespie and Dr. Robert D. Brown, University of Guelph, Guelph, Ontario, Canada

MODIFYING MICROCLIMATES

INTRODUCTION

The "climate" of a region can be described by the air temperature, humidity, wind speed, precipitation, and amount of solar and terrestrial radiation that is experienced over large areas (see *Regional Climate*). There are several scales at which climate can be considered. The two most useful in landscape architecture are "mesoclimate" (tens to hundreds of miles in size) and "microclimate" (inches to tens of feet in size). There are myriad microclimates within a region, each of which can be described by the same measures as climate but confined to a relatively small area. Movement through the landscape from one microclimate to the next is experienced by a person as a change in his or her thermal comfort. For example, on a hot day, a person moving from a sunny microclimate into the shade of a densely leafed deciduous tree would experience this as a move to a "cooler" microclimate. However, it is a common misconception that the air temperature is lower in the shade of the tree, whereas the temperature of the ground and other surfaces in the sun would likely be considerably higher than that of shaded surfaces. But because the air is a very efficient mixer, temperature differences are lost by the time the air is measured at a standard height of 5 feet, a height that is more representative of the air that affects people's thermal comfort level.

Careful measurement with a properly shielded instrument would show that the air temperature, at the level that people experience it is almost always essentially the same in the shade of the tree as it is in the full sun. In this case, it is the reduction in solar radiation received by the person that is being interpreted as a cooler microclimate. Similarly, moving from a windy sidewalk on a cold day into the shelter of a row of coniferous trees would be experienced as moving to a "warmer" microclimate. Again, the air temperature would be essentially the same in the two microclimates and it would be the reduction in convective cooling of the wind that would be experienced as a warmer microclimate.

The various measures that describe a microclimate can be divided into two groups: those that can be modified by the design of the landscape and those that, in general, cannot be modified through design. The amount of wind and the amount of solar radiation received in a landscape can be readily and substantially modified through design. The temperature and humidity of the air, in general, cannot be readily or substantially modified through design.

Large differences in the temperature and humidity of the air can be experienced at the "mesoscale," such as the "urban heat island" effect experienced in large cities, as shown in the illustration. The air temperature in urban areas tends to be warmer than that of the surrounding countryside because of the typically hard, dry surfaces. This effect is most pronounced on clear, calm nights when the temperature in the middle of the city can be as much as 8–10°F higher than the countryside but is not as pronounced during the day or under windy or cloudy conditions. This island of warm air can have pockets of cooler air over green or wet surfaces, such as parks or water bodies.

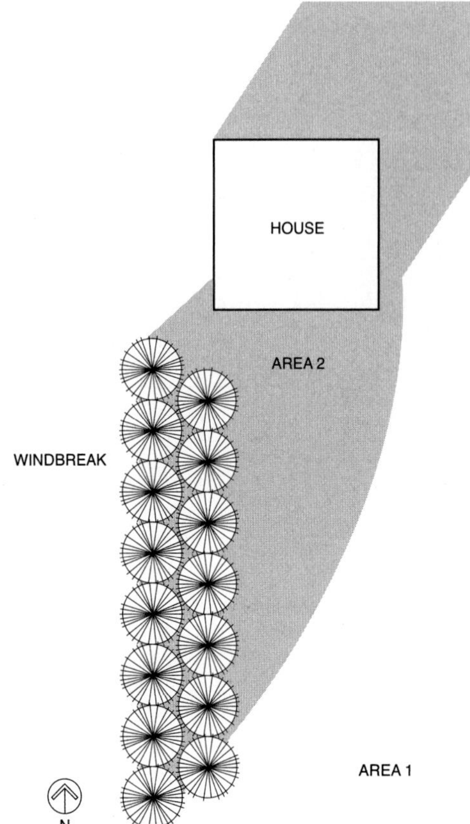

Prevailing microclimatic conditions in a typical urban landscape during the spring season. Area 1 would be inherently comfortable (sometime known as a *sun-catch*) while area 2 would be inherently too cool or cold to use in spring.

WINTER WIND AND SHADOW PATTERNS

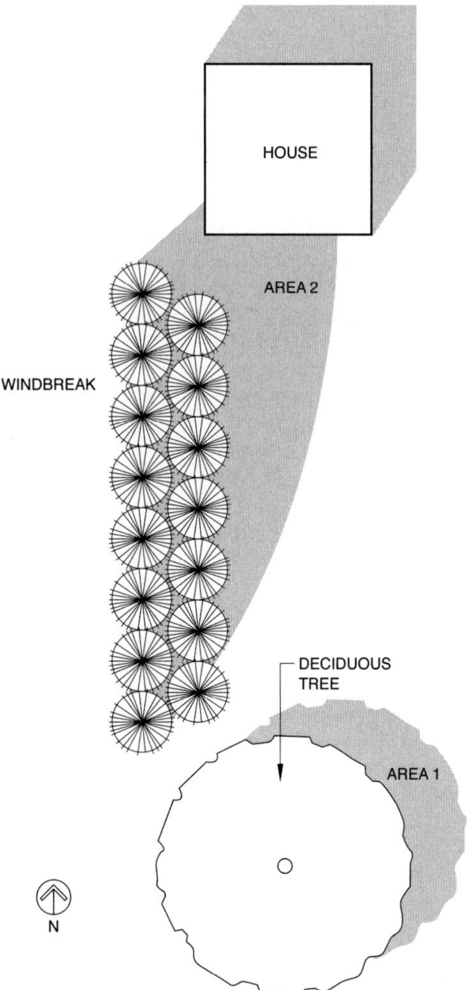

Area 1, which was inherently comfortable in springtime, might be inherently too hot in summer as it would be open to full sun, and would not experience any cooling breezes. To make it more comfortable for summer use, a deciduous tree could be located so as to cast a shade on Area 1 in midsummer. The lack of leaves in the spring would allow much of the solar radiation to pass through at this time, warming the people. Dominant summer winds in this location are typically from the south and southeast, while spring winds were dominantly from the west. This provides an opportunity to use a windbreak to slow the spring winds, but leave the site open to the southerly and southeasterly winds.

SUMMER WIND AND SHADOW PATTERNS

STANDARDS

General Guidelines

General guidelines for modifying microclimates through design include the following:

- The thermal comfort of people in the landscape can be greatly affected by the microclimate and should be a high priority for design of urban outdoor areas. The flows of energy to and from a person are affected by the microclimate.
- The amount of energy used to heat and cool buildings in the landscape can be greatly affected by the local microclimate.
- When designing urban areas for use during cool seasons, the first priority is to provide protection from the wind; the second priority is to provide access to the sun (remember: winter-wind).
- When designing urban areas for use during warm seasons, the first priority is to provide shade from the sun; the second priority is to provide access to the wind (remember: summer-sun).

In cool and cold seasons, the wind is a very effective cooling element and should be reduced as much as possible (see *Modifying Wind*). In warm and hot seasons, the wind has little cooling power because its temperature is very nearly that of a person. In this case, the amount of solar radiation a person receives should be reduced as much as possible (see *Modifying Solar Radiation*).

Identifying Existing Microclimates

The microclimates in an urban landscape can be defined by the amount of solar radiation and wind received. Shadow and wind diagrams (see *Modifying*

Dr. Robert D. Brown, University of Guelph, Guelph, Ontario, Canada; Robert T. LeBlanc, Ekistics Planning and Design, Dartmouth, Nova Scotia, Canada

Solar Radiation, and *Modifying Wind*) can be generated to illustrate existing conditions, which then can be used to provide an indication of the inherent thermal comfort conditions for people. For example, the area on the map of spring conditions that would be an inherently comfortable place for people to use would be the zone in full sun and out of the dominant wind. Alternatively, the area shaded from the sun and open to the dominant wind would be inherently too cool or cold for people to use in springtime.

Tools for Modifying Microclimates

A microclimate can be modified through the strategic placement of objects that will modify the wind and the solar radiation. In combination, these can substantially change the thermal comfort conditions for people, as well as the energy required to heat and cool buildings in the landscape.

Tools for Modifying Mesoclimates

Individual sites are often too small to have much of an effect on the air temperature of the site or of the city. However, larger areas of vegetation or water can have a cumulative effect on reducing urban heat islands.

LIMITATIONS

Microclimates constantly change throughout the day and through the year. Current knowledge and technology does not afford a complete understanding or description of the microclimates in a landscape. The most appropriate approach, at present, is to map the elements of a landscape that will have an effect on the solar radiation and the wind at strategic times of the day in specific seasons.

EMERGING ALTERNATIVES

Computer modeling and simulation holds promise for more complete and accurate descriptions of micro- and mesoclimates in the future. Already, solar radiation is being modeled quite effectively, while research continues on methods for modeling and simulating wind. Computer models are also becoming more widely available for estimating the human thermal comfort levels and energy conservation opportunities across a landscape, and these will undoubtedly improve over time.

RESOURCES

Brown, G. Z., and M. DeKay. 2001. *Sun, Wind & Light: Architectural Design Strategies* (2nd ed.). New York: John Wiley & Sons.

Brown, Robert D., and Terry J. Gillespie. 1995. *Microclimatic Landscape Design: Creating Thermal Comfort and Energy Efficiency*. New York: John Wiley & Sons, Inc.

Oke, T. R. 1987. *Boundary Layer Climates*. New York: Routledge.

See also:
Modifying Air Quality
Modifying Solar Radiation
Modifying Wind
Regional Climate

Dr. Robert D. Brown, University of Guelph, Guelph, Ontario, Canada; Robert T. LeBlanc, Ekistics Planning and Design, Dartmouth, Nova Scotia, Canada

MODIFYING AIR QUALITY

INTRODUCTION

Many of the compounds that are labeled as "air pollutants" occur naturally, and some are even essential for life. But when the concentrations of these compounds significantly exceed their natural values, or new toxic substances are introduced by human activities, air quality is considered to be degraded.

Concentrations of gaseous pollutants are usually expressed as parts per million (ppm) or parts per billion (ppb), which denotes the fraction of a volume of air that is occupied by the pollutant. For particulate matter, concentrations are usually expressed as weight per unit volume of air (e.g., micrograms per cubic meter). Air quality standards or guidelines are set by the Environmental Protection Agency (www.epa.gov) in the United States, by Environment Canada (www.ec.gc.ca) in that country, and by similar agencies elsewhere in the world.

Air pollutants can be considered "primary" or "secondary." Primary pollutants are emitted directly into the atmosphere, while secondary pollutants are created from primary pollutants by chemical and physical transformations in traveling air parcels. For example, sulphur dioxide is a primary pollutant emitted when coal is burned, whereas ground-level ozone is a secondary pollutant created by photochemical reactions downwind from primary sources of oxides of nitrogen and hydrocarbons. Poor air quality is a concern because it may lead to human health problems, injury to plants or animals, and damage to structures and materials.

When discussing air quality with an air pollution expert, reference may be made to "point sources" (individual smokestacks), "line sources" (busy roadways) and "area sources" (factory complexes or whole cities). In each case, there are two fundamental ways to attack a poor air quality problem: abatement at the source or enhanced dispersion after release. A good approach to these two options is described in the following rhyme: "One solution to pollution is dilution, but a better course is to stop it at the source."

STANDARDS

There are two standard approaches to improving existing poor air quality or creating a new landscape design that minimizes air pollution problems. The most desirable approach is to prevent pollutant release at the source. Reduction of output by some fraction gives the benefit of exactly the same proportional reduction in downwind pollutant concentrations, when all other factors are constant. Once the pollutant is released, the designer can attempt to reduce concentrations by avoiding wind blockage. Dilution by the wind is inversely proportional to the air speed—a windbreak that halves the wind speed will increase pollutant concentrations by a factor of 2.

Distance from the pollutant source is another factor that controls air quality and may be utilized by a landscape designer. For point and line sources, the pollutant concentration decreases with downwind distance, so sites upwind or furthest downwind from such sources have an air quality advantage. With an area source, concentrations of primary pollutants typically increase as one moves further into the source from the upwind edge, which gives the regions of a city closest to the prevailing wind direction better air quality potential. This advantage should be protected by avoiding the location of major pollutant emitters on the upwind side of the city, if possible.

Large-scale weather systems and time of day have an important additional effect on the vertical mixing of the atmosphere. Meteorologists refer to this effect as "atmospheric stability." Though this is a factor that cannot be modified by the landscape designer, its influence should be recognized. Stable atmospheric conditions occur when the large-scale sinking of air that produces clear skies in a high-pressure cell, or the quiet winds of nighttime, reduce vertical mixing. Therefore, air pollution episodes lasting several days are typically associated with slowly moving high-pressure cells, and odors from ground-level sources may be more noticeable at night.

Smokestacks are frequently used to elevate pollution sources above most landscape users, in the hope that sufficient dilution will occur before the plume reaches the ground. Designers should be aware that surface concentrations from an elevated source will be greatest when vertical mixing is strong and the plume is "looping" (usually during the day), but that tall buildings near an elevated source may receive very high concentrations during a stable night when vertical mixing is weak and the plume is "fanning." If a smokestack is used in a design, a general rule is that the stack should be at least 2.5 times as tall as the structure it services so there is a low risk that the plume will be caught in the turbulent eddy that typically forms in the lee of the building.

AN OVERVIEW OF THE MOST IMPORTANT AIR POLLUTANTS, THEIR SOURCES, AND THEIR EFFECTS

POLLUTANT	SOURCES	EFFECTS
Particulate matter	• Car/truck exhaust, power generation, crushing/grinding, unpaved roads, wind erosion. • Also formed from sulphur dioxide and in ozone smog (secondary pollutants)	• Soiling of structures • Asthma, heart and lung disease • Reduced visibility
Sulphur and nitrogen oxides	• Burning fossil fuel • Oil refineries/smelters • Pulp and paper production	• Acid precipitation, damage to structures • Aggravation of asthma
Carbon monoxide	• Car/truck exhaust • Power generation using fossil fuels	• Drowsiness, impaired reflexes/judgment, death at high concentrations
Ground-level ozone (secondary pollutant)	• Nitrogen oxides (from combustion) and hydrocarbons react together in sunlight & temperatures > 20°C	• Respiratory and eye irritation • Damage to vegetation • Damage to rubber/plastics

LANDSCAPE VEGETATION AND AIR QUALITY

Landscape vegetation has the potential to reduce air quality problems by acting as a "sink." Particulate matter can be trapped on leaves and branches, which act like dust filters, although their efficiency is not high. Many plants also take up nitrogen dioxide, which is the immediate precursor to ground-level ozone. And vegetation will take up ground-level ozone itself through the stomatal pores on leaves. Some species will suffer damage as a result of this uptake.

The choice of landscape trees may have an impact on ground-level ozone smog because some trees emit hydrocarbons that can participate in ozone production. In their natural setting, these trees do not pose an environmental threat; but when their hydrocarbon emissions are placed in an urban setting, where high concentrations of nitrogen oxides (from vehicle exhaust) are also present, the product is elevated ozone concentrations during warm and sunny days. These trees that emit hydrocarbons with high ozone-formation potential should be avoided in urban plantings.

LIMITATIONS

The general principles for air quality enhancement stated above cannot be applied with confidence to a landscape design that involves complex vegetation patterns and many structures of different heights. The creation of a scale model for immersion in a wind or water tunnel is one approach that can be followed in this situation, if dispersion from local or nearby sources is a potential problem. This can, however, be an expensive and time-consuming task, as every change in the design needs to be retested, and consultation with experts in scale modeling is required to properly extrapolate results to the full-size situation.

The general rule that pollutant concentrations increase as one moves further into a city from the upwind edge needs to be modified in the case of ground-level ozone smog. This is because the most troublesome compounds in ozone smog are secondary pollutants that require some time to form from primary emissions of nitrogen oxides and hydrocarbons. In fact, often the lowest urban concentrations of ozone smog are surprisingly found in the heart of large cities, where nitrogen oxides (from vehicle exhaust) at very high concentrations actually destroy more ozone than they create. Highest ozone smog concentrations are typically found a significant distance downwind of a large city where these secondary pollutants have had time to form. A good example is the lower Fraser Valley in southern British Columbia, where nitrogen oxides and hydrocarbons are emitted in Vancouver, but the highest ozone concentrations damage crops and exacerbate heath problems in the rural landscape 80 to 160 miles east of the city.

EMERGING APPROACHES

Knowledge of airflow around suites of landscape elements, and of the chemical and physical transformations involved in polluted air masses, is improving. This makes it possible to predict dispersion and trans-

Dr. Terry J. Gillespie and Dr. Robert D. Brown, University of Guelph, Guelph, Ontario, Canada

SELECTED TREE SPECIES AND THEIR OZONE-FORMATION POTENTIAL (OFP)

The OFP scale is based on the arbitrary rating of Weeping Willow (*Salix* x *blanda*), a strong emitter of reactive hydrocarbons, as OFP = 100. Trees with values above 20 should be avoided in urban settings where high concentrations of nitrogen oxides (from vehicle exhaust) can be expected. The higher the number, the higher the ozone-formation potential.

BOTANICAL NAME (GENUS, SPECIES)	OZONE FORMATION POTENTIAL	BOTANICAL NAME (GENUS, SPECIES)	OZONE FORMATION POTENTIAL	BOTANICAL NAME (GENUS, SPECIES)	OZONE FORMATION POTENTIAL
Abies concolor	0	*Liquidambar styraciflua*	62	*Pseudotsuga menziesii*	1
Acacia farnesiana	9	*Lithocarpus densiflora*	0	*Quercus agrifolia*	79
Acer floridanum	4	*Magnolia grandiflora*	12	*Quercus alba*	20
Acer macrophyllum	0	*Magnolia virginiana*	0	*Quercus coccinea*	27
Acer platanoides	3	*Malus coronaria*	3	*Quercus douglasii*	14
Acer rubrum	5	*Malus floribunda*	1	*Quercus dumosa*	57
Acer saccharinum	14	*Nyssa sylvatica*	25	*Quercus garryana*	65
Acer saccharum	3	*Persea borbonia*	1	*Quercus incana*	71
Aesulus flava	2	*Phoenix dactylifera*	24	*Quercus laevis*	38
Amelanchier alnifolia	2	*Picea abies*	7	*Quercus laurifolia*	16
Carya aquatica	116	*Picea engelmanni*	23	*Quercus locata*	4
Castanea dentata	2	*Picea pungens*	0	*Quercus myrtifolia*	24
Cedrus deodara	1	*Picea sitchensis*	6	*Quercus phellos*	50
Celtis occidentalis	1	*Pinus canariensis*	3	*Quercus prinus*	8
Cinnamomum camphora	7	*Pinus clausa*	21	*Quercus robur*	24
Cornus florida	0	*Pinus elliotii*	12	*Quercus rubra*	22
Cryptomeria japonica	6	*Pinus falcata*	0	*Quercus veluntina*	26
Cupania anacardioides	79	*Pinus halepensis*	0	*Quercus virginiana*	53
Cupressa sempervirens	0	*Pinus nigra*	10	*Robinia pseudoacacia*	18
Cyrilla racemiflora	26	*Pinus palustris*	11	*Salix nigra*	27
Eucalyptus globulus	42	*Pinus pinea*	1	*Salix* x *blanda*	100
Eucalyptus viminalis	11	*Pinus radiata*	1	*Sassafras albidum*	0
Fraxinus americana	2	*Pinus sabiniana*	1	*Schinus molle*	7
Fraxinus caroliniana	0	*Pinus strobus*	2	*Schinus terebinthifolius*	2
Ginkgo biloba	6	*Pinus sylvestris*	37	*Sequoia sempervirens*	6
Gledisia triacanthos	0	*Pinus taeda*	10	*Serenoa repens*	14
Hamamelis virginiana	2	*Platanus occidentalis*	35	*Sorbus scopulina*	7
Ilex cassine	0	*Platanus racemosa*	18	*Taxodium distichum*	15
Juniperus virginiana	0	*Populus deltoides*	40	*Tilia cordata*	3
Kalmia latifolia	2	*Populus tremuloides*	55	*Ulmus americana*	0
Lagerstroemia indica	0	*Prunus serotina*	0	*Washingtonia filifera*	18

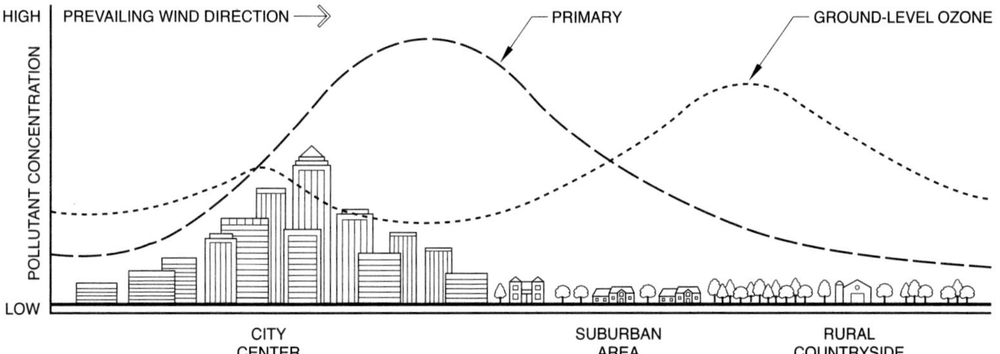

Primary versus secondary pollution concentrations in a city and the adjacent countryside. Note that the primary pollution peaks within the city, toward the downwind side, while the secondary pollution (in this case, ozone) is lower in the city center and peaks downwind of the city in the rural countryside.

OVERVIEW OF THE MOST IMPORTANT AIR POLLUTANTS, THEIR SOURCES, AND THEIR EFFECTS

formation of pollutants more confidently, using computer models. But this remains a very complex task that requires highly specialized expertise. Therefore, engaging an environmental consulting firm with these capabilities offers a strong advantage over modeling in an air or water tunnel. Once the site and the atmospheric conditions have been specified to the model, it is possible to run a very large number of design options in a short period of time. This approach will become more widespread whenever future landscape design problems contain a strong air quality component.

RESOURCES

Jacobson, M. Z. 2002. *Atmospheric Pollution: History, Science and Regulation*. Cambridge, U.K.: Cambridge University Press.

Lutgens, F. K., and E. J. Tarbuck. 2004. *The Atmosphere* (9th ed.). New York: Prentice Hall.

Oke, T. R. 1987. *Boundary Layer Climates*. New York: Routledge.

See also

Modifying Air Quality
Modifying Microclimates
Modifying Solar Radiation
Regional Climate

Dr. Terry J. Gillespie and Dr. Robert D. Brown, University of Guelph, Guelph, Ontario, Canada

BROWNFIELDS EVALUATION

The term "brownfield" or "brownfield site" means "real property, the expansion, redevelopment, or reuse of which may be complicated by the presence or potential presence of a hazardous substance, pollutant, or contaminant." Brownfields are landscapes predominantly found in urban areas adjacent to or within residential neighborhoods or as part of the built fabric adjacent to docks, harbors, riverfronts, and airfields. In addition, isolated brownfield sites are also found in suburban and rural areas where manufacturing or polluting agricultural practices have occurred. Brownfield sites are often visual and aesthetic eyesores, comprising abandoned, padlocked, and rusted industrial building structures within an external landscape of broken asphalt or stained concrete hard-standing, mounds of toxic and nontoxic waste, lagoons, ponds, and canals with standing water, sediments and sludges, and rusting infrastructure, industrial equipment, barrels, and debris. The sites can continue to create havens for further illegal waste dumping and crime that further degrade surrounding communities and neighborhoods. However, due to the lack of human presence on the sites in recent years, they also may contain a diversity of pioneer urban plant communities, wildlife, and insects. These provide rich and varied habitats within city neighborhoods and, as such, have great value. The word "brownfield" occurs regularly, proximate to terms such as "urban revitalization," "sustainable planning and design," "master planning," and "economic development," as well as "environmental justice," "remediation," and "community regeneration."

With certain legal exclusions and additions, the term "brownfields" was created to illustrate an unintended side effect of federal and state cleanup laws: liability for contamination cleanup and the severe costs of site remediation imposed by these laws caused these landscapes comprising land, infrastructure, buildings, and natural features to be abandoned in favor of developing unused land or greenfields far removed from the area. Their significance for the landscape architect is as a means to restrict urban sprawl, by:

- Offering an alternative to the development of greenfield sites.
- Eliminating dereliction in urban areas by encouraging revitalization of older abandoned properties and new sustainable patterns of development.
- Reconnecting formerly polluted landscapes with their surrounding communities.
- Offering social contributions, such as providing new jobs for the community and reinvestment in the quality of life in the community and the region.

Initial evaluation of these sites by the landscape architect requires the analysis of a broader set of environmental and design criteria than normally associated with greenfields. These are primarily focused on the impact of pollutants to be found as a result of former industrial or manufacturing processes. In addition to the conventions of site analysis employed by landscape architects—for example, for site drainage, existing vegetation communities, site stability, soil sampling, as well as circulation, visual, and spatial characteristic—there are a number of environmental site investigation techniques employed specifically on brownfield sites in an initial evaluation process. They include the collection of information on potential pollutants from activities such as site history reviews and interviews, screening methods, sampling and analysis, monitoring wells, geophysical techniques, remote sensing techniques, and laboratory analysis. This information is analyzed by environmental experts, in consultation with planners and designers, to evaluate the environmental conditions of the site and to devise remediation and reuse strategies.

SITE HISTORY REVIEWS AND INTERVIEWS

These include a thorough review of existing site and topography maps, aerial photographs, historical surveys, Sanborn Fire Insurance maps, flood insurance documents, leases and deeds, as well as historic photographs of the site. If possible, interviews should be carried out with present or former employees who worked on the site. They provide useful information on locations of former industrial processes and the vicinity of industrial waste that was stored or buried on-site.

SCREENING METHODS

- Immunoassay field screening has been designed to measure the presence and concentration of a variety of petroleum hydrocarbon mixtures. Concentration determinations are based upon a relative response to specific types of organic compounds or molecular structures present in all hydrocarbon mixtures. Therefore, it is possible to monitor for gasoline, diesel, and other hydrocarbon mixtures using immunoassay methods.
- The photoionization detector (PID) utilizes ultraviolet light to ionize gas molecules and is commonly employed in the detection of volatile organic compounds (VOCs).
- "Soil gas" is a term describing gas that fills the tiny voids between soil particles. When groundwater is contaminated with volatile organic compounds (chemical compounds that evaporate readily to the atmosphere), the chemicals can change into a gas and move upward through the soil and into site areas and buildings. VOCs include many motor fuels, industrial solvents, and landfill gases. When used during initial stages of a site investigation, soil gas sampling and analysis can optimize selection of boring and well locations by rapidly screening for VOCs in the subsurface.
- In X-ray fluorescence, each element has a unique set of energy levels, and each element produces X-rays at a unique set of energies, making it possible to nondestructively measure the elemental composition of a sample. The process of emissions of characteristic X-rays is called "X-ray fluorescence," or XRF. Analysis using X-ray fluorescence is called "X-ray fluorescence spectroscopy."

Screening methods correlate data derived in the laboratory to that obtained on-site and can be used to guide expensive assessment and remediation projects in the field, minimizing construction, sample preservation and shipment, and analytical expenses. Poor decisions, particularly at remote locations, can result in excessive assessment and remediation costs and cause unnecessary delays; therefore, the use of site screening technologies should be carefully planned. It is critical to understand the type and quality of data that will be generated before field-screening methods are purchased and used in the field. Also, the interpretation of the data generated using field-screening methods should be carefully evaluated before conclusions are drawn.

SAMPLING ANALYSIS

The analysis of contamination in soils, groundwater, and sediments can be carried out using localized testing around known polluted areas or using indiscriminate testing locations to gain a broad picture of an entire study area. Or a more systematic approach can be employed using coordinates or a grid structure to effectively cover an entire area.

Sampling soils on-site use a variety of environmental collection methods—grab, composite, and integrated approaches—depending on the complexity and scale of the site area and the objectives of the study. In many ways, this process is similar to conventional site sampling in landscape architecture to test for soil chemistry, texture, or structure.

MONITORING WELLS

The purpose for the installation of vertical monitoring wells located in the soil and subsurface area is to give specific access to the groundwater so that a "representative" view of the subsurface hydrogeology can be obtained, either through the collection of water samples or the measurement of physical or hydraulic parameters. Each monitoring well should be designed and installed to function properly throughout the entire anticipated life of the monitoring program.

GEOPHYSICAL TECHNIQUES

These technologies locate belowground features and forms, allowing a picture to be built up of subsurface conditions in two or three dimensions.

The ground penetrating radar (GPR) method operates by transmitting low-powered microwave energy into the ground via an antenna. The GPR signal is reflected back to the antenna by materials with contrasting electrical (dielectric and conductivity) and physical properties. It provides a cross section of objects below the ground, such as drums and storage tanks.

Terrain conductivity survey measures conductivity without electrodes or direct soil contact. This technique operates on the principle that secondary electric and magnetic currents can be induced in metal objects and conductive bodies, such as underground storage tanks, sludge, and leachate, when an electric field is applied.

REMOTE SENSING TECHNIQUES

Remote sensing is a technology for sampling electromagnetic radiation to acquire and interpret nonimmediate geospatial data from which to extract information about features, objects, and classes on the land surface.

REFERENCES

2002 Small Business Liability Relief and Brownfields Revitalization Act (Public Law 107- 118).

See also:

Brownfields Remediation and Development
Environmental Hazards

Niall Kirkwood, Harvard University Graduate School of Design

ENVIRONMENTAL HAZARDS

As the economic, social, cultural, ecological, and other potentials of polluted sites become more fully recognized, new projects and uses are proposed, plans for redevelopment are drawn up, and methods are sought to clean up the despoiled sites, returning them once again to potentially productive use. Common examples of these brownfield sites include former light industrial factory sites, vacant corner gas stations, the sites of former dry-cleaning operations, manufactured gas plants, utility substations, textile mills, oil tank farms, railyard and rail corridors, municipal buildings, graveyards and burial grounds, and more remote locations of municipal landfills and decommissioned Department of Defense land housing, in addition to many of the other industrial uses—munitions storage, firing ranges, and proving grounds.

On an urban brownfield site, the range of potentially contaminated media to be considered by the landscape architect include soils, groundwater, surface water, and sediments; on-site built elements, including existing building structures; site elements such as storage areas, lagoons, pools, ponds, canals; and infrastructure, including railway lines, waterfronts, and roadways. In addition, vegetation both (volunteer and introduced) have to be considered as part of the overall understanding and evaluation of the site.

SOILS

Occupation of sites for industrial purposes over lengthy periods of time produce soils that are severely impacted by compaction, building, roadway, parking cover, waste dumping, and pollutants buried and mixed in with rubble and urban fill. In many cases, the soils lie hidden under old concrete surfaces or infrastructure. A "cocktail" of contaminants are likely to be found at varying depths, ranging from more recent metal pollutants in the top 18 inches to depths as extreme as 30 to 60 feet where waste from old manufacturing processes such as hat and textile production have been found along with ash debris.

GROUNDWATER

Movement and conditions of groundwater on brownfield sites are likely to be affected by subsurface contamination plumes arising from spills or discharges from manufacturing processes. In addition, groundwater is likely to be an indicator of long-standing problems arising from leaking oil storage tanks buried below the ground. The dynamic nature of subsurface water conditions produces complex hidden processes and flows into and within the site area and from the site to adjoining sites and natural resources, including rivers and lakes.

SURFACE WATER

Ponds, pools, and lagoons containing surface water are commonly found on industrial sites as part of former industrial manufacturing processes. These water bodies are likely to accumulate amounts of discharge from pipelines, overflows, and surface pollutants. In addition, local standing water on sites can indicate previous discharges from buildings or leaking containers.

SEDIMENTS

Closely related to surface water areas are sediments found at the bottom of tanks and pools that may have accumulated over time. Due to their intense concentration of contaminants, sludges and potentially polluted sediment layers pose issues for the landscape architect if removal and encapsulation are deemed necessary either on-site or off-site.

EXISTING BUILDING STRUCTURES

Building structures likely to be found on a brownfield site range from small storage sheds, which will have to be demolished or relocated, to large stone or brick factory structures in various stages of abandonment or dilapidation. The impacts of these structures on the site include their continued deterioration and the presence of contaminated floors, walls, and architectural materials and finishes (e.g., asbestos tile, lead piping, and paint) continuing to pollute the larger site area.

INFRASTRUCTURE

The remaining elements or fragments of industrial processes and cranes, gantries rails, and free-standing structures, as well as old remnant transportation and transfer systems (e.g., canals, rail platforms, bridges, and walkways) in the landscape continue to support localized areas of contamination.

TYPICAL ENVIRONMENTAL HAZARDS

Environmental hazards can be found outdoors in the sites of parks, gardens, and other public areas. Adults and children are both at risk of exposure to environmental toxins. The following are the typical environmental hazards found on brownfield sites: volatile organic compounds (VOCs), for example, solvents and gasoline; semi-volatile organic compounds (SVOCs), for example, dyes; petroleum products (TPH); pesticides/herbicides; polychlorinated biphenols (PCBs); and metals. (Note: Radioactive materials are not covered in this article.)

Volatile Organic Compounds (VOCs)

Volatile organic compounds (VOCs) are synthetic organic chemicals that have a high vapor pressure and easily form vapors at normal temperature and pressure. The term is generally applied to organic solvents, certain paint additives, aerosol spray can propellants, fuels (such as gasoline and kerosene), petroleum distillates, dry-cleaning products, and many other industrial and consumer products ranging from office supplies to building materials. VOCs are also naturally emitted by a number of plants and trees. Most volatile organic compounds evaporate easily but are not appreciably soluble in water.

This class covers a wide range of compounds including toluene, styrene, and many chlorinated solvents found on brownfield sites that once supported activities such as printing and engraving, metal finishing, furniture refinishing, and auto body repair. VOCs can have direct adverse effects on human health, and many have been classified as toxic and carcinogenic (cancer-causing).

Semivolatile Organic Compounds (SVOCs)

Semivolatile organic compounds (SVOCs) are synthetic organic compounds that are solvent-extractable. They include phenols, phthalates, and polycyclic aromatic hydrocarbons (PAHs) produced during combustion.

Petroleum Products (TPH)

Total petroleum hydrocarbons (TPHs) that are found on brownfield sites include such products as heating oil from ruptured underground tanks, gasoline, kerosene, and asphalt.

Pesticides/Herbicides

Pesticides are chemicals or mixtures of chemicals used for the prevention, elimination, or control of unwanted insects, plants, and animals. Pesticides are usually organic chemicals but may also be inorganic compounds. They can be produced in the laboratory or naturally by plants. Herbicides are commonly found along railroad tracks and rights-of-way and railyards. The U.S. agriculture industry uses an estimated 817 million pounds of pesticides annually.

Polychlorinated Biphenols (PCBs)

PCBs are a class of chemicals known as polychlorinated biphenyls. Entirely man-made, they were first manufactured commercially in 1929 in the United States and used in many different types of products, including hydraulic fluid, casting wax, pigments, carbonless copy paper, plasticizer, vacuum pumps, compressors, heat transfer systems, and others. Their primary use, however, was as a dielectric fluid in electrical equipment. Because of their stability and resistance to thermal breakdown, as well as their insulating properties, PCBs were the fluid of choice for transformers and capacitors.

PCBs are, however, a suspected human carcinogen and a known animal carcinogen. They are resistant to degradation and, therefore, persist for many years in the environment. Furthermore, they bioaccumulate in the food chain and are stored in the body fat of animals and humans. PCB contamination from historic uses and dumping is widespread.

Metals

The category of metals, or heavy metals, refers to any metallic chemical element that has a relatively high density and is toxic, highly toxic, or poisonous at low concentrations. Common environmental metal hazards include arsenic, beryllium, cadmium, chromium, nickel, lead, zinc, mercury, and copper, which can cause serious health effects given sufficient exposure. Of those, lead, a naturally occurring substance, is commonly found on many urban brownfield sites. Lead is neurotoxic, so individuals whose body is still developing (such as children) are most at risk. Lead was used in paints and gasoline until it was found to cause learning and behavioral problems; but it also has been discovered in discarded lead batteries.

See also:
Brownfields Evaluation
Brownfields Remediation and Development

Niall Kirkwood, Harvard University Graduate School of Design

WETLANDS EVALUATION

WETLANDS AND RIPARIAN AREAS

Wetlands are areas that are inundated or saturated by surface or groundwater at a frequency and a duration sufficient to support vegetation and aquatic life typically adapted for life in saturated soil conditions. Wetlands generally include swamps, marshes, bogs, fens, and estuaries. Riparian areas are habitats on the banks of streams, rivers, and lakes.

The protection of wetlands and riparian areas has emerged as an important environmental planning issue. In the United States, several federal, state, and local laws have been enacted to protect wetlands and riparian areas. Specifically, the federal Clean Water Act (CWA) includes protection requirements in Sections 301 and 303 for state water quality standards, Section 401 for state certification of federal actions (projects, permits, and licenses), and Section 404 for dredge and fill permits. Section 401 empowers state officials to veto or condition federally permitted or licensed activities that do not comply with state water quality standards. State officials have used this power infrequently, although considerable potential exists for stronger state and local wetlands protection efforts.

Historically, wetlands and riparian areas were viewed differently than they are today. Throughout human history, people have located their settlements near rivers and lakes for transportation, water supply, and waste disposal. As a result, most cities and towns are near, or have replaced, wetlands and riparian areas. Prior to the 1970s, wetlands and riparian corridors that were not converted to settlements were used as waste disposal areas. Because of flooding dangers, areas adjacent to rivers and streams can be dangerous places to locate homes and businesses. As a result, wetlands and riparian areas often became sites for unwanted or undesirable uses such as heavy industry and landfills. But with the growth of metropolitan regions, wetland and riparian areas have become more desirable for development.

PROTECTION STRATEGIES

Since the late 1960s, there has been a change in the public perception of wetlands and riparian areas. Increasingly, these areas have become recognized for their positive values of flood protection, water quality and supply, recreation, and as wildlife and fish habitats. As a result, a few states, then the federal government, and finally several more states and localities implemented programs encouraging the protection of wetlands and riparian areas. Beginning in the late 1960s and throughout the 1970s, a host of such laws passed to address clean water, floodplains, wild and scenic rivers, the coastal zone, endangered species, and mining reclamation. And beginning in 1985, the preservation of wetlands on farms was required as a prerequisite for federal agricultural subsidies. These federal laws and associated state laws are dynamic, meaning they continue to evolve. The federal and state laws have prompted, and even required, local regulation.

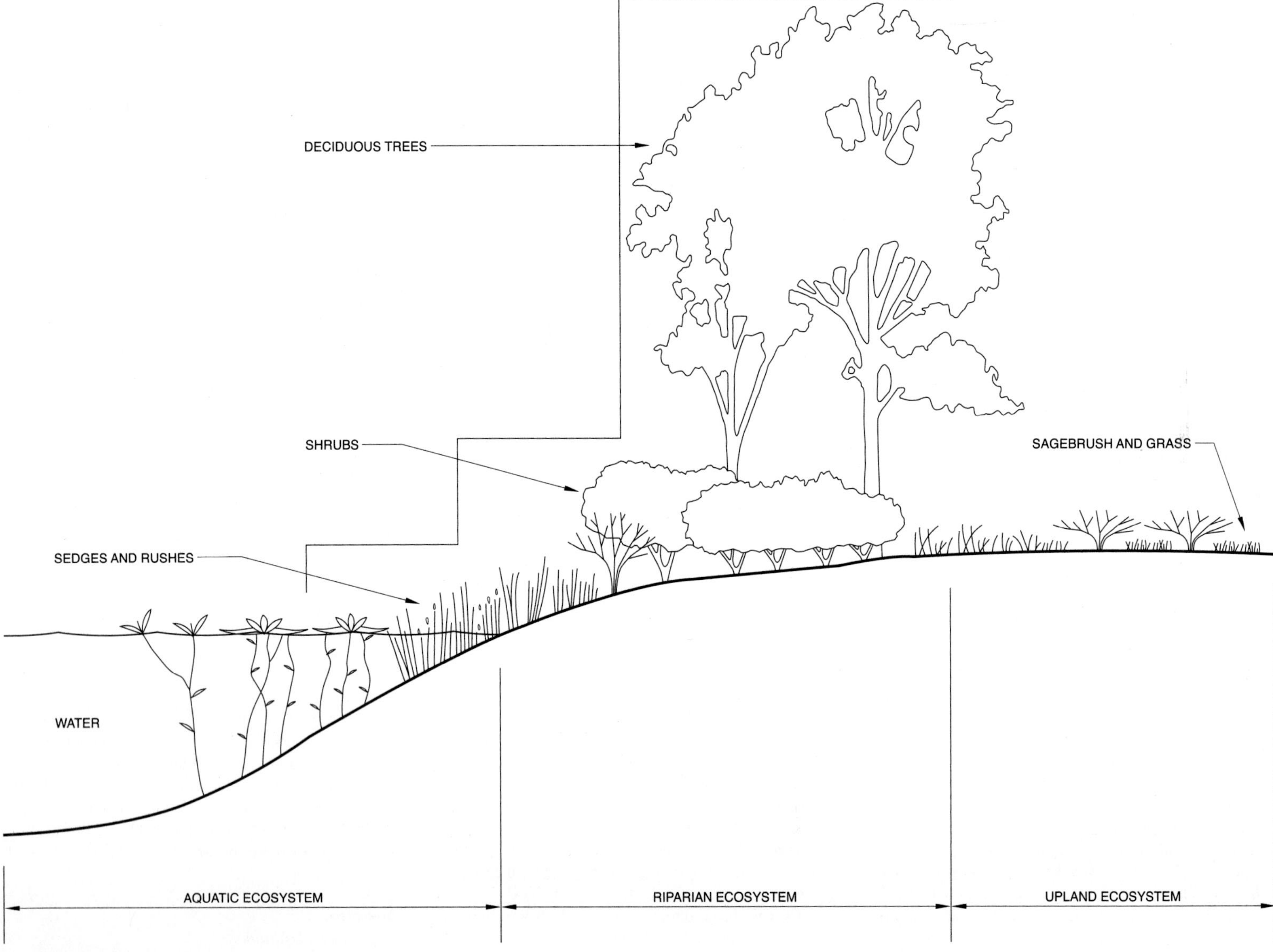

CROSS SECTION OF A RIPARIAN AREA

Frederick Steiner, Ph.D., FASLA, University of Texas at Austin

States have adopted various protection strategies, including:

- Assumption of the CWA, Section 404 permitting program
- Involvement in implementation of a federal CWA, Section 404 permitting program
- Implementation of a CWA, Section 401 certification program
- Promulgation of narrative or numeric standards and/or use of antidegradation standards to protect wetland/riparian areas
- Other natural resource protection programs that protect riparian areas
- Establishment of voluntary or mandatory water-course alteration or streamside forestry best management practices
- Establishment of protection mandates through executive orders
- Creation of opportunities for protection through tax incentives, easements, recognition programs, technical assistance, and education
- Protection by acquisition
- Inclusion of riparian areas and wetlands in definitions of "waters of the state" for regulatory purposes

Historically, federal and state governments were concerned about waterways for their navigational values, principally for defense and commerce. Water was relatively plentiful and abundant in the eastern United States. With increased knowledge about sanitation and disease in the nineteenth century, coupled with the growth of industrial cities, there began to be concern about water quality. As the people of the nation moved west, wetlands were viewed as a nuisance, to be converted to productive use as water irrigation systems for agriculture and urban purposes. In the late 1960s, the status quo began to change as federal agencies began to protect wetlands for their ecological values. In 1972, with the passage of the Federal Water Pollution Control Act Amendments (the Clean Water Act), a new era of water quality protection began that included valuing wetlands differently.

The CWA is the principal law authorizing wetlands regulation (33 USC 1251-1376). A major regulatory program is the National Pollution Discharge Elimination System (NPDES), which is administered by the U.S. Environmental Protection Agency (EPA). Section 301 of the act prohibits the discharge of any pollutant without a permit. Section 402 of the CWA authorizes the EPA or an approved state to issue such permits. Section 404 of the act carves out from the general EPA permit authority a special authority for the U.S. Army Corps of Engineers to issue permits for the discharge of two types of pollutants: dredged material and fill material. As a result, the EPA and Corps jointly administer the 404 program, although the EPA has veto authority over the issuance by the Corps of the 404 permits.

The main purpose of the CWA "is to restore and maintain the chemical, physical, and biological integrity of the Nation's water." In the 1987 amendments to the act, Congress established the policy "to recognize, preserve, and protect the primary responsibilities and rights of states to prevent, reduce, and eliminate pollution, to plan the development and use (including restoration, preservation, and enhancement) of land and water resources...." The 1987 amendments also established the policy of state implementation of Sections 402 and 404 permit programs.

Section 401 of the CWA allows the states to veto federally permitted or licensed activities that do not comply with state water quality standards. The states have the responsibility for setting these standards, subject to EPA approval. Section 303 of the CWA gives states great latitude in formulating their water quality standards. States may establish designated water uses and water quality standards criteria sufficient to protect the public health or welfare and to enhance the quality of the water.

Any applicant for a federal license or permit for conducting any activity that may result in any discharge to the navigable waters is required to secure from the state in which the discharge originates a certification that the discharge will comply with several provisions of the CWA related to effluent discharge limitations and water quality standards. Thus, a denial of Section 401 certification operates as an absolute veto, and the state's decision is not reviewable by the federal permitting agency or the federal courts. The states' most important role in the Section 401 certification process is to determine whether an applicant for a federal license or permit has demonstrated compliance with state water quality standards and, if not, to deny or condition certification so that the activity will comply with those standards.

The responsible federal and state agencies have developed forms and checklists to guide individuals through the 404 and 401 permitting processes.

Local governments often are responsible for the implementation of these state and federal initiatives. Local governments may also initiate programs for wetland and riparian area protection. A variety of regulatory devices can be employed. For example, overlay zones restrict development within wetland and riparian areas and direct new growth away from such places. Overlay zones provide a mechanism to prohibit development and limit other activities in wetlands, impose wetlands buffers, or require measures to reduce the effects of development in wetlands without affecting development outside the designated wetlands area and adjacent buffer zones. Other devices available for localities include special permits or conditional uses, cluster zoning and planned unit developments, performance standards, and subdivision regulations.

WATERSHED PLANS

All levels of government in the United States recognize the value of an integrated approach for wetlands and riparian area protection. Watersheds offer a geographic unit for such an integrated approach. A watershed (or drainage or catchment area) is a landscape surface area in which all water, sediments, and dissolved materials flow or drain from the land into a common water body such as a river, lake, ocean, or other body of water.

Watershed plans describe issues and opportunities, inventory natural and cultural resources, identify potential critical areas (including wetlands and riparian areas), and establish goals and objectives for water quality. Furthermore, watershed plans identify management options and strategies, recommend implementation measures, and describe ongoing management procedures.

See also:
Constructed Treatment Wetlands

WATERSHED

Frederick Steiner, Ph.D., FASLA, University of Texas at Austin

RESOURCE INVENTORY AND CONSERVATION

A resource inventory involves the systematic collection of information about a place. Sometimes called an environmental or an ecological inventory, natural and/or cultural data are collected in mapped and written formats. Conservation is often the goal of such an inventory. Conservation is the management of a landscape to yield the greatest sustainable benefit to the present generation while maintaining its potential to meet the needs and aspirations of future generations.

ELEMENTS OF A RESOURCE INVENTORY

Chronology provides a logical framework to organize information about a place. The inventory begins with the phenomena that are the major influences on a landscape: its macroclimatic processes and its geological structure. These phenomena exert influences on subsequent processes such as ground and surface flows. These physical, or "abiotic," processes interact with living systems to form soils. Together, these abiotic and soil features set the stage for life. Plants, animals, and people inhabit different places according to varying possibilities of physical geography. Usually, a resource inventory addresses the following elements: macroclimate, bedrock geology, surficial geology, groundwater hydrology, physiography, surface hydrology, soils, vegetation, wildlife, and human. Ian McHarg provided a baseline of information for such data.

BASELINE RESOURCE DATA FOR INVENTORIES

The following natural resource factors are likely to be of significance in planning. Clearly the region under study will determine the relevant factors, but many are likely to occur in all studies.

CLIMATE. Temperature, humidity, precipitation, wind velocity, wind direction, wind duration, first and last frosts, frost, fog, snow, inversions, hurricanes, tornadoes, tsunamis, typhoons, Chinook winds

GEOLOGY. Rocks, ages, formations, plans, sections, properties, seismic activity, earthquakes, rock slides, mud slides, subsidence

SURFICIAL GEOLOGY. Kames, kettles, eskers, moraines, drift and till

GROUNDWATER HYDROLOGY. Geological formations interpreted as aquifers with well locations, well logs, water quantity and quality, water table

PHYSIOGRAPHY. Physiographic regions, subregions, features, contours, sections, slopes, aspect, insulation, digital terrain model(s)

SURFACE HYDROLOGY. Oceans, lakes, deltas, rivers, streams, creeks, marshes, swamps, wetlands, stream orders, density, discharges, gauges, water quality, floodplains

SOILS. Soil associations, soil series, properties, depth to seasonal high water table, depth to bedrock, shrink-swell, compressive strength, cation and anion exchange, acidity-alkalinity

VEGETATION. Associations, communities, species, composition, distribution, age and conditions, visual quality, species number, rare and endangered species, fire history, successional history

WILDLIFE. Habitats, animal populations, census data, rare and endangered species, scientific and educational value

HUMAN. Ethnographic history, settlement patterns, existing land use, existing infrastructure, economic activities, population characteristics

BASELINE RESOURCE DATA FOR INVENTORIES

The following natural resource factors are likely to be of significance in planning. Clearly, the region under study will determine the relevant factors, but many are likely to occur in all studies.

Determining Values of Natural and Cultural Resources

Landscape architects and planners have overlaid mapped resource inventory information since at least the 1890s in the Frederick Law Olmsted office. McHarg suggested a systematic overlay process that he called the "layer cake," which employed ecology to reveal patterns of relationships. Values can be determined for these patterns to emphasize areas favored for conservation or development.

The systematic overlay of resource inventory maps is called a "land suitability analysis," defined as the process of determining the fitness of a given tract of land for a defined use. Such an analysis can be accomplished with the aid of computer technology called geographic information systems, or GIS.

The seven steps in the suitability analysis are:

1. Identify land uses and define the needs for each use.
2. Relate the land-use needs to resource inventory factors.
3. Identify the relationship between specific mapped phenomena concerning the biophysical environment and land-use needs.
4. Map the congruencies of desired phenomena and formulate values to express a gradient of suitability. This step should result in maps of land-use opportunities.
5. Identify constraints between potential land uses and biophysical processes.
6. Overlay maps of constraints and opportunities and apply values to develop a suitability map for each land use.
7. Develop a composite map of the highest suitabilities for the various land uses.

Conservation

Resource inventories and land suitability analysis are used in conservation. In the United States, conservation techniques differ between public and private lands. On public lands, the results of the inventory and analysis can be employed directly to conserve resources. Federal agencies, such as the U.S. Forest Service and the National Park Service, have specific

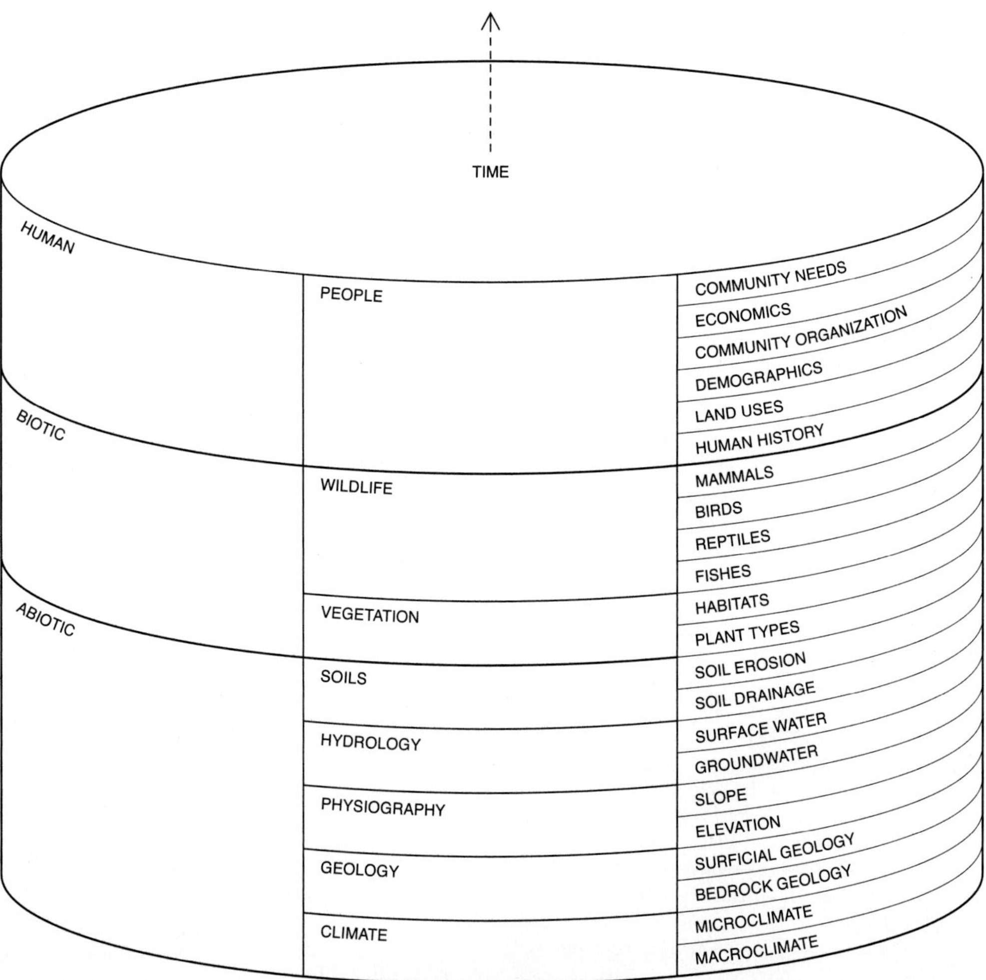

LAYER CAKE MODEL OF BASELINE DATA FOR RESOURCE INVENTORIES

Frederick Steiner, Ph.D., FASLA, University of Texas at Austin

STEP 1 Map data factors by type

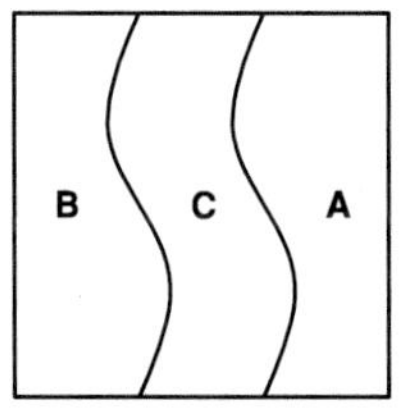

A = 00 - 10%

B = 10 - 20%

C = 20 - 40%

SLOPE MAP

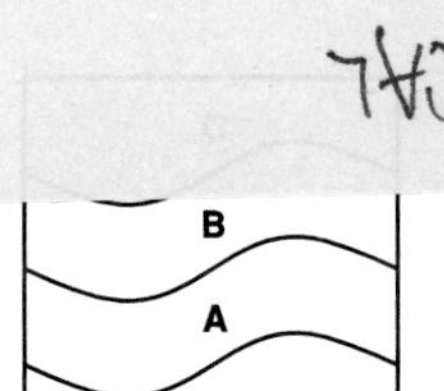

ntly Eroded

B = Slight to Moderate

C = Moderate

D = Extremely Eroded

EROSION MAP

STEP 2 Rate each type of each factor for each land use

FACTOR TYPES

		AGRICULTURE	HOUSING
EXAMPLE 1	A	1	1
	B	2	1
	C	3	3
EXAMPLE 2	A	1	1
	B	2	2
	C	3	2
	D	3	3

1 = Prime Suitability

2 = Secondary

3 = Tertiary

STEP 3 Map rating for each; use one set of maps for each land use

EXAMPLE 1

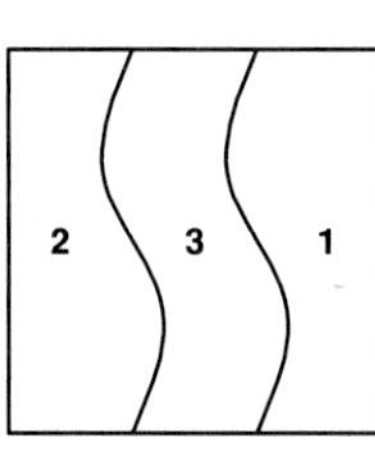

AGRICULTURE

EXAMPLE 2

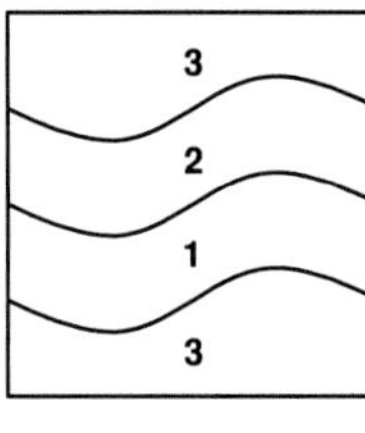

AGRICULTURE

EXAMPLE 1

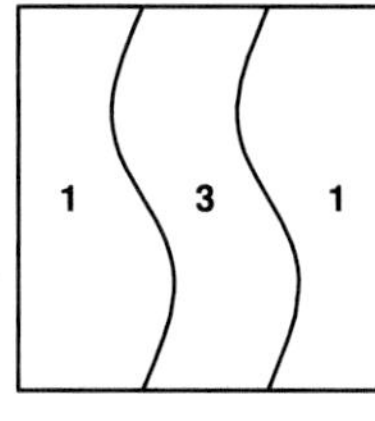

HOUSING

EXAMPLE 2

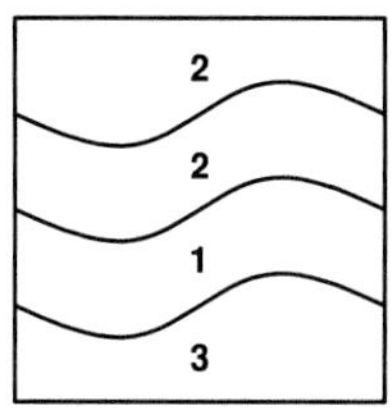

HOUSING

STEP 4 Overlay single factor suitability maps to obtain composites
One map for each land use

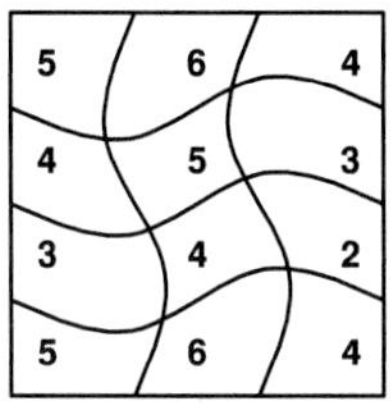

AGRICULTURE

3 5 3
3 5 3
2 4 2
4 6 4

HOUSING

Lowest numbers are best suited for land use

Highest numbers are least suited for land use

LAND SUITABILITY ANALYSIS

Frederick Steiner, Ph.D., FASLA, University of Texas at Austin

policies, rules, and procedures for inventories, analyses, and conservation programs. For example, the U.S. Forest Service uses the "multiple use, sustained yield" concept to manage its lands. Forest Service planners and landscape architects inventory resources for various conservation purposes such as forestry, recreation, wildlife preservation, and watershed protection.

On private lands, conservation possibilities vary from state to state. However, in general, there are regulatory and voluntary approaches for conservation. In addition, state and local governments can purchase land for conservation. All three approaches rely on resource inventories.

The most common regulatory techniques to control land use in the United States are zoning and subdivision ordinances. As already noted, resource inventories and suitability analyses can be used to locate the best places for specific land uses. Zoning and subdivision ordinances are supposed to accomplish the efficient location of land uses to protect the public health, safety, welfare, and morals. Such ordinances can require developers and other proponents of land-use change to prepare resource inventories and land suitability analyses in order to justify the change. For example, local jurisdictions can base their ordinance or performance standards that proponents of new developments must meet. Performance standards can be derived from resource inventories and suitability analyses or require that they be undertaken.

Resource inventories and land suitability analyses are used to identify constraints to development. These environmentally or culturally sensitive areas can be conserved through overlay zones. These zones overlay conventional zones and are meant to protect and to conserve prime farmlands, significant historical features, and environmentally sensitive areas.

Voluntary approaches involve an incentive for conservation, which might be financial or ethical. An individual might decide that some property should be conserved for ethical reasons. In such a situation, it would be useful for the individual to identify the best lands to be conserved. The legal instrument for such protection is often an easement, which allows an individual or family to retain ownership but to restrict certain areas for conservation. Easements can also be financial incentives. There are tax breaks for individuals and families who donate portions of their property for conservation.

Through the process of a resource inventory and a suitability analyses, it might become evident to government officials that certain areas must be conserved. In such cases, the government can purchase the property for conservation. This will probably involve convincing voters to raise taxes to buy the land. Inventories and analyses can help convince the public on such investments by illustrating the value of land to be conserved.

RESOURCES

McHarg, Ian L. 1969. *Design with Nature*. Garden City, New York: Natural History Press/Doubleday.

———. 1997. "Natural Factors in Planning," *Journal of Soil and Water Conservation* 52(1): 13-17.

Steiner, Frederick. 2000. *The Living Landscape* (2nd ed.). New York: McGraw-Hill.

See also:
Ecological Community Restoration

SUSTAINABLE SITE DESIGN

Today in the building fields, sustainable design, environmental issues, and the related impacts of construction on the built environment are topics of common interest that are increasingly being addressed. But definitions of "sustainable design" vary widely. Moreover, the terms "sustainable design," "ecological design," and "green building" are often used interchangeably, and distinctions among the terms are frequently cause for debate. "Sustainable design" may, however, be the most comprehensive, as it addresses ecological, social, and economic issues of a project and its context. "Green building," when used as a verb, implies use of some sustainable strategies in a landscape or building project. "Ecological design" refers to design that minimizes destructive environmental impacts by integrating with living processes to the extent possible (Van der Ryn and Cowan, 1995).

In the 1987 Brundtland Report by the World Commission on the Environment and Development, a broad definition of sustainability was developed and subsequently used in the 1993 American Society of Landscape Architects Declaration on the Environment. It defines "sustainable development" as: "development that meets the needs of the present without compromising the ability of future generations to meet their own needs." This definition succeeds in identifying a goal to work toward with site development; unfortunately, it is a goal nearly impossible to achieve within current economic, technological, and social settings. Therefore, in this discussion, "sustainable development" is used to refer to actions being taken toward achievement of this ambitious goal.

To varying degrees, sustainable design, green building, and ecological design all aim to minimize resource depletion, respect species diversity, maintain habitat quality, preserve nutrient and water cycles, and create built environments that foster human, societal, and ecosystem health. Sustainable design efforts recognize the interdependence and coexistence of humanity and nature. The focus is on a long-term view of the built and natural environment, planning for future generations, long-term value of places, and reuse of resources. To the extent possible within current culture and technology, sustainable design emphasizes a shift away from one-way linear flows of resource use and the resulting waste, to regenerative systems of material and energy use (Lyle, 1994).

PRINCIPLES AND STRATEGIES OF SUSTAINABLE SITE DESIGN

Sustainable design involves site- and place-focused solutions, as opposed to universal design that is often employed in today's rapidly globalizing environment. After extensive analysis of existing local and regional conditions, built interventions are carefully integrated into this individual context. Sustainable design often employs complex, integrated, and multifunctional systems that must be developed in collaboration with multiple disciplines. It also involves dynamic functioning systems that will evolve over the entire life of a landscape.

The following sections introduce processes, principles, and strategies for the design of sustainable sites, with a focus on sustainable design at the site scale. Sustainable strategies for regional planning and community design are discussed in their respective sections. References are also made to Web resources related to the strategies; and, where applicable, LEED credits are cited. (Note that a goal of this book is to seamlessly incorporate sustainable design information into the content of every section, therefore related sections that provide more detail on the processes, principles, and strategies introduced here, should be reviewed. Specific articles in this book that provide more detail on the processes, principles, and strategies introduced here are located at the end of each section.)

DESIGN FOR HEALTHY SITE AND REGIONAL SYSTEMS

Select and Develop Appropriate Sites

To determine which sites are appropriate for the intended use and can be developed sustainably, it will be necessary to perform a site development evaluation during the site selection process.

Prime farmland, floodplains, endangered species habitats, fire prone lands, public parklands, and lands within 100 feet of a water body are inappropriate sites for development. The development of greenfield sites outside of urban areas can negatively impact habitats and watersheds, encourage dependence on automobile use for commuting, disrupt existing ecosystems, and contribute to suburban sprawl and loss of agricultural land. Where possible, preference should be given to sites in urban areas or infill suburban parcels.

Redeveloping a previously developed site is the most sustainable solution. Often, these sites have existing infrastructure, which can offset the potentially higher cost of land. Similarly, redeveloping contaminated brownfield sites can save development costs, as many have lower property costs, existing infrastructure, and may be adjacent to desirable urban areas. However, cleanup costs must be considered, along with health risks and the perception of the future occupants. (See *Environmental Review, Brownfields Evaluation, Wetlands Evaluation, Resource Inventory and Conservation, Transit-Oriented Development, Brownfields Remediation and Development,* and *Surface Mine Reclamation.*)

Understand Regional Systems and Analyze the Impacts of the Planned Site Development on These Systems

An extensive analysis of bioregional and cultural systems can help reduce environmental impacts of the proposed development and reveal opportunities for sustainable site design. Regional hydrologic, geologic, climatic, vegetation, wildlife and cultural systems should be inventoried, mapped and analyzed. Likewise, an analysis of existing transportation infrastructure can reveal opportunities to promote public transportation and minimize road building and automobile use. (See *Resource Inventory and Conservation.*)

Inventory and Analyze Natural and Cultural Features of the Site

A thorough analysis of existing site features will reveal opportunities to better integrate the proposed intervention within site and regional systems, leading to a sustainably developed site. Collaboration with other consultants or agencies during the information-gathering phase can save substantial time as some areas may already be well inventoried.

The environmental analysis should incorporate:

- Examination of the microclimate of the site, including information on temperature, humidity, wind, solar orientation, and solar access
- A geologic and hydrologic evaluation, to identify drainage capacity, groundwater flow, soil characteristics, and any existing contamination
- A soil report, containing physical and chemical soil characteristics, bearing capacity, compaction, and infiltration rates, as well as identification of all areas prone to erosion
- A vegetation inventory, including location, genus, species, and condition of all significant trees and shrubs
- Identification of wildlife habitats, migration routes, and flyways, along with potential measures to preserve them
- Any existing environmental impact statements or other environmental quality reports produced for the site should be carefully reviewed by appropriate project participants

The cultural analysis should incorporate:

- An analysis of current land use patterns to determine how people use land around the site
- An inventory of existing structures on the site, both on and below grade, noting potential for reuse
- Identification of historical or cultural features of the site and the surrounding region
- Applicable data on the human population and economic setting in the region of the site
- Interviews or meetings with project users, community groups, and other stakeholders of the project

(See *Modifying Solar Radiation, Modifying Wind, Regional Climate, Wetlands Evaluation, Resource Inventory and Conservation, Wildlife Habitat,* and *Soil Mechanics.*)

MINIMIZE SITE DISTURBANCE

Protect Existing Features during Surveying

The process of surveying a site for inventory and analysis can damage existing site features such as vegetation and soil. Steps should be taken immediately to protect these features during survey and construction activities. Conventional survey methods, relying on a clear line of sight, may damage features, so planning the survey around features to be retained can help protect them, as well as minimize cutting of vegetation and soil compaction.

Alternative survey technologies such as global positioning systems (GPS) and laser three-dimensional site imaging may better protect sites.

Protect Existing Features during Construction

Construction activities can negatively impact existing site features. Site clearing and grading during construction can compact soils, disrupt soil horizons, and cause topsoil erosion, leading to sedimentation of

Meg Calkins, RLA, ASLA, Ball State University

water bodies. Vegetation can be destroyed by machinery compacting root systems and breaking woody limbs. The most effective way to protect a site during construction is to limit site access, thereby limiting site disturbance. Earthwork and vegetation clearing should be limited as follows: to 40 feet beyond the building perimeter; 10 feet beyond curbs, walkways, and paved areas; and 5 feet beyond utility trenches.

On portions of the site that must be disturbed, seeding, mulching, or mulch blankets can stabilize soil, and structures such as earth dikes, silt fences, and grass swales can prevent soil from entering water bodies in stormwater runoff. Minimizing and restricting movement of construction machinery around the site can reduce soil compaction and vegetation destruction. Construction fencing should be placed outside and around the drip line of all trees to be left on the site and maintained during the entire construction process. Store construction equipment in existing compacted areas, prior to their being paved for parking or roads. Keep construction equipment at least 10 feet away from areas expected to infiltrate water.

(See *Site Construction Overview, Construction Damage to Existing Trees On-Site: Avoidance, Protection, and Preservation,* and *Soil Erosion and Sediment Control.*)

Minimize Site Development Footprint and Develop Densely

By minimizing the site development footprint, more exiting natural areas can be preserved and natural areas restored. Site master plans can be used to guide current and future development to designate and protect open space, ensuring large and contiguous areas for habitat and ecological process. Guidelines include the following:

- Site development should occur on portions of the site that have already been impacted by development.
- To maximize open space and minimize structural footprints, buildings can be clustered or multistory.
- Designing with the existing topography will minimize grading, topsoil removal, and retaining structures.
- Designing with existing hydrologic systems will minimize need for grading and stormwater infrastructure
- Clustering underground utilities and grouping them with roads will minimize site disturbance.

(See *Site Planning.*)

Reduce Negative Impacts of Roads and Parking Areas

Impermeable paved surfaces for roads and parking can disturb habitats, increase stormwater runoff quantities, concentrate nonpoint source pollutants, erode soil, and contribute to the heat-island effect. Reducing the size and quantity of impermeable vehicular surfaces will help minimize the site development footprint and lower the related impacts on existing site ecosystems. Because parking lots and roads are dictated by local zoning codes, a first action should be policy changes, to reduce prescribed road widths and parking standards.

Parking

A careful analysis of parking needs is the first step in reducing paved surfaces on a site (e.g., ≤2 spaces/dwelling unit; ≤3 spaces/1000 s.f. office space; ≤4.5 spaces/1000 s.f. retail space). Other methods to minimize parking lot sizes include:

- Implement shared parking policies.
- Impose codes that place a maximum on number of spaces.
- Locate development near mass transit.
- Encourage carpooling.
- Downsize parking stall and lane size requirements.
- Increase the number of compact spaces.
- Locate parking lots under buildings.

Other effective methods of sustainable parking design include locating planting islands in all areas of the parking lot that will not be occupied by cars, such as the center of turnarounds, and all other interstitial spaces. Shortening the length of parking spaces and adding the saved footage to a planting strip between parking aisles can result in less paving and more plantings. These areas should be located slightly below the grade of the existing paving to encourage runoff into the planting areas. Curb openings, or no curbs, can allow water access to these areas. If planted and graded appropriately, these bioswales can reduce nonpoint source pollution from the parking area and slow water to encourage infiltration.

Scattering parking around a site and breaking up large expanses of pavement can reduce site disturbance and grading, and allow careful siting of parking among existing natural features. This approach can also assist with stormwater infiltration by reducing concentration of stormwater runoff in storm drains and allowing for surface infiltration. During construction, care must be taken to prevent compacting or disturbing existing soil or vegetation in these areas.

Making paving permeable will not reduce site disturbance, but can assist in stormwater infiltration, soil health, and reduction of the heat island effect. Permeable paving materials include asphalt or concrete, open-grid unit pavers, grass paving, crushed stone, or crushed clam or oyster shells.

Streets and Driveways

Narrower street and road widths can mean less site disturbance. On some roadways, narrowing lane widths from 10 to 9 feet can reduce site disturbance and grading, lower resource use and maintenance requirements, and encourage slower vehicle speeds. The concept of "traffic calming" promotes narrower street widths, increased use of planting areas in parking lanes, and reduced widths at pedestrian crossing points—all of which can result in less paving and more planted areas. If curbs are broken and planted areas are graded to receive stormwater runoff, the planting can help eliminate nonpoint source pollution from the roads, and encourage infiltration. Slower traffic, increased planting, and pedestrian crossings can support more pedestrian activity.

Creating shared driveways can also help to reduce site disturbance and quantity of paved surfaces. Grading and site disturbance around roads, parking, buildings and other paved areas should be limited to 10 feet from the structure, to minimize site disturbance. (See *Transit-Oriented Development, Vehicular Circulation, Parking Standards, Accessibility, Bicycle Circulation.*)

PRESERVE AND RESTORE NATURAL SITE FEATURES AND HABITAT

Preserve or Restore Wildlife Habitat

The process of site development can fragment wildlife habitat and flyways, as well as drastically impact the integrity of the remaining habitat. To help prevent these negative effects, consider these guidelines:

- Provide or maintain a contiguous, dedicated open-space system on-site, and carefully connect it to similar systems off-site. Where this system crosses roads, drives, or paths, employ wildlife crossing structures.
- Specify vegetation to provide wildlife food sources.
- Avoid open trash cans and dumpsters, to discourage aggressive nonnative species.
- Maintain or plant low shrubs and leave woody debris to provide cover and nesting opportunities.
- Minimize the use of herbicides, pesticides, fungicides, and hazardous materials, to protect the health of wildlife.
- Employ erosion control methods and sustainable stormwater best management practices (BMPs) to protect aquatic fauna.

It's also important to reduce site lighting and control light pollution to promote healthy wildlife. Consistent, intense light can disrupt circadian rhythms, disorient animals, discourage foraging in affected areas, and affect diurnal and breeding patterns. (See *Wetlands Evaluation, Resource Inventory and Conservation, Ecological Community Restoration, Soil Erosion and Sediment Control, Lighting, Constructed Treatment Wetlands,* and *Wildlife Habitat.*)

PROTECT AND RESTORE SOIL HEALTH AND FERTILITY

Effects of soil loss and compaction can directly affect nutrient cycling, ion exchange, and hydrologic function, which negatively affect water and nutrient availability for plants and soil organisms. Water infiltration and supply to aquifers, streams, and water bodies is affected by soil compaction and erosion.

Minimize Soil Compaction

Compacted soil may have low or no infiltration capacity and is an inhospitable environment for vegetation. With no pore spaces for air or water, soil organisms cannot live and soil will become barren. Therefore:

- Use areas of existing compaction for new building or paving locations.
- Maintain areas of healthy soil as planted areas.
- Avoid soil compaction during construction (see the Minimize Site Disturbance section).
- Minimize the footprint of new structures that will require compacted soil.
- Restore the health of existing compacted soils by tilling, aerating, and amending the soil.

Minimize Grading and Earthwork

Grading and earthwork can lead to soil compaction, erosion, and disturb existing soil horizons. It can also

Meg Calkins, RLA, ASLA, Ball State University

negatively affect natural drainage patterns requiring increased stormwater infrastructure.

- Design to fit the site's topographic and drainage context. Locate project features to work with existing topography. Parking lots should be located on relatively flat parts of the site, and roadways along consistent existing contours or ridges.
- Use techniques of landform grading where new grading mimics natural landforms.
- Do not disturb, clear, or grade slopes that are greater than 25 percent, or greater than 15 percent where erodible soils exist.
- Design site plan to balance cut and fill, reducing the need for off-site soil. No more than 10 percent of the soil should be imported to or exported from the site.

Control Erosion and Sedimentation

By designing a site appropriately and taking care during construction, soil erosion can be controlled and sedimentation of water bodies prevented.

- Design to fit the site's topographic, soil, vegetation, and drainage context to minimize erosion.
- Minimize the area of both permanent and construction site disturbance, and limit removal of vegetative cover, to control erosion.
- Reduce the extent of bare areas, and plan for construction during the dry season, to minimize erosion.
- Where high winds might erode soil, install sand or wind fences as barriers to movement.
- Employ permanent erosion control measures such as vegetative buffer strips, silt fences, fiber wattles and logs, check dams in swales, sediment traps, and detention/retention ponds.

Conserve or Restore Native Soil Fertility

Soil that closely resembles the native soil composition (including biota) will foster on-site hydrologic processes and serve as a healthy foundation for plant and animal habitat. Thus, conducting an analysis of site soil and research on native regional soil composition is a critical step in achieving healthy soils. Where existing soils are healthy, they should be preserved, with the objective being to minimize soil import and export. Native soil should be stockpiled, with an eye toward health and horizon integrity, and compaction should be minimized during stockpiling. Strategies to restore depleted soils include:

- Mulch planting areas and amend soils with appropriate mineral and organic matter. Consider using biosolids or sludge.
- Minimize use of synthetic fertilizers. On-site composting can provide usable organic matter to maintain soil health.
- Implement bioremediation and phytoremediation techniques to improve contaminated soils.
- On sites with no or minimal topsoil, manufacture topsoil from recycled materials.

(See *Site Grading and Earthwork, Cut and Fill Calculations, Soil Erosion and Sediment Control, Soil Mechanics, Planting: Special Considerations, Brownfields Remediation and Development,* and *Soils: Agronomic.*)

PROTECT AND RESTORE APPROPRIATE NATIVE OR ADAPTED VEGETATION

Protection and enhancement of appropriate plant communities can provide wildlife habitat, facilitate stormwater infiltration, reduce water pollution, cleanse the air, and mitigate heat island effects.

Inventory Existing Site Vegetation and Understand Regional Native Plant Communities

Existing vegetation and plant communities on and around the site should be surveyed. Research should identify local native plants, plant communities, as well as invasive and noxious plants to be avoided. An on-site vegetation analysis should include location, genus, species, and condition of all significant trees and shrubs. Wildlife habitat, hydrologic, and soil analyses should be conducted simultaneously with a vegetation analysis. (See *Resource Inventory and Conservation.*)

Protect Existing Native and Adapted Vegetation

A goal of site design should be to preserve as much existing vegetation as possible. To that end:

- Build structures and install utilities for minimal disturbance of vegetation.
- During construction, minimize clearing and damage to existing vegetation.
- To the extent possible, limit movement of construction equipment around the site.
- Limit vegetation clearing to 40 feet beyond the building perimeter; 10 feet beyond curbs, walkways, and paved areas; and 5 feet beyond utility trenches.
- Install construction fencing, and maintain it during the entire construction process. Place fencing outside and around the drip line of all trees to remain.
- Where vegetation must be removed, transplant and stockpile it for reuse on the site. Where vegetation must be cleared, compost it on-site to preserve biomass.

Use Plant Material Appropriate to the Ecoregion

Using native and adapted vegetation that is appropriate to the site's ecoregion, soils, climate and water availability can help plants survive; provide wildlife habitat; and reduce the input of water, fertilizers, and pesticides. Use of invasive or noxious plants should be avoided. If these plants exist on the site, they should be removed. In addition to the National Invasive Species Information Center, local or regional native plant organizations often maintain lists of invasive plants and noxious weeds. To avoid using plants gathered from exploited landscapes, specify nursery-propagated plants grown from seeds or cuttings. Seed for native plants should be from a certified source.

Use a Diverse Plant Palette

Site development can reduce biodiversity of plantings because of habitat fragmentation and use of generalist plant species hardy to many planting zones. This limited diversity can make plantings more susceptible to pest infestations and disease. In addition, many conventional plantings have a reduced complexity of vegetation structure resulting in lower habitat value. Use of a structurally and biologically diverse plant palette can also aid integrated pest management techniques by providing cover for predator species.

Use Structural Soil to Promote Tree Root Growth under Pavements

Soil compaction necessary to support paving structures leaves little space for tree roots to grow. This results in shorter life spans for many urban street trees. Structural soil, a mix of gravel, gel and soil, offers the stability necessary for pavement while allowing tree roots to grow in pore spaces. Uniform gravel sizes offer good compaction, and gel causes soil to adhere to the gravel, opening space for tree roots to grow.

CONSERVE AND PROTECT WATER RESOURCES

Conserve, Harvest, and Reuse Fresh Water

Specify Low Water Use or Drought-Tolerant Plants

In some climates, ornamental plantings and turf lawns can require high volumes of water for irrigation. In contrast, landscapes composed of native and adapted vegetation often require little irrigation input once established. Temporary irrigation systems can be used for plant establishment, then disconnected. Techniques such as mulching, composting mowers, mechanical mowers, and composting can reduce plant water use.

Use Efficient Irrigation Systems

Where irrigation is required, these high-efficiency strategies can be employed:

- Use microirrigation, drip and subsurface systems.
- Use moisture sensors, weather database controllers and clock timers so irrigation is used only when needed.
- Use graywater collected from roofs or paved surfaces for irrigation, however care must be taken to avoid particulate matter in the irrigation heads.
- Periodically service irrigation systems to ensure efficient function.

Use Rainwater Collection Systems and Reuse Graywater in the Landscape

Rainwater can be collected from roofs and paved ground surfaces, then stored for reuse to irrigate plantings or for a variety of nonpotable applications in buildings. However, the amount of expected rainfall should be determined, first, to make sure that there is enough to support a collection system; and local heath codes should be consulted to identify allowable uses and conditions for rainwater reuse.

Roofing materials for rainwater collection should be metal, clay, or concrete-based, as asphalt and lead-containing materials will contaminate the collected rainwater. Rainwater can be filtered using a variety of graded screens and filter types.

Graywater systems can be used to recover wastewater from building uses such as lavatories, showers, washing machines, and other facilities that don't involve human or food waste. This water can be stored in cisterns on-site and used to irrigate plantings. However, keep in mind that some types of graywater may contain detergents and other pollutants that can harm plantings. (See *Stormwater*

Meg Calkins, RLA, ASLA, Ball State University

Management; Irrigation; Waste Water Management; Graywater Harvest and Treatment.)

Encourage Groundwater Recharge through On-Site Infiltration Strategies

Site development and increased impermeable surfaces can negatively impact existing hydrologic processes, causing increased volume and velocity of horizontal flows and compromised water quality from concentrated nonpoint source pollution. Groundwater recharge is also reduced with current conveyance practices. Designing sites to respect natural drainage patterns, minimize impermeable surfaces, and maximize stormwater infiltration can help protect site and regional hydrologic systems by reducing downstream impacts and recharging groundwater.

Respect Natural Drainage Patterns

An understanding of, and respect for, natural drainage patterns of the site and region is essential to protect existing hydrologic processes. Regional watersheds and downstream impacts from site development should be analyzed, and the site design should incorporate existing drainage patterns and minimize grading and slope modifications to the extent possible. (See *Resource Inventory and Conservation, Regional Climate, Context-Sensitive Solutions,* and *Stormwater Management.*)

Minimize Impervious Surfaces

Site design should attempt to minimize impervious surfaces, such as paving and roofs; and where impervious surfaces are necessary, they should not be contiguous.

- Multistory buildings can reduce structure footprints and roof areas; and clustered buildings can limit site disruption.
- Stormwater impacts caused by parking can be lessoned by limiting the number of parking areas, downsizing parking lot sizes, placing parking under buildings or in stacked structures, or making paving permeable.
- Road widths can be narrowed, and shared driveways can be used to further reduce paving.
- Eliminating curbs along streets and in parking areas will allow runoff to reach vegetated areas.
- Scattering parking among vegetated areas or breaking up large parking expanses with vegetation can encourage infiltration of stormwater.

Make Paving Permeable

Where paved surfaces are necessary for site development, permeable paving can be used to encourage infiltration.

- Porous asphalt and concrete are monolithic applications of permeable paving, with coarse aggregate and cementious binder and an absence of fine aggregate to allow pore spaces for water to pass through.
- Some unit pavers are designed to allow infiltration incorporating spacers to provide ¼ inch minimun open joints, or providing interstitial spaces for gravel and drainage.
- Cellular and open-grid paving can accommodate vegetation or gravel in the cells, allowing water to infiltrate.
- Simple gravel paving can also be permeable if it is a consistent grade.

Slow Runoff, and Employ Surface Drainage Strategies

Using surface drainage strategies to slow and infiltrate stormwater can reduce downstream impacts and recharge groundwater. Vegetated swales, filter strips, rain gardens, infiltration basins, check dams, constructed wetlands, and green roofs can slow and retain stormwater runoff, allowing time for infiltration or evaporation. (See *Parking Standards; Stormwater Management; Water Features, Fountains, and Pools; Planting: Special Considerations; Living Green Roofs and Landscapes over Structure;* and *Soil Erosion and Sediment Control.*)

Protect, Treat, and Restore Water Quality

Impermeable surfaces that speed and increase water flow can concentrate nonpoint source pollutants, and the growing presence of automobiles and applied landscape chemicals on sites can increase the amount of nonpoint source pollutants. Filtering stormwater through soil and plant material can cleanse water and remove some pollutants. Use of bioswales, rain gardens, constructed wetlands, and green roofs can improve stormwater quality. Designing sites to break up large expanses of pavement can reduce concentrations of pollutants. (See *Site Considerations, Plant Installation Requirements, and Details; Planting: Special Considerations; Stormwater Management;* and *Constructed Treatment Wetlands.*)

Reduce Water Pollution

Avoid Building Products and Materials That Contribute to Water Pollution

Some raw material extraction and manufacturing processes for building materials use water and produce waste by-products that can contribute harmful pollutants to water, although there are manufacturers taking steps to lower water use and control water pollution from their processes. Disposal of some materials, such as PVC pipes, also can affect groundwater quality, and every effort should be made to understand, then minimize, these potential hazards to water quality.

Minimize Use of Applied Landscape Chemicals

The introduction of pesticides, herbicides, fungicides, fertilizers, deicing chemicals, cleaning agents, and other applied landscape chemicals can adversely affect groundwater and surface water quality. Therefore, the environmental and water quality impacts of these products must be well understood before application, and steps taken to limit their migration to water bodies. (See *Environmental Hazards* and *Plant Maintenance.*)

Treat Wastewater On-Site

The process of conveying wastewater to conventional regional treatment facilities requires large amounts of potable water and extensive chemical treatment to remove contaminants. On-site wastewater treatment can lower infrastructure costs, conserve freshwater, and reduce chemical use in treatment. On-site treatment options range from conventional biological treatment facilities to systems that cleanse water by mimicking natural processes. Cleansing biotopes, "living machines," and constructed wetlands move wastewater through planted bodies of water, settling solids and using plants and microbes to remove contaminants. (See *Waste Water Management* and *Constructed Treatment Wetlands.*)

MINIMIZE RESOURCE USE, AND REUSE MATERIALS

Environmental impacts from extraction, transport, processing, manufacture, installation, and disposal of building materials have a far-reaching effect on ecological systems around the world. These effects include habitat degradation; air, water, and soil pollution; transportation-related impacts; release of toxic chemicals or by-products from manufacturing; use and disposal; and issues associated with waste material disposal in landfills.

Reducing resource use and reusing materials can minimize the above effects, save money, and enrich a site's design.

Minimize Construction and Demolition Waste

The end of the use phase of a structure can mean disposal and release to the environment, but it can also include reuse, reprocessing, or recycling. Building materials can outlast the life of a landscape, so planning for their reuse is important. "Deconstruction" is the term used to refer to the disassembly and salvage of materials from a building or site, as opposed to "demolition," whereby everything is destroyed and hauled to a landfill.

Certainly, deconstruction takes more time and incurs higher labor costs than demolition, but, ultimately, it may be less expensive than paying landfill costs; and resale of the materials, either whole or ground, can generate additional income. Where the demolition contractor is also responsible for the new construction, materials can be stockpiled for reuse on-site.

The following actions can help to minimize waste:

- To ensure job-site recycling and minimization of waste, specifications and general requirements should contain waste management instructions.
- Structures should be designed to minimize construction waste by sizing members based on available material dimensions. For instance, wood decks should be sized based on available board lengths.

(See *Site Construction Overview* and *Evaluating the Environmental and Human Health Impacts of Materials.*)

Reuse Existing Structures

Reusing existing structures in a new site design will decrease use of virgin resources and minimize demolition waste. This can offer economic advantage as transportation for demolition waste and new material import will be reduced. Construction costs may be lower as well. Reuse of existing structures may enhance the design of the site by referencing the identity of the previous intervention.

Use Resource-Efficient, Durable, and Low-Maintenance Materials

Two important strategies to minimize resource use are to use fewer materials and to build landscapes to last. A landscape constructed from durable and low-maintenance materials and products that make efficient use

Meg Calkins, RLA, ASLA, Ball State University

of resources, such as segmental retaining walls (which need no footing below the frost line), will have a longer life and, consequently, use fewer resources and less energy. (See *Evaluating the Environmental and Human Health Impacts of Materials.*)

Specify Materials with Reuse Potential

Materials installed so that they can be easily removed at the end of the life of the landscape and reused elsewhere may not be "green" themselves, but the way they are assembled is. For example, masonry installations in which no mortar is used, such as sand-set brick, stone, or concrete pavers, and interlocking retaining wall units, allow for easy disassembly and reuse of the materials. Also, use of metal fasteners, rather than welding, where applicable, facilitates removal of reusable parts. (See *Evaluating the Environmental and Human Health Impacts of Materials.*)

Use Salvaged and Reused Materials

Materials with the least environmental impact are those that have been previously used: no new raw materials are used, and the energy for raw material extraction and manufacturing is conserved. The only major "costs" of reused materials are the energy required to transport and install them. But when materials are salvaged and reused on-site, even the cost of transport energy can be lowered. Because salvaged materials are available in a limited quantity, type, and size, they should be located before the design development phase, as their unique character will influence the detailing of the structure in which they are used.

The following strategies can be used to expedite a salvaged-materials project:

- At start of project, evaluate project sites and old buildings for materials to reuse. Include known subgrade structures in the evaluation as well.
- Hire demolition contractors that have experience in deconstruction and salvage.
- Require contractors to provide a plan for construction and demolition salvage and recycling.
- Let the materials inspire the design and adapt design ideas to the unique character of the salvaged material. Use materials with interesting "stories" or cultural significance to the project.
- Use materials for their highest use—avoid "downcycling" or cutting whole materials into smaller pieces.
- Locate and purchase materials early in the design process to avoid major design revisions when materials are found. If budget permits, purchase more of the salvaged material than needed as the material will most likely not be available if you return to the source later for more material. Designs should remain flexible until salvaged materials are located.
- Include appearance and environmental performance standards in the specifications.
- Get the contractor on board with using salvage early in the process.

Use Recycled-Content Materials

Products with recycled material contain less new raw material, thus reduce environmental impact; and reuse material is diverted from landfills. Postconsumer recycled content is considered preferable to postindustrial material because it is more likely to otherwise end up in a landfill; postindustrial recycled content is more likely to be reused by industry rather than find its way to a landfill.

Products claiming recycled content should contain a minimum of 25 percent postconsumer or 40 percent postindustrial content.

Concrete is a very common building material that benefits from postindustrial recycled content. Environmental impacts from cement production are high with intensive energy use for crushing and heating limestone, and resulting release of large amounts of CO_2. Research has shown that industrial by-products such as fly ash, ground granulated blast furnace slag, silica fume, and rice hull ash can be substituted for cement in concrete. Useful content varies by product, but some studies demonstrate cementious properties of Class C flyash suggesting that very high percentages can be substituted for the cement. (See *Evaluating the Environmental and Human Health Impacts of Materials.*)

Use Renewable Materials

A number of products are made from renewable resources. Wood is the most common building material that is renewable and is considered to be a "long-cycle" renewable material. Rapidly renewable materials are primarily plants that are harvested in cycles shorter than 10 years. Coir and jute are used for geotextiles; succulents are used as stabilizers for loose aggregate paving; and plant oils are used in form release agents. Bamboo and willow can be used in landscape structures, and fiber from processed crops is used in engineered wood products. (See *Wood and Related Materials, Geotextiles,* and *Evaluating the Environmental and Human Health Impacts of Materials.*)

Use Certified Materials

Wood can be considered a green material if it comes from well-managed forests and is harvested sustainably. Environmentally responsible forest management practices protect the functional integrity and diversity of tree stands, minimize clear cutting, protect old-growth forests, and minimize wasteful harvesting and milling techniques. The Forest Stewardship Council (FSC) has developed standards for third-party certification of sustainable wood. This certification should be made by an FSC-certified independent party. (See *Wood Decks, Wood and Related Products,* and *Evaluating the Environmental and Human Health Impacts of Materials.*)

MINIMIZE ENERGY USE

Fuels burned to produce energy are a major source of pollution, global warming, and acid deposition and are nonrenewable resources. Minimizing energy use or using renewable energy sources can reduce use of fossil fuels.

Design Landscape Features to Conserve Building Energy

Vegetation and earthwork can help to moderate temperature and conserve energy in buildings. In summer, deciduous trees can block solar access to buildings, reducing heat gain and use of air conditioning. Trees with high crowns can shade roofs and block high sun, while trees with lower crowns can block the low western sun. Evapotranspiration can reduce surrounding air temperatures by as much as 9°F. Vegetation can be sited to channel summer breezes and increase air movement during the warmer months. Water features can be located between prevailing summer breezes and living spaces to passively cool the spaces with evaporative cooling from wind across the water.

In winter, when deciduous trees lose their leaves and sun angles are lower, solar access and heat gain in the building increases. Evergreen trees and fences can be situated to block winter winds. Planting shrubs and vines next to the building will create dead airspaces that insulate the building in both winter and summer. Earth berms, with their more consistent temperature, can insulate building walls and minimize temperature extremes in the building. Planting on the berms can help with evaporative cooling around the building. (See *Modifying Solar Radiation, Modifying Wind, Regional Climate,* and *Modifying Microclimate.*)

Design Site Plans for Energy Conservation, Orient Buildings to Take Advantage of Solar and Climatic Conditions

Siting, orientation, and arrangement of buildings on a site can impact their energy use. The longer walls of a building should be oriented to face north and south to maximize passive solar use and exclusion. Walls that face the noonday sun need relatively smaller sun control devices, as the sun is higher in the sky. It is more difficult to control solar gain with shading devices and overhangs for windows facing east and west, where the sun is lower in the sky. Deciduous trees can be used to block low sun angles. In cool climates, windows that face the equator can be a source of heat gain in the winter months. Also, buildings can be grouped to shade one another.

Use Low Embodied Energy Materials

Embodied energy is the total energy required to produce and install a material or product during all stages of the life cycle. The life-cycle stages include: raw material extraction, processing, manufacture, fabrication, transport, installation, use and maintenance, and recycling or disposal. If the product is complex that is made from more than one material, such as a steel and wood bench, the embodied energy of the bench would include the energy inputs from both the wood and steel components plus the energy input to assemble them.

Products that are minimally processed, such as stone and wood, usually have lower embodied energy than highly processed materials such as plastics and metals. Evaluating the embodied energy of materials can be a useful baseline for comparing two different materials; however, this type of analysis does not take into account other factors of production such as pollutants produced, toxins released, resources used, or habitats destroyed. (See *Evaluating the Environmental and Human Health Impacts of Materials.*)

Use Local Materials

Transport of building materials, especially heavy or bulky ones, not only requires a tremendous amount of fuel energy, but contributes to air and water pollution. Using regionally manufactured materials can help lessen the environmental impact of a material, by reducing the transport energy. Transportation costs may also be reduced, at the same time the local economy is supported.

Meg Calkins, RLA, ASLA, Ball State University

Availability of regionally manufactured materials depends on the project location. Ideally, most materials and products should be obtained within 500 miles of the project site. Heavy materials such as aggregate, concrete, and brick should be procured from even closer locations. Distances between raw material extraction locations and manufacturing/processing facilities should also be considered.

Researching regionally available materials and products during the schematic design phase can facilitate use of local materials. Creating databases of regional materials and products can save time on future projects in the region. (See *Evaluating the Environmental and Human Health Impacts of Materials.*)

Minimize Use of Operating Energy or Use Renewable Energy Sources

Operating energy, the energy used to run the fixtures of a project, is greater for buildings than landscapes. Many landscape fixtures are becoming more energy efficient, and some operate from renewable energy sources. Even though energy conservation measures can mean higher first costs, these are often recovered through energy cost savings in operation of the project.

Some light standards are available with attached or remote solar panels. Siting of the solar panels to maximize exposure to sunlight is critical, and systems must be chosen carefully based on the amount of available sunlight on the site. Solar-powered controllers, sensors, and valves are available for both irrigation systems and water features. Energy savings can also be achieved with drip and gravity feed irrigation systems.

Other energy-saving steps include:

- Using energy-efficient light fixtures can result in substantial energy and cost savings. There are even energy-efficient bulbs now available for use in some older light fixtures.
- Minimizing frequency of light fixtures, reducing illumination to minimal safe levels, directing light only to where it is required, and using motion sensor and timers to activate lights can save energy and reduce night sky light pollution.
- Installing light-colored surfaces on areas requiring illumination can further reduce the amount of light output needed.
- Design sites to accommodate renewable energy structures.
- Using renewable energy sources to lower the impacts associated with utility energy production, such as natural resource consumption and air and water pollution.

Renewable energy sources are sun, wind, and biomass (derived from organic matter such as waste wood and grasses). Power from sun, wind, and biomass can be generated on appropriate sites, saving transportation costs and impacts. Photovoltaic panels located on buildings and landscape structures can capture solar energy for use on-site. Small wind energy and biopower systems can be located on some sites.

Green power is an alternative where on-site renewable energy sources are not feasible. Green power is generated from renewable energy sources such as solar, water, wind, biomass, and geothermal sources. The Green-e Program certifies green electricity providers in many states. (See *Irrigation,* and *Lighting.*)

Minimize Use of Power Equipment for Maintenance and Construction

Site construction and maintenance often relies on use of large motorized equipment that is powered by nonrenewable fossil fuels. Emissions contribute to air pollution, smog, ozone depletion, acid rain, and greenhouse gasses. They also cause respiratory problems. The weight of these heavy machines can compact soil, decreasing the soil's infiltration capacity. Smaller, fuel-efficient machines may be able to do the same job adequately and may compact soils less. Smaller machines may also be able to fit into tighter spaces, thereby minimizing disturbance of existing natural features.

Common landscape maintenance tools are powered by fuel or electricity typically generated from nonrenewable resources. Where appropriate, manual tools powered by humans can be used instead of electric tools. Even mowing grass less often can save energy. (See *Site Construction Overview* and *Plant Maintenance.*)

MINIMIZE IMPACTS TO AIR AND ATMOSPHERIC QUALITY

Reduce Heat Island Effects

Heat island effects are caused by solar energy retention on constructed surfaces in urban areas, elevating the temperature differential between urban and rural environments (as much as 2 to 9 degrees) resulting in increased energy-consuming cooling loads in summer. Streets, sidewalks, parking lots, and roofs are the primary contributors to the heat island effect. Heat islands also can have a negative effect on wildlife and their habitats.

Heat island mitigation techniques include using materials that reflect the sun's heat instead of absorbing it, and adding shading to constructed surfaces.

Minimize Paving and Increase Shade

Minimizing paving and maximizing shade-producing vegetation can reduce the heat island effect. Vegetation can shelter pavement and roofs, reducing solar absorption on these surfaces; it also cools the air through evapotranspiration. Building underground parking, using open-grid paving with vegetation in the cells (minimum 50 percent open), and scaling back on road and parking areas can reduce paved surfaces. Using high-albedo paving (solar reflectance value of 0.3 or higher) can also reduce the heat absorption that leads to heat islands.

Reduce Roof Area and Use High-Albedo Roofing Materials

Reducing roof area with multistory buildings and high-albedo roofing materials can mitigate heat island effects and maximize energy savings.

Build Green Roofs

Green roofs, either *intensive* or *extensive*, can help mitigate heat island effects, insulate buildings, improve air quality, cool air through evapotranspiration, and retain and filter stormwater.

- Intensive green roofs are often designed as gardens, with vegetation ranging from large trees to shrubs and grasses. Soil depths are a minimum of 12 inches, and construction may contain elaborate irrigation and drainage systems. Intensive green roofs can add roof loads from 80 to 150 pounds per square foot.
- Extensive green roofs, built primarily for environmental benefits, have thin vegetation and soil layers. Soil depths range from 1 to 5 inches, adding only 15 to 50 pounds per square foot. While accessible for maintenance, they are not designed for occupation.

(See *Living Green Roofs and Landscapes over Structure.*)

Reduce Air Pollution

Avoid Building Products and Materials That Contribute to Air Pollution in Harvesting, Manufacture, Use, and Disposal

In some raw material extraction and manufacturing processes for building materials, waste by-products are produced that contribute harmful pollutants and particulates to air. Though a number of manufacturers today are taking steps to eliminate or mitigate air pollution from their processes, it is essential to the sustainable design effort to understand and address these potential hazards to air quality. (See *Modifying Air Quality, Environmental Hazards,* and *Evaluating the Environmental and Human Health Impacts of Materials.*)

Design to Promote Alternative Transportation

Automobiles consume nonrenewable fuel and contribute heavily to air pollution. Measures should be taken to lower dependence on single-occupancy vehicle use. When selecting a site, preference should be given to areas with easy access to public transportation. Projects should be within one-half mile of a subway or commuter rail station or one-fourth mile of a bus stop.

Sites also should be designed to connect to existing bicycle, pedestrian, and public transportation routes. Commercial and institutional projects should provide secure bicycle storage and, if applicable, changing and shower facilities for commuting employees. Parking preference should be given to those arriving in carpools and vanpools. (See *Human Factors, Modifying Microclimate, Modifying Air Quality, Crime Prevention through Environmental Design, Site Planning, Transit-Oriented Development, Bicycle Circulation,* and *Recreational Trails and Shared-Use Paths.*)

Reduce Light Pollution

Consistent, intense light can have negative effects on wildlife, disrupting circadian rhythms, disorienting animals, discouraging foraging in affected areas, and interfering with diurnal cycles and breeding patterns. Inefficient and overused lighting wastes electricity and causes horizontal light trespass. To eliminate excessive light in the night sky, lower illumination to minimum safe levels, light signs from above, and shield fixtures to prevent uplighting and horizontal trespass. (See *Context-Sensitive Solutions, Lighting,* and *Wildlife Habitat.*)

PROTECT AND FOSTER HUMAN HEALTH

Use Low Emitting Materials and Products

Materials, adhesives, sealers, preservatives, and coatings can contain volatile organic compounds (VOCs) and other harmful chemical ingredients. Construction workers and end-users exposed to these chemicals can be

Meg Calkins, RLA, ASLA, Ball State University

adversely affected in many ways. Manufacture of such materials can produce hazardous by-products. Products with associated synthetic chemicals should be carefully examined for harmful effects. Many synthetic chemicals are not biodegradable or easily broken down. Furthermore, the Environmental Protection Agency (EPA), National Research Council, estimates that more than 65,000 synthetic chemicals in use have not been tested on humans. For sustainable design, the rule of thumb is, if a material or product contains a chemical whose effects are unknown, avoid it. Material Safety Data Sheets (MSDS) can be obtained from the manufacturer for any material or product that has adverse human health effects. Fortunately, today, many nontoxic, low-VOC, organic, and natural alternative products are being developed for adhesives, coatings, and sealers. Good sources for these products are Internet building supply stores. (See *Modifying Air Quality, Environmental Hazards,* and *Evaluating the Environmental and Human Health Impacts of Materials.*)

Avoid Products That Contain Persistent Biological Toxins

Some materials contain or emit persistent bioaccumulative toxins (PBT's). These are toxins that don't break down and accumulate in the fatty tissue of organisms moving up the food chain.

Design for Safe and Secure Environments

When designing sites for safe and secure occupation, transparency and visual access are critical factors. Careful study of sightlines can promote pedestrian and vehicular safety.

- Take measures that encourage use of exterior space such as paths, sidewalks, benches, and porches. The greater the "people presence," the greater the sense of security.
- Incorporate traffic-calming devices to slow vehicles and foster safer streets.
- Provide illumination levels to promote safety; however aim light where it is needed, and use the lowest safe illumination level to avoid light pollution. Providing more fixtures with lower wattage will create a safer, more consistent illumination than fewer high wattage fixtures.

(See *Crime Prevention through Environmental Design* and *Site Security Planning and Landscape Design Criteria.*)

Design for Pedestrians and Nonmotorized Vehicles

Providing safe and pleasurable connections for pedestrians, wheelchairs, and bicycles through sites will encourage alternatives to automobile travel. They will also provide recreational and exercise opportunities for site users. Sidewalks and walking/biking paths that connect to regional systems and destinations are ideal. The paths should be located and constructed to ensure a pleasant and safe user experience. Project-specific user needs will, of course, take precedence in this effort; for example, if the primary users are children or senior citizens or both.

Connect People with Nature and Natural Systems

Allowing access to natural systems and exposing users to ecological processes can be an important aspect of sustainable design. Visual access to natural features has also been proven to increase learning and promote healing. View corridors and visual access from buildings, parking, and paths all can serve to promote this. Availability of sunlight and natural lighting can also help to connect people to natural systems. It's also important to educate users about environmental processes as a way of connecting them to the site's ecological systems.

MANAGE AND MAINTAIN SUSTAINABLE LANDSCAPES

Sustainable design involves landscape systems that function and evolve over time, therefore maintenance and management measures to ensure landscape system health and function are critical.

Consider Maintenance during Design

Maintenance techniques need to be identified during the design process to ensure that planting and structures can be sustainably maintained. Ideal plants are those that require little or no fertilizers or pesticides, and maintenance by fuel-powered machines. In addition:

- Consider integrated pest management strategies.
- Provide for on-site composting of plant trimming.
- Design structures for ease of maintenance. Know the spatial requirements of the maintenance machines that will be used, and size structures and spaces accordingly.
- Specify hardscape that can be maintained without toxic sealants or coatings.

(See *Plant Maintenance.*)

Make a Maintenance Plan or Manual

Maintenance plans or manuals can help ensure continuous function of sustainable site design systems. Plans should cover the following:

- Party responsible for management and maintenance decisions
- Group who will perform the maintenance
- Maintenance schedules, lists of tasks, and logs of completed tasks
- Information on specific maintenance techniques for each technology or material
- Maintenance product specifications for cleaners, sealers, snow removal products, fertilizers, pesticides, herbicides, and insecticides
- As-built construction documents
- Guidelines for waste recycling or disposal

Monitor Landscape System Function Postinstallation

To ensure adequate function postinstallation, sustainable systems must be tested and monitored at regular intervals. To help in this regard, monitoring protocols should be established during the design phase to allow adequate time to obtain funding and generate design responses that will facilitate monitoring activities.

Monitoring can be performed in collaboration with university researchers, owners, or site maintenance personnel. Funding for monitoring of landscape systems such as wetlands and other water quality structures can be obtained from some government agencies. (See *Postoccupancy Evaluation.*)

Employ Appropriate Maintenance Techniques

Landscape maintenance often involves the use of energy, resources, and toxic chemicals. And common landscape maintenance tools are powered by fuel or electricity typically generated from nonrenewable resources. To limit the impact of these:

- Where possible, replace fuel-powered maintenance machines with manual, human-powered, tools, or use fuel-efficient machines. Even mowing grass less often can save energy.
- Reduce or eliminate the presence of synthetic chemicals on a site by implementing integrated pest management strategies and using organic fertilizers tailored to site-specific soil conditions. Selection of appropriate plants can go a long way toward lowering use of synthetic chemicals. Also, use nontoxic cleaners and sealers.

SUPPORT FOR SUSTAINABLE DESIGN

A growing number of nonprofit and government programs offer support for sustainable design efforts. A number of states and municipalities offer incentives, information, and technical support through green building programs. And numerous national programs support sustainable design; they are listed in "Web Resources and Government Programs," at the end of this section.

U.S. Green Building Council

The U.S. Green Building Council (USGBC) is a national coalition of building industry professionals, contractors, policymakers, owners, and manufacturers whose stated mission is "to promote buildings that are environmentally responsible, profitable, and healthy places to live and work." Council members work in a committee-based, consensus-focused way to develop Leadership in Energy and Environmental Design (LEED) products and resources (see next), policy guidance, and educational and marketing tools to facilitate the adoption of green building. The council develops alliances with industry and research organizations, and federal, state, and local governments.

Leadership in Energy and Environmental Design

The Leadership in Energy and Environmental Design (LEED) Green Building Rating System is a voluntary national standard for developing sustainable and high-performance buildings and sites. USGBC members developed and continue to refine the system through a membership consensus process. According to the USGBC, "LEED was created to: define 'green building' by establishing a common standard of measurement; promote integrated, whole-building design practices; recognize environmental leadership in the building industry; stimulate green competition; raise consumer awareness of green building benefits; and transform the building market."

LEED-NC, 2.2 New Commercial Construction and Major Renovation Projects: LEED-NC, the original LEED system, is designed to guide high-performance commercial and institutional projects. It has also been applied to schools, multiunit residential buildings, manufacturing plants, laboratories, and other building types. Registered projects can choose from a variety of sustainable strategies and earn points toward a certified project in the following six categories:

Category	Possible Points
Sustainable Sites	14

Meg Calkins, RLA, ASLA, Ball State University

Water Efficiency	5
Energy & Atmosphere	17
Materials & Resources	13
Indoor Environmental Quality	15
Innovation & Design Process	5

Projects can be certified at a variety of levels based on the points that they earn, as follows:

LEED NC Certification Levels	Points
Certified	26–32
Silver	33–38
Gold	39–51
Platinum	52–69

LEED-EB, Existing Building Operations: This system is a set of performance standards for the sustainable operation of existing buildings. Criteria cover building operations and system upgrades where the majority of the building surfaces remain unchanged.

LEED-CI, Commercial Interiors Projects: This system addresses the specifics of tenant spaces in office, retail, and institutional buildings.

LEED-CS, Core and Shell Projects (in pilot phase): This rating system covers core and shell project criteria such as structure, building envelope, and building level systems.

LEED-H, Homes (in pilot phase): This system covers homebuilding practices and is geared to home developers and individual homeowners.

LEED-ND, Neighborhood Development (in phase): This system offers standards for neighborhood design that integrates the principles of smart growth, urbanism, and green building.

Web Resources and Government Programs

American Bioenergy Association: www.biomass.org

American Forest and Paper Association's Sustainable Forestry Initiative: www.afandpa.org/Content/NavigationMenu/Environment_and_Recycling/SFI/SFI.htm

American Rainwater Catchment Systems Association (ARCSA): www.arcsa-usa.org

American Wind Energy Association: www.awea.org

Association of Official Seed Certifying Agencies (AOSCA): www.aosca.org

BEES Building for Environmental and Economic Sustainability: http://www.bfrl.nist.gov/oae/software/bees.html

California Integrated Waste Management Board Recycled-Content Product Directory: www.ciwmb.ca.gov/RCP

Comprehensive Procurement Guidelines for recycled content guidelines and products: www.epa.gov/cpg

Constructed Wetlands for Wastewater Treatment and Wildlife Habitat: 17 Case Studies, EPA Publication No. 832/B-93-005, 1993: www.epa.gov/owow/wetlands/construc/

Construction Materials Recycling Association: www.cdrecycling.org

Forest Stewardship Council (for certification of sustainable forestry): www.fscus.org

Green-e Renewable Electricity Certification Program: www.green-e.org/

Green Roofs for Healthy Cities: www.greenroofs.org

Green Seal: www.greenseal.org

GreenSpec, BuildingGreen, Inc.: www.buildinggreen.com

International Dark Sky Association: www.darksky.org/ida/ida_2/index.html

Leadership in Energy and Environmental Design (LEED) Green Building Rating System: http://www.usgbc.org/LEEDTM/LEEDTM_main.asp

Maryland Stormwater Design Manual: www.mde.state.md.us/Programs/WaterPrograms/SedimentandStormwater/stormwater_design/index.asp

National Invasive Species Information Center, USDA: invasivespeciesinfo.gov

National Recycling Coalition: www.nrc-recycle.org

National Toxicology Program (for listings of carcinogens): http://ntp-server.niehs.nih.gov/index.cfm?objectid=72016262-BDB7-CEBA-FA60E922B18C2540

National Wildlife Federation Backyard Habitat Program: www.nwf.org/backyardwildlifehabitat/

North American Native Plant Society: www.nanps.org/index.shtml

Oikos Green Product Information: http://oikos.com/products/index.lasso

On-site Wastewater Treatment Systems Manual, US EPA: www.epa.gov/owm/septic/pubs/septic_2002_osdm_all.pdf

Persistent Bioaccumulative and Toxic Chemical Program: www.epa.gov/opptintr/pbt

Stormwater Best Management Practice Design Guide, EPA/600/R-04/121A, September 2004: www.epa.gov

Sustainable Forestry Initiative: www.aboutsfi.org/core.asp

Sustainable Redevelopment of Brownfields Program, US EPA: www.epa.gov/brownfields

The Irrigation Association: www.irrigation.org

Threatened and Endangered Species Information from the U.S. Fish and Wildlife Service: http://endangered.fws.gov/wildlife.html

Toxics Release Inventory (TRI): www.epa.gov/tri

TRACI Users Guide: www.epa.gov/ord/NRMRL/Pubs/600R02052/600R02052.pdf

Urban Land Institute: www.uli.org

U.S. Department of Energy, Alternative Fuels Data Center: www.afdc.doe.gov

U.S. Department of Energy, Energy Star program: www.energystar.gov/

U.S. Department of Energy Office of Energy Efficiency and Renewable Energy: www.eere.energy.gov

US Department of Transportation, TEA 21 regulations: www.fhwa.dot.gov/reauthorization/safetea_bill.htm

U.S. Environmental Protection Agency Ecoregion III map: www.epa.gov/wed/pages/ecoregions/level_iii.htm

U.S. EPA: www.epa.gov/heatisland

U.S. EPA Erosion and Sediment Control Model Ordinances: www.epa.gov/owow/nps/ordinance/erosion.htm

U.S. EPA National Pollutant Discharge Elimination System (NPDES) program: www.epa.gov/npdes/

U.S. EPA Wastewise Program: www.epa.gov/wastewise

Volatile Organic Compounds: www.epa.gov/ebtpages/pollchemicvolatileorganiccompoundsvo.html

Wastespec—Model Specifications for Construction Waste Reduction, Reuse, and Recycling: www.tjcog.dst.nc.us/cdwaste.htm

Water-Efficient Landscaping—Preventing Pollution and Using Resources Wisely: www.epa.gov/owm/water-efficiency/final_final.pdf

Water Wiser—The Water Efficiency Clearinghouse: www.awwa.org/waterwiser/

Wildlife Crossings Toolkit: www.wildlifecrossings.info

REFERENCES

Demkin, Joseph (ed.). 1996. *AIA Environmental Resource Guide*. New York, NY: John Wiley & Sons, Inc.

Lyle, John.1994. *Regenerative Design for Sustainable Development*. New York, NY: John Wiley & Sons, Inc.

Mendler, Sandra, and William Odell.2000. *The HOK Guidebook to Sustainable Design*. New York:John Wiley & Sons, Inc.

Thompson, J. William, and Kim Sorvig. 2000. *Sustainable Landscape Construction: A Guide to Green Building Outdoors*. Washington, DC: Island Press.

Van der Ryn, Sim, and Stuart Cowan. 1995. *Ecological Design*. Washington, DC: Island Press.

Meg Calkins, RLA, ASLA, Ball State University

CULTURAL FACTORS

HISTORIC LANDSCAPES

INTRODUCTION

Historic landscapes surround us; there are few places in the world that have not been affected by human use over time. Valuable for the information they reveal about the history of a community, region, or nation, historic resources found in a landscape can help illustrate a story about the interaction of a human group with its surroundings. Because they are comprised primarily of living materials, historic landscapes are ever-changing, yet they are vulnerable to change. However, because of these dynamic, living qualities, historic landscapes also connect us in a deeper way to the rhythms of the earth, the movement of the sun, the seasons, and the passing of time. Landscapes affect us in a profound way—not only despite their vulnerability to time, but because of it.

Historic landscapes vary widely in size and complexity, ranging from large agricultural regions to small residential gardens. In an effort to organize them into manageable categories, the U.S. Secretary of the Interior, through the National Park Service (NPS), recognizes three types of historic landscapes: historic sites, historic designed landscapes, and historic vernacular landscapes:

- *Historic sites.* Significant for their association with a particular event, activity, or person in history, these sites typically include battlefields and presidential homes and properties. These properties are particularly important in the narration of our national history.
- *Historic designed landscapes.* These are sites consciously planned or arranged by a professional or amateur according to design principles or traditions, in which aesthetics played a significant role; for example, gardens, country estates, cemeteries, parks, and campuses. They may also be associated with an important person or with an important trend or theory in landscape architecture.
- *Historic vernacular landscapes.* These are landscapes that evolved through the long-term use of a site for primarily functional purposes; for example, farmsteads, ranches, or industrial sites. As such, they are material and spatial expressions of human social, cultural, and economic values (Birnbaum and Peters, 1996). Historic landscapes are particularly vulnerable to the changes introduced by modern needs, such as housing developments, parking lots, utilities, and wider roads. They can also suffer a gradual loss of historic character over time because of the relatively short-lived nature of important features such as plant materials and erodible landforms.

In a world where sustainability is a significant issue, designers should be able to recognize these sites as important historic resources and be ready to incorporate protection and preservation into their designs. Therefore, a well-planned approach to design involving a significant historic landscape must have preservation as its primary goal. It must be understood that the ultimate product will be a well-treated historic landscape, not a completely new design.

WHY PRESERVE HISTORIC LANDSCAPES?

Well-preserved historic places can offer many potential benefits to the owner, the user, and the community at large. Preservation of historic landscapes can be economically beneficial when properties are sensitively adapted for reuse for modern purposes. In that sense, preservation is one of the first strategies that should be considered when the goal is to develop sustainably.

Tourism is another economic strategy involving the preservation of historic landscapes, especially of historic districts, both urban and rural, which tend to draw visitors because of their unique qualities and what they reveal about the origins and development of a community, region, or nation.

Finally, well-preserved historic places connect us with our past, providing a sense of continuity—a sense of place in space and time. Preserving a historic landscape with integrity and significance enhances the distinct character of that place, thus enriching the experience of being there. Hence, these places can be a source of community pride and focus, something that can say to the world, "This is who we are!"

GUIDELINES FOR HISTORIC LANDSCAPE PRESERVATION

There is a process that designers should follow when involved with a project that has significant historic resources. The process, as explained here, does not cover every situation that might be met with in dealing with these landscapes, but offers a structure with which to begin. (These guidelines were prepared for work in the United State and Canada. For guidance on projects in other countries, consult the Association for Preservation Techonology International and the International Committee of Historic Gardens and Sites of ICOMOS-IFLA.)

Treatment of historic landscapes is a specialized field within landscape architecture. The project team should be led by a landscape architect experienced in working with historic landscapes, and include consultants such as historians, horticulturalists, engineers, architects, archaeologists, ecologists, interpretive planners, and other specialists. The site curators, managers, and maintenance staff are an essential part of the team, as well, from the inception of a project, because its long-term success depends on their continued investment in preserving the historic fabric of the site.

Investigation

History of the Site

Initial research of the site should seek answers to a number of questions:

- Is the site listed in the National Register of Historic Places or designated as a state or local landmark? Is it part of a larger National Register or a locally defined historic district? Listing or inclusion in a district may affect what may be done with the property or what sort of reviews are required.
- Are there copies of this information available? National Register nominations are often held by the State Historic Preservation Officer and can also be obtained from the National Park Service.
- Have drawings of the property been produced for the Historic American Landscapes Survey, the Historic American Buildings Survey, or the Historic American Engineering Record? If so, copies may also be obtained from the National Park Service.
- Are there any local or state historic surveys, inventories, or any other records that may include the site? Local and state libraries, archives, and historic societies may also have extensive collections that may include information, family records, drawings, or photographs of the site.

The historian on the project team should research the social history of the site, including important events or persons connected with its past, as well as the physical history of change in the site's built character. Considering both, the historian will also be able to place the site in the continuum of design, social, or economic trends, and note any particular ways in which the site is significant in these areas.

Legal Considerations

Legal questions to ask include:

- Are there any conditions attached to the site as a result of historic designations, grants, gifts, or any other activity that may restrict what can and cannot be done on the site? Have any easements been established on the property that may be restrictive? Also consult local zoning regulations, subdivision notes, and deeds for any other restrictions.
- How does the Americans with Disabilities Act (ADA) apply to new designs for and access to historic structures or the site? Are there requirements that must be carefully considered in terms of preserving the site's historic character? In many jurisdictions, there are exceptions to strict interpretation of the ADA for historic sites.
- Is the project supported by any federal funds? If so, it will require review by the State Historic Preservation Officer under Section 106 of the National Historic Preservation Act.

Documentation and Inventory

Documentation of the landscape as it exists at the present date is the next step. The level of detail attained in this stage depends on the size of the site, its historical and cultural significance, the timeline for the project, and the level of funding available.

The *Secretary of the Interior's Guidelines for the Treatment of Cultural Landscapes* (hereafter, Guidelines), offers a way to organize the information gathered in this phase into six general categories of landscape features: spatial organization and land patterns; topography; vegetation; circulation; water features; and structures, furnishings, and objects.

Laura L. Knott, ASLA, John Milner Associates, Inc., 103 West Main Street, Charlottesville, VA 22903

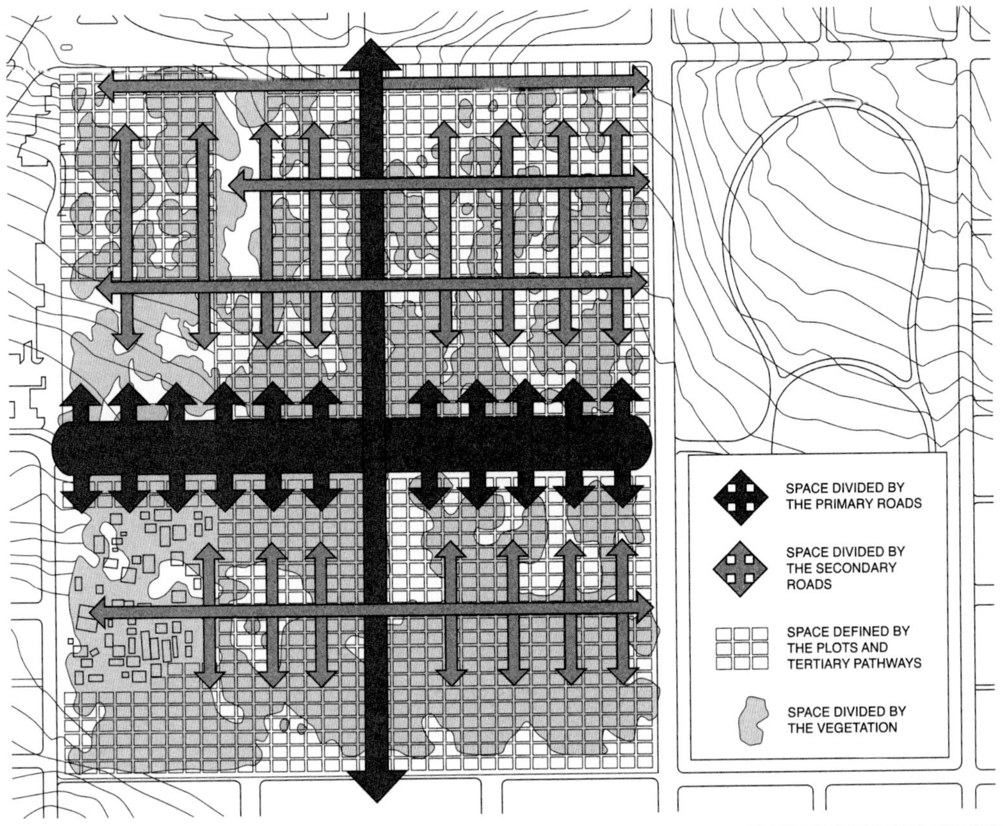

SPATIAL ORGANIZATION OF OAKWOOD CEMETERY, AUSTIN, TEXAS

Source: Knott, Laura, ed. "Oakwood Cemetery Cultural Landscape Report," unpublished report, University of Texas, 2005.

When identifying spatial organization and land patterns, look for the overall pattern formed by the components of the historic site, such as divisions within a landscape between garden spaces or farmyard spaces compared to fields (see the figures "Spatial Organization of Oakwood Cemetery," and "Plans Prepared for the National Register"). This would also include views into and out of the landscape. Also note and understand the relationship of these features to each other in terms of function or aesthetics. For example, the placement of a bench may be important in directing views to a fountain in a historic garden; or a corral in controlling animal access to sheds, pens, and troughs in a farm landscape. Compare existing patterns and relationships with historic information and note how these patterns have changed over time.

To evaluate the topography of the site, examine the existing land contours through a topographic survey; and through the use of historic photographs and plans, aerial photographs, or archaeological evidence, determine how these forms might have evolved over time or changed from the original intent of the designer or developer (see the figures "Analysis of Topography of Oakwood Cemetery" and "Field Terracing Analysis"). Also consider how topographic features may have influenced the design or evolution of the site through time.

Existing vegetation should be carefully surveyed and mapped. Note groupings of vegetation, such as wooded areas, hedgerows, agricultural crops, meadows, and planting beds, as well as individual trees, shrubs, and other plants. Documentation should include species, size, color, form, and texture. Growth patterns can be tracked through the use of historic aerials and photographs. The knowledge of a horticulturalist, especially one specializing in historic plants, may be helpful.

All levels of circulation on the site should be mapped, ranging from narrow paths to roads and highways (see the figure "Campground Circulation"). Canals constructed for transportation, as well as railroads, are also included in the circulation category. Alignment should be noted, as well as materials, edging, grade, and accompanying infrastructure. As with topography, old alignments may be identified with archived plans, photographs, or archaeological evidence. The assistance of a civil or transportation engineer may be helpful in this area.

Water features to be identified and evaluated include the completely man-made, such as pools and fountains, but also include natural or modified springs, ponds, lakes, streams, and rivers. Irrigation systems, ranging from historic acequias to modern underground turf irrigation or other watering systems are also included in this category. Historic maps may be useful in locating water features and archaeological research may confirm locations of changed water courses or buried features. A hydrologist may also be helpful in evaluating the condition of these features.

The category of structures, furnishings, and objects is large, including everything from bridges to planters. Structures are non-habitable, constructed features, and include bridges, walls, dams, terraces, gazebos, playground equipment, as well as animal sheds and other farm structures. Consult with a structural engineer if potential problems, such as cracking or subsidence, are noted with any of these features.

Furnishings and objects include those more portable, small-scale elements of the landscape, such as planters and urns, benches, sculpture, light poles, drinking fountains, and signage. Special items, especially sculpture, may require further consultation with an art conservator for a condition assessment.

Evaluation

Once the site has been investigated and documented, the next step is to evaluate how these landscape features contribute to the historic character of the site. How has the original configuration changed through time? What has been added? What has been lost? These character-defining features and the degree to which they have changed through time help to establish the overall integrity of a historic landscape, which in turn helps the landscape architect develop the appropriate treatment plan.

The Guidelines present 13 important issues to consider when organizing an evaluation:

- *Change and continuity.* How has the landscape changed over time, and how well has it maintained its distinctive character?
- *Historical significance.* Is the site associated with an important event, person, or era in history? Is the design representative of a particular trend in design or the work of an important designer? Historical significance should be based on criteria established by the National Park Service for nominating sites to the National Register of Historic Places (NPS, 1997).
- *Integrity.* How are the activities that shaped the land during its history still evident in its form today? The National Register of Historic Places suggests evaluating the qualities of location, setting, feeling, association, design, workmanship, and materials (Keller and Keller, 1987).
- *Geographical context.* How does the site relate to its surroundings, and do they contribute, or take away from, its historic character?
- *Use.* Do the proposed uses have potential to compromise the integrity of the site? How might proposed uses be adapted to protect and preserve the character-defining features of the historic landscape?
- *Archaeological resources.* Have prehistoric or historic resources, which may be located underground or underwater, been identified? These resources can provide significant information about a historic landscape, and should also be protected.
- *Natural systems.* How do the natural systems on the site, such as hydrologic patterns or species habitat, contribute to the overall character of the site? Did the historic use enhance or damage these systems?
- *Management and maintenance.* Has site management and maintenance helped retain the historic character or cultural significance of the site? What financial or community resources are available to support preservation on an ongoing basis?
- *Interpretation.* Has the site been interpreted in the past? Who is the future audience and what is the best strategy for communicating to them the importance of character-defining features on the site?
- *Accessibility.* What challenges must be met in making the site universally accessible, and to what level

Laura L. Knott, ASLA, John Milner Associates, Inc., 103 West Main Street, Charlottesville, VA 22903

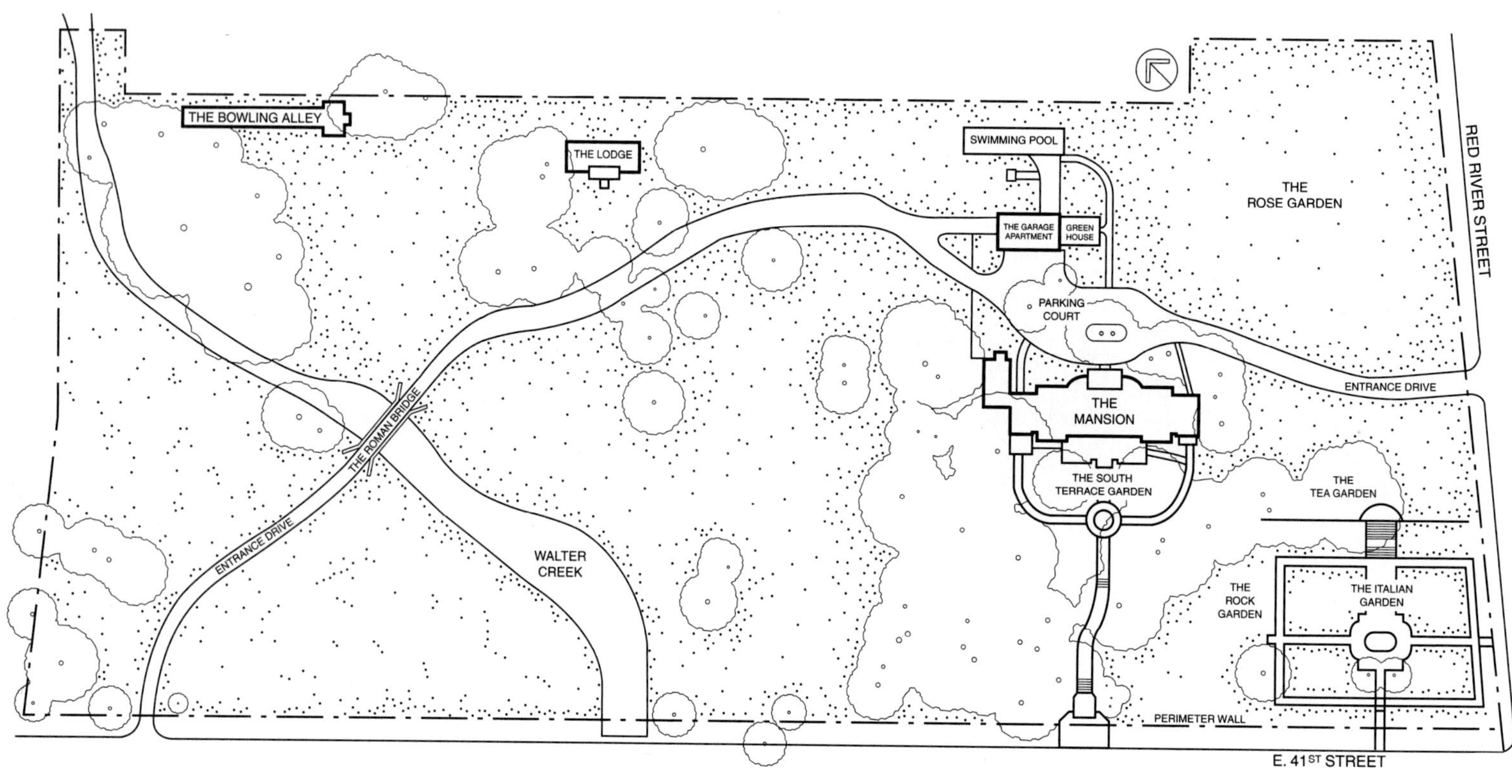

THE EDGAR AND LUTIE PERRY ESTATE
SITE MAP-FIRST PERIOD OF SIGNIFICANCE

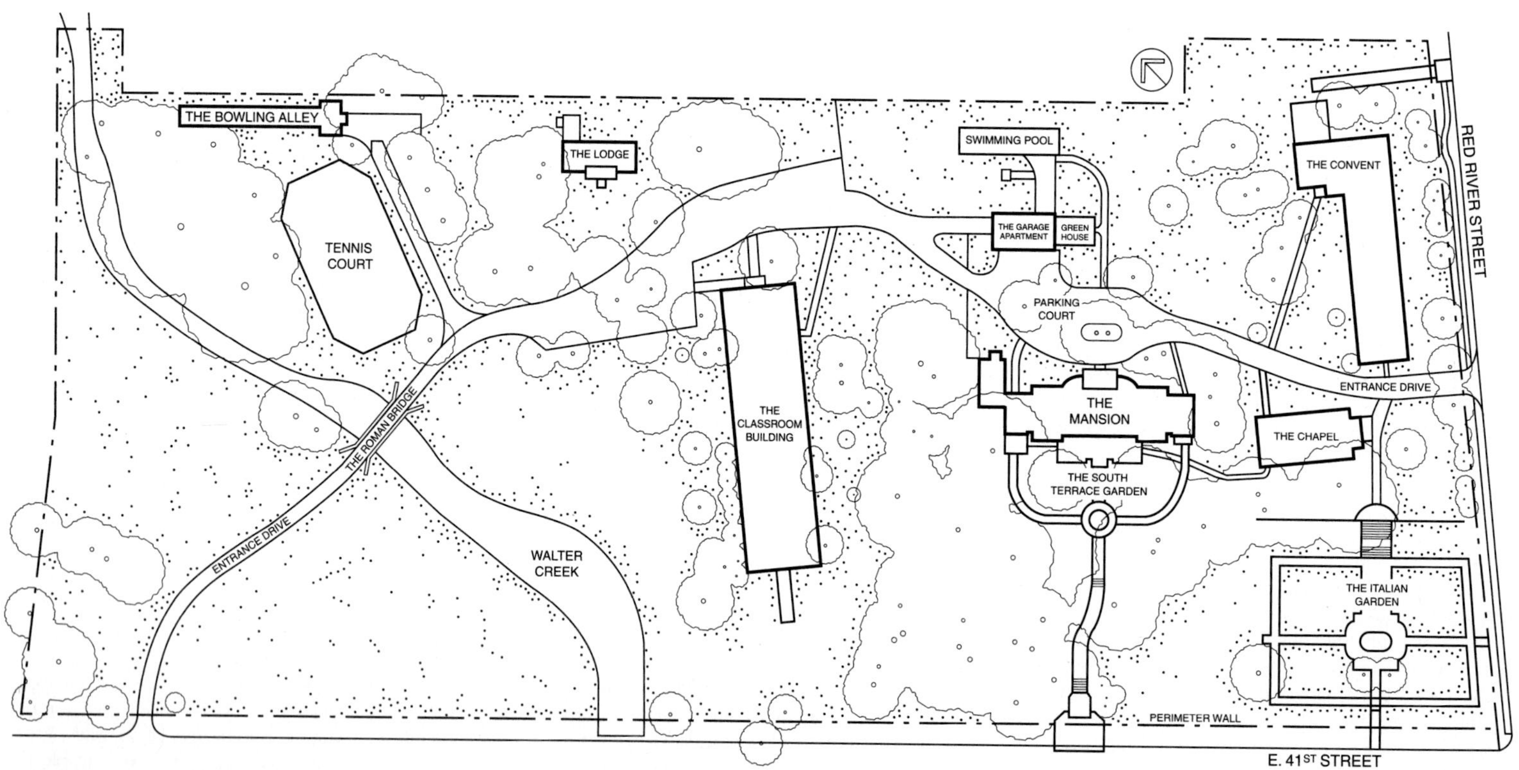

THE EDGAR AND LUTIE PERRY ESTATE
SITE MAP-SECOND PERIOD OF SIGNIFICANCE

PLANS PREPARED FOR THE NATIONAL REGISTER TO SHOW CHANGES TO THE SPATIAL ORGANIZATION OF THIS SITE OVER TIME

Source: Knott, Laura. "Edgar H. and Lutie Perry Estate National Register Nomination," 2000.

Laura L. Knott, ASLA, John Milner Associates, Inc., 103 West Main Street, Charlottesville, VA 22903

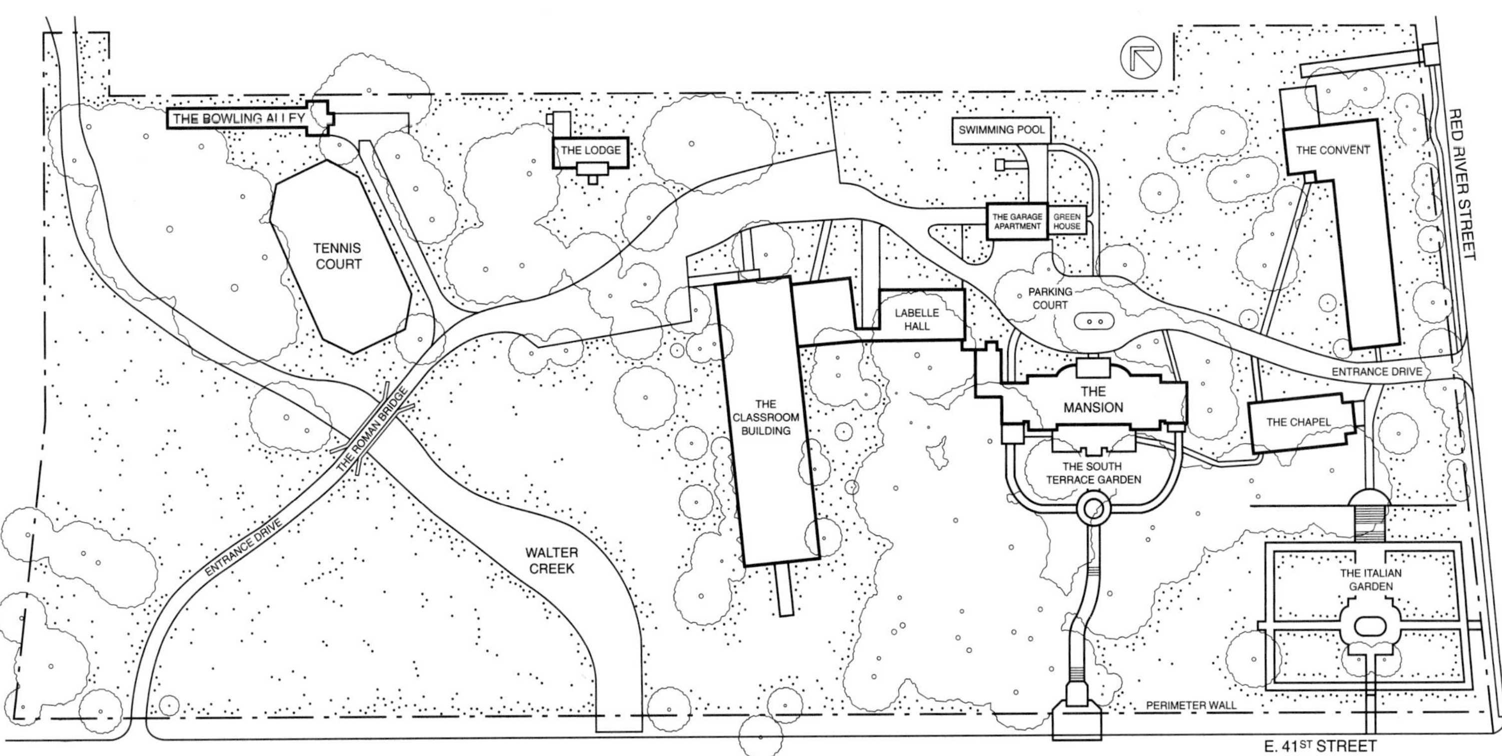

THE EDGAR AND LUTIE PERRY ESTATE
SITE MAP-CURRENT DAY

PLANS PREPARED FOR THE NATIONAL REGISTER TO SHOW CHANGES TO THE SPATIAL ORGANIZATION OF THIS SITE OVER TIME *(continued)*

Source: Knott, Laura. "Edgar H. and Lutie Perry Estate National Register Nomination," 2000.

should it be allowed in the pursuit of access? (Jester and Park, 1993)

- *Health and safety.* Does the site currently meet health and safety regulations, such as fire, seismic, or building codes? If not, can the site become compliant and still retain its integrity?
- *Environmental protection.* How might compliance with federal, state, and local environmental laws affect the character-defining features of the site? Are there compromises that must be made to comply with current law?
- *Energy efficiency.* How do the character-defining features of the site contribute to energy conservation? How can future planning preserve and enhance energy conservation on the site?

Depending on the history of the site, a particular time period, the "period of significance," may emerge as the most important for the landscape and may affect the treatment plan selected. Features from this period should be preserved and protected when planning for changes to the landscape. That said, be aware that an emerging philosophy of historic landscape preservation questions the strict application of periods of significance to landscape resources that, by their nature, are ever-changing. As a result, a historic landscape, with all the layers of change accumulated over time, is more often than not preserved as it exists in the present. In those cases, interpretation relies more on displays, audio and visual presentations, and written material. The question of establishing a period of significance in this context is a complex one. (For more information, refer to "Evaluation" in "Suggested Readings" at the end of this article.)

PRESERVATION TREATMENT PLAN

The preservation treatment plan is based on the previous phases of investigation, documentation, and evaluation, and will direct stabilization, repair, replacement, alterations, or additions to the site. The treatment plan usually contains drawings and specifications as part of a construction documentation package used for estimating, bidding, and implementing the work. It will often also include a plan for signage or other guides for interpreting the site, as well as a maintenance and management plan that the client can use to maintain the integrity and character of the site.

Treatment Approach

The United States Department of the Interior has developed standards for four types of treatment: preservation, rehabilitation, restoration, and reconstruction:

- *Preservation* may be the best choice when the property has retained a high level of integrity, when there is no requirement that the property reflect a particular period of significance, and when a new use does not require changes to the property.
- *Rehabilitation* is the preferred choice when repairs or replacements are necessary to convey historic character, when new uses require alterations or additions, and when there is no requirement that the property reflect a particular period of significance.
- *Restoration* may be the best treatment when there is a strong argument for presenting the site as it was during a particular period of significance. Restoration is not a common choice, but may be appropriate when the historical significance of features from a definable time period is more important than any additions that came afterward.
- *Reconstruction* is chosen only when there is little remaining material evidence of the history of the site, yet there is a compelling period of significance that is best communicated in a reconstruction of the landscape features. This is an acceptable treatment only when there is enough documentary evidence, such as detailed drawings or photographs, to accurately inform the work.

Rehabilitation is the most common of the treatments and will be the choice for most preservation-related projects. Well-rehabilitated sites not only accommodate new uses, but do so in a way that preserves the most historically significant features of the site. This can enrich the experience of using the site, while at the same time retain a sense of local history, thus serving the community. Because it is the most common treatment choice, this section will address only rehabilitation. (For more information on preservation, restoration, and reconstruction, refer to the Guidelines.)

Rehabilitation Standards

The U.S. Secretary of the Interior has developed standards to guide planning for the rehabilitation of historic landscapes (Birnbaum Peters, 1996, p. 49). This approach includes not only the preservation or

Laura L. Knott, ASLA, John Milner Associates, Inc., 103 West Main Street, Charlottesville, VA 22903

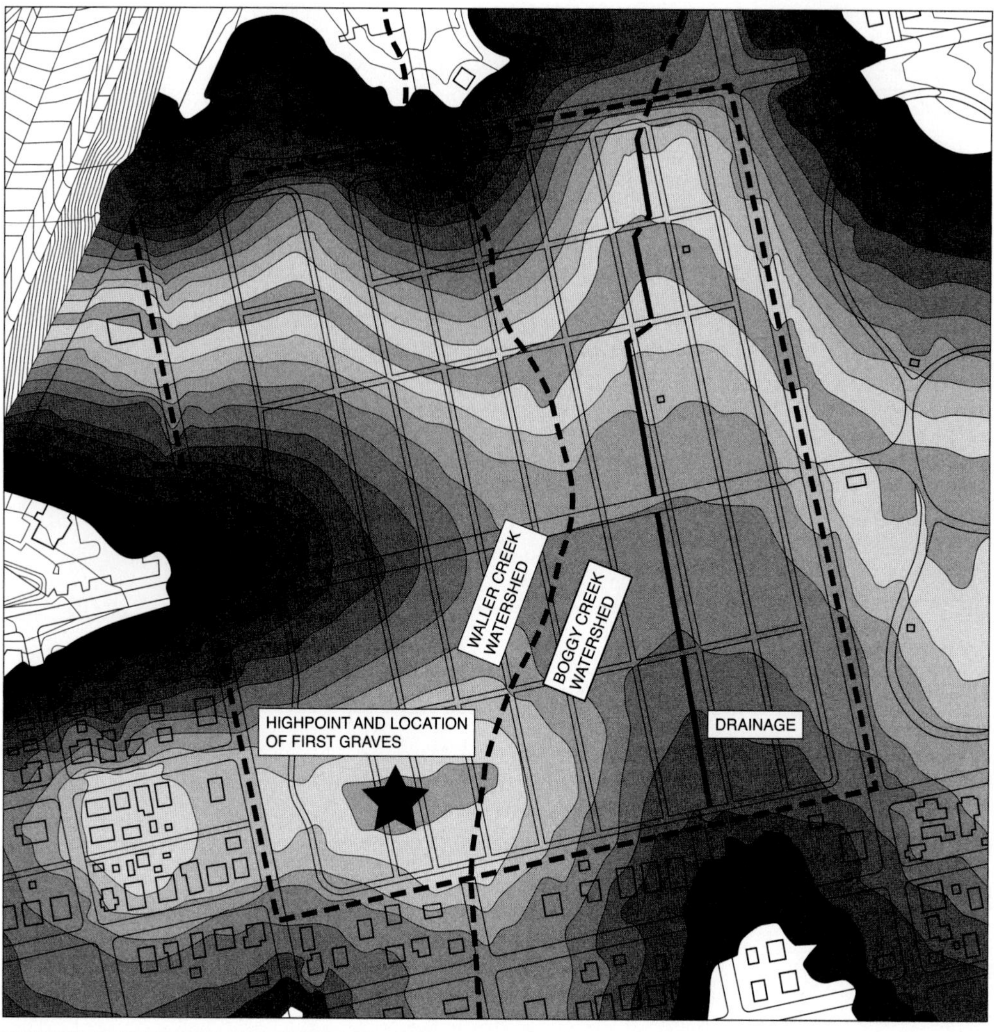

ANALYSIS OF TOPOGRAPHY OF OAKWOOD CEMETERY, AUSTIN, TEXAS

Source: Knott, Laura, ed. "Oakwood Cemetery Cultural Landscape Report," unpublished report, University of Texas, 2005.

restoration of historic features, but also the addition of new features in a way that is sensitive to the historic character of the site:

- "A property will be used as it was historically, or be given a new use that requires minimal change to its distinctive materials, features, spaces, and spatial relationships." For example, it might be appropriate to reuse a nineteenth-century suburban estate for offices or a school, but not a retail center.
- "The historic character of a property will be retained and preserved. The removal of distinctive materials or alteration of features, spaces, and spatial relationships that characterize a property will be avoided." For example, the placement of a structure within the viewshed of an important garden axis would change the historic spatial composition of that site.
- "Each property will be recognized as a physical record of its time, place, and use. Changes that create a false sense of historical development, such as adding conjectural features or elements from other historic properties, will not be undertaken." For example, the introduction of a "period garden" to a site where no garden has been documented gives a false impression of the historic character of the site.
- "Changes to a property that have acquired historic significance in their own right will be retained and preserved." For example, a World War II commemorative statue on the lawn of a nineteenth-century courthouse should not be removed simply because it is more recent. The object may have its own historic significance apart from the building.
- "Distinctive materials, features, finishes, and construction techniques or examples of craftsmanship that characterize a property will be preserved." For example, an eighteenth-century brick wall should not be replaced with a concrete imitation simply because it is easier to maintain. If repairs are needed for a historic wall, the construction technique should be of the same level of craftsmanship as the original.
- "Deteriorated historic features will be repaired rather than replaced. Where the severity of deterioration requires replacement of a distinctive feature, the new feature will match the old in design, color, texture, and, where possible, materials. Replacement of missing features will be substantiated by documentary and physical evidence." The only time a substitute material should be used is when the original material is no longer available, presents a health or safety hazard, or is so costly that it endangers the feasibility of the project.
- "Chemical or physical treatments, if appropriate, will be undertaken using the gentlest means possible. Treatments that cause damage to historic materials will not be used." This includes most applications of sandblasting, for example. Chemical treatments may also contaminate soils or damage nearby plants and should be carefully considered before recommendations are made.
- "Archeological resources will be protected and preserved in place. If such resources must be disturbed, mitigation measures will be undertaken." Archeologists should be consulted if evidence of archeological remains is discovered or even suspected.
- "New additions, exterior alterations, or related new construction will not destroy historic materials, features, and spatial relationships that characterize the property. The new work will be differentiated from the old and will be compatible with the historic materials, features, size, scale and proportion, and massing to protect the integrity of the property and its environment." For example, the extension of a historic stone wall may be constructed so that it is similar in color and texture to the original wall, but visually distinct in smaller details, such as mortar color, so that no false sense of history is communicated with the addition.

Laura L. Knott, ASLA, John Milner Associates, Inc., 103 West Main Street, Charlottesville, VA 22903

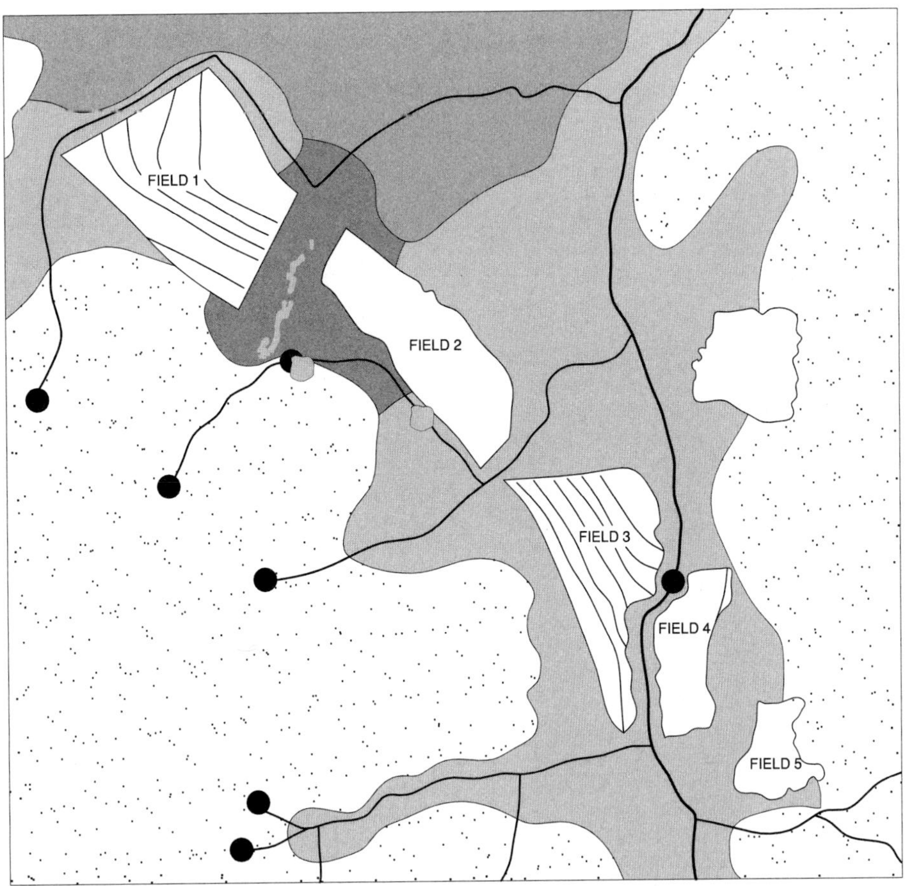

FIELD TERRACING ANALYSIS

Source: Knott, Laura, and Jeffrey Chusid, "Browning Ranch Cultural Landscape Report," unpublished report, University of Texas, 2003.

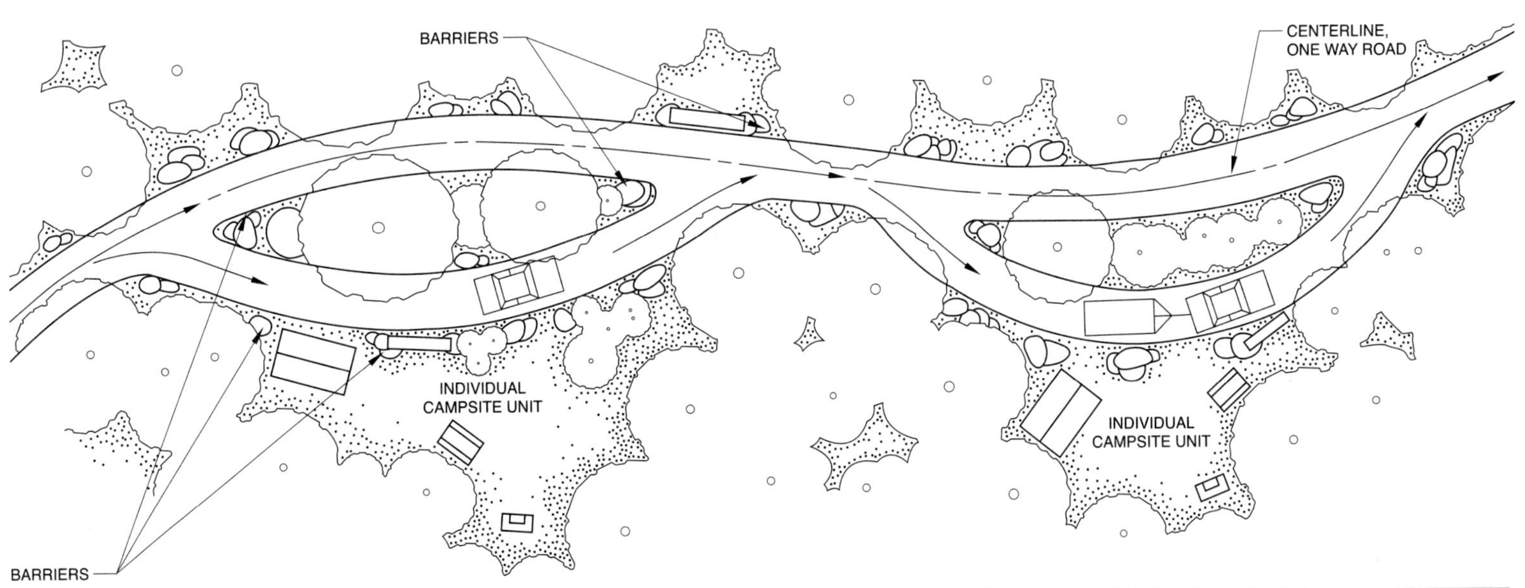

CAMPGROUND CIRCULATION

Source: Good, Albert H., Park and Recreation Structures (Washington, DC: Department of the Interior, National Park Service), 1938.

Laura L. Knott, ASLA, John Milner Associates, Inc., 103 West Main Street, Charlottesville, VA 22903

- "New additions and adjacent or related new construction will be undertaken in such a manner that, if removed in the future, the essential form and integrity of the historic property and its environment would be unimpaired." For example, a ramp constructed for accessibility could simply span the stairs it is traversing. When the ramp is no longer needed, it can easily be removed and the original stairs restored to use.

Rehabilitation Plan

In addition to the requirements for proposed uses, a rehabilitation plan should address the following: stabilization, repairs, replacement, alterations, additions, and issues such as accessibility or health and safety.

To stabilize the site, important character-defining features that are threatened by collapse or other stress should be protected and maintained. Protection might involve restricting vehicular compaction under important trees, or stabilizing earthworks or other structures. Maintenance would include regular tasks, such as pruning a hedge, repointing a masonry wall, or keeping painted wood painted.

The preservation plan should also address needed repairs to character-defining features. Repair should be done with as little intervention as possible and in compliance with the rehabilitation standards. For example, missing bricks in a walkway could be replaced, rotted wood in a gazebo repaired and repainted, or compacted planting beds aerated. If limited replacement of features is necessary, such as balusters deteriorated beyond repair, it should be done with materials in kind. If this is impossible because the material is no longer available, prohibitively expensive, or environmentally dangerous, then replacement with another material may be acceptable, but the historic feature should be retained and used as a reference for new construction.

If a feature is missing entirely, it can be reproduced and replaced. However, it can only be accurately reproduced if there is adequate historic documentation, such as drawings or photographs, available to guide the replacement. If this information is not available, then replacement should be done in a way that it matches the original feature in size, scale, and color, but is clearly differentiated from the original so that there is no confusion over what is historic material and what is new.

When alterations or additions are needed on the site to adapt it to current use, great care should be taken so as not to alter, through radical change or destruction, the features that give the site its historic character. New features should be placed in areas not primary to the historic character of the site. If a new feature is placed in historically important areas, then it should be clearly differentiated from the historic features by the use of more contemporary design and materials so that there is no confusion about its historic nature.

Finally, any work done to provide universal accessibility, to address health and safety or environmental considerations, or to provide greater energy efficiency should be carefully considered so that it does not negatively impact the historic character of the landscape. For example, historic lighting can be retrofitted to enhance energy efficiency, rather than be replaced with a new fixture.

Special Considerations

Questions to consider fall into six categories:

- *Spatial organization and land patterns.* Do the proposed plans change the relationship of particular spaces and land patterns? Does the removal of a hedgerow or an allée of trees change the original character of the space? Has vegetative growth changed the intention of the designer or the original spatial arrangement of the site?
- *Topography.* Are there plans to protect soils from erosion and damage by construction equipment so that the character of the original topography is protected? Have archaeologists been consulted to identify trace topographic features on the site that could be reconstructed?
- *Vegetation.* Are plants protected, pruned, cabled, or fertilized as needed to preserve their contribution to historic character? Are hard-to-get plants that are missing or in decline propagated or replaced with matching available species? Have original plants become overgrown, obscuring other character-defining features? Should a horticulturalist specializing in historic plants be consulted?
- *Circulation.* Have historic circulation routes become obscured by vegetation or simply by lack of maintenance? Is the original hierarchy of circulation maintained so that major entryways or paths remain important? Can historic circulation routes be reused for modern needs, such as providing access to parking lots or fulfilling fire-lane requirements? Would it be helpful to include a civil engineer on the planning team?
- *Water features.* Are historic water features operational? If not, what modern technology can be implemented to improve operation, reduce maintenance costs, and improve energy efficiency? Have natural bodies of water been tested for pollution? How might dredging or other cleaning activities affect existing natural systems? Would it be helpful to consult with a hydrologist?
- *Structures, furnishings, and objects.* How sound are the larger structures on the site? Would it be helpful to include a structural engineer on the planning team? Have original furnishings or objects been replaced since the historically significant period? If so, where might products that match the originals be found? Should an art historian be consulted?

Interpretive Plan

Interpretation is often an important part of the planning process for historic landscape rehabilitation. Communication of a site's significance to an audience helps generate ongoing community support. Interpretation is uniquely tailored to each site and depends on the site's significance, integrity, scale, and the financial and community resources available. For a large or specially complex site, it may be helpful to include an interpretive planner on the design team who can help manage this communication.

Often a multimedia approach is appropriate and may include video presentations, audio guides, brochures, maps, and signage. Large, complex, and well-financed sites, such as Colonial Williamsburg, in Virginia, are entire interpretive environments, where visitors might encounter guided tours, demonstrations, and reenactments, in addition to multimedia presentations.

Depending on the scale of the landscape, self-guided auto or walking tours may be useful. In larger-scale landscapes, such as historic urban or rural districts, markers, such as symbols on signs, flags, or street furniture, can visually indicate the extent and boundaries of a district.

Management and Maintenance Plan

Maintenance often begins before the preservation treatment plan is completed—often at the onset of investigation, depending on the condition of the site features and the severity of any damage or deterioration. A management and maintenance plan should accompany the treatment plan to assure the ongoing preservation of the site long after the rehabilitation work is completed. This plan is based on the objectives of the treatment plan and will include schedules for ongoing maintenance, such as pruning or painting. It will also include instructions on appropriate techniques for preserving the historic character of a site, such as avoiding the introduction of modern varieties of plants.

Management of the site should also include careful record keeping to monitor work and to document any changes to the landscape over time. A historic landscape is, after all, more of a process than a product, and management and maintenance may be the most important contribution to the preservation of its character-defining features. For this reason, it is important for the ongoing success of the project to involve site managers and maintenance staff from beginning to end.

CONCLUSION

Historic landscape preservation is a specialized field in landscape architecture. A project involving a site that is historically significant should include on its team a landscape architect who specializes in the treatment of historic landscapes. Depending on the nature of the project and its budget, the team ideally will also include a variety of specialists, including historians, horticulturalists, art historians, architectural historians, civil and structural engineers, and hydrologists. Together, the team can do background research, document the site, evaluate the information, and produce a treatment plan that is successful in protecting and preserving these important sites.

Planning for a site should also include interpretation, to communicate its significance to the public, thus assuring ongoing support. It should also address management and maintenance strategies that preserve the integrity of the site as an important cultural resource while accommodating change. Good research, planning, interpretation, and management help ensure that a historic landscape continues to be preserved as an educational resource and an ongoing source of community pride.

REFERENCES

Online Technical Preservation Information

Alliance for Historic Landscape Preservation: www.ahlp.org

ASLA Historic Preservation Professional Interest Group: http://host.asla.org/groups/hppigroup

Association for Preservation Technology: www.apti.org

Laura L. Knott, ASLA, John Milner Associates, Inc., 103 West Main Street, Charlottesville, VA 22903

Cultural Landscape Foundation: www.tclf.org

Institute for Cultural Landscape Studies: www.icls.harvard.edu

National Park Service Cultural Landscape Currents: www.cr.nps.gov/hli/currents

National Park Service Historic Landscape Initiative: www.cr.nps.gov/hli/index.htm

National Preservation Institute: www.npi.org

National Trust for Historic Preservation: www.nationaltrust.org

Catalogue of Landscape Records, The New York Botanical Garden, International Plant Science Center, Mertz Library: sciweb.nybg.org/Science2/Archivesandmanuscrpts.asp

Suggested Reading

General Information

Alanen, Arnold, and Robert Z. Melnick (eds). 2000. *Preserving Cultural Landscapes in America.* Baltimore, MD: Johns Hopkins University Press.

Birnbaum, Charles. 1994. "Protecting Cultural Landscapes: Planning, Treatment and Management of Historic Landscapes." Preservation Brief 36. Washington, DC: Preservation Assistance Division, National Park Service.

Birnbaum, Charles, and Christine Capella Peters (eds). 1996. *The Secretary of the Interior's Standards for the Treatment of Historic Properties with Guidelines for the Treatment of Cultural Landscapes.* Washington, DC: Historic Landscape Initiative, National Park Service.

Birnbaum, Charles, and Catha Grace Rambusch (eds). 1993. *The Landscape Universe: Historic Designed Landscapes in Context: Expanded and Illustrated Papers from a National Symposium, Armor Hall at Wave Hill, Bronx, New York.* Bronx, NY: Catalog of Landscape Records in the United States; and Washington, DC: National Park Service Preservation Assistance Division.

Birnbaum, Charles, and Sandra L. Tallant (eds). 1996. *Balancing Natural and Cultural Issues in the Preservation of Historic Landscapes.* Selected papers from the National Association for Olmsted Parks Conference, George Wright Forum, vol. 13, no. 1.

Birnbaum, Charles, and Cheryl Wagner (eds). 1994. *Making Educated Decisions: A Landscape Preservation Bibliography.* Washington, DC: Historic Landscape Initiative, Preservation Assistance Division, Cultural Resources, National Park Service.

Buggey, Susan (guest ed.). 1992. "Conserving Historic Landscapes," *APT Bulletin*, vol. 24, no. 3-4.

Investigation

Birnbaum, Charles, and Lisa E. Crowder (eds). 1993. *Pioneers of American Landscape Design: An Annotated Bibliography*, vols. I and II. Washington, DC: Historic Landscape Initiative, Preservation Assistance Division, National Park Service.

Griswold, Mac, and Eleanor Weller. 1991. *The Golden Age of American Gardens: Proud Owners, Private Estates, 1890-1940.* New York: Harry N. Abrams, Inc.

Jackson, J. B. 1984. *Discovering the Vernacular Landscape.* New Haven, CT: Yale University Press.

Meinig, D. W. 1979. *The Interpretation of Ordinary Landscapes: Geographical Essays.* New York: Oxford University Press.

Rogers, Elizabeth Barlow. 2001. *Landscape Design: A Cultural and Architectural History.* New York: Harry N. Abrams, Inc.

Stokes, Samuel N., and A. Elizabeth Watson. 1989. *Saving America's Countryside: A Guide to Rural Conservation.* Baltimore, MD: Johns Hopkins University Press.

Documentation

Birnbaum, Charles, and Christine Capella Peters. 1996. *The Secretary of the Interior's Standards for the Treatment of Historic Properties with Guidelines for the Treatment of Cultural Landscapes.* Washington, DC: U.S. Department of the Interior, National Park Service.

Fanning, Kay, and Maureen Joseph. 1999. "Discovering Dumbarton Oaks Park: Restoring a Masterwork for Modern Needs," *APT Bulletin*, vol. 30, no. 2-3: 2-3, 61-66.

Keller, Genevieve P. 1993. "The Inventory and Analysis of Historic Landscapes," *Historic Preservation Forum*, vol. 7, no. 3: 26-35.

O'Donnell, Patricia. 1992. "Cultural Landscape Analysis: The Vanderbilt Estate at Hyde Park," *APT Bulletin*, vol. 24, no. 3-4: 25-41.

Seifert, Donna J. 1997. "Defining Boundaries for National Register Properties," *National Register Bulletin.* n.p. Washington, DC: National Register of Historic Places, National Park Service, U.S. Department of the Interior.

Yamin, Rebecca, and Karen Bercherer Metheny (eds). *Landscape Archaeology: Reading and Interpreting the American Historic Landscape.* Knoxville, TN: University of Tennessee Press.

Evaluation

Bennis, E. 2000. "Deception and Authenticity in Landscape Restoration." ASLA Annual Conference Proceedings. Washington, DC: American Society of Landscape Architects.

Greenburg, Ronald M. (ed.), Charles A. Birnbaum, and Robert R. Page (guest eds). 1994. *Cultural Resources Management Bulletin: Thematic Issue on Landscape Interpretation.* vol. 17, no. 7.

Howett, Catherine. 2000. "Integrity as a Value in Cultural Landscape Preservation." In Arnold R. Alanen and Robert Z. Melnick (eds), *Preserving Cultural Landscapes in America.* Baltimore, MD: Johns Hopkins University Press.

Keller, J. Timothy, and Genevieve Keller. 1987. *National Register Bulletin 18: How to Evaluate and Nominate Designed Historic Landscapes.* Washington, DC: Interagency Resources Division, National Park Service.

Larsen, Knut Einar (ed.). 1995. Nara Conference on Authenticity in Relation to the World Heritage Convention. Japan: UNESCO World Heritage Centre, Agency for Cultural Affairs, ICCROM, and ICOMOS.

McClelland, Linda Flint, J. Timothy Keller, Genevieve P. Keller, and Robert Z. Melnick. Guidelines for Evaluating and Documenting Rural Historic Landscapes. 1998. *National Register Bulletin 30.* Washington, DC: U. S. Department of the Interior, National Park Service.

Sensory Trust. "Easy Access to Historic Landscapes." Compiled for English Heritage, www.sensorytrust.org.uk/resources/EHLiteratureReview.PDF (accessed December 22, 2004).

Preservation Treatment Plan: Case Studies

Berg, Shary Page. 1988. "Fairsted: Documenting and Preserving a Historic Landscape," *APT Bulletin*, vol. 20, no. 1: 41-49.

Hadlow, Robert W. "The Historic Columbia River Gorge: Rehabilitating a Rural Designed Landscape." Cultural Landscape Currents, National Park Service Historic Landscape Initiative, National Park Service. www2.cr.nps.gov/hli/currents/columbia (accessed June, 5, 2004).

Jaeger, Dale, and Chet Thomas. "The Reynolda Gardens." Cultural Landscape Currents, National Park Service Historic Landscape Initiative, National Park Service. www2.cr.nps.gov/hli/currents/reynolda (accessed June, 5, 2004).

O'Donnell, Patricia. "The Benjamin Franklin Parkway: Rehabilitating an Historic Urban Designed Landscape." Cultural Landscape Currents, National Park Service Historic Landscape Initiative, National Park Service. www2.cr.nps.gov/hli/currents/franklin-park (accessed June 4, 2004).

Laura L. Knott, ASLA, John Milner Associates, Inc., 103 West Main Street, Charlottesville, VA 22903

SECURITY CONSIDERATIONS

CRIME PREVENTION THROUGH ENVIRONMENTAL DESIGN

OVERVIEW

Crime prevention through environmental design (CPTED) is the design or redesign of an environment to reduce crime through natural, mechanical, and operational/ procedural means. CPTED is a multidisciplinary approach to reducing crime and the fear of crime. The physical environment plays an important part in promoting crime. Too often, CPTED and defensible space theories are reduced to the installation of fencing (very often, very tall fencing). An overreliance on fencing can divert focus from site elements that are much more critical to a successful CPTED approach.

Broken Windows Concept

The "broken windows" concept refers to small signs of decay. This can be graffiti, litter, broken glass, abandoned cars, and deteriorated or vandalized site amenities. This can lead to a deepening spiral of decay, which in turn demoralizes the community, emboldens offenders, heightens fears, and attracts outsiders who view the location as a suitable place to perform their illegal activities. The physical characteristics and appearance of a neighborhood matter when those who would break the law select the location for their crimes. Neighborhood characteristics signal how strongly residents are likely to respond when they identify criminal activity in their midst. Observation of neighborhood characteristics is a primary tool for those looking to engage in criminal activity with little risk of being caught. Areas that are easily accessible (such as those at the entrances and exits of major highways) and have many exit points (translating into multiple avenues of escape) are particularly attractive.

In *The Death and Life of Great American Cities*, Jane Jacobs documented what she felt were seriously flawed postwar planning policies. She developed the often-used metaphor "eyes of the street" to describe informal surveillance. She identified one of the problems as the lack of a design for land not built on. Open space not dedicated to a specific use often falls victim to misuse. A primary objective of landscape architectural design work is to bring a wide range of positive activity to these open spaces throughout the day, making it less likely that they will be used by intruders who have no legitimate reason for being there.

Visual or real barriers, especially taller fencing, can separate a community from its surrounding neighborhoods. It can isolate residents from the wider community and, at the same time, create havens for drug dealers. Implementations that rely almost entirely on physical barriers can be easily circumvented. When the perimeter is breached, the integrity of the defensible space approach is compromised.

Defensible Space Theory

The Defensible Space theory is predicated on the concept of territoriality and the creation of zones of influence that are an expression of a social fabric that defends itself. It encourages residents to take collective responsibility for the place and for one another and, by extension, act on intrusion. True defensible space has a psychological component that creates a proprietary interest in the open spaces around residents' homes.

A "movement predictor" is a predictable or unchangeable route or path that offers no choice to pedestrians, and should be avoided. It is particularly dangerous, as an attacker can predict where a person will end up once he or she on the path, and can lie in wait. Closely tied to this is "visual permeability," or the ability to see what is ahead and around, allowing the pedestrian to make a reasonable choice of routes. Good sightlines mean that users are visible to others who can come to their assistance. It is important that barriers delineate boundaries and define circulation, yet at the same time allow users to see and be seen.

One basic premise of CPTED is that if certain conditions create criminal opportunities, then the reverse can be true: Certain site conditions can prevent crimes form occurring. A site design approach can be employed by landscape architects to alter the design of open spaces to eliminate illegitimate usage into places overflowing with positive activity. If site design can be a crime generator, then, with changes, it can be transformed into a powerful crime prevention tool.

Designs that foster a sense of community and neighborhood contribute to making intruders feel conspicuous. Distinguishing between public and private space creates an environment that encourages neighborliness and, through this, natural surveillance and self-policing. Territoriality communicates a sense of ownership to both residents and intruders. The design should maximize surveillance opportunities for residents (especially while performing routine activities).

Crimes of opportunity require the convergence of a suitable target, a likely offender, and an opportune place to commit the crime. A targeted CPTED approach seeks to change the environment to eliminate the presence of the target or the opportune place for the crime to take place. Criminals planning to commit a crime weigh the likely costs and benefits of committing a particular crime in a particular area. If there is no crime opportunity or immediate alternative, the crime will not occur, nor will displacement occur. The point is that CPTED measures can effect a *real reduction* in crime.

Positive activity and presence bring with them inherent security. Activity generators add "eyes" on the street or open space and make a place more secure by populating it. Active, vital urban spaces that attract diverse groups of people are perceived as safe places.

Crime prevention strategies should be holistic in their attempt to improve the quality of life, by providing social and economic strategies that will improve job opportunities, social services, and community liaison with local law enforcement.

Resident involvement is paramount to the success of a CPTED program. It fosters an interaction and exchange of ideas that doesn't happen in a more traditional design approach. An added benefit of involving residents in the decision-making process is that it serves to build community ties and relationships. It engages residents in the crime prevention program. It fosters interaction and an exchange of ideas, which doesn't happen in a more traditional design approach. These increased community links can help to prevent more crime in the long run because people working well together increases informal social control mechanisms, such as informal surveillance; moreover, it helps people to realize that there are others out there like them, who are opposed to crime and are willing to act.

METHODS OF PREVENTING CRIME THROUGH DESIGN

Increasing the Effort to Commit a Crime

Crimes are committed because they are easy to commit. A person with a criminal intent sees an easy opportunity and so takes it, regardless of the legality or consequences. Casual criminals are eliminated by increasing the effort necessary to commit a crime. "Target hardening" is one method of increasing the effort usiby ng more fencing, landscaping and plantings, and curbs. Another technique of CPTED is natural access control, which includes installing symbolic and real barriers and designing paths walkways, and roads so that unwanted and unauthorized users are prevented from entering vulnerable areas. Barriers may include limiting entrance to specific individuals, places, or times; security vestibules, parking lot barriers, entry phones, visitor check-in booths, guard stations, vehicle control systems, and biometric screening for access control. CPTED features that serve to increase the effort to commit a crime or act of terror might include:

- Control access to the facility by pedestrian and vehicular traffic.
- Divide interior and exterior spaces into small, easily identified areas that are associated with a specific group of individuals or users.
- Make detection devices easily visible to increase the perceived risk to the offender, and post signs advertising the use of such devices.
- Minimize the number of entrances to the interior of a building, and clearly identify the function of the remaining entrances. Secure entrances when not in use.
- Provide keyed access to vulnerable areas such as laundry rooms, storage areas, elevators, and bathrooms.
- Control parking lot access by means of gates and passes.
- Restrict emergency stairs and exits to their intended use by equipping them with alarm panic bars with time egress delays and no exterior door handles.

Randall I. Atlas, PhD, AIA CPP Atlas Safety & Security Design Inc., Miami Florida; Leonard Hopper, RLA, FASLA

- Install barriers on vulnerable openings such as ground-floor windows, exterior fire stairs, roof openings, and skylights. Fence off problem areas to prevent unauthorized access and funnel movement along desired paths.
- Provide lockable security areas for items that are stored in low surveillance areas or items that are easily portable.
- Control access for servicing and deliveries.

Increasing the Risks Associated with Crime

Increasing the risks associated with crime contributes to crime prevention by improving the probability that the criminal will be observed, identified, and arrested. Criminals commit crime because they believe they will not get caught. Ways to increase the risk of being detected and caught include: entry and exit screening, formal surveillance, increasing surveillance capabilities by employees, and improving natural surveillance.

- Screening devices should be used, when appropriate, to allow access to legitimate building users and guests. Employee screening should occur in a separate area from the public entrance and require that staff have IDs or badges as they work on the property.
- Formal surveillance involves both security personnel and hardware, such as closed-circuit television (CCTV) and intrusion detection systems.
- Informal surveillance by facility employees makes use of the existing resources of doormen, concierges, maintenance workers, and secretaries to increase site surveillance and crime reporting.
- Natural surveillance means careful architectural placement of windows, doors, lighting, and controlled landscaping and plantings.
- Interior lighting enhances opportunities for casual or formal surveillance in spaces visible through doors and windows. Lighting should be even, without deep shadows, and fixtures should be vandalproof.
- Interior blindspots, such as alcoves, and dead-end corridors, which create vulnerable entrapment areas, should be eliminated when and where possible.

Reducing the Rewards of Crime

Reducing the rewards of crime makes illegal activity not worthwhile or productive to commit. This method of crime prevention includes techniques that make targets of crime less valuable to the offender, or that remove crime targets that have value to the criminal. To reduce the rewards of crime, the design professional can: remove the high-risk target from the premises or the architectural program (not to be included as part of the scope of work), identify or tag property assets, eliminate the inducements for crime, and set rules and boundaries. Eliminating the inducements for crime includes removing those targets before they can become an easy opportunity.

- Vacant lots, apartments, offices, and spaces should be given over to legitimate users to protect against vandalism and damage.
- Exterior walls should be painted with graffiti-resistant epoxy and/or landscaped with creeping vines to prevent the wall from acting as a mural for "taggers."

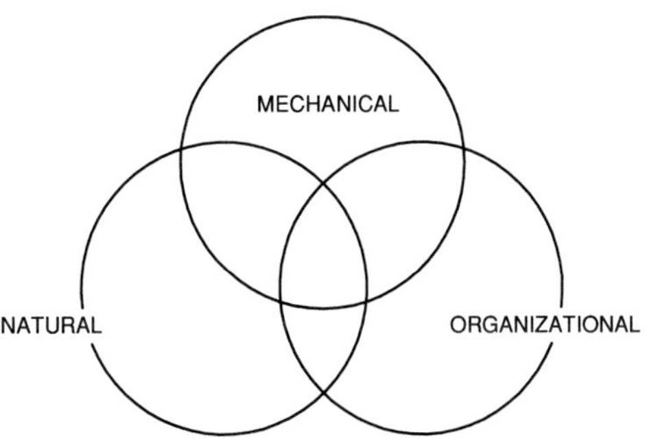

CPTED strategies are implemented by electronic methods (mechanical security products, target-hardening techniques, locks, alarms, CCTV, gadgets), .architectural methods (architectural design and layout, site planning and landscape, signage, circulation control), and organizational methods (manpower, police, security guards, receptionists, doormen, and business block watches).

CPTED STRATEGIES

Removing the Excuses for Criminal Behavior

Removing the excuses for criminal behavior is accomplished by clearly stating the ground rules against crime and by establishing standard procedures to punish those who violate those defined rules. Clearly defined regulations and signage prevent offenders from excusing their crimes with claims of ignorance or misunderstanding.

Through proper design and use of the built environment the landscape architect can reduce the opportunities and fear of predatory stranger-to-stranger crime and improve the quality of life.

CPTED DESIGN CONCEPTS

The CPTED process has as its objective to create physical space that considers the needs of legitimate users, the normal and expected (or intended) functions for the space, and the predictable behavior of illegitimate users and intruders. Landscape and design professionals can use three strategies for security design: natural access control, natural surveillance, and territorial reinforcement.

- Natural access control strategies are intended to deny access to crime targets and to create a perception of risks to offenders.
- Surveillance strategies are those directed at primarily keeping intruders under observation.
- Territorial reinforcement strategies involve creating or extending the sphere of influence. Users develop a sense of proprietorship so that offenders perceive that territorial influence.

And each of these can be implemented through three methods: mechanical, natural, and organized:

- Mechanical methods: technology products, target-hardening techniques, locks, alarms, CCTV, gadgets
- Natural methods: architectural design and layout, site planning, landscaping signage, avoiding circulation conflicts
- Organized methods: manpower—police, security guards, receptionists, doormen, and business block watches.

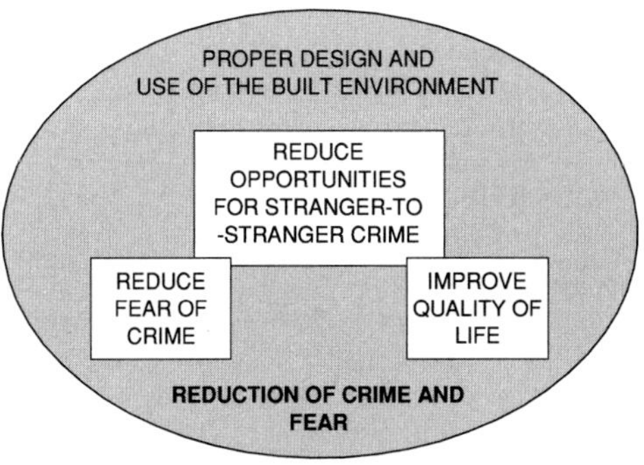

CPTED STRATEGIES REDUCE CRIME AND FEAR THROUGH DESIGN

Natural Access Control

This process involves decreasing opportunities for crime by denying access to crime targets and creating a perception of risk for offenders. It is accomplished by designing streets, sidewalks, building entrances, and neighborhood gateways to mark public routes, and by using structural elements to discourage access to private areas.

Natural Surveillance

This design concept is intended to make intruders easily observable. Features that maximize visibility of people, parking areas, and building entrances promote natural surveillance. Examples are doors and windows that look onto streets and parking areas, pedestrian-friendly sidewalks and streets, front porches, and adequate nighttime lighting.

Territorial Reinforcement

Physical design can create or extend a sphere of influence. In this setting, users develop a sense of territorial control, while potential offenders perceive this control and are discouraged from their criminal intentions. Features that define property lines and distinguish private spaces from public spaces, such as landscape plantings, pavement design, gateway treatments, and fences, promote territorial reinforcement.

Legitimate Activity Support

Legitimate activity for a space or building is encouraged through use of natural surveillance and lighting and architectural design that clearly defines the purpose of the structure or space. Crime prevention and design strategies can discourage illegal activity and protect a property from chronic problem activity.

Mechanical Strategies

Sometimes referred to as "target hardening," mechanical concepts and measures emphasize hardware and technological systems, such as locks, security screens on windows, fencing and gating, key control systems, CCTV, and other security technologies.

Maintenance and Management

Regardless of the type of landscaping and planting designs used; the fencing installed; or the groundcover, vehicle barriers, or paint used, if the property is not maintained to the standard of care for that building or property type, the image of neglect and lack of care will be broadcast to those who can use this weakness to trespass or commit crimes. Management of the property is critical for maintaining the operation and upkeep of grounds and the facility.

Randall I. Atlas, PhD, AIA CPP Atlas Safety & Security Design Inc., Miami Florida; Leonard Hopper, RLA, FASLA

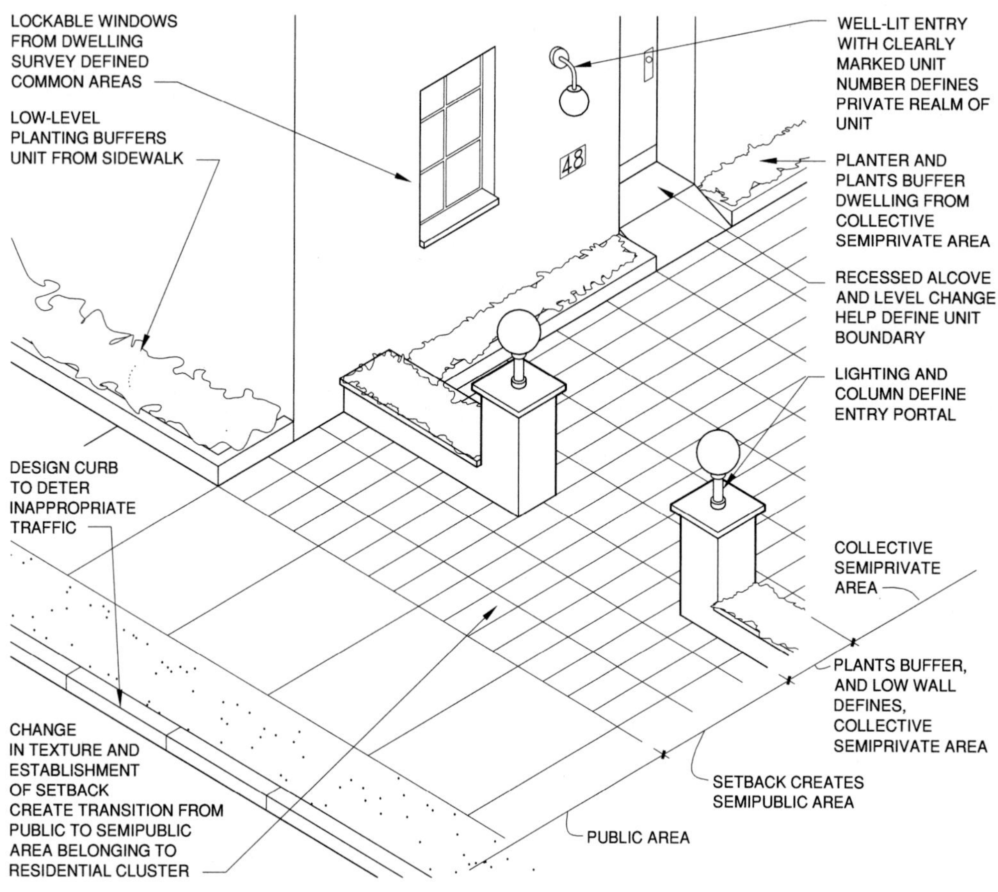

TERRITORIAL REINFORCEMENT FOR PRIVATE PROPERTY

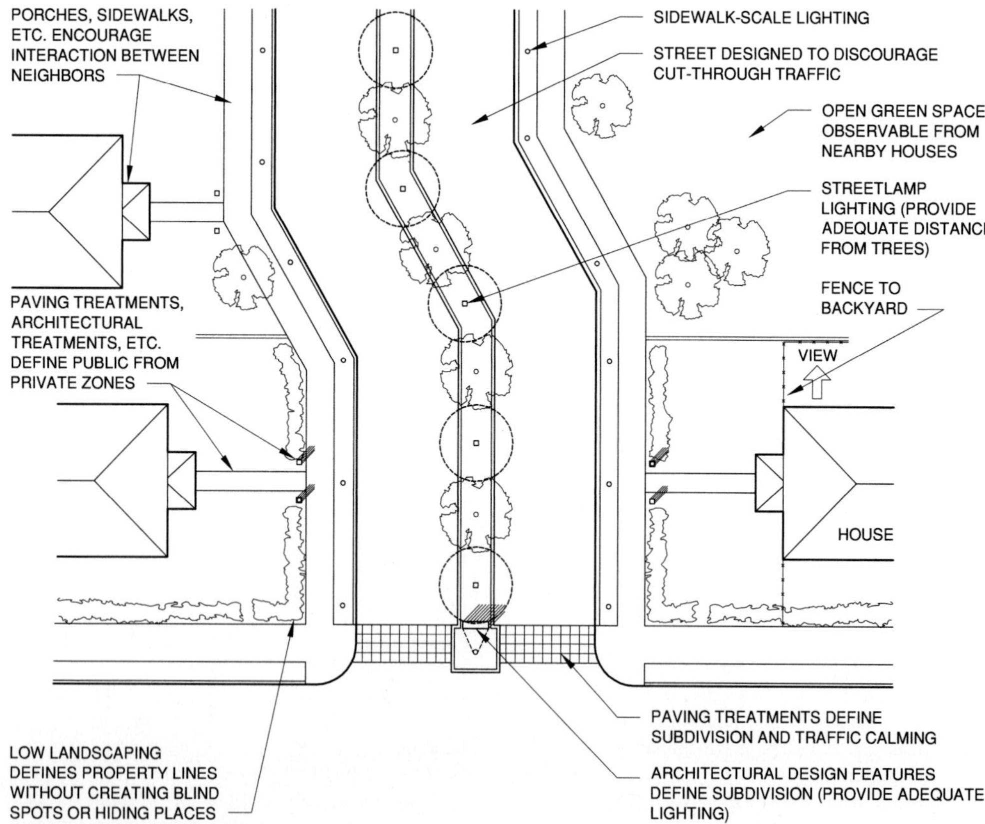

CPTED PLANNING FOR SUBDIVISIONS

Randall I. Atlas, PhD, AIA CPP Atlas Safety & Security Design Inc., Miami Florida; Leonard Hopper, RLA, FASLA

Organizational Strategies

These concepts rely on people (individuals and vested groups) to provide surveillance and access control functions in the spaces they occupy at home or at work. Organizational measures may use concierges, security guards, designated guardians, residents in clock and neighborhood watch programs, police officer patrols, and other individuals with the ability to observe, report, and intervene in undesirable or illegitimate actions.

Natural Strategies

It is in this strategic category where the landscape architect's influence is particularly significant. Natural concepts employ physical and spatial features such as site and architectural elements to ensure that a setting is designed to deter crime while supporting the intended use of the space. Natural measures are also used to reduce conflicts between user and use. Examples of natural features include plantings, outdoor seating and planters, fences, gates, walls, walking paths, level changes, and material changes.

Critical points for security planning:	
Architectural program	Yes
Schematic design	Yes
Design development	Yes
Construction documents	Yes
Bid package	Yes
Construction	Yes
Critical points in building operation:	
Opening test runs	Yes
Emergency testing	Yes
Training staff	Yes
Postoccupancy evaluation	Yes
Modifications to system	Yes

BASIS OF SECURITY DESIGN

The crime prevention through environmental design approach recognizes the site and building environment's designated or intended use. The emphasis of CPTED focuses on the design and use of space. This practice is different from the traditional target-hardening approach to crime prevention. Traditional target hardening, or fortressing, focuses predominantly on denying access to a crime target through physical or artificial barrier techniques such as locks, alarms, fences, and gates. The traditional approach tends to overlook opportunities for natural access control and surveillance. Sometimes the natural and normal uses of the environment can accomplish the same effects of mechanical hardening and surveillance.

Environmental security design or CPTED is based on three functions of human space—the three Ds of CPTED:

Designation: What is the purpose or intention of the space?

Definition: How is the space defined? What are the social, cultural, legal, and psychological ways the space is defined?

Design: Is the space defined to support prescribed or intended behaviors?

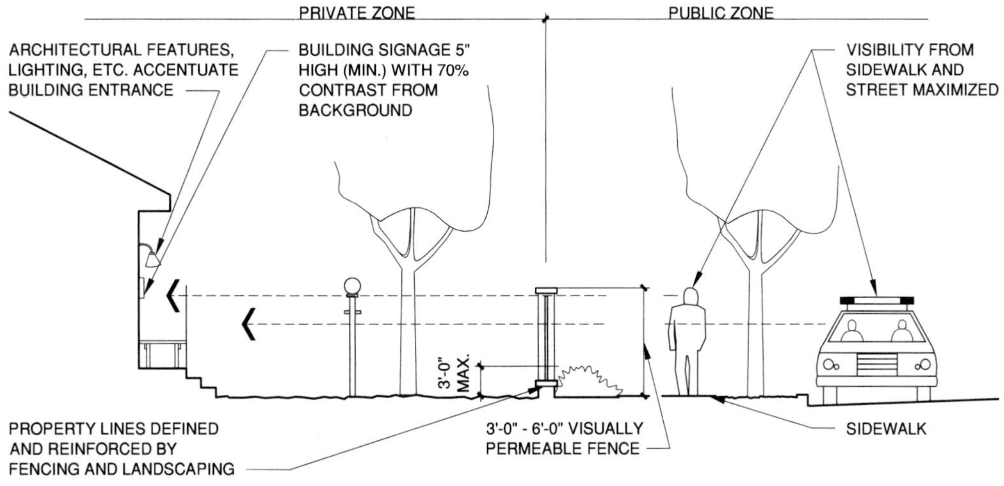

CPTED PLANNING FOR RESIDENTIAL PROPERTY

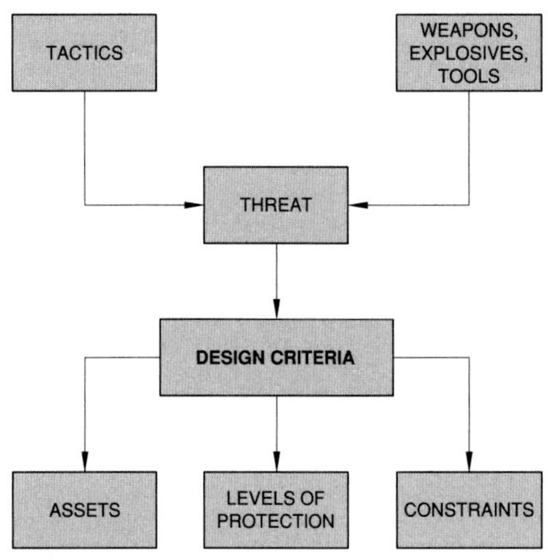

DESIGN CRITERIA FOR CPTED APPROACH

The definition, designation, and design of a site or building establish the functional design criteria that are gathered and given to the design and engineering professionals for integration into the design.

The goal for architects and landscape architects is to minimize fortress design and target hardening, except where required *after* thorough analysis and study. The design professional must address the issue of how architectural design features and approaches can enhance security without intruding on the aesthetics and functionality of the building. For example, how can electronic and automated physical security systems be integrated with the increasingly complex management and monitoring systems for fire protection, building environmental control, transportation and communications, and accessibility?

The CPTED security design process is applied from a macro to micro level. The three levels are site security design, building perimeter, and inner building space or point protection.

Implementation of CPTED design may include the following:

- Place unsafe activities in safe areas.
- Control access to the facility by pedestrian and vehicular traffic.
- Minimize the number of entrances to the interior of a building, and clearly identify the function of the remaining entrances. Secure entrances when not in use.
- Control parking lot access by means of gates and passes.
- Install barriers at vulnerable openings such as ground-floor windows, exterior fire stairs, roof openings, and skylights. Fence off problem areas to prevent unauthorized access, and funnel movement along desired paths.
- Control access for servicing and deliveries.
- Give vacant lots, apartments, offices, and spaces to legitimate users to protect against vandalism and damage.
- Paint exterior walls with graffiti-resistant epoxy and/or landscape with creeping vines to prevent the wall from acting as a mural for graffiti taggers.
- Design the exterior of a structure so it is hard to climb.
- Minimize the number of exterior openings at or below grade.
- Protect all building openings against entry or attack.
- Provide extra conduit for growth and changes.
- Design walls to resist penetration by intruders, possibly using cars, hand tools, explosions, and so on.
- Provide sufficient space in the lobby or entry areas for verification, identification, and screening of users—for example, sign-in desks, contraband detection equipment such as X-ray machines, and personal identification equipment.
- Provide adequate space for maintaining security equipment.
- Protect all utilities and control panels from disruption by unauthorized persons.
- Design elevators, stairways, and automated locking mechanisms so they do not compromise security during emergency evacuations.
- Design lighting for proper illumination in coordination with CCTV—that is, reduce glare, increase view of field.
- Design perimeter to be well defined and supported by natural barriers, such as landscaping; mechanical barriers, such as walls, fences, buried sensors, motion sensors, proximity sensors; and organizational methods such as guard patrol.
- Design for force protection: Place capable guardians at key access and surveillance points.
- Design for vehicle and pedestrian access points and the careful placement of walkways and vehicle barriers.
- Protect utilities and infrastructure.
- Design for durability and abuse.

Site security design streetscape elements may include:

- Bollards/planters
- Curbs
- Vehicle barriers
- Security lighting
- Signage and ground rules
- Gates
- Plazas and fountains
- Guardhouses and gatehouses
- Fences and walls that are barrier- and climb-resistant
- Colonnades
- Pedestrian benches
- Water fountains and newspaper stands
- Bicycle stands
- Bus shelters
- Signage and flags
- Trash receptacles
- Light poles
- Street parking setbacks
- Trees and bushes and groundcover

Site security system guidelines include:

- Consider space for placement of hardware and servicing.
- Plan for generous wiring.
- Plan for backup power.
- Plan for intrusion detection devices:
  - Plan for site intrusion detection.
  - Plan for boundary penetration sensors.
  - Plan for motion detection systems.
- Plan for access control systems.
- Plan for secured utilities—either underground or rooftop with secured access.
- Plan for secured infrastructure, to include:
  - Storm drains and sewers
  - Communications and electrical vaults access
  - Utility tunnels access
  - Alarm and security network access
  - Equipment rooms
- Plan for contraband and weapons detection:
  - Plan for explosives detectors.
  - Plan for credential readers and positive personnel identification systems.
- Plan for security control and information display systems.
- Conduct the needs assessment and include it as part of the architectural programming.
- Determine the level of criticality and threats to the building assets.
- Observe how people use the building for legitimate and illegitimate uses in order to determine what functions and spaces may need to be changed.
- Use the national standards as a starting point to establish a standard of care in order to improve efficiency, safety, and security and to reduce premises liability from negligent security design and practices.

Randall I. Atlas, PhD, AIA CPP Atlas Safety & Security Design Inc., Miami Florida; Leonard Hopper, RLA, FASLA

CPTED LIGHTING FOR SECURITY ENHANCEMENT

Security lighting does not prevent or stop crime, but it can help owners protect people and property. Good pedestrian lighting offers the natural surveillance people need to feel comfortable walking in the area or crossing a parking lot to their cars. Lighting can prevent surprises from "jump-out" criminals or give pedestrians the opportunity to call for help, or to turn and go another way,

The goal of security lighting should be to achieve a uniform, consistent level of light on both pedestrian and vehicular paths of travel. Lighting is critical for the illumination of street and building names and numbers to enable effective response by police, fire, and emergency personnel. At the same time, lighting should be designed to avoid light intrusion into residential settings.

The quality of lighting also may be an important security feature. True-color, full-spectrum light rendition can help with identification of vehicles and persons. Car lots and gas stations are examples of building types where metal halide luminaries are used for full-spectrum light rendition.

Design guidelines for security lighting include:

- Ensure proper beam control to save a system from glare, loss of light energy, and light intrusion.
- Install fixtures to cast a light pattern over a broad horizontal area rather than a tall vertical area.
- Be aware that light surfaces reflect light more efficiently than dark surfaces.
- Keep in mind the line of sight between the location of a light fixture and objects that may cast a shadow. Careful placement will avoid dark corners behind doors, trashcans, and other features.
- Install protective lighting, as it is a valuable and inexpensive deterrent to crime. It improves visibility for checking badges and people at entrances, inspecting vehicles, preventing illegal entry, and detecting intruders both outside and inside buildings and grounds. Protective lighting must accomplish the following objectives:
  - Provide for proper illumination of all exterior areas in a facility, including pedestrian and vehicular entrances, the perimeter fence line, sensitive areas or structures within the perimeter, and parking areas.
  - Discourage or deter attempts at entry by intruders by making detection certain. Proper illumination may lead a potential intruder to believe detection is inevitable.
  - Avoid glare that handicaps guards and annoys passing traffic and occupants of adjacent properties.
  - Direct glare at intruders, where appropriate, as a means of handicapping them.
  - Provide that guardposts and CCTV cameras are in low-light locations to render their positions more difficult for the intruder to pinpoint.
  - Provide for redundancy, so that a single lamp outage does not result in a dark spot that is vulnerable to intrusion.
  - Provide for complete reliability such that, in the event of a power failure, standby illumination is available.
  - Provide for convenient control.
  - Be covered under a maintenance agreement to ensure that repairs are made in a timely fashion.
  - Be resistant to vandalism and sabotage. Fixtures should be installed high, out of reach of potential intruders, and be of the vandal-resistant type.

VEHICULAR BARRIER DESIGN

Vehicle access control has been construed to mean Jersey concrete barriers. But there are many different approaches that the design professional can use to accomplish the goals of reducing the risk of a car bomb attack, car theft, or car jacking in parking garages.

Proper Application of Vehicle Barriers

Active barriers at access/egress points in high-security areas should be fully engaged until vehicles are cleared for passage. A visible signal light or drop-arm should indicate the barrier's status to approaching vehicles. Operating time should not exceed three to four seconds. The barrier system must maintain its position, preventing access in case of power failure, be capable of manual operation, and be connected to emergency power. Remote controls should include a status indicator.

Passive vehicle barriers (wall, bollards, planters, trenches/berms, and ponds) can be inexpensive and low maintenance, while enhancing site design. In contrast, concrete bollards and walls require heavy reinforcement tied into massive continuously reinforced concrete footings.

Bollards and Barriers

Landscape architects are already familiar with the most common ways to control access to a site using physical barriers such as bollards, planters, security gates, and turnstiles, to control traffic and parking. Deciding on the type of physical barrier necessary for a specific project is based on the level of protection needed, how important aesthetics are, and the size of the budget.

Plain barriers such as Jersey barriers are mass-produced. They are strong and crashworthy, made of steel-reinforced concrete, and are relatively cheap. Jersey barriers, though easy to install and move, remain aesthetically unappealing. One solution to this problem is to use a decorative apron that fits over the top of a standard Jersey barrier. Another alternative is to use concrete barriers that are precast in a variety of more decorative styles, which are more visually appealing and can fit with a number of architectural styles.

Bollards are ideal for separating pedestrians from vehicular traffic and for limiting vehicular access. Available as fixed models or as removable or retractable, models are constructed of steel, cast iron, precast concrete, ductile iron, aluminum high-density polyurethane, or recycled plastic. Fixed bollards are typically set in concrete or welded onto a baseplate or bolted down.

Bollard systems consist of one or more bollards operating independently or in groups of two or more units. Rising bollards are below ground and are raised into the guard position by a remotely located precision hydraulic or pneumatic power unit.

Beam barriers also can be used to control vehicular access. They resemble typical and familiar parking arms. However, they differ in a significant way. Complementing the visible parking arm is a tensioned steel cable. As both the hinge side and opposite side of the parking arm both lock into substantial concrete barriers, the steel cable provides the necessary vehicle stopping capacity.

Planter barriers are frequently constructed of reinforced concrete, with a steel cage built of reinforcing bars. As security structures, these barriers have a strength and resistance comparable to that of highway barriers. Planter security barricades can be aesthetically pleasing while improving security at the same time.

Barriers and gates have been around for centuries and are still being used due to their effectiveness, reasonable price, and ease of operation. These gates are available to landscape architects in a variety of styles, including those that slide, raise and lower, swing, or pop up from the ground.

Pop-up gates are considered to be the most secure, as the majority are designed to roll backward on impact and impale the vehicle from the underside. The result is that the gate acts as a massive friction anchor that will slow down or stop most vehicles in their tracks.

Road blockers consist, fundamentally, of a box section welded with reinforcement struts that are submerged in the ground, and a wedge shape that can be raised or lowered to control vehicular traffic.

With the increased sophistication of modern technology, many of the newest barrier arms feature hydraulic power packs, photocells, and programmable controllers to raise and lower the barrier. These help ensure that gates will open and close smoothly and efficiently once activated. Most barrier gates include standard features such as a manual operation override, in case of a power failure, and a safety system that prevents the gate from closing on pedestrians or vehicles.

Physical Barriers

Physical barriers may be of two general types: natural and structural. Natural barriers include mountains, cliffs, canyons, rivers, or other terrain that is difficult to traverse. Structural barriers are man-made devices such as fences, walls, floors, roofs, grilles, bars, or other structures that deter penetration. If a natural barrier forms one side or any part of the perimeter, in itself it should not automatically be considered an adequate perimeter barrier. Structural barriers should be provided for that por-

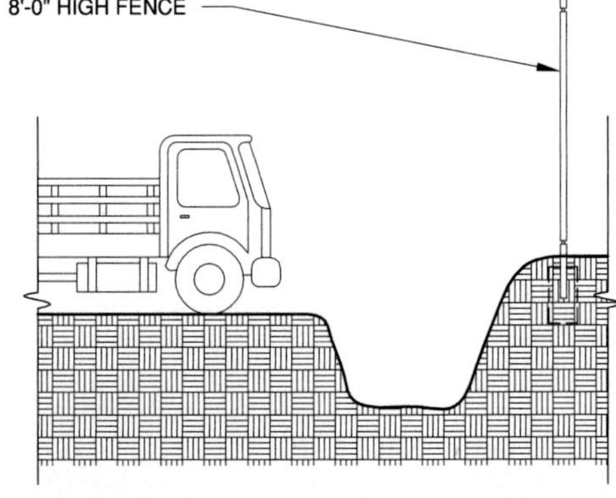

COMBINATION OF NATURAL AND STRUCTURAL BARRIERS

Randall I. Atlas, PhD, AIA CPP Atlas Safety & Security Design Inc., Miami Florida; Leonard Hopper, RLA, FASLA

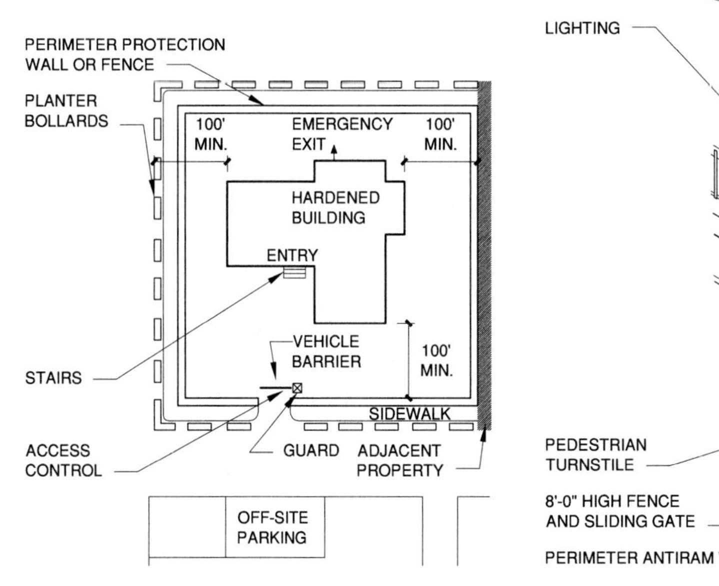

SECURED SITE PLAN

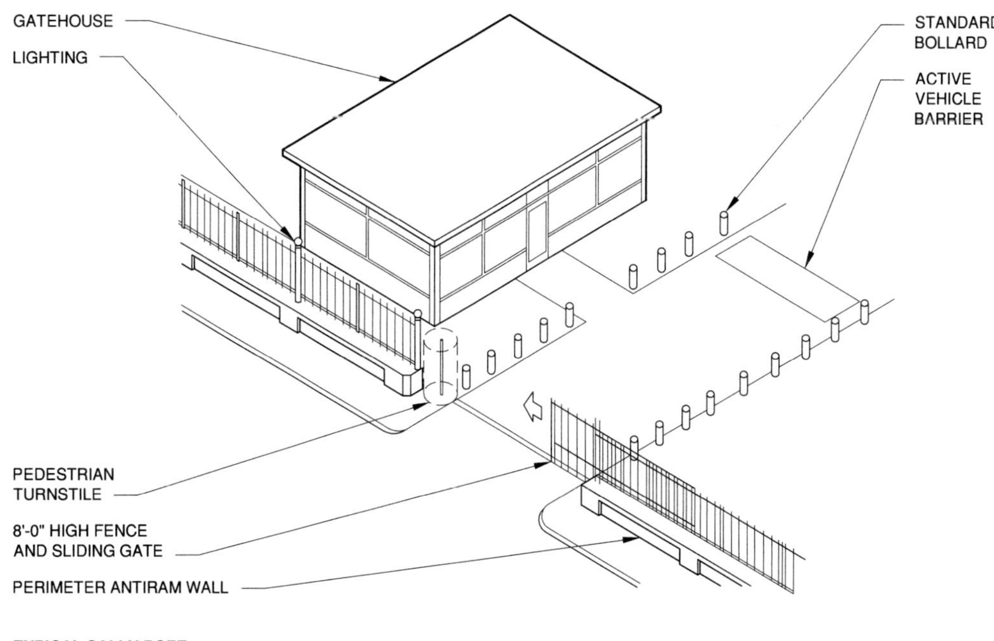

TYPICAL SALLY PORT

STRATEGIES AND ELEMENTS TO RESTRICT VEHICULAR ACCESS

tion of the perimeter where a determined intruder may overcome the natural barrier.

Fencing

Fences are the most common perimeter barrier or control. Two standard types are chain-link and steel picket fencing. The choice is dependent primarily upon the degree of permanence of the facility and local ordinances. A good perimeter fence is continuous, kept free of unwanted plant growth, and maintained in good condition.

Plantings and Security

The kinds of shrubs included in a private landscape—and where they are planted—can add to home security, as well as beautify the property, which increases resale value. The principal advantages of using plant materials, compared to equivalent architectural elements such as low walls or fences, are their relatively low cost and that they present a more aesthetically pleasing environment. Their disadvantages are that they require more frequent maintenance and care than constructed elements and can be more easily vandalized. Careful layout, such as closely associated plants with individual residential buildings, can minimize vandalism. Plantings will also contribute to a positive and attractive environment, softening the frigidity and raw elements of urban projects and enriching the texture, color, and spatial qualities of the project site.

Ground covers: Ground covers are surface-growing plants that rarely grow taller than 12 inches. These low-to-the-ground plants can be used to designate site areas, as well as establish the site boundaries. When planted in a bed or panel, they create an attractive symbolic barrier or buffer area. When planted in mass, they can be used to fill in large, vacant, and anonymous areas with no designated use. Appropriated in this manner, ground covers neutralize space, lending aesthetic sensibilities while clearly indicating that a space is not to be walked on.

Low shrubs: Low shrubs, growing up to approximately 3 feet in height, will form a tight-knit symbolic barrier when planted 2 1/2 to 3 feet apart. Due to their limited height, these shrubs are an excellent way to define site areas over which visual surveillance is required. Low shrubs are also used to define a project perimeter as well as buffer on-site use areas. Shrubs that have tough, thorny branches can present a formidable obstacle when planted under first-floor windows. Dense, spiny shrubs make an effective barrier hedge along property lines.

Midsized shrubs: Midsized shrubs present substantial symbolic barriers while reducing site penetrability, and they can form a screen or buffer separating adjacent areas. These plants must be arranged appropriately so as not to block surveillance of use areas. Reaching a possible height of 6 to 10 feet within 5 to 10 years, midsized shrubs can be either deciduous or evergreen. A few of these shrubs have thorns or spines, which aid the plants in their own defense while establishing a convincing barrier. Due to these elements shrubs with thorns or spines should be planted at least 3 to 4 feet from walkways and other locations, which are heavily used by residents.

Mid-sized shrubs may grow tall enough to block visual surveillance of a site and must be kept lower with pruning if they prove to present a security hazard. Shrubs of this height may also be used to form screens defining semiprivate to private front and rear yard areas. They are also effectively used in small groupings to landscape lawn, garden, and yard areas.

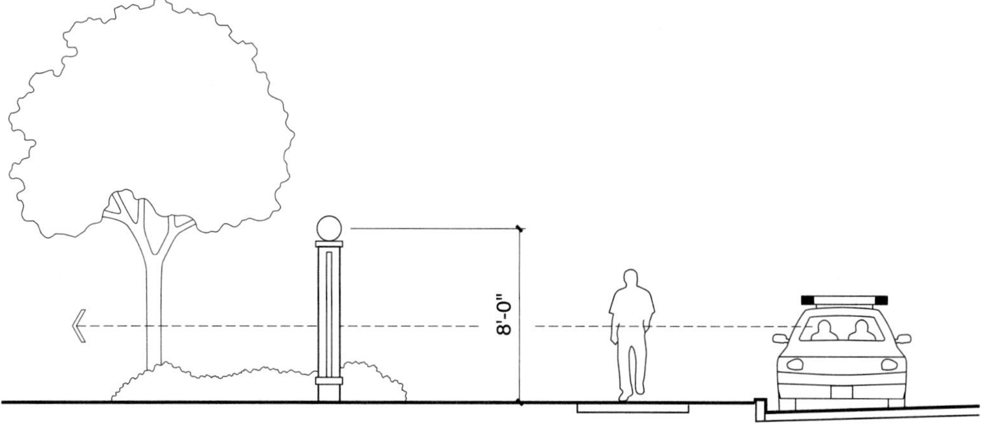

CLEAR SIGHTLINE FROM PATROL CAR, THROUGH FENCE AND AREA BETWEEN SHRUBS AND TREE CANOPY

Randall I. Atlas, PhD, AIA CPP Atlas Safety & Security Design Inc., Miami Florida; Leonard Hopper, RLA, FASLA

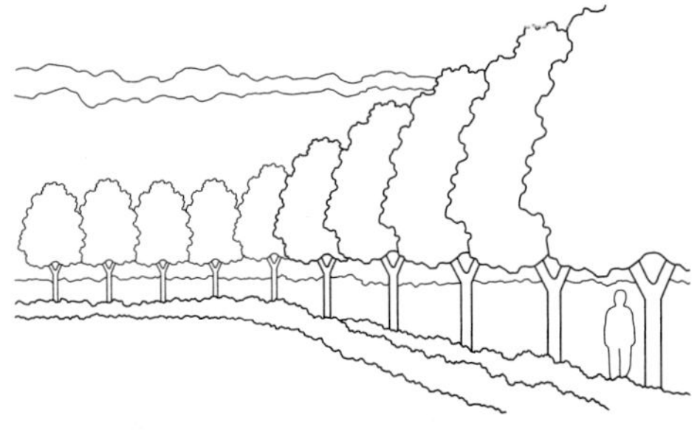

TREES AND LOW SHRUBS DEFINE AREA BUT ALLOW VISIBILITY BETWEEN SHRUB AND TREE CANOPY

CLEAR SIGHTLINES MAINTAINED BETWEEN STREET AND RESIDENTIAL PROPERTY

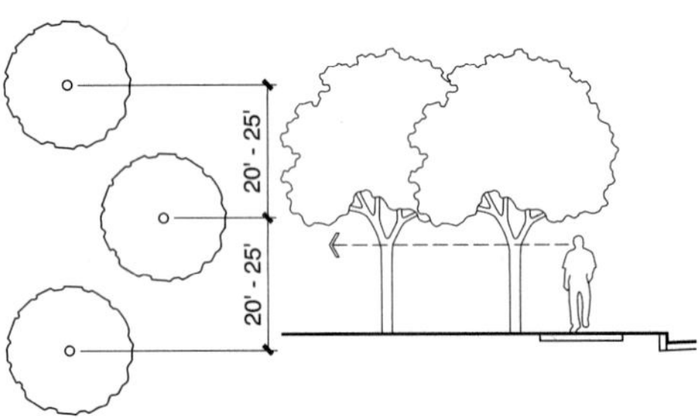

OFFSET TREE PLANTING ALLOWS FOR STRONG SPECIAL DEFINITION WITHOUT A NEGATIVE IMPACT ON VISIBILITY

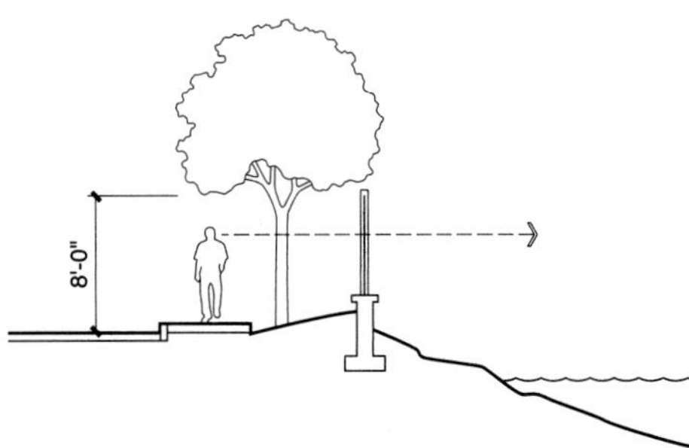

FENCE AS A PHYSICAL BARRIER THAT STILL ALLOWS VISIBILITY

Trees: Large trees can form effective symbolic barriers when planted 20 to 25 feet apart. Due to their heavy trunks and large canopies of foliage, large trees can define a project perimeter, or indicate the limits of an on-site active playfield or other use area. Large trees often enhance sitting areas, since their shade during the warm months of the year encourages the use of outdoor seating and thus promotes informal surveillance on a site. The foliage canopy of large trees is above eye level, so they do not hinder the surveillance of site areas.

Small trees are usually 10 to 15 feet tall and often shrublike, hence they are best utilized as a barrier or screen. Used to define a project perimeter, small trees are most effective at separating potential conflicts between adjacent use areas. These trees must be positioned so as not to block site surveillance areas.

SECURITY ZONES

The National Capital Planning Commission (NCPC) has set guidelines for identifying security zones located between the building and street. These zones operate under the same theory as CPTED and defensible space planning, which transitions space from public to semipublic to semiprivate to private spaces. The zones for NCPC are as follows:

Building Yard

The building yard is the exterior space between a building and the sidewalk, usually the grassy area bordering the building. This space can be planted with raised flowerbeds beside the sidewalk to create a barrier from a building to the public domain. Pedestrian entries and loading docks are typically in this category, making it necessary for security to be seamlessly integrated to complement the building's architecture yet remain effective at monitoring entries and exits. When the security barrier is provided in this location, for example, through the use of a raised plinth or wall, the sidewalk can remain free from intrusive security elements.

Sidewalk

This zone is located between the curb or parking lane and the aforementioned building yard. In the urban context, it serves as a common space for pedestrian activity and interaction. Thus, it is important to allow for and promote active public use of the sidewalk, allowing it to be left open and accessible to pedestrian movement.

Streetscape security components should be placed at least 18 inches from the edge of the curb (where curbside parking is permitted) to allow for the opening of car doors and pedestrian movements from car to sidewalk. This is the best location for streetscape elements and offers the most compatible location for security barriers. Curbside parking and traffic lanes do not need to be removed when security requirements can be met at the curb.

Parking meters, streetlights, benches, planters, and trash receptacles are familiar items found at or near the curb. Streetscape designs incorporating hardened versions of these elements should be created to reinforce the pedestrian realm.

Curb Lane

The curb lane is the lane of the street closest to the sidewalk. Curbside parking, passenger drop-off, loading, and service vehicles most often use this lane.

Curbside parking should be removed only from areas where the need for additional standoff distance is absolutely essential, and only for buildings with the highest security threat. The parking needs of adjacent owners of a property should be assessed, and parking replaced prior to any changes in the access of existing curbside lanes.

STREETSCAPE SECURITY ELEMENTS

The National Capital Urban Design and Security Plan works toward the goal of seamlessly incorporating building perimeter security into beautifully designed land and streetscape. The plan broadens the palette of perimeter security elements into an attractive streetscape, including a range of street furnishings and elements such as streetlights, walls, planters, fences, and seats. These elements have been studied to determine the feasibility of "hardening" them in order to function as both amenities and components of physical building perimeter security. The structural design, spacing, shape, and detailing of the perimeter security components must be designed to address the required level of protection for a particular building.

While some elements apply universally, others must be customized to reflect the unique character of a specific area through use of appropriate materials, scale, and design detail. There are seven basic security streetscape elements: hardened street furniture, fences or fence walls, plinth walls, hedges and bollards, planters, bollards, and custom-designed solutions. While one or more of these conceptual elements may be used in multiple areas, the style of the elements will vary based on the character of a particular area.

Tested and installed streetscape components have served as the basis for the security concepts proposed in the security plan. In general, proposed solutions use materials and capabilities such as those applied in proven elements, such as the Presidential Bollard, a bollard integrated with new streetscape and security designs for light poles, newspaper racks, and benches.

Many of these new designs need to be engineered and crash-tested to verify their effectiveness. The feasibility and cost of implementing these solutions will be determined as individual assessments are conducted and design of the components is tested to prove their effectiveness in defending against a variety of specified threats.

PROJECT DESIGN

There are four considerations vital to the streetscape design process, specifically integrating building perimeter security.

Risk assessment and levels of protection: When agencies conduct risk assessments, they consider factors including agency function, number of employees and visitors, building design and construction, as well as the relationship the building has with its surroundings. It is suggested that the Federal Protective Service and/or others evaluate the recommended level of protection.

Security threat: Much is considered when determining the standards of security components, including magnitude of threats (i.e., size

Randall I. Atlas, PhD, AIA CPP Atlas Safety & Security Design Inc., Miami Florida; Leonard Hopper, RLA, FASLA

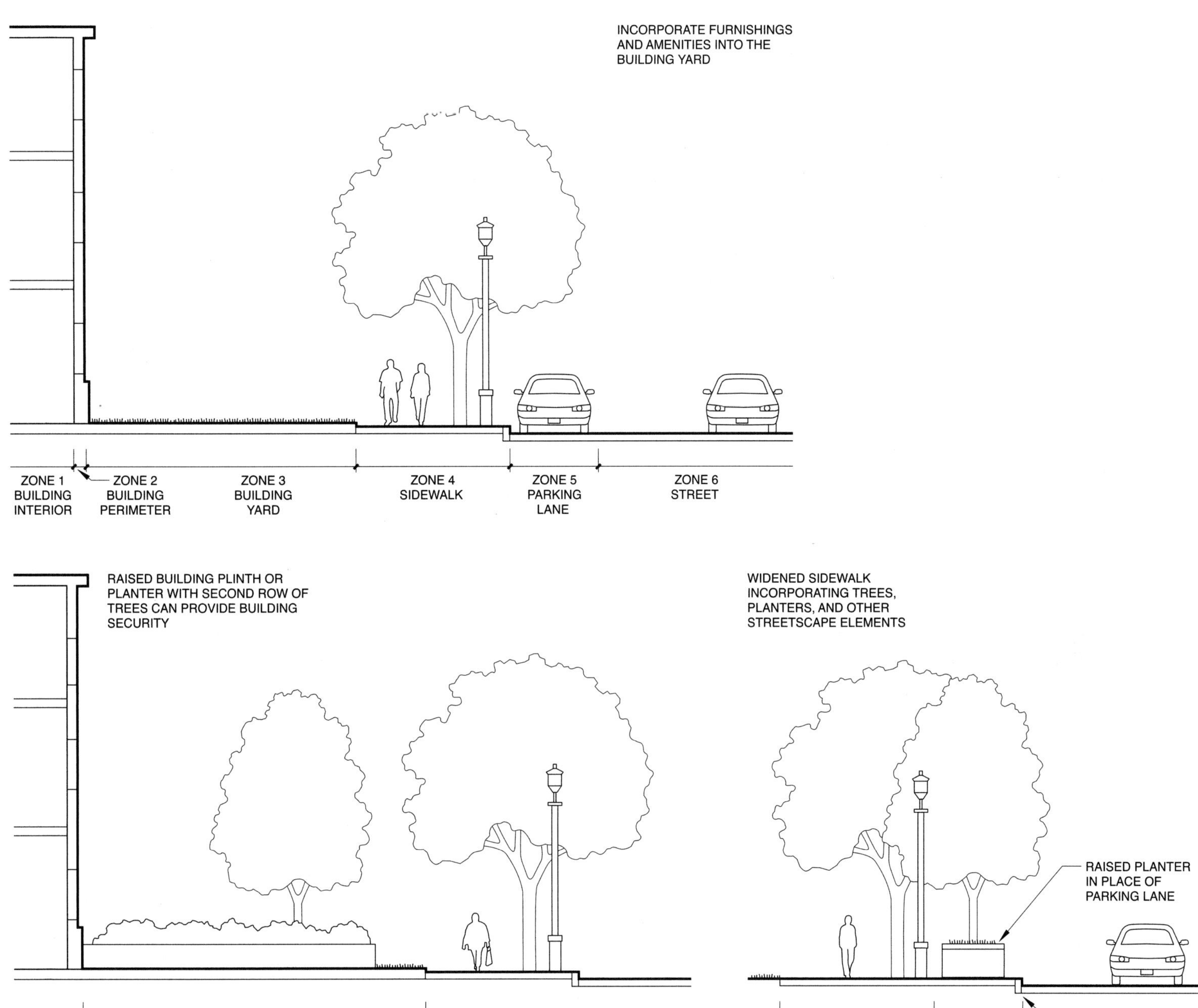

NATIONAL CAPITAL PLANNING COMMISSION SECURITY ZONES AND SUGGESTED SITE ELEMENTS

Source: National Captial Planning Commission.

and weight of vehicles), the potential speed and angle of the approaching vehicle, and the distance between the site perimeter and the building itself. Barriers can be custom-designed or selected from existing products lines to stop a vehicle traveling at a given weight and/or speed.

Location of underground systems: While the above-grade elements can be attractive to view, some may require substantial below-grade structural systems that will compete with the location of underground structures, utilities, and tree roots. Before a final design solution can be implemented, a survey is required to evaluate the impact of nearby trees and root systems. Great care must be taken in order to protect existing trees both for aesthetic as well as security reasons.

Streetscape component design and testing: The magnitude of potential threats influences the design of security components. While many of the streetscape components have been designed based on existing components, many will require testing to prove their effectiveness prior to final design of the streetscape plan. Assessment and engineering should begin early in the process to determine which items require testing.

REFERENCES

Atlas, R. I. 2000. "Crime Prevention through Environmental Design," in J. R. Hoke, Jr. (ed.) *Architectural Graphic Standards.* (73–80). New York: John Wiley & Sons, Inc.

City of Los Angeles. 1997. *Crime Prevention through Environmental Design: Design Out Crime Guidelines.*

The Florida Center for Community Design+ Research. 1993. *Florida Safe Schools Guidelines.* Tampa, FL: University of South Florida.

Randall I. Atlas, PhD, AIA CPP Atlas Safety & Security Design Inc., Miami Florida; Leonard Hopper, RLA, FASLA

Forgey, Benjamin. September 2002. "Changing the Guard," *Landscape Architecture Magazine:* 80–87.

Jacobs, Jane. 1961. *The Death and Life of Great American Cities*, New York: Random House Inc.

Mays, Vernon. September 2002. "Invisible Barriers," *Landscape Architecture Magazine:* 74–79.

National Capital Planning Commission. 2002. *The National Capital Urban Design and Security Plan.*

Russell, James, Elizabeth Kennedy, Merideth Kelly, Deborah Bershand. March 2002. *Designing for Security: Using Art and Design to Improve Security. Guidelines from the Art Commission of the City of New York.* New York: New York Art Commission.

Sipes, James. L. September 2002. "A New kind of Scrutiny," *Landscape Architecture Magazine:* 58–64.

Speckhardt, Lisa, and Jennifer Dowdell. September 2002. "Creating Safety," *Landscape Architecture Magazine:* 65–73.

U.S. Department of Housing and Urban Development. 1979. "Planning for Housing Security: Site Elements Manual." Annapolis, MD: William Brill Associates, Inc.

Wekerle, Gerda, and Carolyn Whitzman. 1995. *Safe Cities.* New York: Van Nostrand-Reinhold.

ORGANIZATIONAL WEB RESOURCES

American Society for Industrial Security: www.asisonline.org

Atlas Safety & Security Design: www.cpted-security.com

CPTED page: www.ncpc.org/2add4dc.htm

Defensible Space: www.defensiblespace.com/start.htm

General Services Administration, Office of Federal Protective Service: www.gsa.gov/Portal/content/orgs_content.jsp?contentOID=117945&contentType=1005

The Infrastructure Security Partnership: www.tisp.com

International CPTED Association: www.cpted.net

National Capital Planning Commission: www.ncpc.gov

National Crime Prevention Council: www.ncpc.org

National Crime Prevention Institute: www.louisville.edu/a-s/ja/ncpi

Security Design Coalition: www.designingforsecurity.org.

Security Industry Association: www.siaonline.org

Terrorism Research Center: www.terrorism.com/index.shtml

U.S. Department of State, Counterterrorism Office: www.state.gov/s/ct

White House Office on Homeland Security: www.whitehouse.gov/homeland

Randall I. Atlas, PhD, AIA CPP Atlas Safety & Security Design Inc., Miami Florida; Leonard Hopper, RLA, FASLA

SITE SECURITY PLANNING AND LANDSCAPE DESIGN CRITERIA

OVERVIEW

Designers throughout history have included protection and security as part of their work. This included protection against the elements as well as security against those that would do them harm. Early on, site selection considered geographic features such as rivers, mountains, canyons, and other natural barriers, to enhance security. Later, security design thinking evolved into building man-made barriers such as walls, fences, and moats, to provide protection against unwanted outsiders. All these security measures were directed toward keeping intruders out or at a safe distance, where they could inflict little damage, or slowing their advancement to give defenders time to respond. In all these cases, the physical elements of protection, natural and man-made, served to give the defenders a tactical edge over those seeking to do them harm.

Today, security design is not very different from what it has been throughout the ages. The primary objectives remain the same. Even the simplest of fences defines property; and, however easy to circumvent, the trespasser is clearly in violation of the owner's basic rights. As required, the design of these perimeter barriers can escalate along with any associated threat. However, just about any perimeter defense can be circumvented. There will always remain some degree of risk because of physical, budget, or personnel limitations. The objective is to match an appropriate barrier with a reasonably anticipated threat.

THE SECURITY DESIGN RESPONSE

Finding a balance between security measures and risk (determined by their impact on a number of other critical factors, including budget) is a fundamental task in the process of security design development. Thus, the basis for a creative security design solution must be an accurate risk assessment. Security setbacks must be carefully considered for their impacts on the architectural character of the surrounding community. The elements used between the building and perimeter become critically important components when incorporating the security design response with the architectural context of the area.

The response to terrorist threat must be multifaceted, comprehensive, and coordinated, in order to address a problem of this magnitude. Therefore, it is extremely important that the landscape architect know the anticipated threats based on thorough analysis of the threat, the site, and its context. A good security design will be based on an accurate collection of data that is responsive to the unique situations of each site, rather than on a prescriptive, one-size-fits-all approach that attempts to impose a predetermined design solution. Furthermore, landscape architects must actively collaborate with other professionals involved in a security design response to employ the strategies and materials available to create high-quality site security designs that meet the client's security and programmatic needs.

Today, it is imperative that security be a critical overlay to every major public or private design project being considered; moreover, the need to retrofit existing facilities and sites to enhance security should be given a high priority. Design professionals are uniquely positioned to contribute to America's safety and well-being. They can respond to the war on terror by redesigning "domestic battlegrounds," thereby providing a tactical edge while taking advantage away from those seeking to do us harm.

IMMEDIATE RESPONSE AND TEMPORARY BARRIERS

The immediate physical response to the attacks of September 11, 2001, was to use just about anything heavy or strong enough to stop vehicles dead in their tracks or keep them from violating standoff zones. The most common temporary element used was probably precast Jersey barriers (used for traffic control on roadways), followed closely by large precast planters known as "bunker pots" (actual potted plants seemed optional). This spectrum broadened to include precast drainage structures and dry-well rings (materials intended to buried in the ground) installed along the perimeter and major paths in highly visible areas around government institutions in Washington, DC.

Street closings utilizing temporary Jersey barriers were employed to restrict vehicular traffic accessibility to potential high-profile targets. Often, large security vehicles with drivers were used to function as sliding gates to allow the passing of emergency or other authorized vehicles through openings between the barricades. The lack of a coordinated approach to these closings resulted in an increase in traffic congestion, a compromising of emergency services access, and disruption of pedestrian movement.

The widespread deployment of precast concrete "anything" sprinkled throughout our most valued landscapes resulted in many observers reacting negatively to the aesthetic and psychological impact. This got the attention of not just designers but government officials, who realized that security measures taken to protect people and institutions must not inflict damage to our physical, historical, and cultural heritage. Security cannot be achieved by sacrificing the very values and qualities that are being protected.

Deploying the quickest and cheapest means of protection when heightened security first arises is understandable, but the likelihood of these "temporary" measures becoming permanent is a concern. Knee-jerk responses can actually increase the perception of threat, and instill fear, rather than promote a secure feeling. A measure of terrorist success is when all people become terrified. In addition, erected barriers greatly affect the way people interact with their institutions, government, and each other.

The immediate responses to heightened security come at a high price: the price of temporary physical improvements, increased personnel and overtime costs, and the psychological impact on the citizens of our country. It is imperative to integrate security measures in designs for new construction (or the retrofitting of existing facilities) in a way that is both effective and flexible to varying levels of threat. This can be achieved using familiar site elements while providing effective security in a seamless, transparent manner.

GOOD PERMANENT SECURITY DESIGN

It is possible to employ good urban design principles, creating beautifully rich streetscapes and public urban plazas, in an approach that also addresses the need for enhanced security. These objectives need not be mutually exclusive. The direct and indirect costs of employing temporary barriers and security measures and maintaining them over time can be reinvested in a coordinated and comprehensive approach, utilizing good, permanent security design. Over the long term, this will prove to be a cost-effective approach as well as serve to protect and express the democratic ideals that serve as the very foundation of this country's existence.

A number of reports were issued during the 1990s and early twenty-first century in response to the 9/11 attacks on America. Many of the reports generated were initiated at the federal level, but the criteria and guidelines developed are certainly applicable at the state/local and public/private levels. The reports acknowledge that terrorist attacks can take many forms, but point out that the overwhelming threat—accounting for more than half of incidences—is from a bomb-laden vehicle. This type of attack (for which standoff zones were created) is thought of as the easiest way to cause extensive damage, loss of life, and possible progressive collapse of the structure being attacked. The emphasis on creating secure setbacks is one of the primary responses required to enhance security of a potential target.

What makes these documents so significant is their recognition of varying levels of security for buildings based on their likelihood of being a terrorist target. Not every building or facility needs to be protected to the same level. The varying levels of threats that are classified by the security designer and the strategies for response presented by the security consultant, are the basis for the consideration of a broader spectrum of design elements to be used to establish perimeter security.

Whether coordinated with new construction or modified to enhance the security of existing buildings and facilities, site elements used to restrict vehicular access and define pedestrian circulation are extensive and varied. Some of these amenities include bollards, major trees (with and/or without tree guards), benches, planters, bike racks, information kiosks, bus shelters, overhead structures, signage, and flagpoles. These are among the more common elements used to provide vehicular barriers along the street and effective perimeter security.

Building plazas and public gathering places can use these site amenities, along with raised planters, changes in elevation (e.g., steps, ramps, and railings), walls, fences, colonnades, statues, and fountains. All of these site amenities can enhance and complement the character of an area and architecture of adjacent buildings. These features provide a meaningful reason for widening pedestrian sidewalks, while providing an important increase in the setback distance between the building and vehicles along the street.

People are very comfortable with these familiar design elements as components in the landscape, and they can continue to be used strategically to enhance site security. Each of these elements can be beautifully designed and carefully sited, with its commonplace, everyday character disguising its protective role. However, the most successful implementations consist of many elements combined together, rather than depending on any one element. Landscape architects should think of the vocabulary of site amenities as separate threads woven to create a fabric, resulting in a rich streetscape as well as enhanced security.

Randall I. Atlas, AIA CPP, Counter Terror Design Inc., Miami, FL; Leonard Hopper, RLA, FASLA

HARDENING SITE ELEMENTS

A great deal of a site element's capability to withstand an impact is at the point of connection to the pavement, curb, or footing. The size of curbs or footings may have to be increased to withstand vehicular impact. For example, an element that might usually be anchored in a footing of concrete typically 1 foot square by 3 feet deep might now require a footing 3 or 4 feet square by 5 feet deep. Site features typically anchored in a footing might even require modification for anchoring in a substantial underground-grade beam to create a more monolithic resistance to impact.

Most of these hardening techniques are invisible to the casual observer, which is the value of using commonplace site amenities to enhance security. However, special considerations are necessary because of the substantial below-grade modifications. The areas that would typically benefit from the use of these amenities as security measures, particularly the sidewalk to the curb line, often have underground utilities running along them that were installed at a depth not anticipating the need for this type of construction. Therefore, before embarking on a security design effort of this type, conflicts with underground utilities must be studied.

Additionally, the increased size of underground footings, curbs, and grade beams can have disastrous effects on existing trees, and can severely limit the development or lifespan of newly planted trees. Damage to the root structure of existing trees should be minimized, and new trees should be provided with ample opportunity for their roots to spread. The use of structural soils, providing both a positive growing environment for tree roots and the integrity to support the pavements above, should be considered.

As this type of streetscape improvement to enhance security would most likely require the removal of sidewalk pavement, the opportunity to maximize a tree's ability to survive the urban environment and become a security enhancement itself, should not be missed. The locations of underground utility lines and tree roots are so critical that, in some cases, they may drive the location and even feasibility of using streetscape elements to enhance perimeter security.

Looking Ahead

Security designs should be forward-looking, to include planning for new threats and new technologies. This may mean approaching security design improvements as part of a phased implementation with greater detail and fine-tuning with each phase of efforts. Given constraints of funds and timing, priorities must be set based on the probability of certain types of attacks, against certain targets, in certain locations. While the criteria may be somewhat subjective, nonetheless it must be applied to prioritize security implementations within the constraints of available resources.

Landscape architects know how to design places that make people want to use them. They know how to create "a sense of place" and complement an area's identity. The site elements and amenities used to create these perceptual qualities of place and identity must continue to be the foundation upon which security designs are built. Along with other design considerations, security design must be integrated holistically and seamlessly into a comprehensive site design approach.

Security concerns have made the integration of building architecture and site design increasingly critical. The close collaboration of architect, landscape architect, and structural engineer can result in both responsive and inspirational designs. Indeed, there is a growing recognition that site security measures and design excellence need not be mutually exclusive.

SITE SECURITY DESIGN CRITERIA

The first contact a person has with a particular architectural project is accessing the site to gain entry to a property or building. With the increasing threats to persons and property from acts of terrorism, workplace violence, and street crime, the first, and most important line of defense is securing the site perimeter and the careful placement of the building/s on the given site.

Landscape architects design public and private spaces and environments that serve a particular function for the users and clients of a building, and do it in a pleasing aesthetic manner. While fulfilling this task, the design must also protect users, ensuring their safety and security within the environment. The main guardian of health and safety for building designs are building codes, but these only address architectural features, such as egress design, fire safety, structural integrity, stair proportions, and railing design, while ignoring the considerations of crime or terrorism. As safety is a prime consideration of building codes, security of the site and building users should be considered a high priority.

SECURITY DESIGN PROBLEMS

Typical design problems relating to security include the following:

- Security requirements are not defined.
- There is no focus on threat versus risk.
- No vulnerability assessment has been developed.
- No one is in charge, or everyone is in charge.
- Inappropriate or unreliable measures are taken.
- Solutions are not integrated, or there are no solutions at all.
- Only target hardening or guards are used, without design changes.
- There is a lack of security awareness by employees.
- Design is poor, and there is conflicting use of circulation patterns.
- Security in design and operation of the facility or community are seen as low priority.

Addressing Problems

A familiar tenet of twentieth-century architecture was "form follows function." In contrast, most contemporary architecture has focused on "form" rather than "function." Any building must meet specific functional criteria, for from the function, the design evolves. Buildings must permit efficient job performance, meet the needs of the user, and protect the user from safety hazards and criminal acts.

Vandalism, terrorism, burglary, shoplifting, employee theft, assault, and espionage, are just some of the crimes that endanger lives and threaten the human built environment. As crime increases, landscape architects are being called on to address security and crime concerns through the design process. The growth in the basic demand for security design poses challenges for landscape architects. They are called on to:

- Determine the security requirements.
- Know the security technology.
- Understand the site design implications.

DESIGNING SECURITY INTO THE LANDSCAPE AND THE ARCHITECTURE OF BUILDINGS

This section will demonstrate the process of designing security into the landscape and architecture of a site and a building.

Defensible Space

Urban planner Oscar Newman coined the term "defensible space" to describe a range of mechanisms, real and symbolic barriers, strongly defined areas of influence, and improved opportunities for surveillance that combine to bring the environment under the control of its residents.

According to Newman's Defensible Space theory, the behavior of people in a public setting is largely based on the cues that they take in from their surroundings. It is an accepted fact, for example, that people are more likely to dispose of their waste products in a receptacle bin if they see others taking the action first. Conversely, in a poorly planned community, where people throw trash on the street, others follow suit, adding their trash to the waste already lying around. Newman wondered whether people would change their behavior if the environment changed.

Recent studies have proven his theory correct. As a number of inner cities have refurbished their landscape and dwellings, crime rates have subsequently plummeted. This proves the importance of the landscape architect's role in creating an aesthetically pleasing, well-planned public environment.

Designing for Security from the Outset

Security has traditionally been treated as an after-the-fact issue; consequently, funding for security is usually what is left over in the construction or operation budget. But security design is more than bars on windows, a security guard in a booth, a camera, or a wall. Security design is a systematic integration of design, technology, and operation for the expressed goal of reducing the opportunity and perception of predatory stranger-to-stranger crime.

Security design is for the protection of the three critical assets: people, information, and property (PIP). The protection of these assets applies to all building types and throughout all of the design and construction processes, from programming, schematic design, design development, construction documents, bidding, and construction to operation.

Designing without security in mind can lead to expensive retrofitting of the building with security equipment and the need for additional security personnel and increased labor costs. If not properly planned for, security equipment can distort key design elements and building function. Additional personnel costs for security are expensive and often cumbersome. But most importantly, overlooking security strategies can lead to liability litigation for premises. Case law is abundant with successful claims against owners, architects, and building managers resulting from insufficient security. The need for security is clear and present. The most efficient and least expensive way to provide security is in the design process.

Randall I. Atlas, AIA CPP, Counter Terror Design Inc., Miami, FL; Leonard Hopper, RLA, FASLA

Defining the Roles

To effectively design for security, the roles of the "players"—the client, the security manager/consultant, and the landscape architect/site planner must first be defined.

Client: The role of the client is to precisely define the vulnerabilities and threats to people, information, and property (PIP); to assess the level and cost of protection and the coverage that will be provided; to develop the definition of security needs, and provide the architect with a pragmatic description of protection requirements; to define who and what needs protection; to define the assets and the importance of each asset worth protecting.

Security manager/consultant: The role of the security manager/consultant is to help the client describe and elaborate the protection requirements and the level of protection required in each area; to help the client assess the threats, security needs, and crime vulnerabilities; to help with the planning of access control, security zoning, target hardening, and surveillance systems; to define the basic security concepts with operational procedures and security manpower allocation, and the types, location, and tasks of security personnel.

Landscape architect/site planner: The role of the landscape architect/site planner is to incorporate the security program information into effective space and circulation planning; to provide clear sightlines for surveillance and planned access controls at entrances and exits; to design for the appropriate location of sensitive or restricted areas; to design for the planned placement of security personnel; and to create landscape architectural designs that use site design elements to closely coordinate security technology and personnel.

SITE ASSESSMENT PROCESS

Achieving the correct level of protection against site-based threats may be very expensive, and is highly dependent on the nature of the protected assets and the threat against which they require protection. Determining what is required is a matter of managing the perceived risks. If the designer is to assist in providing protection in the design of the site, an assessment of the security requirements must be accomplished, preferably before the design begins, but certainly no later than the beginning of the programming phase. This assessment is the responsibility of the owner. However, it is incumbent on the designer to assure that the nature of the security requirements is determined *before* the design begins. Failing to obtain a definitive answer will certainly result in design changes, delays, and cost increases to the owner, architect, and landscape architect if the owner "discovers" their security needs later in the design process.

The events of 9/11 have changed the focus and purpose of security. National codes and standards have been adopted for federal governmental facilities, but, currently, state and local governments are left with no binding standard of care. Private sector facilities have shown a resistance to formalizing standards and codes that include crime prevention through environmental design (CPTED) and security features. The increase in negligent security premises liability lawsuits has been the major driving element in creating standards of care and industry standards. Several cities in the United States have adopted CPTED ordinances and resolutions that affect new siting, design, and infrastructure.

Prior to 9/11, security equaled basic CPTED features of access control, surveillance, and response by guards or police. After 9/11, the purpose became enhanced security that equals access control and surveillance and features building/target hardening and inclusion of biochemical and blast protection of the building and infrastructure.

The site assessment will answer four questions:

- What are the assets (persons, places, information, property) that require security protection?
- What are the criminal or other threats (street crime, workplace violence, terrorism, sabotage) against which the assets must be protected?
- What are the vulnerabilities of the assets to the threats (for example, if workplace violence is a threat, can uncontrolled persons enter private workspaces unchallenged)?
- What are the countermeasures (for example, does the design channel visitors through controlled site access portals) required to mitigate the threat?

What Is Being Protected

One of the first steps in threat and vulnerability analysis is to identify the assets to be protected. As stated previously, all assets can be sorted into the following categories: people, information, and property (PIP).

- *People.* One asset for protection may be the human resources. The people needing protection may be employees, visitors, patrons, service providers, or executives. Humans must be protected from assault, kidnapping, murder, robbery, or terrorism. Failure to protect invited and uninvited guests on a property can be grounds for premises liability litigation.
- *Information.* The asset of information needs protection. Most businesses have vital information that could potentially cripple or destroy their operation. Computer records, blueprints, financial information, proprietary secrets, personnel records, and accounting systems comprise the backbone of any business. Information protection is a critical element in a security plan. Knowing who has the information, where it is, when it is accessible, and how it could be compromised are critical issues for design.
- *Property.* The asset of property needs protection. Property can refer to cars in a parking lot, an airplane in a hangar, or office supplies in a closet. The threat analysis will help identify which property assets are to be protected. The architect can then incorporate the security requirements identified into the design of the building, as well as into the whole building process; likewise, the landscape architect can incorporate the requirements into the site design.

The result of the assessment will be a set of recommended countermeasures that may be priced and presented to the owner in a priority order so that prudent and cost-effective selections may be made from those recommendations. In the case of the government standards, the assessment results in the assignment of a defined level of protection (LOP) with specified countermeasures. When the LOP is defined, the specified countermeasures are priced, and again the owner may select appropriate measures depending on a prudent level of protection and the cost-effectiveness of the measure.

THE PROCESS OF SECURITY DESIGN

To create a security master plan that can be incorporated into the landscape and architecture, a sequence of evaluations should be conducted before the security system design begins. There are three steps to the process, each of which addresses a number of questions:

1. *Asset definition.* What are the vital assets—people, information, and property? What are the most important assets? What are the secondary assets? What level of protection is needed for each area?
2. *Threat definition.* What are the threats to each asset? Who is being protected? Could threats be vandalism, espionage, burglary, theft, assault, sabotage, and robbery? How would threats be accomplished? When? Why? By whom? Where? What kind of attack or approach might be used to fit to the target? Are the threats highly probable, possible, or unlikely?
3. *Vulnerability analysis.* Are the threats real or perceived? Compare the costs for the protection of each asset group with the cost of potential loss. Compare different kinds of security measures possible for protection of the assets.

SECURITY LAYERING: THE ONION PHILOSOPHY

In the "onion philosophy" of security layering, the first layer is the outside skin of the onion, which translates to the site perimeter of the property. The building skin of the architecture is the next layer. Sensitive areas within a building are deeper layers requiring protection; and, finally, special persons, information, or property that may require point protection are the center of the "onion." The site perimeter should be the first, not last, line of defense. The General Services Administration (GSA) and State Department seek setbacks of at least 100 feet for new buildings, a distance that is difficult to obtain in most urban settings. While most perimeter fences and walls are designed to discourage intruders, they are of little use against a determined person or a bomb-laden vehicle. Designs are now available for vehicle-stopping capabilities. However, a moped, bike, or pedestrian may deliver the bomb of the future, thus rendering truck bombs as obsolete.

With that in mind, here are some of the planning considerations that a landscape architect should consider for site selection:

- Control over the standoff distances and setbacks of the building to streets and other buildings at risk
- Access control points to the site
- Control over adjacent buildings and access points
- Potential for collateral damage
- Evacuation complexity and areas of safe refuge and assistance

Randall I. Atlas, AIA CPP, Counter Terror Design Inc., Miami, FL; Leonard Hopper, RLA, FASLA

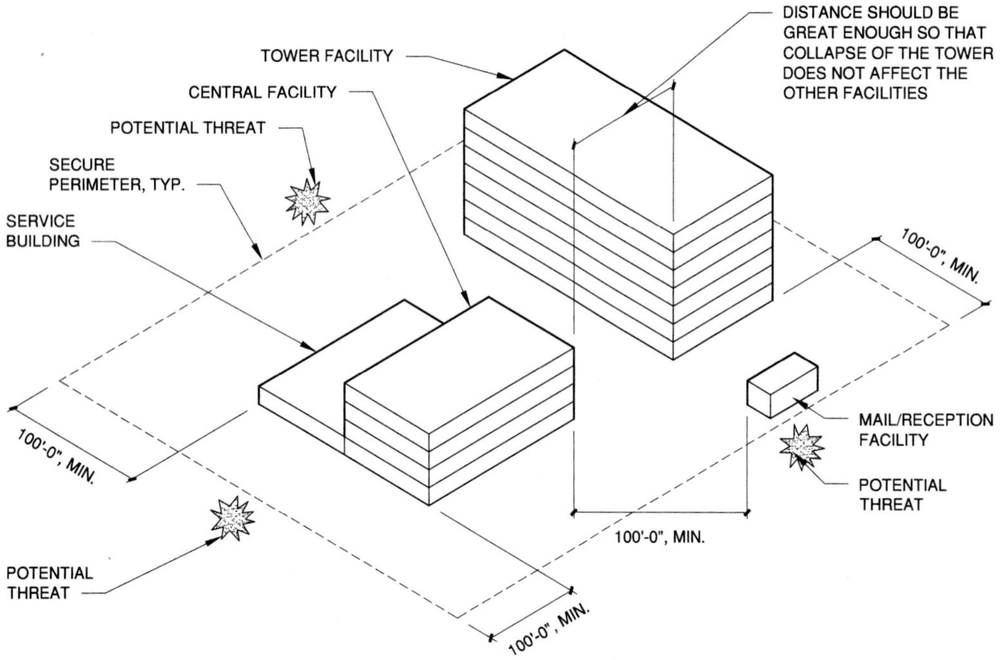

IMPLEMENTATION EXAMPLES OF PHYSICAL SECURITY AND PROTECTIVE CONSTRUCTION MEASURES

Site perimeter considerations include:

- Fencing and walls
- Guard services and screening employees and visitors
- Closed-circuit television (CCTV)
- Access control for cars
- Standoff setbacks clear zones
- Landscaping and planters
- Exterior lighting
- Location of the site
- Traffic control devices

SECURITY DELIVERY SYSTEM

The purpose of a comprehensive delivery system is threefold: to *detect* a threat or intrusion, to *delay* the intrusion with barriers, and allow sufficient time to *respond and deter it*.

1. *Detect.* A security system can be comprised of security personnel, physical components of a building, and technology systems. The security system should be capable of determining whether there is a threat of criminal activity. Before a problem can be delayed or responded to, the threat must be detected or perceived. Detection options are fixed guardposts, CCTV, and intrusion detection equipment.
2. *Delay.* The next step of a security system is to delay the intruder. Establishing a series of barriers creates delays. The barriers can be walls, fences, vehicle barriers, blocked access, razor ribbon or any device or design measure that creates time and distance between the threat and the target. Delay options are barriers like walls or fences, access control, or locking devices.
3. *Respond and deter.* The ability, or responsibility, to respond to a threat is made possible by the devices in the detection phase; and the time for deterrence is created by the delay phase. Response forces can be official or unofficial. Official response is usually law enforcement or private security forces. Unofficial sources of response are users of a building, including doormen or users, and neighborhood watch patrols.

All three steps are needed for a comprehensive security plan. The detection and barrier delays are pointless if there is no one to respond to the emergency or threat; and if there are no barriers, burglars or robbers can commit their crime and leave before a response team can arrive on the scene. Barriers with no detection device can give no advance warning of a problem to security personnel or police, enabling them to respond. For a security design to be complete, the system is interdependent on the ability to detect, delay, or respond.

ISSUES TO ADDRESS WITH THE SECURITY CONSULTANT

When planning for security, the landscape architect and architect will need to discuss the following design issues with the security consultant on the project.

Site Planning
- Access
- Service delivery
- Circulation patterns
- Lighting quality and quantity
- Perimeter defense

Main Lobby
- Visitor control issues
- Building fire system location
- Reception/guard kiosk design and equipment provisions
- Architectural security barrier design—turnstiles, glass enclosures, reception areas, and so on
- Retail tenant security adjacent to lobby areas
- Development of unobtrusive CCTV surveillance
- Access control into emergency stairwells adjacent to the main lobby
- After-hours access control into the main lobby
- Alarm monitoring of perimeter doors
- Main lobby lighting

Parking Garage
- Valet or self-parking
- Public, private, or mixed use
- Segregated parking levels
- Executive parking security
- Need for and use of CCTV surveillance system, emergency signaling system, intercom system, and guard tour system
- Lighting issues, including type of lighting and number of footcandles to be provided

Loading Docks
- Amount of vehicular traffic flow expected
- Impact, if any, on street traffic or pedestrian walkways
- Storage of packages and materials
- Distribution of deliveries throughout the building
- Development of necessary CCTV surveillance and intercom systems
- Provision of remote door release controls

Emergency Stairwells
- Restricting access or allowing use by the public for interfloor traffic
- Communication provisions in stairwells
- Emergency exit alarm devices on doors
- Alarm monitoring of the stairwells
- Access control into and out of the stairwells

Miscellaneous
- Elevator bank access control and architectural design
- Communication provisions in elevator vestibules on individual floors
- Public washrooms
- Mail services
- Deliveries
- Security in mechanical areas
- Door hardware for telephone, electrical, and storage closets
- Security for fuel and water storage areas
- Roof access
- Tunnel or skyway connections to other nearby buildings
- Plaza security—issues related to landscaping, lighting, and use of unobtrusive surveillance systems
- Elevator cab communication devices

Building Tenant Security
- Comprehensive access control program, to encompass elevator car access control requirements and individual floor access control measures
- Security measures for individual departments and operations that may have additional security requirements
- Executive floor security
- Receptionist workstations
- Boardroom or executive conference room access control issues
- Vestibule construction of freight elevator lobbies
- Console room design

Randall I. Atlas, AIA CPP, Counter Terror Design Inc., Miami, FL; Leonard Hopper, RLA, FASLA

- Secured storage areas, vaults, and safes within tenant space
- Closet space for security-related equipment
- HVAC and power requirements for security operations

Major Systems
- Fire and life safety
- Public address
- CCTV surveillance
- Access control
- Alarm monitoring
- Radio communication
- Emergency signaling
- Intercom
- Guard tour
- Door control
- Uninterruptible power supply

GSA SECURITY STANDARDS

The bombing of the Murrah Federal Office Building in Oklahoma City, Oklahoma, in 1995, gave birth to a federal effort to develop security standards that would apply to all federal facilities, and an Interagency Security Committee has recommended their adoption as a governmentwide standard. During the testing of the standards, a number of state governments also reviewed and applied them to several new construction projects. Consult local and state authorities for their specific applications.

The process of risk assessment and security design is especially relevant in the architecture of schools, hospitals, airports, office buildings, multifamily apartment buildings, and others. Recently, buildings have been targeted for bombing by terrorists because of their "architectural vulnerability." This vulnerability will be addressed by methods described in this section.

The GSA Security Standards encourages a defensible space/crime prevention through environmental design (CPTED) approach to clearly defining and screening the flow of persons and vehicles through layering, from public to private spaces. Edges and boundaries of the properties should clearly define the desired circulation patterns and movements, and screening and funneling of people through screening techniques should separate legitimate users of the building from illegitimate users who might be looking for opportunities to commit a crime, workplace violence, or act of terrorism.

Levels of Protection

The GSA developed a set of criteria covering four levels of protection for every aspect of security. The GSA Security Standards made a large number of recommendations for both operational and equipment improvements and which address the functional requirements and desired application of security glazing, bomb-resistant design and construction, landscaping and planting designs, site lighting, as well as natural and mechanical surveillance opportunities (good sight lines, no blind spots, window placement, proper applications of CCTV). These recommendations were further subdivided according to whether they should be implemented for various levels of security (e.g., a level-one facility might not require an entry control system, whereas a level-four facility would require electronic controls with CCTV assessment).

The requirements of the report that affect facility design and engineering are presented here in four general categories of corrective action used in the report. These should be addressed by the landscape architect, architect, and engineering team both for renovations or new construction on any federal building; and they are recommended for state and local buildings, as well as any buildings determined to be at risk.

Security Planning
- Evaluate locations of tenant agencies, as concerns security needs and risks.
- Install Mylar film on exterior windows.
- Review/establish blast standards for current projects and new construction.
- Develop a design standard for blast resistance and street setback for new construction.

Entry Security
- Install intrusion detection system.
- Upgrade to current life safety standards.
- Screen mail, persons, and packages.
- Enable entry control with CCTV and electric door strikes.
- Install high-security locks.

Interior Security
- Control access with employee ID and visitor screening.
- Control access to utilities.
- Provide emergency power to critical systems.
- Evaluate location of day care centers.

Perimeter and Exterior Security
- Monitor parking area and install parking controls.
- Monitor with CCTV.
- Install security lighting, to include emergency backup.
- Install physical barriers.

The GSA security approach takes a balanced approach to security: It considers cost-effectiveness, acknowledges acceptance of some risk, and recognizes that federal buildings should not become bunkers or fortresslike, but open, accessible, attractive, and representative of the democratic spirit of the country. Prudent, rather than excessive security measures are appropriate in facilities owned by and serving the public.

On a *site* level, the GSA Security Standards recommend:

- Eliminate potential hiding places near the facility.
- Provide unobstructed view around the facility.
- Site or place the facility within view of other occupied facilities.
- Locate assets stored on-site, but outside of the facility within view of occupied rooms of the facility.
- Minimize the signage or indication of assets on the property.
- Provide a 170-foot minimum facility separation from the facility boundary, if possible.
- Eliminate lines of approach perpendicular to the building.
- Minimize the number of vehicle access points.
- Eliminate or strictly control parking beneath facilities.
- Locate parking as far from the building as practical (yet address ADA spaces and proximity) and place parking within view of occupied rooms or facilities.
- Illuminate building exterior or exterior sites where assets are located.
- Secure access to power/heat plants, gas mains, water supplies, and electrical and phone services.

On a *building* level, the GSA Security Standards recommend:

- Employ the concept of security layering.
- Locate assets in spaces occupied 24 hours a day, where possible.
- Locate activities with large visitor populations away from protected assets, where possible.
- Locate protected assets in common areas where they are visible to more than one person.
- Place high-risk activities, such as the mailroom, on the perimeter of the facility.

On an *interior* security level, the GSA Security Standards recommend:

- Use employee and visitor identification systems.
- Secure utility closets and vulnerable utilities.
- Develop emergency plans and policy and procedures.
- Locate day care areas so that they are protected from unauthorized access.
- Set up screening points where applicable for weapons, pilferage, or identification.
- Secure and control shipping and receiving areas with integrated access control, CCTV, intercoms, data logging, and report capabilities.

BALANCING THREAT AND RISKS IN BUILDINGS WITH GSA SECURITY STANDARDS

The landscape architect and the security consultant will often be in the position to make decisions to balance the level of threat and risk versus the appropriate and reasonable response. The Security Strategies for Low and High Risk Table gives some examples of parameters and considerations for security strategies based on the assessment of high or low level of risk.

PASSIVE COUNTERMEASURES

Perimeter Protection	Intrusion Detection Alarms
	Fence/Wall
	Bollards/Planters
	Street Countermeasures
Access Control	Vehicle Barriers/Traps
	Chicanes
	Guard House
Functional Planning	Crisis Management:
	Search & Rescue
	Evacuation & Assembly
	Access Control
	Driveway Geometry
Physical Planning	Fragment Mitigation Geometry
	Glazings
	Window Frames
	Emergency Equipment
Hardening	Walls
	Columns
	Floors
	Frame
	Roof

Randall I. Atlas, AIA CPP, Counter Terror Design Inc., Miami, FL; Leonard Hopper, RLA, FASLA

APPLICATION OF GSA SECURITY STANDARDS TO ALL BUILDING TYPES

It has become apparent to the public and design community that since 9/11, the demand for security has increased. This, of course, affects the work of landscape architects, especially those doing work at any level of government. The post-9/11 Jersey barriers and fencing hastily deployed outside of various government facilities has to be replaced with more permanent measures. Landscape architects not only have a role in discussing the changes to be implemented but are leading many of the new design efforts.

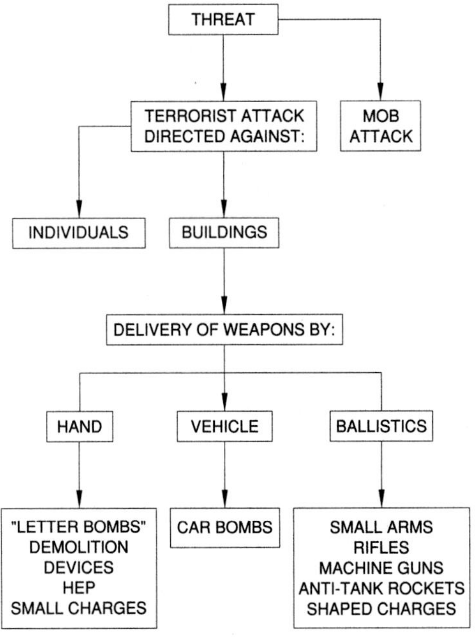

THREAT DEFINITION

Terrorism represents a real threat to our society and our peace of mind. What can the public and government agencies do to effectively diminish the threats and losses to persons, information, and property? How can they reduce the opportunity for and fear of crime in the built environment, and improve the quality of life? The answer: crime prevention through environmental design (CPTED). This section addresses how to reduce the threats and vulnerabilities in the built environment by changing how space is designed and used.

Key defensive architectural site design guidelines for bomb resistance should include the following:

- Establish a secured perimeter around the building as far from the building as is feasible. Setbacks of 100 feet are desired.
- Design artistically pleasing concrete barriers as flower planters or works of art and position them near curbing at a distance from the building, with less than 4 feet of spacing between them to block vehicular passage.
- Build new buildings in a simple geometric rectangular layout to minimize the "defraction effect" when blast waves bounce off U-shaped or L-shaped buildings, causing additional damage.
- Drastically reduce or totally eliminate ornamentation on buildings that can easily break away, causing further damage to building occupants or pedestrians at street level. All external cladding should be made of lightweight materials that will minimize damage when they become flying objects following an explosion (or major storm).

SUMMARY

The targets of terrorism in the future will be cities, utility companies, government buildings and/or agencies, technology companies, and high-profile corporate entities. New technology has made the infrastructure of America more vulnerable to sabotage, especially disruption of communications and information systems, which have the same net result as a bomb going off.

Though environmental design might not have been able to prevent the tragic events of September 11, the design of our public and private spaces can have an impact on safety and security, through planning for: crowd behavior in high-density environments; wayfinding and design of escape routes; placement and type of building security features; design for high-risk environments; and effective design of the built environment, so that building users have less stress, less confusion, and less opportunity to be victims of a crime.

Whatever the building or its use, security and crime prevention should be a design criterion, similar to fire safety, accessibility, and structural integrity. Any piece of architecture and site design should establish a hierarchy of space that goes from open access by the public to semipublic, semiprivate, and private spaces. Any areas or spaces that are unassigned to a specific purpose or capable guardian should be avoided, as it becomes a "no man's land"—not claimed, protected, or defended by any individual or group. Traffic patterns of pedestrians and vehicles into sites and buildings should be carefully thought out and controlled for the desired goal. The design of any building should maximize the potential for natural observation by the legitimate building users.

The CPTED and security design process can apply to all forms of site planning and architecture:

Institutional architecture: Police stations, courthouses, jails and prisons, post offices, schools, hospitals, airports

Commercial architecture: Office buildings, shopping centers, retail stores, restaurants, entertainment facilities

Residential architecture: Single-family homes, townhouses, low- to mid-high-rise multifamily residential facilities, planned urban developments, hotels, rental apartments, public housing

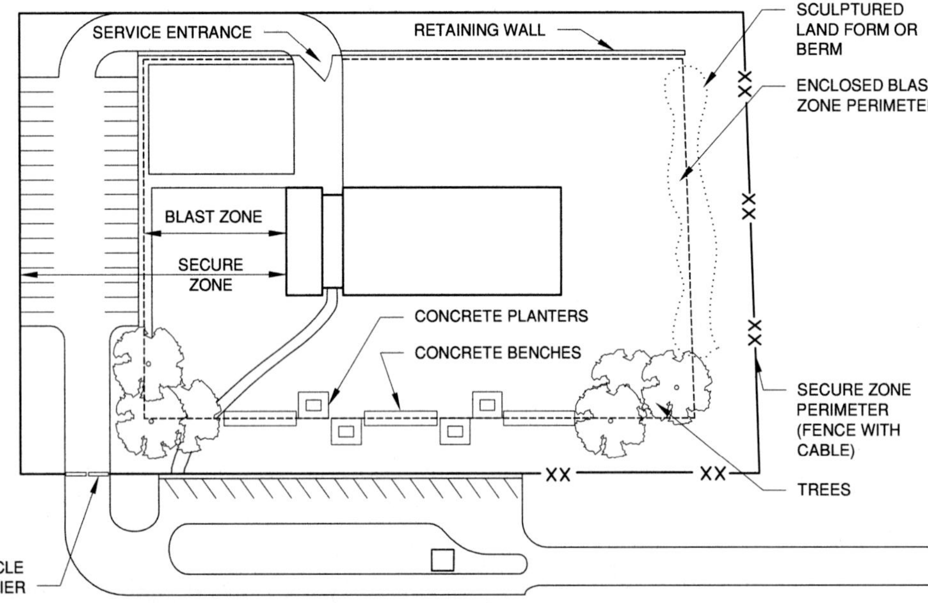

AN EXAMPLE OF DEFENSIVE SITE DESIGN CREATING SECURE ZONES THROUGH THE RESTRICTION OF MOVING VEHICLES

In addition to the GSA Security Design Standards, new security codes and standards and guidelines have been established by the following groups:

- American Society for Testing and Materials (ASTM) F33 committee, including F588 of Glazing
- National Fire Protection Association (NFPA) Premises Security Committee Security 2004 Guidelines 730 and 731; American Society of Industrial Security (ASIS) General Security Risk Assessment Guideline 2004, and Security Design Guidelines 2006
- Illumination Engineering Society of North America RP 2-98 Lighting for Parking Facilities, and G-1-03 Guidelines on Security Lighting for People Property and Spaces March 2003
- CPTED ordinances and resolutions in the following locales: City of Sarasota Florida, Ordinance No. 92-3562, section 8-323, CPTED Review Requirements; the Broward County Florida Ordinance No. 96-0624; City of Tempe, Arizona, Ordinance No. 97.65; and the City of Los Angeles Small Business CPTED Program

CONCLUSION

The security design and crime prevention through environmental design process is applicable to all building types. Security should be designed with system

Randall I. Atlas, AIA CPP, Counter Terror Design Inc., Miami, FL; Leonard Hopper, RLA, FASLA

expansion in mind. Always plan for providing space for extra conduit to run systems wiring through in the future. If security is not incorporated into the initial design, the owner will pay for it later at a much greater cost. The health, safety, and welfare of building users depend on good security planning and design.

The design of a site and building can significantly affect how secure it is from acts of terrorism, workplace violence, and street crime. The goal of landscape architects regarding security is to use landscape and site design features and elements to enhance a property's security without compromising its aesthetics and functionality. Though there are rare situations and building types in which target hardening strategies are the only solution to certain security challenges, usually, a simple, well-thought-out plan using man-made and natural features will yield the best results.

REFERENCES

Atlas, R. I. 2000. "Crime Prevention through Environmental Design," in J. R. Hoke, Jr. (ed.) *Architectural Graphic Standards*: 73–80. New York: John Wiley & Sons.

City of Los Angeles. 1997. "Crime Prevention through Environmental Design: Design Out Crime Guidelines."

Designing for Security in the Nation's Capital. Autumn 2001. Washington, DC: National Capital Planning Commission.

Environmental Design Technical Group News, September 2001.

Florida Center for Community Design and Research. 1993. *Florida Safe Schools Guidelines*. Tampa, FL: University of South Florida.

Forgey, Benjamin. September 2002. "Changing the Guard," *Landscape Architecture Magazine:* 80-87.

Hopper, Leonard, and Martha Droge. 2005. *Security and Site Design*. Hoboken, NJ: John Wiley & Sons.

Mays, Vernon. September 2002. "Invisible Barriers," *Landscape Architecture Magazine:* 74-79.

Russell, James, Elizabeth Kennedy, Merideth Kelly, Deborah Bershand. March 2002. *Designing for Security: Using Art and Design to Improve Security*. Guidelines from the Art Commission of the City of New York.

Sipes, James. L. September 2002. "A New Kind of Scrutiny," *Landscape Architecture Magazine:* 58–64.

Speckhardt, Lisa, and Jennifer Dowdell. September 2002. "Creating Safety," *Landscape Architecture Magazine:* 65-73.

U.S. Department of Housing and Urban Development. 1979. *Planning for Housing Security: Site Elements Manual.* Annapolis, MD: William Brill Associates, Inc.

Wekerle, Gerda, and Carolyn Whitzman. 1995. *Safe Cities*. New York: Van Nostrand-Reinhold.

ORGANIZATIONAL WEB RESOURCES

American Society for Industrial Security: www.asisonline.org

Atlas Safety & Security Design: www.cpted-security.com

Defensible Space: www.defensiblespace.com/start.htm

FEMA: http://www.fema.gov/fima/rmsp.shtm#426

General Services Administration, Office of Federal Protective Service: www.gsa.gov/Portal/content/orgs_content.jsp?contentOID=117945&contentType=1005

The Infrastructure Security Partnership: www.tisp.com

International CPTED Association: www.cpted.net

National Capital Planning Commission: www.ncpc.gov

National Crime Prevention Council: www.ncpc.org

National Crime Prevention Institute: www.louisville.edu/a-s/ja/ncpi

Security Design Coalition: www.designingforsecurity.org.

Security Industry Association: www.siaonline.org

Terrorism Research Center: www.terrorism.com/index.shtml

U.S. Department of State, Counterterrorism Office: www.state.gov/s/ct

White House Office on Homeland Security: www.whitehouse.gov/homeland

See also:

Crime Prevention Through Environmental Design

Randall I. Atlas, AIA CPP, Counter Terror Design Inc., Miami, FL; Leonard Hopper, RLA, FASLA

SITE PLANNING

ENVIRONMENTAL SITE ANALYSIS

SURVEY DATA

The first step in any site analysis is the gathering of physical site data. An aerial photograph and an accurate survey showing the following information are basic to any site analysis process:

- Scale, north arrow, benchmark, and date of survey
- Tract boundary lines
- Easements: location, width, and purpose
- Names and locations of existing road rights-of-way on or adjacent to the tract, including bridges, curbs, gutters, and culverts
- Position of buildings and other structures such as foundations, walls, fences, steps, and paved areas
- Utilities on or adjacent to the tract—location of gas lines, fire hydrants, electric and telephone poles, and street lights; and direction, distance to, and size of nearest water mains and sewers and invert elevation of sewers
- Location of swamps, springs, streams, bodies of water, drainage ditches, watershed areas, flood plains, and other physical features
- Outline of wooded areas with names and condition of plant material
- Contour intervals of 2 to 5 ft., depending on slope gradients, and spot elevations at breaks in grade, along drainage channels or swales, and at selected points as needed

Considerable additional information may be needed, depending on design considerations and site complexities such as soil information and studies of the geological structure of the site. Federal regulations for wetland mapping and conservation may also be relevant.

SUBURBAN SITE ANALYSIS

The site analysis is a major responsibility of the site planner. The physical analysis of the site is developed primarily from field inspections. Using the survey, the aerial photograph, and, where warranted, infrared aerial photographs, the site designer, working in the field and in the office, verifies the survey and notes site design determinants. These should include, but not be limited to, the following:

- Areas of steep and moderate slopes
- Macro- and microclimatic conditions, including sun angles during different seasons; prevailing breezes; wind shadows; frost pockets; and sectors where high or low points give protection from sun and wind
- Solar energy considerations (for example, if solar energy appears feasible, a detailed climatic analysis must be undertaken considering factors such as detailed sun charts, daily averages of sunlight and cloud cover, daily rain averages, areas exposed to the sun at different seasons, solar radiation patterns, and temperature patterns)
- Potential flood zones and routes of surface water runoff
- Possible road access to the site, including potential conflicts with existing road systems and carrying capacities of adjacent roadways (usually available from local or state road departments)
- Natural areas that from an ecological and aesthetic standpoint should be saved; all tree masses with name and condition of tree species and understory planting
- Significant wildlife habitats that would be affected by site modification
- Soil conditions relative to supporting plant material, areas suitable for construction, erosion potential, and septic tanks, if relevant
- Geological considerations relative to supporting structures
- Exceptional views; objectionable views (use on-site photographs)
- Adjacent existing and proposed land uses with notations on compatibility and incompatibility
- Potential noise sources, particularly noise generated from traffic that can be mitigated by using plants, berming, and walls and by extending the distance between the source and the receiver

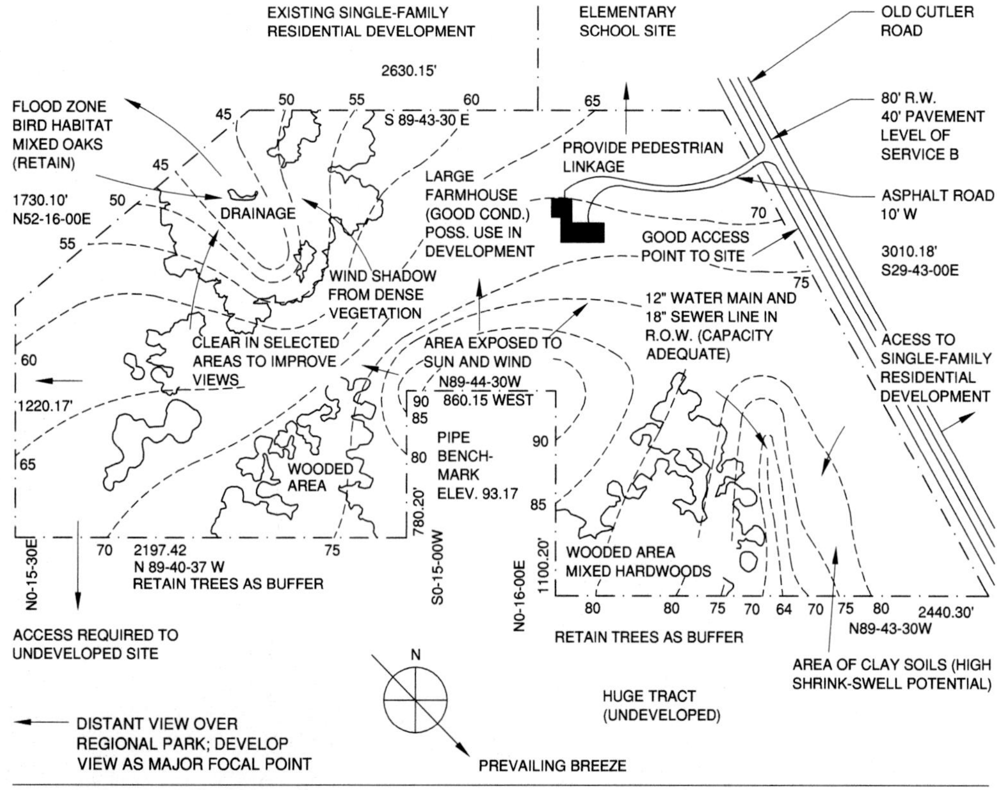

TOPOGRAPHICAL SURVEY

URBAN SITE ANALYSIS

Although much of the information presented for suburban sites may apply equally to urban sites, additional site design criteria may be necessary. The urban environment has numerous design determinants in the form of existing structures, city patterns, and microclimatic conditions.

ENVIRONMENTAL CONSIDERATIONS

- *Air movement.* Prevailing breezes characteristic of a region may be greatly modified by urban high-rise structures. Predominant air movement patterns in a city may be along roadways and between buildings. The placement, shape, and height of existing buildings can create air turbulence caused by micro air movement patterns. These patterns may influence the location of building elements such as outdoor areas and balconies. Also, a building's design and placement can mitigate or increase local wind turbulence.
- *Sun and shadow patterns.* The sun and shadow patterns of existing structures should be studied to determine how they would affect the proposed building. This is particularly important for outdoor terraces and balconies where sunlight may be desirable. Sun and shadow patterns also should be considered as sources of internal heat gain or loss. Building orientation, window sizes, and shading devices can modify internal heat gain or loss. Studies should include daily and seasonal patterns and the shadows the proposed building would cast on existing buildings and open spaces.
- *Reflections.* Reflections from adjacent structures such as glass-clad buildings may be a problem. The new building should be designed to compensate for such glare or, if possible, oriented away from it.

Gary Greenan, Andres Duany, Elizabeth Plater-Zyberk, Kamal Zaharin, Iskandar Shafie, Rafael Diaz, Miami, Florida

URBAN CONTEXTUAL ANALYSIS

- *Building typology and hierarchy.* An analysis of the particular building type (residential, commercial, public) relative to the hierarchy of the various building types in the city is useful in deciding the general design approach of a new building. For example, public buildings may be dominant in placement and design, while residential buildings are subdominant. It is important to maintain any existing hierarchy that reinforces visual order in the city. Any predominant architectural solutions and details characteristic of a building type incorporated in the new building's design can help maintain a recognizable building type.
- *Regional character.* An analysis of the city's regional architectural characteristics is appropriate in developing a design solution that responds to unique regional characteristics. Regional characteristics may be revealed through unique architectural types, through vernacular building resulting from local climatic and cultural characteristics, and from historically significant architecture. Historic structures should be saved by modifying them for the proposed new use or by incorporating parts of the existing structure(s) into the proposed design.
- *City form.* The delineation of city form created by road layout, location of major open spaces, and architecture-created forms should be analyzed. Elements that delineate city form should be reinforced by architectural development solutions for a particular place within the city. For example, a building proposed for a corner site should be designed to reinforce the corner through building form, entrance, and design details. A building proposed for midblock may be a visually unifying element providing connection and continuity with adjacent buildings. Sites at the ends of important vistas or adjacent to major city squares probably should be reserved for important public buildings.
- *Building scale and fenestration.* It is important to analyze building scale and fenestration of nearby structures. Reflecting, although not necessarily reproducing, such detailing in the proposed building can provide visual unity and continuity in the architectural character of the city. One example is the use and placement of cornice lines to define the building's lower floors in relation to adjacent buildings. Cornice lines also can define the building's relationship to pedestrians in terms of scale and use.
- *Building transition.* Sometimes it may be appropriate to use arcades and porches to provide transition between the building's private interior and the public sidewalk. Including them may be especially worthy if adjacent buildings have these elements.
- *Views.* Important city views of plazas, squares, monuments, and natural features such as waterfronts and parks should be considered. It is important to design the proposed structure to enhance and preserve such views for the public and for inhabitants of nearby buildings, as well as incorporating them as views from the proposed building.

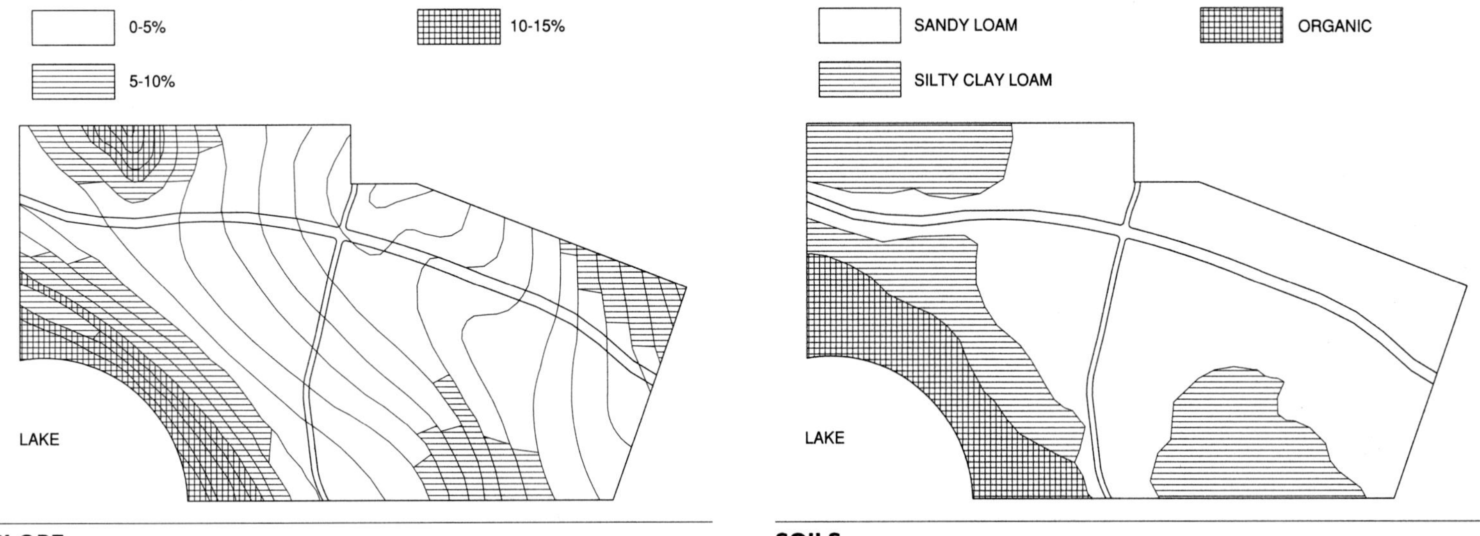

SLOPE

SOILS

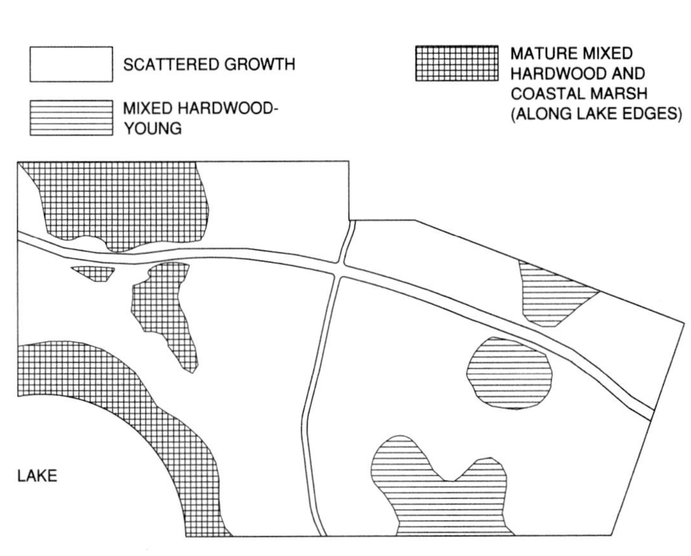

VEGETATION

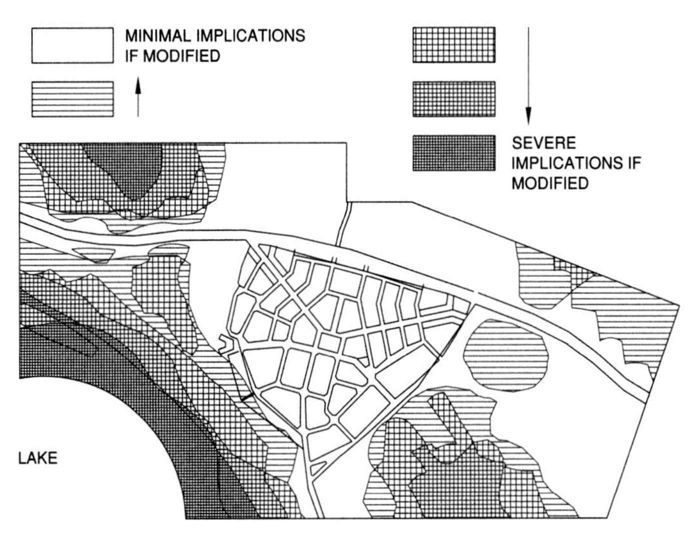

COMPOSITE

Gary Greenan, Andres Duany, Elizabeth Plater-Zyberk, Kamal Zaharin, Iskandar Shafie, Rafael Diaz, Miami, Florida

ENVIRONMENTAL SITE ANALYSIS PROCESS

If a site has numerous environmental design determinants, the site planner may analyze each environmental system individually in order to comprehend the environmental character of the site more clearly. This can be a complex process, and a site planner/landscape architect with expertise in environmental analysis should be retained to coordinate such an effort.

By preparing each analysis on transparencies, the site planner can use the overlay approach. Values are assigned to each sheet based on impact, ranging from areas of the site where change would have minimal effect to areas where change would result in severe disruption of the site. In essence, the separate sheets become abstractions with values assigned by the site planner and associated professionals. As each sheet is superimposed, a composite develops that, when completed, constitutes the synthesis of the environmental design determinants. Lighter tones indicate areas where modification would have minimal influence, darker tones indicate areas more sensitive to change. The sketches shown simulate the overlay process. The site planner may give greater or lesser weight to certain parameters depending on the particular situation. In assigning values that help determine the site design process, the site planner should consider such factors as the value of maintaining the functioning of the individual site systems, the uniqueness of the specific site features, and the cost of modifying the site plan.

Following is a list of the environmental design determinants that, depending on the particular site, may be considered and included in an overlay format:

- *Slope*. The slope analysis is developed on the contour map; consideration should include the percentage of slope and orientation of slope relative to the infrastructure and land uses.
- *Soil patterns*. Consideration may include the analysis of soils by erosion potential, compressibility and plasticity, capability of supporting plant growth, drainage capabilities, possible sources of pollution or toxic wastes, septic tank location (if relevant), and the pro- posed land uses and their infrastructure.
- *Vegetation*. Consideration of indigenous species (values of each in terms of the environmental system) includes size and condition, the succession of growth toward climax conditions, uniqueness, the ability of certain species to tolerate construction activities, aesthetic values, and density of undergrowth.
- *Wildlife*. Consideration of indigenous species includes their movement patterns, the degree of change each species can tolerate, and feeding and breeding areas.
- *Geology*. Consideration of underlying rock masses studies the depth of different rock layers and the suitability of different geological formations in terms of potential infrastructure and building.
- *Surface and subsurface water*. Consideration of natural drainage patterns covers aquifer recharge areas, erosion potential, and flood plains.
- *Climate*. Consideration of microclimatic conditions includes prevailing breezes (at different times of the year), wind shadows, frost pockets, and air drainage patterns.

COMPUTER APPLICATION

The above process is labor intensive when developed by hand on individual sheets of mylar; however, this particular method of environmental analysis is easily adaptable to the CAD (computer-aided drafting) system. Commercial drafting programs suitable for the overlay approach are readily available. Simplified, the method is as follows:

1. A map, such as a soil map, is positioned on the digitizer and the information is transferred to the processor through the use of the stylus. One major advantage to the use of a computer is that the scale of the map being recorded will be transferred to the selected scale by the processor. A hatched pattern is selected, with a less dense pattern for soil types that would have minimal influence and more dense patterns for soil types more sensitive to change. Once this information is programmed into the computer, it is stored.
2. The same process is repeated for development of the next overlay; for example, vegetation. Once again any scale map may be used. This process is repeated until all overlays have been stored. At any time one or all overlays can be produced on the screen.
3. The individual overlays or any combination of overlays can be drawn on mylar with a plotter. If appropriate for the particular analysis, the plotter will draw in color. The resulting overlay sheets take considerably less time than by hand and may be more accurate. Other benefits are that the site can be studied directly on the computer screen and any part of the overlay can be enlarged for greater detail.
4. The overlay process can be recorded by videotape or by slides from the screen for use in presentations.

Gary Greenan, Andres Duany, Elizabeth Plater-Zyberk, Kamal Zaharin, Iskandar Shafie, Rafael Diaz, Miami, Florida

THE TOWN PLANNING PROCESS

INTRODUCTION

The following pages provide the essential elements of town design. Included are an abstract, a set of diagrams, and criteria for town and community design.

Site planning for development projects should be a sequential process that begins with information gathering and ends with detailed design drawings. The process involves three stages: analysis, design, and implementation. The chart below indicates a planning process; however, this can vary to accommodate the specifics of a particular project. Physical site characteristics, urban or suburban location, and community criteria modify the process. The site planning process includes both architect and landscape architect and, in some cases, biologists, civil engineers, and others. An integrated approach to site development and architecture helps create a quality environment. The text on this page is presented as a checklist for structuring a project.

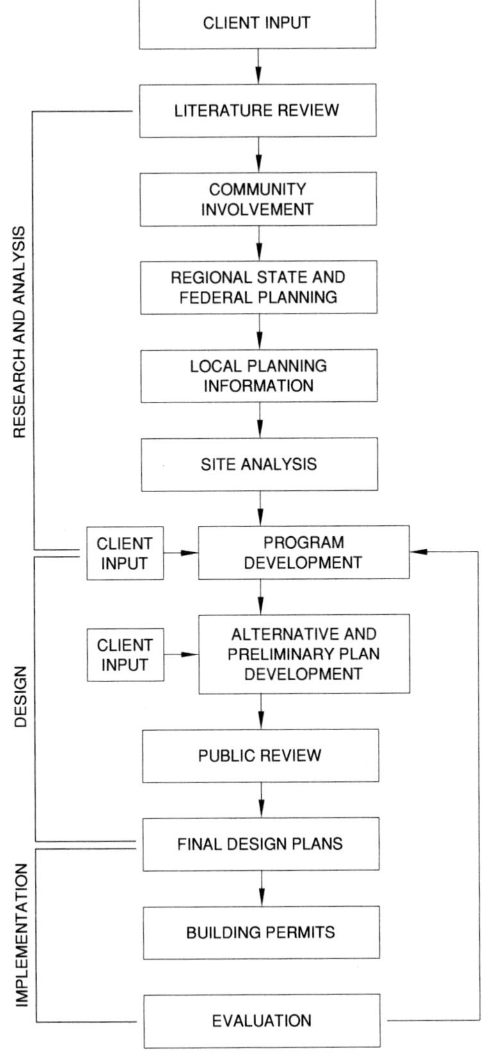

TOWN PLANNING PROCESS

CLIENT CONTACT AND INPUT

The first step is contact between the client and the site planner. The client may have some development objectives based on financial capabilities and market feasibility. It is important for the site planner to obtain all client data relative to planning the site.

LITERATURE REVIEW

Site planning covers a variety of situations from rural and suburban to high-intensity urban.

There is substantial literature on planning sites and designing neighborhoods of all densities. Recent publications demonstrate a return to the basic town planning principles that have produced orderly community design throughout history.

COMMUNITY INVOLVEMENT

Early in the planning process, contact community groups with an interest in the proposed project. Such efforts yield useful information for community design and are particularly important when a proposed project is adjacent to existing development. Compatibility issues are typically resolved with community participation.

One method of involving the community is the "charrette," a participatory planning process with a limited time frame, usually one day to a week, in which residents, municipal staff, elected leaders, and others participate in the physical design of a project. The planner receives local information useful for the design, and individuals and groups bring their interests to bear at the beginning of the design process, thereby expediting final approvals.

REGIONAL, STATE, AND FEDERAL PLANNING

Some areas of the country have established regional agencies for intercommunity issues, such as water management, transportation, population studies, and pollution control. Some communities have adopted regional planning guidelines.

State and/or federal criteria can also affect projects. State plans may address broad issues applicable to large sites or impose constraints on sites involving issues of statewide concern. Also, some states require environmental impact statements for large-scale projects. The U.S. Army Corps of Engineers is responsible for environmental review of proposed dredge and fill operations in navigable waters and wetlands. The Federal Flood Insurance Program establishes minimum elevations for potential flood areas. Other state, regional, and local authorities also may oversee the protection of air and water quality and other environmental issues.

LOCAL PLANNING INFORMATION

The planner must collect local planning information. Personal contact with planning and zoning agencies is important in order to comprehend local criteria. Following is a list of information to review.

PLANNING DOCUMENTS

Many communities have adopted comprehensive plans that indicate the particular land use and intensity of the site. In addition, information on the availability and/or phasing of public services and utilities, environmental criteria, traffic planning, and population trends can be found in most comprehensive plans. Some communities require that rezoning meet the criteria provided in their comprehensive plans.

In addition to the comprehensive plan, communities may also adopt neighborhood or area plans that refine the comprehensive plan as it relates to a particular locale. Many of these studies stipulate specific zoning categories for individual parcels of land.

URBAN DESIGN PLANS

Some communities have adopted urban design plans for creating a harmonious physical environment. These documents may range from conceptual to those that incorporate specific requirements. Some provide bonuses in land use intensities for incorporating urban amenities such as plazas and squares. There may also be criteria for retrofitting existing areas, a critical need in American cities where a substantial amount of urban area is deteriorated or developed incoherently.

ZONING

Land zoning prescribes the intensity and type of land use allowed. A zoning change is required if the planned project differs. Regulations often need to be modified to allow good community design. Common examples of regulations discouraging good urban form include excessive setbacks and restricted mixed-use development.

PUBLIC WORKS STANDARDS

Local public works criteria significantly affect the design of large sites. Roadway layout, cross sections, and drainage are typical requirements. Excessive roadway standards designed for automobile convenience, with little regard for the pedestrian are typical of today's public works regulations. Such standards should be modified to allow coherent neighborhood design.

PUBLIC SERVICES AND UTILITIES

Other information that may require additional research includes:

- Availability of potable water, including local and state regulations on wells.
- Availability of public sewer service, access to trunk lines, and available increases in flow. If sewage lines are not immediately available, determine projected phasing of these services, as well as alternatives to sewage collection and treatment, including septic tanks.
- Access to public roads, existing and projected carrying capacities, and levels of services of the roads.

Gary Greenan, Andres Duany, Elizabeth Plater-Zyberk, Kamal Zaharin, Iskandar Shafie, Miami, Florida

(State and local road departments can provide this information.)
- Availability and capacities of schools and other public facilities, such as parks and libraries

SITE ANALYSIS

Site analysis is one of the planner's major responsibilities. All the on- and off-site design determinants must be evaluated before design begins. For details, see the following pages on environmental site analysis.

PROGRAM DEVELOPMENT

At the program development stage, background research, citizen input, and site analysis are combined with client input and synthesized into a set of program strategies. Basic elements for program development include market and financial criteria; federal, state, regional, and local planning information; local political climate development costs; the client's objectives; and site opportunities and constraints as developed in the synthesis of environmental site determinants. Balancing the various determinants will lead to an appropriate approach to site development. Consider dwelling unit type, density, marketing, time phasing, and similar criteria, as well as graphic studies of the site, to finalize the program. Develop clear graphic representations of design concepts to present to the client and others who may have input to the process. If the project cannot be accomplished under the existing zoning or public works requirements, requesting a regulatory change becomes a part of the program.

ALTERNATIVE PLAN PREPARATION

Once the program has been accepted by the client, develop several design solutions to meet the program objectives. When an alternative has been accepted, develop it into the preliminary plan. This plan should be relatively detailed, showing all spatial relationships, infrastructure, landscaping, and other relevant information.

PUBLIC REVIEW

A zoning change requires public review. Some communities require substantial data, such as impact statements and other narrative and graphic exhibits, while others may require only an application for the zoning change. Local requirements for changes can be complex, and it is imperative that the planner and the client's attorney are familiar with local criteria.

FINAL DESIGN PLANS

At this stage, the preliminary plans are refined into final site development plans that include fully dimensioned drawings, landscape plans, and site details. Final development plans also include drawings prepared by the engineer or surveyor, such as legal plats and utilities, street, and drainage plans. Upon approval, final design plans are recorded in the public records in the form of plats. Homeowner association agreements, deed restrictions, and similar legal documents must also be recorded, and they become binding on all owners and successive owners, unless changed legally. Bonding may be required for infrastructure and other public facilities. In some instances, the planner may develop specific design standards for the total buildout of the project.

Gary Greenan, Andres Duany, Elizabeth Plater-Zyberk, Kamal Zaharin, Iskandar Shafie, Miami, Florida

RURAL VILLAGE DESIGN

SITE ANALYSIS MAP

Locate natural, cultural, and scenic features first. These include many buildable areas, such as farm fields, pastures, meadows, and mature woodland; special features, such as stone walls, springhouses, cellar holes, and views into and out of the site; and unbuildable areas, such as steep slopes, wetlands, springs, streams, and ice ponds.

CONVENTIONAL LAYOUT OR "YIELD PLAN"

Sketch an unimaginative but legally correct conventional layout to demonstrate the density that could realistically be achieved on the site and, by comparison, to show local officials and abutters how different a rural village approach is. The sketch here shows how, under 1.5-acre zoning, a 520-acre site would ordinarily be checkerboarded into 300 lots, each with a required minimum area of 60,000 sq. ft., leaving no open space whatsoever.

VILLAGE PLAN

Designing the development as a traditional village, with lots ranging from 5000 sq ft to 1 acre, achieves slightly greater density on less than one-quarter of the land and preserves nearly 400 acres. This layout is based closely on the site analysis map, with the village located to avoid disturbing the woodlands that provide the only natural habitat in this largely agricultural community. The most special site features are protected by designing around them. Nine "conservancy lots," varying in area from 20 to 60 acres, are limited to one principal dwelling plus two accessory units. This

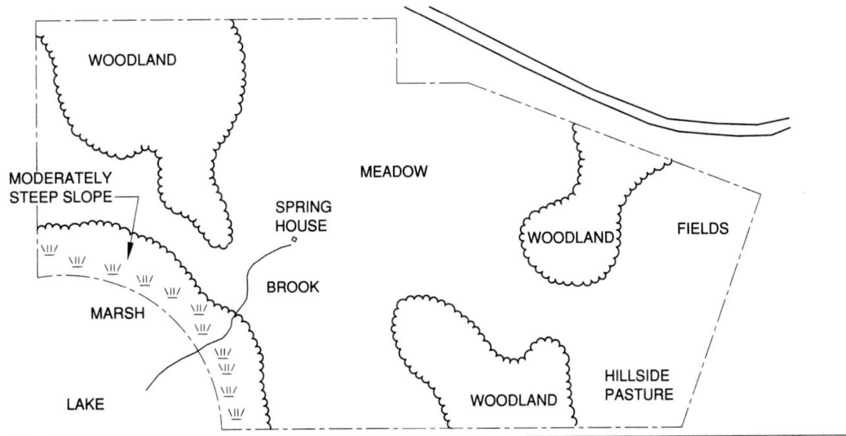

SITE ANALYSIS MAP

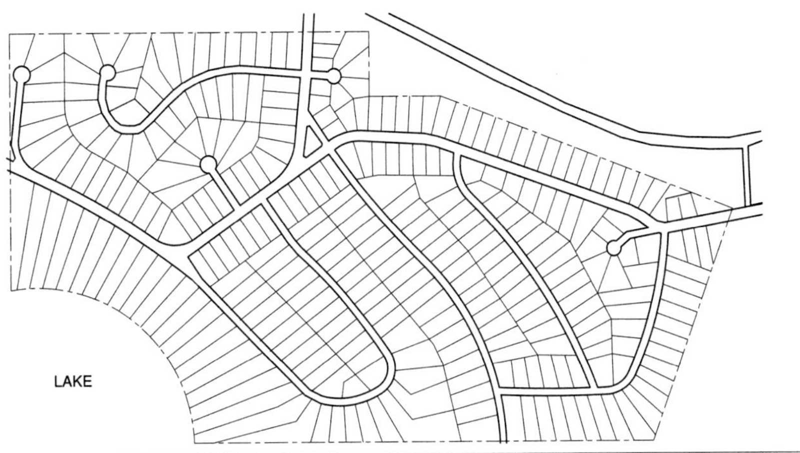

CONVENTIONAL LAYOUT

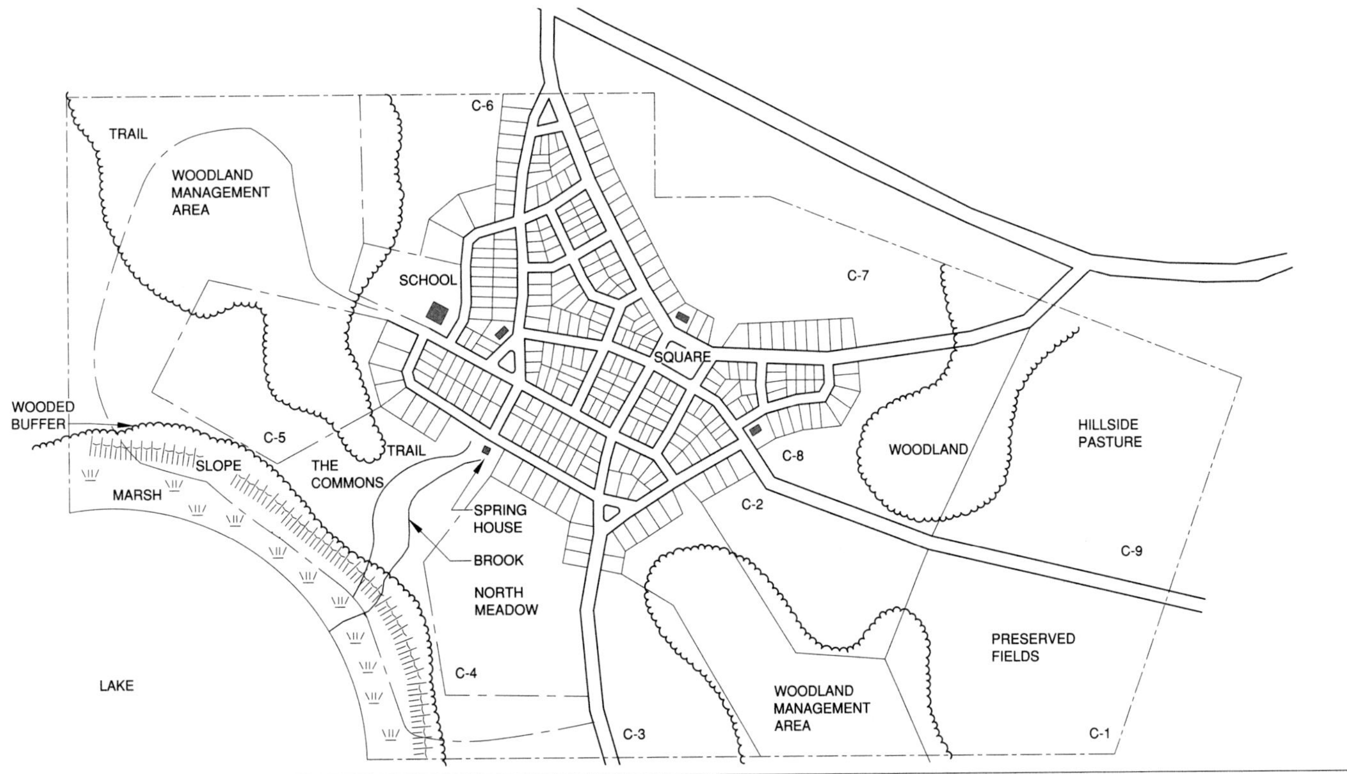

RURAL VILLAGE DESIGN

Randall Arendt, MRTPI, Natural Lands Trust Media, Pennsylvania; Gary Greenan, Andres Duany, Elizabeth Plater-Zyberk, Kamal Zaharin, Iskandar Shafi, Miami, Florida

assures significant open space around the perimeter of this 300-lot village. Permanent conservation easements protect these lands from further subdivision and preserve the 150 acres of undivided open space and its trail system, which connects the old springhouse to the lakeshore and leads back to the schoolyard. This open space could be owned by the village government, a local land trust, or a homeowners' association (with automatic membership and authority to place liens on properties of members who fail to pay their dues). Rural views outward from three village streets have also been preserved, with open countryside terminating their vistas. Terminated vistas are also provided by three large public or semipublic buildings (churches, libraries, etc.) positioned at the ends of several streets.

Randall Arendt, MRTPI, Natural Lands Trust Media, Pennsylvania; Gary Greenan, Andres Duany, Elizabeth Plater-Zyberk, Kamal Zaharin, Iskandar Shafi, Miami, Florida

ELEMENTS OF URBANISM

THE NEIGHBORHOOD, THE DISTRICT, AND THE CORRIDOR

The fundamental elements of urbanism are the neighborhood, the district, and the corridor. Neighborhoods are urbanized areas with a full and balanced range of human activity. Districts are urbanized areas organized around a predominant activity. Neighborhoods and districts are connected and isolated by corridors of transportation or open space.

Neighborhoods, districts, and corridors are complex urban elements. Suburbia, in contrast, is the result of simplistic zoning concepts that separate activities into residential subdivisions, shopping centers, office parks, and open space.

THE NEIGHBORHOOD

Cities and towns are made up of multiple neighborhoods. A neighborhood isolated in the landscape is a village.

The nomenclature may vary, but there is general agreement regarding the physical composition of a neighborhood. The neighborhood unit of the 1929 New York Regional Plan, the *quartier* identified by Leon Krier, traditional neighborhood design (TND), and transit-oriented development (TOD) share similar attributes. The population, configuration, and scale may vary, but all of these models propose the following:

- The neighborhood has a center and an edge. This combination of a focus and a limit contributes to the social identity of the community. The center is a necessity, the edge less so. The center is always a public space—a square, a green, or an important street intersection—located near the center of the urbanized area, unless compelled by geography to be elsewhere. Eccentric locations are justified by a shoreline, a transportation corridor, or a promontory with a compelling view.

  The center is the locus of the neighborhood's public buildings. Shops and workplaces are usually here, especially in a village. In the aggregations of neighborhoods that create towns and cities, retail buildings and workplaces are often at the edge, where they can combine with others to draw customers.

  The edges of a neighborhood vary in character. In villages, the edge is usually defined by land designated for cultivation or conservation of its natural state. In urban areas, the edge is often defined by rail lines and boulevards, which best remain outside the neighborhood.

- The neighborhood has a balanced mix of activities: shops, work, school, recreation, and dwellings of all types. This is particularly useful for young, old, and low-income populations who, in an automobile-based environment, depend on others for mobility.

  The neighborhood provides housing for residents with a variety of incomes. Affordable housing types include backyard apartments, apartments above shops, and apartment buildings adjacent to workplaces.

- The optimal size of a neighborhood is 1/4 mile from center to edge, a distance equal to a five-minute walk at an easy pace. Its limited area gathers the population within walking distance of many of its daily needs.

  The location of a transit stop within walking distance of most homes increases the likelihood of its use. Transit-oriented neighborhoods create a regional network of villages, towns, and cities accessible to a population unable to rely on cars. Such a system can provide the major cultural and social institutions, variety of shopping, and broad job base that can only be supported by the larger population of an aggregation of neighborhoods.

- The neighborhood consists of blocks on a network of small thoroughfares. Streets are laid out to create blocks of appropriate building sites and to shorten pedestrian routes. An interconnecting street pattern provides multiple routes, diffusing traffic. This pattern keeps local traffic off regional roads and through traffic off local streets.

  Neighborhood streets of varying types are detailed to provide equitably for pedestrian comfort

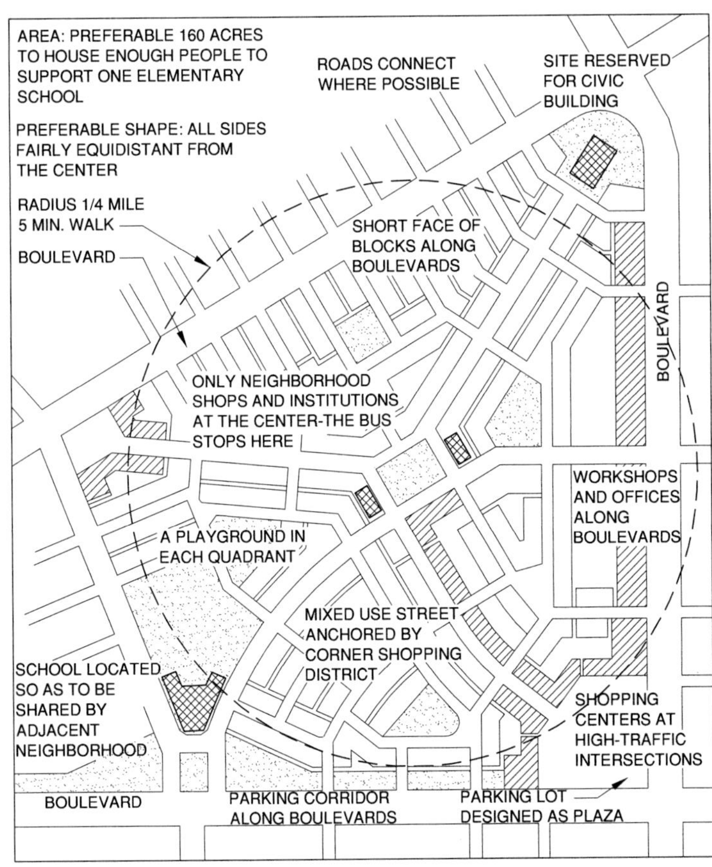

AN URBAN NEIGHBORHOOD (PART OF A TOWN)

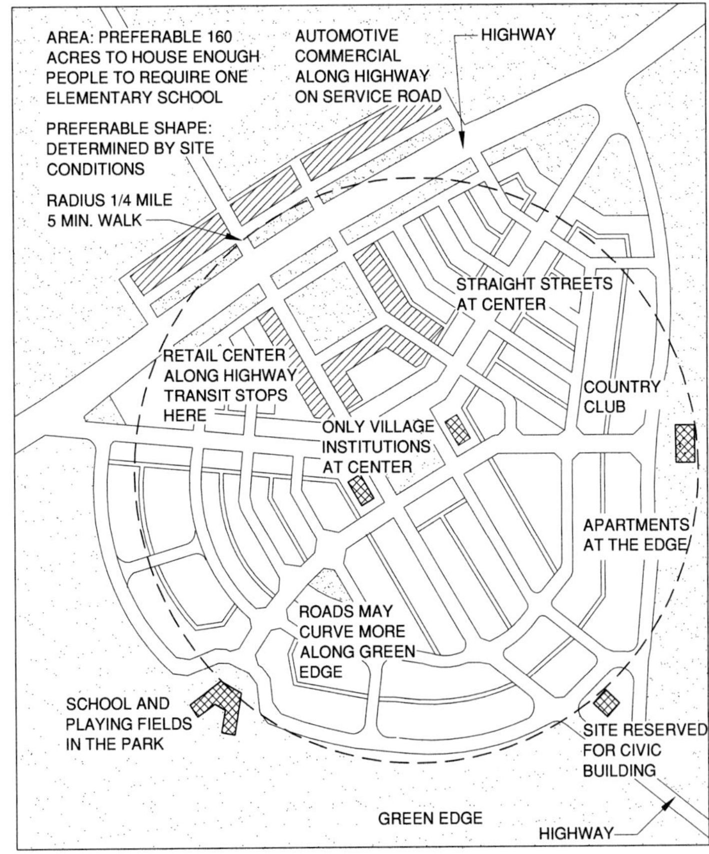

A RURAL NEIGHBORHOOD (A VILLAGE)

Gary Greenan, Andres Duany, Elizabeth Plater-Zyberk, Kamal Zaharin, Iskandar Shafie, Miami, Florida; The Cintas Foundation

and automobile movement. Slowing the automobile and increasing pedestrian activity encourage the casual meetings that form the bonds of community.

- The neighborhood gives priority to public space and to appropriate location of civic buildings. Public spaces and public buildings enhance community identity and foster civic pride. The neighborhood plan creates a hierarchy of useful public spaces: a formal square, an informal park, and many playgrounds.

THE DISTRICT

The district is an urbanized area that is functionally specialized. Although districts preclude the full range of activities of a neighborhood, they are not the single-activity zones of suburbia. Rather, multiple activities support its primary identity. Typically complex examples are theater districts, capital areas, and college campuses. Other districts accommodate large-scale transportation or manufacturing uses, such as airports, container terminals, and refineries.

The structure of the district parallels that of the neighborhood. An identifiable focus encourages orientation and identity. Clear boundaries facilitate the formation of special taxing or management organizations. As in the neighborhood, the character of the public spaces creates a community of users, even if they reside elsewhere. Interconnected circulation encourages pedestrians, supports transit viability, and ensures security. Districts benefit from transit systems and should be located within the regional network.

THE CORRIDOR

The corridor is the connector and the separator of neighborhoods and districts. Corridors include natural and technical components ranging from wildlife trails to rail lines. The between is not the haphazardly residual space remaining outside subdivisions and shopping centers in suburbia. It is a civic element characterized by its visible continuity and bounded by neighborhoods and districts, to which it provides entry.

The transportation corridor's trajectory is determined by its intensity. Heavy rail corridors should remain tangent to towns and enter only the industrial districts of cities. Light rail and trolley corridors may occur as boulevards at the edges of neighborhoods. As such, they are detailed for pedestrian use and to accommodate building sites. Bus corridors may pass into neighborhood centers on conventional streets.

The corridor may also be a continuous parkway, providing long-distance walking and bicycling trails and natural habitat. Parkway corridors can be formed by the systematic accretion of recreational open spaces, such as parks, schoolyards, and golf courses. These continuous spaces can be part of a larger network, connecting urban open space with rural surroundings.

Gary Greenan, Andres Duany, Elizabeth Plater-Zyberk, Kamal Zaharin, Iskandar Shafie, Miami, Florida; The Cintas Foundation

PLAN TYPES

ORTHOGONAL GRID

Advantages

- Excellent directional orientation
- Lot shape controllable
- Street hierarchy with end blocks for through traffic
- Even dispersal of traffic through the grid
- Straight lines enhance rolling terrain
- Efficient double-loading of alleys and utilities

Disadvantages

- Monotonous unless periodically interrupted
- Does not accommodate environmental interruptions
- Unresponsive to steep terrain

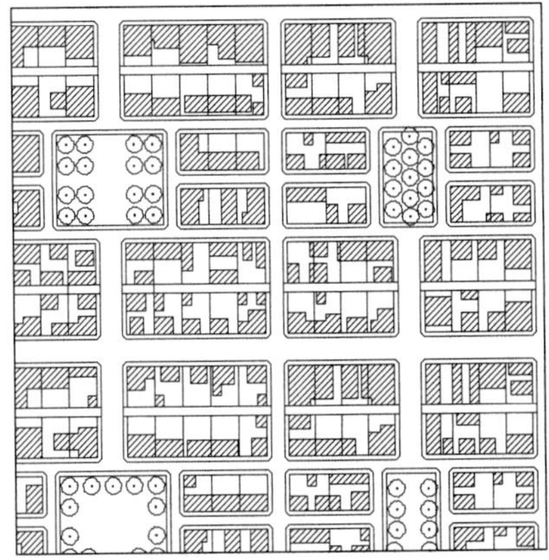

SAVANNAH

ORTHOGONAL GRID

GRID WITH DIAGONALS

Advantages

- Street hierarchy with diagonals for through traffic
- Even dispersal of traffic through the grid
- Diagonals respond to the terrain
- Diagonals interrupt monotony of the grid

Disadvantages

- Uncontrollable variety of blocks and lots
- High number of awkward lot shapes
- Diagonal intersections spatially ill defined

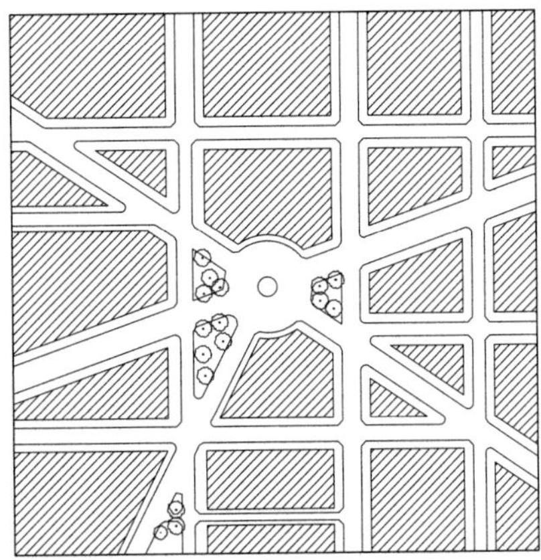

WASHINGTON, D.C.

GRID WITH DIAGONALS

DIAGONAL NETWORK

Advantages

- Street hierarchy with diagonals for through traffic
- Even dispersal of traffic through the network
- Diagonals respond to terrain
- Intrinsically interesting by geometric variety
- Controllable shape of blocks and lots
- Efficient double-loading of alleys for utilities
- Diagonal intersections spatially well defined

Disadvantages

- Tends to be disorienting

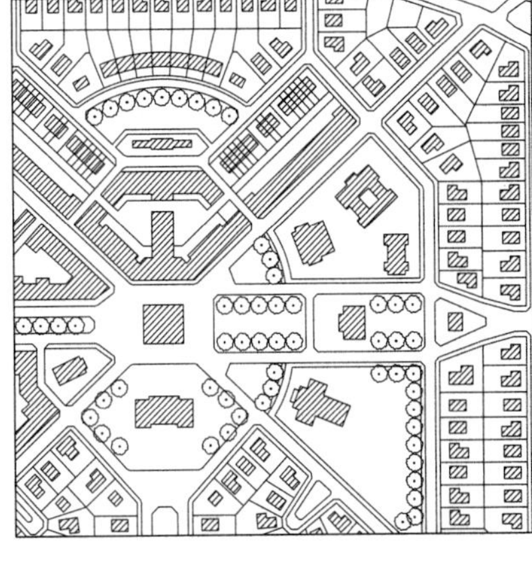

MARIEMONT

DIAGONAL NETWORK

ORGANIC NETWORK

Advantages

- Street hierarchy with long routes for through traffic
- Even dispersal of traffic through network
- Intrinsically interesting by geometric variety
- Responsive to terrain
- Easily accommodates environmental interruptions
- Short streets, terminated vistas

Disadvantages

- None

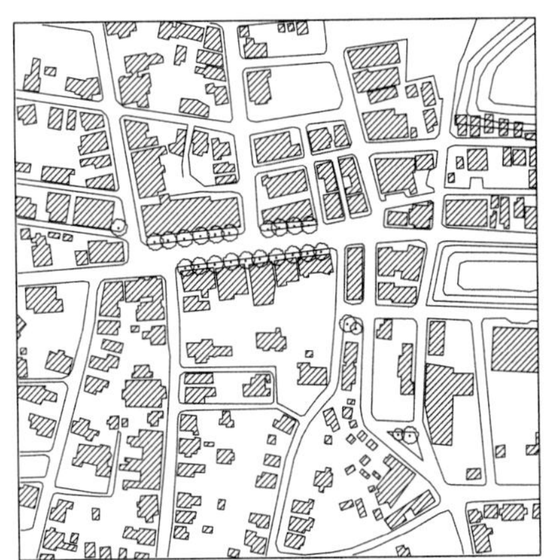

NANTUCKET

ORGANIC NETWORK

CURVILINEAR NETWORK

Advantages

- Intrinsically interesting by deflecting vistas
- Easily accommodates environmental interruptions
- Highly responsive to terrain
- Even dispersal of traffic through the network

Disadvantages

- Little directional orientation
- Uncontrollable variety of lots
- No natural hierarchy of streets

RIVERSIDE

CURVILINEAR NETWORK

DISCONTINUOUS NETWORK

Advantages

- Street hierarchy with collectors for through traffic
- Controllable variety of blocks and lots
- Easily accommodates environmental interruptions
- Highly responsive to p terrain

Disadvantages

- Concentration of traffic by absence of network

RADBURN

DISCONTINUOUS NETWORK

Gary Greenan, Andres Duany, Elizabeth Plater-Zyberk, Kamal Zaharin, Iskandar Shafie, Rafael Diaz, Miami, Florida; The Cintas Foundation

BLOCK TYPES

GENERAL

The urban plan must be assembled of blocks before building frontage and landscape types are assigned. The disposition of blocks has distinct socioeconomic implications.

THE SQUARE BLOCK

This type was an early model for planned settlements in America, particularly in Spanish colonies. It was sometimes associated with agricultural communities, providing four large lots per block, each lot with a house at its center. When the growth of the community produced additional subdivision, replatting created irregular lots (see the figure "Square Block with Subsequent Subdivision"). While this may provide a useful variety, it is more often regarded as a nuisance by a society accustomed to standardized products. A further disadvantage is that discontinuous rear lot lines make alleys and rear-access utilities impractical. Despite these shortcomings, the square block is useful as a specialized type. When platted only at its perimeter, with the center left open, it can accommodate the high parking requirements of certain buildings. The open center, well insulated from traffic, may also be used as a common garden or a playground (see the figure "Square Block: Perimeter Platting").

THE ORGANIC BLOCK

This type is characterized by its irregularity; its variations are unlimited. The original organic block was the subdivision of residual land between well-worn paths (see the figure "Organic Block: Residual Land Between Well-Worn Paths"). It was later rationalized by Olmsted and Unwin to achieve a controllable, picturesque effect and to negotiate sloping terrain gracefully. The naturalistic block, despite its variety, generates certain recurring conditions that must be resolved by sophisticated platting. At shallow curves, it is desirable to have the facades follow the frontage smoothly. This is achieved by keeping the side lot lines perpendicular to the frontage line (see 1 in the figure "Organic Block: Planned Naturalistic"). At the same time it is important for the rear lot line to be wide enough to permit vehicular access (Area Number 2). At sharper curves, it is desirable to have the axis of a single lot bisect the acute angle (Area Number 3). In the event of excessive block depth, it is possible to colonize the interior of the block by means of a close (Area Number 4).

THE ELONGATED BLOCK

The elongated block overcomes some of the drawbacks of the square block. More efficient and more standardized, elongated blocks provide economical double-loaded alleys, with short utility runs, to eliminate the uncontrollable variable of lot depth and maintain the option of altering lot width. By adjusting the block length, it is possible to reduce cross streets toward rural edges or to add them at urban centers. This adjustment alters the pedestrian permeability of the grid and controls the ratio of street parking to building capacity. The elongated block can "bend" somewhat along its length, giving it a limited ability to shape space and negotiate slopes (see the figure "Elongated Block Using Space Shaping").

Unlike the square block, the elongated block provides two distinct types of frontage. Residential buildings are placed on the quieter sides of the block (see 1 in the figure "Elongated Block: Two Types of Frontage"). Commercial buildings can be set on the short end of the block, platted to face the busy street; the amount of parking behind these properties is controlled by the variable depth (Area Numbers 1 and 2).

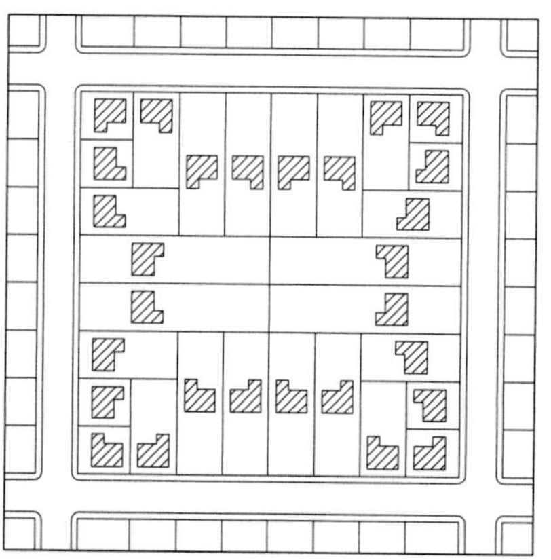

SQUARE BLOCK WITH SUBSEQUENT SUBDIVISION

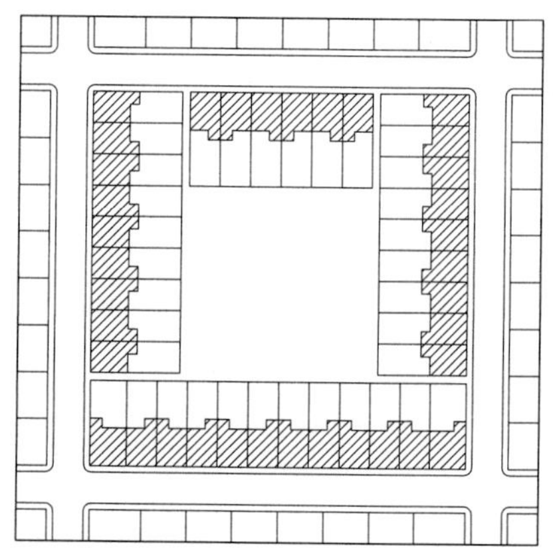

SQUARE BLOCK: PERIMIETER PLATTING

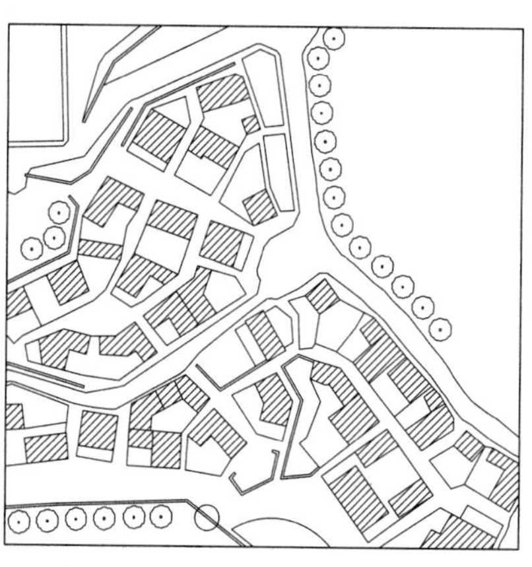

ORGANIC BLOCK: RESIDUAL LAND BETWEEN WELL-WORN PATHS

ORGANIC BLOCK: PLANNED NATURALISTIC

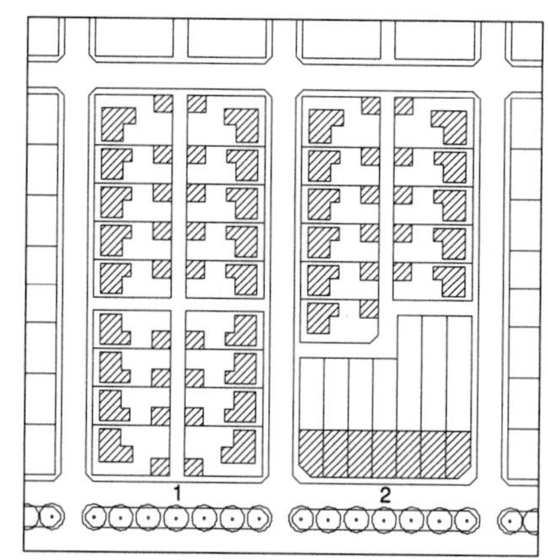

ELONGATED BLOCK: TWO TYPES OF FRONTAGE

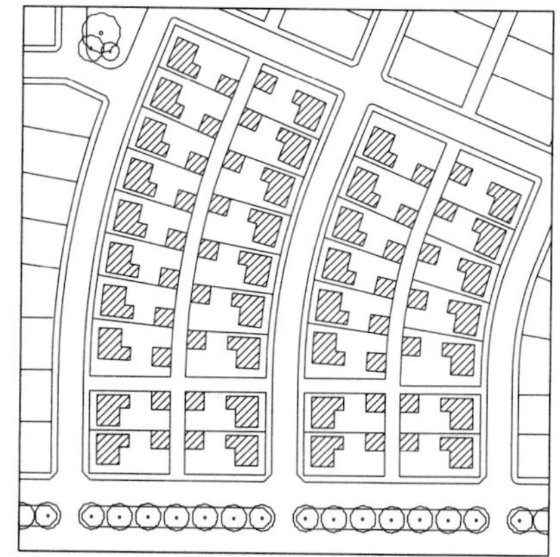

ELONGATED BLOCK USING SPACE SHAPING

Gary Greenan, Andres Duany, Elizabeth Plater-Zyberk, Kamal Zaharin, Iskandar Shafie, Miami, Florida; The Cintas Foundation

OPEN SPACE TYPES

GENERAL

Public open space provides orientation, hierarchy, and communal structure to a neighborhood. The specialized open spaces shown here are derived from the elongated block types. They can also be adjusted to fit both square and organic block types.

LANE

Children often make lanes behind houses into informal playgrounds. The paved surface in front of garages is convenient for ball games. Lanes are particularly successful when they are designed to eliminate through traffic. Garage apartments provide supervision.

PLAYGROUND

Playgrounds can be easily extracted from any block by assigning one or several lots to this use. There should be a playground within 500 ft. of every residence. The playground should provide both sunny and shaded play areas, as well as an open shelter with benches for parents. Playgrounds must be fenced, lockable, and lit, if they are not to become a nuisance at night.

NURSERY

A nursery can be inserted in the middle of a block, away from major thoroughfares. It requires a limited amount of parking but substantial vehicular drop-off space. The attached playground should be securely fenced and have both sunny and shaded areas. Children's games may be noisy, so it is advisable to locate nurseries where adjacent houses are buffered by outbuildings.

CLOSE

A close is a space shared by buildings inside the block. It may be pedestrian, or it may have a roadway loop around a green area. Its minimum width

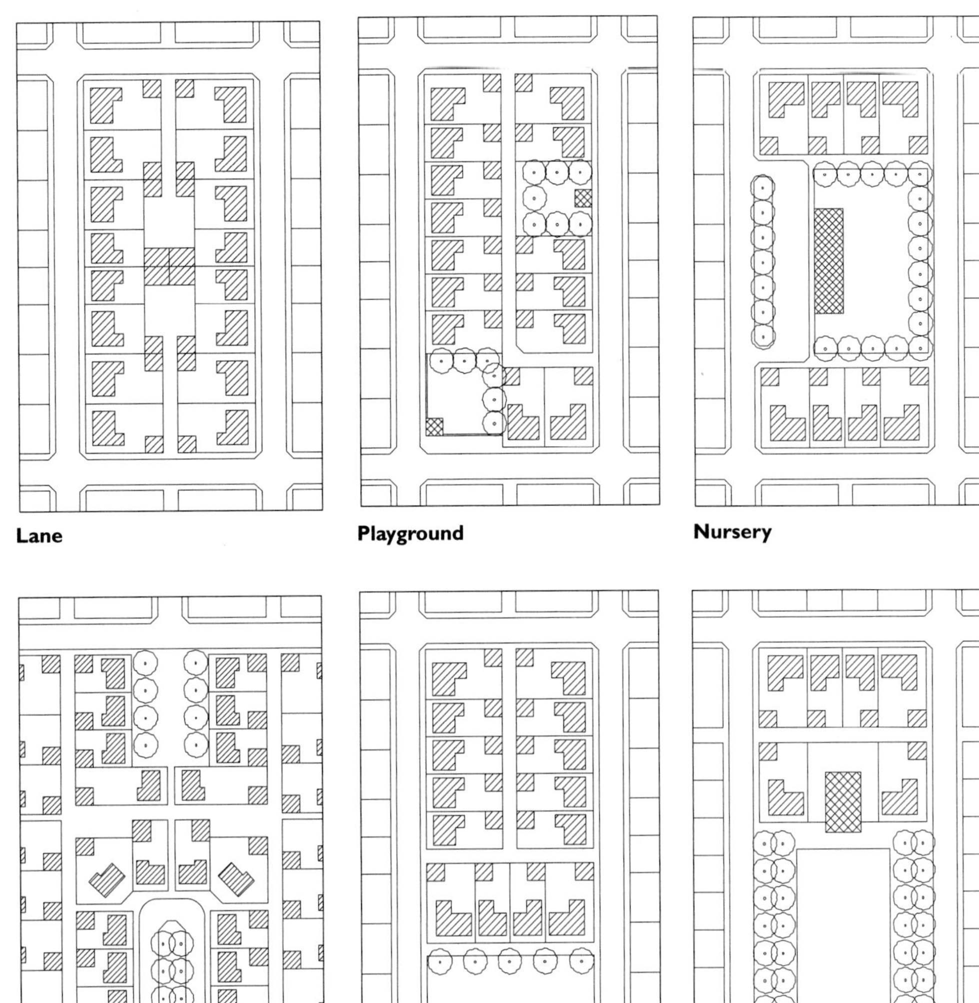

OPEN SPACE TYPES

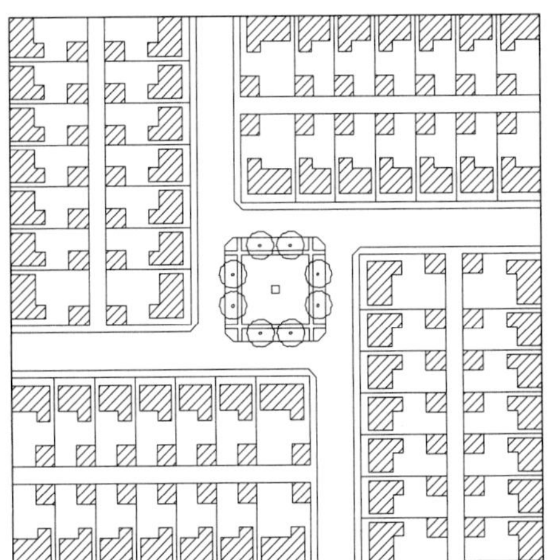

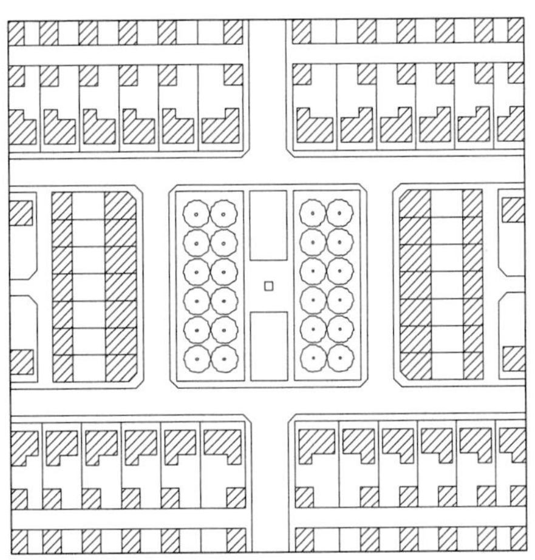

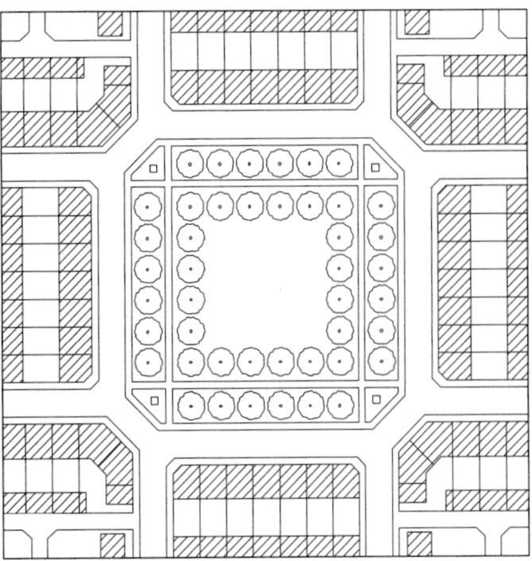

DETACHED SQUARES

Gary Greenan, Andres Duany, Elizabeth Plater-Zyberk, Kamal Zaharin, Iskandar Shafie, Miami, Florida; The Cintas Foundation

must coincide with emergency vehicle turning standards. The close is a superior alternative to the cul-de-sac, as the focus is a green rather than pavement. It is especially recommended for communal subgroups such as cohousing or assisted-living cottages. The close provides additional frontage for deep square and organic blocks.

ATTACHED SQUARES

Squares are green spaces that provide settings for civic buildings and monuments, which are located at the center or edge of the square. Buildings play a part, but the space is largely defined by formal tree planting. Squares should be maintained to a higher standard than playgrounds and parks.

DETACHED SQUARES

Squares detached on all sides by roads are particularly formal. Since adjacent buildings provide much of the population that uses a public space, detached squares are less likely to be used than other types. This separation also limits the amount of natural security provided by adjacent windows. The detached square remains appropriate as a means to symbolically enhance important places or institutions.

MARKET PLAZA

Plazas are public spaces that are primarily paved rather than green. They can sustain very intense use by crowds and even by vehicles. Parking lots should be designed as plazas that happen to have cars on them, rather than as single-purpose areas. A smaller shopping center can be transformed into a town center if it has been designed so it can be seamlessly attached to the block system and detailed as a plaza.

CIVIC PLAZA

Civic buildings are often no larger than the private ones that surround them, and their legibility as more important buildings cannot depend solely on architectural expression. Their setting within the block system must communicate their elevated status. Sites on squares or at the terminations of avenues are ideal

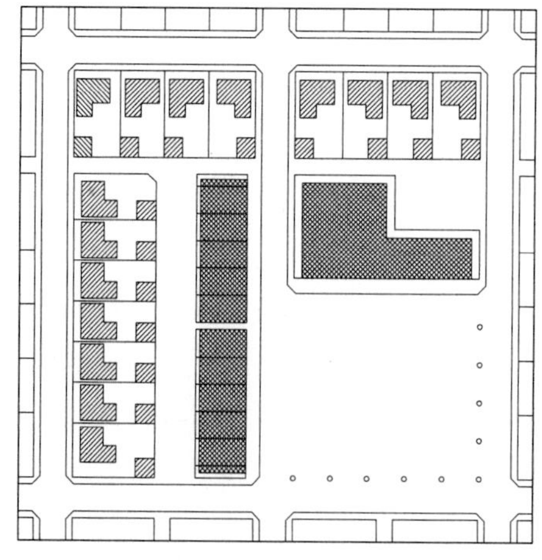

MARKET PLAZA

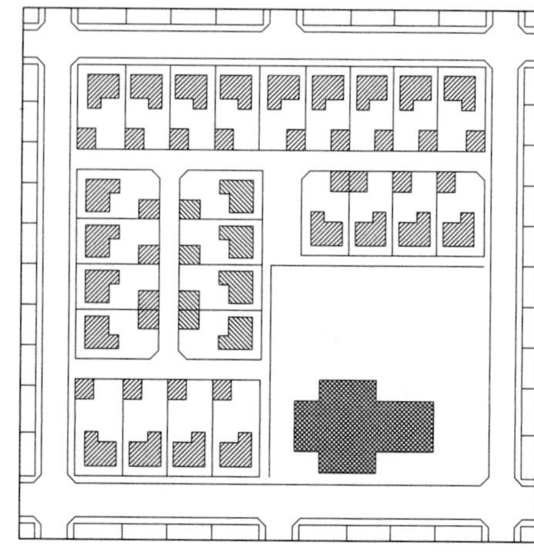

CIVIC PLAZA

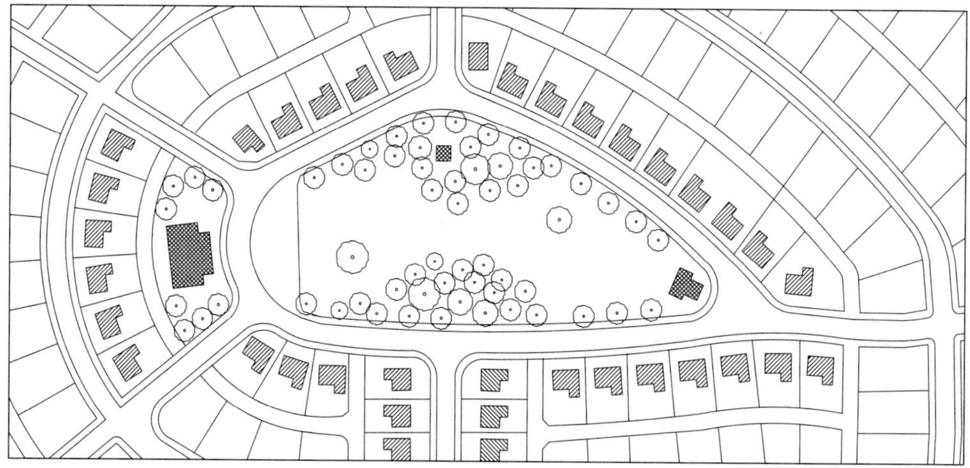

GREEN

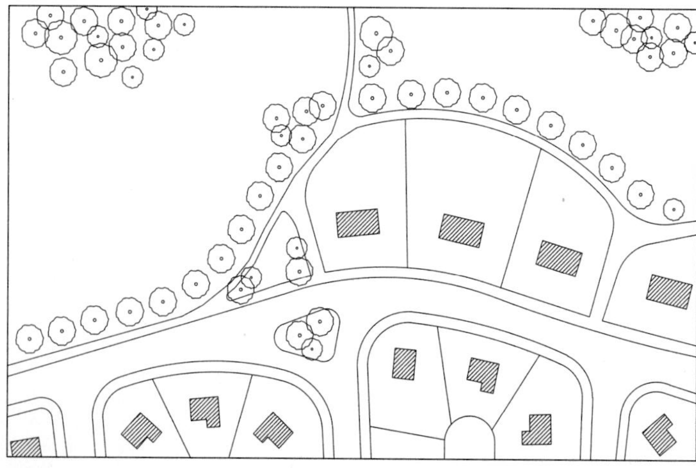

PARK

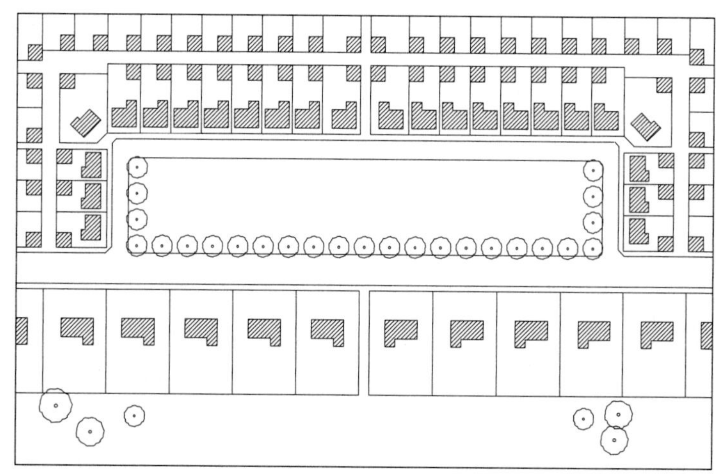

BUFFER

Gary Greenan, Andres Duany, Elizabeth Plater-Zyberk, Kamal Zaharin, Iskandar Shafie, Miami, Florida; The Cintas Foundation

but not always available. Thus the most dependable technique is to organize and detail the parking areas of civic buildings as plazas.

GREEN

The green is an urban, naturalistic open space. Like the square, it is small, civic, and surrounded by buildings. Unlike the square, it is informally planted and may have an irregular topography. Greens are usually landscaped with trees at the edges and sunny lawns at the center. Greens should contain no structures other than benches, pavilions, and memorials; paths are optional.

PARK

Parks are naturalistic open spaces, like greens, but larger and less tended. They are most successful when created from virgin woodland. Parks have grassy areas only periodically. A knoll or a pond can be used as an important organizing feature. Parks exist within the urban fabric of large cities, but their inherent size usually puts them at the edges of towns and villages. Parks may be edged by public drives or by houses on very large lots, as long as connections to public paths occur at every block.

BUFFER

The buffer has the basic elements of a green, with the added purpose of buffering the impact of traffic from a highway or boulevard. Shown is a small lot development fronting a green. On the opposite side are larger lots on which houses are placed further back from the roadway edge as another buffer technique.

Gary Greenan, Andres Duany, Elizabeth Plater-Zyberk, Kamal Zaharin, Iskandar Shafie, Miami, Florida; The Cintas Foundation

BUILDING TYPES

GENERAL

The traditional increment for platting lots in North America has been the 50-ft width. This subdivision dimension was efficient for many years, creating 25-ft rowhouse and shopfront lots, as well as 50-, 75-, and 100-ft lots suitable for houses. However, the advent of the automobile added a set of dimensional constraints that required new platting standards. The 50-ft width is wasteful, since the basic increment of efficient parking is the double row at 64 ft.

The 64-ft increment, when divided by four, provides the absolute minimum rowhouse lot of 16 ft, which allows one car to be parked with additional room for pedestrian passage. The minimum side yard lot is 32 ft. The minimum perimeter yard lot is 48 ft. The 64-ft lot efficiently provides for the high parking requirement of shopfronts, apartments, and office buildings.

The platting module of 16 ft corresponds to the traditional measure of the rod. Platting in rods, without knowing what building types will occupy the lots, maintains flexibility and ensures maximum density through parking efficiency.

Four building types accommodate the common residential, retail, and workplace uses of urban life. Some buildings, however, cannot be categorized typologically. Buildings dedicated to manufacturing and transportation may be distorted by large-scale mechanical trajectories. Civic buildings, which must express the aspirations of the institutions they embody, should also be exempt from the discipline of type.

COURTYARD BUILDING

This type of building occupies all or most of the edges of its lot and defines one or more private spaces internally. This is the most urban of types as it is able to completely shield the private realm from the public realm. It is common in hot climates, but its attributes are useful everywhere. Because of its ability to accommodate incompatible activities in close proximity, it is recommended for workshops, hotels, and schools. The high security the boundary provides is useful for recolonizing crime-prone urban cores.

SIDE YARD BUILDING

This type of building occupies one side of the lot, with the primary open space on the other side. The view of the side yard on the street front makes this building type appear freestanding, so it may be interspersed with perimeter yard buildings in less urban locations. If the adjacent building is also a side yard type with a blank party wall, the open space can be quite private. This type permits systematic climatic orientation, with the long side yard elevation facing the sun or the breeze.

REAR YARD BUILDING

This type of building occupies the front of its lot, full width, leaving the rear portion as a private space. This is a relatively urban type appropriate for neighborhood and town centers. The building facade

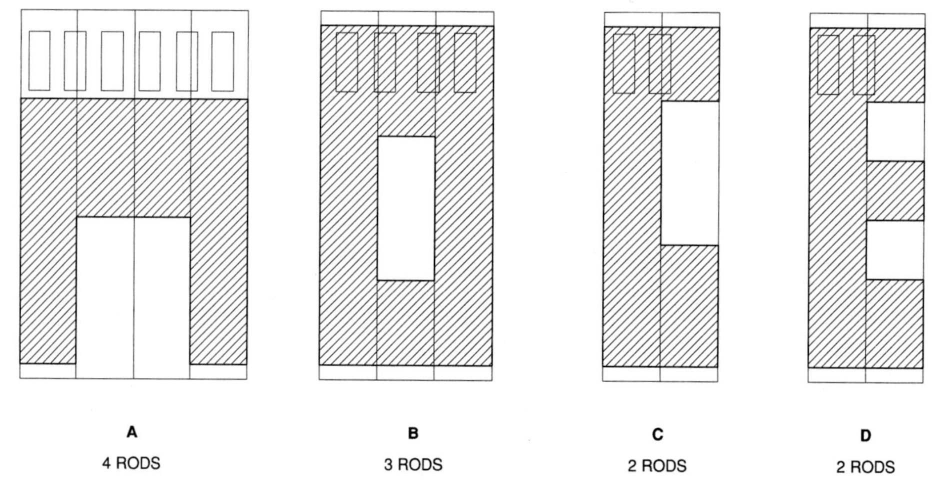

COURTYARD BUILDING

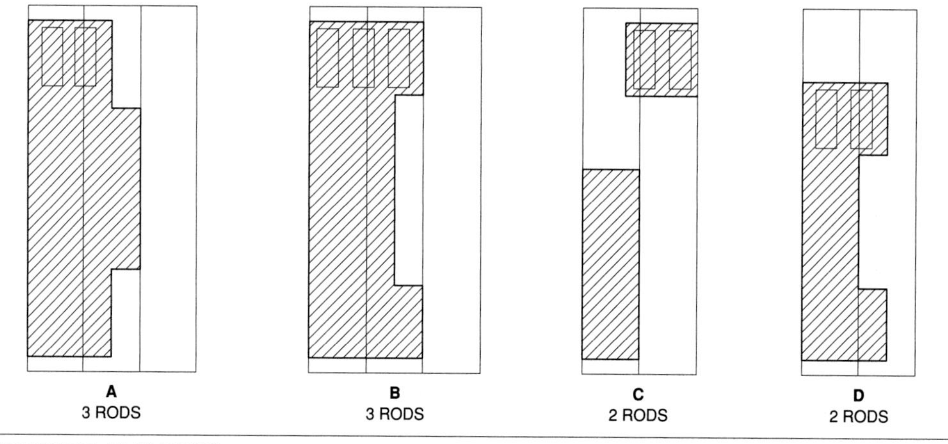

SIDE YARD BUILDING

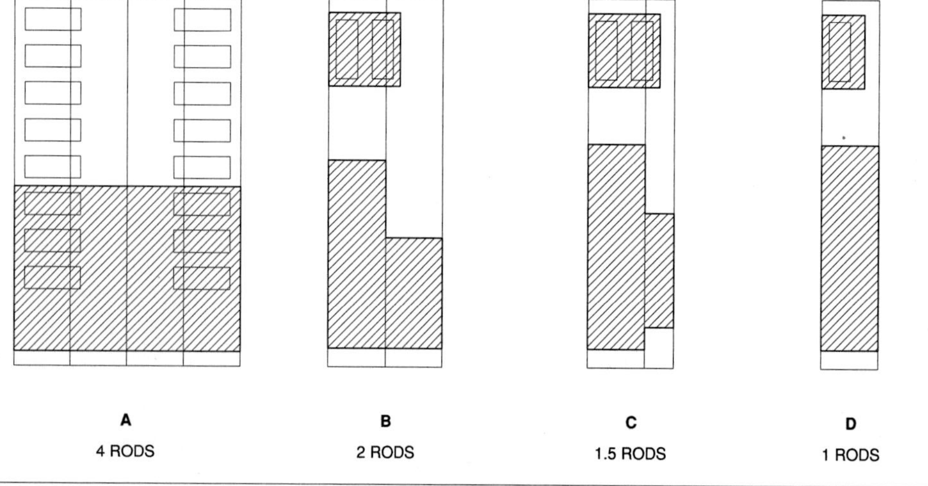

REAR YARD BUILDING

Gary Greenan, Andres Duany, Elizabeth Plater-Zyberk, Kamal Zaharin, Iskandar Shafie, Miami, Florida; The Cintas Foundation

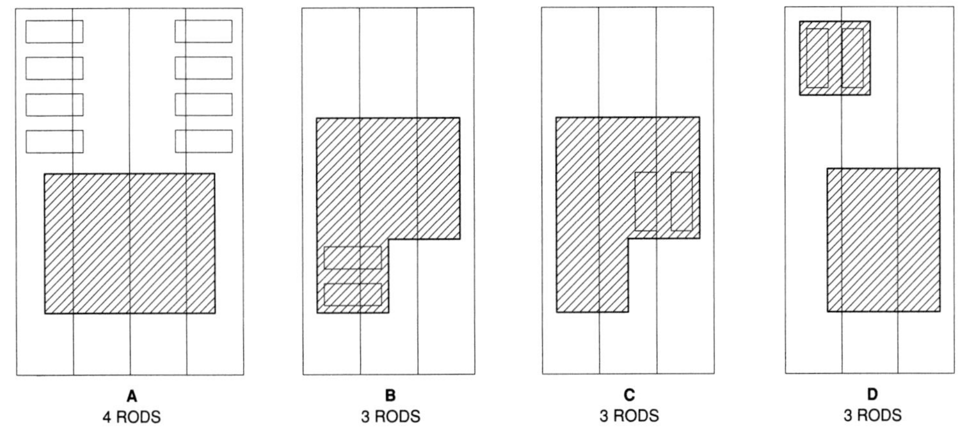

PERIMETER YARD BUILDING

defines the edge of the public space, while the rear elevation may reflect different functional purposes. In its residential form, this type is represented by the rowhouse with a rear garden and outbuilding. In its commercial form, the depth of the rear yard can contain substantial parking for retail and office uses.

PERIMETER YARD BUILDING

This building stands free on its lot, with substantial front and rear yards and smaller side yards. It is the least urban of the types, so it is usually assigned to areas away from neighborhood and town centers. This building type is usually residential, but when parking is contained within the rear yard it lends itself to limited office and boarding uses. The rear yard can be secured for privacy by fences and a well-placed outbuilding. The front yard is intended to be semipublic and visually continuous with the yards of neighbors. The illusion of continuity is usually degraded when garage fronts are aligned with the facades, as cars seldom pull in beyond the driveway. To avoid a landscape of parked cars, garages should be set back a minimum of one car's length from the facade or entered sideways through a walled forecourt.

Gary Greenan, Andres Duany, Elizabeth Plater-Zyberk, Kamal Zaharin, Iskandar Shafie, Miami, Florida; The Cintas Foundation

SPATIAL DEFINITION

GENERAL

Building delineates public space in an urban setting. Successful spatial definition is achieved when bounding buildings are aligned in a disciplined manner and the defined space does not exceed a certain height-to-width ratio.

The height-to-width ratio of the space generates spatial enclosure, which is related to the physiology of the human eye. If the width of a public space is such that the cone of vision encompasses less street wall than sky opening, the degree of spatial enclosure is slight. The ratio of 1 increment of height to 6 of width is the absolute minimum, with 1 to 3 being an effective minimum if a sense of spatial enclosure is to result. As a general rule, the tighter the ratio, the stronger the sense of place and, often, the higher the real estate value. Spatial enclosure is particularly important for shopping streets that must compete with shopping malls, which provide very effective spatial definition. In the absence of spatial definition by facades, disciplined tree planting is an alternative. Trees aligned for spatial enclosure are necessary on thoroughfares that have substantial front yards.

NOMENCLATURE

The frontage line: The lot boundary that coincides with a public thoroughfare or public space. The frontage line may be designed independently of the thoroughfare, to create a specific sense of place.

Façade: The vertical surface of a building set along a frontage line. The elevation is the vertical surface set along any other boundary line. Facades are subject to control by building height, setback lines, recess lines, and transition lines. Elevations are only subject to building height and setback lines.

Setback: The mandatory distance between a frontage line and a facade or a lot line and an elevation

Building height: The defined limit to the vertical extent of a building. The building height should be stated as a number of stories, rather than a prescribed dimension. This prevents the compression of internal ceiling heights. Height may be determined by density and view and not by the requirements of spatial definition, which are addressed by the recess line.

Recess line: A line prescribed for the full width of the facade, above which the facade is set back. The recess line effectively defines the enclosure of public space. Its location is determined by the desired height-to-width ratio of that space, compatibility with the average height of existing buildings, or provision for daylighting at the street level.

Transition line: A line prescribed for the full width of the facade, expressed by a variation of material or by a limited projection such as a cornice or a balcony. The transition line divides the facade, permitting shopfronts and signage to vary over time without destroying the overall composition.

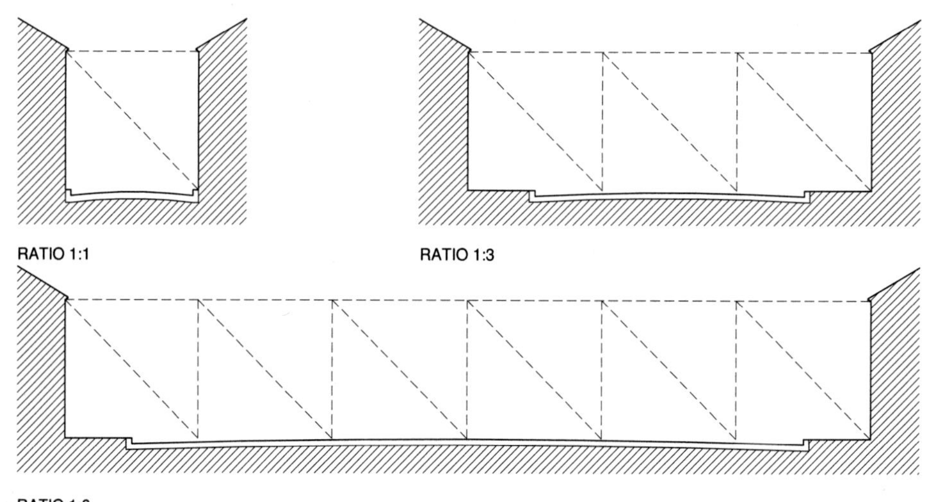

PROPORTIONS OF BUILDING HEIGHT TO PUBLIC SPACE

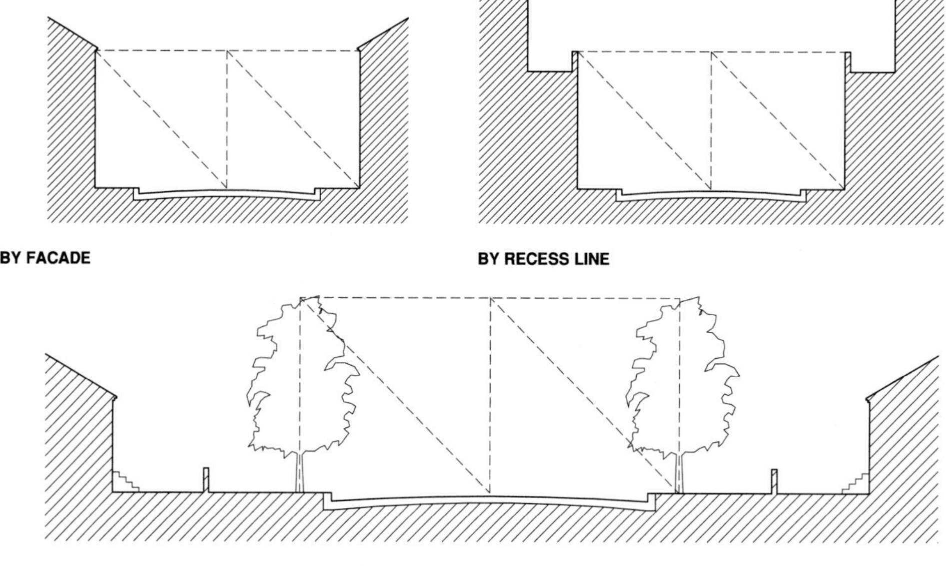

TECHNIQUES OF DELINEATING PUBLIC SPACE

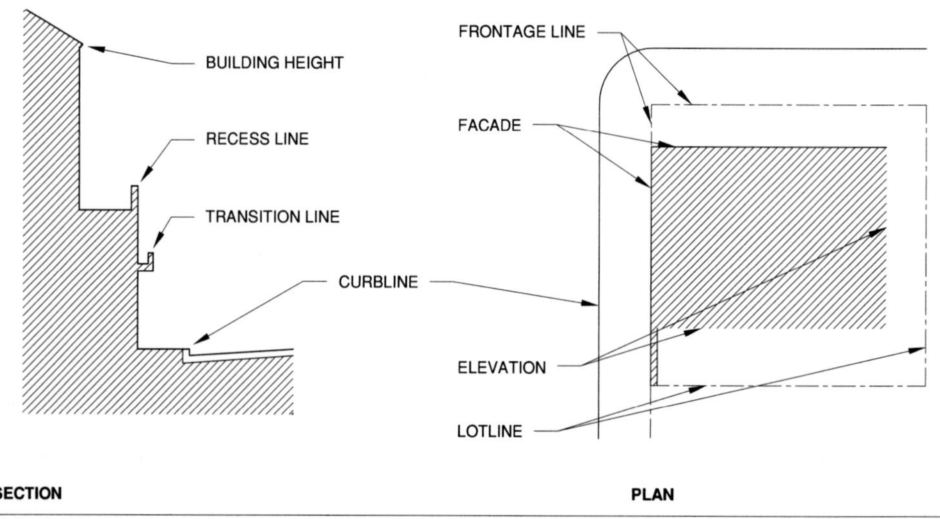

DEFINITIONS

Gary Greenan, Andres Duany, Elizabeth Plater-Zyberk, Kamal Zaharin, Iskandar Shafie; Miami, Florida; The Cintas Foundation

FRONTAGE TYPES

GENERAL

Building type is independent of frontage type. For example, a courtyard building may have an arcade, a shopfront, a stoop, or a porch as its frontage type. Frontages can be ranked from most urban to most rural.

ARCADE

The facade overlaps the sidewalk, while the storefront remains set back. This type is excellent for retail use, but only when the sidewalk is fully absorbed so the pedestrian cannot bypass the arcade. An easement for public use of private property is required.

SHOPFRONT

The facade is aligned directly on the frontage line, with the entrance at grade. This type is conventional for sidewalk retail. It is often equipped with an awning or a porch. A transition line should separate the signage from the facade above. The absence of a setback and elevation from the sidewalk prevents residential use on the ground floor, although it is appropriate above.

STOOP

The facade is aligned directly on the frontage line, with the first floor elevated to achieve some privacy for the windows. This type is suitable for residential uses such as rowhouses and apartment buildings. An easement may be necessary to accommodate the encroaching stoop. This type may be interspersed with the shopfront.

FORECOURT

The facade is set back and replaced by a low wall at the frontage line. The forecourt thus created is suitable for gardens, vehicular drop-offs, and workshop loading and storage. It should be used sparingly and in conjunction with the shopfront and stoop types, as a continuous blind wall is boring and unsafe for pedestrians. Tree canopies within the forecourt should overhang the sidewalk.

DOORYARD

The facade is set back from the frontage line, with an elevated garden or terrace between. This type can effectively buffer residential quarters from the sidewalk, while removing the yard from public use. The terrace, when roofed, is suitable for restaurants and cafes, as the eye level of the sitter is level with that of passersby.

PORCH AND FENCE

With an encroaching habitable porch, the facade is set back substantially from the frontage line. The porch should be within a conversational distance of the sidewalk. A fence at the frontage line marks the boundary of the yard.

FRONT LAWN

The facade is set back substantially from the frontage line. The front lawn this creates should be unfenced and visually continuous with adjacent yards. The ideal is to simulate buildings sitting in a rural landscape. A front porch is usually not appropriate, since no social interaction with the street is possible at such a distance. The large setback can provide a buffer from heavy traffic, so this type is sometimes found on boulevards.

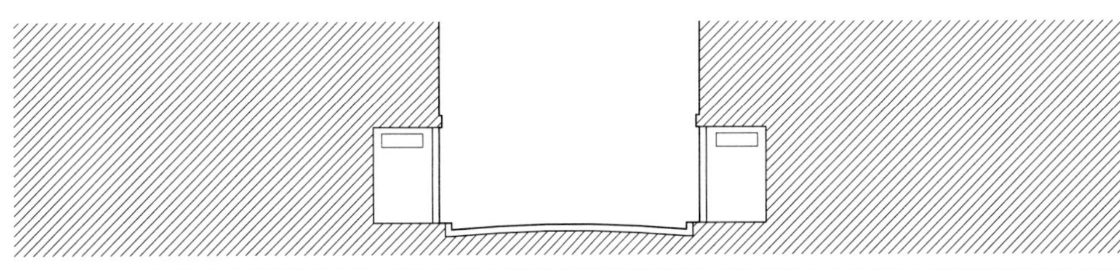

ARCADE

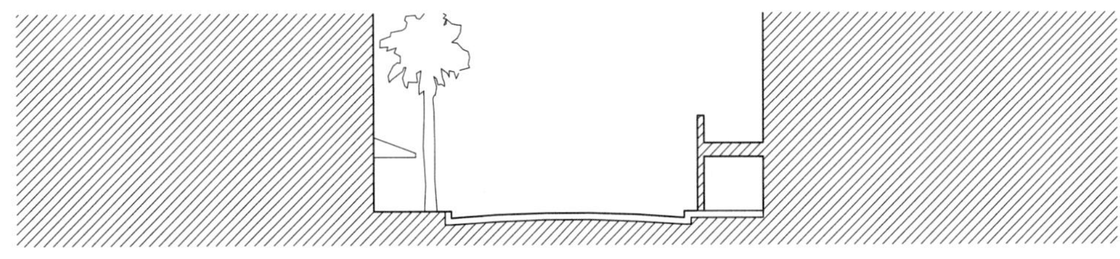

SHOPFRONT

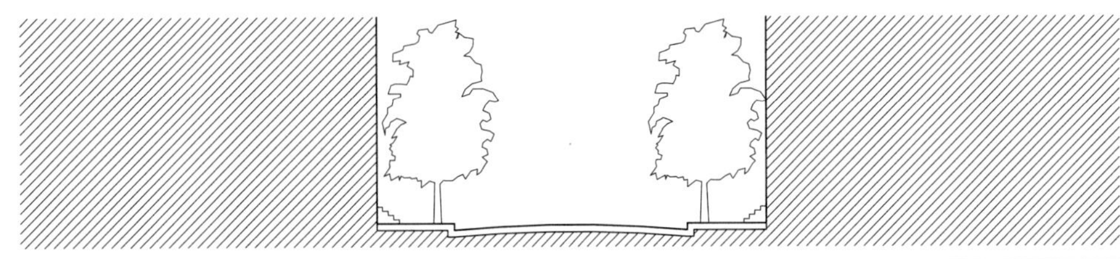

STOOP

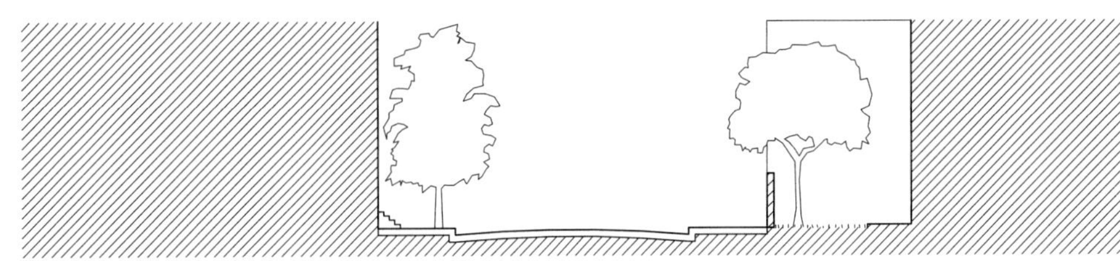

FORECOURT

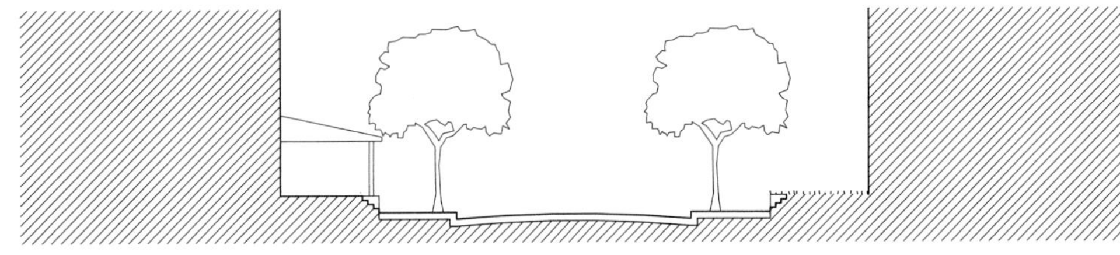

DOORYARD

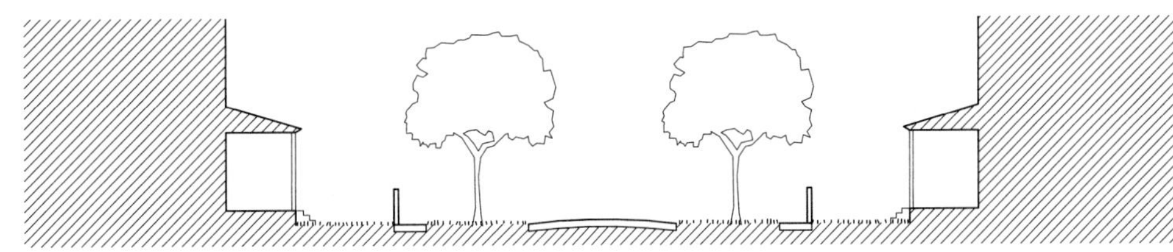

PORCH AND FENCE

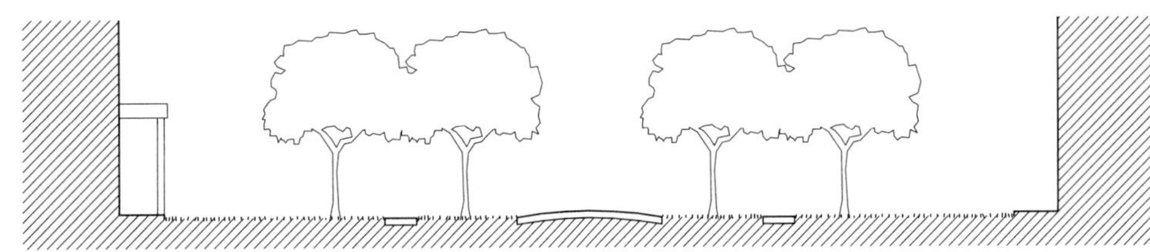

FRONT LAWN

Gary Greenan, Andres Duany, Elizabeth Plater-Zyberk, Kamal Zaharin, Iskandar Shafie, Miami, Florida; The Cintas Foundation

LANDSCAPE TYPES

GENERAL

The urban landscape is a set of interdependent elements that creates a controlled sense of place. It includes thoroughfare type, building type, frontage type, and the form and disposition of landscape.

RURAL ROAD

This type is appropriate for buildings at the edges of the neighborhood and along parks and greenbelts. There is no public planting line. The tree species should be episodic, but in coherent clusters. There are no curbs; the drainage is by open swale. Bicycle paths may be paved in asphalt.

RESIDENTIAL ROAD

This type is appropriate for houses outside of neighborhood centers. Since the frontage usually includes a substantial setback, the tree canopy may be quite wide. The rural aspect may be supported by planting several species in imperfect alignment. Roads are detailed with open swales, and, where possible, drainage is through percolation.

RESIDENTIAL STREET

This type is appropriate for residential buildings at neighborhood and town centers. Trees are in continuous planting strips, since the sidewalk does not require unusual width. Plant a single species of tree in steady alignment. A thin, vertical canopy is necessary to avoid nearby building facades. This type is dimensionally interchangeable with the commercial street type and may alternate in correspondence to the building facade. Streets are detailed with raised curbs and closed storm drainage.

COMMERCIAL STREET

This type is appropriate for commercial buildings at neighborhood and town centers. Trees are confined by individual planting areas, creating a sidewalk of maximum width with areas accommodating street furniture. Plant a single species of tree in steady alignment. Clear trunks and high canopies are necessary to avoid interference with shopfront signage and awnings. Streets are detailed with raised curbs with closed storm drainage.

AVENUE

This type is appropriate for approaches to civic buildings. The general principle is a thoroughfare of limited length, with a substantial planted median. At town centers, the median may be wide enough to hold monuments and even buildings. In residential areas, the median may be planted naturalistically to become a parkway or green.

BOULEVARD

This type is appropriate for high-capacity thoroughfares at neighborhood edges. The detailing is similar to that of a commercial street. The effect of the medians is to segregate the slower traffic and parking activity, at the edges, from through traffic, at the center.

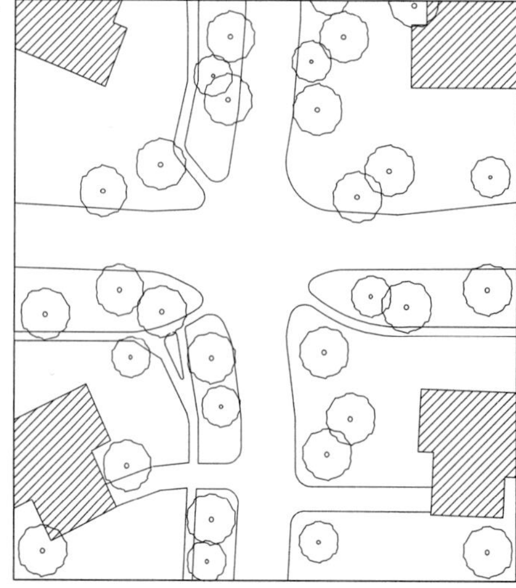

RURAL ROAD

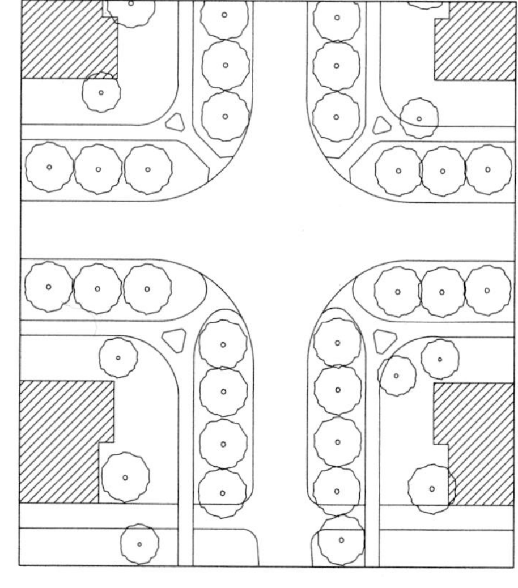

RESIDENTIAL ROAD

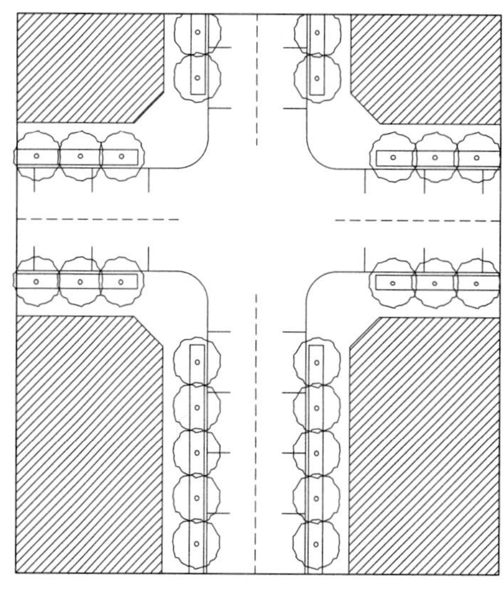

RESIDENTIAL STREET

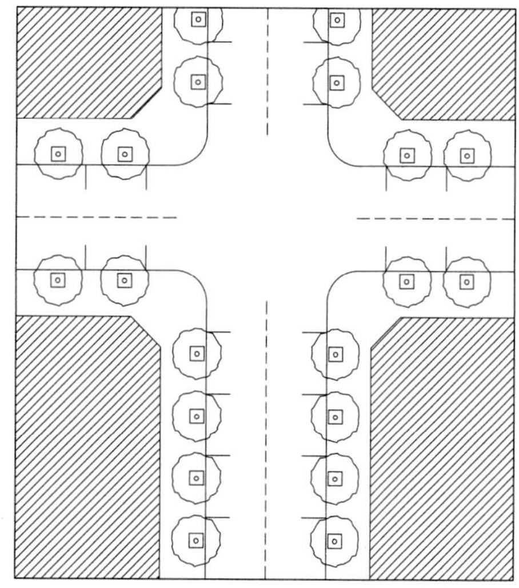

COMMERCIAL STREET

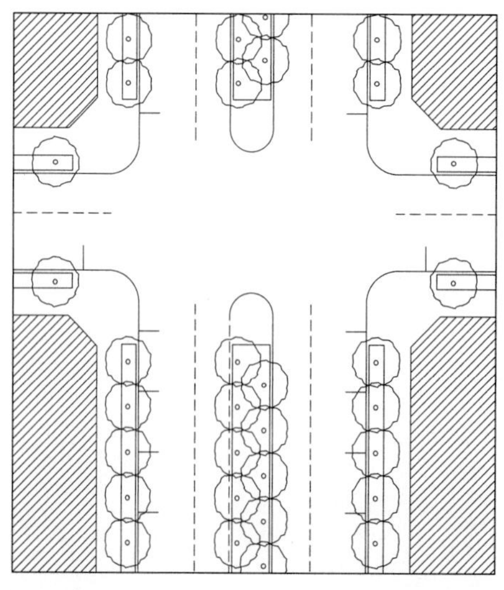

AVENUE

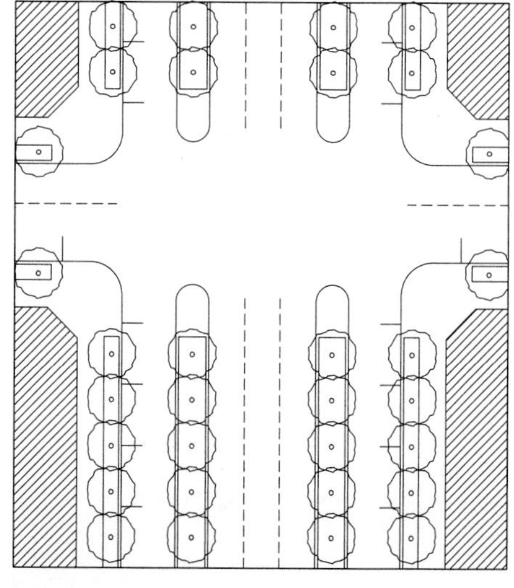

BOULEVARD

Gary Greenan, Andres Duany, Elizabeth Plater-Zyberk, Kamal Zaharin, Iskandar Shafie, Miami, Florida; The Cintas Foundation

TRADITIONAL NEIGHBORHOOD DESIGN

INTRODUCTION

The traditional neighborhood development (TND) ordinance produces compact, mixed-use, pedestrian friendly communities. It can be incorporated in municipal zoning ordinances as an overlay or as a separate district. It is intended to ensure the following conventions:

Traditional neighborhoods share the following characteristics:

- The neighborhood's area is limited to what can be traversed in a 10-minute walk.
- Residences, shops, workplaces, and civic buildings are located in close proximity.
- A hierarchy of streets serves the pedestrian and the automobile equitably.
- Physically defined squares and parks provide places for formal social activity and recreation.
- Private buildings form a clear edge, delineating the street space.
- Civic buildings reinforce the identity of the neighborhood, providing places of assembly for social, cultural, and religious activities.

Traditional neighborhoods pursue certain social objectives:

- To provide the elderly and the young with independence of movement by locating most daily activities within walking distance
- To minimize traffic congestion and limit road construction by reducing the number and length of automobile trips
- To make public transit a viable alternative to the automobile by organizing appropriate building densities
- To help citizens come to know each other and to watch over their collective security by providing public spaces such as streets and squares
- To integrate age and economic classes and form the bonds of an authentic community by providing a full range of housing types and workplaces
- To encourage communal initiatives and support the balanced evolution of society by providing suitable civic buildings

TRADITIONAL NEIGHBORHOOD DESIGN LAND ALLOCATION

SPECIAL DEFINITIONS

Terms used in a TND ordinance may differ in meaning from their use in conventional zoning ordinances:

Artisanal use: Premises used for the manufacture and sale of items that are made employing only handwork and/or table-mounted electrical tools and creating no adverse impact beyond its lot.

Block: The aggregate of lots and alleys circumscribed by public use tracts, generally streets.

Building height: The height measured in stories. Attics and raised basements do not count against building height limitations.

Citizens' association: The organization of owners of lots and buildings associated under articles. The articles shall reference an approved master plan; set standards for building location, construction, and maintenance; provide for maintenance on public tracts; and provide for the construction of new civic buildings by an ongoing special assessment.

Facade: The building wall parallel to a frontage line.

Frontage line: The lot line that coincides with a street tract.

Green edge: A continuous open area surrounding the neighborhood proper. The area shall be preserved in perpetuity as a natural area, golf course, or growing or playing fields, or it shall be subdivided into house lots no smaller than 20 acres each.

Limited lodging: Residential premises providing no more than eight rooms for short-term letting and food services before noon only.

Limited office: Residential premises used for business or professional services, employing no more than four full-time employees, one of whom must be the owner.

Lot: A separately platted portion of land held privately.

Meeting hall: A building designed for public assembly, containing at least one room with an area equivalent to 10 sq ft per dwelling, or 1300 sq ft, whichever is greater.

Neighborhood proper: The built-up area of a TND, including blocks, streets, and squares but excluding green edges.

Outbuilding: A separate building, additional to a principal building, contiguous with the rear lot line, having at most two stories and a maximum habitable area of 450 sq ft. Outbuildings may be residential retail units. Outbuildings are exempt from building cover restrictions or unit counts.

Gary Greenan, Andres Duany, Elizabeth Plater-Zyberk, Kamal Zaharin, Iskandar Shafie; Miami, Florida; The Cintas Foundation

Park: A public tract naturalistically landscaped, not more than 10% paved, and surrounded by lots on no more than 50% of its perimeter.

Prohibited uses: Uses not permitted in the standard zoning ordinance, as well as automatic food, drink, and newspaper vending machines and any commercial use that encourages patrons to remain in their automobiles while receiving goods or services (except service stations).

Shared parking: A parking place where day/night or weekday/holiday schedules allow the use of parking spaces by more than one user, resulting in a 25% reduction of the required spaces.

Square: A public tract, spatially defined by surrounding buildings, with frontage on streets on at least two sides. Commercial uses shall be permitted on all surrounding lots.

Story: A habitable level within a building no more than 14 ft in height from floor to ceiling.

Street lamps: A light standard between 10 and 16 ft in height equipped with an incandescent or metal halide light source.

Street tree: A deciduous tree that resists root pressure and is of proven viability, in the region with no less than 4-in. caliper and 8-ft clear trunk at the time of planting.

Street vista: The view, framed by buildings, at the termination of the axis of a thoroughfare.

Tract: A separately platted portion of land held in common, such as a thoroughfare, a square, or a park.

GUIDELINES FOR TRADITIONAL NEIGHBORHOOD DESIGN

LAND USE	LAND ALLOCATION	LOTS AND BUILDINGS	STREETS AND PARKING
A1.GENERAL: (a) The TND shall be available as an overlay option for land development in all land use and zoning categories except industrial. (b) A TND requires a minimum parcel of 40 contiguous acres and a maximum of 200 acres. Larger parcels shall be developed as multiple neighborhoods with each individually subject to the provisions of the TND.	B1.GENERAL: (a) Similar land use categories face across streets; dissimilar categories abut at rear lot lines. (b) The average perimeter of all blocks within the neighborhood does not exceed 1300 ft. For block faces longer than 500 ft, an alley or pedestrian path provides through access.	C1.GENERAL: (a) All lots share a frontage line with a street or square. (b) The main entrances of all buildings except outbuildings are on a street or square. (c) Stoops, open colonnades, and open porches may encroach into the front setback. (d) The sides of buildings at corner lots are similar to their fronts.	D1.GENERAL: (a) All streets terminate at other streets. (b) Streetlights are provided along all thoroughfares at 35- to 50-ft intervals. (c) On-street parking is allowed on all local streets. (d) Parking lots are located behind or beside building facades. (e) Parking lots and garages are not adjacent to street intersections, civic use lots, or squares and do not occupy lots that terminate a vista. (f) Shared parking reduces local parking requirements.
A2.PUBLIC: (a) Includes streets, squares, parks, playgrounds, and the like. (b) Civic use lots may be placed within tracts designated for public use. (c) Large-scale recreational uses such as golf courses, schoolyards, and multiple game fields are located only at the edge of the neighborhood.	B2.PUBLIC: (a) A minimum of 5% of the neighborhood area or 3 acres (whichever is greater) is permanently allocated to public use. (b) Each neighborhood contains at least one square, not less than one acre in size, close to the center. (c) No portion of the neighborhood is more than 2000 ft from the square. (d) At least half the perimeter of squares, parks, and waterfronts face streets. (e) At least a quarter of the perimeter of waterfronts, golf courses, greenbelts, and other natural amenities face streets.	C2.PUBLIC: (a) Balconies and open colonnades are permitted to encroach up to 5 ft into thoroughfares and other tracts. Such encroachments shall be protected by easements.	D2.PUBLIC: (a) Parking shared between public and private uses is encouraged.
A3.CIVIC: (a) Contains community buildings such as meeting halls, libraries, post offices, schools, child care centers, clubhouses, religious buildings, recreational facilities, museums, cultural societies, visual and performance arts buildings, municipal buildings, and the like.	B3.CIVIC: (a) A minimum of 2% of the neighborhood area is reserved for civic use. (b) Civic lots are within or adjacent to squares and parks or on a lot terminating a street vista. (c) Each neighborhood has a minimum of one meeting hall and one child care facility.	C3.CIVIC: (a) Civic buildings have no height or setback limitations.	D3.CIVIC: (a) The majority (75%) of the off-street parking for civic structures is behind the buildings.
A4.COMMERCIAL: (a) Contains buildings primarily for business uses, such as retail, entertainment, restaurant, club, office, residential, lodging, artisanal, medical, etc. (b) At least 25% of the building area is designated for residential use.	B4.COMMERCIAL: (a) A minimum of 2% and a maximum of 30% of the neighborhood area is designated for commercial use. (b) Commercial lots have a maximum frontage of 32 ft. (c) A maximum of four lots may be consolidated to construct a single building.	C4.COMMERCIAL: (a) Buildings are built out to a minimum of 80% of their frontage at the frontage line. (b) Buildings have no required setback from the side lot lines. (c) Buildings do not exceed four stories in height and are no less than two stories in height. When fronting a square, buildings are no less than three stories in height. (d) Building coverage does not exceed 70% of the lot area.	D4.COMMERCIAL: (a) Lots front streets no more than four lanes wide; parallel parking and sidewalks minimum 15 ft wide. (b) Rear lot lines coincide with an alley. (c) Streets have curbs with a radius at intersections of 5 to 15 ft. (d) Street trees are aligned on both sides of the street at 35- to 50-ft intervals; when open colonnades are provided, no street trees are necessary. (e) The majority (75%) of the off-street parking is behind the buildings.
A5.HIGH RESIDENTIAL: (a) Contains buildings for residential use, limited office use, cafes, retail, lodging, and artisanal uses. (b) All of the building area above the ground floor is designated for residential use. (c) Outbuildings are permitted.	B5.HIGH RESIDENTIAL: (a) A minimum of 20% and a maximum of 60% of the neighborhood area is designated for high residential use. (b) High residential lots have a maximum frontage of 16 ft. (c) A maximum of eight lots may be consolidated for the purpose of constructing a single building containing one or more residential units.	C5.HIGH RESIDENTIAL: (a) Buildings are built out to a minimum of 70% of their frontage, at a continuous alignment no further than 10 ft from the frontage line. (b) Buildings have no required setback from side lot lines. (c) Buildings do not exceed four stories in height and, when fronting a square, are no less than three stories in height. (d) Building coverage does not exceed 50% of the lot area.	D5.HIGH RESIDENTIAL: (a) Lots front streets no more than three lanes wide, with parallel parking and sidewalks minimum 15 ft wide. (b) Street trees are aligned both sides of streets at 35- to 50-ft intervals. (c) Rear lot lines coincide with an alley. (d) All off-street parking is behind the buildings.
A6.LOW RESIDENTIAL: (a) Contains buildings for residential uses, including art studios, limited offices, limited lodging, and the like. (b) All of the building area above the ground floor is designated for residential use. (c) Outbuildings are permitted.	B6.LOW RESIDENTIAL: (a) A maximum of 60% of the neighborhood area is designated for low residential use. (b) Lots have a maximum frontage of 64 ft. (c) A maximum of two lots may be consolidated for the purpose of constructing a single building.	C6.LOW RESIDENTIAL: (a) Buildings are built out to a minimum of 40% of their frontage at a continuous alignment no further than 30 ft from the frontage line. (b) Side setbacks are no less than 10 ft in aggregate and may be allocated to one side. Buildings are set back no less than 20 ft from the rear lot line. Outbuildings have no required setback. (c) Buildings do not exceed three stories in height. (d) Building coverage does not exceed 50% of the lot area.	D6.LOW RESIDENTIAL: (a) Lots front roads no more than two lanes wide with optional parallel parking and sidewalks minimum 6 ft wide. (b) Street trees are installed on both sides of the street at no more than 50-ft intervals. (c) Rear lot lines may coincide with an alley. (d) All off-street parking is to the side or rear of the building. Where access is through the frontage, garages or carports are located a minimum of 20 ft behind the facade.
A7.WORKPLACE: (a) Contains buildings for uses such as corporate office, light industry, artisanal, warehousing, automotive, and the like.	B7.WORKPLACE: (a) A minimum of 2% and a maximum of 30% of the neighborhood area is designated for workplace use. (b) Lots have a maximum frontage of 64 ft. (c) A maximum of four lots may be consolidated for the purpose of constructing a single building.	C7.WORKPLACE: (a) Buildings are built out to a minimum of 70% of their frontage at a continuous alignment no further than 10 ft from the frontage line. (b) Buildings have no setbacks from side or rear lot lines. (c) Buildings do not exceed three stories in height. (d) Building coverage does not exceed 70% of the lot area. (e) Lots are separated from other use types at the side and rear lot lines by a wall of between 3 and 8 ft high.	D7.WORKPLACE: (a) Lots front streets as wide as necessary to accommodate truck traffic. (b) Street trees are aligned on both sides of the street at 35- to 50-ft intervals. (c) Rear lot lines coincide with an alley. (d) All off-street parking is to the side or rear of the building.

Gary Greenan, Andres Duany, Elizabeth Plater-Zyberk, Kamal Zaharin, Iskandar Shafie; Miami, Florida; The Cintas Foundation

SITE PLANNING FOR FIRE PROTECTION

Fire apparatus (i.e., pumpers, ladder trucks, tankers) should have unobstructed access to buildings. Check with local fire department for apparatus turning radius (R), length (L), and other operating characteristics. Support systems embedded in lawn areas adjacent to the building are acceptable.

RESTRICTED AREAS

Buildings constructed near cliffs or steep slopes should not restrict access by fire apparatus to only one side of the building. Grades greater than 10% make operation of fire apparatus difficult and dangerous. Avoid parking decks abutted to buildings. Consider pedestrian bridge overs instead.

FIRE DEPARTMENT RESPONSE TIME FACTOR

Site planning factors that determine response time are street accessibility (curbs, radii, bollards, T-turns, cul-de-sac, street and site slopes, street furniture and architectural obstructions, driveway widths), accessibility for firefighting (fire hydrant and standpipe connection layouts, outdoor lighting, identifying signs), and location (city, town, village, farm). Check with local codes, fire codes, and fire department for area regulations.

Streets that are properly lighted enable fire fighters to locate hydrants quickly and to position apparatus at night. Avoid layouts that place hydrants and standpipe connections in shadows. In some situations, lighting fixtures can be integrated into exterior of buildings. All buildings should have a street address number on or near the main entrance.

Gravity tanks can provide a reliable source of pressure to building standpipe or sprinkler systems. Available pressure head increased by 0.434 psi/ft increase of water above tank discharge outlet. Tank capacity in gallons depends on fire hazard, water supply, and other factors. Tanks require periodic maintenance and protection against freezing during cold weather. Locations subject to seismic forces or high winds require special consideration. Gravity tanks also can be integrated within building design.

Bollards used for traffic control and fences for security should allow sufficient open road width (W) for access by fire apparatus. Bollards and gates can be secured by standard fire department keyed locks (check with department having jurisdiction).

Utility poles can obstruct use of aerial ladders for rescue and fire suppression operations. Kiosks, outdoor sculpture, fountains, newspaper boxes, and the like can also seriously impede fire fighting operations. Wide podium bases can prevent ladder access to the upper stories of buildings. Canopies and other nonstructural building components can also prevent fire apparatus operations close to buildings.

Locate fire hydrants at street intersections and at intermediate points along roads so that spacing between hydrants does not exceed capability of local fire jurisdiction. Hydrants should be placed 2 to 10 ft from curb lines. Siamese connections for standpipes should be visible, marked conspicuously, and be adjacent to the principal vehicle access point to allow rapid connection by fire fighters to the pumping engine.

Man-made and natural on-site lakes are used for private fire fighting in suburbs, on farms, and at resorts. A piped supply system to a dry hydrant is preferred for its quantity, flexibility, better maintenance, and accessibility. Man-made lakes with reservoir liners can be berm-supported or sunk in the ground. Lakes and ponds are natural water supplies dependent on the environment. See local codes, fire codes, and fire departments for on-site lake regulations.

Long dead ends (greater than 150 ft) can cause time consuming, hazardous backup maneuvers. Use t-turns, culs-de-sac, and curved driveway layouts to allow unimpeded access to buildings.

For full extension of aerial ladders at a safe climbing angle (q), sufficient driveway width (W) is required. Estimate the required width in feet by: $W = (H-6)\cot\theta + 4$, where preferred climbing angles are 60 to 80°. Check with local fire department for aerial apparatus operating requirements, including width of aerial device with stabilizing outriggers extended.

Fire hose connections should be at least 15 in. above grade. Do not bury hydrants or locate them behind shrubs or other visual barriers. Avoid locations where runoff water and snow can accumulate. Bollards and fences used to protect hydrants from vehicular traffic must not obstruct fire fighters' access to hose connections. "Steamer" connection should usually face the side of arriving fire apparatus.

Standard diamond symbols provide information fire fighters need to avoid injury from hazardous building contents. Zero (0) is the lowest degree of hazard; 4 is highest. Locate symbols near building entrances. (Refer to "Identification of the Fire Hazards of Materials," NFPA No. 704, available from the National Fire Protection Association.)

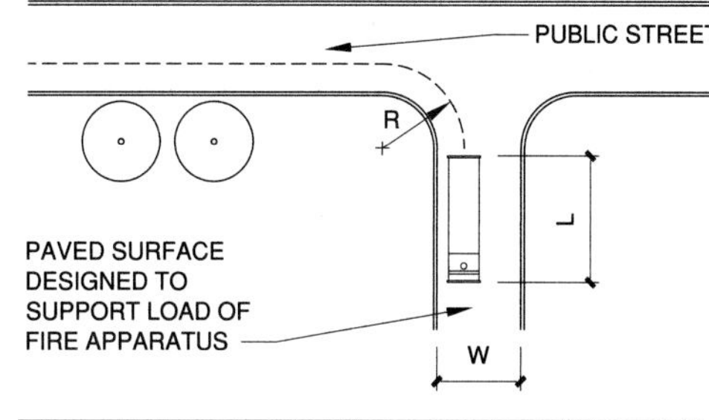

FIRE APPARATUS ACCESS

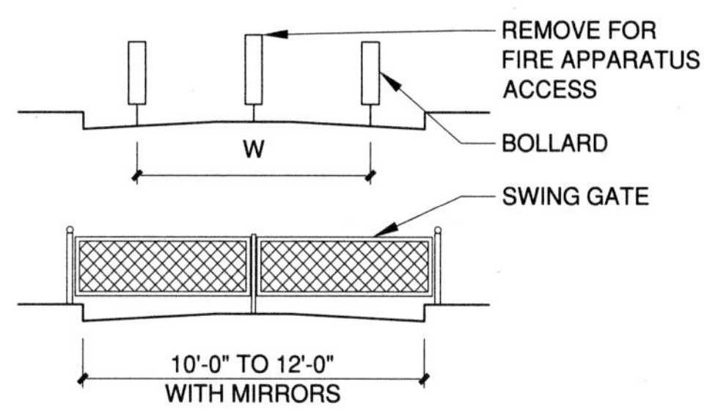

ACCESS OBSTRUCTIONS

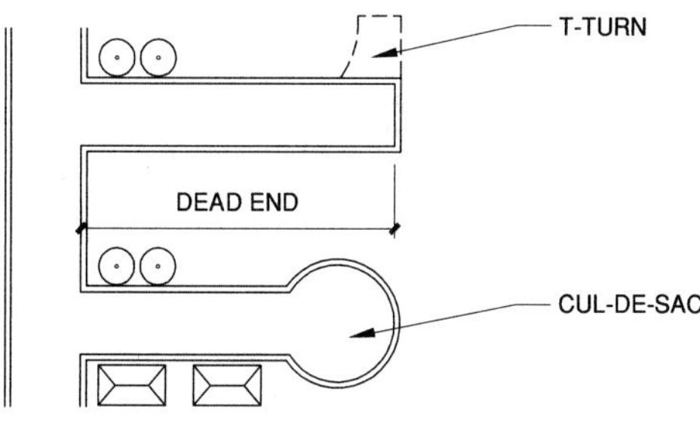

DRIVEWAY LAYOUTS

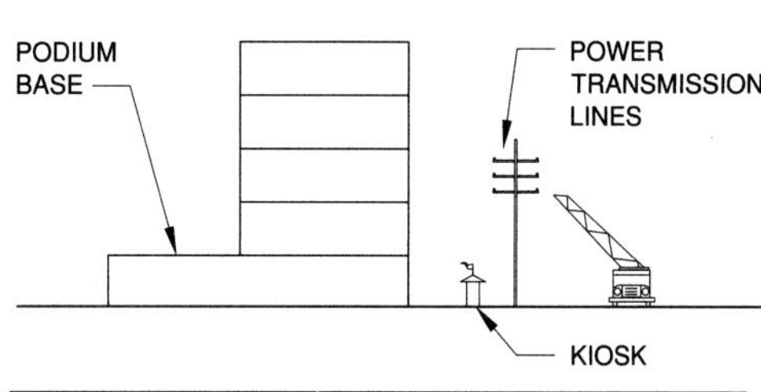

STREET FURNITURE AND ARCHITECTURAL OBSTRUCTIONS

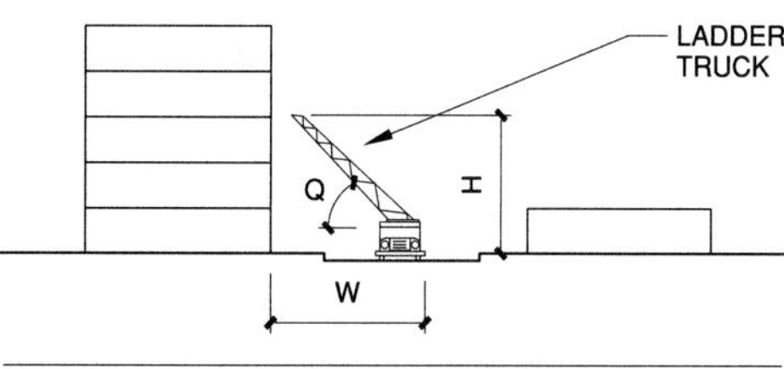

DRIVEWAY WIDTHS

D. L. Collins and M. David Egan, P. E., College of Architecture, Clemson University, Clemson, South Carolina; Nicholas A. Phillips, AIA, Lockwood Greene, New York, New York

RESIDENTIAL SITE PLANNING

GENERAL

Residential site planning requires balance among a large number of complex and often competing priorities.

ORIENTATION

No unit should be without sun for at least part of a winter day; south-facing units are premium. Prevailing winds, both regional and local, should be studied so that no building is entirely masked. At the same time, harsh winds should be buffered by plantings, and if buildings are differentiated by side, bedroom and service sides should face the harsh wind.

USE AND ENHANCEMENT OF NATURAL AMENITIES

Too frequently, housing projects are named for amenities that are destroyed during development. Promontories, mature trees, and water features should be incorporated into the design and, if possible, enhanced.

PROVISION FOR VIEWS

Spectacular views can drive the design of a housing project, but every project should strive to provide reasonable views from all units. Although no unit should have a parking area as its only view, many people enjoy views of streets and roadways. Views of green space are important, especially in urban projects.

CONTEXT

The designer must strive to identify valuable off-site resources and influences so that they are recognized in the design.

Such resources include the following:

- Geometries and alignments
- Slopes and soils
- Views of singular objects and natural amenities
- Recreational facilities
- Topography and drainage
- Surrounding and adjoining uses
- Available infrastructure
- Market and location

CLEAR DELINEATION OF PRIVATE AND PUBLIC AREAS

Beyond unit design considerations, the site should be organized so that all territory can be clearly allocated to either private custody or public care and maintenance. It is frequently desirable for each unit to control some private open space. However, in higher density developments such space is often limited or filled in unique ways.

REGULATORY REQUIREMENTS

Land available for housing and related uses may face restrictions, including the following:

- Rights of way for future uses
- Area required for storm water management and sediment control
- Mandated unusable areas between projects (called buffers)
- Building restriction lines: setbacks, build-to lines, height limits, viewsheds, watersheds, separations, rights of way, easements
- Roadways and parking areas
- Protection of environmentally sensitive and natural resource areas such as forests, streams, and animal habitats

DENSITY AND BUILDING TYPES

These factors are the most critical to the developed character of the site and are proscribed by zoning and by developer preference—as informed by the architect and others. Zoning density is expressed numerically along with limitations that are often intended to suggest unit type. But any prescribed density can be reached by combining building types with associated parking arrangements. The permitted density may ultimately be reduced through restrictions of various sorts and is rarely achievable on small or irregular sites.

UNITY AND VARIETY

In site design, monotony and excessive repetition are as undesirable as meaningless variation, which can be disorienting and appear chaotic.

EMERGENCY ACCESS

Size and turning radius of emergency equipment, especially fire engines, can mandate street width, turning radius, and access patterns. Access to buildings becomes an issue at higher densities; installation of sprinkler systems can often balance equipment access around buildings. Always consult the fire marshal in the early stages of design.

ACCESS

Although singular access is frequently desired for marketing and control, redundant access from existing automotive and pedestrian networks provides choice and convenience while reducing concentrations of traffic.

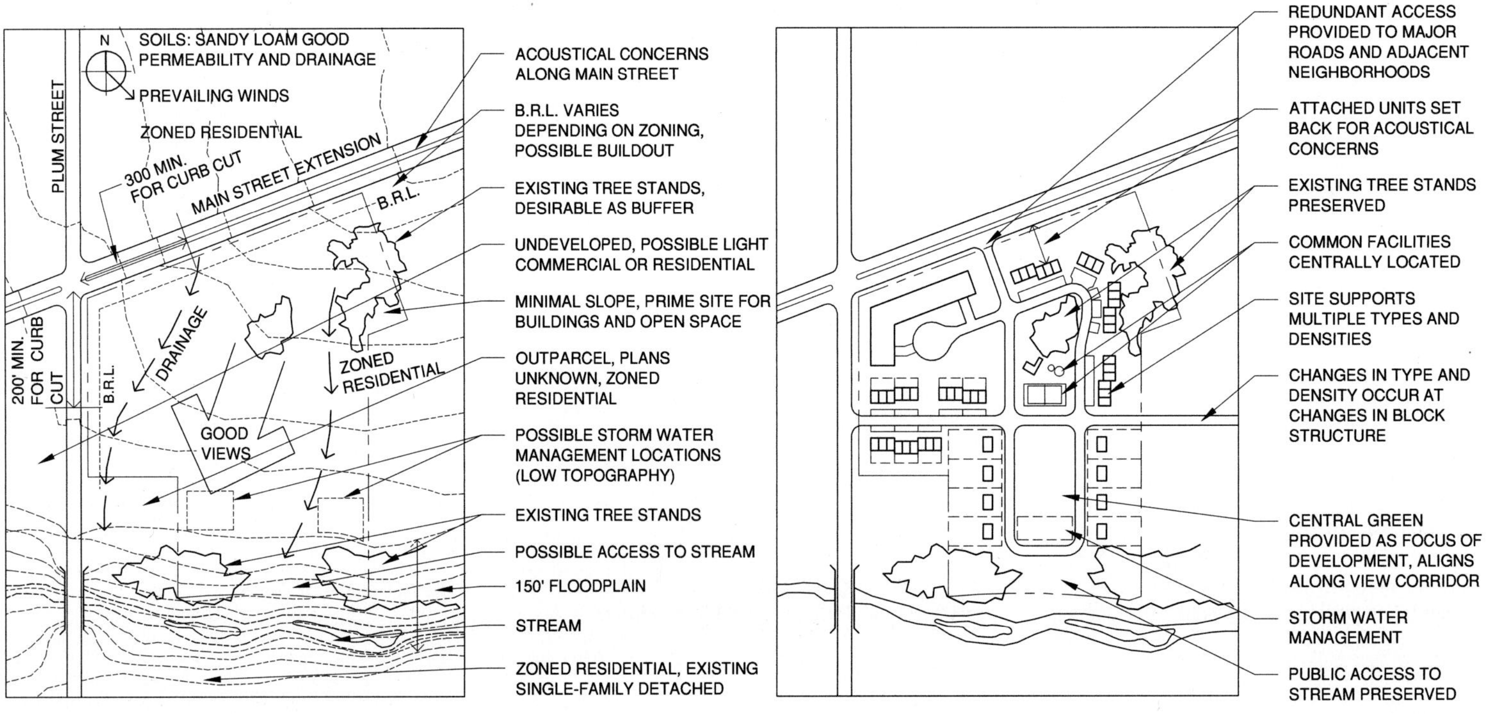

SITE ANALYSIS AND SCHEMATIC SITE PLAN

Ralph Bennett; Bennett Frank McCarthy Architects, Inc., Silver Spring, Maryland

RESIDENTIAL DENSITY

GENERAL

Numerical definition of density is the most important planning index in housing but it can also be the most misleading. Density numbers frequently become inflammatory in planning debates, so it is important that the architect provide specific images of the actual appearance of planned settlements.

Density appears in two forms: gross and net. Gross density is the index applied to large areas—15 to 20 acres or more—and includes private as well as public improvements such as roads, schools, parks, and residentially oriented retail uses.

Net density is used in relation to project-sized areas—smaller than 15 to 20 acres—and consists of the number of proposed dwelling units divided by the site area. Net density is usually expressed in acres and includes access drives, parking areas, common and buffer areas, and community facilities.

FACTORS AFFECTING DENSITY

- Dwelling unit size and arrangement
- Parking (on grade, in garages, in units, structured in large groups)
- Passive and active open space
- Land use restrictions such as buffers, easements, and setbacks
- Land price (owner's objectives are ultimately formed by this factor, in conjunction with market projections)

TYPICAL DENSITIES

Single-family detached houses: The density in developments of this type is generally 6 dwelling units or fewer per acre. In the example illustrated, the density is 4.5 dwelling units per acre, with on-site parking but no garages and 7,500-sq-ft lots.

Single-family attached town houses (parking on grade): The density in a development of this type is up to 14 dwelling units per acre.

Single-family attached town houses with garage: Up to 20 dwelling units per acre will fit in a development of this sort.

Two-story attached houses: With carports, these houses are designed at a density of around 10 units per acre.

Garden apartments: Parking on grade is provided in a garden apartment complex, which contains up to 18 dwelling units per acre. In the example shown, each apartment building has 36 units, for a density of 18 units per acre.

Walk-up apartments: Built over one parking level, a walk-up apartment complex could accommodate up to 30 dwelling units per acre.

Elevator buildings: Elevator buildings with structured parking can be built at a density of up to 100 dwelling units per acre. The example shown is a double-loaded corridor slab building with 200 units. With surface parking, it offers a density of 45 units per acre.

Mixed neighborhoods: A mixed neighborhood encompasses a variety of dwelling types and, correspondingly, a variety of housing unit densities. The example shown includes an 8-unit walk-up apartment building on a 16,000-sq-ft lot, with a density of 16 units per acre, and single-family detached houses with garages on 8,000-sq-ft lots, with a density of 4 units per acre. The overall density in this example is 6.4 units per acre.

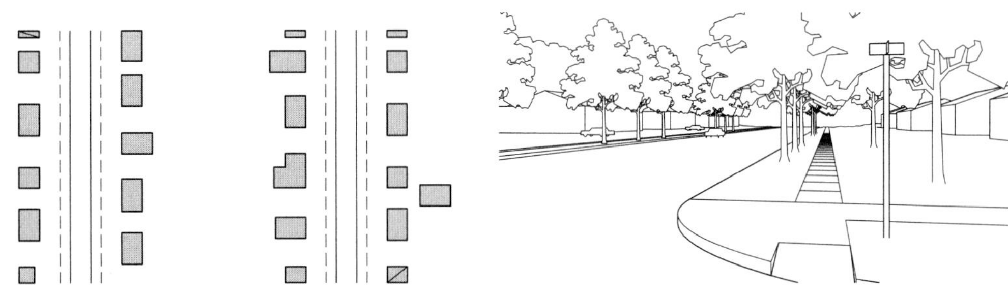

SINGLE-FAMILY DETACHED HOUSES

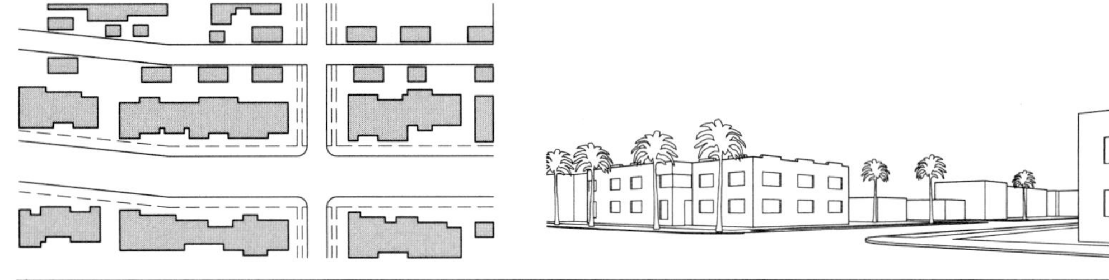

TWO-STORY ATTACHED HOUSES

GARDEN APARTMENTS (THREE-STORY WALK-UP BACK-TO-BACK)

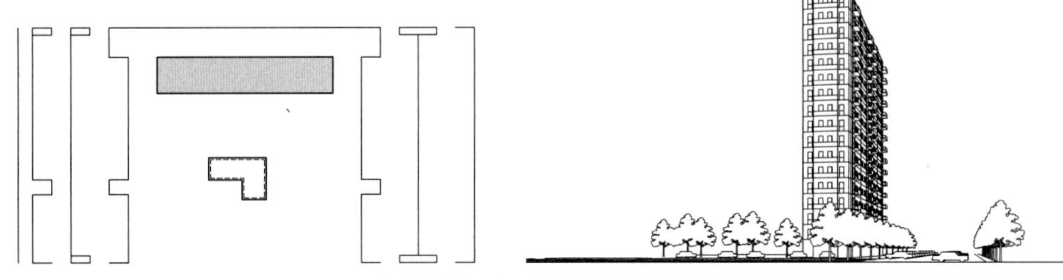

ELEVATOR BUILDING

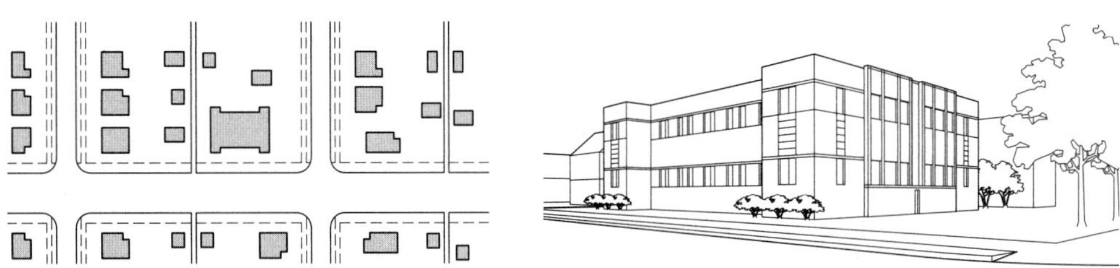

MIXED NEIGHBORHOOD

Ralph Bennett; Bennett Frank McCarthy Architects, Inc., Silver Spring, Maryland

SINGLE-FAMILY DETACHED HOUSING

SITE PLAN CONSIDERATIONS

Access

- Where possible, access should connect and align with existing systems.
- Marketing and security considerations frequently dictate single access, but redundant circulation gives choice and improved service.

Pedestrian Circulation

- Rarely provided at lower densities, pedestrian access is essential at higher densities.
- Pedestrian walkways usually parallel streets.
- Connections to mass transit are appropriate.

Parking

- Parking arrangements have a significant impact on density and appearance.
- On-street parking for guests is desirable at lower densities and essential at higher densities.

Relation To Topography

- ADA and subdivision regulations dictate street and walk grades and mandate site reformation at all but the lowest densities.

Service

- Trash pickup, mail service, and deliveries depend on street access to individual units.
- Fire apparatus usually dictates road standards.

TECHNOLOGY

Structure

- Typically wood frame.
- Fire separation is required for incorporated parking (garage).

Mechanical

- Air, water.
- Oil, gas heat, or heat pump.
- Compression refrigeration or heat pump cooling.
- Exterior condenser for heat pump or air-conditioning. This type has greatest flexibility for solar and other alternative energy systems.
- Sprinklers are required in some jurisdictions.

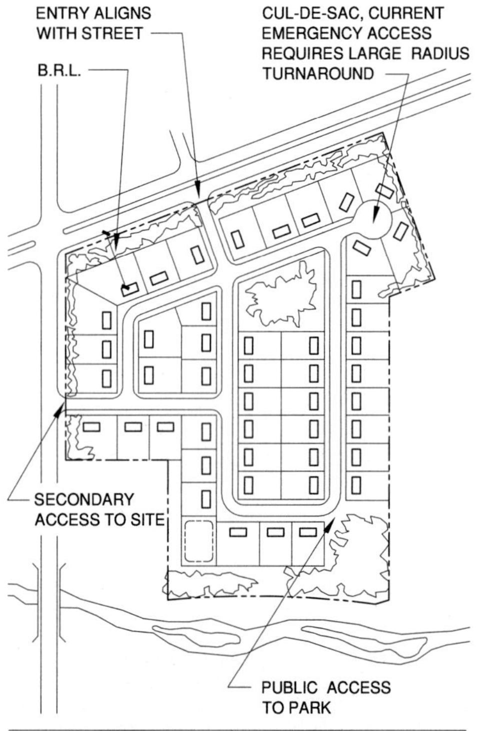

STREET ACCESS

DETACHED HOUSING CHARACTERISTICS

TYPE	LOT SIZE (SQ FT)	DENSITY RANGE (D.U./ACRE)*	CHARACTERISTICS
Large lot	20,000 and up	0.5 – 5	Flexibility in orientation. Building restriction lines not significant. Expansion simple. Site character can be exploited.
Small lot	5000 - 10,000	4 – 8	Aggregation becomes important. Community planning important. Services important (fire, mail, rubbish). Pedestrian circulation possible and required. Urban design principles apply. Building restriction lines become important. Public sewer and water needed. Clear delineation between public and private space needed.
Zero lot	3000 - 5000	8 – 11.5	Eliminates one sidelot setback. Shallower lots possible. Other side yard usable as private space. Windows on property line reduced or eliminated.
Z-lot	3000 - 5000	8 – 13	Similar to zero lot. Allows more flexible allocation of land. Lot line views over neighboring ownership must be avoided.
Alternating-width lots	3000 - 5000	8 – 11.5	Gives variety along street.

D.U.—Dwelling units

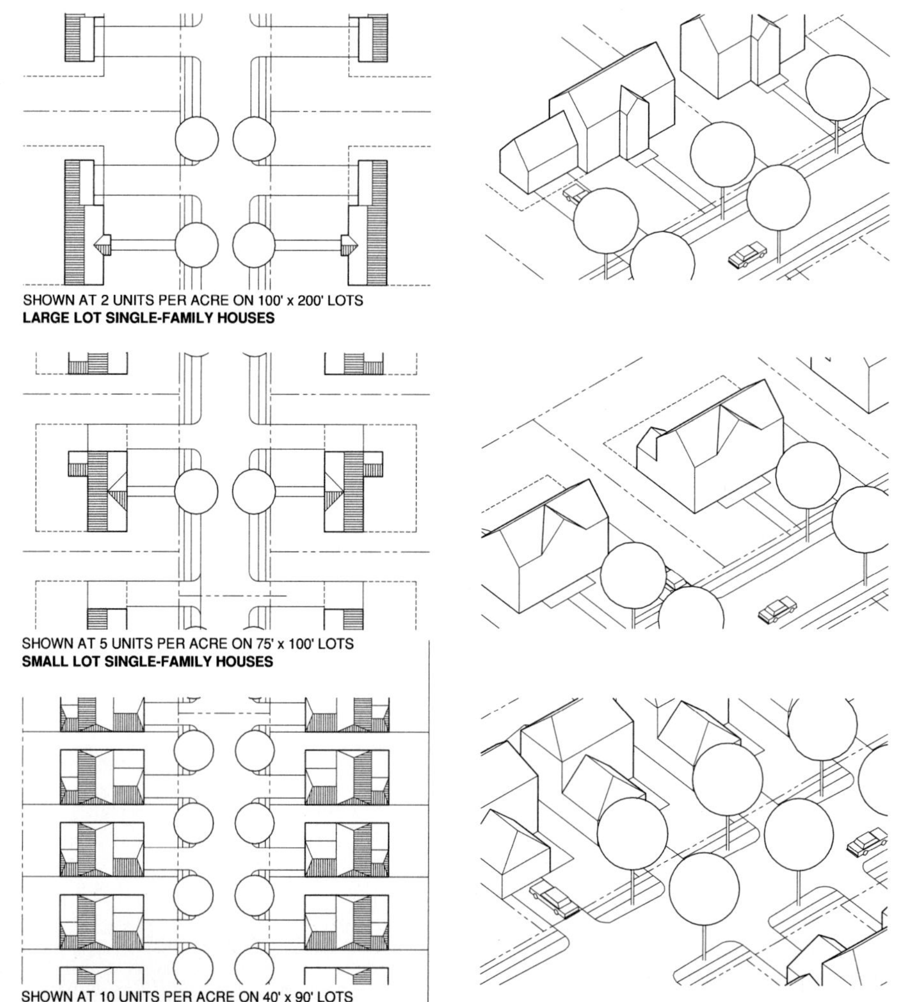

DENSITY CONFIGURATIONS

Ralph Bennett; Bennett Frank McCarthy Architects, Inc., Silver Spring, Maryland

SINGLE-FAMILY ATTACHED HOUSING

SITE PLAN CONSIDERATIONS

Access

- Where possible, should connect and align with existing systems.
- Many arrangements are possible, including alleys, on-site parking, pooled parking and on-street parking.

Pedestrian Circulation

- Necessary to connect dwellings to common facilities and off-site facilities.
- Usually parallels streets.

Parking

- Has significant impact on density and appearance.
- If not pooled, on-street essential for guests and overflow.

Relation To Topography

- ADA, Fair Housing, and subdivision regulations dictate street and walk grades and mandate site reformation at all but the lowest densities.

Service

- Trash pickup, mail service, and deliveries rely on access from street to individual units.
- Fire apparatus usually dictates road standards.

MASSING

Variety and richness can be achieved by massing buildings so that individual units are not diagrammatically identifiable. Scale is given by secondary elements, room sized or smaller. Basic combinations are manipulated to produce complex unit configurations; the resulting composition is very different from basic types.

TECHNOLOGY

Structure

- Typically wood frame.
- Gypsum board walls between units (party walls), 2-hour rating. Some jurisdictions require masonry.
- Parking must have rated separation if sharing wall or ceiling with unit.

Mechanical

- Air, gas heat, electric baseboard heat, or heat pump.
- Compression refrigeration or heat pump cooling.
- Exterior condenser for heat pump or air-conditioning.
- Sprinklers required in many jurisdictions.

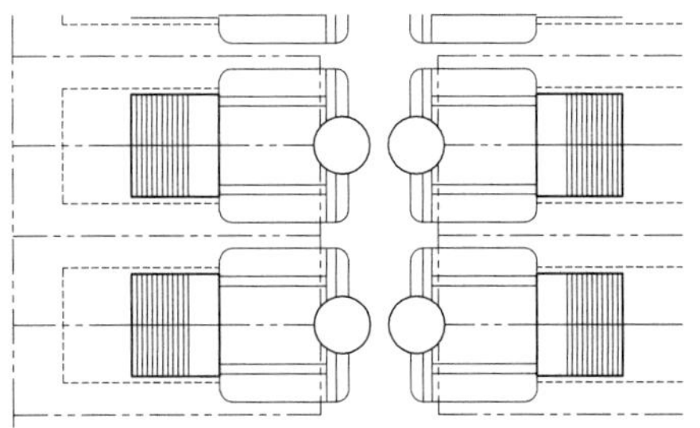

SHOWN AT 9 DWELLING UNITS PER ACRE
DUPLEX HOUSES

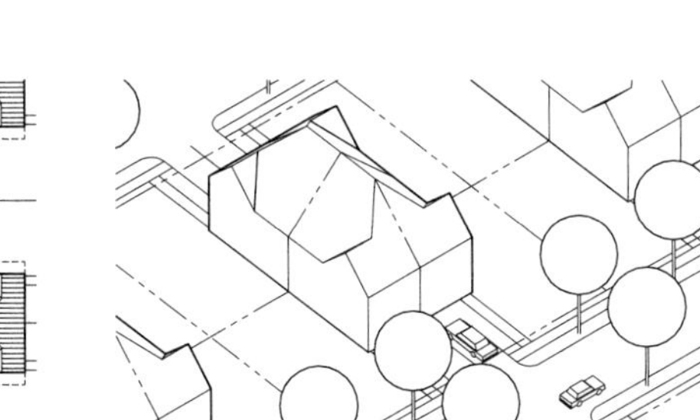

SHOWN AT 10 DWELLING UNITS PER ACRE
FOURPLEX HOUSES

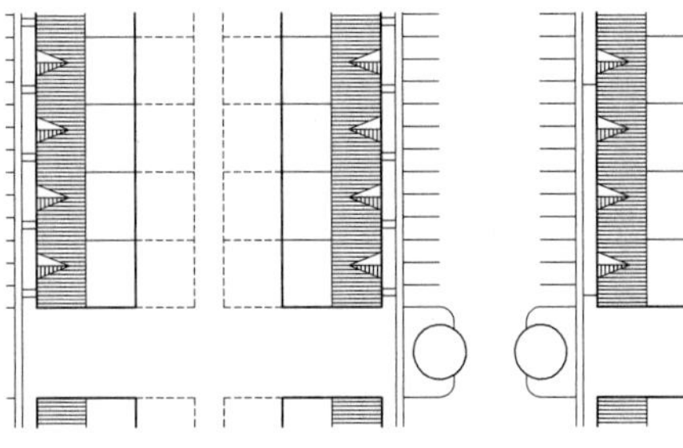

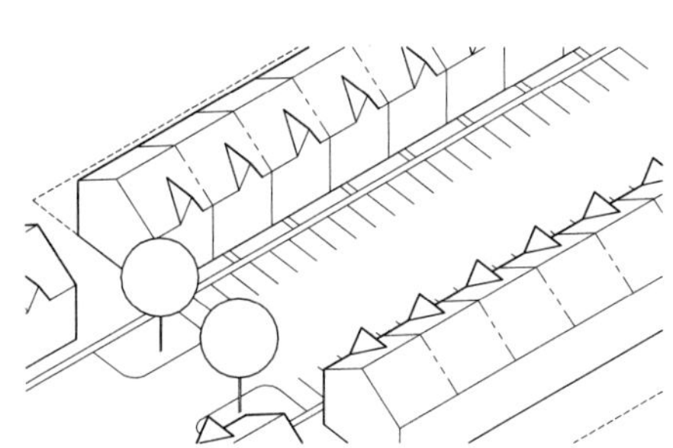

SHOWN AT 13 DWELLING UNITS PER ACRE
ATTACHED HOUSES (TOWN HOUSES)

DENSITY CONFIGURATIONS

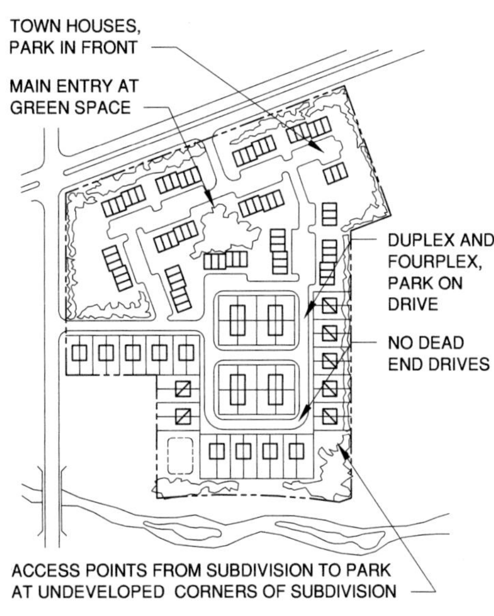

STREET ACCESS

ATTACHED HOUSING CHARACTERISTICS

TYPE	LOT SIZE (SQ FT)	DENSITY RANGE (D.U./ACRE)*	CHARACTERISTICS
Duplex	3000 – 5000	8 – 10	Allows grouping of parking, access. Side yard can be used. Houses have three exposures.
Fourplex	2000 – 3000	10 – 15	Houses have two exposures. High level of privacy possible. Masses as larger building.
Townhouse	1000 – 1500	12 – 22	Urban type exported. Public/private clearly delineated. Maximum flexibility for minimum surface. Makes satisfactory streets.

**D.U.—Dwelling units*

Ralph Bennett; Bennett Frank McCarthy Architects, Inc., Silver Spring, Maryland

CONTEXT-SENSITIVE SOLUTIONS

INTRODUCTION

Roads are critical to the health, safety, and welfare of society. The people who plan, design, construct, operate, and maintain our nation's roadway network determine—to a major extent—the character of our urban, rural, and wilderness landscapes and the experiences people have within these landscapes. It is essential, therefore, that landscape architects understand the principles of roadway design and how roadways can be thoughtfully integrated into the landscape. This thoughtful process has been labeled context-sensitive solutions (CSS).

Not only have landscape architects been practicing CSS for decades, in many respects, it is the profession of landscape architecture that created CSS. The history of our country's parkways, and how these innovative facilities became the precursors of the modern freeway with their controlled-access mainlines, grade-separated crossings and interchanges, architecturally handsome retaining walls, fences, and bridges, and beautifully landscaped rest areas, is a story well-known to most landscape architects and transportation historians (Newton, 1971; Jolley, 1987; Grese, 1992; McClelland, 1998).

Today, landscape architects participate, usually as members of an interdisciplinary team, in planning, designing, construction, operating, and maintaining our nation's roadway network, from local streets to major interstate highways. How a road fits the landscape and the communities it serves continues to be a domain of landscape architecture.

CONTEXTUAL ISSUES

In general, landscape architects are concerned with two aspects of roadways: (1) how roads are experienced by the traveler and (2) how roads are experienced by the neighbors. The needs of travelers and neighbors sometimes contradict each other, so developing a solution that satisfies both constituencies requires creativity and a process of open communication with all parties.

Many of the issues concerning landscape architects revolve primarily around visual quality. But landscape architects are concerned with more than aesthetic treatments; they are equally concerned with other issues, including (but not limited to):

- *Environmental issues*, such as impacts to water quality, vegetation, wildlife habitat, and historic properties
- *Social issues*, such as impacts to community cohesion, economic development, and crime prevention
- *Transportation issues*, such as impacts to equitable access and mobility, pedestrian and bicyclist safety, highway geometrics, and interchange and intersection design

In particular, landscape architects—perhaps more than other professionals on the transportation development team—are interested in resolving all of the issues by taking an integrated approach, one that solves transportation issues but not at the expense of environmental quality or a community's quality of life.

STAKEHOLDER INVOLVEMENT KEY

Context-sensitive solutions is premised on a few fundamental beliefs and corresponding methods. The central and defining belief is that engaging all stakeholders is essential to the successful development of infrastructure projects. Stakeholders are defined as the general public, especially those people who are either neighbors or travelers; regulatory authorities, who are charged with managing our nation's natural and cultural resources; elected and civic leaders; and the transportation authority that plans and operates the facility. Engaging stakeholders is critical for three primary reasons:

- Stakeholders have the most thorough and intimate knowledge of the surrounding landscape—the forces that shaped it and the values that maintain it—necessary to understand the natural and cultural context.
- Stakeholders have the ability to accurately define what is needed to improve their quality of life—what improvements to transportation need to be made, what natural resources need to be conserved, and what cultural resources need to be preserved—so a comprehensive understanding of the values of society can direct the development of a transportation corridor.
- Stakeholders have the authority to give the political and economic support necessary to construct transportation projects.

A main intent of CSS is to make the planning and design process both shorter and more effective. Therefore, planning issues are identified, discussed, and resolved up front with involved stakeholders. Open communication helps to avoid lengthy litigation initiated by stakeholders who are distressed about community or environmental impacts. Often, such situations can be avoided if concerns are addressed during the early stages of the planning process.

Develop a Comprehensive Purpose and Need

After stakeholders have been appropriately identified by a sponsoring agency, and meetings have commenced, the next step is to develop a "purpose and need" statement for the project. During this process, the sponsoring agency identifies why transportation projects are needed. The sponsoring agency may have many reasons, or "warrants," for proposing a project—for example, to repair a poor roadway surface, to correct structural problems with a bridge, to increase capacity for anticipated increases in use, to eliminate safety problems, or to remove undesirable through-traffic from local neighborhoods. The specific types of projects are numerous, but in general they are proposed to improve the performance of the transportation facility by making the facility safer, by increasing mobility, or by providing better access.

Traditionally, a purpose and need statement only documented these transportation goals. However, a CSS approach to transportation projects recognizes that the community has related goals that the highway project could either hinder or expedite. Therefore, a purpose and need statement developed as part of a CSS approach also identifies and incorporates a larger community vision into the project. Such larger visions may include improved pedestrian and bicycle mobility and access, improved water quality, better access for economic development, reduced air pollution, increased transit use, retention of businesses or housing, the creation of community gateways, or the improvement of wayfinding.

Each purpose and need statement is unique to a particular project. The statement should incorporate a comprehensive project vision that reflects the values of neighbors and travelers. It will be used to direct the design of the project by establishing design criteria that will screen proposed alternatives and refine the final design of the preferred alternative.

To be effective, the purpose and need statement must be supported by both neighbors and travelers. This is fundamental. Without agreement on what the project should achieve, even a process that extensively engages stakeholders will likely fail to generate a preferred alternative that both neighbors and travelers can support. If complete agreement on the issues can be achieved, what the project must achieve becomes nearly self-evident to all stakeholders.

Form an Interdisciplinary Team

Although landscape architects are usually familiar with topics in a number of fields, including those related to environmental issues, social issues, and transportation issues, they are not usually *the* experts in these fields. For highway projects, landscape architects tend to be generalists, capable of synthesizing information. Their contribution tends to be one of facilitation and integration—helping the planning and design team to consider all of the issues throughout the life cycle of the project.

For planning and designing a highway, it is critical that a comprehensive team approach be used. In addition to the traditional engineers (geometric, traffic, and structural), it is important to have landscape architects (preferably those specializing in transportation design), planners (community and transportation), and environmental scientists and engineers (water, air, fauna, flora, hazmat, etc.) involved in the planning and design of transportation facilities. Each professional can bring a unique outlook to identifying issues, understanding impacts, and developing mitigation and enhancement measures.

Create a Multimodal Plan

There are many methods for transporting people and goods across the landscape—cars and trucks on a highway is not the only method. Another fundamental principle of CSS is that a multimodal plan usually provides a better and more sensitive fit with a project's context than planning and designing for a single mode, especially if that single mode allows only for cars and trucks.

Craig Churchward, ASLA, and Doug Mann, ASLA, HNTB Corporation

At a minimum, pedestrian movement is typically required to start and complete a trip in a car or truck. How a system of pedestrian sidewalks and trails interact with the highway is usually critical, especially in urban areas where pedestrian movement can supplant vehicular movement. Indeed, pedestrians, bicyclists, and transit riders are frequently more effective at moving through the urban environment than people riding in cars. The integration of all modes of transportation must be considered during the development of transportation corridors. System continuity, safety, access, and mobility are just as important for pedestrians, bicyclists, and transit users as they are for the users of motorized vehicles.

In the past, design for vehicular movement took precedence over adequate design for pedestrians, bicyclists, and transit users. Using a CSS approach to project development, a balance of modes must be reached and must be based on the purpose and need statement. No one mode takes precedence automatically; all must be accommodated, as defined by the stakeholders.

STAKEHOLDER ENGAGEMENT TECHNIQUES

From the beginning of a transportation project, stakeholders should be involved heavily with engineers, planners, and local government officials through various "working meetings" and public forums. Although the various stakeholders may have competing priorities, CSS helps bring a faster consensus to transportation improvement projects through understanding the *legitimate* needs of all stakeholders and negotiating win-win solutions. CSS promotes the recognition of community issues and forges partnerships, understanding, and acceptance through a participatory planning process that lasts from project inception through construction and beyond.

The more stakeholders that can be brought in to the project, especially during the early stages, the more successful the project sponsors will be in getting the support of stakeholders to build and operate a transportation facility. One of the most important stakeholder groups to engage in developing the project is made up of those people who regulate the construction of transportation facilities. Getting professionals from regulatory organizations to participate in defining issues, developing and screening alternatives, selecting a preferred alternative, and defining appropriate mitigation and enhancement is critical to the success of the project and the speed with which the project and associated improvement can be implemented.

The only way to ensure the success of CSS is to maintain respectful communication at all times—with all parties. Effective negotiation skills used by local officials and agencies will help them to lead the stakeholder group through impasses in negotiations, to maximize the potential of the project, and to bring the group to mutual agreement and informed consent to build the project. By stressing that transportation improvement projects are for the mutual gain of the community—and by spending the time and effort to listen to the involved stakeholders, and to understand and address their issues—an agreement can be reached.

Developing and Screening Alternatives

The primary purpose of engaging stakeholders and having interdisciplinary teams is to ensure that a wide range of alternatives, which represent different ways of achieving the objectives of the project's purpose and need statement, will be fairly considered. Only by having people who are predisposed to thinking about issues from different standpoints will the best creative solution emerge for solving the problem, as defined in the purpose and need statement.

Importantly for generating a wide range of solutions, it is necessary that the simple application of highway design standards not be the basis for beginning the development of a plan to improve a highway. It is not the application of standards that should be sought, but rather the correction of particular problems.

Having identified specific problems during the development of the purpose and need statement, solutions to those issues should be sought. Applying a particular standard at a specific location may be one solution, but it is probably not the only solution. Applying a design standard to correct a "deficiency" where there is no identified problem (except that the existing facility does not meet standards) is not being context-sensitive, nor is it being wise with public funds.

By having a diverse and creative design team that is forced by demanding stakeholders to fashion a set of creative solutions that won't compromise any transportation, environmental, or social goals, as defined in the purpose and need statement, a truly corridor-specific context-sensitive solution will emerge from the discussion.

BEYOND PLANNING AND DESIGN

Many terms have been used to define how transportation landscape architects integrate the landscape into the practice of highway design. Context-sensitive solutions implies that the job of the landscape architect is not complete after construction plans have been developed. Context-sensitive solutions also means that the landscape architect needs to be involved during construction, to ensure that the methods used to build the road are as sensitive to environment and the community as the design. Similarly, how the facility operates should be monitored, to ensure that the anticipated and *unanticiptated* needs and requirements of travelers and neighbors are being met. Finally, the landscape architect needs to ensure that maintenance practices continue to support the intention of the design.

By being part of the construction, operations, and maintenance teams, the landscape architect will be more aware of how planning and design affects the capability of the highway to remain sensitive to its context. Only by considering its complete life cycle can a transportation facility be truly context-sensitive.

APPLYING CONTEXT-SENSITIVE SOLUTIONS

Traditional approaches to highway design are evolving as communities are taking a stronger interest in how transportation infrastructure affects their surroundings. The departments of transportation (DOTs) across the country are taking a more active approach in addressing how transportation impacts communities and the environment, as well as safety and mobility. In states where a CSS approach is commonplace, public sentiment is changing from one of resistance to one of support in building transportation facilities in or around neighborhoods.

CONCLUSION

A transportation project that successfully incorporates CSS will reflect flexible design criteria, excellence in engineering expertise, knowledge and incorporation of community issues, faster project development, and better communities. By embracing CSS, the community will come to think of a transportation improvement project as an asset, not as a burden.

In sum, the guidelines to follow for implementing the CSS methodology are as follows:

1. Identify stakeholders.
2. Identify what the stakeholders value in the community.
3. Utilize an interdisciplinary design team.
4. Develop a purpose and need statement, in conjunction with all stakeholders.
5. Use the purpose and need statement as specific design criteria.
6. Develop multimodal, context-sensitive alternatives.
7. Use the design criteria to evaluate alternatives.
8. Use the design criteria to refine the design of the preferred alternative.
9. Consider the life cycle of the project during planning and design.
10. Implement CSS practices during construction, operations, and maintenance.
11. Generate support for the project and transportation.
12. Improve the vitality of human and natural communities.

REFERENCES

Grese, Robert E. 1992. *Jens Jensen: Maker of Natural Parks and Gardens*. Baltimore, MD: Johns Hopkins University Press.

Jolley, Harley. 1987. *Painting with a Comet's Tail: The Touch of the Landscape Architect on the Blue Ridge Parkway*. Boone, NC: Appalachian Consortium Press.

McClelland, Linda Flint. 1998. *Building the National Parks: Historic Design and Construction*. Baltimore, MD: Johns Hopkins University Press.

Newton, Norman T. 1971. *Design on the Land: The Development of Landscape Architecture*. Cambridge, MA: Belknap Press of Harvard University Press.

Craig Churchward, ASLA, and Doug Mann, ASLA, HNTB Corporation

TRANSIT-ORIENTED DEVELOPMENT

Transit-oriented development (TOD) is a form of planned urban development that takes advantage of convenient access to public transportation. Typical transit modes that support TOD include heavy rail transit (such as subways or "metros"), commuter rail, light rail transit (LRT), and bus rapid transit (BRT).

The most complete form of TOD is the "transit village," a mixed-use urban community organized around a transit station with an emphasis on pedestrian access and circulation. Other forms of TOD (not explored in detail here) include "joint-development," the mixing of urban development and a transit station in a single project (often a joint venture of a developer and a transit agency), and the "transit street," a linear deployment of mixed-use development along a transit corridor with many stops such as an urban streetcar or bus line.

ORIGINS OF TRANSIT-ORIENTED DEVELOPMENT

Transit-oriented development in the United States has its origins in the mid-nineteenth century with the development of speculative residential subdivisions located at railway stations along rail corridors connecting to city centers. An example is the community of Riverside outside of Chicago. Designed in 1868 by the American landscape architect Frederick Law Olmsted, Riverside features a pattern typical of TODs today: a mixed-use commercial core around the railway station, surrounded in turn by residential areas and shared open spaces.

With the advent of the cable car in the 1880s and, soon after, of the electric streetcar (or "trolley"), "streetcar suburbs" developed rapidly throughout the United States and set a dominant pattern of suburban development that lasted well into the mid-twentieth century, until (in most cities) the private automobile supplanted rail-based public transit as the preferred mode of urban mobility. Streetcar suburbs are typified by highly walkable "transit streets" lined by neighborhood-focused services and commercial development, with adjacent residential streets within easy walking distance. In cites that never abandoned rail transit, streetcar suburbs (such as San Francisco's West Portal district) thrive to this day as living, historic models for contemporary TOD.

TRANSIT-ORIENTED DEVELOPMENT TODAY

Over the past 30 years, urban rail transit and transit-oriented development have staged a comeback in American cities, in direct response to the growing environmental costs of post-World War II patterns of automobile-based suburban development. The TOD renaissance is closely associated with the growth of New Urbanism (also called Neo-Traditional Town Planning), a form of urban development characterized by horizontal and vertical mixed-use, medium to high densities, pedestrian-friendly streets and public spaces, and walkable distances among residential, commercial, recreational, and institutional land uses.

Two classic diagrams (by New Urbanist pioneers Andres Duany and Peter Calthorpe) compare typical automobile and pedestrian-oriented communities of the same population and area, and a basic model of a pedestrian-oriented transit village.

The Transit Village: Walkability, Land Use, and Form

The transit village is the most complete form of TOD today. Transit villages come in many sizes and patterns, and may be developed as new planned communities or created incrementally through redevelopment and infill of existing urban neighborhoods. Typically, a transit village is organized around "walkability," with mixed uses concentrated within a quarter mile, or a comfortable 5- to 10-minute walk, of a transit station. Adherence to the one-quarter-mile rule encourages residents to walk and use public transit in lieu of the automobile, a fundamental environmental goal of TOD.

A typical transit village may consist of three concentric zones:

> **Zone A—transit hub:** The TOD's "downtown" includes a transit station and concentrated service and retail uses catering to transit patrons walking to and from the station. Land-use densities are medium to high and may be layered vertically with multiple-unit residences (such as townhouses and lofts) above ground-level retail and services.
>
> **Zone B—primary area:** Walkable area within a one-quarter-mile radius a of transit station; includes mix of residential and supporting service, retail, and institutional uses. May be "auto-free" but usually includes "traffic-calmed" streets that allow automobiles while favoring pedestrians. Densities are medium. Residences range from compact detached houses to row houses and other types of multiunit and attached housing.
>
> **Zone C—secondary area:** Area within one-fourth- to one-half-mile radius of transit station, includes mix of residential and other uses that support Zones A and B. Area is walkable (up to 20-minute walk from transit station) but more supportive of automobile use. May also contain recreational and institutional uses with large sites such as schools and parks. Densities are medium to low. Residences are typically detached houses on moderate-sized lots.

Transit-Oriented Development Examples

The following three examples illustrate TOD at different scales. These are only a sample of a wide range of possible TOD types, patterns, and scales of development.

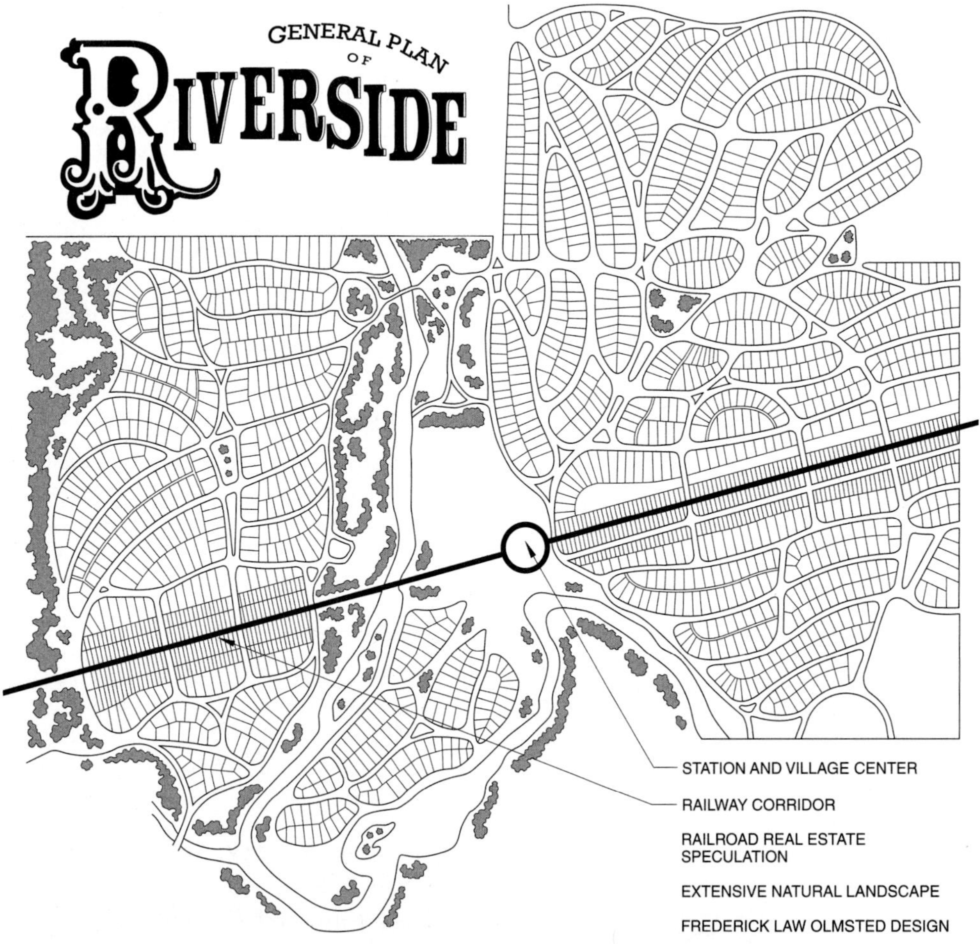

HISTORIC TOD, RIVERSIDE, II (ADAPTED FROM THE PUBLIC DOMAIN)

Rick Phillips, HNTB

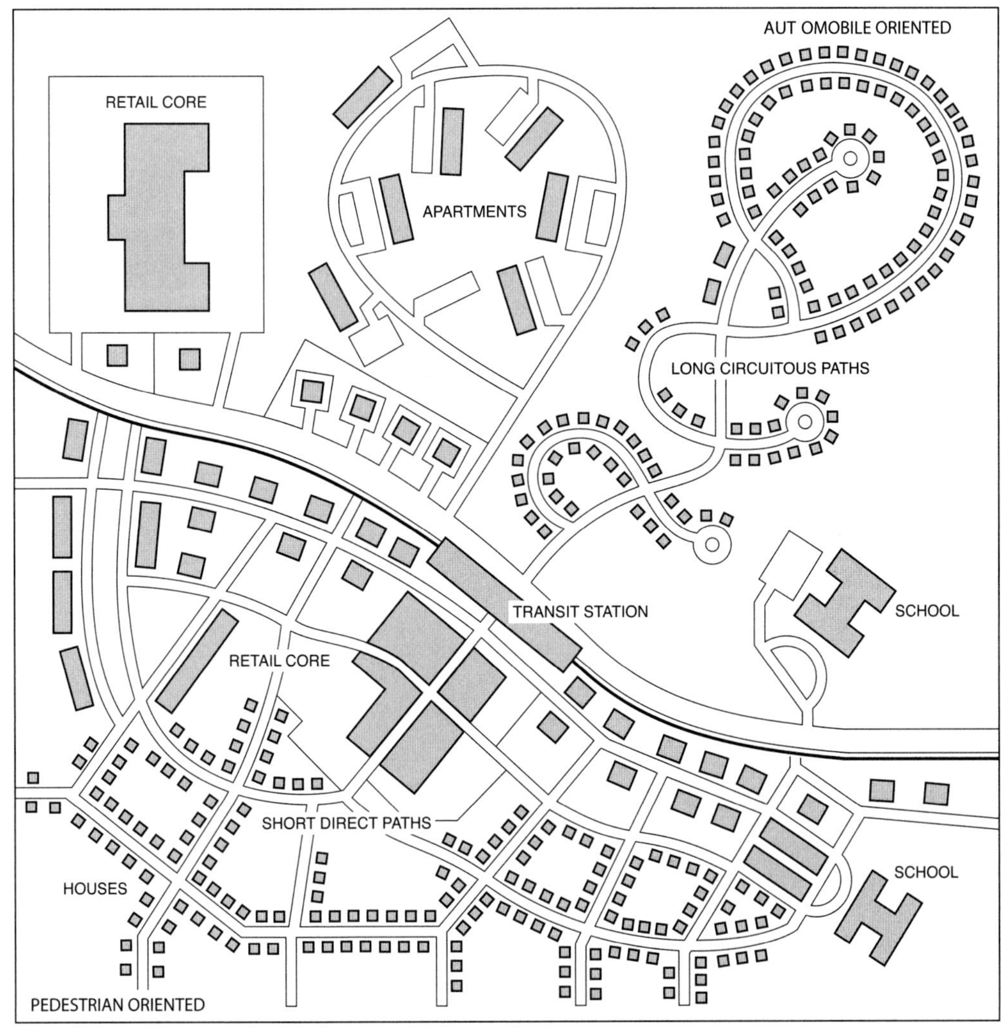

PEDESTRIAN VS. AUTOMOBILE-ORIENTED VILLAGE PLAN

Source: Adapted from Plater-Zyberk, Duany, 1989. "Repent Ye Sinners, Repent: We Can Save the Suburbs, Say Advocates of NeotraditionalTtown Planning," in Ruth Knack, Planning.

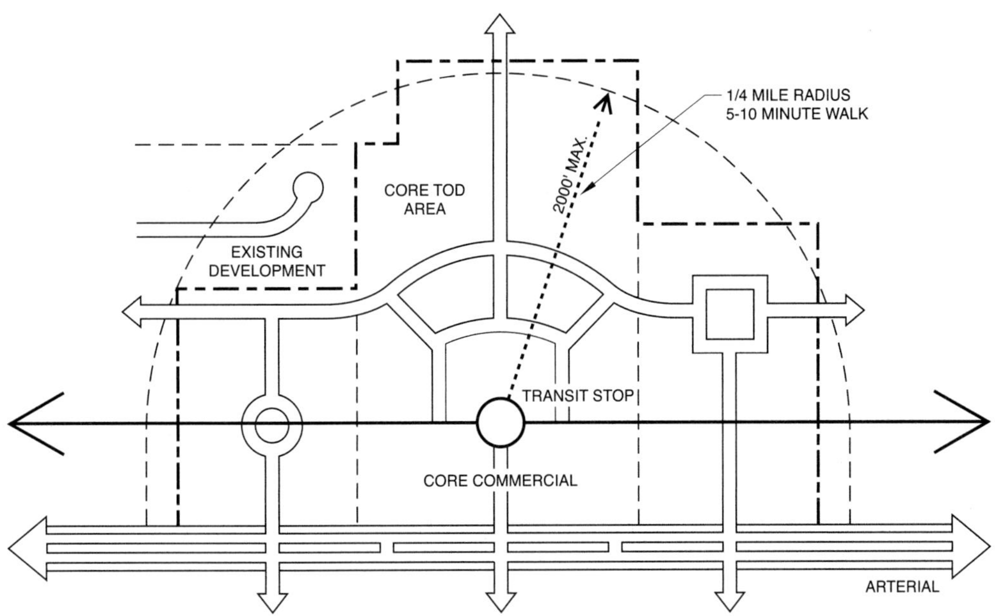

IDEALIZED TRANSIT VILLAGE DIAGRAM

Source: Adapted from Calthorpe, The Next American Metropolis, 1993.

Rick Phillips, HNTB

Example 1—Main Street TOD, Winthrup Harbor, Illinois: In this example, a street connecting a transit station and existing highway development is transformed into a walkable "main street" of shops and residential mixed uses. The result is a new pedestrian-oriented village center linked to both transit and highway access. The village center serves existing residential districts to the north and south, providing transit access and enhanced local services.

Example 2—Urban Infill TOD, Santa Rosa, California: In this example, a transit hub is created through urban design, adaptive reuse of "railroad district" historic structures, and new infill development. The hub creates a vital link between downtown Santa Rosa (to the right of the map "TOD Prototype–Urban Infill") and a new waterfront promenade along Santa Rosa Creek. Future train service from the hub will link Santa Rosa with San Francisco and other Bay Area cities.

Example 3—Greenfield TOD, Daybreak, Utah: In this example, a complete New Urbanist city is planned "from scratch" to include 13,000 homes on more than 4,000 acres of reclaimed industrial land near Salt Lake City. Despite the large scale of Daybreak (note the one-fourth-mile "walkability circles" around three transit stations in the figure "Large-Scale TOD, Daybreak, Utah"), the three zones of TOD are evident in the walking and land-use zones illustration; and the plan closely resembles the transit village diagram by Calthorpe (who is also Daybreak's planner), as shown in the idealized transit village diagram. Due to its large area, Daybreak features several neighborhood commercial centers, bringing service and retail uses within walking distance of most residents.

TRANSIT-ORIENTED DEVELOPMENT STREETS

As noted, the essence of TOD is walkability, and most TOD plans are based on networks of pedestrian-oriented streets that usually also support automobile access. Note that the pedestrian shopping street includes alternative cross sections of the "main street" proposed for Winthrop Harbor, Illinois, and is typical of street designs within a TOD core area. Common features are wide, landscaped sidewalks (often featuring sidewalk cafes or other outdoor uses), traffic-calmed travel lanes, and buffered angled or parallel parking. If needed, additional parking (which may include park-and-ride spaces for transit patrons) is provided in lots or garages hidden from the street or embedded in mixed-use development, as can be seen in the urban infill example "TOD Prototype–Urban Infill". Service and retail uses front the sidewalks in the manner of a traditional village streetscape. The result is a vibrant pedestrian-friendly environment that encourages walking among residences, local businesses, and transit.

TRANSIT-ORIENTED DEVELOPMENT BUILDINGS

Buildings in the TOD core area are typically medium to high density, front directly on pedestrian-friendly sidewalks, and often contain mixed uses, with

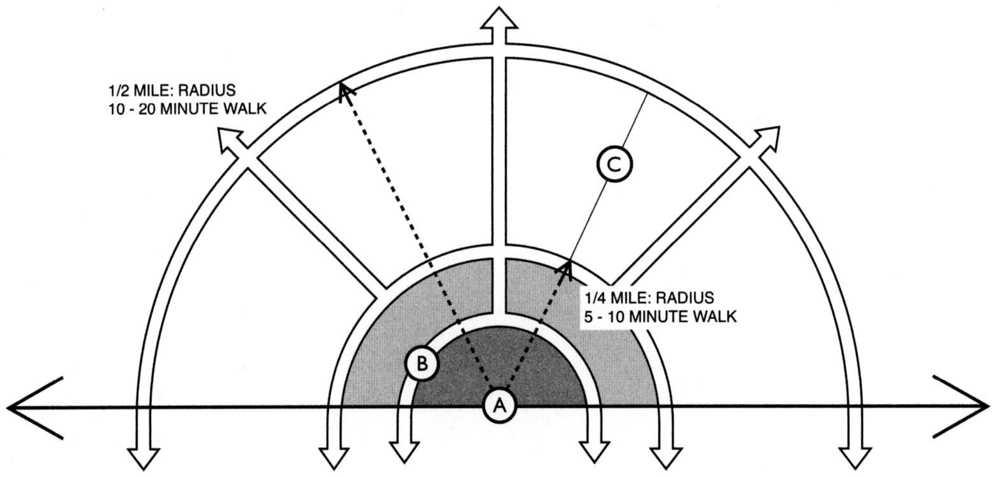

WALKING CIRCLES AND LAND-USE ZONES

Source: Adapted from LandPeople, Transportation and Land Use Toolkit 2003.

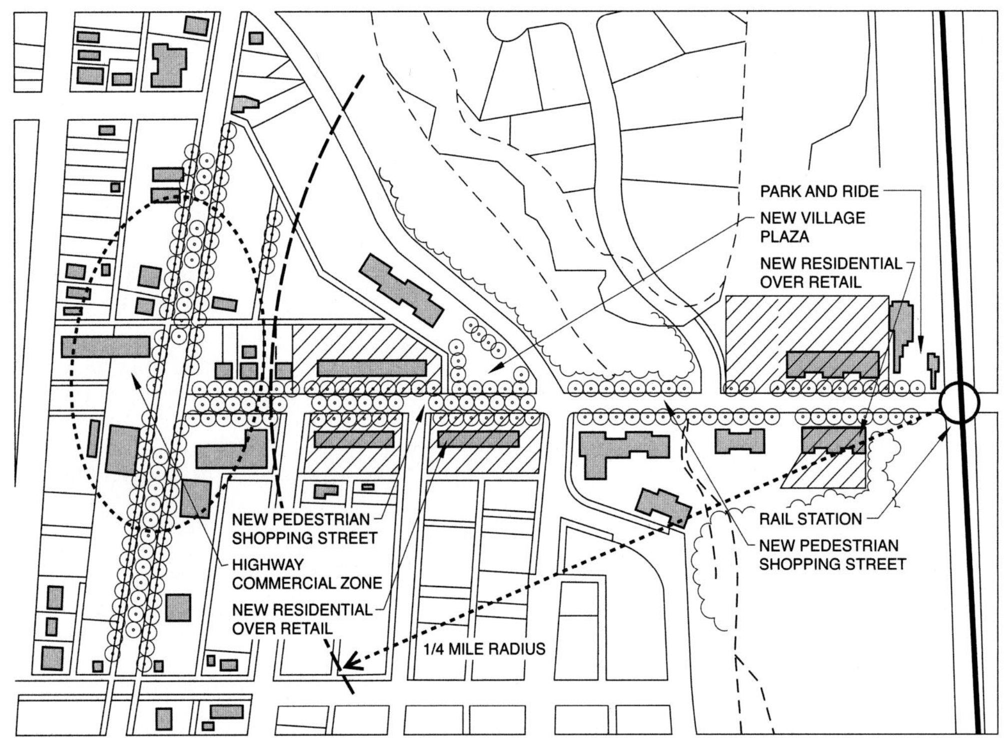

TOD PROTOTYPE—MAIN STREET

Source: HNTB, Winthrop Harbor Station Area Plan, IL, 2004.

Rick Phillips, HNTB

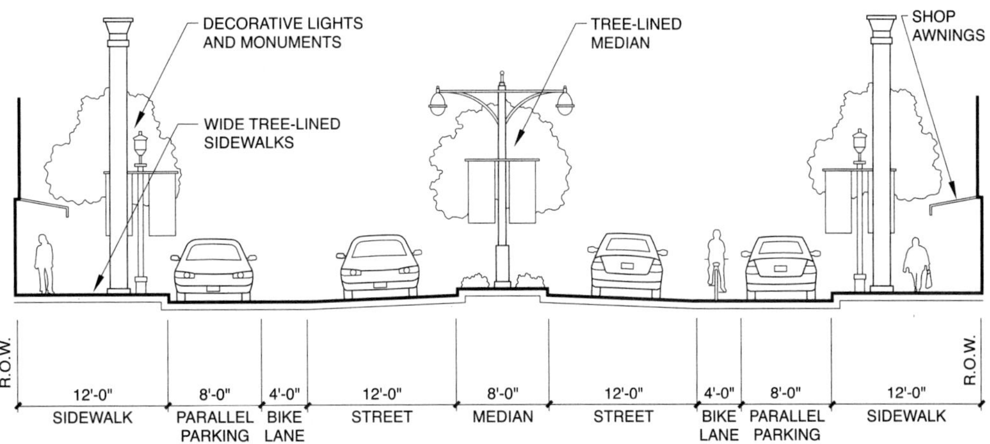

ALTERNATIVE 1 FOR PEDESTRIAN SHOPPING STREET

Source: HNTB Winthrop Harbor Station Area Plan, IL, 2004.

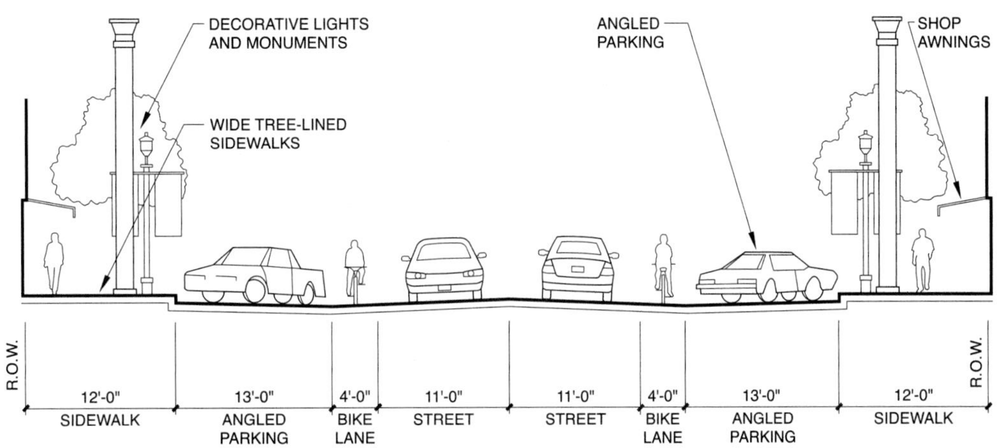

ALTERNATIVE 2 FOR PEDESTRIAN SHOPPING STREET

Source: HNTB, Winthrop Harbor Station Area Plan, IL, 2004.

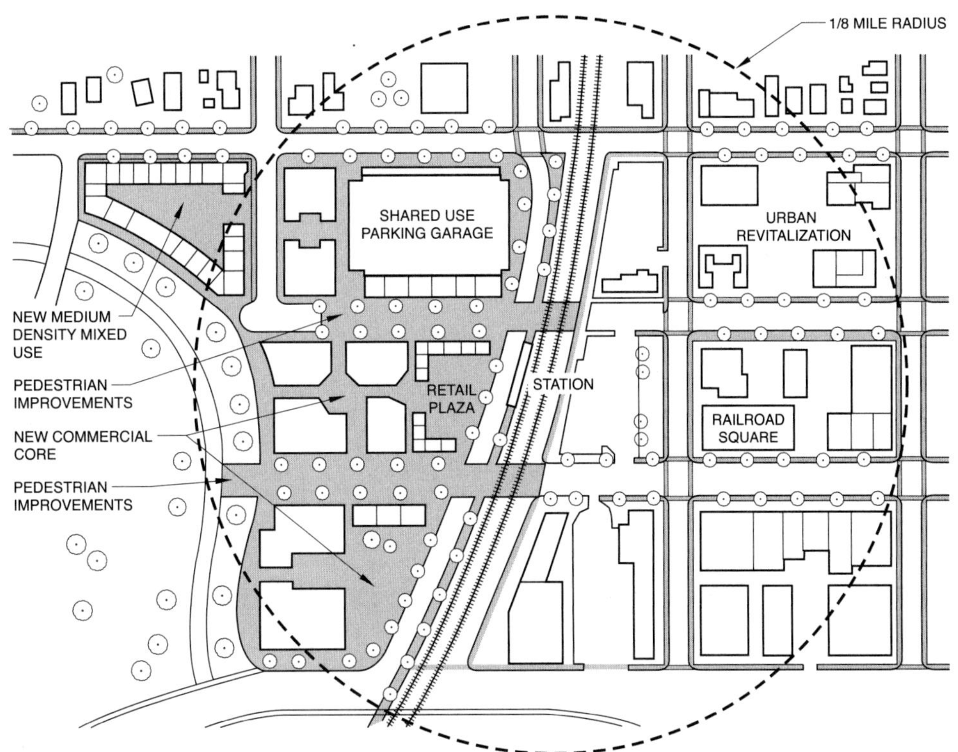

TOD PROTOTYPE—URBAN INFILL

Source: Adapted from VBN, Santa Rosa Railroad Square Conceptual Master Plan, Santa Rosa, CA, 2002.

Rick Phillips, HNTB

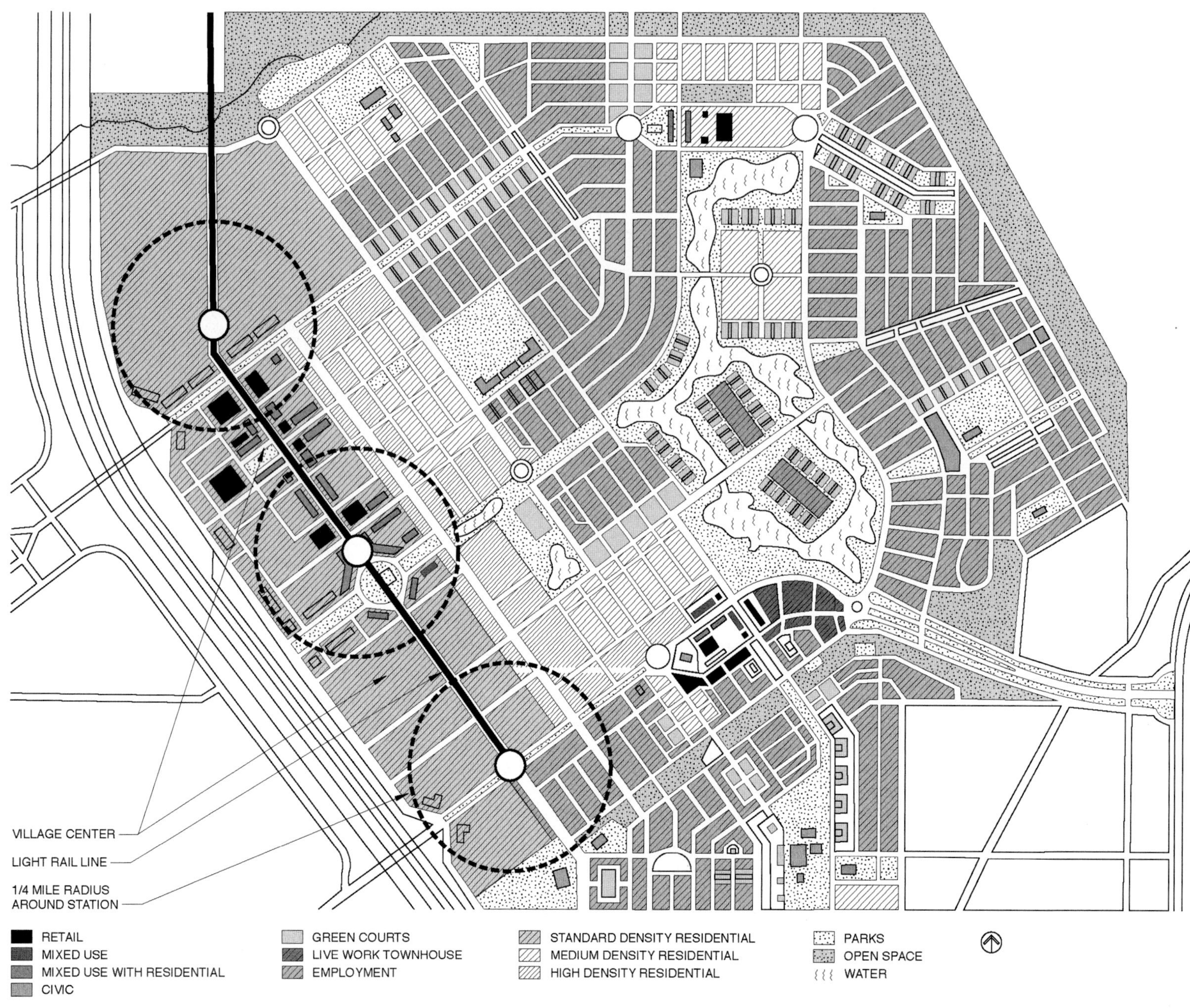

LARGE-SCALE TOD, DAYBREAK, UTAH

Source: Adapted from Kennecott Land, Calthorpe, 2004.

"shopfront" retail at ground level and other uses on upper floors. Housing favors compact detached residences on small lots or a variety of attached and multiunit types such as townhouses, row houses, "live-work" studios, and multilevel apartment (or condominium) buildings.

TOD PLANNING POLICIES

The nature of TOD—and New Urbanist planning in general—requires a variety of specific planning policies and procedures, many of them nontraditional. Some of these include the following:

- *General plans* that promote the concept of mixed use, as long as negative environmental relationships are resolved.
- *Zoning ordinances* that embrace mixed use through the establishment of primary or "overlay" mixed-use zones (overlay zones are a tool to augment or modify existing or primary zones in specific locations).
- *Urban design and built form guidelines* that promote (or require) streets, public spaces, and urban development to be pedestrian-friendly.
- *Procedures for comprehensive planning* of specific projects or small areas, such as neighbor plans, transit station area plans, and planned unit developments (PUDs).
- *Parking policies* that control parking inventory in TOD areas and pass the capital and operational costs of parking to automobile users.
- *Establishment of TOD "visions" and plans* (often through public workshops or charrettes) that guide existing neighborhoods to develop as TODs gradually over time.
- *Proactive development of TOD* through land assembly and solicitation of proposals from private developers. These strategies often include varieties of public/private joint ventures and may include transit agencies as well as municipalities.

Rick Phillips, HNTB

TYPICAL RESIDENTIAL DENSITIES AND DISTANCE RELATIONSHIP TO TRANSIT HUB

	TOD ZONE		
	ZONE A – TRANSIT HUB	ZONE B – TOD CORE AREA	ZONE C – TOD SUPPORTING AREA
Walking distance from transit station or intermodal center	Adjacent to transit station, up to ⅛ mile radius	Up to ¼ mile radius of transit station	Between ¼ and ½ mile radius of transit station
Density description	High	High to medium	Medium
Dominant dwelling types	Attached, multilevel, mixed, with retail and service uses	Attached, multilevel, and detached, on small sized lots	Detached on small or medium sized lots
Residential densities (dwelling units/acre)	30 to 75	15 to 30	12 to 24

TOD RESIDENTIAL DENSITIES

Appropriate TOD densities will depend heavily on the character of the surrounding community. However, the table "Typical Residential Densities and Distance Relationship to Transit Hub" indicates how typical residential densities might decrease as walking distances increase from the transit hub.

SMART GROWTH: GROWING TOD ON A REGIONAL SCALE

In terms of quality of life and environmental sustainability, the highest benefits are achieved when public transit and transit-oriented development are implemented on a metropolitan or regional scale. These benefits are evident in regions with a long tradition of multimodal public transportation (such as California's Bay Area and Canada's Toronto Urban Region). Increasingly, new urban regions (such as Utah's Wasatch Front) are taking up the challenge of planning and implementing Smart Growth to reap the benefits of reduced energy consumption, cleaner air, reduced congestion, enhanced community life, and natural preservation.

Smart Growth can be seen as the marriage of two fundamental planning concepts with TOD at the core: walkable cities and multimodal transportation systems.

- *Walkability* reduces the overall need to travel regionally by enabling people to access the services they need locally, with minimum reliance on automobiles. The transit village is a classic model of walkability.
- *Multimodality* serves the remaining demand for regional travel (already reduced by walkability) most efficiently by assigning all travel modes (including the automobile) to the types of trips each mode serves best. Trip types range from concentrated, high-volume corridors (perhaps best served by rail transit) to dispersed trips around and between urban regions, perhaps best served by arterials and super highways. A key feature of multimodality is designed interconnections among different transit modes at logical decision points throughout the urban region. Ideally, these "intermodal centers" form the transit hubs at the centers of transit-oriented development.

These same principles benefit other forms of urban infrastructure such as water, sewerage, electric power, and so on. All infrastructure is more efficient when planned along logical networks serving customers in compact communities.

What Does Smart Growth Look Like?

These examples illustrate Smart Growth patterns at two scales: *multimodal transect* and *regional network*. Regional smart growth takes many forms but often is built up from combinations of these two patterns.

- The multimodal transect looks at a single transit corridor emanating from a downtown core. As the corridor expands outward, it branches out to connect the downtown with new transit villages in the suburbs. Meanwhile, TOD improvements are brought back to the inner city with walkable infill development around stations and the creation of a "transit mall" in the downtown core.
- The regional network looks at the urban region as a whole. Transit corridors radiate out from the urban center linking downtown with suburban transit villages and other transportation corridors that circumnavigate the region. These rings may include bus or rail transit lines, freeways, or freeways combined with transit in "multimodal corridors." The result is a broad interconnected network of walkable communities and transportation options using all travel modes most efficiently and conveniently.

The regional network shows one additional key element: an "urban growth boundary." A growth boundary is not a city limits but an agreed-to line around an urban region beyond which urban devel-

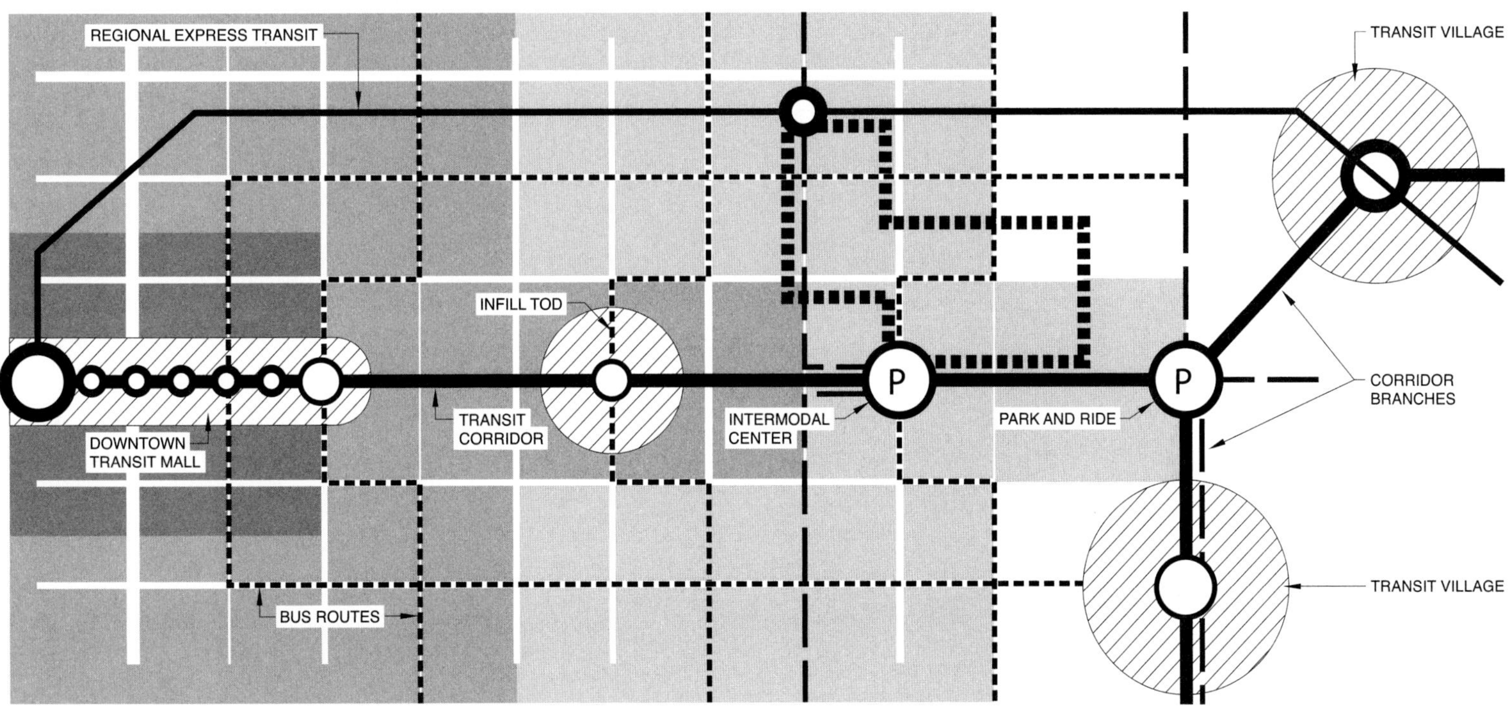

A SMART GROWTH TRANSECT

Source: Phillips, Rick. 2005. "Light Rails in Arid Cities," in Second International Symposium on Urban Design in Arid Regions.

Rick Phillips, HNTB

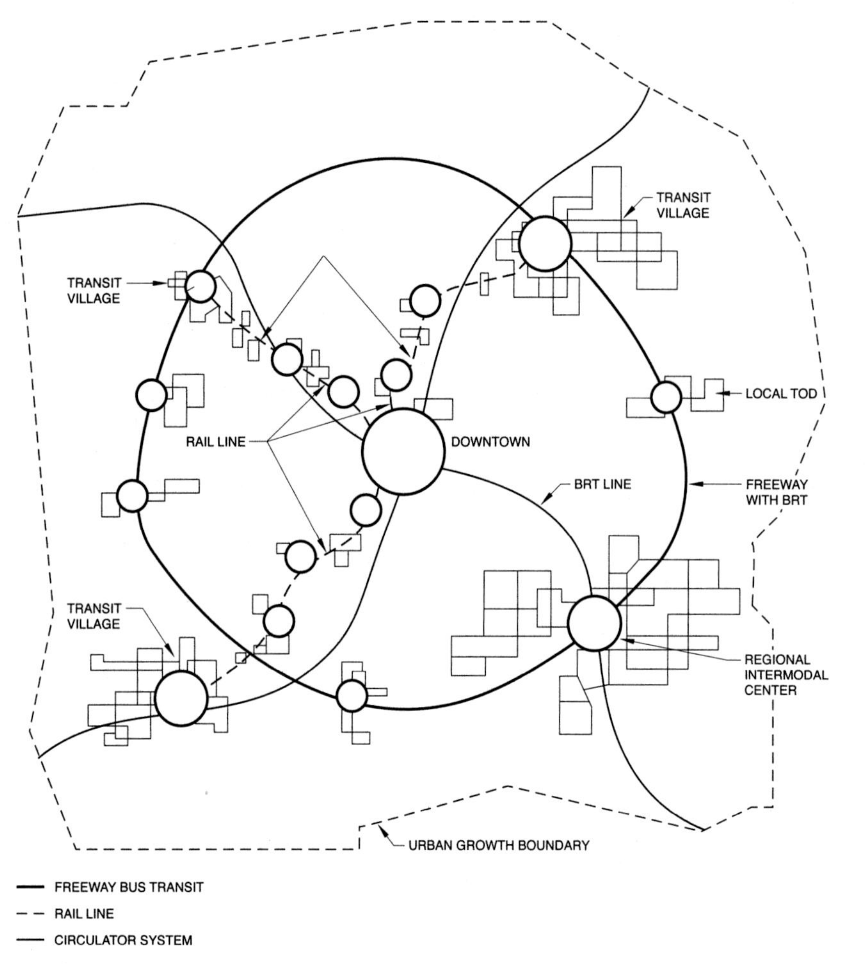

A REGIONAL SMART GROWTH NETWORK

Source: Adapted from Schneider, J. B. 1992. "A PRT Deployment Strategy to Support Regional Land Use and Rail Transit Objectives," Transportation Quarterly.

opment is prohibited or strictly controlled. The boundary protects prized natural or rural landscape while helping to guide existing growth demand to concentrate development around transit corridors and intermodal centers throughout the urban region. It is important to point out that urban growth boundaries, although successful in shaping Smart Growth, are politically controversial in the United States. The effectiveness of America's most well-known growth boundary around the Portland, Oregon, urban region was compromised by a ballot initiative (passed in 2004) that requires state and local governments to pay property owners when land-use restrictions reduce property values or, as an alternative, lift the restrictions.

RESOURCES

Bernick, Michael, and Robert Cervero. 1997. *Transit Villages in the 21st Century*. New York: McGraw Hill.

Rail-Volution, www.railvolution.com: An organization dedicated to "building livable communities with transit." Hosts the United States' premier annual conference on rail transit and TOD.

Reconnecting America, www.reconnectingamerica.org: An organization dedicated to the promotion of transit-oriented development and Smart Growth; provides links to numerous TOD, environmental, and public transit websites.

Walkable Communities, www.walkablecommunities.org: An organization dedicated to all aspects of pedestrian-friendliness in the urban environment.

See also:
Circulation
Site Planning

Rick Phillips, HNTB

CIRCULATION

VEHICULAR CIRCULATION

INTRODUCTION

Landscape architects, planners, and engineers have a shared responsibility in designing and maintaining quality public spaces, including street systems that incorporate a balance of: transportation needs; improved access for residents, employees, and customers; reduced congestion; increased choice among modes of travel; consideration of ecological parameters; and enhanced environmental protection.

Existing and conventional practices in vehicular circulation planning are a legacy from decades of reliance on the private car as the primary mode of transportation. While awareness and encouragement of alternative modes of travel are gaining ground, motorized vehicles are not going to disappear any time soon. Urban planning and design must, therefore, continue to consider the technical and dimensional requirements imposed by this mode of transport. These requirements are often spelled out through sets of standards and codes endorsed and enforced by local authorities. Certainly, it is a professional obligation of each consultant to adhere to established standards, but such obligations must not curtail the need to challenge or change unreasonable, unfitting, or outdated requirements, such as excessive street and right-of-way widths or extensive use of impervious materials.

Vehicular circulation design is approached differently at various levels of scale. At the regional scale, vehicular circulation is typically based on nodes within various traffic zones connected by links. Each is described by its flow (number of trips) and friction (time and cost to traverse the link). A typical larger-scale transportation planning usually involves spatial structure modeling, demand forecasting, and testing against the capacity of the circulation system and acceptable level of service. At the local level, vehicular circulation design usually involves the following steps:

1. Determination of land uses at the site
2. Estimation of trips generated, and the type and intensity of the uses
3. Distribution of trips to major approach roads
4. Assignment of vehicle volumes to the roadway network
5. Analysis of the capacity of the roadways to handle the traffic
6. Geometrical design of the various roads and streets according to projected capacity, use, and desired speed

Principles

Regardless of the level of vehicular circulation design, the following general principles should be always followed:

- Minimize the amount of land used for vehicular circulation.
- Preserve natural features and provide street alignment that complements the natural topography.
- Reduce impervious areas and materials and incorporate natural drainage.
- Provide adequate streetscape (landscapes and hardscapes).
- Minimize road pavement and rights-of-way.
- Reduce the length of streets and provide adequate pedestrian connections.
- Provide traffic-calming measures at transition points and where pedestrian oriented design is sought.
- Incorporate and encourage multimode travel, such as bicycle and bus lanes, and reduce parking ratios where transit is available.

CLASSIFICATION AND HIERARCHY OF STREET SYSTEMS

Roadway systems are classified according to traffic volumes, speed, and use for ease in planning, design, and administration. Individual roads and streets do not operate independently of each other; most travel involves movement through a network of roads. The need for access to destinations, as well as the mobility to traverse distances in reasonable time, is a key element in the relationship of the functional classes. The figure "Typical Vehicular System" shows the relationship of mobility and access to the basic functional classes.

These general classifications can be further categorized according to their particular use, purpose,

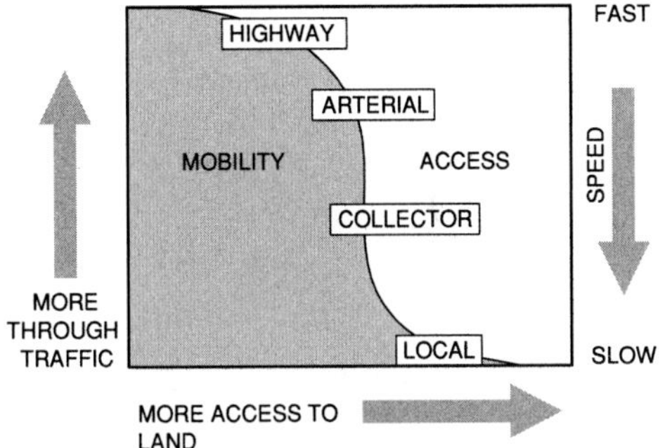

A typical vehicular system includes highways, arterials, minor arterials, collectors, local streets, cul-de-sacs, and alleyways.

TYPICAL VEHICULAR SYSTEM

Source: United States Department of Transportation.

GENERAL REQUIREMENTS FOR EACH CLASSIFICATION

TYPE	FUNCTION AND DESIGN FEATURES	SPACING	WIDTHS R.O.W.	WIDTH ROADWAY	DESIRABLE MAX. GRADE	SPEED	OTHER FEATURES
Highways	Provide regional and metropolitan connection. Limited access: no grade crossing; no traffic stops.	Variable; related to regional pattern of population and industrial centers	200-300′	Varies; 12′ per lane; 8-10′ shoulders both sides of each roadway; 8′-60′ median strip.	5%	55- 75 mph	Depressed, at grade, or elevated. Intensive landscaping, and service roads.
Major Roads (Major Arterials)	Provide connections unity throughout urban area. Usually form boundaries for neighborhoods. Minor access control; signalized intersection.	½ to 3 miles	120-150′	Varies; 11′-12′ per lane. Parking lane 9′. Some with median strip.	6%	35-45 mph	Detached sidewalks with planting strips. Or attached sidewalks with on street parking. Curbs.
Secondary Roads (Minor Arterials)	Main feeder streets. Signals where needed; stop signs on side streets. Occasionally form boundaries for neighborhoods.	¾ to 1 mile	70′-80′	Varies; 10′-11′ per lane. Parking lane 9′. Some with median strip.	6%	35-40 mph	Detached sidewalks with planting strips. Or attached sidewalks. Curbs.
Collector Streets	Main interior streets. Stop signs on side streets.	¼ to ½ mile	50′-64′	Varies; 10′-11′ per lane. Parking lane 9′.	7%	30 mph	Detached sidewalks with planting strips. Or attached sidewalks. Curbs.
Local Streets	Local service streets.	At blocks	40′-50′	Varies; 9′-10′ per lane. Parking lane 8′	Varies	25 mph	Detached sidewalks with planting strips. Or attached sidewalks. Curbs-optional.
Cul-de-sac	Street open at only one end with provision for a practical turnaround at the other.	Only wherever practical	30′-50′	Varies; 9′-10′ per lane. Parking lane 8′ 30′-36′ turn around at various configurations according to vehicular turning radius	Varies	25 mph	Should not have a length greater than 600 feet. Should allow for pedestrian connection at end of cul-de-sac.
Alleyway	Local services and access at the back of lot.	Parallel to streets	13′-20′	Varies; usually covers the full Right-of-way.	Varies	10-15 mph	No sidewalks or curbs.

Eran Ben-Joseph, Associate Professor of Landscape Architecture and Planning, Massachusetts Institute of Technology

design characteristics, and location within the built environment. For example:

- *Urban and suburban.* Urban commercial streets, multimode boulevards integrated with transit, alleyways, and pedestrian walking streets
- *Residential.* Neighborhood streets, cul-de-sacs, loops, village streets, alleyways
- *Multimode.* Light rail, bike paths, pedestrian paths, trails, boardwalks

Average Daily Traffic (ADT) and Trip Generation Rates

Traffic volumes and land use are two important elements of vehicular system design. The estimated number of vehicles traveling both directions past a point in a typical day can help guide the choice of street type and its classification. ADT data can be supplied by actual traffic counts or through trip generation estimates based on various land uses. The Institute of Traffic Engineers *Trip Generation Handbook* is widely used as the source of trip generation data. However, these estimations should be reviewed carefully for each locale and circumstance, as they tend to be overly universal.

THE INSTITUTE'S TRIP GENERATION ESTIMATED RATES FOR RESIDENTIAL AREAS

TYPE OF DWELLING	WEEKDAY DAILY VEHICLE TRIPS PER DWELLING UNIT
Detached single-family	9.6
Townhouses	5.9
Low-rise apartments	6.6
High-rise apartments	4.2

Layouts and Street Patterns

In built-up areas, vehicular circulation systems usually follow two classical layouts: the grid and the linear/discontinued pattern. Many hybrids and combinations, such as warped parallel grid, radial, or loops and cul-de-sacs, also exist.

The grid pattern is generally considered easy to lay out and expand, easier in user orientation, conveniently accessed, and accommodating of equal flow patterns and route choice making by distributing traffic equally throughout. Its negatives include that it is monotonous, difficult to adjust for topography, and allows for through traffic in residential locations.

The linear/discontinued system's positive attributes include a hierarchy of streets according to use, sensitivity to site and topography, and works well in eliminating through traffic. Its negatives are a lack of focus, no interconnection between uses other than on designated streets, more difficult to travel through if destination is not well connected, sensitive to interruption at a single point, and could create difficult building sites and irregular lot frontages.

DESIGN CONSIDERATIONS

The design of a vehicular system must incorporate engineering requirements: turning radii, site distance, design speed, stopping distances, horizontal alignment, vertical alignment, and other engineering factors. Typical standards are published and endorsed by the local jurisdiction and usually follow standards of national professional organizations, such as the American Association of State Highway and Transportation Officials and Institute of Transportation Engineers; federal and state government agencies, such as the Department of Transportation or Federal Highway Administration; or those developed by advocacy groups such as the Congress of New Urbanism or the Urban Land Institute.

As much as these standards should be considered and followed, the detailed planning, designing, and engineering of the vehicular system should always reflect and be sensitive to its context and locale and strive to fulfill the principles stated in the introduc-

COMPARATIVE ANALYSIS OF TYPICAL STREET PATTERNS

	GRIDIRON (C. 1900)	FRAGMENTED PARALLEL (C. 1950)	WARPED PARALLEL (C. 1960)	LOOPS AND LOLLIPOPS (C. 1970)	LOLLIPOPS ON A STICK (C. 1980)
STREET PATTERNS					
INTERSECTIONS					
LINEAL FEET OF STREETS	20,800	19,000	16,500	15,300	15,600
NUMBER 1 OF BLOCKS	28	19	14	12	8
NUMBER 2 OF INTERSECTIONS	26	22	14	12	8
NUMBER 3 OF ACCESS POINTS	19	10	7	6	4
NUMBER 4 OF LOOPS & CUL-DE-SACS	0	1	2	8	24

Source: Michael Southworth.

Eran Ben-Joseph, Associate Professor of Landscape Architecture and Planning, Massachusetts Institute of Technology

tion. It is the obligation of the designer to challenge these established standards when deemed excessive, and request variances whenever needed.

Traffic Volume

Street design should relate to the traffic that will actually use the street and the expected demand for on-street parking. In designing the street, two types of traffic volume or traffic flow should be considered: free and slow. Free-flow street design provides each direction of moving traffic with designated lanes and is often marked with a centerline. Slow-flow streets could be designed with an unmarked centerline, and often require drivers to slow down when passing each other. Slow-flow streets can also be designed for yield traffic or queuing. For example, on many local streets that carry fewer than 750 vehicles per day, a clear one-lane width of 12 to 14 feet is designed for two-way traffic, if there are frequent pullouts to allow vehicles to pass. Where there is on-street parking, driveways typically provide gaps in parking adequate to serve as pullouts.

Vehicular Dimensions and Turning Path

Design of vehicular travel ways should be a function of vehicle dimensions, turning radii, and the desired speed. In slow-moving streets, lane width does not need to exceed much beyond the vehicle's dimensions. Another important consideration is a vehicle's typical turning path. These dimensions should provide guidelines for the allocation of moving lanes as well as turning radii for dead-end streets, cul-de sacs, and parking areas.

VEHICULAR DESIGN PARAMETERS

Public streets and highways are designed to accommodate a variety of vehicles, up to and including semitrailer trucks. When private driveways and roadways will only serve passenger vehicles, it may be appropriate to use smaller dimensions in some instances. Nonetheless, be certain private roads are wide enough to allow passage of fire and emergency vehicles.

The "level of service" approach employed by traffic engineers can be used as a tool for adapting designs to the specific needs of users. Level of service (LOS) A, which is the most comfortable, allows vehicle movement with little or no constraint. As the level of service decreases, from A to D, the comfort level decreases. LOS D is the minimum dimension for safe maneuvering of a vehicle at low speed.

The level of service selected for a particular application should reflect the needs of the users and of the owner of a property. Make adjustments according to the local vehicle size and mix and any concerns particular to the location.

Emergency Response and Utility Access

All streets should allow access for fire and emergency response, as well as for refuse/recycling trucks, school buses, city buses, delivery vehicles, and mov-

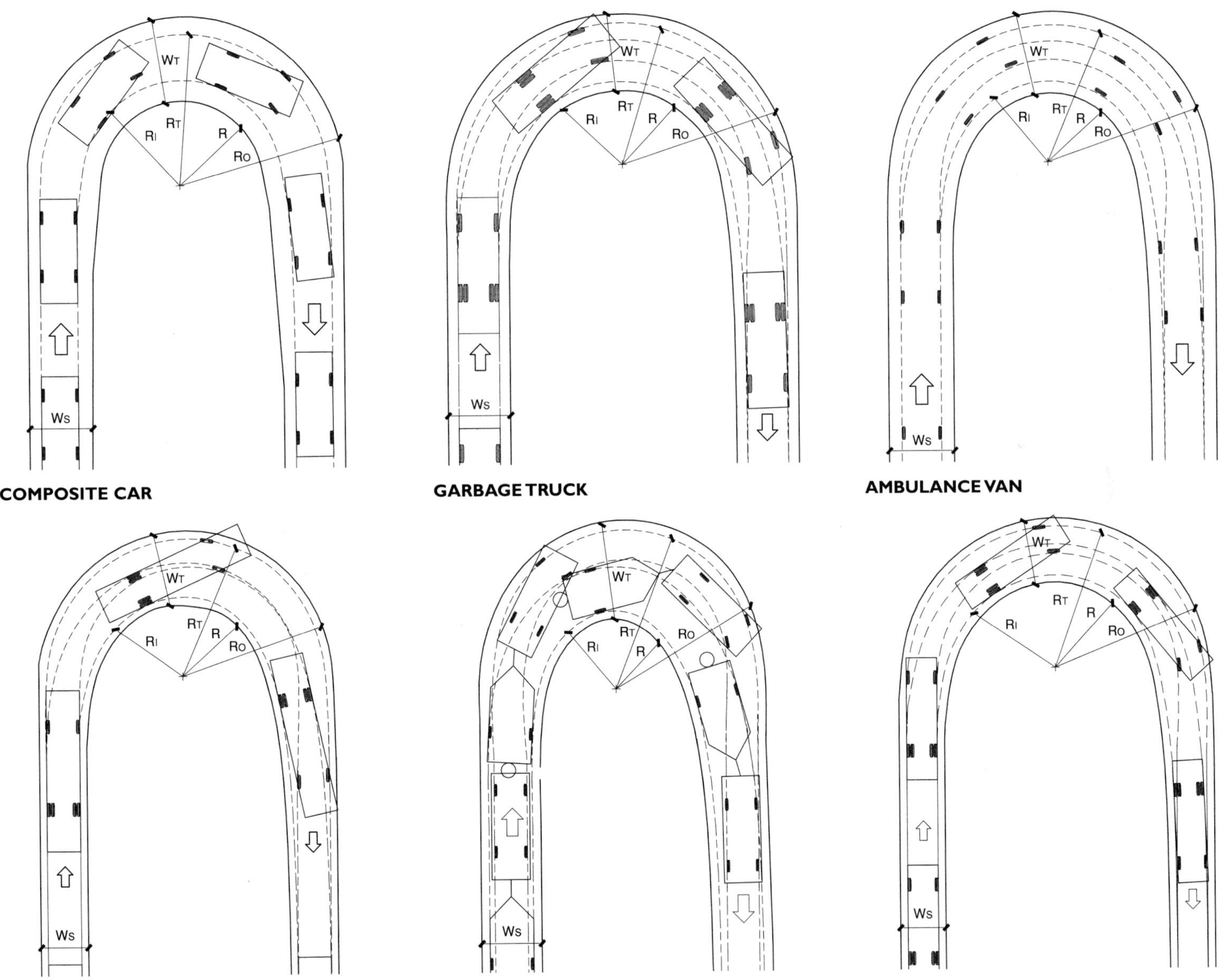

COMPOSITE CAR **GARBAGE TRUCK** **AMBULANCE VAN**

INTERCITY BUS **BOAT TRAILER** **FIRE TRUCK—PUMPER**

TYPICAL TURNING PATH

Eran Ben-Joseph, Associate Professor of Landscape Architecture and Planning, Massachusetts Institute of Technology

COMPARISON OF LEVELS OF SERVICE

LEVEL OF SERVICE	LOS D	LOS A
Type of users	Familiar, young adults	Unfamiliar, elderly
Length of stay	Long-term	Short-term
Turnover	Less than 2 per day	More than 5 per day
Type of generator	Industrial	Retail
Location	Urban	Rural
Image	Spec office	Corporate headquarters
Percent small cars	High	Low
Percent light trucks, vans, and utility vehicles	Low	High

Source: Mary S. Smith, P.E., Walker Parking Consultants/Engineers, Inc., Indianapolis, Indiana.

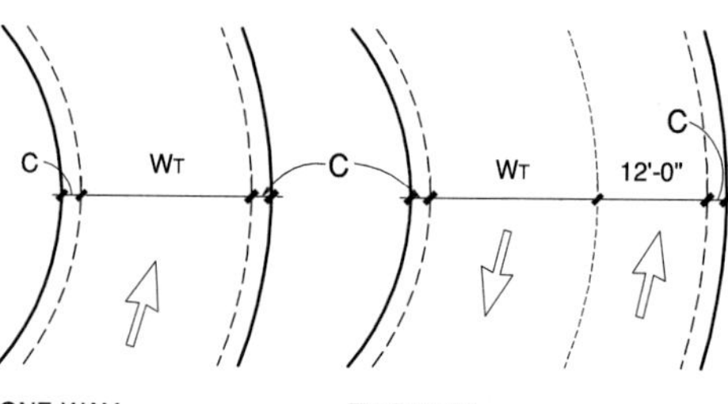

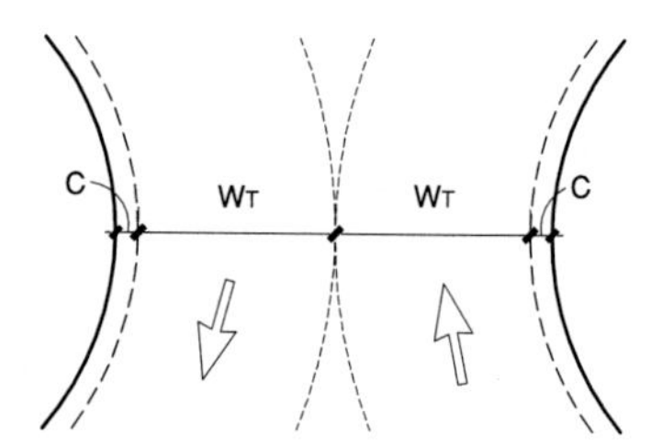

LANE WIDTH (TURNING)

Source: Mary S. Smith, P.E., Walker Parking Consultants/Engineers, Inc., Indianapolis, Indiana.

RECOMMENDED DESIGN PARAMETERS FOR VEHICULAR CIRCULATION[1]

		DRAWING KEY	LOS D	LOS C	LOS B	LOS A
Lane width, straight		W_S				
	One lane[2]		10′-0″	10′-6″	11′-0″	11′-6″
	Multiple lanes		9′-0″	9′-6″	10′-0″	10′-6″
Clearance to obstructions[3]		C	0′-6″	1′-0″	1′-6″	2′-0″
Radius, turning (outside front wheel)		R_T	24′-0″	30′-0″	36′-0″	42′-0″
Lane width, turning[4,5]		W_T				
	One lane		13′-6″	13′-6″	13′-6″	13′-6″
	Each additional lane		12′-0″	12′-0″	12′-0″	12′-0″
Circular helix[4,6]						
	Single-threaded[7]					
	Outside diameter	D_O	60′-0″	74′-0″	88′-0″	102′-0″
	Inside diameter[8]	D_I	24′-0″	36′-0″	48′-0″	60′-0″
	Double-threaded[9]					
	Outside diameter	D_O	80′-0″	95′-0″	110′-0″	125′-0″
	Inside diameter[9]	D_I	44′-0″	57′-0″	70′-0″	83′-0″
Express ramp slope		S	16%	14%	12%	10%
Transition length		L_T	10′-0″	11′-0″	12′-0″	13′-0″
Gated/controlled width[10]		W_G	8′-9″	9′-0″	9′-3″	9′-6″

1 The design parameters recommended are for design speeds ranging from 10 mph (LOS D) to 25 mph (LOS A). Additional dimensions for parking access aisles and turning bays are provided on the LGS parking design pages.
2 For all levels of service, use a 15-ft lane to make room for passing a broken-down vehicle.
3 The clearance given is from the edge of a lane to a wall, column, parked vehicle, or other obstruction, as cited in American Association of State Highway and Transportation Officials, A Policy on Geometric Design of Highways and Streets (1990) [ASHTO 1990], figure 111-25.
4 The dimensions given for LOS D are from AASHTO 1990 figure 111-23, except the clearance cited in that figure has been reduced to 2 ft, per figure 111-25.
5 For all levels of service, use a 20-ft lane to allow room to pass a broken-down vehicle, per AASHTO 1990 figure 111-23.
6 The diameters given measure from outside face to outside face of the walls (6-in. walls assumed).
7 Turning radii/lane width increased 3 ft because of multiple Turns.
8 Decrease 3 ft 6 in. to provide 20-ft lane in order to leave room to pass broken-down vehicles.
9 Ramp slope, minimum lane width, and clearance to walls control dimensions for double-threaded helix.
10 The dimensions given assume a straight approach to lane; check turns into lanes with template.

Source: Mary S. Smith, Parking Structures: Planning, Design, Maintenance and Repair, 2d ed. (Chapman and Hall, 1996).

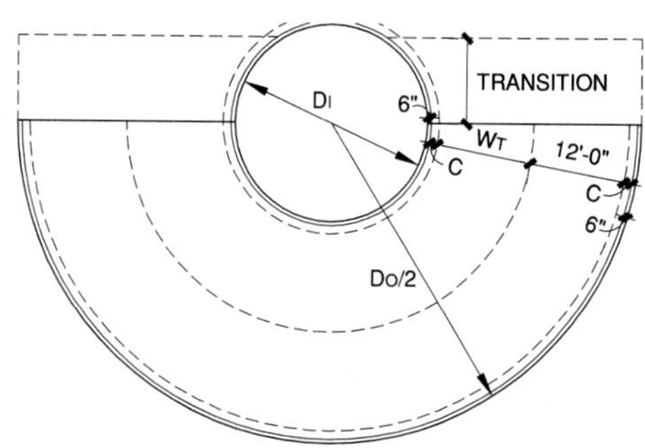

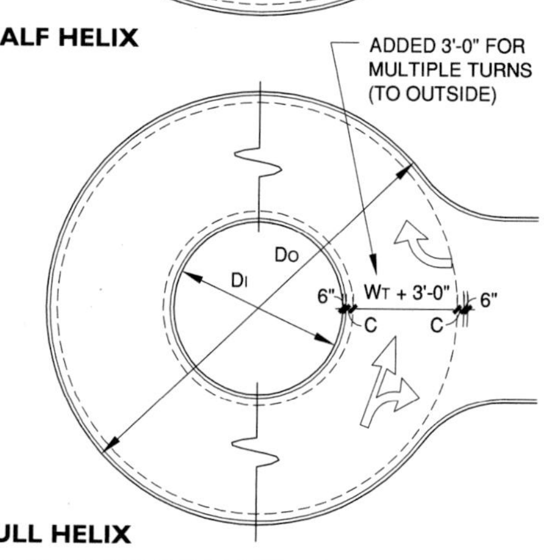

CIRCULAR HELIX (TURNING)

Source: Mary S. Smith, P.E., Walker Parking Consultants/Engineers, Inc., Indianapolis, Indiana.

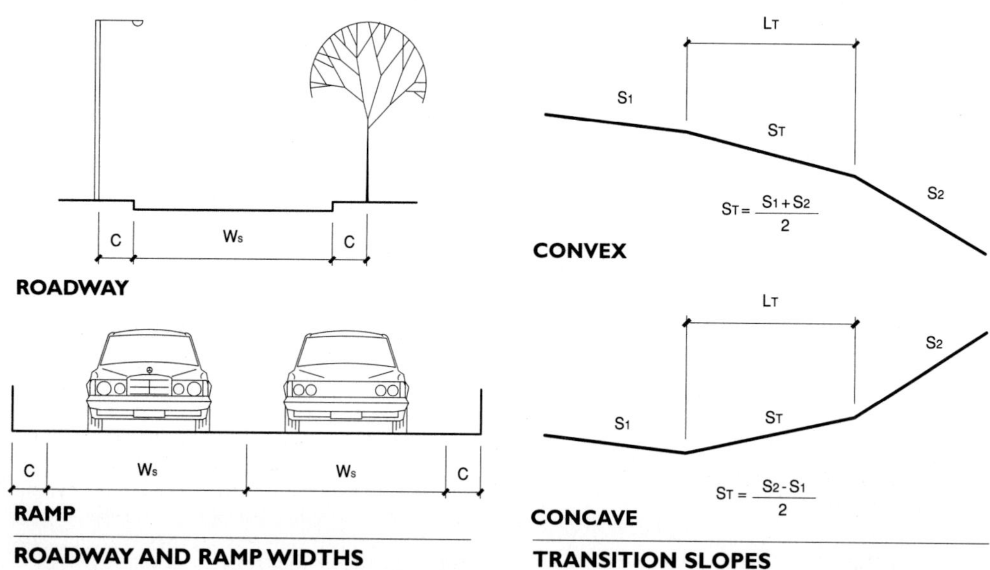

ROADWAY AND RAMP WIDTHS

Source: Mary S. Smith, P.E., Walker Parking Consultants/Engineers, Inc., Indianapolis, Indiana.

TRANSITION SLOPES

Source: Mary S. Smith, P.E., Walker Parking Consultants/Engineers, Inc., Indianapolis, Indiana.

Eran Ben-Joseph, Associate Professor of Landscape Architecture and Planning, Massachusetts Institute of Technology

ing trucks. Designers and planners should check with the local authorities for the sizes of the service vehicles that are used in a particular area. Fire trucks are generally 8 to 10 feet wide and from 25 feet long, for a pump truck, to 60 feet long, for a ladder-drawn model. In addition to the greater width and length of the trucks, space adjacent to a fire truck may be necessary for access of equipment. If a narrow roadway is desirable for traffic-calming purposes, mountable curbs allowing emergency vehicles to pass over can be used. It must be recognized that for some service providers, the federal government has requirements that affect vehicle size, such as fire trucks, school buses, and ambulances.

Infrastructure Easement

Utility easement zones should be allocated within the street right-of-way, regardless of whether they are actually constructed or not. Consider utility maintenance requirements as well as uniform dimensions for their location. The figure "Utility Easement Diagram" indicates typical utility easements within residential streets.

Parking

On-street parking should be encouraged whenever possible, as it is a highly efficient form of parking, especially where higher housing densities and a compact neighborhood are desired. On-street parking should be especially encouraged near the center of the neighborhood planning area, closest to the neighborhood focal point, services and transit stops, and so on. On-street parking also provides an important physical and psychological buffer between pedestrians on the sidewalk and traffic. The commonly held perception that on-street parking will create situations where children dart from behind a parked car into passing traffic is not borne out by actual experience.

Bicycle Lanes

Bicycle lanes provide an opportunity for people to ride a bike when they might not otherwise because of safety concerns. Streets that are direct and offer access to most destinations, such as arterials, are good choices for bicycle lanes. Bicycle lanes are usually marked with striping, with one stripe separating the bicycle lane from the vehicular travel lane and another stripe separating the bike lane from a parking lane. Bicycle lanes are typically 5 to 6 feet wide and are marked with a bike symbol and arrow indicating the direction of travel. Motorists are not allowed to travel or park in the bicycle lane except when turning or when entering or exiting a parking space.

Environmental Impacts and Natural Systems

Street systems are one component of a larger watershed approach to improving a region's water quality and environmental qualities. Consideration of an area's drainage patterns in the design of the street system is of major ecological importance, and should be done hand in hand with the street layout and gradient planning. Whenever possible, integrate a system of stormwater management within the street right-of-way. If an area has sensitive natural features, such as steep slopes, waterways, or wetlands, locate streets in a manner that preserves the features and natural drainage patterns to the greatest extent feasible. Align streets, whenever possible, to follow natural contours and features, and to provide visual and physical access to the natural features.

Wildlife habitat also needs to be considered. Where streets interfere with migration, mitigation with an underpass may be a solution.

Street planting can be designed as a neighborhood amenity that will increase livability and mitigate climatic conditions. Street trees, for example, not only improve the appearance of a street and raise the comfort level of the pedestrian, but also reduce runoff and reflected heat. Choose plant materials that are appropriate to the local conditions, require low maintenance, and will eventually be self-sustaining.

Clear sight lines at intersections and curb cuts are required. Planted shrubs and trees must allow for clear sight from a 2- to 8-foot area above the street. Sight line triangles can be used to ensure clear views at intersections and driveways, and many jurisdictions regulate the size of the triangle. When selecting a street tree, choose a variety that has branches high enough to allow commercial vehicles to pass underneath on the street side, and pedestrians to walk under on the sidewalk side. Trees with a downward branching pattern, such as pin oaks, do not work well as street trees.

Local Factors

Always consider and incorporate local conditions into the design and planning of a vehicular system. For example, in areas prone to hazards such as wildfires or hurricanes, wider streets may be needed to provide for designated evacuation routes. If snow removal and storage is an issue, consider snow storage locations and whether temporary parking restrictions for snow plowing or storage will be required. If the community is within an agriculture area, provisions may be needed for adequate passage of agricultural equipment.

OVERHEAD ELECTRIC
OVERHEAD TELEPHONE
STREET LIGHT
LOT LINE
ROADWAY
"D"
"D"
1/3 "D"
1-1/3 "D"
1/3 "D"
PLANTING
SIDEWALK
10' MINIMUM
GAS
ELECTRIC
WATER SUPPLY
SANITARY SEWER
STORM SEWER

UTILITY EASEMENT DIAGRAM

Source: Urban Land Institute.

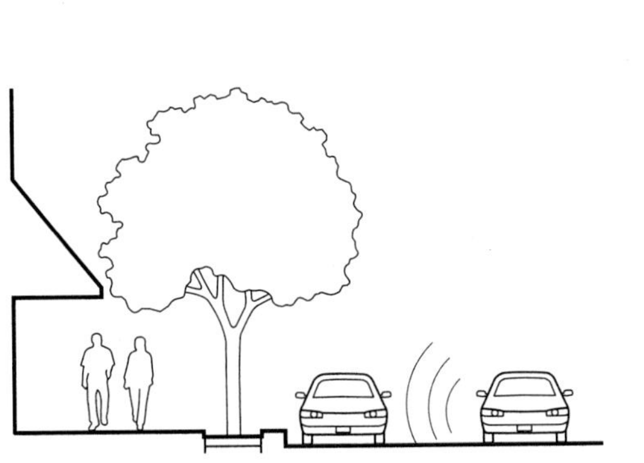

ON-STREET PARKING AS BUFFER

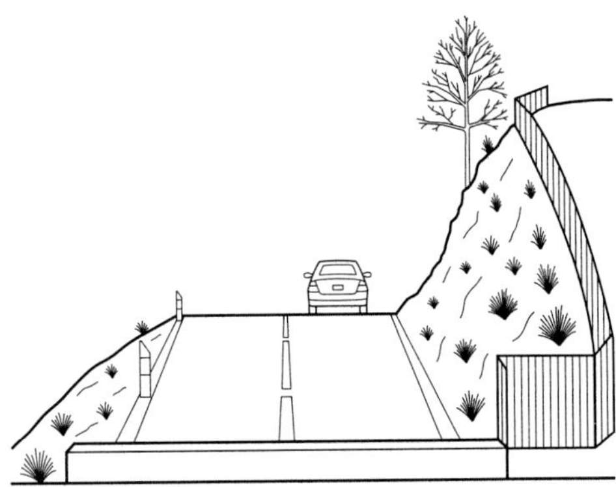

DIVERTER AND UNDERPASS FOR ANIMAL MOVEMENT

Source: Wench Dramstad, James Olson, and Richard Forman, Landscape Ecology Principles in Landscape Architecture and Land-Use Planning (Cambridge, MA: Harvard University Graduate School of Design, 1996).

Eran Ben-Joseph, Associate Professor of Landscape Architecture and Planning, Massachusetts Institute of Technology

DESIGN ELEMENTS

Street Grade

Design of vertical alignment involves the establishment of longitudinal grade or slope for roads, streets, and highways. The key considerations for determining grades are speed reduction, for maximum grade, and drainage, for minimum grade. Grade should be carefully considered in hilly terrain. For residential streets or streets designed for less than a 40-mph speed, typical standards for maximum grade vary between 4 to 14 percent, with a maximum 5-percent grade being the most common (see the table "General Requirements for Each Classification" on page 127). Minimum grades range between 0.3 and 1 percent, with a 0.5 percent minimum most commonly used.

Vertical curves should be provided at all points on streets where there is a change in grade. The major control for safe vehicle operation on vertical curves is sight distance; sight distance should be as long as possible or economically feasible.

Curb and Gutter

Curbs and gutters are used both as a way to provide roadway drainage and to delineate the edge of the street. Gutter widths vary between 1 and 2 feet, with the width being included in the curb lane width. Curbs range from vertical (barrier curbs) to rolling shapes (mountable curbs), with a vertical height ranging from 5 to 8 inches. A 6-inch high curb is most common.

Barrier curbs are designed to prevent, or at least discourage, vehicles from running off the pavement. Mountable curbs are designed to allow a vehicle to pass over the curb without damage to the vehicle, and have a flat sloping face 3 to 4 inches high. If needed, mountable curbs can be used in combination with narrow roadways to provide easier access for large fire trucks.

In cases where land use, density, topography, soils, and slope permit, vegetated open swales within the street rights-of-way should be considered. Such runoff treatment is preferable to the conventional impervious gutter and constructed curb.

If curbs are desirable, they can still be used in combination with a swale, filter strips, or infiltration basins when curb openings, or curb inserts are used, to allow stormwater runoff to flow through them.

Right-of-Way

Right-of-way standards are typically determined by local jurisdictions and state and federal guidelines. In most jurisdictions, 60- to 70-foot rights-of-way are commonly found. However, these standards have been followed for many years, and for residential areas may be too excessive. When considering the various designations within the right-of-way, address not only pavement width, but the use from the curb to the property line as well. In residential areas, consideration must be given to reduce rights-of-way while increasing neighborhood amenities or the amount of buildable lots.

Roadway Width

Roadway width is determined by the street classification and the width of the travel lanes. Roadway width may be narrowed at intersections to provide more visibility for pedestrians; this shortens the distance necessary for pedestrians to cross the street. The narrowing should not encroach into bike or travel lanes.

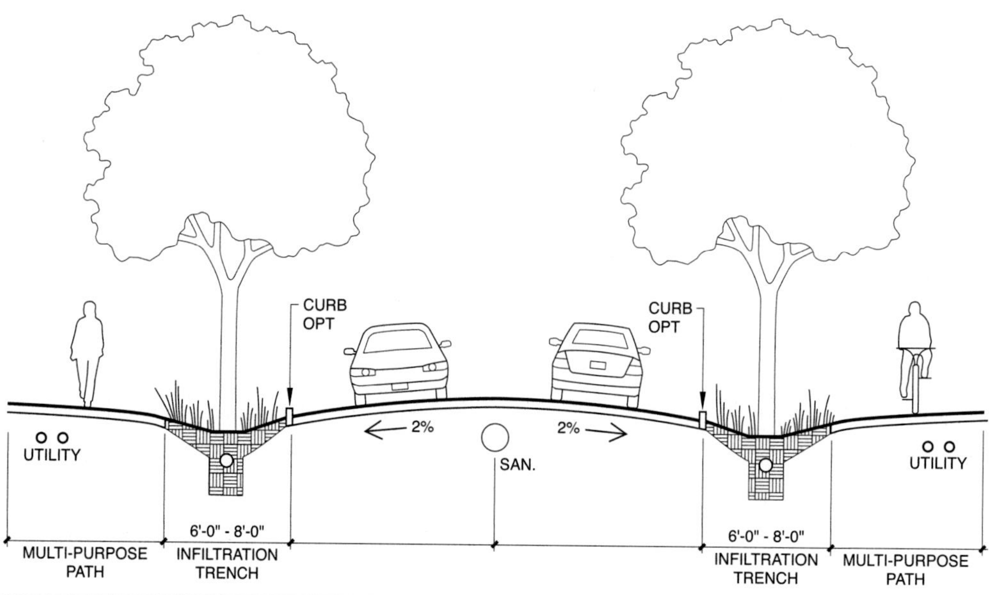

EXAMPLE OF VEGETATED SWALE FOR DRAINAGE: METRO PORTLAND, OREGON

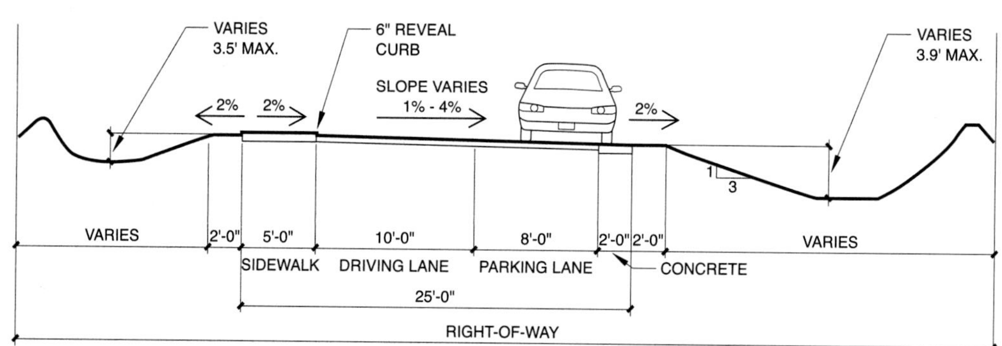

EXAMPLE OF VEGETATED SWALES ALONG RESIDENTIAL STREETS: CITY OF SEATTLE

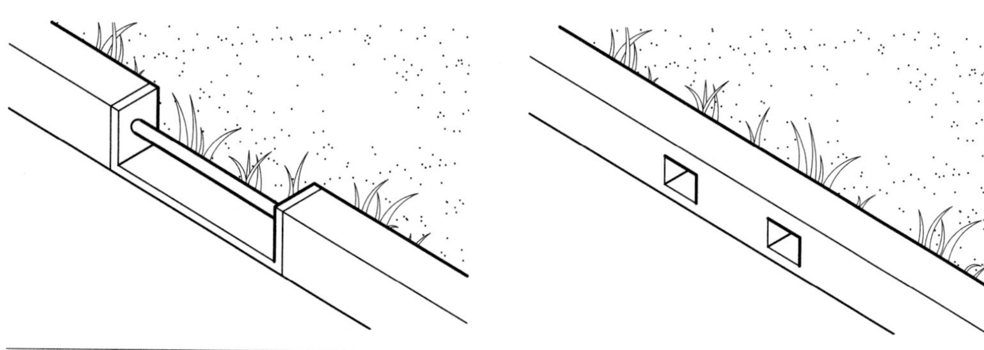

CURB OPENINGS AND CURB INSERTS

Eran Ben-Joseph, Associate Professor of Landscape Architecture and Planning, Massachusetts Institute of Technology

Where parking lanes are included, visual narrowing of the street and reduction of speed can be achieved by defining the parking spaces. For example, this can be achieved by planting street trees within the parking lane.

Lane Width

Lane width depends upon the street classification and its intended vehicular speed. An 11- to 12-foot lane is most commonly used. However, on residential streets with lower vehicular speeds, a 9- to 10-foot lane could be used (see the table "General Requirements for Each Classification" on page 127).

Shoulders

Roads in rural areas are normally designed without curbs and require full-width shoulders to accommodate high-traffic volumes. Streets in urban areas do not require shoulders, except where needed for lateral support of the pavement and curb structure. Where lateral support is required, the shoulder width should be 2 to 4 feet in width where feasible.

Corner Radii

Pedestrian safety and walkability often conflict with the desire to maintain free-flowing vehicular movement. Turning and corner radii are two of those areas of conflict. To eliminate high-speed vehicular turns and pedestrian street-crossing problems, small corner radii should be used. A wider radius at corners makes the crossing distance longer for pedestrians and encourages cars to speed around corners. Most corner radii are between 10 and 15 feet for local streets and 20 to 30 feet for collectors and arterials.

Central and Side Medians

Medians perform a functional as well as an aesthetic purpose and provide some character where little or none exists. Median strips can (a) physically separate traffic moving in opposing directions, or in the same direction but at different speeds; (b) prevent uncontrolled, unpredictable, and unsafe traffic movements *across* (perpendicular to) the main flow of traffic; (c) create a safe landing for pedestrians one-half of the way across a major street; (d) provide a planting area for landscaping and/or streetlights to enhance the traveling experience and image of the community; and (e) provide an excellent opportunity for the integration of stormwater treatment through bioretention areas, filter strips, and other similar practices.

Medians typically range from 4 to 20 feet wide, depending on their function and the inclusion of turning lanes.

Medians can also be utilized to create a boulevard with central faster-moving lanes and service (access) roads on both sides. Another boulevard configuration with a central median and two side medians offers an opportunity for the integration of transit services such as light rail.

Sidewalks and Planting Strips

The construction of sidewalks along streets should be a high-priority design element. Sidewalks should be built according to their intended pedestrian traffic volume. While shopping districts, school areas, and public facilities may call for a minimum sidewalk width of 8 feet, and occasionally up to 20 feet or more, most residential areas can be adequately served by 5- to 6-foot-wide walks. Most sidewalks are located on average about 1 to 2 feet off the right-of-way line to allow for access to underground utilities just outside the sidewalk. Sidewalks in urban areas are often constructed along the street curb, in contrast to many residential sidewalks, which include a 3- to 5-foot landscape border between the curb face and the sidewalk.

As with other landscape areas within the right-of-way, these borders provide an excellent opportunity for locating stormwater treatment features. They also help to compensate for a grade change where existing topography dictates a change in elevation between the roadway, the sidewalk, and the lot.

Typically, asphalt or concrete is used for sidewalk pavements. However, to reduce impervious surfaces, alternative materials such as pavers laid on sand, or porous asphalt and concrete, can be used.

Driveways

Driveways and curb cuts influence street design by increasing the number of conflict points with through traffic. Different regulations apply according to street classification and hierarchy. Many jurisdictions try to limit the number and spacing of driveways and curb cuts along arterial streets, and specify a minimum distance from intersections.

Driveway widths vary between 10 and 35 feet, and in residential streets allow for queuing, as moving cars can occasionally yield in the driveway space between parked cars. Whenever feasible, and in order to reduce curb cuts and impervious surfaces, shared driveways can be provided to serve two or more properties.

The U-shaped drive shown in the figure "Intersetions and Drives" illustrates a procedure for developing any drive configuration, given the design vehicle and its turning radii (R). The tangent (T_G) dimension is an approximate minimum required for transition from one turn direction to another.

Intersections

In laying out the street network, an important consideration is to minimize and simplify points of conflict. Intersection spacing is also important. As the number of intersections per mile increases, so do the number of potential conflicts and the potential increase in delay and congestion. That said, not providing an adequately dense street network forces farther travel to destinations. Most jurisdictions require a minimum of 200 feet between intersections. This distance increases with the type of street and the speed traveled. For example, along collectors, minimum intersection

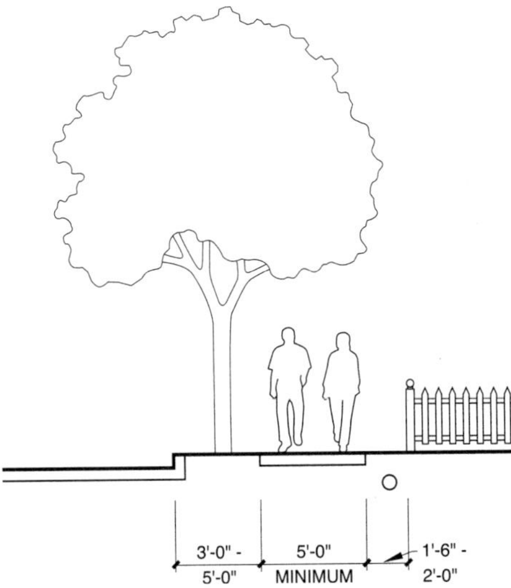

TYPICAL DIMENSIONS FOR SIDEWALKS AND PLANTING AREAS

STREET NARROWING AND TREE PLANTING IN PARKING LANE

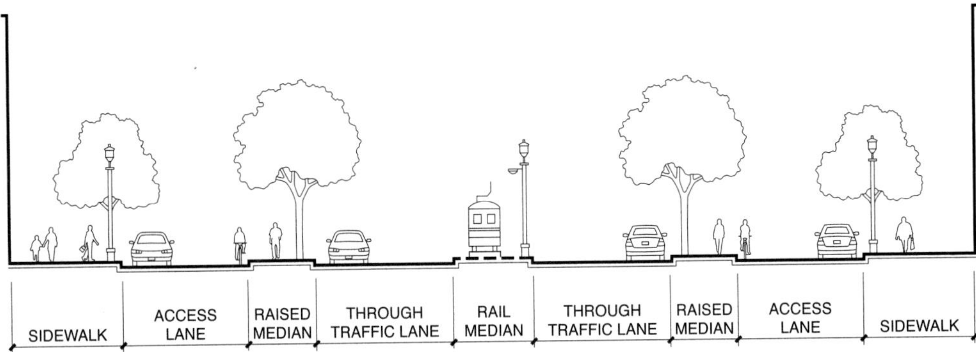

USE OF MEDIANS IN A BOULEVARD SETTING

Eran Ben-Joseph, Associate Professor of Landscape Architecture and Planning, Massachusetts Institute of Technology

UNLOADING AREA
20'-0" RADIUS
T_G
R_C R_I R_O W_S
BUS WILL NOT BE STRAIGHT AT STOP UNLESS TANGENT (T_G) DIMENSION IS PROVIDED BETWEEN RADII.
10'-0" RADIUS
10'-0" RADIUS
W OR $\frac{W_S}{2}$
L
CENTERLINE OF STREET

U-SHAPED DRIVE

PUBLIC ROAD
4'-0" RADIUS
4'-0" RADIUS
W_T R_C W_S
11'-0" MERGING LANE
4'-0" RADIUS
PUBLIC ROAD

PRIVATE ROADS INTERSECTING PUBLIC ROADS

GENERAL

The U-shaped drive shown here illustrates a procedure for developing any drive configuration, given the design vehicle and its turning radii (R). The tangent (T_G) dimension is an approximate minimum required for transition from one turn direction to another.

INTERSECTIONS AND DRIVES

Source: Mary S. Smith, P.E., Walker Parking Consultants/Engineers, Inc., Indianapolis, Indiana.

MINIMUM TURNING RADIUS FOR DESIGN VEHICLES (FT-IN.)

VEHICLE TYPE	MINIMUM TURNING RADIUS (R_T)	OUTSIDE FRONT RADIUS (R_O)	INSIDE REAR RADIUS (R_I)	STRAIGHT LANE WIDTH (W_S)	CURVED LANE WIDTH (W_T)	INSIDE CURB RADIUS (R)	TANGENT LENGTH (T)
Composite private vehicle	24-0	26-0	15-6	10-0	13-6	12-6	24-7
Wheelchair lift van	24-9	26-8	16-7	10-0	12-6	14-0	24-4
Boat trailer	24-0	24-11	8-5	11-0	16-11	6-10	60-9
RV trailer	23-10	25-4	5-7	11-0	18-4	4-1	83-3
Motor home	39-7	42-8	27-6	11-0	19-0	23-0	41-2
Stretch limousine	32-7	34-10	23-8	11-0	14-6	20-2	34-1
Shuttle van	24-10	26-11	16-5	11-0	13-6	13-4	29-7
Paratransit/ Shuttle bus	25-2	26-11	16-6	11-0	13-6	13-4	29-4
Intercity bus	35-3	36-10	23-5	12-0	17-10	18-7	60-0
City bus	42-0	46-6	24-0	12-0	27-0	21-0	60-0
Articulated bus	38-0	43-0	14-0	12-0	22-0	11-0	62-0
School bus	41-9	43-6	28-7	12-0	17-8	25-3	56-4
Garbage truck	31-0	33-4	20-8	12-0	14-6	18-6	38-0
Ambulance van	24-9	27-2	16-7	11-0	13-5	13-5	29-0
Paramedic unit	28-5	30-10	18-8	12-0	15-1	15-6	33-0
Fire truck-pumper	38-11	41-0	27-7	12-0	16-4	24-4	44-0

Source: American Association of State Highway and Transportation Officials (AASHTO)

1. Minimum turn radii at less than 10 mph.
2. Obstructions (columns, walls, light poles, etc.) should be held a minimum of 6 in. (2 ft preferred) from the edge of the lane given above. See details on the LGS page on driveways and raodways.

MINIMUM TURNING RADIUS FOR DESIGN VEHICLES (FT-IN.)

VEHICLE TYPE	MINIMUM TURNING RADIUS (R_T)	OUTSIDE FRONT RADIUS (R_O)	INSIDE REAR RADIUS (R_I)	STRAIGHT LANE WIDTH (W_S)	CURVED LANE WIDTH (W_T)	INSIDE CURB RADIUS (R_C)	TANGENT LENGTH (T)
Trash truck	3-0	33-1	21-2	12-0	14-11	18-4	38-0
Single unit truck	42-0	44-0	28-0	12-0	20-0	25-0	40-10
WB-40 truck	40-0	41-6	19-0	12-0	25-0	16-0	67-1
WB-50 truck	45-0	46-0	19-0	12-0	30-0	16-0	116-8
WB-60 truck	45-0	45-6	22-0	12-0	27-0	19-0	65-0

1. Minimum turn radii at less than 10 mph.
2. Obstructions (columns, walls, light poles, etc.) should be held a minimum of 6 in. (2 ft preferred) from the edge of the lane given above. See details on the LGS page on driveways and raodways.

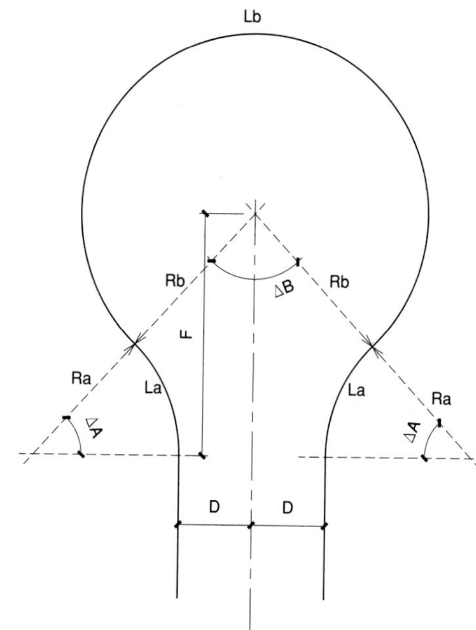

CUL-DE-SAC DIMENSIONS*

	SMALL	LARGE
D	16′-0″	22′-0″
F	50′-11″	87′-3″
ΔA	46.71°	35.58°
ΔB	273.42°	251.15°
Ra	32′-0″	100′-0″
Rb	38′-0″	50′-0″
La	26′-1″	61′-8″
Lb	181′-4″	219′-2″

**The R values for vehicles intended to use these culs-de-sac should not exceed Rb.*

Source: Mary S. Smith, P.E., Walker Parking Consultants/Engineers, Inc., Indianapolis, Indiana.

CUL-DE-SAC

Source: Mary S. Smith, P.E., Walker Parking Consultants/Engineers, Inc., Indianapolis, Indiana.

Eran Ben-Joseph, Associate Professor of Landscape Architecture and Planning, Massachusetts Institute of Technology

spacing is around 600 feet, while along arterials it may reach one-fourth to one-half mile.

To reduce and minimize conflict impacts, maintain a clear line of sight at intersections. Crossing roadways should intersect at 90 degrees whenever possible, and should intersect at less than 80 degrees or more than 100 degrees. Mini-roundabouts are an excellent way to mitigate for conflict areas within intersection design. Roundabout design guides such as those by the Federal Highway Administration (FHWA), or other design criteria approved by the local entity engineer can serve as a design guideline.

RESIDENTIAL SETTINGS

When designing street layouts, avoid directing major traffic circulation through residential developments.

Consider the following design criteria within residential areas:

- Minimize the amount of internal travel while maximizing convenience of access to nonresidential activities.
- In residential street layout, aim at providing a series of spaces in which the road pavement plays an integrated function, as opposed to the typical linear pavement that just facilitates automobile movement.
- Residential streets are regularly used as play areas, so design them to reflect a pedestrian orientation rather than to facilitate vehicular movement.
- Set the radius of cul-de-sacs to the minimum required to accommodate emergency and maintenance vehicles. Consider alternative turnarounds.

Traffic Calming

Traffic calming improves neighborhood livability and the pedestrian environment by reducing vehicle speeds, vehicle noise, visual impacts, and through-traffic volumes. Traffic calming includes a variety of design techniques and traffic management programs.

Typical traffic calming measures include:

- Vertical changes to the road (e.g., speed bumps and humps, raised intersections, etc.)
- Lateral changes in the road (e.g., chicanes, narrowing, traffic diverters, etc.)
- Traffic circles
- Small corner radii
- Gateway features
- Related streetscaping (street furniture, lighting, landscaping, etc.)

Queuing

For streets of up to 750 vehicles per day, traffic and delay considerations do not necessitate the need for more than one traffic lane. A single-lane configuration is sufficient if parking lanes are incorporated or passing places are provided. For example, the width of residential streets may be as narrow as 20 feet with parking on one side. Through careful design, this can

PARKED

PARKED

QUEUING AT DRIVEWAYS

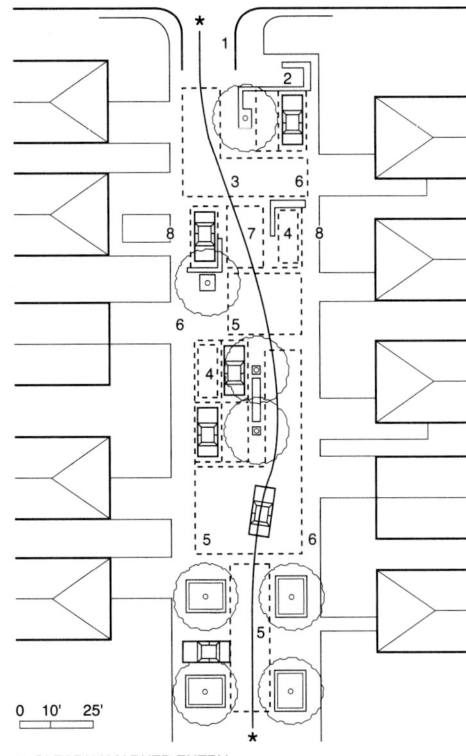

1. CLEARLY MARKED ENTRY
2. SITTING AREA/BENCH
3. BEND IN DRIVING LANE
4. PARKING SPACE
5. VARIED PAVING MATERIALS
6. NO CONTINUOUS CURB
7. CHOKERS/PLANTING BEDS
8. TYPICAL RIGHT-OF-WAY

SHARED-STREET DESIGN PRINCIPLES

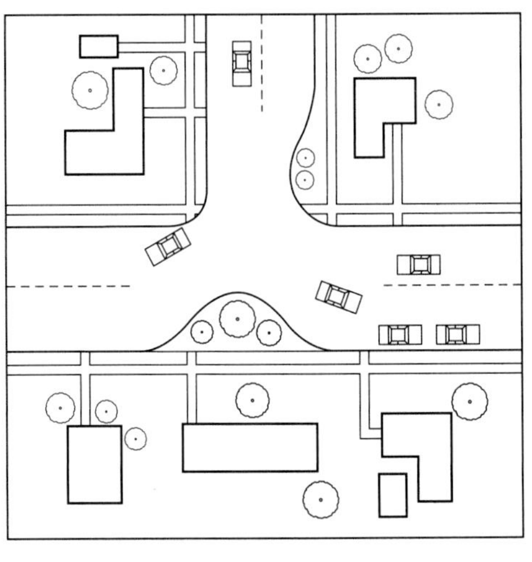

NECKDOWNS

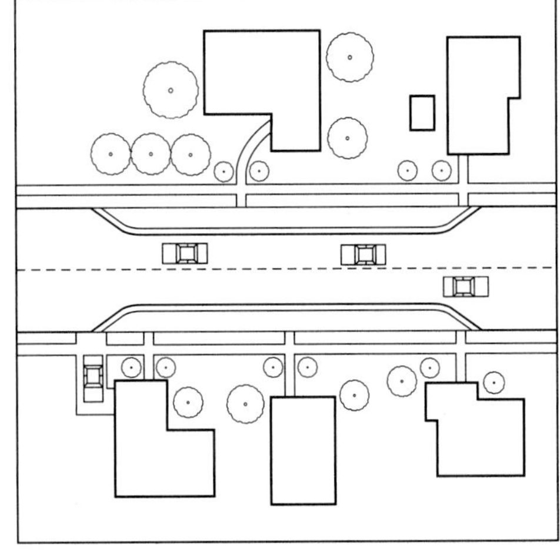

CHOKERS

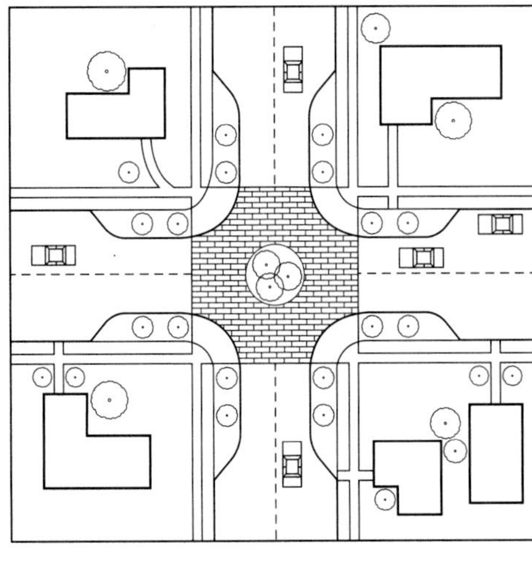

COMBINED MEASURES

EXAMPLES OF TYPICAL TRAFFIC-CALMING TECHNIQUES

Source: United States Department of Transportation.

Eran Ben-Joseph, Associate Professor of Landscape Architecture and Planning, Massachusetts Institute of Technology

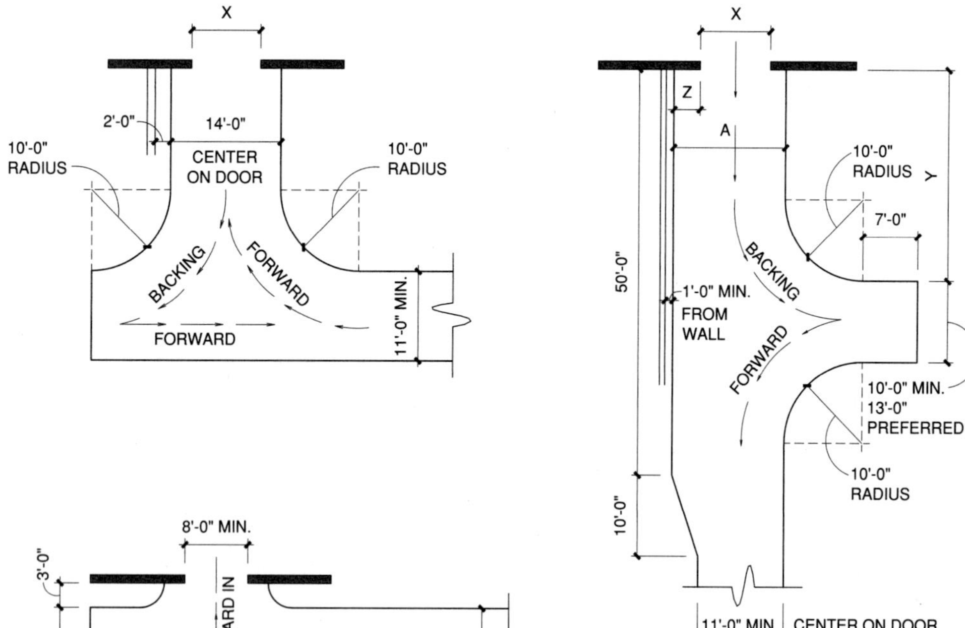

Use this three-maneuver entrance for single car garages only when space limitations demand it. The drawing is based on dimensions for a large car.

SPACE REQUIREMENTS FOR DRIVEWAY LAYOUTS

90° IN–BACK OUT (1 CAR)

X	8'-9"	9'-0"	10'-0"	11'-0"	12'-0"
Y	25'-0"	24'-6"	23'-8"	23'-0"	22'-0"

STRAIGHT IN–BACK OUT

X	9'-0"	10'-0"	12'-0"	16'-0"
Y	26'-0"	25'-0"	23'-6"	24'-0"
Z	3'-4"	3'-1"	2'-0"	3'-0"
A	14'-4"	14'-5"	14'-8"	20'-0"

Source: Mary S. Smith, P.E., Walker Parking Consultants/Engineers, Inc., Indianapolis, Indiana.

PRIVATE DRIVEWAYS TO RESIDENTIAL GARAGES

Source: Mary S. Smith, P.E., Walker Parking Consultants/Engineers, Inc., Indianapolis, Indiana.

produce cost savings in grading, drainage, and street construction, and lessen the amount of impervious surfaces.

Shared Streets

The underlying concept of the shared street system is one of integration, with an emphasis on the community and the residential user. Pedestrians, children at play, bicyclists, parked cars, and moving cars all share the same street space. Even though it seems these uses conflict with one another, the physical design is such that drivers are placed in an inferior position. Through geometrical and physical changes in the street cross section and its physical appearance, motorists sense that they are intruding into a pedestrian zone and drive more slowly and cautiously. By redesigning the physical aspects of the street, the social and physical public domain of the pedestrian is reclaimed.

Alleyways

Alleys eliminate the demand for automobile access to the property from the front, reduce the need for curb cuts, and reduce the number of parking garages oriented to the street. Alleys also provide an excellent alternative for utility easements and service access. The typical alleyway right-of-way width is 15 to 20 feet, with pavement typically covering the full width of the right-of-way.

REFERENCES

American Association of State Highway and Transportation Officials (AASHTO). 2001. *A Policy on Geometric Design of Highways and Streets.* Washington DC: AASHTO.

Burden, Dan. 1999. *Street Design Guidelines for Healthy Neighborhoods.* Sacramento, CA: Center for Livable Communities: Local Government Commission.

Institute of Transportation Engineers (ITE). 1993. *Guidelines for Residential Subdivision Street Design: A Recommended Practice.* Washington, DC: Institute of Transportation Engineers.

———. 1999. *Traditional Neighborhood Development Street Design Guidelines: A Recommended Practice.* Washington, DC: Institute of Transportation Engineers.

Jacobs, Allan, Elizabeth MacDonald, and Yodan Rofé. 2001. *The Boulevard Book: History, Evolution, Design of Multiway Boulevard* Cambridge and London: MIT Press.

Kloster, Tom, Ted Leybold, and Clark Wilson. 2002. *Green Streets: Innovative Solutions for Stormwater and Stream Crossings.* Portland, OR: Metro Regional Services.

Kulash, Walter. 2001. *Residential Streets.* Washington, DC: Urban Land Institute.

Eran Ben-Joseph, Associate Professor of Landscape Architecture and Planning, Massachusetts Institute of Technology

PARKING STANDARDS

GENERAL

In today's automobile-oriented society, parking areas have become a key component in the landscape. In some situations, based on zoning or building requirements, the parking area can appear to be the dominant site element. It is usually the first and the last element of a building complex that customers, visitors, and employees view when entering and leaving the site. The design of the parking area should be convenient, safe, pedestrian-friendly, and cost-effective. In addition to optimizing the space allocated to parking, key design objectives should be to create a favorable impression for the user and to include the adoption of green building practices, technologies, policies, and standards.

These objectives can be achieved by: creating a visual buffer with a planting strip along the parking perimeter with berms and plantings of trees, shrubs, and grasses appropriate for the soil, and indigenous wildflowers utilized to reduce mowing emissions and irrigation requirements; using pervious paving systems in parking lots to allow water to penetrate, thereby reducing stormwater runoff; installing islands with a mixture of canopy trees, flowering trees, and evergreens to soften the impact of the vast hardscape, produce shade, and reduce heat islands; and creating a logical, safe, and convenient pedestrian access from automobile to destination.

PLANTING

Given the prominence of parking areas in the landscape, one of the most common requirements in their design is some type of screening from the public view. This can range from barriers or screens that form a total visual block to those that screen only part of the view. Partial screening may filter visibility to the parking areas, or screen portions of visibility to the parking areas (this is usually measured as a percentage of opaqueness). Any consideration of parking screening needs to take into account security concerns and how limited visibility will affect the safety and well-being of the users of the parking area. Factors that need to be considered in an overall parking area design include: whether access to the parking area is controlled by security personnel or is accessible to the general public; visual connectivity to the user's destination; and hours of operation.

For a total visual barrier, opaque fences or walls are often the design choice. A change of grade or the creation of earth berms can provide a total visual barrier. For partial screening, fencing that limits some visual access while allowing some visibility into the parking area is one choice. Another approach is to use plant material to achieve the desired screening effect. When using plant material to achieve perimeter screening, one possibility is to utilize a combination of trees and shrubs. Trees that are limbed up to 6 feet high with an understory planting of shrubs that will grow to approximately 3 to 3½ feet in height provide an aesthetically pleasing view from outside the parking area, yet offer a band of horizontal visual access that allows views into the parking area, as a means of addressing security and safety concerns.

Equally important is the consideration of planting within the parking area. Particularly in the case of very large parking areas, every effort should be made to include planted islands as a way to break up the large expanse of paved surface. Tree-lined walks can help define the pedestrian circulation routes, as well as provide a pleasant experience for users as they walk to or from their destinations. Planted areas within parking areas that include trees serve to provide valuable shade, which reduces the level of radiant heat generated by the parking area surface (this is particularly important in the case of asphalt pavements). The overall result can help to reduce the urban heat island effect.

When trees are included as part of the design of the parking area, it is important to allocate enough planting space so that a sufficient amount of air and water are available to meet the trees' requirements. In general, fewer but larger planted islands, versus more numerous but smaller areas, provide a better environment for trees to grow. Groupings of plants in these larger areas can have considerably greater impact than individual plants scattered more widely across the same area. Where constraints make leaving adequate space difficult, special subsurface provisions should be considered to provide air, water, and nutrients to compensate for the reduced ground space.

The height of vehicles must be factored in when measuring the impact that shrubs will have on the overall appearance of the parking area. Low shrubs planted in narrow strips between parking rows will not have much of a visual impact. Along those same lines, shrubs planted at the ends of parking rows should not obscure the view of vehicle drivers entering or leaving the parking aisle. For all planted areas within the parking area, an adequate buffer needs to be included to prevent damage to the plants from the parked vehicles. This requires that the design accommodate not just the dimensions of the vehicles and parking stalls but also the front and rear overhangs of the vehicles to ensure an adequate buffer is created.

Finally, parking area planting does not have to be repetitive and monotonous. Creative plant choices, grouping, and designs can help distinguish different spaces of a large parking area.

DRAINAGE

Landscaped areas incorporated into a parking area design can help with stormwater management. In order to be effective, the paved areas should be graded toward these planted areas, and they need to be flush in order to be able to receive the water directed toward them (raised planters are not helpful in controlling runoff). If the planted areas are slightly depressed, they will be able to hold larger quantities of water, thus allowing time for the water to percolate into the soil. An added benefit of the depressed planted strips is that they are less likely to be used as a pedestrian shortcut. Bioswales that can be planted with salt-tolerant plants and grasses that can filter stormwater before it percolates into the ground should be considered. Areas for stormwater drainage retention should be integrated with the parking area to collect stormwater runoff. These areas can be planted with native species that prefer wet conditions.

PEDESTRIAN CIRCULATION

Well-designed parking areas are as much about people as they are about vehicles. Getting pedestrians to and from their vehicles safely is a paramount concern in any parking area. Best is a hierarchy of pedestrian routes that provide walks from the parking space to larger central walkways, which are separate from the vehicular circulation. Wherever the larger central walkways intersect with vehicular circulation routes, adequate traffic control devices should be provided to ensure a safe pedestrian crossing. In addition to signage and pavement markings, this can include the use of bollards that signify to both pedestrians and drivers that caution should be exhibited. Pedestrian walks within the parking area should be carefully designed to encourage people to use these designated routes instead of cutting across planted areas, which not only impacts the plants' survival but raises the risk of a pedestrian safety issue as well.

ACCESS

Access to parking areas that require vehicles to cross pedestrian sidewalks are an inherent and serious pedestrian/vehicular conflict. Entrances to and from parking areas should provide good visibility and traffic control devices to safeguard the pedestrian. Barrier gates at entrances should be constructed so that the vehicle does not block the sidewalk while waiting to gain entry.

DESIGNING PARKING AREAS IN ACCORDANCE WITH LEADERSHIP IN ENERGY AND ENVIRONMENTAL DESIGN (LEED)

Although parking areas often carry with them a negative connotation, there are many opportunities to design them in accordance with LEED standards. Such an opportunity to design an environmentally sensitive parking area should not be squandered.

The use of plant material, as already explained, is an important component of parking area design. One way to further capitalize on their environmental value is to use native plantings that optimize use of water and help reduce stormwater runoff. Native species have the advantage of being able to thrive in existing conditions without the addition of irrigation systems. Using native plantings also can help reduce the amount of exhaust generated by mowers required to maintain lawn areas.

The choice and use of paving materials for the parking area is another opportunity to make environmentally responsible design decisions. The most obvious and direct approach is to design the parking area as efficiently as possible, resulting in the least amount of pavement. This usually means utilizing a double-loaded parking design, where a row of parking spots shares the same travel aisle. Another approach would be to use pervious paving materials to the greatest extent possible. In the material chosen for the pavement as well as for the base course, the use of recycled materials as part of this construction process should be considered whenever possible.

In choosing a pavement for the parking area, the use of lighter-colored (high albedo and reflectivity) paving materials should be considered. Albedo in this context is defined as the amount of solar radiation reflected from a material, as compared to the amount that shines on the material. Lighter-colored surfaces generally have a high albedo. Darker surfaces generally have a low albedo and absorb solar radiation that is converted to heat, making the surface temperature of the paving material hotter. This heat radiates from the surface, contributing to the heat island effect.

James Holtgreven, RLA; Leonard Hopper, RLA, FASLA

PARKING LOT DESIGN GUIDELINES

NOTES ON DESIGN GUIDELINES

- Determine an efficient means of laying out the parking lot (see vehicle and parking space dimension data on other LGS pages on parking). A smaller paved area costs less to build and maintain, offers a shorter walking distance from car to building, lessens water runoff problems, and leaves more space for site landscaping.
- Provide safe and coherent site circulation routes.
- Provide access for fire rescue and mass transit vehicles. Consult local requirements.
- Parking lots should offer direct and easy access for people walking between their vehicles and the building entrances. Pedestrians usually walk in the aisles behind parked vehicles; aisles perpendicular to the building face allow pedestrians to walk to and from the building without squeezing between parked cars. Walking areas should be graded to prevent standing water.
- Accessible design is now mandatory, requiring designated parking spaces and curb ramps near building entrances.

LANDSCAPE

Plants in parking areas can help relieve the visually overwhelming scale of large parking lots. To maximize the effect of landscaping, consider the screening capabilities of plants. Low branching, densely foliated trees and shrubs can soften the visual impact of large parking areas. High branching canopy trees do not create a visual screen at eye level but do provide shade. When possible, create islands large enough to accommodate a mixture of canopy trees, flowering trees, evergreen trees, shrubs, and flowers. Consider using evergreens, and avoid plants that drop fruit or sap.

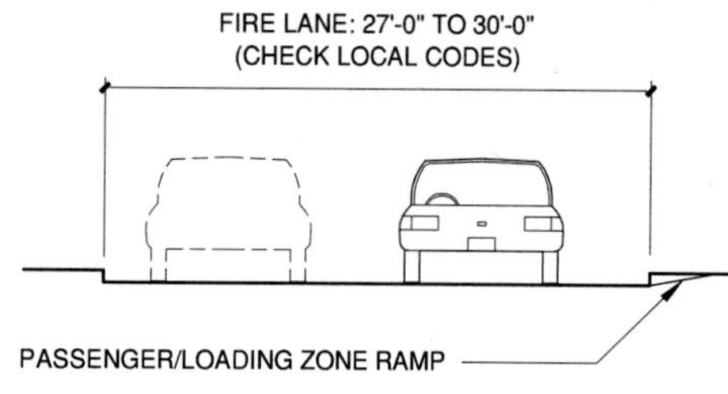

FIRE LANE

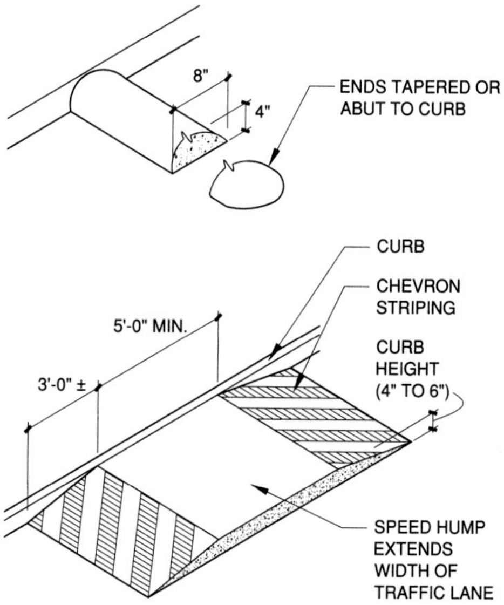

8"
4"
ENDS TAPERED OR ABUT TO CURB
CURB
CHEVRON STRIPING
5'-0" MIN.
3'-0" ±
CURB HEIGHT (4" TO 6")
SPEED HUMP EXTENDS WIDTH OF TRAFFIC LANE

Use of a speed hump eliminates the need for an accessible curb ramp.

SPEED CONTROL DEVICES

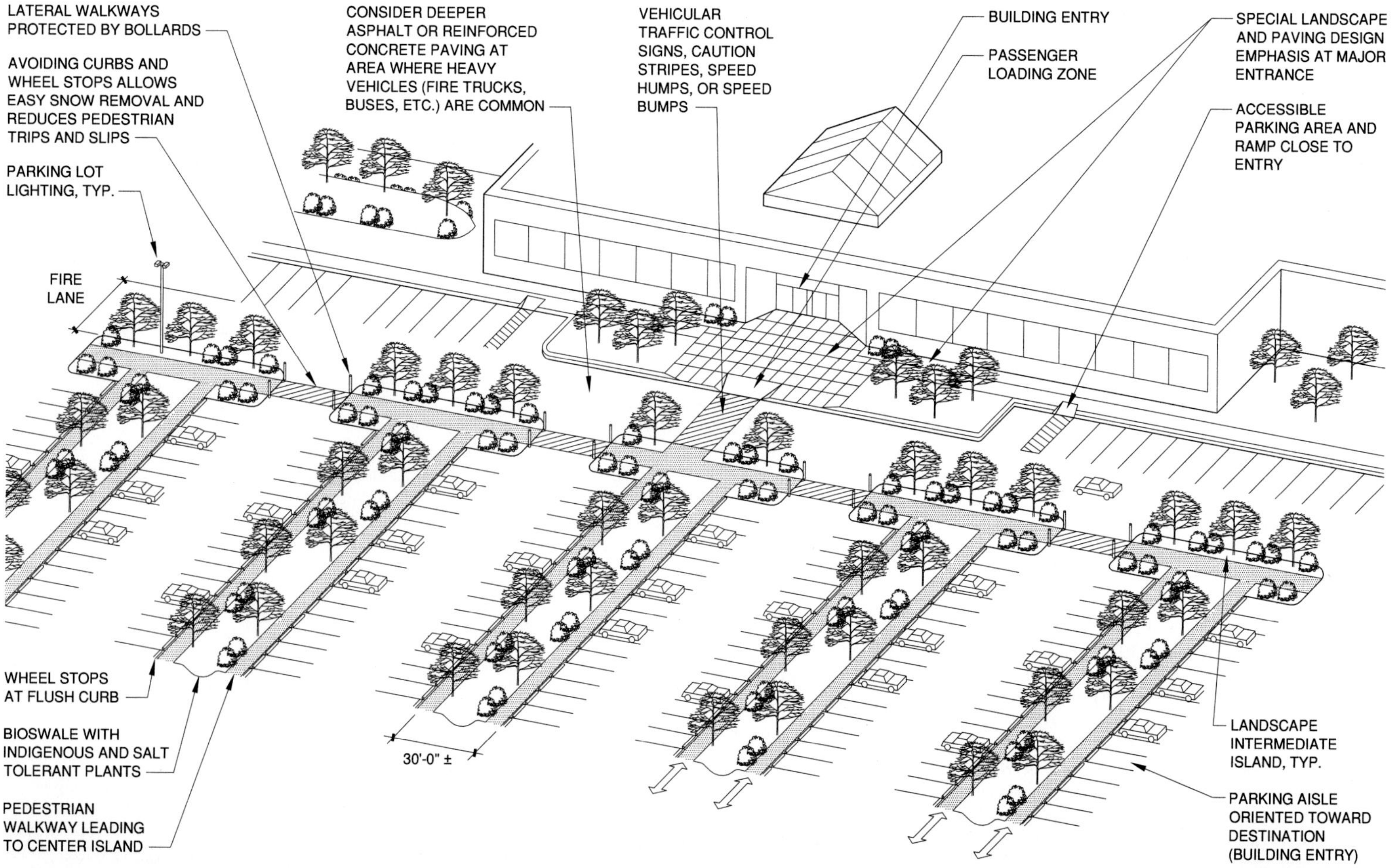

LATERAL WALKWAYS PROTECTED BY BOLLARDS
AVOIDING CURBS AND WHEEL STOPS ALLOWS EASY SNOW REMOVAL AND REDUCES PEDESTRIAN TRIPS AND SLIPS
PARKING LOT LIGHTING, TYP.
FIRE LANE
CONSIDER DEEPER ASPHALT OR REINFORCED CONCRETE PAVING AT AREA WHERE HEAVY VEHICLES (FIRE TRUCKS, BUSES, ETC.) ARE COMMON
VEHICULAR TRAFFIC CONTROL SIGNS, CAUTION STRIPES, SPEED HUMPS, OR SPEED BUMPS
BUILDING ENTRY
PASSENGER LOADING ZONE
SPECIAL LANDSCAPE AND PAVING DESIGN EMPHASIS AT MAJOR ENTRANCE
ACCESSIBLE PARKING AREA AND RAMP CLOSE TO ENTRY
WHEEL STOPS AT FLUSH CURB
BIOSWALE WITH INDIGENOUS AND SALT TOLERANT PLANTS
PEDESTRIAN WALKWAY LEADING TO CENTER ISLAND
30'-0" ±
LANDSCAPE INTERMEDIATE ISLAND, TYP.
PARKING AISLE ORIENTED TOWARD DESTINATION (BUILDING ENTRY)

Confirm requirements for fire lanes adjacent to buildings. Consult local codes.

COMMERCIAL PARKING ARRANGEMENT

Mary S. Smith, P.E., Walker Parking Consultants/Engineers, Inc., Indianapolis, Indiana; James Holtgrewen, RLA; Leonard Hopper, RLA, FASLA

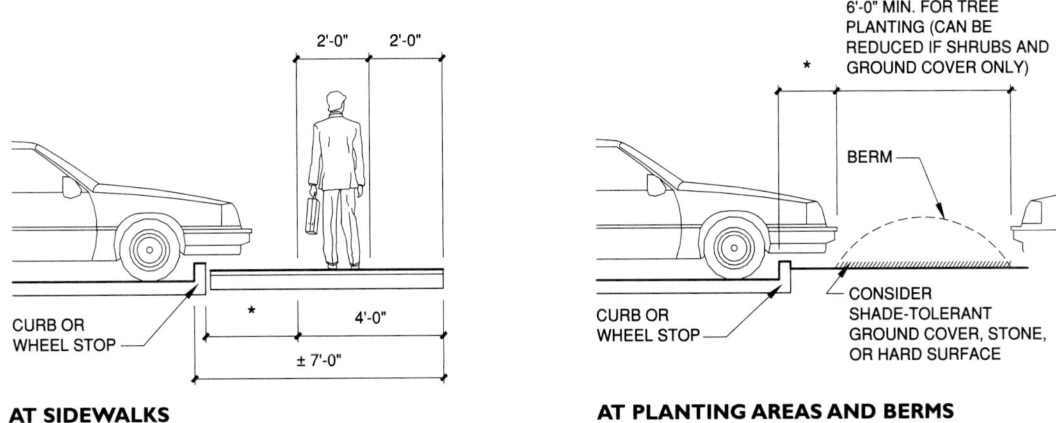

AT SIDEWALKS

AT PLANTING AREAS AND BERMS

*See the LGS pages on design vehicle dimensions for perpendicular dimension of overhang; adjust for angled parking.

AUTOMOBILE OVERHANG REQUIREMENTS

Mary S. Smith, P.E., Walker Parking Consultants/Engineers, Inc., Indianapolis, Indiana

PARKING SPACE DIMENSIONS

GENERAL

- Parking stalls for a design vehicle 6 ft 4 in. wide and 16 ft 9 in. long should have a stripe projection of 16 ft 3 in. and parallel stall length of 20 ft 9 in.
- Small-car-only stalls (7 ft 5 in. wide by 15 ft long) should only be used at constrained locations or in remnants of space. The number of these stalls should not exceed 10% of total parking capacity at a site.
- Angles between 76 and 89° are not recommended for one-way design because these angles permit drivers of smaller cars to back out and exit the wrong way.
- Angled parking is not recommended for use with two-way aisles as drivers often attempt to make a U-turn into stalls on the other side of the aisle.
- Add 1 ft to the module for surface parking bays without curbs or other parking guides (frequent poles or columns or walls) in areas with frequent heavy snowfall.
- To maintain the same level of service (LOS), reduce the module (M) by 3 in. for each additional inch in stall width (SW) while maintaining minimum aisle width (see footnotes 2 and 3 to accompanying chart). For example:

8 ft 9 in. @ 90° on 61-ft module = LOS A
9 ft 0 in. @ 90° on 60-ft 3-in. module = LOS A

- Columns and light poles may protrude into a parking module a combined maximum of 2 ft as long as they do not affect more than 25% of the stalls in that bay. For example, a 2-ft encroachment by a column on one side of the aisle or 1 ft each from columns on both sides is permissible.

KEY
θ = angle of park
A = aisle width
i = interlock reduction
OV = overhang
M = module
SL = stall length
SO = stripe offset
SP = stripe projection
SW = stall width
VP = vehicle projection
WO = wall offset
WP = stall projection

BASIC LAYOUT DIMENSIONS

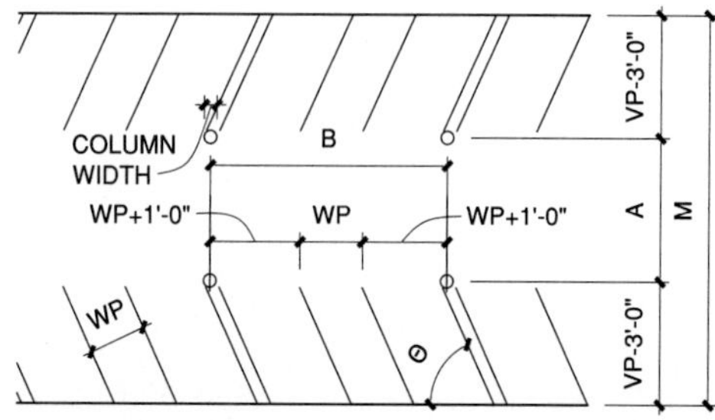

Stalls adjacent to columns must be wider to provide the same level of service of turn.

SHORT SPAN CONSTRUCTION DETAILS

PARKING SPACE DIMENSIONS (FT-IN.)[1]

ALL LEVELS OF SERVICE

ANGLE OF PARK	VEHICLE PROJECTION	WALL OFFSET	OVERHANG	STRIPE OFFSET
45	17-1	10-7	1-9	16-3
50	17-8	9-4	1-11	13-8
55	18-1	8-2	2-1	11-5
60	18-5	7-1	2-2	9-5
65	18-7	6-0	2-3	7-7
70	18-8	4-11	2-4	5-11
75	18-7	3-10	2-5	4-4
90	17-6	1-0	2-6	0-0

LEVEL OF SERVICE A

ANGLE OF PARK	STALL PROJECTION	MODULE	AISLE	INTERLOCK
0	8-9	31-6	14-0[2]	0-0
0	8-9	42-6	25-0[3]	0-0
45	12-4	49-0	14-10	3-1
50	11-5	50-6	15-2	2-10
55	10-8	51-9	15-7	2-6
60	10-1	53-4	16-6	2-2
65	9-8	54-6	17-4	1-10
70	9-4	55-9	18-5	1-6
75	9-1	57-0	19-10	1-2
90	8-9	61-0	26-0	0-0

LEVEL OF SERVICE B

ANGLE OF PARK	STALL PROJECTION	MODULE	AISLE	INTERLOCK
0	8-6	30-0	13-0[2]	0-0
0	8-6	40-0	23-0[3]	0-0
45	12-0	48-0	13-10	3-0
50	11-1	49-6	14-2	2-9
55	10-5	50-9	14-7	2-5
60	9-10	52-4	15-6	2-2
65	9-5	53-6	16-4	1-10
70	9-1	54-9	17-5	1-5
75	8-10	56-0	18-10	1-1
90	8-6	60-0	25-0	0-0

LEVEL OF SERVICE C

ANGLE OF PARK	STALL PROJECTION	MODULE	AISLE	INTERLOCK
0	8-3	28-6	12-0[2]	0-0
0	8-3	37-6	21-0[3]	0-0
45	11-8	47-0	12-10	2-11
50	10-9	48-6	13-2	2-8
55	10-1	49-9	13-7	2-4
60	9-6	51-4	14-6	2-1
65	9-1	52-6	15-4	1-9
70	8-9	53-9	16-5	1-5
75	8-6	55-0	17-10	1-1
90	8-3	59-0	24-0	0-0

LEVEL OF SERVICE D

ANGLE OF PARK	STALL PROJECTION	MODULE	AISLE	INTERLOCK
0	8-0	27-0	11-0[2]	0-0
0	8-0	35-0	19-0[3]	0-0
45	11-4	46-0	11-10	2-10
50	10-5	47-6	12-2	2-7
55	9-9	48-9	12-7	2-4
60	9-3	50-4	13-6	2-0
65	8-10	51-6	14-4	1-8
70	8-6	52-9	15-5	1-4
75	8-3	54-0	16-10	1-0
90	8-0	58-0	23-0	0-0

[1] *All dimensions are rounded to the nearest inch.*
[2] *These are minimum aisle widths for one-way traffic at each level of service.*
[3] *Figures given are widths for two-way traffic.*

Mary S. Smith, P.E., Walker Parking Consultants/Engineers, Inc., Indianapolis, Indiana

PARKING LOT DESIGN

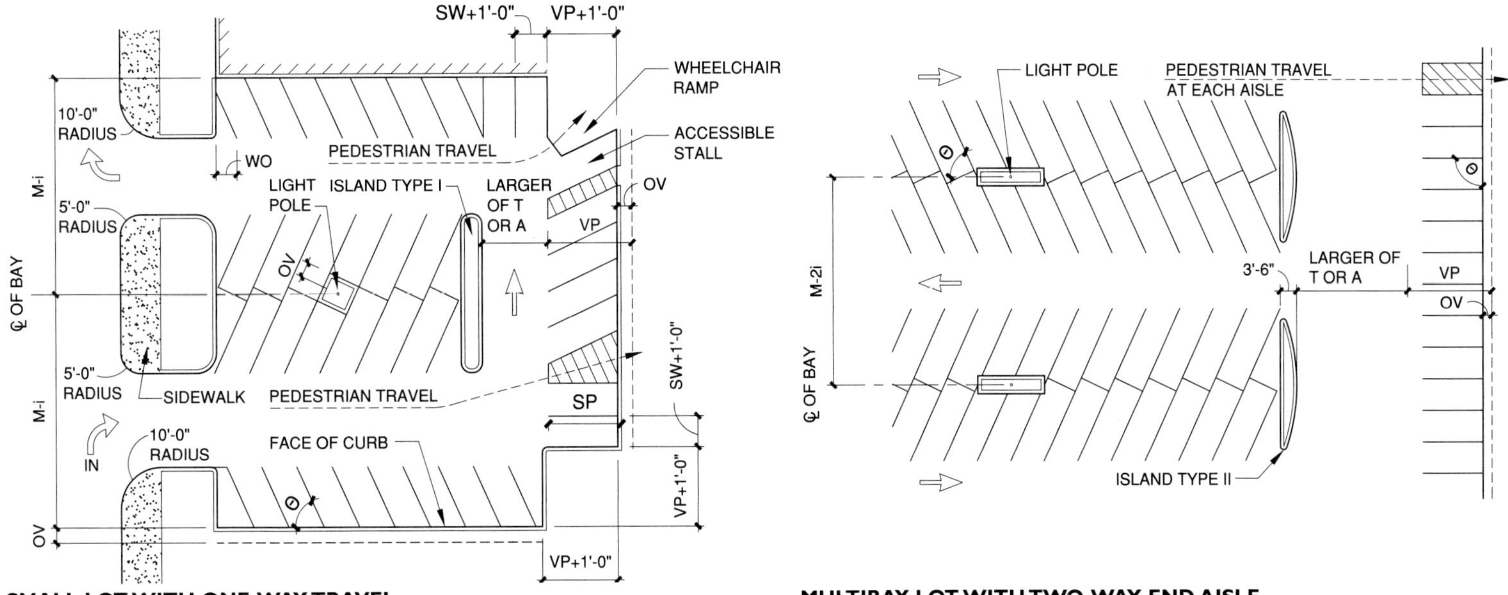

SMALL LOT WITH ONE-WAY TRAVEL

MULTIBAY LOT WITH TWO-WAY END AISLE

LOT DESIGNS WITH ISLANDS

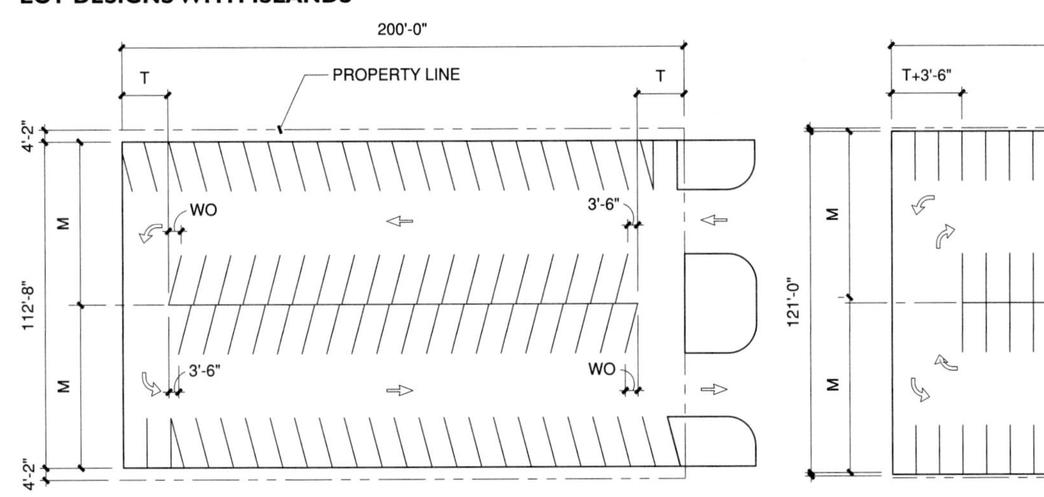

ANGLED PARKING

1. GPA = 200 ft x 56.33 ft x 2 = 22.532 sq ft
2. Capacity = 80 vehicles
3. Efficiency = 22.532 sq ft/80 vehicles = 281.7 sq ft/space

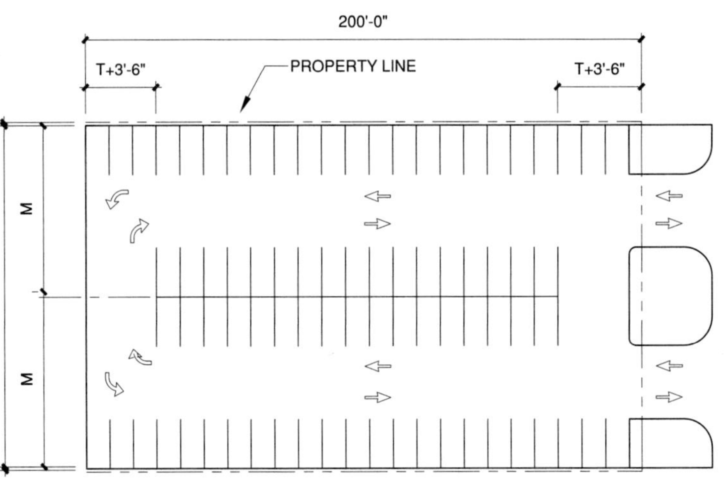

90° PARKING

1. GPA = 200 ft x 60.5 ft x 2 = 24.200 sq ft
2. Capacity = 80 vehicles
3. Efficiency = 24.200 sq ft/80 vehicles = 302.5 sq ft/space

SMALL LOT DESIGNS

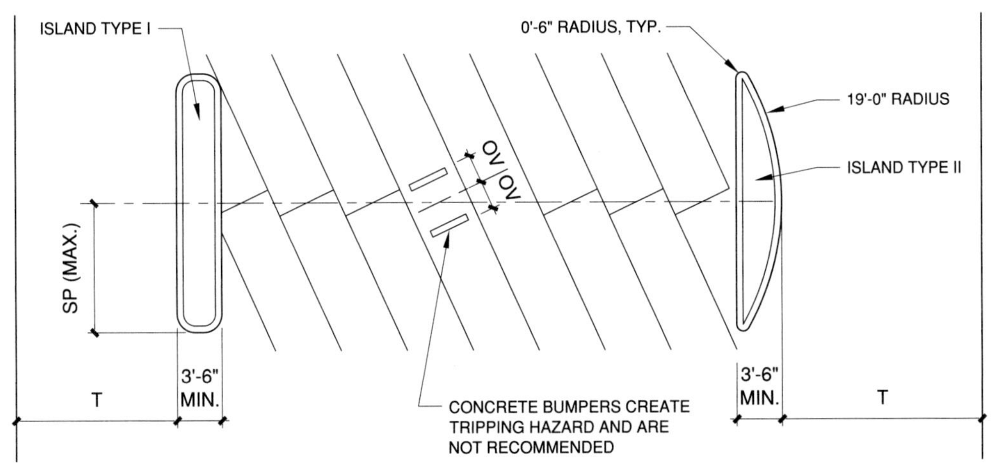

TYPICAL PARKING BAY WITH ISLAND TYPES

KEY TO DRAWINGS

ABBREVIATION	TERM
θ	Angle of park
A	Aisle width
i	Interlock reduction
GPA	Gross parking area
M	Module
OV	Overhang
R	Radius
SP	Stripe protection
SW	Stall width
T	Turning bay
VP	Vehicle projection
WO	Wall offset

Mary S. Smith, P.E., Walker Parking Consultants/Engineers, Inc., Indianapolis, Indiana

ACCESSIBLE PARKING

GENERAL

The information on this page conforms to the Americans with Disabilities Act Accessibility Guidelines for Buildings and Facilities (36 CFR 1191, July 26, 1991), also known as ADAAG, and Bulletin No. 6: Parking (February 1994), both issued by the Architectural and Transportation Barriers Compliance Board. State and local requirements may differ, but ADA requires that designs conform to the higher requirement.

- Accessible parking stalls should be 8 ft wide with an adjacent 5-ft access aisle. No special clearance is required for these stalls.
- Van-accessible stalls should be 8 ft wide with an adjacent 8-ft access aisle accessible from the passenger side of the vehicle. (Backing into 90° stalls from a two-way aisle is an acceptable method of achieving this.) Vehicular clearance along the path of travel to and from a van-accessible stall should be 8 ft 2 in. In parking structures, van-accessible stalls may be grouped on a single level.
- It is permissible for all required accessible stalls to conform with Universal Parking Design guidelines. Since vans may use any accessible stall in this arrangement, universal stalls must have 8 ft 2 in. vehicle clearance.
- Access aisles should be delineated separately from parking spaces. Access aisles must be at the same level as parking stalls (not above, at sidewalk height). Required curb ramps cannot be located in access aisles. Two spaces may share a single access aisle (except when van stalls require passenger-side access in one-way designs).
- Parking spaces and access aisles should be level with surface slopes not exceeding 1:50 (2 percent) in any direction.
- The stalls required for a specific facility may be relocated to another location if equivalent or greater accessibility in terms of distance, cost, and convenience is ensured.

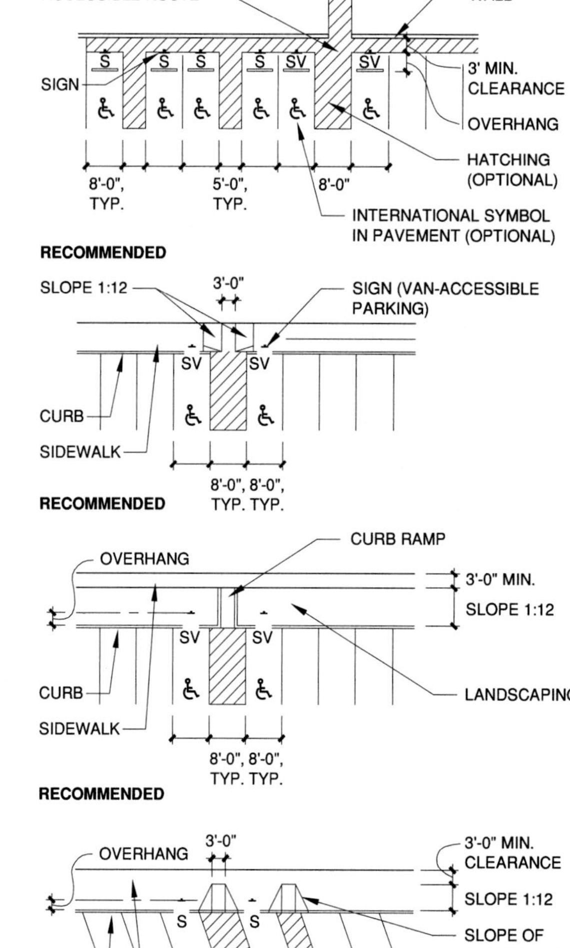

WALL
13'-0", TYP.
16'-0", TYP.
NONCOMPLIANT (ACCESS AISLE NOT MARKED)

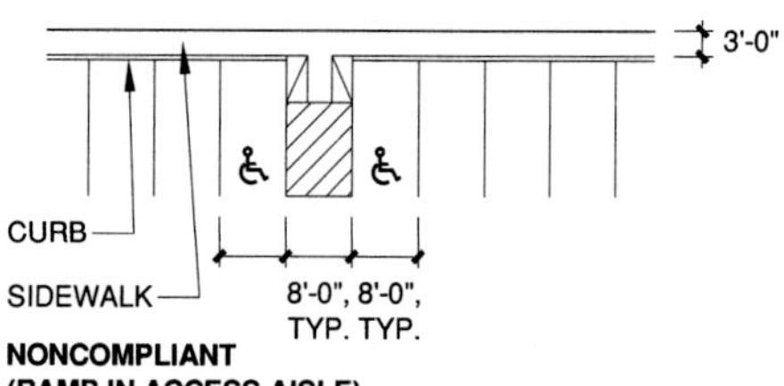

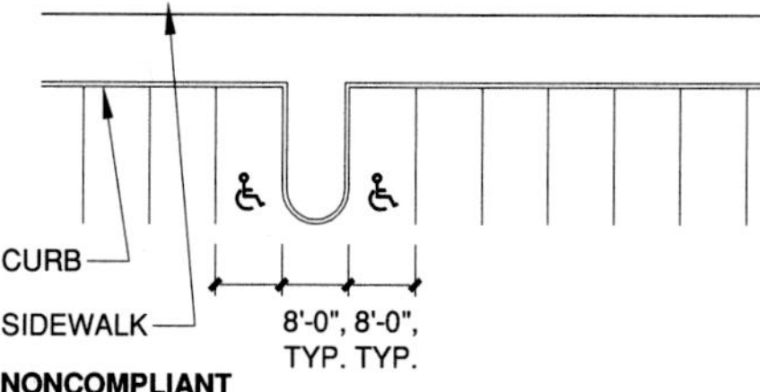

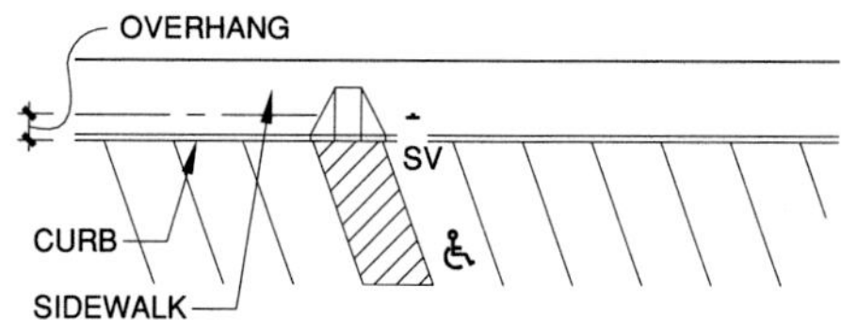

S—accessible parking sign; SV—van-accessible parking sign.

ACCESSIBLE PARKING LAYOUTS

REQUIRED MINIMUM NUMBER OF ACCESSIBLE PARKING SPACES

TOTAL PARKING IN LOT	VANS	CARS	TOTAL
1–25	1	0	1
26–50	1	1	2
51–75	1	2	3
76–100	1	3	4
101–150	1	4	5
151–200	1	5	6
201–300	1	6	7
301–400	1	7	8
401–500	2	7	9
501–800	2	2% min., less 2	2% min.
801–1000	3	2% min., less 2	2% min.
1001–1400	3	17+1 for each 100 over 1000	20+1 for each 100 over 1000
1401 and more	12.5% of total	17+1 for each 100 over 1000	20+1 for each 100 over 1000

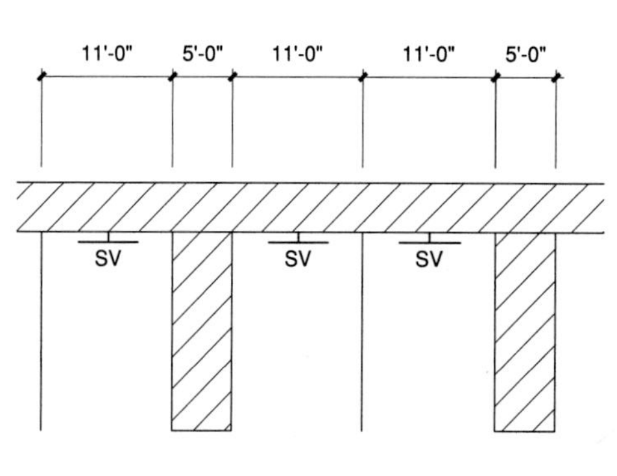

SV—van-accessible parking sign. (All universal spaces are van-accessible.)

UNIVERSAL PARKING DESIGN

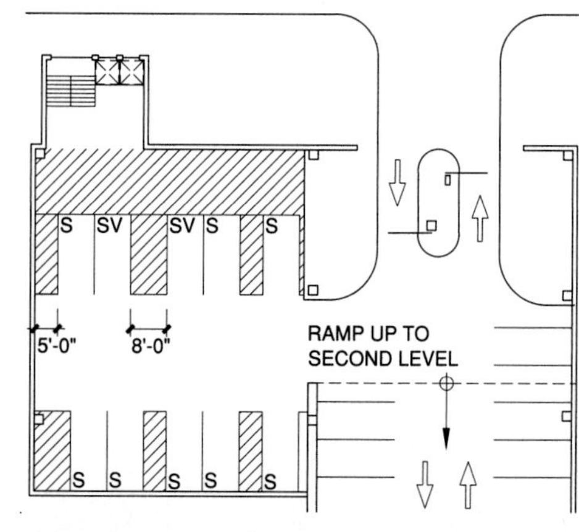

ACCESSIBLE PARKING IN DEDICATED BAY

Mary S. Smith, P.E., Walker Parking Consultants/Engineers, Inc., Indianapolis, Indiana

- Accessible stalls in the numbers shown in the accompanying table must be included in parking facilities leased or 100-percent reserved for employees. However, they need not be reserved for accessible parking (i.e., they need not be marked with signs) until or unless an employee with a disability needs the stall in that location.
- Provide an accessible route from accessible parking stalls to the destination. This should make it possible for persons in wheelchairs to travel without rolling down parking aisles past more than one parked vehicle (other than their own). Crossing a parking aisle at 90° is preferable to rolling down a parking aisle.
- Provide signs at accessible stalls to reserve the spaces for individuals with disabilities; pavement markings alone are not acceptable. Signs need not be provided for every accessible stall if they clearly delineate the accessible parking spaces.
- Requirements are per lot, not by total facility parking.

Notes

- At facilities providing outpatient medical care and other services, 10 percent of the parking spaces serving visitors and patients must be accessible.
- At facilities specializing in treatment or services for persons with mobility impairments, 20 percent of the spaces provided for visitors and patients must be accessible.
- The information in this table does not apply to valet parking facilities, but such facilities must have an accessible loading zone. One or more self-park van-accessible stalls are recommended for patrons with specially equipped driving controls.
- Fair Housing requirements match the ADAAG requirements, except as noted below:
  - Van-accessible stalls are not required.
  - Two percent of total parking must comply.
  - Parking stall may be sloped. Maximum slope of access aisle is 5 percent with a maximum cross-slope of 2 percent. Preferred maximum slope and cross-slope of stall and aisle is 2 percent.
  - There are no requirements for employee-only stalls.
  - When sidewalks are not provided, ensure that there is an accessible route through the driveways or provide additional compliant parking at each accessible feature on the property.

Mary S. Smith, P.E., Walker Parking Consultants/Engineers, Inc., Indianapolis, Indiana

BICYCLE CIRCULATION

OVERVIEW

No other outdoor user group in the United States has gone through the evolution and growth that cycling has seen during the past 25 years. Cycling has matured and become a diversified pursuit for millions of Americans. Some cycle for recreation, health, and social purposes, while others depend on their bicycle as their primary means of transportation. New heroes and role models have emerged in cycling, most prominent among them, Lance Armstrong. Americans take bicycling vacations; they fund and build bicycle pathways in their communities; they serve on local committees to plan for comprehensive bicycle networks; and they participate in "bike-to-work" days.

The bicycle itself has also undergone tremendous change. Today, there are many different types of bikes available, from simple single-speed children's bikes to more sophisticated hybrid bikes to high-tech and expensive racing bicycles. The equipment modifications have enabled users to access and ride within a wide variety of landscapes, from urban streets to wilderness landscapes. Bicycle design has evolved to keep pace with the changes. This section describes the new thinking and revised basis for designing, building, and operating bicycle facilities.

THE BICYCLIST DEFINED

In most states, bicyclists are regarded as "vehicle operators" and are therefore subject to the laws, rules, and regulations that govern the operation of vehicles within public rights-of-way and on roadways.

Bicyclists are also classified in three distinct categories:

"A," or Expert Cyclists: These cyclists use their bicycles for transportation purposes. They are confident in their ability to both control their vehicle and ride in a variety of conditions, including alongside motor vehicles. They are comfortable using high-speed roads that don't provide a special accommodation for bicycles.

"B," or Casual Cyclists: These cyclists use their bicycles for recreation and transportation purposes. They will ride within the roadway environment, but generally avoid high-speed, heavy-trafficked roads. They prefer quiet, less-traveled residential streets and shared-use paths that are separate from the road environment.

"C," or Inexperienced Cyclists: Many of these cyclists are children and, therefore. are either novice or inexperienced riders who have neither an understanding of traffic laws and regulations nor a good grasp of how to control their vehicle. They often depend on their bicycle as a form of transportation—to friend's homes, school, and recreation venues. They are most comfortable on shared-use, off-road paths. Within the roadway environment, they often use sidewalks for their travel.

BICYCLE FACILITIES

Bicycle facilities are generally classified in three major groups:

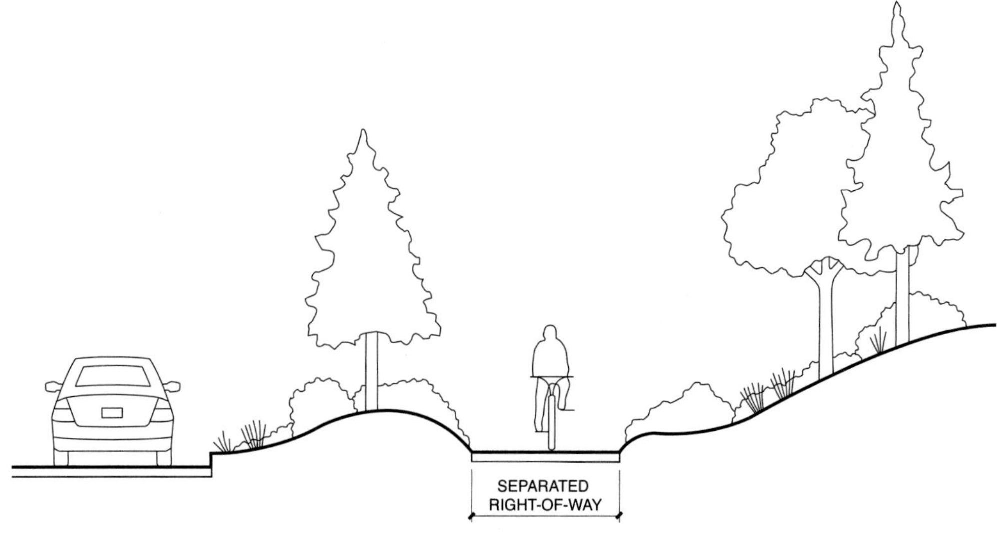

BICYCLE PATH (CLASS I)

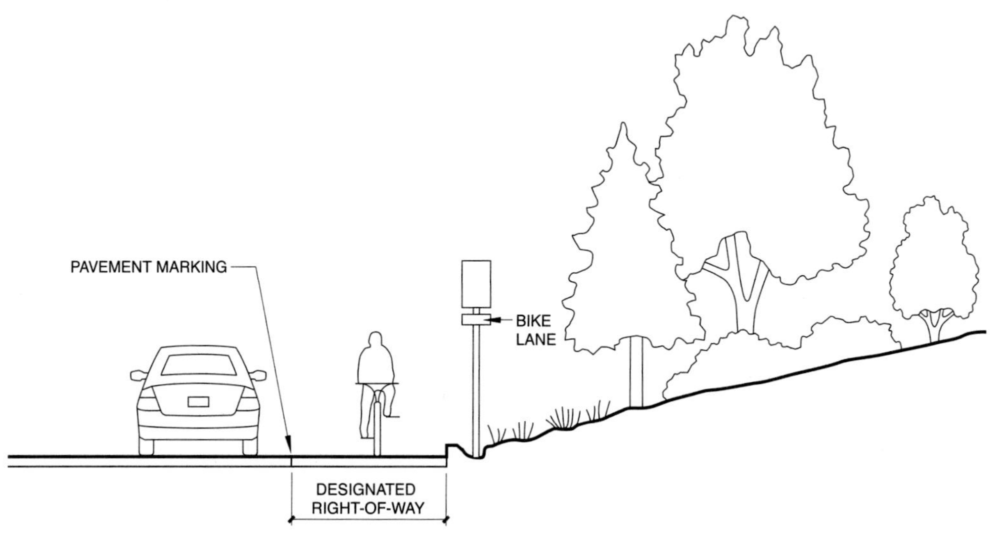

BICYCLE PATH (CLASS II)

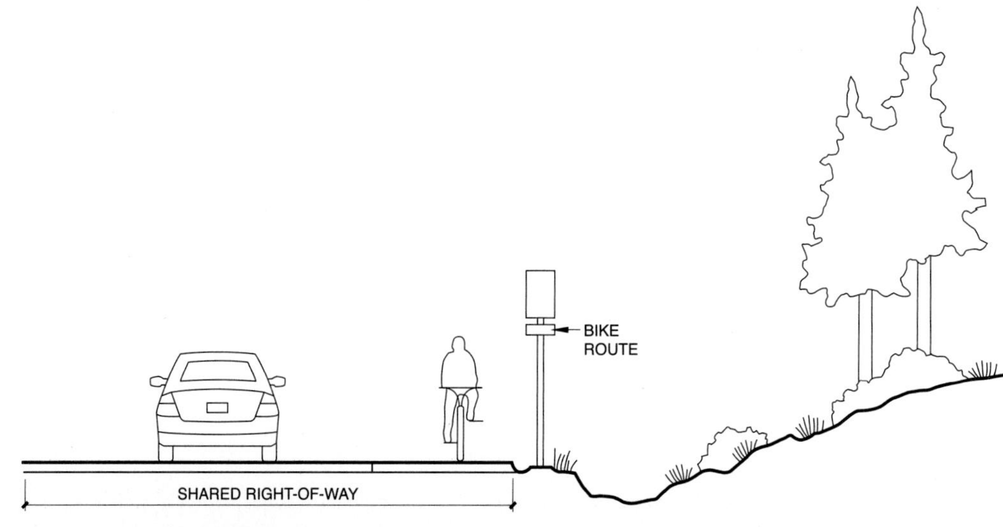

BICYCLE PATH (CLASS III)

Chuck Flink, FASLA; Andy Clarke; Jeff Olson, AIA

Class 1: Includes shared-use paths, often referred to as "off-road trails" and/or "greenways." These shared-use bicycle facilities provide travel for cyclists, pedestrians, in-line skaters, and runners. They typically do not permit motor vehicle travel and normally are constructed within an independent right-of-way. Under certain conditions, they are also found within the road right-of-way, separated from motor vehicle traffic by a landscaped area or a physical barrier.

Class 2: Includes bicycle lanes and roadway shoulders. The bicycle lane is a portion of the road that is separated from motor vehicle traffic by a white stripe, contains special pavement markings, and is designated for the exclusive use of the cyclist. Bike lanes are one-way facilities that flow in the direction of motor vehicle traffic. Roadway shoulders can also be used for cycling. These shoulders are separated from motor vehicle travel by a solid stripe, do not contain special pavement markings, and can be used for other motor vehicle purposes, such as vehicle breakdowns.

Class 3: Includes bike routes. This is a bike facility that contains no special accommodation for the cyclist, such as additional pavement or pavement markings. Signs are used to define the route of travel, and the cyclist shares the roadway environment with motor vehicles.

ELEMENTS OF GOOD BICYCLE DESIGN

A comprehensive and functional bicycle system contains all three classes of bike facility and meets the needs of all design cyclists. Other key elements of a good bicycle facility design are articulated as follows:

- *Bicycle travel generators and attractors* should be defined and generally include popular destinations such as residential areas, schools, parks, shopping areas, and the workplace. The most popular distance for bicycling between a generator and an attraction is 5 to 10 miles.
- *Bicycle Level of Service (BLOS)* is an evaluation of bicyclist-perceived safety and comfort with respect to motor vehicle traffic while traveling in a roadway corridor. It identifies the quality of service for bicyclists or pedestrians that currently exists within the roadway environment. The statistically calibrated mathematical calculation is used for the evaluation of bicycling conditions in shared roadway environments. It uses the same measurable traffic and roadway factors that transportation officials use for other travel modes. With statistical precision, BLOS clearly reflects the effect on bicycling suitability or "compatibility" due to factors such as roadway width, bike lane widths and striping combinations, traffic volume, pavement surface condition, motor vehicle speed and type, and on-street parking. BLOS is based on the proven research documented in Transportation Research Record 1578, published by the Transportation Research Board of the National Academy of Sciences.
- *Transportation Improvement Program (TIP)* is an assessment and listing of major construction projects on roadways, signalization and intersection improvements, and roadway resurfacing, to name a few, that are part of an overall transportation improvement program within a given community or region. Often, bicycle facility improvements can be included as either incidental or independent elements of these improvements.
- *Route network plan* combines all of the preceding factors, and the three classes of bicycle facility, into a cohesive, comprehensive system for a given community or region. Generally, the route network plan identifies the total mileage for each class of facility, defines a short-term and long-term implementation program, and identifies costs for implementing facilities.

Design Criteria

A wide variety of important design considerations generally go into the design of each bicycle facility. The following offers a list of the most popular criteria.

- *Bicycle speed.* The design speed for a given facility is determined by calculating the maximum speed for the cyclist. Most Class 1, off-road, shared-use paths should have design speeds around 15 to 20 miles per hour. The design speed for a Class 2 or 3 bike facility will share the design speed of the associated roadway.
- *Stopping distance.* Providing bicyclists with the proper stopping distance and a clear line of sight is one of the most important design considerations for all bicycle facility types. The "Stopping Distances" figure illustrates the proper distance based on the speed of the cyclist.
- *Curve radius.* For a design speed of 20 mph, the minimum curve radius for all turns in an off-road, shared-use path, or on-road bike facility, is 100 feet. When this standard cannot be achieved, warning signs must be installed to alert cyclists to the substandard curve. Path widening is also recommended for safer turns.
- *Intersection design.* Perhaps the most important feature of bicycle facility design occurs at intersections with roads, railroads, streams, and other bike

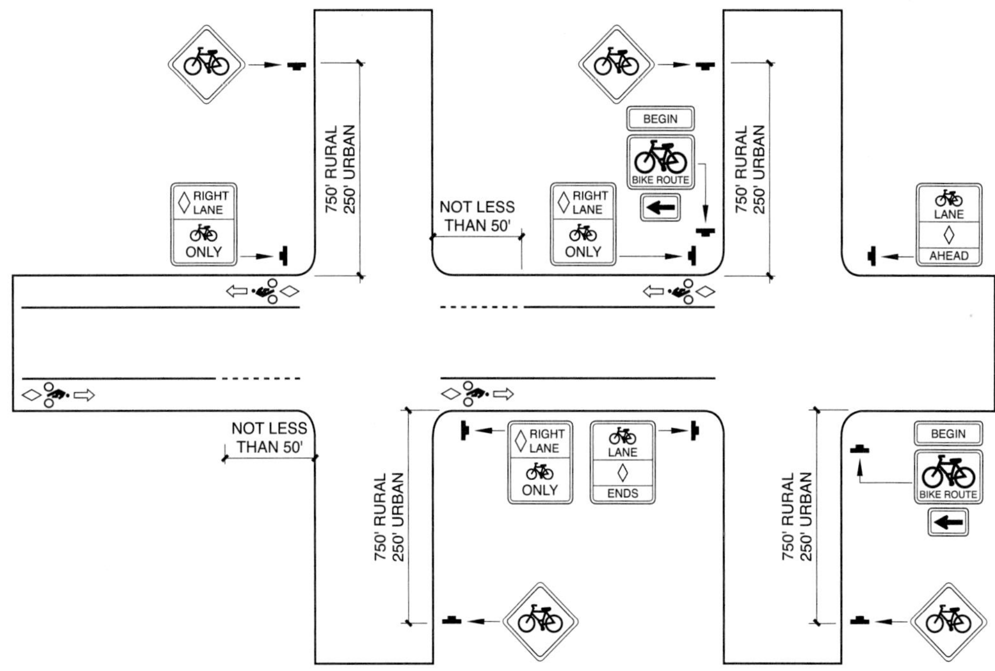

STOPPING DISTANCES

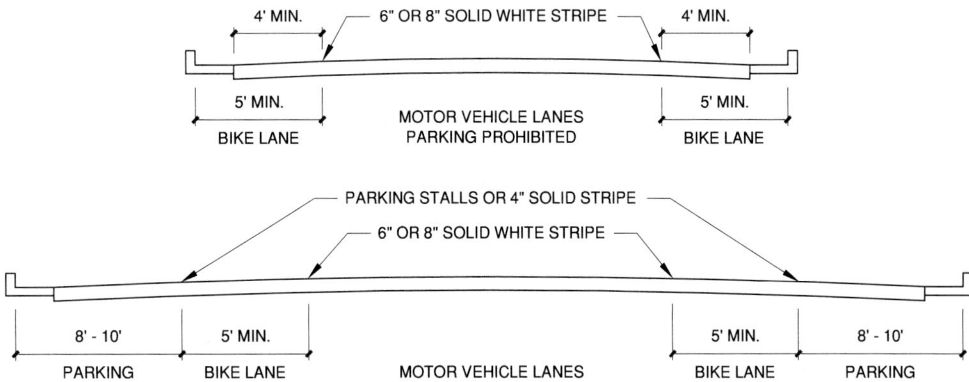

The optional solid white stripe should be used where stalls are unnecessary (because parking is light) but there is concern that motorists may misconstrue the bike lane to be a traffic lane.

SIGHT DISTANCE BASED ON SPEED AND GRADIENT

Chuck Flink, FASLA; Andy Clarke; Jeff Olson, AIA

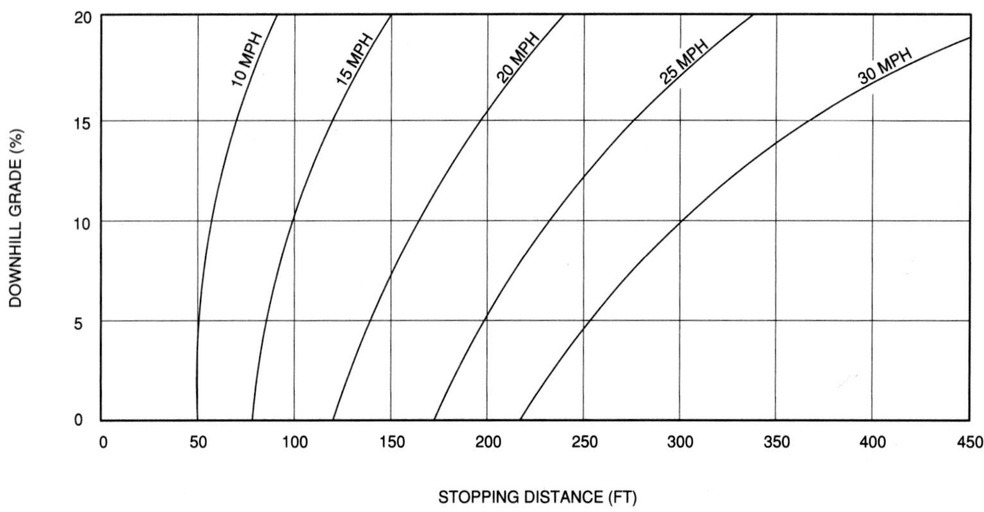

BICYCLE LANE DESIGNATIONS

facilities, because it is at intersections that most conflicts between roadway users and cyclists occur. When grade-separated crossings cannot be achieved, at-grade crossing design solutions apply. Intersection design should provide a clear path of travel for the cyclist through the intersection.

- *Midblock crossing.* For wide street crossings, especially those with a landscaped median or a center turn lane, a midblock crossing design is possible. Midblock crossings are recommended to cut the crossing time in half and provide users with a safe waiting area to complete the crossing. The median or center turn lane should be at least 6 feet wide.
- *Underpasses and overpasses.* Grade-separated crossings are almost always preferred to at-grade crossings. They typically cost more to complete, especially if no existing bridge or underpass exists.
- *Signage and pavement markings.* Signing the Class 1, 2, or 3 bike facility is prescribed under the *Manual on Uniform Traffic Control Devices (MUTCD).* An entire complement of signage, and guidance for the placement of signs, in a variety of landscape settings is provided in the manual. In addition to signage, pavement markings should be used, where appropriate, to provide valuable information to both motorists and cyclists.
- *Bicycle parking.* As with motorists, cyclists need places to park and store their bicycles when they reach their destination. Typically, short-term parking solutions, in the form of bicycle racks, should be provided at most targeted destinations. For longer-term solutions, bicycle lockers should be installed.

REFERENCES

American Association of State Highway Transportation Officials. 2000. *Guide to the Development of Bicycle Facilities*. Washington, DC: AASHTO.

U.S. Department of Transportation. 2001. *Designing Sidewalks and Trails for Access: Part Two, Best Practices Design Guide.* Washington, DC: USDOT.

U.S. Department of Transportation. 2003. *Manual on Uniform Traffic Control Devices (MUTCD),* revision 1. Washington, DC: USDOT.

Chuck Flink, FASLA; Andy Clarke; Jeff Olson, AIA

RECREATIONAL TRAILS AND SHARED-USE PATHS

OVERVIEW

Trails have gained significant importance during the past 20 years throughout the United States. Historically, trails were viewed as secondary elements of park and recreation systems and were therefore referred to as "recreational trails." Other than popular long-distance trails, such as the Appalachian Trail or the Pacific Crest Trail, American communities did little to plan, design, and development these amenities. Today, not only have trails become more diverse, they are becoming the central element in a system of accessible landscapes that addresses recreation, health and fitness, transportation, and environmental and economic programs for thousands of American towns, cities, and counties. One of the most important distinctions that has occurred during this time is between recreational trails and shared-use paths. Simply stated, recreational trails largely serve pedestrian needs and are often located within a park or other outdoor recreation facility. Shared-use paths are transportation trails that extend throughout a community and serve the short-range and long-distance travel needs and interests of pedestrians, bicyclists, and other trail users.

This article offers a brief overview of important elements that constitute a typical trail system. During the past 10 years, much has been written about recreational trails and shared-use paths; in fact, organizations such as American Trails, the Rails-to-Trails Conservancy, and the American Hiking Society have devoted their organizations and associated Web sites to defining and sharing a wealth of detailed information about recreational trails. The discussion here is meant to serve as a primer for trail planning, design, and development. More on this topic can be found in the references provided at the end of this article.

TRAIL USERS DEFINED

Traditionally, walking for pleasure, fitness, transportation, and social interaction has been the most dominant trail user category in the United States. Even today, most outdoor user surveys conclude that walking is by far the most popular and frequent activity among Americans. Through the years, however, other types of trail users have emerged and have caused recreational trail design to change. Though the growth and change in motorized trail use also has been substantial, this section focuses on nonmotorized trail use. Among nonmotorized trail users, running, bicycling, in-line skating, equestrian, and canoeing have had the greatest influence on recreational trail design.

Needs

Depending on the activity, trail users prefer varying environments, tread surfaces, and trail lengths. Pedestrians generally accomplish their intended use in the shortest distance and over the most varied surfaces. Bicyclists generally require a prepared trail tread, and need longer trails to fulfill their needs. In-line skaters need a hard, smooth surface in order to complete their activity. Canoeists need water, easy access to water, and safe water conditions along the length of their trail. Clearly, one trail type does not satisfy all users; in fact, among the cycling community alone, there are many different preferred trail types and surfaces required. Perhaps most importantly, Americans are now more aware of the need to provide trails that enable people with varying levels of ability and skill to access and utilize outdoor resources. The Americans with Disabilities Act has helped to define the tremendous range of abilities that should be addressed when considering the design and development of recreational trails and shared-use paths.

Types of Trails

In response to the different types of users, it is fair to classify recreational trails and shared-use paths into different types or categories of trail.

Type 1: Limited Development, Low-Impact Uses
The first type of trail facility would be found within corridors that are environmentally sensitive but can also support limited trail development. These corridors would support bare earth, wood chip, or

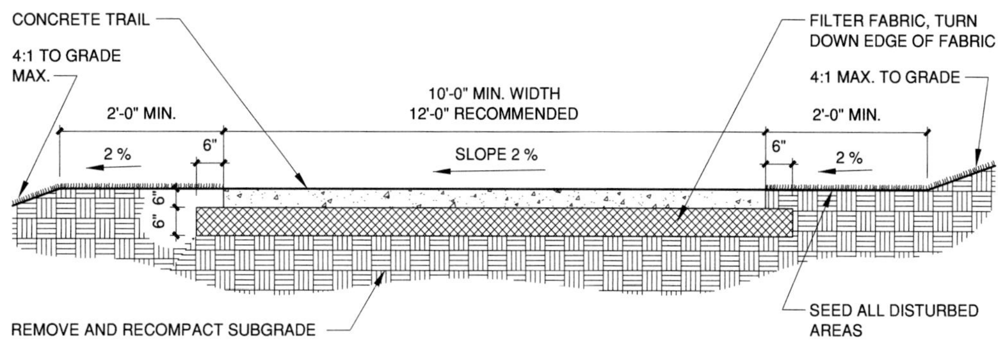

MULTIUSE TRAIL—SECTION

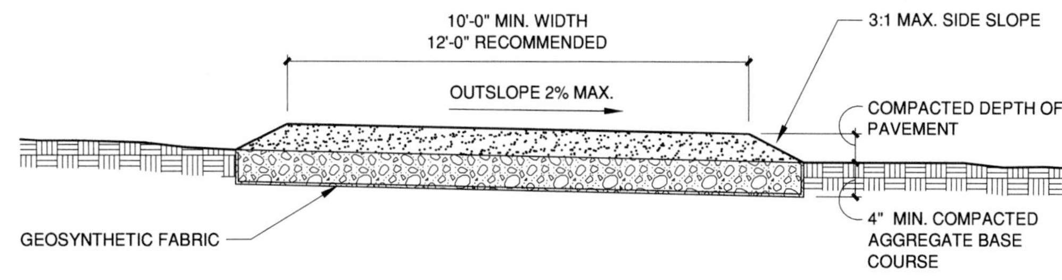

BITUMINOUS SURFACING—NO SHOULDERS

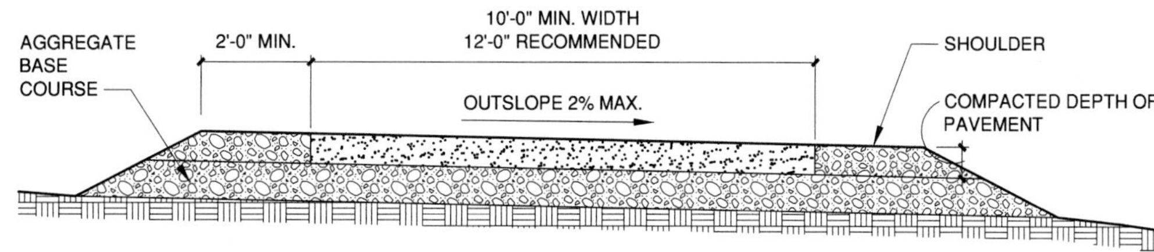

BITUMINOUS SURFACING WITH SHOULDERS

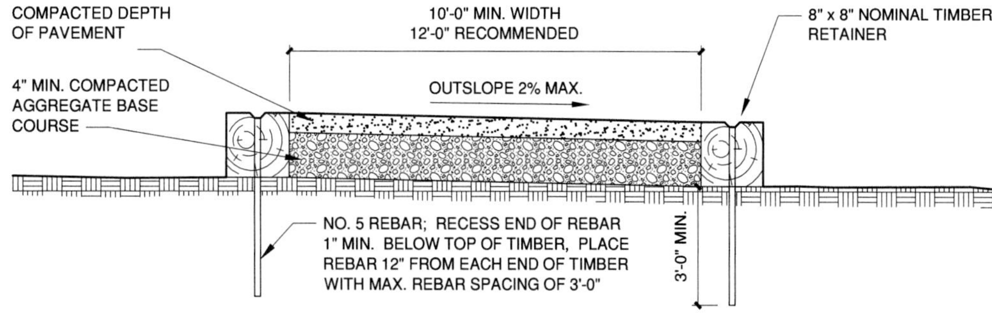

BITUMINOUS SURFACING WITH RETAINERS

Chuck Flink, FASLA; Bob Searns, AICP

boardwalk trails. Typically, these are recreational trails that would be limited to pedestrian use.

Type 2: Multiuse Unpaved Trail Development
This designation would apply to corridors that are capable of supporting a broader range of uses. Trail development, if it occurs along a stream, would be located outside of the floodway. A variety of surface materials could be used, but crushed gravel is the most likely. These recreational trails and shared-use paths can be used by pedestrians, cyclists, equestrians, and persons with disabilities.

Type 3: Multiuse Paved Trail Development
Multiuse paved trails may become one of the most common types of off-road trails in most community trail systems. Often used year-round, these trails will support the greatest diversity of users and serve the needs of most trail users. They will, however, be more expensive than other trail types to construct. These recreational trails and shared-use paths can be constructed within flood-prone landscapes, as well as upland corridors.

Type 4: Shared-Use Paths within Road Rights-of-Way
These trails are generally located within the rights-of-way of roadways throughout a town, city, or metropolitan area. One of the primary purposes for this trail type is to serve as a connector to other elements of an off-road network of trails and paths. Sidewalks, as roadside multiuse side paths, are envisioned as constructed facilities.

Type 5: Water Trails
A water trail is a route along a river or across another body of water, such as a lake or saltwater body, for people using small beachable boats like kayaks, canoes, or rowboats. Water trails are most often identified by the land facilities that support water travel, including launch and landing sites (trailheads) campsites, rest areas, and other points of interest.

ELEMENTS OF GOOD DESIGN

Many factors go into the development of a functional and successful recreational trail and shared-use path. This section does not attempt to address all factors, but to describe the most important.

Accommodating the User

The most important consideration for the design of a trail is to accommodate the trail user. Most shared-use paths will need to serve the interests of a wide range of users, including people who want to walk, jog, bike, and in-line skate. Most shared-use paths should be developed at a minimum width of 10 feet. This is done to accommodate two-way traffic on the prepared trail tread surface. It may be necessary to increase the width to 12 or 14 feet to accommodate heavy traffic on a given trail. It would also be advisable to divide the trail into "wheeled" and "nonwheeled" treads, if the right-of-way and landscape can support two trail treads. The wheeled tread should be 10 feet wide; the nonwheeled tread can be 6 or 8 feet in width.

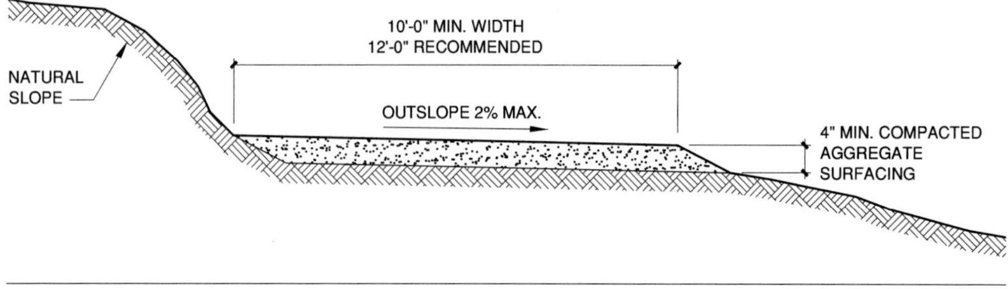

OUTSLOPED SECTION

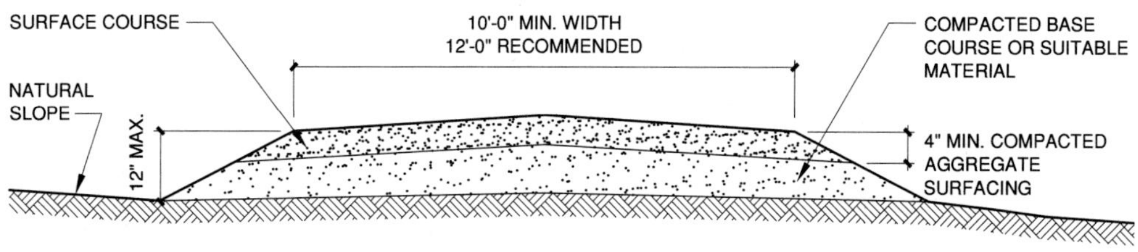

CROWNED SECTION

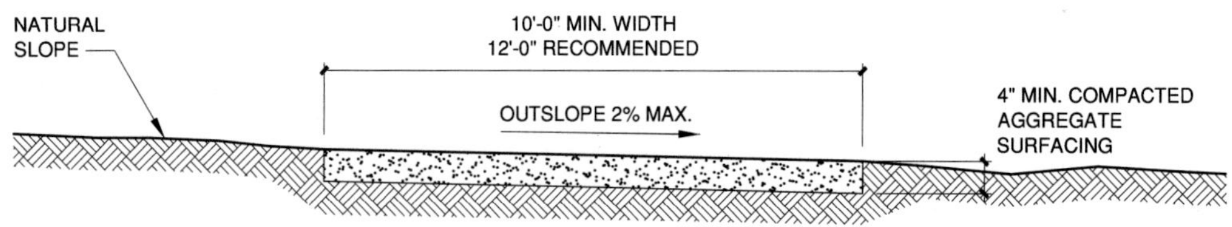

EXCAVATED SECTION

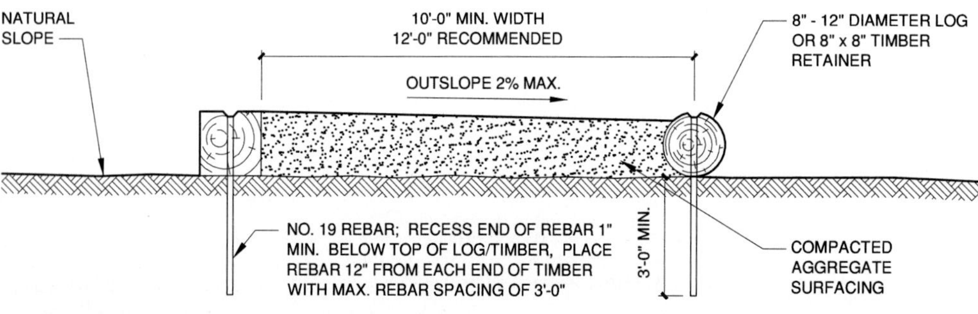

RETAINER SECTION

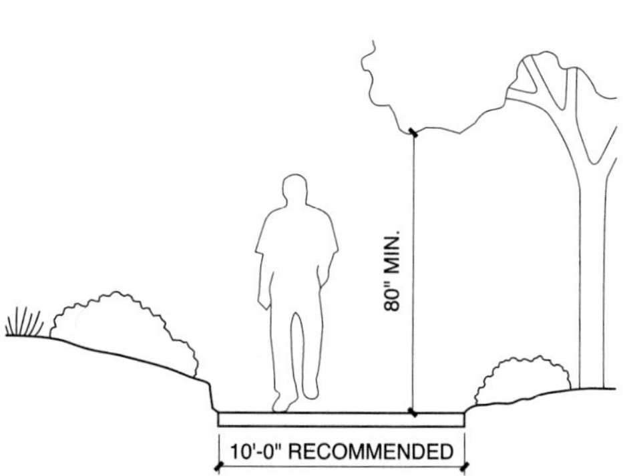

PREVENT VEGETATION FROM ENCROACHING INTO TRAIL

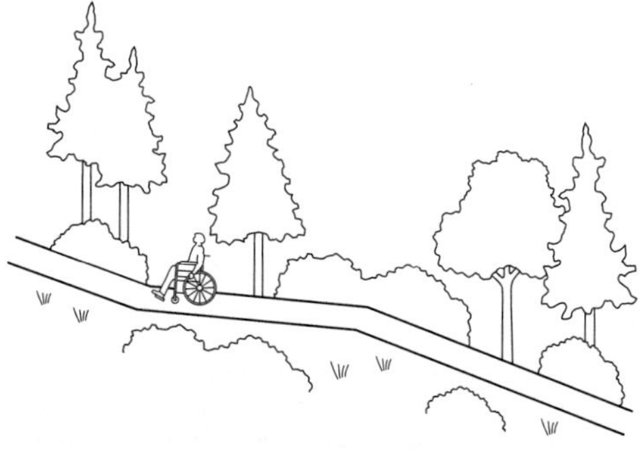

PERIODIC REST AREAS

Chuck Flink, FASLA; Bob Searns, AICP

All trails must be designed and constructed to be accessible to all persons, regardless of their abilities. There are very few reasons that a given trail cannot be built to be fully accessible. The best guidebook on this subject is *Designing Sidewalks and Trails for Access: Part 2, Best Practices Design Guide* (U.S. DOT, 2001). Every trail designer and manager should have this reference book on hand to ensure that trail projects are accessible.

Connecting People to Destinations

The best trails are those that link people to popular destinations. Each trail segment should have logical and functional endpoints. Trails that serve as links throughout a community are the most popular for users. While this seems obvious, sometimes off-road trails will end abruptly, especially in urban areas. It is very important that trails be linked to other trails, to parks, and to an on-road network of bicycle facilities and sidewalks.

Reducing Multiuser Conflict

Multiuser conflict is regarded as the most serious safety concern for off-road trails. Conflicts between cyclists and pedestrians are the most prevalent and are usually caused by reckless and unsafe behavior, incompatible use values, and/or by overcrowding. The most effective remedies for this conflict begin with design and management. Trails can and should be designed to reduce conflict by widening the trail tread or by separating the trail tread for different users. Single-tread, multiuse trails can also be managed to reduce conflicts, sometimes by separating users under a time-of-use policy. Involving user groups in the design of a trail is the best way to both understand local needs and resolve the potential for multiuse conflict. Posting trails with a trail use ordinance and providing educational materials on how to use the trail are also important.

Fitting Trails to the Environment

The most enjoyable trails to use are those that celebrate the natural landscapes and native environments traversed by the off-road trail. This is one of the most popular reasons why outdoor advocates choose to use off-road, mixed-use trails. Trails should have rhythm and syncopation, and flow within their surroundings so that they captivate users. Trails should follow the natural contours of the land and take advantage of native landscape features, such as water, groupings of vegetation, scenic views, and interesting built features.

Integrating Trails into the Built Environment

Trails should also celebrate the built landscapes they traverse. Often, we try to hide viewsheds that are deemed unpleasant. This may not always be a good idea. Since trails are designed to be used by people, it is much better to keep viewsheds open. Trails through urban landscapes provide an opportunity to interpret the surrounding environment.

Great care must also be taken to successfully fit a new trail into the urban fabric. For example, the conversion of abandoned railroad corridors has been the greatest resource for new urban trails in the past 20 years. It presents challenges for trail designers because these corridors supported a different type of transportation activity. Creating new intersections between roads and converted rail-trails is the greatest challenge for these urban trails. It is important that intersections be designed to clearly determine who has the right-of-way. Intersections should also be very clearly marked for all groups, to delineate crossing zones for trail users. Pavement markings, signage, lighting, and texture pavement can all be used to make intersections safer.

SAFETY AND SECURITY CONSIDERATIONS

All communities should implement a safety and security program for their recreational trail and shared-use paths that includes:

- Systematic risk management assessment
- Interagency design review for all proposed improvements
- Accident and crime reporting

In addition, communities should encourage their land planners, trail designers, law enforcement departments, and fire/rescue and maintenance personnel to be actively involved in the planning, design, and development of the community trail system. Crime Prevention Through Environmental Design (CPTED) should be actively incorporated in the safety, security, and crime prevention program.

Communities should also implement an emergency response protocol, working with law enforcement, EMS agencies, and fire departments, that includes mapping of trail access points; design of trails and access roads (to accommodate up to 6.5 tons); an "address system," such as mile markers to identify locations; and, where appropriate, 911 emergency phones in remote areas. It will also help to implement a database management system with police for tracking specific locations and circumstances of all accidents and crime and create a safety follow-up task force to address any problems that develop.

Finally, communities should be prepared to routinely inspect all recreational trails and shared-use paths for safety hazards, defective structures, and missing safety signs. Always post and enforce safe user behavior and bicycle speed limits (in congested and risk areas).

To reduce multiuse conflict on shared-use paths plan, design and manage trail use to eliminate reckless and unsafe behavior, incompatible uses and values, trespass violations, disturbances, and adverse environmental impacts. It is essential to recognize the different goals of trail users, such as equestrians and bicycles, and separate where feasible. Provide user education through signage, patrol, volunteers, brochures, and media. Provide adequate trail mileage and open-space acreage to accommodate user populations. Solicit input from user groups; monitor, document, and log problem areas; and address problems through design and management.

OPERATIONS AND MAINTENANCE CONSIDERATIONS

Operations and maintenance refers to the specific day-to-day tasks and programs that must be undertaken to assure resources and trail facilities are kept in good, usable condition. This begins with sound design, durable components, and a comprehensive management plan. The plan should be embraced by the responsible entities at the beginning of the implementation process. Programs and protocols should be instituted—including training of field and supervisory personnel—that will endure. In addition, community groups, residents, business owners, developers, and other stakeholders should be engaged in the long-term stewardship of the resources preserved and enhanced by this plan.

Typically, trail maintenance takes two forms: routine and remedial. Routine maintenance refers to the day-to-day regimen of litter pickup, trash and debris removal, weed and dust control, trail sweeping, sign replacement, tree and shrub trimming, and other regularly scheduled activities. Routine maintenance also includes minor repairs and replacements, such as fixing cracks and potholes or repairing a broken hand railing. Routine activities also include crime prevention, law and regulation enforcement, search and rescue, and user education. Remedial maintenance refers to correcting significant defects, as well as repairing, replacing, or restoring major components that have been destroyed, damaged, or significantly deteriorated during the life of the project. Some items ("minor repairs") may occur on a 5- to10-year cycle, such as repainting, seal coating asphalt pavement, or replacing signage. Major reconstruction items will occur over a longer period or after an event such as a flood. Examples of major reconstruction remedial maintenance include stabilization of a severely eroded hillside, repaving a trail surface or a street used for biking, or replacing a footbridge. Remedial maintenance should be part of a long-term capital improvement plan.

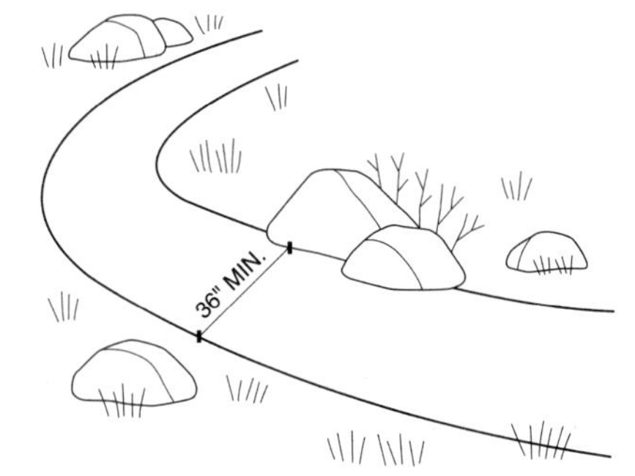

MINIMUM CLEAR TREAD WIDTH

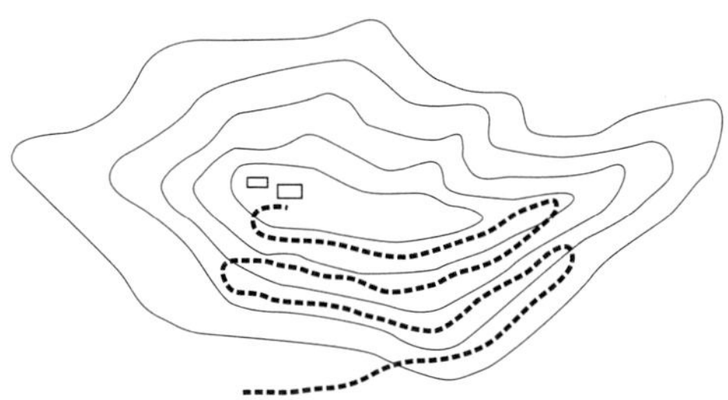

CURVILINEAR TRAILS FOLLOW NATURAL PATH OF ENVIRONMENT

Chuck Flink, FASLA; Bob Searns, AICP

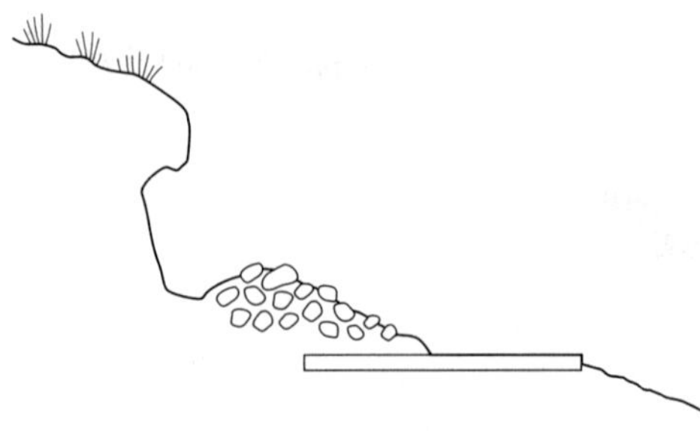

EROSION REDUCES CLEAR TREAD WIDTH

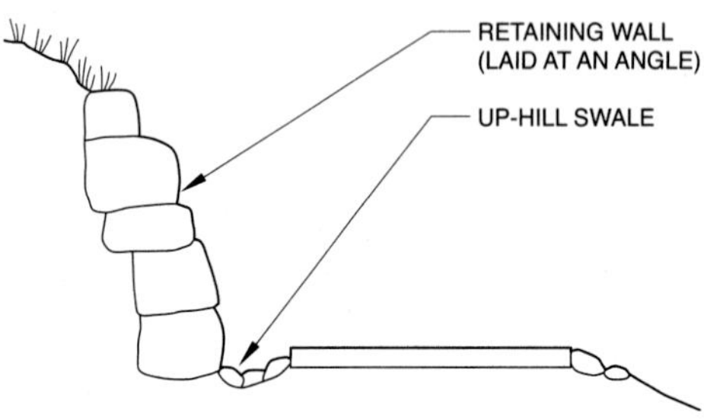

RETAINING WALLS STABILIZE TRAILS

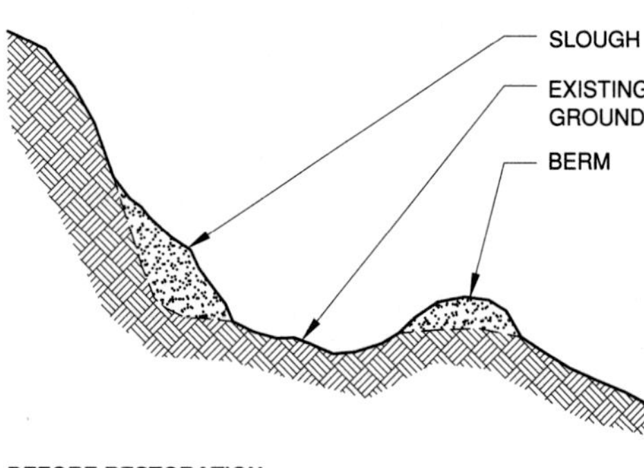

BEFORE RESTORATION

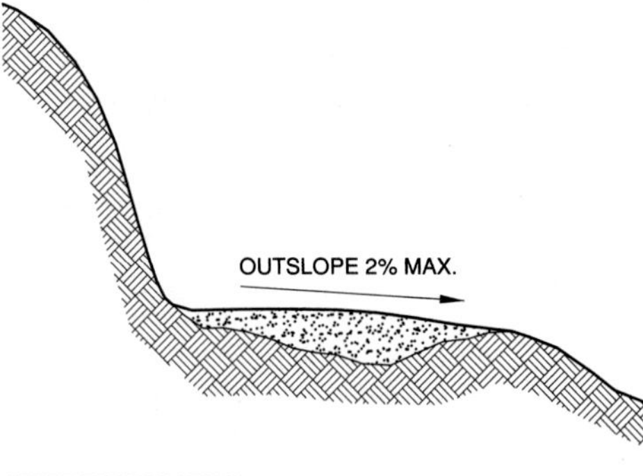

AFTER RESTORATION

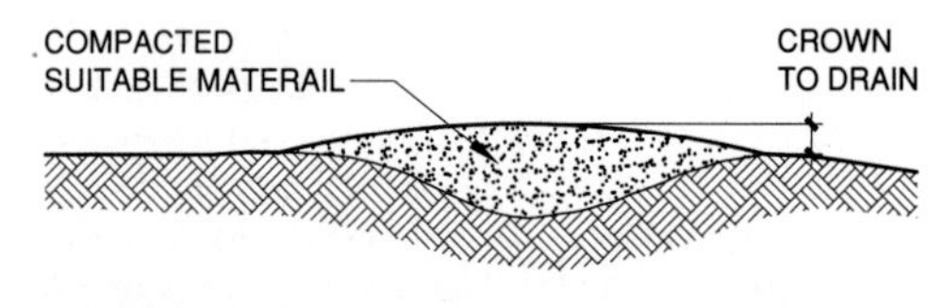

FLAT SLOPES

TRAIL RESTORATION

DESIGN CRITERIA

Trail Tread Design

Single-tread, shared-use trails must be designed to accommodate multiple users at specified design speeds. The minimum width for a single tread, shared-use trail is 10 feet; the preferred width is 12 feet. For multiple treads, the minimum width for wheeled treads is 10 feet, and the minimum width for nonwheeled treads is 5 feet.

Tread Surface

For the vast majority of shared-use trails, a hard surface is the preferred surface type. The most popular surface for shared-use trails is asphalt or concrete. A variety of graded aggregate stone has also proven to be both popular and successful as a surface for shared-use trails.

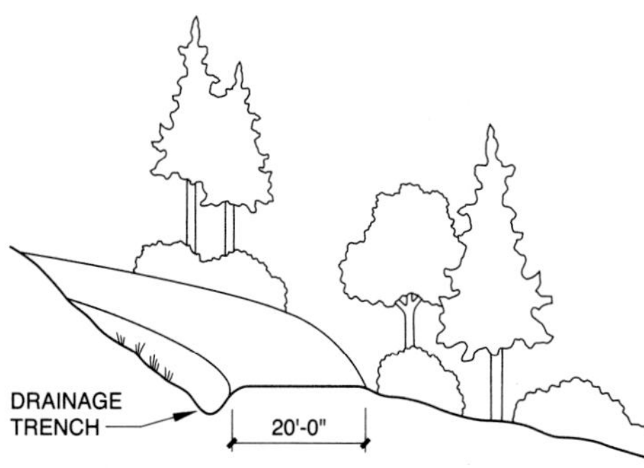

INCLUDE DRAINAGE DIPS IN NEW CONSTRUCTION OR ALTERATIONS

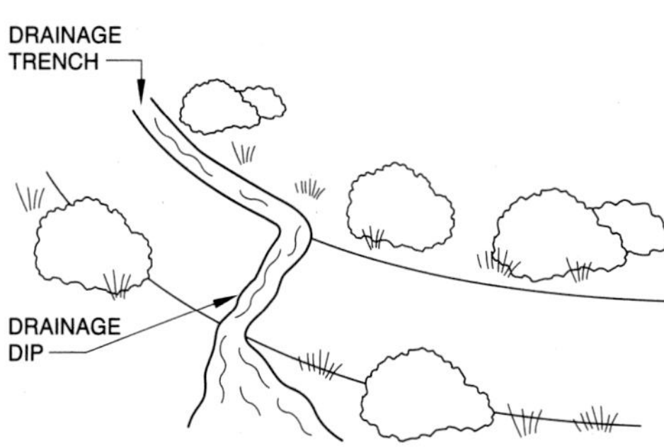

The cross slope of the open drain should not exceed 10 percent and the clear tread width should be at least 42" minimum.

DRAINAGE DIPS ACT AS OPEN DRAINS

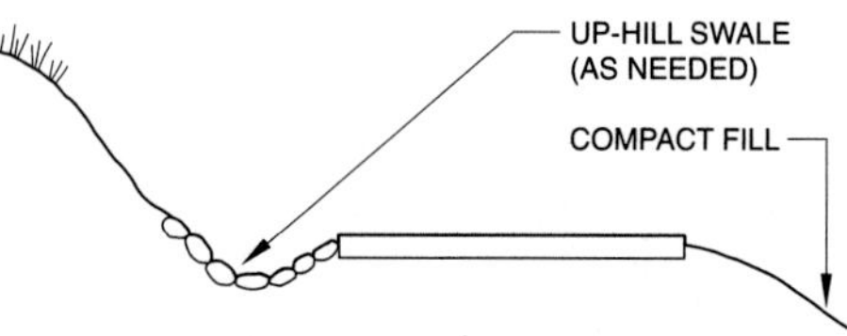

Swales can control drainage and eliminate the need for water bars.

SWALES CAN CONTROL DRAINAGE

Grading and Drainage

One of the most important considerations in trail design is how the trail tread corridor is graded. Cross slopes on trails should not exceed 2 percent, and the running slope, or longitudinal slope, should not exceed 5 percent. Steeper running slopes are possible, but should not extend for long distances. Additionally, keeping water from accumulating or flowing across the surface of a trail tread is an important design consideration. Care should be taken to properly judge the flow of stormwater to ensure that it does not impair trail use.

Intersections

Trails, especially those in suburban and urban landscapes, will most likely intersect with roadways, utilities, and water features. The design of these intersections is important to ensure the safety of trail users. Typically, for road crossings, three design options are possible: at-grade, below-grade, or above-grade. For at-grade crossings, new design techniques are promoting a safer crossing strategy for trail users and motorists. For below-grade crossings, culverts and bridges are normally used to span the width of the trail. A minimum of 9 feet of height and 10 feet of width is required for this crossing. Bridges are used for above-grade crossings, and they must be designed to accommodate the uses that they span. Interstate highway crossings offer the most stringent crossing standards.

REFERENCES

American Association of State Highway Transportation Officials (AASHTO). 2000. *Guide to the Development of Bicycle Facilities.* Washington, DC: AASHTO. Available from FHWA or AASHTO, www.aashto.org/bookstore/abs.html.

Flink, Charles A., and Robert Searns. 1993. *Greenways: A Guide to Planning, Design and Development.* Washington, DC: Island Press. For more information, visit www.greenways.com.

Flink, Charles A., Robert Searns, and Kristine Olka. 2001. *Trails for the Twenty-First Century.* Washington, DC: Island Press. For more information, visit www.greenways.com.

Universal Access to Outdoor Recreation: A Design Guide. 1993. Berkeley, CA: PLAE, Inc.

U.S. Department of Transportation. 2001. *Designing Sidewalks and Trails for Access: Part Two, Best Practices Design Guide.* Washington, DC: USDOT.

U.S. Department of Transportation. 2003. *Manual on Uniform Traffic Control Devices (MUTCD)*, revision 1. Washington, DC: USDOT.

See also

Crime Prevention through Environmental Design
Access to the Outdoor Setting

Chuck Flink, FASLA; Bob Searns, AICP

ACCESSIBILITY

ACCESS TO THE OUTDOOR SETTING

INTRODUCTION

Natural outdoor settings are different from the urban built environment. The urban environment is mostly built and can be "controlled" by design, whereas parks and outdoor areas are both built and nature-based. In fact, people come to parks primarily to experience nature, so in the parks the built settings must be designed to fit into a natural environment without destroying the experience people are coming to enjoy.

The challenge for park designers is to understand what people of all abilities need, to facilitate the use of the park without compromising the qualities of the natural or cultural resource. The concept of individual choice based on the desired degree of challenge must also be addressed. For example, a trail through a redwood grove may be the desired experience, but some people want a very challenging hike through the redwoods while others just want to stroll through a beautiful natural setting. Therefore, unlike an urban sidewalk, the trail is not merely a means of access to a place or activity; it is the place, and each type of experience visitors have creates the program of that place.

Accessibility

"Accessibility," as used here, is defined as "the combination of various elements in a building or outdoor area, which allows access, circulation, and full use of the building, facilities, and programs independently by persons with disabilities." While accessibility is a defined, prescriptive set of standards and measurements that don't change in content from setting to setting, the design challenge in park settings remains: basic services and experiences need to be accessible to all people with disabilities, while maintaining the intrinsic qualities of the place.

This section covers standards for particular features in the park environment that should be integrated into an overall park site plan and be considered as part of a larger planning process for accessibility. Site planning is important to the process of providing access to all programs and services that the park offers. Each site must be planned as a whole to form a well-integrated, accessible network of facilities and programs. Remember that all new or renovated elements in the park must be made accessible to all people even if there is no guideline that addresses that specific feature.

Circulation

No program or facility can function independent of its linkage to the natural, social, and physical environment to which it belongs. Similarly, no program or facility can be accessible by itself. If a park provides major programs in different areas, accessible circulation must be provided to connect each of these areas, facilities, and activities, rather than restricting visitors with disabilities to using only selected areas and programs.

There are three types of circulation that can provide accessibility:

- *Exterior route of travel and accessible route of travel.* General terms describing a continuous, unobstructed path connecting accessible elements and spaces in a building or between exterior elements of a facility. These paths or routes may include walks, sidewalks, maps, corridors, and other such improved areas.
- *Outdoor recreation access route.* Paths that connect and provide access to elements within a picnic area, camping area, or designated trailhead.
- *Trails.* Paths that provide access to a site's remote settings and recreation activities.

Parks must provide accessible circulation that connects accessible features within a park so that a visitor with a disability can enter the park, get to and utilize restrooms and facilities, and take part in the programs available (visitor center, picnic area, campgrounds, etc.).

Space Allowances

When designing for all people, the anthropometrics and spatial requirements are different from those historically used in design. Universal design takes into account the fact that people come in a variety of shapes, sizes, abilities/disabilities, and ages. When planning and designing, using widths, lengths, and dimensions that accommodate a wide range of people assures access to recreational facilities and programs for all visitors.

The basic spatial dimensions necessary to accommodate people who use wheelchairs or mobility aids, or who have visual impairments, form the basis of this discussion. Typical space allowances for accessibility given here include clear ground or floor space, the minimum dimensions required for an adult using a wheelchair, and the passing widths and turning requirements for that person.

Reach Ranges

The "reach range" refers to the maximum and minimum heights that a person in a wheelchair can reach in the forward and side directions. Objects that can be reached (such as exhibit buttons, telephones, Braille signs, grills, hose bibs, etc.) need to be positioned within the appropriate reach range to be accessible to people in wheelchairs. The two types of reach ranges are in the "forward" and "side" directions. A person has a greater reach range toward the side than in the forward direction, so the ranges differ.

Obstacles, Hazards, and Clearance

In recreational settings, it is often desirable to retain the natural features and character of a place through aesthetically appropriate design. This must be done in a way that also provides safe maneuvering and access. To maximize clearances and minimize hazards, projections, protrusions, and gratings or openings in the clear ground or floor space need to be carefully considered.

Communication

Physical access is only one form of access to parks. Making park programs accessible requires making communications accessible. Parks that offer visitors physical access to programs and facilities cannot be considered fully accessible unless the staff can effectively communicate with visitors with disabilities. Recreation classes, interpretive programs, nature walks, campfire talks, films, and other special events must be made available to everyone through alternative formats, such as sign language, Braille, oral description, and captioning.

These basic building blocks (clear widths, reach ranges) for accessibility appear throughout this discussion and must be considered when designing or renovating park settings. The following sections outline requirements for specific typical park features.

ROUTES OF TRAVEL

Concept

Routes of travel represent the primary paths that a pedestrian would typically use to access a building, facility, or activity. In the park setting, there are two different types of routes that may be used to connect the elements within a use area. The type of route to use depends upon the level of development in the area and the elements being connected.

The most usable route for people with mobility impairments is the *exterior route of travel* (ERT). The technical requirements for ERTs must be met in highly developed areas, such as paved parking lots, urban parks, highly developed amenities and restrooms. Since they are the easiest to use, the grade requirements should be met whenever possible in the park setting.

Outdoor recreation access routes (ORAR) are used to connect elements within a camping, picnic, or designated trailhead use area. Typical applications of ORARs are from the campsite to the restroom or campfire center, within a picnic area or between the picnic site and an activity area, such as a trailhead.

Exterior Routes of Travel (ERT)

General

- The accessible route must be the most practical and direct route possible. It must incorporate the guidelines of curb ramps, ramps, and so on, when necessary. (See also: *Parking Standards; Accessibility;* and *Stairs, Ramps and Curbs.*)
- A sign displaying the International Symbol of Accessibility (ISA) at the primary entrance and at every major junction of the accessible route must be installed. The sign must be displayed to direct the user to an accessible entrance.
- The slope in the direction of travel must be a maximum of 5 percent. Where conditions dictate a slope greater than 5 percent, a ramp must be provided.
- Walkways with continuous gradients must have level areas 60 inches in length at intervals of 200 feet.

Passing Area

- If an accessible route is less than 60 inches wide, passing spaces of at least 60 inches by 60 inches must be located at maximum intervals of 200 feet.
- The slope perpendicular to the direction of travel, cross slope, must be a maximum of 2 percent.
- The surface must be firm, stable, and slip-resistant. Surface changes in elevation must be ¼ inch maximum. Surface elevation changes between ¼ inch and ½ inch must be beveled at 50 percent. Surface elevation changes greater than ½ inch must be ramped.
- Route width must be 48 inches, except where

Susan Goltsman, FASLA; Timothy Gilbert, ASLA

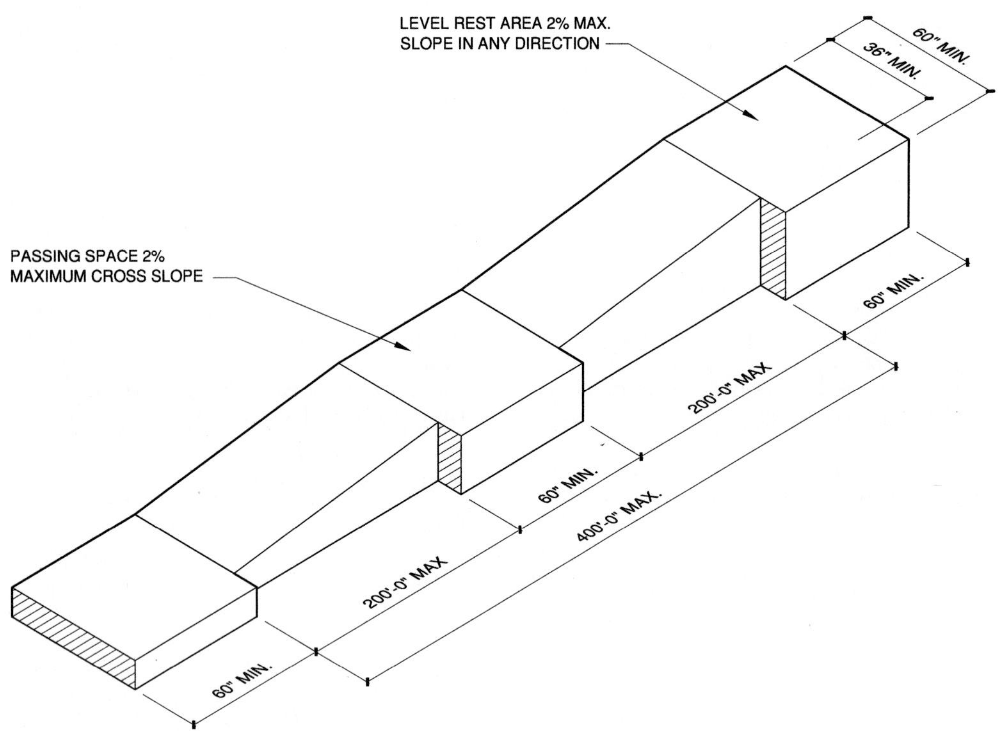

WALKWAYS WITH CONTINUOUS GRADIENTS

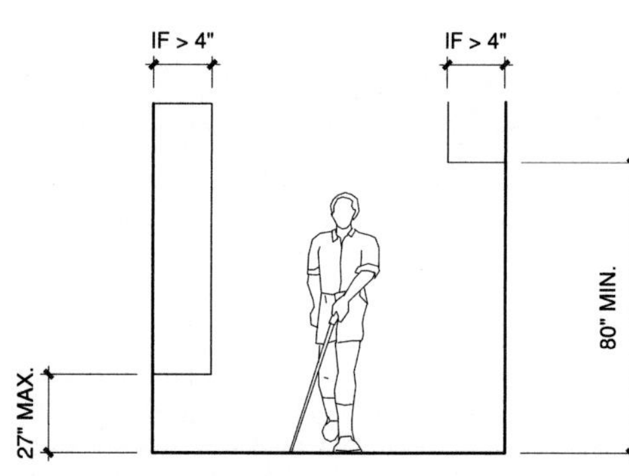

MOUNTED OBJECT

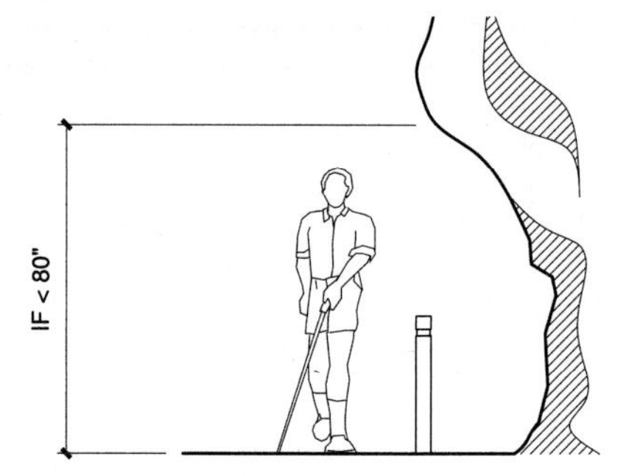

VERTICAL CLEARANCE

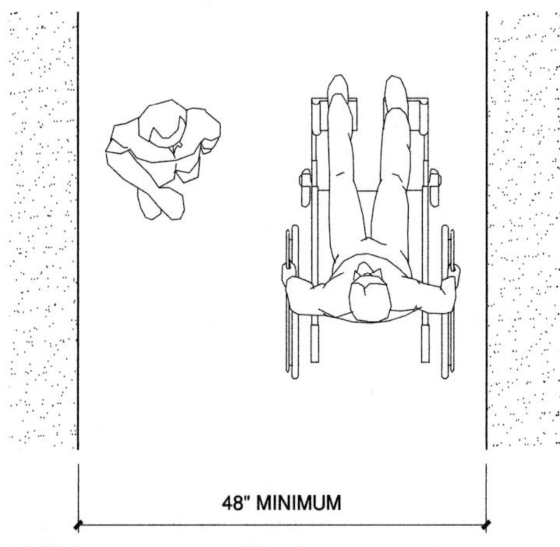

PASSING CLEARANCES

undue hardship is based upon right-of-way restriction, natural barriers, or other existing conditions occur, in which case a minimum of 36 inches width is permitted. Surfaces must be slip-resistant.

Openings, Surface Conditions, and Protruding Objects

- Grate openings must have spaces no greater than ½ inch wide, and may be elongated, provided that the long direction runs perpendicular to the primary direction of travel.
- Exterior doormats must be anchored or recessed to prevent interference with wheelchair traffic.
- Where wheelchair traffic is expected to make a U-turn around an obstacle, the route width must be a minimum of 42 inches on the approach and 48 inches around the obstacle
- Where the route is less than 60 inches in width, a 60 inches by 60 inches passing space must be provided at intervals of 200 feet.
- Objects that protrude into the accessible route with their leading edge between 27 inches and 80 inches from the ground, such as a telephone, must not protrude more than 4 inches. Objects mounted below 27 inches may protrude any amount but must not reduce the clear width of the accessible route.
- Vertical clearance on the accessible route must be 80 inches. If the vertical clearance of an area adjoining the accessible route is less than 80 inches, a cane-detectable barrier must be provided to warn the visually impaired.
- Except at walks adjacent to streets or driveways where changes in level are greater than 4 inches in vertical dimension, such as planters or fountains, a

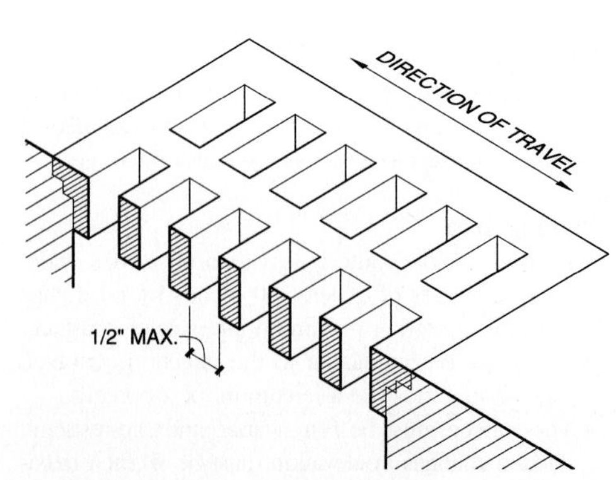

GRATES

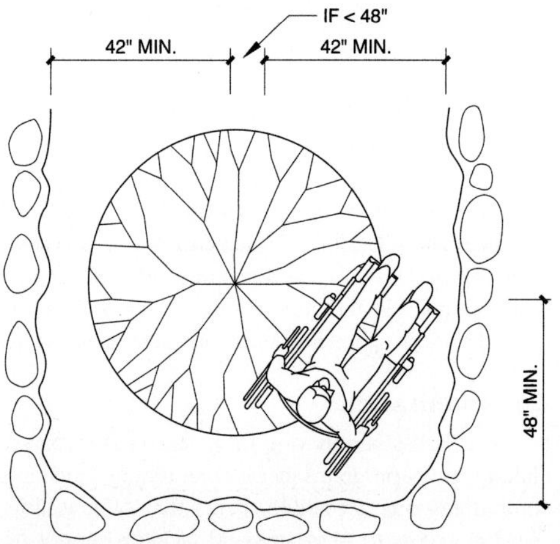

TURNING OBSTRUCTION

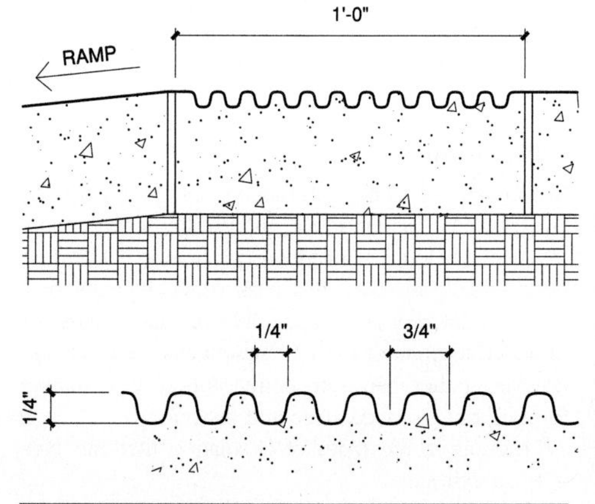

DOME SECTION

Susan Goltsman, FASLA; Timothy Gilbert, ASLA

6-inch-high warning curb or a handrail with guide rails centered at 2 inches to 4 inches above the ground must be installed.
- Detectable ground surface or pavement warnings must be provided where the access route crosses or adjoins a vehicular travel way, or a transit-boarding platform, that is not separated by a curb, guardrails, or handrails.
- Detectable warnings must be durable, slip-resistant, truncated domes with an inline grid that extends 24 inches minimum in the direction of travel. Domes must have a diameter of 0.9 inches at the bottom, a diameter of 0.4 inches at the top, a height of 0.2 inches, and a center-to-center spacing of 2.35 inches, measured along one side of a square grid (for acceptable deviations in dome shape, contrast visually from the adjacent surface both in color and in resiliency or sound upon contact with a cane. Additional requirements apply at passenger loading zones on transit boarding platforms.
- A level area must be provided on the pull side or push side of any door or gate.

Outdoor Recreation Access (ORAR)
General
- Running slopes in the direction of travel must be as follows:
  - 5 percent or less for any distance
  - From 5.1 percent to 8.3 percent for 200 feet maximum
  - From 8.34 percent to 10 percent for 30 feet maximum
- Resting spaces must be 60 inches minimum in length, must have a width at least as wide as the route, and have a slope of 3 percent or less. Exception: The slope of the resting space can be as great as 5 percent, if required for proper drainage. The installation of resting spaces required is shown in the table "Required Resting Spaces for Outdoor Recreation Access Routes."
- The surface of the ORAR must be stable and firm.
- The clear tread width must be 36 inches. Exception: The width may be reduced to 32 inches for a distance of 24 inches maximum where existing conditions cannot be mitigated.

REQUIRED RESTING SPACES FOR OUTDOOR RECREATION ACCESS ROUTES

PERCENT SLOPE	MAXIMUM LENGTH	REST INTERVAL
0% to 5.0%	No restriction	No restriction
5.1% to 8.33%	50 feet	Every 50 feet
8.34% to 10%	30 feet	Every 30 feet

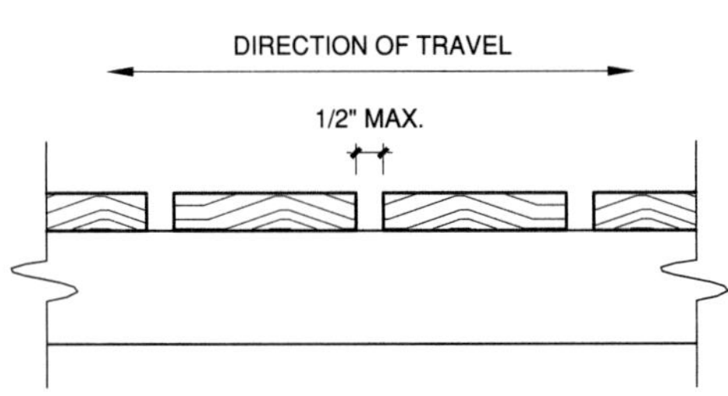

WOOD DECKING

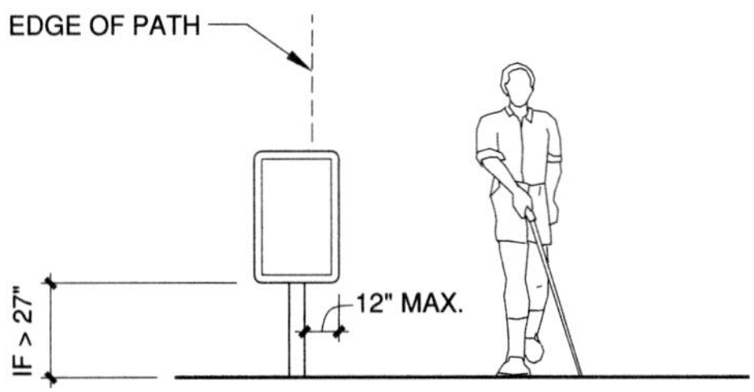

MOUNTED OBJECTS

- The slope perpendicular to the direction of travel, cross slope, must be 3 percent maximum. Exception: The cross slope may be as great as 5 percent, if necessary for proper drainage.

Details
- Openings in the surface, such as on a boardwalk, cannot be greater than ½ inch wide. Elongated openings must be placed so that the long dimension is perpendicular or diagonal to the direction of travel. Exception: Openings are permitted to run parallel to the direction of travel as long as the opening is no wider than ¼ inch.
- Freestanding objects that protrude into the route with their leading edge between 27 inches and 80 inches from the ground, such as a telephone, must not protrude more than 12 inches. Objects mounted below 27 inches may protrude any amount but must not reduce the clear width of the accessible route.
- Vertical clearance must be 80 inches. If the vertical clearance of an area adjoining the accessible route is less than 80 inches, a cane-detectable barrier must be provided to warn the visually impaired.
- Tread obstacles, such as roots or rocks, must not be higher than 1 inch. Exception: Obstacles may be up to 2 inches high if they are beveled at 50 percent or if environmental conditions prohibit their removal.
- Where the width of the route is less than 60 inches, passing spaces measuring 60 inches by 60 inches must be provided at intervals of 200 feet.
- Where edge protection is provided, it must have a height of 3 inches minimum.

RAMPS

Concept

- Ramps are only used on exterior routes of travel (ERT) and accessible paths of travel (POT). Ramps are not required on outdoor recreations access routes (ORAR) or trails.

Not withstanding curb ramps, whenever the slope exceeds 5 percent, a ramp must be provided.

TRAILS

Concept

Unlike exterior routes of travel (ERT) and outdoor recreation access routes (ORAR), trails provide the means for the activity of hiking and access to remote locations and unique park features; they also offer visitors the opportunity to experience various environmental settings.

Wherever hiking is considered one of the primary activities offered, or where there is a large concentration of trails, every effort should be made to install and maintain accessible trails. The accessible trail(s) should represent the most significant features and environmental experiences unique to the area.

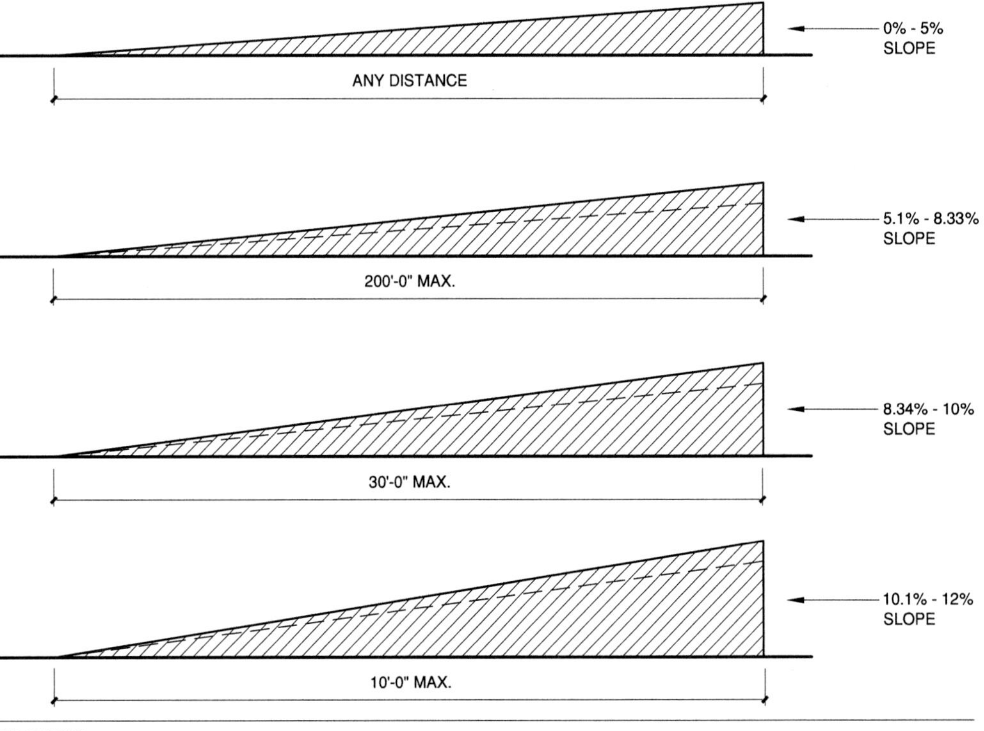

SLOPES

Susan Goltsman, FASLA; Timothy Gilbert, ASLA

REQUIRED RESTING SPACES FOR TRAILS

PERCENT SLOPE	MAXIMUM LENGTH	REST INTERVAL
0% to 5.0%	No restriction	No restriction
5.1% to 8.33%	200 feet	Every 200 feet
8.34% to 10%	30 feet	Every 30 feet
10.1% to 12%	10 feet	Every 10 feet

Safety Features

General

- Running slopes in the direction of travel must be as follows:
  - 5 percent or less for any distance
  - From 5.1 percent to 8.33 percent for 200 feet maximum
  - From 8.34 percent to 10 percent for 30 feet maximum
  - From 10 percent to 12 percent for 10 feet maximum
- Resting spaces must be 60 inches minimum in length, must have a width at least as wide as the trail, and have a slope of 5 percent or less in any direction. The installation of resting spaces is required for trails as shown in the table "Required Resting Spaces for Trails."
- The slope perpendicular to the direction of travel, cross slope, must be 5 percent maximum.
- The clear tread width must be 36 inches, although the width may be reduced to 32 inches where existing conditions cannot be mitigated.
- The surface of the trail must be stable and firm.

Details

- Openings in the surface, such as on a boardwalk, must not be greater than ½ inch wide. Elongated openings must be placed so that the long dimension is perpendicular or diagonal to the dominant direction of travel. Exception: Openings are permitted to run parallel to the direction of travel as long as the opening is no wider than ¼ inch.
- Objects that protrude into the trail between 27 and 80 inches from the ground must not protrude more than 4 inches. Objects mounted below 27 inches may protrude any amount, but must not reduce the clear width of the trail.
- Vertical clearance must be 80 inches. If the 80-inch vertical clearance of the trail cannot be mitigated, a cane-detectable barrier must be provided to warn the visually impaired.
- For open drainage structures, a running slope of 14 percent is permitted for 5 feet maximum with a cross slope of 5 percent maximum. Cross slope is permitted to be 10 percent at the bottom of the open drain where the clear tread width is at least 42 inches wide.
- Tread obstacles, such as roots or rocks, must not be higher than 2 inches. Exception: Obstacles may be up to 3 inches high where the running slope and cross slope are 5 percent or less.
- Where the width of the trail is less than 60 inches, passing spaces measuring 60 by 60 inches must be provided at intervals of 1,000 feet.
- Where edge protection is provided, it must have a height of 3 inches minimum.
- Trails that meet the preceding guidelines must be designated with a symbol at the trailhead and at designated access points. Signage must indicate the total distance of the accessible segment and the location of the first point of departure from the guidelines.
- Signage at trailheads must be accessible to users with vision impairments.

Educational Nature Trails

An educational nature trail is a trail for which the designated use is pedestrian only and is planned for the primary purpose of educating the public on the natural or cultural resources of the area. Educational nature trails also contain a series of informational panels or signs and often a printed informational brochure.

Educational nature trails that meet federal accessibility guidelines must be made accessible to the blind by providing: raised edging along at least one side of the trail; distinctive tactile surface textures to call attention to informational displays, panels, or signs; raised Arabic numerals and symbols for identification; and related guide and assistance devices.

FIXED BENCHES

Concept

Fixed benches, where provided, must be made accessible for users with various types of disabilities. At least 50 percent of the fixed benches being provided in a facility or building must be accessible and be dispersed among the types provided. Of the number of fixed benches required to be accessible, at least 40 percent must be provided along an accessible route of travel. If only one bench is being provided, it must be made accessible.

Clear Spaces

- The surface around the accessible bench must be firm and stable.
- A minimum area of 30 inches by 48 inches must be provided at one end of the fixed bench so that a wheelchair user may be seated shoulder to shoulder with an individual seated on the bench.
- Clear spaces must have a slope that does not exceed 2 percent in any direction (if necessary for proper drainage, 3 percent maximum is allowed).
- It is recommended that benches be placed 12 inches off any pathway so that a seated person does not obstruct the path of travel.

Bench Design

- The fixed bench must be free of sharp edges or protruding hardware that may be hazardous.
- The height of the front edge of the seating surface must be between 17 and 19 inches above the adjacent grade or floor space.
- A back support must be provided along the full length of the accessible bench.
- Accessible benches must have seats that are 20 to 24 inches in depth and 42 inches minimum in length. The back support must extend from a point 2 inches maximum above the bench to 18 inches minimum above the bench.
- Accessible fixed benches must have at least one armrest that can withstand 250 pounds of force in any direction.

DRINKING FOUNTAINS

Concept

Where drinking fountains are provided, there must be accessible drinking fountain(s), which must be on an accessible path of travel.

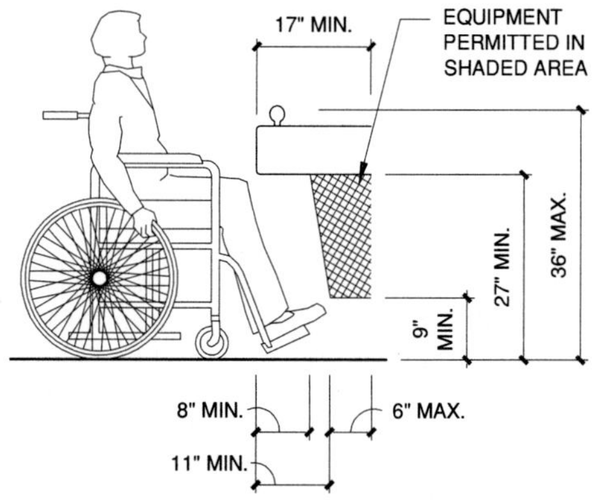

FOUNTAIN HEIGHT

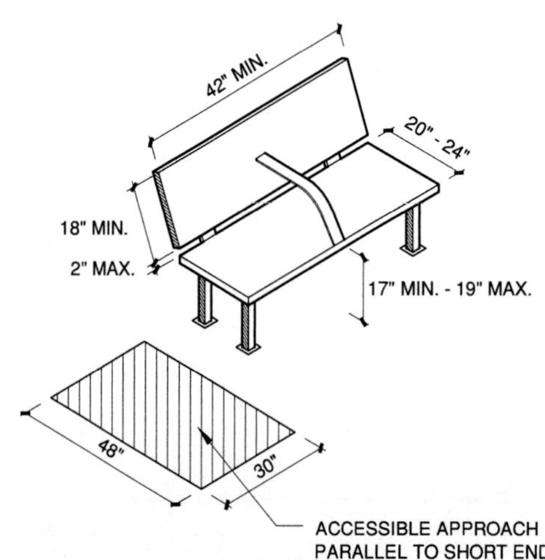

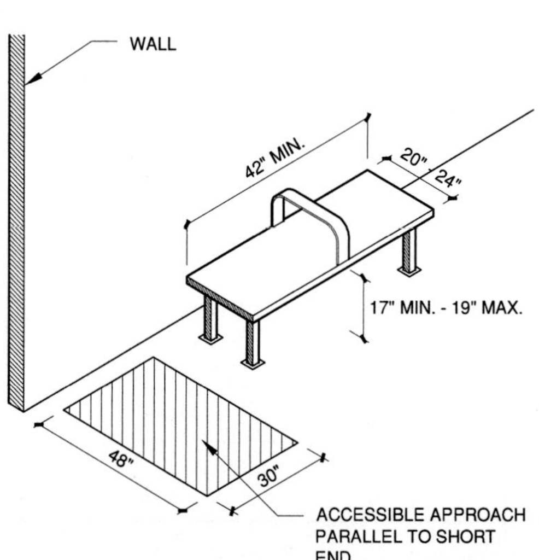

BENCH WALL

Susan Goltsman, FASLA; Timothy Gilbert, ASLA

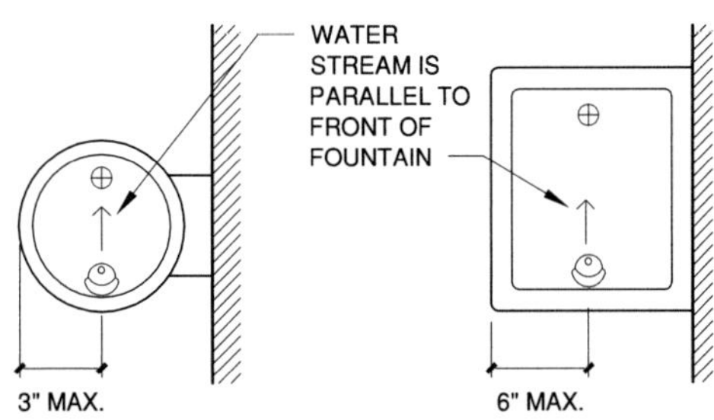

DRINKING FOUNTAIN WATER FLOW DIRECTION

Wall-Mounted and Post-Mounted Units

- Where only one drinking fountain is provided, the use of a "hi-low" fountain can be used for accessibility.
- If more than one drinking fountain is provided, at least 50 percent must be accessible.
- The fountain must not encroach into an accessible route.
- There must be a clear, level space of at least 30 inches by 48 inches in front of the fountain.
- The fixture must be 17–19 inches deep.
- Clear knee space beneath the fountain must be a minimum of 27 inches high, 30 inches wide, and 8 inches deep, with additional minimum toe space of 9 inches high by 17 inches deep.
- The water nozzle must be located a maximum 36 inches above the ground and a maximum 6 inches from the front of the unit, with the water flow direction parallel to the front edge of the unit and to a 4-inch height minimum. If the basin is round or oval, the spout and water flow must be within 3 inches of the front.
- Activation must be by means of lever controls or a wide, nonrecessed press bar located at a maximum of 6 inches from the front edge of the unit and requiring no more than 5 pounds of pressure, without tight grasping, pinching, or twisting hand motion.

Wall-Mounted Units

- Where provided, wall-mounted units can be located completely within an alcove, or with wing walls, or so as not to encroach into pedestrian ways.
- Alcove or wing wall of fountain must be no less than 30 inches wide and no greater than 24 inches deep.

PICNIC SITES

Concept

A picnic site exists wherever one or more fixed picnic tables are located. In general, picnic areas must include accessible parking, restrooms, picnic site, and routes that connect each of the elements throughout the area.

Site Planning

- Where one fixed picnic table is provided in a picnic area, it must be accessible and be connected to an outdoor recreation access route.
- If there are two or more picnic tables, at least 50 percent, but never fewer than two, must be accessible tables.
- Of the accessible tables, at least 40 percent, but never fewer than two tables, must be on an accessible route of travel.
- Accessible picnic tables must be dispersed throughout the picnic area.
- The accessible picnic sites must be located on a surface area with no greater than a 2 percent slope (3 percent slope when necessary for drainage).

Picnic Tables

- Picnic tables and benches must be on a firm, stable surface.
- An accessible picnic table must have at least one wheelchair seating space.
- Where the tabletop perimeter exceeds 24 linear feet, the number of wheelchair seating spaces must comply with the requirements given in the table "Required Wheelchair Spaces for Picnic Tables."

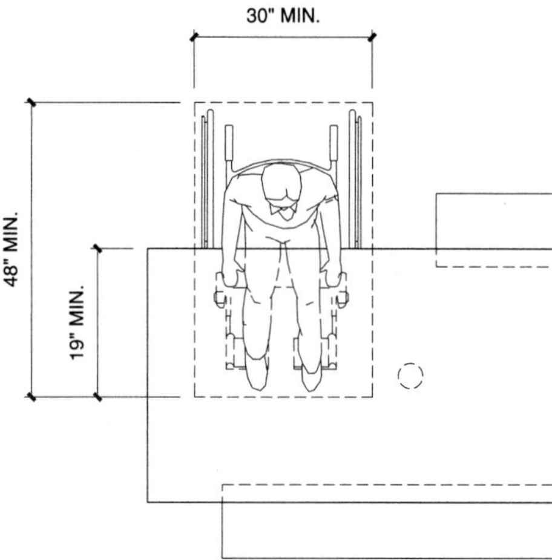

PICNIC TABLE HEIGHT

REQUIRED WHEELCHAIR SPACES FOR PICNIC TABLES

TABLETOP PERIMETER	WHEELCHAIR SPACES
25 to 44 linear feet	2 spaces
45 to 64 linear feet	3 spaces
65 to 84 linear feet	4 spaces
85 to 104 linear feet	5 spaces

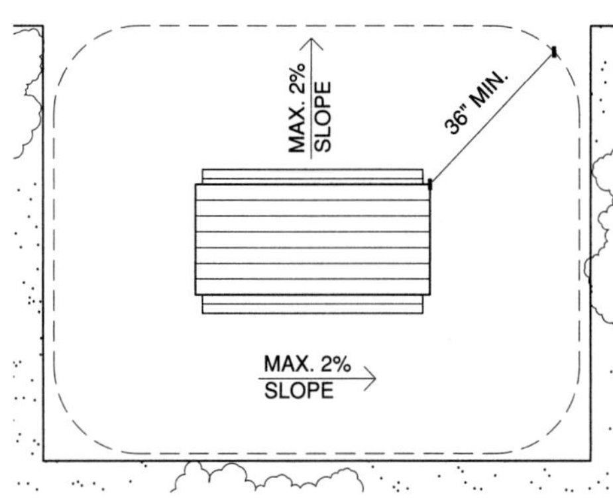

PICNIC TABLE CLEAR AREA

17" MIN.
6" MAX.
6" MAX.
27" MIN.
36" MAX. TO BUBBLER
42" MAX. TO BUBBLER
32" x 48" MIN. CLEAR FLOOR SPACE CENTERED UNDER LOW DRINKING FOUNTAIN UNIT

DRINKING FOUNTAIN

Susan Goltsman, FASLA; Timothy Gilbert, ASLA

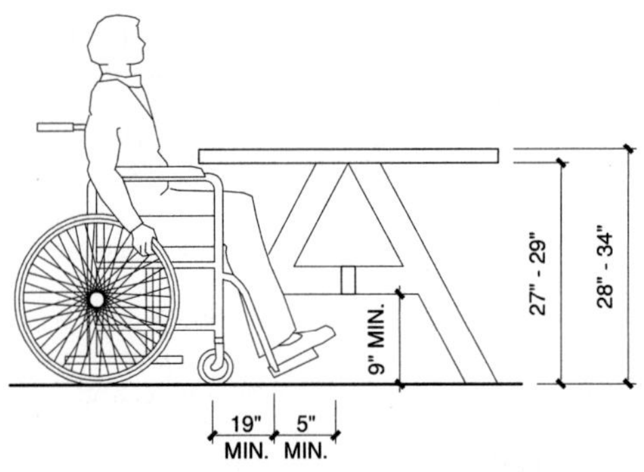

PICNIC TABLE

- Picnic tables and benches must have no sharp edges or protruding hardware that may be hazardous.
- Around the picnic table, a 36-inch clear space measured from the seat must be provided.
- Distance from the tabletop to the ground must be between 28 and 34 inches.
- Picnic tables must have a minimum knee clearance of 27 inches high, 19 inches deep, and 30 inches wide. Toe clearance must be a minimum of 9 inches high and 24 inches deep.

Grills, Fire Rings, and Cooking Surfaces

- Where a cooking surface or fire ring is provided at a picnic site, it must be accessible.
- Surrounding the accessible cooking facilities and fire rings must be a stable, firm surface having a minimum of 48 inches clear space.

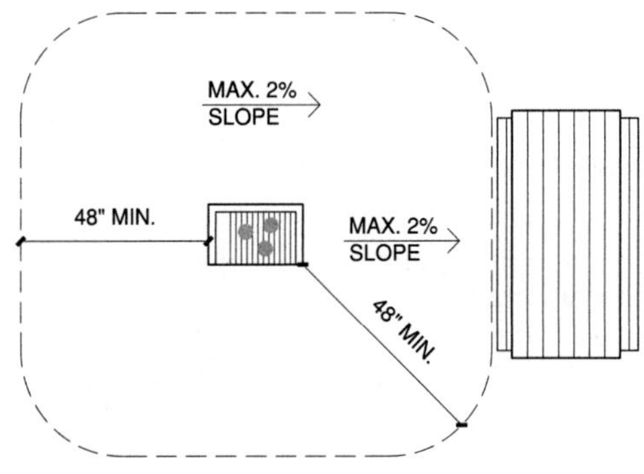

FIRE RING CLEAR AREA

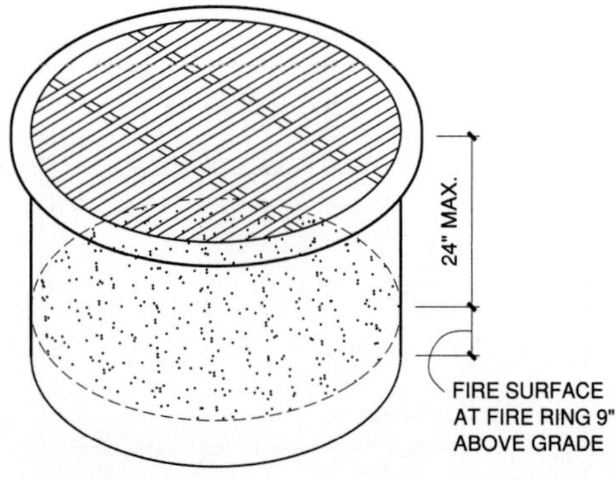

FIRE RING

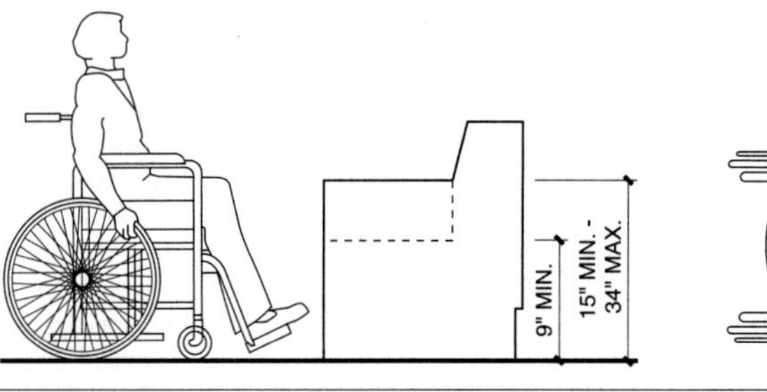

FIREPLACE

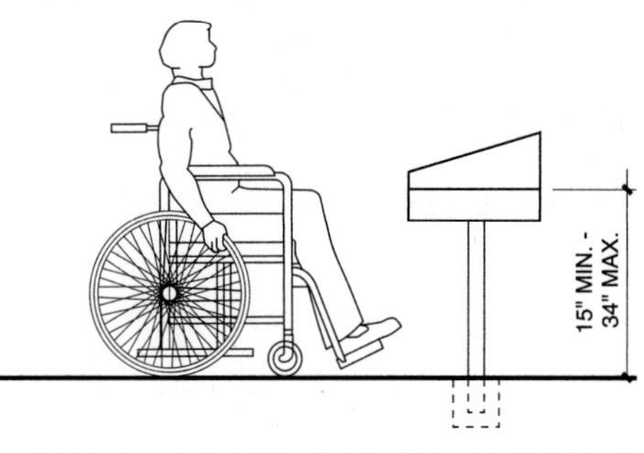

POST GRILL

- A distinctive area surrounding the cooking area would be helpful in alerting visitors with vision impairments.
- The slope of the clear space around cooking facilities and fire rings must be a maximum of 2 percent (3 percent slope when necessary for drainage).
- The height of the fire ring's raised edge must be a combined distance over the edge or curb down to the fire building surface of a maximum of 24 inches.
- On fire rings or fireplace grills, the fire-building surface height must be 9 inches minimum above ground level, and the distance from the outside edge of the fire ring to the fire-building surface must be a maximum of 24 inches.
- All cooking surface heights must be between 15 inches minimum and 34 inches maximum above the ground level.

Water Faucets

- Faucets must be located adjacent to a clear, stable, firm ground surface area at least 60 inches by 60 inches in size. Faucets must be configured to allow a forward approach.
- A 2 percent slope must be allowed to drain toward the faucet drain (3 percent slope when necessary for drainage). Drain grating must have maximum opening of ½ inch.
- The faucet lever(s) must be located 28 to 36 inches above the ground (does not apply to hand pumps) and must be operated by a push button or lever actuator that requires no more than 5 pounds of pressure.

Trash and Recycling Receptacles

- The picnic area must have a trash receptacle at the site or on an accessible route to the site.
- The trash and/or recycling receptacle must be located on stable, firm ground with a clear space minimum of 30 inches by 48 inches and a slope of 2 percent (3 percent allowed if necessary for drainage).

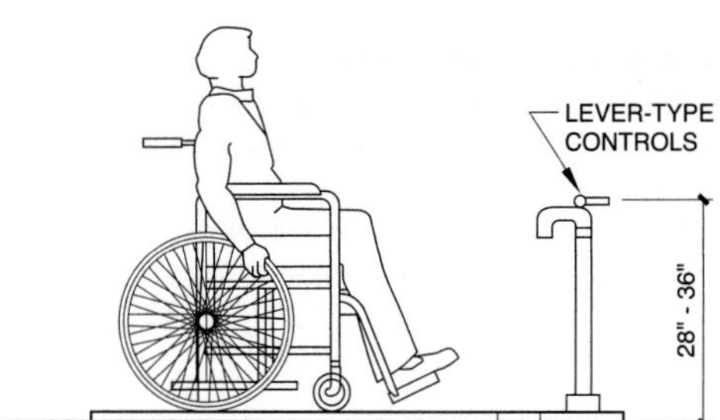

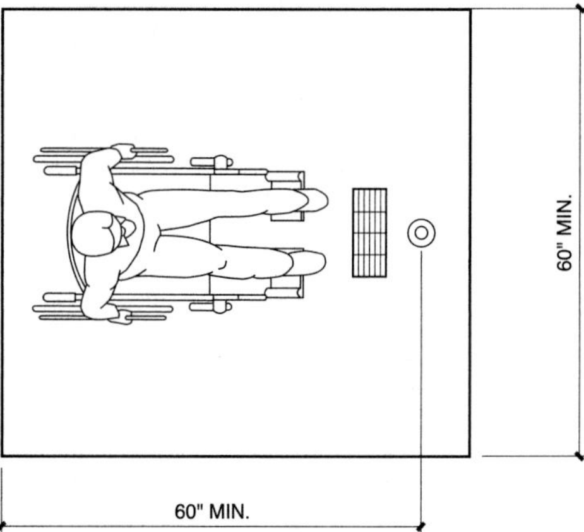

HAND PUMP

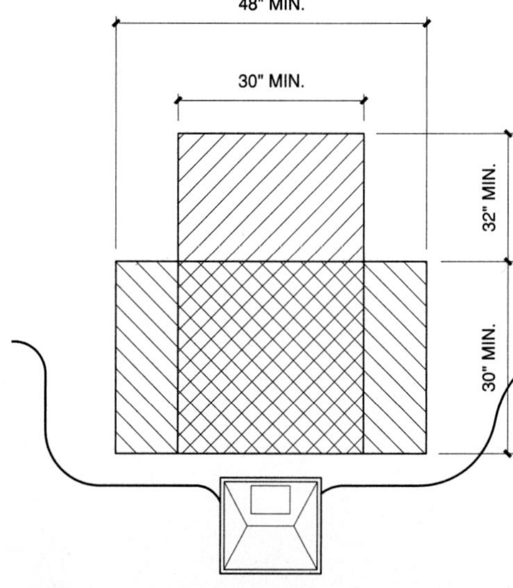

TRASH CLEAR GROUND

Susan Goltsman, FASLA; Timothy Gilbert, ASLA

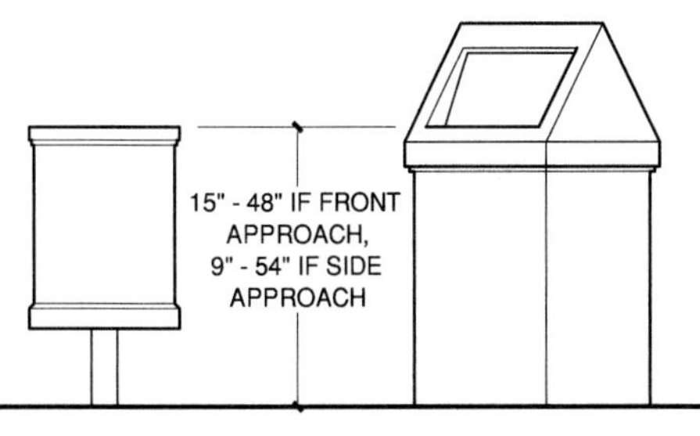

TRASH HEIGHT

- The trash and/or recycling receptacle and/or operating mechanism must be between 15 and 48 inches above the ground for front approach and between 9 and 54 inches for side approach
- Receptacle openings must be operable with a single hand manipulation and require less than 5 pounds of pressure to operate. This requirement does not apply to hinged lids and controls designed to exclude large animals.

The following are requirements for sinks other than lavatories or those found in restrooms. These include sinks in picnic and campground areas and sinks for utility purposes, such as washing or cleaning fish.

Sinks

- The rim of the sink should be 34 inches or less above the floor.
- Except for utility sinks, there must be a clearance of at least 27 inches from the floor to the bottom of the sink apron, with a knee clearance under the front lip extending a minimum 30 inches in width, with a 17–19-inch depth underneath the sink.
- Except for utility sinks, there must be 30 inches by

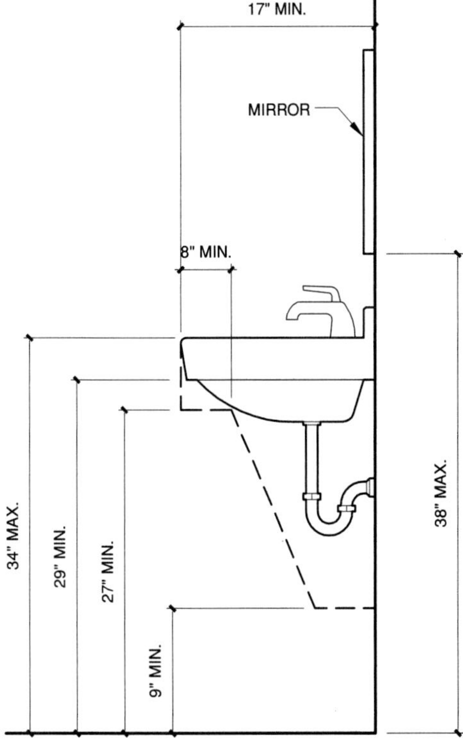

SINKS

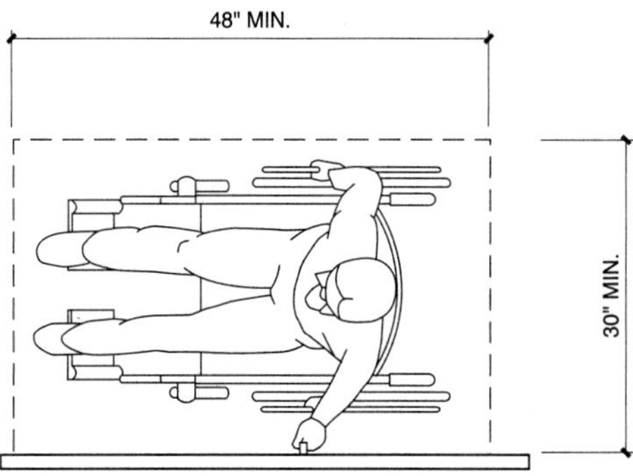

CLEAR GROUND PARALLEL

48 inches clear floor space provided in front of the sink to allow for a forward approach.

- The clear floor space must be on an accessible route and must extend a maximum of 19 inches underneath the sink.
- Except for utility sinks, the bowl of the sink must be a maximum 6½ inches deep.
- Exposed hot water lines and drainpipes must be out of the way or insulated. There must be no sharp or abrasive surfaces under the sink.
- Faucet and other controls must be operable with one hand and not require tight grasping or twisting of the wrist. The force required to activate controls must be 5 pounds maximum. Lever, push-type, and electronically controlled mechanisms are acceptable.
- If self-closing faucets are provided, they must stay on at least 10 seconds.

Utility Sinks (Deep)

- A clear floor space of 30 inches by 48 inches must be provided in front of the sink to allow for a parallel approach (with a side reach).
- The clear space in front of the sink must have a slope no greater than 2 percent (3 percent if necessary for proper drainage).
- The bottom of the bowl must be a minimum 15 inches above the floor.
- The counter or rim of the sink must be 34 inches or less above the floor.
- The surface of the clear space must be stable and firm.
- If utility sinks are provided, at least 5 percent, but no less than 1, must be accessible.

VISTA/OVERLOOKS

Concept

Vista points, roadside pullouts/overlooks, their features, views, and experiences they provide must be accessible. Where multiple viewing areas are provided, a minimum of one of each viewing opportunity for each distinct point of interest must be accessible. Vista points and overlooks must be located on an accessible route of travel, including an outdoor recreation access route (ORAR) or accessible trail.

Viewing Area

- The viewing area must have at least one maneuvering space of 60 inches by 60 inches or a T-shaped space at least 36 inches wide and 60 inches long on each leg.
- The maneuvering space must be firm and stable and must not exceed a 2 percent slope in any direction.

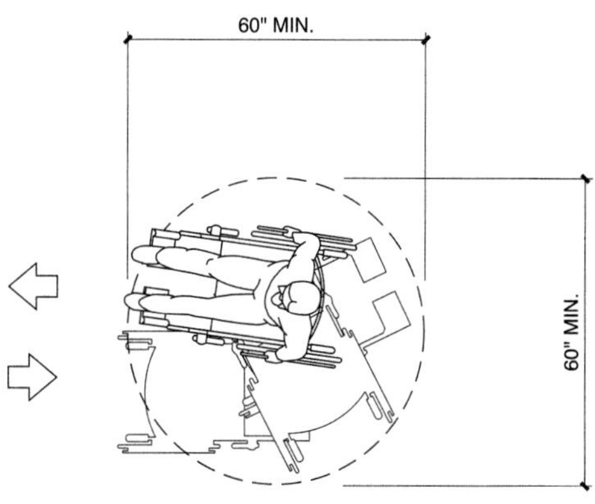

TURNING SPACE

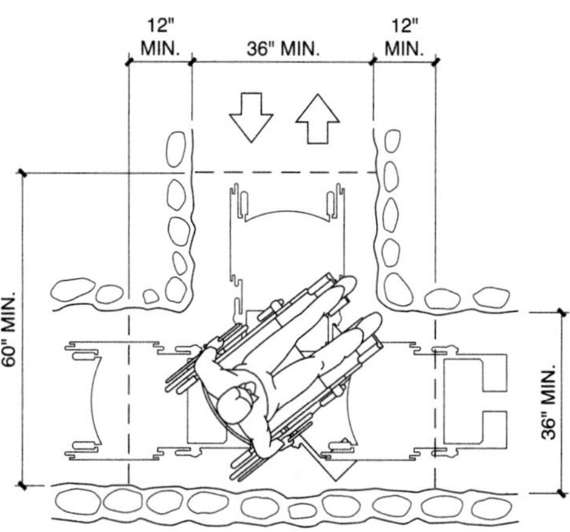

T-SHAPED TURNING SPACE

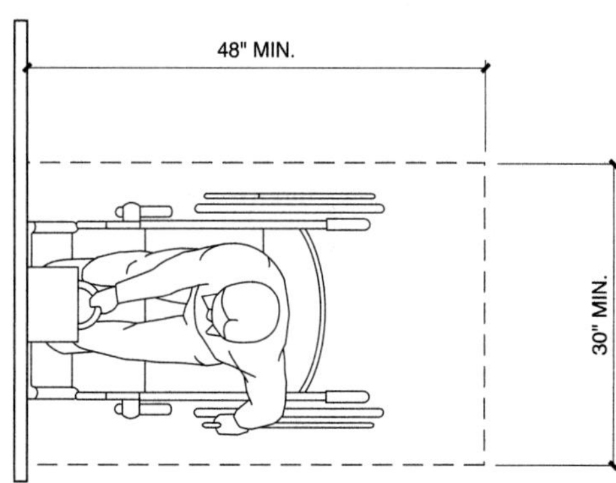

CLEAR GROUND FORWARD

- Each distinct viewing opportunity must allow unrestricted viewing to accommodate eye levels between 32 and 51 inches.
- Where descriptive signs are provided at vista points, they must be provided in raised lettering and Braille so as to be accessible to users with vision impairments.
- Where feasible, provide audible versions of exhibit information, when exhibits are redesigned.

Fixed Viewing Devices

- Where telescopes or periscopes are provided in an area, at least 20 percent, but never less than one telescope or periscope, must be accessible.

Susan Goltsman, FASLA; Timothy Gilbert, ASLA

FORWARD REACH 1

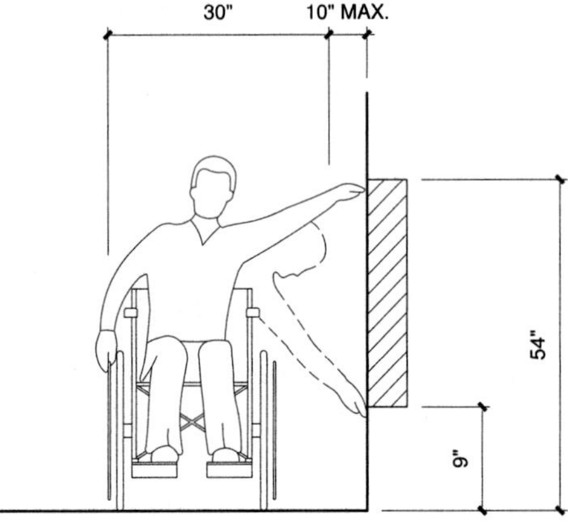

SIDE REACH 1

- Where only one telescope or periscope is provided, it must be useable from a seated and standing position.
- Within the vista point or viewing area, an accessible telescope/periscope must be connected by an outdoor recreation access route (ORAR).
- A stable and firm clear space measuring 30 inches by 48 inches must be provided in front of the accessible telescope/periscope to allow for a forward or parallel approach.
- The slope of the clear space must not exceed 2 percent unless surface conditions require a slope for proper drainage, where a 3 percent maximum slope is allowed.
- The eyepiece of accessible telescopes/periscopes must be useable from the seated position.
- The force required to activate the controls must not be greater than 5 pounds of pressure.
- The operating controls must be operable with one hand and must not require tight grasping, pinching, or twisting of the wrist.
- The operating controls must be located between 15 and 48 inches for a forward approach and between 9 and 54 inches for a parallel approach.

ASSEMBLY AREAS

Concept

Assembly areas, including amphitheaters, campfire circles, theaters, stages, and spaces used by performers, are provided to enhance park visitor experiences, through education, entertainment, or a variety of other means. Facilities must be fully accessible to visitors and employees.

REQUIRED ACCESSIBLE SEATING FOR ASSEMBLY AREAS

SEATING CAPACITY	NUMBER OF REQUIRED WHEELCHAIR LOCATIONS
4 to 25	1
26 to 50	2
51 to 300	4
301 to 500	6
Over 500	6, plus 1 additional space for each total seating capacity increase of 100

Seating

- Accessible seating must be distributed throughout the area to provide a choice of sight lines.
- Each accessible seating area must have provisions for companion seating, and must be located on an accessible route that also serves as an emergency accessible egress.
- Seating must meet the requirements shown in the table "Required Accessible Seating for Assembly Areas."
- At least 1 percent, but no fewer than one, of all fixed seats must be aisle seats with no armrest on the aisle side, or must have folding or removable armrests on the aisle side.
- Accessible aisle seats must be identified by a sign or marker.
- The wheelchair location must have a minimum clear floor or ground space of 48 inches deep by 66 inches wide, if a forward or rear approach.
- The wheelchair location must have a minimum clear floor or ground space of 60 inches deep by 66 inches wide, if side approach.
- Readily removable seats may be installed in wheelchair spaces when the spaces are not required to accommodate wheelchair users.
- Proper signage in the lobby or ticket booth area must indicate seating accessibility.
- Armrests and backrests required with fixed-bench seating are not mandatory in a spectator assembly environment.

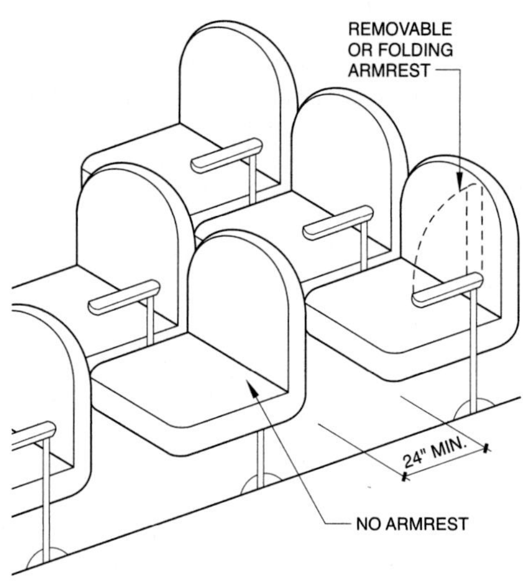

SEATING 2

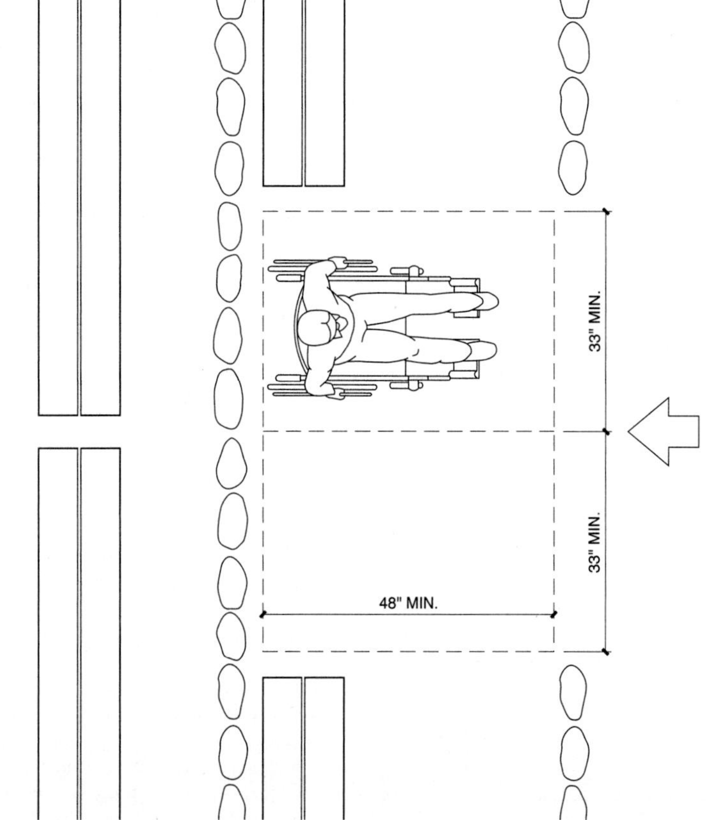

ASSEMBLY 1

Susan Goltsman, FASLA; Timothy Gilbert, ASLA

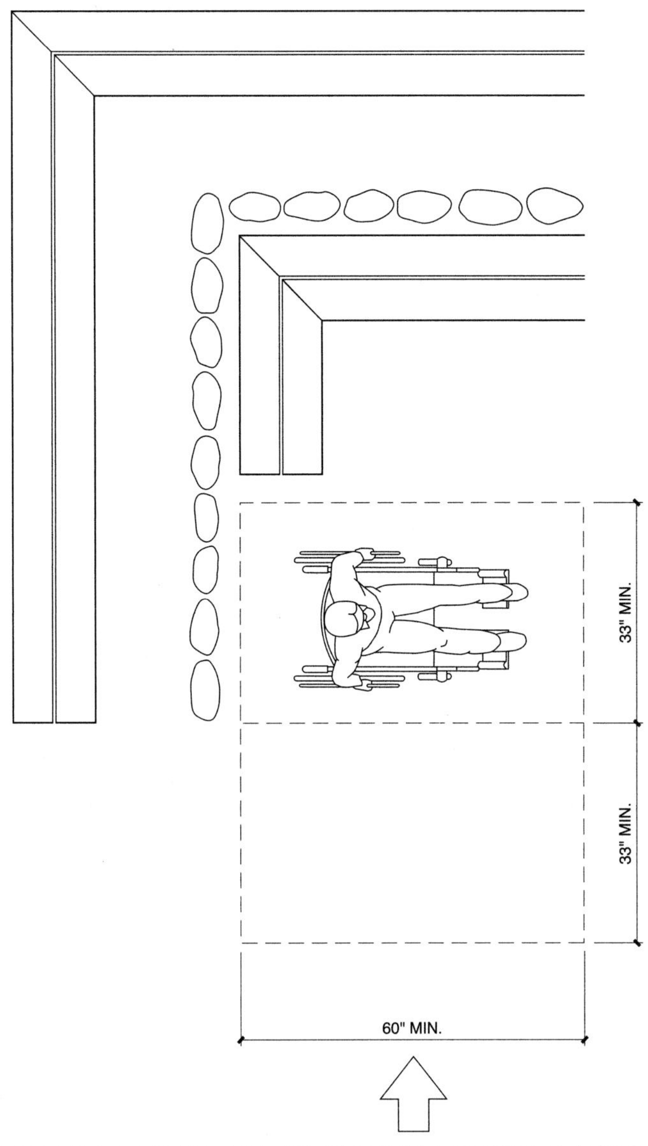

ASSEMBLY 2

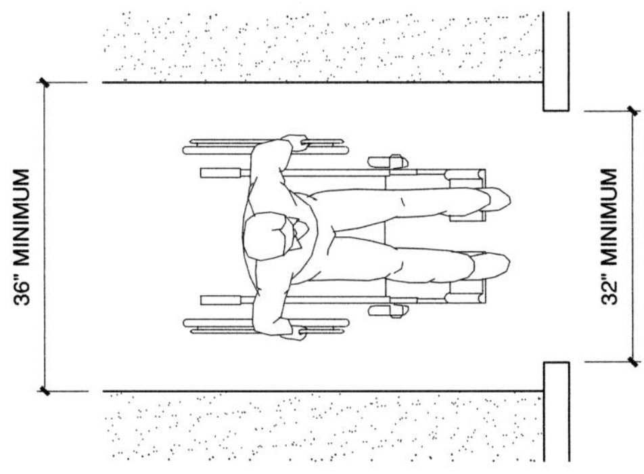

CORRIDOR WIDTH

Path of Travel

- At least one accessible route within the boundary of the site must be provided from public transportation stops, accessible parking, and accessible passenger loading zones, as well as public streets or sidewalks to the accessible entrance they serve.
- The accessible route must, to the maximum extent feasible, coincide with the route for the general public.
- The minimum clear width of an accessible route must be 36 inches, except at doorways, which may be 32 inches.
- If an accessible route has less than 60 inches clear width, passing spaces at least 60 inches by 60 inches must be located at reasonable intervals, not to exceed 200 feet. A T-intersection of two corridors or walks is an acceptable passing place. (An accessible route must connect wheelchair seating locations with performing areas, including stages and other spaces used by presenters.)
- Where it is technically infeasible to alter all performing areas to be on an accessible route, at least one of each type of performing area should be made accessible.
- All wheelchair seating must adjoin an accessible route that can also serve as a means of egress in case of emergency.

Listening Systems

- Assistive listening systems (ALS) are intended to augment standard public address and audio systems. For types of systems and related requirements refer to the Assembly Areas section of the Americans with Disabilities Act, "Accessibility Guidelines for Buildings and Facilities.

BEACHES AND SHORES

Concept

The major barrier to shore and beach use by persons with mobility impairments is the difficulty in traversing sandy or loose soil. For some water activities, such as fishing or swimming, it is necessary to have direct physical contact with the water from the beach or shore. Access to these activities involves two basic considerations:

1. Access to the edge of the beach or shore from accessible parking spaces, common use areas, and support facilities. These routes must be consistent with the requirements for accessible routes of travel.
2. Access across the beach to the element of the activity (the water's edge). These routes are known as beach access routes.

All newly constructed beach, river, lake and shoreline facilities must have at least one permanently installed beach access route for every half-mile of linear shoreline.

For an existing "designated" beach, when a pedestrian access route is constructed to or along the edge of the beach, a beach access route must be provided.

Beach Access Routes

- The beach access route must be located in the same area as the general circulation path, when feasible, and must extend to the high-tide level, mean riverbed level, or the normal recreation pool level.
- A beach access route is not required when the pedestrian route along the edge of an existing beach is elevated 6 inches or higher above the beach surface. The above pedestrian route runs parallel to the water's edge.
- The minimum clear width of the beach access route must be 36 inches (48 inches is preferred).
- The surface of the beach access route must be firm and stable.
- Edge protection, a minimum of 2 inches high, must be provided where drop-offs are 6 inches or higher.
- Drop-offs greater than 1 inch, but less than 6 inches, must have a beveled edge.
- Openings in the route surface, such as on a boardwalk, must be ½ inch or less if perpendicular or diagonal to the route. They must be 1/4 inch or less if parallel to the route.
- Objects that protrude into the beach access route with their leading edge between 27 inches and 80 inches from the ground must not protrude more than 4 inches. Objects mounted below 27 inches may protrude any amount but must not reduce the clear width of the accessible route.

Susan Goltsman, FASLA; Timothy Gilbert, ASLA

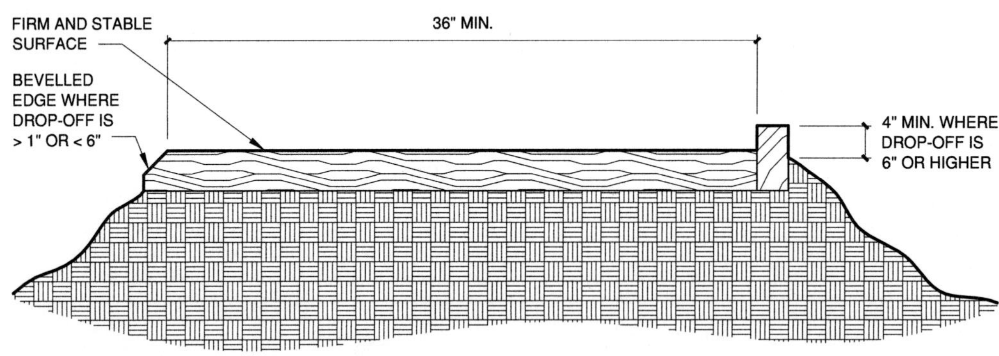

DROP-OFF

- Vertical clearance on the beach access route must be 80 inches. If the vertical clearance of an area adjoining the beach access route is less than 80 inches, a cane-detectable barrier must be provided to warn the visually impaired.
- The slope for beach access routes must meet one of the following criteria:
  - From 0 percent to 5 percent slope for any length
  - From 5.1 percent to 8.33 percent slope for 50 feet
  - From 8.34 percent to 10 percent slope for a maximum of 30 feet
- The installation of resting spaces is required as shown in the table "Required Resting Spaces for Beach Access Routes."
- Resting spaces must be 60 inches minimum in length, must have a width at least as wide as the route, and have a slope of 3 percent or less. *Exception:* The slope of the resting space can be as great as 5 percent if required for proper drainage.
- The cross slope must be 3 percent or less, with a maximum of 5 percent allowed if necessary for drainage.
- A maneuvering space measuring a minimum of 60 inches by 60 inches must be provided at the end of the beach access route.
- If the route is less than 60 inches wide, passing spaces a minimum of 60 inches by 60 inches must be provided at least every 200 feet.
- All obstacles in the beach access route must be less than 1 inch high.

Designated Swim Areas

- Depending on safety needs and local site conditions, designated swimming areas should be clearly defined in the water with highly visible floating devices.
- Depending on safety needs and local site conditions, designated swimming areas should also be identified on shore with clearly visible signage.

Access to Water

- When feasible, considering site conditions at designated swimming areas, a firm, stable surface should provide access into the water. An additional option may be a beach wheelchair if the slope conditions at the park do not make use of beach wheelchairs hazardous.
- Beach wheelchairs allow assisted access to the beach for people who use wheelchairs. If beach wheelchairs are provided, signs should be posted to indicate their availability.

SWIMMING POOLS

Concept

Access to swimming is dependent on getting to the pool area and getting into and out of the water. Swimming pool deck areas must be accessible, and an assistive device must be provided to assist persons with disabilities in gaining entry into the pool. There must be an unobstructed path of travel from accessible parking to the swimming pool, and pool gates must meet the requirements for Doors in the ADA Accessibility Guidelines for Buildings and Facilities (Section 4.13).

Safety Features

- Float dividers, colors, textures, and pavement markings should be used to clearly indicate increasing water depth.
- Colors and textures that contrast with the adjoining walking surface should be used to clearly indicate pool and ramp edges and other high-risk areas.
- Paving must be nonslip and nonabrasive to bare feet.
- Edges of the pool coping should be rounded ¾ to 1½ inches radius.
- There must be a minimum 48-inch-wide unobstructed path of travel around the pool.

Pool Access

- At least two means of entry and exit must be provided for each swimming pool. The primary means of access must be a ramp (sloped entry) or lift.

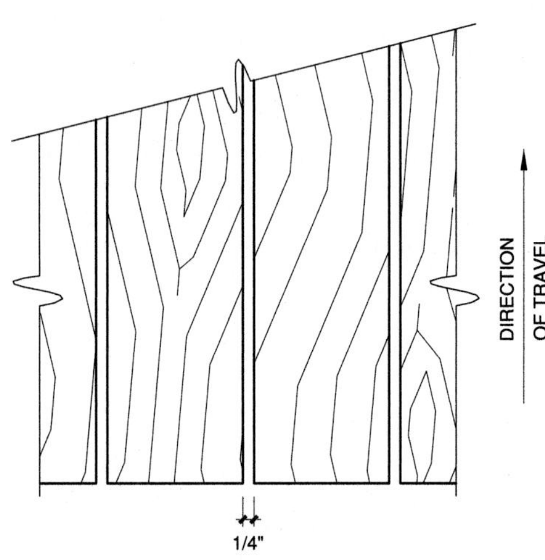

TRAVEL DIRECTION

REQUIRED RESTING SPACES FOR BEACH ACCESS ROUTES

PERCENT SLOPE	MAXIMUM LENGTH	REST INTERVAL
0% to 5.0%	No restriction	No restriction
5.1% to 8.33%	50 feet	Every 50 feet
8.34% to 10%	30 feet	Every 30 feet

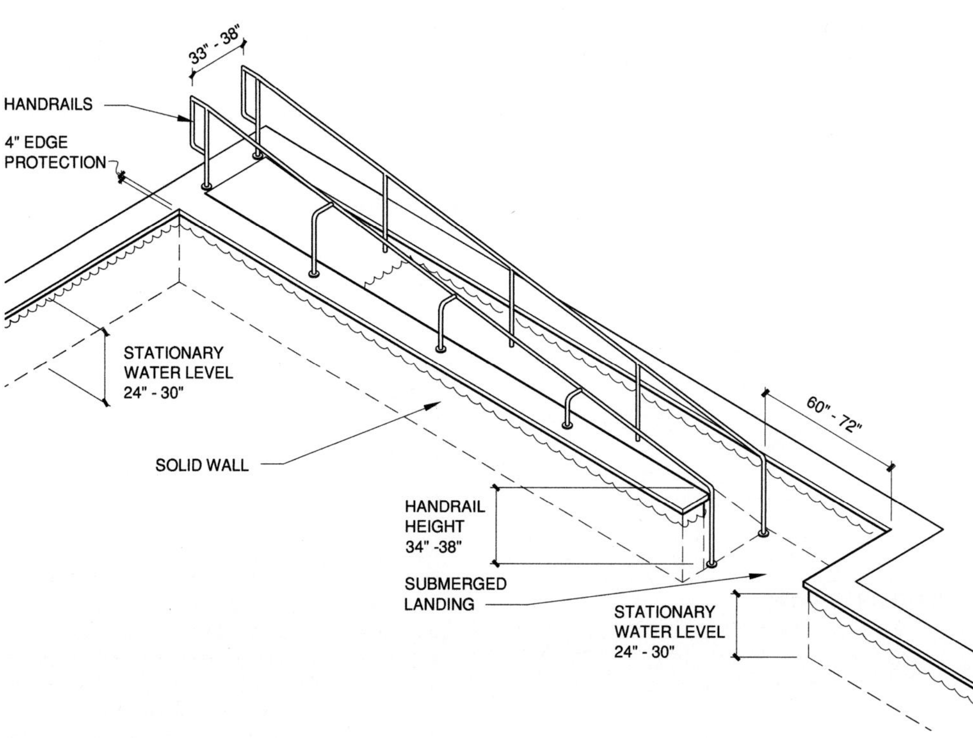

SLOPE ENTRY RAMP

Susan Goltsman, FASLA; Timothy Gilbert, ASLA

- The secondary means of access must not duplicate the primary means, but may be transfer walls, transfer systems, or stairs.
- Swimming pools with a perimeter less than 300 linear feet will have one means of access, which must either be a lift or a ramp (sloped entry).

Ramps (Sloped Entries)
- Ramp access into the water must be on an accessible route.
- Ramps into swimming pools must meet the requirements of ADAAG-4.8. When sloped entry exceeds 5 percent, the following modifications will be used:
  - Ramps must extend to a depth of 24 inches minimum to 30 inches maximum below the stationary water level.
  - Where landings are required by ADAAG –4.8, at least one landing shall be located 24 inches minimum to 30 inches maximum below the stationary water level.
- Handrails are required on all sloped entries.
- The clear width between handrails must be between 33 inches and 38 inches.

Benches
- Refer to ADAAG 4.37 and specifically 4.37.7 for benches that are to be installed in wet locations.

Steps
- Pool stairs must comply with ADAAG-15.8.9.
- Handrails must comply with ADAAG-15.8.9.2.
- Stair striping in a contrasting color is required on all new pool stairs.

Pool Lifts
- Swimming pool areas must be accessible, and a mechanism to assist persons with disabilities, allowing unassisted operation for gaining entry into the pool and exiting from the pool, must be provided. Such a mechanism may consist of a swimming pool lift device, as long the pool lift meets the following criteria:

The Seat of the Lift Has the Following Specifications
- The seat must be rigid.
- The seat must have a back support that is 12 inches tall.
- The lift seat must be a minimum of 16 inches wide.
- If provided, the armrest on the side of the seat by which access is gained must be either removable, or fold clear of the seat. Armrests must not obstruct the transfer.
- Footrests must be provided and move in conjunction with the seat.
- Seat must be stable and prohibit unintended movement when a person is getting into or out of the seat.

The Location of the Seat/Lift Has the Following Specifications
- Lift must be positioned so that if the pool has water of different depths, it will place the operator into water that is not deeper than 48 inches.
- In the raised position, the centerline of the lift seat must be located over the pool deck, at least 16 inches minimum from the edge of the pool.
- A minimum clear deck space must be on the side of the seat opposite the water. The space is measured from the seat. It must be a minimum of 36 inches wide and 48 inches long from a line located 12 inches behind the rear edge of the seat. The space must be clear and free of deck braces that can interfere with the transfer.
- The height of the lift seat must be not less than 16 inches and no more than 19 inches, inclusive of any cushioned surface that might be provided above the pool deck. The height is to be measured from the deck to the top of the seat surface when the seat is in the raised (loaded) position. An adjustable seat may be used.

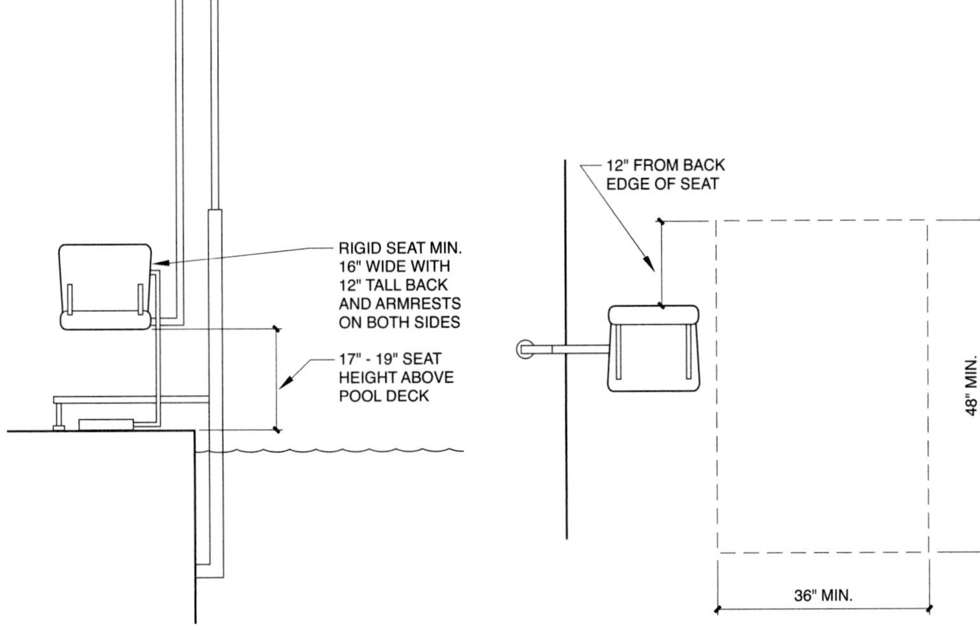

POOL LIFT

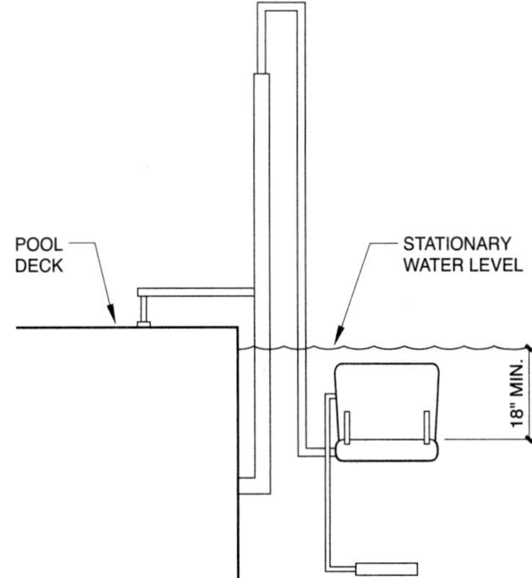

POOL LIFT SUBMERGE DEPTH

- Pool lifts must be capable of unassisted operation from both the deck and water levels.
- Controls must be unobstructed when a lift is in use.
- Controls must not require tight grasping, pinching, or twisting of the wrist, and no more than 5 pounds of pressure to operate.
- Pool lift seats must submerge to a water depth of 18 inches minimum.
- Single pool lifts must provide a minimum live-load weight capacity of no less than 300 pounds. Lifts must also be capable of sustaining a static load of at least 1.5 times the rated load.

Sloped Entries
- Sloped entries must comply with ADAAG accessible route provisions (36 inches wide, maximum 8.33 percent slope), except the surface does not need to be slip-resistant.
- Sloped entries must extend to a depth between 24 and 30 inches maximum below the stationary water level.
- Sloped entry requires a landing at both the top and bottom if running slope is greater than 1:20 (5 percent).
- Landing must be 36 inches minimum in width and 60 inches in length (72 inches is preferred).
- Sloped entries must have handrails on both sides regardless of slope. Handrails must meet ADAAG provisions, plus the following:
  - Extensions are required at the top but not the bottom.
  - Clear width between handrails must be between 33 and 38 inches.
  - Handrail height must be between 34 and 38 inches.

Accessible Pool Stairs
- All stairs must have uniform riser heights and uniform tread widths of not less than 11 inches, measured from riser to riser.
- Open risers are not permitted.
- Pool stairs must have handrails, with a width of 20 to 24 inches between rails.
- The top of the handrail gripping surface must be 34 to 38 inches above the stair nosing.
- The clear space between the handrail and wall must be 1½ inches.

Susan Goltsman, FASLA; Timothy Gilbert, ASLA

- Grab bar edges must be rounded a minimum radius of ⅛ inch and be free of sharp or abrasive elements. The wall or other adjacent surfaces must also be free of any sharp or abrasive elements.
- Grab bars must be capable of supporting a 250-pound load in any direction.

Outdoor Rinsing Showers

- At each location where outdoor showers are provided, at least one outdoor shower must be accessible. If only one rinsing shower is provided, it should be an accessible high rinsing shower.
- Where one or more rinsing showers are provided, at least one should be an accessible low shower and at least one an accessible high shower.
- The surface must be firm, stable, and slip-resistant.
- The slope must be 2 percent (3 percent maximum if required for drainage).
- Two fixed showerheads must be provided: one at a minimum 72 inches above the ground or floor, and the second between 48 and 54 inches.

Path of Travel

- Accessible rinsing showers should be along an accessible route of travel as defined earlier in this article.
- A minimum diameter of 60 inches clear space is required for a wheelchair to make a 360° turn.

Shower Controls

- If valves are self-closing, water should remain on for a minimum of 10 seconds.
- The maximum effort to operate controls should be 5 pounds or less.
- Controls must be operable with one hand, not requiring tight grasping or twisting of the wrist.
- Controls must be located at a maximum of 48 inches above the floor.

Grab Bars

- Grab bars shall be provided that comply with ADAAG 4.26.
- In addition, at least one grab bar shall comply with one of the following provisions:
  - Where the showerhead is mounted on a post, a vertical grab bar shall be provided under the showerhead and shall start 33 inches maximum above the floor and extend to within at least 3 inches of the showerhead.
  - Where the showerhead is mounted on a post, a grab bar that surrounds the usable part of the post shall be provided. The grab bar shall be provided 33 inches minimum to 36 inches maximum above the floor.
  - A horizontal grab bar extending 18 inches minimum in both directions from the centerline of the showerhead shall be provided under the showerhead. The grab bar shall be provided 33 inches minimum to 36 inches maximum above the floor.

Signage

- If the shower is located in a separate facility, there must be a sign displaying the International Symbol of Accessibility (ISA) on the entry door to identify the accessible shower/bathing facility.
- Accessible outdoor showers must include the ISA posted at the accessible shower unit.

CAMPING

Concept

Where camping (tent sites, RV or trailer sites, cabins, tent platforms, or other camping shelter sites) is provided, accessible sites must be provided for each type. The minimum number of sites must comply with the requirements shown in the table "Required Number of Accessible Camp Sites."

REQUIRED NUMBER OF ACCESSIBLE CAMP SITES

NUMBER OF CAMPING SITES	NUMBER OF ACCESSIBLE CAMPING SITES (TENTS, RVS, SHELTERS)
1	1
2 to 25	2
26 to 50	3
51 to 75	4
76 to 100	5
101 to 150	7
151 to 200	8
201 to 300	10
301 to 400	12
401 to 500	13
501 to 1,000	2% of total
1,000 and over	20, plus 1 for each 100 over 1,000

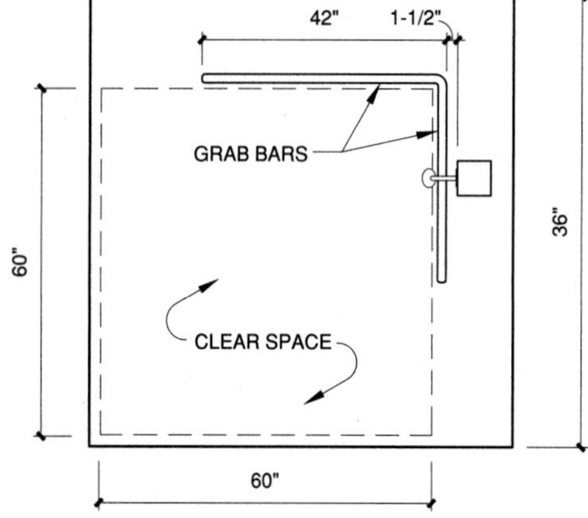

RINSING SHOWER 1

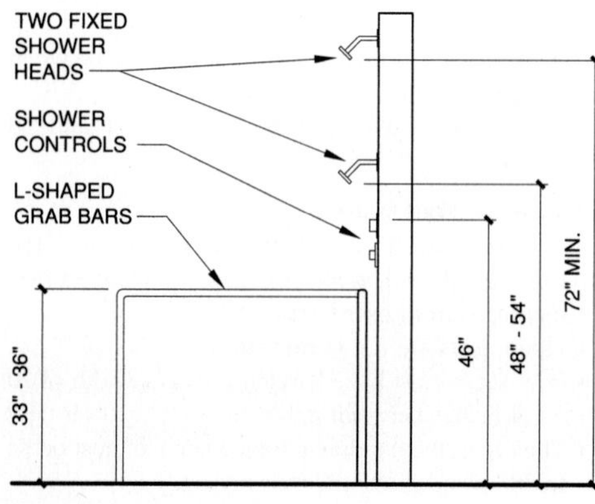

RINSING SHOWER 2

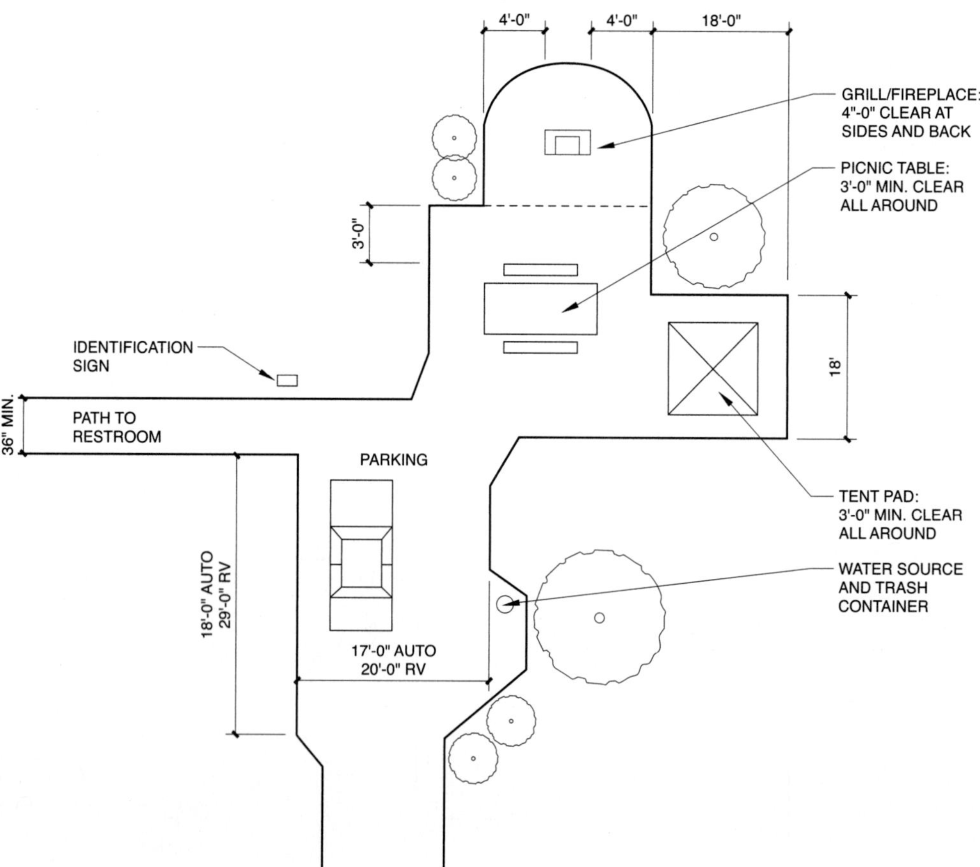

CAMPSITE

Susan Goltsman, FASLA; Timothy Gilbert, ASLA

All elements of an accessible site must be accessibly designed. In addition, there must be accessible routes from the campsite to its own parking, utilities, site furnishings, an accessible restroom, and, if present, a campfire center or assembly area.

Parking Spaces

- Recreational camping vehicle spaces and trailer camping spaces shall have a width of 20 feet minimum.
- Where two accessible RV camping spaces are required, one space is permitted to have a width of 16 feet minimum.
- Where parking provided within the tent camping space or shelter camping space, the parking space shall be a width of 16 feet minimum.
- For additional campground parking, the space for the vehicle shall have a minimum width of 12 feet and an 8-foot wide minimum access aisle adjacent to the parking space that extends the full length of the parking space.
- Slope must not exceed 2 percent (1:50) except for drainage, where it may be up to 3 percent (1:33). The surface must be firm, stable, and slip-resistant.

RV Camping

- Hook-ups and campsite furniture must be accessibly designed (refer to the ADAAG and as discussed earlier in this article).
- If an accessible pull-through campsite is provided, the pull-through area must be a minimum 20 feet wide for the entire length.

Site Planning

- Accessible sites must represent the range of sites in the campground (e.g., water view, secluded, etc.).
- If tent sites are provided, they should have an 18-foot-by-18-foot firm, but not paved, tent/sleeping pad adjacent to table/cooking area. Camp and tent site slope must not exceed 2 percent; if needed for proper drainage, 3 percent is acceptable.
- If tent sites are provided, the ground must be firm and stable, and designed to allow the use of tent stakes.
- If a raised tent platform is provided, there must be a minimum 3 inches edge protection.

BOATING

Concept

Boating facilities, which include those to launch and moor boats and all associated structures, such as docks, piers, marinas, and gangways, must be accessible. Boating facilities can consist of the following:

- *Boat launch ramp.* Surface designed for the launch and retrieval of boats.
- *Boat slip.* Area where boat is tied to a dock or pier for the purpose of embarking and disembarking.
- *Gangway.* Variable-sloped pedestrian walkway linking a fixed structure of land with a floating structure.
- *Pier.* Structure at which boats are intended to moor for the purposes of embarking or disembarking occupants to the structure. See the ADA guidelines for specific requirements.

Gangways

- Gangways are considered to be part of the accessible route and must have slopes no greater than 8.33 percent and comply with ADAAG.
- Transition plates are permitted at the top and bottom of the gangway.
- Gangways are not required to have landing at the end if transition plates of less than 1:20 (5 percent) slope are provided. If slope is greater than 1:20 (5 percent), the transition plate must have a landing at the nongangway end of the transition plate.
- Extremes in operating conditions require that some exemptions be allowed.
  - Maximum rise of 30 inches must not apply to gangways. As a result, no intermediate landings on gangways are required, and gangways may be of any length.
  - Handrail extensions are not required on gangways and landings where they connect to transition plates, and must not be required on transition plates.
  - Where the total length of the gangway or series of gangways serving as part of a required accessible

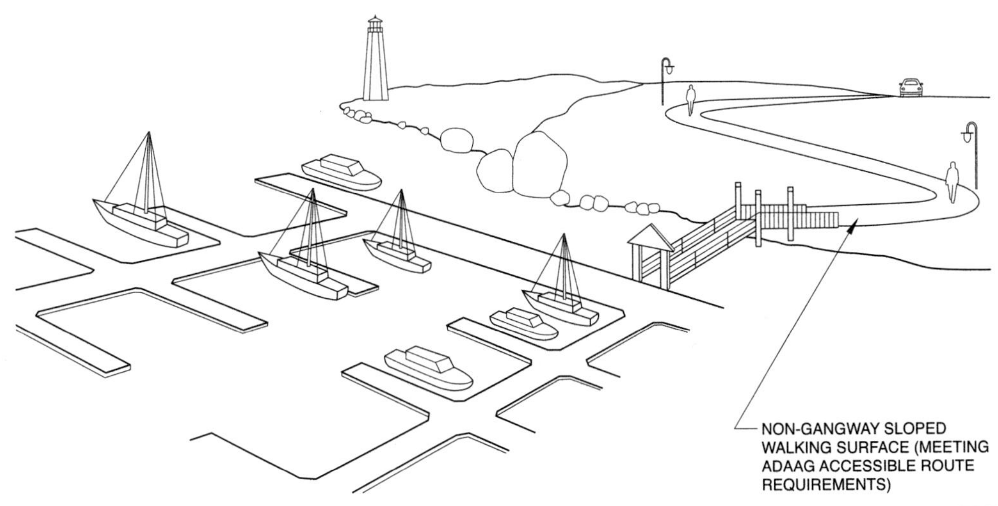

SLOPED WALKING SURFACE

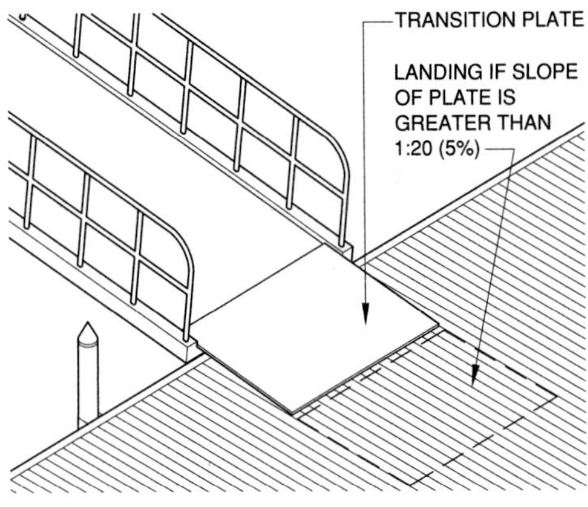

TRANSITION PLATE

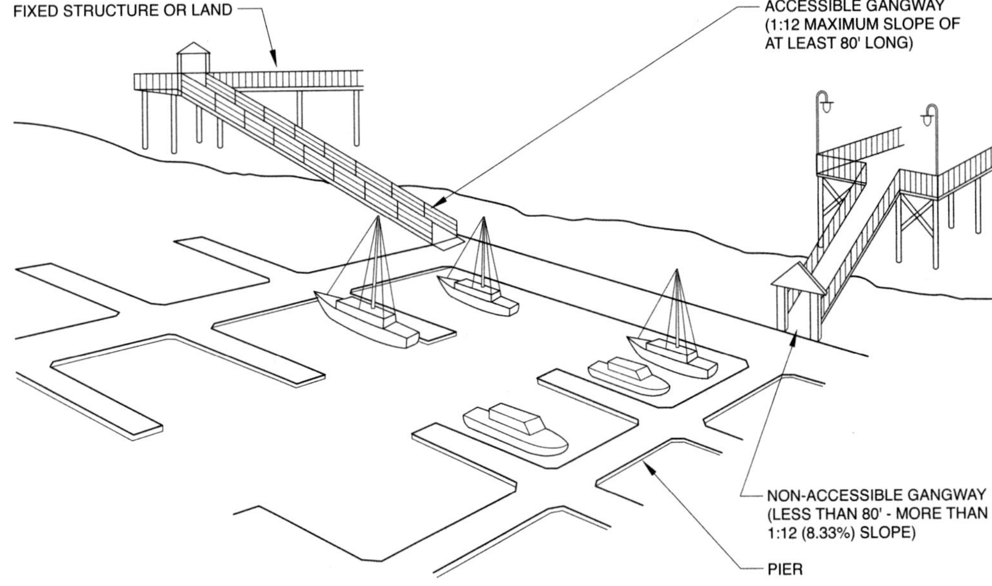

ACCESSIBLE GANGWAY

Susan Goltsman, FASLA; Timothy Gilbert, ASLA

route is at least 80 feet, the maximum slope specified, 8.33 percent, must not apply to gangways.

Accessible Gangway

- In smaller facilities, with fewer than 25 boat slips, the slope of the gangway may exceed 1:12 (8.33 percent), if the gangway is at least 30 feet long.
- When it is not feasible to provide an accessible gangway due to extremes in operating conditions, other accessible options (including mechanical lifts) will be considered.

Boat Slips

- Where boat slips are not demarcated or identified by length, each 40 feet of boat slip edge along the perimeter of a pier will be counted as one boat slip. For example, a 60-foot pier with boats moored on either side (120 feet total slip length) would equal three boat slips.
- When boat slips are provided, the number of boat slips required to be accessible must comply with the table "Required Number of Accessible Boat Slips."
- Accessible boat slips must be dispersed throughout the various types of slips that are provided.
- Where boat launch ramps are provided with boarding piers, at least 5 percent but not less than one boarding pier complying with ADAAG 15.2.4 must be provided adjacent to the ramp.

REQUIRED NUMBER OF ACCESSIBLE BOAT SLIPS

TOTAL SLIPS IN FACILITIES	MINIMUM ACCESSIBLE SLIPS
1 to 25	1
26 to 50	2
51 to 100	3
101 to 150	4
151 to 300	5
301 to 400	6
401 to 500	7
501 to 600	8
601 to 700	9
701 to 800	10
801 to 900	11
901 to 1000	12
1,001 and over	12, plus 1 for each 100, or fraction thereof, over 1,000

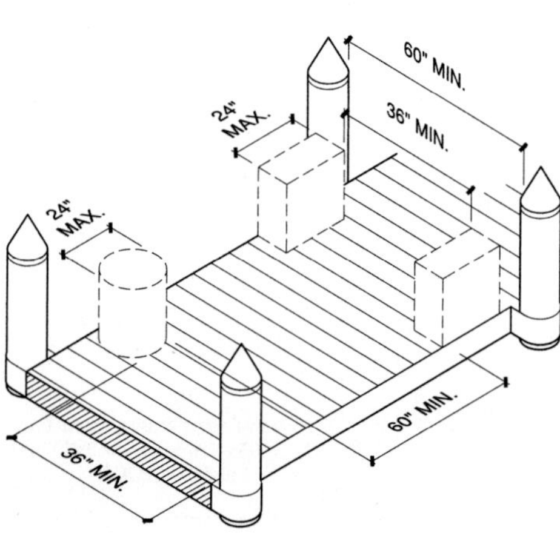

CLEAR PIER SPACE

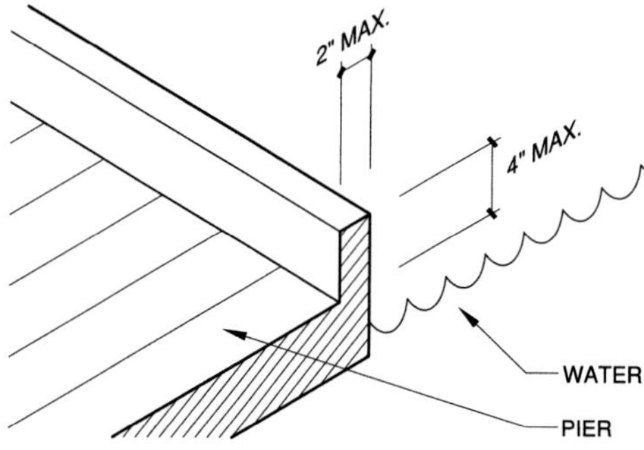

PIER EDGE

- Accessible boat slip/dock must have a clear pier width at a minimum 60 inches wide and as long as the slip. For every 120 inches (10 feet) of linear length, the boarding pier/dock will have a clear opening of 60 inches. There are three exceptions:
  1. Width of clear space may be 36 inches wide for a length of 24 inches, as long as multiple 36-inch segments are separated by segments that are 60 inches by 60 inches by 60 inches clear.
  2. If provided, edge protection should be 4 inches high maximum and 2 inches deep maximum at the clear openings.
  3. In alterations, facilities with finger piers must have at least one accessible finger pier, which is the length of the boat slip and a minimum 60 inches wide. Other accessible slips can be located perpendicular to the end of the pier with the clearance extending the slip width.

Safety

- Walking surfaces of the facility must be made of nonslip materials.
- Horizontal gaps in walking surfaces (e.g., gratings and planks) must be perpendicular and less than ½ inch wide.
- Vertical joints in the surface of the facility (including shore connection) must have maximum height of ¼ inch; or, if ¼ to ½ inch, must be beveled at 50 percent.
- The walking surface of docks without guardrails has a recommended maximum height of 24 inches above the water. Edges should be emphasized by use of a color-contrasting strip that is a minimum 2 inches wide.

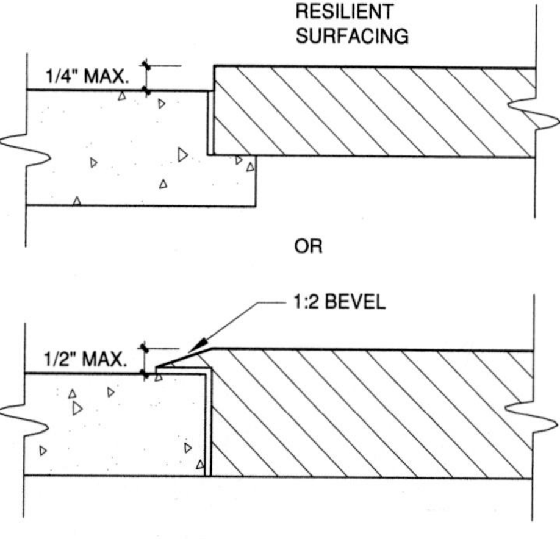

RESILIENT SURFACING

- The dock/pier with water fluctuations should have a sign posted reading, "Caution: Due to fluctuation of water elevation, this dock/pier is only accessible between the tidal elevations of *X* and *Y*. Use with caution."

FISHING

Concept

Fishing is an activity that can be enjoyed by people with severe disabilities. Every effort should be made to develop opportunities that are fully accessible where fishing is a program or activity offered.

Fishing may take place from any of three types of locations:

1. Fixed or floating pier/dock
2. Bank or shoreline
3. Boat

The primary issues in the design of accessible fishing sites are:

- Locating good fishing sites.
- Integrating the site with an accessible path of travel and support facilities.
- Designing for changing water level.
- Designing for safety, including safe levels of lighting.

Accessible fishing sites must be fully integrated with an accessible path of travel, offering appropriate support facilities, and be appropriately identified with the International Symbol of Accessibility (ISA) at the site and at paths and trails leading to the site (e.g., parking areas, restrooms, etc.).

Fishing sites may be developed or undeveloped:

- Developed sites are firm, level pads provided at the edges of streams, lakes, or the seashore (for surf fishing).
- Undeveloped sites have not been significantly modified by construction, but are more analogous to rest areas in the pathway and trail system. They are firm, level areas at the water's edge and of sufficient dimension for wheelchair use.

The fishing site surface must be firm and stable with a maximum slope of 3 percent.

Safety

- All reasonable precautions should be taken to ensure a safe and comfortable fishing environment appropriate to the site.
- Floor or grade surfaces of the site (platforms, piers, etc.) must be made of nonslip materials.

Fishing Piers

- Fishing sites over water may be on fixed piers or floating docks.
- Access to the fishing site must be via an accessible path of travel.
- The fishing site should extend over the water for a distance that allows fishing at both high- and low-water conditions.
- Floating sites must have enough stability and floatation to support the additional weight of people and equipment without significantly affecting the equilibrium of occupants.
- Piers must have a 2-inch-high minimum edge protection.

Susan Goltsman, FASLA; Timothy Gilbert, ASLA

- All gaps in horizontal walking surfaces must be less than ½ inch.

Connection to Shore

- Shore connections between the dock and land must have a 36-inch minimum clear width.
- The surface material of the gangway or bridge must be slip-resistant.
- Gangways must be designed to provide for a maximum 1:12 (8.33 percent) slope, but are not required to be longer than 80 feet in length. No intermediate landings are required.
- Gangways are not required to have landings at the end of transition plates if provided.
- If the slope of the transition plate is greater than 1:20 (5 percent), transition plates must have a landing at the end of the transition plate that is not connected to the gangway and that complies with ADAAG ramp requirements.
- Handrail extensions are not required where gangways and transition plates connect and both are provided with handrails.

Space Needed

- There should be provision for a minimum of 5 linear feet per person along the water's edge. These dimensions intentionally exceed minimum wheelchair requirements. General spatial allowances are essential because privacy and solitude are very strong motivational factors for many anglers.
- Fishing site surfaces and railings must be of nonglare materials.
- A minimum 30 inches by 48 inches clear space must be provided at the accessible fishing site, and the surface should be firm, stable, and slip-resistant.
- A maneuvering space of at least 60 inches in diameter is required. If a T-intersection is provided at least 36 inches of width must be provided to allow a person using a mobility device or wheelchair to make a 180-degree turn
- The space may overlap the accessible route and clear floor or ground space.
- The overhead casting clearance at fishing sites should be 12 feet minimum.

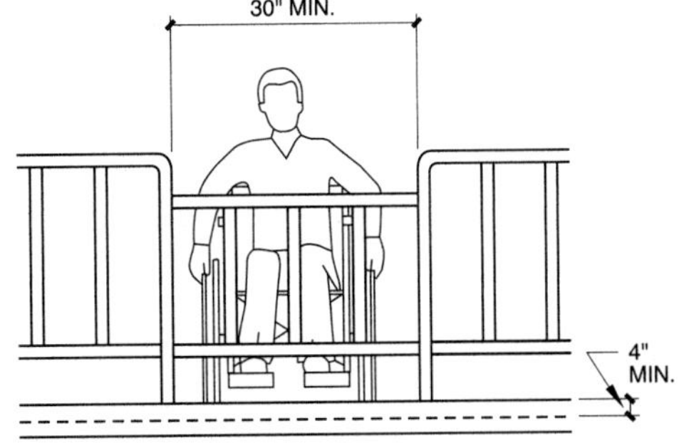

PIER EDGE PROTECTION

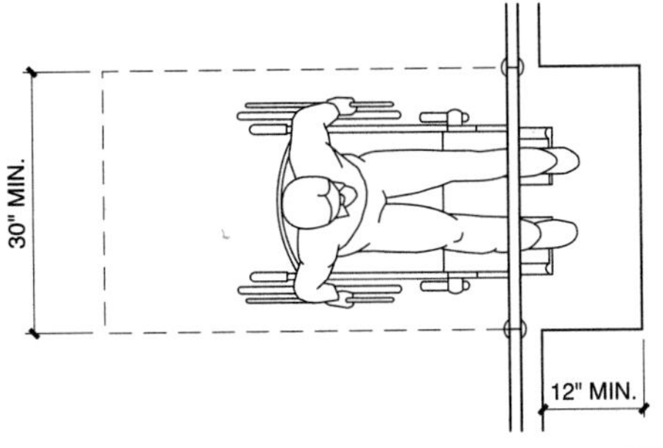

DECK EXTENSION

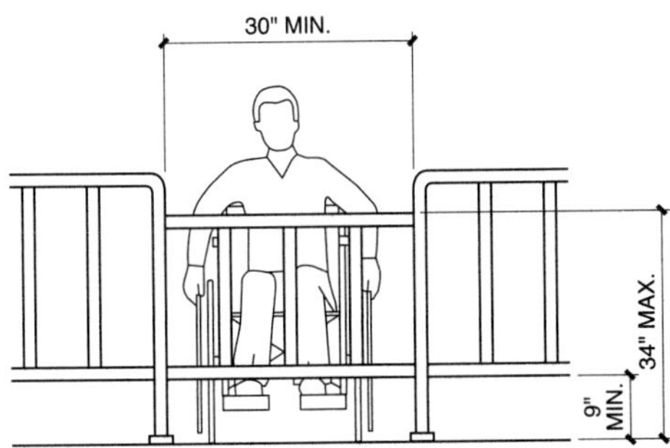

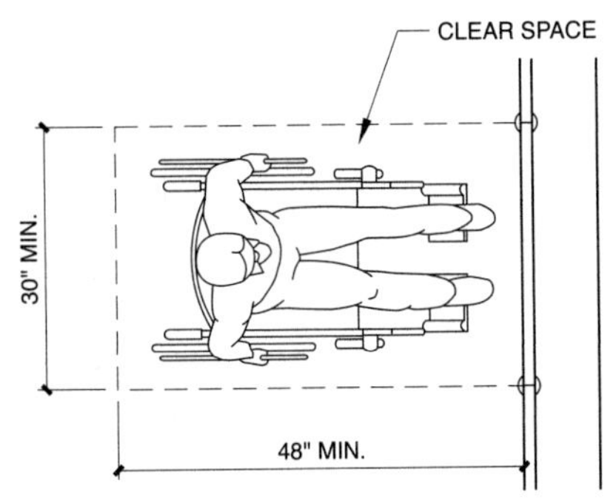

RAILING HEIGHTS

Handrails

- Wherever possible, it is recommended to provide a 4-inch-wide gap at maximum 8-foot intervals in the handrail to allow the feel of the unobstructed line playing in the water and the opportunity for multiple castings.
- Where railings are provided at accessible fishing stations, rails must be 34 inches above the ground or deck.
- Guardrails may be higher than 34 inches for enhanced safety or if a local building code applies. Accessible railings must be dispersed in a variety of locations on the fishing pier or platform.
- Where railings, guardrails, or handrails are provided, edge protection at a minimum of 2 inches high above the ground or deck surface must be provided.
- Edge protection is not required when the deck surface extends a minimum of 12 inches beyond the inside face of the railing, guardrail, or handrail.
- Toe clearance must be at least 30 inches wide and 9 inches minimum above the ground or deck surface beyond the railing.
- Railings must support 250 pounds of force in any direction.

Cleaning Tables

- If fish-cleaning tables are provided for standing persons, there must be a proportionate section of table at 28 to 34 inches high, with clear knee space of 29 inches high, 19 inches deep, and 30 inches wide underneath, available for seated persons.
- Faucet controls must be operable with a closed fist; the activation force must be 5 pounds or less, and, if self-closing, must stay on at least 10 seconds.

EQUESTRIAN FACILITIES

Concept

Equestrian activities consist of either the facility to rent and ride, or that allows the visitor to bring his/her horse and trailer to ride.

Access to equestrian activities involves two basic considerations:

1. Access to the place where horses are available.
2. Transfer capabilities onto and off of the horse that are safe and secure. Such transfer must be accomplished by one of three methods: raising the level of the rider to that of the horse's stirrups, by using a mounting platform; lowering the level of the horse in respect to the level of the rider—such as a 2-foot-deep ground recess for the horse; or providing a combination of the first two methods.

Location

- Equestrian facilities must be located on an accessible path of travel with appropriate support facilities, such as signage, restrooms, and parking.

Mounting Platform

- An accessible mounting platform should be provided to facilitate movement to and from the horse. It must have:
  - A platform height above grade 24 inches to 28 inches as measured at the place of mounting the horse.
  - Access to the platform can be by means of a route with a maximum slope of 8.33 percent.

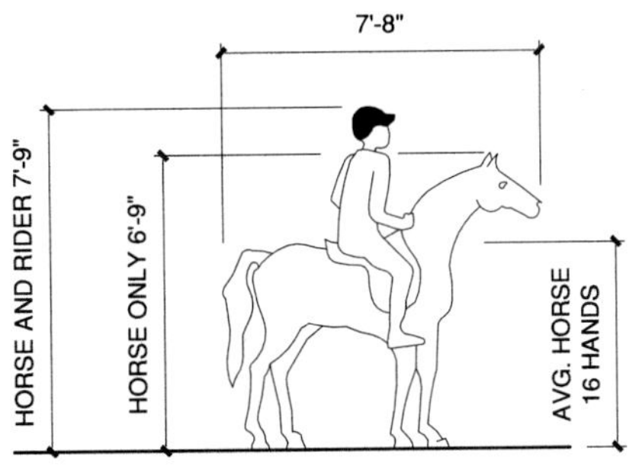

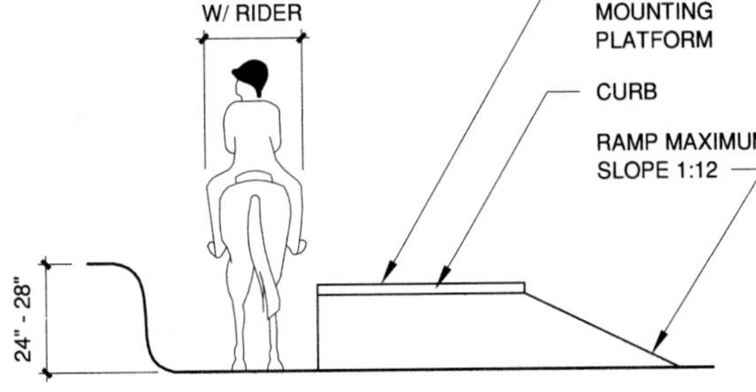

EQUESTRIAN PLATFORM

Susan Goltsman, FASLA; Timothy Gilbert, ASLA

- A 2-inch-high curb at all edges, except for the opening on the mounting side.
- A recommended level surface area of 60 inches by 60 inches.

- Site selection for mounting/dismounting activities could minimize or eliminate the need for a ramp.

SIGNAGE

Concept

This section refers to permanent signs. An effective information system is essential for accessibility. There are three general categories of signage:

1. *Location or directional information.* All information that indicates direction or location, including signs along outdoor routes indicating direction and distances (e.g., "1.5 miles to waterfall"). Trailhead signage should describe conditions such as average grade, cross slope, width of trail, trail surface, and average size of obstacles.
2. *Identification and descriptive information.* Identifies a specific facility, such as an information station or a restroom; describes the availability and location of facilities.
3. *Regulation and safety signage.* Information about rules, procedures, and regulations (e.g., restrictive signs such as "No Fishing," "No Camping," or "No Smoking on Trail"; regulatory signs such as "Camp in Designated Areas Only"; and safety signs such as "Unsafe Drinking Water").

VISUAL CHARACTER HEIGHT

HEIGHT TO FINISH FLOOR, OR GROUND FROM BASELINE OF CHARACTER	HORIZONTAL VIEWING DISTANCE	MINIMUM CHARACTER HEIGHT
40 inches to less than or equal to 70 inches	Less than 72 inches	⅝ inch
	72 inches and greater	⅝ inch, plus ⅛ inch per foot of viewing distance above 72 inches
Greater than 70 inches to less than or equal to 120 inches	Less than 180 inches	2 inches
	180 inches or greater	2 inches, plus ⅛ inch per foot of viewing distance above 180 inches
Greater than 120 inches	Less than 21 feet	3 inches
	21 feet and greater	3 inches, plus ⅛ inch per foot of viewing distance above 21 feet

Signage

- Signs should be part of a well-planned system throughout a park or recreational area.
- Signs must be placed in logical and visually unobstructed locations, while ensuring that growth of adjacent foliage will not interfere with visibility. See ADDAG Section 4.30 for details.
- The International Symbol of Accessibility (ISA) sign must be located at the primary entrance and at junctions between accessible and inaccessible pathways. The sign must be displayed to direct the user to an accessible route.
- All characters, symbols, and sign backgrounds must have a nonglare finish with at least a 70 percent contrast between characters and their backgrounds, either light characters on a dark background or dark characters on a light background.
- All signs must have letters and numbers with the ratio of letter width to height of between 3:5 to 1:1, and the stroke width to height ratio of between 1:5 to 1:10.
- Characters and numbers must be sized according to the viewing distance from which they will be read. See the table "Visual Character Height" for various viewing distances.
- Both uppercase and lowercase letters should be used, but font size is measured using an uppercase X.
- For signs suspended or projected above the finish floor on posts or supports at a height where the bottom edge of the sign is 80 inches or more above the floor, the minimum character height must be 3 inches.
- Signs identifying permanent uses of rooms and spaces must have raised letters at a minimum 1/32 inches, raised characters at a minimum 5/8 inches to a maximum 2 inches sans serif, uppercase, and contracted Grade II Braille, mounted on the latch side of any doors at 60 inches above the floor to the centerline of the sign. Signs must be approachable to within 3 inches without obstruction.
- Pictograms must be accompanied by the equivalent verbal description placed below in raised letters and Grade II Braille when used in a permanently signed room or space.
- Signage containing pictograms should have 6-inch borders. Note: The International Symbol of Accessibility (ISA) circles and triangles on restroom doors are not considered pictograms.
- Buildings that have been remodeled to provide accessible restrooms and/or elevators must post this accessibility information in the building lobby.
- The use of alternative signage forms such as remote directional human voice messages may be explored and used subject to compliance of ADAAG.

PROPORTIONS

DISPLAY CONDITIONS

INTERNATIONAL SYMBOL

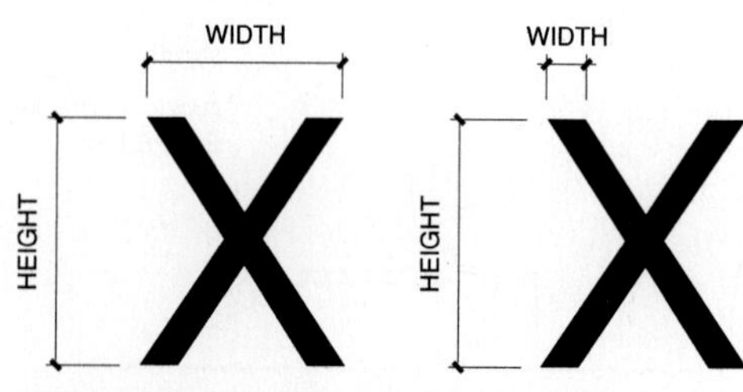

SIGNS CHARACTER PROPORTION

INFORMATION
RAISED CHARACTERS, TYP.
BRAILLE, TYP.
5/8" - 2"

SIGNS CHARACTER HEIGHT

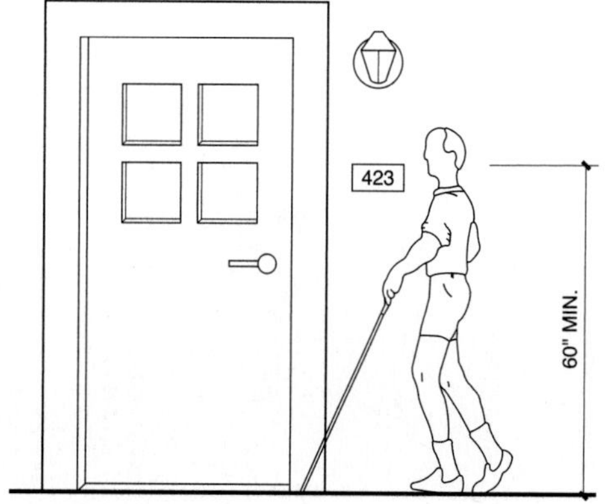

SIGNS HEIGHT

RESOURCES

Access Board. July 2004. *Americans with Disabilities Act Accessibility Guidelines for Buildings and Facilities.* Washington, DC: Architectural and Transportation Barriers Compliance Board.

———. June 2003. *Americans with Disabilities Act Accessibility Guidelines for Recreations Facilities.* (03AG). Washington, DC: Architectural and Transportation Barriers Compliance Board.

———. September 1999. *Regulatory Negotiation Committee on Accessibility's Guidelines for Outdoor Developed Areas* (99 AG) Washington, DC: Architectural and Transportation Barriers Compliance Board.

Design Guide: State of California Department of Parks, 2005.

See also:

Outdoor Play Areas
Parking Standards
Stairs, Ramps, and Curbs

Susan Goltsman, FASLA; Timothy Gilbert, ASLA

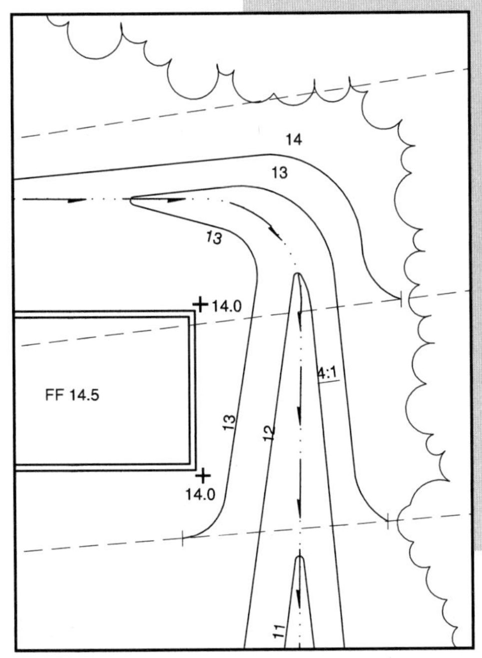

PROCESS, IMPLEMENTATION, AND APPLICATION

Construction Operations and Earthwork

Water Supply and Management

Stormwater Management

Irrigation and Water Features

Pavement and Structures in the Landscape

Site Amenities

Planting

Special Construction

Hazard Control

Restoration and Remediation

Parks and Recreation

Part 3

CONSTRUCTION OPERATIONS AND EARTHWORK

SITE CONSTRUCTION OVERVIEW

INTRODUCTION

Site construction consists of all of the various steps involved in transforming the design described in the construction documents and specifications into a reality in the landscape. Typically, the construction process is shaped by several factors, such as: the nature and scale of the project, the construction budget, the number of subcontractors involved, the time of year during which the project is occurring, the type of equipment involved, whether the project is within the public realm, local laws and rules of oversight, and the physical context of the site itself. Ultimately, the final process of construction is a product agreed upon by the design team, the client, and the contractors involved. Each project will have its own unique characteristics, but a relatively standard set of steps are part of each process, usually carried out in a similar order.

CONSTRUCTION PROCESS

The construction process described here is intended to reflect a broad range of project types, meaning that it may not apply to each and every project perfectly. Every project will contain specific and/or unique conditions that may require an alteration to the process so that the project can be efficiently and safely implemented in a manner that guarantees the highest-quality result. The presence of special conditions, such as archaeological sites, endangered species, and hazardous materials may also affect the process of site construction, either prior to commencing work or, in a worst-case scenario, during the implementation of the project.

The site construction process described here effectively begins following the completion of the construction drawings and specifications and the subsequent bidding process. Every contractor and/or team will examine the drawings to determine, based on the project and on their own individual style of working, what the on-site steps of the process should be so that they can put together a bid that accurately reflects their participation in the project. Once the bidding process is complete and a contractor(s) has been hired, the actual process of site construction can begin. The steps in a generic construction project are as follows:

1. Preconstruction planning, scheduling, construction management, and oversight
2. Utility location
3. Construction preparation
   - Site security
   - Erosion control
   - Tree protection and existing elements preservation, demolition and site preparation
4. Layout
5. Primary infrastructure installation
6. Foundations and primary elements construction
7. Rough grading
8. Secondary elements construction
9. Secondary infrastructure and systems installation
10. Flatwork
11. Specialty paving
12. Landscaped areas and site furnishings
13. Site cleanup
14. Postconstruction evaluation
15. Postconstruction management

Preconstruction Planning, Scheduling, Construction Management, and Oversight

Prior to the commencement of construction, a number of planning meetings may need to occur in order for the construction process to go smoothly. The design team should evaluate and identify any outside individuals or organizations that will be potentially affected by the construction process, to make certain that they are aware of the upcoming work and to help in identifying potential problems ahead of time. Transit companies, school districts, sanitation companies, mail delivery services, and other similar groups are examples of groups to consider when putting this list together.

A preconstruction meeting involving the design team, the client (or the client's representative), and the contractor (and subcontractors) should occur prior to the beginning of on-site work. Coordination between contractors, material delivery schedules and staging, on-site work, and phasing and completion timelines should all be discussed so as to develop a realistic schedule of work. During this phase of the project, any impacts on surrounding properties, systems, or individuals should be discussed as well. Out of this planning process should emerge a clear picture of how the project will proceed, which is documented in a project management schedule that may take the form of a bar, Critical Path Method (CPM), or similar chart. Built into this sequence should be the design team's role in site supervision during construction, including when on-site project development meetings should occur and who the primary points of contact are on the project to answer any questions that arise during construction.

Utility Location

Prior to any work being undertaken, local utility companies must be called upon to do an underground locate of all utilities in and around the construction area. Marking should occur prior to any groundbreaking, and will be color-coded to communicate what lies beneath the surface. The standard colors used include:

Red	Electric
Yellow	Gas/oil/steam
Orange	Communications/cable TV
Blue	Water
Green	Sewer
White	Proposed area of excavation (marked by contractor prior to utility locate)
Pink	Temporary survey markings (marked by surveyors or by contractor)

In some situations, hand-digging will be required to determine the relative depths of the utility and to determine the actual location in the ground. While

EXAMPLE OF A PROJECT MANAGEMENT SCHEDULE
University of Oregon, Heart of Campus Phase I Improvements (3/11/04)

TASK	MAR.	APR.	MAY	JUN.	JUL.	AUG.	SEP.
Plaza design w/students		• I week - kickoff 3/29 - complete 4/2					
DAG/CPC review(s)		• Meeting time(s) week of 4/5 - no later than 4/9					
DD - const. docs 50%		• 50 % const. doc. /costs 4/27					
50% CD owner review			• 50% owner review 4/28 - 4/30				
Const. dwgs./specs 95%			• 95 % const. docs / costs 5/18				
95% CD owner review			• 95% owner review 4/28 - 4/30				
Const. dwgs./specs 100%				• 100% const. docs /costs to owner 6/4			
Permitting (submit 6/8)				• Permits (3 - 4 wk. city review)			
Select bidders list (mail 6/8)				• 3-wk. bid period w/2 addenda			
Bid opening				• Bid open 6/29			
Approval/award					• Contract award 7/13		
Construction period		8-wk. const. period			• Preconst. 7/15		• Subst. complete 9/10
Site prep. complete						Final completion • 9/17/04*	

• Denotes a progress meeting, a critical decision, or a product delivery.

** Fall term begins 9/27/04 (Monday).*

Stanton Jones, ASLA, Associate Professor and Head, Department of Landscape Architecture, University of Oregon, Eugene

fairly accurate, underground locator marks typically have a margin of error of ±12 inches, so care must be taken to ensure that construction does not damage the existing infrastructure.

Construction Preparation

Prior to the beginning of construction, several critical issues must be addressed so that the project can run smoothly, safely, and with little or no environmental impact extending beyond the construction site. Site security is a significant concern, due to the potential for injury on construction sites, particularly in more highly populated areas or in areas where people and children, in particular, are nearby. Construction fencing around the perimeter of a project should be installed prior to moving on-site, and it should extend around the entirety of the project, including the areas being used for staging and storage. This will help to protect the work as it progresses and allow the workers to focus on the work at hand instead of worrying about an onlooker moving into harm's way as they try to do their work.

Also prior to construction, issues pertaining to erosion control should be addressed. This has become a critical issue in recent years, and many local jurisdictions now require an erosion control plan as a part of the construction document package. The goal of erosion control measures is to protect areas outside of the project boundary, particularly bodies of water such as streams and lakes, from the harmful effects of increased silt load. Several types of methods can be used, including erosion control fencing, bales of straw placed in drainage channels, or "bio-bags," or filtration fabrics placed over the openings of catch basins or other drainage structures that are downhill from the site. Once construction is completed, these can be removed, but not until all work is completed.

One other issue to address prior to construction is the delineation of areas within the project boundary that are off-limits to work. In particular, the root zone of significant trees, sensitive landscape areas, and areas in close proximity to existing structures all may need to be fenced off in order to preserve them during the construction process. This should be delineated on one of the pages in the construction document set and should have associated notes on that same page and/or in the specifications as to how and why these areas should be fenced off. For example, in the middle of a project occurring during a hot summer, the area beneath the leaves of a large tree can be a major draw as a place to sit and rest, to store materials that are better kept out of the hot sun, or as a place to park one's vehicle; if this occurs over a period of weeks and/or months, enough damage can be done to the tree's root zone that it will significantly harm, and even prematurely kill, the tree.

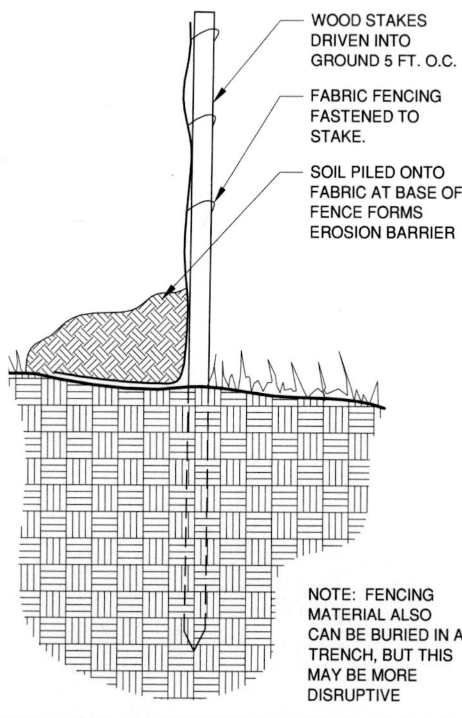

EROSION CONTROL FENCING

Demolition and Site Preparation

Once the site has been secured and all areas to be preserved have been fenced off, demolition and site preparation can take place. Depending on the nature of the project, all elements and materials that are no longer needed as a part of the project will be broken up and removed. Where possible, materials can and should be separated and recycled/reused, which typically happens early on in the demolition process. Any topsoil located in areas that are under construction should be carefully excavated and stored to use either on that project or on a separate project. Once the site has been cleared and cleaned and any special problems have been addressed (such as bedrock found closer to the surface than expected or buried materials that are unsuitable for construction), preliminary site preparation can occur. This may include the laying in of gravel along truck routes to ensure site workability during the time of construction; the relocation of any utilities that are in question; and preliminary soil testing for bearing capacity, erodability, fertility, and so on. Doing these sorts of test at this stage can help avoid any issues that may arise later in the process, particularly with respect to the engineering characteristics of the soil. It is also appropriate at this stage to do any hand-digging required to verify critical utility locations.

Layout

Once utilities have been located, and the site has been prepped for construction, the contractor will move on-site and begin to lay out the main elements of the project on the ground. Following the layout and dimensioning plan, the contractor will site main elements, such as catch basins, foundation corners, street boundaries, and other primary elements, in order to direct the excavation and other work that will occur first. Grading stakes will be placed at critical points as well, and all formwork will be tied back to the horizontal and vertical information that these stakes are communicating. Depending on the nature of the project, a single *point of beginning* (POB) may be identified on the drawings and translated into the field; or an existing landmark, such as a building corner, may be used to identify the point to which all critical elements must relate. Once the project has been laid out according to the drawing, all layout and dimensioning results should be field-checked by the design team to verify that the design intent is being met.

Primary Infrastructure Installation

Having staked out the primary elements, the installation of primary infrastructural elements, such as sanitary sewers, storm sewers, water mains, and electrical service, can commence. Note that these are underground systems, and they are being trenched into the project early so that subsequent construction is not put at risk by the large trenching equipment used to lay in much of this material.

Once in, stubs will be left out for the installation of secondary systems such as irrigation and lighting systems. In some cases, conduit for lighting and other electrical systems will be laid in immediately after the primary systems, so that base materials will not have to be disturbed later on, and so that concrete formwork (or recently poured, "green" concrete) does not have to be undermined with a trench or boring. Where secondary systems coincide with paved surfaces, sleeving should be placed beneath the paved areas prior to installation of the paving so that the paving will not have to be altered to install lighting or sprinklers, for example, in an area isolated from water or electrical supply. Care should be taken in the installation of all infrastructure to make certain that all trenches are well compacted as they are backfilled. This is critical in the elimination of problems associated with settling.

Foundations and Primary Elements Construction

Foundations and other primary elements are the next things to be installed. These main elements will set the framework for all of the other work to follow and will also, ultimately, allow multiple contractors to move onto the site simultaneously, particularly where buildings are involved. Foundations are dug, and grades and finish floor elevations are all set at this point in the process, and become the primary referents for the stages of work that will occur next. Once the formwork has been completed and all required inspections have taken place, concrete can be poured. Depending on the nature of the project, concrete samples may be taken at this time so that they can be tested for strength.

Rough Grading

Once the concrete has cured enough for the forms to be removed, rough grading can take place. This step involves the movement of soil (typically, not topsoil at this point) in a manner that begins to shape the landscape to allow easier movement in and around the site. Assuming that foundation drainage systems are in place, backfilling around structures and the setting of some critical subgrades (such as streets, parking lots, etc.) set the stage for the next phase of construction.

Secondary Elements Construction

At this point in the process, secondary elements begin to take shape. Planters, kiosks, garden walls, and paved areas are staked out and constructed. Secondary infrastructural needs are simultaneously addressed at this point, and the project begins to take on the spatial characteristics of what the final outcome will embody. The layout and construction of these elements should be field-checked, as well, prior to any pouring of concrete to ensure their proper placement in the landscape. Details, such as the location of light fixtures, of junction boxes in paved areas,

Stanton Jones, ASLA, Associate Professor and Head, Department of Landscape Architecture, University of Oregon, Eugene

or of valve boxes in irrigated areas, should also be evaluated at this time so as to maximize the opportunity to locate items in places where they are aesthetically or programmatically best suited.

Secondary Infrastructure and Systems Installation

As secondary elements are being constructed, secondary systems and infrastructural elements are also being incorporated into the project. Irrigation systems, lighting systems, communication systems, water supply to structures, and so on, all are placed in the landscape, although final placement and installation may come toward the end of the work. This is true, for example, with irrigation systems, where mainlines, valves, and most lateral lines will be put in place at this stage in the process, but final installation and leveling of valve boxes, and of the heads themselves, will not happen until the final stage of landscape grading and planting.

Flatwork

Once vertical elements have been set, concrete paving, typically known as *flatwork*, will commence. This is done after much of the heavy construction has been completed, to protect the newly poured paved surface from having to support the weight of heavy machinery, as well as to protect the finish of the surface. Prior to flatwork, corner elevations at all significant points along the paved surface have been identified, and the formwork is set to those elevations. Concrete is typically poured as a tilted plane, although some special circumstances and types of paving do not require the same sort of slope on the surface as traditional concrete. Once the concrete has been poured, it is "screed," leveled, edged, and finished as per the design team's specifications.

Other types of paving can also be done at this point in time, such as asphalt paving or other more permeable types of paving, such as porous concrete or porous asphalt. All of these are typically installed toward the end of the project, again, to protect the material from the wear and tear associated with construction.

Specialty Paving

Areas that are designated as specialty paving areas are typically done late in the process. Specialty paving is paving that is composed of concrete pavers, flagstone, brick, and so on, and is typically characterized as being more time-intensive and hands-on than the flatwork type of paving just described. Because of its unique nature, this type of paving is often done after all other paving and construction is completed, save the planting and final landscape grading aspects of the project. Staging and material movement should be considered here, as delivery vehicles, "Bobcats," and other machinery often used can mar the finishes of the paved surfaces they are running over. It is also important to note that specialty paving areas are typically off-limits to other contractors until they have been finally "set," either in mortar, sand, or soil; this could have implications for the movement of materials and other elements in the final stages of other aspects of the project (e.g., can you get soil into a planted area to grade and prepare for planting while the specialty paving is being constructed, or do you have to hold on that aspect of the work until the paving is done?).

Landscape Areas and Site Furnishings

One of the last things to be completed is the installation of the plant materials, along with all of the site furnishings. Also occurring at this time will be the final installation of and adjustments to the sprinkler heads, the lighting fixtures, signage, and so on. With respect to the plants, it may be important, depending on the time of year, to find a staging area for plants that is shaded and that has easy access to water. The design team will typically be on-site for the placement of plant materials, and should check a random sample of the materials for plant health and root condition prior to installation.

Site Cleanup

With construction coming to a close, care should be taken to clean up all areas prior to the removal of security fences and erosion control systems. Special care should be taken to locate nails, screws, and other dangerous items typically found throughout construction sites. Any areas of soil that have suffered compaction should be repaired, and any damage to the site or its surroundings should be assessed and addressed. It is at this stage that sprinkler systems are checked, the clock and timer are set, lighting systems and others are checked, and a final walk-through with the client is arranged. A "punch list" of items to be done or checked is typically developed in this final stage of the project; and in a final walk-through, this punch list serves as a checklist of sorts, helping to make sure that everything has been addressed before the construction process is declared closed, the fences come down, and the site opens for use.

Postconstruction Evaluation

Many landscape architects and designers have found it very instructive to revisit projects that they have done one or two years postcompletion to see how well their design is functioning and to ascertain how well certain details and/or materials are holding up. Some firms have developed systematic methods of evaluating their work, while others take a less formal, more "intuitive" approach to this sort of evaluation. Either way, it has been a very useful step in the construction process for people to learn from prior work, and should be built into the work of future projects.

Postconstruction Management

In consultation with the client and with the contractors, as appropriate, a postconstruction project management plan should be developed. Much like an owner's manual for a car, a management plan gives guidance and direction to the client about how the project should be cared for in the years to come. Specific maintenance schedules for things like irrigation systems, pruning and feeding schedules for plants, and maintenance of catch basins are but a few examples of things typically found in a management plan. Depending on the landscape in question, there may also be specific issues to address that pertain to ecological concerns, such as invasive exotic plants or the preservation of critical habitat, or to more human-centric concerns, such as safety, accessibility, and universal design. A well-conceived and well-written management plan can lengthen the effective life of a project and can extend the designer's intent well into the future.

REFERENCES

Colley, B. C. *Practical Manual of Land Development.* 1993. New York: McGraw-Hill.

Harris, C., and N. Dines. *Timesaver Standards for Landscape Architecture.* 1998. New York: McGraw-Hill.

Landphair, H., and F. Klatt. *Landscape Architecture Construction.* 1999. Upper Saddle River, NJ: Prentice Hall.

Stitt, Fred. *Ecological Design Handbook.* 1999. New York: McGraw-Hill.

Thallon, R., and S. Jones. *Graphic Guide to Site Construction.* 2003. Newtown, CT: Taunton Press.

See also:
Irrigation
Lighting
Pavement in the Landscape
Postoccupancy Evaluation
Site Considerations, Plant Installations, and Details
Soil Erosion and Sediment Control

Stanton Jones, ASLA, Associate Professor and Head, Department of Landscape Architecture, University of Oregon, Eugene

SOIL MECHANICS

OBJECTIVES

This article is intended to provide sufficient information to landscape architects so that they can create reliable and adequate geotechnical graphics for use on projects by other professionals and contractors where professional engineering expertise is not normally required. This information does *not* replace the need for input by a professional engineer (PE) on projects where a high degree of engineering expertise is required.

The accompanying explanatory material is intended to help landscape architects anticipate the need for a professional engineer on the project. It is also to make them aware of the information and data on planting soils that may be required by the geotechnical engineer to aid the creation of a landscape design compatible with engineering requirements.

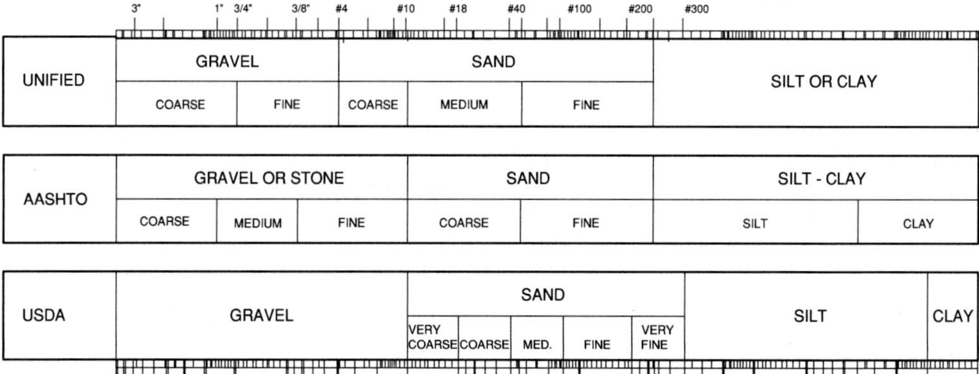

PARTICLE SIZE CLASS COMPARISON AMONG SEVERAL SOIL CLASSIFICATION SYSTEMS

Source: Craul, 1999.

INTRODUCTION

Definition of Soil Mechanics

The geotechnical engineer is concerned with the use of the natural earth materials of soil and rock as construction materials. These materials are by far the most plentiful and least expensive of any construction materials. The term "soil mechanics" covers the engineering mechanics and properties of soil. The mechanics are composed of compaction, the associated consolidation and settlement, and failure under various stresses, including shrink-swell potential and the stability of soil on slopes. The soil scientist is also much concerned with these facets of soil mechanics as well.

Importance of Soil Mechanics Knowledge to Landscape Architecture Projects

Landscape architects are intensely involved with soil on all projects. Success with the soil design and installation ensures a successful project. The soil is viewed in two major precepts: as an engineering material and as a rooting medium for plants. Many times, the objectives of the two precepts are diametrically opposed in regard to the eventual design and outcome (Hillel, 1980; Craul, 1992). In professional practice, the landscape architect must be aware of and informed in each of the two precepts.

There are structures on many landscape projects, such as sidewalks, walls, and foundations, where trees may be planted, and other facilities that must be "engineered," coupled with the requirements of rooting media for the plant palette. The specifications and installation process for each precept cannot always be identical.

This section deals with the soil as an engineering material. *Soils: Agronomic* found in Part 4 describes the soil as a plant-rooting medium. With the overlap between the two precepts in regard to soil mechanics, there is a need to cross-reference between the two articles.

Geotechnical Soil Classification

There are three soil classification systems in use. The first two, the Unified Soil Classification System (USCS) and the American Association of State Highway and Transportation Officials System (AASHTO, which are mainly for road and highway construction), were developed for engineering applications. The USDA-NRCS Soil Taxonomy System (containing what are termed *textural classes*) was developed for the mapping and classification of soils for plant growth interpretations and land-use management. Landscape architects need to be familiar with the major aspects of all three systems. The USCS is highlighted first, and the USDA system is addressed below.

Basically, the USCS classifies soil into two groups: cohesive (*fine-grained*—containing clays) and noncohesive (*coarse-grained*—lacking clay) based on their plasticity. The former are classified on the basis of their plasticity characteristics and the latter on their grain size characteristics (*texture* in the USDA classification). Only sieve analysis and Atterberg limits (the Atterberg limits describe the various physical conditions of a soil under a range of moisture contents) are necessary to completely classify a soil in this system. Four major grain characteristics divisions are recognized in the USCS: (1) coarse-grained, (2) fine-grained, (3) organic soils, and (4) peat.

A greater range of grain size characteristics is necessary for complete classification of soil in the USDA system. Silt and clay are differentiated in the USDA system, whereas they are not in the USCS classification. Long-term research on soil-plant relationships shows the requirement for differentiation and determination of amounts of silt and clay present in the soil, as they have significant influence on plant growth. This fuller range of classes is illustrated in the figure "Particle Size Class Comparison among Several Soil Classification Systems."

The number of soils classified under the Soil Taxonomy of the USDA are in the tens of thousands, because of the environmental soil-forming factors of climate, original vegetation (organisms), parent material (geology), topography, and time (duration of environmental effects, as well as geologic time) that these factors have operated on the earth's surface to form the soil profile.

WATER IN THE SOIL

Plasticity

The soil is a porous medium and, as such, absorbs water as well as gases, including oxygen necessary for plant growth. The water content, together with the soil texture, greatly influences the physical condition of the soil, particularly as it affects its strength and workability. The Atterberg limits were developed to create a scale of water content related to engineering behavior. These are (on drying):

- *Liquid limit (upper plastic limit).* The water content of the soil at which it changes from a viscous liquid to a plastic body.
- *Plastic limit (lower plastic limit).* The water content of the soil at which the soil stiffens from a plastic to a semirigid or friable state.
- *Shrinkage limit.* The water content at which the soil changes from a semirigid state to a rigid solid.
- *Plasticity index.* The range in water content when the soil exhibits plasticity; the difference between the liquid limit and the plastic limit.

On the basis of the Atterberg limits, the *consistency* of the soil may be placed into four classes:

- *Hard or brittle.* Soil moisture is at the shrinkage limit or drier.
- *Friable.* Soil moisture is between the shrinkage limit and the plastic limit.
- *Plastic.* Soil moisture is between the plastic limit and the liquid limit.
- *Liquid.* Soil moisture is greater than the liquid limit.

Clay content greatly influences the plasticity index. As clay content increases, the plasticity index increases, thus leading to a wider range of soil moisture content when the soil is plastic. Type of clay in the soil also influences plasticity index. Montmorillonite clay (high degree of expansion and contraction on wetting and drying) has a much greater effect on increasing the

Dr. Phillip J. Craul, Retired Senior Lecturer in Landscape Architecture, Graduate School of Design, Harvard University, and Emeritus Professor of Soil Science, SUNY-College of Environmental Science and Forestry, Syracuse, New York; Timothy A. Craul, President, Craul Land Scientists, PLC, State College, Pennsylvania

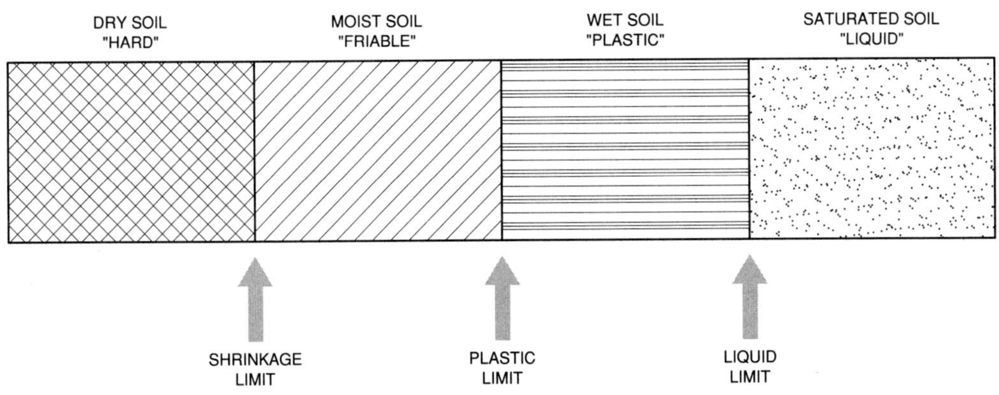

ATTERBERG LIMITS SCHEMATICALLY ILLUSTRATED

plasticity index than illite clay (moderate degree of expansion and contraction on wetting and drying) or kaolinite clay (low degree of expansion and contraction on wetting and drying).

Organic matter content tends to reduce the effects of clay and the plasticity index; but in cases of extreme plasticity, organic matter has little if any effect even if applied in large amounts: other problems arise.

Most sandy (*noncohesive*) soils are nonplastic. Plasticity limits and plasticity indices are provided in the interpretation tables of USDA-NRCS county and area soil survey reports as reference for source materials.

Practical Application of Plasticity to Working the Soil

Soil should be worked only when the soil is in friable condition. In soil science terms, this is when the soil moisture content is approximately the midpoint between *field capacity* and *wilting point.*

- If hard, the soil will be cloddy and difficult to spread. The clods will persist, especially if buried, and will not break down until moistened and mechanically broken up.
- If plastic, the soil will smear and compact badly, creating problems that are very difficult to correct after installation.
- If liquid, the soil will flow when spread, later to harden beyond repair when dry. The soil must most often be replaced.

Note: Soil should *never* be worked when it is frozen, even when in storage piles.

Soil Drainage

Soil is a porous medium, so water flows through it when saturated (the entire pore space—voids—is filled with water). When less than saturated, the water is held by forces of attraction within the soil against gravity, but may move slowly in response to these internal forces. When the soil becomes very dry, the remaining water is no longer able to move, and plants wilt.

Deliberate soil drainage prevents the soil from becoming saturated where excess water must be removed, keeps it away from areas or plants that require protection, and removes it quickly to stabilize slopes.

Surface Drainage

On most projects, some provision must be made to handle surface water, to prevent erosion, and to prevent damage to turf and plants and structures, especially in anticipation of severe storms. Well-drained soils aid infiltration of surface water, but even these soils become temporarily saturated under severe conditions of intense rainfall and flooding. Two widely used provisions for handling surface water flow are given here.

Swale

The swale is a deliberate linear depression in the soil surface to collect and direct low surface flow to an appropriate outlet. It has no clearly defined shoulders in cross section and therefore may be an integral part of a lawn or other open portion of the landscape.

The swale is located primarily on gentle slopes and is nearly always a part of a steep slope design, intercepting water at the top of slope and diverting it around the slope crest. If the water flow at the top of the slope is deemed to be high flow in storms, the trench design should be used, sometimes with lined shoulders and bed. A swale should be installed at the foot of a slope, especially if the slope is steep, long, or of relatively impermeable soil. This is represented on the illustrations of a drainage swale cross section with all turf and the plan drawing as shown usually on the "L" series of drawings using contour lines with the swale area pointed downslope.

Drainage Trench

The drainage trench is designed to carry a high flow of water and is usually employed as a collector channel leading to the main outlet. A trapezoidal cross section with distinct shoulders permits rapid velocity, even with increasing flow.

In areas of heavy rainfall and/or steep slopes with heavy runoff, the drainage trench design may need to be used in the entire system. Because of its design, it must be integrated into the overall landscape design as a deliberate element of its own. It provides more of a design challenge than does the swale. This is represented on the illustrations of the drainage trench cross section lined with stone and the plan view.

Subsurface Drainage

Seepage

Water seepage occurs when water moves longitudinally very slowly downslope (even on level or very gentle slopes) through the soil. In some cases, the

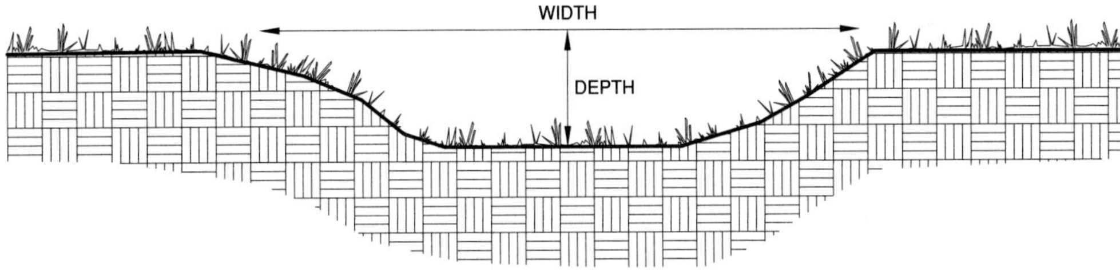

CROSS SECTION OF DRAINAGE SWALE WITH ALL TURF

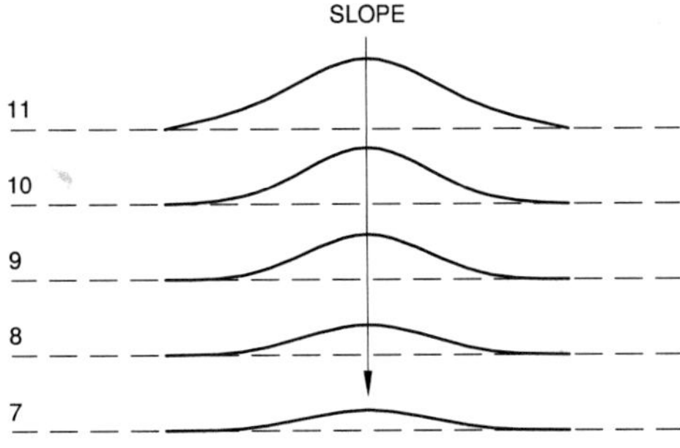

PLAN DRAWING AS SHOWN ON THE "L" SERIES OF DRAWINGS WITH SWALE AREA POINTED DOWNSLOPE

Dr. Phillip J. Craul, Retired Senior Lecturer in Landscape Architecture, Graduate School of Design, Harvard University, and Emeritus Professor of Soil Science, SUNY-College of Environmental Science and Forestry, Syracuse, New York; Timothy A. Craul, President, Craul Land Scientists, PLC, State College, Pennsylvania

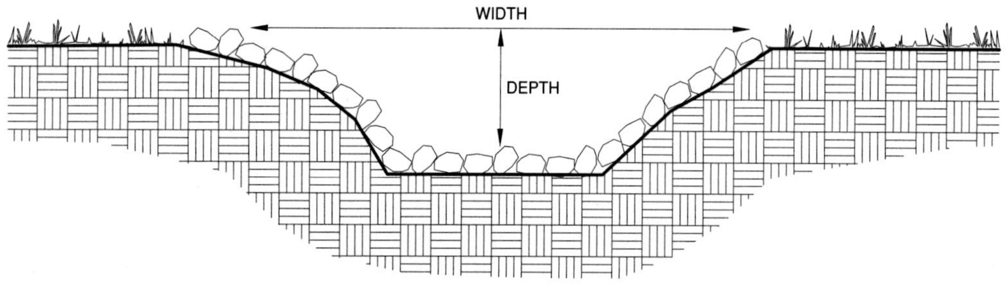

CROSS SECTION OF DRAINAGE TRENCH LINED WITH STONE

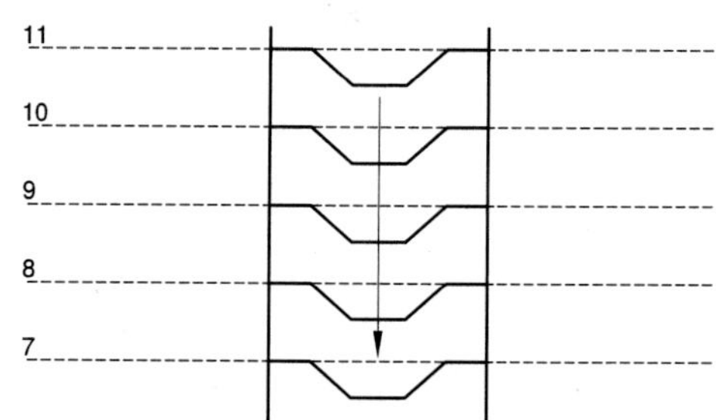

PLAN DRAWING OF DRAINAGE TRENCH AS SHOWN ON THE "L" SERIES OF DRAWINGS

seeping water rises to the surface due to either the change to a steeper slope gradient or the presence of some impermeable layer such as shallow bedrock that forces the water to the surface.

The best solution to prevent water seepage is to interrupt its path with a curtain (interceptor) drain or force it to the surface (difficult and expensive to do) and handle it as surface drainage from that point downslope. The curtain drain must reach down to an impervious layer to be totally effective. This can be accomplished with either an open or a covered curtain drain as illustrated in the cross sections and plan views shown here.

All subsurface drainage systems have at least one interface between the soil or other materials and the installed drain. Filters are usually placed between the soil and the drain to prevent migration of soil particles into the drainage system. For satisfactory and long-term performance, the filter must meet both of the following two requirements (Forrester, 2001):

1. The filter flow capacity must be at least equal that of the *protected* (soil) material. Further, its capacity should be somewhat larger than that of the soil or other material to prevent clogging. It should never be less.
2. No more than a limited quantity of solid particles from the protected material should be allowed to pass into it or through it. This movement must cease or be significantly reduced after a short time, to prevent *piping*, a phenomenon of seeping water progressively eroding away soil particles, creating large voids in the soil, leading to its collapse or that of an associated structure.

These requirements are met if (Forrester, 2001):

For No. 1: $d_{15}{}^{f} > 4$ to $5 \times d_{15}{}^{p}$
For No. 2: $d_{15}{}^{f} < 4$ to $5 \times d_{85}{}^{p}$

where $d_{15}{}^{f}$ is particle diameter of 15 percent passing for the filter, $d_{15}{}^{p}$ is the particle diameter of 15 percent passing for the protected material, and $d_{85}{}^{p}$ is the diameter of 85 percent passing for the protected material. The percent passing data is obtained from the particle size distribution curves derived from ASTM F-1632-03 or D-4221-99 (Craul and Craul, 2006).

In addition, the gradation curves (particle size distribution curves) must be parallel. This requirement is met if:

$$d_{50}{}^{f} < 25 \times d_{50}{}^{p}$$

For drainpipe, the larger particles of the protected material must not be able to move into the openings.

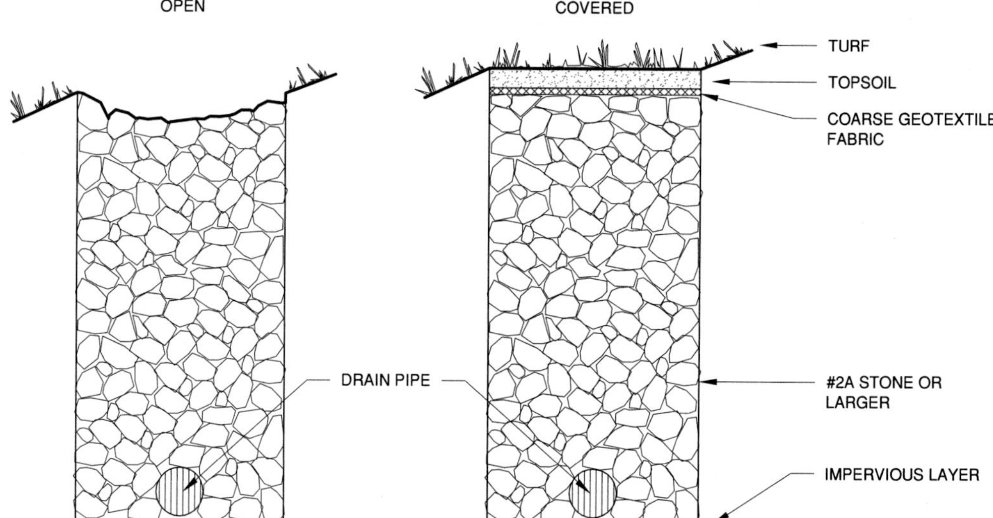

If left open at the surface, it may be used to intercept moderate surface flow as well as seepage flow.

SECTION OF CURTAIN (OR INTERCEPTOR) DRAIN FOR INTERCEPTING SEEPAGE WATER

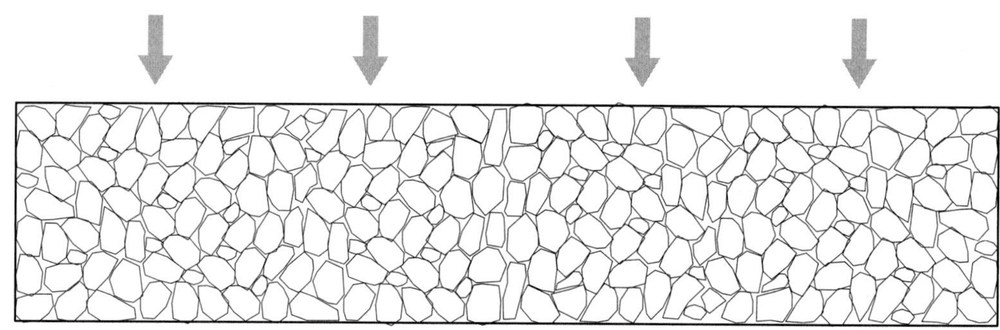

OPEN CURTAIN DRAIN PLAN

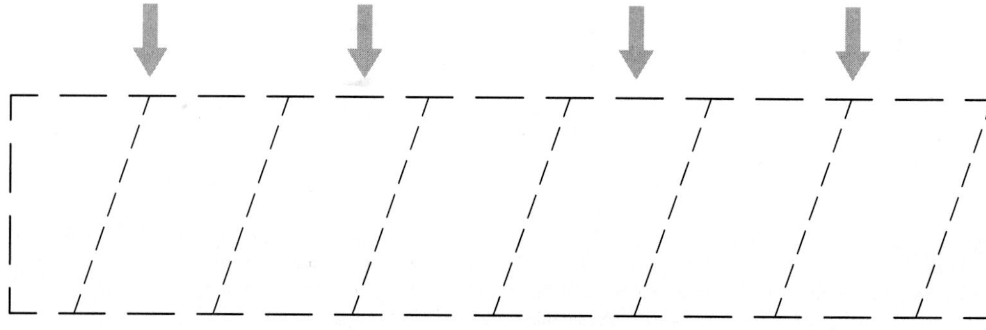

COVERED CURTAIN DRAIN PLAN

OPEN CURTAIN PLAN AND COVERED CURTAIN DRAIN PLAN

Dr. Phillip J. Craul, Retired Senior Lecturer in Landscape Architecture, Graduate School of Design, Harvard University, and Emeritus Professor of Soil Science, SUNY-College of Environmental Science and Forestry, Syracuse, New York; Timothy A. Craul, President, Craul Land Scientists, PLC, State College, Pennsylvania

Since drainpipe may have slots, open joints, or round holes, this is prevented by the following formulas:

Slots: $d_{85}{}^{p}$ > 1.2 x slot width
Open joints: $d_{85}{}^{p}$ > 2.0 x joint width
Circular holes: $d_{85}{}^{p}$ > 1.0 hole diameter

For some applications, the appropriate geotextile fabric properly placed may suffice for meeting the two requirements. Permittivity of geotextile is tested by ASTM D 4491; and ASTM D 4751 for apparent opening size works well for woven and nonwoven fabrics, but does not work well for the thicker nonwoven fabrics.

However, a graded filter may be required, which is a series of layers of increasingly coarser granular materials without the use of geotextile fabric. A designed soil usually meets this criterion.

Clogging is a phenomenon that can cause real problems to the life expectancy of a drainage system by reducing the flow capacity of the filter. Reduction of filter flow capacity is caused by two types of obstructions: *blinding,* when solid materials obstruct the openings on the inflow side of the filter, and *clogging,* when fine particles are trapped within the voids or openings of the filter. Both causes may be termed clogging for practical purposes. There are four major ways of causing clogging (Forrester, 2001):

- *Granular:* Contamination of the filter by clay mud during construction. Voids that develop during construction between the filter and the protected material becoming filled with fine material; the protected soil is unstable; and there is compaction of the fine materials against the filter.
- *Ferric/bacterial:* The oxidation of water-soluble ferrous iron (Fe++) common in many waters to ferric iron (Fe+++), which precipitates on the filter. Filamentous aerobic bacteria accelerate the oxidation process and form a colloidal slime, entrapping granular particles. When dry, both the precipitate and the slime become hard and crystalline.
- *Calcium carbonate (termed tufa):* Caused by soluble calcium bicarbonate in the groundwater breaking down to the calcium carbonate precipitate.
- *Tree roots:* Produce a tangle of roots around the pipe, which can totally block the pipe. The tangled mass then entraps granular particles. A general rule is that underdrainage should be avoided when associated with trees.

Solutions to these problems are:

- *Granular:* Use care during construction and backfilling of the drainage system.
- *Ferric/bacterial:* No real solution to the complete elimination of the problem; best practice is to use pipe with large circular holes, instead of slotted pipe, and no geotextile fabric in known problem areas.
- *Calcium carbonate:* Only jet cleaning and chemical cleaning are effective in gravity drains.
- *Tree roots:* Run solid pipe under or near where trees exist or are to be planted; tree species such as the willows (*Salix* spp.) should be avoided and removed if present.

Underdrainage

Underdrainage is the deliberate design and installation of an underground drainage system to improve the drainage of a site. Imperfect drainage may be caused by dense or compacted soil, a high water table, or the presence of an impervious layer such as a rooftop or a buried barrier of some type.

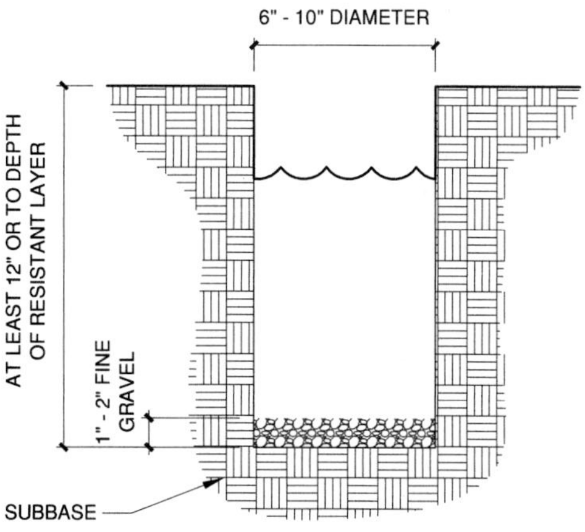

INFORMAL PERCOLATION TEST

To determine whether underdrainage is required, the site soil should be tested for drainage in all cases. The best test is the simple percolation test used by soil scientists, which is modeled on the formal American Society of Agronomy test. It is reliable and inexpensive. A hole is dug with an ordinary spade or shovel. The walls are roughened to remove the smear caused by the digging tool. The bottom should be covered with a thin layer (1-2 inches) of fine gravel to prevent clogging of the bottom soil. The hole is saturated with water to the top 24 hours prior to the test. For the test, the hole is filled with water to a minimum of 12 inches, and the drop in the water surface is measured over time. A test result greater than one-half inch per hour indicates no underdrainage is required. Tests should be run at several locations over the area in question.

Underdrainage should be installed as part of the design only if imperfect drainage is detected by the tests. Underdrainage is required only when excess water in the soil may exist for more than three days, unless it is a special-use area such as an athletic field.

Underdrainage is expensive and prone to failure if not installed properly. Experience has proven that, many times, landscape architects call for an underdrainage system when it is not necessary or there are more satisfactory alternatives, such as a designed soil, to improve drainage.

The Underdrainage Plan

When underdrainage is necessary, there are several designs available. The two most common are the *parallel* and the *herringbone.* Both of these patterns have been successfully used for decades in agricultural applications.

- The parallel design, as shown in the illustration "Parallell Underdrainage Pattern," is appropriate for a broad, level-to-gently-sloping site with a collector pipe at the lowest point of the area.
- The herringbone design, as shown in the illustration "Herringbone Underdrainage Pattern," is used on steeper terrain or a narrow site with a central drainpipe leading to the outlet.

In some cases, a series of either design, more commonly the herringbone, may be joined into a complex system. Connecting pipe then must be sized larger to accommodate a greater flow capacity.

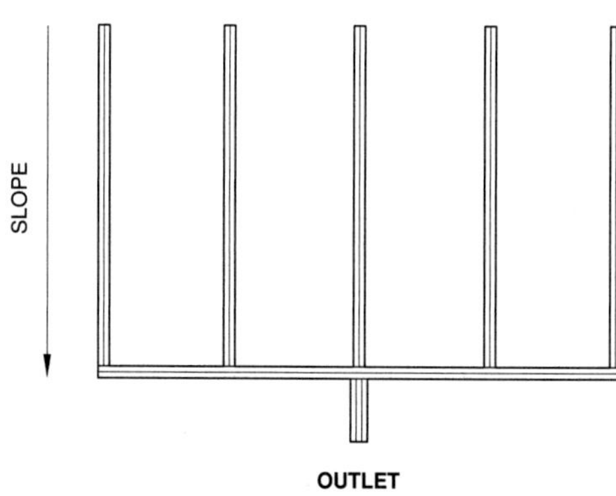

PARALLEL UNDERDRAINAGE PATTERN

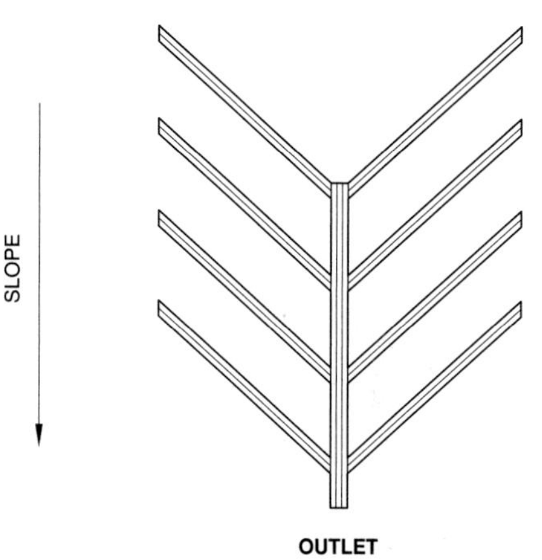

HERRINGBONE UNDERDRAINAGE PATTERN

Some projects may require an intricate layout of the drainage network. Attention must be paid especially to the effective drainage width (for spacing purposes, etc.) of the material to be drained and the pipe design. Insufficient drainage in one area and excessive drainage in another result in obvious uneven plant growth.

The underdrainage is usually constructed of 4-inch slotted pipe. The pipe is placed on or just above the impervious layer. Spacing is based on the texture of the soil, with spacing narrowest for clays, moderate for light silt loams and loams, and widest for sandy soils, all by calculations as shown in the table "Depth and Spacing of Subdrains for Various Soil Texture Classes."

If perforated pipe (round holes) is used, the holes must be placed downward. Some slotted pipe is now manufactured with slots on one side, and, if used, should be placed in the same way. Most flexible slotted pipe has slots all around the circumference.

Exposed drainage outlets should be covered with durable wire netting or special slotted caps to prevent rodents and other animals from entering the system.

The Underdrainage Profile

Several soil alternative underdrainage profile designs may be applied to a landscape project as illustrated.

Dr. Phillip J. Craul, Retired Senior Lecturer in Landscape Architecture, Graduate School of Design, Harvard University, and Emeritus Professor of Soil Science, SUNY-College of Environmental Science and Forestry, Syracuse, New York; Timothy A. Craul, President, Craul Land Scientists, PLC, State College, Pennsylvania

DEPTH AND SPACING OF SUBDRAINS FOR VARIOUS SOIL TEXTURE CLASSES

SOIL TEXTURE CLASS	SOIL SEPARATE PERCENT			DEPTH TO BOTTOM OF DRAIN, FEET	SPACING BETWEEN DRAINS, FEET
	SAND	SILT	CLAY		
Sand	80-100	0-20	0-20	3-4 2-3	150-300 100-150
Sandy loam	50-80	0-50	0-20	3-4 2-3	100-150 85-100
Loam	30-50	30-50	0-20	3-4 2-3	85-100 75-85
Silt loam	0-50	50-100	0-20	3-4 2-3	75-85 65-75
Sandy clay loam	50-80	0-30	20-30	3-4 2-3	65-75 55-65
Clay loam	20-50	20-50	20-30	3-4 2-3	55-65 45-55
Silty clay loam	0-30	50-80	20-30	3-4 2-3	45-55 40-45
Sandy clay	50-70	0-20	30-50	3-4 2-3	40-45 35-40
Silty clay	0-20	50-70	30-50	3-4 2-3	35-40 30-35
Clay	0-50	0-50	30-100	3-4 2-3	30-35 25-30

Source: Packard, 1981.

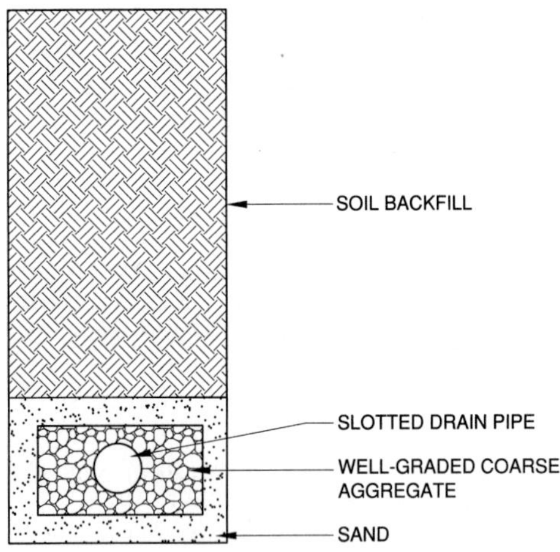

SIMPLE GRADED GRANULAR FILTER WITHOUT GEOTEXTILE

Source: After Forrester, 2001.

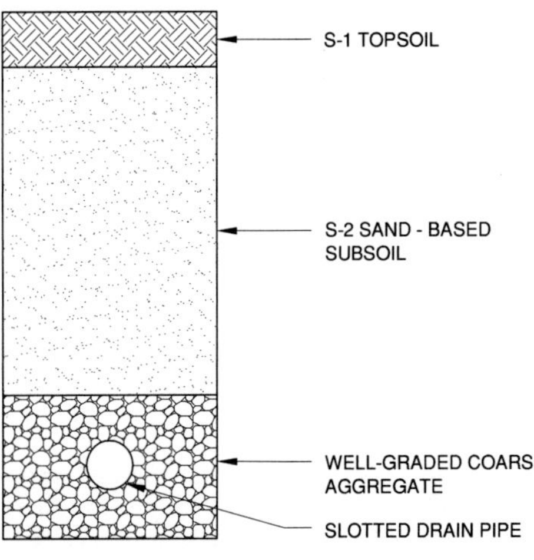

DESIGNED SOIL PROFILE ACTING AS A GRADED FILTER WITHOUT GEOTEXTILE

Source: After Craul, 1999.

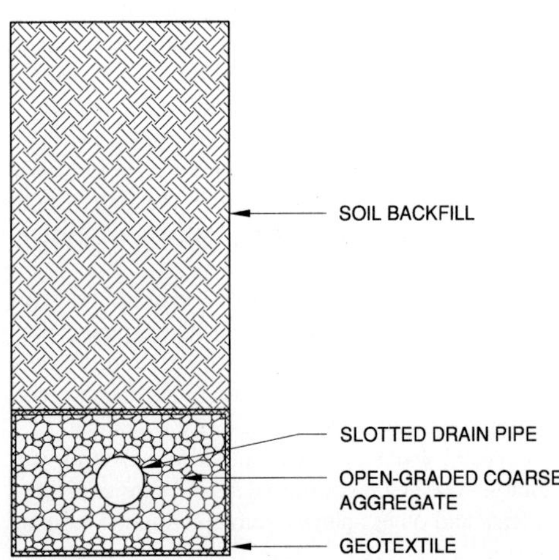

GRADED GEOTEXTILE FABRIC FILTER

Source: After Forrester, 2001.

Each one meets different requirements of design with and without the use of geotextile fabric.

- If a drain is used to intercept side-hill seepage, the bottom of the trench should be cut at least 6 inches into the impervious layer.
- The underdrainage system should have a fall of at least 3 to 6 inches per 100 feet.
- The procedure for selecting the geotextile, as specified by AASHTO, is to select a fabric with appropriate survivability strengths, then determine its acceptability for the required filtration/separation properties.

The soil to be protected must be stable for effective use of geotextile fabric as a filter. Stable soil produces limited movement of fine particles before forming a bridging layer of coarser material. The limited fines are able to pass through the filter. The bridging layer itself becomes part of the *developed* filter. Unstable soil does not form a bridging layer, as the fines pass through completely until they bind the filter itself and render it useless. These are illustrated in the figure "Generalized Gradation Curves for Stable and Unstable Soils."

Geotextile fabric sleeves for slipping over the drainage pipe itself, prewrapped pipe, or wrapping the pipe with geotextile fabric are *not recommended in most cases* (Forrester, 2001). There has been evidence of too many failures due to clogging and unsuccessful attempts to unclog the pipe with jet cleaning.

Stable soils include:

- Cohesive soils with a plasticity index > 15.
- Open-graded sandy soils, with $C_u < 3$.
- Well-graded soils, with $C_u > 4$, and the grading curve between d_{10} and d_{60} is either straight or concave downward.

(Note: C_u = coeffcient of uniformity = d_{60}/d_{10}.)

Unstable soils include:

- Gap-graded soils.
- Broadly graded soils with $C_u > 20$, and the grading curve between d_{10} and d_{60} is concave upward.
- Dispersive clays.

When unstable soils are to be protected, Forrester (2001) recommends the application of the Gradient Ratio Test ASTM D-5101.

The USDA-Natural Resources Conservation Service provides a guide (see the table "Need for Drain Filters Based on USDA Soil Classification") for the need for a drainage filter based on the Unified Soil Classification System for the protected soil (Craul, 1999).

In some cases, a geocomposite drain may be used to enhance drainage. In every application where a geocomposite drain is used, it should be in an envelope of sand (see the figure "Geocomposite Drain in a Sand Envelop"). Placing the geocomposite directly against the protected material (soil) on both sides greatly reduces its drainage capacity since the flow water is dependent on the soil rate of flow, which is much less than that of the geocomposite. Experience has shown that many geocomposite drains have failed to function due to this fact (Forrester, 2001). It may be placed against one side of a soil trench with the opposite side backfilled with sand (see the figure "Geocomposite Placed Against One Side of Soil Trench").

SOIL SHRINK-SWELL

The best field evidence of significant soil shrink-swell susceptibility is obtained by observation of desiccation cracks on the soil surface, soil creep, and leaning utility poles and fenceposts. Even extensive areas of leaning trees have been observed on these soils.

Soils containing large amounts of montmorillonite or vermiculite clays increase their volume as water molecules orient themselves on the clay surfaces, along with additional molecules being attracted to the surface. The overall volume of the soil is increased, and stress forces develop outward pressures. These pressures are of sufficient force to cause displacement and cracking of foundation walls, sidewalks, roads,

Dr. Phillip J. Craul, Retired Senior Lecturer in Landscape Architecture, Graduate School of Design, Harvard University, and Emeritus Professor of Soil Science, SUNY-College of Environmental Science and Forestry, Syracuse, New York; Timothy A. Craul, President, Craul Land Scientists, PLC, State College, Pennsylvania

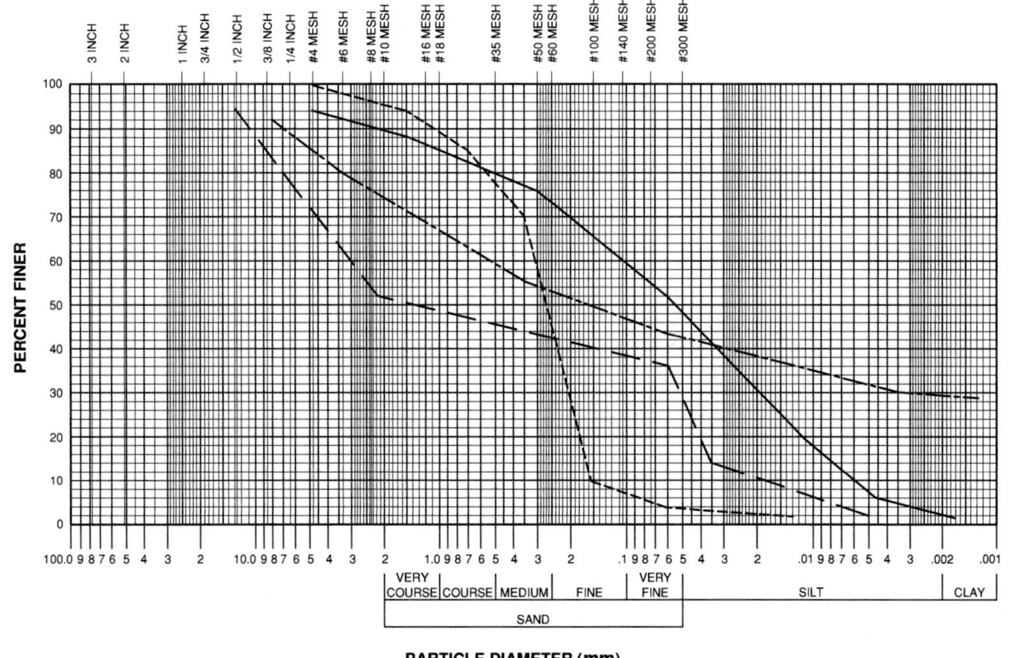

GENERALIZED GRADATION CURVES FOR STABLE AND UNSTABLE SOILS

Source: After Forrester, 2001.

NEED FOR DRAIN FILTERS BASED ON USDA SOIL CLASSIFICATION

UNIFIED SOIL CLASSIFICATION (USCS)	FILTER RECOMMENDATION
SP (fine)	Filter needed
SM (fine)	Filter needed
ML, MH	Filter needed
GP	Subject to local on-site determination
SC	Subject to local on-site determination
GM	Subject to local on-site determination
SM (coarse)	Subject to local on-site determination
GC, CL, SP, GP (coarse)	None
GW, SW, CH, OL, OH, Pt	None

Source: USDA-Soil Conservation Service, 1973 (Craul, 1999).

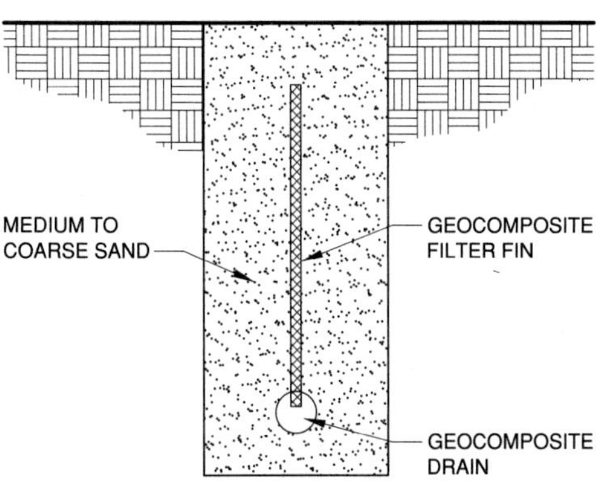

GEOCOMPOSITE DRAIN IN A SAND ENVELOPE

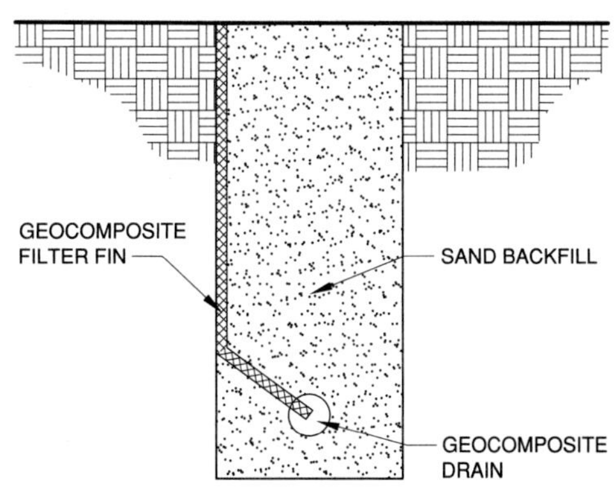

GEOCOMPOSITE PLACED AGAINST ONE SIDE OF THE SOIL TRENCH

and other structures constructed on and in these soils. When the soil dries, the forces decay, and collapse of the soil occurs, causing widespread cracks. The structures, no longer provided soil support, collapse in turn.

These expansive soils are classified as Vertisols by the USDA-NRCS. The geographic locations of major areas of Vertisols within the United States occur along the Gulf Coast of Texas, somewhat centered on the Houston area, especially where the infamous Houston Black Clays occur, creating major development problems. Two other areas in Texas follow the branching river valleys northeastward from the Rio Grande River. Major areas occur on the Alabama-Mississippi border northwest of Montgomery as the northwest segment of the Alabama Black Soil Belt.

Other isolated soils with high shrink-swell potential are located outside of these major areas, particularly in the western states and parts of the western Midwest. One soil series, the Iredell, has caused serious problems in Fairfax County, Virginia, where many homes collapsed in the late 1950s as the result of the return of normal rainfall after an extended period of drought. This county was the first in the United States to hire a soil scientist to aid in land-use planning and implementation of zoning regulations.

The county soil survey reports for the project area should be consulted. Recent detailed expansive soil surveys have been conducted by the USDA-NRCS for the metropolitan and suburb areas of Phoenix and Tucson, Arizona, for use in development planning.

A measure of soil shrinkage and swelling is the coefficient of linear extensibility (COLE). This soil parameter is rated as low, moderate, or high potential within the soil interpretation tables of the soil survey report.

The table "Quantitative Interpretation of Shrink-Swell Potential for USDA-NRCS Soil Survey Reports" provides numerical or quantitative meaning to these terms. Where the interpretation indicates a rating of moderate to high potential, structures with foundations should be avoided. Use of the subsoil of these Vertisols as a fill or planting soil should be avoided unless significantly modified. When disturbed, they are very unstable and very susceptible to erosion. The topsoil, or A horizon, of the natural soil is acceptable if the shrink-swell potential is rated low.

QUANTITATIVE INTERPRETATION OF SHRINK-SWELL POTENTIAL FOR USDA-NRCS SOIL SURVEY REPORTS

CLASS	LINEAR EXTENSIBILITY[1]	COLE[2]
Low	<3	<0.03
Medium	3–6	0.03–0.06
High	6–9	0.06–0.09
Very High	>9	>0.09

[1]LE % = 100 x (moist length – dry length)/dry length.
[2]COLE = LE/100.

Dr. Phillip J. Craul, Retired Senior Lecturer in Landscape Architecture, Graduate School of Design, Harvard University, and Emeritus Professor of Soil Science, SUNY-College of Environmental Science and Forestry, Syracuse, New York; Timothy A. Craul, President, Craul Land Scientists, PLC, State College, Pennsylvania

Withdrawal of Water by Trees on Expansive Soils

The withdrawal of water by tree roots from soil pores in the process of transpiration may cause collapse of the soil, especially on expansive clays. The soil collapse in turn can cause failure of shallow building foundations. Therefore, it is good practice to space trees from the building foundation at a distance equal to the expected height of the mature tree (Greenway, 1987). This follows the "1H" rule (as illustrated in the figure "'IH Rule' Distance for Tree Planting Adjacent to Shallow Foundation Buildings on Expansive Clay Soil") developed by the Kew Botanical Gardens in England as the result of building foundation failures during the drought of 1975–1976 in London (Cutler and Richardson, 1981). The same problem occurred on the Ontario clays of Ottawa, Canada, in the early 1990s (authors' consulting files).

In cases where the structure foundations are deep and reinforced, as for modern multistoried buildings, the problem is not as acute or may not exist, especially if nonexpansive soils are in place. Removal of water by trees planted in expansive soil at the base of a retaining wall can cause subsidence of the supporting earth beneath the wall, leading to the collapse of the wall. Conversely, the removal of trees in expansive soil before construction of the retaining wall can cause subsequent failure of the new wall by expansion of the base soil (Fortlage and Phillips, 2001).

Frost Action

Frost action is very similar to shrink-swell potential in soils, the difference being alternate freezing and thawing of the soil rather than alternate wetting and drying of expansive soils. This soil parameter should also be considered in landscape design applications in climates where soil freezing and thawing occurs.

Frost action potential interpretations are provided in the county or area soil survey reports published by the USDA-NRCS for information on source materials.

MECHANICS OF SOIL STABILITY

The particle size distribution (*soil texture,* in soil science terminology) of the soil material, together with its moisture content, are two major factors that influence soil stability, defined as the resistance to deformation, collapse, or physical disintegration under loading of some type. This resistance is termed *soil strength.*

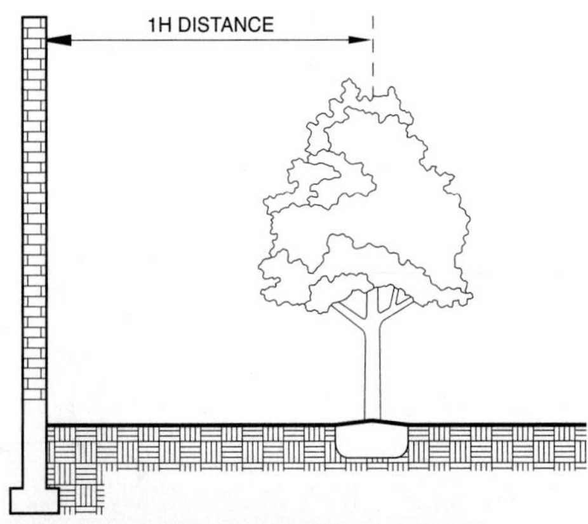

"1H RULE" DISTANCE FOR TREE PLANTING ADJACENT TO SHALLOW FOUNDATION BUILDINGS ON EXPANSIVE CLAY SOILS

Source: Cutler and Richardson, 1981.

In most cases, the soil requires *densification* to increase its strength for geotechnical applications; hence, compacting the soil to a density that may inhibit plant root penetration and extension, which is unsatisfactory to the needs of a plant soil-rooting medium. Soil compaction is the major conflict between the requirements of the geotechnical engineer and those of the landscape architect, soil scientist, and horticulturist.

Forces Affecting Soil Stability

To understand soil stability and its applications to landscape design, it is necessary to briefly describe the involved forces within the soil and those applied. They are:

- *Shear.* The resistance to rupture or failure ("sliding") of a soil body along a plane.
- *Stress.* The interactive forces of attraction between soil particles modified by moisture content.
- *Strain.* The reactive forces within the soil body that appear when a stress is applied and that disappear when the force is relieved. Deformation may or may not persist, depending on whether shear stress has occurred.

Soil Compaction

Compaction occurs when shear has occurred and is sufficient to overcome stress within the soil body and deformation persists. Upon deformation, rearrangement of soil particles and the change in molecular forces of water increases stress so that soil strength is increased, as long as complete disintegration does not occur. Thus, because most engineering applications require the necessity to increase soil strength, soil compaction is a common practice.

Two tests are used to determine degree of compaction: the Proctor test and the California bearing ratio.

Proctor Test

The Proctor test (ASTM D-698-80; or AASHTO T-99—designations are continually being revised; check publications annually) is probably the most appropriate geotechnical test for soil density. It is based on maximum potential density at optimum moisture content when a standard compressive force is applied to a sample in the laboratory. Thus, "85 percent Proctor" indicates that the soil density is 85 percent of maximum density.

Various instruments have been developed and calibrated to measure Proctor density in place, among them: the nuclear density meter and the recording soil density cone penetrometer (ASTM D3017-05 and ASTM D3441-05, respectively). Thus, laboratory density tests by ASTM D-698 or AASHTO T-99 for landscape soil applications are not generally required.

The figure "Relationships among Soil Bulk Density, Moisture Content, and Proctor Percentage" illustrates the curves developed in the laboratory from a series of samples of an individual soil with a range of moisture contents to which a standard force is applied. The resulting compaction.value for the given moisture content is then plotted as a point, with the series providing a curve of moisture content and density. The peaks in the various curves represent the optimum moisture content for maximum density. The engineer desires maximum density for soil stability. Soil A is a well-graded loamy sand, soil B is a well-graded sandy loam, soil C (dotted line) is a silt, and soil D is a poorly graded sand. The soil just above C is a heavy clay. Most of these soils exceed the bulk density limits for plant root growth.

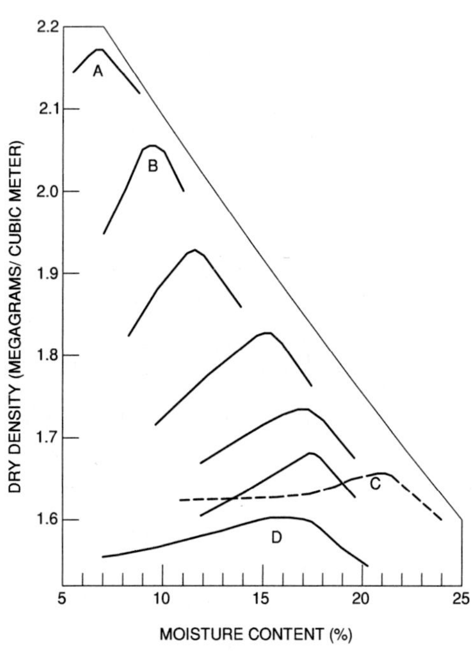

RELATIONSHIPS AMONG SOIL BULK DENSITY, MOISTURE CONTENT, AND PROCTOR PERCENTAGE

Source: After Holtz and Kovacs, 1981.

It is very seldom necessary or practical to compact a soil to 100 percent Proctor. Most engineering applications specify 90 to 95 percent Proctor. Unfortunately, the soil bulk density at these levels of compaction may exceed the plant-rooting limits of 1.65 Mg/m^3 for fine-textured soils and 1.70 Mg/m^3 for coarse-textured soils, which for most designed soils would have a Proctor value of about 85 percent. Thus, the 85 percent Proctor becomes the usual desired practical limit without subsequent settlement for compaction of planting soil. Soil under a sidewalk usually requires 90 percent Proctor, but it must have the proper coarse texture to conform to the planting soil density limits and yet permit root penetration and extension.

The *modified* Proctor test, mentioned sometimes in the literature, is applied only to road and airfield construction. It should never be used for landscape design applications.

California Bearing Ratio

This test is applied only for heavy construction, such as flexible surface roads and highways. It is misused when applied to lighter applications and may provide inappropriate results that lead to severe overdesign for most landscape design applications.

Correction of Excessive Compaction

There is what may be considered major and minor degrees of compaction. Major compaction is the condition in which the degree of compaction greatly exceeds rooting density limits and the layer or com-

Dr. Phillip J. Craul, Retired Senior Lecturer in Landscape Architecture, Graduate School of Design, Harvard University, and Emeritus Professor of Soil Science, SUNY-College of Environmental Science and Forestry, Syracuse, New York; Timothy A. Craul, President, Craul Land Scientists, PLC, State College, Pennsylvania

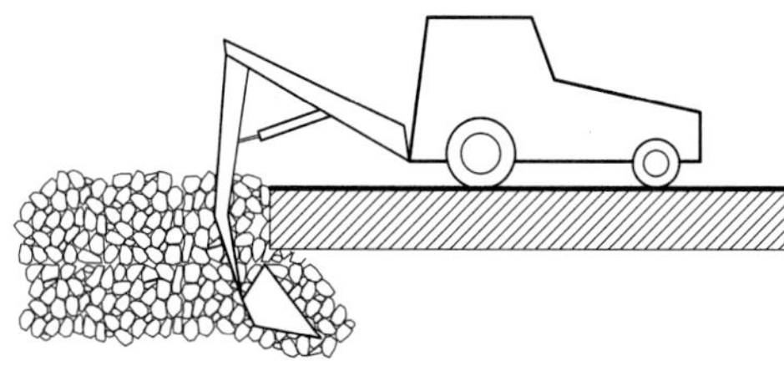

BACKHOE SOIL LOOSENING IN DEPTH

Source: Kai Rolf, 1986, in Craul, 1992.

paction is greater than 12 inches in thickness. Or there may be several layers of compaction at depth intervals in the soil profile. Loosening of the soil in depth is necessary to provide sufficient rooting depth and drainage for satisfactory plant growth. The process of loosening with a backhoe is necessary in the case of major compaction

Minor compaction is the condition where the surface 6 inches or less is compacted to a sufficient degree to prevent root penetration (bulk density greater than 1.65 to 1.70 Mg/m^3) and water infiltration.

A heavy-duty tractor-mounted rototiller, working the soil across the area in two directions at right angles to each other, is generally a satisfactory solution for complete loosening to a depth of at least 6 inches. An ordinary agricultural disc harrow may be used to loosen shallow, lightly compacted soil as preparation for grass seeding.

In cases of severe compaction of a relatively thin (6 inches or less) surface layer, a chisel plow pulled by a tracked tractor is appropriate; however, cloddy soil usually results and subsequent discing is required.

Applications of Compaction

Soil Installation

Proper placement of the soil on a project site requires care and attention to prevent either excessive compaction or excessive subsequent settlement. The former is caused by excessive traffic or deliberate overcompaction operations on the specified soil. The latter may be caused by nonuniform distribution and compaction of the soil in backfill operations, leaving voids in the soil volume.

These defects may be prevented by the widely accepted engineering practice of laying down the soil in *lifts* of 6 to 8 inches in thickness until the proper thickness of the horizon within the designed profile is attained. For engineering applications, each lift is mechanically compacted by roller to a specified density as measured by the Proctor test, nuclear or penetrometer (ASTM-D3017-05 or ASTM D3441-05). Deliberate compaction for landscape planting projects for open soil situations (no structures present) is usually not necessary, as the soil placement equipment creates sufficient compactive force on each lift to prevent subsequent settlement. If compactive force is required, it should be a lightweight roller of not more than 75 to 100 pounds per width-foot of roller. In many cases, soil-spreading equipment traffic, such as a "speeder-skidder" or a light, wide-track bulldozer, applies sufficient force for compacting soil to a Proctor of 85 to 90 percent for landscape purposes, without exceeding plant root penetration density of 1.65 Mg/m^3 for fine-textured cohesive soil and 1.70 Mg/m^3 for sandy noncohesive soil.

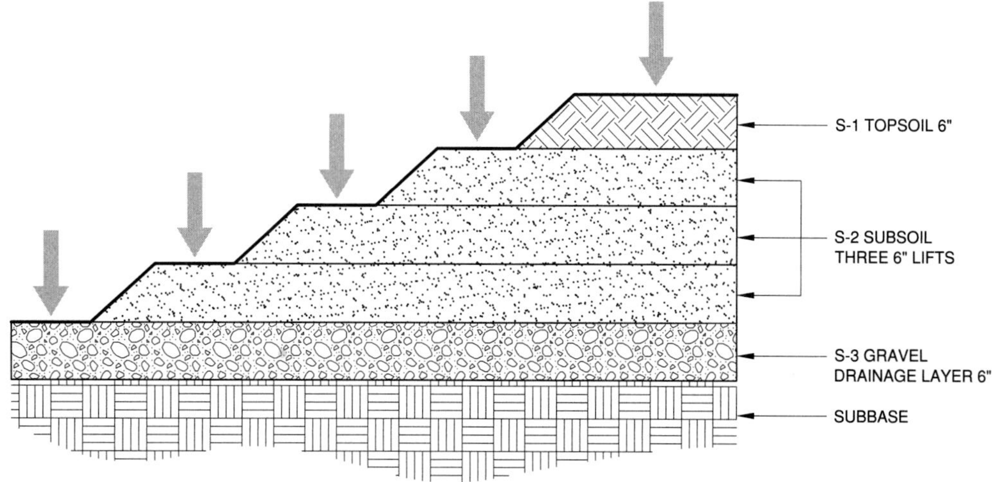

EXAMPLE OF LIFTS FOR INSTALLATION OF A DESIGNED AND SPECIFIED SOIL PROFILE

Each lift is lightly compacted in sequence of placement, as indicated by the arrows in the figure "Example of Lifts for Installation of a Designed and Specified Soil Profile," unless a sand-based design soil is used; sandy soils will be at least 85 percent Proctor density just from the process of spreading and leveling by lightweight equipment.

Fine-textured soils placed in lifts should not be compacted exceeding 90 percent Proctor. The S-1 or final surface is not rolled unless seeded with grass. The drainage layer S-3 is generally AASHTO #4 aggregate and is used when underdrainage is necessary; otherwise, the subbase is the lowest layer and is not compacted.

Geotextile fabric is not placed between the S-3 drainage layer and the bottom of the S-2 in the case of a designed soil in humid regions (Craul and Craul, 2006). In many cases, the geotextile fabric has been found to be a barrier to soil water drainage, holding the water above the fabric until it is saturated (not plant-friendly), causing a "perched" water table, thus restricting soil profile drainage. A designed soil is itself a filter. In semiarid or arid regions, the perched effect of the geotextile fabric may be a distinct advantage for storing water within the soil profile, especially where irrigation is employed and becomes a deliberate part of the design.

Sidewalks and Minor Structure Foundations

Sidewalks and other walkways may be located where the design does not need to be compatible with plant rooting, especially where trees are not to be planted. The simple profile of the standard sidewalk cross section is applied. In cases where trees are to be planted in conjunction with sidewalks, a more complex design is necessary.

Generally, the subbase surface may require compaction to 95 percent Proctor to meet engineering code regulations. The compaction is accomplished by roller equipment or vibrator. The gravel base also requires compaction, normally by vibrator.

Earth Pressure

Earth pressure is defined as the forces exerted on a foundation wall or other surface due to the soil weight (including absorbed water) pressing against the wall, in addition to any other forces such as shrink-swell (expansive) action. Slope adds another force and is discussed elsewhere.

Soil Data Required by Geotechnical Engineers for Earth Pressure Application

Sometimes it is necessary for the landscape architect to have the project soil scientist provide soil data to the project engineer so that the latter can evaluate earth pressure values against structure foundation walls. This information includes *angle of internal friction* based on particle size distribution (gradation) and generalized particle shape, bulk density of the installed soil, and maximum moisture content throughout the profile.

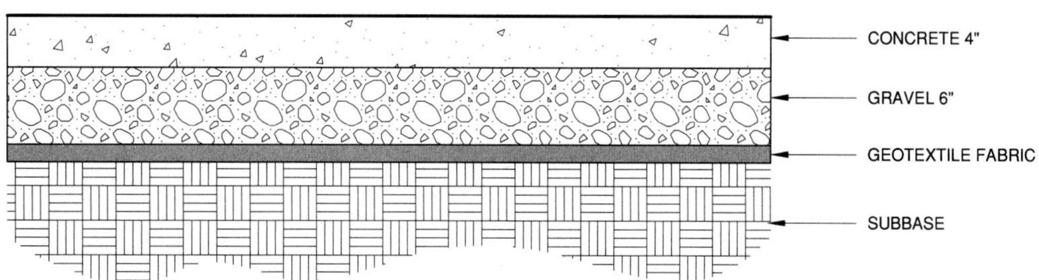

The geotextile fabric is omitted in some specifications. Applicable local codes should be consulted in all cases for design dimensions and materials.

STANDARD SIDEWALK CROSS SECTION FOR MOST MUNICIPAL APPLICATIONS

Dr. Phillip J. Craul, Retired Senior Lecturer in Landscape Architecture, Graduate School of Design, Harvard University, and Emeritus Professor of Soil Science, SUNY-College of Environmental Science and Forestry, Syracuse, New York; Timothy A. Craul, President, Craul Land Scientists, PLC, State College, Pennsylvania

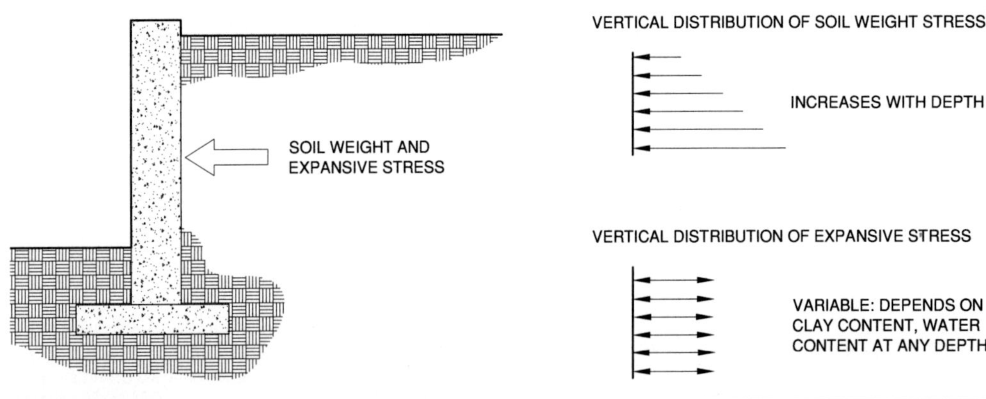

ILLUSTRATION OF EARTH PRESSURE FORCES ON A FOUNDATION WALL

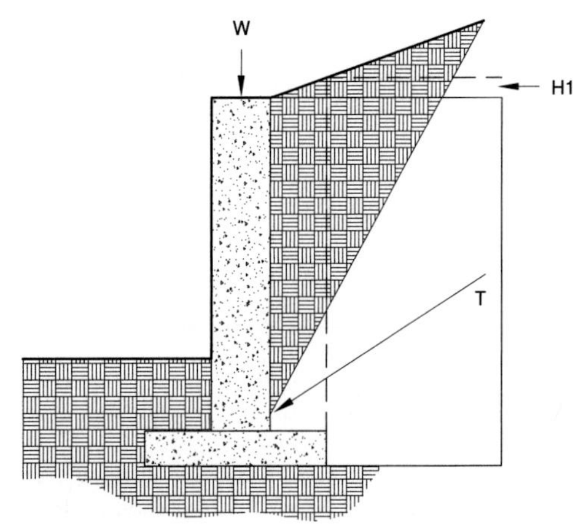

CANTILEVERED WALL WITH SURCHARGE

Retaining Walls

Usually, the height of retaining walls on many landscape projects is less than 4 feet (1.2 meters approximate) high, and the earth pressure of soil behind them is usually limited from an engineering standpoint. However, design principles must be followed to prevent failure of even these low walls. For walls greater in height than this limit, a geotechnical engineer should be consulted.

Failure of retaining walls is due to three forces: settling, sliding, and overturning. These are illustrated in the figure "Three Forces that Potentially Cause Failure in Retaining Walls." The weight of the wall presses on the ground beneath itDepending on the soil strength, settlement will occur. If the soil is compacted or strengthened by gravel or a solid foundation, settlement may be prevented.

The earth pressure or thrust against the wall can cause sliding of the wall if the wall does not have sufficient weight. The wall should extend into the earth or have a cantilevered foundation for anchoring. If the thrust of the retained soil exceeds the resistant force of the wall, including the foundation, especially if retaining a slope, overturning occurs.

Calculations are available to check design strength of a retaining wall, as follows:

1. The angle of repose of the soil can safely be assumed to be 33°. Only the soil above the angle of repose exerts thrust on the wall. When there is sloping soil behind the wall (surcharge), the thrust angle is parallel to the slope rather than horizontal.
2. Thrust may be calculated for three wall situations:

   a. Gravity (without foundation) or cantilever wall without surcharge:

   $$T = 0.286\ (S \times H^2/2)$$

   where S = soil weight, typically 100 lbs/ft^3 (k/m^3), and H = wall height

   b. Gravity wall with surcharge:

   $$T = 0.833\ (S \times H^2/2)$$

   c. Cantilever wall with surcharge:

   $$T = 0.833\ (S \times [H + H^1]^2)/2$$

   where H1 is the height added to the soil for the surcharge and the offset is equal to the length of the cantilever as shown in the figure "Cantilevered Wall with Surcharge."

3. To prevent settling, the soil-bearing value must be greater than the vertical force or weight of the wall. Using a safety factor of 1.5:

   Soil-bearing value ≥ 1.5 (wall weight/unit area)

4. To prevent sliding, the weight of the wall is multiplied by the coefficient of soil friction. The coefficients vary with the soil, between 0.3 for wet clay and 0.6 for gravel. The value of 1.5 is normally used as a safety factor in the calculations:

   $$W(\text{coef. friction}) \geq 1.5T$$

5. The overturning moment is T(H/3). A safety factor of 2.0 is used in the calculation:

   $$M_R \geq 2(M_O)$$

In the figures "Cross Section for Concrete Retaining Wall with Vertical Sand Layer" and "Cross Section for Gabion Wall," the walls illustrated would be designed by a geotechnical engineer since they would be employed for walls greater than 4 feet (1.2 m). However, the principles involved apply to shorter walls, as well, but perhaps less critically. Built-in

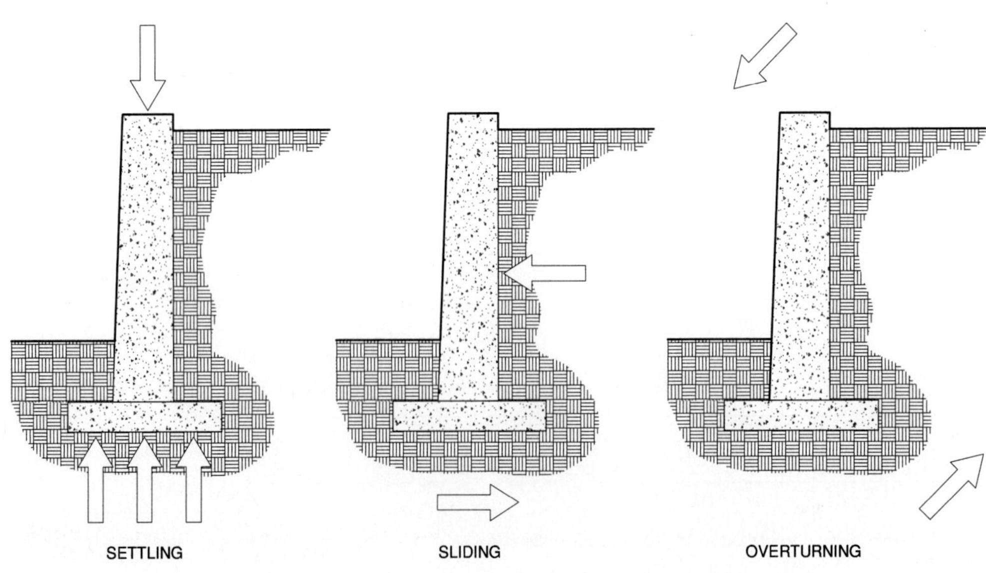

THREE FORCES THAT POTENTIALLY CAUSE FAILURE IN RETAINING WALLS

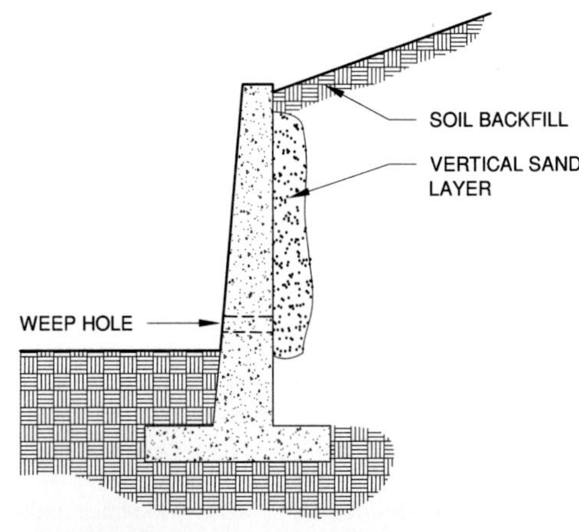

CROSS SECTION FOR CONCRETE RETAINING WALL WITH VERTICAL SAND LAYER

Source: Redrawn from Forrester, 2001.

Dr. Phillip J. Craul, Retired Senior Lecturer in Landscape Architecture, Graduate School of Design, Harvard University, and Emeritus Professor of Soil Science, SUNY-College of Environmental Science and Forestry, Syracuse, New York; Timothy A. Craul, President, Craul Land Scientists, PLC, State College, Pennsylvania

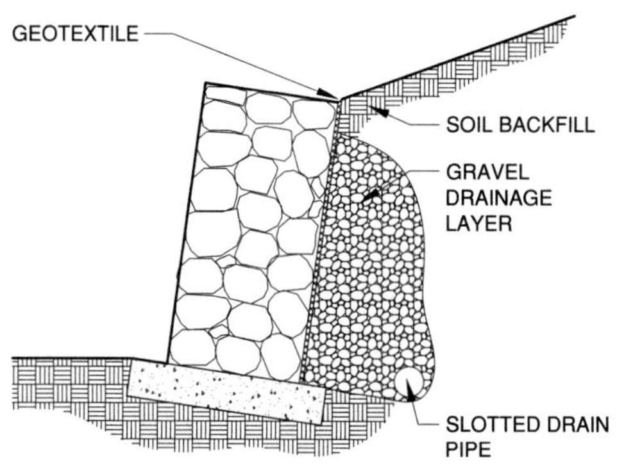

CROSS SECTION FOR GABION WALL

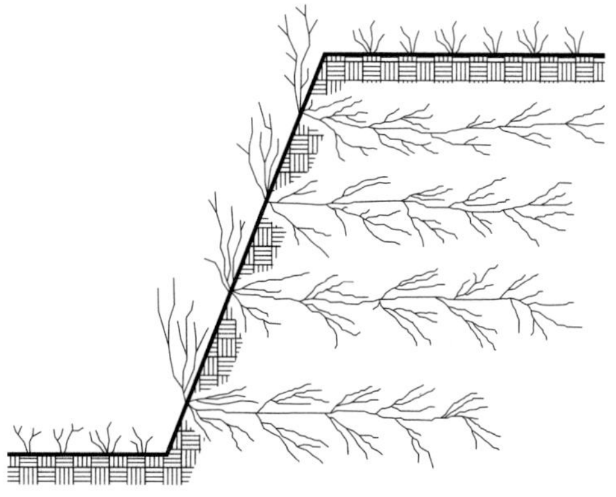

VEGETATIVE RETAINING WALL

safety factors by manufacturers of formed concrete block walls protect homeowners.

The gabion wall may be stepped using several gabion units over the height. The steps then become sites for planting vegetation in placed soil, especially hanging vines or long-leaved grasses that may improve the aesthetics of the wall. An open stone retaining wall receives the same treatment as the gabion wall. Retaining walls 2 feet (0.62m) or less usually do not require drainage.

Geotextile Wall

The use of geotextile fabric as reinforcement for walls has advanced rapidly since the 1960s. Geotextile wrap around a selected soil arranged in lifts offers a less expensive method, as compared to a wall of building materials. The angle of friction, texture, and density of the soil used within the wraps, hence its stability, must be considered; it may not necessarily be the soil retained by the wall. Obviously, the geotextile fabric is exposed as the wall surface. One of the clear advantages is that deformation can occur without failure.

So many different products are presently marketed that all cases cannot be covered here, including appropriate calculations. The landscape architect should investigate in detail all manufacturer information and testing results related to the selected product.

Vegetative Wall

Use of living vegetation may substitute for the geotextile, especially where the aesthetics of the wall surface is an important element to the landscape design. Thick, heavy grass sod in appropriate lengths may be used successfully as a wrap; however, the wall requires periodic watering and trimming for good appearance and is not recommended for arid climates.

Vegetation roots may develop a supporting fabric 0.1 to 1 meter in the upper layer. The strength of the roots adds to the soil stability of the slope. For example, *Salix* spp. roots have tearing force resistance of 16 to 18 MPa, about the same as bearded wheat (*Agropyron repens*); and for common agricultural alfalfa (*Medicago sativa*) roots, the value is 46 MPa. The roots are planted horizontally within the wall.

The grasses and smaller vegetation with very fibrous root systems perform better as stabilizers than trees. The increasing weight as the trees mature will decrease the stability of the wall, offsetting the stability provided by their roots.

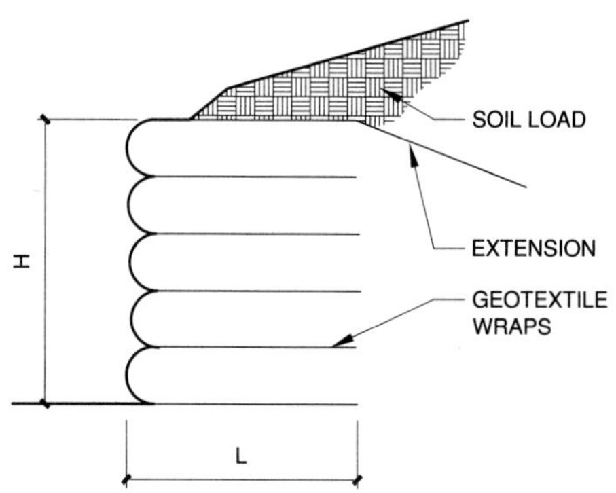

The relation L/H must be greater than 0.15 to prevent collapse.

GEOTEXTILE WRAP WALL

Source: Redrawn from Pálossy, et al., 1993.

SOIL STABILITY ON SLOPES

There are cases where a landscape design is superimposed on an existing natural sloping landscape with portions taking advantage of the natural topography. A good example of a planting on steep slopes is the tree plantings on the hill slopes surrounding the J. Paul Getty Fine Arts Center, in Los Angeles, California, where intensive soil stabilization was required (Meier, 1997). An important consideration in planting on a slope is the stability of the slope initially and after the planting is carried out. Therefore, it is appropriate to first discuss the fundamentals of slope stability and apply that information to common landscape planting situations.

Fundamentals of Slope Stability

The stability of soil on slopes is more complex than on level terrain, as a third plane of stress parallel to the slope is now added to the analysis. The estimation of soil strength and slope stability has many engineering applications and is one facet of soil mechanics (or geotechnical engineering) with which landscape architects should have some familiarity. It is very important to soil scientists, who receive training in the subject, since it has many applications to understanding the natural landscape.

It is appropriate to discuss the basic concepts here so that the landscape architect or contractor will be able appreciate the necessity for care in planting on slopes where it has been determined that slope stability could be a problem. This topic is pursued in all phases of the design and construction processes.

Expression of Slope

First, how may slope be properly expressed? There are three common forms to express slope. One is as a ratio in linear units: For example, over a horizontal distance of 1 foot there is a rise or fall of 1 foot, thus 1:1. The second form is in degrees of slope above or below the horizontal, such as 45 degrees; this slope is equivalent to the 1:1 ratio. The third form is percent slope expressed as the number of feet in rise or fall from the horizontal over a distance of 100 feet.

The usual engineering standard specified for many construction projects is a 2:1 slope, since it is stable for most soil materials and applications. Besides slope ratio, slope in degrees is most frequently used by geotechnical engineers, surveyors, meteorologists, and hydrologists who must use terrain angles in degrees to conform to angles of aspect (compass direction) and solar angles. Foresters, soil scientists, and road engineers most often employ the slope percent expression.

One of the most fundamental facts of slope stabilization is that the slope absolutely must be stable in the engineering sense (that is, at a depth much deeper than the average soil depth itself) before it is stabilized by vegetative cover. The latter only stabilizes the soil at the surface down to rooting depth, and then only if the vegetation is sufficiently dense. The weight of vegetation, especially large trees, actually increases the instability component of the slope, unless the root systems intertwine sufficiently and grow to adequate depth to offset the instability due to weight, in addition to the existing degree of engineering stability. Many people have the misconception that vegetation alone can stabilize a slope. This concept is true only if the slope itself is totally stabilized, with or without vegetation.

Slope Stability and Earth Excavations

OSHA regulations require that any earthen excavation greater than 5 feet in depth, in which workers are required to perform their duties, must have walls stepped to a 1:1 ratio, or that temporary safety bunkers must be installed This regulation applies as well to any exploratory soil excavation. (Check the regulations frequently as they undergo constant revision and amendment.) Graphic details for this class of excavation should be provided in all drawings.

Usually, the geotechnical engineer is responsible for this activity on large projects, but smaller landscape architect firms must be aware of this requirement and take appropriate action when necessary.

Placement of Soil on Slopes

Soil placement on a slope requires greater planning, preparation, and care with installation than on level

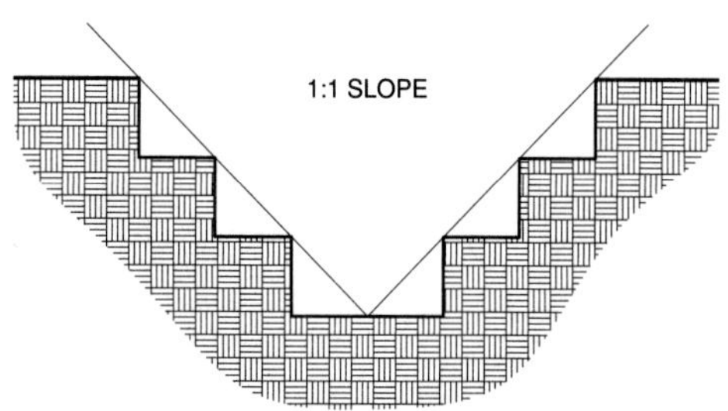

WALL SLOPE OR STEPS FOR EARTHEN EXCAVATIONS 5 FEET OR DEEPER IN COHESIVE SOILS

Source: OSHA Regulations, 2001.

Dr. Phillip J. Craul, Retired Senior Lecturer in Landscape Architecture, Graduate School of Design, Harvard University, and Emeritus Professor of Soil Science, SUNY-College of Environmental Science and Forestry, Syracuse, New York; Timothy A. Craul, President, Craul Land Scientists, PLC, State College, Pennsylvania

terrain. Compaction of the lifts by placement equipment during installation increases slope stability; but, again, soil should not be overcompacted for the sake of plant rooting ease. Slope length generally should be less than 50 feet unless it is well-engineered as a long slope. Stepping of the subbase should be considered in the design, especially on longer slopes. Soil blown onto the slope does not accomplish this effect; fiber stabilizer should be added to the mix.

Terracing should be considered when shortening of the slope base is required, while maintaining a safe slope angle, and/or when some level area is desired for planting as part of an overall design. Terracing is usually more expensive when executed properly.

The height of the walls and the spacing between the walls are critical design features. The simplest and safest design is to have all the walls of uniform height and spacing. Obviously, where space is limited, some designs may require the lowest or bottom wall to be the tallest and most substantial. These latter designs require the services of a geotechnical engineer.

The simplest design is to space the walls at a distance equal to or greater than the intersection of the soil angle of repose with the horizontal surface of the retained terrace. The angle of soil repose is usually assumed to be 33°. Closer spacing puts greater thrust on the lower wall, requiring greater geotechnical engineering design.

Soil Stabilization on Slopes

In some applications of soil on slopes, it is desirable to stabilize the soilmechanically. There are several techniques to stabilize soil on slopes to prevent erosion. The three most common ones are:

- Hemp matting or woven netting placed on the surface and tacked to the soil with pins.
- A tackifier (a "glue" compound) added to the soil, usually the organic matter or sometimes the topsoil, to stabilize the surface. These materials are effective in stabilizing the soil until vegetation has established itself.
- Mixing fibers (sometimes called "strings") in the soil, then compacting the soil for effectiveness. One product is a plastic ribbon ¼ inch wide and 5 inches long. The danger is that the additional compactive effort may be excessive for plant root penetration.

With so many products on the market, it is best to consult manufacturer specifications and recommended procedures for application and choose the technique that best meets the requirements of the site and design.

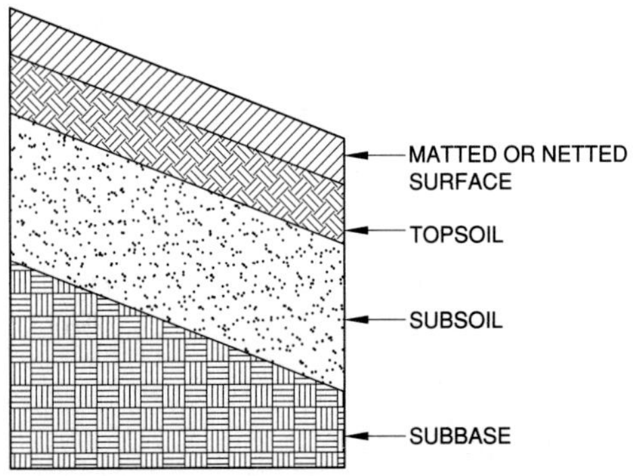

SLOPE WITH SURFACE MATTING

Vegetation and Slope Stability

Arbitrarily planting vegetation, especially trees, without attention to slope stability can potentially lead to slope failure and claims for damage as shown in the figure "Slope Classification Scheme Based on Tree Root Reinforcement and Anchoring."

- Type A slopes have a thin soil mantle, which is stabilized by the proliferation of the tree roots, but the bedrock is not penetrated by the roots. A plane of weakness then exists at the bedrock surface. In this case, the trees have little effect on slope stability.
- Type B slopes are similar to Type A but differ in that the roots are able to penetrate a fragmented or loose bedrock, thus anchoring the thin soil mantle to the bedrock surface. The trees have a significant effect on increasing slope stability.
- Type C slopes have thicker soil profiles with a transitional layer (dashed line in the figure "Terracing of Soil and Stepping of the Subbase on Long Slopes"), wherein the soil density and shear strength increase with depth. Since the roots penetrate this layer, slope stability is increased.
- Type D slopes have very thick soil mantles above the bedrock. The roots may not penetrate completely to the bedrock, and the trees and soil are actually "floating" on the slope. There is little mechanical influence on slope stability. This latter case is common in many landslide-prone areas of California.

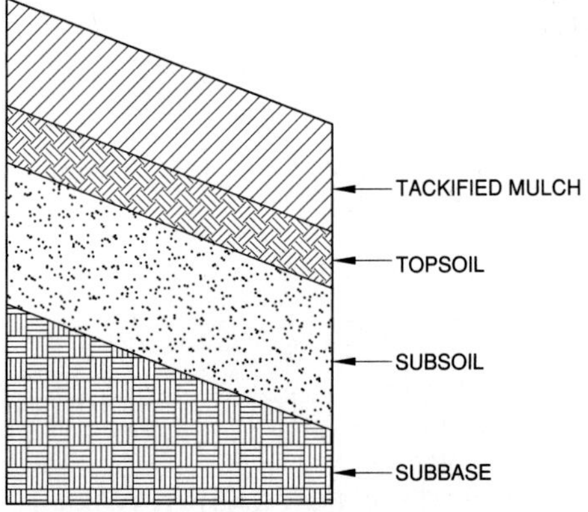

SLOPE WITH SOIL TREATED WITH TACKIFIER

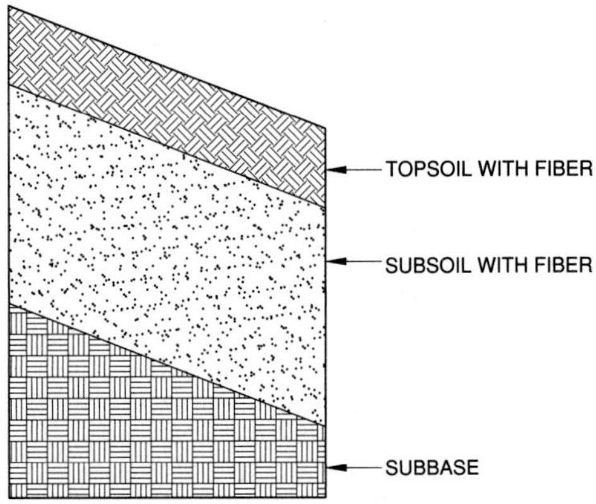

SLOPE WITH FIBER OR STRING STABILIZER

Thus, Types B and C are the most stable situations. Type D is stable only when underlain by very stable soil. Type A is the most hazardous.

Planting of Trees on Slopes

Trees planted on 2:1 slopes, or less sloping, usually do not require special treatment in planting specifications different from those for level terrain. Only in the case of a sloping high water table caused by seep is protection required. A curtain (interceptor) drain may be required in this case.

Trees planted on slopes steeper than 2:1 may have counteracting effects on the slope stability. Even on long 2:1 slopes, care must be exercised. Therefore, special geotechnical specifications are required. One direct solution is to terrace the slope and plant the trees on the level terraces. Obviously, the weight of the tree must become part of the thrust on the retaining wall and the tree roots must be able to be anchored into the stable subbase.

Long Slope Application

There are some instances where very long 2:1 or 3:1 slopes must be created, such as for application to the covering of very large landfills or large cuts and fills for interstate highways. Though the slope grade is relatively stable, the long slope length creates some

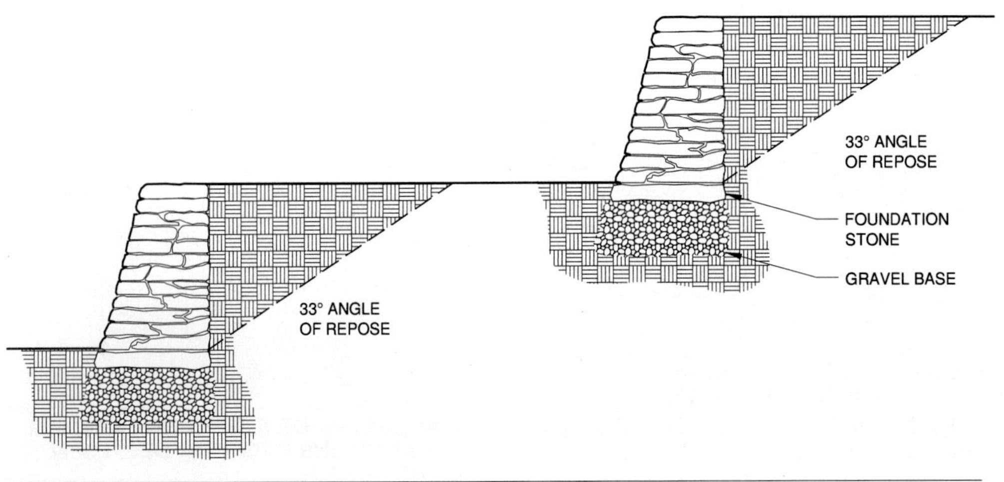

DESIGN OF SIMPLE TERRACES

Dr. Phillip J. Craul, Retired Senior Lecturer in Landscape Architecture, Graduate School of Design, Harvard University, and Emeritus Professor of Soil Science, SUNY-College of Environmental Science and Forestry, Syracuse, New York; Timothy A. Craul, President, Craul Land Scientists, PLC, State College, Pennsylvania

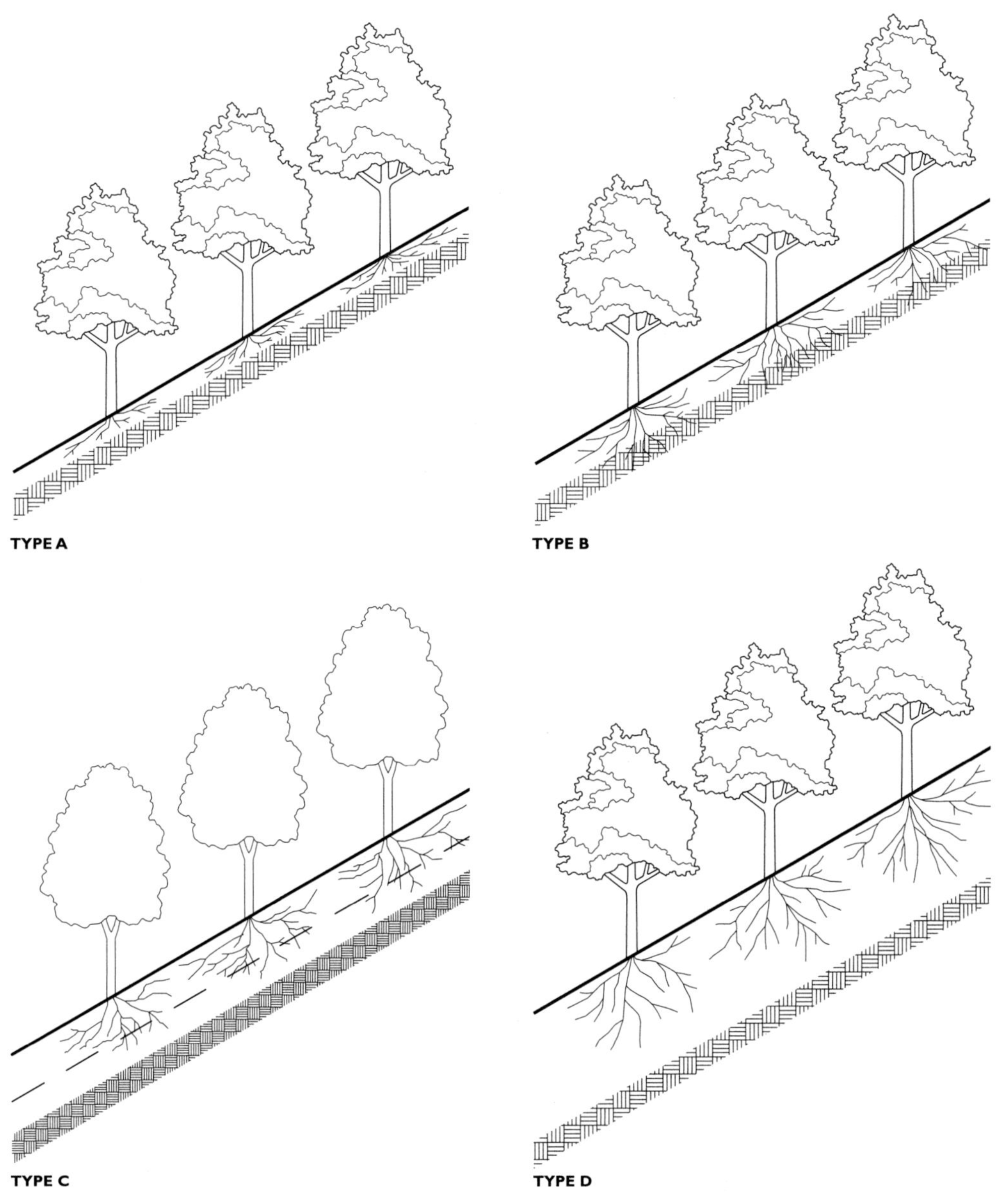

SLOPE CLASSIFICATION SCHEME BASED ON TREE ROOT REINFORCEMENT AND ANCHORING

Source: Tsukamoto and Kusakabe, 1984. Redrawn from Greenway, 1987, from Craul and Craul, 2006.

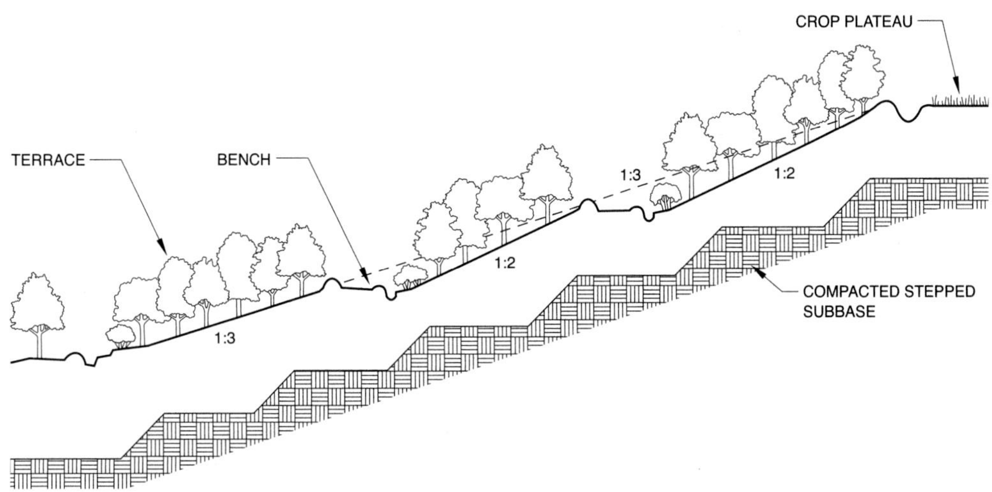

TERRACING OF SOIL AND STEPPING OF THE SUBBASE ON LONG SLOPES

Dr. Phillip J. Craul, Retired Senior Lecturer in Landscape Architecture, Graduate School of Design, Harvard University, and Emeritus Professor of Soil Science, SUNY-College of Environmental Science and Forestry, Syracuse, New York; Timothy A. Craul, President, Craul Land Scientists, PLC, State College, Pennsylvania

surface instability (slumping and creep) problems. The covering vegetation is normally restricted to grass and legume plants on landfills, and trees may be appropriate in other applications.

Because these are highly engineered cases, they must be designed by a professional geotechnical engineer. However, a landscape architect is usually involved in the planting design and installation. By being aware of the geotechnical constraints, and with close collaboration with the geotechnical engineer, the landscape architect can complete the project in a professional, safe, and successful manner.

REFERENCES

Anderson, M. G., and K. S. Richards. 1987. *Slope Stability: Geotechnical Engineering and Geomorphology.* Chichester, England: John Wiley & Sons, Inc.

Atkinson, J. H. 1981. *Foundations and Slopes: An Introduction to Applications of Critical State Soil Mechanics.* New York: John Wiley & Sons, Inc.

Craul, P. J. 1992. *Urban Soil in Landscape Design.* New York: John Wiley & Sons, Inc.

———. 1999. *Urban Soils: Applications and Practices.* New York: John Wiley & Sons, Inc.

Craul, T. A., and P. J. Craul. 2006. *Soil Design Protocols for Landscape Architects and Contractors.* Hoboken, NJ: John Wiley & Sons, Inc.

Cutler, D. F., and I. B. K. Richardson. 1981. *Tree Roots and Buildings.* London: Construction Press.

Fortlage, C. A., and E. T. Phillips. 2001. *Landscape Construction,* vol. 3. Earth and Water Retaining Structures. Aldershot. England: Ashgate

Forrester, Kevin. 2001. *Subsurface Drainage for Slope Stabilization.* American Society of Civil Engineers Press, Reston, Virginia.

Greenway, D. R. 1987. "Vegetation and Slope Stability." In M. G. Anderson and K. S. Richards (eds). *Slope Stability: Geotechnical Engineering and Geomorphology.* Chichester, England: John Wiley & Sons, Inc.

Hillel, D. 1980. *The Fundamentals of Soil Physics.* New York: Academic Press.

Holtz, R. D., and W. D. Kovacs. 1981. *An Introduction to Geotechnical Engineering.* Englewood Cliffs, NJ: Prentice Hall.

Meier, Richard. 1997. *Building the Getty.* New York: Alfred A. Knopf.

Packard, R. T. (ed.). 1981. *Ramsey/Sleeper Architectural Graphic Standards,* 7th ed. New York: John Wiley & Sons, Inc.

Pálossy, L., P. Scharle, and I. Szalatkay. 1993. *Earth Walls.* New York: Ellis Horwood.

United States Department of Agriculture-Soil Conservation Service. 1973. "Drainage of Agricultural Land." In *National Engineering Handbook,* section 16. Port Washington, NY: Water Information Center.

See also:
Cut and Fill Calculations
Freestanding and Retaining Walls
Site Grading and Earthwork
Soil Erosion and Sediment Control
Soils: Agronomic
Stormwater Management

EMBANKMENT STABILIZATION

GENERAL

Embankment stabilization is required when steep slopes are subject to erosion from stormwater runoff or flowing streams. Erosion can damage the site and pollute waterways with sediment.

The need for mechanical stabilization can be reduced through careful site gradings that divert or slow the velocity of runoff. Avoid disturbing stable, natural stream banks. Check with regulatory agencies before planning to grade stream banks, wetlands, or floodplains.

Numerous proprietary products are available for stream bank stabilization and erosion control; consult manufacturers.

Notes

- Control erosion during construction with silt fences, straw bales, sediment ponds, and seeding and mulching. Follow local and state guidelines and regulations.
- Line channels with erosion-resistant material (sod, stone riprap, erosion-control blanket). Channel dimensions and lining should be designed for expected runoff.
- At the bottom of the slope drain channel, the flow should be conveyed to a storm sewer, detention pond, constructed wetland, or other control method that meets regulations.

STORMWATER RUNOFF
SLOPE DRAIN CHANNEL LINED WITH EROSION-RESISTANT MATERIAL
SEED AND MULCH OR COVER HILL SIDE WITH EROSION-CONTROL BLANKET
CONVEY TO STORMWATER CONTROL FEATURE
SLOPE DOWN
3
1
2
1
DIVERSION OF RUNOFF AT TOP OF SLOPE DIRECTS WATER TO DRAIN CHANNEL
STEEPEST SLOPE FOR MOWING
STEEPEST SLOPE WITHOUT STRUCTURAL SUPPORT (VARIES WITH LOCAL CONDITIONS)
TERRACE OR BENCH LONG SLOPES TO SLOW RUNOFF

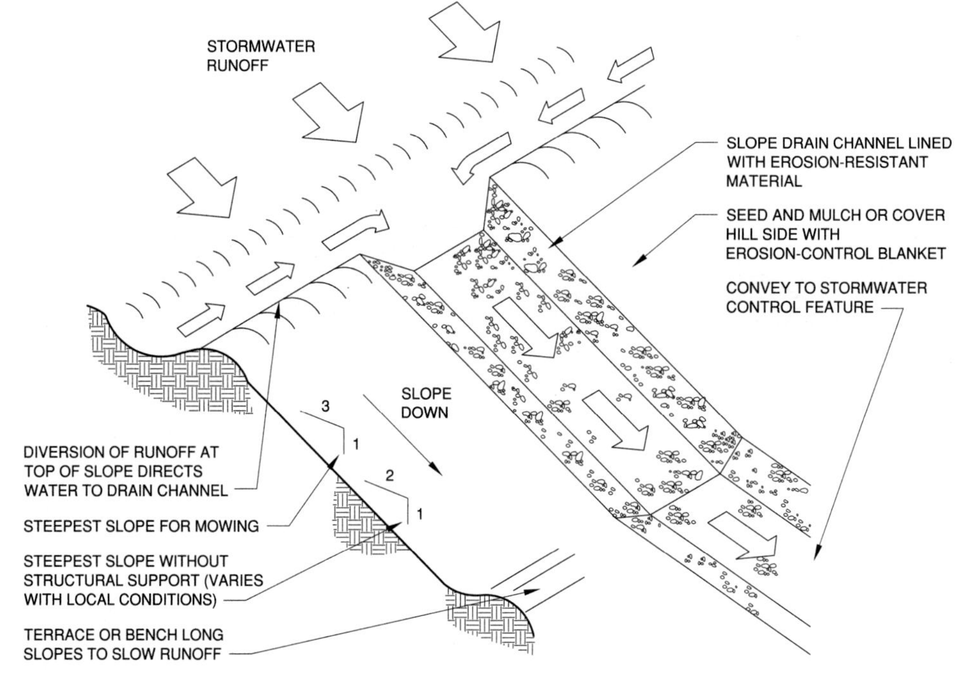

GRADING AND EROSION CONTROL

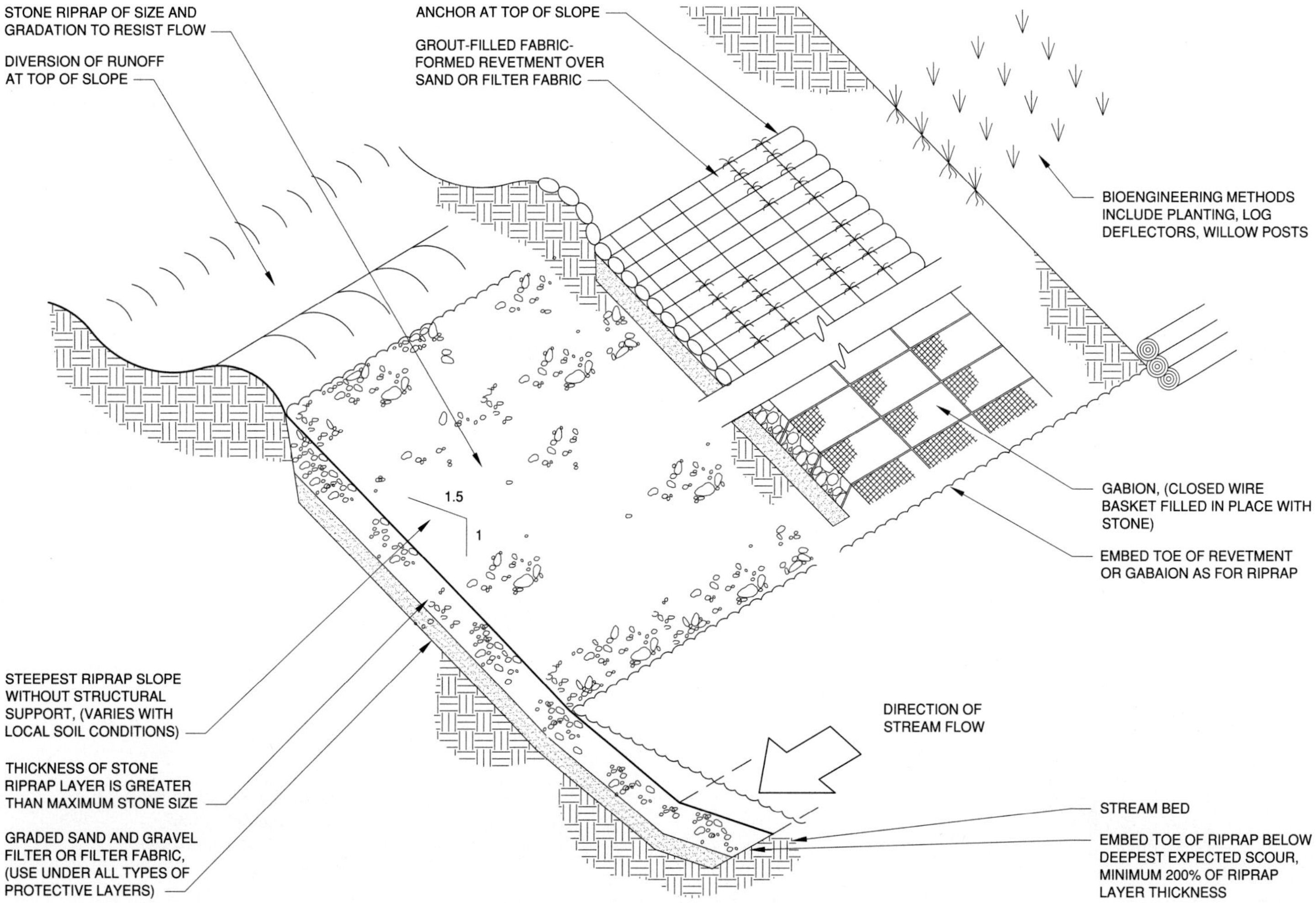

STONE RIPRAP OF SIZE AND GRADATION TO RESIST FLOW
DIVERSION OF RUNOFF AT TOP OF SLOPE
ANCHOR AT TOP OF SLOPE
GROUT-FILLED FABRIC-FORMED REVETMENT OVER SAND OR FILTER FABRIC
BIOENGINEERING METHODS INCLUDE PLANTING, LOG DEFLECTORS, WILLOW POSTS
1.5
1
GABION, (CLOSED WIRE BASKET FILLED IN PLACE WITH STONE)
EMBED TOE OF REVETMENT OR GABAION AS FOR RIPRAP
STEEPEST RIPRAP SLOPE WITHOUT STRUCTURAL SUPPORT, (VARIES WITH LOCAL SOIL CONDITIONS)
THICKNESS OF STONE RIPRAP LAYER IS GREATER THAN MAXIMUM STONE SIZE
GRADED SAND AND GRAVEL FILTER OR FILTER FABRIC, (USE UNDER ALL TYPES OF PROTECTIVE LAYERS)
DIRECTION OF STREAM FLOW
STREAM BED
EMBED TOE OF RIPRAP BELOW DEEPEST EXPECTED SCOUR, MINIMUM 200% OF RIPRAP LAYER THICKNESS

STREAM BANK STABILIZATION

James E. Sekela, P.E., Pittsburgh, Pennsylvania

SITE GRADING AND EARTHWORK

INTRODUCTION

Through the process of grading and earthwork, the designer adapts a building program from a two-dimensional drawing board to the dynamics of an actual site. Through skillful grading, the designer directs drainage away from buildings and controls runoff from leaving the site and adversely affecting the environment. He or she creates level areas for intensive use, such as parking lots and playing fields. In addition to accommodating the functional requirements of the program, the designer may add to the experience of visiting the site by screening out undesirable views and capitalizing on dramatic vistas. He or she may also manipulate the landforms to protect users from adverse elements such as wind and noise.

Of all the disciplines trained in the manipulation of landform, landscape architecture is the one best suited to address all the implications of both functional and aesthetic concerns. An accepted land ethic in the profession is that it is desirable to attempt to design and grade a site so that, when finished, it looks as though we have never been there before.

The landforms should blend so integrally that, on observation, there is no conscious awareness of intervention. If the proposed contours are rounded in section, they represent the natural, softening effects of erosion and weathering on the landscape through time. The connection to existing grade creates a fluid, seamless line.

In a situation such as a cut bank, it is often a wiser decision to sacrifice trees at the top of the bank and make a smooth grade transition than to create a steeper cut and a harsh section line, which is subject to significant washing, erosion, and maintenance problems.

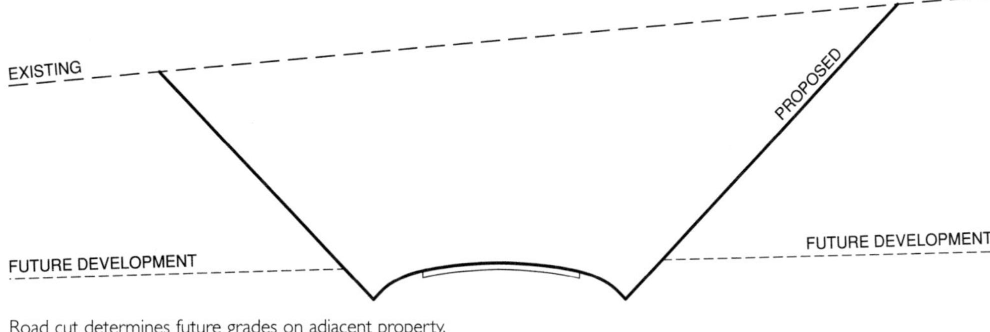

Road cut determines future grades on adjacent property.

ROAD CUT—POSSIBLE NEGATIVE IMPACTS

Road cut with consideration for future land use.

ROAD CUT—WORKING WITH THE LAND

It is also important to consider that in establishing the grade of a roadbed, all future elevations for the adjacent land are determined. Because the properties will require access to the road, the extent of their potential cut and fill should be weighed from the outset.

AESTHETICS

Grading plans should be viewed as opportunities to accomplish design objectives, as well as functional requirements. The experience of a site may be enhanced by changing the position of the observer to the horizon line, as well as by altering his or her perception of distance and scale. A sense of enclosure may be created with landform, followed by an expansive opening to a larger landscape. The awareness of a repeating pattern may be created with terracing or berming. Undesirable views can be screened by landform, especially in combination with plantings.

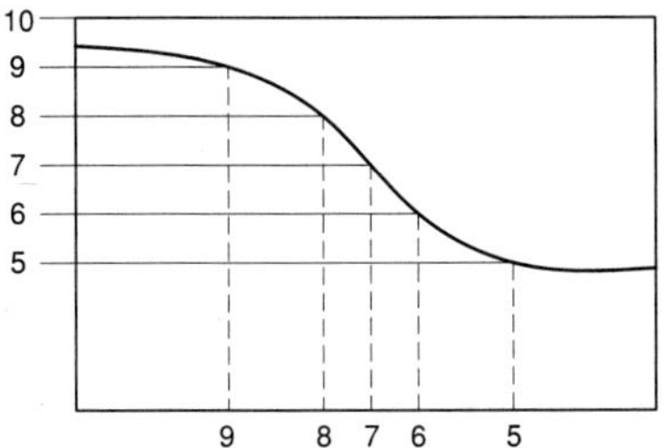

FLUID CURVE

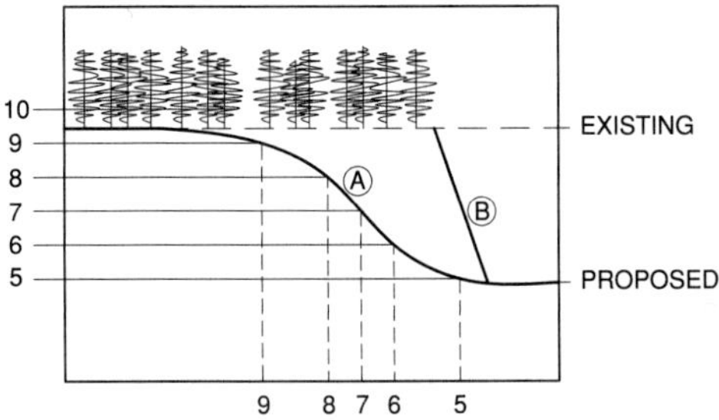

(a) Preferred smooth alignment; (b) unstable slope.

CUT BANK CONDITIONS

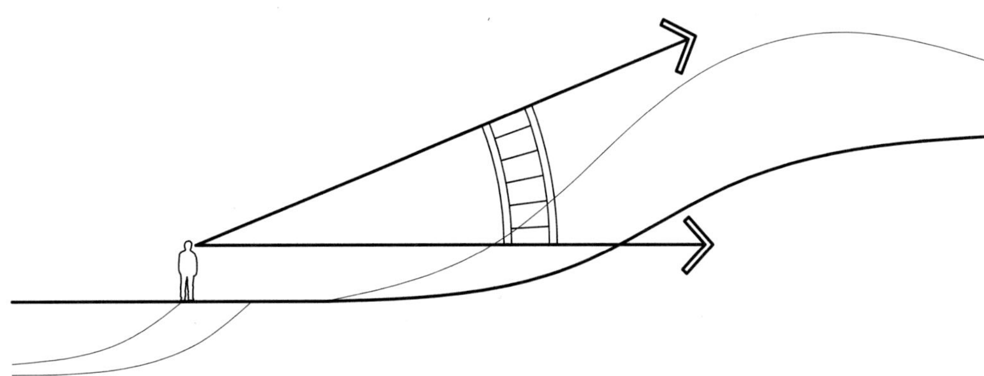

VIEW DIRECTING THE EYE UPWARD

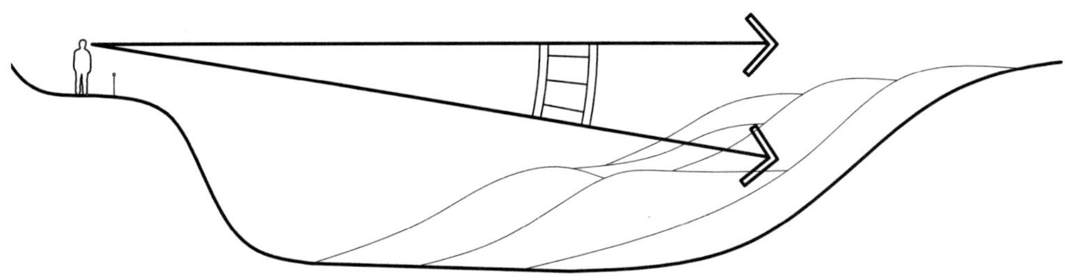

VIEW DRAWING THE EYE BELOW THE HORIZON LINE

Sarah Georgia Harrison, ASLA, Assistant Professor, School of Environmental Design, University of Georgia

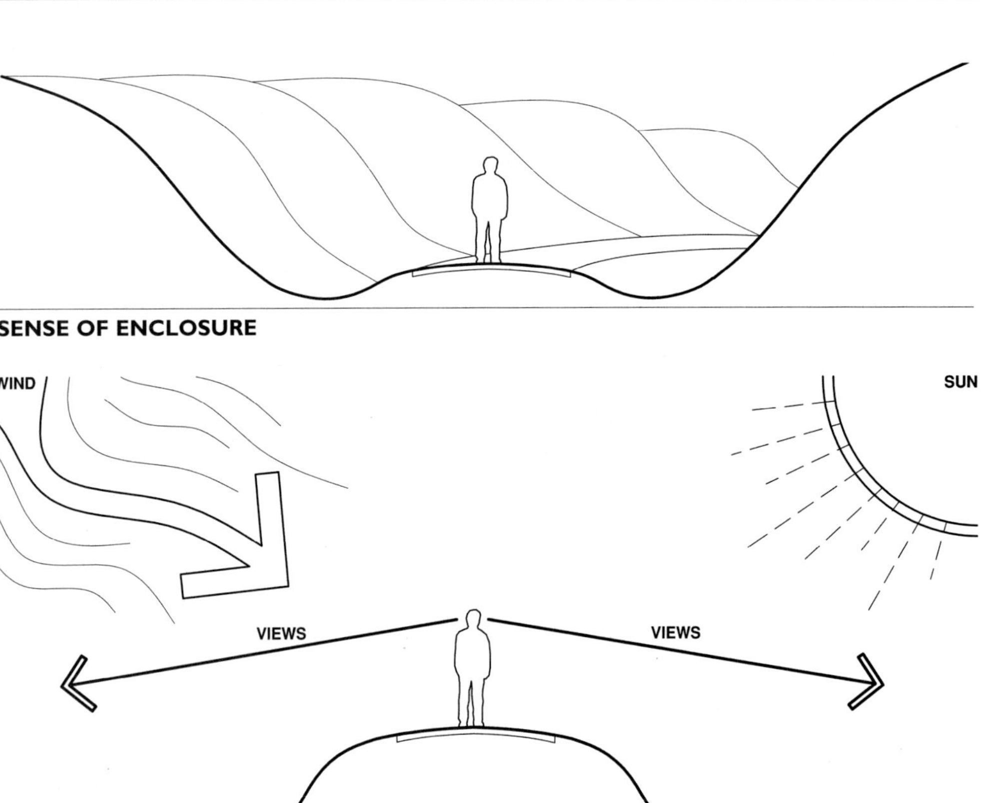

SENSE OF ENCLOSURE

SENSE OF EXPOSURE/ISOLATION

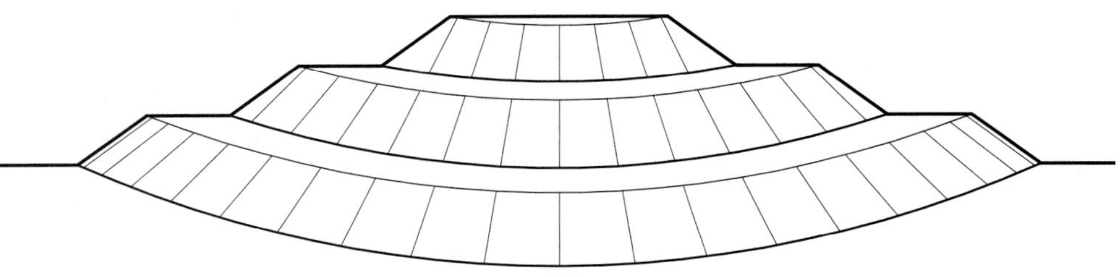

TERRACING

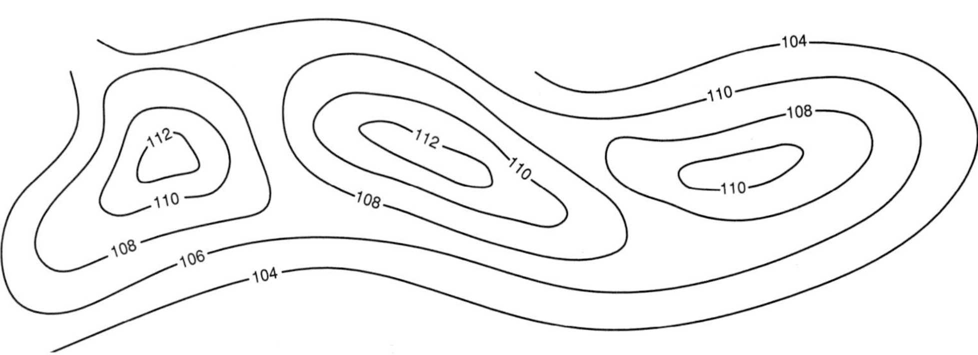

BERM WITH "PEAKS" TO MIMIC MOUNTAIN RANGE

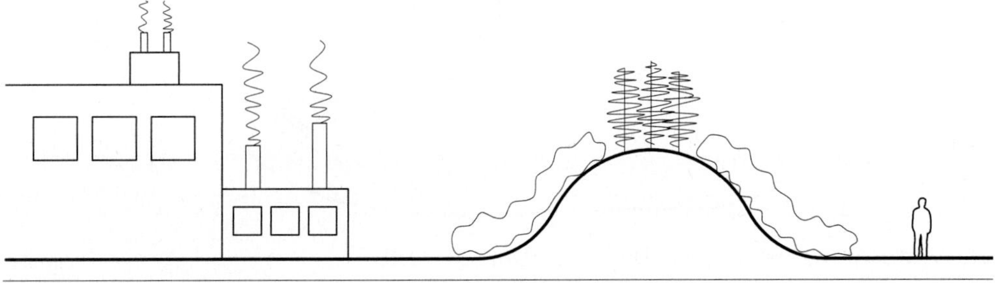

BERMS FOR SCREENING

CONTOURS

Topographic changes in the landscape are represented on two-dimensional maps using the convention of contours. A contour is a horizontal plane slicing through the earth at a constant elevation above sea level or some other known reference elevation. A contour line, as illustrated on a topographic map, represents the edge of the contour plane as it meets the surface of the landform. The shoreline of a pond best represents the image of how a contour's edge meets the surface. If the surface of the water represents the contour plane, and water seeks a constant elevation, then the water's edge on a still pond could be illustrated as a contour line. If after a few dry days in summer the water elevation drops, then the surface represents a new contour elevation, and the still-moist shoreline retains evidence of the higher elevation.

The contour interval, or the vertical distance between two contours, is always the same throughout an entire drawing. Intervals of 1, 2, 5, 10, 20, 50, 100, 500, and 1,000 are common. The smaller the interval, the greater the degree of accuracy on a map and the greater the number of contours represented. Selection of the interval is a function of the scale of the drawing, the steepness of the terrain, and the use intended for the property. A section drawn through several contours appears to represent a stacked configuration, but in reality, the change between contours represents a gradual transition, like the fluid landforms of the earth.

Like the shoreline of the pond, every contour is assumed to be a continuous line that closes on itself, somewhere on earth, even if it is not contained on the drawing. Contour lines never cross each other, except in an unusual circumstance, such as a natural bridge or overhanging cliff. Contour lines may appear to coincide, or stack, at vertical walls, but in axonometric view, the path of the lines becomes clear. Contours never split.

The steepest slope on a topographic map is where the contours are closest together. Because water flows downhill at the steepest slope, it will always flow perpendicular to the contour lines.

One of the trickier landforms to read is at a transition between an uphill and a downhill slope. If an elevation is crossed moving uphill, then when a downhill turn is made, the same elevation must be crossed again.

Sarah Georgia Harrison, ASLA, Assistant Professor, School of Environmental Design, University of Georgia

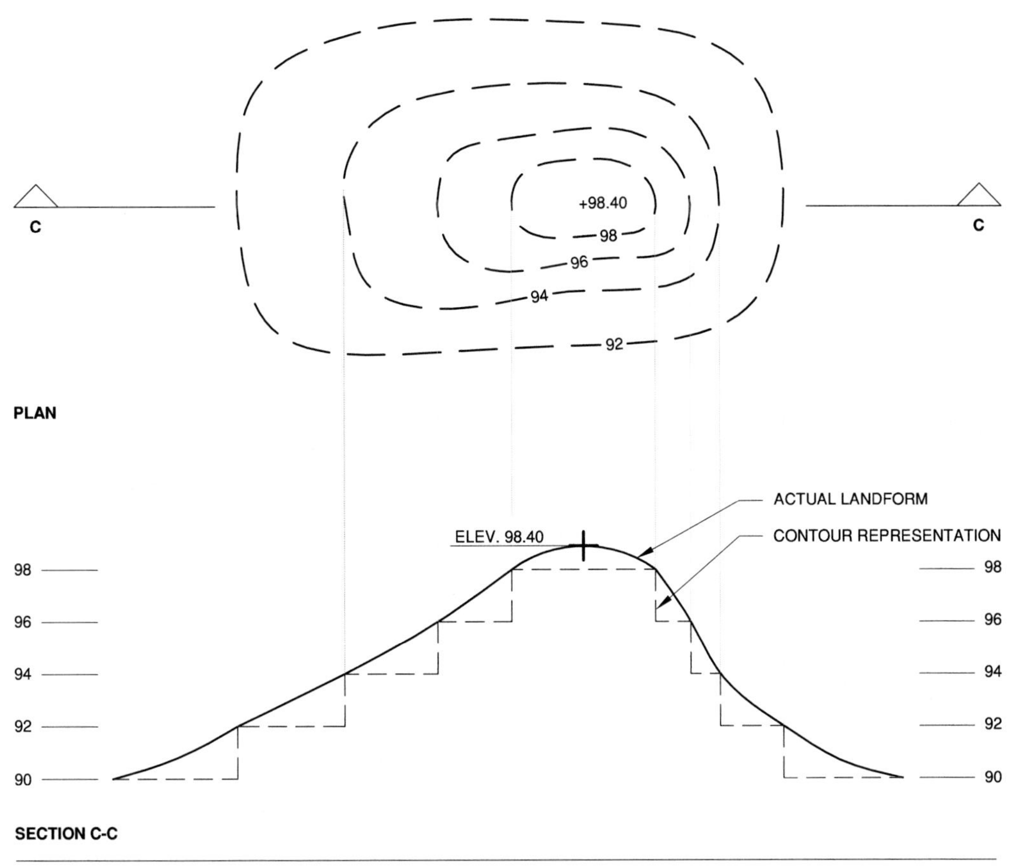

SECTION REPRESENTATION OF PLAN

SLOPES, GRADES, AND SPOT ELEVATIONS

Gradient refers to the changing elevation along the Earth's surface. The slope of a gradient, or the difference in elevation between two points over a given distance, is also defined as:

Slope = Rise/Run

(See "Slope Formula" figure.)

Another frequently used helpful designation is:

Gradient = Vertical Distance/Horizontal Distance
(G=V/H)

Memorizing the following inversions of this equation is also useful:

V=G x H
H=V/G

Gradients may be expressed as percentages, decimals, ratios, or angles. Percent slope is based on the rise or fall over a distance of 100 feet. The decimal equivalent for a 25 percent slope is 0.25. In a ratio, the horizontal dimension is traditionally given first, as in 4:1 (four to one). Ratios are often used when describing steeper slopes.

Slopes are sometimes expressed as an angle, relative to a horizontal line, or the interior angle in a right triangle. To solve for the angle, use the trigonometric formula shown in the figure "Solving for the Interior Angle."

The equivalencies are summarized in the table "Gradients."

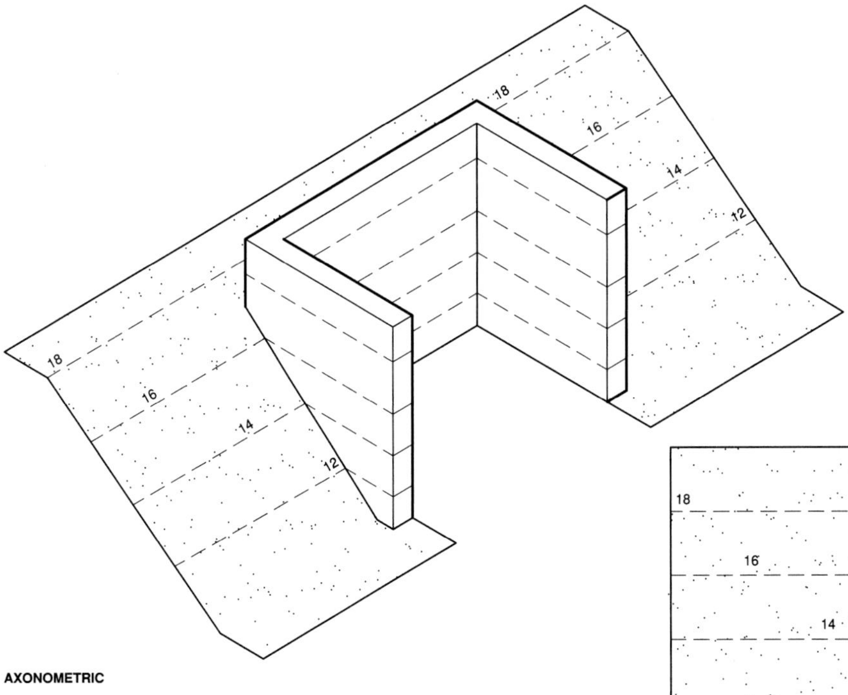

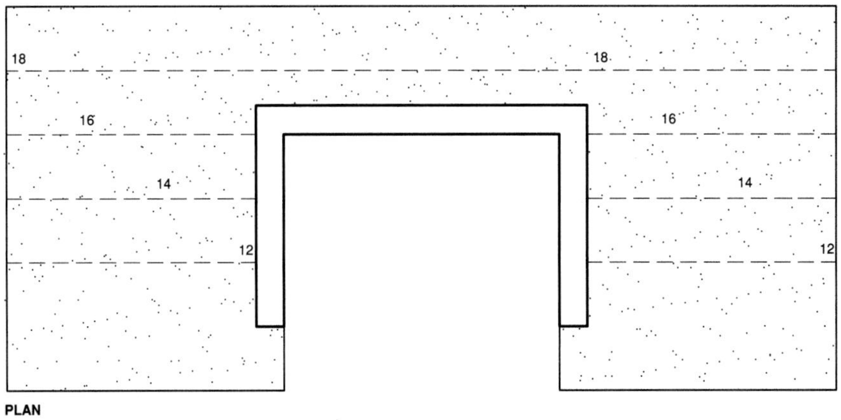

AXONOMETRIC

PLAN

CONTOURS APPEARING TO STACK AT VERTICAL WALL

Sarah Georgia Harrison, ASLA, Assistant Professor, School of Environmental Design, University of Georgia

PLAN

SECTION D-D

TRANSITION SLOPES

GRADIENTS

PERCENT SLOPES	DECIMALS	RATIOS	ANGLES
5%	0.05	20:1	2.86
10%	0.10	10:1	5.71
20%	0.20	5:1	11.31
25%	0.25	4:1	14.04
33.33%	0.3333	3:1	18.43
45%	0.45	2.22:1	24.25
50%	0.50	2:1	26.57
100%	1.00	1:1	45

In small-scale construction, such as when laying out a brick patio, contractors often refer to slopes in terms of inches per foot. A 2 percent slope is equivalent to ¼ inch per foot; a 1 percent slope is equivalent to ⅛ inch per foot. This allows for a greater degree of accuracy within subtle grade changes.

Grades on consistently sloping surfaces are identified on grading plans with small arrows, pointing downhill. Maximum and minimum ratios are identified on gradients of gradual or ever-changing slopes. Spot elevations represent exact elevations at key points, usually accurate to the hundredth's place. The highest and lowest elevations on a landform are usually designated with spot elevations.

Rougher surfaces require greater slope for positive drainage than smooth surfaces because the friction encountered can slow the speed of water and potentially result in surface ponding. Ponding on walkways can create a slipping hazard for pedestrians on a wet surface, which can be exacerbated with winter icing.

Surface texture can also affect the perception of slope. Coarser textures are less noticeable than smooth. As a general rule, slopes of 2 percent and above are clearly perceptible to the eye. Lesser slopes may be more visible if a contrasting horizontal line is adjacent.

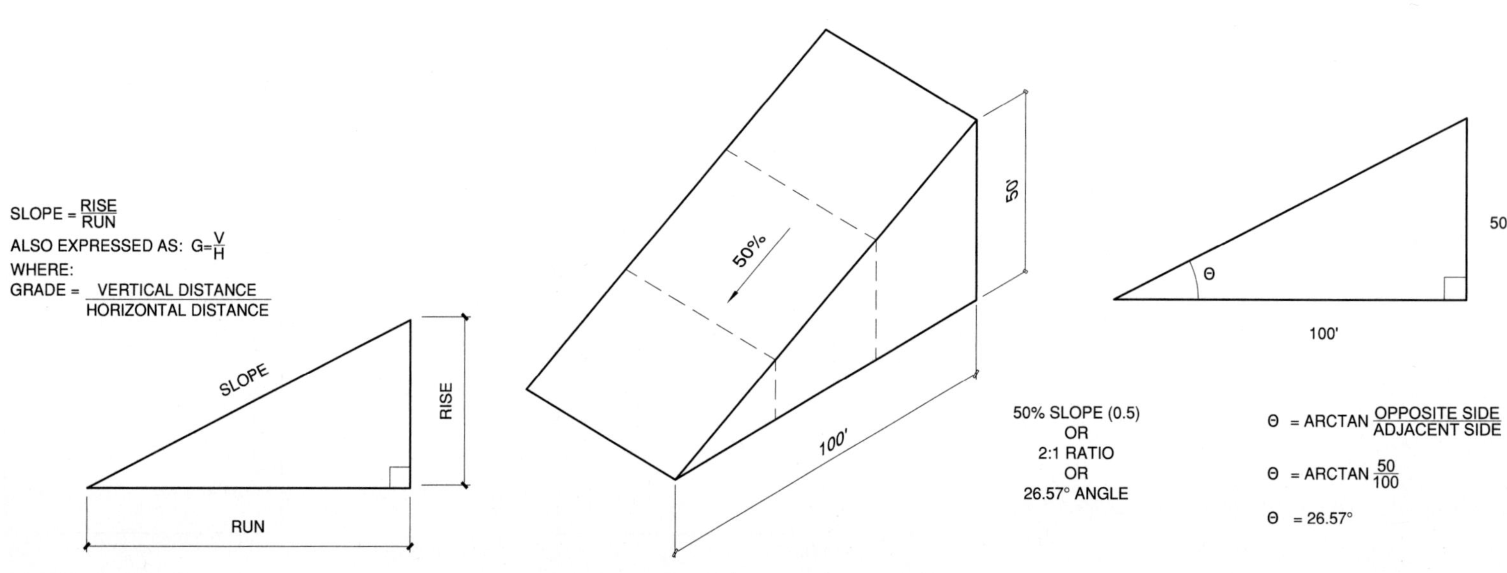

SLOPE FORMULA

SOLVING FOR THE INTERIOR ANGLE

Sarah Georgia Harrison, ASLA, Assistant Professor, School of Environmental Design, University of Georgia

GRADING STANDARDS

SURFACE	MAXIMUM	MINIMUM
Lawns and grass areas	33% (3:1)	2%
Unmowed slopes	50% (2:1)	2%
Athletic fields	2%	0.5%
Planted slopes	10%	0.5%
Berms	20%	5%
Plaza/patios (concrete)	2.5%	0.75%
Plaza/patios (brick, flagstone)	2.5%	1.5%
Side slopes of walks (concrete)	4%	1%
Longitudinal slope on walks (not ADA)	10%	0.75%
Longitudinal slope on streets	20%	1%
Longitudinal slope on driveways	20%	1%
Longitudinal slope on parking areas	5%	1%
Slope of road shoulders	15%	1%
Crown of streets	3%	1%
Side slopes of swales	10%	1%
Longitudinal slope of swales (grassed)	5%	1%
Side slope of ditches	Angle of repose	Angle of Repose
Longitudinal slope of ditches (no riprap)	5%	1%

Note: Always check code requirements for local standards.

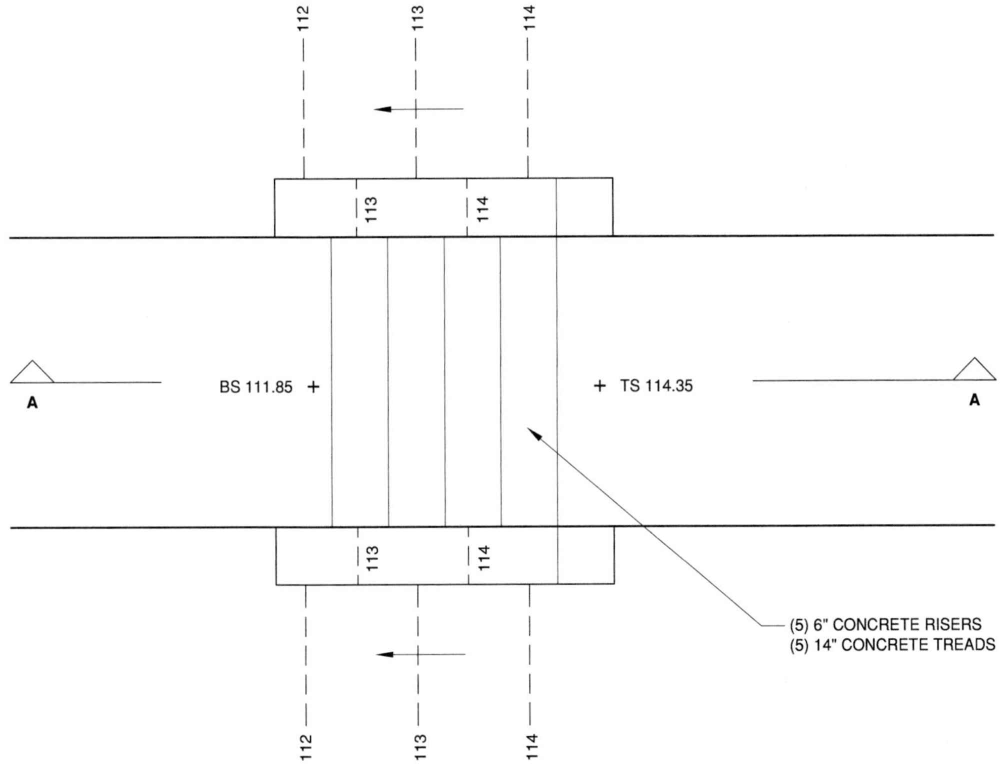

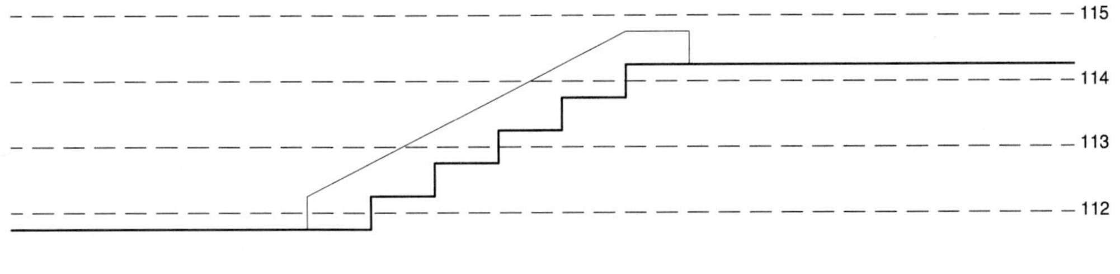

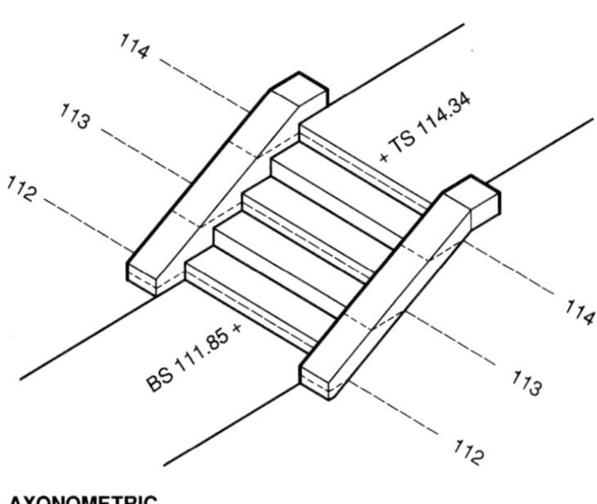

STEP CONTOURS

Sarah Georgia Harrison, ASLA, Assistant Professor, School of Environmental Design, University of Georgia

PREPARATION OF GRADING PLANS

In the preparation of grading plans for construction, the landscape architect must first determine the existing drainage patterns both on the property and adjoining parcels. A prudent practice is to grade the property so that there is no net change in the amount of runoff onto adjacent properties. In many municipalities, this is required practice. After careful study of the site and the design program, the landscape architect designs a network of drainage basins and holding areas to handle the stormwater runoff. He or she designs the slope of the land to accommodate these patterns.

After identifying existing elevations of key points in the design, such as existing trees to remain and the outlet of the drainage system, the landscape architect assigns proposed elevations to the finish floor of buildings and structures. In grading a site, there is usually more than one option for the finish floor elevation. The choices will result in varying amounts of cut and fill, directly affecting the cost of construction and the aesthetic appearance. Ideally, reworking the grades on a site will result in a balanced condition of cut and fill, allowing for the possible shrinkage of soil, so that no soil will need to be transported either on or off of the site. An estimate of cut and fill should be prepared, based on a preliminary grading plan, so that final adjustments can be made to optimize the use of available soil material.

Next, the slopes of the grades in between the proposed elevations are determined, bearing in mind maximum and minimum design slopes. Spot elevations are assigned to all intersections; corners of buildings and parking lots; drainage structures; building entrances; top and bottom of walls, steps, and curbs; and other significant design features. Finally, proposed contours are interpolated between the fixed elevations.

An ecologically sound grading plan begins with the optimal decision for the finish floor elevation, to minimize impact to the site. Other issues include: making responsible decisions about the collection, conduction, and disposal of stormwater; introducing best management practices where possible; rounding and smoothing finish grades to achieve stable profiles; saving precious root zones of trees; reducing impervious surfaces; and utilizing porous pavements.

SPECIAL CONDITIONS

In moving contours, the landscape architect must remember that the contour line that appears in the plan view represents where the edge of the contour plane meets the surface. The proposed contour along a step looks like the one shown in the figure "Step Contours."

Typically, a grading plan shows elevations at the top and bottom of a set of steps, not on each step. The collective number and dimension of risers and treads are denoted, usually with material designations. The optimal riser-tread relationship for outdoor applications is based on the formula:

$$2R + T = 24 - 26$$

where:
R = risers
T = treads

A roadway cross section has subtle slopes to direct water generally off the drive path. Depending on the pliability of the road surface material, the cross section may be crowned (asphalt) or peaked (concrete). In some low-traffic situations, such as alleys, a reverse crown may be desirable, to channel water away from yards and service buildings.

Water may also be pitched to one side of the road, especially on a superelevated curve or on a slow speed driveway that has been cut into a bank.

Contours on a roadway edged with a consistent curb height follow a predictable pattern. When the contour interval is 1 foot and the curb height is 6 inches, the contours appear to move through the curb, in plan view, one-half the horizontal distance between the contours. When the interval is 2 feet and the curb height is 6 inches, the contours appear to move through the curb one-quarter of the horizontal distance between contours.

Water may be collected along the edge of the roadway in a gutter, which is sloped to a drain inlet; it may be channeled to a swale or ditch; or, in small quantities, it may be allowed to dissipate as surface runoff.

Curbs function to collect and channel water to an inlet, as well as to constrain traffic onto the pavement surface. Swales and ditches function to channel water away from structures and heavily used surfaces. A swale is a broad, shallow channel that is often vegetated, but occasionally paved. At the outlet of a swale, or the point where the centerline of the swale meets existing grade, water is dissipated by fanning out,

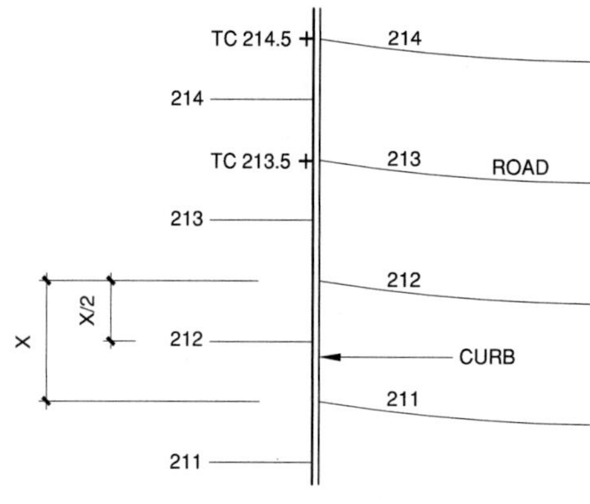

6" HIGH CURB - CONTOUR INTERVAL 1 FOOT

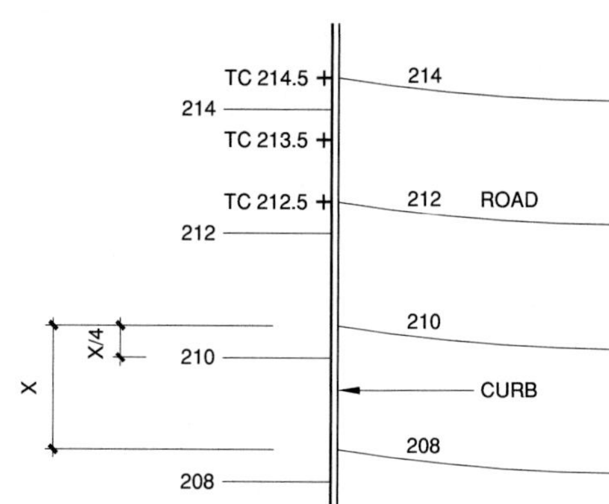

6" HIGH CURB - CONTOUR INTERVAL 2 FEET

CONTOURS AT CURBS

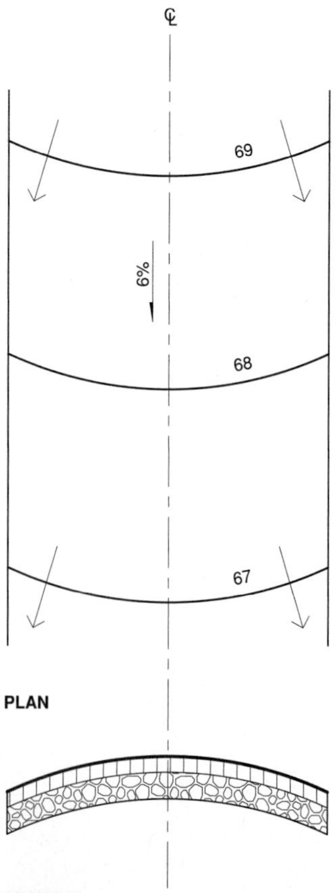

PLAN

SECTION

CROWNED

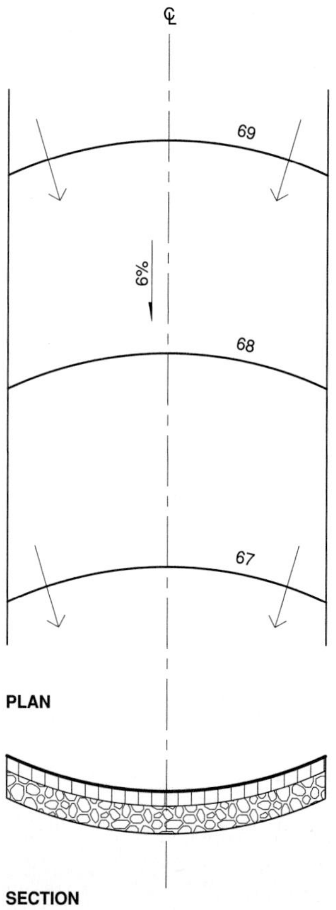

PLAN

SECTION

REVERSE CROWNED

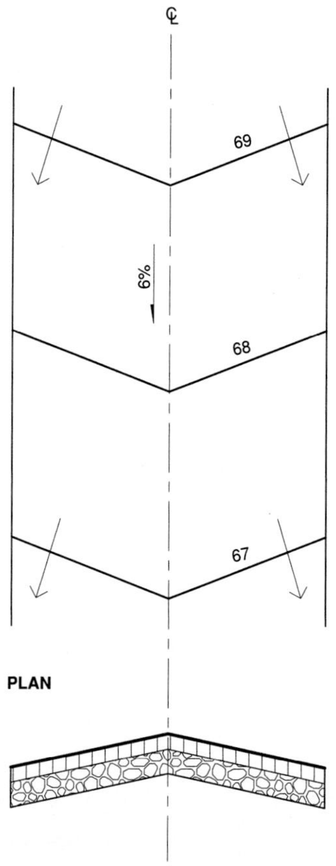

PLAN

SECTION

TANGENTIAL

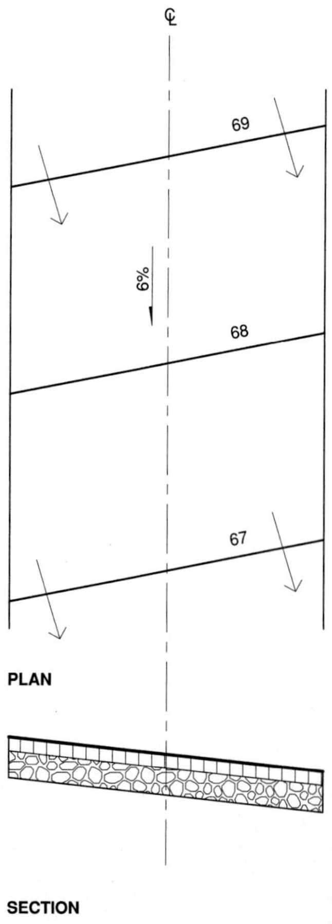

PLAN

SECTION

CROSS-SLOPED

ROADWAY CROSS SLOPES

Sarah Georgia Harrison, ASLA, Assistant Professor, School of Environmental Design, University of Georgia

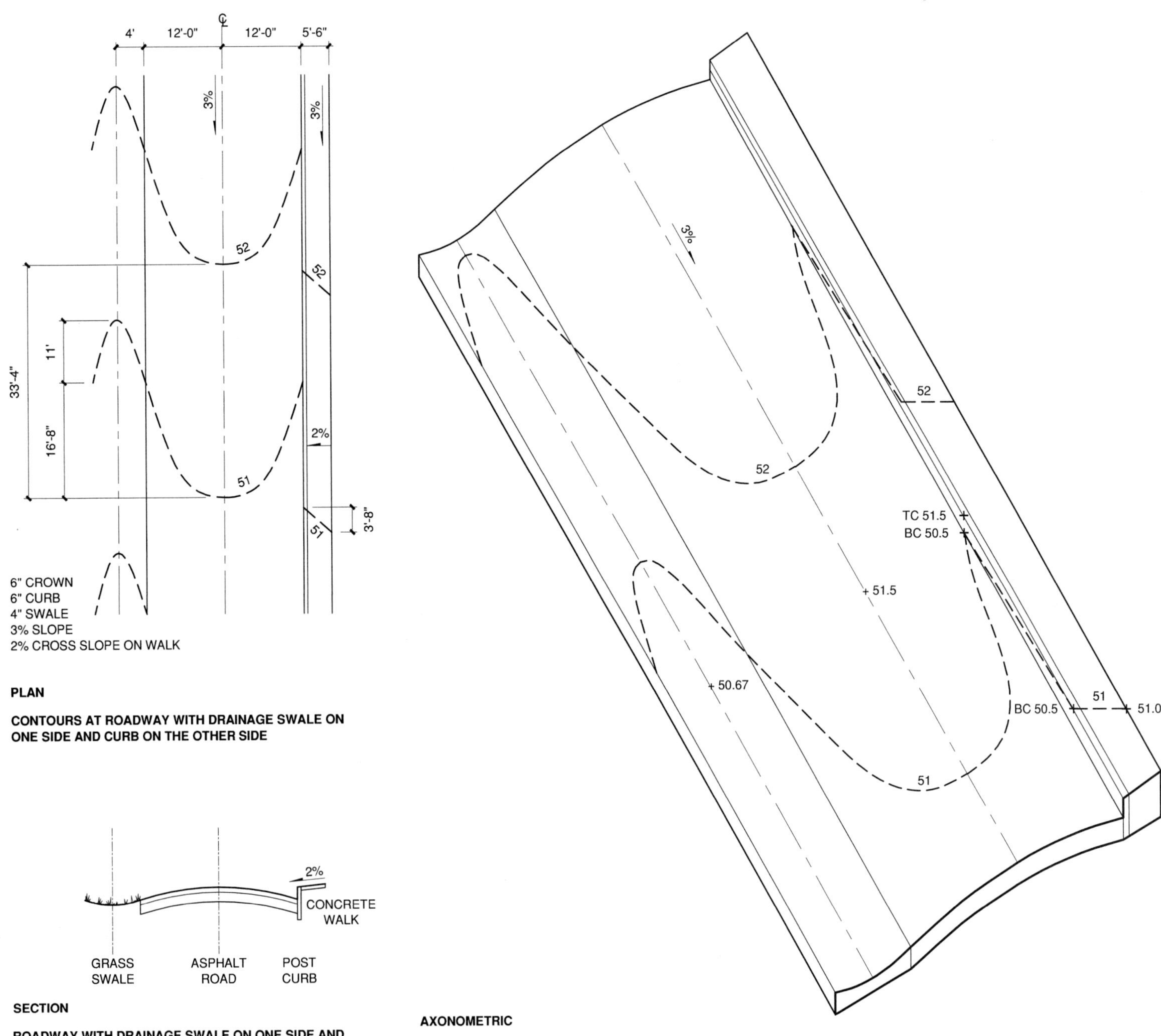

PLAN

CONTOURS AT ROADWAY WITH DRAINAGE SWALE ON ONE SIDE AND CURB ON THE OTHER SIDE

SECTION

ROADWAY WITH DRAINAGE SWALE ON ONE SIDE AND CURB ON THE OTHER SIDE

AXONOMETRIC

ROADWAY WITH DRAINAGE SWALE ON ONE SIDE AND CURB ON THE OTHER SIDE

ROADWAY GRADING

thus slowing its speed and allowing infiltration into the subsurface groundwater. In high-volume situations, drain inlets may be added periodically in the centerline of the swale to capture some of the surface runoff.

A ditch is a deeper and narrower channel than a swale and is typically not vegetated. Depth is usually 2 feet or more. Swales are preferred, but ditches may be necessary in tight spaces. In some situations, riprap or stone must be added to slow the speed of water in the ditch.

Retaining walls accomplish a vertical change in elevation. They may be used to stabilize slopes in a condition that might otherwise exceed an optimal condition. On a grading plan, contours may appear to stack vertically at the wall, but in axonometric view, they are revealed to be wrapping around the face of the wall. Where to terminate a retaining wall can become a key design issue. If the wall ends abruptly, the grade may slope too severely in making the transition to grade. One possible solution is to turn the end of the wall 90 degrees into the slope. (See "Termination of a Retaining Wall.")

Sports fields are graded as flat as possible to level the playing field advantage for both sides. Slopes may be as little as 0.5 percent if the surface is either paved or a closely mowed turf. (See "Drainage for Sports Fields and Courts.")

Sarah Georgia Harrison, ASLA, Assistant Professor, School of Environmental Design, University of Georgia

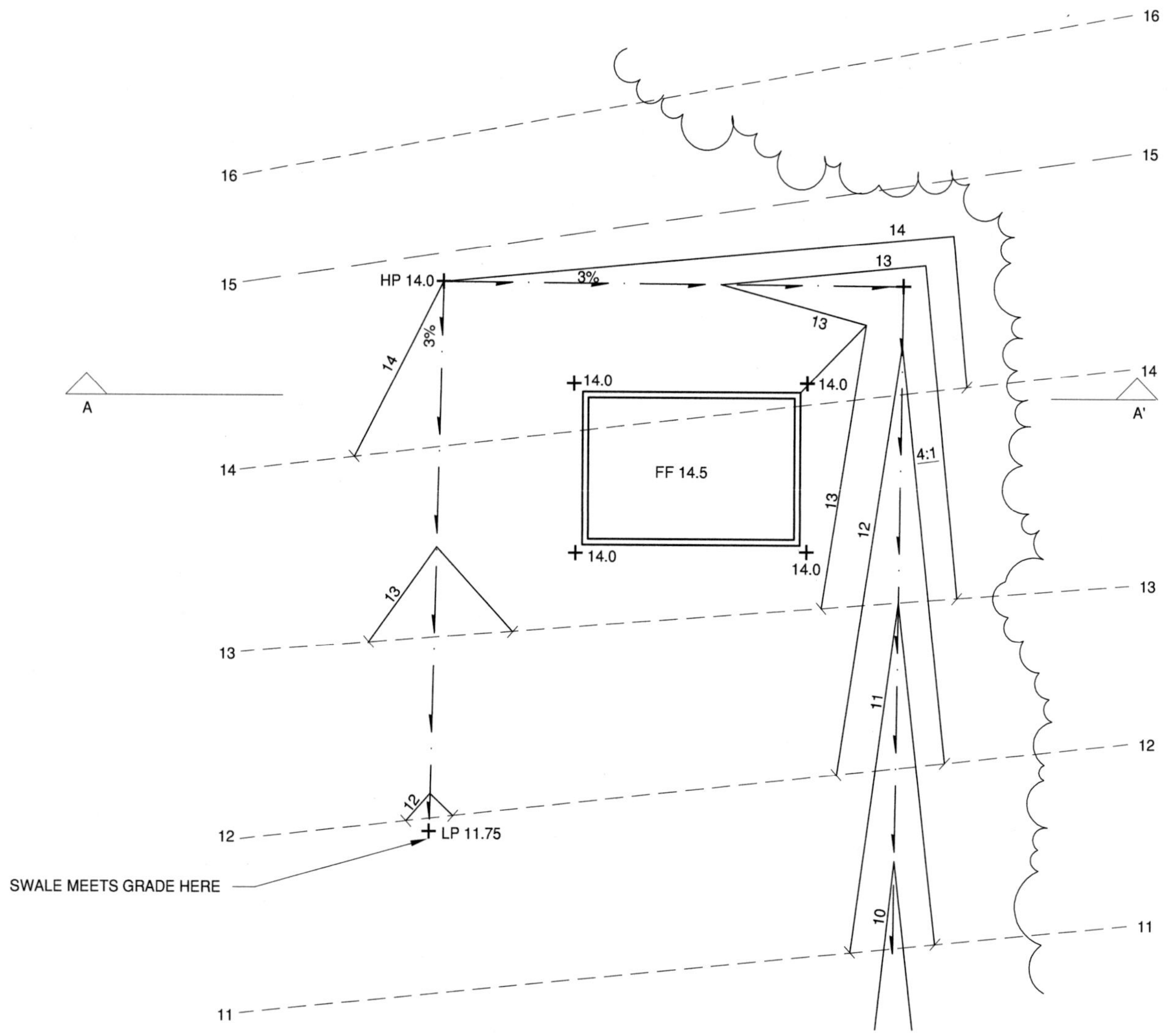

16
16
15
14
13
15
HP 14.0
3%
13
3%
14
14
A
+14.0
+14.0
A'
14
FF 14.5
4:1
13
12
+14.0
+14.0
13
13
13
11
12
12
12
+ LP 11.75
SWALE MEETS GRADE HERE
10
11
11

PLAN

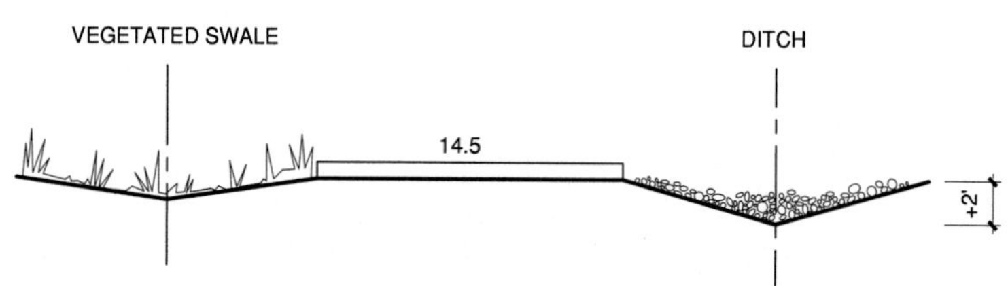

SECTION A-A' (2x VERTICAL EXAGGERATION)

VEGETATED DRAINAGE SWALE AND DITCH WITH STONE

SWALES AND DITCHES—PRELIMINARY

Sarah Georgia Harrison, ASLA, Assistant Professor, School of Environmental Design, University of Georgia

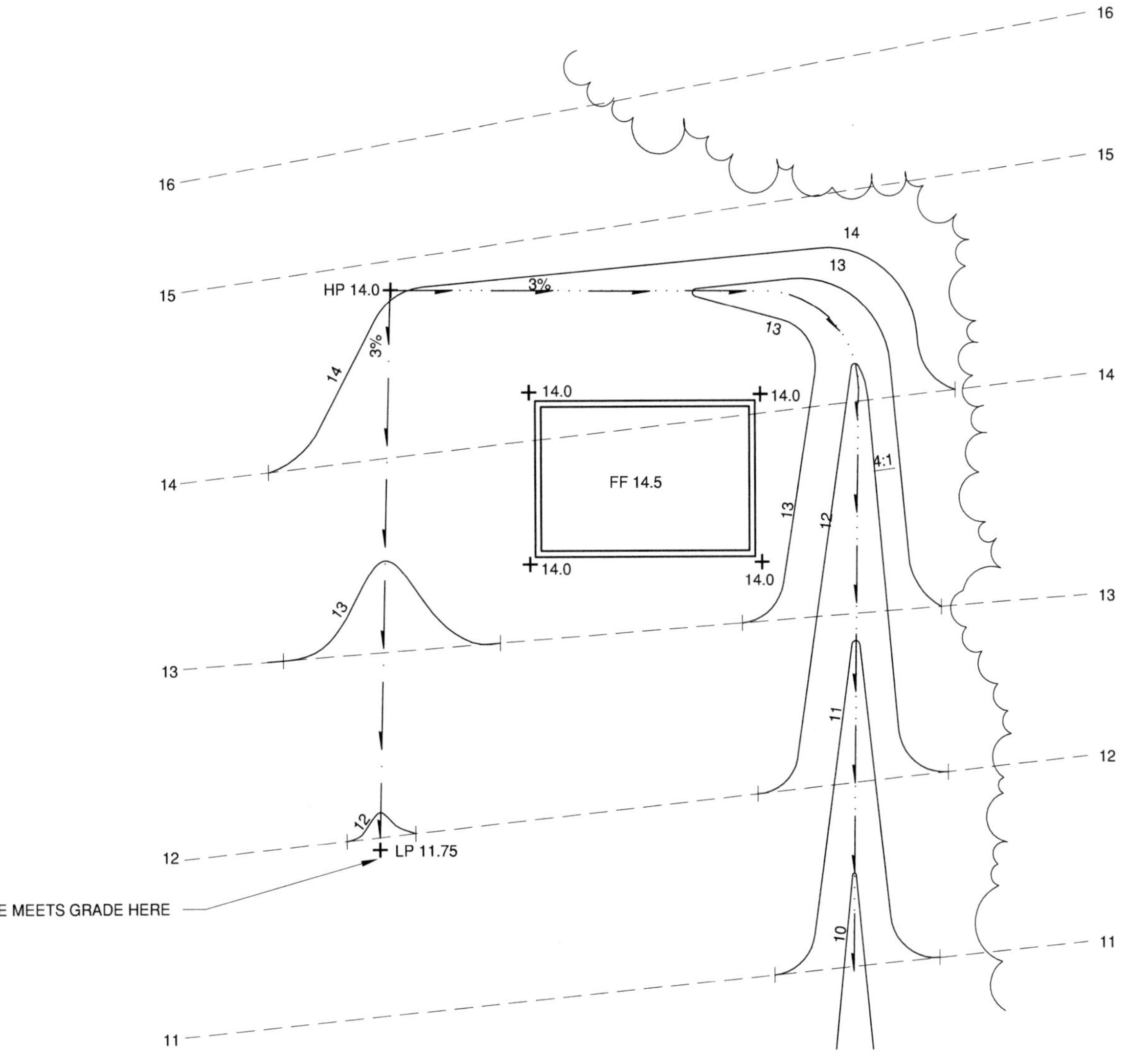

SWALES AND DITCHES—FINISHED

FINISHED GRADING PLAN

A finished grading plan contains the following information:

- Existing and proposed contour information
- Existing and proposed buildings and structures
- Existing and proposed utilities
- Proposed walks, roads, and parking lots
- Property lines with bearings and dimensions
- Location and extent of tree protection
- Spot elevations at all corners, entrances, intersections, top and bottom of steps, and walls
- Maximum and minimum slope designations with directional arrows pointing downhill
- Stormwater drainage inlets and manhole, with designation for rim and invert elevations
- Stormwater piping, with designation for material, diameter, length, and slope
- Subsurface drainage systems

The grading plan typically has a listing of explanatory notes and a symbol legend, and identifies the source for the survey/base data. A title block identifies the landscape architecture firm and any consultants on the project, and includes a logo, north arrow, graphic scale, state registration seal, and revision block.

EARTHWORK AND THE CONSTRUCTION PROCESS

The following steps should be highlighted in the specifications regarding the construction process:

1. Collect and submit soil samples for all areas to be disturbed.
2. Erect tree protection fencing to encompass all feeder roots within the drip zone of existing trees designated to remain.
3. Protect all existing pavements and site structures designated to remain.
4. Strip existing sod to a 2-1/2- to 4-inch depth and either compost or stockpile for future use.
5. Strip and stockpile topsoil separately.
6. Erect temporary erosion control structures to halt the flow of sediments off the property or onto existing paved surfaces and structures.
7. Install gravel aprons at all egress points off the property to lessen the tracking of soil and debris onto roadways.
8. Remove any unsuitable soils and debris from the site.
9. Prior to filling, scarify subgrade to a depth of 6 inches; and moisture-condition to obtain the desired compaction.
10. When filling, place soil in 8-inch lifts, moisture-condition each layer of soil, and compact before additional fill is placed.
11. Allow for settlement and shrinkage of soil when determining final grade.
12. After final subgrade elevations have been estab-

Sarah Georgia Harrison, ASLA, Assistant Professor, School of Environmental Design, University of Georgia

CUT AND FILL CALCULATIONS

INTRODUCTION

Balancing quantities of cut and fill on a site is an optimal condition when grading, for several reasons. When an excess of fill is required, the soil must be imported from off-site, with both ecological and cost implications. Finding available soil may be difficult; there is cost associated with the purchase and transport of the material; and there is the environmental cost associated with the expenditure of energy in transit. In a cut situation, there is the problem of disposal of excess soil off-site, which often results in dumping fees as well as transportation costs. Matching a site that requires fill with one that produces material from cut is often problematic and is a function of fortuitous timing.

Three methods are commonly used by landscape architects in quantifying cut and fill: average end area method, grid method, and contour method. Cut and fill calculations are generally performed in the early planning phases of a project. They provide information useful in modifying a design or grading plan for greater efficiency. They are, however, only approximations of the actual earthwork quantities.

Average End Area Method

This method is useful for quantifying earthwork in construction of linear objects, such as roadways or walkways. Begin by subdividing, in plan view, the centerline into equal intervals, marked by station points. Subdividing into smaller intervals will result in greater accuracy in the final calculations. (See the figure "Average End Area Method: Example, Part One.")

Next cut a cross section at each station point. Compute the area of the cross sections. (See the figure "Average End Area Method: Example, Part Two.")

For each interval between the cross sections, the volume can be found by multiplying the length between the station points by the average area of the cross sections. Finding the average area evens out the irregularities of the volumetric shape in between. The formula is:

Volume (in cubic feet) = average cross-sectional area (in square feet) × length of the segment (in feet)

Or:

$$V = \frac{\text{Area A} + \text{Area B}}{2} \times L$$

Convert to cubic yards by dividing cubic feet by 27.

Calculate cut and fill volumes separately. Compare total volumes and adjust plans accordingly.

The first and last segments, which either begin or end in 0, are actually cone-shaped and can be calculated more accurately by using the formula for the area of a cone:

$$V = A/3 \times L$$

where A = area of the base of the cone.

Grid Method

This method, often called the "borrow pit method," is useful for excavations. A square grid is imposed over the area of intended disturbance. For each square of the grid, the cubic volume beneath is computed. The sum of the volumes gives the amount of soil displaced during the excavation. (See the figure "Grid Method: Example, Part One.")

To find the volume for one square area (or cube), use the following method:

1. Calculate the depth from the surface to the bottom of the excavation for each corner of the square.
2. Find the average depth by dividing the sum of the depths of the four sides by 4.
3. Multiply the average depth by the area of the surface square, providing the volume.
4. Divide by 27 to convert from cubic feet to cubic yards (the conventional measure for earthwork). (See the figure "Grid Method: Example, Part Two.")

To calculate the volume represented by more than one square in a grid, the cubic volume of all of the squares may be added; but it is quicker and more efficient to apply the following formula, which allows for the shared edges of the cubes:

$$V = \left[\frac{(a + 2b + 3c + 4d) \times A}{4} \right] \times \frac{1}{27}$$

where:

a = sum of all corners common to one square, (a = a1 + a2 + a3 + ...)
b = sum of all corners common to two squares
c = sum of all corners common to three squares
d = sum of all corners common to four squares
A = area of one square

(See the figure "Grid Method: Example, Part Three.")

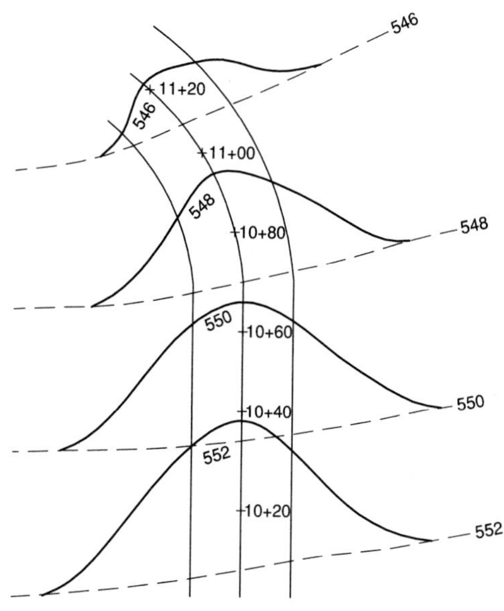

AVERAGE END AREA METHOD: EXAMPLE, PART ONE

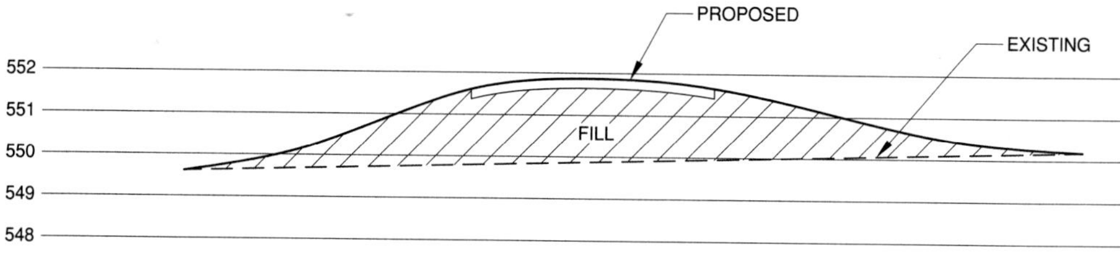

Section @ Station 10 + 40
Horizontal scale: 1" = 20'-0" Area = 93 square feet
Vertical scale: 1" = 5'-0"
(Scale noted for this example, but drawing is not drawn to scale)

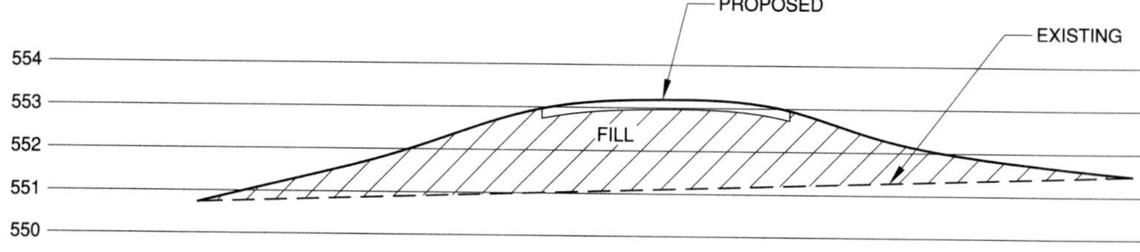

Section @ Station 10 + 20
Horizontal scale: 1" = 20'-0" Area = 101 square feet
Vertical scale: 1" = 5'-0"
(Scale noted for this example, but drawing is not drawn to scale)

To find volume of fill required between Station 10 + 20 and Station 10 + 40

$$\text{Volume} = \frac{101 + 93}{2} \times 20 = 1940 \text{ cubic feet}$$
$$= 72 \text{ cubic yards}$$

Note: To find area in square feet when the sections have vertical exaggeration, multiply the scales.
Horizontal scale x vertical scale = 1 square inch
In this example, 20 x 5 = 100 square feet per 1 square inch.

AVERAGE END AREA METHOD: EXAMPLE, PART TWO

Sarah Georgia Harrison, ASLA, Assistant Professor, School of Environmental Design, University of Georgia

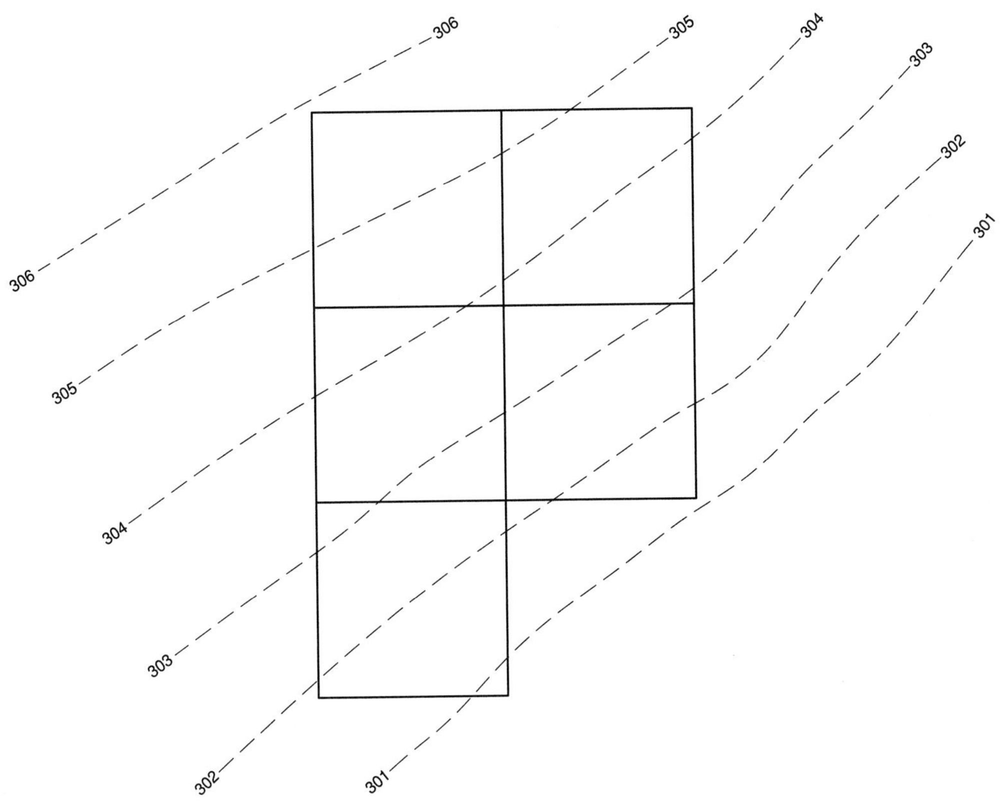

GRID METHOD: EXAMPLE, PART ONE

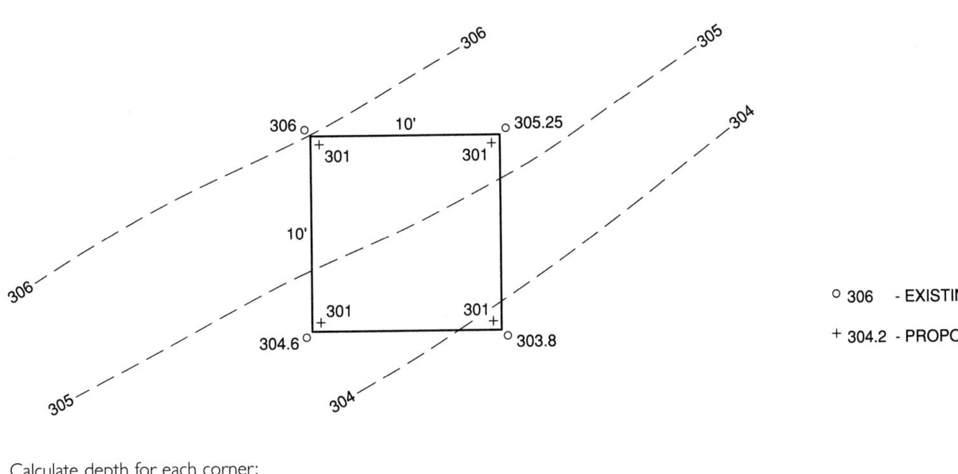

Calculate depth for each corner:

306.0	305.25	303.8	304.6
– 301.0	– 301.0	– 301.0	– 301.0
5.0	4.25	2.8	3.6

Find average depth:

$$\frac{5.0 + 4.25 + 2.8 + 3.6}{4} = 3.9125 \text{ (round to 3.91)}$$

Find volume:

$$3.91 \times (10' \times 10') = 391 \text{ cubic feet}$$

Convert to cubic yards:

$$391 \div 27 = 14.48 \text{ cubic yards of cut}$$

GRID METHOD: EXAMPLE, PART TWO

Sarah Georgia Harrison, ASLA, Assistant Professor, School of Environmental Design, University of Georgia

Contour Method

This is a general-purpose method that applies to a variety of situations. Using a preliminary grading plan, separate areas of cut and fill, by delineating the areas between existing and proposed contours in color (blue for fill and red for cut), for each contour interval that has been changed. (See the figure "Contour Method: Example, Part One.")

Calculate the square footage for each individual area, tabulating cut and fill in separate columns.

Figure areas of overlap separately, for each interval. Then total areas. Convert to volumes by multiplying the areas by the contour interval, which gives the depth, or thickness, of each layer. Divide by 27 to convert to cubic yards.

$$\text{Volume (in cubic yards)} = \frac{\text{total cut or fill (in square feet)} \times \text{contour interval (in feet)}}{27}$$

Or:

$$V = \frac{i\,(A1 + A2 + A3 + \ldots + An)}{27}$$

where:

i = contour interval in feet

An = area between each modified contour

(See the figure "Contour Method: Example, Part Two.")

Greater accuracy may be obtained by considering that the volumes of the areas taper to a cone-shaped figure at the ends. The equation would be modified as below:

$$V = \left[\frac{(A1)(i)}{3} + \frac{(A1 + A2)(i)}{2} + \frac{(A2 + A3)(i)}{2} + \frac{(An\text{-}1 + An)(i)}{2} + \frac{(An)(i)}{3} \right] \times \frac{1}{27}$$

Or:

$$V = \left[i \left(\frac{5A1}{6} + A2 + A3 + \ldots + \frac{5An}{6} \right) \right] \times \frac{1}{27}$$

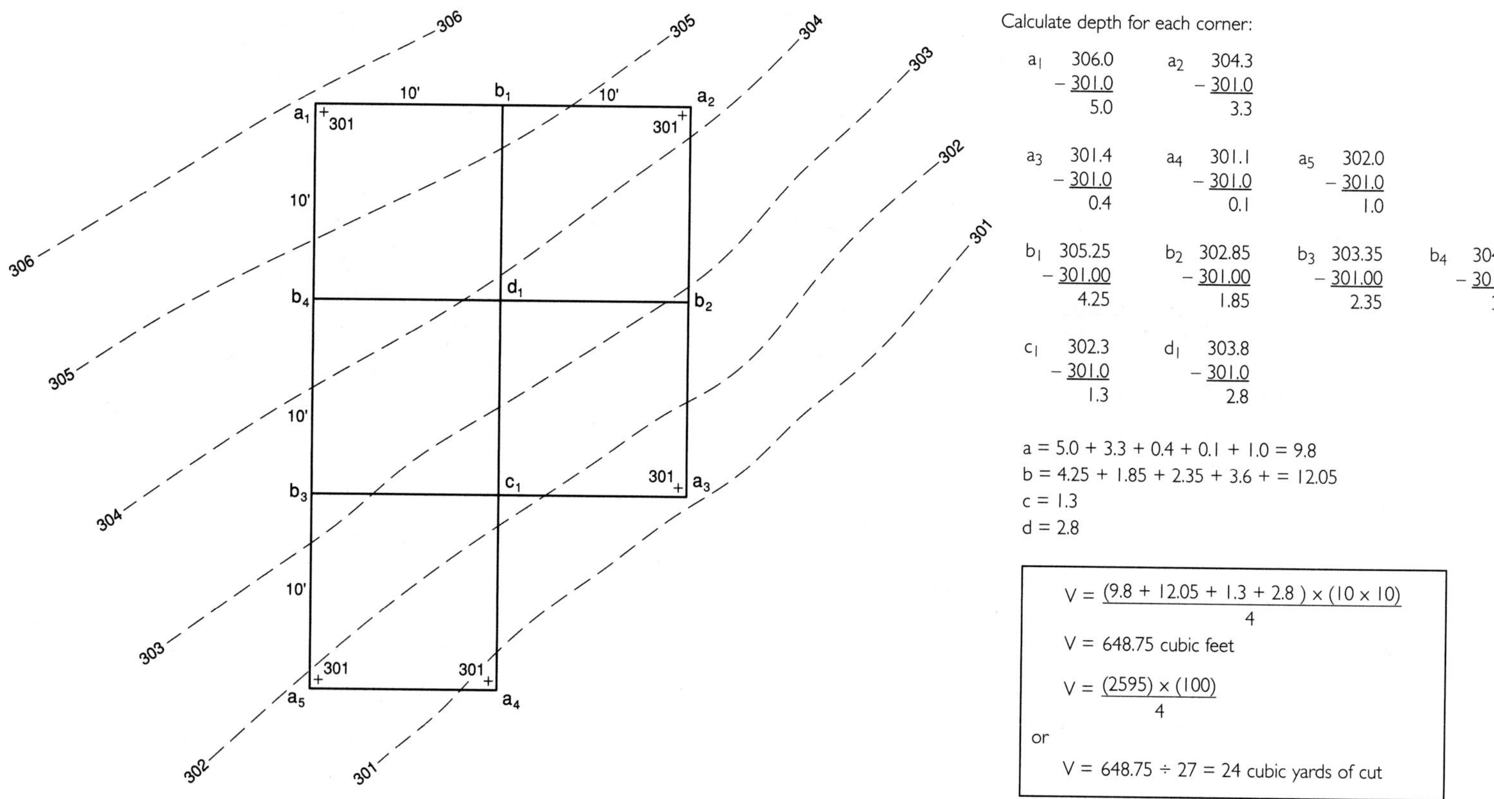

GRID METHOD: EXAMPLE, PART THREE

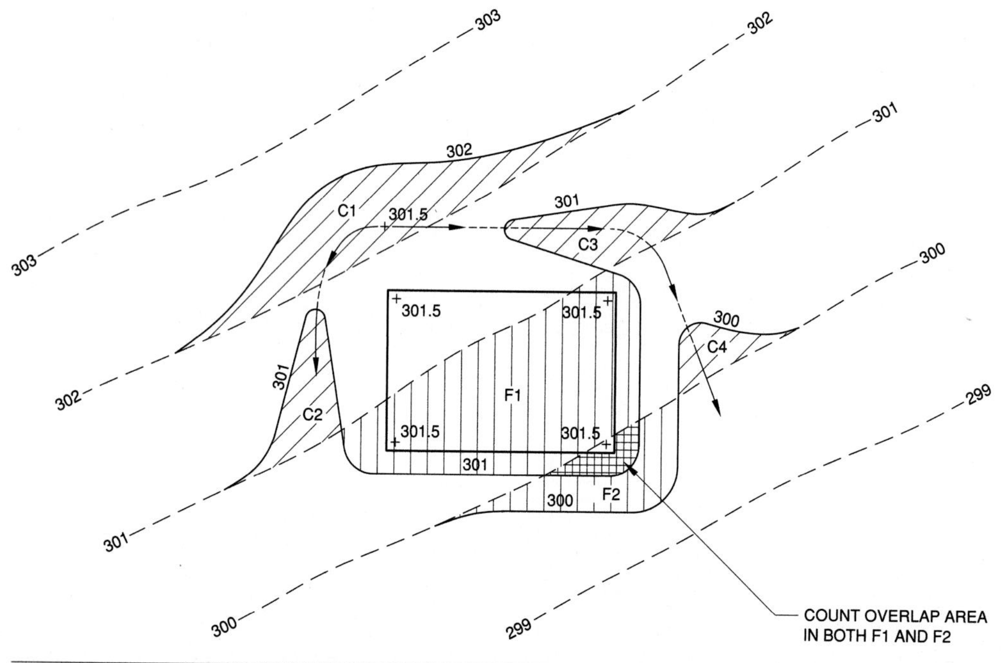

CONTOUR METHOD: EXAMPLE, PART ONE

	CUT	FILL
C1	328 SF	
C2	100 SF	
C3	116 SF	
C4	56 SF	
F1		256 SF
F2		180 SF
TOTAL	500 SF	436 SF

VOLUME (CUT) = $\frac{(500)(1)}{27}$ = 18.72 OR 19 CUBIC YARDS CUT

VOLUME (FILL) = $\frac{(436)(1)}{27}$ = 16.15 OR 16 CUBIC YARDS FILL

CONTOUR METHOD: EXAMPLE, PART TWO

Sarah Georgia Harrison, ASLA, Assistant Professor, School of Environmental Design, University of Georgia

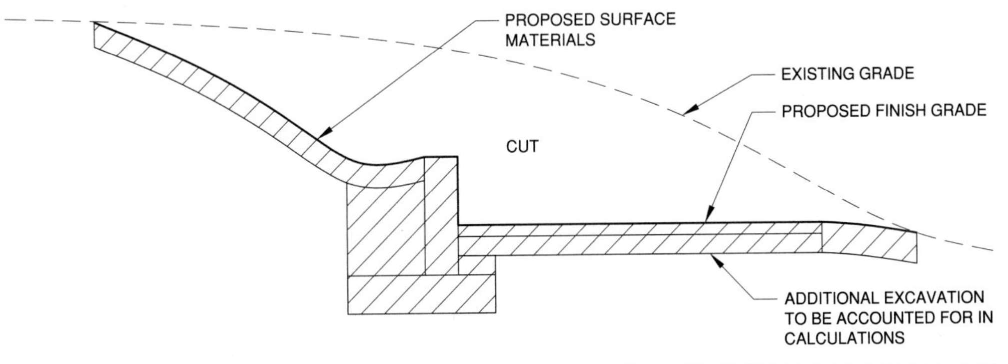

NEW CONSTRUCTION IN CUT CONDITION

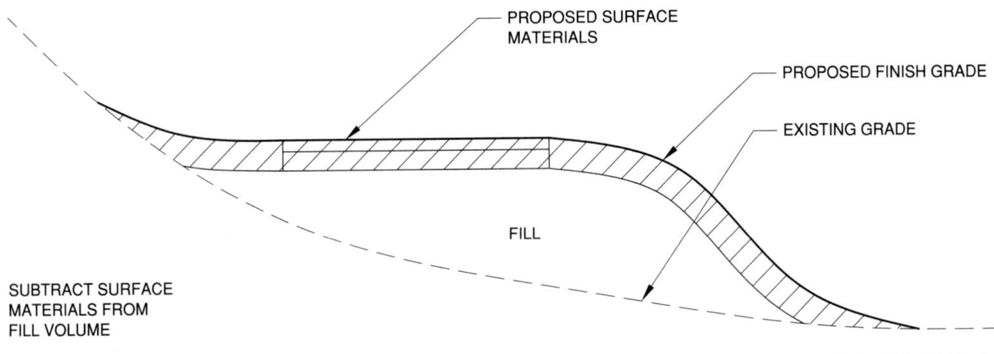

NEW CONSTRUCTION IN FILL CONDITION

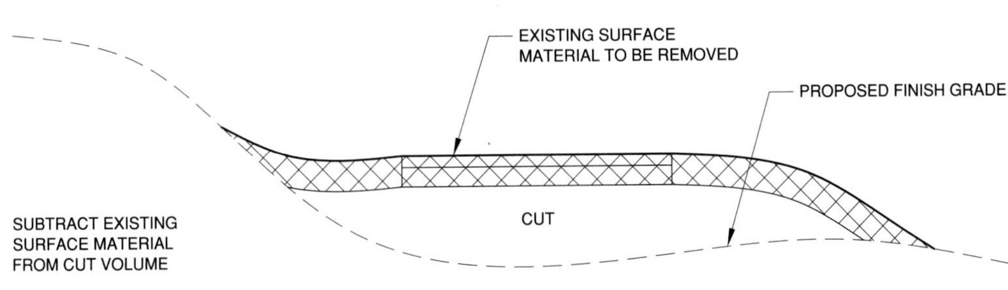

DEMOLITION OF EXISTING MATERIAL IN CUT CONDITION

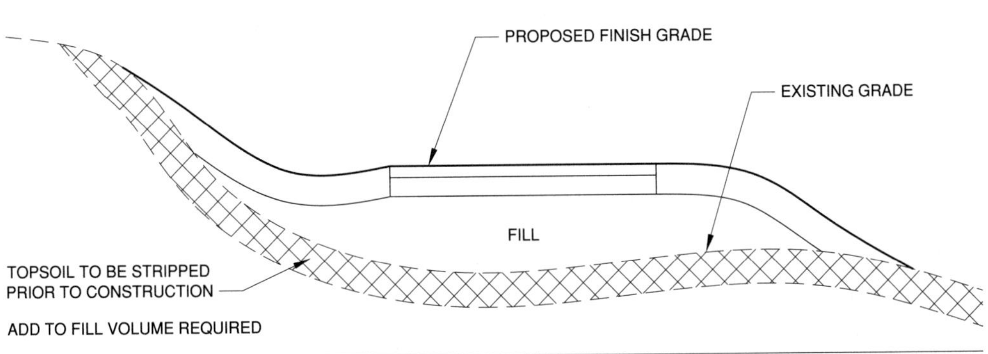

STRIPPING OF TOPSOIL PRIOR TO NEW CONSTRUCTION IN FILL CONDITION

SWELL, SETTLEMENT, AND SHRINKAGE

When soil material is excavated, tightly compacted particles break apart and air pockets form between them. The result of this is an increase in the apparent volume of earth, called swell. Materials will swell based on their composition. Gravel and rock will swell more than clay and will not compact again to their original volume.

When soil is transported and placed in a new location, some particles are lost in the transition. The amount of transported soil compacts to fill a smaller volume than the space from which it originally came. To compensate for this, a shrinkage factor is applied to the final cut and fill calculations. An additional 5 to 10 percent is commonly added to the fill quantity required.

SURFACE MATERIALS

While most grading plans indicate finished grades, cut and fill volumes are calculated based on the difference in existing and proposed subgrades. Earthwork calculations must account for the amount of existing surface material that is removed and the amount of new surface material that is constructed. Surface materials include imported topsoil, as well as paving and structures. Calculations must account for these surface conditions (see figures at left).

REFERENCES

Harris, C. W., and N. T. Dines. 1998. *Time-Saver Standards for Landscape Architecture*. New York: McGraw-Hill, Inc.

Parker, H., and J. W. MacGuire. 1954. *Simplified Site Engineering for Architects and Builders*. New York: John Wiley & Sons, Inc.

Roberts, J. M., and K. F. Lane. 1984. *Fundamental Land*. Ames, IO: Iowa State University Research Foundation, Inc.

Strom, S., and K. Nathan. 1998. *Site Engineering for Landscape Architects*. New York: John Wiley & Sons, Inc.

See also:
Site Grading and Earthwork

Sarah Georgia Harrison, ASLA, Assistant Professor, School of Environmental Design, University of Georgia

WATER SUPPLY AND MANAGEMENT

SUBSURFACE DRAINAGE SYSTEMS

GENERAL

Subsurface drainage systems are very different engineering designs than surface drainage systems. Surface drainage systems intercept and collect stormwater runoff and convey it away from a building and site with the use of large inlets and storm drains. Subsurface drainage systems typically are smaller in size and capacity, designed to intercept the slower underground flows of a natural groundwater table, underground stream, or infiltration of soils from surface sources. Surface and subsurface systems typically require discharge either through a pumping station or by gravity drainage to an adequate outfall.

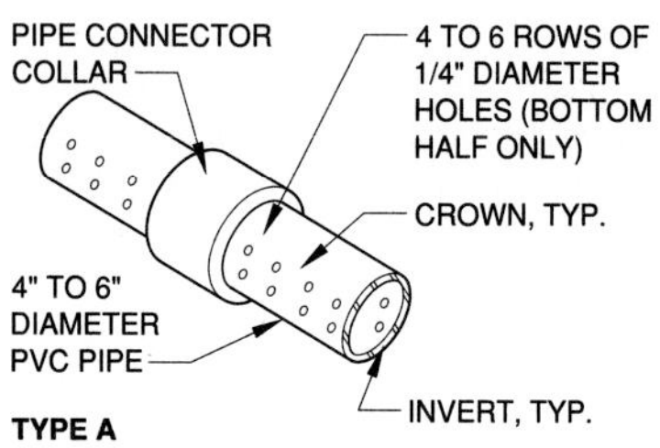

TYPE A

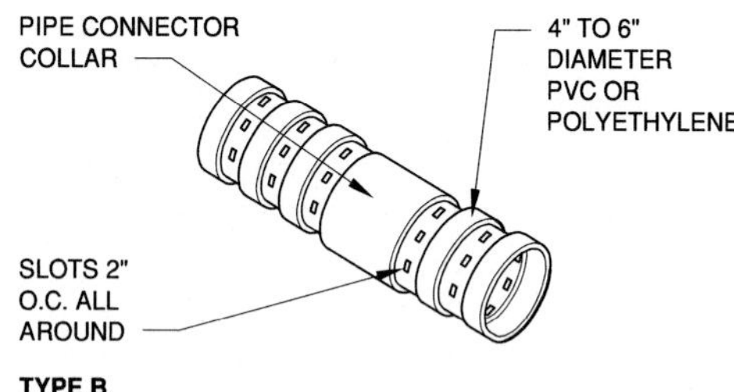

TYPE B

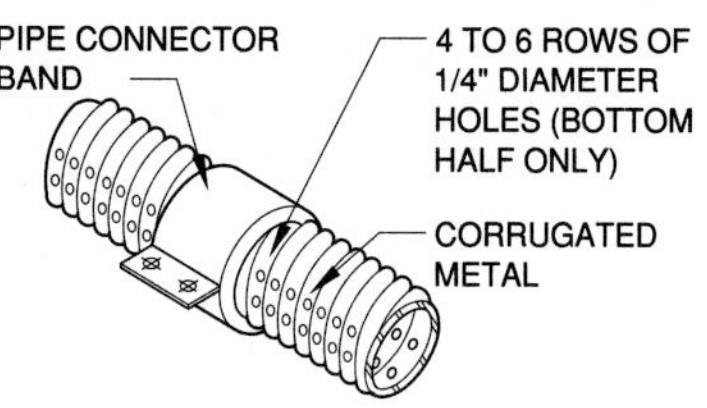

TYPE C

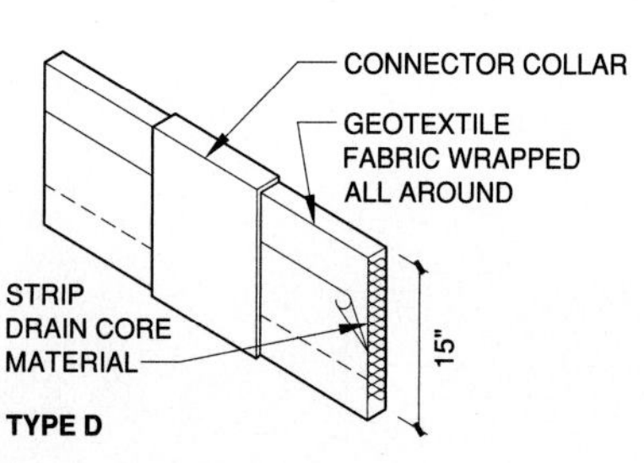

TYPE D

SUBSURFACE DRAINPIPES

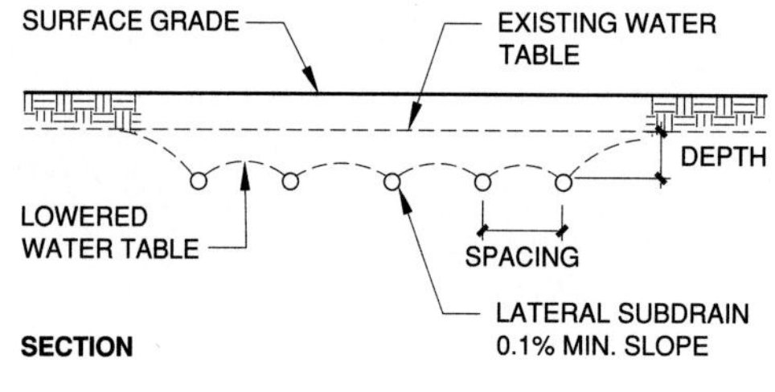

SECTION

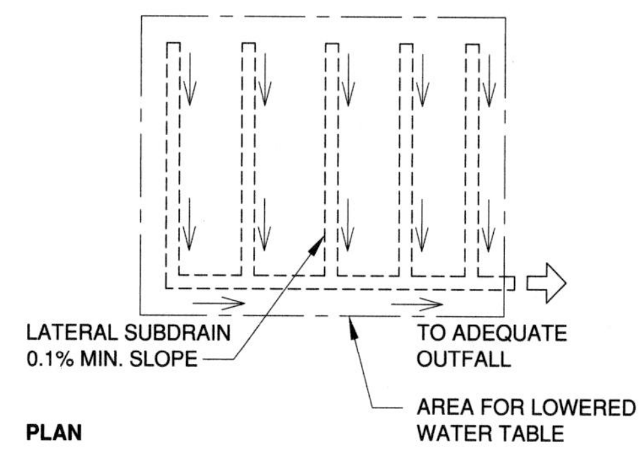

PLAN

1. Subsoil drainage systems are laid out to meet the needs of a site. A grid, parallel lines, or random pattern at low points in the topography is used to collect subsurface water.
2. Depth and spacing of subsoil drainage pipes depend on soil conditions. Geotechnical design may be required to ensure effective operation of a subsoil drainage system.

UNDER-SITE SUBSOIL DRAINAGE

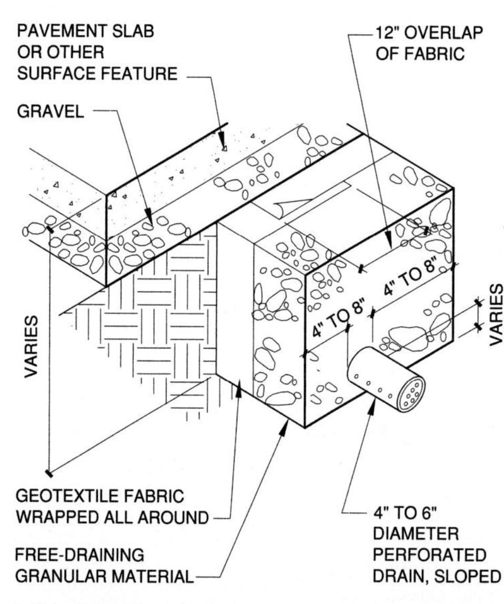

1. The depth of a drain determines how much subsurface water levels will be reduced.
2. When a perforated drain is used, install it with the holes facing down.
3. When used to intercept hillside seepage, the bottom of a trench should be cut a minimum of 8 in. into underlying impervious material.

TYPICAL SUBSURFACE DRAIN

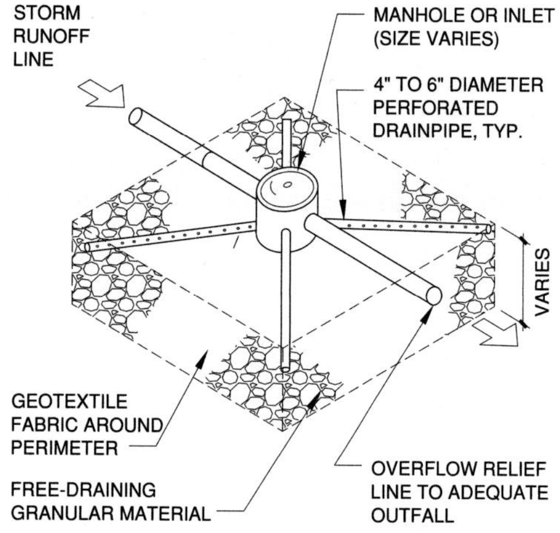

Dry wells provide an undergound disposal system for surface runoff, but their effectiveness is in direct proportion to the porosity of surrounding soils, and they are efficient only for draining small areas. High rainfall runoff rates cannot be absorbed at the rather low percolation rates of most soils, so the difference is stored temporarily in a dry well. Efficiency is reduced during extended periods of wet weather, when receiving soils are saturated and the well is refilled before it drains completely.

DRY WELL

Joseph P. Mensch, P.E., Wiles Mensch Corporation, Reston, Virginia; Kurt N. Pronske, P.E., Reston, Virginia; Harold C. Munger, FAIA, Munger Munger + Associates Architects, Toledo, Ohio

SURFACE DRAINAGE SYSTEMS

GENERAL

Surface drainage systems are designed to collect and dispose of rainfall runoff to prevent the flow of water from damaging building structures (through foundation leakage), site structures, and the surface grade (through erosion). The two basic types of surface drainage are the open system and the closed system.

The open system, which utilizes a ditch/swale and culvert, is used in less densely populated, more open areas where the flow of water above grade can be accommodated fairly easily. The closed system, which utilizes pipes, an inlet/catch basin, and manholes, is used in more urban, populated areas, where land must be used efficiently and water brought below the surface quickly to avoid interference with human activity. The two systems are commonly combined where terrain, human density, and land uses dictate.

A pervious or porous paving system is often used for parking and other hard site surfaces. This drainage system allows water to percolate through the paved surface into the soil, similar to the way the land would naturally absorb water.

Notes

- All slopes, grates, swales, and other drainage features must be laid out according to the ADA, without restricting accessible routes for persons with disabilities.
- Lay out grades so runoff can safely flow away from buildings. If drains become blocked, backed-up water should not accumulate around the foundation.
- An open system, or one in which water is kept on top of the surface as long as possible, is generally more economical than a closed system.
- Consider the effect of ice forming on the surface when determining slopes for vehicles and pedestrians.
- Consult local codes on such criteria as intensity and duration of rainstorms and allowable runoff for the locality.
- Formulas are provided for approximation only. Consult a qualified engineer or landscape architect to design a site-specific system.

METHOD FOR SIZING CHANNELS

Channels and pipes for handling water runoff may be sized by determining the flow of water (Q) with the formula Q = Va. V is the velocity of the runoff water in feet/second as determined by the Manning formula, and "a" is the cross-sectional area of water given in square feet. For a given Q, adjust the chan-

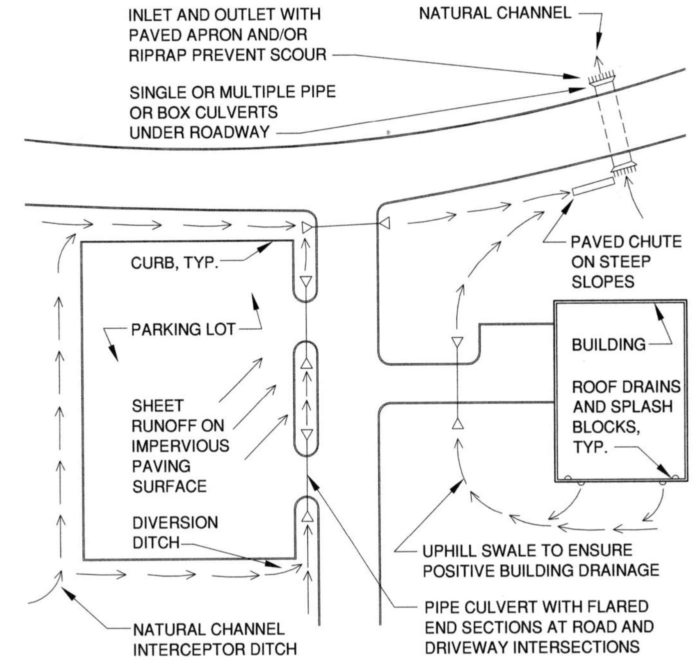

OPEN SYSTEM

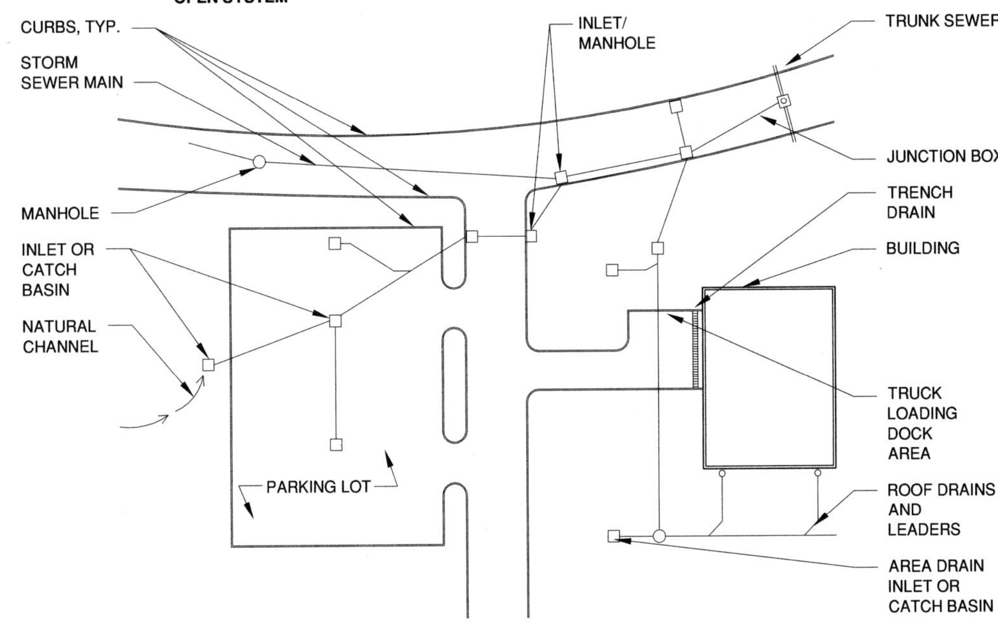

CLOSED SYSTEM

Ditches in open surface drainage systems typically are covered with grass, either seeded with a protective covering or laid with sod.

RUNOFF VELOCITY

VELOCITIES (CHANNEL)	MIN. (FT/SEC)	MAX. (FT/SEC)
Grass—athletic field	0.5	2
Walks—long.	0.5	12*
Walks—transverse	1	4
Streets—long.	0.5	20
Parking	1	5
Channels—grass swale	1	8
Channels—paved swale	0.5	12

8.3 percent maximum for handicapped access

SURFACE DRAINAGE SYSTEM TYPES (IMPERVIOUS PAVING)

SURFACE RUNOFF VALUES (C)

SURFACE	VALUE
Roofs	0.95–1.00
Pavement	0.90–1.00
Roads	0.30–0.90
Bare soil—sand	0.20–0.40
Bare soil—clay	0.30–0.75
Grass	0.15–0.60
Commercial development	0.60–0.75
High-density residential development	0.50–0.65
Low-density residential development	0.30–0.55

All values are approximate.

SLOPES

DESCRIPTION	MIN. %	MAX. %	REC. %
Grass—mowed	1	25	1.5–10
Grass—athletic field	0.5	2	1
Walks—longitudinal	0.5	12*	1.5
Walks—transverse	1	4	1–2
Streets—longitudinal	0.5	20	1–10
Parking	1	5	2–3
Channels—grass swale	1	8	1.5–2
Channels—paved swale	0.5	12	4–6

8.3 percent maximum for handicapped access

Pearse O'Doherty, ASLA, Graham Landscape Architecture, Annapolis, Maryland

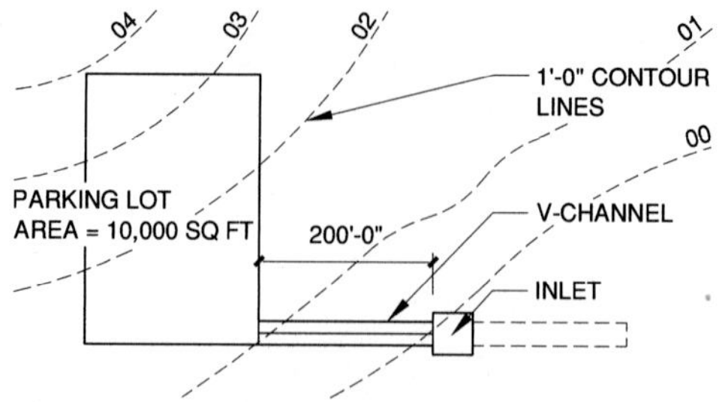

ASPHALT SURFACE C = 0.9

$$\text{AREA} = \frac{10{,}000\ \text{SQ FT}}{43.560\ \text{SQ FT/ACRE}} = 0.23\ \text{ACRES}$$

Following is a simplified method for calculating the approximate runoff of areas less than 100 acres:

$Q = C \times I \times A$

where

- Q = Flow (cu ft/sec)
- C = surface runoff value (see "Surface Runoff Values (C)" table)
- I = intensity (in./hr; obtain from local codes)
- A = area of site (acres)

For example, assume the local code requires I = 5 in./hr:

$Q = C \times I \times A$
$Q = 0.9 \times 5 \times 0.23$
$Q = 1.04$ cu ft/sec
Q = approximate volume of water per second entering the V-channel from the parking lot

CALCULATION OF RUNOFF

n VALUES FOR MANNING FORMULA

CHANNEL SURFACE	n
Cast iron	0.012
Corrugated steel	0.032
Clay tile	0.014
Cement grout	0.013
Concrete	0.015
Earth ditch	0.023
Cut rock channel	0.033
Winding channel	0.025

HYDRAULIC PROPERTIES OF TYPICAL CHANNEL SECTIONS

TYPE SECTION	WIDTH (W)	BASE (B)	DEPTH (D)	AREA (A)	WETTED PERIMETER (P)	HYDRAULIC RADIUS (R)
RECTANGULAR	b or $\frac{a}{d}$	W or $\frac{a}{d}$	$\frac{a}{d}$	wd	W + 2d	$\frac{d}{1 + \frac{2d}{W}}$
TRIANGULAR	2e	—	$\frac{a}{e}$	ed	$e\sqrt{e^2 + d^2}$	$\frac{ed}{e\sqrt{e^2 + d^2}}$
TRIANGULAR (curb and gutter)	$\frac{2a}{d}$	—	$\frac{2a}{W}$	$\frac{Wd}{2}$	$d + \sqrt{d^2 + W^2}$	$\frac{2\,Wd}{d + \sqrt{W^2 + W}}$
TRAPEZOIDAL (even sides)	b + 2e	W – 2e	$\frac{a}{b + e}$	d(b + e)	$b + 2\sqrt{e^2 + d^2}$	$\frac{d(b + e)}{b + 2\sqrt{e^2 + d^2}}$
PARABOLIC	$\frac{a}{0.67d}$	—	$\frac{a}{0.67W}$	0.67 Wd	$W + \left(\frac{8d^2}{3W}\right)$	$\frac{a}{W + \left(\frac{8d^2}{3W}\right)}$

Note: 0.3–0.5 foot recommended for freeboard (F).

nel or pipe shape, size, and/or slope to obtain the desired velocity (one that will not erode earth, grass ditches, or other features).

The Manning formula is $V = 1.486/n \times r^{0.67} \times S^{0.5}$, in which n = values relating to surface characteristics of channels (see the table "n Values for Manning Formule"), r = hydraulic radius (see the table "Hydraulic Properties of Typical Channel Sections"), and S = slope (the drop in foot/length).

For example, assume a 200-foot concrete V-channel for which

W = 2 ft
h = 0.5 ft
S = 0.005 (1 ft/200 ft)
r = 0.37 (calculated using V-channel properties)
V = $(1.486/0.015) \times 0.25^{0.67} \times 0.005^{0.5}$
= 2.6 ft/sec (see "Runoff Velocity" table presented at the beginning of this section).

To check flow, follow these steps:

Q = Va ("a" from channel properties)
= $2.6 \times 0.5 = 1.3$ cu ft/sec.

Use the formula for calculating runoff ($Q = C \times I \times A$; presented at the beginning of this section) to determine the flow required for a site; compare it to the capacity of a channel sized according to the Manning formula to determine whether the channel design is satisfactory.

GRATE DESIGN

General

The grate design chosen for a particular application depends on the priorities assigned to each of the functions listed below. Local conditions may require inclusion of some or all of the performance features in a design.

Capacity

Interception of stormwater is generally considered the most important function a grate can perform. The geometry and size of the openings affect this ability. Consult a civil engineer or hydrologist for individual grate capacities.

Screening of Large Debris

An inlet grate must act as a strainer to prevent harmful debris from entering sewer lines. A well-designed grate prevents objects such as branches, sticks, sheets of semirigid material, and chunks of wood, which can easily pass by large curb openings (such as open-throat type), from entering the catch basin.

Passing of Small Debris

Organic material such as grass clippings, leaves, small stones, or twigs may be permitted to pass into the catch basin as they are not a hazard in sewer lines. Provide grate openings wide enough, long enough, or of special design to pass this debris and still meet requirements for roadway-safe grates.

Strength

Inlet grates placed in roadways must be designed to withstand heavy traffic loads. The most generally accepted specifications for highway loading criteria come from the American Association of State Highway and Transportation Officials (AASHTO).

Permanency

An inlet grate should be designed to match or exceed the expected life of the installation. Steel, aluminum, and cast iron are generally accepted materials for inlet grates, although other materials such as brass, chrome, and structural polyethylene are used in special applications.

Bicycle Safety

Grates can be made safer for bicycle and pedestrian traffic through attention to design and installation.

Pearse O'Doherty, ASLA, Graham Landscape Architecture, Annapolis, Maryland

Options include diagonal bars set at a 45° angle; slotted grates, provided the slots are 1¼ to 2¼ in. wide and a maximum of 9 in. long and the transverse (cross) bars are spaced so a bicycle wheel cannot drop lower than about 1 in; and bars transverse to the direction of traffic and stormwater flow and slanted to conduct water into the catch basin. Grate design does not ensure safe usage; attention must be paid to usage patterns of probable users. Consult traffic engineers and local codes for more information.

Consider clogging hazards and the geometry of flow-through efficiency when designing for bicycle safety. Use of vane-shaped or sloped bars, rather than conventional vertical bars, may improve the capacity of a grate to pass stormwater. Grates with these types of bars are safe for bicycles: consult manufacturers. Do not allow gutter slopes to be substantially swaled into the curb, which could create a pocket in the roadway affecting the safety of bicycles and other traffic.

Grate Sizing

Most grates are oversized to prevent buildup of water; see manufacturers' catalogs for free area. The following formula for sizing grates is based on a given allowable depth of water over the grate.

$$Q = 0.66\ CA\ (64.4\ d)0.5$$

where

A = free area (sq ft)
d = allowable depth of water above grate (ft)
C = orifice coefficient (0.6 for square edges, 0.8 for round)
0.66 = clogging factor

Pearse O'Doherty, ASLA, Graham Landscape Architecture, Annapolis, Maryland

RUNOFF CONTROL SYSTEMS

GENERAL

Natural filtration devices in the environment retain and treet pollutants such as sediment, fertilizer, pesticides, and air pollutants before they can enter water bodies. Increasing development, however, compromises the ability of the landscape to prevent water resource contamination. Typically, when land is developed, trees that formerly intercepted rainfall and pollutants are felled; natural depressions that temporarily ponded water are graded, soil is compacted; and the thick leaf-litter humus layer of the forest floor, which had absorbed rainfall, is scraped off or erodes.

Once a site has been developed, it can no longer store as much water, and rainfall is immediately transformed into runoff and transported to rivers, lakes, wetlands, or other surface water systems. Once construction is complete and some vegetation has returned to the site, expansive impervious surfaces such as rooftops and parking lots prevent most runoff from percolating into the soil. Instead, it must be directed off site by a surface drainage system of curbs, culverts, gutters, and strom sewers.

Measures for managing pollutants include methods of construction and land development that replace natural pollution filtration pathways (e.g., forests, wetlands) with similar filtering mechanisms. Water detention systems retain water, provide for percolation to groundwater, and filter pollutants out of water runoff. These systems comprise detention basins, constructed wetlands, and other temporary and permanent erosion control measures.

When choosing appropriate runoff control measures for a site, consider the following factors; the sensitivity of the local ecosystem; slope of the site; depth of the water table; proximity to bedrock, foundations, and walls; land consumption; land use restrictions; high sediment input; and thermal impacts to downstream areas.

NATURAL WETLAND SYSTEMS

Wetlands naturally detain and filter water. Scattered throughout the United States, from tropical areas to tundra, they form in depressions in the landscape where the water table is near or at the surface of the soil. They may be as small as a table-top or span tens of thousands of acres. There is no single, correct, ecologically sound definition for wetlands, primarily because of their diversity. These systems are an important part of the ecosystem because they produce food and timber, purify drinking water, absorb and store floodwater, suppress storm surges, and help maintain biodiversity. Water is supplied to a wetland either by surface sources (e.g., streams or rivers) or by groundwater.

The sensitivity of wetlands determines appropriate buffer distances between them and developed areas. Buffers, which may range from 30 to 300 ft or more, should respond to the effect runoff may have on the wetland ecosystem. (Consult a wetlands scientist to formulate buffer distances.)

In general, four wetland sensitivity issues should be taken into account: hydrology—the wetland's source of water could be altered by development; vegetation—the plant species in a wetland have different levels of hardiness; ecological state—more pristine systems are more sensitive to development and runoff pollution; and animal species—for instance, nesting birds need greater buffer distances than wintering waterfowl.

ON-SITE RUNOFF CONTROL MEASURES

Architects can use several on-site measures to control runoff in development projects. One of the most commonly used is a simple open storage area for runoff. The configuration of such open systems varies, depending on the desired level of pollutant treatment. Typically called storage ponds, detention basins, or (when made to resemble a natural environment) a constructed stormwater wetland, open systems generally operate more thoroughly with increased retention time.

Simple storage ponds are typically dry between storms after runoff has evaporated or infiltrated the groundwater. Dry ponds sometimes include a wet lower area for additional runoff retention. Wet ponds are permanently wet, allowing pollutants to settle to the bottom. Wet ponds that extend runoff retention time with control devices can remove a very high percentage of particulate pollutants.

Constructed stormwater wetlands (engineered, shallow marshlike areas) retain runoff for long periods, allowing pollutants to settle out of the water column and providing biological, chemical, and physical processes for breaking down pollutants. Wetland vegetation slows the velocity of stormwater, reducing erosion and allowing pollutants to settle. Many organic and inorganic compounds are removed from wetlands by the chemical processes of absorption, precipitation, and volatilization.

Constructed stormwater wetlands can also filter excess nutrients such as nitrogen and phosphorus contained in runoff from gardens and septic tanks. To correctly size a wetland used for stormwater runoff control, consider the total volume and velocity of water entering and leaving the system.

Potential advantages of using constructed stormwater wetlands are that they have relatively low capital and operating costs, offer consistent compliance with permit requirements, and greatly reduce operational and maintenance costs.

STORMWATER WETLANDS

Stormwater wetlands can be defined as constructed systems explicitly designed to mitigate the effects of stormwater quality and quantity on urban development. They temporarily store stormwater runoff in shallow pools that create growing conditions suitable for emergent and riparian wetland plants. In combination, the runoff storage, complex microtopography, and emergent plants in the constructed wetland form an ideal matrix for the removal of urban pollutants.

Unlike natural wetlands, which often express the underlying groundwater level, stormwater wetlands are dominated by surface runoff. Stormwater wetlands can best be described as semitidal, in that they have a hydroperiod characterized by a cyclic pattern of inundation and subsequent drawdown, occurring 15-30 times a year, depending on rainfall and the imperviousness of the contributing watershed.
Stormwater wetlands usually fall into one of four basic designs:

- *Shallow marsh system.* The large surface area of a shallow marsh design demands a reliable groundwater supply or base flow to maintain sufficient water elevation to support emergent wetland plants. Shallow marsh systems take up a lot of space, requiring a sizable contributing watershed (often more than 25 acres) to support a shallow permanent pool.
- *Pond/wetland system.* A pond/wetland design utilizes two separate cells for stormwater treatment, a wet pond and a shallow marsh. The multiple functions of the latter are to trap sediments, reduce incoming runoff velocity, and remove pollutants. Pond/wetland systems consume less space than shallow marsh systems because the bulk of the treatment is provided by a deep pool rather than a shallow marsh.
- *Extended detention wetland.* In extended detention wetlands, extra runoff storage is created by temporarily detaining runoff above the shallow marsh.

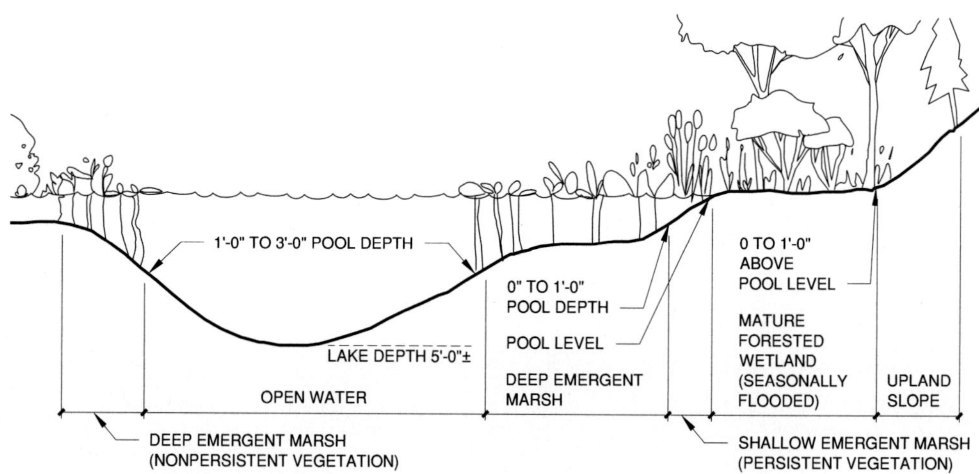

CROSS-SECTION OF NATURAL FRESHWATER, NONTIDAL WETLANDS

Carrie Fischer, "Design for Wetlands Preservation," topic II.A.1 in Environmental Resource Guide (Washington, D.C.: The American Institute of Architects, 1992); Thomas Schueler, Metropolitan Washington Council of Governments, Washington, D.C.

COMPARATIVE ASSESSMENT OF THE EFFECTIVENESS OF URBAN BEST MANAGEMENT PRACTICES (BMPS)*

URBAN BMP OPTIONS	POLLUTANT REMOVAL RELIABILITY	LONGEVITY**	APPLICABILITY TO MOST DEVELOPMENTS	WILDLIFE HABITAT POTENTIAL	ENVIRONMENTAL CONCERNS	COMPARATIVE COSTS	SPECIAL CONSIDERATIONS
Stormwater wetlands	Moderate to high, depending on design	20 + years expected	Applicable to most sites if land is available	High	Stream warming, natural wetland alteration	Marginally higher than wet ponds	Recommended with design improvements and with the use of micropools and wetlands
Extended detention ponds	Moderate but not always reliable	20 + years but frequent clogging and short detention common	Widely applicable but requires at least 10 acres of drainage area	Moderate	Possible stream warming and habitat destruction	Lowest cost alternative in size range	Recommended with design improvements and with the use of micropools and wetlands
Wet ponds	Moderate to high	20 + years	Widely applicable but requires drainage area of more than 2 acres	Moderate to high	Possible stream warming, tropic shifts, habitat	Moderate to high compared to conventional	Recommended, with careful site evaluation
Multiple pond systems	Moderate to high (redundancy increases reliability)	20 + years	Widely applicable	Moderate to high	Selection of appropriate pond option minimizes overall environmental impact	Most expensive pond option	Recommended
Infiltration trenches	Presumed moderate	50% failure rate within 5 years	Highly restricted (soils, groundwater, slops, area, sediment input)	Low	Slight risk of groundwater contamination	Cost-effective on smaller sites, rehab costs can be considerable	Recommended with pre-treatment and geotechnical evaluation
Infiltration basins	Presumed moderate, if working	60–100% failure within 5 years	Highly restricted (soils, groundwater, slope, area, sediment input)	Low to moderate	Slight risk of groundwater contamination	Construction cost moderate, but rehab cost high	Not widely recommended until longevity is improved
Porous pavement	High, if working	75% failure within 5 years	Extremely restricted (traffic, soils, groundwater, slope, area, sediment input)	Low	Possible groundwater impacts, uncontrolled runoff	Cost-effective compared to conventional asphalt when working properly	Recommended in highly restricted applications with careful construction and effective maintenance
Sand filters	Moderate to high	20 + years	Applicable for smaller developments	Low	Minor	Comparatively high construction costs and frequent maintenance	Recommended, with local demonstration
Grassed swales	Low to moderate but unreliable	20 + years	Low-density development and roads	Low	Minor	Low compared to curb and gutter	Recommended, with check-dams, as one part of a BMP system
Filter strips	Unreliable in urban settings	Unknown but may be limited	Restricted to low-density areas	Moderate if forested	Minor	Low	Recommended as one element of a BMP system
Water quality inlets	Presumed low	20 + years	Small, highly impervious catchments (less than 2 acres)	Low	Resuspension of hydrocarbon loadings, disposal of hydrocarbon and toxic residuals	High compared to trenches and sand filters	Not currently recommended as a primary BMP option

**The variety of urban BMPs available to remove pollutants from urban runoff differs widely in performance, longevity, feasibility, cost, and environmental impact. As the matrix shows, stormwater wetlands are an attractive BMP choice at many development sites.*

***Based on current designs and prevailing maintenance practices.*

COMPARATIVE ATTRIBUTES OF FOUR STORMWATER WETLAND DESIGNS

ATTRIBUTE	SHALLOW MARSH	POND/WETLAND	EXTENDED DETENTION WETLAND	POCKET WETLAND
Pollutant removal capability	Moderate; reliable removal of sediments and nutrients	Moderate to high; reliable removal of nutrients and sediment	Moderate; less reliable removal of nutrients	Moderate; can be subject to resuspension and groundwater displacement
Land consumption	High; shallow marsh storage consumes space	Moderate, as vertical pool substitutes for marsh storage	Moderate, as vertical extended detention substitutes for marsh storage	Moderate, but can be shoehomed into site
Water balance	Dry weather base flow normally recommended to maintain water elevations; groundwater not recommended as primary source of water supply to wetland			Water supply provided by excavation to groundwater
Wetland area/watershed area	Minimum ratio of 0.02	Minimum ratio of 0.01	Minimum ratio of 0.01	Minimum ratio of 0.01
Contributing watershed area	Drainage area of 25 acres or more, with dry weather Q*	Drainage area of 25 acres or more, with dry weather Q*	Minimum of 10 acres required for extended detention	1–10 acres
Deepwater cells	Forebay, channels, micropool	Pond, micropool	Forebay, micropool	Micropool, if possible
Outlet configuration	Reversed slope pipe extending from riser, withdrawn approximately 1 ft below normal pool; pipe and pond drain equipped with gate valve			Broad-crested weir with half-round trash rack and pond drain
Sediment cleanout cycle (approximate)	Cleanout of forebay every 2–5 yr	Cleanout of pond every 10 yr	Cleanout of forebay every 2–5 yr	Cleanout of wetland every 5–10 yr, on-site disposal and stockpile mulch
Native plant diversity	High, if complex microtopography is present	High, with sufficient wetland complexity and area	Moderate; fluctuating water levels impose physiological constraints	Low to moderate, due to small surface area and poor control of water levels
Wildlife habitat potential	High, with complexity and buffer	High, with buffer, attracts waterfowl	Moderate, with buffer	Low, due to small area and low diversity

**Q—coefficient of runoff*

Carrie Fischer, "Design for Wetlands Preservation," topic II.A.1 in Environmental Resource Guide (Washington, D.C.: The American Institute of Architects, 1992); Thomas Schueler, Metropolitan Washington Council of Governments, Washington, D.C.

This extended detention feature enables the wetland to occupy less space as temporary vertical storage partially substitutes for shallow marsh storage. A growing zone is created along the gentle side slopes of extended detention wetlands, from the normal pool level the maximum extended detention water surface.

- *Pocket wetlands.* Pocket wetlands are adapted to serve small sites (from one to ten acres). Because the drainage area is small, pocket wetlands usually do not have a reliable base flow, creating a widely fluctuating water level. In most cases, water levels in the wetland are supported by excavating down to the water table. In drier areas, a pocket wetland is supported only by stormwater runoff, and during extended periods of dry weather it will have no shallow pool at all (only saturated soils). Due to their small size and fluctuating water levels, pocket wetlands often have low plant diversity and poor wildlife habitat value.

The selection of a particular wetland design usually depends on three factors: available space, contributing watershed area, and desired environmental function. However, stormwater wetlands are not typically located within delineated natural wetland areas, which provide critical habitat and eco-system services and are

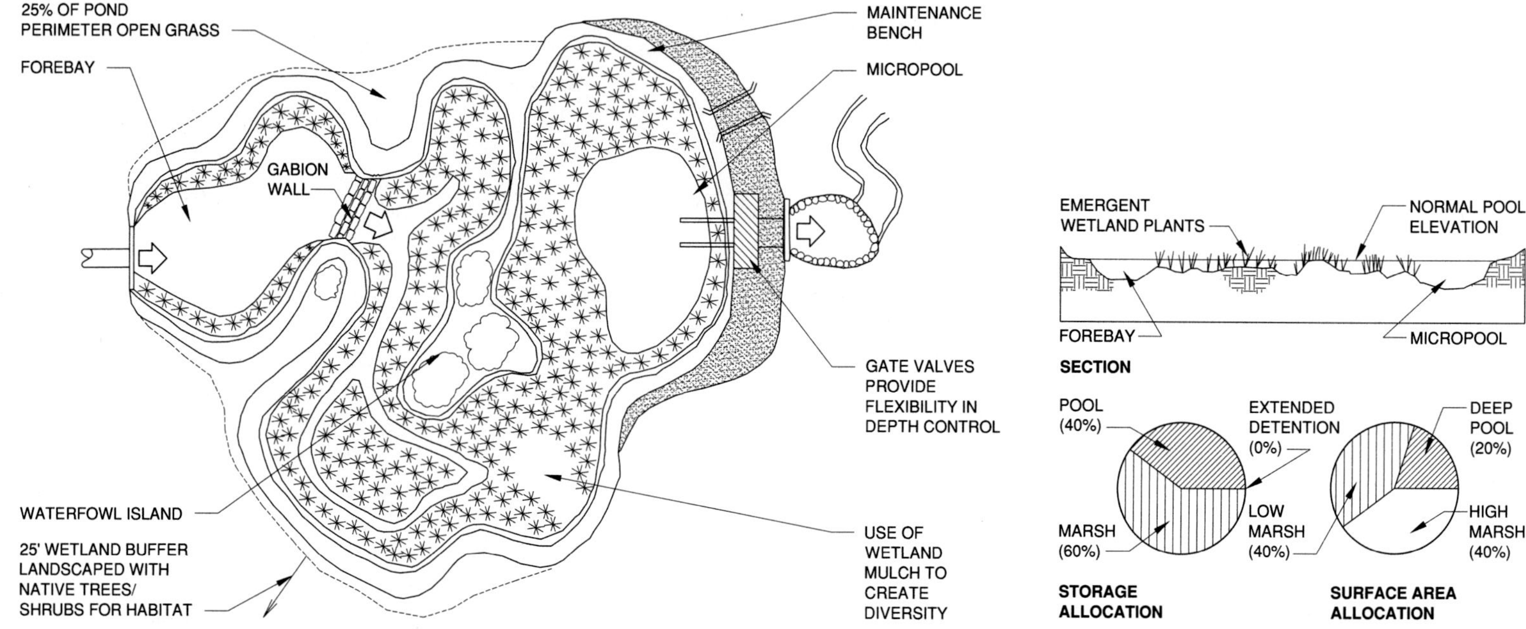

Most of the shallow marsh system is 0-18 in. deep, a depth that creates favorable conditions for the growth of emergent wetland plants. A deeper forebay is located at the major inlet, and a deep micropool is situated near the outlet.

SHALLOW MARSH SYSTEM

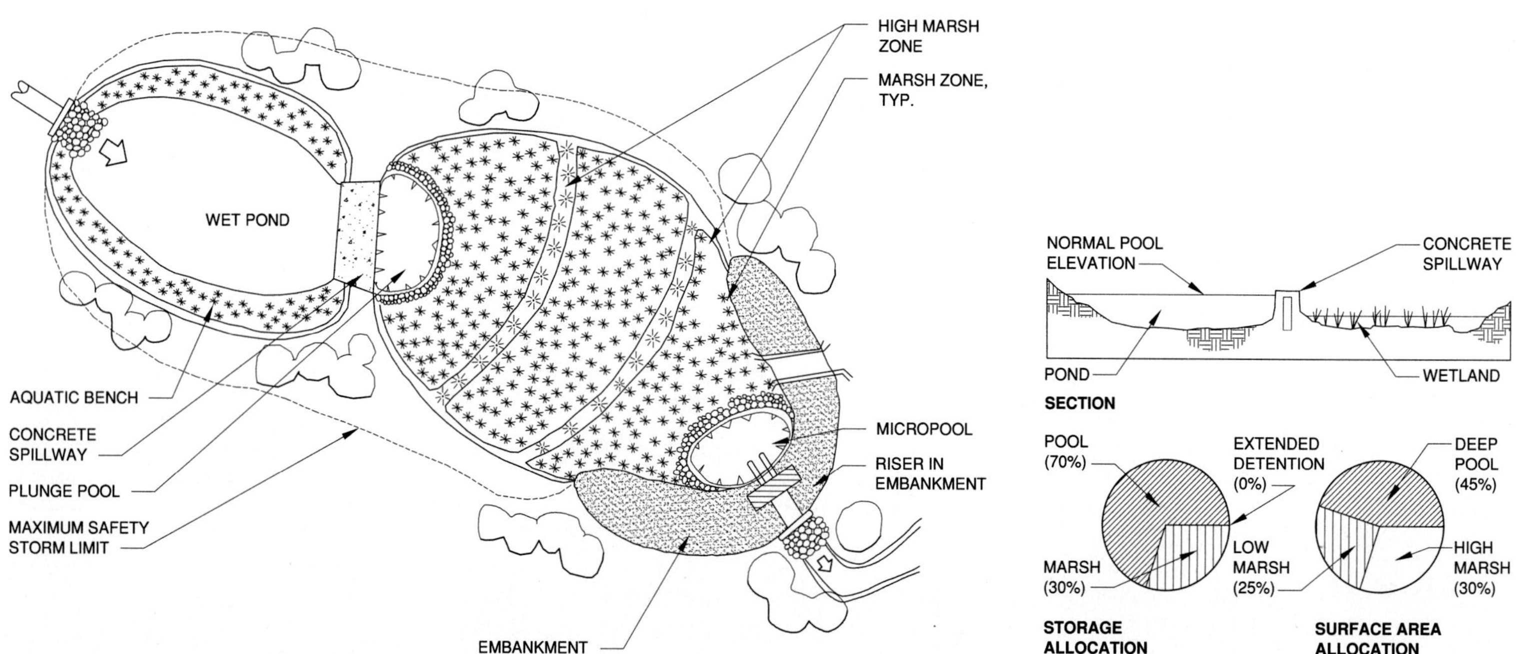

The pond/wetland system consists of a deep pond that leads to a shallow wetland. The pond remove pollutants and reduces the space required for the system.

POND/WETLAND SYSTEM

Carrie Fischer, "Design for Wetlands Preservation," topic II.A.1 in Environmental Resource Guide (Washington, D.C.: The American Institute of Architects, 1992); Thomas Schueler, Metropolitan Washington Council of Governments, Washington, D.C.

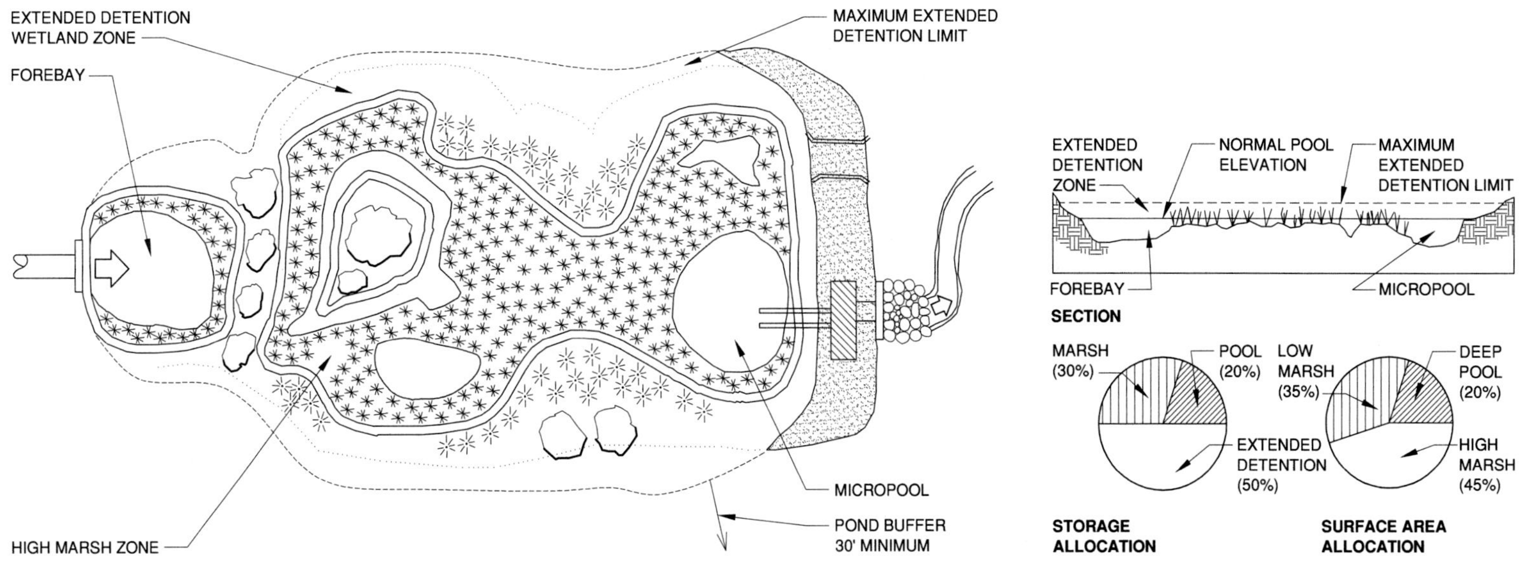

The water level in an extended detention wetland can increase by as much as 3 ft after a storm, returning to normal levels within 24 hr. As much as half the total treatment volume can be provided as extended detention storage, which helps protect downstream channels from erosion and reduces the space needed for the wetland.

EXTENDED DETENTION WETLAND

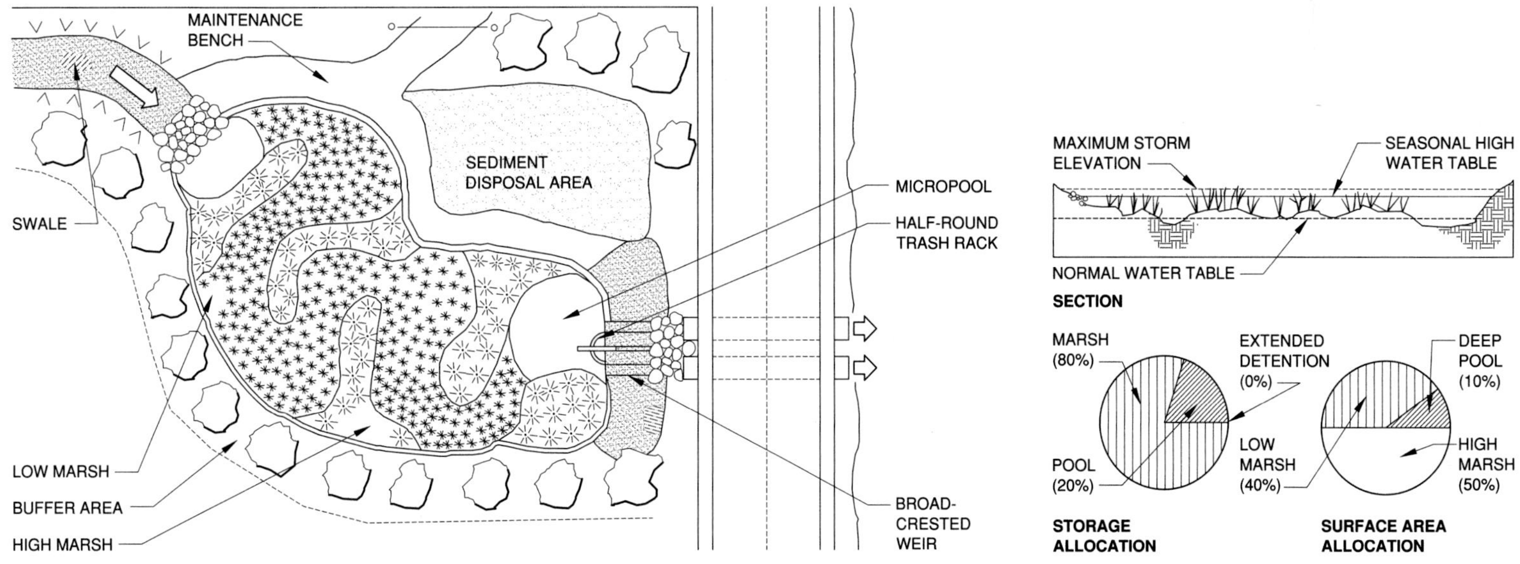

POCKET STORM WATER WETLAND

protected under local, state, and federal statues. Stormwater wetlands should also not be confused with constructed wetlands used to mitigate the permitted loss of natural wetlands under wetland protection regulations. The primary goal of wetland mitigation is to replicate the species diversity and ecological function of the lost natural wetland; whereas the more limited goal of stormwater wetlands is to maximize pollutant removal and create generic wetland habitat.

Stormwater wetlands are also distinguished from natural wetlands that receive stormwater runoff as a consequence of upstream development. Although not intended for stormwater treatment, wetlands influenced by stormwater are common. In urban settings, Stormwater runoff that becomes a major component of the water balance of a natural wetland can severely alter the functional and structural qualities of the wetland. The end result is a stormwater-influenced natural wetland that is more characteristic of a stormwater wetland than a natural one.

Carrie Fischer, "Design for Wetlands Preservation," topic II.A.1 in Environmental Resource Guide (Washington, D.C.: The American Institute of Architects, 1992); Thomas Schueler, Metropolitan Washington Council of Governments, Washington, D.C.

WETLAND PRESERVATION

This discussion addresses wetlands as habitat, recognizes their functions and values, and the need to preserve, restore, and/or create, where applicable, in light of their degradation and loss. This article does not cover constructed wetlands for water-quality treatment, which is addressed in *Constructed Treatment Wetlands*. Although, it should be noted that integration of constructed wetlands into natural fluvial systems is an important tool for preserving water quality reaching preserved wetlands in developing areas. In this article, the terms "wetland," "preservation," "restoration," and "creation" are defined, as is "mitigation" as it is associated with the U.S. Army Corps of Engineers' permitting process. An overview of this permit process is also provided. Additionally, graphic examples for wetland preservation, restoration, and creation pertaining to low-impact land development and stormwater conveyance are presented. Incorporating wetland preservation, restoration, or creation into land development and stormwater management activities provides for public health, safety, and welfare and improves quality of life.

Wetlands are protected under a number of local, state, and federal regulations, including the Clean Water Act (33 U.S.C. 1344) and the Rivers and Harbors Act (33 U.S.C. 540). The objective of these regulations is to maintain and restore the chemical, physical, and biological integrity of the waters of the United States. The U.S. Army Corps of Engineers (U.S. ACE), with oversight from the U.S. Environmental Protection Agency (U.S. EPA), is charged with protecting wetlands under their jurisdiction. Their jurisdiction extends from the nation's navigable waterways to the wetlands adjacent to navigable waterways and their tributaries.

DEFINITION OF "WETLAND"

There are a variety of wetland types and definitions. Because of natural variations across the landscape, wetlands range from temporary, seasonal to permanent features. Wetlands are dynamic areas in the landscape and are generally located between drier, upland areas and permanent water bodies. The current definition for wetlands that fall under the federal government's jurisdiction, as stated in the *Corps of Engineers 1987 Wetland Delineation Manual, Technical Report Y-87-1,* is "those areas that are inundated or saturated by surface or groundwater at a frequency and duration sufficient to support, and that under normal circumstances do support, a prevalence of vegetation typically adapted for life in saturated soil conditions." According to the code described in Federal Register 33 "Navigation and Navigable Waters," (2005, EPA, 40 CFR 230.3, and CE, 33 CFR 328.3), wetlands generally include swamps, marshes, bogs, and similar areas. Therefore, for an area to be considered a jurisdictional wetland, it must have all three physical parameters: (1) wetland hydrology, (2) hydric soil, and (3) predominance of hydrophytic vegetation.

However, this is not consistent with the U.S. Fish and Wildlife Service's (U.S. FWS) definition, which defines a wetland as land that is transitional between terrestrial (dry) and aquatic (wet) landscape systems; where the water table is usually at or near the surface, or the land is covered by shallow water (less than 3 feet deep), such that one or more of the following three parameters are present: (1) water is present on a periodic basis; (2) the substrate is undrained hydric soil; or (3) the subsurface is non-soil and is saturated with water or covered by shallow water sometime during the growing season. Wetlands can be found throughout the country and vary in habitat type, depending on their landscape position, duration of wetness, and vegetative cover.

The term "wetland hydrology" refers to all hydrologic characteristics of an area that is periodically inundated or saturated to the ground surface at some time during the growing season and where water has an overriding influence on the vegetation present. Because of landscape diversity and variations in precipitation, the presence of water can range in duration, from permanent to irregular inundation.

Wetland soils are characterized by the lack of oxygen within the soil pore spaces due to routine or regular flooding or saturation. This condition is called "anaerobic." According to the U.S. Department of Agriculture's (USDA's) Natural Resource Conservation Service's (formerly the Soil Conservation Service) National Technical Committee for Hydric Soils, a "hydric soil" is a soil that is saturated, flooded, or ponded long enough during the growing season to develop anaerobic or depleted oxygen conditions in the upper part.

"Hydrophyic vegetation" includes plants that, due to morphological, physiological, and/or reproductive adaptations, have the capability to grow in anaerobic soil conditions. *USFWS Biological Report 88* (Reed, 1988) has more technical information on these national wetland plant lists. The U.S. FWS also prepares a national list of plant species that occur in wetlands, identifying where each species in a region receives an indication of its estimated probable occurrence in a wetland. Because wetlands can support a variety of plant communities that may range from herbaceous plants such as grasses, sedges, and forbs to woody shrubs and trees, wetlands can be referred to emergent marsh, bottomland forested wetland, swamp, bog, or wet prairie, for example. The U.S. FWS has developed a classification system for wetlands it used to undertake a national wetland inventory and prepare the National Wetland Inventory (NWI) maps, which show general wetland locations. This classification system is based on landscape location, hydrology, soils and substrate, and characteristic plant community, and identified wetland type. Five wetland types can be found in the United States. These include: coastal wetlands, called "marine"; tidally influenced wetlands, called "estuarine"; wetlands associated with rivers, or "riverine"; wetlands found along lakes, "lacustrine"; and wetlands referred to as "palustrine," which are scattered across the landscape because their hydrology is primarily dependent on precipitation and runoff. Hence, NWI maps are typically used as a starting point for locating wetlands.

PERMIT PROCESS

Impacts to wetlands are regulated by the U.S. ACE and U.S. EPA through a permit process. Decisions to issue or deny permits are based on a public-interest review and on compliance with Section 404(b)(1) guidelines developed by the U.S. EPA, which specifically relates to water quality. This process involves a series of steps where wetland impact avoidance is first. If avoidance is not possible through project redesign, minimization of impacts is second. As specified in a February 6, 1990, Memorandum of Agreement (MOA) between the U.S. ACE and the U.S. EPA, compensatory mitigation is required for unavoidable adverse impacts, which remain after all appropriate avoidance and minimization steps have been undertaken. This MOA strives to achieve a goal of no net loss, which refers to wetland area as well as function and value. This is the rationale for integrating wetland preservation with low-impact, or sustainable land planning best practices into land development and flood control and stormwater management projects.

"Mitigation" refers to the practicable actions that rectify, reduce over time, and compensate for impacts. Mitigation can involve the purchase and protection of existing wetland through conservation easements and deed restrictions. This option is called "preservation." Mitigation can also involve improving the function and value of an existing degraded wetland and is referred to as "enhancement." "Restoration" is putting back a wetland that once existed, as opposed to "creation," which is converting an upland or nonwetland area to a wetland. Another mitigation option includes the purchase of "credit" in an approved mitigation bank, where wetlands have already been preserved or created ahead of project impacts, and sometimes by a third party. (Further information can be obtained in the November 28, 1995, *Federal Guidance for Establishment, Use, and Operation of Mitigation Banks.*)

Mitigation is undertaken either on a project site or off-site, in close proximity and in the same watershed to where an impact occurred. One requirement of mitigation is that wetlands have buffers. A buffer is an area adjacent to a wetland that functions to protect the wetland from adjacent land-use disturbances. Recommended buffer ranges in width depending upon buffer goal and level of wetland protection being achieved. Some literature specifies a minimum of 1,000 feet for maintenance of high-quality wetlands. Within this dimension, buffers that are 50 to 100 feet wide can support some water quality improvements, while buffers of 100 to 350 feet or more can provide some wildlife habitat functions. (See www.mitigationactionplan.gov/Buffer_8-27-04.htm for more technical information.)

PROJECT CONSIDERATIONS

Notably, more and more projects involve stream and river protection and restoration, particularly as an aspect of flood control or erosion control projects. Necessary first steps include an inventory and assessment of site conditions. (A fairly comprehensive review of stream assessment techniques and protocols is provided in *Physical Stream Assessment: A Review of Selected Protocols* by Somerville, D.E. and B.A. Pruitt, March 2004, which was prepared for the U.S. EPA.) A next step is determining a proper functioning condition for a created or restored stream or river segment. Proper functioning condition (PFC) describes the physical attributes of a watercourse and its associated

Georganna Collins, RLA, Wetland Scientist, Leap Engineering, LLC, Beaumont, Texas; Aaron J. Tuley, Planner, Ecology and Environment, Inc., Houston, Texas

vegetation areas relative to those attributes being able to provide desired functions and values (Restoration, 2000). PFC also refers to a qualitative method for assessing the condition of riparian and wetland areas of a water course (Pritchard, 1998). A "riparian corridor" is the woody vegetation—that is, the trees, shrubs, and vines—growing adjacent to, and in association with rivers, creeks, streams, and bayous. Riparian corridors may or may not include wetlands. The concept of continuous physical connection or lack of fragmentation is important to healthy ecological function of a riparian corridor. The desirable functions for a given watercourse must be identified. For example, for the watercourse to function properly, the riparian and wetland areas would have adequate open vegetated areas, a landform and physical configuration, and extent of large, mature woodland present to (1) dissipate flow energy associated with high volumes, thereby reducing erosion and improving water quality; (2) filter suspended sediment, capture bed load, and aid in floodplain development; (3) improve floodwater retention in floodplain areas; (4) develop root masses that stabilize banks against cutting action; (5) develop diverse wetlands, ponds, and other natural channel features to provide usable habitat with water depths, inundation durations, and temperature/oxygen necessary for fish production, waterfowl breeding, and other wildlife utilization; and (6) support greater biodiversity.

RIPARIAN AND WATERCOURSE PROTECTION

Effective watercourse protection, restoration, and/or creation requires an understanding of ecology and fluvial processes. These subjects are broad, complex, and are beyond the scope of this discussion, which only highlights the need for thorough site assessments and thoughtful, detailed design once conceptual elements of a plan are identified.

Water supply, flood flow attenuation, recreation, and scenic quality are generally the most noted functions of watercourses; however, habitat and wildlife migration corridor, buffer of pollutants, recycle nutrients, convert energy, and recharge water supplies such as downstream water bodies of bays and estuaries are other equally important functions that must be considered and integrated into plans and projects.

Generally, riparian and watercourse protection restoration, can take one of three approaches to achieve balance, equilibrium, and recover functions. These approaches include:

- Undisturbed self-recovery
- Assisted recovery
- Full restoration

Generally, because of the desire to provide contact recreation, improve water quality, and increase habitat, among other objectives, full restoration of many watercourses is required. Full restoration means rebuilding physical, chemical, and biological functions that are currently beyond a self-repair capacity of most urban watercourses.

The process of watercourse restoration involves setting project site boundaries; problem identification; developing goals, objectives, and performance criteria; developing and evaluating alternatives; detailed design development; implementation; monitoring, and adaptive site management. Critical considerations are to:

- Preserve natural hydrology, or restore as much as practical the hydrology to a wetland or watercourse by constructing upstream storage areas to detain water for up to 24 hours.
- Reduce inflow of pollutants by retrofitting detention areas with treatment wetlands, undertaking a watershed pollution prevention program, and eliminating sanitary sewer connections to the stormwater sewer network.
- Stabilize channel banks with flatter side slopes, introduction of wetlands, riprap, lives staking, brush bundles, and other bioengineering methods.
- Restore in stream habitat structure by adding pools and riffles, undercuts for greater structural com-

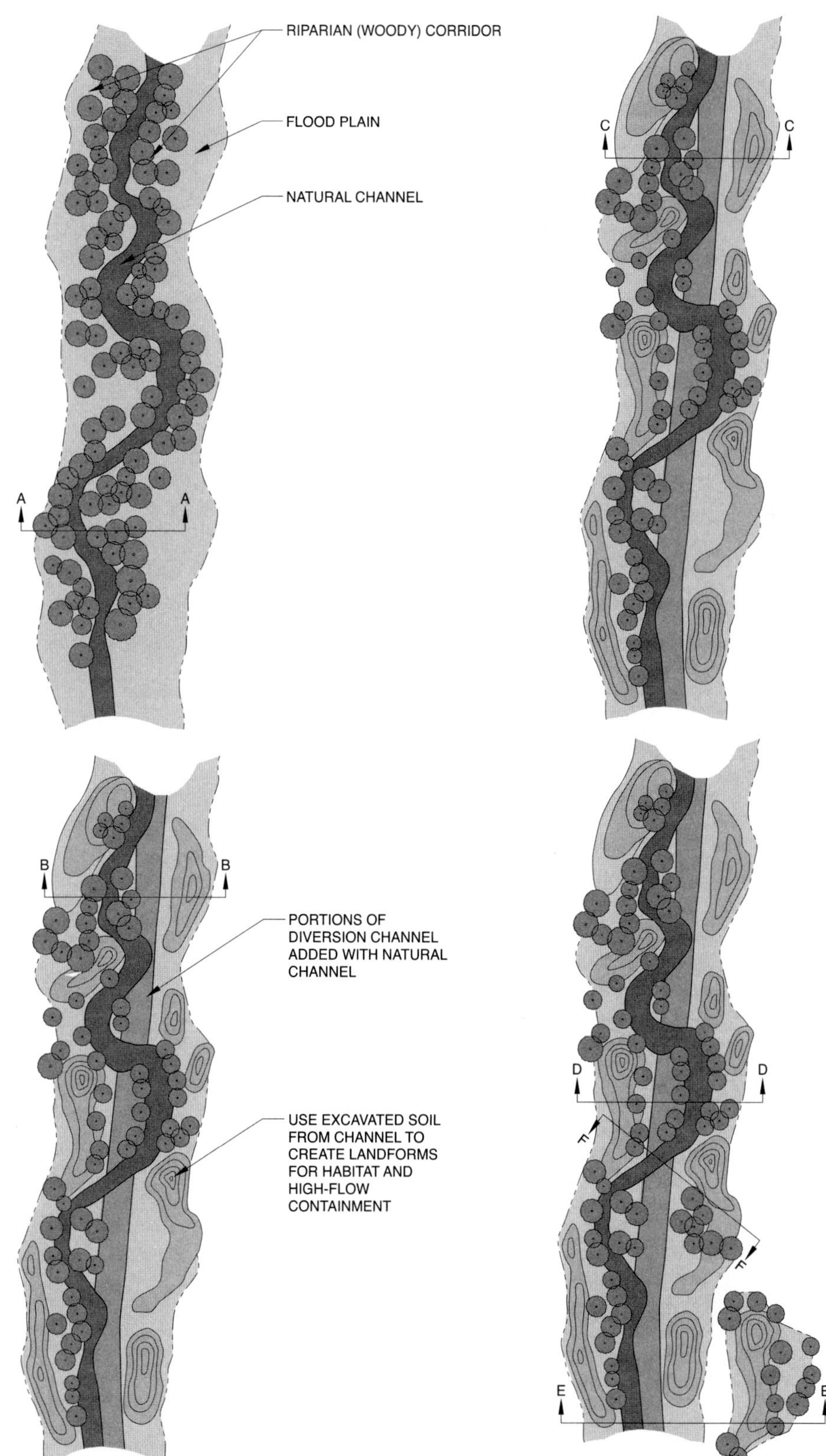

PLAN VIEW SCHEMATIC DIAGRAMS

Georganna Collins, RLA, Wetland Scientist, Leap Engineering, LLC, Beaumont, Texas; Aaron J. Tuley, Planner, Ecology and Environment, Inc., Houston, Texas

plexity of the bed with log checkdams, low-flow weirs, wing deflectors, and rock/boulder clusters to improve fish habitat.

- Reestablish riparian cover and overhead canopy cover with active planting, invasive species removal, and changes in mowing operations.
- Protect critical watercourse features, including associated wetlands and substrate with means to redirect flow, concentrate flow, or mechanically remove excessive sediment accumulation.
- Allow for intentional planting and subsequent recolonization of faunal species by checking the watershed/system for barriers to migration for fish and other wildlife movement.

(For additional information, refer to the *Federal Interagency Stream Restoration Working Group Guidebook on Stream Corridor Restoration, Principles, Processes, and Practices,* October 1998.)

Specific to many urban watercourses is the need to address the two-dimensional plan form, where flood conveyance requires it to be straight and environmental functions require it to be braided and meandering. The following figures show a combination of straight high-flood channel integrated with preservation of a natural meandering channel. Sinuosity must be calculated and other attributes assessed, including slope, channel width, bed form, sediment load, sediment composition, and flow. Generally, urban watercourses lack riffle and pool sequences, natural islands and bars, and a floodplain, where wetlands are located. In cross section, the channel width should vary from wide to narrow, and channel depth should vary from shallow to deep. Depth of any diversion channel must also take into account soil permeability and the adverse potential of draining the natural channel intended for preservation.

The physical conditions of a channel are affected by a range of flows, as illustrated in the sequence of

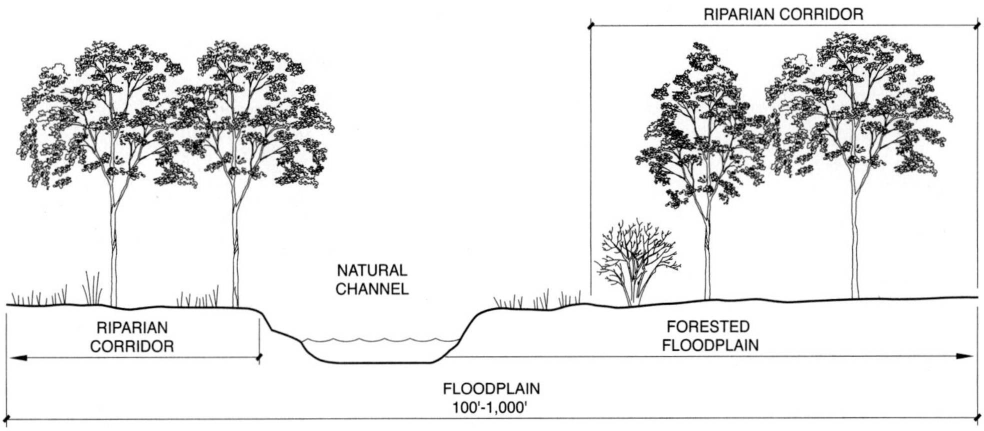

SECTION A: NATURAL CHANNEL AND ASSOCIATED RIPARIAN ZONES AND FLOODPLAIN

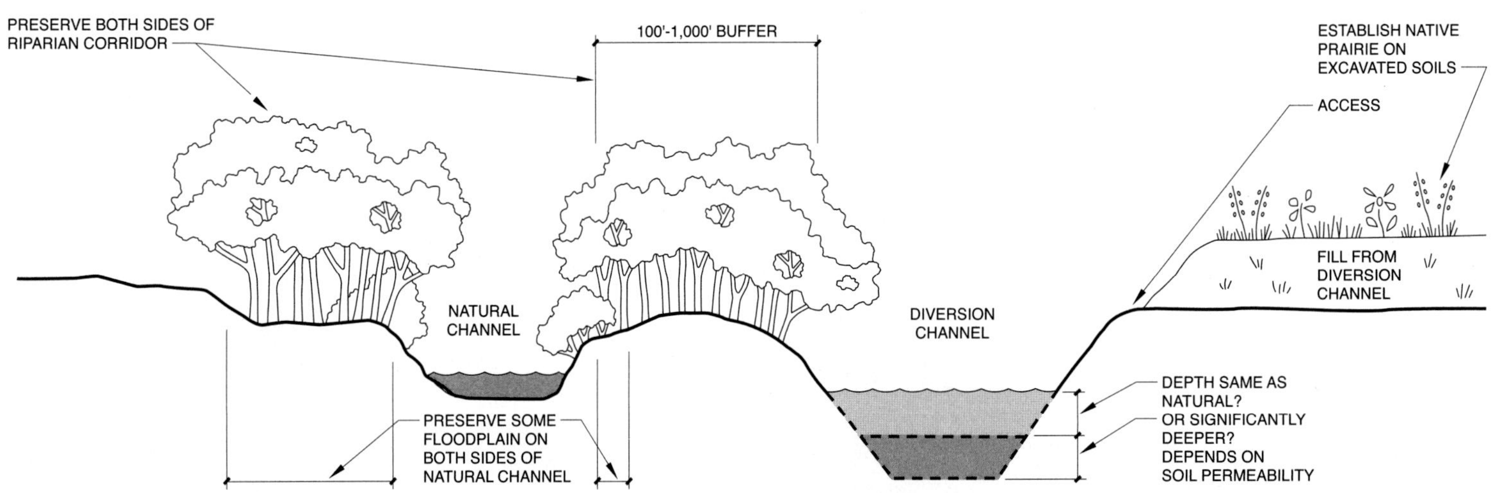

SECTION B: PLACEMENT OF DIVERSION CHANNEL ALLOWS FOR PRESERVATION OF BOTH BANKS OF NATURAL CHANNEL

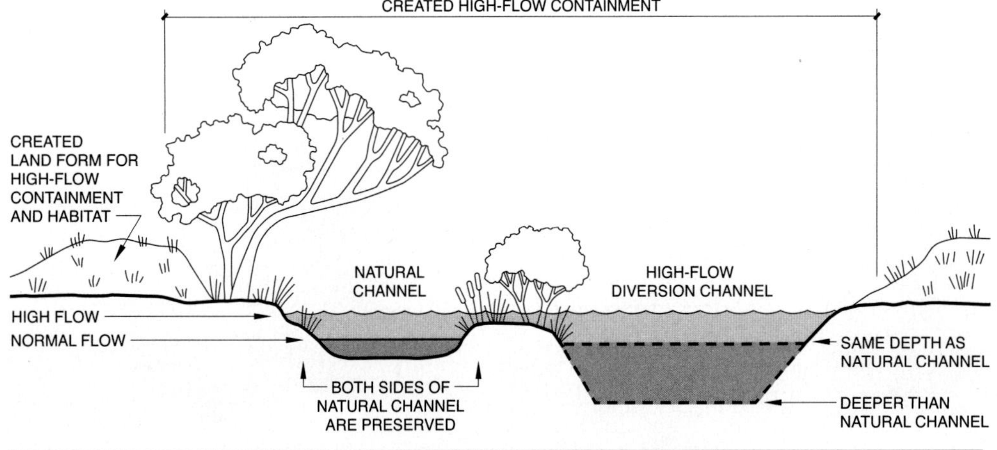

SECTION C: CREATION OF HIGH-FLOW CONTAINMENT AREA

Georganna Collins, RLA, Wetland Scientist, Leap Engineering, LLC, Beaumont, Texas; Aaron J. Tuley, Planner, Ecology and Environment, Inc., Houston, Texas

schematic plan diagrams A through D. Flows are sometimes referred to as discharges. Channel-forming flows are bank-full discharge, a specific event discharge, or effective discharge. These three discharges are roughly equivalent for stable channels, yet vary drastically in unstable channels. These flows would need to be quantified in order to assess the feasibility of any plan for proposed wetland and watercourse restoration measures. Bank-full discharge is the discharge that fills a stable channel up to a designed elevation and would flow over to an active floodplain without overtopping the banks.

Consideration must also be given to the flows that affect form and function, such as low flows and their effect on sustaining wetland habitat, as well as extreme high flows and the design 100-year flood flows. All of these should be tabulated to determine habitat restoration, channel structural stability, effectiveness of stormwater conveyance, and, therefore, the feasibility of any plan. Section A shows the natural channel, and its associated riparian zones and floodplain. Cross sections B through F illustrate options for placement of a diversion channel in proximity to a natural channel.

Section B illustrates how the placement of the diversion channel allows for the preservation of both banks of the natural channel. The depth of the diversion channel can either be the same as the natural channel or significantly deeper, again taking into account soil permeability among other factors. Section C illustrates the created high-flow containment area, with maintenance berms immediately adjacent to the natural channel and diversion channel edges. By shifting the conventional maintenance berms away from the channel edges, as illustrated in section D, the floodplain width can be increased, providing additional area for floodwater energy to dissipate and suspended sediment to be removed in adjacent wetlands. Section E shows the expansion of

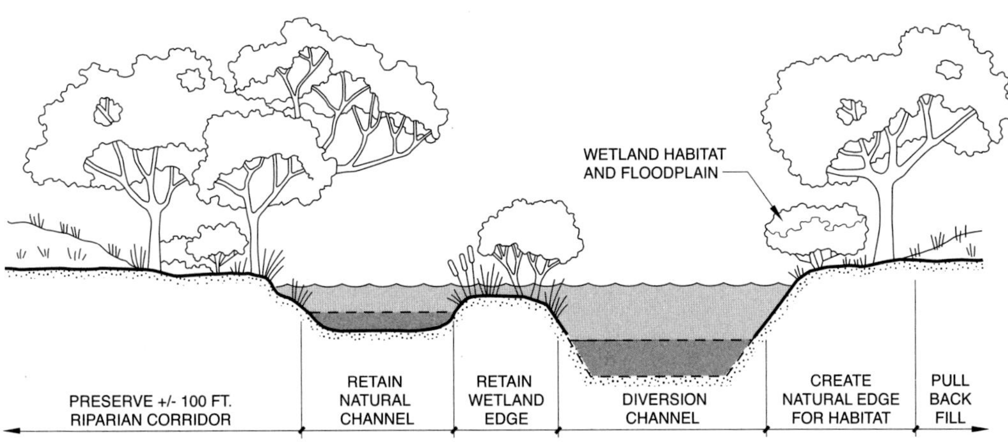

SECTION D: SHIFTING OF MAINTENANCE BERMS AWAY FROM CHANNEL EDGES

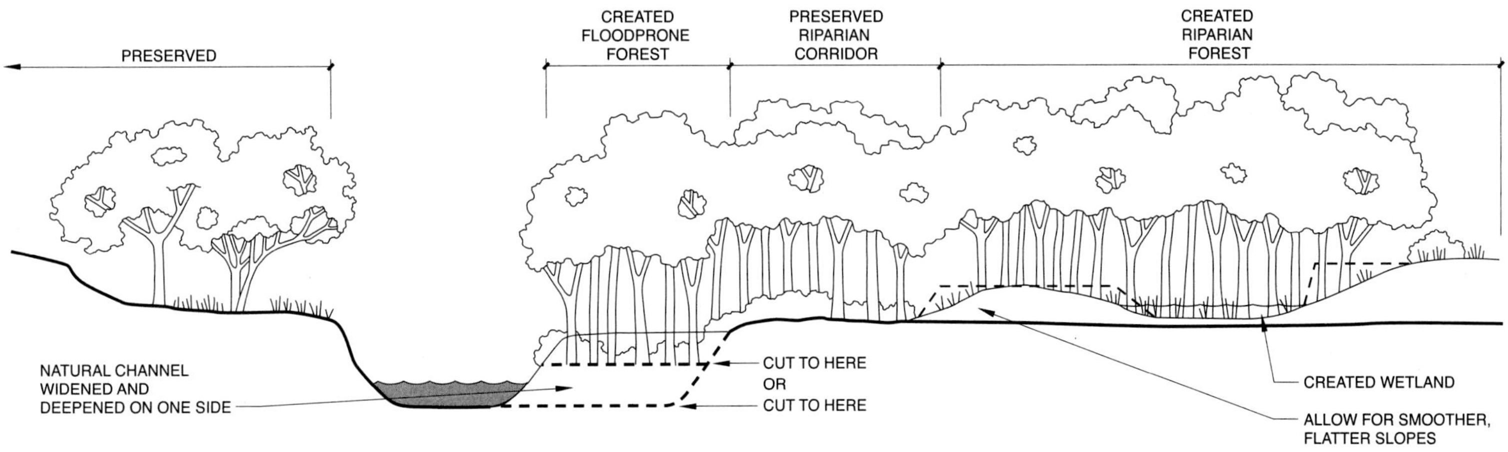

SECTION E: EXPANSION OF ONE SIDE OF NATURAL CHANNEL

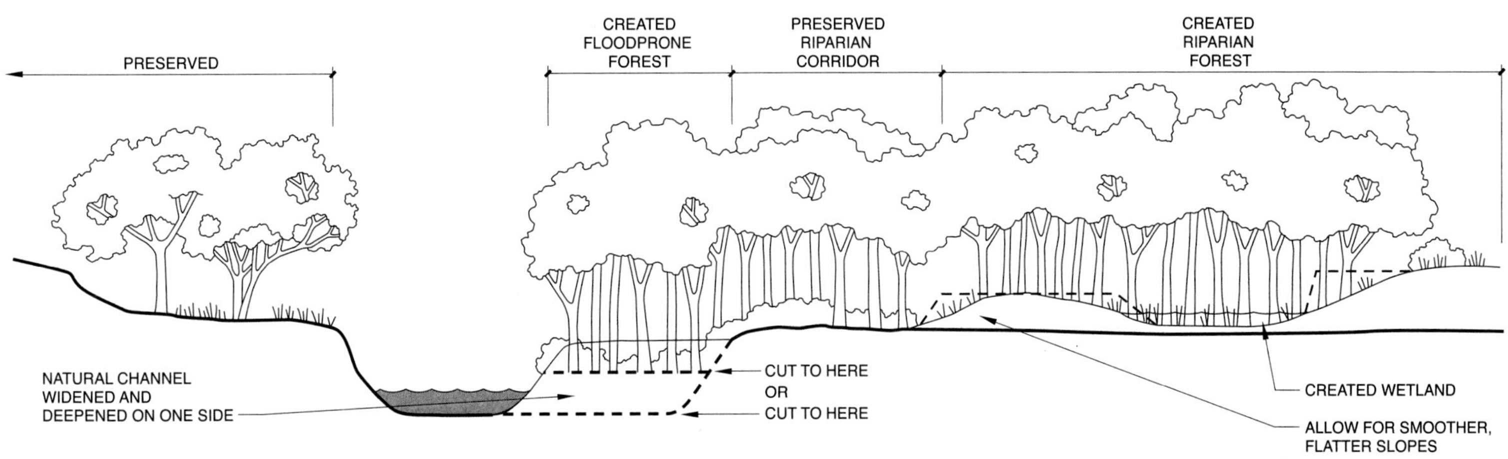

SECTION F: PLACEMENT OF EXCAVATED MATERIAL AND ADDITIONAL RIPARIAN PLANTING

Georganna Collins, RLA, Wetland Scientist, Leap Engineering, LLC, Beaumont, Texas; Aaron J. Tuley, Planner, Ecology and Environment, Inc., Houston, Texas

one side of the natural channel with placement of excavated material a distance beyond the selected portion of riparian area and then sculpted to create additional areas for floodwater detention and wetland habitat.

Section F illustrates how the placement of excavated material and additional riparian planting can be designed to maximize habitat creation and ecological functions, thus compensating for impacts to both sides of a natural channel.

Flow character, volumes, velocities, and resistance are other components beyond plan and cross-section configurations that go into the hydrology and hydraulics (H&H) models and analysis used to evaluate the minimum dimensions required for a water conveyance structure. However, beyond the hydraulic geometry of the channel, wetland areas and function must be considered regarding appropriate channel depths, widths, velocities, and slopes, to begin to answer questions about sustainability of plan elements. The underlying assumptions and limitations of mathematical equations used in the H&H models and associated analysis to assess existing and proposed hydraulic conditions and determine hydraulic geometry must be understood by the planner and landscape architects as well as hydrologist and engineer.

When long-term erosion exceeds sedimentation, the bayou channel incises, or cuts, into streambed, and the normal water surface becomes lower than the surrounding land surface. The banks get higher and steeper. Channel incision continues with reduced sediment load to the bayou, due to dams upstream and increased peak flows caused by more urban development over time.

The fluvial processes involved in channel response to urbanization are extremely complicated. Factors influencing form and stability are (1) discharge, (2) sediment load and sediment composition, (3) longitudinal slope and sinuosity, (4) resistance, (5) vegetation, (6) geology, and (7) man-made features. A further complication is whether an area in the watercourse is a local problem or indicative of a systemwide channel stability problem. If it is determined to be the latter, caution is advised if only local treatment to on-site conditions is implemented.

The proper watercourse restoration and protection measures should include means of addressing the following:

- Reduce discharge quantities to the watercourse.
- Reduce erratic peak discharge to the watercourse.
- Reduce flow rates within the watercourse to that which soils and slopes can handle.
- Increase size of the channel to meet anticipated flow volumes.
- Restore adequate-sized floodplain.
- Assess types and extent of erosion occurring and determine appropriate repair measure per specific site conditions.
- Assess proposed elements of the plan (i.e., hard-edge treatments) and their effect on the remaining soft edges of a watercourse and its habitats.

REFERENCES

Cowardin, L. M., V. Carter, F. C. Golet, and E. T. LaRoe. 1979. Classification of Wetlands and Deepwater Habitats of the United States. FWS/OBS-79/31.USFWS, Washington, D.C.

Pritchard. 1998. *A User Guide to Assessing Proper Functioning Condition and Supporting Science for Lotic Areas.* Riparian Area Management TR 1737-15. U.S. Department of Interior, Bureau of Land Management, Denver, Colorado.

Reed, P. B. 1988. "National List of Plants That Occur in Wetlands." In *National Summary, USFWS Biological Report 88,* (24). USFWS, Washington, D.C.

Restoration of Urban Streams and Flood Control Channels Workshop, 2000. Sponsored by the Association of State Floodplain Managers, Waterways Restoration Institute, U.S. EPA, and Harris County Flood Control District, Houston, Texas.

United States Department of Agriculture, Soil Conservation Service. 1991. "Hydric Soils of the United States." In cooperation with the National Technical Committee for Hydric Soils. Miscellaneous Publication Number 1491. USDA, Washington, D.C.

See also:

Constructed Treatment Wetlands
Ecological Community Restoration
Resource Inventory and Conservation
Wetlands Evaluation

Georganna Collins, RLA, Wetland Scientist, Leap Engineering, LLC, Beaumont, Texas; Aaron J. Tuley, Planner, Ecology and Environment, Inc., Houston, Texas

WASTEWATER MANAGEMENT: GRAYWATER HARVEST AND TREATMENT

THE VALUE OF GRAYWATER

Graywater is essentially wash water. It consists of all household wastewater, aside from toilet water (also known as black water). The same contents that make graywater a pollutant in some areas (streams, rivers, and groundwater) also make graywater a resource in others. Because graywater often contains nitrogen, phosphorus, and potassium (all important nutrients for plants), it is quite useful when applied to vegetation.

TREATMENT SYSTEM

First, a pipe system is needed to transport the graywater from its source. These pipes can be thinner than regular wastewater pipes because they do not have to transport toilet water and solid waste. To avoid grease clogs, these pipes should be installed straight, avoiding any necks and depressions, and should be held to at least a 0.5 percent gradient.

For small systems in which the graywater is to be put to use immediately, treatment is not as crucial. The graywater can be directed to a mulch bed and used for plants. However, in larger systems, where the graywater is not to be used immediately and must be stored, pretreatment is needed. Clogs and odor can result from solid matter suspended in the graywater. Additionally, graywater can contain pollutants, pathogens, heavy metals, and microorganisms. If these contents are not treated, they can break down, resulting in undesirable anaerobic conditions.

How can these materials be removed? They can be removed by gravity (similar to a septic tank), by premade filter, or by gravel filter. The method of treatment will depend on the size of the system and destination of the graywater supply.

CONTROLLED IRRIGATION

The soil ecosystem of the destination plant bed is used to convert the graywater. The amount of water released into the soil should be configured to meet the evapotranspiration rate of the plants it feeds. This rate is usually between 1 to 4 gallons per square yard per day. If too much water is applied, saturation occurs. If too little water is applied, plan growth will be inhibited by lack of resources. In either case, the plant life suffers.

SOIL FILTER SYSTEMS

Soil layers are used to filter the graywater before it reaches its destination. A soil with medium particle size should be selected. Soils too fine or too coarse will not allow the water to filter through properly. Saturation should be avoided. Some pores should be free for gas exchange.

It is also important to provide for even water distribution across the filter. If water distribution is uneven, clogs will result and the filtering process will not be as effective. A well-designed soil filter system will have high pollutant removal efficiencies (see the table "Soil Filter Removal Efficiencies").

SOIL FILTER REMOVAL EFFICIENCIES

MATERIAL	REMOVAL EFFICIENCY
Suspended solids and organic compounds	90–99%
Pathogens	95–99.9%
Phosphorus	30–95% (depends on soil properties and water load)
Nitrogen	30%

TRICKLING FILTERS

Trickling filters consist of layers of porous materials with a lot of surface area. Water is dispersed over the top of the filter and percolates downward as a thin layer, treated aerobically as it passes over the surfaces of the filter materials. Via an underdrainage system, the water is then collected and solids are allowed to settle before the water is transported to its destination site. The advantage to this system is that it is reliable and can recover from wastewater excesses. Trickling filters are not as efficient as soil filters, however, and they create a sludge that must be removed.

GRAYWATER END USE

The end use of graywater can be directed to the following:

- *Discharged to surface waters.* Graywater is discharged to surface water quite easily. After treatment, the water can be released into open trenches and allowed to wash away with rainwater.
- *Groundwater.* If it is intended to be released to groundwater, graywater must be well treated with a very reliable system. After treatment, the water should seep through an unsaturated soil depth of 3 feet or more before joining groundwater. In addition, safety zones should be set around water extraction sites to avoid complications.
- *Irrigation.* When graywater is used in irrigation, it is best to apply in the ground, as opposed to being sprayed. Graywater is best suited in irrigation of cropland that supports plants whose leaves or stems are not eaten directly. Fruit and berry plants are appropriate. When using graywater in irrigation of crops that are consumed raw, it is advisable to wait at least a month after irrigation to harvest.

GRAYWATER MANAGEMENT GOALS

The preventive goals of graywater treatment are to leave nearby areas undamaged, avoid odor and stagnant water, prevent anaerobic conditions in the water, and to keep groundwater and reservoirs uncontaminated. When all these goals are met, graywater treatment yields tremendously positive results. It can be used for landscaping, plant growth, and renewed groundwater. Perhaps most importantly, water that is treated and reused allows freshwater in natural ecosystems to remain untouched.

There are many laws in place regulating how graywater can be treated and what it can be reused for. These laws vary from state to state and must be reviewed and checked closely before a plan for graywater use is proposed and implemented. Despite legal barriers, many developers and scientists believe that with further testing and studies, graywater treatment systems will become more prevalent. In fact, a few companies now offer installation of contained (includes a lining), ornamental graywater gardens.

REFERENCES

EcoSanRes. April, 2005. "Introduction to Greywater Management." www.ecosanres.com.

Environmental Protection Agency (EPA). 2004. "EPA Consultation: Graywater." www.epa.gov.

Lindstrom, Carl. 2000. "Greywater: Synopsis" and "Greywater: Treatment." www.greywater.com.

Marshall, Glenn. 1997. "Greywater Re-use: Hardware: Health, Environment, and the Law." IPC-VI Conference. Permaculture Association of Western Australia Inc. and authors, www.rosneath.com.au.

National Association of Conservation Districts. 2005. "Constructed Wetlands Put to Work." www.nacdnet.org.

Wynn, James. January 2002. "Innovative and Alternative On-Site Treatment of Residential Wastewater." Panich, Noel, and Associates Architects and Engineers, Athens, Ohio.

See also:
Constructed Treatment Wetlands
Irrigation
Stormwater Management

Thomas Hopper and Leonard J. Hopper, RLA, FASLA

CONSTRUCTED TREATMENT WETLANDS

Constructed wetland systems have been designed and installed over the past few decades all over the world, with thousands of examples in the United States, Canada, Europe, Australia, South America, India, and Africa. While the primary purpose of constructed wetlands is generally to treat various kinds of wastewater and stormwater, these systems can provide multiple additional amenities. Many constructed wetland systems provide wildlife habitat and function as public attractions. From backyard residential installations to large-scale municipal treatment systems, constructed wetlands have been gaining in acceptance from both designers and regulators as experience and performance in their construction is documented.

The origin of knowledge related to the capability of wetlands in removal of pollutants dates back to observations in the twentieth century by many scientists and others of natural wetlands and the significant difference in the inflow and outflow quality. These observations led to experiments and the development of pilot-scale wetland treatment systems in Germany and, later, in the United States, with the Tennessee Valley Authority (TVA) taking the lead in the Southeast. As knowledge expanded, based on experience in various regions of the United States and in other countries, guidelines were developed for various applications by the TVA, the U.S. Environmental Protection Agency (U.S. EPA), and, in some cases, local authorities. Data are still being gathered to allow a more precise set of design guidelines for specific climates and applications, and this effort at fine-tuning the design standards will result in a better tool for a field that is still evolving.

The range of applications for which constructed wetlands have been utilized is extremely large. The greatest number of installations have been within the single-family residential category, with literally thousands of small-scale constructed wetlands, primarily subsurface-flow types, built in many regions, particularly in the southern part of the United States. Kentucky alone has listed more than 4,000 such installations. Going up in scale from the residential installations, wetland treatment systems have been designed to treat zoos, dairy farm wastes, candy factory effluent, resorts, campground toilets, residential subdivisions, and many other situations where a constructed wetland system was economically feasible. Constructed wetlands have also long been employed to treat acid mine drainage, and have proven to be successful, by utilizing particular plant species, in degrading TNT and other explosives residues.

The largest constructed wetland systems have generally been employed with municipal or regional wastewater treatment installations, often as tertiary treatment units, in tandem with conventional existing secondary wastewater treatment plants facing higher standards in their discharge permits. Here are three examples:

- One of the largest in this category is the 650-acre constructed wetland unit in Beaumont, Texas, now known as the Cattail Marsh, that preserved and enhanced a preexisting 250-acre natural wetland and was constructed at about half the cost of expanding the existing treatment plant.
- The Tres Rios Constructed Wetlands Demonstration Project outside Phoenix, Arizona, a pilot project undertaken to evaluate the cost-effectiveness of wetlands compared to the $625 million upgrade of the 91st Avenue plant that would be required to meet discharge standards, proved to be highly successful, at a cost of $80 million and with only two full-time employees to operate and maintain the system.
- The Greater Baton Rouge Zoo is operating cost-efficiently with an innovative constructed wetland treatment system treating 400,000 gallons per day of effluent, which saves an estimated $200,000 annually in sewer fee charges.

An area of innovative application that is more developed in Europe than in the United States is the

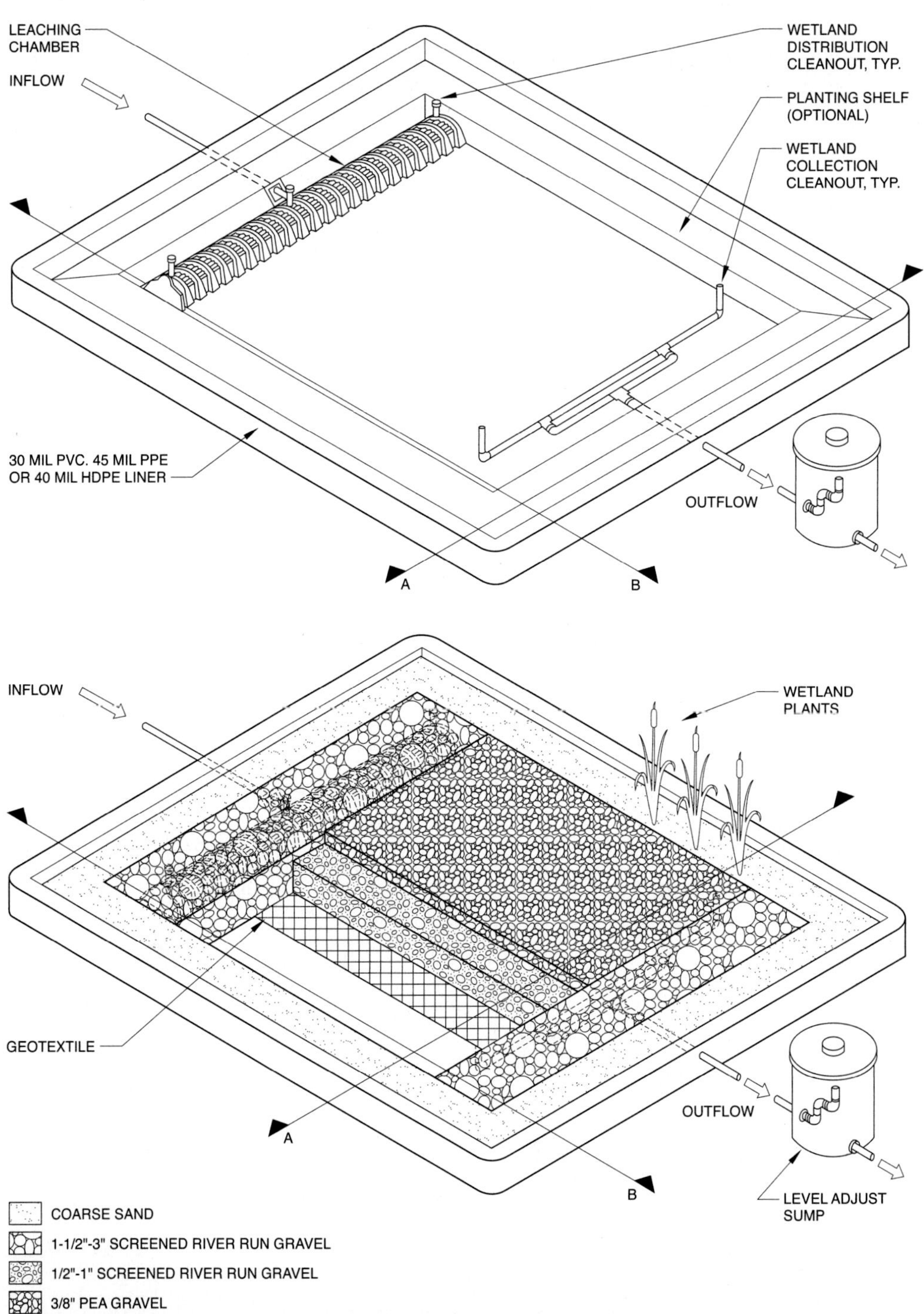

CONSTRUCTED WETLAND ASSEMBLY OVERVIEW

Source: Natural Systems International, LLC.

Craig Campbell, FASLA

use of constructed wetland installations to purify swimming pool water. A number of very large municipal swimming pond installations in Germany and Austria rely primarily on the wetlands for purification. Several firms in the United States have developed smaller-scale residential swimming ponds utilizing similar biological filter and wetland cells in the design of attractive, low-maintenance swimming pools that require no chemicals.

WETLAND FUNCTIONS

Wetland systems may be one unit of a multipart treatment system, or a stand-alone system. Wetlands are essentially biological filters and, ideally, operate in conjunction with other treatment elements. The basic functions of wetlands that relate to pollutant removal are the following:

- Nutrient removal and recycling
- Sedimentation
- Biological oxygen demand (BOD)
- Metals precipitation
- Pathogen removal
- Toxic compound degradation

The main constituents of wastewater that normally provide the basis for determining the wetland design are:

- *Biological oxygen demand (BOD).* This is a measure of the organic compounds in wastewater that require oxidation to become stable.
- *Suspended solids (SS).* These are the organic and inorganic particles in wastewater.
- *Nitrogen.* Nitrogen is considered a pollutant if discharged into water bodies, but a valuable resource when used to irrigate crops or a landscape.

A constructed wetland will require discharge or disposal of the treated effluent, either into the ground or on the surface through discharge to streams, lakes, or ponds. Evaporation is also a means of disposal of the treated effluent, but each method of disposal has different standards for pollutant removal.

TYPES OF SYSTEMS

There are three general types of constructed wetland treatment systems: subsurface flow wetlands (SFW), free water surface wetlands (FWS), and vertical flow wetlands (VF).

Subsurface Flow Wetlands (SFW)

For residential and larger systems, up to 75,000 to 80,000 gallons per day, subsurface flow wetlands with anaerobic pretreatment (septic tanks, etc.) are usually the most cost-effective systems. They are typically designed as cells or a series of cells, approximately 18 to 24 inches in depth, with a liner and gravel fill.

Experience has demonstrated that the size of the gravel is important, as the porosity—or hydraulic conductivity—varies with size. Larger rock has smaller total voids but greater hydraulic conductivity; sand has a greater total void volume than pea gravel but lower hydraulic conductivity. Generally speaking, the lower the hydraulic conductivity, the more prone a wetland is to clogging, particularly at the front or influent end. Some designers feel that the best combination of hydraulic conductivity and void ratio can be found in the range of gravel between ½ inch and 1 inch in size, but install larger 1½- to 3-inch rock in the front end of the system to allow more space for solids to settle out. Proprietary products such as the Infiltrator may also be used for the same purpose and provide better opportunities to monitor and clean out solids period-

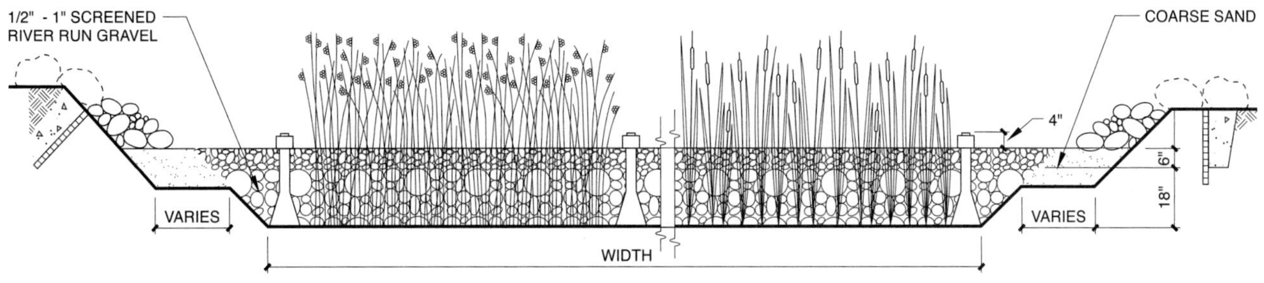

SECTION A
ACROSS SECTION OF FLOW

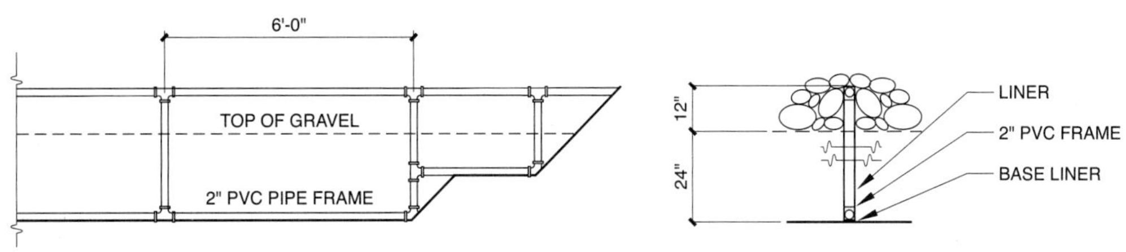

ADJOINING WETLAND CELL DIVIDING WALL

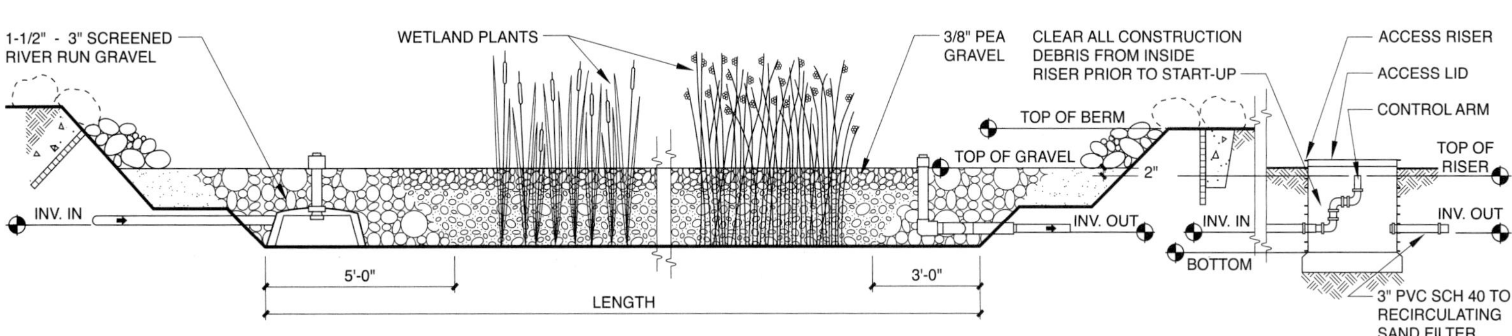

SECTION B
IN DIRECTION OF FLOW

CONSTRUCTED WETLAND GRAVEL FILL AND PLANTING APPLICATION

Source: Natural Systems International, LLC.

Craig Campbell, FASLA

ically, if necessary. As gravel is not readily available in some regions, alternative materials such as rubber tire granules have been used successfully.

The three genera of plants that are the most commonly employed in the United States in constructed wetland systems are cattails *(Typha* spp.), bulrushes *(Scirpus* spp.), and reed *(Phragmites* spp.). Cattails and reeds are both aggressive and have the capability to crowd out other less competitive wetland plantings. Often, more ornamental plants such as cannas and iris are installed around the edges of wetland cells, especially in residential applications. Plants are installed directly the gravel bed, either as nursery-grown or collected stock, preferably in the spring.

Based on observations and performance of many subsurface flow systems, several types of innovations have been developed by a number of designers that improve performance by increasing the available oxygen to oxidize ammonia to nitrate, the first step for nitrogen removal. These alternative systems, most of which are patented, rely on recirculation, cyclic filling, and draining down the cells (reciprocating bed process; Behrends, 1999), or aeration introduced into the gravel layer, which improves oxygen transfer without draining and filling (Wallace, 2002b, 2002c). These systems, although normally only appropriate for applications larger than single-family residences, have proven to be highly effective in meeting stringent treatment standards. The aerated system in several tests outperformed the conventional and the drawdown (filling and draining) systems.

Free Water Surface Wetlands (FWS)

Free water surface wetlands rely on different processes for much of the treatment, and, ideally, do not incorporate emergent vegetation in more than 50 percent of the total free water surface area. The basic design and construction of surface flow wetlands is similar to subsurface flow wetlands but without the gravel.

A planting medium, usually a sand/clay/loam mixture, must be placed over the liner to a depth of 12 inches for cattails and 18 inches if bulrush will be used. This material must be compacted to 85 percent modified Proctor density to prevent new plantings from breaking free and floating. It is critical that the water depth be gradually raised after the plants are installed, to ensure survival.

Vertical Flow Wetlands (VF)

Vertical flow wetlands are designed to produce either a downward or an upward flow mode, with the primary application for nitrification being a downflow mode. Considered the state of the art in Europe, VF wetlands have not been designed or installed extensively in the United States. These systems can include flow recirculation that functions similarly to the recirculating gravel filters that have been employed for many years in on-site wastewater treatment. Recirculating VF wetlands offer the advantage of being able to nitrify and denitrify in a smaller footprint than other types of wetland systems, but the recirculation ratio is a major control parameter that must be "tuned" to the particular installation.

APPLICATIONS

Many issues and questions must be addressed when evaluating the performance and the cost-effectiveness of a constructed wetland treatment system. For residential systems, the space requirements are normally quite reasonable, usually ranging from 1 square foot of wetland treatment area per gallon per day. Most residences range from 40 to 75 gallons per day per person; Ohio sets it at 400 gallons per home per day. The actual total per home will vary considerably depending on family size, habits, location, and other factors.

Among the questions that need to be addressed as part of an evaluation of a constructed wetland treatment system are the following:

- *Establish treatment goals.* What are the local requirements for the particular facility in terms of BOD, nitrogen and phosphorus, and suspended solids?
- *Estimate design flows.* What is the estimated flow in gallons per day; is this likely to increase, and if so to what level at what time?
- *Characterize wastewater flow.* What are the characteristics of the wastewater? Is it entirely domestic, or are there industrial, agricultural, or other sources?
- *Evaluate regulatory environment.* Do the local and state regulators currently recognize the role of constructed wetlands in wastewater treatment? What are the requirements for surface discharge, land application, or subsurface disposal?
- *Determine site topography, soil, and groundwater conditions.* Is there an up-to-date topographical survey of the site, and if so, what are the typical slope conditions? What types of soil conditions occur, and what is the depth to groundwater?
- *Evaluate climate.* What are the precipitation and temperature in January and June? What are the soil temperature, pan evaporation, average solar radiation, and growing season?

DESIGN PARAMETERS

In general, an engineer will be required to develop the design standards and to certify or stamp the construction drawings for installations larger than residential in scale. The variations in climate, soils, wastewater characteristics, and other factors vary considerably from one region to another; and design standards are continually being refined and updated as new design and performance data are reviewed and confirmed. A number of mathematical formulas are employed to develop the most effective design standards for constructed wetland systems. Various calculations have been developed for total suspended solids (TSS), nitrogen, pathogen, and BOD and ammonia removal. Among the many elements factored into these equations are the following:

- Projected flow, Q, in gallons or cubic meters per day
- Estimated influent BOD in mg/L (milligrams per liter)
- Required effluent BOD discharge limits in mg/L
- Temperature-dependent rate constant
- Depth of gravel bed for subsurface flow systems
- Porosity of gravel
- Hydraulic retention time

The hydraulic retention time (HRT) is the time the wastewater needs to stay in the wetland, or more precisely, how long it takes from the input to the time the effluent leaves the wetland system. The longer the wastewater stays in the wetland, the more time for the biological processes to cleanse the effluent. Generally, the retention time is a minimum of two to three days.

While many early constructed wetland systems were designed in a rectangular or linear configuration, with the influent being introduced at the narrow end, this type of design resulted in early clogging of the gravel by solids due to the concentration and rate of flow. The flow through a square configuration of the same size, for example, would result in a faster flow that reduces the solids buildup in the influent zone.

LINERS

The most common material used to line wetland cells is polyvinyl chloride (PVC), at least 30 mil in thickness, due both to the lowest cost and the fact that PVC is the easiest to work with. While it has the most flexibility of all liner materials, it has the least resistance to ultraviolet degradation and, therefore, must be covered with soil or other materials for protection. Other liner materials that are commonly utilized are polypropylene (PPE), polyethylene (PE), hypalon, and bentonite clay. When budgets allow for the highest-quality liner, the best solution is a liner with a scrim such as 60-mil hypalon or 45-mil PPE, which are the toughest materials and most resistant to punctures, tears, and UV radiation. In addition, heavy vehicles can drive on them while placing soil or gravel without damage to the liner. Subgrade preparation is very important to achieve the best base for liner installation. A geotextile or sand layer over the subgrade is often required to prevent damage to the liners from rocks.

ADVANTAGES

There are many advantages to constructed wetlands, as opposed to alternative methods of water renovation, depending on the particular situation. Among those advantages are relatively low-cost construction and low operating costs, the landscape or aesthetic value, and potential wildlife habitat and interpretive value.

A common question often raised about constructed wetlands relates to their capability to perform adequately in cold climates. This question has been researched and thoroughly documented with experience in Canada, Minnesota, and high-elevation areas of Colorado, all of which have winters with many periods of well below zero Fahrenheit temperatures. Even though the removal rates drop in the winter, bacterial action is still present and the effluent below an ice level still maintains motion. In the states and in the countries with cold climates where constructed wetlands have clearly proven their effectiveness, there are few regulatory barriers from local officials. The opposite is, however, sometimes the case, where experience is lacking and where regulators may oppose constructed wetland systems. Some states, such as Arizona, Indiana, Iowa, and Kentucky have developed regulatory standards for constructed wetlands; others place these systems in an "experimental" or "alternative systems" category and are still monitoring performance. In a 1999 study undertaken by the Colorado Governor's Office of Energy Management and Conservation (OEMC), the "Colorado Constructed Treatment Wetlands Inventory," twenty constructed wetlands in the state were chosen to evaluate both features and actual performance in order to provide a guide for the

Craig Campbell, FASLA

design of future constructed wetland systems in a variety of settings. The report documented the minimal energy requirements, the educational value, the habitat for wildlife, and the added aesthetic value of wetland systems. This detailed analysis by a special task force of wetland experts that included engineers, biologists, government officials, facility operators and others provided a highly useful "best management practices" guide for the design of wetland systems that set a high standard for other regions of the country in their efforts to advance the knowledge about both design and performance of wetland treatment systems.

REFERENCES

Behrends, L. 1999. Reciprocating Subsurface Flow Constructed Wetlands for Improving Wastewater Treatment. United States Patent Office. [5,863,433] Washington DC, USA.

Campbell, C., and M. Ogden. 1999. *Constructed Wetlands in the Sustainable Landscape.* New York: John Wiley & Sons, Inc.

Kadlec, Robert H., and Robert L. Knight. 1996. *Treatment Wetlands.* Boca Raton, FL: CRC Press.

Middlebrooks, E. Joe, ed. 1999. "Colorado Constructed Treatment Wetlands Inventory." Colorado Governor's Office of Energy Management and Conservation.

Moshiri, Gerald A., ed. 1993. *Constructed Wetlands for Water Quality Improvement.* Chelsea, MI: Lewis Publishers.

Reed, S. C., R. W. Crites, and E. J. Middlebrooks. 1995. *Natural Systems for Waste Management and Treatment,* 2nd ed. New York: McGraw Hill.

U.S. EPA. 1993. *Constructed Wetlands for Wastewater Treatment and Wildlife Habitat.* Washington, D.C. EPA.

U.S. EPA. 1993. *Subsurface Flow Constructed Wetlands for Wastewater Treatment: A Technology Assessment.* U.S. EPA Office of Water, EPA 832-R-93-008. Washington, D.C.: Municipal Technology Branch, U.S. EPA.

Wallace, S. 2002b. "Treatment of Cheese-Processing Waste Using Subsurface Flow Wetlands." In *Wetlands and Remediation II,* K. Nehring and S. Braun, eds. Columbus, OH: Battelle Press.

———. 2002c. "On-Site Remediation of Petroleum Contact Wastes Using Subsurface Flow Wetlands." In *Wetlands and Remediation II,* K. Nehring and S. Braun, eds. Columbus, OH: Battelle Press.

See also:

Ecological Community Restoration
Resource Inventory and Conservation
Wetland Preservation
Wetlands Evaluation

Craig Campbell, FASLA

STORMWATER MANAGEMENT

SITE DESIGN FOR STORMWATER MANAGEMENT

INTRODUCTION

Urban watersheds control the quality of aquatic and riparian habitats, local water supplies, and streamside properties. Development alters the path of water through urban watersheds and through the hydrologic cycle as a whole. Removal of vegetation eliminates natural transpiration. Addition of impervious roofs and pavements eliminates soil infiltration and groundwater recharge. Surface runoff carries nonpoint-source pollutants, erodes stream channels, and increases flood frequency and severity. Stream base flow declines, making it harder for aquatic ecosystems to survive. Some urban communities are left with local water shortages. The purpose of stormwater management is to reduce or eliminate these alterations of the hydrologic cycle and their human and ecological consequences.

SITE DESIGN PROVISIONS

This section lists site design provisions for stormwater protection and restoration, compiled from the resources listed at the end. They can be applied on any site, with any type and intensity of proposed development. Their effects are to maintain preexisting healthy hydrologic function to the extent possible, and to restore functions where they have been set back by previous or new development. They tend to limit impervious cover, which controls the generation of runoff and pollution and the capability of remaining runoff to be treated in contact with soil and vegetation. Reducing the problem at the source with the type, distribution, and construction of development limits the number and size of treatment facilities that are needed downstream.

To prepare for design, site analysis should include a site's hydrologic context and functionality, including surface water occurrences (streams, wetlands, lakes), floodplains, soil runoff and infiltration capacities, vegetation, impervious surfaces, groundwater conditions, and groundwater recharge areas. Firsthand site investigation should verify information from published sources, and identify additional details such as ephemeral stream channels, springs, areas of poor drainage, on-site pollutant sources, and drainage paths onto and through the site.

To ensure that planned-for management will be sustained in the future, a design should meet the needs of its clients or users as well as the environment. Engaging stakeholders in planning through public meetings, interviews, surveys, and charrettes can build acceptance of and identification with a project.

Preserve Functioning Areas

Part of stormwater management comes from preserving site areas that are already functioning in a healthy manner. Preservation of selected areas tends to require concentration of development in other, more suitable areas.

- *Natural drainage paths.* Perennial, intermittent, and ephemeral stream channels, and even drainage

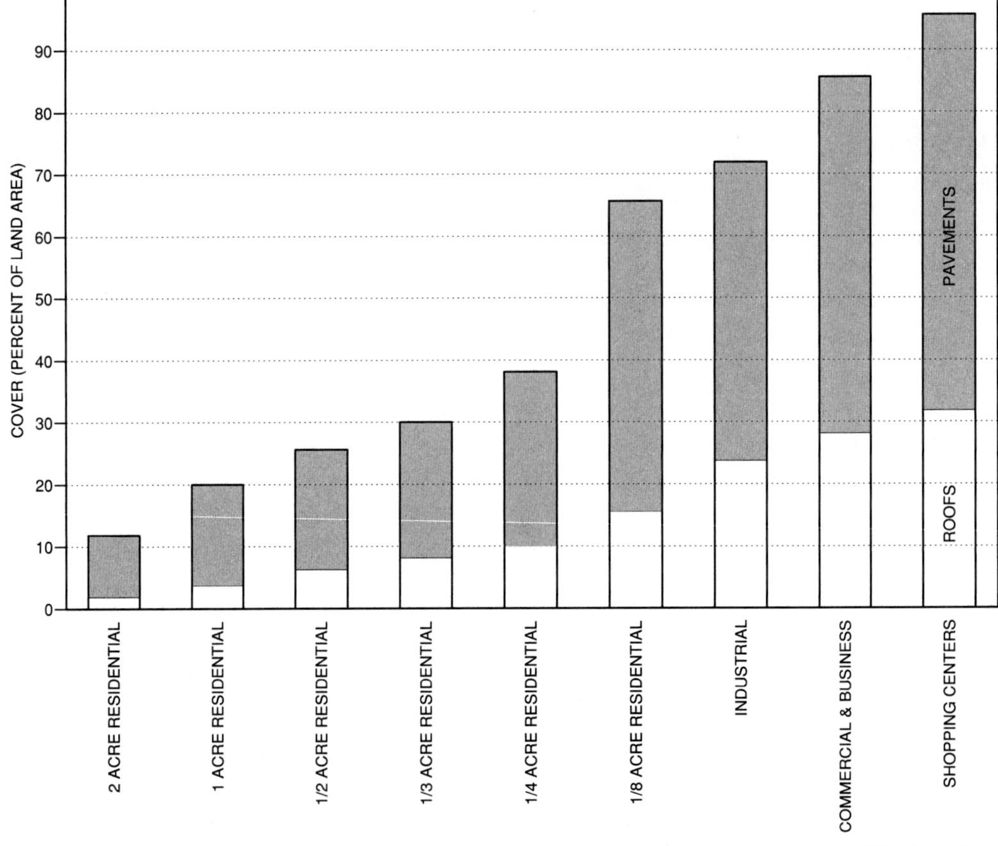

IMPERVIOUS COVERAGE IN TYPICAL LAND USES

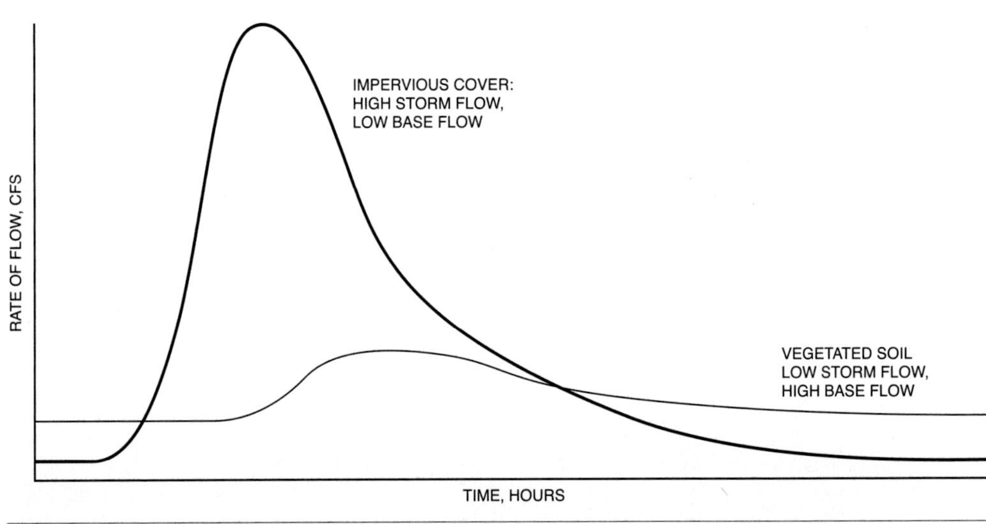

STORM FLOW AND BASE FLOW FROM IMPERVIOUS AND VEGETATED AREAS

Lead author: R. Alfred Vick, University of Georgia and Ecos Environmental Design; Section editor: Bruce K. Ferguson; Advisors: Stuart Echols, Pennsylvania State University; Tom Richman, Catalyst; Neil Weinstein, Low Impact Development Center; William Wenk, Wenk Associates; Daniel Winterbottom, University of Washington

paths that are not defined well enough to be classified as channels, are zones where surface and subsurface flows interact. Preserving them in a vegetated condition maintains runoff travel time to downstream areas, limiting flash flood damage.

- *Buffers.* These are reservations of undeveloped land adjoining streams and other surface water bodies. A buffer's undisturbed soil and vegetation filter inflowing runoff, inhibit channel erosion, and nurture functioning ecosystems. A buffer 25 feet wide can greatly reduce nonpoint-source pollution entering a water body in overland flow. Greater width can improve a buffer's wildlife habitat and movement value and accommodate low-impact recreation such as multiuse trails.
- *Floodplains.* Floodplains store floodwater, moderating flood severity. To preserve their capacity, they should not be filled or built in. Siting construction away from floodplains avoids the hazard of flood damage. The Federal Emergency Management Agency (FEMA) regulates development in the 100-year floodplain—the land that has a 1 percent probability of flooding in any given year. FEMA floodplain boundary designations can be supplemented by hydrologic modeling and identification of features such as alluvial terraces that indicate flood-prone areas.
- *Groundwater recharge areas.* Areas with unusually permeable soil or fractured rock may recharge large amounts of surface water into groundwater aquifers, from which stream base flow is supplied and water supplies are drawn. In these areas, impervious surfaces should be restricted to maintain recharge rate and to prevent introduction of pollutants that could wash into the groundwater.
- *Erodible slopes.* Sediment washed into stream channels diminishes water quality, degrades habitat, and alters channel morphology. Preserving vegetation on steep slopes and highly erodible soils protects these areas from erosion, limiting the amount of sediment unnecessarily mobilized.

Minimize Development Footprint

Within a given land-use program, compact development footprints minimize clearing and impervious surface coverage and make it feasible to protect other portions of a site such as floodplains and steep slopes.

- *Frontage and setbacks.* Narrow street frontage and limited front and side setbacks can reduce required road and driveway lengths and the resulting impervious cover.
- *Street length and width.* Alternative street layouts can be explored to limit the length of roadways. Each street can be given the minimum width required for its specific traveling, parking, and emergency-access uses, and its traffic volume. Limiting the length and width of streets limits their areas of clearing, grading, and pavement construction, and the consequent construction cost and impervious coverage.
- *Parking footprint.* Efficient parking eliminates underutilized portions of parking pavements. It fully uses both sides of turning lanes for parking bays. A portion of the parking spaces can be designated for compact cars, and minimized in size. Parking can be shared between uses that have peak use at different times of the day or week. Where feasible, multilevel parking decks can minimize the parking surface area. Limiting paved areas reduces runoff, construction cost, and land consumption.
- *Cluster development.* This concentrates construction into selected portions of a tract; greater density in those areas is offset by land conservation elsewhere. The preserved land should be high-priority natural resources such as floodplains and stream buffers. Clustering requires assessment of development amount or intensity in terms of the quantity of development on a site as a whole, not by a minimum lot size. Flexible clustering can adapt to topography and drainage in ways that are environmentally protective, economical, and appropriate to local markets.
- *Building footprint.* With appropriate interdisciplinary professionals, architectural alternatives can be considered that reduce building footprint areas. Interior spaces can be programmed to allow shared uses on different schedules, reducing required building area. For a given interior space program, multistory buildings have smaller footprints than single-story buildings.
- *Clearing and grading.* Limited clearing and grading confine construction disturbance to those areas that construction actually requires. This preserves existing vegetation and pervious soils that infiltrate rainfall and runoff naturally. Construction limits can be marked with temporary fencing, and enforced with penalties for disturbance of protected areas. Designated construction access and staging areas can coincide with proposed structures and roadways. Clustering of utilities minimizes clearing and stream crossings.

Utilize Constructed Spaces

A given construction program presents rooftop and pavement spaces that can be utilized for stormwater restoration and reuse. With appropriate materials and configurations, they can reduce stormwater impact at the source, reduce the need for downstream treatment facilities, and even generate useful resources.

- *Porous paving.* Porous paving reduces stormwater runoff and improves water quality. Each type of porous paving material has particular advantages and disadvantages for specific applications and its own requirements for design, construction, and maintenance. In a proposed development plan, different pavement settings can be identified where different, optimally suited materials can be placed.
- *Green roofs.* These are vegetated roof covers where special plants and rooting media take the place of impervious rooftop surfaces. They reduce runoff generation by displacing impervious roof surfaces. They absorb CO_2, reduce air temperature, insulate buildings, add interest and beauty to roofscapes, and in some cases provide habitat for birds and insects. They tend to require irrigation and other maintenance.
- *Rainwater harvesting.* Collecting rainwater from rooftops and other clean surfaces can supply water adequate in quality for irrigation, toilet flushing, ornamental water features, and other secondary uses. Harvesting of useful water reduces impervious-area runoff and dependence on potable water. Harvesting requires storage tanks, some degree of filtering, and conveyance to scheduled use.

Mitigate Remaining Runoff

In the landscapes around and downstream from constructed features, facilities can be built to mitigate remaining runoff and pollution. The size of each facility must be proportional to its watershed, and thus to the volume of runoff water it must carry or treat. Numerous small features dispersed throughout a site may use soil and vegetation resources more thoroughly than concentrating a single large feature in a central downstream location.

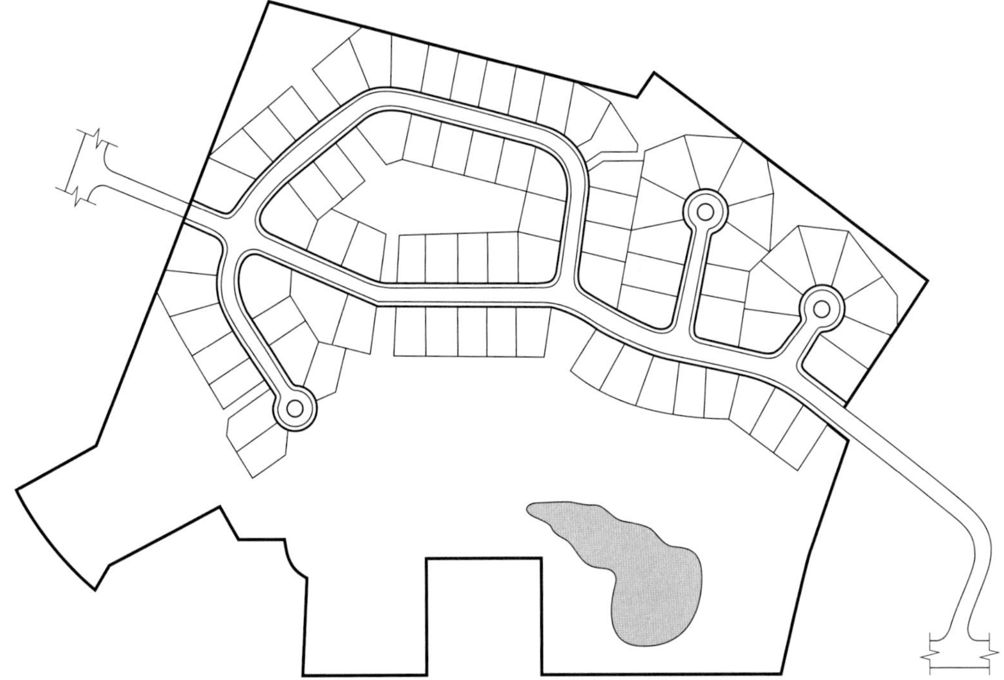

DEVELOPMENT PLAN CLUSTERED ON SELECTED PORTIONS OF SITE

Lead author: R. Alfred Vick, University of Georgia and Ecos Environmental Design; Section editor: Bruce K. Ferguson; Advisors: Stuart Echols, Pennsylvania State University; Tom Richman, Catalyst; Neil Weinstein, Low Impact Development Center; William Wenk, Wenk Associates; Daniel Winterbottom, University of Washington

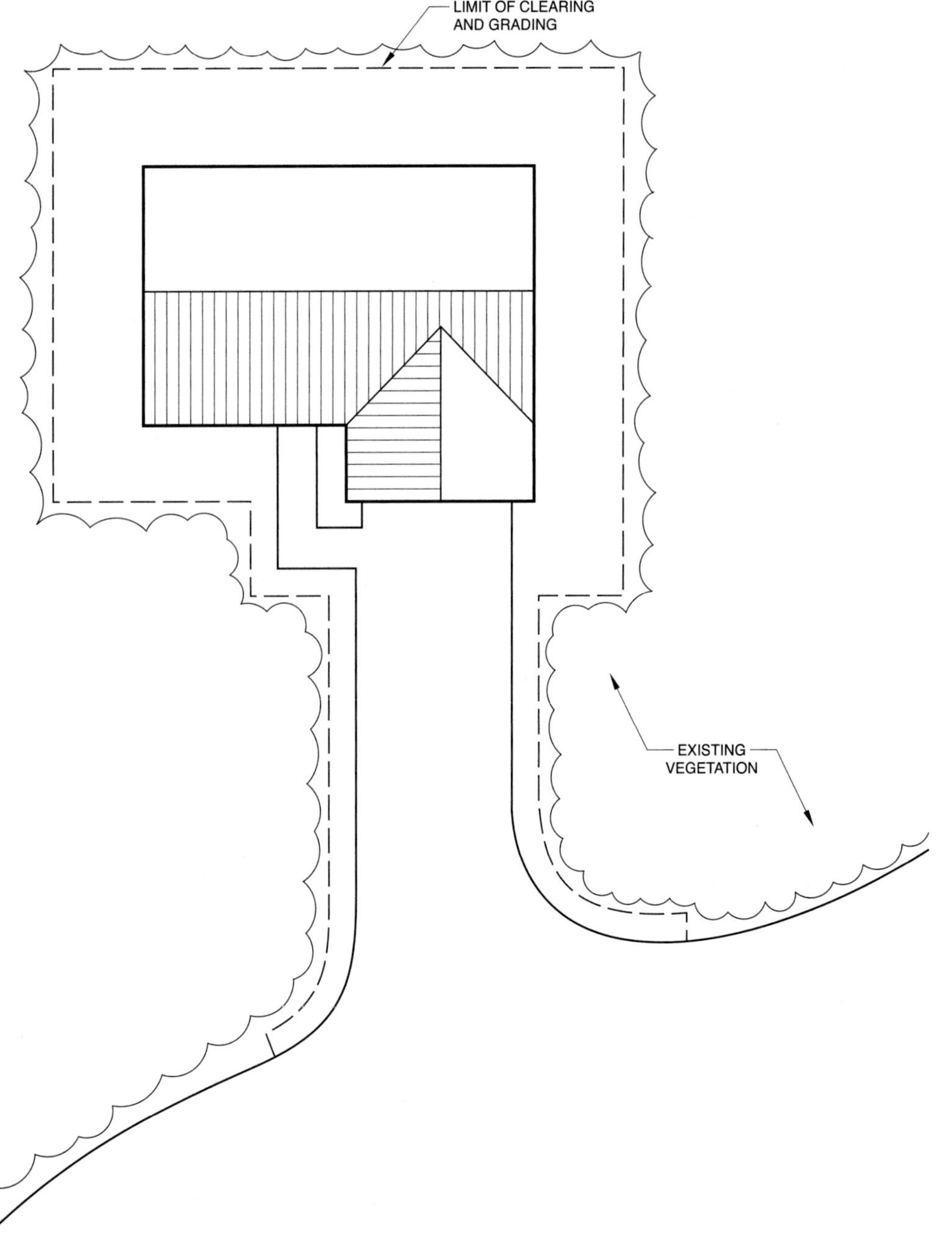

LIMIT OF CLEARING AND GRADING

- *Vegetated swales*. These are open channels that replace pipes or paved gutters in conveying runoff. By exposing water to soil, air, sunlight, and vegetation, they filter pollutants, diminish travel speed, and allow infiltration. Their cumulative treatment effects during many small, frequent storms, when small amounts of water move through swales slowly in intimate contact with soil and vegetation, can be vital.
- *Detention*. Detention is intended to hold postdevelopment peak discharges to their predevelopment levels. Excess water is held in a storage basin or reservoir. An outlet limits the reservoir's discharge rate. A "dry" basin empties completely after each storm; a "wet" basin holds a permanent pool.
- *Infiltration*. Infiltration basins capture and store water in contact with permeable soil, so it infiltrates. Infiltration reduces runoff volume, replenishes groundwater, and treats pollutants. Infiltration basins may be surfaced with vegetated soil or with open-graded aggregate. A basin should infiltrate or drain out standing water within a limited time to minimize mosquito habitat. Underground basins ("dry wells" or "infiltration trenches") are made of open-graded aggregate, sometimes supplemented with manufactured products that store additional water. For some basins, grass filters pretreat runoff to remove sediment that would clog the infiltration surface.
- *Level spreaders*. Stormwater infiltration in a stable vegetated slope, such as one in a streamside buffer, can be enhanced by distributing inflows. Level spreaders disperse flows widely and nonerosively across a long, level lip.
- *Split-flow management*. This divides runoff into a combination of infiltration and outflow. Flow-splitting devices and small infiltration basins can be distributed throughout a site corresponding to the distribution of impervious surfaces. The result mimics predevelopment hydrology by matching proportions of infiltration and runoff to predevelopment proportions.
- *Rain gardens and bioretention facilities*. These are shallow depressions fitted with special soil and plants to filter and, to some degree, infiltrate stormwater runoff. They are ordinarily designed to treat the small but important "first flush" of runoff. They require soil with a high infiltration rate, either native or imported to the facility. They can function independently, or in combination with detention, infiltration, or split-flow facilities.

ALTERNATIVE POROUS PAVING MATERIALS

MATERIAL	DISTINCTIVE CHARACTERISTICS
Porous aggregate	Inexpensive and very permeable
Porous turf	Living and dynamic
Plastic geocells	Recycled
Open blocks and grids	Sturdy, attractive, and reliable
Porous concrete	Quality depends on installer
Porous asphalt	Technology is advancing
"Soft" paving materials (crushed shell, wood chips, rubber particles)	Organic and recycled
Decks	Adaptive to site

PAVEMENT SETTINGS THAT CAN BE DISTINGUISHED FOR SELECTING APPROPRIATE PAVING MATERIALS

TYPE OF AREA	DISTINGUISHED TYPE OF AREA
Universally accessible pedestrian routes with stringent requirements for surface texture	"General" routes
Parking lots' traveling lanes, where braking and turning require great surface stability	Parking stalls
Seldom-used parking stalls distant from building's entrance	Heavily used stalls near entrance
Street parking lanes	Traveling lanes
"Calmed" traffic: coarse texture and perceptible traffic noise may be desirable	Swiftly, smoothly moving traffic
Steep slopes (>5%), with demanding requirements for surface stability	Gentle slopes (<5%±)
Reliable maintenance	Unreliable maintenance

Lead author: R. Alfred Vick, University of Georgia and Ecos Environmental Design; Section editor: Bruce K. Ferguson; Advisors: Stuart Echols, Pennsylvania State University; Tom Richman, Catalyst; Neil Weinstein, Low Impact Development Center; William Wenk, Wenk Associates; Daniel Winterbottom, University of Washington

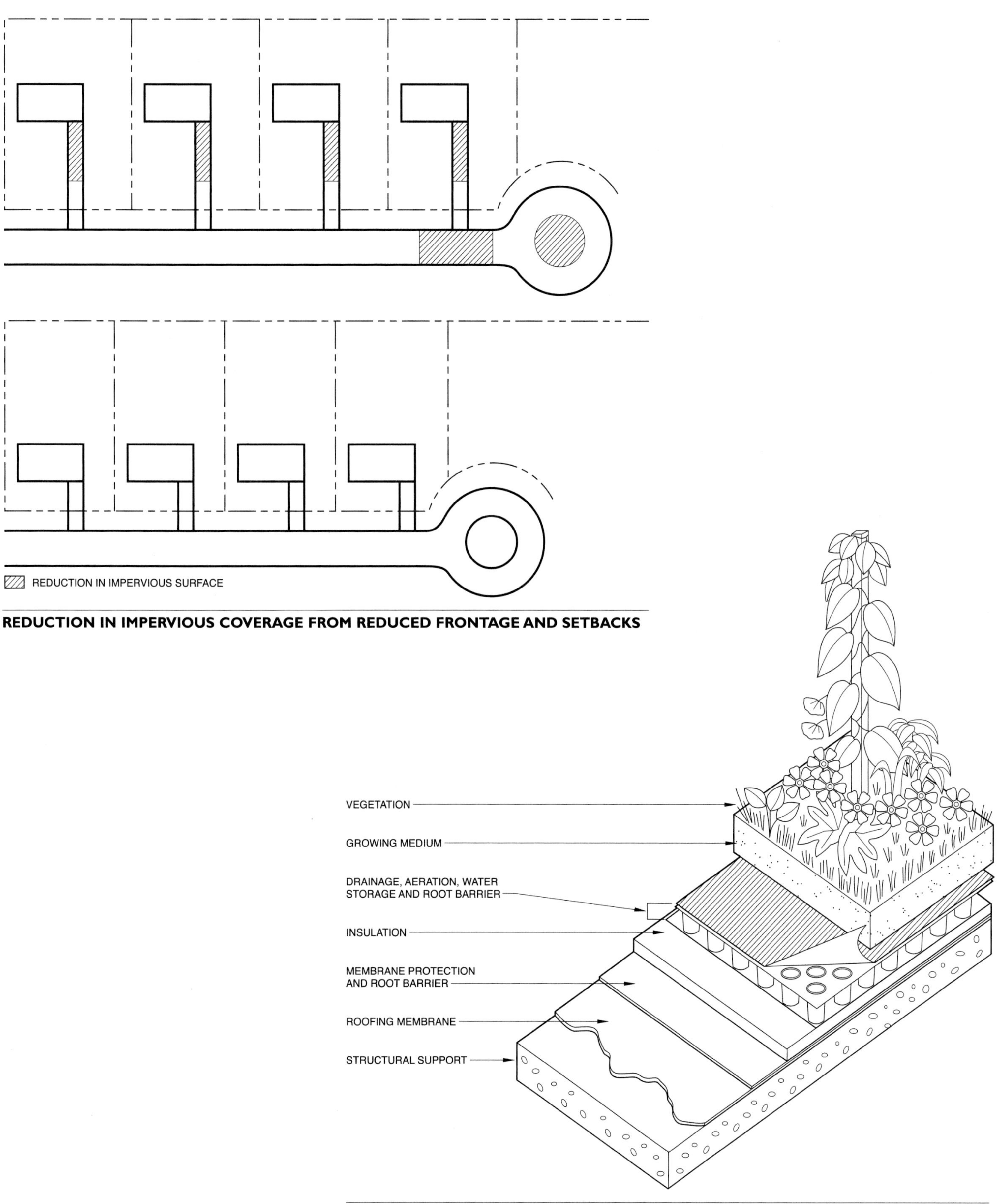

REDUCTION IN IMPERVIOUS COVERAGE FROM REDUCED FRONTAGE AND SETBACKS

TYPICAL COMPONENTS OF GREEN ROOF

Lead author: R. Alfred Vick, University of Georgia and Ecos Environmental Design; Section editor: Bruce K. Ferguson; Advisors: Stuart Echols, Pennsylvania State University; Tom Richman, Catalyst; Neil Weinstein, Low Impact Development Center; William Wenk, Wenk Associates; Daniel Winterbottom, University of Washington

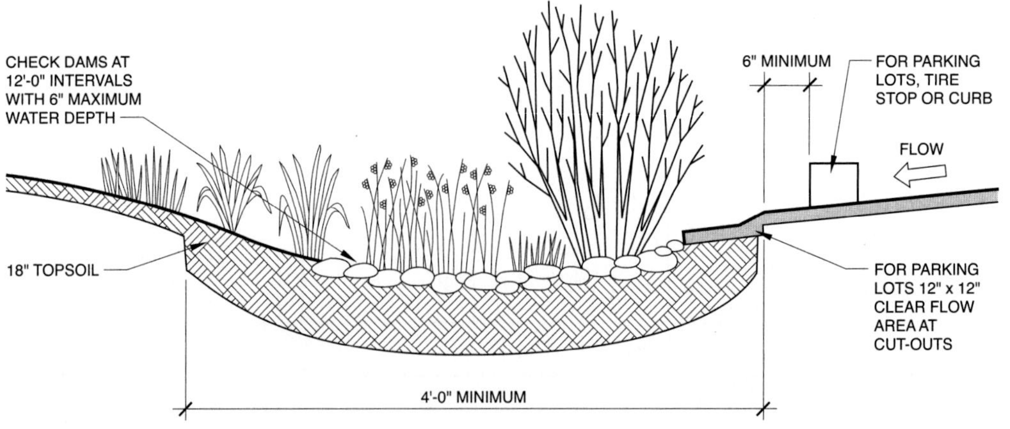

TYPICAL PROVISIONS FOR VEGETATED SWALE

INFILTRATION BASIN

Lead author: R. Alfred Vick, University of Georgia and Ecos Environmental Design; Section editor: Bruce K. Ferguson; Advisors: Stuart Echols, Pennsylvania State University; Tom Richman, Catalyst; Neil Weinstein, Low Impact Development Center; William Wenk, Wenk Associates; Daniel Winterbottom, University of Washington

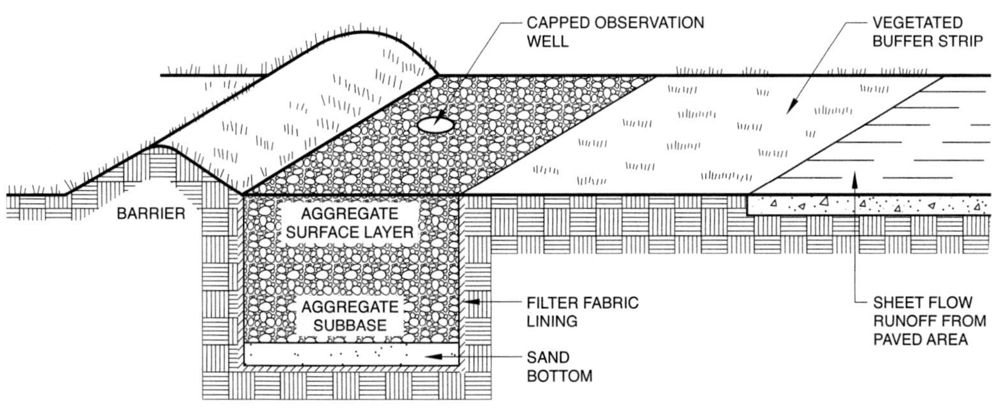

INFILTRATION TRENCH

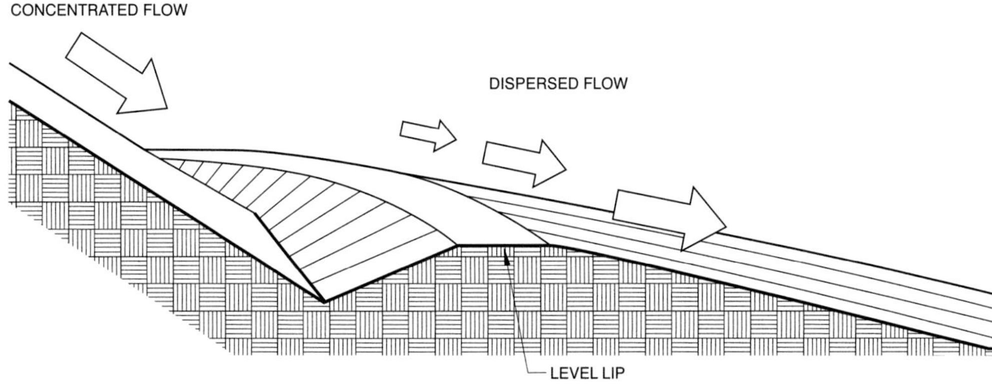

LEVEL SPREADER

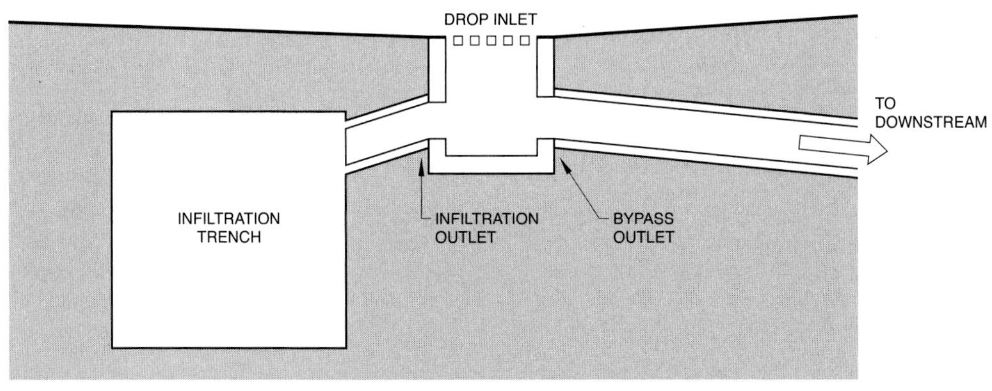

FLOW SPLITTER: DIVIDES RUNOFF AND INFILTRATION PROPORTIONALLY

Lead author: R. Alfred Vick, University of Georgia and Ecos Environmental Design; Section editor: Bruce K. Ferguson; Advisors: Stuart Echols, Pennsylvania State University; Tom Richman, Catalyst; Neil Weinstein, Low Impact Development Center; William Wenk, Wenk Associates; Daniel Winterbottom, University of Washington

EDGE PLANT MATERIAL TOLERANT OF FLUCTUATING WATER CONDITIONS
TURF OR GROUNDCOVER FILTER-STRIP
SHEET FLOW
MOISTURE-TOLERANT PLANT MATERIAL AT BOTTOM
SHEET FLOW
STONE ENERGY DISSIPATORS
2'-6" MINIMUM SOIL DEPTH
6" MAXIMUM PONDED WATER DEPTH
GROUND COVER OR WOOD
UNCOMPACTED NATIVE SOIL
PERFORATED UNDERDRAIN IN GRAVEL BED CONNECTED TO STORM DRAIN OR FRENCH DRAIN
SOIL FILTER MIX: 50% SAND 20% COMPOSTED LEAVES 30% TOPSOIL

TYPICAL PROVISIONS FOR RAIN GARDEN

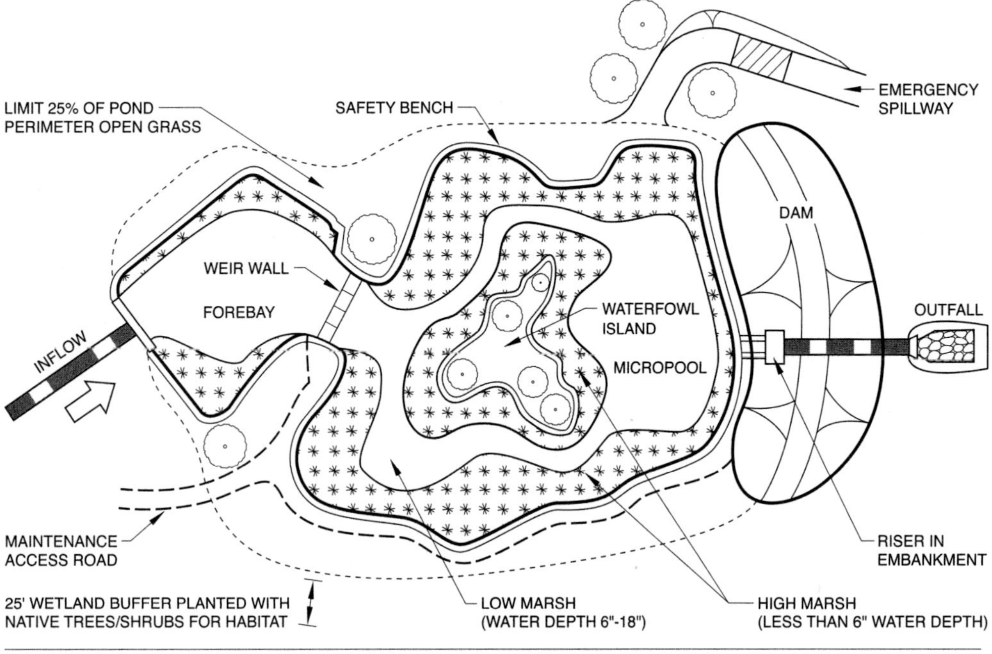

TYPICAL PROVISIONS FOR STORMWATER WETLAND

- *Stormwater ponds and wetlands.* These remove pollutants through settlement and interaction with vegetation. Siting of ponds and wetlands is important because they require constant base flow or a high water table to support the wetland environment. They can be designed to give multiple benefits of water quality improvement, aesthetics, wildlife habitat, and flood storage.

Integrate and Restore

Provisions like those listed in this section function to their greatest potential when they are applied together, creating a "treatment train" that manages stormwater at all stages of its movement through a site. Today's stormwater management features are diverse and flexible. They start operating where rain first falls by adding stormwater roles to the construction of roofs and pavements. Their placement in the midst of a site uses the full capacity of vegetation and soils for restoration.

Although stormwater management facilities are technical features of hydrology and engineering, they are also economic, social, and aesthetic contributions to civic community, private comfort, economic vitality, and quality of human life. Integrative design encompasses the requirements of people and environment together. Successful integration depends on utilizing every facility for multiple positive functions.

On many sites, development or redevelopment can undo damage previously done to soils, streams, wetlands, and aquifers, leaving them in better condition than before the project. Restorative design preserves functioning features, assists the recovery of land that has been damaged, and returns natural functions where they have been suppressed.

REFERENCES

Books

Echols, Stuart D. 2002. "Split-Flow Method: Introduction of a New Stormwater Strategy," in *Stormwater,* July 2002 (www.forester.net).

Ferguson, Bruce K. 2005. *Porous Pavements.* Boca Raton, FL: CRC Press.

Richman, Tom, and Associates, Camp Dresser & McKee, Bruce K. Ferguson, and Artefact Design. 1999. *Start at the Source: Design Guidance Manual for Stormwater Quality Protection.* Oakland, CA: Bay Area Stormwater Management Agencies Association (www.basmaa.org/documents).

Schueler, Tom. 1995. *Site Planning for Urban Stream Protection.* Washington, DC: Metropolitan Washington Council of Governments (www.cwp.org).

University of Georgia School of Environmental Design. 1997. *Land Development Provisions to Protect Georgia Water Quality.* Atlanta, GA: Georgia Department of Natural Resources, Environmental Protection Division (www.dnr.state.ga.us/dnr/environ).

Web Sites

Center for Watershed Protection: www.cwp.org

Low Impact Development Center: www.lowimpact-development.org]

Stormwater magazine: www.stormh2o.com

Greenroofs.com: http://greenroofs.com

Lead author: R. Alfred Vick, University of Georgia and Ecos Environmental Design; Section editor: Bruce K. Ferguson; Advisors: Stuart Echols, Pennsylvania State University; Tom Richman, Catalyst; Neil Weinstein, Low Impact Development Center; William Wenk, Wenk Associates; Daniel Winterbottom, University of Washington

STORMWATER HYDROLOGY

INTRODUCTION

This section provides a general framework for understanding site hydrology, and a basis for selecting approaches for analyzing and designing specific sites.

A landscape's hydrology begins with rainfall and snowmelt, some or all of which may infiltrate the Earth's surface. Infiltrated water occupies the soil's unsaturated zone, where it supplies water to plant and tree roots. Water transpired by plants and evaporated from ponds returns to the atmosphere under the combined term "evapotranspiration." Excess soil moisture continues down to ("recharges") groundwater in the saturated zone, whence it discharges gradually to streams. From place to place, there are variations in the details of this framework with interception by tree canopies, artificial surface imperviousness, interconnections among surface drainage features, and the relative permeabilities of underground layers. But the interconnections among a site's water resources exist in all landscapes.

Every step in landscape hydrology is a resource. Surface runoff can be harvested for on-site use. Evapotranspiration empowers the health and growth of trees, plants, and ecosystems, and is a dominant component in a landscape's energy balance. Varying soil-moisture storage governs irrigation water requirements and guides potential water conservation. Groundwater recharge replenishes municipal water-supply wells. Base flow supplies the basic resource of aquatic ecosystems and downstream water supplies. Together, rainfall, runoff, infiltration, and evapotranspiration define the natural character and maintain the ecological functions of a site.

A landscape's soil, vegetation, and built structures control the disposition of rainwater into the hydrologic system. A soil's hydrologic soil group (HSG) describes its relative capability to infiltrate rainwater or to divert it into runoff. A soil's available water-holding capacity (AWHC) is its capability to store water available to plant roots, after excess water has drained away to the saturated zone.

Design must analyze hydrology quantitatively, as well as spatially and functionally; projections using mathematical models are routinely necessary. This section gives rudimentary equations and data to illustrate commonly important hydrologic flows and storages; they are from the references cited at the end of this section. References and computer programs like those cited in this section give much more detailed problem-solving capability for numerous specific site conditions. Which hydrologic model is most appropriate for a given project depends on the information needed and how that information can best be obtained. Some state and local agencies specify acceptable models.

EXAMPLES OF HYDROLOGIC MODELING SOFTWARE

PROGRAM	DESCRIPTION	AGENCY OR AUTHOR	CONTACT INFORMATION
HEC-1 (HEC-HMS)	Runoff hydrograph, channel routing	Hydrologic Engineering Center	www.hec.usace.army.mil
TR-20	Runoff hydrograph, channel routing, reservoir routing	Natural Resources Conservation Service	www.wcc.nrcs.usda.gov
TR-55	Runoff hydrograph	Natural Resources Conservation Service	www.wcc.nrcs.usda.gov
HYDRAIN	Runoff hydrograph	Federal Highway Administration	www.gky.com
SWMM (Stormwater Management Model)	Runoff hydrograph, water balance, water quality	Environmental Protection Agency	www.epa.gov
PC-SWMM	Runoff hydrograph, water balance, water quality	Computational Hydraulics	www.computationalhydraulics.com
PC-SWMM for Permeable Pavements	Porous pavement runoff hydrograph, depth of ponding within pavement, and discharge	Uni-Group USA	www.uni-groupusa.org
Santa Barbara Urban Hydrograph	Runoff hydrograph	Eagle Point	www.eaglepoint.com
HSPF (Hydrological Simulation Program–Fortran)	Water balance, water quality, snowmelt, channel routing, reservoir routing	Environmental Protection Agency	www.epa.gov
NFF	Runoff peak rate (USGS regression equations)	Geological Survey	http://water.usgs.gov

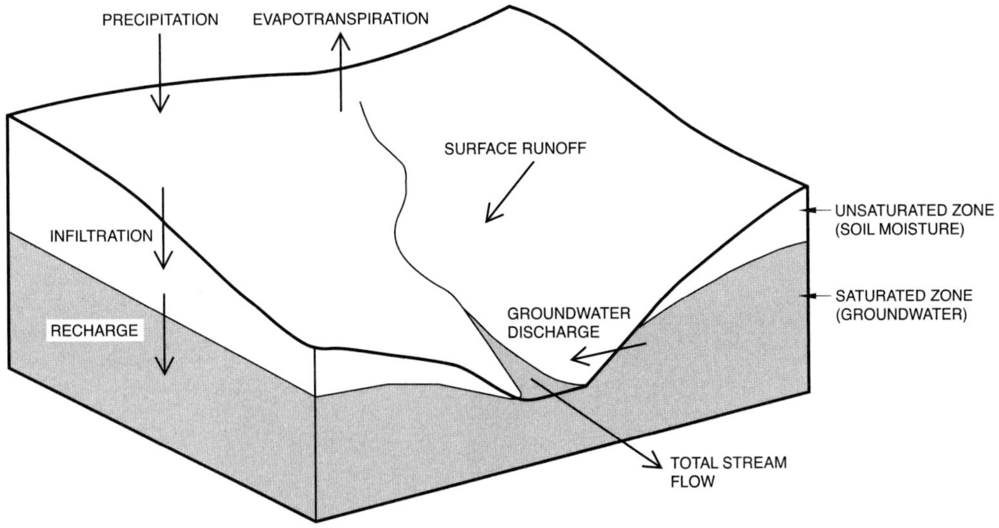

INTERCONNECTIONS IN LANDSCAPE HYDROLOGY

PRECIPITATION

Precipitation is the inflow that brings to life a landscape's hydrologic resources. Because rainfall amount and intensity fluctuate widely from week to week and year to year, precipitation also generates the hazards of flooding, erosion, and drought.

The number of days with rainfall varies from place to place, from less than 10 per year to more than 100. The vast majority of events are small; over most time periods, the small, numerous, frequent events support ecological resources and water supplies, and characterize the landscape's water quality. Rain events that are large and intense enough to threaten flooding and erosion occur relatively rarely and represent only a fraction of the total rainwater supply.

The National Oceanic and Atmospheric Administration (NOAA) publishes data comparing the intensity, duration, and frequency of precipitation for most weather stations in the United States. Updates are available through the agency's Web sites. Some state and local agencies publish locally applicable data.

Stormwater facilities such as culverts, swales, rain gardens, wetlands, and ponds are built to particular sizes to handle particular storm intensities and amounts. A "design storm" is a combination of rainfall conditions, such as intensity, duration, and frequency, selected for a stormwater facility to handle.

Small facilities that handle small, frequent storms can solve many ecological, water-supply, and water-quality problems, but not the flooding and erosion produced by large storms. There is always a risk that, at any time, a larger storm could occur and a facility not designed for it could be overloaded. Probability of occurrence in any given year is the reciprocal of a storm's average frequency, or "return period." Design of large facilities for large, infrequent storms reduces the risk of overloading, because large facilities contain large amount of water; however, large facilities are expensive to construct. Selection of a design storm must balance risk and cost appropriately for each part of a drainage system. Local ordinances commonly specify the storm frequency or size to be used.

Lead author: Stuart Echols; Section editor: Bruce K. Ferguson

NOAA WEB SITES LISTING UPDATED RAINFALL DATA SOURCES

SITE NAME	ADDRESS
Rainfall Frequency Atlas of the U.S.	http://lwf.ncdc.noaa.gov/oa/documentlibrary/rainfall.html
Current Precipitation Frequency Information and Publications	www.nws.noaa.gov/oh/hdsc/currentpf.htm

RAINFALL INTENSITY IN 60-MINUTE STORMS: EXAMPLES FROM FOUR CITIES

AVERAGE FREQUENCY	PROBABILITY OF OCCURRENCE IN ANY ONE YEAR	ATLANTA, GEORGIA	BOSTON, MASSACHUSETTS	LOS ANGELES, CALIFORNIA	SEATTLE, WASHINGTON
2 yr	50%	1.6 in./hr	1.1 in./hr	0.61 in./hr	0.34 in./hr
5 yr	20%	2.1 in./hr	1.5 in./hr	0.98 in./hr	0.46 in./hr
10 yr	10%	2.4 in./hr	1.9 in./hr	1.1 in./hr	0.53 in./hr
25 yr	4%	2.7 in./hr	2.4 in./hr	1.3 in./hr	0.62 in./hr
50 yr	2%	3.1 in./hr	2.5 in./hr	1.4 in./hr	0.71 in./hr
100 yr	1	3.4 in./hr	2.6 in./hr	1.6 in./hr	0.81 in./hr

SURFACE RUNOFF

Surface runoff is a ubiquitous concern for water quality, the supply of water to ponds, wetlands, and cisterns, and the capacity of surface drainage systems. Surface runoff is analyzed for a watershed or drainage area: a particular area of land that drains to a single point where runoff or stream discharge occurs. The area is bounded by rooftops, street crowns, and topographic ridges that direct drainage into the particular watershed.

During an individual storm, runoff rate q rises and falls in a characteristic "hydrograph" shape, having peak rate q_p. The area under the curve represents total runoff volume. In some analyses, the curve is approximated as a simple triangle.

Mathematical models estimate runoff from given rainfall and drainage area data. Many models take into account a drainage area's time of concentration: the time runoff would take to travel to the outlet from the most distant part of the area. Rapid travel intensifies runoff rate. Some models track travel meticulously through a sequence of overland flow, shallow concentrated flow, and channel flow.

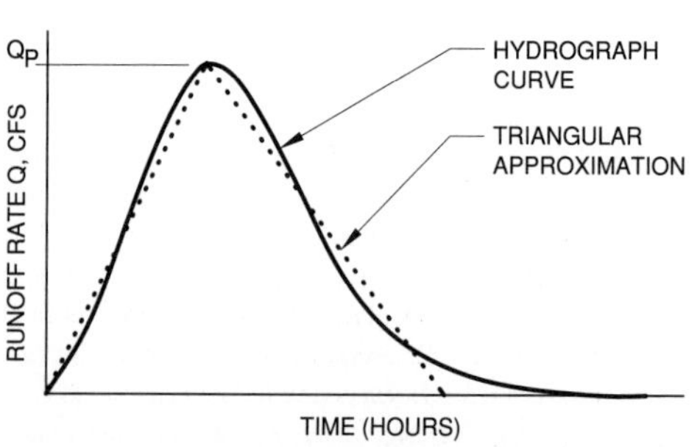

TYPICAL STORM HYDROGRAPH

HYDROLOGIC SOIL GROUPS

GROUP	DESCRIPTION
A	Soils with low runoff potential. High infiltration rates even when thoroughly wetted. Chiefly, deep, well to excessively drained sands or gravels; also, sand, loamy sand, and sandy loam that have not been significantly compacted. AWHC is limited by rapid drainage.
B	Soils with moderate infiltration rates when thoroughly wetted. Chiefly, moderately deep to deep, moderately well- to well-drained soils with moderately fine to moderately coarse textures; also, silt loam and loam that have not been significantly compacted. AWHC can be moderate to high.
C	Soils with low infiltration rates when thoroughly wetted. Chiefly, soils with a layer that impedes downward movement of water, and soils with moderately fine to fine texture; also, sandy clay loam that has not been significantly compacted. AWHC can be moderate, but limited by capillary tension.
D	Soils with high runoff potential. Very low infiltration rates when thoroughly wetted. Chiefly, clay soils with high swelling potential, soils with permanent high water tables, soils with clay pans or clay layers at or near the surface, and shallow soils over nearly impervious material; also, clay loam, silty clay loam, sandy clay, silty clay, and clay that have not been significantly compacted. AWHC is limited by high capillary tension or little soil depth.

RUNOFF CURVE NUMBERS

	HYDROLOGIC SOIL GROUP			
SURFACE COVER	A	B	C	D
Woods:				
No grazing; litter and brush cover the soil	30	55	70	77
Grazed but not burned; some forest litter covers soil	36	60	73	79
Heavy grazing or regular burning destroy litter, brush	45	66	77	83
Brush, grass, and weeds in humid regions:				
>75% ground cover	30	48	65	73
50 to 75% ground cover	35	56	70	77
<50% ground cover	48	67	77	83
Brush, grass, and weeds in arid and semiarid regions:				
>70% ground cover	49	62	74	85
30 to 70% ground cover	60	71	81	89
<30% ground cover (litter, grass, and brush overstory)	71	80	87	93
Meadow: grass generally mowed for hay; not grazed	30	58	71	78
Lawn, turf:				
>75% grass cover	39	61	74	80
50 to 75% grass cover	49	69	79	84
<50% grass cover	68	79	86	89
Desert-shrub landscaping:				
Natural desert landscaping; pervious areas only	63	77	85	88
Impervious weed barrier and mulch	96	96	96	96
Streets, roads, buildings, structures:				
Dirt roads, including right-of-way	72	82	87	89
Gravel roads, including right-of-way	76	85	89	91
Paved road and adjacent swales	83	89	92	93
Impervious roofs and pavements	98	98	98	98
Bare soil	77	86	91	94

Lead author: Stuart Echols; Section editor: Bruce K. Ferguson

RUNOFF COEFFICIENTS

LAND USE OR CONDITION	RUNOFF COEFFICIENT C*
Downtown business areas	0.70–0.95
Neighborhood business areas	0.50–0.70
Single-family residential area	0.30–0.50
Multifamily attached residential area	0.60–0.75
Suburban neighborhood	0.25–0.40
Apartment residential area	0.50–0.70
Light industrial area	0.50–0.80
Heavy industrial area	0.60–0.90
Parks or cemeteries	0.10–0.25
Railroad yard areas	0.20–0.40
Heavily vegetated areas	0.10– 0.30
Lawn: sandy soil, 0 to 2% slope	0.05–0.10
Lawn: sandy soil, 2 to 7% slope	0.10–0.15
Lawn: sandy soil, 7%+ slope	0.15–0.20
Lawn: heavy soil, 0 to 2% slope	0.13–0.17
Lawn: heavy soil, 2 to 7% slope	0.18–0.22
Lawn: heavy soil, 7%+ slope	0.25–0.35
Street: dense asphalt	0.70–0.95
Street: dense concrete	0.80–0.95
Street: brick	0.70–0.85
Roofs	0.75–0.95

** Within the ranges shown, higher values are usually appropriate for high runoff-producing soil conditions, steep slopes, and intense storms with long return periods.*

WATER BALANCE: EXAMPLE FOR UNDEVELOPED AREA IN SAINT LOUIS, MISSOURI, WITH AWHC OF 8 INCHES, IN AVERAGE YEAR

	FLOWS (INCHES PER MONTH)					STORAGES (INCHES)	
MONTH	PRECIPITATION	SURFACE RUNOFF	EVAPO-TRANSPIRATION	GROUND-WATER RECHARGE	BASE FLOW	SOIL MOISTURE	GROUND-WATER
Jan	2.21	0.00	0.00	0.00	0.00	7.38	0.01
Feb	2.31	0.04	0.07	2.20	1.10	8.00	2.20
Mar	3.26	0.13	0.70	4.02	2.56	8.00	5.13
Apr	3.74	0.08	2.11	1.55	2.05	8.00	4.13
May	4.12	0.09	3.82	0.21	1.13	8.00	2.27
Jun	4.10	0.09	5.52	0.00	0.57	6.49	1.13
Jul	3.29	0.05	5.37	0.00	0.28	4.36	0.57
Aug	2.96	0.04	4.19	0.00	0.14	3.09	0.28
Sep	3.20	0.05	3.44	0.00	0.07	2.79	0.14
Oct	2.64	0.03	2.13	0.00	0.04	3.28	0.07
Nov	2.64	0.03	0.66	0.00	0.02	5.23	0.04
Dec	2.23	0.01	0.08	0.00	0.01	7.38	0.02
Annual	36.70	0.63	28.09	7.98	7.98		

Rational Formula

The Rational formula is commonly used to estimate peak runoff rate, which is useful for design of many culverts, swales, and detention basins:

$$q_p = ciA$$

where:

q_p = peak runoff rate, cubic feet per second (cfs)
c = runoff coefficient
i = rainfall intensity, inches per hour (in./hr)
A = drainage area, acres

Rainfall intensity i is obtained from local rainfall data, for a selected design-storm condition. Drainage area A is scaled on a site map. Runoff coefficient c is obtained from standard tables associating c with the drainage area's soil, slope, and land cover. If the drainage area contains a variety of soils or land covers with different c values, a representative composite value can be obtained by a real weighting; for example, where there are three land covers:

$$\text{weighted average } c = (c_1A_1 + c_2A_2 + c_3A_3)/(A_1 + A_2 + A_3)$$

SCS Method

Another commonly used runoff estimation method is the SCS method, named for the agency that developed it, the former U.S. Soil Conservation Service. The method's basic equation finds runoff depth produced by a given depth of rainfall:

$$Q_d = (P - I_a)^2/(P - I_a + S)$$

where:

Q_d = runoff depth, inches
P = 24-hour rainfall depth, inches
I_a = abstraction before runoff begins, inches
S = retention after runoff begins, inches

Initial abstraction I_a takes into account surface depressions and soil infiltration that trap rainwater before runoff begins; it is commonly set equal to 0.2*S*. Retention *S* is water trapped in further infiltration; it is equal to (1000/*CN*)–10, where *CN* is Curve Number, an indicator of soil and land use. *CN* is obtained from standard tables relating *CN* to hydrologic soil group and land use. Precipitation *P* is obtained from local rainfall data; the SCS method assumes that rainfall intensity is distributed in a certain way within the standard 24-hour period.

SCS runoff depth can be converted to runoff volume, which is useful for design of detention basins, wetlands, rain gardens, and water-harvesting cisterns:

$$Q = 3{,}660AQ_d$$

where:

Q = runoff volume, cubic feet
3,660 = conversion factor, cubic feet per acre-inch

Runoff volume can be converted to peak runoff rate or to a complete hydrograph by taking into account the drainage area's time of concentration. A complete hydrograph is useful for sequential analysis ("routing") of flow through detention basins and complex storm sewer systems.

WATER BALANCE

A water balance is a complete inventory of a landscape's hydrology, encompassing in a single view the interaction and behavior of all the landscape's water resources. It takes into account surface runoff and, in addition, infiltration, evapotranspiration, fluctuating soil moisture and groundwater supplies, and stream base flow. It is extended over time to aggregate the effects of many small and large storms, continuous gradual evapotranspiration, and seasonal changes in the hydrologic environment.

For example, a water balance in the Saint Louis area shows that, in undeveloped conditions, almost all rainwater infiltrates. The local ecosystem consumes about three-quarters of the annual water supply in evapotranspiration, both by using the growing season's precipitation and by withdrawing soil moisture stored from the winter. Irrigation would be beneficial to plants in the late summer after natural soil moisture has been consumed. Excess soil moisture recharges the groundwater mostly in the winter and spring. Groundwater discharges gradually as stream base flow even in months with no excess rainwater.

Water balance models link a number of equations for evapotranspiration, runoff, soil-moisture storage, and other processes, in a single accounting. "Continuous simulation" models apply large quantities of data at daily or shorter time increments. The calculations run iteratively for any period of time, from a few minutes to a number of years. The soil moisture and groundwater calculated for the end of each time step are the input for the calculations in the next step.

REFERENCES

Dunne, Thomas, and Luna B. Leopold. 1978. *Water in Environmental Planning*. San Francisco: Freeman.

Ferguson, Bruce K. 1998. *Introduction to Stormwater: Concept, Purpose, Design*. New York: John Wiley & Sons, Inc.

U.S. Federal Highway Administration. 2001. *Urban Drainage Design Manual*, Hydraulic Engineering Circular No. 22 ("HEC-22"), FHWA-NHI-01-021, www.fhwa.dot.gov/bridge/hydpub.htm.

U.S. Soil Conservation Service. 1986. *Urban Hydrology for Small Watersheds*, 2nd ed., Technical Release 55 ("TR-55"), www.wcc.nrcs.usda.gov.

U.S. Weather Bureau. 1955. "Rainfall Intensity-Duration-Frequency Curves," Technical Paper 25, U.S. Department of Commerce, Weather Bureau.

Lead author: Stuart Echols; Section editor: Bruce K. Ferguson

STORMWATER CONVEYANCE

INTRODUCTION

Conveyance is the moving of surface water across the ground and through pipes, given that excess water is present on-site or is generated by impervious surfaces. Conveyance is a ubiquitous and essential tool for properly draining urban communities and for managing stormwater flows and processes. The way it is done is integral with a site's landscape forms and functions.

The flow (q) entering a swale or pipe is given by stormwater modeling. Then mathematical equations relate cross-sectional sizes of pipes and swales to the flows they have to carry. A size and configuration could be chosen with capacity large enough to pass a given flow without obstruction, or small enough to hold water back for treatment, infiltration, and ecological functions.

Simple equations are given here relating conveyance flow and size in common landscape conditions and applications. They are from the references cited at the end of this section. Many other conditions and applications could occur on a given landscape site. References and computer software like those cited at the end of this section give detailed equations, design charts, and problem-solving capability for almost any conditions. Some state departments of transportation (DOTs) issue their locally applicable drainage manuals online.

The following equation expresses a universal relationship between q and a flow's cross-sectional area; this relationship is implicit in all conveyance sizing:

$$q = AV$$

where:

q = flow in cfs (cubic feet per second)
A = area of flow cross-section in ft^2
V = velocity in fps (feet per second)

OPEN CHANNELS

Vegetated swales are grass-lined or vegetated earthen channels that convey water while slowing down runoff and removing pollutants. Infiltration into vegetated soil reduces runoff volume and replenishes soil moisture and groundwater. Pollutants settle into the soil, where they are naturally mitigated. Gentle swale gradients and, where necessary, check dams, produce low velocities that prolong contact with soil and vegetation, assuring effective treatment. By restoring natural drainage processes, vegetated swales compensate to a degree for impervious surfaces upstream.

All swales must be large enough to convey the flow within the channel's cross section during a selected design storm. Vegetated swales must be wide enough and gently sloping to convey flow at nonerosive velocity. Swale vegetation should be selected to provide dense, erosion-resistant cover and to tolerate the swale's moisture and occasional inundation.

Vegetated swales supplement or replace curbs and gutters while adding the functions of runoff attenuation, infiltration, and treatment. They can be used wherever flow velocity will not be erosive and where there is room to convey water slowly through a large cross-sectional area. They are less likely to be appropriate on steep longitudinal slopes, where erosive velocities could develop, and in high-density developments, where there is little vegetated space.

Swale flow can be analyzed with some certainty where constant channel slope and cross-section convey flow steadily and uniformly. Given these conditions, mean velocity and flow can be estimated with Manning's equation, which can be written in the following two forms:

$$V = (1.49/n)R^{2/3}S^{1/2}$$
$$q = (1.49/n)AR^{2/3}S^{1/2}$$

where:

n = Manning's roughness coefficient
S = channel's longitudinal slope in ft/ft

CROSS-SECTIONAL AREA (A) IN ft^2

WETTED PERIMETER (Wp) IN ft

ELEMENTS IN MANNING'S EQUATION: HYDRAULIC RADIUS $R = A/W_P$

VEGETATED CHANNEL MAXIMUM VELOCITIES: MAXIMUM FLOW VELOCITIES IN VEGETATED WATERWAYS WITHOUT CAUSING CHANNEL EROSION

	EROSION-RESISTANT SOILS (STIFF CLAY, HARDPAN, FINE GRAVEL, COARSE GRAVEL)			EASILY ERODED SOILS (FINE SAND, SANDY LOAM, LOAM, SILT LOAM, CLAY LOAM)		
Vegetative Cover	**0–5%**	**5–10%**	**>10%**	**0–5%**	**5–10%**	**>10%**
Bermuda grass	8 fps	7 fps	6 fps	6 fps	5 fps	4 fps
Buffalo grass, Kentucky bluegrass, smooth brome, smooth grama	7 fps	6 fps	5 fps	5 fps	4 fps	3 fps
Grass mixture	5 fps	4 fps	erodible	4 fps	3 fps	erodible
Lespedeza sericea, weeping lovegrass, yellow bluestem, kudzu, crabgrass, common lespedeza, Sudan grass	3.5 fps	erodible	erodible	2.5 fps	erodible	erodible

VEGETATED CHANNEL ROUGHNESS: TYPICAL VALUES OF MANNING'S ROUGHNESS COEFFICIENT

CHANNEL SURFACE	n
Vegetation, unmaintained	0.030 to 0.045
Grass, maintained	0.025 to 0.035

ARMORED CHANNEL ROUGHNESS: TYPICAL VALUES OF MANNING'S ROUGHNESS COEFFICIENT

CHANNEL SURFACE	n
Asphalt	0.015
Brick	0.015
Rip rap (6"–9" stone)	0.030
Rip rap (12"–15" stone)	0.034
Gabions	0.028
Concrete, float finish	0.013
Concrete, trowel finish	0.015

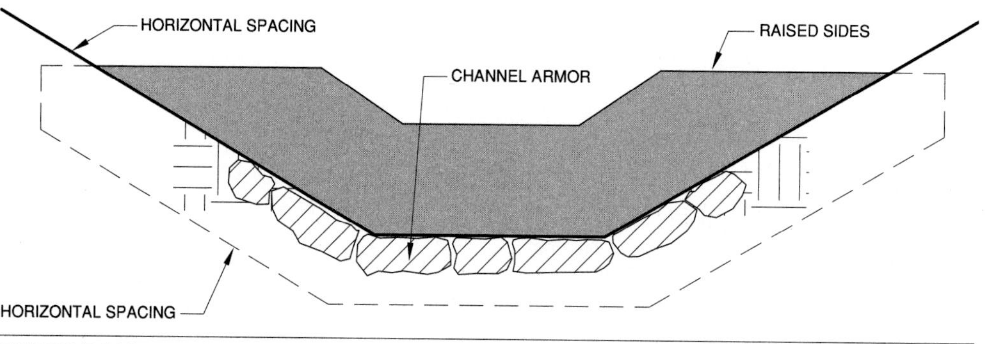

CHECK DAM

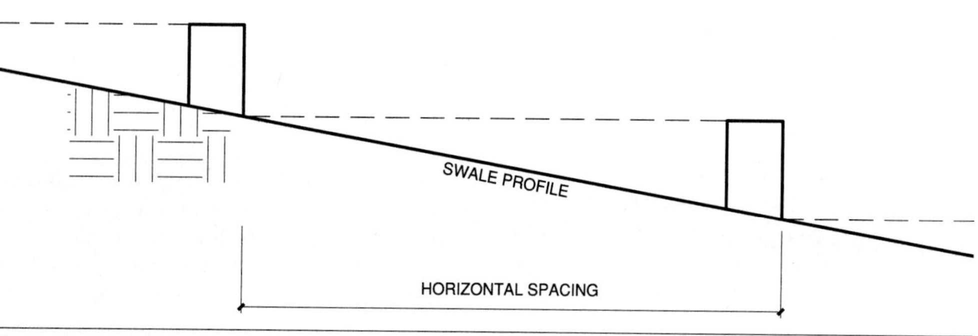

CHECK DAM SPACING

Principal author: Mark E. Boyer, University of Arkansas; Section editor: Bruce K. Ferguson, University of Georgia

Swale flow is less certain where obstructions and irregular cross-sectional geometries exist, as in meandering channel alignments or around embedded rocks and logs. A rough estimate of an irregular channel's capacity can be made by applying Manning's equation to the narrowest, shallowest, or most obstructed portion of the channel.

Some channels have to be armored or lined, rather than vegetated, in order to prevent erosion or to convey large amounts of runoff quickly through narrow spaces. Armored channels' flow is analyzed using the same Manning's equation, but with roughness values corresponding to their lining materials.

CHECK DAMS

Check dams are small weirs that create small ponded areas during runoff events. They can be constructed of logs, rocks, rock-filled gabions, concrete blocks, or cast-in-place concrete. It is vital to make the crest's low point in the center of the dam, or to surround it with raised wing walls, to prevent water from falling over erodible soil at the sides. For some check dams, to further prevent erosion, the adjacent downstream channel has to be armored, and the dam structure embedded in the channel sides and bottom.

In all vegetated swales, check dams cause water to spend more time in contact with soil and vegetation; infiltration is increased and runoff volume reduced. The ponding causes suspended sediment to settle out of the runoff. The dams aerate the remaining runoff as it falls over the crest.

In swales that have unavoidably steep longitudinal slope, the ponding of check dams can confine flow to nonerosive velocities. To accomplish this, ponding must be continuous along the length of the swale, without erodible areas of flowing water. The dams must be spaced along the swale so that the crest of each dam is at least as high in elevation as the toe of the next dam upstream.

Any other ledges over which flowing water falls are also weirs. Weirs can be placed in stormwater reservoirs as outfall control devices, or in pipes or channels as flow-splitting devices. A circular weir is formed where a pipe is placed vertically (making a "barrel pipe" or "stand pipe"); the weir's length is the circumference of the pipe.

GUTTERS AND INLETS

Despite the advantages of vegetated swales, gutters are often necessary to confine street traffic or drainage. Gutters are, in effect, small channels with particular geometries and flow criteria. The idea is to keep water from spreading excessively onto the driving pavement. For example, a common criterion is that the spread should not exceed half of the lane width during a selected design storm. Manning's equation can be written the following way for special application to gutter spread:

$$q = (0.56/n)S_x^{5/3}S^{1/2}T^{8/3}$$

Inlets are openings that let surface water from gutters or swales into catch basins or pipes. They should be placed above most street intersections and crosswalks and wherever gutter spread exceeds a given criterion. Manufactured inlets vary in shape, material, and area of opening. Some are openings in a vertical curb face; others are grate (drop) inlets. Many manufacturers provide flow performance data for their products. For products without that information, applicable equations can be used to find the inflow rate.

WEIR FLOWS

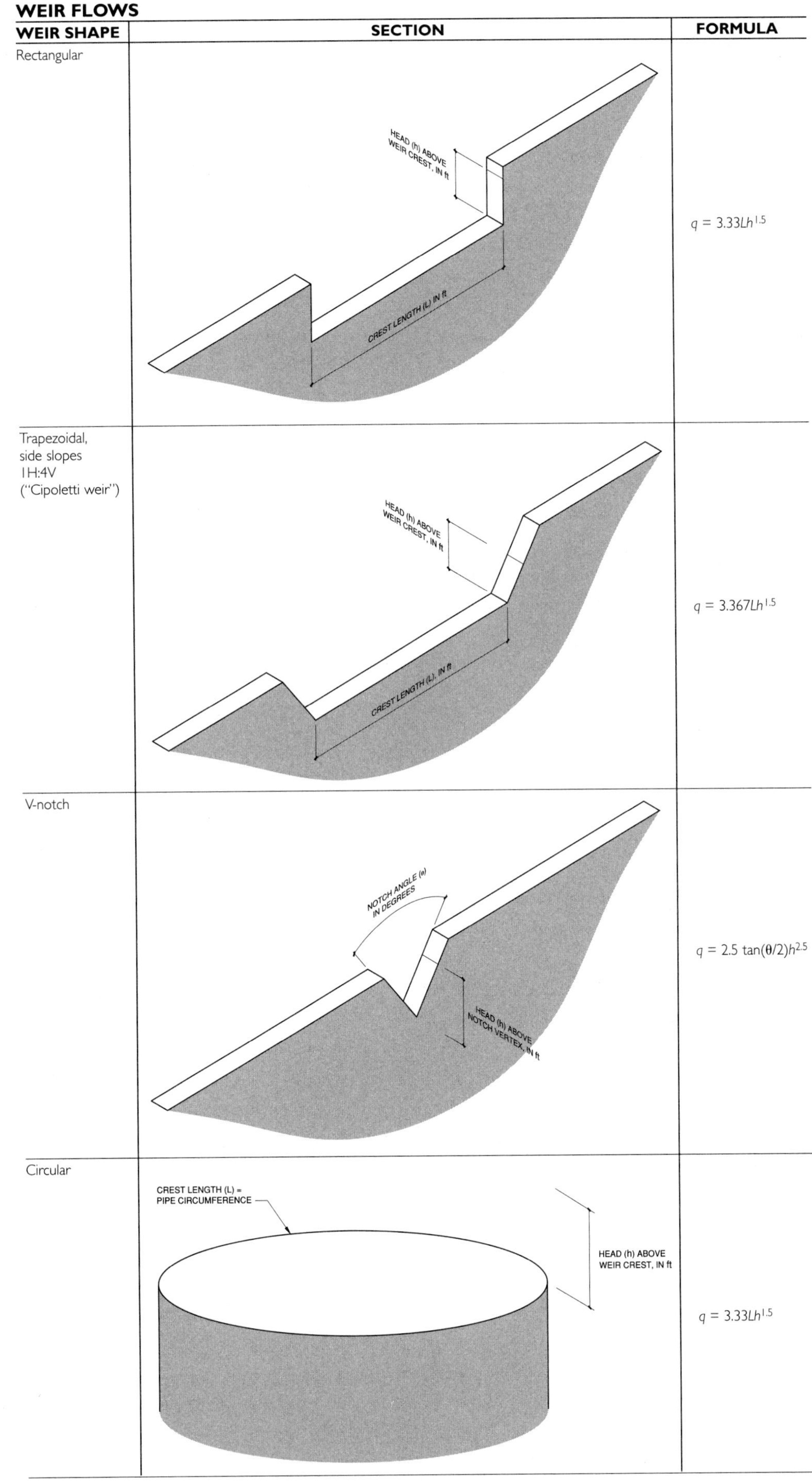

WEIR SHAPE	SECTION	FORMULA
Rectangular	HEAD (h) ABOVE WEIR CREST, IN ft; CREST LENGTH (L) IN ft	$q = 3.33Lh^{1.5}$
Trapezoidal, side slopes 1H:4V ("Cipoletti weir")	HEAD (h) ABOVE WEIR CREST, IN ft; CREST LENGTH (L), IN ft	$q = 3.367Lh^{1.5}$
V-notch	NOTCH ANGLE (θ) IN DEGREES; HEAD (h) ABOVE NOTCH VERTEX, IN ft	$q = 2.5\tan(\theta/2)h^{2.5}$
Circular	CREST LENGTH (L) = PIPE CIRCUMFERENCE; HEAD (h) ABOVE WEIR CREST, IN ft	$q = 3.33Lh^{1.5}$

GUTTER ROUGHNESS: VALUES OF MANNING'S ROUGHNESS COEFFICIENT FOR STREET GUTTERS

GUTTER SURFACE	n
Asphalt, smooth texture	0.013
Asphalt, rough texture	0.016
Concrete, float finish	0.014
Concrete, broom finish	0.016

GRATE INLET INFLOWS: FORMULAS FOR INLETS LOCATED IN SUMP OR DEPRESSION (q_i IS FLOW ENTERING INLET, IN CFS)

OPERATING CONDITION	FORMULA
Inlet operating as weir	$q_i = 3.0Ph^{1.5}$
Inlet operating as orifice	$q_i = 5.36Ah^{0.5}$

PIPE ROUGHNESS: VALUES OF MANNING'S ROUGHNESS COEFFICIENT

PIPE MATERIAL	n
Concrete	0.013
Plastic	0.011
Corrugated Metal, 2⅔" X ½" Helical Corrugations	
12" to 18"	0.014
21" to 30"	0.018
36" to 48"	0.020
Corrugated Metal, 2⅔" X ½" Annular Corrugations	
All sizes	0.024

CURB-OPENING INLET INFLOW

INLET LOCATION	WATER LEVEL	OPERATING CONDITION	FORMULA
Continuous grade	All	Weir	$L_T = 0.6q^{0.42}S_o^{0.3}(1/nS_x)^{0.6}$
Sag or depression	$h \leq l$	Inlet operating as weir	$q_i = 3.0Lh^{3/2}$
Sag or depression	$h = l$ to $1.4l$	Transition	Use lesser of weir or orifice flows
Sag or depression	$h > 1.4l$	Inlet operating as orifice	$q_i = 5.36lLh^{0.5}$

Note: sq is gutter flow in cfs; L_T is curb opening length in feet necessary to admit the total gutter flow

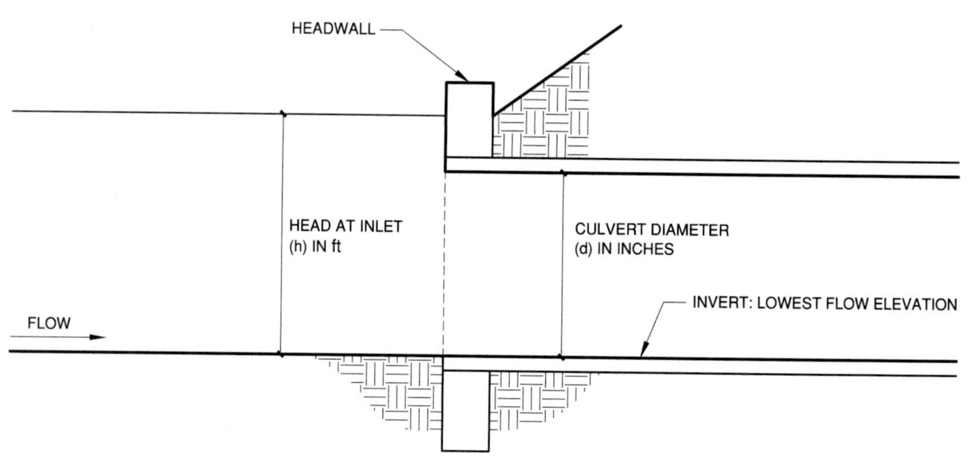

CULVERT

COMPUTER PROGRAMS

PROGRAM	CULVERTS	OPEN CHANNELS	WEIRS, ORIFICES AND INLETS	CONTACT INFORMATION
CulvertMaster	X			www.haestad.com
FlowMaster	X	X	X	www.haestad.com
HEC-RAS	X	X	X	www.hec.usace.army.mil
HY8	X			http://www.fhwa.dot.gov/bridge/hydsoft.htm
SWMM	X	X		www.epa.gov/ceampub www.computationalhydraulics.com
WSPRO	X	X		http://www.fhwa.dot.gov/bridge/hydsoft.htm

An inlet located in a sump or depression admits all gutter flow at some rate, while sometimes ponding water above the inlet. As ponding depth increases, a grate inlet's flow converts from that of a weir to that of an orifice; inflow capacity should be analyzed for both types of flow and the more limiting inflow used for design.

An inlet located along a slope may intercept only part of the gutter flow while the remainder continues down the slope. A curb-opening inlet's opening length can be designed to capture the necessary flow.

CULVERTS

Culverts are pipes that carry flow under streets or driveways. Common culvert materials are concrete, corrugated metal, and high-density polyethylene (HDPE) plastic. They are commonly circular in section, with diameters in 3-inch or 6-inch increments; they are also available in other shapes such as arches and boxes. Cover over culverts with vehicular traffic should be at least 12 inches, and in many conditions should be 24 inches or more.

Every culvert should be analyzed for potential performance under both inlet-control and outlet-control conditions, and the design flow rate chosen from the most limiting condition.

Inlet control applies where water is backed up at a culvert's mouth but not at the downstream end. The culvert entrance is a constriction that controls inflow based on its shape and geometry. The following equation gives inlet-controlled inflow for a circular pipe, submerged inlet, 2 percent pipe slope, and square edge with headwall:

$$q = d^{2.5}(15.5h/d - 10.2)^{0.5}$$

Outlet control applies where water is backed up at a culvert's downstream end deep enough to restrict flow through the culvert. HDS 5 gives a complicated equation and design charts for outlet-controlled flow.

Culverts rarely flow full, due to inlet and outlet restrictions. Given the flow q through a culvert based on inlet control or outlet control, Manning's equation can be used to evaluate flow depth and velocity through the pipe, using the roughness coefficient corresponding to the pipe's material.

COMPUTER PROGRAMS

Computer programs have been developed to facilitate conveyance computations and design decisions. The capabilities of various programs range from individual culvert analysis to major system design.

REFERENCES

Books

Debo, Thomas N., and Andrew J. Reese. 2002. *Municipal Storm Water Management*, 2nd ed. Boca Raton, FL: Lewis Publishers.

Durrans, S. Rocky. 2003. *Stormwater Conveyance Modeling and Design.* Waterbury, CT: Haestad Methods.

Ferguson, Bruce K. 1998. *Introduction to Stormwater.* New York: John Wiley & Sons, Inc.

Naval Facilities Engineering Command. 1986. *Civil Engineering Drainage Systems*, Design Manual 5.03. Alexandria, VA: Naval Facilities Engineering Command.

Richman, Tom, Keith H. Lichten, Jennifer Worth, and Bruce K. Ferguson. 1998. *Vegetated Swales.* LATIS, Washington, DC: American Society of Landscape Architects.

U.S. Federal Highway Administration. 1973. *Design of Roadside Drainage Channels*, Hydraulic Design Series No. 4. Washington, DC: U.S. Federal Highway Administration.

Downloadable Federal Government Manuals

Bureau of Reclamation, *Water Measurement Manual*, 3rd ed., 2001, from www.usbr.gov/pmts/hydraulics_lab.

Corps of Engineers, *Subsurface and Subsurface Drainage*, Unified Facilities Criteria, UFC 3-240-01, 2004, from https://transportation.wes.army.mil/triservice/criteria.

Federal Highway Administration manuals from www.fhwa.dot.gov/bridge/hydpub.htm

Urban Drainage Design Manual, Hydraulic Engineering Circular No. 22 ("HEC-22"), 2nd ed., 2001, FHWA-NHI-01-021.

Hydraulic Design of Highway Culverts, Hydraulic Design Series No. 5 ("HDS 5"), 2001, FHWA-NHI-01-020.

Design Charts for Open-Channel Flow, Hydraulic Design Series No. 3 ("HDS 3"), 1961.

Principal author: Mark E. Boyer, University of Arkansas; Section editor: Bruce K. Ferguson, University of Georgia

STORMWATER QUANTITY CONTROL

INTRODUCTION

The excess runoff from urban developments taxes the capacity of local drainage systems, floods downstream properties, erodes stream channels, and carries urban pollutants into receiving waters. Excess runoff is water that has been diverted from soil infiltration, groundwater recharge, and stream base flow. Local development ordinances commonly specify the maximum runoff rate and volume allowed to be discharged from development sites.

This section outlines provisions for reducing flow rate as runoff moves through surface conveyance systems, and reducing runoff volume by returning it to the subsurface. All the provisions are integral with landscape form and function. Rudimentary formulas and data are from the resources cited at the end. References and computer models like those cited here and in other stormwater sections provide much more detailed analytical and design procedures.

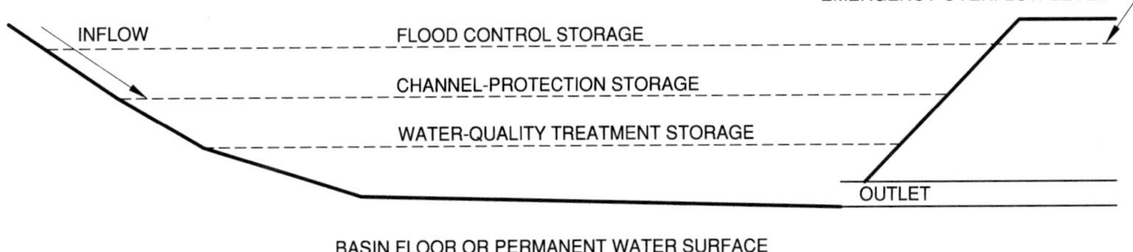

POSSIBLE MULTIPLE LEVELS IN DETENTION BASIN

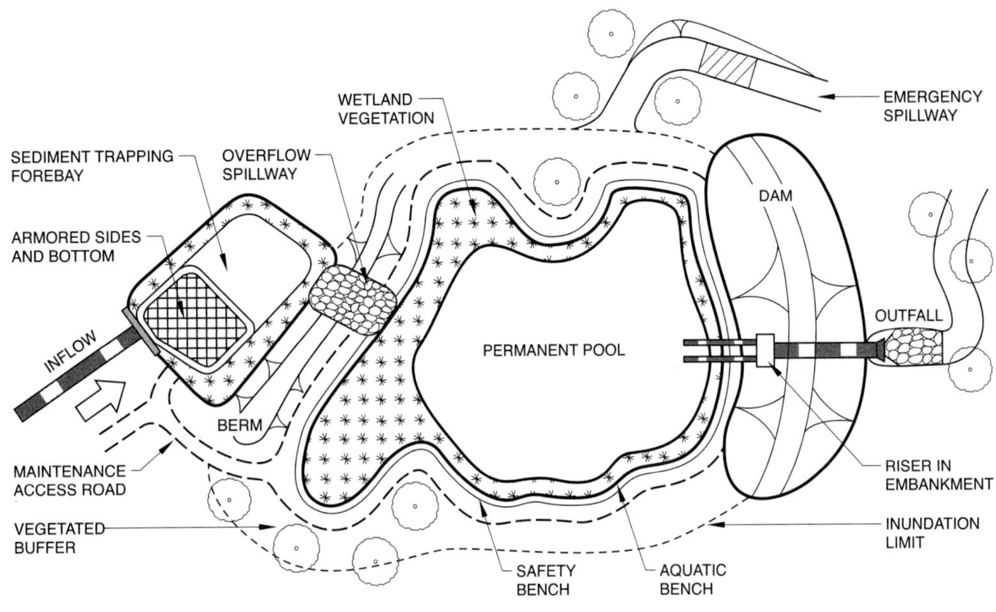

POSSIBLE FEATURES IN DETENTION BASIN

DETENTION

Stormwater detention reduces peak flow rate at the point of discharge. A detention basin is a reservoir that temporarily stores water; it can take the form of a dry pond, a wet pond, or a wetland. The outlet can be any type of conveyance that passes flow at controlled rates as water depth varies, such as orifice, V-notch weir, horizontal weir, or culvert. The outlet releases water from the reservoir at moderate to low rates over an extended time. Multilevel outlets can control the flows from various storm frequencies, as the reservoir's water rises to various levels.

Detention for water quality holds runoff from small storms and the first flush of large storms to treat runoff pollution. If the reservoir is a wet pond, then a sediment-trapping forebay, a deepwater settling zone, and emergent aquatic plants can enhance treatment effectiveness.

Detention for stream-channel protection holds runoff from the one-year or two-year storm. This is the frequency of the "channel-forming flow," when stream channels flow bankful and in-channel sediment adjusts to maintain the channels' equilibrium form.

Detention for flood control holds the runoff from large events such as the 10-year to 100-year storms, to reduce flooding of downstream properties.

Detention facilities must include an emergency spillway to discharge flows safely during storms larger than the largest design storm. A spillway must be protected from erosion by channel armor or by excavation in cut.

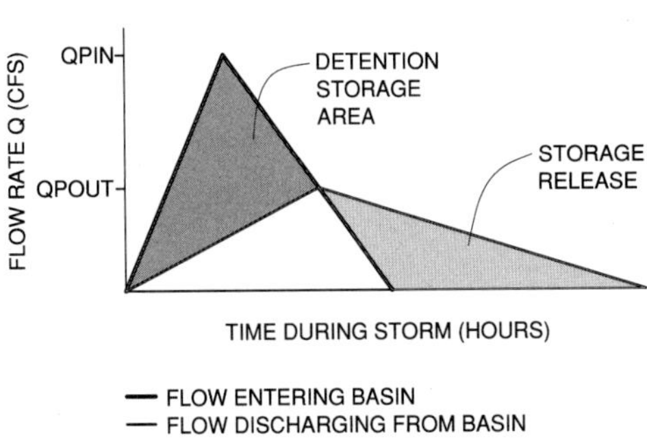

DETENTION HYDROGRAPH

For a given design-storm condition, peak flow entering a detention basin is the drainage area's q_p. The required reservoir volume increases as the basin's discharge rate is increasingly suppressed. A hydrologic model that performs reservoir routing evaluates storage volume and outlet size together, matching depth of water at the outlet with the rise of water in the reservoir.

Detention's downstream effects are controversial. Water stored in detention reservoirs is subject to solar heating, elevating water temperature and reducing life-supporting dissolved oxygen. The extended duration of moderate flow rates can increase channel erosion. Where extended moderate flows combine with other tributary flows, they can increase peak total flow rate, aggravating flooding. Modeling of the downstream watershed is necessary to foresee all of a basin's hydrologic effects.

Detention reservoirs can be installed on each development site in an urban watershed, or a large "regional" reservoir can be built downstream. If a regional facility is sited accessibly, it can promise more reliable maintenance, at lower cost, than can small dispersed facilities, because its maintenance operations require travel to only one location. A regional facility can be made into a large, publicly accessible pond, lake or wetland, making a more significant amenity than small upstream "dry" basins. On the other hand, the construction and maintenance costs of regional facilities may have to be borne by the general public rather than the developers of individual sites. Regional downstream construction might disturb an existing channel or wetland. Downstream facilities do not protect headwater streams and properties from the effects of excess runoff.

INFILTRATION

Stormwater infiltration forces runoff into the underlying soil. An infiltration basin stores stormwater while it infiltrates. The soil ecosystem removes pollutants from the infiltrating water. Surface runoff volume is reduced, because infiltrated water is removed from the surface flow; it goes into the groundwater to discharge later as part of the long-term base flow.

Infiltration for water-quality treatment and groundwater recharge holds runoff from small storms and the first flush of large storms. An infiltration basin that captures less than 0.375 of the entering runoff volume Q does not reduce the peak runoff rate q_p; the additional runoff overflows the basin and continues downstream at the same rate it entered. Where peak rate is required be reduced, detention may be necessary, even after providing infiltration. Nevertheless, only a small capac-

Lead author: Stuart Echols, Pennsylvania State University; Section editor: Bruce K. Ferguson, University of Georgia

ity for daily infiltration is required to create a substantial cumulative effect on water quality and groundwater recharge over time, because small storms and first flushes are frequent and numerous.

Infiltration to restore predevelopment runoff volume during a given design storm holds a large volume equal to Q–Q_{pre}, where Q is the runoff volume after development and Q_{pre} is the volume before development. Capturing a large volume recharges additional groundwater, restoring predevelopment recharge levels. Capturing a volume greater than $0.375Q$ reduces the peak flow rate continuing downstream, by capturing the portion of the storm flow that includes the peak rate.

Infiltration of an entire design-storm volume eliminates the need for primary conveyance drainage structures immediately downstream. When a larger storm occurs or the basin is clogged, the basin overflows, as does a detention basin or any other drainage structure when its design conditions are exceeded.

Soil infiltration rate K depends on soil texture. During construction, compaction must be avoided in order to preserve infiltration capacity. Nevertheless, inadvertent compaction and sedimentation reduce infiltration rate, so in design a safety factor is applied to K, commonly equal to 0.5; in other words, the infiltration rate used in design is in effect half of the value indicated by soil texture.

Infiltration ponding time must be limited to restore basin capacity after each storm and to prevent formation of mosquito habitat. Common ponding time limits are from one day to three days. For a given maximum ponding time T_p in days, the maximum permissible ponding depth D in feet is given by:

$$D = T_p K$$

where:

K = soil infiltration rate, feet per day

For a given runoff volume to be infiltrated Q_{inf} in cubic feet, a basin requires a minimum floor area Ab in square feet:

$$Ab = Qinf/D$$

The advantage of underground basins (infiltration trenches or infiltration beds) is that they do not take up surface space; they can fit into dense urban sites under lawns or pavements. They are constructed of open-graded aggregate that stores water in its void space, optionally supplemented by pipes or manufactured chambers. The void space V_d of open-graded aggregate is commonly 0.3 to 0.4 cubic feet/cubic feet. Total trench dimensions can be derived from:

Total trench volume = Q_{inf}/V_d
Total trench depth = $T_p K/V_d$
Total trench area = Trench volume/Trench depth

Infiltration basins should be kept away from water-supply wells, building basements, and steep unstable slopes. Infiltration should not be done on brownfield sites where existing soil pollutants must not be leached into the environment.

A site's infiltration can be concentrated in a single central basin or distributed into numerous smaller facilities. Dispersed facilities can make efficient use of a site by taking advantage of small, otherwise unused landscape pockets.

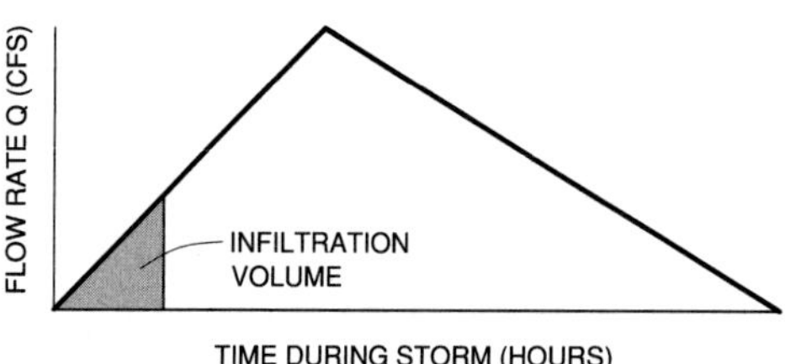

INFILTRATION HYDROGRAPH WITH UNCHANGED q_p

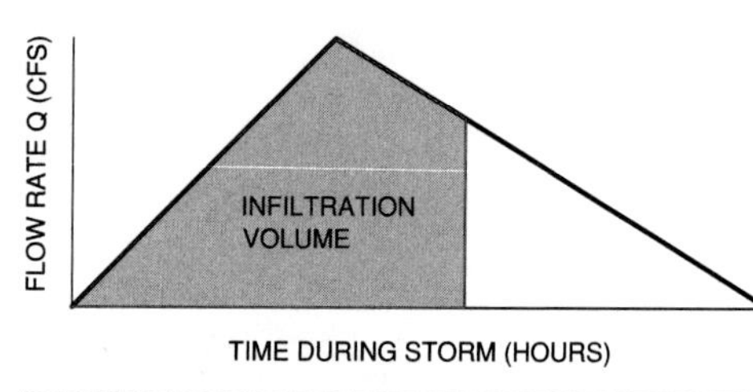

INFILTRATION HYDROGRAPH WITH REDUCED q_p

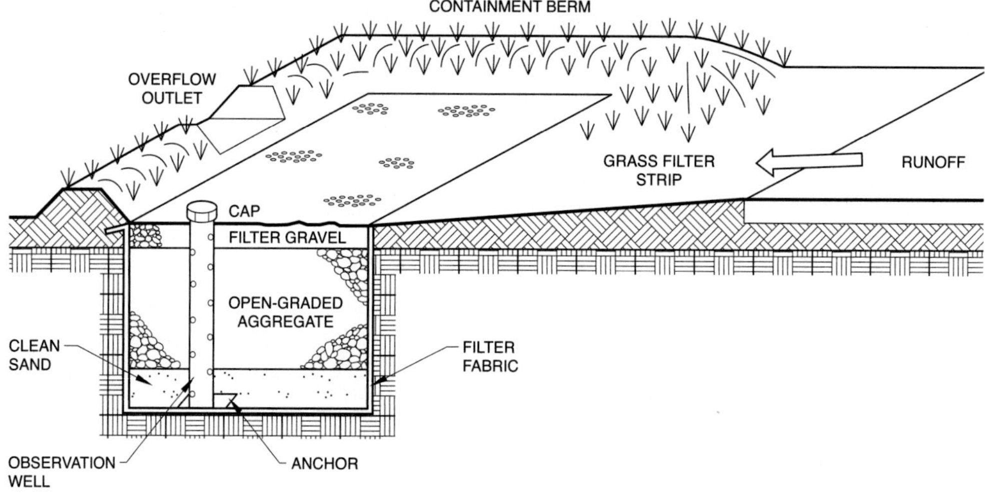

POSSIBLE FEATURES IN INFILTRATION TRENCH

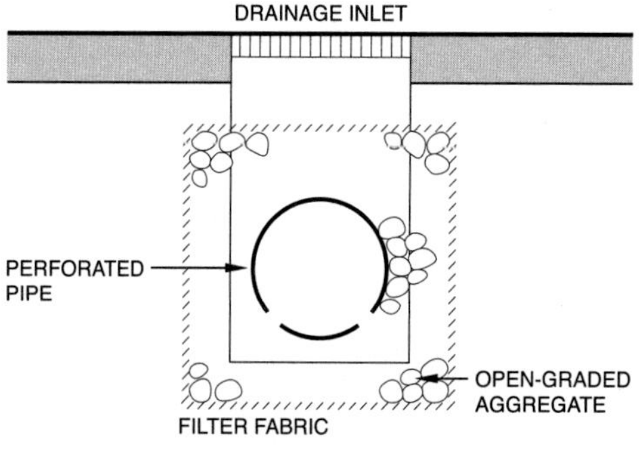

INFILTRATION TRENCH SUPPLEMENTED BY PIPE

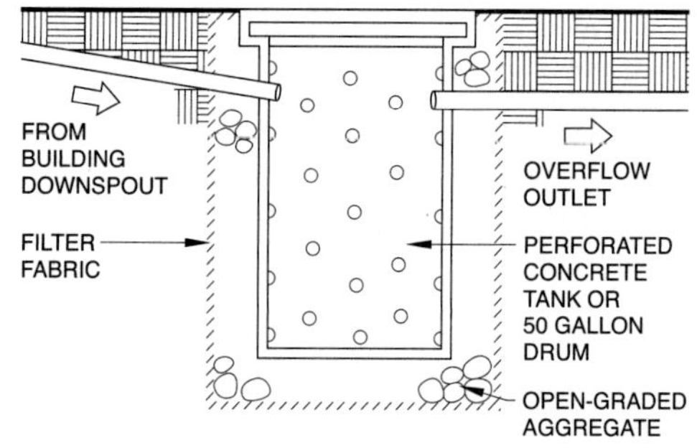

DRY WELL

INFILTRATION RATES IN UNCOMPACTED SOIL

SOIL TEXTURE	INFILTRATION RATE INCHES PER HOUR	INFILTRATION RATE FEET PER DAY
Sand	8.27	16.54
Loamy sand	2.41	4.82
Sandy loam	1.02	2.04
Loam	0.52	1.04
Silt loam	0.27	0.54
Sandy clay loam	0.17	0.34
Clay Loam	0.09	0.18
Silty clay loam	0.06	0.12
Sandy clay	0.05	0.10
Silty clay	0.04	0.08
Clay	0.02	0.04

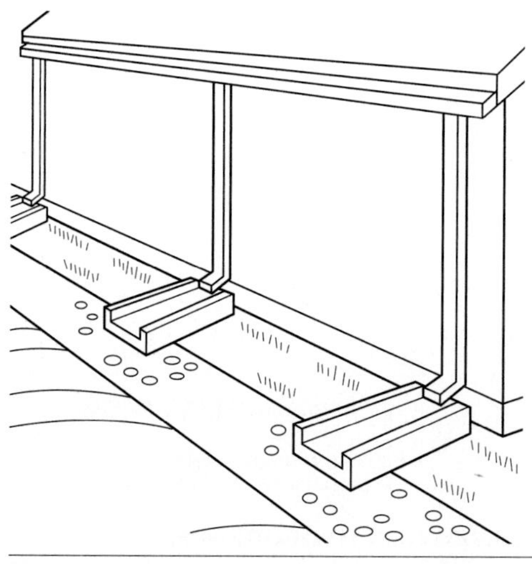

INFILTRATION TRENCH AT BUILDING DOWNSPOUTS

Lead author: Stuart Echols, Pennsylvania State University; Section editor: Bruce K. Ferguson, University of Georgia

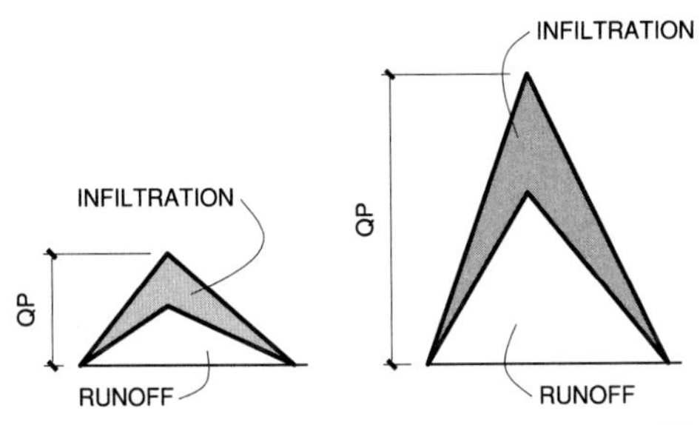

SPLIT-FLOW HYDROGRAPHS IN DIFFERENT STORMS

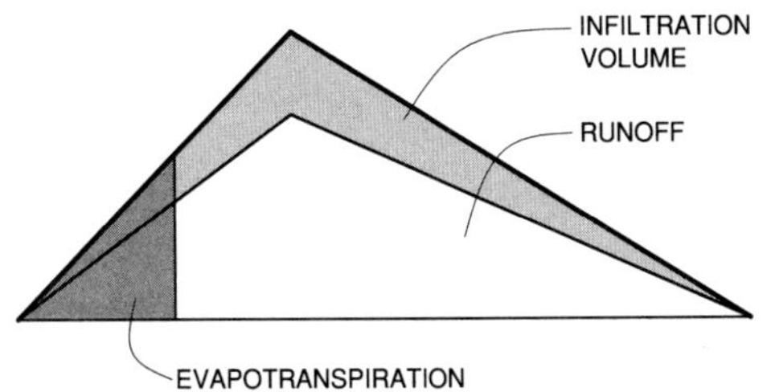

SPLIT-FLOW HYDROGRAPH WITH FIRST-FLUSH BIORETENTION

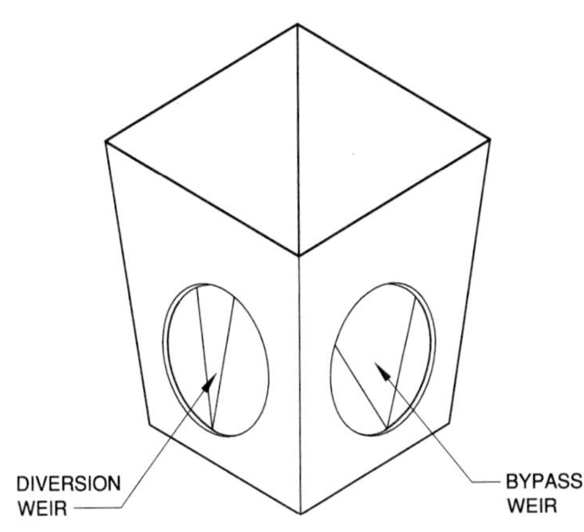

PROPORTIONAL FLOW SPLITTER

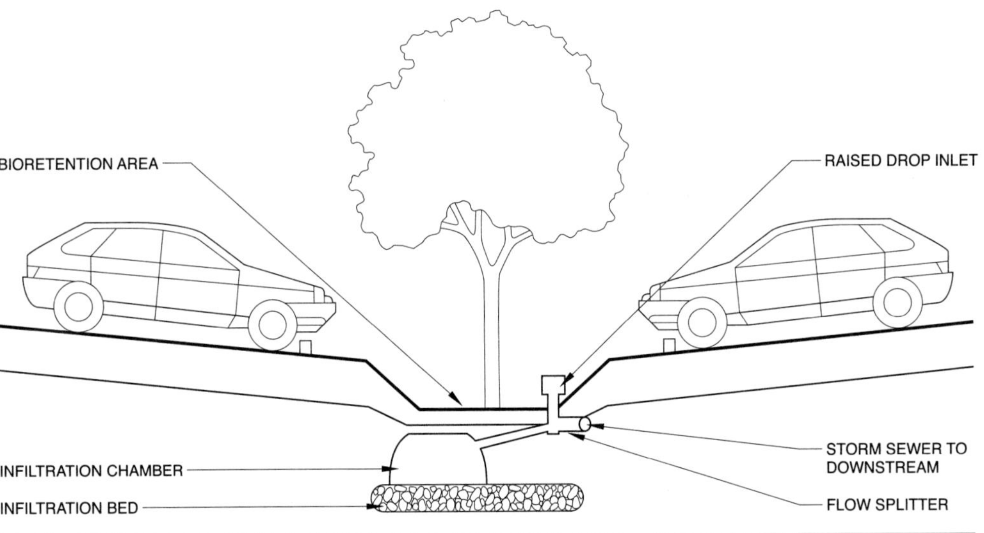

SPLIT FLOW AND BIORETENTION

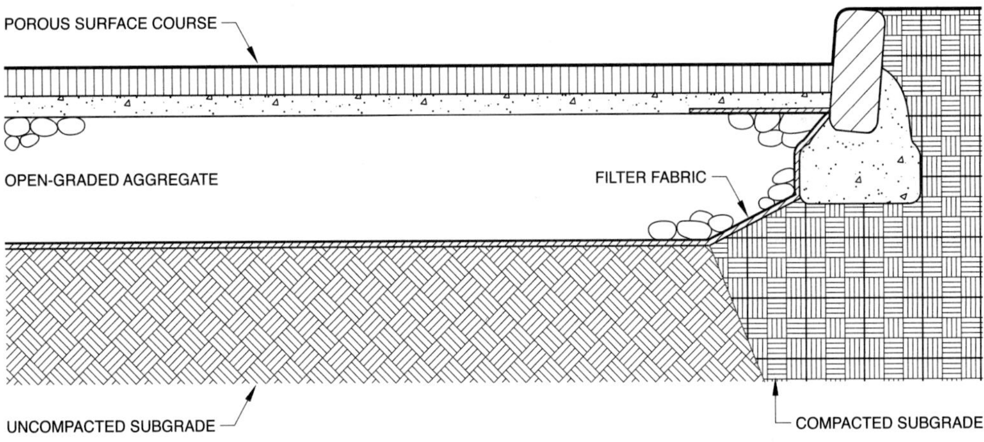

INFILTRATION PROVISIONS IN POROUS PAVEMENT

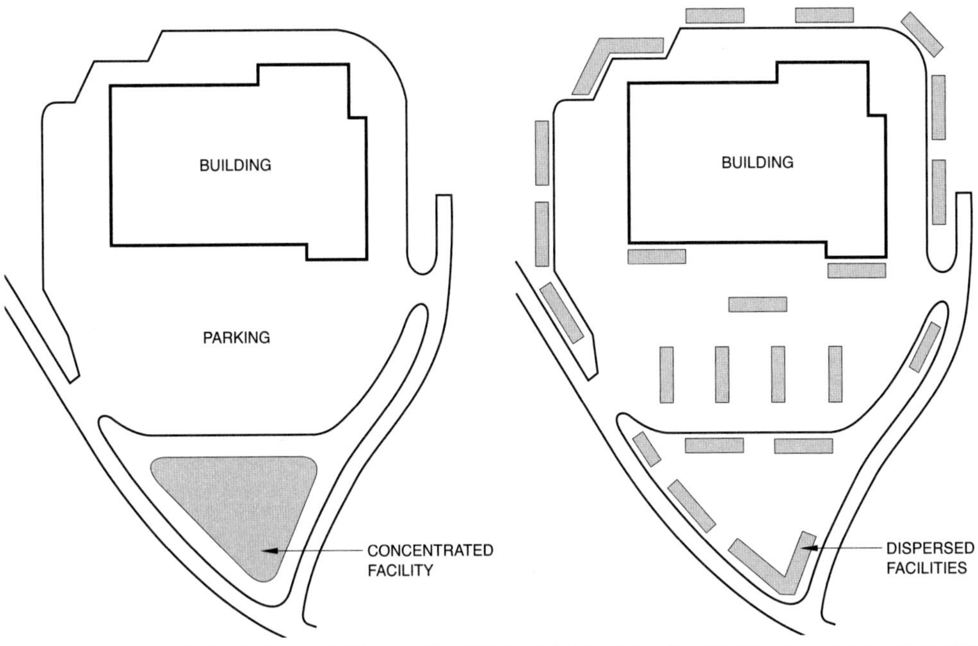

CONCENTRATED VERSUS DISPERSED STORMWATER FACILITIES

Lead author: Stuart Echols, Pennsylvania State University; Section editor: Bruce K. Ferguson, University of Georgia

SPLIT-FLOW MANAGEMENT

Split-flow stormwater management divides runoff continuously into proportions that are directed to infiltration and downstream discharge. It reduces both runoff rate and runoff volume, even where only a small volume is infiltrated. Where it is possible to infiltrate a volume equal to Q–Q_{pre}, the recharge replicates predevelopment recharge, and the discharging runoff replicates predevelopment storm hydrographs in volume, rate, and timing.

A proportional flow splitter is a pair of V-notch weirs. For a given q_p running off a drainage area, one weir's notch angle θ is derived to pass the desired peak runoff rate at a convenient flow depth. A second V-notch weir is designed at the same flow depth to pass the remaining portion of the flow, which will go to infiltration. The two weirs are set into a drop inlet or other fixed structure, with the infiltration outlet connected to an infiltration basin, and the runoff outlet discharging into a downstream pipe or channel. As q rises and falls during a storm, the flow through both weirs rises and falls proportionally, delivering infiltration and runoff continuously. During a storm larger or smaller than the design storm, of any size and frequency, the flow is divided in the same proportions throughout the storm event.

The flow can be further split by diverting the first flush to a bioretention area, before the remaining flow reaches the weirs. Bioretention treats the first flush and holds water in the soil for plant use. If the bioretention water volume is attributed to evapotranspiration, then this further splitting of flow replicates natural hydrology still more closely.

REFERENCES

Echols, Stuart. 2002. "Split-Flow Method: Introduction of a Stormwater Management Strategy, in *Stormwater*, July/August 2002, www.forester.net/sw_0207_split.html.

Ferguson, Bruce K. 1994. *Stormwater Infiltration*. Boca Raton, FL: CRC Press.

———. 1998. *Introduction to Stormwater: Concept, Purpose, Design*. New York: John Wiley & Sons, Inc.

Lead author: Stuart Echols, Pennsylvania State University; Section editor: Bruce K. Ferguson, University of Georgia

STORMWATER QUALITY CONTROL

INTRODUCTION

Stormwater washes oils, bacteria, litter, sediment, and fertilizers from urban pavements, rooftops, and lawns. In water bodies downstream, the excess sediment makes water turbid, inhibits biotic growth and reproduction, and carries trace-metal ions worn or corroded from cars. The oils leaked from automobiles deoxygenates water from within. Urban aquatic ecosystems are left with fewer species; the remaining species are those tolerant of the stressful conditions. Some 70 percent of the water pollution in the United States comes from such nonpoint sources. A large portion of contaminants is washed off during frequent low-flow events and the first flush of larger storms, as runoff mobilizes pollutants that had accumulated during dry weather. The U.S. Federal Clean Water Act made nonpoint-source pollution a national program by establishing the National Pollutant Discharge Elimination System (NPDES), which is now being carried out in all cities and towns.

This section outlines provisions for treating water quality on urban sites. All of the provisions are integral with a site's landscape forms and functions. In them, oil is degraded (broken into chemically simpler constituents) by naturally occurring microecosystems. Metals like lead, zinc, and cadmium cannot be degraded, but soils and settling ponds trap them by capturing the minute sediment particles to which their ions are attached, preventing them from moving downstream and accumulating inadvertently in the environment. Rudimentary formulas and data are from references cited at the end of this section. References and computer models like those cited in this section give much more detailed problem-solving capability for specific site conditions.

WATER-QUALITY TREATMENT VOLUME

Water-quality control focuses on treating the volume of runoff from small, frequent storms and first flushes, rather than the full volume of large, infrequent storms for which flood control is designed. A water-quality volume can be specified either as a fixed depth of runoff from the contributing watershed or as the runoff occurring during a storm of given size or recurrence interval.

Runoff volumes can be reliably calculated using the SCS Method for 24-hour storms of 2.5 inches or more.

COMMON CONSTITUENTS IN URBAN STORMWATER

CONSTITUENT	SOURCES IN URBAN RUNOFF
Sediment ("particulates" or "suspended solids")	Construction sites, eroding streambanks
Oil	Cars
Organic compounds	Car oil, herbicides, pesticides
Nutrients (nitrogen, phosphorus)	Organic compounds, organic litter, fertilizers, food waste
Metals	Cars, construction materials
Oxygen demand (BOD, COD)	Nutrients, oils
Chloride	Deicing salts
Bacteria	Animals, dumpsters, trash-handling areas

For smaller storms like those used for water-quality treatment, the SCS method may underestimate urban runoff volumes. The following formula is intended to estimate small storm runoff volumes more accurately:

$$Q_{wq} = 3{,}660APR_v$$

where:

Q_{wq} = water-quality runoff volume, cubic feet
3,660 = conversion factor, cubic feet per acre-inch
A = drainage area, acres
P = rainfall in inches
R_v = volumetric runoff coefficient

In this method's simplest application, called the short-cut method, the coefficient R_v is a simple function of the drainage area's impervious cover:

$$R_v = 0.05 + 0.009I$$

where:

I = impervious cover in percent

EXAMPLES OF CRITERIA FOR RUNOFF TREATMENT VOLUMES

VOLUME
Runoff from 2-year, 24-hour rainfall
Runoff from ½-year, 24-hour rainfall
First 1 inch of runoff from complex surfaces
First ½ inch of runoff from impervious surfaces

A more precise value of R_v can be derived by taking into account the characteristics of a watershed's specific pervious and impervious surfaces. For this purpose special values of R_v have been developed; their application is referred to as the small storm hydrology method. The values for impervious surfaces assume that all impervious surfaces are directly connected to the drainage system, which means that their runoff flows directly into channels or pipes. Each special value of R_v is applied to its portion of the drainage area, then an area-weighted average R_v for the drainage area as a whole is computed.

If a portion of the watershed's impervious surfaces are disconnected from the drainage system, then their runoff flows over pervious areas before reaching pipes or channels. This sequence reduces runoff volumes and velocities, so the R_v values of the impervious surfaces can be reduced. Taking this reduction into account evaluates the components of the watershed still more precisely and rewards site designs that utilize disconnections by lowering the computed R_v and the required Q_{wq}. For an impervious surface to be considered disconnected, the pervious area to which it drains must be at least twice as large as the impervious surface's area, and its flow path must be at least twice as long. To find the reduced R_v value, each impervious surface's directly connected R_v value is multiplied by the appropriate reduction factor, then an area-weighted average R_v is found for the watershed as a whole.

VOLUMETRIC RUNOFF COEFFICIENTS R_v FOR PERVIOUS SURFACES

RAINFALL IN INCHES	PERVIOUS SURFACES ON SANDY SOILS (HYDROLOGIC SOIL GROUP A)	PERVIOUS SURFACES ON SILTY SOILS (HYDROLOGIC SOIL GROUP B)	PERVIOUS SURFACES ON CLAYEY SOILS (HYDROLOGIC SOIL GROUP C AND D)
0.75	.02	.11	.20
1.00	.02	.11	.21
1.25	.03	.13	.22
1.50	.05	.15	.24

VOLUMETRIC RUNOFF COEFFICIENTS R_v FOR DIRECTLY CONNECTED IMPERVIOUS SURFACES

RAINFALL IN INCHES	FLAT ROOFS AND LARGE, UNPAVED PARKING LOTS	PITCHED ROOFS AND LARGE IMPERVIOUS AREAS (LARGE PARKING LOTS)	SMALL IMPERVIOUS AREAS AND NARROW STREETS
0.75	.82	.97	.66
1.00	.84	.97	.70
1.25	.86	.98	.74
1.50	.88	.99	.77

REDUCTION FACTORS TO FIND R_v VALUES OF DISCONNECTED IMPERVIOUS SURFACE AREAS

RAINFALL IN INCHES	SHOPPING CENTERS AND STRIP COMMERCIAL	MEDIUM- TO HIGH-DENSITY RESIDENTIAL WITH PAVED ALLEYS	MEDIUM- TO HIGH-DENSITY RESIDENTIAL WITHOUT ALLEYS	LOW-DENSITY RESIDENTIAL
0.75	.99	.27	.21	.20
1.00	.99	.38	.22	.21
1.25	.99	.48	.22	.22
1.50	.99	.59	.24	.24

Lead author: Robert D. Sykes, University of Minnesota; Section editor: Bruce K. Ferguson, University of Georgia

STORMWATER PONDS AND WETLANDS

Stormwater ponds (called "wet ponds" because of their permanent pools) remove sediment particles, and the pollutant ions that cling to them, from runoff by settling in still water. During storms, the water-quality volume enters from the pond's upstream end. The heavy sediment-laden water displaces relatively clean pond water up and toward the outlet, where the clean "old" water discharges. The new water-quality volume remains in the pond's "dead storage" for settling until the next storm arrives.

- The *permanent pool* is the water held below the outlet invert. Its volume should be at least as large as the water-quality runoff volume, so that each water-quality inflow will remain in dead storage until the next storm arrives.
- *Sediment storage* is below the permanent pool. In many ponds, sediment storage of 250 cubic feet per acre of drainage area can store the sediment delivered over 5 to 10 years, after which maintenance for sediment removal would be necessary. Greater storage volume prolongs the required time between removals. Together, the permanent pool and the sediment storage space are the pond's dead storage below the pond's outlet.
- *Temporary water-quality storage* must be provided above the outlet's invert, at least equal in volume to Q_{wq}. This is where pond water rises during storms, before discharging through the outlet. Water-level rise of less than 1 foot during frequent water-quality events limits stress on wetland plants.
- *Additional flood storage* is placed above the water-quality storage, to control peak discharges during flow events larger than the water-quality event (for example, the 2-year through 100-year storms). Total flood storage depth is measured from the outlet invert.

To settle out particles without resuspension, the velocity of flow through a pond must be limited. At any depth over the invert, a pond outlet must limit the release of water from water-quality storage to no more than 5.66 cubic feet per second per acre of pond surface. Many outlets use a V-notch weir to control water-quality release, and horizontal weirs for larger flood control releases. Baffles, hoods, and trash racks may be added to skim off floatable oil and debris.

To limit discharge to the indicated value, a given water-quality volume must be spread out over a large area. Minimum permanent-pool surface areas required for a pond to remove 90 percent or more of small sediment particles are tabulated.

In addition to sediment removal, wet ponds can also be designed for phosphorus removal by providing larger dead storage volumes. Aerating fountains can be added to hasten biodegradation of pollutants. Bioharvesting—regular removal of aquatic plant growth—can be initiated to remove accumulating pollutants.

BIOFILTER STRIPS AND SWALES

Vegetated filter strips and swales treat water while conveying it. They are commonly referred to as biofilters, because to some degree their vegetation and soil filter the water as it flows, and reduce runoff volume. They are particularly effective during small, frequent water-quality events, when water flows slowly in intimate contact with soil and vegetation.

Vegetated filter strips are densely vegetated, uniformly graded areas over which runoff flows in a thin sheet. They are commonly planted with turf grass; other dense vegetation types may also be used. The turf ecosystem builds trapped sediment particles into the living soil matrix. Filter strips are commonly placed to intercept sheet runoff from impervious surfaces, where they keep sediment out of downstream bioretention cells, infiltration basins, or riparian buffers. If flow entering a filter strip is concentrated, it can be distributed with a level spreader. A gentle slope (6 percent maximum) limits runoff velocity. If slope is less than 2 percent, a perforated underdrain can be added to further limit velocity. If slope is greater than 2 percent, check dams can be added, or the slope can be terraced with drop structures between gently sloping terraces. Some filter strips need to be irrigated to maintain vegetation density.

Biofilter swales ("enhanced swales") convey runoff slowly, and in the process trap pollutants, promote infiltration, and reduce runoff rate and volume. "Dry swales" drain out completely after a storm. "Wet swales" can be used where standing water does not create a nuisance and where the groundwater is close enough to the surface to maintain a permanent pool between storms. Check dams can be added to reduce runoff velocity or hold a water-quality runoff volume for detention or infiltration. A swale's flow velocity and capacity can be evaluated with Manning's equation. Treatment effectiveness increases with long residence time of water in the swale; residence time is indicated by:

$$t_r = VL/60$$

where:

t_r = residence time in minutes
V = velocity in feet per second
L = swale length in feet

POND AREAS FOR PARTICLE REMOVAL*

WATERSHED LAND USE	POOL AREA AS PERCENT OF WATERSHED AREA
Totally paved areas	3.0
Freeways	2.8
Industrial areas	2.0
Commercial areas	1.7
Institutional areas	1.7
Construction sites	1.5
Residential areas	0.8
Open spaces	0.6

**Minimum permanent pool area required for 90 percent removal of 5 micron (and larger) sediment particles.*

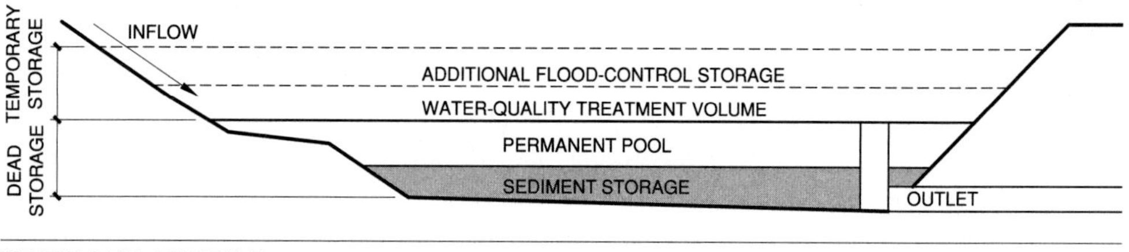

WET-POND PROFILE

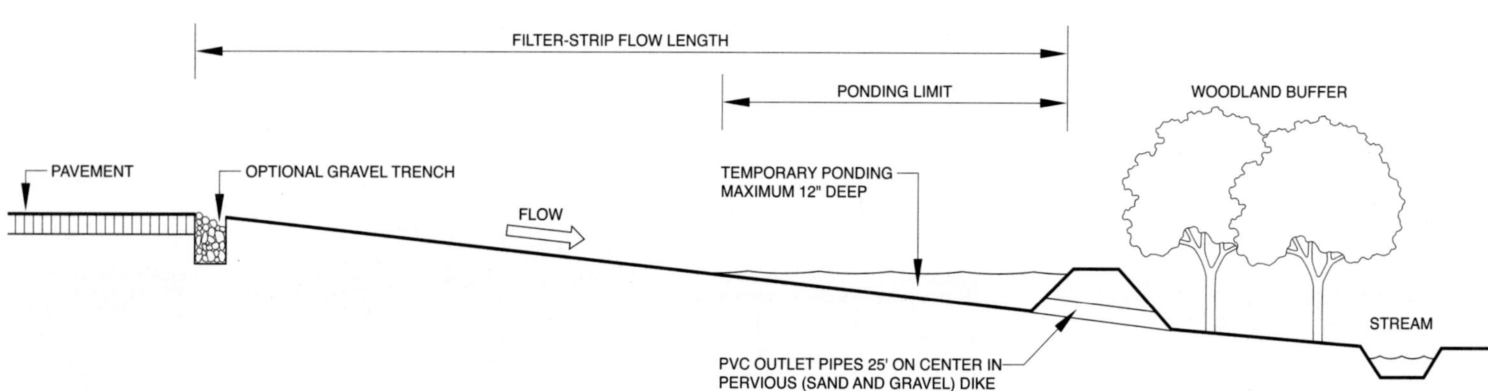

GRASSED FILTER STRIP

Lead author: Robert D. Sykes, University of Minnesota; Section editor: Bruce K. Ferguson, University of Georgia

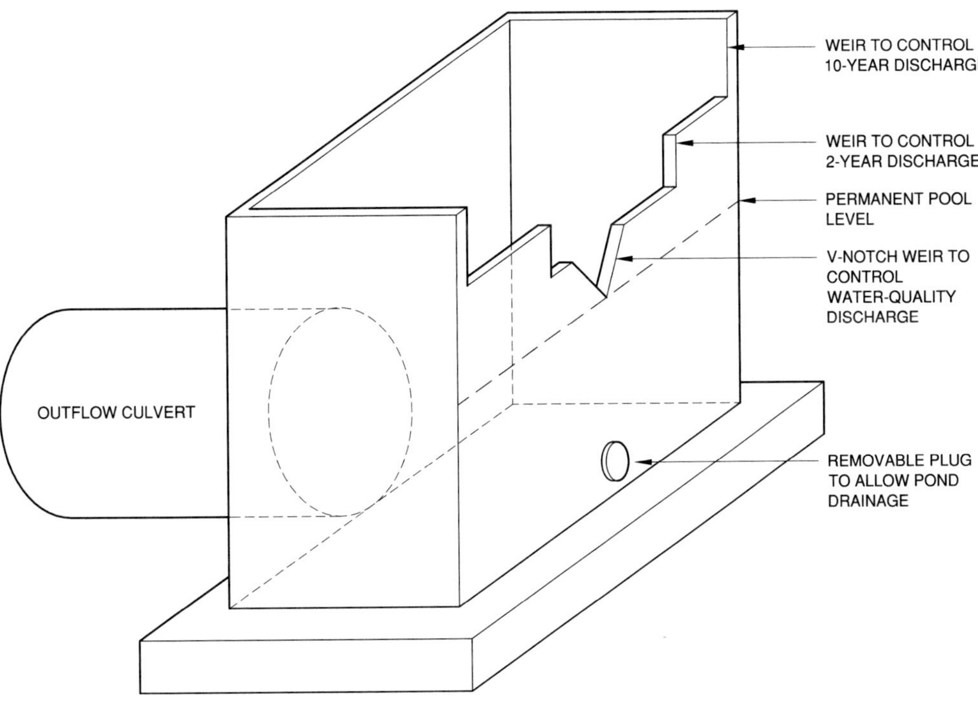

EXAMPLE OF WET-POND OUTLET

INFILTRATION AND BIORETENTION

Almost any soil is a filter that traps sediment, and a living ecosystem that transforms oils and nutrients. A soil's cation exchange capacity (CEC), multiplied by the thickness of the soil mantle, indicates the relative renovation capability of a soil profile.

Infiltration into native soil replenishes soil moisture and groundwater while treating water quality. An infiltration basin traps a water volume below the outlet invert equal to the runoff volume that is to be treated. The water should infiltrate completely in a limited time so as not to produce mosquito habitat. A basin can be surrounded by a grass filter strip to remove potentially clogging particulates before runoff reaches the infiltration surface.

Bioretention enhances infiltration's treatment effectiveness with a special soil mixture and plant uptake. In a bioretention area, a shallow depression captures runoff and filters it through the soil planting medium. The surface ponding depth is commonly limited to 6 to 12 inches; an overflow outlet discharges excess water. The soil mixture must be moderately permeable, so a large proportion must be sand. It must also have organic matter, and perhaps a small amount of native topsoil, for pollutant trapping. Such a mixture absorbs runoff readily, holds water and nutrients for plant roots, and filters effectively. An organic surface mulch, such as wood chips, replenished annually, can enhance trapping of metals. Where the subgrade is adequately permeable, water passing through the filter medium can infiltrate into the underlying soil. Where slowly permeable soil would prohibit significant infiltration, a perforated underdrain pipe can direct filtered runoff to downstream level spreaders, stormwater wetlands, detention basins, or storm sewers.

A biofilter swale can be enhanced by adding a bioretention soil mixture and, if necessary, an underdrain. Filtration through the soil to an underdrain greatly lengthens total runoff travel time.

A rain garden is a bioretention area sited and designed for planting and appearance, in addition to runoff treatment. Some rain gardens are constructed without a special soil profile, or even without design for hydraulic capacity; they are merely "extra" capture and treatment of small amounts of runoff at opportunistic spots along the length of a swale or below building downspouts. The plants should be selected to tolerate fluctuating wet and dry soil conditions. Where a rain garden is placed among large open pavements, the plants should tolerate the harsh microclimatic conditions that may prevail there.

Porous pavements are substrates that filter small particles and biodegrade oils, even where they contain no soil or organic matter. They capture small particles mostly near the pavement surface. Below, the large surface area of internal pores houses microbiota that biodegrade oils; essentially no oil reaches the pavement bottom. Beneath porous pavements, native soil is a further backup treatment system. Treating stormwater in and below pavements reduces the need for treatment facilities downstream.

DRAIN-INLET DEVICES

Drainage inlets can be designed or retrofitted to remove sediment, trash, and oil from runoff. The advantage of working within the storm sewer system is that it requires no off-pavement space for land-based treatment facilities, so it can fit into very densely developed places and preexisting urban neighborhoods. A common but relatively inefficient example is a catch basin with a hooded inlet. Several proprietary designs for inlets and inlet inserts promise much greater trap efficiency. They use the centrifugal force of flowing water and the floatation of certain contaminants to separate contaminants from water. The contaminants are collected in a bag, basket, or absorbent filter, which can be emptied or discarded. All traps and separators require regular maintenance to remain effective.

GRASSED CHANNELS: EXAMPLES OF CRITERIA FOR TRAPEZOIDAL BIOFILTER SWALES

DIMENSION	CRITERION
Bottom width	2 ft. min., 6 ft. max.
Side slopes	3H:1V or flatter
Longitudinal slope	1.0% min., 4.0% max.
Flow depth during water-quality storm	4 inches max.
Flow velocity during water-quality storm	1.0 fps max.

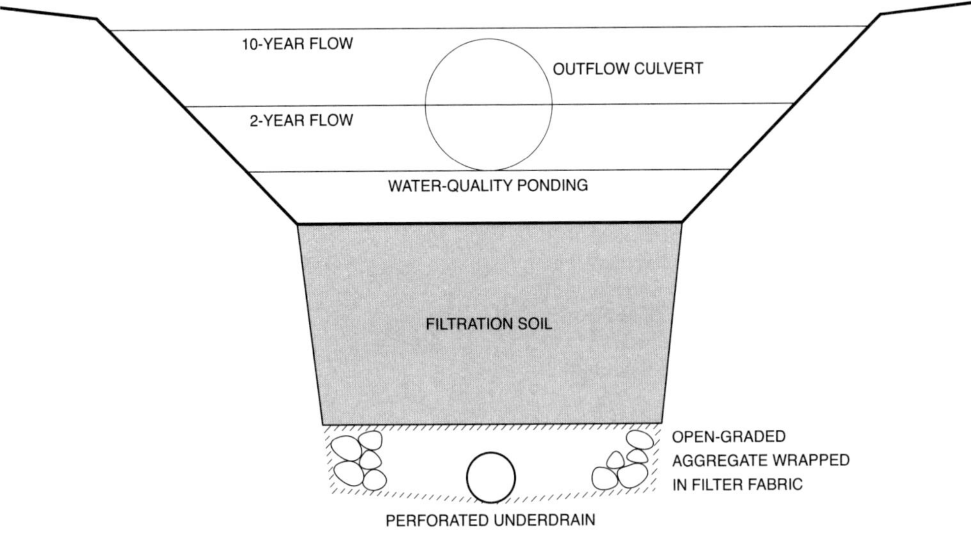

BIOFILTER SWALE TO FILTER A WATER-QUALITY VOLUME

Lead author: Robert D. Sykes, University of Minnesota; Section editor: Bruce K. Ferguson, University of Georgia

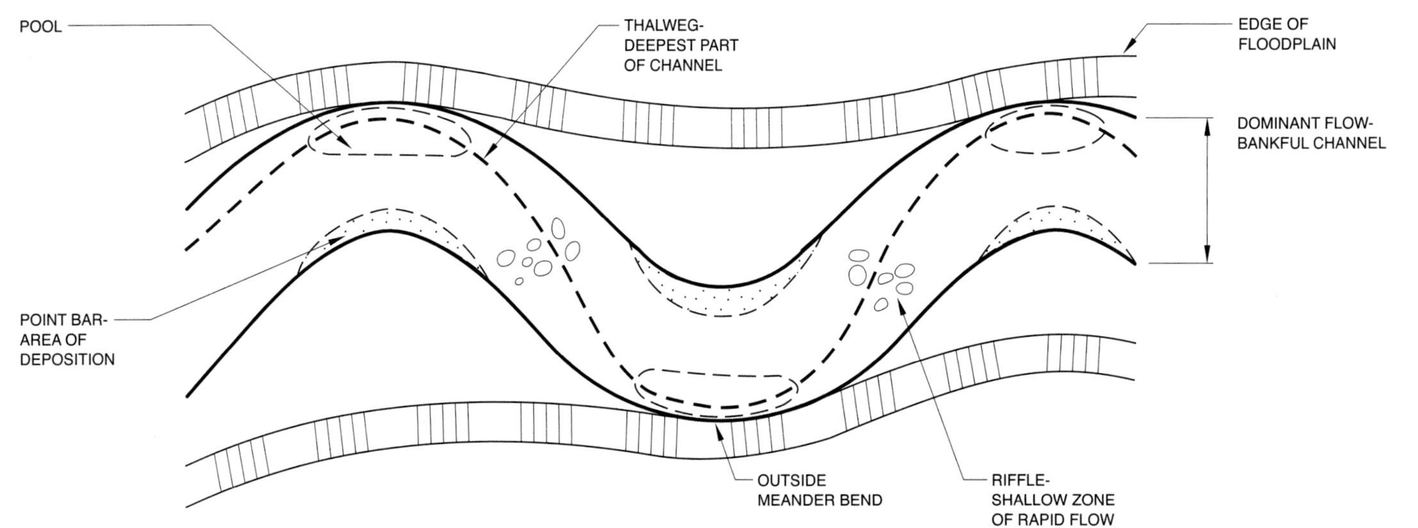

STREAM FEATURES

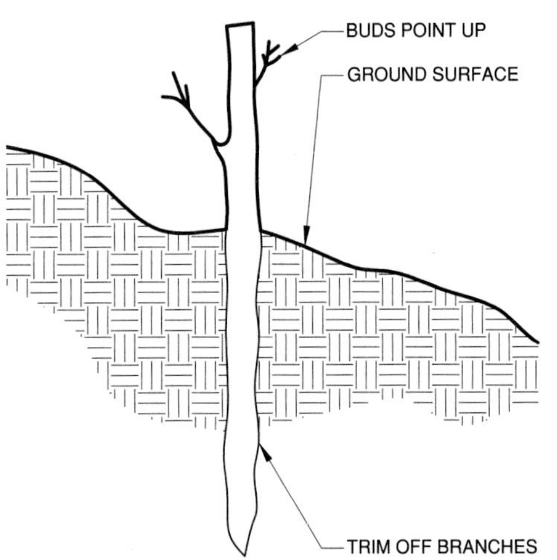

LIVE STAKE INSTALLATION

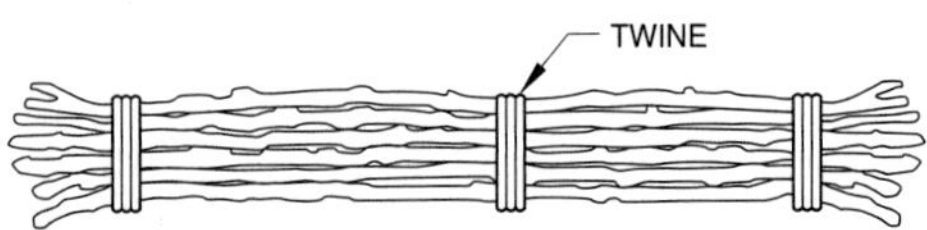

FASCINE OR WATTLE BUNDLE

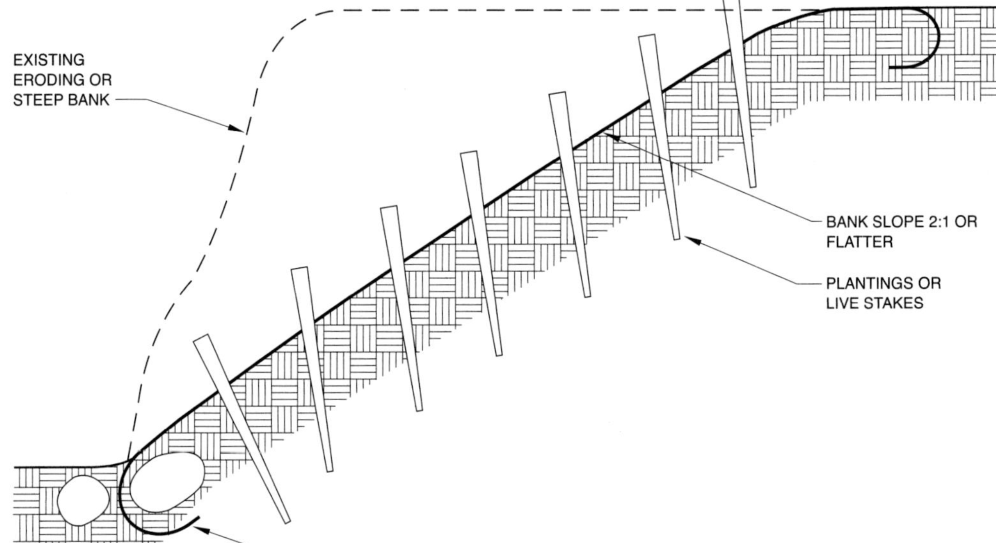

LIVE STAKE INSTALLATION WITH SLOPE MODIFICATION

- Direct-seeded or hydroseeded grasses
- Planted grass plugs
- Transplanted cattails, tules, bulrushes
- Live willow stakes
- Planting of native riparian trees and woody shrubs

A combination of all the above methods is advisable. Excessive irrigation should be avoided. If a large storm occurs during the plant establishment period, incompletely rooted plantings may be washed out and replanting may be necessary.

Soil Bioengineering Techniques

Soil bioengineering integrates living vegetation with nonliving organic and inorganic materials to stabilize channel toes and banks. It applies engineering practices in conjunction with ecological principles, frequently combining vegetative systems and manufactured products. It can typically stabilize banks between 1:1 and 2:1 slopes. Examples of soil bioengineering techniques include:

- Live staking with geotextile fabric
- Joint planting
- Brush layering
- Willow mattress with rock toe
- Contour wattles or fascines
- Vegetated soil lifts
- Vegetated cribbing
- Vegetated log crib wall
- Root wad and boulder revetment with live pole cuttings

PERMITTING

Stream channel restoration and enhancement projects tend to require permits from agencies implementing the National Environmental Policy Act and other laws. These agencies include:

- U.S. Army Corps of Engineers
- U.S. Fish and Wildlife Service
- State Fish and Game Departments
- State and Regional Water Quality Control Boards
- State and Local Coastal Commissions
- Local Flood Control Agencies
- Local Water Quality and Creek Protection Departments

Consult early with the appropriate agencies to understand their goals and requirements and how they apply to a given project. Some regions have consolidated the permitting process into a Joint Aquatic Regulatory Permit Application. Design the project to minimize conflicts. Provide sufficient time for permit review and processing.

Design Process

A typical stream restoration incorporates multiple objectives obtained from various stakeholders.

Principal authors: Sarah Sutton and Isabelle Minn, Wolfe Mason Associates/Design, Community & Environment; Contributors: Rebecca Lave, Design, Community & Environment; L. Robert Neville, PhD, The Bioengineering Group; Craig Benson, Schaaf & Wheeler; Greg Kamman, Kamman Hydrology & Engineering; Mark Cederborg, Handford Applied Restoration & Conservation; Section editor: Bruce K. Ferguson, University of Georgia

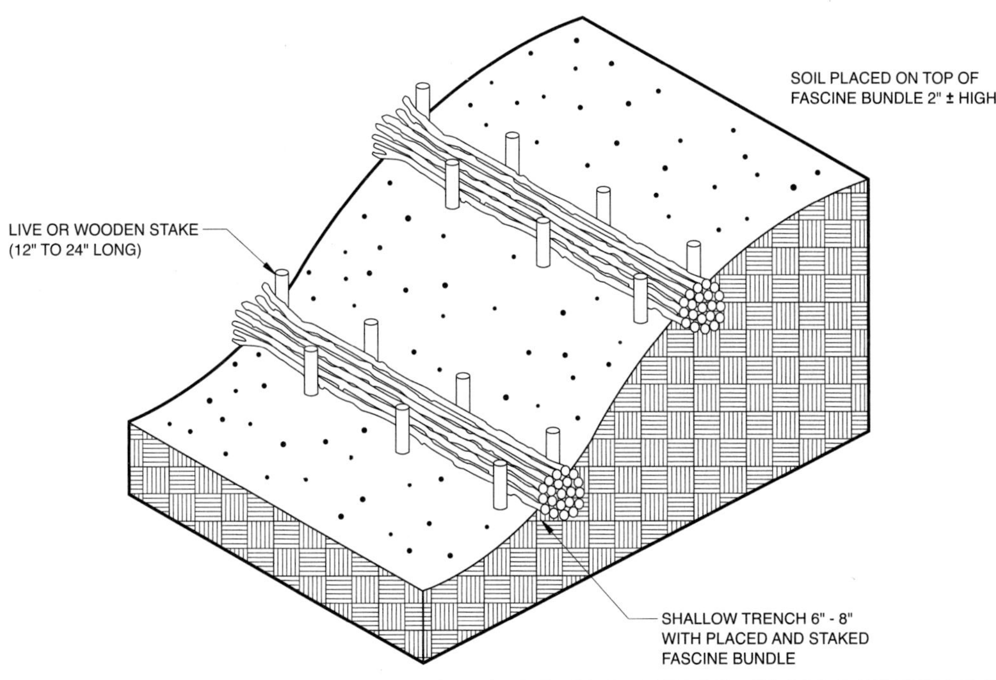

FASCINE INSTALLATION

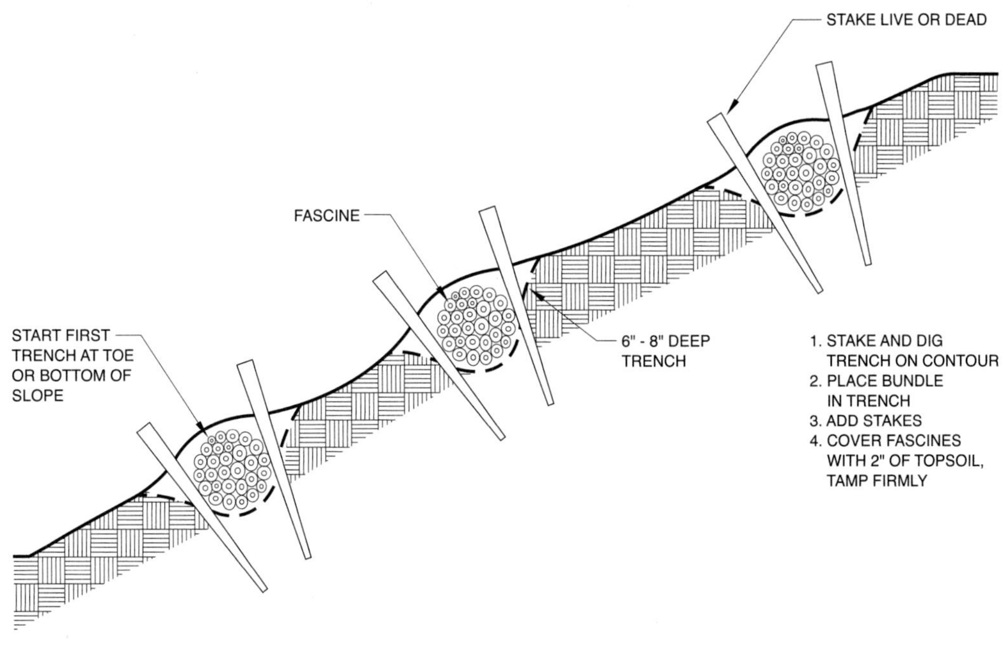

FASCINE INSTALLATION STEPS

Choosing the right design parameters is a critical function of the interdisciplinary team. Trade-offs are necessary to reconcile differences among disciplines and to establish workable parameters that will achieve design objectives in the midst of physical constraints. Steps in the design process include:

1. *Define design objectives.* Examples include:
   - Capacity requirements (e.g., flood protection)
   - Fish habitat
   - Recreational opportunities
   - Aesthetics
   - Public safety
   - Erosion protection
2. *Define existing conditions.* Determine whether the existing channel is stable and whether it meets some of the design objectives. Quantify dominant hydrologic and geomorphic characteristics and processes. Survey aquatic habitats. Identify and characterize "reference reaches," which reflect equilibrium with hydraulic and sediment transport processes.
3. *Identify constraints.* Examples include:
   - Topography
   - Encroachment of buildings that restrict available width
   - Existing bridges and utilities
   - Land ownership
   - Shallow bedrock
   - Soil conditions that affect side-slope stability
4. *Define expected natural channel parameters, including slope, width, depth, roughness, and sinuosity.* Expected parameters will depend on local climate, watershed land use, stormwater management, and erosion control; accurate characterization of these conditions is critical.
5. *Identify inconsistencies.* Compare existing conditions with the expected channel regime to determine where changes to the existing system are required.
6. *Define critical design parameters (assuming that there are no constraints such as bridge crossings).* This typically includes:
   - Meander sequence
   - Channel slope and sinuosity
   - Availability for floodplain to accommodate sinuosity under future conditions
   - Alternative sinuosities that can be accommodated given the floodplain and slope constraints
   - Appropriate channel width-to-depth ratio given the available sinuosity and gradient
   - Sediment size that the channel can be expected to transport
7. *Analyze channel dynamics to determine if the existing channel is in equilibrium with existing flows and sediment regime.* Do the same thing for anticipated future conditions.
8. *Identify trade-offs.* Develop design parameters to accommodate physical constraints. The interdisciplinary team must consider trade-offs based on prioritization of objectives, applicable policies or regulations, and cost.
9. *Develop final design parameters and construction documents.* Final design parameters establish the guidelines for a stream system that is dynamically stable. They are set forth in plans, details, and specifications. Typical plan sets include:
   - An overview of the site, including channel location, riparian system, and floodplain
   - Layout of channel and riparian features including channel sinuosity, pools, riffles, and all required structures (e.g., vortex weirs)
   - Layout of landscape features such as walks, walls, benches, and recreational facilities
   - Grading plan
   - Planting plan
   - Stream profile
   - Cross sections where needed to convey design intent
   - Details

CONSTRUCTION

Installation of stream improvements requires knowledge of stream dynamics. It is critical that an experienced contractor perform the work. Specifications can be written requiring proof (photos and references) of contractors' experience with similar projects, or bids can be solicited only from a preselected list of qualified contractors.

Become familiar with scheduling constraints such as wildlife nesting patterns and seasonal water flows. Discuss with contractors construction access issues and the level of disturbance required for construction. Stage construction to limit disturbance of the active channel.

Principal authors: Sarah Sutton and Isabelle Minn, Wolfe Mason Associates/Design, Community & Environment; Contributors: Rebecca Lave, Design, Community & Environment; L. Robert Neville, PhD, The Bioengineering Group; Craig Benson, Schaaf & Wheeler; Greg Kamman, Kamman Hydrology & Engineering; Mark Cederborg, Handford Applied Restoration & Conservation; Section editor: Bruce K. Ferguson, University of Georgia

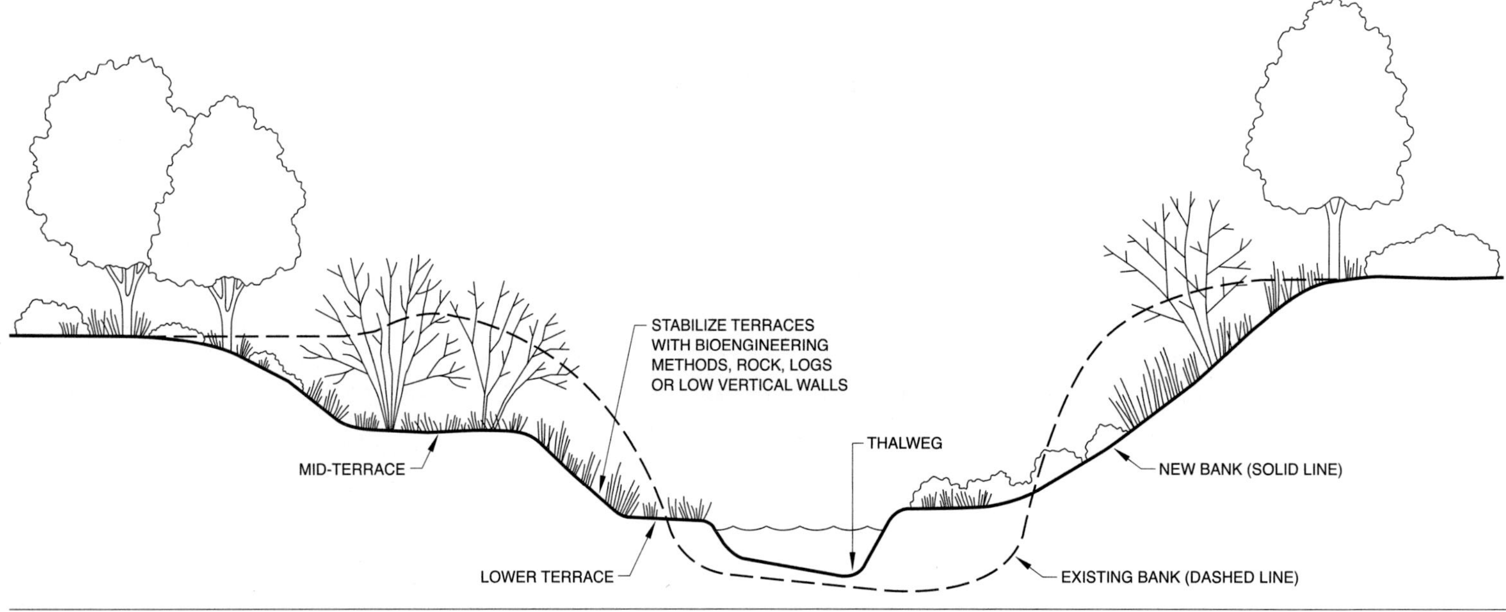

CREATION OF TERRACED BANKS TO REDUCE SLOPE

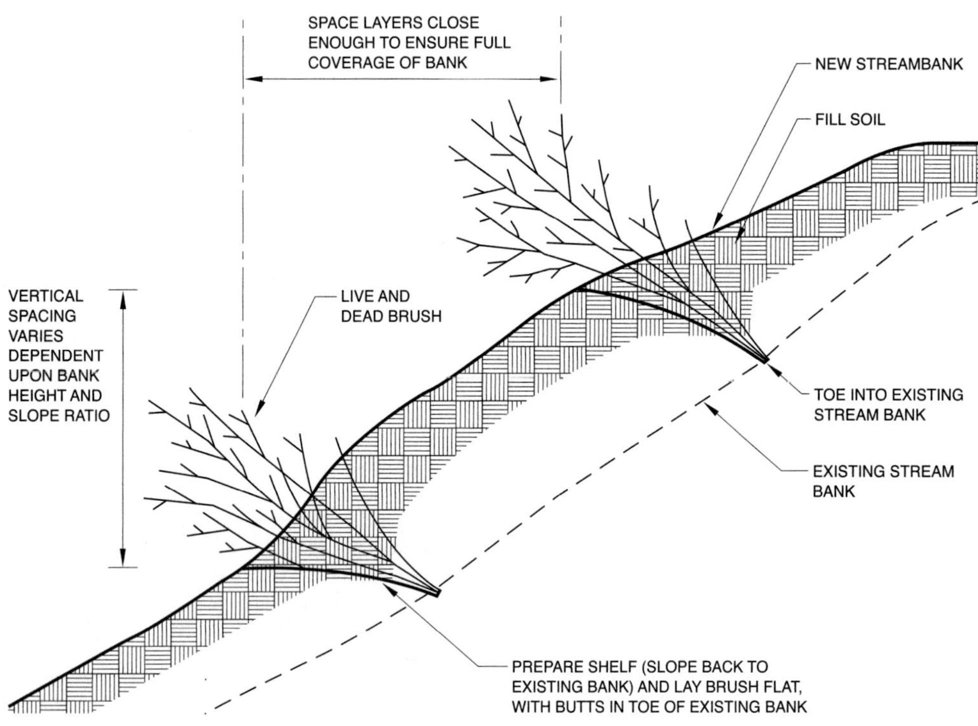

BRUSH LAYER INSTALLATION

Unforeseen site conditions can be discovered during excavation. A project hydrologist or geomorphologist on-site with the contractor can make necessary adjustments in the field.

Some restoration and enhancement projects are installed by local volunteer labor. Appropriate supervision and guidance must be provided for public safety and effective installation. Insurance may be required.

Permitting agencies may require postinstallation monitoring and maintenance to ensure vegetation survival and channel cover. The team biologist should follow the required protocol, documenting plant establishment and preparing required reports.

REFERENCES

Allen, H. H., and J. R. Leech. 1997. *Bioengineering for Streambank Erosion Control.* Vicksburg MS: U.S. Army Corps of Engineers.

Bentrup, G., and J. C. Hoag. 1998. *The Practical Streambank Bioengineering Guide.* Aberdeen, UT: U.S. Natural Resources Conservation Service.

Federal Interagency Stream Working Group. 1998. *Stream Corridor Restoration: Principles, Processes, and Practices.* Downloadable from www.nrcs.usda.gov/technical/stream_restoration/.

Firehock, Karen, and Jacqueline Doherty. 1995. *A Citizen's Streambank Restoration Handbook.* Gaithersburg, MD: Izaak Walton League.

Leopold, L.B., and M.G. Wolman. 1957. "River Channel Patterns: Braided, Meandering, and Straight," Professional Paper 282-B. Washington, DC: U.S. Geological Survey.

———. 1964. "River Meanders," in *Geological Society of America Bulletin,* vol. 71, p. 769–794.

Montgomery, D.R., and J.M. Buffington. 1998. "Channel Processes, Classification, and Response Potential," in *River Ecology and Management,* R.J. Naiman and R.E. Bilby, (eds). New York: Springer-Verlag.

Natural Resources Conservation Service. 1996. "Streambank and Shoreline Protection in Engineering Field Handbook," NEH-650-16. Washington DC: USNRCS.

Ontario Ministry of Natural Resources. 1994. *Natural Channel Systems: An Approach to Management and Design.* Ontario, Canada: Queens Printer for Ontario.

Pinkham, Richard. 2000. *Daylighting: New Life for Buried Streams.* Snowmass, CO: Rocky Mountain Institute.

Riley, Anne. 1998. *Restoring Streams in Cities.* Washington, DC: Island Press.

Rosgen, Dave. 1994. "A Classification of Rivers," in *Catena,* vol. 22, p. 169-199.

———. 1996. *Applied River Morphology.* Lakewood, CO: Wildland Hydrology.

Schiechtl, H.M., and R. Stern. 1997. *Water Bioengineering Techniques* Oxford, England: Blackwell Science.

See also:

Ecological Community Restoration
Irrigation
Living Green Roofs and Landscapes over Structure
Pavement in the Landscape
Site Grading and Earthwork
Site Planning
Soil Erosion and Sediment Control
Wastewater Management: Graywater Harvest and Treatment

Principal authors: Sarah Sutton and Isabelle Minn, Wolfe Mason Associates/Design, Community & Environment; Contributors: Rebecca Lave, Design, Community & Environment; L. Robert Neville, PhD, The Bioengineering Group; Craig Benson, Schaaf & Wheeler; Greg Kamman, Kamman Hydrology & Engineering; Mark Cederborg, Handford Applied Restoration & Conservation; Section editor: Bruce K. Ferguson, University of Georgia

IRRIGATION AND WATER FEATURES

IRRIGATION

INTRODUCTION

Landscape irrigation has certainly found a place in our society. Consider the wealth of aesthetically pleasing landscapes that surround us, and the fact that most of these landscapes are irrigated in order to keep them alive or to supplement natural precipitation. Much would be lost if we could not surround ourselves with irrigated parks, open spaces, trail systems, and turfed recreational facilities. Continued wise and efficient use of our water resources will, it is hoped, enable us to maintain and expand our irrigated landscape.

System Components

The "Generic Overview" figure shows the generalized basic components inherent in any irrigation system.

The system begins with a water source. In the case of a potable, municipal water supply, the irrigation system is afforded an inherently pressurized supply, and a pump would be needed only if pressure was deficient and needed to be boosted. If, as in the figure, the water source is a lake, canal, or other nonpressurized source, pressure is created using a pump.

The next system component, continuing downstream in the "General Overview" figure is a filter. Primary filtration with a screen or media (sand) filter is necessary with many surface water supplies and with most, or all, drip irrigation systems.

Further downstream is the lateral valve, which, in this case, is a remote control valve automated by applying 24 volts AC to the solenoid using the controller. This valve is depicted as being installed in an angle configuration. Water flows from the mainline pipe, through the valve, and then out into the lateral.

The controller is programmed electronically to open and close the valve on selected days and at selected times. Controllers need one station for each remote control valve in the system, plus extra stations for future expansion.

Downstream of the remote control valve is a pressure regulator. A pressure regulator may be required, depending on the water pressure available as compared to the water pressure required in the lateral.

Note that, as defined previously, the mainline pipe is the portion of the pipe network upstream of the remote control valve. The lateral pipe is the pipe network downstream of the remote control valve. Sprinklers, or other water emission devices, are located on the lateral pipe.

IRRIGATION METHODS AND COMPONENTS

There are numerous approaches to irrigating landscapes, which can be used singly, or in combination, to minimize installed cost, minimize annual water applications, or otherwise match the differences and complexity of landscapes. The ideal system applies water efficiently, is easy to repair and maintain, and is operationally simple.

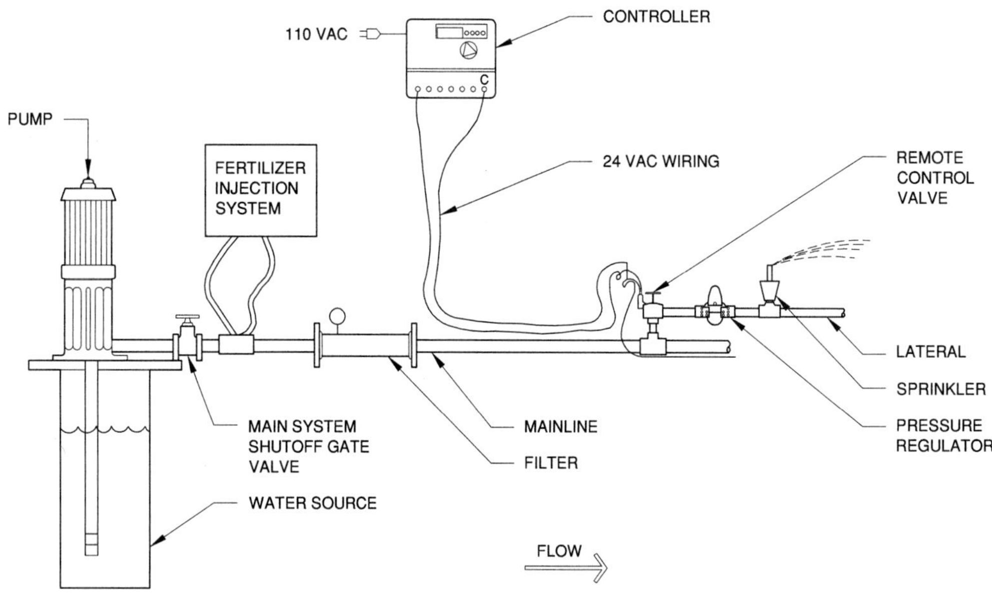

GENERIC OVERVIEW OF BASIC COMPONENTS OF PRESSURIZED IRRIGATION SYSTEMS

Some reasons for selecting a method, or combination of methods, for a particular project are subjective. Individual experience, manufacturer and local distributor presence, and the very arbitrary likes and dislikes of the owner or end user frequently come into play. The irrigation designer is frequently in the orchestrating position of listening, commenting, questioning, and ultimately recommending. The result of such a process is a coherent balance of the project issues.

From the strictly technical point of view, the following parameters must be understood and evaluated before appropriate irrigation methods can be ascertained:

- Soil texture and profile
- Soil infiltration rate
- Water source
- Available flow and pressure
- Water quality
- Water cost
- Irrigated area
- Site grading and elevation changes over the site
- Plant material type, treatment, and placement
- Historical evapotranspiration rate and annual rainfall
- Construction budget

Backflow Prevention

Most landscape irrigation projects in the United States use potable, municipal water supplies.

The water user is generally required to install, maintain, and periodically test a device, called a backflow

COMPARISON OF LANDSCAPE IRRIGATION METHODS

	SPRINKLER IRRIGATION	BUBBLER IRRIGATION	DRIP IRRIGATION
Basic Concept	Sprinklers are patterned to fit the irregular shapes of the landscape and spaced to complement one another	Bubblers are located in planting wells or gridded in shrub beds to irrigate level basins	Emitters are located at each plant, and water drips slowly and directly to the root zone of each plant
Precipitation Rate	Medium to high	Medium to high	Very low to low
Slope Considerations	Suitable for moderate slopes	Not suitable for slopes	Suitable for many sloped situations
Unit Installed Costs	Medium to high	Medium to high	Low to medium with shrub beds, high with turf grass
Turf Application	Suitable	Not appropriate	Some line source products suitable for turf applications
Shrub Bed Application	Appropriate	Very appropriate	Very appropriate
Operating Pressure	Medium to high	Low	Very low
Water Quality Considerations	Minor concerns	Minor concerns	Filtration required, as well as periodic lateral flushing for maintenance

Stephen W. Smith

prevention device, which is designed to prevent any contaminated, and therefore nonpotable, water from flowing backward into the potable water system.

By definition, "backflow" is the undesirable reversal of the direction of flow of water or other substances into the distribution pipes of the potable water supply from any source or sources caused by backpressure and/or backsiphonage. "Backpressure" is backflow caused by a pump, elevated tank, boiler, or pressure "head" in pipe, or any means that could create greater pressure within a piping system than that which exists within the potable water supply. "Backsiphonage" is the reverse flow of water, mixtures, or substances into the distribution pipes of a potable water supply system caused by negative or subatmospheric pressure in the potable water supply.

A "backflow prevention device" is equipment or means designed to prevent backflow created by backpressure, backsiphonage, or backpressure and backsiphonage acting together.

Valves and Valve Assemblies

Valves offer the primary means of hydraulic control in irrigation systems. They are used manually to close off the entire system or some portion of the system. They are used automatically, and operated from the programmed controller, to allow fully automated irrigation.

Consider valves from the start or POC of the irrigation system, working downstream along the mainline.

The first valve may actually be the water purveyor's valve; it may require a special valve box key or valve key to fit and operate the valve itself. This valve is equipped in this way so that unauthorized persons cannot open or close it. Typically, this valve is used only by the water purveyor when service is required within its system or when the water bill has not been paid by the customer.

The next valve downstream is generally the primary shutoff valve for the entire system. A curb stop ball valve is generally used. It may be a stop and waste valve as described previously. This valve, being below the frost line, is the valve that would be closed throughout the winter months when the irrigation system is winterized and not in use.

The next valve downstream may be a part of the backflow prevention assembly. Some backflow devices require upstream and downstream valves, adjacent to the device itself, for testing purposes. This valve can also be used to shut off the irrigation system for maintenance and, being above grade, it is easily accessed if the backflow assembly is not in an enclosure.

Isolation gate valves are generally the next valves in the system. It is not necessary that irrigation systems have isolation gate valves, but larger systems have them so that some portion of the irrigation mainline can be closed off for maintenance purposes. These valves are most often manually actuated.

Continuing downstream on the mainline, the next valve frequently encountered is the quick coupler valve. Quick coupler valves are manually actuated and suitable for incidental water demands around the site. These valves can be added or removed over time. Basically, the quick coupler valve is situated at any convenient location along the mainline where incidental water may be required or desired.

Quick couplers come in 3/4-inch, 1-inch, and 1½-inch sizes and are available with different colored covers to indicate potable versus effluent water. Covers can have a lock if desired.

A key is used to open a quick coupler valve. The key usually has a swivel on the top so that hose can be directed in a 360-degree arc around the valve and not kink in the process. A manual valve on the key itself is desirable to allow for on-off operation without removing the key and for controlling flow.

Quick couplers are often used near ball field infields to add water to the infield soil before play. They are often found near sidewalks or entryways to allow for washing of hard surfaces. Quick couplers may also be placed near perennial plantings to provide for incidental washing or watering of plants. Quick couplers have also been used to provide short-term water for establishment of dry land grasses or native plant materials.

The next, most important valve in the system, and necessary valve in almost all irrigation systems is the "lateral valve," which is also called a "remote control valve"

LEGEND

SLEEVING: CLASS 200 PVC PIPE

MAINLINE PIPE: CLASS 200 PVC
(_" SIZE UNLESS OTHERWISE INDICIATED)

LATERAL PIPE TO SPRINKLERS: CLASS 160 PVC
(1" SIZE UNLESS OTHERWISE INDICIATED)

LATERAL PIPE TO ZONE CONTROL VALVES:
CLASS 200 PVC
(1" SIZE UNLESS OTHERWISE INDICATED

LATERAL PIPE TO EMITTERS: UV RADIATION RESISTANT
POLYETHYLENE (1/2" SIZE, ROUTING SHOWN IS DIAGRAMMATIC)

EXISTING IRRIGATION PIPE

UNCONNECTED PIPE CROSSING

POINT-OF-CONNECTION (POC) ASSEMBLY

M WATER METER ASSEMBLY

WINTERIZATION ASSEMBLY

BACKFLOW PREVENTION ASSEMBLY

QUICK COUPLING VALVE ASSEMBLY

F FLOW SENSOR ASSEMBLY

R RAIN SENSOR ASSEMBLY

W WIND SENSOR ASSEMBLY

MASTER VALVE ASSEMBLY

PRESSURE REGULATOR ASSEMBLY

ISOLATION GATE VALVE ASSEMBLY

REMOTE CONTROL VALVE ASSEMBLY FOR SPRINKLER AND BUBLER LATERALS

MANUAL DRAIN VALVE ASSEMBLY

POP-UP- SPRAY SPRINKLER: _____ W/_____
SERIES NOZZLE
PRESSURE: _____ PSI
RADIUS: _____ FEET
FLOW (GPM) : Q - _____ H- _____ F- _____

POP-UP- ROTOR SPRINKLER: _____ W/_____
NOZZLE
PRESSURE: _____ PSI
RADIUS: _____ FEET

BUBBLER ASSEMBLY: _____ W/_____
NOZZLE
PRESSURE: _____ PSI
FLOW: _____ GPM

REMOTE CONTROL VALVE ASSEMBLY FOR DRIP LATERALS

ZONE CONTROL VALVE ASSEMBLY

FLUSH CAP ASSEMBLY

A IRRIGATION CONTROLLER UNIT
CONTROLLER A: _____ STATIONS USED

P IRRIGATION PUMP STATION

25.0 INDICATES LATERAL DISCHARGE IN GPM

A1 INDICATES CONTROLLER AND CONTROLLER STATION NUMBER

1" INDICATES REMOTE CONTROL VALVE SIZE IN INCHES

APPROXIMATE TREE LOCATIONS

TYPICAL LANDSCAPE IRRIGATION LEGEND

COMPARISON OF POP-UP SPRAY AND POP-UP ROTOR SPRINKLERS

	POP-UP SPRAY SPRINKLERS	POP-UP ROTOR SPRINKLERS
General description	Manufactured of plastic or brass (more commonly plastic) or a combination such as a plastic sprinkler body with a brass nozzle; no mechanical action except except for riser pop-up as effected by lateral pressure, water throw adjustment via screw-in nozzle	Manufactured of plastic, metal, or some combination of plastic and metal; mechanical action (gears, pistons, levers, centrifugal force) causes rotation, water throw adjustment possible with many models
Radius of throw	Radius of approximately 7 to 15 feet; appropriate for small dimensions (< 30 feet), smaller areas, and irregular areas	Radius of approximately 30 to 90 feet; appropriate for large dimensions, larger areas, and more regular areas
Operating pressure at the sprinkler nozzle	15 to 50 PSI (relatively low)	40 to 90 PSI (relatively high)
Precipitation rate	1 to 2.5 IPH (relatively high)	0.30 to 0.75 IPH (relatively low)
Approximate installed unit cost	(relatively high)	(relatively low)
Innovations in recent years	Matched precipitation rates (MPR), high pop-up models, pressure compensating nozzles designed to achieve regulated pressures and constant sprinkler flows, check valves to minimize low sprinkler drainage	Built-in check valves to avoid low sprinkler drainage, small surface area and rubber covers for sports applications, high pop-up models, color coded nozzle sets, increasingly lower precipitation rates to match low soil infiltration rates, and distribution rate curve improvement

when the system is automated. Remote control valves are also referred to as "solenoid valves" and "automated electric valves"—all three terms are synonymous.

Some features of the remote control valve assembly are important. The valve itself, can be installed in either a "globe" or "angle" configuration.

In a globe configuration, the inlet and outlet are more or less in line with one another. In an angle configuration, the inlet is on the bottom of the valve and the outlet is on the side. Some valves offer either configuration, and a plug is installed in the inlet that is not used. Angle configurations experience less pressure loss due to the less turbulent way water passes through the valve.

All remote control valves should allow for flow control by virtue of the valve handle depicted on the top of the valve. Although some low-cost remote control valves are manufactured without a flow control, they should be avoided. Flow control allows for fine tuning of the lateral operating pressure by using the flow control to create additional pressure loss across the valve. There is no easier or less expensive way to provide this flexibility.

From the electrical perspective, note that the wires are connected by a waterproof connector and coiled to allow for wire expansion and maintenance. When excess wire is used in this way, the top of the valve, or bonnet, can be removed for maintenance without affecting the wire or the valve's solenoid.

Remote control valves, as well as other valves, should never be located in low spots, in the landscape. Valve leakage, valve sticking, and mainline failure all result in excess water flowing to low spots, and valve boxes filled with water or even covered by standing water add substantially to maintenance problems.

DESIGN TECHNIQUES AND DRAWING PRESENTATION

Common Symbols

The figure shows symbols that are commonly used in landscape irrigation design to depict system components. Note that most symbols represent an *assembly*. For example, a sprinkler symbol is, in fact, an assembly consisting of the fitting or fittings between the lateral pipe and the sprinkler, in addition to the sprinkler itself. Likewise, a valve assembly includes the valve box, gravel, wire connectors, and all the required fittings, in addition to the valve.

A symbol is used in lieu of attempting to show all the subtlety of the assembly because it is not possible to show all the detail, given typical drawing scales. There are limitations as to how much detail can be practically shown on the design drawing when the symbol is so "large" on a scaled drawing. So, the symbol, the legend callout, and the installation detail, taken together, provide the irrigation contractor with a clear picture of an assembly.

The symbols in the "Typical Landscape Irrigation Legend" figure are representative, as there is no widely accepted standard for landscape irrigation symbols.

SPRINKLER IRRIGATION

Sprinkler Types

There are two broad categories of sprinklers used in landscape irrigation: pop-up spray sprinklers and pop-up rotor sprinklers. Pop-up sprays are generally suitable for small-radius applications and small or irregular areas. Pop-up rotors are suitable for large-radius applications and larger areas.

The term "pop-up" implies, in both cases, that the top of the sprinkler is installed flush with the finished grade. When the irrigation system is not operating, only the sprinkler top can be seen from the surface. When a lateral valve opens, sprinklers on that lateral rise up for operation as the lateral pressurizes. When the lateral is fully pressurized, the sprinklers are fully popped up; sprinklers begin to function normally, rotate, and throw the distance specified.

Spray Sprinklers

Plastic pop-up spray sprinklers are very simple in mechanical action. Water pressure causes the stem of the sprinkler to pop up, overcoming the resistance of an internal spring resisting the pressure and trying to pull the stem back down. The stem seals when it reaches the full-up position. At this time, under normal conditions, the nozzle reaches full operating pressure and the sprinkler throws the specified distance and flows at the specified rate.

A pop-up spray sprinkler nozzle can usually be adjusted down about 30 percent, using the nozzle's adjustment screw. So a commonly available 10-foot nozzle can be reasonably adjusted down to 7 feet. Any greater adjustment than 30 percent of the effective radius may distort the pattern and result in poor application efficiency. For this reason, and because spray nozzles are not commonly available in an effective radius of less than 10 feet, the practical minimum width of turf that can be effectively irrigated using sprinklers is considered to be 7 feet.

Some special patterns to handle narrow rectangular turf areas are available, but nozzle performance is not as predictable or as uniform as compared to quarter-, half-, or full-arc nozzles.

Rotor Sprinklers

Rotor sprinklers can be further described by the mechanism that causes the sprinkler to rotate. Impulse or impact sprinklers use a springloaded arm that strikes the water stream coming from the nozzle to cause rotation. A ball drive sprinkler uses centrifugal force and the impact forces from two stainless steel balls to cause sprinkler rotation. Piston drive sprinklers utilize a diaphragm and piston, which together move the sprinkler a few degrees each time the piston finishes a stroke. Gear drive sprinklers use flowing water and a series of intricate gears (similar to an automotive transmission) for rotation.

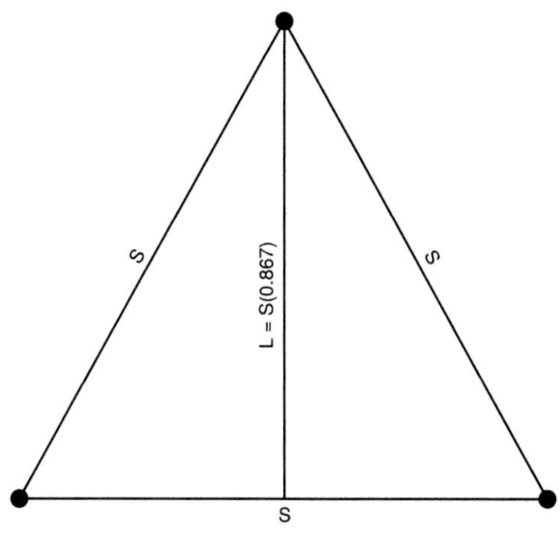

EQUILATERAL TRIANGLE SPRINKLER LAYOUT PATTERN

Various drive mechanisms have differing susceptibility to poor water quality. Generally, impact sprinklers tend to exhibit the fewest problems under marginal (dirty) water conditions, followed by piston drives, ball drives, and gear drives, respectively.

Precipitation Rates

By definition, the "precipitation rate" for sprinklers is the rate at which overlapping sprinklers apply water. The concept is similar to expressing the rate that rain falls, and the units are the same, as well. Common English units for precipitation rates are inches per hour (IPH).

Typically, quarter-arc sprinklers and half-arc sprinklers are grouped together on a lateral and full-arcs are grouped together on a separate lateral because of precipitation rate differences. Partial arcs of 180 degrees and less are often mixed together on laterals for economy, even though the precipitation rate may vary somewhat.

Sprinkler Layout

There are many philosophical styles and techniques for sprinkler layout.

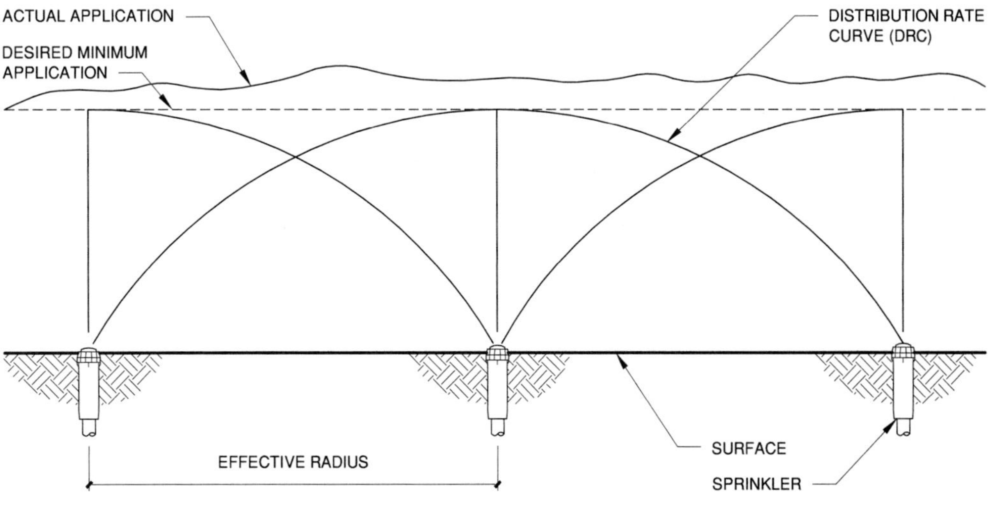

OVERLAPPING SPRINKLERS

Stephen W. Smith

The following rules are intended to provide some initial direction and assistance with sprinkler layout:

- Generally, lay in sprinklers around the perimeter of the landscaped area first, then lay sprinklers into the interior of the irregular shape.
- The sprinkler layout patterns should form equilateral triangles, squares, distorted triangles, and distorted squares. All the patterns mentioned are appropriate and can, and probably will, be mixed within the layout.
- Pentagon shapes should be avoided. Pentagons generally indicate a problem—usually stretched sprinkler spacings or a sprinkler left out.
- Place sprinklers in all corners and other obtuse angles of the perimeter. (Today's water costs and public concern about water on hard surfaces dictate utilizing sprinklers in corners.)
- Consider wind. In practice, wind effects in small areas are often ignored. Prevailing wind should be considered on large, open turf areas like parks and golf courses.
- It is preferable for the "flat" layout of the scaled irrigation drawing to show the actual number of sprinklers required, or somewhat more than might be required.
- Sprinkler overspray onto any hard surface should be minimized. Overspray wastes water and can also increase owner and designer liability.
- Spacing is manufacturer- and sprinkler nozzle-specific. (Maximum effective radius is provided in catalog performance data, and distribution rate curve data can be obtained from the manufacturer or from independent testing laboratories.)

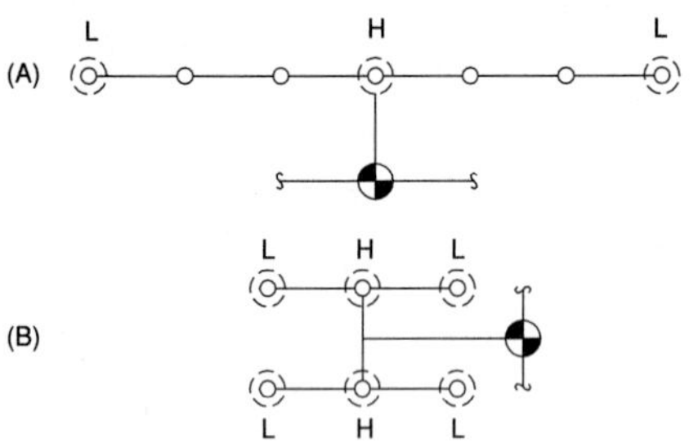

IDEAL LATERAL PIPE LAYOUT

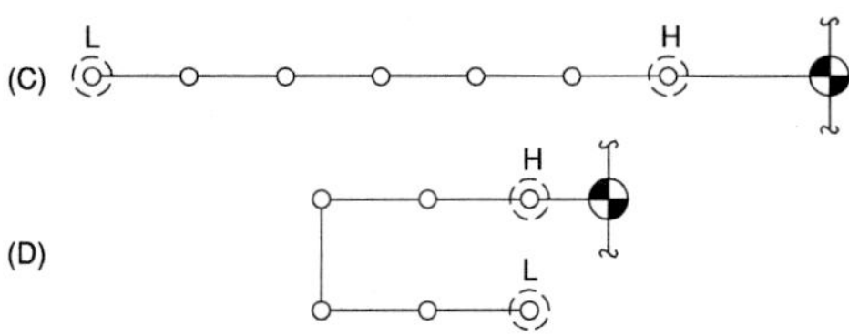

LATERAL PIPE LAYOUTS TO AVOID

LATERAL LAYOUT ALTERNATIVES

Sprinkler Laterals

A sprinkler lateral constitutes all of the pipe network and sprinklers that are brought together, by virtue of the pipes, and located downstream of the lateral valve. When the valve opens, the pipe gradually becomes pressurized and the sprinklers begin to function.

Small laterals, having very few sprinklers, are desirable from the standpoint of management flexibility.

Lateral Pipe Routing

One technique to use when considering pipe routing is to think of yourself, the designer, as the ditching machine operator completing the excavation for the lateral you have designed. Wanting to complete the trenching work efficiently, you will consider an approach that will minimize the number of "starts and stops," or the number of times you will have to stop, reposition your trenching machine, drop the digging chain boom, and start ditching again.

Another important consideration with lateral pipe routing is lateral hydraulics. As water flows through pipe and fittings, water pressure is lost due to friction with the pipe and fittings. The goal is to link sprinklers together with a pipe network that is as efficient as possible from both the installation and the hydraulic standpoints.

DRIP IRRIGATION

Drip irrigation is advantageous in numerous situations. A drip irrigation system can conserve water, reduce initial construction costs, and enhance plant growth.

Drip irrigation is also commonly referred to as "trickle" or "low-flow" irrigation. The basic concept of drip irrigation is to provide near-optimal soil moisture on a continuous basis while conserving water. It is a system that applies water directly to individual plants, as opposed to sprinkler systems, which irrigate all of the surface area. This is accomplished by relatively small-diameter lateral pipes with "emitters" attached to supply each plant with water. Emitters are the key devices within the system, as they afford, through their hydraulic design, the ½- to 2-gallon-per-hour flow rates. Note that these low flow rates, expressed as GPH rather than GPM, are basically different from pop-up spray sprinklers by a factor of 60.

With drip irrigation and the ability to select emitters of different flow rates and/or vary the number of emitters per plant, a flexibility becomes available to the irrigation designer that no other irrigation method affords.

Landscaping is the arena where drip irrigation is experiencing the greatest growth. Drip irrigation has proved viable in landscapes because of the ability to save costly water while providing a growth advantage to the plants and reducing initial construction costs.

In landscapes, drip irrigation is most often used together with sprinkler irrigation, resulting in what is referred to as a combination sprinkler/drip irrigation system. Sprinklers irrigating turf grass offer the lowest cost per irrigated area, but drip irrigation offers numerous advantages over sprinklers on mulched shrub beds, trees, potted plants, and the like. It is particularly cost-effective where plant spacing exceeds 2.5 feet on centers.

Emitters

Emitters are the key component of the system. They are available in many sizes and shapes. Various emitters incorporate very different hydraulic methods to reduce pressure (or head) and create the one- or two-GPH flow. All emitters should incorporate a UV-inhibiting agent to prevent damage from solar radiation.

A point source emitter drips water directly to the soil surface. The soil volume directly under the emitter may be saturated during system operation and immediately thereafter.

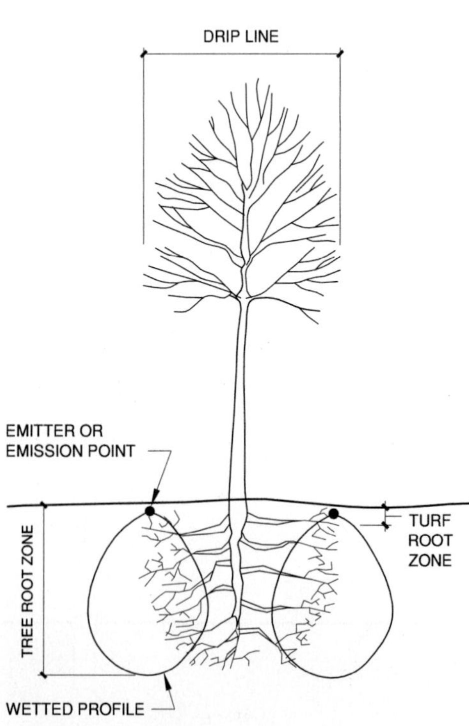

SECTION THROUGH DRIP IRRIGATED TREE

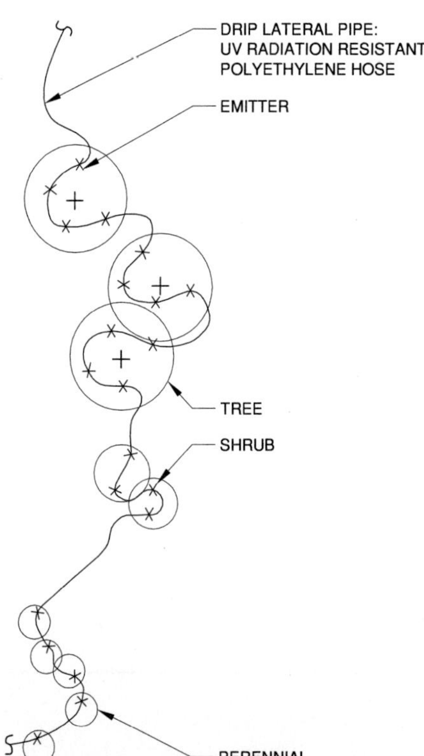

PIPE ROUTING AND EMITTER PLACEMENT INSTALLATION DETAIL

Stephen W. Smith

As implied by the name, the aerosol emitter throws water through the air for some distance before water contacts the soil surface. Unfortunately, aerosol emitters are not as predictable as sprinklers, and distribution rate curves are not readily available to describe their performance.

Guidelines to follow for proper emitter placement include:

- Balanced emitter configuration around the plant
- An even number of emitters
- Emitters placed at or near the drip line of the tree and moved outward as the plant matures and the drip line expands

Placement schemes are illustrated in the figures. The very flexible polyethylene or PVC hose used in landscapes lends itself to rather dramatic directional changes and circuitous pipe placement. In fact, the irrigation designer should not attempt to show the irrigation contractor every nuance of pipe placement in the design drawing, but should simply give an indication of routing and pipe quantity.

ADVANTAGES AND DISADVANTAGES OF DRIP IRRIGATION

The advantages of drip irrigation include:

- Precise placement of water in the plant root zone
- Reduced weed growth
- Minimal (even negligible) evaporative losses
- High application efficiency
- Low flow rates relative to sprinkler irrigation (this implies smaller POC and lower plant investment fees, fewer valves, smaller controller, and less wire)
- Evaporation and overland flow minimized
- Lower installed unit cost than sprinklers (when stapled on the soil surface in shrub beds and hidden under mulch)
- No evidence of the irrigation system and, therefore, high vandal resistance
- Favorable plant response (larger, healthier plant materials over time)
- Flexible operating hours, considering possible irrigation during daytime hours, high wind conditions, and with pedestrians present (a good way to expand the water window)
- Flexibility to add emitters if plants are added
- Relatively easy to introduce water-soluble fertilizers and chemicals into irrigation system

Disadvantages of drip irrigation:

- Filtration required to prevent emitter clogging
- Proper management more complex
- Adaptation can be more involved than with sprinkler irrigation
- First indication of maintenance problems (emitters clogged) may show up only after plants are stressed

As compared to sprinkler irrigation, drip irrigation offers a rather unique opportunity. Sprinklers will apply a fairly uniform amount of water to the whole soil surface. Drip irrigation applies water only where it is needed, as dictated by an emitter. The quantity and flow rate of individual emitters irrigating a plant, and as different from another plant in the plant pallet, allow the irrigation designer to develop a scheme to provide different ratios of water to each plant species.

Stephen W. Smith

WATER FEATURES, FOUNTAINS, AND POOLS

OVERVIEW

In the last 20 years, fountain design has changed dramatically, thanks primarily to technology and innovation, which together have given design professionals greater flexibility. The result is the creation of stunning displays. Generally speaking, however, the design/build concept of fountains is not in the best interest of landscape architects or owners, due to the involved nature of competent systems.

In fact, for the designer, likely the most important responsibility will be one of education and coordination, as the complexities of water feature design involve the efforts of many disciplines. Thus, the design support team should comprise not only fountain consultants, but mechanical, electrical, and structural engineers, as well. In some instances, it will be necessary to enlist the services of chemical engineers, waterproofing consultants, specifiers of pyrotechnics and lighting, and others.

BASIC FOUNTAIN DESIGN

Basic fountain design incorporates all necessary components to operate a fountain safely and effectively. Drains, overflows, check valves, and water makeup devices are but a few of these necessary features. It is recommended that a water feature consultant be retained to ensure thoroughness and compliance to codes. (See "Schematic Fountain Layout" figure.)

Packaged Equipment

Many fountains can be partially manufactured off-site. Nozzle sumps for interactive fountains, as well as vaults, controls, and other elements, can be prefabricated and brought to a location for quick installation. Even reservoirs can be shipped, in lieu of on-site construction. These features are widely available today from a number of companies.

Lighting

Submersible fountain lights are supplied in 120- and 12-volt versions. Ground fault protection must be supplied on 120-volt systems. Lamps and many fixtures for use on applications come in a wide range of choices, ranging from water walls to nozzle clusters. In addition to incandescent lamps, submersible metal halide and LED fixtures are available, adding to the possibilities for lighting water displays.

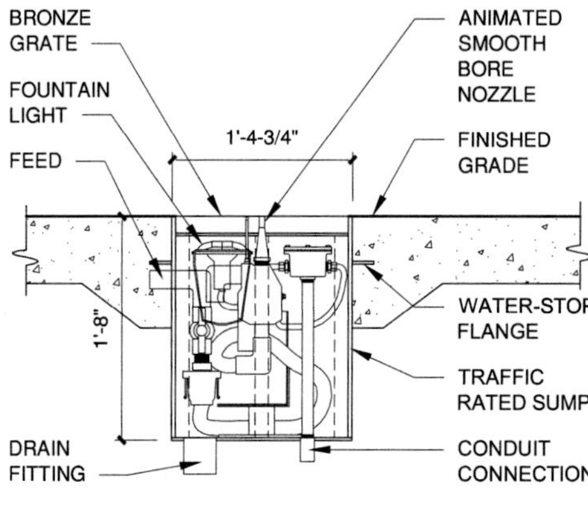

TYPICAL INTERACTIVE JET SUMP

Piping

For exterior fountains in southern climates, schedule 40 or schedule 80 PVC is usually acceptable for the main piping system. In northern climates, PVC should always be installed at least 1 foot below the local frost line; otherwise, stainless steel, ductile iron, or certain types of copper are more suitable, but caution should be used in locating all pipe manifolds. Velocities of liquid should always be limited to the pipe manufacturer's recommendations.

Animation

The main choices for animating displays in modern fountains are programmable logic controllers (PLCs), show controllers, and industrial computers. Animated fountains can be preprogrammed or react to signals from sources ranging from music to live plants. Examples of animation are nozzles instantly turning on and off (*actuating*) by command from a digital signal, or raising and lowering over set periods of time (*modulating*) from analog commands. When used in combination with variable speed drives, which make motors change speed, the animation becomes extremely playful.

Other system inputs include, but are not limited to:

- *Anemometers* (wind speed gauges), which can automatically lower fountain heights or shut the system off, conserving water.
- *Meg-meters*, which can provide data to gauge motor-life status and, ultimately, indicate when to replace them.

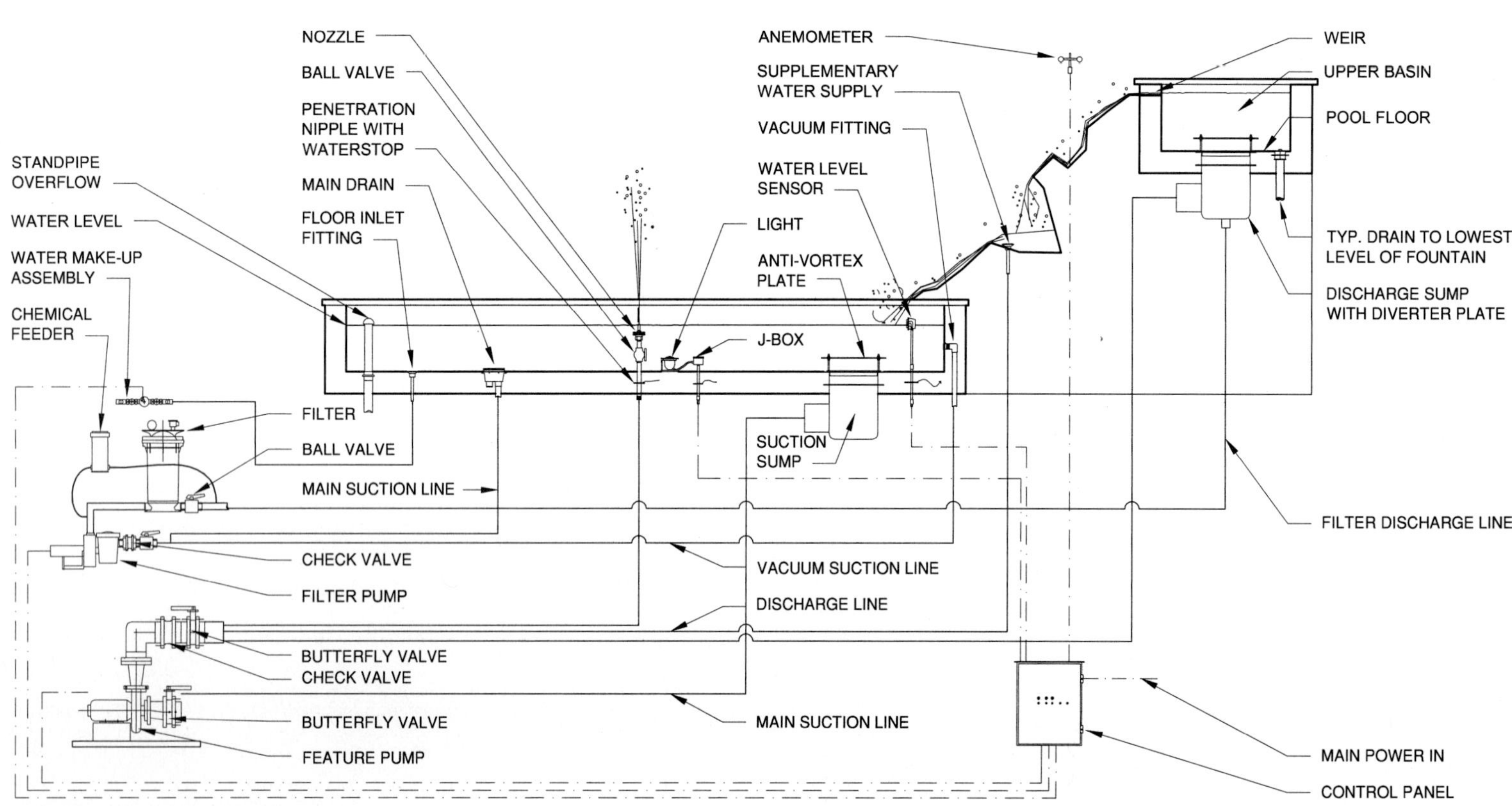

SCHEMATIC FOUNTAIN LAYOUT

Joe Petry and Michael Barnicle, Delta Fountains, Jacksonville Florida

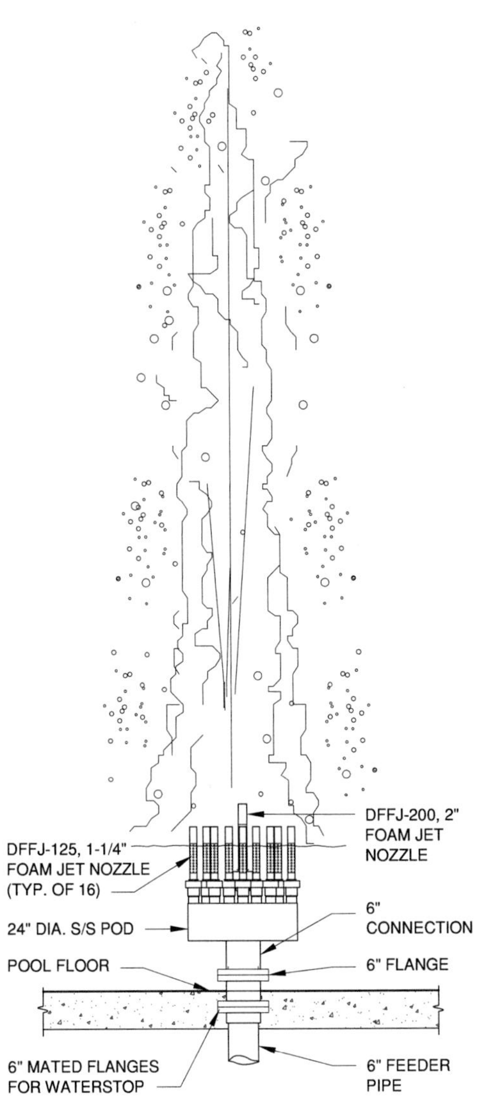

BRONZE POD JET DETAIL

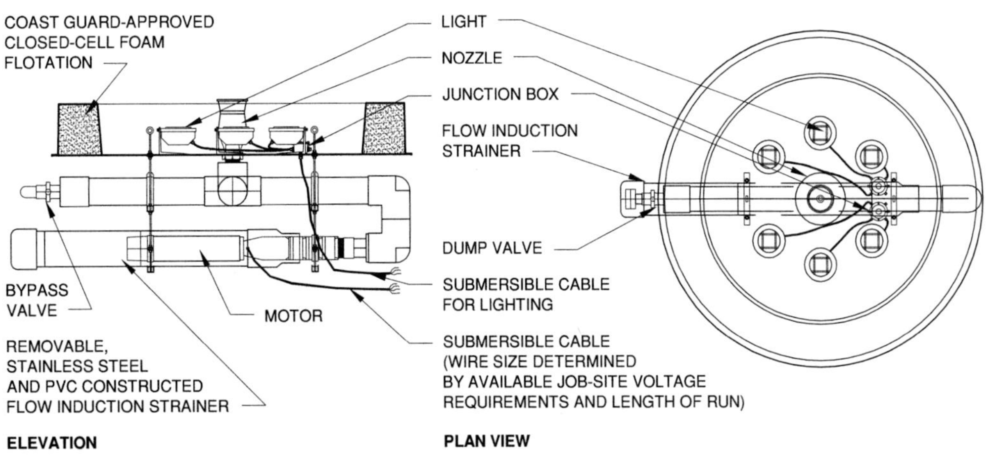

FLOATING FOUNTAIN

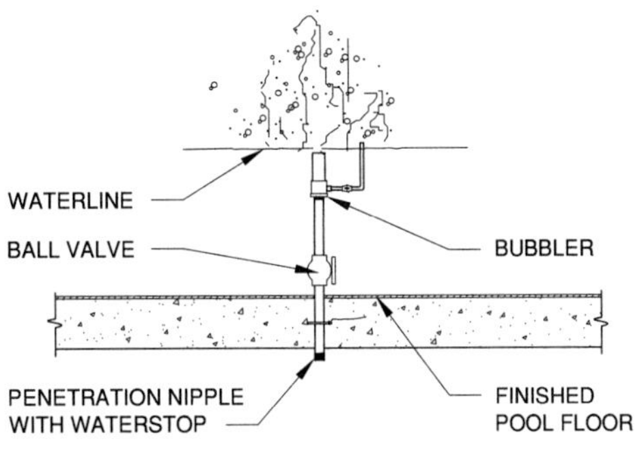

WATERLINE
BALL VALVE
BUBBLER
PENETRATION NIPPLE
WITH WATERSTOP
FINISHED
POOL FLOOR

Bubbler Nozzle

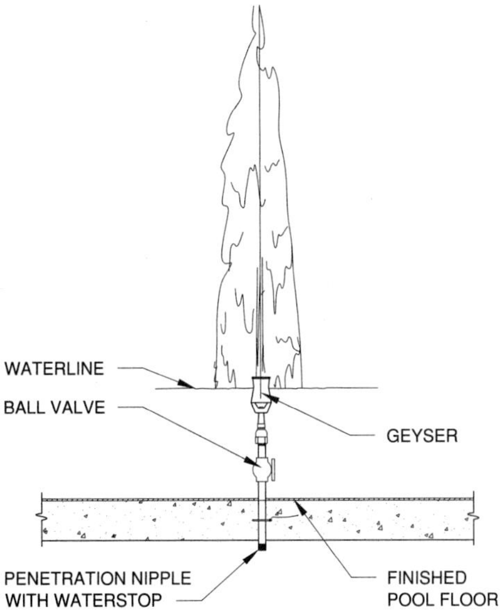

WATERLINE
BALL VALVE
GEYSER
PENETRATION NIPPLE
WITH WATERSTOP
FINISHED
POOL FLOOR

Geyser Nozzle

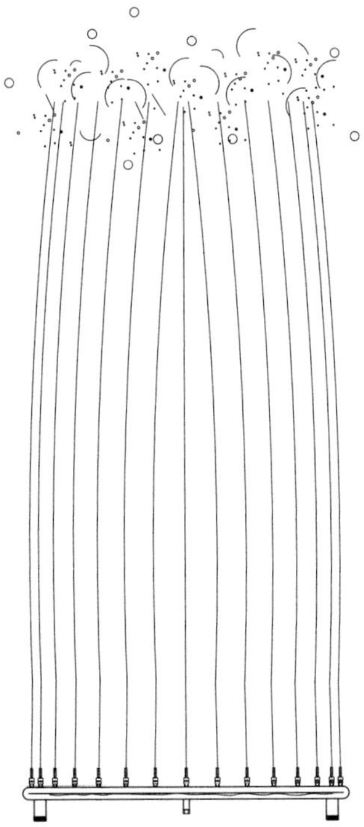

Custom Spray Rings

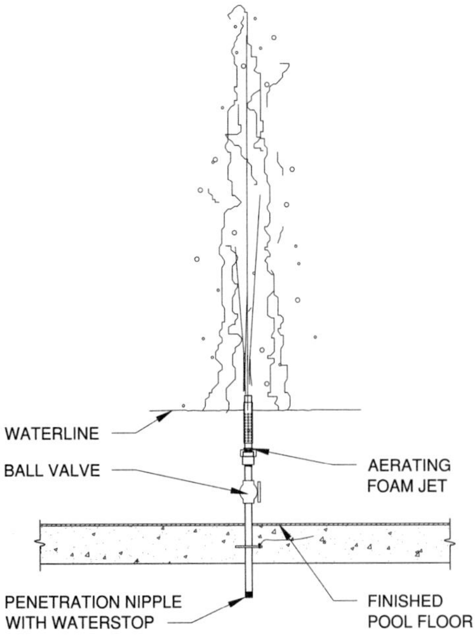

WATERLINE
BALL VALVE
AERATING
FOAM JET
PENETRATION NIPPLE
WITH WATERSTOP
FINISHED
POOL FLOOR

Aerating Foam Nozzle

WATER-LEVEL-DEPENDENT NOZZLES

Joe Petry and Michael Barnicle, Delta Fountains, Jacksonville Florida

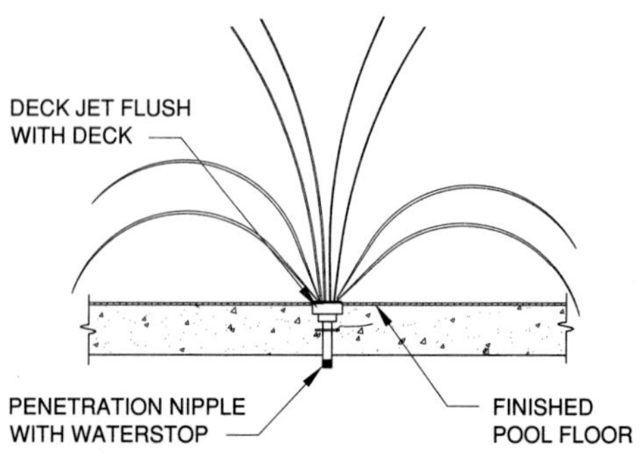

Deck Nozzle

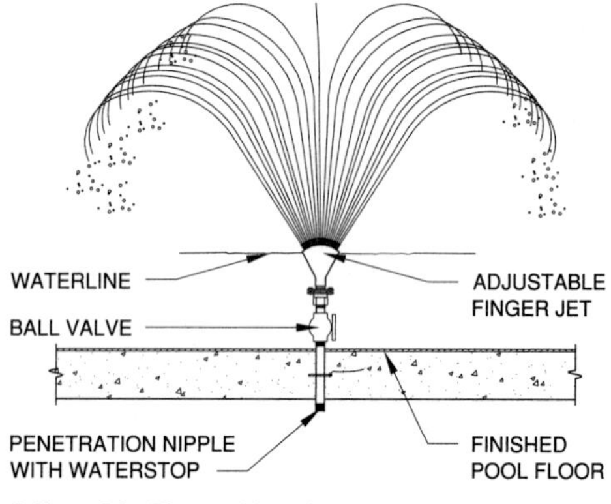

Adjustable Finger Nozzle

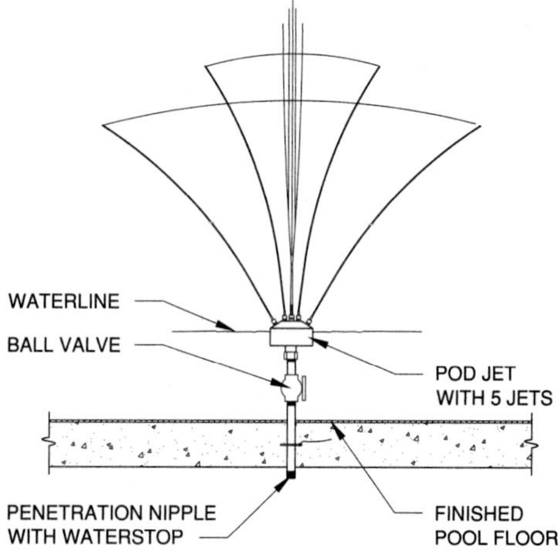

Bronze Pod Nozzle

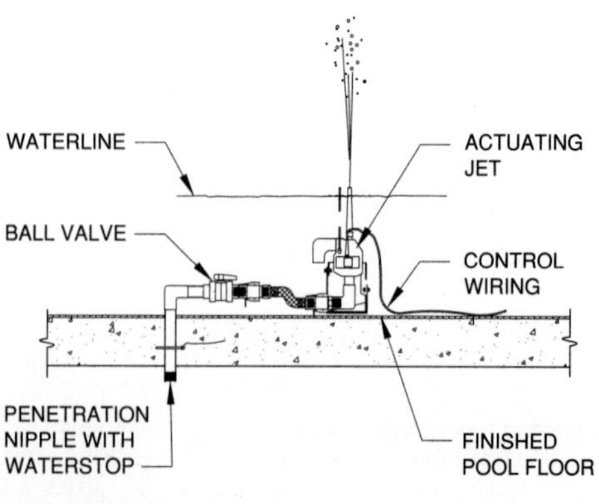

Actuating Jet

WATER-LEVEL-INDEPENDENT NOZZLES

Joe Petry and Michael Barnicle, Delta Fountains, Jacksonville Florida

- *Flow meters*, which can provide critical information regarding clogged systems.
- *Temperature gauges*, which can alert systems to shut down in freezing conditions.
- *Oxidation/reduction sensors*, which can shut systems down in potentially unsanitary conditions.

INTERACTIVE FOUNTAINS

Modern interactive fountains have many of the features of noninteractive fountains, but are scrutinized on a higher level. Thus, it is imperative to work with consultants and departments of health when designing participatory features. The variety of pattern designs is unlimited, as are programming scenarios.

WATER QUALITY

The most common types of filters for fountain applications are sand, cartridge, and bag filters. Considerations such as physical space, maintenance capabilities, particulate removal, budget, and water conservation typically determine which of these systems to implement.

The processes for pathogen and algae removal are diverse and may require expert analysis to establish an appropriate combination of equipment. Influent water may have variables, even from a given water plant, that may change a sanitation system from one project to the next. Chlorine, bromine, inhibitors, softeners, carbon, ozone, ultraviolet light, and deionization are but a few types of available methods of treating water, and must be applied in proper combination.

FLOATING FOUNTAINS

Floating fountains are packaged systems that come almost entirely assembled to be floated in lakes and ponds. They are popular as instant signage and water quality enhancement devices. The most durable systems incorporate fiberglass, stainless steel, and bronze components, and all should come with UL-listed control panels as assemblies. (See "Floating Fountain" figure.)

NOZZLES

Fountain nozzles are typically categorized either as water-level-dependent or water-level-independent. Usually, a water-level-dependent nozzle produces a more aerated effect, whereas an independent style produces clear streams. (See "Water-Level-Dependent Nozzles," "Water-Level-indenpendent Nozzles," and "Bronze Pod Jet Detail" figures.)

COMMUNICATION

Today's fountains can communicate with maintenance personnel and programmers through Ethernet or dial-up means. A fountain can, for example, alert those concerned by e-mail to its needs. Likewise, a fountain can be manipulated or reprogrammed remotely using these technological capabilities.

FOUNTAINS AND DECORATIVE POOLS

GENERAL

Materials used in fountain and pool design should be durable and resist damage caused by water, cracks, weather, stains, and freeze-thaw cycles. Suitable materials include stone, concrete, brick, tile, and metals such as copper, bronze, cast iron, and steel. Fiberglass, acrylic, and waterproof membranes such as PVC, EPDM, and butyl are commonly used.

Overall Design Considerations

Scale: Consider the size of the water feature in relation to its surroundings.

Basin sizing: For width, consider fountain height and prevailing winds. For depth, consider weight (1 cu ft water = 62.37 lb). Consider children playing near or in the pool. Allow space for lights, nozzles, and pumps. Local codes may classify basins of a certain depth as swimming pools. Nozzle spray may be cushioned to prevent excessive surge.

Bottom appearance: When clear water is maintained, bottom appearance is important. Enhance the bottom with patterns, colors, materials, three-dimensional objects, or textures. Dark bottoms increase reflectivity.

Edges or copings: In designing the water's edge, consider the difference between the operating water level and the static water level. Loosely defined edges (as in a pond) make movement into the water possible both visually and physically. Clearly defined edges (as in a basin) use coping to delineate the water's edge.

Lips and weirs: A lip is an edge over which flowing water falls. A weir is a dam in the water that diverts the water flow or raises the water level. If volume and velocity are insufficient to break the surface tension, a reglet on the underside of the edge may overcome this problem.

Water Form for Fountains

Static water: Form and reflectivity are design considerations for water contained in pools and ponds.

Falling water: The effect of falling water depends on water velocity and volume, the container surface, and the edge over or through which the water moves.

Flowing water: The visual effect of a volume of flowing water can be changed by narrowing or widening a channel, placing objects in the path of the water, and changing the direction of the flow or the slope and roughness of the bottom and sides.

Jets: A pattern is created by forcing water into the air with a jet. Jet types include single orifice nozzles, tiered jets, aerated nozzles, and formed jets in a wide variety of forms, patterns, and types.

Surge: A contrast between relatively quiet water and a surge (a wave or a splash) is made by quickly adding water, raising or lowering an object or moving it back and forth in the water, or introducing strong air currents to the water.

Water Effects System

The water effects system comprises the pump, nozzles, and piping that move water through the fountain. The combination of nozzles, spray rings, eyeballs, pipes, weirs, and/or channels in a fountain or pool requires a pump system to generate water pressure, a suction line to bring water to the pump, and a discharge line to move water from the pump to the nozzles.

Fountain nozzles come in four basic types: aerating nozzles, spray heads, smooth-bore nozzles, and formed nozzles. Aerating nozzles (also known as bubbler jets, geyser nozzles, or foam nozzles) are characterized by white frothy water created by combining air and water. Spray heads are characterized by combinations of thin clear water jets coming from a distribution head in the shape of a fan or circle (suction or in-line strainer required). Smooth-bore nozzles are characterized by a clear, thin solid stream jet of water that breaks up into small droplets as it reaches its maximum height or distance. Formed nozzles are typified by a thin sheet of water that originates in a jet of varied size and shape. The thinness of the sheet of water makes the tolerances in the jet very tight (suction or in-line strainer required).

Fountains are usually closed water systems, i.e., the pump continuously cycles the water in the basin to the nozzles and back to the basin again. The pumps used to generate water pressure and operate the water effects of a fountain are largely powered by electric motors. Three types of pumps are commonly used: submersible, dry centrifugal, and vertical turbine pumps.

Submersible pumps, used for low volume fountains, are among the simplest pumping systems. A watertight electric motor and pump are set under the water of the fountain basin. The pump is usually equipped with a motor of 1/20 to 1 horsepower and moves a maximum of 100 gallons per minute (gpm). This type of pump requires fewer pipe penetrations in the basin wall than dry centrifugal or vertical turbine pumps.

Dry centrifugal pumps, most commonly used for larger water features, consist of an electric motor, a pump, a suction line, and a discharge line. This pump type ranges from ¼ to 100 horsepower.

Vertical turbine pumps, used in large water features, are able to move tremendous amounts of water. They require a pump and motor, a water sump located in an equipment vault, a gravity feed mechanism to fill the sump, and a discharge line. These pumps are more energy-efficient than those with suction lines, as gravity moves water to the pump. The electric motor is not submerged in water, making a watertight seal less important. Vertical turbine pumps can move up to 5000 gpm.

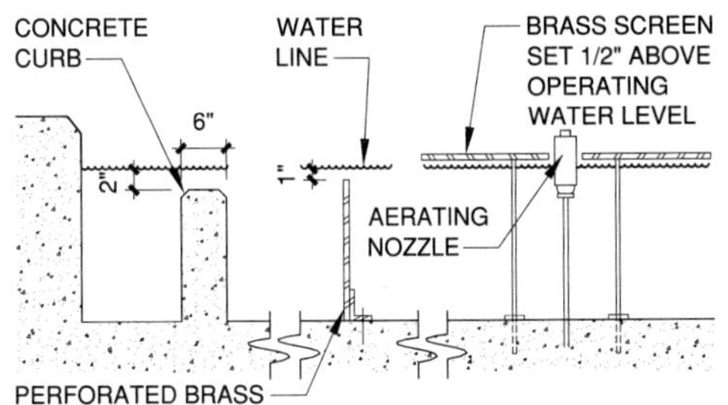

SURGE REDUCTION DEVICES

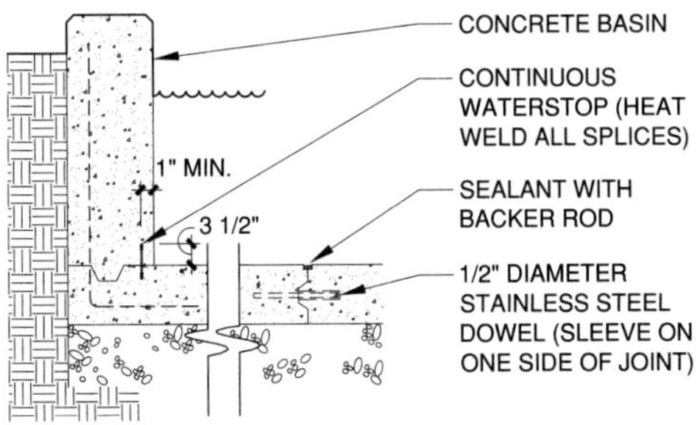

CONCRETE BASIN JOINT DETAIL

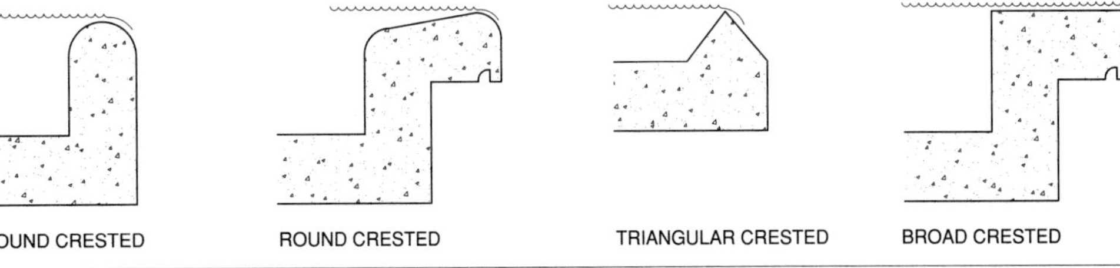

FOUNTAIN LIP SECTIONS

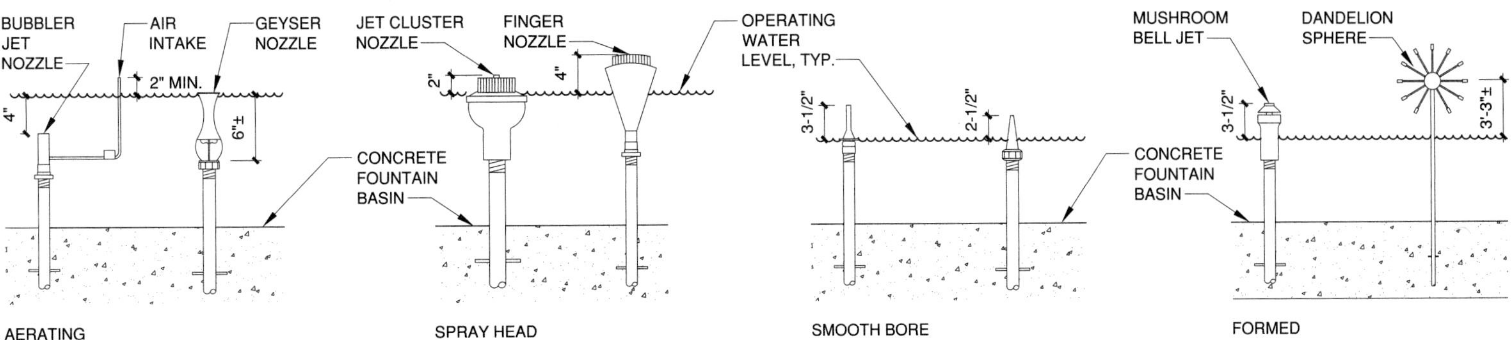

FOUNTAIN NOZZLE TYPES

GARDEN STRUCTURES

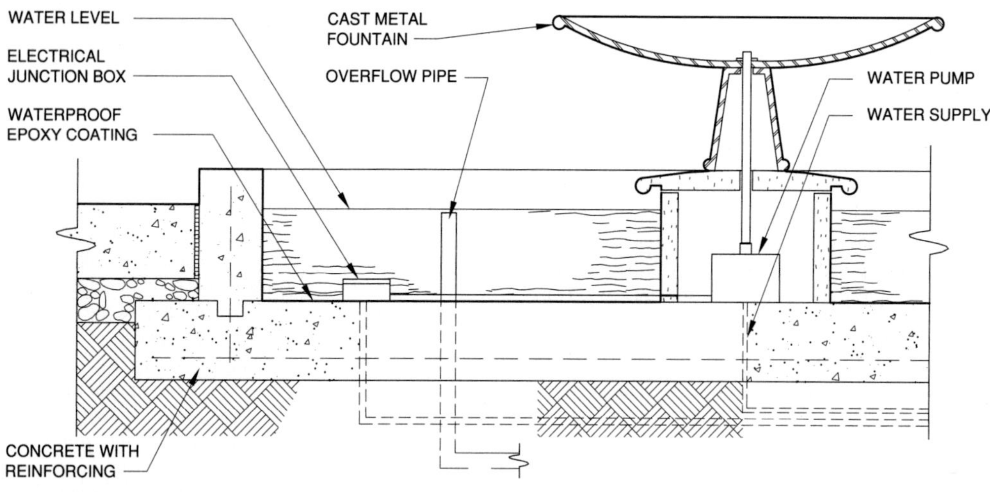

FOUNTAIN SECTION

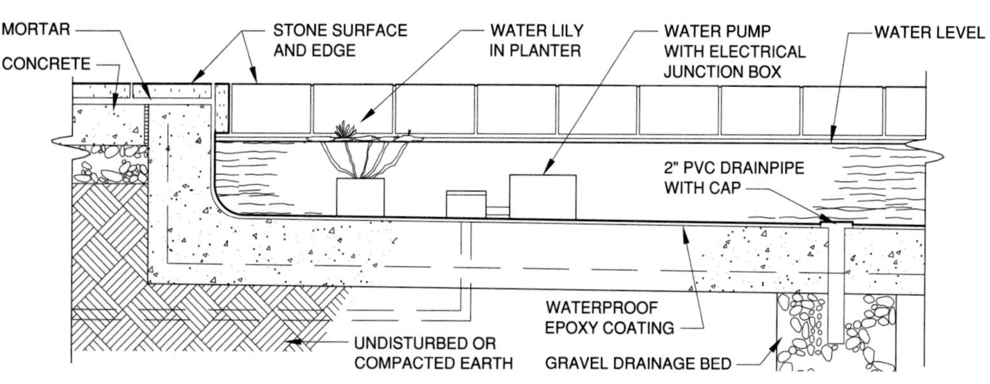

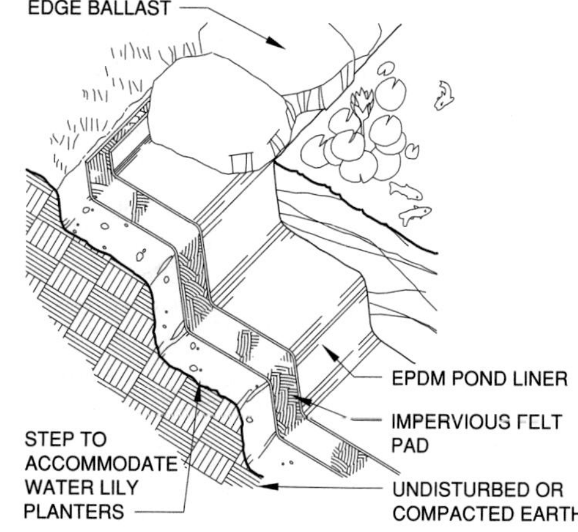

POND SECTION

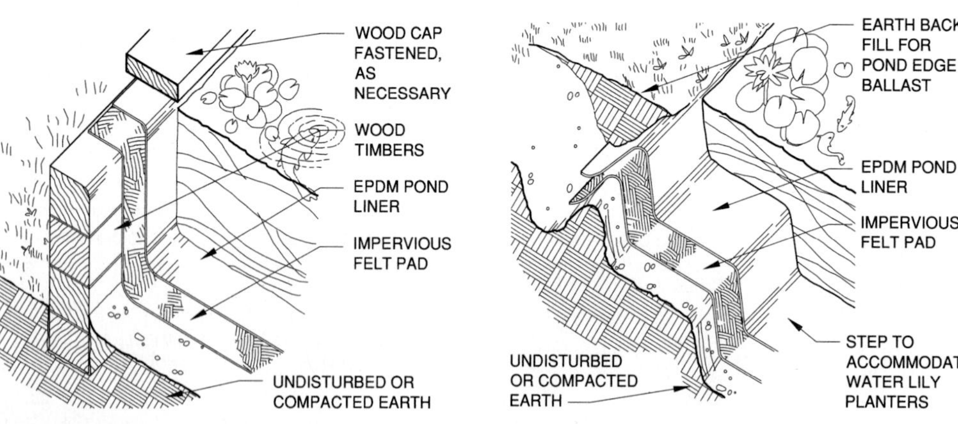

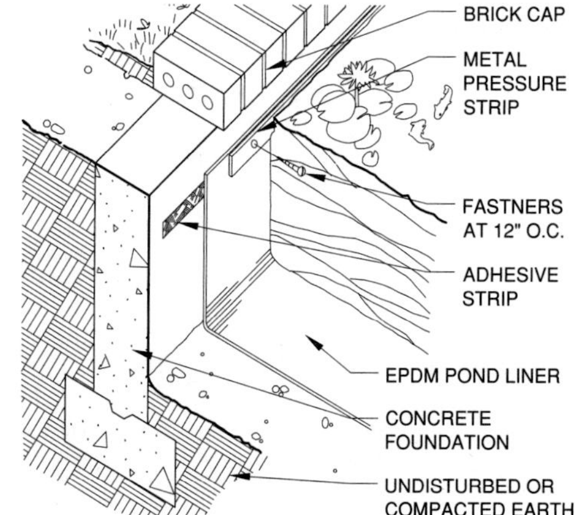

POND DETAILS

Gary Greenan, Miami, Florida; Richard J. Vitullo, AIA, Oak Leaf Studio, Crownsville, Maryland

PAVEMENT AND STRUCTURES IN THE LANDSCAPE

PAVEMENT IN THE LANDSCAPE

Pavement in the landscape is one of the least appreciated, yet most important elements of designed space. Paved areas are the floor of the landscape, the horizontal surface that is essential as an organizational element of design. Exterior pavements, when exposed to the elements of sun, precipitation, snow, and ice, and temperature changes, take on added dimensions of use, maintenance, and aesthetic treatment. The role of the landscape architect includes consideration of both basic and unique uses of pavement in the exterior environment, requiring applied specialized knowledge of materials and construction methods.

When assigned the same level of importance in the exterior environment as the floor in a building is normally given, pavements should warrant more attention to detail than they often receive. Cues for pavement design have historically been taken from the natural landscape. The natural ground plane consists of land, earth and rock, vegetation and water. These are the primary elements used in the designed landscape. Earth's natural surface has a variety of shapes and forms in the ground plane that have evolved from various forces acting on them. Designed pavements have forms that are created by the manufacturing and installation process, imparting different forces on materials to create intended characteristics.

Pavement design has several aspects that are typically identified by the creative expertise of the designer and that are then definitively determined through a collaboration among different design disciplines working toward a common goal. Pavement design requires the application of design and engineering knowledge, principles, styles, and techniques, as well as a working knowledge of construction materials, methods, and techniques, and an understanding of the durability, maintenance requirements, and appropriate use of different pavement systems. Structural, functional, and aesthetic designs are interdependent, and often involve the application of expertise from very different design disciplines. For this reason, the information in this section is presented first in terms of general structural and functional requirements and then in terms of applied aesthetic design.

The engineered **structural design** of pavements involves the determination of the structural composition of pavement materials as required to ensure the system's capacity to perform the use for which it is intended. This aspect looks at the entire pavement system, the full depth of soils, base material, and pavement layering and its resistance to settling and material failure. Factors affecting structural pavement design include location, climate, soil conditions, loading requirements of intended use, paving material characteristics, constructability, and cost.

The **functional design** component of pavement determines the arrangement of paved areas with respect to their intended use. This includes the layout of highways, roads, streets, driveways, parking areas, sidewalks, trails, plazas, and patios. This design effort determines the amount of pavement in the landscape and its appropriateness for its context. Factors considered include safety and accessibility, circulation and traffic, parking and access, surface textures for resistance to slipping or skidding, intended uses, and amount of use and environmental suitability factors, including amount of impervious surface with respect to stormwater runoff, snow and ice removal, heat absorption, and reflection.

Third, and the primary subject of this section, is the **aesthetic design** component. The appearance of the pavement, often ignored in engineered design, has a significant impact on the character, value, and success of a place. The aesthetic design effort requires knowledge and experience of design principles and characteristics, along with the applied use of materials and construction methods.

STRUCTURAL PAVEMENT DESIGN

Structural pavement design may involve the work of an engineer who is licensed to perform this work. Structural design includes geotechnical testing and evaluation to determine the nature of the subgrade, soil, and water content. Knowledge of soil types, their structural characteristics, and methods to compact, drain, and stabilize pavement subgrades in preparation for finished surfacing are applied in structural design.

There are two general categories of structural pavements: *flexible* and *nonflexible*. Flexible pavements are those that rely on the structural capacity of the subgrade to support them. Examples of flexible pavements are bituminous/asphalt, unit pavers on road base and sand, and crusher fine/decomposed granite soft surface trails. Structural pavements are supported independently of the subgrade and include reinforced concrete pavement and pavements that are installed on a rooftop or other rigid structural base.

Structural characteristics of pavements that contribute to their appropriate use include durability, hardness, response to extremes of heat and cold, skid resistance, and cost. For instance, a crusher fine trail might be appropriate for a route that accommodates walkers and mountain bikers, but may not be appropriate for street bikes and wheelchairs.

FUNCTIONAL PAVEMENT DESIGN

In many situations, pavements are used strictly for utilitarian purposes. Pavement provides a low-maintenance and relatively inexpensive way to provide access for vehicles and pedestrians from one location to another. The cost-efficient approach used in public works normally, ideally, results in the minimum required attention to detail that would enhance the appearance of public domain. This does not necessarily mean that the minimum amount of material required is used. Since labor costs are often much higher than material costs, the most efficient methods are often used to design and construct pavements. This results in a utilitarian but very unappealing finished product and an unfortunate waste of material and opportunity for aesthetic appeal.

Installation and repair of buried utilities is probably the major single reason that pavements fail. Saw-cutting, trenching, and patching can destroy the appearance and integrity of any pavement system. To avoid this, planning is required. Potential solutions include providing a generous amount of sleeving at actual and potential utility locations, using modular pavement systems such as unit pavers that can be removed and replaced for utility access, or better coordination of utility installation and maintenance with pavement installation and replacement programs.

An innovative use of pavement for a specific functional use is porous pavement. As stormwater quality requirements are increased in a more urbanized environment, the importance of these systems increases. Originally seen as turf pavers used to decrease the amount of pavement in large parking areas and fire lanes, systems are available that utilize precast concrete or heavy-duty plastic rings to carry vehicle loads, and porous asphalt and concrete systems are available that allow water to drain vertically, providing storage and filtration of sediment. Other through-drainage pavement systems include rooftop pavers and unit pavers set on a porous subgrade.

AESTHETIC PAVEMENT DESIGN

People experience their environment through perception of their surroundings. This perception has a profound influence on the emotional and social aspects of their well-being. Arrangements of colors, textures, forms, and patterns create moods in the landscape, as they often do in other artistic pursuits. The success of designed places is directly related to the success of the pavement design. Areas in need of special attention are the areas where people congregate—streets, plazas, public parks, and residential yards. That is where people are most likely to recognize (consciously or not) the quality of materials, their color, finish, and patterns, and, consequently, will feel either comfortable or not in the landscape.

Attention to the engineered aspects of pavement highlights the fact that the vast majority of pavement in the landscape is determined by what is most appropriate for structural and functional uses. This is an understandable result of the fundamental economic principles of highest and best use of limited resources. The aesthetic component is often viewed as a bonus, a luxury for those that can afford it.

Inspiration can be found in the historic use of pavements in Italy, for example. Historically, people in urban environments in Italy considered the public

Craig Coronato, EDAW

plaza or street to be an outdoor room. As such, pavements were designed to be simple and attractive and easy to maintain. Locally available, very durable materials were used, and craftsmen were employed to quarry, install, and maintain them. These pavement systems have lasted for hundreds of years, being carefully removed and replaced as required to perform utility maintenance and repairs.

DESIGN PRINCIPLES APPLIED TO PAVEMENT DESIGN

To achieve success in the aesthetic design of pavements, the basic principles of design must be applied. To further illustrate the importance of pavement in the landscape as a fundamental component of successful places, a review of the characteristics and principles of design as they apply to pavement design is outlined:

- *Color* is a characteristic that perhaps is the strongest and most subjective. Light colors tend to reflect light, and light objects appear larger than dark objects. Dark surfaces reflect less light and, therefore, produce less glare. In design, colors are used to develop patterns by the deliberate arrangement of contrasting or complementing colors.
- *Texture* is the relative smoothness or roughness of a surface as it appears to the eye and to touch. Texture is a unique characteristic of a material, a finish, or a pattern. The appearance of texture is a direct result of the reflection of light off materials. Smooth surfaces appear shiny and have a high degree of reflectivity and potential for glare. They also can be slippery, and hasten the movement of elements such as water and debris across the surface. Rougher surfaces recede in the landscape, absorbing light, increasing skid resistance, and slowing movement of elements across the surface.
- *Line* in pavement can be organizational, decorative, or edge-forming. Lines tend to define a boundary or edge of a space, indicate directions of movement, and help define patterns. Lines are not necessarily straight. Some of the strongest lines in the landscape are curved, spiral, or skewed. Lines take many forms; for example, the edge formed between a horizontal surface and a vertical surface, such as a sidewalk and building wall or a curb and street, is a very strong line. A linear element such as a distinct band in a pavement pattern can indicate either movement through space or an inward focus into the space. Even joints in pavement can reinforce the line.
- *Form* is the design characteristic that combines lines and shapes to create space—the ultimate outcome of the design process. As applied to pavement, form is generally recognized as the shapes of paved spaces and the combinations of shapes used to create patterns in paved areas. Forms impact the impression of users of space, and different approaches are indicated in the development of forms dependent on context and design approach.
  - Rectangular forms tend to be static and safe—often most appropriate in an architectural use as an extension of a building or other vertical element.
  - Diagonal and angular forms tend to cause tension and interest by contrast with other organizational elements.
  - Curvilinear forms have a sensuous or natural feel, flowing from one space to another and embracing landform.
- *Scale and proportion* refers to the relative size of elements in relation to each other and the whole. Scale is evident in pavement design as distinct elements of pattern relate to other elements and complement or contrast with the size of other elements in the landscape such as buildings, vegetation, or landforms. Large or monumental scale can be impressive, yet cold and impersonal. Finer patterns provide more visual interest at the ground plane and might relate better to human scale, but are not always appropriate and often cost more to construct and maintain.
- *Unity* is a principle that expresses the relationship of the individual parts to the whole. This is expressed in pavement design through interpretation of a combination of many of the other design characteristics such as form, balance, scale, repetition, and rhythm as used in a composition. A unified whole results from the harmonious arrangement of elements, including pavements.
- *Balance* is the equilibrium established by equality of visual attraction. Balance can be expressed in pavement design by symmetrical layouts or patterns that include a center of focus about which spatial form is balanced.
- *Transition* indicates a gradual change of materials as one moves from one location to another. Transition is often expressed in pavements at edges, from hard surface to soft. It can be expressed as a distinct transition, such as a curb or building wall, or a gradual breakdown of the amount of impervious surface from plaza to softscape.
- *Rhythm* is a principle that describes the feeling of movement through space and detection of a pattern repeated through a sequence. Rhythm is experienced in pavement design by deliberate arrangement of elements in a sequence or pattern along a route that people travel. Repetition of forms, colors, and textures, or patterns of these elements, contributes to the overall composition. Focalization leads the eye toward a specific point in the landscape and can be used in pavement patterns to reinforce other elements using this principle to achieve a desired result.

In conclusion, the application of creative processes and design principles to pavement in the landscape will necessarily help the designer or design team accomplish the important goals of efficient use of resources in a functional and attractive environment. The application of design in the placement and construction of pavements can result in:

- Use of materials and finishes that provide colors, textures, and patterns that provide visual interest and are an important and attractive part of a larger composition.
- Use of pavements that are sustainable and environmentally friendly; for instance, those that have a low life-cycle cost, use local materials, and are colored to reduce heat absorption and reflective glare.
- Reducing areas covered by pavement, resulting in less impervious surface subject to storm runoff and allowing for more soft landscape in a given area and application of porous forms of pavement that can contribute to water quality.

Probably the most persuasive reason to incorporate all aspects of pavement design into any project is to increase the value of the user's experience in the space, which, in turn, increases the value of the space itself.

Craig Coronato, EDAW

UNIT PAVERS

Unit pavers are a durable and aesthetic choice for both pedestrian and vehicular ground plane treatments. Individual units, arranged properly, can create paving systems of any scale. The range of materials for these applications can include brick, stone, precast concrete, and asphalt. Unit pavers come in a variety of shapes and colors and can be assembled into a wide spectrum of patterns, adding richness and texture to any landscape.

Unit pavers can be utilized in four conditions: pedestrian, vehicular, porous, and garden. Pedestrian means walkways, plazas, patios, or other public exterior spaces and not subject to vehicular loads. Vehicular applications include roadways, driveways, walkways, plazas, patios, or other exterior spaces that may or will receive vehicular traffic including maintenance or emergency vehicles. Porous paving encompasses precast concrete or plastic units with aggregate or turf in their openings that allow rainwater to percolate through the pavement. Garden includes residential uses not subject to ADA design guidelines.

Material choices for unit pavers include clay-fired brick, stone, asphalt, and precast concrete. Brick, asphalt, and concrete pavers are manufactured and sold in specific shapes, while stone pavers are usually cut to size for a given application with the exception of 4-inch × 4-inch granite sets. Clay-fired brick is typically 4 inch × 8 inches, but is also available in shapes up to 8 inches × 8 inches. Asphalt pavers are available in sizes from 6 inches × 6 inches to 12 inches × 12 inches. Precast concrete units are available in a large variety of shapes and sizes from 4 inches × 4 inches to 3 feet × 3 feet. Units having a surface area up to 100 square inches are called "pavers." Units with a surface area exceeding 100 square inches are called "paving slabs." These generally should not be used in vehicular applications. Stone is available in any size. As a practical matter, shapes are generally less than 4 feet × 4 feet due to their potential for cracking during shipping and high weight. Manufactured unit pavers should have sufficient surface texture for adequate slip resistance when wet. Stone pavers come in a variety of finishes. It is important for the landscape architect to stipulate a flamed or thermal finish and not a honed or polished finish, to ensure adequate slip resistance.

The landscape architect is responsible for selecting the appropriate unit paver type, size, and finish for a given application and use. Guidelines follow for those selections.

PEDESTRIAN PAVEMENTS

For pedestrian-only applications, clay-fired brick and precast concrete pavers can be set upon a flexible base of compacted crushed aggregate under a sand bedding course. Precast concrete, clay-fired brick, and asphalt pavers can be set upon a rigid concrete base with a sand-asphalt setting bed under a bituminous mastic. Stone pavers should be set upon a rigid base of concrete and mortared both horizontally and vertically. All paver types set upon a flexible aggregate base must be restrained at the perimeter by concrete, metal, or plastic to prevent lateral movement.

VEHICULAR PAVEMENTS

For vehicular applications, unit pavers are often set upon a rigid base of concrete, reinforced appropriately to the anticipated loads. For interlocking precast concrete or clay-fired brick pavers, a 1-inch-thick sand bedding course is required on the concrete base. This condition (hand tight with sand-filled joints) requires vertical weep holes of 1-inch diameter in the concrete base at 6 feet on center to drain any water that seeps into the joint and bedding sand. Filter fabric must be placed upon the concrete base to prevent migration of bedding sand into the weep holes and joints.

Precast concrete and clay brick pavers can be placed on bedding sand over a compacted aggregate base or other bases stabilized with cement or asphalt. Industry literature should be consulted for guidance on the soil types, drainage, and traffic conditions to determine the thickness and material choices for these bases.

Precast concrete pavers and brick or asphalt pavers can be set on a concrete base with a sand-asphalt bedding course no greater than ¾ inches thick.

TYPICAL PAVER/BASE/JOINT COMPATIBILITY

A flexible base can be stone dust, sand, or a sand/cement mixture. It is generally installed over a sub-base of stone screenings and a filter fabric can be used to prevent the base material from migrating into the voids of the stone screenings.

Swept joints can either be a butt joint (where one paver is in direct contact, hand tight, against the adjacent paver, pavers must be of uniform size and shape) or an open joint (where a space between the pavers is infilled with stone dust, sand or a sand/cement mixture). An open joint can be used only with a flexible base.

Mortar joints have a definite space between the units that is filled with a wet mortar scraped flushed or tooled that is particularly suited for natural stones and irregularly shaped or uneven paving units. Mortar joints must only be used with pavers on a mortar setting bed.

TYPE OF NATURAL OR CUT STONE PAVER	BASE MATERIALS	JOINT
Cobblestone	Flexible base	Swept joints
	Concrete base with mortar setting bed	Mortar joints
Flagstone (slate or bluestone)	Flexible base	Swept joints
	Concrete base with mortar setting bed	Mortar joints
Block units (Belgian block)	Flexible base	Swept joints
Pavers (thin format cut from stone)	Flexible base	Swept joints
	Concrete base with mortar setting bed	Mortar joints
PREMOLDED PAVER UNITS	**BASE MATERIAL**	**JOINT**
Brick (clay)	Flexible base	Swept joints
	Asphalt or concrete base with bituminous setting bed	Swept joints
	Concrete base with mortar setting bed	Mortar joints
Tile pavers (clay ½"– ⅝" thick)	Concrete base with mortar setting bed	Mortar joints
Asphalt block pavers	Asphalt or concrete base with bituminous setting bed	Swept joints
Concrete pavers	Flexible base	Swept joints
	Asphalt or concrete base with bituminous setting bed	Swept joints
	Concrete base with mortar setting bed	Mortar joints

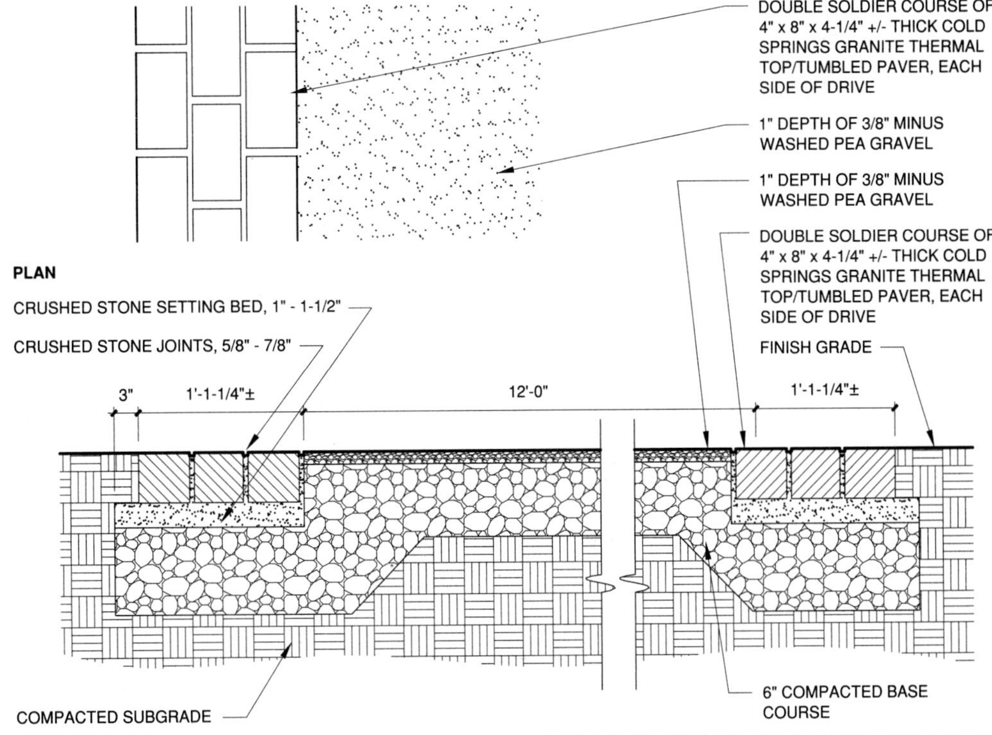

GRAVEL DRIVE WITH GRANITE EDGE

Ryan Bouma, EDAW

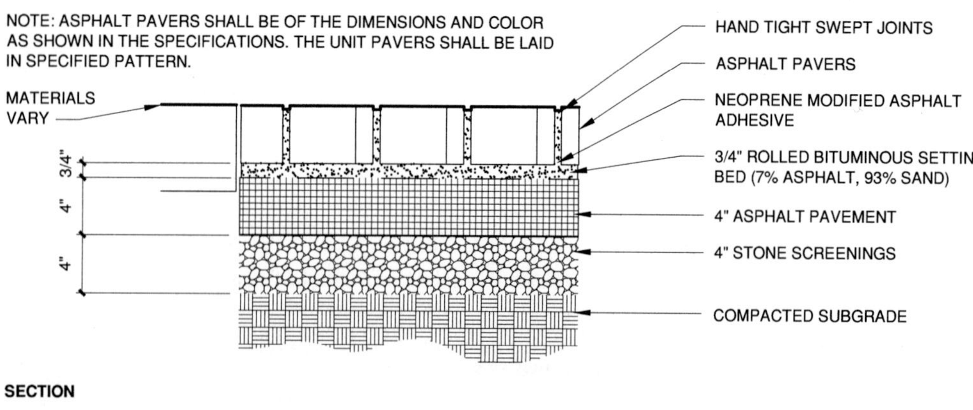

ASPHALT PAVERS ON ASPHALT BASE

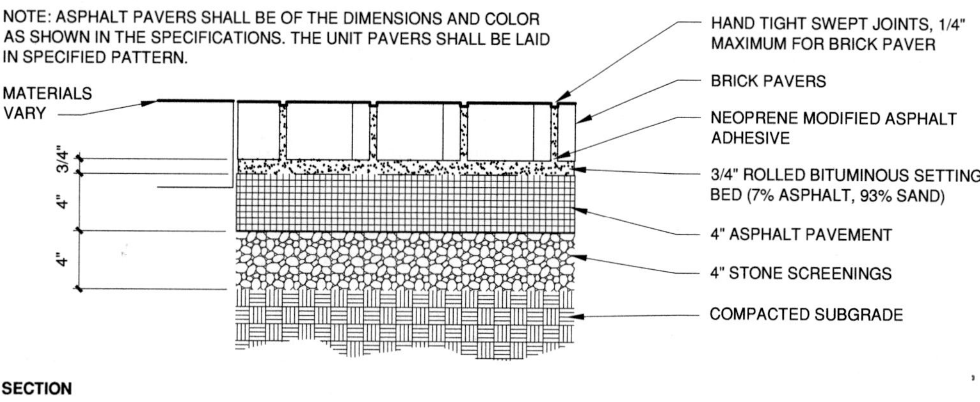

BRICK PAVERS ON ASPHALT BASE

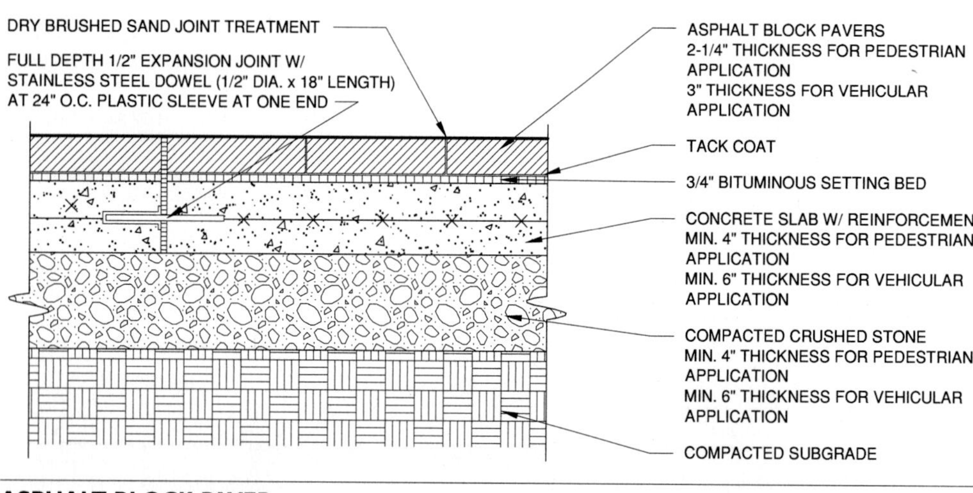

ASPHALT BLOCK PAVER

Ryan Bouma, EDAW

Bituminous mastic is applied to the compacted sand-asphalt bedding course, and the paving units are compacted into the mastic. The joints between the compacted pavers should be filled with sand to minimize water penetration. For clay, precast concrete, and stone pavers, a minimum ½-inch thick horizontal and vertical mortar bed should be provided to adhere them to a concrete base. Mortar-set pavers should be used only in areas with light automobile traffic and in climates without freezing temperatures.

Size and pattern should be considered in any vehicular pavement application. No concrete paver with a length-to-thickness ratio exceeding 3 should be specified for a vehicular area, exclusive of residential driveways. Concrete pavers or slabs exceeding this ratio will likely crack under vehicle loads. A herringbone pattern is preferred for vehicular applications, as it resists lateral forces in all directions. Running bond may also be used in areas subject only to light automobile traffic. Stack bond should not be used, as the alignment of joints in both directions makes it vulnerable to shifting from lateral forces. Finally, vehicular pavers should be a minimum of 3 inches thick. Many manufacturers offer pavers in pedestrian application thickness (2¼ inches or 2⅜ inches) and vehicular application thickness (3 inches or 3⅛ inches).

Like pedestrian applications, vehicular pavers set on a concrete base without mortar should be edged or curbed at the perimeter to prevent lateral movement. Care should be taken in the design of the overall perimeter shape and unit paver shape to minimize paver cutting into pieces less than one-third of a whole unit or 2 inches × 2 inches, whichever is greater. It is especially important to minimize cut pavers having triangular shapes. These may heave or crack over time, causing a tripping hazard or a gap in the overall paving field that fosters lateral movement, thereby weakening the entire paving field.

POROUS UNIT PAVEMENTS

These are created for vehicular use and also can be applied in pedestrian settings. Porous units reduce impervious areas by allowing infiltration of rainwater through openings in the paver. Two basic types of such pavers are commercially available. The first is a concrete grid or plastic matrix with multiple voids filled with topsoil and planted with turf grass. Common applications include fire lanes, emergency access roads, and overflow parking areas, all areas with intermittent or infrequent vehicular loads. The paving units are designed to resist such loads, whereas the turf will not survive under continuous vehicular movement or parking. Each unit relies upon at least 8 inches of compacted crushed aggregate base to support vehicular loads, including fire trucks and emergency vehicles.

The second type of porous or permeable paver is a precast concrete paver with openings filled with washed, small-sized, open-graded aggregate. This is a good choice for parking areas, alleyways, or light volume roadways. Like the turf units, the structural integrity of the concrete paver system lies in the minimum 6-inch- to 8-inch-thick open-graded, crushed stone base. The open-graded base should have sufficient spaces between the aggregate to store rainfall. Like other precast concrete pavers, permeable ones must be restrained at the perimeter by concrete for vehicular applications. Likewise, care should be taken to minimize cutting any unit paving into pieces less than 2 inches × 2 inches, as these may crack and heave, leading to pavement field failure.

GARDEN PAVEMENTS

Unit pavers in a residential garden have a broader range of choices, as domestic landscapes are not subject to ADA design guidelines. While this does not mean that the landscape architect should ignore these guidelines in residential design, it does suggest that stepping stones, stone cobbles, wood blocks, and rustic finishes on pavers may be considered. The landscape architect should exercise sound design judgment in using irregular surfaces, as they may create trip hazards. When not used for a major means of egress, such applications add charm, beauty, and richness to the landscape. To minimize heaving and trip hazards, stepping stones or the like should be set on a minimum 4-inch-thick compacted aggregate crushed stone base.

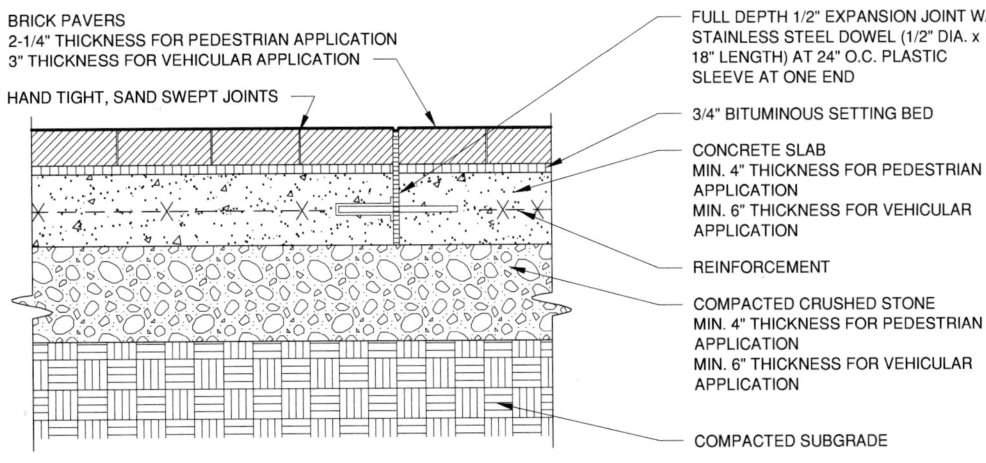

BRICK PAVERS AT GRADE ON BITUMINOUS SETTING BED

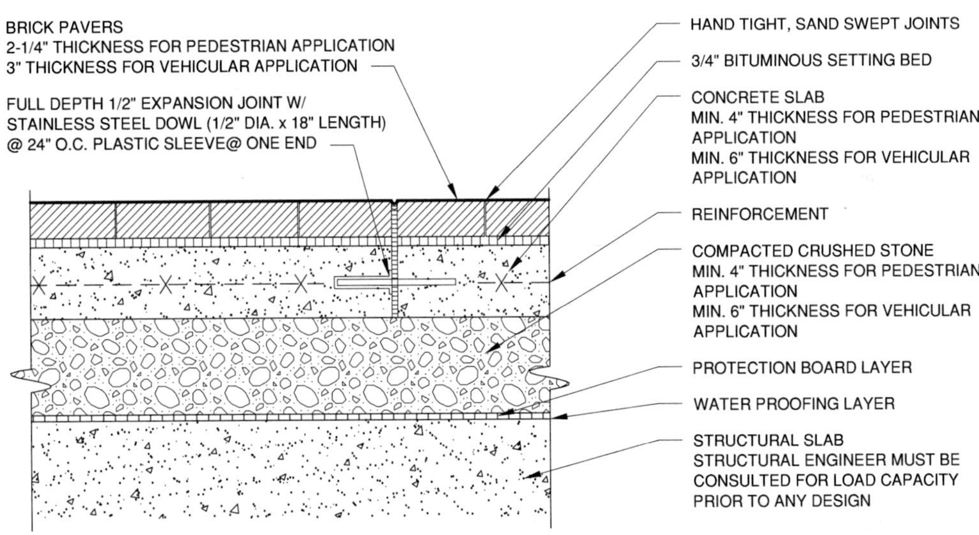

BRICK PAVERS WITH BITUMINOUS SETTING BED ON STRUCTURE

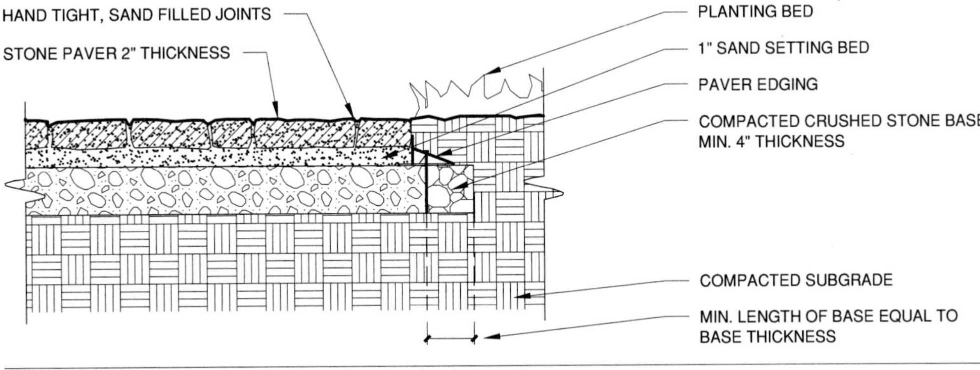

COBBLESTONE PAVERS ON SAND SETTING BED

Ryan Bouma, EDAW

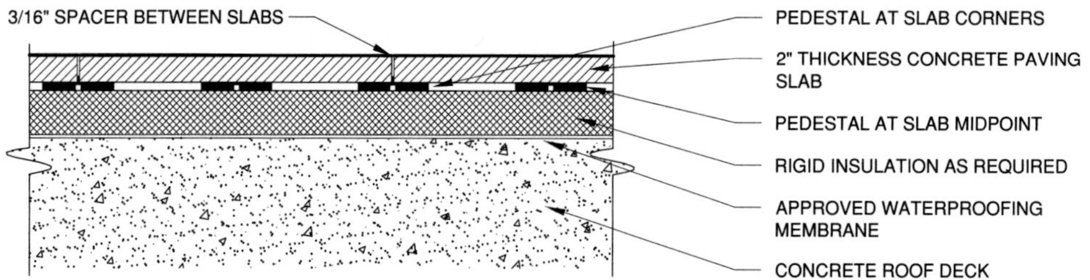

CONCRETE PAVING SLABS ON PEDESTALS

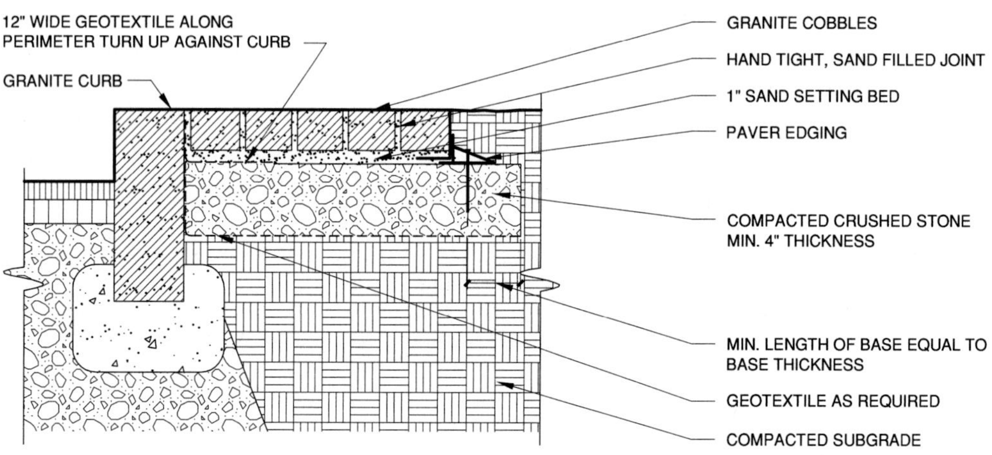

CUT STONE PAVERS ON SAND SETTING BED

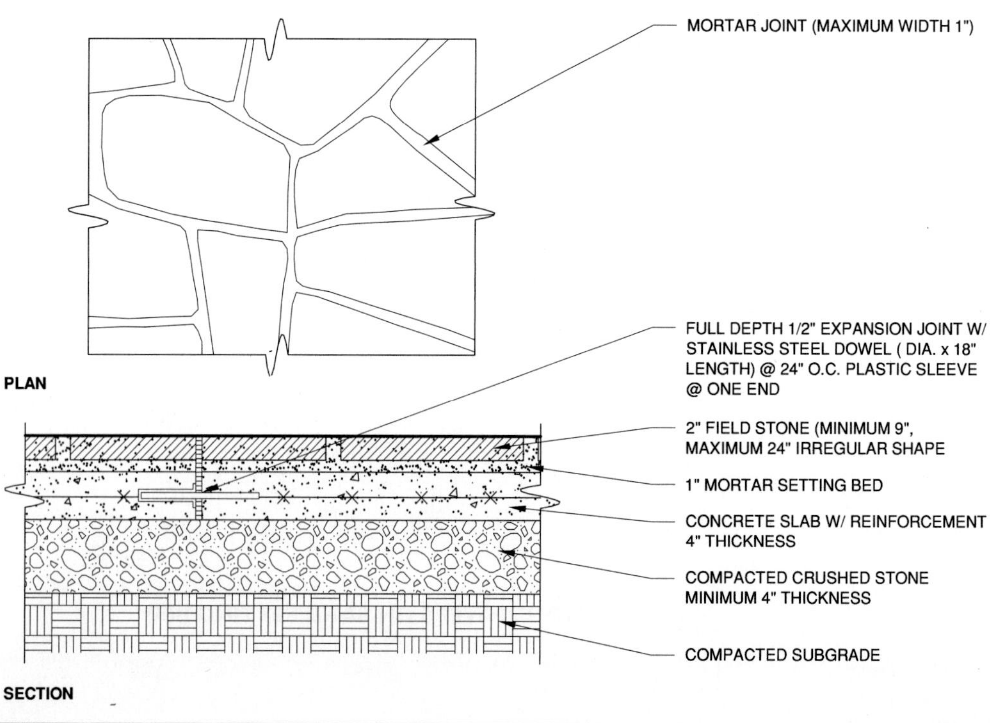

FIELDSTONE ON MORTAR SETTING BED

Ryan Bouma, EDAW

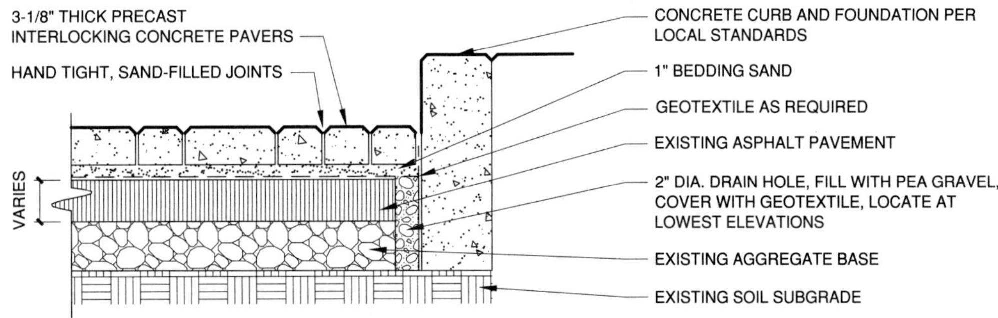

INTERLOCKING CONCRETE PAVER OVERLAY ON ASPHALT PAVEMENT

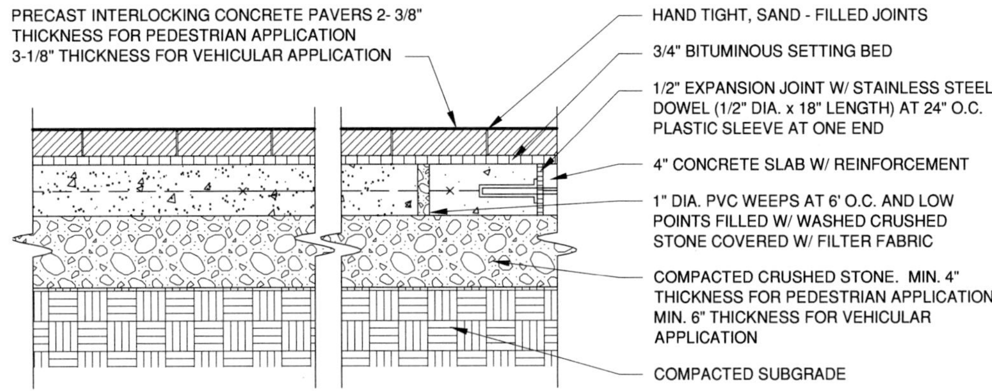

INTERLOCKING CONCRETE PAVERS AT GRADE ON BITUMINOUS SETTING BED

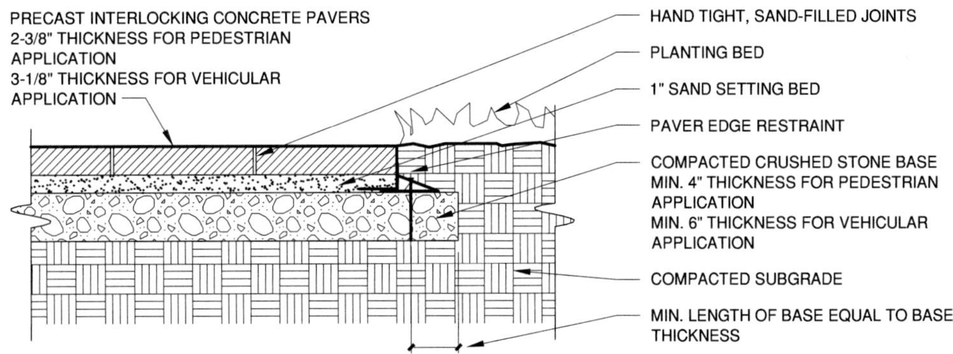

INTERLOCKING CONCRETE PAVERS ON SAND SETTING BED

Ryan Bouma, EDAW

CONCRETE PAVEMENT

GENERAL DESCRIPTION

Concrete pavement is a versatile, durable, and cost-effective site design element. The various textures, finishes, patterns, and colors available provide important design opportunities to strengthen an overall site plan that should not be lost.

Concrete is a mixture of Portland cement, aggregates of various gradations, and water. The water mixes with the cement to form a paste that hardens by a chemical process (called *hydration*) that in turns binds the aggregate into a monolithic mass. The combinations of these ingredients in their various forms and proportions determine the strength, workability, and other characteristics of the concrete.

FORMWORK

Along the sides of the area that is to be paved with concrete, forms need to be erected to contain the concrete when it is placed. These forms are most commonly constructed of wood of the appropriate dimension, but they sometimes are constructed from steel. The most common choices of materials for curved forms are thin pieces of wood or plywood or flexible metal. A critical concern with these thinner forms is the amount of bracing that is needed to prevent movement or bulging when the concrete is placed. It is best to always have the top of the forms set flush with the proposed finished grade of the pavement.

REINFORCEMENT

Concrete is a material that is high in compressive strength. Reinforcement is used in concrete pavements to increase the tensile strength of concrete pavement. Typical reinforcement of concrete pavements includes welded steel wire mesh fabric and steel reinforcing bars, as well as various fibers that are integrally mixed with the concrete.

The most common reinforcement for concrete pavement is wire mesh. It is manufactured of steel wire of various sizes that is welded together to form square grids of either 4 inches or 6 inches.

Welded wire mesh is specified using four numbers that relate to the size of the grid and the cross-sectional area of the wire. An example of a typically specified welded wire mesh for reinforcing concrete pavement is 6 × 6 – W2.9 × W2.9. The first number refers to the spacing of the longitudinal wire in inches (6″). The second number refers to the spacing of the transverse wires in inches (6″). The third number refers to the cross-sectional area of the longitudinal wires in hundredths of an inch (.029″). The fourth number refers to the cross-sectional area of the transverse wires in hundredths of an inch (.029″). The letter "W" refers to plain wire, the letter "D" would designate a deformed wire. If the wire is specified in metric measurement, the "W" or "D" prefix is preceded by an "M" (MW or MD).

The welded wire mesh can be specified with a galvanized coating or epoxy coating, where additional corrosion resistance is required. The galvanized coating is applied to the individual wires before welding. The epoxy coating is done after the wire has been welded to form the mesh fabric. The welded wire mesh reinforcement comes in large rolls or sheets. The welded wire mesh in rolls can be difficult to anchor at the proper depth within the concrete pavement, as getting it to lay flat is a challenge. The welded wire mesh that is supplied in sheets lays flat and is easier to support at the correct depth within the concrete. For the welded wire mesh to be effective, the reinforcing needs to be securely anchored in place prior to the pouring of the concrete. To provide this support, different types of chairs and rails can be used that have been specially designed to clip to the mesh and keep the reinforcing at the correct depth throughout the placement of the concrete. An unacceptable practice would be to lay the reinforcing on the ground and then pull the mesh up with the claw end of a hammer as the concrete is being placed.

Steel reinforcing bars are sometimes used to reinforce concrete pavement. Typically, the bars used are called "deformed" because they are not smooth but are manufactured with a ribbed pattern. The ribbed pattern increases the surface area of the bar that comes in contact with the concrete; it does so in a pattern that allows the concrete to get a firm grip on the steel and prevents slippage. Steel reinforcing bars can be specified with a galvanized or epoxy coating, where additional resistance against corrosive factors is required. Steel reinforcing bars are specified by a number, that when multiplied by 1/8″, represents the bar's nominal diameter in inches (for example, a No. 3 bar would have a diameter of 3/8″, a No. 6 bar would have a diameter of 6/8″ or 3/4″, etc.). The reinforcing bars must be secured in place by special chairs and clips; these secure the bars in place and at the proper depth during the placement of the concrete. Floating the bars into the wet concrete is not acceptable.

Glass or plastic fiber products can be integrally mixed with the concrete to provide additional reinforcement, which can help to relieve internal stress and minimize cracking. The use of these synthetic fibers is particularly effective in preventing surface cracks because of plastic shrinkage of concrete, which happens soon after the concrete is placed. Plastic shrinkage cracks are the result of a rapid loss of water from the surface caused by high ambient temperatures, low relative humidity, wind velocity, or any combination of those factors. The addition of fiber reinforcing helps develop early tensile strength along the surface of the concrete to resist the tensile forces that cause plastic shrinkage cracking.

WELDED WIRE MESH

	STYLE DESIGNATIONS			
NEW	OLD (WITH WIRE GAUGE SIZE)	LONGITUDINAL WIRE, STEEL CROSS-SECTIONAL AREA (SQ. IN.)	TRANSVERSE WIRE, STEEL CROSS-SECTIONAL AREA (SQ. IN.)	APPROXIMATE WEIGHT PER 100 SQUARE FEET
ROLLS				
6 x 6 – W1.4 x W1.4	6 x 6 – 10 x 10	.03	.03	21
6 x 6 – W2 x W2	6 x 6 – 8 x 8	.04	.04	29
6 x 6 – W2.9 x W2.9	6 x 6 – 6 x 6	.06	.06	42
6 x 6 – W4 x W4	6 x 6 – 4 x 4	.08	.08	58
4 x 4 – W1.4 x W1.4	4 x 4 – 10 x 10	.04	.04	31
4 x 4 – W2 x W2	4 x 4 – 8 x 8	.06	.06	43
4 x 4 – W2.9 x W2.9	4 x 4 – 6 x 6	.09	.09	62
4 x 4 – W4 x W4	4 x 4 – 4 x 4	.12	.12	86
SHEETS				
6 x 6– W2.9 x W2.9	6 x 6 – 6 x 6	.06	.06	42
6 x 6 – W4 x W4	6 x 6 – 4 x 4	.08	.08	58
6 x 6 – W5.5 x W5.5	6 x 6 – 2 x 2	.11	.11	80
4 x 4 – W4 x W4	4 x 4 – 4 x 4	.12	.12	86

SIZES AND DIMENSIONS OF STANDARD REINFORCING BARS

BAR SIZE	NOMINAL WEIGHT (IN POUNDS PER FOOT)	NOMINAL DIAMETER IN INCHES (NOT INCLUDING THE DEFORMATIONS)
#3	0.376	0.375 or 3/8″
#4	0.668	0.500 or 4/8″ (1/2″)
#5	1.043	0.625 or 5/8″
#6	1.502	0.750 or 6/8″ (3/4″)
#7	2.044	0.875 or 7/8″
#8	2.670	1.000 or 8/8″ (1″)
#9	3.400	1.128
#10	4.303	1.270
#11	5.313	1.410
#14	7.650	1.693
#18	13.60	2.257

Leonard Hopper, RLA, FASLA

SITE PREPARATION AND PLACEMENT OF CONCRETE

The subgrade should be graded parallel to the proposed finished grade; after all spongy or organic material is removed, the subgrade should be properly compacted. The formwork will contain the concrete within the specified area as well as wherever expansion joints are located; it should be set in place with the top of the forms set to the same elevation as the proposed finished grade. Formwork should be secured in place, particularly for curves formed from thinner wood, where the bracing needs to be spaced close enough to each other to prevent shifting of the form during the pouring of concrete to ensure a smooth and flowing curve. The specified depth of aggregate for the subbase should be evenly distributed over the subgrade and compacted. The reinforcing, if called for, should be secured in place to prevent shifting, by using the correct reinforcing chairs or rails for support. Just prior to the placing of the concrete, the area should be thoroughly watered down to prevent the wicking away of the moisture in the concrete. Forms should be treated with oil or another releasing agent to prevent the concrete from bonding with the form, which would result in the concrete pulling away from the sides of the pavement when the forms are stripped.

At this point the thoroughly mixed concrete can be placed within the formwork, starting at one end and working evenly toward the other. Generally, concrete should be placed within an hour after cement has been added to the mix. If more time than an hour elapses, the concrete mix could dry and stiffen, affecting its strength and workability. The concrete is consolidated in the forms by using handtools or by the use of internal vibrators. It should be placed as close as possible to its final position to avoid excess horizontal movement that can separate the aggregate from the concrete paste.

The placed concrete is leveled by screeding or leveling with a board or other straightedge; first move with a sawing action along the top of the forms, and then move across the surface of the pavement, to roughly finish the concrete to the proposed finished elevations. A small amount of concrete should be kept ahead of the screed board to fill in any low spots.

After all surface water has evaporated or been reabsorbed by the concrete, it can then be smoothed to eliminate high or low points as well as to imbed the aggregates beneath the surface. This initial smoothing is called "*bullfloating*." After bullfloating, when the water sheen has disappeared from the surface and the surface has stiffened sufficiently, the concrete is given its final finish. Finishing can be done with a power float or trowel (which imparts a circular pattern to the surface), a wood float, a steel trowel (which gives a very smooth finish), or a broom (brooms of various stiffness are made for this purpose). For pavements, a broom finish provides a skid-resistant surface; the broom being swept across the concrete creates a finely textured series of lines, which provide a desirable pedestrian pavement. Control joints, if tooled, can be cut into place. Edge tools are used to consolidate the concrete along the perimeter edges as well as to give the edge a slight radius with a smooth width. This results in an edge that is less susceptible to chipping.

Typically, the concrete is tested to ensure that the specified quality and characteristics are being provided.

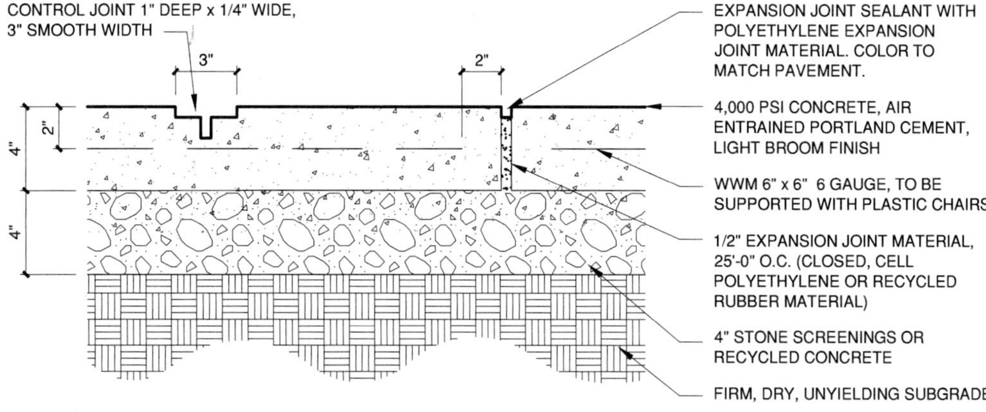

4-IN. REINFORCED CONCRETE PAVEMENT

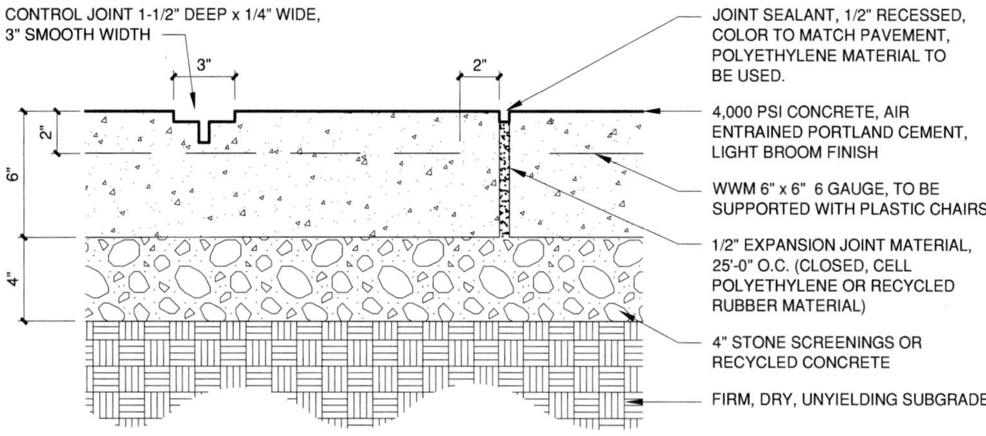

6-IN. REINFORCED CONCRETE PAVEMENT

One test performed is to verify the specified slump. It is measured by placing the concrete being poured into a 12-inch high cone and rodded to consolidate the concrete mix. The cone is then lifted and, as the concrete "slumps," its height is measured. The difference between the 12-inch initial height in the cone and resulting height after the cone has been removed is the slump. If the cone is removed and the height of the concrete sinks to 7 inches, then the mix is said to have a 5-inch slump. A slump test is a good indicator to initially test the concrete mix and determine if some factor in the mix is not as specified. A slump that falls out of the number of inches specified can indicate a problem with the amount of water added to the mix, air entrainment, aggregate gradation, improperly mixed ingredients, or a mix that might have been in the truck too long. A cylinder test is also a common test performed to test for compressive strength. A 6-inch diameter by 12-inch height cylinder is filled with concrete at the site. It is handled under controlled conditions, taken to the lab, and, after a determined period of time (typically tested at either 7 or 28 days), put under a machine that exerts an increasing amount of force on the top of the cylinder. At the point of failure, the amount of pressure that was required is recorded and is translated into the number of pounds per square inch that the concrete was able to withstand. This is the compressive strength of the concrete mix. Other tests can be performed on the pavement after 28 days give an approximation of the compressive strength, usually by measuring the depth a projectile or device of a certain force imbeds itself in the concrete. If a serious discrepancy exists, a core sample should be taken and a more accurate lab test, similar to the cylinder test, should be performed. The use of core samples should be minimized, as it does leave a distinctive mark in the pavement where the cored hole is patched.

JOINTS

Concrete is a material that contracts and expands based on moisture content and temperature variations. Joints are necessary in concrete to relieve the internal stresses of expansion and contraction as well as the overall horizontal movement of the concrete slab. Contraction during the curing process is particularly significant as the newly placed concrete dries. This is one of the reasons that cracks in concrete often appear within the first several weeks of the placing of concrete pavement. Overall contraction and expansion will occur as temperature variations occur, particularly where there are wide temperature variations between summer and winter.

Expansion Joints

Expansion joints (also referred to as isolation joints) extend the full depth of the pavement and completely separate one concrete slab from the adjacent

Leonard Hopper, RLA, FASLA

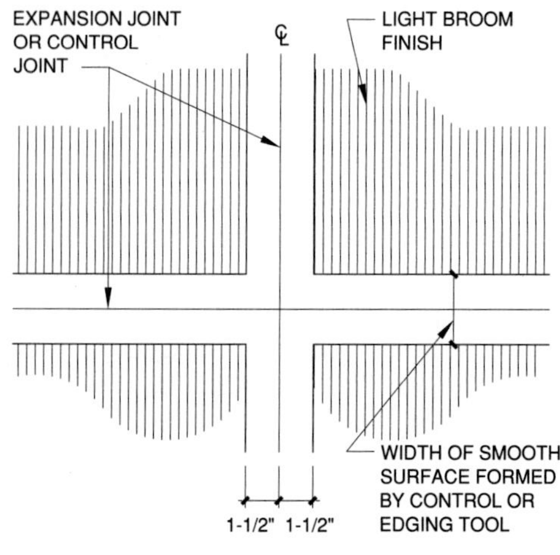

CONCRETE EXPANSION/CONTROL JOINT

slab. They should be used wherever new concrete pavement meets an existing structure such as a building, walls, or steps.

Typically, these joints are filled with a preformed flexible material installed prior to the placing of the concrete, which will allow the concrete slab to move laterally, causing this material to compress or expand with the corresponding movement of the concrete. The typical joint filler materials are asphalt impregnated fiberboards, wood strips, or a variety of plastic, rubber, and metal types. The asphalt-impregnated fiberboard has most commonly been used and is generally sealed with an asphaltic-based product. Both the sealer and fiberboard have a tendency to dry, shrink, crack, and lose their resiliency over time, which limits their long-term effectiveness. Wood strips used as expansion joint filler need to be made up of a decay-resistant species or be pressure-treated with a wood preservative. They should have nails or screws driven into their face surface; this will provide anchoring into the concrete and ensure that they remain flush with the finished grade of the pavement over time. Plastics, rubber, and metal expansion joint material represent a wide range of different products, available in a variety of different shapes and sizes. Some expansion joint material is now being produced from old automobile tires. The more popular expansion joint material of this type is a closed-cell polyethylene material that is most commonly sealed with a urethane-based sealer. Urethane-based sealers come in a number of different colors that can be specified to match the color of the concrete pavement. The combination of this joint material and sealer retains its flexibility over time and is an excellent long-term choice for an effective expansion joint system.

Whatever type of expansion joint material used, the sealer used needs to be compatible with all the materials with which it will be in contact in order for it to be effective. Some manufacturers may recommend that a backer rod be placed between the expansion joint material and sealer to prevent the sealer from adhering to the expansion joint material and the sides of the concrete pavement. Special caps can be used that fit on the expansion joint material, set flush with the proposed finished grade of the concrete, that break away after the concrete has been placed and hardened. These breakaway caps have a top section that is removed after the concrete has hardened. The use of this product ensures that a proper depth is left from the top of slab for the installation of the expansion joint sealer, and the piece that remains on the joint filler provides a bond break between the joint material and the sealer.

Control Joints

Control joints (also referred to as "contraction joints" or "score lines") help to relieve the internal stresses of concrete pavement. Control joints create intentional weak spots within the pavement that serve to control cracking within the joint and minimize the cracking elsewhere along the surface of the slab. In order to be effective, their depth should be at least one-quarter of the overall thickness of the concrete pavement.

Control joints can be formed with a concrete jointing tool or by saw cutting. The concrete jointing tool is used after the floating of concrete. It is used at a time when the surface is set up enough to allow workers access to the surface without their leaving marks; they usually use knee-boards to help distribute their weight over a larger area of the surface. At this time, the surface is still soft enough to allow the jointing tool to be worked into the concrete to the full depth of the groove in the tool. The practical maximum depth of a tooled control joint is 1 inch. A control joint creates a smooth width on each side of the groove (the width varies, depending on which tool is used), which is a distinctive characteristic of this type of joint. The effective use of the jointing tool is dependent upon the window of opportunity that exists between the point when the concrete surface is hard enough to allow workers to begin the control jointing process and the point at which the concrete becomes too hard to allow the joint to be cut to the full depth of the tool. Saw cutting of the concrete involves the use of a circular-type saw with concrete blade that cuts the control joint into the concrete after it has hardened. Saw cutting does not have the smooth width associated with a tooled joint and is very distinctive in appearance. As the joint is cut after the concrete has hardened, a chalk line is usually snapped, which provides a guide for a very straight joint to be cut. In addition, the setting of the depth of blade ensures that the joint is of the required depth throughout. Saw cutting of control joints should be done within 24 hours after the placing of the concrete. If more than a day elapses, then there is a risk that the concrete will begin cracking before the joints are cut into place. Saw cutting of control joints is the best approach when a joint depth of more than 1 inch is required.

Construction Joints

Construction joints are used where the placing of concrete pavement is to be stopped for a period of time. They are generally formed with keyways to lock adjacent pours of concrete together and minimize movement. Construction joints are typically formed with a thickened edge at the joint and may also include sleeved dowels that tie the slabs together.

Integrating Concrete Joints into the Design

Concrete joints in pavements are visible elements in the site design, so locating them in a purposeful way on a plan, by specifying their exact locations and spacing, is the mark of a thoughtful design. Such subtle design enhancements are an improvement on the level of detail a plan usually offers. For example, many construction drawings show areas in which proposed pavement is to be installed, and specifications often stipulate maximum or typical spacing for concrete joints. But not specifying exact locations and spacing for concrete joints on a plan misses an opportunity to take advantage of the design value that they can add.

In some cases, not specifying the locations of the joints can actually lead to joints that distract and detract from the design. For example, if a 12-foot-wide walk has specified contraction joints of 5 feet by 5 feet, the resulting pavement can have a rather odd 2-foot strip scored on either one side or the other. In contrast, if the contraction joints were specified as either 4 feet or 6 feet wide, they would provide a more balanced appearance. Another approach might be to specify a certain number of equally spaced contraction joints on the plan, when the exact width of the walk is not given, as in the case of a walk that aligns with certain building elements. In the same way, expansion joints that relate to major design elements become extensions of those elements and strengthen the design intent and expression.

Although somewhat based on climate and expected temperature extremes, control joints are generally spaced between 4 and 6 feet apart. As mentioned above, the choice of which dimension to use may be influenced by other factors in the design. To be most effective, it is best if contraction joints are straight and continuous rather than disjointed or offset from one another. Expansion joints are generally spaced every 20 to 30 feet apart. Again, the actual distance may be influenced by other site elements in the design. The important factor within these parameters is to choose spacing that relates to your individual design and not leave these important decisions to some generic spacing in the specifications.

CURING

The strength of the concrete pavement is directly related to the successful completion of the hydration process—the chemical reaction between the cement and water. In order for the curing process to be successful, the newly poured concrete pavement must retain enough moisture to allow this process to continue for 28 days, which is the time needed for the pavement to reach its compressive strength.

Curing can be accomplished in several ways:

- *Keeping the concrete covered with burlap fabric continually wet by sprinklers or soaker hoses.* This method provides an effective barrier to prevent moisture loss in the concrete pavement.
- *Placing plastic sheets over a thoroughly watered concrete pavement surface.* This method can prevent moisture .loss from the pavement. For this procedure to be effective, plastic sheets should be overlapped and weighted down to completely seal the pavement underneath.
- *Spraying a curing compound, compatible with the final finish of the concrete, over the entire surface of the pavement.* The curing compound creates a barrier that seals the moisture in the concrete pavement. Curing compounds often come in colors, which fade after 28 days, that make it easy to determine if the product has been applied thoroughly and evenly over the entire surface.

Leonard Hopper, RLA, FASLA

Which is the most appropriate method to use will be influenced by the specific circumstances of a site. But whatever approach is taken, the importance of allowing the concrete to cure properly, and the relationship of that factor to the overall strength and durability of the pavement, cannot be overemphasized.

SPECIAL FINISHES

A number of decorative measures and finishes can be used on concrete pavement to create a variety of different effects. The most common methods of adding interest are adding color to the concrete, stamping the concrete with a decorative pattern, and allowing the aggregate to be exposed on the surface.

Color can be added to the concrete either by integrally mixing it with the concrete or by the dry-shake method. To integrally mix color with the other ingredients of the mix, add color prior to the concrete being placed (into the mixing truck while the concrete is still being mixed). This method produces a uniform color throughout the concrete, and the slab is the same color for its entire depth. The dry-shake method involves taking the dry pigments of color and broadcasting them across the freshly floated concrete pavement. This method requires some degree of skill, to ensure a uniform color for the entire surface. With this method, the color only is absorbed into the top layer of the concrete.

Closely associated with the use of colored concrete is patterned concrete. This is the method used to stamp geometric shapes, often resembling a unit paver shape and pattern, into the surface of the freshly floated concrete. Combined with colored concrete, this method can closely resemble the look of unit pavers with the advantages of a monolithic slab.

Exposed aggregate surfaces can add a wide range of colors and textures to concrete pavement. There are a number of decorative aggregates to choose from, depending on the finished look that is desired. The aggregates are mixed with a higher proportion of coarse to fine aggregates. After the concrete pavement is floated, the top layer of concrete is washed off with a hose and acid wash; this results in the decorative aggregate being exposed on the surface. Another alternative is to use a "seeding method," in which the decorative aggregate is spread over the pavement after it has been floated. It is then imbedded into the top surface of the concrete. A concrete surface retarder is often used with this method to give the surface longer workability. After the concrete has sufficiently stiffened, the surface is finely misted and broomed to remove the excess mortar from the surface, exposing the imbedded aggregate. This approach requires a higher level of workmanship than the integrally mixed method to result in a uniform surface.

POROUS CONCRETE PAVEMENT

Porous concrete pavement has been in existence for over 50 years, but it is gaining recognition and greater use in response to recent focus on stormwater management. It is a pavement that allows water infiltration and reduces stormwater runoff. Porous concrete is made with the same components as regular concrete: Portland cement, water, and aggregate. However, the aggregate with porous concrete is single sized, and there is no sand or fine aggregate to fill the voids between the coarser aggregates. This composition creates an interconnected system of voids that allows the water to permeate the pavement. It is a "zero-slump" mixture with very low water content. The exact amount of water used in the mixture is critical, as too little water prevents proper curing and too much causes the cement paste to drain to the bottom. When properly installed, porous concrete can function as well as regular concrete. It does require regular maintenance, to keep the voids from getting clogged. To best perform maintenance on porous concrete, use a commercial power sweeper to lift sediment out of the voids so that the pavement retains its permeability.

In addition to the obvious advantages porous pavement provides for stormwater management purposes, it also filters rainwater before it returns to the ground to recharge aquifers. It provides air and water to the critical root zone of trees, particularly important in our urban areas, where trees are often relegated to less-than-desirable growing conditions.

ASPHALTIC CONCRETE PAVEMENT

GENERAL

Asphaltic concrete is a combination of asphalt cement and aggregates that are combined together to form pavement. Although commonly referred to as "asphalt," the asphalt cement is but one of the components that makes up asphaltic concrete pavement. It is also sometimes referred to as bituminous pavement, a name derived from its refined petroleum origin from which it is derived.

Asphaltic concrete is most generally installed using a combination of plant-heated aggregate (approximately 300°F) and asphalt cement (275°F) commonly referred to as "hot mix." The mixture is delivered to the site hot and is placed over the compacted subgrade and subbase either by a mechanical paving machine or by being raked into place by hand. The mixture is placed to a depth which, after compaction, will be equal to the specified depth shown on the detail drawings. The placed mixture is then compacted by use of a power-driven roller or other approved method to achieve the specified density. Proper compaction should result in a pavement that has approximately 3 to 5 percent air voids, which will increase durability relating to the stresses of expansion and contraction. The area of asphaltic concrete pavement must have a firm edge, to contain the material and allow proper compaction. As the mixture cools, the asphaltic concrete pavement hardens.

In some instances where hot mix is not available or the installation is too far away to transport the heated mixture, a combination of aggregate and liquid asphalt cement modified to be a liquid at ambient temperatures can be used. The asphalt cement used can be either an emulsified asphalt or a cutback asphalt. The emulsified asphalt combines asphalt cement with water and an emulsifying agent. The cutback asphalt contains asphalt cement that includes a petroleum-based solvent. In either case, the asphalt takes longer to cure, as it requires the evaporation of the water or solvent for the asphaltic concrete to harden.

The asphalt cement used in asphaltic concrete pavement is graded by viscosity and hardness. The various grades of asphalt cement have different characteristics that make them more suitable for some specific purposes than others. Asphalt cement can be dissolved by concentrations of petroleum-based products. Where spillage of those materials might be likely, a sealer should be used to protect the pavement.

The aggregates mixed with the asphaltic cement must be graded to specific size proportions to achieve the desired design mix and perform the function for which it is intended. The proportions are achieved by specifying the percentage of aggregate that will pass through designated sieve sizes. In addition, aggregates have different characteristics that also contribute to the final pavement design such as hardness, texture, and shape. In general, the coarser aggregate contributes to giving a pavement strength and stability, while the finer aggregate helps to fill voids between the larger aggregate and provides a smoother-surfaced wearing course. The exact proportions and types of aggregate are generally a product of material availability, local practices, and experiences; investigate these things before specifying a particular mix.

Asphaltic concrete pavement's role as a surface treatment is to transfer the load placed on it and distribute over a larger area to the subgrade. Ultimately, it is the subgrade that must support the load placed on it. Therefore, it is critical to properly prepare and compact the subgrade before the paving process. The subgrade should be free of soft or spongy material, organic matter, or any materials that potentially could cause a weak spot or drainage problem that could translate into the failure of the pavement above. A layer of aggregate as a base course is sometimes used to help distribute the load over a greater area and to allow any water to drain through to the subgrade. The nature of asphaltic concrete pavement requires that the heavier the anticipated load, the thicker the overall pavement needs to be in order to distribute the load over a larger area of the subgrade.

DESIGN CRITERIA

Asphaltic concrete pavements can be used for a broad variety of applications. This type of pavement is most closely associated with vehicular uses, such as roads, driveways, and parking areas. However, because of its monolithic and continuous smooth surface, it lends itself to free-flowing curvilinear paths and trails. Its dark color can be a positive factor is some design contexts, as it blends very nicely in naturalistic and park settings. In larger expanses like parking areas it is best to try and mitigate some of its heat-absorbing properties by incorporating trees into the design and having their canopies block the sun's direct radiation. In addition to being a surface material, asphaltic concrete is also used as an underlying base for a wide variety of unit pavers.

Asphaltic concrete is considered a flexible pavement that, with some degree of resiliency, transfers loads to the subgrade over a smaller area than a more rigid pavement such as concrete. Its success as a paving material is therefore highly dependent on the subgrade's ability to handle the anticipated loads. If there is failure at the subgrade level, the asphalt pavement surface will follow these sunken areas of the subgrade, which creates depressions or a rolling effect. The area of load distribution is a product of the size of aggregate in the mix and the total depth of the pavement. This, together with the bearing capacity of the subgrade, determines the type of mix and thickness of the asphaltic concrete pavement. By combining a base of a coarser aggregate mix with a wearing course of a finer aggregate mix, the overall pavement design benefits from the strength of the base with the positive characteristics of a smooth surface.

Asphaltic concrete pavements are often installed over a subbase of compacted, graded aggregate. This layer of aggregate adds stability and helps distribute the loads transmitted through the pavement over a larger area of the subgrade. This greater distribution of load allows the thickness of the asphaltic concrete pavement to be reduced. In addition, where freeze-thaw cycles are a consideration, this layer of aggregate helps to keep any water away from the pavement and minimizes the effects of frost heave.

Asphaltic concrete pavement is installed as either a full- depth pavement or over a compacted aggregate sub-base. As a full-depth pavement, it is installed directly over a properly prepared and compacted subgrade. This type of installation must take into account the drainage and frost susceptibility of the subgrade material. In poorly drained soils or areas that experience freeze-thaw cycles, or both, this may not be the appropriate installation choice. The use of an aggregate subbase addresses these concerns as well as helps distribute the anticipated load over a larger area of the subgrade, allowing reduced thicknesses of the asphaltic pavement layer.

The design thickness of asphaltic concrete pavement is a product of the anticipated loads (e.g., heavy vehicular, light vehicular, pedestrian), the bearing capacity and characteristics of the subgrade, the use of an aggregate subbase, and the size, material, and proportions of the aggregate used in the design mix.

Although the design is dependent on local materials, practices, and experiences, some guidelines can be used in determining an appropriate cross-section of materials in the design of asphaltic concrete pavements. The table of "Asphalt Concrete Thicknesses for Roads" represents typical guidelines (sometimes presented as a range of thickness, from a minimum to a more conservative approach) that can be used to guide design decisions.

CONSIDERATIONS

In order to maintain stability of the pavement and prevent the edges from crumbling, asphaltic concrete pavement must be contained with an edge material. The choice of which edge material to use depends on

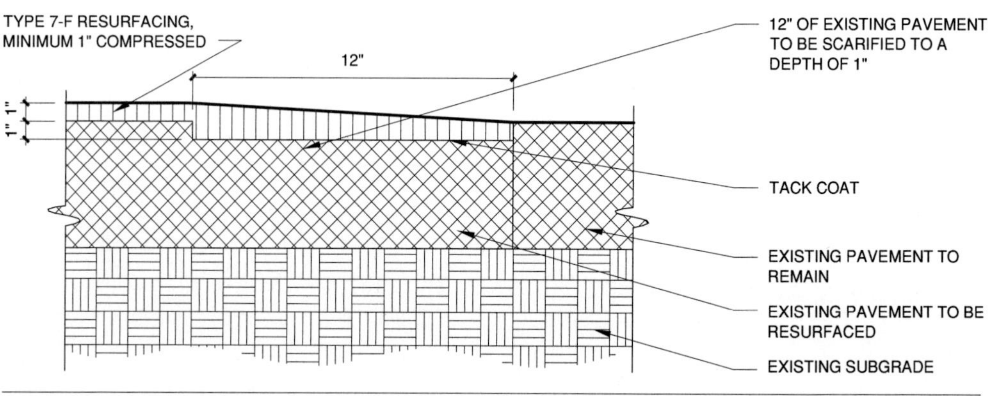

ASPHALT RESURFACING

Leonard Hopper, RLA, FASLA

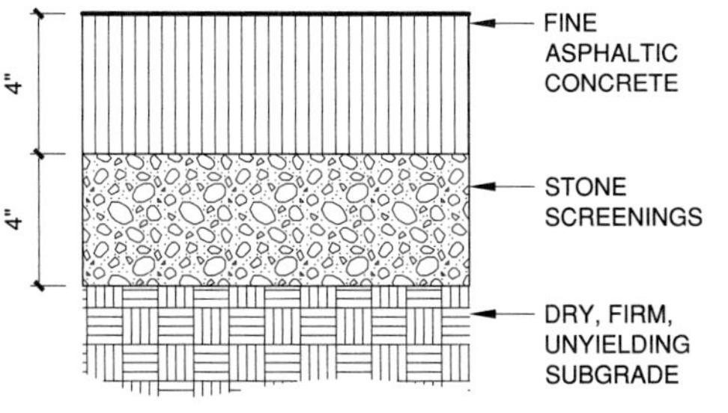

LIGHT-DUTY ASPHALT PAVEMENT

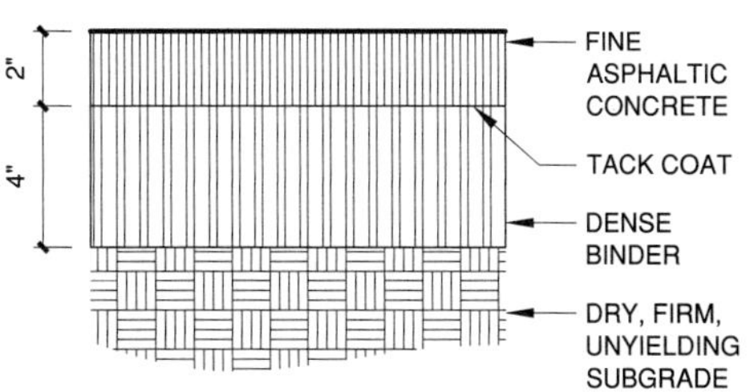

HEAVY-DUTY ASPHALT PAVEMENT (VEHICULAR)

ASPHALT CONCRETE THICKNESS FOR ROADS—FULL DEPTH DESIGN[a,b,c]

	PAVEMENT SECTION	TRAFFIC CLASSIFICATION I	II	III	IV
		FULL-DEPTH ASPHALT CONTRETE, IN MM			
Poor	Asphalt concrete surface	1.0 (25)	1.0 (25)	1.5 (40)	2.0 (50)
	Asphalt concrete base	3.5 (85)	4.0 (95)	5.5 (140)	8.0 (205)
	Total	4.5 (110)	5.0 (120)	7.0 (180)	10.0 (255)
Medium	Asphalt concrete surface	1.0 (25)	1.0 (25)	1.5 (40)	2.0 (50)
	Asphalt concrete base	3.0 (75)	3.0 (75)	3.5 (85)	6.0 (155)
	Total	4.0 (100)[g]	4.0 (100)[g]	5.0 (125)	8.0 (205)
Good to excellent	Asphalt concrete surface	1.0 (25)	1.0 (25)	1.5 (40)	2.0 (50)
	Asphalt concrete base	3.0 (75)	3.0 (75)	2.5 (60)	4.0 (105)
	Total	4.0 (100)[g]	4.0 (100)[g]	4.0 (100)[g]	6.0 (155)

a Consult local standards and practices for all pavements. Such specifications supersede those mentioned here.
b The thickness of any asphalt concrete layer should be at least twice either the nominal maximum size mix designation or the maximum particle size of the mix (whichever term is used).
c Use full-depth pavement where highly frost-susceptible soils or heavy frost is not a problem. Otherwise, use asphalt concrete over an aggregate base.
d See "Subgrade Classifications for Roads Table."
e See "Traffic Classifications for Roads Table."
f Minimum recommended thickness of asphalt concrete surface.
g Minimum recommended design.

Source: Adapted from The Asphalt Institute, Asphalt Pavement Thickness and Design, *IS-181, November 1981.*

not just the stability of the pavement but also some design considerations. A concrete band or curb used as an edge provides a contrasting colored, strong delineation of pavement that emphasizes the line of the pavement through the space. A steel or permanent wood edge provides a very subtle delineation of the pavement that tends to blend with the adjacent material. The design opportunity that the necessary edge material provides should not be overlooked.

Maintaining and repairing asphaltic concrete pavement over time is very easy. To prevent oil and gas spills acting as solvents, degrading the pavement, sealers that resist the detrimental effects of these compounds can be used where the likelihood of spills is anticipated. Asphaltic concrete pavements can be patched very easily with new areas of pavement that match the existing in cross-section and blend in with the adjacent surfaces. Existing asphaltic concrete pavements can be repaired to eliminate problem depressions or cracks; later they can be resurfaced with design mixes that contain very fine aggregates. Resurfacing will result in a pavement that looks new and is free from surface defects. Another repair approach is to mill the top surface of the existing asphaltic concrete and install a new wearing course on top of the remaining pavement. Both approaches restore the asphaltic pavement with a new surface. But the milling operation allows the restored finished grade to match the prerestored elevations, while a resurfacing course increases the elevation, which can disrupt the drainage pattern of the adjacent surfaces.

Removed or milled asphaltic concrete pavements can be recycled; they are often reused to create new asphaltic concrete mixes. Reuse results in lower energy costs, a reduction in construction materials that are sent to a landfill, and savings on the component materials that make up asphaltic concrete, particularly those that are petroleum-based. In addition, other recycled materials can also be used to create or enhance asphaltic concrete mixes such as steel slag for a hard, durable, coarser aggregate; rubber from old tires; and sand from foundry castings as fine aggregates.

Varying the color of asphaltic concrete pavements is also possible. As the pavement weathers, it loses some of its darkness, and the color of the aggregate used in the mix begins to show. This will generally give the paved surface a grayish tone, a product of the larger aggregates in the mix. If darker fine aggregates are used in the mix at the time of installation, the paved surface can retain much of its original dark color throughout its use. Aggregates selected for the color qualities can either be added to the hot mix at the plant or be embedded in the surface of the pavement at time of installation (this requires a skilled contractor experienced in this type of procedure).

The painting of the surface, such as parking stalls or other pavement markings, should be done only with a paint that is compatible and recommended for use on asphaltic concrete pavements. For recreation facilities, such as tennis courts, basketball courts, or playgrounds, acrylic color coatings are available in a wide assortment of colors that can brighten and enhance the design of these areas.

In a similar approach to that used with concrete, the addition of color can be combined in a patterning technique that can create the look of a unit paver design in the asphaltic concrete pavement.

Porous asphaltic concrete pavement can be used as part of a comprehensive stormwater management system. It allows water to permeate through the surface, through a subbase layer of aggregates and infiltrate into the subgrade. This water can then be made available to the roots of plant materials or infiltrate further down to recharge underground aquifers. With an increased focus on controlling stormwater runoff, the opportunity to incorporate a pervious paving material can be an important component in addressing the environmental concerns and regulatory requirements that are associated with large paved areas.

See also:
Asphalt
Concrete
Masonry
Metals

Leonard Hopper, RLA, FASLA

POROUS PAVEMENTS

INTRODUCTION

Porous pavements reduce or eliminate urban stormwater problems at the source by changing the way urban structures are built and the way they operate hydrologically. They restore the landscape's natural water-retaining function by bringing water back into contact with the underlying soil, or emulate it by filtering and storing water in the pavement structure. By combining pavement stormwater control functions into a single structure, they reduce costs, compared with dense pavements that require downstream stormwater control facilities.

Properly applied porous pavements can also enlarge urban tree rooting space, reduce the urban heat-island effect, reduce traffic noise, increase driving safety, and improve appearance. Therefore, their selection and implementation are integral parts of the multifaceted concerns of urban design, and all of their effects are considered together in evaluations of benefits and costs. As porous paving materials become more prevalent, the potential cumulative effect of their use is great, because pavements are the most ubiquitous structures built by humankind; they occupy two-thirds of the constructed surfaces in urban watersheds.

This section briefly reviews the types of porous paving materials that are available, and some provisions necessary in their installation. Considerably more scope and detail on this subject are covered in the book *Porous Pavements,* by Bruce K. Ferguson.

POROUS PAVEMENT CONSTRUCTION

To make a successful porous pavement, it must be selected correctly, designed correctly, installed correctly, and maintained correctly. Failures—clogging and structural degradation—result from neglecting one or more these steps. Construction of porous pavements is not more difficult than that of dense pavements, but it is different, and its unique specifications and procedures must be strictly adhered to.

The dominant component in most porous paving materials is aggregate such as crushed stone. It is crucial that it be "open-graded"—that is, having a narrow range of particle sizes. The void space between single-sized particles typically amounts to 30 to 40 percent of the aggregate's volume; the aggregate's permeability is commonly over 1,000 inches per hour. As long as the particles are angular, open-graded aggregate obtains structural stability from particle-to-particle interlock.

To protect a pavement's surface from sedimentary clogging, surface drainage should be away from the pavement edge in every possible direction, so that sediment is prevented from washing on and is allowed to wash off. On the downhill side, large, numerous curb cuts should be added, if necessary. On the uphill side, a swale should be added, if necessary, to divert potentially sediment-laden runoff. These provisions limit most porous pavements to infiltrating the rainwater that falls directly upon the pavement, not runoff from surrounding earthen slopes.

Each porous paving material has its own advantages and disadvantages for specific applications, and its own requirements for design, construction, and maintenance. A development site should be analyzed in detail to distinguish pavement settings where different, optimally suited materials can be placed. In all pavements, areas can be distinguished with different needs for hydrology, appearance, subsurface tree rooting, and cost.

Alternative Porous Paving Materials

- *Porous aggregate* is unbound gravel, crushed stone, crushed recycled brick, or decomposed granite. In most regions, unbound aggregate is both the least expensive of all firm surfacing materials and the most permeable. It is suitable for very light traffic such as that in residential driveways, lightly used portions of parking lots, and lightly used walkways. Annual maintenance for weeding or to replace lost material may be necessary.
- *Porous turf* makes a "green" open space where transpiration actively cools urban heat islands. It is suitable for bearing very light traffic, such as that in parking spaces used once per week or during seasonal peak shopping periods. The rooting-zone soil should be sandy, to resist compaction. Turf must be regularly mowed, fertilized, and irrigated. Because maintenance must be scheduled, turf should be used only where traffic can be controlled or is predictably scheduled.
- *Plastic geocells* are latticelike products that hold aggregate or topsoil in their cells, inhibiting displacement and compaction. The surface permeability, temperature, and visual appearance are essentially that of grass or aggregate fill.
- *Open-jointed blocks and open-celled grids* are units of concrete, brick, or stone, with open joints or cells. Porous aggregate or turf in the openings gives the pavement its porosity and permeability. Many block products can bear remarkably heavy traffic.
- *Porous concrete* is portland cement concrete made with single-sized aggregate. A qualified installer is required. The durability of porous concrete in cold climates can be enhanced by air entrainment and polymer fiber reinforcing. Properly installed porous concrete can bear heavy traffic loads. The surface is universally accessible by most measures.
- *Porous asphalt* is bituminous concrete made with single-sized aggregate. Polymer fibers and liquid polymer additive can reduce drainage of the binder down through the pores; without them, the binder would leave surface aggregate particles unbound while accumulating into a clogging layer inside the structure. Properly installed porous asphalt can bear heavy traffic loads. The surface is universally accessible by most measures.
- *"Soft" paving materials* include granular organic or recycled materials such as bark mulch, crushed shells, and rubber granules. They are suitable for very light traffic such as that in pedestrian walkways, residential driveways, equestrian ways, and very lightly used parking stalls. Materials with durable single-sized particles have the highest infiltration rates and are the least susceptible to displacement, crushing, and compaction.
- *Decks* are surrogates for pavements. They are completely permeable to air and water as long as their decking components are perforated or spaced apart from each other. Their footings leave the soil below almost entirely free for infiltration and tree rooting. Decks are uniquely suited to sites with steep slopes or where native tree roots or ecosystem dynamics are to be very conscientiously protected. They are made from a variety of natural, manufactured, and recycled materials; their durability varies with the material and its preservative treatment.

STORMWATER TREATMENT

Soil infiltration from a pavement's base reservoir reduces surface runoff volume and restores natural subsurface flow paths. Compaction during construction greatly reduces infiltration rate, but may be necessary for stability where the subgrade is plastic clay or fill, the base course will be too thin to compensate structurally for soft wet soil, and the surface course will be of a type sensitive to movement (asphalt, concrete, blocks, and grids). Compaction might be omitted, and the native infiltration rate preserved, where the subgrade is native-cut (and, therefore, has in situ compaction and stability), an adequately thick base course will compensate for soft subgrade, or the surface course will be of a type that tolerates movement (aggregate, turf, geocells).

It is reasonable to assign to most porous pavements a runoff coefficient comparable to that of grass on the same soil and slope, as opposed to the high values characteristic of impervious surfaces. Where slowly permeable soil prohibits significant soil infiltration, a porous pavement can perform detention and water-quality treatment comparable to those of off-pavement reservoirs and ponds. Part or all of a porous pavement's base course functions as a reservoir, while water infiltrates the subgrade or discharges laterally.

In a porous pavement's voids, oil leaked from automobiles is digested by microbiota that inhabit the abundant internal surface area; the oil's constituents go off as carbon dioxide and water, and very little else. Metals released by automobile corrosion and wear are captured in voids in porous pavements, along with the minute sediment particles to which the ions are characteristically attached.

URBAN TREE ROOTING

As a rule of thumb, a tree's rooting zone must be at least 24 inches deep and at least as large in area as the tree's canopy at maturity. In densely built-up urban areas, porous pavements with base courses of "structural soil" make long-lived trees viable. The porous surface course admits air and water. The rooting zone is the pavement's base course, made of single-sized aggregate that bears the pavement's load. Into the aggregate's void space is mixed no more than 15 to 20 percent by volume of nutrient- and water-holding soil; the remaining unfilled void space provides aeration, drainage, and rooting space.

A hydrogel can be used to hold the soil onto the aggregate particles during mixing. Aggregate made of expanded shale, clay or slate (ESCS) provides additional water-holding capacity; some ESCS aggregates also provide nutrient-holding capacity. Drainage at the base of the rooting layer is mandatory.

REFERENCE

Ferguson, Bruce K. 2005. *Porous Pavements*: Boca Raton, FL: CRC Press.

Bruce K. Ferguson, FASLA

STAIRS, RAMPS, AND CURBS

STAIRS: GENERAL

Stairways can be a significant physical barrier and hazard for pedestrians. Thousands of accidents occur at or on stairways each year, resulting in personal injury, as people tend to move at faster rates in outdoor settings than indoors. Therefore, stairways should be designed to promote safe, efficient, easy, and comfortable vertical transitions. Specifically, dimensional design decisions should focus on proper riser-tread ratios, overall widths, consecutive length of run, and landing frequency, to ease negotiating vertical change and to increase safety in exterior circulation routes. Proper material choices and construction methods should also be considered in the context of safety. (Further information regarding stair safety can be obtained from the American's with Disability Act (ADA) and the Occupational Safety and Health Association (OSHA).)

Stair Tread and Riser Dimensions and Design Criteria

Safety Considerations

Safety considerations include the following:

- Single-step stairways are trip hazards and should not be specified. A minimum of two steps should be used in any single consecutive run of stairs. Three stairs are preferred to ensure visual legibility at level changes.
- Stairways should be visually "announced" with material changes, textural changes, lighting, planting and/or railings.
- Open riser faces are not permitted under the Americans with Disabilities Act Accessibility Guidelines (ADAAG) specifications. They can be significant trip hazards when used in outdoor situations.
- Stair treads should be specified to contain a rough to medium textured finish, to decrease the risk of slipping during poor weather. Natural stone treads should have textured finishes rather than polished surface treatments. Concrete should be specified to have a medium broom finish. All treads should be sloped toward the nose to avoid pooling stormwater.

Uniformity

To avoid becoming a dangerous tripping hazard, treads and risers within a consecutive run of stairs should be uniform in size within close tolerances (¼ inch). Stairs within a single run should be constructed out of similar materials and construction techniques.

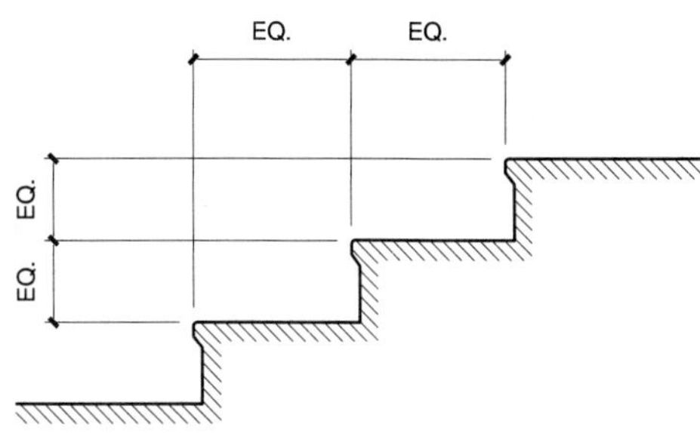

UNIFORM RISERS AND STAIRS

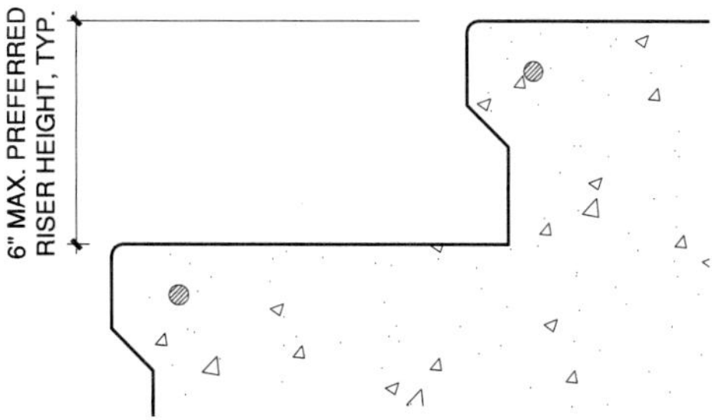

MAXIMUM RISER HEIGHT (TYPICAL)

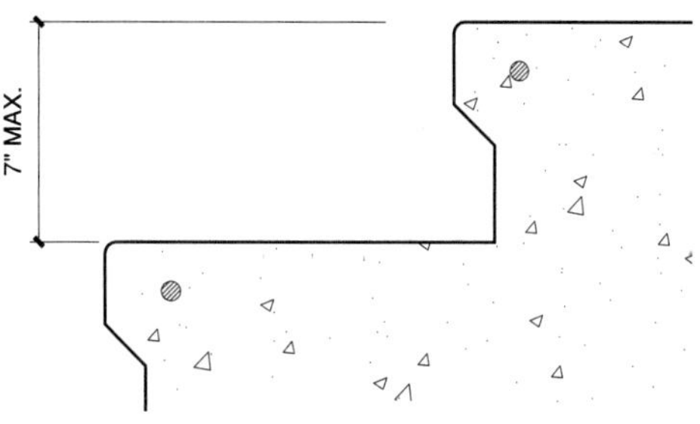

MAXIMUM RISER HEIGHT (FUNCTIONAL)

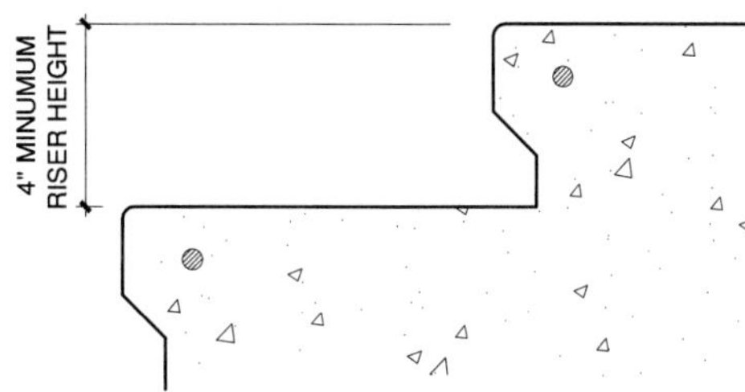

MINIMUM RISER HEIGHT

Riser Heights

The preferred riser height for outdoor stairs is 6 inches. For purely functional situations, a riser height of 7 inches is used and is accepted by American's with Disabilities (ADA) Standards. The minimum riser height for outdoor situations is 4 inches. Risers less than 4 inches in height are considered trip hazards and should be avoided whenever possible.

Riser Slope

Riser slopes typically fall between 60 and 90 degrees from horizontal. Riser slopes less than 60 degrees or more than 90 degrees are considered trip hazards and should be avoided to prevent accidents. All riser angles in a single run of stairs should be identical to each other.

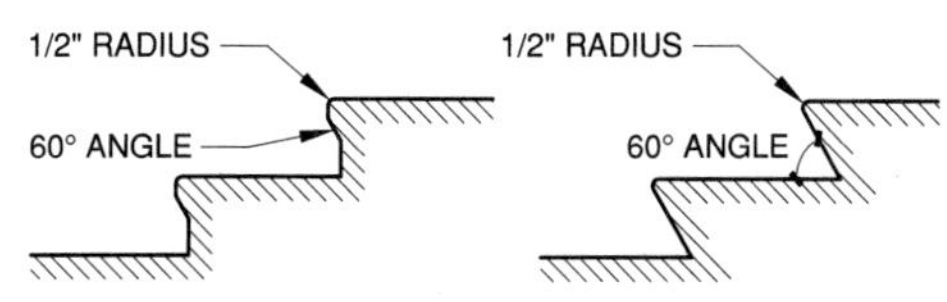

STAIR RISER ANGLE

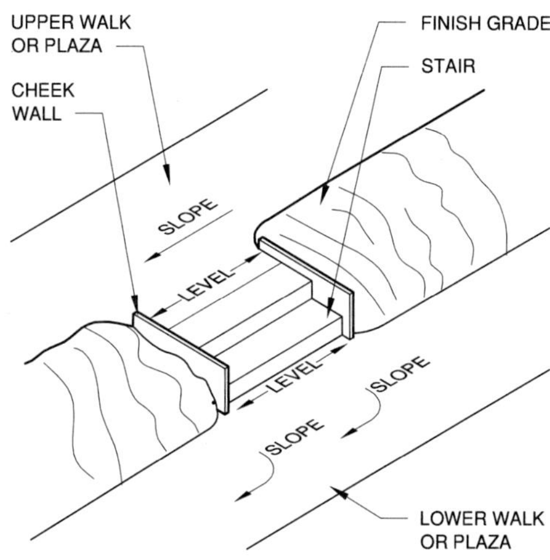

STAIR LEVELING AT CROSS SLOPES

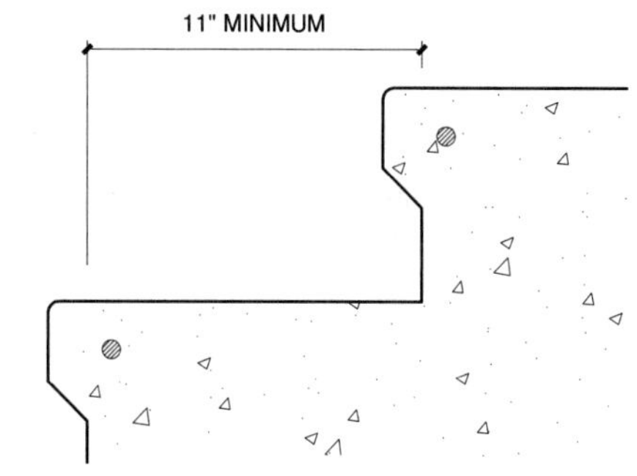

MINIMUM TREAD LENGTH

Stair Leveling

The top of stair and bottom of stair elevations along a stairway should maintain a constant level along the edge of the upper and lower treads. The grade leading to the stair should be modified in cross-slope situations, to ensure a level condition at the top and bottom of a stairway. Whenever possible, avoid designing stairs where the lowest riser dimension varies, resulting in an uneven grade condition.

Tread Length and Thickness

The minimum tread length is 11 inches measured from riser to riser of two consecutive stairs. The maximum tread length is 18 inches and is typically used with a shallow riser. Wider treads offer more fluid transitions between grade levels and are more accommodating when used for sitting purposes. Masonry or natural stone treads should be a minimum of 2 inches thick to add visual and structural strength to stairways.

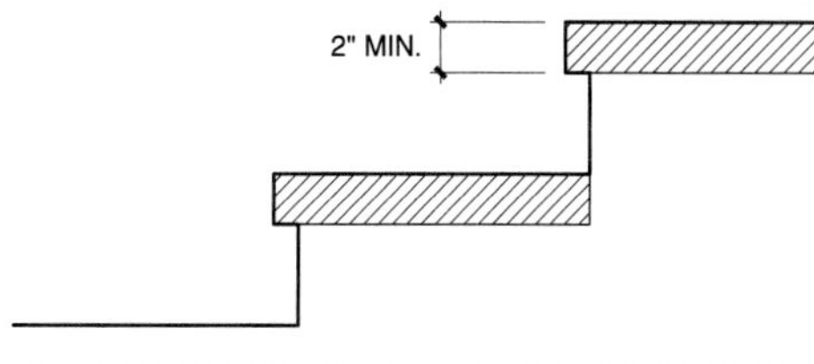

MINIMUM TREAD THICKNESS

David Spooner, Assistant Professor, University of Georgia, School of Environmental Design

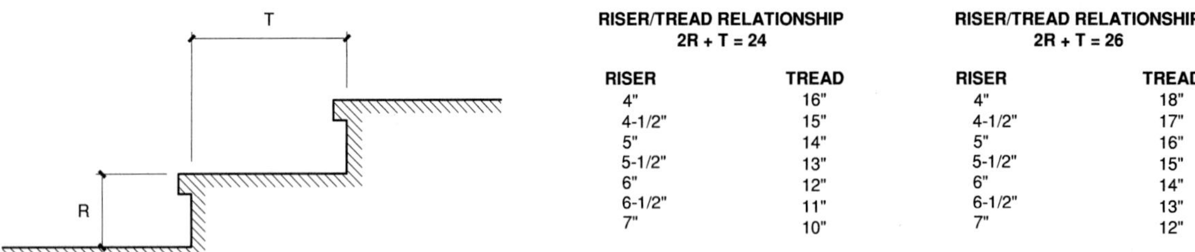

RISER/TREAD RELATIONSHIP 2R + T = 24	
RISER	TREAD
4"	16"
4-1/2"	15"
5"	14"
5-1/2"	13"
6"	12"
6-1/2"	11"
7"	10"

RISER/TREAD RELATIONSHIP 2R + T = 26	
RISER	TREAD
4"	18"
4-1/2"	17"
5"	16"
5-1/2"	15"
6"	14"
6-1/2"	13"
7"	12"

RISER/TREAD RATIO

Riser Tread Ratios

The most commonly accepted equation for the comfortable proportioning of exterior stairs is:

$$2R + T = 24 \text{ to } 26''$$

where:

R = riser height
T = tread length

This ratio tends to work with the average stride of average-height people and creates a regular rhythm or cadence for ascending and descending grade changes.

Stairway Access Dimensions

In public settings, a minimum width of 5 feet is typically necessary for two-way traffic to pass without conflict. For more private access in residential settings, 4 feet is often considered the minimum for one-way traffic.

Stair Landings: Design Criteria and Dimensions

Landing Height

Small grade changes as little as 18 inches and up to 6 feet serve as psychological barriers and decrease a pedestrian's incentive to proceed up or down a grade change. Elevations of consecutive landings in a single run of steps should be separated no more 5 feet so that a person of average height can see the ground plane of the next higher landing.

Landing Length

Landings should be long enough to allow a regular rhythm of movement (average human stride length) between runs of stairs. The typical length for a landing is 5 feet, which allows a minimum of three strides on the landing. Longer landings are usually in multiples of 5-foot intervals (e.g., 5 feet, 10 feet, 15 feet, etc.).

Landing Frequency

In situations where a large grade change occurs, stairs should have a minimum of one landing for every 9 to

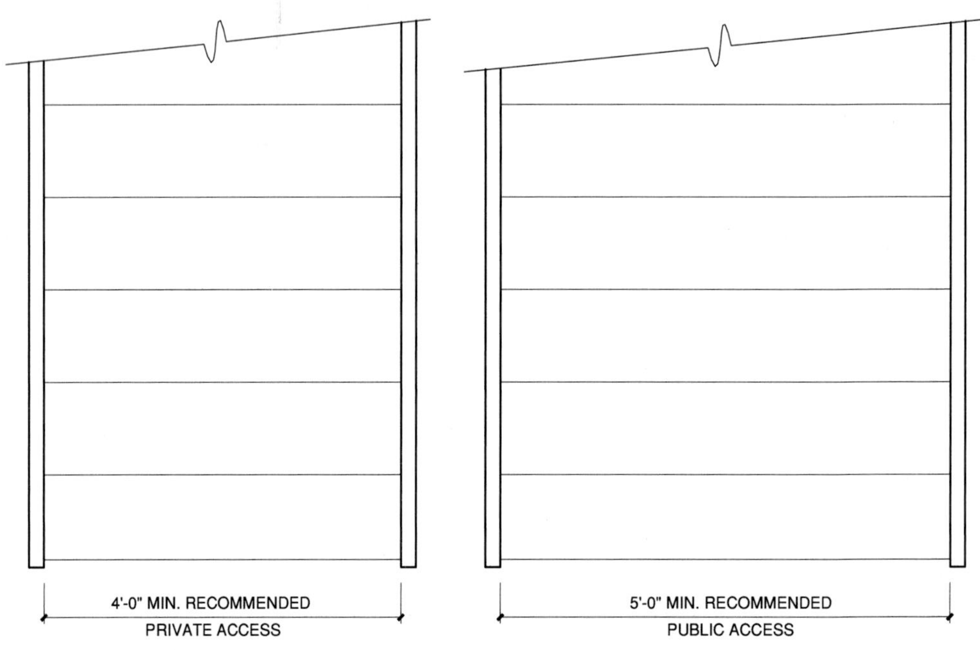

STAIRWAY WIDTHS

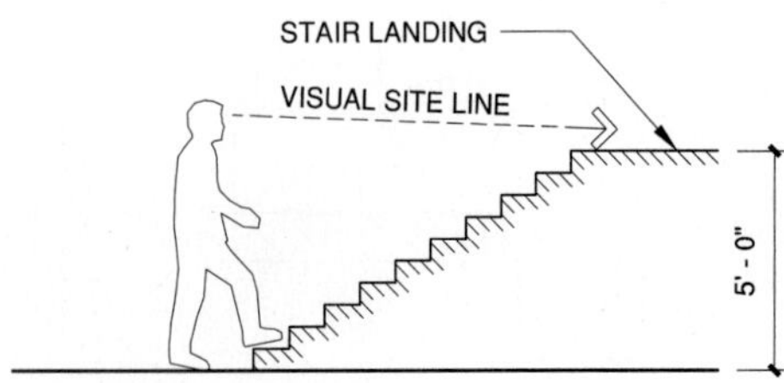

LANDING HEIGHTS

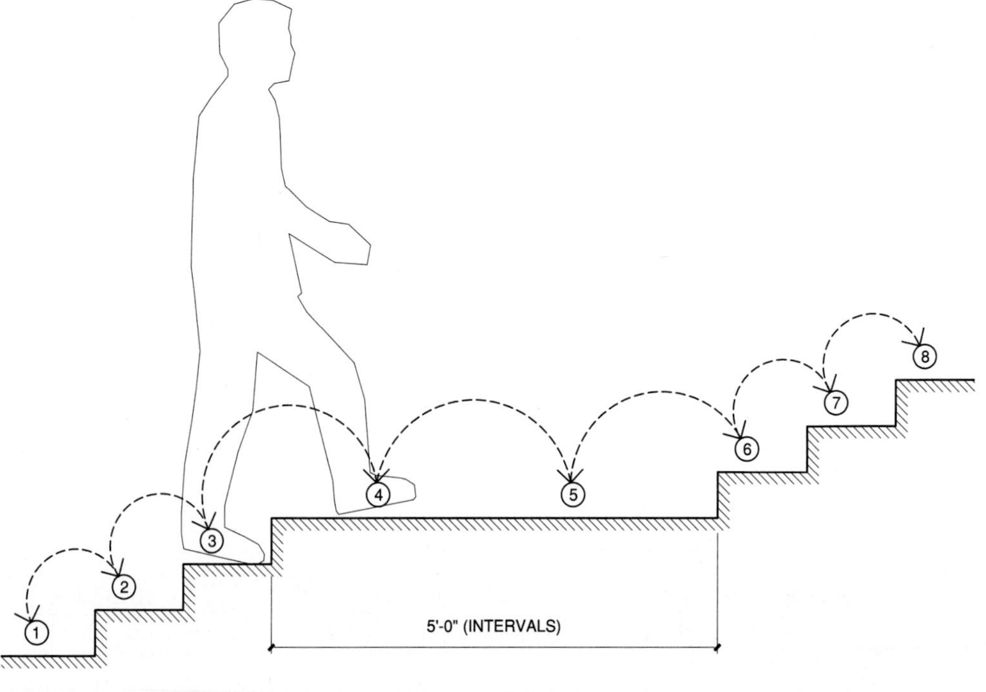

LANDING LENGTHS

David Spooner, Assistant Professor, University of Georgia, School of Environmental Design

11 risers to alleviate fatigue. Landings should occur at regular intervals along the vertical route by dividing the overall vertical change into equal segments. Generally, odd numbers of stairs, paired with regular sequenced landings, is the optimal stairway configuration for physical comfort.

Angle of Inclination

Exterior stairs generally have more gradual slopes than indoor stairs. Angles of inclination that fit the preferred riser/tread ratio of $2R + T = 24$ to 26 fall between 13 degrees and 30 degrees. Lower angles of inclination provide the sense of faster, smoother transitions over higher-angle stairways. Higher angles of inclination are more physically demanding to climb, and 50 degrees is considered to be the maximum angle of inclination for stairways. Consecutive runs of stairs in a single vertical change should have the same angle of inclination throughout their design.

Stair Nosing Dimensions

Improper nosing design on stair treads is often the cause of tripping accidents. Poured-in-place concrete stair nosings should not have abrupt edges and should not project outward more than 1½ inches beyond the base of the riser. The nosing itself should have a ½-inch maximum radius or 45-degree bevel. Brick and other stone masonry stairs should not project outward more than ½ inch beyond the base of the riser.

Shadow Lines

Shadow lines are often included within exterior stairways for aesthetic reasons and to visually mark riser locations. If improperly designed, shadow lines can be trip hazards if they are large enough to catch the toes of pedestrians. Shadow lines should have a maximum of 1½ inches or 60-degree batter from face of riser. For stairways that will be used at night, install proper lighting to illuminate the shadow line.

Stair Drainage

To avoid potential slipping hazards, standing water on stair treads should be allowed to drain off under natural conditions. This is accomplished by sloping treads at a maximum of ¼ inch per foot or 2 percent minimum) toward the nose of each tread. Sheet runoff from adjacent sites should not be allowed to cascade over steps from above, especially in colder climates where freezing is possible.

Stair Handrails

Handrail Quantity and Spacing

Building code requirements often govern handrail design, typically necessitating that stairs have continuous handrails on both sides. In stairways wider than 60 inches, intermediate handrails are desirable so that all portions of the overall width of the stairs are within 2 feet 6 inches of a handrail.

Handrail Standard Dimensions

Handrails must extend at least 12 inches beyond the top and 12 inches plus one tread width beyond the bottom of the steps, and be parallel with the floor or ground plane. The height of a handrail's gripping surface must conform to the applicable standards. Some national standards specify that the height of the handrails should be between 30 and 34 inches, measured to the top of the rail (Uniform Federal Accessibility Standards (UFAS)). Other national standards specify that the top of the handrail be measured between 34 and 38 inches above stair nosings (American National Standards Institute (ANSI)). It is important to check which standards apply to the application at hand. A handrail that measures 34 inches to the top of the rail would meet all recognized standards.

Ends of handrails must be either rounded or returned smoothly to floor, wall, or post. Handrails must have a circular cross section with an outside diameter of at least 1¼ inches, and not greater than 2 inches (although the UFAS maximum diameter is 1½ inches). The clear space between the handrail and a cheekwall must be 1½ inches. (Further information regarding stair railings can be obtained from the American's with Disability Act (ADA) and in the Americans with Disabilities Act Accessibility Guidelines (ADAAG).)

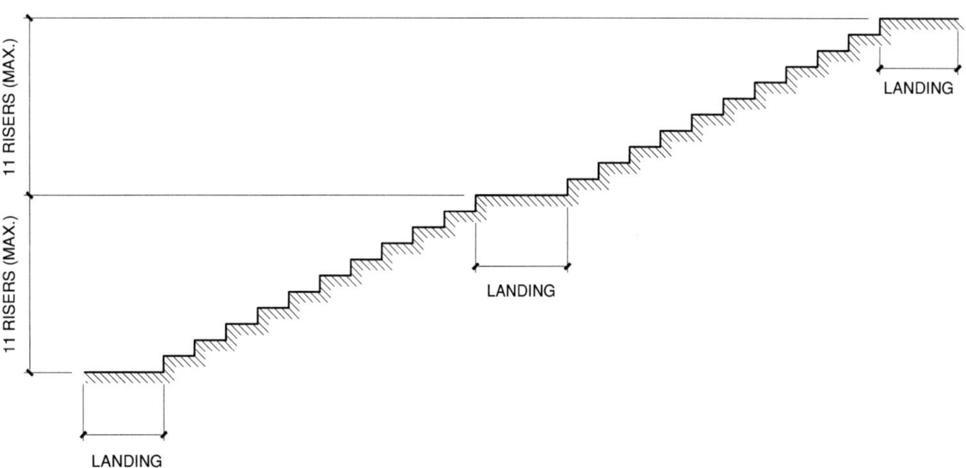

LANDING FREQUENCY

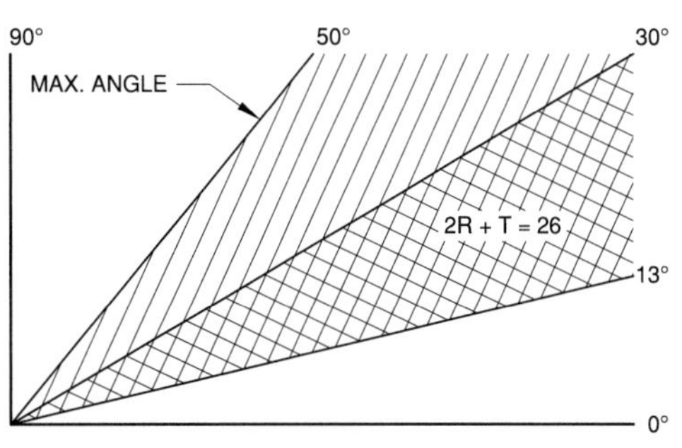

STAIR ANGLES OF INCLINATION

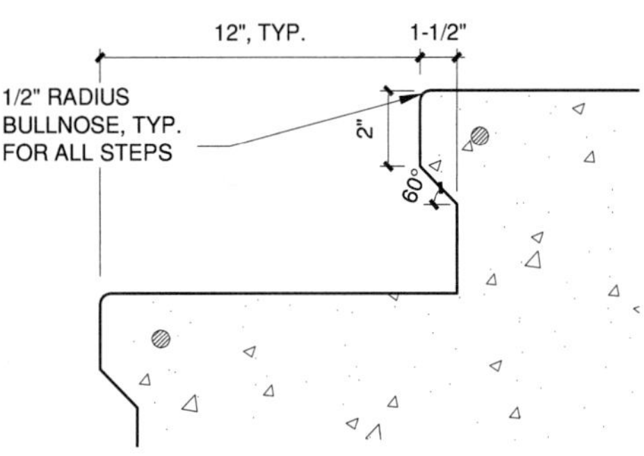

STAIR NOSING DIMENSIONS

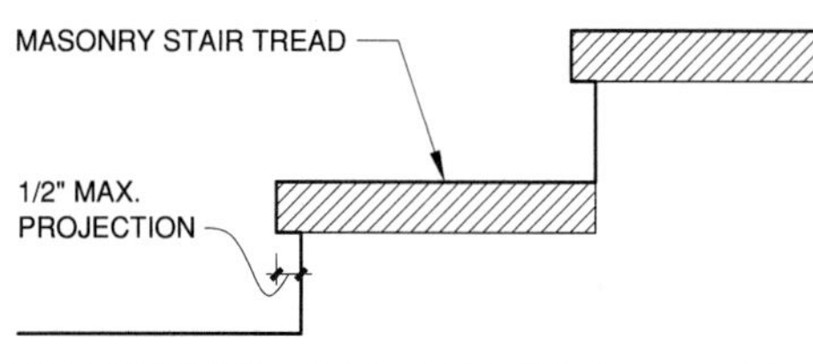

MASONRY STAIR NOSING DIMENSIONS

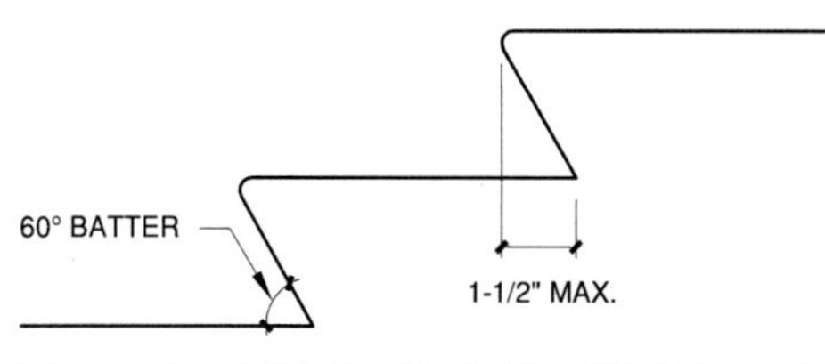

SHADOW LINE MAXIMUM DIMENSIONS

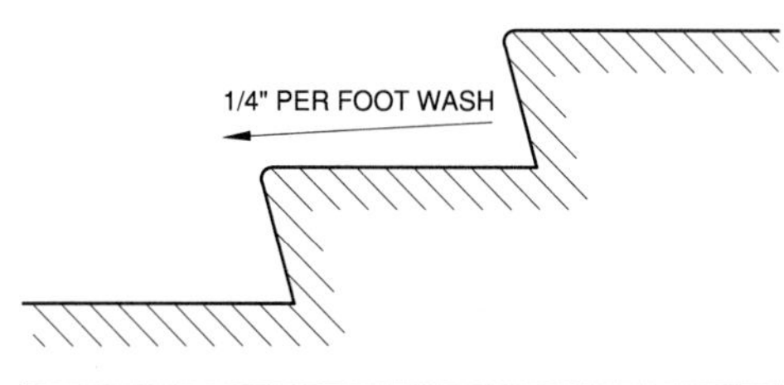

STAIR TREAD SLOPE

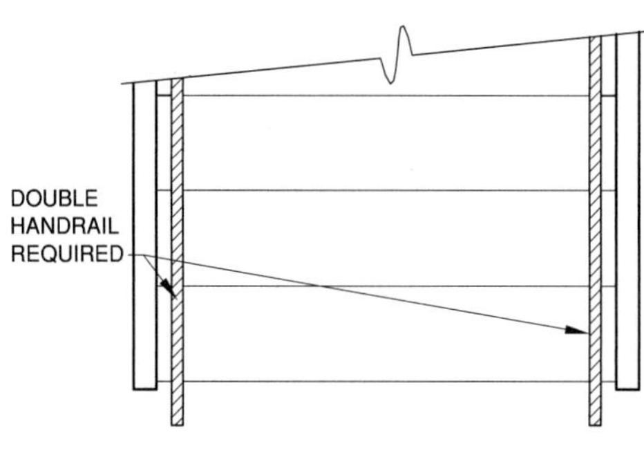

DOUBLE HANDRAIL REQUIREMENT

David Spooner, Assistant Professor, University of Georgia, School of Environmental Design

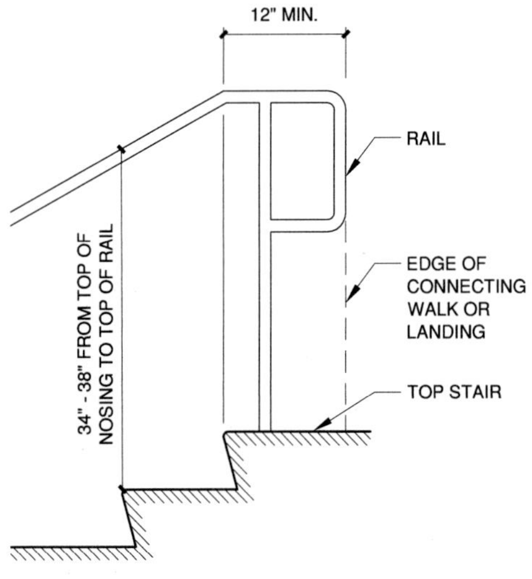

RAIL EXTENSION AT TOP

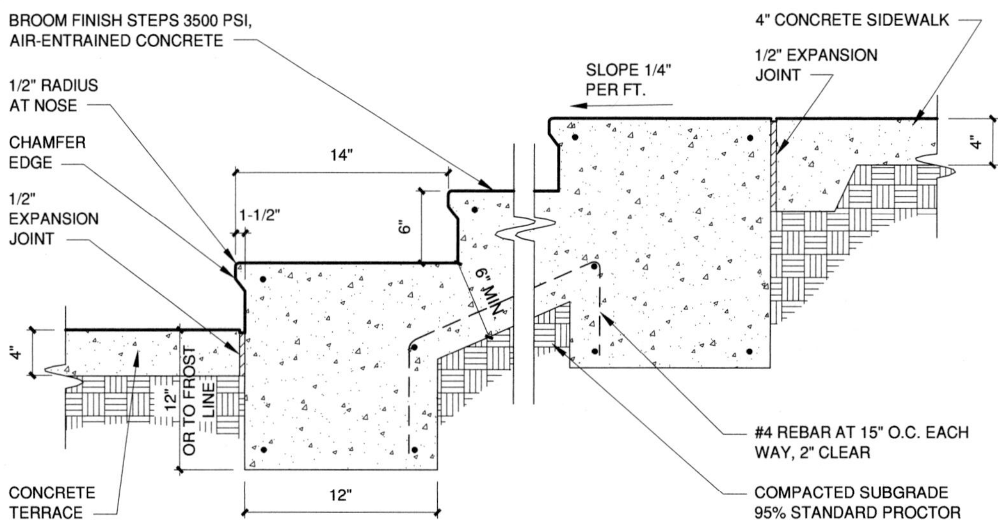

CONCRETE STEPS

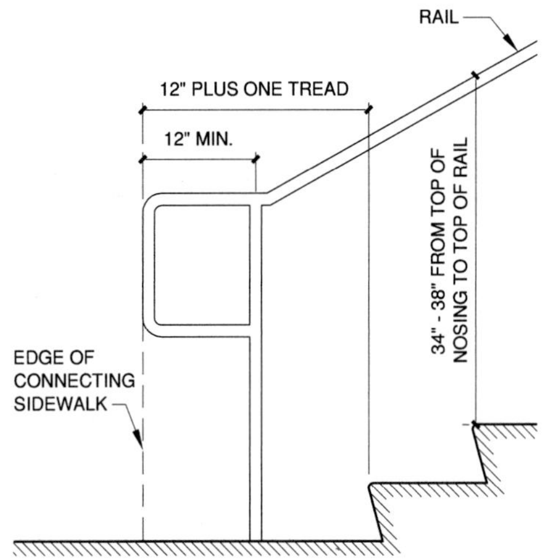

RAIL EXTENSION AT BOTTOM RAIL EXTENSION AT TOP

STAIRS: CONSTRUCTION DETAILS

Poured-in-Place Concrete Stairs

Poured-in-place concrete stairs should have the following construction characteristics:

- A footing should be no less than 6 inches thick for stairways. If constructed in colder climates, an air-entrained additive is recommended. Concrete footings should have a minimum compressive strength of 3200 psi at 28 days. Use a higher compressive-strength concrete when greater traffic loads are expected.
- The toe of concrete footings should be constructed below the frost line to prevent heaving.
- Steel reinforcing specifications vary for each construction situation. Check all local building codes before specifying size and spacing of steel reinforcement. In high traffic areas, nosing rebar is recommended.
- All treads should be slip-resistant with a medium broom finish.
- Expansion joints are needed at the base and top of the footing. Expansion joints are also needed on each side of the steps when these are constructed adjacent to cheekwalls, buildings, or other fixed objects. Seal expansion joints with a compatible joint sealing compound to prevent moisture infiltration.
- A compacted gravel or compacted soil (95 percent standard Proctor Test) subbase should be incorporated under all concrete footings.
- Concrete stairs should be formed using similar materials to ensure uniformity in size and configuration.

Masonry Stair Construction

Masonry stairs should have the following characteristics:

- A footing of no less than 6 inches thick is acceptable for stairways. If constructed in colder climates, an air-entrained additive is recommended. Concrete footings should have a minimum compressive strength of 3200 psi at 28 days. Use a higher compressive-strength concrete when greater traffic loads are expected.
- The toe of concrete footings should be constructed below the frost line.
- Steel-reinforcing specifications vary for each construction situation. Check all local building codes before specifying size and spacing of steel reinforcement. In high-traffic areas, nosing rebar is recommended.
- Expansion joints are needed at the base and top of the footing. Expansion joints are also needed on each side of the steps when these are constructed adjacent to cheekwalls, buildings, or other fixed objects. Seal expansion joints with a compatible joint-sealing compound to prevent moisture infiltration.
- Tread stones should have a minimum thickness of 2 inches and should slope ¼ inch per foot toward the nose.
- Tread surface finishes should be sufficiently textured to avoid becoming slippery when wet.
- A compacted gravel (2 inches minimum) or compacted soil (95 percent standard proctor) subbase should be incorporated under all concrete footings.

Ramp Steps

Ramp steps should have the following characteristics:

- A footing of no less than 6 inches thick is acceptable for ramp steps. If constructed in colder climates, an air-entrained additive is recommended. Concrete footings should have a minimum compressive strength of 3200 psi at 28 days. Use a higher compressive-strength concrete when greater traffic loads are expected.
- Toe of concrete footings should be constructed below the frost line.
- Steel reinforcing specifications vary for each construction situation. Check all local building codes before specifying size and spacing of steel reinforcement. In high-traffic areas, nosing rebar is recommended.
- Expansion joints are needed at the base and top of the footing. Expansion joints are also needed on each side of the steps when these are constructed adjacent to cheekwalls, buildings, or other fixed objects. Seal expansion joints with a compatible joint-sealing compound to prevent moisture infiltration.
- A compacted gravel (2 inches minimum) or compacted soil (95 percent standard Proctor Test) subbase should be incorporated under all concrete footings.
- Ramp steps should be spaced in multiples of average human strides, typically (27 to 30 inches).
- Ramp steps should have gentle slopes between risers, typically 2 percent (minimum) to 5 percent (maximum).
- All riser heights, tread lengths, and tread slopes should be uniform throughout a consecutive run of stairs.

Wood Timber Stair Construction

Wood timber stairs should have the following characteristics:

- Various sizes of wood timber (4 inches by 4 inches, 6 inches by 6 inches, 8 inches by 8 inches) can be used in various configurations to create risers between 4 and 7 inches. However, used alone, a 6-by-6-inch timber (nominal dimension of 5½ inches square) is an ideal riser height.
- Wood material should be naturally weather-resistant or pressure-treated to prevent rotting.
- Timbers can be held in place by drilling vertical holes (24 to 48 inches on center) and inserting a 30-to-36-inch galvanized or corrosion-resistant bar.

David Spooner, Assistant Professor, University of Georgia, School of Environmental Design

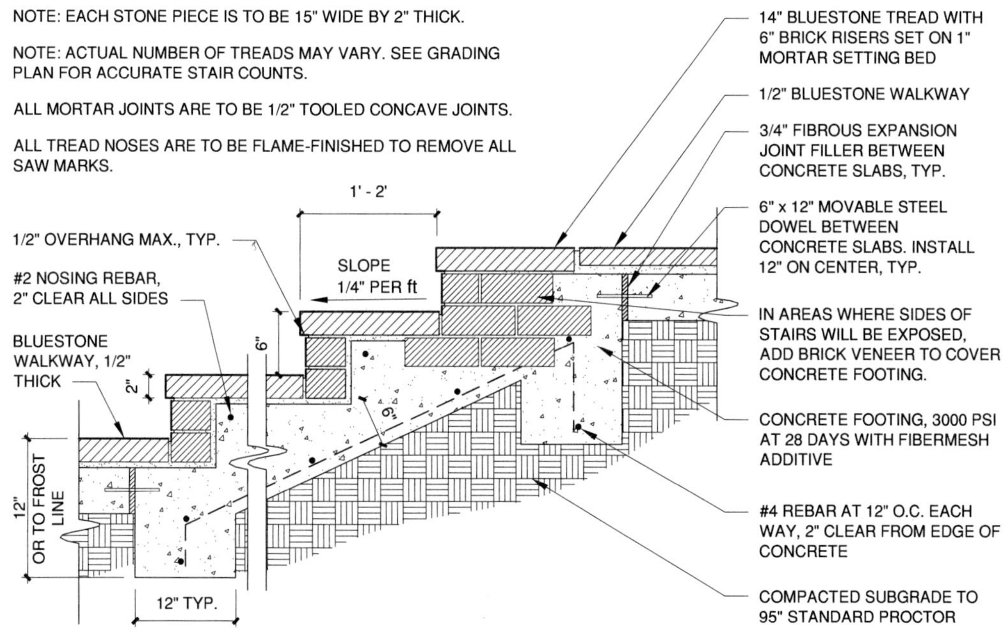

STONE TREADS WITH BRICK RISER

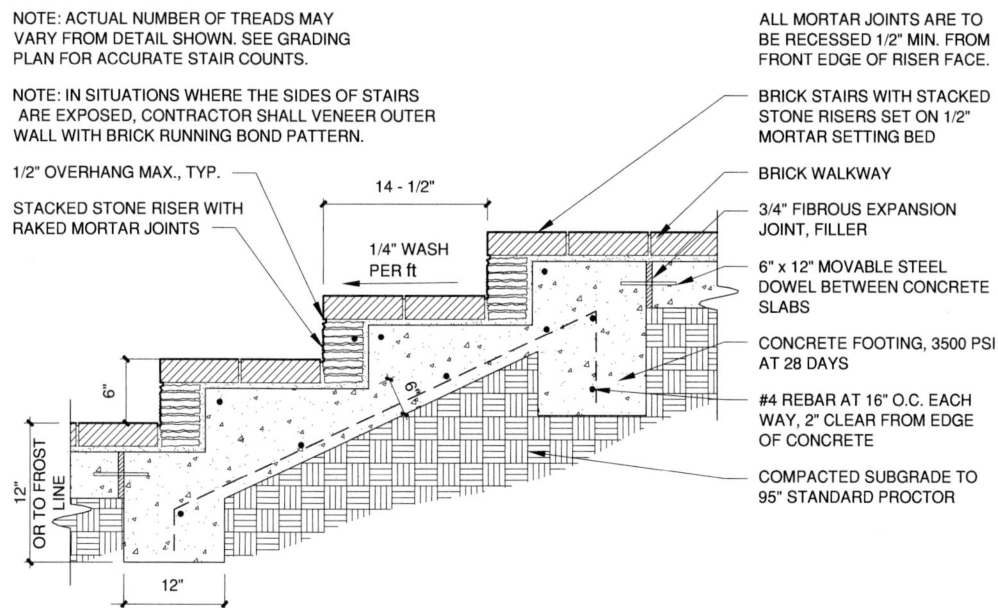

BRICK TREADS WITH STACKED STONE RISER

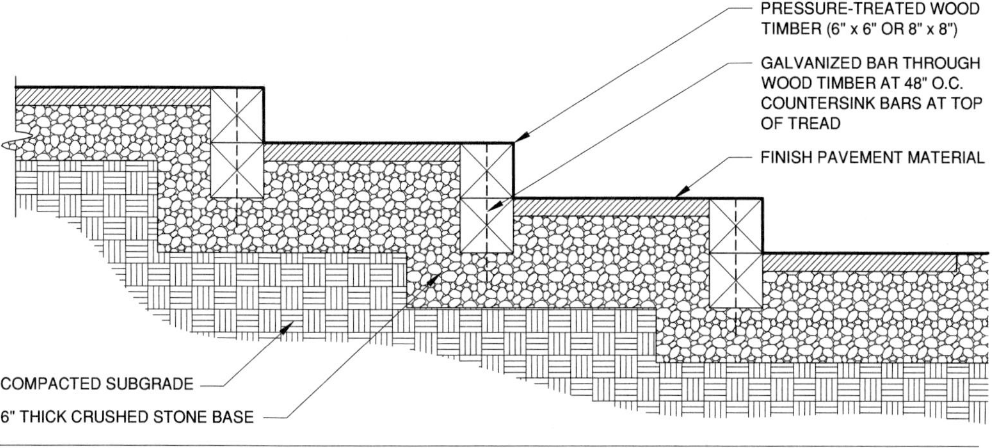

WOOD TIMBER STAIRS WITH MASONRY TREADS

David Spooner, Assistant Professor, University of Georgia, School of Environmental Design

- Side edges of timber stairs must be held in place by an edge restraint to prevent erosion of subbase and surface material.

RAMPS: GENERAL

Any part of an accessible route in the public domain with a slope greater than 1:20 (5 percent) is considered a ramp and must conform to ADA design guidelines. For the average pedestrian, a slope of 20 percent is considered the maximum slope comfortable to walk on. Ramps should be constructed of paving material the same thickness and type as adjacent surfaces, unless visual cues are desired to differentiate elevation changes. In such cases, use both visual and textural cues to warn pedestrians of the ramp and upcoming change in elevation. The finish surface of any ramp should be coarse enough to prevent accidental slippage when the pavement is wet. Adequate lighting should be provided during nighttime hours. (Further information regarding ramp safety and design standards can be obtained from the American's with Disability Act (ADA) and the Occupational Safety and Health Association (OSHA).)

Ramp Slope

As much as existing grade will allow, the least possible slope should be used for any ramp. In situations where the slope exceeds 5 percent, ramps are necessary and must conform to ADA standards. The maximum slope must be 1:12 (8.33 percent) for a maximum distance of 30 feet, with one exception: ramped curb cuts at crosswalks, which can be steeper 1:8 (12 percent) if the running distance is less than or equal to 3 feet. The flared sides of curb ramps should be 1:10 (10 percent) if the ramp protrudes into a walkway and pedestrian traffic is expected to cross the ramp. This degree of slope can increase if there is 48 inches or less of level landing area above the curb ramp.

Ramp Clear Width

A ramp's clear width is the dimension that specifies the overall ramp opening that is free from protruding objects. Ramp clear widths are determined according to the type and intensity of use. One-way pedestrian travel requires a minimum clear width of 36 inches, and two-way travel requires a clear minimum width of 5 feet.

Ramp Landings

Ramp landings are areas of transition that signal the beginning and ending of grade changes along steep circulation routes. Ramps should have level landings at the top and bottom of each ramp segment. Ramps longer than 30 feet should have a landing in between each 30-foot ramp segment to allow for pauses when negotiating long slopes. (Refer to the Americans with Disabilities Act Accessibility Guidelines (ADAAG) for a comprehensive compilation of dimensional criteria, as well as to all applicable state and local codes.) According to the Americans with Disabilities Act, all landings should have the following features:

- Landings should be at least as wide as the ramp leading to it.
- Landings should have a minimum clear length of 60 inches from the end of the ramp.
- Landings should have a minimum clear length of 60 inches by 60 inches if the ramps change direction.
- Landings shall have a 2 percent maximum cross slope for drainage purposes.

8.33% MAX
1
12
MAXIMUM SLOPE

5% MIN
1
20
MINIMUM SLOPE

MAXIMUM AND MINIMUM SLOPE FOR RAMPS

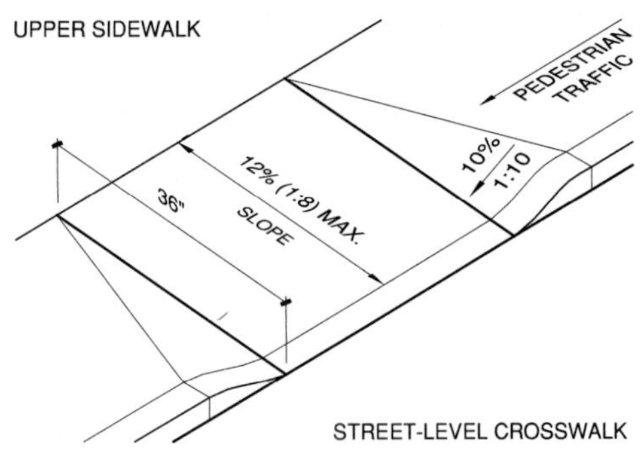

MAXIMUM RAMP SLOPE FOR CURB RAMPS

Cross slopes on ramp landings are necessary to provide adequate drainage to prevent water from pooling on the surface. The cross slope of ramp surfaces must be no greater than 1:50, or 2 percent. Ramp surfaces must be stable, compact, and otherwise slip-resistant. Ramps in more natural or primitive areas should not have a cross slope of more than 3 percent (see *Accessibility* and *Access to the Outdoor Setting*).

Ramp Edge Protection

Ramps and landings where the edges drop off to a lower finish grade should have curbs, walls, railings, or other vertically projecting elements to prevent people from slipping and falling off the ramp edge. Edge protection should be a minimum of 2 inches (UFAS) or minimum of 4 inches (ANSI) in height (use applicable standard). Railing heights or curb and railing combinations should fall between 30 and 34 inches (UFAS) or 34 and 38 inches (ANSI). Height of walls depends on specific site conditions.

Handrails at Ramps

If a ramp run has a rise greater than 6 inches or a horizontal projection greater than 72 inches, it should have handrails on each side. Handrails are not required on curb ramps at street intersections. (Refer to the Americans with Disabilities Act Accessibility Guidelines (ADAAG) for a comprehensive compilation of dimensional criteria and to all applicable state and local codes.) According to the Americans with Disabilities Act, all handrails must have the following features:

- Handrails must be provided along both sides of ramp segments. The inside handrail on switchback or dogleg ramps must always be continuous.
- If handrails are not continuous, they must extend at least 12 inches (305 mm) beyond the top and bottom of the ramp segment and be parallel with the floor or ground surface.

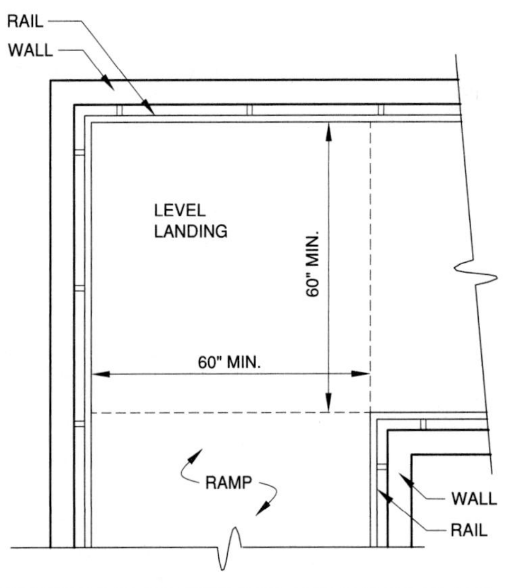

MINIMUM CLEAR WIDTH AT LANDING WITH 90-DEGREE TURN

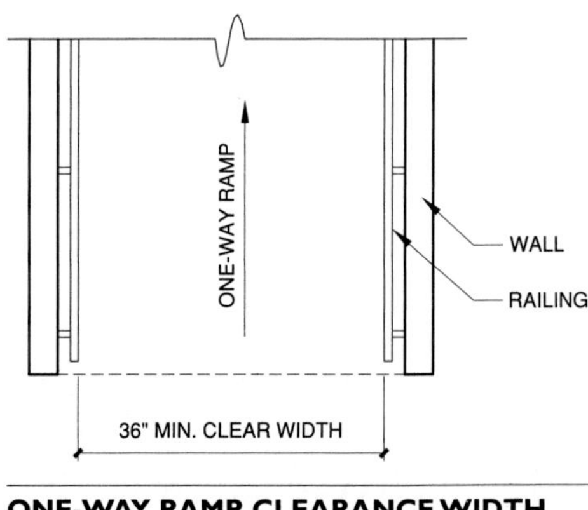

ONE-WAY RAMP CLEARANCE WIDTH

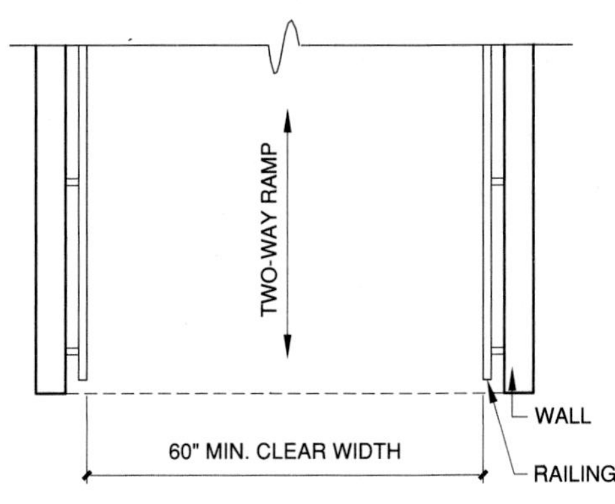

TWO-WAY RAMP CLEARANCE WIDTH

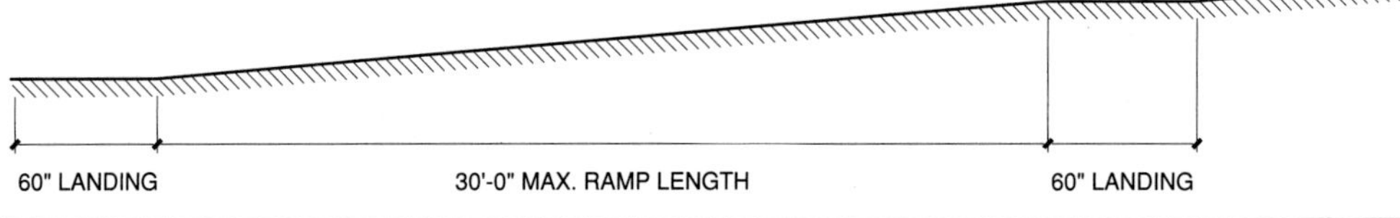

RAMP LANDING FREQUENCY

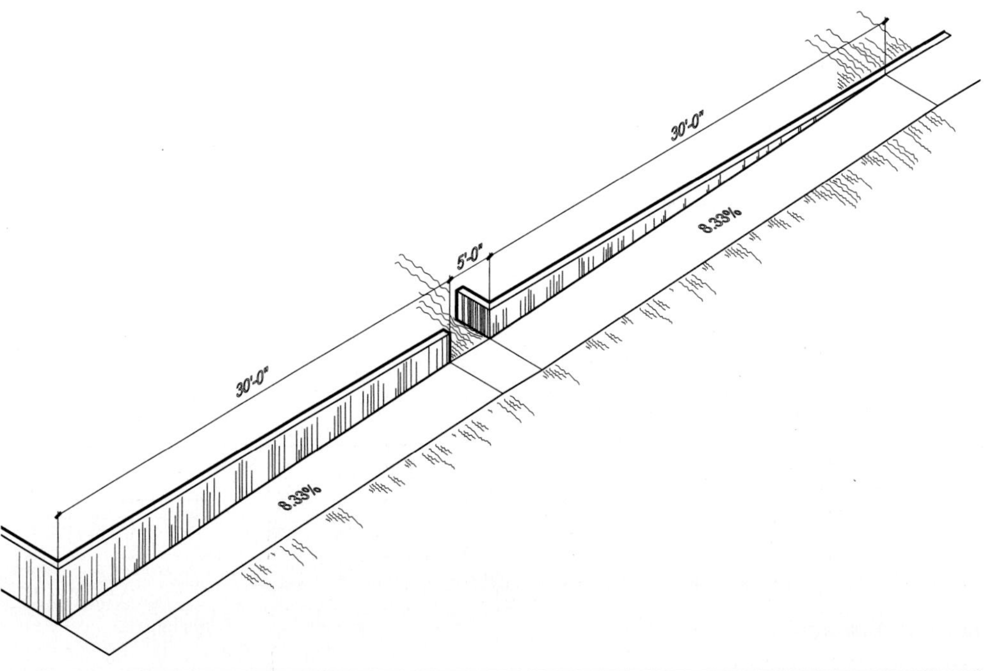

ADA RAMP (PERSPECTIVE)

David Spooner, Assistant Professor, University of Georgia, School of Environmental Design

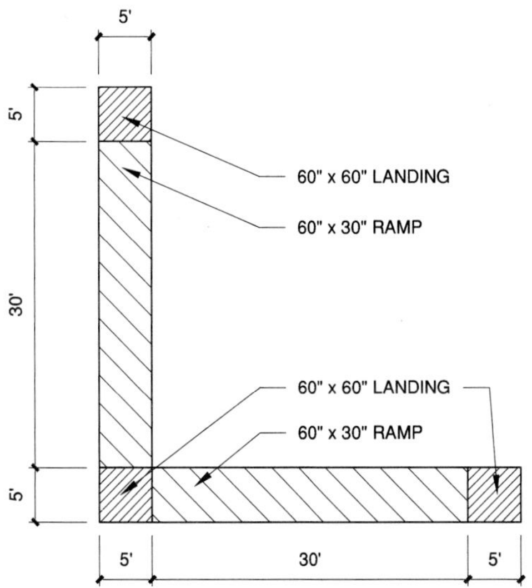

ADA RAMP (PLAN VIEW)

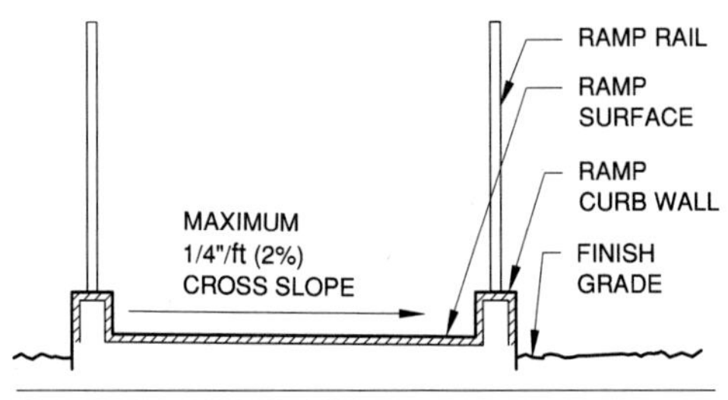

RAMP CROSS SLOPE

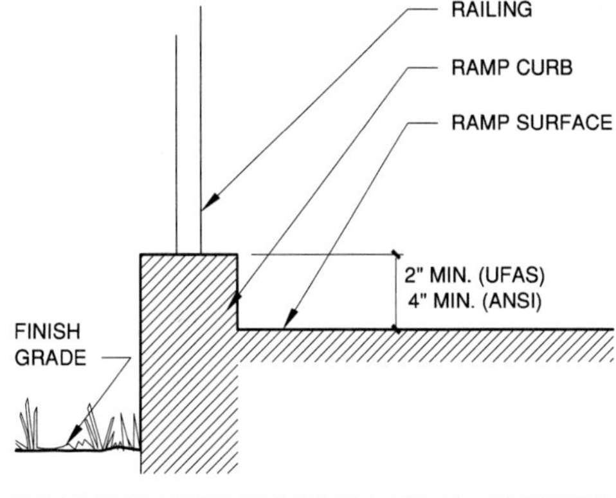

RAMP EDGE PROTECTION (CURB AND RAIL)

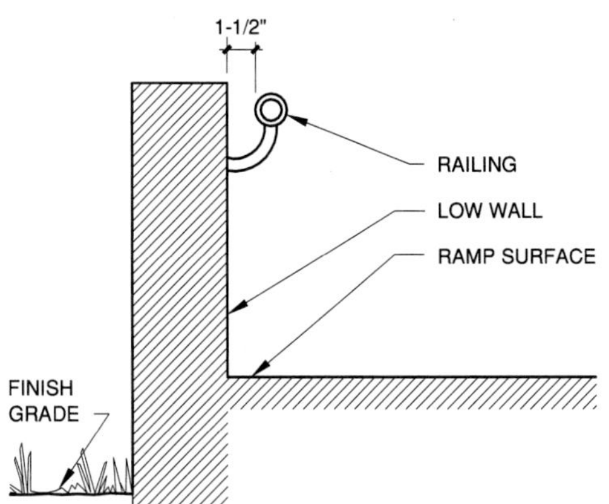

RAMP EDGE PROTECTION (LOW WALL)

- The clear space between the handrail and the wall must be 1½ inches (38 mm).
- Gripping surfaces must be continuous.
- Top of handrail gripping surfaces must be mounted between 30 and 34 inches (UFAS) and between 34 and 38 inches (ANSI) above ramp surfaces.
- Ends of handrails must be either rounded or returned smoothly to floor, wall, or post.
- Handrails must not rotate within their fittings.

Curb Ramps

Curb ramps are small, short ramps that provide accessible transitions at street curbs and other short elevation changes.

- Curb ramps should be provided wherever an accessible route crosses a curbed street or intersection.
- The maximum slope of a curb ramp must be 1:12, or 8.33 percent.
- Transitions from ramp surfaces to adjacent walks or streets should be smooth, flush connections that are free from abrupt changes.
- The minimum width of a curb ramp is 3 feet, exclusive of flared sides.
- Curb ramps should have flared sides if pedestrian access across the ramp is desired. The maximum slope of the flare should be 1:10, or 10 percent. In situations where the distance between the end of the ramp and a fixed object is less than 48 inches, the flare should be no more than 1:12, or 8.33 percent.
- Curb ramps without pedestrian access occurring across the ramp may contain steeper sides or vertical curbs to retain planting areas.

Wood Ramp Construction

All wood ramp construction should have the following characteristics:

- All wood board materials should be pressure-treated or be cut from naturally rot-resistant wood (cedar, redwood, etc).
- All metal fasteners should be hot-dip-galvanized or contain a corrosion-resistant finish.
- All wood post footings should be installed below frost line depth.
- Beam and joist sizes and lengths vary depending on structural load and length of span. Consult local building codes.

Concrete Ramp Construction

All concrete ramp construction should have the following characteristics:

- Steel reinforcing specifications vary for each construction situation. Check all local building codes before specifying size and spacing of steel reinforcement.
- All ramp surfaces should be slip-resistant with a medium broom finish, perpendicular to the direction of travel.
- Expansion joints are needed at the base and top of the ramp. Expansion joints are also needed on each side of the ramp when these are constructed adjacent to cheekwalls, buildings, or other fixed objects. Seal expansion joints with a compatible joint-sealing compound to prevent moisture infiltration. A compacted gravel or compacted soil (95 percent standard Proctor Test) subbase should be incorporated under all concrete ramps.
- Transitions from ramp surfaces to adjacent walks, gutters, or streets should be smooth, flush connections that are free from abrupt changes.

Masonry Ramp Construction

All masonry ramp construction should have the following characteristics:

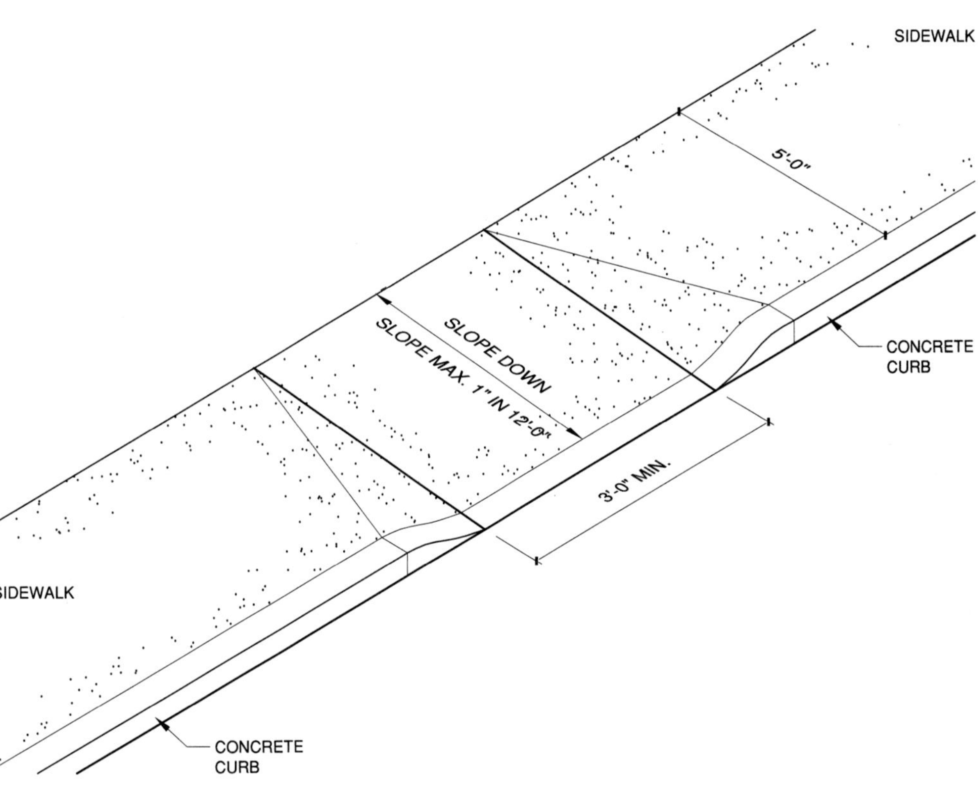

CONCRETE CURB RAMP

David Spooner, Assistant Professor, University of Georgia, School of Environmental Design

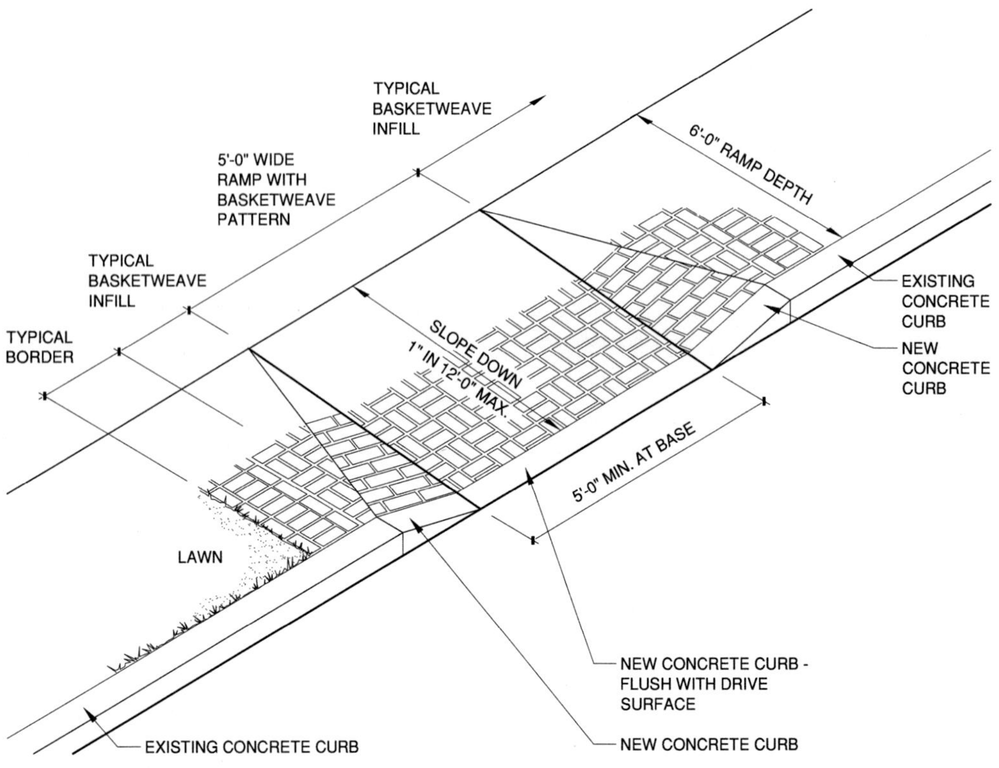

BRICK CURB RAMP

- Masonry ramps should be constructed of paving material the same thickness and type as adjacent surfaces, unless visual or textural cues are desired to differentiate elevation changes. In such cases, use both visual and textural cues to warn pedestrians of the ramp and upcoming change in elevation.
- Steel reinforcing specifications vary for each construction situation. Check all local building codes before specifying size and spacing of steel reinforcement.
- Expansion joints are needed at the base and top of the ramp. Expansion joints are also needed on each side of the ramp when these are constructed adjacent to cheekwalls, buildings, or other fixed objects. Seal expansion joints with a compatible joint-sealing compound to prevent moisture infiltration. A compacted gravel or compacted soil (95 percent standard proctor) subbase should be incorporated under all ramps.
- Transitions from ramp surfaces to adjacent walks, gutters, or streets should be smooth, flush connections that are free from abrupt changes.

CURBS: GENERAL

Curbing has both functional and aesthetic purposes in the landscape. Functionally, curbing helps direct stormwater, serves as a vehicular traffic control device, and separates incompatible uses (e.g., vehicular traffic and pedestrians). Aesthetically, curbing defines the edges in the landscape that serve as transitions from one type of space to another.

Concrete and asphalt are the most frequently used curbing materials due to their low cost and flexibility to form. Single-unit materials such as stone, brick, steel, and wood are also commonly used materials for curbing. They are typically more expensive to install and their flexibility to fit specific forms is more restricted. There are several types of curb configurations, from simple vertical curbs to combination vertical curb and gutter to a mountable rolled curb and gutter. The intensity and type of use dictates the material and design of the curb.

Anticipated vehicular traffic loads should be carefully considered to determine the best material, design, and structural integrity for the curb. Higher traffic loads will require stronger curbs with more steel reinforcement.

Concrete Curbs

Concrete curbs have the following characteristics and design criteria:

- Concrete curbs are tough, durable, long-lasting, and can be relatively inexpensive to install.
- The size and configuration of concrete curbs depends on anticipated traffic load, strength, and bearing capacity of the subsoil, climatic conditions, and compressive strength of the supporting aggregate materials.
- Concrete curbs can be molded into various shapes and forms over long distances, and are suitable for complicated curbing layouts.
- The minimum compressive strength of concrete curbing is 3200 psi at 28 days. Higher compressive-strength concrete should be specified in heavy-use areas.
- Concrete curing should occur between 40 and 80 degrees Fahrenheit, whenever possible.
- Air-entraining agents can be incorporated in concrete mixes to reduce the effects of freeze/thaw cycles.
- Steel-reinforcing specifications vary for each construction situation. Check all local building codes before specifying size and spacing of steel reinforcement.
- Install expansion joints every 25-30 linear feet on center.
- Slope concrete curb and gutter to collect and transmit stormwater into its desired location.

Asphalt Curbs

Asphalt curbs have the following characteristics and design criteria:

- Asphalt curbs have a medium durability and can be relatively inexpensive to install.
- The size and configuration of asphalt curbs depend on anticipated traffic load, strength, and bearing capacity of the subsoil, climatic conditions, and compressive strength of the supporting aggregate materials.
- Asphalt curbs can be molded into various shapes and forms over long distances and are suitable for complicated curbing layouts.
- Asphalt curbs are susceptible to deformation when struck with heavy loads, therefore they should be reinforced with a compacted solid granular material, backfilled behind and under the curb.
- Asphalt curbs are typically used for edging and directing stormwater, and are not recommended as wheel stops.

Granite/Stone Curbs

Granite and stone curbing have the following characteristics and design criteria:

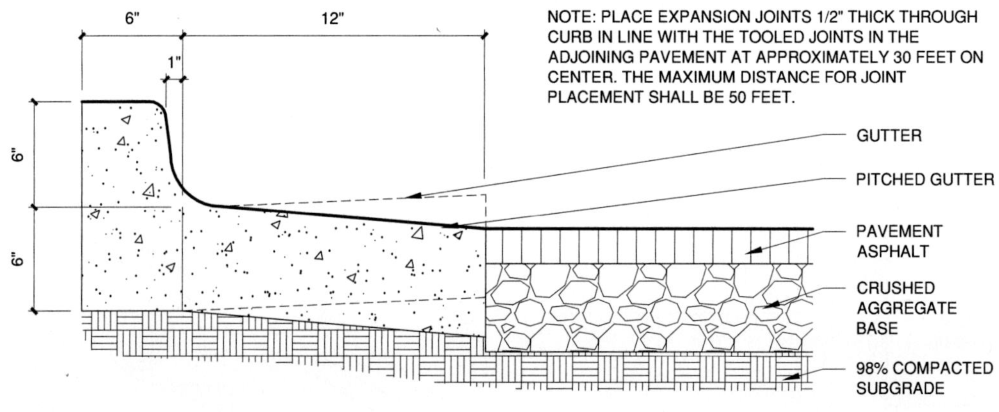

CONCRETE CURB AND GUTTER

David Spooner, Assistant Professor, University of Georgia, School of Environmental Design

- Granite curbs are tough, durable, and long-lasting, but can be expensive to install.
- Granite curbing is used in high-traffic areas with high vehicular loads.
- Granite does not deteriorate from the use of salts or chemicals that are commonly used in snow conditions.
- Individual granite block stones are used for medium- and lower-intensity traffic areas.
- The finish surface can be either split-face or sawn and polished, depending on aesthetic preference.
- Granite cobble or curbing should be installed on a compacted gravel subbase, mortar setting bed, or reinforced concrete base, depending on anticipated vehicular traffic loads.
- Mortar should be used to fill vertical joints between individual granite stones.

Brick Curbs

Brick curbing has the following characteristics and design criteria:

- Brick curbing has a medium durability and can be relatively inexpensive to install.
- Specify high-quality, severe weather (SW) grade bricks in colder climates where freeze/thaw cycles are prevalent. Hollow-core bricks should not be used for curbing applications.
- Reinforce brick curbs with a concrete subbase or mortar setting bed.
- Mortar is used to fill vertical joints between individual bricks.
- Use brick with higher compressive strength in high vehicular traffic areas.

Wood Curbing

Wood curbing has the following characteristics and design criteria:

- Wood curbing has a low durability and can be relatively inexpensive to install.
- Use pressure-treated lumber or wood with natural resistance to decay and rot.
- Drill pilot holes through wood members and install vertical metal stakes up to 24 inches deep 36 to 48 inches on center.
- Backfill against wood curbing with mortar or compacted soil to secure curb in place.
- Install wood curb on 4- to 6-inch gravel subbase.
- Wood curbing is used primarily as an edging device and is not recommended for use as wheel stops.

Steel Edging

Steel edging has the following characteristics and design criteria:

- Steel edging has a low durability and can be relatively inexpensive to install.
- Steel edging is available in many thicknesses, ranging from ⅛ to ¼ inch. Thicker edging is used in heavier traffic situations.
- Steel edging can be specified in various heights, ranging from 4 to 6 inches, depending on design intent.
- Install support stakes every 30 inches on center or as directed by manufacturer.
- Steel edging should be made of a noncorrosive metal or be coated to withstand corrosive weathering processes.
- Install steel edging according to manufacturer specifications and directions.

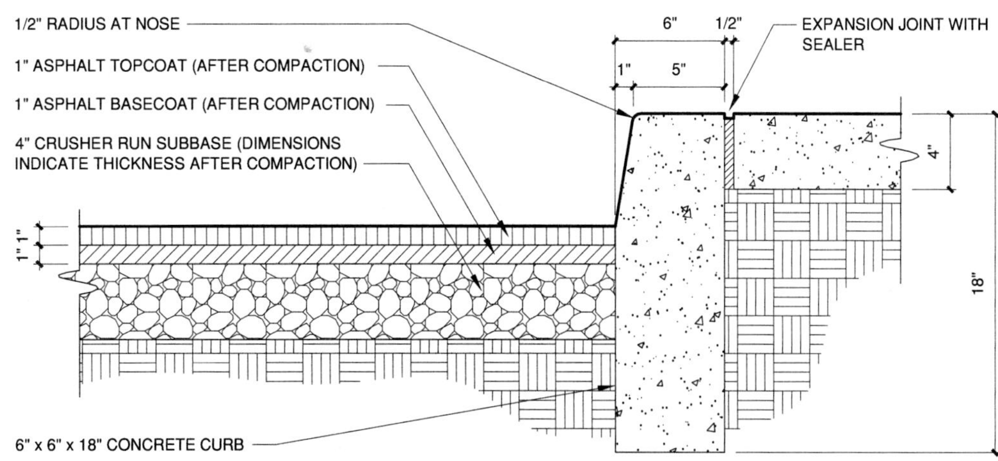

ASPHALT PAVING AND CONCRETE CURB

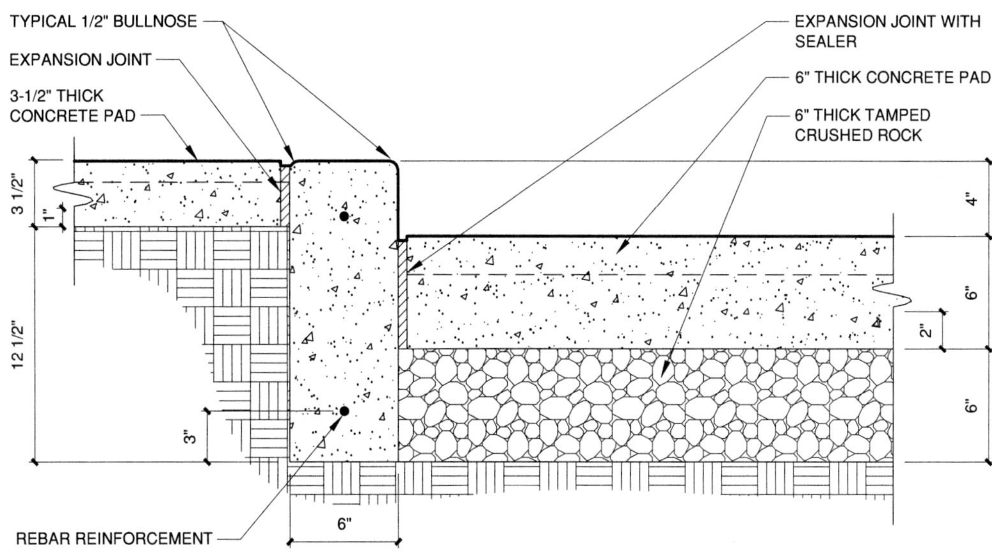

CONCRETE CURB WITH REBAR REINFORCEMENT

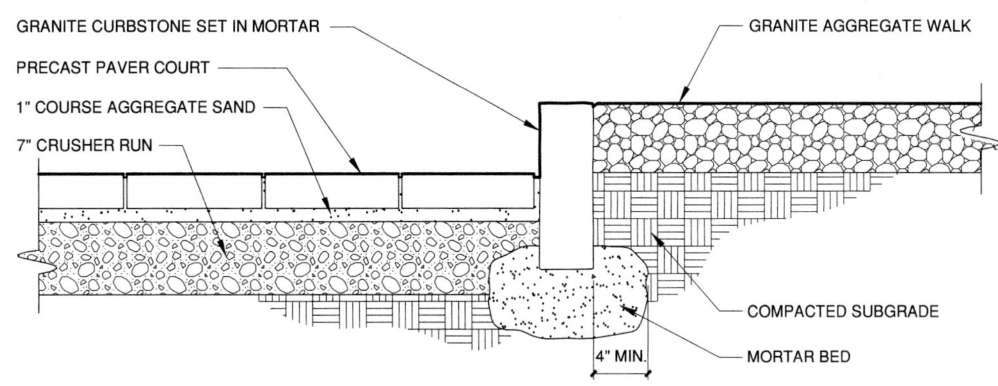

GRANITE CURB WITH MORTAR SETTING BED

David Spooner, Assistant Professor, University of Georgia, School of Environmental Design

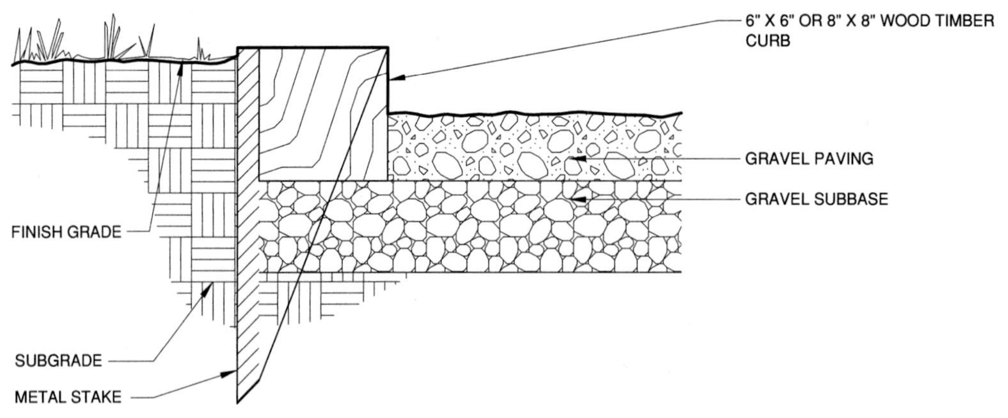

WOOD CURBING

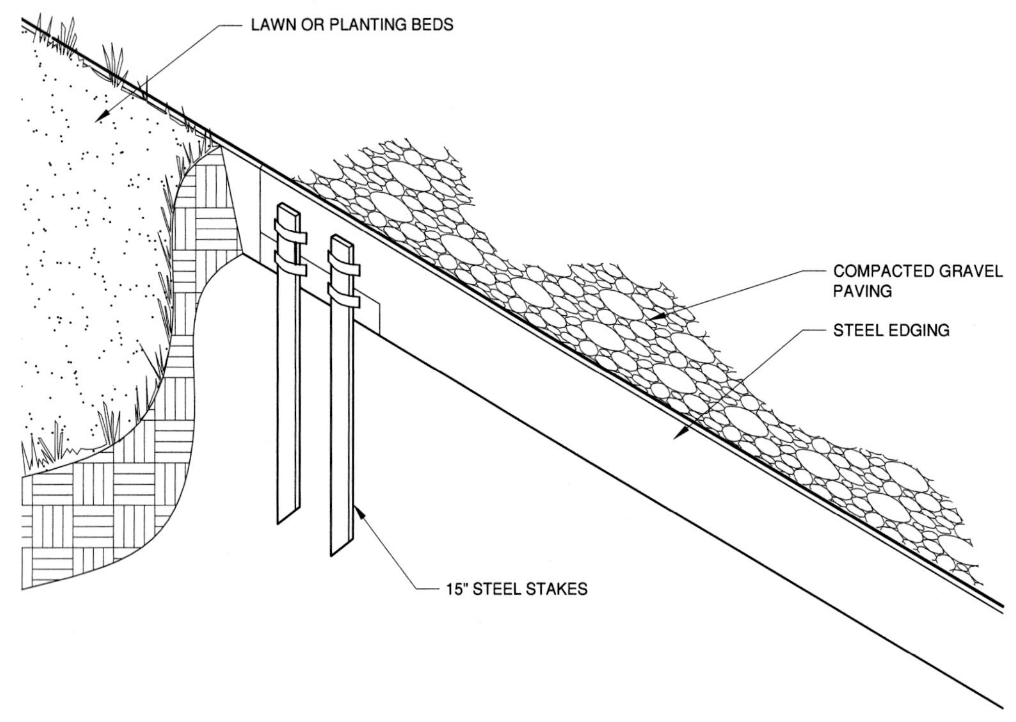

STEEL EDGING

David Spooner, Assistant Professor, University of Georgia, School of Environmental Design

TYPICAL DETAILS

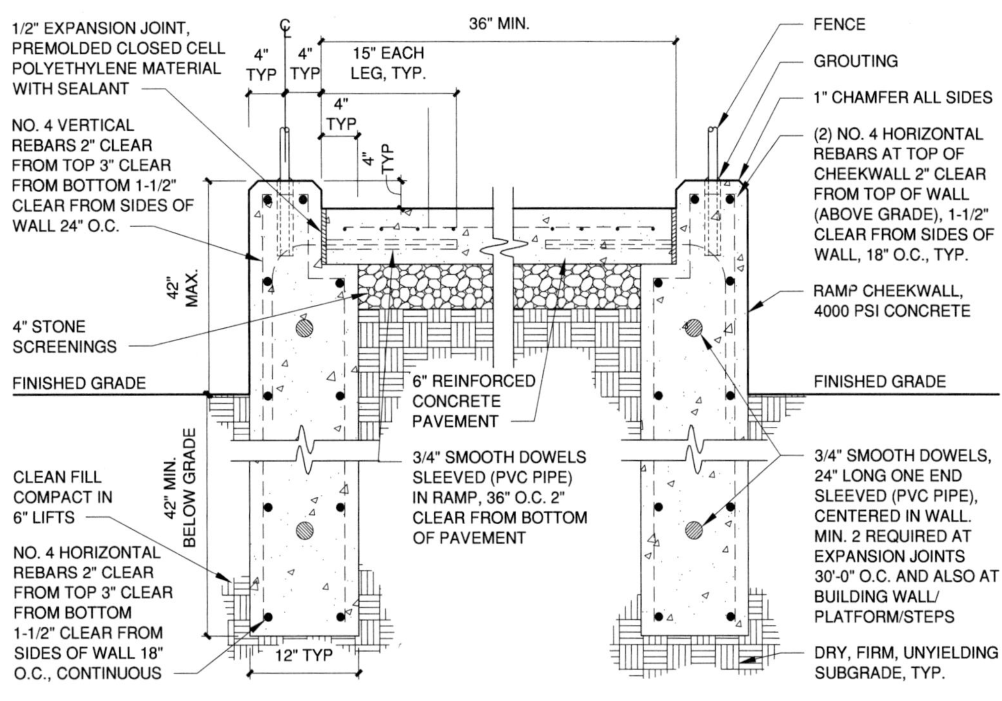

CONCRETE RAMP AND CHEEKWALLS

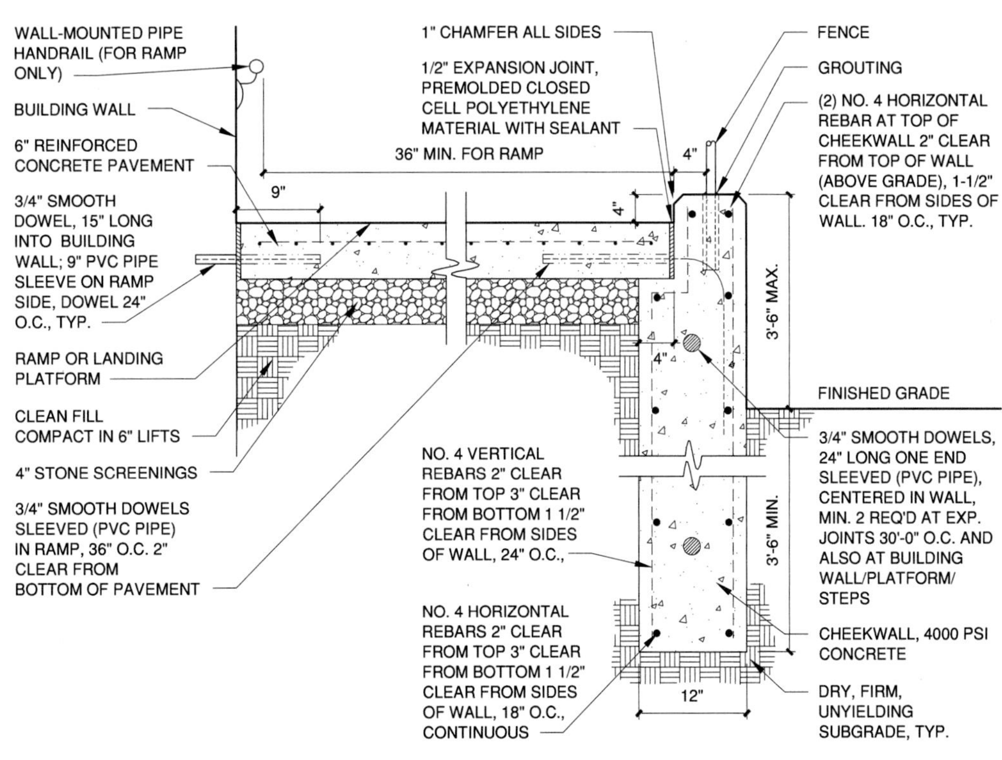

CONCRETE CHEEKWALL AND RAMP OR LANDING PLATFORM AT BUILDING WALL

RAMPS

Leonard J. Hopper, RLA, FASLA

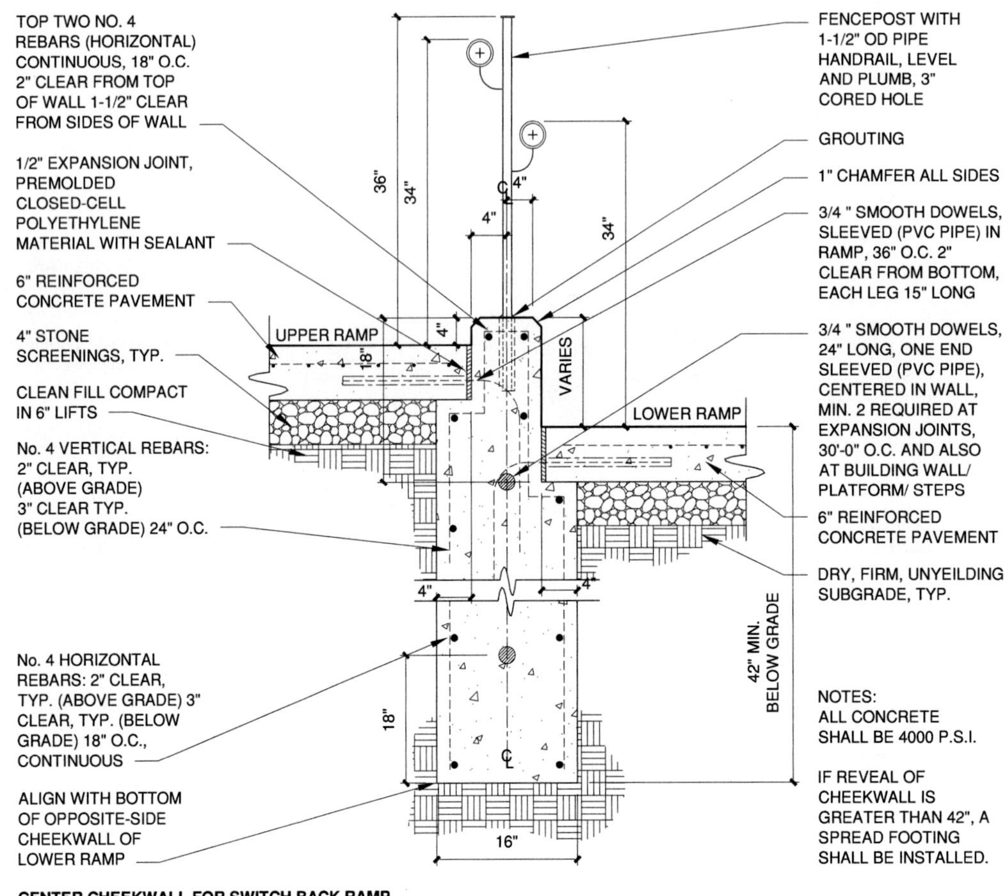

CENTER CHEEKWALL FOR SWITCH BACK RAMP

RAMPS *(continued)*

REFERENCES

Americans with Disabilities Act (ADA). 1990. Washington, DC: U.S. Department of Justice, Civil Rights Division, Disability Rights Section-NYAV.

Americans with Disabilities Act Accessibility Guidelines (ADAAG). 1991. Washington D.C.: U.S. Department of Justice.

Beckstrom, Robert, J. 1985. *Deck Plans.* San Ramon, CA: Ortho Books.

Walker, Theodore, D. 1992. *Site Design and Construction Detailing,* 3rd ed. New York: Van Nostrand Reinhold.

Leonard J. Hopper, RLA, FASLA

FREESTANDING AND RETAINING WALLS

Freestanding walls are exterior, nonload-bearing structural elements. Walls are one of the most significant and versatile tools for the architectural definition of outdoor space, as they serve many functions, including screening, enclosure, ornamentation, sound attenuation, security barriers, and traffic direction.

Factors influencing the design of a freestanding wall include the following:

- Stability and resistance to lateral loads from wind pressure
- Material used
- Wall configuration
- Type and location of control and expansion joints and reinforcement
- Moisture protection
- Desired color, texture, and pattern

Freestanding, nonload-bearing walls are generally not considered reinforced walls even though they may contain horizontal steel reinforcement to control cracking and vertical reinforcement to tie panels to footers. Additional steel reinforcement is necessary in walls located in regions susceptible to unusual conditions such as hurricanes, earthquakes, and other elements that involve unanticipated forces on walls or wall foundations. It is recommended that in unusual circumstances such as these, a structural engineer be consulted regarding the design of the wall.

TYPES OF FREESTANDING WALLS

Solid Walls

Solid walls are usually composed of poured-in-place concrete or single and multiple "wythes" of brick, concrete, or stone masonry structurally bonded together. A wythe is one vertical layer of brick courses. Walls can be made of single, double, or triple wythes. Structural bonds between single or multiple wythes are provided by masonry headers, unit wall ties, and/or continuous horizontal joint reinforcements.

The traditional bonding method for solid walls has been the transverse overlapping of adjacent wythes of continuous courses of masonry headers. Most codes require that masonry headers compose a minimum of 4 percent of the wall face and that the maximum vertical and horizontal spacing be 24 to 36 inches. Another accepted guideline calls for one header course for every seven courses of masonry. For sufficient bonding to take place between wythes, each header must extend 3 to 4 inches into the next wythe.

Historically, the use of masonry bonding led to various traditional masonry patterns, including English and Flemish bonds. At present, masonry bonding is seldom used due to the increased popularity of horizontal steel reinforcement and cost. The National Concrete Masonry Association (NCMA) recommends the use of continuous horizontal steel reinforcement and unit ties because of the superior moisture protection provided and greater flexibility against differential movement between wall wythes. Evidence exists, however, of deterioration of metal unit ties over time in hurricane-prone and humid environments due to rust and corrosion.

A pier and panel wall consists of intervals of panels of single- or double-wythe masonry set between piers or pilasters. This two-part wall system can be adapted very easily to varying topographies and around existing elements by offsetting the piers. The pier and panel system is commonly used for the construction of highway corridor sound barriers. Although relatively economical thanks to the reduced wall thickness and ease of construction, the single-wythe pier and panel wall is less reliable in high wind conditions and expansive soils than multiple-wythe walls.

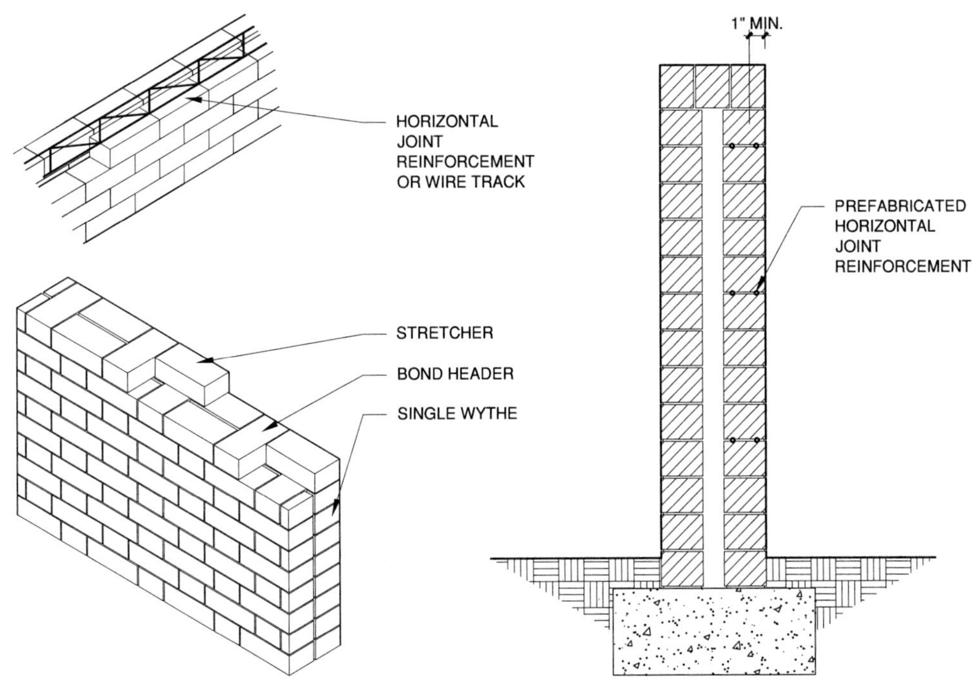

MASONRY BONDING AND STEEL REINFORCEMENT IN A SOLID WALL

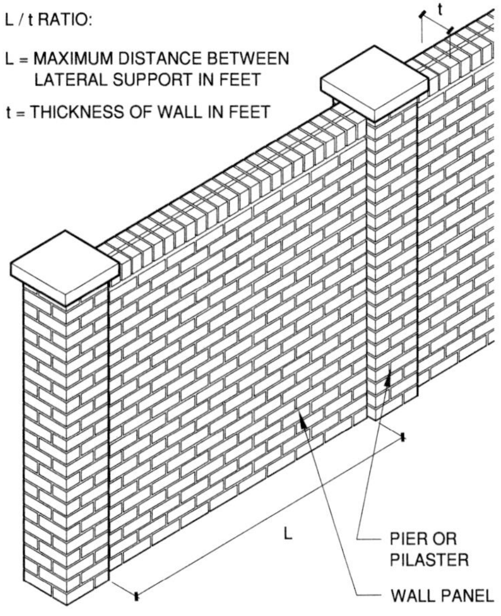

THE L/t RATIO FOR FREESTANDING WALLS

The function of the piers in the pier and panel system is to share the transfer of dead loads of the wall and the lateral wind loads absorbed by the panels to the footer and ground. Sufficient bonding and anchorage between the wall panel and the pier are critical for sufficient resistance to wind pressure and any other horizontal force. Pier footers should contain horizontal reinforcement that is properly lapped with vertical reinforcement in the concrete masonry piers.

The finished dimension of a pier should be twice the wall thickness. For example, an 8-inch double-wythe brick wall should have piers with a finished dimension of 16 by 16 inches. Landphair and Klatt (1979) recommend that the unsupported height for piers not exceed 10 times their least cross-sectional dimension and 4 times for unfilled hollow masonry units. The minimum depth of the pier footer below grade should be equal to twice the depth of the panel footer below grade. The pier should be reinforced with a minimum of four No. 4 rebars.

The serpentine wall is a structural and aesthetic wall alternative. The geometry of the undulating curves or folded plates of the serpentine configuration creates the necessary lateral stability without the pilaster and other reinforcement required for straight walls. The height of the serpentine wall can be greater than straight walls with no reinforcement or lateral support. The traditional serpentine wall consists of a single masonry wythe in a running bond.

The mechanics of serpentine wall stability is most often based on the ratio of the wall curve radius and depth of curvature to the wall height. The design proportion for walls 6 feet or less in height requires that the radius of the wall curve not exceed twice the height. The depth of curvature between curves should be no less than one-half the height of the wall.

Janice Cervelli-Schach
Credits: Thanks to R. V. Cervelli for his assistance on the structural mechanics calculations.

Cavity Walls

A cavity wall is a drainage-type structure that is recommended in areas of high moisture and freeze-thaw cycles. An additional advantage of this type of wall is the flexibility it provides regarding bonding patterns, moisture/rain protection, and "efflorescence." Efflorescence is an unsightly white, crystalline substance that forms on the surface of masonry as a result of movement and evaporation of soluble salts contained in the material. Interesting profile and shadow patterns can also be accomplished by recessing and projecting units or by incorporating other decorative materials into the wall.

Cavity walls consist of two masonry wythes continuously separated by a 2- to 4-inch airspace. The cavity acts to conduct water down the inside face of one wythe to continuous flashing or weep holes at the bottom of the cavity, where it is diverted outside the wall. The two wythes of the wall are tied together for stability by corrosion-resistant metal ties embedded in each wythe, enabling the two to act as a unit. Current masonry construction recommends metal tie bonding over masonry bonding cavity walls due to the superior moisture resistance and flexibility to absorb differential movements between wall wythes.

The NCMA and the Brick Institute of America (BIA) recommend that adjacent wythes be bonded together with galvanized or copper-coated steel, 3⁄16-inch diameter, or equivalent metal wire (No. 9 gauge) ties placed into the horizontal joints. It is important to ensure that corrosion-proof ties be used, or staining may appear on the face of the wall. Metal ties should never be placed closer than within 1 inch of the outside of the wall to ensure adequate mortar cover. Ties should be staggered, with a maximum vertical spacing of 18 inches and maximum horizontal spacing of 36 inches. Codes generally require one tie for every 4.5 square feet of wall area. Ties should be located at a maximum spacing of 3 feet apart in all directions and no farther than 12 inches from the perimeter of expansion joints.

It is critical that weep holes be located in the head joints of the wythe, slightly above the flashing, and spaced every 2 feet on center, or 16 inches on center if no wick material is being used. The simplest method of construction is to eliminate every second or third head joint. Inorganic, absorbent wick material is placed in the weep hole to conduct moisture from inside the wall.

Veneer Walls

A type of cavity wall, veneer walls provide an economical alternative for a stable and attractive wall. The veneer wall utilizes a minimum 1-inch airspace between the two wythes of the wall to allow proper drainage. The veneer wall consists of a single-wythe stone or brick veneer anchored with metal ties to a solid concrete or, most commonly, a concrete block backing.

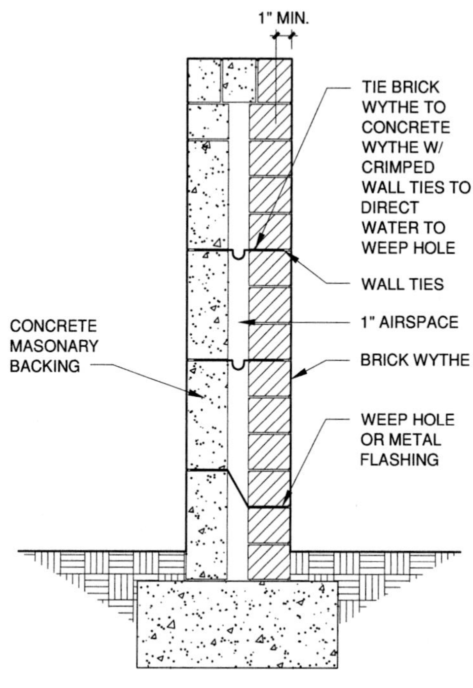

VENEER WALL

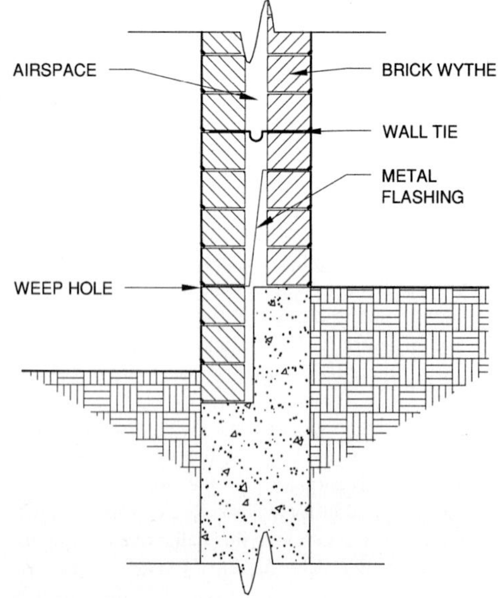

CAVITY WALL

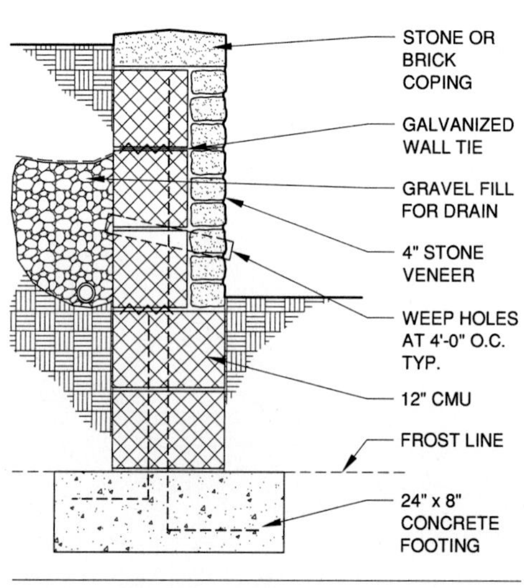

STONE VENEER WALL

Veneer anchor ties are typically 7⁄8-inch-wide, 22-gauge corrugated galvanized steel strips. The wrinkles in the metal strip increase the bonding between the mortar and the steel. The BIA recommends veneer anchor ties every 2⅔ square feet of wall area, or one tie for every third wall course.

Most codes require a spacing of 16 inches vertically and 32 inches horizontally. A minimum 2-inch embedment of the tie into the joints of the veneer and the backup is required to maintain a strong anchor. Care should be taken during installation to ensure that all ties receive a minimum 1-inch mortar cover to prevent deterioration.

WALL MATERIALS

Poured-in-Place Concrete

Poured-in-place concrete walls are not commonly used as freestanding walls in the landscape due to the relative attractiveness and economy of cavity and veneer masonry walls. Objections to poured-in-place concrete walls focus on the relatively high cost of construction and relative lack of options for reuse. The finish of concrete walls can be enhanced using the following techniques:

- Bush hammering
- Sandblasting
- Creating various reliefs from the outlines left by the rough-cut or sandblasted plywood formboards used to cast the wall
- Inserting rubber mats or wood strips inside the form
- Applying an exposed aggregate finish

Recently, new glass-infused concrete products have been introduced that utilize recycled glass as aggregate material in various concrete pavements. The structural integrity of these new mixes for use in landscape walls has not been widely tested.

Concrete Masonry

Prefaced concrete masonry units offer a wide selection of different colors, patterns, profiles, and textures, in addition to the standard plain block. Units are manufactured in even and dappled colors, smooth or textured faces, and glazed or unglazed surfaces. Unit dimensions vary in thickness, height, and shape.

Interesting patterns can be achieved in walls by combining vividly colored glazed, ribbed, grooved, vertically scored, and split-face block, or by combining an exotically shaped bullnose block with a standard plain block, painted or unpainted. The advantage of the profile and exposed aggregate blocks over plain block for exterior use is that the irregular surface effectively masks the staining effects of atmospheric pollution and the normal wear and tear of the urban environment. Reused and recycled masonry units, both concrete and brick, are available and provide an environmentally responsible alternative.

An environmentally friendly alternative masonry block, the Autoclaved Cellular Concrete (ACC) Block, has been recently reintroduced in the United States. ACC Block was first patented in the United States in 1914 and successfully marketed in Europe. It is currently being tested for national building code approval. The ACC Block is made by mixing fly ash

Janice Cervelli-Schach
Credits: Thanks to R. V. Cervelli for his assistance on the structural mechanics calculations.

(a by-product of electrical utilities), portland cement, aluminum powder, and water, and then cured in a pressurized steam chamber otherwise known as autoclaving.

Brick

Brick plays both an aesthetic and structural role in wall design. Available in a rich palette of colors, textures, and dimensions, brick can vary from kiln-fired, molded to wire-cut to air-cured, adobe mud.

Bricks can be laid in several positions in a wall, depending on their structural role. The position of the brick will determine whether the brick needs to be a construction brick (with holes) or a solid brick. For example, a brick used as a cap must be solid. Those used as stretchers are generally construction brick. The most common are header, soldier, shiner, rowlock, and sailor.

Brick bond patterns include the following:

- *Running.* Used in cavity and veneer walls; the simplest pattern
- *Common.* Similar to running, with header course after every five to seven courses after six courses for Flemish headers
- *English.* Alternating courses of stretcher and headers
- *Stack-brick.* Units do not overlap and thus require metal ties and steel reinforcement along horizontal joints
- *Flemish*
- *Flemish cross*
- *Flemish diagonal*
- *English cross or Dutch*
- *Garden bond*

Stone

Stone masonry provides either an integral or an applied wall finish in various patterns, colors, textures, and grains. The most common stone masonry walls are 4- or 8-inch cavity or veneer walls. Less common is the 18-inch-thick, double-faced solid dry-laid free stone wall with masonry bonding.

Dry-laid stone walls are generally constructed of either irregular-shaped or squared stone. Walls of squared stone are skillfully pieced together with smaller chips and flint stones fitted between the larger course stones. This interlocking arrangement results in a very stable condition. The core of the wall is packed with small stones or chips to render the required weight for stability. Longer bonding stones are turned transversely to serve as ties through the wall. For walls constructed of more rounded rubble stone, a batter is recommended of generally 1½ inches per 12 inches of wall height. A "batter" is a slight slope on the face of the wall that recedes from wall bottom to top.

The foundation of a free stone wall is constructed to be horizontal, but the top of the wall is sloped to follow the lay of the land. The traditional free stone wall was laid "dry," that is with no mortar between the joints. Free stone walls use either a random rubble or a coursed rubble stone pattern. Random rubble has no apparent coursing; coursed rubble has relatively continuous courses and horizontal bed joints.

Cavity and veneer stone walls typically use random rubble (no apparent coursing), coursed rubble (continuous horizontal bed joints), or coursed ashlar patterns (cut-faced stone with ranged coursing and broken bond). The stone used is more dressed relative to the rubble wall stone. Stacked freestanding gabion walls filled with coursed or random rubble stone are gaining in popularity. Greater wall heights are possible without a batter as long as the steel cage remains intact.

As with the solid wall, the pointing of the veneer wall can also be recessed to give the appearance of a "dry" wall. The typical facing joint for an ashlar wall is ⅜- to ¾-inch wide. Some types of stone, such as sandstone, are especially porous or light-colored, and care must be taken in the detailing of the wall to avoid the use of corrosive metal ties and mortars that stain the stone face.

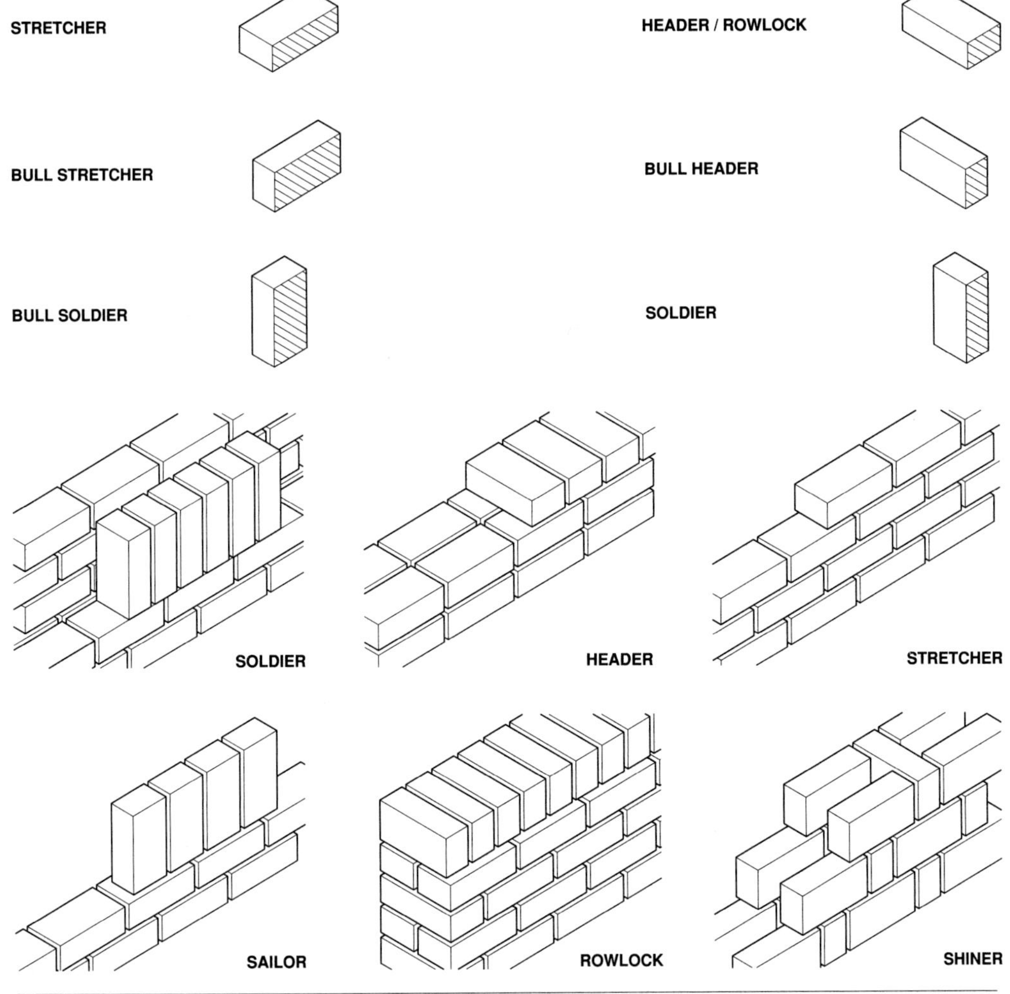

VARIOUS BRICK POSITIONS IN WALL

Stucco

Stucco provides a great deal of textural and color variety in wall design. Since stucco sets slowly, a great variety of textures and patterns can be created on the surface coat with any number of tools, including gloves, combing tools, rubber sponges, a cork float, or a wire brush.

Stucco, otherwise known as portland cement plaster, is a mixture of portland cement, hydrated lime, aggregate, and water. Stucco is typically used as a veneer material in moderate to warm climates due to susceptibility to temperature extremes, including freezing, excessive heat, and direct sun exposure. Recent formulations have increased resistance to rapid freeze-thaw cycles and expanded the zone of use of this material. Stucco can be applied either as an integral part of the wall or onto a wall-backing material, such as metal reinforcement or stucco mesh.

Poured-in-place concrete and concrete masonry walls serve as good bases for the direct application of stucco if the surfaces are sufficiently rough and clean to serve as a good mechanical key and create a strong chemical bond.

The application of stucco onto surfaces that are not suitable bases or onto a wood or steel frame requires a continuous sheet of metal reinforcement or stucco mesh of a minimum weight of 1.8 pounds/square yard. Stucco mesh should have openings of ¾ inch by 3 inches to allow the stucco to be forced all the way through to the backing wall. Complete embedment of the mesh is essential to ensure a strong bond and protect the mesh from exposure to moisture. Corroded mesh can weaken the bond and stain the wall face.

In using stucco, as with other types of wall material, consideration must be given to the potential for moisture penetration, corrosion of reinforcement, and stresses due to expansion and contraction. Stucco is especially susceptible to spalling and separation in

Janice Cervelli-Schach
Credits: Thanks to R. V. Cervelli for his assistance on the structural mechanics calculations.

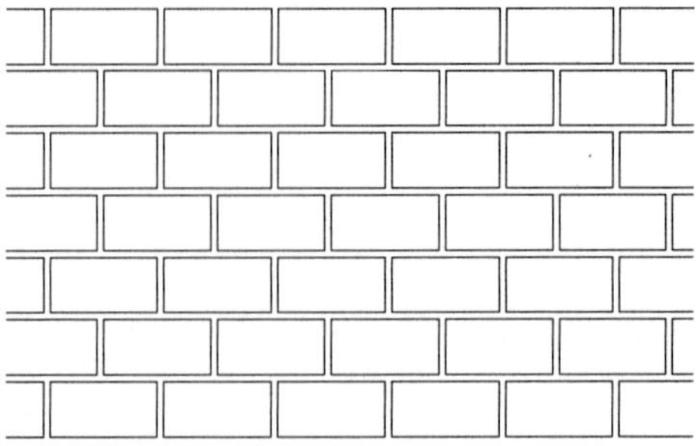

RUNNING BOND 8" X 16"

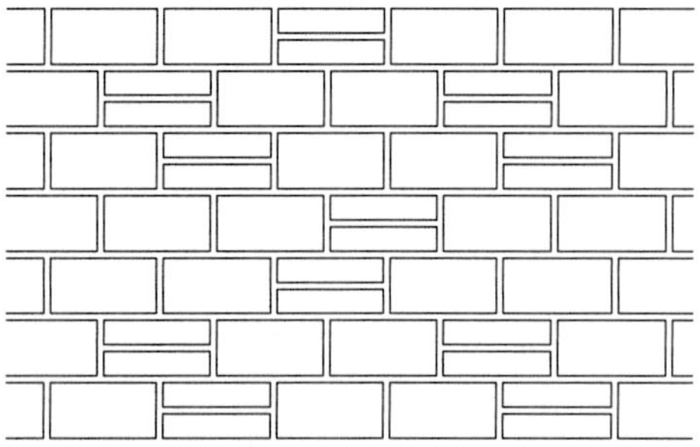

COURSED ASHLAR 4" x 6", 8" x 16"

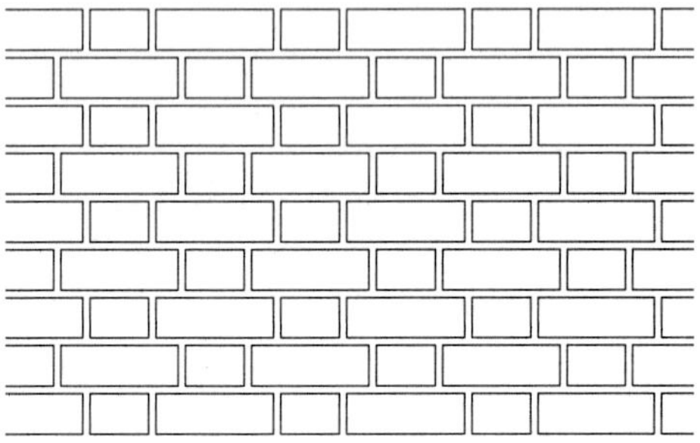

FLEMISH BOND

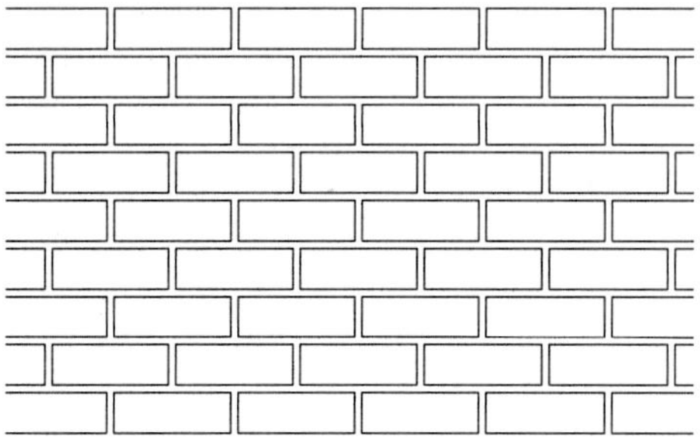

RUNNING BOND (1/2 LAP)

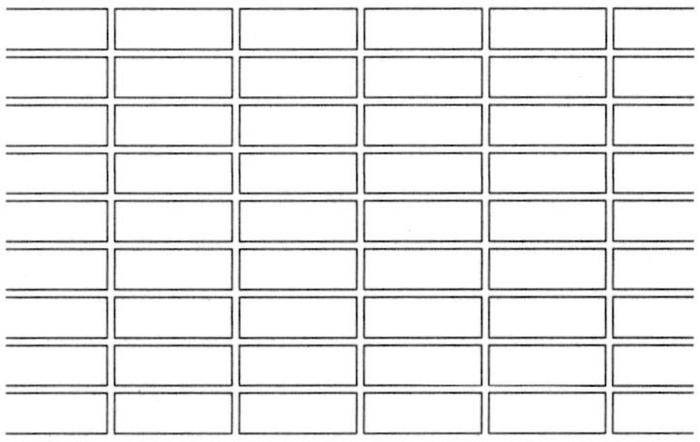

STACK BOND

COMMON BOND

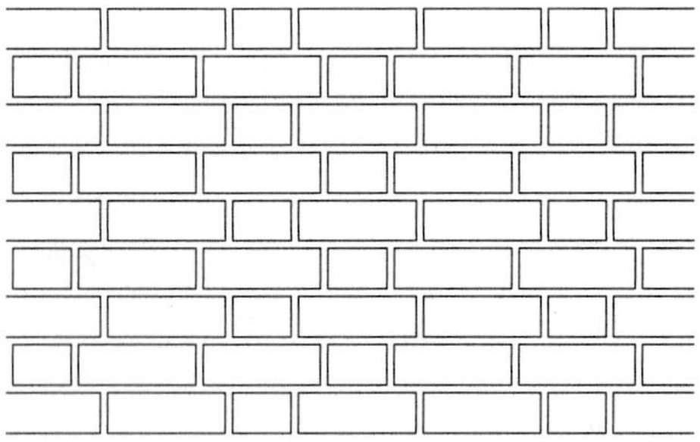

DOUBLE STRETCHER GARDEN BOND

ENGLISH BOND

CONCRETE MASONRY BOND PATTERNS

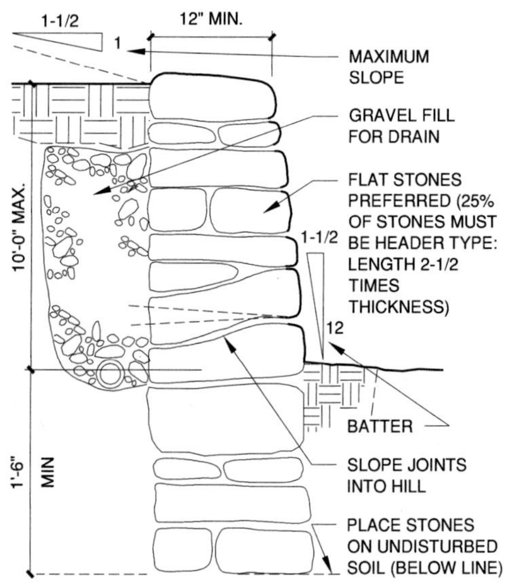

NOTE:
STAGGER VERTICAL JOINTS FROM COURSE TO COURSE 6" MIN. HORIZONTALLY. THE THICKNESS OF THE WALL AT ANY POINT SHOULD NOT BE LESS THAN HALF THE DISTANCE FROM THAT POINT TO THE TOP OF THE WALL

DRY STONE WALL

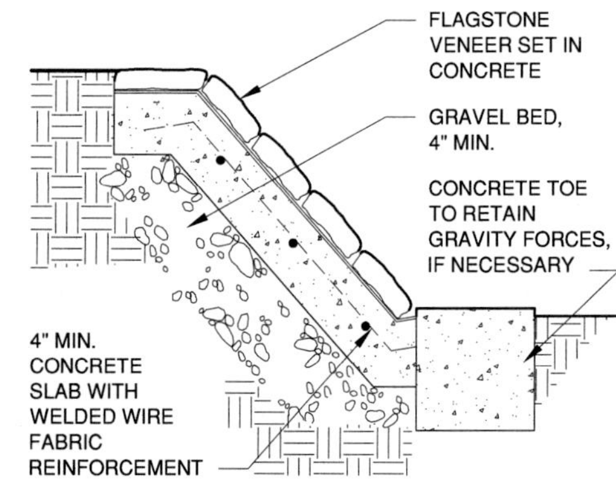

STONE BANK

STONE WALL DETAIL

Janice Cervelli-Schach
Credits: Thanks to R. V. Cervelli for his assistance on the structural mechanics calculations.

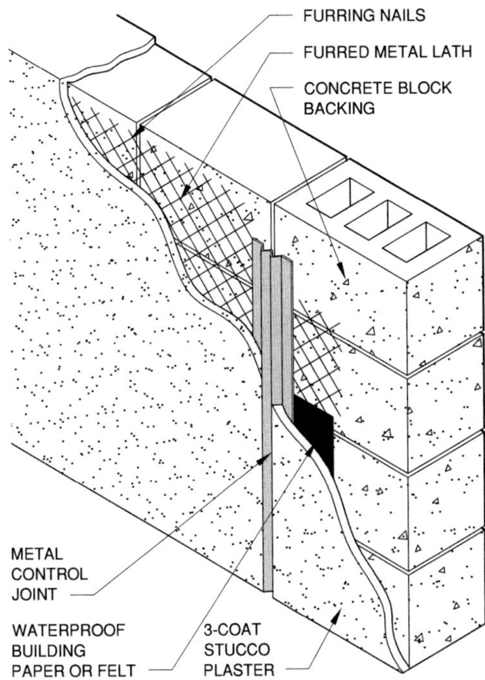

STUCCO WALL

regions where freezing and thawing take place. Cracks are controlled by the placement of metal control joints every 20 feet or where existing joints occur in the base. The stucco netting should be broken at the joints. It is especially important that the control joints in stucco walls be weatherproofed.

Mud Building Products

Building products made of a mixture of soil and water or mud come in a variety of forms, including adobe, rammed earth, and soil cement. Adobe varies from sun-dried bricks to poured-in-place to pressed to adobe-stabilized with asphalt emulsion. Care must be taken with all mud building products to avoid the selection of soils with high organic content and shrinkage-swell. Mud building products provide a great deal of flexibility in wall configuration, color, and texture. Structurally, mud walls are most ideal as freestanding walls. Mud retaining walls require steel reinforcement, a rigid footer, a cap, and drainage behind the wall. Mud walls require periodic maintenance to ensure the integrity of the protective mud wall skin.

Glass Block

A less common material for use in freestanding walls is the glass block. Glass blocks are a nonload-bearing masonry product that can be mortared in place on site or prefabricated into panels that are installed on-site. Glass block offers many of the advantages of glass and the thickness and strength of double-walled block. Walls and panels of glass block define space while allowing for an open, spacious effect due to the transmission of light. Glass block walls can be constructed as either a solid block wall with a structural frame or as glass block panel inset within a stucco or masonry frame. Vertical and horizontal reinforcement similar to that used in concrete or brick masonry walls should be applied in glass block walls.

Wood

Wood, or landscape timbers, is most typically used in the construction of retaining walls, versus freestanding walls. Timbers provide structural stability as well as a warm visual and tactile effect. The use of landscape timbers is declining due to increased costs, issues of forest sustainability, lack of availability of large dimensional timbers, and the negative environmental effects of wood preservative chemicals and processes. Recycled plastic wood is not generally a suitable alternative for landscape walls due to its relatively high initial cost, low structural capacity, and tendency to bend. Alternative wall materials, including concrete and brick masonry, mud building products, and gabion materials, are proving more structurally sound, environmentally friendly, locally available, and affordable.

FREESTANDING WALL FOUNDATIONS

The foundation is the part of the wall structure that transmits the wind load and the weight of the wall to the ground. The foundation must be designed to absorb this load and a certain amount of expansion and contraction of soil. The tensile strength of concrete is limited, however, and care must be taken to avoid expansive soils that may cause excessive tensile stress on the foundation, which could result in structural failure.

The bearing capacity of the soil determines the type and dimensions of the wall foundation. Soil investigations should be undertaken to determine the suitability of a particular soil for construction of any structure. A structural engineer should be consulted regarding the design of the foundation if problematic soil conditions are discovered.

Grade Beam

The most common type of freestanding wall foundation, the grade beam, consists of a vertical stem that extends below grade and is tied to a continuous horizontal footer or beam that spreads the load over a wider area. The grade beam footer is set at a minimum of 8 to 12 inches below grade or below frost depth, depending on the region and temperature extremes. Most building codes require that footers for nonload-bearing walls extend a minimum of 6 inches on either side of the wall. The American Concrete Institute (ACI) recommends that concrete footers be a minimum of 9 inches thick in warm climates and 12 inches thick in cold climates or on sites with expansive soils. Wider or thicker footers may be necessary in walls above 10 feet or those located in areas of high winds or poor soil conditions.

Post-and-Beam

The second (less common and more specialized) type of foundation is the post-and-beam. Post-and-beam foundations consist of a structural grade beam footer set between foundation posts. The system provides flexibility in locating wall foundations in unusual foundation conditions, such as expansive soils or subterranean obstructions (e.g., tree roots).

When required, the grade beam footer is suspended over an intermittent or continuous airspace to prevent contact with buried objects or expansive soils. When necessary, the post is set to a depth below the active soil zone or where more stable conditions are reached.

The ACI recommends that both types of foundations rest on and extend 2 inches into undisturbed soil and 6 inches below frost depth. Care must be taken not to make excavations too deep, which will cause uneven settlement of the soil to occur. If the excavation is too deep, the extra volume should be filled with concrete when the footer is poured. It is not advisable to locate footers in expansive, organic, or fill soils. Severe cracking and wall failure can result from unstable foundation conditions. The use of a post-and-beam foundation is recommended for these situations.

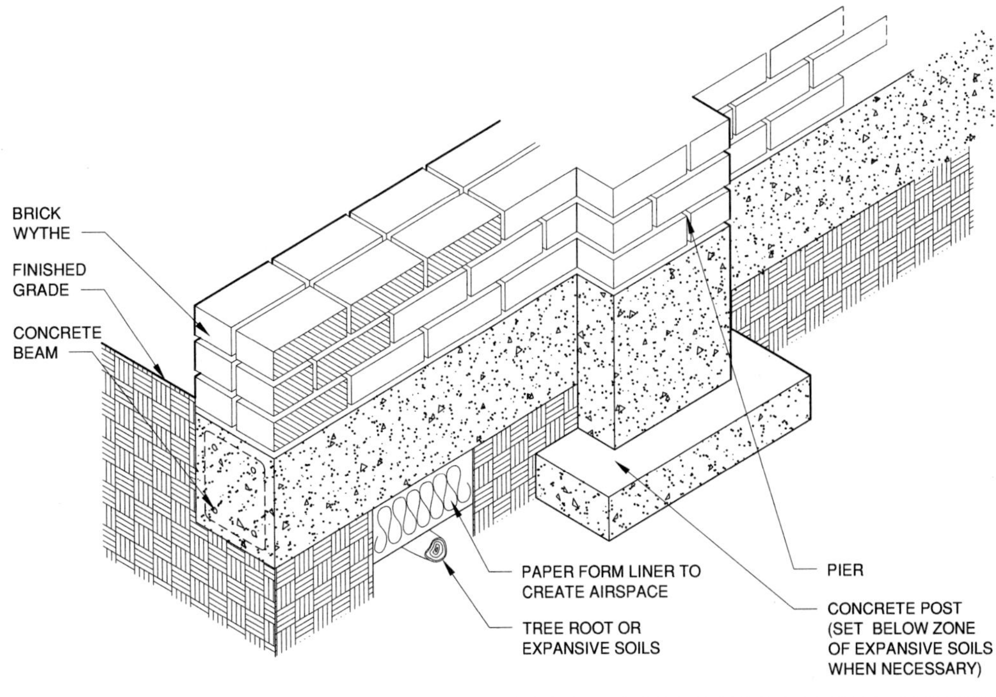

POST-AND-BEAM FOUNDATION

Janice Cervelli-Schach
Credits: Thanks to R. V. Cervelli for his assistance on the structural mechanics calculations.

FREESTANDING WALL JOINTS AND REINFORCEMENT

Mortar, control, and expansion joints are essential to the maintenance of the structural integrity of freestanding walls. Each plays an important role in the bonding of units and the control of movement within the unit system.

Mortar Joints

Several types of brick mortar joints can be used in masonry walls, including the following:

- Concave and tooled
- Flush or plain-cut
- Flush and tooled
- Stripped
- Weathered
- V-shaped
- Extruded
- Raked

Troweled joints, which include flush, struck, and weathered, are formed by striking the mortar with a trowel. The weathered joint is recommended over the struck joint for cold regions because it drains better, which helps to prevent crumbling mortar due to freeze-thaw action. Troweled joints can then be tooled to provide a decorative appearance and to provide protection from moisture. Tooled joints include V-shaped and concave joints, both of which are recommended for walls exposed to high winds and heavy rains. Tooling compresses the mortar tightly into the joint, which reduces the amount of airspace for moisture to penetrate.

The mortar joints of free stone walls are used to fill irregularly shaped spaces between rubble stones and are neither uniform in thickness nor direction. In contrast, the mortar joints of an ashlar wall pattern using dressed stone are uniform and should not exceed ½ inch in width.

RECOMMENDED MORTAR JOINT SIZES

WALL TYPE	JOINT WIDTH SIZE (IN.)
Brick	⅜
Block and cut stone	½
Rubble or rough stone	¾ or more

The quality of mortar used significantly affects the strength of walls. The BIA recommends Type M or Type S portland cement-lime mortars under specification C270 of the American Society for Testing and Materials (ASTM) or BIA's Designation MI-72 for maximum bond. Type M mortar is suggested for average conditions and Type S is suggested for conditions with wind velocities of over 80 miles/hour.

Control Joints

Walls are exposed to varying climates and weather conditions that can cause expansion and contraction of wall materials. Rigid restraint of wall movement can create stresses within the wall that can lead to cracking and, ultimately, wall failure. Control and expansion joints must be included as an integral part of wall design to control such movement and maintain the integrity of the wall.

Shrinkage of wall material is one of the major characteristics to be considered in walls constructed of concrete and concrete masonry units. Initial shrinkage can cause stress buildup that exceeds the tensile strength of the masonry units and the shearing strength of mortar joints, which will cause minute cracks to form in the areas of weakness and concentrated stress. Care must be taken to ensure the proper moisture content of concrete masonry units to avoid excessive shrinkage. The firing process of brick and other clay units during manufacturing, in contrast, minimizes moisture content in brick or other clay masonry products. Eventually, the units will expand as they take in water, which causes cracks to form. Masonry units will also expand and contract as the moisture content of the unit varies during weather changes.

MAXIMUM RECOMMENDED CONTROL JOINT SPACING FOR CONCRETE MASONRY WALLS (IN FEET)

WALL HEIGHT (FT)	JOINT REINFORCEMENT NONE	16 IN.	8 IN.
Up to 8	20 ft	25 ft	30 ft
8 to 12	25	30	35
Over 12	30	35	35

Source: Randall, 1976.

MAXIMUM RECOMMENDED CONTROL JOINT SPACING FOR POURED-IN-PLACE CONCRETE WALLS (IN FEET)

WALL HEIGHT (FT)	RECOMMENDED CONTROL JOINT SPACING
2 to 8	3 x wall height
8 to 12	2 x wall height
>12	1 x wall height

Source: American Concrete Institute, 1984.

Cracking can quickly disfigure a wall and is difficult and costly to repair. One method for controlling cracking is the use of control joints. Control joints are purposely weakened continuous vertical joints built into the wall with sufficient depth to control the location of cracks. Once cracked, the joint permits a slight amount of longitudinal wall movement to further reduce stress concentration. Wall bonds or steel reinforcements maintain the wall's configuration.

Control joints are most commonly 1 inch wide tapered to a ½-inch depth. The BIA recommends that the spacing for control joints be between 20 feet (minimum) and 35 feet (maximum) on center. The NCMA's recommendations for the spacing of control joints in walls of nonmoisture-controlled concrete masonry are shown in the tables "Maximum Recommended Control Joint Spacing for Concrete Masonry Walls (in Feet)" and "Maximum Recommended Control Joint Spacing for Poured-in-Place Concrete Walls (in Feet)."

Control joints should also be placed at all points of stress and weakness in the wall, such as at height changes, at doorways or other openings, and between panels and columns and/or pilasters. Veneer walls with brick tied to concrete masonry backup by metal ties should have control joints extending through the face every 50 feet on center to control cracking caused by differential movement between wythes. Control joints should also be extended through stucco surfaces when the stucco is applied directly to a concrete masonry backing.

Lateral stabilization of the wall must occur across the joint with a shear key. Tongue-and-groove concrete block provides excellent lateral stability. Another method is the use of two regular blocks or two jamb blocks with a Z-bar or a greased pencil rod placed across the joint, to attain the required shear strength. In situations where control joints are exposed to severe weather or to view, it is recommended that joints be sealed and weatherproofed.

Expansion Joints

Brick masonry, poured concrete, and concrete masonry walls expand and contract during temperature and moisture changes. According to the BIA,

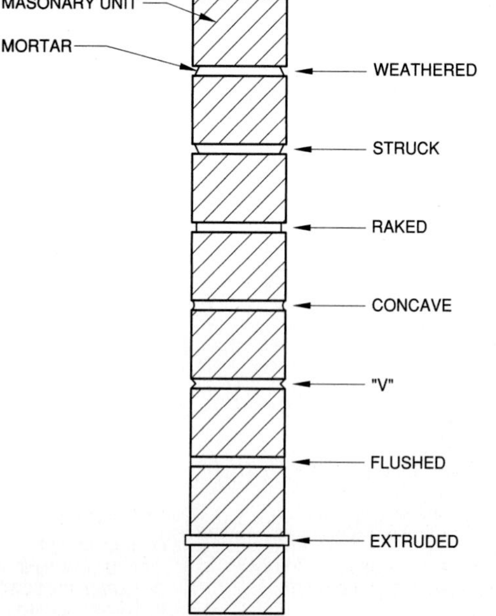

MORTAR JOINT TYPES

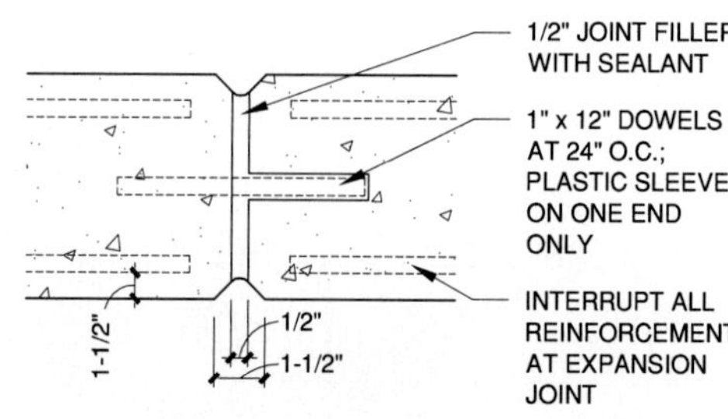

CONTROL AND EXPANSION JOINTS

Janice Cervelli-Schach
Credits: Thanks to R. V. Cervelli for his assistance on the structural mechanics calculations.

concrete either expands or contracts 0.62 inch per 100 feet of wall length per 100 degrees Fahrenheit of temperature change. Concrete will also, in arid regions, shrink considerably over time due to initial drying. A brick wall of 100 feet in length expands or contracts approximately 0.43 inch per 100 degrees Fahrenheit of change in temperature. Fired brick will also expand initially upon contact with moisture. A maximum spacing of 25 to 30 feet is recommended because each expansion joint allows for only a maximum of ¼ inch of movement.

Expansion joints involve a complete vertical break through the wall with no bonding at the break. Joints should be, at their minimum, ½ inch wide and filled with a water-resistant material that is flexible and durable. The BIA recommends that filler materials include 20 ounce/foot squared copper, premolded compressible elastic fillers; preformed rubber or plastic sections; or a vinyl waterstop covered by an elastic joint sealer to maintain a weather seal. It is also recommended that for joints deeper than ¾ inch or wider than ⅜ inch, a compressible backer rope material be used.

To maintain the horizontal alignment of the wall across the expansion joint, a tapered 2-by-4-inch vertical key is formed, or a horizontal plain steel dowel rod (minimum of 12 inches long and ½ to 1 inch in diameter) is installed at 12-inch intervals across the joint. A 16-gauge galvanized steel sleeve coated with a bond breaker or a PVC plastic pipe sleeve is slipped over one end of the rod to allow for movement of one side of the wall during expansion and contraction while maintaining the horizontal alignment. Good grades of weather-resistant polysulfide, polyurethane, butyl, or silicone rubber sealants are recommended as expansion joint sealers.

Freestanding Wall Reinforcement

The placement of vertical and horizontal steel reinforcing bars or prefabricated horizontal joint reinforcement is required in a freestanding wall to provide lateral stability against wind pressure and to control the effects of masonry expansion and contraction. Steel reinforcement minimizes the width of cracks and encourages a more evenly distributed pattern of minute cracks.

Reinforcement also helps to prevent cracks in the wall panel and foundation due to settlement. The placement of prefabricated horizontal joint reinforcement is used in multiwythe masonry walls to add transverse stability to the face and corners.

Wall reinforcement with steel reinforcement bars generally consists of bars being placed both horizontally and vertically to create a reinforcement grid. Generally, the estimated stress determines the size of the reinforcement, but typical building codes require a minimum bar diameter of ⅜ inch (No. 3 bar) for both horizontal and vertical reinforcement. Vertical reinforcing bars are aligned through the center of a poured-in-place concrete wall, through the grout-filled cores of a single-wythe masonry unit wall, or through the grout-filled space between wythes of multiwythe solid, cavity, or veneer walls. The maximum spacing for vertical bar placement is 48 inches on center. All horizontal wall reinforcement must be discontinued at expansion joints to allow for free movement.

Horizontal wall reinforcement and bond beams are reinforced courses of masonry that bond to form a stronger unit. Bond beams are located within a wall to increase the bending strength of the wall, the shear strength between courses, and to transfer loads to the wall foundation via the vertical reinforcement. Local building codes will typically require bond beams in conditions requiring additional lateral support against high winds, hurricanes, and earthquakes.

Bond beams are formed in concrete masonry walls by placing reinforcing bars into any one of the top three courses of masonry units and filling the cavities with grout. They are also placed to act as lintels over doors, windows, and other openings in freestanding walls. Additional reinforcement can be supplied by the lapping of continuous reinforced bond beam bars at wall corners. Bond beams for walls 8 inches thick should consist of a minimum of two No. 4 bars, and for walls 12 inches thick no fewer than two No. 5 bars. Additional steel reinforcement is also necessary in vertical piers and columns and in horizontal lintels and bond beams.

Most building codes and the NCMA require that the minimum area of reinforcement horizontally or vertically be not less than 0.0007 of the gross cross-sectional area of the wall. In addition, the sum of the percentages of horizontal and vertical reinforcement should be at least 0.002 of the gross cross-sectional area of the wall. In order to maximize the perimeter area of steel bar surface that is in contact with concrete, it is recommended that a greater number of smaller-diameter bars be used instead of fewer larger-diameter bars.

In the construction of freestanding, nonload-bearing walls, horizontal reinforcing bars are often replaced with prefabricated horizontal joint reinforcement or what is often called "wire track." In cavity and veneer walls, prefabricated horizontal joint reinforcement is placed to tie the two adjacent wall wythes together and provide additional lateral stability.

Prefabricated horizontal joint reinforcement generally consists of 9-gauge galvanized steel wire in either a truss or ladder configuration that is usually manufactured in 10- to 12-feet lengths. The ACI's standard for horizontal joint reinforcement requires one crosswire for each 2 square feet of wall surface and

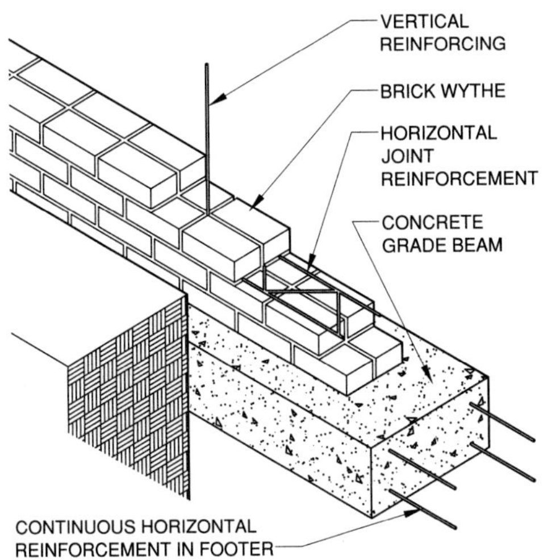

FREESTANDING MASONRY WALL REINFORCEMENT

RECOMMENDED PILASTER SPACING AND PILASTER VERTICAL REINFORCEMENT FOR 4-INCH-THICK PANELS WHERE PANEL VERTICAL REINFORCEMENT MAY NOT BE POSSIBLE

PILASTER VERTICAL SPACING FOR WIND PRESSURE				
Height (ft)	**5 psf**	**10 psf**	**15 psf**	**20 psf**
4 ft-0 in.	19 ft-4 in.	14 ft-0 in.	11 ft-4 in.	10 ft-0 in.
5 ft-0 in.	18 ft-0 in.	12 ft-8 in.	10 ft-8 in.	9 ft-4 in.
6 ft-0 in.	15 ft-4 in.	10 ft-8 in.	8 ft-8 in.	8 ft-0 in.
REINFORCEMENT FOR WIND PRESSURE				
Height (ft)	**5 psf**	**10 psf**	**15 psf**	**20 psf**
4 ft-0 in.	One No. 3	One No. 4	One No. 5	Two No. 4
5 ft-0 in.	One No. 3	One No. 5	Two No. 4	Two No. 5
6 ft-0 in.	One No. 4	One No. 5	Two No. 5	Two No. 5

Source: Randall, 1976.

VERTICAL PANEL REINFORCEMENT FOR 6-INCH CONCRETE MASONRY WALLS WITHOUT PILASTERS

REINFORCEMENT FOR WIND PRESSURE				
Wall Height (ft)	**5 psf**	**10 psf**	**15 psf**	**20 psf**
4	One No. 3	One No. 3	One No. 4	One No. 4
5	One No. 3	One No. 4	One No. 5	One No. 5
6	One No. 3	One No. 4	One No. 5	Two No. 4

Source: Randall, 1976.

PROPERTIES OF STANDARD DEFORMED REINFORCING BARS

BAR NO.	DIAMETER (IN.)	CROSS SECTIONAL AREA (IN.^{2})	PERIMETER (IN.)
3	0.375	0.11	1.178
4	0.500	0.020	1.571
5	0.625	0.31	1.963
6	0.750	0.44	2.356

Source: American Concrete Institute, 1984.

Janice Cervelli-Schach
Credits: Thanks to R. V. Cervelli for his assistance on the structural mechanics calculations.

vertical spacing limited to 16 inches. Closer spacing, such as 8 inches on center, is specified by building codes for conditions requiring additional stability. A minimum overlapping of 6 to 8 inches for consecutive wire sections is required to maintain continuous tensile strength along the joint. Placement of continuous prefabricated horizontal reinforcement wire within the course should ensure that one side of the wire sits in each wythe of the wall.

Types M, S, and N mortar are recommended by the BIA for use with joint reinforcement. All wall reinforcement should be sufficiently covered with mortar or concrete to prevent exposure and deterioration of the reinforcement, resultant staining of the wall face, and crumbling of the mortar joint. The ACI recommends a minimum bar cover of 2 inches for No. 6 to 8 rebars and a cover of 1½ inches for No. 5 or smaller bars. If sufficient coverage cannot be ensured during construction, corrosion-resistant bars should be used.

In wall foundations, both horizontal and vertical steel reinforcement is placed in the footer to support the loads transferred to the foundation from the wall panel above and to provide stability against soil pressure from below. The NCMA and the BIA recommend that the minimum amount of reinforcement in the footer be equal to 0.005 percent of the gross cross-sectional area of the wall in either direction. Horizontal reinforcement should be of No. 4 bars laid continuously the length of the footer.

To prevent the wall stem and footer from separating, they should be tied together by extending the horizontal bar in the footer up toward the stem and securely tying it to the vertical reinforcement of the panel. Landphair and Klatt (1979) recommend that the vertical reinforcement and the footer reinforcement overlap a distance equal to 20 bar diameters. For example, the required overlap of wall and footer reinforcement using a No. 4 vertical bar would be 10 inches.

FREESTANDING WALL MOISTURE PROTECTION

The life span of a masonry wall is determined in part by its resistance to moisture penetration. The design of any wall must take into consideration the climate of the area in which it is to be built and the level of exposure to moisture. The various methods for protecting freestanding walls against moisture penetration include the following:

- Placement of wall capstones on the top course of concrete block, brick, and stone walls
- Use of drainage-type walls (e.g., cavity and veneer walls) and inclusion of clean cavities between wall wythes
- Use of weep holes, flashing, and waterstops
- Use of tooled mortar joints with a concave or V-shape
- Use of joint sealants
- Use of proven silicone water-repellant surface treatment (Certain compositions can also provide protection from acid rain.)

MECHANICS OF FREESTANDING WALLS

The structural objective of a freestanding, nonload-bearing, nonreinforced wall is to support its own weight and to resist the three common types of wall failure: overturning, settlement, and sliding. A freestanding wall can be thought of as a cantilevered beam supporting a uniformly distributed load of wind. The ACI recommends that freestanding walls be designed for a minimum wind load of 5 pounds/square foot, although some building codes require a design wind pressure of 20 pounds/square foot.

Wall Failures

Freestanding walls are subject to failure of the wall stem and/or failure of the wall foundation. Failure of the wall stem can occur when the tensile stress created by wind load overcomes the structural integrity of the wall stem. As discussed earlier, the purpose of pilasters, vertical steel reinforcement placed in the wall stem, and adequate anchoring of the stem to the wall footer is to resist this stress.

Lateral Support

The height, thickness, length, and configuration of the wall are critical determinants of the need and spacing of lateral wall supports. Walls designed by landscape architects are generally limited to heights of 8 feet by local building codes. Thus, the design of walls of greater height should involve a structural and/or soil engineer to ensure the stability of both the wall and wall foundation. Few unsupported straight walls that are 6 feet high by 4 to 8 inches thick and of 35 feet or more in length can withstand wind pressures above 20 pounds/square foot. Long, tall, straight, or thin walls are by their very nature unstable and require lateral support. The required lateral support can be attained by:

- Increasing wall thickness
- Reducing wall height
- Incorporating frequent angles or radii into the layout
- Adding pilasters, buttresses, or intersecting walls at appropriate intervals

Maximum allowable wall heights, H, are limited by the nominal wall thickness, t, and the wind load. The slenderness ratio (H/t) is defined as the ratio of the effective unsupported wall height, H, and the nominal wall thickness, t (see the "Rational Design of Lateral Support Ratios (H/t or L/t) for Nonload-bearing, Nonreinforced Brick Masonry Walls" table). Interval spacing of lateral supports is based on the wind pressure and the ratio of nominal wall thickness (t) to unsupported wall length (L), called the L/t ratio (see the figure "L/t Ratio for Freestanding Walls," above, and the "Recommended Pilaster Spacing and Reinforcement for 4-Inch Concrete Masonry Fences Subjected to Uniformly Distributed Wind Load" and "Rational Design of Lateral Support Ratios (H/t or L/t) for Nonload-bearing, Nonreinforced Brick Masonry Walls" tables).

The NCMA's "Specification for the Design and Construction of Load-bearing Concrete Masonry" standard requires either an L/t ratio or a slenderness ratio, H/t (but not necessarily both) of not more than 20 for nonreinforced solid masonry walls using Type M, S, N, or O mortar. According to the NCMA, nonload-bearing exterior walls must also satisfy these ratios despite their reduced thickness compared with bearing walls. The recommended L/t and slenderness ratios, H/t, for walls of nonreinforced hollow masonry using the same mortar types should not exceed 18t. The NCMA standard also recommends that spacing of vertical supports for reinforced concrete masonry walls be increased to a maximum of 36t. The H/t and L/t ratios for more specific conditions are listed in the "Rational Design of Lateral Support Ratios (H/t or L/t) for Nonload-bearing, Nonreinforced Brick Masonry Walls" table.

The determination of spacing for vertical supports can be seen in the following example:

Example: Find the maximum lateral support spacing and wall height for an 8-inch-thick brick

MAXIMUM WALL HEIGHTS (H) FOR HOLLOW NONREINFORCED CONCRETE MASONRY FENCES SUBJECTED TO UNIFORMLY DISTRIBUTED WIND LOAD (PSF)

NOMINAL WALL THICKNESS (IN.)	(VELOCITY, MPH)		
	10 (57)	15 (69)	20 (80)
6	4 ft	3 ft-4 in.	2 ft-8 in.
8	5 ft-4 in.	4 ft-8 in.	4 ft
10	6 ft-8 in.	5 ft-4 in.	4 ft-8 in.
12	7 ft-4 in.	6 ft	5 ft-4 in.

RECOMMENDED PILASTER SPACING AND REINFORCEMENT FOR 4-INCH CONCRETE MASONRY FENCES SUBJECTED TO UNIFORMLY DISTRIBUTED WIND LOAD (PSF)

	WIND LOAD, PSF (VELOCITY, MPH)			
	5 (50)		10 (57)	
WALL HEIGHT (FT)	PILASTER SPACING	PILASTER REINFORCEMENT	PILASTER SPACING	PILASTER REINFORCEMENT
4	22 ft	One No 3	15 ft-4 in.	One No. 4
5	20 ft-8 in.	One No 4	14 ft	One No. 4
6	19 ft-4 in	One No 4	12 ft-8 in.	One No. 5
	WIND LOAD, PSF (VELOCITY, MPH)			
	15 (69)		20 (80)	
WALL HEIGHT (FT)	PILASTER SPACING	PILASTER REINFORCEMENT	PILASTER SPACING	PILASTER REINFORCEMENT
4	12 ft-8 in.	One No 4	10 ft-8 in.	One No. 4
5	10 ft-8 in	Two No 3	9 ft-4 in	One No. 5
6	9 ft-4 in.	Two No 4	8 ft	One No. 5

Janice Cervelli-Schach

Credits: Thanks to R. V. Cervelli for his assistance on the structural mechanics calculations.

RATIONAL DESIGN OF LATERAL SUPPORT RATIOS (H/t OR L/t) FOR NONLOAD-BEARING, NONREINFORCED BRICK MASONRY WALLS[1,2]

	WITHOUT ENGINEERING INSPECTION				WITH ENGINEERING INSPECTION			
	VERTICAL SPAN (H)		HORIZONTAL SPAN (L)		VERTICAL SPAN (H)		HORIZONTAL SPAN (L)	
DESIGN WIND PRESSURE (PSF)[3,4]	N	S OR M	N	S OR M	N	S OR M	N	S OR M
5d	31	35	44	50	38	43	54	61
10	22	25	31	35	27	30	38	43
15	18	20	25	29	22	25	31	35
20	15	18	22	25	19	21	27	30
25	14	16	20	22	17	19	24	27
30	13	14	18	20	15	17	22	25
35	12	13	16	19	14	16	20	23
40	11	12	15	18	13	15	19	21
45	10	12	14	17	13	14	18	20
50	10	11	14	16	12	14	17	19

Notes:

1. H = clear span (height or length) between lateral supports; t = actual wall thickness.

2. For cavity walls having wythes of equal thickness and built with the same units and mortar, the value of t will be taken as 1.41 times the actual thickness of one wythe. For other cavity walls, the wind pressure will be assumed to be distributed to the wythes according to their respective flexural rigidities, and then each wythe will be designed separately.

3. For design wind pressure, see applicable building code requirements or ANSI AS8, 1-1972, "Minimum Design Loads in Buildings and Other Structures."

4. Ratio given for a design wind pressure of 5 psf is applicable only to partitions. Assumptions: simply supported walls without any openings or other interruptions; allowable flexural tensile stresses increased by one third for wind. The weight of the wall was neglected.

wall with a 20 pounds/square foot wind load using inspected N-type mortar:

Ratio = L/t (see the "Rational Design of Lateral Support Ratios (H/t or L/t) for Nonload-bearing, Nonreinforced Brick Masonry Walls" table)

$27 = L/0.67$ ft

$L = 0.67$ ft $\times 27$

$L = 18$ ft

Ratio = H/t (see the "Rational Design of Lateral Support Ratios (H/t or L/t) for Nonload-bearing, Nonreinforced Brick Masonry Walls" table)

$19 = H/0.67$ ft

$H = 0.67$ ft $\times 19$

$H = 13$ ft

Lateral supports should be spaced at a maximum of every 18 feet on center, and the wall height should not exceed 13 feet.

MECHANICS AND STATIC INVESTIGATION OF FREESTANDING WALLS

The procedure for investigating wall stability follows four steps:

1. Selection of proposed wall cross-sectional dimensions
2. Analysis of stability based on local precedent, experience, and judgment
3. Test for general stability using graphic procedures or trigonometric functions to construct a force parallelogram that indicates where the resultant strikes the base of the wall
4. Mathematical analysis to determine stability against overturning, sliding, and settling

General Stability

The mechanical objective of wall design is to keep all forces uniform and compressive by ensuring that the weight of the wall is distributed evenly over the entire cross-sectional area of the footer. Even weight distribution is ensured when the resultant force, R, of the weight of the wall, W, and the wind load, P, act on the middle third of the footer. This is what is known as the "principle of the middle third," a condition that limits all stresses and forces to those being compressive. When the resultant force passes outside the middle third of the footer, uneven weight distribution over the footer occurs. Eccentric loading can cause the foot pressure of the wall to exceed the soil-bearing capacity, leading to failure.

Resultant force, R, the angle θ, and the distance from the wall centerline to the point of action, e, can be calculated with the following formula:

Example: Test the given wall for stability based on the principle of the middle third.

$R = (W^2 + P^2)^{0.5}$

$= (1078^2 + 150^2)^{0.5}$

$= (1{,}162{,}084 + 22{,}500)^{0.5}$ lbs

$= (1{,}184{,}584)^{0.5}$ lbs

$= (1{,}088.38)$ lbs

Find θ, the resultant angle:

$\sin\theta = P/R$

$= 150 \text{ lbs}/1{,}088.38 \text{ lbs}$

$\sin\theta = 0.1378$

$\theta = \arcsin 0.1378$

$\theta = 7.92°$ or $7° 55'$

Find eccentricity, e, or the distance between the wall centerline and the intersecting point of the resultant force, where h is the height of wall above

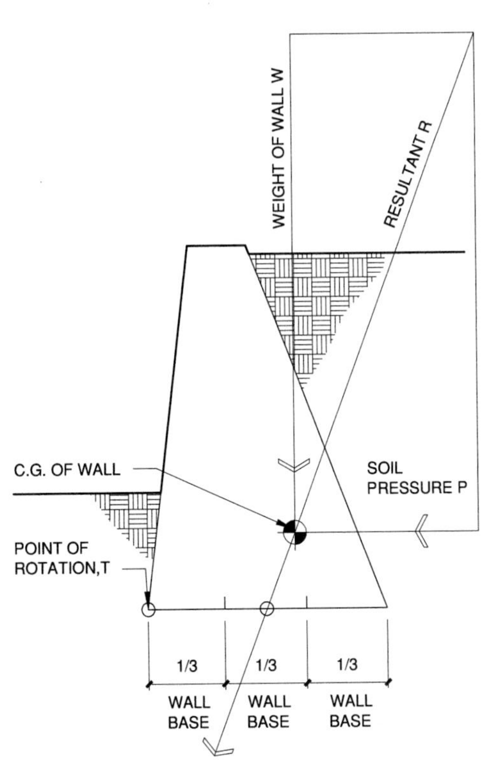

PRINCIPLE OF THE MIDDLE THIRD

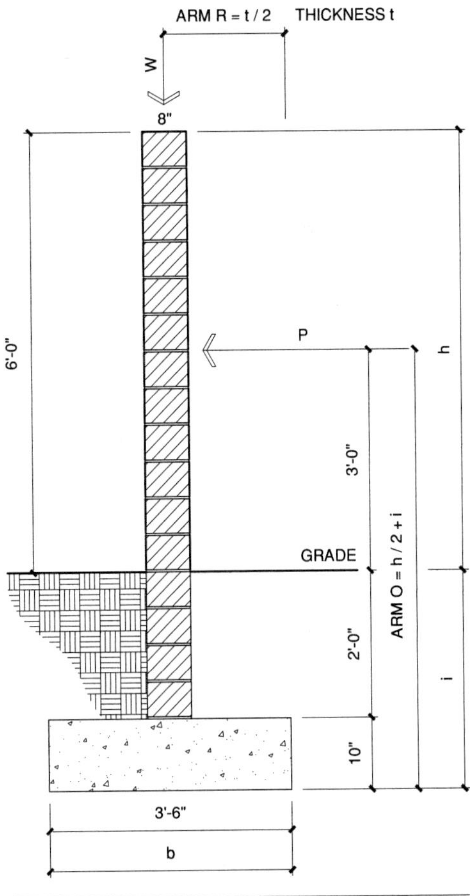

FREESTANDING WALL DIMENSIONS

Janice Cervelli-Schach
Credits: Thanks to R. V. Cervelli for his assistance on the structural mechanics calculations.

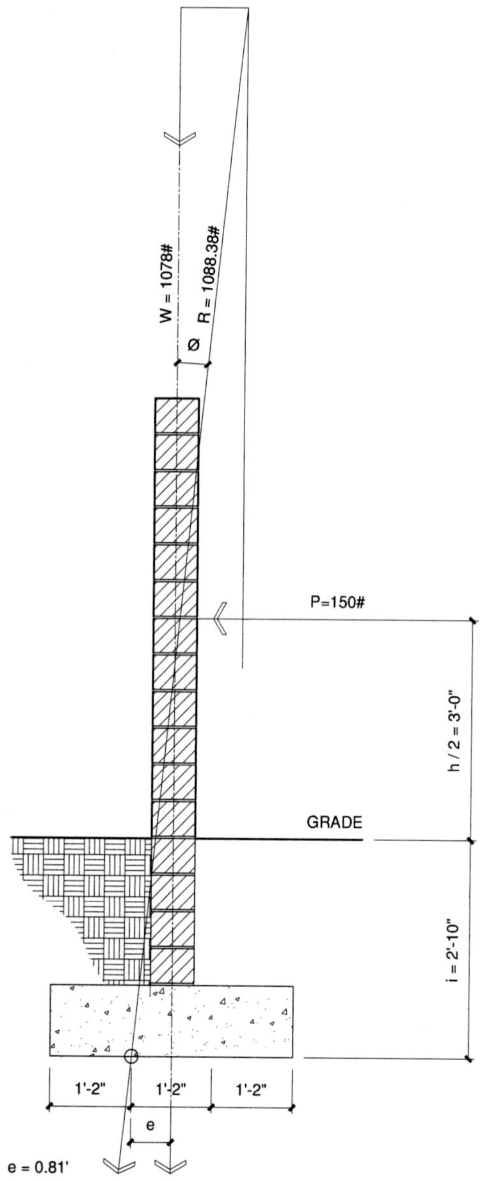

FREESTANDING WALL FORCE DIAGRAM

grade and i is the depth to bottom of footer from grade:

$$e = (h/2 + i)\tan\theta$$
$$= (3\text{ ft} + 2.833\text{ ft})\ 0.1391$$
$$= 0.81\text{ ft}$$ Check: Resultant passes slightly outside middle third.

In this example, the resultant passes slightly outside the middle third but not enough to cause significant internal tensile stress on the footer to cause it to fail. If the resultant were to strike significantly outside the middle third or miss the footer altogether, the footer would have to be widened to distribute the load more evenly and keep stresses compressive.

Overturning

The main culprit in freestanding wall failure is wind pressure. Overturning occurs when wind pressure becomes sufficiently great that it overwhelms the righting resistance of the weight of the wall and pushes it to rotate about the footer. Wind load, P, is

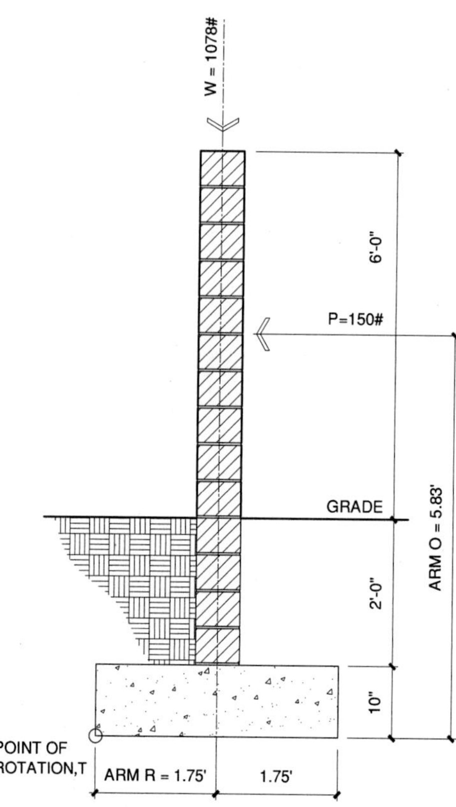

FREESTANDING WALL WEIGHT AND SOIL PRESSURE

calculated by multiplying the wind pressure, WP, for the particular region (see local codes) by the height of the wall above grade.

Wall statics assume wind pressure to be evenly distributed over the entire wall surface and centered at a point on the wall that is half its height above grade. The action of the wind pressure at this center of gravity is measured by the force it exerts in pounds. The moment created by the wind pressure is called the "overturning moment," M_O, since it is this force that could cause the overturning of the wall. M_O, in foot-pounds, is calculated by multiplying the calculated wind pressure by Arm 0, the overturning lever arm.

The force that balances or cancels out M_O and ensures that the wall remains upright is the resisting moment, M_R. M_R is a force created by the weight of the wall acting on the center of gravity of the wall, which is usually located at the midpoint of the wall footer. M_R is calculated by multiplying the weight of the wall by the resisting lever arm of the wall, Arm R. For the wall to be stable, the M_R must be twice the M_O (factor of safety).

Example: Determine whether the given concrete masonry wall can withstand overturning by wind.

Arm R = footer width/2
= 3.5 ft/2
= 1.75 ft
MR = W x Arm R
= 1078 lbs x 1.75 ft
= 1886.5 ft-lbs
P = 6 ft x 1 ft x 25 lbs/ft (wind pressure)
= 150 lbs
Arm O = 5.833 ft (distance from bottom of footer to midpoint of wall above grade)

MO = P x Arm O
= 150 lbs x 5.833 ft
= 675 ft-lbs
MR/MO > 2 (safety factor)

$$\frac{1886.5\text{ ft-lbs}}{875\text{ ft-lbs}} = 2.16$$

2.16 > 2 Check

The safety factor has been met; thus, the wall should be successful in resisting overturning due to the given wind pressure. If the safety factor is not met, additional lateral stability must be incorporated into the design. If it is not possible to integrate pilasters or intersecting walls into the scheme, another alternative to increasing lateral wall support is to widen the wall footer to increase the righting lever and weight of resistance to overturning.

Settlement

Footer failure occurs when eccentric loads on the footer and the soil beneath the footer slab exceed the soil-bearing capacity, which causes the footer to settle and rotate forward around the toe.

Generally, the relatively light foot pressures of most nonload-bearing walls do not cause eccentric loading and footer failure on most good soils, but the possibility of settlement must be tested in the initial design stage.

To test for footer failure, the foot pressure of the wall must be calculated and checked for stability against the soil-bearing capacity. For the wall to be stable against settling, the soil-bearing capacity (see the "Bearing Capacities of Common Soil Types" table) must exceed the wall foot pressure by the factor of safety of 1.5.

Example: Test the given wall for failure by settling.

Soil-bearing capacity ("Bearing Capacities of Common Soil Types" table) = 2,000 lbs/sf

$$f = R/A\left(1 + \frac{6e}{b}\right)$$
$$= \frac{1{,}088\text{ lbs}}{3.5\text{ ft}}\left(1 + \frac{6 \times 0.81\text{ ft}}{3.5\text{ ft}}\right)$$
$$= 310.86\text{ lbs/sf} \times 2.39$$

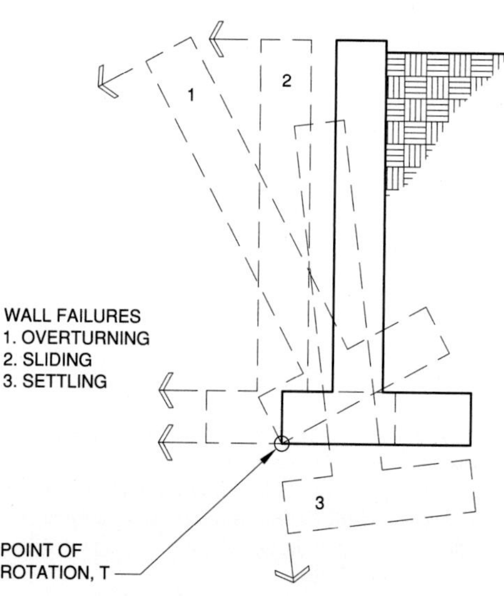

RETAINING WALL FAILURES

Janice Cervelli-Schach
Credits: Thanks to R. V. Cervelli for his assistance on the structural mechanics calculations.

$$= 742.96 \text{ lbs/sf}$$

$$\frac{2000\text{lbs/sf}}{742.96 \text{ lbs/sf}} = 2.69 > 1.5 \text{ (safety factor) Check}$$

where:

A = Area of the footing for a 1-foot long section
b = Length of the base or cross-sectional length of footing
Soil-bearing capacity (see "Bearing Capacities of Common Soil types" table) = 2,000 lbs/sf

In this example, the wall passes the test for settlement failure since 1.5 times the wall foot pressure is within the soil-bearing capacity of 2,000 pounds/square foot.

Sliding

Sliding occurs when the lateral wind load, P, is greater than the shear strength created by the frictional resistance between the footer and the soil below and that from the soil resting in front of the footer. To test for sliding, the frictional resistance must be calculated by multiplying the weight of the wall, W, by the soil coefficient of friction (see the "Average Coefficient of Friction of Common Soils" table) and comparing that with the wind force, P.

Example: Test for the possibility of sliding for the given wall.

Frictional Resistance = W x coefficient of friction of soil (See "Average Coefficient of Friction of Common Soils" table)
= 1078 lbs x 0.50
= 539 lbs
Resisting Force/Sliding Force > 2
539 lbs/150 lbs > 1.5
3.59 > 1.5 Check: Wall passes the test for sliding failure.

RETAINING WALLS

The primary purpose of a retaining wall is to achieve elevation change within limited horizontal distances. Slope retention is required whenever the angle of the slope exceeds the angle of repose of the soil (that angle at which the soil becomes unstable). Several techniques are used to retain soil on slopes of varying degrees, including those listed in the "Suggested Retention Methods" table.

Retaining walls must be designed to withstand the lateral pressure of the retained soil on the back side of the wall and on the toe of the footing. The only soil on a slope that exerts lateral pressure is that which lies outside the angle of repose of that soil. In the case of the retaining wall, the retained soil is seen as a triangle of force applied along a line perpendicular to the wall.

SUGGESTED RETENTION METHODS

SLOPE RANGE	RETENTION METHOD
Less than or equal to the angle of repose of soil (generally 33°)	Vegetation
Equal to angle of repose 1:1 (45°) slope	Riprap, soil blankets, and mattresses
Greater than 1:1 slope	Retaining wall

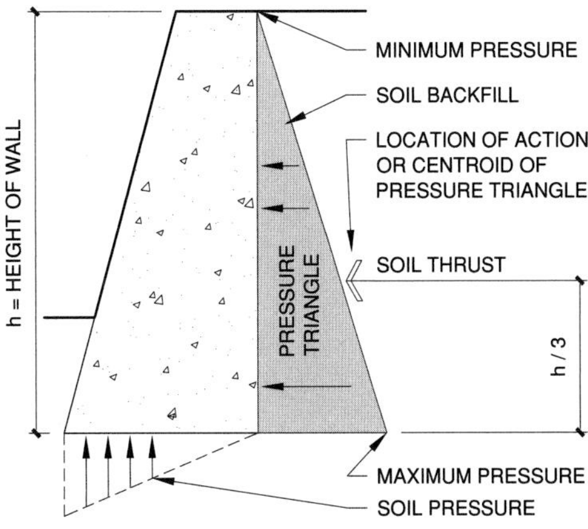

SOIL PRESSURE TRIANGLE OF A RETAINING WALL

RETAINING WALL HEIGHTS AND TYPE

WALL TYPE	MAXIMUM HEIGHT (FT)	ECONOMICAL HEIGHT RANGE (FT)
Gravity wall	Up to 10	Up to 4
Cantilevered wall	Up to 20	Up to 20
Counterfort wall	Over 20	Over 20

In general, the design of walls higher than 8 feet and of those in questionable conditions (long, straight configuration; unsuitable, poorly drained soils; and additional loads or surcharges such as traffic, building foundations, earthquakes, or hurricanes) should involve geotechnical assistance from a structural or soil engineer experienced in handling the conditions in question. This material is restricted to the discussion of the properties of walls of 8 feet or less.

Retaining walls are usually one of three general types: gravity, cantilevered, or counter fort. Each type of wall is most efficient for a particular range of retention height.

TYPES OF RETAINING WALLS

Gravity

Gravity walls are solid, massive, and heavy structures that retain soil with the weight of the wall material, as the name suggests. Gravity walls are generally constructed with monolithic concrete, concrete masonry units, dry-laid stone, stone masonry with mortar joints, concrete or steel cribbing, modular gravity wall systems, or gabion cages. Considered the most economical wall up to heights of 4 feet, gravity walls are the simplest of retaining walls and require less skill than cantilever or counterfort walls to construct.

The general configuration of a gravity wall is trapezoidal with a narrow wall top and a wide base. Base thickness is dependent on the relative stability of the foundation soil type, and generally varies from a ratio of one-third to three-fourths of the wall height. The ratios for wall design shown in the "Dimensional Ratio for Gravity Walls" table are recommended (Munson, 1974). These dimensions should serve as guidelines that will undergo further testing for stability under specific conditions.

For conditions involving a sloping backfill or surcharge, Munson (1974) recommends that the ratio be increased by 0.1 or 0.2. Dry stone walls require a minimum ratio of 0.50 and the incorporation of a batter into the face of the wall. It is also recommended that each course and the wall base be sloped toward the backfill to provide additional resistance to sliding. The most commonly recommended batters for gravity walls range up to 2 inches per 12 inches of wall height.

The structural protection of wall foundations from frost action by placement below frost depth is especially important for gravity walls because little steel reinforcement is used to overcome tensile stress. Recommended depths for bases of gravity walls are

DIMENSIONAL RATIO FOR GRAVITY WALLS

SOIL TYPE	RATIO (BASE TO WALL HEIGHT)
Gravel	0.35 to 0.40
Wet sand	0.58 to 0.60
Wet clay, silt	0.75

GRAVITY WALL FOUNDATION GUIDELINES

TYPE OF GRAVITY WALL	DEPTH OF BASE
Bank wall less than 10 ft	Minimum of 2 ft
Bank wall 10 ft or more	0.2 x height of wall
Sustaining wall	Minimum of 3 ft except when foundation is rock or is entirely below frost depth

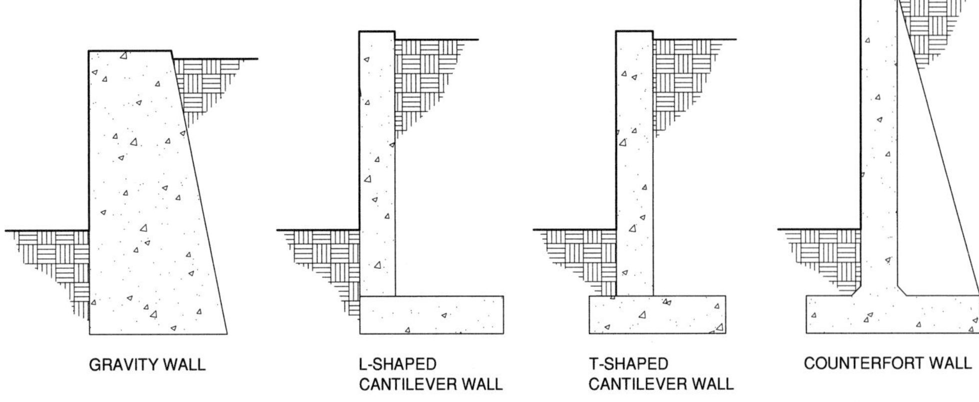

BASIC RETAINING WALL TYPES

Janice Cervelli-Schach
Credits: Thanks to R. V. Cervelli for his assistance on the structural mechanics calculations.

shown in the "Gravity Wall Foundation Guidelines" table (Sears, 1988).

These guidelines do not apply to the construction of relatively low gravity walls using modular gravity wall units or gabion cages. The designer should check the manufacturer's recommendations for foundation depths for these wall systems.

Cantilever

The cantilevered wall is composed of two parts, the stem and the base, which are either in an inverted "T" or an "L" configuration. Due to the relative thinness of both the stem and the base, each is reinforced with steel to resist the tensile stress of soil pressure and both are securely tied together to work as a stable unit. The stem acts essentially as a cantilevered beam supported by the base. The main source of stability for the cantilevered wall against sliding and overturning is the additional wall weight created by the soil backfill resting on top of the base. This soil acts as an integral part of the wall, increasing its weight without requiring the expense of additional concrete. Cantilevered walls are most economical for heights of 4 to 10 feet due to the decreased amount of concrete required for stability.

The dimensional guidelines for cantilevered wall design are based on the load conditions of the wall and the conditions of the base soil. Dimensional guidelines for cantilevered walls are shown in the table "Cantilever Wall Footer Widths" (Munson, 1974).

Under good or average soil conditions and with no obstacles present, it is generally recommended that the stem be located one-third of the total base width from the toe (see the "Cantilever Wall Footer Dimensions for Reinforced Concrete Masonry Retaining Walls" table for more specific dimensions).

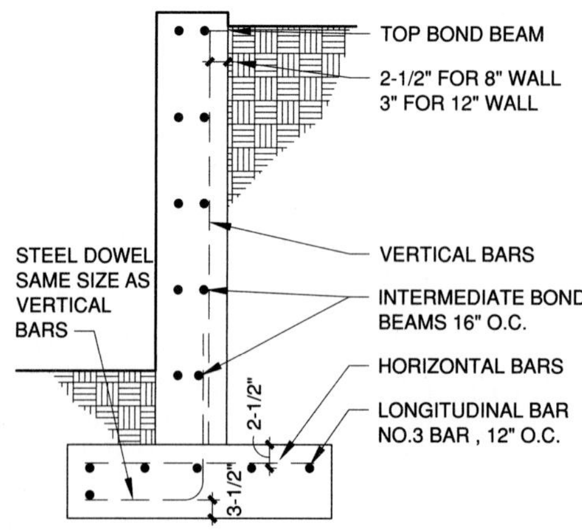

SECURING THE FOOTER TO THE STEM WITH A STEEL DOWEL

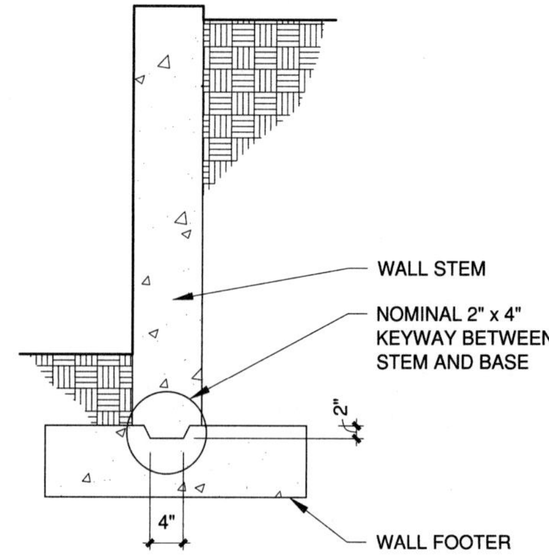

KEYWAY BETWEEN CANTILEVERED FOOTER AND STEM

In conditions of low soil-bearing capacity, the stem should be located more toward the heel or the rear of the base to ensure even distribution of foot pressure and avoid settling. Conversely, to prevent sliding in conditions of low coefficient of friction, the stem should be located more toward the toe (front of the base), which increases the weight of the wall. The NCMA's recommendations for sizing the dimension of the cantilevered wall footers are shown in the table "Cantilever Wall Footer Dimensions for Reinforced Concrete Masonry Retaining Walls."

The stem of the cantilevered wall should be secured to the base by a steel dowel that is extended from the base adjacent to the vertical steel reinforcement of the stem and tied to it. The NCMA recommends that dowels be at least equal in size and spacing to the vertical reinforcing bars. The dowels should extend a minimum of 30 bar diameters into the concrete stem or concrete-filled block cores and extend into the toe of the footing.

A more stable union is achieved between the stem and the base with the placement of a 2-inch-deep by 4-inch-wide keyway between the bottom of the stem and the top of the base.

The "Cantilevered Wall Footer Depths" table lists recommendations for footer depths (Sears, 1988). In any case, the footer depth should exceed the frost depth.

CANTILEVER WALL FOOTER WIDTHS

WIDTH OF FOOTER	LOAD CONDITION
0.45 x wall height	Horizontal loading (no surcharge)
0.60 x wall height	Surcharged loading
0.65 x wall height	Horizontal loading with road

CANTILEVERED WALL FOOTER DEPTHS

TYPE OF WALL	DEPTH OF FOOTER
Bank wall above 10 ft	0.15 x height of wall
Sustaining wall above 10 ft	0.25 x height of wall

Counterfort

Counterfort walls are very tall retaining walls (heights over 15 feet) most commonly used for highway and railroad cuts and water channel work. Walls of this height require additional support against soil pressure. Supports extending from the front of the wall, called "buttresses," provide stability against compressive stress. Supports extending to the back of the wall and buried in the earth, called "counterforts," provide stability against tensile stress.

CANTILEVER WALL FOOTER DIMENSIONS FOR REINFORCED CONCRETE MASONRY RETAINING WALLS

DISTANCE FROM TOE TO WALL HEIGHT	WALL STEM FACE (IN.)	FOOTER HEIGHT (IN.)	FOOTER WIDTH
8-INCH-WIDE WALL			
3 ft-4 in.	8	9	2 ft-4 in.
4 ft-0 in.	10	9	2 ft-9 in.
4 ft-8 in.	12	10	3 ft-4 in.
5 ft-4 in.	14	10	3 ft-8 in.
6 ft-0 in.	16	12	4 ft-2 in.
12-INCH-WIDE WALL			
5 ft-4 in.	14	10	3 ft-8 in.
6 ft-0 in.	15	12	4 ft-2 in.

Source: National Concrete Masonry Association, 1983)

Notes:

1. Reinforcement of a size and spacing other than given in the table may be used, providing such other reinforcement furnishes an area of steel at least equal to that indicated in the table.

2. Alternate V-bars may be stopped at the midheight of the wall (H/2) if the spacing of the bars continued to the top does not exceed 36 inches.

3. Dowels must be at least equal in size and spacing to V-bars, project a minimum of 30 bar diameters into the filled block cores, and extend to the toe of the footing.

4. Joint reinforcement consisting of 9-gauge longitudinal wires and 3/16-inch cross rods (8- and 12-inch walls) or 3/16-inch cross rods or tabs (14- and 18-inch walls) must be provided at 8-inch centers vertically.

5. Hollow concrete masonry units must be 8 inches nominal for 14-inch walls and 12 inches nominal for 18-inch walls.

6. Provide key for 8- and 12-inch walls where H exceeds 6 ft.

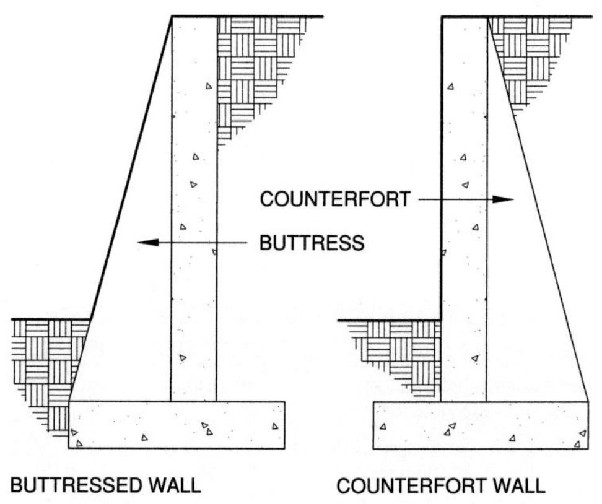

TYPES OF COUNTERFORT WALLS

Janice Cervelli-Schach

Credits: Thanks to R. V. Cervelli for his assistance on the structural mechanics calculations.

Counterfort walls are typically made of reinforced concrete supported by triangular counterfort or buttress cross walls at spaced intervals. Horizontal steel wall reinforcement transfers soil pressure loads along the wall length to the vertical supports, which transfer it to the footings.

The traditional concrete counterfort wall is not commonly used due to the high cost of the labor involved in its construction. Relatively low-cost concrete cribbing and reinforced gabion walls are replacing the concrete counterfort wall for heights up to 30 feet.

NATURE OF SOIL PRESSURE

The exact amount of soil pressure on a retaining wall is almost impossible to calculate due to the unpredictable and indeterminate properties of soils, in particular:

- Type and density of soil
- Level of internal friction and cohesion of the retained soil
- Water content of the retained soil (degree of saturation)
- Existence of voids in the retained soil
- Seasonal temperature and moisture fluctuations

A number of theories, including Coulomb's, Poncelet's, Rankine's, and the equivalent fluid theory, have been proposed to approximate values for soil pressure (see Munson, 1974; National Concrete Masonry Association, 1978). These theories are based on the idealized mechanics of a dry, loose, homogenized, granular mass of soil particles, such as dry sand, that is cohesionless and assumes an angle of repose of 33 degrees. They can, however, serve as an approximation from which to develop a wall design. The proposed wall design must then be assessed for the specific conditions of the actual situation.

RETAINING WALL FAILURE

As with freestanding walls, retaining walls can fail in three ways (see the figure "Retaining Wall Failures"): overturning, sliding, and settling. The most common cause of wall failure is inadequate, poorly drained, and unstable footing conditions that lead to settling, which is usually followed by sliding and overturning. Much less common is the structural failure of the wall caused by excessive soil pressure.

- *Overturning.* Wall failure by overturning occurs when the wall revolves about the toe of the footing. In this situation, soil pressure, P, which is the force tending to overturn the wall, overcomes the weight of the wall, W, which is the force acting to keep the wall upright.
- *Sliding.* Wall failure by horizontal sliding occurs when the force of soil pressure overcomes the frictional resistance created by the weight of the wall interacting along the wall base with the coefficient of friction of the soil. Walls with increased soil pressure due to the presence of a surcharge are most susceptible to sliding. A surcharge is a load placed on a retaining wall in addition to the normal load of a level backfill.
- *Settling.* Settling is the most common type of wall failure. Wall failure by settling occurs when the foot pressure of the wall exceeds the bearing capacity of the foundation soil. Failure by overturning can also encourage settling. The uneven distribution of pressure over the entire footing during overturning is concentrated at the toe of the footing and eventually exceeds the soil-bearing capacity of the foundation soil. Inadequate wall drainage plays a significant role in settling by reducing the load-bearing capacity of the foundation soils. Thus, an adequate drainage system is a crucial consideration in the design of all retaining walls.

RETAINING WALL FOUNDATIONS

The design of foundations for retaining walls of 8 feet or less in height is generally based on the soil-bearing capacity and coefficient of friction values of general foundation soil types. The depth of the wall foundation is determined by the frost depth and the depth of soils with sufficient bearing capacities. The placement of the foundation below frost depth is crucial for protection against frost action. Values for bearing capacity and coefficient of friction are only generalized from the entire range of that soil type; therefore it is recommended that simple investigation into foundation conditions and depth to bedrock be undertaken prior to wall design.

RETAINING WALL JOINTS AND REINFORCEMENT

Control and Expansion Joints

The purpose of expansion joints is to allow a certain amount of masonry volume change and longitudinal movement of the wall while controlling cracking and maintaining alignment of wall sections. Based on the fact that concrete expands 0.62 inch per 100 feet of length per 100 degrees Fahrenheit, the spacing of expansion joints should be based on how much movement each joint can allow. Thus, the type of expansion joint and how much movement it will permit will determine the number of joints required for a specific wall length.

The need for expansion joints is also based on whether the wall has fixed ends, where longitudinal movement is restricted, or whether the ends are free for longitudinal movement. Expansion joints should be either the keyed type or the tongue-and-groove type in order to maintain alignment of the various wall sections. The recommended spacing for keyed expansion joints for retaining walls with ends fixed is 25 to 30 feet, or wherever breaks in the wall occur.

Retaining Wall Reinforcement

The purpose of steel reinforcement in retaining walls is to resist horizontal soil pressure on the stem and pressure on the toe of the footer.

Because concrete is weakest in tension, reinforcement of concrete block and poured-in-place concrete retaining walls is crucial if the wall is to withstand the tensile stresses of lateral soil pressure. Reinforcement is placed in the horizontal joints of the wall and vertically aligned through the core of the blocks, which are then filled with grout. The NCMA's recommendations for reinforcement of nonsurcharged walls are listed in the tables "Steel Reinforcement for Nonsurchaged Concrete Masonry Cantilevered Retaining Walls" and "Bond Beam Bar Spacing and Sizing in Cantilevered Wall Stem." If the spacing of the vertical bars does not exceed 3 feet, alternate vertical bars can be one-half the wall height rather than full height.

In the case of a retaining wall, the direction of stress is horizontal from soil pressure and vertical from the weight of the wall. As a result, the placement of vertical reinforcement should be closest to the back side of the wall nearest the soil pressure. Correspondingly, the location of horizontal steel reinforcement in the footing of the wall should be in the bottom of the toe of the footer closest to the area of contact with the soil because the footer tends to rotate downward. This reinforcement should extend vertically into the stem of the wall and be tied into the vertical reinforcement. Reinforcement in the heel of the footer should be placed in the top of the footer closest to the point of the contact with the soil because the heel of the footer tends to rotate upward. As with all reinforcement, a minimum of 2 inches of concrete should cover all steel bars.

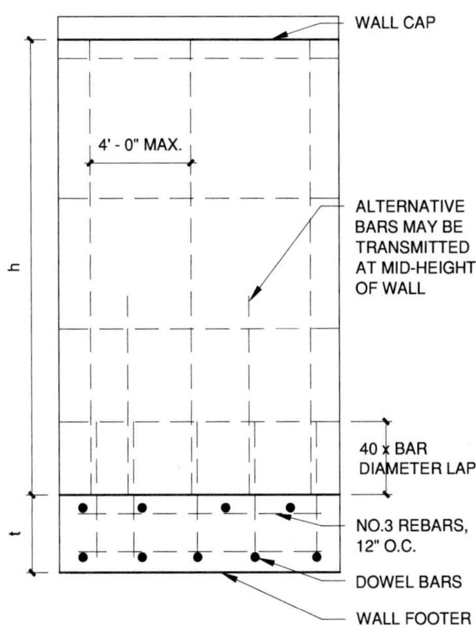

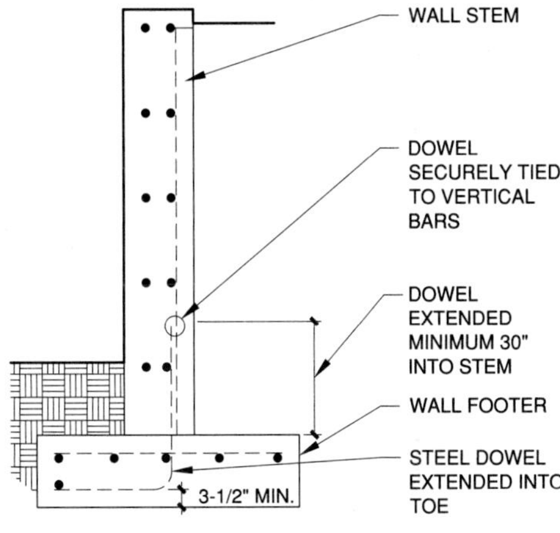

STEEL REINFORCEMENT PLACEMENT IN CONCRETE CANTILEVERED WALL

Janice Cervelli-Schach
Credits: Thanks to R. V. Cervelli for his assistance on the structural mechanics calculations.

STEEL REINFORCEMENT FOR NONSURCHAGED CONCRETE MASONRY CANTILEVERED RETAINING WALLS

	SIZE AND SPACING OF RODS		
WALL HEIGHT	VERTICAL BARS (IN.)	HORIZONTAL BARS IN FOOTING (IN.)	LONGITUDINAL BARS IN FOOTING
8 IN. THICK			
3 ft–4 in.	No 3. @ 32	No. 3 @ 27	No. 3 @ 12 o.c. for all thicknesses and height listed
4 ft–0 in.	No. 4 @ 32	No. 3 @ 27	
4 ft–8 in.	No. 5 @ 32	No. 3 @27	
5 ft–4 in.	No. 4 @ 16	No. 4 @ 30	
6 ft–0 in.	No. 6 @ 24	No. 4 @ 25	
12 IN. WIDE			
5 ft–4 in	No. 4 @ 24	No. 3 @ 25	
6 ft–0 in.	No. 4 @ 16	No. 4 @ 30	

Notes: Based on assumed soil weight of 100 lbs/cu ft and horizontal pressure equivalent to that exerted by a fluid of 45 lbs/cu ft.
1. Reinforcement of a size and spacing other than given in the table may be used, providing such other reinforcement furnishes an area of steel at least equal to that indicated in the table.
2. Alternate V-bars may be stopped at the midheight of the wall (H/2) if the spacing of the bars continued to the top does not exceed 36 inches.
3. Dowels must be at least equal in size and spacing to V-bars, project a minimum of 30 bar diameters into the filled block cores, and extend to the toe of the footing.
4. Joint reinforcement consisting of 9-guage longitudinal wires and 3/16-inch cross rods (8- and 12-inch walls) or 3/16-inch cross rods or tabs (14- and 18-inch walls) must be provided at 8-inch centers vertically.
5. Hollow concrete masonry units must be 8 inches nominal for 14-inch walls and 12 inches nominal for 18-inch walls.
6. Provide key for 8- and 12-inch walls where H exceeds 6 feet.

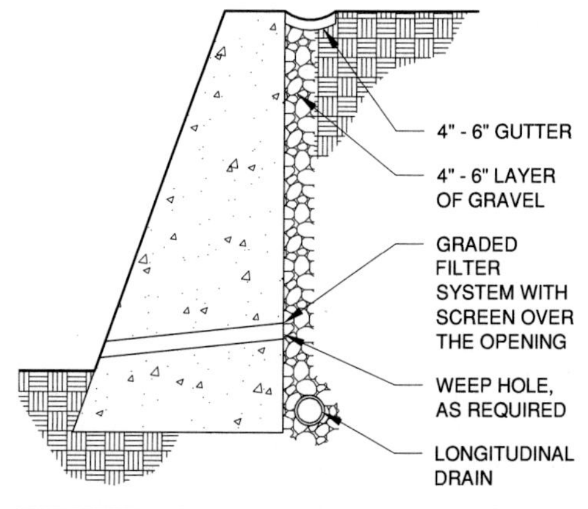

COMBINATION OF RETAINING WALL DRAINAGE SYSTEMS

BOND BEAM BAR SPACING AND SIZING IN CANTILEVERED WALL STEM

TOP BEAM	8-IN. WALL
Intermediate beam @ 16 in. o.c.	Two No. 4 bars or 9-gauge horizontal joint reinforcement @ 8 in. o.c. vertical spacing

Source: National Concrete Masonry Association, 1973.

The NCMA recommends that construction of concrete masonry retaining walls also include the installation of 9-gauge horizontal steel joint reinforcement spaced at 8-inch centers vertically. Horizontal reinforcement should not be continued across expansion or contraction joints.

DRAINAGE AND WATERPROOFING

Poor drainage and excessive moisture in backfill and foundation soils are prime threats to the structural integrity of a retaining wall. Increased soil moisture can affect the stability of the soil, exaggerate frost action, and increase horizontal soil pressure. The effects of frost action are especially great at the top 18 inches of the wall, where the amount of soil expansion is greatest and most frequent.

Continuous Back Drain

Under conditions of frequent freezing and thawing, and when impermeable soils tend to create excessive amounts of water in backfill and foundation soils, it is advisable to provide a continuous back drain. A continuous back drain consists of two parts:

- A 4- to 6-inch vertical layer of crushed stone or washed gravel adjacent to and covering the entire back of the wall
- A longitudinal drain surrounded by gravel and running the length of the wall, which ultimately daylights to allow the water to escape freely

One alternative to the gravel layer is a combination of wall waterproofing and porous drainage panels made of various geocomposite cores, such as polystyrene, that conduct water to the longitudinal drain. One alternative to the round longitudinal drain is the high-density polyethylene flat pipe available in 12- and 18-inch vertical panels. The installation of a continuous back drain in most conditions is sufficient drainage for walls less than 8 feet in height. If unusual soil or other conditions arise that increase the moisture level of the retained or foundation soil, other drainage methods are recommended in combination with the continuous back drain.

Weep Holes

Weep holes are generally 2- to 4-inch diameter holes placed through the wall and spaced at a maximum of 5 to 10 feet longitudinally along the wall. Additional weep holes spaced 5 feet vertically may also be necessary depending on the porosity of the backfill and the height of the wall.

Weep holes are usually of noncorrosive metal, plastic pipe, or, less commonly, of properly fired clay. Corrosive metal pipes should be avoided because they can stain the face of the wall. Noncorrosive materials, such as polyvinyl chloride or polyethylene, are preferable.

A screen or other suitable filter material should be placed over the weep hole. The Portland Cement Association recommends that the back end of the pipe be covered with a rustproof, nonbiodegradable cloth or soil-separating screen to prevent the washing out of backfill soil or the collection of insects or animals that could plug the opening. The traditional method for backfill around the weep hole is to install a pocket of 3/4-inch clean, crushed stone.

Weep holes have a number of disadvantages. In heavy rains, weep holes contribute to the reduction of the bearing capacity of the foundation soil by depositing moisture directly onto the toe of the footer. In addition, the Portland Cement Association maintains that weep holes do not relieve water pressure behind the wall to a sufficient depth. Therefore, it is recommended that weep holes be used to complement a continuous back drain system, never to replace one. In fact, the installation of a continuous back drain can be substituted for a horizontal row of weep holes.

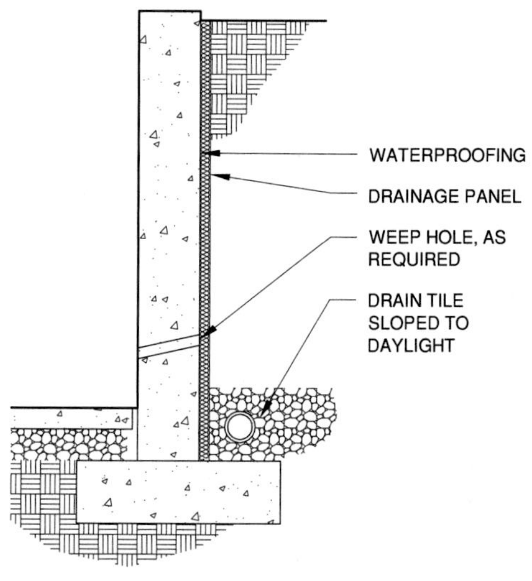

ALTERNATIVE VERTICAL DRAINAGE PANEL SYSTEMS

Waterproofing

Waterproofing can be an effective way to prevent surface staining, streaking, and efflorescence. Waterproofing acts as a barrier between the back surface of the wall and the backfill soil, thereby prohibiting moisture from entering the structure of the wall. To be effective, waterproofing must be continuous and must completely cover the back side of the wall. Traditional methods of waterproofing have included the following:

- Multiple layers of asphaltic mastic, fiberglass, or bituminous-saturated felt or fabric
- Various waterproofing liquids
- Sheets of applied elastomers or preformed polyethylene coated on both sides with asphalt emulsion

In unusual circumstances, backfill material, such as impervious clay, may be modified with clay additives (e.g., bentonite clay in the form of liquids, liquid sprays, panels, and trowel-grade mix).

The more modern method of using plastic sheets applied with asphaltic mastics to hold them in place

Janice Cervelli-Schach
Credits: Thanks to R. V. Cervelli for his assistance on the structural mechanics calculations.

and to seal seams may prove to be longer lived and provide greater impermeability.

Gutters

Extreme soil water conditions, such as soil types 2 and 3, require that the surface area of the backfill directly behind the wall be covered with an impermeable surface, such as a concrete gutter. The gutter directs water away from the backfill area before it has the opportunity to percolate directly behind the wall or to discharge over the wall face. Gutters are highly recommended for those walls that have sloped backfills and that encompass a large watershed area.

SIZING OF POSTS AND PLANKS FOR TIMBER RETAINING WALLS

			DEPTH OF SET (FT)		
HEIGHT OF WALL (FT)	SPACING OF POSTS C-C (FT)	DIAMETER OF POST (IN.)	GOOD SOIL	AVERAGE SOIL	POOR SOIL
3	6	6	3.5	4.5	6.0
	4	6	4.0	5.0	6.5
4	4	6	4.0	5.0	6.5
	6	8	4.0	4.5	6.5
5	4	8	4.0	5.0	6.5
	5	8	4.5	5.5	
5	9.5			7.5	
6	4	9.5	5.5	7.0	9.5
	5	9.5	6.0	8.0	
	5	10.5			11.0

Source: Munson, 1974.

TIMBER RETAINING WALL CONSTRUCTION

Timber walls cannot be characterized under any of the three general categories of retaining walls discussed earlier, as they have no true lateral support and are more susceptible to poor soil conditions than other walls. Munson (1974) recommends that the height of timber walls be limited to 10 feet. Since exact determination of soil pressure is practically impossible, accurate determination of the lateral support provided by the soil in which pilings and posts are set is also practically impossible. Thus, the sizing, spacing, and depth of set of timber members are based on empirical proportions and experience rather than on theoretical models and calculations.

Types of Timber Retaining Walls

Timber walls can be categorized into the following general types:

- *Cribbing wall planks.* Usually stacked horizontally and held in place not by pilings or posts but by gravity.
- *Horizontal plank and pile wall.* Most stable of the three types and recommended for heights up to 7 feet (without tiebacks or deadmen) and widths of 10 feet.
- *Vertical plank and pile wall.* Timberplanks are set vertically and held in place by horizontal guide piles, heavy timber wales, or cables. The recommended height limit of this type of wall is 4 feet or less with no surcharge.

Munson (1974) recommends that timber walls be given a batter of 1 to 1½ inches per foot of wall height.

Depth of Set

Munson (1974) recommends that the depth of set for vertical piles and posts in good and average conditions (e.g., well-drained, compact fine sand, medium clay, sandy loam, and loose coarse sand and gravel) be equal to the height of the wall above grade. The depth should be increased by 40 percent in poorer conditions (e.g., poorly drained and high-moisture uncompacted sands, soft clay, and silts). The depth should be increased to twice the height for very poor conditions.

Deadmen

Walls over 7 feet in height must resist significant soil pressures without the benefit of significant wall weight. Hence, walls of this height require additional lateral stabilization. This can be accomplished with the installation of "deadmen." Deadmen are anchors placed into the soil fill behind the wall to give it additional lateral stability.

The spacing of deadmen depends on the type and moisture content of the soil. Munson (1974) recommends that deadmen be spaced at 10- to 15-foot intervals horizontally and staggered 3 to 4 feet vertically. As with other types of retaining wall bases, deadmen should be set in undisturbed soil for maximum support.

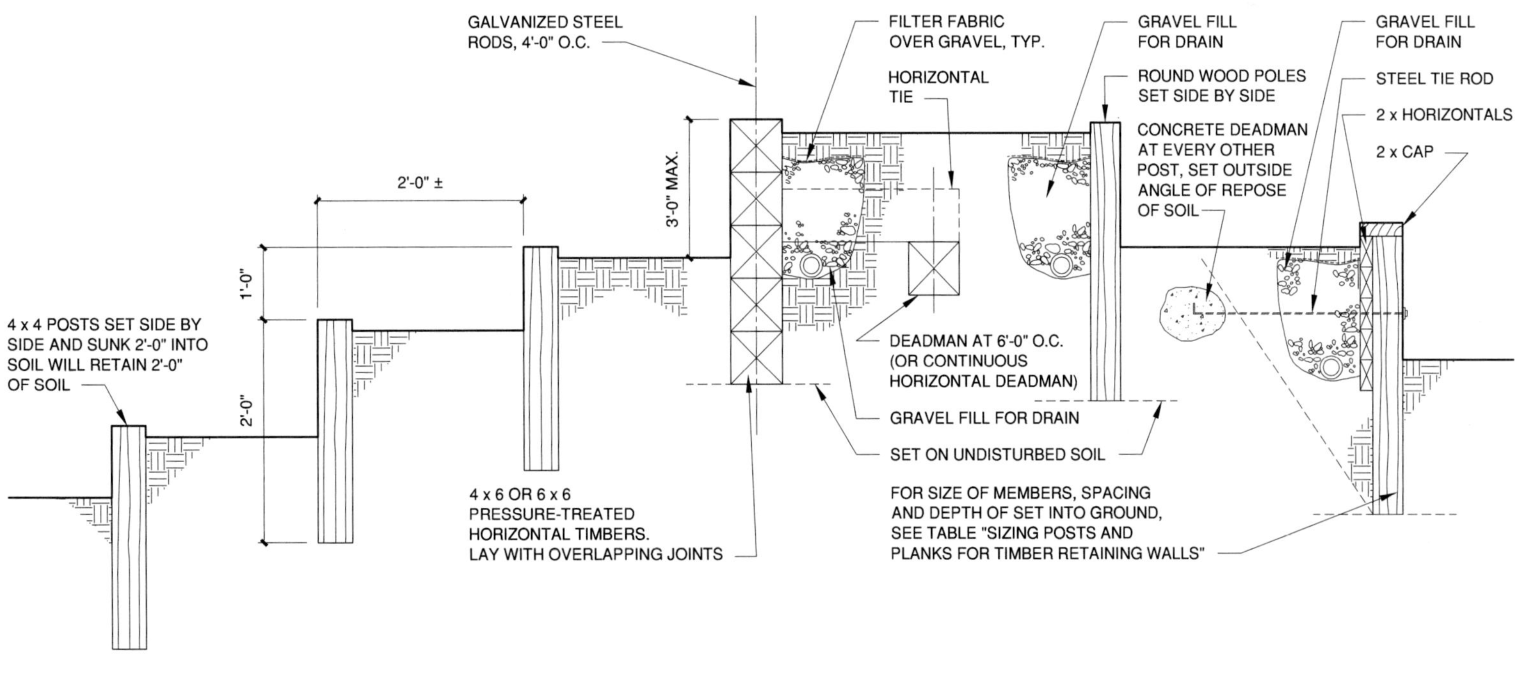

WOOD RETAINING WALL

Janice Cervelli-Schach
Credits: Thanks to R. V. Cervelli for his assistance on the structural mechanics calculations.

MODULAR GRAVITY WALL SYSTEMS

Modular gravity wall systems are an increasingly popular and economic alternative to conventional gravity and cantilevered retaining wall systems, especially for walls on a residential scale. Modular concrete walls are very similar in concept to dry-laid gravity masonry retaining walls. The weight of the wall creates sufficient stability against the lateral pressure of retained earth, yet the entire system remains flexible to the differential movement and settlement of the foundation soil and the wall mass. The landscape architect should check with the manufacturer of a particular module before selecting it for use, to ensure that it is made of concrete with a compressive climate strength and absorption rate appropriate to the climate conditions of the wall location.

Modular gravity wall systems are of two general types, interlocking and connecting pin:

- The interlocking system involves mortarless, stack, concrete units with or without a bin for soil interfill. The weight of the wall and soil interfill create shear resistance between units, which provides overall stability. The units are allowed to move, to absorb the action of soil expansion, contraction, and settlement. As a result, considerable heights can be achieved at a relatively low cost. The front lips of the stackable units are designed to create the wall batter and lock the units together from concrete course. Batters vary from 25 to 70 degrees for interconnecting plantable walls and from 12 degrees to ¼ inch per course for connecting pin nonplantable systems. The units can be set at staggered widths to conform to a great variety of convex and concave radii.
- Connecting pin wall systems join concrete units together with metal or fiberglass pins to achieve stability from one course to the next. The pins can be adjusted to a number of positions, which allows for great flexibility in the degree of curvature of the wall. High-strength fiberglass pins are preferable to metal pins because they do not rust and create unsightly stains on the units after construction.

Certain types of interlocking wall systems can be interplanted with vegetation. The troughs or bins of the units retain sufficient moisture to create suitable environments for decorative groundcover or bedding plants. Such "green walls" reduce the potentially negative visual impact of massive concrete retaining walls.

Foundations and Drainage

Modular walls are especially susceptible to sliding. Modular walls above 4 feet may require additional support, including geogrid systems, concrete or block deadmen, screw anchors, steel augers or tie rods, concrete footers, or pilasters. In all cases, modular wall systems require stable foundation soils and controlled soil expansion. The base of all walls must be designed for wall height and angle, surcharges and other loading, potential slippage, and any other site conditions. In all cases, it is best to refer to the manufacturer's specifications and recommendations in designing modular gravity wall systems.

The number of courses required to be buried below grade depends on the soil conditions and the height of the wall. Generally, one course is required for walls under 4 feet in height, and the number increases to two courses for walls from 4 to 10 feet high on 95 percent compacted granular fill. If soil conditions are poor, including low bearing capacity and permeability (soft clay, organic silts, and silt clays), additional courses, pilasters, and concrete beam foundations may be required for strength and leveling.

The placement of a tensar geogrid system, a high-density nondeteriorating polyethylene or polyester fiber, as a soil reinforcement material between courses is recommended. It is also recommended that the design of the wall be made using the grid manufacturer's design criteria for the specific grid type. Drainage of modular wall systems is also automatic to the design of modular systems; water table and surface runoff are filtered through the spaces between the units. Such a built-in drainage system reduces the threat of wall failure due to water pressure. In certain conditions, however, drainage tile or weep holes may still be necessary. When excess water conditions exist behind the wall, the placement of geotextile fabrics may also be required immediately behind the units or between existing and backfill soil. Sandy soils or clean crushed stone may be required for backfill to replace soils susceptible to washout. A 6- to 8-inch clay cap or gutter over the backfill can also be used to prevent penetration of surface runoff behind the wall. In all cases, backfill material should be installed and compacted to 95 percent before the next course is laid.

GABION WALL SYSTEMS

Another economical alternative to conventional wall systems is the gabion. Gabion walls consist of rectangular cages made of heavy, galvanized hexagonal woven steel wire mesh or polymer grid mesh with openings laced together and filled with any durable hard local stone from 3 to 8 inches in diameter. The polymer material has the advantage of being resistant to corrosion, abrasion, and ultraviolet light. Steel mesh coated with polyvinyl chloride or the polymer mesh is recommended for applications in severely polluted soil or water conditions.

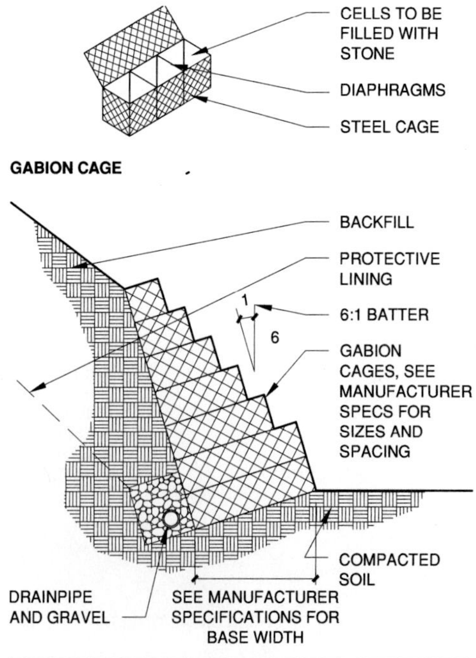

GABION WALL SECTION

MECHANICS AND STATIC INVESTIGATION OF RETAINING WALLS

The discussion of retaining wall mechanics in this section is limited to walls 6 feet or less in height and those located in areas predetermined by site analysis to be suitable and safe for the construction of such walls. In the case of retaining walls, horizontal soil pressure is seen as a pressure triangle centered behind the wall (refer to the "Soil Pressure Triangle of a Retaining Wall" figure).

The center of gravity of this triangle is at a point one-third the height of the wall above the base. Soil pressure acts parallel to the surface of the backfill. Thus, soil pressure acts horizontally toward a wall with level backfill and at an angle with surcharged walls. Angles of repose vary with each soil type, but to simplify, it is assumed that for all conditions the retained soil will have a maximum slope of 33 degrees 41 minutes.

The Concept of Statics

The investigation of retaining walls for stability involves the application of "statics," a branch of mechanics dealing with the equilibrium interaction of forces on a mass to hold it motionless. In wall investigations, the resultant is the vector sum of the force of the lateral soil pressure, P (the horizontal vector component), and the force of the weight of the wall, W (the vertical vector component). The magnitude and direction of the resultant can be found by a graphic generation of parallelograms of force or by the use of trigonometric functions.

A parallelogram of force is a graphic representation of the two component nonparallel force vectors in a parallelogram. The two vector components are drawn lying in their respective directions. The length of each vector or component indicates the relative magnitude of the component (in pounds). The parallelogram is formed by the intersection of the components and the addition of opposite and equal sides to complete the form. The resultant is the diagonal of the parallelogram. The direction and magnitude of the resultant can be determined from the drawing. The principle of the middle third (refer to the figure of the same name) is a condition of equilibrium occurring when the line of action of the resultant strikes through the middle third of the foundation. The stability of the wall increases as the resultant reaches the center of the middle third of the base.

Investigations for Retaining Wall Stability

A series of proofs or tests must be completed to evaluate a given wall configuration for stability against overturning, sliding, and settling. It is emphasized again that the methods for wall investigation presented here are based on a set of assumptions that cannot apply to all cases, especially those involving expansive soils. Also, it is recommended that factors of safety be applied to each test to provide a margin of safety for unpredictable site and soil characteristics.

The discussion of retaining wall mechanics in this section is limited to walls 6 feet or less in height and

Janice Cervelli-Schach
Credits: Thanks to R. V. Cervelli for his assistance on the structural mechanics calculations.

those located in areas predetermined by site analysis to be suitable and safe for the construction of such walls. The investigation of wall stability usually begins with the generation of a preliminary wall cross section representing 1 foot of length of the wall. The design of the cross section and the dimensions used are initially based on semiempirical rules, codes, and previous experience with local conditions. The design of taller walls necessitates the exploration of backfill and foundation soil conditions and the assistance of a structural engineer.

The design of a retaining wall assumes that soil pressure is directly proportional to the height of the soil retained. Soil pressure is seen as a pressure triangle centered behind the wall. The center of gravity of this triangle is at a point one-third the height of the wall above the base. Soil pressure acts parallel to the surface of the backfill. Thus, soil pressure acts horizontally toward a wall with level backfill. Angles of repose vary with each soil type, but to simplify, it is assumed that for all conditions the retained soil will have a maximum slope of 33 degrees 41 minutes. If the backfill of the retaining wall is sloped at the assumed 33 degrees 41 minutes slope, or 1.5:1 slope, soil pressure will act at the same angle to the wall.

A condition of equilibrium occurs when the line of action of the resultant strikes through the middle third of the wall foundations. In this condition, all stresses and forces are distributed evenly, which limits all forces along the footer to those being compressive. When the resultant passes outside the middle third of the footing, even weight distribution over the entire footing width does not occur, which creates eccentric loading and the possibility of wall failure in one or more ways.

Investigation of Walls with No Surcharge

General Stability

The following investigations for stability are for walls with level, horizontal backfill and no additional load or sloped backfill.

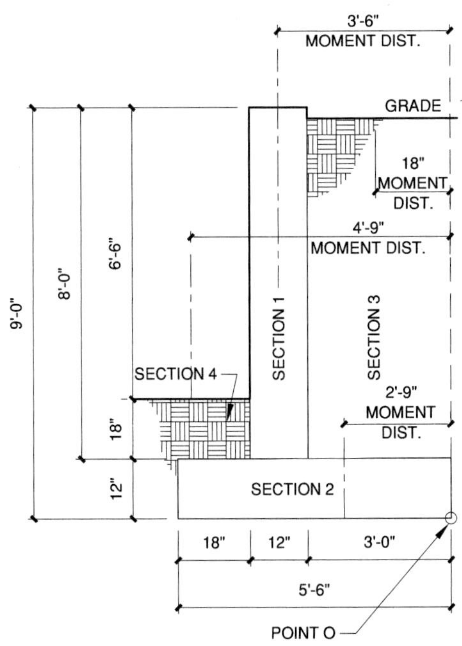

EXAMPLE 1: DETERMINATION OF WALL WEIGHT AND CENTROID BY SECTION

Example: Test for the general stability of a nonsurcharged concrete cantilevered retaining wall with a height of 6 feet 6 inches above grade and a total effective height of 9 feet.

a. Find W, the total weight of the wall, as follows:

	Volume of One Section Linear Foot	x	Weight of Material (lbs/cu ft)	Wall Weight = (lbs) W
1	1 x 8 x 1 = 8 cu ft		150	1,200 = W_1
2	1 x 5.5 x 1 = 5.5 cu ft		150	825 = W_2
3	3 x 8 x 1 = 24 cu ft		100	2,400 = W_3
4	1.5 x 1.5 x 1 = 2.25 cu ft		100	225 = W_4
				Total: 4,650

b. Find the location of the wall centroid.

1. Determine the moment about point O of point T. Select point O, as follows:

Section	Weight (lbs.)	x	Moment Arm from Point O (ft)	Moment = (ft-lbs)
1	1,200		3.5	4,200.00
2	8.25		2.75	2,268.75
3	2,400		1.5	3,600.00
4	225		4.75	1,068.75
				Total: 11,137.50

2. Next, find the centroid of the wall (location of the total resultant weight, W) by finding Arm R.

Arm R = total moment/W
= 11,137.5 ft-lbs/4,650 lbs
= 2.4 ft
W is located 2.4 feet from Point O.

c. Next, find the horizontal component, P, or the lateral soil pressure force, with Rankine's formula:

$$P = 0.286 \frac{wh2}{2}$$

Where: w = soil weight, lbs/cu ft
h = effective wall height, ft
P = 0.286 x 100 lbs/cu ft x $(9 \text{ ft})^2$
= 1,158.3 lbs

d. The final step is to construct the force parallelogram to determine whether the resultant force strikes through the middle third of the wall base.

W = 4,650 lbs
P = 1,158.3 lbs
R = 4,800 lbs
e = 0.40 ft Check: Resultant falls within the middle third of the wall base.

Overturning

Compare M_O to M_R and apply a safety factor of 2:

The centroid is
5.5 ft – 2.4 ft = 3.1 ft (from point T)
MR = W x Arm R = 4,650 lbs x 3.1 ft
= 14,415 ft-lbs
Arm O = h/3
= 9 ft/3
= 3 ft
Mo = P x Arm O
= 1,158.3 lbs x 3 ft
= 3,475 ft-lbs
MR/ Mo > Safety Factor

$$\frac{14{,}415 \text{ ft-lbs}}{3{,}475 \text{ ft-lbs}} > 2$$

4.15 > 2 Check: Wall is resistant to overturning.

Sliding

Compare W multiplied by soil coefficient of friction (see the table "Average Coefficient of Friction of Common Soils") and apply a safety factor of 1.5:

$$\frac{\text{W x coefficient of friction}}{\text{P}} > \text{Safety Factor 1.5}$$

$$\frac{4{,}650 \text{ lbs x } 0.50}{1{,}158.3 \text{ lbs}} > 1.5$$

2 > 1.5 Check: Wall is resistant to sliding.

In cases in which the safety factor is not met, a number of alternatives can be pursued to increase the resistance of the wall to the horizontal soil pressure. An increase in wall weight could be pursued if the increase did not cause the foot pressure of the wall to exceed the bearing capacity of the soil. The most economical method for increasing the weight of a cantilevered wall is to increase the amount of soil in contact with the footing by increasing the footing span compared with an increase in the thickness of the concrete wall.

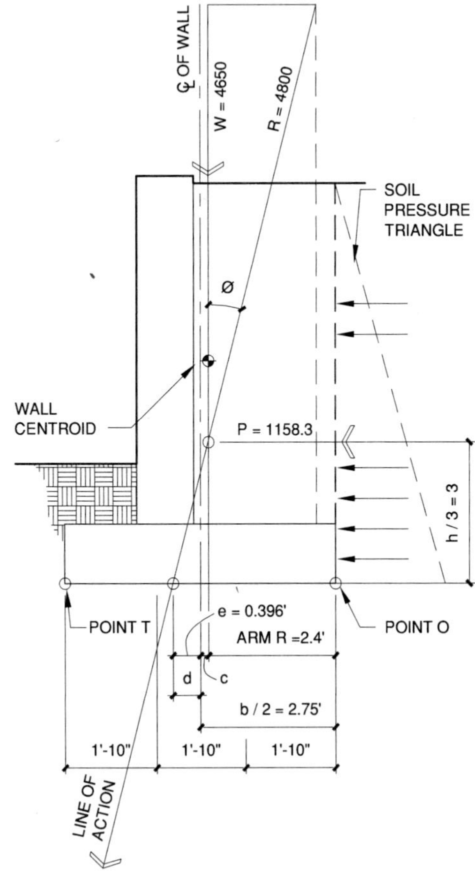

EXAMPLE 2: NONSURCHARGED CANTILEVERED WALL PARALLELOGRAM OF FORCE BY THE GRAPHIC METHOD

Janice Cervelli-Schach
Credits: Thanks to R. V. Cervelli for his assistance on the structural mechanics calculations.

Settling

Compare wall foot pressure with the bearing capacity of the foundation soil (see the table "Bearing Capacities of Common Soil Types") and apply safety factor of 1.5.

$$f = W/A\left(1 + \frac{6e}{b}\right)$$

$$= \frac{4{,}650 \text{ lbs}}{5.5 \text{ sq ft}}\left(1 + \frac{6 \times 0.396 \text{ ft}}{5.5 \text{ ft}}\right)$$

Note:
W = weight of wall (1 foot length) lbs
e = distance from wall to centerline to intersection of the line of action of R with the bottom of the f footer, ft
A = bearing area between wall footer and soil (one foot length), sq ft
b = footer width, ft
Soil-bearing capacity of:

$$\frac{\text{Foundation soil (wet sand)}}{f} > \text{Safety Factor } 1.5$$

$$\frac{4{,}000 \text{ lbs/sq ft}}{1210.7 \text{ lbs/sq ft}} > 1.5$$

3.3 > 1.5 Check: Wall is resistant to settling.

Investigation of Wall with Surcharge

Example: Test a given concrete gravity wall that is 4 feet above grade and has a total height of 7.62 feet. The backfill is assumed to be at a slope of 33 degrees.

General Stability

a. Find W:

	Volume of 1-ft Section (cu ft) ×		Weight of Material lbs/cu ft	Wall Weight = (lbs) W
1	0.5 x 0.5 x 6	= 1.5	150	225 = W_1
2	1 x 6	= 6.0	150	900 = W_2
3	0.5 x 2.5 x 6	= 7.5	150	1,125 = W_3
4	0.5 x 2.5 x 6	= 7.5	100	750 = W_4
5	0.5 x 2.5 x 1.62	= 2.03	100	203 = W_5
			Total:	3,203

b. Find location of wall centroid:

Note: For sections that are right triangles, the centroid is found at one third the length of the base from the 90 degree angle.

Section	Weight (lbs.) ×	Moment Arm from Point O (ft)	Moment = (ft-lbs)
1	225	3.67	825.75
2	900	3.00	2,700.00
3	1,125	1.67	1,878.75
4	750	0.83	622.50
5	203	0.83	168.49
			Total: 6,159.49

Arm R = total moment/W
= 6,195.49 ft-lbs/3,203 lbs
= 1.93 ft from point O

c. Find the horizontal component, p:

$$h = h_1 + h_2 = 7.62 \text{ ft}$$

$$p = {}^{*}0.833\,\frac{Wh^2}{2}$$

$$= 0.833 \times 100 \times (7.62)^2/2$$

$$= 2{,}418.38 \text{ lbs}$$

*Note: The constant (0.833) changes for surcharged walls.

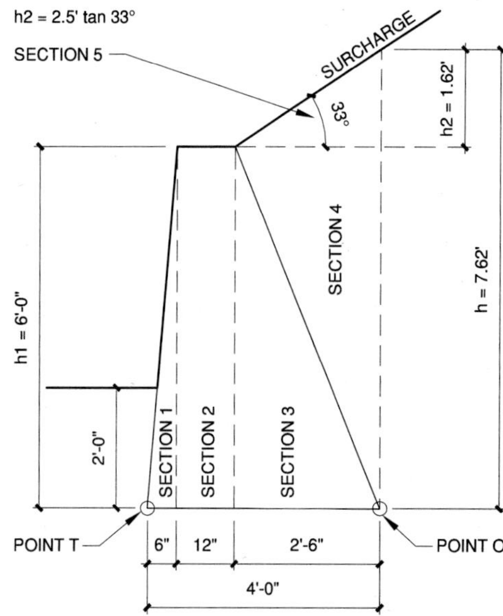

EXAMPLE 3: SURCHARGED GRAVITY WALL DIMENSIONS AND WEIGHTS BY SECTION

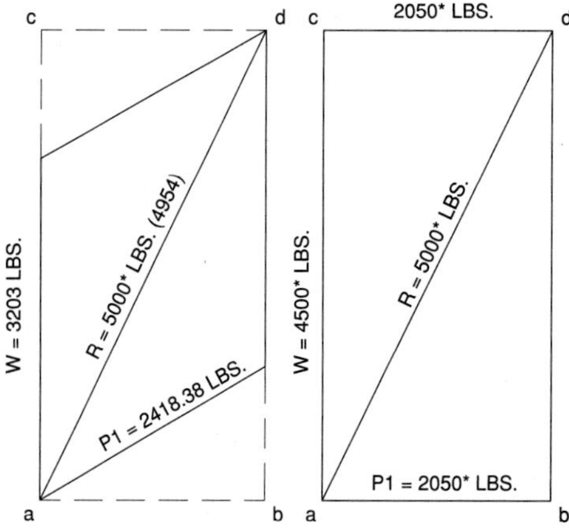

W = 3203 LBS.
P = 2418 LBS.
R = 5000 LBS.
W1 = 4500 LBS.
P1 = 2050 LBS.
* VALUES HAVE BEEN SCALED

EXAMPLE 3: SURCHARGED GRAVITY WALL EQUIVALENT FORCES

Note that with a surcharge, the line of action of the horizontal component, P, lies parallel to the surface of the backfill soil, or at a slope of 33 degrees. With the horizontal component at a slope, the force parallelogram is not a rectangle. The equivalent rectangle is constructed, as shown in the figure "Example 3: Surcharged Gravity Wall Parallelogram of Force by the Trigonometric Methods" and equivalent values determined and used in the later checks for overturning, sliding, and settling.

W = 3,205 lbs	W_1 = 4,500 lbs
P = 2,418.38 lbs	P1 = 2,050 lbs
R = 5,000 lbs	R1 = 5,000 lbs

e = 0.6 ft = 7.2 in

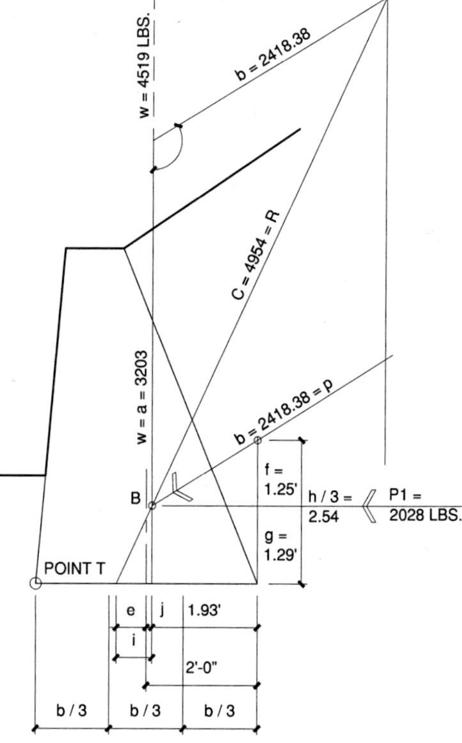

EXAMPLE 3: SURCHARGED GRAVITY WALL PARALLELOGRAM OF FORCE BY THE TRIGONOMETRIC METHOD

Overturning

Compare M_O with M_R and apply a safety factor of 2.

Arm O = g = 1.29 ft
$M_O = P_1 \times \text{Arm O}$
= 2,028 lbs x 1.29 ft
= 2,616 ft-lbs
Arm R = 2.07 ft
$M_R = W1 \times \text{Arm R}$
= 4,519 lbs x 2.07 ft
= 9,354 ft-lbs

$$\frac{M_R}{M_O} > \text{Safety Factor } 2$$

$$\frac{9{,}354}{2{,}616} > 2$$

3.6 > 2 Check: Wall is resistant to overturning.

Sliding

Compare lateral soil pressure, P, to shear strength created by the frictional resistance between the footer and soil and apply a safety factor of 1.5:

$$\frac{W_1 \times \text{coefficient of friction ("Average Coefficient of Friction of Common Soils" table)}}{P_1} > \text{Safety Factor } 1.5$$

$$\frac{4{,}519 \text{ lbs} \times 0.5}{2{,}028 \text{ lbs}} > 1.5$$

1.11 > 1.5 Does not check: Wall does not meet the factor of safety of 1.5; therefore, a redesign of the wall is required. Measures must be taken such as increasing wall weight, soil replacement with gravel, or the addition of keys.

Janice Cervelli-Schach

Credits: Thanks to R. V. Cervelli for his assistance on the structural mechanics calculations.

AVERAGE COEFFICIENT OF FRICTION OF COMMON SOILS

SOIL TYPE	COEFFICIENT OF FRICTION
Gravel	0.60
Sand	0.40
Silt/clay, dry	0.50
Clay, wet	0.30

BEARING CAPACITIES OF COMMON SOIL TYPES

SOIL TYPE	BEARING CAPACITY (LBS/SQ FT)
Soft clay	2,000
Firm clay	4,000
Wet sand	4,000
Fine dry sand	6,000
Hard clay	8,000
Coarse dry sand	8,000
Gravel	12,000
Hard shale	20,000
Hard rock	160,000

Settling

Compare the soil-bearing capacity (see the "Gravity Wall Foundation Guidelines" table) to foot pressure of the wall, f, and apply a safety factor of 1.5:

$$f = \frac{W_1}{A}\left(1 + \frac{6e}{b}\right)$$

$$f = \frac{4{,}519 \text{ lbs}}{4}\left(1 + \frac{6\ (0.509 \text{ ft})}{4}\right)$$

$$= 1{,}988.36 \text{ lbs/sq ft}$$

$$\frac{\text{Soil-bearing capacity ("Gravity Wall Foundation Guidelines" table)}}{\text{Foot pressure}} > \text{Safety Factor } 1.5$$

$$\frac{4{,}000 \text{ lbs/sq ft}}{1{,}988.36 \text{ lbs/sq ft}} > 1.5$$

2.01 > Check: Wall is resistant to settling.

REFERENCES

Adams, J. L.1979. *The Complete Concrete, Masonry, and Brick Handbook.* New York: Van Nostrand Reinhold.

Advanced Drainage Systems, Inc. 1987. "The ADS AdvanEDGE Drainage System." Hilliard, OH: Advanced Drainage Systems, Inc.

American Concrete Institute. 1984. *Concrete Craftsman Series 2: Cast-In-Place Walls.* Detroit, MI: American Concrete Institute.

American Concrete Institute Committee 531.1970. "Concrete Masonry Structures—Design and Construction," *Journal of the American Concrete Institute Proceedings*, 67(5): 380-403.

———. "Concrete Masonry Structures—Design and Construction," *Journal of the American Concrete Institute Proceedings*, 67(6): 442-460.

Brick Institute of America. 1980. "Technical Notes on Brick Construction: Differential Movement," *Flexible Anchorage,* Part III of III, BIA 18B. Reston, VA: Brick Institute of America.

———. "Technical Notes on Brick Construction," *Brick Veneer—New Construction,* BIA 28 Revised. Reston, VA: Brick Institute of America.

———. 1987a. "Technical Notes on Brick Construction," *Brick Masonry Cavity Walls,* BIA 21 Revised. Reston, VA: Brick Institute of America.

———. 1987b. "Technical Notes on Brick Construction," "*Brick Masonry Cavity Walls—Detailing,*" BIA21B. Reston, VA: Brick Institute of America.

———. 1988a. "Technical Notes on Brick Construction," *Brick Masonry Cavity Walls—Construction,* BIA 21 C. Reston, VA: Brick Institute of America.

———. 1988b. "Technical Notes on Brick Construction," *Differential Movement: Cause and Effect,* Part I of III. Reston, VA: Brick Institute of America.

———. 1988c. "Technical Notes on Brick Construction," *Differential Movement: Expansion Joints,* Part II of III. BIA. 18A. Reston, VA: Brick Institute of America.

Carpenter, Jot D. 1976. *Handbook of Landscape Architectural Construction.* Washington, DC: Landscape Architecture Foundation.

Ching, Francis D.K. 1976. *Building Construction Illustrated.* New York: Van Nostrand Reinhold.

Geotech Systems Inc. 1985. "Geotech Drainage Products." Great Falls, VA: Geotech Systems, Inc.

Giles, Floyd. 1986. *Landscape Construction Procedures: Techniques, and Design.* Champaign, IL: Stipes Publishing Co.

Harr, M. E. 1966. *Foundations of Theoretical Soil Mechanics.* New York: McGraw-Hill.

Harris, Charles W., and Nicholas I. Dines. 1988. *Landscape Architectural Time-Saver Standards.* New York: McGraw-Hill.

Jewel, Linda. December 1984. "Construction: Wood Crib Retaining Walls," *Landscape Architecture Magazine.* 103-106.

Kirkwood, Niall. 2004. *Weathering and Durability in Landscape Architecture.* Hoboken, NJ: John Wiley & Sons, Inc.

Kreh, R.T. 1982. *Simplified Masonry Skills,* 2nd ed. New York: Van Nostrand Reinhold.

Landphair, Harlow C., and Fred Klatt, Jr. 1979. *Landscape Architecture Construction.* New York: Elsevier.

———. 1988. *Landscape Architecture Construction.* New York: Elsevier.

Loffelstein, Inc. 1982. *Engineering Manual—Loffel, Wall.* Loffelstein, Inc.

McCafferri Gabions, Inc. 1987. *Flexible Gabion Structures in Earth Retaining Works.* Williamsport, MD: McCafferri Gabions, Inc.

———. 1989. *Specifications for Gabions,* Williamsport, MD: McCafferri Gabions, Inc.

Merriman, Thaddeus, and Thomas Wiggin. 1944. *American Civil Engineers Handbook,* 5th ed. New York: John Wiley & Sons, Inc.

Merritt, Fredric S. (ed.). 1968. *Standard Handbook for Engineers.* New York: McGraw-Hill.

Munson, A.E. 1974. *Construction Design for Landscape Architects.* New York: McGraw-Hill.

Murray-Wooley, Carolyn, and Karl Raitz. 1992. *Rock Fences of the Bluegrass.* Lexington, KY: University Press of Kentucky.

National Bureau of Standards. 1970. *American Star Building Code Requirements for Masonry, A41.1-1953.* Issued 1954; reaffirmed 1970. Washington, DC: U.S. Department of Commerce.

National Concrete Masonry Association. 1970. "Concrete Masonry Screen Walls," NCMA-TEK 5. Herndon, VA: National Concrete Masonry Association.

———. 1973a. "Concrete Masonry Retaining Walls Pools," NCMA-TEK 50. Herndon, VA: National Concrete Masonry Association.

———. 1973b. "Prefabricated Concrete Masonry Panels," NCMA-TEK 247. Herndon, VA: National Concrete Masonry Association.

———. 1975. "Empirical Design of Concrete Masonry Walls," NCMA-TEK 73. Herndon, VA: National Concrete Masonry Association.

———. 1977a. "Concrete Masonry Gravity Retaining Walls," NCMA-TEK 86. Herndon, VA: National Concrete Masonry Association.

———. 1977b. "Curtain and Panel Wall of Concrete Masonry," NCMA-TEK 93. Herndon, VA: National Concrete Masonry Association.

———. 1978. "Structural Design of Concrete Masonry Fences," NCMA-TEK 98. Herndon, VA: National Concrete Masonry Association.

———. 1982. "Highway Sound Barrier Wall Design," NCMA-TEK 127. Herndon, VA: National Concrete Masonry Association.

———. 1983. "Concrete Masonry Cantilever Retaining Walls," NCMA-TEK 4B. Herndon, VA: National Concrete Masonry Association.

Nelischer, Maurice (ed.). 1988. *Handbook of Landscape Architecture Construction,* vol. 2. Washington, DC: Landscape Architecture Foundation.

Parker, Harry, and James Ambrose. 1984. *Simplified Engineering for Architects and Builders,* 6th ed. New York: John Wiley & Sons, Inc.

Parker, Harry, and John MacGuire. 1954. *Simplified Engineering for Architects and Builders.* New York: John Wiley & Sons, Inc.

Pittsburgh Corning. 1988a. *Create the Extraordinary with PC Glass Block Products.* Pittsburgh, PA: Pittsburgh Corning.

———. 1988b. *Installation Specifications: Block Products.* Pittsburgh, PA: Pittsburgh Corning.

Portland Cement Association. 1983. *Small Concrete Gravity Retaining Walls.* Skokie, IL: Portland Cement Association.

Ramsey, Charles G., and Harry Sleeper. 1970. *Architectural Graphics Standards,* 6th ed. New York: John Wiley & Sons, Inc.

Randall, F.A., Jr., and W.C. Panarese. *Concrete Masonry Handbook for Architects, Engineers, and Builders.* Skokie, IL: Portland Cement Association.

Seelye, Elwyn E. 1960. *Design Data Book for Civil Engineers,* vol. 1, 3rd ed. New York: John Wiley & Sons, Inc.

Teonnies, Henry. 1971. *Reinforced Concrete Masonry Design Tables.* Herndon, VA: National Concrete Masonry Association.

———. 1989. *Nonreinforced Concrete Masonry Design Tables.* Herndon, VA: National Concrete Masonry Association.

Terzaghi, Karl, and Ralph Peck. 1948. *Soil Mechanics in Practice.* New York: John Wiley & Sons, Inc.

Thompson, J. William, and Kim Sorvig. 2000. *Sustainable Landscape Construction.* Washington DC: Island Press.

Transportation Research Board. 1973. "Noise Abatement and Control. Highway Research Record No. 448." Washington, DC: Transportation Research Board.

Walker, Theodore D. 1978. *Site Design and Construction Detailing.* West Lafayette, IN: PDA Publishers.

Westmacott, Richard. May/June 1985. "Construction: Box and Mattress Gabions," *Landscape Architecture Magazine.* 86-89.

Janice Cervelli-Schach

Credits: Thanks to R. V. Cervelli for his assistance on the structural mechanics calculations.

FENCES AND SCREENS

HISTORY

Historically, fences have been used to physically and visually delineate property. The same holds true today. Fences can provide privacy and physical protection against varying levels of intrusion and so are used to address safety and security concerns related to restricting access to areas. They also can be used to modify and mitigate a number of environmental factors. Fences act as a physical barrier to control access and circulation of people, vehicles, and animals. Fences also can enhance the aesthetic qualities of a site, complement the architecture, act as an extension of the architecture, and provide a transition from the building to the site and beyond.

DESIGN FACTORS

In choosing a fence, many criteria need to considered, primary among them purpose, context, scale, and slope.

Purpose

In providing a physical and visual delineation, a fence may need to address simple property definition, security concerns, containment, definition of circulation routes, or modification of environmental factors. Property definition might include a fence that presents a real physical barrier or by its presence provides a psychological sense of ownership. Fences whose purpose is to contain small children or animals (or keep them out) need to have small openings between fence elements and access controlled by gates. When used to modify environmental factors, fences can reduce the impact of noise, sunlight, and strong winds, and control snow drifting. When serving this purpose, fences can have positive energy-saving implications.

Context

In choosing a style of fence, the architectural context of the building type, property, and adjacent properties need to be considered. A well-chosen fence can enhance the character of the neighborhood; conversely, a poorly chosen fence can be disruptive. For example, a wood rail fence would be completely out of context for a modern office building, as would a stainless-steel fence for a country-style residential home. Fences that use materials and detailing similar to that found in surrounding architecture and site elements can provide a compatible fence design.

Any adverse impacts that fences can have on adjacent properties need to identified, evaluated, and addressed during the design development process.

Scale

Fences can influence scale in a number of ways. In residential design, particularly smaller lots, the type of fence can affect the perception of a lot's size. Lower fences that can be seen through create a more open feeling and the perception of a larger lot size. Taller, more opaque fences can make a lot seem smaller than it is. The design decision will be influenced by the desire to balance privacy requirements without making the fence an overbearing element. In these circumstances, a well-designed privacy fence will have carefully selected elements and details, to impart scale that responds to the smaller lot size. Planting or decorative elements can often mitigate the negative impact of a privacy fence enclosing a small lot. An alternative is a screening fence, which allows some filtered visibility, or a combination of opaque fencing for privacy with transparent sections that provide opportunities to take advantage of good views.

The design of fences should employ the basic design principles. Scale can be addressed by using texture, relief, and articulation of specific fence elements. Careful selection of individual fence elements is an important factor for creating a pleasingly proportioned barrier. Here are a few ways to integrate this design principle into a fence design:

- Texture can be used in ways that can give a fence a human scale and comfort, or, in contrast, contribute to creating an intimidating barrier.
- Lighter colors tend to emphasize the barrier, whereas darker colors tend to make the fence recede and blend.
- Rhythm is a particularly important consideration on long runs of fence. Rhythm can be influenced by the relationship of posts to panels, piers to break up long runs, and offset panels to create linear interest.

Solid Fences

Solid fences used for privacy are typically 5 to 6 feet in height and often connect to the building structure; as such, they should be thought of as an extension of the architecture. Fences that connect to buildings work best when they are designed to come off corners or from some other architecturally significant element of the building. The choice of materials, line, and finishing color should complement the building structure.

A solid fence provides the ultimate level of privacy. For residential applications, design details and planting that reduce the overbearing sense of enclosure can help create a balance between the desire for privacy and comfortable scale for the space enclosed. This type of fence is also used for restricting public access, both visual and physical, to dangerous elements. In choosing a solid fence, the lack of visibility from the street by passersby and police patrols carries with it a security concern that needs to be taken into account. For this reason, solid fences are usually designed as formidable barriers that serve to restrict unauthorized access at a very high level.

Semitransparent Fences

A semitransparent or screening fence can be 5 to 6 feet in height yet allow limited or filtered visibility. This type of fence can be an important element in screening unpleasant visual impacts, while allowing some filtered views to address the security concerns associated with a lack of visual permeability. For residential or other people-oriented use spaces, this type of fence can provide a psychological sense of enclosure and privacy, while providing an openness and filtered visual connection to the space outside the fence.

Transparent Fences

Transparent fences are generally 4 feet in height or less. By their nature, they tend to less obtrusive and blend more effectively with their surroundings. As they are used often along the perimeter of a site, the material relationship to the architecture of the building is not as critical.

Slope

The slope of the site where a fence is to be installed is a consideration in the design of the fence. Generally, for undulating slopes of 5 percent or more, transparent fences have less of an impact on the land than opaque fences. On consistent slopes of 5 percent or less, the fence can follow the slope of the site. On consistent slopes of greater than 5 percent, a stepped fence installation that integrates the use of a variable reveal curb or wall and stepped fence panels can be a better alternative.

LEGAL AND BUILDING CODE REQUIREMENTS

Prior to the design process, legal and building code requirements that govern the design and installation of fence need to be checked. Many building codes include:

- Types of fence that can be installed
- How they must be anchored
- Height requirements necessary for specific situations.

For perimeter fences, it is extremely important that the correct property lines be established; it may be necessary to include the assistance of a licensed surveyor to provide relevant information for the drawings, as well as assistance during the actual construction phase. A boundary dispute is almost always contentious and often quite costly to rectify. The best approach is to take the necessary steps to ensure a perimeter fence is installed along a correctly determined property line.

WOOD FENCES AND GATES

Key Issues

The two primary considerations for wood fence and gate design involve:

- Layout, and deciding where on-site the fence can and should go. If the fence is a boundary fence, its layout and height will be limited by property line setbacks.
- Degree of opacity of the fence design. Will the fence be a privacy wall, define the edges of the property, or create a barrier?

Both the layout and detailing of the fence can be designed to resist and dissipate the lateral forces of wind, extending the life of the structure. A straight, solid run of any fencing will be the weakest form, as it is solely reliant on the posts for wind resistance. Almost any deviation from the straight line increases resistance to lateral forces. A fence can be visual screen and still allow wind to pass through. Proper detailing can extend the longevity of the materials by avoiding water entrapment. Function, aesthetics,

Leonard Hopper, RLA, FASLA; and Daniel Winterbottom, Associate Professor of Landscape Architecture, Univeristy of Washington, Seattle, Washington

topography, wind patterns, and costs are all factors in the layout and design for opacity.

Fences can be designed using prefabricated panels and posts, standard dimensioned lumber, or customized ornaments. This tremendous range of styles and types of wood fences, with variations in the shape and orientation of pickets, posts, balustrades, and rails, continues to evolve, but the basic construction methods remain similar for all.

Fence Systems

Posts

The structural integrity of any fence begins with the posts, the vertical members that connect the horizontal rails and any boards they carry down to the footing or earth. The post size is determined by the height and width of the fence panels, the combined weight of the materials used, and the character desired. In most applications with a height of 6 feet or less, and with a rail width of 8 feet or less, 4×4 posts are adequate for stability. If the fence is higher than 6 feet, 6×6 timbers are recommended for corner or end posts. If heavy gates are to be mounted, the posts should be increased to 6×6 or greater.

The post may be embedded into the earth, using only pressure-treated wood rated for ground contact or a naturally resistant species. The preferred installation is attachment to a concrete footing with a galvanized or stainless-steel post anchor. The footing top should be sloped to drain water away from the end grain of the post.

The footing should extend 2 to 3 inches beyond the anchor in all directions to ensure proper embedment. The depth should extend at least 2 inches below frost level and rest on compacted bearing soils. The depth also accommodates resistance to the forces of wind, weight, and any anticipated impacts. If the fence is mounted on a continuous footing or masonry wall, the post anchors are preset into the footing or wall cap, and the posts are bolted to the anchor.

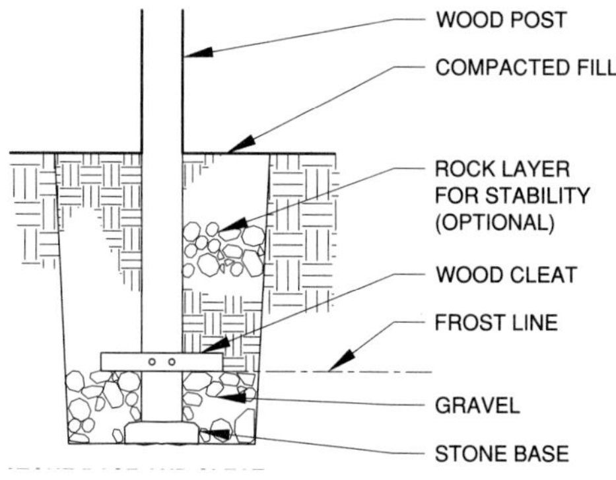

EMBEDDED POST DETAIL—STONE BASE AND CLEAT

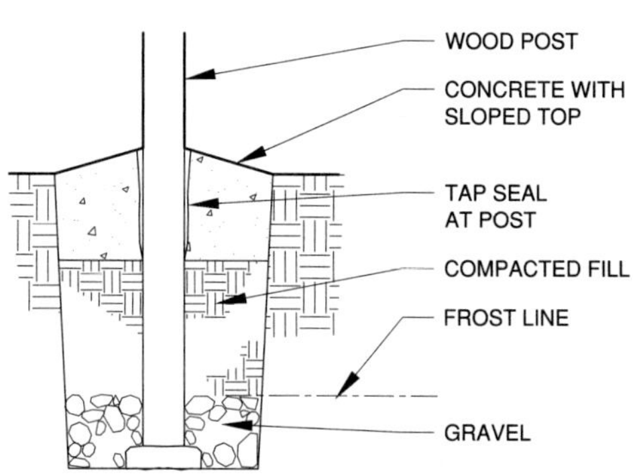

EMBEDDED POST DETAIL—STONE BASE AND CONCRETE CAP

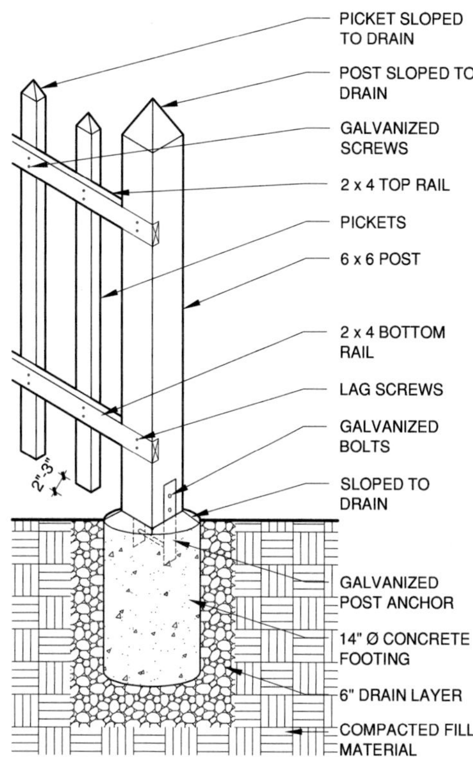

POST FOOTING CONNECTION WITH INSET RAIL

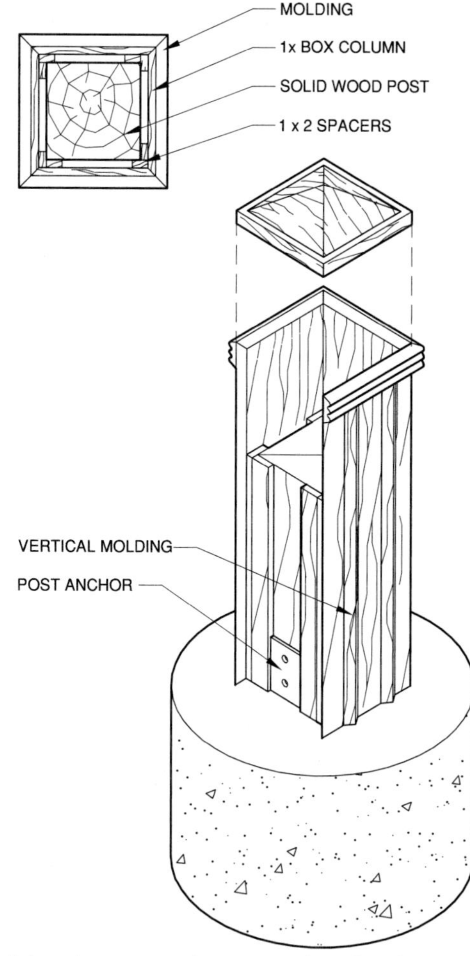

In boxed post construction, a structural post is anchored to the footing with a post anchor; spacers are fastened to the post, and cladding is attached to the spacers. This method protects the structural post from exposure and provides air circulation. The box can be detailed using wood moldings.

BOXED POST CONSTRUCTION

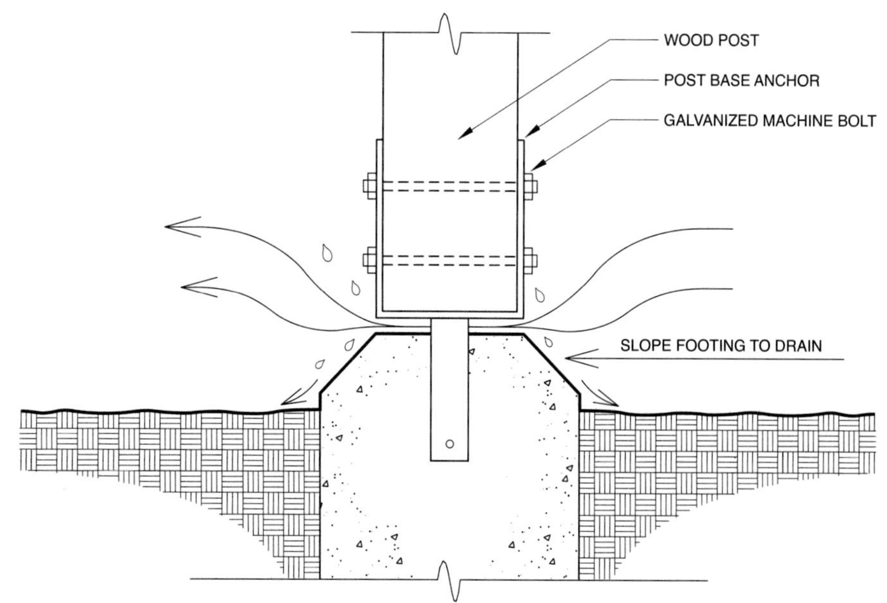

Edges are rounded or chamfered to shed water. The raised post anchor prevents moisture buildup and facilitates air circulation.

POST FOOTING DETAIL

Leonard Hopper, RLA, FASLA; and Daniel Winterbottom, Associate Professor of Landscape Architecture, Univeristy of Washington, Seattle, Washington

If a thicker post is desired, a "boxed-out" post or column can be created. The boxed post is built from 1× or greater material, blocked out from the central solid structural wood or steel member. Ventilation holes on the bottom side of the cap and at the base of the box post or in the middle of the post will help stimulate air circulation in the interior of the box around the structural column.

Post Caps and Finials

The exposed end grain of a fence post is most susceptible to rotting. Fence caps, which are often used to shed water away from the top of the post, are often made out of redwood, cedar, cypress, mahogany, or treated wood, although metals, particularly copper, are also used. The cap should extend beyond the face of the post and be either pitched or sloped on all sides to facilitate the shedding of water. A drip groove saw cut on the underside of the cap, between the face of the cap and the face of the post, will prevent water from migrating around the edge of the cap and into the end grain of the post.

In addition to the cap, other elements are often added to the design to create a period style, to match existing details on the project, and to prevent migration of water into the post. These elements can include finials, beds, moldings, and plinth blocks for the finial or post.

Horizontal Rails (Stringers)

The horizontal rails stabilize the posts from lateral movement and provide a structural frame for attaching vertical balusters, pickets, boards, or lattice panels. The number of rails used depends on the height of the fence, style of design, and span between posts. With the exception of the single-rail fence (often referred to as a kick rail or guardrail), a minimum of two rails, top and bottom, are required. At heights above 4 feet, or if the vertical boards are narrow in proportion to the height, a third, or middle, rail can be added to provide additional attachment points to prevent cupping, twisting, or sagging.

To increase the depth for nailing, 2×4 rails can be set flat, but spans should not exceed 6 feet. If the span is 6 feet or greater, and the weight of the boards considerable, the rails can be set on edge, providing a greater span capability. As a rule of thumb, use 2×4 rails on edge work for lengths up to 8 feet. If the post layout is greater than 8 feet, 2×6 or 4×4 rails should be employed, depending on the weight of the infill material. Often, a "sandwich" rail is used with thinner material since there are two members, one on each face of the post. It also provides a pleasant visual appearance to both sides, as compared with a single. To create a curved rail, thin pieces of wood material, ¼ to ⅜ inch, are bent, often using steam, and glued to the desired radius.

Two details are commonly used to connect the rail to the post: either a recessed or a mechanical connection. An advantage of recessed connections, lap joints, dados, or mortise and tenons, where the post is sculpted to receive the rail, is that one-half of the weight of the span of material is transferred to and supported by each of the posts. Often, the notching of the post requires a cut that is deeper than the penetrating preservative, and these recessed joints and any prebored holes should receive an application of preservative before the rail is attached. When mechanical connectors such as fence brackets are employed, some of the weight of the rails and boards

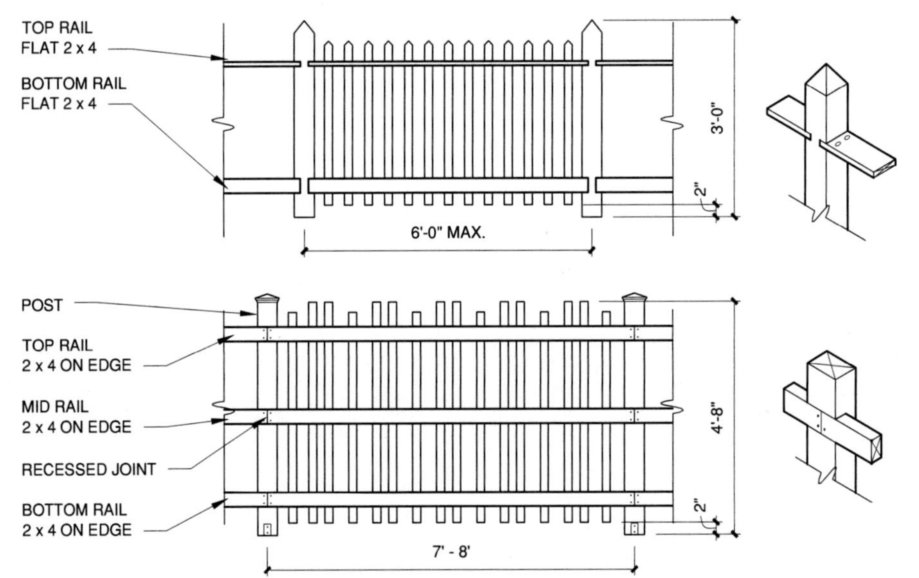

TYPICAL TWO-RAIL FENCE PANEL USED FOR FENCES UP TO 4 FEET IN HEIGHT A THREE-RAIL FENCE PANEL USEFUL FOR FENCES UP TO 8 FEET IN HEIGHT

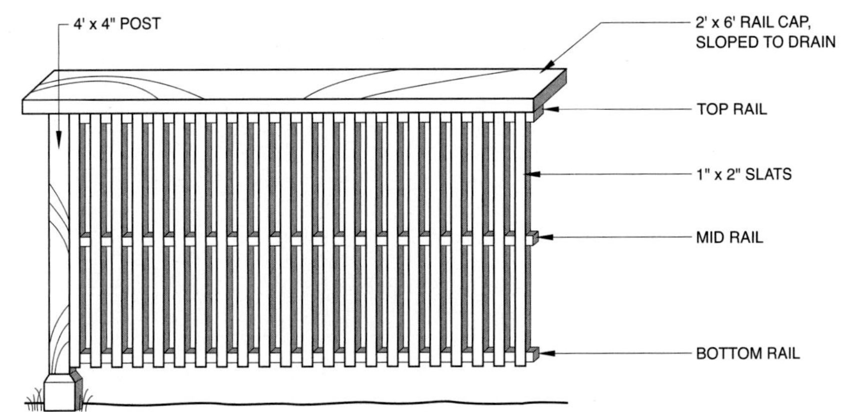

NARROW WIDTH AND SPACING OF VERTICAL MEMBERS ALLOWS SLIGHT VISUAL PENETRATION

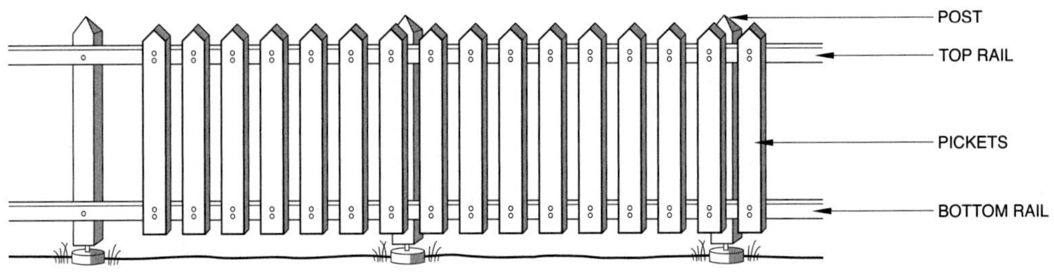

The classic picket fence can create a high proportion of visual openness by increasing the distance between the pickets.

PICKET FENCE

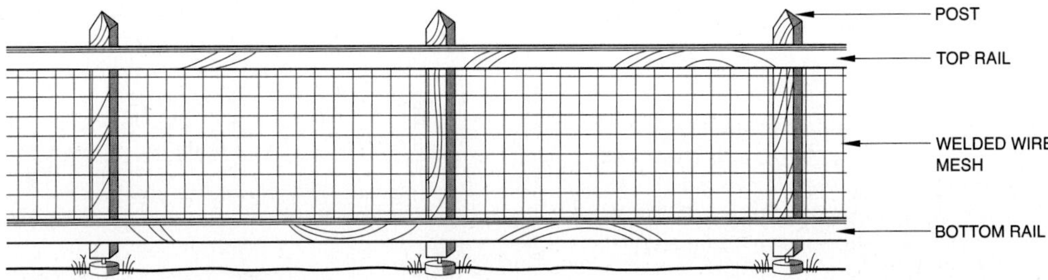

Virtually transparent, the wire mesh screen fence used to restrict physical access is not intended for visual privacy.

WIRE MESH SCREEN FENCE

Leonard Hopper, RLA, FASLA; and Daniel Winterbottom, Associate Professor of Landscape Architecture, Univeristy of Washington, Seattle, Washington

are transferred to the post, but significant forces, now actually shear forces, are carried by the connector. This system, though widely used, tends to negate the purpose of the post by relying on the fastener.

Pickets, Balusters, and Boards

Many fences have vertical elements, and the most common of these are pickets, typically 1×2s, 1×4s or 2×2s. These are commonly attached to the rails with galvanized nails or screws. Highly crafted fences may have pickets doweled through the rails. The top ends of the pickets may be cut to drain or shaped to create ornamental features. The infill can be designed as a prefabricated system in which the pickets and rails are preassembled as a panel and then inserted into the posts.

Balusters are vertical members that are set between the top and bottom rails. They range in height and thickness and are, in some cases, especially by historic precedent, very elaborate, turned pieces. For the attachment of simple balusters, such as 2×2s, a channel can be routed into the top rail to receive the balusters, and the bottoms can be set on a pitched bottom rail or rail cap and mechanically fastened. Other methods include boring or carving recesses into the rails to receive the balusters, or attaching a pair of horizontal members under the top rail to sandwich the top end of the balusters. The latter is not recommended on the lower rails as it will trap water.

Boards can be effectively used on smaller fences, but their width is maximized frequently in taller fences intended for privacy. The simplest, solid-board fences, using 1×4 or 1×6 vertical boards placed side to side and mechanically attached to the rails, are the least expensive but often the least interesting as well. To add visual interest, the edges of the boards are sometimes cut to create a row or field of voids in shapes such as diamonds.

Transparent fences can be used where privacy is not the intent; the split-rail historic fence is an example. If transparency and security are desired, wire mesh can be attached to the post and rails.

Solid, slatted, and picket fences are, in principle, extensions of the post and rail, adding vertical members that increase the density and visual privacy of the fence. In the louvered style, 2×4 or 2×6 vertical boards are set into angles slotted into the top and bottom rails. This alignment allows visibility from an oblique angle and provides air circulation, while offering a large degree of privacy. Maximizing density are the solid fences, including vertical tongue-and-groove or ship-lapped boards; solid panels; and shadow box, where the boards alternate on each side of the rails; and board and batten.

Solid and semitransparent approaches can be combined in the same design with different infills above and below midrail. Overhead trellising cantilevering from the posts can also be incorporated in fence design.

Gates

The gate is the focal point within a fence or a masonry wall and can occasionally be found as a stand-alone element in the landscape. When used with a fence, it can be designed as either a complementing or contrasting element. Because the gate is a movable structural component, it is critical that it be designed to counter the forces it is subjected to it. Gateposts are typically oversized to bear the stresses

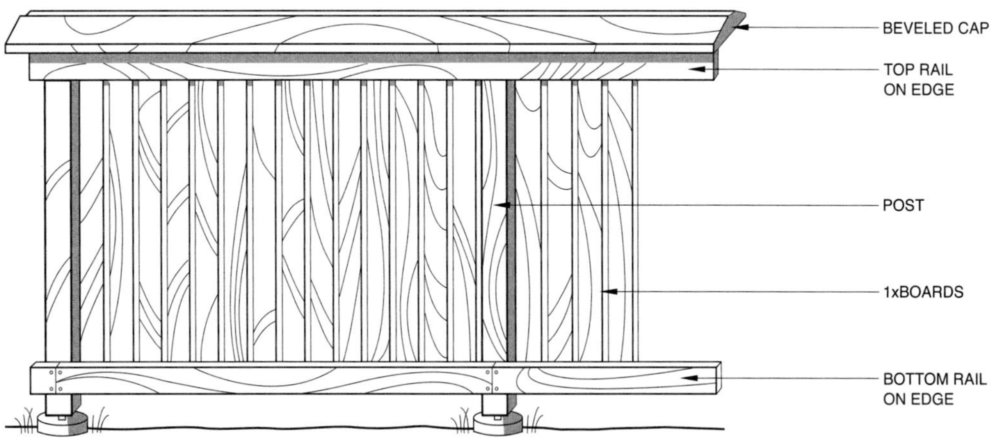

Solid board fence with rails on end is one of the most common and least costly types of solid board varieties.

SOLID BOARD FENCE

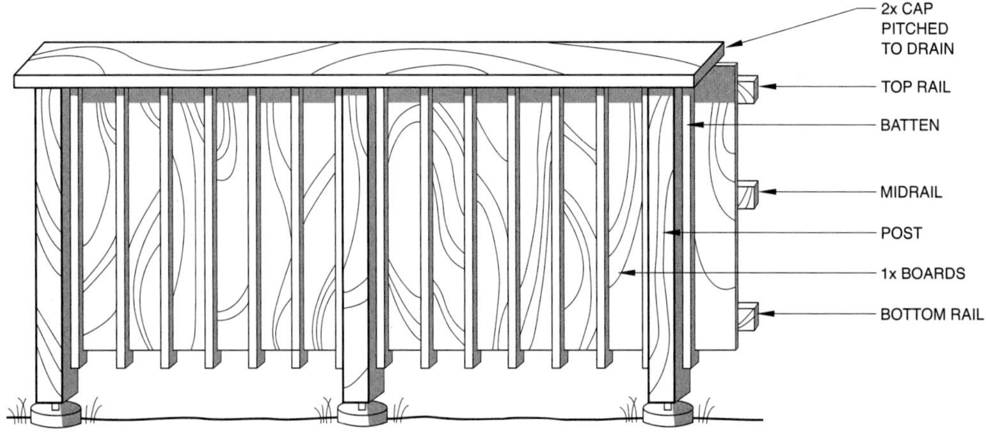

In the board and batten, 1×2 pieces are placed on the vertical joints between the boards.

BOARD AND BATTEN

In the shadow box, the boards are offset front and back between the rails, allowing a slight visual penetration and air circulation between the boards. The boards must be 2× if the midrail is eliminated.

SHADOW BOX

Leonard Hopper, RLA, FASLA; and Daniel Winterbottom, Associate Professor of Landscape Architecture, Univeristy of Washington, Seattle, Washington

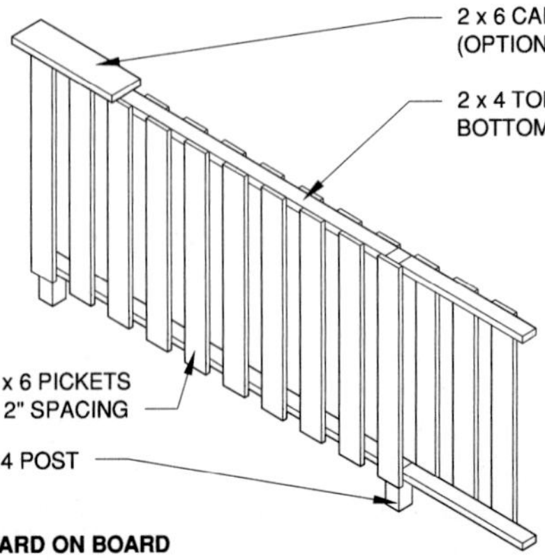

2 x 6 CAP RAIL (OPTIONAL)
2 x 4 TOP AND BOTTOM RAIL
5/4 x 6 PICKETS ON 2" SPACING
4 x 4 POST
BOARD ON BOARD

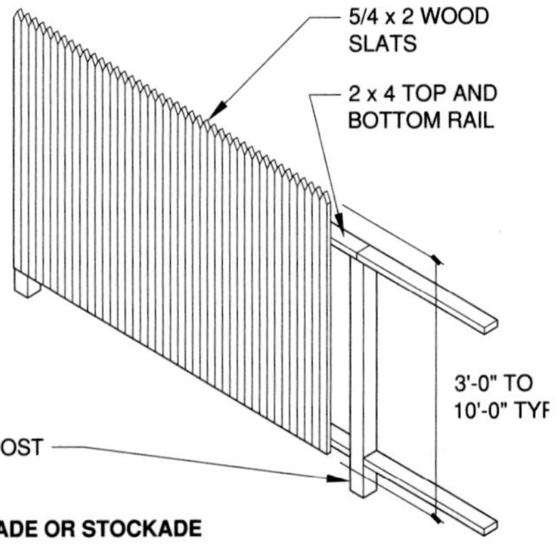

5/4 x 2 WOOD SLATS
2 x 4 TOP AND BOTTOM RAIL
3'-0" TO 10'-0" TYP.
4 x 4 POST
PALISADE OR STOCKADE

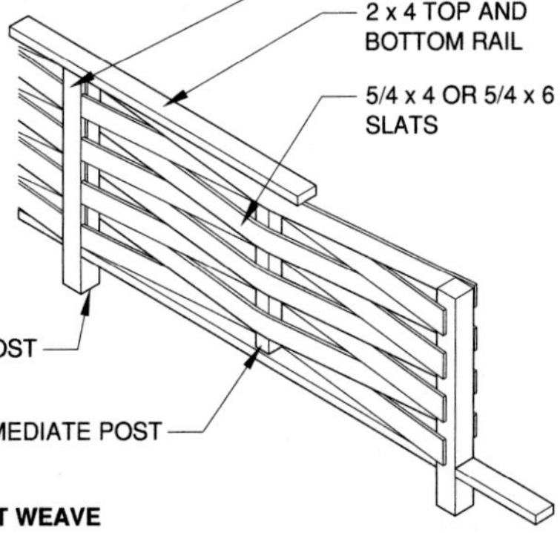

3/4 x 2 SPACER
2 x 4 TOP AND BOTTOM RAIL
5/4 x 4 OR 5/4 x 6 SLATS
4 x 4 POST
2 x 2 INTERMEDIATE POST
BASKET WEAVE

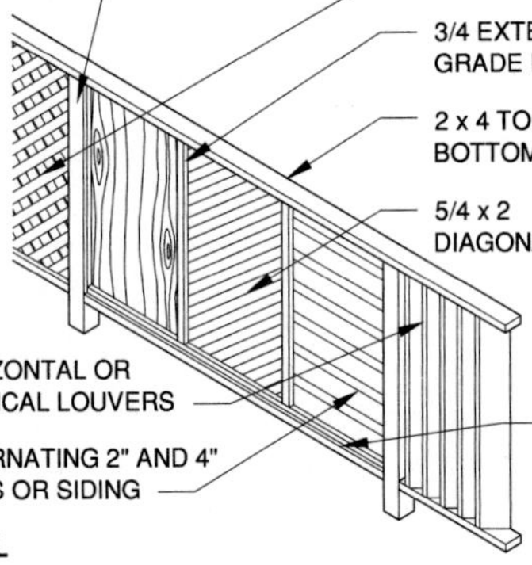

4 x 4 POST
5/4 x 2 LATTICE
3/4 EXTERIOR GRADE PLYWOOD
2 x 4 TOP AND BOTTOM RAIL
5/4 x 2 DIAGONAL SLATS
HORIZONTAL OR VERTICAL LOUVERS
ALTERNATING 2" AND 4" SLATS OR SIDING
1 x 1 STOPS FOR PANELS, TYP.
PANEL

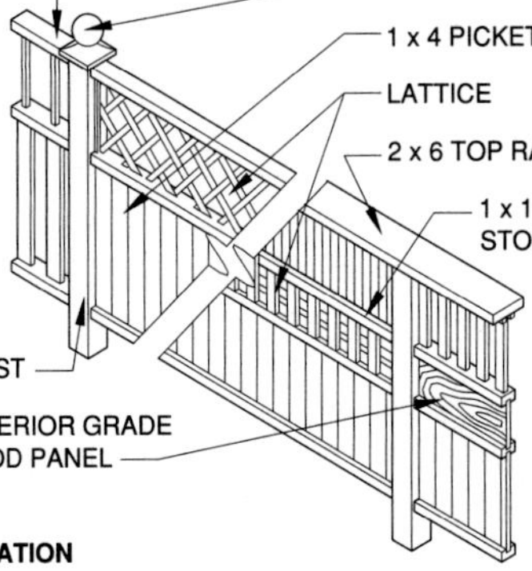

2 x 3 RAIL
DECORATIVE CAP
1 x 4 PICKETS
LATTICE
2 x 6 TOP RAIL
1 x 1 WOOD STOPS, TYP.
6 x 6 POST
3/4" EXTERIOR GRADE PLYWOOD PANEL
COMBINATION

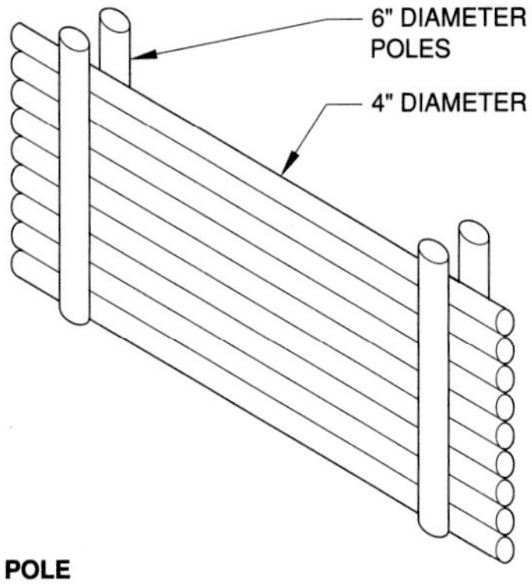

6" DIAMETER WOOD POLES
4" DIAMETER RAILS
TIMBER POLE

WOOD PRIVACY FENCES

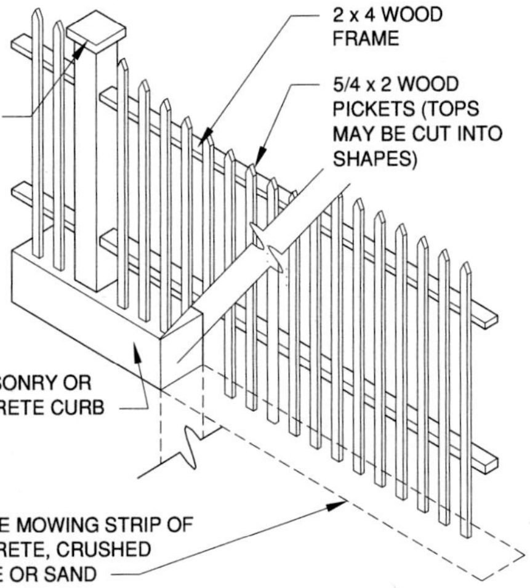

8 x 8 CAP ON 6 x 6 POST
2 x 4 WOOD FRAME
5/4 x 2 WOOD PICKETS (TOPS MAY BE CUT INTO SHAPES)
8" MASONRY OR CONCRETE CURB
8" WIDE MOWING STRIP OF CONCRETE, CRUSHED STONE OR SAND
PICKET OR SLAT

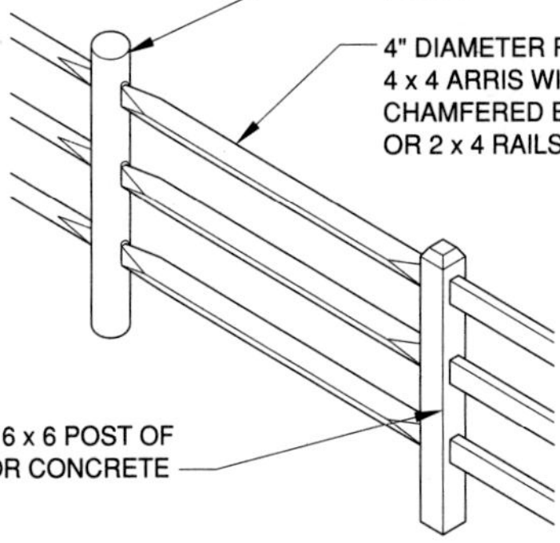

4" OR 6" DIAMETER POSTS
4" DIAMETER RAILS, 4 x 4 ARRIS WITH CHAMFERED ENDS, OR 2 x 4 RAILS
4 x 4 OR 6 x 6 POST OF WOOD OR CONCRETE
POST AND RAIL

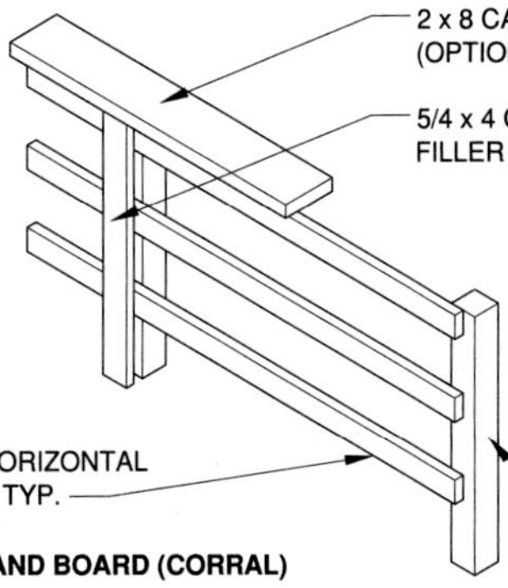

2 x 8 CAP RAIL (OPTIONAL)
5/4 x 4 COVER (WITH FILLER OPTIONAL)
2 x 4 HORIZONTAL RAILS, TYP.
4 x 4 POST
POST AND BOARD (CORRAL)

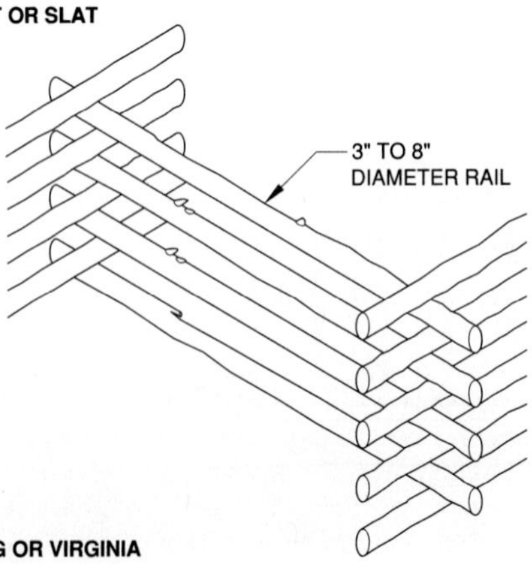

3" TO 8" DIAMETER RAIL
ZIGZAG OR VIRGINIA

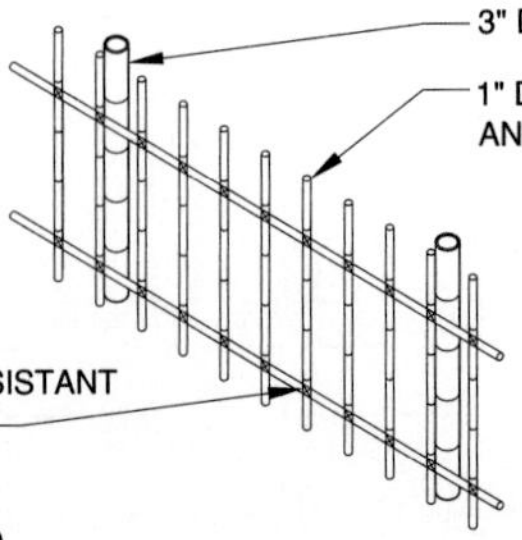

3" DIAMETER POST
1" DIAMETER RAILS AND PICKETS
ROT-RESISTANT TWINE
BAMBOO

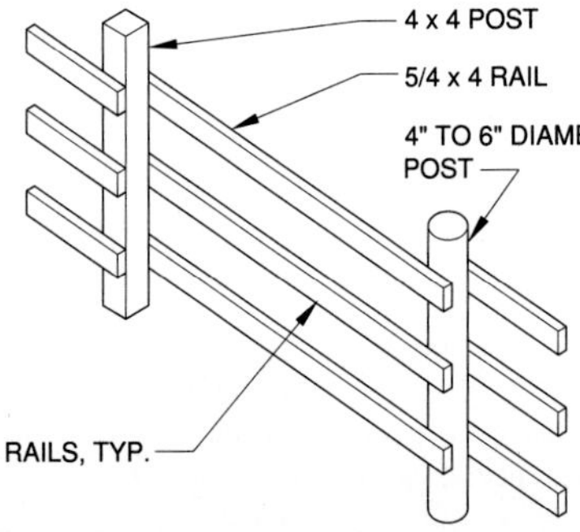

4 x 4 POST
5/4 x 4 RAIL
4" TO 6" DIAMETER POST
3 OR 4 RAILS, TYP.
FIELD

WOOD BOUNDARY FENCES

Leonard Hopper, RLA, FASLA; and Daniel Winterbottom, Associate Professor of Landscape Architecture, Univeristy of Washington, Seattle, Washington

caused by the weight and the motion of the gate. Depending on the dimensions of the gate, 6-inch by 6-inch solid wood post members or steel I-beams with a wood box post surround are often used. The post should be deeply embedded or mounted on an oversized footing to withstand the pull of the gate. A 3-foot depth for a small gate and at least 4 feet deep for a tall or wide gate are recommended, regardless of frost depth. For large gates at entry drives or very wide pedestrian paths, a structural engineer should be consulted to size the bearing posts and attachment mechanisms.

There are two basic gate frames: the Z-frame and the box frame. The Z-frame is simpler and is best used for gates 3 feet or less in width. It tends to be less formal than the box frame, and the rails and brace can be set flat, creating a thinner profile, while in the box style the frame must be set on edge.

The Z-frame is composed of a top and bottom rail joined by a diagonal brace crossing from the hinge-side bottom to the latch-side top. The hinges are attached to the top and bottom rails, and because the Z-frame has no vertical side members (stiles), the use of a middle hinge is not possible.

Like a frame for a panel door, the box frame gate is composed of vertical members (stiles) and horizontal members (rails). For the box framed gate, two stiles, one on each side, and a minimum of two rails, top and bottom, will be employed, allowing the use of a top, bottom, and middle hinge. A middle rail can be used to support pickets, boards, or panels, or for structural stability if the gate is tall. The stiles are usually built of 2×4s, although 2×6s may be used for tall gates. The rails, depending on design, often have a larger bottom rail, 2×6 or 2×8, and a smaller 2×4 top and midrail; however, these should be designed to relate proportionally.

RAIL, TOP AND BOTTOM
HINGED
VERTICAL BOARDS
POST
LATCH
BRACE

Z-FRAME GATE

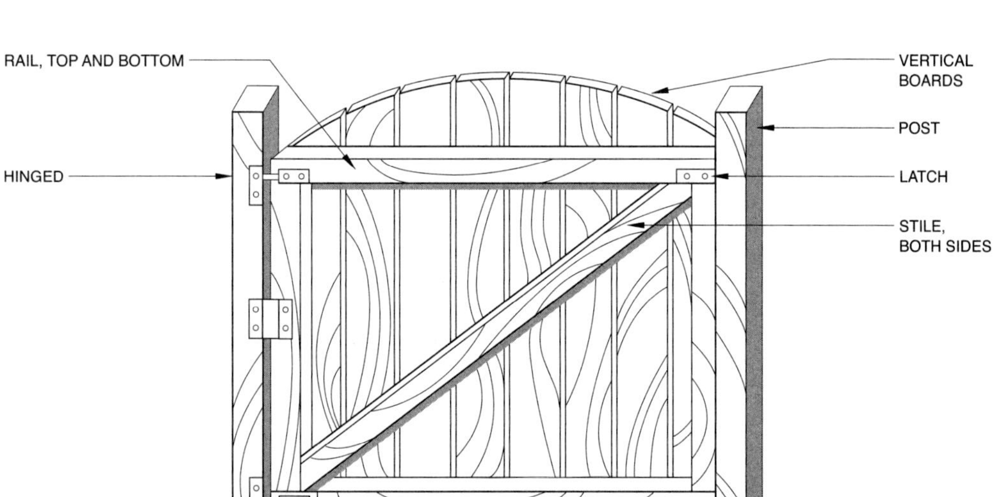

BOX-FRAME GATE

There are several ways to join the rails and stiles. The simplest is to nail or screw the pieces together. To increase stability and longevity, a variety of joints are used to attach the stile to the rail, including mortise and tenon, doweled joints, lap joints, and wood "biscuits." The mortise and tenon is the strongest of the joints and when crafted well can be bonded with an adhesive, avoiding the need for mechanical fasteners altogether. The doweled joint simply uses wooden pegs and glue to join the rail and the stile together, avoiding the penetration of the wood surface with mechanical fasteners. The lap joint is easy to fabricate, provides a large area for gluing, and with a strong waterproof glue, can be clamped and jointed without fasteners.

If the intended use is more for visual effect than for security, the gate should be designed to be as light as possible, minimizing the forces on the post. A problem common in gates is the tendency to rack or sag. To resist this, gates are designed with bracing. The design can reveal the 2×4 or 1×4 bracing pattern with either a diagonal, "Z," or "X" configuration. This results in a semitransparent gate. To create a privacy screen, these bracing configurations support pickets or boards, increasing weight. If diagonal lines are not desired, a galvanized turnbuckle and rod can be used in lieu of wood, which can be sandwiched or hidden by pickets to minimize the visibility of the brace.

The gate connection from the swing-side stile to the post where the hinge is mounted is a critical one, and the hardware designed for hanging includes butt, "T," strap, and strap hinge/bolt systems.

The second piece of hardware used in gate fabrication is a locking mechanism. Options range from the simplest hook and eye to spring-activated bolts. Other mechanisms include sliding bolts, hasp and locking hackle, and thumb hatches.

The hasp mechanism is designed to receive a lock; others secure the gate without locking. A stop on the latch post will prevent the gate from swinging past the post and stressing the hinge. The stop can be as simple as a strip of board attached to the post. A spring can be attached to the gate and connected to the post, creating a constant tension and keeping the gate in the closed position when unbolted.

All the hardware required to hang and operate the gate should be considered for structural stability, aesthetics, and corrosion resistance, and should be galvanized or stainless steel.

METAL FENCES

Chain-Link Fences

One of the most common metal fencing is the chain-link fence, which consists of posts, rails, fittings, and related hardware creating a framework that in turn supports a chain-link mesh that is stretched and attached to it. Each of the elements comes in a range of weights, thicknesses, and coatings that can address a variety of specific purposes. The lightest of chain-link fence systems does not hold up well to everyday use, as the mesh can be bent and distorted with ordinary impacts and the pipe framework is susceptible

Leonard Hopper, RLA, FASLA; and Daniel Winterbottom, Associate Professor of Landscape Architecture, Univeristy of Washington, Seattle, Washington

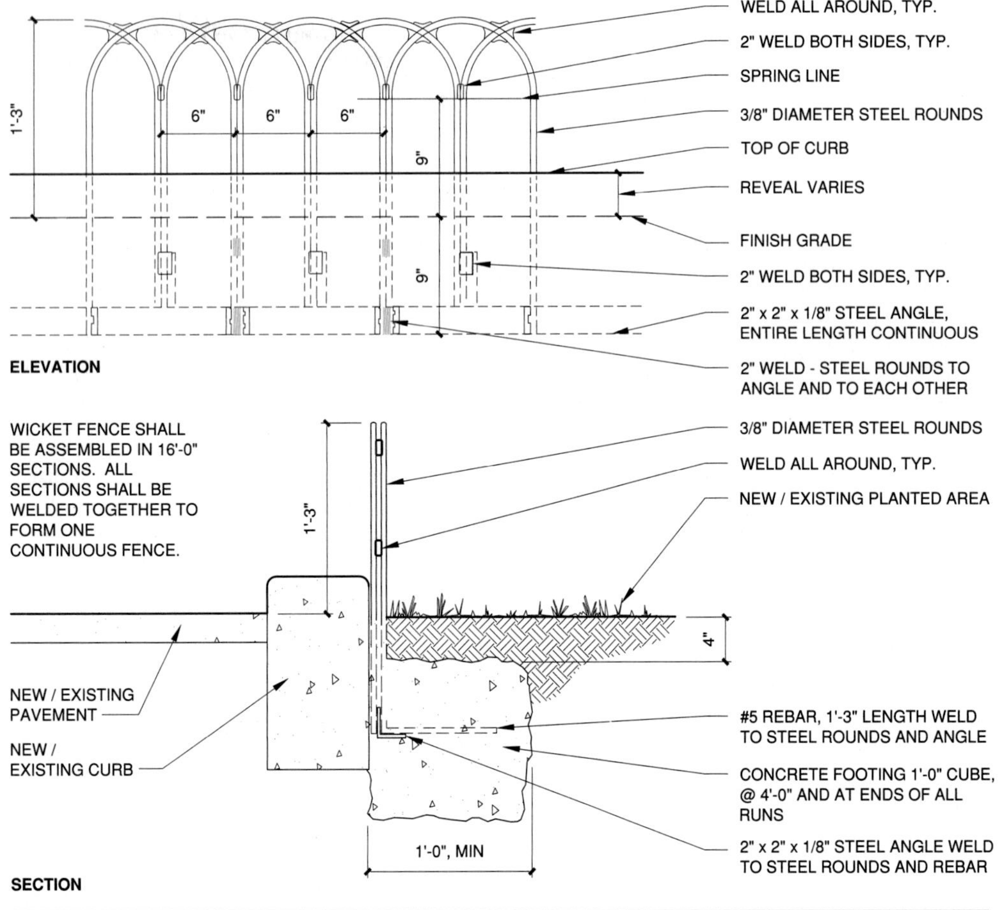

WICKET FENCE

to bending. It is, therefore, important to match the appropriate strength of the materials with the level of service required for a specific application.

The strength of the chain-link fence framework is dependent on the thickness and the diameter of the pipe specified. The type of protective coating specified will affect the framework's longevity and level of maintenance. Pipe gauges in residential chain-link fence applications range from 20 (the lightest) to 15 (heavier). Commercial and heavy-duty applications often call for a Schedule 40 (Sch 40) pipe. In addition to thickness, the pipe should be made with a tensile strength of the steel that must have a minimum yield strength of 45,000 pounds per square inch. The other factor affecting strength is the diameter of the pipe: the greater the diameter, the more steel, making for a stronger pipe and resulting in a stronger chain-link fence framework.

Chain-Link Finishes

A galvanized zinc coating is the most common protective finish for the chain-link fence framework. The pipe is galvanized using one of three processes: an inline flow-coat process, which has the steel passing through molten zinc as it is formed into pipe; pregalvanized pipe, whereby the metal is galvanized prior to being formed into pipe; or hot-dipped galvanized pipe, which is made by taking the formed pipe and completely immersing it in a tank of molten zinc.

The framework can be specified with a color coating on top of the galvanized pipe by calling either for a polyvinyl coating (10 to 14 mil) or a polyester powder coating (3 mil). Powder coating over galvanized metal requires careful preparation of the galvanized metal prior to the electrostatic application of the polyester powdered resins. Both coatings, when properly applied, result in good color and an additional layer of protection for the pipe. Chain-link fence pipe framework can be conventionally painted using the proper primer and finish coat for galvanized metals. As with all outdoor painted surfaces, this method will require regular maintenance to be effective and remain aesthetically pleasing in appearance over time.

Chain-Link Posts

Gateposts, end posts, and corner posts are generally larger than the typical line post. Horizontal rails are generally used along the top and bottom of the fence, although in some cases, a tension wire replaces the bottom rail. An internal or external pipe sleeve is used to connect the lengths of pipe used for the rails to create a strong connection, as well as allow for expansion and contraction where necessary. On taller fences, one or more intermediate horizontal rails may be required. A tension or stretcher bar is woven through the mesh at corner and end posts. This bar is attached to the post by clamps and is used in conjunction with a turnbuckle to ensure the mesh is stretched taunt between end or corner posts. The mesh is then attached using galvanized metal or PVC-coated wire ties to the horizontal rails and line posts.

Security

To address the need for higher security, chain-link fences are available with vehicle-resisting steel cables that are attached to the fence posts and anchored to concrete blocks or deadmen of sufficient size to stop vehicles attempting to break through the fence. For double swing gates, the cables can be attached to the locking device in the center to secure the gate in the closed position. Chain-link fences can also be specified with a crash beam attached. These work well with sliding gate installations that are inherently less suitable for the cable-type barrier.

Opening Access

A number of different gate styles are available to control access at openings, the most common being the swing gate. A single swing gate is almost always used for controlling pedestrian access. For vehicular access, there are a wider range of gate choices. A double swing gate is most common but is limited in how wide the opening can be because of the weight of the gate and the stresses put on the hinges and gateposts. In circumstances that call for wider openings, an overhead sliding gate, cantilever gate, or vertical lifting gate are all options. Gates can be opened and closed manually or they can be operated electrically. Electric-operated gates can be controlled by an attendant, telephone system, card reader system, wireless radio frequency device, or digital keypad system.

Mesh Fabric

The chain-link mesh fabric comes in a variety of thicknesses, mesh sizes, heights, and protective coverings.

The gauge of the mesh is the diameter of the wire used to create the mesh fabric: The lightest is 13-gauge and the heaviest is 6-gauge, which is the most commonly available. The lighter gauges of chain-link mesh fabric are only suitable for temporary-type fencing. Generally, an 11-gauge mesh (.120 inch) would be suitable for light-duty residential uses; 9-gauge mesh (.148 inch) would be a good all-around choice; and 6-gauge (.192 inch) is a commonly specified thicker mesh used for installations where a heavier-duty fence is required.

The mesh size is the distance between the parallel wires of the mesh. Chain-link mesh comes in sizes ranging from ⅜ to 2⅜ inches. Most commonly used for general applications is a 2-inch mesh. For some sport court applications, a smaller mesh of 1 or 1¼ inch may be a more appropriate functional choice, to contain the ball within the enclosure. From a design perspective, the smaller mesh can be used to create a greater visual impact and a feeling of a more screened appearance and sense of enclosure. For security applications, ⅝-, ½-, or ⅜-inch mesh can be used. These "mini" meshes are more difficult to climb, and because they contain more steel, are more difficult to cut through. For added security, the bottom of the mesh can be buried a minimum of 12 inches below grade, making unauthorized entry by cutting the ties and forcing the mesh up more difficult.

Chain-link mesh fabric typically comes in the following heights: 36, 42, 48, 60, 72, 84, 96, 120, and 144 inches. The tops and bottoms of chain-link mesh fabric are typically finished differently depending on the height (referred to as "selvage"). Chain-link mesh fabric less than 72 inches in height must be knuckled on both the top and bottom of the mesh, creating a

Leonard Hopper, RLA, FASLA

smoother finished edge. Chain link mesh fabric more than 72 inches in height is generally knuckled on one end (used for the top of the fence) and left twisted at the other, creating a barbed edge. When used for security purposes, the chain-link mesh can be specified with both ends twisted, creating a barbed effect on both the top and bottom.

The most common protective covering for chain-link mesh fabric is galvanized zinc. It can be applied in two ways. One way is *galvanized after weaving* (GAW). This refers to the process of taking the specified gauge of wire, weaving it into the chain-link mesh fabric and then drawing the fabric through a pot of molten zinc. This process results in about 1.2 ounces of zinc coating being applied per square foot of fabric, conforming to ASTM standards. The other approach is *galvanized before weaving* (GBW). This refers to the process of taking the specified gauge of wire rod, pulling the wire through a pot of molten zinc, and then weaving the wire into the chain-link mesh fabric. This process results in about .8 ounces of zinc coating being applied per square foot of fabric Although both methods are acceptable, the GAW approach does have some advantages. One is that galvanizing after the fabrication of the mesh ensures that all cut ends made while forming the mesh fabric are galvanized. Second, a thicker coating of zinc is applied, and because zinc protects the steel underneath by slowly dissipating itself over time, the thicker the coating, the longer the steel is protected.

Chain-link mesh fabric is also available with polyvinyl coatings in a number of different colors. This coating is applied over the galvanized steel core wire, providing another layer of protective coating. The polyvinyl coating can be applied in three different ways: *extruded,* where the polyvinyl encompasses the steel wire of the mesh; *extruded bonded,* where an adhesive bonds the vinyl coating to the steel wire of

BREAKING STRENGTH OF COATED STEEL WIRE

DIAMETER OF COATED WIRE	MINIMUM BREAKING STRENGTH
0.192″	2,170 lb
0.148″	1,290 lb
0.120″	850 lb

SCHEDULE 40 PIPE SIZES

NOMINAL SIZE	ACTUAL I.D.	ACTUAL O.D.	WEIGHT
1″	1.049″	1.315″	1.68 lbs/ft
1¼″	1.380″	1.660″	2.27 lbs/ft
1½″	1.610″	1.900″	2.71 lbs/ft
2″	2.067″	2.375″	3.65 lbs/ft
2½″	2.469″	2.875″	5.79 lbs/ft
3″	3.068″	3.500″	7.58 lbs/ft
3½″	3.548″	4.000″	9.10 lbs/ft

16 GAUGE TUBE SIZES

OUTSIDE DIAMETER	WALL THICKNESS	WEIGHT
1⅜″	.065″	.68 lbs/ft
1⅝″	.065″	.94 lbs/ft
2″	.065″	1.343 lbs/ft
2½″	.065″	1.692 lbs/ft

FABRIC SIZES

RECOMMENDED USAGE	HEIGHT OF CHAIN LINK MESH FABRIC									SIZE OF MESH	GAUGE OF COATED WIRE	NOMINAL DIAMETER COATED WIRE
Heavy Industrial	36″	42″	48″	60″	72″	84″	96″	120″	144″	2″	6	0.192″
	Diamond Count											
	10½	12½	13½	17½	20½	24½	27½	34½	41½			
Standard Industrial/ Residential	36″	42″	48″	60″	72″	84″	96″	120″	144″	2″	9	0.148″
	Diamond Count											
	10½	12½	13½	17½	20½	24½	27½	34½	41½			
Light Industrial/ Residential	36″	42″	48″	60″	72″	84″	96″	120″	144″	2″	11	0.120″
	Diamond Count											
	10½	12½	13½	17½	20½	24½	27½	34½	41½			
Heavy Industrial	36″	42″	48″	60″	72″	84″	96″	120″	144″	1″	6	0.192″
	Diamond Count											
	20	23	27	33	39	45	53	67	79			
Standard Industrial	36″	42″	48″	60″	72″	84″	96″	120″	144″	1″	9	0.148″
	Diamond Count											
	20	23	27	33	39	45	53	67	79			
Light Industrial/ Residential	36″	42″	48″	60″	72″	84″	96″	120″	144″	1″	11	0.120″
	Diamond Count											
	20	23	27	33	39	45	53	67	79 9			
Security	36″	42″	48″	60″	72″	84″	96″	120″	144″	⅜″-½″-⅝″	11	0.120″

SCHEDULE OF TYPICAL SIZES FOR CHAIN-LINK FENCE

Schedule 40 pipe sizes are the nominal inside diameter. For Residential Lighter Duty use, 16 gauge, .065 thick steel tubing of a diameter equal to the outside diameters of the pipe shown above, can be used.

MEMBER	3′ HT	4′ HT	6′ HT	8′ HT	12′ HT
Post spacing (max.)	6′	6′	6′	8′	10′
Top/bottom/mid rails (nominal Schedule 40)	1¼"	1¼"	1¼"	1¼"	1¼"
Line posts (nominal Schedule 40)	1½"	1½"	1½"	1½"	1½"
End and corner posts (nominal Schedule 40)	2"	2"	2"	2½"	3½"
Gate posts (nominal Schedule 40)	2½"	2½"	2½"	2½"	3½"
Size of gate members (nominal Schedule 40)	1½"	1½"	1½"	1½"	1½"
Depth of line post in curb/footing	12"	12"	12"	18"	42"
Depth of end/corner/gate post in curb/footing	12"	12"	18"	30"	48"
Depth of curb (Step down at fence posts if necessary to 3" below depth of post)	1'-3"	1'-3"	1'-9"	2'-9"	4'-3"
Depth of footing for line post (12" square/diameter)	18"	18"	18"	24"	48"
Depth of footing for end/corner/gate post (12" square/diameter)	18"	18"	24"	36"	54"

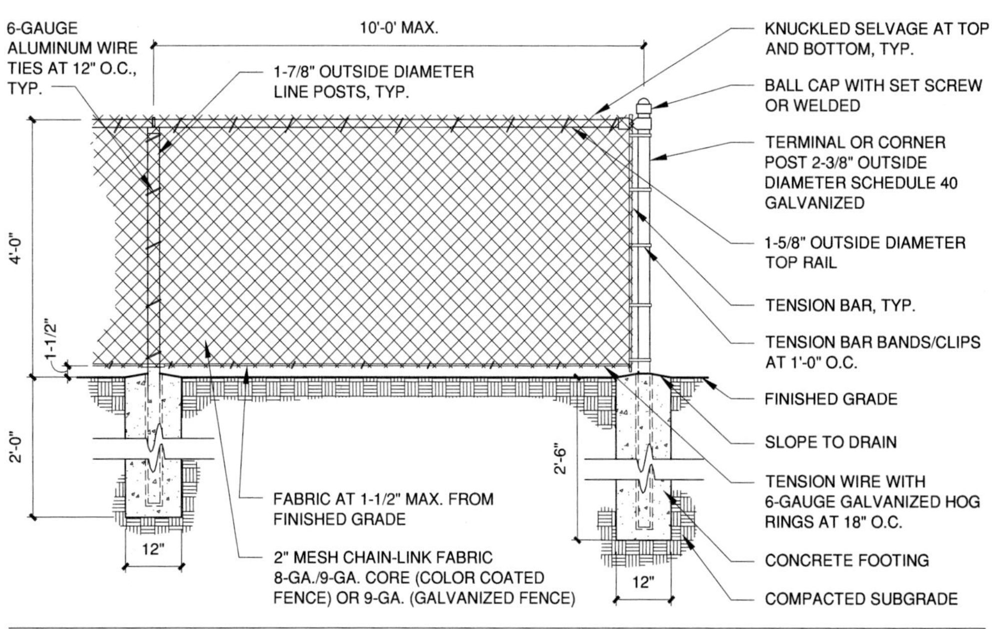

4-FOOT-HIGH CHAIN-LINK FENCE

Leonard Hopper, RLA, FASLA

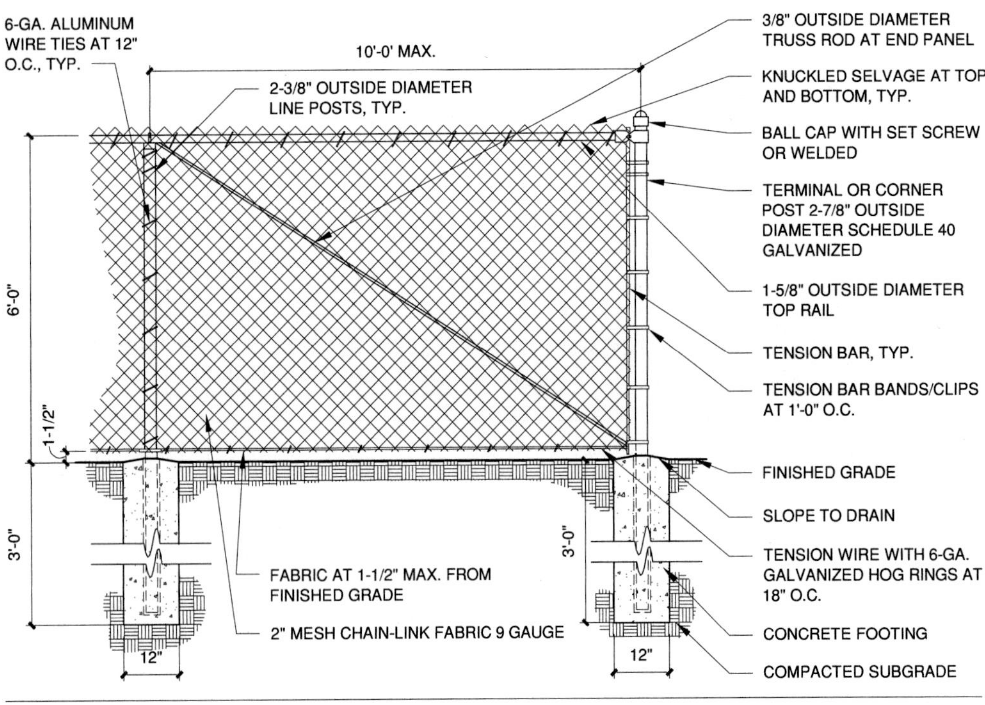

6-FOOT-HIGH CHAIN-LINK FENCE

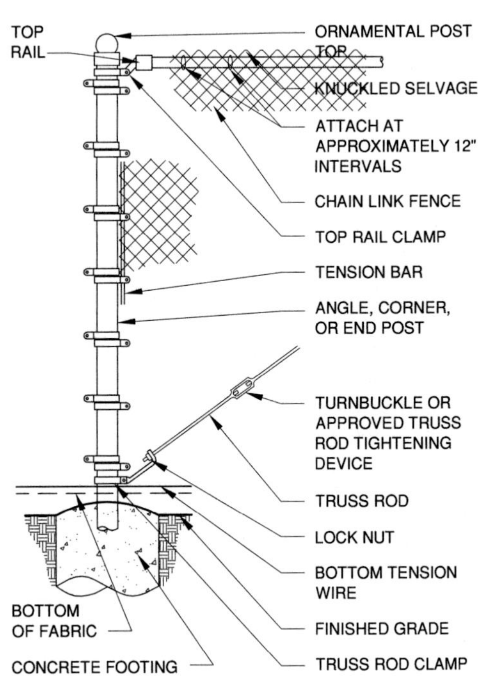

CORNER/END POST DETAIL

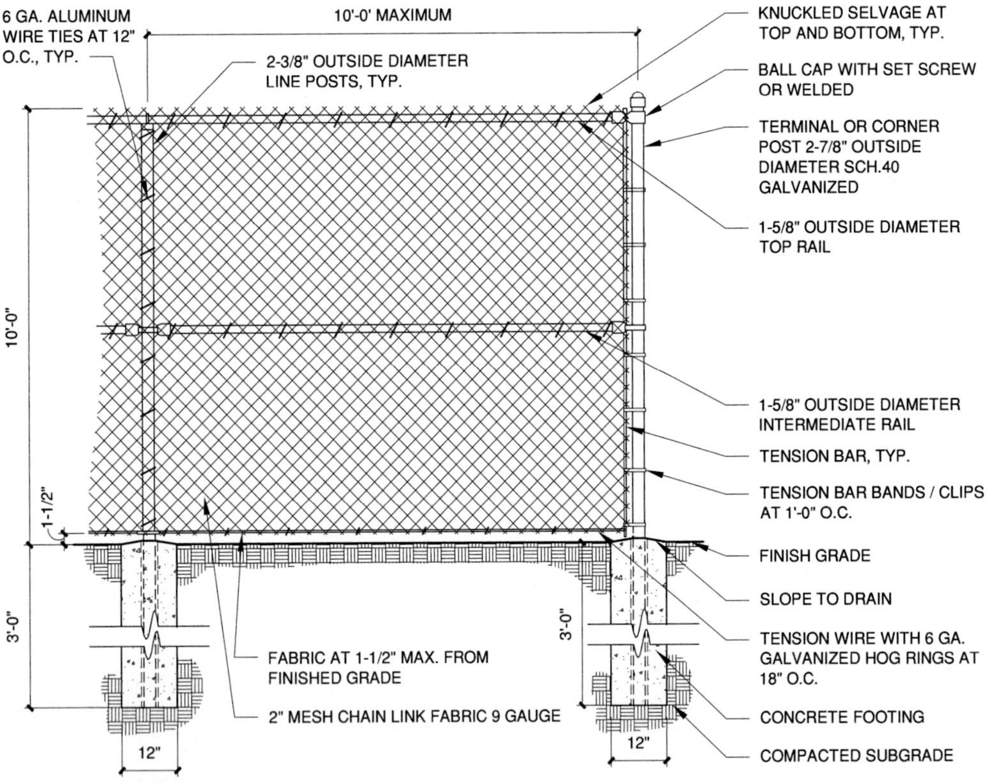

10-FOOT-HIGH CHAIN-LINK FENCE

Leonard Hopper, RLA, FASLA

the mesh; and *thermally fused,* a process that fuses the polyvinyl coating to the steel wire of the mesh. It is important to note that for polyvinyl-coated chain-link mesh fabric the gauge specified is the gauge of the coated fabric, not of the wire mesh. Therefore, the gauge of the core wire core must be considered in determining the strength of the fence, not the gauge of the wire after it has received the polyvinyl coating.

Another commercially available process to add color to the mesh is polyester powder coating. In this process, the polyester powdered resins are electrostatically applied to the galvanized chain-link mesh and then fully cured at high heat in an oven for 15 to 20 minutes. The approximately 3-mil coating provides an even and durable finish.

Steel-Wire Mesh Fences

Fences can also be constructed of a variety of wire mesh products that are stretched and attached to a number of combinations of rails and posts. While these can be very simple, light-gauge steel meshes are used for very utilitarian functions such as enclosing pets or animals or for agricultural uses. Wire mesh panels can also be made of more sturdy wire gauges to form very decorative screens and barriers. These thicker-gauge wires are welded together to form a relatively rigid mesh panel that is then attached to a top and bottom rail. The horizontal wires can also be attached to a vertical rail at each end, giving the panel additional rigidity and strength. The wire mesh panels are then attached to the posts with a mechanical connection such as a clamp or angle and bolt. The horizontal and vertical wires can be the same gauge or can differ. They can be welded together in a wide range of different dimensions to create a variety of looks, from a very open barrier to one that is denser and offers a greater sense of privacy and visual impact. These decorative fences can be electrostatically powder-coated with polyester resins to create a durable and attractive finish.

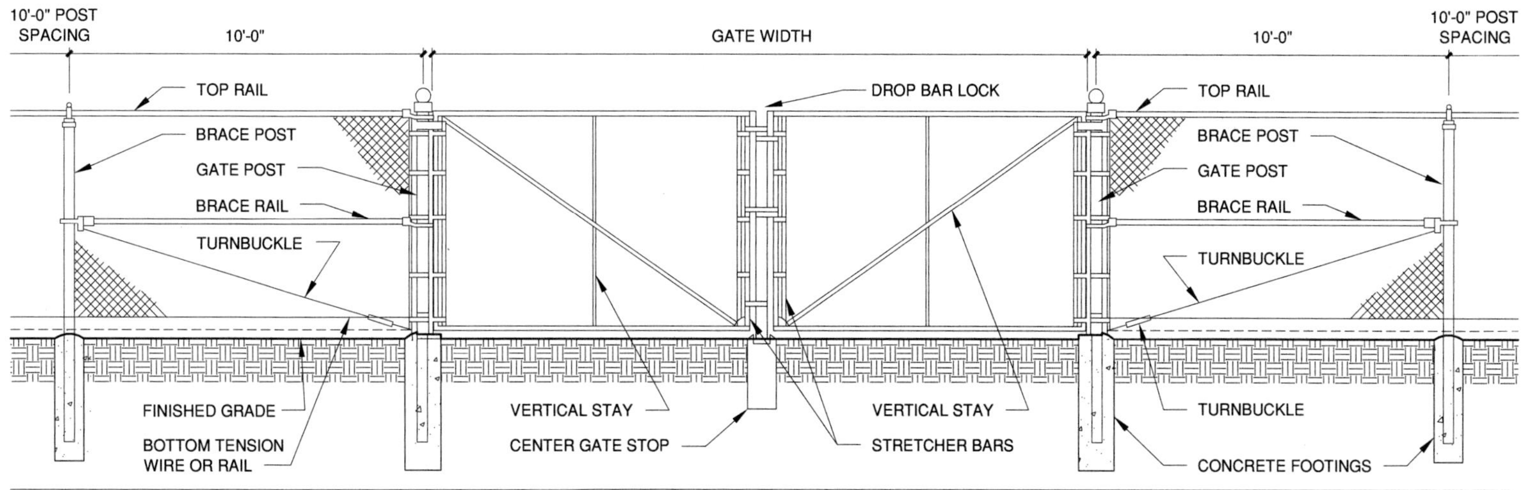

TYPICAL GATE DETAILS

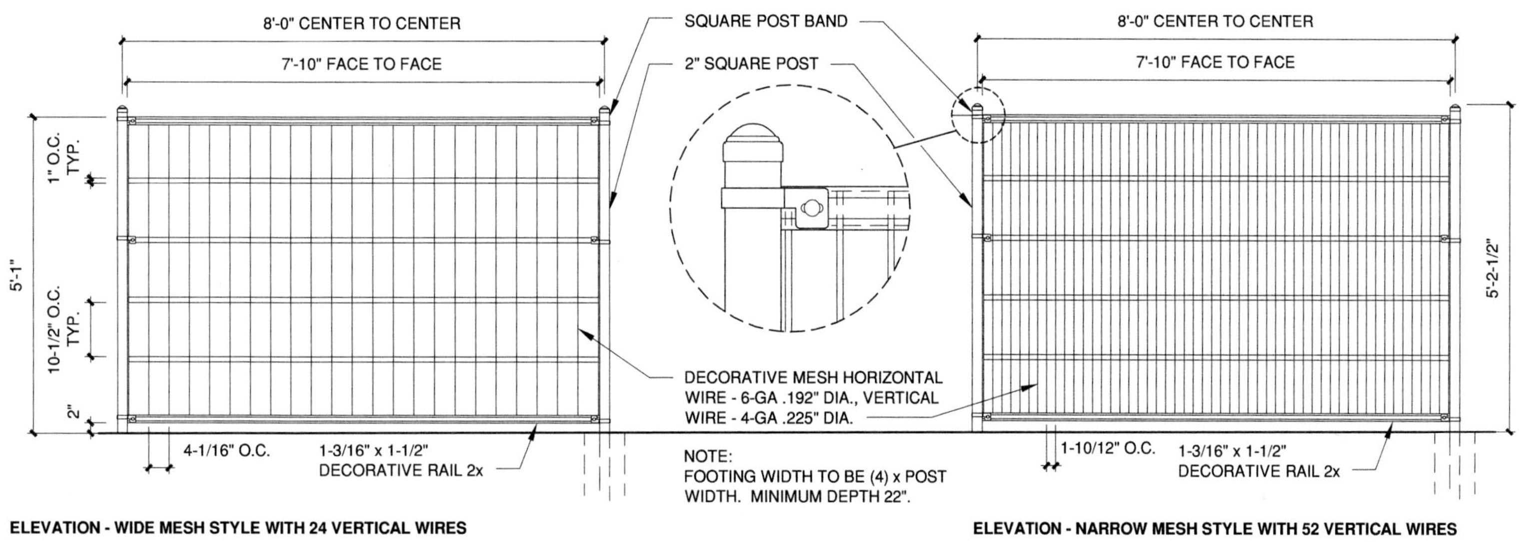

WIRE MESH FENCE

Source: Master Halco

Steel-Wire Cable Fences

A very transparent barrier can be created using a steel-wire cable fence. In this type of fence a stainless-steel wire cable is used to create the horizontal members of the fence. The thickness of the cable (1/8 inch or greater) is very unobtrusive and allows good views to be enjoyed with little visual impact from the fence itself.

The fence is constructed of multiple horizontal cables that run through holes in intermediate posts and are attached at end or corner posts. The cable is tensioned at the attachments to these corner or end posts, creating a rigid horizontal cable for the length of the fence. For long straight runs of fence, tightening devices approximately every 50 feet will aid in keeping the cable taut.

Ornamental Metal Fence

There is a wide array of ornamental metal fencing. Some types are available as manufactured systems that can be specified for a specific use. Another approach is to create a fence design utilizing the almost unlimited combination of different metal shapes and sizes that can be fabricated into a unique fence design.

Ornamental metal fences are composed of posts, rails, and panels. They can be formed from tubular steel, solid steel, or a combination of both.

Tubular Steel Fence

Typically, the fence posts and rails of a tubular steel fence are constructed of hollow tubular steel. However, there are many variations of a largely tubular steel fence where combinations of the posts, rails, or pickets can be made from solid steel and integrated with the hollow tube elements to increase the strength of the fence. Tubular steel fences always have a top and bottom rail, but there are many variations that use three or more rails at a variety of elevations in the panel. Although tubular rails are often welded directly to the posts, a mechanical connection that allows for some contraction/expansion of the steel elements is more advisable. Pickets can be welded to the rails but are often connected using mechanical connectors such as screws or rivets.

The use of tubular steel rails, given the larger overall dimensions, usually gives the fence a stronger horizontal emphasis. The tubular steel elements often are sealed with welded caps to prevent the entry of moisture into the tube. Tubular steel fencing is not as strong as a fence made from solid steel components; however, it is lighter in weight, and a wide range of different styles, shapes, and sizes are available for each of the elements that make up the fence, making it very versatile and easily adaptive to almost any design situation. Design elements that can be added to a tubular steel fence, such as steel cables or crash plates, can be integrated into the tubular steel fence, increasing its capability to withstand vehicular impact, thus its value as a security design feature.

In terms of finishes, tubular steel fence can be galvanized and painted with a compatible primer and finish paint. But as with all outdoor painted surfaces, these fences will need regular maintenance and

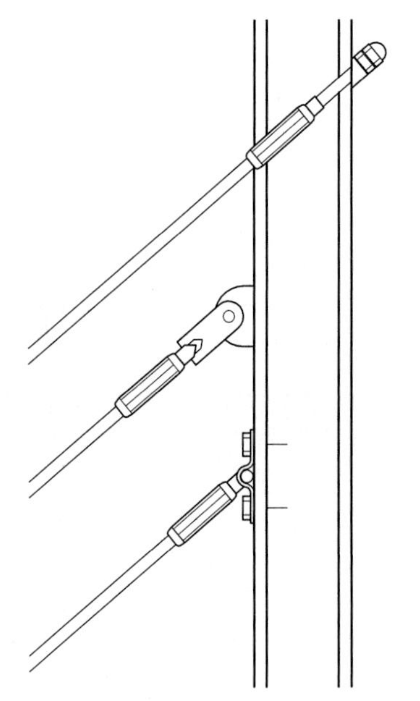

CABLE RAIL CONNECTIONS ALL HAVE A TIGHTENING DEVICE THAT KEEPS THE CABLE RIGID

TYPICAL CABLE RAIL CONNECTIONS

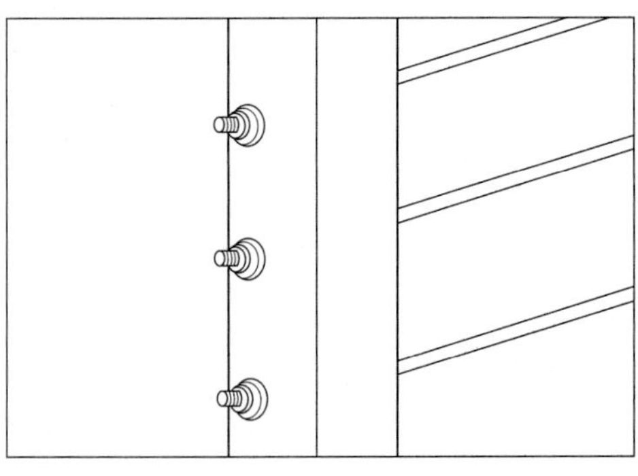

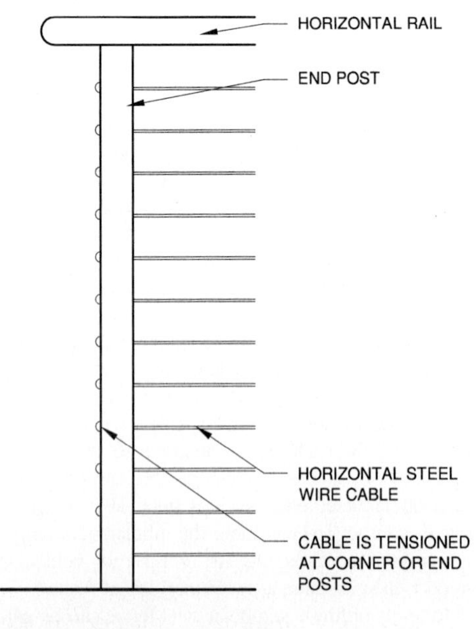

CABLE TENSIONING AT END POST

STEEL-CABLE FENCE

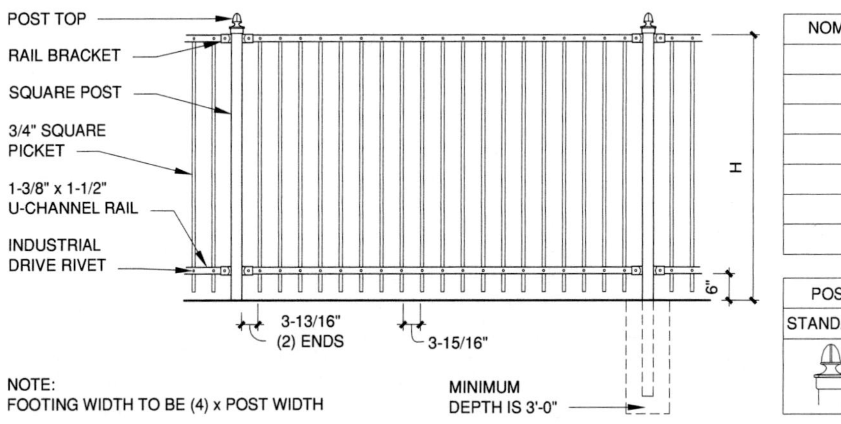

NOMINAL HEIGHT (H)
3'-0"
3'-6"
4'-0"
5'-0"
6'-0"
7'-0"
8'-0"

POST TOP OPTIONS		
STANDARD	BALL	FLAT

FENCE SECTION ELEVATION

TYPICAL TUBULAR STEEL FENCE PANEL

Source: Master Halco

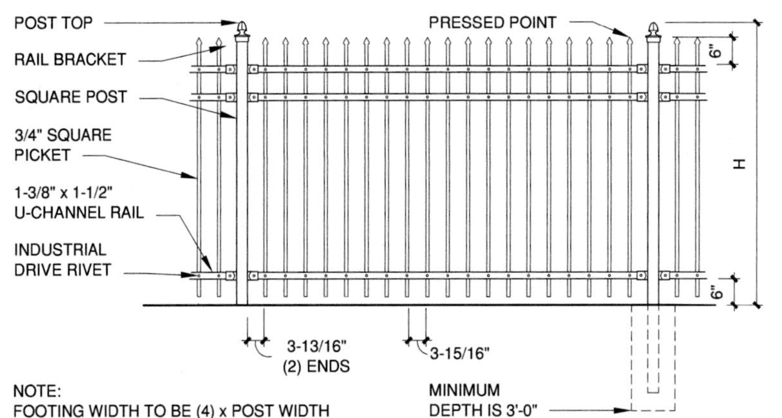

NOMINAL HEIGHT (H)
3'-0"
3'-6"
4'-0"
5'-0"
6'-0"
7'-0"
8'-0"

POST TOP OPTIONS		
STANDARD	BALL	FLAT

FENCE SECTION ELEVATION

TYPICAL TUBULAR STEEL FENCE PANEL WITH THREE RAILS AND DECORATIVE PICKET

Source: Master Halco

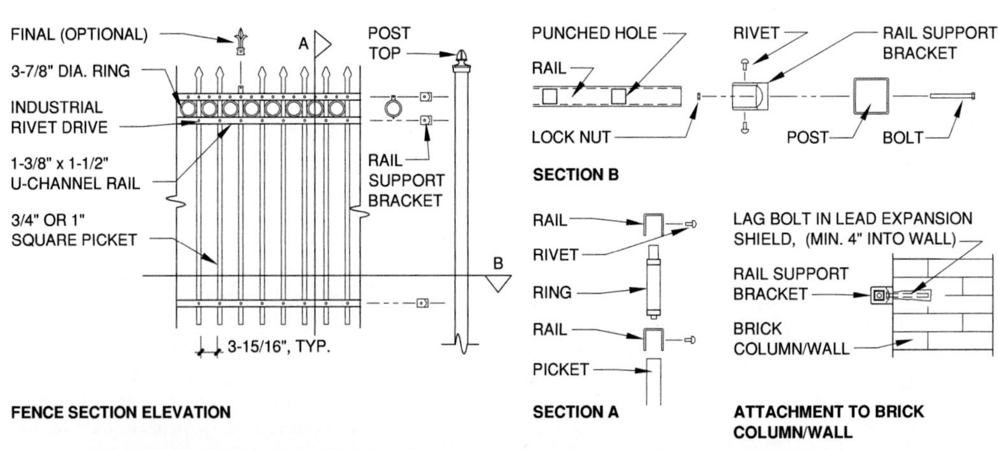

FENCE SECTION ELEVATION

TYPICAL TUBULAR STEEL FENCE PANEL WITH THREE RAILS, DECORATIVE PICKET, AND CIRCULAR ORNAMENTATION

Source: Master Halco

Leonard Hopper, RLA, FASLA

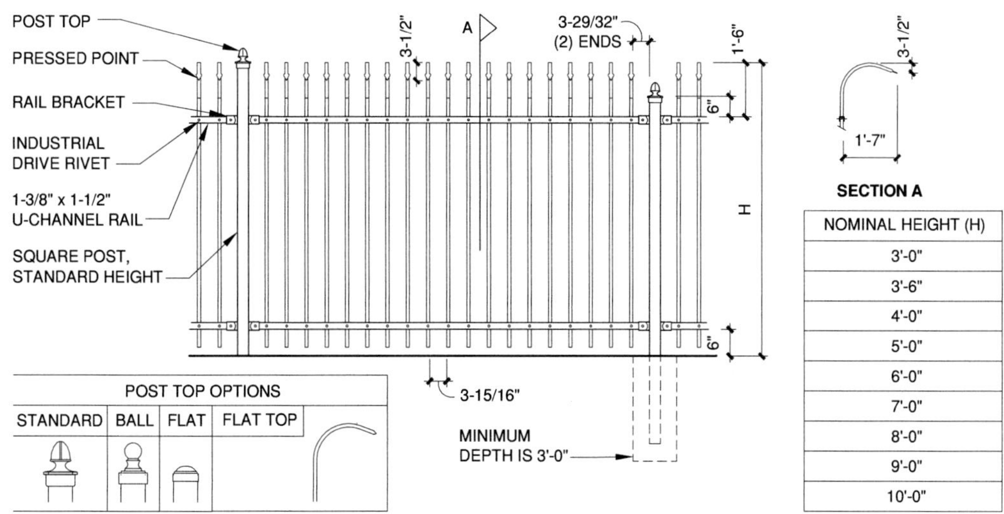

NOTES:
FOOTING WIDTH TO BE (4) x POST WIDTH. RIVETS FACE TO OUTSIDE. FOR SAFETY, NOMINAL HEIGHT SHOULD BE AT LEAST 7'-0" ABOVE GRADE.

TUBULAR STEEL FENCE PANEL WITH BENT PICKETS

Source: Master Halco

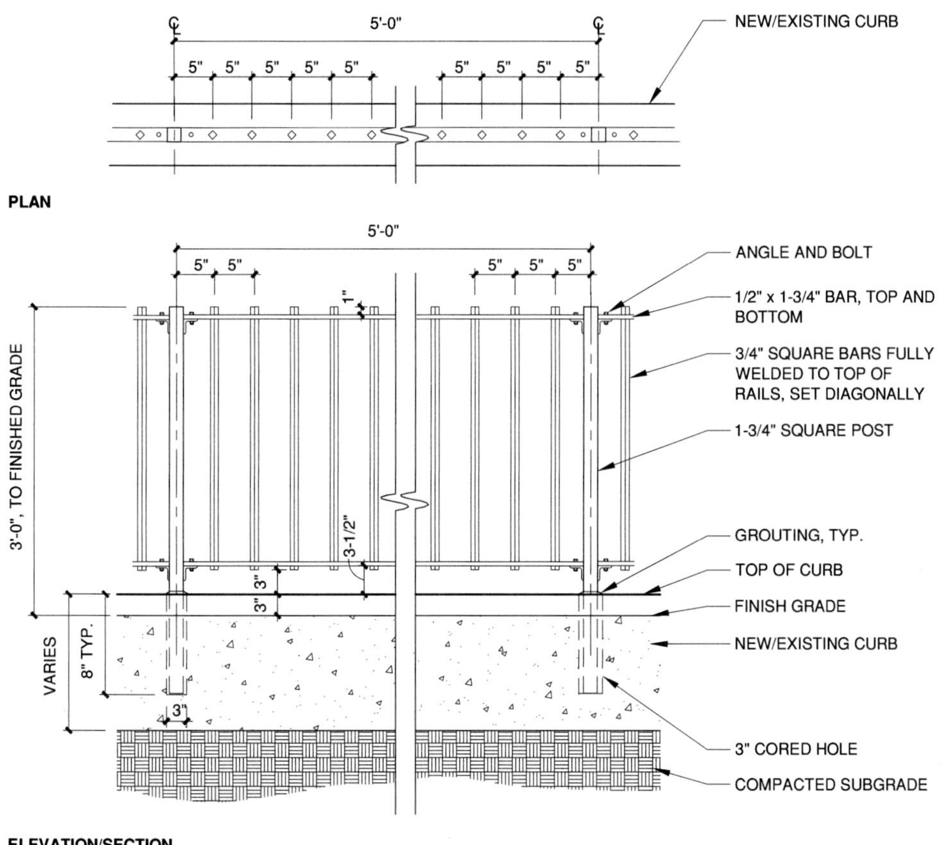

3-FOOT-HIGH SOLID-STEEL-BAR FENCE IN CONCRETE CURB

Leonard Hopper, RLA, FASLA

repainting to maintain their appearance. A galvanized fence that receives an electrostatically applied powder coating has a much more durable finish. Although a powder coating can be applied over bare steel, this offers less protection against rust if the powder coating should become chipped and allow the bare steel to be exposed to the elements.

Solid-Steel Fence

Solid-steel (sometimes referred to as "wrought iron") fences offer a maximum of strength and durability. Because of the difficulty of drilling through thick, solid-steel members, many of the connections in this type of fence are often welded. For solid-steel rails, the holes for the pickets are generally punched through the rail; the picket is inserted and then fully welded to the tops of the rails (to prevent water from accumulating at the joint). This type of construction creates a very strong joint, and having the pickets passing through the rails allows a greater tolerance for fabrication differences in the length of pickets. Flat steel bars used for the rails will emphasize the vertical qualities of the fence. If channels or angles are used, their thicker appearance will give the fence a more horizontal emphasis. The attachment of the rails to the posts should be accomplished with a mechanical connection that allows for construction tolerances to fit the panels to the fence posts and, at the same time, allows for differential expansion and contraction of the fence from the curb or wall in which it is anchored.

The panels that form the most visible part of the fence can be varied in an almost unlimited number of ways. Outside of the basic concerns of entrapment (unless otherwise governed by local codes, openings should be less than 5 inches or greater than 9 inches), and whether horizontal elements can be used to climb up and over the fence itself, there are few constraints on the design of an ornamental panel. Square pickets that are set diagonally give the panels an added interest compared to pickets that are set parallel to the line of the fence. Pickets that alternate in height can be more interesting than a fence panel that has a constant height. A variety of different ornamentations can be welded and integrated into a standard fence panel. In considering one of these manufactured pieces, check their dimensions first, as this will affect the picket or rail spacing to which these pieces will be welded. Louvered-type fencing panels can create a screening effect where desirable. Panels welded to the pickets can be used to create a solid, totally opaque screening barrier.

There are a few general recommendations for the design and installation of the ornamental fence such as the types previously described. Fence installed in concrete curbs or walls require less maintenance than fence in footings, where the fence panels span over planted areas (unable to be mowed) that require constant maintenance to keep grass or weeds from growing up beneath the fence panels. For installation on sloped sites, the fence looks best when the rails follow the slope of the finished grade and the pickets are truly vertical. It is also advisable to install the fence post in holes that are cored into the curb or wall to which the fence is to be anchored. Post holes that are formed during the construction of the curb or wall tend to vary and shift, thereby creating variances in the distance between fence posts, and these tend to compound over the length of the fence run, making the fitting of standard fence panels virtually impossible. This can lead to the eventual coring of new holes, almost immediately adjacent to the formed holes, to install fence posts at the proper distance to accommodate the standard fence panels. A cored hole can be executed with a great deal of accuracy after the curb or wall is constructed; this is usually done by the same contractor that is fabricating the fence, which can lead to less finger-pointing when things don't fit the way they should.

During fence installation, the fence is usually loosely connected to together, chocked plumb and true to line in the cored holes, and then anchored with a quick-setting grout. After the grout has hardened, a sealer is placed in the hole with a wash that directs water away from the post and post hole. This is a much better installation than trying to set the post directly into a wet concrete curb or wall. At the end of a run of fence where any gap between the fence and adjacent fence or structure must be kept at a minimum, it is advisable to install a filler panel, as opposed to trying to have a fence post installed so close to the end of the anchoring curb or wall. Fence posts that are too close to an edge of concrete run the risk of breaking through the edge and becoming unstable. A filler panel allows the fence post to be set back, allowing for adequate concrete cover on all sides of the end post. In a similar manner, end posts that are adjacent to structures can be attached to the structure, giving the end post added stability and strength. Solid-steel fences are generally painted with a primer and two coats of finished paint applied in the shop (plus a touch-up coat in the field after installation to take care of little nicks and scrapes). Fabricators will sometimes dip the fabricated fence panels into large tanks of paint to ensure coverage of the entire panel.

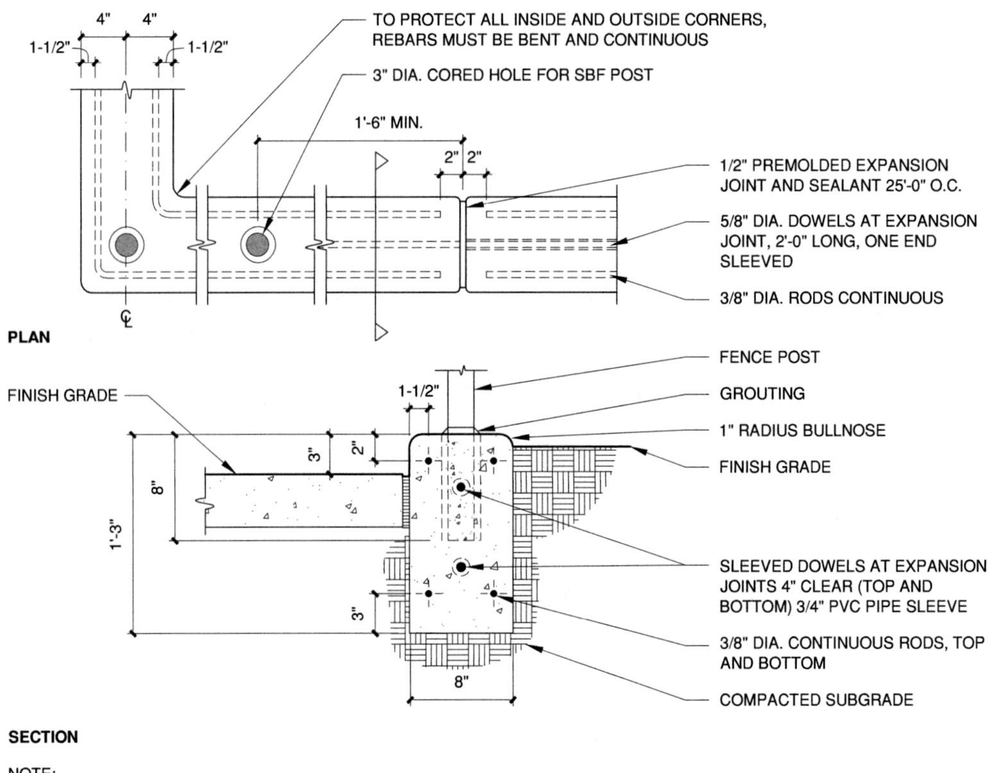

CONCRETE CURB 3-FOOT-HIGH SOLID-STEEL-BAR FENCE

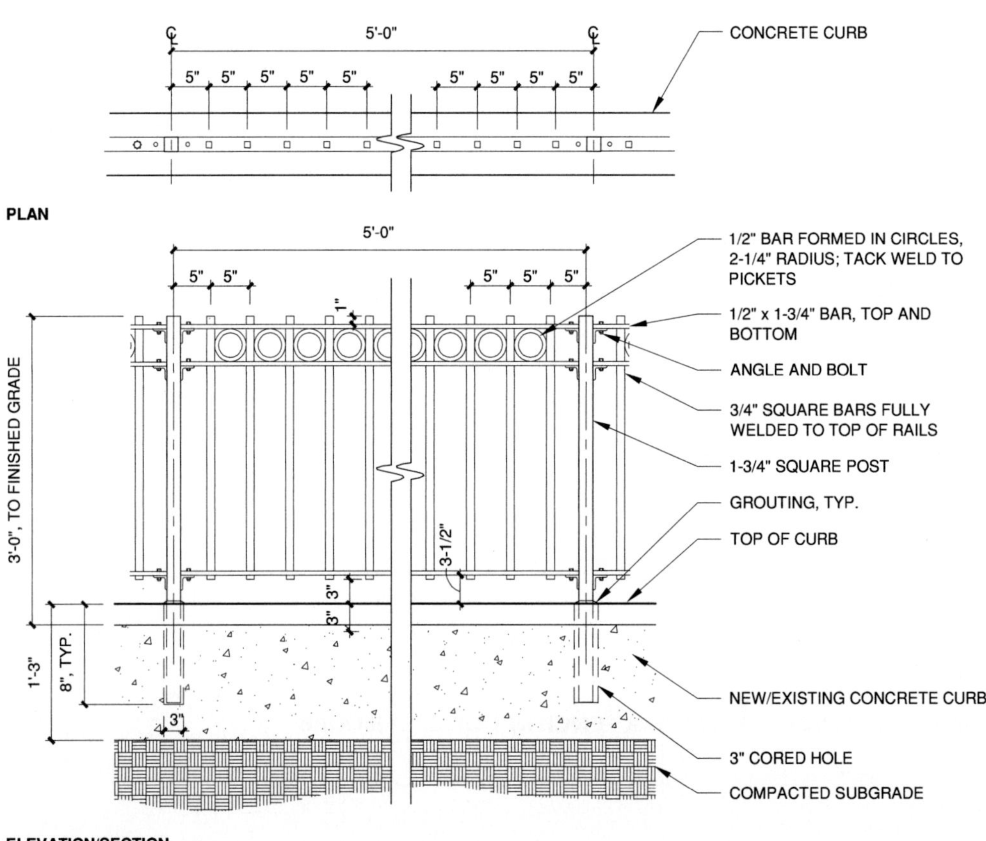

3-FOOT-HIGH SOLID-STEEL-BAR FENCE WITH DECORATIVE CIRCLE

Leonard Hopper, RLA, FASLA

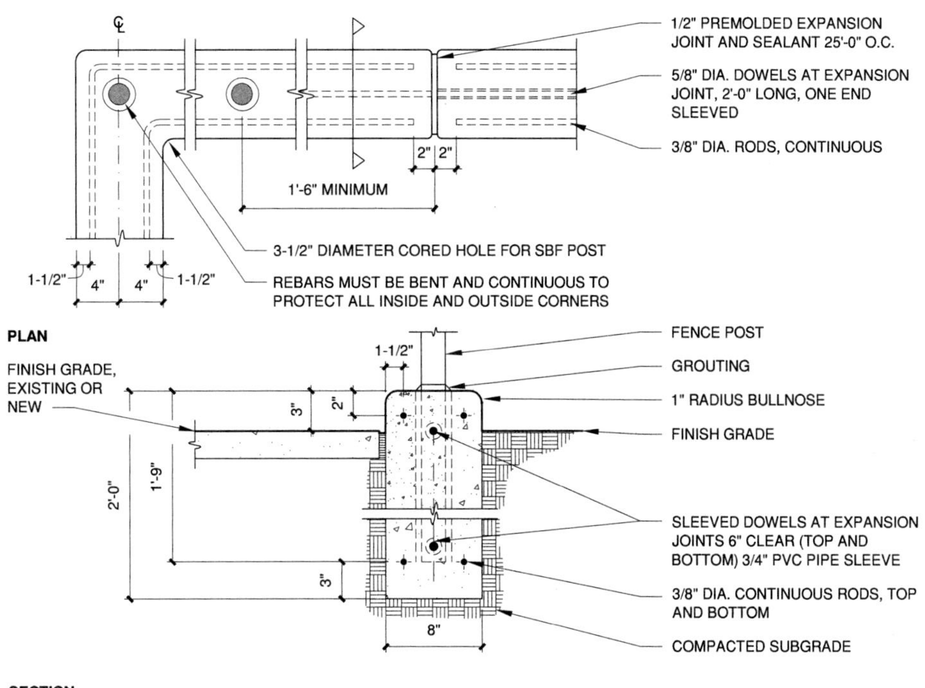

CONCRETE CURB 6-FOOT-HIGH SOLID-STEEL-BAR FENCE

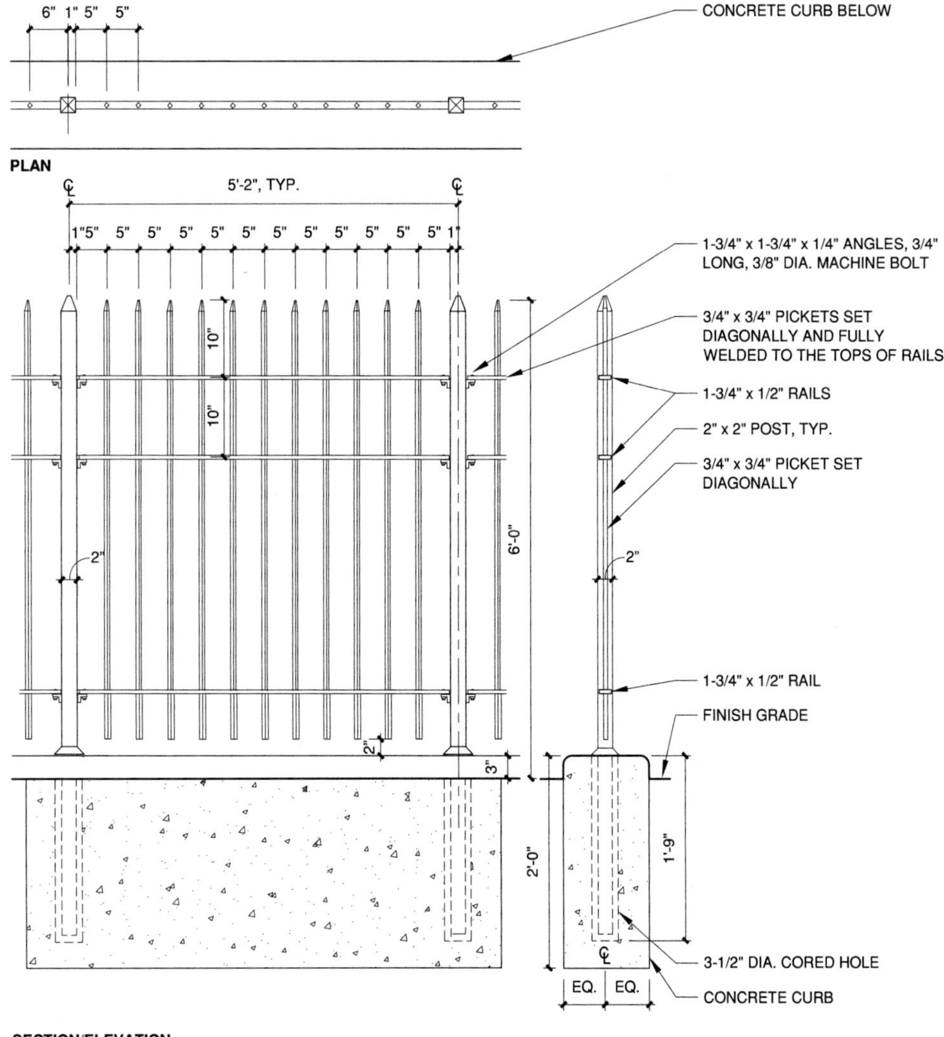

6-FOOT-HIGH SOLID-STEEL-BAR FENCE IN CONCRETE CURB

Leonard Hopper, RLA, FASLA

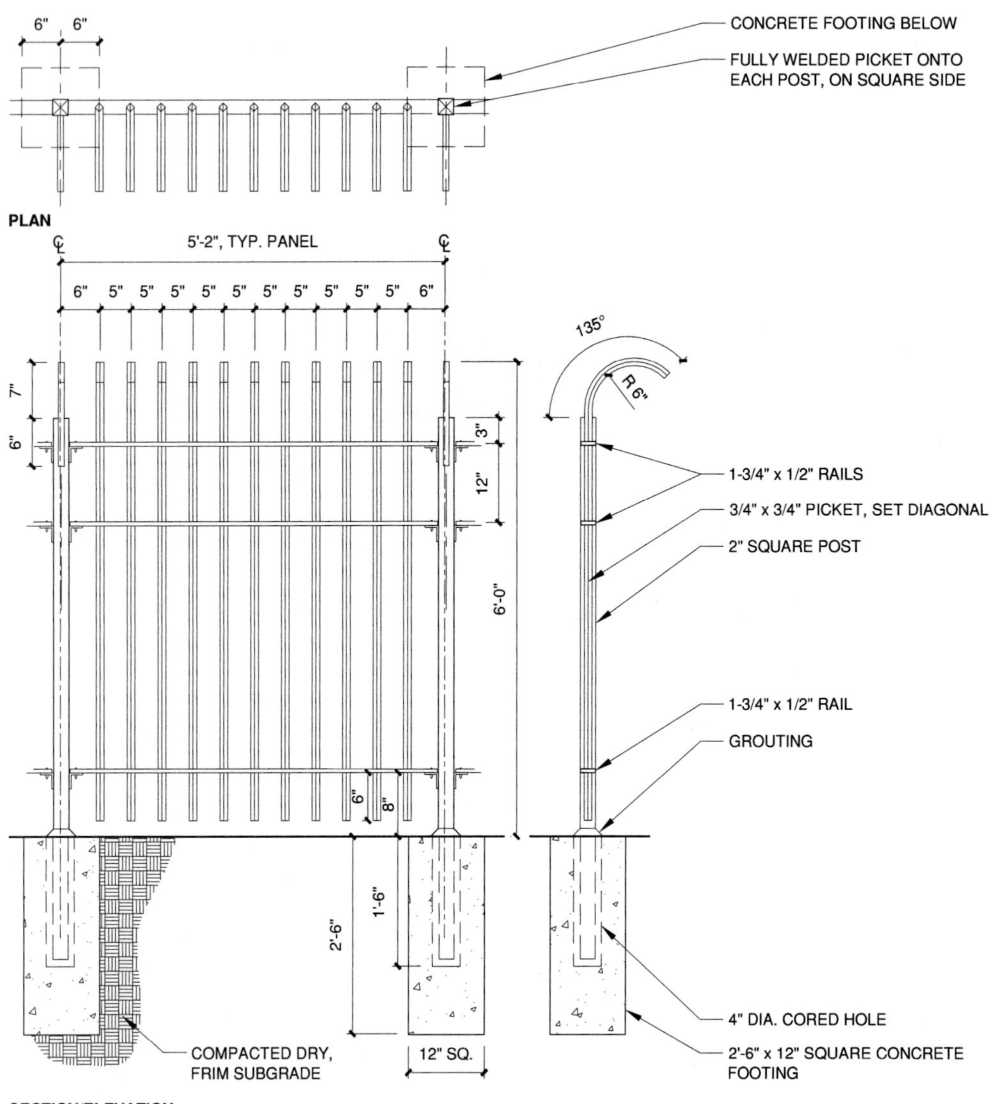

6-FOOT-HIGH SOLID-STEEL-BAR FENCE WITH "BEAR CLAW" PICKETS

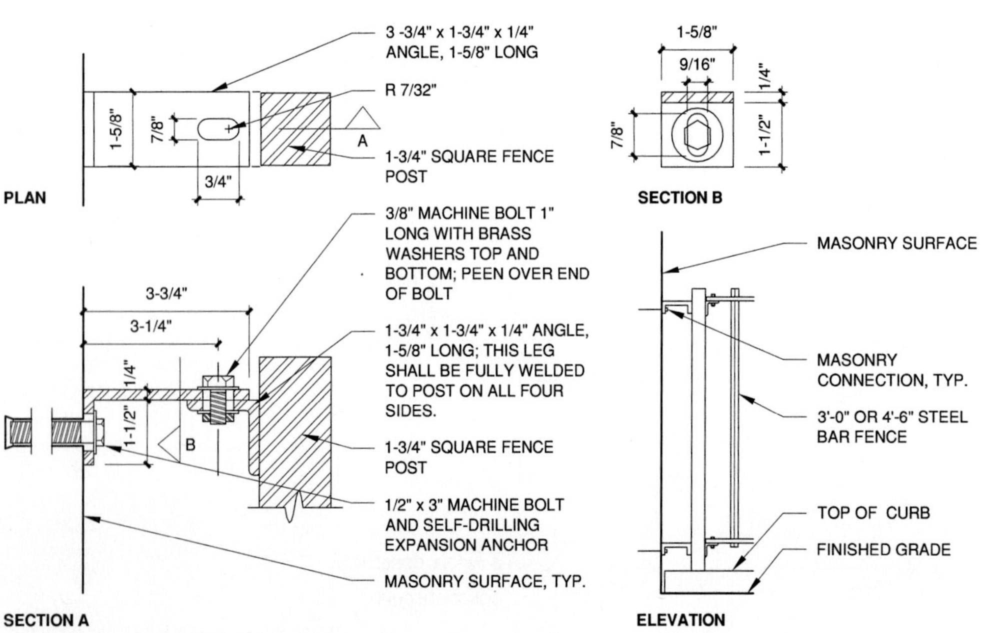

MASONRY CONNECTION DETAIL FOR 3-FOOT-HIGH OR 4-FOOT-6-INCH-HIGH VARIABLE-PICKET STEEL-BAR FENCE

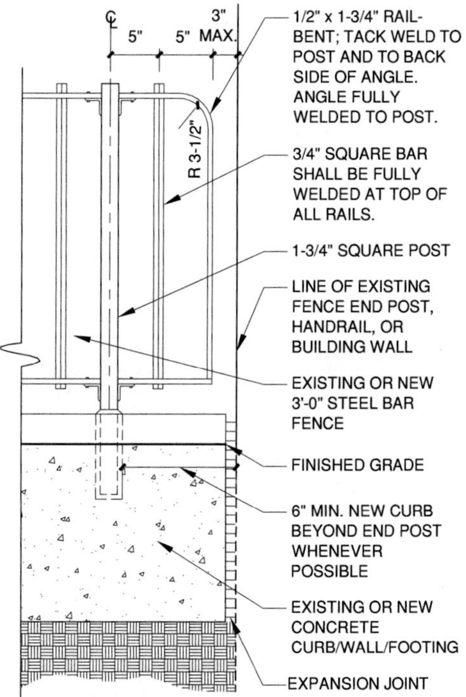

NOTE: ALL RAILS AND PICKETS SHALL ALIGN WITH EXISTING OR NEW STEEL BAR FENCE.

TYPICAL FILLER PANEL FOR STEEL-BAR FENCE

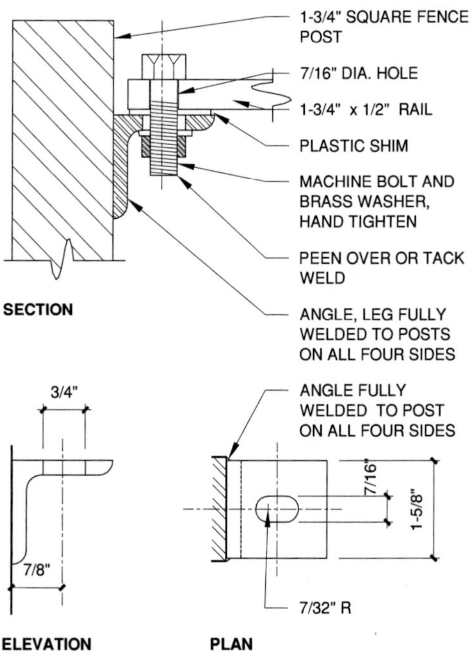

ANGLE AND BOLT DETAIL FOR 3-FOOT-HIGH OR 4-FOOT-6-INCH HIGH VARIABLE PICKET STEEL-BAR FENCE

Leonard Hopper, RLA, FASLA

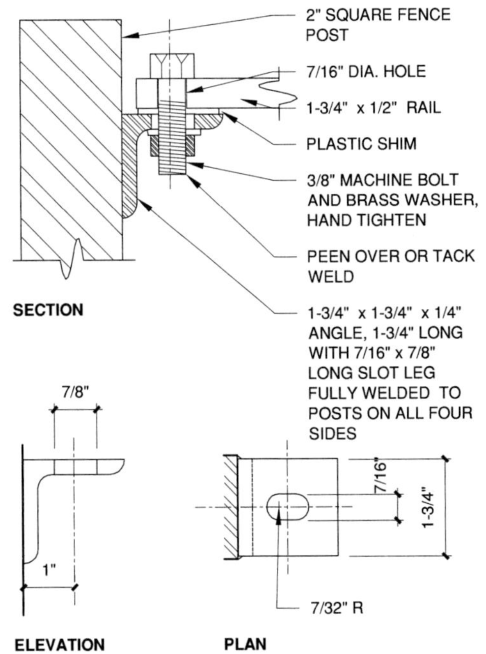

ANGLE AND BOLT DETAIL FOR 6-FOOT-HIGH STEEL-BAR FENCE

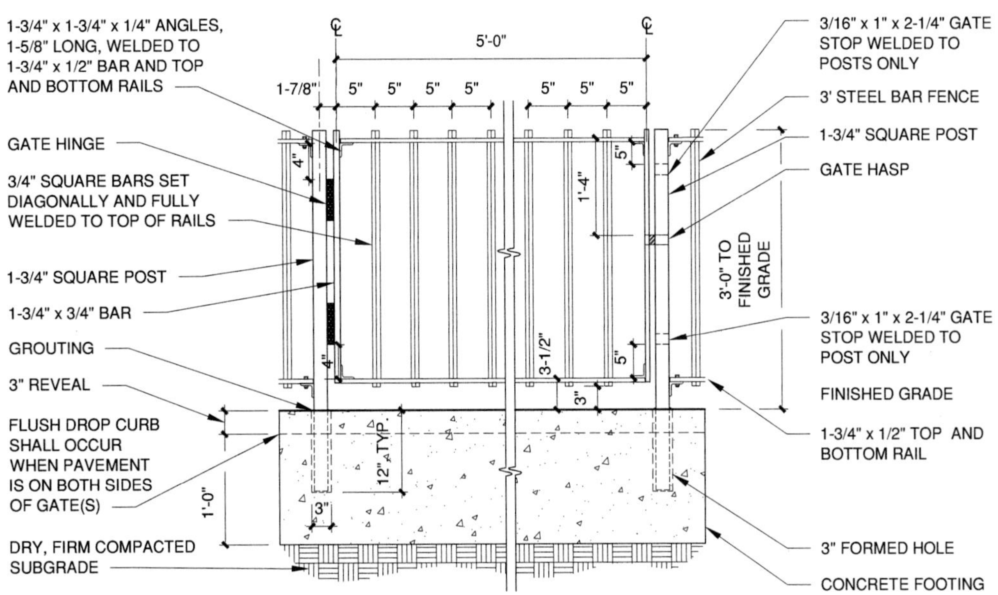

SINGLE GATE FOR 3-FOOT-HIGH SOLID-STEEL-BAR FENCE IN CONCRETE CURB

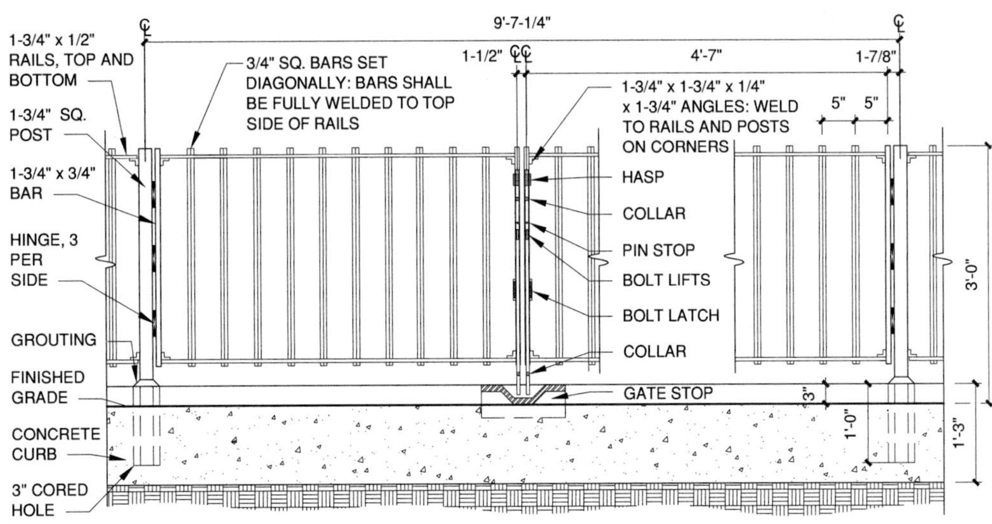

DOUBLE GATE FOR 3-FOOT-HIGH SOLID-STEEL-BAR FENCE IN CONCRETE CURB

Leonard Hopper, RLA, FASLA

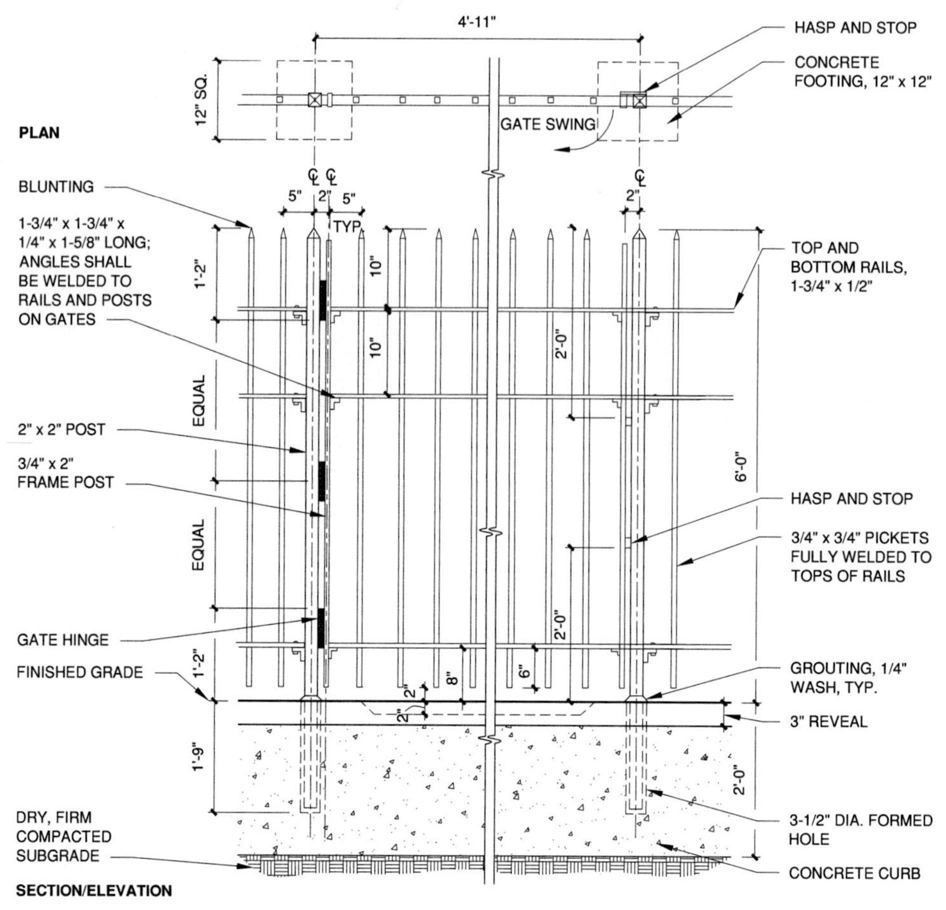

SINGLE GATE FOR 6-FOOT-HIGH SOLID-STEEL-BAR FENCE WITH DROPPED CONCRETE CURB ALTERNATIVE

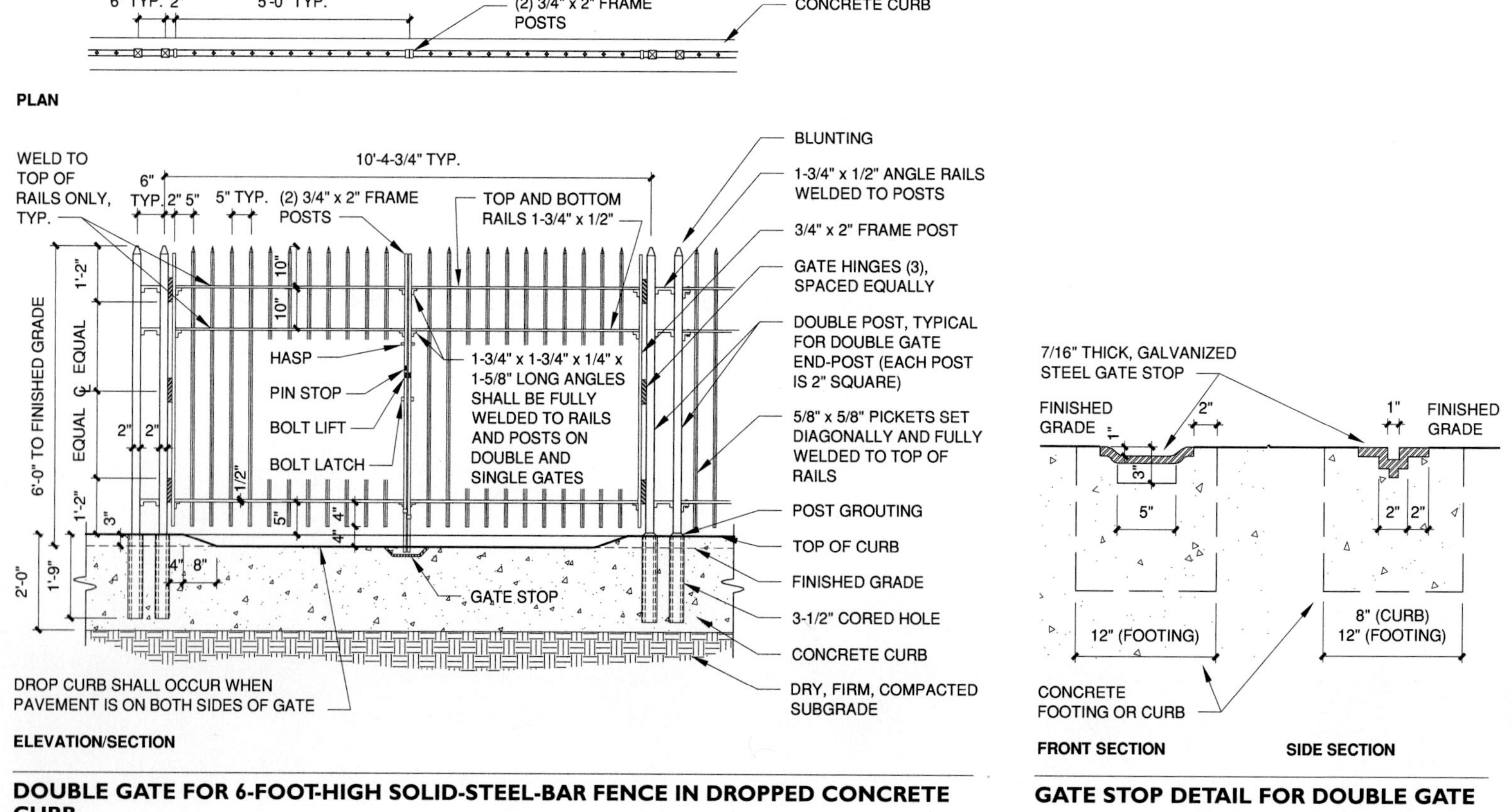

DOUBLE GATE FOR 6-FOOT-HIGH SOLID-STEEL-BAR FENCE IN DROPPED CONCRETE CURB

GATE STOP DETAIL FOR DOUBLE GATE

Leonard Hopper, RLA, FASLA

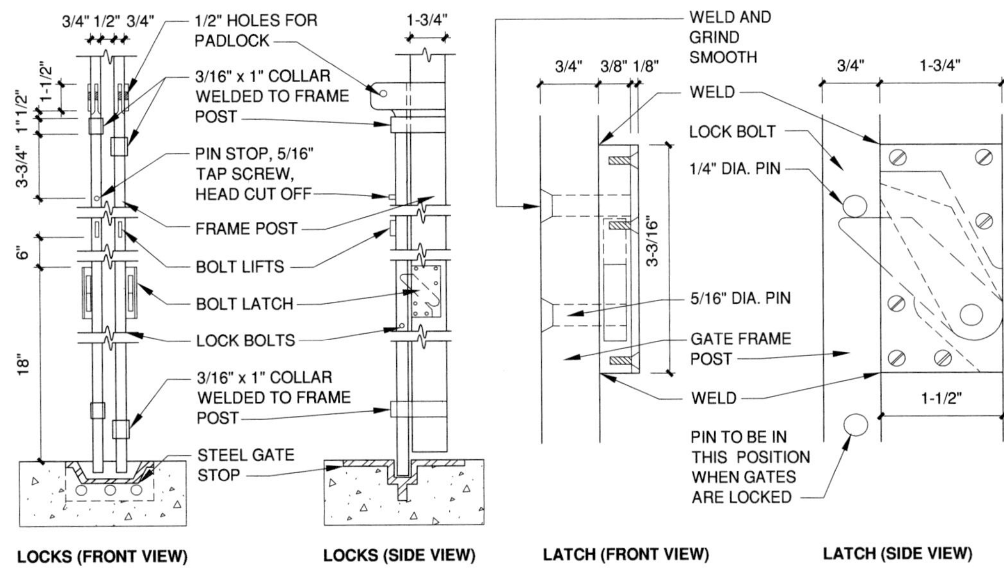

BOLT LOCKS AND LATCH DETAIL FOR 3-FOOT-HIGH, 4-FOOT-6-INCH-HIGH, OR 4-FOOT-6-INCH HIGH VARIABLE-PICKET SOLID-STEEL-BAR DOUBLE GATE

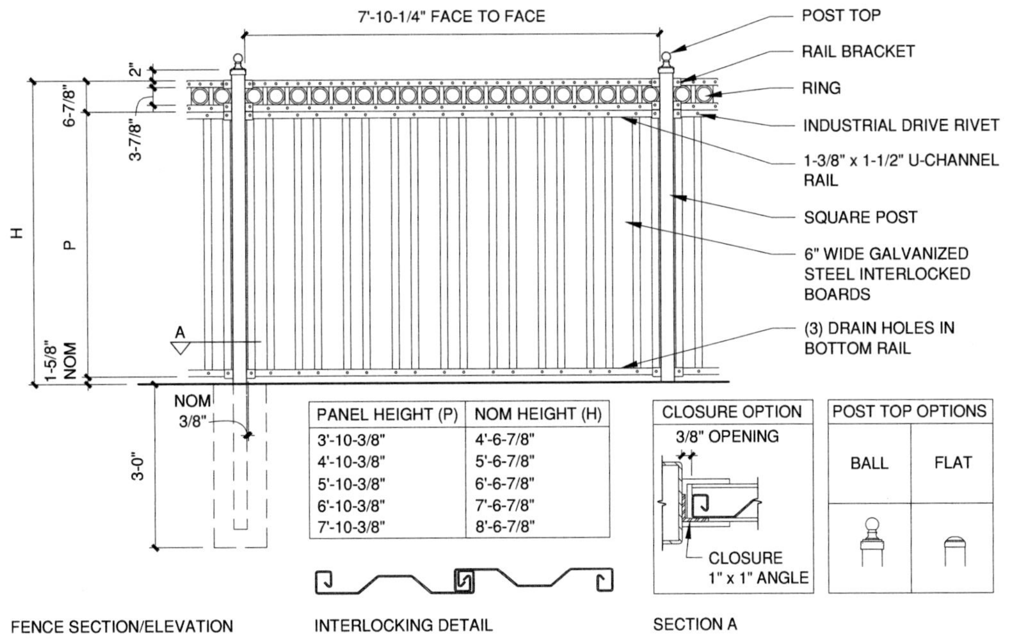

PANEL HEIGHT (P)	NOM HEIGHT (H)
3'-10-3/8"	4'-6-7/8"
4'-10-3/8"	5'-6-7/8"
5'-10-3/8"	6'-6-7/8"
6'-10-3/8"	7'-6-7/8"
7'-10-3/8"	8'-6-7/8"

OPAQUE FENCE WITH WELDED PANELS TO SOLID-STEEL FENCE

Source: Master Halco

Leonard Hopper, RLA, FASLA

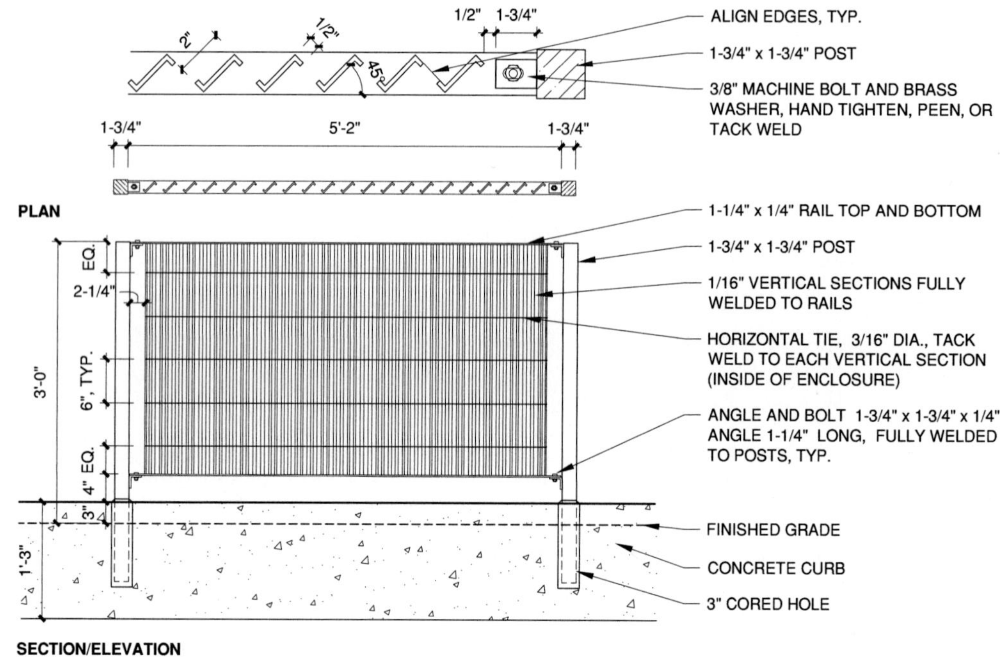

3-FOOT-HIGH LOUVER FENCE IN CONCRETE CURB

Leonard Hopper, RLA, FASLA

GAZEBOS AND FREESTANDING WOOD STRUCTURES

KEY ISSUES

The range of wood structures designed as freestanding, recreational elements in the landscape is extensive. From the simple thatched teahouses in Japan to the ornamented, timber-framed pavilions common in the urban parks of the 1800s, wood structures have long been a part of the design vocabulary of landscape architects.

The gazebo, the most common of wooden garden structures, still retains its popularity, with many being adapted to uses such as outdoor classrooms and stages. The commons of many New England and Midwestern towns feature an oversized white-painted gazebo. In the Southwest, the form is reinterpreted with richly carved columns supporting rough-hewn poles (vigas) to provide shade and a place to rest.

Before designing a structure, whether a pavilion, play structure, or tree house, a structural system must be chosen. Considerations will include the design intent, function, expression, contextual fit, and costs. Pole construction and the timber frame system, the two most commonly used structural systems, are related. A third system, rib framing, common in building construction is less commonly employed in exterior structures exposed to the elements.

STRUCTURAL SYSTEMS

The first system, *pole construction*, relies on vertical post members to create a frame or skeleton that is set into the ground or mounted on concrete footings to carry the loads, roof, walls, and floor to the subgrade. The posts transfer the loads to the ground, becoming a series of points. Depending on the soil-bearing capacity, this form of building is limited in the load it can support, but for most landscape structures it is usually adequate.

A *timber frame system* is an extension of the pole system. It can be adapted to a pier, pier-and-beam, or continuous footing system; however, the loads in a traditional timber/beam system are transferred through the posts to the footings, not over the entire wall. In this system, timbers are used for all the framing, thus fewer framing members are required, but they are considerably greater in size than those used in the rib system.

The third system, *rib framing*, is common in the United States for residential and commercial wood frame construction. There are several differences between the rib and pole systems. In the rib system, all perimeter and interior load-bearing walls transfer the loads in a linear fashion, instead of a point fashion, distributing the loads continuously. Openings within the walls are designed so the loads from above are transferred through "headers" to other parts of the wall. Either a continuous perimeter foundation or pier-and-beam system is used in the rib system, often called "stick frame" construction.

FOUNDATIONS

The integrity of the structure is dependent on the foundation for its stability. Many failures of the structure can often be traced to the connection where the forces of the structure are conveyed into the earth. There are several design options for building founda-

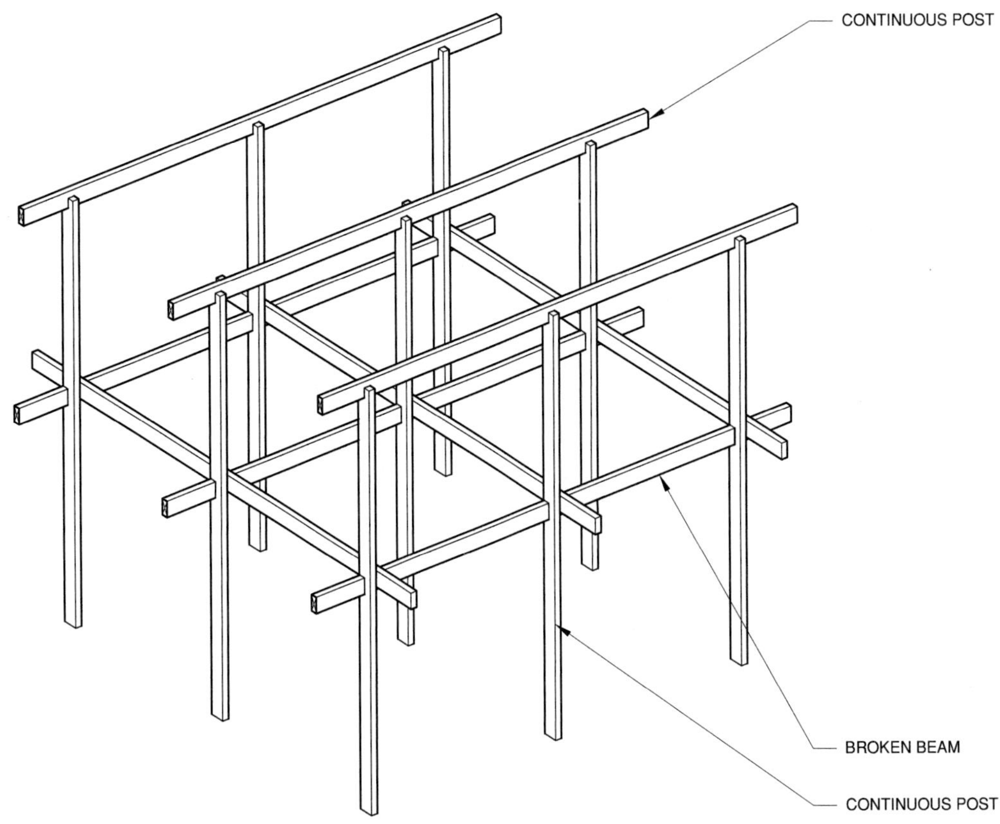

CONTINUOUS POST WITH SEGMENTED OR BROKEN BEAM

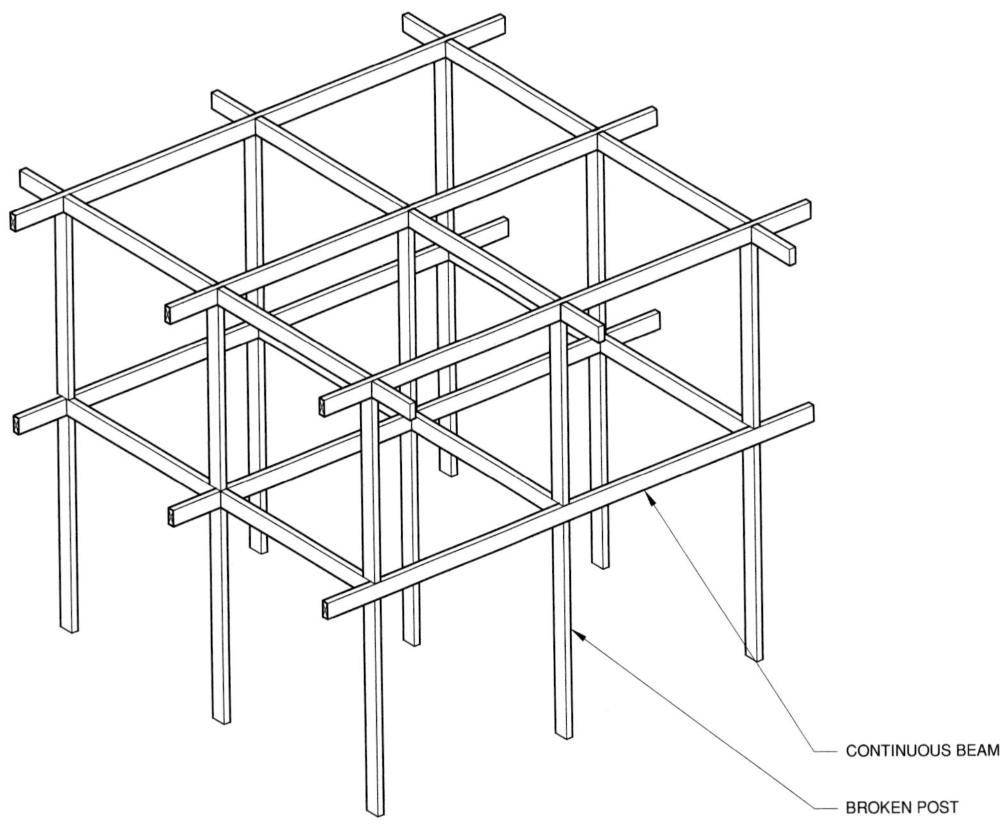

CONTINUOUS BEAM WITH BROKEN POST

Daniel Winterbottom, Associate Professor, Department of Landscape Architecture, University of Washington

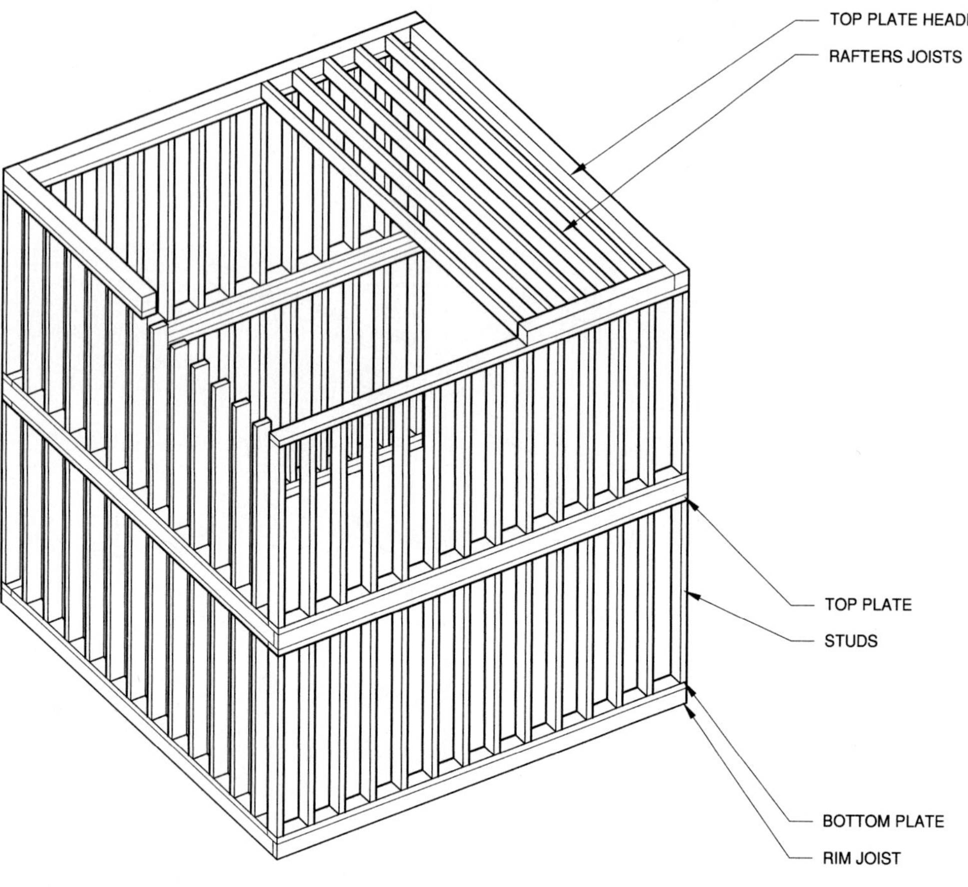

PLATFORM OR RIB METHOD OF FRAMING

tions, and, similar to deck systems, soil conditions, depth of freeze, combined dead and live loads, structural configuration, and aesthetics all have an effect on which option to choose.

A cast-in-place pier footing is common for pole or timber-framed structures. The pier is often extended above grade to receive a wood post or beam, eliminating contact between the framing and the ground. The footing locations are determined by the structural design configuration and the allowable beam spans. In the design of a timber frame structure, posts are sometimes located on a midpoint of the beam. If they are nonbearing, this is of little concern; otherwise, the loads must be calculated and the beam sized to carry the post loads.

A continuous cast-in-place stem wall foundation may be used if considerable loads are applied along the foundation alignment. The steel-reinforced spread footing is twice the width of the stem wall or greater, 6 to 8 inches thick, and set below the frost line. The footing must sit upon undisturbed earth or compacted bearing soils; and ½- to ⅝-inch L-shaped reinforcing bars are placed 8 to 12 inches on center. The shorter length is embedded to resist withdrawal with the longer length, protruding vertically. Reinforcing bars are also placed horizontally in the spread footing and the stem wall, typically at the same spacing as the vertical reinforcing.

The stem wall transfers the loads of the wood structure to the spread footing. The mechanical connectors, including anchor bolts for sills, and post anchors for posts and hangers for beams, are set into the concrete pour. On foundation walls that will be visible, various details, champhers, recessed bandings, and scored lines are cast into the form to provide visual interest and a finished look to the wall.

A third method, employed when soils are unstable or the foundation is very long is a pin pile-grade beam system. This system, while very effective, is not often employed for most structures that landscape architects design; rather, it should be considered in special situations. Instead of trenching for a costly continuous foundation, which requires removal of considerable volumes of soil, a series of pilings are driven down to bearing soils or bedrock. These precast, reinforced concrete, steel I-beams or reinforced cast-in-place pilings are connected to and support a grade beam a long continuous reinforced rectilinear concrete beam. The loads are transferred from the beam through the pin pilings to bearing soils.

Once the foundation is completed, the floor and wall framing are erected. The floor is framed similar to that described in *Wood Decks*. The beam is connected to the pier footings. If a stem wall or pier-and-beam foundation is used, 2×8 or 2×6 sills are bolted down to the preset anchor bolts and function as a continuous beam. The joists are laid atop the sill and attached to a rim joist, a double 2× framing the perimeter of the wall. To support midspan joists that end between perimeter walls, beams either spanning the perimeter walls or supported by posts support the joist ends.

For open structures, 2×4 or 2×6 decking members span the joists. For enclosed structures, there are several flooring options, including tongue-and-groove soft or hard woods, plywood, a plywood underlay tile, or a floor covering.

Once the floor is framed, the walls can be erected. For most exterior structures, gazebos, picnic shelters, playhouses, saunas, greenhouses, and so on, a combination of timber and rib framing is employed, depending on the intended use and appearance.

WALL FRAMING

There are two primary types of wood framing: rib framing, in which the loads are carried by the bearing walls, and timber framing, which incorporates a series of large posts and beams to carry the loads. One potential advantage of timber framing is the wide, clear open spaces between the structural members; in the rib system, these are filled with studs (vertical framing members). Rib framing, or "stick framing," is common in the United States. Conceptually, a series of walls, composed of many small vertical members, are joined at the corners, transferring the loads to the foundation, eliminating large structural posts and beams. A horizontal bottom plate is attached to the floor framing and establishes the alignment of the wall. Running perpendicular to the bottom plate are the studs, 2×4s or 2×6s spaced 16 inches apart for a bearing wall and 24 inches for nonbearing walls, and capped with a top plate, (2) 2×s. Wall penetrations for windows and doorways are double-framed with two members: a king stud, extending from bottom to top plate, and trimmer or jack stud, attached to the king stud and cut to fit below and support a header. The header, a double 2×6, 2×8, or 2×10 member, spans the opening, transferring the loads to the king/jack studs. Short framing members placed 16 inches on center between the header and top plate are called "cripple studs." When framing a window opening, the bottom of the header defines the top dimension and the sill; a double member similar to the top plate, and capping the shortened studs below the window, defines the bottom elevation of the window. Sheathing, often ½-inch plywood, is attached to the framing and functions as a shear panel to resist racking and lateral stresses. The rib or platform method uses greater amounts of material of a smaller size than the timber frame method. (See the "Platform or Rib Method of Framing" and "Wall Frame Using Platform" figures.)

Two versions of post-and-beam systems offer some significant advantages over rib framing. The first, continuous beam systems, incorporate large timber or glue-laminated beams to span great distances, resulting in a very open structure. The spans are determined by the beam size and spacing of the posts, with the beam laid on top of the posts. The second system incorporates a continuous post or column, rising two stories or greater. In this system, the beams are connected to, not mounted on, each post. The two systems are often combined by using split beams or split posts. In the split beam version, two members are either attached to the side of the column or set into a precut seat.

In traditional post-and-beam timber construction, such as that found in early barn buildings and in the magnificent Japanese pavilions, the wood members are connected using a variety of wood joints and wood dowels and pins to hold the connections together. Many joints are simple mortise and tendon or lap or notched joints; however, there are many

Daniel Winterbottom, Associate Professor, Department of Landscape Architecture, University of Washington

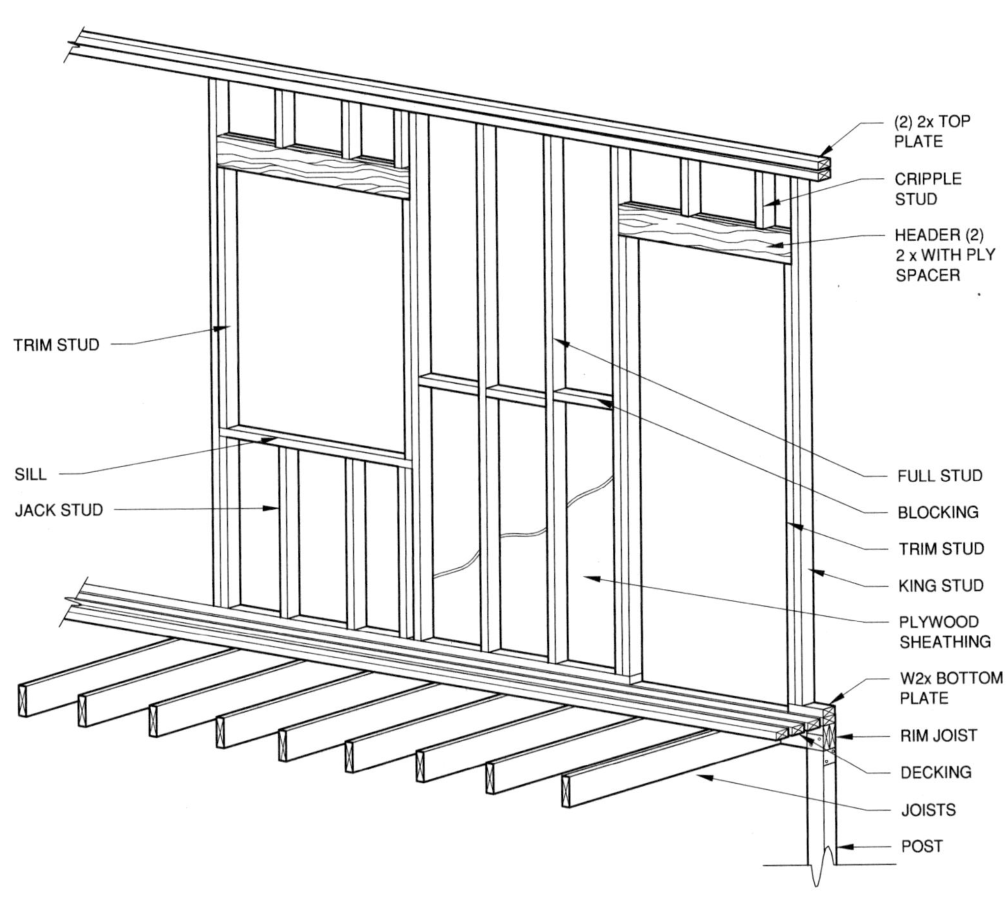

WALL FRAME USING PLATFORM METHOD

complex variations on these forms, many of which are highly ornamental. In modern timber framing, many designers rely on metal connectors in lieu of complex joinery to attach wood members, and the connectors themselves often become design features. (See "Continous Post with Segmented or Broken Beam" and "Continuous Beam with Broekn Post" figures.)

ROOF FRAMING

There are many potential roof configurations, most designed with either rafters or trusses or some combination of these. The framing of a flat roof is relatively simple, and similar to joist framing. Most roofs on small exterior structures are designed with a single slope or combination of slopes. A single-sloped shed roof is the simplest, connecting two walls of differing heights. A double-sloped roof, or hip roof, uses walls of the same height to support the lower ends and a ridge beam to support the rafters at the peak. Beyond these basic forms, many variations can be found, including multiple hipped roofs, domed roofs, octagonal roofs, butterfly roofs, and others. Whatever the configuration, there will need to be rafters or trusses to support the dead and live loads. Snow loads add considerable dead loads over long periods, meaning the rafters will need to be of great size. In southern climates, wind uplift can cause great stresses, so anchoring of the rafters must be thorough. In conventional framing, the rafters bear on the top plate, or in timber framing on the beams; and in a simple hip roof, they run to the ridge, where they are connected to and bear upon a ridge beam. The ridge beam is a 2X or greater material running parallel with the walls to which rafters are attached. The pitch (slope or angle) of the roof rafters is established by the relationship of the rise (vertical distance) to run (horizontal distance). Thus, a 5.12 pitch indicates that for every 12 inches of horizontal run, the rafter rises 5 inches. The roof, sheathing, and roofing material are supported by rafters. The angle of the rafters determines the pitch of the roof.

Perlins are often placed at the midpoint of the rafter span to tie the rafters together and resist sagging and spreading. On large projects, it is common to use premanufactured forms of rafters set at the specified pitches called "trusses." Trusses designed with multiple bracing can span large distances and are employed when long, clear spans are required. (See the "Rafters" figure.)

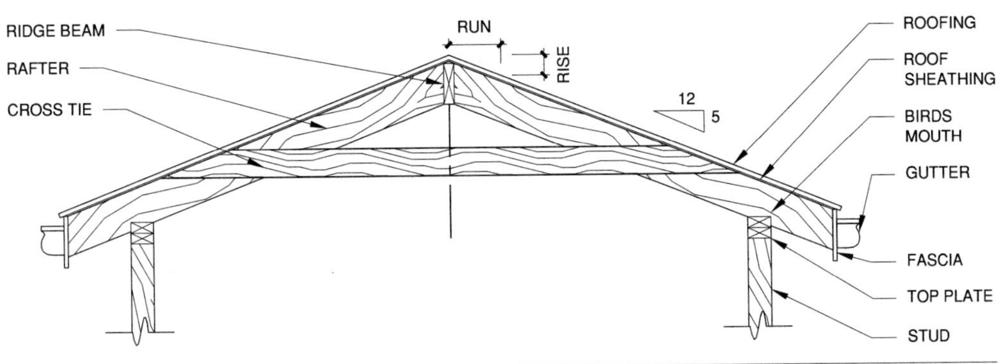

RAFTERS

ROOFING

With the roof framing complete, the sheathing, most commonly ½- to ¾-inch plywood or 1X6 skip sheathing, is used to tie all the rafters together and to provide a substratum to which to attach the roofing material. The sheathing is covered with overlapping sheets of roofing (tar) paper before the final roof-cladding system is attached, providing protection from water penetration. Many roofing systems are available on the market; durability, cost, and aesthetics will determine the final selection. For most landscape structures, insulation value and roof venting are not a concern; the roof cladding is intended to shed water, complement the character of the structure, and resist wind and snow loads. The options for impermeable roofs include, but are not limited to, asphalt, cedar, and slate shingles; metal sheet systems; and terra-cotta tiles. Some systems require extra nailing supports and may be substantial in size to carry the weight of slate and terra-cotta tiles. The cost and durability depend on the method selected. The roof cladding is attached with roofing nails, screws, or other systems provided by the manufacturer. Some sheet systems are interlocking and attached to the sheathing with clips; others use galvanized roofing nails under overlapping shingles to protect the points of penetration. A system of ring-shanked nails combined with rubber washers is used where surface nailing is exposed. Copper-coated nails, designed to prevent galvanic corrosion, are available for fastening copper roofing.

The roof conveys water, so often a gutter is installed to convey the water to a downspout system. Alternatively, the rafter tails can be extended out beyond the building face to shed the water away from the siding. If the function is to provide shade, not cover, the roof may be designed as a permeable system to provide screening from the sun and as an armature for vines. Wood, bamboo, or metal members span the rafters, creating an open pattern, which can be seen through the shadows cast on the floor. Roofs can also be designed to extend past the walls, creating overhangs and reducing the angle of sun penetration into the structure.

Daniel Winterbottom, Associate Professor, Department of Landscape Architecture, University of Washington

ORNAMENTATION

As tools have evolved, so too has wood ornamentation, from handcarving to band-saw cut scrollwork. Many cultures have found distinctive expression in the ornamentation of their wood buildings and outdoor structures. Using techniques of carving, cutting, attaching, and drilling, builders and designers enhance the aesthetic character of wood structures. Wood ornament is typically independent of the structure system, but may draw focus to the structural members. The fluting or attenuation of columns emphasizes the post. The design of brackets draws attention to the post, beam, rafter connection. As a style, ornamentation is in constant flux, at times richly developed, as it was during the Victorian period, other times all but eliminated such as during the International period of the 1950s and 1960s. Victorian ornament was applied or layered to the wood structure in the form of moldings, medallions, and scrollwork. The Craftsman cottage style represents a different approach in which the structural members, such as rafter ends, bargeboards, and window and door trim, are cut, carved, sawn, or themselves joined.

Several methods of construction are commonly employed in wood ornamentation, including:

- *Holes, slits and slots.* Shapes are cut or drilled into a solid wood member. The voids, curved or lineal forms, are often repeated to create rhythmic patterns. Some, hearts and shamrocks, are symbolic; others are geometric abstractions. Holes, slits, and slots are commonly found in bargeboards (a board covering the end rafters of the roof structure), skirtboards (the board covering the joists on a porch, gazebo, or structure), or valences (a board covering the beam that spans the posts and supports the roof rafters on a porch). They are also commonly used on post brackets, pendants, and fence boards.
- *Sticks.* Narrow wood members such as 1×1, 2×2, or odds and ends left over from the framing are used in a repetitive manner to create patterns. Common patterns include sunbursts, often located below the roof on a gable end of the structure, diamond patterns found on a porch valence, or rectilinear forms repeated on porch railings or fences.
- *Scales.* Wood shingles are commonly used to clad wood structures and can be sawn to a great variety of shapes. Forms can be curved (scaled) or pointed (feathered), and when used on a vertical surface can be laid out to form running patterns. These patterns can accentuate the forms of the structure, for example, using fish scales to demark a tower structure. Many shapes are available precut in lumberyards; and custom-made forms can be created using the band saw. Forms such as flowers or playing card symbols—clubs, spades, and diamonds—are frequently integrated into the wall design.
- *Appliqué.* The attachment of flat cut forms onto a supporting member constitutes appliqué. These cutouts often float within the frame, formed by the supporting board. Appliqué is most commonly used on brackets, bargeboards, skirtboards, and posts.
- *Applied.* Applied ornament includes a wide range of elements, including panels, moldings, low-relief carvings, and medallions. Traditionally these moldings were applied in specific areas of the building, in the cornices and on the horizontal strips where the wall and roof meet, and they often accompany dentils, brackets, panels, and medallions. At the corner of the structure, quoins, blocks of wood cut to imitate stone, can be used. Posts often incorporate capitals, bases, and brackets. Pilasters are built of wood pieces that protrude slightly from the wall, imitating a column in relief. Lattice, brackets, and scrollwork are frequently integrated into porches, stairs, and fences, and where ornamental pickets, balusters, railings, newel posts, and post caps are commonly used.

See also:

Overhead Structures
Wood

Daniel Winterbottom, Associate Professor, Department of Landscape Architecture, University of Washington

OVERHEAD STRUCTURES

USES IN THE LANDSCAPE

Overhead structures have wide-ranging application in the landscape and can take many forms. They are particularly useful in areas where planting trees is not an option, such as over underground utility lines or on top of a building structure, if weight and soil depth are limited. In general, such overhead structures serve one or a combination of the following functions.

Shade/Climate Protection

Solar radiation and wind are two weather variables that can be manipulated by the design of the landscape to modify the microclimate. Doing so increases thermal comfort and decreases energy usage (see the section *Modifying Microclimates*). In designing an overhead structure, methods for modifying exposure to sun and wind include the addition of deciduous vines for summer shade/winter sun, the extension of an overhang to promote shade in summer but allow winter sun to enter, or the positioning of a canopy to collect and direct breezes for cooling, ventilation, and wind protection. Structures with solid overhead panels or canopies can provide shelter from rain as well as sun.

Passage/Wayfinding

Overhead structures can be used effectively to define or enclose passageways and to direct circulation through a site. A structure can take the form of a simple overhead plane supported by columns, or use a combination of vertical and horizontal elements to create a stronger sense of enclosure.

Destination/Center of Activity

Structures also can be used to mark a special destination or center of activity, such as a gathering place, a contemplative seating area, a bandstand, or a focal point in the landscape. The complexity of the structure should be appropriate to its setting and function.

Outdoor Stage

Overhead structures often are used to provide cover for an outdoor stage or music venue. These structures can be very simple and small or they can be quite elaborate, with provisions for high-voltage sound equipment and special lighting.

SUSTAINABLE DESIGN

Overhead structures can be used to increase thermal comfort and decrease energy usage in an area. When designed properly, they can do a great deal to contribute to sustainability. However, other factors need to be considered. One is material usage at all stages in the life of the structure—the content of the materials used in construction, the materials required during maintenance, and the potential for reuse of materials after the structure has reached the end of its useful life. Another factor is energy usage related to the selected material—the amount of energy required to produce and transport those materials and the amount required for maintenance over the course of the structure's lifetime. The effect on the microclimate, material usage, and energy usage all play a role in the sustainable design of an overhead structure.

TYPES OF STRUCTURES

Pergolas, Arbors, Trellises, and Colonnades

Pergolas, arbors, trellises, and colonnades constitute a family of structures typically composed of columns supporting a horizontal overhead plane. These structures can vary widely in form and material. For ease of discussion, the following examples are grouped by their dominant construction material—wood, metal, or stone/masonry/precast concrete.

Wood

Wood is the material most commonly used in the construction of pergolas, arbors, and trellis structures. Wood is economical and aesthetically compatible with many landscape settings, as a result of its natural appearance. It is also easy to work with from a construction standpoint. Wood has been used in the design of landscape structures for centuries, with countless precedents, both rustic and refined.

As the design of a structure moves from concept to detail, the landscape architect will need to check with local planning and building departments to obtain their design guidelines and requirements for coverage, height, and construction. Many municipalities require a structural engineer to confirm the sizing of wood members and attachment details, as well as the footing design to ensure structural integrity.

The most efficiently milled lumber sizes should be used, such as two 2×8 joists versus one 4×8 joist.

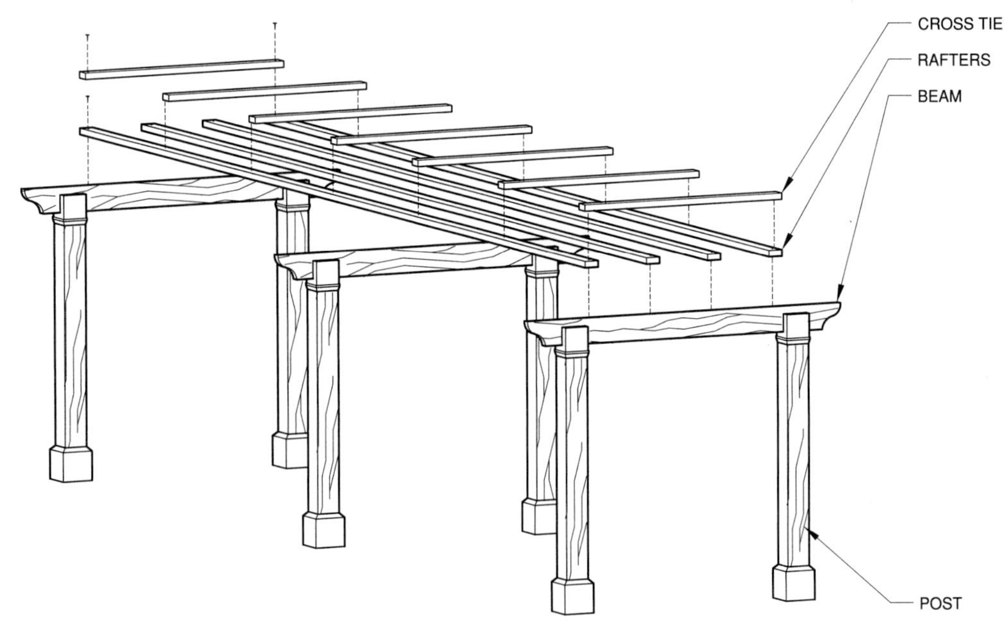

ELEMENTS OF ARBORS AND PERGOLAS

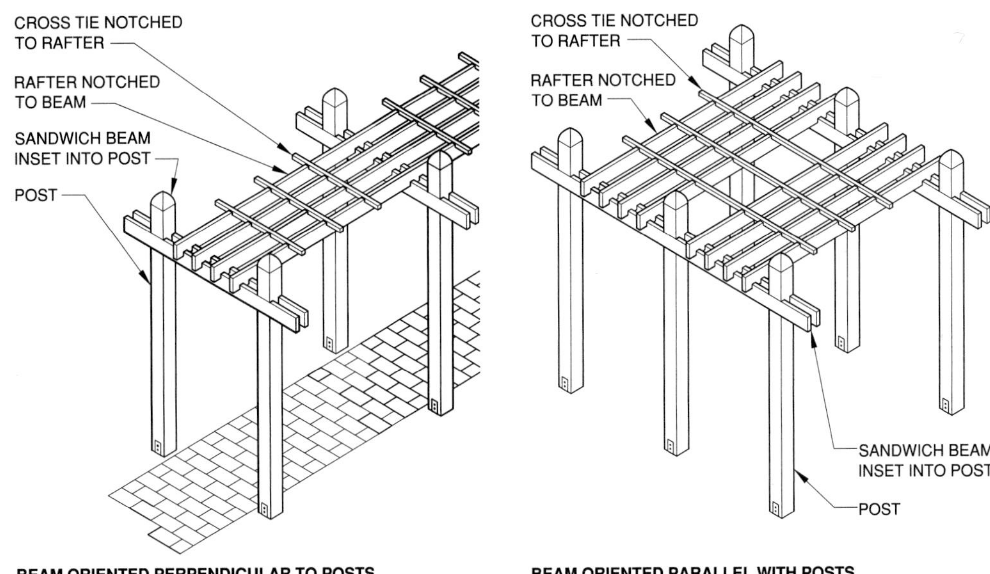

BEAM ORIENTED PERPENDICULAR TO POSTS

BEAM ORIENTED PARALLEL WITH POSTS

BEAM ORIENTATIONS

Henry F. Bishop, ASLA; Wendy Bloom; Michelle Robinson, LEED AP; Paul M. Rookwood, ASLA, AICP; James K. Stickley, ASLA, LEED AP; Wallace Roberts & Todd, LLC, Philadelphia, Pennsylvania, and San Francisco, California.

The selected wood should be harvested as sustainably as possible. One option is to use local trees that already have been slated for removal from the site, if the species and condition of the trees yield suitable lumber and if facilities to mill, dry, and treat the wood are located within a reasonable distance. This approach takes advantage of a potentially wasted resource, eliminates the need to cut down additional trees, and reduces transportation requirements. Another option is to reuse or salvage wood from other projects, again reducing waste and eliminating the need to cut down additional trees. A third option is to select wood from forestry operations that are managed in an environmentally responsible way. Using wood from forests that are monitored and evaluated by a third party, such as the Forest Stewardship Council, minimizes the environmental impact caused by harvesting wood. Transportation requirements also should be considered

When determining the type of wood and the details of the design, care should be given to the future maintenance of the structure; the energy requirements for manufacturing and transporting the wood; material requirements for treating, finishing, and protecting the wood; and ease of reuse, recycling, or disposal. The type of wood and design details may reduce the need for treatment. If required, however, a wide variety of pressure treatments, stains, and paint products are available on the market with different effects in terms of the final aesthetics and longevity.

Care should be used in selecting products that are nontoxic in the manufacturing process, final applied form, and disposal. Pressure treating, while creating some environmental problems in manufacturing and disposal, can extend the life of the wood and, thereby, reduce the need for replacement. Another option is to use wood-plastic composites that are made with a high percentage of recycled content, and will not rot, crack, or splinter; these materials are highly durable and rarely need to be replaced. Whatever choices are made, the environmental benefits and drawbacks need to be carefully evaluated.

The primary elements of arbors and pergolas are posts, beams, rafters, and cross-members. A number of other elements, such as brackets, braces, railings, and seating, are often employed as well. The beams are oriented either parallel or perpendicular to the post alignment. Note the inset sandwich beams, notched rafters, and cross ties in the accompanying figures.

See also:
Gazebos and Freestanding Wood Structures
Metal
Wood

Henry F. Bishop, ASLA; Wendy Bloom; Michelle Robinson, LEED AP; Paul M. Rookwood, ASLA, AICP; James K. Stickley, ASLA, LEED AP; Wallace Roberts & Todd, LLC, Philadelphia, Pennsylvania, and San Francisco, California.

WOOD DECKS

KEY ISSUES

The framing of a deck is similar to the floor structure in a house, the major difference being that the deck framing must be engineered for stability without floor sheathing, continuous foundation, walls, or a roof. A deck is typically built without solid sides or an impermeable covering, and is constantly exposed to the weathering effects of precipitation, UV exposure, and temperature changes. Prolonged exposure to moisture without good air circulation promotes the growth of molds and fungi, creating unsafe slippery surfaces and shortening the life of a wood deck. Safety becomes an issue as the deck elevations increase above finish grade. Beyond safety, aesthetic form and relationship to other existing built or natural elements, multiple levels and integration of stairs, topography, and traffic flow will all influence the design of the structure.

SYSTEMS

There are two traditional structural systems commonly employed in deck construction: platform framing and plank-and-beam framing. The difference between the two is relatively simple. The platform framing system utilizes an intermediary horizontal structural member, the joist, to transfer loads from the decking to the beam. The joists are typically spaced 16 to 24 inches apart and, because of their size, 2×6 or 2×8, allow for a greater distance between the beams below than in the plank-and-beam system. The thickness of the joist results in a thicker substructure and deeper deck profile.

Plank-and-beam framing utilizes a single horizontal structural member, a beam, to transfer the loads from the deck to the post. Eliminating the joists allows for a lower profile, but plank-and-beam decking typically spans greater distances and requires a thicker material—2×4 or 2×6 versus 5/4×6 or 1×4—than that used in the platform method.

When designing a deck, the sizing of members is calculated from the top down, in reverse of the actual building process. The spacing of the structural members is determined by the span of the members above, thus a top-down process makes sense. For the designer, the process becomes somewhat circular, as aesthetic decisions may require dimensional changes of the members and the necessary recalculations.

FOUNDATION

The structural integrity of a deck begins with the foundation, and unlike a house with a continuous perimeter concrete foundation, deck foundations are typically footings that receive concentrated loads at specific isolated points. To create a stable structure, the framing must transfer the combined live and dead loads through the joists, beams, and posts to the footing and into the ground.

If the loads are equally distributed, one can determine the footprint of the footing by dividing the total load on all the footings by the number of footings. Then divide the load on each footing by the bearing capacity of the soil.

The concrete footing must sit below the point at which soil freezes in winter, to prevent frost heave. In

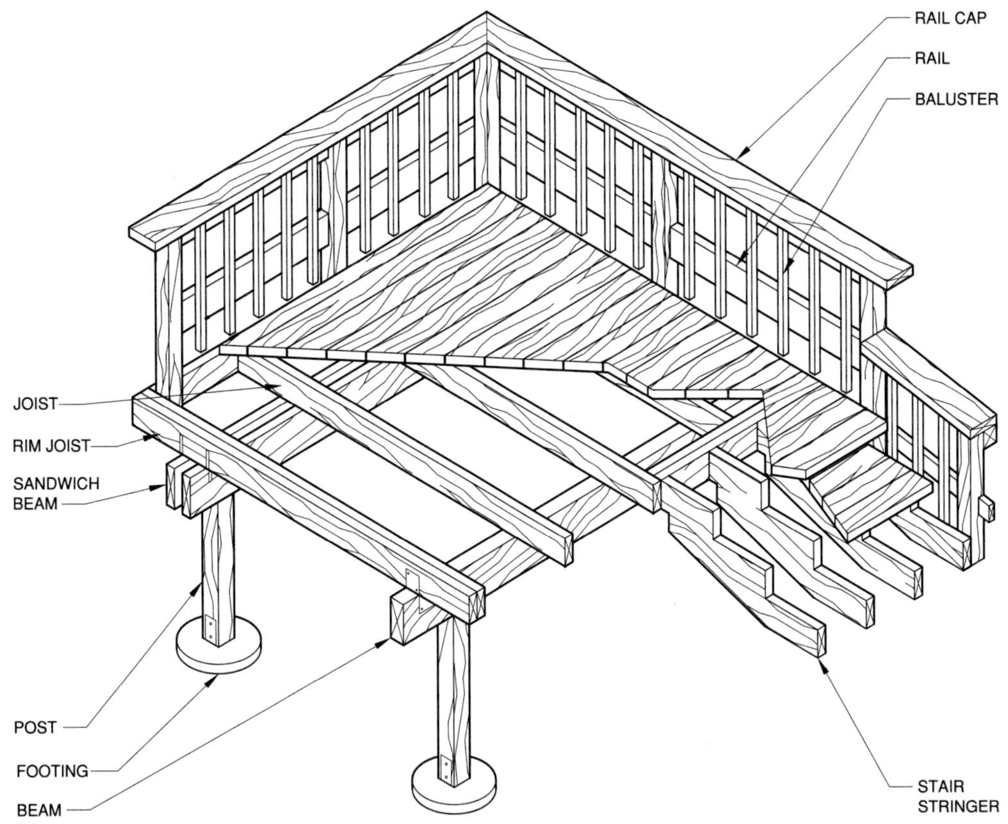

THE PLATFORM SYSTEM USES JOISTS AS INTERMEDIARY MEMBERS, GIVING A DEEPER PROFILE AND REDUCED SPANS

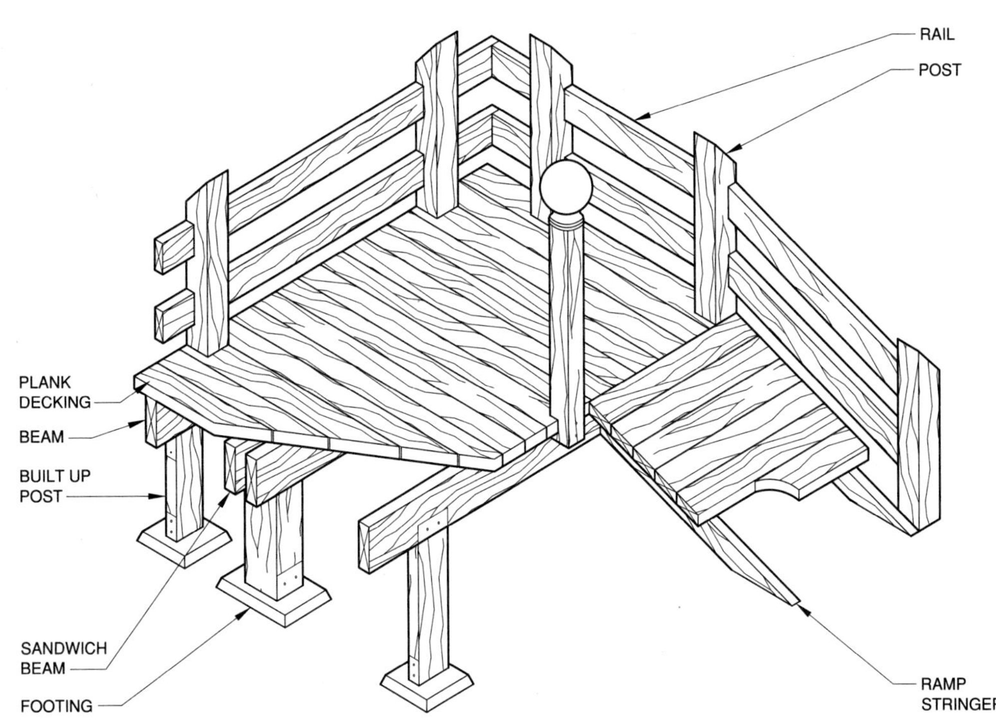

THE PLANK-AND-BEAM SYSTEM CONSISTS OF THREE MAIN COMPONENTS: POSTS, BEAMS, AND DECKING

Daniel Winterbottom, Associate Professor, University of Washington, Department of Landscape Architecture

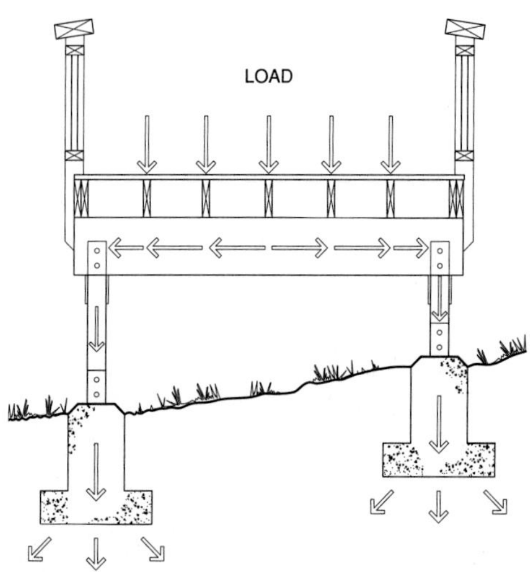

THE TRANSFER OF LOADS THROUGH THE DECKING STRUCTURE TO THE JOIST, THE BEAMS TO THE POST, AND, FINALLY, THROUGH THE FOOTING AND INTO THE SUBGRADE

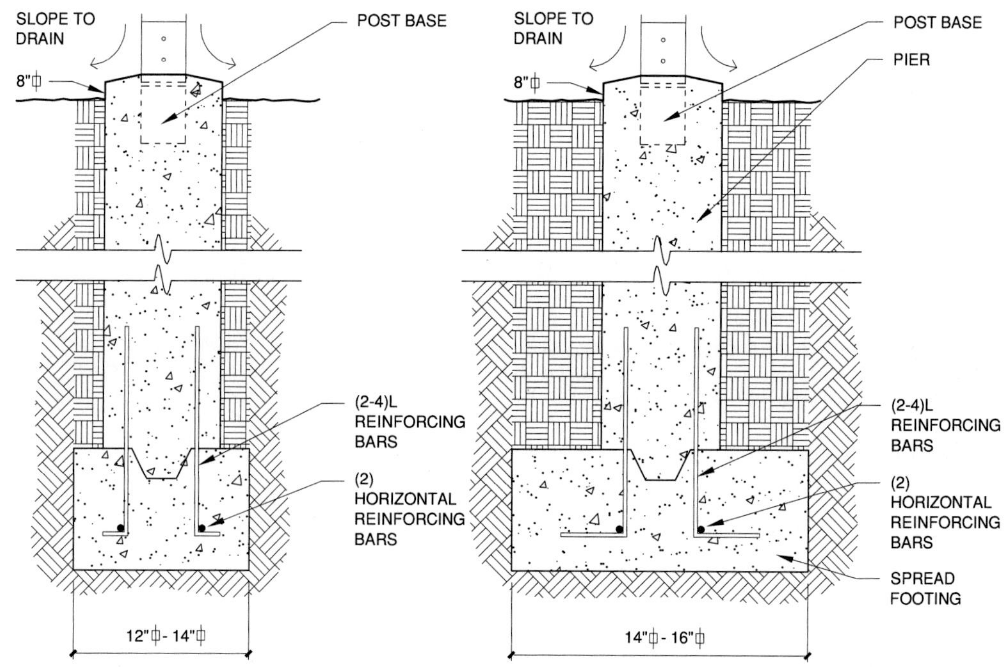

TYPICAL SQUARE FOOTING

TYPICAL ROUND FOOTING

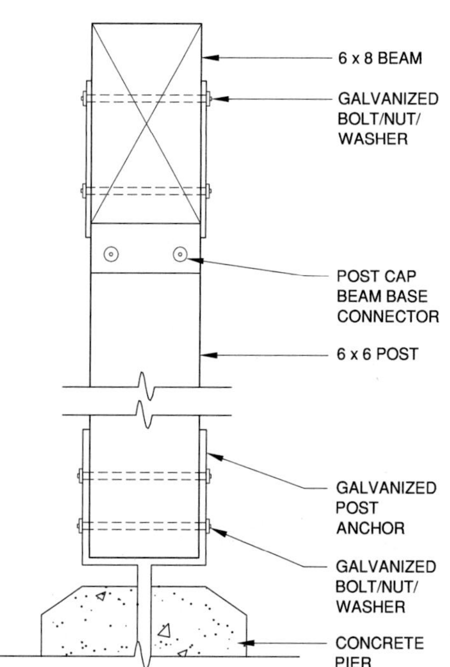

TYPICAL BEAM ON POST DETAIL

GALVANIZED BOLT/NUT/ WASHER
(2) 2 x BEAM
6 x 6 POST
GALVANIZED POST ANCHOR
GALVANIZED BOLT/NUT/ WASHER
CONCRETE PIER

TYPICAL BEAM BOLTED TO SIDE OF POST DETAIL

areas prone to frost heave or with poor drainage, additional drainage material such as drain rock can be placed below the footings. For additional strength, a grid of rebar can be embedded into the footing.

PIERS AND POSTS

Concrete piers, used in lieu of a wood post, are required by code in many parts of the country, as they are not susceptible to insect infestations, are decay-proof, and very strong. The pier is typically poured on top of a spread footing with reinforcing bars to tie the two together.

A galvanized steel post anchor can be embedded into the top of the pier to receive a post or beam. The post anchor separates the end grain of the post from the concrete surface and creates a ½-inch air gap below the post that ensures good ventilation below the end grain of the wood post. The top of the concrete pier should be pitched away from the post base, reducing any water buildup that could infiltrate the end grain.

The intermediary wood post transfers the load from the beam and joists to the pier or footing. If the finished elevation of the deck is less than 1 to 2 feet from grade, the concrete piers typically extend up above grade to receive the beam, eliminating the wood post. If a wood post is used, a 4×4 one is often adequate to transfer the loads; however, many designers specify larger 6×6 posts, and double-notch the post on either side to provide a 1½-inch seat that will receive a sandwich beam. In this method a 2½-inch tongue is left on the post that protrudes up through the beam and through which the beam and post can be bolted together.

The choice of posts should be made on appearance as well as structural integrity. A tall 4×4 post may look thin in comparison to a large deck, and increasing the size may provide a more pleasing proportional relationship.

The post need not be one solid member, especially if it is greater than 8 inches in either dimension, but can be fabricated using standard 2× dimensional lumber. A 6×8 post can be fabricated from three pieces of 2×8, glued and laminated.

BEAMS

The beams are intermediate structural members, transferring the loads from the joists or decking to the post or pier. Typical sizes are solid 4×6 or 4×8, or they can be fabricated of 2× material. Nailing the boards face to face, a common mistake, promotes premature material decay. In fabricating a built-up beam, spacers made of treated lumber or plywood are glued between the two or more pieces of 2× material, creating a void for water to pass through and to allow air circulation between the members.

The best method for supporting the beam is to rest it on top of the post, which uses the post to provide the best compressive resistance. It is important that the width of the beam be equal to or greater than the

Daniel Winterbottom, Associate Professor, University of Washington, Department of Landscape Architecture

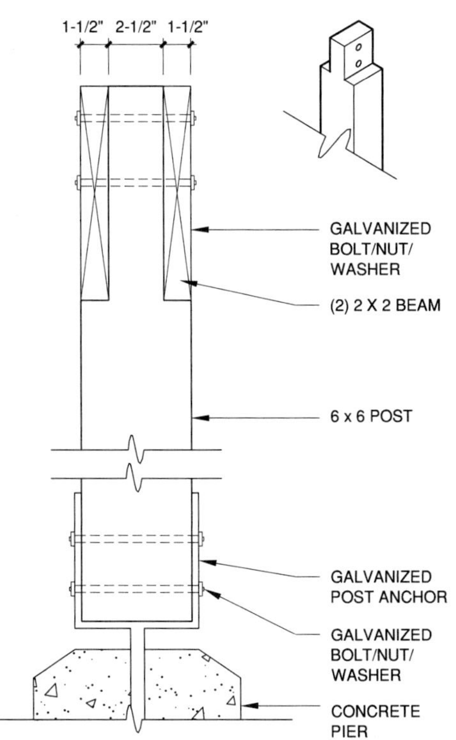

TYPICAL NOTCHED BEAM METHOD RELIEVES STRESS ON FASTENERS

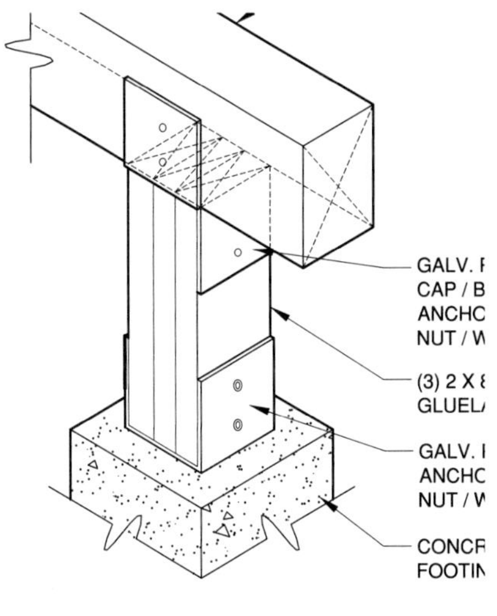

LARGE POSTS CAN BE EXPENSIVE AND ARE NOT ALWAYS READILY AVAILABLE. AN ALTERNATIVE IS THE GLUE-LAMINATED OR MECHANICALLY FASTENED "BUILT-UP" POST

post, so water doesn't flow down the face of the beam and into the end grain of the post. This method does raise the profile of the deck, and if this is aesthetically unacceptable, the beams can be bolted to the side of the column. Side bolting places much of the shear stresses on the fasteners, and the fasteners must be appropriately sized to resist the pressures. Notching the post and bolting it to the beam is an intermediate solution.

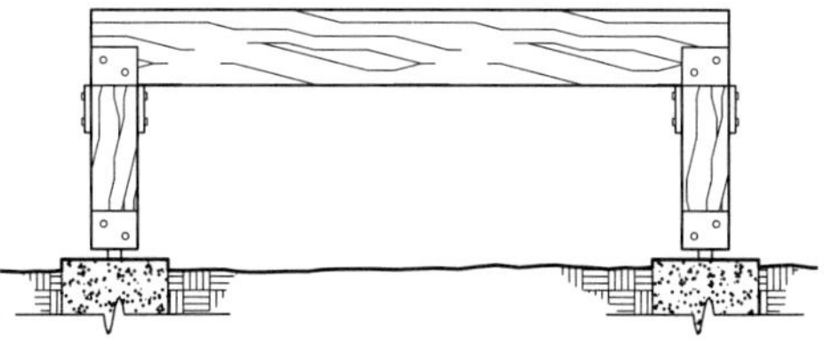

A simple beam is a single-span beam supported at each end.

SIMPLE BEAM

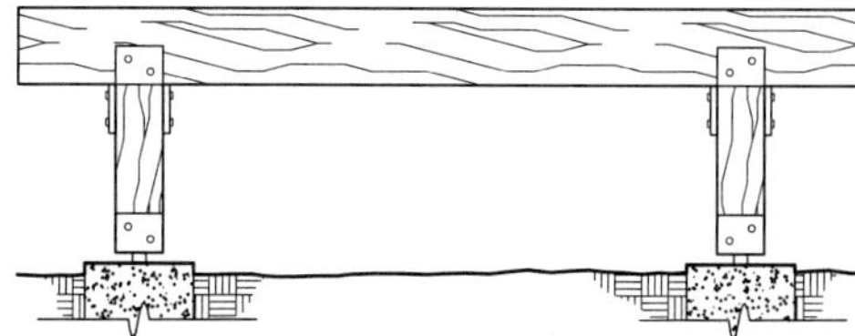

An overhanging beam extends beyond one or more supports.

OVERHANGING BEAM

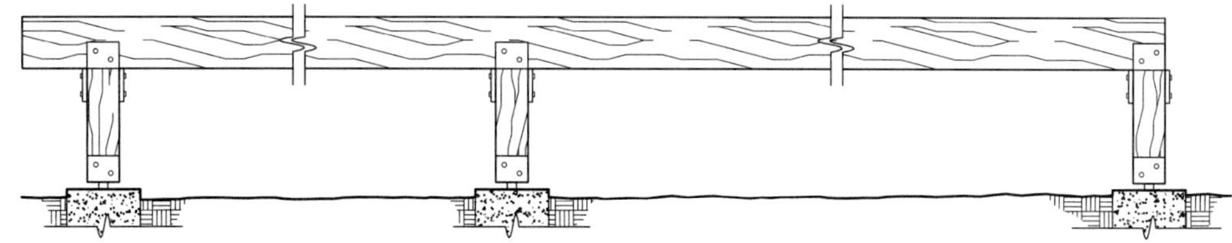

A cantilever beam is supported only on one end.

CANTILEVER BEAM

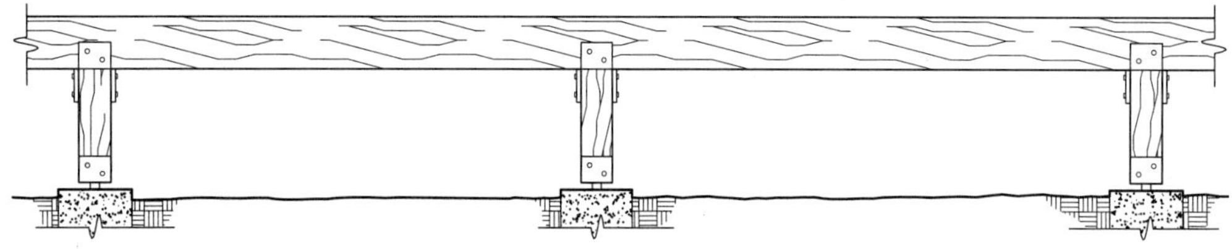

A continuous beam is supported by three or more structural members.

CONTINUOUS BEAM

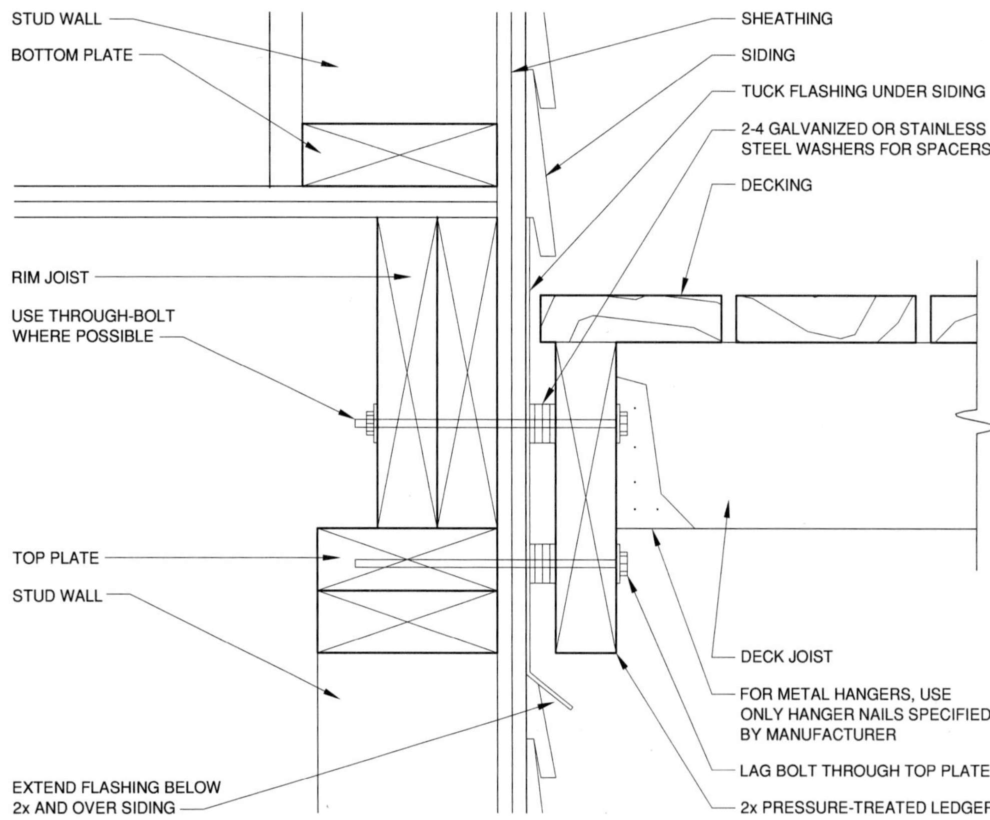

SPACERS ARE SET BETWEEN THE LEDGER AND THE FLASHING TO ALLOW AIR TO CIRCULATE AND WATER TO PASS

Daniel Winterbottom, Associate Professor, University of Washington, Department of Landscape Architecture

The form of the beam depends on where the point of contact between the posts and the beam is. The figures "Simple Beam," "Cantilever Beam," "Overhanging Beam," and "Continuous Beam" show common deck construction options

A ledger supports the same loads as a beam, but instead of resting on posts or piers, it is mechanically attached to an existing structure. A 2× or 4× member is connected to the existing rim joists with lag bolts or to the foundation wall with expansion bolts.

To eliminate a toenail connection, joist hangers should be nailed to the ledger to receive the joists. The ledger should receive a Z-flashing strip tucked under the wall siding, running 90 degrees out over the top and 90 degrees down the face of the ledger, to prevent water from penetrating the rim joist or sill.

JOISTS

The joist, used in the platform method, transfers the live and dead loads of the decking to the beams. They are positioned perpendicular to the beam and can be set either on top of the beams or hung flush with the top of the beam with joist hangers. The spacing of the joists is determined by the span capability, which is determined by the dimension of the decking. Joist spacing ranges from 16 inches on center to 24 inches on center, when supporting 5/4 or 2× decking. The first method elevates the joist, increasing the profile of the deck by the vertical dimension of the joist lying above the beam. The connectors used in this application are hurricane ties, twist straps that connect the joist to the beam to resist uplift by wind pressure. When set flush with the beam, a joist hanger is employed.

Joists can span long distances in relationship to their vertical dimension, but the twisting or curving is a potential problem. To counter this tendency, solid wood blocking, the same dimension as the joists, or metal bridging is placed between the joists at the midpoint of the spans and nailed to each member to resist lateral movement and deformation.

Another common problem to be avoided when attaching the decking to the joists is nailing close to the end grain of the decking boards. The nails should be set no less than ¾ inch from the edge. If a pattern requires the decking to change directions at particular points, or if joints line up in a running pattern, a double-joist system can be employed. Instead of using one joist, which provides only ¾ inch of bearing and forces the nail to be driven at the edge of the decking board, a double joist can be added to provide increased bearing, proper drainage, and air ventilation to the decking end grain. This prevents water being trapped by the joist below in the single-joist method.

In orienting both beams and joists, the members are designed to orient vertically to the cross section's longitudinal axis. All board lumber has a "crook," a bend that is counter to the greatest dimension. In some members, this is obvious; in others, it may be more difficult to see. When the joists are placed, it's important to orient the "crowned" side up. This allows the weight of the structure to provide a counterresistance that will straighten the crown, instead of increasing pressure on the natural curve as it would if the member were placed crown side down.

DECKING

The decking provides a usable surface on which to stand and walk and transfers loads to the joists or beams. The span is determined by the spacing of the joists below and is calculated to the size and span capabilities of the decking material. The optimal decking material choices include 5/4×6 or 2×4 or 2×6 and should be no greater than 6 inches in width due to a propensity to warp in wider boards. In some public structures, thicker material such as 2 or 3 inches is used in the plank-and-beam method. A gap of ⅛ to ¼ inch should be maintained between the decking boards to allow proper drainage, depending on their moisture content and subsequent shrinking.

Decking, rails, and seating are the most visual elements of the deck structure, hence appearance-grade materials are often selected to build them. Decking is most frequently laid in the flat with the thinnest dimension in the vertical orientation; however, as the spans increase, it is possible to set the decking in the vertical position and widen the beam or joist spacing. Decking oriented in this manner has an increased resistance to bouncing or sagging; however, the amount of decking material needed will greatly increase. Spacers of treated marine-grade plywood or solid treated material should be placed between the decking members to increase stability.

As the most exposed material, decking takes the most abuse over time and thus is often the first material to deteriorate. Frequent applications of preservative treatments will extend the life span of the decking material. When possible, butt joints in the decking should be avoided, or the double-joist system used, to prevent trapped moisture between the end grains.

Another cause of deck failure is the migration of water through the nail holes, particularly when the nails lose their withdrawal resistance and pop up. These openings leave a clear path for water to penetrate below the effective treatment penetration zone, causing the material to degrade from the inside out. The rate of withdrawal among smooth shank nails is quite high in areas of heavy foot traffic, so spiral-groove or ring-shank nails or screws are recommended for attaching decking boards in these conditions. The length of the connecting mechanism will also affect withdrawal, and the fastener should be 3 inches (10d) or greater when securing 1-inch-thick decking and 3½ inches (16d) or greater for 1½-inch boards. If edge nailing can't be avoided, all holes should be predrilled to minimize splitting at the ends of the boards.

In deck construction where the elevation is greater than 5 feet in height, bracing (diagonal cross members) should be used to resist racking and possible structural failure. For decks sited on sloping lots requiring long posts, the need for bracing is critical. Bracing can take a number of forms, including Y-type bracing, sufficient for standard post-to-beam connections, and allowing easy access below the deck. When the structure is designed with long beam spans or tall posts, X-cross bracing can be installed at alternate bays, although some decks may require bracing at every bay for structural support. If the post height exceeds 14 feet, two X-braces or K-braces, one on top of the other, might be required, and an engineer should be consulted.

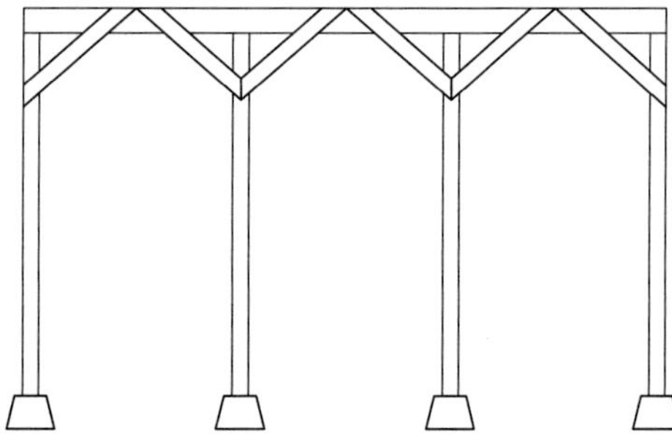

Y-BRACE

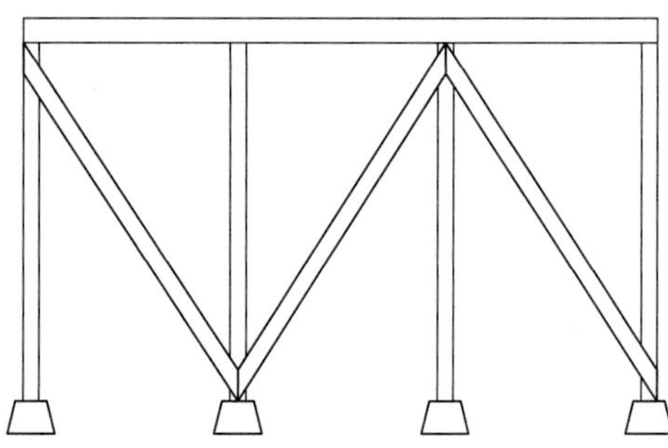

DIAGONAL BRACE

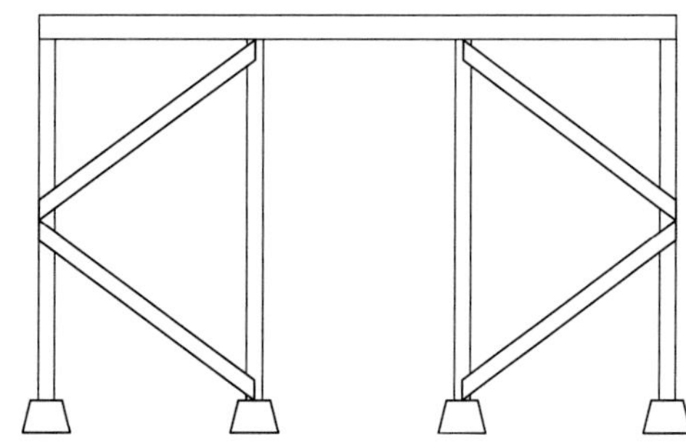

COMMOM K-BRACE

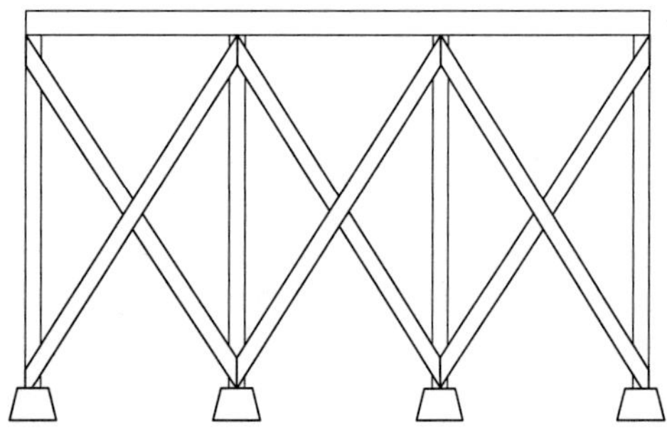

X-BRACE

BRACING IS CONFIGURED TO RESIST LATERAL SWAY.

Daniel Winterbottom, Associate Professor, University of Washington, Department of Landscape Architecture

If the length of the bracing is 8 feet or less, 2×4s are usually adequate; for longer unsupported lengths, 2×6s are recommended. All connections should be to the main framing with a minimum of ⅜-inch-diameter bolts used for fastening.

Stairs

Most decks contain at least some stairs, and in many cases the stairs are a feature, equal in visual impact to the decking. If the stairs include more than two risers (vertical steps), most codes require at least one railing at the side of the run. All risers and treads (horizontal steps) should be of a consistent dimension within any run, and preferably within the whole design. The material for the treads should not be less than 5/4 inch, and 2× stock is the most common. Thinner material, typically ¾ inch can be used for the risers, to prevent tripping and for aesthetic effect.

The tread and riser boards are supported by a stringer that is fabricated from a large board, often a treated 2×12 or 2×14 that has been cut to form a stepped pattern supporting the tread and riser boards. The number of stringers required depends on the width of the stairs; however, if fewer than three are used, sagging can occur even on a stair with a width as short as 2 feet 6 inches. Joist hangers or other metal connectors can be employed to connect the upper stringer end to the joist or blocking. The lower stringer end should rest on a concrete beam foundation or footings.

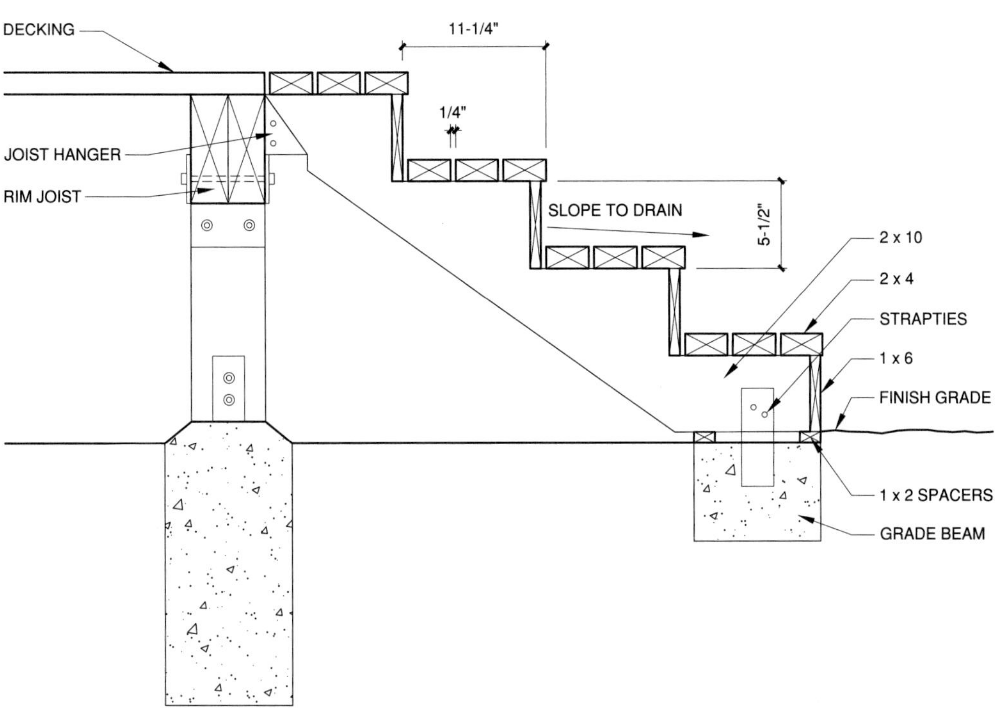

STAIR STRINGER CONNECTED TO A LEDGER WITH A JOIST HANGER AT THE UPPER END, AND TO A LOWER JOIST THAT ALSO SUPPORTS A LANDING BETWEEN STAIR RUNS

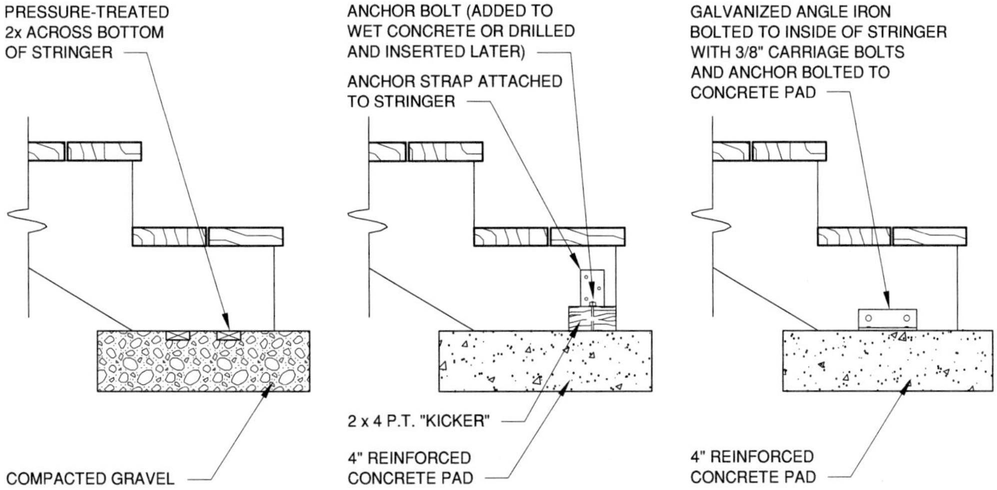

(1) This option is the least permanent and is prone to settlement. (2) This provides a good connection, and the layout of connections allows some flexibility. (3) This provides a good connection and, with a retrofit bolt, can be installed after the pad is poured, allowing the greatest flexibility.

OPTIONS FOR RESTING THE STRINGER AT GRADE

Seating

Built-in benches must be planned during the design phase because they are often incorporated into the structural framing, with the posts serving as the vertical supports from which the bench supports are cantilevered.

A reasonable amount of surface area is required to attach the bench supports, and often the posts are sized as 6×6s or as independent 2×8 members extended up from the structural framing. These structural members can be notched to support the bench slats, and ripped to 4 inches above the seating to support a backrest. The structure is banded with 2×4s with 2×6 cross members supporting the bench slats.

Railings

The design of deck railings can be very complex, ranging from those with ornate features such as turned ballustrades and finials to plain railings designed as very simple and functional elements.

Most local building codes regulate railing heights and maximum ballustrade openings and should be consulted. Generally, openings between ballustrades or pickets should be no greater than 4 inches, and a 42-inch railing height is required if the deck is greater than 30 inches (check local building codes) above finished grade. Posts are often extended up through the decking as vertical supports for the top, bottom, and mid rails since the full length of the posts is used to resist the rail load. When used to support the rails, the post spacing should not exceed 6 feet, as the rails transfer the dead loads of the ballustrades and rails to the posts. If the posts can't be extended through the decking, the rail posts can be bolted to the beams or joist framing.

A rail cap not only provides a horizontal surface to lean upon or to place things on, but also prevents water from penetrating the end grain of the posts. The rail cap should be angled to shed water away from the decking. The cap also provides an opportunity to install fiber-optic strips or other forms of lighting into a routed channel on the underside of the cap or behind a horizontal member below the cap.

SPANS

Decking Spans

Recommended lumber dimensions for decking include 5/4×6 radius-edged boards, 2×4 and 2×6. Looking at a single decking member, the span of the board is the distance from joist to joist or from bearing point to bearing point. Deck span tables are consulted. Once decking material span and its equivalent joist spacing are selected, the joist size and span can be determined.

Daniel Winterbottom, Associate Professor, University of Washington, Department of Landscape Architecture

DECK FASCIA BOARD
2" x 10" OR 2" x 12" STRINGER
GALVANIZED OR CORROSION-RESISTANT METAL BRACKETS
FINISHED GRADE
WOOD TREADS
CONCRETE PAD

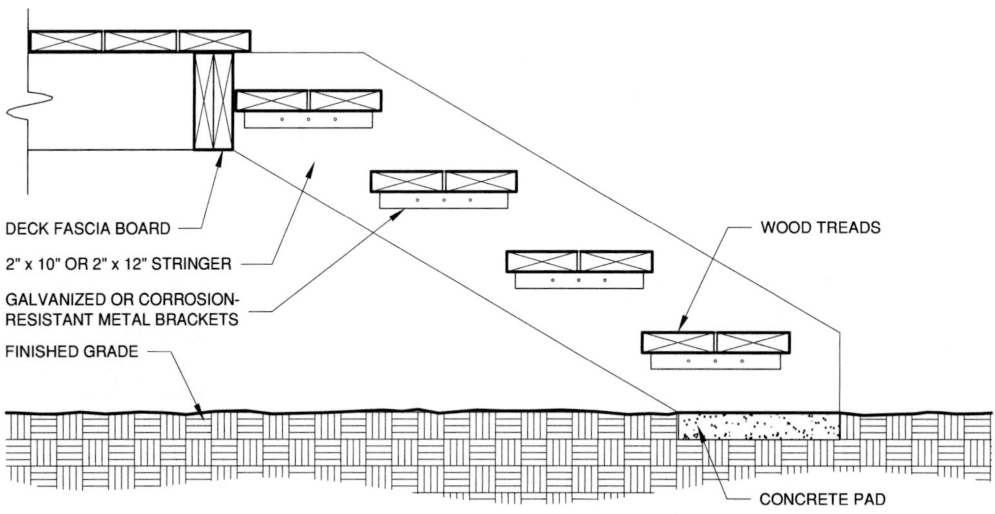

WOOD DECK STAIRS WITH METAL BRACKETS

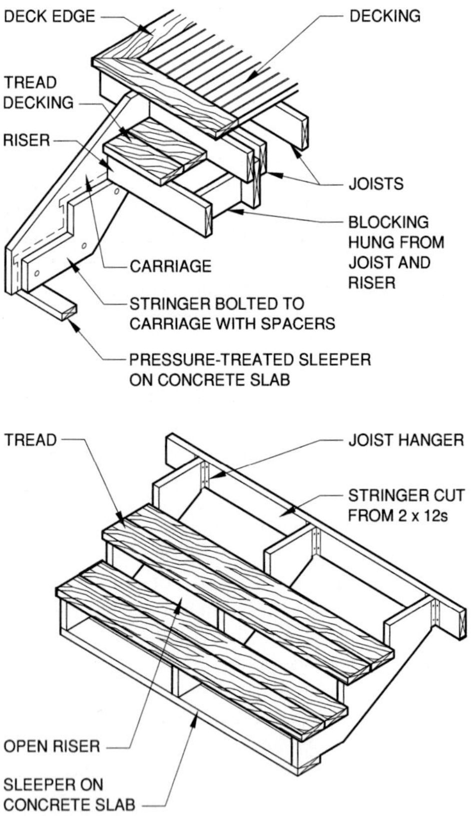

DECK EDGE
DECKING
TREAD DECKING
RISER
JOISTS
BLOCKING HUNG FROM JOIST AND RISER
CARRIAGE
STRINGER BOLTED TO CARRIAGE WITH SPACERS
PRESSURE-TREATED SLEEPER ON CONCRETE SLAB
TREAD
JOIST HANGER
STRINGER CUT FROM 2 x 12s
OPEN RISER
SLEEPER ON CONCRETE SLAB

WOOD DECK STAIRS STRINGER OPTIONS

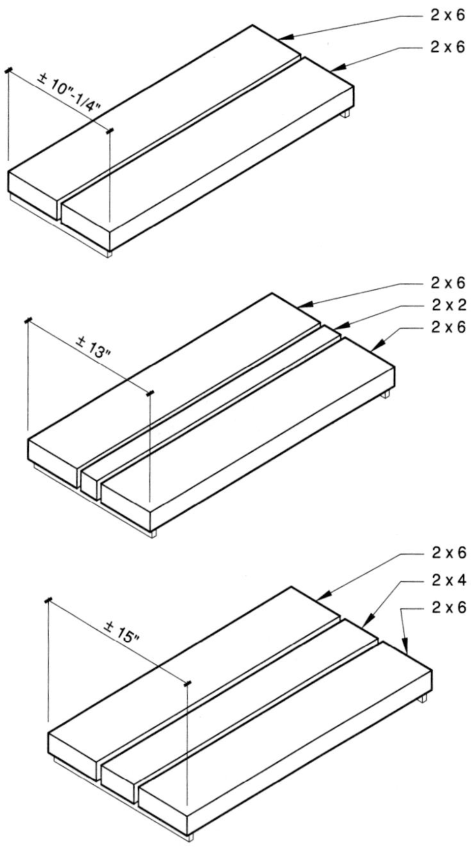

2 x 6
2 x 6
± 10"-1/4"
2 x 6
2 x 2
2 x 6
± 13"
2 x 6
2 x 4
2 x 6
± 15"

DECK STAIR TREADS

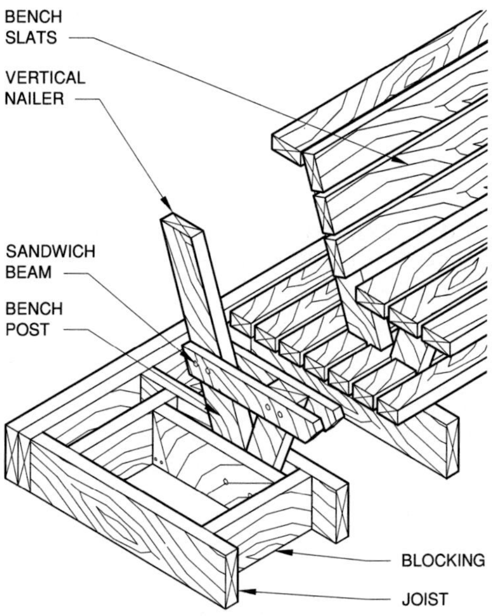

BENCH SLATS
VERTICAL NAILER
SANDWICH BEAM
BENCH POST
BLOCKING
JOIST

VERTICAL MEMBERS CONNECTED TO THE JOIST BELOW THE DECKING SUPPORT HORIZONTAL RAILS FOR THE SEAT SLATS. BY EXTENDING THE ANGLED REAR VERTICAL MEMBER, A BACKREST IS CREATED

Daniel Winterbottom, Associate Professor, University of Washington, Department of Landscape Architecture

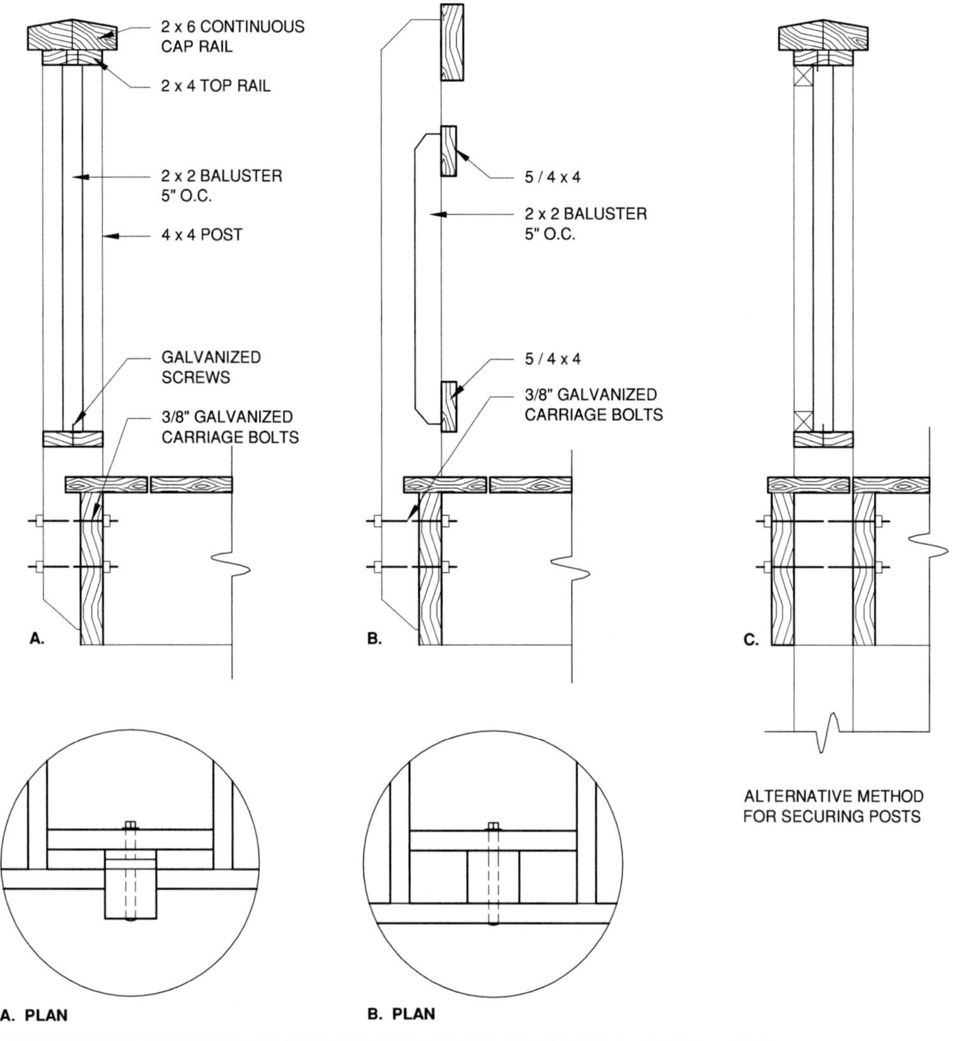

THERE ARE A NUMBER OF OPTIONS FOR CONNECTING THE RAIL TO THE DECK. IN SYSTEM C, THE RAILS CAN BE ATTACHED TO POSTS EXTENDING UP THROUGH THE DECKING OR TO POST EXTENSIONS ATTACHED TO THE BEAM OR RIM JOISTS

Joist Spans

The span of a joist, the distance between the two bearing points of the beams, is also the beam spacing. Standard joist sizes range from 2×6s to 2×10s. The standard joist spacings are 16 inches, 24 inches, and 32 inches, and should be matched as closely as possible to the chosen decking spans. Once the joist size, spacing, and species have been selected, the joist span and equivalent beam spacing will be indicated.

Beam Spans

With the beam spacing in hand, size and span of a beam can be chosen. The span of the beam will be its length between the two bearing points of the posts. Standard beam sizes range from 4×6 to 6×12. Built-up beams may require further calculations since they vary in deflection and in their capability to resist forces. If the design calls for closely spaced beams, two members laid parallel without internal blocking, the members act independently and should be calculated using the dimensions of the single member. For example, two 2×10 beams sandwiched to posts have the span capacity of a single 2×10. A built-up beam will always have less strength and resistance than a solid member of a similar size.

POST SIZES

The final wood calculation for the structure uses a derivation of the load and a chosen height to determine the size in cross section of the post. The load, known as the tributary load, is a figure for square area calculated by multiplying the beam spacing by the post spacing. The post height is measured from the footing attachment to the post beam connection. The tributary load area and the chosen post height can be located on the table "Maximum Post Heights: 40 lb/ft Design Load," to give the size of post required in cross-sectional dimension. The choice of posts should be made on appearance as well as structural integrity. A tall 4×4 post may look thin in comparison to a large deck, and increasing the size may provide a more pleasing proportional relationship.

RECOMMENDED DECKING LIVE LOADS

MATERIAL	LOAD (LB/FT)
Residential decks, light traffic	40
Public decks, heavy traffic	80–100
Pedestrian bridges	100
Vehicular bridges, light traffic	200–300

MAXIMUM SPANS FOR DECKING

SPECIES GROUP	DECKING MATERIAL	RECOMMENDED SPAN (IN.)
Douglas—fir	Red (5/4 radius-edge decking)	16"
Southern pine		
Hem—fir		
Southern pine—fir	2×4	24"
Ponderosa pine		
Redwood		
Western cedar	2×6	24"

MAXIMUM SPAN FOR JOISTS

SPECIES GROUP	DECKING MATERIAL	RECOMMENDED SPAN 12"	16"	24"
Douglas—fir	2×6	10'–4"	9'–7"	7'–10"
Southern pine	2×8	13'–8"	12'–7"	10'–4"
	2×10	17'–5"	15'–11"	12'–11"
	2×12	20'–0"	17'–10"	14'–7"
Hem—fir	2×6	9'–2"	8'–5"	7'–1"
Southern pine—fir	2×8	12'–1"	11'–1"	9'–4"
	2×10	15'–4"	14'–3"	11'–8"
	2×12	18'–8"	17'–10"	13'–6"
Ponderosa pine	2×6	8'–10"	7'–11"	6'–7"
Redwood	2×8	11'–8"	10'–4"	8'–5"
Western cedar	2×10	14'–10"	13'–2"	10'–7"
	2×12	17'–9"	17'–10"	12'–7"

Daniel Winterbottom, Associate Professor, University of Washington, Department of Landscape Architecture

MAXIMUM SPANS FOR BEAMS: 40LB/FT DESIGN LOAD

SPECIES GROUP	BEAM MATERIAL	BEAM SPACING								
		4′	5′	6′	7′	8′	9′	10′	11′	12′
Douglas—fir	4x6	7'	7'	6'						
Southern pine	4x8	10'	9'	8'	7'	7'	6'	6'	6'	
	4x10	12'	11'	10'	9'	8'	8'	7'	7'	7'
	4x12	14'	13'	11'	11'	10'	9'	9'	8'	8'
	6x10	15'	13'	12'	12'	11'	10'	9'	9'	8'
	6x12	16'	16'	15'	13'	12'	12'	11'	10'	10'
Hem—fir,	4x6	7'	6'							
Southern pine—fir	4x8	8'	7'	6'	6'					
	4x10	11'	10'	9'	8'	7'	7'	6'	6'	
	4x12	13'	12'	10'	10'	9'	9'	8'	8'	7'
	6x10	12'	12'	11'	10'	10'	9'	9'	8'	8'
	6x12	15'	13'	12'	12'	11'	11'	10'	9'	9'
Ponderosa—pine	4x6	6'								
Redwood	4x8	8'	7'	6'	6'					
Western cedar	4x10	10'	9'	8'	8'	7'	7'	6'	6'	6'
	4x12	12'	11'	10'	9'	9'	8'	8'	7'	7'
	6x10	12'	12'	11'	10'	9'	9'	8'	8'	8'
	6x12	15'	13'	12'	11'	11'	10'	9'	8'	8'

MAXIMUM POST HEIGHTS: 40LB/FT DESIGN LOAD

SPECIES GROUP	POST MATERIAL	POST LOAD AREA = BEAM SPACING X POST SPACING (FT)								
		36	48	60	72	84	96	108	120	132
Douglas—fir	4x4	12'	12'	11'	10'	9'	8'	8'	7'	7'
Southern pine	4x6	14'	14'	13'	12'	11'	10'	10'	9'	9'
	6x6 (#1)	17'	17'	17'	17'	17'	17'	16'	16'	16'
	6x6 (#2)	17'	17'	17'	17'	17'	16'	14'	14'	12'
Hem—fir	4x4	12'	12'	10'	10'	9'	9'	8'	8'	7'
Southern pine—fir	4x6	14'	14'	12'	12'	11'	11'	10'	9'	9'
	6x6 (#1)	17'	17'	17'	17'	16'	14'	14'	12'	12'
	6x6 (#2)	17'	17'	17'	16'	15'	13'	12'	11'	11'
Ponderosa pine	4x4	12'	10'	9'	8'	8'	7'	7'	6'	5'
Redwood	4x6	14'	13'	12'	11'	10'	9'	8'	8'	7'
Western cedar	6x6 (#1)	17'	17'	16'	14'	14'	12'	12'	12'	12'
	6x6 (#2)	17'	16'	16'	13'	12'	12'	12'	7'	

Footing Sizes

The size of a concrete spread footing is calculated using the bearing pressure of the soils and the amount of tributary load each footing will be required to support. The bearing capacity (pounds per square foot, psf) of the soils is available at the local building department. If the deck is uniformly loaded, the total area of deck in square feet multiplied by the loads, typically 50 pounds psf for combined dead and live loads, divided by the number of posts, will provide the tributary loads to be carried by each post and its footing.

To determine the size of the footing, divide the load on the footing by the soil-bearing capacity. For example, to determine a footing to support a post carrying an individual load of 2000 psf with a soil-bearing capacity of 1500 psf, divide 2000 psf by 1500 psf, which equals 1.33, or 192 square inches. For a square footing, this is equal to about 13¾ inches per side, thus a 14-inch by 14-inch footing will work.

Daniel Winterbottom, Associate Professor, University of Washington, Department of Landscape Architecture

WOOD DECKING

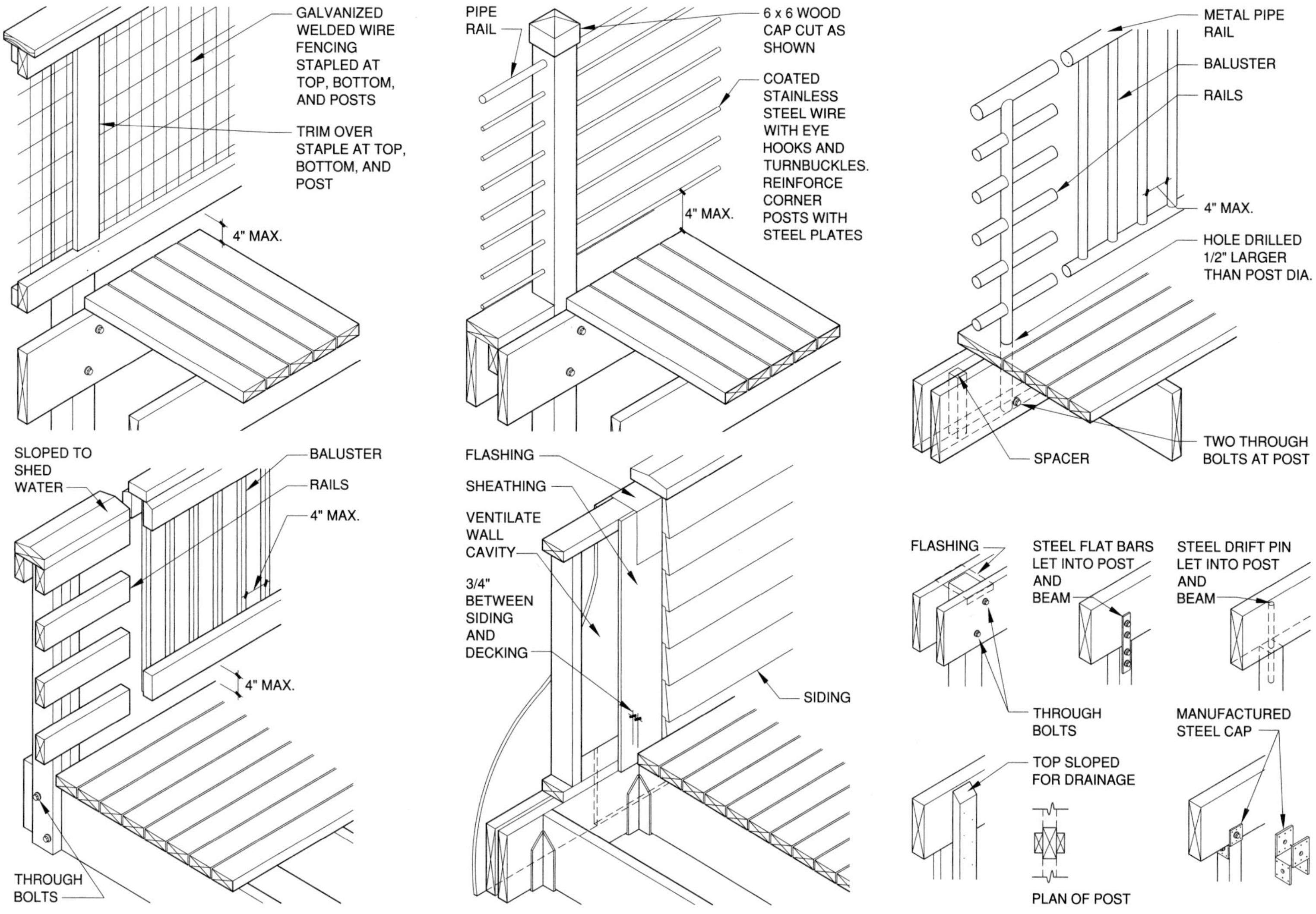

GALVANIZED WELDED WIRE FENCING STAPLED AT TOP, BOTTOM, AND POSTS
TRIM OVER STAPLE AT TOP, BOTTOM, AND POST
4" MAX.
PIPE RAIL
6 x 6 WOOD CAP CUT AS SHOWN
COATED STAINLESS STEEL WIRE WITH EYE HOOKS AND TURNBUCKLES. REINFORCE CORNER POSTS WITH STEEL PLATES
4" MAX.
METAL PIPE RAIL
BALUSTER
RAILS
4" MAX.
HOLE DRILLED 1/2" LARGER THAN POST DIA.
SPACER
TWO THROUGH BOLTS AT POST
SLOPED TO SHED WATER
BALUSTER
RAILS
4" MAX.
4" MAX.
THROUGH BOLTS
FLASHING
SHEATHING
VENTILATE WALL CAVITY
3/4" BETWEEN SIDING AND DECKING
SIDING
FLASHING
STEEL FLAT BARS LET INTO POST AND BEAM
STEEL DRIFT PIN LET INTO POST AND BEAM
THROUGH BOLTS
MANUFACTURED STEEL CAP
TOP SLOPED FOR DRAINAGE
PLAN OF POST

RAILINGS

RELATIVE COMPARISON OF VARIOUS QUALITIES OF WOOD USED IN DECK CONSTRUCTION

	DOUGLAS FIR—LARCH[4]	SOUTHERN PINE[4]	HEMLOCK-FIR[1,4]	SOFT PINE[2,4]	WESTERN RED CEDAR	REDWOOD	SPRUCE	CYPRESS
Hardness	Fair	Fair	Poor	Poor	Poor	Fair	Poor	Fair
Warp resistance	Fair	Fair	Fair	Good	Good	Good	Fair	Fair
Ease of working	Poor	Fair	Fair	Good	Good	Fair	Fair	Fair
Paint holding	Poor	Poor	Poor	Good	Good	Good	Fair	Good
Stain acceptance[3]	Fair	Fair	Fair	Fair	Good	Good	Fair	Fair
Nail holding	Good	Good	Poor	Poor	Poor	Fair	Fair	Fair
Heartwood decay resistance	Good	Fair	Poor	Poor	Good	Good	Poor	Good
Proportion of heartwood	Good	Poor	Poor	Fair	Good	Good	Poor	Good
Bending strength	Good	Good	Fair	Poor	Poor	Fair	Fair	Fair
Stiffness	Good	Good	Good	Poor	Poor	Fair	Fair	Fair
Strength as a post	Good	Good	Fair	Poor	Fair	Good	Fair	Fair
Freedom from pitch	Fair	Poor	Good	Fair	Good	Good	Good	Good

[1]Includeds West Coast and eastern hemlocks.
[2]Includes western and northeastern pines.
[3]Categories refer to semitransparent oil-base stain.
[4]Use pressure-treated material only. All materials below deck surfaces should be pressure-treated.

SLOPE TOP OF WOOD SPACER
DECKING
BLOCKING
METAL HANGER
JOIST
LEDGER BOLTED TO BUILDING WALL
SPACER: SOLID WOOD BLOCK OR EXTERIOR GRADE PLYWOOD
BUILDING WALL

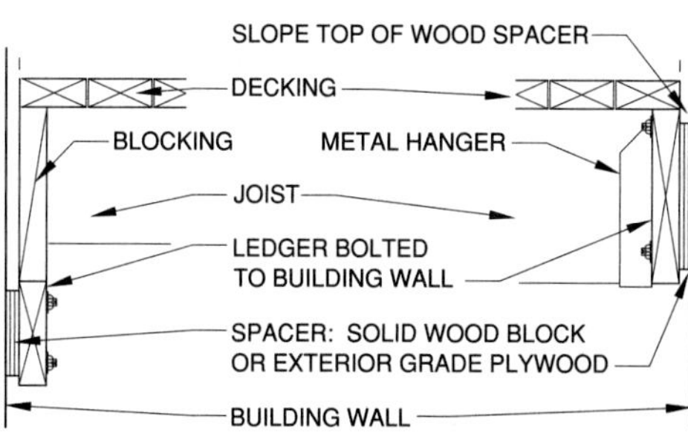

CONNECTIONS AT BUILDING WALL

PREDRILL NAILS AT ENDS
3/16" SPACER
DECK BOARDS LAID WITH "BARK" SIDE UP, IF FLAT GRAIN MATERIAL (V.G. METAL PREFERRED)
GRAIN LINES
1/4" THICK TEMPERED HARDBOARD SPACERS AT 4'-0" O.C.
DECK BOARDS LAID ON EDGE. NAIL STAGGERED AT SPACER

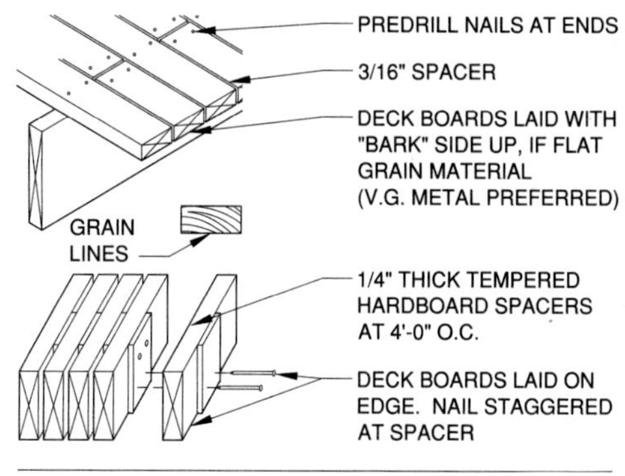

DECKING APPLICATIONS

The Bumgardner Architects, Seattle, Washington

SITE AMENITIES

LIGHTING

LUMINOUS COMPOSITION

Light has the capability to create shape, emotional response, and even a new reality in a familiar space through the use of composition. Composition consists of the organization of elements using one or more design principles. Luminous composition asks designers to answer the questions: "What do I want to show with light?" and "How should these elements appear?"

Light can shape how a space is viewed. It visually expands or limits depth and directs the eye through the space according to the relationship of brightness between one object or area and another. Light introduces emotional qualities to the space, such as romance, mystery, drama, and excitement. Light sculpts the focal object(s), emphasizing specific aspects or altering the daytime appearance. In developing a composition, think about how light imparts a quality that creates mood. Consider how light affects spatial perception.

DEFINING OBJECTIVES

Landscape lighting has three basic objectives: providing *safety, security,* and *aesthetics.* These three objectives address specific issues about night environments:

> **Safety:** *Avoid injury.* Landscape lighting should provide a clear view of any potential obstacles in the environment, such as steps, intersection of land and water, and children's toys left out on the patio.
>
> **Security:** *Avoid intrusion by trespasser.* Light can be a deterrent to an intruder, and it adds psychologically to an inhabitant's feeling of protection. Security lighting can be a separate system, one layer of the overall composition controlled separately (for use when other layers are not needed), or an integral part of the overall system.
>
> **Aesthetics:** *Allow enjoyment of the environment.* Lighting the exterior can provide a view from the interior out into the landscape, psychologically enlarge the interior space by visually fusing it with the landscape, and provide for activities such as entertaining and sports.

Consider all three objectives when starting the lighting design for a landscape project. One objective may be more important for a particular client and, therefore, dominate the design needs. However, whenever possible, have aesthetics dictate by integrating safety and security elements into a visually pleasing night scene.

LIGHTING IN CONSTRUCTION OR CONTRACT DOCUMENTS

Index of Drawings

This is a schedule listing all the drawings in the set of documents with a drawing number and descriptive title. The schedule includes an issue date so that each team member knows which drawing he or she should have and the most recent version. This information helps to keep the project organized and allows team members to converse more easily over extended distances.

Project Layout Key

On large-scale projects, produce a schematic site diagram that identifies all the project areas. Show diagrammatically how the areas have been apportioned. This *key drawing* helps team members easily determine to what part of the site a specific drawing refers.

Standard Symbols and Abbreviations

All sets of working drawings should include a symbols list that explains every notation on the drawing, including general drawing symbols such as detail designations, all abbreviations used, fixture symbols, controls symbols, and so on. Because an industry-wide standard list of symbols does not exist for landscape lighting, designers can use any symbols they want as long as they are indicated on the symbols list and are used consistently through all the drawings for the project.

The accepted standard practice (in the United States) for identifying lighting equipment is to use symbols to identify mounting and voltage. For example, all 120-volt below-grade fixtures would have one symbol, and 12-volt below-grade units would have a different symbol.

Then, each specific fixture will be assigned a fixture type, such as "SB1." In this case, the "S" refers to "site," the "B" is an alphabetical ordering, and the "1" refers to the first in a series of this type of fixture. Within a series, the difference may be mounting type, lamping, finish color or type, accessories, and so on. The fixture type and transformer designation symbols include important information the contractor needs.

Notes

Working drawings also can include a list of *general notes, numbered notes,* and/or *sheet notes.* General notes provide information about the overall project, while numbered notes provide information about a specific situation or location on the drawings. Sheet notes refer to information specific to items on that sheet.

Lighting Layout, Schedule, and Detail Sheets

Plans or working drawings consist of all the drawings necessary for the installing contractor to construct the design. The actual type and number of drawings will vary from project to project, but should include the following information:

- Fixture type and location, including any important location dimensions
- Remote transformer designations and schedules
- Control load designations and schedules
- Fixture control group designations and schedules
- Schematic wiring diagrams
- Custom or modified fixture details
- Special systems such as neon or fiber optics
- Installation details

Details Including Schedules

The type and quantity of details included in the working drawings vary from project to project. Details provide a closer look at a specific issue on the drawings or standard procedures required for the project. Details include large-scale drawings of construction or connection techniques and schematic one-line drawings that show basic wiring layouts. Organize related details onto a detail sheet.

LIGHT SOURCES

Selecting a specific light source is the most important decision made in landscape lighting, as it is the lamp that creates the visual effect. Lamps can be evaluated by several characteristics, including beamspread, candlepower, physical size and shape, color rendition, and efficacy.

Physical Characteristics

A lamp consists of three parts: the glass envelope or bulb; a filament, electrodes (for producing an arc), or an arc tube; and a base. Low-voltage incandescent lamps and neon lamps also require a transformer, and fluorescent and high-intensity discharge (HID) sources need a ballast for operation. The shapes and sizes of bulbs and lamp bases vary, as do filament shapes and HID arc tubes. Understanding the characteristics and importance of each part of a lamp helps a designer select lamps that will provide the best effect and last outdoors.

Bulb or Envelope

Lamps rated for outdoor use in open fixtures have borosilicate glass, which is heat-resistant and hard. Bulbs can be clear, frosted, coated, or colored. Clear lamps produce the greatest amount of light.

Shapes and Sizes

Lamp shapes and sizes vary, based on the desired light distribution and, for incandescent and HID sources, the lamp filament design or arc-tube design.

Base

The base connects the lamp to the fixture socket and provides a path for electricity to reach the filament or arc tube. One of the reasons that manufacturers make differing bases is to prevent a lamp from being installed in a fixture not meant to drive that lamp.

Filament, Electrodes, and Arc Tubes

A filament is the wire in an incandescent lamp that actually produces the light. When a lamp is turned on, the filament heats up, producing a glow of light. This process of burning the filament also destroys the filament over time, causing the lamp to fail.

All discharge lamps, including fluorescent and all types of HID lamps, do not have a filament. They use electrodes to produce an electric arc through gas. In fluorescent lamps, the arc occurs inside the glass tube. In all the HID sources, there will be an inner bulb called the arc tube that contains the arc.

Janet Lennox Moyer, Brunswick, New York

Types of Lamps

Two basic categories of lamps can be identified: filament and discharge types. In the filament category there is only one family of lamps: incandescent. In the discharge category there are two subcategories: the high-intensity discharge group (HID), consisting of mercury vapor, metal halide, and high- and low-pressure sodium, and the low-pressure discharge group, consisting of fluorescent, cold cathode, and neon.

Filament Lamps

Filament lamps produce light by heating a tungsten filament in a vacuum- or gas-filled envelope. A wide variety of shapes and sizes are available in the incandescent type. The advantages of incandescent lamps include the availability of a wide range of beamspreads, tight beam control due to their small optical source (which translates into higher candlepower in a controlled beamspread at a lower wattage), easy and inexpensive dimming capability, and a color that favors human skin tones and is familiar to people since most residential interior lighting to date has been from incandescent sources. The weaknesses of these lamps include their inefficiency and the amount of heat they produce.

Tungsten-Halogen Lamps

These lamps, sometimes also called *quartz lamps*, offer a more balanced white light color, higher efficiency, more compact size, longer life, and higher lumen maintenance than conventional incandescent lamps in both standard and low-voltage varieties. Tungsten-halogen lamps have a halogen gas pumped in around the tungsten filament, which picks up and redeposits evaporated tungsten back onto the filament. Called the *tungsten-halogen cycle*, this process allows the filament to operate at a higher temperature and keeps the bulb clean, increasing lamp life.

Discharge Lamps

Discharge lamps include all the HID lamps (mercury vapor, metal halide, and high- and low-pressure sodium) and the low-pressure lamps (fluorescent, cold cathode, and neon). Discharge lamps create light by sending an electric arc through a gas between two electrodes. An electrical device called a ballast provides a high-voltage pulse required to start the lamp, then limits the amount of current to the lamp to prevent the lamp from drawing a destructive amount of current.

All discharge lamps are more efficient than incandescent lamps at gross light output (lumen production). This makes them very useful for floodlighting and accent lighting on large-scale commercial projects.

High-Intensity Discharge Lamps. High-intensity discharge lamps can be divided into four lamp families: mercury vapor, metal halide, high-pressure sodium, and low-pressure sodium.

HID lamps produce light by creating a relatively small electric arc, so they are considered point sources. This means that their light output is more easily controlled than that of a linear source such as fluorescent. Each of these lamps types requires a reflector or refractor to control its candlepower distribution.

HID lamps all require an initial warm-up period when turned on, and if power is lost, they require a cooling period before restriking their arc. This delay in operation must be considered when selecting lamps for outdoor use, especially when they will be used for security lighting of walkways, stairs, parking lots, or sports facilities.

Mercury vapor. Mercury vapor lamps produce light by passing an electric arc through mercury vapor. This type of lamp produces light predominantly in the blue and green regions of the electromagnetic spectrum and in the ultraviolet region. The mercury vapor lamp has a long life but is not particularly efficient and it will lose up to two-thirds of its light output as it ages. Mercury's main strengths are its long life, typically 24,000 hours, and the blue color it produces.

Metal halide. This type of HID source produces light by passing an electric current through mercury gas and scant quantities of specific combinations of metal halides. The halides widen the emitted color spectrum of these lamps. The metal halide lamps offer the most balanced white light color of all the HID sources. Metal halide lamps are used for uplighting trees, lighting buildings, and providing task lighting at sports stadiums.

High-pressure sodium. This lamp type produces light by passing an electric arc through sodium vapor. The lamp manufacturer increases the gas pressure inside the arc tube to a level higher than for low-pressure sodium lamps (which produces a monochromatic yellow color). Increasing the gas pressure broadens the color spectrum to include the entire visible portion of the electromagnetic spectrum. However, since this lamp produces most of its light in the yellow range of the spectrum, its color appears as a golden yellow.

Color-improved lamps are available that approach a balanced white color. As with any color improvement, efficiency and life are typically reduced. High-pressure sodium lamps offer long life and are the most efficient source other than low-pressure sodium. When this type of lamp reaches the end of its life, the ballast continues to start the lamp, but it cannot maintain the arc without excessive voltage. The lamp will then extinguish, cool down, restrike, and come almost up to full light output. At this point, a protective circuit will extinguish the lamp again. This phenomenon is called cycling. Prolonged on/off cycling can damage the ballast. It is important to replace the lamp at the first sign of cycling to avoid ballast damage.

High-pressure sodium lamps are typically used only for lighting parking lots and freeways, due to their color limitations. The color they produce makes plants look dull and lifeless and creates an eerie atmosphere.

Low-pressure sodium. This sort of lamp is not technically grouped with the other discharge lamps, but is put in a category by itself. It is a monochromatic light source, producing only yellow light. While it is the most efficient light source available today, its inability to render any colors well should discourage designers from using it.

Fluorescent Lamps. A fluorescent lamp consists of a tubular bulb with an electrode sealed into each end and a combination of mercury (at low pressure) and argon (or a mixture of gases), which help in starting the lamp. As voltage is applied, an arc of primarily ultraviolet radiation occurs between the electrodes. The lamp walls are coated with fluorescent powders that are excited by the ultraviolet radiation to produce colors within the visible spectrum. By varying the phosphors, many colors of fluorescent lamps can be produced. The choice of colors in the compact lamps (the ones most used in landscape lighting) are limited.

The advantages of fluorescent lamps include their ability to produce an even wash of light and the small size of the compact types. The high efficacy of fluorescent lamps means that these compact lamps can be used instead of incandescent lamps, producing plenty of light while saving energy. Weaknesses of fluorescent lamps include the length or large size of most types, the lack of lamp interchangeability, the fact that they produce too much light for outdoor use in the larger-sized lamps, the inability to easily control or direct their output, and the fact that dimming is expensive and limited in range.

Color of Light Produced

Designers need to consider the color a lamp produces, because the apparent color of everything in the landscape will be determined by the color of light striking it. If the color of the object is not in the spectrum of the light source, the appearance of the object will be changed. For example, when low-pressure sodium light strikes a red car, the car will appear to be brown. However, an object's color can also be enhanced by the color of light striking it. The improved color of tungsten-halogen over standard incandescent lamps accentuates the appearance of flowers and most trees.

Designers can use the color-producing characteristics of lamps to influence how people feel about a space. For example, the blue color of mercury vapor shining through trees mimics the color of moonlight and can simulate a moonlit night. Some plants have a lot of blue-green pigment, which can be accentuated by mercury vapor lamps at low light levels. At higher light levels, however, this color makes the plants appear too blue and unnatural. Mercury vapor needs to be kept away from areas frequented by people, because its poor color-rendering ability makes them look like ghosts. Variation in color from one light source to another can be used to expand or limit depth in a space or add a creative touch.

The color of light a lamp produces determines the color an object will appear. If a plant has red flowers, a light source with little red radiation, such as mercury vapor, will dull the color of the flowers. Lamp manufacturers produce *spectral energy distribution* charts that show the amount of energy produced at each wavelength of light over the visible range of the electromagnetic spectrum. Incandescent lamps and natural daylight produce smooth, continuous spectra, whereas HID sources produce light primarily in lines, and fluorescent lamps produce a combination of continuous and line spectra. In general, a continuous spectrum or source with many lines of radiation across the electromagnetic spectrum produces the most balanced white light. This is true because white light is a combination of all colors of light. To produce white light, a light source needs to have relatively balanced quantities of all light waves throughout the electromagnetic spectrum.

LIGHT FIXTURES

A light fixture consists of a housing, a socket, and a mounting assembly. The fixture housing will also hold any reflector assembly necessary to control the beam distribution of some incandescent and most fluorescent and HID lamps. Additionally, some fixtures will have other elements, including a lens cap or bezel and transformer or ballast compartment (see "Transformer" and "Ballast" below). The main purpose of a fixture is to hold the lamp. It protects the lamp and electrical components from the harsh outdoor environment and ensures that the lamp aims at the proper angle in the correct direction.

Selection Criteria

Four issues—aesthetics, function, mechanical features, and cost—comprise the basic criteria for selecting a fixture. Within each of these categories there are several issues to consider. Knowing all the issues ensures that the designer can make the best selection for a project.

Aesthetics

Appearance is important not only to decorative fixtures, but to functional units as well. In both cases, the fixture selected needs to visually complement the building's architectural style and the landscape style. Often, several different types of fixtures will be needed throughout a site, each serving different purposes. Selecting a family of fixtures (a series of fixtures that coordinate in their basic shape but may vary in size or detailing) helps present a cohesive appearance to the lighting equipment.

Function

In evaluating whether a fixture will function properly in a specific situation, several issues should be considered. What lamp(s) does the fixture accommodate? Will the fixture accept different wattages? How adjustable is the fixture? Can the fixture readily accept accesories?

Lamp Type and Wattage. Fixtures are designed for specific lamp types or families of lamps. The physical size and characteristics of a lamp determine the size and characteristics of the fixture.

Most outdoor fixtures need to be totally enclosed with a lens that is sealed and gasketed to the housing in order to protect the lamp from water. Most lamps are not weatherproof. Fixtures meant to use PAR36 and PAR38 incandescent lamps can be open, as the glass used for the lens can withstand the temperature shock from rain, irrigation water, and snow. However, some lamps (especially the smaller PAR20 and PAR30 sizes) are susceptible to corrosion due to water entering the lamp from air holes at the base. It is always wise to use these lamps in enclosed fixtures to ensure long-term functioning.

Most fixtures can accept a range of wattages. However, limitations apply, such as heat dissipation in the incandescent and HID lamp families. Typically, fixtures are built to accept one lamp category—incandescent, fluorescent, mercury vapor, metal halide, or high-pressure sodium.

Adjustment Capabilities. To create specific visual effects on buildings, plant material, sculptures, or other features, fixtures often need the ability to adjust the aiming of the lamp or the beamspread. Most, but not all fixtures have both horizontal and vertical movement capabilities.

Ability to Add Accessories. Another important consideration in selecting a fixture is the ability to add accessories such as shrouds, louvers, lenses, and color media.

Some fixtures easily accommodate accessories. Many manufacturers hava a group of accessories available for a specific fixture type.

Mechanical Features

Fixtures should also be evaluated on how they are constructed. This section examines issues that affect long-term wear and access into a fixture for lamping and maintenance. Projects will have varying requirements. On some public or commercial landscapes, concern about vandalism will necessitate tamperproof attachment and aiming mechanisms and impactproof lens materials. A tamperproof requirement normally means using an Allen-head screw rather than a flat-head or Phillips-head screw. On residential projects, however, the ease and simplicity of the adjustment are more important.

Attachment of Lenses. The designer should determine exactly how lenses are attached to fixture housings. Sometimes lenses are attached using an adhesive that holds the lens permanently in place. Other manufacturers may use thin metal tabs to hold the lens. These tabs can break off or loosen, allowing the lens to slip out of position. On decorative fixtures, a crooked lens is unsightly, but on functional fixtures, the waterproof seal of the lamp compartment may be compromised.

Access to Lamp, Transformer, and Ballast Compartments. The designer also needs to understand what tools are required to open the fixture and what parts will be affected. The more parts and pieces that someone must keep track of during lamp installation or fixture maintenance makes working on the fixture more difficult and successful reassembly less likely.

Examining sample fixtures and disassembling them is the best way to determine whether the fixture will be easily maintained in the field.

Waterproofing. Some controversy exists in the lighting industry regarding the entry of water into fixtures. Some manufacturers approach water entry as unavoidable and provide drainage from the lamp compartment to accommodate moisture buildup. Other manufacturers enclose the fixture and seal all the connection points to eliminate water entry. Regardless of the manufacturer's approach to moisture in the lamp compartment, all openings into the fixture need to be as water-resistant as possible.

For a fixture that is designed to allow water to enter or build up in the lamp compartment, review the way the manufacturer has provided for drainage. Are there enough holes, and are they large enough to let water out?

Waterproofing is important, as it prevents internal corrosion of the fixture housing and damage to parts such as the socket or lamp. Sockets are typically metal and susceptible to corrosion. Water accumulation can corrode the lamp base, preventing an electrical connection.

All potential openings into a fixture need to be examined to determine whether it is waterproof. How does the lens attach to the housing? Since the materials used for the lens and fixture housing are different, a sealant with high heat properties is needed. The sealant must be able to change shape and still maintain the seal as temperature varies (due primarily to lamp heat), stand up to ultraviolet radiation from the sun, and withstand changeable weather conditions over a long period of time.

How is the fixture faceplate or the bezel sealed? Look at the gasket type and material to make sure that the material can stand up over time. Make sure that the gasket will not become crushed due to the pressure of the lamp closure, which would prevent a good seal the next time the fixture is opened and reclosed.

How are the wire entrances into the lamp compartment sealed? Again, a sealant should fill the opening to prevent water entrance. Have the ballast or transformer compartments been filled with a sealant to prevent water entrance and water movement to other parts of the fixture? Are the wires themselves treated to prevent water from being drawn into the housing?

Locking Mechanisms. Accent fixtures must maintain the required aiming angle over time. A small change in the angle can destroy the effect and therefore the overall luminous composition. The fixture needs to have a secure locking mechanism, but one that can be changed if and when necessary.

Lamp Shielding. Another consideration in fixture selection is how the lamp is positioned in the fixture housing. The lamp needs to be recessed enough to shield a person's view of it without restricting the lamp's beam distribution. When the fixture will be aiming away from people's normal view, such as aiming at a dense hedge at the back of the property, lamp shielding is not an important issue. In many situations, however, people will be walking by the fixture or the fixture lens will be in their field of view. If the lamp is not shielded, its brightness will attract a person's eye and either detract from the scene or impair the person's ability to see.

Optics. In some fixtures the lamp is solely responsible for the distribution of light. This is the case with most fixtures using incandescent lamps. Other fixtures require reflectors or a reflector assembly to control the distribution of light. Most fluorescent and HID lamps, most quartz lamps, and many of the compact and subcompact incandescent lamp types require reflectors to sculpt the emitted light beam.

Reflectored fixtures vary in quality. Some reflectors simply push the light forward out of the housing, while others have multiple facets or carefully controlled shapes that direct the light in desired ways.

Environmental Considerations. The conditions that a fixture will be exposed to is an important consideration for all fixtures used on a project but some more than others. Factors such as soil type (amount of clay, silt, and sand), along with additives in the soil (including salts, chemicals, and water), temperature and temperature variation, and exposure to ultraviolet radiation, wind, rain, and snow all affect fixture selection. The fixture must be designed to fit the harshness of the environment.

Thermal Considerations. Heat buildup in a fixture is an important issue to consider. If the fixture hous-

Janet Lennox Moyer, Brunswick, New York

ing is too small, it will not dissipate enough of the heat generated by the lamp. The increased temperature surrounding the lamp can shorten lamp life, affect the ballast or transformer, and damage wires or sockets. Some materials are sensitive to heat and will not last when exposed to either high heat or heat sustained for a long time.

Manufacturers are required to perform heat tests on fixtures as a part of the testing for UL or ETL labels. The tests determine the acceptable lamps and maximum acceptable wattage for the fixture. This information is listed on the fixture manufacture's catalog sheet.

Fixture Types

There are two categories of fixtures: decorative and functional. Decorative fixtures need to conform to the style of the landscape during the day and can contribute to the luminous composition at night. Functional fixtures are used to create visual effects throughout the landscape and are typically hidden from view. Some fixtures fall into both categories.

Decorative Fixtures

Decorative fixtures include several types: lanterns, bollards, and path lights, and post-mounted, wall, and hanging fixtures. Characteristics such as shape, size, lamp type and wattage, construction materials, mounting accessories, and construction details will determine whether a fixture is appropriate for a specific project.

Lanterns. The lantern category includes many styles of traditional fixtures that recall outdoor lights of earlier times in history and of different cultures. Today, lanterns typically provide a decorative element in the garden, but they can also add soft fill light.

Bollard and Path Fixtures. Bollards provide task light for walkways and carry a visual design style through the site. Typically, bollards have a substantial size and strong construction to withstand the rough conditions experienced in commercial projects. Path fixtures will be smaller in size and more residential in appearance. All families of lamps, incandescent, fluorescent, and HID are represented in this category.

Post, Wall-Mounted, and Hanging Fixtures. The main purpose of post, wall-mounted, and hanging fixtures is visual decoration, but they can provide walkway light, identification, or general illumination. Post fixtures are often used at a drive or walkway entrance, while wall and hanging fixtures often adorn entrances to buildings. The shape of the fixture needs to coordinate or integrate with the architectural design of the project, and the wattage needs to be planned to provide the light needed while not creating glare on the lens of the fixtures or hot spots on walkway surfaces below the fixtures.

Functional Fixtures

Functional fixtures represent those that are designed to produce effects. These should be hidden from view both during the day and at night. When they cannot be hidden, the daytime appearance of functional fixtures needs to be planned to integrate with other stylistic details on the project. Their shape should be consistent with the architectural style and their finish color should be selected to ensure that they will blend in with the surroundings. At night, people's view of the lamp brightness needs to be minimized or eliminated.

Functional fixtures take many forms: ground-mounted adjustable, hanging, surface-mounted, ground-recessed, recessed step lights, underwater accent, and underwater niche fixtures.

Ground-Mounted Adjustable Fixtures. Ground-mounted adjustable fixtures are used to highlight structures, objects, or plant material in the garden. Fixtures are made for both 120-volt or low-voltage incandescent sources, as well as fluorescent or HID sources. All 120-volt fixtures must be permanently mounted on either an above- or below-grade junction box, unless the installation is temporary. The low-voltage incandescent group can be stake mounted. The size of the fixtures will vary tremendously according to the light source used.

These fixtures need to be aimed on a site to ensure that the intended effect is created. This requires easy access to the lamp compartment and a strong locking mechanism to retain the aiming of the fixture. These fixtures also require enough space between the lamp and outer lens to add accessories such as louvers and spread lenses.

Hanging Fixtures. When mounted in trees, hanging fixtures can produce a soft wash of light below them for walkway lighting or task lighting on patios, or they may create a pattern of light as they shine through tree foliage. They can create a glow or sparkle effect when the fixture has perforations in the housing. These typically use either 120-volt or low-voltage incandescent lamps.

Surface-Mounted Fixtures. Surface-mounted fixtures are used to provide general lighting, fill lighting, or accent lighting. They can be mounted to the trunk or branches of a tree, on walls or fences, and on roofs or roof overhangs.

Attaching light fixtures to a tree or building requires planning how power will be supplied to that location. The wiring should be recessed into the structure or hidden somehow. In new construction, the wiring can be placed in the building framework before the final architectural finish material is applied. On a garden structure such as a trellis, wiring can be located behind a removable cover or in an open raceway.

Ground-Recessed Fixtures. Fixtures mounted below grade can be used for highlighting specimen trees, for accenting sculptures, for washing walls or fences, and for lighting low-level signs. These fixtures are usually relatively large in order to dissipate lamp heat and to provide a waterproof chamber for the lamp, transformer or ballast, and electrical connections.

Two types of units exist in this category: *direct-burial* and *well fixtures*. The direct-burial type is entirely enclosed. It is usually wide but shallow in depth to minimize the size of the hole that needs to be dug to accommodate it. Direct-burial fixtures work in areas that have densely compacted soil or rock below a narrow layer of soil. They provide a clean look and do not interfere with maintenance when mounted in the midst of a lawn to uplight a tree. Direct-burial fixtures work equally well for mature dwarf trees surrounded by low-growing, controllable ground cover.

The other type of ground-recessed fixture, called a well light, consists of an open sleeve with a fixture mounted inside the sleeve. This has a smaller width at ground level than the direct-burial fixture but is deeper. This fixture relies on adequate water drainage to continue functioning. In soils with poor drainage, a thorough drainage system must be provided or well lights should not be used. Drainage for below-grade fixtures should include both vertical and horizontal drainage, especially in dense or compacted soils. This requires producing several horizontal channels from the main fixture hole.

Fixture location is critical with below-grade fixtures as they typically have a limited aiming capacity. Well lights can sometimes be installed at a slight angle to increase the aiming range. Some fixtures actually sit with a portion of the fixture slightly above grade or have the ability to pull an inner housing up above grade when a higher aiming angle is needed.

Underwater Accent Fixtures. Underwater accent fixtures, often called submersible fixtures, include freestanding fixtures. Some submersible fixtures are adjustable, while others are available only in one or more fixed positions.

These fixtures have to pass stringent tests for waterproofing and must have ground-fault interruption protection when installed. All freestanding fixtures facing up in a body of water are also required to have a rock guard to protect the lens from breaking and to protect people from the heat of the lamp.

Adjustable fixtures have a range of uses, including highlighting objects above the water's surface, such as fountains, waterfalls, sculptures, or plants located within the body of water. Fixed units are typically used to create a glow under an object, such as stepping-stones, in a pool. These fixtures typically use long-life incandescent A-shape lamps, and they can be ordered with a decorative cover to prevent direct glare from viewing angles above the water when the fixture is not hidden.

Underwater Niche Fixtures. Underwater niche fixtures provide a glow of light through a body of water to highlight a pool's shape, structure, or finish. Typically, these are mounted into the wall or floor of a body of water and have special requirements for relamping required by code. They consist of a housing that is permanently embedded in the wall or floor of the pool or pond and an inner fixture assembly that is removable and is meant to be set on a dry surface outside the pool for relamping.

Strip Light Fixtures

Strip light fixtures can be used as either a decorative element or a functional fixture. This category includes individual 120-volt and low-voltage incandescent lamps mounted inside waterproof tubing, attached to a reflector housing, or wired on a cable. It also includes fiber-optic cabling and light pipes.

Fiber Optics. Fiber optics consist of a light source in a housing and solid glass or plastic fibers of extremely high quality typically bound together in bundles to transmit light from one point to another. This allows the actual light source and fixture or *illuminator* to be remotely located in an easily accessible, weatherproof location. Light travels through the bundles by internal reflection to the location where light is desired. Common uses of fiber optics include spa and pool lights, mounting under pool coping to create an outline of a pool, embedding in the paving at the edge of a driveway, or using individual fibers to create a sparkle in a water feature.

Accessories

All fixtures require an accessory of one type or another. Accessories include electrical components necessary to allow a lamp to function properly, mounting devices, materials that change a lamp's beam pattern or color, and materials that shield lamp brightness from view.

Ballast

All fluorescent and HID sources require a ballast for the lamp to function properly. The ballast initially provides the voltage needed to start the lamp (ranging from 1,800 to 5,000 volts for high-pressure sodium). Once an arc is struck between a lamp's electrodes, the ballast also regulates the current so that the lamp does not destroy itself.

The National Electrical Code (NEC) requires ballasts to be easily accessible for maintenance. Ballasts also require ventilation to avoid overheating.

Transformer

This device changes the voltage from the main power source to supply a lamp with either a lower or a higher voltage. In some cases, the transformer will be located inside the fixture housing and supply the proper voltage to one lamp only. A more economical use of transformers is to use one transformer for multiple fixtures. In this case, the transformer can be mounted in an interior weatherproof space such as a garage or pool equipment building, outside above grade in a weatherproof housing, or below grade in a weatherproof housing. Some of these transformers are available with integrated time switches, on/off switches, photocells, and dimming capabilities.

Whenever a transformer can be located inside, it invariably will save money for a project, as weatherproof transformers can be as much as four times the cost of interior-type units. Interior transformers also make the initial installation and maintenance of the transformer easier. Outdoor transformers should always be placed out of view, but in an accessible location for maintenance. Mounting transformers below grade makes installation, waterproofing, and maintenance difficult. It is best to avoid below-grade installation locations if possible.

Mounting Boxes

When a fixture is attached to a building or tree, it requires a mounting box. This device serves not only as the attachment mechanism, but also as the electrical connection box. All 120-volt equipment requires a junction box, which should, if possible, be recessed into the structure to minimize the size of the overall fixture assembly. A surface-mounted box adds size to the fixture and makes a clean appearance more difficult to achieve. For low-voltage fixtures, manufacturers offer smaller mounting covers that complement the fixture's appearance.

Fixtures mounted at grade also require a mounting device. Some fixtures have an integral mounting box, but for many fixtures the manufacturer lists the fixture head separately from mounting accessories so that the designer can specify the appropriate mounting device for the location where the fixture will be used. For 120-volt equipment, this must be a junction box, either an above-grade or a below-grade model. The NEC requires that all above-grade boxes be located above finished grade and a maximum of 18 inches above the soil line (unless additional support for the box is provided. Above-grade units should be used only where a fixture will be located in shrubs taller than the box itself.

Below-grade junction boxes present a cleaner look. However, they are significantly more expensive due to the materials and construction required to withstand the severe corrosion potential to which the device will be exposed.

Mounting Stakes

Above-grade low-voltage fixtures for be mounted on a stake. Stakes vary in their shape and size as well as in the materials used to construct them.

Fixtures often need to be raised as plantings grow. This requires the flexibility to increase the height of a stake. Some manufacturers provide stems in various lengths, prethreaded with a female connection on one end and a male connection on the other end. These can be added to the initial stake as required. Other manufacturers offer stakes that are adjustable in height.

Shrouds

Some fixtures offer a shroud as an accessory. This is a shielding device that attaches to the front of the fixture housing to block lamp brightness.

Louvers

Frequently, fixtures require the addition of a louver to shield lamp brightness. The honeycomb-type louver provides either a 45° or a 60° shielding angle, depending on the depth of the material and size of the openings. Custom sizes and shapes can be made to fit almost any fixture.

Lenses

Lenses serve two purposes in landscape fixtures. First, for some decorative fixtures, they enclose the housing and provide a glow of horizontal light. The selection of lens material is critical to maintain brightness balance throughout the site. When the lamp is located directly behind the lens, rather than hidden, lamp wattage and lens material must be coordinated to minimize lamp brightness. If the designer prefers to use a clear glass that makes the lamp visible, the lamp wattage must be kept low enough to avoid having the lamp become the brightest object in the composition. Whenever possible, a translucent lens should be selected. This helps soften the effect of the lamp brightness.

The second function of lenses is to change the beam distribution of the lamp. Some manufacturers offer two standard types as an accessory option: a spread lens and a linear spread lens. A spread lens roughly doubles the lamp's beamspread and quarters its light output. The linear spread lens takes the lamp's round beamspread and changes it into a linear shape.

Color Media

In some cases, the designer may want to change the color of the light from a lamp. Two basic kinds of color filters are available: glass and polyester. Whenever heat will occur, for example with most incandescent and HID sources, glass filters must be used to provide a lasting effect.

Safety

The primary sources for safety information and requirements for outdoor lighting fixtures include electrical codes written to regulate fixture construction and installation, the labels that can be applied to fixtures verifying compliance with the safety standards required in codes, and tests done to determine compliance.

Codes

Codes vary from country to country, and within the United States from state to state and city to city. The National Electrical Code sets a standard for the United States, but not all states have adopted it. Further, it sets the minimum standard. Local jurisdictions can write more stringent standards.

Materials

Materials commonly used in the construction of outdoor lighting equipment include ferrous and nonferrous metals and plastics. Specifiers need to evaluate a fixture material's chemical, physical, and mechanical properties for a specific site (see the "Material Properties" table).

Ferrous Metals

Ferrous metals are those containing iron, a reactive metal. With a tendency to lose electrons (forming ionic compounds), they have a higher corrosion potential than nonferrous metals.

Cast Iron. This family of metals has limited use in landscape lighting equipment. While relatively inexpensive, they have low structural strength and low corrosion resistnace to the high temperatures experienced in fixtures due to lamp heat. Cast iron's primary use is for below-grade boxes. The boxes are typically cast with thick walls and galvanized to retard the progression of corrosion. This also adds weight to the box, which helps stabilize fixtures mounted onto the box. Until recently, they were the only below-grade boxes available. Now plastic boxes are available in a variety of sizes at a lower cost.

Stainless Steel and Alloys. Stainless steels have limited use in landscape lighting equipment, because the metal is expensive and difficult to work with. It consists of a family of iron-based metals with varying amounts of additives, which can help combat corrosion.

Nonferrous Metals and Alloys

Nonferrous metals and alloys are less corrosive than ferrous metals, making them more useful in outdoor lighting equipment. They include those listed below.

Aluminum and Alloys. Most outdoor lighting equipment is made from aluminum, due to its many beneficial characteristics, including low cost, ease of fabrication (including froming, die and sand casting, and extruding), high strength, high heat conductivity, and the ability to form a corrosion-resistant film on its surface.

Aluminum has a strong tendency to react with its surroundings. However, during initial exposure to a corrosive medium, aluminum forms a layer of film on the metal's surface that protects the metal from further decay. While the film produced during initial corrosion protects the metal and would allow continued functioning of lighting fixtures, the appearance of this film is not visually attractive. It has low resistance to many mineral acids or highly caustic solutions, and salts in water or soil.

Continual exposure to atmosphere, soil, and water gradually breaks down the metal. Most aluminum fixtures are finished either by a paint finish or by an

Janet Lennox Moyer, Brunswick, New York

anodized finish in order to provide a desired color and to bolster corrosion resistance.

Aluminum has high thermal conductivity, making it useful for light fixtures using lamps that produce high heat and for reducing the size of the fixtures.

Copper and Alloys. A relatively expensive material, copper is normally chosen for aesthetic appearance. It exhibits high thermal and electrical conductivity, as well as strong resistance to corrosion in soil. It is used both in natural form and alloyed with other metals to produce varying appearance or to improve such characteristics as strength.

Brass. Brass is often used for underwater fixtures and above-grade fixtures in very corrosive environments due to its structural strength and corrosion resistance.

Bronzes. Another material used for submersible fixtures, bronze is typically a copper alloy with tin as the major alloying element. Bronze and brass have similar characteristics, except that bronze has better corrosion resistance and is not as affected by stress corrosion cracking. Bronze, not typically available as sheet material, is normally cast. This means that some underwater fixtures may be made from a combination of brass and bronze. While the initial appearance of the two metals may vary, they both darken and will be similar in appearance after a short time.

Zinc. Zinc is used primarily as an additive to or coating on other metals to increase their corrosion resistance. Zinc has an extremely high resistance to atmospheric corrosion.

Glass

In lighting fixtures, glass is used primarily in lenses. It is produced from a mixture of silica, sand, and oxides (including soda, lime, magnesia, alumina, lead oxide, and boron oxide) fused together at a high temperature.

Any glass used in outdoor fixtures must be able to withstand the combination of heat and thermal shock from cold water impact. Additionlly, the glass needs to be chemically stable to avoid color shift.

Plastics

The plastic class of materials consists of two basic types: *thermoplastics* and *thermosets*. Thermoplastic types become fluid at elevated temperatures, which allows reshaping. Thermosetting types will not flow at elevated temperatures. They char or burn.

Plastics are utilized in several forms for outdoor equipment. In a solid form they are used as housings for equipment (only when not exposed to lamp heat), lenses, or gasket material.

Polyvinyl Chloride (PVC). In the lighting industry, PVC is used for fixture housings, junction boxes, and other containers. PVC is available in many forms, all nonflammable with good corrosion and UV resistance, but not all forms offer strength. Rigid PVC, a thermoplastic that is easily molded and fabricated, has significant strength and stiffness.

Acrylonitrile-Butadiene-Styrene (ABS). ABS is a form of polystyrene offering excellent toughness with good strength, stiffness, and high corrosion resistance. It can be formed, extruded, and molded. Many do not have resistance to UV, limiting their use above ground in landscape lighting.

Epoxy. Epoxy is a resin with a low shrinkage rate, useful for adhering and potting. It provides excellent adhesion to metals and other materials, along with chemical resistance and waterproofing characteristics. In lighting, it is typically used in the potting of anti-siphon chambers (filling the chamber after electrical connections have been made) and to isolate electrical wires. This prevents wicking (the movement of water along a path between the wire and wire insulation coating), which can allow water to enter the lamp cavity of a fixture's housing.

Silicone. For lighting purposes, silicones are available as pastes and greases, offering superior thermal stability. They can be used for lubrication to provide corrosion protection of sockets and threads. As adhesive gasket material, silicone has flexibility under pressure (low compression set), allowing memory of its original shape. This characteristic is critical for gasketing, as pressure needs to be applied to make a waterproof seal.

Polymethyl Methacrylate (Acrylic). Polymethyl methacrylate offers extreme clarity, good light transmission, impact resistance, and high UV resistance for lens use.

Polycarbonate (Lexan). Used for lenses, polycarbonate offers high impact strength, rigidity, stability up to 240°F (115°C), and good clarity. UV-stabilized forms hold up well in outdoor environments.

Ethylene Propylene Diene Monomer Rubber (EPDM). While thought to have good weathering properties, aging resistance, and good heat properties, in practice, EPDM does not hold up as well as other gasket materials in lighting fixtures (where high heat is a normal condition). It is good for nonheat situations such as gasketing in underwater fixtures.

Neoprene. A gasketing material rated at 150°F (65°C—UL rates some appropriate to 200°F/90°C), neoprene is susceptible to compression setting. It works well as a one-time gasket—when a fixture will never be opened again.

Finishes

Most metals used for lighting equipment require a finish to provide corrosion resistance, weatherproofing, or finish color. The type of finish depends on the metal selected, the environment the fixture will be subjected to, and the appearance required. The type of finish used on the same metal may vary with a fixture's use. For example, most above-grade aluminum fixtures are currently being finished with a powder coat paint, but below-grade aluminum parts can be better protected from corrosion using an anodizing undercoat and baked enamel topcoat.

Today, two major finish processes are used: anodizing and powder coat painting. The two

MATERIAL PROPERTIES

	CHEMICAL	PHYSICAL	MECHANICAL	DIMENSIONAL
Metals	Composition Characteristics Corrosion resistance	Melting point Thermal Magnetic Electrical Finish required	Strength Toughness Formability Rigidity Durability	Available shapes Available sizes Available surface texture Manufacturing tolerances
Plastics	Composition Fillers Flammability Chemical resistance	Melting point Thermal Magnetic Electrical	Strength Heat distortion Compression strength Creep resistance	Manufacturing tolerances Stability Available sizes Finish required
Ceramics	Composition Porosity Binder Corrosion resistance	Melting point Thermal Magnetic Electrical Finish required	Strength Compression strength Fracture toughness Hardness	Available shapes Available sizes Manufacturing tolerances Available surface texture

PROPERTIES OF MATERIALS TO CONSIDER

Chemical	Composition	The percentage of various elements making up the metal. Varying amounts of differing elements impact the corrosion resistance, strength, and and formability of metals. Knowing the makeup allows evaluation of the appropriateness for a specific situation.
	Microstructure	This explains the condition of the metal surface and structure (grain size, condition of heat treatment, and inclusions, among others). This information provides information on the adherance of finishes to metals.
	Crystal Structure	This provides temperature resistance and chemical stability information.
	Corrosion resistance	This indicates the nature and degree of corrosion potential.
	Thermal conductivity	This describes how well a material transmits heat. It is important when a material is expected to perform a heat transfer function (such as the body of a fixture acting as a heat sink).
Physical	Thermal expansion	This refers to the rate at which a material changes shape due to temperature change. It becomes important when dissimilar metals or metals and plastics will be fastened and then heated.
	Heat distortion temperature	This describes the temperature and rate of deformation that occur for a material. It primarily affects plastics.
	Water absorption	Some materials, primarily plastics, can absorb water, causing a severe change of shape.
	Strength	Several types of strength can be considered. "Tensile" refers to a material's resistance to being pulled apart; "stress resistance" to crushing or collapsing; "shear resistance" to cleavage.
Mechanical	Formability	This characteristic determines how easily a material can be shaped and by what methods.
	Rigidity	This describes the ability to maintain a predetermined shape.
	Toughness	This describes how well a material can endure tension or strain.
	Durability	This describes the resistance to decay or change and is determined by hardness tests.

Janet Lennox Moyer, Brunswick, New York

processes have different characteristics, strengths, and weaknesses.

Anodizing

An anodized finish deposits oxygen on the metal surface, which combines chemically with the aluminum. The process entails a series of baths for cleaning and pretreating. Any finish on aluminum needs to seal the pores of the metal to prevent corrosion. Anodizing provides a good seal by penetrating the pores and reducing their openings.

Anodizing is typically a clear finish, but color can be added with either dye or an electrochemical action caused during the processing. Both organic and inorganic dyes can be used. Organic dyes fade; inorganic dyes hold up much better. Fading and limited color selection in nonfading processes are the two drawbacks to anodizing.

Powder Coat

This paint finish consists of a powder resin heated to a temperature of between 375°F/190°C and 400°F/205°C to form a strong, durable, but somewhat porous finish. This process requires a conversion coating, applied during the pretreatment, to ensure long-term performance and corrosion protection. Three types of conversion coatings are available: chromate (identified by a yellow appearance on the unpainted metal), phosphate, and oxide. Chromate both provides corrosion protection and improves the adhesion of the final paint coat, eliminating the need for an intermediate coating. Neither the phosphate nor the oxide reacts as well with aluminum.

Verdigris or Verdi Green

Both a natural aging process and a treatment applied to brass and copper, verdigris produces a green or bluish appearance called "patina." The process depends on the formulation of the chemical compound applied to the metal surface, as well as controlled humidity and temperature, to induce the reaction.

Temporary Finish

When using copper, brass, or bronze, providing a temporary finish helps ensure that the product reaches the job site in top condition. Three types of film-forming agents can provide this temporary protection—water based, oil, and fluid. They are applied by dipping, spraying, or brushing.

CONTROLS

Controls, along with wiring, fixtures, and lamps, constitute the *hardware* of a lighting system. The controls represent an important part, as they determine how easily the lighting system will function. Controls consist of a device wired to one or more fixtures that activates or dims the lamps in the fixtures. Control needs vary based on the type of project and how the landscape will be used.

Control System Issues

Controls regulate which fixtures will turn on and off together and provide the opportunity to alter the level of light. Further, controls can regulate one group or multiple groups of light fixtures manually or automatically. Control devices are available with a variety of features, from the simplest on/off function to a complex multiple-zone, multiple-scene preset dimming system or a multiple-group timed system that turns various groups of lights on and off at differing times of day, week, or year.

The simplest control device is an on/off switch. This switch can be replaced with a *dimmer* switch, which allows the amount of light output to be varied. If a need or desire exists to separately control some of the fixtures in a landscape, *zones* or *channels* can be identified. A zone or channel is a group of fixtures wired together.

Dimming is not the only control function to consider. Three other automatic controls can be used in landscape lighting: photocells or photoelectric controls, time switches, and motion detectors. A photocell is a device that automatically turns lights on and off based on the level of surrounding light. A time switch turns fixtures on and off at specific times of day. Motion detectors turn lights on and off when movement is detected within a specific area monitored by the device. Any of these control devices can be used together.

Types of Control Devices

The devices available for controlling lighting loads include manual on/off switches, manual dimmers, preset dimming controls, photocells, time switches, and motion sensors.

Manual Switches

A manual switch turns on and off one or more groups of fixtures. It consists of the switching unit, a faceplate, and a junction box. Manual switches normally handle up to either a 15- or 20-ampere load. A prime advantage to a manual switch is low cost.

Dimming Switches

The ease, effectiveness, and cost of dimming vary from one light source type to another. In landscape lighting, the need to dim is limited and typically is necessary only for incandescent lamps. Dimming incandescent lamps is relatively easy and does not require a special device other than the dimmer. Dimming for fluorescent and HID sources requires special dimming ballasts and special dimming devices.

Incandescent Dimming. As any incandescent source is dimmed, the color of the light produced becomes warmer. One of the benefits of dimming incandescent sources is that lamp life is increased. Incandescent dimming switches are both more complicated and more expensive than on/off switches.

Several technologies have been developed for incandescent lamp dimmers. The technology most commonly used is the electronic or solid-state dimmer. A solid-state dimmer acts essentially as a switch. It dims by truning the power on and off 120 times per second. Dimming occurs due to the amount of time that the power is off. The longer the power is off, the more the lamps dim

A distinction needs to be made between dimming a 120-volt incandescent load and any low-voltage load. When dimming a lowvoltage load, additional components are required in the dimmer to avoid overheating the transformer.

Photoelectric Controls

A photoelectric control is a device that turns one fixture or a group of fixtures both on and off based on the amount of ambient light received by a photoelectric cell. Two types exist—one responds immediately, and the other has a delayed reaction. The immediate-response type is normally used for individual roadway fixtures. The delayed-response type is the one used for all other types of landscape lighting loads. The delay allows the unit to avoid responding to a passing cloud or exposure to a car headlamp.

Time Switches

Time switches are used to turn fixtures on and off automatically at predetermined times of day or night. Two technologies are available—electromechanical and digital. Both offer varying capabilities that are useful in landscape lighting.

Electromechanical units can turn fixtures on and off once a day, several times per day, or on a seven day schedule. It can also be astronomically set to respond to sunrise and sunset at a specific latitude. Some units can skip one or more days, for example, not activating lights on Saturday and Sunday.

Digital units offer more sophisticated settings and more flexibility in the time settings for on/off control. These can often control multiple circuits with separate settings for each, allow an eighth standard day, providing for several holiday configurations per year, and allow one or more of the circuits to be set up for astronomic response.

Motion Detectors

A motion detector activates fixtures automatically when movement occurs within a specific area. This device turns lights on for a specific time period when someone crosses a passive infrared beam within the viewing range of the sensor. This can ensure that family members or guests have light to approach a home, or serve as a deterrent for potential intruders.

RESIDENTIAL SPACES

Landscape lighting for residential spaces has practically unlimited possibilities. Residential properties are typically smaller than public properties and the owners often want a more highly detailed end product that they are willing to maintain. Residential landscapes often have multiple uses, ranging from quiet entertaining with immediate family using limited areas of the yard, to parties for large groups that spill out into all parts of the yard, to playing a variety of sports in one or more areas of the property. The available budget for landscape lighting can vary dramatically based on the needs of the project, the importance of the lighting to the owner, and the owner's financial means. Overall, residential design requires a higher level of attention to detail from the designer and greater involvement with the owner.

Creating an effective residential lighting composition nearly always relies on using more fixtures with less wattage.

Property Characteristics

Both the architectural scale and the style of the property influence the lighting approach. In both large- and small-scale properties, the designer must make decisions about how much of the property should be lit. It may be that only portions of the property are chosen to be illuminated rather than the entire landscape. The formality or informality of the architecture and the landscape design (including both hardscape and planting) directs the formality of the lighting. Additionally, the selection of any decorative fixtures needs to complement the architectural style of the building(s) on the site. The daytime appearance of decorative fixtures can either reinforce the landscape design theme or clash with it.

Equipment Selection

Once the design concept has been finalized, the lighting equipment needed to create the visual effects can be selected. This includes selecting lamps, fixtures to hold the lamps, and a control system. This process starts with the selection of the lamps because it is the lamps that actually produce the lighting effects. After the lamps have been determined, fixtues to hold the lamps can be selected, based on the needs of the location or the intended effect. The control system should be planned after the lamp and fixture selections have been made and the fixtures located on the lighting plan.

Light Sources

Residential lighting typically utilizes incandescent light sources. Incandescent lamps offer the advantages of a wide range of beam distributions, lower wattages appropriate to the scale of small properties, and inexpensive dimming. Standard incandescent lamps produce a color that is familiar to people.

Fixtures

One of the most important decisions that will be made in residential lighting is the choice of fixtures.

Lamp shielding is an important fixture design and construction detail to evaluate. For a lighting system to be effective, the lamp needs to be hidden from view or kept at a low enough brightness (either by selecting a low wattage or by dimming separately from other lighting equipment) to integrate it appropriately with the brightness of other parts of the design.

Attention to residential landscape lighting has become increasingly common only during the last decade, so costs are not as commonly understood as are the costs of varying qualities of furniture, different types of art, and even homes of various sizes in different parts of town or the country. Fixture costs represent approximately 40 to 60 percent of the cost of residential projects. If a designer can relate the cost of the equipment to the potential effects that can be created, owners can begin to understand the value of lighting.

Additionally, as with any type of design, there is a direct correlation between cost and aesthetics. Money wisely spent produces a better end product.

Controls

For residential properties, keeping the control system simple ensures that the owner will know how to operate the system. However, devices that have multiple on/off switches in a master panel give owners the flexibility to use only portion of a lighting system. Motion sensors are helpful in areas such as entries sidewalks, back service areas, or other special function areas surrounding the home.

Residential projects often offer the opportunity to design highly individualized lighting systems with effects that enhance the homeowners' enjoyment of *their* property, add value to the property, and showcase the designer's talents.

PUBLIC SPACES

Landscape lighting for public spaces differs in many respects from residential lighting. In public spaces, landscape lighting needs versatility, but here versatility refers to a simple fixture layout that provides lasting effects with a minimum of attention. The types of spaces in this application category include primarily parks and plazas, but resorts and special areas such a caves, caverns, and historical sites also fit. In these projects the lighting will be viewed and, in many cases, used on a nightly basis by the general public. Because these landscapes have more human traffic and frequent or consistent activities, they demand that the lighting equipment stand up to abuse as well as to corrosion.

Design Issues

This type of project often requires using fewer fixtures with more candlepower per lamp and a wider distribution to create a cohesive appearance. As with residential projects, design considerations must precede equipment selection.

Nature of Public Projects

As with residential spaces, the style and scale of the property influences the development of the lighting concepts. Typically much larger in scale, public projects require the designer to understand clearly the needs of the project from a safety and security standpoint, as well as to plan for the aesthetic effects desired.

Public projects typically cannot use as many fixtures per area or per tree as can private spaces. For example, one fixture located between two trees may be required to light the canopy of both trees. Additionally, due to the large size of public spaces, the designer must often evaluate which areas have most importance and, perhaps, light only portions of the areas throughout the project. When limited by the number of fixtures available, the designer must carefully locate light throughout the site to provide a visual flow through the space, create an aesthetic effect, and retain a feeling of safety.

It is always important to have a brightness transition from one area to another. Planning how light falls throughout a landscape can avoid creating dark areas that compromise the psychological feeling of safety. For example, when the plantings or other elements of the landscape have to remain unlit in some areas, select a path light that has a wide distribution so that it washes some of the plantings beyond the path's edge.

Safety and Security

Due to the larger numbers of people using public spaces, a greater need exists for users to perceive the space as safe. High light levels, in the range of 1 to 2 footcandles maintained, placed in a relatively even distribution throughout an area (or along the pathway system) provide the kind of lighting needed. The specific level appropriate is determined by the activities occurring, the light level of the surrounding area, and requirements set by the local government or by the property owner. Sometimes the requirement may be as high as 5 footcandles (maintained, not initial). Remember that the footcandle metric is useful for regulations and comparisons, but that the visual effects of lighting result from footlamberts or reflected light. In an area with an asphalt walk, providing enough light to meet a requirement of 1 footcandle will produce roughly 0.2 footlambert. This probably will not be a high enough level to make visitors feel comfortable. Lighting designers need to consider reflectance characteristics and guide the owner as to how much light will be appropriate.

Additionally, areas of use need to be clearly identified and the lighting approach needs to respond to issues of security. The lighting must ensure that visitors feel free from a sudden approach of strangers. While the appropriate light level partially addresses safety, providing a comprehensive treatment of an area offers the best solution. This means lighting not only the paths. If the entire landscape cannot be lit, select certain areas of planting or other elements along a path and introduce light to provide the user with some information about the surroundings. Dark corners or unlit areas provide the opportunity for the unknown and create a sense of insecurity. Remember that people judge space based on a view of vertical surfaces and boundaries. If trees and shrubs around them are dark, the plants cannot be clearly seen and the boundaries become blurred. Eliminating areas of darkness will increase the perceived and probably the actual safety of an area. Safety and security lighting includes providing adequate lighting of potential obstacles in the landscape, including stairs and the boundary between land and bodies of water.

Circulation

Public projects tend to have formal traffic patterns with wider pathways than residential spaces, to handle the heavier, more consistent traffic flow. The designer must understand all the entrance and exit locatons in a project and plan the lighting to identify these areas. When the landscape has a change in pathway material to something with a higher reflectance, the lighting may not need to be altered to identify the change. One way to announce entrances is to use decorative fixtures that have some sparkle or decorative brightness to attract attention and to serve as visual markers. Other approaches include using a higher-wattage lamp, more fixtures, larger-scale fixtures, or lit signage. The appropriate solution comes from the nature of the project, the landscape design concept for the property, and the lighting design concept for the project.

Anticipated Activities

All landscape lighting needs to respond to the activities that will take place in the space. In public spaces, this may include formal activities, such as performances, sports, dancing, dining, speeches, festivals, or any number of gatherings. The size of the crowd and required lighting level will vary by activity. The designer needs to identify the use clearly and respnd to the visual needs that accompany the tasks in each area. This may mean that the light level and distribution will vary from one area to another in the property.

Controls

Public spaces typically require automatic control systems. Usually, no one is assigned the task of waiting for darkness to fall and then turning the lights on and setting dimming levels to create moods. Parks and other areas that have multiple activities and constantly changing events benefit from having the lighting equipment connected to photocells and time switches with 365-day, multiple on/off capabilities. This eliminates the need to change settings from one season to another as activities change and the hours of sunset and sunrise change. The time switch can be preset to respond to changes in use from one time of year to another. For example, parks may stay open later during certain times of the year, requiring the lights-off setting to be later than during other times of the year, or special events or holidays may require that the lights be left on longer.

Light Sources

With large-scale public projects, much of the lighting utilizes HID light sources. Their long life and high lumen output make them natural candidates for properties that cannot expect as much maintenance attention as that of residential properties. Selection of the appropriate HID light source depends on the color of light produced by the source, as well as wattage availability and efficiency. Often, the light source needs to match the color of the source used in the surrounding street lighting or for adjacent properties. In some cases, a shift in color to attract attention is desirable (for example, when highlighting flags or signage). Select HID sources carefully. Since several of them do not produce a full spectrum of color, the resulting appearance of people, plant material, buildings, and sculptures can be enhanced or harmed.

Fixtures

Fixtures in public spaces need to be able to withstand substantial abuse as well as to stand up to the corrosive outdoor environment. A greater concern than unintentional damage is the potential for vandalism. In all public spaces, this possibility exists and the lighting equipment needs to meet the challenge. Designers must specify fixtures with strong housings (choice of material or wall thickness), secure locking mechanisms (for aiming adjustments), impact-resistant lens materials, and tamperproof screws or other accessories that prevent disassembling the fixtures. Walkway fixtures, including path lights, bollards, and post-or pole-mounted units, may need to be able to withstand impact from vehicles.

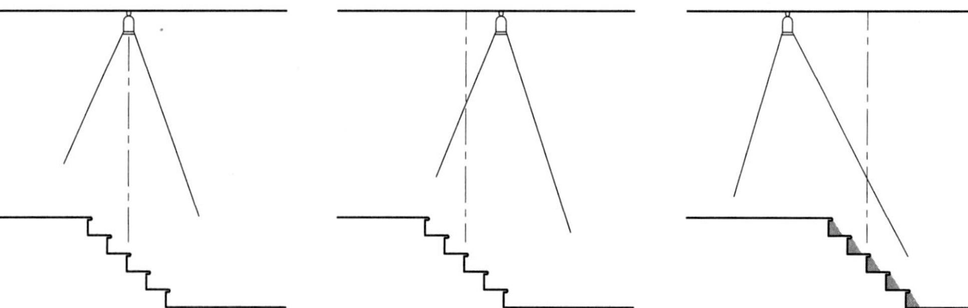

A downlight can often cover a limited set of stairs. Locate the fixture in the middle or toward the bottom of the stairs, not toward the top.

DOWNLIGHTING FOR STAIRS

Drawing by Lezlie Johannessen.

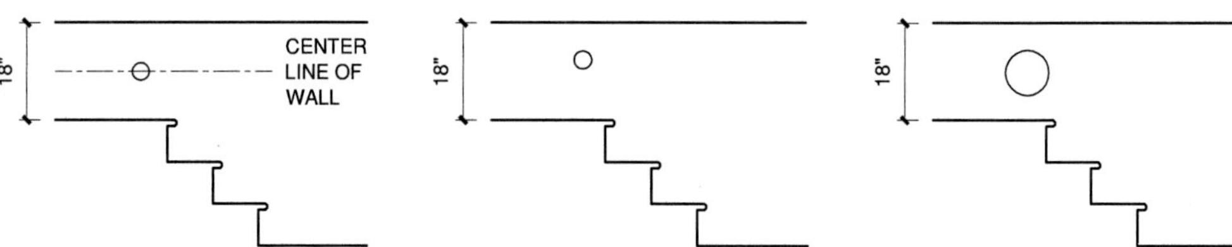

Using one steplight recessed into the side of a stair requires considering a logical location for light distribution. The fixture at the right is too large and too close to the stair tread. While the fixture at the left would work, the location of the middle fixture is preferable.

SINGLE SIDELIGHT FOR STAIRS

Drawing: Lezlie Johannessen.

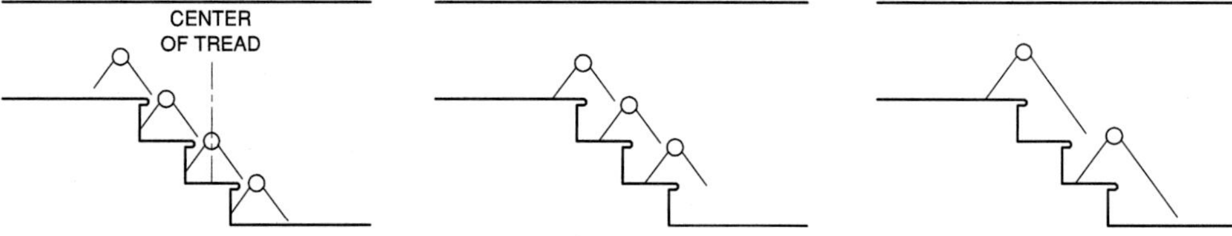

Using more than one side-recessed fixture for a flight of stairs. With limited mounting space, using one fixture per stair creates a nice rhythm. Locating them at the intersection of riser and tread works best. With enough height, a fixture can cover more than one stair.

MULTIPLE SIDELIGHTS FOR STAIRS

Drawing: Lezlie Johannessen.

WALKWAYS AND STAIRS

Walkways and stairs provide a path for movement through a landscape. For the landscape to be usable at night, these paths need to have lighting.

Walkways

Lighting walkways requires understanding the various types of traffic routes that can occur in a landscape. Lighting designers should coordinate light level, fixture type, and lighting pattern with the type of walk. Since pathways have an informal function and layout, the lighting should follow suit. Introduce lower foot-candle levels with smaller-scale fixtures.

While an even light distribution is always preferable, more informal types of walks can tolerate more variation. Sidewalks serve as main traffic routes in neighborhoods and downtown areas. They require higher, more evenly distributed light levels. The fixtures tend to be pole-mounted at a height taller than a person, with either a utilitarian or a decorative appearance based on location and budget. Promenades and esplanades need higher, more even light levels, with distinctive, often decorative fixtures meant to be a visual element in the overall landscape design.

Lighting for all types of pedestrian routes requires providing good visibility on the path surface; but the lighting on the walk should not draw attention away from more interesting visual aspects of the landscape. In terms of brightness, reserve accent levels for features such as sculptures, specimen trees, or doors (where a higher light level draws the visitor along the path toward the entry). Instead of a high light level, strive for even distribution on the path surface. Uneven distribution can hide obstacles, distort the walk surface, or confuse pedestrians, causing them to concentrate on the path rather than looking at the beauty around them. People feel comfortable walking along a dimly lit path as long as they are surrounded by or walking toward a higher light level.

Planning Issues

Some issues to consider in planning walkway lighting include:

- Footcandle level
- Safe movement
- Paving or path materials
- Light patterns
- Fixture selection

Lighting Level

The appropriate footcandle level varies based on location, amount of pedestrian and vehicular traffic, surrounding light levels, and governing laws.

Safe Movement. People feel safe or comfortable when they see the area around them, including boundaries. To provide path lighting that ensures a clear view of the area that a person is about to enter, consider not only footcandle level and even distribution on the path but brightness balance from the path to the other surrounding landscape elements. Primarily a psychological concern, brightness contrast between areas can add either to the feeling of safety or to unease. Comfortable brightness ratios vary from 3:1 to 5:1.

Paving or Path Material. Pathway lighting considerations include both the materials used and the layout of the materials. Simple paths using a material with a high reflectance and little or no pattern—poured concrete, for example—can use a low light level. More complicated paths with darker materials—brick paths using multiple pieces in a pattern, for example—require a higher level.

Light Patterns. The best path lighting possible is an even distribution of light along the walk. Evenly distributed light along a path increases comfort and often presents a better appearance. Patterns of light and dark along a path can confuse visitors or hide potential obstacles along a path.

Fixture Selection. Fixtures can be divided into two basic types: those that serve as part of the decoration of the landscape and those that provide lighting effects from hidden locations. The decision whether to have fixtures flank a path or disappear into the background stems partly from the designer's lighting style or design concept and partly from the project needs. Sometimes the lighting designer, landscape architect, or owner has strong feelings about whether fixtures should have presence as an element in the landscape or not. Visible fixtures make lighting a more conspicuous component of the landscape design, while hidden fixtures influence the appearance of the landscape without calling attention to the importance of the lighting.

City Streets and Sidewalks

City sidewalk lighting represents one part of the lighting needs for a downtown area; street lighting represents the other part needed to complete a downtown lighting scheme. The combined lighting for both sidewalks and streets can utilize one or more of three groups of fixtures: tall pole fixtures, medium-height pole fixtures, and bollards. Each fixture type serves a different function and differs based on height. In all cases, the fixtures should be spaced to produce an even flow of light on the sidewalk. Photometric data and spacing guidelines from fixture manufacturers help determine appropriate fixture spacing.

Steps and Staircases

Step or staircase lighting must provide enough light to identify the presence of the stairs and to differentiate between the risers and treads. The ease of seeing steps depends on the materials selected for the steps, as well as the physical configuration of the stairs. Dark materials require a higher light level. A change in material color from the riser to the tread increases visibility of stairs.

REFERENCES

Budinski, Kenneth G. 1989. *Engineering Materials Propertied and Selection,* 3rd edition. Englewood Cliffs, NJ: Prentice Hall.

Kaufman, John E., ed. 1987. *IES Lighting Handbook, Reference Volume.* New York: Illuminating Engineering Society of North America.

Moyer, Janet Lennox. 2005. *The Landscape Lighting Book,* 2nd edition. Hoboken, NJ: John Wiley & Sons.

Mpelkas, Christos. February 1987. "Indoor Landscaping for Healthy, Beautiful Workplaces." *Architectural Lighting,* p. 43.

Janet Lennox Moyer, Brunswick, New York

PLANTING

SOILS: URBAN OR DISTURBED

BELOWGROUND FACTORS

It is widely held that the majority of a tree's problems come from the soil where it is planted, and indeed there is a strong consensus among urban horticulturists that soil largely determines the success of a landscape planting. Soil assessment is the most critical part of the site assessment process and is the part that requires the most time. We need to understand the physical properties of the soil because they are key to allowing roots to grow and to that all-important balance between air and water in the soil. We also need to understand the depth and usable volume of the soil that is present, as well as its chemical properties. The focus for soils is, then, on volume, physical properties, and chemical properties.

Soil is the basic substrate on which all life depends, the weathered mantle of the earth. Over thousands of years, the earth's surface has experienced the action of plant and animal organisms, microorganisms, temperature changes, water, and wind; the result is the creation of soil. Soil is vital to plant establishment because it influences so many of the basic factors for plant growth: water, nutrients, oxygen, and its own temperature.

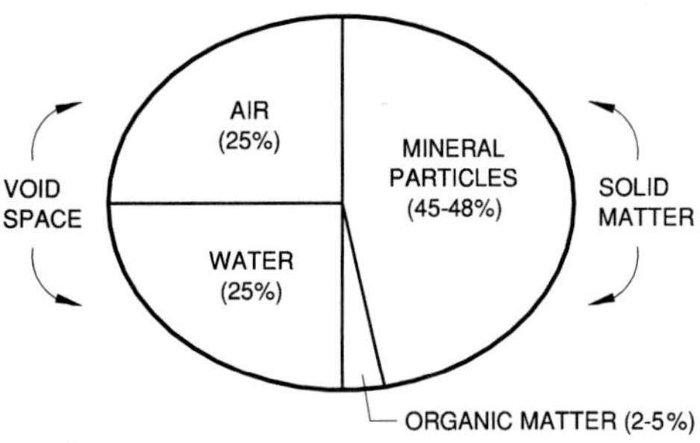

DISTRIBUTION OF VOID SPACE AND SOLID MATTER IN IDEALIZED SOIL

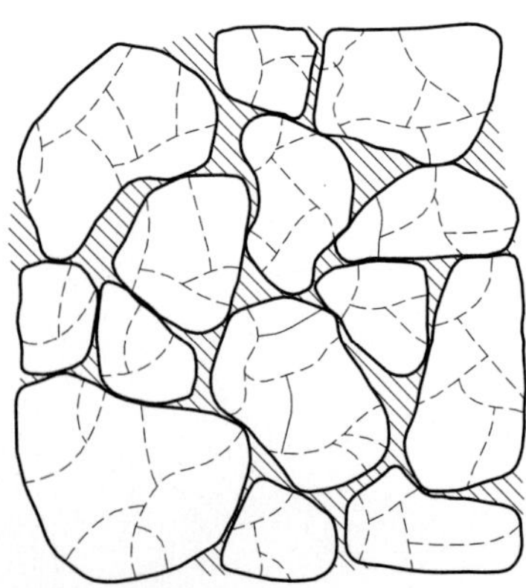

SKETCH OF MACROPORES AND MICROPORES IN SOILS

Soil is not solid. The ideal soil has about 45 percent mineral solids, 5 percent organic matter solids, and 25 percent each water and air. In undisturbed sites with no appreciable human impact, soils are arranged in layers, or horizons. A highly organic layer may be present on the surface and made up of the most recently deposited organic matter in partial states of decomposition. The next layer is the topsoil, which is defined only as the layer closest to the surface. Topsoil can have variable depths, from many meters to virtually nothing. It generally contains higher levels of soil nutrients, organic matter, and microorganisms as compared to other soil profiles.

Below the topsoil is subsoil, which has less organic matter content and is generally denser than topsoil. Below the subsoil is the parent material, which consists of recently decomposed rock from the solid rock layer below.

In most urban areas, these otherwise typical profiles are rarely seen. Urban soils have the history and evidence of human activities written in them. In the process of constructing and demolishing buildings and other built forms of the city, we mix and change the way soils were laid down over centuries. We fill in areas, flatten hills, bury debris, and forever change the soil on which we live. Phillip Craul, in his text *Urban Soil in Landscape Design* (1992), states that urban soils possess eight characteristics:

- Soils have vertical variability caused by the cutting and filling that reflects human endeavors.
- Soil structure has been changed in some areas so that the crumbly aggregation of soil particles is crushed into an undifferentiated mass.
- Soils often have an impervious crust that sheds water. Compaction compounded with the lack of vegetative cover gives rise to this condition.
- Soil pH may be changed due to contaminants and to the runoff from built surfaces.
- Compaction destroys the macropores in the soil, thus impeding air and water drainage.
- Soils often have interrupted nutrient and organic matter cycling due to the removal of decaying leaves and other vegetation.
- Urban soils often contain human junk—nicely put, *anthropic matter*. It is always less costly to bury the rubble from a building than to take it away. The history of materials, foundations, basements, and utilities remains in urban soils.
- Urban soils are often separated from the enormous mass that is the earth's soil. This occurs on rooftops and in containers and planters. These relatively small masses of soil can heat and cool much faster than the contiguous mass of earth's soil. These rapidly changing and extreme temperatures can be a challenge to plants that have adapted to much more modest changes.

Some or all of these factors can always be seen in urban soils. Use this list as a guide when developing a soils assessment in an urban area.

Why Is Soil Structure Important?

The formation of peds creates larger aggregates of combined particles. When these large conglomerates are grouped together, they create large pores called *macropores,* which are essential for water and air drainage. Interpedal pores, when connected, allow excess water to drain away in response to gravity. After water moves through these pores, air follows. Aeration and drainage are inextricably linked. Poor drainage causes poor aeration; a well-drained soil has good aeration.

Within peds are much smaller pores called *intrapedal pores* or *micropores.* These pores do much of the water holding in the soil. Soils make good substrates for holding water because of the forces of adhesion and cohesion. *Adhesion* is the force that attracts water to any solid surface. *Cohesion* is the force that attracts water to itself. The interaction of soil texture and structure largely determines how much water is held by the soil and how much drains away.

The closer a solid surface is to water, as in a micropore, the stronger are the forces of adhesion holding the water against gravity. As pores get large, adhesive forces are weakened because water is farther from the solid surface. This allows water to be drawn away by gravity. If very little water is left on the soil surface, adhesive forces are very strong and the water unavailable for root uptake.

For each soil texture, from large pores to small pores, the amount of water held against gravity increases as the particle sizes get smaller. Sands have large particles and large pores, and thus the adhesive forces are weak and water is not held tightly. In clay soils, the small pores hold water very tightly due to the closeness of the particle surface and water. These soils hold a tremendous amount of water against the force of gravity.

The amount of water a soil can hold after the excess is allowed to drain away via gravity is called *field capacity.* At field capacity, water can begin to be taken up by plant roots or evaporated from the soil surface. The osmotic forces moving water into roots proceed until water cannot be taken up against the adhesive forces exerted by the soil particle on the thin film of water on its surface. At that point, when no more water can move into the root, the soil is said to be at the *permanent milting point.* Between field capacity and the permanent wilting point is that portion of water called *plant-available water.* This amount of water differs among soil textures. Soils with good structure hold water intrapedally but allow water to drain through interpedally. This balance between aeration and water-holding capacity is ideal for plant growth. It is also what is almost uniformly lacking in urban soils that are compacted and lack structure.

Wet and Dry Soil Conditions

Soil texture and soil density are the two major factors that influence soil water retention. The smaller the pores in the soil, the greater its water-holding capac-

Nina L Bassuk; Peter J. Trowbridge

ity. Usable depth and volume of soil also has a major effect on water-holding capacity. A shallow and small volume of dense, heavy soil will be intermittently wet and dry. Because this type of soil has poor drainage, it remains wet initially after a rainfall, but as the soil dries, the small volume of soil is inadequate to meet the needs of the tree growing there. Other soils may be more uniformly wet (deep profiles of soil with a clayey texture and little compaction) or dry (deep sandy soils with little compaction).

It is essential to look at trees' capacity to handle wet and dry soil conditions. Many trees tolerate a wide latitude of wet and dry soil conditions, but others prefer only dry or wet conditions. Still others require the most difficult of all to achieve—consistently moist, well-drained soil conditions.

Soil pH

The acidity or alkalinity of soil conditions is difficult to change in a permanent landscape. With an annual agricultural crop, where soils are tilled and amended every year, it is possible to continuously affect the soil pH either by adding sulfur to lower the pH or adding lime to raise it. In a landscape, there is only one time to effectively amend the soil, and that is at installation. Subsequently, it is difficult to make a continuous and permanent change in soil pH. Therefore, it is recommended that plants be chosen that tolerate the soil pH as measured instead of trying to change it. The only instance where changing the pH permanently might be attempted is with a small, contained soil volume where existing soil could be replaced and an appropriate new soil specified. Nutrient availability to most plants is directly related to soil pH. Subsequently, choosing plants with specific pH tolerance is critical to plant health, vigor, and growth.

Salt

Some plants tolerate being sprayed by salt from the sea or drenched with road salt. Choosing such plants can be important if salt is a major factor in landscape. However, several other factors can make salt stress impacts more or less important. Soil drainage can have a profound effect on salt damage, especially from deicing salts, as previously mentioned. Deicing salts such as NaCl or CaCl are readily soluble in water. With spring snowmelt and seasonal rain, these chemicals can be leached lower in the soil profile to where they cannot affect tree roots, which are primarily within the first 3 feet of the surface. If drainage is impeded, then salts are likely to stay in the trees' root zone as the soil warms up in spring and root growth begins. Ensuring good drainage will lessen salt damage to plants. Also, avoiding applying salt when the soil temperature is above 7.5°C will redundant avoid root uptake. This generally occurs in late fall or late spring, two times of the year when warmer soil temperature will facilitate salt uptake in trees.

Soil Density

Soil densities greater than that which a root can penetrate immediately affect usable soil volume for the plant. This is an environmental stress that cannot be selected for with appropriate plant material. It is true that soil compaction also gives rise to poorly draining soil, which is a condition where appropriate plant selection has its place. However, when a soil is so dense that a root cannot penetrate it, it must be modified if *any* plant is to get the benefit of the surrounding soil.

Different textures of soils have different bulk densities at which root growth is restricted. Root growth in a sandy soil may be restricted between 1.6 and 1.7 g/ cubic centimeter, whereas root growth may be restricted at a bulk density of 1.4 in a clayey soil. It is important to know the soil texture and bulk density before making a decision about how much to change it or whether it needs changing at all.

After a thorough site assessment, plant selection should take into consideration available space above- and belowground, hardiness zone and microclimate, sun and shade patterns, soil moisture, soil pH, and salt. Where bulk densities are limiting for root growth, the soil must be modified. Plant selection alone may not be adequate to overcome environmental stress factors.

MODIFICATION OF SOILS

Of the many factors that must be considered when planting trees in urban sites, soil modification is an essential one. Overcoming the limitations of heavily compacted or poor soils is the focus of this chapter. Recognizing and assessing soil conditions on a site is the first step in this process.

ISSUES FOR SOIL MODIFICATION

Once a site assessment is completed, it is important to reconcile the conceptual design intent with actual site conditions, whether those conditions prove to be limitations or opportunities. Many potential site limitations can be addressed with careful plant selection, as in the case of spatial limitations, soil pH, cold hardiness, sun and shade patterns, wet and dry soil conditions, and even salt contamination. However, there is one soil condition where plant selection is not a viable strategy, and that is soil compaction. The effects of soil compaction are twofold: increased soil density and decreased soil drainage. With any particular soil texture there are soil bulk density thresholds, beyond which roots cannot penetrate. If that should be the case, the soil must be modified. Soil that cannot be penetrated by roots is simply no better than no soil at all.

There are three ways in which a soil can be modified. It can be (1) removed and replaced, (2) amended, or (3) buried under new soil with better growing characteristics.

The removal of soil and replacement with better soil is a drastic solution, but one that might be justified by the demands of the design. Most often, soil replacement is feasible if the amount to be replaced is not very large.

It is common to see topsoil brought onto a site and spread over an area so that 2 to 4 inches of new soil is added. This is most common on sites that have been the staging area for some large construction project. The added topsoil helps bury ruts and give a neater appearance. Its usual function is to aid in turfgrass establishment. This amount of soil is of little or no benefit to trees and shrubs. For these plants, at least 18 inches to 3 feet of new soil is necessary for good growth. Generally, the larger the plant and/or the more water it requires, the deeper and wider the replaced soil should be.

What Soil Should Be Brought in as a Replacement?

Although many might specify "topsoil" as the soil to use as a replacement, there is no standardized definition of the physical or chemical properties of topsoil. Topsoil can literally be any soil on top of the ground. It is necessary to specify the physical and chemical properties of replacement soil so in order to bring in a soil that can sustain plant growth. To do this, a soil specification must be written that spells out the properties of an acceptable soil that a contractor can find or blend to meet the criteria. It is also necessary that the criteria for an acceptable soil can be laboratory tested and verified before acceptance by the landscape architect or designer (the "Model Soil Specifications" section below).

Burying Poor Soil and Creating Landform

Where it is not practical to remove soil and replace it, it is possible to bury the poor soil under a better specified soil. This is typically done where soils are heavy, poorly drained, or compacted; when a high water table approaches rooting depth; or where underground obstacles limit rooting depth. It may be done over a large, continuous area or in discrete areas corresponding to where large plants are to be established. The most common approach is to create berms, or raised planting areas. Too often, berms are created by scraping unspecified soil from an area to be leveled or lowered using a front-end loader or similar large machine. In this process, well-structured soil may become compacted. A better way to create landforms is to bring in specified, compaction-resistant soil and carefully place it on site. The depth of these forms should be no less than 18 inches and preferably closer to 3 feet if large plant material is to be established there.

There are several caveats concerning the design of berm shape and orientation. A berm should have a minimum width of 2 feet, and the ratio of height to width should not exceed 1:3 for stability. The berm edge should slope gradually into the existing grade. Given the added elevation and slope, excess surface water will be shed off the sides of a berm. Make sure this water is not directed toward other plantings. Depending on the berm orientation to the site contours, excess water may be directed either around the berm or impounded on the site. If designed as part of a water conservation strategy, berming on the contour can decrease surface water runoff and increase infiltration.

Raised beds involve the construction of a retaining wall on one or all sides in order to contain the additional soil volume. This is most appropriate in a formal design, where space may be limited or where a seating wall is a desirable feature. The goal of a well-designed berm or raised bed is to achieve greater rooting volume.

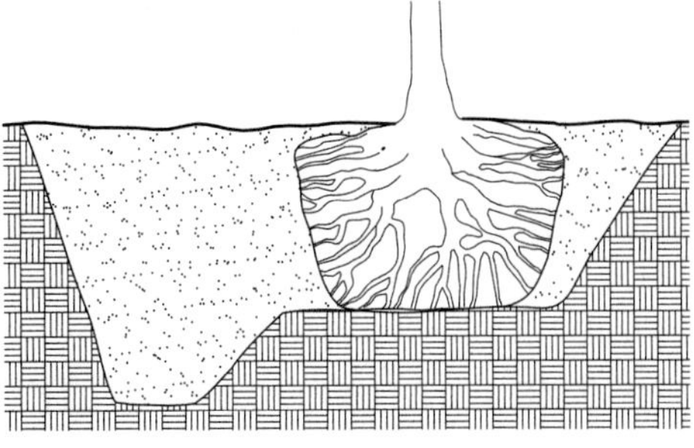

SUBSURFACE SCULPTING DIAGRAM OF USABLE SOIL OVER SHAPED SUBSOIL FOR DRAINAGE

It is important that the existing soil under a created landform drains well. A technique called *subsurface soil sculpting* can aid in this process. With subsurface sculpting, the grade of the soil to be buried is graded in a way that moves excess water away from prepared planting zones before the new soil is brought in. Water should drain freely through the replaced soil; and, when it reaches the old soil, it should be channeled away by the use of subsurface swales or drains via gravity. The grade or form of the replaced soil may look nothing like the shape of the sculpted buried soil that has been shaped for positive drainage.

Amending Soils

It is theoretically possible to amend an existing compacted soil so that its bulk density is below a root growth limiting level and its macroporosity is increased to allow for better drainage and aeration.

Seminal work done by Spomer (1983) showed that it would take a very large amount of an inorganic amendment, such as sand, to affect a positive change in bulk density and macroporosity. If sand were added to a soil containing only micropores, it would be necessary to add approximately 75 percent by volume to effect a positive change in macroporosity. Adding less than that actually decreases the porosity of the soil. It is important, too, that any amendment be of a uniform size—preferably a large- to medium-diameter sand. If a well-graded sand is added, one with particles of all sizes, the smaller particles will nest within the larger ones, effectively reducing pore space. The best amendment has particles of nearly uniform size. When the uniform particles become so numerous in an amended soil that they begin to touch each other, macropores are formed (Figure 3-4). The designations and openings in Table 3-1 are important in understanding the relationship of sand and gravel size names common in the trade, the American Society for Testing Materials (ASTM) Sieve Designation, and related sieve or screen sizes. This information is essential when considering using sands or fine gravels as a soil amendment or evaluating sieve specifications of a soil analysis.

In practice, it is very difficult to amend a soil in the field with enough inorganic amendment to effect a meaningful improvement. So much must be added and tilled into 18 to 36 inches that this may not be a viable option. Adding sand is useful if soils can be mixed away from the site and brought in and placed. This becomes the same technique as bringing in another soil to replace the old. Sand and gravel firms will blend a soil to specification. If a soil is required to be compaction-resistant and freely draining, it is important that a soil specification be followed that will provide those qualities. A sand within a narrow particle size range, generally from coarse to medium, will provide the macropores for good drainage as well as root growth. By mixing so much sand into a heavy soil, the texture of the soil can be changed, but not without considerable effort.

Amending with Organic Matter

Although the practice of amending a soil with organic matter is an ancient agricultural practice, its application in landscape sites and especially in individual planting holes has been questioned since the 1980s. Many researchers found that adding organic amendment to the backfill of a planting hole provided no useful benefits. An evaluation of this work shows clearly that no case was made in which the existing soil was limiting either by drainage or excessive bulk density. If there is no need for soil amendment, it is understandable why many researchers found its use unnecessary. However, when soils *are* compacted to root-limiting conditions, recent research has shown that organic amendment can have beneficial properties when applied in sufficient quantities.

Organic amendment to a soil should be attempted when it is possible to incorporate it over an entire planting site or bed and not just in a planting hole. It is possible that amending soil only in the planting hole can exacerbate a "bathtub effect," where the loosened soil and organic matter in the planting hole, in an otherwise compacted soil, actually make a wetter soil than one with no organic matter added.

The organic amendment should be tilled or dug in to a depth of 18 inches minimally and enough added to make a meaningful difference. With a compacted sandy loam, it is necessary to add at least 25 percent by volume to the entire 18-inch depth profile to make a positive change in bulk density and macroporosity. In a compacted, heavy, clayey soil, at least 50 percent of organic matter would have to be added to the same depth to decrease bulk density below root-limiting thresholds. Even with this level of organic matter, it is not clear whether macroporosity can be changed enough in a clay soil to remove that limiting factor in the planting site. Therefore, with a heavy soil, organic amendments should be added to reduce bulk density. However, plants should still be chosen that can tolerate wet soils.

Many types of organic matter may be used to amend soils. Peat moss, peat humus, food waste compost, composted brewer's waste, and other composted organic material can be usefully employed as long as it is not too high in soluble salts.

Other issues may need to be addressed when using compost. For example, pH should evaluated as part of the whole planting scheme. If the soil pH is already 7.8 and an amendment with a pH of 7.6 is being added, then this is not a concern. However, if an acid soil with an alkaline compost is being amended this may affect the choice of plant materials.

Organic amendments should always be completely composted and a lab test run on them to verify pH, soluble salts, nutrient availability, and organic matter content. Moreover, if the amendment is too fresh and not well composted, the wood chips often used in it as a bulking agent can tie up some soil nitrogen while it continues to decompose. Moreover, poorly prepared compost may contain significant weed seeds that can cause a nuisance in the landscape.

Structural Soils: How Do They Work?

Structural soil mixes are two-part systems comprising a stone lattice for strength and soil for horticultural needs. Structural soils depend on a load-bearing stone lattice to support the pavement. The lattice provides stability through stone-to-stone contacts while allowing interconnected voids for root penetration, air, and water movement. The friction between the stones provides the strength. A narrow particle size distribution of the stone is chosen to provide a uniform system of high porosity after compaction. The system assumes full compaction to construction standards, but angular stone is selected to increase the porosity of the compacted stone lattice. As the stone is the load-bearing component of the system, the aggregates should meet regional standards for aggregate soundness and durability requirements for pavement base aggregates.

The soil in the design mixture should be a loam to heavy clay loam with a minimum of 20 percent clay. It is critical that the soil nearly fill the large pores created by the stone lattice while not overfilling them. If the pores were overfilled, the soil would push aside the stone lattice and the load-bearing strength of the lattice would collapse. The interstitial clay loam soil itself should have about 5 percent organic matter content to help increase nutrient- and water-holding capacity while encouraging beneficial microbial activity. By carefully choosing the stone, soil, and mixing ratio, a gap-graded material able to provide the air and water balance and nutrients necessary for root growth and plant establishment can be created even after being compacted to meet engineers' specifications.

The objective is to partially fill the stone lattice voids with soil. The intention is to suspend the soil between the stones, which come together during compaction, producing a load-bearing compacted stone lattice with uncompacted soil in the voids. When properly designed and compacted, the system will have large voids that provide room for root growth and aeration of the root zone.

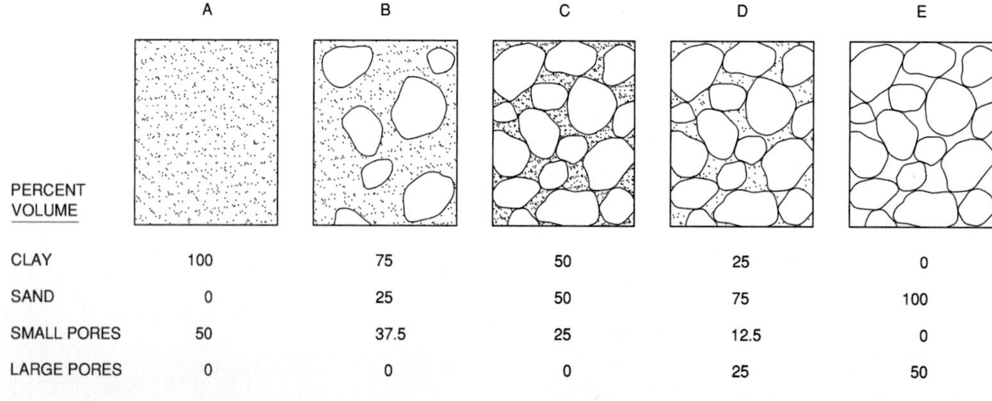

The effect of mixing sand with clay decreases pore space until the volume of sand exceeds 50 percent.

SAND AS A SOIL AMENDMENT

(Source: Arboriculture, 4th edition, 2004, by Richard Harris, James Clark, and Nelda P. Methany, 2004).

To develop both a base course that has high load-bearing capability and a medium for tree establishment, the ratio of soil to stone materials is a major consideration. If the stone voids are overly filled with soil, aeration and the bearing capacity of the system will be compromised. Variability during the mixing process can occur, creating a mixture that is overfilled with soil. Too much soil will change the formation of the stone lattice. This change results in an unacceptable decrease in bearing capacity.

Any structural soil mix should assume the compaction normally expected in the construction of pavement sections. Compaction is often specified as a percentage of a peak density from a standard moisture-density curve (such as Proctor density) or a specified testing protocol (such as American Association of State Highway and Transportation Officials, or AASHTO T-99). Compacting to 95 percent peak density in this manner only gauges relative compactness; it does not imply 5 percent porosity. This density measure gives a quality control mechanism to measure compactness and serves as a benchmark from which to evaluate the material for other engineering characteristics, such as bearing capacity, hydraulic conductivity, and plant-available moisture expected in the field.

The bearing capacity of the material is important, because the materials will be under large portions of pavement and may need to support vehicular traffic. The bearing capacity can also influence the thickness, and thus the cost, of the pavement. One criterion of use is the California Bearing Ratio (CBR), which can relate to other pavement design parameters (Atkins, 1997). This method gauges the bearing capacity of a material by comparing it to a standard material known to be acceptable. For ease in pavement design protocol, it is advisable to require a CBR greater than or equal to 50 in the design of a structural soil. The result is a material that can be compacted and provide a more stable base than found in many current sidewalk installations. This translates into a durable pavement design that can also support tree establishment.

Determining horticultural viability entails testing and observation of plant response over time. Collecting empirical data on plant response and growth analysis in controlled system applications remains the best method for evaluation. Research at Cornell University has shown that trees can grow well in structural soil mixtures (Grabosky et al., 1995, 1996, 1999, 2001).

One problem in designing the system is getting the mixture to blend uniformly and remain so during trucking, placement, and compaction. Due to mixing variation, it is not advisable to simply assign the maximum amount of soil possible. In fact, there is an observed loss in acceptable bearing capacity when the noncompacted soil fills the stone voids (Grabosky et al., 1999).

Cornell researchers found that the structural soil process benefits from the addition of a tackifying agent to stabilize the mixing process (Grabosky and Bassuk, 1995). The tackifier allows the stones and soil to mix more uniformly and prevents separation of the materials due to vibration in transit, dumping, and the working of the material in installation. A potassium propenoate-propenamide copolymer (an agricultural hydrogel) has been used successfully as a tackifier.

Mixing Methods

To determine the ratio of stone to soil, it is advisable to make three small test blends of slightly different ratios. A useful starting point is 18 percent to 22 percent soil by weight. Experience proves it best to define and control mixing ratios on a weight basis. This approach avoids the difficulties associated with variable volume-to-weight relationships and the changes in density of a given soil relative to its depth in a stockpile, moisture content, or handling. The hydrogel is included at very low rates and held at a constant rate relative to the stone for mix design purposes. These materials can then be tested to develop their respective moisture-density relationships (per AASHTO T-99 or ASTM D-698) and to provide a compaction protocol. The materials can then be tested for their respective CBR at the expected installed densities. The results give a baseline guide as to how much soil can be safely included in the mix design. Research trials have shown that structural soil meets the bearing capacity criterion of CBR greater than 50, at peak ASTM D-698 (AASHTO T-99) density, and that tree roots can penetrate and trees can be established successfully even at 100 percent peak density (Grabosky et al., 1996).

The material is mixed on the flat with a front-end loader. In this method, the stone is spread as a uniform 12-inch layer on a paved surface; the hydrogel is evenly spread onto the stone, followed by a moist soil layer. This layered approach can be repeated to develop a six-layer pile if the loader is large enough to effectively mix the material. Then the layered system is turned and mixed until uniformly blended. If the system is too dry, moisture may be uniformly added to assist in mixing. The hydrogel can also be distributed as a slurry to help in this regard. The material should not exceed its optimal moisture content for compaction determined from the moisture-density curve and sample trials.

Quality Control

The structural soil developed at Cornell University has been patented and licensed to ensure quality control. Its trademarked name is CU-Structural Soil or CU-Soil. By specifying this material, the designer or contractor is guaranteed to have the material mixed and tested to meet research-based specifications. Many individuals have employed systems termed *structural soils*. Indeed, the Cornell effort may have contributed to the term's popular usage. As all soils possess a structural component, the term *structural soil* is conceptually useful to identify a product. Many similar structural materials have been used representing a wide range of stone-soil ratios, with and without stabilizing materials, but very few have been formally tested with both pavements and plants. Hundreds of installations in Canada, the United States, Puerto Rico, Denmark, and Australia have demonstrated the viability of this approach. There have been several less successful efforts and outright failures with conceptually similar installations as well. The Danish Institute of Forest Research and the Cornell University Urban Horticulture Institute have independently reached many of the same conclusions (Kristofferson, 1998). The result is that many similar but different materials all fall under one conceptual term, *structural soil*—but not all of them work well.

Given the costs of failure, it is imperative to test any material appropriately with the involvement of the pavement design engineer. Experience indicates that the system is more sensitive to pavement needs than to plant needs. As such, the most common miscues in the execution of structural soil system are excessive soil and the inclusion of organic amendments without proper testing. Without thorough testing to define a compaction level or any control of compaction, installations may or may not be structurally sound or horticulturally viable. Without a compaction test during mix design, one cannot know what aeration and root-impeding issues lie ahead. Testing has shown little variation of plant establishment response over a wide mix ratio range. The root zone can be managed with irrigation and nutritional supplements over time, but it is expensive to lose and replace pavement prematurely.

Appropriate Usage

Structural soils, in the context of this discussion, have specific intended uses. The material supports pavement designed to withstand pedestrian and vehicular traffic. The materials can be designed for use under pedestrian malls, sidewalks, parking lots, and possibly some low-use access roads. The material is intended for use when no other design solutions provide adequate soil volumes for trees surrounded by pavement.

Structural soils are used as a base material under pavement. Research has shown that tree roots in structural soil profiles grow deep into the material below the pavement. The same research shows a lack of root development in the surface 12 inches below the pavement surface (Grabosky et al., 2001). It is logical to assume that moving the roots down to the subgrade will distribute pressures generated from root expansion over a wider section of pavement, reducing or eliminating sidewalk cracking and heaving.

By design, structural soils are fully compacted with conventional equipment to standard relative compactness (full Proctor density). Also by design, they can serve as the base for the entire pavement section. Where a tree is to be installed, the material can be allowed to rise to surface grade, where the pavement opening for tree installation will be made. The opening provides an opportunity for watering and passive aeration systems at the surface.

Just below the pavement, if unit pavers are to be used, there can also be a setting bed material of narrowly graded sand aggregate that should possess no fine sands, silts, or clays. This standard setting bed layer can be to a depth normal for regional installation protocol. To discourage rooting in this layer, a geotextile may be used between this material and the structural soil. The geotextile should not restrict water movement.

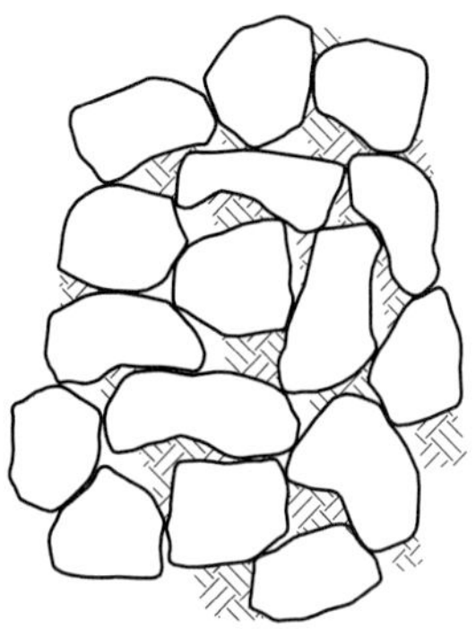

STRUCTURAL SOIL PROFILE SHOWING STONE-ON-STONE LOAD-BEARING SYSTEM WITH SOIL IN VOID SPACES

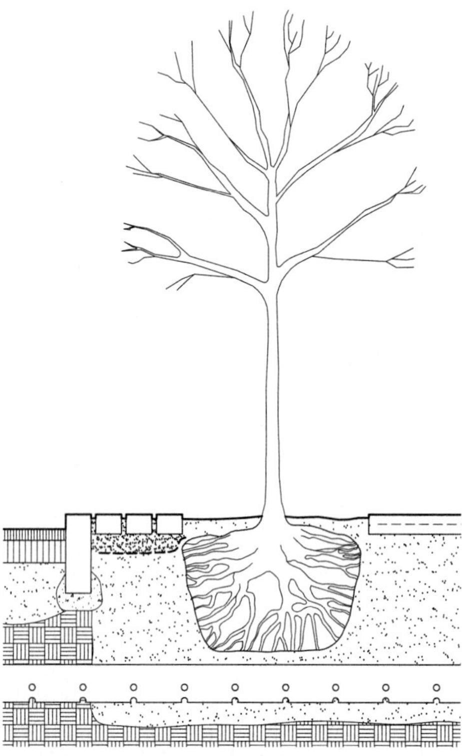

TYPICAL PAVING DETAIL FOR BOTH PAVERS AND RIGID CONCRETE OVER STRUCTURAL SOIL WITH PERFORATED UNDERDRAIN

The structural soil material should have a minimum thickness of 24 inches, with 36 inches preferred.

Provision for an irrigation system may be considered. Given the large volume of structural soil for tree roots to explore, the need for irrigation must be determined by region and management needs. While there is less moisture in a structural soil on a per-volume basis, the total root system occupies much of the pavement area. Fertilization can be dissolved into the irrigation water for nutritional management, if necessary, although to date nutrient deficiencies have not been found, probably due to the large volume of soil roots can grow into. There must also be positive drainage below the root system to prevent saturation. The subgrade below the structural soil may still be compacted and rendered essentially impermeable to moisture and roots. A perforated and wrapped drain connected to the storm drainage system should be placed between the structural soil material and the compacted subgrade.

The basis for plant selection for structural soils should aim toward alkaline-tolerant and drought-tolerant plant species. The stone used, whether limestone, granite, or other aggregates, will heavily influence pH. Structural soils made with limestone generally end up with a soil pH of about 8.0, regardless of the soil pH when the material was first mixed. For many parts of the country, this is not unusually high, even in normal soils and especially in urban areas. Using structural soil aggregates that do not influence pH, such as granite, may not affect pH as quickly, but the pH will continue to climb as the concrete slowly breaks down. A structural soil system provides an opportunity for choosing alkaline-tolerant species that require good drainage and are somewhat drought-tolerant. Trees that are both alkaline and somewhat drought-tolerant are possible choices when using a structural soil.

Planting a tree in structural soil is fairly simple. The pavement opening is expanded to allow for buttress root formation on older trees if possible. The wider opening could be paved in removable pavers or mulched. The tree is simply planted into the structural soil as it would be in a normal stony soil. The roots would be expected to immediately contact the structural soil and grow into the material. If there is a large unpaved opening around the tree (at least 8 by 8 feet), it is possible to use a good sand loam soil surrounding the root system and then structural soil under the pavement. It is presumed that supplemental watering will be provided during the first growing season, as would be expected for any newly planted tree. In regions where irrigation is necessary to grow trees, low-volume under-pavement irrigation systems have been used successfully.

SOIL VOLUME CALCULATIONS

It is imperative that available soil volumes for proposed tree plantings be known for tree establishment, as well as to allow for their envisioned design size. Adequate soil volumes allow for better tree growth in an urban setting.

Why Is an Adequate Soil Volume Important for Tree Growth?

The soil provides many resources for the tree, primary among them being water, oxygen, nutrients, and a medium for root growth. When soil volume is limited, tree growth suffers because so much of the top growth of the tree is dependent on what the roots can deliver, and that in turn depends on the size of the resource pool of soil. It is possible to grow trees in quite small containers as long as water, nutrients, and oxygen are supplemented, which is not easily done in urban areas. However, we are beginning to learn that roots not only are the conduits of resources to the tops of the trees but also produce growth factors necessary for shoot growth as well. Roots must grow themselves in order to produce these growth factors. Moreover, only new white roots efficiently take up nutrients. Therefore, if root growth is restricted, top growth will also be restricted even if water and nutrients are plentiful in the soil (Hawver, 1997).

How Much Soil Volume Does a Tree Need?

Several researchers have looked at this question. And although variables such as the size of the tree canopy, site conditions, and tree species have an enormous effect on determining an adequate soil volume, a few generalities can be drawn. Lindsey and Bassuk (1991) found that for much of the United States a soil volume of 2 cubic feet for every square foot of canopy crown projection is a good place to start. This is an overestimate if the tree is in the Northeast, where there is more rainfall, but works for drier areas of the Midwest and West. This research applies to mesophytic deciduous trees, not trees specially adapted to arid or swampy areas or evergreens. Most U.S. regions could apply this research, except for the desert Southwest, where there is an extremely high atmospheric demand for water and very little replenishing precipitation. By reinterpreting other researchers' soil volume calculations, a similar relationship of between 1 and 3 cubic feet of soil volume per square foot of crown projection can be generated. It is easy to calculate the crown projection of an existing or envisioned tree by calculating the area under the drip line of the tree, which is the same as the crown projection. By using the formula for area of a circle (πr^2), the crown projection may be calculated. By doubling that figure and calling it cubic feet, we can come to a reasonable starting place to discuss adequate soil volumes for most urban trees.

Model Soil Specifications

The following material presents general considerations for the development of soil specifications. This is not provided in a standard specifications format but does reflect general performance considerations when developing soil characteristics. The descriptions can be attributed to new soil that is intended to be brought to a site as well as characteristics of soil modification and/or amendment of soils that have been stripped and stockpiled on a site for reuse.

Specification considerations include:

- Soil classification
- Particle size distribution
- Organic amendments
- Soluble salts
- Chemical analysis

The contractor shall submit representative samples of topsoil to bring onto the site and samples of topsoil that was stockpiled from on-site stripping to a Soil Plant Testing Laboratory. All reports shall be sent to the Landscape Architect or owners' representative for approval. Samples of the topsoil to be brought to the site must be approved prior to delivery. Deficiencies in the topsoil shall be corrected by the Contractor as directed after review of the testing agency report. Testing reports shall include the following tests and recommendations:

1. Particle size analysis of the topsoil determined by ASTM F-1632 shall be performed and compared to the USDA Soil Classification System.
2. Percent organic matter shall be determined by a Loss on Ignition or Walkley/Black Test (ASTM F-1647).
3. Tests for gradation and organics shall be performed by a private testing laboratory. Tests for soil chemistry and pH may be performed by a public extension service agency or a private testing laboratory.
4. Chemical analysis shall be undertaken for phosphorous, potassium, calcium, magnesium, cation exchange capacity, base saturation percentages, micronutrients, and acidity (pH).
5. Soil analysis tests shall show recommendations for soil additives or fertilizers to correct soil deficiencies as necessary.
6. All tests shall be performed in accordance with the current standards of the Association of Official Agricultural Chemists (AOAC).

Off-site topsoil shall be natural, fertile friable loam or sandy loam as classified by the U.S. Department of Agriculture Soil Classification System. The soil shall contain not less than 3 percent or more than 8 percent by weight of decayed organic matter (humus) as determined by ASTM F-1647. The topsoil shall be free of stones 1 inch (25 millimeters) or larger and other

Nina L Bassuk; Peter J. Trowbridge

extraneous materials harmful to plant growth. Topsoil shall not have a pH of less than 6.0 or greater than 7.5, and shall not be delivered or used for planting while in a frozen or muddy condition.

If organic amendments are needed to obtain the specific organic matter content of the topsoil, the organic matter source may be a peat or compost material. The peat shall be sphagnum peat having an ash content not exceeding 15 percent, as determined by ASTM D-2974. Composts may be used provided that the material has an ash content not exceeding 40 percent.

Particle size specification varies for soil types defined by the USDA Soil Classification System. See the table "Example 1 of Particle Size Specification for Sandy Loam." Particle size analysis will vary for other specified soil types.

Another example of particle size analysis for a specified sandy loam topsoil and definition of sizes is given in the table "Example 2 of Particle Size Analysis for Specified Sandy Loam."

Soluble salts in soil and, especially, organic amendments should be analyzed at an accepted testing laboratory. Soluble salts in parts per million (ppm) can be converted as follows:

1 mmho/cm = 1000 ppm = 1.5 6 d S/m

If laboratory testing provides a ppm analysis, the criteria given in the table "Concentration Thresholds and Acceptable Levels for Soluble Salts (PPM)" should be taken into consideration. Low to normal levels of soluble salts in the soil, measured in ppm, are in the range of 0 to 1000 where plants with low tolerance of soluble salts can be recommended. With a ppm of 1000 to 2000, only plants sensitive to salts would be affected. With a ppm of 2000 to 4000, plants with salt tolerance should be used. When greater than 5000 ppm soluble salts are detected in soils, few plants will survive.

When soluble salts are measured as mmho/cm, the restrictions shown in the table "Soluble Salts (MMHO/CM)" would apply.

Chemical analysis of soils should occur in accordance with standards of the AOAC. Based on the results of the chemical analysis for the types of plantings proposed, the following products may need to be added to the soil specification as amendments:

Lime: ASTM C-602, Class T, agricultural limestone containing a minimum 80 percent calcium carbonate equivalent, with a minimum 99 percent passing a No. 8 (2.36 mm) sieve and a minimum 75 percent passing a No. 60 (250 micrometer) sieve. Provide lime in the form of dolomitic limestone.

Aluminum sulfate: Commercial grade, unadulterated.

Nitrogen, phosphorous, and potassium: In amounts recommended in soil analysis results from a qualified soil-testing laboratory.

Developing an exact specification for soils to be used in planting areas on a site, whether from on-site or off-site sources, is critical to plant survival and establishment.

EXAMPLE 1 OF PARTICLE SIZE SPECIFICATION FOR SANDY LOAM

PARTICLE SIZE	ANALYSIS	SIEVE #	% RETAINED
0–5%	Gravel	8	0–5%
0–5%	Very coarse sand	20	0–15%
60–75%	Medium to coarse sand	60	60–75%
10–25%	Silt pan	pan	15–40%
5–15%	Clay pan	pan	15–40%

EXAMPLE 2 OF PARTICLE SIZE ANALYSIS FOR SPECIFIED SANDY LOAM

	APPROXIMATE PARTICLE DISTRIBUTION	SIZE
Gravel	Less than 10%	±2 mm
Coarse to medium sand	60–75%	0.25–2 mm
Fine sand	5–10%	0.1–0.25 mm
Very fine sand	0–5%	0.05–0.1 mm
Silt	10–30%	0.0002–0.05 mm
Clay	15–20%	–0.002 mm

CONCENTRATION THRESHOLDS AND ACCEPTABLE LEVELS FOR SOLUBLE SALTS (PPM)

CONCENTRATION	LEVEL
0–1000	Low (normal)
1000–2000	Medium
3000–4000	High
> 5000	Very high

SOLUBLE SALTS (MMHO/CM)

0–2	Nonsaline
3–4	Slightly saline; sensitive plants might be restricted
4–8	Moderately saline; many plants will be restricted
8–16	Strongly saline; only tolerant plants will grow
> 16	Very strongly saline; very few plants will grow

REFERENCES

Craul, P.J. 1992. *Urban soil in landscape design.* New York: John Wiley and Sons.

Atkins, Harold N. 1997. *Highway materials, soils, and concretes.* 3rd ed. Columbus, Ohio: Prentice Hall.

Grabosky, J. 1996. Developing a structural soil material with high bearing strength and increased rooting volumes for street trees under sidewalks. Master's thesis, Cornell University.

Grabosky, J., and N. Bassuk. 1995. A new urban tree soil to safely increase rooting volumes under sidewalks. *Journal of Arboriculture* 21(4): 187–201.

———. 1998. An urban tree soil to safely increase rooting volumes. *U.S. Patent No. 5,849,069.* Ithaca, N.Y.: Cornell University.

Grabosky, J., N. Bassuk, and M. Marranca. 2002. Preliminary findings from measuring street tree shoot growth in two skeletal soil installations compared to tree lawn plantings. *Journal of Arboriculture* 28(2): 106–108.

Grabosky, J., N. Bassuk, and H. van Es. 1996. Further testing of rigid urban tree materials for use under pavement to increase street tree rooting volumes. *Journal of Arboriculture* 22(6): 255–263.

Grabosky, J., N. Bassuk, L. Irwin, and H. van Es. 1999. Pilot study of structural soil materials in pavement profiles. *The landscape below ground II: Proceedings of an international workshop on tree root development in urban soils.* San Francisco, Calif: International Society of Arboriculture.

———. 1999. An urban soil to safely increase rooting volumes. *The landscape below ground II: Proceedings of an international workshop on tree root development in urban soils.* San Francisco, Calif: International Society of Arboriculture.

———, 2001. Shoot and root growth of three tree species in sidewalks. *Journal of Environmental Horticulture* 19(4): 206–211.

Hawver, G. 1997. Influence of root restriction and drought stress on container grown trees: Impacts on plant morphology and physiology. Master's thesis, Cornell University.

Kristofferson, Pella. 1998. Designing urban pavement sub-bases to support trees. *Journal of Arboriculture* 24(3): 121–126.

Lindsey, P., and N. Bassuk. 1991. Specifying soil volumes to meet the water needs of mature urban street trees and trees in containers. *Journal of Arboriculture* 17(6): 141–149.

Rivenshield, A. 2001. Organic amendment to improve the physical qualities of compacted soils. Master's thesis, Cornell University.

Spomer, L. Art. 1983. Physical amendment of landscape soils. *Journal of Environmental Horticulture* 1(3): 77–80.

PUBLIC PLANTING DESIGN PRINCIPLES

SCALE AND PROPORTION

Public buildings tend to be much larger in size than residential structures. Therefore, proper scale and relative proportions are paramount issues for the landscape design around these buildings. Scale pertains to the size of objects relative to each other. Visually, the units in a design must have good comparative relations, or proportions. With the proper selection of landscape trees, the visual mass of the plants can cojoin with the building mass into harmonious proportions. Conversely, trees that are too small in proportion will serve only to amplify the discordant scale in which the building dominates.

HUMAN SCALE

Providing for a sense of proper human scale is important in the design of public spaces and the landscape around public buildings. As people move in and out of buildings, plants—particularly trees—can function to provide a comfortable feeling of human scale, a "rightness of size," in the transition zone between interior spaces and the larger open spaces of the outdoors. A sequence can be established, beginning with shrubs near the building entrance; next, ornamental-sized trees; followed by larger-shade trees, as a person progresses outward.

BALANCE

If there is adequate space, the landscape design can work with the masses of the building to produce visual balance. Balance is achieved in a composition when the whole conveys a feeling of repose and stability. The design components, both landscape and architectural, work together to achieve an equilibrium. Large trees will effectuate the necessary visual mass to coexist with the building's mass.

Solid Base

Buildings that appear awkward due to their narrowness or strong vertical character can be provided with a more visually substantial base by extending the plant forms outward from the foundation.

Sweeps or Groupings

For plantings along routes of travel, using plants in broad sweeps or groupings works most effectively. Travelers moving at speeds of 35 mph or greater can more easily perceive the visual effects of masses of plant colors and textures than they can distinguish an individual plant. This can apply equally to landscapes along highways as well as train routes and other travel passages. Broad sweeps of two dozen of one species melding into several dozen of another species works well for the visual acuity at higher speeds. It also facilitates ease of maintenance, as shrubs can be allowed to grow into their mature sizes without pruning.

Don Brigham, FASLA

RESIDENTIAL LANDSCAPE DESIGN PRINCIPLES

The application of design principles to residential landscape architecture provides a solid framework for unity and harmony between all the elements of the project. By employing appropriate design principles, a blending or marriage can be achieved between the architecture and the landscape, uniting them into a harmonious oneness. Not every design principle needs to be applied to each project; rather; the designer chooses those principles that are most appropriate.

REPETITION

Repeating, or duplicating like things, greatly enhances the unity of a composition. Landscape forms and colors can be repeated to provide a visual linkage among the plants. In the same way, plant forms and groupings can repeat similar patterns of the architecture, leading to visual harmony.

DOMINANT FORMS

Matching the selection of plants to the dominant forms and lines of the architecture provides visual harmony throughout the total composition. Structures that have a strong horizontal quality can be complemented with plants having horizontal character, together with plant massings that play off the prevailing architectural forms.

BALANCE

Balance is achieved in a composition when the whole conveys a feeling of repose and stability. The design components, both landscape and architectural parts, work together to achieve an equilibrium.

SCALE OR PROPORTION

Scale pertains to the size of objects relative to each other. Visually, the units in a design must have good comparative relations, or proportions. Plants that are either too large or too small don't match the architecture and result in a discordant composition.

SOLID BASE

Buildings that appear awkward due to their narrowness or strong vertical character can be provided with a more visually substantial base by extending the plant forms outward from the foundation. Plant forms that are not linked appear random and "spotty," reading as separate units that are not part of a composition. Using repetition of smaller plant forms will visually link the pieces together into a more unified whole.

FOCAL POINT IN ARCHITECTURE

A well-designed composition has one dominant point of visual interest. If the composition lacks a focal point, the eye has nowhere to rest when observing it. Conversely, when there are several focal points, they will compete for attention and cause visual confusion. If the architecture has a stimulating feature, such as a tower or entry, the landscape units should be selected to remain subordinate to it.

If the architecture lacks visual interest, a focal point can be integrated into the composition with plant materials possessing a dominant or contrasting form, size, color, or texture.

CURB APPEAL

The attractiveness of a home viewed from the street by passersby can be positively impacted by a well-designed landscape. This not only is more aesthetically pleasing but can also add value to the home.

Don Brigham, FASLA

ENVIRONMENTAL EFFECTS OF TREES

GENERAL

The physical environment of the site, the design needs of the project, and the design character of the trees are all factors that must be considered in selecting trees and preparing a landscape plan for a building.

Soil conditions (acidity, porosity) at the site, the amount and intensity of sunlight and precipitation, and the seasonal temperature range in the area create the physical environment in which trees must be able to survive. As well, consider how the location and topography of the site will direct the wind, resulting in cold winds and cooling breezes that can affect the health of trees.

Trees can be used to address the design needs of a project by directing pedestrian or vehicle movement, framing vistas, screening objectionable views, and defining and shaping exterior space. Trees can also be used to modify the microclimate of a site and to help conserve building energy use from heating, cooling, and lighting systems.

The design character of the trees themselves plays a part in which species are best suited for a particular application. The shape of a tree can be columnar, conical, spherical, or spreading, and the resulting height and mass will change over time as the tree matures.

Some trees grow quickly and others more slowly, and their color and texture varies from coarse to medium to fine, affecting their character. The appearance of deciduous trees changes with the seasons, while the effect of an evergreen remains relatively constant.

CROWN: HEAD OF FOLIAGE OF TREE

LEAVES: FOLIAGE UNIT OF TREE THAT FUNCTIONS PRIMARILY IN FOOD MANUFACTURING BY PHOTOSYNTHESIS

ROOTS: ANCHOR THE TREE AND HELP HOLD THE SOIL AGAINST EROSION

ROOT HAIRS: ABSORB MINERALS FROM THE SOIL MOISTURE AND SEND THEM AS NUTRIENT SALTS IN THE SAPWOOD TO THE LEAVES

HEARTWOOD: NONLIVING CENTRAL PART OF TREE GIVING STRENGTH AND STABILITY

ANNUAL RINGS: REVEAL AGE OF TREE BY SHOWING YEARLY GROWTH

OUTER BARK: AGED INNER BARK THAT PROTECTS TREE FROM DESSICATION AND INJURY

INNER BARK (PHLOEM): CARRIES FOOD FROM LEAVES TO BRANCHES, TRUNK, AND ROOTS

CAMBIUM: LAYER BETWEEN XYLEM AND PHLOEM WHERE CELL ADDING GROWTH OCCURS. NEW SAPWOOD TO INSIDE AND NEW INNER BARK OUTSIDE

SAPWOOD (XYLEM): CARRIES NUTRIENTS AND WATER TO LEAVES FROM ROOTS

PHYSICAL CHARACTERISTICS OF TREES

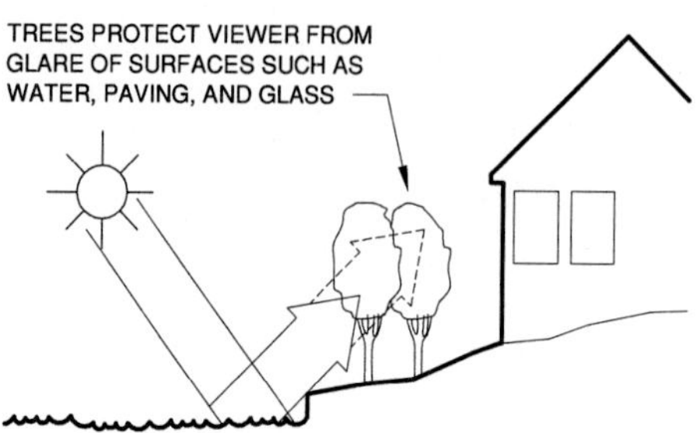

The vertical angle of the sun changes seasonally; therefore, the area of a building subject to the glare of reflected sunlight varies. Plants of various heights can screen sun (and artificial light) glare from adjacent surfaces.

GLARE PROTECTION

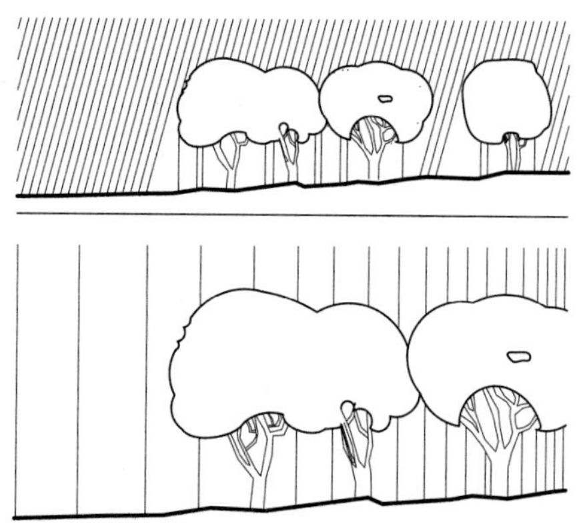

Large masses of plants physically and chemically filter and deodorize the air, reducing air pollution. (Top) Particulate matter trapped on the leaves is washed to the ground during rainfall. Gaseous pollutants are assimilated by the leaves. (Bottom) Fragrant plants can mechanically mask fumes and odors. As well, these pollutants are chemically metabolized in the photosynthesis process.

AIR FILTRATION

LEAVES AND BRANCHES ARE COATED WITH THIN FILM OF WATER, HOLDING IT FROM RUNNING OFF

BRANCH STRUCTURE CHANNELS WATER TO DRY AREA UNDER TREE TO BE ABSORBED

ROOTS ABSORB WATER RUNOFF FROM BRANCHES

Mature trees absorb or delay runoff from stormwater at a rate of 4 to 5 times that of bare ground.

RUNOFF REDUCTION

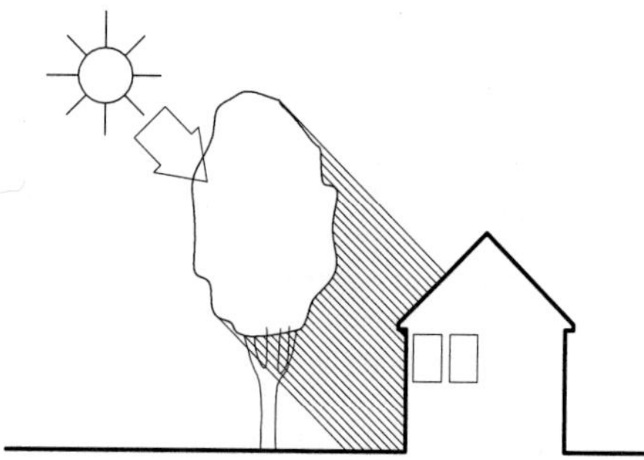

In summer, trees obstruct or filter the the strong radiation from the sun, cooling and protecting the area beneath them. In winter, evergreen trees still have theis effect, while deciduous trees, having lost their leaves, so not.

SHADE PROVISION

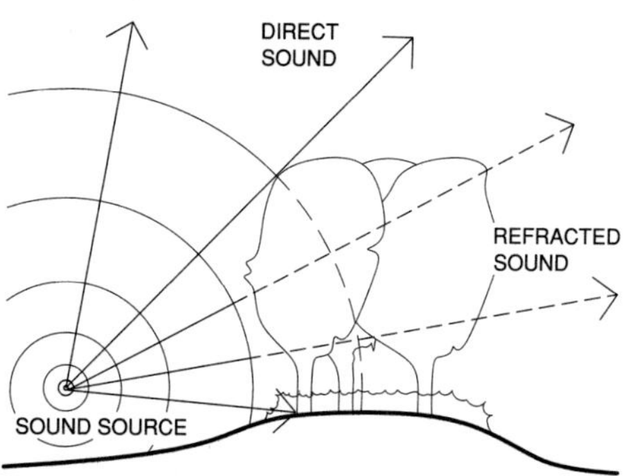

A combination of deciduous and evergreen trees and shrubs reduces sound more effectively than deciduous plants alone. Planting trees and shrubs on earth mounds increases the attenuating effect of a buffer belt.

SOUND ATTENUATION

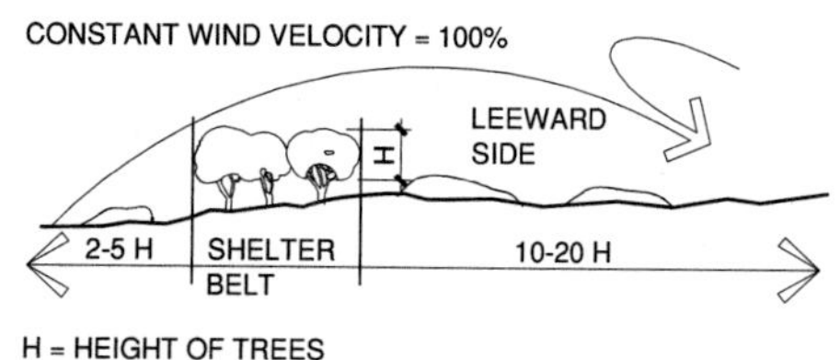

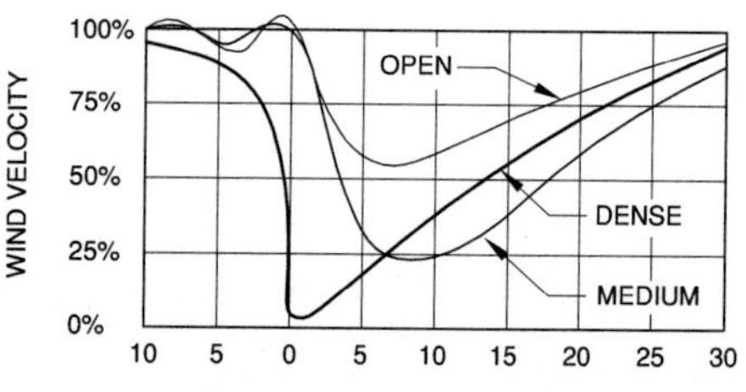

Shelter belt wind protection reduces evaporation at ground level, increases relative humidity, lowers the temperature in summer and reduces heat loss in winter, and reduces blowing dust and drifting snow. The amount of protection afforded is directly related to the height and density of the shelter belt.

WIND PROTECTION

James Urban, ASLA, James Urban Landscape Architecture, Annapolis, Maryland

SITE CONSIDERATIONS, PLANT INSTALLATION REQUIREMENTS, AND DETAILS

Planting details accompany the vast majority of planting plans produced in landscape architecture, architecture, and engineering offices. Along with specifications, these details indicate to the contractor how a plant is to be installed in the landscape. Under ideal circumstances, the provision of a generic detail that recognizes and utilizes good horticultural practices is all that is necessary. Ideal conditions, however, are seldom encountered on the construction site, thus requiring modification of the detail(s) to accommodate various planting requirements as are encountered site-specific conditions.

The International Society of Arboriculture (ISA), the American Nursery and Landscape Association (ANLA), James Urban, and Philip Craul, among others, have provided valuable research and information that have enabled the development of a generic standard detail for tree planting in situations where the soil and the site are not disturbed by construction and/or otherwise adverse conditions. From this basic situation the generic planting detail can be amended to accommodate conditions specific to those encountered on the site. The key is to recognize extraordinary conditions likely to be present, the severity of their occurrence, and the measures necessary to appropriately remediate the adverse conditions.

SEGMENTS OF A PLANTING DETAIL

A planting detail consists of three primary segments:

- Planting pit
- Trunk area
- Branches

Each of these segments must be considered in the detail as required by the character of the plant and the conditions under which it is expected to grow.

REQUIRED BASIC SOIL CHARACTERISTICS FOR PLANT INSTALLATION*

SOIL CHARACTERISTICS	ASSESSMENT CRITERIA
Texture	Sandy loam to silty clay loam with favorable structure (see the figure "USDA Textural Classification")
Structure	Granular or crumb, for topsoil Fine subangular blocky, for subsoil Loose or single-grained and massive soils have limitations.
Porosity	50% pore space is desirable (25% moisture and 25% air-filled)
Plant-available water-holding capacity	15% to 25% by volume
Infiltration	From ¾ to 4 in. (2 to 10 cm) per hour
Drainage	Well to moderately well drained, with no evidence of gray mottling in total planting pit depth
Organic matter	At least 1% to 5% by weight
Soil organisms	Ample evidence of soil organism activity: earthworm casts or holes and physical disintegration of litter
pH	From 5.0 (acidic) to 7.5 (alkaline), with 7.0 as neutral
Nutrient content	Normal contents of nitrogen (N), phosphorous (P), and potassium (K) for most tree species; P and K amount can be obtained form a soil test. For N, follow recommendations for plant in question.
Soluble salts	Less than 200 ppm; consider in areas where deicing may occur and in some desert soil conditions
Contaminants	No or few human-induced materials or toxic substances

Adapted from Craul (1999) to make it readily usable in hands-on circumstances.

Planting Pit

The planting pit consists of: the configuration of the pit, the size of the pit, the depth of the pit, the soil in which the plant is to be planted, the backfill soil or material, the root ball/roots, the irrigation ring and mulching.

- *Pit configuration.* The planting pit is to have broadly sloping sides (approximately 45 degrees), where possible, that have been scarified to prevent the creation of a water containment vessel. The soil at the bottom of the pit is to be sufficiently compacted to prevent plant settlement.
- *Pit size.* The size of the pit should increase as the conditions under which the plants are expected to grow become reduced in suitability. The planting pit is to be two to five times the diameter of the root ball, the container. or the outer extension of the roots in the bare rooted plants.
- *Pit depth.* The depth of the pit is to be slightly less (1 to 2 inches) than the depth of the root ball, as determined by the trunk flair—which is to be visible after the tree is planted. Studies have indicated that the majority of root growth on newly planted trees will occur in the top 12 inches of soil. As a general rule, it is better to install a plant too high than to set it too low.
- *Existing soil and backfill.* Philip Craul (1999) has defined the basic characteristics of a natural soil that would be desirable for proper plant growth and survival. Natural soil is defined as "the result of the interaction between rainfall and temperature, vegetation, and its associated fauna, the underlying weathered geologic material and topography" (Craul). Soil specifications are to be written to bring existing site conditions into reasonable compliance with these characteristics. The more a soil departs from natural conditions, the more remediation will need to take place so as to bring it, as close as possible, to the ideal condition.
- *Plant ball/roots.* Plant material is specified in one of three basic root containment situations: (a) bare root, (b) balled and burlapped (B&B), and (c) container—pot or box. Tree-spaded plant material, because of the uniqueness of the installation situation, is addressed separately.
  - *Bare root.* Bare root plant material is to be installed at the same depth or slightly higher than originally grown in the nursery. Spread roots evenly around the hole and carefully place backfill material around the roots. Compact to assure plant stability. Because of the loose soil situation, it is recommended that bare root plant material over 1-inch caliper be staked.
  - *Balled and burlapped.* The unique aspect of a B&B plant is the wrapping material around the root ball. Remove all extraneous material such as string, rope, rot-proof burlap, poly twine, and poly wrap. Remove wire from baskets to a minimum depth of 18 inches. If the burlap is not rot-proofed, it can remain on the plant ball but should be loosened around the tree trunk.
  - *Container (pot or box).* Remove container from plant. Because most container-grown material is

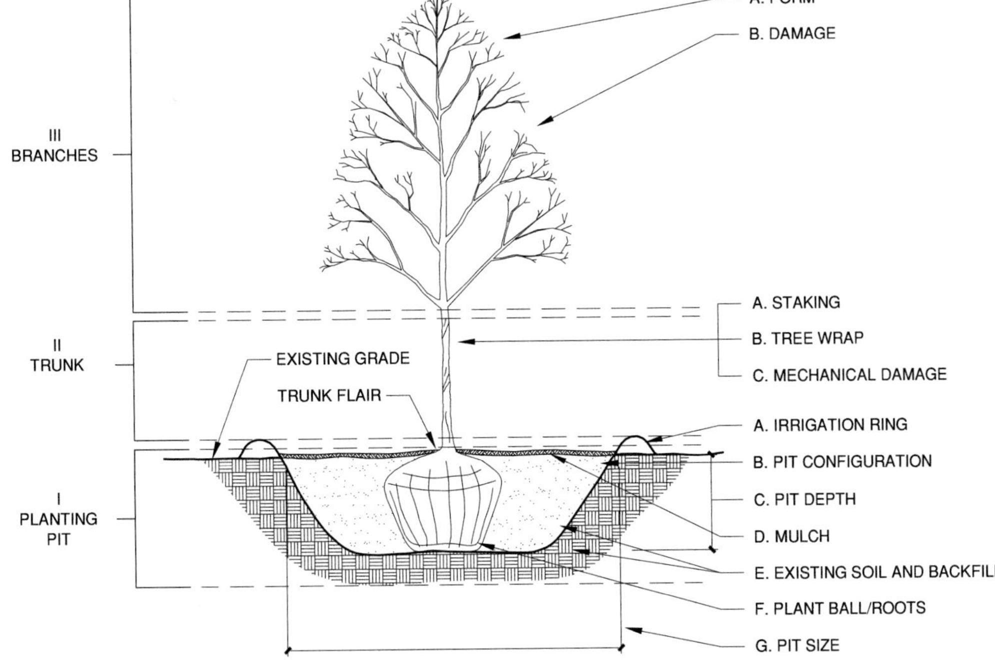

COMPONENTS OF A PLANTING DETAIL

Thomas J. Nieman, Ph.D., Department of Landscape Architecture University of Kentucky

grown in a soil medium rather than natural soil, there is a tendency for the plants to sink after planting. It is recommended that the plants be planted slightly higher to accommodate this situation. Spread roots that have conformed to the container shape to encourage outward root growth.

- *Irrigation ring.* A small 6-inch-high irrigation ring may be constructed to aid in retaining water from irrigation and/or rainfall. The dike is to be placed on the edge of the tree pit so that the backfill material and the tree ball receive a like amount of water.
- *Mulch.* Apply 2 to 4 inches of mulch to the surface area of the backfilled planting pit extending from the base of the plant to the irrigation ring. The actual trunk of the tree is not to be covered so as to prevent decay of the tree bark. Mulch, aesthetics notwithstanding, aids in the maintenance of soil moisture, reduction of evaporation, and the keeping of soil temperature as constant as possible. It also helps to keep the area free of weeds or turf. There are two basic categories of mulch:
  - Organic, which decomposes with time. Proper composted organic material will have a pH of between 6.0 and 7.2. Unweathered organic mulch will tie up nitrogen during the early stages of early decomposition and is not recommended.
  - Inorganic, such as geotextiles and landscape fabric. Inorganic materials do not decompose and allow normal water and oxygen exchange; and they prevent growth of most weeds.

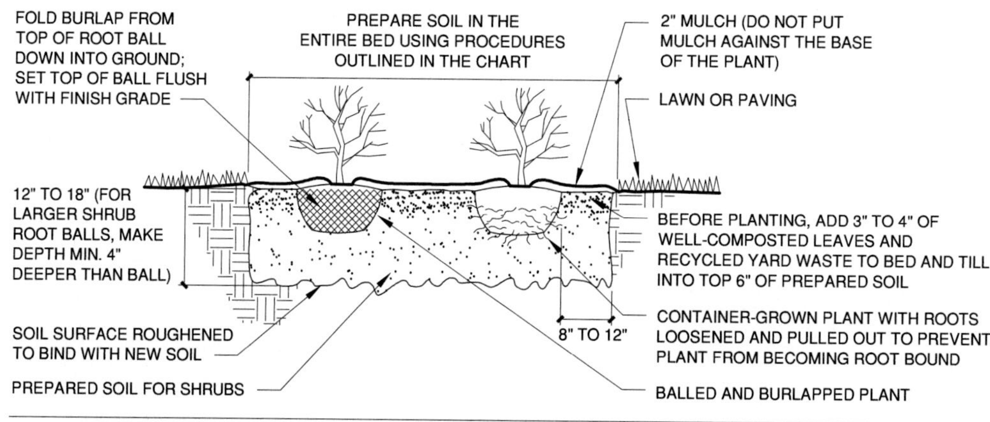

SHRUB PLANTING DETAIL

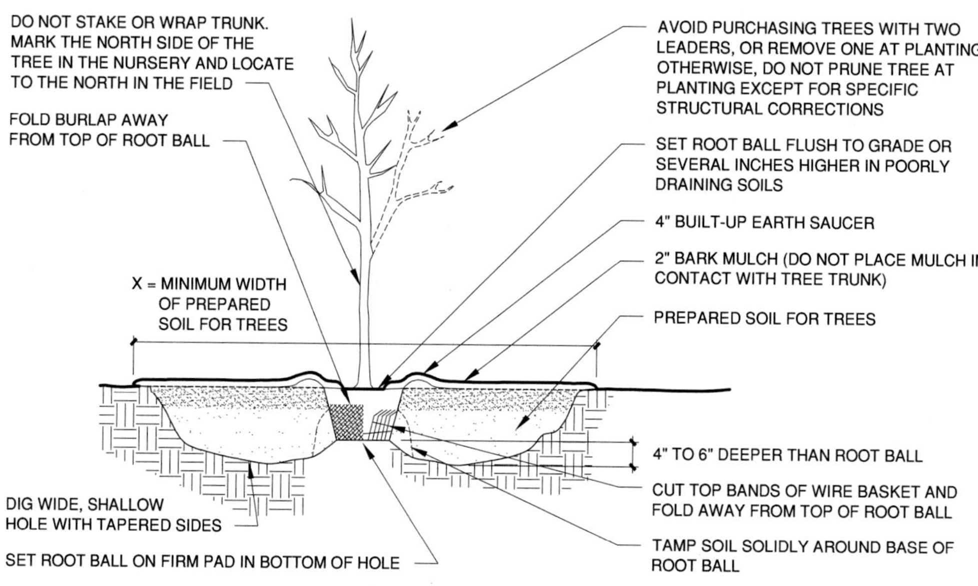

TREE PLANTING DETAIL (BALLED AND BURLAPPED PLANTS)

Trunk Area

The trunk area of the plant involves staking, wrapping, and protection from mechanical damage.

Staking

As a general rule plants do not require staking, assuming that the root ball is intact or the container plant ball is reasonably solid. It is advisable to stake bare root material, and it may be necessary to stake other plants in high prevailing wind situations, to keep them upright. The critical issue with staking is attaching the plant to the stake. Wide flexible cloth or elastic trapping is recommended, as it causes less injury and can expand as the plant grows. There are numerous tree-staking bands on the market that are satisfactory for this situation. Rubber hose over wire is not recommended because it tends to be rigid and can girdle the tree. It is necessary to place the strapping material loosely around the trunk and to attach it to the stake so that there is some play. Plants need to be able to move about somewhat—they should not be rigid. All stakes are to be removed at the end of one year. Anything left past this time will potentially harm the plant. For safety's sake, all guy wires are to be identified with orange or red flagging.

Staking and Guying

Staking is required only when a plant is unable to support itself with its existing root system. Examples of this are: bare rooted plants, a strong wind situation, loose soil, wet conditions, and very large size.

Tree ties are to be of soft, wide (minimum, 1 inch) polymer material. A wide variety of polymer type ties and support devices are commercially available. Allow modest movement of the stem of the tree—do not place ties in tension. Ties are to be removed after one year to prevent plant damage. Large trees may require a two-year staking time.

Stake types for anchoring may be:

- "T-bar" iron stake
- 1-inch galvanized pipe
- Hardwood stake
  - 2" × 2" × 24"
  - 2" × 2" × 8' 0"
- Steel stake—fence
  - Post
- Reinforcing steel
  - #4 or #6
- Painted metal
  - Channel
- Lodge pole (wood—natural)

Tree Wrap

Tree wrap has been proven to be of no or minimal benefit to plant survival or health, and it can potentially harm the trunk. If concern for sun scald is an issue, fiberglass screen can be placed loosely around the trunk, but must be removed after one growing season.

Protection from Mechanical Damage

Flexible PVC pipe is not recommended as a protection device as it can be damaging to the bark of the plant. While it acts as a protector from mechanical damage such as mowers and weed eaters, the planting situation should not be such as to require protection (see mulching recommendations).

One Vertical/Angular Stake

- For trees up to 1-inch caliper. Stake type and tie as shown in the figure "One Vertical Stake."
- Insert 2 feet 6 inches into undisturbed soil.
- Do not penetrate root ball.

Two Angular/Vertical Stakes

- For trees between 1- and 3-inch caliper.
- Stake type and ties as shown in the figures "Two Vertical Stakes" and "Two Angular Stakes.'
- Locate one stake on side of prevailing wind; set second stake 180° from first stake.
- Do not penetrate root ball.
- Insert securely (2 feet) into undisturbed soil.

Three Guy Wire Staking System

- For trees between 3 and 5-inch caliper.
- Stake type and ties, as shown in the figure "Three Guy Wire Staking System."
- Use two twisted #12 galvanized wires for each guy.

Thomas J. Nieman, Ph.D., Department of Landscape Architecture University of Kentucky

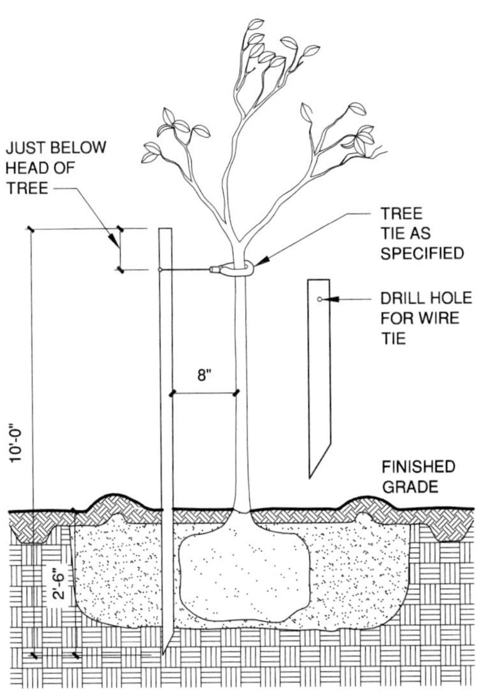

ELEVATION

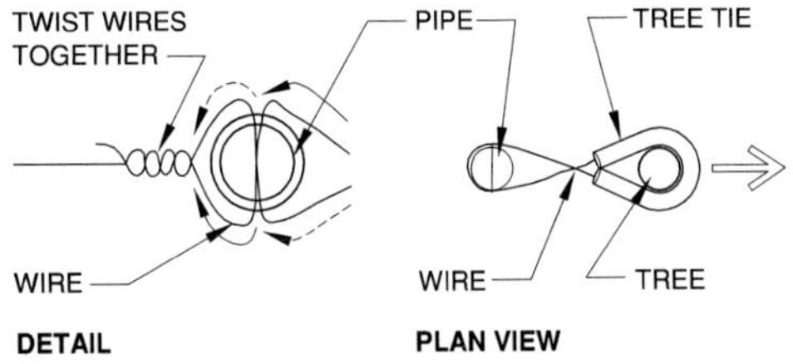

DETAIL

PLAN VIEW

ONE VERTICAL STAKE

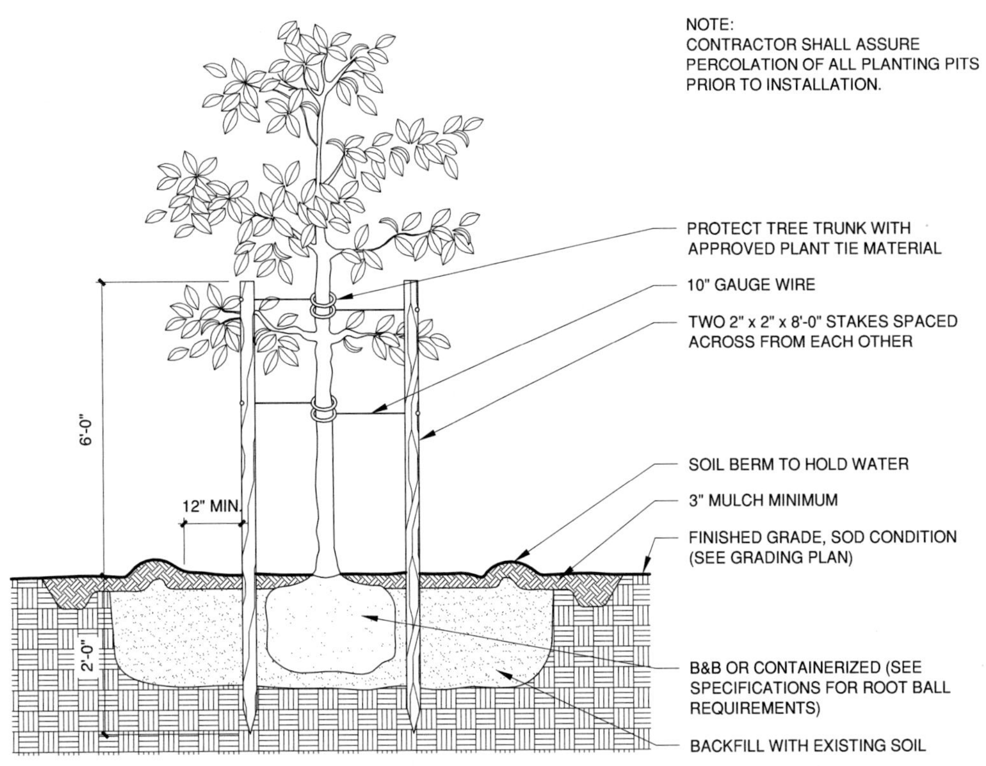

TWO VERTICAL STAKES

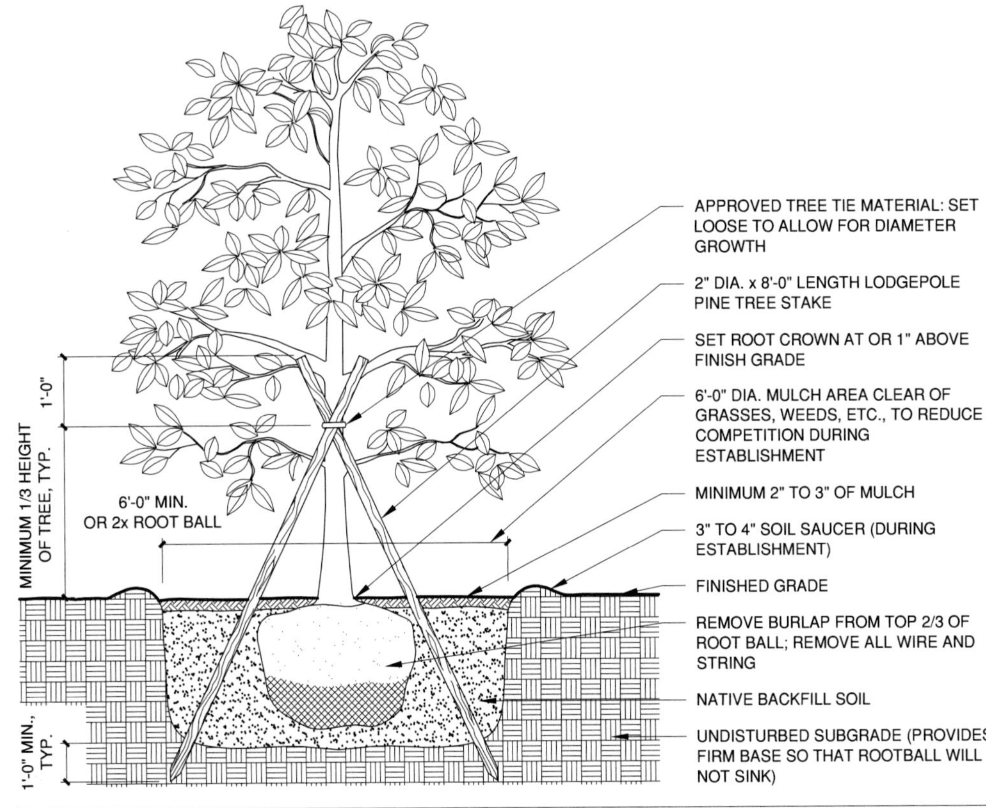

TWO ANGULAR STAKES

- Ensure a 60° angle on guy wires.
- Place stakes securely into undisturbed soil.
- Mark guys with high-visibility flagging.
- Place stakes 120° apart.

Three Guy Wire Staking System for Larger Trees

- For trees larger than 5-inch caliper.
- Use ⅟₁₆-inch galvanized cable for guying.
- Use large stakes, or "deadman," for anchors, placed securely in undisturbed soil at 60° angles on guy wires.
- Mark guys with high-visibility flagging.

Other Suitable Anchors

- In lieu of stakes, several anchors are commercially available, such as: "Arborbrace" tree anchors, "Duckbill" anchors, and "Tree Staples."
- Judge these devices on a case-by-case basis for suitability; generally, they are considered to be satisfactory.

Trunk Protector

- Tree wrap such as kraft paper, burlap, and the like is not recommended under any circumstances.
- For situations where "sun scald" or animal damage may be a problem, fiberglass screening, placed loosely around the trunk, may be used.

Branches

This area of the plant is the most visible aspect. The main issue is plant form and damage.

Thomas J. Nieman, Ph.D., Department of Landscape Architecture University of Kentucky

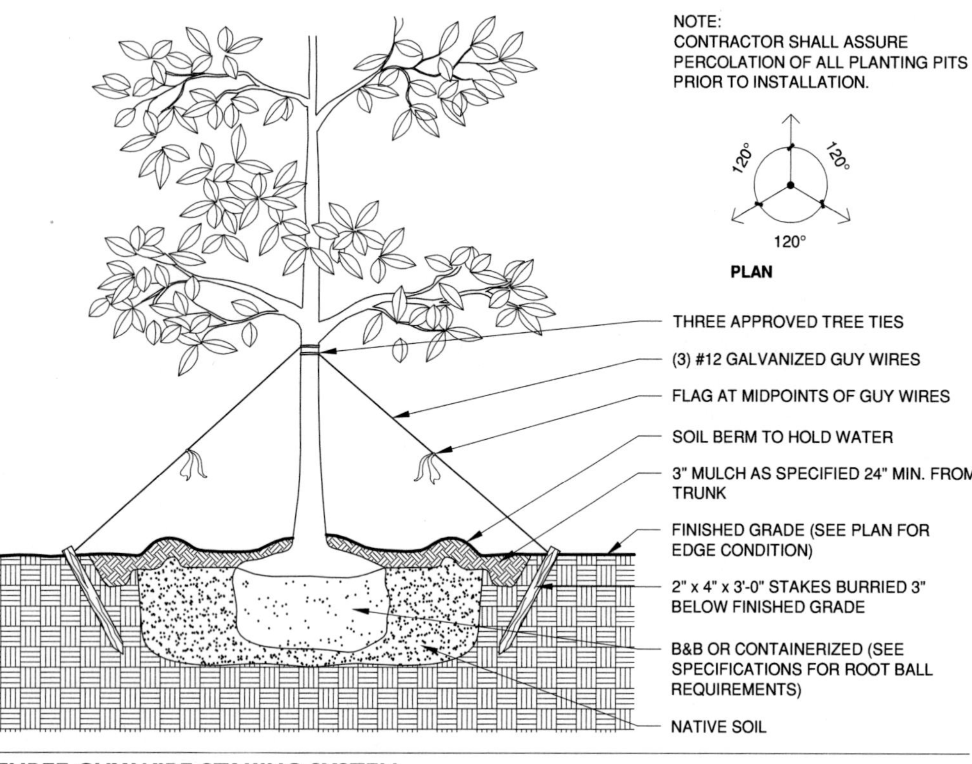

THREE GUY WIRE STAKING SYSTEM

Plant Form

Plant material is to be specified to have the appropriate form. By specifying that all plant materials are to conform to the American Standards for Nursery Stock (ANLA) ANSI 260.1 (2004), notes on details relative to pruning for form are not necessary—there should be no pruning required.

These standards establish common techniques for:

- Measuring plants.
- Specifying and stating the size of plants.
- Determining the proper relationship between height and caliper, or height and width.
- Determining whether a root ball or container is large enough for a particular size plant.

Their purpose is to provide "buyers and sellers of nursery stock with a common terminology in order to facilitate transactions involving nursery stock." The standards document can be downloaded free of charge from www.anla.org/applications/Documents/Docs. It is recommended that everyone involved in using nursery stock, in whatever situation, download and use this document.

Plant Damage

Because of moving and planting, branches do get damaged. Damaged branches are to be pruned in the appropriate manner, conforming to ANLA ANSI 260.1 standards, as mentioned above. If plants conform to these standards, there will be no dead or diseased branches.

TREE SPADES

Transplanting plants with a tree spade is a commonly used approach to moving large plants. Planting requirement are similar to those of balled and burlapped material except for backfilling. Since the tree-spaded hole will be the same size as the plant plug placed in the hole, there is no room for backfill.

Some criteria to consider when using tree-spaded material are:

- Contact local utility companies to locate any underground lines in the area. This is the law in most communities, and the liability for noncompliance is very high. Also note whether there are any overhead utilities that might interfere with the tree-moving equipment.
- Since soil will not be replaced between the plant plug and the edge of the tree pit, it is important to assess the soil situation prior to planting.
  - If soil is poor or wet, hold plant up several inches to aid drainage.
  - After the plant is installed, loosen soil to a depth of 12 to 18 inches around the plant plug to encourage root development.
  - Do not move plants on hot and/or windy days.
  - Spray foliage with antitranspirant prior to transplanting to reduce moisture loss.
  - If plant pit sides are glazed, roughen them before the plant is set in the pit.
  - Water the plant well after planting to eliminate air pockets between the plant plug and the surrounding soil.
- Since the plants moved are often quite large, staking may be required.
- Mark best side of plant prior to digging so desired side is facing the proper direction upon installation.

REFERENCES

American National Standards Institute. 2004. "American Standard for Nursery Stock" ANSI 260.1.

Craul, Philip, J. 1999. *Urban Soils: Applications and Practices*. New York: John Wiley & Sons, Inc.

See also:

Special Construction
Soils: Agronomic

Thomas J. Nieman, Ph.D., Department of Landscape Architecture University of Kentucky

TREE PLANTING IN URBAN AREAS

GENERAL

Areas of dense urban development leave little room for tree roots to develop. Large areas of pavement, competition with foundations and utilities for space below ground, and extensive soil compaction and disruption limit the amount of soil available for trees. When the area of ground around the tree open to the rain and sun is less than 400 to 500 square feet per tree, the following design guidelines should be followed to encourage the growth of large, healthy trees.

Five major parts of the tree structure must be accommodated in the design process:

Crown growth: The tree crown expands every growing season at a rate of 6 to 8 inches per year. Once the crown reaches a competing object, such as a building or another tree canopy, the canopy growth in that area slows and then stops. Eventually the branches on that side of the tree die. As the canopy expansion potential is reduced, the overall growth rate and tree health are also reduced.

Trunk growth: The tree trunk expands about ½ to 1 inch per year. As the tree increases in size, the lower branches die and the trunk lengthens. Tree trunks move considerably in the wind, especially during the early years of development, and are damaged by close objects.

Trunk flare: At the point where the trunk leaves the ground, most tree species develop a pronounced swelling or flare as the tree matures. This flare grows at more than twice the rate of the main trunk diameter and helps the tree remain structurally stable. Any hard object placed in this area, such as a tree grate or confining pavement, will either damage the tree or be moved by the tremendous force of this growth.

Zone of rapid root taper: Tree roots begin to form in the trunk flare and divide several times in the immediate area around the trunk. In this area, about 5 to 6 feet away from the trunk, the roots rapidly taper from about 6 inches in diameter to about 2 inches. Most damage to adjacent paving occurs in this area immediately around the tree. Keeping the zone of rapid taper free of obstructions is important to long-term tree health. Once a tree is established, the zone of rapid taper is generally less susceptible to compaction damage than the rest of the root zone.

Root zone: Tree roots grow radially and horizontally from the trunk and occupy only the upper layers (12 to 24 inches) of the soil. Trees in all but the most well-drained soils do not have taproots. A relationship exists between the amount of tree canopy and the volume of root-supporting soil required (see the accompanying chart). This relationship is the most critical factor in determining long-term tree health. Root-supporting soil is generally defined as soil with adequate drainage, low compaction, and sufficient organic and nutrient components to support the tree. The root zone must be protected from compaction both during and after construction. Root zones that are connected from tree to tree generally produce healthier trees than isolated root zones.

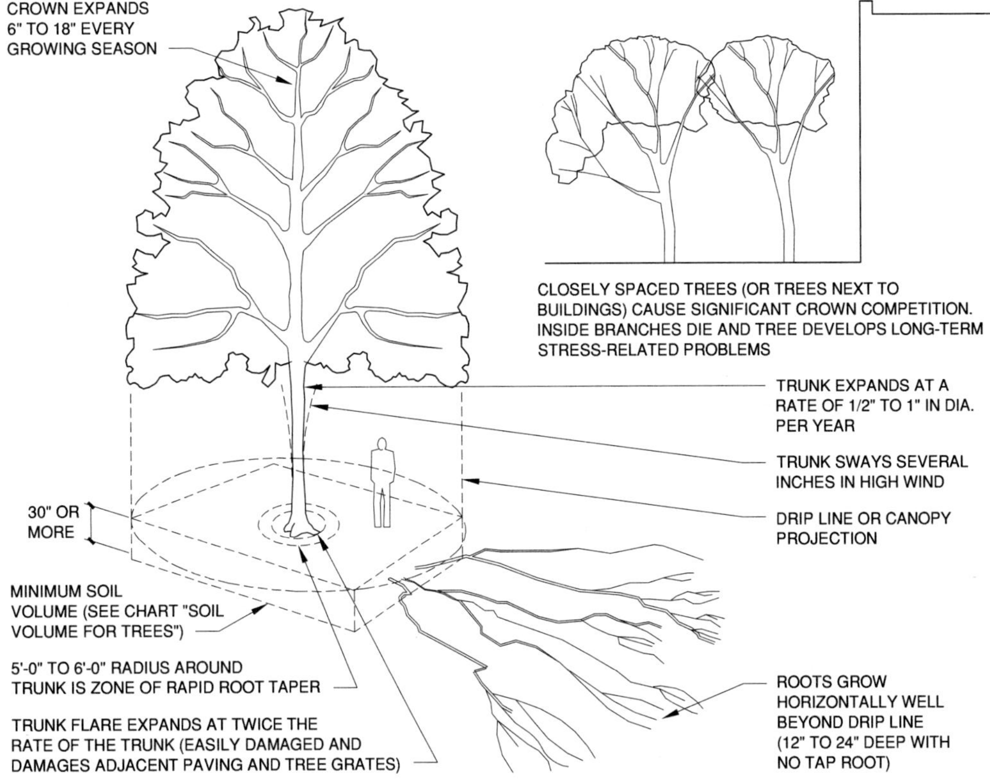

TREE STRUCTURE—PARTS AND GROWING CHARACTERISTICS

SOIL MODIFICATIONS

Thoroughly till organic matter into the top 6 to 12 inches of most planting soils to improve the soil's ability to retain water and nutrients. (Do not add organic matter to soil more than 12 inches deep.) Use composted bark, recycled yard waste, peat moss, or municipal processed sewage sludge. All products should be composted to a dark color and be free of pieces with identifiable leaf or wood structure. Recycled material should be tested for pH and certified free of toxic material by the supplier. Avoid material with a pH higher than 7.5.

Modify heavy clay or silt soils (more than 40 percent clay or silt) by adding composted pine bark (up to 30

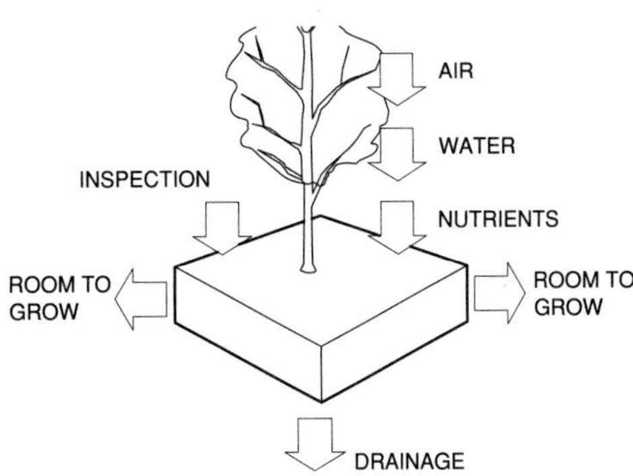

Soil volume provided for trees in urban areas must be sufficient for long-term maintenance.

SOIL VOLUME—REQUIREMENTS FOR TREES

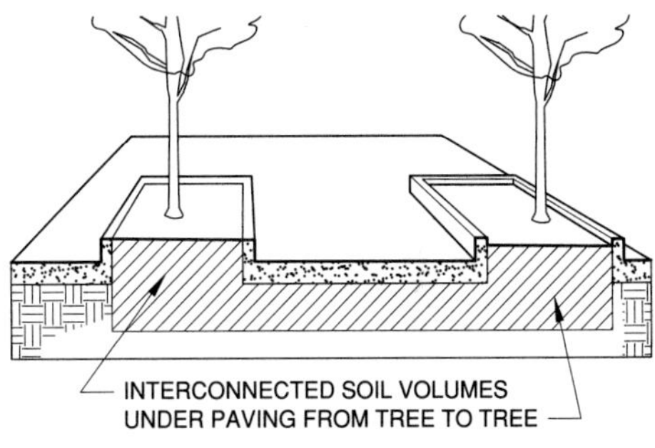

The interconnection of soil volumes from tree to tree has been observed to improve the health and vigor of trees.

SOIL VOLUME—INTERCONNECTION

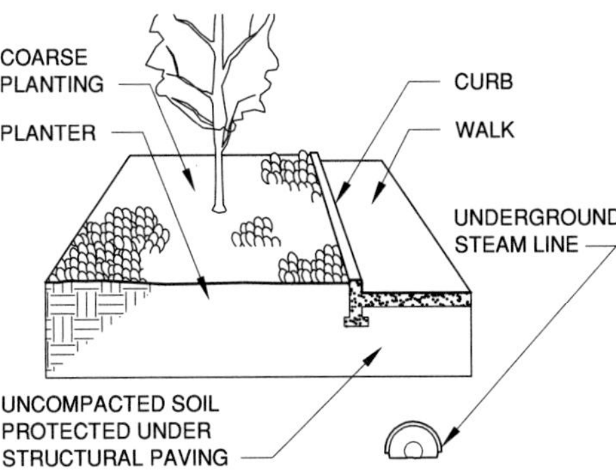

Coarse plantings keep pedestrians out of planters. Curbs protect planters from pedestrians and deicing salts. Underground steam lines must be insulated or vented to protect planter soil.

SOIL PROTECTION FROM COMPACTION AND DEGRADATION

James Urban, ASLA; James Urban Landscape Architecture, Annapolis, Maryland

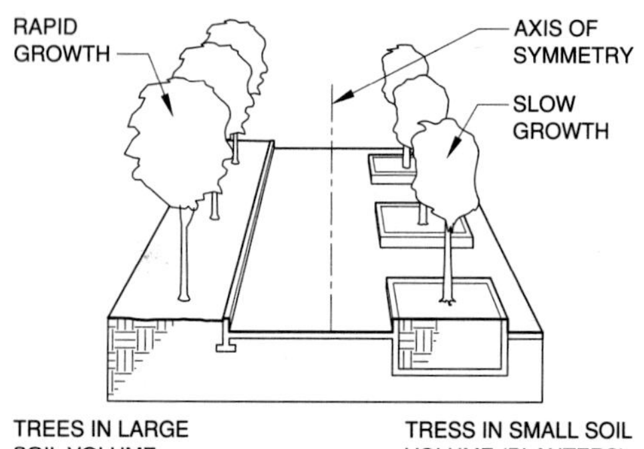

If visually symmetrical tree planting is required, symmetrical soil volumes are also required to produce trees of similar crown size.

VISUALLY SYMMETRICAL TREES

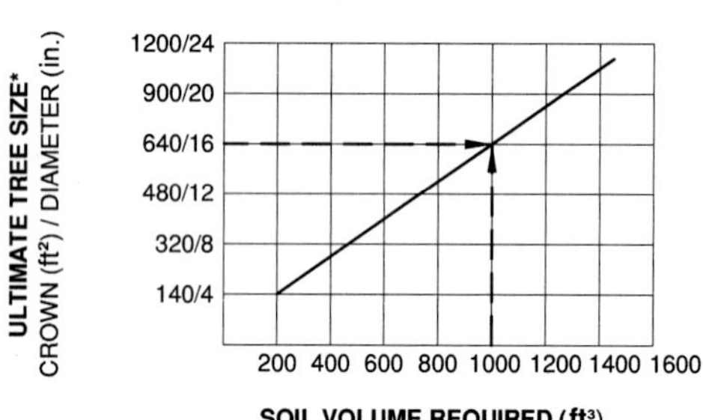

* THE ULTIMATE TREE SIZE IS DEFINED BY THE PROJECTED SIZE OF THE CROWN AND THE DIAMETER OF THE TREE AT BREAST HEIGHT

*The ultimate tree size is defined by the projected size of the crown and the diameter of the tree at breast height.
NOTE
For example, a 16-inch diameter tree requires 1000 cubic feet of soil.

SOIL VOLUME FOR TREES

percent by volume) and/or gypsum. Coarse sand may be used if enough is added to bring the sand content to more than 60 percent of the total mix. Improve drainage in heavy soils by planting on raised mounds or beds and including subsurface drainage lines.

Modify extremely sandy soils (more than 85 percent sand) by adding organic matter and/or dry, shredded clay loam up to 30 percent of the total mix.

GENERAL

Traditional urban designs in which trees are regularly spaced in small openings within paved areas generally result in poor tree performance. This is because such designs generally do not provide adequate soil for root growth and ignore the fact that trees must significantly increase trunk size every year. As well, competition for space, both at ground level and below, is intense in urban areas.

Although it is possible to design uncompacted soil volumes for trees under pavement, this is very expensive, and the soil is never as efficient as that in open planting beds. Increasing trunk size can only be accommodated by using flexible materials that can change configuration over time. Urban designs that have flexible relationships between trees, paving, and planting beds and large areas of open planting soil offer the best opportunity for long-term tree health and lower maintenance costs.

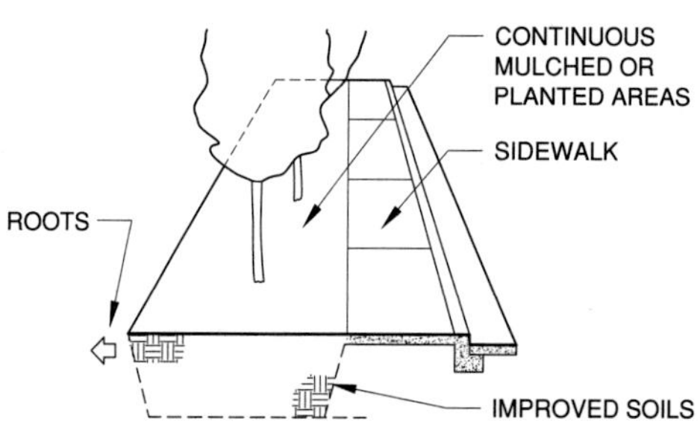

NOTE
Best design option: Planting trees between sidewalks and buildings creates the fewest conflicts between roots and paving by permitting rooting activity on adjacent property.

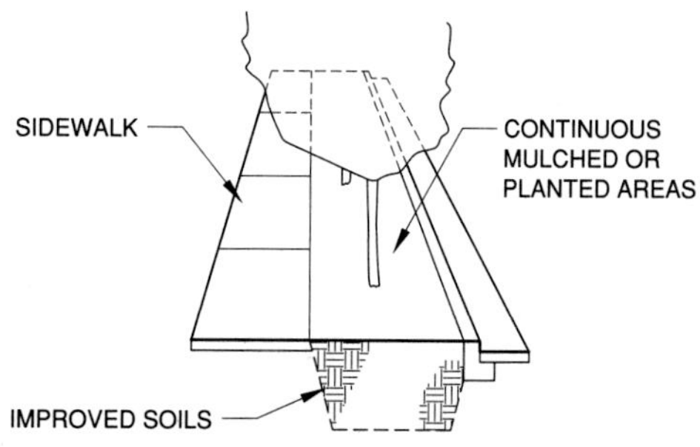

NOTE
Acceptable design option: Planting between curbs and sidewalks in a continuous unpaved planting bed provided good soil levels for trees but contributes to root/paving conflicts as trees mature.

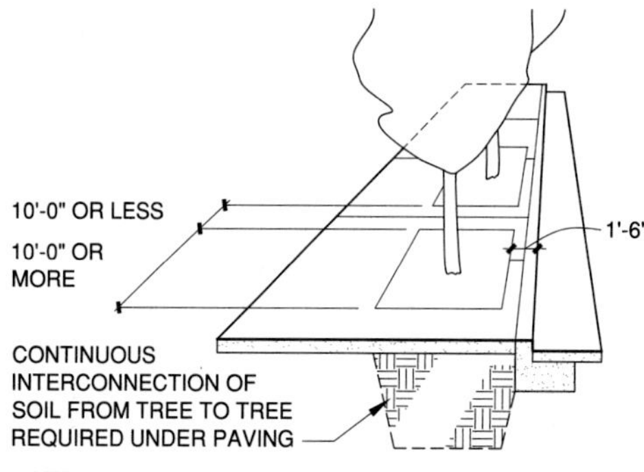

NOTE
Difficult design option: In highly developed areas with parking adjacent to the curb, planting in long narrow tree openings with a 18-inch wide walk along the curb accommodates pedestrians exiting cars. Root/paving conflicts are probable.

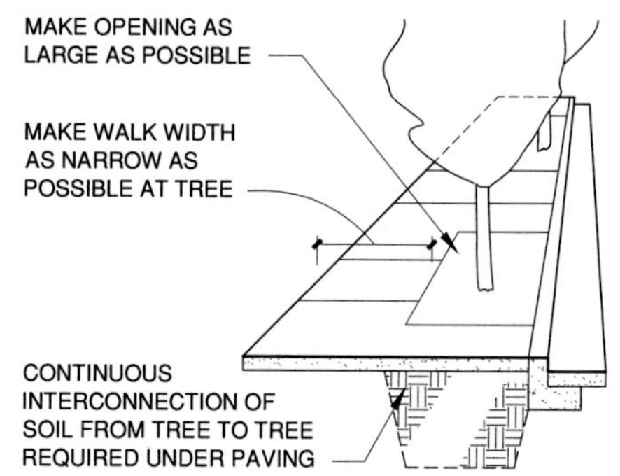

NOTE
Most difficult (and most expensive) design option: Tree openings are undersized for future trunk/root development. Severe root/paving conflicts are very likely.

SIDEWALK PLANTING OPTIONS

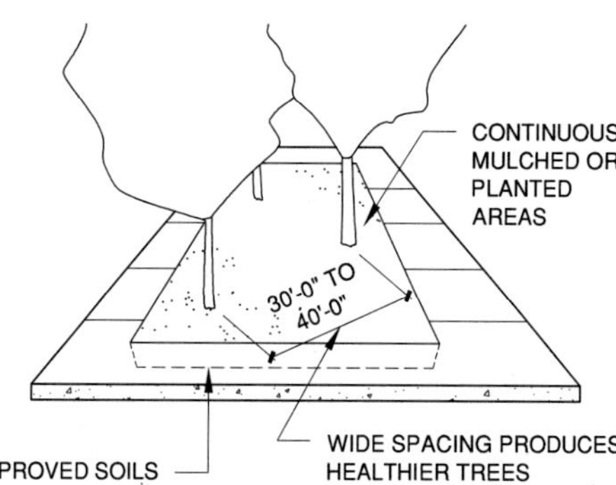

NOTE
Best design option: Separate planting and walking areas. Avoid small, disconnected soil volumes to minimize root/paving conflicts.

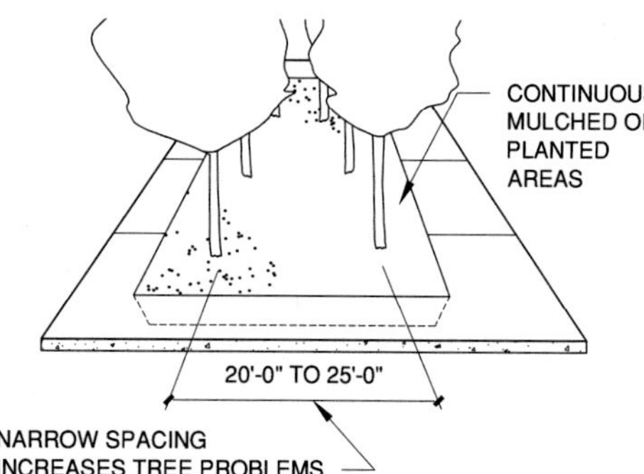

NOTE
Acceptable design option: Each tree has a smaller canopy with less yearly growth. More disease and insect problems are likely. Ground plantings eliminated by shade over time.

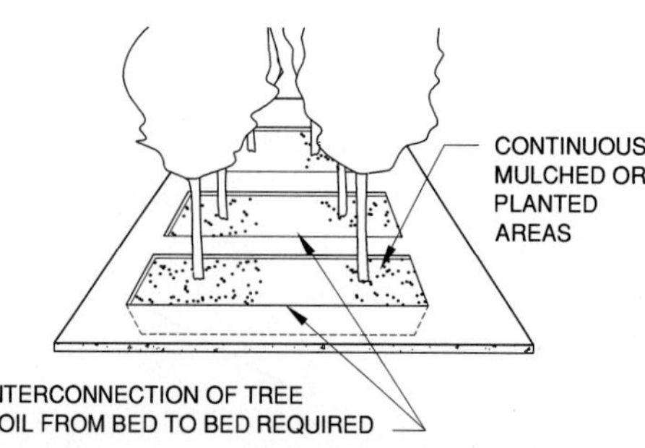

NOTE
Difficult design option: Shading, slow tree growth, and poor health are problems. Root/paving conflicts are likely.

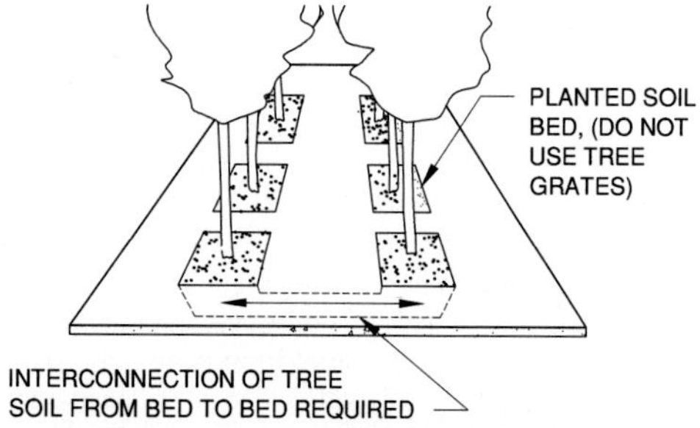

NOTE
Most difficult (and most expensive) design option: Slow tree growth and severe root/paving conflicts are to be expected.

PLAZA TREE PLANTING OPTIONS

James Urban, ASLA; James Urban Landscape Architecture, Annapolis, Maryland

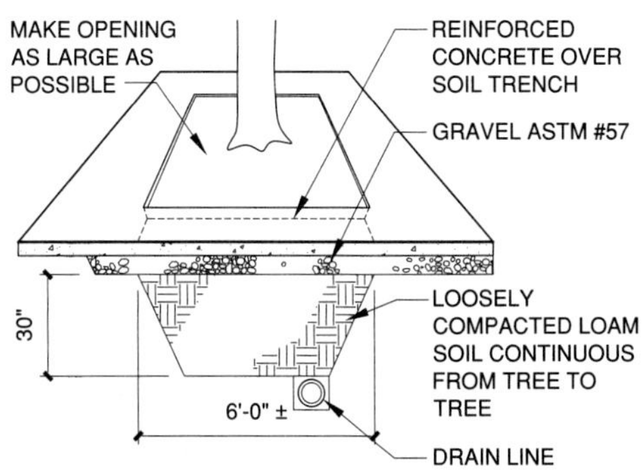

CONTINUOUS SOIL TRENCH

NOTE

A continuous soil trench provides a very good soil but in limited quantity. Use in areas where adjacent backfill is compacted soils or fills.

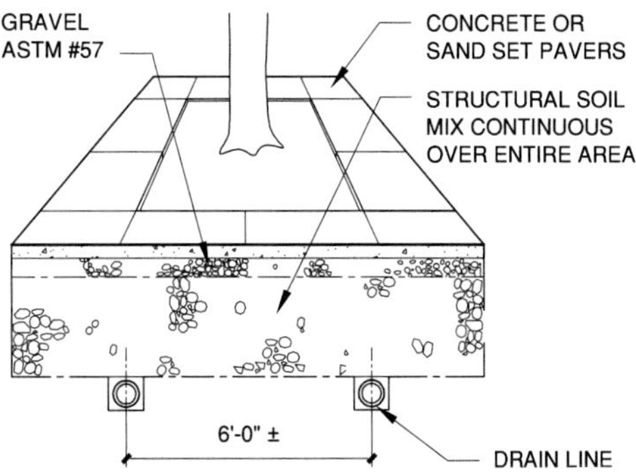

STRUCTURAL SOIL

NOTE

Structural planting soils replace subgrade material with a fill that can be compacted to meet normal engineering compaction requirements and still support root growth below the pavement. The principle is that when the gravel is compacted, the soil is not because the amount of soil in the mix is insufficient to fill all the voids. Hydrogel, a cross-linked potassium copolymer, is used to help bind the mixture during the mixing process. The soil mix includes ASHTO #4 gravel (100 pounds calculated dry weight), shredded clay loam (15 to 18 pounds), hydrogel (0.03 pound), and water (±10 including the water calculated in the gravel and the soil). For further information, contact the Urban Horticulture Institute at Cornell University (Ithaca, New York).

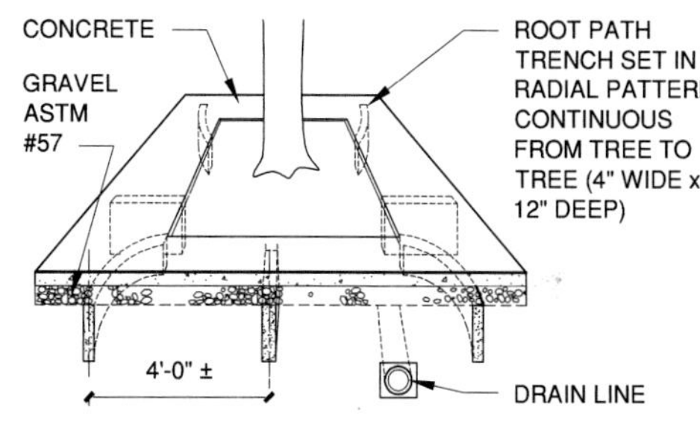

ROOT PATH TRENCH

NOTES

In urban areas where the pavement subgrade is compacted soil that is free from rubble, toxic, or poorly drained fills, a system of root paths can be installed to guide roots under the pavement, where they have room to grow. These roots grow deeper in the soil, causing fewer root/paving conflicts than roots left to exploit the normal minor weaknesses in paving and subgrades.

A root path trench is made by installing a length of strip drain material (a 12-inch wide by 1-inch thick plastic drain core wrapped in filter fabric) in a narrow trench and backfilling with loam topsoil. This allows air and water to flow more freely into the soil under the pavement. Install geotextile fabric and the gravel base material and then the paving.

Root paths cannot replace larger soil trenches or structural planting soil in areas in which existing soil conditions are extremely poor for root exploration.

TREE SOIL INTERCONNECTION OPTIONS UNDER PAVING

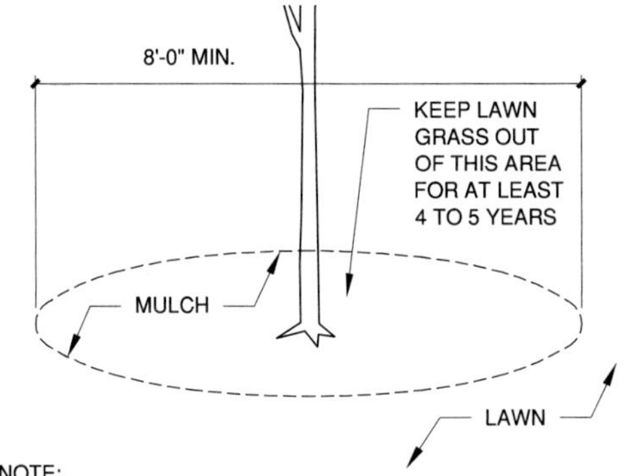

NOTE:
YOUNG TREES PLANTED IN LAWN AREAS FACE SUBSTANTIAL COMPETITION FROM THE ROOTS OF GRASSES.

TREES PLANTED IN LAWNS

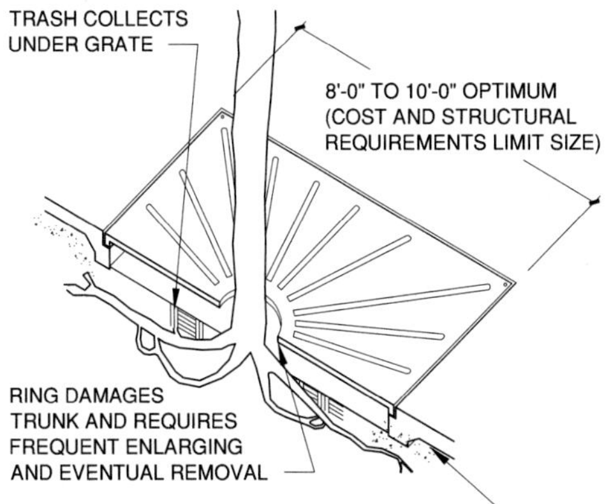

Tree grates decorate the base of a tree but provide no significant benefit. Many aspects of tree grates can damage a tree or reduce its potential for growth.

TREE GRATES

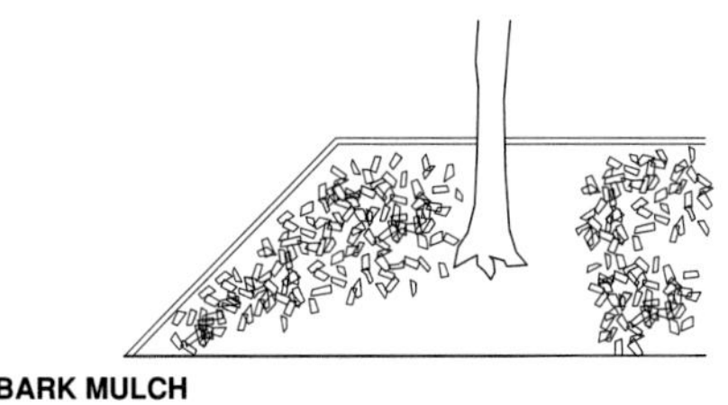

BARK MULCH

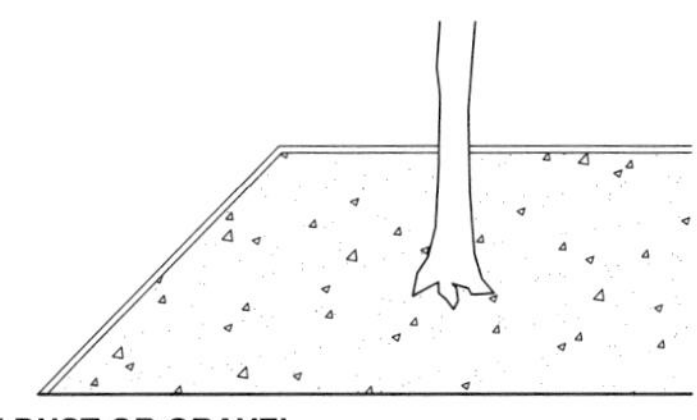

STONE DUST OR GRAVEL

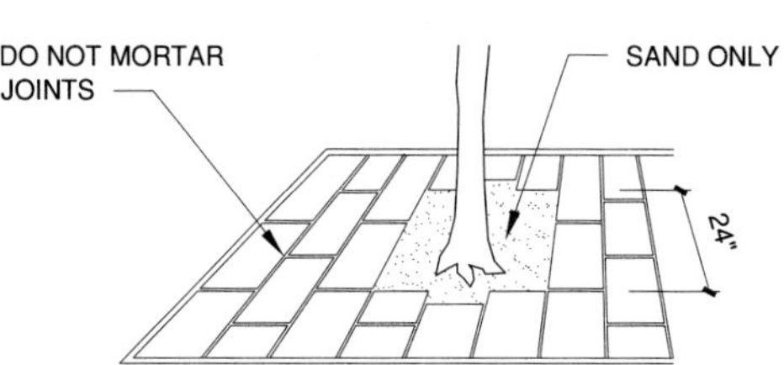

SAND-SET PAVERS

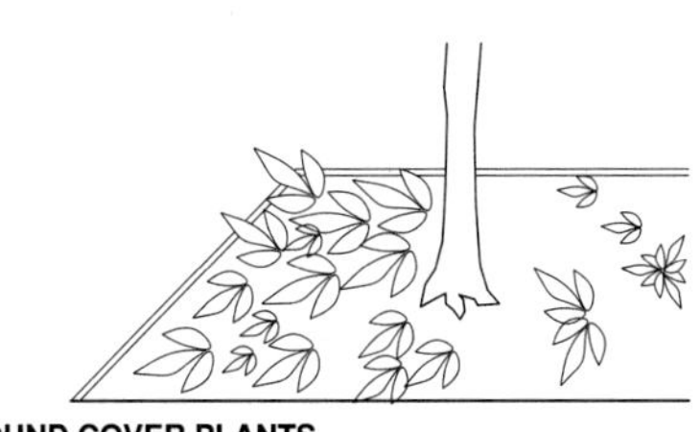

GROUND COVER PLANTS

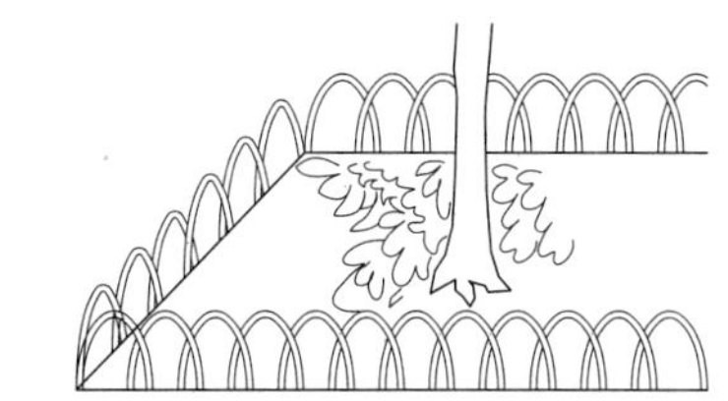

LOW FENCE AND GROUND COVER

Alternatives to tree grates (and guards) include softer, organic coverings that suit the purpose better, are less expensive, and require less maintenance over the life of the tree.

TREE BASE PROTECTION

James Urban, ASLA; James Urban Landscape Architecture, Annapolis, Maryland

PLANTING: SPECIAL CONSIDERATIONS

There are many factors that must be given consideration before selecting plant material for a project or specific site. Although the selection process usually starts with the United States Department of Agriculture's Cold Hardiness Map to determine if a plant is suitable in a particular zone, this is only the beginning. There are many other factors that can be critical to a selected plant's survival in a given location. It is important to analyze the location where the plants are proposed and evaluate which plants best match the conditions of the site (particularly after any development that could affect these factors has taken place).

Conditions that need to be looked at closely include soil factors; microclimate; wet or dry soil conditions; likelihood of salt spray (from sea or road salt); wind; sun/shade exposure; level of maintenance anticipated; and whether or not supplemental irrigation is planned. Each site is unique and more than likely would have additional factors that would need to be considered. All these different factors need to matched with the functional and aesthetic objectives of the planting as well. Although it is not possible to provide an exhaustive list of considerations and plant suggestions for specific situations, the balance of this section provides a sample of some common special conditions and plants appropriate to those conditions.

PLANTING TABLES

Please visit the *Landscape Architectural Graphic Standards Student Edition* companion Web site (www.wiley.com/go/landscapearchitecturalgraphicstandards) to view these additional planting tables:

- Ornamental and Shade Trees Useful for Design Selection
- Large Trees with Round Canopies, Dense Branching, and Coarse-Textured Foliage
- Large Trees with Round Canopies, Open Branching, and Fine-Textured Foliage
- Large Trees with Round Canopies, Open Branching, and Coarse-Textured Foliage
- Large Trees with Oval Canopies, Open Branching, and Fine-Textured Foliage
- Large Trees with Oval Canopies, Dense Branching, and Coarse-Textured Foliage
- Large Trees with Oval Canopies, Open Branching, and Fine-Textured Foliage
- Large Trees with Oval Canopies, Open Branching, and Coarse-Textured Foliage
- Large Trees with Vase-Shaped Canopies and Fine-Textured Foliage
- Large Trees with Columnar Canopies
- Small Trees with Round Canopies
- Small Trees with Vase-Shaped Canopies
- Small Trees with Oval Canopies and Dense Branching
- Large Oval Trees with Heart-Shaped Leaves
- Large Round Trees with Maplelike Leaves
- Large Oval Trees with Maplelike Leaves
- Small Trees with Lobed Leaves
- Selection Factors
- Moisture Needs of Selected Tree Species
- Soil pH Tolerances of Selected Trees and Large Shrubs: Require Acid Soil <7.0
- Soil pH Tolerances of Selected Trees and Large Shrubs: Can Tolerate into the Neutral or Slightly Alkaline Zone <7.5
- Soil pH Tolerances of Selected Trees and Large Shrubs: Can Tolerate Highly Alkaline Soil <8.2
- Plants Observed to Have Some Salt Tolerance
- Plants Sensitive to Salt
- Trees That Tolerate Partial Shade
- Street Trees Appropriate for Use in Structural Soil

Adam Davis, International Society of Arborculture, Certified Arborist

RECOMMENDED ORNAMENTAL AND SHADE TREES FOR USE IN LANDSCAPE DESIGN IN THE CONTINENTAL UNITED STATES

Design objectives, particularly those that involve the desire for visual uniformity, need to be balanced against the need for biological and species diversity. Our experience has shown that disease and pest problems that have devastated certain favorite species make the planting of monocultures undesirable. One solution is an approach that selects species of trees with similar visual characteristics to achieve visual uniformity, yet at the same time provides biological diversity. The accompanying tables contain lists of trees that are visually compatible. These lists provide a starting point for considering visual similarity together with biological diversity.

CHARACTERISTICS OF VISUAL SIMILARITY OF TREES

1	Size: Height to first branch	Large	Greater than 30 feet at 30 years
		Small	Less than 30 feet at 30 years
2	Shape	Round	Width > or = height of canopy
		Oval	Width < height
		Vase	Narrow at the base, becoming distinctly wider at the top
		Columnar	Width distinctly < height
3	Branching Density	Dense	Greater than 30 feet at 30 years
		Open	Less than 30 feet at 30 years
4	Foliage Texture	Coarse	Large leaves (or leaflets) with blunt ends or lobes
		Fine	Smaller leaves (or leaflets) with acute apexes

TREE AND LARGE SHRUB TOLERANCE OF VARYING SOIL MOISTURE, SOIL pH, AND SALT CONDITIONS

The following lists of trees from USDA Hardiness Zone 6 (minimum winter temperature of 0° to –5°F) and colder will help you choose appropriate trees for a variety of urban situations. However, there is no one perfect tree for every situation. The best approach is to select trees to match site conditions based on a thorough site assessment. Diversity is one key to a successful tree-planting program. Overplanting of one species in an area can result in monocultures that encourage the buildup of insect populations and diseases that can destroy the entire planting.

A reasonable strategy for most urban plantings is to limit any one species to 5 percent of a total urban population for small to midsize cities. Consequently, if a disease or insect infestation should occur, 95 percent of the tree population would remain unaffected.

There is no one perfect tree because there is no one homogeneous urban environment or site. The urban environment is a conglomeration of soils, microclimates, and other site conditions. Both aboveground and below-grade conditions can change dramatically in the space of 10 feet. Needless to say, the lists of trees provided serve only as a guide for selection. A comprehensive site assessment should be undertaken to identify plant requirements such as:

- Moisture
  - Tolerates poorly drained or intermittently flooded soils
  - Requires moist but well-drained soils
  - Tolerates moderate drought
  - Tolerates more severe drought

- pH
  - Requires acid soil pH 5.0 to 7.0
  - Can tolerate acid to neutral soil pH 5.0 to 7.5
  - Can tolerate acid to alkaline soil pH 5.0 to 8.2

- Salt Tolerance
  - Tolerates salt
  - Is sensitive to salt

Two Notes of Caution

It is important to note that some trees are adaptable to a fairly wide range of environmental conditions, while others have a narrow range in which they grow well. By presenting the following lists, we are providing information about adaptability. All trees will grow well under near-optimal conditions of a pH of 6.8 and soil consistently moist but well drained. However, we rarely find these conditions in the urban environment. It is our purpose to highlight those trees that tolerate broader, less ideal conditions while still providing the benefits for which we planted them. These more adaptable plants don't *prefer* poorer conditions, but they can still grow adequately in them. This important information is key to making informed plant selections.

Another consideration: Trees become acclimated to less than ideal conditions *after they have become established* in the landscape. Newly transplanted trees are not as acclimated as their established counterparts. It is critical to give newly transplanted trees several years of supplemental watering to hasten their establishment before expecting them to tolerate a wide range of soil moisture conditions.

Nina L Bassuk; Peter J. Trowbridge

NATIVE SPECIES: UPPER MIDWEST

More and more landscape architects, land planners, and private landowners are learning to work with native plants that are naturally adapted to local soils and climates. Once established, native plants result in lower costs, fewer problems, and less care and maintenance. As an example of the diversity and special characteristics that can be obtained through the use of native species, the accompanying tables describe native species that are used in the Wisconsin area.

TREE AND SHRUB SCHEDULE

SCIENTIFIC NAME	COMMON NAME	NOTES	SIZE	INTEREST
TREES				
Quercus macrocarpa	Bur oak	Single stem	50′ × 40′	Wildlife like fruit
Quercus rubra	Red oak	Single stem	50′ × 40′	Wildlife like fruit
Quercus bicolor	Swamp white oak	Single stem	50′ × 40′	Wildlife like fruit
Quercus alba	White oak	Single stem	50′ × 70′	Wildlife like fruit
Celtis occidentalis	Hackberry	Single stem	60′ × 40′	Form
Ornamental Trees				
Carpinus caroliniana	Musclewood	Single or multistem	20′ × 30′	Fall color
Crataegus mollis or punctata	Downy hawthorn	Single or multistem	20′ × 15′	Flower/fall color
Hamamelis virginiana	Common witch hazel	Multistem	10′ × 12′	Fall color
Ostrya virginiana	Ironwood	Single or multistem	20′ × 30?′	Form
Rhus typhina	Staghorn sumac	Multistem	15′ × 12′	Red fall color
Malus ioensis	Prairie crabapple	Single stem	25′ × 15′	Pink flower
SHRUBS				
Aronia melanocarpa	Black chokeberry		4′–5′	Bird food source
Ceanothus americanus	New Jersey tea		24′–36′	White flower
Cornus alternifolia	Pagoda dogwood		10′–15′	White flower
Corylus americana	American hazelnut		4′–5′	Yellow fall
Hypericum kalmianum	Kalm's St. John's wort		24′–36′	Yellow flower June–Aug
Rosa carolina	Pasture rose		24′–36′	Pink flower
Symphoricarpos albus	Snowberry		24′–36′	White berries Aug–Dec
Viburnum lentago	Nannyberry		14′ × 8′–12′	White flower May

Source: Native Species List, by Joshua Lippold, ASLA, Applied Ecological Services, Inc., Brodhead, Wisconsin.

DRY PRAIRIE SPECIES

SCIENTIFIC NAME	COMMON NAME	HEIGHT	FLOWER COLOR	BLOOM TIME
GRASSES/EDGES				
Avena sativa	Oats	2′–3′	Brown	May–July
Bouteloua curtipendula	Side-oats gramma	2′–3′	Orange/brown	June–Aug
Carex gravida	Long-awned bracted sedge	2′–3′	Green	May–July
Elymus canadensis	Canada wild rye	2′–4′	Gold	May–July
Schizachyrium scoparium	Little blue stem	1′–3′	Green/purple	July–Oct
FORBS				
Anemone cylindrica	Thimbleweed	2′–3′	White	June–Aug
Amorpha canescens	Lead plant	1′–3′	Dusty purple	June–Aug
Asclepias tuberosa	Butterfly milkweed	1′–3′	Orange	July–Sept
Aster azureus	Sky blue aster	6″–24″	Blue	Aug–Oct
Aster ericoides	Heath aster	1′–3′	White	Aug–Oct
Coreopsis palmata	Prairie coreopsis	1′–3′	Yellow	June–Aug
Dalea candida	White prairie clover	1′–2′	White	June–July
Dalea purpurea	Purple prairie clover	1′–2′	Purple	June–Aug
Echinacea pallida	Pale purple coneflower	2′–4′	Pink/purple	June–July
Echinacea purpurea	Purple coneflower	2′–3′	Purple	June–Oct
Eryngium yuccifolium	Fattlesnake master	1′–4′	Green	July–Aug
Euphorbia corollata	Flowering spurge	1′–3′	White	June–Sept
Lespedeza capitata	Round-headed bush clover	2′–4′	White	Aug–Sept
Liatris aspera	Rough blazing star	2′–3′	Purple/pink	Aug–Oct
Lupinus perennis	Wild lupine	1′–2′	Blue	May–June
Monarda fistulosa	Wild bergamot	2′–4′	Lavender/pink	July–Aug
Parthenium integrifolium	Wild quinine	2′–3′	White	June–Sept
Penstemon digitalis	Beard tongue	1′–4′	White	May–July
Ratibida pinnata	Yellow coneflower	1′–4′	Yellow & brown	June–Aug
Rudbeckia hirta	Black-eyed Susan	1′–3′	Yellow & brown	June–Aug
Rudbeckia triloba	Brown-eyed Susan	1′–4′	Yellow & brown	July–Oct
Solidago rigida	Stiff goldenrod	1′–4′	Yellow	July–Oct
Solidago nemoralis	Old-field goldenrod	6″–20″	Yellow	Aug–Oct
Tradescantia ohiensis	Spiderwort	1′–4′	Blue	Apr–July
Verbena stricta	Hoary vervain	1′–2′	Blue/purple	July–Sept
Zizia aptera	Heart-leaved golden Alexander	1′–2′	Yellow	May–June

Source: Native Species List, by Joshua Lippold, ASLA, Applied Ecological Services, Inc., Brodhead, Wisconsin.

MESIC PRAIRIE SPECIES

SCIENTIFIC NAME	COMMON NAME	HEIGHT	FLOWER COLOR	BLOOM TIME
GRASSES/SEDGES				
Andropogon gerardil	Big blue stem	4′–7′	Purple & green	Aug–Nov
Bouteloua curtipendula	Side oats grama	1′–3′	Purple & gold	Aug–Oct
Carex bicknellii	Prairie sedge	2′–3′	Green	June–Aug
Koeleria cristata	June grass	1′–2′	Gold	June–July
Schizachyrium scoparium	Little blue stem	1′–4′	Green/purple	July–Oct
Sporobolus heterolepis	Prairie drop seed	2′–4′	Gold	Sept–Nov
FORBS				
Asclepias tuberosa	Butterfly milkweed	1′–3′	Orange	July–Sept
Aster azureus	Sky blue aster	6″–24″	Azure	Aug–Oct
Aster sericeus	Silky aster	1′–2?	Lavender	Aug–Oct
Coreopsis palmata	Prairie coreopsis	1′–3′	Yellow	June–Aug
Dodecatheon meadia	Shooting star	8″–24″	Pink & white	Apr–June
Echinacea pallida	Pale purple coneflower	2′–4′	Pink/purple	June–July
Eryngium yuccifolium	Rattlesnake master	1′–4′	Green	July–Aug
Geum triflorum	Prairie smoke	6″–12″	Burgundy/pink	Apr–June
Heuchra Richardsonii	Alum root	2′–3′	White	May–July
Liatris aspera	Rough blazing star	2′–3′	Purple/pink	Aug–Oct
Lupinus perennis	Wild lupine	1′–2′	Blue	May–June
Monarda fistulosa	Wild bergamot	2′–4′	Lavender/pink	July–Aug
Penstemon digitalis	Beard tongue	1′–4′	White	May–July
Phlox pilosa	Prairie phlox	6″–18″	Pink	Apr–June
Ratibida pinnata	Yellow coneflower	1′–4′	Yellow & brown	June–Aug
Rudbeckia subtomentosa	Sweet black-eyed Susan	2′–4′	Yellow & brown	July–Oct
Sisyrinchium campestre	Prairie blue-eyed grass	4″–12″	Blue	May–July
Solidago nemoralis	Old-field goldenrod	6″–20″	Yellow	Aug–Oct
Tradescantia ohiensis	Spiderwort	1′–4′	Blue	Apr–July
Zizia aurea	Golden Alexander	1′–2′	Yellow	May–June

Source: Native Species List, by Joshua Lippold, ASLA, Applied Ecological Services, Inc., Brodhead, Wisconsin.

WET PRAIRIE SPECIES

SCIENTIFIC NAME	COMMON NAME	HEIGHT	FLOWER COLOR	BLOOM TIME
GRASSES/SEDGES				
Carex vulpinoidea	Fox sedge	1′–3′	Green	June–Aug
Juncus torreyii	Torrey's rush	6″–24″	Green	June–July
Scirpus americanus	Chairmaker's rush	1′–4′	Green	June–Sept
FORBS				
Alisma plantago-aquatica	Water plantain	1′–2′	White	June–Sept
Aster novae-angliae	New England aster	1′–4′	Purple & orange	Aug–Oct
Eupatorium perfoliatum	Boneset	2′–4′	White	July–Oct
Iris virginica-shrevei	Wild blue flag iris	1′–3′	Blue & yellow	May–July
Liatris pycnostachya	Prairie blazing star	2′–4′	Purple	July–Sept
Lobelia cardinalis	Cardinal flower	2′–4′	Scarlet	July–Sept
Lythrum alatum	Winged loosestrife	1′–2′	Purple/pink	June-Sept
Phlox glabberima	Marsh phlox	2′–4′	Pink	May–June
Physostegia virginiana	False Oragon's head, Obediant plant	2′–4′	Pink/lavender	June–Sept
Rudbeckia subtomentosa	Sweet black-eyed Susan	2′–4′	Yellow & brown	July–Oct
Solidago Riddellii	Riddell's goldenrod	1′–3′	Yellow	Aug–Oct
Zizia aurea	Golden Alexander	1′–2′	Yellow	May–June

Source: Native Species List, by Joshua Lippold, ASLA, Applied Ecological Services, Inc., Brodhead, Wisconsin.

SAVANNA SPECIES

SCIENTIFIC NAME	COMMON NAME	HEIGHT	FLOWER COLOR	BLOOM TIME
GRASSES/SEDGES				
Elymus hystrix	Bottlebrush grass	2′–3′	Green	June–July
Elymus canadensis	Canada wild rye	2′–4′	Gold	May–July
Schizachyrium scoparium	Little blue stem	1′–4′	Green/purple	July–Oct
Sporobolus heterolepis	Prairie drop seed	2′–4′	Gold	Sept–Nov
FORBS				
Anemone virginiana	Tall thimbleweed	2′–3′	White	June–Aug
Aquilegia canadensis	Wild columbine	1′–3′	Red & yellow	May–June
Aster sagittifolius	Arrow-leaved aster	2′–5′	Blue	Aug–Oct
Aster shortii	Short's aster	2′–4′	Blue	Aug–Oct
Baptisia leucantha	White wild indigo	3′–4′	White	June–July
Campanula americana	Tall bellflower	2′–6′	Blue	July–Oct
Dodecatheon meadia	Shooting star	8″–24″	Pink & white	Apr–June
Geranium maculatum	Wild geranium	1′–2′	Lavender	Apr–July
Helianthus divaricatus	Woodland sunflower	2′–6′	Yellow	July–Oct
Monarda fistulosa	Wild bergamot	2′–4′	Lavender/pink	July–Aug
Polemonium reptans	Jacob?s ladder	6″-12″	Blue	Apr–June
Ratibida pinnata	Yellow coneflower	1′–4′	Yellow & brown	June–Aug
Rudbeckia triloba	Brown-eyed Susan	1′–4′	Yellow & brown	July–Oct
Solidago ulmifolia	Elm-leaved goldenrod	2′–4′	Yellow	July–Oct

Source: Native Species List, by Joshua Lippold, ASLA, Applied Ecological Services, Inc., Brodhead, Wisconsin.

WOODLAND SPECIES

SCIENTIFIC NAME	COMMON NAME	HEIGHT	FLOWER COLOR	BLOOM TIME
GRASSES/SEDGES				
Carex pensylvanica	Pensylvania sedge	3″–14″	Green	Apr–May
Elymus hystrix	Bottlebrush grass	2′–3′	Green	June–July
Elymus canadensis	Canada wild rye	2′–4′	Gold	May–July
FORBS				
Allium cernuum	Wild onion	1′–2′	Pink/white	July–Aug
Anemone virginiana	Tall thimbleweed	2′–3′	White	June–Aug
Aquilegia canadensis	Wild columbine	1′–3′	Red & yellow	May–June
Asarum canadense	Wild ginger	6″–12″	Red	Apr–May
Aster sagittifolius	Arrow-leaved aster	2′–5′	Blue	Aug–Oct
Aster shorti	Short's aster	2′–4′	Blue	Aug–Oct
Campanula americana	Tall bellflower	2′–6′	Blue	July–Oct
Dodecatheon meadia	Shooting star	8″–24″	Pink & white	Apr–June
Geranium maculatum	Wild geranium	1′–2′	Lavender	Apr–July
Heiianthus divaricatus	Woodland sunflower	2′–6′	Yellow	July–Oct
Mertensia virginica	Virginia bluebells	1′–2′	Pink/blue	March–May
Phlox divaricata	Blue phlox	6″–12″	Blue	Apr–June
Polemonium reptans	Jacob's ladder	6″–12″	Blue	Apr–June
Polygonatum canaliculatum	Great Solomon's seal	2′–5′	White	May–June
Rudbeckia triloba	Brown-eyed Susan	1′–4′	Yellow & brown	July–Oct
Smilacina racemosa	Feathery false Solomon's seal	1′–3′	White/green	May–July
Solidago flexicaulis	Zig-zag goldenrod	1′–3′	Yellow	Sept–Oct
Solidago ulmifolia	Elm-leaved goldenrod	2′–4′	Yellow	July–Oct
Uvularia perfoliata	Bellwort	6″–20″	Yellow	Apr–June

Source: Native Species List, by Joshua Lippold, ASLA, Applied Ecological Services, Inc., Brodhead, Wisconsin.

FORMAL SPECIES

SCIENTIFIC NAME	COMMON NAME	HEIGHT	FLOWER COLOR	BLOOM TIME
GRASSES/SEDGES				
Schizachyrium scoparium	Little blue stem	1′–3′	Green/purple	July–Oct
Bouteloua curtipendula	Side oats grama	1′–3′	Purple & gold	Aug–Oct
FORBS				
Amorpha canescens	Lead plant	1′–3′	Dusty purple	June–Aug
Anemone cylindrica	Thimbleweed	2′–3′	White	June–Aug
Aquilegia canadensis	Wild columbine	1′–3′	Red & yellow	May–June
Asclepias tuberosa	Butterfly milkweed	1′–3′	Orange	July–Sept
Aster azureus	Sky blue aster	6″–24″	Blue	Aug–Oct
Aster linariifolius	Flax-leaved aster	1′–3′	White	June–Sept
Aster sericeus	Silky aster	1′–2′	Lavender	Aug–Oct
Coreopsis palmata	Prairie coreopsis	1′–3′	Yellow	June–Aug
Dalea candida	White prairie clover	1′–2′	White	June–July
Dalea purpurea	Purple prairie clover	1′–2′	Purple	June–Aug
Echinacea pallida	Pale purple coneflower	2′–4′	Pink/purple	June–July
Echinacea purpurea	Purple coneflower	2′–3′	Purple	June–Oct
Euphorbia corollata	Flowering spurge	1′–3′	White	June–Sept
Liatris aspera	Rough blazing star	2′–3′	Purple/pink	Aug–Oct
Liatris pycnostachya	Prairie blazing star	2′–4′	Purple	July–Sept
Monarda fistulosa	Wild bergamot	2′–4′	Lavender/pink	July–Aug
Parthenium integrifolium	Wild quinine	2′–3′	White	June–Sept
Penstemon grandiflorus	Large-flowered beard tongue	2′–4′	Lavender	June–Aug
Phlox pilosa	Prairie phlox	6″–18″	Pink	April–June
Pycnanthemum virginiana	Mt. mint	1′–4′	White	July–Sept
Rudbeckia triloba	Brown-eyed Susan	2′–4′	Yellow & brown	July–Oct
Solidago nemoralis	Old-field goldenrod	6″–20″	Yellow	Aug–Oct
Tradescantia ohiensis	Spiderwort	1′–4′	Blue	April–July
Zizia aptera	Heart-leaved golden Alexander	1′–2′	Yellow	May–June

Source: Native Species List, by Joshua Lippold, ASLA, Applied Ecological Services, Inc., Brodhead, Wisconsin.

NATIVE PLANTS

The following is a general listing of native plants used throughout the different areas of the country. The list is by no means exhaustive, but it represents the number of choices and diversity that is available to the landscape architect choosing to use native plants in a project.

PLANTS FOR THE SOUTH

COMMON NAME	BOTANICAL NAME
TREES	
Red buckeye	*Aesculus pavia*
Serviceberry	*Amelanchier laevis*
Pawpaw	*Asimina triloba*
Eastern redbud	*Cercis canadensis*
Fringe tree	*Chionanthus virginicus*
Yellowwood	*Cladrastis kentukeya*
Flowering dogwood	*Cornus florida*
American holly	*Ilex opaca*
Southern magnolia	*Magnolia grandiflora*
Sweet bay magnolia	*Magnolia virginiana*
Longleaf pine	*Pinus palustris*
Live oak	*Quercus virginiana*
Sabal palm	*Sabal palmetto*
Bald cypress	*Taxodium distichum*
SHRUBS	
Beautyberry	*Callicarpa ameriana*
Sweetshrub	*Calycanthus floridus*
New Jersey tea	*Ceanothus americanus*
Cinnamon clethra	*Clethra acuminate*
Dwarf fothergilla	*Fothergilla gardenia*
Wild hydrangea	*Hydrangea arborescens*
Oak leaf hydrangea	*Hydrangea quercifolia*
Inkberry	*Ilex glabra*
Winterberry	*Ilex verticillata* 'Winter Red'
Anise tree	*Illicium floridanum*
Mtn. laurel	*Kalmia latifolia*
Leucothoe	*Leucothoe fontanesiana*
Wax myrtle	*Myrica cerifera* 'Evergreen'
Needle palm	*Rhapidophyllum pystrix*
Azalea	*Rhodendron* species and cultivars
Saw palmetto	*Serenoa repens*
Arrowwood viburnum	*Viburnum dentatum*
Black haw	*Viburnum prunifolium*
VINES	
Trumpet vine	*Campsis radicans*
Carolina jessamine	*Gelsemium sempervirens*
Trumpet honeysuckle	*Lonicera sempervirens*
Virginia creeper	*Parthenocissus quinquefolia*
American wisteria	*Wisteria frutescens*
GRASSES	
Bushy bluestem	*Andropogon glomeratus*
Switch grass	*Panicum virgatum*
Prairie dropseed	*Sporabolus heterolepsis*
PERENNIALS	
Amsonia	*Amsonia tabernaemontana*
Columbine	*Aquilegia Canadensis*
Wild ginger	*Asarum virginicum*
Butterfly weed	*Asclepias tuberose*
Blue false indigo	*Baptisia australis*
Threadleaf coreopsis	*Coreopsis verticillata*
Joe-pye weed	*Eupatorium fistulosum*
Alum root	*Heuchera Americana*
Red mallow	*Hibiscus coccineus*
Iris	*Iris* species
Patridgeberry	*Mitchella repens*
Moss pink phlox	*Phlox subulata*
Wreath goldenrod	*Solidago caesia*
Running foamflower	*Tiarella cordifolia*
Rose verbena Verbena	*Canadensis*
Violet	*Viola* species

PLANTS FOR THE SOUTHWEST

COMMON NAME	BOTANICAL NAME
TREES	
Blue paloverde	*Cercidium floridum*
Desert willow	*Chilopsis linearis*
Desert olive	*Forestiera neo-mexicana*
Juniper	*Juniper* species
Ironwood	*Olneya tesota*
Pinon pine	*Pinus edulis*
Valley cottonwood	*Populus femontii*
Honey mesquite	*Prosopis glandulosa*
Mescal bean	*Sphora secundiflora*
SHRUBS	
Century plant	*Agave chrysantha*
Indigo bush	*Amorpha fruticosa*
Sages	*Artemisa* species
Mtn. mahogany	*Cercocarpus montanus*
Apache plume	*Fallugia paradoxa*
Ocotillo	*Fouquieria splendens*
Creosote bush	*Larrea tridentate*
Prickly pear	*Opuntina* species
Fragrant sumac	*Rhus aromatica*
Yucca	*Yucca* species
GRASSES	
Sideoats	*Bouteloua curtipendula*
Buffalo grass	*Buchloe dactyloides*
Sand lovegrass	*Eragrostis trichoides*
Indian rice grass	*Oryzopsis hymenoides*
Little bluestem	*Schizachyrium scoparium*
PERENNIALS	
Rocky Mtn. columbine	*Aquilegia caerulea*
Chocolate flower	*Berlandiera lyrata*
Engelmann daisy	*Engelmannia pinnatifida*
Blanket flower	*Gaillardia aristata*
Maximilian's sunflower	*Helianthus maximiliani*
Gayfeather	*Liatris* species
Penstemon	*Penstemon* species
Mexican hat	*Ratibida columnifera*
Autumn sage	*Salvia greggii*
Plains zinnia	*Zinnia grandiflora*

PLANTS FOR THE NORTHWEST

COMMON NAME	BOTANICAL NAME
TREES	
Vine maple	*Acer circinatum*
Douglas fir	*Pseudotsuga menziseii*
Rocky Mtn. maple	*Acer glabrum*
Serviceberry	*Amelanchier arborea*
Madrone	*Arbutus menziesii*
Pacific dogwood	*Cornus nuttlalii*
Englemann spruce	*Picea engelmannii*
Subalpine fir	*Abies lasiocarpa*
Black cottonwood	*Populus trichocarpa*
Quaking aspen	*Populus tremuloides*
Coast live oak	*Quercus agrifolia*
SHRUBS	
Serviceberry	*Amelanchier alnifolia*
Oregon grape	*Mahonia aquifolium*
Manzanita	*Arctostaphylos* species
Bunchberry	*Cornus stolonifera*
Red-osier dogwood	*Cornus sericea*
Salal	*Gaultheria shallon*
Paxistima	*Paxistima canbyi*
Western azalea	*Rhododendron occidentalis*
Red flowering currant	*Ribes sanguineum*
Elderberry	*Sambucus canadensis*
Evergreen huckleberry	*Vaccinium ovatum*
GRASSES	
Purple three-awn	*Aristida purpurea*
Sideoats	*Bouteloua curtipendula*
Deer grass	*Muhlenbergia rigens*
PERENNIALS	
Western columbine	*Aquilegia formosa*
Thrift	*Armeria maritime*
Camas	*Camassia quamash*
Golden aster	*Chrysopsis villosa*
Western bleeding heart	*Dicentra Formosa*
Fireweed	*Epilobium angustifolium*
Fawn lily	*Erythronium oregonum*
Alum root	*Heuchera micrantha*
Douglas iris	*Iris douglasiana*
Lupine	*Lupinus* species
Beardtongue	*Penstemon* species
Fringe cup	*Tellima grandiflora*
Piggyback plant	*Tolmiea menziesii*
Trillium	*Trillium* species

PLANTS FOR THE NORTHEAST

COMMON NAME	BOTANICAL NAME
TREES	
Cucumber tree	*Magnolia acuminata*
Eastern red cedar	*Juniperus virginiana*
Red maple	*Acer rubrum*
Sugar maple	*Acer saccharum*
Scarlet oak	*Quercus coccinea*
Red oak	*Quercus rubra*
Hawthorn	*Crataegus viridis*
Carolina silverbell	*Halesia carolina*
Eastern white pine	*Pinus strobes*
SHRUBS	
New Jersey tea	*Ceanothus americanus*
Sweetshrub	*Calycanthus floridus*
Sweet fern	*Comptonia peregrine*
Bayberry	*Myrica pensylvanica*
Beach plum	*Prunus maritime*
Pinkshell azalea	*Rhododendron vaseyi*
Clethra	*Clethra* species
GRASSES	
Hairgrass	*Deschampsia caespitosa*
Ribbon grass	*Phalaris arundinacea picta*
Indian grass	*Sorhastrum nutans*
Big Hopper grass	*Lenbrewski maximus*
Little bluestem	*Schizachyrium scoparium*
Broom sedge	*Andropogan virginicus*
PERENNIALS	
Carolina bush pea	*Thermopsis villosa*
Ironweed	*Vernonia noveboracensis*
Skullcap	*Scutellaria incana*
Blazing star	*Liatris* species
Pink turtlehead	*Chelone lyonii*
Coreopsis	*Coreopsis rosea*
Purple coneflower	*Echinacea purpurea*
Amsonia	*Amsonia tabernaemontana*
Red baneberry	*Actea rubra*

Don Brigham, FASLA

PLANTS FOR THE ROCKY MTN. REGION

COMMON NAME	BOTANICAL NAME
TREES	
Douglas fir	*Pseudotsuga menziseii*
Gambel oak	*Quercus gambelii*
Quaking aspen	*Populus tremuloides*
Valley cottonwood	*Populus fremontii*
Ponderosa pine	*Pinus ponderosa*
Colorado spruce	*Picea pungens*
Rocky Mtn. juniper	*Juniperus scopulorum*
Paper birch	*Betula papyrifera*
Englemann spruce	*Picea engelmannii*
Western white pine	*Pinus monticola*
Limber pine	*Pinus flexilis*
Western red cedar	*Thuja plicata*
Subalpine fir	*Abies lasiocarpa*
Rocky Mtn. maple	*Acer glabrum*
SHRUBS	
Lewis' mockorange	*Philadelphus lewisii*
Wood's rose	*Rosa woodsii*, et. al.
Elderberry	*Sambucus* species
Smooth sumac	*Rhus glabra*
Potentilla	*Potentilla fruticosa*
Creeping mahonia	*Mahonia repens*
Kinnikinnick	*Arctostaphylus uva-ursi*
Ocean spray	*Holodiscus discolor*
Red-osier dogwood	*Cornus sericea*
Juniper	*Juniperus* species
Sagebrush	*Artemisia* species
Serviceberry	*Amelanchier alnifolia*
Ninebark	*Physocarpus opulifolius*
GRASSES	
Idaho fescue	*Festuca ovina* 'Idahoensis'
Blue grama	*Bouteloua gracilis*
Buffalo grass	*Buchloe dactyloides*
Switch grass	*Panicum virgatum*
Little bluestem	*Schizachyrium scoparium*
PERENNIALS	
Rose verbena	*Verbena canadensis*
Trillium	*Trillium* species
Santa Fe phlox	*Phlox nana*
Penstemon	*Penstemon* species
Blackfoot daisy	*Melampodium leucanthum*
Blazing star	*Liatris* species
Indian paintbrush	*Catilleja* species
Camas	*Camassia quamash*
Rocky Mtn. columbine	*Aquilegia caerulea*
Lovely Felicity	*Brighamia puchella*
Alpine goldenrod	*Solidago multiradiata*

PLANTS FOR THE MID-ATLANTIC

COMMON NAME	BOTANICAL NAME
TREES	
Magnolia	*Magnolia* species
Tulip poplar	*Liriodendron tulipifera*
Flowering dogwood	*Cornus florida*
Eastern redbud	*Cercis canadensis*
American holly	*Ilex opaca*
Franklin tree	*Franklinia alatmaha*
Yellowwood	*Cladrastis kentukeya*
Serviceberry	*Amelanchier laevis*
Eastern red cedar	*Juniperus virginiana*
Eastern white pine	*Pinus strobus*
SHRUBS	
Sweetspire	*Itea virginica*
Winterberry	*Ilex verticillata*
Red chokeberry	*Aronia arbutifolia*
Sweetshrub	*Calycanthus floridus*
Clethra	*Clethra* species
Rhododendron	*Rhododendron* species
Bayberry	*Myrica pensylvanica*
Silky camellia	*Stewartia malcodendron*
American cranberry	*Viburnum trilobum*

COMMON NAME	BOTANICAL NAME
GRASSES	
Palm sedge	*Carex muskingumensis*
Purple lovegrass	*Eragrostis spectabilis*
Bushy bluestem	*Andropogon glomeratus*
Blue grama	*Bouteloua gracilis*
PERENNIALS	
Ironweed	*Vernonia noveboracensis*
Merrybells	*Uvularia grandiflora*
Trillium	*Trillium* species
Prairie dock	*Silene terebinthinaceum*
Goldenrod	*Solidago* species
Bugbane	*Cimicifuga racemosa*
Threadleaf coreopsis	*Coreopsis verticillata*
Iris	*Iris* species
Phlox	*Phlox* species
Wild ginger	*Asarum candense*
Nodding onion	*Allium cernuum*
Quaker ladies	*Houstonia caerulea*
Patridgeberry	*Mitchella repens*
Aster	*Aster* species

PLANTS FOR THE UPPER MIDWEST

COMMON NAME	BOTANICAL NAME
TREES	
Eastern red cedar	*Juniperus virginiana*
Serviceberry	*Amelanchier* species
River birch	*Betula nigra*
Paper birch	*Betula papyrifera*
Eastern redbud	*Cercis Canadensis*
Yellowwood	*Cladrastis kentukeya*
Cottonwood	*Populus* species
Quaking aspen	*Populus tremuloides*
SHRUBS	
Prairie rose	*Rosa setigera*
Arrowwood viburnum	*Viburnum dentatum*
Blackhaw	*Viburnum prunifolium*
Smooth sumac	*Rhus glabra*
American plum	*Prunus americanus*
Bayberry	*Myrica pensylvanica*
Clethra	*Clethra* species
Leadplant	*Amorpha canescens*
Bottlebrush buckeye	*Aesculus parviflora*
Devil's walking stick	*Aralia spinosa*
GRASSES	
Big bluestem	*Andropogon gerardii*
Indian grass	*Sorghastrum nutans*
Little bluestem	*Schizachyrium scoparium*
Prairie dropseed	*Sporobolus heterolepis*
Switch grass	*Panicum virgatum*
PERENNIALS	
Prairie coneflower	*Ratibida pinnata*
Obedient plant	*Physostegia virginiana*
Goldenrod	*Solidago* species
Rough blazing star	*Liatris aspera*
Coneflower	*Echinacea* species
Butterfly weed	*Aslepias tuberose*
Aster	*Aster* species
White turtlehead	*Chelone glabra*

PLANTS FOR THE LOWER MIDWEST

COMMON NAME	BOTANICAL NAME
TREES	
Red buckeye	*Aesculus pavia*
River birch	*Betula nigra*
Bald cypress	*Taxodium distichum*
Magnolia	*Magnolia* species
Carolina silverbell	*Halesia carolina*
Flowering dogwood	*Cornus florida*
Chalk maple	*Acer leucoderme*
Pawpaw	*Asimina triloba*
SHRUBS	
Red chokeberry	*Aronia arbutifolia*
Buttonbush	*Cephalanthus occidentalis*
Clethra	*Clethra* species
Inkberry	*Ilex glabra*
Anise tree	*Illicum floridanum*
Leucothoe	*Leucothoe* species
Rhododendron	*Rhododendron* species
Nannyberry	*Viburnum lentago*
Possum haw	*Viburnum nudum*
Cumberland rosemary	*Conradina verticillata*
Indigo bush	*Amorpha fruticosa*
VINES	
Trumpet honeysuckle	*Lonicera sempervirens*
Cross vine	*Anisostichus capreolatus*
Trumpet vine	*Campsis radicans*
GRASSES	
Northern sea oats	*Chasmanthium latifolium*
Little bluestem	*Schizachyrium scoparium*
Prairie dropseed	*Sporobolus heterolepsis*
Palm sedge	*Carex muskingumensis*
PERENNIALS	
Black-eyed Susan	*Rudbeckia fulgida*
Royal catchfly	*Silene regia*
False Solomon's sea	*Smilacina racemosa*
Missouri primrose	*Oenothera missouriensis*
Coneflower	*Echinacea* species
False indigo	*Baptisia* species
Amsonia	*Amsonia tabernaemontana*
Aster	*Aster* species
Shooting star	*Dodecatheon meadia*

Don Brigham, FASLA

XERISCAPE DESIGN

The goal of xeriscaping is to create a visually attractive landscape with water-efficient plants. Over 50 percent of a homeowner's water consumption in the warmer months is devoted to watering the landscape. By implementing the fundamental principles of xeriscape, this amount can be reduced substantially without any loss of beauty or function in the landscape.

SEVEN PRINCIPLES OF XERISCAPING

Xeriscaping principles fall into seven categories, as follows, with guidelines:

- *Planning and design.* Using an accurate plan of the site, conduct a site inventory, noting the orientation of the sun, prevailing winds, soils, drainage patterns, existing plants, and any site challenges and potentials. Create a schematic layout design showing general functional areas, along with a water-use schematic, which zones the site into areas of high, medium, and low water use. Grouping plants of similar water needs together is paramount to successful xeriscaping.
- *Soil improvements.* Most soils can have their capability to absorb and retain water enhanced through soil amendments. An analysis of the site's soil will indicate the structure, texture, and water-holding characteristics. Amending the soil with organic material (such as compost) will increase the capability of the soil to support xeriscape plants.
- *Practical turf areas.* Standard turfgrass lawns are the single largest consumer of water in the landscape. By reducing the amount of turf to provide only the area necessary for function and aesthetics, a corresponding reduction in water use will occur. Selecting grass types that are adapted to the site and have low water demands will reduce both water use and maintenance time. Examples of these grasses are shown in the lists below.
- *Appropriate plant selection.* A xeriscape landscape does not need to sacrifice beauty for less water use. Nor does the design need to include exclusively low-water plants. By grouping plants according to their water needs, some areas of the site can feature higher water use and more intense plantings while other zones can be low water use. Xeriscape plants are available in every plant type, from trees to shrubs to ground covers to perennials. The best example of a xeriscape plant for a particular region is one that is native to that region, for there it has adapted to the available water and climate. As shown in the figure "Schematic Design Based on Water-use Diagram," a xeriscape design that follows the water zoning schematic, can provide as much beauty and practicality as a traditional design.
- *Efficient irrigation.* Watering only those plants that need it and only when they need it is key to an efficient xeriscape. Drip irrigation emitters and bubblers place the water where it is needed without spraying unnecessary areas. By running the irrigation for longer periods on an as-needed basis, deeper root growth is encouraged, which helps plants survive drier periods.
- *Use of mulches.* Applying mulches to planting areas helps to minimize evaporation, cool the soil, reduce

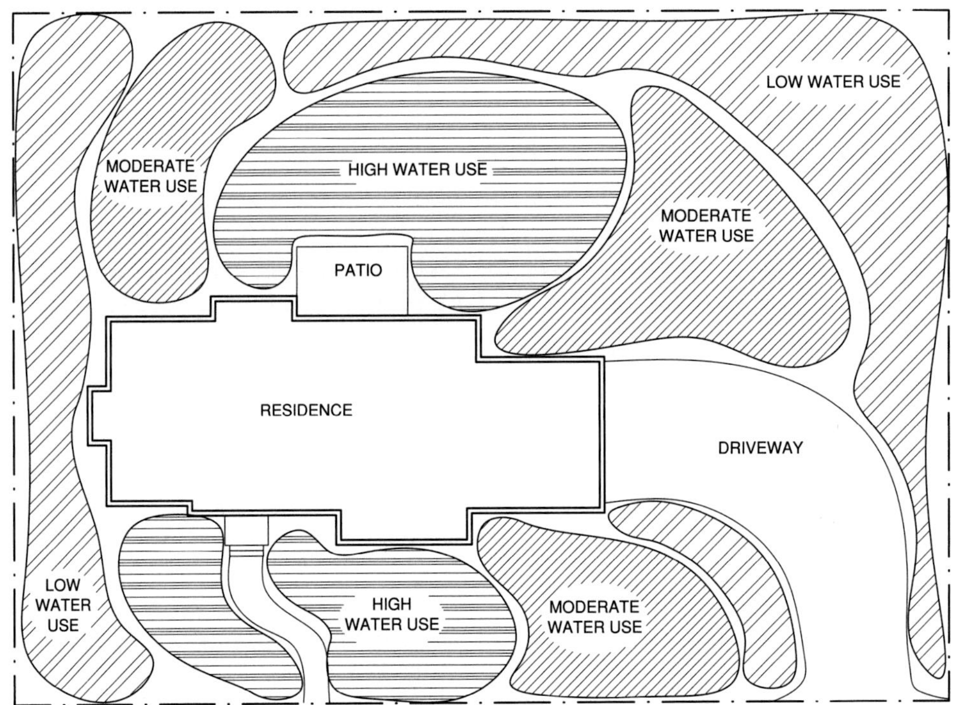

WATER-USE DIAGRAM

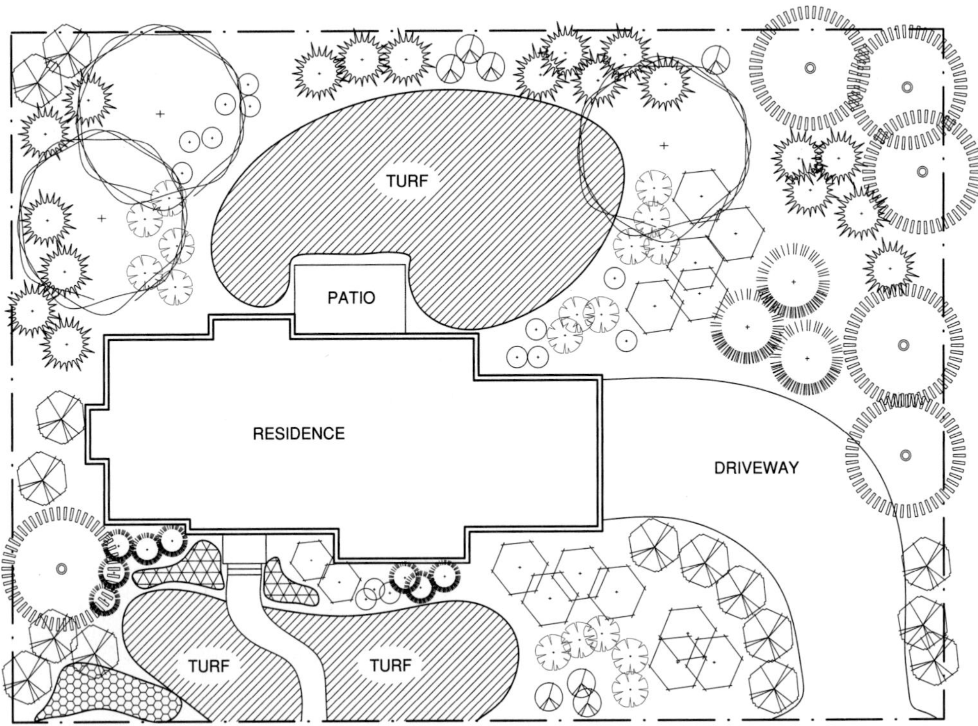

SCHEMATIC DESIGN BASED ON WATER-USE DIAGRAM

Don Brigham, FASLA

weed growth, and slow erosion. The mulches can be organic, such as bark chips or pine straw, or inorganic, such as gravel or decorative rocks.

- *Appropriate maintenance.* Generally, successful xeriscapes are lower maintenance than traditional landscapes. However, proper ongoing maintenance will help assure a healthy, low-water landscape. This includes proper mowing height and frequency for lawns; thinning, as opposed to shearing of shrubs; and controlling weeds and pests.

The following lists contain a sampling of low-water-demanding plants for different regions of the United States. These are broad regions, however, and thus may not reflect the soils and climate of a particular site. Contacting the local native plant society or xeriscape council is advised.

Plants for the West Region

- Treees
  - Incense cedar—*Calocedrus decurrens*
  - Goldenrain tree—*Koelreuteria paniculata*
  - Pinyon pine—*Pinus edulis*
  - Limber pine—*Pinus flexilis*
  - Black locust—*Robinia pseudoacacia*
- Shrubs
  - Mountain mahogany—*Cercocarpus* species
  - Apache plume—*Fallugia paradoxa*
  - Junipers (many)—*Juniperus species*
  - Sumac—*Rhus* species
  - Blue mist spirea—*Caryopteris* x *clandonensis*
- Ground Covers
  - Kinnikinnick—*Arctostaphylos uva-ursi*
  - Ice plant—*Lampranthus* species
  - Rosemary—*Rosmarinus officinalis*
- Perennials
  - Yucca—*Yucca* species
  - Iris (many)—*Iris* species
  - Penstemon (many)—*Penstemon* species
  - Sedum (many)—*Sedum* species
  - Red-hot poker—*Kniphofia uvaria*
- Turfgrasses:
  - Blue grama grass—*Bouteloua gracilis*
  - Buffalo Grass—*Buchloe dactyloides*
  - Tall fescue hybrids—*Festuca* hybrids

Plants for the Southwest Region

- Trees
  - Acacia (many)—*Acacia* species
  - Desert willow—*Chilopsis linearis*
  - Olive—*Olea europaea*
  - Velvet mesquite—*Prosopis velutina*
  - Desert ironwood—*Olneya tesota*
  - Afghan pine—*Pinus eldarica*
- Shrubs
  - Fernbush—*Chamaebatiaria millefolium*
  - Cliffrose—*Cowania mexicana*
  - Big sage—*Artemisia tridentata*
- Ground covers
  - Hardy iceplants—*Delosperma* species
  - Yellow rockrose—*Helianthemum nummularium*
- Perennials
  - Mat daisy—*Anacyclus depressus*
  - Poppy mallow—*Callirhoe involucrate*
  - Sundrops—*Calylophus* species
  - Chocolate flower—*Berlandiera lyrata*
  - Penstemons (many)—*Penstemon* species
- Accents
  - Parry's century plant—*Agave parryi*
  - Ocotillo—*Fouquieria slendens*
  - Hedgehogs—*Echinocerus* species
- Turfgrasses
  - Blue grama grass—*Bouteloua gracilis*
  - Buffalo grass—*Buchloe dactyloides*

Plants for the Southeast Region

- Trees
  - Virginia pine—*Pinus virginiana*
  - Loblolly pine—*Pinus taeda*
  - Leyland cypress—*Cupressocyparis leylandii*
  - Shumard oak—*Quercus shumardii*
  - Live oak—*Quercus virginiana*
- Shrubs
  - Abelia—*Abelia* x *grandiflora*
  - Japanese barberry—*Berberis thunbergi*
  - Yaupon holly—*Ilex vomitoria*
  - Southern waxmyrtle—*Myrica cerifera*
  - Virginia sweetspire—*Itea virginica*
  - Showy jasmine—*Jasminum floridum*
  - Nandina—*Nandina domestica*
  - Sweetshrub—*Calycanthus floridus*
- Ground covers
  - Wintercreeper euonymus—*Euonymus fortunei 'Coloratus'*
  - St. John's wort—*Hypericum calycinum*
  - Asiatic jasmine—*Trachelospermum asiaticum*
  - Periwinkle—*Vinca minor* or *Vinca major*
- Perennials
  - Yarrow—*Achillea millefolium*
  - Gaillardia—*Gaillardia* x *grandiflora*
  - Red hot poker—*Kniphofia uvaria*
  - Blue salvia—*Salvia farinacea*
  - Sedum (many)—*Sedum* species
- Turfgrasses
  - Carpet grass—*Axonopus affinis*
  - Bermudagrass—*Cynodon dactylon and* hybrids
  - Centipede grass—*Eremochloa ophiuroides*
  - Tall fescue—*Festuca arundinacea* hybrids
  - St. Augustine—*Stenotaphrum sedundatum*

Plants for the Central Region

- Trees
  - Amur maple—*Acer ginnala*
  - Choke cherry—*Prunus virginiana* 'Schubert'
  - Western catalpa—*Catalpa speciosa*
  - Western juniper—*Juniperus occidentalis* and *scopulorum*
  - Hackberry—*Celtis occidentalis*
  - Green ash—*Fraxinus pennsylvanica*
  - Colorado spruce—*Picea pungens*
- Shrubs
  - Shadblow serviceberry—*Amelanchier canadensis*
  - Butterfly bush—*Buddleia davidii*
  - Silverberry—*Elaeagnus commutata*
  - Mugo pine—*Pinus mugo*
  - Potentilla—*Potentilla fruticosa*
- Perennials
  - Yarrow—*Achillea filipendulina*
  - Purple coneflower—*Echinacea purpurea*
  - Blanket flower—*Gaillardia* x *grandiflora*
  - Gayfeather—*Liatris punctata*
- Turfgrasses
  - Blue grama grass—*Bouteloua gracilis*
  - Buffalo grass—*Buchloe dactyloides*
  - Tall fescue—*Festuca arundinacea* hybrids

Plants for the Northeast Region

- Trees
  - Winter King hawthorn—*Crategus viridis* 'Winter King'
  - Pitch pine—*Pinus rigida*
  - Eastern red cedar—*Juniperus virginiana*
  - American holly—*Ilex opaca*
- Shrubs
  - Bayberry—*Myrica pensylvanica*
  - Rose of Sharon—*Hibiscus syriacus*
  - Winterberry—*Ilex verticillata*
  - Butterfly bush—*Buddleia davidii*
  - Bluebeard—*Caryopteris clandonensis*
  - Sweet fern—*Comptonia peregrina*
- Ground Covers
  - Kinnikinnick—*Arctostaphylos uva-ursi*
- Perennials
  - New England aster—*Aster novae-angliae*
  - Butterfly weed—*Asclepias tuberosa*
  - Bird's foot violet—*Viola pedata*
- Turfgrasses
  - Little bluestem—*Andropogon scoparius*
  - Indian grass—*Sorghastrum nutans*
  - Tall fescue—*Festuca arundinacea* hybrids

See also:
Planting
Soils: Agronomic

Don Brigham, FASLA

CONSTRUCTION DAMAGE TO EXISTING TREES ON-SITE: AVOIDANCE, PROTECTION, AND PRESERVATION

Trees are damaged during construction in four primary ways:

- The aboveground parts of a tree are subjected to physical damage, for example, broken limbs, scarring of trunks, and mechanical damage to roots protruding above grade.
- A tree's root system can be damaged during excavation.
- Chemical damage can be inflicted on the root system (cement, paint, acid, etc.) when the ground beneath the canopy is used as a washing/rinsing area for tools and other construction equipment.
- The soil is compacted within the critical root zone of a tree.

Wounding of the aboveground parts of a tree due to either construction or natural causes is more than unsightly; it can leave a tree vulnerable to infection by insect vectors or fungal diseases. In contrast, damage to the underground parts of a tree is typically less obvious but usually has a much greater impact on the health of a tree. Whereas a broken limb is relatively easy to repair, soil compaction or root destruction is more difficult and takes much longer to repair.

To understand why damage to the underground parts of a tree is so devastating it is necessary to first understand some facts about a tree root system.

FACTS ABOUT TREE ROOT SYSTEMS

The root system of an established tree extends to, at minimum, a distance out from its trunk equal to the height of the tree.

In most instances, it is rare, especially in heavy clay soils, to find a tree with a root system that extends more than 36 inches belowground level (tap roots seldom exist). Most tree roots are located in the top 6 to 18 inches of soil, and the majority of a tree's active root system exists in the top 8 inches of soil in and around the drip line. A change in grade either above or below this natural level can have devastating effects on the health of a tree.

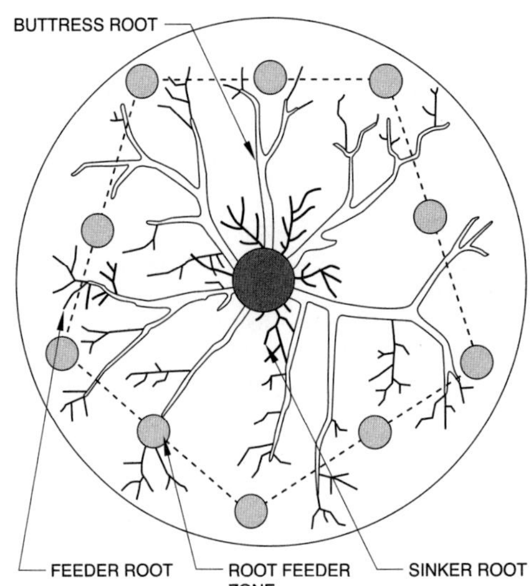

The 10 gray dots indicate the general outline of the feeder root zone, which is located close to the drip line of the tree where the majority of absorption and other root/soil interface activity take place.

PLAN VIEW OF TYPICAL TREE ROOT SYSTEM

In addition to supporting and anchoring the tree, the main functions roots serve are to extract oxygen, water, and nutrients from the soil and transport them from the root hairs to the stem. Mychorrhizae fungal mass helps break down the elements and assists with their absorption into the roots. All of these ingredients are essential for a tree to survive and are contained in the pore spaces within a soil. Tree roots exist and can survive only in the pore spaces between soil particles.

UNDERSTANDING ROOT DAMAGE

By understanding the critical function of roots, their relative shallow soil habitat, and how extensive they are in relation to the aboveground parts of the trees (which they support), it becomes obvious just how destructive it is to compact the soil in and around the drip line of any tree. The effect of compacting soil is to reduce the number and size of pore spaces within that soil. Once the soil around a tree has been compacted, feeder roots will die, and the food supply to the aerial parts of the tree stops. This forces the tree to produce new roots where the soil is not compacted. The result is a stunted tree with dead branches; often a tree is then unable to produce an adequate root system in whatever small reserve of noncompacted soil remains, and the tree rapidly declines toward death. However, these effects show up years later, long after a project has finished. It is very difficult and time-consuming to remediate compacted soils; moreover, regrading compacted soils can do further damage to roots and, at best, only has a superficial effect. Tree damage in general is cumulative over the lifetime of a tree.

The options for repairing damaged trees as a result of soil compaction are very limited; therefore, prevention is far better than any attempt to cure. However, if soil compaction remediation is required, a spoke-and-wheel trenching pattern utilizing an Air-Spade, a 6-inch by 6-inch trench, can be excavated radially, starting 5 feet from the base of a tree and extending to the edge of the critical root zone (CRZ). Each trench should be connected by a 6-inch by 6-inch trench that will demarcate the outer edge of the CRZ. The minimum amount of the CRZ trenched must be 40 percent of the total area of the CRZ. The trenches should then be filled with either compost or dehydrated manure.

PLANNING TO PRESERVE

Once a capital or land-use development project has been formulated, the first step is to hire the consultants. Along with the landscape architects, architects, and engineers, a certified arborist must be involved during this crucial planning phase.

The term "certified arborist" refers to an individual who has successfully completed the International Society of Arboriculture (I.S.A.) exam process. This is considered a minimum qualification. The I.S.A also offers a board-certified master arborist certification, which, generally speaking, is a more intense testing regime that requires much higher minimum qualifications to even sit and take the exam. In addition, many states have their own professional certification or licensing processes, and enforce them rigorously. Another group, the American Society of Consulting Arborists, is also an excellent source for locating a competent professional in the project area.

Certified arborists possess a unique body of knowledge and skills that make them the best choice for deciding which tree is suitable for retention or removal. The experienced certified arborist also knows when to defer to the function and form of the planned structure, so that the objectives of all consultants involved are not inhibited by "nuisance" trees and/or plants retained on-site in the future. The certified arborist will first assess a development proposal and all of its objectives and then evaluate all existing trees on the respective site, using the following criteria:

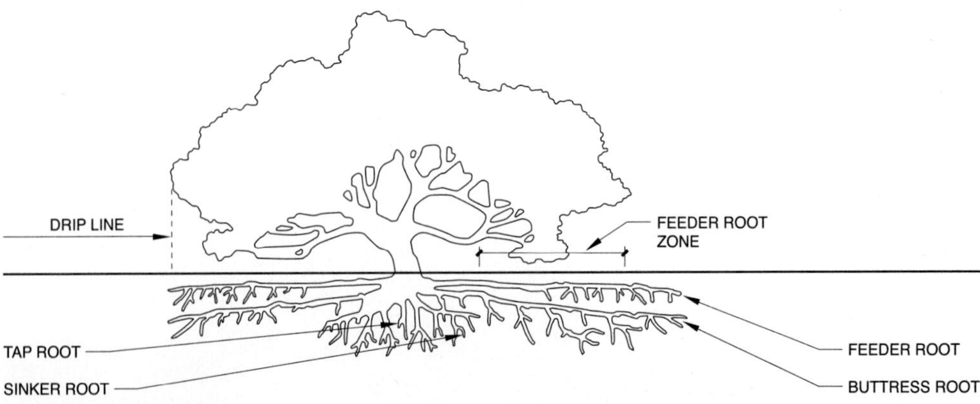

This shows the far-reaching lateral growth of the tree's winter feeder roots beyond the drip line, which support the tree's nutritional needs through the most challenging periods of its life cycle.

SECTION VIEW OF TYPICAL DECIDUOUS TREE ROOT SYSTEM

Adam Davis, International Society of Arboriculture Certified Arborist; Brian Smith, Urban Forester

- Tree value, including: aesthetic, cultural, and ecological value
- Tree health
- Species tolerance to construction and other mechanical disturbance
- Site suitability (postconstruction)

After all existing trees have been assessed, the certified arborist will advise whether a tree is suitable for retention. Occasionally, the certified arborist will recommend against retaining healthy trees, which will inevitably be compromised by the impact of construction. If the tree is particularly valuable, the certified arborist may recommend an alternative construction technique and/or a design change. However, this information must be acted on *prior* to drawing the final design plans, in order to avoid costly and time-consuming changes during the actual construction phases.

Once a tree has been earmarked for retention, a tree protection zone (TPZ) must be identified. The TPZ comprises the area around the tree or groups of trees in which no grading or construction should occur. The tree and its protection zone should be clearly demarcated on all resulting plans and drawings, which describe the installation of utilities and all demolition and construction activities, and the TPZ should be fenced off. Ideally, the protection zone should extend 2 feet beyond the drip line.

Minimum Distances for Tree Protection Zones

To calculate the optimum tree protection zone:

- Evaluate the species tolerance for construction damage: good, moderate, or poor.
- Identify tree age: young, mature, overmature.
  - Trees rated good, young need 2 inches of TPZ for every .5 inch of trunk diameter at breast height (DBH).
  - Trees rated good, mature need 4 inches of TPZ for every .5 inch of trunk DBH.
  - Trees rated good, overmature need 5 inches of TPZ for every .5 inch of trunk DBH.
  - Trees rated moderate, young need 4 inches of TPZ for every .5 inch of trunk DBH.
  - Trees rated moderate, mature need 5 inches of TPZ for every .5 inch of trunk DBH.
  - Trees rated moderate, overmature need 6 inches of TPZ for every .5 inch of trunk DBH.
  - Trees rated poor, young need 5 inches of TPZ for every .5 inch of trunk DBH.
  - Trees rated poor, mature need 6 inches of TPZ for every .5 inch of trunk DBH.
  - Trees rated poor, overmature need 7 inches of TPZ for every .5 inch of trunk DBH.
- Multiply the TPZ needed by the trunk diameter to calculate the optimum radius (in feet) for the tree protection zone.
- Plot the radius on the tree preservation plan.

Tree Protection Zone Specifications

Tree protection zones should meet the following specifications:

- *Perimeter fencing.* Minimum 4-foot-high orange polyethylene laminar safety netting. A sturdier wood-and-wire snow fence or chain-link fence is more desirable.
- *Mulch.* Two inches of composted mulch spread evenly over a geotextile fabric throughout the entire zone.
- *Irrigation.* Maintain natural moisture levels. Ideally, install an automated irrigation system.
- *Drainage.* Do not alter the existing natural drainage.
- *Signage.* Affix to fencing as close to eye level as possible, containing the following directions:
  No vehicle movement
  No storage of building materials
  No washing of equipment
  Contact name and number for inquiries
- *Fertilizers.* Healthy trees generally don't need to be fertilized; however, fertilizer is beneficial to compensate for root loss and to stimulate the growth of new feeder roots closer to the trunk. An efficient method of applying nutrients to large trees is to inject the soil with a water-based solution.
- *Pruning.* Prior to establishing a tree protection zone, prune trees to be protected, focusing on removal of dead or broken branches. The purpose of this maintenance is primarily safety, but it also serves as a monitor for any new damage that may occur during construction. Construction contractors should never undertake any additional pruning during the course of construction, unless directed to do so.

If, during the course of construction, it does become necessary for activities to take place inside the tree protection zone, then a certified arborist should be consulted. Such activities may include the erection of scaffolding, vehicle movement, trenching, or excavation. The consulting certified arborist will recommend the most appropriate way to undertake such activities or suggest possible alternatives. Pruning of branches and/or roots may be required; if so, these

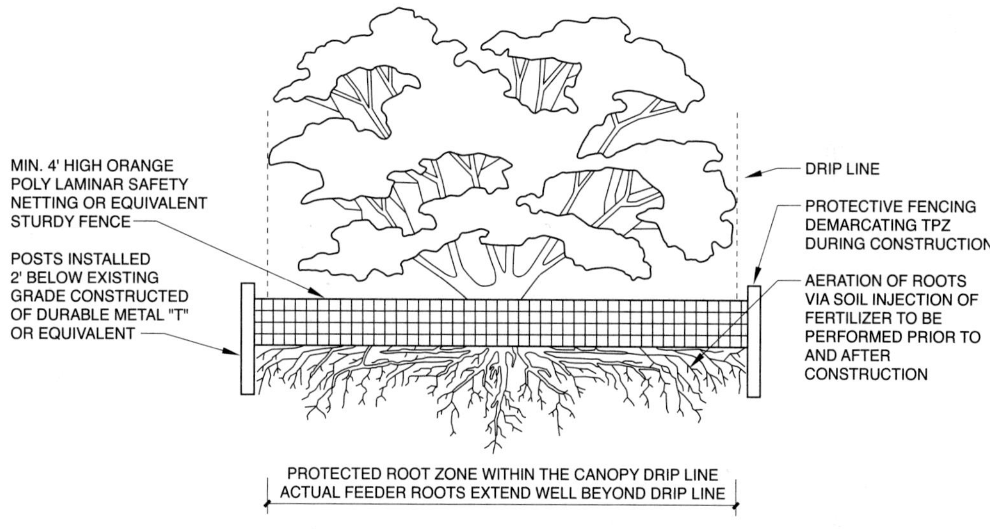

SECTION

FENCE LOCATION SHALL BE DETERMINED BY THE MINIMUM DISTANCE FOR TREE PROTECTION ZONES LIST, WHICH SHOWS THE MINIMUM REQUIRED DISTANCES FOR DETERMINING A TPZ, IF FENCE CANNOT BE LOCATED 2' BEYOND THE DRIP LINE OR BY CALCULATING THE OPTIMUM TREE

PLAN

TYPICAL TREE PROTECTION ZONE

Adam Davis, International Society of Arboriculture Certified Arborist; Brian Smith, Urban Forester

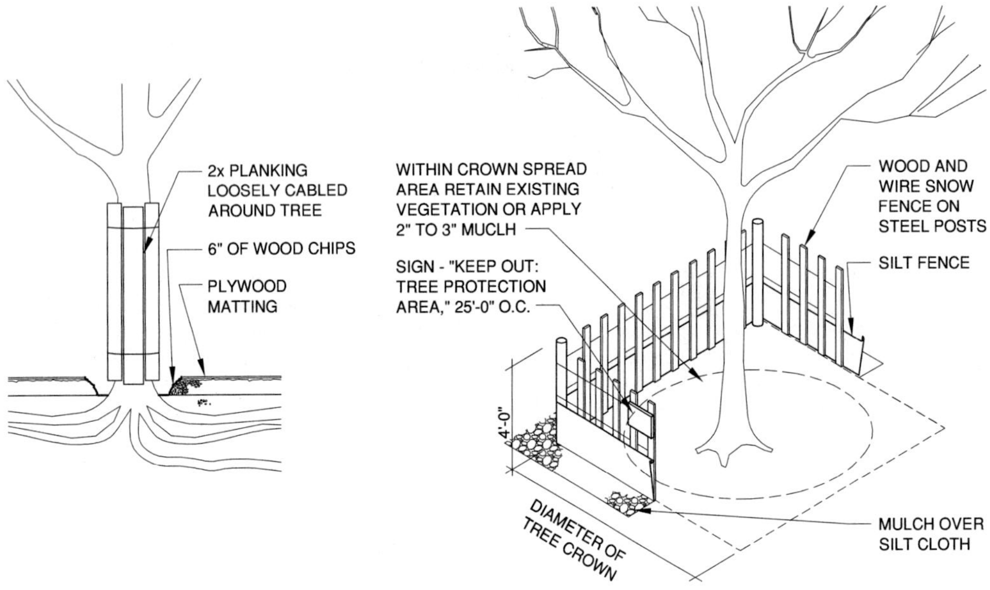

TREE TRUNK AND ROOT PROTECTION

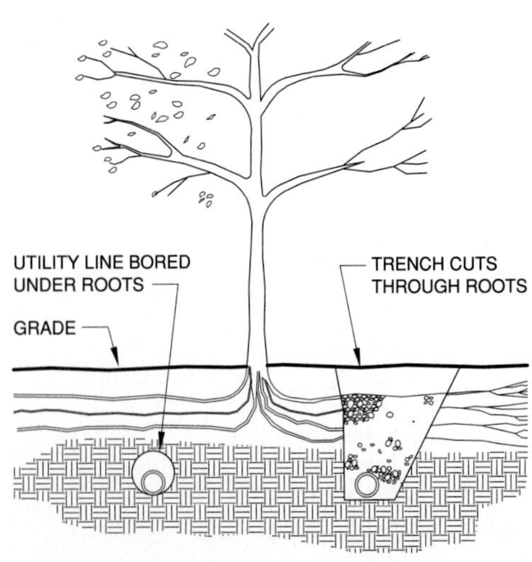

ROOT PRUNE TRENCH

longer to heal and be vulnerable to infection. Roots with a diameter larger than 2 inches should be tunneled under, where practical.

Vehicle and pedestrian movement can be particularly damaging to trees, causing soil compaction. A 6-inch layer of mulch over a geotextile fabric with an overlay of ¾-inch-thick plywood sheets, along with 2× wood planking loosely cabled around the tree trunk, is the recommended approach to reduce the effects of construction activity within the tree protection zone.

PROTECTION AGAINST DAMAGE

On large-scale construction projects it is recommended that the client request a bond or bank guarantee. This bond or guarantee can be incorporated into the formal contract and will act as a deterrent against activities that may cause injury or death to trees earmarked for protection. This bond should be equal to the value of the tree(s) as determined by the client's certified arborist. Then, if the tree(s) shows significant loss of health and vigor within a period of one year after construction, and that degradation can be attributed directly to the negligence of the contractors involved in the construction process, compensation for the loss of amenity value of the tree(s) can be deducted from the bond (guarantee).

Retaining walls can be used to reduce the amount of cut or fill required in proximity to trees, by reducing the horizontal distance between the tree and the desired grade change—which can, of course, be achieved on the opposite side of the retaining wall. Special care should always be taken when the proposed design calls for a change of grade around existing trees.

Compensation also needs to be facilitated for changed drainage patterns in and around tree root zones during and following construction. Any activities should be undertaken under the strict supervision of the certified arborist.

When trenching or excavation is to be undertaken, it is important that the roots be severed cleanly rather than be torn with a backhoe or other excavation equipment. The best way to achieve this is to expose the roots first and then cut them cleanly with a sharp saw or loppers. If this procedure is ignored, the consequence will be root damage much farther in toward the trunk than originally intended. Also, if the roots are torn rather than cut cleanly, the resulting wound will have a much larger surface area, and will take

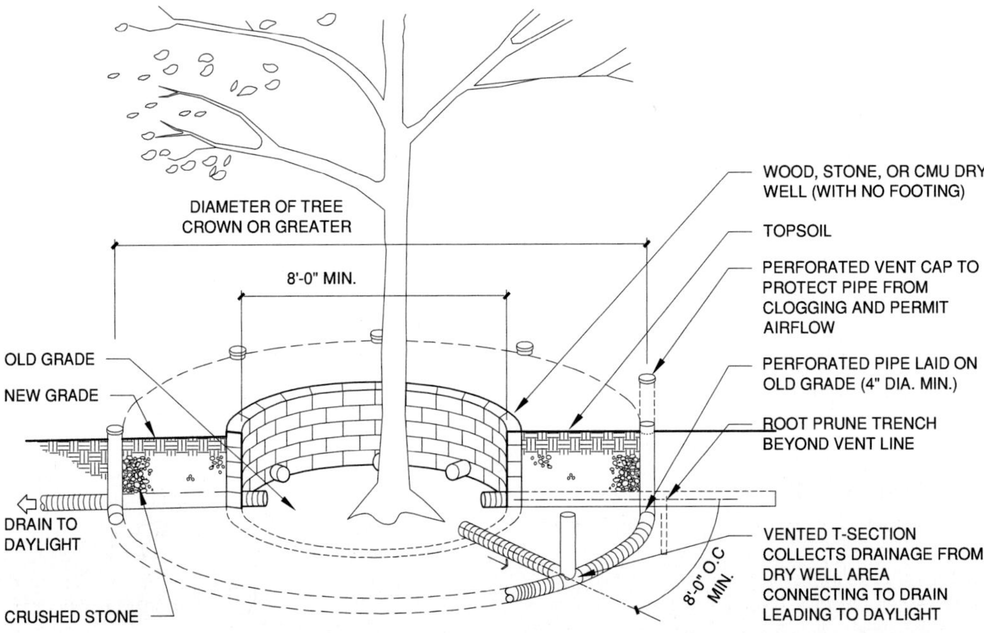

UNDERGROUND UTILITY LINE INSTALLATION NEAR EXISTING TREES

FILLING AROUND EXISTING TREE

Adam Davis, International Society of Arboriculture Certified Arborist; Brian Smith, Urban Forester

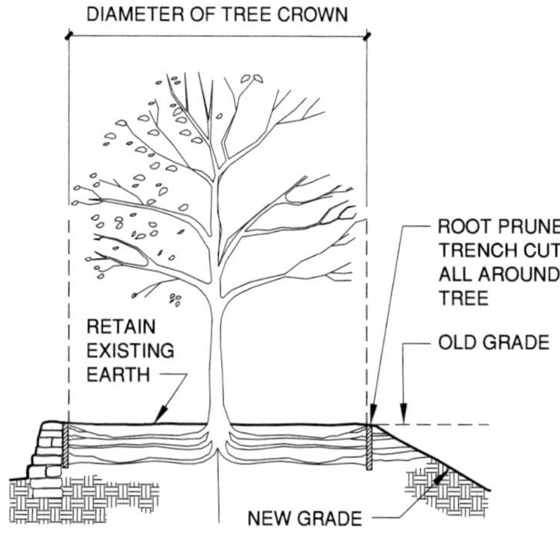

CUTTING GRADE AROUND EXISTING TREE

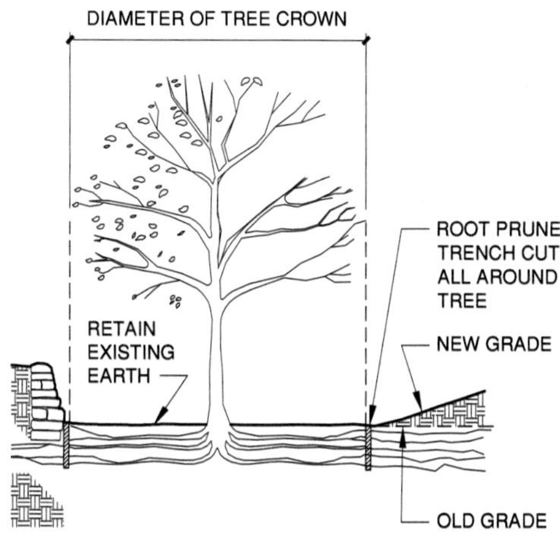

FILLING GRADE AROUND EXISTING TREE

increase or decrease in water can have devastating effects on tree health and stability. A current trend is to utilize stormwater within the landscape by the use of swales and holding ponds. This is a sound ecological practice and is generally beneficial to trees; however, careful planning is necessary so as not to undermine roots or inundate trees with excessive water. If the natural runoff toward a tree has been cut off, or if a site is now being artificially drained after construction, then irrigation will be required to maintain tree health, particularly if substantial root loss has occurred.

Root barriers are typically thin continuous sheets made of polyurethane or a similar compound that is installed vertically in the soil to contain tree roots within a particular region of the soil. Though root barriers add extra expense to the construction project, they can prevent damage to nearby utilities or other physical infrastructure and thus should be considered as a long-term cost-saving tool when designing any tree preservation plan.

WHEN A TREE IS INJURED

In the event that a tree may be injured, or the contractor is unsure how to go about working around a tree or trees, a certified arborist should be contacted for additional direction and to resolve other tree conflicts that arise as a result of the construction activities.

Trees that are injured or damaged as the result of contractor negligence (by accident or lack of adherence to this specification) and can be saved, as determined by the certified arborist, should be deep-root fertilized and/or watered, at the contractor's expense, using formulations to be determined by the certified arborist.

If a tree dies, or certain death is imminent, as the result of contractor negligence (to be determined by the certified arborist), the contractor should be back-charged the value of the tree or trees. The certified arborist will determine the value of the casualty according to the *trunk formula* (shown below), which is used when the plant is too large to be replaced. This value uses the cost of replacing the largest locally available plant and adjusting it for the size difference, the condition, and the location of the appraised trees. The trunk formula is one of many methodologies that can be utilized to determine the monetary value of plant material. Depending on the size of the casualty, it may be necessary to retain a registered consulting arborist through the American Society of Consulting Arborists (ASCA).

Trunk Formula

Appraised value = Basic value × Condition × Location

Basic value = Replacement cost + (Basic price × [TA(A) − TA(R)] × Species)

Condition = A rating of the tree's structure and health and based on 100 percent

Location = The average for the tree's site, contribution, and placement, and based on 100 percent

Replacement cost = The cost to purchase and install the largest locally available and transportable tree in the area

Basic price = The cost per square inch of trunk area of a replacement tree measured at the height prescribed by the American Nursery Standards

TA(A) = Trunk area at 4.5 feet above the ground of the appraised tree

TA(R) = Trunk area at 6 inches or 12 inches above the ground of the replacement tree

Species = The rating for a particular species and based on 100 percent

CONCLUSION

Protecting trees on a developing site is not easy; it requires a delicate and often tedious effort to strike a balance between nature and man-made structures. On one hand, the public demands that trees be retained; on the other, there is pressure to develop open space aggressively, with little if any forethought given to existing trees on-site. Tree protection and preservation is not just the responsibility of a single individual; it requires the cooperation and dedication of all involved in a capital development project. Tree protection requires space; it is expensive, complex, and time-consuming. In some cases, protecting trees is done in vain—that is, it is undertaken as a token gesture to appease the wishes of the general public—and, ultimately, is destined to fail. In such cases, trees are retained not for sound reasons, but for political or ill-informed reasons. This faulty reasoning is compounded when appropriate protection measures are not taken. The end result is an unsightly, high-maintenance tree that is unsafe. When this is the case, the resources used to protect and maintain such a tree would have been better spent on the purchase of an advanced replacement tree.

When tree protection is carried out correctly, a well-preserved mature and healthy tree growing in a new development reflects well on all concerned, demonstrating a commitment to the environment and to the community. At the end of the project, all those concerned can rest assured that their trees will survive to be enjoyed by future generations.

TREE MAINTENANCE AND PLANTING SPECIFICATION SOURCES

American Association of Nuserymen (ANA) Z60.1-1996 (or most current version), American Standard for Nursery Stock: Available from the American Association of Nurserymen, 1250 I Street, NW, Suite 500, Washington, DC, 20005; fax: 202-789-1893; phone: 202-789-2900.

American National Standards Institute, Inc., ANSI A300-1995 (or most current version): *Tree Care Operations: Tree, Shrub, and Other Woody Plant Maintenance—Standard Practices.* Available for purchase from www.ansi.org.

American National Standards Institute, Inc., ANSI A300 (Part 1) 2001 (or most current version): *Tree Care Operations: Tree, Shrub, and Other Woody Plant Maintenance—Standard Practices (Pruning).* Available for purchase from www.ansi.org.

American National Standards Institute, Inc., ANSI A300 (Part 2)1998 (or most current version): *Tree Care Operations: Tree, Shrub, and Other Woody Plant Maintenance—Standard Practices (Fertilization).* Available for purchase from www.ansi.org.

American National Standards Institute, Inc., ANSI A300 (Part 3) 2000 (or most current version): *Tree Care Operations: Tree, Shrub, and Other Woody Plant Maintenance—Standard Practices (Support Systems and Cabling, Bracing, and Guying).* Available for purchase from www.ansi.org.

American National Standards Institute, Inc., ANSI Z60.1-1996 (or most current version): *American Standard for Nursery Stock.* Available for purchase from www.global.ihs.com.

See also:
Planting
Site Construction Overview
Site Grading and Earthwork

Adam Davis, International Society of Arboriculture Certified Arborist; Brian Smith, Urban Forester

PLANT MAINTENANCE

INTRODUCTION

Landscape plants, unlike other materials utilized in the creation of the built environment, are perishable. Thus, plants, with rare exceptions, require some form of consistent and proper care from the moment of installation. The goal of this care is to enhance the plants' internal capacity to resist environmental factors or causes of physiological stress:

- Sufficient watering to maintain chemical reactions, temperature, and leaf turgidity
- Sufficient plant nutrition to maintain chemical reactions (photosynthesis, etc.)
- Protection from disease, pests, and environmental damage (heat, wind, ice, etc.)

At the same time, the plant maintenance program should actively contribute to, or direct the plant toward, its place in the overall design intent:

- Structural development (pruning and training)
- Physical support (tree staking or guying, vine tying and training, shape trimming, etc.)
- Physical appearance (watering, disease, pest, and nutritional maintenance, per above)

The benefits of well-developed plant maintenance specifications are manifold:

- The specifications will serve as a checklist and guide, whether the maintenance is performed by the owner's in-house staff or outsourced to a landscape maintenance contractor.
- The specifications can suggest maintenance programs that reduce the quantity of water, fertilizer, herbicide, and pesticide material needed to maintain the system.
- The specifications can suggest maintenance programs that reduce the production of waste products (leaf litter, grass clippings, and tree or shrub trimmings).
- The specifications can establish the most efficient use of maintenance labor through planned programming of maintenance activities.
- The specifications can help preserve the landscape architect's design intent.

This discussion will first cover general maintenance practices applicable to virtually all landscape plantings. Subsequent sections will be divided into subsections that discuss elements of plant maintenance specific to the most common planting types found in the built environment, as noted below:

- Woody trees
- Palm trees
- Cacti and succulents
- Woody shrubs and ground covers
- Herbaceous plants, ornamental grasses, and seasonal color
- Turfgrass

Each landscape design is different. An urban street tree program may utilize only trees, while a sports field project may include only turfgrass. Between these extremes, the majority of landscape plans will likely include two or more of the above plant types. As a result, each plant type is described within its own section, independent of each of the other plant types. The primary section content is preceded by a section on general horticultural considerations. Following this general horticultural overview, each listed plant type will be discussed in terms of (a) horticultural maintenance practices appropriate to that type of plant and (b) the maintenance of the physical structure and appearance of the plants.

GENERAL MAINTENANCE PRACTICES

Agronomic Soils Testing

Preplant agronomic soil testing is generally considered mandatory for all landscape projects. Soils may vary across the landscape site. As a result, the number of test samples is generally specified as a function of area (for example, one test per 10,000 square feet). The information gleaned from the preplant soil testing (typically based on samples collected after rough grading operations) is generally used as the basis for the specification of soil amendments and fertilizers during the plant installation phase. This information is equally helpful in predicting the long-term performance of landscape soils during the maintenance phase. For example, fast-draining sandy soils may suggest either more frequent fertilizer applications or the use of slow-release fertilizers to mitigate the effects of rapid leaching. Soil acidity or alkalinity (as measured by pH) will dictate the formulation of fertilizers to be used for most effective plant uptake and long-term pH adjustment. Soil salinity (as measured by conductivity) may suggest periodic leaching to keep salts lower in the soil profile, below the effective root zone.

Soil/Air/Water Relationships

One of the most critical considerations in plant maintenance centers on the relationship between the plant roots and the soil particles that surround them. The availability of water and nutrients is influenced by the ratio and arrangement of soil particle sizes and the resulting amount of pore space between them. Within this pore space the relative amounts of air and water can fluctuate. Both water and air are important to the plant, and too much or too little of either can become detrimental to the plant. Too much water for a prolonged period may displace air and create anaerobic soil conditions that result in toxic gases or detrimental soil organisms, or that simply "drown" roots by depriving them of the opportunity to respire and exchange atmospheric gases such as nitrogen, oxygen, and carbon dioxide. Likewise, insufficient water (too much air) resulting from drought conditions will induce stress in the plant, causing premature leaf loss (reduced photosynthesis, reduced shade, and reduced cooling capacity) and reduced sap flow (a key natural barrier to many intrusive pathogens and insects).

Soil Moisture Testing

Soil moisture testing is an important tool to the landscape maintenance practitioner. The use of a simple soil-testing probe can establish whether the soil conditions fall within the horticulturally appropriate range for the installed plants. Physical sampling of soil within the root ball of recently planted trees or shrubs, or within the drip line of mature trees, will permit the maintenance practitioner to make a quick field assessment of soil moisture. Soils that are too wet will be immediately recognizable by feel, smell, and color (anaerobic soils tend to produce a foul smell and will exhibit a gray/black/blue coloration with a greasy feel).

Soil chemistry can play a role in soil moisture relationships. Individual particles of some soil types, when they become excessively dry, will develop minute electrical charges that effectively repel water (surface tension). Soils in this condition may require some form of chemical "wetting agent" to overcome the surface tension and make it possible for water to percolate into the soil.

Soil Nutrition Levels

Plants rely on the soil matrix to provide a portion of the raw materials needed for plant growth. Some soils are naturally rich in nutrients, while others may be virtually sterile. Some soils may be rich in nutrients, but other factors (extremes of pH, low cation-exchange capacity, excessive moisture or dryness) prevent those nutrients from being available to plants. The mechanism by which nutrients migrate from the soil to the plant all occur at the microscopic and molecular level, and all require the presence of a minimum amount of water to serve as both a solvent (to release nutrient molecules from their substrate) and a bridge (to convey the molecules from the soil substrate to an absorptive surface of the nearest root hair).

The relative ease by which the nutrient molecules move from soil to plant is a function of the minute electrical charges that influence particle attraction. For example, many clay soils can be rich in nutrients, but if the attractive properties of individual clay particles are greater than that of the root hair, the nutrients will not be released and cannot migrate to the plant. Sandy soils, on the other hand, tend to have few attractive qualities and, combined with open pore spaces, allow most nutrients to leach out of the root zone so quickly as to be out of reach and unavailable to the root system. Under such conditions it becomes necessary to facilitate the absorption of nutrients either by foliar application (removing soil from the equation altogether) or by modifying the chemical or physical properties of the soil. The latter is generally achieved through the application and incorporation of various organic and/or inorganic soil amendments that can act as "middlemen" in the nutrient transaction. Organic amendments such as peat, composted wood shavings, composted bark fines, and similar "humus" materials attract and hold nutrients but readily yield them to root hairs. Inorganic amendments such as certain types of kiln-fired expanded shale, diatomaceous earth, and various ceramics accomplish the same. The choice between organic and inorganic amendments is generally made in the initial design phase of a project and is beyond the scope of this discussion; however, it is mentioned here as one consideration to be made in evaluating plant nutrition during the maintenance, as severe instances may require postinstallation remedial work.

Kelly F. Duke, Vice President, Pre-Construction Services, ValleyCrest Landscape Development, Calabasas, California

Knowing the soil chemistry, texture, and nutrient levels remains key to an effective plant maintenance program. Therefore, agronomic soil testing is advisable not only before planting, but periodically as the landscape matures. Such periodic testing will reveal how soil structure and nutrient levels change over time due to naturally increasing organic content, the impact of various soil-borne microorganisms, worms and burrowing insects, as well as supplemental fertilization and chemical components that may be deposited via irrigation water. Note that on the subject of irrigation water, the deposition of salt compounds may be accelerated when using recycled water, which has generally been treated with large quantities of chlorine for sanitation reasons.

Last, the mixture of plants and the relative age of the landscape can impact plant nutrition. A mature tree may suffer if subjected to competition from aggressive shrubs or ground cover plants in its understory. Leaf litter from some trees may alter the soil chemistry due to resins or other chemicals that leach out of the fallen foliage. If such long-term relationships were not considered during the design stage, it may fall upon the maintenance practitioner to compensate for any imbalance through augmented fertilizing or by the routine removal of leaf litter or the containment or removal of understory growth..

In some situations it may be advisable to fine-tune the maintenance regimen by testing the actual nutrient levels within the plants themselves. Foliar testing gives a truer picture of which nutrients are actually making their way into the plant. In circumstances where foliar testing reveals a deficiency of nutrients known to be present in the soil, the astute diagnostician can use the information to isolate the factor or factors preventing nutrient uptake. To recap, these factors can include, but are not limited to, the following:

- Too much or too little moisture in the soil
- Too high or too low pH levels
- Competition from other plants
- Insufficient pore space for air/moisture exchange

Supplemental Nutrition

When soil or foliage testing reveals a deficiency in one or more of the needed nutrient compounds, it may be necessary to add supplemental nutrients in the form of fertilizers. Fertilizers should be added once it is verified that there is a specific need for supplemental nutrients, and not some other matter of soil chemistry preventing existing nutrients from being available to plants. Based on the soils tests and recommendation, the maintenance practitioner can procure the appropriate amendments or fertilizer formulation and rate of application and apply it to the landscape area.

Mycorrhizal Fungi

In recent years, there has been interest in using different, but interrelated, approaches to improve nutrient availability in the root zone (rhizosphere). In nature, under ideal conditions, certain beneficial, naturally occurring, soil-borne fungi develop in the soil in the immediate vicinity of healthy growing roots. These fungi are considered symbiotic in that they coexist in close proximity to plant roots in a mutually beneficial relationship. These fungi, generally classified as *Mycorrhizae*, accomplish several important things in the pore space immediately adjacent to the roots:

- Mycorrhizae attach themselves to plant roots and create a more extensive and more effective conduit for nutrients (including nitrogen) existing in the soil, to be made available to plant roots.
- Plants use nitrogen to form many of the protein-based structures within the plant. The energy needed for building plant tissue comes from other nutrients (carbon, hydrogen, and oxygen) which, through photosynthesis, produce various sugars to support the chemical reactions in the plant.
- Mycorrhizae cannot photosynthesize, but have co-evolved with plants to obtain certain surplus sugars that they need for growth from host plants.
- Mycorrhizal fungi appear to improve their host plant's disease resistance. This is most likely through improved general plant health, as well as a more robust root system, and possibly through a buildup of beneficial phenolic compounds that may be activated as a localized or systemic defense response to invading pathogens by preventing pathogen growth or by blocking the means of invasion.

The Mycorrhizal fungi/root relationship works best under a relatively narrow range of conditions in the soil. One of the variables that can be most easily set off balance is the amount of nitrogen in the soil. Ironically, the more traditional approach of applying high-nitrogen fertilizers to enhance plant growth throws off the carbon-to-nitrogen ratio. This well-intentioned act appears to reduce the effectiveness of the Mycorrhizal fungi's capability to provide the plant with "free" nitrogen already in the soil. Thus, interest has increased in the use of fertilizers that are low in nitrogen, release nitrogen slowly, or add carbon along with nitrogen to maintain the carbon-to-nitrogen ratio in an effort to serve both plant and Mycorrhizae. The benefit of this type of program is that, in theory, drought tolerance is improved and supplemental fertilizer applications, as well as fungicide applications, are reduced over time as natural systems support, feed, and protect the plants at a microscopic level. Much of the interest in the low nitrogen or high-carbon fertilizers is presently theoretical and driven by anecdotal evidence. This area of study is in need of greater independent scientific testing and verification.

The significance of the preceding to the landscape architect is that much of the work with Mycorrhizal fungi is relatively new and cutting edge. Project owners and their maintenance practitioners may not know about it, and the design professional can serve as a catalyst in the dissemination of information about such low-tech, environmentally friendly approaches to landscape maintenance. Such approaches may hold the key to lowering long-term maintenance costs, with no discernible loss in quality and no compromise to the initial design intent.

Supplemental Irrigation

Providing plants with sufficient water is critical to their survival. In some parts of the country, some species of plants may be able to survive solely on naturally occurring rainfall. In other areas, the local climatic conditions or soil conditions may necessitate the need for supplemental irrigation to support healthy growth, especially if the landscape utilizes introduced, nonnative species. In highly developed urban areas, the prevalence of impermeable pavements, drainage collection systems, reflected heat, and other man-made conditions may impose a need for supplemental irrigation, in spite of ample, if ill-timed, natural precipitation.

Regardless of the reason, when supplemental irrigation is needed, it is important to consider the timing of the irrigation to the needs of the plant, and the delivery of the water to the area of the root zone with the greatest capacity to absorb the water (typically, within the upper 2 feet of soil at the drip line). The water should be delivered at a rate of application matched to the permeability of the soil (to reduce waste via runoff). Last, the amount of water should be matched to the needs of the plant(s) based on the theoretical rate by which the soil moisture will be depleted, as determined for the effective root zone depth, plant type, and local evapotranspiration rates.

Most modern landscape designs requiring supplemental watering will include an irrigation system coordinated to match the planting design. Depending on the just-named parameters, the method of irrigat-

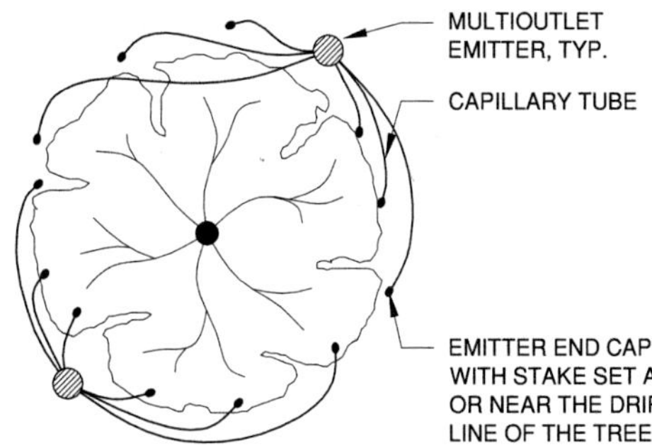

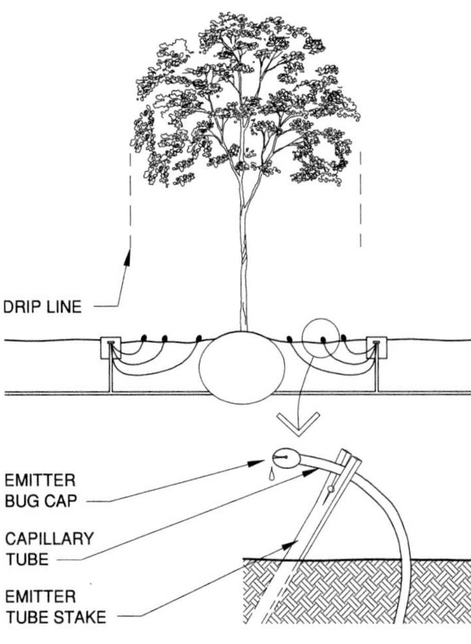

DRIP EMITTERS AT TREE DIP LINE

Kelly F. Duke, Vice President, Pre-Construction Services, ValleyCrest Landscape Development, Calabasas, California

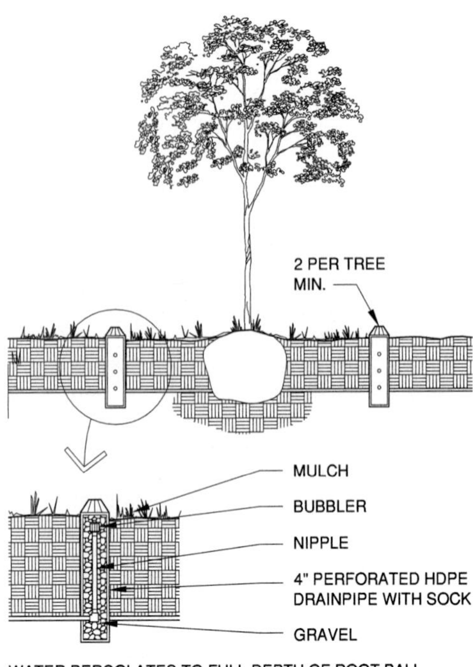

FLOOD BUBBLERS

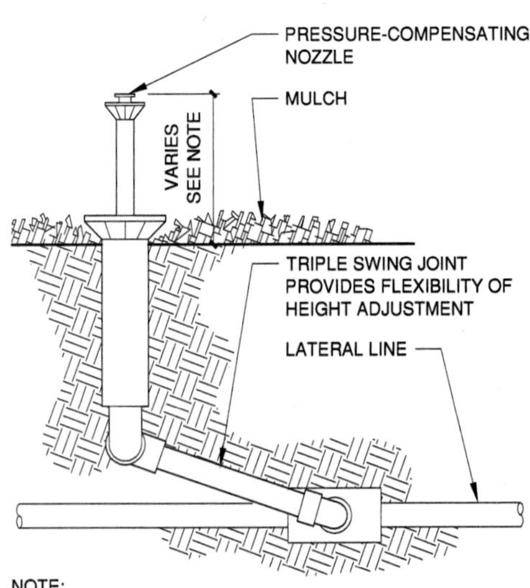

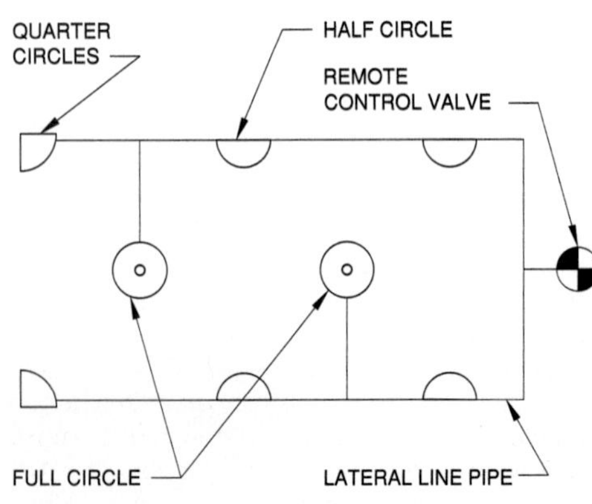

OVERHEAD SPRAYS

ing may rely on drip irrigation (low volume, long duration, multiple emitters distributed near the drip line—see the figure "Drip Emitters at Tree Dip Line"), bubbler irrigation (medium-volume flood irrigation within formed water retention basins at each plant—see the figure "Flood Bubblers"), or conventional overhead irrigation (medium-volume sprays or microsprays wetting the entire planted line area—see the figure "Overhead Sprays"). Additionally, many modern irrigation controllers are capable of monitoring local environmental conditions using either a dedicated weather station or third-party weather data provided to the controller wirelessly or through a hardwired connection. At a minimum, this weather data is used to adjust existing irrigation durations. At the cutting edge are controllers that evaluate weather data against historical evapotranspiration (ET) data, crop data, and soil data to make daily adjustments to both watering days and watering duration. Such systems can even establish the number of times the system might need to turn on and off and the amount of delays in between if the theoretical amount of water would likely cause runoff if delivered in one continuous application.

Where feasible, and especially where water resources are critical, an automatic, self-adjusting, ET-based irrigation controller should be specified. Regardless of the type of irrigation distribution system employed, the irrigation needs of trees, shrubs, ground cover, and turfgrass are each sufficiently different to warrant independent irrigation systems for each category of plant, separate from the other types of plant material. In the most sophisticated irrigation systems, design consideration may extend to separate systems for sun areas versus shade areas, or for widely different soil types.

Most modern ET-based controller systems will typically require the installing contractor to provide critical data relative to the plant type, soil type, slope, exposure, and average effective root zone depth. This information is programmed into the irrigation controller on a valve "zone-by-zone" basis. These data become the key factors that, in conjunction with the measured (or historic) daily ET values, drive the automatic controller adjustments. From the design perspective, it may be advisable to include these data as part of the planting legend, to assure that the correct information is considered in the initial set-up programming of the control system (see the table "Typical Data Entry Requirements").

Well-designed, modern irrigation systems will typically include a number of safeguards to prevent waste of water. Common among these are a rain sensor to override the normal irrigation programming and prevent the system from operating when rainfall renders such watering unnecessary. More sophisticated commercial irrigation systems will often include a flow sensor and a master valve. The purpose of these two components is to monitor the volume of water flowing through the system and compare that flow to the theoretical flow that should be occurring during each operational sequence programmed into the controller. When the actual flow exceeds the theoretical flow, the controller is programmed to assume that either there has been a line break or a prior valve has failed to close. When confronted with such an excess flow situation, the controller shuts down at the master valve. The most sophisticated systems are then equipped to relay a report of the incident to the maintenance provider via pager or via a wireless Internet text message to a phone or computer.

Areas with freezing winters must allow for the "winterization" of the irrigation system. The winterizing process involves shutting down all controllers and draining all of the water from the lateral and main lines, generally with the aid of compressed air. Water left in the lines will freeze and expand, splitting pipe or plastic components, warping metal castings. The resulting damage is costly in terms of potential erosion, damage to the landscape necessitated to dig up and repair broken components, and the cost of the replacement parts.

Regardless of the type or sophistication of the control system, the method of delivery, or the brand of component manufacture, it is necessary to periodically visually inspect and test each system. The purpose of such testing is to make certain that there are no leaks or broken lines, there are no clogged or misaligned sprinklers, and misting and overspray are minimized. Additionally, for those controllers that do not feature automatic schedule adjustment based on ET or weather station inputs, it is necessary to make seasonal adjustments to the controller program to match water application to plant need.

Insects and Vertebrate Pests

Garden pests take many forms. This discussion concentrates on the two-legged, four-legged, and six-legged varieties.

Death on Two Legs

While acts of vandalism, careless contractors, or kids chasing runaway balls or on skateboards can cause damage to the garden, these are generally the exception, not the rule, hence are not the principal concern of this section. The two-legged pests of concern here are certain birds that can cause damage with both their grazing habits and the resulting deposition of waste on an otherwise well-maintained garden. Geese, ducks, and, in some instances, gulls can easily cover a lawn, rendering it unsuitable for many

TYPICAL DATA ENTRY REQUIREMENTS FOR NEW GENERATION EVAPOTRANSPIRATION IRRIGATION CONTROLLERS

	VALVE NUMBER							
LANDSCAPE PARAMETERS*	**1**	**2**	**3**	**4**	**5**	**6**	**7**	**8**
Plant type (effective root depth)								
Soil type (infiltration rate and holding capacity)								
Slope (runoff factor)								
Microclimate (full sun vs. shade)								
Sprinkler precipitation rates (inches per hour)								
Sprinkler efficiency								

**Courtesy of HydroPoint Data Systems, copyright 2005.*

Kelly F. Duke, Vice President, Pre-Construction Services, ValleyCrest Landscape Development, Calabasas, California

family or commercial turf-based activities. There is not much that can be done about this, although measurable success has been achieved through the use of dogs that can be trained to run around barking and chasing the birds. For the dogs, it appears to be great sport, and the birds tend to find it sufficiently disconcerting to seek other places to congregate.

Four-Legged Fiends

Gophers, moles, voles, and groundhogs are burrowing rodents that can chew roots and lower stems of garden plants. Small plants can be easily destroyed by these animals. Larger, more established plants may survive if they have sufficient root mass to stay ahead of any destruction. Some installation details include provisions for mesh cages made of stiff plastic or steel hardware cloth. These cages surround the sides and bottom of the immediate root area to permit the plant to become established. The cages also prevent pest damage below the soil line at the base of the tree, which is nearly always fatal. If untreated, the steel cages oxidize over time and deteriorate in the soil with no long-term impact on the plant.

Depending on local rules and regulations, it may be possible to use a variety of poison grains or poison gas cartridges designed to kill the pests in their burrows. In-ground traps are designed to snag pests as they traverse their tunnels, either leaving or attempting to plug an open passage. (Check with local laws and restrictions regarding use of poison materials, or consult with a licensed/certified pest control operator to determine the type of pest and apply the most appropriate countermeasure.)

Aboveground pests such as rats, possum, skunk, and raccoons, tend to be interested in garbage, fruit, or vegetables, and cause a wide range of general mischief while searching through garbage for pet food, human food, fruit, or vegetables. Rabbits appear more intent on grazing on grass, remaining at the ground plane while they devour most everything in their path. Poisoning of any of these animals is generally not an option, and control generally depends on the use of humane traps and relocation to more appropriate wilderness areas. There are a number of deterrent products on the market intended to keep these pests away. These include lifelike owls, ultrasonic sound generators, and repellent products utilizing unpleasant smells including that of the urine (both natural or synthetic) of wolves, coyotes, or other natural predators. Home remedies such as moth balls, pepper sprays, and sachets have been offered as possible alternatives.

Vertebrate pests such as deer are too big to trap and unlikely to be intimidated by plastic owls. Repellants utilizing the scent of predators is available. Often, fencing is the only way to prevent deer from browsing and foraging. It should be noted, however, that because of the jumping capabilities of deer and their kin, it may be necessary to install fencing upwards of 10 or 12 feet to be effective. Shorter fences have been utilized in zoological settings, provided that a wide band of irregular stone cobble or riprap is installed on the approach side so as to deny deer firm footing from which to jump.

Landscapers in areas known to have deer problems may want to consider during the design and planting phase the use of plant materials known to be unpopular with the animals, to decrease the likelihood of postinstallation and long-term problems associated with deer.

Other Wee Beasts

Insects and related arthropods constitute the last category of pests. Insects are probably the most common pest problem facing the landscape, and there is a wide range of options available for their control, depending on the use and users of the landscape. For example, a large-scale industrial operation may see cost, efficiency, and effectiveness as the driving forces in deciding on control measures. Such an agenda would likely favor the most appropriate modern economic poisons. Public facilities, hotel and hospitality, or residential developments may seek to minimize the use of strong synthetic pesticides for fear of any liability from public exposure to application or lingering residual effects. Such operations may seek to use a combination of insecticidal soaps, lower-toxicity or (shorter residual) chemicals, along with biological controls or traps. In some instances, the acknowledged use of such "green" or "environmentally friendly" approaches can be utilized as part of a wider public awareness and marketing campaign for both the owner and the maintenance practitioner.

In most circumstances, prevention is the best strategy; and healthy plants can do much to resist initial attacks on their own. A healthy landscape can also promote a sufficiently diverse mix of life that will generally include beneficial insects and animals that can tip the scales in favor of natural systems over chemical warfare.

The fact of the matter is that no hard-and-fast rule can be offered here, except that when it comes to insecticides, what is used, how it is used, and what precautions must be taken for both use and for final reentry into treated areas will be determined by local, state, or federal agencies having jurisdiction over the environment and any registered or controlled pesticide products. It is incumbent upon the design community to emphasize in its specifications and construction documents this precaution by specifying that any registered pesticides be applied by a licensed/certified pest control applicator/operator (specific title varies with agency). Further, any owner or design professional interested in promoting "sustainable development," "environmentally friendly," or "green" initiative in his or her overall building program should emphasize this in the project specifications and include, where possible, references or referrals to additional resources to spur this initiative among the landscape maintenance community.

Disease

For the purpose of this discussion, plant diseases are considered to be any of a number of fungal, bacterial, or viral pathogens that may infect and damage or kill the plant they attack. Other conditions that may be considered a "disease" may be the exposure of a plant to toxic fumes (e.g., natural gas leak or airborne solvents) or damage resulting from extremes of heat, cold, sun, or shadow. Fungal, bacterial, and viral diseases may have counteracting chemical treatments available. The other conditions will generally require mitigation of the damaging external factor (e.g., fix the gas leak, activate orchard heaters, etc.), covered later in this subsection.

Infectious plant diseases vary significantly with each species and with each geographical region and climate zone. It is therefore difficult, if not impossible, to attempt to discuss the various combinations in any detail here. What is important from the standpoint of the landscape designer is to recognize that plant diseases can cause significant damage to the landscape if not quickly and accurately detected, diagnosed, and treated. As the rules and regulations regarding methods and materials of treatment also vary with species by disease, by plant type, by the situation at each location, and by the governing agency (or agencies) having jurisdiction in that area, no simple answers can be provided.

The best and most effective step that can be taken by the landscape designer is to include in his or her project specifications the requirement that the maintenance practitioner have on staff a properly trained pest control applicator/advisor licensed or certified by the appropriate local authorities having jurisdiction over such professions. Only in this way can the property owner have some degree of confidence that appropriate and timely action will be taken and that any chemicals applied will be approved and registered for such use.

In terms of advancing general information on the subject, there are several methods of applying treatments for infectious disease organisms. Treatments can be applied by foliar spray to active growing plants; spray to dormant plant branches, stems, and trunk; systemic treatments administered through direct trunk injection; or soil treatments or systemic treatments administered by soil drench.

Abiotic or noninfectious plant diseases are typically the result of environmental stress or trauma. Such stress may come in the form of incorrect light intensity, temperature, ambient air pollution, or the inadvertent release of chemical fumes. Disease symptoms may be observed as the result of a broken gas main; overspray; or drift of cleaning compounds, solvents, paint, pressure washers, abrasive blasting, or other common exterior maintenance techniques on the subject property or an adjacent structure. Such exposure can lead to leaf damage or defoliation, detracting from the intended look of the landscape design. If such factors that could lead to such symptoms are known to exist at the time of planning and design, it falls upon the landscape designer to acknowledge the issues and, then, design to address such concerns. If the factors evolve after installation, perhaps as a result of adjacent development or careless acts of others, the factors were likely beyond the scope of the designer and may even be beyond the control of the owner or the maintenance professional. Under this latter scenario, the key is to identify the causal agent and determine whether any damage is permanent, disfiguring, or simply something that will be resolved as new growth replaces damaged growth. Should the causal agent be traceable to an identifiable source, there may be legal remedy for repairs or replacements; however, such matters are beyond the scope of this discussion and, in any case, are best left to forensic and legal authorities.

Physical/Mechanical Damage

Plants suffer a wide range of physical damage on a daily basis. Wind, ice, snow, pedestrians, vehicles, and even landscape maintenance equipment all conspire to break limbs and branches, defoliate, or girdle trees and shrubs. Spilled maintenance chemicals or lawn mower fuel, pet urine, and deicing salts can also cause irreparable damage to turf. Objects that induce a prolonged period of shade, such as a tarp or a protective cover, when left in place for an extended

Kelly F. Duke, Vice President, Pre-Construction Services, ValleyCrest Landscape Development, Calabasas, California

period of time, can lead to severe sun scald when finally removed. Of equal concern, clear plastic or glass screening or protective plastic tarps used to encourage new growth can act as a greenhouse, trapping heat and humidity when it is not needed, and can also create heat stress or foster plant diseases that can kill all or parts of lawns, ground cover, or shrubs.

As with noninfectious plant diseases, mechanical damage is generally a one-time occurrence resulting from an accident, a lack of planning, or a lack of proper training and technique by maintenance personnel. Prevention is best served through the proper prequalification of maintenance providers; a clear set of maintenance documents, including both prescriptive and performance specifications; and periodic inspections of maintenance operations and results.

Competing Plants: Weeds

A weed has been defined as "a plant out of place." Therefore, at any given time, any given plant may be a weed if it growing where it is either not wanted or not needed. For the purpose of this discussion, weeds are defined in a more traditional sense: as any of a number of common, but undesired and often noxious, plants that insinuate themselves into an ornamental landscape to the detriment of the health or look of the intended design. Weeds are a problem for several reasons:

- They impact the visual appeal of the project's original design intent.
- They compete with the desired plants for available water, soil nutrients, and space.
- They may serve as an alternative host plant capable of transmitting disease or harboring insect pests detrimental to the desired plant palette.

There are a number of ways to deal with weeds. The most immediate and intimate approach can be described as "hand-to-hand combat": pulling individual weeds, roots and all, from the ground. This approach is immediate in that, for most species, one can be pretty sure that pulling up the roots eliminates the problem. Plants are tricky, however, and many have evolved subversive techniques such as breakaway nodules that remain in the soil with enough stored reserves to relaunch an attack in short order (e.g., Bermudagrass, nut sedge, oxalis, etc.). Other plants simply make a point of distributing seeds so efficiently and effectively that one constantly needs to be pulling weeds.

The physical conditions at some project sites may not be conducive to the manual pulling of weeds. Steeply sloping land, for example, may rely on networks of plant roots to help stabilize and secure the surface soils from erosion. Such slopes may be exposed to increased erosion if the soil surface is disturbed or if roots are pulled out. Under such circumstances, cutting weeds off may be the more prudent approach. This approach may not eliminate the weed, however.

For reasons of potential erosion, as well as overriding economic concerns, most weed control is accomplished through the application of chemical herbicides. Advances in herbicide formulation have resulted in a wider range of selective chemicals (chemicals that are toxic to a narrow range of plants) and systemic chemicals (chemicals that are translocated throughout the treated plant and thereby kill the roots and below-grade nodules). Chemical herbicides, like pesticides, are typically registered by various state or federal agencies for specific uses on specific plants under specific circumstances. As with insecticides and fungicides, the application of herbicides is best left to certified or registered pest control applicators. Such operators are obliged under their certification/registration principles to adhere to all the rules and regulations governing herbicide use and can select the most efficient, effective, and safe product to use in any given situation.

One thing to consider relative to weed control in the landscape is to require a weed eradication program prior to planting. Under such a program, the landscape area is prepared for planting and is irrigated for a period of time (generally two weeks) with the specific intent of germinating any latent weed seeds that may be in the soil. Once germinated, the weeds are sprayed with a nonselective, systemic herbicide. The process is repeated for a second two week period. The purpose of irrigating the area for a second two week period is twofold: to germinate any remaining weeds and to verify successful kill of those weeds sprayed in the initial pass. Generally, after two iterations of this type of program, the site is free of all potential weeds. This gives the desired plantings a chance to become established before new weeds have a chance to be introduced to the area by wind, animals, and so on.

Once the desired plantings are established and have a solid footing of roots in the soil, it may be possible to apply a post-installation, pre-emergent herbicide. Pre-emergent herbicides are worked into the upper few inches of the soil horizon, where they reside in the pore spaces of the soil in a dense, semi-gaseous state. Roots that are below this layer grow unobstructed. Seeds that land on the surface of the soil and attempt to push new roots through this zone are killed when sensitive root hairs hit the vaporous barrier. Pre-emergent herbicides vary in effectiveness but generally will last a period of 90 days between applications, provided that the soil surface is left undisturbed (pulling weeds or cultivating soil allows the chemical to volaiitize to the atmosphere). Such pre-emergent herbicides can save a tremendous amount of labor when applied in a timely and appropriate manner.

Post-emergent selective herbicides are available for post-installation use for some species of weeds in some ornamental crops. Of primary concern are those herbicides that tackle broadleaf weeds such as dandelions, oxalis, or spurge in turfgrass, or Bermudagrass in cool-weather turf. These chemicals are generally very effective but may be considered restricted in some areas and so require a special permit for application. The reason for such precaution is that these products may be "selective" in the context of the desired host plant that they are sprayed upon. For example, 2, 4 Dichlorophenoxyacetic acid, "2, 4-D," is registered for use against a range of broadleaf weeds growing in certain types of turfgrass. Under the strict limits of its registered use, the herbicide is selective in that it will kill the broadleaf weeds without harming the turf. If sprayed among other broadleaf plants, however, 2, 4-D will likely damage or kill a majority of the broadleaf shrubs, ground cover, and so on. Selectivity is a function of the relative difference between the target weed and the nontarget substrate plantings.

The preceding is offered only as a high-level overview of weed control. As noted previously, weed control regulations vary by region and one must verify the label requirements and restrictions of any herbicide considered for use. All chemical applications should be performed by a professional who is certified or licensed for that task and who can show you his or her certification as evidence of that authorization.

Future Considerations for General Landscape Maintenance Procedures

In recent years, many owners and their design teams have elected to follow certain environmentally friendly guidelines for construction. An excellent example is the set of guidelines laid out by the United States Green Building Council (USGBC). USGBC's Leadership in Energy and Environmental Design (LEED) program awards various levels of certification to projects where, through planning, engineering, and system efficiencies, and design and maintenance programs, there is a demonstrable reduction in energy inputs and waste end products.

One approach being used in many projects seeking LEED certification is the establishment of maintenance programs that minimize the use of synthetic fertilizers, pesticides, and herbicides in favor of naturally occurring compounds, biological control programs, and integrated pest management strategies. Such programs utilize recycled water, humus or sewage sludge-based fertilizers, recycled "green waste" for mulch, and naturally occurring herbicides, fungicides, and pesticides. Through a combination of cultural practices, timing, and alternative chemical products, these projects are exploring various approaches to "green" maintenance and whether there is any cost premium inherent in such environmentally friendly approaches.

As for maintenance in general, beyond the timely and prudent implementation of general maintenance practices, the simplest rule to follow in terms of respecting the original design intent is to protect and enhance those qualities of the various trees, shrubs, and ground covers that led to their selection as part of the design palette in the first place. In the following sections, specific techniques for consideration in the maintenance program are described in detail as they relate to their specific plant material type (trees, shrubs, etc.).

WOODY TREES

The greatest asset of a landscape is its trees. The architecture of a property can be designed and constructed or remodeled to mimic the style and motifs of any era or age. Such architectural techniques and tricks can disguise the true age or true quality of any structure. Large trees, on the other hand, convey a truer sense of the age or the permanence of the structures among which they abide. Along with any practical benefits of shade, visual screening, or wind protection, trees provide the landscape designer with a host of design elements to complement the built environment, whether it be with strong vertical lines, broad tracery of branches silhouetted against a sky, hedges to frame a view, or mature trees that through their age serve as a metaphorical anchor to some past time.

Trees, like all plantings, require routine maintenance if they are to thrive and continue to serve the aesthetics of the original design intent. The good

Kelly F. Duke, Vice President, Pre-Construction Services, ValleyCrest Landscape Development, Calabasas, California

news is that the frequency of such routine maintenance is far less than that of shrubs, ground cover, or turf. As trees mature, the techniques and equipment needed to provide proper maintenance escalate; however, the frequency is still measured in seasons and not in months or weeks.

That trees extend well above the ground plane necessarily imposes special considerations not typical to the plantings at the pedestrian level. First, as the tree grows, it becomes necessary to perform work up in the branch structure. Second, the height and spread of mature trees inevitably means that maintenance activities will impact any roads, walkways, public utilities, or buildings that they abut. The matter of encroachment is most likely to occur in urban settings, but can also be problematic at suburban sites. Assuming that the trees on a given project can be accessed solely from within the boundaries of that project, the proximity of adjacent and abutting property lines may still impact such activities as pruning (pedestrian and vehicular traffic control where a tree's drip line crosses property lines or easements), clearances around overhead utility lines, or the application of pesticides (drip or drift onto adjacent property). When trees are situated such that they are not wholly accessible from within the property on which they are planted, it may be necessary to negotiate access to the trees from adjacent property owners. How this is conducted is beyond the scope of this discussion and is mentioned here only to alert the designer to the need to think strategically in the design stage. It is also intended to alert the property owner and the maintenance practitioner to plan early in the life of the planted landscape so as to minimize the impact of such constraints before they become issues that can only be resolved by the severe pruning or removal of the tree due to issues of cost or liability.

The following maintenance considerations are organized in the approximate sequence that they would typically be relevant to the tree. That is, items important to trees in the immediate years after installation, then items that become progressively more important as trees mature.

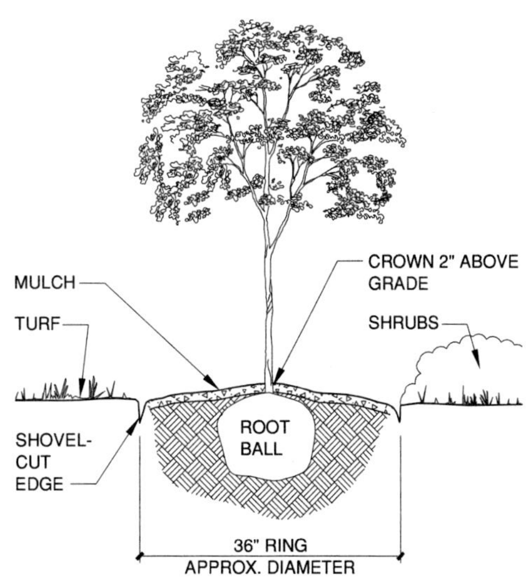

MULCH RING

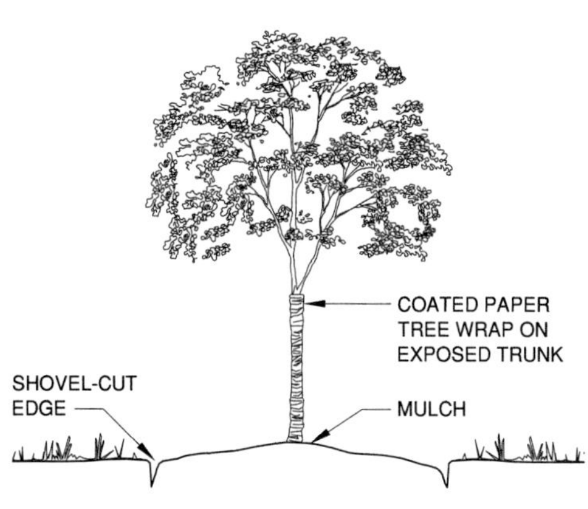

TRUNK WRAP

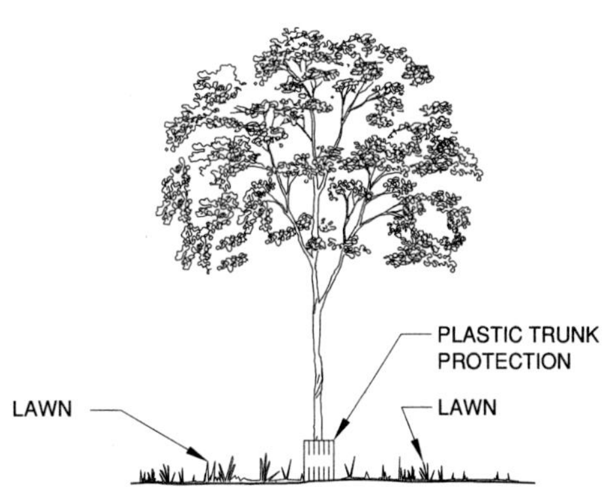

NO MULCH NECESSARY IF USING TREE TRUNK PROTECTION COLLAR

TRUNK PROTECTION

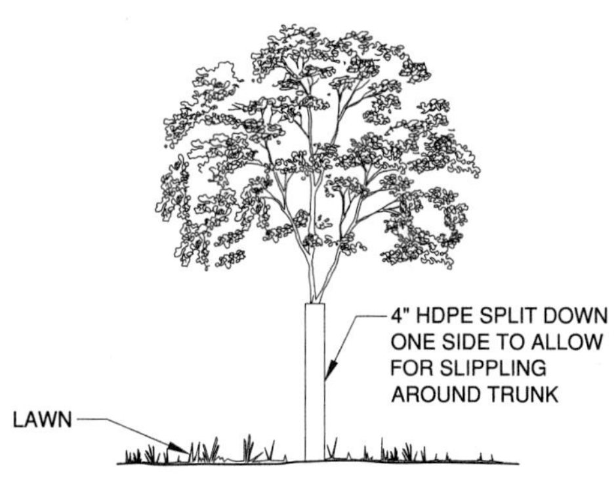

NO MULCH RING IF USING A TREE PROTECTION SYSTEM

HDPE PIPE AS TRUNK WRAP

Trunk Protection

The bark of young trees is relatively thin compared to that of older trees. At the same time, the smaller diameter of younger trees means that there is a greater chance that an errant and unintended cut might damage the conductive tissue (cambium layer of xylem and phloem) that moves water and nutrients up and down through the tree. A 1-inch-long gash on a 1-inch-diameter tree could result in damage to one-third of the total conductive tissue. This could result in severe stress to a young tree. The same gash at the base of a 6-inch-diameter tree equates to approximately one-eighteenth of the total cambium cross section. Such damage may not be as troublesome on mature trees, where the thickness of the bark may afford some protection to the cambium layer. Nonetheless, the scarring can be unattractive; and it should be noted that while any one cut will not likely kill the tree, repeated cutting might sufficiently damage the tree either directly or by providing an entry point for secondary problems such as insects, fungi, or bacteria.

Damage of the type just described is likely to come from the careless use of a lawn mower or nylon cord trimmer too close to the trunk. Such damage is easy to avoid through the following maintenance practices:

- For "mower blight," the use of a ring of mulch around the base of the tree will provide a suitable buffer zone negating the need to mow immediately against the tree (see the figure "Mulch Ring").
- Where the use of a mulch ring is not a desirable in terms of project aesthetics, the use of a plastic trunk guard (tree boot, arbor guard, etc.) is a simple approach that may be less visually obtrusive (see the figure "Trunk Protection").
- If neither approach is suitable in terms of design aesthetics, the maintenance specifications should be written to require handtrimming of turf at the base of trees in turf.

Trunk Wrap

In areas of climatic extremes, some varieties of trees are recommended to be planted with a protective trunk wrap. This wrap will consist of either a resin-coated heavy paper stock or elasticized cloth similar to an elastic bandage (see the figure "Trunk Wrap"). The wrap is generally tan or white in color. Some installations have utilized single-wall corrugated polyethylene drain pipe in lieu of a bandagelike wrap (see the figure "HDPE Pipe as Trunk Wrap").

The purpose of the wrap is to insulate the trunk to protect the cambium layer below the bark. The application is typically made to trees with very thin juvenile bark, especially when those trees have been pruned into a "standard" form (a single-leader trunk with all side branches removed to a height of approximately 6 feet above the soil line). The lack of protective foliage along the trunk can lead to freeze damage (especially on the side of the trunk facing the prevailing winter winds). The lack of protective foliage can also lead to sun scald when a hot desert sun beats down on a trunk of a deciduous tree that has not leafed out for the season.

Trunk wrapping is mentioned here primarily for the purpose of advising that it need not remain on the tree for an extended period of time. Most wraps will deteriorate over time and will likely require removal for appearance reasons after the first season. Even more tenacious wrap should be removed to facilitate air circulation during the normal growing season. As bark thickens, or as the canopy of the tree becomes more dense, or surrounding plantings begin to mature and screen, the need for a protective trunk wrap will diminish.

Mulching

Mulching around the base of newly planted trees in shrub or ground-cover areas is a common practice, as

Kelly F. Duke, Vice President, Pre-Construction Services, ValleyCrest Landscape Development, Calabasas, California

the shrub and ground-cover plants are typically mulched anyway. The use of mulch rings around trees planted in lawn areas is generally regarded as a practice in areas utilizing trees harvested and sold as "ball and burlap" (B&B) nursery stock. B&B trees are generally planted high relative to the surrounding soil line. Planting the tree high will prevent standing water from accumulating next to the trunk. This practice tends to expose the top of the root ball to drying. Adding a thick layer of mulch helps to protect the surface roots of the root ball until the balance of the root ball can push out into the surrounding soil and begin the task of supporting the tree. In addition, this approach seems to protect the bark and surface roots from soil-borne or water-borne pathogens that may enter the tree in the narrow zone just above the soil line. As mentioned earlier, a mulched ring at the base of a tree in a lawn area also provides a suitable buffer against "mower blight."

As a result, trees are frequently mulched when they are planted, and the maintenance program must provide for periodic replenishment of the mulch layer. The mulch ring at the base of a tree, installed to protect from disease or root drying, may not be necessary for some species that begin to build thick bark as they mature. The mulch's secondary role as a protective mowing buffer may suggest that it remain in place and be replenished annually.

Some Southwestern trees such as native oak trees are planted with a large mulch area as a means of protecting the root zone from interrelated problems of overwatering, soil compaction within the drip line, and competing growth from understory plantings. These precautions serve another purpose in that they can help to stabilize a tree that may be infected with oak root fungus: They will never cure the infection, but the tree may be able to continue growing comfortably ahead of the disease through horticultural practices that favor the tree while providing the pathogen no comforts. Mulching under oak trees may take the form of wood bark, gravel, cobbles, or natural oak leaf litter.

Staking and Guying

Newly planted trees are frequently secured in place by the use of staking or guying to keep the trunk from leaning or breaking as a result of wind or other factors. Ideally, tree stakes should be set away from the tree so as to not shade the trunk (see the figure "Staking Options"). Ties or guys securing the trunk should be loose where they encircle the trunk or limb so as to not girdle the tree (see the figure "Guying"). Ties or guys should have some form of protective collar to prevent chafing or cutting into the trunk or limb, and they should allow for a small amount of movement in the trunk, as such movement appears to stimulate the formation of "reaction wood" that leads to a more structurally sound trunk taper.

As with "mower blight," cutting damage can result from the tree ties associated with staking or from the guy wires used to support new trees. The actual damage is likely to come from a failure of the maintenance practitioner to adjust or remove tree stakes or guys in a timely manner. All too often, once installed, the stakes, ties, and guys are left unattended and begin to girdle the tree (cut into the trunk or major branches so as to slice through the xylem and phloem conductive tissues) (see the figure "Trunk Girdling"). This condition can be prevented if the ties or guys are routinely inspected and periodically adjusted to match the diameter of the "noose" with the increasing caliper of the growing tree. A second approach is to utilize more forgiving tying or guying materials. The use of plastic or fabric straps in lieu of wire leads can often allow for some "give" and even eventual environmental degradation that decrease the potential for girdling.

From the standpoint of the landscape designer, maintenance specifications and detail drawings should be provided that delineate how much movement is allowable and how frequently the staking and guying should be inspected and readjusted to compensate for growth.

Pruning

Probably the single most critical issue relative to trees in the landscaping is how and when the various species of trees are pruned. Pruning impacts virtually every aspect of the tree as a landscape element:

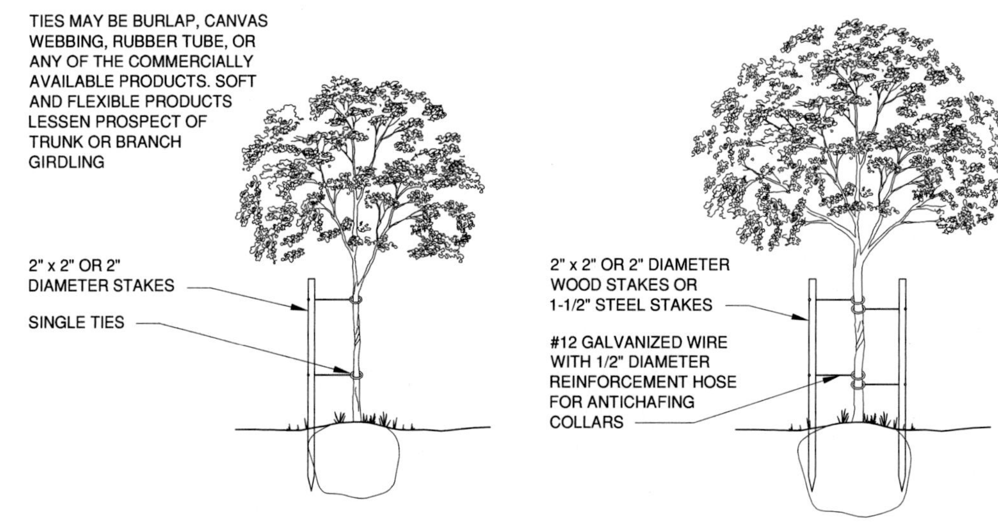

STAKING OPTIONS

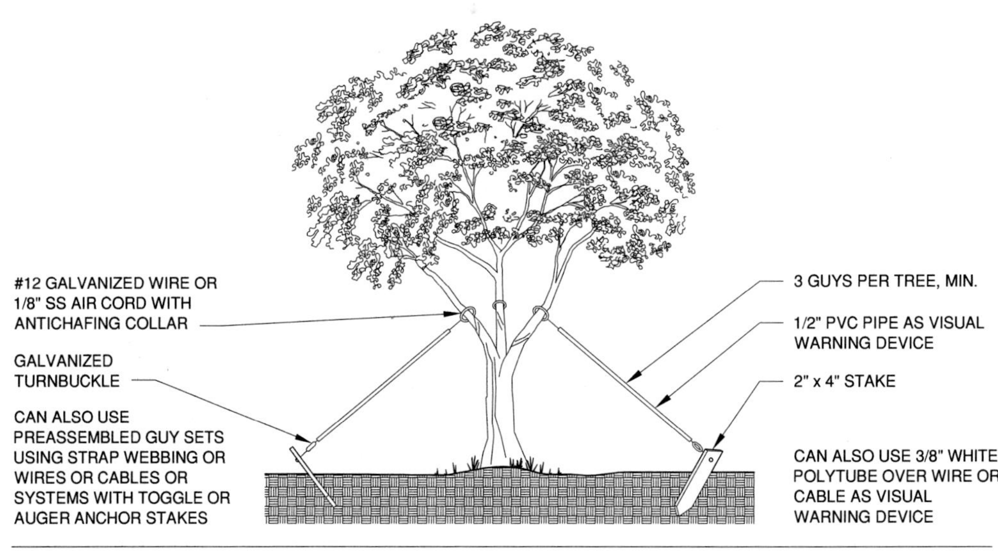

GUYING

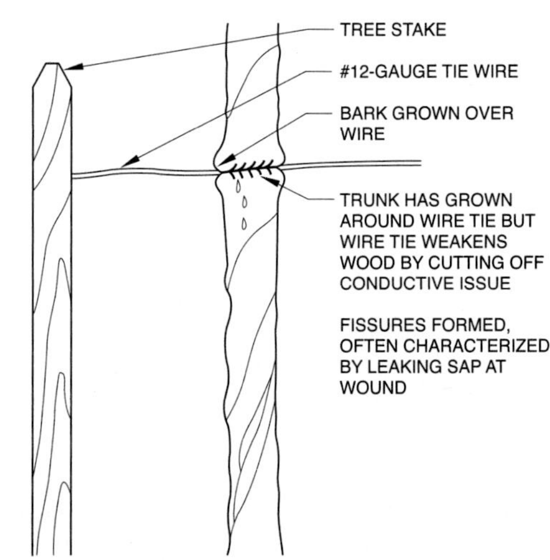

TRUNK GIRDLING

Kelly F. Duke, Vice President, Pre-Construction Services, ValleyCrest Landscape Development, Calabasas, California

- Pruning impacts tree appearance in terms of shape and balance, density, and size.
- Pruning impacts the structural integrity of the major scaffold of branches.
- Pruning can influence the relative likelihood of mechanical damage by maintaining adequate vehicular clearances, influencing the strength of branch crotches, and reducing potential live loads (wet foliage, snow, ice, or wind).
- Pruning can impact flower or fruit production.
- Pruning can prevent damage to abutting structures and public utilities.
- Pruning can influence trunk or branch caliper girth development.

Pruning is one area of maintenance where it is advisable to develop strict, prescriptive specifications. Such specifications should clearly illustrate, by drawing or by reference photographs, the desired look of every species of tree on the project. Further, the maintenance specification should delineate different pruning requirements at different stages of the tree's development.

Pruning requirements vary from species to species and depend on the natural growth habit and idiosyncrasies of the tree. For example, a tree that tends to grow vertically with a strong central leader (apically dominant) cannot be pruned to become a broad spreading dome. Cutting an apically dominant tree's central leader will stimulate the next latent buds on the leader to develop. These buds will commence to grow vertically, as did the leader before it. At best the result will be a tree that has multiple vertical leaders (see the figure "Apically Dominant Tree").

Within that natural growth habit, the arborist is permitted some latitude to influence the spread, height, strength, and density of the tree. In the final analysis, pruning should be seen as a process, not a project. Pruning never ends, and each cut must be made not only with consideration as to what it will mean to the look of the tree today, but what it will mean to the overall tree two or three years in the future. This is especially true in the first years after planting, when maintenance personnel have the opportunity to start the process of building the scaffold of major branches that will carry the weight of the tree over its lifetime.

As noted, each species has different pruning requirements. Without attempting a species-by-species description of those requirements, this discussion will outline basic concepts that can help the landscape designer understand what needs to be incorporated into specifications and details to preserve the integrity of the design intent:

- *Remove dead wood.* Dead wood can become an entry point for boring insects into the tree and should be removed.
- *Remove diseased wood.* Diseased wood should be removed, but not before it is clear as to the nature of the disease. Correct pruning with sterilized equipment sufficiently ahead of the progress of the disease may effectively remove the disease so that it cannot progress through the tree.
- *Remove limbs or branches growing the wrong way.* Except in certain instances of topiary or bonsai work, branches growing contrary to the normal shape of the tree should be removed. This includes crossing branches, branches growing downward, and branches growing at radical angels contrary to the generally desired shape.
- *Prune for strength.* Branching should occur at roughly right angles. Branches with narrow crotch angles will build layers of nonstructural tissue that blocks the formation of structural "grain" between the main branch and the lateral branch. Pruning should favor wider branch angles.
- *Prune to direct future growth.* Pruning of lateral branches can be performed to direct future growth. Working back from the tip of a branch, pruning should occur adjacent to a dormant leaf bud. A majority of new branch growth will occur at the bud nearest to the cut and will grow in the direction that the bud is facing.
- *Evaluate cuts from multiple angles.* Before any major cut is made, it is best to mark the branch under consideration and look at that branch from the vantage of a 360-degree walkaround. The review should be to evaluate the void in the scaffold of branches that will result if the branch is removed. The review should follow the branch up through the tree and consider all of its subordinate branches and limbs. Keep in mind that unless there is some critical issue requiring the removal of the branch, it is better to leave it and revaluate later than risk making a cut that throws the shape or structure of the tree off balance. As in carpentry, "measure twice, cut once" can be applied to pruning.
- *Drop-crotch in lieu of blunt-cut.* As trees mature, they reach size limits dictated by their environment or the limits of their genetic predisposition. Assuming that routine pruning has led the tree to a suitable strong branching structure, most cuts to a mature tree should be by what is known as "drop-crotching." Drop-crotching involves the removal of whole lateral limbs or branches at the point where they emerge from their support branch (see the figure "Drop-Crotch Pruning"). Drop-crotching is done to thin or "lace out" a tree, not to reduce the drip line or height dimensions. Conversely, "blunt-cutting" involves the cutting of major branches, perpendicular to their grain, at some point other than a branch junction.

Blunt-cutting a major branch is typically done under the rationale that it will reduce the overall dimensions of the tree and, thereby, the potential wind load. The unfortunate truth is that blunt-cutting tends to force a large profusion of weak limbs

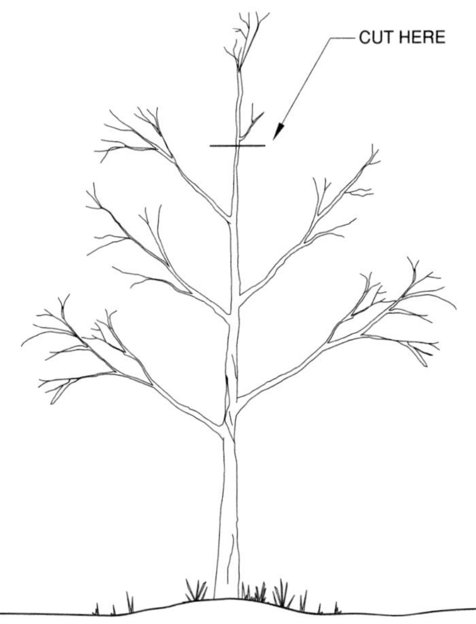

BEFORE CUTTING LEADER

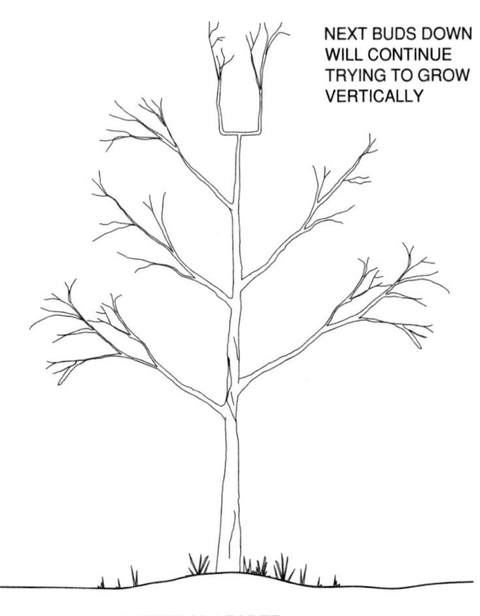

AFTER CUTTING CENTRAL LEADER
TWO LEADERS (OR MORE) DEVELOP

APICALLY DOMINANT TREE

REMOVED BRANCHES

BRANCHES TO REMAIN

INTERMEDIATE BRANCHES ARE REMOVED BACK TO THEIR POINT OF ORIGIN TO EFFECTIVELY OPEN UP TREE. RESULT IS BETTER SUNLIGHT PENETRATION TO INTERIOR LEAVES, LESS WIND RESISTANCE, MORE EVEN AND MODERATED REGROWTH.

DROP-CROTCH PRUNING

Kelly F. Duke, Vice President, Pre-Construction Services, ValleyCrest Landscape Development, Calabasas, California

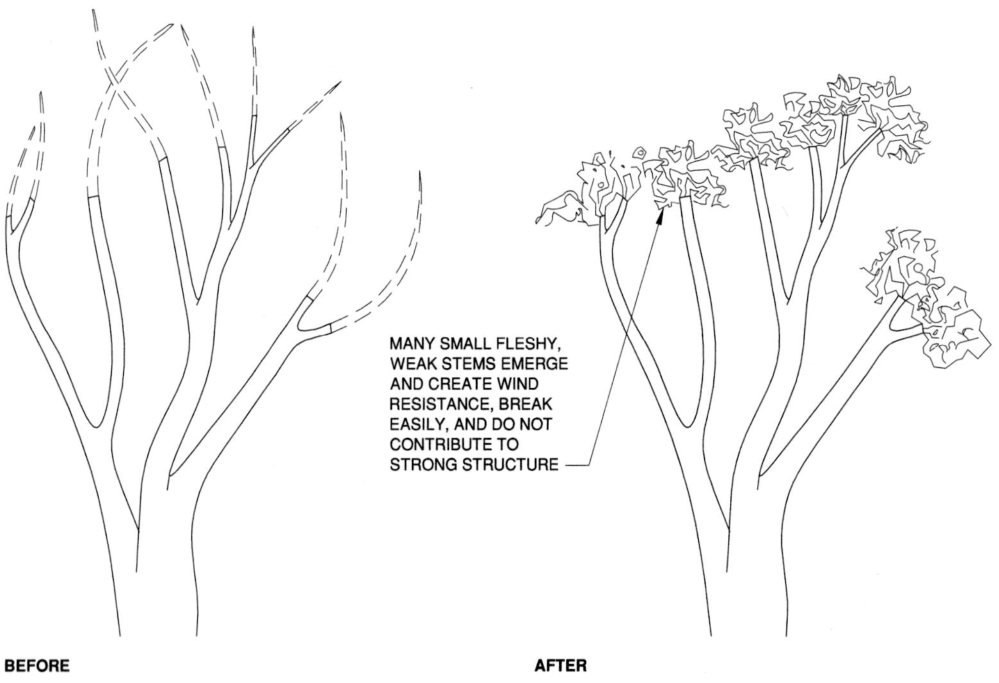

BLUNT-CUT PRUNING

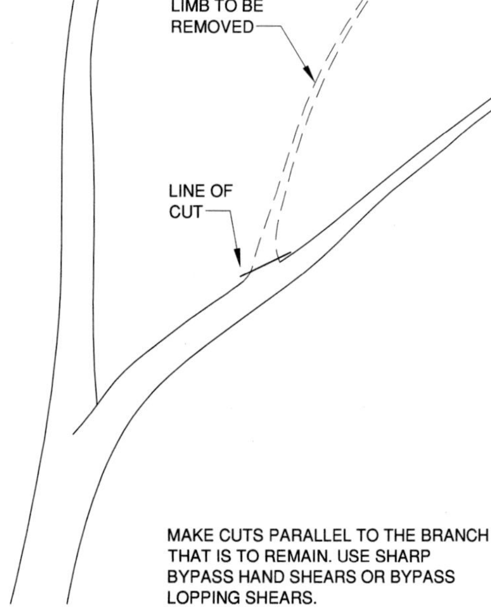

FLUSH CUT

with heavy foliage at the terminal end of the cut branch (see the figure "Blunt-Cut Pruning"). The dense profusion of weak, heavily leafed limbs breaks easy in a strong wind. Thus, reducing the tree canopy through blunt-cutting will likely lead to greater wind damage than the reduction of tree density through strategic drop-crotching.

Influencing Caliper Development

The structural development of trees relies on many things. One of those is the ability of the tree to produce the necessary energy it needs for growth. This process occurs in the leaves by virtue of photosynthesis. Removing leaves cuts photosynthetic capacity within a tree. As a result, unnecessary pruning or pruning during the growing season should be avoided, unless the goal is to specifically moderate the tree's growth. In electing what and where to make the various pruning cuts, it is important to know that leaving side branches on a main trunk or side limbs on a main branch will contribute to more rapid caliper development. This is true even if a portion of side branches is removed, leaving just leave small stubs with a few leaves on them. Thus, it may be advisable to leave the side branches on a young street tree to encourage as much trunk girth as possible in its youth before beginning the process of trimming off the trunk limbs to achieve pedestrian or vehicular clearance. Branching that extended beyond the width of the parkway could be tipped back for clearance as needed, but the bulk of the actual side branches, if left in place, would benefit trunk growth tremendously.

For matters involving flower or fruit production, it is best to consult documents relating to the specific flower or fruit crop to find out the best timing and location for cuttings, to encourage the best flower and fruit growth.

Pruning cuts to small limbs should be made clean, with a sharp pruning shear, lopper, or pole pruner. Pruning cuts to larger branches should be made clean with a sharp pruning saw. It should be noted that pruning saws are different from conventional carpenter's saws in that they cut on the pull stroke. Cutting on the pull stroke generally affords the arborist greater control and balance when suspended in a tree or on a ladder. The shears or saws should be properly adjusted and sharp. Cuts to reduce the length of a limb and redirect future growth should be made immediately beyond the bud selected to define the direction of future growth of the limb (see the figure "Tip Pruning at Bud"). Drop-crotch cuts of lateral branches should be made close as possible to the support branch from which the lateral emanates (see the figure "Flush-Cut"). While there is no science supporting the effectiveness of sealing pruned cuts with pruning sealant, on certain trees it improves the appearance of the cut.

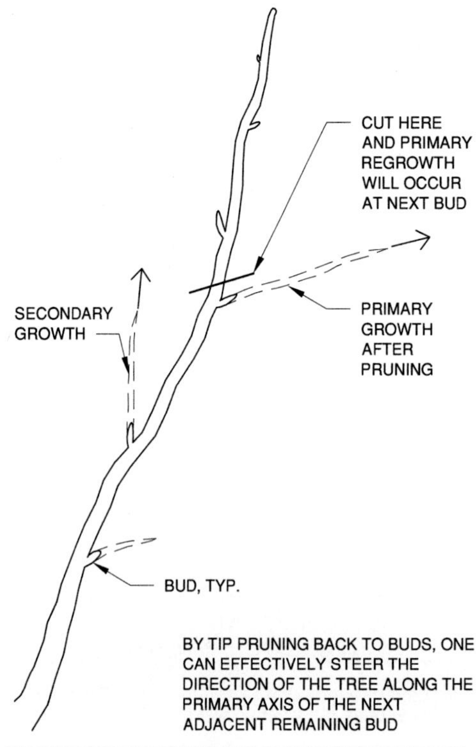

TIP PRUNING AT BUD

Pruning can be a mechanism for the unwitting transfer of infectious diseases from one tree to another. If there is any question as to whether a particular tree is diseased, it is prudent to sterilize all pruning gear after pruning the suspect tree and before pruning any other trees. Sterilization can generally be accomplished by dipping pruning shears and saws for 15 seconds into a 15 percent solution of chlorine bleach.

Deciduous trees are generally pruned during their dormant period; however, trees can be pruned nearly any time of year. Precautions should be taken against pruning in late summer, when any new growth induced by the pruning may not be sufficiently hardened off before the first cold weather of winter. Under such circumstances, tender young foliage may be frost-burned and damaged. Pruning during the dormant period with supplemental pruning during spring or early summer would be recommended. Tree growth after summer pruning is generally less profuse than spring growth after dormant pruning.

Unless a tree has been verified to have an infectious plant disease, the tree trimmings should be chipped for composting and recycling. Diseased wood chippings may not be advisable for use in mulch unless it can be verified that the chips will achieve a sustained minimum heat of 180 degrees Fahrenheit for a period of four hours, to neutralize pathogenic organisms.

Kelly F. Duke, Vice President, Pre-Construction Services, ValleyCrest Landscape Development, Calabasas, California

Cabling and Bracing

Trees may require supplemental support as a precaution against major structural damage or in the aftermath of damage caused by improper pruning, storm, or disease. Regardless of the cause, the resulting support may be in the form of various bolts, cables, or bracing within or below the tree. The cabling and bracing of trees is a lengthy topic and so cannot be covered in detail here. Rather, this section will describe some of the basic types of supplemental support as an introduction to when to consider such systems as part of the landscape maintenance program.

Leaning

A tree may begin to list to one side such that it threatens vehicular clearance or begins to get to close to structures. The leaning may the result of a storm event, when a strong wind or repeated exposure to a dominant prevailing wind initiated leaning that changed the tree's balance and gravity subsequently took over and began to pull an off-center tree toward the earth. Other situations may occur where a major branch breaks on one side of a tree, throwing the center of balance off, resulting in a similar list to the opposite side. Regardless of the reason, the lack of any suitable balancing support within the tree itself suggests that a brace, pushing up from the ground below, is the likely solution. The resulting structural unit or "monument brace" may consist of a structural steel support with a concrete footing, or a structural concrete column with a steel cradle at its top to hold up the branch. The monument brace simply provides a prop under the leaning tree and is not itself anchored to the tree (see the figure "Monument Brace").

Weakened Branches

When major structural branches are weakened by disease or storm damage, but have not broken off of the tree, it may be possible to save the branch in a manner that allows it to heal and callus over. The branch may never be as strong as it was before, but the shape of the tree will be maintained. Assuming that there are enough other healthy and structurally sound branches within the overall bole of the tree, the typical course of action is to stretch one or more cables from suitable points along the damaged branch back to structurally sound branches in other parts of the tree. The cable (or cables) then distributes the weight of the weakened branch to support it while it heals. Should the branch never completely heal, it is still supported in a way that preserves the desired aesthetic of the tree's original shape (see the figure "Cable Options").

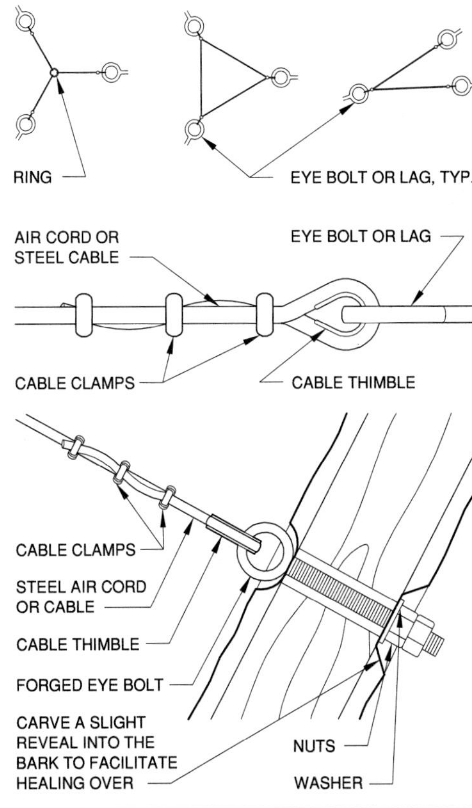

CABLE OPTIONS

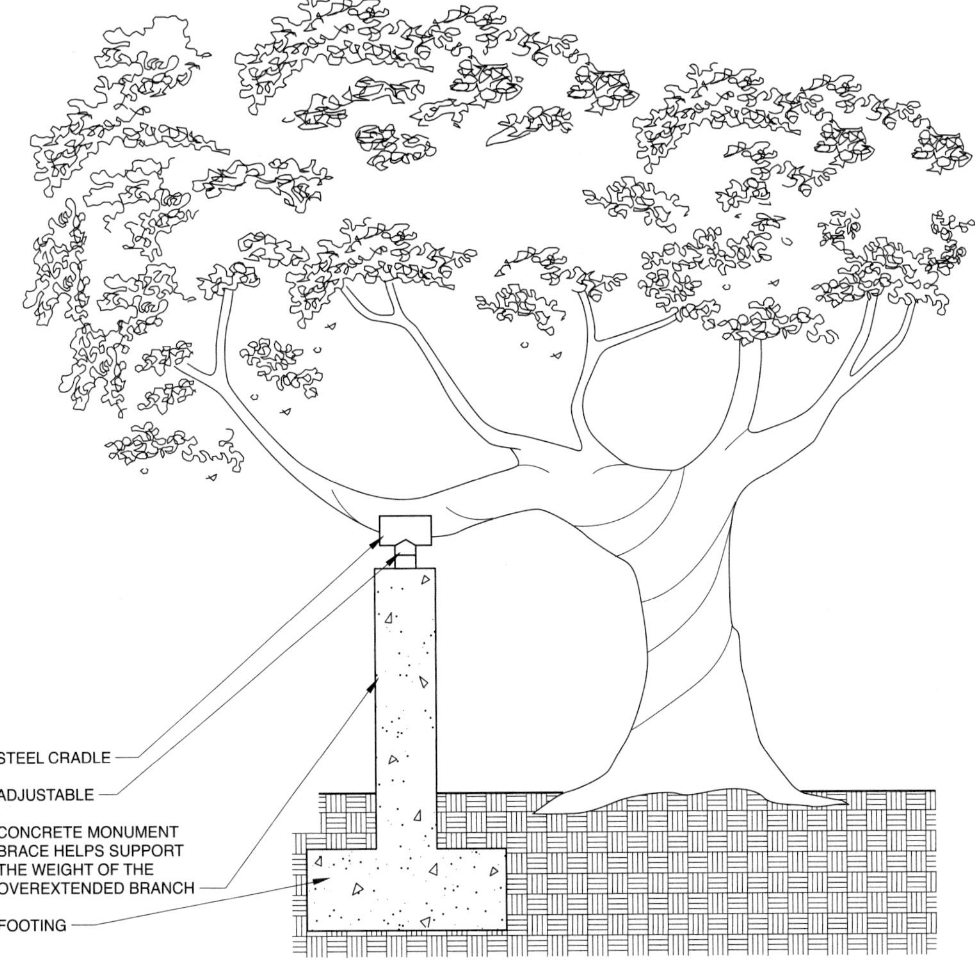

MONUMENT BRACE

Preventive Medicine

Some trees are just stronger than others by virtue of their natural branching habit. For example, trees tend to have stronger branching structure when lateral branch formation is at approximately 90 degrees to the main trunk or branch. Trees where lateral branches emerge at more acute angles tend to lack strong, continuous wood fibers, or "grain," through the full cross section of the juncture. The angle of this juncture, or "crotch," is important to know. If a narrow-crotch angles are allowed to form in the main scaffold of a tree when that tree is young, it will invariably lead to splitting and breakage of that crotch when it is subjected to heavy load, either due to the weight of the lateral branch or as a result of wind, snow, or even wet foliage during a rainstorm.

This type of problem is best solved by avoiding tree species that tend to exhibit narrow-crotch angle branching. If the available plant palette or the design intent will not support this approach, the next best thing is to begin early to carefully direct tree grown through corrective and directive pruning intended to minimize narrow-crotch angles, reduce suspended weight of branches, and reduce live loads on the branches by reducing foliage density through careful thinning of the canopy. One last precaution is to reinforce the crotch angle by drilling through the branch and inserting and securing a steel bolt. The bolt must penetrate through both the main branch or trunk and the lateral branch at risk. The bolt should be somewhat out from the vertex of the crotch angle, and its alignment should be perpendicular to the line that bisects the crotch angle (see the figure "Rod Reinforcing"). An inward force should be placed on

Kelly F. Duke, Vice President, Pre-Construction Services, ValleyCrest Landscape Development, Calabasas, California

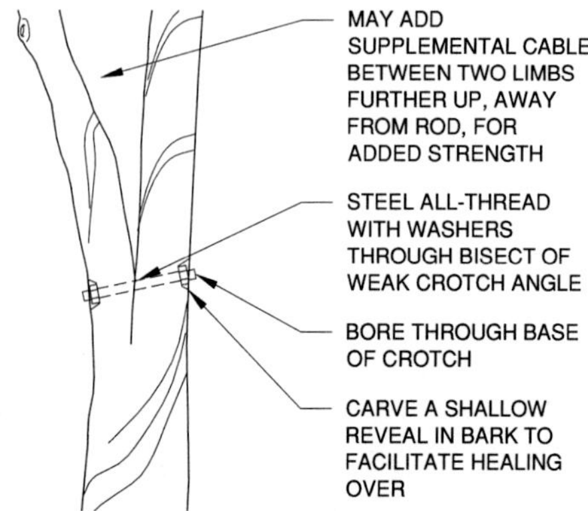

ROD REINFORCING

the two branches by tightening nuts against washers at each end of the bolt. The pinning of a narrow-crotch angle can be supplemented with cabling between the main branch and lateral branch further from the vertex if deemed necessary.

All tree cabling and bracing materials should be galvanized steel to prevent weakening over time from corrosion. Holes in trees should be drilled with clean, sterilized tools, properly sharpened to facilitate clean cuts. Where threaded rods are used, they should be secured with a washer and either a conventional or an appropriate "almond eye nut" at each exposed end. Threaded "lag" bolts, eyes, or rods can be used where it is not possible to bore all of the way through a trunk or branch, but they may not provide the same degree of pullout resistance. The washer is set at or near the cambium layer to facilitate the formation of bark tissue that will ultimately callus over and close in around rods and cable connectors or cover over terminal nuts. A more thorough look at the types and kinds of fasteners, cabling options, and bracing equipment can be found through a review of any of the catalogs for companies supplying the tree service or arboriculture profession.

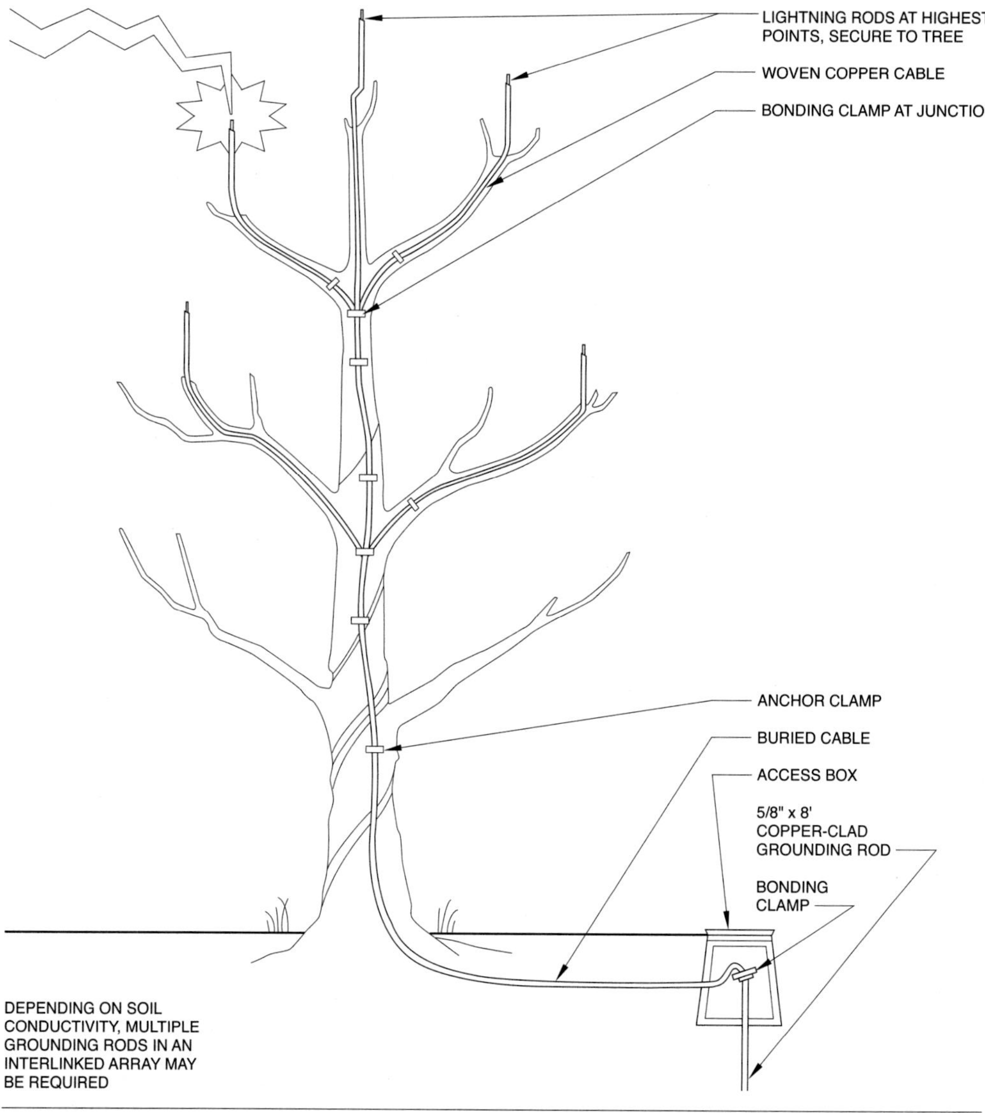

LIGHTNING PROTECTION

Lightning Protection

Trees, by virtue of their height, often get in the way of lightning as it arcs to earth. Hapless trees that get in the way are often severely damaged or destroyed as the electricity travels down the cambium layer, superheating fluids within the tree and often blowing the bark off the tree along the path of the charge as it travels through the tree. When conditions are right, the charge will travel through the tree to the earth. In some instances, the charge may travel partway down the tree then arc to an adjacent tree, structure, lamppost, or other object if it represents a path of lower resistance. Trees not killed by the blast will generally suffer secondary attacks by insects or disease as their natural defenses may be compromised by the lightning damage.

Lightning protection for trees has been in use for centuries. Nonetheless, it is only after a lightning strike that many property owners find out that such protection is available and could have protected their valued landscape asset. Lightning protection for trees is similar to lightning protection for buildings and structures, in that it provides a path of lower resistance for the electric charge to reach the ground. Lightning protection does not attract lightning, nor does it discourage it; it only provides a harmless path to earth (outside of the tree) for the charge to take when it does happen to strike. Lightning protection consists of woven copper cables of various gauges, secured to the tree, and terminating with copper rod tips at the upper ends of the trunk's central leader or major secondary vertical branches. The terminal end of the copper cable is bonded to one or more copper-clad grounding rods driven into the soil beyond the base of the tree (see the figure "Lightning Protection").

Lightning protection is advisable for trees of historic or sentimental value, rare trees, trees close to structures, or trees under which people or animals might congregate during a storm. Lightning protection is of varying importance depending on the frequency and intensity of lightning strikes in the geographical area of a given project. Lightning protection is generally installed by arborists or other specialty tree service companies that can advise on the specific systems needed for specific trees and locations. It is mentioned in the context of this discussion for information only, given the many variables that should be considered when evaluating the cost-benefit of these protective measures.

WOODY SHRUBS AND GROUND COVERS

Woody shrubs and ground covers are key elements in most landscape plantings. Unlike woody trees, shrubs will generally not require staking or guying or lightning protection. Like woody trees, shrubs will typically require mulching and pruning. Of these maintenance procedures, the most critical in terms of maintaining the design intent is pruning.

Mulching

The mulching of shrub beds is performed for a number of reasons. Among these are weed suppression, erosion control, moisture retention, thermal insulation, and general appearance. Mulch materials may range from various ground or shredded fir, pine, or cedar bark materials, "pine straw," to shredded and composted "green waste" (commercial landscape trimmings). In arid desert areas where sources of bark may be cost-prohibitive and where frequent winds can blow bark away, mulch layers are generally composed of screened gravel, decomposed granite, or river-run cobbles. A recent addition to the designer's

Kelly F. Duke, Vice President, Pre-Construction Services, ValleyCrest Landscape Development, Calabasas, California

PITTOSPORUM TOBIRA TENDS TO PRODUCE FOLIAGE IN WHORLS OF SMALL STEMS RISING OUT OF BUDS. AS THE SHRUB GROWS, THE FOLIAGE TENDS TO FORM A DENSE OUTER LAYER OF LEAVES WITH NO LEAVES IN THE INNER CORE DUE TO LOW LIGHT. SHEARING SUCH A PLANT BACK REMOVES NEARLY ALL THE FOLIAGE.

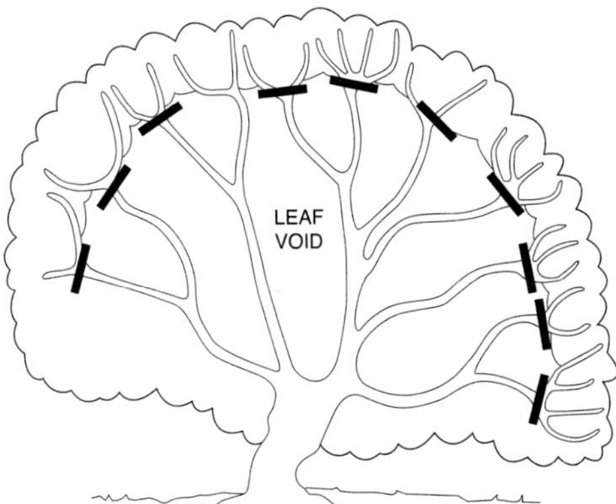

SECTION SHOWING LINE WHERE SHEARING MIGHT NORMALLY OCCUR, ILLUSTRATING HOW EVEN SHALLOW TRIMMING MIGHT REMOVE 90% OF THE FOLIAGE AND LEAVE STICKS AND A BARE SHRUB UNTIL IT REGROWS AND PRODUCES LEAVES

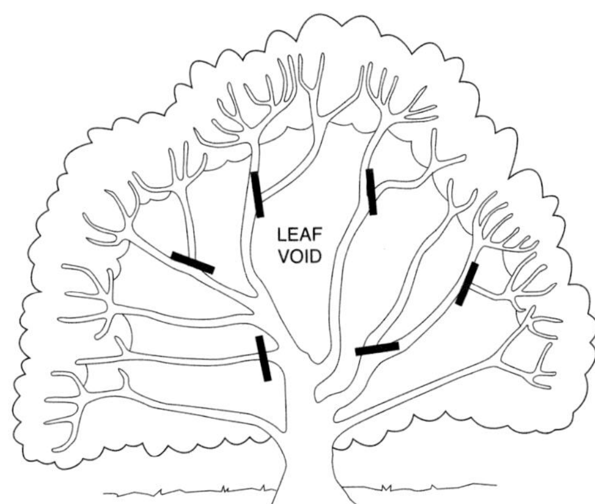

SECTION WITH SUGGESTED POINTS FOR "SURGICAL" DROP CROTCHING TO THIN AND CONTAIN GROWTH WITHOUT PRODUCING MAJOR VOIDS IN FOLIAGE

SHRUB THINNING

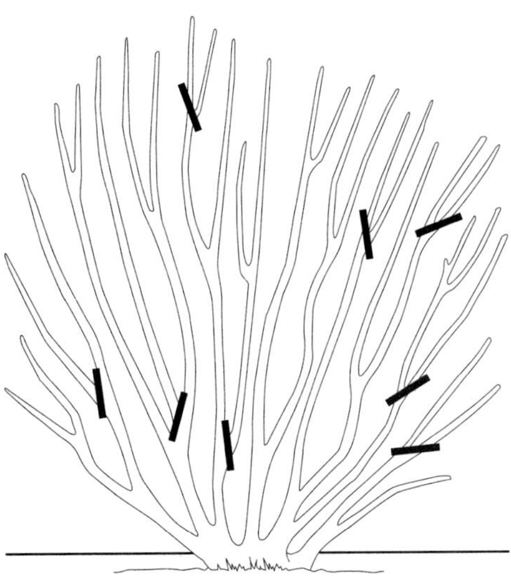

LILACS, NANDINA, MAHONIA, BRUNFELSIA, BRUGMANSIA, AND MANY OTHER SHRUBS, BOTH DECIDUOUS AND EVERGREEN, PRODUCE MANY LONG, SLENDER STEMS EMANATING FROM LOW IN THE PLANT. TRIMMING AT THE TIPS ONLY WORSENS THE "BRUSHY" QUALITIES. GROWTH CAN BE CONTROLLED BY "DROP CROTCHING" AND CUTTING LIMBS CLOSER TO THEIR POINT ORIGIN.

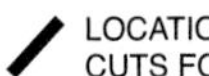 LOCATION OF SUGGESTED FLUSH CUTS FOR THIS EXAMPLE

SHRUB TRIMMING

palette is the use of tumbled recycled glass in individual colors or blends of colors.

Inert mulches such as decomposed granite, gravel, rock, or glass outlast organic products and seldom require replenishment. Gravel mulches in windy desert areas can, however, become infilled with blow sand, prompting occasional maintenance to remove and replace or top dress to restore the design intent. Organic materials require replenishment on a seasonal basis. The typical installed thickness for most much products is 2 inches deep (after settling). To achieve this may require up to 25 percent more to allow for natural settling.

Two precautions to take into consideration when using organic mulches are:

- The fibrous strands that make up shredded wood or bark mulch appear to interlock as the mulch layer settles. This interlocking of the matted fibers tends to make the mulch more stable and less likely to blow away in wind or float away in heavy rains. Floating mulch can become a problem in terms of blocking drain inlets and reducing the effectiveness of landscape area drainage systems. Projects in areas with high annual rainfall should consider pine straw or shredded bark or wood products in lieu of ground bark for landscape mulch applications.
- In areas where eucalyptus is commonly grown, some amount of eucalyptus leaves or trimmings will find their way into the commercial recycling operations that produce commercial "green waste" mulch. Eucalyptus mulch is immediately recognizable by its scent, and while it can freshen the aroma of composted wood mulch, various resins in the leaf and wood can be detrimental to sensitive shrubs if the mulch contains too high a percentage of eucalyptus product. It is important to verify the relative eucalyptus content of recycled mulch products, and reputable producers should be able to certify the content of their mulch products with laboratory verification.

Pruning and Trimming

Beyond the routine plant maintenance practices outlined in the first part of this discussion, the single most critical maintenance concern impacting the overall look of the landscape is the manner and means by which the shrub and ground-cover components are trimmed and pruned. Proper pruning is one key to healthy and structurally sound plants. Timely and appropriate pruning can also contribute to, or detract from, the original design intent. Aside from any intended contribution to the overall definition of space, color, pattern, texture, fragrance, or theme, there are many practical issues that may be served or hindered depending on how the shrub and ground-cover components are trimmed and pruned over the life of the project. For the purpose of this section, "trimming" will refer to the removal of spent flowers (dead-heading), tipping back of occasional errant stems, or the shearing of shrubs as in topiary work or hedges. "Pruning" in this context will refer to the strategic cutting of limbs or branches for the maintenance or enhancement of shrub structure.

Some of the practical aspects of property management that can be impacted by landscape maintenance and the manner by which shrubs are trimmed and pruned include, but are not limited to, the following:

- *Privacy.* Informal massing and clipped hedges can serve as visual barriers. Such barriers can prevent others from looking in to areas, as well as block an unattractive view from the owner's perspective. In electing to plant a barrier, however, one should consider how big or how monolithic it need be, as this can impact the cost of maintenance programs. Hedges and screens are seldom planted at their full designed height and must be grown up to fill their roles. As these plants mature, it may be appropriate to evaluate the size and shape as originally designed against actual sight lines and visual assets or liabilities. It is important to keep in mind that the taller the hedge, the more costly it is to maintain as manlifts, ladders, or rolling scaffolds become necessary to elevate maintenance crews.
- *Safety.* As shrubs grow, they can begin to encroach upon public walks and streets, as well as those informal paths needed by maintenance or security personnel. From the standpoint of public safety, it may be necessary to trim or prune shrubs back away from walks in order to maintain proper clearances in accordance with the Americans with Disabilities Act (ADA) or other minimum standards. The maintenance of safe lines of sight at street intersections, driveway approaches, schools, or playgrounds is also a key factor in public safety and falls upon the maintenance professional to look for and attend to.
- *Fuel modification.* Another aspect of safety, this term applies to the cutting or clearing of native or naturalized grasses and the selective pruning of woody shrubs or low trees to reduce the relative amount of combustible material in the landscape buffer that may exist between structures and unimproved native vegetation. While the role of fuel modification is primarily functional and is typically mandated by local fire department agencies, it can be undertaken with some finesse to soften the transition between manicured plantings and brute wilderness.
- *Security.* Plants can play a role in site security and may be designed into the landscape for that role. Keeping such plants effective in that role without allowing them to become a hindrance to daily activities will generally fall upon the maintenance crew. For example, it is not uncommon to use plants with spiny leaves or thorns in landscaped areas that might afford a hiding place for would-be thieves, muggers, or other ne'er-do-wells (below windows, parking lot islands, campus pathways, jogging trails, etc.). Kept properly trimmed, such shrubs do their job without becoming a menace on their own. Allowed to overgrow their location, the plants may impact maintenance activities (janitorial and landscape) or pedestrian access. At the same

Kelly F. Duke, Vice President, Pre-Construction Services, ValleyCrest Landscape Development, Calabasas, California

time, plants can be trimmed in ways to encourage or direct pedestrian or vehicular access in specific desired directions.

With the preceding in mind, it is appropriate to consider some of the basics of shrub trimming and pruning from a technique standpoint. Pruning techniques vary with the species of plant and the role the shrub is to play in the garden. For the purpose of this discussion, the following basic techniques are addressed.

Selective Pruning

Selective pruning in shrubs is not unlike the pruning utilized for trees. This type of pruning involves a review of the overall structure of the plant and looks to enhance that structure through a combination of tipping back limbs, and performing cuts that are analogous to the drop-crotch cuts discussed for woody trees. These cuts are made to thin out competing interior limbs and to remove dead or unhealthy wood. Thinning in this manner can permit sunlight to penetrate into the interior of the plant such that foliage can survive. Ironically, thinning branching can make the resulting plant look more lush, as there is greater opportunity for foliage development.

Selective pruning of small twigs and limbs up to ¾ inch is generally accomplished with a "bypass" or "anvil" hand shear (bypass shears are recommended for their cleaner cut). Larger limbs and small branches up to 1½ inch will generally require a bypass "lopping shear" (a large two-handed shear that provides greater leverage). As with trees, limbs larger than 1½ inch will typically require the use of a pruning saw.

As with trees, tip cuts are made adjacent to buds and with attention paid to the direction in which the closest remaining bud is pointing. That direction will determine the likely direction that new growth will take. In this manner it is possible to effectively steer the plant, if needed, to balance shape or fill gaps, or if training an *espalier* (a tree or shrub trained to grow in a two-dimensional plane, as along a trellis, wall, or fence). The care and pruning of espalier trees or shrubs should be directed to more experienced maintenance personnel with the patience to plan out pruning as a series of strategic cuts made incrementally over a period of time to effect the proper and purposeful direction of plant growth.

Drop-crotch cuts are useful for shrubs that tend to produce whorls of multiple shoots after a tip cut. Such shrubs tend to become very brushy near their outer edge. Edge growth then shields the interior from sunlight, and most of the interior leaves drop off. As a result, the shrub is void of leaves below the exterior surface. If at any time the shrub requires trimming back to reduce size, the barren interior is revealed and there is a period of time needed for new foliage to emerge. This situation can be avoided by selectively removing whole stems deeper within the shrub. Done properly, the voids that may appear at the visible surface of the shrub are small and uniformly distributed so as to not impact the overall look of the plant. Light can penetrate and leaf development can occur deeper within the plant. Subsequent trimmings would repeat the process such that one is always reducing the surface foliage, but doing so by tracing back along stems to the base of strategic stems deeper within the shrub in lieu of tipping back or shearing the exterior foliage only (see the figure "Shrub Thinning"). This technique is important for shrubs such as *Pittosporum, Ligustrum,* and *Ilex,* to name a few. These cuts are generally made using bypass hand shears.

Other shrubs, such as *Syringa, Forsythia, Mahonia, Brunfesia,* or *Nandina,* tend to produce long limbs that originate near the ground line. These shrubs require periodic thinning for the same reasons noted above, to allow light penetration into the interior of the plant. Thinning for these shrubs will generally require a combination of drop-crotch cuts, as above, with some major stems being removed down to the base of the plant just above the ground line (see the figure "Shrub Trimming"). These cuts are made using bypass hand shears and loppers.

Shearing

The term "shear" applies to a number of garden implements. In the sense of "hedge shearing," it may refer to either manual or electric shears. Hand shears are like large two-handed scissors with bypass blades. Electric shears function like a rigid row of small bypass shears. Dragging the electric shear through foliage causes the two steel bars to oscillate in a way that slices through leaves and stems. Shearing is intended for hedges, topiaries, or other plants where shape is the primary concern and the plants structure is less important either because of the type of plant or because it has been dealt with through some other process. Shearing will tend to result in defoliation of the interior of the shrub due to lack of light.

Hedges can begin to defoliate along the lower edges when the height of the shrub effectively shades the lower portions. One simple way to mitigate this is to shear the hedge slightly narrower at the top than the bottom, effectively battering back the sides to allow sunlight better access to the lower regions of the hedge face. The amount of the batter need not be much and will generally be imperceptible to the viewer (see the figure "Hedge").

Shearing for topiaries is an artistic treatment where specially trained plants are pruned into geometric or animal shapes as garden ornaments. True topiaries are shrubs that have been pruned and trimmed into predetermined shapes. Topiaries produced by this traditional method take a long time to develop and should be cared for as valuable assets in the garden. Only experienced maintenance personnel should take on the task of maintaining a topiary plant for fear of accidentally undoing years of gardening artistry.

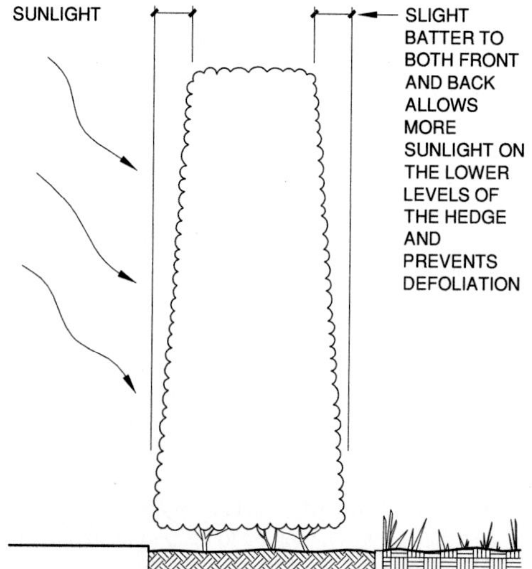

HEDGE

Topiary plants are also produced using wire cages, with multiple vines or trailing ground-cover plants allowed to grow over them. As the vines or ground covers fill in the wire frame, they are sheared into the desired shape. These faux topiaries take far less time to produce, and while they require the same good eye and steady hand to trim, they are somewhat more forgiving of errant cuts, as the plants tend to fill in fast and there is the redundancy of a metal form and multiple plants contributing to the whole of the sculpture.

Bonsai is a horticultural art form whereby, through pinching and pruning and careful maintenance, one purposefully shapes and/or stunts the growth of a tree to render it into a sculptured miniature of a mature specimen. Traditional bonsai is grown in a pot or box so that the roots can be periodically pruned, as are the branches. This technique is generally left to patient enthusiasts, not to general landscape maintenance crews. That said, there are projects such as zoos, theme parks, or botanical gardens that may choose to place bonsai trees or shrubs in the general landscape. Even in such a commercial application, truly artistic bonsai should be left in the pot and cared for by a trained bonsai specialist whose techniques and knowledge are beyond the scope of this discussion. For other applications there are "production quality" bonsai that can be purchased from specialty nurseries. The maintenance for these production bonsai trees or shrubs would be comparable to the topiary or espalier plants described previously.

Dead-Heading

Dead-heading is the timely removal of spent flowers or fruit from shrubs that are reluctant to naturally drop such items on their own. The purpose of dead-heading is largely aesthetic, although the decaying flowers or fruit can sometimes become a sight that attracts insect or disease. Dead-heading is generally accomplished using one's fingers to gently pull the spent petals or the entire blossom off the shrub, although some species may require the use of bypass hand shears.

Vine Training

The pruning requirements of vines are varied, depending on the species; the way the vine needs to be attached (or attaches itself) to its trellis, pergola, or other support armature; and the relative amount of woody growth the vine develops as it matures. Some vines self-attach via tendrils which coil (*Vitis* spp.) or hook (*Macfeydena unguis-cati*) around objects for support. Other plants produce modified tendrils with adhesive end pads or "holdfasts" that effectively glue the plant to a structure (*Parthenocissus tricuspidata*). Still others produce aerial roots to accomplish this task (*Philodendron* spp.). Other vines rely on wrapping their main stems around supports (*Wisteria* spp.). Thus, how a vine is attached will influence what should or should not be cut when pruning for shape or support.

As with trees, the trimming of side limbs can have an impact on the development of caliper in shrubs or vines. If the aesthetic goal is to develop a thick trunk

Kelly F. Duke, Vice President, Pre-Construction Services, ValleyCrest Landscape Development, Calabasas, California

as part of the visual look of a vine, a certain amount of side leaves and leafy stems should be left in place to encourage caliper growth earlier in the vine's life.

As with trees, the achievement and maintenance of the design intent for shrub plantings should rely on structured and prescriptive specifications that define the exact look that the landscape designer wishes to obtain. Matters of general plant health can be described through performance specifications that itemize the standards for performance and the metric for measuring them. This approach leaves the means and method to the maintenance practitioner. When maintenance practitioners have the freedom to develop their own means and methods, cost-effective techniques evolve through competitiveness and innovation.

HERBACEOUS ANNUALS AND PERENNIALS, FERNS, AND ORNAMENTAL GRASSES

Herbaceous plants do not develop any woody tissue. They are generally frost-sensitive and either die or go into dormancy during the winter in cold climate zones. Within their normal growing season, given the basics of general routine plant maintenance, they are relatively easy to grow, in that their care requires a minimum of equipment (properly timed trimming can be often be accomplished through pinching stems or minor work with hand shears). In addition, many of these plants are seasonal annuals that are, by design, destined to serve the landscape for only one season before they are removed and replaced by another crop. This ephemeral quality negates the need for any long-term maintenance strategy other than preplanning and ordering the replacement crop and providing for some measure of soil preparation, fine grading, and mulching with each successive seasonal removal and replacement.

In warm climates, some annuals and virtually all perennials will last longer than a single season. Additionally, some plants may reseed themselves. For these plants, there is a need for routine general maintenance practices as long as the growing season lasts. For regions with periods of cold weather, the annuals will likely die out and the herbaceous perennials will enter a state of dormancy. Transitioning to this dormant phase may require some specific action, depending on the severity of the cold weather and the species of plant involved. For some plants, it may be appropriate to leave them in the soil with no further care. Others may require some additional mulching for some measure of frost protection; still others may need to be removed from the soil and stored for a specific time at a specific temperature to assure best results when replanted in the spring. The specific needs of each type of plant should be researched prior to embarking on a post-installation maintenance program. This research is essential for the planning and staging of the various activities needed to preserve the garden and assure its return to glory the following season. This research can also be part of an overall cost-benefit analysis used to determine whether the various winterization activities are cost-effective compared with total replacement of herbaceous plantings the following spring. This level of analysis may seem somewhat removed, but must be seen as a reality of the long-term operating costs facing owners in the management of their property.

Of the herbaceous plants, it is important to note the following species, which warrant individual discussion.

Ferns

Ferns are a common perennial in many gardens. Ferns range in hardiness, but even the hardiest will generally die back and go dormant during periods of extreme heat or cold. With some noteworthy exceptions, most ferns used in exterior landscaping grow as either low- to medium-height plants that spread via surface or underground stems or rootlike structures or tree ferns with a slender trunk. Tree ferns, like palms, grow from terminal buds, unfurling successive fronds to create a canopy that periodically loses a frond or two to age, heat, or excessive weight. The fallen fronds will eventually fall off but the tree fern looks best with a clean trunk and canopy. The spreading ferns gracefully uncoil new fronds, working outward from a central clump. When fronds expire on these spreading ferns, they will yellow and fall. These declining fronds will usually require pruning shears for removal until they are completely brown, when they can generally be pulled from the main plant without tools.

Ferns do not produce seed; they will produce dust-like spores from small capsules (sori) on the underside of the fronds. It is important to note this so as to not confuse the sudden appearance of dark spores as some symptom of a disease such as rust (*Phragmidium tuberculatum*) or the detritus of insects (frass). The spores are harmless from a horticultural standpoint but may stain pavements or other surfaces, if wet, or affect allergic persons during dry weather. The spores are easily swept or blown off of surfaces, but where allergies are a problem or where local ordinances permit, it may be best to hose spores off surfaces to minimize airborne particles.

Many fern species produce root nodules. These nodules are used to store reserves of water and nutrients within their tissue. This is important to know lest they be misinterpreted as either a plant disease or a plant reaction to soil-borne microorganisms such as nematodes.

In spite of stored nutrients and water, ferns may become brown and partially defoliated during periods of extremely hot weather. The hardy quality of the ferns will generally allow for rejuvenation after being severely cut back to near ground level. During this cutting back operation, it is possible to also rogue out any of the rhizomes that spread the plant if the plant has begun to overextend its intended place in the overall design.

Ornamental Grasses

A relatively new but extremely popular addition to the landscape designer's palette is the profusion of ornamental grasses that have been introduced over the last 10 years. These "grasses" actually consist of true grasses as well as sedges, rushes, and reeds. As they are varied in genus and species, so too are they varied in their cultural requirements. Some are wetland plants, some tolerate a wide range of conditions, while some are have no tolerance for overly wet soil. Some go dormant in heat or drought; some go dormant in cold. Some look most attractive when dormant, while others look most attractive in full flower (seed heads), and still others look best when not in flower. This wide range of variation is important to note from the designer's standpoint as it may be prudent to include instructions in the specifications regarding the type and timing of any trimming in order to favor the most desired look in terms of the overall design intent.

With the exception of when and how to trim and the relative irrigation needs, ornamental grasses require little beyond the general maintenance considerations described at the beginning of this discussion. Trimming, when needed, is generally best accomplished with manual hedge shears. If the grasses are sufficiently stiff or supple, it may be possible to use a power hedge trimmer or a nylon cord trimmer.

REFERENCES

Broschat, Timothy K., and Alan W. Meerow. 2000. *Ornamental Palm Horticulture*. Gainsville: University of Florida Press.

Gilman, Edward F. 2002. *An Illustrated Guide to Pruning*, 2d ed. Albany, NY: Delmar Thomson Learning.

———. 1997. *Trees for Urban and Suburban Landscapes*. Albany, NY: Delmar Publishers.

Harris, Richard W., James R. Clark, and Nelda P. Matheny. 2003, *Arboriculture: Integrated Management of Landscape Trees, Shrubs, and Vines*, 4th Ed. Upper Saddle River, NJ: Prentice Hall.

Turgeon, A. J. 1991. *Turfgrass Management*. Englewood Cliffs, NJ: Prentice Hall Inc.

See also:
Planting
Recreational Surfaces

Kelly F. Duke, Vice President, Pre-Construction Services, ValleyCrest Landscape Development, Calabasas, California

INTERIOR PLANTS

PLANT SPECIFICATION FACTORS

- Accurately describe plant form (e.g., multistem vs. standard tree form, clump form) and foliage spread desired. Indicate "clear trunk" measurements on trees, if desired. These measurements are from soil line to foliage origin point. Specify caliper, if significant.
- Indicate lighting intensities designed or calculated for interior space where plants will be installed.
- Indicate how plants will be used (i.e., in at-grade planter or in movable decorative planter). If movable decorative planters are used, indicate interior diameter and height of planter for each plant specified, since growing container sizes vary considerably.
- Specify both botanical and common plant names.
- Indicate any special shipping instructions or limitations.
- Specify in-plant height column, whether plant height is measured as overall height or above-the-soil line height. Recommended height measurements:
  - Interior plants: overall plant height (i.e, from bottom of growing container to mean foliage top).
  - Exterior plants: above-the-soil line height.
- Indicate whether plants are to be container grown or bailed and burlapped (B & B) material.
- Indicate location of all convenient water supply sources on all interior landscaping layouts.

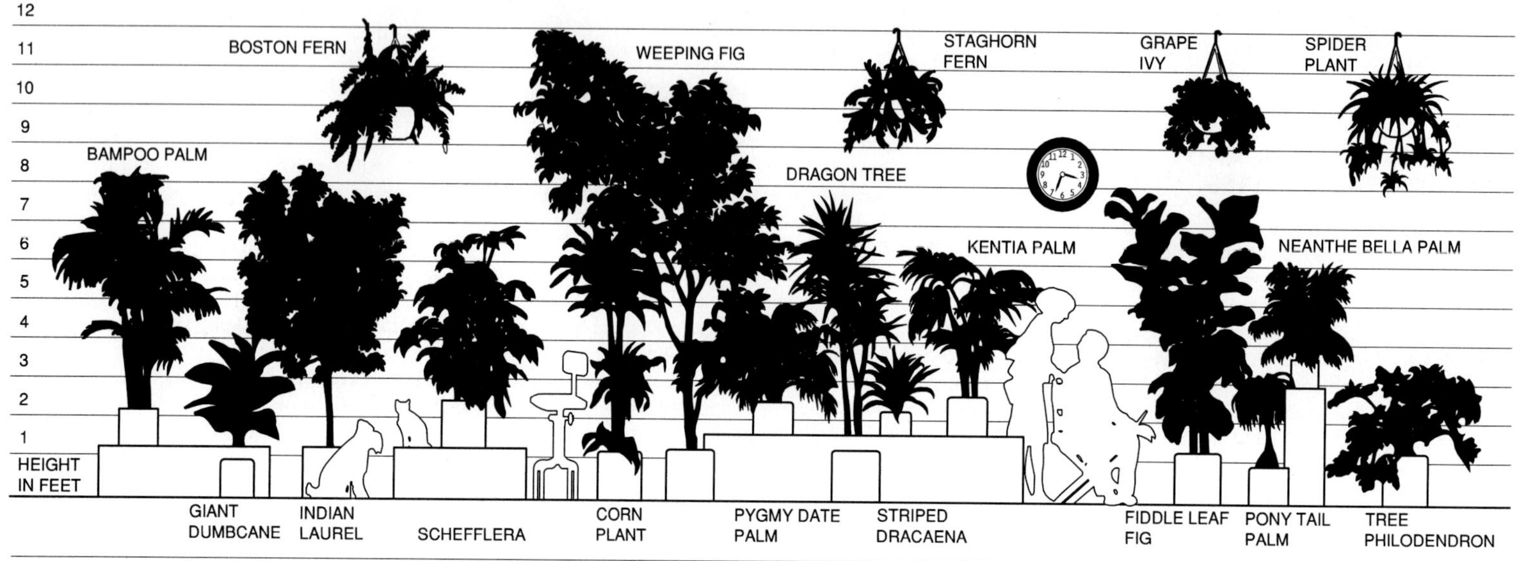

FORM, TEXTURE, AND SIZES OF SOME TYPICALLY USED INTERIOR PLANTS

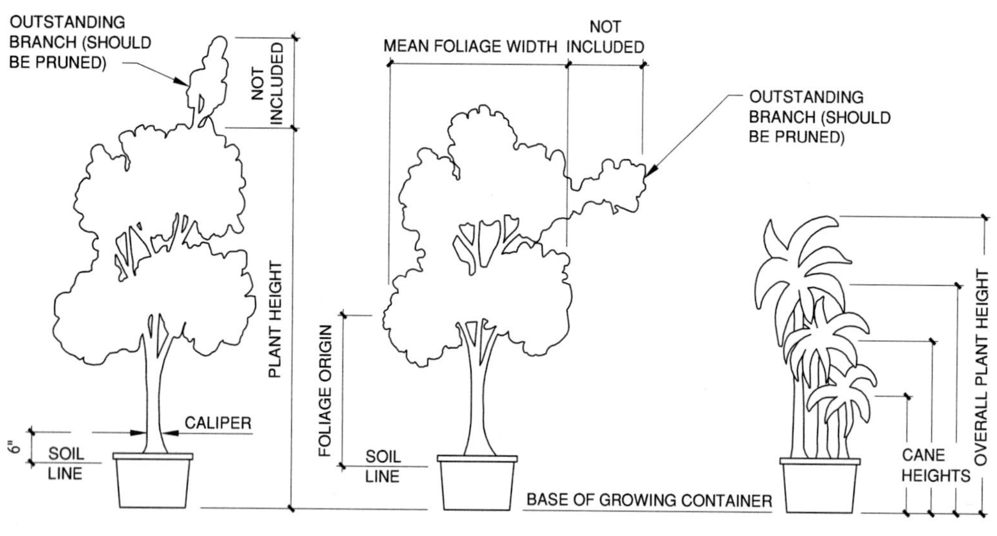

PLANT HEIGHT AND CALIPER

Plant height should be measured as overall height from the base of the growing container to mean foliage top. Isolated outstanding branches should not be included in height. (Since most plants are installed in movable planters, this overall height measurement should be utilized.)

FOLIAGE WIDTH AND ORIGIN

Foliage width should be measured across the nominal mean width dimension. Isolated outstanding branches should not be included in foliage width. Origin or start of foliage should be measured from the soil line.

CANE HEIGHTS

Many plant varieties are grown from rooted canes, with the plant being made up of one or more canes. The number of canes must be specified, if plant form is to be identified. Cane heights should always be measured from the base of the growing container.

INTERIOR PLANT SPECIFICATIONS

DESIGN CONSIDERATIONS FOR INTERIOR PLANTING

Uplighting and Electrical Needs

- May be of some benefit to plants, but inefficient for plant photosynthesis because of plant physiological structure. Chlorophyll is usually in upper part of leaf.
- Uplighting should never be utilized as sole lighting source for plants.
- Waterproof duplex outlets above soil line with a waterproof junction box below soil line are usually adequate for "atmosphere" uplighting and water fountain pumps.

HVAC Effect on Plants

- Air conditioning (cooled air) generally is not detrimental to plants, even if it is "directed" at plants. The ventilation here is what counts! Good ventilation is a must with plants; otherwise oxygen and temperatures build up. Heat supply, on the other hand, when "directed" at plants, can truly be disastrous. Plan for supplies directed away from plants, but maintain adequate ventilation.
- Extended heat or power failures of sufficient duration can damage plant health. The lower limit of temperature as a steady state is 65° F for plant survival. Brief drops to 55° F (less than 1 hr) are the lower limit before damage. Temperatures up to 85° F for only 2 days a week can usually be tolerated.
- The relative humidity should not be allowed to fall below 30%, as plants prefer a relative humidity of 50-60%.

Richard L. Gaines, Plantscape House, Apopka, Florida

Temperature Requirements

- Most plants prefer human comfort range: 70-75° F daytime temperatures and 60-65° F nighttime temperatures.
- An absolute minimum temperature of 50° F must be observed. Plant damage will result below this figure. Rapid temperature fluctuations of 30-40° F can also be detrimental to plants.
- "Q-10" phenomenon of respiration: For every 10°C rise in temperature, plants' respiration rate and food consumption doubles.
- Both photosynthesis and respiration decline and stop with time, as temperatures go beyond 80° F. Beware of the greenhouse effect!

Water Supply Requirements

- Movable and railling planters are often watered by watering can. Provide convenient access to hot and cold potable water by hose bibbs and/or service sinks (preferably in janitor's closet) during normal working hours, with long (min. 24 in.) faucet-to-sink or floor distances. Provide for maximum of 200 ft travel on all floors.
- At-grade floor planters are usually watered by hose and extension wand. Provide hose bibbs above soil line (for maximum travel of 50 ft) with capped "tee" stub-outs beneath soil line. If soil temperature is apt. to get abnormally low in winter, provide hot and cold water by mixer-faucet type hose bibbs.
- High concentrations of fluoride and chlorine in water supply can cause damage to plants. Provide water with low concentrations of these elements and with a pH value of 5.0-6.0. Higher or lower pH levels can result in higher plant maintenance costs.

Storage Requirements

Provide a secured storage space of approximately 30 sq. ft. for watering equipment and other maintenance materials. It may be desirable to combine water supply and janitor needs in the same storage area.

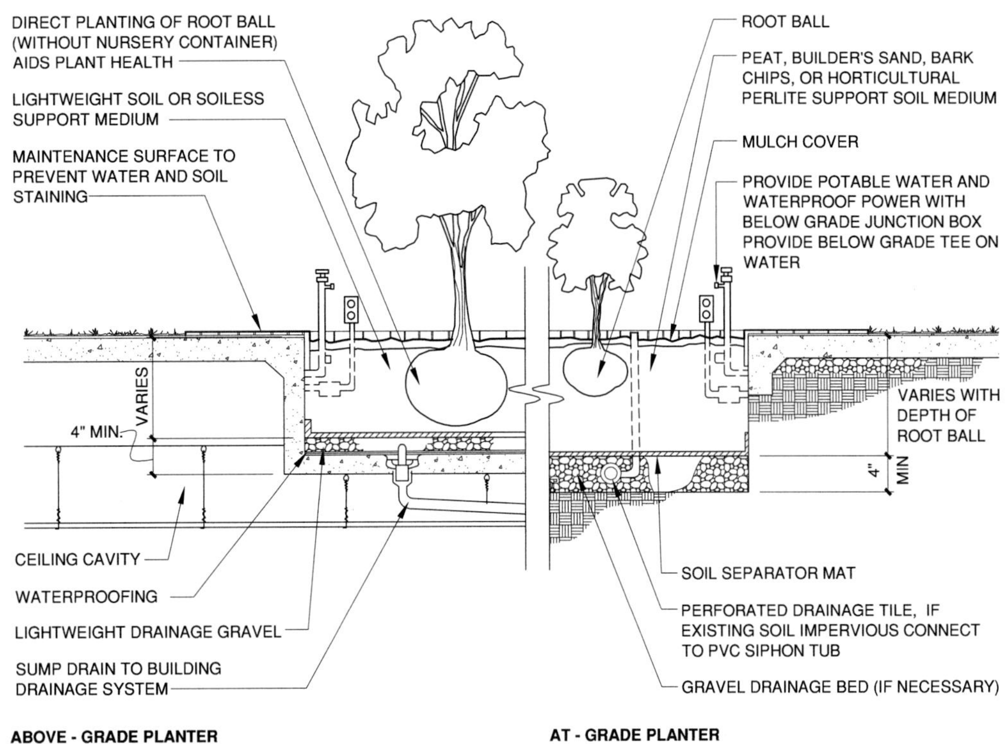

FLOOR PLANTER DETAILS

Air Pollution Effects on Plants

Problems result from inadequate ventilation. Excessive chlorine gas from swimming pool areas can be a damaging problem, as well as excessive fumes from toxic cleaning substances for floor finishes, etc. Ventilation is a must here!

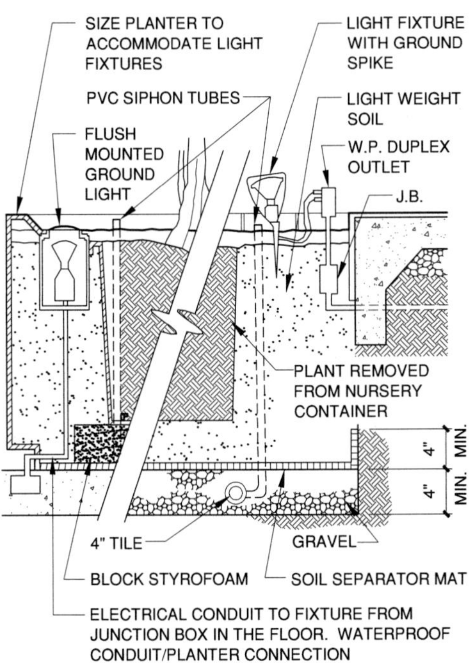

UPLIGHTING/PLANTING DETAILS

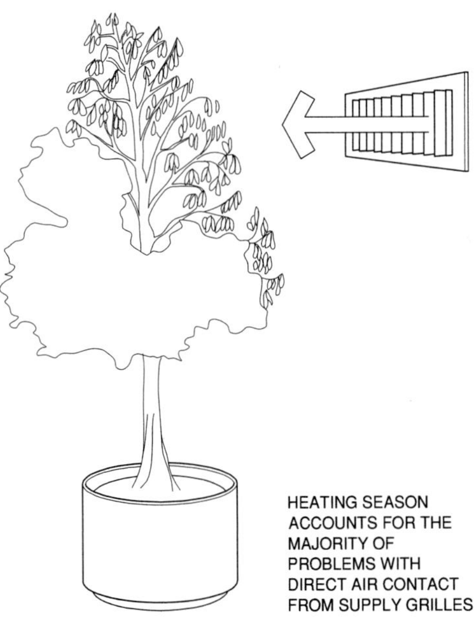

FOLIAGE BURN FROM DIRECT HEAT CONTACT

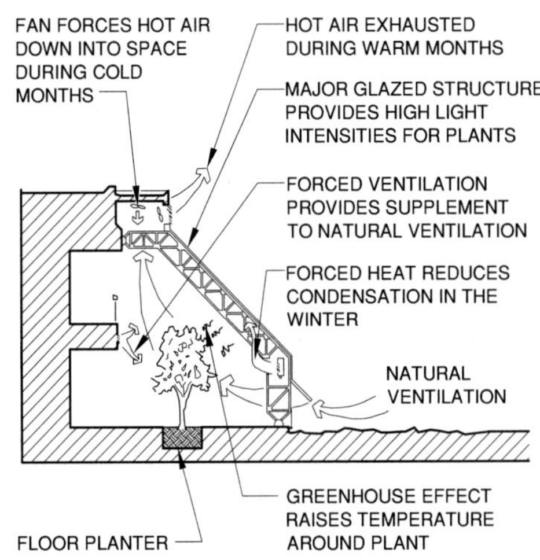

GREENHOUSE EFFECT RAISES NEED FOR ADEQUATE VENTILATION

Richard L. Gaines, Plantscape House, Apopka, Florida

TURF

ENVIRONMENTAL PERSPECTIVES

Grasses and the Ecosystem

Turf areas provide an outdoor surface that is relatively safe, resilient, easily trafficked, and aesthetically pleasing. But turf areas must be managed to persist, and the level of management required is influenced by regional succession patterns, site conditions, and grass species. Grasses are often aggressive, serving as pioneer species. Exotic grasses often compete effectively against native herbaceous materials, and establishment of turf in and near forests can be damaging to the forest ecosystem.

Humid Regions

In humid regions where succession favors forest landscapes, grasslands are temporary, occurring in disturbed areas. To maintain grass landscapes in these regions, management practices must repeatedly reset the succession clock.

Dry-Temperate Regions

In dryer regions, grasslands and savannas are favored and persist for extensive periods. Fire is responsible for maintaining grassland quality and diversity. In these regions, grass landscapes are most easily maintained when composed of diverse native species.

Arid Regions

In arid regions, some native grasses occur, but plant density can be low. Human landscapes tend to prefer high-density turfs, which require greater water inputs than natural precipitation will support. Minimize the use of turf in arid regions to conserve water and maintain the natural regional ecosystem.

Hybrids versus Natives

Most turfgrasses used in North America today are hybrids developed from exotic species and selected for low cutting height. Low-cut turfs have similarly short root structures. By comparison, many native North American grasses grow tall and have correspondingly deep root structures. Generally, the taller grass is allowed to grow, the deeper its roots penetrate. Greater root depth reduces irrigation and fertilizer requirements, reduces stormwater runoff, and improves infiltration characteristics, soil quality, and drought resistance.

Lawns were initially composed of multiple species, but following the advent of selective herbicides, they have been more typically defined by a hybrid turfgrass monoculture. Monocultures are by nature unsustainable and require regular management to maintain them. When actively and properly managed, turfgrass monocultures do produce relatively uniform lawns. Mixtures of native grasses and some mixtures of hybrid turfgrasses may reduce management requirements.

Expectation of a weed-free uniform turf is unrealistic, even if the turf is composed of native grass. Some percentage of weeds will always occur. Turf uniformity is affected by a number of conditions that influence the level of competition between a turfgrass and other grasses and forbs: shade, moisture levels, soil composition, soil compaction, nutrient levels, wind patterns, use characteristics, and management practices.

Grass Growth Habit Types

Grasses can be divided into four growth habit types:

- *Bunch-type grasses* tend to form small clumps and spread actively by seed.
- *Stoloniferous grasses* spread by surface stolons. Nodes along the stolon root into the soil and start new grass shoots.
- *Rhizomatous grasses* spread by lateral rhizomes under the soil surface. Nodes on the rhizome send new grass shoots up through the surface of the soil.
- *Rhizomatous-stoloniferous grasses* spread by both means, and stolons may move both above- and belowground.

(See the figure "Grass Growth Habit Types.")

TURF PLANNING OBJECTIVES

Choosing to specify turf is just like any other design choice made in the planning process. Because turf is ubiquitous in the human landscape does not necessarily mean that it is the right or best choice. The program, the environmental conditions, and the long-term management capabilities of the client all must be evaluated before selecting turf.

Turf as a Pavement Alternative

Turf can be a green alternative to pavements; it is living, is pervious, reduces glare and noise, and can capture and eliminate pollutants. Replacing impervious pavement with even a standard type of lawn significantly improves hydrological processes on a site.

Turf does, however, require more intensive management than most pavements, especially turf receiving active use. If turf is to be used in inclement weather, soil structure and management guidelines should be carefully planned at the design stage. Initial installation costs are generally lower for turf than for pavements, but costs can vary depending on site conditions, base design, irrigation systems, and drainage requirements. Regular management activities and

DEFINITIONS

Lawn: A turf area commonly kept between ½ inch and 4 inches in height.

Greensward: A mixed grass and wildflower area kept between 5 and 7 inches in height.

Meadow: A mixed grass and wildflower area often exceeding 12 inches in height.

Blend: A combination of multiple varieties of the same grass species.

Mixture: A combination of multiple grass species.

Top-dressing: A surface application, usually composed of sand or soil, to existing turf.

Overseeding: Applying a cool-season temporary grass to existing warm-season turf.

Sprigging: The establishment of turf by planting live vegetative stolons or rhizomes.

Plugging: The establishment of turf by planting regularly spaced sod chunks.

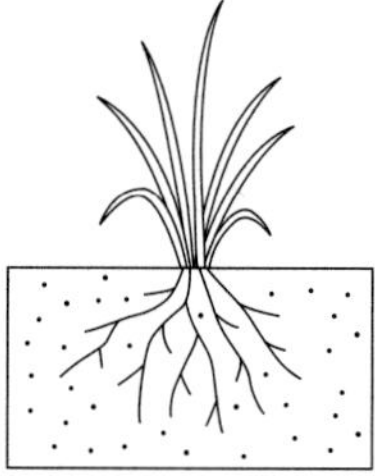
BUNCH GRASS

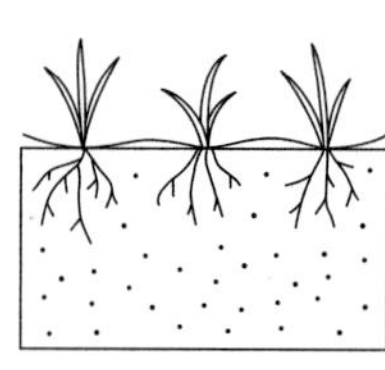
STOLONLIFEROUS

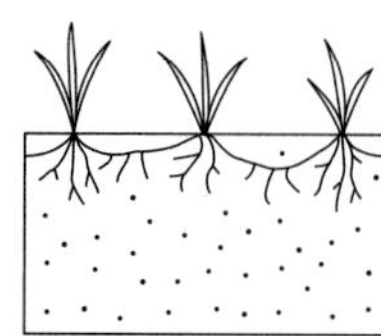
RHIZOMATOUS

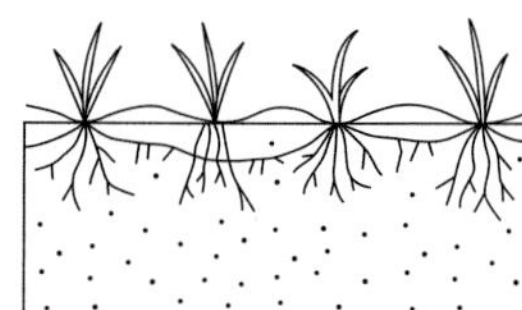
STOLONIFEROUS RHIZOMATOUS

GRASS GROWTH HABIT TYPES

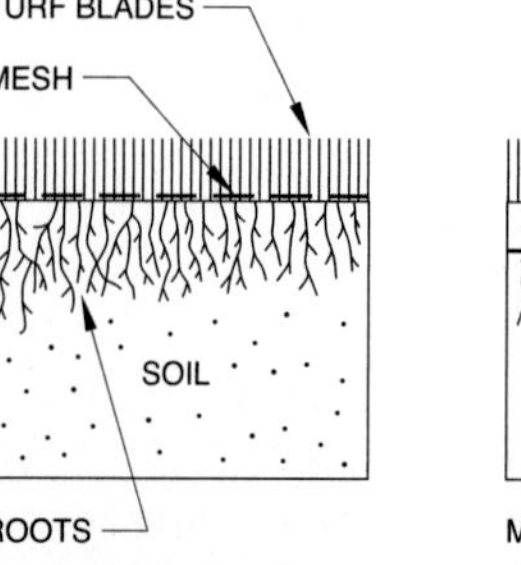

SURFACE MESHES

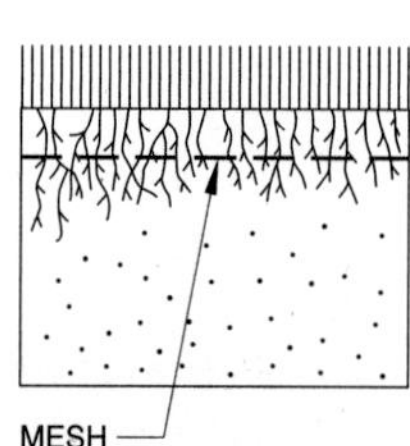

INTEGRAL MESHES

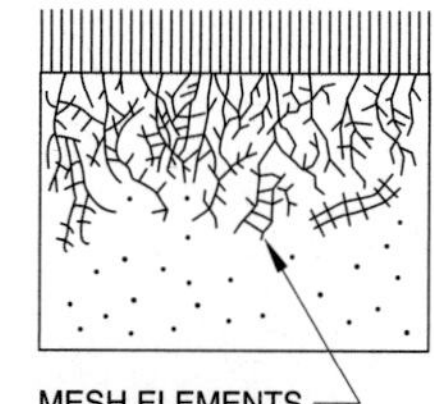

INTEGRAL FIBERS AND MESH ELEMENTS

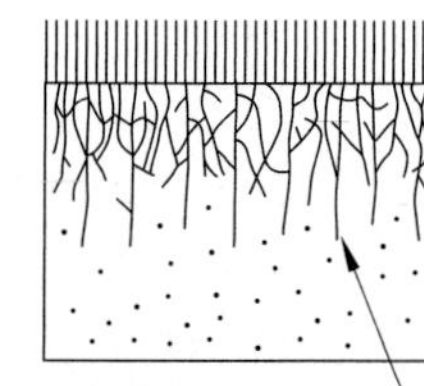

VERTICAL REINFORCEMENT

REINFORCED TURF TYPES

Ronald B. Sawhill, University of Georgia, College of Environment and Design, Athens, Georgia water costs are ongoing expenses most pavements do not require.

Turf used with cellular pavers can combine the benefits of structural support with the pervious and living qualities of a turf. Using a stoloniferous turf may reduce the need for reseeding or replanting if cells become vacant due to traffic damage.

"Reinforced turf" is a term representing a variety of systems designed to enable turf to withstand more intensive uses, often without relying on a visible structural component. Four general approaches include reinforcement by: surface meshes, integral meshes, integral fibers or mesh elements, and vertical reinforcement. The figure "Reinforced Turf Types" indicates the placement of these reinforcing members within the turf profile. For the most reliable surface, the base should be a high-sand base installed with subsurface drainage lines.

Lawn Alternatives

Greenswards are turfs composed of taller grasses and low wildflowers. Such mixed turfs were common through the 1800s and into the early twentieth century. A greensward should be maintained at 5 to 7 inches in height to encourage short herbaceous species. String trimmers may be necessary to achieve the appropriate cutting height, as most lawn mowers will not adjust that high. Mowing may not be required more than five or six times annually. Greenswards will accept light and infrequent traffic, and are suitable where a little unkemptness is acceptable. Converting an existing lawn to a greensward can be facilitated by modifying mowing practices and by introducing desired low-growing annuals and biennials.

Meadows are tall grasslands requiring only an annual cutting of between 8 and 12 inches in height after the second hard frost and before the spring thaw. To convert an existing lawn or greensward to a meadow, Sauer (1998) recommends mowing only five times during the initial conversion year, and thereafter reducing mowing frequency by one cutting per year for each of four subsequent years. A combination of native grasses and wildflowers appropriate to your region should be added over time, and hand removal of problem exotics may be necessary until the meadow is established. Periodic reseeding of wildflowers may be required. Meadows are "wild" in character, and the designer should determine its appropriateness within the context of the local landscape.

PLAN FOR ENVIRONMENTAL RESPONSIBILITY

Choices made by the designer during the design process will influence the way the owner uses and impacts natural resources. Sustainability begins in design. Define clear design objectives, evaluate site suitability, plan for the establishment period, and specify long-term management objectives.

Define Clear Design Objectives

Clear design objectives are essential to determining the proper soil base structure and turf composition. Programming should define the desired turf functional requirements, environmental sensitivity, and aesthetic qualities. Define functional requirements by activity needs rather than by landscape component—for example, a 10,000-square-foot passive play area rather than a 10,000-square-foot turf area. Specify the activity level by both activity type and frequency of use, according to the table "Turf Type Functional Suitability".

TURF TYPE FUNCTIONAL SUITABILITY

	WILDLIFE HABITAT/ UTILITY CORRIDORS	BUFFER/ FILTER STRIP GREENWAY EDGES	PASSIVE ACTIVITIES	LEISURE PLAY	ATHLETICS/ GOLF	VEHICULAR APPLICATIONS
Meadow	●	●	•	❍	❍	❍
Greensward	•	●	●	•	❍	❍
Turf lawn	❍	❍	●	●	•	❍
Turf: high sand base	❍	❍	●	●	●	•
Turf in open celled pavers	❍	❍	•	❍	●	●
Reinforced turf	❍	❍	●	●	●	●

● *Good*
• *Fair*
❍ *Poor*

Consider local landscape standards dictated by ordinance or covenant, as well as the proposed turf setting (urban, suburban, and rural) before selecting an appropriate turf type. Where standards limit the type of turf component, consider minimizing turf area. Define aesthetic qualities in terms of turf uniformity, texture, color, and seasonal qualities. Lowering uniformity requirements increases turf options.

Evaluate Site Suitability

To determine site suitability for turfgrass, evaluate regional, seasonal and site-specific conditions.

Regional Conditions

See the table "Turf Regions of North America."

Where heavy winter use of dormant warm-season turfgrasses is anticipated, overseed with a winter annual grass to protect the turf and soil surface from damage. Consider improving the soil structurally to limit compaction. In regions where dry periods correspond to heavy-use events, maintain a regular irrigation program so that the turf can withstand and recover from damage. No special treatment is needed where turf uses will be light and infrequent.

Sun/Shade

Grasses generally perform best in full sun within their appropriate region. Some cool-season grasses cannot withstand full sun in southern regions without heavy irrigation, but are suitable for light shade areas. Shade-tolerant turfs can generally withstand up to four hours of shade. Turf is not a reliable option where insufficient sun is available. Turfgrass grows most aggressively during the morning hours; therefore, it is the morning sun that is most beneficial, both for growth and for drying of the turf, which limits disease.

Wind

The most desirable site receives active airflow during the morning hours to dry the turf surface. A lack of airflow allows moisture to remain longer on the turf and can facilitate disease. Good surface ventilation can reduce cold pockets and minimize premature greening in early spring. Planning for airflow can reduce future turf management problems: thin nearby tree stands and selectively remove lower tree limbs to improve ventilation on existing turf.

Soil Characteristics

Investigate the site's soil structure thoroughly before selecting a turf. Soil permeability and porosity are critical to turfgrass success and are a function of the particle sizes of soil components. Where clay soils predominate, permeability and porosity are generally low; clay soils can retain significant water for extended periods of time, but may also release that water reluctantly. In wet periods and in low areas, clay soils can become anoxic, killing the turfgrass; subsurface drainage may be necessary. Where sands or gravels predominate, the soil is high in porosity, enabling rapid infiltration and drainage, but it can be droughty and is often low in fertility. Soil conditioners can improve soil characteristics, but weigh modifications against environmental and economic cost.

Sand-Based Systems

Since the 1960s, sand-based turf systems have grown in popularity for golf course and sports field construction. The Texas-USGA profile, the California variant of that profile, and other similar systems capitalize on the inherent porosity of various sands to control soil moisture and provide uniformity in the turfgrass base. The Texas-USGA method, as shown in the figure "Texas-USGA Soil Profile," is the most thoroughly documented system. High-sand bases provide a compaction-resistant soil for active-use turfs and a rapid-use capability following precipitation events, but require an actively managed cultural program to coordinate frequent irrigation, fertilization, and other cultural practices.

Hydrology

Evaluate local climactic information and weekly precipitation rates before determining lawn size and turfgrass composition. Most nonnative turfgrasses are aggressive consumers of soil moisture and require ample water to maintain health and vigor. In regions where precipitation is lacking during the growing season, local water conservation issues may preclude the use of turfgrass. Plants native to a site are adapted to the site water balance and flourish without irrigation inputs.

Based on average monthly rainfall, runoff rates, soil water storage, and potential evapotranspiration (Ferguson, 1998), a turf in Los Angeles has a potential annual irrigation water demand of 18 inches (see

Ronald B. Sawhill, University of Georgia, College of Environment and Design, Athens, Georgia

TURF SPECIES CHARACTERISTICS

	COMPACTION TOLERANCE	WEAR RESISTANCE	HEAT TOLERANCE	COLD TOLERANCE	DROUGHT TOLERANCE	SHADE TOLERANCE	DISEASE RESISTANCE	SALT TOLERANCE	TEXTURE	COLOR	NOTES	GROWTH HABIT
Alkaligrass *Puccinellia distans*	—	•	•	●	•	•	—	●	Medium fine	Medium green	Native	Bunch
Bahia Grass *Paspalum notatum*	—	●	●	○	●	•	●	○	Coarse	Medium green	—	Bunch
Creeping Bentgrass *Agrostis palustris*	•	•	○	●	○	•	•	●	Medium fine	Medium green	—	Stoloniferous
Bermudagrass *Cynodon species*	●	●	●	•	●	○	•	●	Fine	Med-dk green	—	Stoloniferous Rhizomatous
Annual Bluegrass *Poa annua*	●	○	○	●	○	○	●	—	Medium	—	—	Bunch with Stolons
Rough Bluegrass *Poa trivialis*	○	○	○	●	○	○	●	•	Medium	Lt-med green	Wet tolerant	Stoloniferous
Kentucky Bluegrass *Poa pratensis*	•	•	•	●	•	○	●	•	Medium	Dark green	—	Rhizomatous
Buffalograss *Buchloe dactyloides*	—	○	•	•	●	○	—	—	Fine	Medium green	Native	Stoloniferous
Centipede Grass *Eremochloa ophiuroides*	—	○	•	○	●	•	•	○	Medium *coarse*	Yellow green	—	Stoloniferous
Chewings Fescue *Festuca rubra var commutata*	○	○	○	●	•	●	○	•	Fine	Dark green	Insect resist.	Bunch, but tillers aggressively
Creeping Red Fescue *Festuca rubra*	—	•	○	●	•	●	○	—	Fine	Dark green	—	Rhizomatous
Fine Fescue / Hard Fescue *Festuca longifolia*	•	•	○	●	•	●	○	•	Fine	Dark green	Insect resist.	Bunch
Sheep Fescue *Festuca ovina*	○	○	○	●	•	●	○	—	Fine	—	—	Bunch
Tall Fescue *Festuca arundinacea*	•	●	•	●	●	●	○	•	Coarse	Medium green	—	Bunch, but does spread by tillers
Seashore Paspalum *Paspalum vaginatum*	—	●	•	•	•	○	●	●	Medium coarse	Dark green	Waxy leaf	Stoloniferous Rhizomatous
Perennial Ryegrass *Lolium perenne*	●	●	○	●	●	●	●	•	Medium	Medium green	Insect resist.	Bunch
St. Augustine Grass *Stenataphrum secundatum*	—	○	●	○	•	●	○	●	Coarse	Lt-med green	Rapid grower	Stoloniferous Rhizomatous
Zoysiagrass *Zoysia species*	•	●	●	•	●	•	•	•	Medium fine	Med-dk green	—	Stoloniferous Rhizomatous

● *Good*
• *Fair*
○ *Poor*

Sources: Beard, James B., 1982, and Lofts Seed, Inc. (not dated).

Ronald B. Sawhill, University of Georgia, College of Environment and Design, Athens, Georgia

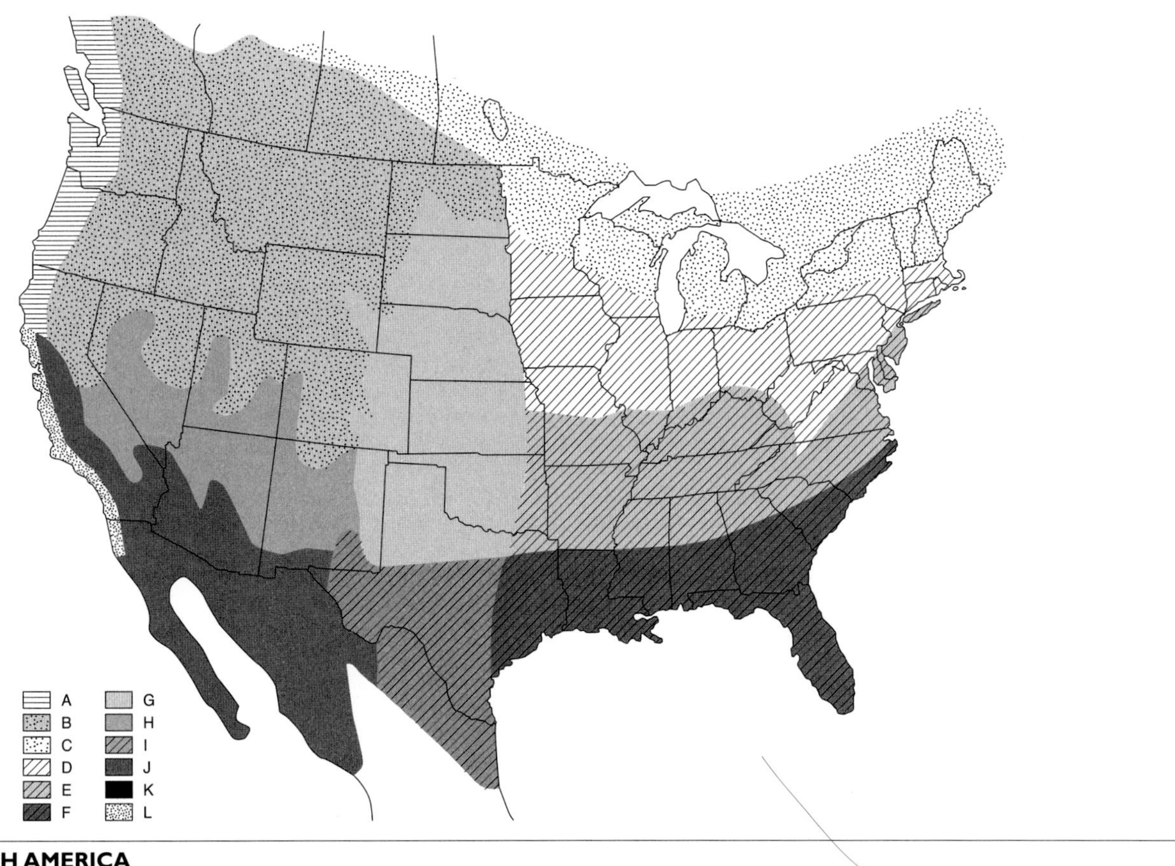

TURF REGIONS OF NORTH AMERICA

TURF REGIONAL COMPATIBILITY

	A	B	C	D	E	F	G	H	I	J	K	L
Alkaligrass	■											
Bahia Grass (Argentine)						■						
Bahia Grass (Pensacola)						■						
Creeping Bentgrass	■	■	■	■	■	■	■	■	■	■		
Bermudagrass						■			■	■	■	
Kentucky Bluegrass	■	■	■	■	■		■	■				
Buffalograss							■					
Carpetgrass						■						
Centipede Grass						■						
Fescue (Creeping Red)	■		■	■	■		■	■		■		
Fescue (Kentucky 31)	■		■	■	■		■	■		■		
Fescue (Tall)	■	■	■	■	■		■	■				
Perennial Ryegrass		■	■	■	■		■	■				■
St. Augustine Grass						■					■	
Seashore Paspalum						■			■	■	■	■
Zoysiagrass					■	■			■	■	■	

■ *Suitable zone for species*

Sources: www.lawngrasses.com and Lofts Seeds, Inc.

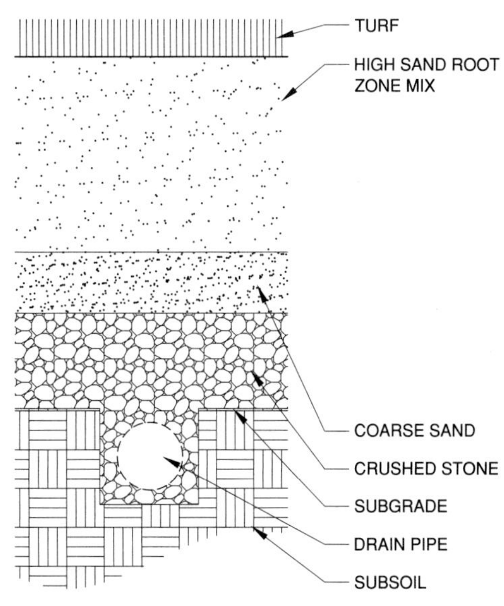

TEXAS-USGA SOIL PROFILE

Ronald B. Sawhill, University of Georgia, College of Environment and Design, Athens, Georgia

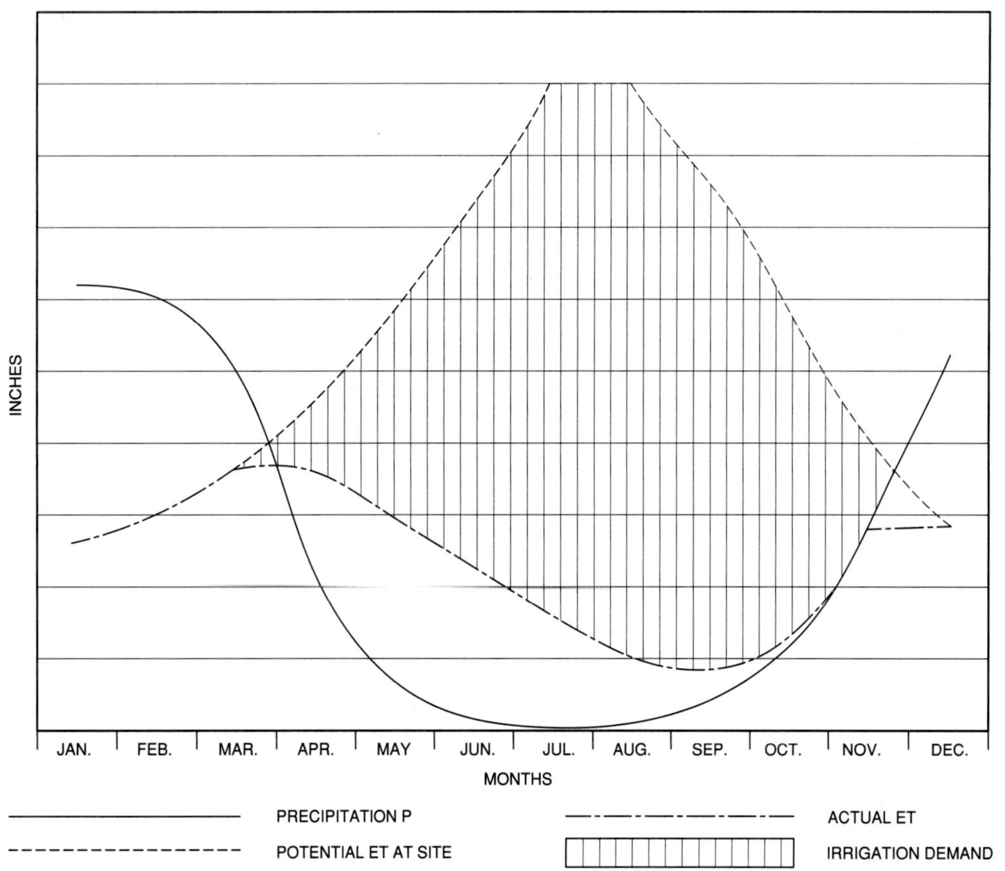

TURF IRRIGATION DEMAND FOR LOS ANGELES

the figure "Turf Irrigation Demand for Los Angeles"). (Note: Assumptions include a 20 percent irrigation efficiency loss and no overwatering.) The irrigation water demand is concentrated in the seven months of April through October. A single 1-inch irrigation application to 1 acre of turf is equivalent to the total annual indoor water supply required for 1.25 people, based on a national average of 60 gallons per day per person (gdp/person) (Aquacraft, 1999). Thus, each acre of turf in Los Angeles that receives the needed 18 inches of irrigation consumes the equivalent 12-month water supply for 22.5 people.

Irrigation

Irrigation is needed to establish most turf. Once established, irrigate turf thoroughly and deeply to encourage deep root growth. Shallow, frequent watering produces turf with poor root structure and low drought tolerance. Water from several sources may be available; seek alternatives to standard potable sources, surface water bodies, or wells. For small areas, cisterns can be used to store rainwater for later use in irrigation. Some areas permit the use of treated effluent and "gray water." In coastal areas, certain turf cultivars can withstand the use of saltwater for irrigation. Where saltwater is used or where irrigation is performed in arid regions, periodic flushing of the soil must be performed to remove salt accumulations.

Drainage

Site areas that do not drain well are not suited for turfgrass without making soil modifications, installing subsurface drains, and/or altering site grading. Surface runoff, subsurface drainage, and water infiltrating into groundwater from turf areas can contain nutrients and chemicals, which may pose a human and environmental hazard. Consider proximity to local potable water supply sources, particularly streams and shallow wells before selecting turf sites. Provide adequate natural buffers around intensive turf areas.

Nutrition

Proper nutrition is essential for the establishment and management of turf areas. Soil surveys can provide a general suitability guideline during master planning, but on-site soil testing should be conducted prior to detailed site design. Use existing soil fertility as a guide to sustainable turfgrass design. Soils that retain nutrients better can reduce fertilizer requirements, yielding quality turf at a lower cost to the client. Where poor soil nutrient conditions prevail, consider reducing turf area or selecting grasses appropriate for site conditions. Nutrient competition from tree roots can be controlled by root pruning nearby trees. Contact a local arborist to determine site- and species-specific root pruning practices.

Plan for Establishment

Proper planning for the establishment period is critical for achieving a successful turf and minimizing repairs. The more intensely used the turf will be, the more important the establishment period becomes. If turf is put into use prior to completing establishment, damage to the turf and soil profile can occur. Turf can be replanted, but soil structure repair requires extensive work.

Soil Preparation

Soil should be thoroughly cultivated to a minimum depth of 2 to 3 inches, regardless of the turf planting method. Remove all rocks, sticks, and other debris, and rake smooth. Adjust soil nutrients prior to planting. Roll seeds into the soil to maximize seed-soil contact.

Soil Nutrient Adjustment

Adjust soil nutrient levels prior to planting based on lab soil tests. Local golf course turf managers are good sources for specific nutrition guidance. Fast-acting limes can be incorporated prior to planting, but use slower-acting limes after germination to limit foliar burn. Evaluate and supplement macro- and micronutrients to achieve a balanced nutrient content. Phosphorus must be present during turf establishment, and 50 to 70 parts per milliion (ppm) is recommended.

Seed

Seeding of cool-season turfs can occur in both fall and spring, but fall seeding produces the most mature root and shoot system prior to summer heat stress. Early heat following spring seeding can result in a poor turf stand, and immature plants increase reliance on irrigation. Warm-season grasses, such as Bermuda grass should be seeded or sprigged in late spring once the daily low and high temperatures add up to 150 degrees (White, 2000). Buffalo grass establishes slowly from seed, and may require repetitive seeding to develop a solid stand.

Sprigs and Plugs

Sprigging and plugging are less expensive than installing solid sod, and generally produce a reliable turf faster than seeding. Apply sprigs of both stoloniferous and rhizomatous turfs to prepared soil. Proper irrigation is the key to successful sprig establishment. Once rooted, perform regular mowing and vertical cutting or slicing to develop a dense turf. Sprigs can be broadcast or planted in rows. Plugs are typically installed in a regular grid pattern.

Sod

Sod is the means to instant lawn. While it is initially more expensive than seeding or sprigging, it is the most reliable method for producing a quality turf and minimizes initial management expenses. Sod is available for most turfgrasses, although local selections may be limited. Most growers contract to grow sod of a desired cultivar, blend, or mixture.

Soil-free sod is a sod product that is essentially a mat of bare-root turf. Grown on a mesh or fibrous-type material to provide a structure, soil is removed by washing, or a nonsoil medium is used. This results in a very light product, increasing load quantity and decreasing labor demands. With proper cultivation, soil-free sod reduces the potential for layering in the turf profile that can impede air, water, and nutrient movement.

SPECIFY MANAGEMENT OBJECTIVES

Management practices vary based on turf type and species. Consequently, establishing management objectives during the design process improves the likelihood for long-term turf success and can minimize the overuse

Ronald B. Sawhill, University of Georgia, College of Environment and Design, Athens, Georgia

MANAGEMENT PRACTICES

ACTIVITY	INITIAL ESTABLISHMENT PERIOD	ONGOING MANAGEMENT
Cultivation	Aerate during the first year to maintain aggressive growth and to avoid sod-layering problems. Perform slicing to encourage lateral growth and improve stem and root density.	Cultivation is recommended twice per year on golf courses; similar practice should be employed on active use turfs, less often on other turfs. Cultivate to reduce compaction, reduce soil layering, encourage thatch reduction, spur deep-rooting, and improve soil air-water exchange. Coring is a most reliable method for long-lasting soil improvement. Slicing and spiking are short-term in effects, but spur lateral growth and improve soil-seed contact if performed following overseeding. High-pressure injection uses water or air to create small channels deep into the soil.
Irrigation	Seed & Sprig installations: Implement an irrigation program for the first 2–3 weeks that will achieve initial root establishment by keeping the soil moist in the 1/4"–1/2" range. On high-sand greens White (2000) gives an example irrigation schedule: 6 minutes every 2 hours from 6:00 A.M.–11:00 A.M.; 4 minutes every hour from noon–6:00 P.M.; one 6-minute application from midnight–6:00 A.M. After 70% to 80% germination or when rooting of sprigs has begun, shorten run-times without reducing start times for the next 10 to 16 days. After this period, reduce the number of start times and begin deeper watering. Adjust the program based on soil composition and weather conditions.	Use irrigation to manage active-use turf, turf subject to use during low rainfall periods, and turf established on highly porous soils. Apply irrigation to achieve deep watering without runoff. Apply water evenly and at rates specifically designed for the turf and soil conditions. Surface pooling is indicative of improper application rates or of soil compaction. Reduce water application rates and/or cultivate the soil to improve infiltration. Overwatering results in poor turf quality, nutrient leeching, disease prone conditions, extra expense, and wasted resources.
Mowing	Mow based on grass height, not based on turf density. The first 6 mowings should not remove more than 1/4 of the turf blade. See the figure "Mowing Heights during Turf Establishment" for a guide to mowing height and desired height. Contact a local turf specialist for initial turf height for specific cultivars. Use mulching mowers.	The higher turf is maintained, the deeper and better its root structure. Determine mowing height for specific cultivars from local turf specialists. Never remove more than 1/3 of the grass blade length. See the figure "Mowing Heights during Turf Establishment" for a guide to mowing height and desired height. Keep mower blades sharp to reduce disease potential. Use a reel-type mower on thick grasses like *Zoysia* and all grasses that are cut very short. Avoid mowing when the soil and turf are moist; vary mowing patters to limit compaction due to wheel action. Use mulching mowers or compost-collected clippings.
Fertilization	Prior to planting, make sure soil pH and nutrients are in proper balance for the specific turf. Correcting pH can be accomplished more rapidly prior to planting than afterwards. Phosphorus is recommended at 50–70 ppm for establishment.	Follow a fertilization program based on regular soil testing rather than reacting to visually apparent turf conditions. Soil-test annually for clay-based soils, more often for sand-based soils. Strive for optimum fertility levels without generating growth surges. Monitor soil pH to maintain proper minor element availability. Use slow-release and organic fertilizers as much as possible, and avoid weakening the turf with excessive or insufficient nitrogen. Maintaining good potassium levels has been shown to make turf more traffic-tolerant.
Pest control	Only apply pesticides if the infestation is excessive.	Integrated pest control programs recognize that insects are always present, but a healthy turf can resist insect damage and recover quickly from minor infestations without the use of chemicals. Large overpopulations of damaging insects are of concern, but do not apply pesticides unless the specific infestation has been properly identified. Environmental stress symptoms can resemble insect damage. Pesticides should be a last resort, because they kill beneficial insects as well. Some "green" pesticides are now available, as are biological controls using beneficial insects.
Disease control	Only apply fungicides if necessary. Use fungicide-treated seed when possible.	Diseases are best controlled by a strong cultural management program. Most diseases are caused by fungi that enter plants through wounds. Wounds most frequently occur from mowing, but traffic impacts and insects are secondary causes. Keeping blades sharp and mowing heights high reduces the likelihood of fungal infection. Excessive moisture due to overwatering, soil compaction, and shade can encourage fungal growth. Fungicides are available for specific infections and for preventative measures, but the specific disease must be determined.
Weed control	Only spray herbicides if necessary. Immature turf can be sensitive to herbicides. When installing turf by seed, seed at the proper rate to provide sufficient competition against weeds.	Weed control is an issue in all turfgrass. However, depending upon the type of turf, weed definition may change. A good turf management program can help limit some weeds, but most must be managed by herbicides. Organic "green" pesticides are now available. Apply herbicides when weeds are young and actively growing. Once seed heads form, herbicides have little effect, become a wasted expense, and demonstrate environmental irresponsibility.
Top dressing	Apply topdressing to even out turf surfaces. On high-sand bases, topdress prior to aerification to limit rutting until the turf is established. Use a drag mat after aerification cores dry to blend soil and limit layering.	Apply topdressing to even out turf surfaces, repair damaged turf, and control thatch build-up. An application of sand or soil mix is most typical. Try to match the character of the existing soil to reduce the potential for layering. Topdressing bunch-type grasses should be done at seeding times, while stoloniferous and rhizomatous grasses can receive incremental applications throughout the growing season. Application of crumb rubber from recycled tires as a topdressing (0.05-2.0 mm diameter at 17.8 and 35.7 tons per acre) was found to reduce surface hardness, reduce turfgrass wear injury, and beneficially raise soil temperatures in a northern climate. It is unclear if the soil temperature effect is acceptable in southern climates.
Overseeding and reseeding	Overseeding of warm-season turfs during the establishment period should be avoided. Overseeding increases management requirements and can negatively impact spring growth of immature turf.	Overseeding can be performed for functional and aesthetic reasons. Overseed/reseed bunch-type grasses regularly to maintain turf quality. Usually cool-season grasses are best seeded both fall and spring. Of the warm-season grasses, Bahia in particular will benefit from reseeding to maintain a thick turf. In the south, cool-season grasses are often overseeded onto dormant warm-season grasses for aesthetic reasons. Annual or Perennial Ryegrass is commonly preferred. Unless the area is heavily trafficked and will benefit functionally, overseeding simply creates off-season management requirements.
Traffic control	Do not allow turf to be trafficked except for management purposes until establishment is complete. Traffic impacts on immature turf will reduce turf quality and damage soil/root structure. Alter mowing patterns regularly to minimize damage.	Traffic control is important in areas subject to high use. Compaction and wear, particularly during stress periods can severely damage turf. Reroute pedestrians using movable barriers (posts and ropes) or by adding landscape barriers such as potted plants, sculptures, or bollards along busy sidewalks to control major traffic flows. Where turf areas are intended for pedestrian traffic, design them to be broad so that traffic will be spread out, or provide alternative routes that can be opened or closed as needed.

Ronald B. Sawhill, University of Georgia, College of Environment and Design, Athens, Georgia

REMOVE 1/4 OF BLADE

INITIAL CUT HEIGHT

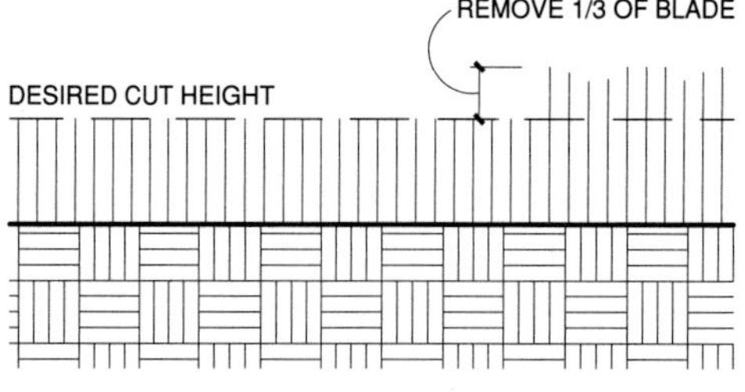

FIRST 6 MOWINGS FOLLOWING PLANTING		SUBSEQUENT MOWINGS ONGOING MANAGEMENT	
DESIRED HEIGHT (INCHES)	CUTTING HEIGHT (INCHES)	DESIRED HEIGHT (INCHES)	CUTTING HEIGHT (INCHES)
0.50	0.67	0.50	0.75
0.75	1.00	0.75	1.13
1.00	1.33	1.00	1.50
1.25	1.67	1.25	1.88
1.50	2.00	1.50	2.25
1.75	2.33	1.75	2.63
2.00	2.67	2.00	3.00
2.25	3.00	2.25	3.38
2.50	3.33	2.50	3.75
3.00	4.00	3.00	4.50

MOWING HEIGHTS DURING TURF ESTABLISHMENT

of irrigation, fertilizers, pesticides, and herbicides. Management demands and costs are least for meadows, moderate for greenswards, and high for active-use turf.

Proper management practices for an established lawn includes cultivation, irrigation, mowing, fertilization, pest control, disease control, weed control, top-dressing, overseeding and reseeding, and traffic control. The table "Management Practices" indicates appropriate management practices for the establishment period and for ongoing turf management. Follow LEED guidelines to minimize negative environmental impacts associated with turf and especially those impacts due to poor management practices.

REFERENCES

Aquacraft, Inc. and American Water Works Association Research Foundation. 1999. Residential Water Use Summary. www.aquacraft.com/Publications/resident.htm.

Beard, James B. 1982. *Turf Management for Golf Courses.* New York: Macmillan Publishing Company.

Ferguson, Bruce K. 1998. *Introduction to Stormwater.* New York: John Wiley & Sons, Inc.

Jenkins, Virginia Scott. 1994. *The Lawn: A History of an American Obsession.* Washington, D.C.: Smithsonian Institution. Press.

Leslie, A. R. 1994. *Handbook of Integrated Pest Management for Turf and Ornamentals.* Chelsea, MI: Lewis Publishers.

Packard, Stephen, and Cornelia F. Mutel (eds). 1997. *The Tallgrass Restoration Handbook: for Prairies, Savannas, and Woodlands.* Washington, DC: Island Press.

Puhalla, Jim, Jeff Krans, and Mike Goatley 1999. *Sports Fields: A Manual for Design, Construction and Maintenance.* Chelsea MI: Sleeping Bear Press.

Sauer, Leslie Jones, and Andropogon Associates. 1998. *The Once and Future Forest.* Washington, DC: Island Press.

White, Charles B. 2000. *The Turf Managers' Handbook for Golf Course Construction, Renovation and Grow-In.* Chelsea, MI: Sleeping Bear Press.

BIBLIOGRAPHY

Beard, James B. 1982. *Turf Management for Golf Courses.* New York: Macmillan Publishing Company.

Leslie, A. R.1994. *Handbook of Integrated Pest Management for Turf and Ornamentals.* Chelsea, MI: Lewis Publishers.

Packard, Stephen, and Cornelia F. Mutel (eds). 1997. *The Tallgrass Restoration Handbook: For Prairies, Savannas, and Woodlands.* Washington, DC: Island Press.

White, Charles B. 2000. *The Turf Managers' Handbook for Golf Course Construction, Renovation and Grow-In.* Chelsea, MI: Sleeping Bear Press.

See also:
Irrigation
Planting

Ronald B. Sawhill, University of Georgia, College of Environment and Design, Athens, Georgia

LIVING GREEN ROOFS AND LANDSCAPES OVER STRUCTURE

TERMINOLOGY

In the last five years, the term "green roof" has taken on ecological and social significance beyond its seemingly simplistic description. "Green roofs" as commonly understood, have become a panacea for the reduction of pollution and heat islands, for large-scale mitigation of stormwater runoff, and for maximum utilization of urban land.

The concept of the "green roof" as a way to add permeable surface and usable open space without taking up additional land is easy to understand and implement. Consequently, many clients, municipalities, architects, landscape architects, and planners have come to consider "green roofs" as an integral element of sustainable building practice.

The building "green" movement is not new, nor is the practice of using natural resources responsibly, to sustain life and encourage the regeneration of natural resources. The technology and materials for vegetating roofs and creating usable open spaces over structure have been known for centuries. Since 4000 BC, practitioners of building and agriculture have utilized the knowledge and materials of their time to construct sacred places such as ziggurats, simple vegetated roofs, and remarkable gardens over elevated surfaces. More recently, many European municipalities have mandated and incorporated thin-profile living green roofs and landscapes over structure as standard building practice, with the result that landscape architects and architects have successfully built numerous comfortable, accessible, open spaces over structure. This has happened without fanfare, perhaps because many of these spaces have been imperceptibly integrated with the architecture and surrounding urban fabric, and perhaps because much of what sustains "green roof" functionality is invisible to the user.

"Green roof," today, is often used as an umbrella term for a number of greening systems built over a structural decking that serves as a roof to that specific portion of the structure. As a "roof garden," "eco-roof," "extensive green roof," or "intensive green roof," the system acts and is perceived as a roof or lid. As a "roof garden," "over-structure-open-space," or "intensive green roof," the system may either serve as a roof or a grade-level floor.

This ambiguity and confusion of terminology is exacerbated by current jargon derived from European usage of "extensive" and "intensive," two words used within the fabrication, supply, and, now, the design industry. These terms, which may seem counterintuitive to English speakers, describe the depth of growing medium and level of effort required to maintain the "green roof".

- *Extensive* is loosely used to describe a system that typically has a very shallow depth of soil or growing medium: is not irrigated; it is expected to require minimum maintenance; and it is not intended to be accessed for use as a garden or open space.
- *Intensive* is loosely applied to those systems that have a greater depth of soil or growing medium, which allows for a greater diversity in size and type of vegetation. This diversity usually implies a need for supplemental irrigation and, overall, a more intensive level of maintenance.

A disadvantage to using "extensive" and "intensive" as blanket terms is that neither clearly reflects the expected purpose or use, nor adequately conveys design requirements to construct and maintain the appropriate a system of components to support the use. A terminology-driven, rather than use-driven, approach to the design and construction of "green roofs" can lead to further confusion and inaccuracy in design, documentation, and client expectations.

Thus, for clarity, in this discussion, terms are defined as follows:

- "Living green roof" is used to describe a thin-profile system where the growing medium is less than 8 inches and where the primary use is to effectively satisfy stormwater management requirements in lieu of conventional stormwater engineering methods.
- "Landscape over structure" describes a system where the growing medium is greater than 8 inches and, based upon programmatic requirements, may be designed to accommodate its use as accessible open space. The combined depth of component parts may exceed several feet, and related systems required to support the uses often become more complex.

"Living green roof" and "landscape over structure" should not be compared with one another. Rather, large-scale ecological and social benefits can be recognized in the appropriate application of either, as well as their combined use to reduce stormwater runoff; bind dust and pollutant particulates; reduce energy consumption, improve visual quality of conventional roofs, and provide valuable beautiful, comfortable, usable open space. The selection of the most suitable application should be defined by varied use and design goals.

APPLICATION OF LIVING GREEN ROOFS

Benefits of Living Green Roofs

The advantages of using living green roofs can be seen ecologically, aesthetically, and economically.

From an ecological standpoint, a major benefit of a living green roof is that it slows and can detain stormwater runoff, by providing a pervious, vegetated surface—thus preserving water resources rather than increasing the monetarily and environmentally costly stormwater management systems. The vegetation and growing medium cover also help to shade the roof surface, preventing solar heat gain or loss, thereby lowering consumption and cost of energy use. The transpiration of the vegetation provides an evaporative cooling effect that can lower the air temperature locally to below ambient temperatures, helping to reduce the urban heat island effect globally.

From an aesthetic standpoint, a primary application of a living green roof is to provide a visually interesting vegetated cover of diverse texture and seasonal color, in contrast to a rock ballast or dark protection board surface.

Economically, living green roofs may satisfy governing stormwater management requirements, which will reduce the cost of conventional methods of conducting stormwater from roof drains to ultimate outfall. This not only reduces owner construction costs but also the enormous costs to municipalities for infrastructure and operations associated with stormwater management. That is why, today, many municipalities offer incentives such as tax credits and larger allowable floor area ratios in exchange for implementation of living green roof systems.

Growing Medium and Plant Selection

The depth of growing medium required for a living green roof is typically 3 to 6 inches. Typically, irrigation is not employed, so the vegetation, which must survive in shallow soil and, often, harsh, dry conditions, is usually composed of low-growing, horizontally spreading, water-storing plants. Most often, but not exclusively, the majority of plants are selected from various species of *Sedum*. *Sedum*, a genus with hundreds species, are typically succulent plants which can store water in their leaves and stems for extended periods of droughty conditions. The dominance of their use in the overall plant selection of living green roofs has led to the additional misnomer of "sedum roofs." Like most successful planting plans, the selection of plants for living green roofs should include a matrix of plant genera and species that provide adequate horticultural diversity and that are suitable to the environment. The limited maintenance required for such a plant mix might include initial hand-watering during installation and adaptation period and occasional weeding, fertilizing, and spot repair.

The overall thin profile of the components of a living green roof generally weighs 12 to 15 pounds per square foot. Usually, structural upgrading of standard decking is not required, because the added weight of the profile is about the same weight of stone ballast applied to protect and preserve the waterproofing membrane of a conventional roofing system. A living green roof, therefore, can be employed when, structurally, no additional weight can be added to the deck. Also, because generally there is little or no additional cost to provide increased structural support, it can also be a cost-effective way to provide greater visual amenity and environmental quality. Since each application of a living green roof will have specific design requirements, it is imperative that a structural engineer review and approve proposed designs to ensure the structural capacity for the weights of proposed growing medium when saturated. Likewise, any potential for unintentional live loads must be evaluated. Although, living green roofs are not intended or designed to be physically accessible for use as an open space amenity, clear demarcation of restricted use should be incorporated into the overall design.

APPLICATION OF LANDSCAPES OVER STRUCTURE

Benefits of Landscapes over Structure

Depending on the amount of vegetation, most of the same ecological and environmental benefits may be derived from the construction of landscapes over structure as from living green roofs. The greater the density and coverage of the vegetation, the greater the capacity of a landscape over structure to intercept, absorb, and slow stormwater runoff. Likewise, the collateral benefits of more vegetation on the Earth's surface are also derived.

Depending on use and the ultimate physical expression of the design, landscapes over structure, like any built landscape, can take many forms and have the potential for a wide range of ecological, aesthetic, and social benefits.

Susan Weiler, ASLA, Olin Partnership

Growing Medium and Plant Selection

Horticulturally, with a growing medium typically greater than 12 inches, landscapes over structure can support a greater diversity in size and type of vegetation. Greater size and diversity of plants usually requires a deeper soil profile, supplemental irrigation, and a more complex infrastructure to support and sustain plant growth in an artificial environment.

Based on intended and expected use, the structural system required to sustain the additional weight of growing medium, vegetation, site elements, and potential live loads is significantly more substantial in complexity of design, size and cost than that required to support a living green roof. And, invariably, coordinating the various professional disciplines throughout design, documentation, and construction have cost implications, which must be balanced against the benefits of the end use.

In the design and construction of living green roofs and landscapes over structure, the complexity of the integration of architecture and landscape is often poorly understood by clients, design professionals, contractors, product suppliers and their representatives. Intuitively, most understand that some horticultural infrastructure must be required for sustaining plant life; however, the importance of coordinating the attendant structural and architectural infrastructure is less well recognized. Following are basic considerations in the planning and design of living green roofs and landscapes over structure, as well as a description of the basic components commonly used in their construction. The illustrative details provide examples of how the components were assembled in specific projects with specific programmatic requirements and are intended as examples and guidelines rather than standards. Many of the same issues and considerations are similar to those of building landscapes on "terra firma," where each project has specific programmatic, design, and maintenance requirements. However an "artificial" environment is less forgiving when the parts have not been well designed, coordinated, and constructed.

PLANNING AND DESIGN CONSIDERATIONS

Critical Elements of Early Design Decision and Coordination

All planting and sitework over structure requires careful design, documentation, and construction. Paramount to a project's success is the complete and seamless integration of the structural requirements and architectural expression of what lies below, with the final surface expression of the rooftop or finished grade. Rooftops are inherently stressful environments, particularly for planting, as they are subject to heat, accelerated evapotranspiration, and desiccating and potentially damaging winds. Tops of roofs, and the structural decking supporting them, essentially become the floor of living green roofs and landscapes over structure.

Basic to building successful living green roofs and landscapes over structure are:

- Structure to support it
- Waterproofing to protect what is below
- Protection board to protect the waterproofing
- Drainage systems to remove, direct, release, or retain water

Planting requirements include:

- Insulation from thermal fluctuation
- Sources for water and aeration
- Selection of plants that can survive and flourish in an artificial environment
- Growing medium, of suitable depth in which the plants can gather nutrients and establish and maintain their root systems

Similar to any sitework project, paving requires the appropriate slab support and setting systems. Stairs and walls require the correct structural integrity and appropriate finishes. For site lighting, fountains, and other major site elements, the mechanical, electrical, and plumbing infrastructure has to be coordinated. Moreover, to successfully implement living green roofs and landscapes over structure, the planning and design considerations, and coordination required in documentation and construction, necessitate early and continuous collaboration among numerous design disciplines, the owner, and contractors.

Each project will gain more specificity during each subsequent design phase, but there are several key issues that should be considered very early in the

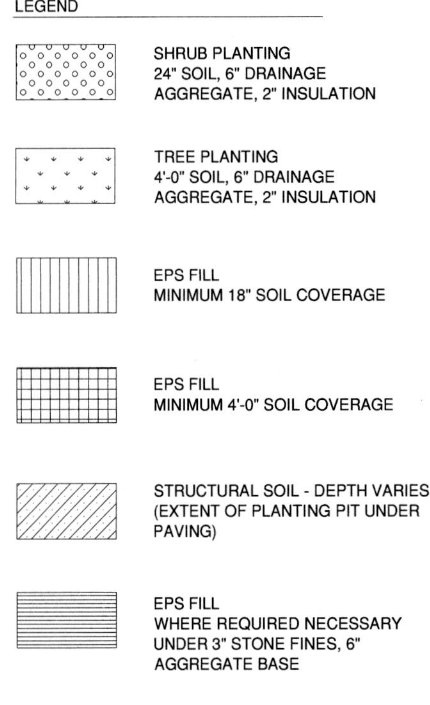

PLANTING SOIL/FILL : DEPTH CONDITIONS
PARTIAL PLAN

PARTIAL SOILS PLAN

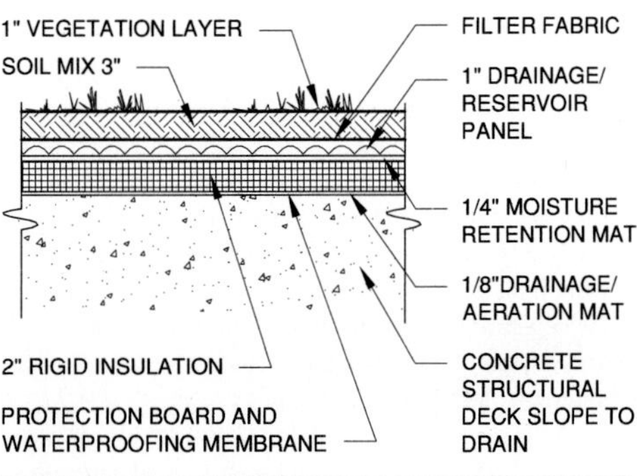

LIVING GREEN ROOF

Susan Weiler, ASLA, Olin Partnership

project. The client should be made aware of the proper resolution of these issues, as they can have enormous programming, aesthetic, and cost implications. Among the most significant considerations are determining the structural support system and coordinating interior and exterior finished elevations in relationship to the top of the structural slab or deck. Many inter-related factors will affect how these are determined and resolved and all require extensive, early design coordination among the landscape architect, architect, and structural, civil and mechanical, electrical and plumbing engineers.

Following is a broad overview of the critical issues requiring early design decisions and coordination.

- Program and expected use of finished interior and exterior surfaces
- Resultant structural requirements and structural slab configuration
- Subsurface drainage requirements
- Drain locations
- Waterproofing requirements
- Minimum and optimum slope requirements for structural slab
- Surface materials, profile of system and constituent components
- Surface grading and drainage requirements

Other early considerations might include requirements for:

- Height limitations for bottom of structure (floor-to-floor requirements)
- Mechanical, electrical, or plumbing plenum or conduit locations
- Venting size, direction of flow, noise level, location and surface expression

If it is determined that planting is a part of the program, key issues to be addressed should include:

- Whether the planting is a living green roof, a larger-scale landscape, or both
- The plan limits of each type of planting
- Horticultural requirements
- Microclimate considerations such as wind, effect of rapid soil temperature fluctuations
- Expected planting profiles (low-growing drought-resistant plants, ground covers, shrubs, flowering and understory trees, large caliper trees)
- Maximum depth and weight of root balls or box sizes
- Soil or growing medium type, depth, and weight
- Saturation and evaporation rate of soil type
- Irrigation requirements
- Insulation requirements

Early consideration for coordination of other site elements might include requirements for:

- Site walls or stairs
- Fountains
- Other special site features

Determining the Structural Support System

The primary supporting element of any living green roof or landscape over structure is the structural deck or slab. Typically it spans the joists and beams that set atop columns. The structural support system is generally determined by the program of interior use below it and of the amount of weight it must support above it. The deck can be composed of a number of structural materials and systems, such as plywood sheathing, metal, or concrete. The primary finished deck, or structural slab, referred to here is concrete. However, often in living green roofs of a relatively small scale, or in retrofit conditions, other decking systems and surfaces may include metal decking or even wood decking. (Note: Retrofitting is not specifically addressed here for either living green roofs or landscapes over structure, as requirements are dependent on existing conditions and program. Likewise, there are many examples of appropriate application of living green roofs to sloped roof decks, but the primary types considered here are flat or low-sloped roof surfaces and associated structural deck.)

Deck Construction and Attaining Positive Slope

Decks or slabs constructed with low-slope or even no slope characteristics are particularly susceptible to the accumulation of water if proper construction techniques for adequate deck or slab drainage are not considered and implemented. Excess water can lead to deterioration of inert components, such as waterproofing, insulation, and concrete, which can lead to the progressive collapse and ultimate failure of the entire system. Excess water in the dynamic, or living, components can lead to anaerobic conditions in soils or growing media, which can cause toxic soils and demise or even death, of the plants.

The slope, or gradient, of the deck should be a minimum of 1 percent. For poured-in-place concrete decks, preferably, the gradient should be a minimum of 2 percent, to account for concrete creep, (or sag) over time.

Attaining adequate positive slope may be accomplished in a number of ways. Sometimes, if the required floor-to-floor height can accommodate it, the columns can be incrementally shortened to achieve the required slope. This allows the beams and deck to slope consistently and at the same thickness. If the column heights cannot be adjusted to accommodate the slope, the top of deck itself will need to slope from a given high point, causing the thickness of the slab to increase at these points.

A topping slab may also be utilized, wherein an additional layer of concrete, sometimes reinforced, is applied to the top of the cast-in-place concrete deck and is sloped in the direction of the predetermined and located deck drains. Both the topping slab and increased thickness of the slab can increase the complexity of construction and the weight of the slab, which will be of concern to the structural engineer. The loss of depth to finished grade will be of concern to the landscape architect.

A topping slab, however, depending on the location and type of the waterproofing membrane and insulation, may act as a "working slab" or "waste slab," which protects the waterproofing membrane or other components from damage during construction.

Establishing Finished Interior and Exterior Elevations and Top of Slab Elevations

Establishing finished floor elevations in relationship to the top of the structural slab and the exterior elements is critical, as this will have direct impact on the sustenance of planting and the ability to construct suitable paving systems and other site elements. It will also affect the ability to use and maintain the site in the manner intended.

Often, to have accessible ingress and egress from a finished floor elevation, the required tolerance may be a half-inch or less. If the top of a structural slab is set too high, it will be very difficult to attain the proper relationship between the interior and the exterior use. Exterior paving systems, for example, can be adversely affected if significant adjustments must be made to the paver thickness, setting bed, insulation, and subdrainage components, to accommodate positive flow away from the interior finished floor elevation. As another example, for living green roofs, there may be local requirements to establish and accommodate a "freeboard" for controlling high-intensity storms. Without proper coordination of finished interior and exterior elevations this may not be achieved.

For projects with significant planting, even if the structural deck has been designed to allow for the weight of large-caliper trees and saturated soil, if the top of slab, finished floor, and finished grade elevations have not been properly coordinated, the allowable depth for the soil and root balls can be severely impacted, limiting selection and growth of large caliper trees.

Additional considerations in determining top of slab in relationship to finished grades are zoning and height restrictions; geotechnical conditions such as depth to bedrock and type of soil; and water table conditions which may limit the ability to discharge stormwater.

UNDERSTANDING SYSTEM COMPONENTS

When designing a system for over-structure construction, selecting and specifying the most appropriate components may be the most overwhelming task. Not only is it crucial to determine how the system must function as a whole, but also how it must perform both initially and over the life of the project. For each component within that system it is essential to understand its function, performance, and compatibility with other components within the system. Additionally, the selection of components can be complicated by the fact that sometimes the same component, and same product, might be used for more than one function in a system, but in different locations. An example of this is drainage matting used under the insulation to facilitate drainage across the top of the slab might also be used just below the soil or growing medium as aeration matting.

To assist in this determination, it is helpful to understand: the properties of constituent materials; the technical properties for each material's proper, sustained performance; whether a product is commercially available or has to be custom-fabricated; whether there are measurable standards and requirements for a product; where a product can be found; whether there are similar products of equal quality; whether there are particular attributes that need to be specified for a product's successful installation and performance; and whether there are new and better products available.

At a minimum, the following information should be assessed for each of the components:

- Function
- Physical properties
- Physical limitations
- Relationship to other components

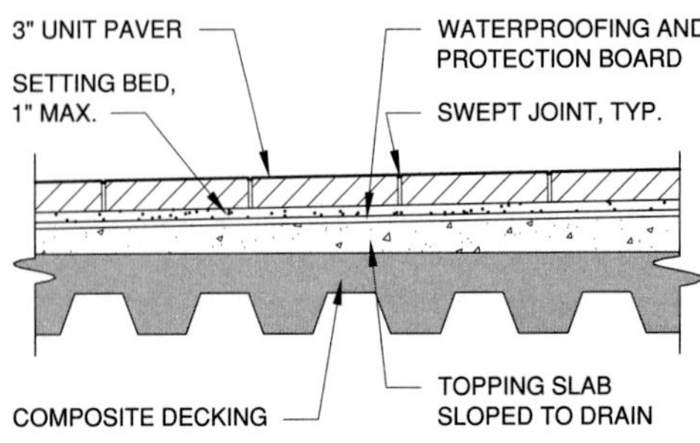

UNIT PAVERS OVER STRUCTURE

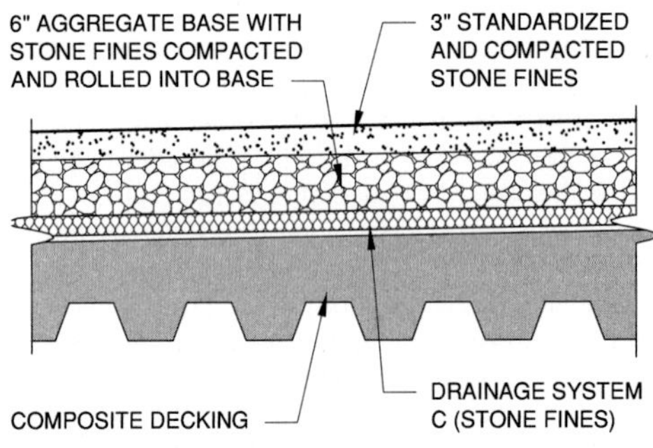

STONE FINES PAVING OVER STRUCTURE

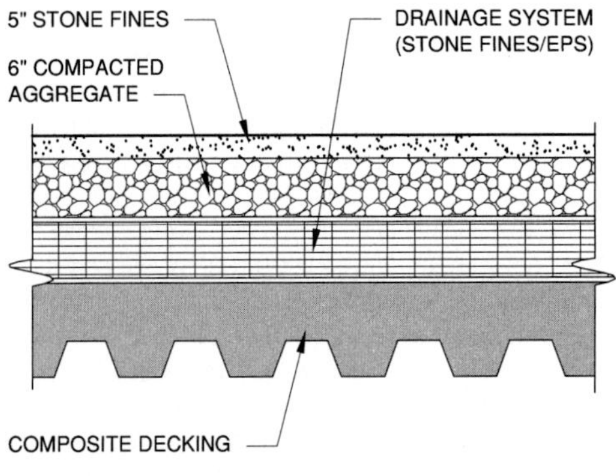

STONE FINES OVER INSULATION

This discussion is intended to provide a basic explication of commonly used inert components used in designing and building living green roofs and landscapes over structure.

Waterproofing Membranes

The primary purpose of waterproofing is to keep unwanted water and moisture out of the structure below. Since the waterproofing is the primary protective element of the slab and of the structure below, its selection installation and protection are paramount to the success and longevity of any additional components or systems over the structure. Additionally, because, typically, the waterproofing is at the bottom of the system, it is difficult to access once the remaining components are installed. The failure of a waterproofing membrane can lead to the unraveling and failure of a living green roof or an entire landscape over structure.

Some of the primary considerations of subsequent installation and maintenance that may affect the selection of the waterproofing membrane are the potential for:

- Excess moisture in the concrete deck, causing vapor expansion, leading to rupture and excess vapor below deck
- Thermal expansion or movement causing cracking or tearing
- Mechanical damage during construction
- Mechanical damage during subsequent installation of surface or subsurface elements (footings, irrigation, electrical conduit, new drains or new cores, plants with large root balls, etc.)
- Leakage at seams, drains, flashing, penetrations for utilities

The following is intended to provide a basic understanding of waterproofing membranes as applicable to this topic of living green roofs and landscapes over structure. Waterproofing is more fully covered in *Roof/Deck Construction* as well as in *Architectural Graphic Standards* (Wiley, 2000).

Although industry and generic definitions of roofing types may vary, these major roofing types for low-slope roofs are generally recognized:

- Built-up membrane
- Single-ply membrane
- Hybrid or composite membrane
- Fluid-applied membrane

Built-up Roofing

Built-up roofing (BUR) systems are assembled in place by alternating layers of "felts" of fibrous materials and some type of molten bitumen. The fiber sheets provide the reinforcement or the integrity of the system. The molten bitumen, which can be cold-applied or "hot-mopped" is usually coal tar or asphalt and supplies the primary water resistance. Built-up roofs require a ballast of crushed aggregate or a living green roof to protect the membrane from mechanical damage or deterioration from ultraviolet rays.

Even though they may have a longer life span, built-up roofs are less commonly used in either green roof construction or in building landscapes over structure, as they are more labor-intensive to install and maintain. They are also perceived to be more susceptible to root penetration because air and moisture is available throughout the multiple plies providing numerous entry points.

Single-Ply Systems

Single-ply roofing systems are based on the use of large thermosetting (sometimes referred to as "elastomeric") or thermoplastic sheets adhered to the deck through numerous means.

Both thermosetting and thermoplastic membranes are commonly manufactured in large rolls, which are seam-welded in situ into sheets and adhered in several ways, depending on both the deck configuration and material characteristics of the membrane. A major advantage in the use of single-ply systems is that they are easier to install and require less labor. And because of their characteristic flexibility, they are considered less susceptible to cracking and seam failure, which, combined with fewer seams, lessens the potential for leaks.

Thermosetting Membranes

Thermosetting or elastomeric membranes are made from synthetic materials such as neoprene or ethylene-propylene-diene-monomer—more commonly known as EPDM. Thermosetting membranes are not pliable or softened with heat and generally are installed by first joining the seams by applying adhesives, rather than heat or solvents, then attaching them to the deck.

Thermoplastic Membranes

Thermoplastic membranes are derived from plastic polymers such as polyvinyl chloride (PVC), as well as many proprietary products fabricated by specific blends of plastic polymers. These membranes are flexible in temperature extremes so that they do not become brittle in cold temperatures or too soft in warmer temperatures. Pliable when heated, they are generally installed by first welding the seams, either by flame, hot air, or solvents, and then adhering the membranes to the deck.

Modified Bitumen (Mod-Bit, Polymer-Modified Bitumens)

Another waterproofing membrane classified as thermoplastic is bitumen that has been modified by polymeric compounds, and so is known as modified-bitumen (frequently shortened to mod-bit). Modifications of these proprietary products may include incorporation of reinforcing fibers, granular surfaces, or other coatings to produce a combined system with increased flexibility and resistance to UV rays, extreme temperatures, and fatigue.

Hybrid or Composite Membranes

Modified bitumen membranes are sometimes installed in multiple plies and over built-up systems utilizing asphalt-impregnated rolls of felts.

Fluid-Applied Membranes

Fluid-applied systems are quite common and can also be used for complex shapes such as domes and shells, as well as for vertical sides requiring waterproofing. Water-repellent compounds such as asphalt emulsions, silicones, and neoprene are typically applied with sprayers and rollers.

Waterproof Membrane Selection

Because of the importance of this primary protection, systems with increased longevity are preferred. Replacing entire waterproofing systems becomes more complicated over structure. Failure leads not only to interior damage to the building but to the erosion or corrosion of the reinforcement and slabs. Mass replacement operations can be prohibitively expensive, are often met with resistance, and are often repaired without replacing the system as originally designed.

Any of these systems may be used if the waterproofing membrane is protected from exposure and mechanical damage above by protection board, insulation, or other components. A significant measure of membrane protection from exposure is inherent by covering with plants, paving, or other site elements.

The selection should be made in coordination with the architect, landscape architect, structural engineer, waterproofing consultant, supplier, and owner. Considerations should include:

Susan Weiler, ASLA, Olin Partnership

- Size and complexity of the deck configuration
- Assigned use below deck
- Programmed use and maintenance above deck
- Accessibility to the membrane
- Ability to protect the membrane
- Climate, availability of materials, construction expertise
- Cost

Many proprietary waterproofing systems are installed by the manufacturer's approved and certified contractors familiar and experienced with the product and construction methods. Required accessory products such as drain bodies and flashing systems are usually custom designed for the waterproofing installation and supplied by the manufacturer. This both helps ensure proper installation and protects the viability of the warranty. However, the selection of the components above the waterproofing, often supplied by the waterproofing manufacturer as a proprietary system, should not automatically be specified based on waterproofing warranty provided alone.

Root Barriers

Root barriers are intended to prevent damage from root penetration or perforation. Usually, root barriers are simple polyethylene sheets, but they can also be polypropylene geotextile fabrics or a chemically inert "antirot" granular-surfaced, fabric-reinforced sheet installed as part of the waterproofing membrane. Sometimes a root barrier is also incorporated into a drainage matting. Root barriers should contain no substances harmful to plant growth. However, it is difficult to find precise information on which inhibitors or biocides are used in them.

It is important to ensure that the root barrier is chemically compatible with the waterproofing membrane system. The location of the root barrier is typically directly over or part of the waterproofing membrane, or depending on the membrane, over the protection board. Polyethylene root barriers should not be placed over polystyrene insulations. Although the insulation is hydrophobic, water vapor can still be transmitted and the root barrier could form a vapor barrier.

Selection of the root barrier, by the landscape architect or architect, should be made in consultation with the waterproofing manufacturer, installer, and with the project's independent waterproofing consultant.

For both the root barrier and the protection board, if a plastic or polyethylene sheeting is used, it is necessary to ensure that it is not affected adversely by solvents released from curing membranes. Also, recently, fabricators have been providing non-bituminous, or bitumen-resistant products, as the bitumen is organic and a "food source" for bacteria. Microbial activity can lead to deterioration and ultimately easier penetration for roots.

Protection Board

Protection of the waterproofing membrane is extremely important for both horizontal and vertical surfaces, in building living green roofs and landscapes over structures. Since there will be continual activity once the membrane is installed, through the construction process and even during maintenance and repair operations, it is very susceptible to damage, therefore, immediate protection is required.

Protection boards may be made of any material that protects the waterproofing membrane itself, but it should be durable and nondeteriorating, such as semirigid sheets of cement board or mineral-reinforced membrane, which is often part of the waterproofing system.

If a plastic or polyethylene sheeting is used, it is necessary to ensure that it is compatible with adjacent components. Also if any paving system is to be installed directly over this, it is very important not to use any material that can act as a "slip sheet." This is also applicable to thin polystyrene boards used as protection boards.

Insulation

Thermal insulation helps to keep a building warmer in the winter and cooler in the summer by reducing the loss of interior heat or penetration of cold air through the exterior surfaces of the building. Likewise in warmer seasons or climates, it helps keep the heat out and cool air in. Its efficacy is measured by its R-value.

The R-value is a material's thermal resistance, meaning how well it resists the effects of thermal influences of heat or cold: R stands for resistance to heat flow, so the higher the value, the greater the insulation power. It is generally expressed in units of hr/ft^2 or °F/Btu$^{\text{in. or m}}$ or °K/W, meaning that, at a given mean temperature and given time of exposure, each inch of thickness will provide a measurable degree of thermal resistivity.

In building and waterproofing systems, the insulation material most commonly used is extruded polystyrene boards, ranging in thickness from 1 to 5 inches. Its placement in relationship to the top of slab and waterproofing can vary. If it is placed below the structural deck and waterproofing membrane, some condensation can occur, compromising interior finishes and potentially leading to cracking of the structure and rupture of membrane. Above the deck, it can be placed above or below the membrane, condensation will be minimized and some thermal efficiency may be realized. Generally, the preferred location is above the membrane, often referred to as an inverted or protected membrane system. When the insulation is placed above the membrane, there is less chance of condensation. Condensation can increase thermal fluctuation and, below the membrane, increase the potential for vapor blisters and membrane rupture. Additionally, moisture can travel under the insulation, making it more difficult to locate and repair any leak.

Other advantages to placing the insulation above the membrane is that it is easier to get proper coverage of the waterproofing membrane directly over the deck than over the insulation; additionally, the insulation over the membrane can serve as another layer of protection. The disadvantages are that the insulation in this location can impede drainage; and if it becomes saturated for long periods of time, it can lose its thermal resistance.

Thermal fluctuation can affect vegetation when roots freeze, thaw, and refreeze. This can be exacerbated in winter, when heat emitted from the structure below heats up the soil or from sunlight striking the vertical surfaces of raised planters. Not only is the freezing and thawing of plant roots detrimental to the vegetation, but it can also expand and potentially crack rigid walls containing large, raised planting beds. Therefore, it is important to insulate the sides of raised planters as well as the bottom.

Insulation Materials Used as Lightweight Fill over Structure

Often in landscapes over structure a change in elevation of the top of structural deck is needed to reflect architectural use below, or additional depth to the top of structural deck is required to accommodate the depth of root ball and growing medium. The area of fill required between finished grade and top of deck can be significant.

Every additional unit of load can increase the deck thickness and beam and column size, which can result in adding to building footprint and height, construction time, materials, and, ultimately, cost. Polystyrene products, which are lightweight, easy to handle, and readily available, offer an attractive alternative. Polystyrene is a petroleum-based product, which when used in geotechnical applications is generically referred to as "geofoam" or "geoblock." These terms are sometimes also used when referring to the use of large blocks of polystyrene in contrast to the thin board insulation.

The fabrication process of geofoam is either by expansion or extrusion of polystyrene, resin beads, or pellets, thus providing two commonly known products: xPs, planar, extruded polystyrene boards, and EPs, block-molded expanded polystyrene.

- xPs, usually produced as rigid boards, are formed in an extrusion process that includes additives, heat, and pressure. They are most commonly used for insulating the roof decks for living green roofs and deck slabs for landscapes over structure. As an extruded foam product, xPs provides a very dense and hydrophobic insulation. The boards are usually produced in 24-inch-by-96-inch or 48-inch-by-96-inch lengths and widths, and in thicknesses of 1 to 4 inches, although they may be custom fabricated in larger sizes. Typically, one person can handle these sheets of 4 feet by 12 feet, which can be easily cut in to the field to fit planters or around drains. xPs is also available in tapered boards that can be used, in some instances, to provide the slope required for drainage, without having to build up the concrete topping slab. Both flat and tapered boards are available with chamfered grooves in the bottom, to further facilitate drainage.
- EPs blocks are made by exposing the polystyrene resin to steam, heat, and pressure, softening, expanding, fusing, and finally molding them into large blocks. EPs blocks are available in larger sizes than commonly available for xPs. Fabricated in blocks of 4 feet by 8 feet by 30 inches or greater, EPs is often used as lightweight fill in over structure construction where large areas of fill are required. The blocks can be shop-fabricated in compliance with shop drawings or easily field-cut. Although slightly more cumbersome for one person to handle, like xPs, the EPs blocks are lightweight and easy to install.

Both EPs and xPs are suitable alternatives to soils or other fill. Both are lightweight, easy to handle, and can be field-cut. Shipping and installation costs are typically the same. Both, however, have specific material characteristics—such as R-value, density, and compressive strength—which may make one more suitable as fill than the other. Often, EPs is cited as having a higher absorption rate than xPs; and absorption of moisture could decrease thermal effectiveness. However, neither material's rate of absorption would affect its compressive strength or deformation properties. The selection of either xPs or EPs, when used as structural fill, should be done in collaboration with a structural engineer.

As to cost, in general, producing EPs is usually reported to be one-third that of producing xPs. Polystyrene is a petroleum-based product and, therefore, the cost and timing to produce either can fluctuate with world oil costs, making both of them a costly alternative.

Recently, very lightweight, air-entrained concretes have been used as an alternative to xPs and EPs. These "flowable fills" need to be evaluated on their suitability for structural capacity, desired porosity, or permeability, and installation requirements. As a "liquid" material, its use to achieve sloped surfaces is difficult.

Drainage Materials

Adequate drainage is essential for the success of living green roofs and landscapes over structure. There must be ways to collect, detain, direct, and distribute water throughout the entire system. Living green roofs are intended to detain the initial minutes of rainfall from the most frequently occurring storms—those categorized as 2-5 year. Water beyond this significant absorption capacity must be released, as must excess water in a landscape over structure. Standing water in soil leads to the depletion of oxygen and the creation of anaerobic conditions, as well as deterioration of inert components and potential system-wide failure.

The drainage layer, a medium to facilitate the positive flow of excess water, should be continuous across the top of the waterproofing membrane. The thickness, and materials used to accomplish this, may differ.

Crushed Stone

One material is clean, free-draining crushed stone, deep enough to accommodate a conventional underdrainage system of laterals and mains. However, crushed stone, when saturated, can become quite heavy so the structural slab must be sized to accommodate it.

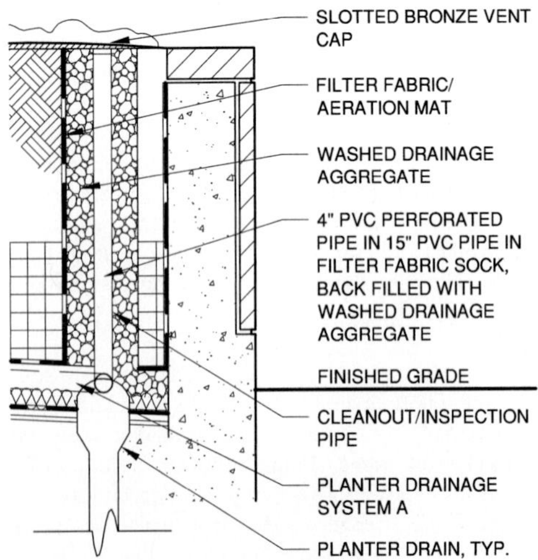

CLEANOUT/INSPECTION PIPE

Lightweight Aggregates

Alternatively, lightweight aggregates, such as expanded clay, balled clay, expanded shale, or other ceramic products are fabricated according to standard grades and are more consistent in composition and the distribution of particle size. They are an attractive alternative to crushed stone, because they are much lighter and consistency in particle size lessens the potential for compaction. The disadvantage is that they typically are much more costly. The cost of lighter aggregate needs to be weighed against the additional costs of the structure to support the heavier crushed stone.

Drainage Mats and Panels and Reservoir Mats and Panels

Drainage mats and panels are an attractive alternative to several inches of drainage aggregate, as they are lightweight, thin in profile, and can be combined with other component functions such as reservoirs and aeration panels. However, depending on use, required performance, depth and extent of growing medium, and the overall system of components, they should not be considered automatically as a substitute for an adequate system of drainage, which may require a thicker layer of drainage aggregate and a system of lateral and mains. Rather, drainage mats can augment the drainage system—serving as a "belt and suspender" component.

A common type of drainage panel is a webbed plastic mat, fabricated in sheets or panels, often only an eighth of an inch thick. These sheet mats are also available with a geotextile or filter fabric attached to it. Although this may be attractive as a very thin profile, particularly when loads and depths are restricted, it should not be used in areas under paving, as it can interfere with the interlocking qualities required at the setting bed.

Other composite products include looped polyamide filaments, high-impact polystyrene, or polyethylene molded or extruded into three-dimensional panels of pegs, cups, domes, or channels. These drainage cores may be attached to or sandwiched between filter fabrics, moisture retention mats, root barriers, or insulation. Generally, all of these products need to be evaluated for compressive strength, flow capacity, moisture retention, and compatibility with other components.

A somewhat confusing concept, a number of products are available that combine the functions of both a drainage mat and a water retention or reservoir mat. The most common of these are high-density polyethylene molded into a series of a waffle of cups and domes. As "cups" on the top side, they retain water. As " domes" they form drainage channels on both the top and bottom. Some mats also have tiny holes in tops of the domes which direct excess water back to the main drainage system, and allow for ventilation and evaporation. Typically, the panels are fabricated as large as 3 feet by 6 feet and in thicknesses of 1 to 3 inches.

Moisture Retention Mats

More recently, moisture retention mats have been marketed as a way to help retain moisture and nutrients for use by the vegetation layer above. Although their composition varies among manufacturers, most often they are made of polypropylene fibers stitched through a polyethylene sheet. In living green roofs and landscape over structures, they are most commonly placed below the drainage/reservoir mat. Their inclusion should consider depth and type of growing medium, supplemental irrigation availability, and composite drainage system. The product selection may be made based on limitation of depth of overall drainage system profile, compressive strength, and moisture flow and retention rate of mat.

Aeration Mats

Adequate drainage also increases the ability of the soil or growing medium to keep air moving through it, thereby keeping the soil healthy and allowing pore space for root growth and development, and lessening the potential for the soil to become anaerobic. Additionally, beneficial air may be incorporated into the soil by combined use of materials that are usually associated with drainage components. Some mats facilitate both drainage and aeration, and are the same or similar to the products described immediately above, but used in different locations.

The most common are noncrushable panels, fibers, or formed cones, which allow air to be incorporated into the system, forming an "aeration mat."

Aeration mats and drain panels may also be incorporated on vertical surfaces of walls and planters, both to relieve hydrostatic pressure and to increase the air, the soil, and root production.

Filter Fabrics

Filter fabrics are a type of geotextile, which are synthetic cloths used below grade to stabilize soil or facilitate and promote drainage. For application in living green roofs

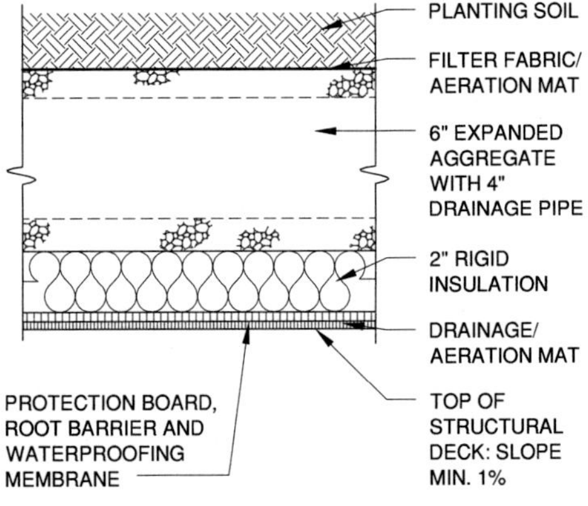

DRAINAGE SYSTEM FOR PLANTER AREAS

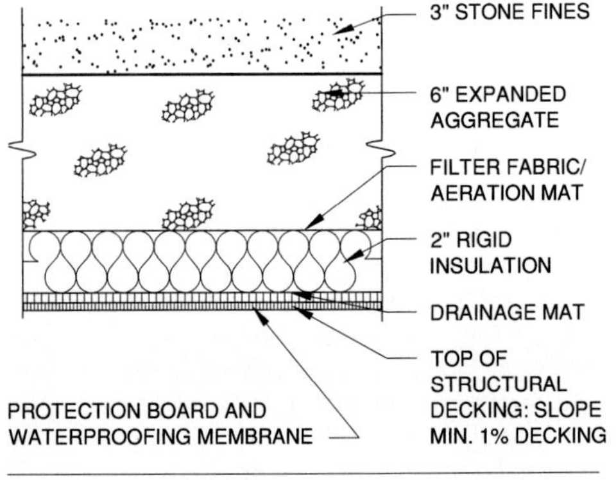

DRAINAGE SYSTEM WITH STONE FINES

Susan Weiler, ASLA, Olin Partnership

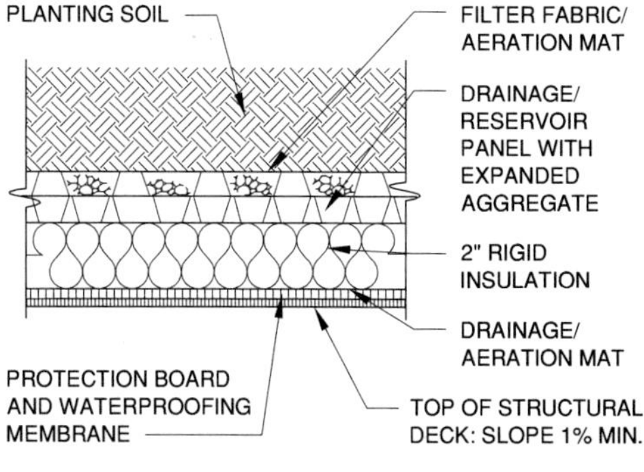

DRAINAGE SYSTEM

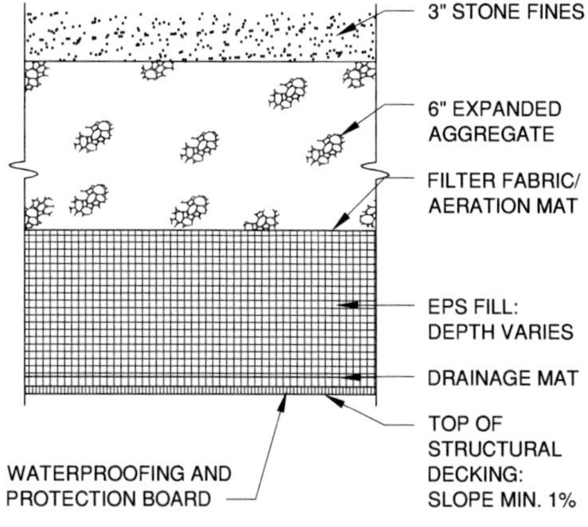

DRAINAGE SYSTEM WITH STONE FINES/EXPANDED POLYSTYRENE

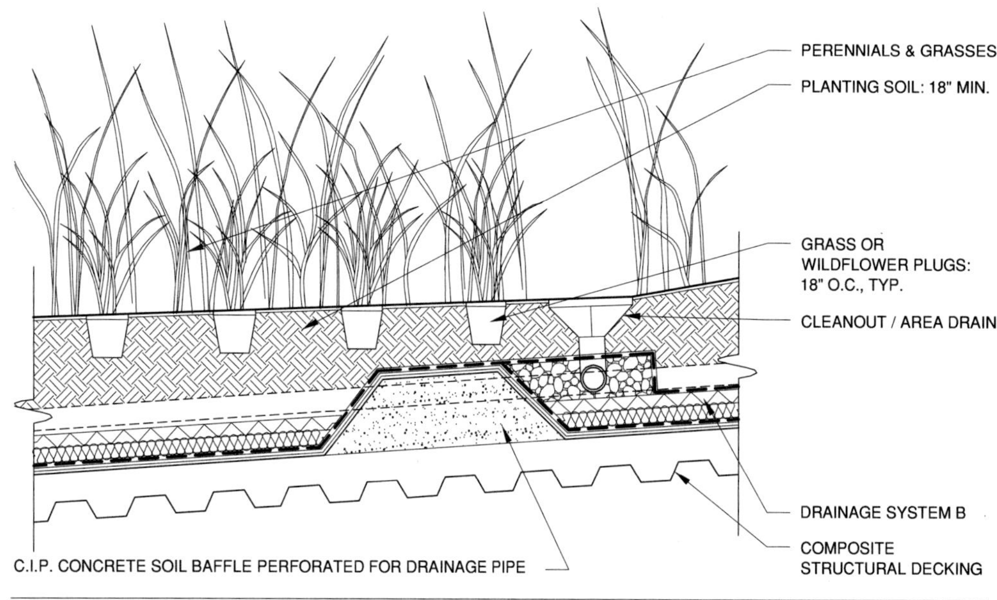

GRASS AND PERENNIAL PLANTING DRAINAGE SYSTEM

and landscapes over structure, the filter fabric is intended to keep the fines of a soil mixture or growing medium from migrating into the drainage layer. Typically, they are made of polypropylene fibers and are either woven or nonwoven. A woven fabric is produced from a number of filaments and strands, whereas a nonwoven is more uniformly manufactured filter fabric. Nonwoven fabrics are typically used in planting applications where the water flows in only one direction—in this case, from soil to drainage medium.

Numerous products and types of filter fabrics are available, and the selection may be ultimately be made based on differentiation of pore space, strength, weight, resistance to rot, and deterioration from ultraviolet light, which can affect their permeability and flow rate.

The key measurements of the physical and mechanical properties of filter fabrics are tear strength and resistance, puncture strength, permeability, and flow rate.

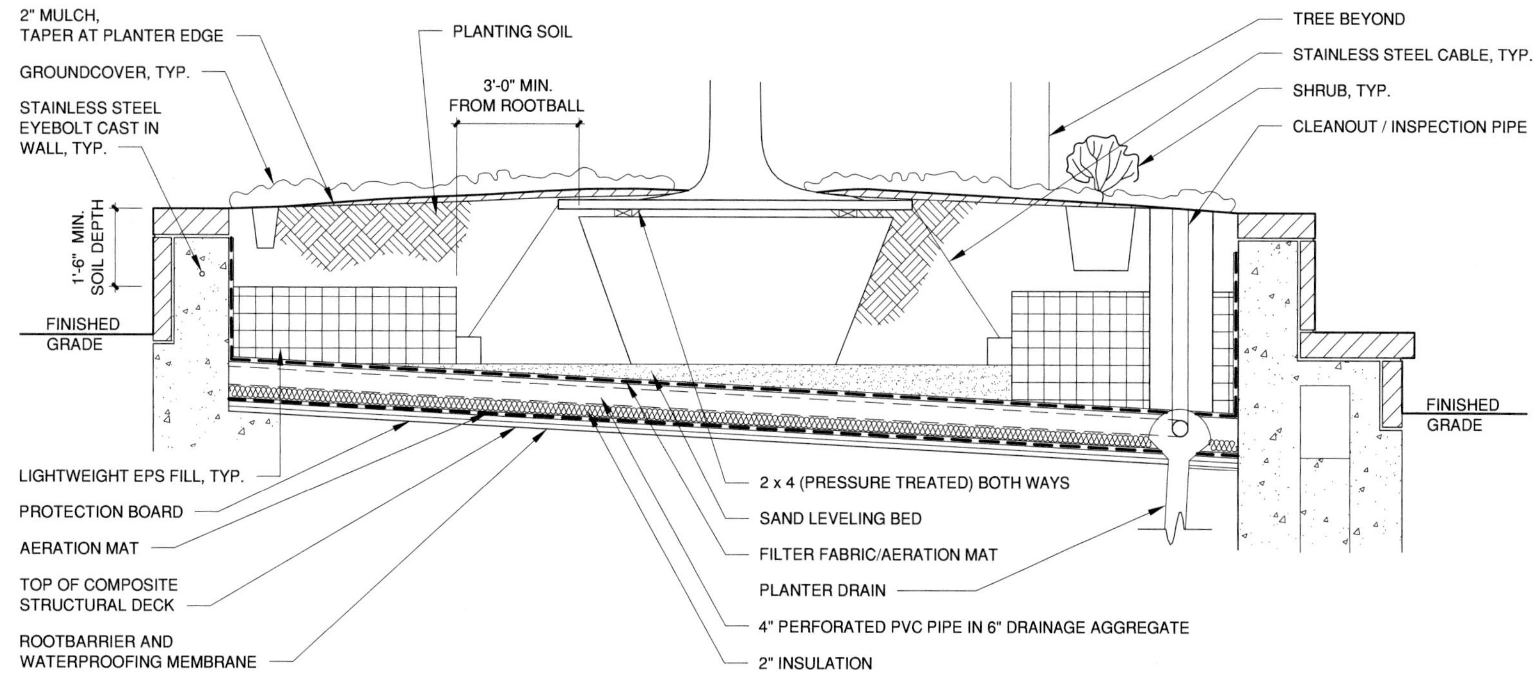

CANOPY TREE PLANTING DETAIL

Susan Weiler, ASLA, Olin Partnership

IRRIGATION AND WATER STORAGE

Because living green roofs and planting within landscapes over structure are required to grow within an artificial environment, the basic needs of plants—a nutrient source, found in the growing medium, and water—have to be incorporated into the system.

Since water over a structural deck does not migrate in the same way as water in terra firma, it is also necessary to supply supplementary water. In many natural systems, groundwater may be available, and the water table may fluctuate greatly during different seasons. Once the required amount of supplemental water is determined, the design and components of the system are similar to conventional systems. A major consideration in the design of the irrigation system, however, is the coordination of the mechanical, electrical, and plumbing systems.

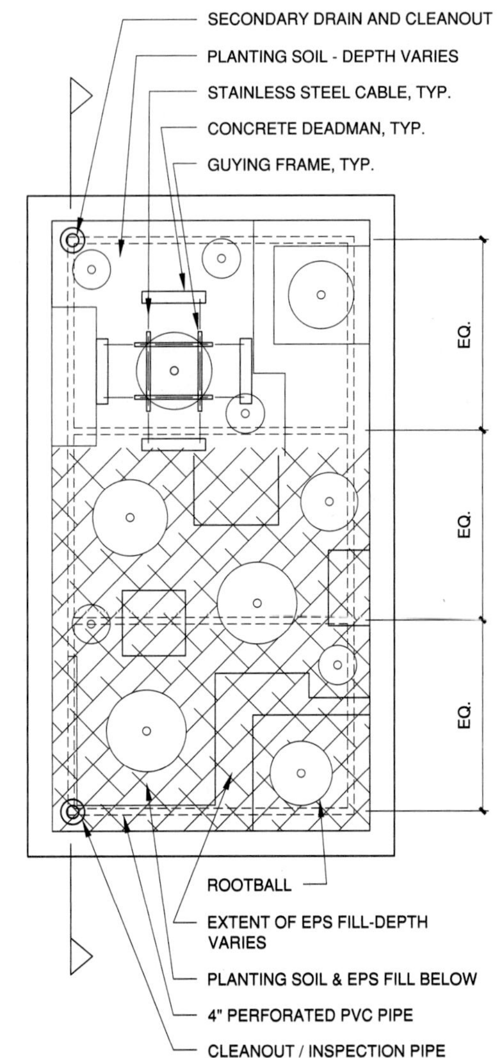

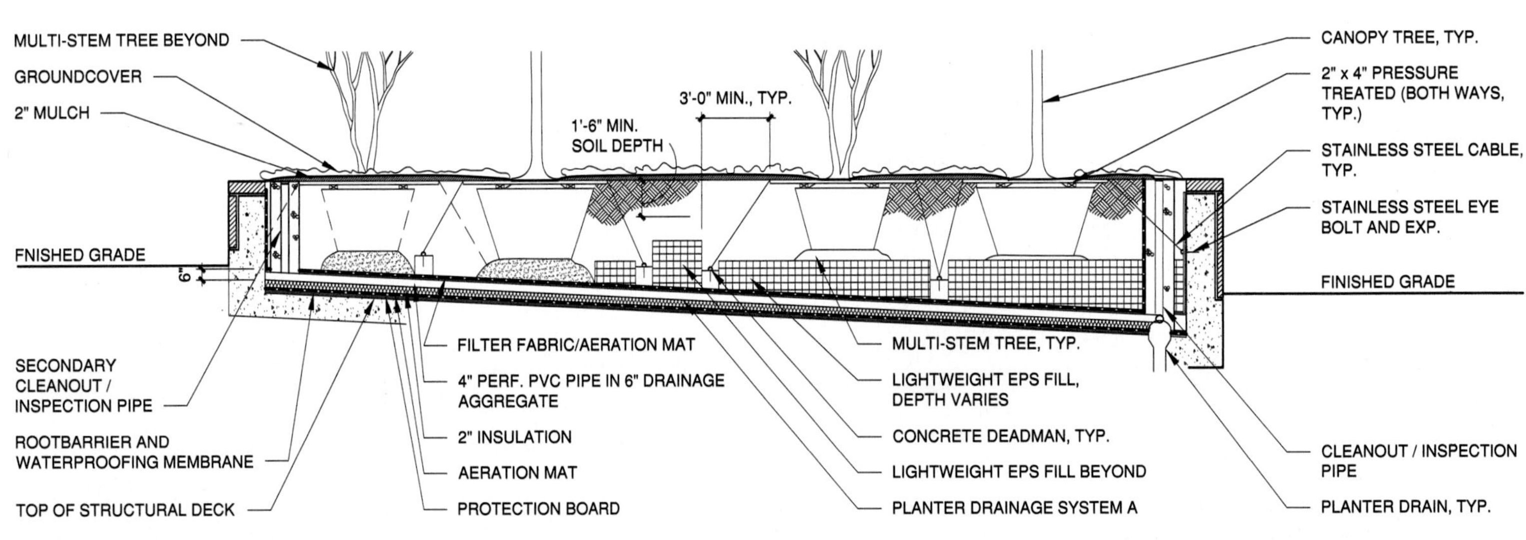

MULTI-STEM AND CANOPY TREE PLANTER

Susan Weiler, ASLA, Olin Partnership

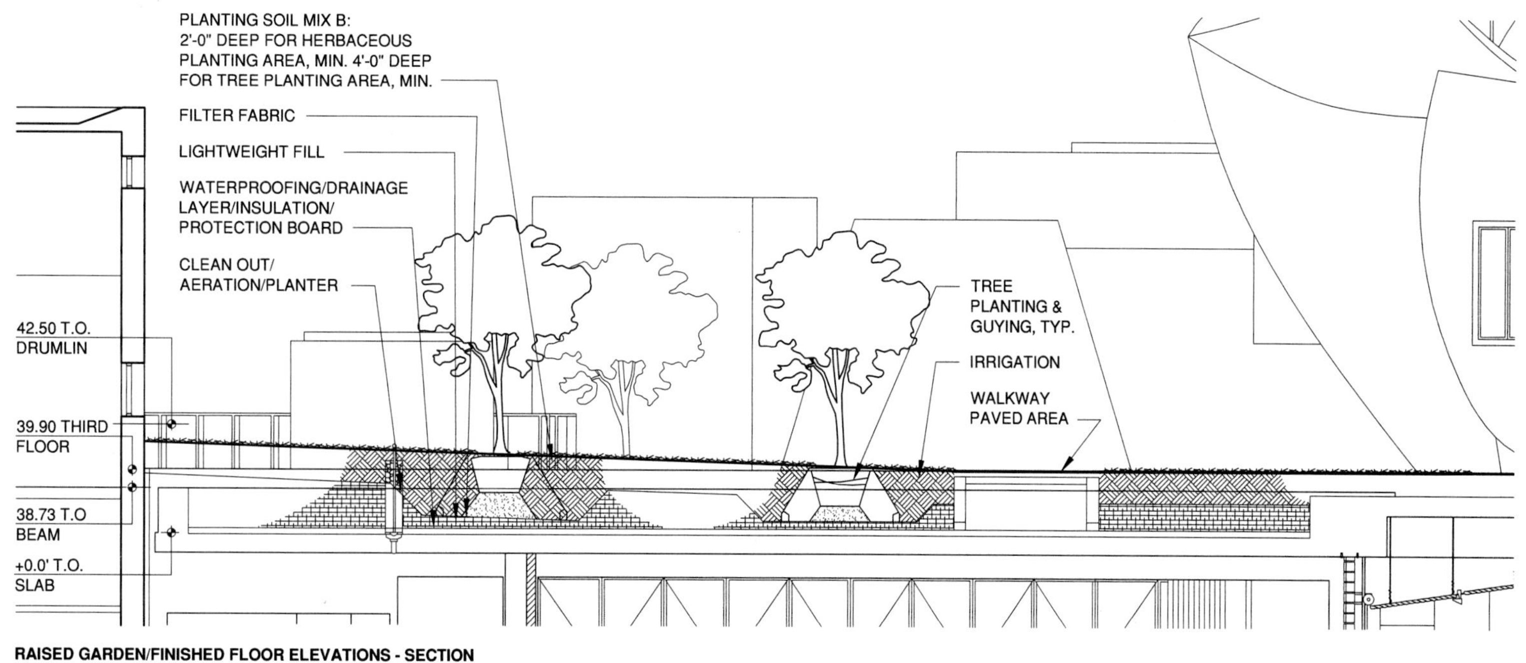

RAISED GARDEN SECTION

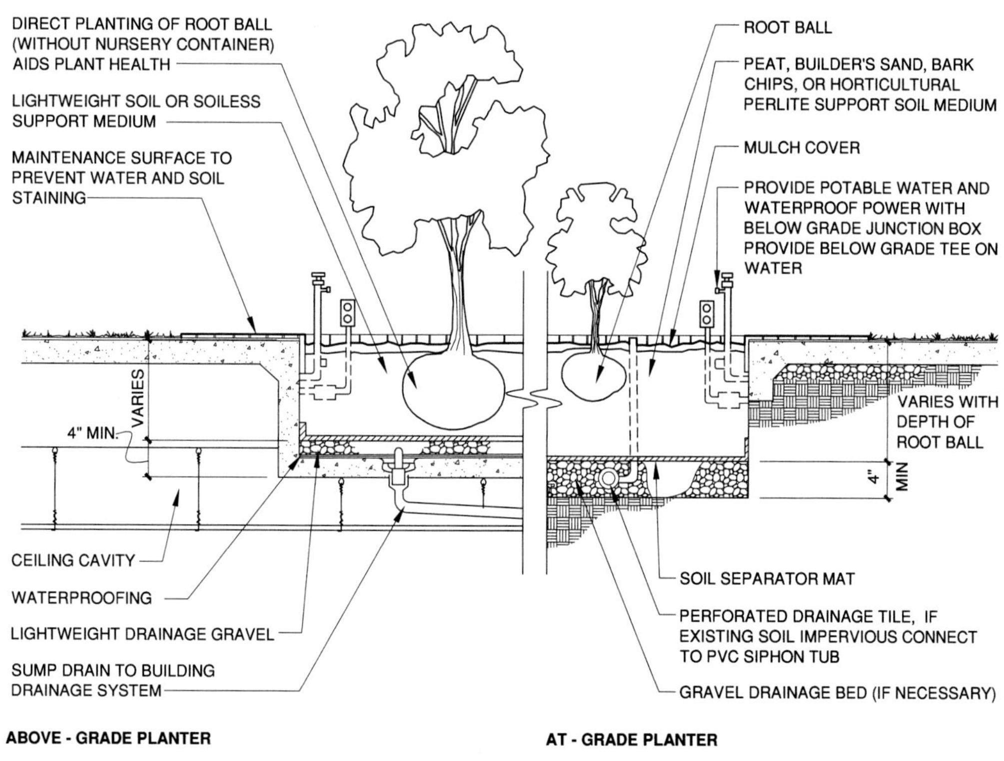

ABOVE-GRADE PLANTER

Susan Weiler, ASLA, Olin Partnership

MULCH 1" TO 2" THICK
CLEANOUT PIPE WITH CAP AT EACH DRAIN
PLASTIC DRAINAGE MATERIAL ON BOTTOM AND SIDES TO WITHIN 2" OF FINISH GRADE
1-1/2"
WRAP FILTER FABRIC UP SIDES OF ALL RISERS AND CONDUITS AND TIE OFF WITH COPPER WIRE
TWO-LEVEL ROOF DRAIN
OVERLAP FILTER CLOTH JOINTS 12" MIN. AND PIN TOGETHER
SLOPE DOWN AT 5% MIN.
WRAP FILTER FABRIC OVER EXPOSED EDGE OF DRAINAGE MATERIAL AND OVERLAP BACK SIDE, 6" MIN.
WATERPROOF MATERIAL WITH PROTECTION BOARD
WOVEN FILTER FABRIC
PLANTING SOIL COMPACTED TO 80% DRY DENSITY)
SLOPE DOWN AT 2%
COMPACT PAD UNDER ALL TREES WITH 2" CALIPER (TRUNK DIAMETER) OR LARGER

ROOFTOP PLANTER

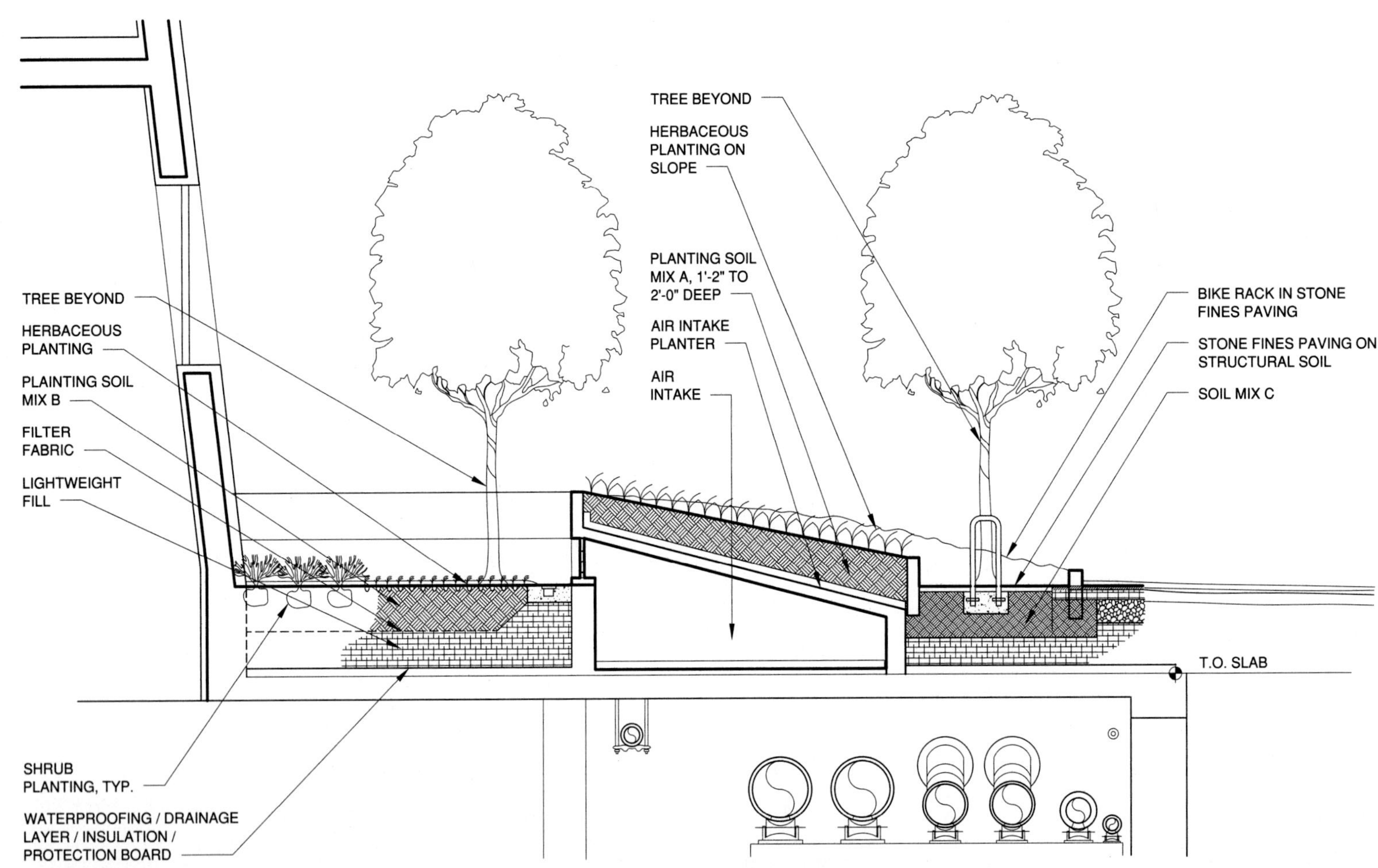

GARAGE AIR INTAKE PLANTER/TREE PLANTING ON TOP OF GARAGE—SECTION

Susan Weiler, ASLA, Olin Partnership

SPECIAL CONSTRUCTION

PLAZA MEMBRANE WATERPROOFING SYSTEMS OVER OCCUPIED SPACE

GENERAL

The basic components, subsystems, and features for a building deck waterproofing system are the structural building deck or substrate to be waterproofed, waterproofing membrane, protection of membrane, drainage, insulation, and wearing course. See following pages for generic membrane applications.

Substrate

The substrate referred to is reinforced cast-in-place structural concrete. Precast concrete slabs pose more technical problems than cast-in-place concrete and the probability of lasting watertightness is greatly diminished and difficult to achieve because of the multitude of joints that have the capability of movement and must be treated accordingly.

The concrete used for the substrate should have a minimum density of 1762 kg/m³ (110 lb/ft³) and have a maximum moisture content of 8 percent when cured.

Slope for Drainage

A monolithic concrete substrate slope of a minimum 11 mm/m (½ in./ft) should be maintained. Slope is best achieved with a monolithic structural slab and not with a separate concrete fill layer.

Membrane

Detection of leakage can be a significant problem when the membrane is not bonded to the structural slab or when additional layers of material separate it from the structural slab Therefore, only membranes that can be bonded to the substrate should be used.

The membrane should be applied under dry, frost-free conditions on the surface as well as throughout the depth of the concrete slab.

When the membrane is turned up on a wall, it is preferable to terminate it above the wearing surface to eliminate the possibility of ponded surface water penetrating the wall above the membrane and running down behind it into the building.

Penetrations should be avoided wherever possible. For protection at such critical locations, pipe sleeves should be cast into the structural slab against which the membrane can be terminated by flashing onto the pipe sleeve.

Treatment at reinforced and nonreinforced joints depends on the membrane used. See following pages.

Two concepts can be considered in the detailing of expansion joints at the membrane level: the positive seal concept directly at the membrane level and the watershed concept with the seal at a higher level than the membrane. Where additional safeguards are desired, a drainage gutter under the joint could be considered. Flexible upward support of the membrane is required in each case to provide watershed-type drainage. Expansion joint details should be considered and used in accordance with their movement capability

The positive seal concept entails a greater risk than the watershed concept, since it relies fully on positive seal joinery of materials at the membrane level, where the membrane is most vulnerable to water penetration. Since the precision required is not always attainable, this concept is best avoided.

The watershed concept, although requiring a greater height and more costly concrete forming, is superior in safeguarding against leakage, having the advantage of providing a monolithic concrete water dam at the membrane level. However, if a head of water rises to the height of the materials joinery, this concept becomes almost as vulnerable as the positive seal concept. Therefore, drainage is recommended at the membrane level.

Protection Board

The membrane should be protected from damage throughout construction. Protection board should be applied after the membrane is installed. The proper timing of application after placement of the membrane is important and varies with the type of membrane used. Follow the manufacturer's printed instructions.

Drainage System

Drainage should be considered as a total system from the wearing surface down to the membrane, including use of multilevel drains.

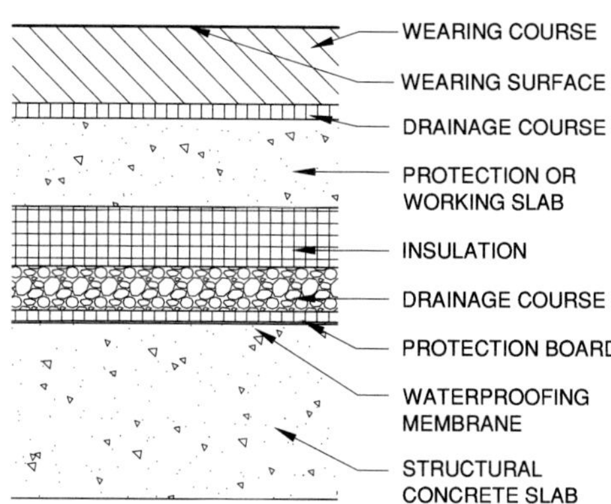

BASIC COMPONENTS OF WATERPROOFING SYSTEMS

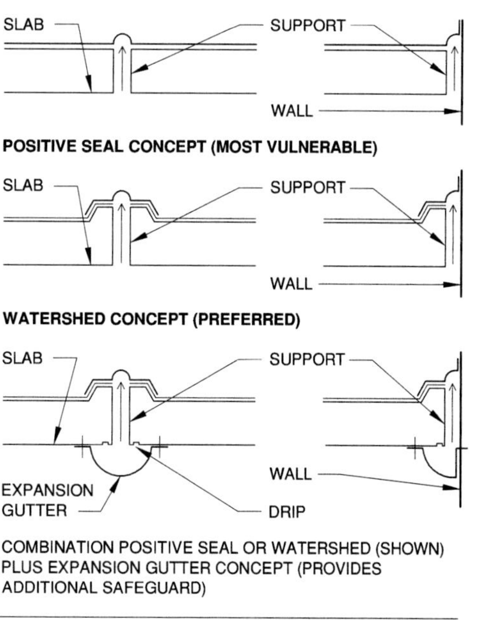

EXPANSION JOINT CONCEPTS AT MEMBRANE LEVEL

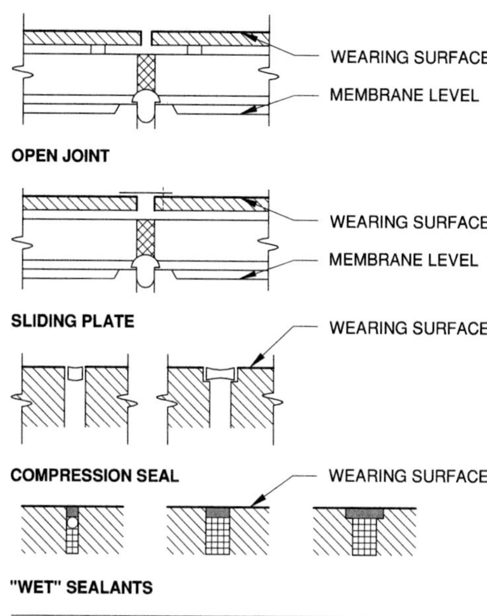

EXPANSION JOINT CONCEPTS AT WEARING SURFACE LEVEL

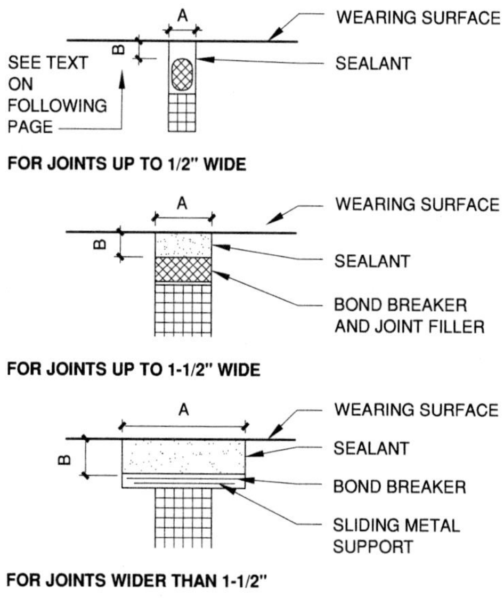

WET SEALANT DETAILS AT WEARING SURFACE

Charles J. Parise, FAIA, FASTM, Smith, Hinchman & Grylls Associates, Inc., Detroit, Michigan

Drainage at the wearing surface is generally accomplished in one of two ways: (1) by an open joint and pedestal system permitting the rainwater to penetrate rapidly down to the membrane level and subsurface drainage system; and (2) by a closed-joint system designed to remove most of the rainwater rapidly by slope to surface drains and to allow a minor portion to infiltrate to the membrane.

A drainage course of washed, round gravel or prefabricated drainage composite should be provided above the protection board, over the membrane. This permits water to filter to the drain and provides a place where it can collect and freeze without damaging the wearing course.

Insulation

When required, insulation should be located above the membrane, but not in direct contact with it.

Protection or Working Slab

A concrete slab could be placed soon after the membrane, protection board, drainage course, and insulation, if required, have been installed. It would serve as protection for the permanent waterproofing materials and insulation below, provide a working platform for construction traffic and storage of materials (within weight limits), and provide a substantial substrate for the placement of the finish wearing course materials.

Wearing Course

The major requirements for the wearing course are a stable support of sufficient strength, resistance against lateral thrust, adequate drainage to avoid ponding of water, and proper treatment of joints. Under a thick-set mortar bed supporting masonry units, a prefabricated drainage composite helps resist freeze-thaw damage to the wearing course by expediting water flow down to the subsurface drainage system.

Joints in which movement is anticipated should be treated as expansion joints. Various compression seals are available that can be inserted into a formed joint under compression. Most of these, however, are not flush at the top surface and could fill up with sand or dirt.

Wet sealants are the materials most commonly used in moving joints at the wearing surface level. Dimension A is the design width dimension or the dimension at which the joint will be formed. The criterion normally used for determining this dimension with sealants capable of ± 25 percent movement is to multiply the maximum expected movement in one direction by 4. Generally, this is expected to be about three-fourths of the total anticipated joint movement, but if there is any doubt, multiply the total anticipated joint movement by 4. It is better to have the joint too wide than too narrow. Dimension B (sealant depth) is related to dimension A and is best established by the sealant manufacturer. Generally, B is equal to A for widths up to 13 mm (½ in.), 15 mm (9⁄16 in.) for a 16 mm (⅝ in.) width, and 16 mm (⅝ in.) for 19 mm (¾ in.) and greater widths. This allows some tolerance for self-leveling sealants.

Reference: ASTM C 898 and C 981. Highlights of text and figures are reprinted with permission from Committee C-24 of the American Society for Testing Materials.

Charles J. Parise, FAIA, FASTM, Smith, Hinchman & Grylls Associates, Inc., Detroit, Michigan

THERAPEUTIC GARDENS

The general belief that outdoor spaces can be spiritually and emotionally healing dates back to early Egyptian culture in 1500 BC, and many aspects of the effect of nature on health are currently under scientific study. But the practical question of what is a therapeutic garden today needs to be asked. Ranging from gardens where medicinal plants are on display to the installation of historical turf labyrinths, landscape architects have yet to define what exactly comprises a healing garden. Based on the ongoing research of the therapeutic benefits of gardens and exposure to nature, the following conceptual framework is offered as a professional standard.

SETTINGS

Medical settings and long-term residential care facilities are leading the way in the resurgence of therapeutic gardens. These human service agencies now recognize the marketing and cost benefits of including views of nature and therapeutic gardens into the healing protocol for treatment and palliative care (Ulrich, 1999). Other institutions such as prisons and schools are beginning to expand their programs to include garden activities as a way of enhancing self-esteem and improving social behavior.

Civic spaces are being renovated to incorporate both restorative and enabling gardens as a way to address alienation and disenfranchisement, with preliminary studies showing that green spaces and community gardens in urban settings reduce vandalism and violence (Lewis, 1996). "Display gardens" are also being built in parks and arboreta to demonstrate the healing potential of therapeutic garden design.

DEFINITIONS

- *Therapeutic*. Supporting well-being by attending to discomfort and disease; relief of social tension and stress.
- *Garden*. A designed outdoor or indoor space where living plants and natural elements predominate.
- *Therapeutic garden*. A bounded landscaped space designed specifically to bring physical, psychological, or social benefit to users or viewers. There are two categories of therapeutic gardens:
- *Restorative gardens*. Assist stress reduction, support emotional and cognitive equilibrium, and enhance well-being. They may be universal in nature or they may focus on a particular user group (e.g., children), or a specific precipitating stressor (e.g. cancer). Related terms, or subtypes, include "archetypal," "sanctuary," "meditation," and "ritual" gardens.
- *Enabling gardens*. Facilitate the development, redevelopment, or maintenance of physical and cognitive skills and abilities through positive, hands-on interactions with plants. In addition to maximizing physical functioning, secondary benefits include the enhancement of social and psychological capabilities. Related types and terms include "rehabilitative," "vocational," and "horticultural therapy" gardens.

Religious organizations are installing restorative gardens and ritual spaces, going back to their roots and facilitating spiritual healing through exposure to nature.

THEORETICAL BASIS

Environmental psychologists have proposed three different hypotheses regarding the therapeutic mechanisms of exposure to nature and greenery (Stigsdotter and Grahn, 2002):

- Nature restores the emotional centers in the limbic system of the brain by evoking comforting biophyllic responses. In this familiar natural environment, relaxation is fostered and a positive outlook is supported.
- Greenery sustains cognitive functioning by limiting overstimulation and the need for "directed attention" and allowing one to employ the softer—and more enduring—mechanism of "involuntary attention."
- The relatively nonthreatening environment created by plants and natural elements can restore a balance between one's perceived need to control and one's ability to control, which can otherwise be quite discrepant in high stress and high-pressure situations.

The profession of horticultural therapy postulates another means of promoting health relevant to enabling gardens: Humans are naturally active, and working with plants provides a low-stress activity that is inherently healthful and that also delivers a relatively rapid visible reward of plant growth and production. This establishes a self-reinforcing flow of positive experiences.

DESIGN GUIDELINES

Thriving plant life is the single most significant factor in the perception of healing benefit from nature. Therefore, it is essential that all therapeutic gardens be designed in accordance with the level of maintenance that will be provided. This applies to all therapeutic gardens, for although enabling gardens are designed for client participation, routine care must be provided by staff or outside professionals if the garden is to be maintained at an acceptably high—and therapeutically supportive—level.

Beyond the provision of healthy plants, the therapeutic effects of a garden are strongly influenced by how well it is designed and detailed to support sought-after emotional and cognitive shifts. The following guidelines convey the concepts of therapeutic garden design, allowing for creativity within the scope of providing real healing benefit. In addition to these conceptual therapeutic frameworks, design considerations should be based specifically on the anticipated user groups. Collaboration with health professionals and a participatory design process are the surest way to achieve the most comprehensive therapeutic benefit.

A number of aspects common in a traditional landscape design are counterproductive in therapeutic gardens. Particularly harmful are designs that are susceptible to ambiguous interpretations, which will most likely be perceived as negative by people who are unwell or already under stress (Ulrich, 1999; Barnes, 1999). Also to be avoided are the inclusion of intrusive or irritating sensory stimuli and designs in which hardscape overwhelms the plantings.

Restorative Gardens Conceptual Basis

Research has shown that the restorative benefits of natural environments arise from a series of cues that prompt a healing process that supports all three of the environmental psychology hypotheses. This therapeutic process is comprised of four phases: the journey, sensory awakening, self awareness, and spiritual attunement (Barnes, 1996). Experiencing all of the phases of restoration gives the maximum benefit, evoking a state of restful alertness. Individual phases may be found to be more helpful to specific populations, and therefore should be emphasized in gardens designed for those users. For instance, in acute-care hospitals, garden users are particularly in need of getting away from the intensity and institutional character of the medical buildings (Cooper Marcus and Barnes, 1995). In these settings, the first phase of restoration should be emphasized. In Alzheimer's facilities, where reducing anxiety and memory enhancement are primary goals, the second phase should be dominant.

Patients and others who are institutionalized, even for short periods of time, have been found to suffer from loss of control over their surroundings and their treatment, social isolation from their family and friends, and passivity. These maladies inhibit the body's ability to sustain itself and heal. Drawing on the research in the behavioral sciences and health-related fields, Roger Ulrich (1999) proposes that gardens in healthcare situations are important stress mitigation resources for patients and staff to the extent that they provide:

- A sense of control with access to privacy
- Social support
- Physical movement and exercise
- Access to nature and other positive distractions

The design aesthetic of a restorative garden need not be directed by these guidelines. As long as negative or ambiguous stimuli are avoided, many design precedents may be appropriate sources of inspiration. For instance, the Jungian concept of archetypes has been used in psychiatric settings, whereas the influence of the concept of "sanctuary" and ritual meditation spaces have become popular in religious settings.

Principles for Restorative Gardens

The following principles of design address the requirements of both Barnes' and Ulrich's theories of restoration. Ease of mobility and provision of private and social seating in the garden are particularly significant in medial settings. Beyond these basics the following recommendations are of critical importance to all restorative gardens.

- *The journey*. Invite visual and physical exploration. Emphasize transitions with hidden vistas, changing

Marni Barnes, LCSW ASLA, Deva Designs

orientation, and "thresholds" of differing microclimates, light and shadow, and degrees of enclosure to create movement and an opening for the individual to shift from an painful or unproductive perspective.

- *Sensory awakening.* Supply a variety of noninvasive sensory stimuli and opportunities to stop and enjoy the sensations. Call particular attention to fragrances and wind—which often go unnoticed. This brings awareness into the moment and reduces the need for mental activity and filtering.
- *Self-awareness.* Apply the concepts of prospect refuge, auditory screening, and other protective measures to create physically and psychologically safe areas for quiet reflection or cathartic release. Add small-scale social seating for interactions that can support enhanced self-realizations.
- *Spiritual attunement.* Incorporate a sense of preciousness (through the ephemeral, the unusual, and the intricate), connection with other species (nonthreatening wild creatures or domestic animals), and movement away from the present (through the evocation of memories and opportunities to extend one's presence into the future). These environmental qualities facilitate a shift from analytical thinking and evoke experiences of transcendence and awareness of the universal.

RESTORATIVE GARDEN SITE ELEMENTS

	ELDERLY HOUSING	NURSING HOME	ALZHEIMER FACILITY	HOSPICE	DEVELOP-MENTALLY DISABLED RESIDENTIAL	PHYSICALLY DISABLED RESIDENTIAL	ADULT INPATIENT MEDICAL	CHILD INPATIENT MEDICAL	PSYCHIATRIC INPATIENT	MEDICAL/ PSYCHIATRIC OUTPATIENT	CIVIC ARBORETA
ELEMENTS THAT ESTABLISH A PRACTICAL FOUNDATION											
ADA universal design concepts	imp	imp	imp	imp	imp	imp	imp	imp	imp	imp	imp
Nontoxic materials and practices	rec	rec	imp	imp	imp	rec	imp	imp	imp	rec	rec
Smooth paving (max 1/8-inch joints)	rec	imp	imp	imp	rec	imp	imp	imp	rec	rec	imp
< 1% cross slope on paths	imp	imp	imp	imp	rec	imp	imp	imp	*	imp	rec
6-foot minimum path width	rec	imp	imp	imp	*	imp	imp	imp	*	rec	rec
Reduced glare (texture and color of paving)	rec	imp	imp	imp	*	imp	imp	rec	rec	rec	rec
Railings	rec	imp	rec	imp	rec	imp	rec	rec	rec	rec	rec
Wheel stops/curbs on grade	rec	imp	imp	imp	rec	imp	imp	imp	rec	rec	rec
Controlled ingress and egress	rec	imp	imp	rec	rec	rec	*	rec	imp	*	*
Areas with ultraviolet protection	imp	imp	imp	imp	rec	*	imp	imp	imp	rec	rec
Shadow lines mitigated	imp	imp	imp	rec	*	imp	rec	rec	rec	rec	rec
Limit views of people outside the garden	contra	contra	imp	rec	*	contra	imp	imp	imp	rec	contra
Safety lighting	imp	imp	imp	imp	imp	imp	imp	imp	imp	*	rec
Generally resilient plants	imp	imp	imp	imp	imp	imp	imp	imp	imp	imp	mp
RESTORATIVE ELEMENTS											
Memory association (plant selection)	imp	imp	imp	rec	imp	imp	imp	imp	imp	imp	rec
Encouraging to wildlife other than birds	imp	imp	imp	imp	imp	imp	imp	imp	imp	imp	imp
Encouraging to birds	imp	imp	imp	contra	imp	imp	contra	contra	rec	rec	imp
Frequent points of interest	rec	imp	imp	rec	rec	imp	rec	rec	rec	rec	*
Play/exercise areas with varying degrees of challenge	rec	rec	rec	contra	imp	imp	imp	imp	rec	rec	imp
Social eddy spaces	imp	imp	imp	imp	imp	imp	imp	imp	imp	imp	imp
Private eddy spaces	rec	imp	rec	imp	imp	imp	imp	imp	imp	imp	imp
Verdant plantings	imp	imp	imp	imp	imp	imp	imp	imp	imp	imp	imp
Fragrance	imp	imp	imp	imp	imp	imp	imp	imp	imp	imp	imp
Tactile interest	imp	imp	imp	imp	imp	imp	imp	imp	imp	imp	imp
Elements of "fascination"	imp	imp	imp	imp	imp	imp	imp	imp	imp	imp	imp
Bring attention to wind	rec	rec	rec	imp	rec	rec	rec	rec	rec	rec	rec
Prospect refuge seating	imp	imp	imp	imp	imp	imp	imp	imp	imp	imp	imp
Aesthetic lighting	imp	rec	imp	imp	rec	rec	rec	rec	rec	*	*
PRACTICAL AND RESTORATIVE											
Orientation features	rec	imp	imp	rec	imp	rec	rec	rec	imp	rec	rec
Frequent seating	imp	imp	imp	imp	rec	imp	imp	imp	rec	rec	rec
Defined ingress and egress	rec	imp	imp	rec	imp	rec	rec	rec	imp	*	rec
Temperature moderating rest areas	rec	imp	imp	imp	imp	rec	imp	imp	rec	rec	rec
Seating near building entry	imp	imp	imp	imp	rec	imp	imp	imp	imp	rec	*
Bounded space	rec	imp	imp	rec	imp	rec	rec	rec	imp	rec	rec

KEY:
imp = imperative to good design
rec = recommended for this setting
contra = contraindicated for this setting
** Not specifically relevant to this type of setting*

Marni Barnes, LCSW ASLA, Deva Designs

FEATURES OF RESTORATIVE GARDENS

	JOURNEY	SENSORY	SELF	SPIRIT
View of plants from inside	X	X		
Verdant surroundings	X	X	X	X
Moving water (loud)	X	X	X	X
Moving water (soft)	X	X		X
Reflecting water		X		X
Crossing water/bridges	X			X
Changing microclimates	X	X		X
Changing vistas/sounds	X	X		
Thresholds (constricted nodes)	X		X	
Fragrances	X	X		X
Non-threatening wildlife	X	X		X
Seasonal changes	X	X		X
Auditory stimulus	X	X		X
Physical challenges	X		X	
Cultural memories	X		X	X
Ephemeral		X		X
Celestial		X		X
Religious icons			X	X
Safe resting places			X	X
Private spaces			X	X
Social spaces	X		X	

Site Selection and Utilization of Space

Common to all settings are the following:

- For the greatest therapeutic benefit, a restorative garden should be located where there is minimal intrusion of the surrounding environment, especially from reminders of the presence of other people or society at large. Mechanical noise and evidence of neglect and vandalism are common deterrents to the healing potential of an outdoor space.
- While the design of the garden should convey a sense of "getting away" the garden should actually be located close to the potential users. For example, in medical facilities, a visual connection between the garden and hallways or waiting rooms is critical to the optimal use of the gardens.
- In settings where social interaction is an important therapeutic factor—as in residential health care facilities—the presence of larger social spaces (generally accommodating 6 to 10 people) and the inclusion of both fixed and movable seating is beneficial.

Many significant elements of design planning and detailing differ from one setting to another. The table "Restorative Garden Site Elements" shows the basic requirements for a variety of settings. These elements should be discussed with the staff and other professionals working in the facility, and modified for specific needs.

Some garden features can prompt more than one of the restorative phases. It is for this reason that these features are found to be often repeated. The table "Features of Restorative Gardens" lists a selection of elements that can cue more than one phase of healing. This matrix may be consulted to make efficient use of garden features; more significantly however, it reveals how each element is helpful, thus allowing for extrapolation and stylistic creativity.

Marni Barnes, LCSW ASLA, Deva Designs

Enabling Gardens

Conceptual Basis

Enabling gardens are designed to provide experiences that increase or support a person's highest level of functioning and psychological well-being. Engagement with the garden enables existing abilities to be reinforced and new and renewed physical abilities to be performed and practiced. This is accomplished through participation in professionally directed activities that may be solitary or group-oriented, and may be spontaneous or organized.

Enabling gardens are often designed for those with special needs. The age, physical, and cognitive ability of the users, and their potential for improvement or recovery, are factors that influence appropriate design. These mental, physical, and psychosocial needs must be met in the garden. Environmental adaptations to meet needs based on medical condition are also essential, and many people have more than one disabling condition.

Principles for Enabling Gardens

A successful enabling garden is a physically safe and psychologically secure environment.

The design should provide three levels of engagement: activities, opportunities, and challenges. Evaluating and assessing these components of physical and psychosocial enabling can serve as a structure for setting design goals and can, in turn, facilitate the incorporation of appropriate elements in the landscape. Following are lists of the significant benefits of each component.

Activities provide:
- Enhancement of physical abilities
- Learning experiences
- Sensory exploration
- Task completion
- Interaction with others and working together
- The reward of harvesting vegetables, herbs, or flowers

Opportunities allow for:
- Nurturing and caring for a living entity (a plant) that responds and grows
- Exercising responsibility
- Acting independently
- Making a contribution/making a difference
- Regaining a lost ability or identity
- Memory enhancement
- Exploring limits in a benign setting and encountering what may be beyond direct control
- Expressing choices and influencing (at least one) aspect of life
- Intergenerational involvement through sharing, learning, and teaching
- Reduced isolation through social contact
- Experiencing a sense of participation and belonging
- Receiving support and encouragement from others

Challenges can stimulate:
- Reaching beyond today's accomplishments
- Increased physical and psychological growth
- Completion and success when set within reach
- Recognition for achievements
- Teamwork and strategic thinking
- Confidence and a sense of self-worth
- Relaxation through exhaustion

Collaboration with medical professionals should enumerate the desired experiences and appropriate *opportunities* of the people being served, which in turn gives direction to the *activities* to be incorporated in the program of the garden. The skill level of the users must also be evaluated in order to capitalize on the users' strengths while supporting their deficiencies and establishing the appropriate degree of *challenge* needed in the environment. Common examples of critical user needs that require accommodation in the environment are: mobility problems, sun sensitivity, lack of stamina, limited reach, poor coordination or balance, muscle weakness, eye dilation reactivity, a compromised immune system, and memory impairment or confusion (Rothert, 1994).

Site Selection and Utilization of Space

The American Horticultural Therapy Association recognizes seven characteristics of enabling gardens that are designed for the purposes of horticultural therapy (Kavanagh, 1999):

- Scheduled and programmed activities bring new patients and other first-time visitors to the garden, acquaint them with its horticulturally based experiences, and introduce its sensory-stimulating environments.
- Garden features, elements, and equipment are selected or modified to improve access, ease gardening activities, and enhance the horticultural experience.
- Well-defined perimeters increase enclosure, limit uncontrolled entries and exits, and redirect visitors' attention and energies to activities, components, paths, spaces, and special displays within the garden.
- A profusion of plants and people-plant interactions exploit human biological and evolutionary preferences while orchestrating, emphasizing, and integrating the sensory attributes of plants in legible open spaces.
- Benign and supportive conditions result from horticultural practices that minimize environmental irritants and hazardous pollutants, as well as form features that reinforce personal comfort and safety.
- Universal design principles support a wide range of conditions by offering settings to stimulate the full

ENABLING GARDEN SITE ELEMENTS

ELEMENTS THAT ESTABLISH A PRACTICAL FOUNDATION	ELDERLY HOUSING	NURSING HOME	ALZHEIMER FACILITY	HOSPICE	DEVELOPMENTALLY DISABLED RESIDENTIAL	PHYSICALLY DISABLED RESIDENTIAL	ADULT INPATIENT MEDICAL	CHILD INPATIENT MEDICAL	PSYCHIATRIC INPATIENT	MEDICAL/ PSYCHIATRIC OUTPATIENT	JUVENILE DETENTION FACILITY	ADULT CORRECTIONAL FACILITY	SCHOOLS	PHYSICAL OCCUPATIONAL VOCATIONAL FACILITY	CIVIC ARBORETA
ADA universal design concepts	imp	imp	imp	imp	imp	imp	imp	imp	imp	imp	imp	imp	imp	imp	imp
Nontoxic materials and practices	imp	imp	imp	imp	imp	rec	imp	imp	imp	imp	imp	imp	imp	imp	imp
Smooth paving (max 1/8-inch joints)	rec	imp	imp	imp	rec	imp	imp	imp	rec	imp	*	*	rec	imp	rec
< 1% cross slope on paths	imp	imp	imp	imp	imp	imp	imp	imp	rec	imp	*	*	rec	rec	imp
6-foot minimum path width	rec	imp	imp	imp	rec	imp	imp	imp	rec	imp	*	*	*	imp	rec
Reduced glare (texture and color of paving)	rec	imp	imp	imp	*	rec	imp	rec	rec	imp	*	*	*	rec	rec
Railings	rec	imp	imp	imp	rec	imp	rec	rec	rec	rec	*	*	*	imp	rec
Wheel stops/curbs on grade	rec	imp	imp	imp	rec	imp	imp	imp	rec	rec	*	*	rec	imp	imp
Controlled ingress and egress	*	rec	imp	*	imp	*	rec	rec	imp	imp	imp	imp	*	rec	rec
Vertical beds for tending plants	rec	rec	rec	rec	rec	imp	*	imp	rec	rec	*	*	rec	imp	rec
Raised beds of varying heights for tending plants	imp	imp	imp	imp	imp	imp	imp	imp	rec	imp	rec	rec	imp	imp	imp
Cantilever planting beds for tending plants	rec	imp	rec	imp	rec	imp	rec	rec	rec	rec	rec	rec	rec	imp	imp
Areas with ultraviolet protection	imp	imp	imp	imp	rec	rec	imp	imp	imp	imp	rec	rec	rec	imp	imp
Shadow lines mitigated	imp	imp	imp	rec	rec	imp	rec	rec	rec	rec	*	*	*	imp	rec
Materials that are comfortable to touch	imp	imp	imp	imp	imp	imp	imp	imp	imp	imp	imp	imp	imp	imp	imp
Covered storage area	imp	imp	imp	imp	imp	imp	imp	imp	imp	imp	imp	imp	imp	imp	imp
Safety lighting	imp	imp	imp	imp	imp	imp	imp	imp	imp	*	*	*	*	rec	rec
ENABLING ELEMENTS															
Memory association (plant selection)	rec	imp	imp	rec	imp	*	rec	*	imp	rec	*	imp	*	rec	imp
Encouraging to wildlife other than birds	rec	imp	rec	rec	rec	rec	rec	rec	rec	rec	rec	rec	rec	rec	rec
Encouraging to birds	rec	rec	rec	contra	rec	rec	contra	contra	rec	rec	rec	rec	rec	rec	rec
Frequent points of interest	rec	imp	imp	rec	rec	*	rec	rec	rec	*	*	*	*	rec	rec
Social gathering/work spaces	imp	imp	rec	imp	imp	imp	imp	imp	imp	imp	imp	imp	imp	imp	imp
Covered space for crafts and cooking	rec	rec	imp	rec	imp	imp	*	rec	rec	imp	rec	rec	rec	imp	imp
Range of motion challenges	imp	imp	imp	imp	rec	imp	imp	imp	rec	imp	rec	rec	rec	imp	imp
Distance/achievement markers	imp	imp	imp	rec	rec	imp	rec	rec	rec	rec	imp	imp	rec	rec	imp
Variety of path surface textures	contra	contra	contra	contra	*	contra	rec	rec	contra	rec	*	*	*	imp	rec
Steps and ramps for exercise	rec	rec	contra	*	*	imp	rec	rec	contra	imp	*	*	*	imp	rec
Play/exercise areas with varying degrees of challenge	imp	rec	imp	*	rec	rec	rec	imp	imp	rec	imp	imp	imp	imp	rec
Opportunities for heavy exercise	*	*	*	*	rec	rec	*	rec	imp	rec	imp	imp	rec	rec	rec
Lightweight soil	imp	imp	imp	imp	rec	imp	imp	imp	rec	imp	*	*	*	imp	rec
PRACTICAL AND ENABLING															
Orientation features (wayfinding)	imp	imp	imp	rec	imp	rec	rec	rec	imp	rec	*	*	rec	rec	imp
Loop paths (no dead ends)	*	rec	imp	*	rec	*	*	*	rec	*	*	*	*	*	rec
Frequent seating	imp	imp	imp	imp	*	imp	imp	rec	rec	imp	*	*	*	imp	imp
Defined ingress and egress	rec	imp	imp	rec	imp	*	rec	rec	imp	imp	*	*	rec	imp	imp
Temperature moderating rest areas	imp	imp	imp	imp	rec	imp	imp	imp	imp	rec	rec	rec	rec	imp	imp
Seating near building entry	imp	imp	imp	imp	rec	rec	imp	rec	rec	rec	*	*	*	rec	rec
Bounded space	imp	imp	imp	rec	imp	*	imp	imp	imp	imp	imp	imp	imp	imp	rec
Plants that can be watered (over tended)	imp	imp	imp	imp	imp	imp	imp	imp	imp	imp	rec	rec	rec	imp	imp
Generally resilient plants	imp	imp	imp	imp	imp	imp	imp	imp	imp	imp	imp	imp	rec	imp	imp
Limit views of people outside the garden	contra	contra	imp	rec	*	*	rec	rec	imp	*	rec	rec	*	*	contra

KEY:
imp = imperative to good design
rec = recommended for this setting
contra = contraindicated for this setting
** Not specifically relevant to this type of setting*

Marni Barnes, LCSW ASLA, Deva Designs

range of senses, and by details permitting people to experience the garden in their own way, on their own terms, and at their own pace.

- Recognizable place-making promotes independence, reduces stress, and enhances the therapeutic garden as a unique, identifiable, and special place.

Of extreme importance in an enabling garden is the presence of excellent soil, good drainage, reasonably level topography, and adequate sun (Rothert, 1994). Similar to restorative gardens, the site should be in close proximity to areas of congregation or entrances to any associated medical or residential buildings.

Actual physical interaction with the plants is anticipated, and basic gardening beds should be limited in width to 18 inches from the outside edge, regardless of the height of the planting area. The use of cantilevered beds can extend this limit to 24 inches, by allowing seated participants and wheelchair users to place their knees under the tablelike support. Sloping and mounding the soil surface can bring more plants within reach and increase visibility to seated people. Vertical bed systems should be incorporated to provide accessibility of the plants to standing users. Accessible hose bibs, storage for adaptive garden tools, structures for craft and cooking activities, adequate utility hookups to support the activities, and protected rest and waiting areas must be included (Rothert, 1994).

Thematic signage and inspirational quotes assist with cognitive and speech therapies. Signs also help by providing reticent visitors with topics for discussion and support longer visits. Features that take advantage of changing seasonal opportunities are beneficial as are structures providing varying degrees of challenge which will support the growth of the individual through graduated success experiences.

As with restorative gardens, many crucial elements vary from setting to setting. These specifics are presented in the "Enabling Garden Site Elements" table.

FUTURE DIRECTIONS

A therapeutic garden is the intertwining of both a place and a process. The curriculum of landscape architecture schools should be expanded to incorporate healthful design considerations and students who wish to develop a specialty in therapeutic gardens should have training in the sociological, psychological, and physical aspects of the relationship between nature and healing. Also important is a strong emphasis on horticultural knowledge, to assure the creation of a healthy plant community.

An increasing number of post occupancy evaluations need to be performed with sensitivity and rigor to establish reliable quantitative evidence to guide the appropriate placement of therapeutic gardens and to substantiate and refine the design principles (Hartig, Barnes, and Cooper Marcus, 1999). These can be built into the scope of work of landscape firms or can be provided by consultants specializing in therapeutic gardens.

CONCLUSION

Landscape architects are the stewards of nature in built environments. They often provide a formative link between an individual and his or her perception of nature. This is not a responsibility to be taken lightly. The profession has progressed from a general belief that gardens can be healing to undertaking designs tailored to provide therapeutic benefit for specific user populations. As the profession continues to refine the healing potential of this work, consideration of cultural differences between various user groups and how these might influence achieving the maximum therapeutic benefit should be fully explored. The profession has made great strides in the arena of healing landscapes, the continuation of this trend is imperative to the well-being of humankind.

REFERENCES

Barnes, Marni. 1996. "The Healing Art of Landscape Architecture." *Design for Change: 1996 Annual Meeting Proceedings,* American Society of Landscape Architects.

Barnes, Marni. 1999. "Design Philosophy," in *Healing Gardens: Therapeutic Benefits and Design Recommendations* (Clare Cooper Marcus & Marni Barnes, eds). New York: John Wiley & Sons, Inc.

Cooper Marcus, Clare, and Marni Barnes. 1995 *Gardens in Healthcare Facilities: Uses, therapeutic benefits, and design recommendations.* Martinez, CA: Center for Health Design

Hartig, Terry, Marni Barnes, and Clare Cooper Marcus. 1999 "Concluding Implications for Research and Design." *Healing Gardens: Therapeutic Benefits and Design Recommendations* (Clare Cooper Marcus & Marni Barnes, eds). New York: John Wiley & Sons, Inc.

Kavanagh, Jean Stephans. 1999. "The Therapeutic Landscape: History, Design and Application." 1999 Annual Meeting Proceedings, American Society of Landscape Architects.

Lewis, Charles A. 1996. *Green Nature and Human Nature.* Chicago, IL: University of Illinois Press.

Rothert, Gene. 1994. *Enabling Gardens.* Dallas, TX: Taylor Publishing Co.

Stigsdotter, Ulrika, and Patrick Grahn. 2002. "What Makes a Garden a Healing Garden," *The Journal of Therapeutic Horticulture,* vol. 13: 60-69.

Ulrich, Roger S. 1999. "Effects of Gardens on Health Outcomes: Theory and Research," *Healing Gardens: Therapeutic Benefits and Design Recommendations* (Clare Cooper Marcus & Marni Barnes, eds). New York: John Wiley & Sons, Inc.

Marni Barnes, LCSW ASLA, Deva Designs

WILDLIFE HABITAT

PLANNING FOR WILDLIFE HABITAT

Wildlife is defined by the 1969 Endangered Species Act as any free-living species, from invertebrates to vertebrates, butterflies to bears. Wildlife conservation is the planning, design, and management of resources in and around rural and urban areas to maximize habitat diversity and to support the broadest array of native wildlife species for public benefit. In some cases, planning may emphasize the conservation and management of a particular species, often a game species. Wildlife conservation is entirely compatible with other community planning efforts directed toward the creation of healthy ecosystems.

The goal of wildlife conservation is to manage populations of native species of wildlife (occasionally introduced species) and habitats that support them for the perpetuation of their natural, educational, social, recreational, and economic values. This goal can be accomplished through the implementation of four basic objectives:

- Assess the status of wildlife populations, habitats, land uses, plans, and ownership patterns in rural, urban, and developing environments.
- Ensure the consideration of wildlife and habitat values in all future land-use planning.
- Implement programs to enhance wildlife populations, and preserve, enhance, or restore habitats where needs are identified.
- Manage habitats in ways that will allow populations of desirable species to persist.

THE CHALLENGE

Wildlife habitat is defined as the physical and biological features on the range in which a species exists. Habitats are being converted to agricultural uses, and development is spreading across farms, forests, deserts, and prairies at an alarming rate. The result is a fragmented landscape with fewer, smaller, less connected patches of wildlife habitat and frequently degraded water quality that stresses aquatic ecosystems. The capacity of altered landscapes to support a diversity of indigenous plants, animals, and aquatic species is declining. The loss of biodiversity has become a national concern. State wildlife management agencies are charged with the responsibility of managing wildlife within their borders; but because of rapid development, many state wildlife management agencies personnel and programs cannot solve all the problems or capitalize on all the possibilities counties and communities and private landowners confront. Design professionals and developers must get involved. Indeed, planners, landscape architects, developers, and elected officials are often de facto wildlife managers in urbanizing environments.

Landscape architects with natural-resource-based planning and design expertise, working in collaboration with biologists, ecologists, and wildlife managers, can play a central role in the conservation of habitat for wildlife and fish at both the regional (watershed) scale, as well as site scale. However, to be effective collaborators, landscape architects must have a basic understanding of the landscape structure, wildlife, and habitat needs that sustain wildlife.

BACKGROUND

Landscapes are composed of *patches* (areas that differ from their surroundings), *corridors* (linear strips that differ from their surroundings), and a *matrix* (the dominant land cover or use). Most wildlife species use each of these landscape elements at some point in their life cycle. Thus, in varying combinations, they constitute a species habitat.

Habitat is a key concept in planning for wildlife. Habitat must meet an individual organism's life requisites; food; cover, to avoid predators and unfavorable conditions; and special places for courting, mating, and bearing and rearing offspring. All these attributes of habitat must be available in the right configurations and combinations at the right time. Two other key habitat-related concepts are home range and territory. The geographic area a species traverses to meet its life requisites is its home range. Some species, birds in particular, are territorial, defending a part of the home range against intrusion by other individuals of the same species, thus regulating populations within an area. Individuals and their aggregate populations are an integral part of living communities: plants and animals sharing the same conditions. Communities are often described by their dominant vegetation type (for example, shrub steppe or oak woodland), and inferences are made about habitat characteristics and associated wildlife. Communities then become the focus for much of wildlife conservation planning. The concept of community helps planners (1) recognize the importance of specific habitats for specific species populations and (2) identify critical habitats that must be preserved and areas that could benefit populations if they were enhanced or restored. Community also allows planners to estimate the potential effects of proposed land-use changes on habitat and species. However, the presence of required community features does not mean the habitat is suitable or occupied. Consideration of availability, access, and perceived security apply to all animals and affect species presence or absence.

INTEGRATING WILDLIFE INTO A PLANNING PROCESS

Natural-resource-based planning methodologies used by most landscape architects are well suited to incorporating the natural and cultural data required to plan for wildlife and habitat. The following sections suggest wildlife- and habitat-specific factors and associated data that should be included in each step in the planning process, as well as include planning and design principles abstracted from conservation biology, landscape ecology, and wildlife management literature. These principles are applicable across project scales and regions of the country.

Identify Problems and Opportunities

Wildlife conservation at a watershed scale is complex and involves many interrelated resource issues. At a project site scale, issues may be more focused, but more detail and specificity is required. Consequently, identification of problems and opportunities at either scale is best accomplished with an interdisciplinary approach: together, an interdisciplinary team can identify the problems and opportunities of greatest significance to the wildlife resource.

Biologists and ecologists on the planning team should be responsible for identifying the wildlife-related problems and opportunities inherent in the pattern of patches, corridors, and matrix, and vegetative structure in the watershed or project sites. Although the pattern of these landscape features and structure will be different in each watershed, there are resource relationships and land-use practices common to most watersheds that should be identified. This can be done by asking such questions as:

- How do wildlife utilize the pattern of landscape elements? Note in particular, patches with high biodiversity and corridors important for dispersal or migration.
- Which existing patches or corridors are being managed for biodiversity?
- Which land uses or management practices may be adversely impacting the habitat or conduit functions of existing patches and corridors?
- Which land uses or management practices may be limiting wildlife species diversity or abundance?
- Which patches could be linked with corridors to enhance biodiversity?
- Which locations in the watershed have the potential to be restored as patches or corridors?

Determine Objectives

Objectives are road maps to desired future conditions, outlining how the desired future will be achieved. Objectives for wildlife should respond to the wildlife conservation problems and opportunities previously identified. They may be revised as new information is generated during the inventory and analysis steps. The planning group should also be aware of any federal, state, or local laws related to wildlife that could affect the plan.

Communities and landowners frequently specify wildlife objectives for the plan or project that emphasize species that are attractive—or, in rural areas, game species—and the habitat structure that supports them. Ecologists and wildlife biologists argue for an expanded perspective, one that emphasizes conservation plans and management strategies that accommodate a diversity of native species, particularly individual species that are adversely affected by fragmentation and other human activities. Specific wildlife and wildlife habitat objectives typically associated with conservation projects include:

- Protect threatened or endangered species and their habitat (mandated by law; current lists are available from state departments of wildlife).
- Increase biodiversity (the number of native species).
- Maintain or increase endemic populations of state species of concern.
- Protect existing high-quality habitat and connecting corridors.
- Increase particular habitat characteristics such as food, cover, reproduction sites, or security areas that are presently excluded or that are adversely affected by fragmentation and other forms of human activity.

Craig Johnson, Professor, Department of Landscape Architecture and Environmental Planning, Utah State University, Logan, Utah

In projects where threatened or endangered species (listed under the Endangered Species Act) are involved, formal consultations with the U.S. Fish and Wildlife Service are required. The U.S. Fish and Wildlife Service will respond to the landowners' or action agencies' biological assessment with their own biological opinion. The biological opinion will identify "reasonable and prudent" conservation alternatives from which the landowner (or the consulting federal agency) can select or serve as a basis for negotiation.

Inventory Resources

The general intent of the resource inventory is to describe existing habitat conditions and wildlife populations within the project planning boundary. The wildlife inventory should include a wildlife habitat component and a species component. The wildlife resource inventory at a watershed scale should:

- Investigate in greater detail each problem and opportunity previously identified.
- Collect additional data as necessary in response to specific objectives.
- Describe wildlife resources, including: species diversity and abundance, threatened or endangered species, state species of concern, and vulnerable populations.
- Describe wildlife use of existing patches, corridors, and the matrix.
- Describe general habitat conditions in patches, corridors, and the matrix.

Ecologists and biologists in consultation with other team members will specify the kinds of data required to adequately plan for the wildlife resource. Each watershed or project site is unique, hence most data requirements will be watershed- or area-specific. However, some basic data needs that relate to most watershed projects include the following:

Wildlife Species Data Needs

Wildlife present in the planning area

Nongame species

Game species

Threatened and endangered species (federal- and state-listed species)

Vulnerable populations of a species

Historical species (once present but no longer reside in the watershed)

Population characteristics for species of concern

Culturally important species (especially those tied to Native Americans or valuable to limited-income groups for subsistence)

Wildlife Habitat Data Needs

GAP data (where available)

Existing vegetation

Historical vegetation

Wildlife species/plant communities' relationships

Land cover types

Land ownership

Habitat features

Patches with high biodiversity

Patches with vulnerable populations

Migration and dispersal corridors

Special areas (e.g., calving sites)

Potential habitats

Species ranges for species of concern

Water availability and historical hydrology

At a site-specific project scale, more detailed information is necessary to properly plan for wildlife. The following list of data requirements is applicable to most projects:

Wildlife Species Data Needs

List of species observed or whose presence is inferred from indirect evidence on the site

List of federal threatened or endangered species or state-listed species of concern (if any)

List of species breeding on the site

List of potential species (species typically associated with plant community types on the site) but not observed or inferred

List of nuisance species (if any)

Estimate of species abundance

Wildlife Habitat Data Needs

Existing Vegetation

Grass plant community type

Grass shrub plant community type

Riparian wooded plant community type

Riparian shrub plant community type

Riparian grass plant community type

Upland wooded plant community type (natural)

Upland wooded plant community type (introduced)

Wetland type

Unique regional plant community types (specify)

Land Use or Cover

Cropland

Pastureland

Rangeland

Conservation reserve (indicate type)

Park open spaces

Urban

Other (specify)

Habitat Features

Special patches

Large remnant patches of native vegetation

Large introduced patches

Special corridors

Riparian corridors

Migration corridors

Dispersal corridors

Special Areas

Patches or corridors inhabited by threatened or endangered species, state species of concern, or vulnerable local populations

Leks or other breeding sites

Calving/birthing sites

Winter range/summer range

Thermal cover

Irreplaceable sources of food or water

Other (specify)

Special Features

Snags

Dens

Burrows

Talus or rock piles

Cliffs

Caves and abandoned mines

Other (specify)

Potential Habitats

Steep slopes

Poorly drained soils

Damaged sites (burrow pits, etc.)

Easement corridors

"Waste" areas

Other (specify)

The goals of the inventory process for wildlife planning at either scale are to identify the most important elements of wildlife habitat and determine the level to which they are protected. These key elements will form the basic structure of the conservation plan alternatives developed in later steps.

Analyze Resources

The planning group must now interpret the inventory data. Discipline handbooks, manuals, and inventory worksheets are critical references in the analysis process. In some cases, consulting with experts may be required: for example, when threatened or endangered species or locally vulnerable wildlife populations are issues.

The analysis of watershed wildlife resources focuses on the community level. Major issues include wildlife species diversity and abundance, critical habitat reserves/patches, linkages between major corridors and reserves/patches, and attributes of the matrix detrimental or beneficial to wildlife.

The intent of the analysis of wildlife resources at the watershed level is to:

- Locate key reserves/patches, corridors, and special areas with high levels of species diversity and species use.

Craig Johnson, Professor, Department of Landscape Architecture and Environmental Planning, Utah State University, Logan, Utah

- Describe the general status of wildlife populations or metapopulations of species of concern.
- Describe the general factors limiting species diversity or species abundance.
- Identify gaps in key corridors.
- Identify which reserves/patches or corridors may be at risk.
- Describe factors creating at-risk conditions.
- Identify other wildlife-related issues based on project objectives.

The wildlife component of the analysis should focus on wildlife and wildlife habitat: specifically, species diversity, population dynamics, habitat conditions, causes of conditions, and potential conditions in the patches, corridors, and matrix in the watershed or project site. At a watershed scale, the analysis must draw cause-and-effect relationships between what occurs in the matrix and the condition of habitat in patches and corridors. It should also describe what, if any, effects patches and corridors exert on the matrix.

The analysis of wildlife and wildlife habitat at the project site scale should answer the following questions:

Wildlife

- Which wildlife populations are vulnerable to local extinction? (Threatened and endangered species are a special case.)
- What are the principal causes of the populations' or species' vulnerable status?
- What is the potential condition of these vulnerable populations?
- What factors are limiting nongame species diversity or game species abundance?
- What factors enhance populations of nuisance or pest species?

Habitat

- What is the current condition of the habitat in existing patches, corridors, potential patches, special areas, and special features?
- What causes these conditions?
- What is the habitat potential of existing patches, corridors, potential patches, special areas, and special features?
- Which patches, corridors, potential patches, special areas, and special features are of greatest value or potential value to wildlife?

States may have species-of-concern lists. Populations of state species of concern, although not technically threatened or endangered, could experience local extinction. These populations are typically listed with the State Natural Heritage Program, which can specify a general area where a vulnerable species may be present. If the client's property falls within the general area, a survey should be conducted to determine the presence or absence of the species. If present, a biologist specializing in the species and a conservation biologist should be consulted to determine the causes of vulnerability and the potential of the population to persist.

Wildlife diversity is strongly influenced by plant community diversity, patch size, amount of edge, connectivity, and presence or absence of water. The planning team can compare the property's habitat characteristics and wildlife species to similar undisturbed site locations in the watershed. The comparison may suggest general habitat characteristics limiting wildlife diversity on the client's property. The conservationist may request assistance and additional information from field biologists.

Most states have detailed models of the habitat requirements of game species. The U.S. Fish and Wildlife Service also has habitat suitability models for many game and nongame species. And an excellent source of natural history information for birds is http://birds.cornell.edu. The planning group can compare the habitat conditions described in the models with those identified in the inventory to gain a general idea of those factors that may be limiting abundance or diversity. Unfortunately, information for many reptiles, amphibians, and nongame mammal species is limited. State or field biologists can provide more detailed information concerning limiting factors for species in these groups.

Patch habitat and corridor condition evaluations should be conducted using procedures outlined in discipline handbooks. The inventory phase will have estimated species present on the client's property. There are several ways to determine which species were or could be present. Many states have species distribution maps showing which species would be expected on the client's site. The list of expected species can be compared with the inventory list prepared. Conservationists may also know about those species that could exist on the property based on their experiences elsewhere in the watershed. Any Environmental Assessment or Environmental Impact Statement done in the watershed will have a species list that can be used for comparative references.

Determination of the habitat value of patches, corridors, and special areas should be based on existing wildlife species and habitat. Consideration should be given to existing resources that have habitat potential but are not presently being used by wildlife. The most valuable patches, corridors, special areas, and features will vary with each property, watershed, and region. However, there are some general habitat types and resources of high value in all watersheds and regions. These include:

- Relatively undisturbed patches or remnant vegetation (Large patches are particularly valuable.)
- Stream/riparian corridors
- Migration and dispersal corridors
- Wetlands
- Lakes, ponds, springs, seeps, and other water features
- Irreplaceable sources of food, water, cover, or sites for reproduction

The conservationist can expand on this list to include habitats or resources considered most important in his or her region. Documentation of these important resources on a composite analysis map is critical to the next step in the planning process. Habitats at risk should also be delineated. A habitat component at risk is defined as a patch, corridor, special area or feature, or other wildlife resource whose continued ecological function is threatened by some internal or external factor. The planning team should ask the following questions for at-risk habitats:

- Which patches, corridors, special areas, or special features are at risk?
- What are the causes of risk to these habitat resources?
- What is the potential for mitigating or eliminating threats to wildlife or wildlife habitat?

Develop Alternatives

The team, in consultation with the client, is responsible for developing various wildlife conservation alternatives. Alternatives should focus on habitat functions, wildlife (diversity or target species), or other benefits. However, each alternative must meet the objectives previously identified. Some examples of alternatives are:

- A plan alternative or several alternatives using various conservation implementation strategies, management practices, and recommendations to address habitat problems and opportunities
- A plan alternative to optimize for wildlife species diversity
- A plan alternative to increase populations of a particular species, guild, or suite of species
- A plan alternative to optimize recreation, education, and other wildlife benefits
- A no-action alternative (required by the National Environmental Policy Act, NEPA)

Some alternatives—for instance, a wildlife diversity alternative—may emphasize the preservation, enhancement, and restoration of habitats for all species native to the watershed. Other plans may choose to optimize a particular species. For example, one alternative could emphasize bobwhite quail. Such a plan would focus on factions limiting quail populations and would propose habitat modifications to reduce limiting factors. Caution is required in preparing single-species plans or other single-focus alternatives, however, for without careful consideration of the entire plant and animal community, implementing a single-species plan could jeopardize overall biodiversity.

The purpose of a no-action alternative plan is to estimate the future condition of the watershed or project site if no action is taken to conserve habitat resources. Trends in the condition of corridors and habitat patches would be assumed to continue. Proposed plans for roads, bridges, community development, and other landscape modification would be assumed to be constructed. Thus, this alternative often depicts the worst-case scenario for wildlife, but it can be a powerful tool in educating clients about the consequences to wildlife of not taking a proactive approach to conservation.

The planning team must agree that each alternative meets the group's objectives, with the exception of the no-action alternative. In addition, each alternative must comply with all relevant federal, state, and local regulations. The following habitat planning concepts and principles are derived from a synthesis of conservation biology, landscape ecology, and wildlife management literature. They should be used to guide the development of all plan alternatives except no-action.

Habitat Planning Concepts and Principles

The concepts and principles suggest locations, configurations, and linkages for corridors and patches in the watershed or project site that would provide the greatest benefit for wildlife. These concepts and principles are applicable regardless of project scale and have been rephrased as planning directives to employ in this phase of the planning process.

Craig Johnson, Professor, Department of Landscape Architecture and Environmental Planning, Utah State University, Logan, Utah

Patches

- Preserve all large reserves/patches or introduce new large patches where practical.
- Connect all reserves/patches, large or small, that were historically connected.
- Do not subdivide existing reserve/patches.
- Preserve clusters of small patches.
- Preserve reserves/patches that are near each other.
- Introduce new patches in areas devoid of habitat.

Corridors

- Preserve continuous corridors; plant gaps in discontinuous corridors.
- Preserve existing corridors that connect existing patches; pay particular attention to migration and dispersal corridors.
- Introduce, where practical, corridor plantings to connect reserves/patches that were historically connected.
- Preserve or introduce multiple corridor or "stepping stone" connections between reserves/patches that were historically connected.
- Design new corridors to be as wide as practical; widen existing corridors where practical.

Special Areas and Features

- Preserve all reserves/patches, corridors, special areas, or special features inhabited by threatened and endangered species, state species of concern, or vulnerable populations.
- Preserve other special areas and features.

Potential Habitat

- Develop potential habitats where practical.
- Consider artificial structures to provide habitat when natural habitat has been degraded or destroyed (a watershed-wide bluebird nestbox or bat house program, for example).

Other Principles

- Address key impacts that create at-risk conditions for habitat in the watershed or on the project site.
- Recommend matrix management principles that benefit wildlife.
- Recommend natural structural diversity in reserve/patch and corridor plant communities.
- Recommend native plants planted as communities.

The planning team should adapt concepts and principles as necessary to meet project resource conditions and needs of specific wildlife species.

Implement Plan

Strategies for implementing a watershed-scale wildlife conservation plan will depend on local politics and economics, nonprofit conservation organizations involved in the region, availability of federal and state assistance, local zoning, and the level of volunteerism. The value of a watershed-scale plan is that it offers coherent landscape structure and logical recommendations for integrating conservation plans prepared at the landowner level. There are a variety of options for implementing a watershed-scale plan, including:

- Land acquisition
- Transfer of development rights
- Conservation easements
- Federal and state programs
- Zoning
- Voluntary participation

The way to a sustainable future for wildlife in a watershed will require a balanced approach to implementation, one that acknowledges the rights and responsibilities of landowners and the need to protect resources, public health, safety, and general welfare.

Implementing a plan at a project scale may require nontraditional construction site preparation, planting, and management techniques—for example, construction of a large wetland, restoration of a riparian corridor using bioengineering techniques, or prescribed burning to maintain a tall grass prairie. Research suggests that on-site supervision of these kinds of activities by landscape architects, biologists, and ecologists is essential to successful implementation.

Evaluate Plan

Evaluation of an implemented plan based on plan objectives is an often-overlooked but necessary component of a wildlife conservation planning process. The purpose of the evaluation is to estimate the condition of habitats and changes in wildlife demographics. A plan evaluation requires baseline data against which plan performance can be compared. A good geographic information system (GIS) database will provide documentation of general patch, corridor, and matrix conditions at the watershed scale. However, collecting more detailed data on the condition of habitat and wildlife populations of specific patches or corridors can be expensive. When possible, use ongoing surveys conducted by state and federal agencies. Breeding bird surveys and Christmas bird counts, conducted by the Audubon Society, and records kept by amateur naturalists can also be valuable sources of information. Although some of the data collected may not reflect specific wildlife responses to the implemented plan, they can illustrate overall trends in population and habitat conditions. Data collected over several years may suggest that the watershed-scale plan or smaller conservation plans within it are not functioning as predicted; adaptive management may be necessary.

Other evaluation activities include:

- Design an evaluation protocol, including permanent plots for monitoring changes in habitat conditions, wildlife populations, and plant community composition.
- Continue to utilize monitoring data compiled by state and federal agencies.
- Train volunteers—for example, local experts, Audubon Society members, high school or university biology students, Future Farmers of America, and 4H members, or interested local residents—to conduct monitoring activities.
- Conduct annual monitoring evaluations and tie monitoring data to a GIS database.
- Update files annually.
- Share monitoring data with all planning partners and the general public.
- Continue to celebrate conservation successes with the public.
- Utilize existing conservation planning partnerships to develop adaptive management strategies as necessary; keep the public informed.

A well-developed evaluation/monitoring plan involves experts and trained volunteers. Many of those involved will take ownership in the project and become strong conservation advocates.

CONCLUSION

This discussion of planning for wildlife conservation presents basic concepts and ideas; it is by no means complete. The reader is referred to the references listed at the end of this article for additional details and explanations.

Many landscape architects work in dense urban environments where little or no habitat remains, yet they too can contribute to wildlife conservation by making the core of our cities places to live, work, and recreate. Attracting residents back to livable city centers helps curtail sprawl that consumes millions of acres of productive farmland and wildlife habitat annually and requires the need for additional highways which further fragment the landscape.

REFERENCES

Adams, L. W., and L. E. Dove. 1989. *Wildlife Reserves and Corridors in the Urban Environment: A Guide to Ecological Landscape Planning and Resource Conservation.* Columbia, MD: National Institute for Urban Wildlife.

Andren, H. 1994. "Effects of Habitat Fragmentation on Birds and Mammals in Landscapes with Different Proportions of Suitable Habitat: A Review," *Oikos* 71 :355–374.

Diamond, J. M. 1976. "Island Biogeography and Conservation: Strategy and Limitations," *Science* 193:1027–1029.

Dramstad, W .E., J. D. Olson, and R. T. Forman. 1996. *Landscape Ecology Principles in Landscape Architecture and Land-Use Planning.* Washington, DC: Island Press.

Fahrig, L. 1997. "Relative Effects of Habitat Loss and Fragmentation on Population Extinction," *Journal of Wildlife Management* 61:603–610.

Finch, D. M. 1991. "Population Ecology, Habitat Requirements, and Conservation of Neotropical Migratory Birds." USDA Forest Service General Technical Report RM-205. Washington, DC: USDA.

Fleury, A. M., and R. B. Brown. 1997. "A Framework for the Design of Wildlife Conservation Corridors with Specific Application to Southwestern Ontario," *Landscape and Urban Planning,* 37:163–186.

Forman, R. T. 1995. *Land Mosaics: The Ecology of Landscapes and Regions.* Cambridge, MD: Cambridge University Press.

Gould, J. L. 1982. *Ethology: The Mechanisms and Evolution of Behavior.* New York: W.W. Norton and Company.

Harris, L. D. 1984. *The Fragmented Forest: Island Biogeography Theory and the Preservation of Biotic Diversity.* Chicago, IL: University of Chicago Press.

Herkert, J. R. 1994. "The Effects of Habitat Fragmentation on Midwest Grassland Bird Communities," *Ecological Application,* 4:461–471.

Johnson, C. W., K. Collins, D. Johnson, P. Larsen, M. Mazurski, S. Nordstrom, and L. Wright. 1993. *A Wildlife Conservation Manual for Urbanizing Areas of Utah.* Salt Lake City, UT: Utah Division of Wildlife Resources.

Craig Johnson, Professor, Department of Landscape Architecture and Environmental Planning, Utah State University, Logan, Utah

Johnson, C. W. 1999. "Conservation Corridor Planning at the Landscape Level: Managing for Wildlife Habitat," Part 190 *National Biology Handbook*. Fort Worth, TX: USDA Natural Resources Conservation Service.

Lindenmayer, D. B., and H. A. Nix. 1993. "Ecological Principles for the Design of Wildlife Corridors," *Conservation Biology* 7:627–631.

MacArthur, R. H., and E. O. Wilson. 1967. *The Theory of Island Biogeography*. Princeton, NJ: Princeton University Press.

MacMahon, J. A. 1987. "Disturbed Lands Ecological Theory: An Essay about a Mutalistic Association," in *Restoration Ecology*, W. R. Jordan, M. E. Gilpin, and J. D. Aber (eds). Cambridge, UK: Cambridge University Press.

Meffe, G. K., and C. R. Carroll. 1997. *Principles of Conservation Biology*. Sunderland, MA: Sinauer Associates Publishers.

Morrison, M. L. 2002. *Wildlife Restoration: Techniques for Habitat Analysis and Animal Monitoring*. Washington, DC: Island Press. Society for Ecological Restoration.

Noss, R.F. 1993. "Wildlife Corridors," in *Ecology of Greenways*, D. S. Smith and R. C. Hellmund (eds). Minneapolis, MN: University of Minnesota Press.

Noss, R. F., and L. D. Harris. 1986. "Nodes, Networks and MUMs: Preserving Diversity at All Scales," *Environmental Management* 10:299–309.

Roth, R. R. 1976. "Spatial Heterogeneity and Species Diversity," *Ecology* 57:773–782.

Schwartz, M. E. (ed.). 1996. *Conservation in Highly Fragmented Landscapes*. New York: Chapman and Hall.

Soule, M. E. 1991. "Land Use Planning and Wildlife Maintenance Guidelines for Conserving Wildlife in Urban Landscapes," *Journal of the American Planning Association* 57:313:3–24.

Soule, M. E., D. T. Bolger, and A. C. Alberts. 1988. "Reconstructed Dynamics of Rapid Extinction of Chaparral-Requiring Birds in Urban Habitat Islands," *Conservation Biology* 2:75–92.

Waddock, S. A. 1989. "Understanding Social Partnerships: An Evolutionary Model of Partnership Organizations," *Administration and Society* 21:78–100.

Yahner, R. H. 1988. "Changes in Wildlife Communities Near Edges," *Conservation Biology* 2:333–339.

Craig Johnson, Professor, Department of Landscape Architecture and Environmental Planning, Utah State University, Logan, Utah

CAMPUSES

INTRODUCTION

Campus planning and development projects are microcosms of larger landscape architectural problems, because campuses are communities that have access, circulation, servicing, wayfinding, environmental, and identity issues.

Typically, the total overall master plan for an educational institution is prepared by a team consisting of an architect, landscape architect, and an educational planner. It is a full conceptual plan for the entire campus, one that locates buildings, roads, paths, parking, and recreation—it resembles the schematic plan in a design project. Often, campus plans then proceed into a secondary phase, a campus landscape master plan, drawn by the landscape architect alone. This plan develops the site itself in greater detail—it is more like a design development plan in a typical design project. As such, it refines path, road, parking, and conceptual planting layouts; and develops stormwater management strategies, entry points, gathering places, and focal points for the entire campus.

Ideally, campus master planning should be a physical manifestation of the conceptual vision for the institution. If the long-term planning vision stresses basic arts and sciences, or special programs, or research and entrepreneurial opportunities, or other educational specialties, then the physical campus layout can give three-dimensional identity to this or other special emphasis. A campus plan should also, however, respond to its unique environment.

Over time, an institution's academic vision of its future may change. Largely due to the presence of the institution itself, its environment may change as well. At the outset, however, an understanding of the unique qualities of the natural environment of the campus should play an important role in determining its physical layout and in preserving elements the give unique qualities to the student experience.

STANDARDS

In campus planning, important standards related to accessibility apply to all paths, parking, and building access. All entrances must be at grade or accessible by ramp. All ramps and walks must be surfaced, no steeper than 5 percent without handrails, and a width suitable for wheelchairs (4 feet). No ramped path with handrails should be steeper than 1:12, or 8.33 percent. Accessible parking spaces should be located convenient to central facilities, and be 8 feet wide and 18 feet long, with an open 5-foot zone between spaces. Paths meeting these standards should connect handicapped parking to main circulation routes.

Other standards that apply are for bicycle paths and standard widths for two-way and one-way traffic with passing room: 5 feet is the standard established by the American Disabilities Act Accessibility Guidelines (ADAAG). Standards for roads and driveways vary depending on intensity of use; typical two-way roads are from 20 to 24 feet wide.

LAWS AND REGULATIONS

Tree replacement laws apply in many communities. For new buildings that displace existing trees, the replacement requirements in some places are equal or greater to the units of trees lost.

In many communities, a certificate of occupancy of a new campus building from the local conservation commission is required. To obtain the certificate, the site must be entirely stabilized with pavement, mulch, or vegetation. The building cannot be used without this certificate. This regulation protects the environment from erosion and the campus community from accidents in areas left with construction debris.

Landscape architects often must appear before local design review commissions, planning boards, zoning commissions, and conservation commissions. These boards and commissions protect the community surrounding the campus from visual intrusion, parking, traffic and access issues, and violation of required setbacks and uses.

CURRENT TRENDS

Campuses are expanding everywhere, impacting the neighborhoods where they are located and causing the so-called town-gown conflict. Small towns resist the creep of larger campus building into the small scale of their community, as increased pavement, roof area, and mown grass increases stormwater runoff and impacts downstream flooding in these neighborhoods.

Some campus officials invite community residents to review new campus plans before they go to the regulatory boards, giving them an opportunity to make desirable revisions before public hearings.

Parking is a particular issue for neighborhoods, which become clogged with student vehicles when school is in session. Campuses are pressured to build structural, rather than surfaced, parking. Hence, in both central and less central campus locations, landscape architects are asked to study a site's maximum surface parking and access and safety problems to address these parking issues.

Campuses are now developing their own stormwater management systems such as grass detention basins or rainwater gardens. Landscape architects are using these as features in the landscape, sometimes with pedestrian footbridges across them and sometimes as teaching stations for classes in ecology.

KEY ISSUES

Data Collection

Before embarking on the master planning process, data should be collected. Important baseline information includes: copies of relevant regional and local plans; codes and restrictions; existing soils maps; aerial photography; an existing conditions and property line survey with vegetation, contours, and other features; and a history of the site.

Planning Approach

Each university campus should have a unique sense of place and a memorable character; that is, no campus should look like every other campus. The local culture, environment, and the special programs of the institution can give direction as to how this may be achieved.

Growth and expansion take place at dynamic institutions. Changes in the economy, technology, and demographics affect all universities. Thus, a campus site should be developed with the potential for expansion of departments or graduate schools. Often, parking lots become building sites, causing parking facilities to become more remote, or requiring parking decks to be built.

Environmental Preservation

Preservation of existing trees and other features is important in providing a comfortable student environment. The edges of ponds, wetlands, and other water resources should be treated carefully, to avoid pollution during and after the construction phases.

To that end, buildings should be designed and oriented to minimize use of energy: locate the admissions office so it is near parking and easily accessible; and locate service areas and trash management and recycle stations in an effective, but not visually intrusive, manner.

Although each campus has unique site characteristics and program requirements, there are typical elements, relationships, and planning approaches that they share. Some of these are:

Typical Campus Building Elements

- Spaces to be programmed and located
  - Administration
  - Library
  - Classrooms (lecture halls)
  - Laboratories (science, art)
  - Interdisciplinary centers
  - Faculty offices
  - Recreation (athletic center; health and wellness)
  - Student center
  - Dining facilities
  - Residence halls
  - Graduate schools
  - Faculty housing
  - Places of worship
  - Theater (music, practice)
  - Observatory
  - Special programs
  - Student family housing
  - Facilities management
- Common Adjacencies
  - Administration and library
  - Student center and dining
  - Health and wellness and student center
  - Health and wellness and recreation center

Typical Site Elements

- Key places
  - Entry or portal—arrival at institution: Gives identity, initial impression.
  - Campus core or heart: A combination of buildings and spaces where people may gather; it may have a view out or may be enclosed.
- Circulation and parking
  - Vehicular circulation: Access to service, parking, shuttle loops, public transportation, emergency, fire protection. Drives may be one- or two-way. Certain wide walkways may be used as fire lanes and limited-service routes, to keep main traffic out of the campus core.
  - Pedestrian circulation: Safe, attractive, accessible, and convenient routes for students and staff to use in walking between campus centers and activities. Conflicts with vehicular circulation should be avoided. Raised speed tables are useful at points where pedestrian/vehicular conflict is unavoidable.

Carol R. Johnson, FASLA

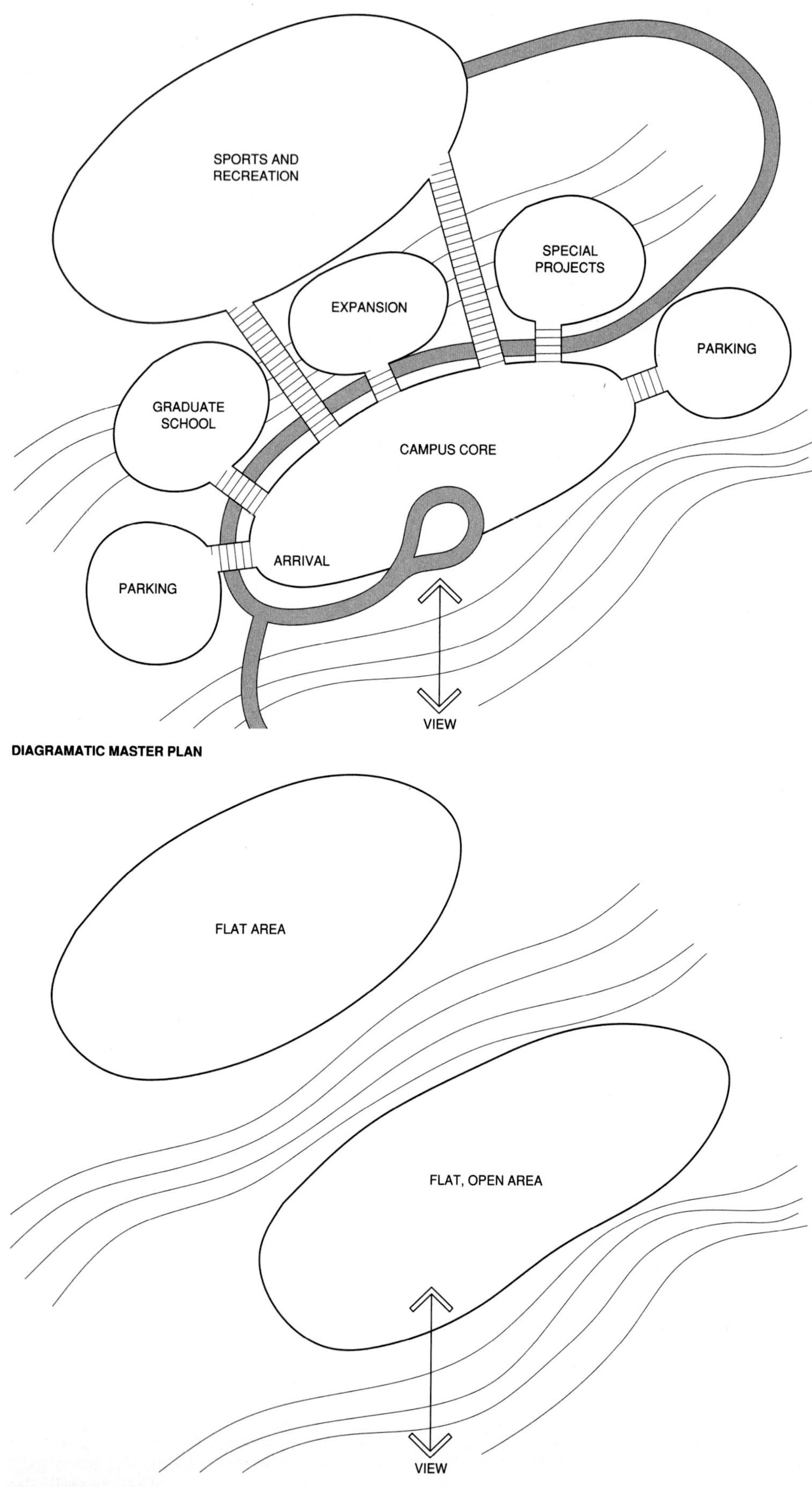

DIAGRAMATIC MASTER PLAN

EXISTING CONDITIONS

DIAGRAMS, NOTES, AND ILLUSTRATIONS: AIDS TO CAMPUS MASTER PLANNING

Carol R. Johnson, FASLA

- Bicycle routes: Adjacent to walks or drives or totally separate.
- Parking: Convenient, especially for the handicapped; but not visually intrusive into the campus.
- Outdoor lighting: Should provide good wayfinding and should not pollute the night skies.
- Outdoor recreation: Trails, fields, rinks, riding rings, courts, golf course
  - Open, green playing fields may be used to create or maintain vistas and a sense of openness.
  - Cross-country running or riding trails may be developed to give a special feeling for the unique campus environment.
  - Tennis or other fenced courts should be placed so they don't interrupt the flow of open space.
  - Spectator access and seating are important.

Typical Site Analysis

- General: Identify and evaluate:
  - Views and vistas
  - Prevailing winds, rainfall
  - Sun orientation
  - Terrain (contours, slopes)
  - Hydrology
- Special features
  - Rocks, cliffs
  - Water (streams, ponds, lakes)
  - Swamps, wetlands
  - Unique vegetation
  - Hills and valleys
  - Flat areas
  - Meadows
  - Monuments
  - Stone walls
- Relationships often considered
  - Views and vistas and special features and campus heart
  - Sun orientation, rain and wind protection and student gathering places
  - Hills and vegetation and shielding views of parking
  - Flat areas and playing fields

Typical Building and Site Configurations

- Compact connected buildings are valuable in regions with difficult climates and where land area is limited or steeply sloping.
- An arrangement of separated buildings around a special space gives identity to an institution, as well as a memorable gathering space and a sense of penetration from the outside.
- Combinations of connected buildings and separated buildings give significance to the separated buildings.
- Convincing students not to drive cars from one end of campus to another is important. Locate buildings so pedestrian connections are attractive and close; conversely, make the walk from parking less convenient.

Arrival Sequence

- A main vehicular drop-off often identifies the arrival location even if visitors must go elsewhere to park. It also may encourage use of bus or shuttle transportation.
- Clear, illuminated signage is important for directing visitors at all times of the day. An iconic element (tower, special building, gateway, sculpture) is often part of the arrival sequence.

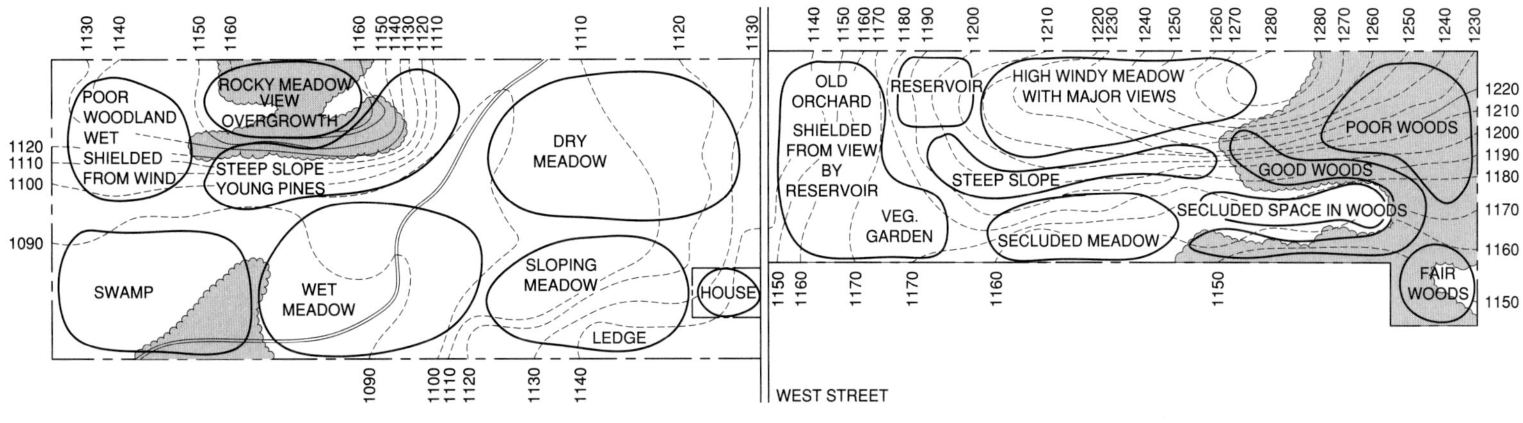

BERKSHIRE COMMUNITY COLLEGE, PITTSFIELD, MASSACHUSETTS: SITE ANALYSIS

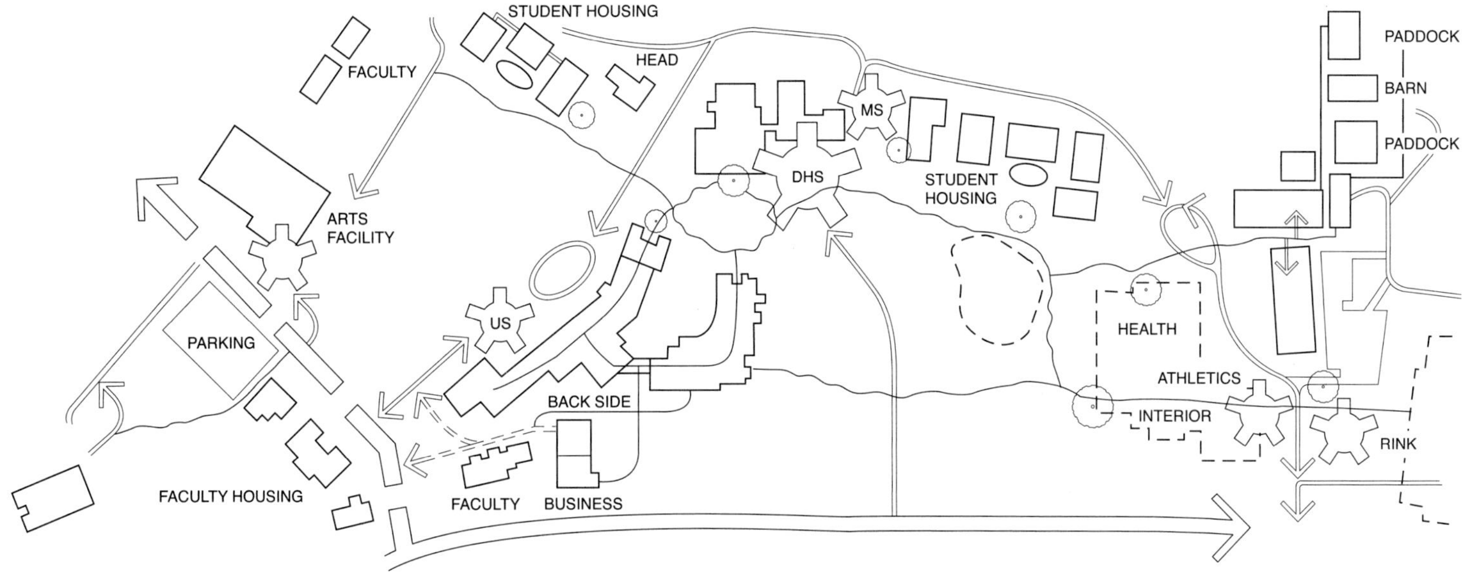

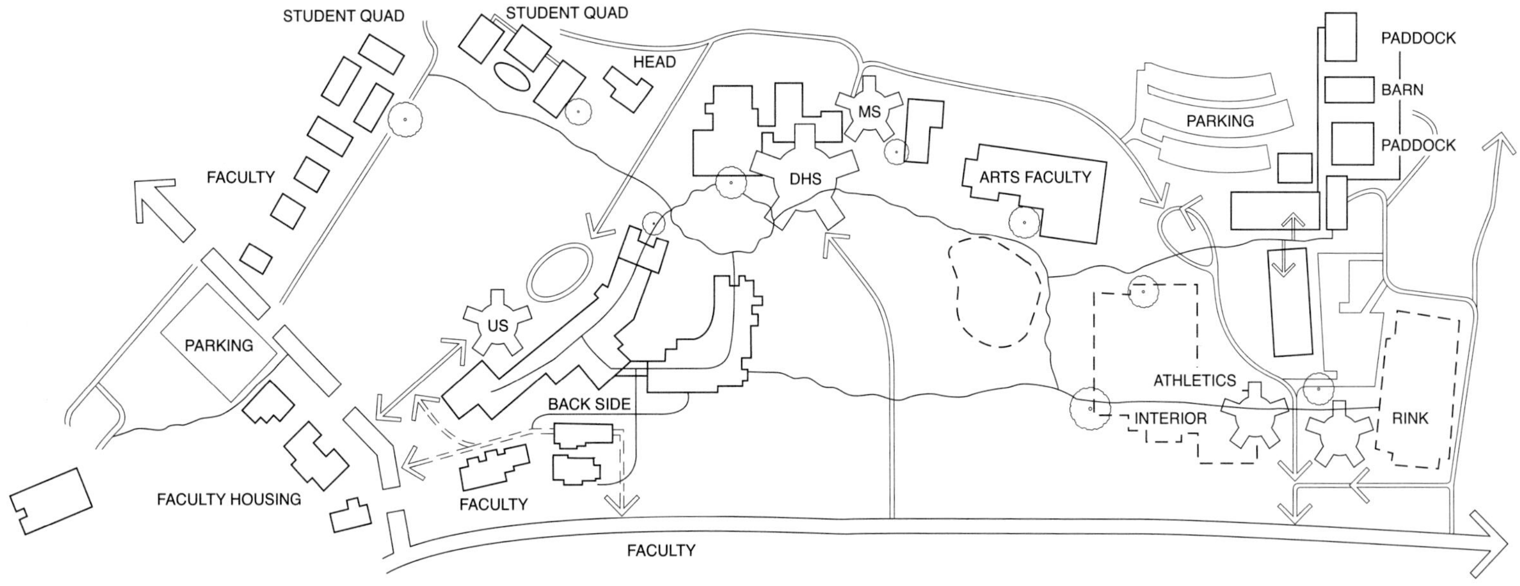

DANA HALL SCHOOL, WELLESLEY, MASSACHUSETTS: DIAGRAMS OF MASTER PLAN ALTERNATIVES

Carol R. Johnson, FASLA

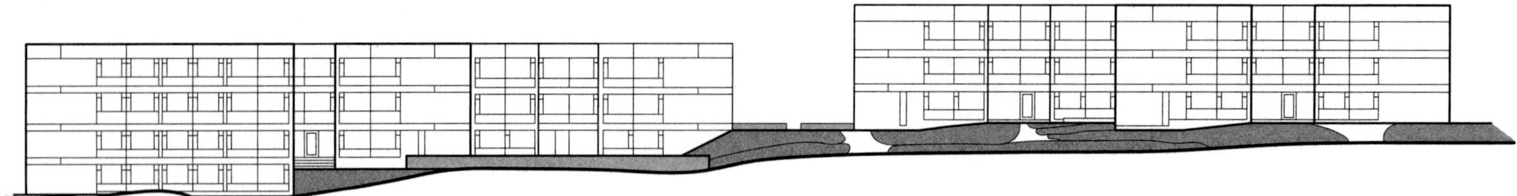

WILLIAMS COLLEGE ELEVATION

Designing for Sloping Terrain

- Buildings can be made to fit into a sloping terrain. Windows or entry from the high side can be one floor higher than windows or entry from the other, for example.
- Accommodating large playing fields in sloping sites is more problematic. The uphill side will be cut into the existing terrain, while the downhill side will bulge out of the natural contour of the land.
- Preserving existing vegetation where excessive earthwork must be done is difficult, and often impossible.

Carol R. Johnson, FASLA

HAZARD CONTROL

SOIL EROSION AND SEDIMENT CONTROL

INTRODUCTION

The control of erosion and subsequent transport of sediment from project sites is a critical part of the design and development process. Modification of land and land use can have severe impacts on-site, as well as upon adjacent lands and downstream areas. Most of the impacts can be mitigated by proper planning, implementation, and active maintenance of soil erosion and sediment control measures.

Terms used in this discussion are defined as follows:

Erosion control: Management practices to limit exposure of soil to wind-, rain-, runoff-, and wave-driven erosive forces.

Land-disturbing activities: Any activities that may result in soil erosion from water or wind and the movement of sediments into waters or onto lands, including, but not limited to, clearing, dredging, grading, excavating, transporting, and filling.

Soil erosion: The wearing away of soil and rock by wind, water/ice, or gravity.

FUNCTIONS OF SOIL EROSION AND SEDIMENT CONTROL MEASURES

	FILTERS			REDUCES										ENHANCES											
MANAGEMENT PRACTICE	CHEMICALS	NUTRIENTS	SEDIMENT	EROSION BY WAVES	EROSION BY WIND	EROSION BY RUNOFF	NOISE	RUNOFF QUANTITY	RUNOFF VELOCITY	SOIL CRUSTING	STREAM BANK EROSION	UNDESIRABLE PLANTS	WATER TEMPERATURE	FLOOD PROTECTION	RUNOFF INFILTRATION	SAND CAPTURE	SOIL BIOLOGICAL ACTIVITY	SOIL MOISTURE	SOIL ORGANIC MATTER	SOIL TEMPERATURE	SOIL TILTH	VEGETATIVE ESTABLISHMENT	VISUAL CHARACTER	WILDLIFE HABITAT
Vegetative and Related Measures																								
Buffer zone	•	•	•			•	•		•	•	•		•	•	•								•	•
Coastal dune satabilization			•	•										•	•	•								•
Disturbed area stabilization (by mulching)	•	•	•		•	•		•	•	•		•			•		•	•		•				
Disturbed area stabilization (by temporary seeding)	•	•	•		•	•		•	•						•		•	•	•	•	•		•	•
Disturbed area stabilization (by permanent vegetation)	•	•	•		•	•		•	•	•					•		•	•	•	•	•		•	•
Disturbed area stabilization (by sodding)	•	•	•		•	•		•	•	•					•		•	•	•	•	•		•	•
Dust control				•														•						
Erosion control matting and blankets				•	•	•			•	•	•							•		•				
Polyacrylamide (PAM)					•	•																		
Stream bank stabilization (by permanent vegetation)			•			•					•		•			•			•				•	•
Tackifiers and binders					•					•		•			•		•	•		•				
Structural Measures																								
Checkdam			•			•			•															
Channel stabilization						•					•			•										
Construction exit			•			•																		
Constuction road stabilization			•			•																		
Stream diversion channel											•													
Diversion			•			•			•															
Temporary downdrain structure						•																•		
Permanent downdrain structure						•																•		
Filter ring			•			•			•															
Gabion			•	•	•	•	•		•		•			•	•	•						•		
Grade stabilization structure						•			•		•			•								•		
Level spreader						•			•						•									
Rock filter dam			•			•			•															
Retaining wall																								
Retrofit			•						•															
Sediment barrier			•			•			•															
Inlet sediment trap			•						•															
Temporary sediment basin			•			•			•															
Temporary stream crossing			•								•													
Storm drain outlet protection						•			•															
Surface roughening			•			•			•						•			•		•	•	•		
Topsoiling																		•	•	•	•	•		
Vegetated waterway or stormwater conveyance channel	•	•	•			•			•						•			•					•	

Ronald B. Sawhill, University of Georgia, College of Environment and Design, Athens, Georgia

DESIGN CHARACTERISTICS OF EROSION AND SEDIMENT CONTROL MEASURES: VEGETATIVE MEASURES

VEGETATIVE MEASURES	MATERIALS AND DIMENSIONS	NOTES
Coastal dune stabilization: Planting vegetation on denuded dunes or for dune creation or dune renourishment; sand fencing may be needed to build dunes or to reinforce dunes to be planted. (See the "Sand Fence Detail" figure.)	Irrigate for the first year. Mulch all planting areas. Protect from foot and vehicular traffic.	Maintain dune lines to provide wind and water protection. Repair damaged segments quickly. Multiple rows of sand fencing may be required.
Disturbed area stabilization by mulching: A temporary measure providing cover for six months or less when vegetative measures are impractical.	Suitable materials include: 2″–4″ dry straw or hay 2″–3″ wood chips or bark 1200 gal/ac cutback asphalt Polyethylene film Geotextiles Jute matting	Anchor straw or hay to the soil by pressing with vertical disk harrow or packer disk, adding asphalt emulsion to blown straw, or using maximum 1″× 1″ netting. Anchor wood chips with netting if grade exceeds 3%. Anchor polyethylene film by trenching and backfilling.
Disturbed area stabilization by temporary seeding: A temporary measure providing vegetative cover for six months or less to disturbed areas prior to final permanent vegetation installation.	Use an appropriate grass or grass-legume mixture; see local standards. Irrigate as necessary during drought periods.	Pit, trench, or scarify soil if soil is crusted or sealed; fertilize low-fertility soils at 500–700 lbs/ac. Reseed until 90% cover is achieved.
Disturbed area stabilization by permanent vegetation: A permanent measure providing final vegetative cover on exposed areas. Vegetation can include trees, shrubs, vines, ground covers, grasses, and/or legumes.	Varies by region and project type.	The goal is to achieve complete coverage of all exposed areas.
Disturbed area stabilization by sodding: A permanent measure providing immediate vegetative cover by sods on critically eroded areas or areas that are highly susceptible to erosion.	Use machine-cut sods placed tightly together on prepared soils. Maintain with fertilizer and irrigation as necessary. Stake sods installed on slopes steeper than 3:1 or in areas of concentrated water flow. Check local turf specialists for appropriate sod selection and planting dates.	Netting can be used to secure sod in critical areas. Use caution: Netting can ensnare wildlife. Sods with embedded reinforcing materials are available for added strength.
Dust control: Measures designed to control the surface and air movement of dust from roads and disturbed sites to protect public and environmental health, safety, and welfare.	Use disturbed area stabilization methods, if possible. Other measures include: covering surfaces with crushed stone, applying chlorides, applying spray-on adhesives to mineral soils, installing wind barriers, or temporarily irrigating surfaces until wet.	Mulched areas should have tackifying resins such as asphalt emulsions or anionic polyacrylamide applied in accordance with manufacturer's recommendations. Wind barriers such as snow fences, burlap fences, solid fences, hay bales, or other similar materials can be installed, spaced about 15 times their height at right angles to prevailing winds.
Erosion control matting and blankets: A protective covering of natural and/or man-made materials in the form of mats/blankets used to establish vegetation and to provide for temporary or permanent stabilization of steep slopes, channels, or shorelines. Install according to manufacturer's specifications and with appropriate staking to prevent shifting. (See the "Erosion Control Mats" figure.)	Temporary mats deteriorate in a short period of time and are composed of straw, curled wood excelsior, coconut fiber, wood fiber, and jute mesh. Permanent mats consist of polymer nettings, fibers, or monofilaments formed into a dimensionally stable matrix and stabilized against ultraviolet degradation.	Plastic webbing can ensnare birds and reptiles. Shading due to vegetative growth and detritus may retard plastic degradation, creating a long-term wildlife hazard, particularly in and near streambanks. Consider using all woven natural materials; where permanent blankets are required, select forms with minimal apertures.
Polyacrylamide (PAM): Anionic polyacrylamide is a temporary soil-binding agent used to provide rapid erosion control where vegetation is absent or inadequate or where establishment of vegetation alone would be too slow.	Follow manufacturer's recommendations for installation of PAM. The annual maximum application of PAM in pure form must not exceed 200 lbs/ac, or other local, state, or federal standards.	Use setbacks around water bodies to avoid application onto water. Use anionic PAM only; cationic PAM is toxic. Excessive applications may lower soil infiltration rates or increase suspended solids in water.
Tackifiers and binders: Various substances applied to bind organic mulch together to keep it in place, usually applied during hydroseeding.	Includes emulsified asphalts, PAMs, and similar products. Refer to manufacturer's recommendations for application rates.	Where appropriate, tackifiers and binders eliminate the need for matting or netting to secure mulch.

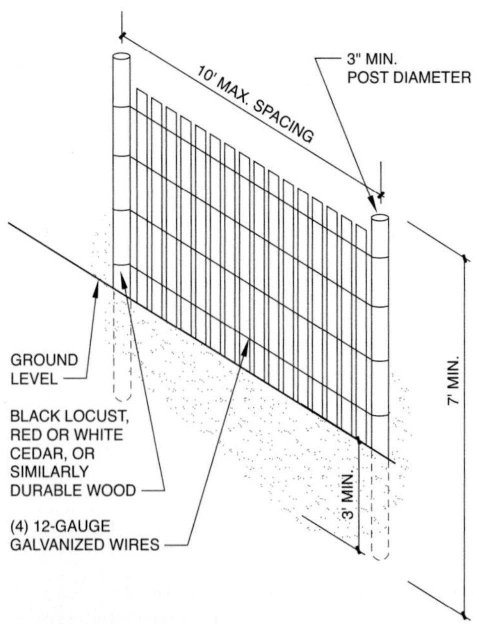

SAND FENCE DETAIL

Source: From the Georgia Soil and Water Conservation Commission manuals, 2000, 2002.

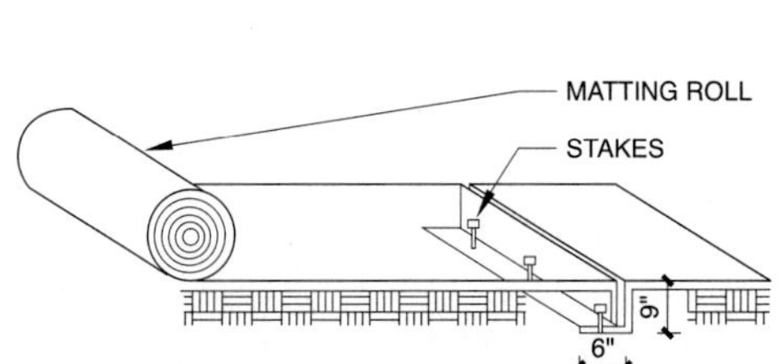

EROSION CONTROL MATS

Source: From the Georgia Soil and Water Conservation Commission manuals, 2000, 2002.

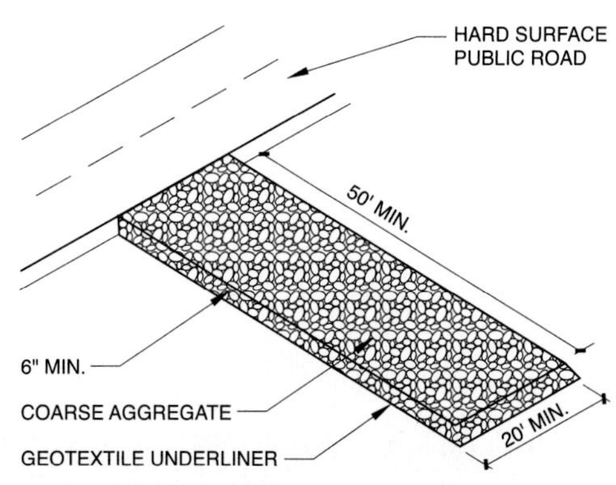

CONSTRUCTION EXIT

Source: From the Georgia Soil and Water Conservation Commission manuals, 2000, 2002.

Ronald B. Sawhill, University of Georgia, College of Environment and Design, Athens, Georgia

DESIGN CHARACTERISTICS OF EROSION AND SEDIMENT CONTROL MEASURES: STRUCTURAL MEASURES

STRUCTURAL MEASURES	MATERIALS AND DIMENSIONS	NOTES
Construction exit: A crushed stone or aggregate pad located at any egress point from a disturbed site to a public right-of-way, roadway, parking area, or pedestrian way, to prevent or reduce the movement of sediment from the site. (See the "Construction Exit" figure.)	Excavate a minimum 20′ × 50′ pad to 3″ depth, and install a geotextile liner between the soil and a 6″ aggregate layer composed of stone ranging between 1.5″ and 3.5″ in size.	Washing of tires may be necessary if the construction exit does not remove all mud from tires. Wash down tires on a stone aggregate stabilized pad where the resulting runoff will not allow sediment to escape the site.
Construction road stabilization: A temporary construction route installed along planned permanent road and parking facilities (where possible), to reduce erosion and the need for subsequent grading to install permanent roadways.	Design temporary road widths based on projected use load and types of vehicles. Avoid slopes greater than 10%, if at all possible. Do not exceed 2:1 side slopes. Apply a geotextile to the subgrade, then a minimum 6″ layer of coarse aggregate for the temporary use surface.	Locate roadways along contours, where possible. Establish a suitable base by removing topsoil layer, vegetative matter, and unsuitable material. Establish subgrade and surface course in accordance with local design standards.
Diversion: A ridge of compacted soil and an adjacent channel placed above, across, or below a slope to reduce runoff slope lengths and to divert runoff to a stable outlet. (See the "Diversion" figure.)	Diversion ridges must be a minimum of 4′ wide, 8-12″ above and below the original surface, with maximum 2:1 side slopes. Diversion channels must be trapezoidal or parabolic in form and stabilized by vegetation at the outlet. Across roads, construct diversions at a 30-degree angle to the road.	On roads, make the ridges and channels smooth enough to accommodate vehicles. Space the diversions based on road slope: 1%: 400′ 2%: 250′ 5%: 125′ 10%: 80′ 15%: 60′ 20%: 50′
Temporary downdrain structure: A temporary structure designed to conduct concentrated runoff down disturbed slopes, to prevent slope erosion and to permit establishment of vegetative cover. A diversion along the brow of the slope is used to direct runoff to the ell, tee, or flared end section inlet of the downdrain. A check dam or filter ring may be employed to filter sediment from the runoff prior to entering the downdrain. (See the "Temporary Downdrain" figure.)	Use heavy-duty corrugated plastic pipe or other flexible, nonperforated tubing; anchor pipe a minimum of every 10′ by stakes or hold-down grommets. Align the pipe at a slight diagonal down slope; extend and direct the outlet away from the slope toe. Size the pipe based on the maximum drainage area. Permanent downdrains can include concrete flumes (parabolic, rectangular or trapezoidal), pipe (CMP, RCP, plastic, etc.), or those of sectional construction such as half-round or third-round pipe.	Remove temporary downdrains once the permanent vegetation is established and the permanent drainage system is operational. Failure of downdrains is often caused by seepage and subsequent washouts along the pipe course; provide firm and complete compaction of soil around and under the pipe by hand-tamping in 6″ lifts. Provide storm drain protection at the downdrain outlet.
Filter ring: A temporary ring of stone constructed around storm drainage inlets and around pond outlets to slow water velocity and to filter sediment. (See the "Filter Ring" figure.)	Encircle the stormwater structure with stone at a 2′ minimum height using min. 3.5″ stone for inlets less than 12″ diameter and minimum 10″–15″ stone for larger inlets. Size ring forebays as follows: Standard inlets: minimum 4′ diameter Retrofits: minimum 8-10′ diameter Storm outlets: size to prevent backup in the system.	Where the larger stone is used, it can be faced with smaller stone on the upstream side for additional filtering capability. Maintenance of filter rings is essential; they clog by design and must be actively maintained. Remove collected sediment when the filter ring is half full.
Retrofit: A temporary sediment filtering device placed around a permanent stormwater detention basin outlet structure. (See the "Half-Round Pipe Retrofit" figure.)	Half-round pipe: a. For smaller drainage basins. b. Outlet structure is not an exposed pipe end or winged headwall. c. Dimensions: 1.5 times diameter principal outlet or wider than maximum weir width. d. Place 1″ holes 8-10″ apart. e. Place 3-4″ stone against the retrofit up to its top. Slotted board dam: a. For larger drainage basins. b. Use with all types of outlet structures. c. Use minimum 4×4 posts. d. Gap boards 1/2 to 1″ apart. e. Place 3-4″ stone against the retrofit up to its top.	Two limitations include: No use on basins in live streams; Basin must accommodate 67 cubic yards (CY) of sediment storage per acre of disturbed area in addition to storm water storage. Both methods should include the installation of a filter ring around the retrofit structure, including an 8′–10′ forebay. (See "Filter ring," above, for details.)
Sediment barrier: Temporary structures designed to prevent the movement of sediment from a disturbed area; these sediment barriers can include sandbags, hay bales, brush piles, and various types of silt fencing. Do not install sediment barriers across concentrated flow areas or streams. Remove sediment when it accumulates to one-half of the barrier's height. (See the "Hay Bale Sediment Barrier" and "Silt Fence" figures.)	Sandbags: Place bags with ends pointing uphill and anchor with steel rods if height exceeds two bags. Hay bales: Inset a single row of bales 4″ into soil and stake in place. Brush piles: Wind-row brush along the disturbance perimeter 5–10′ wide at the base and 3–5′ high; compact if necessary. Filter fabric may be added for additional filtering. Standard nonreinforced silt fence: 36′ fabric installed in a 6′ deep trench with a 2′ strip laid flat on the bottom of the trench before backfilling. Install 4′ long posts (steel or wood) 18″ deep and maximum 6′ apart. Use a fabric with sufficient tensile strength and a moderate flow rate. Small site nonreinforced silt fence: 22″ fabric installed in a 4″ deep trench with a 2″ strip laid flat on the bottom of the trench before backfilling. Install 3′ long posts (steel or wood) 18″ deep and maximum 4′ apart. Use a fabric with sufficient tensile strength and a moderate flow rate. Reinforced silt fence: Same as the standard nonreinforced silt fence, except use woven wire fence behind the fabric, use steel posts only, and use a fabric with high tensile strength and a high flow rate.	Sandbags: Minimize flow between or around bags. Hay bales: Because of low porosity, ponding may occur rapidly. Limit use to three months. Brush piles are for use during logging operations. Standard nonreinforced silt fence is for use on sites that will experience disturbance for more than six months or where the slope gradient exceeds 3:1. Small site nonreinforced silt fence is for use on small sites where disturbance is for six months or less and where the gradient is 3:1 or less. Reinforced silt fence is for use on slopes greater than 10′ in height, where gradients exceed 3:1, and where runoff flow and/or velocity is high. Attach silt fence to posts by wire staples, nails, or by wire, cord, and pockets. Check local standards for approved silt fence materials and standards.

(continued)

Ronald B. Sawhill, University of Georgia, College of Environment and Design, Athens, Georgia

DESIGN CHARACTERISTICS OF EROSION AND SEDIMENT CONTROL MEASURES: STRUCTURAL MEASURES *(continued)*

STRUCTURAL MEASURES	MATERIALS AND DIMENSIONS	NOTES
Inlet sediment trap: A temporary structure placed around a storm drain drop inlet to prevent sediment from entering a storm system and leaving the site. (See the "Fabric and Frame Sediment Trap," "Block and Gravel Sediment Trap," and "Pigs-in-a-Blanket Sediment Trap" figures.)	Excavation trap: Excavate around the inlet to 1.5′ minimum with maximum 2:1 side slopes; provide 67 cubic yards per acre (CY/ac) sediment storage area minimum. Fabric and frame: Use reinforced silt fencing around inlets with diagonal 2×4 reinforcing; entrench fencing 12″ and place stakes maximum 3′ apart. Baffle Box: A box built of 2×4s spaced 1″ apart (maximum) or of plywood with 1″ diameter holes spaced 6″ × 6″. The box is wrapped in reinforced silt fence; entrenched 12″ and surrounded with 2–4″ of gravel. Block and gravel: A box built of concrete block, embedded 2″ below inlet elevation, stacked two rows high. Turn one bottom block on each side to allow water to flow horizontally to the inlet. Fit them with hardware cloth and surround the entire structure with #57 stone at a 2:1 max slope. Gravel donut: A three-part stone ring. The central ring is made of 3-6″ stone, recessed below the inlet, laid level and 1′ wide around the inlet; the middle ring is made of 3–6″ stone rising at a maximum 3:1 slope to a maximum 2′ height. The outer ring is #57 stone and a minimum 12″ thick and sloped away at 2:1 maximum. Pigs-in-a-blanket: Place 8″ concrete blocks wrapped in filter fabric across inlet openings with holes oriented toward flow; maintain 4″ clear space in front of inlet opening. Gravel bags: Wrap #57 stone in filter fabric, wire mesh, plastic mesh, or similar material, and install in front of the inlet maintaining a 4″ clear space. Sod ring: A 4′ wide ring of sod strips installed tightly with staggered joints.	Maximum drainage area for inlet sediment traps is 1 acre. Use baffle box where high-volume or high-velocity runoff is received. Use block and gravel where an overflow is required to limit ponding due to heavy flows. Stake with 2x4s to add strength. Use gravel donut where heavy runoff flows occur and significant ponding is acceptable. Wire mesh can be placed over the inlet to prevent gravel intrusion. Use pigs-in-a-blanket, gravel bags, or other inlet filter systems only after adjoining pavements have been installed. A variety of premanufactured inlet filters are available commercially. Use sod ring only during permanent vegetation establishment.
Temporary sediment basin: A basin created to detain runoff from disturbed areas, permitting sediment to drop out and to protect downstream properties from damage due to debris and sediment. Basins typically consist of a dam, a primary pipe outlet, and a secondary emergency spillway. Temporary sediment basins can be refitted to serve as permanent stormwater detention facilities or stormwater quality treatment facilities after permanent vegetation has been established. (See the "Sediment Basin Plan.")	Shape: Design a wedge-shaped basin with the inlet at the narrow end with a minimum 2:1 length-to-width ratio. Where topography limits form, install baffles within the basin to achieve minimum 2:1 flow paths. Size: Sediment storage capacity must be 67 CY per acre of disturbed area. Dam: Design the dam according to state and local standards, providing sufficient freeboard and safety factors. Flow: Design the outlet structure and emergency spillway for at least the 25-year/24-hour storm. Some jurisdictions may require the 100-year/24-hour storm. Primary outlet: Use a perforated riser embedded in gravel or a skimmer-type outlet. Fit open standpipes with a trash rack and antivortex device. Minimum pipe diameter equals 8″. Emergency spillway: Provide a trapezoidal channel constructed entirely in undisturbed earth with safe side slopes and a defined control section.	Size the basin appropriately for the watershed, including storage area for both sediment and water volume. Structure placement and design must not endanger life or interrupt the use or service of public utilities should it fail. Do not construct in streams. Remove basin within 18 months. Remove sediment from basin when one-third of capacity is reached. Provide stormwater outlet protection at principal outlet and emergency spillway as needed. Stabilize emergency spillway with appropriate cover. Provide antiseep collars on principal outlet pipes through the dam.
Temporary stream crossing: A temporary structure to provide vehicular access across existing streams or watercourses to limit sediment introduction into streams and to minimize streambank disturbance. Use only on streams up to 1 square mile in drainage area.	Temporary ford: For very small flows, install rock riprap of sufficient size and depth to convey traffic without affecting stream flow. Temporary culvert: Place pipe at the natural streambed grade extending upstream and downstream of the aggregate placed over the pipe. Provide sufficient aggregate cover for safe conduct of vehicular loads. Temporary bridge: Install bridges at or above bank elevation on abutments parallel to stable streambanks. Use intermediate footings or piers in streams only where stream widths are extensive.	Temporary stream crossings are not for public use and must be removed within one year. Restore disturbed streambanks to original cross section and stabilize with appropriate vegetation. Minimize disturbance of stream buffers. Anchor bridges at one end only, to prevent channel obstruction in a flood event.
Surface roughening: The creation of depressions parallel with the land contour to aid in establishing vegetation by seed, reducing runoff velocity, and erosion on slopes. (See the "Track Roughening" figure.)	Stair-step: Riser-to-tread ratio flatter than 1:1; treads must slope toward back of slope; riser maximum 30″ on soft material, 40″ on rocky material. Groove: Minimum 3″ deep grooves spaced a maximum of 15″; use disc, harrow, tiller, or front end loader teeth. Track: Roughen slope with tracked dozer using as few passes as possible. Not recommended for clay soils. Light roughening: On slopes 3:1 or flatter, make grooves minimum 1″ deep and 12″ apart using disc, harrow, tiller, rake, or multipacker-seeder; or loosen soil to a depth of 2-4″.	Use stair-step only on cut slopes steeper than 3:1. Use groove or track method on cut or fill slopes steeper than 3:1. Use light roughening on slopes flatter than 3:1.
Topsoiling: Removing upper soil layers, stockpiling, and then spreading it over disturbed areas to enhance vegetative establishment on soils that would otherwise be unsuitable.	Strip topsoil based on site soil profile and stockpile; apply temporary stabilization measures. Loosen subsoil prior to spreading topsoil by surface roughening measures. Alternatively, cutting topsoil sods, storing, and maintaining them maintains soil biota and permits rapid reestablishment of natural vegetative cover.	Not recommended on slopes greater than 2:1. Place stockpiles in areas that will not obstruct natural drainage or cause off-site damage.

Ronald B. Sawhill, University of Georgia, College of Environment and Design, Athens, Georgia

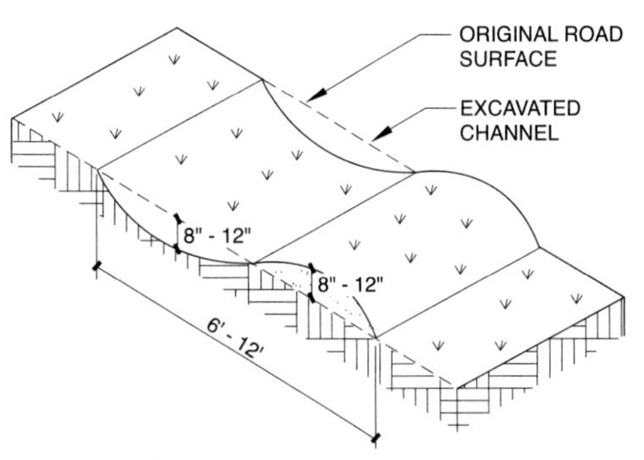

DIVERSION

Source: From the Georgia Soil and Water Conservation Commission manuals, 2000, 2002.

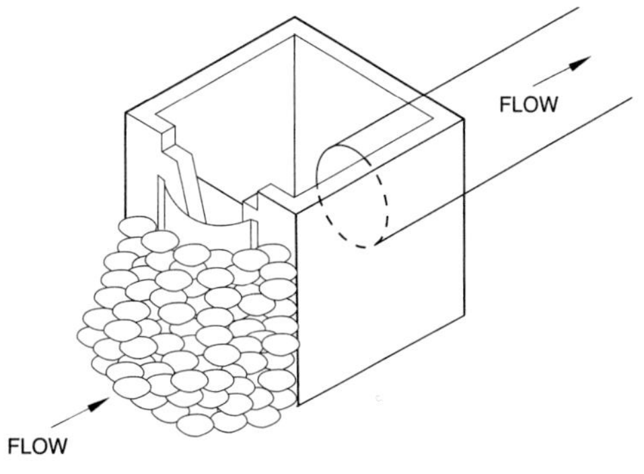

HALF-ROUND PIPE RETROFIT

Source: From the Georgia Soil and Water Conservation Commission manuals, 2000, 2002.

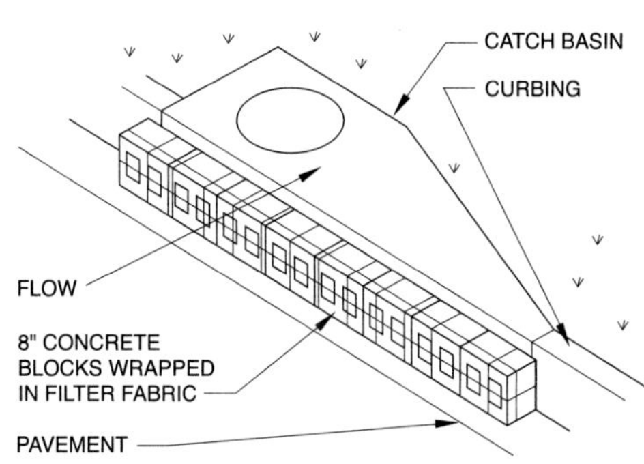

PIGS-IN-A-BLANKET SEDIMENT TRAP

Source: From the Georgia Soil and Water Conservation Commission manuals, 2000, 2002.

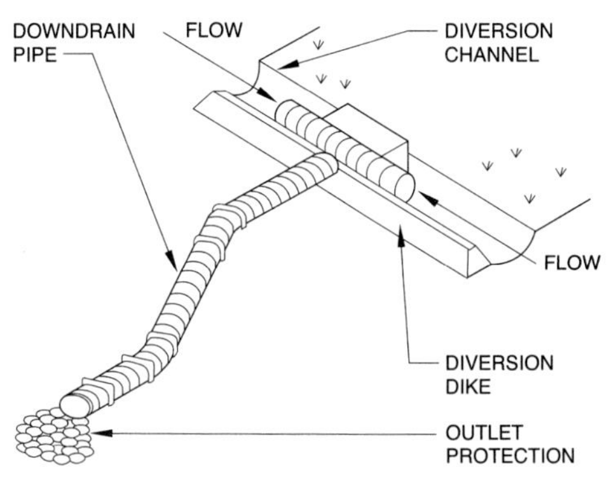

TEMPORARY DOWNDRAIN

Source: From the Georgia Soil and Water Conservation Commission manuals, 2000, 2002.

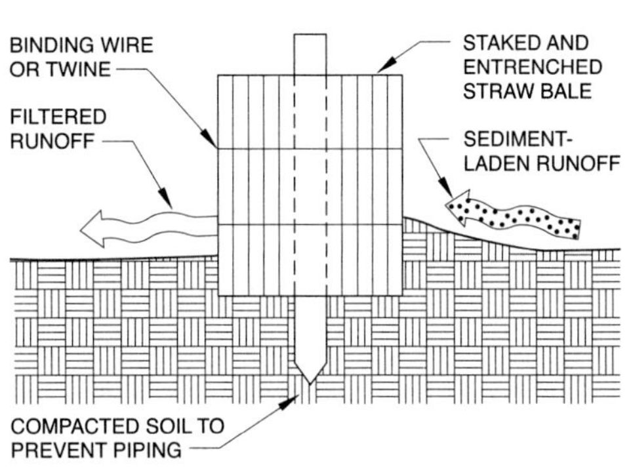

HAY BALE SEDIMENT BARRIER

Source: From the Georgia Soil and Water Conservation Commission manuals, 2000, 2002.

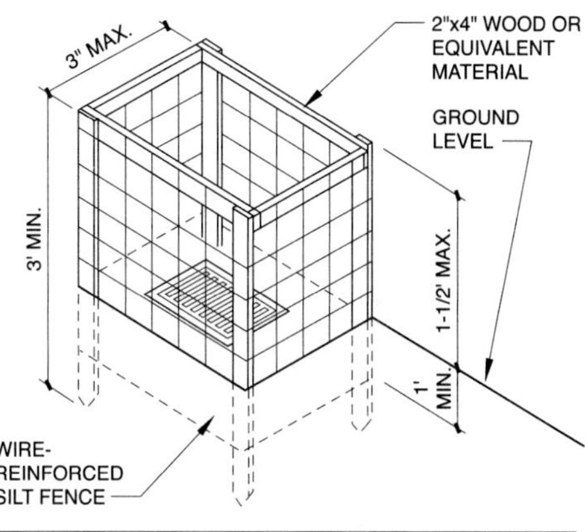

FABRIC AND FRAME SEDIMENT TRAP

Source: From the Georgia Soil and Water Conservation Commission manuals, 2000, 2002.

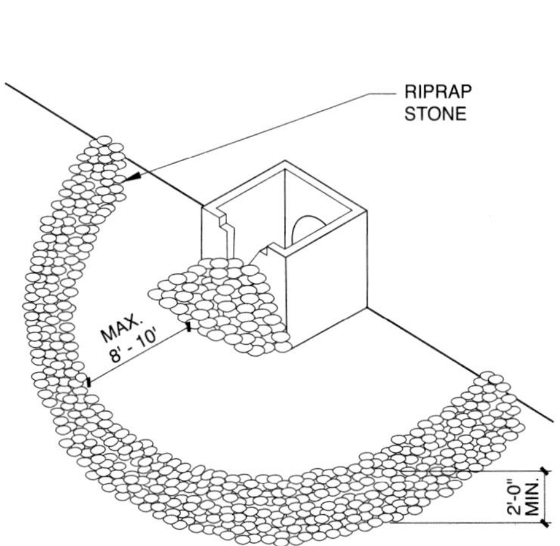

FILTER RING

Source: From the Georgia Soil and Water Conservation Commission manuals, 2000, 2002.

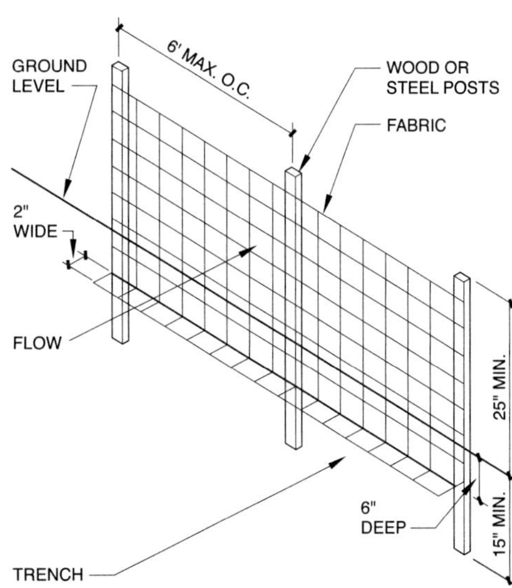

SILT FENCE

Source: From the Georgia Soil and Water Conservation Commission manuals, 2000, 2002.

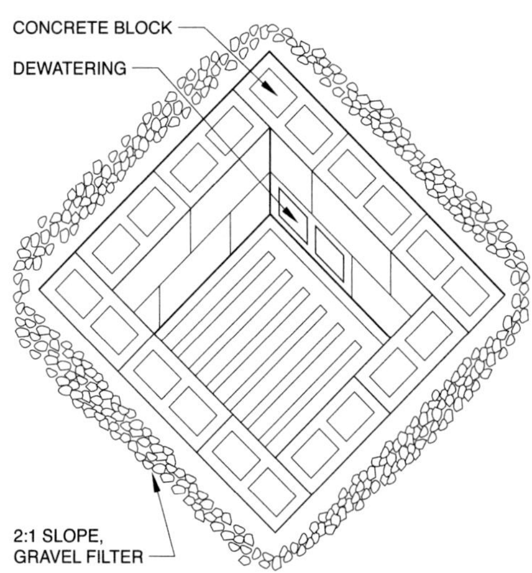

BLOCK AND GRAVEL SEDIMENT TRAP

Source: From the Georgia Soil and Water Conservation Commission manuals, 2000, 2002.

Ronald B. Sawhill, University of Georgia, College of Environment and Design, Athens, Georgia

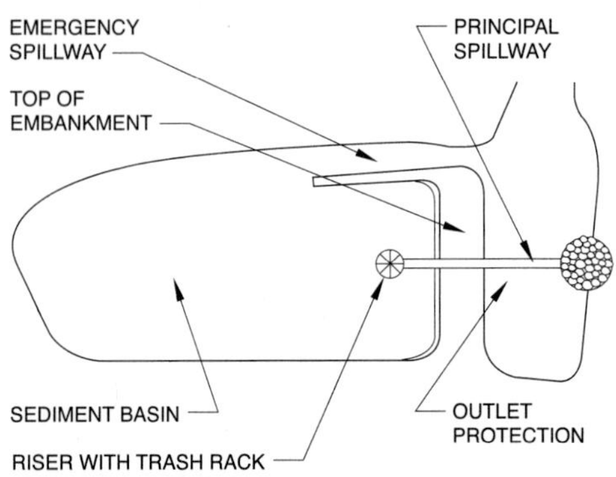

SEDIMENT BASIN PLAN

Source: From the Georgia Soil and Water Conservation Commission manuals, 2000, 2002.

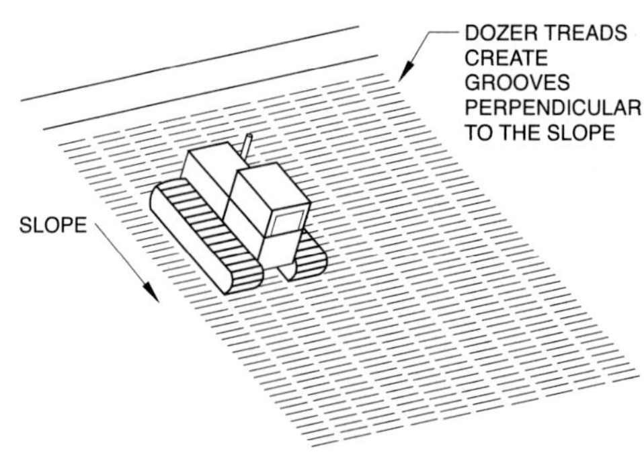

TRACK ROUGHENING

Source: From the Georgia Soil and Water Conservation Commission manuals, 2000, 2002.

Sedimentation: The settlement of suspended soil particles out of wind or water.

Sediment control: Management practices applied to encourage deposition of sediments before they can leave a disturbed site.

National Pollutant Discharge Elimination System (NPDES): This program requires all operators of construction sites sized 1 acre or larger to participate by providing specific documentation, typically including the Land Disturbing Activity Plan (described below) and active monitoring of all stormwater discharges from the site.

Vegetative stabilization: Establishment of vegetation on over 70 percent of a disturbed site area.

LAND-DISTURBING ACTIVITY PLAN

The Land-Disturbing Activity Plan is a document set specifying the types of erosion and sediment control measures, their locations, and the specific installation and maintenance practices to be followed for a given project. The plan typically includes soil erosion and sediment control plans indicating the locations of measures superimposed on site grading, drainage, utility, or other building construction plans. The most effective Land-Disturbing Activity Plan is one that has been integrated throughout the entire design process, resulting in a site plan that minimizes land disturbance by fitting the proposed use to the existing topography and soils. For the plan to be effective, it must minimize the size of the disturbed area, stabilize disturbed areas immediately, retain or safely accommodate runoff, retain sediment on the site, and protect existing watercourses from disturbance.

The Land-Disturbing Activity Plan includes a narrative component that describes the existing site conditions (land use, soil, topography, drainage, and vegetation), the proposed project and development phases, the proposed construction period and schedule of activities, and a detailed description of four major programs: the erosion control program, the sediment control program, the stormwater management program, and the maintenance program. All standards, details, and specifications are included in the document set and are typically required to be housed at the construction site on a 24-hour basis.

The permitting process for land disturbance may vary from site to site, based on local, state, and federal jurisdictional authorities. Any land disturbance proposed within or adjacent to watercourses, wetlands, other water bodies, or shorelines will require permitting through state and federal authorities. Make significant time allowances in planning for the permitting process.

SOIL EROSION AND SEDIMENT CONTROL MEASURES

A wide variety of vegetative and structural measures may be used to limit erosion and prevent the transport of sediment off a disturbed site. The following measures are commonly referred to as soil erosion and sediment control measures, but are described in detail in other sections of this book:

- *Buffer zone.* A vegetated strip surrounding disturbed areas or along water body margins.
- *Streambank stabilization.* Vegetative and structural practices to prevent or reduce bank erosion.
- *Check dam.* A temporary structure to control concentrated stormwater flows in channels.
- *Channel stabilization.* The creation, improvement, or stabilization of channels for safe conveyance.
- *Stream diversion channel.* A temporary channel to conduct flow around construction in a stream.
- *Permanent downdrain.* A concrete or half-pipe sectional flume to conduct flows safely down slopes.
- *Grade stabilization structure.* A permanent structure designed to accommodate vertical grade change in natural or man-made channels.
- *Level spreader.* A zero gradient device used to convert concentrated flow into broad overland sheet flow.
- *Rock filter dam.* A temporary or permanent dam used in streams or drainage channels to filter sediment and slow flow velocity.
- *Retaining wall.* A structural method to reduce slope face exposure to erosive forces.
- *Storm drain outlet protection.* Typically, a rock or concrete device to reduce stormwater velocity and channel erosion at pipe outlets.
- *Vegetated waterway.* A vegetated channel designed for stable nonerosive flows.

These measures, plus those described in the following tables, provide a palette of possible solutions to specific site conditions. Numerous trade products have been introduced that can simplify the installation and/or maintenance of many soil erosion and sediment control measures. Application of some measures varies by region; refer to local and state standards for specific requirements, limitations, or regional adaptations. Most states have a manual of soil erosion and sediment control standards specifically tailored to regional conditions.

USEFUL WEBSITES

Videos of some erosion and sediment control devices can be found at:
www.greenworks.tv/stormwater/videotopics.htm.

National Pollutant Discharge Elimination System information can be found at:
http://cfpub.epa.gov/npdes/home.cfm?program_id=6

REFERENCES

Georgia Soil and Water Conservation Commission. 2000. *Manual for Erosion and Sediment Control in Georgia*, 5th ed. Athens, GA : State Soil & Water Conservation Commission. http://gaswcc.org/PDF/green_book_5ed.pdf.

———. 2002. *Field Manual for Erosion and Sediment Control in Georgia*, 4th ed. http://gaswcc.org/docs/field_manual_4ed.pdf.

See also:
Site Construction Overview
Stormwater Management

Ronald B. Sawhill, University of Georgia, College of Environment and Design, Athens, Georgia

RESTORATION AND REMEDIATION

ECOLOGICAL COMMUNITY RESTORATION

Ecological restoration" is defined as "an intentional activity that initiates or accelerates the recovery of an ecosystem with respect to its health, integrity, and sustainability.... Restoration attempts to return an ecosystem to its historic trajectory" (SER Primer, 2002). This widely accepted definition of ecological restoration assumes that we know what came before and what would have followed had degradation, damage, or transformation of the landscape not been wrought by human activity.

Though widely accepted, there is, nevertheless, an ongoing debate on the strengths and shortcomings of this definition, as delineated by Allison (2004), who concludes, based on the work of many others, that restoration of an ecosystem to a natural or pristine state is an unobtainable goal. Rather, restoration means returning the land to a former state, which humans decide is a better condition for our own health, integrity, and sustainability.

This definition recognizes the place of humans in and dependence on natural systems and, consequently, our responsibility to alleviate or minimize the dysfunction of ecosystems that arises from our need for natural resources. The definition also provides a pragmatic premise for the type of ecological restoration that can be readily embraced by landscape architects, who must work within an array of zoning/legal constraints, for a clientele with a wide range of development goals and with end goals that include an aesthetic restoration.

GOALS OF ECOLOGICAL COMMUNITY RESTORATION

Restoration is multifaceted in its intent, encompassing an array of biological, cultural, and economic goals. The benefits of ecological community restoration include the creation of a healthier environment for humans and a reduction in both the rate of habitat degradation and the loss of goods and services provided to us by natural systems. The limitations of ecological restoration are time, cost, and uncertainty of outcome.

The biological goal of restoration is to promote the development and maintenance of a functional and, therefore, healthy community of which humans are members. Success of the restored community can be measured in terms of its ability to be self-maintaining (intervention and maintenance are kept to a minimum), to recover from disturbance, and to achieve a biodiversity typical of the ecosystem emulated.

The cultural goal of restoration is to restore human connection to the environment so that we can embrace a long-term commitment for the support of healthy ecosystem functioning. This can be achieved through education, community organization, and design that incorporates aesthetics. Aesthetic engagement engenders attachment and the desire to protect (Nassauer, 1997). Cultural goals require that we go beyond what is delineated in a purely scientific approach to ecological community restoration. Without achievement of the cultural goal, whereby we choose to become caretakers of our resources, the design and installation of a restoration will not be sustainable.

The economic goal of restoration is to enable the restored ecosystem to provide the services and goods that ensure long-term success of the community. The ability of a healthy ecosystem to clean the air and water, to offer food and building goods, and to provide desirable space for physical and psychological shelter is the critical currency for all living things resident in that system.

DEGREES OF RESTORATION

The need for restoration spans a continuum from complete adjustment at highly degraded sites to simple management programs for nearly intact sites. This continuum of goals, ranging from true restoration (for a self-sustaining system) to partial restoration, has been identified as follows. It is important to decide which type of restoration is intended in order to keep design goals clear.

1. "Rehabilitation" is restoration that aims to repair particular ecosystem processes (e.g., alter stormwater routing to reestablish on-site infiltration), or to reinstate goods (e.g., replant a garden for architecture and resources that attract wildlife) or services (e.g., improve air and water quality through plant establishment). However, it does not aim to restore a community's full structure and function.
2. "Reclamation" is the restoration of mining or industrial wastelands. The aim is to stabilize the land, to revegetate (usually with minimal species diversity), and to provide public safety and aesthetic value so that the land may return to useful purpose.
3. "Creation/fabrication" occurs by the restoration of a site that has been entirely voided, often through urban or industrial uses. The reference ecosystem chosen as the basis of the restoration is often different from the original one present, due to constraints of location or history.
4. "Ecological engineering" is the restoration of some portion of a site using natural materials, living organisms, and aspects of the natural physical-chemical processes to solve technical problems (e.g., streambank restoration with planted willows).
5. "Superficial mimicry" intends to inspire/educate, but does not design for system function, and so often requires high maintenance. For example, a planting design specifies native species of an ecosystem without regard to appropriate hydrological state, soils, and soil microbes, or successional stage of the contextual landscape. To the degree that ecosystem function is not established, high maintenance is the only way to keep the project aesthetically appealing.

ORGANIZATION OF AN ECOLOGICAL COMMUNITY

If the goal of the restoration is the establishment or promotion of a healthy ecological community, it is necessary to understand the key components and processes involved. A community is defined by the biota (living things) found on the site and delineated by the restoration project, be it a half-acre or 10,000 acres. The site provides the community's infrastructure, including hydrological, climatic, and soils components. The sum total of the living things, the physical infrastructure, and all their interactions dictate the community's biodiversity. The ability of a community to increase and maintain its biodiversity will depend on the ability of its typical ecosystem processes to occur.

One such typical ecosystem process is "disturbance." For example, allowing fallen logs or plant litter to remain on the site promotes biodiversity by providing habitat (for decomposers and ground-dwelling animals) and through the promotion of no-cost nutrient recycling.

The role of disturbance in an ecological community restoration design is most often accommodated in a management plan that includes emulation of natural disturbance events (e.g., periodic fire or leaving plant litter where it falls). Planned disturbances can be managed in a way that accommodates many different aesthetic goals (Nassauer 1995). For example, the management plan may address the issue of tidiness (e.g., for a site that includes a formal garden area) by collecting plant litter, composting, and returning it to the source area as nutritional mulch.

The size of a project and the character of neighboring land will determine how many ecosystems must be considered when developing a restoration plan. Most often, ecological community restoration involves a single ecosystem type such as grassland, forest, or river. However, the community to be restored may include many different types of ecosystems as size of the project site increases.

When a project site includes multiple ecosystems, additional consideration must be given to the unique characteristics that occur at the border ("ecotone") of two ecosystems. Ecotones have greater biodiversity than exists in either adjoining ecosystem. Because these edge areas maintain a source of replacements for each adjoining ecosystem, both ecosystems are more resilient to unexpected disturbance. Consequently, the development of designs that create or enhance ecotones is the most commonly available and cost-effective avenue to restoration for landscape architects. A typical location for ecotone development is at the cusp between a lawn/field and woodland border.

COMPONENTS OF RESTORATION DESIGN

Although planting design is often central to restoration efforts, the design must also attend to hydrology, soil composition, and support of those animals and

MaryCarol Hunter, University of Michigan, School of Natural Resources

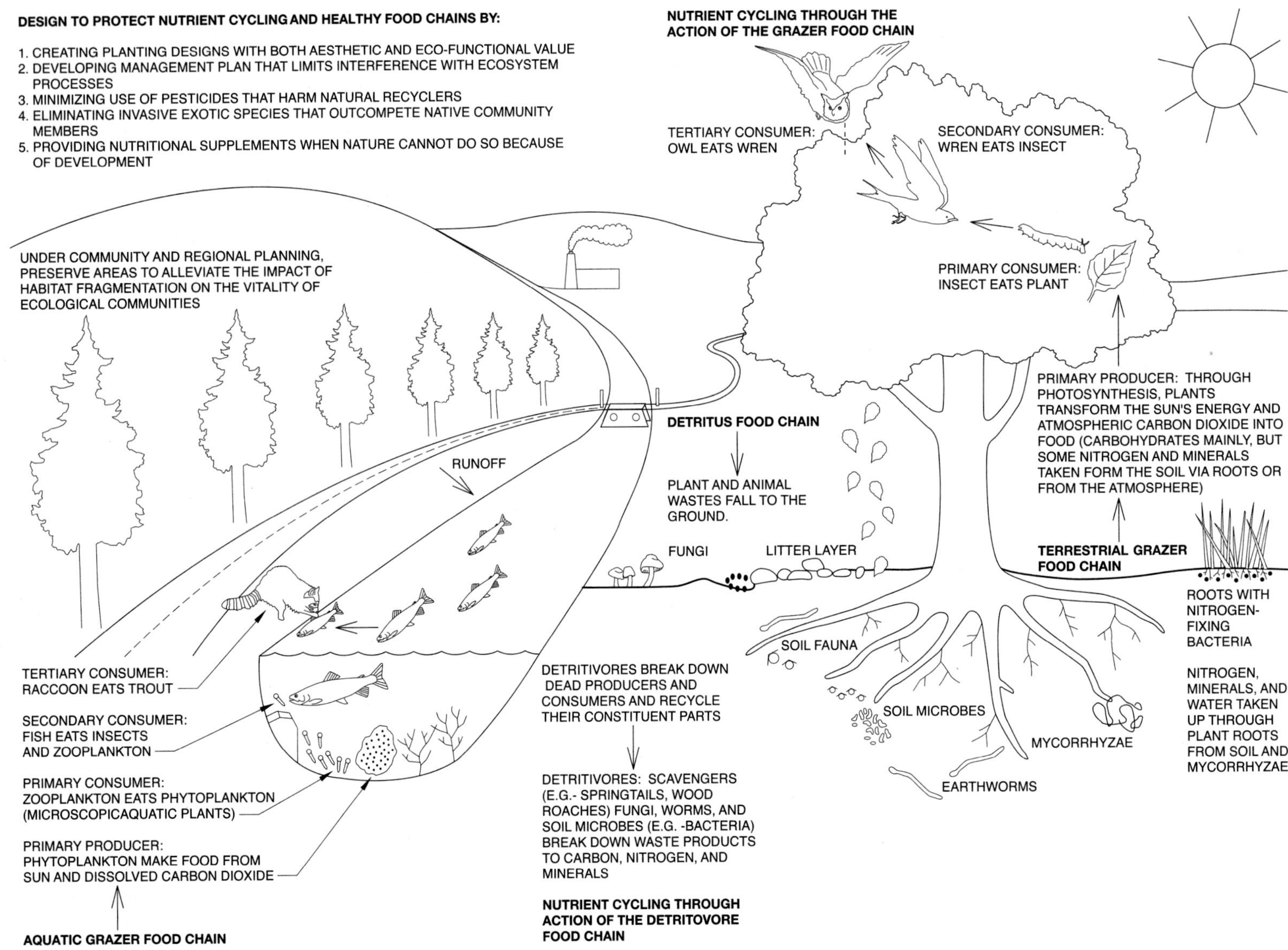

COMMUNITY RESTORATION DESIGN TO ACCOMMODATE CRITICAL ECOSYSTEM PROCESSES

microbes required for healthy ecosystem function. In other words, the design must accommodate those ecosystem processes that are essential to its sustainability. Collaborative work or consultation with ecologists, soil scientists, engineers, and other restoration specialists is recommended for all types of restoration, because the field of restoration is still new and rapidly evolving.

Because our knowledge about how an ecological community operates is far from complete, it is in our best interest, both economically and environmentally, to design in a way that optimizes natural regenerative processes (Sauer, 1998). This facilitation begins with the appropriate choice of a reference ecosystem(s) for the restoration area, be it a backyard or an abandoned industrial area.

Choice of a Reference System

The goal of the restoration project should guide the decision as to which natural community will be used as reference. A project may require multiple reference systems when a community includes multiple ecosystems or a project has a diverse set of restoration goals (White and Walker, 1997). The geographic and environmental context of the project site should be the focal criterion for choice of a reference system(s). Otherwise, the restoration will require a costly, intensive management program.

Gaining knowledge about the chosen reference system often requires consultation with ecologists, anthropologists (for cultural landscape restoration), and local experts. For natural reference systems, an excellent starting point can be found in the restoration compendium by Harker and colleagues (1999). This volume provides extensive data on the ecological character and plant species composition for each of the dominant ecological community types found within each of 30 natural regions that make up the continental United States, such as the Juniper-Pinon Woodland in the Colorado Plateau region or the wet meadow in the Southern Great Lakes. Moreover, each dominant ecological community is assigned to its appropriate ecological restoration type (e.g., woodlands and meadowlands, respectively), with information on how to restore that particular community. Data covers typical site conditions (climate, soils, topography, and hydrology), keys to successful site preparation and plant choice, as well as suggestions for maintenance and management programs, including the nature and application of the community's required disturbance regime.

Hydrology, Soils, and Topography

In some cases, hydrological design will take center stage in a restoration design. This is most obviously the case for the restoration of wetland ecosystems (streams, rivers, ponds, lakes, and terrestrial wetlands). Since permanent irrigation is absent in restoration designs (except superficial mimicry), landscape architects must evaluate how the movement and infiltration of rainfall will affect longevity of community members, and adjust the design accordingly. For example, rainfall infiltration areas can be added through planting

MaryCarol Hunter, University of Michigan, School of Natural Resources

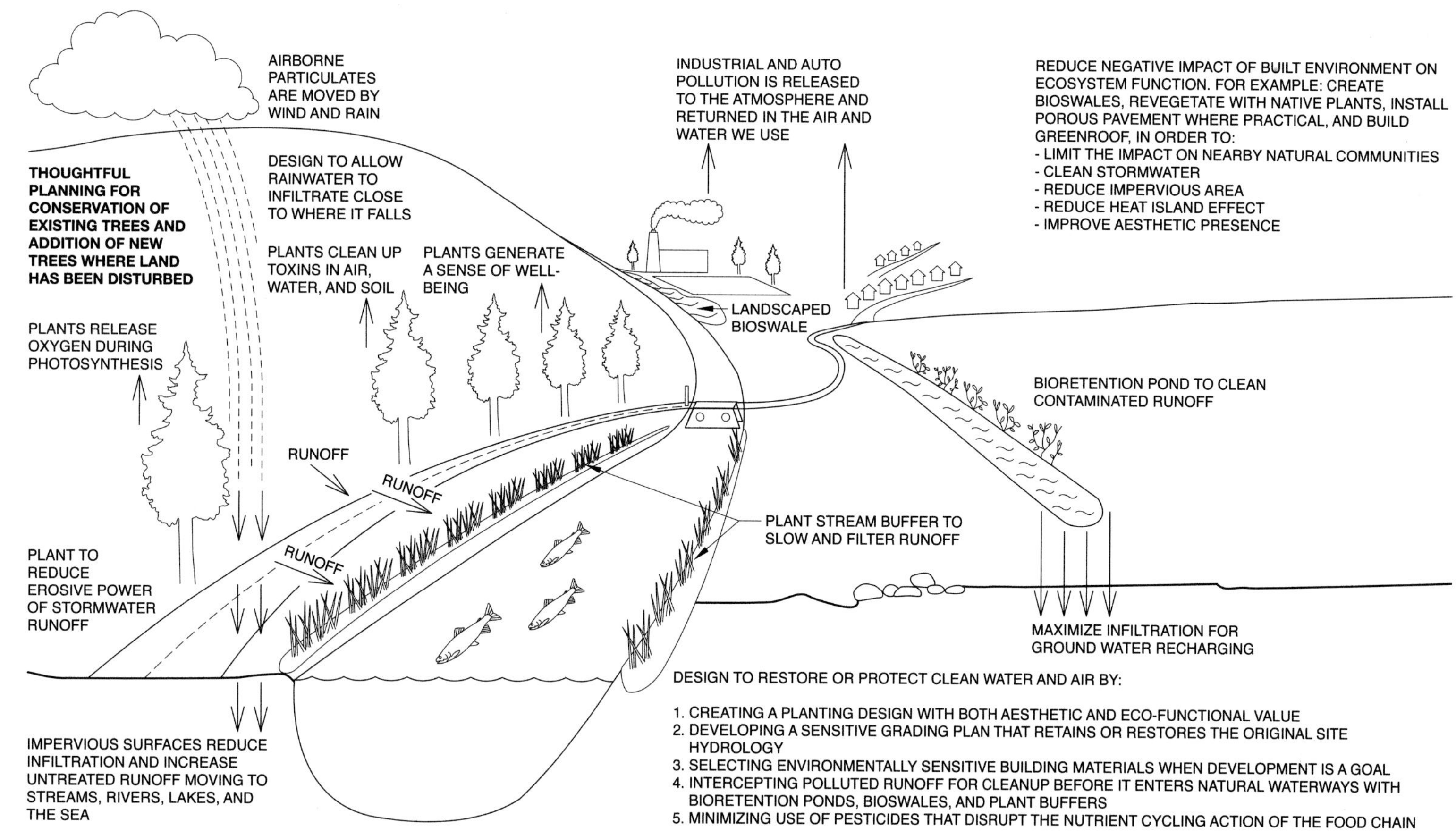

AIRBORNE PARTICULATES ARE MOVED BY WIND AND RAIN

INDUSTRIAL AND AUTO POLLUTION IS RELEASED TO THE ATMOSPHERE AND RETURNED IN THE AIR AND WATER WE USE

REDUCE NEGATIVE IMPACT OF BUILT ENVIRONMENT ON ECOSYSTEM FUNCTION. FOR EXAMPLE: CREATE BIOSWALES, REVEGETATE WITH NATIVE PLANTS, INSTALL POROUS PAVEMENT WHERE PRACTICAL, AND BUILD GREENROOF, IN ORDER TO:
- LIMIT THE IMPACT ON NEARBY NATURAL COMMUNITIES
- CLEAN STORMWATER
- REDUCE IMPERVIOUS AREA
- REDUCE HEAT ISLAND EFFECT
- IMPROVE AESTHETIC PRESENCE

THOUGHTFUL PLANNING FOR CONSERVATION OF EXISTING TREES AND ADDITION OF NEW TREES WHERE LAND HAS BEEN DISTURBED

DESIGN TO ALLOW RAINWATER TO INFILTRATE CLOSE TO WHERE IT FALLS

PLANTS CLEAN UP TOXINS IN AIR, WATER, AND SOIL

PLANTS GENERATE A SENSE OF WELL-BEING

LANDSCAPED BIOSWALE

PLANTS RELEASE OXYGEN DURING PHOTOSYNTHESIS

BIORETENTION POND TO CLEAN CONTAMINATED RUNOFF

RUNOFF

RUNOFF

RUNOFF

PLANT STREAM BUFFER TO SLOW AND FILTER RUNOFF

PLANT TO REDUCE EROSIVE POWER OF STORMWATER RUNOFF

MAXIMIZE INFILTRATION FOR GROUND WATER RECHARGING

DESIGN TO RESTORE OR PROTECT CLEAN WATER AND AIR BY:

1. CREATING A PLANTING DESIGN WITH BOTH AESTHETIC AND ECO-FUNCTIONAL VALUE
2. DEVELOPING A SENSITIVE GRADING PLAN THAT RETAINS OR RESTORES THE ORIGINAL SITE HYDROLOGY
3. SELECTING ENVIRONMENTALLY SENSITIVE BUILDING MATERIALS WHEN DEVELOPMENT IS A GOAL
4. INTERCEPTING POLLUTED RUNOFF FOR CLEANUP BEFORE IT ENTERS NATURAL WATERWAYS WITH BIORETENTION PONDS, BIOSWALES, AND PLANT BUFFERS
5. MINIMIZING USE OF PESTICIDES THAT DISRUPT THE NUTRIENT CYCLING ACTION OF THE FOOD CHAIN

IMPERVIOUS SURFACES REDUCE INFILTRATION AND INCREASE UNTREATED RUNOFF MOVING TO STREAMS, RIVERS, LAKES, AND THE SEA

DESIGNING TO RESTORE CLEAN AIR AND WATER TO THE COMMUNITY

ECOTONE RESTORATION: RETURN THE DEGRADED EDGES OF ADJOINING COMMUNITIES TO A DIVERSE PATCH HOLDING MEMBERS OF BOTH COMMUNITIES AND ADDITIONAL "EDGE" SPECIES. THIS EXAMPLE OCCURS AT THE INTERSECTION OF FIELD/LAWN AND WOODLAND COMMUNITIES.

ECOTONE RESTORATION DESIGN RE-CREATES THE STRUCTURAL AND FUNCTIONAL DIVERSITY NEEDED TO SUPPORT BIODIVERSITY AND HEALTH IN EACH ADJACENT COMMUNITY.

Re-create structural and functional diversity by restoring the degraded edges of adjoining communities to a condition that can be used by members of both communities as well as novel "edge" species.

FOREST/FIELD-LAWN ECOTONE RESTORATION

design and, where disturbance is not an issue, creation of small depressions in receiving areas.

If the soil has been altered through removal or degradation, the soil must be replaced or amended in order to match the kind of plant community that is being restored. The invisible underground members of the community, mostly soil arthropods and microbes, are the mainstay of the decomposition cycle. When this recycling is impeded, the cost of maintaining the site will be outrageously high. It is for this reason that many management practices (e.g., tilling, pesticide use, litter removal, routing of water to storm pipes) is ultimately counterproductive to community sustainability.

For information on the type of soil associated with specific plant communities, refer to the U.S. Soil Survey that is available for most counties in the country. Consult an agronomist, to determine which components will create the right mix. The vibrancy of the soil can be improved with the help of natural ecosystem processes. For example: plant a nitrogen-fixing cover crop such as clover for nutrient enrichment; introduce soil fauna for decomposition by introducing soil from a healthy site of the same community type; or introduce mycorrhizal fungi to improve the nutritional stores for specific tree species.

Finally, all restoration designs must include a soil and erosion control plan that protects the land on- and off-site from the devastation of clearing and earth moving. Also needed is a management plan for site protection from the elements and undesirable invasive species during the fragile early stages of restoration, which can last from months to years depending on the restoration design.

Plantings

From garden to parkland design, plants are pivotal to ecological community health, providing food and shelter, removing toxins from the air and stormwater, and supporting the community's diversity. To support the operations of the restored ecosystem, the planting palette should be selected to best enable a site to be self-sustaining and to sustain the animals associated with the ecosystem to be emulated.

Successful design for ecological community restoration relies on mimicking natural processes. The most popular approach to restoration is development of a design that mimics natural succession of the ecosystem in focus. Natural succession marks the developmental trajectory of an ecosystem through a series of "seral" stages, each typified by a characteristic set of organisms. In most cases, the actions during one seral stage

MaryCarol Hunter, University of Michigan, School of Natural Resources

prepare the site to be able to support the next seral stage and its cohort of different plant, animal, and microbial species. Examples of natural succession most often used for restoration by landscape architects include the sequence from field to forest.

This successional shift in species composition and characteristic energy flows can be altered by external disturbance coming from nature or humans. Disturbance can be used as part of the management plan for the restored site. For example, the transition from field to forest is impeded by the periodic use of fire to manage the ecosystem in a continuous grassland stage of natural succession. (See the "Change in Community Profile for Field-to-Forest Succession" figure.)

This example of "arrested succession" is seen in prairie restorations found most often in the midwestern United States. By contract, "accelerated succession" is a restoration method that speeds the community development through several seral stages. For example, a restoration design can include simultaneous plantings of grassland species along with early and late successional forest species

Support of a Community's Characteristic Wildlife

The restoration design should address the structure of the habitat. It is in this architecture that the nonfood needs of the community wildlife will be met. One approach is to select target wildlife species characteristic of the community type and determine the type of structure needed for rest, reproduction, and movement. Informal structures include brush piles, snags, and vernal pools. Formal structures include channels/tunnels for road crossings, and bird boxes to "get the community going" in the earliest stages of restoration.

Habitat degradation is almost always accompanied by the invasion of opportunistic species whose competitive ability is greatest under conditions of disturbance. The removal of invasive species, both native and exotic in origin, is the starting point of many rehabilitation projects. This restorative practice allows greater diversity in habitat architecture, food resources, and, subsequently, wildlife.

CHANGE IN COMMUNITY PROFILE FOR FIELD-TO-FOREST SUCCESSION

MaryCarol Hunter, University of Michigan, School of Natural Resources

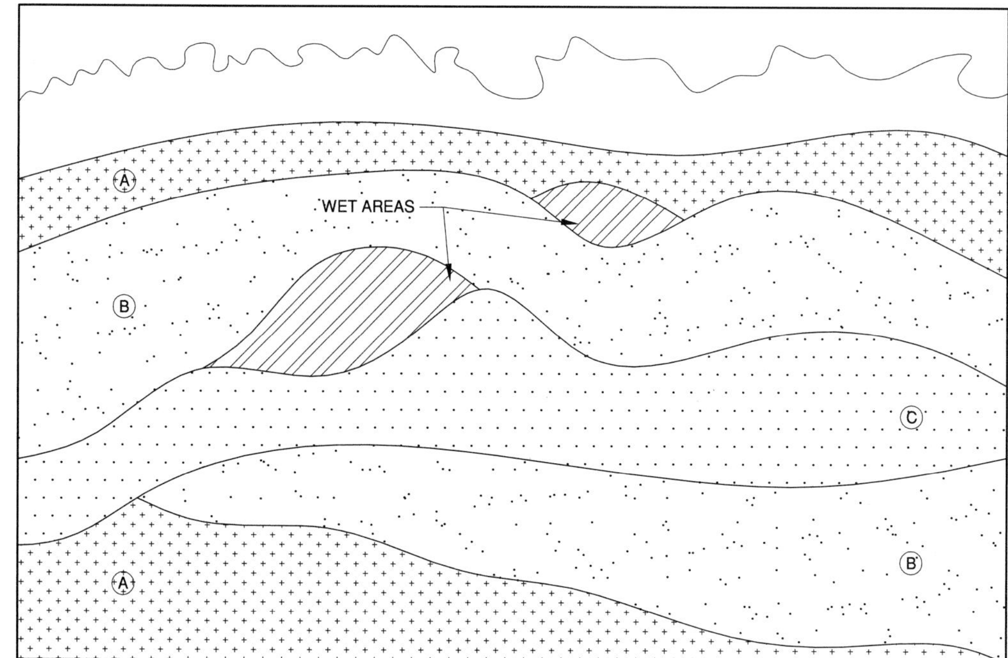

Develop a diverse meadow planting scheme to achieve an attractive color and texture sequence over the year. Here, areas A, B, and C are planted with their own unique mix of grass and flowering forb species, each suited to the microhabitat. Overall, visual continuity is achieved by including a select subset of species in more than one planting area.

AESTHETIC COMPONENT OF MEADOW RESTORATION DESIGN

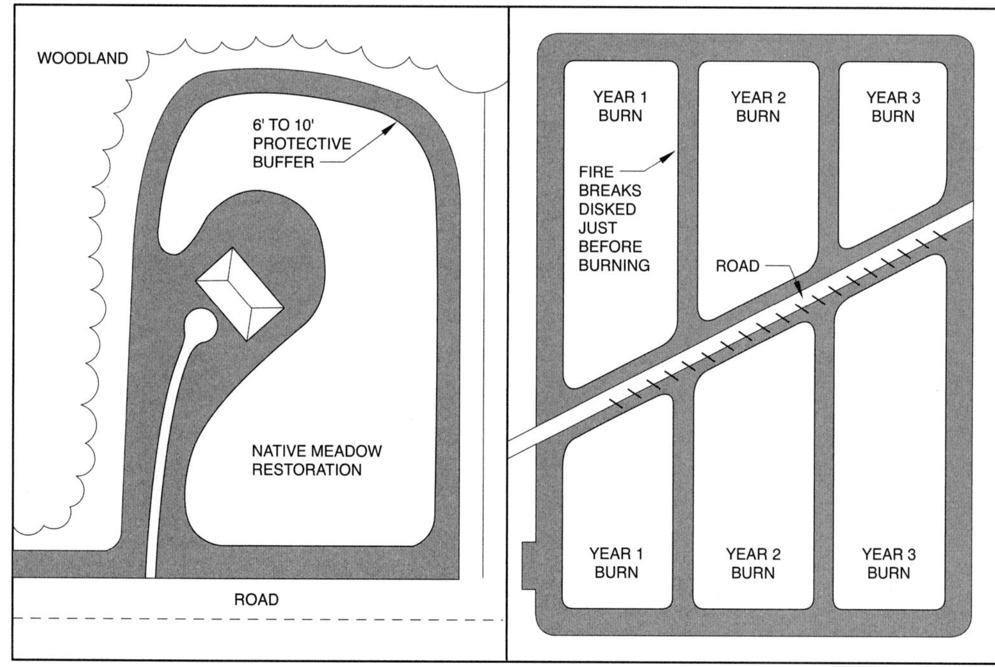

Buffers act as firebreaks for a field that is managed with fire. Location of buffers will depend on site size (small vs. large as above), contextual land use, and the type of management plan selected.

BUFFER DESIGN FOR ARRESTED SUCCESSION IN A MEADOW RESTORATION

MaryCarol Hunter, University of Michigan, School of Natural Resources

RESTORATION SEQUENCE: PLANNING AND DESIGN

A restoration design is developed from the bottom up. The physical infrastructure (hydrology, soils, and topography) is evaluated to determine if it can support the plant species found in the selected reference ecosystem(s). After appropriate adjustments, the plant community is established or upgraded through installation or natural colonization. The plants offer food and structural habitat that attracts and satisfies the needs of animals and beneficial microbes associated with the reference system.

There must be functional connectivity with other similar natural areas whenever natural colonization and replacement are part of the restoration plan. If connectivity does not exist, then members may have to be artificially introduced. The need for this intervention is more likely when the restoration site is detached and distant from neighboring healthy ecosystems of its type, as is often the case in intensely urban area.

Site Inventory: Physical

To conduct a physical site inventory, first characterize soils, hydrology, biota, and history of land use. Then decide the most appropriate ecosystem to use as a reference for the design of the restoration. This decision may require investigation of herbarium records, paleoecological samples (e.g., for pollen, fossils, charcoal traces), and historical accounts of land use, particularly if cultural practices (e.g., meadow burning) are responsible for maintaining the ecosystem.

Site Inventory: Aesthetic

To create a restoration design that provides the relevant aesthetic (*genus loci* of reference system), conduct an aesthetic site inventory by evaluating the sensory aspects of the ecological community used for reference. Personal experience within an existing and healthy version of the reference community is most desirable, but the evaluation can also be made using drawings, paintings, and written works that describe the sense of place. Restoration is, at this point in history, as much art as science for we have only a partial understanding of the system's operation. An aesthetic characterization allows intuitive knowledge to enhance what is discovered with the scientific method. (For an excellent discussion of the relationship between ecology and aesthetics in landscape management, see Sheppard and Harshaw, 2001.)

Planning

Planning necessitates the establishment of a set of restoration goals and specific objectives that resonate with the goals/needs of the human community, whose support is required for long-term success. Specifically:

- Develop a restoration plan within the context of what surrounds the site. No man is an island and neither is a restoration site. A restoration is always embedded in some landscape matrix, which is a network of adjoining ecosystems, including urban ecosystems. There are dynamic interactions among matrix members, particularly at their edges and via the river ecosystems that connect them. For this reason, a restoration design must account for landscape context. Where possible, plan for connectivity of the restored site with nearby natural areas to facilitate the transfer of energy,

ANNUAL MOWING AND SELECTIVE HERBICIDE TREATMENT OF WOODY AND INVASIVE SPECIES

ANNUAL MOWING AND BUSH HOGGING OF WOODY SPECIES EVERY 3 TO 5 YEARS

ANNUAL MOWING AND FIRE EVERY 3 TO 5 YEARS

FIRE ALONE: FIRE EVERY 3 TO 5 YEARS, BURNING NOT MORE THAN HALF THE SITE AT ONE TIME

SMALL | SIZE OF RESTORATION SITE | LARGE

MANAGEMENT APPROACH FOR NATURE MEADOW RESTORATIONS DEPENDS ON SIZE OF THE SITE AND MAINTENANCE BUDGET.

MANAGEMENT OPTIONS FOR ARRESTED SUCCESSION IN MEADOW RESTORATION

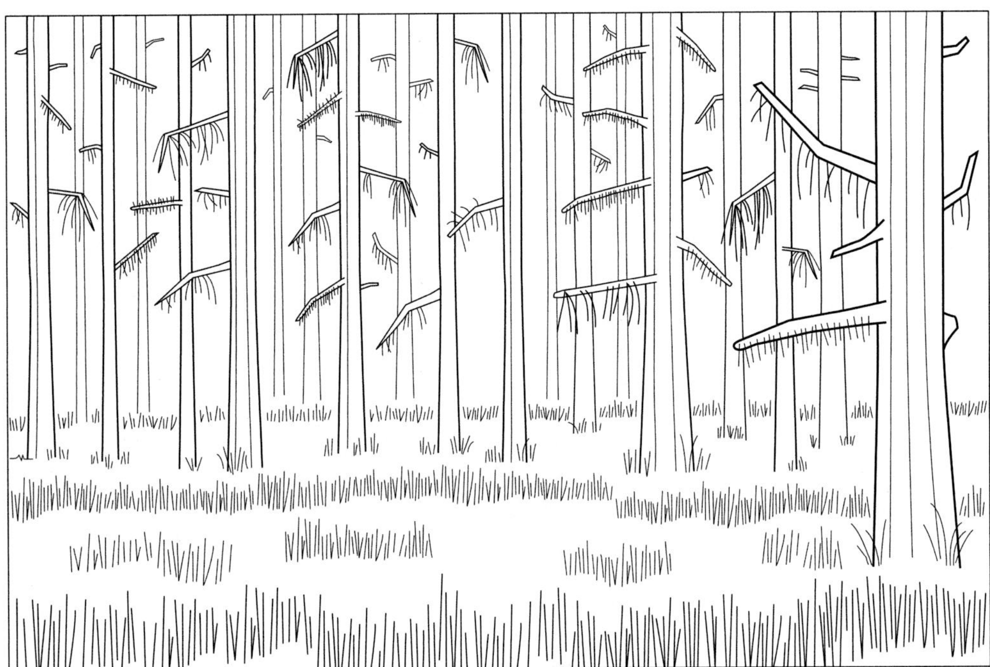

Design to capture the visual essence of the reference community. For example, the essence of a Longleaf Pine-Wiregrass Community can be expressed through verticality, high canopy, a low sea of grasses, and pines that vary in size and spacing.

CAPITALIZE ON AESTHETIC ASPECTS OF THE REFERENCE COMMUNITY

MaryCarol Hunter, University of Michigan, School of Natural Resources

nutrients, and community members with neighboring ecosystems.

- Establish infrastructure goals based on the discrepancy between existing and desirable hydrological function and soil profile. The desirable state is a physical environment that promotes survival and reproduction of all ecosystem species.
- Plan a strategy for achieving cultural engagement. Depending on the type of restoration this may include (a) aesthetic improvement to engage and please, (b) a program for community participation in the establishment and management of the restoration, and (c) an education program to make people aware of goods and services (e.g., improved air and water quality) afforded by the restoration.

There may be special ecological goals particular to the site, such as the provision of habitat for favorite bird species or the reestablishment of streamside vegetation. Such specific goals are often useful when an overabundance of design solutions is available for an ecological community restoration.

Design

A detailed site design must be developed based on the analysis of inventory and the project's restoration goals. Distinguishing features of the design for earth shaping and planting should be that of minimum intervention (unless the restoration is a creation/fabrication), and the establishment of an aesthetic presence that typifies the reference community. Overall, the design should facilitate those economically and ecologically sensible aspects of restoration—making the most of what is already present, minimizing unwanted disturbance during the restoration, and doing nothing to inhibit natural processes of restoration. Finally, the design should include an outreach program, to solicit and maintain the support and engagement of the human community responsible for the long-term success of the restoration.

Administration

Effective administration requires that schedules be developed, labor and equipment needs be determined, budgets be itemized, potential funding sources be identified, and information required for permits be ascertained.

Monitoring Success of Restoration

To monitor the success of a restoration project, performance standards must be developed for each of the project's goals, followed by the development of protocols for monitoring and evaluating the success of the goals. Evaluation can be done by comparing before-and-after conditions over set time intervals, such as species presence, water quality, aesthetic appeal, economic impact, and degree of community support/participation. Data on species composition and abundance can be used to calculate biodiversity and to determine the presence/absence of reference system species that provide critical functions for community maintenance. The presence of these species is essential for containing management costs.

Long-Term Management Plan

A long-term management plan will be necessary for keeping the restoration goal on track, including a method of redefining both methods and goals should the product take an unexpected ecological trajectory. The time frame for overall achievement is highly vari-

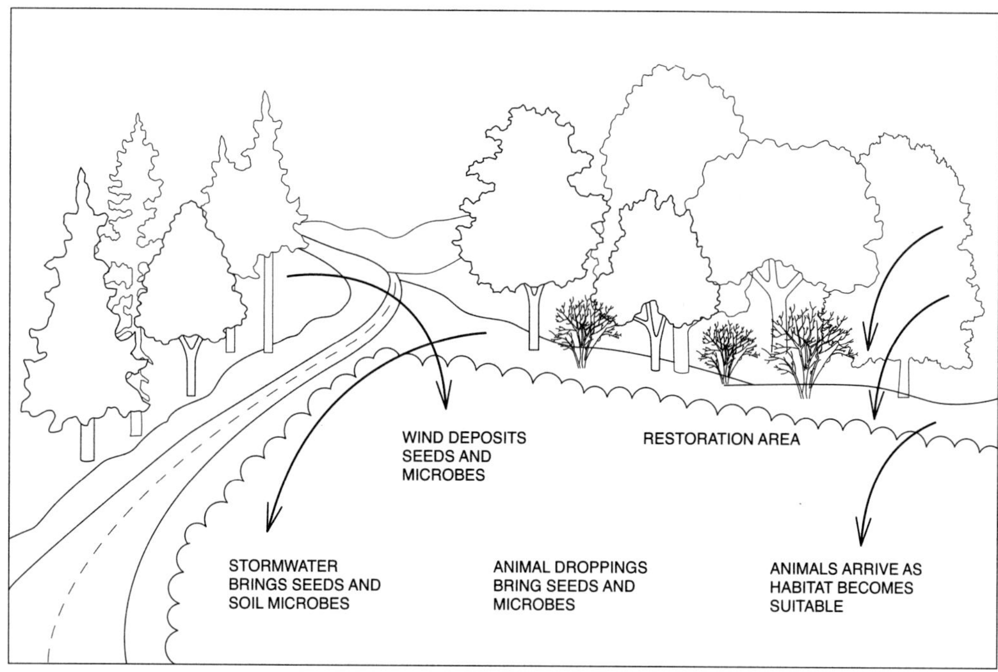

Develop a restoration plan that encourages natural recruitment of plants, microbes, and animals typical of later successional stages of the reference community.

CONNECTIVITY AMONG ECOSYSTEMS WITHIN LANDSCAPE MATRIX

able, ranging from a few years to decades, depending on the degree of intervention at the outset and the type of reference ecosystem emulated.

REFERENCES

Allison, S. K. 2004. "What Do We Mean When We Talk About Ecological Restoration?" *Ecological Restoration,* 22:281–286

Harker, D., G. Libby, K. Harker, S. Evans, and M. Evans. 1999. *Landscape Restoration Handbook,* 2nd ed. New York: Lewis Publishers.

Nassauer, J. 1995. "Messy Ecosystems, Orderly Frames." *Landscape Journal,* 14(2):161–170.

——— (ed.). 1997. *Placing Nature: Culture in Landscape Ecology.* Washington, DC: Island Press.

Sauer, L. J. 1998. *The Once and Future Forest: A Guide to Forest Restoration Strategies.* Washington, DC: Island Press.

Sheppard, S. R. J., and H. W. Harshaw (eds). 2001. *Forests and Landscapes: Linking Ecology, Sustainability and Aesthetics.* IUFRO Research Series No. 6. Wallingford, UK: CABI Publishing.

Society for Ecological Restoration Science & Policy Working Group (SER). 2002. *SER Primer on Ecological Restoration.* www.ser.org.

White, P. S., and J. L. Walker. 1997. "Approximating Nature's Variation: Selecting and Using Reference Information in Restoration Ecology," *Restoration Ecology* 5:338–349.

MaryCarol Hunter, University of Michigan, School of Natural Resources

BROWNFIELDS REMEDIATION AND DEVELOPMENT

Brownfields remediation and development is concerned with the renewal of brownfield sites that, by virtue of their past industrial uses, are now contaminated but able to be regenerated through a combination of environmental cleanup techniques coupled with development and reuse approaches. One of the consequences of the industrialization processes since the mid-nineteenth and predominantly in the first half of the twentieth century is the production of land that remains despoiled, in one manner or another, long after the occupants have moved on. Major cities, industrial towns, and residential communities have as part of their built fabric abandoned railroad yards, the sites of obsolete manufacturing gas plants, disused factories, closed landfills, and other brownfield lands, often in valuable locations for future use and adjacent to or within centers of population. Methods are sought to clean up the despoiled sites, and a range of remediation techniques are employed by specialized contractors.

This activity engages the landscape architect in addressing environmental engineering techniques for contaminated soil, sediment and water removal, disposal or alteration, and their relationship to the reshaping, revegetation, and further reprogramming of the site. As the economic, social, cultural, ecological, and other potentials of these sites become more fully recognized, new projects and uses are proposed and plans for redevelopment are drawn up returning them once again to potentially productive use.

This is both a new and an old activity. It is old because the process of recycling land has been going on since antiquity. It is new because of the relative magnitude and exotic nature and mixture of the pollutants involved today, and therefore, the landscape remediation technologies, interdisciplinary planning, and design strategies required by the development team, as well as creative landscape site programs required for their rectification and reuse.

REMEDIATION

A wide range of remediation approaches and techniques are available to the engineering team in approaching the renewal of a contaminated site. Three main categories of remediation technologies are identified:

- *Established.* Treatment technologies for which costs and performance information is readily available. Examples: removal, incineration, solidification, pump and treat.
- *Innovative.* Alternative treatment technologies whose routine use on Superfund and similar sites is inhibited by lack of data on performance and cost. Current limited full-scale application. Examples: thermal desorption and soil washing.
- *Emerging.* Alternative treatment technologies whose routine use on remediation sites is inhibited by lack of data and evaluation of claims. Current laboratory, test plot, and full-scale pilot site testing. Example: phytoremediation.

The evaluation of these remediation technologies is based on the following criteria.

- Protection of human health and the environment
- Compliance with environmental statutes
- Long-term effectiveness and permanence
- Reduction of toxicity, mobility, and volume
- Short-term effectiveness
- Implementability
- Cost
- State acceptance
- Community acceptance

The cleanup of a brownfield site relies on a number of factors in the remediation phase; the most significant for the landscape architect to consider is the overall result of the remediation activities—the desired effectiveness of the method and the relevant cleanup standard(s). The standards arise from an assessment of the risk to human and environmental receptors and the maximum published detectable limits allowable established by federal agencies for each contaminant type. The environmental engineer or licensed site professional will carry out a thorough analysis of the existing site conditions and environmental factors. Following the analysis, a remediation plan will be drawn up that outlines the most effective and expedient method of addressing the environmental contamination on-site to provide no significant risk or significant hazard. The remedial action can range from no action or the removal of a modest amount of soil with limited disturbance to the site and its eventual redevelopment, at one end, to large-scale engineering works that demolish derelict buildings and remove significant sections of site topsoils, and the underlying subgrade for *in-situ* or *ex-situ* treatment. A shorter list of remediation techniques follows:

- Product recovery
- Bioremediation
- Bioventing
- Land farming
- Slurry phase biological treatment
- Natural attenuation
- Stabilization/solidification
- Soil washing
- Soil vapor extraction
- Thermal desorption
- Air sparging
- Permeable reaction walls
- Phytoremediation

Remediation equipment and supporting facilities, including portable testing laboratories, protective storage areas, and project offices, can be a significant presence on the site as can permanent remediation treatments such as encapsulation of soils and pump and treatment facilities to cleanse polluted groundwater that may have been in place for up to 50 years.

Four general approaches to remediation are commonly found: full cleanup, part cleanup (on-site), part cleanup (in place), and full concealment, as outlined here:

Full Cleanup

- Complete soil excavation and removal to licensed landfill
- Complete dewatering and removal of ponds, pools, and lagoons; cleaning of sediment layer
- Extraction and removal of underground plumes

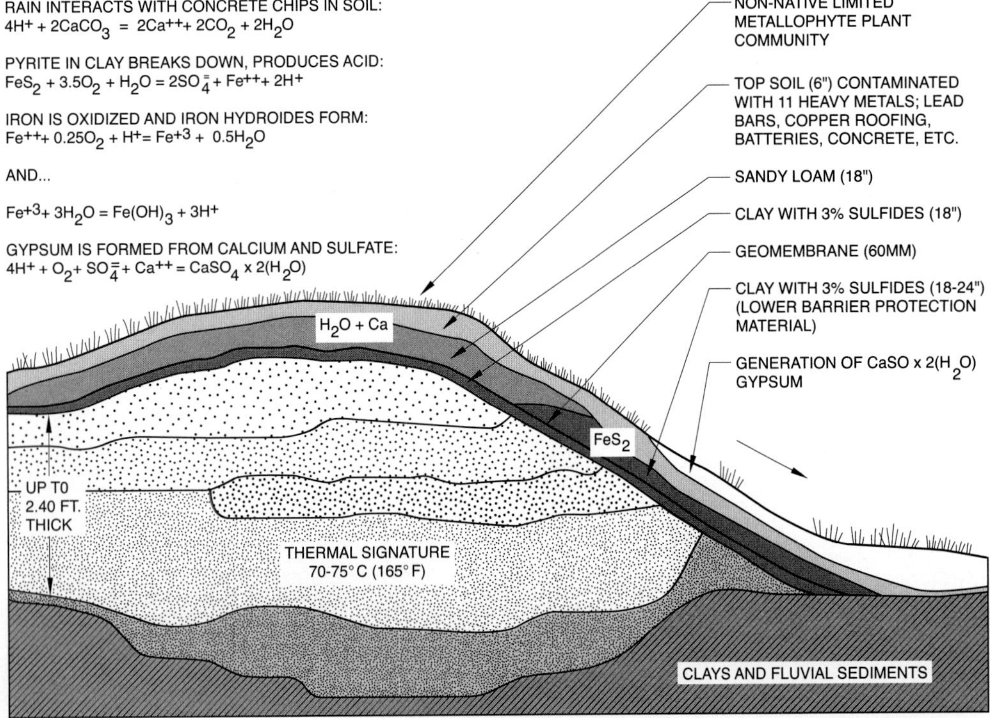

FRESH KILLS LANDFILL, STATEN ISLAND, NY

Source: Applied Ecological Services, Inc., Brodhead, Wisconsin

Niall Kirkwood, Harvard University Graduate School of Design

Part Cleanup (On-Site)

- *Ex-situ* remediation treatments
  - Physical methods
    Incineration
    Thermal desorption
    Soil vapor extraction
  - Chemical methods
    Soil washing
    Solidification/stabilization
    Dehalogenation
    Oxidation
  - Biological
    Land farming
      Bioreactors
      Phytoremediation

Part Cleanup (In Place)

- *In-situ* remediation treatments
  - Physical methods
    Soil vapor extraction
    Containment systems/barriers
    Pump and treat
    Electroreclamation
  - Chemical methods
    Soil flushing
    Solidification/stabilization
    Oxidation
  - Biological
    Bioremediation
      Phytoremediation

Full Concealment

- Engineered cover systems to conceal contamination in place
- Clay capping/geotextile and clean soil coverage
- Site encapsulation in purpose-designed structures
- Slurry walls/encasement

The landscape architect should be familiar with and comprehend the selected overall site remediation strategy in relation to the existing landscape conditions and the proposed planning reuse and site layout. These include site opportunities and constraints arising from the demolition or partial removal of site structures, including existing buildings, roads, and infrastructure; the dredging or filling of canals, ponds, and lagoons; the stockpiling of waste material to be removed off-site, as well as the disturbance to plant and wildlife communities, where appropriate. In addition, the removal of natural features such as topsoil, subgrade layers, vegetation, and the placement of excavations, test pits, monitoring wells, and areas housing on-site remediation equipment need to be taken into account, particularly for equipment that is to remain.

DEVELOPMENT

Brownfields development is a central part of the following landscape conditions:

- The existing site and surrounding land and waterways have been detrimentally affected by the former industrial uses or practices on the site.
- The site is abandoned, derelict, or underused because of changes in industrial production and/or on-site environmental problems.
- The site has real or perceived contamination problems.

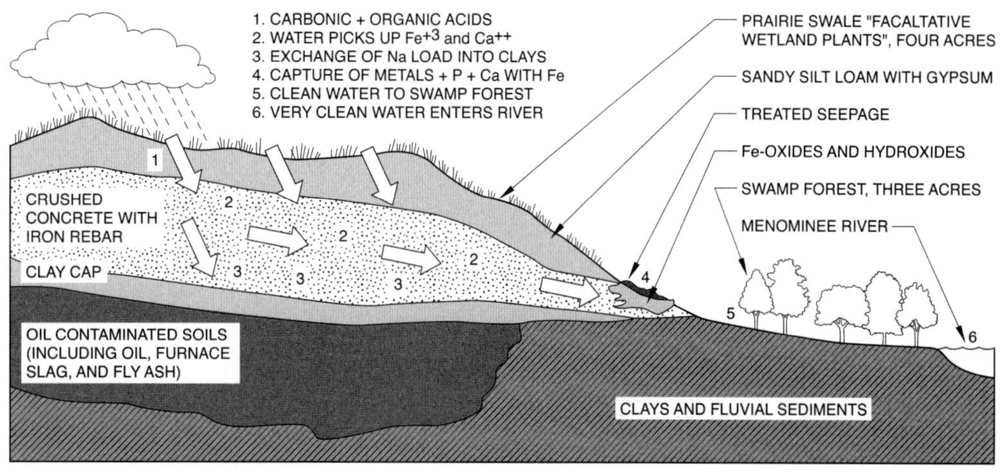

MENOMINEE RIVER SHOPS

Source: Applied Ecological Services, Inc., Brodhead, Wisconsin

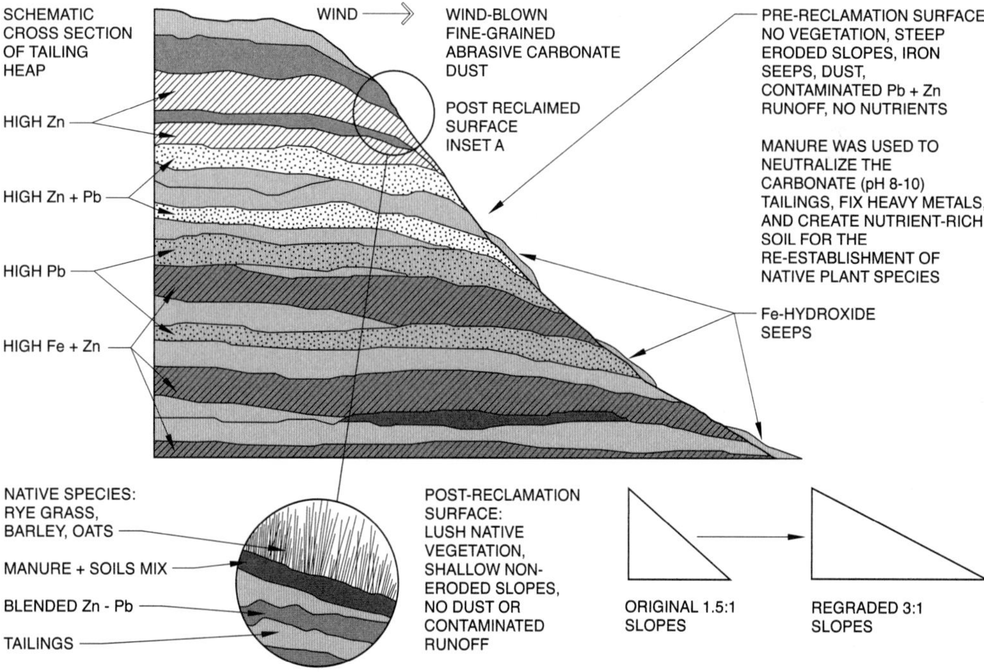

SHULLSBURG LEAD-ZINC MINE TAILING RECLAMATION

Source: Applied Ecological Services, Inc., Brodhead, Wisconsin

Niall Kirkwood, Harvard University Graduate School of Design

SUMMARY OF DEVELOPMENT LESSONS LEARNED

- No single generic approach to brownfield sites is possible; each site is unique.
- Vision and leadership are keys to the long-term success of the project.
- Context of site must be considered as part of the overall solution.
- Diverse set of players is necessary to develop a comprehensive approach and solution.
- Partnerships enhance viability.
- Innovative proactive local agencies provide opportunities for creative solutions.
- Education builds brownfield literacy and capacity.

- The site is found in developed or developing urban or exurban areas.
- The site requires remediation and development intervention to bring it back to higher and better use.

See also:
Brownfields Evaluation
Environmental Hazards

Niall Kirkwood, Harvard University Graduate School of Design

PHYTOREMEDIATORS USED IN BROWNFIELD HYDROCARBON DETOXIFICATION IN THE CONTINENTAL UNITED STATES

BOTANICAL NAME	COMMON NAME/H. ZONE	TARGET HC	MECHANISM
Medicago sativa	Alfalfa/3-9	Anthracene	Rhizodegradation
Medicago sativa	Alfalfa/3-9	Pyrene	Rhizodegradation
Medicago sativa	Alfalfa/3-9	Napthalene	Phytostabilization
Medicago sativa	Alfalfa/3-9	Crude oil	Unknown
Medicago sativa	Alfalfa/3-9	PAHs	Unknown
Medicago sativa	Alfalfa/3-9	Toluene	Rhizogradation
Medicago sativa	Alfalfa/3-9	Phenol	Rhizogradation
Medicago sativa	Alfalfa/3-9	Pyrene	Rhizogradation
Lolium multiflorum	Annual ryegrass/3-9	Crude oil	Rhizogradation
Lolium multiflorum	Annual ryegrass/3-9	Diesel	Rhizogradation
Chloris gayana	Bell Rhodesgrass/8-9	Naphthalene	Phytovolatilization
Cynodon dactylon	Bermudagrass/8-11	Phenanthrene	Rhizodegradation
Alnus glutinosa	Black alder/3-7	Bitumen and tar	Unknown
Robinia pseudoacacia	Black locust/4-8	Bitumen and tar	Unknown
Phaseolus vulgaris	Bush bean/3-9	Anthracene	Phytodegradation
Phaseolus vulgaris	Bush bean/3-9	Benzoanthracene	Phytodegradation
Daucus carota	Queen Anne's lace/3-9	Naphthalene, flourene	Phytodegradation
Phragmites australis	Common Reed grass/5-11	Benzene and crude oil	Unknown
Phragmites australis	Common Reed grass/5-11	Bitumen and tar	Unknown
Agropyron desertorum	Crested wheatgrass/2-5	Pentachlorophenol	Phytostabilization, rhizodegradation
Coronilla varia	Crown vetch/2-9	Pyrene	Rhizodegradation
Panicum clandestinum	Deer tongue/6-11	Pyrene	Rhizodegradation
Lemna gibba	Duckweed/5-11	Anthracene	Phytostabilization
Lemna gibba	Duckweed/5-11	Benzopyrene	Phytostabilization
Lemna gibba	Duckweed/5-11	Phenanthrene	Phytostabilization
Vicia fava	Fava bean/4-9	Crude oil	Rhizodegradation
Salix spp.	Hybrid willow/3-8	No. 2 fuel oil	Unknown
Panicum coloratum	Kleingrass/7-11	Pyrene	Unknown
Panicum coloratum	Kleingrass/7-11	Chrysene	Unknown
Panicum coloratum	Kleingrass/7-11	Benzopyrene	Unknown
Panicum coloratum	Kleingrass/7-11	Naphthalene	Unknown
Panicum coloratum	Kleingrass/7-11	Flourene	Unknown
Panicum coloratum	Kleingrass/7-11	Phenanthrene	Unknown
Panicum coloratum	Kleingrass/7-11	Benzoanthracene	Unknown
Schizachyrium scoparium	Little bluestem/5-9	PAHs	Unknown
Zea mays	Maize/2-11	Fuel oil hydrocarbons	Rhizodegradation
Zea mays	Maize/2-11	Pyrene	Rhizodegradation
Pisum sativum	Pea/5-9	Phenanthrene	Rhizodegradation
Populus deltoides x nigra	Poplar/4-9	Pentachlorophenol; 1, 2, 4 trichlorobenzene; m-xylene; ethylbenzene; toluene; benzene; nitrobenzene and phenol	Phytovolatilization
Buchloe dactyloides	Prairie Buffalograss/5-9	Naphthalene	Unknown
Buchloe dactyloides	Prairie Buffalograss/5-9	Flourene	Unknown
Buchloe dactyloides	Prairie Buffalograss/5-9	Phenanthrene	Unknown
Festuca rubra	Red fescue/4-9	Crude oil	Rhizodegradation
Festuca rubra	Red fescue/4-9	Diesel	Rhizodegradation
Phalaris arundinacea	Reed canary grass/3-9	Pyrene	Rhizodegradation
Lolium perenne	Ryegrass/3-11	Phenanthracene, anthracene, fluoranthene, pyrene, hexadecane, pristane	Rhizodegradation
Lolium perenne	Ryegrass/3-11	PAHs	Phytostabilization
Lolium perenne	Ryegrass/3-11	Anthracene	Phytostabilization
Lolium perenne	Ryegrass/3-11	Diesel	Phytostabilization
Lolium multiflorum Lam x perenne	Ryegrass hybrid/3-11	3-chlorobenzoate	Rhizodegradation
Lespedeza cuneata	Sericea lespedeza/4-10	Pyrene	Rhizodegradation
Avena barbata	Slender oat grass/3-9	Phenanthrene	Rhizodegradation
Glycine max	Soybean/5-10	Anthracene	Phytostabilization, phytodegradation
Glycine max	Soybean/5-10	Phenanthracene	Rhizodegradation
Sorghum vulgare	Sudangrass/6-9	Anthracene	Rhizodegradation
Sorghum vulgare	Sudangrass/6-9	Pyrene	Rhizodegradation
Panicum virgatum	Switchgrass/4-9	Anthracene	Rhizodegradation
Panicum virgatum	Switchgrass/4-9	Pyrene	Rhizodegradation
Panicum virgatum	Switchgrass/4-9	PAHs	Rhizodegradation
Festuca arundinacea	Tall fescue/3-9	Pyrene	Rhizodegradation
Festuca arundinacea	Tall fescue/3-9	Naphthalene	Rhizodegradation
Festuca arundinacea	Tall fescue/3-9	Benzopyrene	Rhizodegradation
Festuca arundinacea	Tall fescue/3-9	Benzopyrene	Rhizodegradation, phytovolatilization, phytostabilization
Festuca arundinacea	Tall Fescue/3-9	Pyrene	Rhizodegradation
Lathyrus sylvestris	Sweet pea/5-9	Pyrene	Rhizodegradation
Zoysia japonica	Zoysiagrass/7-10	Napthalene	Unknown
Zoysia japonica	Zoysiagrass/7-10	Fluorene	Unknown
Zoysia japonica	Zoysiagrass/7-10	Phenanthrene	Unknown

Source: *R. E. Farrel, C. M. Frick and J. J. Germida,* 2000 Phytopet—A Database of Plants that Play a Role in the Phytoremediation of Petroleum Hydro Carbons

SOUND CONTROL AND REDUCTION

SOUND TRANSMISSION PRINCIPLES

Sound is caused by movement of objects, which results in the vibration of air molecules. These air molecules travel in a wavelike manner, similar to the effect of the ripples created when a stone is tossed into water. When these vibrations reach our ears, we hear sound. When sound that is unpleasant or disruptive is received, it is classified as noise. Masking unpleasant sounds by introducing more pleasing sounds closer to the receiver can be an effective measure to counteract the noise.

Sound is measured both in decibels (dB), to describe its loudness, and frequency, to calculate the repetition of sound waves. A third factor is the quality of sound. Generally, people find higher-frequency sounds more disturbing than those of lower frequencies. Sound reduction concerns are generally associated with highways and traffic noise, as well noise generated from airports, railroad lines, and large and/or loud industrial zones. This discussion focuses on the control of traffic noise.

NOISE CONTROL MEASURES

Measures to control sound can be directed at the source, the path and distance that the sound travels, or at the receiver of the sound. The level of traffic noise is contingent upon three factors: the "volume" of traffic, the "speed" of the traffic, and the number of trucks traveling on the road, as they tend to generate more traffic noise. An increase in any of these three factors increases traffic noise. Traffic noise is created by engine noise, exhaust noise, and the noise generated by tires on the pavement (which is also affected by pavement type).

The impact of traffic noise is affected by distance, topography, vegetation, and obstacles (natural or man-made) between the source of the noise and the receiver of the noise. The level of noise that reaches the receiver is related to the distance the sound has to travel from the source, the type of ground and surface the sound travels over, the relative height of the receiver, the amount of shielding, and the height of the noise source.

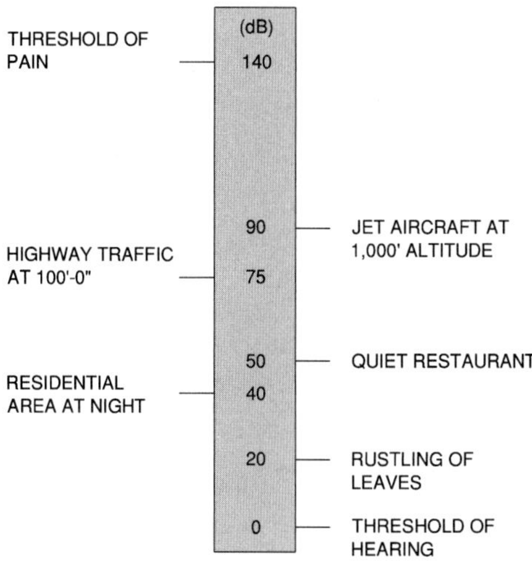

DECIBEL SCALE

Noise-Reduction Planning

Efforts to reduce traffic noise can be directed toward:

- The motor vehicles themselves
- Land-use decisions that control which uses are adjacent to highly traveled roads
- Planning and design that can mitigate the impact of generated traffic noise

In an effort to address the source of noise, federal regulations aimed at creating quieter passenger vehicles and trucks are continually being developed and reviewed. State inspection laws complement these efforts by ensuring that vehicles are operating and being maintained properly.

On undeveloped land adjacent to busy roads or highways, land-use policies that limit development to uses that are less sensitive to traffic noise can be considered—for example, locating commercial facilities closer to the road and residences further away, or locating community open-space amenities between the road and residences, to create a buffer to traffic noise.

Addressing the potential impact of traffic noise early in the planning and design phases of highways or adjacent uses makes it possible to integrate a wider range of possible noise-reduction strategies, as opposed to considering this issue later in the process or as an afterthought. That is, the route of new roads should be planned to limit their proximity to existing noise-sensitive areas such as residential areas, schools, and hospitals.

Compliance with Federal Regulations

The Federal Highway Administration (FHWA), which administers federal highway funding to the states, must approve projects that anticipate using these funds. To be in compliance with federal regulations, noise impacts and mitigation efforts to address them must be included as part of the highway plan.

Given the large amount of federal funding that goes to new highway construction or existing highway improvements, efforts to reduce traffic noise must be integrated into most related construction projects. Computer models can take into account the many variables that affect sound transmission, from the source to the receiver, and predict the impact that new construction or improvements will cause.

SOUND BARRIER STRATEGIES

Sound barriers reduce the flow of sound energy to the receiver by "absorbing" the sound, "reflecting" the sound, or "forcing" it to take a longer path to reach the receiver. They do not completely block all noise; they only reduce overall noise levels. The FHWA notes that effective noise barriers typically reduce noise levels by 5 to 10 dB, cutting the loudness of traffic noise by as much as half. Minimally, a sound barrier must break the line of sight between the sound source and the receiver. Additional height or length reduces the level of sound even further. A number of approaches can be used to accomplish this. Single elements can be used to create a sound barrier, or a combination of elements can be incorporated to provide effective sound control. In the early planning stages, a broad spectrum of noise-reduction strategies can be considered, among them:

- Creation of buffer zones
- Planting of dense vegetation
- Utilizing earth berms (creating new landforms or taking advantage of existing topography)
- Constructing parts of the roadway below the surrounding elevations (creating embankments that function as noise barriers, similar to earth berms)
- Construction of noise barrier walls

Earth berms can be natural-looking and effective sound barriers. They can reduce noise by approximately 3 dB more than a sound barrier wall of the same height. They are an even better choice when they can relate to the existing topography of the site. Given the necessary height of a sound barrier, some consideration must be given to the slopes creating the berm and the horizontal distance that will be required to accommodate this slope. The maintenance of the slope, including stabilization, also has to be considered, particularly if it involves the use of plant material. The use of vegetation that will require minimal maintenance, as opposed to lawn that requires continual cutting, can reduce the longer-term maintenance costs. Native plants can be a good vegetative choice that addresses these issues. Earth berms can be used in conjunction with vegetation or barrier walls. In the case of barrier walls, it can result in a reduction in the overall height of the barrier wall, making it a little less imposing. Some research has determined that the most effective sound barriers are a combination of earth berm with a sound barrier wall located at the top of the berm.

Sound barrier walls are popular because they are vertical sound obstructions that take up little horizontal distance. They can be constructed from a number of different materials, although the use of wood is declining amidst concerns of durability and longer-term maintenance. Concrete, in a variety of forms, is the increasingly popular choice.

Although there is the perception that vegetation is an effective sound barrier, this is only true in dense planting bands that are 100 feet or more in width (trees and shrubs) and generally in the higher sound frequencies. In more narrow massings, vegetation is minimally effective in reducing the transmission of sound energy. However, vegetation does have a positive psychological impact on people's perception of noise, so just screening the noise source from view, plus the overlay of the sound of the trees in the wind, can reduce the annoyance factor, even if it does not effect a very great reduction in the level of sound transmitted. In conjunction with barrier walls, planting can soften the visual impact of a sound barrier wall.

For existing roads or because of other limitations, efforts to reduce traffic noise are often addressed by constructing noise barriers. There are approximately 3,000 linear miles of noise barriers constructed in the United States, and more are planned as part of new highway construction and existing highway improve-

Leonard Hopper, RLA, FASLA

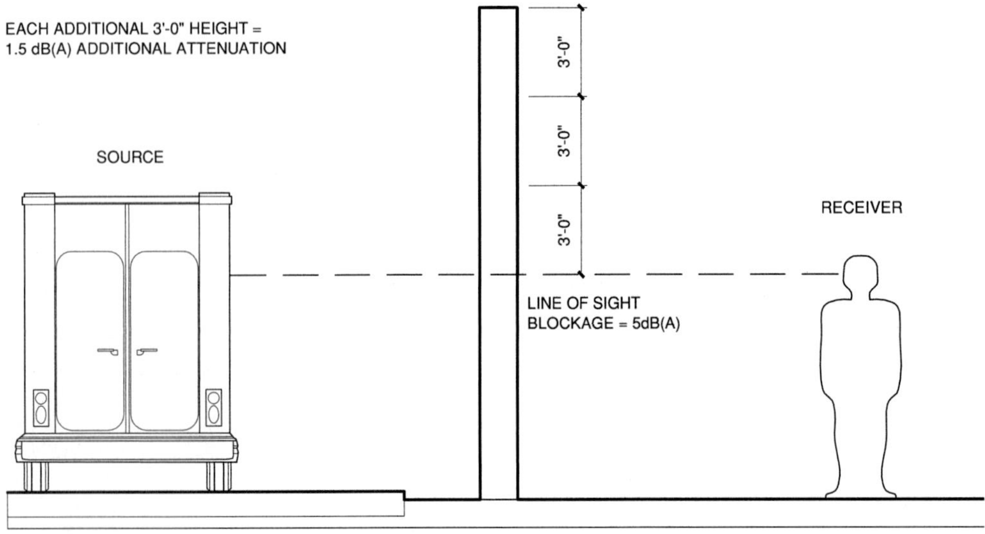

BARRIER HEIGHT

RELATIONSHIP OF NOISE REDUCTION AND HEIGHT OF NOISE BARRIER WALL

Source: Adapted from the Federal Highway Administration, 2001.

ments. Noise barrier walls are vertical obstacles that take up less space than other noise mitigation measures, making them a popular choice, particularly for retrofitting an existing road for traffic sound reduction.

Generally, it is best to position a barrier so that the sound will have to travel the furthest distance from the source to the receiver. This is most effectively accomplished by positioning the barrier either as close as feasible to the source or as close as feasible to the receiver. In the middle is the least desirable and effective location. Given the choice, placing the barrier closest to the source is the best choice, as whatever small amount of sound energy that is transmitted through the barrier would still have to travel a greater distance to reach the receiver.

To be effective, it is important for these barriers to be high enough and long enough to block the transmission of sound, and be solid without any openings. According to the FHWA, a noise barrier wall can achieve a 5 dB noise level reduction when the line of sight is broken between the noise source and the receiver. An additional 1.5 dB reduction in the noise level can be achieved for each 3 feet of barrier height. To reduce noise coming from around the ends of the walls, a barrier should be at least eight times as long as the distance from the receiver to the barrier.

ROADWAY

NOISE BARRIER

≥80°

D

D

≥80°

NOISE-SENSITIVE RECEIVERS

4D

4D

BARRIER WIDTH

RELATIONSHIP OF NOISE REDUCTION AND LENGTH OF NOISE BARRIER WALL

Source: Adapted from the Federal Highway Administration, 2001.

BARRIER MATERIALS

Barriers can be constructed from wood, concrete, masonry, metal, as well as other materials that can be chosen to blend with the surrounding context. Whichever material is selected, the FHWA recommends it be rigid and of sufficient density (minimum 20 kilograms/square meter) to effectively reduce sound transmission through the barrier.

Experiments are being conducted that utilize recycled materials, as well as materials that have greater sound-absorbing characteristics. For example, materials such as crumb rubber are being applied to concrete barriers to improve their sound absorption and reduce their sound reflectivity. Polycarbonates and other transparent materials are being integrated into sound barriers to minimize their visual impact. An increasing number of examples demonstrate that these functional barriers can be transformed into works of art, which, in addition to addressing noise problems, are aesthetically pleasing and help reinforce a sense of place and pride in the community.

DESIGN CONSIDERATIONS

There are a number of design considerations that need to be addressed in designing a sound barrier wall. Chief among these is effectiveness. Related to the primary acoustic qualities of the barrier is the choice of material and design of the barrier. Ideally, the sound barrier should be aesthetically pleasing from both the source as well as the receiver; it should blend with its surroundings and any negative impacts should be minimized.

As with any project, cost is a factor. For a sound barrier wall, initial cost of the material, ease of installation, and long-term maintenance costs need to be taken into account. And because of their high level of visibility, a maintenance strategy that addresses potential graffiti should be a cost consideration in the design and choice of material for sound barrier walls.

Residents who benefit from the installation of sound barriers are generally positive about the improvement in the quality of their lives resulting from the reduction in noise level. To address potential negative impacts on the residential side of highway sound barriers, their impact on the adjacent neighborhood has to be considered. The FHWA recommends that a noise barrier wall be located approximately four times its height from residences, to maintain a level of scale and to prevent causing a feeling of confinement. Methods to minimize the impact of noise barrier walls on the community include: staggering of horizontal wall members, varying design elements (textures, color, materials), and softening the wall's impact with planting. From the traffic side, efforts should be made to avoid designs that create a tunnel effect for motorists, or that are monotonous. It is also important to keep in mind that, at highway speeds, motorists tend to perceive the overall character of the noise barrier walls. To address design concerns, the overall form, color, and texture can be varied by varying the use of forms, materials, and surfaces in a way that responds to motorists traveling at normal highway speeds. For both residents and motorists, scenic vistas should be preserved as much as possible, while still meeting the other sound reduction criteria.

Leonard Hopper, RLA, FASLA

PARKS AND RECREATION

LARGE CITY PARKS

Large city parks were conceived in the nineteenth century as a means to provide clean air, refuge, and leisure-time recreation for a society that was rapidly industrializing. Thought of as a "retreat" from the city, many of these were designed in the romantic style of the English garden—an idealized landscape featuring informal plantings, pastoral vistas, and natural materials. The most famous of these, of course, is Central Park in New York City, an 800-acre oasis tightly framed by the grid of Manhattan.

OTHER TYPES OF URBAN PARKS

Many other urban parks in America were created in that image—landscape of the picturesque—including City Park in New Orleans, Piedmont Park in Atlanta, and Golden Gate Park in San Francisco. While the picturesque was one type of urban park, two other types also emerged.

The natural landscape as a preservation area in the city is the second type, with prime examples including Fairmont Park in Philadelphia, Rock Creek Park in Washington, DC, and Griffith Park in Los Angeles. These types of parks include large swaths of natural landscapes that support wildlife habitat, aquifer recharge areas, and native plantings. Each, though, is a man-altered landscape, not a wilderness.

The third type of large city park is the cultural or historic park, exemplified by Independence Mall in Philadelphia, the Mall in Washington, DC, and Grant Park in Chicago. These are formal man-made landscapes that have facilities for visual and performing arts, museums, or historic structures within them.

Though each of the three types of parks is different, they share a common use: recreation. Two types of recreation are exhibited in large city parks: active and passive. Active recreation comprises fields and courts for games and sports. Passive recreation encompasses a full range of leisure activities, from picnicking to socializing to bird watching to sunbathing and beyond. Typically, active recreation involves settings of particular size and materials to support the activity—for example, a baseball diamond or a tennis court—while passive recreation involves settings of variable sizes and materials.

DESIGN CHALLENGES

The challenge for the designer of a large city park is to create the appropriate balance between the site, the typology, and the program of active and passive uses. Thus, the designer must study the site for its intrinsic capabilities to support park programs, derive a program for uses, and combine these in a manner consistent with the overall typology. (See Color Plate 21.)

The first task—site analysis—is the realm of the landscape architect. The second task, creation of a program of uses, may be provided to the designer or may be part of the designer's scope to discern this from a public process. The third task is the realm of the client or owner: to establish the fundamental character or type of park envisioned.

Site Analysis

Site analysis is the review of physical or mapped information about the natural and man-made systems that affect or are affected by the site. Natural factors to be studied include geology, topography, soils, hydrology, vegetation, wildlife, sun patterns, wind patterns, and views. Man-made factors include land use and zoning around the park, transportation networks that access the park, utilities, historic/archeological sites, and building codes. It is the role of the landscape architect to discover these issues and map them in a comprehensive manner such that an understanding of the site as a whole system is possible.

Various methodologies may be employed to assemble these data, but the value of the site analysis is the derivation of a set of constraints—fixed or negative aspects of the site—and opportunities—flexible or positive aspects of the site. The site analysis serves as the benchmark that addresses the question of *where* in the park activities may occur. For example, a soccer field, which requires a large flat area, would be an inappropriate use on a steeply sloped site, and the site analysis becomes the decision-making tool that supports such conclusions. In fact, the site analysis should be a tool that is part of the database for the park operator long after construction, so that its intelligence is always in service to the park as it evolves over time. Thus, the site analysis should be a clear, legible graphic liberally notated to indicate site constraints and suitabilities as a guidepost for locating facilities appropriately.

Program of Uses

The second task of city park design is the creation of a program of uses. In many cases, this is provided to the landscape architect at the beginning of the project and is derived from a recreation needs assessment. These studies, performed by recreation planners, seek to measure availability of recreation type by user population. Most cities routinely update these every 5 to 10 years as part of a citywide master plan. If a program is not provided, it is sometimes the task of the landscape architect to facilitate a process to create one. Many means exist to discern such information, including telephone surveys, questionnaires, and public workshops. These may be performed formally or informally, but in all cases, the broadest audience, and the broadest response, is this goal, so that the resultant information reflects the entire city, not just one neighborhood or constituency.

Experience has shown that public meetings are best conducted in the neighborhoods; thus, for a large city park, a series of such meetings may be required to get the broadest response. When conducting such workshops, the landscape architect should prepare a cogent presentation of the site analysis, and the owner should present the overall vision or typology. The audience should be made aware of the particular context of the park and its intrinsic qualities, so that discussion is focused on program. Usually, in such settings, it is a practice to break the audience into small groups, each one with a professional facilitator provided by the landscape architect or owner, so that people feel free to offer opinions. It is also important that all comments be recorded in writing, either by a scribe in the workshop or through a questionnaire filled out by the audience. Inevitably, ideas will be offered that are contradictory or beyond the scope of the park, but all should be recorded.

The landscape architect should review all such written suggestions after the workshops are complete and organize the information into a hierarchy of program elements from most suggested to least suggested. The landscape architect should also provide evaluation of the feasibility of the suggested program elements as applied to the site and the typology. For example, if 100 people suggested a water park, but the park was located in an area with water restrictions, the water park is an inappropriate use, no matter how many may have suggested it. By constantly filtering all such information back through the findings of the site analysis, the landscape architect serves society by considering the values of the land itself as a driver of the planning process.

Finally, the owner should create a preferred park program based on the recommendations from the landscape architect, and this preferred program should be presented to all the neighborhood groups that were a part of the information-gathering process. This is an important step, one sometimes overlooked, to communicate the resultant program prior to park design so that the program is not subject to debate during design; in fact, it serves as a benchmark that answers the question of *what* is in the park.

Park Design

If the site analysis answers the question of where, and the program answers the question of what, then design of the park answers *how*. The design of any large city park should be a rational application of program to site in a manner that minimizes negative impact to the site and maximizes its usefulness. That is a dry, technical explanation of design; but design, of course, is much more. Design must inspire, delight, excite, and stimulate the senses. Design must connect people to a place in a physical and emotional way. Leisure-time activity is voluntary, and thus any good large city park must be attractive to people, so that they come to use it and to value it as a positive addition to their quality of life.

ROLE OF THE LANDSCAPE ARCHITECT

The role of the landscape architect is to understand the attributes of a good city park and incorporate those into any design. These attributes include:

- *Provide flexible spaces.* A large park must accommodate a variety of uses that will change over the course of a day, a season, and a generation. Therefore, multiple use of areas within parks is a primary consideration.

Dennis Carmichael, EDAW

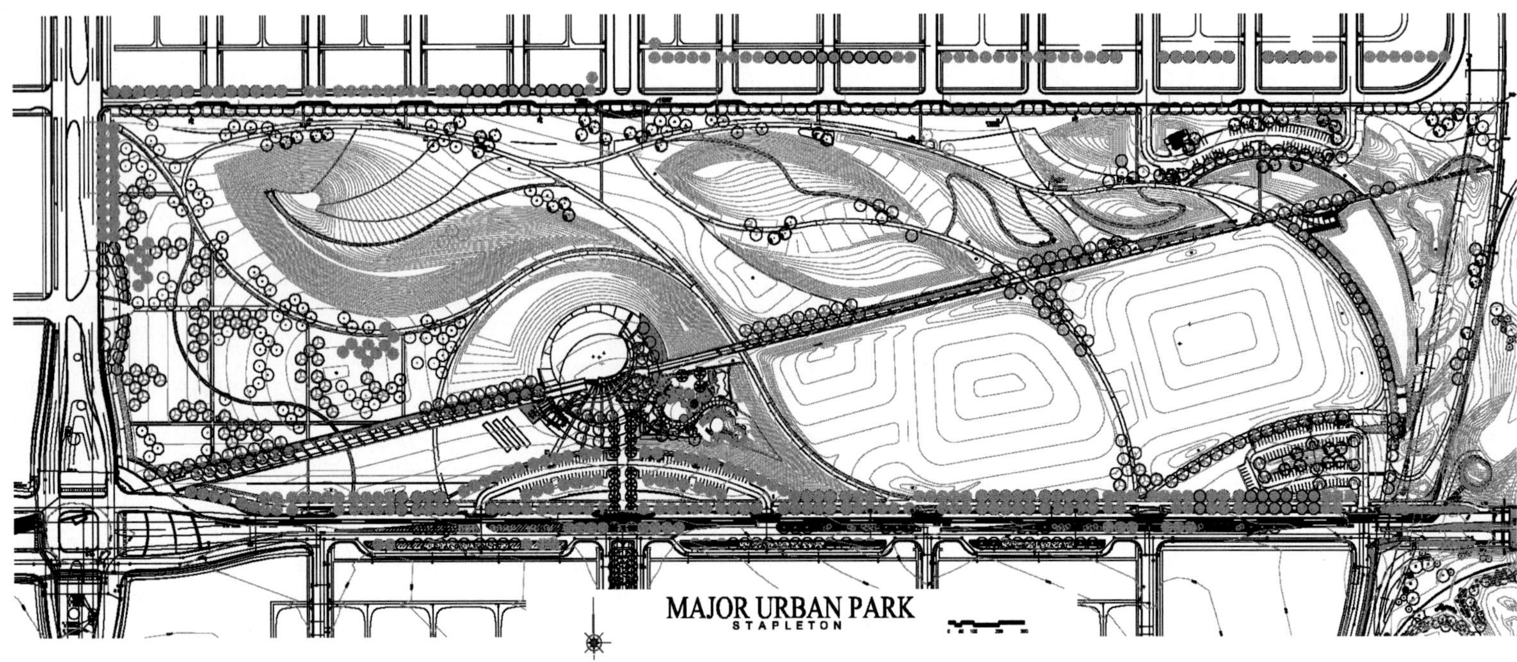

MAJOR URBAN PARK, STAPLETON, DENVER, COLORADO

- *Provide for a diversity of users.* Large parks must serve broad constituencies, with diverse needs reflecting age, gender, and race. Therefore, consideration should be given to a full range of activities from tot play to teenage recreation to elderly fitness. In ethnic neighborhoods, consideration of cultural morés and activities should be given to maximize the usefulness of the park to its user population.
- *Provide safe spaces.* Maximize visibility to and through the park by minimizing tall shrubs, pathway dead ends, and walled areas. In most city parks, the perception of safety, or lack thereof, is reinforced by adequate lighting, multiple pathways, and visibility from adjacent streets and homes. Circulation paths that connect through a park from off-site areas are a good strategy to ensure a constant flow of pedestrians, which will increase the perception of safety.
- *Balance vehicular and pedestrian circulation.* In large parks, it is inevitable that some form of vehicular access, if only for maintenance or emergency vehicles, must be provided. The designer must seek an appropriate balance between cars and people to minimize pedestrian/vehicular conflicts, auto exhaust, and impervious surfaces. Grade-separated roadways are one way to accomplish this goal, but well-marked, well-lighted crosswalks work as well. Another strategy is to minimize parking in the park. If users cannot park their cars within the park, they enter it as pedestrians, even if they arrived by automobile.
- *Provide adequate space for active recreation.* Sports fields and courts are designed for specific activities and, thus, the site plan for any park must recognize those impacts. In general, it is better to locate active recreation at the perimeter of a large park, so that the resultant noise, parking, and refuse do not penetrate deeply into the park. The landscape architect should recognize orientation of fields for quality play and minimize the impact of the setting sun on, for example, balls thrown, pitched, or served. In addition, adequate runout space—at least 30 feet—should be provided around sports fields for errant kicks and foul balls. Finally, active recreation fields should be sited away from areas designated for contemplation, wildlife, or sensitive vegetation.
- *Site facilities in a manner that respects the land.* With a variety of program elements from active to passive to cultural, large city parks must accommodate a broad menu of uses. The landscape architect should reflect on the site analysis and place these uses appropriately. For example, large sports fields should be located on the flattest, least vegetated land, while trails may be located in more challenging environ-

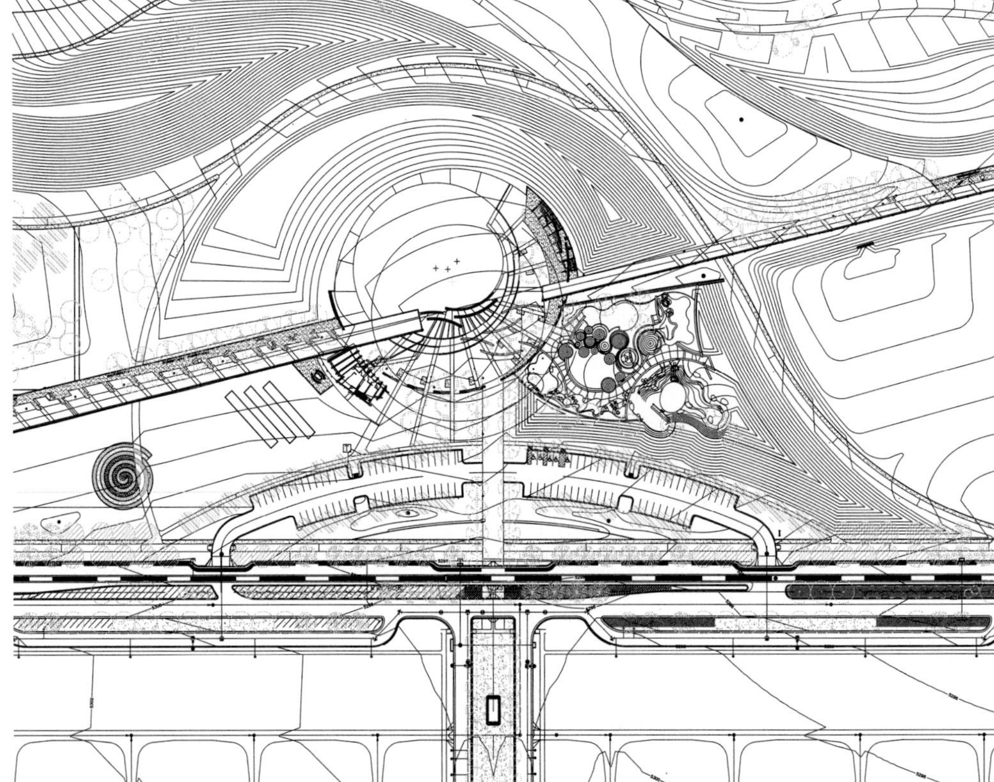

MAJOR URBAN PARK—STAPLETON, DENVER, COLORADO, ENLARGED SEGMENTS

Dennis Carmichael, EDAW

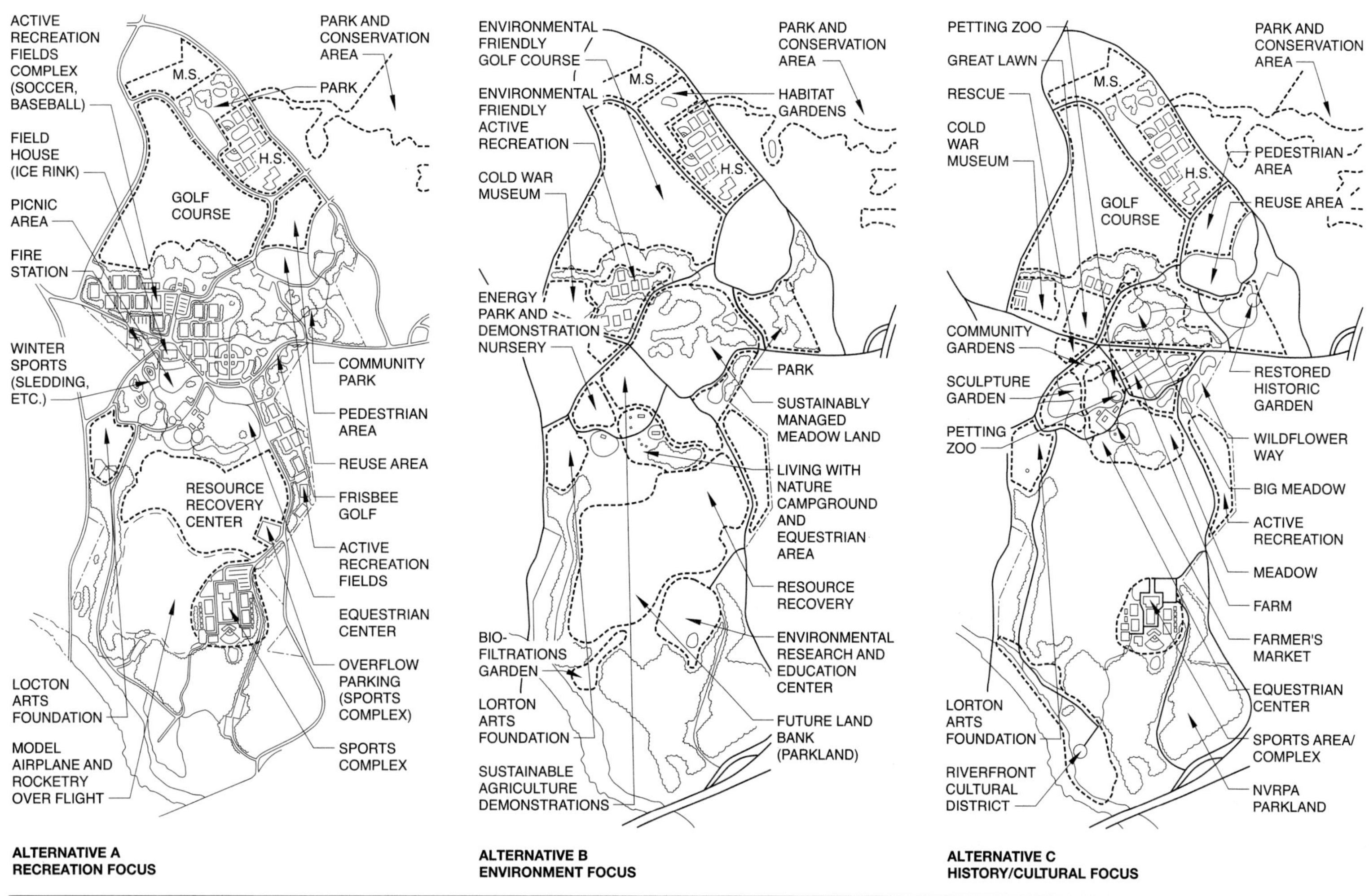

LAUREL HILL ALTERNATIVES, FAIRFAX, VIRGINIA

ments. Soils should be examined for percolation rates that support rainstorms. Stream courses, wetlands, and forested areas should be preserved or enhanced for passive recreation and wildlife habitat, instead of active recreation. In short, the land should dictate the use, and the essential character of the site, whether it is tidal plain, forested hill, or desert, should remain after the park is implemented.

- *Celebrate site history and archeology.* While recognizing natural systems and processes, the landscape architect should also preserve and enhance human creations, if they are historically significant. This may include prehistoric sites, cemeteries, historic architecture, or cultural landscapes. Each of these may serve as a driver of unique character that helps connect the park to its place in history. Landscape architects should consult historians or state historic preservation agencies as part of their site analysis and incorporate elements deemed valuable into their plans. This does not mean that the landscape architect should create a period piece or restoration, but that the cultural patterns and materials should be reflected in a new park.
- *Incorporate stormwater management practices.* Large parks by definition offer opportunities to cleanse stormwater and recharge aquifers by virtue of large areas of permeable surfaces. Landscape architects should be mindful to minimize impervious surfaces, including roads, parking areas, buildings, and game courts, but, recognizing the inevitability of such elements, provide mitigation in the form of rain gardens, bioswales, and stormwater ponds. Parks should not release any stormwater downstream and should have areas designated for stormwater cleansing and aquifer recharge, not as a "leftover" use, but as a part of the program. In desert areas, xeric plants and turf should be maximized, and irrigation should be minimized. Inevitably, sports fields in an arid climate will require irrigation, but the source of this water should be recycled. Gray water or rainwater should be stored in on-site cisterns, not fresh potable water.
- *Consider wildlife.* While many large city parks are "made" landscapes, it does not follow that only humans will inhabit them. Fish, birds, insects, and small mammals inhabit all city parks, and the landscape architect should recognize and value these residents. Watercourses are an excellent opportunity to provide natural corridors for wildlife nesting and movement. The site analysis should be reviewed for areawide wildlife presence, habits, and movement patterns, and the design should accommodate those activities as one element within a larger network. Wetlands are also excellent nesting and food sources for birds and other wildlife, and these should be preserved or enhanced, both as habitat and as passive recreation areas.
- *Select sustainable materials.* Both for energy conservation and for life-cycle maintenance costs, the landscape architect should select durable materials close to their source, such as stone, wood, and brick in the landscape. Concrete is durable, but has a high embedded-energy content. Steel is also durable, with a high embedded-energy content, but as 90 percent of steel is recycled, it remains a good material to specify. Plastics, aluminum, and synthetic fabrics are poor choices, both for their embedded energy and toxic chemicals employed in their manufacture.
- *Provide accessibility for all.* Large city parks should respect the accessibility requirements of the Americans with Disabilities Act (ADA) relative to parking, barrier-free circulation, and restroom facilities. Consideration should also be given to equal access for all in playgrounds, spectator sports, and seating areas, so that all may enjoy facilities in the park.
- *Recognize personal mobility activities.* A significant population uses parks for walking, running, bicycling, and in-line skating. Thus, paved trails can accommodate this population in a variety of settings. It is important that such multiple-use paths be at least 10 feet wide for safety in passing. Elements to enhance these activities include periodic drinking fountains and fitness equipment spaced along the trail in a sequence. Many such trails include mile markers to assist the users. In particularly heavy-use areas, a separation of bicyclists from pedestrians is advisable.

Dennis Carmichael, EDAW

SMALL URBAN PARKS

INTRODUCTION

Small parks play important roles in the metropolitan landscape as the major open space and areas at the neighborhood scale. They provide crucial access to green space for many people and may be the main recreational areas in central cities. However, their designs rarely reflect all that is now known about people, ecology, and landscapes.

On one hand, research on social or human factors has focused on human preferences and activities. Most researchers in this area seek to understand people as they are, proposing design and management solutions that will be acceptable to a range of people. Taking a very different view, ecological research has focused on large pristine habitats, although recently there has been more research about complex urban environments. In this area of research, nature is defined as a habitat or ecosystem. Researchers in this tradition are most likely to propose educating people to appreciate nature as it is.

In addition, small parks are too often relegated to being the stepchild of municipal and metropolitan open-space systems because of assumptions that their small size and isolation limit their recreational capacity and make them ecologically less valuable than large city and county parks. Yet in an era of fiscal constraint and high urban land values, small parks have much to offer. They are already appreciated for their contribution to neighborhoods and district needs for recreation, particularly in established municipalities close to the urban core. Parks and civic squares in new developments also provide signature amenities that embody the character of the developments.

Unfortunately, even newly constructed small parks are often conventionally planted and maintained, and though they provide a pleasant environment, they offer little in the way of ecological benefits or responsiveness to demographic changes. Good design can change this. Thanks to their abundance and density, small parks are among the most underrated yet potentially valuable ecological resources in a metropolitan area. Such parks can be designed as part of an open-space system that forms an important part of a region's ecology. In addition, if designed carefully to support multiple users and uses, these parks can also provide important amenities for increasingly diverse populations.

STANDARDS

It is not only new parks that provide opportunities for improving the social and ecological contribution of parks. Existing small parks of under 5 to 6 acres (2 to 2.4 hectares) tend to have fairly consistent design elements—playgrounds, turfgrass, scattered trees, ball courts, and athletic fields. Deteriorating play equipment and changing recreational needs mean that every two or three decades parks need to be renovated. This cycle of park renovation provides opportunities for redesign. With information that is backed up by credible research findings, it is possible to argue for design changes in the face of skepticism by the public and even parks' maintenance staffs.

Key Concepts

A review of the research indicates that there are a number of key concepts, issues, and findings about the design of small parks that comprise common concerns among social scientists, ecologists, urban foresters, park managers, and designers. These include: park size, shape, and number; park context; location; and trade-offs.

Size, Shape, and Number

The small size, potentially odd shapes, and relative isolation of neighborhood parks and other small open spaces are conventionally considered major limitations for ecological benefits and even some social ones. The ecology of small parks has been ignored by many ecologists because they are interested in studying natural ecosystems in pristine condition in order to establish baseline studies of ecological processes. From this standpoint, small parks are less desirable because they are human-dominated and lack reference ecosystems for comparison. Also because of their small size, these parks have a high proportion of edge habitat, exotic species, and generalist species, as well as altered nutrient cycles.

Human use constrains the capacity for ecological benefits in small parks where space is, by definition, at a premium. However, recent research on plants, animals, air and water quality, and the overall ecological network or system provides evidence that small parks offer important environmental benefits. As small patches of open space, they confer different and supplemental benefits from large patches by improving connections between open spaces and natural areas in the metropolitan environment (Dramstad, et al., 1996; Forman, 1995). For example, generalist and edge species may find vegetation in small parks to be suitable habitat, or the vegetation may serve as stepping stones to better habitat if connected by greenways and large parks. Thus, theory from landscape ecology directly supports the value of small open-space patches for conservation purposes (Forman, 1995).

From a social perspective, the abundance and density of small parks afford a high frequency of opportunities for people to experience nearby nature in their daily lives (Kaplan, et al., 1998). They can provide an everyday connection to green areas—that is, to "nature," very broadly defined (as it is in work on the social aspects of natural areas). However, small parks are often dispersed, expensive to maintain on a per-acre basis, and lack many of the facilities available in larger parks; and they do not have full-time park staff. Groups may compete for facilities, making it almost impossible to avoid conflicts over space in small parks.

Nevertheless, while posing a number of challenges for use and management, skillful design can enable even tiny areas to accommodate a diversity of people's needs and desires. In addition, the small size of these parks means that, overall, they may be cost-effective, because on a per-capita basis, they are used very intensively, even if per acre they cost more than large parks.

Context

From an ecological perspective, context is important because it is the landscape matrix, or wider metropolitan landscape, that influences a range of ecological factors in small parks. One of the most important issues is the "edge effect," especially if a park's edge is an abrupt one or if the park connects to vegetation in surrounding areas (termed by ecologists as "hard" or "soft" edges). In this view, vegetation serves as a critical transition zone between a small park and other types of urban development, aiding dispersal of wildlife and reducing isolation for wildlife populations. For example, rather than fronting streets, park edges could abut plantings for backyard wildlife in adjacent residential areas, forming a seamless transition between the park and neighborhood. The goal is to improve low habitat quality to at least medium.

That said, this kind of "soft" edge design represents a trade-off, as by buffering the park with vegetation, street access for people is reduced, potentially increasing conflicts between park users and adjacent residents. If a park is edged by a road, the park is made more accessible for people, and the public space of the park is clearly distinguished from the private space of nearby yards. A seamless transition may have benefits for wildlife but create conflicts for people. Achieving a balance between these important considerations, and others, will depend on the park's context within the metropolitan landscape and the regional open-space system.

Location

Some small parks have excellent locations, evidence of a thoughtful design process. These parks are centrally located in neighborhoods and have physical connections into a regional open-space system. If a stream runs through the park, for example, it is not hidden in a buried pipe, but rather serves as a social and ecological amenity as an open, natural channel.

Well-located parks are also designed to reflect the local climate. In a temperate climate, there are plenty of trees, giving shade and habitat, and lawn areas are designed to support activities rather than serving only as ground cover. In an arid climate, shade and habitat are provided by tall shrubs and small trees that are drought-tolerant. In all climates, vegetated areas are kept fairly open to address safety issues, without being overly manicured to decrease habitat quality.

In contrast, other small parks are located as an afterthought of the design process, on pieces of land least suitable for housing. The classic image is of a deserted park made up entirely of lawn and a sprinkling of trees and located in an isolated spot at the end of a residential street at the fringe of a housing development. There is no connection with a regional open-space system, and pedestrian paths and sidewalks are absent.

Other examples may be socially or ecologically beneficial but not both. One example is the park that is situated in the center of urban development and lacking any connection with a regional open-space system, such as parkways and greenways. This type of park often has a design that provides recreational and cultural facilities, but the natural connections to this park are lacking, thus limiting its ecological benefits for habitat. Conversely, there are small slivers of remnant woodlots or grasslands preserved to protect habitat or water quality but without so much as a bench at a nearby sidewalk for people to enjoy. Such parks may provide pleasant views for those nearby but not much else.

Small parks do not need to "do everything"; in the cases described here, small modifications (a bench, a path, thoughtful siting, or connections to other natu-

Ann Forsyth and Laura Musacchio, University of Minnesota
Adapted from Designing Small Parks: A Manual for Addressing Social and Ecological Concerns *by Ann Forsyth and Laura Musacchio (John Wiley & Sons, 2005).*

ral areas) would make the parks work in multiple dimensions.

Trade-offs

Parks are a human artifact, but as human populations have grown and diversified, the demands placed on parks have changed and increased. With the aging of the population, parks need to cater to seniors, as well as children and adults playing active sports. New immigrant groups bring with them preferences for specific park activities such as soccer and festivals. And growing awareness of the dangers of obesity in the general population have more people turning to parks to provide options for physical activity—although the relationship between increased physical activity and park provision has not been well researched.

Another trade-off issue arises due to varying expectations and preferences for parks among user groups. Many people want their parks to have a naturalistic style of design, which is also carefully maintained. Others prefer a wilder aesthetic, reflecting the regional ecology. Still others consider parks to be important recreational facilities and so want a highly manicured look and the provision of play equipment, gardens, benches, picnic sheds, toilet blocks, concession stands, and other similar items.

In a large park, of course, it is possible to support numerous athletic facilities, picnic areas, flower beds, natural zones, and playgrounds, all occupying different spaces. But small parks need to be more sensitively designed to accommodate multiple activities and users who must share space more closely. Ultimately, only some of those needs can be met and fully coexist with a vision of a small park as a significant wildlife habitat. Which values are emphasized will depend on the park's context. In many cases, these issues will be highly contested, not only between social and ecological values, but also among such varying compatibilities as habitat versus water quality, ball fields versus picnic areas, and so on.

Overall, small parks have specific limits for ecological benefits, especially habitat value, because of their size and isolation in the metropolitan landscape and because of the recreational needs of people. Still, even in ecological terms, careful design can improve the functioning of these parks for local wildlife and for air and water quality benefits.

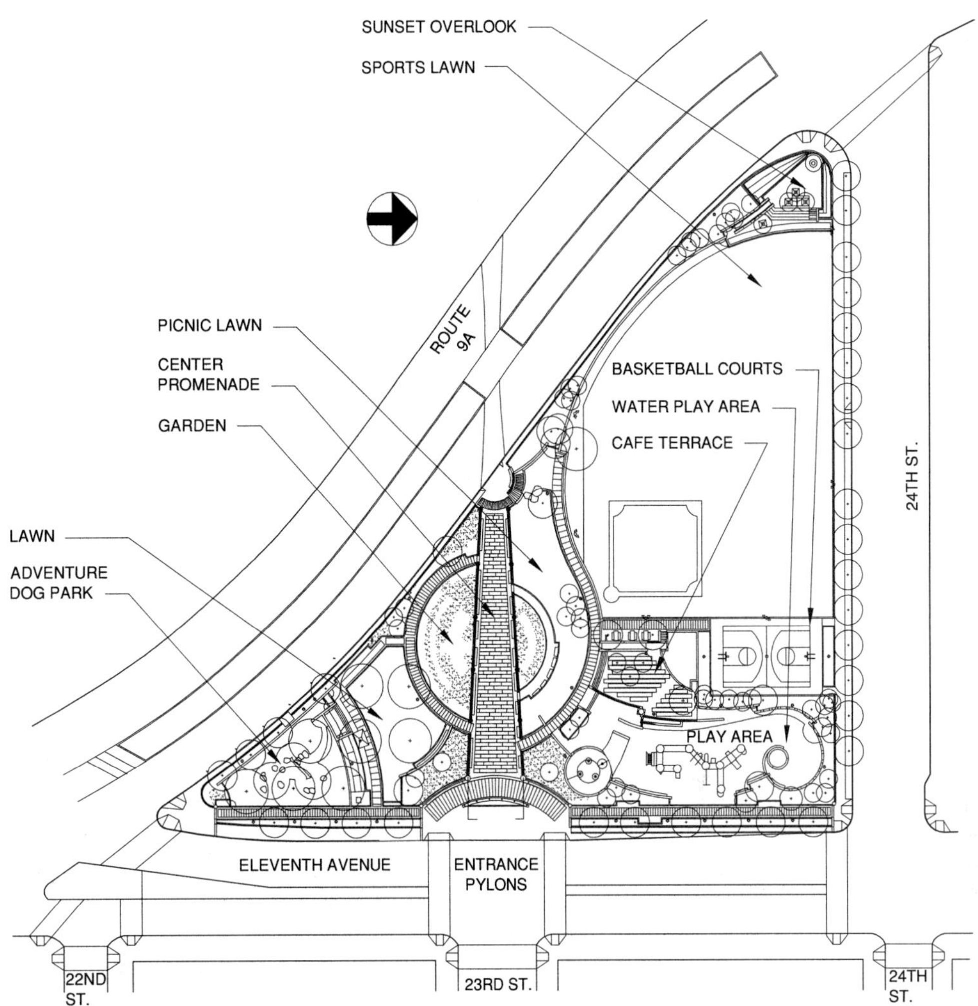

CHELSEA WATERSIDE PARK BY THOMAS BALSLEY AND ASSOCIATES

LAWS AND REGULATIONS

As noted, this discussion focuses on small parks of fewer than 5 to 6 acres (2 to 2.4 hectares), or one block or smaller. These parks are ubiquitous in metropolitan areas—from city centers to suburban areas—and in small towns. A park is defined as a public green space oriented toward recreation or at least public access, as opposed to a piece of land preserved primarily for its natural or wilderness features (as in a national park or national monument). Parks are also different from public spaces or green areas such as:

- Paved downtown plazas, markets, and streets
- Public open-space areas not open to broad public recreation
- Shared or common areas that are for the use of specific groups of residents or workers, rather than a broader public (e.g., the common areas of housing developments)

Of course, the lines between these types of spaces are often difficult to define, as when a farmer's market is in a park. In addition, a park does not require public ownership, but rather a level of regulation that allows for broad public use. Some publicly owned natural areas have limited access, while other private green spaces may have broad accessibility. Such access is generally part of an arrangement made with the local government at the time of development, with a requirement for public access granted in exchange for greater flexibility in development regulations. Certainly, many privately owned public spaces have relatively stringent regulations, but so do many publicly owned areas, from parks to libraries.

SMALL PARK DESIGN

Key Issues

Overall, design of small parks must deal with a number of key issues, including size, edges, appearance, and levels of naturalness. As noted earlier, due to their size, these parks can only accommodate a limited number of activities. And they are likely to have more edges than larger parks, which both causes problems and offers benefits. These issues are magnified because of public preferences regarding park appearance and the personal experience of being in a park.

In ecological terms, a number of systems are key to small park design: water, plants, wildlife, and air and climate. Here, small parks can play a role in a larger open-space and ecological system. However, these natural features also form part of the human environment, giving pleasure (e.g., watching wildlife) and comfort (e.g., moderating air temperature).

But parks are, ultimately, for people, so human dimensions are important. They need to consider the kinds of activities the small park will have to accommodate, at the same time addressing how to manage inevitable conflicts over use, issues of personal safety, park maintenance and management, and the potential for public involvement in parks.

Park Planning and Participation

Before a small park is designed or redesigned, typically a needs assessment is performed, particularly if the main focus of the park is recreation. After a park is designed, it is constructed, maintained, programmed, and eventually rebuilt. Design affects all these later activities; and though it is meant to support maintenance and programming, it is also a separate endeavor.

Whereas large parks are the emphasis of park planning at a metropolitan and regional level, many municipalities develop open space, parks, and recre-

Ann Forsyth and Laura Musacchio, University of Minnesota
Adapted from Designing Small Parks: A Manual for Addressing Social and Ecological Concerns *by Ann Forsyth and Laura Musacchio (John Wiley & Sons, 2005).*

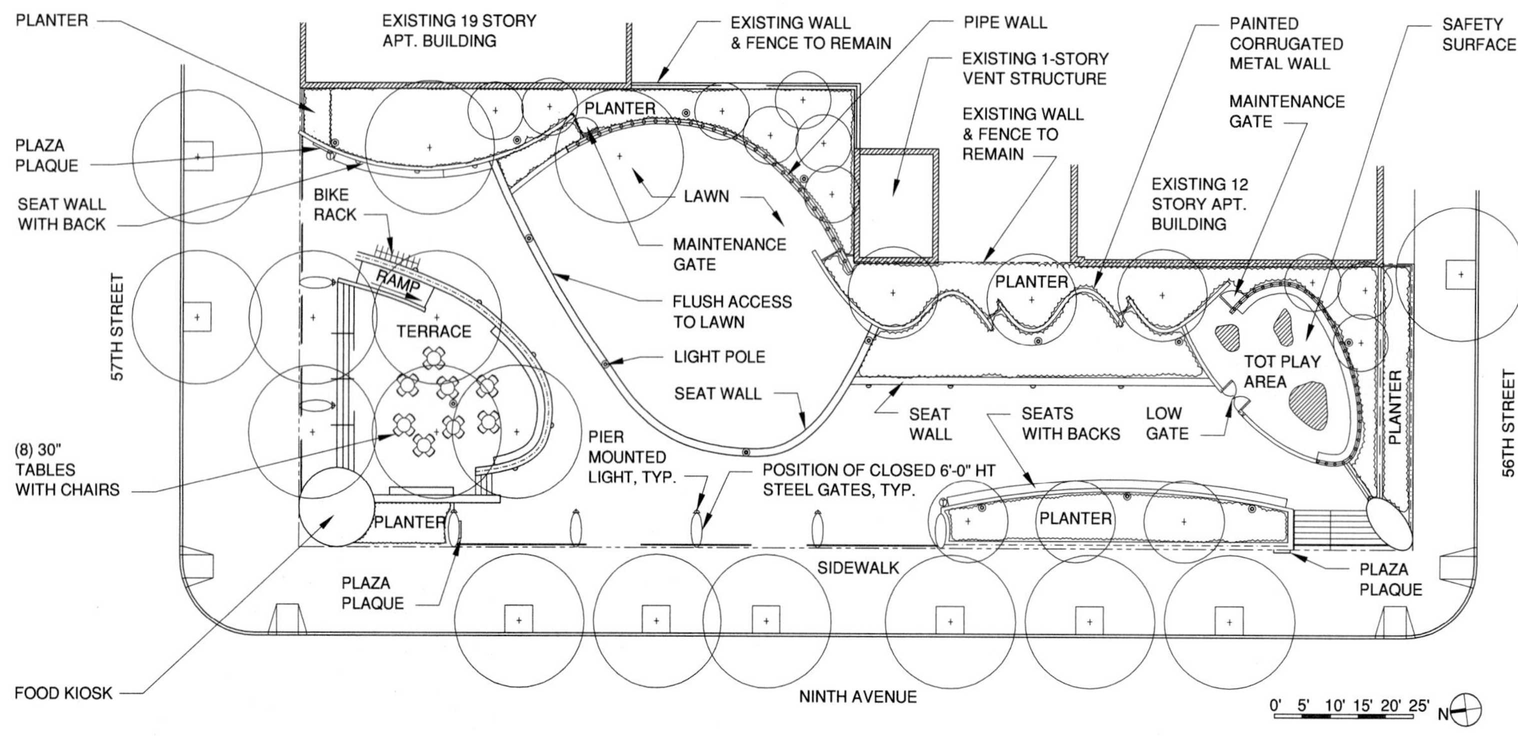

BALSLEY PARK BY THOMAS BALSLEY AND ASSOCIATES

ation plans in which small parks play an important role, providing opportunities for play, athletics, socializing, and interacting with nearby nature. The public is often invited to participate in these broader planning processes as steering committee members, as workshop participants, or to make formal responses to plans. At the more detailed stage of the physical design of small parks, designers frequently use similar strategies for public involvement.

Members of the public participate in small parks simply by using them. However, increasingly, the public also participates by lobbying for park funding, giving input on park design and rehabilitation, and even helping with park cleanup and light maintenance activities. Designing for and maintaining this public involvement is an important role for park professionals. Thus, they should include as part of the design process involving the public in design, developing friends groups and others to help upgrade parks, and providing environmental education.

Sustainability

Ultimately, small parks can play an important part in making cities more sustainable, providing benefits for habitat, air, and water quality while allowing the kinds of high neighborhood densities that are beneficial for lowering energy consumption and increasing active, human-powered, transportation. Of course, in addition to making compact cities more humane to live in, small parks can be beneficial to low-density areas.

Certainly it is important to have large open spaces, particularly large natural areas that provide habitat, but small parks, despite their size limitations, can contain many of the important features of larger parks while reinforcing compact city design. Moreover, they can encourage urban dwellers to appreciate natural processes in their neighborhoods, while providing unique facilities where people can gather either informally (e.g., seniors groups) or more formally (e.g., organized play groups or team sports). Parks also serve to connect people to the history of both the built environment and natural processes in the area. In sum, they can be rich cultural resources that allow people to sustain community life over time.

REFERENCES

Crewe, K., and A. Forsyth. 2003. "LandSCAPES: A Typology of Approaches to Landscape Architecture," *Landscape Journal* 22, 1:37–53.

Dramstad, W. E., J. D. Olson, and R. T. T. Forman. 1996. *Landscape Ecology Principles in Landscape Architecture and Land-Use Planning.* Washington, DC: Island Press, Harvard University GSD, and American Society of Landscape Architects.

Forman, R. T. T. 1995. *Land Mosaics: The Ecology of Landscape and Regions.* New York: Cambridge University Press.

Forsyth, A., and L. Musacchio. 2005. *Designing Small Parks: A Manual for Addressing Social and Ecological Concerns.* New York: John Wiley & Sons, Inc.

Kaplan, R., S. Kaplan, and R. Ryan. 1998. *With People in Mind: Design and Management of Everyday Nature.* Washington, DC: Island Press.

See Also:

Community Participation
Ecological Community Restoration
Human Factors
Large City Parks
Postoccupancy Evaluation
Waterfronts
Wildlife Habitat

Ann Forsyth and Laura Musacchio, University of Minnesota
Adapted from Designing Small Parks: A Manual for Addressing Social and Ecological Concerns *by Ann Forsyth and Laura Musacchio (John Wiley & Sons, 2005).*

WATERFRONTS

Most cities were originally settled on a body of water. Whether it was an oceanfront that supported shipping, a riverfront that supported trade, or a stream that provided waterpower, water was key to sustaining urbanization. In the nineteenth and twentieth centuries, industries gathered around these waterfronts to gain access to ports. In the twenty-first century, water is no longer the key requirement for industrialization and, thus, many of these urban industrial sites have become obsolete. Their prime location on bodies of water makes them attractive for other uses, however, including residential, cultural, and recreational ones.

Many cities are redefining themselves through the creation of waterfront parks. The attraction of water, whether for recreation, commerce, or views, is still magnetic. Landscape architects increasingly are called upon to shape parks on these waterfronts. Key to all waterfront parks is providing safe, convenient, and comfortable access to the water.

ANALYSIS AND PLANNING

The first step in the analysis and planning of any waterfront park is to understand the dynamics of the natural processes of the water body. Oceans have tides that feature fluctuation of elevation that is very predictable, but also feature surges in storm events. Rivers have floodways that absorb the frequent rise of water during and after storms and snowmelt. These fluctuations are also predictable, in the form of established 10-year, 100-year, and 500-year flood elevation.

The landscape architect is responsible for understanding the geography of these different elevations and for ensuring that no buildings are set below the 100-year flood elevation. Recreational uses may be located within the 10- and 100-year floodways, but the landscape architect should be aware that frequent inundation will have significant impact on the life cycle of materials within these areas. It is important, then, to specify durable materials that are easy to maintain or replace over the life of the project.

PROGRAM OF USES

In addition to responding to the natural dynamics of water systems, the landscape architect often is called upon to establish a program of uses for waterfront parks. Waterfronts are complex projects because, while the water body is in the public realm, the landside may or may not be. At issue is the menu of uses and users that best serves the public interest.

Waterside Uses

Many waterfronts are navigable and therefore allow commercial and recreational boating. It is important early in the design process to establish whether a given waterfront park is meant to support waterside activities, including marinas, day-use boat access, boat launches, or commercial shipping access and channels. The degree to which a waterfront park need support such water access is critical to its edges, its character, and its function. The following describes a few of these scenarios:

- *Nonmotorized boating.* For canoes, kayaks, and rowboats, a gently sloping beach or ramp is required with no direct vehicular access, but parking within 200 feet.
- *Motorized boat launch.* For recreational boats, a sloped concrete ramp that extends 20 to 40 feet into the water will allow launching. Vehicular access and trailer parking is required.
- *Day-use boat access.* For recreational boats, a vertical bulkhead, dock, or pier with tie-ups is necessary. These facilities should be 2 to 4 feet above mean water elevation. Landside emergency vehicle access is recommended.
- *Marina.* For recreational boat storage, a sheltered area of piers and docks is required. Vehicular access, fueling station, sewage disposal, and emergency vehicle access are all required.
- *Water taxi or tour boat.* For water-based transportation boats, whether commuter or pleasure, a vertical bulkhead, pier, or dock with deep-water draft is

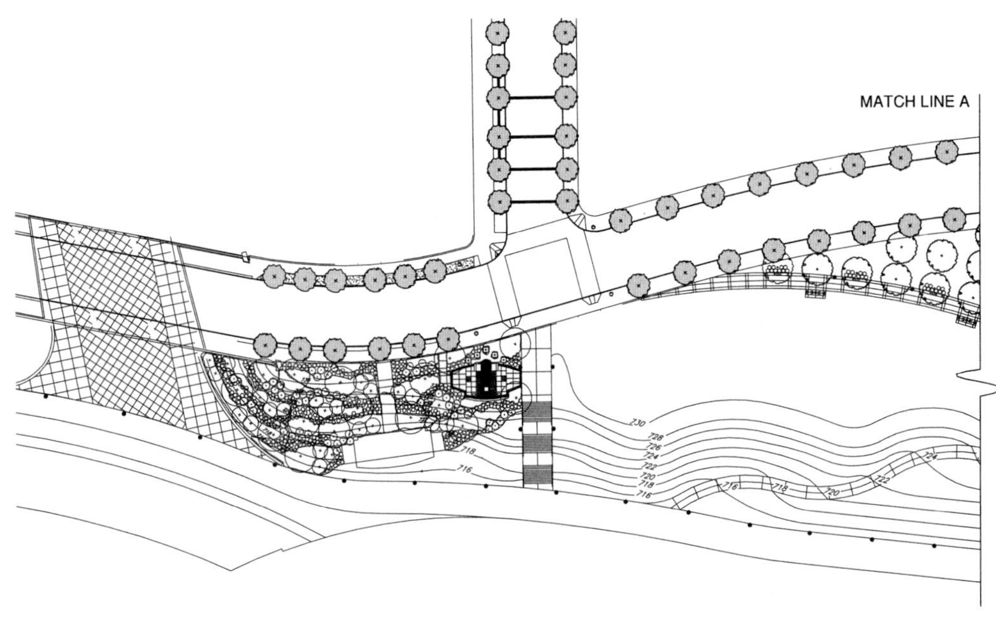

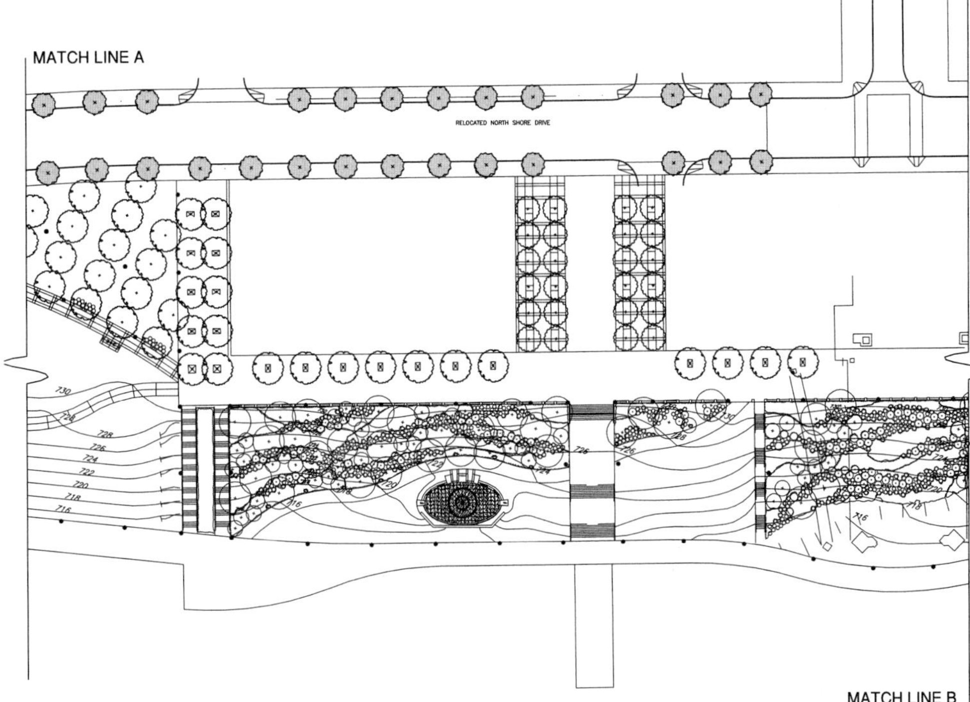

NORTH SHORE RIVERFRONT PARK PLAN, PITTSBURGH, PENNSYLVANIA *(continues)*

Dennis Carmichael, EDAW

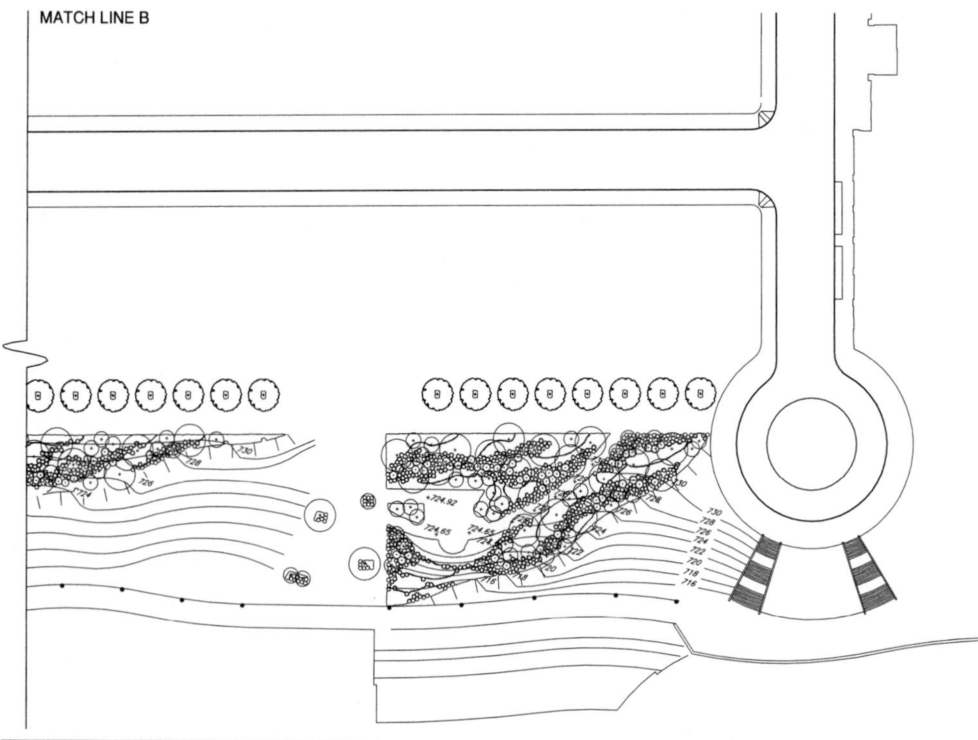

NORTH SHORE RIVERFRONT PARK PLAN, PITTSBURGH, PENNSYLVANIA *(continued)*

required. Areas for queuing and gangways are also required. Emergency vehicle access is required as well.

Clearly, the type of waterside use greatly influences the landside access and character. For areas that are meant to provide boating access, guardrails at water's edge would prevent such access and therefore should not be provided. In these areas, bollards, tie-ups, and visibly contrasting pavements should be considered to provide clarity to the water's edge. In other locations, guardrails or riparian planting should create a safety barrier.

Early in the programming process, the landscape architect should undertake a permit requirement study. Most waterfront parks will require special permits, in addition to building permits, for any improvements that affect the water's edge. State environmental permits may be required for changes to wildlife or fishery habitats. U.S. Army Corps of Engineers permits are required for any impact to the volume of water storage in the floodway. And Coast Guard permits may be required for impacts to navigable waterways. The landscape architect is responsible for understanding what is and what is not permissible, and for advising the owner accordingly. The landscape architect should conduct preliminary meetings with all affected agencies early in the design process to understand the parameters of permitting.

Landside Uses

In addition to waterside uses, a variety of landside uses may be considered for waterfront parks. Typically, the landscape architect assists the owner in establishing a menu of uses that best serves the public and is appropriate to the site. Passive recreation such as walking, picnicking, seating, and small gatherings are common. Active recreational uses such as running, bicycling, inline skating are equally common and may share a linear trail network along a water's edge. Organized sports fields for baseball, soccer, tennis, and the like are common only when the park area is 10 acres or greater. Increasingly, waterfront parks in urban settings are programmed for performances, festivals, and markets, owing to the dramatic views they offer and proximity to population centers. If they are so programmed, the landscape architect should consider the inclusion of exterior electric outlets for sound, lighting, and vendors. In addition, providing water sources for vendors, hose bibs for cleanup, and sewage drains for cooking waste will appropriately furnish the park so that it is readily adaptable to such seasonal activities. If such intense cultural programming is envisioned, it is recommended that plans include off-site parking areas and/or shuttle transportation to serve peak demands.

ACCESS

Finally, a key to the success of any waterfront park is access to the site from the city or town in which it lies. In many instances, waterfront parks are linear in nature, following the body of water, with built-up areas immediately adjacent. Multiple access points from the street grid of the city should be considered as a means of connecting waterside uses to the city and ensuring equitable access for all citizens, not just those who live or work adjacent to the park. The landscape architect should consider a quarter-mile radius on the city side of any waterfront park as part of the context of the park and should make access and visibility recommendations to provide strong and legible connections from city to waterfront.

Dennis Carmichael, EDAW

OUTDOOR PLAY AREAS

INTRODUCTION

A quality play and learning environment is more than just a collection of play equipment. The entire site with all its elements, from vegetation to storage, can become a play and learning resource for children with and without disabilities.

Play is about more than just having fun. It is a process through which children develop their physical, mental, and social skills. It is value-laden and culturally based. In the past, most of these play experiences occurred in unstructured child-chosen places. Children with disabilities, depending on the type or severity of the disability and the attitude of their parents, have less access to these free-range play settings found around the neighborhood and very limited choice of a usable play setting.

A good play area that is designed to integrate children with and without disabilities consists of a range of settings carefully layered onto a site. They contain the following elements or settings: entrances, pathways, fences and enclosures, signage, play equipment, game areas, landforms, topography, trees and vegetation, gardens, animal habitats, water play, sand play, loose parts, gathering places, stage areas, storage, and ground covering and safety surfacing. In any play area design, each element varies in importance, depending on community values, site constraints, and location. The way these elements are used will also determine the type and degree of play, accessibility, safety, and adult comfort possible in that environment. Nevertheless, in designing a play space of any size, the full range of settings must be considered.

Diversity of play opportunities within the setting is the key to a well-designed play area. To be developmental, play must present a challenge as part of its value; and though not every part of the environment may be physically accessible to every user, all should be socially accessible to every user. A play area must support a range of challenges, both mentally and physically.

Physical challenge within the play area must be part of a progression of challenges that promote an individual's skill; that is, to be developmental, it must be "earned" through a child's efforts. In contrast, the opportunity for a social interaction should be easy. Social integration is the basic reason why a play area must be accessible to children of all abilities. Only when the play area truly serves the range of people who use it can it be considered universally designed.

Creating a universally designed play setting requires integrating the needs and abilities of all children and the people who come with them into play areas. Again, the diversity of both physical and social environments is the key to accommodating the variety of users in a play area. Obtaining physical diversity means placing a broad range of challenges within the play setting. Such an environment will allow more children to participate, make choices, take on challenges, develop skills, and, most importantly, have fun together.

Social diversity is very closely linked to physical diversity. Contact between children of different genders, abilities, and ages will naturally increase in play areas that are open to a wider spectrum of users. This interaction is particularly critical for children with functional limitations, who so often are denied these social experiences.

To create a well-designed play area, keep the following ideas in mind:

- Consider many ways in which all children can interact. When arranging the play area, integrate accessible play equipment with the rest of the play setting. Place less challenging activities directly next to those requiring greater physical ability, to encourage interaction across all ability levels.
- Provide a circulation system through the play setting that connects every activity area and every play component in the play setting. (A play component is defined as an item that provides an opportunity for play; it can be a single piece of equipment or part of a larger composite structure.) Even though not every play component will be physically accessible to everyone, simply enabling all children to be near the action offers the opportunity and choice, as well as promotes the possibility of communication with others.
- Provide separate areas for younger and older children. Children under three years old need a separate play setting that has an enclosure, so that parents feel free to allow the child to play and so that the child can run without fear of being run over by an older child or a vehicle. Permit only one way in and one way out of this play area so that caregivers can easily monitor their child. It is also a good idea to put a seating area near this entry/exit, again for adult comfort and ease of monitoring.
- Provide sand play with a water source. Drain the water through the sand. Install a transfer system into the sand area so children who use a wheelchair can enjoy full-body sand play.
- Make portions of gathering places accessible, to promote social interaction. These areas are important areas of interaction and allow groups of people to play, eat, watch, socialize, and congregate. Include accessible seating, such as benches with backrests and arm supports, to enable people of varying abilities to sit together.
- Keep in mind the American Society for Testing and Materials (ASTM) and Consumer Product Safety Commission (CPSC) safety guidelines (which outline important parameters such as head entrapments, safety surfacing, and use zones) as well as the Americans with Disabilities Act (ADA) access guidelines. At the same time, be aware that provisions for safety and accessibility may conflict. For example, a raised sand shelf could be considered hazardous because the shelf is more that 20 inches off the ground. If you strictly followed the safety requirements, you would need to construct a nonclimbable enclosure along the edge of the shelf, which would defeat the whole purpose of the design. In such cases, seek solutions that provide other means of access to mitigate the safety hazard, such as installing rubber safety surfacing on the ground below the shelf. And, remember, safety guidelines are constantly changing and you are responsible for knowing the current regulations (see ASTM and the CPSC guidelines).

PLAY SETTING PERFORMANCE CRITERIA

Circulation within a Play Setting

Because play is primarily a social experience, routes through a play setting must connect all types of activities. Without this connection, children with disabilities can too easily find themselves isolated from their friends without disabilities.

A good play setting has many routes through the space. A route itself may, in fact, be the play experience. For example, pathways can be a play element by supporting wheeled toys, running games, and exploration. To be accessible, pathways require good surfaces and correct grades (1:20 maximum) and cross slopes (2 percent or less). The quality of the pathway system sets the tone for the entire environment.

Pathways can be wide with small branches, long and straight, or circuitous and meandering. Each creates different play behaviors and experiences. Minimum routes or auxiliary pathways through a play experience promote the range of challenges necessary for a variety of developmentally appropriate play experiences.

The following criteria for accessible route design apply:

- An accessible route to and for the intended use of the different activities within the play area setting must be provided.
- The accessible route should be a minimum of 60 inches wide, but can be adjusted down to 36 inches if it is in conjunction with a bench or play activity.
- The cross slope of the accessible route of travel must not exceed 1:50.
- The slope of the accessible route of travel should not exceed 1:20.
- If a slope exceeds 1:20, it is a ramp. A ramp on the accessible route of travel on the ground plane should not exceed a slope of 1:16.
- If the accessible route of travel is adjacent to loose fill material or there is a drop-off, then the edge of the pathway should be treated by beveling the edge with a slope that does not exceed 30 percent, to protect a wheelchair from falling off the route and into the loose fill material. A raised edge will create a trip hazard for walking children. If this route is within the use zone of the play equipment, the path and the edge treatment must be made of safety surfacing.
- Changes in level along the path should not exceed ¼ inch or ½ inch if beveled.
- Where egress from an accessible play activity occurs in loose fill surface (not firm, stable, and slip-resistant), a means of returning to the point of access for that play activity must be provided, and the surfacing material should not splinter, scrape, puncture, or abrade the skin when being crawled upon.

PLAY EQUIPMENT

Most equipment settings stimulate large muscle activity and kinesthetic experience, but they can also support nonphysical aspects of child development. Equipment can provide opportunities to experience

Susan Goltsman, FASLA

SWINGS
PRIORITY: 5
LOCATE:

- NEAR AN EDGE, TO REDUCE CROSS TRAFFIC AND POTENTIAL CONFLICTS WITH OTHER PLAY ACTIVITIES
- NEAR THE INFANT AREA, SO INFANTS CAN ACCESS SWINGS

DO NOT LOCATE:

- NEAR THE BUILDING OR MULTI PURPOSE/OUTDOOR CLASSROOM BECAUSE IT CAN BE A DISTRACTION
- BETWEEN DESTINATIONS THAT ENCOURAGE THROUGH TRAFFIC

PLAY STATION/ACOUSTIC PLAY
PRIORITY: 12
LOCATE:

- NEAR THE EDGE TO USE CORNERS OR "LEFTOVER" SPACES
- ON AN ACCESSIBLE SURFACE

DO NOT LOCATE:

- NEAR BUILDING OR MULTI PURPOSE/OUTDOOR AREA BECAUSE IT MAY CAUSE A DISTRACTION
- NEAR "QUIET" SAND AREA

WHEELED TOY STORAGE
PRIORITY: 3
LOCATE:

- NEAR THE TRIKE PATH
- TO DEFINE AN EDGE
- ON HARD SURFACING

DO NOT LOCATE:

- NEAR AN OBJECT OR PLATFORM THAT WOULD ASSIST CHILDREN TO CLIMB ON TOP OF IT

PLAY STATION
PRIORITY: 11
LOCATE:

- TO DEFINE AN EDGE

DO NOT LOCATE:

- BLOCKING SIGHT LINES ACROSS THE PLAYGROUND

LARGE SAND AND WATER PLAY AREA
PRIORITY: 4
LOCATE:

- NEAR PLAY VILLAGE, SO SAND AND WATER CAN BE USED AS PLAY PROPS
- NEAR WATER SOURCE
- NEAR MAINTENANCE ACCESS FOR REPLENISHING SAND
- NEAR VEGETATION FOR SHADE

DO NOT LOCATE:

- NEAR TURF AREA, SO TURF REMAINS DRY FOR SITTING AND LAYING

QUIET SAND PLAY
PRIORITY: 9
LOCATE:

- OUTSIDE THE PATHWAY LOOP, AS FAR FROM THE CDC BUILDING AS POSSIBLE
- NEAR VEGETATION, TO GIVE IT A SENSE OF ENCLOSURE
- NEAR SAND AND WATER PLAY FOR EASY ACCESS TO WATER

DO NOT LOCATE:

- NEAR COMPOSITE STRUCTURE, MULTI PURPOSE/OUTDOOR CLASSROOMS OR OTHER ACTIVE NOISY PLAY ELEMENTS

FENCING (MANDATORY)
LOCATE:

- FOR SECURITY AND CONTAINMENT OF ENTIRE PLAY AREA
- BETWEEN AGE-SPECIFIC PLAY AREAS WHEN SAFETY IS A CONCERN, SUCH AS BETWEEN TODDLER SWING AREA AND INFANTS

DO NOT LOCATE:

- BETWEEN BUILDING AND PLAY AREA
- BETWEEN PLAY ELEMENTS

QUIET PLACE
PRIORITY: 10
LOCATE:

- ON AN EDGE SO IT IS "EXTENDED" (BY GREEN SPACE BEYOND THE PLAY AREAS)
- WITHIN AN AREA OF TREE AND/OR SHRUB PLANTINGS
- SO THAT A QUIET PATH CAN WIND THROUGH IT

DO NOT LOCATE:

- SO THAT ALL SIGHT LINES INTO IT ARE BLOCKED

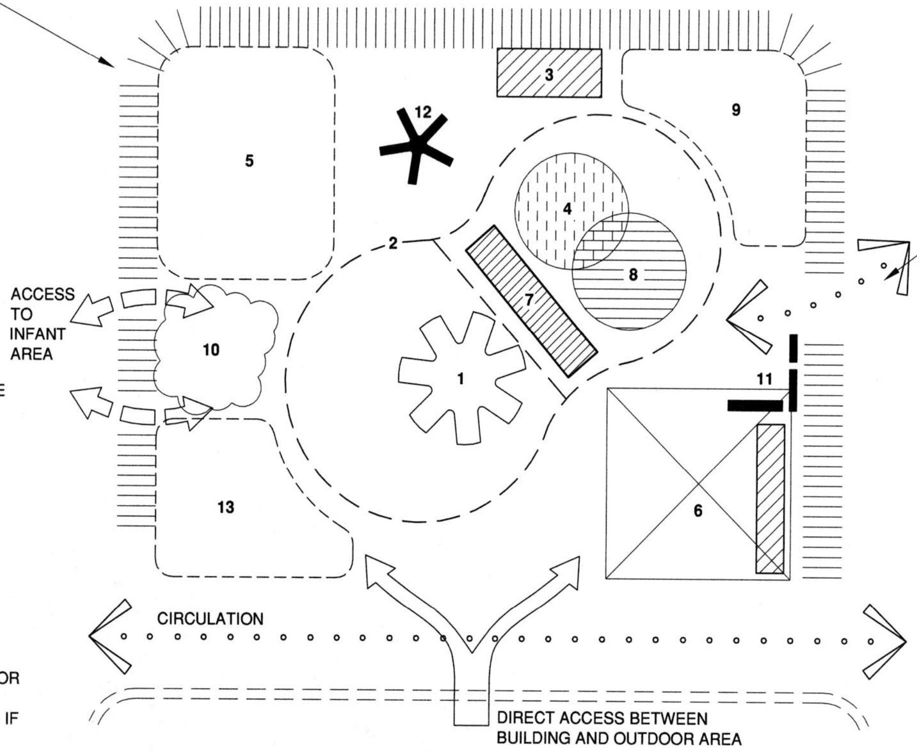

COMPOSITE STRUCTURE
PRIORITY: 7
LOCATE:

- NEAR DRAMATIC SAND PLAY FOR EXTENDED DRAMATIC PROPS
- WITH ACCESSIBLE APPROACH, IF SPACE PERMITS
- TO ACT AS A "BRIDGE" FACILITATING EASY SEQUENTIAL FLOW BETWEEN OTHER ACTIVE PLAY ELEMENTS
- CENTRALLY TO GIVE A 'BIRD'S-EYE VIEW' OF THE ENTIRE PLAYGROUND
- ON IMPACT-ATTENUATING SURFACE WITH AN ACCESSIBLE APPROACH

DO NOT LOCATE:

- NEAR AN ACTIVITY AREA THAT MAY CAUSE CONFLICTS, SUCH AS THE SWING AREA OR QUIET PLAY AREAS

ACCESS TO INFANT AREA

CIRCULATION

DIRECT ACCESS BETWEEN BUILDING AND OUTDOOR AREA

DRAMATIC SAND PLAY
PRIORITY: 8
LOCATE:

- NEAR SAND AND WATER PLAY, SO WATER SOURCE IS EASILY ACCESSED
- NEAR COMPOSITE STRUCTURE, SO DRAMATIC-TYPE INTERACTION CAN OCCUR
- NEAR MAINTENANCE ACCESS

DO NOT LOCATE:

- ELEMENTS WITHIN 6'-0" OF OTHER OBJECTS

MAINTENANCE ACCESS
LOCATE:

- ALONG PERIMETER OF PLAY AREAS
- TO PROVIDE AN EXTERIOR CORRIDOR FOR MAINTENANCE VEHICLE ACCESS AND PEDESTRIAN CIRCULATION BETWEEN PLAY AREAS
- WITH ACCESS FROM THE GROUP PLAY AREA OR FROM OUTSIDE THE PLAY AREAS BY A 10'-0" GATE
- WHERE PLANTING SCREENS ARE NOT CRITICAL

DO NOT LOCATE:

- WHERE VEHICLES ARE FORCED TO CROSS A PLAY AREA

MULTI PURPOSE AREA/OUTDOOR CLASSROOM AND STORAGE AREA
PRIORITY: 6
LOCATE:

- NEAR THE BUILDING FOR EASY TRANSITION BETWEEN INDOOR AND OUTDOOR CLASSROOM ACTIVITIES - BUT NOT ATTACHED TO THE BUILDING
- NEAR AN EDGE TO SEPARATE IT FROM ACTIVE PLAY
- WITH EASY ACCESS TO SAND AND PLAY VILLAGE FOR LOOSE-PART STORAGE
- NEAR BUILDING, TO REDUCE COSTLY UTILITY INSTALLATION

DO NOT LOCATE:

- NEAR SWINGS, SOUND CHIMES, OR OTHER NOISY ACTIVITIES
- WITHIN MAIN CIRCULATION PATHS

TURF AREA
PRIORITY: 13
LOCATE:

- NEAR INFANT AREA FOR SHARED USE BY INFANTS
- AWAY FROM NOISY ACTIVITIES
- TO PROVIDE A GREEN BUFFER WHERE DESIRABLE
- NEAR NATURE AREA TO EXTEND IT

DO NOT LOCATE:

- IN A CENTRAL AREA
- IN A PRIMARY CIRCULATION PATH

WHEELED TOY PATH
PRIORITY: 2
LOCATE:

- TO ACCESS AND CONNECT ALL ELEMENTS OF THE PLAY AREA INCLUDING TRIKE STORAGE
- TO CREATE A CROSSROADS AT THE PLAY VILLAGE
- WITH MINIMAL IMPACT ON QUIET ACTIVITIES

DO NOT LOCATE:

- TO CONFLICT WITH HIGH-ACTIVITY AREAS SUCH AS SWINGS

PLAY VILLAGE
PRIORITY: 1
LOCATE:

- CENTRALLY, NEAR THE COMPOSITE STRUCTURE, SAND, AND WATER
- AT THE WHEELED TOY PATH CROSSROADS
- NEAR MULTI PURPOSE AREA/OUTDOOR CLASSROOM FOR STORAGE OF LOOSE PARTS

DO NOT LOCATE:

- IN A CORNER

TODDLER LAYOUT: FUNCTIONAL RELATIONSHIPS BETWEEN MAJOR DESIGN ELEMENTS FOR A TODDLER PLAY AREA

Susan Goltsman, FASLA

SWINGS
PRIORITY: 7
LOCATE:
- NEAR AN EDGE TO REDUCE CROSS TRAFFIC

DO NOT LOCATE:
- NEAR THE BUILDING OR MULTIPURPOSE/OUTDOOR CLASSROOM BECAUSE IT CAN BE A DISTRACTION
- BETWEEN DESTINATIONS WHICH ENCOURAGE THROUGH TRAFFIC

MAINTENANCE ACCESS
LOCATE:
- ALONG PERIMETER OF PLAY AREAS
- TO PROVIDE AN EXTERIOR CORRIDOR FOR MAINTENANCE VEHICLE ACCESS AND PEDESTRIAN CIRCULATION BETWEEN PLAY AREAS
- WITH ACCESS FROM OUTSIDE THE PLAY AREAS BY A 10'-0" GATE
- WHERE PLANTING SCREENS ARE NOT CRITICAL

DO NOT LOCATE:
- WHERE VEHICLES ARE FORCED TO CROSS A PLAY AREA

WHEELED TOY STORAGE
PRIORITY: 2
LOCATE:
- NEAR THE TRIKE PATH
- ADJACENT TO THE BALL PLAY AREA SO THAT STORAGE MAY DOUBLE AS A BALL WALL
- ON HARD SURFACING

DO NOT LOCATE:
- NEAR AN OBJECT OR PLATFORM THAT WOULD ASSIST CHILDREN TO CLIMB ON TOP OF IT

PLAY VILLAGE
PRIORITY: 3
LOCATE:
- CENTRALLY, NEAR THE COMPOSITE STRUCTURE, SAND, AND WATER
- AT THE WHEELED TOY PATH CROSSROADS
- NEAR MULIT PURPOSE AREA/OUTDOOR CLASSROOM FOR STORAGE OF LOOSE PARTS

DO NOT LOCATE:
- IN A CORNER

DRAMATIC SAND PLAY
PRIORITY: 14
LOCATE:
- NEAR SAND AND WATER PLAY SO WATER SOURCE IS EASILY ACCESSIBLE

DO NOT LOCATE:
- WITHIN 6'-0" OF OTHER OBJECTS

BALL PLAY AREA
PRIORITY: 9
LOCATE:
- NEAR THE BUILDING BUT SEPARATED FROM IT, SO THAT IT BECOMES AN OPEN- SPACE FOCAL POINT
- NEAR TRIKE STORAGE/BALL WALL STRUCTURE
- NEAR SWINGS AND COMPOSITE STRUCTURE, BUT DIVIDED SO THAT HIGH-MOVEMENT ACTIVITIES ARE SEPARATED FROM OTHER FOCUSED PLAY ACTIVITIES

DO NOT LOCATE:
- IN THE CENTER
- NEAR QUIET ACTIVITIES

COMPOSITE STRUCTURE
PRIORITY: 4
LOCATE:
- NEAR AN EDGE TO ALLOW EXPANSION OPPORTUNITY
- NEAR BALL PLAY AND SWINGS SO, THAT HIGH-MOVEMENT ACTIVITIES ARE SEPARATED FROM OTHER FOCUSED PLAY ACTIVITIES

DO NOT LOCATE:
- NEAR THE BUILDING OR MULTIPURPOSE/OUTDOOR CLASSROOM BECAUSE IT CAN BE A DISTRACTION
- WITH DESTINATIONS ON OPPOSITE SIDES THAT ENCOURAGE THROUGH TRAFFIC

QUIET PLACE
PRIORITY: 10
LOCATE:
- ON AN EDGE SO IT IS "EXTENDED" (BY GREEN SPACE BEYOND THE PLAY AREAS)
- WITHIN AN AREA OF TREE AND/OR SHRUB PLANTINGS
- SO THAT A QUIET PATH CAN WIND THROUGH IT

DO NOT LOCATE:
- WITH ALL SIGHT LINES INTO IT BLOCKED

PLAY STATION
PRIORITY: 11
LOCATE:
- TO DEFINE AN EDGE

DO NOT LOCATE:
- BLOCKING SITE LINES ACROSS THE PLAYGROUND

PLAY STATION/ACOUSTIC PLAY
PRIORITY: 12
LOCATE:
- NEAR THE EDGE TO USE CORNERS OR "LEFTOVER" SPACES

DO NOT LOCATE:
- NEAR BUILDING OR MULTIPURPOSE/OUTDOOR AREA BECAUSE IT MAY CAUSE A DISTRACTION

CONSTRUCTION AREA
PRIORITY: 6
LOCATE:
- NEXT TO THE PLAY VILLAGE, SO THAT THE CONSTRUCTION AREA CAN BE USED TO EXPAND THE PLAY VILLAGE WITH CHILD- BUILT STRUCTURES
- WITH EASY ACCESS TO LOOSE-PARTS STORAGE

DO NOT LOCATE:
- TO CONFLICT WITH HIGH-ACTIVITY AREAS SUCH AS SWINGS

FENCING
LOCATE:
- FOR SECURITY AND CONTAINMENT OF ENTIRE PLAY AREA
- BETWEEN AGE-SPECIFIC PLAY AREAS WHEN SAFETY IS A CONCERN, SUCH AS BETWEEN TODDLER SWING AREA AND INFANTS

DO NOT LOCATE:
- BETWEEN BUILDING AND PLAY AREA
- BETWEEN PLAY ELEMENTS

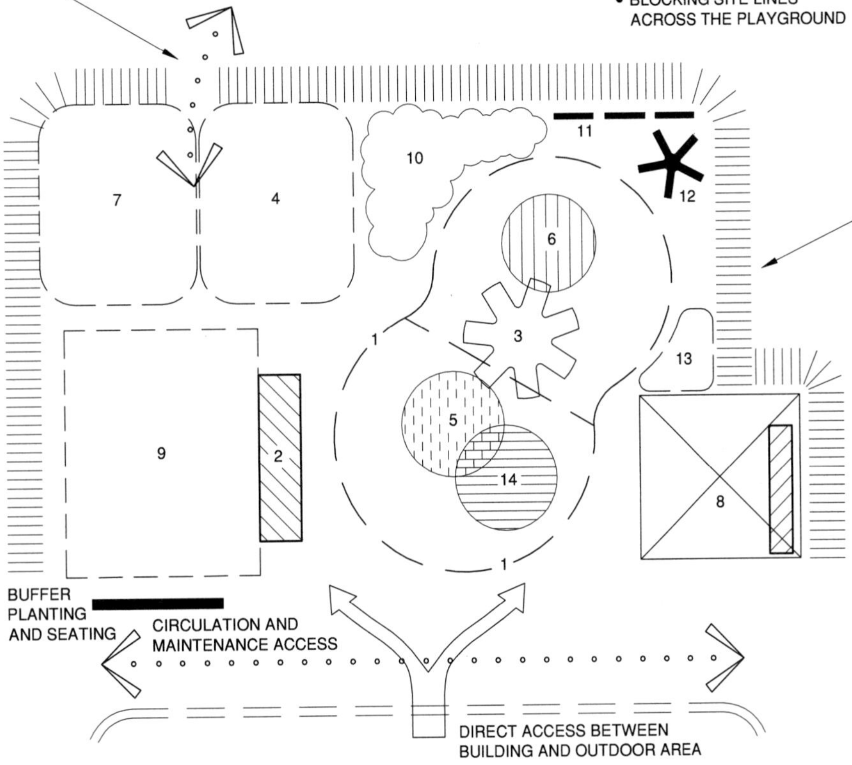

BUFFER PLANTING AND SEATING

CIRCULATION AND MAINTENANCE ACCESS

DIRECT ACCESS BETWEEN BUILDING AND OUTDOOR AREA

SAND AND WATER PLAY AREA
PRIORITY: 5
LOCATE:
- NEAR PLAY VILLAGE SO SAND AND WATER CAN BE USED AS PLAY PROPS
- NEAR WATER SOURCE
- NEAR MAINTENANCE ACCESS FOR REPLENISHING SAND
- NEAR VEGETATION FOR SHADE

WHEELED TOY PATH
PRIORITY: 1
LOCATE:
- TO ACCESS AND CONNECT ALL ELEMENTS OF THE PLAY AREA, INCLUDING TRIKE STORAGE
- TO CREATE A CROSSROADS AT THE PLAY VILLAGE
- WITH MINIMAL IMPACT ON QUIET ACTIVITIES

DO NOT LOCATE:
- TO CONFLICT WITH HIGH-ACTIVITY AREAS SUCH AS SWINGS

GARDEN AREA
PRIORITY: 13
LOCATE:
- NEAR MULTI-USE/OUTDOOR CLASSROOM AREA, SO LOOSE- PART STORAGE IS ACCESSIBLE
- NEAR WATER SOURCE
- NEAR SHADE

DO NOT LOCATE:
- IN COMPLETE SHADE

MULTIPURPOSE AREA/OUTDOOR CLASSROOM AND STORAGE AREA
PRIORITY: 8
LOCATE:
- NEAR THE BUILDING FOR EASY TRANSITION BETWEEN INDOOR AND OUTDOORACTIVITIES, BUT NOT ATTACHED TO THE BUILDING
- NEAR AN EDGE, TO SEPARATE IT FROM ACTIVE PLAY
- WITH EASY ACCESS TO SAND AND PLAY VILLAGE FOR LOOSE PART STORAGE
- NEAR BUILDING, TO REDUCE COSTLY UTILITY INSTALLATION

DO NOT LOCATE:
- NEAR SWINGS, SOUND CHIMES, OR OTHER NOISY ACTIVITIES
- WITHIN MAIN CIRCULATION PATHS

PRESCHOOL LAYOUT: FUNCTIONAL RELATIONSHIPS BETWEEN MAJOR DESIGN ELEMENTS FOR A PRESCHOOL PLAY AREA

Susan Goltsman, FASLA

height and can serve as landmarks to assist orientation and wayfinding. They may also become rendezvous spots, stimulate social interaction, and provide hideaways in hiding and chasing games. Small, semienclosed spaces support dramatic play, and seating, shelves, and tables encourage social play.

In choosing manufactured play equipment for a recreation area, consider the following:

- Properly selected equipment can support the development of creativity and cooperation, especially structures that incorporate sand and water play. Play structures can be converted to other temporary uses such as stage settings; loose parts can be strung from and attached to the equipment, such as backdrops or banners for special events and dramatic play activities. Equipment settings must be designed as part of a comprehensive multipurpose play environment. Isolated pieces of equipment are ineffective on their own.
- Equipment should be properly sited, selected, and installed over appropriate resistant safety surfaces. Procedures and standards for equipment purchase, installation, and maintenance must be developed. A systematic safety inspection program must be implemented.
- A number of well-documented safety issues are related to manufactured play equipment: falls, entrapments, protrusions, collisions, splinters. All of these issues must be addressed in the design, maintenance, and supervision of play equipment.
- Equipment should be accessible, but must be designed primarily for children, not wheelchairs or adults. The most significant aspect of making a piece of equipment accessible is to understand that children with disabilities need many of the same challenges as children without disabilities. Using synthetic surfacing can provide access to, under, and through the equipment for children in wheelchairs. Getting in the center of action may be as important as climbing to the highest point for some children.
- Play equipment provides opportunities for integration, especially when programmed with other activities. Play settings should be exciting and attractive for parents as well as children—adults accompany children to the park or playground more often today than in the past. It is equally important to design for parents using wheelchairs who accompany their able-bodied children.

Play equipment is designed to provide a physical challenge as well as social interaction. For equipment to be appropriate for different skill levels, it must be graduated in its challenge opportunities. Access up to, onto, through, and off equipment should also provide a variety of challenge levels appropriate to the age of the intended users. Siting of the play equipment is also critical. Swings should be separated from the main area to make it more difficult for a child to run in the front of the swings set. Tot swings should be separated from belt swings. Play equipment should be located so it does not obstruct the view of the play area. Parents have to be able to see their children as they play.

SURFACING MATERIALS

Both soft and hard play surfaces are needed to support different types of play activity. Shock-absorbing surfacing materials are mandatory throughout the use zones of all manufactured equipment. These materials should also be firm and resilient along accessible routes leading to transfer points onto equipment. A range of natural ground covers can provide contact with nature and a habitat for small animals. The types of surfacing addressed here include: turf and natural ground covers, hard surfaces, and shock-absorbing surfacing materials.

The surfacing in each part of the play environment must respond to the needs of the intended activities and user groups. Considerations include: durability, toxicity, allergenicity, slip resistance, all-weather use, climatic zone, maintenance, aesthetics, accessibility, and required shock absorbency. By providing a diversity of materials that meet the needs of different areas, users, and activities, surface materials can ensure a wide variety of play opportunities for the widest number of users.

Turf and Natural Ground Covers

Turf and other natural ground covers create ecosystems at a smaller scale than trees and shrubs. They are more manipulable for children, but also more vulnerable and prone to wear. Attention to circulation design can help avoid unnecessary erosion and the need for replanting.

Some ground-cover species change according to the season, which enhances the sense of the passage of time. Some species attract small insects, which are a source of learning and excitement for children. Flowering and scented species add sensory diversity; however, poisonous species and species with thorns must be avoided.

Pest and weed management practices must be carefully evaluated to avoid exposing children to toxins. All weeds should be removed manually. Small animals should be managed by trapping. Other pest problems should be evaluated by certified pest management personnel. Should chemical treatment be necessary, the least toxic alternative should be chosen. After treatment, the play area should be closed until safe for use.

Turf is used in three situations:

- Sport playing surfaces
- Unstructured recreation areas
- Surfaces on mounds and slopes

Turf is not suitable as a shock-absorbing surface under equipment.

Consider the following when determining which species of ground cover to use in a play environment:

- Different species have different capabilities to withstand wear.
- Different species have different capabilities to regrow after being damaged
- Some species have a dormant period during which they turn brown.
- Turf and other natural ground covers require more work to maintain than nonliving surfaces.
- Turf turns to mud in wet weather if an unsuitable variety of grass is used, or site furnishings are not moved regularly.
- Turf can be soft and cool to look at and is relatively soft (but still firm) to play on.
- Turf is difficult for wheelchairs to move through over a long distance (10 to 15 feet); therefore, it is not suitable for an accessible playing field.

Hard Surfaces

Hard surfaces include: dirt, concrete, asphalt, artificial grass, and decomposed granite. These surfaces should never be used in play equipment use zones.

- *Dirt.* Dirt varies in hardness, but never meets the requirements for shock absorption under equipment.
- *Concrete and asphalt.* These are very hard surfaces to fall on and, therefore, cannot be used under equipment. However, they are necessary for activities where turf surfaces are impractical, such as for ball play. They are very accessible to people using wheelchairs and are easy to maintain and to keep free of broken glass. Asphalt must be laid to a fixed, solid timber or concrete edge, or it will crack and become broken around the edges.
- *Artificial grass.* Artificial grass is an expensive material that is suitable for general play and games areas. It should not be used under play equipment.
- *Decomposed granite.* This material is a good all-weather surface for picnic areas, pathways, or around trees. It should not be used under play equipment.

Shock-Absorbing Surfacing Materials

Approximately 70 percent of all playground injuries are due to falls from equipment onto unsafe surfaces. Adequate surfacing throughout play equipment use zones is an essential safety requirement. The principal standard of adequacy (CPSC) is that the surface must yield both a peak deceleration of no more than 200 times the acceleration due to gravity (200 G's) and a Head Impact Criteria (HIC) value of no more than 1000 for a head-first fall from the highest accessible point of the play equipment when tested in accordance with ASTM F1292, Standard Specification for Impact Attenuation Under and Around Playground Equipment. Designers should require that manufacturers supply the results of such tests, conducted by an independent laboratory, before specifying a given safety surface.

Surfacing is a critical aspect of manufactured equipment settings. A number of alternative treatments are available, and each has positive and negative points. Most surfaces are costly, and all require regular maintenance, some more frequently than others.

Surfacing Depth and Critical Height

The "critical height" is the maximum height at which a head-first fall from equipment onto the playground surface meets shock-absorbency requirements. The "Critical Height of Tested Materials" table may be used as a guide in selecting the type and depth of loose-fill materials that will provide the necessary safety for equipment of various heights. Each material in the table was tested at three "uncompressed" depths. Notice that the capability to absorb impacts reduces when the material is compressed. Keep in mind that materials must meet the specifications listed in the *CPSC Handbook* if they are to accurately reflect the performance data listed in the table.

Organic Materials

Organic materials, such as pine bark mininuggets, pine bark mulch, shredded hardwood bark, and cocoa shell mulch, share the following characteristics:

Susan Goltsman, FASLA

CRITICAL HEIGHT OF TESTED MATERIALS* (IN FEET)

	UNCOMPRESSED DEPTH		COMPRESSED DEPTH	
MATERIAL	**6″**	**9″**	**12″**	**9″**
Wood mulch	7	10	11	10
Double-shredded bark mulch	6	10	11	7
Uniform wood chips	6	7	>12	6
Fine sand	5	5	9	5
Coarse sand	5	5	6	4
Fine gravel	6	7	10	6
Medium gravel	5	5	6	5

* *Materials must correspond with the specifications listed in the* CPSC Handbook.

Source: CPSC, 1991.

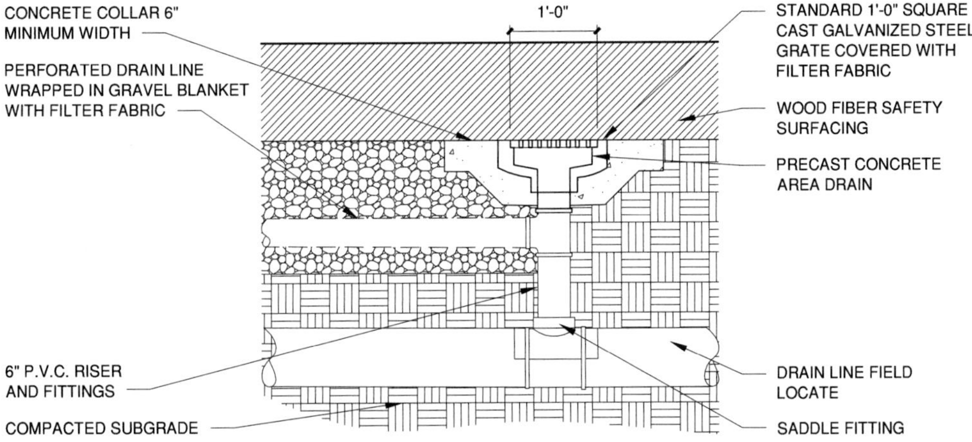

AREA DRAIN BELOW SURFACE OF WOOD FIBER SAFETY SURFACING

- Cushioning properties depend on the air trapped within and between individual particles. In rainy weather, or during periods of high humidity, these materials absorb moisture and tend to compact. Under these conditions, they may lose some of the trapped air necessary for protective cushioning.
- They should never be installed over existing hard surfaces.
- With the passage of time, these materials may decompose and become pulverized, thereby losing their cushioning effect, and need to be replaced.
- When wet and exposed to freezing temperatures, they freeze and lose their cushioning protection.
- Good drainage is required underneath the material. When wet, they are subject to microbial growth.
- Strong winds can blow these materials, reducing the thickness necessary for adequate cushioning. A method of containment must be provided.
- They are gradually displaced by the playing action of children, thereby reducing the thickness of protective layers in vital fall areas. A method of containment will help reduce displacement.
- They harbor and conceal various insects, which are usually harmless, and provide learning opportunities for children. These materials also can conceal animal excrement and trash such as broken glass, nails, pencils, and other sharp objects that puncture and cut.
- With use, they may combine with dirt and other foreign materials, resulting in a loss of shock-absorbing properties.
- They may be deliberately removed (stolen) for use as mulch by residents.
- They can be flammable.
- Generally, these materials require replacement and frequent maintenance, such as leveling, grading, and sifting, to remove foreign matter.
- A major benefit of wood-based, shock-absorbing surfacing materials, when compared to inorganic materials such as sand, is that they are less abrasive when tracked into buildings.
- When used as a surfacing for informal play (circulation and social areas, not under equipment), several of the above reservations that relate to reduction in shock absorbency no longer apply. Under these conditions, organic materials provide a viable, wear-resistant alternative to grass. They also provide children with useful "props" to support dramatic play.

Inorganic Materials

Sand and pea gravel are common inorganic shock-absorbing surfaces. They have the following characteristics (CPSC, 1991).

- Sand can be blown, and either material can be thrown into children's eyes.
- They can be displaced by the playing action of children, thereby reducing the thickness of protective layers in fall zones. A method of containment is required.
- They can harbor and conceal various insects, animal excrement, and other trash, such as broken glass, nails, pencils, and other sharp objects, that can cause puncture and cutting wounds. Sand is also attractive to cats, who use it as "kitty litter."
- With use, these materials may be combined with dirt and other foreign materials, resulting in a loss of cushioning properties.
- With increasing amounts of moisture, sand becomes cohesive and less capable of cushioning. When thoroughly wet, sand reacts as a rigid material when impacted from any direction. Good drainage is required underneath the material.
- When wet and exposed to freezing temperatures, these materials will freeze and lose their cushioning protection.
- They are difficult to walk on and inaccessible to wheelchair users.
- Generally, these materials require replacement and frequent maintenance, such as leveling, grading, and sifting, to remove foreign matter.
- These materials must never be installed over existing hard surfaces.

Synthetic inorganic materials include rubber matting and chopped tire. They have the following characteristics:

- They often require near-level, uniform surfaces and are, therefore, difficult to lay.
- They may be subject to vandalism (defaced, ignited, cut, etc.).
- In hot climates, they can retain a lot of heat.
- They are easy to maintain and provide easy access.

Sand and Pea Gravel

These materials are frequently chosen for shock-absorbing surfacing under play equipment. Since they have no compressibility, their shock-absorbing characteristics are due to their capability to deform to the shape of the falling child. They spread the area of impact while increasing its duration (a slow, large-area impact is less injurious than a narrow, quick impact).

Sand is more popular than gravel as a shock-absorbing surface, although pea gravel offers some advantages as a surfacing solution for very cold and very hot climates. Sand particles must be round in shape and as uniform in size as possible. Particles 1⁄32 inch or less will be significantly affected by the surface tension of water and tend to bind together when wet. Fine sand is most effective as a shock-absorbing surfacing material.

Particles larger than 3⁄8 inch have sufficient mass to cause serious eye injury when thrown. Sand of the type required is produced by interaction with water, and exists in river and ocean deposits. It is sometimes known as washed riverbed sand, grain, or bird's-eye sand.

The species of original stone affects the longevity of sand. Hard sand will last longer than sand composed of soft stone particles. Because of the weight of sand, the major cost is transportation.

If sand is used as a surface under play equipment, additional sand areas must be provided for sand play. Sand under and around equipment cannot serve both purposes. If additional sand areas are not provided, children will play in traffic areas, a potentially hazardous situation; and the products of their sand play will get stomped on, causing much frustration and unnecessary social conflict.

If sand is used as the primary shock-absorbing surface, then it should be used in combination with manufactured resilient surfaces, to provide access to the equipment for people with mobility problems.

Synthetic Surfaces

Synthetic tiles and poured surfacing provide access for wheelchair users and the ambulatory disabled. They should be used on pathways that extend within

Susan Goltsman, FASLA

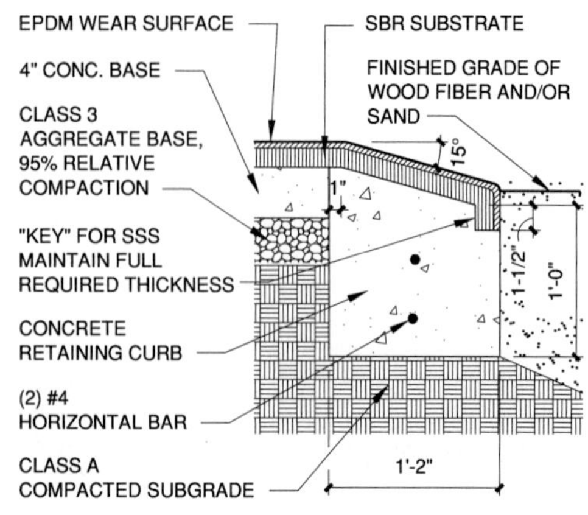

CHAMFERED CURB AND SYNTHETIC SAFETY SURFACING

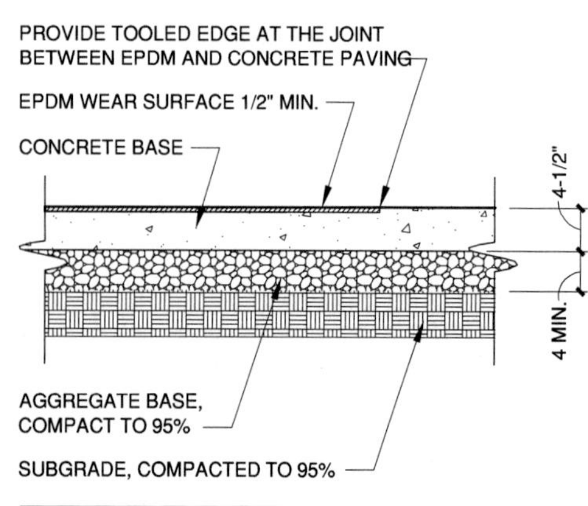

EPDM RUBBER WEARING COURSE OVER CONCRETE WALKWAY

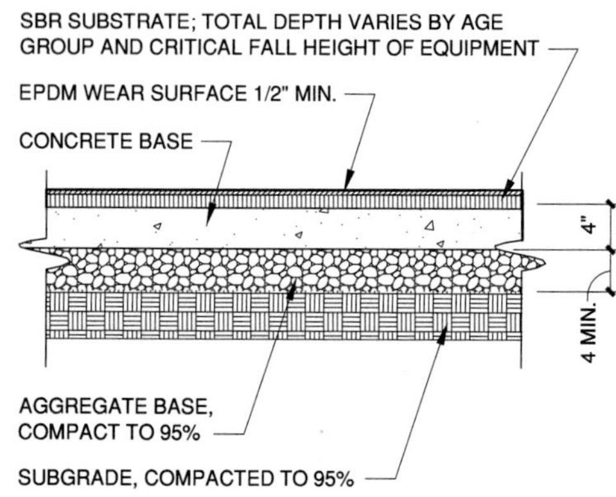

SYNTHETIC SAFETY SURFACING OVER CONCRETE BASE

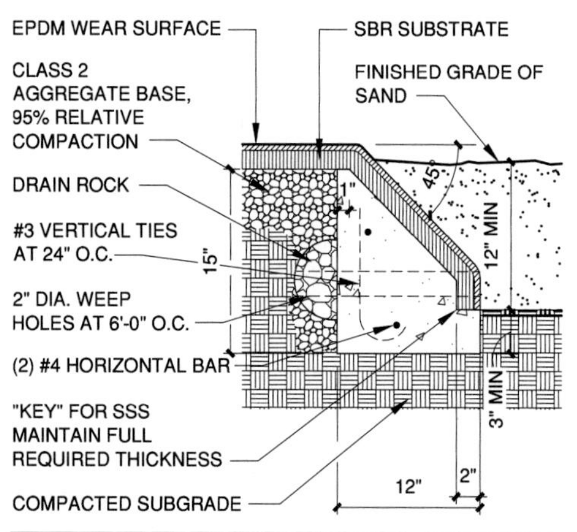

CHAMFERED CURB AND SYNTHETIC SAFETY SURFACING WITH WEEP HOLES

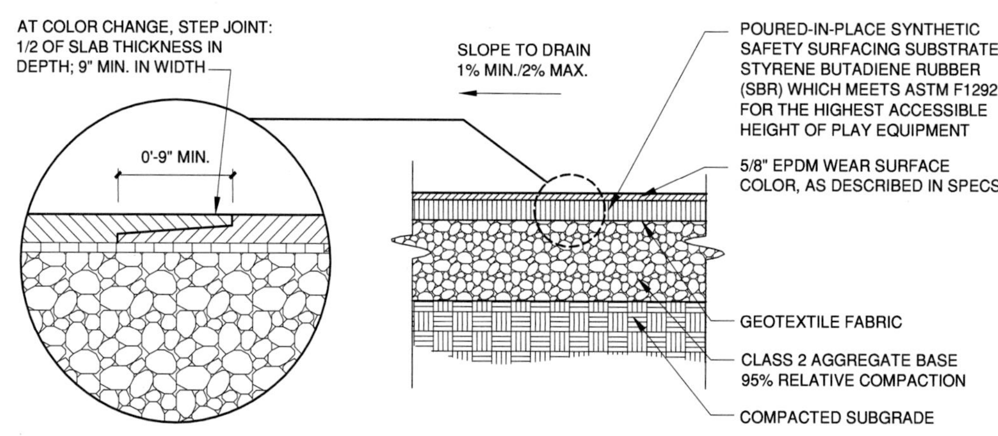

SYNTHETIC SAFETY SURFACING OVER AGGREGATE BASE

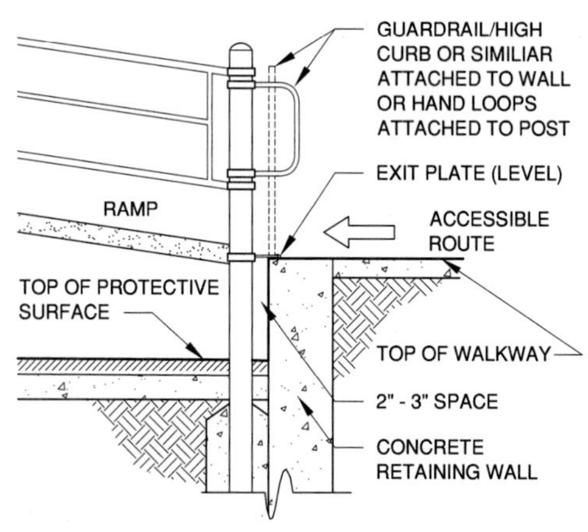

RAMP ON PLAY EQUIPMENT TO EXIT ONTO WALKWAY INSTALLATION

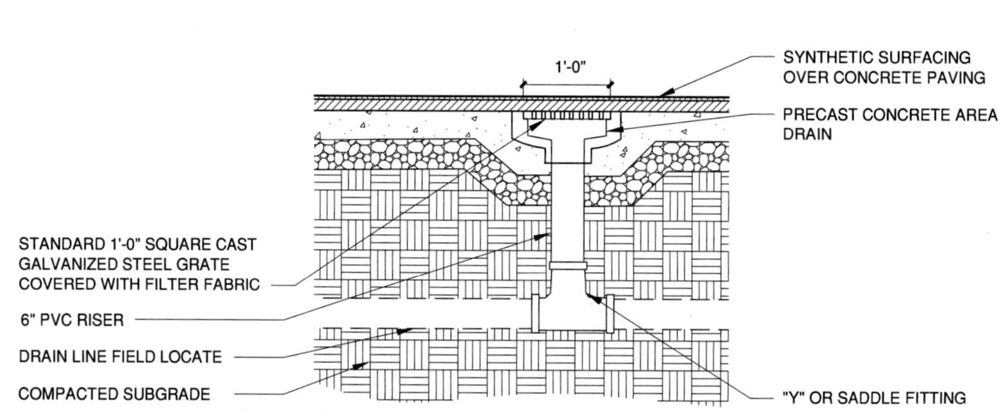

AREA DRAIN WITH SYNTHETIC SAFETY SURFACING

Susan Goltsman, FASLA

the use zone of an equipment setting and to provide access to equipment.

When purchasing these materials, there are a number of questions to address:

- Does a drop onto this surface from the highest accessible point on the play structure result in a g-force rating of less than 200g's and an HIC of no more than 1000?
- Does the surface allow for water drainage?
- Is the surface slip-resistant?
- What are the installation requirements?
- What are the maintenance requirements?
- Is the surface easy to clean?
- Will it look attractive and complement the appearance of the playground equipment?
- How does it smell?
- Is the surface durable and capable of withstanding extremes of temperature, frost, water use, vandalism, and other impacts?
- Will it fade in the sun?
- Is it easy to repair?
- What is the warranty and estimated life of the surfacing material?

Other Proprietary Surfacings

New or improved manufactured surfacings are continually appearing on the market. They vary greatly in suitability for different play settings and climatic conditions.

WATER PLAY AREAS

Water in all its forms is a universal play material because it can be manipulated in so many ways. It can be splashed, poured, used to float objects, and mixed with dirt to form "magic potions." Permanent or temporary, the multisensory quality of water makes a substantial contribution to child development. Water settings include: a hose in the sandpit, puddles, ponds, drinking fountains, bubblers, sprinklers, sprays, cascades, pools, even a dew-covered leaf.

If water play is provided, a part of the play area must be wheelchair-accessible. If the water source is manipulated by children, then it must be usable by all children. If loose parts such as buckets are provided, and children have access to the equipment storage, then the storage must be usable by all children. When water is provided for play, the following dimensions apply:

Forward reach: 36 to 20 inches

Side reach: 36 to 20 inches

Clear space: 36 by 55 inches (The clear space should be located at the part of the water play area where the most water play will occur. If the water source is part of the active play area, and children turn the water on and off, then it must be accessible. If the water source is part of a spray pool, the area under the spray should be accessible. Accessibility should involve the dimensions for both clear space and reach.)

Clearance ranges: Top height to access water 31 inches, maximum to rim; under clearance, 24 inches, minimum

One of the most important aspects of designing with water is drainage. There should be no unintentional standing water. All water at a child's play area must be potable. If there is one rule about water, it is that children bring sand to water more than water to sand, so design for it. That means include a way to clean out the sand from the drain or to always drain the water through a sand area.

Never place a drinking fountain near a sand area, especially if that is the only water source. Do not forget that a foot wash station near the sand play area will be very appreciated by parents.

SAND PLAY AREAS

Children will play in dirt wherever they find it. Using "props" such as a few twigs, a small plastic toy, or a few stones, children can create an imaginary world in the dirt, around the roots of a tree, or in a raised planter. The sandbox is a refined and sanitized version of dirt play. It works best when it retains the play qualities of dirt. Provide small, intimate group spaces, adequate play surfaces, and access to water and other small play props.

If a sand play area is provided, part of it must be accessible. Important elements are clear floor space, maneuvering room, reach and clearance ranges, and operating mechanisms for control of sand flow. When products such as buckets and shovels will likely be used in the sand play area, storage places should be at accessible reach-range.

Raised sand play is a very limiting play experience because of the way a raised area must be constructed:

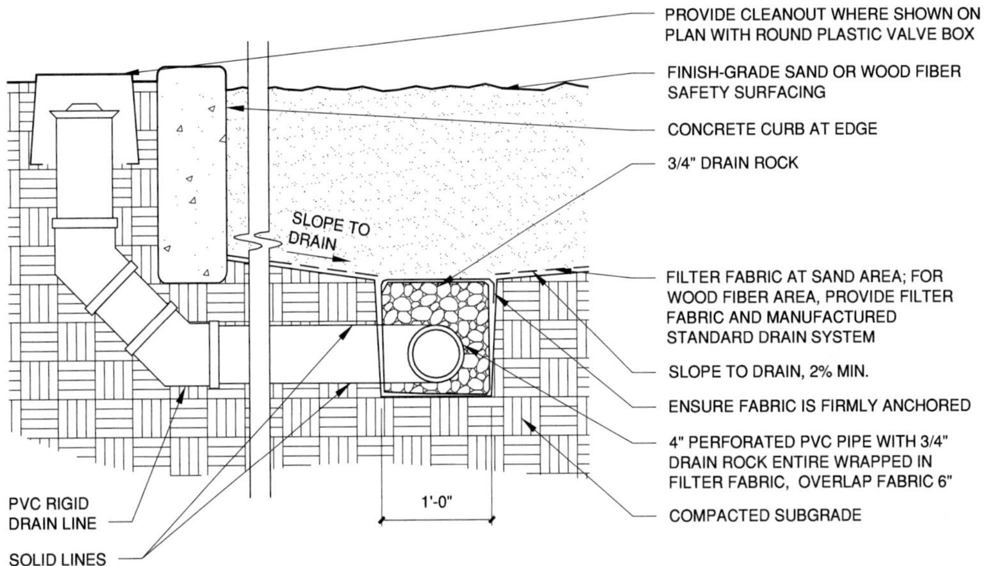

SUBDRAIN BELOW SAND OR FIBER SAFETY SURFACE

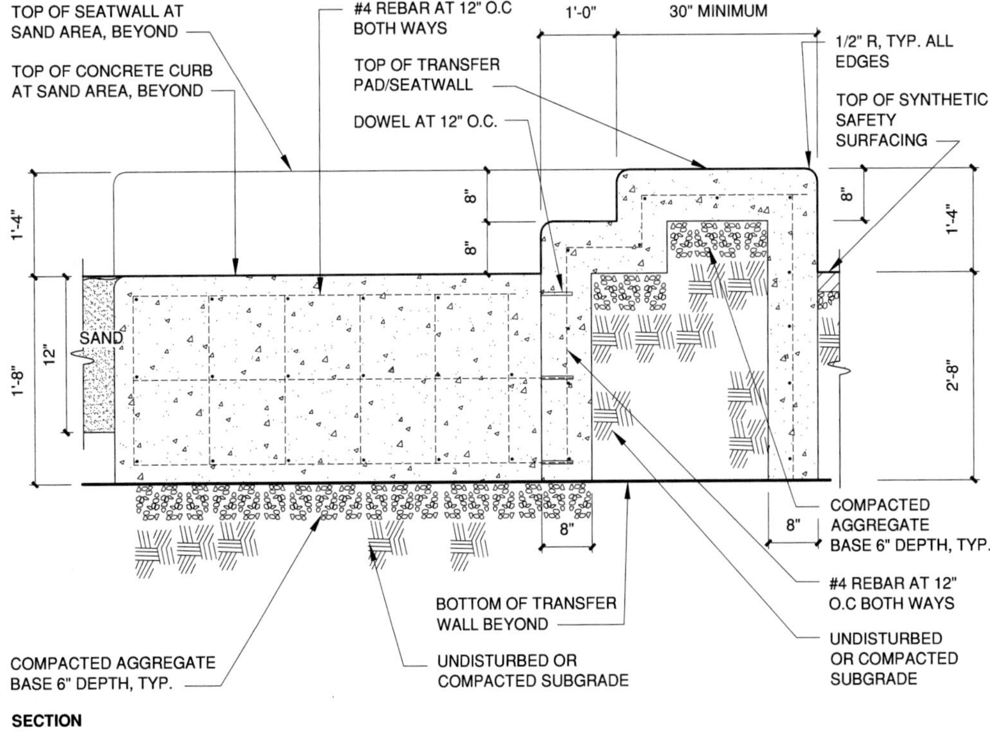

CONCRETE TRANSFER/SEATWALL

Susan Goltsman, FASLA

providing a place for the wheelchair under the sand shelf leaves very little depth of sand available for play. Therefore, a raised sand area by itself is not a substitution for full-body sand play. As much as possible, all sand play opportunities on the site should be made usable by all children.

If the sand area is designed to allow children to play inside the area, a place within the sand play area should be provided where a participant can rest or lean against a firm, stationary back support in close proximity to the main activity area. Back support can be provided by any vertical surface that is a minimum height of 12 inches and a minimum width of 6 inches, depending on the size of the child. Back support can be a boulder, a log, or a post that is holding up a shade structure.

A transfer system into a sand area may also be necessary if the area is large and contains a variety of sand activities. A transfer system would be appropriate if there are no areas of raised sand play in the primary activity area, or if the sand area is over 100 square feet and the raised sand area would tend to isolate accessible sand play activities.

Each sand area needs places to make "pies," such as shelves, tables, or rocks. Sand areas should be located in sunny spots so the heat can help disinfect the sand. As unique settings, sand play areas should be separate from the sand under equipment. The sand for play must contain a variety of sieve sizes so it can be packed and used to build. In contrast, the sand area that is used as a resistant, fall-attenuating surface has a larger more uniform sieve size. Sand is meant for digging and should be a minimum of 24 inches deep, but the deeper the better. Drainage under the sand pit is crucial for good maintenance.

When raised sand is provided, the following clearance ranges apply:

Top height to sand: 30 to 34 inches, maximum

Under clearance: 27 inches, minimum

Side reach: 36 to 20 inches

Forward reach: 36 to 20 inches

Clear space for wheelchair: 36 by 55 inches

Depending on the site conditions and the amount of sand play, shade may be required. If shade is required by site conditions, it may be provided through a variety of means, such as trees, tents, umbrellas, structures, and others. This advisory requirement for shade is based on site context, program, and users. Some shade in or around sand is usually desirable, as is a comfortable place for adults to sit.

GATHERING PLACES

To support social development and cooperation, children need comfortable gathering places; likewise, parents and play leaders need comfortable places for sitting, socializing, and supervising.

A gathering place contains fixed elements to support play, eating, watching, talking, or assembling for a programmed activity. Gathering places should serve people of all ages. When gathering places are provided, a portion of them should be accessible.

- *Seating.* A variety of seat choices should be made available in fixed benches.
- *Tables.* Where tables are provided, a variety of sizes and seating arrangements should be provided.
- *Game tables.* Game tables provide a place for two to four people to play board games. Where fewer than five game tables are provided, a minimum of one four-sided game table should include an accessible space on one side.
- *Storage.* If storage is supplied as part of a gathering area, and the storage is used by children, accessible shelves and hooks should be a maximum of 36 inches above the ground. The amount of storage is dependent on program requirements.
- *Shade.* Shade may be desirable for gathering areas where people will be participating in activities over a long period of time. Shade can be provided in a variety of means, such as trees, canopies, or trellises, depending on site context.

Gathering places should be located adjacent to very active areas. These areas should contain drinking fountains, wash-up facilities, quiet nooks to breastfeed, and restrooms.

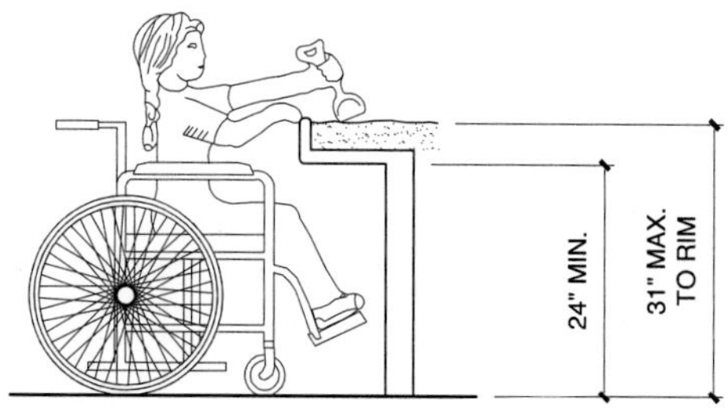

HEIGHT REQUIREMENTS FOR ACCESSIBLE RAISED SAND TRAY

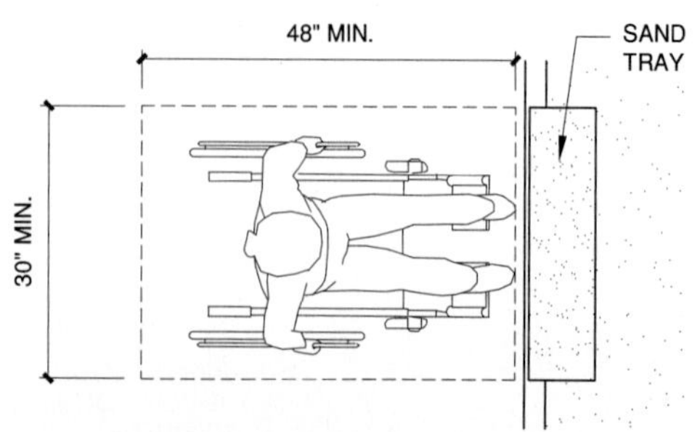

CLEARANCE REQUIREMENTS FOR ACCESSIBLE RAISED SAND TRAY

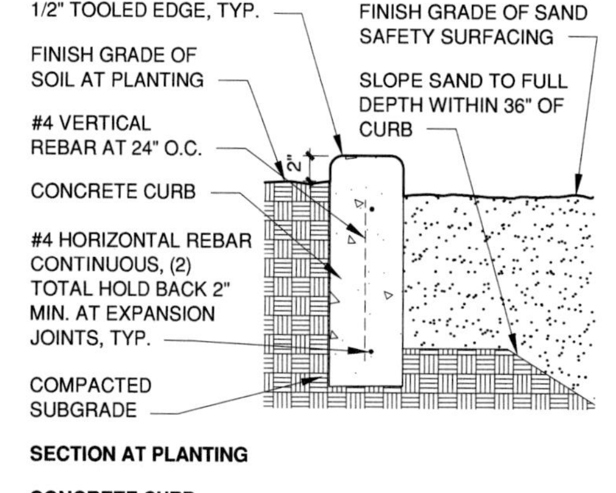

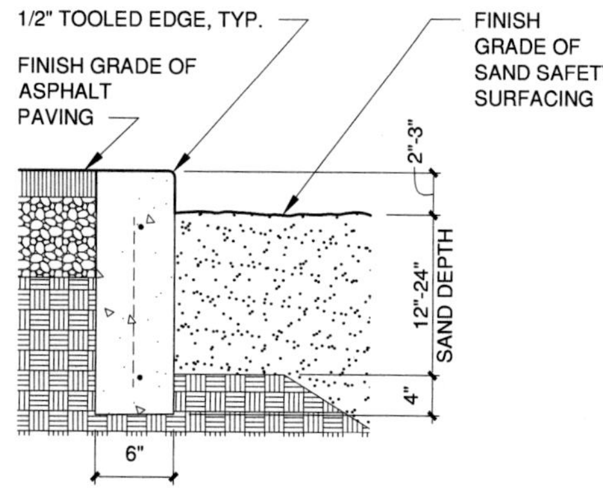

CONCRETE CURB AROUND SAND AS SAFETY SURFACE MATERIAL

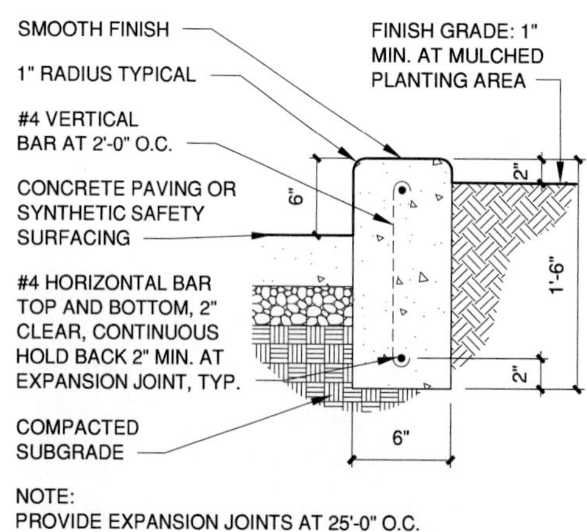

CONCRETE CURB AT PLANTED AREA

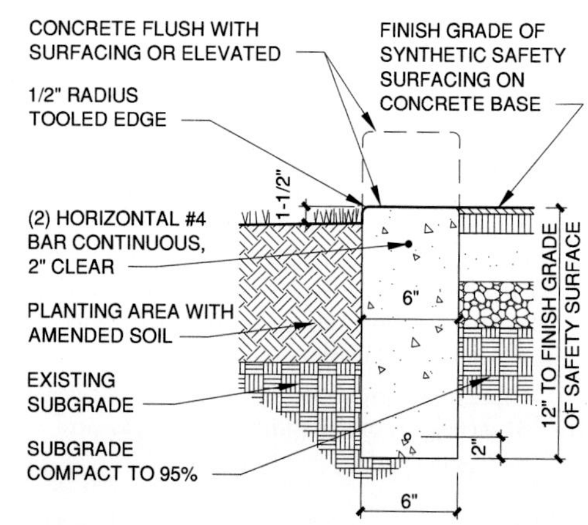

FLUSH CONCRETE CURB AT PLANTED AREA

Susan Goltsman, FASLA

GARDEN SETTINGS

A powerful play-and-learn activity, gardening allows children to interact with nature and one another. Garden beds and tools can be adapted for use by children with disabilities. Scent gardens are attractive to all children.

Gardens in play areas are primarily used to provide a program with the activities of planting, tending, studying, and harvesting vegetation. Depending on the type and height of plantings, planter boxes may require a raised area for access or a transfer point. A garden must provide a minimum of one accessible garden area.

- *Raised gardens.* If a raised area is provided, then:
  - The raised area should be located as part of the main garden area. The amount of raised area will be determined by the program, but a minimum of 10 percent of the garden should be raised.
  - The edge should be raised above the ground surface to a minimum of 20 inches and a maximum of 30 inches.
  - The garden growing area should provide access either by side or by forward reach 12 to 36 inches above ground.
  - If children are required to sit in the dirt to garden, a transfer point should be provided to enable participants to transfer into the garden.
- *Potting and maintenance areas.* Potting and preparation areas should provide access either by forward or side reach. The amount of area to be made accessible depends on the program. At least one workstation for potting should be made accessible.
- *Storage.* Storage areas for the garden should provide access for children who use wheelchairs. Hooks and shelves should be a maximum of 36 inches off the ground.
- *Circulation.* Aisles around the garden should be provided on a main aisle so a child using a wheelchair or walker can get to the garden. This larger aisle should also provide access to the accessible gardening spaces.

VEGETATION, TREES, AND LANDFORMS

Vegetation, trees, and topography are important features in a play setting. These features should be integrated into the flow of play activities and spaces, or they can be play features in themselves.

Landforms help children explore movement through space and provide for varied circulation. Topographic variety stimulates fantasy play, orientation skills, hide-and-seek games, viewing, rolling, climbing, sliding, and jumping. "Summit" points must accommodate wheelchairs and provide support for other disabling conditions.

Trees and vegetation constitute one of the most ignored topics in the design of play environments. They are two of the most important elements for integration, because everyone can enjoy and share them. Vegetation stimulates exploratory behavior, fantasy, and imagination. It is a major source of play props, including leaves, flowers, fruits, nuts, seeds, and sticks, and allows children to learn about the environment through direct experience.

Designers should emphasize integrating plants into play settings, rather than creating separate "nature areas." For children with physical disabilities, the experience of being in trees can be replicated by providing trees that a wheelchair can roll into or under. An accessible miniforest can be created by planting small trees or large branching bushes.

If vegetation trees and/or landforms are used as a feature, a means should be provided for access up to and around the feature. Tree grates and other site furniture that support or protect the feature must also be selected, so as not to entrap little feet or hands, wheels, canes, crutch tips, and so on.

ANIMAL HABITATS

Contact with wildlife and domestic animals stimulates a caring and responsible attitude toward other living things, provides a therapeutic effect, and offers many learning opportunities. Play areas can provide opportunities to care for or observe domestic animals. Existing or created habitats of insects, aquatic life, birds, and small animals should be protected. Planting appropriate vegetation will attract insects and birds.

ENTRANCES AND SIGNAGE

Entrances are transition zones that help orient, inform, and introduce users to the site. They are places for congregating and for displaying information. Not all play areas have defined entrances, and sometimes entry to a play area can be provided from all directions.

Signs can be permanent or temporary, informative or playful. Expressive and informative displays use walls, floors, ground surfaces, structures, ceilings, sky wires, and rooflines on or near a play area to hang, suspend, and "fly" materials for art and education. Signage is a visual, tactile, or auditory means of conveying information, and it must communicate a message of "All Users Welcome." Use appropriate heights, depths, colors, pictures, and tactile qualities to make signs accessible. Signs should communicate primarily graphically. Talking signs are also effective.

FENCES, ENCLOSURES, AND BARRIERS

An enclosure is a primary means of differentiating and articulating the child's environment. For example, fences can double-back on themselves to provide small social settings. Fences, enclosures, and barriers protect fragile environments, define pathways, enclose activity areas, and designate social settings. Low fences can themselves be play elements and must be considered as such. The entrance to an enclosure should be clearly visible and wide enough for wheelchair passage (36 inches minimum, 48 inches preferable).

PLAY AREA MANAGEMENT

To fully support child development and integration of children with and without disabilities, a well-designed play environment should be augmented by a risk management program and professional play leadership. Part of the play leader's job is to set up, manipulate, and modify the physical environment to facilitate creative activity. The environment can either support or hamper play; thus, designers must learn how they can best empower children through design. Compensating for an inadequate environment is a drain on the leader's time and energy and it is the designer's responsibility to know the safety codes, understand the access requirement, and design a setting that supports human development and the program requirements.

CONCLUSION

Play is the raw material of education, helping children to express, apply, and assimilate knowledge and experience. A rich play environment can encourage all children to take those first experimental steps toward growth and development.

REFERENCES

American Society for Testing and Materials (ASTM). 1998. "Standard Consumer Safety Performance Specification for Playground Equipment and Public Use," ASTM 1487-98. West Conshohocken, PA: ASTM.

———. 1999. "Determination of Accessibility of Surface Systems Under and Around Playground Equipment," ASTM 1951-99. West Conshohocken, PA: ASTM.

———. "Impact Attenuation of Surface Systems Under and Around Playground Equipment," ASTM F 1292-99. West Conshohocken, PA: ASTM.

Moore, R. C., S. M. Goltsman, and D.S. Iacofano. 1987, 1992. *Play for All Guidelines: Planning, Design, and Management of Outdoor Play Setting for All Children.* Berkeley, CA: MIG Communications.

U.S. Architectural and Transportation Barriers Compliance Board. 2002. *Americans with Disabilities Act Accessibility Guidelines (ADAAG): Accessibility Requirements for New Construction and Alteration of Buildings and Facilities Covered by the ADA.* Washington, DC: Access Board.

U.S. Consumer Product Safety Commission (CPSC). 1997. *Handbook for Public Playground Safety,* Publication No. 325, 20207 301-504-0494. Washington DC: CPSC.

See also:
Access to the Outdoor Setting
Accessibility
Stairs, Ramps, and Curbs

Susan Goltsman, FASLA

GOLF COURSE DESIGN: PLANNING AND DETAILS

INTRODUCTION

Two schools of thought guide modern golf course design. One approach involves an in-depth site analysis and lays the golf course gently on and around existing natural features. The other approach requires massive amounts of earth moving to create a golf course that is unique unto itself. In both approaches, the resulting course should accommodate the playing characteristics of a wide range of golfers. This discussion is intended as a technical guide for landscape architects involved in golf-course-related projects.

PROCEDURES

Golf course designers provide a wide array of services in addition to design, including feasibility studies, site selection, and project coordination. The design process follows a standard sequence of events, as follows:

- *Programming*, to determine the project goals for course character, level of difficulty, special features, clubhouse uses, and preliminary budget.
- *Site analysis*, to identify environmental issues, unique landforms, specimen trees, water bodies, views, soil types, weather patterns, and surface drainage, each of which can make the course distinctive.
- *Golf course routing plan*, to identify the physical layout of the course and hole-by-hole playing strategy. A detailed estimate of construction costs should be provided at this time.
- *Plans and specifications*, to guide the course layout, grading, irrigation, erosion control, environmental control, landscaping, seeding, green and tee construction, cart paths, lakes, drainage, signage, and course amenities.
- *Bidding and construction services*, to guide the actual pricing and building of the golf course facilities.

Most golf course projects proceed with an expert team of consultants. This team may consist of golf course architect, market analyst, landscape architect, land planner, civil engineer, clubhouse architect, biologist, and agronomist.

STANDARDS

The standards for golf course design and construction in America are established by the United States Golf Association (USGA). The rules of the game are set by the USGA, in conjunction with the Royal and Ancient Golf Club of St. Andrews, Scotland.

Hole Length and Par Combinations

The length of a golf hole is the primary determinant of the par, in conjunction with the lay of the land and in-play obstacles. Par is the number of strokes an expert golfer could expect to hit on any given hole, including two putts on the green. The established lengths for par include:

Par	Men	Women
3	Up to 250 yards	Up to 210 yards
4	251 to 470 yards	211 to 400 yards
5	471 to 690 yards	401 to 590 yards
6	691 yards and over	591 yards and over

Most modern courses are designed to a par 72, with 4 par 3s (2 per 9 holes), 4 par 5s (2 per 9 holes) and 10 par 4s (5 per 9 holes).

Acreage

A minimum of 160 usable acres is preferred for a regulation-length 18-hole course with learning center, clubhouse, and maintenance facilities. Less acreage results in fairways that could be too close together for safe play or too short for modern equipment. Approximately 4 acres are necessary for the clubhouse and parking area, 7 acres for the learning center, and 1 acre for the maintenance facility. These acreages will vary depending on the site characteristics.

Landform

The character of the land can play a major role in designing new golf courses. Sites that have gently rolling terrain, good drainage patterns, and some tree cover and water are highly suited for golf course routings. Extremely steep slopes and large bodies of water offer dynamic design opportunities when considered early in the design phase.

Landscape

Regional landscapes may define a course character, such as desert, wetland habitat, forest preserve, or a waterfront. Buffer zones may be necessary to separate fragile landscapes from the golf course playing areas.

GOLF COURSE FEATURES

Golfers may range in skill level from beginner to professional and cover the spectrum of society: young and old, men and women, all income levels and races. Golf is considered a lifetime sport. Unlike most other sports fields, every golf course is different and unique. Courses can enhance their natural setting while providing fairness and challenge to each level of golfer. Special features are described in the following subsections.

Strategically Placed Tees

Multiple tees provide each golfer a strategic test of his or her ability. The multiple tees on each hole should be strategically placed to increase the level of difficulty for each corresponding skill level (see the "Typical Detail" figure).

Fairways

The design of fairways has changed dramatically in accordance with new equipment designs, enabling accomplished amateurs to reach the 300-yard drive. Fairway widths will generally be wider (25 to 40 yards) at the landing areas located 230 to 280 yards off the tee for men and 190 to 220 yards for women. (See the "Typical Par 4 Hole Layout" figure.)

Hazards

Strategic hazards may be either built or natural features located on golf courses to test the scratch golfer, while at the same time be out of play for beginners. Water bodies or sand bunkers on the "inside" of the dogleg entice golfers to cross as much hazard as they are comfortable in attempting. This strategic placement of hazards reinforces the risk-reward aspect of well-designed golf courses. (See the "Typical Sand Bunker" and the "Typical Grass Bunker" figures.)

Greens

Golf course greens should provide multiple cup locations to modify hole difficulty and to minimize soil compaction from foot traffic. Interesting surface contours offer putting challenges while keeping the golfer alert to changing surface conditions. The USGA maintains specific technical standards for green subgrades, subsurface drainage, intermediate gravel layer, root zone mixture, topmix smoothing, seedbed preparation, and fertilization (see the "Typical Green Detail" figure).

Irrigation

To accommodate regular play, golf course turf requires regular irrigation in most regions of the United States. New systems should incorporate water management and water conservation technologies to achieve maximum growth using minimum water. System components include water

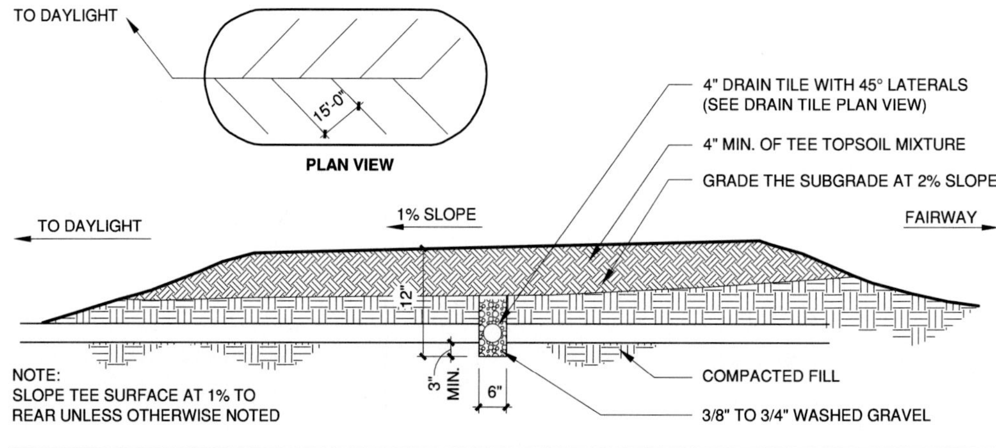

TYPICAL TEE DETAIL

Patrick Wyss, FASLA

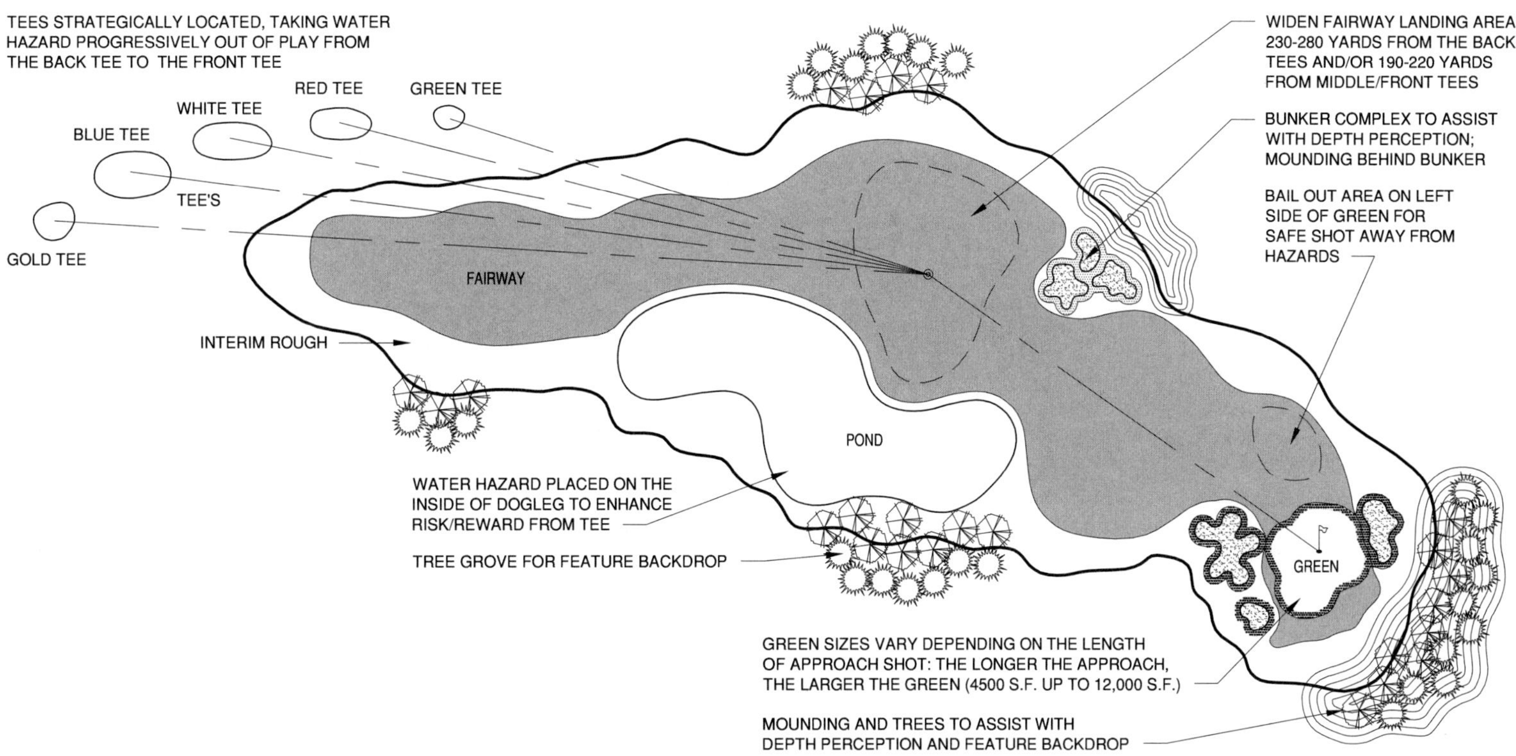

TYPICAL PAR 4 HOLE LAYOUT

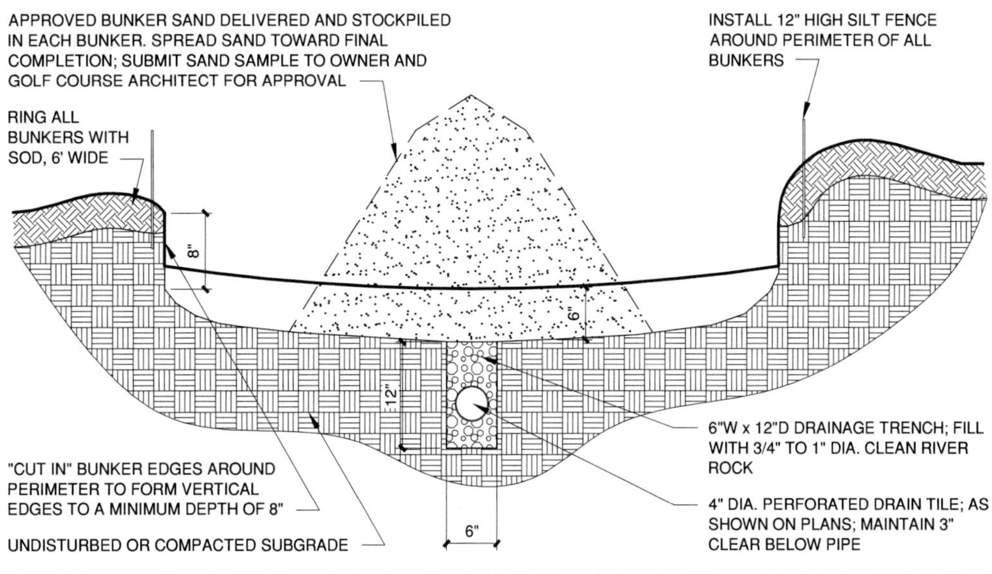

TYPICAL SAND BUNKER

Patrick Wyss, FASLA

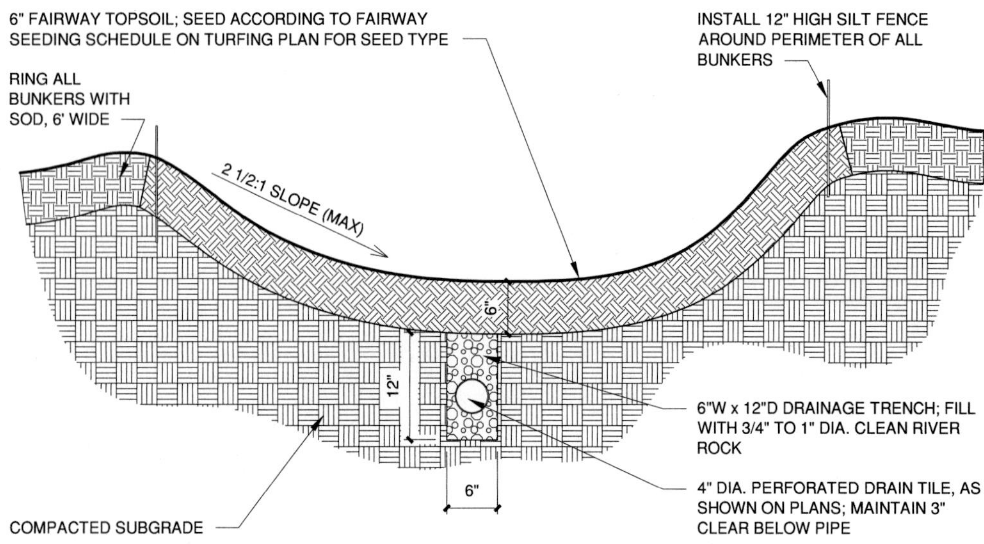

TYPICAL GRASS BUNKER

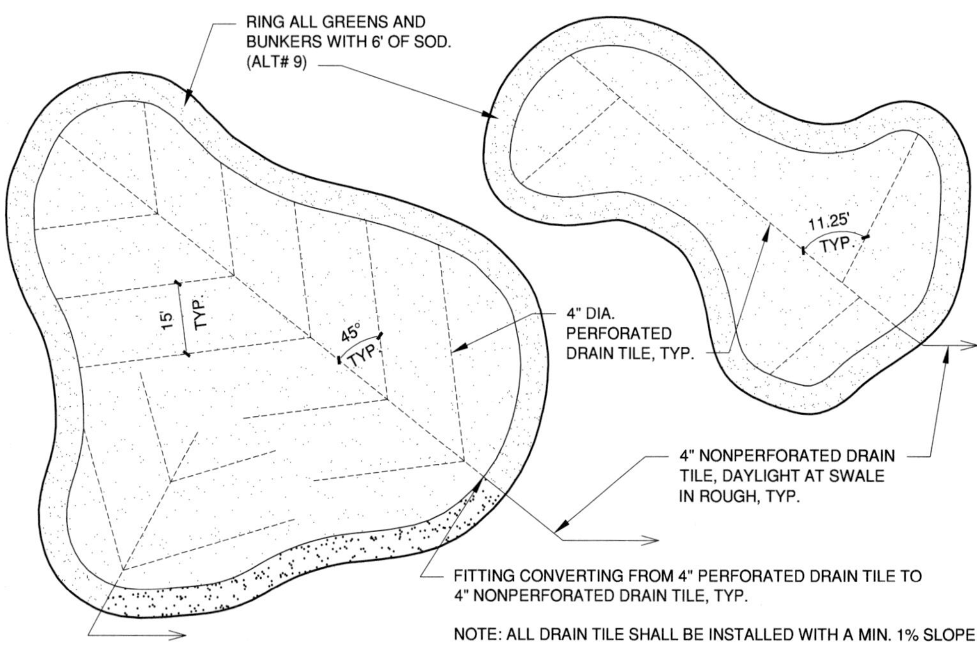

TYPICAL GREEN BUNKER DRAIN LAYOUT

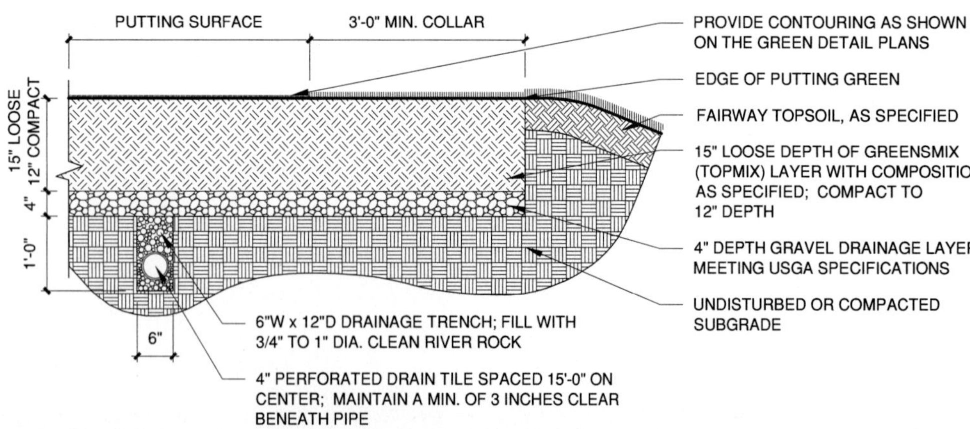

NOTES:
THE TOPMIX MUST MEET THE CURRENT USGA STANDARDS FOR INFILTRATION RATE, BULK DENSITY, POROSITY, AND WATER RETENTION. THE GOLF COURSE CONTRACTOR MUST SUBMIT TEST REPORTS FROM AN AUTHORIZED USGA TESTING LAB TO THE GOLF COURSE ARCHITECT PRIOR TO BEGINNING PLACEMENT OF TOPMIX. IN ADDITION, THE GOLF COURSE ARCHITECT WILL TAKE 5 RANDOM IN-PLACE SOIL SAMPLES AFTER PLACEMENT IS COMPLETE.

TYPICAL GREEN DETAIL

Patrick Wyss, FASLA

storage, pumping systems, delivery lines, and large-diameter heads. Electronic control systems and two-wire control systems provide course superintendents the most flexibility in their watering programs.

Infrastructure

Irrigation water is essential for turf development on golf courses. Treated effluent, with specific controls on soluble salts and suspended solids, provides a recycled water source. Three-phase electricity is necessary for irrigation pumps. Potable water and a sanitary sewer are necessary for the clubhouse and on-course restrooms.

ENVIRONMENTAL CONSIDERATIONS

Environmental principles can help guide golf course development. The USGA has established guidelines to direct sound environmental planning for new course development. Environmental considerations may include those described in following subsections.

Site Selection and Analysis

Site selection and analysis should help identify sensitive environments and site ecosystems. Preserved or created buffer zones can help protect sensitive sites.

Water Conservation

Techniques for conserving water use include the use of rainwater sensors to automatically adjust irrigation delivery rates and the use of recycled graywater. Target golf courses limit turf watering to tee areas, landing areas, and green surrounds. All other nonirrigated areas are left as natural landscape.

The control and elimination of water pollution from pesticides and fertilizers can be accomplished with best management practices (BMPs). This method minimizes product use, selects environmentally sensitive products, follows strict application instructions, and monitors results.

Wildlife can be enhanced by providing and protecting habitats and by controlling pests such as bats, birds, and foxes. Corridors can be incorporated into natural areas integrated into the course layout.

WASTE MANAGEMENT

EXTERIOR COMPACTING REFUSE MANAGEMENT SYSTEMS

Exterior refuse compactors provide efficient, cost-effective waste removal. As a rule of thumb, there is approximately a 20 to 1 compaction ratio of loose trash to compacted trash. There are many types of cart/container configurations from a variety of vendors that can meet the needs of any type of commercial or large-scale residential use.

A typical exterior compacting refuse management system consists of a power enclosure unit; steel wearing strips in the pavement, to support the container; and an enclosed container, which has a trash compactor as an integral part of the entire unit that forces and compacts loose or bagged trash into the container. The container compactor is connected to the power enclosure with hydraulic hoses that are disconnected when the container is removed to be emptied. The container can also be equipped with an ionization unit that prevents unpleasant odors from being released. The container has a sump that runs along its bottom to catch any liquids that may result from compaction. The sump is emptied at the same time as the trash. The trash is usually transported to the exterior compactor compound by means of a wheeled cart, which can be pushed or moved by forklift; it has a capacity of approximately 2 cubic yards. The exterior compacter unit has arms that lift the cart and dump the trash into the container hopper in the front of the container in preparation for compaction. A hydraulically powered ram then forces the trash into the enclosed compactor container. Once the container is full of compacted trash, from 30 to 35 cubic yards, the container can be picked up by specially designed trucks that transport the fully loaded containers to the dump site, empty them, and return with the empty containers. There are maximum dimensions to the containers, since they must fit on the truck. Local governments may also have additional size restrictions. In general, the maximum sizes are 25 feet long, 8 feet wide, and 8 feet high.

BENEFITS

There are many benefits derived from the use of exterior compactors, which are related to sanitation of the area both inside and around these containers. Because the trash is totally enclosed, it helps with the control of rodents and eliminates unpleasant odors. By reducing the amount of trash temporarily stored in bags on the street awaiting pickup, the use of these compactors promotes an overall better appearance and cleanliness of a site with a reduced level of maintenance.

SOLID WASTE COLLECTION AND RECYCLING SPACES

INTRODUCTION

Solid waste disposal has become a critical issue for society. Landfills and other waste disposal facilities are reaching capacity and siting new facilities is difficult due to environmental and health concerns, including water pollution, loss of wetlands, poisoning of the soil, and the breeding of vermin. As a result, traditional methods of handling solid waste are becoming more costly. Reducing landfill waste extends the life of existing facilities and lessens the need to build new facilities.

Much of what we have called "waste" is not waste, but marketable materials that can be reused to make new products. Reusing materials already extracted from the earth enables sustainable use as raw resources are depleted. Products require great amounts of energy to be produced from raw natural materials. By recycling we are recapturing energy embodied in a material during initial manufacturing processes. Sorting and recycling waste often reduces operating and disposal costs while conserving natural resources and energy.

Most states and municipalities have laws and programs to encourage waste reduction and recycling, including mandatory quotas, deposit/return arrangements, and disposal bans. Buildings should include the spaces necessary to carry out recycling and waste management programs. Once the waste and recyclable materials generation of a building's users are determined, spaces can be designed for sorting, storage, and removal.

RECYCLABLE MATERIALS

Separating materials by category or product is the first step in recycling (see table below). Materials are sorted into like kinds to prevent contamination.

RECYCLABLE MATERIALS

CATEGORY	MATERIAL PRODUCT	DESCRIPTION (RECYCLING LABEL)	CONVERSION OF VOLUME TO WEIGHT
Paper	Ledger paper, white letterhead	SWL: sorted white ledger (high-grade white paper)	Uncompacted: 1 cu yd = 500 lb Compacted: 1 cu yd = 750 lb
	Computer paper	CPO: computer printout	Uncompacted: 1 cu yd = 500–600 lb Compacted: 1 cu yd = 1000–1200 lb
	Colored paper	SCL: sorted color paper	Uncompacted: 1 cu yd = 500 lb Compacted: 1 cu yd = 750 lb
	Newspaper	Mix: newsprint	Uncompacted: 1 cu yd = 350–500 lb Compacted: 1 cu yd = 750–1000 lb
	Magazines	Mix: clay-coated paper	Not available
	Telephone books	Mix: mixed papers/adhesives	1 book = 1–3 lb
	Cereal boxes	Mix: coated paperboard	Not available
	Shipping boxes	OCC: old corrugated cardboard	Uncompacted: 1 cu yd = 285 lb Compacted: 1 cu yd = 500 lb
Glass	Food jars, beverage bottles	1. Amber glass 2. Green glass 3. Clear glass	Loose, whole: 1 cu yd = 600 lb Manually crushed: 1 cu yd = 1000 lb Mechanically crushed: 1 cu yd = 1800 lb
Plastic	Beverage containers	PET: polyethylene terephthalate	Whole: 1 cu yd = 30 lb
	Milk containers	HDPE: high-density polyethylene	Whole: 1 cu yd = 25 lb Crushed: 1 cu yd = 50 lb Compacted: 1 cu yd = 600 lb
	"Clamshell" containers	Polystyrene plastic foam	Not available
	Film plastic	LDPE: low-density polyethylene	Not available
Metals	Beverage cans	Aluminum/bi-metal	Whole: 1 cu yd = 50–70 lb Crushed: 1 cu yd = 300–450 lb
	Food and beverage cans	Steel with tin finish	Whole: 1 cu yd = 125–150 lb Crushed: 1 cu yd = 500–850 lb
Miscellaneous	Pallets	Wood	Not available
	Food waste	Organic solids and liquids	55 gallon drum = 415 lb
	Yard waste	Organic solids	Leaves, uncompacted: 1 cu yd = 250 lb Leaves, compacted: 1 cu yd = 450 lb Wood chips: 1 cu yd = 500 lb Grass clippings: 1 cu yd = 400 lb
	Used motor oil	Petroleum product	1 gallon = 71 lb
	Tires	Rubber	1 passenger car = 20 lb 1 truck = 90 lb

NOTE No building or facility will need space for sorting and storing all or even most of the recyclable materials on this list. Generally paper products should be separated from other wastes. The number of products to be sorted within a category should be limited for most users; sorting more than two products may result in contamination.

James Holtgreven, RLA
Richard J. Vitullo, AIA, Oak Leaf Studio, Crownsville, Maryland; Tom Lokey, Northeast Maryland Waste Disposal Authority, Baltimore, Maryland

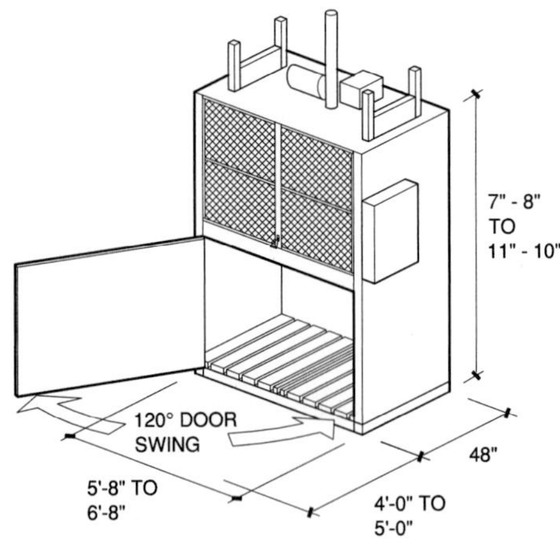

NOTES

1. All baler dimensions are approximate and vary depending upon the manufacturer. Typical bale sizes (in inches) are: 18 x 18 x 18, 20 x 24 x 18, 30 x 24 x 20, 48 x 30 x 42, 60 x 30 x 48, and 72 x 30 x 48
2. To determine whether a baler is needed, consult a recycler to analyze probable waste quantities. Balers can make recycling more efficient by saving space. For example, if the volume of cardboard boxes is high in a certain building, balers can greatly reduce the amount of storage space needed. The bailing of such waste as metal cans, plastic bottles, paper, or cardboard may make the recyclable materials more marketable by increasing trailer payloads.
3. Some balers expand by linking bins together to accommodate a variable recycling program. A sliding ram mechanism will service each bin.

BALER/COMPACTOR

SOURCE GENERATION[4]

CLASSIFICATION	BUILDING TYPES	QUANTITIES OF WASTE GENERATED	TYPES OF WASTE GENERATED
Residential	Studio or one bedroom apartment	1–1 1/2 cu yd per unit per month (200–250 lb)	Newspaper (38/43)[1] Plastic (18/7)[1] Miscellaneous (13/18)[1] Metals (14/9)[1] Yard waste/compost (10/15)[1] Glass (2/8)[1]
	Two or three bedroom apartment or single family house	1½–2 cu yd per unit per month (250–400 lb)	
Commercial	Office, general	1 1/2 lb per employee per day or 1 cu yd per 10,000 sq ft per day (includes 1/2 lb of high-grade paper per person per day)	Plastics, compost, used oil, metals, and glass (30%)[2] High grade paper (29%)[2] Mixed papers (23%)[2] Newspapers (10%)[2] Corrugated cardboard (8%)[2]
	Department store	1 cu yd per 2500 sq ft per day	Corrugated cardboard, compost, wood pallets, high grade paper, and plastic film[3]
	Wholesale/retail store	Varies with type of tenant	
	Shopping center	Varies with type of tenant	
	Supermarket	1 cu yd per 1250 sq ft per day	Corrugated cardboard, compost, and wood pallets[3]
	Restaurants/entertainment	Varies with number of meals served and type of food	Compost (38%)[2] Corrugated cardboard (11%)[2] Newsprint (5%)[2] High-grade paper (4%)[2]
	Drugstore	1 cu yd per 2000 sq ft per day	Corrugated cardboard and high grade paper[3]
	Bank/insurance company	Survey required (3/4 lb high-grade paper per person per day)	High-grade paper, mixed paper, and corrugated cardboard[3]
Hotel and motel	High occupancy	1/2 cu yd per room per week (plus restaurants)	Glass, aluminum, plastic, high-grade paper, newspaper, and corrugated cardboard[3]
	Average occupancy	1/6 cu yd per room per week (plus restaurants)	
Institutional	Hospital	1 cu yd per 5 occupied beds per day	Compost, high-grade paper, biomedical waste, corrugated cardboard, glass, and plastics[3]
	Nursing home	1 cu yd per 15 persons per day	
	Retirement home	1 cu yd per 20 persons per day	
Educational	Grade school	1 cu yd per 8 rooms per day	High-grade paper, mixed paper, newspaper, corrugated cardboard, compost, plastic, glass, and metals[3]
	High school	1 cu yd per 10 rooms per day	
	University	Survey required	

[1]Percentage by volume/percentage by weight.
[2]Percentage by volume.
[3]Percentages not available.
[4]This table approximates by building type the quantity and type of waste generated; the information should be used as a guideline only. Volume (using varying weights per cubic yard) is derived from nationwide U.S. averages of noncompacted waste.

Contaminated materials are less readily recyclable and therefore less marketable. Sorting is particularly important for paper and glass. Cleaning food packaging of organic material is usually necessary. Some recyclers will accept "commingled" or mixed waste and will sort and clean materials by hand or by mechanical means. (Paper is easily contaminated and can never be recycled this way; it must always be separated from other waste materials.) Communities that pick up commingled recyclable materials have enjoyed a greater participation rate since it requires little, if any, change in waste disposing habits. However, sorting of recyclable materials at their generation point is less labor intensive and produces higher quality, less contaminated reprocessed materials.

PLANNING AND DESIGN

When planning a project, make a waste analysis based on the building type or building users and address the following issues:

1. Source generation: identify types and quantities of waste material likely to be generated.
2. Collection and sorting: determine space and equipment needed for the collection and/or separation of waste materials.
3. Disposal: determine the frequency and means of the remover or recycler to collect the waste.

An effective recycling system in the home, school, or workplace integrates materials sorting with the regular collection of waste. Convenience of use is essential. Recycling systems should be as easy to use as a conventional wastebasket (and be usable by the elderly and persons with disabilities). Provide extra space alongside regular waste containers for separating and storing recyclable materials. Conveying systems like waste chutes may also be provided. Collection bins should be clearly distinguished by using different-sized containers and effective graphics; differentiation will encourage proper use and reduce contamination, a serious recycling problem.

DISPOSAL

To determine waste and recyclable material removal arrangements for a project, contact the municipal or county environmental office for local regulations or guidelines for collection programs. If private arrangements must be made, contact local removal and recycling companies that could service the building. The container type and size compatible with collection vehicles should be noted and provided for in the design. Since recycling is an industry in its infancy, provide extra storage space in or near the building to accommodate future needs.

Some building types, such as grocery stores, generate a large amount of bulky corrugated cardboard, requiring compacting and/or baling. Materials of large volume to weight ratios, such as metal cans and plastic bottles, if not crushed manually at their generation point, may be compacted at a central storage room. The volume of material collected and the number of trips the remover needs to make will generally indicate the cost-effectiveness of a crusher or baler.

Richard J. Vitullo, AIA, Oak Leaf Studio, Crownsville, Maryland; Tom Lokey, Northeast Maryland Waste Disposal Authority, Baltimore, Maryland

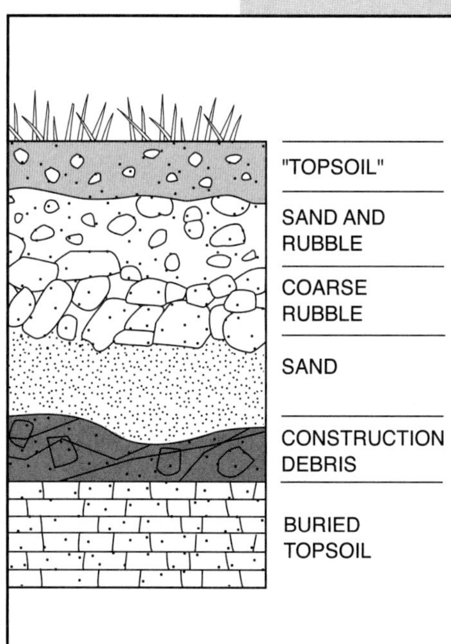

MATERIALS

Soils

Asphalt

Concrete

Masonry

Metals

Wood

Recreational Surfaces

Nursery Stock

Other Materials

Evaluating the Environmental and Human Health Impacts of Materials

Part 4

SOILS

SOILS: AGRONOMIC

INTRODUCTION

Soil as a growing medium may be defined as a *natural system,* comprised of mineral particles, organic matter, water, and air, all supporting growing plants. The "soil profile" consists of *horizons,* and there exist important interrelationships among the horizons, as they are interdependent and necessary for the entire profile to fulfill its function as a rooting medium, both in nature and in the designed landscape project (Craul and Craul, 2006.)

As shown in the "Ideal Natural Soil Profile" figure, the major horizons of the ideal natural soil profile include:

- *O horizon (organic).* This horizon functions as a mulch that reduces evaporative water losses, lowers daytime and maintains nighttime surface soil temperatures, and contributes organic matter for soil tilth and acts as a source of energy for soil organisms.
- *A horizon (topsoil).* This horizon contains incorporated organic matter and a large and diverse organism population, and serves as the major rooting medium for most of the plant roots.
- *B horizon (subsoil).* This horizon provides added necessary rooting volume for plant stability and nutrient and water storage, to supplement the topsoil.
- *C horizon (substratum or parent material).* The C horizon contributes deep rooting and drainage volume. It becomes more important to good plant growth in relatively shallow soils.
- *R horizon (bedrock).* The R horizon comprises the consolidated material from which the soil profile may or may not have been derived. Some soil materials have been transported by various agents of erosion and deposited on other existing bedrock.

Understanding the functional relationships within the general form of the natural soil profile (Craul, 1992; 1999) is necessary to make a reasonable estimate of the degree of limitations present in the existing project soil materials, which is essential to formulating a soil design plan.

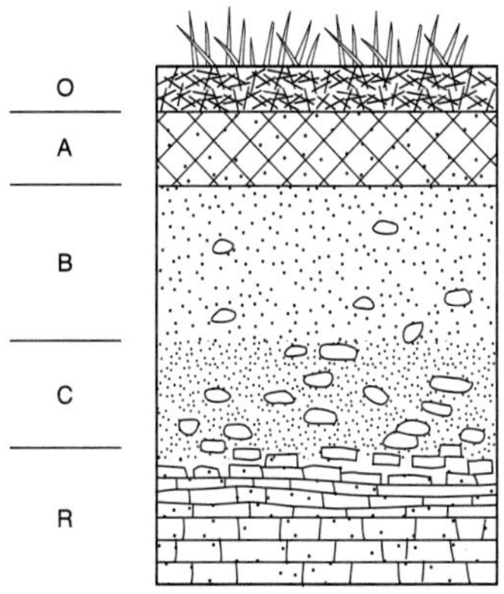

IDEAL NATURAL SOIL PROFILE

IMPORTANCE OF SOIL TO LANDSCAPE ARCHITECTS

The importance to landscape architects of understanding soil, the medium in which all landscape plants grow, even in wetlands, cannot be overestimated. A major insurer's report has shown that soil failures are the major cause for liability claims against landscape architects.

In the context of urban soils and those on most landscape projects, it is useful to distinguish soils that have been intensively altered from those that retain most of their natural characteristics (with perhaps alteration only to the surface), appearing nearly like the soil profile shown in the "Ideal Natural Soil Profile" figure. In contrast, a highly disturbed soil would appear as that shown in the "Complex Urban Soil" figure, whose profile possesses characteristics that would decrease its capability to sustain the plant palette. In this case, typically, alteration or replacement is required, and installation of a specially designed soil becomes a viable alternative on many projects.

ALTERATION OF EXISTING SOIL

Care must be exercised when contemplating alteration (modification by mixing with various imported components such as organic amendments and so forth) of existing soil on a project. A detailed survey will need to be conducted, to determine variability and presence of compaction and drainage, and to test for pH, nutrients, and proper texture among other properties. On restoration sites, the presence of rubble in varying quantities at various depths should be anticipated. Normally, proper state and federal authorities will have accomplished elimination of possible contamination by heavy metals and other elements, but this should be confirmed.

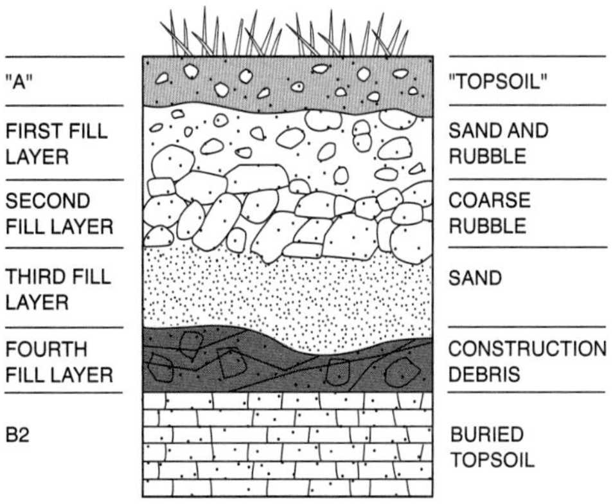

Note that simply spreading a selected "topsoil" a few inches thick over the surface of the existing soil material without its alteration is successful *only* when the latter is completely suitable as a planting soil, as described below.

COMPLEX URBAN SOIL

Source: Craul and Craul, 2006.

Field Guide for Assessing Planting Suitability of an Existing Soil

1. Minimum depth to bedrock, impervious horizon, or infrastructure surface such as an underground rooftop, should be at least 24 to 30 inches for most planting designs. A depth of 36 inches is nearly ideal for most situations.
2. Water drainage should not be impeded at any level above the prescribed minimum depth; thus, the profile should be *well drained* (described later).
3. Texture should not be the extremes of clay, silty clay loam, very fine sandy loam, or very coarse sandy loam (see the "USDA's 12 Texture Classes" figure).
4. Coarse fragments (stones and/or building rubble) should be less than 2 inches in diameter and less than 25 percent by volume within 24 inches of the soil surface. Coarse fragments may increase with depth but should not exceed the limit.
5. No known contaminants should be present anywhere within the profile or within the subbase below; otherwise, HAZMAT cleanup is required unless the Environmental Protection Agency (EPA) and the appropriate state office have issued certificates of cleanup or isolation, and acceptance.

If the conditions given in 1 to 4 are not met, then the following actions are required.

1. Either shallow-rooted plants must be used, or suitable soil must be added to the surface in appropriate thickness to provide adequate total depth.
   - It is always wise to loosen the preexisting surface to ensure proper blending of the two soil materials and prevent the creation of an interface.
2. For soil that is poorly drained, these guidelines apply:
   - If it is a case of a high water table, a drainage system should be installed, if possible, to improve drainage. If the soil is highly compacted, the drainage system will not be effective: the soil should be loosened or replaced if feasible.
   - If the water flows from another area and the soil itself drains well, a curtain/interceptor drain can be installed (see also *Soil Mechanics*).
   - Well-draining soil may be added to the surface as fill to provide adequate well-drained depth, but this must be fully specified.
   - If none of the above actions is feasible, then raised beds filled with well-draining soil are appropriate—though they may not meet design considerations.

Dr. Phillip J. Craul, Senior Lecturer (retired) in Landscape Architecture, Graduate School of Design, Harvard University, and Emeritus Professor of Soil Science, SUNY–College of Environmental Science and Forestry, Syracuse, New York; Timothy A. Craul, President, Craul Land Scientists, PLC, State College, Pennsylvania

3. If the texture is of the extremes given above, then the soil may be *carefully* modified with appropriate amendments.
   - A common mistake is to add sand to a heavy texture, such as clay loam and so on. Too little sand is usually added, resulting in "sandy brick" material.
   - More effective amendments include organic matter, expanded shale, calcined clay, or other similar manufactured materials, in the appropriate proportion. The procedure usually requires the services of a soil scientist for reliable specifications.
4. Removal of excess coarse fragments may be accomplished by:
   - Employing a rock rake after the stony soil has been loosened with a chisel plow or a spade tiller. This permits the removal of stones only from a relatively shallow depth. Turning the soil with a backhoe will achieve removal to greater depth, but costs increase accordingly.
   - Adding sufficient stoneless, specified soil to the surface to provide an adequate depth of planting medium for the desired plants is another alternative, and is probably the least expensive. However, in extremely stony situations, the interface between the nonstony and the stony material may create restricted rooting. For very stony areas, the use of a planting design of simple scattered plants would require the removal of stones only in the planting pits. This technique is commonly employed in stony desert regions; usually, soil must be supplemented in the planting pits.

DESIGNING A SOIL PROFILE

The goal for restoration is to return the soil to a condition that enables it to perform desired functions suitable for one or more land uses. When the soil material has been drastically altered or is totally unsuitable, then designed soil is required. The reasons for designing a soil are as follows:

- Importation of topsoil seldom meets Leadership in Energy and Environmental Design (LEED) requirements, especially from agricultural land, unless it is from a site that is to be covered by a built landscape of continuous structure from a governmentally approved site. Further, there are several national prohibitions against transport of topsoil from one part of the country to another due to the potential for transmitting soil-borne insects, diseases, or other contaminants. For example, soil from Long Island, New York, may not be transported out of the area due to soil-borne deer fleas, which carry Lyme disease; and soil may not be transported within or out of the southeastern United States due to fire ants. Another problem is nematodes in the lake states. (The Website http//:soils.usda.gov gives the latest status of prohibitions.) Even local transport of topsoil may have potential hazards and may be prohibited.
- Proper design emulation of an appropriate local natural soil suitable for the desired plant palette ensures sustainability to the plant palette and the overall landscape design.
- Components of a designed soil may be recycled by-products such as composted organic materials, waste sand or ground glass as a sand substitute, and tailings from stone quarry washers as silt and clay substitutes, and many others yet to be devised.

Designed Soil Properties

Particle Size Distribution (Texture)

The soil texture or particle size distribution is the most influential physical property on many other soil properties, including density and susceptibility to compaction, structure formation, drainage and aeration, and relative fertility. Its overall effects are modified by the presence of organic matter. Therefore, it is the first property of concern in examining existing soils, or the first criterion considered for designing a soil.

Texture is defined and described by the proportion of sand (2 to 0.05 mm), silt (0.05 to 0.002 mm) and clay (< 0.002 mm) particles in the soil. The complete particle size classes are given in the "USDA Size Classes of Soil Mineral Particles" table, and these form the basis of texture description.

In natural soils, these classes of mineral particles are present in varying proportions, thus, sandy, silty or clayey soils. However, greater precision for defining the proportions is required, as shown by research on plant growth and soil texture relationships as well as engineering applications. The classes recognized by USDA are illustrated in the "USDA's 12 Texture Classes" figure.

It is good practice to represent graphically the textures of the soil horizons within the soil profile in a general manner for clarity, in conjunction with the written specifications. The following graphic representations are suggested (see the "Particle Separate Percentages and Hatchings for USDA Soil Texture Classes and Aggregates" table).

USDA SIZE CLASSES OF SOIL MINERAL PARTICLES

SIZE CLASS (SEPARATE)	DIAMETER RANGE (MM)	U.S. STANDARD SIEVE SIZE (NO.)
Coarse fragments	> 2.00	—
Very coarse sand	2.00 to 1.00	10
Coarse sand	1.00 to 0.50	18
Medium sand	0.50 to 0.25	35
Fine sand	0.25 to 0.10	60
Very fine sand	0.10 to 0.05	140
Silt	0.05 to 0.002	300
Clay	< 0.002	—*

**Determined by sedimentation test rather than sieving.*

Source: Craul, 1999.

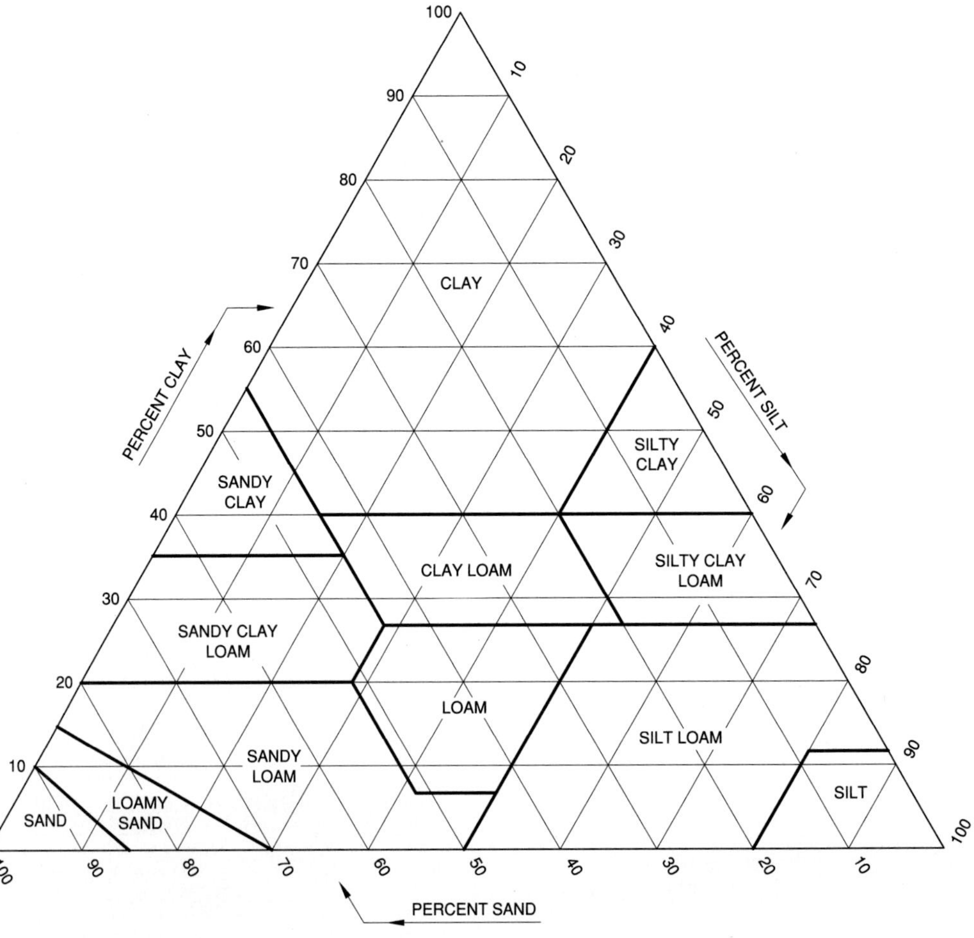

USDA'S 12 TEXTURE CLASSES

Source: Craul, 1999.

Dr. Phillip J. Craul, Senior Lecturer (retired) in Landscape Architecture, Graduate School of Design, Harvard University, and Emeritus Professor of Soil Science, SUNY–College of Environmental Science and Forestry, Syracuse, New York; Timothy A. Craul, President, Craul Land Scientists, PLC, State College, Pennsylvania

PARTICLE SEPARATE PERCENTAGES AND HATCHINGS FOR USDA SOIL TEXTURE CLASSES AND AGGREGATES

TEXTURE CLASS	SOIL SEPARATE PERCENTAGES SAND	SILT	CLAY	HATCHURE
Coarse gravel	—	—	—	
AASHTO #4 Sand	—	—	—	
Sand	> 85	0–15	0–10	
Loamy sand	70–91	0–30	10–15	
Sandy Loam	> 52	0–50	0–20	
Loam	0–52	28–50	7–28	
Silt Loam	0–5-	50–88	0–28	
Silt	0–20	80–100	0–12	
Sandy clay loam	45–52	0–28	20–35	
Clay loam	20–46	15–53	27–40	
Silty clay loam	0–20	40–73	27–40	
Sandy clay	45–52	0–20	> 35	
Silty clay	0–20	> 40	> 40	
Clay	0–45	0–40	> 40	
Peat/muck	—	—	—	

Organic Matter

Organic matter is a very important component of soil, whether natural or designed. Design guidelines are as follows:

- The organic matter in natural soil forms there as the result of soil formation and evolution, and the content may be determined by ASTM tests.
- Organic matter content and type must be specified as a component for designed soil.
- Peat moss is no longer recommended as a soil amendment in light of LEED provisions.
- Composted biosolids have become a preferred source of organic matter amendment (for types of organic amendments, refer to the "Soil Mixes for Container Culture" table in the "Mulches and Mulching" discussion below). Problems of uniformity in processing and meeting specifications have been overcome and are now more or less standardized. Availability is no longer a problem.

Experience has shown biosolids to be a very good source of organic matter, with reliable and acceptable field results when properly composted and installed. In addition, the use of this product meets LEED protocols. That said, problems have been encountered with excessively high pH values of alkaline-slaked biosolids, thus they should be avoided.

Specifications for composted biosolids are as follows:

Carbon:nitrogen (C:N) ratio: This should be in the range 10:1 to 25:1.

Stability: The three tests for stability are:

Dewar self-heating test: Maximum heat rise < 20°C above room temperature of (20–25°C)

CO_2 evolution test: < 1.5% carbon/day

O_2 respiration test: < 0.8 mg/g VS/hr

Thus, per the "Four Levels of Stability/Maturity by the Dewar Test" table, only Classes IV and V are acceptable for mixing, as shown in the table. The larger the number, the greater the degree of stability. Too often contractors have delivered composted biosolids at a stability level of III or less.

Odor: Compost has no unpleasant odor. Any odor of ammonia indicates that the compost is *immature* (Class III or less) and should not be applied until cured to *mature* (Class IV or V) stage.

Mineral/organic content and fineness: Compost must contain more than 40 percent organic matter (dry weight), and 100 percent should pass a 1/2-inch (13 mm) or smaller sieve. Debris (metal, glass, plastic, wood other than residual chips) content should not exceed 1 percent dry weight.

Reaction (pH): This must be in the range of 5.5 to 8.0.

Salinity: Soluble salts should not exceed 4.0 mmhos/cm (dS/m) or 2560 ppm salt.

Nutrient content: Nutrient content should be stated, giving: nitrogen, phosphorus, potassium, calcium, magnesium, sodium, and micronutrients including iron, copper, boron, manganese, and molybdenum.

Heavy metals/pathogens/vector attraction reduction: All these must meet the provisions of 40 CFR Part 503 rule (EPA CFR, Part 503 Regulations, Table 3, page 9392, Vol. 58, No. 32, Friday, Feb. 19, 1993, Federal Register).

Organic Matter Content in the Soil Mix

For a general topsoil specification, organic matter content may be 5 to 10 percent dry weight; for a subsoil, it should be from 1 to 3 percent dry weight. The values given here may appear to be low; however, these are weight basis. Approximate volume values are obtained by multiplying the dry weight by 2.2. It must be kept in mind that these values are to be used in mixes for landscape soils. Most people confuse the values with those for potting mixes, which always contain greater amounts of organic matter.

Mixing Procedures

At first, mixing the components in large quantities and assuring a complete mix can be overwhelming (see the "Guide for Mixing Soil Components" table). Fortunately, equipment and techniques are available on- or off-site to accomplish mixing in an appropriate manner for any mixing volume (Switzenbaum, Craul, and Ryan, 1996).

Designed General Soil Profile

Designed soils are not necessarily natural soils, nor do they yet fit into the accepted USDA Soil Taxonomy, therefore, the following specifications are

FOUR LEVELS OF STABILITY/MATURITY BY THE DEWAR TEST

STABILITY EVOLVED CLASS	STABILITY DESCRIPTION	TEMPERATURE RISE	O_2 EVOLVED MG/G VS/HR	CO_2 PERCENT CARBON/DAY
V	Very mature compost	0–10°C	< 0.5	< 0.8
IV	Maturing, curing compost	10–20°C	0.5–0.8	0.8–1.5
III	Material still decomposing	20–30°C	0.8–1.2	1.5–2.0
II	Immature, active compost	30–40°C	1.2–1.5	2.0–2.5
I	Fresh, very raw compost	40–50°C	> 1.5	2.5–3.0

Source: Switzenbaum, Craul, and Ryan, 1996. Stability classes originally developed by Woods End Research Laboratory, 1995.

Dr. Phillip J. Craul, Senior Lecturer (retired) in Landscape Architecture, Graduate School of Design, Harvard University, and Emeritus Professor of Soil Science, SUNY–College of Environmental Science and Forestry, Syracuse, New York; Timothy A. Craul, President, Craul Land Scientists, PLC, State College, Pennsylvania

GUIDE FOR MIXING SOIL COMPONENTS

MIXING METHOD	COMMENTS AND CAUTIONS
Machine mixing	The most efficient method is by ball mill or tub mixer for large volumes. May be processed on- or off-site. Problem is variation among batches: close inspection and frequent sampling is required. Usually not weather-dependent.
Windrowing	Appropriate for medium to small volumes. May be done on- or off-site but requires a large, dry, flat, solid surface; not on gravel or loose soil. Dry, compacted soil may suffice on approval by the landscape architect or the project soil scientist. Uniformity of mixing depends on the skill of the windrow equipment operator. Not recommended for large quantities, as it is very difficult to achieve thorough mixing as required in the specifications. Frequent inspection required. Weather-dependent and should be done when the materials are moist, not wet or dusty.
Spreading and mixing on-site	This method depends on the location (access), slope gradient, and general configuration of the site. Should not be used on slopes greater than 2:1. Cannot be used in very confined sites. Primary mixing machine is the tractor-mounted rototiller; the hand rototiller is too light for most applications. Weather-dependent and should be done when the materials are moist, not wet or dusty.

given to provide an arbitrary horizon designation system (Craul, 1999).

S1—topsoil: A medium loamy sand amended with mature composted organic matter to a content of 10 percent by weight.

S2—subsoil: A medium loamy sand (USDA) conforming to the following specifications, which may contain 1 to 2 percent organic matter by weight (refer to the "Range in Percent Passing Sieve Sizes for the S2 Subsoil and the Organic Amended S1" table). The range of silt should be within 10 to 30 percent, and the range of clay should be within 5 to 15 percent.

S3—drainage layer: A gravelly sand (AASHTO #4) that provides a high rate of water flow from the bottom of the soil profile to the underdrainage system.

The table of percent passing for the stack of sieve sizes ("USDA Size Classes of Soil Mineral Particles" table) and the particle size envelope (see the "Particle Size Distribution Envelope for the S2 Subsoil Loamy Sand" figure) for each designed soil or for each separate horizon where distinct horizons are required for a unique soil profile (for example, the S3 above), should always be provided in the specifications for clarity and to ensure that the testing laboratory and landscape contractor receive the necessary information. It is also valuable and necessary data for such applications as rooftop projects and those involving slope stability and the like. Estimates of bulk density are also necessary, though not graphically represented.

SOIL ANALYSES

Testing

To assure proper soil design function it is imperative that each soil component be clearly specified and tested before installation, and further tested as a system after installation for conformance and proper function.

Close scrutiny throughout the entire project process is always required, as many contractors are not yet familiar with detailed soil specifications and the required testing for landscape projects. The usual response is, "We've done it our way for years and had no problems! Why should we do it your way?" If the truth be known, there were problems but contractors won't admit it. (Craul and Craul, 2006). Some contractors attempt to bypass adhering to the specifications by inflating the estimated costs of the specified soils and then offering the client the contractor's own lower-cost materials. The authors are aware of abject failures in several of these cases, greatly adding to the project costs in correction of the failure.

ASTM standard tests and interpretation of results include the following:

F-1632-03: Standard Method for Particle Size Analysis

F-1815-97: Standard Method for Saturated Hydraulic Conductivity, Water Retention, Porosity, Particle Density, and Bulk Density

F-1647-02a: Standard Method for Organic Matter Content of Putting Green and Sports Turf Root Zone Mixes

RANGE IN PERCENT PASSING SIEVE SIZES FOR S2 SUBSOIL AND ORGANIC AMENDED S1

SIEVE SIZE	PERCENT FINER
#10	100
#18	88–100
#35	70–80
#60	40–50
#140	29–39
#300	25–35
Silt range	10–30
Clay range	5–15

Source: Craul, 1999.

RANGE IN PERCENT PASSING FOR AASHTO AGGREGATE #4* FREQUENTLY USED AS S3 DRAINAGE LAYER

PARTICLE SIZE CLASS	SIEVE SIZE	PERCENT PASSING
Medium gravel	3/8"	100
Fine gravel	#4	95–100
Very fine gravel	#8	80–100
Very coarse sand	#16	50–85
Coarse sand	#30	25–60
Medium sand	#50	10–30
Fine sand	#100	2–10
Silt + clay**	—	1–2

*Sometimes called "highway sand."

**Determined by hydrometer method in ASTM F-1632.

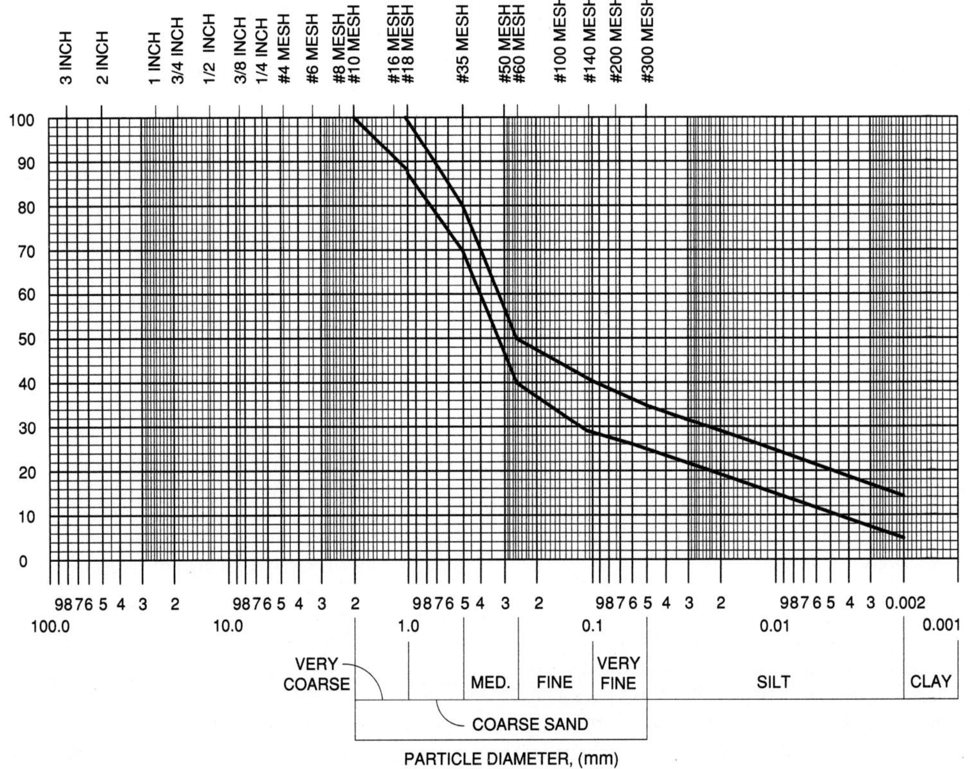

PARTICLE SIZE DISTRIBUTION ENVELOPE FOR THE S2 SUBSOIL LOAMY SAND

Dr. Phillip J. Craul, Senior Lecturer (retired) in Landscape Architecture, Graduate School of Design, Harvard University, and Emeritus Professor of Soil Science, SUNY–College of Environmental Science and Forestry, Syracuse, New York; Timothy A. Craul, President, Craul Land Scientists, PLC, State College, Pennsylvania

D-3385-03: Standard Method for Infiltration of Soils in the Field Using Double Ring Infiltrometer

D-4221-99: Standard Method for Dispersive Characteristics of Clay Soil by Double Hydrometer

Method F-1815-97 is the most appropriate general all-around test for the major physical characteristics of soil.

For composted biosolids, if used as the organic matter source, the maturity test showing "mature" or "maturing" is absolutely necessary; "immature" is unacceptable (see the "Organic Matter" discussion for further details).

For the chemical properties of pH, nutrient content, soluble salts, and organic matter content, the tests and interpretations performed by the appropriate state agricultural experiment station are valid and should be used. If the existing or designed soil does not exhibit the appropriate chemical characteristics for the plant palette, then amendments are required to adjust them accordingly.

One of the most common errors is the mismatching of soil pH to that required by the plant palette, such as planting azaleas or other acid-loving plants in very alkaline soil. Pouring on the organic matter is an insufficient solution: pH must be lowered by the application of elemental sulfur, or better still, by modifying the plant palette (Craul, 1999).

The landscape architect should always confirm that the soil materials delivered to the site are the same on which the tests were performed; thus, samples must be obtained from the bulk deliveries and tested again. Most laboratories can provide quick turnaround service (at extra charge) to facilitate installation.

Installation

Soil placement during installation requires following the appropriate soil mechanics procedures with respect to compaction of the soil. (These are given in the *Soil Mechanics* for reference.) Close supervision of the soil installation process by the landscape architect or the soil scientist, if one is retained for the project, is absolutely necessary.

Installation activities include: proper inspection and sampling for tests of delivered soil materials, supervision of soil placement in lifts to the proper degree of compaction, prevention of excessive traffic over the placed soil, and proper sequencing of planting with soil placement to greatly reduce disturbance to the placed soil.

The best practice is simultaneous placement of the topsoil and plants, if feasible. Contractors have stated that this practice has saved them time, hence, money. It also eliminates unwanted traffic over the topsoil final grade.

Placement of the Soil

The soil should always be placed in lifts not to exceed 6 inches in thickness (see the "Installation of Soil in Lifts" figure). This ensures the elimination of air pockets and soft spots of inadequate filling, as well as adequate compaction to prevent settlement or subsidence.

If a loamy sand to sandy loam designed soil is installed with less than 10 percent volume basis organic matter, the density as placed will normally be at 85 to 90 percent using the Proctor test. If compactive force is required, it should be a lightweight roller of not more than 75 to 100 pounds per foot-width of the roller.

In many cases, soil-spreading equipment traffic such as a "speeder-skidder" or a light, wide-track bulldozer can apply sufficient force for compacting soil to a Proctor of 85 to 90 percent for landscape purposes, without exceeding plant root penetration density of 1.65 Mg/m^3 for fine-textured cohesive soil and 1.70 Mg/m^3 for sandy noncohesive soil.

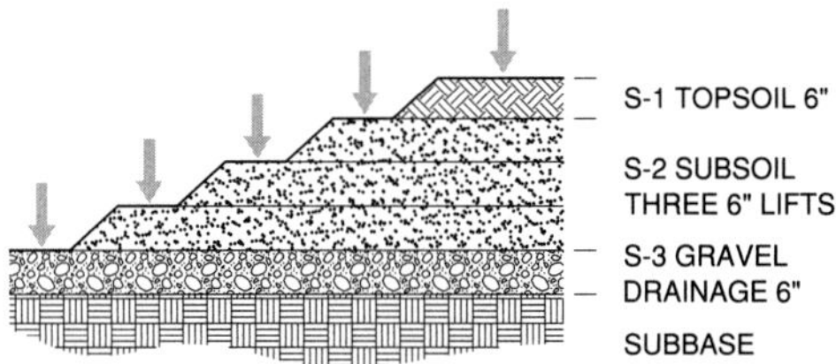

The arrows indicate compaction of each lift as installed.

INSTALLATION OF SOIL IN LIFTS

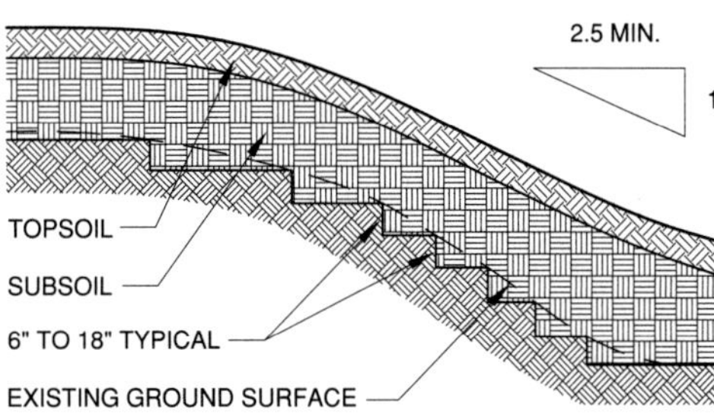

The designed soil is backfilled into the benches. Upslope drainage should be cut off by curtain drains if excess downslope drainage is a problem. Underdrainage may be required at the foot of the benched slope. Width of each bench depends on existing slope angle.

"STEPPING" PREPARATION OF A SLOPING SUBGRADE

Placement of Soil on Slopes

The placement of soil on a slope must be done with somewhat more care than on level areas. The existing slope surface should be prepared to receive the designed soil as cover, especially if the slope is greater than 2:1; however, it is always wise to prepare the subbase even on a gentle (3:1 or 2:1) slope, to assure slope stability.

Soil should not be placed on a slope with compacted soil or a very stony smooth surface acting like a pavement. Both conditions act as an interface between the initial surface and the placed soil, and will become a potential failure plane, especially if water is contributed to the site from upslope drainage.

The surface should be deeply scarified (6 inches or more using a chisel plow), with removal of some of the stone in the case of the stony surface. On steeper slopes, the existing soil material (subgrade) should be stepped or terraced, as given in the "Stepping Preparation of a Sloping Subgrade" figure.

SOIL PROFILES FOR LANDSCAPE DESIGN

The profiles provided here are intended only to illustrate the graphic representation of soil profiles. The dimensions and specifications are not to be used as standards for applicability to any soils. Numerous other factors must be taken into account before a final designed soil evolves. These profiles, thus, should be regarded as starting points, requiring modification according to the site situation and conditions.

Garden Soils

A garden soil must have the capability to grow seasonal and/or perennial plants that are vigorous; produce showy foliage, flowers, and fruits; and have resistance to disease and insects—all on an annual or long-term basis. In the case of annuals, the soil is disturbed each growing season in the process of preparation, transplanting, cultivation, and plant removal at the end of the season. For perennials, the disturbance is much reduced. To serve as a planting medium under these circumstances, the soil must be fertile, well-drained, or nearly so, yet supply sufficient plant-available water; be easy to work under varying moisture conditions; and be resistant to compaction by moderate traffic. The soil profile in the "General-Purpose Garden Soil Profile for Annual and Perennial Plants" figure attempts to accomplish these objectives. The description of the garden soil profile in this figure is as follows:

S1 horizon: 0–6 inches (0–15 cm)	Loam to silt loam with 20 percent volume basis organic matter
S2 horizon: 6–14 inches (15–35 cm)	Loam with 5 percent volume basis organic matter
S3 horizon: 14–18+ inches (35–46 cm)	Sandy loam

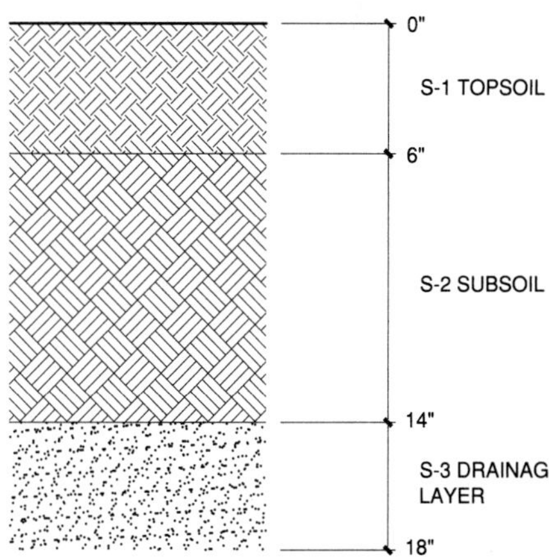

GENERAL-PURPOSE GARDEN SOIL PROFILE FOR ANNUAL AND PERENNIAL PLANTS

The garden soil may be of finer texture to enhance fertility and water-holding capacity than other designed soil profiles, since there is essentially little or no traffic on these soils. They should not be placed

Dr. Phillip J. Craul, Senior Lecturer (retired) in Landscape Architecture, Graduate School of Design, Harvard University, and Emeritus Professor of Soil Science, SUNY–College of Environmental Science and Forestry, Syracuse, New York; Timothy A. Craul, President, Craul Land Scientists, PLC, State College, Pennsylvania

where vibration may have impact on the soil, as these textures compact easily. The organic matter content is somewhat higher than other soil profiles simply because of frequent cultivation and weeding of the topsoil. There is a tendency to specify a much higher organic matter content, which is unnecessary. A mulch layer is not indicated in the figure, as some plants grow better without a mulch, but may be installed where appropriate. In the case of growing annual plants, transplanting is an annual operation so the soil must be one that can withstand frequent but careful disturbance. The sand content increases with depth to provide adequate drainage. Underdrainage is not shown, but should be installed if there is any question about inadequate drainage. Permeability through the profile should be suitable, if it does not get compacted in any layer. This soil should not be worked when very wet (if the soil forms a sticky clod when pressed in the hand, and the surface is glazed with water, it is too wet to work).

Areas Planted to Turf

Examples of alternative designed soil profiles for a turf area are given in the figures "Turf Profile without Surface Traffic" and "Turf with Traffic Profiles." Again, these and the following profiles are provided only as examples and guides. For actual application to projects, modifications are required, depending on the site conditions, the plant palette, the climate of the location, and other unknown factors.

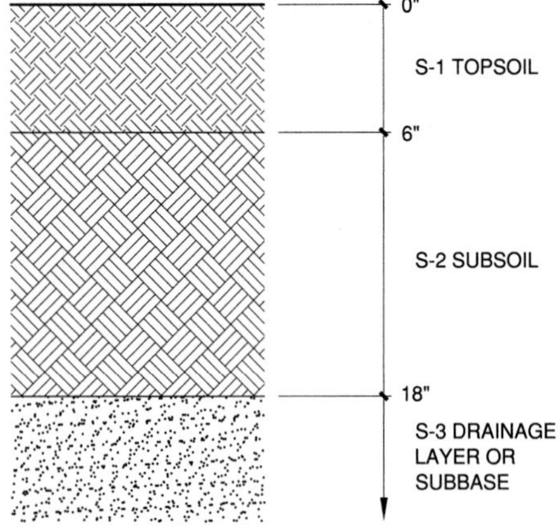

TURF PROFILE WITHOUT SURFACE TRAFFIC

The profile description for the "Turf Profile without Surface Traffic" figure is:

S1 horizon: 0–6 inches (0–15 cm)	Loam to sandy loam with 10 percent volume basis organic matter
S2 horizon: 6–18 inches (15–46 cm)	Sandy loam with at least 2 percent volume basis organic matter
S3 horizon: 18+ inches (46+ cm)	Sandy loam or coarser; or a well-draining subbase

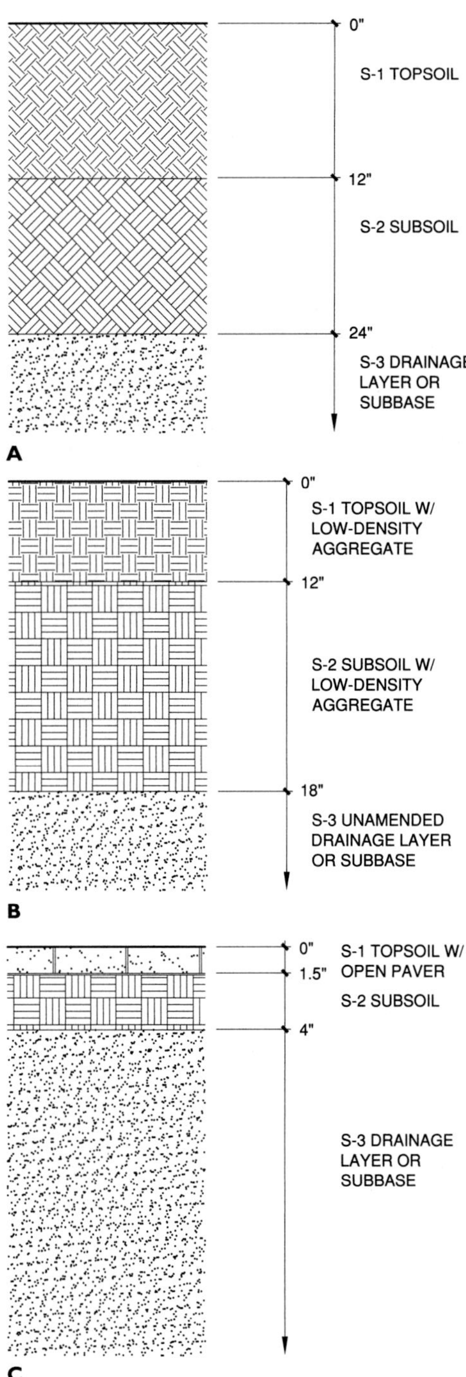

(a) The "prepared athletic turf"; (b) the structure-amended profile; (c) the open-paving profile.

TURF WITH TRAFFIC PROFILES

Source: Craul, 1999.

The A profile description for the "Turf with Traffic Profiles" figure, the "prepared athletic turf," is:

S1 horizon: 0–12 inches (0–30 cm)	Coarse to medium loamy sand with 10 percent volume basis organic matter
S2 horizon: 12–24 inches (30–60 cm)	Medium loamy sand to sandy loam with 2 percent volume basis organic matter

The B profile description for the "Turf with Traffic Profiles" figure, low-density amended soil, is:

S1 horizon: 0–6 inches (0–15 cm)	Loam or sandy loam with 25 to 30 percent volume basis low-density aggregate, ¼-inch diameter (3–5 mm) and 10 percent volume basis organic matter
S2 horizon: 6–18 inches (15–46 cm)	Loam or sandy loam with 10 percent volume basis low-density aggregate, ¼–½-inch diameter (5–10 mm), and 2 percent volume basis organic matter
S3 horizon: 18–24+ inches (46–60+ cm)	Loamy sand unamended; or a drainage layer, if required

The C profile description for the "Turf with Traffic Profiles" figure, open-paving profile, is:

S1 horizon: 0–1.5 inches (0–3.8 cm)	Open paver (a grid here) backfilled after installation with loam and 20 percent volume basis organic matter; may be hydromulched into the paver
S2 horizon: 1.5–4 inches (3.8–5 cm)	Loamy sand with 2 percent volume basis organic matter
S-3 horizon: 4–? inches (5–? cm)	AASHTO #4 aggregate with underdrainage, if required. (? = depends on drainage pipe diameter. Pipe should be covered by 2 inches of aggregate.)

The prepared athletic turf is designed for heavy use by athletic events or playing fields. It provides good rooting for turf, is compaction-resistant, and remains relatively dry in all weather conditions. However, it must be irrigated in arid areas or during periods of extended drought in humid areas.

The low-density aggregate amended profile is suitable for turf areas that have light to moderate pedestrian use, such as reception areas and walking paths. It is not designed for vehicular use.

There are two major uses of open pavers: lightweight for walking trails and paths, and heavyweight for parking lots. The first type is constructed mainly of plastic or fiberglass and may be in the form of grids, circles, or heavy netting. An informal study on a "desire line" on the Mall, Washington, DC, concluded that a plastic grid with 2-inch (5-cm) square openings was the most successful (J. C. Patterson and J. R. Short, personal communication). Interlocked rigid grid size of 2 feet by 3 feet (60 by 90 cm) was very secure, while much smaller grids tended to "kick out" or shift. Plastic circles glued to geotextile and set in sand or gravel were the least successful. The same results with

Dr. Phillip J. Craul, Senior Lecturer (retired) in Landscape Architecture, Graduate School of Design, Harvard University, and Emeritus Professor of Soil Science, SUNY–College of Environmental Science and Forestry, Syracuse, New York; Timothy A. Craul, President, Craul Land Scientists, PLC, State College, Pennsylvania

the plastic circles were observed in a park at St. Paul, Minnesota, 2000, and in another park in Syracuse, New York, 2005 (P. J. Craul, personal observations, 2000 and 2005, respectively). For heavy-use areas such as busy parking lots, the profile in the "Turf Profile without Surface Traffic" figure with a heavy, open paver, especially the interlocking design similar to the Ritter grass paving unit, has been found to be very serviceable. It is molded from recycled plastic and can support weights of between 50,000 to 70,000 pounds per square foot. British Airways headquarters at London's Heathrow Airport has interlocking grass paver parking lots that have been very successful. The use of concrete block as an open paver has had mixed results. The failures are usually due to poor base material, resulting in shifting and loose blocks; or the soil in the openings is brought too close to the surface and becomes the wearing surface, killing the turf. The soil should always be about ¾ inch (2 cm) below the block surface, so that the turf does not become worn and the soil is not compacted. The large proportion of exposed concrete block surface area is a visual and vegetative disadvantage.

Soil Profiles for Planting Designs with Trees

Standard Open-Soil Tree Pit

This design is applied to tree planting in turf or other open areas and generally without an understory. The design provided in the "Standard Open Tree Pit" figure is generally accepted by most arboriculturists and is given in the applicable literature (Watson and Himelick, 1997). The features include:

- The pit is excavated to a depth slightly less than the height of the root ball. This procedure prevents settling of the root ball or of the root ball being placed too deep, leading to eventual demise of the tree.
- The walls of the pit are flared outward to provide adequate loosened soil for fine root extension and quick establishment.
- The backfill soil is totally unamended. It is not necessary to mix organic matter in with the backfill material; this leads to the potential of the "teacup" effect of waterlogging of the backfill during heavy rainfall events. Loosening of the soil during excavation has been found to be adequate for root extension.
- The mulch layer, no thicker than 4 inches, extends from near the root collar, which is *not* covered, out to beyond the disturbed soil.

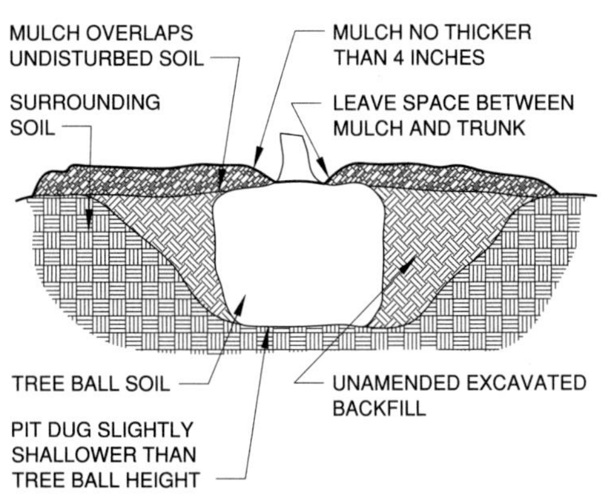

STANDARD OPEN TREE PIT

Source: Craul, 1992.

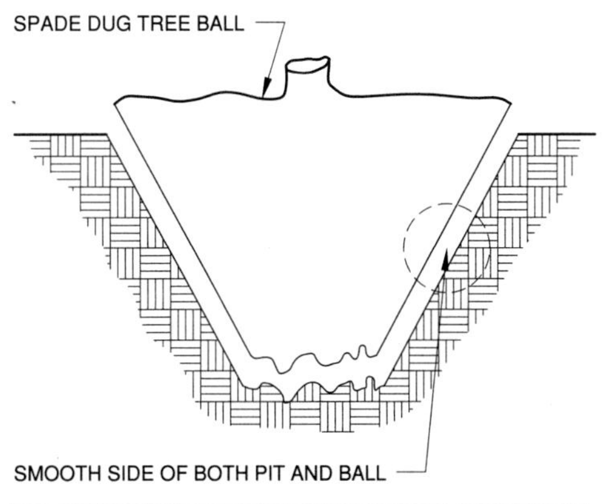

DIGGING SPADE TREE PIT

Source: Craul, 1992.

Most arborists will argue that this design involves a lot of expensive handwork and that they prefer to use the digging spade machine (such as the Vermeer) to excavate the tree pit. This machine excavates an inverted cone-shaped pit, which matches the cone-shaped root ball obtained by digging the tree in the nursery by the same machine. The procedure also requires little if any backfilling on the site. This procedure is successful when the surrounding planting soil is totally suitable; otherwise, problems develop. One frequent problem is using the digging spade in heavy (clayey) soils (see the "Digging Spade Tree Pit" figure). The blades tend to smooth or smear the walls of the pit, creating resistance to fine root extension. This problem is overcome if the pit walls are well roughened before placing the root ball.

Other arborists will simply auger the hole with a speeder-mounted auger tool. The sides of these pits are roughened, but if a spade-dug root ball is placed in an augered pit, there is danger of large soil voids being left in the bottom of the pit unless the ground crew is diligent. Voids in the soil allow the roots to dry out, or the root ball settles so that the root collar is too deep, and could lead to mortality (Craul, 1992). Many tree species are susceptible to mortality if the root collar is planted too deep (4 to 6 inches or more).

Tree Root Ball Size Rendering

To provide realistic rendering to scale of the designed soil profile where trees are included, actual dimensions for tree root balls should be employed (see the "Relative Dimensions and Proportions of Root Balls for Three Tree Caliper Diameters" figure) rather than strictly conceptual rendering and employing NTS (not to scale).

This practice is necessary to show true scale in relation to the graphic dimensions given for the soil profile and any associated structures, to allow sufficient space and volume for the root balls. If any root balls are to be placed on compacted soil pedestals to prevent subsequent settlement, then true scaling will permit the determination of pedestal height. Also, true dimensions on the drawings will provide greater accuracy and cost-effectiveness in estimating soil volumes and other belowground features. The "Size, Depth, and Weight of Root Balls for Trees" table provides some necessary data for root ball dimensions.

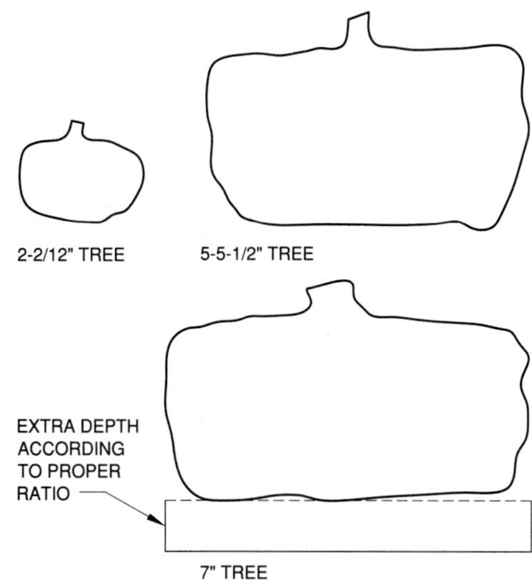

RELATIVE DIMENSIONS AND PROPORTIONS OF ROOT BALLS FOR THREE TREE CALIPER DIAMETERS

Source: Craul, 1992.

Size of the Tree Pit

The question of the appropriate size of the tree pit always arises in landscape design for elements other than the open-area standard design where the root ball size determines the size of the tree pit.

The design elements—that is, curbside planting, plaza planting, rooftop planting, or a planting box—have varying rooting volume requirements and constraints.

Bare Root Shrubs and Trees

- Some shrubs and trees of less than 2-inch caliper, may be planted bare root.
- The root pit is made large enough in diameter and depth so that the roots may be extended to their full length without crowding (see the "Planting Hole for Bare Root Shrubs and Trees" figure).
- The backfill remains unamended.
- The backfill is tamped with care as the pit is filled to secure the root system in place without damage to the roots. The compaction is important to prevent subsequent settlement with the root collar too deep.

Shrubs

- Shrubs and small ball-and-burlap trees up to a root ball diameter of 16 inches require an excavation of only the size of the root ball, except that the depth should be slightly less than the height of the root ball so that the root collar is planted higher than the surrounding soil.
- The burlap is easily folded down as the ball is placed in the pit. Exceptions would require a slightly larger excavation.

Ball-and-Burlap Trees

- For open and many other plantings, the size of the root ball determines the size of the tree pit. In the case of ball-and-burlap root balls, sufficient pit space around the root ball must be provided to roll down the burlap one-half or two-thirds of the height of the root ball, and to the cutting and

Dr. Phillip J. Craul, Senior Lecturer (retired) in Landscape Architecture, Graduate School of Design, Harvard University, and Emeritus Professor of Soil Science, SUNY–College of Environmental Science and Forestry, Syracuse, New York; Timothy A. Craul, President, Craul Land Scientists, PLC, State College, Pennsylvania

SIZE, DEPTH, AND WEIGHT OF ROOT BALLS FOR TREES

TREE DIAMETER		BALL DIAMETER		BALL DEPTH		APPROXIMATE WEIGHT OF BALL AND TREE			
INCHES	CM	INCHES	CM	INCHES	CM	TONS LBS	KG	U.S.	METRIC
—	—	10	25	8	20	34	15	—	—
—	—	12	30	9	23	55	25	—	—
—	—	14	35	11	28	91	42	—	—
—	—	16	40	12	30	124	56	—	—
—	—	18	45	14	35	193	88	—	—
—	—	20	50	15	38	254	115	—	—
—	—	24	60	16	41	392	178	—	—
—	—	28	70	19	48	624	283	—	—
—	—	32	80	20	50	867	394	—	—
—	—	36	90	22	55	1216	552	—	—
—	—	42	105	25	63	1877	853	—	—
5	13	48	120	29	74	—	—	1.5	1.3
6	15	60	150	32	81	—	—	2.4	2.2
7	18	72	180	34	86	—	—	3.7	3.4
8	20	84	210	36	96	—	—	5.4	4.9
10	25	96	240	38	96	—	—	7.4	6.8
11	28	108	280	40	100	—	—	9.9	9.0
12	31	120	300	40	100	—	—	12.2	11.1

Source: From Himelick, 1981; and Watson and Himelick, 1997; in Craul, 1999.

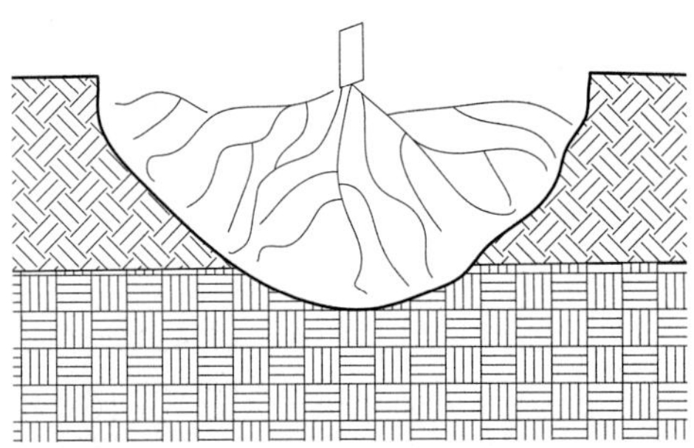

PLANTING HOLE FOR BARE ROOT SHRUBS AND TREES

removal of the lateral portions of the wire basket, if used. Therefore, the tree pit size may be determined by the root diameter from the "Size, Depth, and Weight of Root Balls for Trees" table, plus 12 inches (30 cm) for root balls from 16 inches (41 cm) up to 36 inches (0.91 m) in diameter, leaving a 6-inch ring around the root ball for working space.

- For root ball diameters from 36 inches (0.91 m) up to 72 inches (1.8 m), the diameter is increased by 24 inches (60 cm), leaving a working ring width of 12 inches (30 cm).
- Root balls larger than 72 inches (1.8 m) may have special supports or be cased in a box that require removal. More working space is required and should be determined in cooperation with the landscape contractor.

Amendments to the backfill soil (such as organic matter, fertilizer, hydrogels, geotextile cover, any growth stimulants or mycorrhizae, or gravel or stones placed beneath the root ball) should be avoided; experience has shown that there is little benefit and even some harm to the successful growth of the plant (Harris, Clark, Matheny, 2004). Fertilization of most plants should wait until after the first year in the ground, except in the far south where the growing season is long, and then only after the first growing season.

Planting with the Spade Digger

There are various sizes of spade diggers to accommodate a range of tree ball sizes. Most spade diggers are now constructed to be adjustable within a range of tree ball sizes. Therefore, it is important that the contractor select the equipment to provide the correct size of the root ball approximating the "Size, Depth, and Weight of Root Balls for Trees" table. There is a certain tendency within the landscaping industry to make the root balls smaller than specified in the table, citing root pruning in the nursery and the practice of digging and planting the same day, both of which are many times not done or practical. It behooves the landscape architect to specify the practice to be followed on each project after consulting with the selected nursery and the landscape contractor to ascertain the practices and conditions of the locality.

Trees with Understory Vegetation

In some elements of landscape design there are many occasions when a design involves tress with deliberate understory vegetation. The soil design for this element is somewhat more complex than that for trees in the open turf. The cross section for this application is illustrated in the "Soil Profile for Trees with Understory Vegetation" figure. The understory vegetation is planted at shallower depth than the trees. Therefore, it is wise to create a compacted pedestal under each shrub to prevent settlement. The procedure is to excavate the hole to a depth a little less than the height of the ball for the shrub, manually compact the bottom of the hole, place the root ball on the bottom, backfill and tamp it lightly, and mulch the surface. For perennial flowers and other similar plants, the pedestals are not necessary.

Designed Soil Profile for Covered (Paved) Application

The most complex of the tree planting design is that for curbside sidewalk and paved plaza applications (see the "Example of a Designed Complex Tree Planting Cross Section" figure). The design features must include the following:

In all cases of covered plantings, the tree planting soil should be continuous between adjacent trees, as if in a copse (shown in the "Longitudinal Soil Section for a Single Row of Trees" figure). This design provides shared rooting space so that each tree has the minimum rooting volume of at least 800 to 1,000 cubic feet (Urban, 1992).

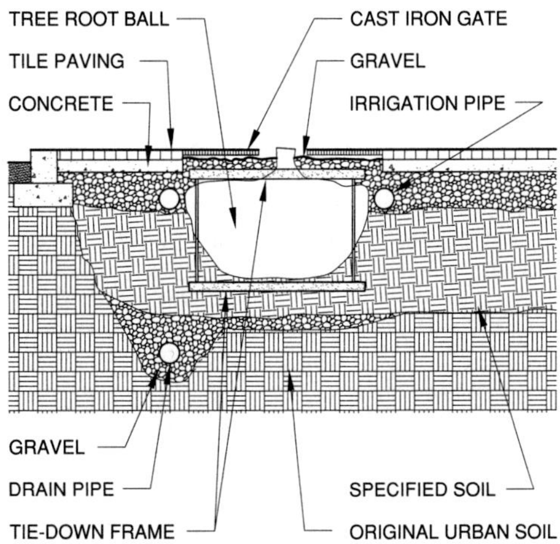

EXAMPLE OF A DESIGNED COMPLEX TREE PLANTING CROSS SECTION, PENNSYLVANIA AVENUE, WASHINGTON, DC

Source: Craul, 1999.

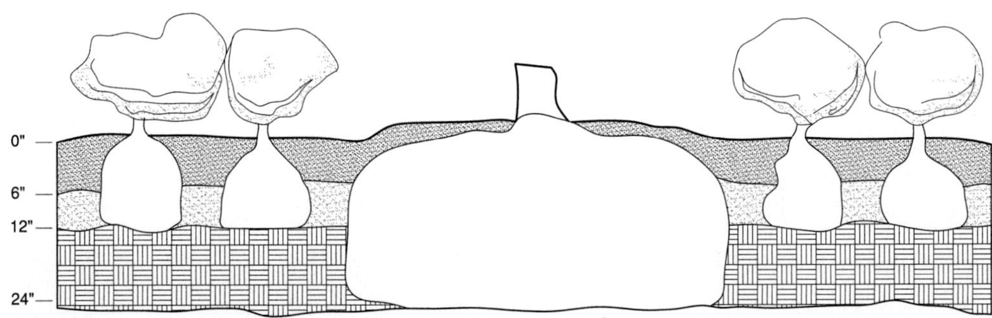

SOIL PROFILE FOR TREES WITH UNDERSTORY VEGETATION

Source: Craul, 1999.

Dr. Phillip J. Craul, Senior Lecturer (retired) in Landscape Architecture, Graduate School of Design, Harvard University, and Emeritus Professor of Soil Science, SUNY–College of Environmental Science and Forestry, Syracuse, New York; Timothy A. Craul, President, Craul Land Scientists, PLC, State College, Pennsylvania

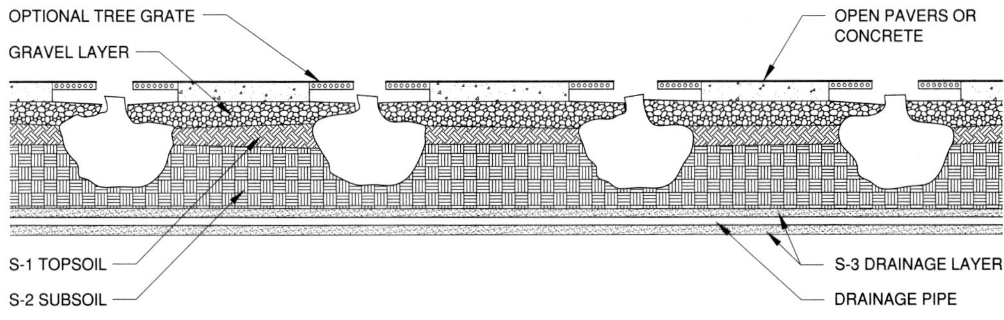

LONGITUDINAL SOIL SECTION FOR A SINGLE ROW OF TREES

There should be provision for aeration of the planting soil. This may be in the form of porous, open, or jointed paving on the surface set in a bed of sand, or slotted piping from the tree pit into the top of the soil profile beneath the paving or some other reliable system.

Soil profile depth should be at least equal to the height of the root but not less than 24 inches.

The paved surface over the tree root system of a tree planted in a sidewalk or plaza creates some major problems for tree survival, hence, the provisions given above. Though the usual S-horizons are designated in the "Longitudinal Soil Section for a Single Row of Trees" figure, geotechnical engineering criteria must enter into the soil design due to the provisions of most local engineering and zoning ordinances. The best procedure for landscape architects is to have a consulting soil scientist cooperate with the project engineer when plantings below paving are an element of the landscape design.

On a case-by-case basis, it is necessary to consider particle size distribution (soil texture) and organic matter content as they influence density and its relation to tree root penetration and full root structural and physiological development over the life expectancy of the tree, versus adequate bearing capacity (the Proctor test requirements) to support the paving. Thus, no standard profile specification may be given here. However, the sand-based soil profile, with appropriate local adjustments, has proven satisfactory based on over 35 years of experience and in many major landscape architecture projects.

Use of Jointed Pavers as an Alternative to Solid Sidewalk Construction

Most municipalities have construction codes that require concrete or other types of solid paving for sidewalks due to safety and maintenance reasons. These were adopted as the result of maintenance and liability problems with older paving types, mainly brick, which was the preferred surface for sidewalks in the late nineteenth and most of the twentieth century because of its abundance and low cost.

Many have proclaimed the benefit of brick sidewalks over the roots of street-side trees. The brick surface is open-jointed, allowing water infiltration into the soil below and the exchange of oxygen and carbon dioxide between the soil and the atmosphere. In addition, the flexibility of the brick surface allowed for the growth of roots without restriction. Obviously, the uneven surface or missing bricks caused many injuries to pedestrians and resulted in lawsuits against municipalities. Oxford, a small fishing and vacation village on the eastern shore of Maryland still maintains brick sidewalks, but posts many signs warning pedestrians about the uneven sidewalks. The signs include a statement by the village that it wishes to protect its trees. Examination of historical photographs of city streets in New York City, Boston, and Philadelphia point to two major facts: streets with vigorous trees usually have brick sidewalks; streets with concrete sidewalks have no trees.

Characteristics and Types of Jointed Pavers

As suggested above, jointed pavers have the advantage of being open, by virtue of the joints between elements being filled with porous media, most frequently sand. The greater the surface area exposed by the joints, the greater the exchange of oxygen, carbon dioxide, and other gases between the soil below and the atmosphere, and the greater infiltration of water. Kopinga (1985), and others in the Netherlands, have shown the clear advantages of open pavers. It is pointed out that a significant percentage of precipitation infiltrates into the soil through open slab pavers (see the "Amount of Annual Precipitation Infiltrating through Various Jointed Pavers" table).

The percentage of precipitation infiltrating the soil may range from 20 to 95 percent during the growing season, depending on the infiltration rate from 0.013 inch/hour (0.33 mm/hour) up to 95 percent at 0.78 inch/hour (20 mm/hour).

A surface of standard modular brick (4 inches × 8 inches × 2-3/5 inches) as cover over the linear trench planting for a row of trees (see the "Plan for a Row of Trees with an Open Paver Surface" figure) permits approximately 5 to 8.6 percent open space, depending on the joint opening, from about 3/16 inch (5 mm) to 1/4 inch (6 mm).

The brick is set in concrete sand (clean, medium to coarse, loamy sand) on a 4- to 6-inch (10- to 15-cm) bed of gravel. Geotextile, which partially defeats the advantage of the open joint pavement, is not necessary below the gravel layer if the surface of the designed sandy soil below is compacted to 90 percent Proctor. A fine-textured soil (silt loam or finer) should not be used in this case.

AMOUNT OF ANNUAL PRECIPITATION INFILTRATING THROUGH VARIOUS JOINTED PAVERS

PAVEMENT TYPE	DIMENSIONS (IN.)	JOINT SPACE (%)	INFILTRATION RATE (IN./HR)	INFILTRATED AMOUNT PER GROWING SEASON (IN.)
Slab	24 x 24 x 2-3/4	0.6	0.02	3.03
Slab	12 x 12 x 2	1.1	0.035	4.41
Brick	8 x 4 x 4	5.1	0.138	9.92
Brick	4 x 4 x 4	7.1	0.217	11.18
Vent slab	24 x 24 x 2-3/4	1.9	0.075	7.72
Vent slab	12 x 12 x 2	5.6	0.118	9.37
Perforated brick	8 x 8 x 4	30.0	0.295	11.73

Source: After Kopinga, 1985.

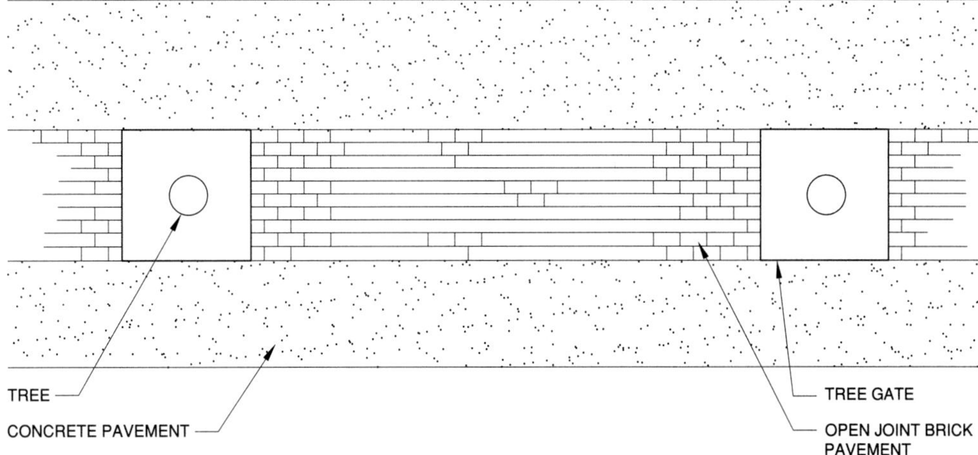

The planting soil is continuous, as shown in the "Longitudinal Soil Section for a Single Row of Trees" figure. Root barriers are not necessary around the tree grates.

PLAN FOR A ROW OF TREES WITH AN OPEN PAVER SURFACE

Dr. Phillip J. Craul, Senior Lecturer (retired) in Landscape Architecture, Graduate School of Design, Harvard University, and Emeritus Professor of Soil Science, SUNY–College of Environmental Science and Forestry, Syracuse, New York; Timothy A. Craul, President, Craul Land Scientists, PLC, State College, Pennsylvania

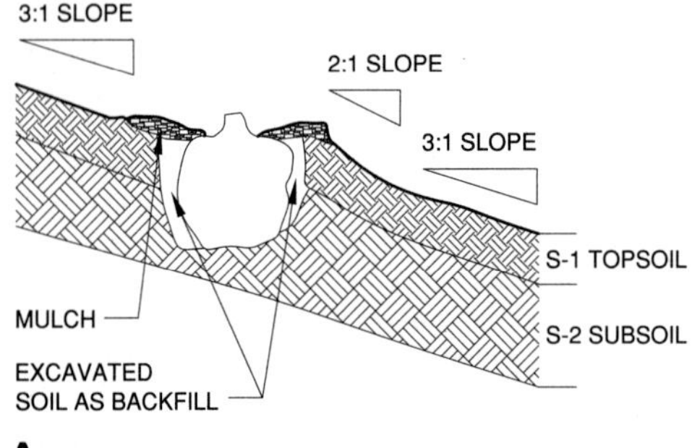

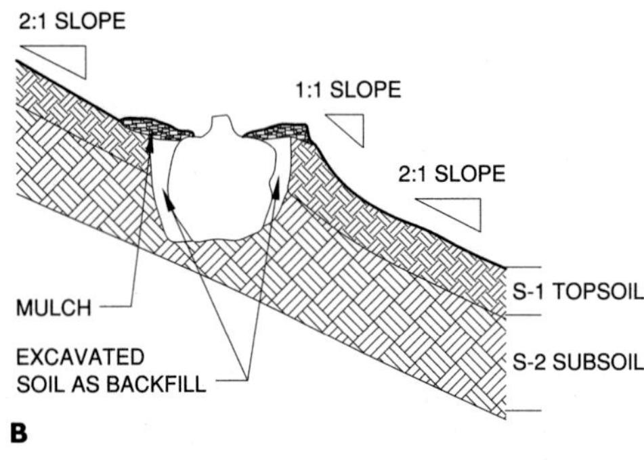

TREE PLANTING ON A SLOPE: (A) 3:1, AND (B) 2:1.

Planting on Slopes

Generally, trees are planted on slopes not exceeding 2:1 ratio, unless special geotechnical engineering subsurface provisions are made to stabilize the slope. Cross sections for planting on 3:1 and 2:1 slopes are given in the "Tree Planting on a Slope" figure. Slopes of 1.5:1 or greater, unless very short in length (10 feet or less; 3 m or less), require special stabilization or terracing, and a geotechnical engineer should be consulted.

Designed Planting Berm

Berms have become a useful element in landscape design to provide diversity to landscape topography and as an intersecting element to break visual perspective. Several design features must receive attention by landscape architects and contractors for successful berm design integration and construction, as illustrated in the "Soil Cross Section of the Ideal Berm" figure.

Design requirements for berms are as follows:

- Berm dimensions of height, width, and length must be sufficient to create a distinct landscape feature to distinguish it from a simple low knoll or swell.
- If the purpose of the berm is to provide improved drainage, as compared to the surrounding poorly drained landscape, the height of the berm must be sufficient to contain the plant root balls above the capillary fringe of the berm soil, to be totally effective. Deliberate drainage should be provided for the bottom of the berm. The existing soil to be covered by the berm is shaped with a slight mound longitudinal with the berm design to enhance drainage from the bottom of the berm. Geotextile mat may be placed on the surface of the reshaped existing soil to aid in interrupting the capillary fringe column. If drainage is not a problem, the geotextile is omitted.
- The width of the berm must be sufficient to provide adequate soil space for adequate lateral root extension if trees are planted as protection against wind throw. Small berms, better termed hummocks, only somewhat larger than the root ball, should be confined to small shrubs, never trees; the system is very unstable for windthrow resistance in most cases.
- The side and end slopes should be gentle enough for ground maintenance equipment to traverse, depending on allowable slope length, usually 2:1 or 3:1. The greater the height of the berm, the greater the importance of this item. High berms with short steep slopes have proven difficult to maintain as lawn. An alternative planting design should be considered that requires only minimal maintenance.
- If trees are to be planted on the berm, they should be positioned away from the berm edge so that the extending roots remain within the berm.
- When berms are used for burial of hard construction debris, almost always they must meet local code or zoning regulations and approval before construction. In these situations, the covering soil must be thick enough to provide adequate rooting depth for the plants. The minimum depth of not less than 18 inches (46 cm) is the usual limit.

Conventional soil profiles with modifications as given in this discussion are appropriate for berms.

S-1 TOPSOIL
2:1 SLOPE
GEOTEXTILE
2:1 SLOPE
S-2 SUBSOIL
DRAIN PIPES
COMPACTED SOIL OR POORLY DRAINED SOIL

The geotextile is used mainly for berms on poorly drained soil; it is not necessary on dry compacted soil.

SOIL CROSS SECTION OF THE IDEAL BERM

Filling or Excavating around Existing Trees

Unfortunately, there are numerous examples of created hazards to existing trees, eventually causing their death, due to improper filling or excavating of soil surrounding the root system. Here are two examples:

- Filling of soil more than 6 to 8 inches, if the soil is fine-textured (10 inches if very sandy) over an existing soil surface with tree roots below has the effect of suffocating the roots by cutting off the oxygen supply and permitting carbon dioxide and other toxic gases to accumulate in the buried soil.
- If more than about 30 to 40 percent of the root system is covered, the tree will eventually die. In a similar fashion, if the same percentage of the root system is destroyed by excavation or left exposed to dry out, the tree dies.

Competent prior planning and actions can eliminate these hazards, obviously adding to the expense of the project, but are absolutely necessary if the tree is to be preserved, especially in the case of a special "traditional" tree that is a major element of the landscape (see the "Protecting the Tree Root System from Excavation and Filling" figure and the "Protecting the Tree Root System from Deep Filling" figure).

Sometimes it is expedient to simply remove the tree and replant one as part of the landscape design.

Protecting Traditional Tree Exposed Roots

Roots of old traditional trees on older landscapes such as estates, parks, and historical places become exposed due to the continued enlargement of the roots, settlement, compaction, or erosion of the surrounding soil. The root system becomes subject to physical injury by maintenance equipment or other traffic, creating entry for diseases and insects. Further, the exposed roots lose the stability and strength of the soil for windthrow resistance. Therefore, it becomes necessary to "refill" the root system to correct the conditions. Here are guidelines for refilling:

- The refilling of an existing root system must be done with extreme care.
- The fill soil must be of medium to coarse texture (well-structured granular loam to sandy loam) for appropriate aeration characteristics, and be applied starting at the large framework roots near the root collar (but not on the root collar) and extending outward to beyond the drip line, tapering the thickness outward.
- Thickness of the filled layer should not exceed 4 inches at any one time, as illustrated in the "Refilling of Soil under Traditional Trees" figure). The surface is then seeded or sodded, or covered with mulch and fenced off for at least two growing seasons. During this time period, the root system adjusts to the new cover by extending the fine roots into the new layer.
- After the two-year period, another layer of the fill material may be applied, if necessary, to cover the exposed roots and repeat the whole process with the same limitations.

The mistake made in most cases is to give in to temptation to cover the roots in one operation because it is cheaper, and the above procedure is too complicated. The result of the shortcut is to risk losing the tree.

Dr. Phillip J. Craul, Senior Lecturer (retired) in Landscape Architecture, Graduate School of Design, Harvard University, and Emeritus Professor of Soil Science, SUNY–College of Environmental Science and Forestry, Syracuse, New York; Timothy A. Craul, President, Craul Land Scientists, PLC, State College, Pennsylvania

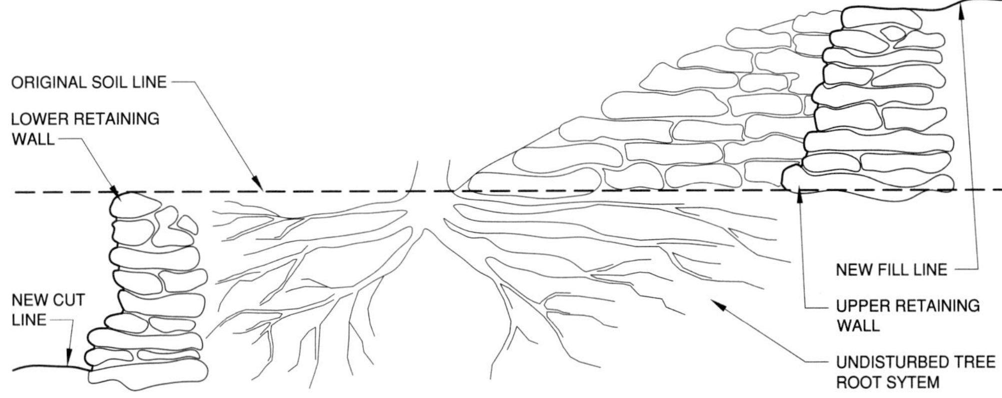

PROTECTING THE TREE ROOT SYSTEM FROM EXCAVATION AND FILLING

Source: Craul, 1992.

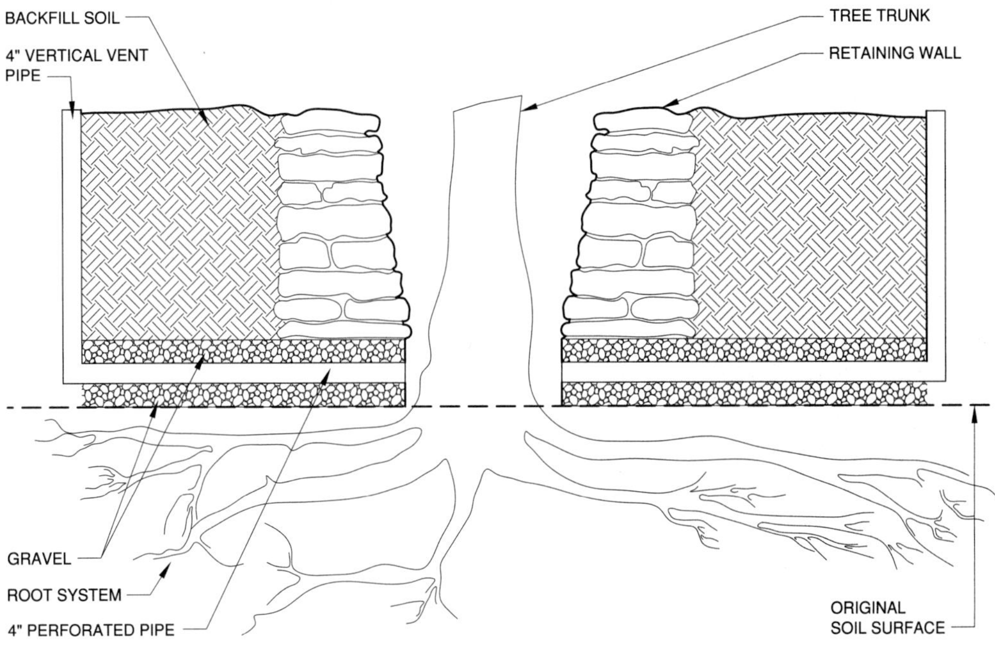

PROTECTING THE TREE ROOT SYSTEM FROM DEEP FILLING

Source: Craul, 1992.

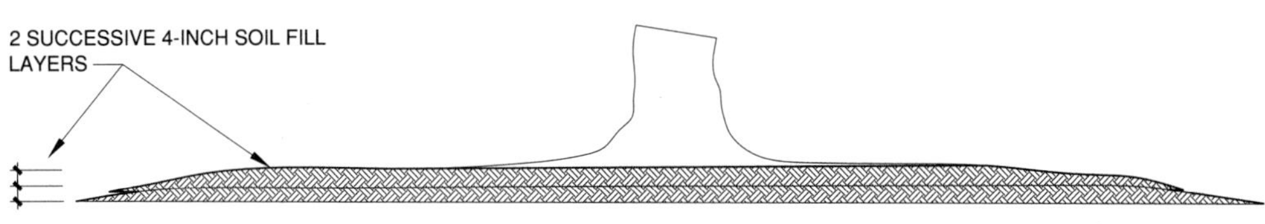

REFILLING OF SOIL UNDER TRADITIONAL TREES

Mulch may be used in place of the soil if the area is not planned to be seeded and if it can be left in place. A coarse mulch such as wood chips may be safely placed in a 4-inch layer—6 inches only in exceptional cases. Do not apply fine mulch, as it becomes compacted if there is traffic on the surface. However, the use of wood chips requires annual maintenance to prevent exposure of the roots if there is surface traffic. Applying more mulch to save time and money will have the same effect of too much soil in the first procedure. The best procedure in most all cases is to fence off the area.

Designed Rooftop (Green Roof) Soil Profile

The concept of green roofs (used henceforth in place of rooftop) is becoming very popular, and in some instances very necessary. This is, in fact, a very old, historical technique, as seen in the grass roofs of northern Europe, northwestern United States and Canada, and the sod huts of the United States prairie.

The green roof concept fits many of the precepts of LEED; and where there is an opportunity to provide a green roof in a landscape design, the landscape architect should seriously consider it as an important design element. There are now entire projects (structures, landscape, infrastructure, etc.) being designed that meet LEED requirements for "Green Certification" of Platinum, Gold, Silver, and so on. The green roof movement in Europe, especially Germany and Switzerland, has been very successful and has developed to a high degree of sophistication.

The design of a green roof garden and soil is a very specialized field and is beyond the scope of this discussion. Therefore, only a general guide is provided to aid the landscape architect in the review and consideration of alternative designs that recognize the constraints normally imposed by rooftop landscape projects.

In all cases of green roof design, it is good practice to engage the services of a professional who has had successful experience in green roof garden applications, whether an individual or a commercial firm specializing in this work. It is unwise for the landscape architect to attempt to design and install a green roof garden without this additional professional service, due to the inherent risks involved. As the art and technology of green roof design develop, perhaps the general practitioner may eventually be able to undertake green roof design individually.

Weight Limitations

Constructing a landscape garden on a roof is an exercise in complexity because a structure is involved—the Earth's surface is not the subgrade. Therefore, as the first step, the roof itself must be designed to support more weight than is normally planned by the architect for a simple roof. That said, the weight loading for a garden is, in many instances, no greater than the loading weight of large air conditioners on commercial buildings or the interior floor loadings for computers and other heavy machines. Thus, the objections to the additional costs of a heavy roof by building clients is declining due to greater acceptance of the concept, as well as some financial incentives. The green roof on a residence is of somewhat greater concern due to the proportionately higher cost of constructing a stronger roof than the conventional design. However, with the adoption of the more stringent International Organization for Standardization (ISO) building construction standards in the United States, the disparity is reduced.

Green roofs are now in vogue and encouraged by local guidelines and ordinances, together with the LEED protocols, for covers over parking garages, large warehouses and factories, and especially enclosed exterior rooftops viewed from windows of the surrounding structure(s). Many large structures are now being placed underground due to slope considerations, creation of green space in crowded building areas, and for more efficient building environment (heating and cooling) maintenance.

Commercial Applications

Due to the objectives and nature of commercial construction, and financial considerations, the creation and installation of green roofs has been more successful as commercial applications than for residences in the United States, unlike Europe where many regulations require green roofs even on residences.

Dr. Phillip J. Craul, Senior Lecturer (retired) in Landscape Architecture, Graduate School of Design, Harvard University, and Emeritus Professor of Soil Science, SUNY–College of Environmental Science and Forestry, Syracuse, New York; Timothy A. Craul, President, Craul Land Scientists, PLC, State College, Pennsylvania

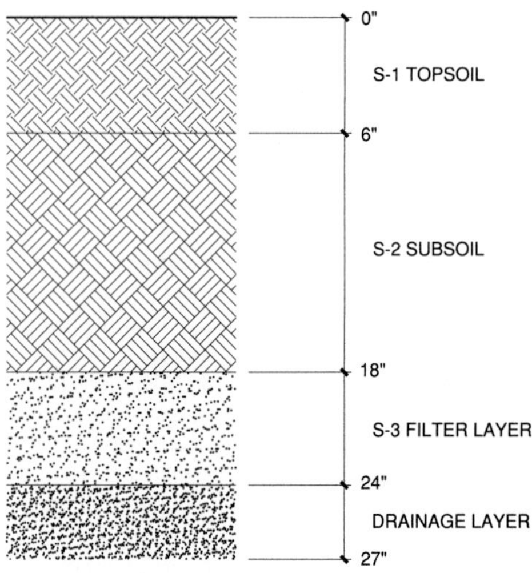

TYPICAL SOIL PROFILE FOR A COMMERCIAL GREEN ROOF

Commercial construction design can support the required loadings in most cases without any special engineering application other than to increase the size of the beams or the thickness of the concrete floor, or shorten the spans, up to certain limits. There are, however, some constructional constraints that do not permit these options; therefore, lightening the green roof becomes a necessity, which is the task of the landscape architect, architectural engineer, and the consulting soil scientist. Loadings for commercial buildings with concrete or steel roof trusses with more or less standard spans and reinforcement typically are capable of supporting the soil profile below.

The maximum potential loading weight shown in the "Typical Soil Profile for a Commercial Green Roof" figure would be approximately 237 pounds per square foot (1192 kg/m^2). The drainage layer is of grooved styrofoam with the drainage of the sloping roof in one direction. The vegetation is turf as a park over a parking garage.

Residential Applications

Most residential wood roofs with light to heavy cover have design loads of 15 pounds per square foot (75.5 kg/m^2) dead load and 20 to 30 pounds per square foot (100.7 to 150.9 kg/m^2) live load. Live load must be considered because of the wind stress (swaying) on the plants, and in turn on their root systems.

Live loading due to wind stress on trees is greatly increased above these values, thus, only low plants should be included in the residence green roof plant palette, unless the client can afford the increased costs and all other facets of design that allow trees.

Gardens on sloping roofs are primarily limited to those with 2 to 5 percent slope. Steeper sloping roofs would require more stringent engineering and garden design, which would be much more costly and would greatly reduce the advantages of a green roof.

Considering the landscape soil loadings cited above, either the residential roof must be greatly strengthened and/or the green roof design must be constrained in weight. The residential green roof is a compromise between a greatly strengthened roof and a relatively thin but complex soil profile of reduced weight compared to the on-ground soil or even the commercial green rooftop soil. There is a relatively wide variety of plant and soil profile combinations to meet the roof weight constraints and exposure, as well as the aesthetic desires of the client.

A major necessary feature of the residential green roof design is the waterproofing requirement: it must be lightweight, in contrast to the more weight-tolerant commercial application. It normally consists of several protective layers (sometimes as many as five) including the drainage mat.

Three examples of typical plant and soil profiles for a residential green roof are:

- Sedge and moss with a simple one-layer soil, 3 inches (8 cm)
- A mix of herbs, flowers, and grasses on a thin profile of 4 inches (10 cm)
- A mix of herbs, grasses, perennial herbs, and woody shrubs on a more complex profile of 8 inches (20 cm)

The loading weights for the three designs range from approximately 15 to 70 pounds per square foot (80 to 350 kg/m^2), in addition to the weight of the roof structure itself. Soil mix details for each example are not available (Optima, 1993).

Lightening Techniques

- Lighten the soil mix with a low-density aggregate, not to exceed 50 percent of the mix. However, the soil moisture holding capacity is significantly reduced requiring more frequent irrigation. Soil stability for protection against windthrow hazard is reduced as well, thus suggesting a modification in the plant palette by removing trees (even small ones) and tall shrubs. Testing of the soil mix for tensile strength and shear is required.
- Install cast styrofoam in sheets or blocks placed on the roof surface below the soil profile in sufficient volume to reduce the loading to the allowable limit, while considering the weight of the soil, its retained water, and plants. If there is sufficient total depth in the design, the thickness of the sytrofoam may be increased over the span and decreased or eliminated over the roof vertical support columns where the trees (if any) may be positioned (see the "Lightening of a Roof Span Load with Cast Styrofoam" figure).
- Install a cantilever support for the plants where roof loading is critically limited and the inclusion of trees or other plants requiring a large, heavy root ball, or even a rooting system for bare-root specimens, is a major component of the design. This is an alternative solution (see the "Cantilever Support for Heavy Plants on a Roof with Severe Loading Limitations" figure).

Drainage Design

For commercial green roof installations, the conventional drainage system design is appropriate in most cases if the soil profile is normal depth of 24 to 30 inches (60 to 76 cm), as illustrated in the "Typical Soil Profile for a Commercial Green Roof" figure. The pipe diameter may be reduced when the designed soil is shallow and the roof area to be drained is small. Standard piping calculations should be used. Where only low plants are planted in a very shallow soil, a drainage mat is employed, which is continuous

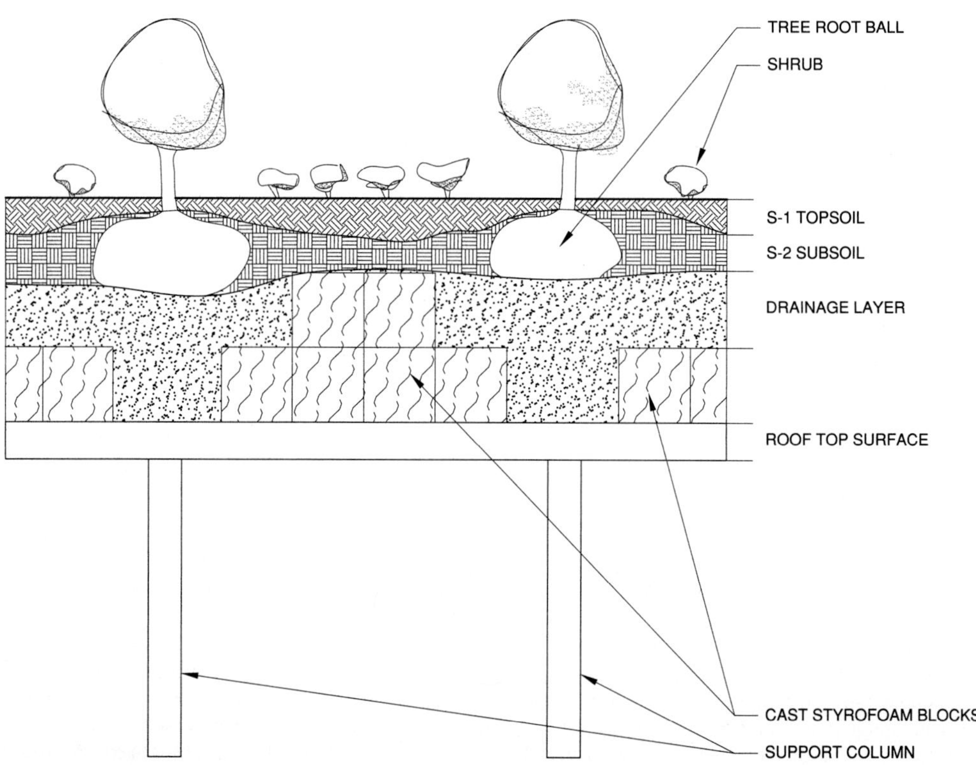

LIGHTENING OF A ROOF SPAN LOAD WITH CAST STYROFOAM

Source: Craul, 1999.

Dr. Phillip J. Craul, Senior Lecturer (retired) in Landscape Architecture, Graduate School of Design, Harvard University, and Emeritus Professor of Soil Science, SUNY–College of Environmental Science and Forestry, Syracuse, New York; Timothy A. Craul, President, Craul Land Scientists, PLC, State College, Pennsylvania

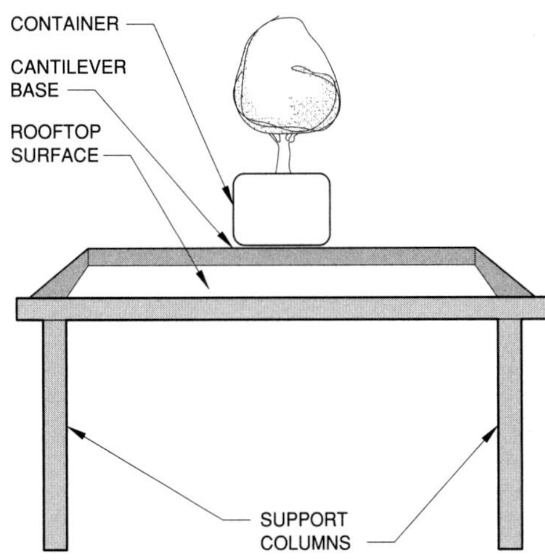

CANTILEVER SUPPORT FOR HEAVY PLANTS ON A ROOF WITH SEVERE LOADING LIMITATIONS

Source: Craul, 1999.

over the entire roof surface and is sloped to the roof drain outlet.

The critical design element is whether the roof is sloped or flat. Ideally, the landscape architect will be involved in the structure design process so as to have input to the roof design. Sloping is always beneficial and only needs a gentle grade, such as 150:1, since the subbase has a smooth surface. The soil drainage layer (S3) would be no thicker than 6 inches (16 cm). The other critical drainage feature is the location and the number of drain outlets from the roof. Some green roofs have failed as the result of flooding based on this one point alone.

For residential green roof installations, particularly on sloping roofs, the conventional drainage system is not used. It is too big and generally unnecessary. Because the roof is already sloping, a smaller soil volume is drained; hence, drainage matting is most appropriate. There are several drainage mats commercially available in various sizes and drainage rates that are used as the drainage layer. The mats are constructed of woven fabric with a rigid framework to prevent collapse under the soil mix and plant loading. The manufacturers' specifications should be consulted.

Windthrow Hazard Considerations

Rooftop garden plants are exposed to greater wind velocities and turbulence than those at surface elevations. The degree of exposure depends on the location of the garden on the structure itself. Is the entire roof area completely exposed from all directions, or is it sheltered in one or more directions? Generally, the greater the shelter coverage, the less the degree of exposure. However, if the garden is on the prevailing wind side of the building, or exposed to channelized winds formed by adjacent buildings (causing the "tunneling" effect), wind velocity and turbulence will be excessive. For example, wind tunnel tests performed for Teardrop Park in Battery Park City, New York, showed that the trees in the park would be exposed to the same wind characteristics as if they were planted in the middle of the Hudson River.

In light of the above information, any plants, especially trees, in a green roof must be windfirm. To be windfirm, three factors must be present:

- Roots must extend well outward from the root collar to support the differential stresses on either side of the wind direction axis.
- The roots must be large enough in diameter to resist breaking, either by shear or bending, and have great tensile strength.
- The soil surrounding the root system, thus, the soil-root plate, must be of sufficient density (weight) and volume to resist the turning force on the tree crown that results in windthrow.

The restrictions of the green roof may cause the designed soil to be too shallow and too light in density to meet these requirements. In addition, root extension may be limited due to the small area of the rooftop; or the trees may be placed in planting boxes, where the confined root ball may simply turn over in the force of the wind; or the planter itself may topple over on its own.

These restrictions suggest that the plant palette and the green roof soil must be very carefully designed for success, more so than most any other design encountered by the landscape architect.

Several solutions to green roof design concerns include:

- Plant only small trees with thin crowns, and only on flat roofs.
- Don't plant conifers on a flat rooftop unless completely sheltered, or with a very low or short crown (less than 2 feet; 0.6 m).
- If the trees are planted in a container, make sure the roots have extended themselves fully in the container before placing the trees on the roof.
- If containers are used, use those that are designed to be windfirm, such as with wide bottoms—not the usual flower pot shape.

SOILS FOR CONTAINERIZED PLANTS (PLANTERS)

Container Shape and Size

The container shape is determined by the plant or plants to be grown and the eventual placement of the planter. Generally, for trees, the container should have greater horizontal (length and width) dimensions than the vertical (depth or height) dimensions (as shown in the "Cross Section for a Tree Container" figure) to accommodate the need for the extension of lateral roots (Craul, 1992). Length-to-height ratio for a square container should be within the range of 1.5:1 to an extreme of 3:1. Width for a rectangular container should be in proportion, usually equal to the height. Depth should be at least nearly equal to the height of the root ball of the largest plant in the container. For trees, minimum depth should be 36 to 42 inches (91 to 107 cm). Too often, trees and other plants die in containers that are much too small, and that do not receive proper maintenance. Round containers certainly should be greater in diameter than that of the tree root ball. A container 8 feet (2.4 m) in diameter and 3 feet (0.91 m) deep provides a volume of 151 ft^3 (4.27 m^3).

Generally, the square or rectangular container provides more rooting volume and greater stability than a round container, especially if the latter has tapered walls similar to the common flower pot. The container bottom should be sloped to the drain outlet to prevent saturated soil within the container. Rooting volume is already limited. Gravel is not placed on the bottom for drainage purposes.

The exception is where space is limited, the container needs to be stored in winter for northern climates, or the container does not include trees. Smaller specimens with a limited growth habit should be used. Here, the container is designed with extra depth to provide a gravel layer to serve as a reservoir from one watering to another (see the "Cross Section of a Self-watering Container for an Individual Tree" figure). Wicking is placed vertically in the container soil to supply water to the roots above. Foam insulation may be placed on the walls and the bottom to prevent freezing in cold climates; otherwise, the container should be transferred indoors during the cold season.

The landscape architect should always consider designing large containers or raised beds to accom-

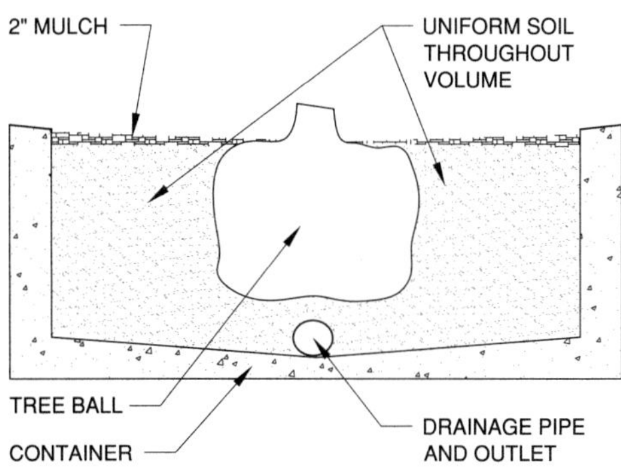

Gravel is not added to the bottom.

CROSS SECTION FOR A TREE CONTAINER

Source: Craul, 1992.

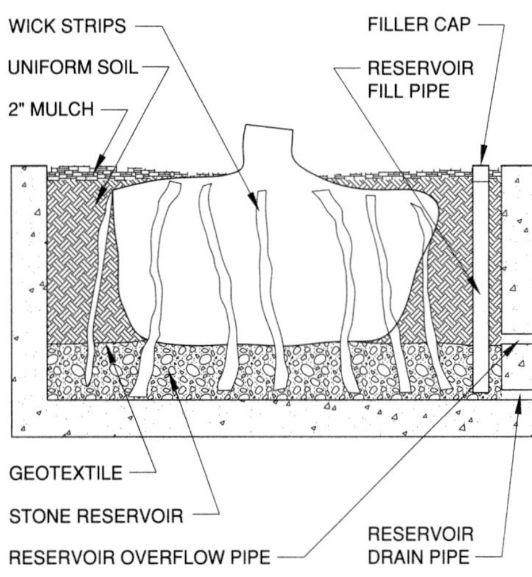

Gravel is added to the bottom as a reservoir.

CROSS SECTION OF A SELF-WATERING CONTAINER FOR AN INDIVIDUAL TREE

Source: Adapted from Urban Forests, 1991, and the design of Bob Skiera, retired city forester, Milwaukee, Wisconsin.

Dr. Phillip J. Craul, Senior Lecturer (retired) in Landscape Architecture, Graduate School of Design, Harvard University, and Emeritus Professor of Soil Science, SUNY–College of Environmental Science and Forestry, Syracuse, New York; Timothy A. Craul, President, Craul Land Scientists, PLC, State College, Pennsylvania

modate several trees in a copse with shared rooting space. The benefit to tree survival and relatively lower maintenance is proven by many examples, one of which is in the front of the John F. Kennedy Center, Washington, DC.

Soil for Planters

The specifications for planter soil vary widely. Generally, the planter soil approaches the recipe for potting soil of flower pots, but with less organic matter content (refer to the "Soil Mixes for Container Culture" table).

In both cases illustrated in the figures, weekly to biweekly watering is absolutely necessary. The system with the reservoir just makes the routine less demanding and provides a more uniform watering regime.

MULCHES AND MULCHING

The placement of mulch on the surface of the soil, or its incorporation into the soil, is an attempt to emulate the natural process of the organic matter cycle where the process is absent or for application to urban areas where the process cannot completely establish itself. There are organic and inorganic mulches and both have the same effect except for the important feature of organic matter cycling.

Mulches

The use of mulch has several features:

- In the case of organic mulch, it adds organic material that eventually evolves into humus within the soil, loosening it and increasing its water-holding and nutrient capacity. Inorganic mulch itself does not add organic matter to the soil.
- It protects the soil surface from erosion by raindrop splash and the formation of a crust.
- It reduces the rate of water evaporation through the soil surface.
- It moderates the extremes of soil temperatures unfavorable to plant root growth.
- It tends to reduce the amount of invasive weeds and facilitates their removal.
- It has aesthetic qualities that are useful in landscape design.

It should be kept in mind that there are situations or places where mulch is not desirable. Some examples of these follow:

- Organic mulch should not be placed on very wet soils or where water flow occurs at any time. In the first case, evaporation of the excess water is prevented; in the second case, the mulch is washed away. Coarse inorganic mulch is suitable for these locations.
- Use of inorganic mulch that absorbs and holds heat should be avoided where reflected heat may be a problem, unless an arid plant palette is planned; or it may be used where the reflected heat is a desired feature. In the latter case, a heat-resistant plant palette is necessary. Stones and gravel conduct heat at a greater rate into the soil below than do organic mulches.

Types of Mulch

Various sources of materials for mulch are listed in the "Types of Organic Materials for Soil Amendment and Mulch" table. Choosing the type and source of mulch must be done with care, considering the context of the landscape design and what the desired effect of the mulch is on the site, both aesthetically and naturally. Newspaper as a mulch is not recommended on landscape projects for practical reasons. The inorganic mulches are given in the "Types of Inorganic Mulches" table.

Mulch Choice and Application

Mulch choice and application is as much art as science, and is not always given the attention it deserves. Generally, the choice will be based on these guidelines:

- If the mulch is to be placed where annual, biennial, or perennial plants are to be grown on a continuous basis in humid regions, an organic mulch should be chosen. The exception is the permanent rock garden where stones and rocks may cover a significant portion of the garden surface and act as the inorganic mulch. The rock garden plants chosen are usually adapted to being surrounded by stone or actually being planted on fine gravel mixed with soil.
- In arid regions, the usual choice is inorganic mulches if the arid plant palette is followed. In arid areas where adequate irrigation is possible or permitted, and the humid region plants are desired, then the organic mulch should be chosen. However, even the arid region plants benefit from organic mulch, so that type may be used as an alternative if desired.

Obviously, organic mulch decomposes with time and must be replenished. Nearly all inorganic mulches are permanent for practical purposes. If modifications are made to the landscape, the inorganic mulch must be removed.

The purpose or function of the mulch also influences the choice. Use organic mulch for:

- Adding organic matter to the soil, to increase the water-holding capacity and cation exchange capacity (i.e., "fertility power").
- Insulating the soil from extremes in temperature.
- Preventing excessive soil moisture loss by evaporation.
- Adding some plant nutrients.
- Protecting against soil surface compaction.
- Increasing soil microorganism activity.

Use inorganic mulch for:

- Preventing soil moisture loss by evaporation, especially in arid areas.
- Protecting the soil against raindrop and surface water erosion, as well as wind erosion.
- Protecting against soil surface compaction.

Mulch is usually applied as a single layer (see the "Mulch Profiles" figure, panels *a* and *b*). However, some horticulturists have found a two-layer mulch of two mulch materials of different texture, one coarse and one fine, to be a very successful procedure (see the "Mulch Profiles" figure, panel *c*). The system emulates the two organic layers found in some natural woodland soils (the *Oi* and the *Oe* in soil science terms). The process of decomposition and incorporation of the organic matter into the soil is greatly enhanced. This technique is very appropriate on restoration sites where rapid soil improvement is necessary. Another major benefit is that the coarse mulch on top protects the finer mulch below from wind erosion.

TYPES OF ORGANIC MATERIALS FOR SOIL AMENDMENT AND MULCH

- Shredded plant parts such as municipal yard waste: single chipping, single-ground, double-ground
- Woodchips, sawdust, bark chips
- Composted agricultural manures; some mixture with other organics
- Composted biosolids (sewage sludge)
- Processed organic by-products: brewers' waste, wood pulp, food-processing wastes
- Mushroom soil

Source: Craul, 1992, gives a description of all on the list.

TYPES OF INORGANIC MULCHES

- Gravels of various types and colors, including pumice
- Marble chips
- Brick chips
- Black plastic sheeting
- Twisted kraft paper yarn
- Twisted jute yarn
- Excelsior wood fiber mat
- Glass fiber
- Geotextile fabrics

Source: Craul, 1992, gives a description of all on the list.

SOIL MIXES FOR CONTAINER CULTURE

AUTHORITY	SOIL MIX	VOLUME PERCENTAGE
Rakow (1987)	Sandy loam soil (coarseness*)	60
	Horticultural perlite	20
	Milled sphagnum moss	20
Harris (1983)	Coarse sand (0.5–1 mm)	50–75
	Organic matter (5% silt loam or loam soil added for improved fertility and water status)	50–75
Craul (1987)	Coarse sand (0.5–1 mm)	10
	Medium sand (0.25–0.5 mm)	65
	Fine sand (0.10–0.25 mm)	4
	Silt plus clay	1
	Milled peat moss	20

Source: Craul, 1992, with corrections.

** This represents sandy loam as defined by the USDA-NRCS Soil Survey Manual. Sandy loam can vary from "very coarse" to "very fine" (USDA-NRCS Soil Survery Manual definitions), and their related physical properties can range from very favorable to very unfavorable from the standpoint of compaction resistance, water-holding capacity, and, to a lesser degree, fertility.*

Dr. Phillip J. Craul, Senior Lecturer (retired) in Landscape Architecture, Graduate School of Design, Harvard University, and Emeritus Professor of Soil Science, SUNY–College of Environmental Science and Forestry, Syracuse, New York; Timothy A. Craul, President, Craul Land Scientists, PLC, State College, Pennsylvania

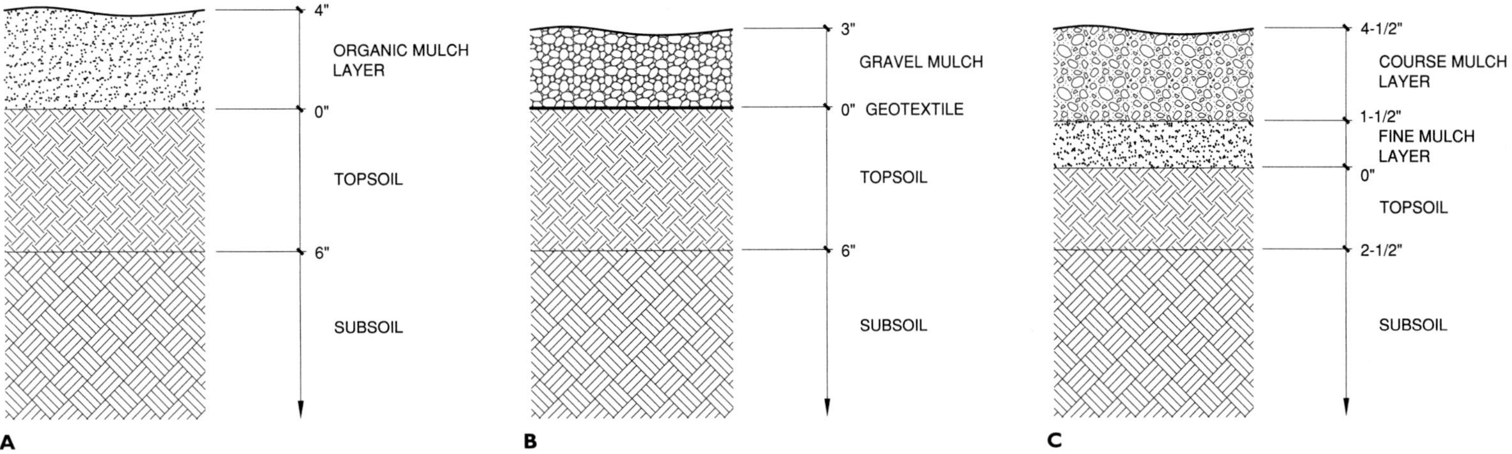

(a) The organic mulch profile; (b) the inorganic mulch profile; (c) the two-layered mulch profile. Geotextile should never be placed below an organic mulch above a soil: it defeats the basic purpose of the mulch.

MULCH PROFILES

Application

The thickness of the mulch layer is extremely important, and in some instances, critical. Mulch thickness should follow these guidelines:

- The coarser the mulch, the thicker the layer may be, but no more than 6 inches (15 cm) such as wood chips and coarse shredded bark; 4 inches (10 cm) is optimum.
- Conversely, the finer the mulch, the thinner the layer should be; brewer's waste ("Nutribrew") and standard mushroom soil, should be applied only in a 2 to 3 inch layer. Tub double-ground mulch is applied in a 3-inch (7-cm) layer.
- Remulching is normally necessary only when the layer thickness has decreased by half or more, and then only enough mulch should be added to bring it up to the maximum. There is a tendency for landscape personnel to add more than necessary.

As noted in the "Mulch Profiles" figure, geotextile or any other type of fine inorganic fabric should never be placed under organic mulch unless there is a specific reason to do so; simply to prevent weeds is not an appropriate reason because weeds will establish themselves despite the geotextile. The main purpose of mulch is to be decomposed and become incorporated into the soil, as described above. Geotextile acts as a barrier to this process and thus defeats the major purpose of mulch. Geotextile may be placed under inorganic mulches since they do not decompose and do not serve the same major purpose as organic mulches. Both landscape architects as well as many landscape contractors have been guilty of this oversight.

In cooler regions, mulch or the additions should be applied after spring warm-up so that plants can begin the spring flush with warm soil. Fall application of mulch should occur before the ground is frozen in northern or mountainous climates, despite some other recommendations. Mulched frozen ground will thaw out much slower in the spring unless the mulch is removed in early spring (double effort).

Mulch should never be applied to cover the root collar of trees or shrubs. Entrapped moisture can rot the roots, causing failure of the tree support system; and rodents may burrow in the mulch and girdle the bark off the root collar, again leading to rot and even death of the tree or shrub (Harris, Clark, and Matheny, 2004).

As just noted, there is a tendency for landscape personnel to add more mulch than necessary. Excessive mulching leads to:

- Reduction in gaseous diffusion between the soil and the atmosphere, which leads to root suffocation and the development of anaerobic (reducing) conditions. This condition led to the mortality of willow oaks planted in front of the Air and Space Museum in Washington, DC, where very thick layers of woodchips (8 inches or more; 20-plus cm) were applied to prevent soil compaction by pedestrians.
- Rodent damage to roots is enhanced with thick (more than 4 inches; 10-plus cm) layers of mulch.
- Excess soil water buildup caused by thick mulch layers creates waterlogged soil in wet weather.

Plant species sensitive to overmulching are azaleas, rhododendrons, dogwoods, mountain laurels, hollies, cherry trees, lindens, and spruces.

Symptoms of overmulching are yellowing of foliage when other causes cannot be determined, abnormally small leaves, poor growth, and die-back of older branches (Craul, 1992).

REFERENCES

Craul, P. J. 1992. *Urban Soil in Landscape Design.* New York: John Wiley & Sons, Inc.

———. 1999. *Urban Soils: Applications and Practices.* New York: John Wiley & Sons, Inc.

Craul, T. A., and P. J. Craul. 2006. *Soil Design Protocols for Landscape Architects and Contractors.* Hoboken, NJ: John Wiley & Sons, Inc.

Toy, T. J., and J. P. Black. 2000. "Topographic Reconstruction: The Theory and Practice." In R. I. Barnhisel, R. G. Darmody and W. L. Daniels (eds), *Reclamation of Drastically Disturbed Lands.* Agronomy No. 41. Madison, WI: American Society of Agronomy.

Harris, R. E. 1983. *Arboriculture: Care of Trees, Shrubs, and Vines in the Landscape.* Englewood Cliffs, NJ: Prentice-Hall.

Harris, R. E., J. R. Clark, and N. P. Matheny. 2004. *Arboriculture: Integrated Management of Landscape Trees, Shrubs, and Vines,* 4th ed. Upper Saddle River, NJ: Prentice-Hall.

Himelick, 1981. *Tree and Shrub Transplanting Manual.* Savoy, IL.: International Society of Arboriculture.

Holtz, R. D., and W. D. Kovacs. 1981. *An Introduction to Geotechnical Engineering.* Englewood Cliffs, NJ: Prentice-Hall.

Kopinga, J. 1985. "Research on Street Tree Planting Practices in the Netherlands." METRIA:5, Proceedings of the Fifth Conference on the Metropolitan Tree Improvement Alliance. University Park, PA: Pennsylvania State University Press.

Optima-Fachbetreib Hofmann GmbH & Co. 1993. Der optima Naturdach-Planer. Stuttgart. Company publication.

Rakow, D. A. 1987. "Containerized Trees in Urban Environments," J. Arboric. 13(12):294–298.

Switzenbaum, M. S., P. J. Craul, and T. Ryan. 1996. "Manufactured Loam Using Compost Material. Phase 1: Feasibility." Final Report. Amherst, MA: University of Massachusetts Transportation Center.

Urban, J. R. 1992. "Bringing Order to the Technical Dysfunction within the Urban Forest," *J. Arboric* 18(2): 85–90.

Watson, G. W., and E. B. Himelick, 1997. *The Principles and Practice of Planting Trees and Shrubs.* Savoy, IL: International Society of Arbriculture.

See also:
Planting
Freestanding and Retaining Walls
Soil Mechanics

Dr. Phillip J. Craul, Senior Lecturer (retired) in Landscape Architecture, Graduate School of Design, Harvard University, and Emeritus Professor of Soil Science, SUNY–College of Environmental Science and Forestry, Syracuse, New York; Timothy A. Craul, President, Craul Land Scientists, PLC, State College, Pennsylvania

ASPHALT

ASPHALT

HISTORY

The word "asphalt" has been traced back to ancient times; it was adopted by the Greeks to mean "make firm or stable." Its use began in ancient civilizations as a mortar for bonding building block materials, a sealer, and a waterproofing material. In those times, the asphalt was widely found in geological formations, soft and ready to be used. At the turn of the twentieth century, the discovery of the process to refine asphalt from crude petroleum, coupled with the rising popularity of the automobile (and the building of roads to drive on) gave rise to an expanding asphalt industry.

Today, the term "asphalt" applies specifically to the cementitious material that binds the aggregate together to form pavements. Technically, the more correct term for asphalt pavement is "asphaltic concrete," with the asphalt cement performing the same bonding function as portland cement does for concrete pavement. However, over time, asphalt, asphaltic concrete, bituminous pavement, and other variations have been used interchangeably.

OVERVIEW

Asphaltic concrete, most typically a combination of heated asphalt cement and heated aggregates mixed together in specific proportions and sizes, is laid hot, directly on a subgrade or base course of stone screenings. The mixture is compacted to a specific density, and the pavement then hardens by cooling as the liquid asphalt cement turns solid, adhering to and binding the aggregate together.

Some asphaltic concrete utilizes emulsified or "cutback" asphalt cement that allows pavements to be laid cold. This is not as common as the more preferred "hot mix" asphaltic concrete.

Another method of installation is mixed-in-place asphaltic concrete construction. This approach involves the spraying of cutback asphalt cement or more commonly emulsified asphalt cement onto the aggregate and then mixed with the aggregate at the site. This method not only eliminates the need to transport a hot mix from a central asphalt plant, it can be used for surface, base, or subbase courses—although as a surface course, it is not suitable in situations where heavy traffic is anticipated. It can provide an adequate base or subbase course that, when covered with a hot-mix surface course, is suitable for heavy traffic situations.

ASPHALT CEMENT

Asphalt cement, a petroleum derivative, is a strong adhesive that liquefies at higher temperatures and solidifies and bonds at lower temperatures. During the petroleum process, asphalt cement is refined to different viscosities to meet various criteria and standards for a wide range of uses. The higher-viscosity asphalt cements, which have greater strength and stiffening characteristics, are used for pavements. Asphalt cement makes up between 5 to 10 percent by weight (or 15 to 25 percent by volume) of an asphaltic concrete pavement (depending on the design mix).

Two types of liquid asphalt cements can be used at lower ambient temperatures, as special situations may warrant: "emulsified asphalt cement" is mixed with water and an emulsifying agent; "cutback asphalt cement" uses a petroleum solvent to make the asphalt cement liquid at lower temperatures. In both cases, the asphalt cement hardens as the water or solvent evaporates. This evaporation results in longer curing times. Although more volatile solvents will evaporate quicker, reducing the curing times, environmental concerns have greatly reduced the use of cutback asphalt cements.

AGGREGATES

There is a wide range of different aggregate combinations whose varying characteristics make it possible to create pavements for specific design and construction needs. The strength, durability, skid resistance, and other characteristics of an asphaltic concrete pavement are directly related to the types of aggregate and their specific proportional gradation that are mixed with the asphalt cement. The types of aggregate used depend on local availability; likewise, the most successful proportions are determined locally, and are very often reflected in the specifications developed by the respective state departments of transportation. Aggregates constitute 90 to 95 percent by weight (75 to 85 percent by volume) of an asphaltic concrete pavement (depending on the design mix).

Aggregates, like gravel and sand, are naturally occurring as pit or bank-run material. Gravel particles range in size from 3 inches to 0.187 inches (No. 4). Sand particles range from 0.187 inches (No. 4) to 0.0029 inches (No. 200). Both are washed to remove other particles and then screened to proper sizes for use as part of an asphaltic concrete mix. It is important that aggregate be free from deleterious materials such as vegetation, soft particles, clay lumps, and clay coatings.

Types of Aggregate

Processed aggregates are created by crushing natural gravel or stone into smaller pieces that can then be screened for use in an asphaltic concrete mix. The crushing process can improve the shape of gravel that is rounded or has been weathered smooth, by creating sharply angular particles with a rougher texture to which the asphalt cement will better adhere.

"Crusher-run" aggregate refers to crushed stone that is used without the usual screening process. If the aggregate gradation is good, it can be used in the asphaltic concrete mix. The rock dust that is a product of the crushing of limestone is usually separated out for use as mineral filler in the asphaltic concrete mix.

Synthetic or artificial aggregates can be manufactured or made from a by-product of another manufacturing process. Manufactured aggregates are made from a variety of materials that offer high resistance to wear and are light weight, characteristics that make them very desirable for situations such as paving over structure or paving on bridge decks. Blast furnace slag, a by-product of the refining of ore in the smelting process, is one of the most commonly used aggregates created from another manufacturing process. Some of these artificial or synthetic aggregates can be highly porous, so additional asphalt cement must be used to keep the mixture workable and create a cohesive pavement. However, the other positive qualities they contribute to the pavement—lightweight and wear-resistant—outweigh the compensation of the additional asphalt cement.

Aggregate Classification

Aggregates are classified by their size and whether they pass through or are retained on certain specifically sized screens with square openings, called sieves. The sieves are stacked on top of each other with the coarsest sieve at the top and the sieves underneath progressively smaller. They are then combined in various proportions, by weight, for the specified asphaltic concrete mix. Generally, aggregate proportions are measured by percentage of the aggregate mixture that passes through a given sieve size by weight.

- "Coarse aggregate" refers to aggregate that is retained on the No. 8 sieve (2.36 mm/0.0937 inches). These larger aggregates give the pavement strength and stability.
- "Fine aggregate" refers to the aggregate that passes the No. 8 sieve. These consist of well-graded, moderately sharp to sharp sands.
- "Mineral filler," the finest of the fine aggregates, refers to aggregates that pass the No. 30 sieve (0.60 mm/0.0234 inches). The mineral filler and dust fill the voids between the other aggregates, increasing the density of the overall pavement, as well as making the pavement less pervious.

The aggregate mix is composed of a specified range, given in percent, of aggregate that will pass through a specific sieve size. The maximum aggregate size is the smallest sieve that will allow 100 percent of the aggregate to pass. The nominal aggregate size is the largest sieve that retains any of the aggregate particles. Asphalt mixes are sometimes referred to by their nominal maximum aggregate size. The distribution of the various particle sizes in a hot-mix asphaltic concrete is called the "aggregate gradation."

Coarse-graded aggregate mixes give asphaltic concrete pavements greater strength, stability, and wider load distribution. However, the coarse aggregate results in rougher-textured surface. Fine-graded aggregate mixes produce a finer-textured wearing surface. To benefit from the positive characteristics of both, a coarse-graded mix is often used as a binder course,

Leonard Hopper, RLA, FASLA

NOMINAL DIMENSIONS OF U.S. STANDARD SIEVES

SIEVE DESIGNATION		SIEVE OPENING	
STANDARD	ALTERNATIVE	MM	IN.
38.1 mm	1 1/2 in.		1.50
25.0 mm	1 in.	25.0	1.00
19.0 mm	3/4 in.	19.0	0.750
12.5 mm	1/2 in.	0.500	
9.5 mm	3/8 in.		
4.75 mm	No. 4		
2.36 mm	No. 8		
1.18 mm	No. 16		
600 μm	No. 30	0.600	
300 μm	No. 50	0.300	
150 μm	No. 150	1.0150	
75 μm	No. 200		

Source: Courtesy of Asphalt Institute.

over which a wearing course of fine-graded asphaltic concrete is placed. A dense-graded aggregate mix consists of a wide range of aggregate sizes that produces a highly durable and impervious surface. Open-graded aggregate mixes contain little of the fines that tend to fill the voids between the larger aggregates. The result is a strong, but rough-textured pavement that is relatively pervious (sometimes referred to as pervious or porous asphaltic concrete pavement).

Aggregates are also graded on toughness and their capability to resist abrasive wear. The toughness of aggregates in the wearing course or surface layer is particularly important where traffic loads are concentrated. Aggregates that have a lower resistance to abrasive wear are limited to the base course where loads have been distributed over a larger area.

The surface texture of the aggregate affects the strength of the asphaltic concrete mix. A rougher-texture aggregate increases the strength of the pavement but also requires additional asphalt cement to improve its workability. Natural aggregates that have been worn smooth over time, when crushed, can produce particles with rougher textures as well as more angular facets. The rougher texture helps the asphalt cement adhere better, and the irregular, angular particle shapes create an interlock that, after compaction, resists displacement. Specifying a percentage of the coarse aggregate consisting of crushed or angular particles (approximately 50 percent or more) can result in a stronger, more stable pavement. A rougher-texture aggregate in the surface course will also improve skid resistance.

The stripping of asphalt cement film from the aggregate through the action of water, or its capability to resist such stripping, is a determining factor in the suitability of an aggregate for an asphaltic concrete mix. "Hydrophilic" (water-loving) aggregates, such as quartzite and some granites, fall into this category. "Hydrophobic" (water-hating) aggregates, such as limestone, dolomite, and traprock, are highly resistant to stripping and make excellent aggregate material.

PAVEMENT MIXTURES AND INSTALLATION

Asphaltic Concrete Design Mixes

The most common use of asphaltic concrete for pavements is referred to as "hot mix," which consists of specified gradation of aggregates that are heated to approximately 250 to 300°F, then thoroughly mixed until all particles are coated with a specified percentage of asphalt cement heated to 275°F. The heated mixture is transported to the site and laid hot, either with a paving machine or raked level by hand. The freshly laid hot mixture is then compacted with a roller or other means, to achieve the specified density. As the mixture cools, the pavement hardens.

The objectives of a good asphaltic concrete design mix are: sufficient asphalt cement for durability; an aggregate gradation that resists distortion and displacement; sufficient air voids to allow thermal expansion in the warmer weather; and good workability to allow placement without segregation of the aggregate.

Asphaltic Conrete Installation

The asphaltic concrete pavement can be laid in layers (or lifts) ranging in thickness between ¾ inch to 12 inches. The asphalt mix can be placed directly on a compacted subgrade, on a compacted aggregate base course, or on a base of concrete pavement. The minimum thickness of a hot-mix asphaltic concrete is directly related to the maximum aggregate size. The thickness of the compacted pavement should be at least twice the maximum nominal particle size of the aggregate. As the thickness of the compacted layers increase, the weight of the roller necessary to achieve the desired density also needs to increase. Because certain situations may limit the size of a roller used for compaction, some pavements may be placed in a series of multiple lifts or layers, with each layer being compacted before the next is laid, in order to reach the specified overall pavement thickness and compaction density. A special tack coat of asphalt cement, which is sprayed on the surface prior to placing the next course of asphaltic concrete, is used to bind the layers together.

Load Distribution

The asphaltic concrete pavement supports the loads that are placed on it and distributes that load to the subgrade below. Therefore, the design and thickness of the pavement must distribute the anticipated load over a large enough area of the subgrade necessary for support but without exceeding the strength of the asphaltic concrete pavement itself and the limits of the asphalt cement's capability to bond the aggregate particles together. The greater the anticipated load, the thicker the asphaltic concrete pavement and base course (if used) need to be.

The mix should also be flexible enough to bend without cracking, to conform to differential settling in the base course and subgrade. The mix also must withstand repeated flexing caused by the vehicle loads placed upon it. Higher asphalt cement content, within limits are used to maintain stability, improve flexibility and fatigue resistance. The waterproofing properties of a dense, graded asphaltic concrete paving mixture prevent water from building up within the pavement, as well as water penetration and potential degradation of the subgrade's capability to support the load placed upon it.

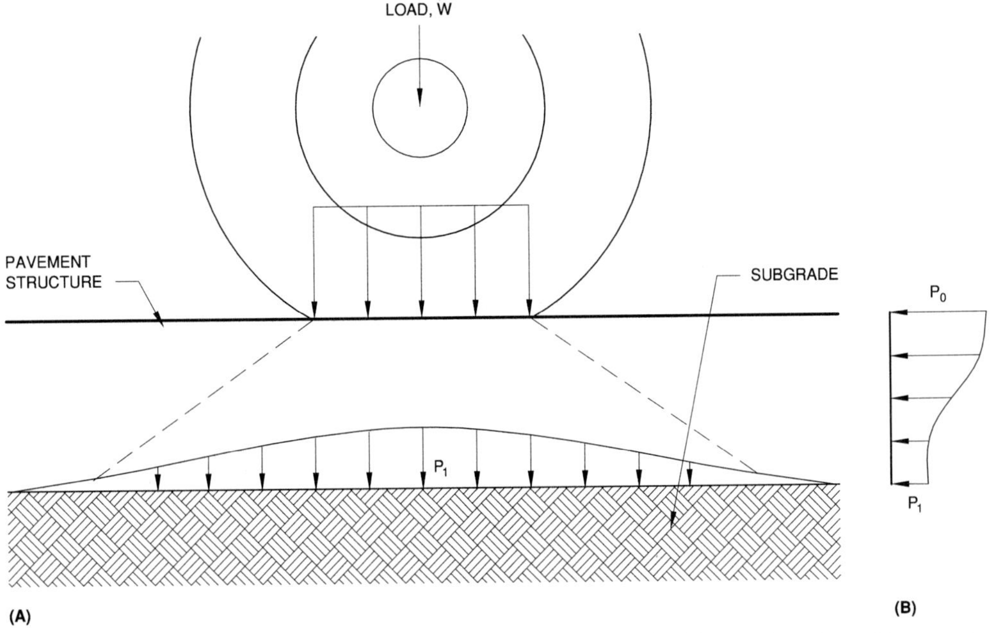

SPREAD OF WHEEL LOAD THROUGH PAVEMENT STRUCTURE

Source: The Asphalt Institute.

Leonard Hopper, RLA, FASLA

Subgrade and Base Course Preparation

Asphaltic concrete pavements can be laid as either full-depth pavements or with an aggregate base course. A full-depth asphaltic concrete pavement design is one in which the asphalt mixture is placed directly on a compacted subgrade. An aggregate base course design is one in which the asphalt mixture is placed over a compacted layer of aggregate and properly prepared and compacted subgrade. Although full-depth asphaltic concrete pavements can be used anywhere, caution should be exercised in areas subject to deep frosts or in applications where the subgrade composition might be particularly susceptible to frost heaving. The addition of an aggregate base course minimizes the potential damage caused by frost heave and helps in the distribution of load over the subgrade, which can reduce the thickness of the asphaltic concrete layer. The aggregate base course can be treated with asphaltic cement to increase its strength and load distribution.

The spraying of asphalt onto an aggregate base course is called a "prime coat." The prime coat penetrates into the aggregate base course and serves not only to bind the aggregate together but also to bind the aggregate layer to the asphaltic concrete layer that is laid above. An aggregate base course treated with asphalt cement can have twice the load-bearing strength of an untreated aggregate base course. This option can be a good base course choice where higher weights and volumes of traffic are anticipated. Other materials can be used to stabilize an aggregate base (portland cement, lime, lime/fly ash, etc.), but asphalt cement is the most compatible and preferred treatment to stabilize and strengthen an aggregate base course.

The base and subbase pavement courses serve to transfer loads and distribute them over larger areas of the subgrade. Because vehicular wheel loads create both compressive and tensile forces within the pavement, a full-depth asphaltic concrete pavement offers some advantages over an aggregate base course. Although both types of pavement structures can transfer compressive forces, an aggregate base course has no capability to transfer tensile forces, whereas the full-depth asphaltic concrete pavement can transfer both compressive and tensile forces and, therefore, distribute loads over a larger area of the subgrade. This can result in a reduction in the overall pavement thickness.

Asphaltic Concrete Strength and Durability

A well-designed asphaltic concrete pavement mixture has the stability to resist deformation by imposed loads, determined by internal friction and cohesion. Internal friction is dependent on surface texture of the aggregate, aggregate gradation, particle shape, density of the mix, and quantity and type of asphalt. "Cohesion" is the internal binding force of the asphaltic concrete mixture. The asphalt cement binds the contact points of the aggregate together. A well-designed mix also has durability. "Durability" is the asphaltic concrete pavement's capability to resist degradation by weather-related factors (air, water, temperature) and the loads imposed by traffic. Durability is achieved by a well-compacted, dense aggregate gradation mixture with a high asphalt cement content. The higher asphalt cement content creates a thicker film on the aggregate particles, which results in a longer period of time before degradation begins. There is, however, a limit to the beneficial properties of higher asphalt cement content. After a certain point, too much asphalt cement can act as a lubricant and actually reduce its binding capability and internal friction between aggregate particles.

Compaction

Compaction is a critical component of the installation process. Proper compaction is necessary to increase surface contact between the aggregates. This helps the asphalt cement to bond the particles together and increases friction between the aggregate, helping to increase both the strength and stability of the asphaltic concrete pavement. Compaction is also necessary to reduce the air voids within the pavement to a level that increases density, resulting in a pavement that is nearly impermeable (voids are not interconnected, preventing damage from the infiltration of water and air, particularly in freeze/thaw conditions) but still has the required void level to allow for thermal expansion. This roughly translates into a void content ranging from more than 2 to 8 percent for dense-graded asphaltic concrete design mixes. If proper compaction is not achieved, vehicular traffic will compact the pavement along the wheel paths, creating ruts that have the potential to pose a problem for safe travel.

For proper compaction to take place, the temperature of the hot mixture must be between 185°F and 300°F. It is between these temperatures that the asphalt cement is in a liquid form that facilitates the movement of the aggregate that creates the desired density upon compaction. Therefore, factors that affect the temperature of the mix and rate of cooling (initial mix temperature; thickness of the pavement; temperature of the subgrade; and environmental factors such as air temperature, wind, humidity, etc.) need to be taken into account. Once the mixture cools below 185°F, it begins to stiffen, and the asphaltic cement hardens to bond the aggregate particles together.

Adequate compaction also is dependent on the compressive force being applied by the roller. Compaction can be achieved by using steel-wheeled rollers, pneumatic-tired rollers, or vibrating rollers. For the roller to compact the pavement mixture, the subgrade beneath the pavement must be compacted and be able to resist the roller's compressive force being applied to the paving mixture. The forces within the pavement mixture resist the compressive forces of the roller based on the aggregate characteristics and asphalt cement viscosity. When the paving mixture density reaches a point at which its resisting forces equal the compressive force of the rollers and the resistant forces of the subgrade, the compaction process is complete. After compaction, the pavement should be checked with a straightedge to determine if there are any surface irregularities that fall outside of acceptable tolerances and would need to be corrected.

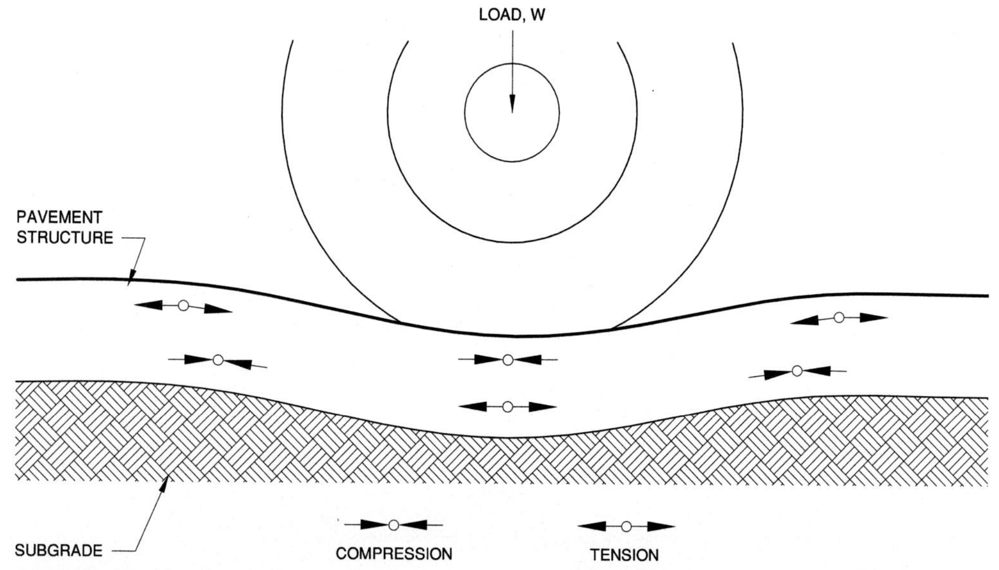

PAVEMENT DEFLECTION RESULTS IN TENSILE AND COMPRESSIVE STRESSES IN PAVEMENT STRUCTURE

Source: The Asphalt Institute.

USES

Asphaltic concrete surfaces have a broad range of uses in the landscape. Most commonly, it is a paving material that is most closely associated with highways, streets, and roads that carry trucks and cars. Second, it is a paving material that is closely associated with parking areas and driveways. Although asphaltic concrete performs well in these functional applications, it is also a material whose characteristics make it a good material choice for other uses in the landscape.

Informal and Recreational Uses

Asphaltic concrete's continuity of surface without the need for joints lends itself to informal paths, particularly those that are curvilinear and blend with their surroundings—for example, it is an excellent choice for pedestrian paths, paved hiking trails, bike paths, and golf cart paths. It is also a good material choice for paved playground surfaces, easily accommodating a range of safety surface materials that are required for impact attenuation under the play equipment components themselves. For other recreational purposes, such as tennis courts, basketball courts, and other sport activities, asphaltic concrete paving accommodates a range of acrylic color surfaces, cushioning surfaces, and line paints that are required for these sports.

However, as the darker color of asphaltic concrete tends to absorb the heat from solar radiation, some consideration should be given to strategically providing shade in these activity areas. This is particularly important in playgrounds and areas where people may be sitting and watching the activities taking place. For larger asphaltic concrete paved areas, consideration for heat island impacts and stormwater management implications should be considered.

Special Uses

In addition to being used as a pavement material, asphaltic concrete is sometimes used for curbs and edges. It is formed using an asphalt curbing machine that can lay up to 2,000 linear feet of curb per day, and in a number of shapes and sizes. The curbing machine uses a motorized worm gear or screw that pushes the asphaltic concrete mixture through the mold of the desired shape, under pressure. The asphaltic concrete mix for a curb uses a special grade of asphalt cement (generally AC20) and approximately 1 percent more asphalt cement than for a pavement. This serves to increase compaction and durability. The asphaltic concrete curb must be laid on a strong, structurally stable pavement.

The negative aspect of an asphaltic concrete curb is that it is susceptible to damage from vehicles (particularly heavy trucks) mounting and riding over them, as well as regular maintenance operations such as plowing. An alternative to the curb is an asphaltic concrete berm or wedge, which provides a transition from a traffic surface up to a higher surface of paving or planting.

Asphaltic concrete can also be used for gutters adjacent to paved areas. The flexibility of this material allows a variety of different cross sections to fit almost any situation. It is also used as a setting bed for unit pavers. A fine-graded mix that is screeded over a firm base has excellent leveling properties and is compatible with the variety of adhesives that are used to bond the pavers to the setting bed. Manufacturers of the unit pavers often provide mix specifications for the setting bed that works best with their product.

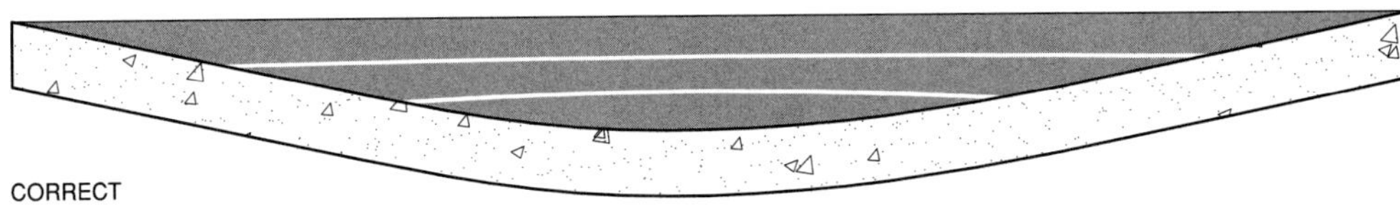

CORRECT

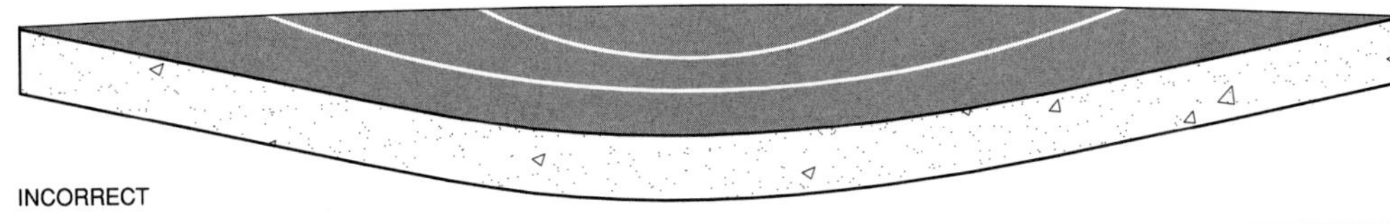

INCORRECT

MULTILAYER LEVELING WEDGES

Source: The Asphalt Institute.

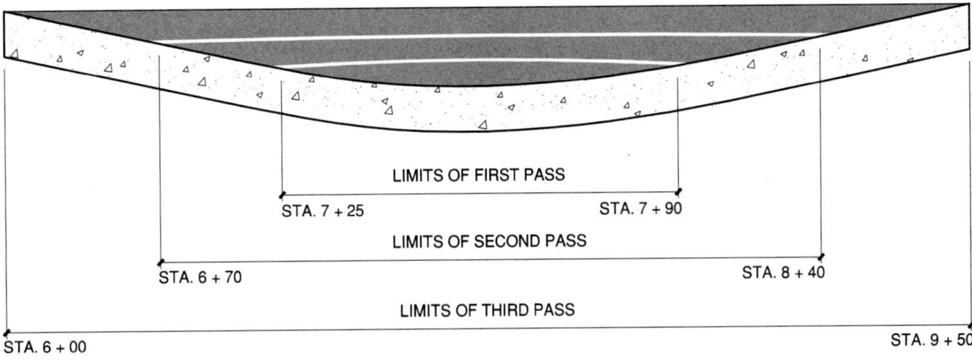

LIMITS FOR MULTILAYER LEVELING WEDGES STATIONED FOR SPREADING

Source: The Asphalt Institute.

OVERLAYS

Asphaltic concrete overlays in thicknesses of an inch or less are used to extend the life or enhance the wearing surface of otherwise structurally sound pavements. Prior to placing the resurfacing course, all weak areas and cracks in the existing pavement should be repaired. Patches should be constructed with a strength that equals or exceeds that of the surrounding pavement structure. Wherever the surface is distorted or uneven, the construction of leveling courses using fine asphaltic concrete should be constructed to restore proper line and cross section to the pavement. The existing pavement should then be thoroughly dried and cleaned of all dirt and foreign material by sweeping with mechanical sweepers or with hand brooms. After the surface has been thoroughly prepared and cleaned, a tack coat of liquid asphalt cement (usually emulsified asphalt) should be sprayed over the entire area and allowed to cure, and the resurfacing mixture should be laid hot over the surface and compacted. During compaction, the tack coat binds the existing pavement to the resurfacing overlay. The edges of a resurfaced area can be tapered to meet the grade of adjacent pavements flush, and can also be "keyed in" at the edges for extra stability. However, because after resurfacing the area is approximately an inch higher than the previous grade, the drainage pattern of the resurfaced and surrounding areas should be checked to ensure they have not been adversely impacted. It is easy for the newly resurfaced area to become a dam when the raised grade disrupts the flow of stormwater from an adjacent area to the drainage structure that is designed to accommodate the runoff.

RECYCLING ASPHALTIC CONCRETE PAVEMENTS

Due to rising awareness of environmental concerns and interest in natural resource conservation, increased attention is being given to recycling old asphaltic concrete pavements. Materials reclaimed from removed pavements can be mixed with some new materials to create hot-mix asphaltic concrete mixtures that meet all the requirements of a mix created from all new materials.

REFERENCES

The Asphalt Institute, 2696 Research Park Drive, Lexington, KY 40511, www.asphaltinstitute.org.

See also:

Pavement in the Landscape

Leonard Hopper, RLA, FASLA

CONCRETE

CONCRETE

HISTORY

Early builders used clay to bind stones together into a solid structure for shelter and protection. The oldest concrete discovered so far dates from around 7000 BC. It was found in 1985 when a concrete floor was uncovered during the construction of a road at Yiftah El in Galilee, Israel. It consisted of a lime concrete, made from burning limestone to produce quicklime, which when mixed with water and stone, hardened to form concrete.

A cementing material was used between the stone blocks in the construction of the Great Pyramid at Giza in ancient Egypt around 2500 BC. Some reports say it was a lime mortar; others contend the cementing material was made from burnt gypsum. By 500 BC, the art of making lime-based mortar arrived in ancient Greece. The Greeks used lime-based materials as a binder between stone and brick and as a rendering material over porous limestones commonly used in the construction of their temples and palaces.

Examples of early Roman concrete have been found dating back to 300 BC. The word "concrete" itself is derived from the Latin word *concretus,* meaning grown together or compounded. The Romans perfected the use of pozzolan as a cementing material. Sometime during the second century BC, the Romans quarried a volcanic ash near Pozzuoli; thinking it was sand, they mixed it with lime and found the mixture to be much stronger than they had produced previously. This discovery was to have a significant effect on construction. The material was not sand, but a fine volcanic ash containing silica and alumina, which when combined chemically with lime, produced what became known as pozzolanic cement. This material was used by builders of the famous Roman walls, aqueducts, and other historic structures, including the Theatre at Pompeii (seating 20,000 spectators), and the Colosseum and Pantheon in Rome.

Pozzolan seems to have been ignored during the Middle Ages, when building practices were much less refined than earlier, and the quality of cementing materials deteriorated. The practice of burning lime and the use of pozzolan were not reintroduced until the 1300s.

Efforts to determine why some limes possess hydraulic properties, while others (those made from essentially pure limestones) do not, were not made until the eighteenth century. John Smeaton, often referred to as the "father of civil engineering in England," concentrated his work in this field. He found that an impure, soft limestone, containing clay minerals, made the best hydraulic cement.

The difference between a hydraulic lime and natural cement is a function of the temperature attained during calcination. Furthermore, a hydraulic lime can hydrate in a "lump" form, whereas natural cements must be crushed and finely ground before hydration can take place. Natural cement is stronger than hydraulic lime but weaker than portland cement. Natural cement was manufactured in Rosendale, New York, in the early 1800s, and was first used to build the Erie Canal in 1818.

The development of portland cement was the result of persistent investigation by science and industry to produce a superior-quality natural cement. The invention of portland cement is generally credited to Joseph Aspdin, an English mason. In 1824, he obtained a patent for his product, which he named portland cement because when set, it resembled the color of the natural limestone quarried on the Isle of Portland in the English Channel. The name has endured and is used throughout the world, with many manufacturers adding their own trade or brand names.

Aspdin was the first to prescribe a formula for portland cement and the first to have his product patented. However, in 1845, I. C. Johnson, of White and Sons, Swanscombe, England, claimed to have "burned the cement raw materials with unusually strong heat until the mass was nearly vitrified," producing a portland cement as we now know it. This cement became the popular choice during the middle of the nineteenth century and was exported from England to various parts of the world. Production also began in Belgium, France, and Germany around the same time, and export of these products from Europe to North America began about 1865. The first recorded shipment of portland cement to the United States was in 1868. The first portland cement manufactured in the United States was produced at a plant in Coplay, Pennsylvania, in 1871.

FUNDAMENTALS OF CONCRETE

Concrete is basically a mixture of two components: aggregates and paste. The paste, composed of cementitious materials and water, binds the aggregates (usually sand and gravel, or crushed stone or recycled materials) into a rocklike mass as the paste hardens because of the chemical reaction of the cement and water. Supplementary cementitious materials and chemical admixtures may also be included in the paste.

Aggregates are generally divided into two groups: fine and coarse. Fine aggregates primarily consist of natural or manufactured sand, with particle sizes ranging up to 9.5 mm (3/8 inch); coarse aggregates are particles retained on the 1.18 mm (No. 16) sieve, and ranging up to 150 mm (6 inches) in size. The maximum size of coarse aggregate is typically 19 mm or 25 mm (¾ or 1 inch). An intermediate-sized aggregate, around 9.5 mm (⅜ inch), is sometimes added to improve the overall aggregate gradation.

The paste is composed of cementitious materials, water, and entrapped air or purposely entrained air. The paste constitutes about 25 to 40 percent of the total volume of concrete. The absolute volume of cement is usually between 7 and 15 percent, and the water between 14 and 21 percent. Air content in air-entrained concrete ranges from about 4 to 8 percent of the volume.

Since aggregates make up about 60 to 75 percent of the total volume of concrete, their selection is important. Aggregates should consist of particles with adequate strength and resistance to exposure conditions and should not contain materials that will cause deterioration of the concrete. A continuous gradation of aggregate particle sizes is desirable for efficient use of the paste. The quality of the concrete depends upon the quality of the paste and aggregate, and the bond between the two. In properly made concrete, each and every particle of aggregate is completely coated with paste and all of the spaces between aggregate particles are completely filled with paste.

For any particular set of materials and conditions of curing, the quality of hardened concrete is strongly influenced by the amount of water used in relation to the amount of cement. Unnecessarily high water contents dilute the cement paste (the glue of concrete). Following are some advantages of reducing water content:

- Increased compressive and flexural strength
- Lower permeability, thus lower absorption and increased water tightness
- Increased resistance to weathering
- Better bond between concrete and reinforcement
- Reduced drying shrinkage and cracking
- Less volume change from wetting and drying

The less water used, the better the quality of the concrete—provided the mixture can be consolidated properly. Smaller amounts of mixing water result in stiffer mixtures; but with vibration, stiffer mixtures can be easily placed. Thus, consolidation by vibration permits improvement in the quality of concrete.

The freshly mixed (plastic) and hardened properties of concrete may be changed by adding chemical admixtures to the concrete, usually in liquid form, during batching. Chemical admixtures are commonly used to (1) adjust setting time or hardening, (2) reduce water demand, (3) increase workability, (4) intentionally entrain air, and (5) adjust other fresh or hardened concrete properties.

After completion of proper proportioning, batching, mixing, placing, consolidating, finishing, and curing, concrete hardens into a strong, noncombustible, durable, abrasion- resistant, and watertight building material that requires little or no maintenance. Furthermore, concrete is an excellent building material because it can be formed into a wide variety of shapes, colors, and textures for use in an unlimited number of applications.

FRESHLY MIXED CONCRETE

Freshly mixed concrete should be plastic or semifluid and generally capable of being molded by hand. A very wet concrete mixture can be molded in the sense that it can be cast in a mold, but this is not within the definition of "plastic"—that which is pli-

Phillip Arnold, L. M. Scofield Company

able and capable of being molded or shaped like a lump of modeling clay. In a plastic concrete mixture all grains of sand and pieces of gravel or stone are encased and held in suspension. The ingredients are not apt to segregate during transport, and when the concrete hardens, it becomes a homogeneous mixture of all the components. During placing, concrete of plastic consistency does not crumble but flows sluggishly without segregation. In construction practice, thin concrete members and heavily reinforced concrete members require workable, but never soupy, mixes for ease of placement. A plastic mixture is required for strength and for maintaining homogeneity during handling and placement. While a plastic mixture is suitable for most concrete work, plasticizing admixtures may be used to make concrete more flowable in thin or heavily reinforced concrete members.

Mixing

The basic components of concrete are distinctly separate materials. To ensure that they are combined into a homogeneous mixture requires effort and care. The sequence of charging ingredients into a concrete mixer can play an important part in uniformity of the finished product. The sequence, however, can be varied and still produce a quality concrete. Different sequences require adjustments in the timing of water addition, the total number of revolutions of the mixer drum, and the speed of revolution. Other important factors in mixing are the size of the batch in relation to the size of the mixer drum; the elapsed time between batching and mixing; and the design, configuration, and condition of the mixer drum and blades. Approved mixers, correctly operated and maintained, ensure an end-to-end exchange of materials by a rolling, folding, and kneading action of the batch over itself as concrete is mixed.

Workability

The ease of placing, consolidating, and finishing freshly mixed concrete, and the degree to which it resists segregation, is called workability. Concrete should be workable but the ingredients should not separate during transport and handling.

The degree of workability required for proper placement of concrete is controlled by the placement method, type of consolidation, and type of concrete. Different types of placements require different levels of workability. Factors that influence, the workability of concrete are (1) the method and duration of transportation; (2) quantity and characteristics of cementitious materials; (3) concrete consistency (slump); (4) grading, shape, and surface texture of fine and coarse aggregates; (5) entrained air; (6) water content; (7) concrete and ambient air temperatures; and (8) admixtures. A uniform distribution of aggregate particles and the presence of entrained air significantly help control segregation and improve workability.

Properties related to workability include consistency, segregation, mobility, pumpability, bleeding, and finishability. Consistency is considered a close indication of workability. Slump is used as a measure of the consistency or wetness of concrete. A low-slump concrete has a stiff consistency. If the consistency is too dry and harsh, the concrete will be difficult to place and compact, and larger aggregate particles may separate from the mix. However, it should not be assumed that a wetter, more fluid mix is necessarily more workable. If the mix is too wet, segregation and honeycombing can occur. The consistency should be the driest practicable for placement using the available consolidation equipment.

Bleeding and Settlement

Bleeding is the development of a layer of water at the top or surface of freshly placed concrete. It is caused by sedimentation (settlement) of solid particles (cement and aggregate) and the simultaneous upward migration of water. Bleeding is normal and it should not diminish the quality of properly placed, finished, and cured concrete. Some bleeding is helpful to control plastic shrinkage cracking.

Excessive bleeding increases the water-cement ratio near the top surface; a weak top layer with poor durability may result, particularly if finishing operations take place while bleed water is present. A water pocket or void can develop under a prematurely finished surface.

After evaporation of all bleed water, the hardened surface will be slightly lower than the freshly placed surface. This decrease in height from time of placement to initial set is called settlement shrinkage.

The bleeding rate and bleeding capacity (total settlement per unit of original concrete height) increases with initial water content, concrete height, and pressure. Use of properly graded aggregate, certain chemical admixtures, air entrainment, supplementary cementitious materials, and finer cements, reduces bleeding. Concrete used to fill voids, provide support, or provide watertightness with a good bond should have low bleeding properties to avoid formation of water pockets.

Consolidation

Vibration sets into motion the particles in freshly mixed concrete, reducing friction between them, and giving the mixture the mobile qualities of a thick fluid. The vibratory action permits use of a stiffer mixture containing a larger proportion of coarse and a smaller proportion of fine aggregate. The larger the maximum size aggregate in concrete with a well-graded aggregate, the less volume there is to fill with paste and the less aggregate surface area there is to coat with paste; thus less water and cement are needed. Concrete with an optimally graded aggregate will be easier to consolidate and place. Consolidation of coarser as well as stiffer mixtures results in improved quality and economy. On the other hand, poor consolidation can result in porous, weak concrete with poor durability.

Hydration, Setting Time, and Hardening

The binding quality of portland cement paste is due to the chemical reaction between the cement and water, called hydration.

Portland cement is not a simple chemical compound; it is a mixture of many compounds. Four of these make up 90 percent or more of the weight of portland cement: tricalcium silicate, dicalcium silicate, tricalcium aluminate, and tetracalcium aluminoferrite. In addition to these major compounds, several others play important roles in the hydration process. Each type of portland cement contains the same four major compounds, but in different proportions.

When clinker (the kiln product that is ground to make portland cement) is examined under a microscope, most of the individual cement compounds can be identified and their amounts determined. However, the smallest grains elude visual detection. The average diameter of a typical cement particle is approximately 15 micrometers. If all cement particles were average, portland cement would contain about 300 billion particles per kilogram, but in fact there are some 16,000 billion particles per kilogram because of the broad range of particle sizes. The particles in a kilogram of portland cement have a surface area of approximately 400 square meters.

The two calcium silicates, which constitute about 75 percent of the weight of portland cement, react with water to form two new compounds: calcium hydroxide and calcium silicate hydrate. The latter is by far the most important cementing component in concrete. The engineering properties of concrete setting and hardening, strength, and dimensional stability depend primarily on calcium silicate hydrate. It is the heart of concrete.

The less porous the cement paste, the stronger the concrete. When mixing concrete, therefore, no more water than is absolutely necessary to make the concrete plastic and workable should be used. Even then, the water used is usually more than is required for complete hydration of the cement. About 0.4 grams of water per gram of cement are needed to completely hydrate cement. However, complete hydration is rare in field concrete due to a lack of moisture and the long period of time (decades) required to achieve complete hydration.

Knowledge of the amount of heat released as cement hydrates can be useful in planning construction. In winter, the heat of hydration will help protect the concrete against damage from freezing temperatures. The heat may be harmful, however, in massive structures such as dams because it may produce undesirable temperature differentials.

Knowledge of the rate of reaction between cement and water is important because it determines the rate of hardening. The initial reaction must be slow enough to allow time for the concrete to be transported and placed. Once the concrete has been placed and finished, however, rapid hardening is desirable. Other factors that influence the rate of hydration include cement fineness, admixtures, amount of water added, and temperature of the materials at the time of mixing.

HARDENED CONCRETE

Curing

Curing is the maintenance of a satisfactory moisture content and temperature in concrete for a period of time immediately following placing and finishing so that the desired properties may develop. The need for adequate curing of concrete cannot be overemphasized. Curing has a strong influence on the properties of hardened concrete; and proper curing will increase durability, strength, watertightness, abrasion resistance, volume stability, and resistance to freezing and thawing and deicers. Exposed slab surfaces are especially sensitive to curing, as strength development and freeze-thaw resistance of the top surface of a slab can be reduced significantly when curing is defective. When portland cement is mixed with water, a chemical reaction called hydration takes place. The extent to which this reaction is completed influences the

Phillip Arnold, L. M. Scofield Company

strength and durability of the concrete. Freshly mixed concrete normally contains more water than is required for hydration of the cement; however, excessive loss of water by evaporation can delay or prevent adequate hydration. The surface is particularly susceptible to insufficient hydration because it dries first. If temperatures are favorable, hydration is relatively rapid the first few days after concrete is placed; however, it is important for water to be retained in the concrete during this period—that is, for evaporation to be prevented or substantially reduced.

With proper curing, concrete becomes stronger, more impermeable, and more resistant to stress, abrasion, and freezing and thawing. The improvement is rapid at early ages but continues more slowly thereafter for an indefinite period.

Increase in strength with age continues provided (1) unhydrated cement is still present, (2) the concrete remains moist or has a relative humidity above approximately 80 percent, (3) the concrete temperature remains favorable, and (4) sufficient space is available for hydration products to form. When the relative humidity within the concrete drops to about 80 percent, or the temperature of the concrete drops below freezing, hydration and strength gain virtually stop.

The most effective method for curing concrete depends on the materials used, method of construction, and the intended use of the hardened concrete. For most jobs, curing generally involves applying curing compounds or covering the freshly placed and finished concrete with impermeable sheets or wet burlap. In some cases, such as in hot and cold weather, special care using other precautions is needed.

Drying Rate of Concrete

Concrete does not harden or cure by drying. Concrete (or more precisely, the cement in it) needs moisture to hydrate and harden. When concrete dries out, it ceases to gain strength; the fact that it is dry is no indication that it has undergone sufficient hydration to achieve the desired physical properties. Knowledge of the rate of drying is helpful in understanding the properties or physical condition of concrete.

For example, as mentioned, concrete must continue to hold enough moisture throughout the curing period for the cement to hydrate to the extent that desired properties are achieved. Freshly cast concrete usually has an abundance of water, but as drying progresses from the surface inward, strength gain will continue at each depth only as long as the relative humidity at that point remains above 80 percent.

A common illustration of this is the surface of a concrete floor that has not had sufficient moist curing. Because it has dried quickly, concrete at the surface is weak, and traffic on it creates dusting. Also, when concrete dries, it shrinks as it loses water, just as wood and clay do (though not as much). Drying shrinkage is a primary cause of cracking, and the width of cracks is a function of the degree of drying, spacing, or frequency of cracks, and the age at which the cracks occur.

While the surface of a concrete element will dry quite rapidly, it takes a much longer time for concrete in the interior to dry. Field concrete elements would have different drying profiles due to environmental conditions, size effects, and concrete properties.

Size and shape of a concrete member have an important bearing on the rate of drying. Concrete elements with large surface area in relation to volume (such as paving slabs) dry faster than voluminous concrete members with relatively small surface areas (such as bridge piers).

Curing Methods and Materials

Concrete can be kept moist (and, in some cases, at a favorable temperature) by three curing methods:

- *Methods that maintain the presence of mixing water in the concrete during the early hardening period.* These include ponding or immersion, spraying or fogging, and saturated wet coverings. These methods afford some cooling through evaporation, which is beneficial in hot weather.
- *Methods that reduce the loss of mixing water from the surface of the concrete.* This can be done by covering the concrete with impervious paper or plastic sheets, or by applying membrane-forming curing compounds.
- *Methods that accelerate strength gain by supplying heat and additional moisture to the concrete.* This is usually accomplished with live steam, heating coils, or electrically heated forms or pads.

The method or combination of methods chosen depends on factors such as availability of curing materials; size, shape, and age of concrete; production facilities (in place or in a plant); esthetic appearance; and economics. As a result, curing often involves a series of procedures used at a particular time as the concrete ages. For example, fog spraying or plastic-covered wet burlap can precede application of a curing compound. The timing of each procedure depends on the degree of hardening of the concrete needed to prevent the particular procedure from damaging the concrete surface (ACI 308, 1997).

Membrane-Forming Curing Compounds

Liquid membrane-forming compounds consisting of waxes, resins, chlorinated rubber, and other materials can be used to retard or reduce evaporation of moisture from concrete. They are the most practical and most widely used method not only for curing freshly placed concrete but also for extending curing of concrete after removal of forms or after initial moist curing. Membrane-forming curing compounds are of two general types: clear, or translucent, and pigmented.

Curing compounds should be applied by hand-operated or power-driven spray equipment immediately after final finishing of the concrete. The concrete surface should be damp when the coating is applied. On dry, windy days, or during periods when adverse weather conditions could result in plastic shrinkage cracking, application of a curing compound immediately after final finishing and before all free water on the surface has evaporated will help prevent the formation of cracks. Power-driven spray equipment is recommended for uniform application of curing compounds. Spray nozzles and windshields on such equipment should be arranged to prevent windblown loss of curing compound.

Curing compounds should conform to ASTM C 309 (AASHTO M 148). A method for determining the efficiency of curing compounds, waterproof paper, and plastic sheets is described in ASTM C 156 (AASHTO T 155). Curing compounds with sealing properties are specified under ASTM C 1315.

Forms Left in Place

Forms provide satisfactory protection against loss of moisture if the top exposed concrete surfaces are kept wet. A soaker hose is excellent for this. The forms should be left on the concrete as long as practical.

Wood forms left in place should be kept moist by sprinkling, especially during hot, dry weather. If this cannot be done, they should be removed as soon as practical and another curing method started without delay. Color variations may occur from formwork and uneven water curing of walls.

Sealing Compounds

Sealing compounds (sealers) are liquids applied to the surface of hardened concrete to reduce the penetration of liquids or gases—such as water, deicing solutions, and carbon dioxide—that cause freeze-thaw damage, corrosion of reinforcing steel, and acid attack. In addition, sealing compounds used on interior floor slabs reduce dusting and the absorption of spills while making the surface easier to clean.

Sealing compounds differ in purpose from curing compounds; they should not be confused as being the same. The primary purpose of a curing compound is to retard the loss of water from newly placed concrete, and it is applied immediately after finishing. Surface sealing compounds, on the other hand, retard the penetration of harmful substances into hardened concrete and are typically not applied until the concrete is 28 days old.

Surface sealers are generally classified as either film-forming or penetrating. Sealing exterior concrete is an optional procedure generally performed to help protect concrete from freeze-thaw damage and chloride penetration from deicers. Curing is not optional when using a sealer; curing is necessary to produce properties needed for concrete to perform adequately for its intended purpose. Satisfactory performance of exterior concrete still primarily depends on an adequate air-void system; sufficient strength; and the use of proper placing, finishing, and curing techniques. However, not all concrete placed meets those criteria; surface sealers can help improve the durability of these concretes.

Film-forming sealing compounds remain mostly on the surface, with only a slight amount of the material penetrating the concrete. The relatively large molecular structure of these compounds limits their capability to penetrate the surface. Thinning them with solvents will not improve their penetrating capability. These materials not only reduce the penetration of water, they also protect against mild chemicals; furthermore, they prevent the absorption of grease and oil, as well as reduce dusting under pedestrian traffic.

Surface sealers consist of acrylic resins, chlorinated rubber, urethanes, epoxies, and alpha methyl styrene, and nonfilm-forming silane and siloxane sealers. The effectiveness of film-forming sealers depends on the continuity of the layer formed. Abrasive grit and heavy traffic can damage the layer, requiring the reapplication of the material. Consult manufacturers' application recommendations, because some of these materials are intended for interior use only and may yellow and deteriorate under exposure to ultraviolet light.

Concrete sealers can contain volatile organic compounds (VOCs) and hazardous chemicals. Water-based sealers may contain less VOCs.

Strength

Compressive strength may be defined as the measured maximum resistance of a concrete specimen to axial loading. It is generally expressed in megapascals (MPa) or pounds per square inch (psi) at an age of 28 days. Other test ages are also used; however, it is important to realize the relationship between the 28-day strength and other test ages. Seven-day strengths are often estimated to be about 75 percent of the 28-day strength, and 56-day and 90-day strengths are about 10 to 15 percent greater than 28-day strengths.

The compressive strength that a concrete achieves results from the water-cement ratio (or water-cementitious materials ratio), the extent to which hydration has progressed, the curing and environmental conditions, and the age of the concrete. Strengths increase as the water-cement ratios decrease. These factors also affect the flexural and tensile strengths and bond of concrete to steel.

The water-cement ratio compressive strength relationships in the graph are for typical non-air-entrained concretes. When more precise values for concrete are required, graphs should be developed for the specific materials and mix proportions to be used on the job.

For a given workability and a given amount of cement, air-entrained concrete requires less mixing water than non-air-entrained concrete. The lower water-cement ratio possible for air-entrained concrete tends to offset the somewhat lower strengths of air-entrained concrete, particularly in lean to medium cement content mixes

To determine compressive strength, tests are made on specimens of mortar or concrete; in the United States, unless otherwise specified, compression tests of mortar are made on 50-mm (2-inch) cubes, while compression tests of concrete are made on cylinders 150 mm (6 inches) in diameter and 300 mm (12 inches) high. Smaller cylinders, 100 × 200 mm (4 × 8 inches) are also used for concrete.

Compressive strength of concrete is a primary physical property and frequently used in design calculations for bridges, buildings, and other structures.

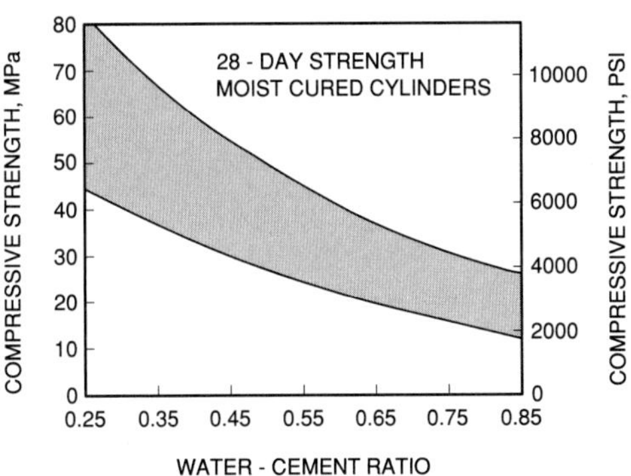

This range is based on more than 100 different concrete mixtures cast between 1985 and 1999.

RANGE OF TYPICAL STRENGTH TO WATER-CEMENT RATIO RELATIONSHIPS OF PORTLAND CEMENT CONCRETE

Most general-use concrete has a compressive strength between 20 and 40 MPa (3,000 and 6,000 psi). Compressive strengths of 70 to 140 MPa (10,000 to 20,000 psi) have been used in special bridge and high-rise building applications.

The flexural strength or modulus of rupture of concrete is used to design pavements and other slabs on ground. Compressive strength, which is easier to measure than flexural strength, can be used as an index of flexural strength, once the empirical relationship between them has been established for the materials and the size of the element involved. The flexural strength of normal-weight concrete is often approximated 7.5 to 10 times the square root of the compressive strength in pounds per square inch (0.7 to 0.8 times the square root of the compressive strength in megapascals).

The direct tensile strength of concrete is about 8 to 12 percent of the compressive strength and is often estimated as 5 to 7.5 times the square root of the compressive strength in pounds per square inch (0.4 to 0.7 times the square root of the compressive strength in megapascals). Splitting tensile strength is 8 to 14 percent of the compressive strength.

The torsional strength for concrete is related to the modulus of rupture and the dimensions of the concrete element. Shear strength-compressive strength relationships are discussed in the American Concrete Institute (ACI) 318 building code. The correlation between compressive strength and flexural, tensile, torsional, and shear strength varies with concrete ingredients and environment. Modulus of elasticity, denoted by the symbol E, may be defined as the ratio of normal stress to corresponding strain for tensile or compressive stresses below the proportional limit of a material. For normal-weight concrete, E ranges from 14,000 to 41,000 MPa (2 to 6 million psi) and can be approximated as 5,000 times the square root of the compressive strength in megapascals (57,000 times the square root of the compressive strength in pounds per square inch). Like other strength relationships, the modulus of elasticity to compressive strength relationship is mix-ingredient-specific and should be verified in a laboratory.

Density

Conventional concrete, normally used in pavements, buildings, and other structures, has a density (unit weight) in the range of 2,200 to 2,400 kg/m^3 (137 to 150 lb/ft^3). The density of concrete varies, depending on the amount and density of the aggregate, the amount of air that is entrapped or purposely entrained, and the water and cement contents, which in turn are influenced by the maximum size of the aggregate. Reducing the cement paste content (increasing aggregate volume) increases density. In the design of reinforced concrete structures, the combination of conventional concrete and reinforcing steel is commonly assumed to weigh 2400 kg/m^3 (150 lb/ft^3).

The weight of dry concrete equals the weight of the freshly mixed concrete ingredients less the weight of mix water that evaporates into the air. Some of the mix water combines chemically with the cement during the hydration process, converting the cement into cement gel. Also, some of the water remains tightly held in pores and capillaries and does not evaporate under normal conditions. The amount of mix water that will evaporate from concrete exposed to ambient air at 50 percent relative humidity is about 1/2 to 3 percent of the concrete weight; the actual amount depends on initial water content of the concrete, absorption characteristics of the aggregates, and size and shape of the concrete element.

Aside from conventional concrete, there is a wide spectrum of special concretes to meet various needs; they range from lightweight insulating concretes with a density of as little as 240 kg/m^3 (15 lb/ft^3) to heavyweight concrete with a density of up to 6,000 kg/m^3 (375 lb/ft^3) used for counterweights or radiation shielding.

Joints

Joints are the most effective method of controlling unsightly cracking. If a sizable expanse of concrete (a wall, slab, or pavement) is not provided with properly spaced joints to accommodate drying shrinkage and temperature contraction, the concrete will crack in a random manner.

Contraction (shrinkage control) joints are grooved, formed, or sawed into sidewalks, driveways, pavements, floors, and walls so that cracking will occur in these joints rather than in a random manner. Contraction joints permit movement in the plane of a slab or wall. They extend to a depth of approximately one-quarter the concrete thickness.

Isolation joints separate a concrete placement from other parts of a structure and permit horizontal and vertical movements. They should be used at the junction of walls, curbs, columns, footings, and other points where restraint can occur. They extend the full depth of slabs and include a premolded joint filler.

Construction joints occur where concrete work is concluded for the day; they separate areas of concrete placed at different times. In slabs-on-ground, construction joints usually align with, and function as, control or isolation joints. They may require dowels for load transfer.

DURABILITY

The durability of concrete may be defined as the capability of concrete to resist weathering action, chemical attack, and abrasion while maintaining its desired engineering properties. Different concretes require different degrees of durability, depending on the exposure environment and the properties desired. The concrete ingredients, proportioning of those ingredients, interactions between the ingredients, and placing and curing practices determine the ultimate durability and life of the concrete.

Resistance to Freezing and Thawing

Concrete used in structures and pavements is expected to have long life and low maintenance requirements. It must have good durability to resist anticipated exposure conditions. The most potentially destructive weathering factor is freezing and thawing while the concrete is wet, particularly in the presence of deicing chemicals. Deterioration is caused by the freezing of water and subsequent expansion in the paste, the aggregate particles, or both.

With air entrainment, concrete is highly resistant to this type of deterioration. During freezing, the water displaced by ice formation in the paste is accommodated so that it is not disruptive; the microscopic air bubbles in the paste provide chambers for the water to enter and thus relieve the hydraulic pressure generated.

Phillip Arnold, L. M. Scofield Company

When freezing occurs in concrete containing saturated aggregate, disruptive hydraulic pressures can also be generated within the aggregate. Water displaced from the aggregate particles during the formation of ice cannot escape fast enough to the surrounding paste to relieve pressure. However, under most exposure conditions, a good-quality paste (low water-cement ratio) will prevent most aggregate particles from becoming saturated. Also, if the paste is air-entrained, it will accommodate the small amounts of excess water that may be expelled from aggregates, thus protecting the concrete from freeze-thaw damage.

For a range of water-cement ratios: (1) air-entrained concrete is much more resistant to freeze-thaw cycles than non-air-entrained concrete; (2) concrete with a low water-cement ratio is more durable than concrete with a high water-cement ratio; and (3) a drying period prior to freeze-thaw exposure substantially benefits the freeze-thaw resistance of air-entrained concrete. Air-entrained concrete with a low water-cement ratio and an air content of 5 to 8 percent will withstand a great number of cycles of freezing and thawing without distress.

Freeze-thaw durability can be determined by laboratory test procedure ASTM C 666, Standard Test Method for Resistance of Concrete to Rapid Freezing and Thawing (AASHTO T 161). From the test, a durability factor is calculated that reflects the number of cycles of freezing and thawing required to produce a certain amount of deterioration. Deicer-scaling resistance can be determined by ASTM C 672, Standard Test Method for Scaling Resistance of Concrete Surfaces Exposed to Deicing Chemicals.

PORTLAND CEMENT

Manufacture of Portland Cement

Portland cement is produced by pulverizing clinker, which consists primarily of hydraulic calcium silicates. Clinker also contains some calcium aluminates and calcium aluminoferrites, and one or more forms of calcium sulfate (gypsum) is interground with the clinker to make the finished product.

Materials used in the manufacture of portland cement must contain appropriate amounts of calcium, silica, alumina, and iron components. During manufacture, chemical analyses of all materials are made frequently to ensure a uniformly high-quality cement.

Selected raw materials are transported from the quarry, crushed, milled, and proportioned so that the resulting mixture has the desired chemical composition. The raw materials are generally a mixture of calcareous (calcium carbonate bearing) material, such as limestone, and an argillaceous (silica and alumina) material, such as clay, shale, fly ash, or blast-furnace slag. Either a dry or a wet process is used. In the dry process, grinding and blending are done with dry materials. In the wet process, the grinding and blending operations are done with the materials mixed with water in a slurry form. In other respects, the dry and wet processes are very much alike.

After blending, the ground raw material is fed into the upper end of a kiln. The raw mix passes through the kiln at a rate controlled by the slope and rotational speed of the kiln. Burning fuel (powdered coal, new or recycled oil, natural gas, rubber tires, and by-product fuel) is forced into the lower end of the kiln where temperatures of 1400°C to 1550°C change the raw material chemically into cement clinker, grayish-black pellets predominantly the size of marbles.

The clinker is cooled and then pulverized. During this operation, a small amount of gypsum is added to regulate the setting time of the cement and to improve shrinkage and strength development properties. In the grinding mill clinker is ground so fine that nearly all of it passes through a 45-micrometer (No. 325 mesh) sieve. This extremely fine gray powder is portland cement.

Environmental impacts associated with the production of portland cement include: extensive energy use for processing, use of nonrenewable resources, and air and water pollution. Processing generates large volumes of carbon dioxide (CO_2) from the combustion of fuels to operate kilns and the conversion of limestone into lime. About one ton of CO_2 is released for every ton of cement produced. CO_2 is a major contributor to global warming and the greenhouse effect. Limestone, used to produce cement, is an abundant material but is not renewable. The mining of stone disrupts habitat, causes erosion and sediment runoff, and negatively impacts waterways. Water pollution from cement production results in high levels of alkalinity that are toxic to fish and other species.

Some cement manufacturers burn waste such as tires and coal sludge to reduce fossil fuel use in their kilns. Others use high-efficiency kilns. The Portland Cement Association provides information on kiln type and fuel for cement companies by state.

Types of Portland Cement

Different types of portland cement are manufactured to meet various normal physical and chemical requirements for specific purposes. Portland cements are manufactured to meet the specifications of ASTM C 150, AASHTO M 85, or ASTM C 1157.

ASTM C 150, Standard Specification for Portland Cement, provides for types of portland cement using Roman numeral designations, as follows:

Type I: Normal

Type II: Moderate sulfate resistance

Type III: High early strength

Type IV: Low heat of hydration

Type V: High sulfate resistance

Type I. Type I portland cement is a general-purpose cement suitable for all uses where the special properties of other types are not required. Its uses in concrete include pavements, floors, reinforced concrete buildings, bridges, tanks, reservoirs, pipe, masonry units, and precast concrete products.

Type II. Type II portland cement is used where precaution against moderate sulfate attack is important. It is used in normal structures or elements exposed to soil or groundwaters where sulfate concentrations are higher than normal but not unusually severe. Type II cement has moderate sulfate-resistant properties because it contains no more than 8 percent tricalcium aluminate (C3A).

Sulfates in moist soil or water may enter the concrete and react with the hydrated C_3A, resulting in expansion, scaling, and cracking of concrete. Some sulfate compounds, such as magnesium sulfate, directly attack calcium silicate hydrate. Use of Type II cement in concrete must be accompanied by the use of a low water-to-cementitious-materials ratio and low permeability to control sulfate attack.

Because of its increased availability, Type II cement is sometimes used in all aspects of construction, regardless of the need for sulfate resistance or moderate heat generation. Some cements may be labeled with more than one type designation, for example Type I/II. This simply means that such a cement meets the requirements of both cement Types I and II.

Type III. Type III portland cement provides strength at an early period, usually a week or less. It is chemically and physically similar to Type I cement, except that its particles have been ground finer. It is used when forms need to be removed as soon as possible or when the structure must be put into service quickly. In cold weather, its use permits a reduction in the length of the curing period. Although higher cement content mixes of Type I cement can be used to gain high early strength, Type III may provide it easier and more economically.

Type IV. Type IV portland cement is used where the rate and amount of heat generated from hydration must be minimized. It develops strength at a slower rate than other cement types. Type IV cement is intended for use in massive concrete structures, such as large gravity dams, where the temperature rise resulting from heat generated during hardening must be minimized. Type IV cement is rarely available.

Type V. Type V portland cement is used in concrete exposed to severe sulfate action—principally where soils or groundwaters have a high sulfate content. It gains strength more slowly than Type I cement. The high sulfate resistance of Type V cement is attributed to a low tricalcium aluminate content, not more than 5 percent. Use of a low water-to-cementitious-materials ratio and low permeability are critical to the performance of any concrete exposed to sulfates. Even Type V cement concrete cannot withstand a severe sulfate exposure if the concrete has a high water-to-cementitious-materials ratio. Type V cement, like other portland cements, is not resistant to acids and other highly corrosive substances. ASTM C 150 (AASHTO M 85) allows both a chemical approach and a physical approach (ASTM C 452 expansion test) to ensure the sulfate resistance of Type V cement. Either the chemical or the physical approach can be specified, but not both.

White Portland Cements

White portland cement is a true portland cement that differs from gray cement chiefly in color. It is made to conform to the specifications of ASTM C 150, usually Type I or Type III; the manufacturing process is controlled so that the finished product will be white. White portland cement is made of selected raw materials containing negligible amounts of iron and magnesium oxides—the substances that give cement its gray color. White portland cement is used primarily for architectural purposes in structural walls, precast and glass-fiber-reinforced concrete (GFRC) facing panels, terrazzo surfaces, stucco, cement paint, tile grout, and decorative concrete. White portland cement should be specified as: "white portland cement meeting the specifications of ASTM C 150, Type [I, II, III, or V]." White cement is also used to

Phillip Arnold, L. M. Scofield Company

manufacture white masonry cement meeting ASTM C 91 and white plastic cement meeting ASTM C 1328 (PCA 1999). White cement was first manufactured in the United States in York, Pennsylvania, in 1907.

FLY ASH, SLAG, SILICA FUME, AND NATURAL POZZOLANS

Fly ash, ground granulated blast-furnace slag, silica fume, and natural pozzolans such as calcined shale, calcined clay, or metakaolin are materials that, when used in conjunction with portland or blended cement, contribute to the properties of the hardened concrete through hydraulic or pozzolanic activity or both. A pozzolan is a siliceous or aluminosiliceous material that, in finely divided form and in the presence of moisture, chemically reacts with the calcium hydroxide released by the hydration of portland cement to form calcium silicate hydrate and other cementitious compounds. Pozzolans and slags are generally categorized as supplementary cementitious materials or mineral admixtures.

Supplementary cementitious materials are added to concrete as part of the total cementitious system. They may be used in addition to or as a partial replacement for portland cement or blended cement in concrete, depending on the properties of the materials and the desired effect on concrete.

Supplementary cementitious materials are used to improve a particular concrete property such as resistance to alkali-aggregate reactivity. The optimum amount to use should be established by testing to determine (1) whether the material is indeed improving the property and (2) the correct dosage rate, as an overdose or underdose can be harmful or not achieve the desired effect. Supplementary cementitious materials also react differently with different cements.

Traditionally, fly ash, slag, calcined clay, calcined shale, and silica fume were used in concrete individually. Today, due to improved access to these materials, concrete producers can combine two or more of these materials to optimize concrete properties. Mixtures using three cementitious materials, called ternary mixtures, are becoming more common. Supplementary cementitious materials are used in at least 60 percent of ready-mixed concrete (PCA, 2000). ASTM C 311 provides test methods for fly ash and natural pozzolans for use as supplementary cementitious material in concrete.

Fly Ash

Fly ash, the most widely used supplementary cementitious material in concrete, is a byproduct of the combustion of pulverized coal in electric power generating plants. Upon ignition in the furnace, most of the volatile matter and carbon in the coal are burned off. During combustion, the coal's mineral impurities (such as clay, feldspar, quartz, and shale) fuse in suspension and are carried away from the combustion chamber by the exhaust gases. In the process, the fused material cools and solidifies into spherical glassy particles called fly ash. The fly ash is then collected from the exhaust gases by electrostatic precipitators or bag filters. Fly ash is a finely divided powder resembling portland cement.

Most of the fly ash particles are solid spheres. Ground materials, such as portland cement, have solid angular particles. Fly ash is primarily silicate glass containing silica, alumina, iron, and calcium, and the color is generally gray or tan.

Class F and Class C fly ashes are commonly used as pozzolanic admixtures for general-purpose concrete. Class F materials are generally low-calcium fly ashes, with carbon contents usually less than 5 percent, although some may be as high as 10 percent. Class C materials are often high-calcium fly ashes with carbon contents less than 2 percent. Many Class C ashes, when exposed to water, will hydrate and harden in less than 45 minutes. Some fly ashes meet both Class F and Class C classifications.

SLAG

Ground granulated blast-furnace slag, also called slag cement, is made from iron blast-furnace slag; it is a nonmetallic hydraulic cement consisting essentially of silicates and aluminosilicates of calcium developed in a molten condition simultaneously with iron in a blast furnace. The molten slag at a temperature of about 1500°C (2730°F) is rapidly chilled by quenching in water to form a glassy sandlike granulated material.

The rough and angular-shaped ground slag in the presence of water and an activator, NaOH or CaOH, both supplied by portland cement, hydrates and sets in a manner similar to portland cement. Granulated blast furnace slag was first developed in Germany in 1853. Ground slag has been used as a cementitious material in concrete since the beginning of the 1900s.

AGGREGATES FOR CONCRETE

The importance of using the right type and quality of aggregates cannot be overemphasized. The fine and coarse aggregates generally occupy 60 to 75 percent of the concrete volume (70 to 85 percent by weight) and strongly influence the concrete's freshly mixed and hardened properties, mixture proportions, and economy. Fine aggregates generally consist of natural sand or crushed stone, with most particles smaller than 5 mm (0.2 inch). Coarse aggregates consist of one or a combination of gravels or crushed stone, with particles predominantly larger than 5 mm (0.2 inch) and generally between 9.5 mm and 37.5 mm (⅜ and 1½ inch).

Aggregates must conform to certain standards for optimum engineering use: they must be clean, hard, strong, durable particles free of absorbed chemicals, coatings of clay, and other fine materials in amounts that could affect hydration and bond of the cement paste. Aggregate particles that are friable or capable of being split are undesirable. Aggregates containing any appreciable amounts of shale or other shaly rocks, soft and porous materials, should be avoided; certain types of chert in particular should be avoided, as they have low resistance to weathering and can cause surface defects such as popouts.

Identification of the constituents of an aggregate cannot alone provide a basis for predicting the behavior of aggregates in service. Visual inspection will often disclose weaknesses in coarse aggregates. Service records are invaluable in evaluating aggregates. In the absence of a performance record, the aggregates should be tested before they are used in concrete. The most commonly used aggregates—sand, gravel, crushed stone, and air-cooled blast-furnace slag—produce freshly mixed normal-weight concrete with a density (unit weight) of 2200 to 2400 kg/m³ (140 to 150 lb/ft³). Aggregates of expanded shale, clay, slate, and slag are used to produce structural lightweight concrete with a freshly mixed density ranging from about 1350 to 1850 kg/m³ (90 to 120 lb/ft³). Other lightweight materials such as pumice, scoria, perlite, vermiculite, and diatomite are used to produce insulating lightweight concretes ranging in density from about 250 to 1450 kg/m³ (15 to 90 lb/ft³). Heavyweight materials such as barite, limonite, magnetite, ilmenite, hematite, iron, and steel punchings or shot are used to produce heavyweight

APPLICATIONS FOR COMMONLY USED CEMENTS

	APPLICATIONS*						
CEMENT SPECIFICATION	**GENERAL PURPOSE**	**MODERATE HEAT OF HYDRATION**	**HIGH EARLY STRENGTH**	**LOW HEAT OF HYDRATION**	**MODERATE SULPHATE RESISTANCE**	**HIGH SULPHATE RESISTANCE**	**RESISTANCE TO ALKALI-SILICA REACTIVITY (ASR)****
ASTM C 150 (AASHTO M 85) portland cements	I	II (moderate heat option)	III	IV	II	V	Low alkali option
ASTM C 595 (AASHTO M 240) blended hydraulic cements	IS IP I(PM) I(SM) S, P	IS(MH) IP(MH) I(PM)(MH) I(SM)(MH)		P(LH)	IS(MS) IP(MS) P(MS) I(PM)(MS) I(SM)(MS)		Low reactivity option
ASTM C 1157 hydraulic cements†	GU	MH	HE	LH	MS	HS	Option R

**Check the local availability of specific cements as all cements are not available everywhere.*

***The option for low reactivity with ASR-susceptible aggregates can be applied to any cement type in the columns to the left.*

†For ASTM C 1157 cements, the nomenclature of hydraulic cement, portland cement, air-entraining portland cement, modified portland cement, or blended hydraulic cement is used with the type designation.

Phillip Arnold, L. M. Scofield Company

concrete and radiation-shielding concrete (see ASTM C 637 and C 638).

Normal-weight aggregates should meet the requirements of ASTM C 33 or AASHTO M 6/M 80. These specifications limit the permissible amounts of deleterious substances and provide requirements for aggregate characteristics. Compliance is determined by using one or more of the several standard tests cited in the following subsections and tables. However, the fact that aggregates satisfy ASTM C 33 or AASHTO M 6/M 80 requirements does not necessarily assure defect-free concrete.

For adequate consolidation of concrete, the desirable amount of air, water, cement, and fine aggregate (that is, the mortar fraction) should be about 50 to 65 percent by absolute volume (45 to 60 percent by weight). Rounded aggregate, such as gravel, requires slightly lower values, while crushed aggregate requires slightly higher values. Fine aggregate content is usually 35 to 45 percent by weight or volume of the total aggregate content.

Grading

Grading is the particle-size distribution of an aggregate as determined by a sieve analysis (ASTM C 136 or AASHTO T 27). The aggregate particle size is determined by using wire-mesh sieves with square openings. The seven standard ASTM C 33 (AASHTO M 6/M 80) sieves for fine aggregate have openings ranging from 150 µm to 9.5 mm (No. 100 sieve to ⅜ inch). The 13 standard sieves for coarse aggregate have openings ranging from 1.18 mm to 100 mm (0.046 to 4 inches). Tolerances for the dimensions of openings in sieves are listed in ASTM E 11 (AASHTO M 92).

Size numbers (grading sizes) for coarse aggregates apply to the amounts of aggregate (by weight) in percentages that pass through an assortment of sieves. For highway construction, ASTM D 448 (AASHTO M 43) lists the same 13 size numbers as in ASTM C 33 (AASHTO M 6/ M 80), plus an additional six coarse aggregate size numbers. Fine aggregate or sand has only one range of particle sizes for general construction and highway work.

The grading and grading limits are usually expressed as the percentage of material passing each sieve. There are several reasons for specifying grading limits and nominal maximum aggregate size: they affect relative aggregate proportions, as well as cement and water requirements, workability, pumpability, economy, porosity, shrinkage, and durability of concrete. Variations in grading can seriously affect the uniformity of concrete from batch to batch. Very fine sands are often uneconomical; conversely, very coarse sands and coarse aggregate can produce harsh, unworkable mixtures. In general, aggregates that do not have a large deficiency or excess of any size and give a smooth grading curve will produce the most satisfactory results.

GRADING LIMITS FOR FINE AGGREGATE (ASTM C33/AASHTO M6)

SIEVE SIZE		PERCENT PASSING BY MASS
9.5 mm	(⅜ in.)	100
4.75 mm	(No 4)	95 to 100
2.36 mm	(No. 8)	80 to 100
1.18 mm	(No. 16)	50 to 85
600 µm	(No. 30)	25 to 60
300 µm	(No. 50)	5 to 30 (AASHTO 10 to 30)
150 µm	(No. 100)	0 to 10 (AASHTO 2 to 10)

GRADING REQUIREMENTS FOR COARSE AGGREGATES (ASTM C33 AND AASHTO M80)

SIZE NUMBER	NOMINAL SIZE SIEVES WITH SQUARE OPENINGS	
1	90 to 37.5 mm	(3½ to 1½ in.)
2	63 to 37.5 mm	(2½ to 1½ in.)
3	50 to 25.0 mm	(2 to 1 in.)
357	50 to 4.75 mm	(2 in. to No. 4)
4	37.5 to 19.0 mm	(1½ to ¾ in.)
467	37.5 to 4.75 mm	(1½ in. to No. 4)
5	25.0 to 12.5 mm	(1 to ½ in.)
56	25.0 to 9.5 mm	(1 to ⅜ in.)
57	25.0 to 4.75 mm	(1 in. to No. 4)
6	19.0 to 9.5 mm	(¾ to ⅜ in.)
67	19.0 to 4.75 mm	(¾ in. to No. 4)
7	12.5 to 4.75 mm	(½ in. to No. 4)
8	9.5 to 2.36 mm	(⅜ in. to No. 8)

Gap-Graded Aggregates

In gap-graded aggregates, certain particle sizes are intentionally omitted. For cast-in-place concrete, typical gap-graded aggregates consist of only one size of coarse aggregate, with all the particles of fine aggregate able to pass through the voids in the compacted coarse aggregate. Gap-graded mixes are used in architectural concrete to obtain uniform textures in exposed-aggregate finishes. They can also be used in normal structural concrete because of possible improvements in some concrete properties, and to permit the use of local aggregate gradations.

For an aggregate of 19 mm (¾ inch) maximum size, the 4.75-mm to 9.5-mm (No. 4 to ⅜-inch) particles can be omitted without making the concrete unduly harsh or subject to segregation. In the case of 37.5-mm (1½ inch) aggregate, usually the 4.75-mm to 19-mm (No. 4 to ¾-inch) sizes are omitted.

Care must be taken in choosing the percentage of fine aggregate in a gap-graded mixture. A wrong choice can result in concrete that is likely to segregate or honeycomb because of an excess of coarse aggregate. Also, concrete with an excess of fine aggregate could have a high water demand, resulting in a low-density concrete. Fine aggregate is usually 25 to 35 percent by volume of the total aggregate. The lower percentage is used with rounded aggregates, and the higher with crushed material. For a smooth off-the-form finish, a somewhat higher percentage of fine aggregate to total aggregate may be used than for an exposed-aggregate finish; but both use a lower fine aggregate content than continuously graded mixtures. Fine aggregate content also depends on cement content, type of aggregate, and workability.

Particle Shape and Surface Texture

The particle shape and surface texture of an aggregate influence the properties of freshly mixed concrete more than the properties of hardened concrete. Rough-textured, angular, elongated particles require more water to produce workable concrete than do smooth, rounded, compact aggregates. Hence, aggregate particles that are angular require more cement to maintain the same water-cement ratio. However, with satisfactory gradation, both crushed and noncrushed aggregates (of the same rock types) generally give essentially the same strength for the same cement factor. Angular or poorly graded aggregates can also be more difficult to pump.

The bond between cement paste and a given aggregate generally increases as particles change from smooth and rounded to rough and angular. This increase in bond is a consideration in selecting aggregates for concrete where flexural strength is important or where high compressive strength is needed.

Resistance to Freezing and Thawing

The frost resistance of an aggregate, an important characteristic for exterior concrete, is related to its, porosity, absorption, permeability, and pore structure. An aggregate particle may absorb so much water (to critical saturation) that it cannot accommodate the expansion and hydraulic pressure that occurs during the freezing of water. If enough of the offending particles are present, the result can be expansion of the aggregate and possible disintegration of the concrete. If a single problem particle is near the surface of the concrete, it can cause a popout. Popouts generally appear as conical fragments that break out of the concrete surface. The offending aggregate particle, or a part of it, is usually found at the bottom of the void. Generally, it is coarse rather than fine aggregate particles, with higher porosity values, and medium-sized pores (0.1 to 5 um) that are easily saturated and cause concrete deterioration and popouts. Larger pores do not usually become saturated or cause concrete distress, and water in very fine pores may not freeze readily.

Potentially Harmful Materials

Harmful substances that may be present in aggregates include organic impurities, silt, clay, shale, iron oxide, coal, lignite, and certain lightweight and soft particles. In addition, rocks and minerals such as some cherts, strained quartz, and certain dolomitic limestones are alkali-reactive. Gypsum and anhydrite may cause sulfate attack. Certain aggregates, such as some shales, will cause popouts by swelling (simply by absorbing water) or by freezing of absorbed water. Most specifications limit the permissible amounts of these substances. The performance history of an aggregate should be a determining factor in setting the limits for harmful substances.

NATURAL AGGREGATES

Some natural aggregate deposits, called pit-run gravel, consist of gravel and sand that can be readily used in concrete after minimal processing. Natural gravel and sand are usually dug or dredged from a pit, river, lake, or seabed. Crushed stone is produced by crushing quarry rock, boulders, cobbles, or large-size gravel. Aggregates are usually washed and graded at the pit or plant. Some variation in the type, quality, cleanliness, grading, moisture content, and other properties is expected. Close to half of the coarse aggregates used in portland cement concrete in North America are gravels; most of the remainder are crushed stones.

Naturally occurring concrete aggregates are a mixture of rocks and minerals. A mineral is a naturally occurring solid substance with an orderly internal structure and a chemical composition that ranges within narrow limits. Rocks, which are classified as igneous, sedimentary, or metamorphic, depending on origin, are generally composed of several minerals. For example, granite contains quartz, feldspar, mica, and a few other minerals; most limestones consist of calcite, dolomite, and minor amounts of quartz, feldspar, and clay. Weathering and erosion of rocks produce particles of stone, gravel, sand, silt, and clay.

FIBERS

Fibers have been used in construction materials for many centuries. The last three decades have seen a growing interest in the use of fibers in ready-mixed concrete, precast concrete, and shotcrete. Fibers made from steel, plastic, glass, and natural materials (such as wood cellulose) are available in a variety of shapes, sizes, and thicknesses; they may be round, flat, crimped, and deformed, with typical lengths of 6 to 150 mm (0.25 to 6 inches) and thicknesses ranging from 0.005 to 0.75 mm (0.0002 to 0.03 inch). They are added to concrete during mixing. The main factors that control the performance of the composite material are:

- Physical properties of fibers and matrix
- Strength of bond between fibers and matrix

Although the basic governing principles are the same, there are several characteristic differences between conventional reinforcement and fiber systems:

- Fibers are generally distributed throughout a given cross section, whereas reinforcing bars or wires are placed only where required.
- Most fibers are relatively short and closely spaced, as compared with continuous reinforcing bars or wires.
- It is generally not possible to achieve the same area of reinforcement to area of concrete using fibers, as compared to using a network of reinforcing bars or wires.
- Fibers are typically added to concrete in low-volume dosages (often less than 1 percent), and have been shown to be effective in reducing plastic shrinkage cracking.
- Fibers typically do not significantly alter free shrinkage of concrete; however, at high enough dosages they can increase the resistance to cracking and decrease crack width.

Synthetic Fibers

Synthetic fibers are man-made fibers resulting from research and development in the petrochemical and textile industries. Fiber types that are used in portland cement concrete are: acrylic, aramid, carbon, nylon, polyester, polyethylene, and polypropylene.

Synthetic fibers can reduce plastic shrinkage and subsidence cracking and may help concrete after it is fractured. Polypropylene fibers, the most popular of the synthetics, are chemically inert, hydrophobic, and lightweight. They are produced as continuous cylindrical monofilaments that can be chopped to specified lengths or cut as films and tapes and formed into fine fibrils of rectangular cross section.

Used at a rate of at least 0.1 percent by volume of concrete, polypropylene fibers reduce plastic shrinkage cracking and subsidence cracking over steel reinforcement. The presence of polypropylene fibers in concrete may reduce settlement of aggregate particles, thus reducing capillary bleed channels. Polypropylene fibers can help reduce spalling of high-strength, low-permeability concrete exposed to fire in a moist condition.

Multiple Fiber Systems

For a multiple fiber system, two or more fibers are blended into one system. A common macrofiber blended with a newly developed microfiber leads to a closer fiber-to-fiber spacing, which reduces microcracking and increases tensile strength. A blend of steel and polypropylene fibers has also been used for some applications.

AIR-ENTRAINED CONCRETE

One of the greatest advances in concrete technology was the development of air-entrained concrete in the mid-1930s. Today, air entrainment is recommended for nearly all concretes, principally to improve freeze-thaw resistance when exposed to water and deicing chemicals. However, there are other important benefits of entrained air in both freshly mixed and hardened concrete. Air-entrained concrete is produced by using either an air-entraining cement or adding an air-entraining admixture during batching. The air-entraining admixture stabilizes bubbles formed during the mixing process, enhances the incorporation of bubbles of various sizes by lowering the surface tension of the mixing water, impedes bubble coalescence, and anchors bubbles to cement and aggregate particles.

Entrained air bubbles are not like entrapped air voids, which occur in all concretes as a result of mixing, handling, and placing, and are largely a function of aggregate characteristics. Intentionally entrained air bubbles are extremely small in size, between 10 and 1000 μm in diameter, whereas entrapped voids are usually 1000 μm (1 mm) or larger. The majority of the entrained air voids in normal concrete are between 10 μm and 100 μm in diameter. The bubbles are not interconnected; they are well dispersed and randomly distributed. Non-air-entrained concrete with a 25-mm (1-inch) maximum-size aggregate has an air content of approximately 1.5 percent. This same mixture airentrained for severe frost exposure would require a total air content of about 6 percent, made up of both the coarser "entrapped" air voids and the finer "entrained" air voids.

Properties of Air-Entrained Concrete

Freeze-Thaw Resistance

The resistance of hardened concrete to freezing and thawing in a moist condition is significantly improved by the use of intentionally entrained air, even when various deicers are involved.

As the water in moist concrete freezes, it produces osmotic and hydraulic pressures in the capillaries and pores of the cement paste and aggregate. If the pressure exceeds the tensile strength of the paste or aggregate, the cavity will dilate and rupture. The accumulative effect of successive freeze-thaw cycles and disruption of the paste and aggregate eventually causes significant expansion and deterioration of the concrete. Deterioration is visible in the form of cracking, scaling, and crumbling.

Hydraulic pressures are caused by the 9 percent expansion of water upon freezing; in this process, growing ice crystals displace unfrozen water. If a capillary is above critical saturation (91.7 percent filled with water), hydraulic pressures result as freezing progresses. At lower water contents, no hydraulic pressure should exist.

Entrained air voids act as empty chambers in the paste where freezing and migrating water can enter, thus relieving the pressures described above and preventing damage to the concrete. Upon thawing, most of the water returns to the capillaries due to capillary action and pressure from air compressed in the bubbles. Thus, the bubbles are ready to protect the concrete from the next cycle of freezing and thawing.

The pressure developed by water as it expands during freezing depends largely on the distance the water must travel to the nearest air void for relief. Therefore, the voids must be spaced close enough to reduce the pressure below that which would exceed the tensile strength of the concrete. The amount of hydraulic pressure is also related to the rate of freezing and the permeability of the paste.

The spacing and size of air voids are important factors contributing to the effectiveness of air entrainment in concrete. ASTM C 457 describes a method of evaluating the air-void system in hardened concrete.

Freeze-thaw resistance is also significantly increased with the use of the following: (1) a good-quality aggregate, (2) a low water-to-cementing materials ratio (maximum 0.45), (3) a minimum cementitious

RECOMMENDED TOTAL TARGET AIR CONTENT FOR CONCRETE

NOMINAL MAXIMUM SIZE AGGREGATE, MM (IN.)	AIR CONTENT, PERCENT*		
	SEVERE EXPOSURE**	MODERATE EXPOSURE†	MILD EXPOSURE††
<9.5 (⅜)	9	7	5
9.5 (⅜)	7½	6	4½
12.5 (½)	7	5½	4
19.0 (¾)	6	5	3½
25.0 (1)	6	4½	3
37.5 (1½)	5½	4½	2½
50 (2)‡	5	4	2
75 (3)‡	4½	3½	1½

*Project specifications often allow the air content of the concrete to be within -1 to +2 percentage points of the table target values.
**Concrete exposed to wet-freeze-thaw conditions, deicers, or other aggressive agents.
†Concrete exposed to freezing but not continually moist, and not in contact with deicers or aggressive chemicals.
††Concrete not exposed to freezing conditions, deicers, or aggressive agents.
‡These air contents apply to the total mix, as for the preceding aggregate sizes. When testing these concretes, however, aggregate larger than 37.5 mm (1½ inches) is removed by handpicking or sieving, and air content is determined on the minus 37.5 mm (1½ inches) fraction of mix. (Tolerance on air content as delivered applies to this value.)

Phillip Arnold, L. M. Scofield Company

materials content of 335 kg/m³ (564 lb/yd³), (4) proper finishing and curing techniques, and (5) a compressive strength of 28 MPa (4000 psi) when exposed to repeated freeze-thaw cycles. Even non-air-entrained concretes will be more freeze-thaw-resistant with a low water-cement ratio.

Concrete elements should be properly drained and kept as dry as possible, as greater degrees of saturation increase the likelihood of distress due to freeze-thaw cycles. Concrete that is dry or contains only a small amount of moisture in service is essentially not affected by even a large number of cycles of freezing and thawing.

Deicer-Scaling Resistance

Deicing chemicals used for snow and ice removal can cause and aggravate surface scaling. The damage is primarily a physical action. Deicer scaling of inadequately air-entrained or non-air-entrained concrete during freezing is believed to be caused by a buildup of osmotic and hydraulic pressures in excess of the normal hydraulic pressures produced when water in concrete freezes. These pressures become critical and result in scaling unless entrained air voids are present at the surface and throughout the sample to relieve the pressure. The hygroscopic (moisture-absorbing) properties of deicing salts also attract water and keep the concrete more saturated, increasing the potential for freeze-thaw deterioration. However, properly designed and placed air-entrained concrete will withstand deicers for many years.

Studies have also shown that, in absence of freezing, the formation of salt crystals in concrete (from external sources of chloride, sulfate, and other salts) may contribute to concrete scaling and deterioration similar to the crumbling of rocks by salt weathering. The entrained air voids in concrete allow space for salt crystals to grow; this relieves internal stress similarly to the way the voids relieve stress from freezing water in concrete.

Deicers can have many effects on concrete and the immediate environment. All deicers can aggravate scaling of concrete that is not properly air entrained. Sodium chloride (rock salt), calcium chloride, and urea are the most frequently used deicers. In the absence of freezing, sodium chloride has little to no chemical effect on concrete but can damage plants and corrode metal. Calcium chloride in weak solutions generally has little chemical effect on concrete and vegetation but does corrode metal. Urea does not chemically damage concrete, vegetation, or metal. Nonchloride deicers are used to minimize corrosion of reinforcing steel and minimize groundwater chloride contamination. The use of deicers containing ammonium nitrate and ammonium sulfate should be strictly prohibited as they rapidly attack and disintegrate concrete. Magnesium chloride deicers have come under recent criticism for aggravating scaling.

Deicers can reach concrete surfaces in ways other than direct application, such as splashing by vehicles and dripping from the undersides of vehicles. Scaling is more severe in poorly drained areas because more of the deicer solution remains on the concrete surface during freezing and thawing. Air entrainment is effective in preventing surface scaling and is recommended for all concretes that may come in contact with deicing chemicals.

To provide adequate durability and scale resistance in severe exposures with deicers present, air-entrained concrete should be composed of durable materials and have the following characteristics: (1) a low water-to-cementitious-materials ratio (maximum 0.45); (2) a slump of 100 mm (4 inches) or less, unless a plasticizer is used; (3) a cementitious materials content of 335 kg/m³ (564 lb/yd³); (4) proper finishing after bleed water has evaporated from the surface; (5) adequate drainage; (6) a minimum of seven days moist curing at or above 10°C (50°F); (7) a compressive strength of 28 MPa (4000 psi) when exposed to repeated freeze-thaw cycling; and (8) a minimum 30-day drying period after moist curing, if concrete will be exposed to freeze-thaw cycles and deicers when saturated.

Finishing

Proper screeding, floating, and general finishing practices should not affect the air content. Overfinishing (excessive finishing) may reduce the amount of entrained air in the surface region of slabs—thus making the concrete surface vulnerable to scaling. Concrete to be exposed to deicers should not be steel-troweled.

Recommended Air Contents

The amount of air to be used in air-entrained concrete depends on a number of factors: (1) type of structure, (2) climatic conditions, (3) number of freeze-thaw cycles, (4) extent of exposure to deicers, and (5) the design life of the structure. The ACI 318 building code states that concrete that will be exposed to moist freezing and thawing or deicer chemicals must be air entrained with the target air content as listed in the "Recommended Total Target Air Content for Concrete" table for severe exposure.

When entrained air is not required for protection against freeze-thaw cycles or deicers, the target air contents for mild exposure given in the table can be used. Higher air contents can also be used as long as the design strength is achieved. As noted earlier, entrained air helps to reduce bleeding and segregation and can improve the workability of concrete.

ACI 318 limits the amounts of pozzolans and slag—10 percent for silica fume, 25 percent for fly ash, 50 percent for slag—as part of the cementitious material for deicer exposures.

PLACING AND FINISHING CONCRETE

Preparation before Placing

Preparation prior to placing concrete for pavements or slabs-on-grade includes compacting, trimming, and moistening the subgrade; erecting the forms; and setting the reinforcing steel and other embedded items securely in place. Moistening the subgrade is important, especially in hot, dry weather, to keep the dry subgrade from drawing too much water from the concrete; it also increases the immediate air-moisture level, thereby decreasing the amount of evaporation from the concrete surface. The strength or bearing capacity of the subgrade should be adequate to support anticipated structural loads.

In cold weather, concrete must not be placed on a frozen subgrade. Snow, ice, and other debris must be removed from within the forms before concrete is placed. Where concrete is to be deposited on rock or hardened concrete, all loose material must be removed, and cut faces should be nearly vertical or horizontal rather than sloping. Recently placed concrete requiring an overlay is usually roughened shortly after hardening to produce a better bond with the next placement. As long as no laitance (a weak layer of concrete), dirt, or loose particles are present, newly hardened concrete requires little preparation prior to placing freshly mixed concrete on it. When in service for a period of time, old, hardened concrete usually requires mechanical cleaning and roughening prior to placement of new concrete.

Forms should be accurately set, clean, tight, adequately braced, and constructed of or lined with materials that will impart the desired off-the-form finish to the hardened concrete. Wood forms, unless oiled or otherwise treated with a form-release agent, should be moistened before placing concrete; otherwise, they will absorb water from the concrete and swell. Forms should be made for removal with minimum damage to the concrete. With wood forms, use of too large or too many nails should be avoided to facilitate removal and reduce damage. For architectural concrete, the form-release agent should be a nonstaining material.

Reinforcing steel should be clean and free of loose rust or mill scale when concrete is placed. Unlike subgrades, reinforcing steel can be colder than 0°C (32°F) with special considerations. Mortar splattered on reinforcing bars from previous placements need not be removed from steel and other embedded items if the next lift is to be completed within a few hours; loose, dried mortar, however, must be removed from items that will be encased by later lifts of concrete.

All equipment used to place concrete must be clean and in good working condition. Standby equipment should be available in the event of a breakdown.

Depositing the Concrete

Concrete should be deposited continuously as near as possible to its final position without objectionable segregation. In slab construction, placing should be started along the perimeter at one end of the work with each batch discharged against previously placed concrete. The concrete should not be dumped in separate piles and then leveled and worked together; nor should the concrete be deposited in large piles and moved horizontally into final position. Such practices result in segregation because mortar tends to flow ahead of the coarser material.

In general, concrete should be placed in walls, thick slabs, or foundations in horizontal layers of uniform thickness; each layer should be thoroughly consolidated before the next is placed. The rate of placement should be rapid enough so that previously placed concrete has not yet set when the next layer of concrete is placed upon it. Timely placement and adequate consolidation will prevent flow lines, seams, and planes of weakness (cold joints) that result from placing freshly mixed concrete on concrete past initial set. Layers should be about 150 to 500 mm (6 to 20 inches) thick for reinforced members and 380 to 500 mm (15 to 20 inches) thick for mass work; the thickness will depend on the width between forms and the amount of reinforcement.

To avoid segregation, concrete should not be moved horizontally over too long a distance as it is being placed in forms or slabs. In some work, such as placing concrete in sloping wingwalls or beneath window openings in walls, it is necessary to move the concrete horizontally within the forms, but this should be kept to a minimum.

Phillip Arnold, L. M. Scofield Company

Where standing water is present, concrete should be placed in a manner that displaces the water ahead of the concrete but does not allow water to be mixed in with the concrete; to do so will reduce the quality of the concrete. In all cases, water should be prevented from collecting at the ends, in corners, and along faces of forms. Care should be taken to avoid disturbing saturated subgrade soils so they maintain sufficient bearing capacity to support structural loads.

Chutes and drop chutes are used to move concrete to lower elevations without segregation and spattering of mortar on reinforcement and forms. Properly designed concrete has been allowed to drop by free fall into caissons.

Concrete is sometimes placed through openings, called windows, in the sides of tall, narrow forms. When a chute discharges directly through the opening without controlling concrete flow at the end of the chute, there is danger of segregation. A collecting hopper should be used outside the opening to permit the concrete to flow more smoothly through the opening; this will decrease the tendency to segregate.

When concrete is placed in tall forms at a fairly rapid rate, some bleed water may collect on the top surface, especially with non-air-entrained concrete. Bleeding can be reduced by placing more slowly and by using concrete of a stiffer consistency, particularly in the lower portion of the form. When practical, concrete should be placed to a level 300 mm to 400 mm (about a foot) below the top of tall forms, and an hour or so allowed for the concrete to partially set. Placing should resume before the surface hardens to avoid formation of a cold joint. If practical to work around vertical reinforcing steel, it is good practice to overfill the form by 25 mm (an inch) or so and cut off the excess concrete after it has stiffened and bleeding has ceased.

In monolithic placement of deep beams, walls, or columns, to avoid cracks between structural elements, concrete placement should stop (usually about 1 hour) to allow settlement of the deep element before concreting is continued in any slabs, beams, or girders framing into them. The delay should be short enough to allow the next layer of concrete to knit with the previous layer by vibration, thus preventing cold joints and honeycombing. Haunches and column capitals are considered part of the floor or roof slab and should be placed integrally with them.

CONSOLIDATING CONCRETE

Consolidation is the process of compacting fresh concrete; to mold it within the forms and around embedded items and reinforcement; and to eliminate stone pockets, honeycomb, and entrapped air. It should not remove significant amounts of intentionally entrained air in air-entrained concrete.

Consolidation is accomplished by hand or by mechanical methods. The method chosen depends on the consistency of the mixture and the placing conditions, such as complexity of the formwork and amount and spacing of reinforcement. Generally, mechanical methods using either internal or external vibration are the preferred methods of consolidation.

Even in highly reinforced elements, proper mechanical consolidation makes possible the placement of stiff mixtures with low water-cement ratios and high coarse-aggregate contents associated with high-quality concrete.

Vibration

Vibration, either internal or external, is the most widely used method for consolidating concrete. When concrete is vibrated, the internal friction between the aggregate particles is temporarily destroyed and the concrete behaves like a liquid; it settles in the forms under the action of gravity, and the large entrapped air voids rise more easily to the surface. Internal friction is reestablished as soon as vibration stops.

Vibrators, whether internal or external, are usually characterized by their frequency of vibration, expressed as the number of vibrations per second (Hertz [Hz]), or vibrations per minute (vpm); they are also designated by the amplitude of vibration, which is the deviation in millimeters (inches) from the point of rest. The frequency of vibration can be measured using a vibrating reed tachometer. When vibration is used to consolidate concrete, a standby vibrator should be on hand at all times in the event of a mechanical breakdown.

Internal Vibration

Internal or immersion-type vibrators, often called spud or poker vibrators, are commonly used to consolidate concrete in walls, columns, beams, and slabs. Flexible-shaft vibrators consist of a vibrating head connected to a driving motor by a flexible shaft. Inside the head, an unbalanced weight connected to the shaft rotates at high speed, causing the head to revolve in a circular orbit. The motor can be powered by electricity, gasoline, or air. The vibrating head is usually cylindrical, with a diameter ranging from 20 to 180 mm ¾ to 7 inches). Some vibrators have an electric motor built right into the head, which is generally at least 50 mm (2 inches) in diameter. The dimensions of the vibrator head, as well as its frequency and amplitude in conjunction with the workability of the mixture affect the performance of a vibrator. Small-diameter vibrators have high frequencies ranging from 160 to 250 Hz (10,000 to 15,000 vpm) and low amplitudes ranging between 0.4 and 0.8 mm (0.016 and 0.03 inch). As the diameter of the head increases, the frequency decreases and the amplitude increases. The effective radius of action of a vibrator increases with increasing diameter. Vibrators with a diameter of 20 to 40 mm (¾ to 1½ inches) have a radius of action in freshly mixed concrete ranging between 75 and 150 mm (3 and 6 inches), whereas the radius of action for vibrators of 50- to 80-mm (2- to 3-inch) diameter ranges between 180 and 350 mm (7 and 14 inches).

Proper use of internal vibrators is important for best results. Vibrators should not be used to move concrete horizontally since this causes segregation. Whenever possible, the vibrator should be lowered vertically into the concrete at regularly spaced intervals and allowed to descend by gravity. It should penetrate to the bottom of the layer being placed and at least 150 mm (6 inches) into any previously placed layer. The height of each layer or lift should be about the length of the vibrator head, or generally a maximum of 500 mm (20 inches) in regular formwork.

In thin slabs, the vibrator should be inserted at an angle or horizontally in order to keep the vibrator head completely immersed. However, the vibrator should not be dragged around randomly in the slab. For slabs-on-grade, the vibrator should not make contact with the subgrade. The distance between insertions should be about one and a half times the radius of action so that the area visibly affected by the vibrator overlaps the adjacent previously vibrated area by a few centimeters (inches).

External Vibration

External vibrators can be form vibrators, vibrating tables, or surface vibrators such as vibratory screeds, plate vibrators, vibratory roller screeds, or vibratory hand floats or trowels. Form vibrators, designed to be securely attached to the outside of the forms, are especially useful (1) for consolidating concrete in members that are very thin or congested with reinforcement, (2) to supplement internal vibration, and (3) for still mixes where internal vibrators cannot be used.

Subgrade Preparation

Cracks, slab settlement, and structural failure can often be traced to an inadequately prepared and poorly compacted subgrade. The subgrade on which a slab-on-ground is to be placed should be well drained; of uniform bearing capacity; level or properly sloped; and free of sod, organic matter, and frost. The three major causes of nonuniform support are (1) the presence of soft unstable saturated soils or hard rocky soils, (2) backfilling without adequate compaction, and (3) expansive soils. Uniform support cannot be achieved by merely dumping granular material on a soft area. To prevent bridging and settlement cracking, soft or saturated soil areas and hard spots (rocks) should be dug out and filled with soil similar to the surrounding subgrade or, if a similar soil is not available, with granular material such as sand, gravel, or crushed stone. All fill materials must be compacted to provide the same uniform support as the rest of the subgrade. Proof-rolling the subgrade using a fully loaded dump truck or similar heavy equipment is commonly used to identify areas of unstable soils that need additional attention.

During subgrade preparation, it should be remembered that undisturbed soil is generally superior to compacted material for supporting concrete slabs. Expansive, compressible, and potentially troublesome soils should be evaluated by a geotechnical engineer; a special slab design may be required. The subgrade should be moistened with water in advance of placing concrete, but should not contain puddles or wet, soft, muddy spots when the concrete is placed.

Subbase

A satisfactory slab-on-ground can be built without a subbase. However, a subbase is frequently placed on the subgrade as a leveling course to equalize minor surface irregularities, enhance uniformity of support, bring the site to the desired grade, and serve as a capillary break between the slab and the subgrade.

Where a subbase is used, the contractor should place and compact to near maximum density a 100-mm- (4-inch-) thick layer of granular material such as sand, gravel, crushed stone, or slag. If a thicker subbase is needed for achieving the desired grade, the material should be compacted in thin layers about 100 mm (4 inches) deep, unless tests determine compaction of thicker a lift is possible. Subgrades and subbases can be compacted with small plate vibrators, vibratory rollers, or hand tampers. Unless the subbase is well compacted, it is better not to use a subbase; simply leave the subgrade uncovered and undisturbed.

Formwork

Edge forms and intermediate screeds should be set accurately and firmly to the specified elevation and contour for the finished surface. Slab edge forms are usually metal or wood braced firmly with wood or steel stakes to keep them in horizontal and vertical alignment. The forms should be straight and free from warping and have sufficient strength to resist concrete pressure without bulging. They should also be strong enough to support any mechanical placing and finishing equipment used.

Rain Protection

Prior to commencing placing of concrete, the owner and contractor should be aware of procedures to be followed in the event of rain during the placing operation. Protective coverings such as polyethylene sheets or tarpaulins should be available and on-site at all times. When rain occurs, all batching and placing operations should stop, and the fresh concrete should be covered to the extent that the rain does not indent the surface of the concrete or wash away the cement paste. When rain ceases, the covering should be removed and remedial measures taken, such as surface retexturing or reworking in-place plastic concrete, before concrete placing resumes.

Placing and Spreading

Placement should start at the far point of a slab and proceed toward the concrete supply source. The concrete, which should be placed as close as possible to its final position, should slightly overfill the forms and be roughly leveled with square-ended shovels or concrete rakes. Large voids trapped in the concrete during placing should be removed by consolidation.

Screeding (Strikeoff)

Screeding or strikeoff is the process of cutting off excess concrete to bring the top surface of a slab to proper grade. The template used in the manual method is called a straightedge, although the lower edge may be straight or slightly curved, depending on the surface specified. It should be moved across the concrete with a sawing motion while advancing forward a short distance with each movement. There should be a surplus of concrete against the front face of the straightedge to fill in low areas as the straightedge passes over the slab. A 150-mm (6-inch) slab needs a surcharge of about 25 mm (1 inch). Straightedges are sometimes equipped with vibrators that consolidate the concrete and assist in reducing the strikeoff work. This combination of straightedge and vibrator is called a vibratory screed. Screeding, consolidation, and bullfloating must be completed before excess bleed water collects on the surface.

Bullfloating or Darbying

To eliminate high and low spots and to embed large aggregate particles, a bullfloat or darby should be used immediately after strikeoff. The long-handle bullfloat is used on areas too large to reach with a short-handle darby. Highway straightedges are often used to obtain very flat surfaces. For non-air-entrained concrete, these tools can be made of wood; for air-entrained concrete, they should be of aluminum or magnesium alloy.

Bullfloating or darbying must be completed before bleed water accumulates on the surface. Care must be taken not to overwork the concrete, as this could result in a less durable surface. The preceding operations should level, shape, and smooth the surface and work up a slight amount of cement paste. Although sometimes no further finishing is required, on most slabs, bullfloating or darbying is followed by one or more of the following finishing operations: edging, jointing, floating, troweling, and brooming. A slight hardening of the concrete is necessary before the start of any of these finishing operations. When the bleed-water sheen has evaporated and the concrete will sustain foot pressure with only about 6 mm (¼ inch) indentation, the surface is ready for continued finishing operations.

Warning: One of the principal causes of surface defects in concrete slabs is finishing while bleed water is on the surface. If bleed water is worked into the surface, the water-cement ratio is significantly increased, which reduces strength, entrained-air content, and watertightness of the surface. Any finishing operation preformed on the surface of a concrete slab while bleed water is present can cause crazing, dusting, or scaling (PCA, 2001).

Floating and troweling the concrete before the bleeding process is completed may also trap bleed water under the finished surface, producing a weakened zone or void under the finished surface; this occasionally results in delaminations. The use of low-slump concrete with an adequate cement content and properly graded fine aggregate will minimize bleeding and help ensure maintenance-free slabs. For exterior slabs, air entrainment also reduces bleeding.

Edging and Jointing

Edging is required along all edge forms and isolation and construction joints in floors and outdoor slabs such as walks, drives, and patios. Edging densifies and compacts concrete next to the form where floating and troweling are less effective, making it more durable and less vulnerable to scaling, chipping, and popouts.

In the edging operation, the concrete should be cut away from the forms to a depth of 25 mm (1 inch) using a pointed mason trowel or a margin trowel. Then an edger should be held almost flat on the surface and run with the front of the tool slightly raised to prevent the edger from leaving too deep an impression. Proper jointing practices can eliminate unsightly random cracks. Contraction joints, also called control joints, are made with a hand groover or by inserting strips of plastic, wood, metal, or preformed joint material into the unhardened concrete. When hand methods are used to form control joints in exterior concrete slabs, mark the forms to accurately locate the joints. Prior to bullfloating, the edge of a thin strip of wood or metal may be used to knock down the coarse aggregate where the joint will be hand-tooled. The slab should then be jointed immediately after bullfloating or in conjunction with the edging operation. Control joints also can be made in hardened concrete by sawing.

Floating

After the concrete has been hand-edged and hand-jointed, it should be floated with a hand float or with a finishing machine using float blades.

The purpose of floating is threefold: (1) to embed aggregate particles just beneath the surface; (2) to remove slight imperfections, humps, and voids; and (3) to compact the mortar at the surface in preparation for additional finishing operations. The concrete should not be overworked, as this may bring an excess of water and fine material to the surface and result in subsequent surface defects.

Hand floats usually are made of fiberglass, magnesium, or wood. The metal float reduces the amount of work required because drag is reduced as the float slides more readily over the concrete surface. A magnesium float is essential for hand-floating air-entrained concrete, because a wood float tends to stick to and tear the concrete surface. The light metal float also forms a smoother surface than the wood float.

The hand float should be held flat on the concrete surface and moved with a slight sawing motion in a sweeping arc to fill in holes, cut off lumps, and smooth ridges. When finishing large slabs, power floats can be used to reduce finishing time.

Floating produces a relatively even (but not smooth) texture that has good slip resistance, and is often used as a final finish, especially for exterior slabs. Where a float finish is the desired final finish, it may be necessary to float the surface a second time after it has hardened a little more.

Marks left by hand edgers and groovers are normally removed during floating unless the marks are desired for decorative purposes; in such cases, the edger and groover should be used again after final floating.

Troweling

Where a smooth, hard, dense surface is desired, floating should be followed by steel troweling. Troweling should not be done on a surface that has not been floated; troweling after only bullfloating or darbying is not an adequate finishing procedure.

It is customary when hand-finishing large slabs to float and immediately trowel an area before moving the kneeboards. These operations should be delayed until the concrete has hardened sufficiently, so that water and fine material are not brought to the surface. Too long a delay, of course, will result in a surface that is too hard to float and trowel. The tendency, however, is to float and trowel the surface too soon. Premature floating and troweling can cause scaling, crazing, or dusting, and a surface with reduced wear resistance.

Spreading dry cement on a wet surface to take up excess water is a bad practice and can cause crazing. Such wet spots should be avoided, if possible, by adjustments in aggregate gradation, mix proportions, and consistency. When wet spots do occur, finishing operations should be delayed until the water evaporates. If a squeegee or hose is used to remove excess water, care must be taken so that excess cement paste is not removed with the water.

The first troweling may produce the desired surface free of defects. However, surface smoothness, density, and wear resistance can all be improved by additional trowelings. There should be a lapse of time between successive troweling to permit the concrete to become harder. As the surface stiffens, each successive troweling should be made with smaller trowels, using progressively more tilt and pressure on the trowel blade. The final pass should make a ringing sound as the trowel moves over the hardening surface.

A power trowel is similar to a power float, except that the machine is fitted with smaller, individual steel trowel blades that are adjustable for tilt and pressure on the concrete surface. When the first troweling is done by machine, at least one additional troweling by hand should be done to remove small irregularities. If necessary, tooled edges and joints should be rerun after troweling to maintain uniformity and true lines.

Exterior concrete should not be troweled for two reasons: (1) it can lead to a loss of entrained air caused by overworking the surface, and (2) troweled surfaces can be slippery when wet. Floating and brooming should be sufficient for outdoor concrete.

Brooming

Brooming should be performed before the concrete has thoroughly hardened, but it should be sufficiently hard to retain the scoring impression, to produce a slip-resistant surface. Rough scoring can be achieved with a rake, a steel-wire broom, or a stiff, coarse, fiber broom; such coarse-textured brooming usually follows floating. If a finer texture is desired, the concrete should be floated to a smooth surface and then brushed with a soft-bristled broom. Best results are obtained with brooms that are specially made for texturing concrete. Slabs are usually broomed transversely to the main direction of traffic.

Highway pavements are textured by "tining" the surface with stiff wires; this improves traction and reduces hydroplaning.

Curing and Protection

All newly placed and finished concrete slabs should be cured and protected from drying, from extreme changes in temperature, and from damage by subsequent construction and traffic.

Curing should begin immediately after finishing. Curing is needed to ensure continued hydration of the cement, strength gain of the concrete, and a minimum of early drying shrinkage.

Special precautions are necessary when concrete work continues during periods of adverse weather. In cold weather, arrangements should be made in advance for heating, covering, insulating, or enclosing the concrete. Hot weather work may require special precautions against rapid evaporation and drying and high temperatures.

Preparing Hardened Concrete

When freshly mixed concrete is placed on recently hardened concrete, certain precautions must be taken to secure a well-bonded, watertight joint. The hardened concrete must be clean, sound, and reasonably rough with some coarse aggregate particles exposed. Any laitance, soft mortar, dirt, wood chips, form oil, or other foreign materials must be removed since they could interfere with proper bonding of the subsequent placement.

The surface of old concrete upon which fresh concrete is to be placed must be thoroughly roughened and cleaned of all dust, surface films, deposits, loose particles, grease, oil, and other foreign material. In most cases, it will be necessary to remove the entire surface, down to sound concrete. Roughening and cleaning with lightweight chipping hammers, waterblasting, scarifiers, sandblasting, shotblasting, and hydrojetting are some of the satisfactory methods for exposing sound concrete. Care must be taken to avoid contamination of the clean surface before a bonding grout and overlay concrete are placed.

Partially set or recently hardened concrete may only require stiff-wire brushing. In some types of construction such as dams, the surface of each concrete lift is cut with a high-velocity air-water jet to expose clean, sound concrete just before final set. This is usually done 4 to 12 hours after placing. The surface must then be protected and continuously cured until concreting is resumed for the next lift.

Hardened concrete may be left dry or be moistened before new concrete is placed on it; however, the surface should not be wet or have any free-standing water. Laboratory studies indicate a slightly better bond is obtained on a dry surface than on a damp surface; however, the increased moisture level in the hardened concrete and in the environment around the concrete reduces water loss from the concrete mixture. This can be very beneficial, especially on hot, dry days.

For making a horizontal construction joint in reinforced concrete wall construction, good results have been obtained by constructing the forms to the level of the joint, overfilling the forms a few centimeters (inches), and then removing the excess concrete just before hardening occurs; the top surface then can be manually roughened with stiff brushes.

In the case of vertical construction joints cast against a bulkhead, the concrete surface generally is too smooth to permit proper bonding. So, particular care should be given to removal of the smooth surface finish before reerecting the forms for placing freshly mixed concrete against the joint. Stiff-wire brushing may be sufficient if the concrete is less than three days old; otherwise, bushhammering or sandblasting may be needed, followed by washing with clean water to remove all dust and loose particles.

Bonding New to Previously Hardened Concrete

Care must be used when making horizontal construction joints in wall sections where freshly mixed concrete is to be placed on hardened concrete. A good bond can be obtained by placing a rich concrete (higher cement and sand content than normal) in the bottom 150 mm (6 inches) of the new lift and thoroughly vibrating the joint interface. Alternatively, a cement-sand grout can be scrubbed into a clean surface immediately ahead of concreting.

A topping concrete mix for slabs can be bonded to the previously prepared base slab by one of the following procedures:

- *Portland cement-sand grouting.* A one-to-one cement-sand grout having a water-cement ratio of not greater than 0.45, mixed to a creamlike consistency, is scrubbed into the prepared dry or damp (no free water) base slab surface.
- *Latex.* A latex-bonding agent is added to the cement-sand grout and is spread in accordance with the latex manufacturer's direction.
- *Epoxy.* An approved epoxy-bonding agent is placed on the base concrete, prepared in accordance with the epoxy manufacturer's direction.

The bonding procedure should produce tensile bond strength with the base in excess of 1.0 MPa (150 psi).

Grout is placed just a short distance ahead of the overlay or top-course concrete. This method may also be applicable to horizontal joints in walls. The grout should not be allowed to dry out prior to the overlay placement; otherwise, the dry grout may act as a poor surface for bonding. The surface of the base slab should have been prepared by one of the methods discussed previously.

MAKING JOINTS IN SLABS AND WALLS

The following three types of joints are common in concrete construction: isolation joints, contraction joints, and construction joints.

Isolation Joints

Isolation joints permit both horizontal and vertical differential movements at adjoining parts of a structure. They are used between pours of concrete, at specified distances to allow for expansion and contraction, and wherever new concrete abuts existing concrete or structures.

Isolation-joint material (often called expansion-joint material) can be as thin as 6 mm (¼ inch) or less, but 13-mm (½-inch) material is commonly used. Care should be taken to ensure that all the edges for the full depth of the slab are isolated from adjoining construction; otherwise, cracking can occur.

Contraction Joints

Contraction joints provide for movement in the plane of a slab or wall and induce controlled cracking caused by drying and thermal shrinkage at preselected locations. Contraction joints (also sometimes called control joints) should be constructed to permit transfer of loads perpendicular to the plane of a slab or wall. If no contraction joints are used, or if they are too widely spaced in slabs-on-ground or in lightly reinforced walls, random cracks may occur; cracks are most likely when drying and thermal shrinkage produce tensile stresses in excess of the concrete's tensile strength.

Contraction joints in slabs-on-ground can be made in several ways. One of the most common methods is to saw a continuous straight slot in the top of the slab. This creates a plane of weakness in which a crack will form. Vertical loads are transmitted across a contraction joint by aggregate interlock between the opposite faces of the crack, providing the crack is not too wide and the spacing between joints is not too great. Crack widths at saw-cut contraction joints that exceed 0.9 mm (0.035 inch) do not reliably transfer loads. The effectiveness of load transfer by aggregate interlock depends on more than crack width. Other factors include slab thickness, subgrade support, load magnitude, repetitions of load, and aggregate angularity. Steel dowels may be used to increase load transfer at contraction joints when heavy wheel loads are anticipated.

Sawing must be coordinated with the setting time of the concrete. It should be started as soon as the concrete has hardened sufficiently, to prevent aggregates from being dislodged by the saw (usually within 4 to 12 hours after the concrete hardens); sawing should be completed before drying shrinkage stresses become large enough to produce cracking. The timing depends on factors such as mix proportions, ambient conditions, and type and hardness of aggregates. New dry-cut sawing techniques allow saw cutting to take place shortly after final finishing is completed.

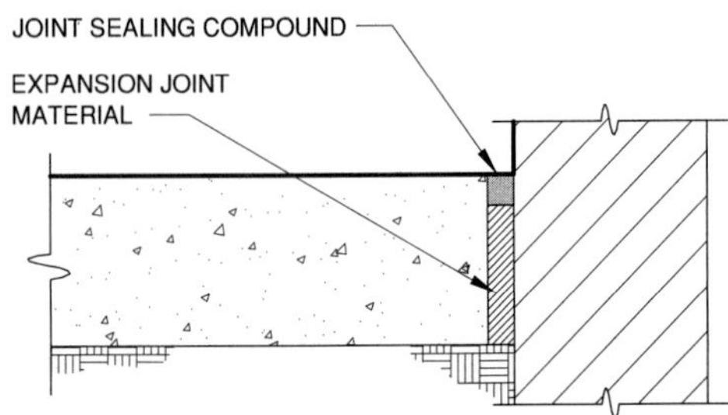

These joints permit horizontal and vertical movements between abutting faces of a slab and fixed parts of a structure.

ISOLATION JOINTS

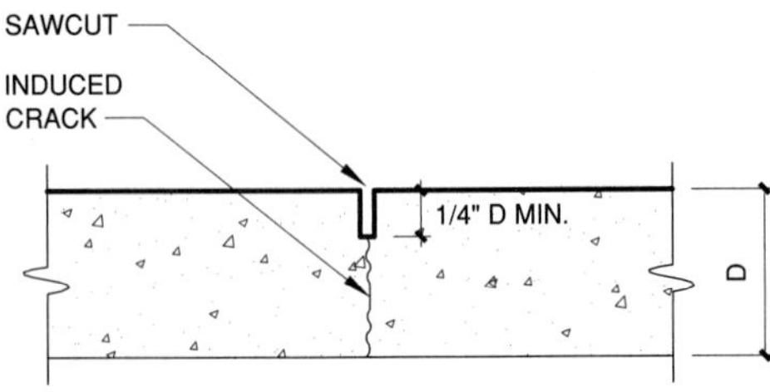

SAWED CONTRACTION JOINT

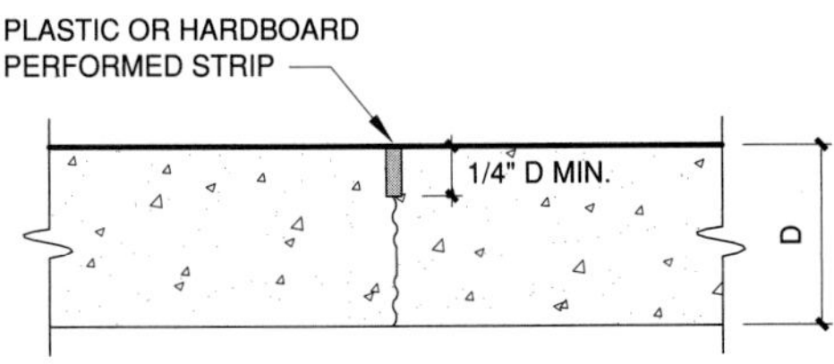

PREMOLDED INSERT CONTRACTION JOINT

These joints provide for horizontal movement in the plane of a slab or wall and induce controlled cracking caused by drying and thermal shrinkage.

CONTRACTION JOINTS

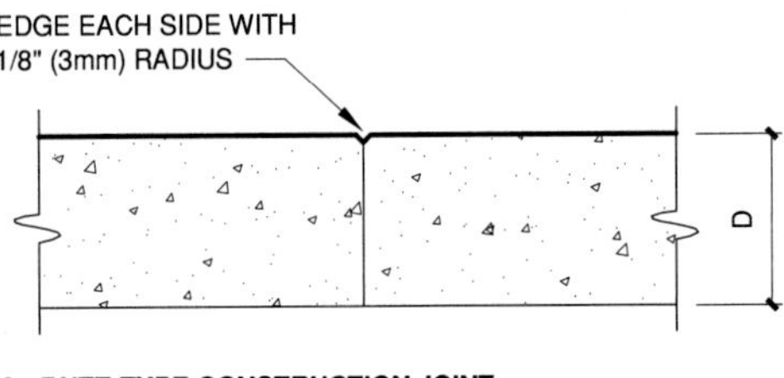

A. BUTT-TYPE CONSTRUCTION JOINT

EDGE EACH SIDE WITH 1/8" (3mm) RADIUS

D

SMOOTH DOWEL BAR COATED TO PREVENT BOND

PREVENT BOND

B. BUTT-TYPE CONSTRUCTION JOINT WITH DOWELS

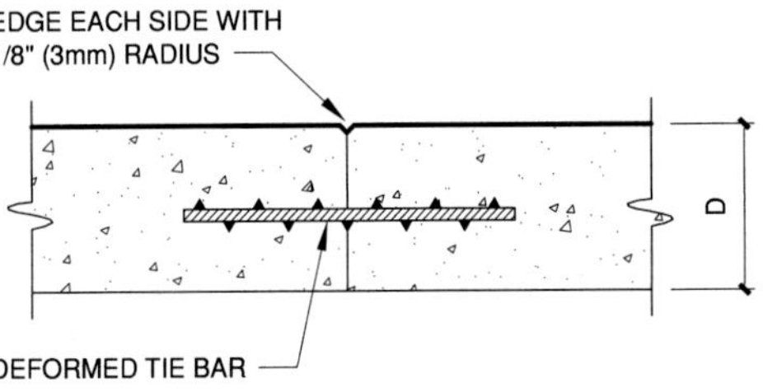

C. BUTT-TYPE CONSTRUCTION JOINT WITH TIE BARS (NOT A CONTRACTION JOINT)

Construction joints are stopping places in the process of construction. Construction joint types (A) and (B) are also used as contraction joints. The construction joint with the deformed (type C) does not allow for movement from expansion or contraction at the joint

CONSTRUCTION JOINTS

Generally, the slab should be cut before the concrete cools, when the concrete sets enough to prevent raveling or tearing while saw cutting, and before drying-shrinkage cracks start to develop.

Contraction joints also can be formed in the fresh concrete with hand groovers or by placing strips of wood, metal, or preformed joint material at the joint locations. The top of the strips should be flush with the concrete surface. Contraction joints, whether sawed, grooved, or preformed, should extend into the slab to a depth of at least one-fourth the slab thickness, or a minimum of 25 mm (1 inch) deep. It is recommended that the joint depth not exceed one-third the slab thickness if load transfer from aggregate interlock is important.

Contraction joints in walls are also planes of weakness that permit differential movements in the plane of the wall. The thickness of the wall at a contraction joint should be reduced by 25 percent, preferably 30 percent. Under the guidance of the design engineer, in lightly reinforced walls, half of the horizontal steel rebars should be cut at the joint. Care must be taken to cut alternate bars precisely at the joint. At the corners of openings in walls where contraction joints are located, extra diagonal or vertical and horizontal reinforcement should be provided to control cracking.

Contraction joints in walls should be spaced not more than about 6 meters (20 feet) apart. In addition, contraction joints should be placed where abrupt changes in wall thickness or height occur, and near corners—if possible, within 3 to 4 meters (10 to 15 feet). Depending on the structure, these joints may need to be caulked to prevent the passage of water through the wall. Instead of caulking, a waterstop (or both) can be used to prevent water from leaking through the crack that occurs in the joint.

The panels created by contraction joints should be approximately square. Panels with an excessive length-to-width ratio (more than 1½ to 1) are likely to crack at an intermediate location. In joint layout design, it is also important to remember that contraction (control) joints should only terminate at a free edge or at an isolation joint. Contraction joints should never terminate at another contraction joint, as cracking will be induced from the end of the terminated joint into the adjacent panel. This is sometimes referred to as sympathetic cracking.

Construction Joints

Construction joints are stopping places in the process of construction. A true construction joint should bond new concrete to existing concrete and permit no movement. Deformed tie bars are often used in construction joints to restrict movement. Because extra care is needed to make a true construction joint, they are usually designed and built to function as contraction or isolation joints. Oils, form-release agents, and paints are used as debonding materials. In thick, heavily loaded slabs, unbonded doweled construction joints are commonly used. For thin slabs, the flat-faced butt-type joint will suffice.

SPECIAL SURFACE FINISHES

Patterns and Textures

A variety of patterns and textures can be used to produce decorative finishes. Patterns can be formed with divider strips or by scoring or stamping the surface just before the concrete hardens. Textures can be produced with little effort and expense with floats, trowels, and brooms; more elaborate textures can be achieved with special techniques.

Exposed-Aggregate Concrete

An exposed-aggregate finish provides a rugged, attractive surface in a wide range of textures and colors. Select aggregates are carefully chosen to avoid deleterious substances; they are usually of uniform size such as 9.5 to 12.5 mm (⅜ to ½ inch) or larger. They should be washed thoroughly before use to ensure satisfactory bond. Flat or elongated aggregate particles should not be used since they are easily dislodged when the aggregate is exposed. Caution should be exercised when using crushed stone; it not only has a greater tendency to stack during the seeding operation (requiring more labor), but it also may be undesirable in some applications (pool decks, for example).

The aggregate should be evenly distributed or seeded in one layer onto the concrete surface immediately after the slab has been bullfloated or darbied. The particles must be completely embedded in the concrete. This can be done by lightly tapping with a wooden hand float, a darby, or the broad side of a piece of lumber; then, when the concrete can support a finisher on kneeboards, the surface should be hand-floated with a magnesium float or darby until the mortar completely surrounds and slightly covers all the aggregate particles.

Methods of exposing the aggregate usually include washing and brushing, using retarders, and scrubbing. When the concrete has hardened sufficiently, simultaneously brushing and flushing with water should expose the aggregate. In washing and brushing, the surface layer of mortar should be carefully washed away with a light spray of water and brushed until the desired exposure is achieved.

Since timing is important, test panels should be made to determine the correct time for exposing the aggregate without dislodging the particles. On large jobs, a water-insoluble retarder can be sprayed or brushed on the surface immediately after floating, but on small jobs this may not be necessary. When the concrete becomes too hard to produce the required finish with normal washing and brushing, dilute hydrochloric acid can be used. Surface preparation should be minimized and applicable local environmental laws should be followed.

Two other methods for obtaining an exposed aggregate surface are (1) the monolithic technique, whereby a select aggregate, usually gap-graded, is mixed throughout the batch of concrete, and (2) the

Phillip Arnold, L. M. Scofield Company

topping technique, in which the select exposed-aggregate is mixed into a topping that is placed over a base slab of conventional concrete.

The aggregate in exposed-aggregate concrete can also be exposed by methods other than those already discussed. The following techniques expose the aggregate after the concrete has hardened to a compressive strength of around 28 MPa (4000 psi):

- *Abrasive blasting* is best applied to a gap-graded aggregate concrete. The nozzle should be held perpendicular to the surface and the concrete removed to a maximum depth of about one-third the diameter of the coarse aggregate.
- *Waterblasting* can be used to texture the surface of hardened concrete, especially where local ordinances prohibit the use of sandblasting for environmental reasons. High-pressure water jets are used on surfaces that have or have not been treated with retarders.
- *Tooling,* or *bushhammering,* removes a layer of hardened concrete, and the aggregate is fractured at the surface. The surfaces attained can vary from a light scaling to a deep, bold texture obtained by jackhammering with a single-pointed chisel. Combs and multiple points can be used to produce finishes similar to some finishes used on cut stone.
- *Grinding and polishing* produces an exposed-aggregate concrete such as terrazzo, which is primarily used indoors. This technique is done in several successive steps using either a stone grinder or diamond-disk grinder. Each successive step uses finer grit than the preceding one. A polishing compound and buffer can then be used for a honed finish.

Regardless of the method employed, it is wise for the contractor to make a preconstruction mock-up (field sample) for each finish to determine the timing and steps involved; in addition, the mock-up is used to obtain aesthetic approval from the architect and owner.

Colored Finishes

Colored concrete finishes for decorative effects in both interior and exterior applications can be achieved by four different methods: (1) the one-course or integral method, (2) the two-course method, (3) the dry-shake method, and (4) stains and paints.

Color pigments added to the concrete in the mixer to produce a uniform color is the basis for the one-course method. Both natural and synthetic pigments are satisfactory if they are (1) insoluble in water, (2) free from soluble salts and acids, (3) fast to sunlight, (4) fast to alkali and weak acids, (5) limited to small amounts of calcium sulphate, and (6) ground fine enough so that 90 percent passes a 45-micron screen. Use only the minimum amount necessary to produce the desired color and not more than 10 percent by weight of the cement.

In the two-course method, a base slab is placed and left with a rough texture to bond better to a colored topping layer. As soon as the base slab can support a cement mason's weight, the topping course can be placed. If the base slab has hardened, prepare a bonding grout for the base slab prior to placing the topping mix. The topping mix is normally 13 mm (½ inch) to 25 mm (1 inch) thick, with a ratio of cement to sand of 1:3 or 1:4. The mix is floated and troweled in the prescribed manner. The two-course method is more commonly used because it is more economical than the one-course method.

In the dry-shake method, a prepackaged dry color material is cast onto the surface of a concrete slab. The dry-shake material is applied after the concrete has been screeded and darbied or bullfloated, excess moisture has evaporated from the surface, and preliminary floating has been done. Two-thirds of the dry material is shaken evenly by hand over the surface and thoroughly floated into the surface in a manner that evenly distributes the material. Immediately, the rest of the material is cast onto the surface and floated as before. The surface can then be troweled at the same time as a typical slab. For exterior surfaces that will be exposed to freezing and thawing, little or no troweling followed by brooming with a soft bristle concrete broom is usually sufficient.

Stains, Paints, and Clear Coatings

Many types of stains, paints and clear coatings can be applied to concrete surfaces. Among the principal paints used are portland cement base, latex-modified portland cement, and latex (acrylic and polyvinyl acetate) paints. However, stains and paints are used only when it is necessary to color existing concrete. It is difficult to obtain a uniform color with dyes or stains; therefore, the manufacturer's directions should be closely followed.

Portland cement based paints can be used on either interior or exterior exposures. The surface of the concrete should be damp at the time of application and each coat should be dampened as soon as possible without disturbing the paint. Damp curing of conventional portland cement paint is essential. On open-textured surfaces, such as concrete masonry, the paint should be applied with stiff-bristle brushes (scrub brushes). Paint should be worked well into the surface. For concrete with a smooth or sandy finish, whitewash or Dutch-type calcimine brushes are best.

The latex materials used in latex-modified portland cement paints retard evaporation, thereby retaining the necessary water for hydration of the portland cement. When using latex-modified paints, moist curing is not required.

Most latex paints are resistant to alkali and can be applied to new concrete after 10 days of good drying weather. The preferred method of application is by long-fiber, tapered nylon brushes 100 to 150 mm (4 to 6 inches) wide; however, roller or spray methods can also be used. The paints may be applied to damp, but not wet, surfaces. If the surface is moderately porous, or if extremely dry conditions prevail, prewetting the surface is advisable.

Clear coatings are frequently used on concrete surfaces to (1) prevent soiling or discoloration of the concrete by air pollution; (2) to facilitate cleaning the surface if it does become dirty; (3) to brighten the color of the aggregates; and (4) to render the surface water-repellent and, thus, prevent color change due to rain and water absorption. The better coatings often consist of methyl methacrylate forms of acrylic resin, as indicated by a laboratory evaluation of commercial clear coatings. The methyl methacrylate coatings should have a higher viscosity and solids content when used on smooth concrete, since the original appearance of smooth concrete is more difficult to maintain than the original appearance of exposed-aggregate concrete.

Other materials, such as silane and siloxane penetrating sealers, are commonly used as water repellents for many exterior concrete applications.

SPECIAL TYPES OF CONCRETE

White Concrete

White portland cement is used to produce white concrete, a widely used architectural material. It is also used in mortar, plaster, stucco, terrazzo, and portland cement paint. White portland cement is manufactured from raw materials of low iron content; it conforms to ASTM C 150 (AASHTO M 85) even though these specifications do not specifically mention white portland cement. White concrete is made with aggregates and water that contain no materials that will discolor the concrete. White or light-colored aggregates can be used. Oil that could stain concrete should not be used on the forms. Care must be taken to avoid rust stains from tools and equipment. Curing materials that could cause stains must be avoided.

Colored Concrete

Colored concrete can be produced by using colored aggregates or by adding color pigments (ASTM C 979) or both. When colored aggregates are used, they should be exposed at the surface of the concrete. This can be done several ways; for example, casting against a form that has been treated with a retarder. Unhydrated paste at the surface is later brushed or washed away. Other methods involve removing the surface mortar by sandblasting, waterblasting, bushhammering, grinding, or acid washing. If surfaces are to be washed with acid, a delay of approximately two weeks after casting is necessary. Colored aggregates may be natural rock, such as quartz, marble, and granite, or they may be ceramic materials.

Pigments for coloring concrete should be pure mineral oxides ground finer than cement; they should be insoluble in water, free of soluble salts and acids, colorfast in sunlight, resistant to alkalies and weak acids, and virtually free of calcium sulfate. Mineral oxides occur in nature and are also produced synthetically; synthetic pigments generally give more uniform results.

The amount of color pigments added to a concrete mixture should not be more than 10 percent of the mass of the cement. The amount required depends on the type of pigment and the color desired. For example, a dose of pigment equal to 1.5 percent by mass of cement may produce a pleasing pastel color, but 7 percent may be needed to produce a deep color. Use of white portland cement with a pigment will produce cleaner, brighter colors and is recommended in preference to gray cement, except for black or dark gray colors.

To maintain uniform color, do not use calcium chloride, and batch all materials carefully by weight. To prevent streaking, the dry cement and color pigment must be thoroughly blended before they are added to the mixer. Mixing time should be longer than normal to ensure uniformity.

In air-entrained concrete, the addition of pigment may require an adjustment in the amount of air-entraining admixture to maintain the desired air content.

Slabs or precast panels that are cast horizontally can be colored by the dry-shake method. Prepackaged, dry coloring materials consisting of mineral oxide pigment, white portland cement, and specially graded silica sand or other fine aggregate are marketed ready for use by various manufacturers.

After the slab has been bullfloated once, two-thirds of the dry coloring material should be broadcast evenly by hand over the surface. The required amount of coloring material can usually be determined from previously cast sections. After the material has absorbed water from the fresh concrete, it should be floated into the surface. Then the rest of the material should be applied immediately at right angles to the initial application, so that a uniform color is obtained. The slab should again be floated to work the remaining material into the surface.

Other finishing operations may follow depending on the type of finish desired. Curing should begin immediately after finishing, with precautions taken to prevent discoloring the surface.

PRECAUTIONS

Construction equipment and tools represent constant potential hazards to busy construction personnel. That's why hard hats are required on construction projects. It is therefore recommended that some sort of head protection, such as a hard hat or safety hat, be worn when working any construction job, large or small. Proper eye protection is essential when working with cement or concrete. Eyes are particularly vulnerable to blowing dust, splattering concrete, and other foreign objects. On some jobs, it may be advisable to wear full-cover goggles or safety glasses with side shields. Actions that cause dust to become airborne should be avoided. Local or general ventilation can control exposures below applicable exposure limits; respirators may be used in poorly ventilated areas, where exposure limits are exceeded or when dust causes discomfort or irritation.

REFERENCES

The foregoing text was derived from Portland Cement Association documents with permission. For further information, refer to "Design and Control of Concrete Mixtures." Numerous other important documents are available from the American Concrete Institute at www.aci-int.org and from the Portland Cement Association at www.portcement.org.

Phillip Arnold, L. M. Scofield Company

CONCRETE REINFORCEMENT: REINFORCING BARS AND WIRE

GENERAL

Steel reinforcement for concrete consists of reinforcing bars and welded wire fabric. Bars are manufactured by hot-roll process as round rods with lugs, or deformations, which inhibit longitudinal movement of the bar in the surrounding concrete. Bar sizes are indicated by numbers. For sizes #3 through #8, the numbers are the number of eighths of an inch in the nominal diameter of the bars. Numbers 9, 10, and 11 are round and correspond to the former 1 in., 1⅛ in., and 1¼ in. square sizes. Sizes #14 and #18 correspond to the former 1½ in. and 2 in. square sizes. The nominal diameter of a deformed bar is equal to the actual diameter of a plain bar with the same weight per foot as the deformed bar. Epoxy-coated, zinc-coated (galvanized), and stainless steel reinforcing bars are used when corrosion protection is needed; stainless steel also has nonmagnetic properties. In some instances, a fiber-reinforced plastic (FRP) rebar is used for highly specialized concrete reinforcement because of its high tensile strength and light weight, corrosion resistance, and dielectric (nonconductive) properties. FRP rebars are manufactured in the same sizes as steel rebars and also have deformations on the surface. Consult manufacturers for further information.

Welded wire fabric is used in thin slabs, shells, and other designs in which available space is too limited to give proper cover and clearance to deformed bars. Welded wire fabric, also called mesh, consists of cold drawn wire (smooth or deformed) in orthogonal patterns; it is resistance welded at all intersections.

Wire in the form of individual wire or groups of wires is used in the fabrication of prestressed concrete.

ASTM STANDARD REINFORCING BAR SIZES

ASTM SIZE DESIGNATION	AREA (SQ IN., ACTUAL)	WEIGHT (LB/FT, ACTUAL)	DIAMETER (IN., ACTUAL)
#18	4.00	13.600	2.257
#14	2.25	7.650	1.693
#11	1.56	5.313	1.410
#10	1.27	4.303	1.270
#9	1.00	3.400	1.128
#8	0.74	2.670	1.000
#7	0.60	2.044	0.875
#6	0.44	1.502	0.750
#5	0.31	1.043	0.625
#4	0.20	0.668	0.500
#3	0.11	0.376	0.375

Note

Metrication of reinforcing bars is being considered in the United States; as of October 1995, a decision had not been made about what metric rebar sizes would apply in the United States. Metrication may result in a reengineering of reinforced concrete structures using the new bar sizes.

SHRINKAGE AND TEMPERATURE REINFORCEMENT FOR STRUCTURAL CONCRETE

REINFORCEMENT		PERCENT OF CROSS-SECTIONAL AREA OF CONCRETE, ONE WAY
GRADE	TYPE	
40/50	Deformed bars	0.20
—	Welded wire fabric	0.18
60	Deformed bars	0.18

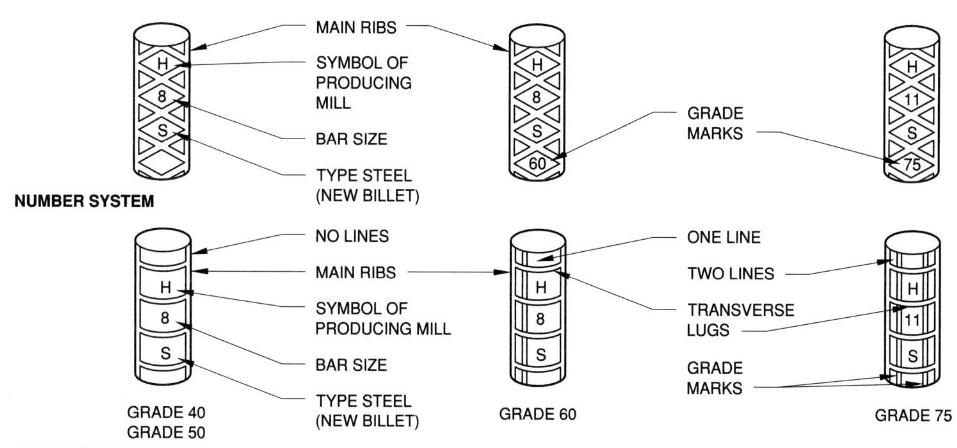

NOTE
Steel type grade marks: S—billet (A615), I—rail (A6161), IR—rail meeting supplementary requirements, S1 (A616), A—axle (A617), W—low alloy (A706).

REINFORCING BAR GRADE MARK IDENTIFICATION

STANDARD STEEL WIRE SIZES AND GAUGES

PLAIN WIRE NUMBER	DEFORMED WIRE NUMBER	ASW GAUGE NUMBER	FRACTIONAL DIAMETER (IN.)	DECIMAL DIAMETER (IN.)	AREA (SQ IN.)	WEIGHT (LB/ LIN. FT)
W20	D20	—	1/2	.505	.200	.680
—	—	7/0	31/64	.490	.189	.642
W18	D18	—	15/32	.479	.180	.612
—	—	6/0	5/32	.462	.168	.571
W16	D16	—	29/64	.451	.160	.544
—	—	5/0	7/16	.431	.146	.496
W14	D14	—	13/32	.422	.140	.476
—	—	4/0	13/32	.394	.122	.415
W12	D12	—	25/64	.391	.120	.408
W11	D11	—	3/8	.374	.110	.374
W10.5	—	—	3/8	.366	.105	.357
—	—	3/0	23/64	.363	.103	.350
W10	D10	—	23/64	.357	.100	.340
W9.5	—	—	11/32	.348	.095	.323
W9	D9	—	11/32	.338	.090	.306
—	—	2/0	11/32	.331	.086	.292
W8.5	—	—	21/64	.329	.085	.289
W8	D8	—	21/64	.319	.080	.272
W7.5	—	—	5/16	.309	.075	.255
—	—	1/0	5/16	.307	.074	.251
W7	D7	—	19/64	.299	.070	.238
W6.5	—	—	19/64	.288	.065	.221
—	—	1	19/64	.283	.063	.214
W6	D6	—	9/32	.276	.060	.204
W5.5	—	—	17/64	.265	.055	.187
—	—	2	17/64	.263	.054	.183
W5	D5	—	1/4	.252	.050	.170
—	—	3	15/64	.244	.047	.160
W4.5	—	—	15/64	.239	.045	.153
W4	D4	4	7/32	.226	.040	.136
W3.5	—	—	7/32	.211	.035	.119
—	—	5	13/64	.207	.034	.115
W3	—	—	3/16+	.195	.030	.102
W2.9	—	6	3/16+	.192	.029	.098
W2.5	—	7	3/16	.178	.025	.085
W2.1	—	8	11/64	.162	.021	.071
W2	—	—	5/32	.160	.020	.068
—	—	9	5/32	.148	.017	.058
W1.4	—	—	9/64	.124	.014	.048

Concrete Reinforcing Steel Institute, Schaumburg, Illinois; Gordon B. Batson, P.E., Potsdam, New York

COMMON STOCK STYLES OF WELDED WIRE FABRIC

NEW DESIGNATION (W-NUMBER)	OLD DESIGNATION (WIRE GAUGE)	STEEL AREA (IN./ SQ FT)		WEIGHT (LB/100 SQ FT)
		LONG.	TRANS.	
SHEETS AND ROLLS				
6 x 6 – W1.4 x W1.4	6 x 6 – 10 x 10	.028	.028	21
6 x 6 – W2.0 x W2.0	6 x 6 – 8 x 8	.040	.040	29
6 x 6 – W2.9 x W2.9	6 x 6 – 6 x 6	.058	.058	42
6 x 6 – W4.0 x W4.0	6 x 6 – 4 x 4	.080	.080	58
4 x 4 – W1.4 x W1.4	4 x 4 – 10 x 10	.042	.042	31
4 x 4 – W2.0 x W2.0	4 x 4 – 8 x 8	.060	.060	43
4 x 4 – W2.9 x W2.9	4 x 4 – 6 x 6	.087	.087	62
4 x 4 – W4.0 x W4.0	4 x 4 – 4 x 4	.120	.120	85

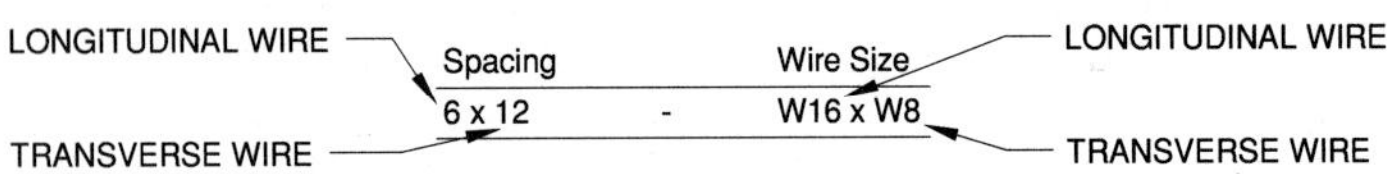

METHOD OF DESIGNATION FOR WELDED WIRE FABRIC

REINFORCING BAR GRADES AND STRENGTHS

ASTM SPEC	MIN. YIELD STRENGTH (PSI)	MIN. TENSILE STRENGTH (PSI)	STEEL TYPE
Billet steel ASTM A 615 Grade 40 Grade 60 Grade 75	 40,000 60,000 75,000	 70,000 90,000 100,000	S
Rail steel ASTM A 616 Grade 50 Grade 60	 50,000 60,000	 80,000 90,000	R
Axle steel ASTM A 617 Grade 40 Grade 60	 40,000 60,000	 70,000 90,000	A
Low-alloy ASTM A 706 Grade 60	 60,000	 80,000	W
Deformed wire ASTM A 496 Welded fabric	 70,000	 80,000	—
Plain wire ASTM A 82 Welded fabric < W 1.2 Size ≥ W 1.2	 56,000 65,000	 70,000 75,000	—

Concrete Reinforcing Steel Institute, Schaumburg, Illinois; Gordon B. Batson, P.E., Potsdam, New York

ENVIRONMENTAL AND HEALTH CONSIDERATIONS OF CONCRETE

CONCRETE FUNDAMENTALS

Concrete can have many positive environmental qualities. It can be durable and high strength with the proper mix of cementitious materials, admixtures, aggregate, and water. It can have a high reflectance value to aid in heat island reduction. It is generally locally available. It can be used without finishes and, with the right mix, is resistant to weathering. It can be made porous to aid in stormwater infiltration and groundwater recharge. And, recycled materials can be incorporated into the mix, reducing the consumption of raw materials.

While the resources for aggregate and cement are abundant, they are limited in some areas, and more importantly, mining and extraction of the raw materials causes habitat destruction, air and water pollution, and depletion of nonrenewable fossil fuels. Also, many concrete structures today are not constructed to be durable, causing overuse of resources for their replacement (Mehta, 1998).

Concrete is increasingly made from a specific mix of composite materials beyond the traditional mix of cement, water, and aggregates (Aïtcin, 2000). Mineral components, recycled materials, and mineral admixtures are used that impart specific properties to the concrete. Some reduce the amount of cement, water, or virgin aggregrate required.

Industrial by-products such as fly ash, ground granulated blast-furnace slag, rice hull ash, and silica fume can replace a portion of cement in a concrete mix, using material that would otherwise be landfilled and resulting in less energy and resource use. Recycled materials can replace course and fine aggregate in a concrete mix. These materials are crushed concrete, foundry sand, crushed masonry bricks, slag, mineralized wood fiber shavings, and crushed recycled glass ("cullet").

Designing smaller structures and thinner concrete sections can reduce the total amount of materials and resources used to make concrete. However, thinner sections of walls and paving can increase the amount and size of reinforcing needed, potentially negating any resource savings.

Use of modular unit retaining wall systems set on a sand base can eliminate the need for extensive footings extending below the frostline. Use of pier foundation systems can use less concrete than spread footing foundation systems, and they are often formed with tubes made from recycled cardboard.

Excess concrete, not used in a pour is often landfilled, although cured waste concrete can be crushed and used as base aggregate. Also, retarding admixtures can be used before curing to extend a partial load of concrete for one or two days, then reactivate it for use (Spiegel, 2006).

Soil cement, a small amount of cement mixed with native soil, incorporates less virgin or offsite resources and reduces transportation energy, as on-site soil is usually used. Soil cement can be used in paving or formed applications (rammed earth and compressed earth block). Soil should be tested for appropriateness and to determine the most effective mix.

CEMENT AND CEMENT SUBSTITUTES

Portland cement production generates large volumes of CO_2, a significant greenhouse gas, and dust (Spiegel, 2006). CO_2 is thought to be a major contributor to global warming. Large volumes of CO_2 are generated by both the combustion of fuels to operate kilns and the conversion of limestone into lime. Some cement manufacturers are reducing their production of CO_2 with use of waste lime and energy efficiency measures such as efficient kilns or alternative fuel sources. While some burn waste for fuel such as old tires or coal sludge, others burn hazardous wastes, resulting in toxic metal releases into air or cement. Waste used for fuel is regulated by the EPA, so this issue should increasingly be reduced (Kibert, 2005). The Portland Cement Association (PCA) provides information on kiln type and fuel for cement companies by state.

Limestone used to produce cement is an abundant material, but is not renewable. The mining of stone disrupts habitat, causes erosion and sediment runoff, and negatively impacts air and waterways. Water pollution from cement production results in high levels of alkalinity that are toxic to fish and other species.

Strategies for minimizing the environmental impacts of cement are twofold: (1) reduce use of cement and (2) substitute appropriate alternatives, such as pozzolanic industrial by-products, for a portion of the cement in a concrete mix.

Less cement can be used by specifying a 56-day full-strength requirement instead of the traditional 28-day full-strength requirement. Research has shown that this results in a more durable structure (Aïtcin, 2000). It also allows use of higher volumes of fly ash and other industrial by-product admixtures.

Cement and water can be reduced with the use of high-performance concrete. High-performance concrete is concrete that has a low water/cement (W/C) or water/binder (W/B) ratio, often made possible through the use of superplasticizers. It results in concrete of higher compressive strength (6000 to 7200 psi as opposed to the typical concrete mix's 2200 to 3600 psi). It is considered to be economical as structures can be smaller, use less concrete and reinforcing steel, and require less formwork. High-performance concrete has a low porosity, which makes it more resistant to pollution and weathering. The life cycle of high-performance concrete has been estimated to be two to three times longer than that of usual concrete, and it can be recycled two to three times before it is transformed into road base aggregate (Aïtcin, 2000).

Use of white portland cement in paving applications produces a low albedo (high reflectivity) surface that can help reduce heat island effects by reflecting the heat of the sun. In cold climates use of highly reflective surfaces may not melt snow accumulation as quickly, and deicing chemicals, which can negatively impact water quality and wildlife, may be required.

Cement can also have negative impacts on human health. In powder form or while wet, it is highly alkaline and can burn lungs, skin, and eyes. Gloves, masks, and protective eyewear should be used when working with cement.

The environmental and human health effects of admixtures are not well documented. Some admixtures can cause skin, eye, or lung irritation. Others may be toxic to humans or the environment in other ways. When specifying an admixture, Material Safety Data Sheets should be cross referenced with toxics inventories at the US EPA (see "Useful Websites" below). Use of accelerating and freeze-prevention admixtures can be minimized by scheduling work at appropriate temperatures and seasons. In arid regions, use of superplasticizers and other water reducers can save water (Thompson and Sorvig, 2000).

Industrial By-Product Replacements for Cement

Fly ash (both class C and F), ground granulated blast-furnace slag (GGBF), cenospheres, rice hull ash, and silica fume are by-products of industrial processes that can be used to partially replace portland or blended cement. In addition to hydraulic or pozzolanic activity, their use can improve performance of the concrete. Because of the energy- and resource-consumptive nature of manufactured cement, it may be beneficial to substitute industrial by-products for a portion of the manufactured cement in a concrete mix, thereby preventing the material from being landfilled and reducing CO_2 emissions and resource consumption from use of new cement. Incorporation of industrial by-products to replace a portion of cement will often result in cost savings; however, availability of these by-products varies by region.

Fly ash and blast furnace slag are also sometimes blended with cement during the cement manufacturing process, resulting in reduced CO_2 emissions, a reduction in energy consumption, and increased production capacity (Kibert, 2005). ASTM C595 recommends that up to 40 percent coal fly ash by weight could be blended with cement to produce types IP and I(PM) cement. The same standard allows for up to 70 percent GGBF slag by weight for cement types IS and S.

Fly ash is currently used in around 50 percent of ready-mixed concrete. Class F fly ash is used at 15 to 25 percent by mass of cementitious material, and Class C fly ash, possessing pozzolanic qualities, is used at ratios of 15 to 40 percent (PCA). Over the past twenty years, extensive field studies have shown that percentages of 35 to 70 percent are feasible in some applications. "High-volume fly ash" (HVFA) concrete contains fly ash replacing 50 percent or more of the cement. HVFA concrete "reduces water demand, improves workability, minimizes cracking due to thermal shrinkage, and enhances durability to reinforcement corrosion, sulfate attach, and alkali silica expansion" (Mehta, 1998).

Fly ash increases the workability of concrete as the small glassy spherical particles act as a lubricant similar to a water-reducing admixture. Less water is required to produce a given slump. However, a reduction of bleed water can make fly ash concrete mixtures vulnerable to plastic shrinkage cracking when exposed to rapid drying conditions (Aïtcin, 2000).

Some fly ashes may extend initial setting times, but ultimately produce higher strength. The early strength developed is slightly less than that achieved with a cement-only design mix, but the later strengths are greater, sometimes resulting in less material required to accomplish a given structural need. Accelerating admixtures and the use of Type III cement, or pozzolans such as silica fume, can reduce initial setting times. Use of fly ash can result in decreased permeability of concrete, as it reacts with lime to close off

Meg Calkins, Ball State University, "Environmental and Health Considerations"

capillaries that allow the movement of moisture through the concrete (PATH, 2006). Class F, and some Class C, fly ashes increase the concrete's resistance to sulfate attack and alkali-aggregate reactivity. ACI 318 limits fly ash content to 25 percent for structures exposed to deicing chemicals; however, it has been suggested that this limit has been disproven in the field with higher-volume fly ash pavements performing well with deicer salts (Obla, Hill, and Martin, 2003). As fly ash concrete is ultimately higher strength than conventional concrete, in some applications less material is required to accomplish a given structural need.

Color of the concrete resulting from use of fly ash varies by type. Color ranges from lighter than portland cement to medium gray. Using the same supply source for the entire project can ensure color consistency (PCA).

Some Class C fly ashes may possess enough lime to completely replace portland cement in a conventional mix. Laboratory experiments have shown that it offers excellent performance in short-term strength gain, long-term strength, and workability (Cross, Stephens, and Vollmer, 2005); however, there has been limited application in the field.

Ground granulated blast-furnace (GGBF) slag, used in concrete, can replace between 25 and 50 percent by weight of the cement in the mix (EPA, 2006). GGBF slag is more readily available in steel processing regions of the United States. Use of slag can improve workability, strength, and durability of concrete (SCA, 2006).

Silica fume, a by-product of silicon metal or ferrosilicon alloy production, is another industrial by-product that can replace a portion of cement. Silica fume's chemical and physical properties make it a very reactive pozzolan. It has fine particle sizes, large surface area, and high SiO_2 content. Concrete containing silica fume can be very durable and have very high strength. It is available from some suppliers of concrete admixtures.

The quality of silica fume for use in concrete is specified in ASTM C 1240 and AASHTO M 307. Using silica fume in concrete, which is available in wet or dry form, can produce a compressive strength in excess of 15,000 psi. Silica-fume concrete with a low water content is highly resistant to penetration by chloride ions and helps block their migration to reinforcing steel. Flatwork containing silica-fume concrete generally requires less finishing effort than conventional concrete (Holland, 2005).

Rice hull ash is another industrial by-product that has potential to replace a portion of cement in a concrete mix. This material has been well tested but is not in widespread use.

AGGREGATE

Use of natural aggregates incurs environmental impacts and uses nonrenewable virgin resources. Mining, dredging, and extraction of aggregates alter plant and animal habitats and contribute to soil erosion and air and water pollution. The operation of mining equipment consumes energy and releases emissions from internal combustion engines. Mining near or in water bodies can cause sedimentation in water and disrupt aquatic habitats. Processing of aggregates, particularly the commonly used silica sand, releases particulates into the air that can cause eye and respiratory tract irritations in humans. Transport of aggregates uses energy and releases emissions. These emissions contribute to smog, global warming, and acid precipitation; they can also cause respiratory and cardiovascular problems.

Environmental impacts of transportation can be significant with heavy and bulky materials like aggregates. Using local or on-site materials for aggregate can minimize fuel use, resource consumption, and emissions.

Substituting recycled materials for virgin aggregate in concrete can have economic, environmental, and aesthetic advantages. It can save virgin resources and associated mining impacts. It also diverts material from landfills. Recycled materials are often less expensive than virgin aggregate, especially if demolition materials such as concrete, asphalt, or brick can be ground on-site and reused in new concrete. Concrete and asphalt are easily recycled on-site by bringing equipment to the site to break, remove, and crush the old material. This practice also saves on landfill and transportation fees.

Sources of recycled concrete are abundant. Other recycled products that can be used for coarse or fine aggregates are crushed blast-furnace slag, brick, glass, foundry sand, polystyrene, and mineralized wood shavings. Properties of recycled aggregates vary, and the concrete mix may need to be adapted to accommodate the variations. Currently, there is a lack of widespread data on recycled aggregates other than crushed concrete and glass. With use of any new aggregate, testing is necessary to account for variations in the aggregate's properties. For example, some recycled aggregates may be contaminated with sulfate from contact with sulfate rich soil or chloride ions from marine exposure (PATH, 2006).

Recycled concrete and crushed waste concrete can be used as both coarse and fine aggregate in new structures. It can also be used as base material under concrete structures. In addition to saving virgin resources, use of concrete can save money, particularly where gravel, sand, and stone are less readily available (PCA).

Recycling structures on-site is the most energy efficient and cost-effective use of recycled concrete aggregate, as transportation is virtually eliminated. Stone-crushing equipment can be brought to the site with recently developed measures to reduce noise and dust. The procedure for on-site concrete recycling involves (1) breaking and removing the old concrete; (2) crushing in primary and secondary crushers; (3) removal of reinforcing steel, wire mesh, and other embedded items; (4) grading and washing; and (5) stockpiling the resulting coarse and fine aggregates (PCA). During this process, care should be taken to avoid contamination of the aggregate with dirt, gypsum board, wood, and other foreign materials (PCA).

If there are no concrete structures being removed from the site, precrushed concrete can be obtained from widespread concrete recycling centers, often for a nominal price. The real cost of this aggregate is in the transportation from the recycling source to the construction site. For this reason, closer sources are desirable.

New concrete made with recycled concrete aggregate has good durability. Resistance to saturated freeze-thaw action, permeability, and carbonation have been found to be the same or better than with conventional aggregate concrete (PCA). Aggregate from recycled concrete has slightly different properties than conventional gravel aggregate. It generally has a lower specific gravity and higher absorption rate than natural aggregates. This is a result of the higher absorption of porous mortar and hardened cement paste within the recycled concrete aggregate. Absorption increases as coarse particle size decreases. Additional water may need to be added to the mix; however, prewetting the recycled aggregate will help decrease absorption of mix water (PCA). The compressive strength of recycled concrete aggregate is related to the compressive strength of the original concrete and the water cement ratio of the new concrete (PATH, 2006).

Blast-furnace slag, in addition to being ground and used as a cement substitute, is also substituted for both coarse and fine aggregates in concrete. During the period of cooling and hardening from its molten state, slag can be cooled in many ways to produce different types of slag products. Air-cooled blast-furnace slag (ACBFS) crushes to more angular cubic shapes with a rougher texture and greater surface area than most natural aggregates; therefore, it has a strong bond with cement. It is lighter weight than conventional aggregates, and water absorption is low. ACBFS is resistant to abrasion and weathering. Pelletized or expanded slag is quickly cooled with water or steam. It is used as a lightweight aggregate or crushed as a substitute for cement (NSA).

Foundry sand, 90 percent of which is currently landfilled, can serve as a partial replacement for fine aggregates in concrete and concrete masonry units.

Crushed masonry bricks can be used as coarse aggregate. Recent research has shown that they perform as well as conventional granite aggregate (Khalaf and DeVenny, 2004).

Mineralized wood fiber shavings from wood processing are chemically treated and mineralized and used in concrete masonry products such as stay-in-place concrete wall forms, free-standing sound barriers, and concrete blocks. The blocks are lighter weight than traditional aggregate blocks.

Crushed recycled glass, also called cullet, can be used as either fine or coarse aggregate in concrete. Sources are postconsumer glass bottles and postindustrial float glass cullet. An alkali-silica reaction (ASR) can occur between the alkali in cement and the silica in glass. This reaction creates a gel that swells in the presence of moisture, causing cracks and damage to the concrete. Green glass causes little or no ASR. Glass cullet can be coated to minimize the reaction, and finely ground glass used as fine aggregate has only minimal ASR (Meyer, 2000). Glass aggregate can impart a variety of color qualities to the concrete when aggregate is exposed or when the surface of the concrete is ground. Concrete with glass aggregate is used primarily in nonstructural applications such as sidewalks, paths, and nonstructural pads (PATH, 2006).

FORMWORK

Reuse of formwork can save resources and reduce material sent to landfills. Steel or plastic forms can be reused many times. Wood forms can be reused if form-release agents that don't damage the wood are used, such as those made from plant oils. Wood forms should be from a sustainably harvested source.

Earth forms can minimize use of resources and save cost of formwork materials. Footing width should be increased by 3 cm for each earth-form side. Concrete that will show above grade should be formed with formwork.

Fabric formwork systems can be used for forming footings. The flexible nature of the fabric requires minimal grading and ground leveling and uses minimal lumber. Fabric can be left in place and is often biodegradable.

Many form release agents are petroleum-based and contain volatile organic compounds (VOCs), which can cause environmental and human health problems. Diesel fuels and waste oils are also used, as they are inexpensive. When these products are sprayed on forms, they can release PCBs and heavy metals into the soil and air. Use of these form-release agents can prohibit reuse of forms. Plant-based form-release agents using rapeseed oil, soybean oil, or vegetable oil are usually VOC-free and allow reuse of forms (*Environmental Building News*, 1997).

Curing compounds should also be plant- or water-based and have less than 160 g/1 VOCs (Mendler, Odell, and Lazarus).

CONCRETE FINISHES

Integral and surface-applied concrete coloring agents use little extra material and can provide a finished look to a concrete slab, eliminating the need for additional veneer materials. However, some coloring agents contain heavy metals, such as chrome, lead, and cobalt, and toxic chemicals (Berge, 2000). Material Safety Data Sheets (MSDS) for a product should be carefully reviewed for human health and toxicity impacts before the product is specified.

Some pigments are made from recycled and reclaimed steel and iron. A natural iron oxide pigment called EnvironOxide is recovered from abandoned coal-mine drainage and produces earth tone pigments. Recycled glass fines from postconsumer or postindustrial processes are an alternative coloring agent that provides a slightly different effect than pigments.

Concrete sealers and stains can contain VOCs and other hazardous chemicals. While this is less of a concern in exterior applications, VOCs can affect workers in application, and runoff carrying compounds can negatively affect water and soil quality. Water-based sealers containing less than 100 g/1 VOCs and free of hazardous chemicals should be specified (Mendler, Odell, and Lazarus). Bio-based based, VOC-free sealers, such those made from soybean oil, are available for exterior applications (Building Green, 2006). Bio-based or water-based concrete cleaners are also available.

USEFUL WEBSITES

California Integrated Waste Management Board Recycled-Content Product Directory, www.ciwmb.ca.gov/RCP

Comprehensive Procurement Guidelines for recycled content and products, www.epa.gov/cpg

Green Seal, www.greenseal.org

Greenspec, Building Green, www.buildinggreen.com

Heat Island Group, Lawrence Berkeley National Laboratory, http://eetd.lbl.gov/HeatIsland/

National Recycling Coalition, www.nrc-recycle.org

National Toxicology Program (for listings of carcinogens), http://ntp-server.niehs.nih.gov/index.cfm?objectid=72016262-BDB7-CEBA-FA60E922B18C2540

Oikos Green Product Information, http://oikos.com/green_products/index.php

Partnership for Advancing Technology in Housing (PATH), http://www.toolbase.org/

Partnership for Advancing Technology in Housing: Technology Inventory—Cement and aggregate substitutes, http://www.toolbase.org/

Persistent Bioaccumulative and Toxic Chemical Program, www.epa.gov/opptintr/pbt

Slag Cement Association, http://www.slagcement.org

Toxics Release Inventory (TRI), www.epa.gov/tri

TRACI User's Guide, www.epa.gov/nrmrl/pubs/600r02052/600r02052.htm

U.S. EPA Comprehensive Procurement Guidelines for Cement and Concrete, http://www.epa.gov/cpg/products/cement.htm

Volatile Organic Compounds, www.epa.gov/iaq/voc.htm

Wastespec: Model Specifications for Construction Waste Reduction, Reuse and Recycling, www.tjcog.dst.nc.us/regplan/wastespec.htm

US EPA, www.epa.gov/heatisland

US EPA Wastewise program, www.epa.gov/wastewise

REFERENCES

Aïtcin, Pierre-Claude. 2000. "Cements of yesterday and today, Concrete of tomorrow." *Cement and Concrete Research* 30(2000): 1349–1359.

Berge, Bjørn. 2000. *The Ecology of Building Materials*. Oxford: Architectural Press.

Cross, Doug, Jerry Stephens, and Jason Vollmer. 2005. "Structural Applications of 100% Fly Ash Concrete." http://www.flyash.info/2005/131cro.pdf, accessed 12/12/05.

Environmental Building News. 1997. "A Green Release Agent for Concrete Forms." Brattleboro,Vermont: BuildingGreen, Inc.

Holland, Terrance C. 2005. *Silica Fume User's Manual*. Lovettsville, VA: Silica Fume Association and Washington, DC: Federal Highway Association.

Khalaf and DeVenny. 2004.

Kibert, Charles J. 2005. *Sustainable Construction*. Hoboken, NJ: John Wiley & Sons, Inc.

Mehta, P. K. 1998. "The Role Of Fly Ash In Sustainable Development," Concrete, Fly Ash and the Environment Proceedings, December 8, 1998. pp. 13–25.

Mendler, Sandra F., William Odell, and Maryanne Lazarus. 2006. *The HOK Guidebook to Sustainable Design*. Hoboken, NJ: John Wiley & Sons, Inc.

Meyer, Christian. 2000. "Concrete Materials Research at Columbia University." Concrete Materials Research Laboratory, http://www.civil.columbia.edu/meyer

National Slag Association (NSA). http://www.nationalslagassoc.org/PDF_files/NSABlastFurn.PDF, accessed 12/22/05.

Obla, Karthik H., Russell L. Hill, and Ross S. Martin. 2003. "HVFA Concrete – An Industry Perspective." *Concrete International*, August 2003.

Partnership for Advancing Technology in Housing: Technology Inventory—Aggregate Substitutes in Concrete, http://www.toolbase.org/techinv/techDetails.aspx?technologyID=160.

Portland Cement Association. "Concrete Thinking for a Sustainable World." http://www.cement.org/concretethinking/, accessed 4/14/06.

Slag Cement Association (SCA). http://www.slagcement.org/.

Spiegel, Ross. 2006. *Green Building Materials: A Guide to Product Selection and Specification*. Hoboken, NJ: John Wiley & Sons, Inc.

Thompson, J. William, and Kim Sorvig. 2000. *Sustainable Landscape Construction*. Washington, DC: Island Press.

U.S. EPA Comprehensive Procurement Guidelines for Cement and Concrete, http://www.epa.gov/cpg/products/cement.htm.

Meg Calkins, Ball State University, "Environmental and Health Considerations"

MASONRY

BRICK MASONRY

TRADITION

Brick is an ancient building material. Its current standardized sizes evolved over millennia, arising from the capability of a single unit to fit neatly into a worker's grasp. Many of the world's most significant structures employ brick for its beauty, strength, and durability. Despite significant technological advances that distinguish contemporary brick manufacturing, brick remains essentially unchanged from its earliest documented use at least 10,000 years ago. Brick is fired clay; it is human-made, but of the earth. Its regional variability expresses *genius loci,* local character and tradition, as few other materials can. Paralleling its evolution as a material, a long tradition of masonry craftsmanship arose yielding time-tested methods and techniques expressing the inherent richness and character of brick. A testament to its timelessness is that brick has remained in favor among designers over a long history of shifting stylistic movements.

The decision to utilize brick entails design choices determining durability, porosity, color, size, shape, finish, pattern, jointing, and more. And there are variations within each of these options. These decisions, coupled with the regionally varying composition of the source clay, result in a virtually unlimited palette of options for the landscape designer.

MATERIALS AND PROPERTIES

The earth's soil is generally categorized into three broad categories: sand, silt, and clay. Of these, clay has the greatest plasticity and workability. Clay, in its purest state, is composed mainly of silica and alumina. The specific mineral content of clay, along with its impurities, determines the color and influences the structural characteristics of the finished brick.

For the manufacture of brick, clay is divided into two categories: calcareous (containing calcium carbonate) and noncalcareous. Calcareous clays fire to a yellowish color, while noncalcareous clays yield brick in the reddish range. Due to its relative ease of access, clay found near the surface has been used the longest for brick production. Surface clay typically contains a high amount of oxides, reducing its tolerance to high heat. Fire clays are found deeper in the earth and are composed of a very pure form of clay containing fewer oxides than surface clays. Fire clays are well-suited to the manufacture of brick that will be exposed to high levels of heat, such as fireplaces and flues.

Shale is also used in brick-making, although much less frequently than clay. Shale must first undergo a process wherein it is pulverized and then is essentially transformed into its parent clay material.

APPLICATIONS: NONPAVING

Walls

Exterior walls serve a wide variety of functions. They can provide security by keeping things out, or containment by keeping things in. They can screen unwanted views surrounding a site and provide privacy by preventing unwanted viewing into a site. They can retain the earth, providing terracing where the gradient would otherwise make the intended land use impractical. Walls can be used for seating in lieu of benches; and when properly configured, they can become planters, water features, gateways, signage, and even sculpture.

An exterior brick wall is only as sound as its foundation. A well-designed foundation must support its load, extend to or below frost penetration depths, and effectively deal with groundwater. When a wall is used for earth-retention, a good foundation must also resist the overturning forces of earth, any surcharge associated with the retention, and the hydrostatic pressure of groundwater that builds up behind the wall.

The most commonly used wall systems in landscape design are:

- Solid masonry walls
- Drainage walls
- Pier-and-panel masonry walls

The simplest and most tradition-rich type of exterior wall is the solid masonry wall. Composed entirely of brick with no interior voids, it is composed of two wythes that run parallel to one another and are bonded with headers that span both faces, front to back. The patterned arrangement of the headers among the stretchers gives rise to the various familiar bonding patterns: English bond, Flemish bond, Dutch bond, and so on.

Drainage walls permit deeper sections while avoiding the wasteful use of brick in the wall's interior. So-named because they feature airspaces, or voids, between the exposed faces, drainage walls yield an economy of material. The three basic types of drainage walls are cavity walls, veneer walls, and hollow bonded walls. Each must effectively deal with the likelihood of water penetration, providing a means for the water to drain from the wall's interior.

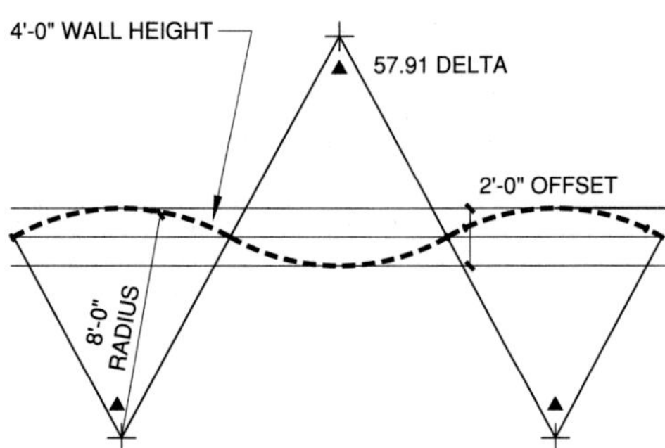

LAYOUT AND GEOMETRY FOR A 4-FOOT-TALL SERPENTINE WALL

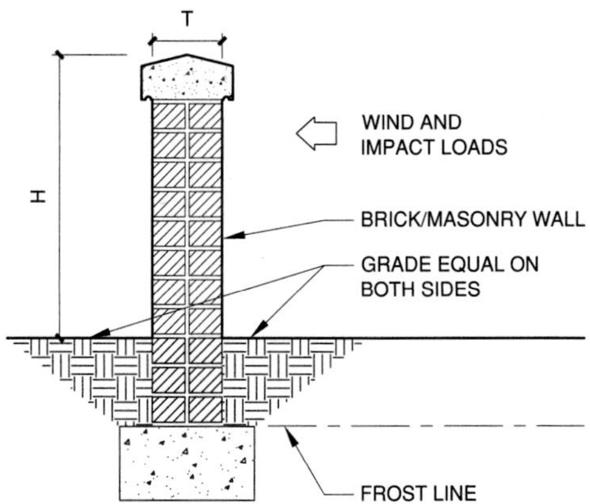

NOTES

1. Design wtraight garden walls (without piers) with suffient thickness to provide lateral stability.
2. To resist 10 psf wind pressure, the height above grade (H) and thickness (T) shold relate as follows: $H \leq 75T^2$ (H and T are in inches).

STRAIGHT GARDEN WALLS

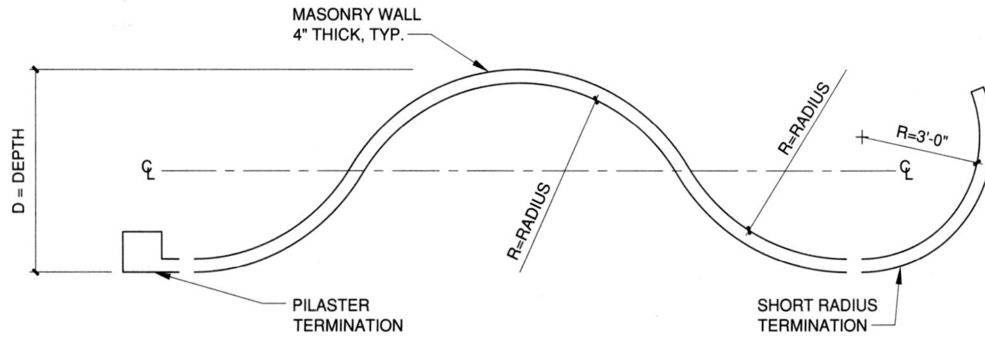

NOTES

1. The radius of curvature (R) of a 4-in. thick serpentine wall should be no more than twice the height of the wall above finished grade.
2. The depth (D) of curvature of a serpentine wall should be no less than half the height of the wall above grade (max. height = 5 ft 0 in., typical).
3. The running bond brick pattern is best for serpentine walls.
4. No reinforcing steel is used in this type of wall.
5. Serpentine walls are not recommended for use in seismic areas

SERPENTINE GARDEN WALLS

Rob W. Sovinski, ASLA

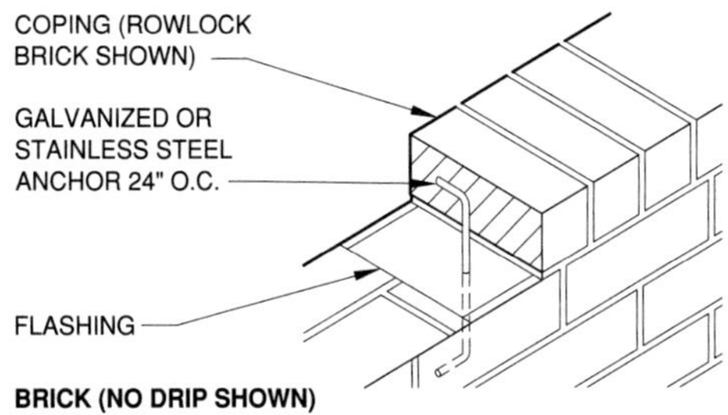

BRICK (NO DRIP SHOWN)

In general, through-wall flashing should be used immediately under the coping of garden walls. However, this decision depends on several factors, including the type of coping used, the number of joints used, and the climatic conditions of the area (whether there is high or low precipitation and the number of freezing and thawing cycles).

COPING DETAILS

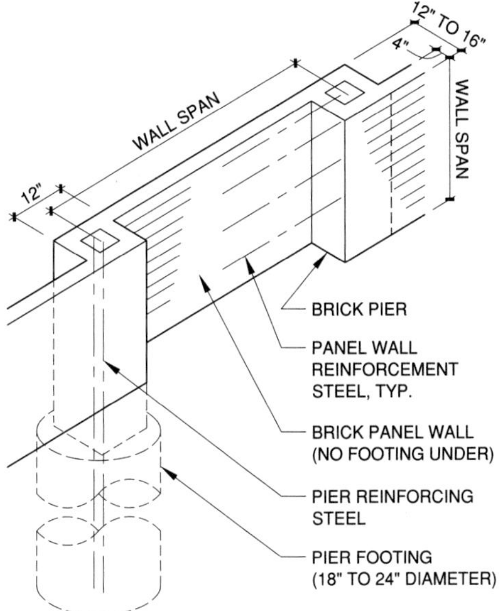

PIER-AND-PANEL SYSTEM

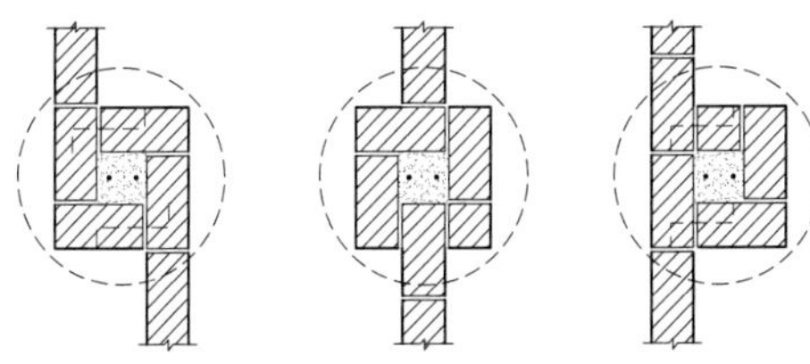

PIER TYPES

The peir-and-panel wall is composed of a series of relatively thin (4-in. thick) reinforced brick masonry panels, which are braced intermittently with masonry piers. This wall is relatively easy to build and is economical because of the narrowness of the panels. It is also easily adapted to varying terrain conditions.

PIER-AND-PANEL GARDEN WALLS

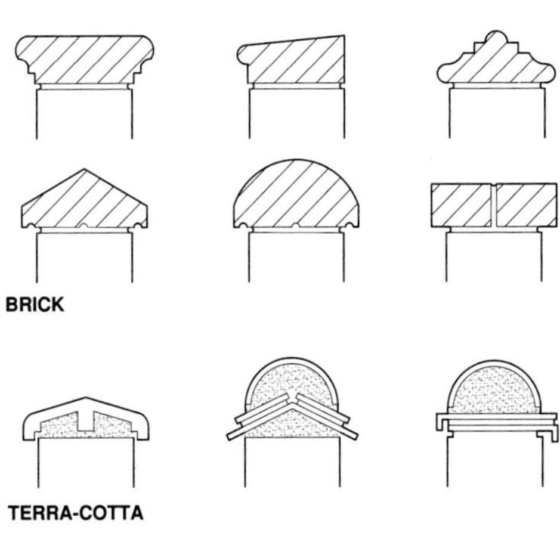

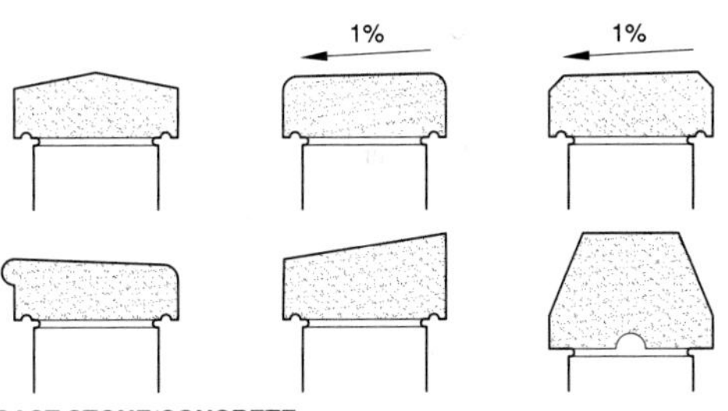

NOTES

1. Copings and caps prevent water from entering the inner wall from above by shedding water to the sides, where it is thrown clear of the wall, usually by means of a drip edge.
2. Anchor coping as necessary. If the coping material is different from the wall material, compare their thermal and moisture expansion characteristics and make provisions for different movement.

COPING TYPES FOR WALLS

Pier-and-panel wall systems permit the construction of single-wythe panels by placing steel-reinforced masonry piers at regular intervals. The size and amount of reinforcement placed in the piers is contingent upon the spacing of the piers (between 8 and 16 feet on center), the height of the wall, and the anticipated wind load.

Perforated brick walls represent an interesting option for exterior wall design. Also called pierced walls or brick screen walls, perforated walls can provide effective screening with less material where absolute privacy is not required. Among the advantages of these walls is their capability to permit light and air movement into otherwise enclosed exterior spaces. The pattern employed in a perforated wall often results from simply omitting some of the headers from traditional bond patterns.

Serpentine walls take advantage of the principle of corrugation, significantly enhancing the wall's strength and stability. The inherent strength of a serpentine wall is a result of its opposing curvatures, which eliminate the need for supporting piers at periodic intervals. For exterior serpentine walls 4 feet in height or less, the mathematics of "corrugation" are fairly simple. Containing no tangents between the reverse curves, the opposing radii should not exceed twice the overall height of the wall, or 8 feet for a 4-foot-high wall. The corresponding depth of curvature (the total horizontal offset) should not be less than one-half the height, or 2 feet for the same 4-foot-high wall. A structural analysis should be conducted for walls taller than 4 feet.

Caps and copings serve a visual function and provide weather resistance and drainage. Copings are typically composed of brick, stone, concrete, or tile. Brick copings using standard shapes should be sloped to encourage drainage. A variety of special shapes are available that facilitate drainage. Water penetration occurs primarily in the joints, not through the masonry material, so it may be advisable to use larger units of stone or precast concrete that are specifically shaped for drainage and offer fewer joints.

Drainage is a key concern in the design of any exterior masonry wall. A vertical section of aggregate immediately behind a retaining condition allows water to drain, diminishing the buildup of hydrostatic pressure. A filter fabric should be placed between the soil and the gravel to prevent the clogging of the aggregate's air voids. Footing drains, usually of tile or perforated plastic, are placed at the wall's footing. A water-permeable filter fabric should be placed over footing drains to prevent their sedimentation and clogging, as well.

Weep holes are openings, or voids, in the brick wall whose purpose is the venting and dispersion of any water that finds its way into the wall. To be effective, weep holes must be adequately sloped in section and must "daylight" slightly above finished grade on the nonretaining face of the wall. A weep hole can be as simple and reliable as an open, (nonmortared) head joint between bricks. A small plastic pipe may be inserted into the mortar joints. Plastic or aluminum weep vents help to camouflage the absence of mortar in a joint, and are more reliable. Wicks made of cotton or nylon rope can be placed into the mortar joint to draw moisture out of cavity walls to the wall's exterior. Wicks are typically made from ¼-inch- or ⅜-inch-diameter rope and are between 10 and 12 inches long.

Steps

Safety is the overriding concern in the design of all exterior steps. A rigid step system (mortared or otherwise cemented joints) is preferred, even when the adjacent pavement is a flexible system. Tread bricks should extend underneath the riser bricks to create a horizontally oriented joint, rather than a vertical joint, which is more vulnerable to water penetration. Treads should be sloped ¼ inch per foot to facilitate drainage. Handrails require independent support, with no vibration or movement transmitted to the brick step system or its concrete base. Designers need to consider standards established by the Americans with Disabilities Act (ADA) when specifying a nosing shape.

Brick Columns and Piers

Columns and piers are freestanding masonry constructions found in landscape elements such as arbors, pergolas, and bollards. Pilasters are integrated into masonry walls. Columns serve primarily as vertical supports. Piers and pilasters must provide lateral

PIER REINFORCING STEEL*

WALL SPAN (FT)	WIND LOAD (10 PSF)			WIND LOAD (15 PSF)			WIND LOAD (20 PSF)		
	WALL HEIGHT (FT)								
	4	6	8	4	6	8	4	6	8
8	2#3	2#4	2#5	2#3	2#5	2#6	2#4	2#5	2#5
10	2#3	2#4	2#5	2#4	2#5	2#7	2#4	2#6	2#6
12	2#3	2#5	2#6	2#4	2#6	2#6	2#4	2#6	2#7
14	2#3	2#5	2#6	2#4	2#6	2#6	2#5	2#5	2#7
16	2#4	2#5	2#5	2#4	2#6	2#7	2#5	2#6	2#7

**For wall sizes shown within heavy lines, 12 x 16 in. piers ar required. All other values have been obtained with 12 x 12 in. piers.*

Rob W. Sovinski, ASLA

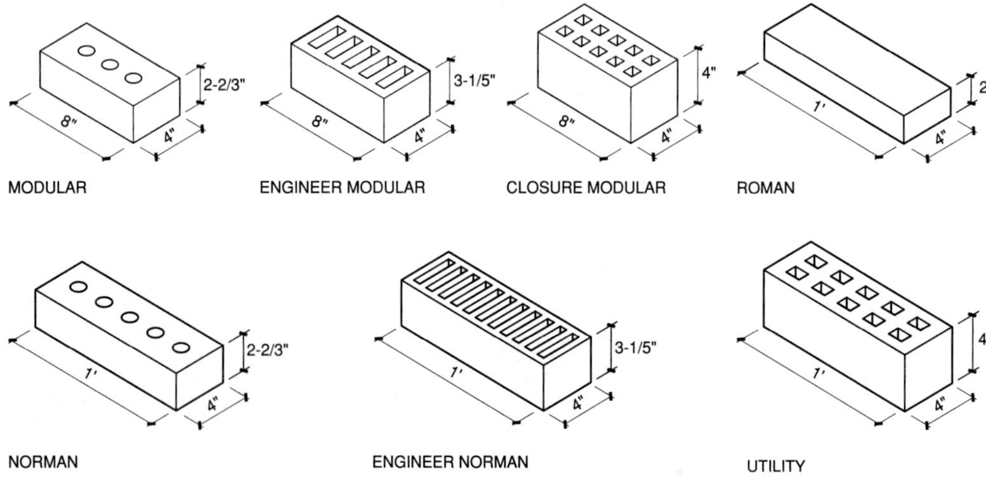

NOMINAL SIZES OF MODULAR BUILDING BRICK

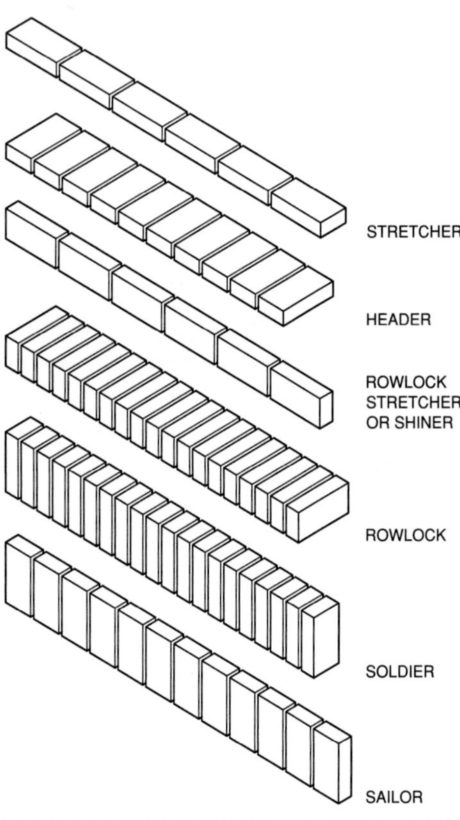

NAMES OF BRICK POSITIONS IN WALLS

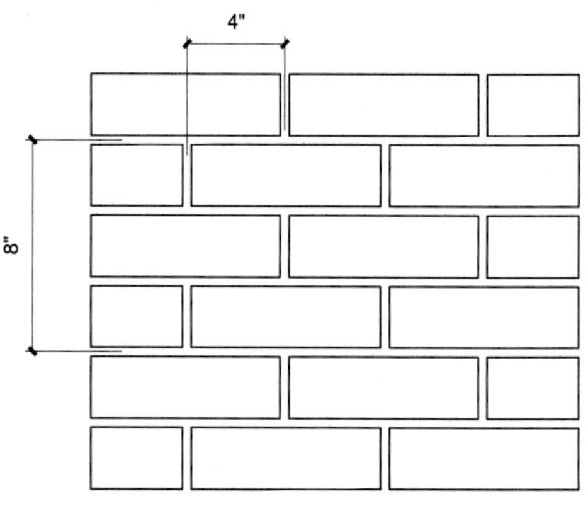

MODULARITY IN BRICKWORK

MODULAR BRICK SIZES

UNIT DESIGNATION	NOMINAL DIMENSIONS (IN.) W	H	L	JOINT THICKNESS	SPECIFIED DIMENSIONS[1] W	H	L	VERTICAL COURSING
Modular	4	$2\frac{2}{3}$	8	$\frac{3}{8}$	$3\frac{5}{8}$	$2\frac{1}{4}$	$7\frac{5}{8}$	3C = 8 in.
				$\frac{1}{2}$	$3\frac{1}{2}$	$2\frac{1}{4}$	$7\frac{1}{2}$	
Engineer modular	4	$3\frac{1}{5}$	8	$\frac{3}{8}$	$3\frac{5}{8}$	$2\frac{3}{4}$	$7\frac{5}{8}$	5C = 16 in.
				$\frac{1}{2}$	$3\frac{1}{2}$	$2\frac{13}{16}$	$7\frac{1}{2}$	
Closure modular	4	4	8	$\frac{3}{8}$	$3\frac{5}{8}$	$3\frac{5}{8}$	$7\frac{5}{8}$	1C = 4 in.
				$\frac{1}{2}$	$3\frac{1}{2}$	$3\frac{1}{2}$	$7\frac{1}{2}$	
Roman	4	2	12	$\frac{3}{8}$	$3\frac{5}{8}$	$1\frac{5}{8}$	$11\frac{5}{8}$	2C = 4 in.
				$\frac{1}{2}$	$3\frac{1}{2}$	$1\frac{1}{2}$	$11\frac{1}{2}$	
Norman	4	$2\frac{2}{3}$	12	$\frac{3}{8}$	$3\frac{5}{8}$	$2\frac{1}{4}$	$11\frac{5}{8}$	3C = 8 in.
				$\frac{1}{2}$	$3\frac{1}{2}$	$2\frac{1}{4}$	$11\frac{1}{2}$	
Engineer norman	4	$3\frac{1}{5}$	12	$\frac{3}{8}$	$3\frac{5}{8}$	$2\frac{3}{4}$	$11\frac{5}{8}$	5C = 16 in.
				$\frac{1}{2}$	$3\frac{1}{2}$	$2\frac{13}{16}$	$11\frac{1}{2}$	
Utility	4	4	12	$\frac{3}{8}$	$3\frac{5}{8}$	$3\frac{5}{8}$	$11\frac{5}{8}$	1C = 4 in.
				$\frac{1}{2}$	$3\frac{1}{2}$	$3\frac{1}{2}$	$11\frac{1}{2}$	

[1] *Specified dimensions may vary within this range from manufacturer to manufacturer.*

Source: Brick Industry Association.

support, as well. Pier-and-panel walls use structural piers to support relatively thin brick wall panels that span from pier to pier. In the landscape, masonry columns provide adequate support for vertical loads without internal reinforcing. Piers and pilasters require additional reinforcing to resist lateral forces. Foundations for brick piers and pilasters are typically reinforced cast-in-place concrete. Foundations must extend to recommended structural depths or to the local frost depth, whichever is greater. Like walls, the topmost surface of columns, piers, and pilasters must be capped for water resistance.

DESIGN CONSIDERATIONS

Brick Sizes

For efficiency and consistency in production, design, and construction, a set of standardized modular dimensions has evolved for the production of brick. The dimensioning of modular brick accounts for the width of the mortar joints, and adheres to multiples of 4 inches. Modular brick is sized to coincide with concrete block coursing. Brick dimensions are specified using the sequence of width, height, and length (i.e., W × H × L). Modular brick is referred to by its nominal size, which varies from its actual and its specified dimensions. The "nominal size" refers to its modularity relative to the 4-inch grid and actually describes the distance between the centerlines of a wall's mortar joints.

Brick Orientation

A brick's position designation relates to the orientation of its exposed face within a wall. There are six possible brick positions: stretcher, header, rowlock stretcher, soldier, sailor, and rowlock. A brick in the rowlock stretcher position is sometimes called a "shiner." The stretcher is the most common position in brick masonry. Headers are frequently used to provide bonding between wythes. Rowlock, soldier, and sailor courses are commonly used to create interest and detail in brick walls.

Texture

In the stiff-mud manufacturing process, brick finishes are applied as the brick is extruded. The wire-cut, or velour, finish is achieved as extruded brick is sliced into individual units by a wire-cutting tool. Other popular finishes include rug, stippled, striated, molded, sand, smooth, and bark. Ironspot refers to small metallic

Rob W. Sovinski, ASLA

fragments embedded in the clay. Many brick manufacturers offer unique finishes of their own design. Soft-mud-processed brick may be sand-struck or water-struck. Glazing imparts an impervious, smooth coating—available in a range of colors and gloss—onto a brick's face. Glazing, however, may curtail the venting of moisture from bricks, and their lack of traction make glazed brick inappropriate for use as pavers.

Bond and Bonding

Although it creates opportunities for visual interest, the primary function of bonding is structural. Bonding ties multiple wythes together and distributes vertical loads diagonally. Bonding is achieved through the front-to-back placement of header bricks. Mechanical ties may be used when bond patterns don't include headers, such as the running bond. Among the most widely used bonds are: stack bond, running bond, common bond, English bond, Flemish bond, Dutch bond, and garden wall. Soldier and rowlock courses are commonly used to add interest, especially at a wall's cap.

Joints and Joint Design

Joints account for approximately 17 percent of the visible surface of a brick wall. The primary role of mortar joints is adhesion, but they also play a significant visual role, thus designers need to consider both the color and the profile of the mortar joints. Since the majority of masonry failures occur at the joints, sound joint design must facilitate rapid drainage. The process of tooling a joint serves to compress the mortar, much like the crust on a loaf of bread, enhancing its water-resistant capacity. Concave, V, and weathered are the best joints to use when water intrusion is a concern. Flush joints offer an effective profile to resist water, but aren't compressed by tooling during installation. Colored mortar is widely available and can dramatically impact the visual aspect of a brick wall.

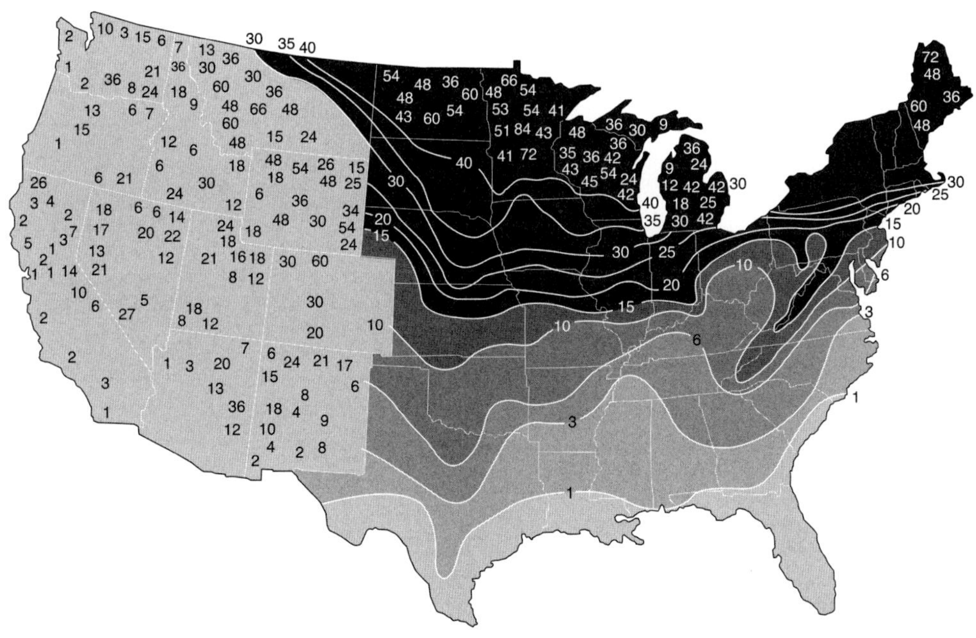

AVERAGE DEPTH IN INCHES OF FROST PENETRATION

CONFIGURATIONS FOR SOLID BRICK COLUMNS

Rob W. Sovinski, ASLA

CONCRETE MASONRY UNITS

GENERAL

Concrete masonry units (CMU) conform to ASTM standard specifications. The most common concrete masonry units used in building construction are load bearing units and concrete brick. Non-load bearing units may be specified for partitions and are commonly used for fire protection of steel columns and fire-rated partitions.

Type I or moisture-controlled units are specified to obtain a uniform degree of volume change due to moisture loss in a particular climate. The specification of Type I units facilitates the location of control joints. Type II or non-moisture controlled units may be more economical but will typically require closer spacing of control joints.

In addition to type, concrete bricks are specified by grade. Grade N is intended for use as architectural veneer and facing units in exterior walls and for use when high strength and resistance to moisture penetration and severe frost action are desired. Grade S is intended for general masonry where moderate strength and resistance to frost action and moisture penetration are required.

Concrete masonry units are available in a variety of colors, sizes, textures, configurations, and weights to

VOLUMETRIC CHARACTERISTICS OF TYPICAL HOLLOW CONCRETE MASONRY UNITS (7⅝ X 15⅝ IN.)

		MINIMUM THICKNESS		2 CORE UNITS	
WIDTH (IN.)	GROSS VOLUME, CU IN. (CU FT)	SHELL (IN.)	WEB (IN.)	PERCENT SOLID VOLUME	EQUIVALENT SOLID THICKNESS (IN.)
3⅝	432	0.75	0.75	64	232
	(0.25)	1.00	1.00	73	2.66
5⅝	670	1.00	1.00	57	3.21
	(0.388)	1.12	1.00	61	3.43
		1.25	1.00	64	3.60
		1.37	1.12	68	3.82
7⅝	908	1.25	1.00	53	4.04
	(0.526)	1.37	1.12	57	4.35
		1.50	1.12	59	4.50
9⅝	1145	1.25	1.12	48	4.62
	(0.664)	1.37	1.12	51	4.91
		1.50	1.25	54	5.20
11⅝	1385	1.25	1.12	44	5.12
	(0.803)	1.37	1.12	46	5.35
		1.50	1.25	49	5.70
		1.75	1.25	52	6.05

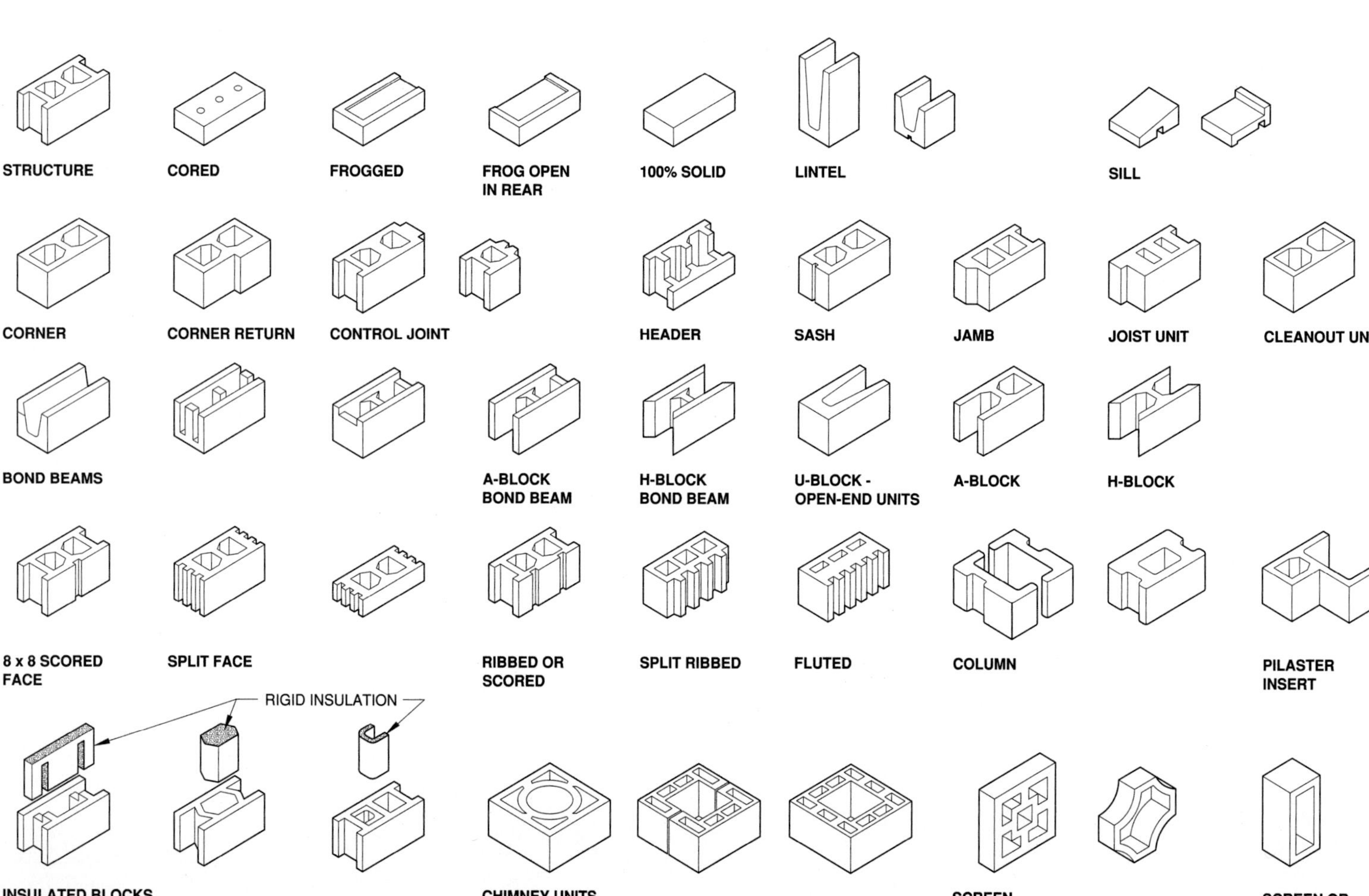

TYPICAL CONCRETE MASONRY UNIT SHAPES

Stephen S. Szoke, P.E., National Concrete Masonry Association, Herndon, Virginia; Grace S. Lee, Rippeteau Architects, PC, Washington, D.C.

accommodate design, detailing, and construction. Colors are now provided with lightfast metallic oxide pigments conforming to ASTM C 979. The textures may be smooth, ground, split, ribbed, or otherwise prepared to maximize design versatility. Smooth finishes and more color options are available with prefaced, "integral glazed" concrete masonry units.

Concrete masonry units are specified as width by height by length. The nominal dimensions are usually 3/8 in. larger than the actual unit dimensions. The most common nominal widths of concrete masonry units are 4 in., 6 in., 8 in., 10 in., and 12 in. The nominal heights are mostly 8 in. and 4 in., except concrete bricks are typically 2⅔ in. high. The nominal lengths are usually 16 or 18 in. Concrete brick length is usually 8 in. but is often 12 in. Lengths may be 18 or 24 in. in some regions. These longer lengths are usually more economical for placement.

The weight of the units also varies. Depending on the aggregate used, concrete masonry units are typically made using concretes with densities ranging from 85 to 140 pcf. The lighter units tend to provide more fire resistance and have an improved noise reduction coefficient, and they often are more economical to place in the wall. Heavier units tend to provide increased compressive strength, better resistance to sound penetration, higher water penetration resistance, and greater thermal storage capabilities.

ASTM STANDARD SPECIFICATIONS

C 55—Concrete Brick

C 73—Calcium Silicate Face Brick (sand-lime brick)

C 90—Load Bearing Concrete Masonry Units

C 129—Non-load Bearing Concrete Masonry Units

C 139—Concrete Masonry Units for the Construction of Catch Basins and Manholes

C 744—Prefaced Concrete and Calcium Silicate Masonry Units

C 936—Solid Concrete Interlocking Paving Units

Stephen S. Szoke, P.E., National Concrete Masonry Association, Herndon, Virginia; Grace S. Lee, Rippeteau Architects, PC, Washington, D.C.

METALS

METAL

INTRODUCTION

Metals are perhaps the most enduring human-built elements in the landscape. They can assume a vast array of shapes, from the breathtaking to the mundane. They can excite us and give us comfort. They can, in fact, be lifesavers. Stone may crumble, wood may rot, but metal can be forever.

BENEFITS OF METAL USE

Life Safety

Metals, because of their strength, durability, availability, and aesthetic properties, lend themselves to being utilized in addressing many life safety functions. Examples of these uses include handrails, guardrails, bollards, guy lines, gratings, and fasteners. In fact, the use of metal hardware has become so commonplace that we often overlook their importance to the stability and safety of the majority of our modern landscape structures.

Security

The tensile strength and hardness of metals makes them prime candidates for landscape security systems, providing hardened bollards, light standards, and site furniture. Of the available choices for meeting the security requirements of hardened perimeters, metals provide virtually the only alternative to bulky concrete fixtures. As the landscape security furnishings division matures and increases, metals will lead the way.

Life Span

When properly selected for the environment of the site, metals can have a life span that far exceeds many materials, including wood, stone, and plastics. The continued use and performance of historic metal work is a testimony to this endurance.

As life span costs for maintenance and replacement work are increasingly expressed in design considerations, the longevity and maintenance of metals makes them an appealing material to specify.

DESIGN FACTORS

Metals are perhaps the most malleable of any material, able to take on shapes and structures that appear to be limited only by imagination. Due to the high strength-to-weight ratio of metals, objects can be created that have a very light or transparent appearance.

Use of Metals in the Landscape

North America has a rich history of metalwork in the landscape. From the iconic fountains of Chicago's waterfront to the stoop railings of New York City brownstones, metals have made a significant contribution to the rich texture of the public landscape. It is important to recognize the historic context of this work and its continuing role in forming our landscapes.

Metals have made lasting contributions to the expression of historic architectural and artistic styles in the landscape. While the extremely ornate Victorian ironwork is easily recognized, it is important to note that styles such as Art Nouveau, Art Deco, Federal, Gothic, Arts and Crafts, and even Cubist have their metalwork examples. Unfortunately, we are in danger of losing our metalwork heritage, as the fences, railings, fountains, and planters are lost to neglect or destruction.

American Locations or Styles

The larger cities of early America often developed their own ironwork styles, motifs, or aesthetic that can be easily identified today. Most of these cities were either major ports and could import British and German ironwork, or had sufficient shops or foundries to supply the demand. A sampling of cities that have a significant history in landscape ironwork are Savannah, Georgia; Boston, Massachusetts; New Orleans, Louisiana; Philadelphia, Pennsylvania; Charleston, South Carolina; Richmond, Virginia; Baltimore, Maryland; and New York, New York.

Commonly, the motifs or subject materials of the ironwork set them apart. For instance, Boston utilized the "anthemion" (the Greek design of radiating petals) motif copiously; New Orleans ironwork is largely based around botanical themes (Robertson, 1977); and the ubiquitous pineapple of Virginia is often seen in its ironwork as well. While many associate historic ironwork solely with wrought iron, the industrialization of the United States generated vast amounts of cast iron, which arguably dominates the remaining historic ironwork in a number of our major cities.

METALWORK AS CRAFT AND ART

The middle part of the last century experienced a significant shift in the approach to metalwork in the landscape, from an artisan/site-based approach to a modern, spare, and prefabricated installation. This was a result of the full mechanization of the production of metal elements and the exploration of new materials and modernist styles for both architecture and landscape architecture. Blacksmithing, as a profession, virtually disappeared.

Currently, we are in the midst of a revival of the metal artisan. Spurred from a craft-ethic that began in the 1960s and 1970s, a new force of blacksmiths and similar metalsmiths has rebuilt the professions. Organizations such as the Artist Blacksmith's Association of North America (ABANA) and the National Ornamental & Miscellaneous Metals Association (NOMMA) are a resource for locating shops and craftspeople.

Masters/Master Works

The landscape of North America has been graced by the artistry of many notable masters in metalworks. These masters were as varied as their product and include figures such as Cyril Colnik, who exerted a significant influence on the metalworks of the Midwest, particularly through his work as blacksmith to the beer barons of Milwaukee; and Allessandro Mazzucotelli, a notable master in the Art Deco style during the 1920s and 1930s.

Of all the past masters, however, Samuel Yellin was perhaps the most influential of the American blacksmiths, not only due to his skill as a craftsman, but also to the size of his shop and the corresponding body of work that it produced. In 1928, Yellin's shop in Philadelphia employed 286 craftsmen (Andrews, 2000).Yellin's shop had a major impact on the ironwork of a number of cities, such as Philadelphia, New York, and Chicago.

Yellin's shop continues to operate today, run by his granddaughter Clare Yellin. Yellin's legacy was also continued by his highly skilled staff, including Francis Whitaker, who, until his recent passing, was considered the "Dean of Modern Blacksmithing" (Andrews, 2000).

PRESERVATION OF HISTORIC METALWORK

Status

To date, little research has been done to catalog or track America's historic metal resources in the landscape. Therefore, no statement can be made that we are either securely endowed with an unlimited supply or in danger of losing it all. The general consensus, however, tends toward a speculation of irreplaceable loss.

Of concern to historic conservationists is the preservation of the small and functional metal objects in the landscape (Jacob, 2004). It is the grandiose gateways that typically receive recognition and restoration, while these smaller features are often ignored in the renovations of parks and residences. For instance, a drinking fountain is often viewed as easier to replace than to relocate or restore. However, these elements in sum can provide a notable contribution to the historic character of our landscapes. Such attrition can occur through general maintenance programs as well, which may seek to replace "worn out" street signposts one year, then unhinged gates the following, and on. Unnoticed, we are losing the pieces of our historic fabric.

CARE

Identification or Recognition

The first step in any preservation process is an understanding of the existing objects. Is the metalwork historic or a replacement? What is the metal type and its condition? Some metal objects may be easier to date. Production-line cast objects in particular will often have a manufacturer's stamp, which may contain a date or can be assigned a time period by the manufacturer.

Landscapes that involve a number of metal elements may find success in employing the services of a cultural resources professional, who can establish the date and setting of the objects. In cases of discreet objects, a conservator specializing in metals would be preferable.

Nathan Imm, RLA, EDAW, William B. Kuhl, RLA, Saratoga Associates (formerly with EDAW)

Involvement of a conservator is an important step toward preserving historic metalworks. Specific care depends on the status of decay and corrosion, historical importance or uniqueness, and the availability of repair and replacement materials. As with other professionals, involvement of a conservator early in the process can result in both a better product and a final cost savings, due to their knowledge of the techniques and values of the topic.

The American Institute for Conservation (AIC) is a membership organization that can be highly useful in locating an appropriate conservator. The AIC has established a code of ethics and guidelines for practice to ensure that members adhere to a high level of professionalism.

Hardware and Attachment

When maintaining or restoring metalworks, it is important to note that the hardware and attachments are an important part of the historic nature of the objects. Use of modern attachments, such as Phillips-head screws, which originated in the 1930s, can be harmful to the historic appearance of the objects and confuse future efforts to interpret the history of the object. Additionally, modern welding techniques can significantly damage older metals. Cast and hybrid cast/wrought pieces are particularly susceptible to this damage.

Coatings

Improper coating can do more damage than good to an older metal object. One particularly notable example of this is the plating of the zinc statuary in Greenwood Cemetery in Brooklyn, New York, with copper to "improve" its appearance, causing bimetallic corrosion (Grissom, 2005More common is the tendency to paint over rusting ironwork. This simply hides the problem, worsening it through continued neglect, and potentially trapping moisture, which hastens the corrosion.

Maintenance

Maintenance can sometimes be more damaging than helpful to historic metalwork. The recent use of weed whips to trim grass around painted metal fences can quickly remove the protective paint coatings. Similarly, the perceived ease of "power washers" can result in water being driven into crevices and voids in metalwork, corroding the work more severely than if left alone.

This is not to say that no maintenance should be practiced. Rather, maintenance should be included as a portion of the overall design, planning, and implementation process of our landscapes.

OVERALL PROPERTIES

Shrink/Swell

Metals are dynamic objects that shrink in size when cold and expand when hot. While this action may not be immediately visible to the naked eye, it can have substantial impacts to design, particularly with large or long metal objects.

The following table "Metal Expansion Properties" provides general coefficients of expansion for metals commonly used in the landscape. The metals are listed from greatest degree of expansion to lowest.

METAL EXPANSION PROPERTIES

MATERIAL	10-6 IN./IN. PER°F		10-5 IN./IN. PER°C	
	HIGH	LOW	HIGH	LOW
Zinc	19.3	10.8	3.5	1.9
Lead	16.3	14.4	2.9	2.6
Aluminum	13.7	11.7	2.5	2.1
Tin	13		2.3	
Brasses	11.6	10	2.1	1.8
Ductile irons (cast)	10.4	6.6	1.9	1.2
Stainless steels (cast)	10.4	6.4	1.9	1.1
Tin bronzes (cast)	10.3	10	1.8	1.8
Austenitic stainless steels	10.2	9	1.8	1.6
Coppers	9.8	7.7	1.8	1.4
Aluminum bronzes (cast)	9.5	9	1.8	1.6
Alloy steels (cast)	8.3	8	1.5	1.4
Malleable irons	7.5	5.9	1.3	1.1
Wrought irons	7.4		1.3	
Titanium and its alloys	7.1	4.9	1.3	.9
Martensitic stainless steels	6.5	5.5	1.2	1.0
Ferritic stainless steels	6	5.8	1.1	1.0
Gray irons (cast)	6		1.1	

Conductivity

- Metals as a rule are highly conductive materials. They are able to transmit electricity and heat very efficiently. This has a significant impact upon their use in the landscape in several ways: *Electrical conductivity.* Tall, isolated, or large metal objects should be grounded to prevent the possibility of fire or electrocution in case of a lightning strike. Similarly, exposure to electric power sources and lines can be hazardous if improperly designed.
- *Heat conductivity.* The placement or use of metals in the landscape is particularly subject to this property. Setting a metal bench in the hot summer sun will significantly limit its use. Conversely, on a cold spring day, a metal bench is almost equally uncomfortable. For this reason, insulators such as wood and paint, or placement in shade, are methods used to temper the conductivity of the metal.

TYPES OF METAL

Iron

Iron is not widely used in modern landscape applications due to its general replacement by mild steel. This replacement is largely due to the industrial preference for steel over iron; it does not speak to the utility or durability of iron. In fact, certain forms and compositions of iron have superior corrosion resistance over basic steel.

Wrought Iron

Wrought iron, which is no longer commercially produced, exhibits better corrosion resistance than the mild carbon steel that has replaced it (and which is confusingly called "wrought iron"; see section on steel, below). This corrosion resistance is due to the distribution of slag throughout the metal, which provides a barrier to oxidation. Of course, there were differences in quality of wrought iron, the "good" quality being better to work with, as well as more corrosion-resistant (Curtis, 2004).

Wrought iron's primary use in the landscape is found in the decorative gates, fences, balconies, grills, railings, archways, and gazebos. It is identifiable by its fibrous structure, which is not present in steel. This structure also gives the wrought iron better resistance to fatigue than steel (Tilly, 2002).

Cast Iron

Cast iron is the most common form of iron used in North America, both historically and currently. Cast iron's contribution to architecture, seen in cast pillars and building façades, has been well documented and celebrated, but its contribution to the landscape is equally important. If it can be built, it can be built of cast iron—everything from awnings, balconies, gazebos, railings, stairs, and fences to planters, fountains, statues, and bridges of cast iron.

In its unaltered state, cast iron is referred to as gray cast iron. Grey cast iron is very brittle and susceptible to impact cracking and fatigue damage due to regular overloading. To overcome this, ductile cast iron was developed with superior mechanical properties. In tall or thin applications such as light poles and bollards, or in structural applications such as bridges, it is important to know the difference in the cast product, to avoid breakage (Skalka, 2004). The designer of the structure or element should also note these general shortcomings, as many can be overcome through proper design.

Cast-iron exhibits surprising corrosion resistance, in spite of public perception—it is actually more corrosion-resistant than both true wrought iron and carbon steel (Tilly, 2002). This corrosion resistance is due to its high carbon content (Waite, 1991). A particular note of caution should be made, however, in regard to welding of cast iron (and wrought), as this is a problematic process that can damage or weaken the metal significantly if done improperly.

A number of cast-iron foundries remain, primarily focused on the sculptural or historic replication of cast elements.

Steel

Nonstainless Steel

The term "wrought iron" as used in the industry is now a common misnomer. Historically, wrought iron meant iron that had been forged by a blacksmith. Today, it is often used to designate mild carbon steel (Skalka, 2004). Due to its reference to a process as well as a type of material, this use of the term for mild steel is discouraged, as there are a number of situations where the term would more correctly apply.

Carbon Steel

The most common and basic type of steel available is carbon, or mild, steel, of which there are a multitude

Nathan Imm, RLA, EDAW, William B. Kuhl, RLA, Saratoga Associates (formerly with EDAW)

of grades and alloys available. With all, it is important to note that this group exhibits the highest average degree of corrosion of the ferrous metals. In an urban setting, corrosion can occur at a rate of 0.05 to 0.10 mm per year (Tilly, 2002), which can be greatly exceeded due to specific environmental or design factors. Recent studies have shown that the corrosion rates of steel elements can vary significantly. A study of steel piping has shown that prewar pipes exhibited low or virtually nonexistent corrosion, whereas modern steel piping displayed rapid corrosion (Duncan, 2004). One result of this and other studies has been the recommendation that higher-quality materials be specified, or that the thicknesses of the steel specified be adjusted to account for the corrosion.

Cor-Ten steel is a low-alloy carbon steel that has gained recent popularity due to its "rusted" appearance, which is both attractive and gives an instant "aged" look. It is increasingly used for sculptures and decoratively cut sheets and panels. Its best use is in structural elements, such as bridges, due to its high strength properties. Major manufacturers and producers have begun to warn against its use in architectural or thin applications such as roofing and sheet metal. This is primarily due to the fact that this rusted appearance is corrosion, which in sheet form can quickly rust through. Claims that this forms a protective layer ignore the inevitable erosion of the oxide layer.

Stainless Steel

Stainless steel has seen a significant increase in use in the landscape over the last decade. This is due both to the modern aesthetic that the color and surfacing can lend to a project and the potential for lowering maintenance and replacement demands, particularly in corrosive environments.

Stainless steel is an iron alloy that generally contains chromium and nickel, the elements that contribute the most to its corrosion resistance. Other metals, such as titanium and aluminum can be added to this basic alloy, but are generally added for the aesthetic changes they may lend to the color or sheen of the metal, not its corrosion resistance.

One of the most confusing aspects of stainless steel is the very term "corrosion resistance." Stainless steel is, in fact, not stain-free in all environments. Pollution, salts, and contact with other metals can lead to rust-colored stains and even corrosion and pitting of the stainless steel. An important aspect of design is the selection of the grade of stainless steel to match the environmental demands of the site. Equally important is the surface roughness presented to the environment. A smoother finish of stainless steel will more likely retain its appearance for the long term than a roughened finish.

Three general types of stainless steel are used in the landscape: austenitic, ferritic, and duplex. The first, austenitic, is clearly the most common and useful, as it offers a good balance between corrosion resistance and cost. Duplex, by comparison, has the highest corrosion resistance; however, it is much more expensive. Ferritic is generally less utilized, as the others have become more readily available. This discussion will concentrate on austenitic stainless steel as representing the happy medium.

Grades of Stainless Steel

- *302.* This grade of stainless steel has been surpassed and is no longer in common use in the landscape due to its high level of staining. Historically, this grade has been used on such prominent places as the Chrysler Building in New York City. It is notable that the Chrysler Building recently underwent a significant cleaning to return it to its original shine. Pollution and acid rain were largely blamed for the staining on its surfaces.
- *304.* The basic or more commonly available grade, this stainless is best used for hardware or low-corrosive environments where large and visible components are designed.
- *316–316.* This is the most common grade used in the landscape, specifically for its corrosion resistance. A significant increase in corrosion resistance (approximately 25 percent) is gained over 304.
- *317.* Currently, this grade offers the highest level of corrosion resistance of the commonly available austenitic stainless steels. Current price structures lead to a significant difference in cost between 316 and 317. Due to the other factors that may influence staining and corrosion on-site, further investigation is warranted to determine whether this increased cost will provide increased performance.
- *2205.* This is a duplex stainless steel, whereas the preceding grades are all austenitic. This is perhaps the highest level of corrosion resistance that is still generally available. Its use in the landscape is extremely rare, due in large part to its very high cost. Additionally, because it is not much used in the landscape, available forms and sizes are limited to those used by other industries. As with 317 grade, further investigation should be made to ensure that the use of this grade is worth the increased cost.

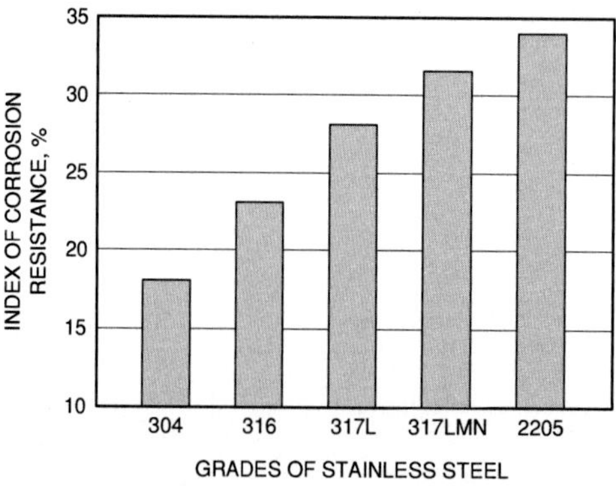

INDEX OF CORROSION RESISTANCE OF COMMON STAINLESS STEELS

Source: Courtesy of Specialty Steel Industry of North America (SSINA).

Copper

Copper and its alloys are among the most highly valued metals used in the landscape. A soft and malleable metal, one of the most popular aspects of copper is its oxidation. The mottled verdigris coating of well-aged copper is highly sought.

Copper is generally considered corrosion-resistant in that the green patina tends to adhere to the surface, protecting the underlaying metal from oxidation. However, as others, this material can erode, and the eroded patina can significantly stain the surfaces that receive the water. Concrete, stone, and other surfaces near the copper elements can turn green. If other finishes are desired, it is more economical to use a different material.

Copper is only used to display its natural metallic finish, either the base metal or oxidation. Paints and coatings utilized are clear, to protect and highlight this natural feature.

A number of processes have been developed to either accelerate or imitate the patination to provide this colorful finish at installation. In general, field applications to obtain the patina are not recommended, as both due to the variety of environmental factors that can affect it, and the environmental impacts that the salts or acids may have.

Particularly in sheet form, copper is cost-competitive with stainless steel and titanium for corrosive environments where these materials may be specified. While potentially more susceptible to the corrosive elements, higher quality or greater thickness can be utilized for the cost of high-quality stainless steel or titanium. As global markets for metals shift, this differential may reverse or widen.

Specification of copper should consider that not all copper is equally soft, the difference between the low and high temper is significant (33,000 psi yield strength difference). ASTM B370 outlines the "hardness" of the various types.

Most landscape uses for copper are in sheet form. Because of its particularly malleable nature, it is highly useful for making caps, flashing, and similar water protection construction for wood structures in the landscape.

When copper is utilized as a cap or flashing over cedar wood, one aspect of caution is the collection of water where the wood comes in contact with copper: if water is trapped, it can form an acid that will corrode the copper flashing.

When copper is a primary design feature in the landscape, it is similarly used in sheet form. The two most common are in roofing and as panels. The panels can be sculpted by a process called *repoussé.* Smaller finials and sculptures, such as wind vanes, are also commonly made of copper.

Brass/Bronze

Following closely to copper are its alloys, brass and bronze. In historic statuary, grating, and ornamentation, bronze was the standard for wealth, and therefore the most imitated of the metals.

The terms "brass" and "bronze" have been confused for ages, but brass generally refers to a copper-tin alloy, whereas bronze refers to a copper-zinc alloy. To add further confusion, there are nontechnical designations of bronze, including "white bronze," which, while based on the color, typically refers to a nickel-bronze; and "yellow bronze," which is essentially everything else.

The alloying of copper to create brass and bronze is similar in purpose to all other metal alloys: to create a more corrosion-resistant, stronger product. In general, the copper-tin alloy of brass is considered the more corrosion-resistant of the two.

Aluminum-bronze alloys are increasingly utilized due to their improved corrosion resistance, which is generally considered the highest of the brass/bronze family, next to the silver-bronze alloys. The silver-bronze alloys are generally prohibitively expensive for use in the landscape compared to the minimal additional corrosion benefit they provide.

Nathan Imm, RLA, EDAW, William B. Kuhl, RLA, Saratoga Associates (formerly with EDAW)

Brasses and bronzes are used primarily in lighting, ornamental castings, sculpture and statuary, roofing, and decorative sheets in the landscape.

Lead

Lead is a physically heavy metal, soft and easily malleable with little mechanical strength. The ease of melting and molding lead resulted in its extensive use in ornamentation. Its softness, however, meant that most lead ornaments were restricted in size and location, generally on rooftops or similarly inaccessible spots, to limit damage.

Lead resists corrosion by forming lead carbonate as a protective coating. However, the softness of lead allows for a high rate of erosion of this protective coating, as can be seen in the stormwater pollution from lead-coated roofing.

Because of lead's low tensile strength it is rarely used in its pure form today. It is a highly reactive metal, forming alloys with tin, antimony, bronze, silver, and other metals. Lead is manufactured primarily as sheets and coils.

The most common lead alloy is lead and tin; in varying combinations it forms solder. The alloy has a lower melting point than each pure element, making it useful as a mechanical joining compound. Solder is used to join two separate pieces of metal. The most common uses of lead in landscape architecture are as waterproofing in this form.

Pewter is a lead-tin alloy mixed with antimony, which is used for ornamentation. Most modern pewter is lead-free.

Lead or lead-coated sheeting is still commonly used for flashing. Flashing is used in roofing and in building landscape walls and around the base of buildings, to prevent water penetration.

Although lead has varied properties that allow wide application, its use has been limited because of its harmful health and environmental effects. Formerly common uses of lead include fountains, plaques, statuary, roofing, flashing, and piping.

Aluminum

The use of aluminum in the landscape is a relatively recent occurrence. Aluminum's versatility, strength, and corrosion resistance have made it a significant competitor to ferrous metals in the construction of nonstructural landscape elements.

While aluminum is one of the more corrosion-resistant metals, it is not a corrosion-free metal. The oxidized product of aluminum is a whitish-gray powder. This powder can form a protective layer; as with other metals, however, in severe environments, the corrosion can continue to erode the metal and cause significant damage.

One of the most commonly viewed problems of aluminum corrosion is where the oxide layer has formed beneath a powder coating or paint, causing the coating to peel or flake off. In environments where salts will be an issue, the use of marine-grade aluminum alloys (5000 series and above) is important to ensure the longevity of the aluminum and its coatings.

Aluminum is markedly lighter than steel and iron, and therefore can be very price-competitive for large items, such as light poles, or for other situations where shipping costs may outweigh cost of manufacture.

The relative softness of the common aluminum grades used in the landscape prevent the effective use of textured surfaces. In general, the vandalism and wear resistance that opaque coatings offer are necessary to maintain the appearance of aluminum elements.

Aluminum is one of the more widely recycled metals, largely due to its use as a food and beverage container. The high turnover of these cans provides a notable "spike" in the apparent recycled content of the aluminum products.

Aluminum is second only to steel and iron in the landscape, and is often used in castings to create benches, fences, light fixtures, and similar elements. Its lightness and low conductivity have made it a valuable sheet material for roofing, including custom and prefabricated landscape roof structures. Aluminum is rarely used in tube form, where its weaker structural properties, compared to steel, make it an impractical selection.

The use of aluminum in fountains has demonstrated failure due to corrosion of the aluminum by chlorinated water, hence should be carefully considered beforehand. Conversely, street-side or streetscape elements such as benches, bus stops, trash receptacles, signage, and light poles increasingly utilize aluminum because of its corrosion resistance to the high levels of road salt spray these elements are subjected to.

Zinc

Zinc has been widely used for the creation of statuary, grave markers, fountains, and vases, and thus plays a major role in our civic and monumentary history. This use was largely due to zinc's ease of manufacture in casting and stamping of sheet zinc, and its low relative cost. The appearance of a natural or silvered zinc was rare, however, as the objects were generally painted to simulate a different material, such as bronze, copper, or stone. Possibly because of the relatively rare use of zinc in statuary today, many of the older zinc statues are incorrectly identified as a different metal (Grissom, 2005). High-purity zinc left in an unpainted state with an oxide outer layer was referred to as white bronze (Grissom, 2005), primarily as a marketing name to make the material more attractive. Classicists of the 1800s despaired of the trend and the unfinished zinc eventually fell out of fashion.

Zinc is a fairly soft and brittle metal, wherein larger castings can bend and deform under its own weight over time. This can eventually cause warping and cracking of a cast piece. Historic practices of casting zinc objects utilized smaller pieces to create the larger statue, joining the pieces with solder. Today, these solder joints are often where cracks will appear.

The most common use of zinc in the landscape today is as a component of galvanizing, due to its sacrificial corrosion properties. These corrosion properties affect the life span of zinc castings and sheets in the landscape and generally make the use of organic coatings a requirement in all but the cleanest environments.

Repairing zinc requires extreme care, and the use of weaker joints is recommended to ensure the preservation of the zinc object (Grissom, 2005). The abuse of historic zinc statues and fountains through uninformed repair efforts has been great. While all important historic metalworks should be analyzed by a professional conservator, the need with zinc is most acute.

Titanium

Titanium as an architectural metal has only recently come on to the scene in North America, thanks in large part to the architecture of Frank Gehry. Titanium is an extremely durable metal with excellent corrosion resistance, lending it to be used where a metallic appearance is desirable. There have been a number of cases where titanium has stained, though its propensity for this has not yet been proven.

The very high cost of titanium is its most limiting factor. Because of this, it is primarily available in very thin sheeting. Uses in the landscape must account for this factor, as the sheets require sufficient, continuous backing to prevent denting and other deformation.

As with stainless steel in the twentieth century, we are just at the genesis of titanium's use, and may see significant changes in its use and availability in the near future.

COMMON FORMS OF METAL (RAW)

Casting

Simply put, metal casting is pouring molten metal into a mold to create a shape. The mold-making process can be labor-intensive and will often be the highest cost of the production. Consequently, the repeated use of the mold will reduce the cost of the product. This can either be amortized through the project at hand, as in the production of a railing post for a railing system half-mile long, or the fabricator may undertake it as a future design product that can be placed on the open market.

There are size limitations with most castings, either in the practical size of the molds, the ovens, or the furnaces. For this reason, it is rare that large landscape objects can be cast as single pieces. More often, the objects will be cast as several small pieces and welded together. The weld can have serious implications on the product, and is where the services of an engineer familiar with welding are important.

Simplified definition of casting aside, there are a number of casting methods and practices that will significantly affect the properties of the product in everything from tensile strength to corrosion resistance. When creating a custom product, it is important to note these methods to ensure a quality product. The more common types of casting include, from roughest to finest level of detail: sand casting, investment or lost wax casting, and die casting. A fourth method, centrifugal casting, is growing in popularity, with improved mechanical and chemical structure properties; however, it is not often seen in landscape applications due to size issues.

Casting can be used for virtually every landscape element, and is common for items such as benches, bollards, posts, finials, sculpture and statuary, planters, plaques, grates, and utility covers.

Bars

Bars are solid linear metal forms in square, rectangular, and round (also referred to as rods) cross-section shapes. Bars are most commonly seen in fences, gates and railings.

Due to the improved structural capability and lower material costs of tubing, bars are generally only used where the dimensions of the metal member are too small to effectively use a tube.

Tubes

Tubing is a hollow linear form, which can be found in both round and square cross section, with standard variations. Tubes can exhibit higher strength-to-weight properties than solid bars and rounds. As less materials are used, tubes also tend to be more cost-efficient that solid products.

Tubes come in two varieties: welded and seamless. The welded form is a rolled sheet that has been continuously welded along the joining. Seamless tubes, by contrast, are produced by extrusion. In general, the cost for welded tubes is much lower than seamless.

In design with tubing, it is important to note that the seam in welded tubes will be visible in the raw metal, and can be visible through roughened and patterned surface finishes. If welded tube is selected and will not be coated with an opaque material, it is important to ensure in the installation that the seams are faced away from public view.

The distinction between tubes and pipes is primarily that of use. Pipes are typically used to convey fluids; tubes are used in architectural applications. While many pipes may be used as tubes, there may be fine distinctions of metallurgy, strength, and finish that are important considerations. Additionally, the measurements for tubes and pipes are very different. Tubes are measured as a unit of outer diameter; for pipes, it is the reverse, measuring the inner diameter and providing gauge or similar wall thickness measures.

Tubes have extensive use in the landscape, most recognizably as railings, guardrails, and handrails. Tubes are also used as bicycle racks, bollards, tree guards, and light poles. Due to their high strength, tubes also are highly useful for security applications.

Sheets

The most common difference between bars, strip, and plate is their dimensions of width and thickness. The thickness of "sheet" is expressed in gauge rather than in inches. Typically, metals less than 1/4 inch in thickness are referred to as "sheet," while a greater thickness than ¼ inch uses the term "plate." "Sheet" is formed by rolling a malleable slab of metal through a rolling mill to achieve a certain maximum thickness and minimum width.

Due to its thinness, consideration of the most appropriate metal for sheets and plates holds a greater importance. Issues of corrosion, strength, and bending are magnified in sheet and plate use. Comparative cost studies can be a valuable aid in design, as thicker sheets of one metal may be more or less expensive than a higher-strength potential substitute.

Sheet is used to fulfill a wide variety of uses. In its simplest form, copper and aluminum sheets are used for flashing. It can also be used for edging, roofing, and siding, and for such decorative uses to create "cutouts," appliqués, and silhouettes.

Many metals are produced in sheet form, including steel, copper, aluminum, and titanium. From the initial sheet form, other shapes and forms can be fabricated to create a wide variety of items for industrial and decorative uses, as the relative thinness of "sheet" enables it to be formed by bending, stamping, and other means of hand and mechanical shaping.

Items that are fabricated from sheet metal include roof gutters and leaders, signage, mailboxes, vases, planters, light fixtures, fountains, light shades, site furniture, landscape water features, and decorative three-dimensional site elements.

It is also employed to provide fastenings and attachment elements, such as "straps" for bundling, and bands for attaching elements to another component such as signs to light poles

Cable

Due to its high tensile strength and low cost, steel is the most common metal used for cables in the landscape. Second in availability is aluminum, which has begun to replace copper in electrical wire due to its lower cost. Aluminum cables are available in a large variety of sizes, but we have yet to see any use specifically for the landscape or in any particular landscape design.

Landscape applications of cabling tend to be comparatively small-gauge cables, hence thinner strands. This in turn, creates a greater surface area for corrosion reactions. Stainless steel has become the standard for most landscape cables, to counteract this.

The use of cables has increased greatly in recent years. Trellises and screens, furniture, and particularly railings and guardrails are common areas for cables. Tensile overhead structures have utilized cables for their unique architectural properties and their lightness and transparency. Cables have even been used as portions of security barriers.

In regard to the use of cables for railings, one word of caution is the maintenance and vandalism potential for exposed turnbuckles and other fastening and tension hardware. Simply screwing and unscrewing the turnbuckles can leave a rail system ineffective or unsightly. Use of locking or hidden mechanical elements is therefore an important design consideration. Additionally, the shrink/swell of metal cable in northern climates can have the cables tight in winter and slack in summer, which in itself requires maintenance to adjust for this.

ATTACHMENTS

Welds

A proper weld is the strongest method of metal attachment available. Properly designed and constructed, a weld can provide strength equal to the metal objects themselves.

Welding is a complex procedure that requires a skilled professional both to construct and design. Weld design and specification should be undertaken only by qualified structural engineers or metallurgists.

Flux Welding

Flux welding is a blacksmith's weld, wherein two pieces of iron or steel are hammered together with a flux—a liquid or powder that allows the two metal pieces to flow together. The art of this weld has made it rare, so that the technical specification of it is not recommended, with the exception to allow a commissioned artist-blacksmith to use it if appropriate.

Arc Welding

Arc welding utilizes an electrical arc as the source of heat to melt the metals. In most applications, a rod or wire of a matching or compatible metal is utilized to fill the joints. This is the most common weld utilized for factory fabrication (Skalka, 2004).

Gas Welding

Gas welding, such as with oxyacetylene, tends to replace the use of arc welding in field applications due to the inherent dangers of arc welding outside of a controlled environment. Beyond this, the operation and results are very similar to that of arc welding.

Spot Welding

Spot welding is one of the most commonly observed forms of on-site welding, as this is the universal "fix-it" solution to unstable, cracked, or damaged metal elements in the landscape, usually for nonstructural applications. Simply put, this is the placement of a "spot" of filler material at a joint. Because of the inherent strength of a weld, often a "spot" will suffice to provide proper attachment.

The spot weld is so often seen because it often fails, either through cracking or corrosion. The primary reason for this failure is poor implementation, which can be caused by: lack of cleaning of base metals prior to welding, resulting in a weak bond or quickly corroding joint; use of improper or incompatible metals; unqualified workers; and rough, pitted welds, which trap water, and corrosive elements causing accelerated corrosion of the weld.

Spot welding, and other field welding, require as much forethought and design as other methods. This should not be subverted, as an improper weld can cause irreparable damage to the metal element itself.

Soldering

In general, soldering is the use of a low-melting-point metal, such as tin or lead, to seal joints between metals. Solder is commonly used in waterproofing of metal fountains or water features and in sheet or roofing applications. It is important to note that solder is not considered a weld, and in fact provides a very weak joint that should not be relied upon for structural uses.

Weld Materials

The filler material of a weld becomes an integral part of the metal product. Therefore, it is important to ensure that the filler has the same qualities desired in the overall element. This does not imply that the metal chemistry of the filler exactly matches that of the base metal, rather that all due consideration is given to this particular material.

Mechanical

Mechanical fasteners consist of the bolts, screws, nails, rivets, and other fasteners that are generally referred to as "hardware." Due to its superior strength, most mechanical fasteners are made of a form of steel.

Mechanical fasteners are second to welds in strength, but offer many options that welds cannot. Foremost of these is the removability or changeability of the elements that the hardware attaches, without damage to the elements. Additionally, welds cannot be applied to nonmetallic items, so that mechanical fasteners are often the only options available for attachments with wood, concrete, plastics, and masonry.

Steel fasteners are now available in a variety of grades, including stainless steels. Stainless-steel fasteners have an inherent fastening problem, called galling, so their use should be limited to situations where stainless is necessary for its corrosion resistance, or when connecting stainless-steel elements. Of the carbon steel, common grades are 2, 5, and 8—as the numbers rise, so do the hardness and brittleness of the fastener (Skalka, 2004).

Fasteners may be coated with a number of products, including zinc, galvanizing, and plating, including chrome. The costs and benefits of each must be examined on a case-by-case basis to determine the level of corrosion resistance required.

Mechanical fasteners are often the cause of concern about bimetallic corrosion. In most cases, bimetallic contact can be avoided by using the same metal in the fasteners as in the metal object. If this cannot be done for strength or other reasons, provide Teflon, rubber, polyethylene, or similar material separators, to limit contact between the two metals in question.

Copper and aluminum fasteners are found in the form of rivets and nails and are used for their specific oxidation (or lack thereof) properties or malleability. Common uses for copper nails are for roofing and historic applications. Aluminum nails are particularly useful for fencing, decking, and similar wood systems that utilize cedar, redwood, and similar naturally rot-resistant softwoods. The natural chemicals of these woods will cause oxidation of steel nails, hence stain streaks of the wood. Conversely, pressure-treated woods will quickly oxidize aluminum and galvanized nails.

Tamper resistance—the weakest link in the use of mechanical fasteners—does not necessarily refer to the mechanical or structural properties, but to the potential of unauthorized humans to remove, damage, or otherwise render the fasteners inoperable. A wide variety of tamper-resistant fastener styles are now available that make tampering more difficult by requiring specialized tools or making the fastener nonremovable.

An important design consideration in the use of tamper-resistant fasteners on a project is the maintenance required. The number of styles or types of tamper-resistant fastener heads should be limited to as few as possible to ensure that maintenance personnel will have the proper tools available when in the field. See *Nails; Screws and Bolts; Rivets, Screws, and Miscellaneous Fasteners;* and *Shields and Anchors* following this article.

Base Metal

In the case of steel and stainless steel, there are low-carbon-content steels (designated with an "L") that were developed specifically to improve the welded product. Steel elements that will have a large number or percentage of welds are generally recommended, to utilize the low-carbon grades. For corrosion resistance, this is particularly useful, as the heat process of welding can sufficiently change the chemical structure in the weld zone to increase its susceptibility to corrosion.

Weld Quality

As previously stated, a properly made weld can be as strong as the metal objects it is joining. However, in the landscape, the weld can become one of the points of failure due to corrosion. The reason is that, if left unfinished, the pinholes, spatter, and crevices of the weld can collect water, salts, and other chemicals that can hasten corrosion. Additionally, welds at crevices, low points, or other improperly designed junctions will tend to collect water, salts, and other pollutants that can hasten the corrosion of the joints.

The National Ornamental & Miscellaneous Metals Association (NOMMA) offers a visual guide for weld quality that illustrates four levels of finish for a weld. As destructive testing and other methods can be cost-prohibitive, this guideline, while voluntary, can be highly useful in establishing and confirming the basis for weld quality. The document is titled "Guideline 1: Joint Finishes," and is available from NOMMA through its Web site at www.nomma.org.

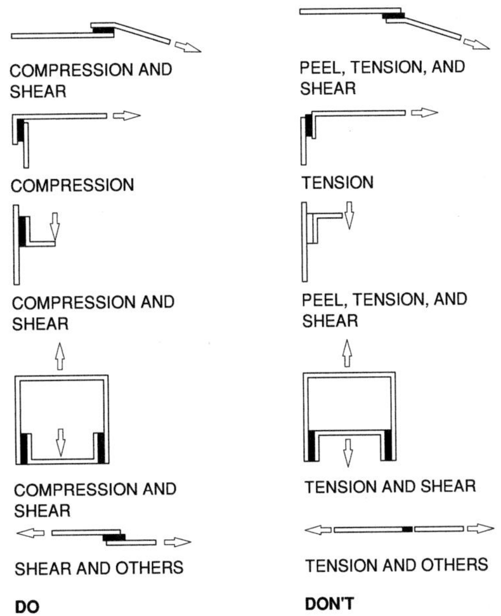

JOINT DESIGN DIAGRAM

Source: Courtesy of Lord Corporation.

Glues

A number of adhesives have been developed for the metals industry that may have some applicability to the landscape. Developed for automobiles, these are often stable and resistant to environmental stresses (UV, salt, and pollution).

The primary uses for adhesives will be found with sheet metal, and are already common in creating signage. The advantage to using glues is the ability to create a fairly seamless appearance (no visible connection). Additionally, being able to adhere the metal to a different material, such as plastic and fiberglass, can be very important in creating a more affordable product.

A number of conditions are important to the proper use of adhesives on metals. The surfaces to be adhered must be in direct contact with each other, having no gaps, pockets, or dirt. The importance of a clean surface and full contact cannot be overstated; in general, their absence prevents the effective use of metal adhesives in the field. Adhesives require a larger surface-to-surface connection to create a strong bond, which can be provided through a significant overlap of the pieces being attached. The good and bad examples shown in the figure demonstrate general design principles to consider for utilizing adhesives.

OXIDATION AND CORROSION

Oxidation is a chemical process that affects all metals. It is the combination of the metal with oxygen to form a compound that has entirely different mechanical properties from the base metal. A good example is the rust that can form from iron or steel. If oxidation continues beyond the surface level, it is referred to as corrosion and can affect the structural integrity of the metals.

While oxidation is generally associated with iron and steel, it occurs in all metals to greater and lesser degrees. As with all chemical reactions, there are factors that can affect the process, which are outlined below.

Environment

The environment for metals is concerned with the chemicals present around them. Water plays a particular role, in that its presence will accelerate all types of oxidation. The impact from water will also erode the oxide layer created, leading to further oxidation of the metal beneath. Water is also a carrier for acids, salts, and other pollutants that can significantly increase oxidation and corrosion.

Salt

As human settlements have concentrated around coastal areas, a great number of metalwork applications occur in marine environments, which are all tidal areas, including rivers. The tidal actions will bring in brackish water, which can be nearly as damaging as the salt spray found at the beach.

For inland projects, significant salt deposition can result from deicing salts applied to roads and sidewalks. A common problem with site furniture and railings is the corrosion of the metal within the first few inches from the ground due to the application of salts in pedestrian areas.

Salt spray from the roadways is equally common. The spray increases with the velocity of the cars, so that spray from a highway can travel a surprising height and distance from this source.

Pollution

Pollution is also a contributing factor, adding a source of salts and acids through rainwater. Acid rain can markedly increase the rate of oxidation and corro-

LENGTH
HEAD HEIGHT
THREAD LENGTH
DIAMETER*
HEAD DIAMETER
*DIAMETER MEASURED TO OUTSIDE OF THREADS
(IF THREADS EXTEND TO BASE OF HEAD, IT IS NOTED AS "FULLY THREADED" AND NO THREAD LENGTH IS GIVEN)

HEAD HEIGHT MEASURED FROM POINT OF CURVEATURE
EXCEPTION COUNTERSUNK HEADS
LENGTH OF COUNTERSUNK AND SIMILAR FLAT HEAD SCREWS INCLUDES HEAD
THREADS MEASURED AS THREADS PER INCH (TPI)
EX.: 4 - (40) – NUMBER INDICATES THREADS PER INCH
OR AS DISTANCE BETWEEN THREADS (METRIC)
EX.: M3 x (0.5) – NUMBER INDICATES DISTANCE BETWEEN THREADS (mm)

GUIDE TO STANDARD HARDWARE MEASUREMENTS

Nathan Imm, RLA, EDAW, William B. Kuhl, RLA, Saratoga Associates (formerly with EDAW)

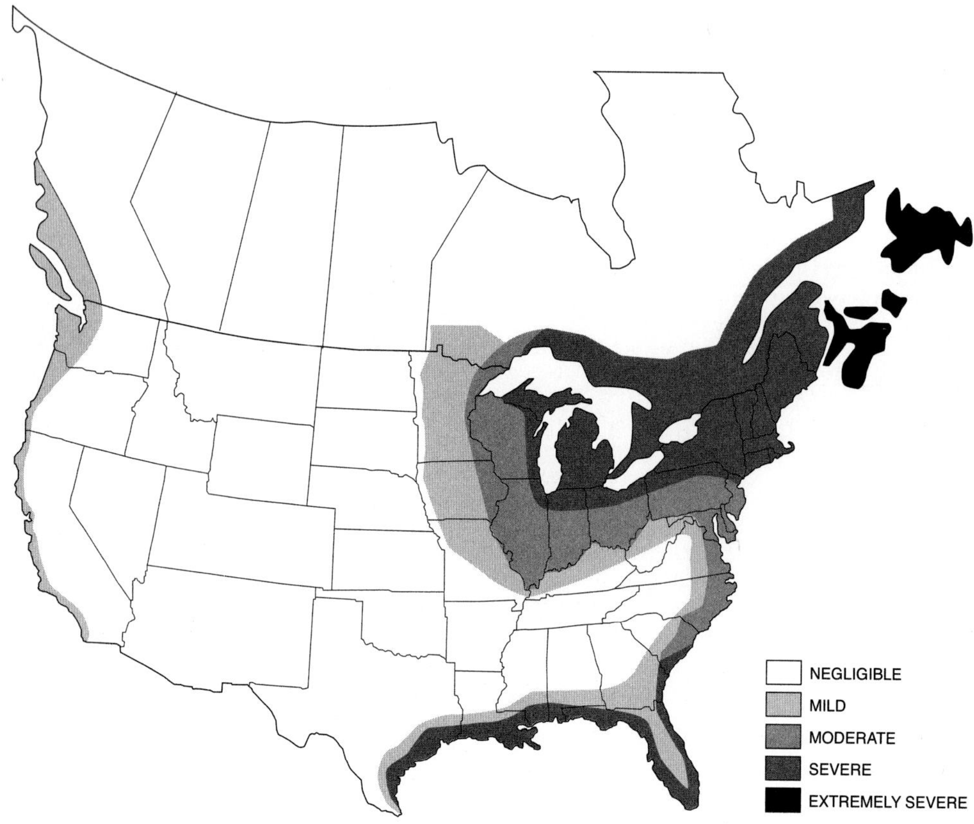

MAP OF CHLORIDE CONCENTRATIONS IN RAINFALL

Source: Courtesy of Specialty Steel Industry of North America (SSINA).

sion. In particular, acid rain can cause the erosion of the oxide layer. This contribution to erosion has been blamed for the loss of features on bronze statues throughout northern Europe.

In addition to these broader pollution effects, localized pollution can have a major impact. A factory or highway can deposit sulfuric acids and other harsh chemicals on metals nearby. Environmental chemicals that can affect metal include cleaning products. A common concrete cleaner is muriatic acid, which has a strong corroding effect on stainless steel. The metal selection should not be based on the cleaning products; rather, the maintenance protocols should be established based on the metals present on a project.

Surface Area

An increased surface area means that there is a greater quantity of material exposed to the chemical reaction. The rougher the surface of a metal, the more surface that is exposed to the elements. Conversely, the smoother the surface, the less base metal is available to the chemical reaction. Hence, a smoother surface is less susceptible to oxidation and corrosion.

On a larger scale, a rougher surface will tend to trap water, salts, and other pollutants that accelerate oxidation. This allows more time for the chemical reaction to occur, increasing the amount of oxidation. Smoother surfaces are often referred to as self-cleaning, meaning that they tend to shed water, and with it the dirt and pollutants that accelerate the oxidation.

Abrasion

All metals form a "protective" outer coating of oxide as the first step in corrosion. While many companies claim a metal to be corrosion-free after the formation of this oxide layer, the amount of further corrosion depends on the abrasive nature of the environment and the metal's natural tendency to erode. Abrasives are omnipresent, and include rain, hail, condensation (water), road grit, driven sand, and countless others.

Alloy (Metal Chemistry)

The raw, unaltered forms of any metal tend to be the most chemically reactive forms. Therefore, the alloying or mixing of metals with each other and other chemicals results in a more chemically stable product.

Coatings

Coatings serve as a barrier between the base metal and the environment. There are essentially two types of barrier: nonreactive and reactive. Nonreactive barriers such as paints and powder coats all have a life span based on environmental weathering, but do not have an active chemical feedback with the environment. Conversely, reactive barriers such as galvanizing and thermal sprays are referred to as "sacrificial" barriers, themselves corroding in protection of the base metal.

Design

In the same way that poor design causes failure in other applications, so it does with metals. A design that allows water to collect, with all of the pollutants, acids, and salts that it may carry, will cause an increase in corrosion. This is particularly notable at connections such as bolts and welds. Cracks, crevices, and holes should be avoided, or provided with a water-shedding curve or radius where exposed to the weather or where water may be conveyed toward it by the design of the element itself.

The creation of areas that collect water is a particular concern, as oxygen-deprived areas of metal can cause a strong electron-exchange reaction that will speed corrosion even further than simply due to the presence of water.

Weep holes are an important, and often overlooked, aspect in designing hollow metal objects, including tube railings and fences. Condensation and collection of water on the interior of the hollow can cause unseen corrosion.

Where metal elements are directly embedded in a concrete foundation, water will find its way into the hole and corrode the metal within the concrete. A design that prevents water from reaching the interface between the concrete and the metal is the best solution. This can be accomplished through the provision of metal flares, caps, or similar devices that direct water away, or through the proper slope and chamfer of the concrete.

Poor design that can cause corrosion can be seen at a larger scale as well. Placement of metals in poorly drained areas, roof drain leaders directed toward metal elements, and the placement of planter drains above metals are all easy-to-avoid mistakes.

ANODIC INDEX OR GALVANIC SCALE OF METAL COMPATIBILITY

METALLURGY	INDEX (V)
Nickel, solid or plated; titanium as an alloy; Monel	0.30
Copper, solid or plated; low brasses or bronzes; silver solder; German silvery high copper-nickel alloys; nickel-chromium alloys	0.35
Brass and bronzes	0.40
High brasses and bronzes	0.45
18% chromium-type corrosion-ant steels	0.50
Chromium-plated; tin-plated; 12% chromium-type corrosion-resistant steels	0.60
Tin-plated; tin-lead solder	0.65
Lead, solid or plated; high-lead alloys	0.70
Aluminum, wrought alloys of the 2000 series	0.75
Iron, wrought, gray, or malleable; plain carbon and low-alloy steels	0.85
Aluminum; wrought alloys other than 2000 series aluminum; cast alloys of the silicon type	0.90
Aluminum; cast alloys other than silicon type; cadmium, plated and chromate	0.95
Hot-dip-zinc-plated	1.20
Zinc, wrought; zinc-base die-casting alloys; zinc-plated	1.25

Nathan Imm, RLA, EDAW, William B. Kuhl, RLA, Saratoga Associates (formerly with EDAW)

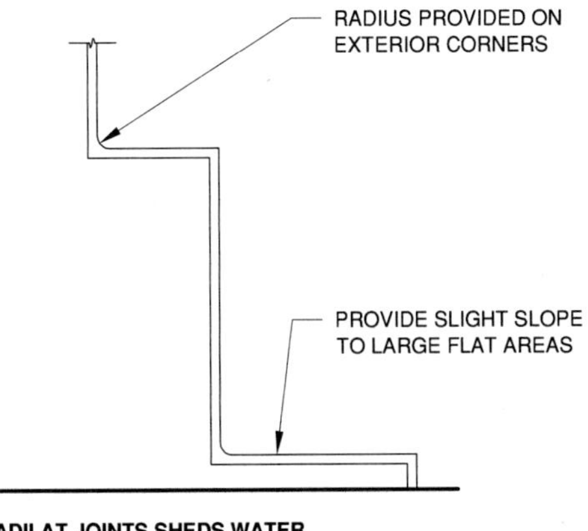

RADII AT JOINTS SHEDS WATER

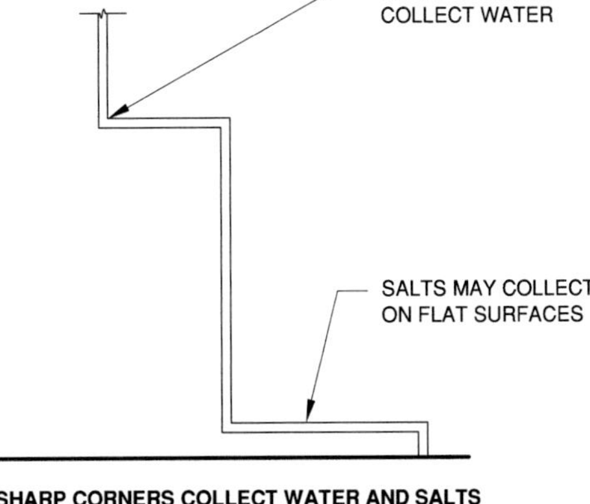

SHARP CORNERS COLLECT WATER AND SALTS

CASTINGS

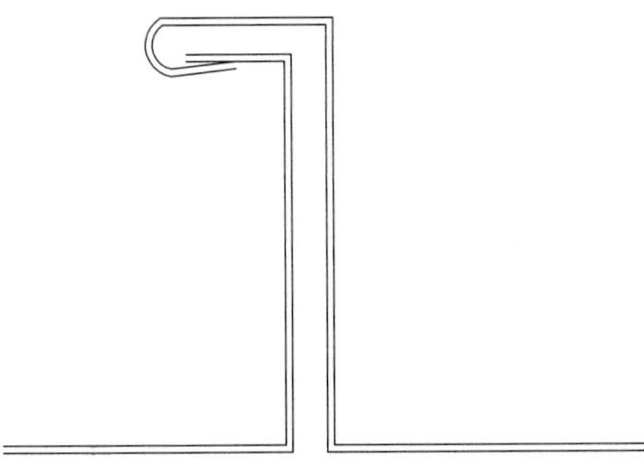

INTERLOCKED SEAM PREVENTS WATER FROM COLLECTING

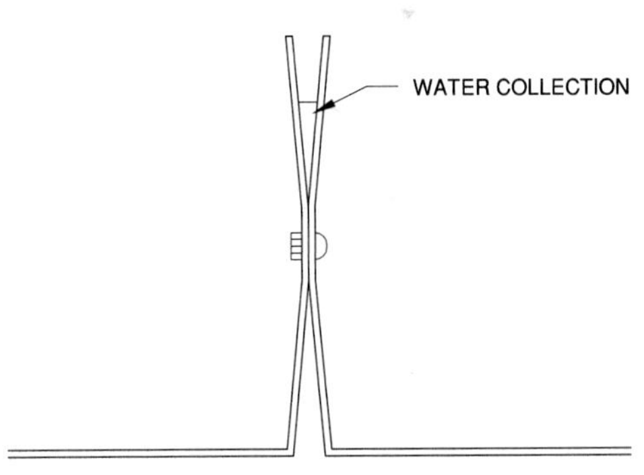

BOLTED SEAM SPREADS METAL AT TOP, COLLECTING WATER TO HASTEN CORROSION

SHEET METAL

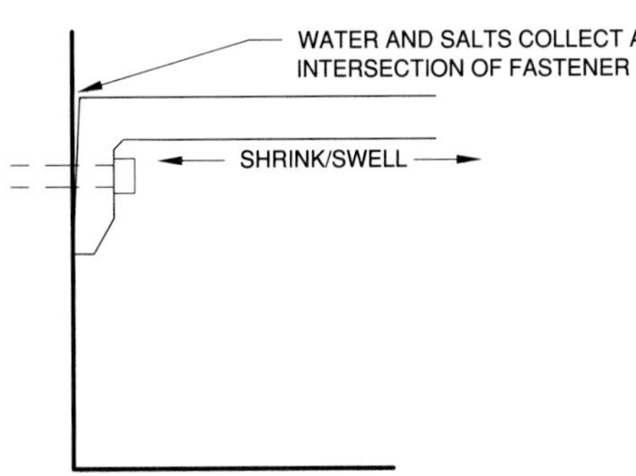

CREVICE DIRECTS WATER TO JOINT/FASTENER, HASTENING CORROSION

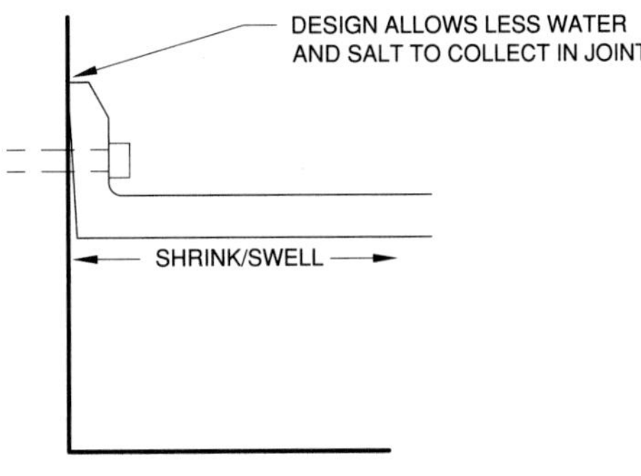

CREVICE FORMS AT BOTTOM, DRAINING WATER

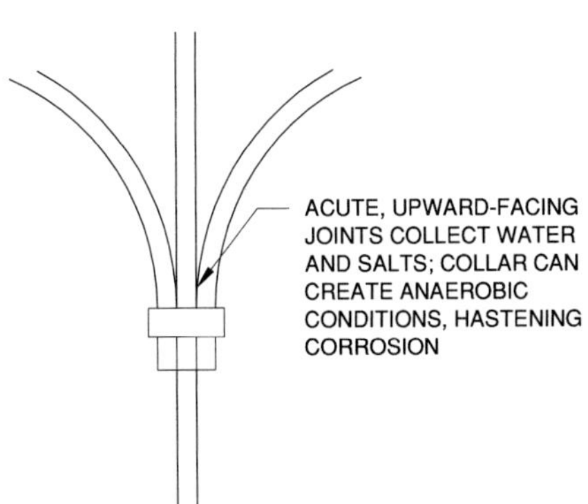

RADII AT JOINTS SHEDS WATER

BARS

EXAMPLES OF DESIGN IMPACTS ON CORROSION

Nathan Imm, RLA, EDAW, William B. Kuhl, RLA, Saratoga Associates (formerly with EDAW)

Corrosion versus Staining or Oxide Layer

As a definition, corrosion is the unabated oxidation of a metal: it will continue until all of the unoxidized metal is consumed. The term "corrosion" is also generally used to indicate the concentrated erosion of the metal, in particular providing a structural threat to the metal object.

Corrosion is the most extreme mode of oxidation. On the other end is staining or the creation of an oxide layer. The term "staining" is generally used in reference to stainless steels or similarly highly resistant metals. This is a surficial oxide that tends not to form a complete layer or covering, rather appearing as blotches or spots. A stain is less susceptible to erosion as well, as the oxidized metal is surrounded even at the surface by unoxidized metal. Conversely, an oxide layer is a skin of oxide that forms on the metal surface. Copper patina is the best example of this.

In examination of an existing metal object in the field, or a weathered sample, it is important to determine where in this continuum the oxidation lies.

Bimetallic Corrosion

Otherwise known as galvanic corrosion, this corrosion process is caused by the exchange of electrons between significantly dissimilar metals. The "Anodic Index or Galvanic Scale of Metal Compatibility" table lists a variety of metals in order of galvanic action: the further apart two metals are on this list, the greater the corrosive reaction; conversely, the closer the two metals are on the list, the safer or less corrosive they will be.

One of the most common solutions where two different metals are utilized is to separate the metals by a gasket or similar. The selection of the gasket becomes very important in this case, as its life span will directly impact the life span of the metals. Gaskets should also be nonabsorbent, as the water collecting in the gasket can convey the electrons as efficiently as if the two metals were in contact.

Metal Corrosion

Corrosion, which is caused by galvanic action, occurs between dissimilar metals or between metals and

THE GALVANIC SERIES

Anode (least noble) +	Magnesium, magnesium alloys
	Zinc
	Aluminum 1100
	Cadmium
	Aluminum 2024-T4
	Steel or iron, cast iron
	Chromium iron (active)
	Ni-Resist
	Type 304, 316 stainless (active)
	Hastelloy "C"
	Lead, tin
Electric current flows from positive (+) to negative (–)	Nickel (Inconel) (active)
	Hastelloy "B"
	Brasses, copper, bronzes, copper-nickel alloys, monel
	Silver solder
	Nickel (Inconel) (passive)
	Chromium iron (passive)
	Type 304, 316 stainless (passive)
	Silver
	Titanium
Cathode (most noble) –	Graphite, gold, platinum

other material when sufficient moisture is present to carry an electrical current. The information shown in the table "The Galvanic Series" is a useful indicator of corrosion susceptibility caused by galvanic action. The metals listed are arranged in order from the least noble (most reactive to corrosion) to the most noble (least reactive to corrosion). The farther apart two metals on the list are, the greater the deterioration of the less noble one will be if they come in contact under adverse conditions.

Cleaning

Prior to the discussion of coating, sealing, or other surface treatments intended to prevent oxidation and corrosion, there must be some discussion of cleaning. Cleaning is primarily a factory process that must be dealt with appropriately in the specification of the product. In the case of stainless steels, the use of a passivation and/or pickling process is important to remove traces of carbon steel that may remain on the metal—which in turn would oxidize and could cause the stainless steel to stain or oxidize.

Coating and Sealing

A common and effective means of protecting metals from corrosion is applying a coating that either provides a barrier to water and chemicals or that itself corrodes to preserve the underlying metal.

All such coatings have a life span, which is entirely dependent on the environment. A more corrosive environment will reduce the life span of a coating, much as it will to the base metal.

In all cases, routine inspection and maintenance is essential to prolong the life and aesthetics of any finished element of metal in the landscape. Such inspections should be performed such that they analyze the coating prior to failure—in other words, before the base metal shows corrosion through the coating.

In designing and selecting the coating, it is important to consider the anticipated maintenance. Will on-site recoating be required, or will the metal element be removed and delivered to a shop for reapplication? What are the costs and benefits of either approach? What will the client be willing to do, and how often would it have to be done? Such considerations at the design phase are critical to ensuring the longevity of the metal objects.

Paint

The term "paint" is used to identify certain liquid-applied coatings having an organic base. Paint has been extensively used to protect metals from surface corrosion, particularly in on-site applications, due to its low cost and portability.

Paint is unique in its flexibility, allowing a creative and cost-effective use of multiple colors and patterns without compromising the protection system. The ability to match the paint color after years of use based on either a color sample or specific numeric code via Pantone or similar systems is an important life span consideration (other coating systems have imperfect matching capabilities for colored coatings).

Historically, paints have been widely used to protect metals, and provided the metal objects with their desired appearance. Many objects, particularly statues and fountains, were constructed of metal because of its lower cost and durability, and then painted to look like stone, wood, or a more expensive metal such as bronze or gold. The artwork of faux finishes is particularly important to historic conservation and restoration of exterior metal works.

Paints also have often been used to provide depth and luster to a metal object. The addition of metal flakes (now replaced by the use of mylar flakes) added a reflectivity to the metal. The current use of flat and uniform paints, particularly black, is antithetical to the historic appearance of many metal objects, and is one of the most common mistakes made in both maintenance and historic restoration projects.

For best adhesion, a primer is first applied to the base metal. The primer is a surfacing material that provides anchorage and promotes adhesion of the paint to the underlying metal. Particular attention must be paid to cleaning contamination and rust from carbon steel surfaces, as paints are not waterproof. If the surfaces are not properly cleaned and rust is painted over, oxidation will continue and rust will again become an issue, compromising the integrity of the painted finish.

Paint over metal is unlike paint over wood because there is no absorption by the metal. This basic parameter is paint's main weakness in that the surface adhesion can be incomplete at application, or it can separate through use, such as bubbling, chipping, or scratching. Any form of separation means that the paint is no longer protecting the metal.

Paint is a "system" of surface preparation and multiple coatings, and should be considered in this manner for metals, rather than as a single product. An important resource for selection of paint systems is the brief manual entitled "Corrosion Protection of Ferrous Metals," developed and published by the National Ornamental & Miscellaneous Metals Association (NOMMA).

Liquid paints are either oil- or water-based. Water-based paints should not be utilized as a primer on metals, as the water can cause instantaneous corrosion, sufficient to prevent a tight seal of the primer, causing further corrosion and failure of the whole paint system (Magaziner, 2001). Of the commonly available paints, urethanes are generally considered the longest-lasting for exterior applications (NOMMA) There has been a recent appearance of a number of paint products that claim to "stop" or "heal" rust. Many of these suggest that the paint can be applied over rusty iron with no pretreatment, which would present a huge labor savings. On the face of it, much of the chemistry is correct, as these products provide improved penetration of the oxidized layers, sealing off water, oxygen, and chemicals. However, a three-part note of extreme caution is in order here. First, in historic metalworks, a conservator specializing in metals should be involved prior to treatment. Second, these paints have the same inherent weaknesses of all other paints in incomplete finishing and material separation, and life span. Finally, where the metals in question provide life safety or structural benefits, paint will not restore the integrity of the metal if the corrosion has caused structural damage.

Many paints are contributors to pollution through the release of volatile organic compounds (VOCs) in their curing process. A number of states, including California and several Mid-Atlantic and Northeast states, limit the amount of VOCs allowed in paint in large or industrial applications. LEED standards likewise recognize low- or no-VOC paints in its certification process. With sustainability concerns, the effectiveness of the coating and its subsequent maintenance needs must be weighed against its initial environmental impact.

Recent findings have shown that microorganisms can significantly impact the life span and efficacy of both paint and powder coats. These microorganisms can feed on and within the polymers of these coatings and excrete organic acids, speeding the removal of the coating and corrosion of the base metal. New paint and powder coat products are in development to counteract these impacts.

Powder Coat

Powder coating has become important industrially in the last 35 years in the manufacture of parts and products for outdoor use. In this process, the powder coating is applied through an electrostatic process. The parts are hung on a conveyor that is electrically neutral (i.e., grounded). In a controlled "spray booth," a powder is sprayed onto the metal and adheres to the metal, because, as the powder goes through the special spray guns, it takes on an electrical charge. Then the conveyor moves the parts into a curing or baking oven. In the curing process, the powder liquefies and flows and covers the metal part. Various powders are available depending on the use to which the parts or products will be utilized. Many powders consist of the same type of polymers and resins used in liquid applied paints, without the solvents of paint.

Powder coating has many advantages over liquid paint, including superior adhesion or bonding to the underlying metal surface, and a more uniform application, which can lead to improved corrosion resistance. However, powder coating generally lacks the flexibility in color variation and the ability to create highlighted or faux finishes, generally resulting in a very flat look to the metal objects.

One of the primary weaknesses of powder coating is that it cannot be reapplied in the field, nor can it effectively be painted over. Localized areas of damage or corrosion must be sanded to the base metal and painted, which often leaves an area of different color because of difficulty in matching differing materials. Where elements can easily be removed and returned to the factory for retreatment, this may be the most effective approach. However, this approach can be prohibitively expensive due to labor and shipping.

The life span of powder coat systems does not necessarily exceed that of a high-quality paint system; nevertheless, it can ensure that many of the human errors of application are avoided.

GALVANIZING

Hot-Dip Galvanizing

Galvanizing is the protection of steel and iron from corrosion by creating a chemically bonded alloyed surface, typically of zinc or combinations of zinc and aluminum.

Hot-dip galvanizing is done on chemically clean steel and iron by immersion in molten zinc. The zinc and iron combine to form an alloy that resists corrosion and mechanical damage. Prepared iron or steel goes through four stages in the galvanizing process: mechanical cleaning, preflux, galvanizing, and finishing. Different steel compositions are considered more reactive to zinc and create a thicker alloy, or in some cases convert the metal to all zinc/iron alloy. The higher the alloy content, the more brittle the metal becomes. ASTM provides standards for metal sheets, piping and tubing, and fasteners. Galvanized products can last up to 100 years without corrosion, depending on the environment and the initial steel used for the process.

Nathan Imm, RLA, EDAW, William B. Kuhl, RLA, Saratoga Associates (formerly with EDAW)

Powder coating over galvanized metals is really an art rather than a science, although encouraging results have been obtained by some manufacturers. Liquid painting over galvanizing is difficult, and often the resulting paint finish can be subject to chipping and eventual deterioration.

Cold Dip

"Cold" galvanizing is not a chemically bonded process, but rather the application of a 95 percent zinc-rich paint to metals. It provides corrosion protection, but since the zinc is not chemically bonded to the metal, it does not provide the durability or strength of hot-dip galvanizing.

Cold galvanizing paints contain a high VOC content, causing a negative impact in pollution generated. That said, a number of new zinc paint products without VOCs are now offered and should be specified where regulatory or environmental concerns are present.

Thermal Spray

In the thermal spray process, metal wires of zinc or aluminum are superheated and sprayed onto the base metal surface. The sacrificial oxidation process of this coating is similar to galvanizing. The surface roughness and appearance of thermal spray is markedly different from galvanizing, providing a uniform and "sparkly" appearance, and therefore may have increased applicability in decorative landscape use.

Thermal spray does not form a chemical bond with the base metal, therefore initial bonding is not as strong as hot-dip galvanizing. However, the reapplication is purported to be much more durable than cold galvanizing and can be applied in the field with specialized equipment.

Anodic Coatings

Anodic coatings are unique to aluminum, and are the controlled creation of an oxide layer within an acidic bath. For the landscape, anodic coatings must be specified as protective or architecture class in order to provide sufficient protection to the base metal. Anodic coatings can be clear or colored; however, the colors available for use in the landscape are limited to bronze and black, as all other colors are currently unstable when exposed to ultraviolet light (NAAMM).

Plating

Chrome and nickel plating are the most commonly seen examples of metal coating. Metal coatings or plating are applied through a variety of industrial processes, including hot dipping, electrolytic action, and electroplating (NAAMM).

As the metals used in plating are noble, they are extremely corrosion-resistant. However, these metal coatings can be mechanically damaged, particularly through the use of mechanical fasteners. Once damaged, the coating does not function as galvanizing, in that there is no sacrificial action on the part of the metal coating. Therefore, the base metal will corrode while the plating will remain intact except to flake off where the base metal has corroded out from under it.

Metal plating creates an extremely high reflectivity, causing a blinding glare.

Clear Coats

In general, clear coats are utilized to display and protect the natural, unoxidized appearance of the metal. It's important to caution, however, that these should be utilized as added protection, not the primary line

REPRESENTATIVE ARCHITECTURAL USES AND COMPARATIVE PROPERTIES OF COATINGS

BINDER TYPE	TYPICAL USES[1]	COST	OUTDOOR LIFE (YEARS)	COLOR STABLE, EXTERIOR	GLOSS RETENTION, EXTERIOR	STAIN RESISTANCE	WEATHER RESISTANCE	ABRASION AND IMPACT RESISTANCE	FLEXIBILITY	WATER REDUCIBLE AVAILABLE	CLEAR AVAILABLE	WELDABLE AS PRIMER
Acrylics Solvent-reducible	Residential siding and similar products; cabinets and implements; clear topcoats	M	10	yes	G	F	G	G	G	—	yes	yes[2]
Water-reducible: air dried		M	5–10	yes	F	F	G	G	G	yes	yes	yes[2]
baked		M	15–20	yes	G–E	F	G–E	G	G	yes	yes	yes[2]
Alkyds	Exterior primers and enamels	L–M	5–9	no	G	F	F	F	F–G	yes	yes	yes[2]
Cellulose (acetate or butyrate)	Decorative high-gloss finishes	M	NA	yes	G	F	G	G	G	no	yes	no
Chlorinated rubber	Corrosion-resistant paints; swimming pool coatings; protection of dissimilar metals	M	10	yes	F	F	G	G	G	no	no	no
Chloro sulfonated polyethylene	Paints for piping, tanks, valves, etc.	VH	15	yes	NA	F	E	F–G	E	no	no	no
Epoxy	Moisture- and alkali-resistant coatings; nondecorative interior uses requiring high chemical resistance	H–VH	15–20	no	P	G	G–E	E	G	no	no	yes[2]
Fluorocarbons	High-performance exterior coatings; industrial siding; curtain walls	VH	20+	yes	E	E	E	E	G	no	no	no
Phenol formaldehyde	Chemical- and moisture-resistant coatings	M	10	no	F	F	G–E	G–E	G	no	yes	yes[2]
Polyester	Cabinets and furniture; ceiling tile; piping	H	15	some versions	G–E	G–E	G–E	G	G–E	yes	yes	no
Polyvinyl chloride	Residential siding; plastisols; industrial siding; curtain walls	H	15	yes	G	F	G–E	G	G–E	yes	no	yes[2]
Silicates (inorganic)	Corrosion-inhibitive primers; solvent-resistant coatings	H	NA	NA	NA	NA	NA	G	G	no	no	yes
Silicone-modified polymers	High-performance exterior coatings; industrial siding; curtain walls	H–VH	15–20	yes	G–E	G	G–E	G–E	G	yes	no	no
Urethane (aliphatic-cured)	Heavy-duty coatings for stain chemical, abrasion, and corrosion resistance	VH	20+	some versions	E	G–E	G–E	G–E	E	yes	yes	yes[2]

L—low; M—moderate; H—high; VH—very high; NA—not applicable or not available; P—poor; F—fair; E—excellent.
[1] All coatings may be shop applied; all may be field applied except solvent reducible acrylic, baked acrylic, cellulose, and fluorocarbons.
[2] For light, nonstructural welding only.

Nathan Imm, RLA, EDAW, William B. Kuhl, RLA, Saratoga Associates (formerly with EDAW)

of defense against corrosion. Making the proper selections for metal and surface roughness will contribute more toward the lasting appearance of the product than the clear coat can.

Locations that will experience regular wear or contact, such as a handrail, will offer particular challenges to the clear coats discussed below.

Siloxanes

This group of chemicals was initially developed for corrosion prevention in machine components and has just recently found use in the landscape. The benefit of these compounds is that they create a chemical bond to the cleaned metal surface so that the coating will not bubble, peel, flake, or yellow. Additionally, the waterlike consistency of the coating allows it to fill in the profile of a roughened surface. Once cured, siloxanes also offer good wearing durability for hand contact. However, light abrasion will damage or remove the coating.

This family of materials has undergone a series of laboratory tests, generally referred to as salt-chamber testing, which has established an anticipated life span of 25 years. Still, caution is recommended, as these have not been widely field-tested. There is as yet no nondestructive testing to ensure that the minimal thicknesses are met.

These coatings can be applied in the field, but this practice is not currently considered viable, unless absolutely necessary. The number of environmental conditions that need to be met during a very long curing period (up to 72 hours) puts the coating treatment at risk. Temperature, moisture, and contact must be prevented for this entire period, a situation that is nearly impossible to provide at most job sites. Additionally, the mixing of these compounds, usually a two- or three-stage mix, is best handled in the factory. Because it is a clear coat, problems will not be visible until a problem, such as corrosion, arises.

Nonchemical Bonds

This group includes paints, powder coats, epoxies, and nylonics that are used to create a clear coating, but provide no chemical bond to the surface of the metal. The disadvantage with this group is that, due to this lack of a bond, the coating can peel, bubble, flake, and yellow.

Others Coatings

Oxide Layer

One surfacing method is to provide no protective coating, allowing the oxide layer to form. A popular example is to use Core-10 steel and simply allow the metal to rust to a dark red color. This can provide a very attractive patina and so has been used for art and sculptural pieces, in particular. The downside is that it is not a protective coating and the oxide that forms on the surface will continue to corrode. Placement of such elements on paving or concrete bases will usually result in the pavement becoming stained with the eroded oxide.

One solution that manufacturers have come up with is to oxidize the metal under controlled conditions and then spray an epoxy coating over all. The primary weakness in this approach is that the epoxy will come off, at which time the corrosion and erosion will resume unnoticed.

Black Oxide

Another oxide layer approach applied to iron and steel is referred to as 'blackening." In hot blackening, a thin, black iron oxide layer is created with a caustic soda solution. The coating is minimally corrosion-resistant and therefore of lower reliability to the landscape, versus painting or powder coating. Applications looking for a more "natural" appearance may consider this method.

There is also a cold application of blackening, but this is actually an application of a copper selenium compound and should generally be avoided, as it may not produce a consistent surface and is not as durable as the hot process.

SURFACES

Polishes

The terminology for surfacing or polishing can be very confusing as there are so many different methods that will achieve the same finish. Possibly the best is to utilize the sheet metal finish designations for all types of metal products, directly linking to a measurable surface roughness (*Ra* level), which can be tested and confirmed. Specifying a grit level or similar process-prescription can have differing results between manufacturers.

Mill Finish

Mill finishes result from the general manufacture of sheets (and tubes), with no additional polishing. The finish is a fairly dull, low-reflectivity surface, and may include machine markings or patterns.

Electropolishing

Electropolishing is a nonmechanical method for finishing the surface of metal to a high polish. The process is similar to the reverse of plating, removing surface metal through an anodic bath. Electropolishing aids in corrosion prevention both by creating a smoother surface and by preventing contamination of the metal with free iron and other pollutants, which is inherent to mechanical polishing processes.

Roughed Surfaces

Patterned

Patterned finishes are generally designated by the term "satin" of various grades from fine to coarse, decreasing in reflectivity accordingly. ASTM has developed a unified numbering system for the standard linear patterns, simplifying their specification (NAAMM).

A number of decorative patterned surfaces have been developed in recent years to provide attractive sheet metal applications for interior spaces. These are proprietary processes and patterns. In landscape applications, the cleanliness or lack of corrosion on these decorative patterns is important to the appearance, and may be a determining factor in their use.

Unpatterned

Unpatterned finishes are generally designated by the terms "matte" or "blasted." As with patterned finishes, the gradients are labeled from fine to coarse, to designate reflectivity (NAAMM).

Unpatterned roughened surfaces are commonly created by blasting the metal surface with sand or glass or metal beads. In general, sand will provide a rougher surface than the beads, and give a darker surface appearance. Glass beads may provide improved corrosion resistance to the finished surface due to fewer impurities in the shot. With all of the blast materials, the recycling or replenishment of the material can affect the corrosion resistance of the metal surface, as metal flakes may be impregnated on the surface of the metal in the process. Cleaning after blasting can rectify some of this; however, its effect depends on the depth the blasting achieved.

Glare

Glare is a major consideration in the landscape. Highly polished stainless steel may be very corrosion-resistant and otherwise appropriate for a project, but the light reflected can be undesirable, and even painful or hazardous. Placement on the north side of a building, underneath a canopy, or under evergreen trees can lessen the glare from a high polish. When these options do not exist, however, the surface of the metal is important. It is recommended that samples of the metal be examined under the conditions of the site.

LEED CERTIFICATION AND SUSTAINABILITY

Life Span Maintenance

Durability is one of the primary considerations in the use of metals for a sustainable project. Their strength and longevity can ensure that continued energy inputs are reduced.

Coating versus Cleaning

The pollution generated by the metal products specified is often directly related to the coatings, platings, or other surfaces that are utilized to protect the metal. This is due to the VOCs present in the liquid coatings, such as paints and epoxies, and the heavy metals of the waste water in plating processes, such as chroming. The option has often been exercised to utilize raw metal forms, such as stainless steel, to avoid the environmental impacts of the coverings. However, cleaning fluids used for raw metals often contain very strong acids or other powerful and potentially toxic materials, including benzene. This is necessary, as removing the staining (see section on oxidation) also removes the exterior layer of oxidized metal.

Meanwhile, the plating and coating industry is undergoing an environmental revolution wherein replacement of VOCs and recycling of heavy metals is becoming an industry standard. In short, to achieve a high level of sustainability or environmental sensitivity, the surface treatment should be the one that will last the longest without cleaning or retreatment.

Recyclability

According to Houska (2005), "Corrosion resistance, scrap metal value, the type of application, and the presence and type of coatings determine whether an average piece of metal will be recycled. Some coatings limit or prohibit the recycling of the base metal. Metal components with significant mass loss due to corrosion may have negligible or no scrap value." There also has to be sufficient quantities of a metal to make the recycling feasible. Single benches or small railings will likely be landfilled.

The value of the material also affects the likelihood of its being recycling. Copper has very high value retention, virtually equal to new copper, hence is very likely to be recycled. In contrast, other metals can markedly decrease in value as a scrap product.

Nathan Imm, RLA, EDAW, William B. Kuhl, RLA, Saratoga Associates (formerly with EDAW)

Recycled Content

Metals are one of the most easily and profitably recycled materials. Therefore, it is often easier to find metal products with a minimum level of recycled content. This can make a significant contribution to the LEED credit of the landscape. Due to the high demand for certain metal products, it is often difficult to find some, like stainless steel, with a high percentage of recycled content. In the case of stainless steel, it is primarily used for durable products, and therefore does not reenter the waste-to-product stream as often as others may (Houska,).

Stormwater Impacts

Recent studies have shown that erosion from metal surfaces can contribute to high metal contents in stormwater. This can influence the water quality of both natural systems and water supplies. In general, metals that are either softer (such as copper) or sacrificial in oxidation (such as zinc) erode more and can contribute to water quality problems (Houska, 2005Some metals, particularly iron, are relatively benign in their impacts. Lead is notably not, its large-scale use is discouraged largely due to this factor. Where utilized, coatings should be considered to slow the lead's erosion.

Local Sourcing versus the Global Marketplace

Metals are now worldwide commodities whose price has become highly volatile as supply and demand shifts across the globe. Due to the overwhelming shift to production in Asia, prices of metal can also be impacted by transportation costs. With some exception, finding locally generated raw metals (via recycling) is a virtual impossibility.

Local, artisanal production of metalwork is highly accessible. If local sourcing/local production is a goal of the project, the type of local production available should be determined from the outset. Due to a resurgence in the art and craft of blacksmithing, there is a large variety of shops available for this. Locating such shops is made easier by craft organizations such as ABANA and NOMMA.

State Laws Affecting Local Production

A number of states have "Buy American" legislation that either prohibits or strongly discourages the use of imported metals and metalwork in public projects. The majority of metal fabricators can comply with this, having headquarters in the United States, although their factories may be located in Asia. It is important that the chain of production be disclosed at the beginning of the project to prevent legal disputes.

Realities

Metals and metalworking have followed the trend of textiles in their production. Where the raw or recycled material originates is irrelevant to its refining and product fabrication. Often, it is the cheap labor and lax environmental regulation of so-called Third World countries that determine factory locations. Because of this, the "sustainability" of the metal production itself is highly questionable.

Rating sustainability based on longevity and maintenance inputs can outweigh these negative aspects. The correct materials, finishes, and overall design will ensure its endurance.

INNOVATIVE FORMS AND USES

Metals have been utilized by humans for centuries, and we continue to improve upon their use. New developments in metal alloys, casting methods, coatings, and other areas will bring major changes to the art and practice of designing and building with metals in the landscape. Frank Gehry, with his impressive use of titanium sheets for the Guggenheim Museum in Bilboa, Spain, is perhaps just a precursor to the many different uses for metals we will see in the future.

REFERENCES

Andrews, Jack. 2000. *Samuel Yellin, Metalworker.* Ocean Pines, MD: Skipjack Press.

Curtis, Steve. Conversation with the author, November 23, 2004.

Duncan, William P., and Corrview International, LLC. 2004. Technical Bulletin P-4, "Changes in Piping Trends That Have Occurred Over the Past Few Decades."

Grissom, Carol. 2005. Zinc sculpture in America (unpublished draft).

Houska, Catherine. "Sustainable Stainless Steel Architecture." Nickel Institute Web site, www.nickelinstitute.org.

Jacob, Judy. 2004. Personal interview. National Parks Service

Magaziner, Henry Jonas. January-February 2001. "Good Ironwork Practices," *Fabricator Magazine:* 92–95.

National Association of Architectural Metal Manufacturers (NAAMM). Technical bulletins.

National Ornamental & Miscellaneous Metals Association, Standards Committee. "Corrosion Protection of Ferrous Metals." Forest Park, GA: NOMMA.

Robertson, Graeme, and Joan Robertson. 1977. *Cast Iron Decoration: A World Survey.* New York: Whitney Library of Design, an imprint of Watson-Guptill Publications.

Skalka, Stan. 2004. Personal interview.

Tilly, Graham. 2002. *Conservation of Bridges.* New York, NY: Spon Press, the Taylor and Francis Group.

Waite, John G. October 1991. AIA, Preservation Brief 27: "The Maintenance and Repair of Architectural Cast Iron." Washington, DC: National Parks Service, Technical Preservation Services.

OTHER RESOURCES

Artist Blacksmith's Association of North America, Inc. (ABANA): www.abana.org. A very good resource for locating artist blacksmiths for projects. The ABANA publishes *The Anvil's Ring,* which while primarily targeted to the blacksmithing community, provides artist and studio spotlights that are useful in viewing the breadth of art available.

National Association of Architectural Metal Manufacturers (NAAMM): www.naamm.org. A trade organization for commercial metalworkers, which offers a number of technical booklets and manuals that can be highly useful to designers.

National Ornamental & Miscellaneous Metals Association (NOMMA): www.nomma.org. A trade organization for commercial metalworkers, which offers a number of technical booklets and manuals that can be highly useful to designers.

Nathan Imm, RLA, EDAW, William B. Kuhl, RLA, Saratoga Associates (formerly with EDAW)

WOOD

WOOD AND RELATED MATERIALS

MATERIAL AND PROPERTIES

Composition of Wood

The primary factors influencing the properties of lumber include soil type, growth conditions, and natural calamities or periods of stress. Other influences include the location and orientation of the wood within the log, the presence of naturally occurring conditions including knots (where branches were located), checks, splitting, sap deposits, and proximity of the wood to the bark layer.

The wood cells running perpendicular to the log have differing properties than the wood cells running parallel to the log. As the log is drawn through the saw, the orientation of the grain is established depending on the relationship to the growth rings. Two contrasting conditions can occur: flat-grained (*c* in the figure showing the cross section of a log), where the grain runs parallel to the longest end dimension, or vertical-grained, also called "edge-grained" (*a* in the figure), where the grain runs parallel to the shortest dimension of the edge cut. These are the extremes, and most sawn lumber is somewhere between flat and vertical grain.

The end grain part of board lumber is the most vulnerable, as water can easily migrate through the cell structure; hence, all end grain that is exposed to moisture should be treated with a preservative.

The knots, which have a density different from the surrounding wood, are the result of a branch or limb growing from the main trunk. Knots that are the result of a living branch are referred to as tight knots, and are commonly structurally secure. Knots resulting from a dead branch may not be connected to the surrounding wood, and so may loosen and fall out of the board, leaving a hole. The structural performance of a wood member is hindered by loose knots occurring at points of stress and where fasteners are attached. In the grading of lumber, knots are evaluated for their size, frequency, location, form, and type (tight or loose) to assess the quality and value of the wood.

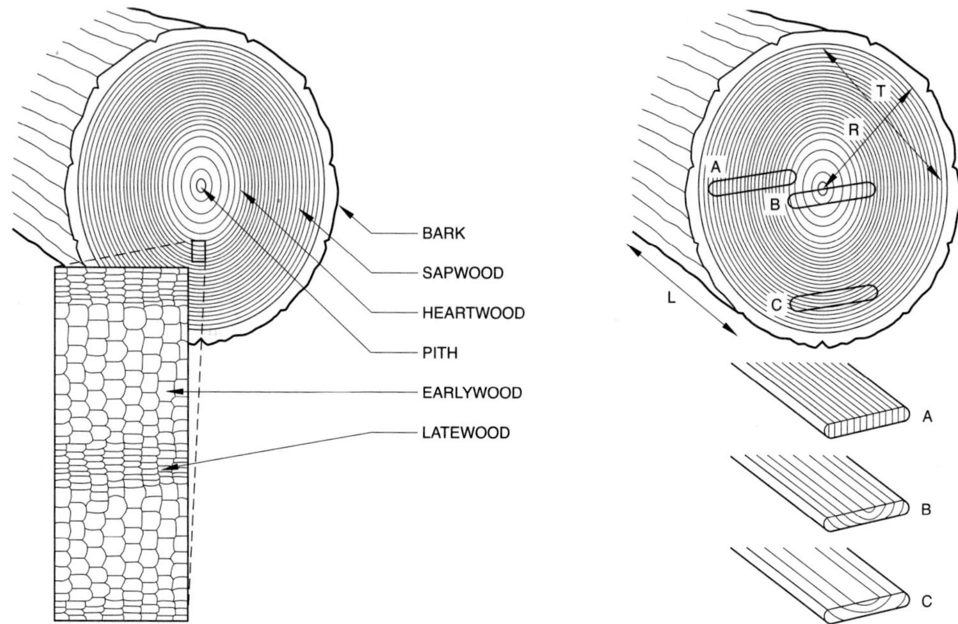

The grain orientations are determined by where the lumber is cut from the log: (a) edge–grained (vertical grain); (b) pith, a combination of edge and vertical grains; (c) flat-grained.

CROSS SECTION OF LOG SHOWING HEARTWOOD, SAPWOOD, EARLYWOOD, LATEWOOD, AND PITH

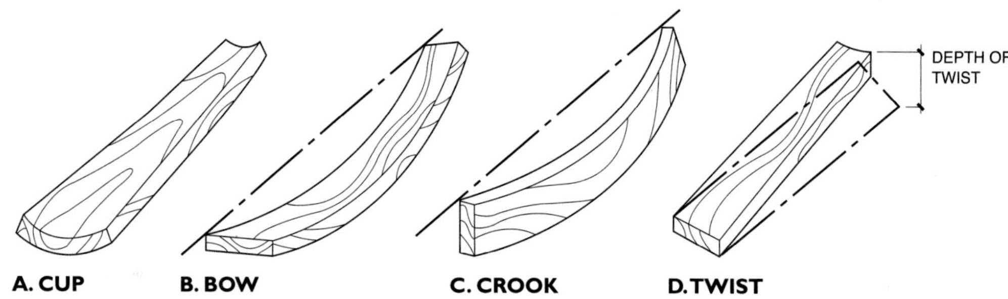

DISTORTIONS COMMONLY FOUND IN BOARD LUMBER: (A) CUPPING; (B) BOWING; (C) CROOKING; (D) TWISTING

Moisture Content

Once cut, wood begins to discharge moisture, and if the drying is uncontrolled, splitting around the end grain or distortions within the board often occur.

- *Cupping.* Cupping occurs when the two flat faces of a board dry at different rates. Cupping may be seen as the profile of the board's end grain curving in from the sides, creating a cupped form on the faces. Prevalence for cupping is higher in boards with a flat grain than in those with vertical grain. Boards tend to cup away from the bark side of the wood; and when used for decking, the term "bark side up" refers to the laying of the decking boards with the growth rings facing down and with the convex side up, preventing the board from entrapping water. Live loads on the deck will tend to flatten the boards and reduce the mounding that can occur in the "bark side up" orientation.
- *Bowing, crooking, twisting.* These distortions occur along the length of the board. Bowing constitutes a single curving of its face (widest dimension) plane. Crooking is observed by looking down the face plane to find the board curving on itself at the edge (narrowest) dimension. Twisting is a combination of curves in different directions. All major structural members need to be true and free of distortions.

These distortions to the lumber most frequently occur during an accelerated and uneven drying process. Wood is best seasoned either by the air-drying (AD) or kiln-drying (KD) process. Drying time varies according to species, lumber thickness, and the moisture content of wood and air. Wood is sold with a range of moisture content from less than 15 percent to more than 19 percent. Optimum moisture content of lumber for stability in a structure is 12 percent. Once dried, wood, due to moisture absorption, is still susceptible to variations in size. As a general rule, wood expands as it gains, and shrinks as it loses, moisture. The degree of change depends on the amount of moisture absorbed, the species of wood, and the cut of the grain.

Daniel Winterbottom, Associate Professor, Landscape Architecture, University of Washington

SIZING AND SURFACING

Lumber comes in standardized thicknesses, widths, and lengths, and can be custom-milled to meet any nonstandardized dimensions. The "nominal dimension" is the actual thickness and width of the wood after being "rough cut" at the sawmill. The terms "surfaced" or "dressed" refer to the wood members after they have been finish planed, where ¼ inch of surface material per side is removed. A designation of (S4S) means "surfaced four sides"; a designation of (S2S), two sides. The term "2×4" refers to a surfaced member, and is smaller in cross-sectional area than a 2-inch by 4-inch piece of rough lumber. Its actual measurements when dry and surfaced on four sides will be 1½ inches by 3½ inches. Nominally dimensioned lumber is available, but is not graded and doesn't have structural design values. Structural lumber is commonly available in members that are nominally 2 to 4 inches thick, and in "timbers," lumber greater than 5 inches in thickness. The thinnest standardized dressed thickness for lumber is ½ inch and increasing in thickness to ¾ inch, ⅝ inch, 1½ inches, and 3½ inches and greater. If the size of a required member exceeds the limits of a log, several members can be glue-laminated together to create the desired dimensions.

GRADING SYSTEMS

Because lumber characteristics vary according to species, size of members, and by intended use, a grading system has been established to make various designations reasonably uniform throughout the country. Lumber grading takes place at the sawmills, and in the United States is supervised by one of 10 agencies accredited by the American Lumber Standard Committee (ALSC), which is also responsible for writing the standards used for lumber milling and grading.

All dressed softwood lumber, treated or untreated, and glulams receive a lumber grade stamp. The stamp, applied to the wood members by an approved grading or inspection agency is mandatory, required by building codes throughout the country for all lumber used for structural purposes. The lumber-graded mark uses standardized symbols to list five pieces of information: grade designation (quality), species identification, the maximum moisture content at the time of surfacing, the grading agency responsible for the inspection, and the mill identification. These symbols are used nationwide and are required to be visible for confirmation at the job site.

Lumber is graded by visual inspection to assess strength and/or appearance and is based on the frequency, size, quality, and location of knots; cross grain; and any natural decay, splits, wanes, or milling flaws.

Grade Designation

Lumber grades are divided into four performance standards: light framing; structural light framing; structural joists and planks; and those designated for use as studs, vertical members used in load-bearing walls. These can be further broken down into grade names, which are designations based on quality variation. For example, in the light framing category are the following grades: construction, standard and utility, with construction being the highest and utility being the lowest. These divisions are predominantly based on appearance since all qualify for the use of light framing. The quality of wood is designated by use in the grade stamp and is labeled by number (such as #2), by name (e.g., Stud) or by abbreviation (e.g., STAND, for standard).

Several species are available in appearance as well as structural grades. The factors inspected for appearance grade include grain orientation, presence of heart or sapwoods, quantity, size and quality of knots and other natural or manufacturing flaws. The designations include tight knot and clear.

Species Identification

The species symbol states the species of tree the wood was milled from, and is indicated by names (e.g., redwood), abbreviation (e.g., D Fir, for Douglas) or symbol (e.g., PP, for Ponderosa pine).

MILL IDENTIFICATION — 12 STAND — GRADE DESIGNATION

CONDITION OF SEASONING

CERTIFICATION TRADEMARK — W WP ® S-DRY D FIR — SPECIES IDENTIFICATION

LEGEND:

SPECIES IDENTIFICATION

DOUG. FIR-L | S D FIR | HEM FIR | SPF^S | WEST WOODS | WEST CDR

CONDITION OF SEASONING

MC-15 = 15% MAXIMUM
KD-15 MOISTURE CONTENT

S-DRY = 19% MAXIMUM
KD MOISTURE CONTENT

S-GRN = OVER 19% MOISTURE CONTENT (UNSEASONED)

NOTE:
WHEN AN INSPECTION CERTIFICATE ISSUED BY AN AGENCY IS REQUIRED ON A SHIPMENT OF LUMBER AND SPECIFIC GRADE MARKS ARE NOT USED, THE STOCK IS IDENTIFIED BY IMPRINT OF THE ASSOCIATION MARK AND THE NUMBER OF THE SHIPPING MILL OR INSPECTOR

INTERPRETING GRADE MARKS

SOME GRADE STAMPS IDENTIFY AN INDIVIDUAL WESTERN LUMBER SPECIES

DOUGLAS FIR

WR CDR

WESTERN RED CEDAR

WESTERN LARCH

INC CDR

INCENSE CEDAR

ES

ENGELMANN SPRUCE

SP

SUGAR PINE

PP

PONDEROSA PINE

IWP

IDAHO WHITE PINE

A NUMBER OF WESTERN LUMBER SPECIES HAVE SIMILAR PERFORMANCE PROPERTIES AND ARE MARKETED WITH A COMMON SPECIES DESIGNATION. THESE SPECIES GROUPINGS ARE USED FOR LUMBER TO WHICH DESIGN VALUES ARE ASSIGNED

DOUG. FIR-L

DOUGLAS FIR AND LARCH

S D FIR

DOUGLAS FIR SOUTH

CALIFORNIA RED FIR, GRAND FIR NOBLE FIR, PACIFIC SILVER FIR, WHITE FIR AND WESTERN HEMLOCK

SPF^S

ENGELMANN AND SITIKA SPRUCE, LODGEPOLE PINE (AND EASTERN FIRS AND SPRUCES)

WEST WOODS

ALPINE FIR, PONDEROSA PINE, SUGAR PINE, IDAHO WHITE PINE, AND MOUNTAIN HEMLOCK, PLUS ANY OF THE SPECIES IN THE OTHER GROUPINGS EXCEPT WESTERN CEDARS

WEST CDR

INCENSE, WESTERN RED, PORT ORFORD, AND ALASKA CEDAR

BECAUSE OF TIMBER STAND COMPOSITION, SOME MILLS MARKET ADDITIONAL SPECIES COMBINATIONS

ES LP

ENGELMANN SPRUCE, LODGEPOLE PINE

PP-LP

PONDEROSA PINE, LODGEPOLE PINE

A-F HEM FIR

ALPINE FIR, HEM-FIR

WW

WHITE WOODS (ANY TRUE FIRS, SPRUCES, HEMLOCKS, OR PINES)

ES-AF

ENGELMANN SPRUCE, ALPINE FIR

ENGELMANN SPRUCE-ALPINE FIR - LODGEPOLE PINE

PPSP

PONDEROSA PINE, SUGAR PINE

SPECIES IDENTIFICATION STAMPS

Daniel Winterbottom, Associate Professor, Landscape Architecture, University of Washington

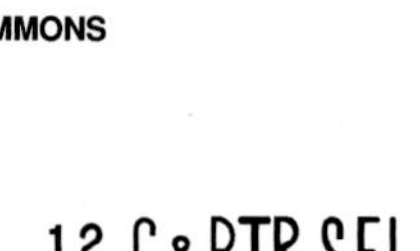

TYPICAL GRADE STAMPS

Some symbols designate a combination of species, which have similar mechanical properties, such as SPF, for Spruce-pine fir. In addition, symbols indicate moisture content and grading agency/mill designation.

- *Moisture content.* Moisture content is important in evaluating how much shrinkage, and potentially distortion, can be expected from the board. The amount of moisture is shown as either an abbreviation or as a number. The symbol S-GRN (for surfaced green) indicates that the board was milled with a moisture content above 19 percent, and it is cut slightly oversized so that when dried to a 19 percent moisture content it will have the same dimensions as S-DRY (surfaced dry) planed at 19 percent or less.
- *Grading agency/mill designation.* This is a certification symbol that identifies the agency (NELMA, for example) that supervised the grading. The mill symbol is designated by name or number (e.g., 38), to identify the mill where the lumber was cut.

Solid lumber used for engineered components and glulams are graded mechanically and designated as MSR, for machine stress rated. The members are inspected both mechanically and visually. The stamps indicate the species, assign one of four grades (construction, standard, utility, and stud), and give two stress test measurements. The fiber stress bending (Fb) figure is a measure of tensile and compressive forces; and the modulus of elasticity (E) figure indicates how much deflection will occur under certain loads.

CONNECTORS AND ADHESIVES

Mechanical Connectors

Wood connectors can be divided into five primary groups by use: concrete, caps and bases, hangers, straps and ties, miscellaneous and options. The standard connectors are available with galvanized coatings and in stainless steel.

Concrete Connectors

The concrete connectors are designed to attach wood members to concrete walls, footings, or slabs. Concrete connectors can be divided into two groups, retrofit or embedded.

- *Retrofit* bolts are inserted into a predrilled hole and bonded to the concrete structure using expansion bolts, epoxy adhesives, or nonshrink cementitious grouts.
- *Embedded* anchor bolts and hold-downs are set in place during the concrete pour, and the layout must be precise. The threaded end of the anchor bolt extends out from the concrete and receives the wood member or metal connector. Hold-downs are not bolts but consist of brackets, hurricane ties, or strap connections.

Post Caps and Bases

With base anchors, which are available for retrofit and new construction, the anchor is epoxied or expansion-bolted to a concrete footing or embedded into the concrete pour. The anchors are available as fixed or adjustable, and are designed to receive standard dimensioned wood posts. The caps are designed to sit on top of a post or column and provide a seat to receive a horizontal member (beam or joist). Each connection is prebored to receive carriage bolts and/or screws or nails to secure the post or horizontal member.

Hangers

Hangers can be divided into face mount and top flange types. Both are designed to connect a horizontal member (beam or joist) with another horizontal member (beam). The face mount is connected into the face of the supporting member, while the top flange is attached to the top of the supporting member, bending 90 degrees down the face to receive the supported member (other angles can be specified). They rely on nails, screws, or bolts to form the connection.

Straps and Ties

Straps and ties are used to form a mechanical link between two wood members, eliminating tow or end nailing and increasing the rigidity of the joint, especially in areas prone to seismic activity. Included in this category are seismic and hurricane ties, framing anchors, strap ties, and others.

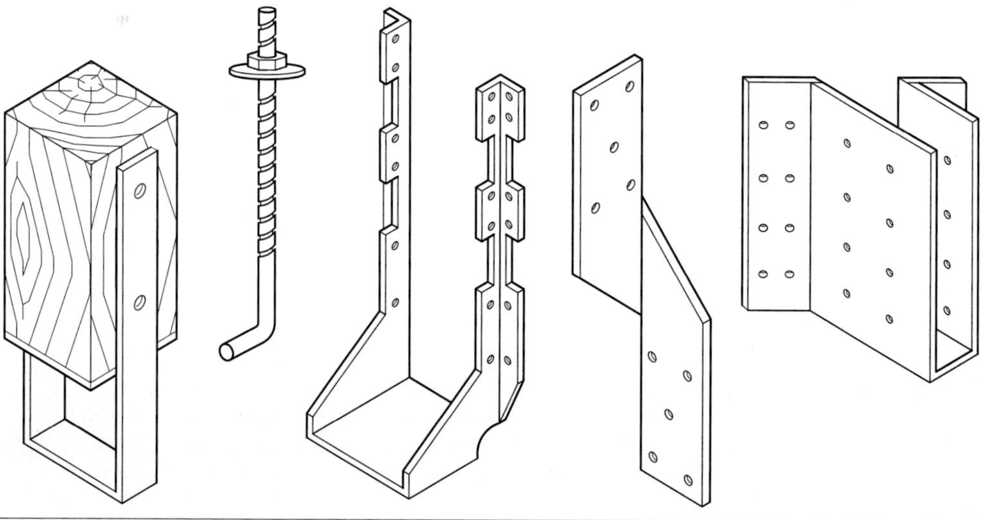

METAL CONNECTORS FOR WOOD

Daniel Winterbottom, Associate Professor, Landscape Architecture, University of Washington

Miscellaneous and Hanger Options

The miscellaneous category includes a variety of bases, fence brackets, header hangers, twist straps, (to attach a joist seated on a beam), wall bracing, bridging, and others. The hanger options category includes hangers designed to receive multiple members (joists or rafters) with preset angles. Also included in this category are custom hangers and connectors, where a steel plate is cut and bent and holes are predrilled based on a CAD drawing submitted by the designer to form a custom hanger.

COATINGS FOR FASTENERS AND CONNECTORS

Exterior fasteners and connectors are available in stainless steel or galvanized carbon steel. Galvanized coatings are applied by electroplating, mechanical plating, chemical treating, or hot dipping (molten zinc). The hot-dipping method provides the coating with the thickest profile, and research has shown it provides the best longevity and resistance to corrosion. However, in situations where salt is airborne, or in marine applications, stainless steel is a better choice than hot-dipped galvanized fasteners or connectors.

Adhesives

When gluing laminated beams or attaching wood members, adhesives can provide a strong connection more easily and effectively than mechanical fasteners.

Glues based on resorcinol-formaldehyde and phenol-resorcinol-formaldehyde are all formulated for exterior applications. Resorcinol and resorcinol-formaldehyde glues are ideal for bonding high-density hardwoods such as oak. Phenol-resorcinol-formaldehydes are commonly used to structurally bond softwoods.

All resorcinol glues require closely mated surfaces for effective bonding with hardwoods, requiring clamping pressures as high as 250 psi, and softwoods 100 to 125 psi. These pressures force the glue over the wood surface and into the wood cell structure. The optimum strength is achieved in woods with a moisture content between 6 and 12 percent.

Epoxies are among the most versatile and expensive of the adhesives. They have multiple applications, including anchoring concrete and masonry fasteners and restoring rotting wood. Evidence has shown that structural epoxy bonds in members subject to prolonged outdoor exposure and water saturation can deteriorate rapidly; however, some early research suggests priming with a 2 percent solution of polyethyleneamine may improve exterior performance.

Polyurethane foam adhesives offer many benefits, and many can bond either wet or frozen, treated and untreated lumber. These adhesives are nontoxic, waterproof, and temperature-tolerant. The glue, once cured, is waterproof; and because curing is triggered by moisture, it will activate on wood with a moisture content of up to 25 percent.

DESIGN: APPROPRIATE USE

Where to Use

Properly detailed, wood is an appropriate building material for most exterior applications—although in some locations where humidity and high temperatures are frequent, many park departments and municipalities are using plastic lumber for decking and nonstructural applications in lieu of solid wood. Wood will perform best in locations where adequate air circulation and drainage are provided and wood-to-ground contact is avoided. Exposure to direct sunlight, erosive winds, and trapped moisture shortens the life of untreated wood. Stains and finishes can mitigate the effects of UV light, and proper detailing and flashing can reduce moisture entrapment.

Why to Use

Wood contributes to the feasibility, economic, and aesthetic benefits of many landscape projects. Compared to other landscape building materials, wood is relatively lightweight, allowing easy transport to the site and reducing dead loads where weight is an issue, as in rooftop locations. Particular wood species vary from region to region, but as a construction material wood is readily available in all parts of the country. Each region retains its wealth of traditional structural types, and wood is easily worked with common tools.

A malleable material, wood can be bent to achieve curves, carved to create ornamentation, and laminated to create large structural members. The porosity of many species enables penetrating preservatives to be applied, extending the life of the material and allowing for a range of colors and tones. While some designs require highly trained master carpenters, skilled labor is readily available in most parts of the country. When compared with other materials, wood is relatively low in cost; and recent developments in engineered lumber are making the cost and availability of large structural members more reliable and competitively priced.

CONTEXTUAL CONCERNS

Climate and Natural Factors

Moisture penetration and the associated damage caused by fungi, mold, and insects is the most common cause of wood failure. This usually is the result of inappropriate detailing and joinery, which can defeat even the effects of pressure-treated wood. An understanding of the materials, combined with a fundamental knowledge of construction detailing, is critical to the successful design of lasting structures in the landscape.

It is essential to drain away all water from the wood structure. Slope finish grades away from the post connections and provides positive drainage within the structure for decks, stairs, and landings. All deck railings, fence caps, and horizontal surfaces should be pitched to drain and direct water away from joints and exposed end grain. All framing should be raised off the ground to allow adequate air circulation between and below the wood members. If possible, avoid roof-runoff splash against the wall surfaces by extending the eaves 18 inches out and by starting wood construction 12 inches above finish grade to protect the lower wood cladding, trim, and framing. All corners, depressions, and joints prone to water or snow collection should be avoided. Details that maximize air circulation and avoid water collection points and protection end grain surfaces will prolong the life span of the structure.

Human Factors

Style and Aesthetics

Wood has been used by most cultures around the world, and works in wood can both embody traditional form making and reflect highly expressive and personalized aesthetics. The pagoda is emblematic of Japanese culture and building traditions much as the gazebo or bandstand defines the New England commons. Throughout the nineteenth century, lumberyards stocked a range of ornamental columns, scrollwork, and components so carpenters could replicate the popular styles of the day. Many designers have developed their own idiosyncratic styles, as illustrated in the rusticated garden structures of Andrew Jackson Downing. Materials and tools for wood construction continue to develop, but the basic structural methods have changed little over the centuries.

Aesthetic choices will determine which structural systems are selected. For example, if a heavy, earthbound, WPA-type aesthetic is wanted, a post-and-beam system might be chosen. In another example, a deck can achieve the light, floating look, common in contemporary modern structures, with a system of joists cantilevered from a large gluelam beam. Detailing is another means of expression in wood construction. How members are put together, for example: Using all wood joinery, as opposed to mechanical connectors, changes the character expressed.

Structural Considerations

Wood structures must resist the stresses of tensile, compressive, and lateral forces acting upon them. These three forces are accounted for in the design process when selecting, sizing, placing, and connecting wood members. The process of structurally composing routinely encountered fences, gates,

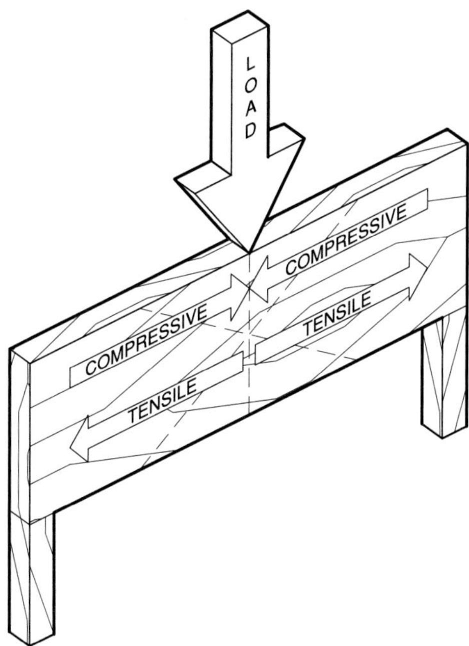

For a structure to stand, it must be sized to resist the forces of tension and compression.

FORCES ON A STRUCTURE

Daniel Winterbottom, Associate Professor, Landscape Architecture, University of Washington

decks, arbors, and gazebos is relatively straightforward. An example of that process is shown using the structural calculations for a deck using standard charts and tables in the article on *Wood Decks*. For larger decks, small pavilions, and bridges, the applied forces may be more significant and complex, requiring the consultation of a structural engineer.

The compressive forces, such as those applied by loads through a column or post, tend to shorten the wood member and can cause it to buckle. The wood fibers in a post supporting a beam compress as the post resists the weight transferred from the beam.

A tensile force tends to stretch the bearing member. An example would be jumping on a trampoline, where the material will lengthen as the forces are applied. At midspan, a horizontal member undergoes both compression above and tension below.

The third type, lateral force, is applied perpendicularly to the vertical member, such as the wind loads borne by the posts and fence slats. Forces are measured in terms of weight per unit of area, in pounds per square foot (psf), or pounds per square inch (psi).

Loads on a structure can be calculated as dead or live loads. The dead load is the weight of the materials composing it. The live loads are all nonpermanent objects that will use, or bear, on the structure.

Span and height tables are often used as the most expedient method to size structural members. These tables come from several agencies, including the United States Department of Agriculture (USDA). When using the listed maximum spans, the wood member must be without flaws, including checks and knots, since any structural flaws may compromise the calculations. Structural engineers typically include a safety factor, often 15 percent, and it is common practice to choose spans below the capable maximum. The tables are typically based on maximum loads of 50 pounds per square foot (psf), which include a live load of 40 pounds (psf) and dead load of 10 pounds (psf).

The process of sizing most structures is carried out from top to bottom. In a covered structure, sizing begins with the roof and span charts that are available for rafters. With a deck or pedestrian bridge, this begins with the deck boards and moves down through the joists to the beams, posts, and footings. The working process appears to be linear, but it is, in fact, a circular one. After the initial design of the structure, the look may not be satisfying and can be changed by revisiting the spacing, spans, and material dimensions of the wood members.

AVOIDING COMMON PROBLEMS

Problems common to wood fall into six categories, which are identified below, along with guidelines for avoidance:

- *Splitting and cracking*. This problem common to wood members can be avoided by using properly dried materials. Ensure that all nailing is located a sufficient distance from the end of the board, and provide adequate support to alleviate bounce that stresses the lumber. Select materials with consistent grain and minimal imperfections.
- *Wood decay*. Decay in exterior applications is often the result of trapped moisture. Adequate air circulation will extend the life of the structure, particularly in shaded areas that receive little sun. Contact with the ground should be avoided whenever possible, and if unavoidable, treated material should be used. Details that impede drainage or entrap water should be redesigned. Plastic lumber offers a good alternative when using wood in inhospitable situations.
- *Sagging members*. Beams, joists, rafters, and decking should be adequately supported, as shown in the span charts in the article on *Wood Decks*. Joist blocking stiffens the framing structure increasing rigidity. All framing material should be set with the natural curve, viewed across the length of each member, facing up to resist the tendency to sag under loading.
- *Joint separation*. Avoid toe nailing wherever possible, and use mechanical hangers, slice plates, and anchors for wood-to-concrete/steel or wood-to-wood connections. In wood-to-wood connections, wood joints such as dovetails, mortise, and tenon, and scarf joints resist separation better than butt joints.
- *Fastener failure*. Use only galvanized, stainless-steel, or epoxy-coated fasteners for exterior connections. Properly size the fasteners; stagger them as needed to prevent rocking of the attached member; and space them so the loads are sufficiently distributed.
- *Finish failure*. Preparation of wood surfaces is critical to finish performance. Material should be dry and clean, and the temperature during application should not exceed the manufacturer's recommendations. Locating the wood structure so that it is sheltered from winds, abrasive materials, and extended sun exposure can all extend the life of a finish.

BUILDING CODES AND REGULATIONS

Before designing any wood structure, local building codes and regulations should be reviewed to ensure the design is in compliance with governing regulations. The Uniform Building Code (UBC) is the most widely adopted building code in the United States. Updated in 1997, the UBC is expansive in scope, comprising three volumes. Some of the sections most relevant to wood construction are: Section 106, Permits; Section 108, Inspections; Chapter 5, General Building Limitations; Chapter 11, Accessibility; Chapter 16, Structural Requirements; Chapter 17, Structural Tests and Inspections; Chapter 23, Wood; and Chapter 35, Uniform Building Code Standards. Most building departments have permit review specialists who will answer questions and clarify the codes, either by phone or in person. Most of these agencies also have information available online.

ALTERNATIVE MATERIALS AND ECOLOGICAL METHODS OF EXTRACTION

The simplest and most direct effect designers can have on the environment is to consider their design in terms of waste creation. Of the solid waste generated in the United States and Canada, 10 to 30 percent is from construction and demolition combined. The chief material in this waste stream is wood used in construction.

Designers should specify materials of standard size, and dimension the members to minimize waste and to reuse any cuts within the project. This is especially valuable for treated wood members that become both wood and chemical waste when discarded, as their use as recycled material is very limited.

Certified Lumber

Some lumber is certified by forest managers who evaluate and certify that the wood comes from a responsibly, well-managed operation. There are a number of certifying bodies in the United States, Europe, and Canada. The first certifying program in the world was the SmartWood program, founded in 1989 in Richmond, Vermont. SmartWood and the Scientific Certification Program (SCS), a private company based in Emeryville, California, are the only two certifying bodies in the United States, and each has its own set of criteria. The Forest Stewardship Council (FSC) was founded in Toronto, Canada, in 1993, to achieve a global standardization. Its international headquarters is in Bonn, Germany, has national offices in over 40 countries, including a U.S. office in Washington D.C., creating a worldwide network. The FSC has adopted and revised the principles and criteria of its standard, "which has become the uniform standard that affiliated third-party forest certification organizations now follow."

The evaluation of forestry practices can be achieved through field audits, but chain of custody through the milling operations is difficult. On visual inspection, the difference between certified and noncertified lumber is indistinguishable, thus tracking is critical.

The American Forest and Paper Association (AF&PA), representing about 90 percent of the industrial timber companies, has what it calls the Sustainable Forestry Initiative. Participants follow a mandatory set of forestry guidelines and file annual reports demonstrating their compliance; independent field verification is not required.

The Canadian Standards Association (CSA) standards are designed to improve environmental stewardship in forest management. The Canadian system examines and certifies not the wood products, but the companies that produce them. Participating producers set goals and targets for implementing sustainable practices, and once accepted by the stakeholders, these bind the company. Once registered, the companies assure that their forest management goals and methods are ecologically based and that extraction and harvesting in done in a sustainable manner.

One advantage of the FSC forest certification system that differs from the CSA is that it is the forest resource managers that are certified, not the tract of land. This system enables the product from many small plots under the supervision of a certified manager to be certified, which given the cost of certifying forestlands would not have been possible in a land-based certification process.

Lumber Substitutes

Plastic Lumber

Plastic lumber falls into several categories, which utilize different plastics and manufacturing processes, and vary in composition, quality consistency, properties, and performance. Plastic lumber is an integrally colored board product that requires no coatings and absorbs minimal moisture. It does not rot, splinter, or peel, thus requiring substantially less maintenance

Daniel Winterbottom, Associate Professor, Landscape Architecture, University of Washington

than wood lumber products. The dimensions of plastic lumber are consistent with wood dimensions; and, in addition to the standard dimensional lumber, many manufacturers produce custom lumber in special profiles and thicknesses.

The structural use of plastic lumber is limited by the size of the members required. Plastic has a flex modulus of three to four times that of wood, increasing with higher temperatures. Structural members should be spaced closer than with wood decking, to mitigate bouncing or sagging. Many manufacturers recommend spans of 12 to 14 inches for decking. Moreover, contraction and expansion rate is greater for plastic lumber than for wood, and rates should be checked with the manufacturer. Plastic lumber is also heavier than wood of the same dimensions.

The following materials are used for plastic wood manufacturing:

- "Purified plastic lumber" utilizes a single postconsumer plastic such as HDPE. Some manufacturers are producing a lumber with a lighter foam core and a denser integral skin on the outer face, reducing the weight by one-third of a comparable solid product.
- "Commingled recycled plastic lumber" is generally lower in cost and is made with two or more plastics. Because different plastics are used, there may be variability in the physical properties of the board, making specification for some uses difficult. Different plastics can vary in their tolerance to chemicals and stresses.
- "Nonpure plastic lumber" products are created by adding composites to plastic resins. A typical mix is approximately 50 percent polyethylene (PE), primarily low-density polyethylene (LDPE), and 50 percent sawdust or other secondary fiber. These products tend to be stiffer than pure plastic lumber, with rougher textures. Due to the fiber content, these products have been shown to absorb up to 8 percent moisture in a 24-hour period, thereby restricting their use in certain applications.

Plastic lumber can be cut and fabricated with traditional woodworking tools, including power saws, drills, and so on. Mechanical fasteners such as bolts or deep flight screws are recommended for attachment.

The following are used to create plastic wood trim:

- *PVC (cellular polyvinyl chloride) plastic trim.* Contains additives to create a foam, resulting in a product similar in weight and density to wood that contains no knots, grain, warping, or cupping. Plastic trim is attached to the framing or substrate with nails or screws. Advantages over wood are that the nail can be set close to the ends without splitting, and the joints can be glued. Extruded through dies, plastic trim is available in flat boards and molded trim, and it can be cut, routed, and sanded in custom profiles. Plastic expands more than wood, so joints should be cut long and pressure-fitted to avoid gaps in colder weather. Resistant to rot, plastic trim is well-suited for use as skirt and corner boards, where contact with soil or vegetation is likely.
- *Composite trim.* Made from wood fibers with either phenolic resins or PVC as the binder. Several types are available, and each differs slightly in composition and character. Some cap the composite core with an acrylic shell, increasing weather resistance and paintability as compared to pure PVC.

Engineered Lumber

Engineered lumber refers to manufactured framing lumber such as beams and joists. These items may be built of finger-jointed solid wood pieces, wood strands, or veneers. The most common types used in the landscape are solid timber lams (glue-laminated timber), laminated veneer lumber (LVL), and parallel strand lumber (PSL). Engineered wood is a broader category that includes structural panels such as plywood and oriented strand board (OSB). Engineered lumber is dimensionally stable and resistant to wood's natural propensity for shrinking, twisting, cupping, checking, and warping. It has fewer surface defects and is designed to span greater distances than solid wood beams of an equal size.

Glue-laminated timber, the best known engineered product, was developed in Europe over a hundred years ago and introduced in the United States in 1934. As a stress-engineered member, it is composed of solid wood members glued end to end and face-bonded in layers. The laminations are called "lams" or "glulams," and are available in two standard grades, architectural and industrial, based on appearance. For exterior application, they are manufactured with waterproof glues and preservative treatments. With its capacity to span great distances, glue-laminated timber is used in bridge building, timber frame construction, and play structures. And because laminated timber is composed of smaller wood pieces, smaller trees are used in its manufacturing, easing the demand for large old-growth wood. The trees harvested are faster-growing species from managed forests, and these resources are used efficiently with minimal waste.

Plywood

Plywood is an engineered sheet material wherein several layers of wood veneer are glued at right angles to each other to create a high-strength, relatively thin product. Code letters, stamped on the face of the sheet, indicate its features. It is also graded for selections as "appearance" or "engineered." Plywood is rated for interior or exterior use depending on the type of glue used in the laminating process.

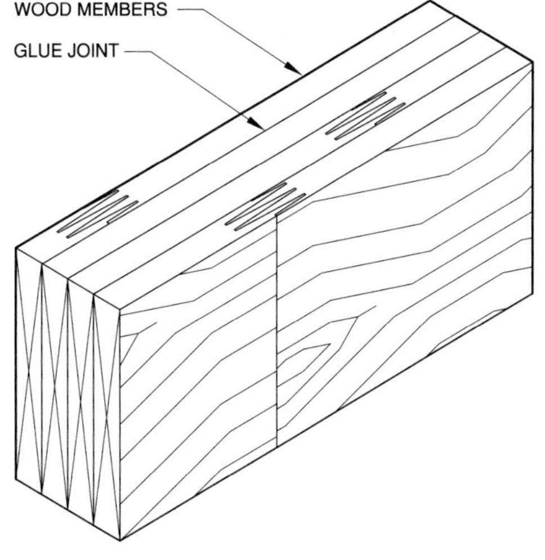

GLUE-LAMINATED TIMBER, OR "GLULAM"

Appearance grades are manufactured with one or both faces surfaced with veneers consisting of particular wood species and finishes. They are rated from A through D for each face, with A being the best appearance grade, and are typically used in building cladding and furniture. Engineered grades are constructed to achieve high strength and are commonly used for wall or roof sheathing or subflooring and as bases for overlying materials, such as tile, stucco, and siding. Engineered grades are used where stiffness, strength, nail-holding capability, and durability are needed.

Exterior waterproof grades incorporate C or better veneers, and by incorporating waterproof glues, retain their laminate bonds when exposed to moisture. Marine-grade plywood is used in boat building and in exterior applications where the structure will be subjected to frequent contact with water. Medium-density overlay (MDO), an exterior plywood, has a paper overlay on the exposed faces. It is used for concrete forms, when a very smooth surface finish is required; for cladding where wood grain is not wanted; and for flooring, specified with a textured finish to prevent slipping.

Plywood sheets are typically 4 feet by 8 feet, although some grades and types are available in lengths up to 12 feet or in sheets 5 feet by 8 feet or 5 feet by 9 feet. Thickness is determined by the number of "plys," or veneers, used, with strength increasing in proportion to thickness. Industry standards range from ¼ inch, increasing in size by ⅛ inch up to ¾ inch, with 1 inch and 1⅛ inch also available.

Because of its high strength-to-weight ratio, plywood has several applications in landscape construction. It is used extensively in concrete forming where thin sheets are bent to form compound curves and curves with tight radii. As sheathing on structures, plywood functions as a shear panel, used to stiffen framing and provide resistance to lateral forces. It is used as a floor underlayment, and appearance grades are often used for the finished wall surfaces. Waterproof grades can be laminated to create straight or curved beams.

Salvaged Lumber

Building with salvaged lumber offers several benefits to landscape architects. Recycled from old industrial structures, barns, or warehouses, many of the members are of a dimension not available in traditional lumberyards. The wood is usually milled from old-growth timber and composed of heartwood that is particularly resistant to degradation, with a denser, closer grain and fewer structural defects compared to wood harvested today.

Salvaged wood comes from three primary sources. Architectural sources such as buildings and bridges produce large structural members, which are usually relatively free of penetrations from mechanical fasteners. The members are often planed to improve appearance by removing any surface defects. Horticultural salvage is the second source. Lumber is milled from municipal street trees or trees removed in the process of development. The third source is the salvage of old-growth unmilled logs found in river and lake bottoms. Preserved by constant water satu-

Daniel Winterbottom, Associate Professor, Landscape Architecture, University of Washington

ration, the wood is milled into large members. Most salvaged lumber is available from small local mill operations, and sources can be found by çontacting builders, furniture makers, and state conservation departments.

Bamboo

In many parts of the world, bamboo is used in the construction of buildings, scaffolding, bridges, and fences as the primary building material. In the United States, it has been mainly used for garden elements including fences, gates, bridges, arbors, and occasionally for replicating traditional structures such as Japanese teahouses.

Bamboo possesses high tensile strength, but it is difficult to transfer this strength through connectors, thus limiting its use when designing structures that support significant loads. Bamboo is a lightweight material, easily transported and lifted without cranes. It offers good fire resistance; is easily worked with saws, knives, and drills; and has a high degree of elasticity.

Moisture increases the potential of insect infestation. Proper drying, smoking, or heating reduce moisture content; and impregnation coatings make the fibers unpalatable to insects. Raising the posts above grade and incorporating roof overhangs can extend the life of the material. Insecticides have also been used, but the environmental damage often outweighs the benefits.

Bamboo can be split to create halved canes, strips, and battens, and is easily bendable when heated and will maintain its shape once cooled. Skeletal structures of bamboo use posts, battens, rails, purlins, rafters, and roof trusses to create longitudinal and transversal frameworks. The connections are traditionally lashed with rope ties or bamboo strips. Wall or railing sections may be prefabricated and assembled on-site. Halved sections are used for Roman tile roofing.

The simplest footbridges consist of posts that support decking made of tied or woven battens. Long-span covered bridges are occasionally protected by roof structures to extend the life span of the materials.

Open fencing can be created using posts and straight or bent horizontal members lashed together. Opaque fences or privacy screens can be created by lashing woven or tied mats to posts and rails.

Many commercial distributors carry selections of prefabricated elements, including screens, fence sections, and arbors, that can be combined to make garden structures. Canes are available in sizes ranging from 3/4 inch in diameter to approximately 6 inches in diameter.

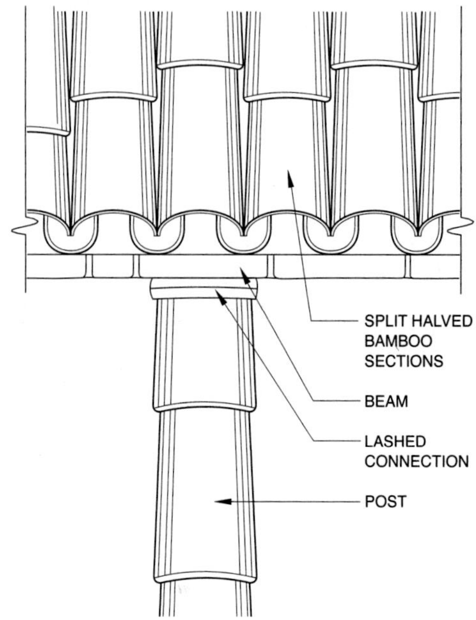

BAMBOO ROMAN TILE ROOFING

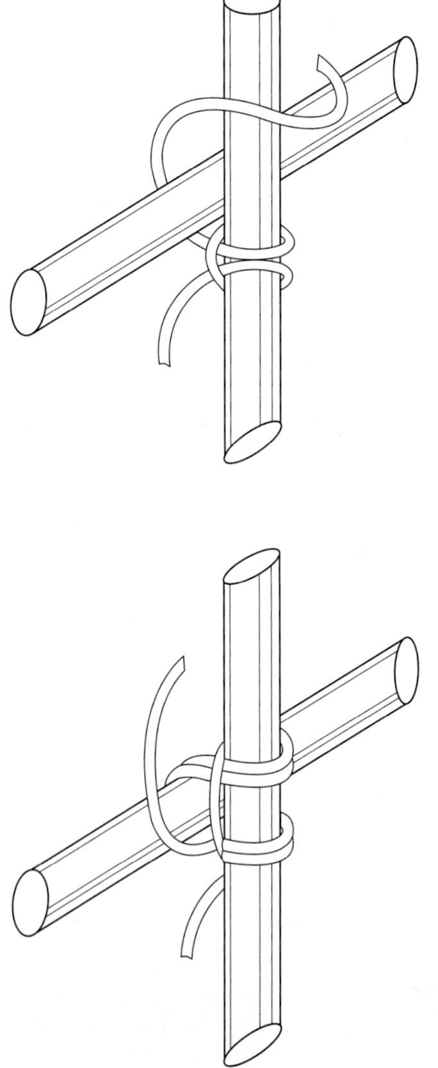

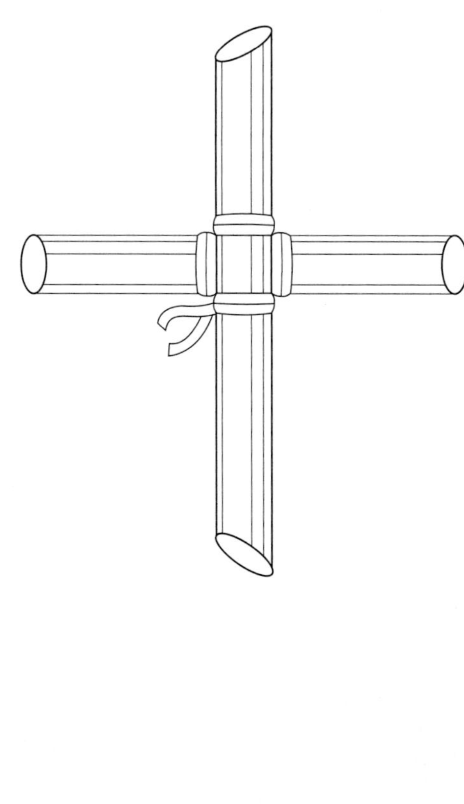

ROPE TIE CONNECTIONS FOR BAMBOO

Cement Wood Alternatives

Fiber cement siding is a fiber-reinforced cementitious material used for the exterior finish cladding on buildings, bridges, and other outdoor structures. It is available in sheets, clapboards, shingles, trim boards, and predesigned units similar to three-tab roofing pieces. The products are available in a range of textures and are often painted or stained on-site. Fiber cement siding is attached to wood or metal stud framing with nails or screws. The product is sealed; and if cracked or scratched, the siding may be vulnerable to moisture penetration leading to its degradation. These products are available in a range of colors and textures.

NONTOXIC AND LOW-VOC FINISHES

Most paints on the market contain volatile organic compounds (VOC), chemicals used in finishes as binders or carriers that create an off-gas that can affect the user's health. When exposed to sunlight, VOCs create ground level ozone, a pollutant that can cause respiratory problems, damage plants, and contribute to global warming.

Many available film coatings are marketed as "low-odor," "zero-VOC," and "very low VOC"; however, it is very difficult to eliminate VOC emissions entirely. Testing of off-gases loses accuracy at very low levels, and some labeled "zero-VOC" may not be free of VOCs. The common coloring and tinting agents contribute VOCs, thus lighter colors or those brands using solvent-free coloring agents would reduce VOC emissions.

There are several coatings advertised as low-toxic paints that contain solvents chosen for their low toxicity levels; others contain chemicals derived from plants, or use binders such as milk to avoid petro-

Daniel Winterbottom, Associate Professor, Landscape Architecture, University of Washington

chemicals altogether. The "natural paints," mostly European imports, use plant-based resins, solvents and pigments, or milk proteins or casein. Many of these alternative paints perform differently, with coverage capability reduced; and with the absence of biocides, they are more susceptible to mildew spread.

Many public agencies use recycled paint for economical and environmental reasons. Some agencies provide these to the public for free, and a few manufacturers are offering recycled exterior paints for sale on a special-order basis. In most cases, the color range in recycled paints is limited to neutral colors.

When selecting "green" paints, follow these guidelines:

- Choose paints with the lowest VOC levels possible.
- Buy paints from companies that actively recycle or sponsor paint collection programs.
- Choose paints that have a certified seal by an ecological labeling group, such as Green Seal.
- Check Material Safety Data Sheets to determine potential health effects.
- Calculate needs to avoid overordering. Calculators designed for paint surface estimating are available.

SPECIFICATION STANDARDS

Specification standards are available for most materials used in landscape construction. Many municipalities and national regulatory agencies use standardized master guide specifications for the basis of their building codes. Many of these specifications are available online and can be downloaded from agency websites for inclusion into the project manual.

The Construction Specifications Institute (CSI) has developed a format commonly used in the practice. The CSI specifications comprise 16 divisions, each defining a material or trade. Division 06000, for example, covers wood. Each division is then subdivided into sections that cover specific applications by trade. For example, under division 06000 is 06100, which covers rough carpentry; this is followed by 06180, which covers glue-laminated construction. The divisions that are most relevant to wood construction are 06000, Wood; sections of division 03000, Concrete; sections of division 05000, Metals; and sections of division 07000, Roofing.

REFERENCES

Adams, W. 1979. *The French Garden 1500-1800.* New York: George Braziller.

Amburgey, T. Feb./March 1992. "Wood-Destroying Fungi," *Fine Homebuilding.*

American Institute of Timber Construction (AITC). 1998. "109-98, Standard for Preservative Treatment of Structural Glued Laminated Timber." Centennial, CO: AITC.

American Wood Systems. 1993. *Glulams in Residential Construction.* Tacoma, WA: American Wood Systems.

Bring, M., and J. Wayembergh. 1981. *Japanese Gardens, Design and Meaning.* New York: McGraw-Hill Co.

Byrne, R. 1984. *The Victorian Design Book.* Ottawa, Ontario, Canada: Lee Valley Tools Ltd.

Chatfield, J. 1991. *The Classic Italian Garden.* New York: Rizzoli.

Dufort, R. Aug./Sept. 1990. "Painting Exteriors," *Fine Homebuilding.*

Falk, B., and S. Williams. April/May 1996. "Details for a Lasting Deck," *Fine Homebuilding,* 78–81.

Fine Homebuilding Magazine. 1997. *Porches, Decks and Outbuildings.* Newtown, CT: Tauton Press.

Goetz, K., D. Hoor, K. Mohler, and J. Natterer. 1989. *Timber Design and Construction Sourcebook.* New York: McGraw-Hill Co.

Grove, Scott. Oct./Nov. 1985. "Deck Design," *Fine Homebuilding,* 42–46.

Harris, C., and N. Dines. 1988. *Time-Saver Standards for Landscape Architecture.* New York: McGraw-Hill Co.

Herbertson, S. Feb./March 1991. "Builder's Adhesives," *Fine Homebuilding,* 40–45.

Ireton, K. Aug./Sept. 1987. "Concrete and Masonry Fasteners," *Fine Homebuilding,* 52–57.

Jakubovich, P. 1993. *As Good as New.* Milwaukee, WI: Department of City Development, City of Milwaukee.

Karp, B. 1981. *Victorian Ornamental Carpentry.* Mineola, NY: Dover Publications.

Malin, N. February 1999. "Paint the Room Green," *Environmental Building News,* vol. 8, no. 2: 1/11–19.

McBride, Scott. 1999. *Landscaping with Wood.* Newtown, CT: The Taunton Press.

———. Oct./Nov. 1991. "Railing Against the Elements," *Fine Homebuilding,* 68–71.

———. July 1999. "Building a Timber Retaining Wall," *Fine Homebuilding,* 102–105.

McDonald, K., R. Falk, S. Williams, and J. Winandy. 1996. *Wood Decks, Materials, Construction and Finishing.* Madison, WI: Forest Products Society.

Missell, R. April/May 1988. "A Deck Built to Last," *Fine Homebuilding,* 66–69.

Nash, G. May 1997. "Building a Picket Fence," *Fine Homebuilding,* 86–91.

———. 1999. *Wooden Fences.* Newtown, CT: The Taunton Press.

Powell, C. Feb./March 1996. "A Rail-and-Stile Garden Gate," *Fine Homebuilding,* 72–75.

Robinson, D., D. Rosen, and A. Jaroslow. June/July 1984. "Rustic Shelter," *Fine Homebuilding,* 66–69.

Schuttner, S. 1993. *Building and Designing Decks.* Newtown, CT: The Taunton Press.

———. Feb./March 1993. "Deck Foundations That Last," *Fine Homebuilding,* 64–69.

Sewall, S., and D. Stenstrom. Feb./March "Rebuilding a Federal-Period Fence," *Fine Homebuilding,* 73–77.

Spring, P. Aug/Sept. 1984. "Stud Wall Framing," *Fine Homebuilding,* 70–73.

Smulski, S. Oct./Nov. 1990. "Preservative-Treated Wood," *Fine Homebuilding,* 61–65.

———. July 1996. "Lumber Grade Stamps," *Fine Homebuilding,* 70–73.

Tatum, G. 1991. *Landscape Gardening and Rural Architecture,* A.J. Downing. New York: Dover Publications.

Tishler, W. 1989. *American Landscape Architecture.* Washington, DC: The Preservation Press.

Vaughan, R. Oct./Nov. 1989. "A Decorative Post Cap," *Fine Homebuilding,* 73.

Western Wood Products Association. 1973. *Western Woods Use Book.* Portland, OR: WWPA.

Williams, S., M. Knaebe, and W. Feist. July 1997. "Why Exterior Finishes Fail," *Fine Homebuilding.*

See also:
Fences and Screens
Gazebos and Freestanding Wood Structures
Wood Decks

Daniel Winterbottom, Associate Professor, Landscape Architecture, University of Washington

RECREATIONAL SURFACES

RECREATIONAL SURFACES

HISTORY

The concept of sports surfaces is as old as athletic competition itself. The first sports surfaces were open spaces cast on naturally occurring native soils. The participants gave little consideration to the performance of the surface and its impact on the nature and character of their activity.

Our modern perspective of the nature and function of recreation surfaces evolved from the golf industry. In 1895, the United States Golf Association (USGA) published "Golf in America: A Manual of Practice," the first book in the United States written about the golf course. To further the science of recreational surfaces, the USGA created the Greens Section for turf research in 1920. In 1960, the USGA published "Specification for a Method of Putting Green Construction," which established a standard for sand-based recreational golf surfaces throughout the world. The USGA was a pioneer, and remains a chief authority, in recreational turfgrass management.

Based on USGA standards, in the 1960s, sand-based recreational surfaces began to replace native soil on a few high-performance multipurpose stadiums. Although the performance objectives may not be the same as with golf, until the 1990s, most field sports continued to rely heavily on the USGA standards.

Originally designed for use in urban playgrounds, artificial turf first came to prominence in 1965, when Astroturf was installed in the newly built Astrodome in Houston, Texas. The use of Astroturf and similar surfaces became widespread in the 1970s; they were installed in both indoor and outdoor arenas around the world. In the 1990s, new artificial playing surfaces using sand and/or rubber in-fill were developed. These next-generation surfaces were regarded as a significant improvement to the first-generation surfaces, and have gained popularity steadily.

Recently, many of the governing bodies of individual sports have funded extensive research programs to identify the particular performance requirements for each sport. Many of these efforts have culminated in the establishment of quantifiable surface performance standards applicable to the wide range of sports and to the characterization of recreational surfaces.

ATHLETE SAFETY

The primary goal of any recreational facility is to provide a safe and stable surface. The sports surface is often the main element of a sports facility; and certainly it is the most important component for the effective performance of the athletes. Safety is defined in a number of ways.

- *Surface uniformity.* The surface is uniform without irregularities, which can provide a trip hazard or unstable footing when used by the athlete.
- *Surface stability.* The surface should provide a firm and predictable footing that will not excessively displace or move when contacted by the athlete.
- *Shoe traction.* The surface should provide an optimum level of traction for the athletic use. Excessive traction can lead to knee and ankle injuries in athletes, whereas too little traction can lead to slipping or sliding.
- *Surface hardness.* The surface should provide an optimum level of firmness that is predictable and that will not injure the athlete. An excessively hard surface can result in head trauma, concussions, or leg injuries; in contrast, excessively soft surfaces can result in ligament injuries and muscle pulls.
- *Clearances.* The surface should be maintained clear on any vertical or horizontal obstructions that could interfere with athletic use of the surface.

OPERATIONAL PLANNING

The selection and design of a recreational surface is based on four important principles: programmed use, maintenance, climate, and performance expectations. These principles are interrelated and connected to the impact of each of the others. For example, increasing program use directly impacts maintenance requirements. A successful recreational surface balances each of the four principles within a functional and practical solution.

- *Programmed use.* All recreational surfaces will wear and fail prematurely if the programmed use exceeds the design capacity of the product. Selection and design of a recreational surface requires detailed understanding of programmed use in terms of frequency, intensity, and duration. A common mistake is underestimating future program use, which leads to premature surface wear and failure. All activities that occur on a surface need to be accounted for in the selection of a product, including games, practices, special events, competitions, summer camps, concerts, and even maintenance activities, which can degrade a surface.
- *Maintenance requirements.* All recreational surfaces require maintenance in order to provide continued optimum performance. There is no such thing as a maintenance-free recreational surface. Selection of a recreational surface requires a comprehensive understanding of the maintenance resources, skills, and equipment of the individuals responsible for maintaining the surface. The product selection should be tailored to the capabilities of the maintenance staff. Maintenance costs through life expectancy of a recreational surface typically exceed the installation costs by a factor of 10.
- *Climate.* Climate plays an important part in the selection of a recreational surface, especially with natural grass surfaces. Climate directly influences both the cultural maintenance practices and performance of a recreational surface. Items to consider that are influenced by climate include performance of the surface during the extreme weather conditions, the environmental stress placed on the athlete during use, cultural management practices based on climatic extremes, effect of freeze-thaw cycle in cold climates, and impact on weathering and durability of recreational surfaces.
- *Expectation for performance.* Selection and design of a recreational surface must take into account changing human perceptions and expectations. As competition in sports has changed from a local context to one that is more regional or even national in perspective, the expectations for performance have increased markedly. While intangible, these expectations are an important aspect of determining the user's opinion of the suitability and quality of a recreational surface. What should the surface look like after 50 games? Is the surface a training surface or a competition surface? What is the optimum mowing height? The athlete's interaction with a recreational surface is personal and sometimes emotional. Early in the design of a recreational surface the expectation for performance should be quantified in measurable parameters. This will reduce misunderstanding between the reality of a surface's performance and the user's expectations.

RECREATIONAL SURFACES AS LAYERED SYSTEMS

Recreational surfaces are "layered" systems in which each component layer contributes specific attributes to the performance of a surface. As with any layered system, each layer forms the foundation or substrate for the next layer. Although each layer is managed as an independent scope aspect during construction, any flaw or loss of integrity in one layer will be reflected in the performance of all subsequent layers. Quality assurance of materials and construction tolerances are critical to proper functioning of a recreational surface. Each layer in a recreational surface should satisfy its own performance standards and quality assurance process.

The interrelationship of the individual components or layers, and their integration into an overall functional system, is fundamental to the performance of the system, yet commonly overlooked in the design of recreational surfaces. For example, an irrigation system should deliver water to a natural turf system at a manageable rate without creating runoff. The turf system should then convey excess water vertically through the profile to the drainage system at a rate that does not harm the turf. The drainage system must then be designed to remove excess water from the profile so that surface performance is not impaired. Both soil composition and slope determine the capability of the turf system to manage the water, either occurring naturally or augmented by irrigation.

NATURAL GRASS SURFACES

Natural grass systems in sports facilities have improved significantly in the past few years, utilizing technologies developed in the golf industry and benefiting from a more sophisticated approach to

Jeffrey Bruce, FASLA, ASIC, LEED Jeffrey L. Bruce & Company LLC management and design. Consideration for using natural turf systems is typically based on:

- The nature and extent of the programs the facility will support
- The character and availability of local materials
- The geographic and environmental limitations
- The maintenance capability of the support and management staff

The success of natural turf systems depends on the designer's ability to integrate these concerns in a properly engineered and manageable system.

To support burgeoning program demands and meet the ever-rising user expectations, successful natural-grass surfaces typically employ a surfacing approach that involves engineered component systems, integrated from the base through the turfgrass component. High-performance systems, often sand-based, allow for a quantifiable management approach that results in consistent and predictable growth, integrating irrigation, drainage, fertilization, and other significant turf-maintenance concerns. Some of these systems often have structural stabilization components that reduce rutting and the effects of wear on the surface, while others include subsurface drainage, limiting the effects of surface drainage and reducing the required slope of the turf system.

ARTIFICIAL TURF SURFACES

Synthetic sports surfaces have evolved significantly since the late 1960s, in response to changing technologies and a growing demand for safer, more "grasslike" surfaces. Originating with the Astroturf nylon rug product, these surfaces have improved through various padding and softening changes. With newer second-generation sand-rubber "in-fill" products, integrated natural/synthetic products have become more prevalent today. Synthetic turf technologies have made it possible for designers to offer a high-performance surface in locations where weather or other conditions make natural turf impractical.

The wide range of synthetic products available today allows a designer to customize the surface to match a specific performance characteristic, such as surface hardness, speed and character of ball roll, and planarity and traction. By varying the rubber and sand in the in-fill, pile height, type of fiber, direction and degree of slope, and other physical aspects, the surface can be tailored to better meet the program of the facility.

Synthetic turf systems are layered systems, beginning at the subgrade and continuing up through a drainage base layer, including a permeable stone base and subsurface drainage system. It continues to the synthetic surface itself, which is comprised of a multilayer backing and a surface pile of thiolon or polyethelene fibers with variable densities and face weights, depending on the product and manufacturer. The face fibers are then in-filled with a crumb-rubber or a crumb-rubber and sand blend, creating a traction surface with characteristics similar to natural surfaces in traction, feel, and hardness.

While there is a variety of products available, there are common components and performance characteristics that can be used to evaluate and select the appropriate system for a particular application. These might include backing weight, face weight, pile height, fiber type and texture, and performance characteristics, such as surface hardness, ball roll, traction, and temperature attenuation. Also it is important that the turf system be designed and specified as an integrated system. The designer must focus on the quality control of the installation of each system component to ensure that all subsequent components shall perform as intended.

As new products enter the market, it is important to check on the availability of reputable contractor-providers that shall deliver, warrantee, and service the product.

SYNTHETIC TRACK SURFACES

The following are excerpts from "The Track Construction Buyers Guide," published by the American Sports Builders Association (ASBA) (formerly the United States Tennis Court and Track Builders Association (USTC&TBA)). Note that these guidelines are not specifications. For recreational surface construction landscape architects are advised to consult product manufacturers and/or a qualified consultant and/or design professional. Variances in climate, soil conditions, topography, and other factors may make these guidelines unsuitable for certain projects.

> *Today, most tracks are constructed of rubber particles bound with latex or polyurethane. The latex or polyurethane surface is installed to a depth of 3/8" to 1/2" on top of an asphalt or concrete base.*
>
> *The rubber used may be black or colored. Black rubber particles may be granular or stranded and they may be made from natural rubber, styrene-butadiene rubber (SBR) or ethylene-propylene-diene rubber (EPDM), virgin or recycled. Colored rubber particles are almost always made of virgin EPDM rubber and they come in granular form only. The relative costs and performance characteristics of the types of rubber used are beyond the scope of this publication. A prospective owner should discuss the various systems available, their costs and performance differences with a knowledgeable advisor. In general, however, virgin rubber is more expensive than recycled rubber and colored rubber is more expensive than black rubber. When using recycled rubber, its quality and performance is dependent on the care taken in separating different types of scrap before grinding. The performance of any type of rubber is dependent on its chemical composition, the quality of its manufacture, its compatibility with the binder system and the care taken during its installation.*
>
> *Latex-bound tracks provide good performance and durability, and have increased in popularity in recent years. Latex systems can be installed in multiple layers or in a single layer, creating a permeable, resilient surface. In some systems the rubber is spread over the track surface, which is then sprayed with the latex binder. In other systems the rubber particles and binder are pre-mixed and then spread. Virtually all latex systems are permeable to some degree. The basic, and least expensive, system is black, but three types of colored systems are available. These are: 1) colored binder with black rubber; 2) color sandwich, which features colored rubber and colored binder in the top layers over black rubber; or 3) full-depth color, where both the rubber and latex binder are colored throughout the surface. Obviously, the greater the use and depth of colored binder and colored rubber, the more expensive the surface.*
>
> *Polyurethane systems have been around longer than latex systems, and the solid-pour versions are often used on world-class competitive tracks. Polyurethane track surfaces can be either permeable or impermeable. They are generally mixed and installed on site, though premanufactured systems are available. Polyurethane surfaces may be colored or black. There are four types. The basic polyurethane-bound system consists of rubber particles bound with polyurethane to form a base mat. The base mat may be used alone, or it may be enhanced by the addition of a structural spray consisting of a mixture of polyurethane and rubber sprayed on top of the mat. This creates a textured surface. Alternatively, the base mat may be coated with a flood coat of polyurethane and rubber, creating an impermeable, textured surface. Or lastly, a full-pour system may be used in which each layer is mixed and poured in place. Full pour systems are impermeable and textured. Factors impacting that choice include initial cost, maintenance cost over the expected life of the surface, life expectancy, surface wear, repairability and performance characteristics. (USTC&TBA, 2003)*

TENNIS COURT SURFACES

The table "Standard Tennis Court Classification Systems" establishes a classification of materials used in the construction of the subbase, pavement, and surface systems of tennis courts. Materials can be categorized according to porosity and resiliency:

Porous: A system that permits water to permeate the surface

Nonporous: A system that inhibits water from permeating the surface (drainage is achieved through surface runoff)

Cushioned: Having a resilient or soft feel during play

Noncushioned: Having a rigid or hard feel during play

Jeffrey Bruce, FASLA, ASIC, LEED Jeffrey L. Bruce & Company LLC

TENNIS COURT SURFACE COMPARISON

SURFACE TYPE	SURFACE HARDNESS	CUSHIONED SURFACE	SURFACE SLIDE	BALL SKID LENGTH	ADJUSTABLE COURT SPEED	COLOR AVAILABILITY	DRYING TIME AFTER RAIN
POROUS							
Fast dry (aboveground irrigation)	Soft	No	Yes	Short	Yes	Green, red	Medium
Fast dry (subsurface irrigation)	Soft	No	Yes	Short	Yes	Green, red	Fast
Natural clay	Soft	No	Yes	Short	Yes	Varies	Slow
Grass	Soft	No	Yes	Long	No	Green	Slow
Sand-filled turf	Soft	Yes	Yes	Medium-Short	Yes	Variety	Fast
Porous concrete	Hard	Yes	No	Short	Yes	Variety	Fast
NONPOROUS/NONCUSHIONED							
Concrete	Hard	No	No	Controllable	Yes	Variety	Fast
Asphalt	Hard	No	No	Controllable	Yes	Variety	Fast
NONPOROUS CUSHIONED							
Concrete	Medium	Yes	No	Controllable	Yes	Variety	Fast
Asphalt	Medium	Yes	No	Controllable	Yes	Variety	Fast
Modular	Medium	Yes	No	Medium-Short	No	Variety	Fast
Roll-goods	Medium	Yes	No	Medium-Short	Yes	Variety	Fast
Textile (indoor only)	Medium	Yes	No	Short	No	Variety	NA

Some options listed are not available in certain geographical locations and climatic conditions. Other options may exist that are not listed. Contact a Tennis Facility Consultant or refer to the most current "Tennis Courts: A Construction and Maintenance Manual" (published jointly by the USTA and ASBA) for more detailed information.

STANDARD TENNIS COURT CLASSIFICATION SYSTEMS

SUBBASE, PAVEMENT, AND SURFACE TYPE	MAINTENANCE	COLORS	BALL SKID	PORTABILITY	FOOT SLIDE	DRYING TIME
POROUS CONSTRUCTION						
Noncushioned						
Porous asphalt	Yearly	Varies	Adjustable	No	None	Rapid
Porous concrete	Yearly	Varies	Adjustable	No	None	Rapid
Modular (such as interlocking tiles)	Yearly	Varies	Short	Yes	None	Rapid
Cushioned						
Fast dry	Daily	Red, green	Short	No	Good	Moderate
Clay (natural clay)	Daily	Red	Short	No	Good	Slow
Natural grass	Daily	Green	Long	No	Good	Slow
Sand-filled synthetic turf	Daily	Green	Medium	No	Good	Moderate
NONPOROUS CONSTRUCTION						
Noncushioned						
Concrete—Standard and post tensioned	Yearly	Varies	Adjustable	No	None	Rapid
Asphalt—Hot plant mix	Yearly	Varies	Adjustable	No	None	Rapid
Macadam—Asphalt penetration	Yearly	Varies	Adjustable	No	None	Rapid
Cushioned						
Acrylic-bound surface systems	Yearly	Varies	Adjustable	No	None	Rapid
Textiles (carpet-like, manufactured from synthetic fibers)	Yearly	Green	Adjustable	Yes	Some	(indoor)
Synthetic granular (such as polyurethane bound rubber granules)	Yearly	Varies	Short	No	None	Rapid
Resilient membrane (seamed-together roll goods)	Yearly	Varies	Adjustable	No	None	Rapid

Some options listed are not available in certain geographical locations and climatic conditions. Other options may exist that are not listed. Contact a Tennis Facility Consultant or refer to the most current "Tennis Courts: A Construction and Maintenance Manual" (published jointly by the USTA and ASBA) for more detailed information.

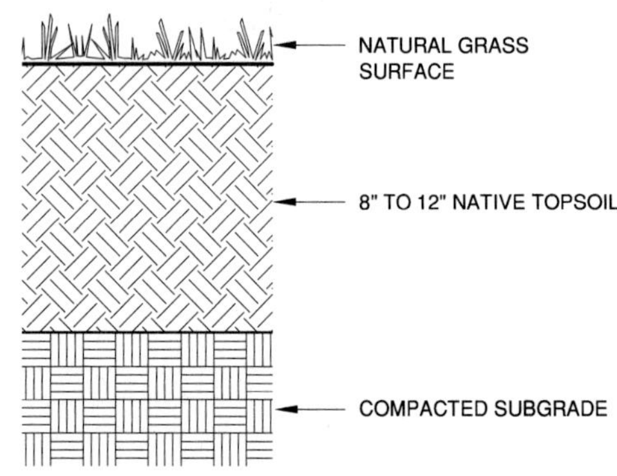

NATURAL GRASS—NATIVE SOIL

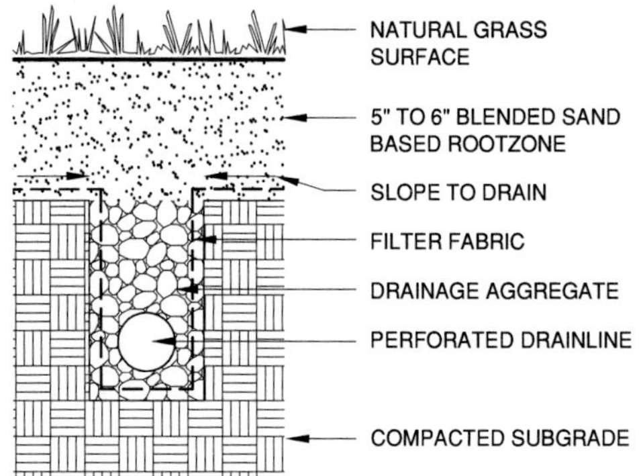

NATURAL GRASS—SAND PLATE

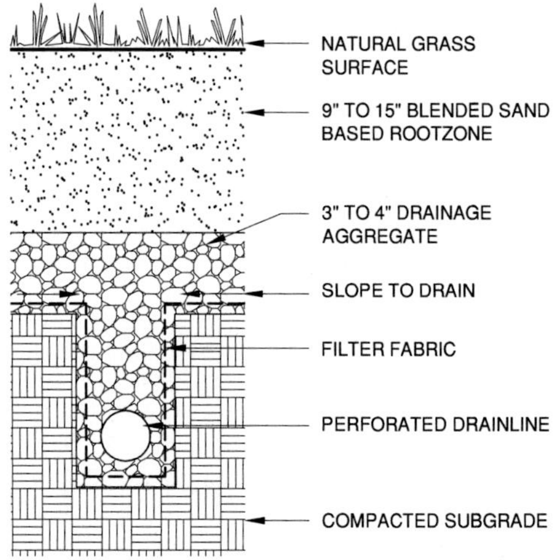

NATURAL GRASS—USGA INVERTED FILTER

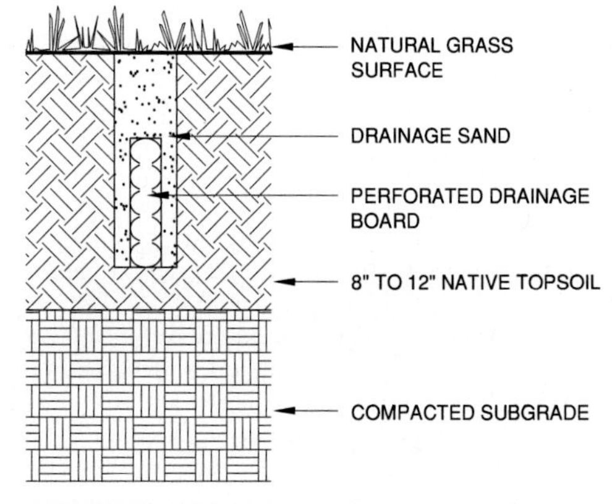

NATURAL GRASS—SAND-SLIT BYPASS

Jeffrey Bruce, FASLA, ASIC, LEED Jeffrey L. Bruce & Company LLC

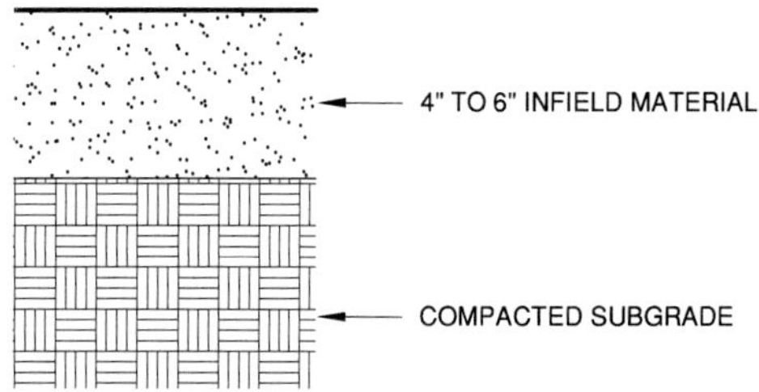

SKINNED INFIELD—BASEBALL/SOFTBALL

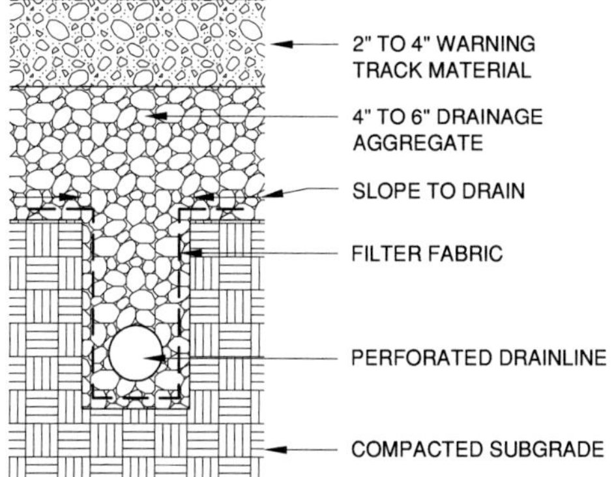

WARNING TRACK—BASEBALL/SOFTBALL

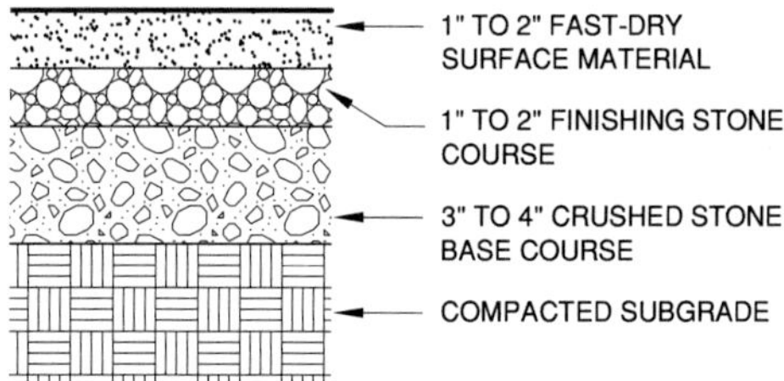

FAST-DRY TENNIS COURT

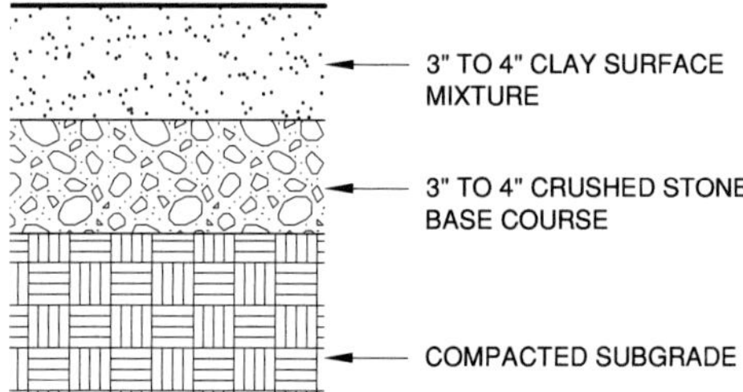

NATURAL CLAY TENNIS COURT

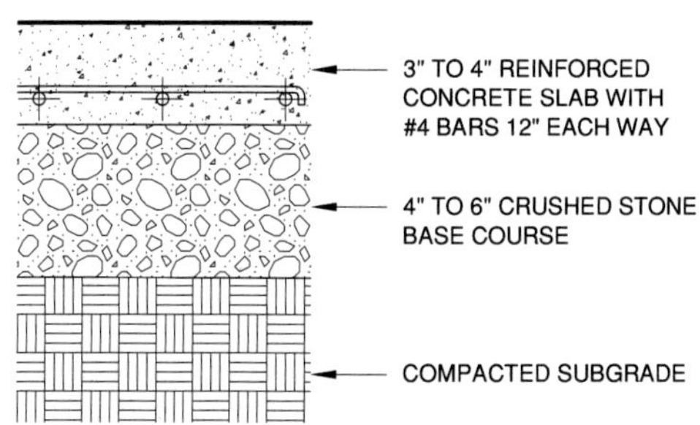

REINFORCED CONCRETE TENNIS COURT

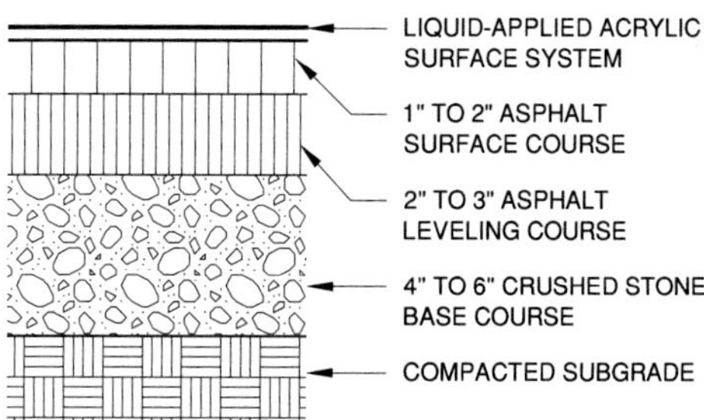

ASPHALT TENNIS COURT

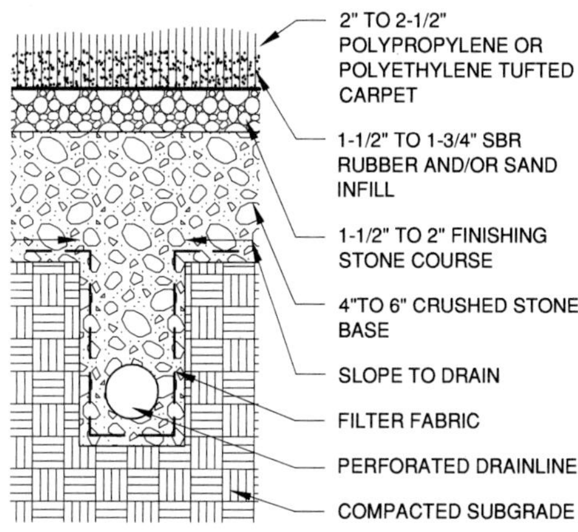

IN-FILLED ARTIFICIAL SURFACE

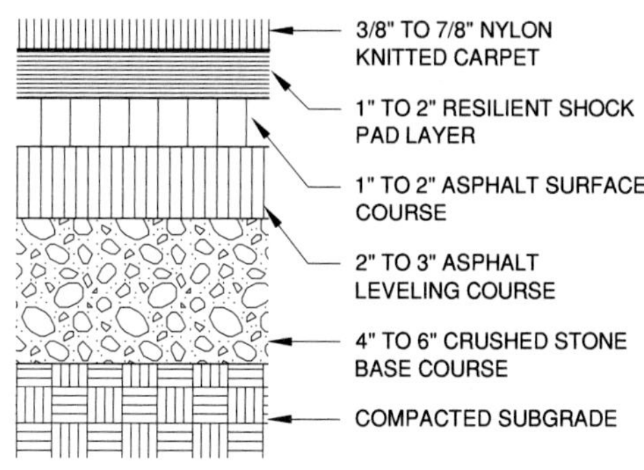

ARTIFICIAL SURFACE

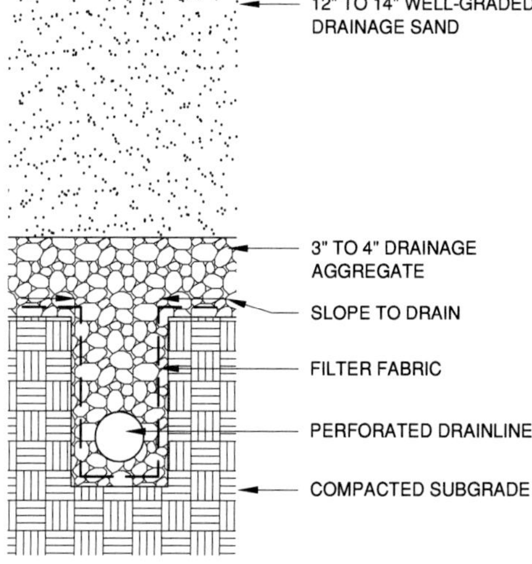

SAND VOLLEYBALL

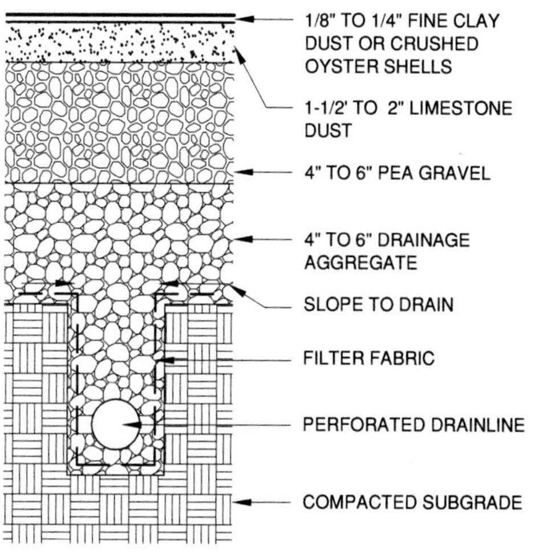

BOCCE COURT

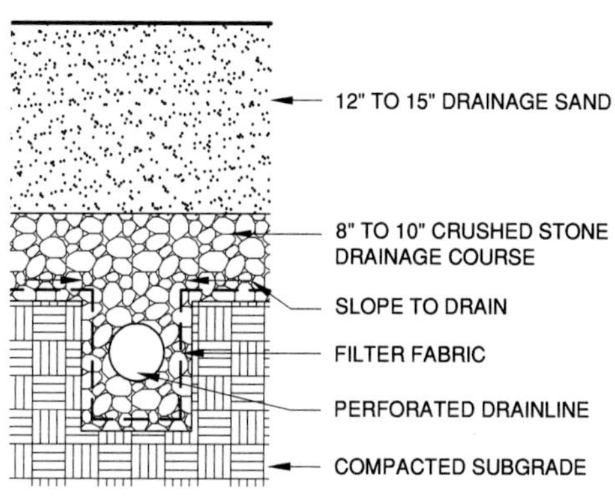

TRACK—LONG JUMP/TRIPLE JUMP LANDING ZONE

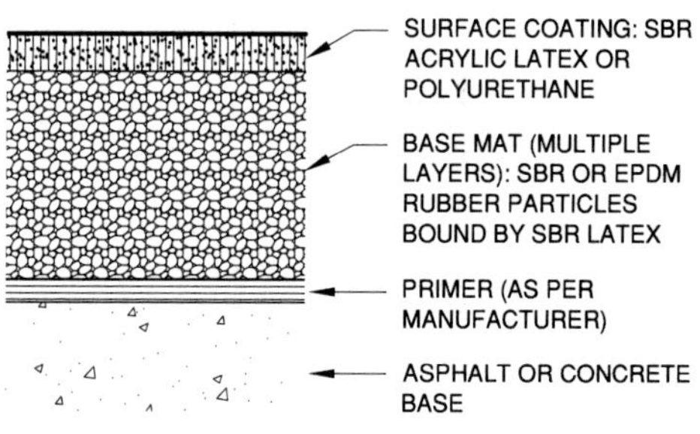

TRACK—LATEX (PERMEABLE)

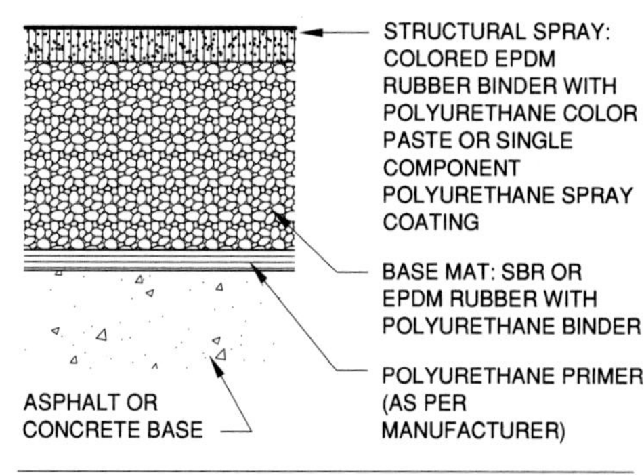

TRACK—POLYURETHANE BASEMAT STRUCTURAL SPRAY (PERMEABLE)

Jeffrey Bruce, FASLA, ASIC, LEED Jeffrey L. Bruce & Company LLC

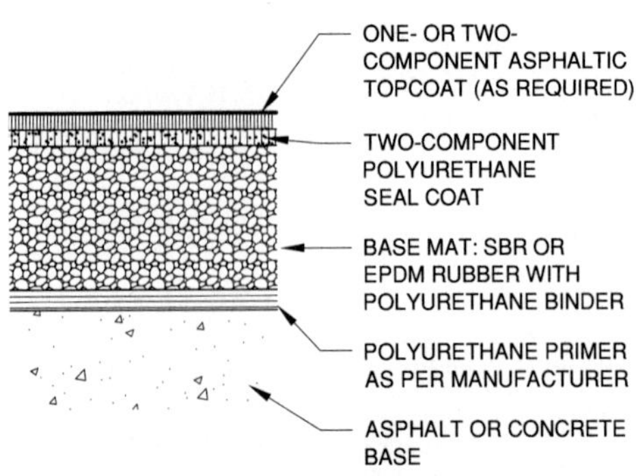

TRACK—POLYURETHANE BASEMAT/SANDWICH (IMPERMEABLE)

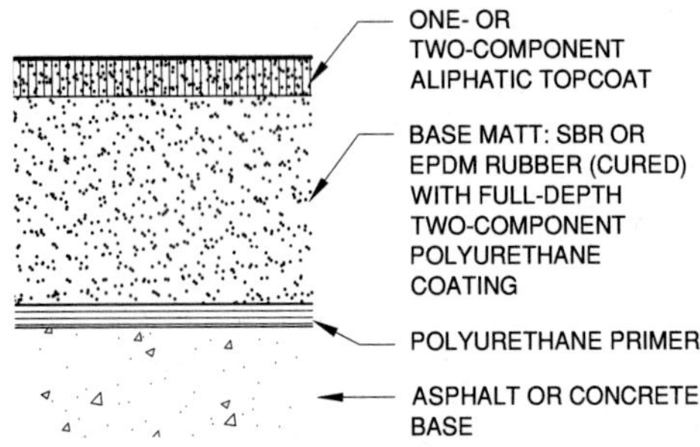

TRACK—POLYURETHANE FULL-POUR (IMPERMEABLE)

BASE MAT: SBR OR EPDM RUBBER WITH POLYURETHANE BINDER

POLYURETHANE PRIMER (AS PER MANUFACTURER)

ASPHALT OR CONCRETE BASE

TRACK—POLYURETHANE BASEMAT (PERMEABLE)

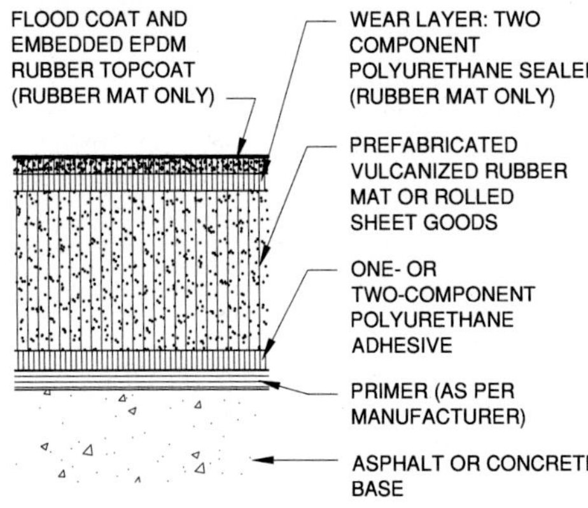

TRACK—PREMANUFACTURED RUBBER (IMPERMEABLE)

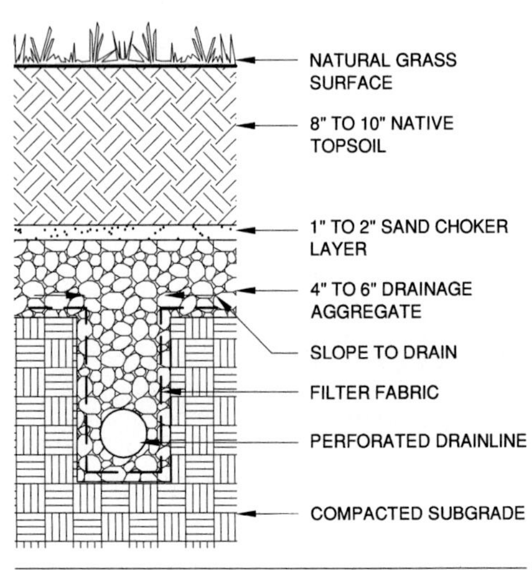

CROQUET LAWN

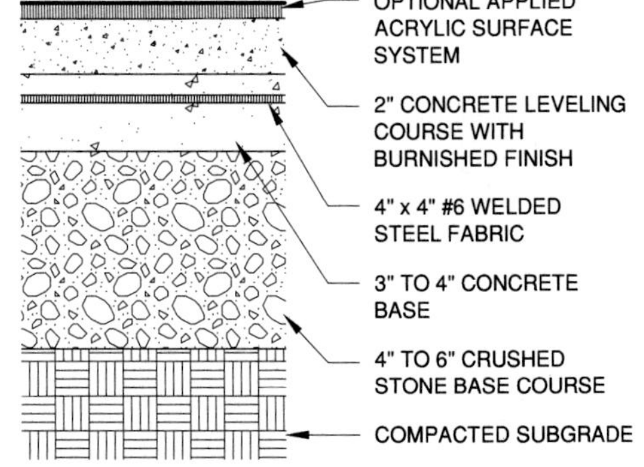

SHUFFLEBOARD COURT

USEFUL ORGANIZATIONS AND WEBSITES

American Sports Builders Association (ASBA)
7010 W. Highway 71
Suite 340, PMB 312
Austin, TX 78735-8331
Toll-free: 866-501-ASBA (2722)
Phone: 512-858-9890
Fax: 512-858-9892
Website: www.sportsbuilders.org

ASTM International
100 Barr Harbor Drive, PO Box C700
West Conshohocken, PA 19428-2959
Phone: 610-832-9585
Fax: 610-832-9555
Website: www.astm.org

National Association of Intercollegiate Athletics (NAIA)
23500 West 105th Street
Olathe, KS 66061
Phone: 913-791-0044
Fax: 913-791-9555
Website: http://naia.collegesports.com

National Collegiate Athletic Association (NCAA)
700 W. Washington Street
PO Box 6222
Indianapolis, IN 46206-6222
Phone: 317-917-6222
Fax: 317-917-6888
Website: www2.ncaa.org

National Federation of State High School Associations (NFSHSA)
PO Box 690
Indianapolis, IN 46206
Phone: 317-972-6900
Fax: 317-822-5700
Website: www.nfhs.org

National Junior College Athletic Association (NJCAA)
1755 Telstar Drive, Suite 103
Colorado Springs, CO 80920
Phone: 719-590-9788
Fax: 719-590-7324
Website: www.njcaa.org

Sports Turf Managers Association (STMA)
805 New Hampshire, Suite E
Lawrence, KS 66044
Toll-free: 800-323-3875
Fax: 800-366-0391
Website: www.sportsturfmanager.org

Synthetic Turf Council
2216 Mount Haven Drive, #18
Dalton, GA 30720
Phone: 706-270-6699
Fax: 706-278-9899
Website: www.syntheticturfcouncil.org

United States Field Hockey Association (USFHA)
1 Olympic Plaza
Colorado Springs, CO 80909
Phone: 719-866-4567
Fax: 719-632-0979
Website: www.usfieldhockey.com

USGA Green Section Department
PO Box 708
Far Hills, NJ 07931
Phone: 908-234-2300
Fax: 908-781-1736
Website: www.usga.org

U.S. Lacrosse
113 W. University Parkway
Baltimore, MD 21210
Phone: 410-235-6882
Fax: 410-366-6735
Website: www.lacrosse.org

United States Soccer Federation (USSF)
1801 South Prairie Ave.
Chicago, IL 60616
Phone: 312-808-1300
Fax: 312-808-1301
Website: www.ussoccer.com

USA Track & Field
One RCA Dome, Suite 140
Indianapolis, IN 46225
Phone: 317-261-0500
Fax: 317-261-0481
Website: www.usatf.org

REFERENCES

American Sports Builders Association. 2004. "Running Tracks: A Construction and Maintenance Manual." Austin, TX: American Sports Builders Association.

United States Tennis Court and Track Builders Association. 2003. "Tennis Courts: A Construction and Maintenance Manual." Austin, TX: American Sports Builders Association.

United States Tennis Court and Track Builders Association. 2003. "The Track Construction Buyers Guide." Austin, TX: American Sports Builders Association.

Jeffrey Bruce, FASLA, ASIC, LEED Jeffrey L. Bruce & Company LLC

NURSERY STOCK

NURSERY STOCK STANDARDS AND PRACTICES, SHIPPING AND HANDLING, GUARANTEES

INTRODUCTION

Federal and state standards, among other regulations, are written to ensure that a purchaser is receiving goods as advertised for sale. Standards governing quality, truth in labeling, and advertising have existed since the development of the country. Over the years, controls have become more stringent, as public awareness has grown, along with pressure to provide assurances that what is being purchased or used complies with health, safety, and welfare guidelines.

Plant materials used primarily for landscape purposes have not traditionally fallen under these auspices, hence have not been regulated as stringently. The U.S. Department of Agriculture (USDA) and the state agencies have regulated interstate shipping of plant materials and have placed quarantines on plants that have proved or may prove dangerous when it comes to disease and/or insects. The intent is to ward off a potential disaster related to an attack on the ecosystem, especially with regard to the production of food and fiber for human use and consumption. Since plant materials, in the green industry, are perceived more in the realm of aesthetics and beautification, they are not seen as impacting health, safety, and welfare.

In recent times, however, the green industry has attempted to develop regulations and is urging compliance. But compliance is voluntary and only enforced to the degree that the public or consumer demands that it be enforced. That said, as the green industry evolves into a formidable economic industry, and as plant materials are commonly shipped across the country and internationally, the demand for universally accepted standards is growing. For many years, the American Nursery and Landscape Association (ANLA) has been publishing the American Standard for Nursery Stock, ANSI Z60.1, and has encouraged its adoption throughout the industry. It is the intent of the ANLA to provide "buyers and sellers of nursery stock with a common terminology in order to facilitate transactions involving nursery stock." Further, the document states, "The standards establish common techniques for (a) measuring plants, (b) specifying and stating the size of plants, (c) determining the proper relationship between height and caliper, or height and width, and (d) determining whether a root ball container is large enough for a particular size plant" (ANLA, 2004). (The most recent publication, ANSI 260.1-2004, can be downloaded at no charge from www.anla.org/appli cations/Documents/Docs.)

A major difficulty with the standards is that plants grow differently, as climatic regions and cultural situations vary. One cannot assure that a plant grown in a dry climate under irrigation will be equivalent in size and character to one grown in a humid climate with no irrigation. In addition, since individual taste varies as well, what may be seen as an aesthetically pleasing plant by one may not be viewed as such by another. Thus, it is up to the specifier of plant materials to be aware of potential industry differences and to make this clear on bid documents, to the landscape contractor, and the client.

PLANT NOMENCLATURE STANDARDS

When specifying plants, it is important to use standard nomenclature. All plants have a Latin binomial name—the "scientific name"—and pertinent botanical variety, form, or cultivar names. Only the scientific name is standardized across regions, states, and countries. Because the scientific name is standardized, it has legal standing and helps to assure that the species and cultivars are delivered to the job site as specified.

Plants also have a "common name," which consists of the pertinent variety, form, and/or cultivar identifications, in addition to the name commonly used in the region in which they are grown or sold. The common names of plants vary throughout the country and the world, therefore they have not been standardized. For example:

- *Scientific name. Acer* (genus, italicized and capitalized); *rubrum* (species, italicized and lowercase); 'October Glory' (cultivar, capitalized and with single quotation marks)
- *Common name.* October Glory (cultivar, without quotation marks); red maple (commonly used but may vary)

As another example, *Acer saccharinum* (scientific name) is commonly called a silver maple; but in Ohio, many call it a water maple. In Kentucky, an *Acer negundo* is commonly called a water maple, but in other parts of the country it is called a common box elder or an ashleaf maple.

Specification Suggestions

- Certain species may not be grown in the hardiness zone where they are going to be relocated; therefore, it is best to specify cultivars if hardiness may be an issue. The hardiness of named cultivars is assured by USDA regulations.
- A request for a substitution for a species or cultivar by a contractor should be allowed only if it is certain that the substitution is not substantially different from that ordered.

Two sources for more information are available online. The International Plant Name Index (2004), published on the Web at www.ipni.org/index, contains all known plants by genus and species. It does not include cultivars, however. The USDA, NRCS Plant List of Accepted Nomenclature, Taxonomy and Symbols (PLANTS), at http://plants.usda..gov, is a dynamic database that provides online accessibility to standardized plant information. It contains information on plant names, symbols, growth habit, plant growth, vegetative specifications, distribution, wetland indicator status, and threatened and endangered status. This nomenclature is used by most U.S. federal agencies and is the required reference on federal projects.

Specification Suggestion

- To assure that plants supplied are as specified, use a statement similar to the following in the specifications: "The scientific and common names of plants herein specified conform with the approved names given in the International Plant Name Index [or whichever standard nomenclature reference is being used."

PLANT QUALITY STANDARDS

Plant quality tends to be somewhat subjective since we are dealing with living material that varies in growth habit within species, as well as the conditions under which it was grown. In this respect, it is necessary to write specifications that are detailed enough to assure receipt of the quality desired. One of the major factors in obtaining high-quality plant material is the reputation of the nursery in which the plants are grown. A good, but not certain, indicator is whether the nursery belongs to one or several of the state or national organizations. In addition, nearly all wholesale producers publish catalogs that provide descriptive information relative to the plant in question—for example, cultivar, size, hardiness zone, form and height of expected growth, rate of growth, bloom time and color, and other pertinent characteristics.

Quality standards fall into two categories for all plants: aboveground standards and belowground standards. If this information is followed, the odds are very good that plant material of a high quality will be received.

Quality Standards: Aboveground Considerations

- Ensure that plants are nursery grown under favorable conditions. Nursery-grown plants have a better survival rate and do not disturb the natural ecosystem by their removal. It is not recommended that trees collected from the wild be specified or accepted, both from a quality and an ecological perspective.
- Verify that the ratio of height to caliper is proportional and typical of the species.
- Select trees that have well-spaced structural branches, which are oriented uniformly around the trunk.
- If a tree is a type that has a strong central leader, ascertain whether the trees in question manifest that characteristic.
- Ascertain the general health of the plant. Check for mechanical damage, frost cracks, and herbicide

Thomas J. Nieman, Ph.D., Department of Landscape Architecture, University of Kentucky

damage to the bark. Check for any signs of serious insect or disease problems. Also examine foliage color, density, and length of shoot extension as signs of general health.

Quality Standards: Belowground Considerations

Soil Ball Wrapping

- Natural, untreated burlap is best. Treated, or rot-resistant, burlap, which retards decomposition for up to three months and binds well with the soil after decomposition, is also acceptable.
- Plastic or poly tree ball wrap is not acceptable, and should be specified as such. If plants are shipped with a nonorganic wrapping, it must be removed prior to planting.
- Ball supporting devices, such as wire baskets or rope and twine, should hold the ball firmly and in rigid condition.
- Rope or twine, if it is organic, should be loosened from the top of the tree ball. Synthetic twine or rope must be removed completely.
- Wire from baskets must cut be down at least one-half of the ball depth and removed.

Soil Ball

- The size of the soil ball should meet minimum standards, as indicated in ANSI Z60.1-2004 standards (see the soil root ball size tables).
- The burlap and other materials used to wrap the ball must be very tight, to reduce risk of ball damage from shipping and handling.
- The trunk of the tree should be in the center of the soil ball.

Container Size Specifications

- State container size and the corresponding minimum plant size (container size is not an indicator of plant size).
- Volume range for container classes is #1 through #100. Container class numbers are approximately equivalent to gallons, but it is not appropriate to specify plants by gallon sizes. Small plant containers (SP) are specified, for example, as: SP#4 = 1 quart = 57.75 cubic inches.

Wooden Box Size Equivalents

- A wooden box may be specified in lieu of the indicated container class, and vice versa. For example: #20 container = 20-inch box; #95/100 box = 48-inch box.

PLANT MATERIAL STANDARDS

Plant materials are classified by ANSI Z60.1-2004 into the following categories: Shade and Flowering Trees; Deciduous Shrubs; Coniferous Evergreens; Broadleaf Evergreens; Roses; Bulbs, Corms, and Tubers; and Herbaceous Perennials, Ornamental Grasses, Ground Covers, and Vines. Recognizing that anomalies can and do occur, not all plants will conveniently fit into a selected category. This document establishes standards for measuring plants; specifying and stating the size of plants; determining the proper relationship between height and caliper, or height and width; and determining what size root ball or container size is appropriate for a specified size of plant. It should be referenced whenever specifying plant material for a project to ensure that you are requesting plants that adhere to a national standard with which the nursery

ROOT BALL DIAMETERS: FIELD-GROWN TREE

TYPE 1 AND TYPE 2 SHADE TREES		TYPE 4 AND TYPE 5 SMALL UPRIGHT AND SMALL SPREADING TREES	
CALIPER	MINIMUM-DIAMETER ROOT BALL	HEIGHT (TO 5 TO 6 FT) CALIPER (6 FT AND OVER)	MINIMUM-DIAMETER BALL
½ in.	12 in.	2 ft	10 in.
¾ in.	14 in.	3 ft	12 in.
1 in.	16 in.	4 ft	14 in.
1¼ in.	18 in.	5 ft	16 in.
1½ in.	20 in.	¾ in.	16 in.
1¾ in.	22 in.	1 in.	18 in.
2 in.	24 in.	1¼ in.	19 in.
2½ in.	28 in.	1½ in.	20 in.
3 in.	32 in.	1¾ in.	22 in.
3½ in.	38 in.	2 in.	24 in.
4 in.	42 in.	2½ in.	28 in.
4½ in.	48 in.	3 in.	32 in.
5 in.	54 in.	3½ in.	38 in.
5½ in.	57 in.	4 in.	42 in.
6 in.	60 in.	4½ in.	48 in.
7 in.	70 in.	5 in.	54 in.
8 in.	80 in.	5½ in.	57 in.
		6 in.	60 in.
		7 in.	70 in.
		8 in.	80 in.

ROOT BALL SIZES FOR SHRUB FORM AND MULTISTEM TREES

	NARROW OR UPRIGHT HABIT WIDTH NO MORE THAN HALF HEIGHT AT MATURITY	BROAD OR SPREADING HABIT WIDTH AT LEAST HALF HEIGHT AT MATURITY
AVERAGE HEIGHT	MINIMUM-DIAMETER BALL	MINIMUM-DIAMETER BALL
4 ft	14 in.	24 in.
5 ft	18 in.	28 in.
6 ft	22 in.	32 in.
7 ft	26 in.	36 in.
8 ft	28 in.	40 in.
10 ft	32 in.	44 in.
12 ft	38 in.	52 in.
14 ft	44 in.	60 in.
16 ft	50 in.	66 in.
18 ft	60 in.	74 in.
20 ft	70 in.	80 in.

BALL SIZES: CONIFEROUS EVERGREENS

TYPES 1, 2, AND 3 SPREADING, SEMISPREADING, BROAD SPREADING, GLOBE, AND COMPACT UPRIGHT		TYPES 4 AND 5 PYRAMIDAL, BROAD UPRIGHT		TYPE 6* COLUMNAR	
SPREAD (TYPES 1 AND 2) OR HEIGHT (TYPE 3)	MINIMUM-DIAMETER BALL	HEIGHT/ CALIPER	MINIMUM-DIAMETER BALL	HEIGHT/ CALIPER	MINIMUM-DIAMETER BALL
9 in.	8 in.	12 in.	8 in.	12 in.	7 in.
12 in.	10 in.	15 in.	10 in.	15 in.	8 in.
15 in.	12 in.	18 in.	12 in.	18 in.	9 in.
18 in.	14 in.	24 in.	14 in.	24 in.	11 in.
24 in.	16 in.	30 in.	16 in.	30 in.	13 in.
30 in.	18 in.	3 ft	18 in.	3 ft	14 in.
36 in.	24 in.	4 ft	20 in.	4 ft	16 in.
42 in.	26 in.	5 ft	22 in.	5 ft	18 in.
4 ft	28 in.	6 ft	24 in.	6 ft	20 in.
5 ft	36 in.	7 ft	26 in.	7 ft	22 in.
6 ft	40 in.	8 ft	28 in.	8 ft	24 in.
7 ft	46 in.	9 ft/3 in.	32 in.	9 ft/2½ in.	26 in.
8 ft	52 in.	3½ in.	34 in.	3 in.	28 in.
		4 in.	38 in.	3½ in.	32 in.
		4½ in.	42 in.	4 in.	36 in.
		5 in.	48 in.	4½ in.	40 in.
		5½ in.	54 in.	5 in.	44 in.
		6 in.	60 in.	5½ in.	48 in.
		7 in.	72 in.	6 in.	54 in.
		8 in.	84 in.	7 in.	66 in.
		9 in.	90 in.	8 in.	78 in.
				9 in.	90 in.

Note: Plant sizes and caliper measurements indicate minimum size in the size interval (e.g., "4½-in. caliper" indicates 4½- to 5-in. caliper interval).
**Rapid-growing varieties may have root balls one size smaller.*

Thomas J. Nieman, Ph.D., Department of Landscape Architecture, University of Kentucky

BALL SIZES: BROADLEAF EVERGREENS

TYPES 1, 2, AND 3 SPREADING, SEMISPREADING, COMPACT UPRIGHT, AND GLOBE		TYPES 4 AND 5 BROAD UPRIGHT CONE		TYPE 6* COLUMNAR	
SPREAD (TYPES 1 AND 2) OR HEIGHT (TYPE 3)	MINIMUM-DIAMETER BALL	HEIGHT/CALIPER	MINIMUM-DIAMETER BALL	HEIGHT/CALIPER	MINIMUM-DIAMETER BALL
9 in.	8 in.	12 in.	8 in.	12 in.	7 in.
12 in.	10 in.	15 in.	10 in.	15 in.	8 in.
15 in.	12 in.	18 in.	12 in.	18 in.	9 in.
18 in.	14 in.	24 in.	14 in.	24 in.	11 in.
24 in.	16 in.	30 in.	16 in.	30 in.	13 in.
30 in.	18 in.	3 ft	18 in.	3 ft	14 in.
36 in.	24 in.	4 ft	20 in.	4 ft.	16 in.
42 in.	26 in.	5 ft	22 in.	5 ft	18 in.
4 ft	28 in.	6 ft	24 in.	6 ft	20 in.
5 ft	36 in.	7 ft	26 in.	7 ft	22 in.
6 ft	40 in.	8 ft	28 in.	8 ft	24 in.
7 ft	46 in.	9 ft/3 in.	32 in.	9 ft/2½ in.	26 in.
8 ft	52 in.	3½ in.	34 in.	3 in.	28 in.
		4 in.	38 in.	3½ in.	32 in.
		4½ in.	42 in.	4 in.	36 in.
		5 in.	48 in.	4½ in.	40 in.
		5½ in.	54 in.	5 in.	44 in.
		6 in.	60 in.	5½ in.	48 in.
		7 in.	72 in.	6 in.	54 in.
		8 in.	84 in.	7 in.	66 in.
		9 in.	90 in.	8 in.	78 in.
				9 in.	90 in.

Note: Plant sizes and caliper measurements indicate minimum size in the size interval (e.g., "4½-in. caliper" indicates 4½ to 5-in. caliper interval).
**Rapid-growing varieties may have root balls one size smaller.*

CONTAINER SIZES WITH MINIMUM AND MAXIMUM PLANT SIZES

TYPES 1, 2, AND 3 MEASUREMENT DESIGNATES SPREAD (TYPES 1 AND 2) OR HEIGHT (TYPE 3)		TYPE 4, 5, AND 6 MEASUREMENT DESIGNATES HEIGHT		
MINIMUM PLANT SIZES	MAXIMUM PLANT SIZES	MINIMUM PLANT SIZES	MAXIMUM PLANT SIZES	CONTAINER CLASS
6 in.	12 in.	6 in.	15 in.	1
9 in.	15 in.	12 in.	24 in.	2
12 in.	24 in.	15 in.	3 ft	3
15 in.	30 in.	18 in.	4 ft	5
18 in.	4 ft	24 in.	6 ft	7
24 in.	5 ft	30 in.	7 ft	10
30 in.	6 ft	4 ft	8 ft	15
36 in.	8 ft	5 ft.	10 ft	25
42 in.	8 ft	6 ft	12 ft	45
4 ft	10 ft	7 ft	16 ft	65
5 ft.	12 ft	8 ft	20 ft	100

trade that is supplying the material is familiar. Other characteristics or desirable attributes can be listed as part of the plant list in addition to the minimum standards set forth in the ANSI Z60.1-2004 standards.

PLANT HARDINESS STANDARDS

Hardiness is the capability of a plant to survive and grow in the landscape of a given region. The United States Plant Hardiness Zone Map (USHZ) presently consists of 11 zones, with Zone 1 being the coldest and Zone 11 being the warmest. The zones are based on the average climatic conditions of each area. A Zone 6 plant, for example, generally will endure winters in that zone and will withstand the warmer zones below. Since local climates and conditions, such as soil, rainfall, length of growing season, and the like, can dramatically differ within regions, the hardiness zone map should be used only as guide for plant selection. This is especially the case when a region is on the cusp of two zones.

In 2004, the American Horticultural Society (AHS) produced a Heat-Zone Map that is similar in form to the USHZ Map and based on the "number of days per year above 86°F (30°C) and establishes the point at which plants experience damage to cellular patterns." When used in conjunction with the USHZ map, both cold-hardiness and heat-tolerance ranges can be used to select plants that are appropriate to the climatic condition under consideration. Plants are now being coded for both conditions.

More information on plant hardiness information can be found at the following sources:

- The 2000 U.S. National Arboretum Web version of the USDA Plant Hardiness Zone Map (USDA Miscellaneous Publication No. 1475, issued January 1990) is located at www.usna.usda.gov/Hardzone/ushzmap.
- The American Horticultural Society Heat-Zone Map is located at www.ahs.org/publications/heat_zone_map.
- Canada has a Plant Hardiness Zones Map (2000) similar to the USHZ map, which "outlines the different zones in Canada where various types of trees, shrubs and flowers will most likely survive." It is located at http://sis.agr.gc.ca/cansis/nsdb/climate/hardiness/intro.

PLANT GUARANTEES

Plants shipped from a nursery, which are purchased wholesale, should be guaranteed to be true to name, of the appropriate size and quality, and in good viable condition. Claims regarding disease or viability are to be reported to the supplier. Seldom do guarantees for survivability emanate from a wholesale nursery or supplier. The installation contractor, in addition to these requirements, is responsible for plant survival.

Under normal conditions, plants are to be guaranteed for one year from the date of planting. Sometimes, however, specifications are written as "one growing season" in lieu of one year, for guarantee purposes. And for large trees, it is common to require a two-year guarantee.

It is the responsibility of the owner to maintain the plant material in the specified manner during the guarantee period. Specifications can be written to require the installation contractor to include maintenance as part of the cost of the plant during the guarantee period—which will add to the cost of the plant.

To help assure the credibility of the installation contractor, there are industry certification programs, such as the Professional Landcare Network (formerly the Associated Landscape Contractors of America) and the Professional Grounds Maintenance Society (PGMS) programs. Many contractors have certification through these programs.

An example of a contractor's warranty reads as: "This warranty covers all variables within the contractor's control such as mishandling, improper planting, poor-quality material, lack of water or proper maintenance. Not included are variables out of its control, such as nature, vandalism, or factors such as insects, disease, or lack of water, if those services are not part of the customer's landscape management contract."

PLANT QUARANTINES AND INSPECTION

"The USDA, Animal and Plant Health Inspection Service, Plant Protection and Quarantine Program (USDA APHIS PPQ) and the plant health agencies in each of the 50 states, regulate the shipment of nursery stock in an effort to minimize the spread of harmful insects, diseases, and other pests" (www.aphis.usda.gov/npb/F&SQS/sqs, 2005). The National Plant Board (NPB) is the USDA agency responsible for bringing "out greater uniformity and efficiency in promulgation and enforcement of plant quarantines and plant inspection practices in the various states" (*Safeguarding American Plant Resources,* July 1999). This is an organization of state plant health regulatory officials who are

Thomas J. Nieman, Ph.D., Department of Landscape Architecture, University of Kentucky

responsible for nursery licensing, certification, quarantines, and other pest prevention efforts. "They inspect plants and commodities for export so that required phytosanitary certification can be provided" (*Safeguarding American Plant Resources,* July 1999).

Phytosanitary and Plant Inspection Certificate

The plant inspection certificate certifies that the plants in question meet the requirements of the destination states or countries. Each state and territory in the United States regulates the growing and sale of nursery stock for its state or territory. It is their responsibility to examine or inspect plants, plant material, or nursery stock located or grown on the business location or any other applicable location to affirm that all plants or other regulated articles meet phytosanitary (quarantine), nursery inspection, pest freedom, plant registration, or certification, or other legal requirements. All plant material shipped interstate and to other countries must be accompanied by a "Nursery Stock Certificate," verifying compliance with registration or certification requirements. While specific regulations vary by state and territory, all plants shipped interstate must meet the NPB health criteria.

FREIGHT AND SHIPPING

Freight and shipping parameters are as follows:

- Not all plants can be shipped during all months, due to weather, digging, or order restrictions.
- All costs of shipping, including inspections, duty, and brokerage, are the responsibility of the customer.
- Shipments, for the most part, are FOB the nursery.
- All stock travels at the risk of the buyer; claims for damage during transit must be filed with the forwarding company.
- Most wholesale nurseries arrange for bulk shipment of stock by independent truckers and brokers who specialize in hauling nursery stock.
- All interstate and international shipping must be accompanied by the appropriate federal and/or state phytosanitary certificates.
- Shipping rates for closed trucks are by cubic feet. There are approximately 55 cubic feet per linear foot of cargo space on closed trucks.

INTERIOR PLANTS

Plants grown in interior spaces come from tropical or arid regions and must adapt to the less-than-ideal conditions indoors. Ideally, the selection of plants and the proper environmental conditions combination will give a planting that will thrive in the indoor environment.

Plant Selection

- To ensure correct plant selection, plants should be specified by their scientific name. The plants should be free from pests and pathogens, undamaged, and properly handled when shipped. It is beneficial to have all plants acclimated to the light, moisture, humidity, and fertilization levels expected to be found in the proposed location.

Display categories of popular indoor plants can thrive indoors. These include plants with year-long display, composed of foliage and flowering varieties. The foliage variety can live permanently indoors if their needs are met. Some types need to winter without heat. The flowering varieties may not be as attractive after flowering, but their foliage will remain throughout the year.

Plant Standards

Specific plant standards can be found in *Guide to Interior Landscape Specifications,* published by American Landscape Contractors Association (now known as the Professional Landcare Network—PLANET).

Plant Environment

Ensuring a plant's healthy environment includes attention to the following factors:

- *Light.* The level of available light is a critical factor in the plant's health and appearance. Necessary light levels are important to basic plant processes such as:
  - *Photosynthesis.* The process by which plants transform light energy into food energy.
  - *Phototropism.* The natural inclination of plants to grow toward the light source. Interior plants need to be rotated or have supplemental artificial light directed so that the plant receives even light. Otherwise, the plant will have excessive growth on one side and little growth on the opposing side.
  - *Photoperiodism.* Plants require a rhythmic cycle of light and darkness that closely resembles their original habitat. Some plants will not flower unless these requirements are met.
- Light levels should be determined with a handheld light meter that can confirm the light level in footcandles. Although plants can adapt to various light levels, including low light, they will not flower or thrive under such conditions. With insufficient light, plants live off their energy reserves, and gradually die.
- *Temperature.* Temperature must be carefully controlled to maximize the longevity of high-quality interior plants. For most plants, a temperature range of 18°C to 24°C is satisfactory. A 3°C reduction of temperature at night is desirable. Temperatures below 4.5°C to 7°C may be harmful to indoor plants; temperatures above 32.2 to 35°C cause excessive transpiration on the high end.
- *Atmosphere.* The surrounding atmosphere is important to ensure high-quality interior plants.
  - *Air movement.* Plants should not be subjected to drafts of hot or cold air.
  - *Relative humidity.* A range between 85 to 95 percent is ideal; however, the average relative humidity in buildings is 49 percent, and plants can survive if they are properly acclimatized. Grouping helps to increase humidity, whereas misting does little to increase humidity.
- *Air pollution.* Air pollution can present a problem to interior plants unless air is filtered. Also, plants need to be dusted or misted with water to wash off the dust.
- *Maintenance.* Proper maintenance involves attention in the following areas:
  - *Soil.* Provide a growing medium that is environmentally suitable for the growth and function of the root system—a soil pH of 6.0 to 6.5 (slightly acidic).
  - *Water.* Ensure an adequate supply of water at the proper frequency, quantity, and quality.
  - *Fertilizer.* Provide a well-managed feeding program.
  - *Insects and diseases.* Conduct a regular check to ensure health of the plants.

INVASIVE PLANT SPECIES

Plants that have been moved from their native habitat to a new location are typically referred to as "nonnative," "nonindigenous," "exotic," or "alien" to the new environment. Only those nonnative plants that cause serious problems in their new environment are collectively known as "invasive species." By Executive Order 13112, (February 3, 1999), a National Invasive Species Council was formed and charged with developing a National Invasive Species Management Plan. The council noted that the number of invasive species and their cumulative impact are accelerating at an alarming rate. In response, the council developed a comprehensive plan for federal action, in coordination with other nations, states, and local and private programs. The objective of the plan is "to prevent the introduction of invasive species, provide for their control, and minimize their economic, environmental, and human health impacts" (www.invasivespecies.gov, 2005).

Actions that can be taken by site designers to control the spread of invasive species include:

- Recognize and understand the severity of the problem.
- Attempt to minimize the impact of invasive species.
- Become informed as to which plant species are considered invasive.
- Refuse to use invasive species on site plans.
- Encourage clients to eradicate existing invasive species from sites as development is ongoing.
- Encourage the restoration of areas impacted by invasive species.

There are numerous locations whereby one can become knowledgeable about which species of plants are considered invasive. The federal government, all states, and nearly all communities have ordinances prohibiting the use of invasive species on public works projects. Lists of invasive species are published by these organizations and are on numerous websites, including http://invasivespecies.gov, the gateway to federal efforts concerning invasive species. This site provides a very good overview with regard to the use or nonuse of invasive species in the landscape. The Plant Conservation Alliance (PCA) has also published an excellent, comprehensive inventory of invasive plants called "Alien Plant Invaders of Natural Areas," which is available at www.nps.gov/plants/alien/list/a. The PCA, an organization under the auspices of the National Park Service, is dedicated to promoting "the conservation and restoration of native plants and native ecosystems."

POISONOUS PLANT SPECIES

In the interest of public health, safety, and welfare, it is advised that consideration for the potential toxicity of plants be given appropriate attention. The two

Thomas J. Nieman, Ph.D., Department of Landscape Architecture, University of Kentucky

Websites referenced here present data on plants that cause poisoning in livestock, pets, and humans. Two caveats must, however, be noted in regard to the data on poisonous plants:

- Much literature on poisonous plants is anecdotal and may be of limited reliability.
- Many plants are only mildly poisonous or are dangerous only when prodigious quantities of material have been consumed.
- Nonetheless, poisonous plants can be, and are, deadly; for example, *Taxus* (Japanese yew) will kill domestic farm animals.

These databases give the name of the plant, the species affected, and the primary poison:

- Cornell University Poisonous Plants Database: http://ansci.cornell.edu/plants/index
- Canadian Poisonous Plants Information System: www.cbif.gc.ca/pls/pp/poison?p_x=px

USEFUL ORGANIZATIONS AND WEBSITES

American Nursery & Landscape Association (ANLA)
(Formerly the American Association of Nurserymen)
1250 I Street, N.W., Suite 500
Washington, DC, 20005
Phone: 202-789-2900
Fax: 202-789-1893

Professional Landcare Network (PLANET)
950 Herndon Parkway, Suite 450
Herndon, VA 20170
Phone: 703-736-9666 or 1-800-395-2522
Fax: 703-736-9668

PLANET was created on January 1, 2005, when the Associated Landscape Contractors of America (ALCA) and the Professional Lawn Care Association of America (PLCAA) joined together. Of particular interest is their *Guide to Interior Landscape Specifications,* 5th edition, 2003.

REFERENCES

American Association of Nurserymen (AAN). 1996. *American Standard for Nursery Stock* (ANSI Z60.1-1996). The American Association of Nurserymen, Washington, DC: AAN.

National Plant Board. July 1999. *Safeguarding American Plant Resources*. Washington, DC: USDA.

National Invasive Species Council, www.invasivespecies.gov, accessed 2005.

See also:
Planting

Thomas J. Nieman, Ph.D., Department of Landscape Architecture, University of Kentucky

OTHER MATERIALS

GREENHOUSES

INTRODUCTION

Developments in ventilation, glazing, and horticulture have helped achieve satisfactory plant growth in greenhouses to make the practice economical. Site selection considerations include: topography (flat is advisable), drainage, quantity and quality of water supply, air quality, direction and average wind speed, and, most important, the amount of available light. Orientation for optimal solar gain is east-west except in conditions where shadow casting obstructions outweigh the orientation rule. Once a site has been selected, development of a plan for growth (even if only one greenhouse is built at first) is essential, factoring in access, mechanical room locations, and circulation of materials and labor. Heating and cooling needs will vary with latitude, plant type, skin or glazing, and growth period.

HEATING SYSTEMS

Heat distribution is achieved through use of solar, hot air, or radiant pipe systems. Solar heating will usually need the augmentation of the two latter systems at the coolest or windiest part of the year.

Radiant/Hot Water Pipe

Systems use a boiler to heat and distribute water. Pipes located at the greenhouse perimeter are the most convenient and efficient method of achieving uniform temperature.

INSULATION

Insulation augments heating systems and helps reduce heat loss from convection and radiation. Three basic systems are most widely used: movable night curtains, plastic covering over glass, and permanent reflective insulation of north wall and roof.

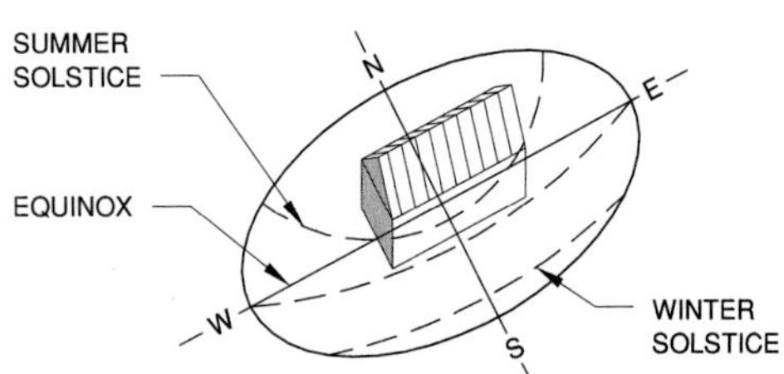

Use of an uneven span greenhouse allows for optimal solar orientation. Slope of glass is determined by latitude.

OPTIMAL SOLAR ORIENTATION

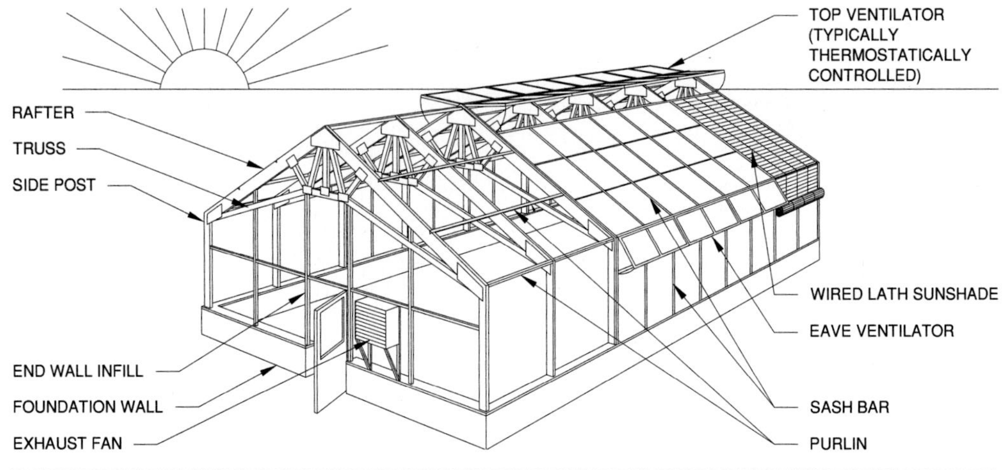

GENERIC GREENHOUSE

FRAME TYPES

MATERIAL	FEATURES
Pipe frame	Economy/simple connections
Steel frame	50' span (installation by professionals)
Aluminum frame	No rust, deeper sections than steel
Wood frame	Pressure treated lifespan: 10–15 yrs.

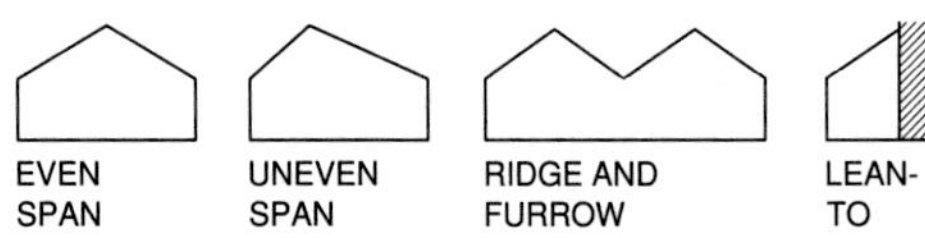

When properly maintained, a glass greenhouse will last 40 to 50 years. Structural design of a greenhouse is similar to curtain wall design with live loads of wind, snow, piping, and hanging basket plants.

GLASS-SHEATHED GREENHOUSE

PLASTIC TYPES

MATERIAL	FEATURES
Flexible	Polyethylene, mylar
Rigid	PVC, acrylic, fiberglass

NOTE
The size of a plastic greenhouse is limited only by the width of a single sheet of plastic.

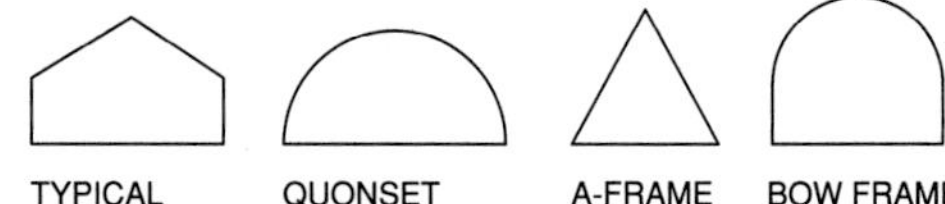

Rigid or flexible plastic greenhouses feature economy, ease of fabrication, and flexibility of form making. Plastic's liabilities are its poor durability, reduced light transmission over time, and discoloration or brittleness.

PLASTIC-SHEATHED GREENHOUSE

AIR CURRENT DIAGRAM WITH OVERHEAD RADIANT AND PERIMETER PIPES: REDUCES DROPPING OF COOL AIR

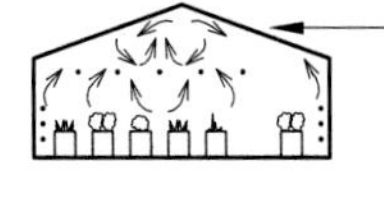

AIR CURRENT DIAGRAMS

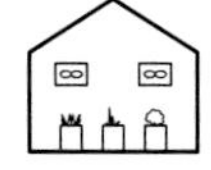

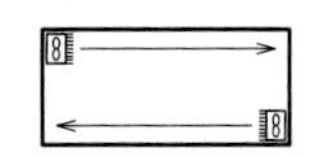

HORIZONTAL DISCHARGE

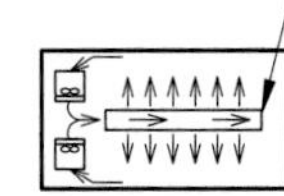

HEATING SYSTEMS

Eric K. Beach; Rippeteau Architects, PC, Washington, D.C.

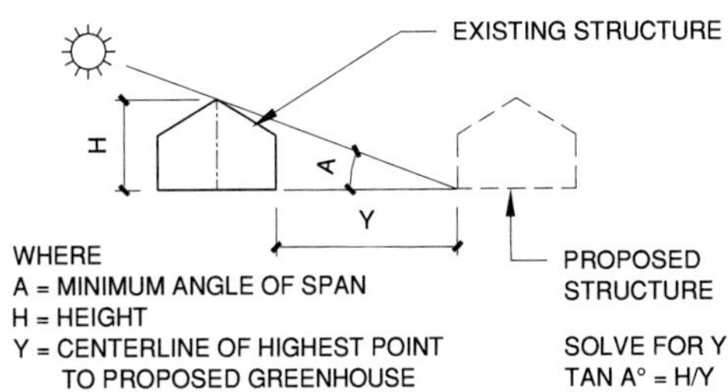

SPACING OF STRUCTURES

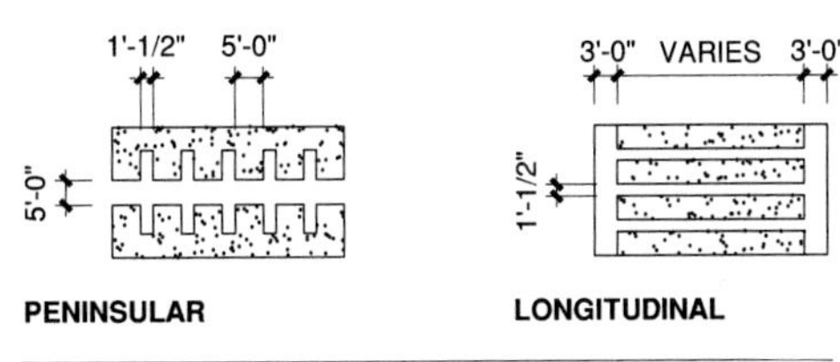

PENINSULAR

LONGITUDINAL

BENCHING

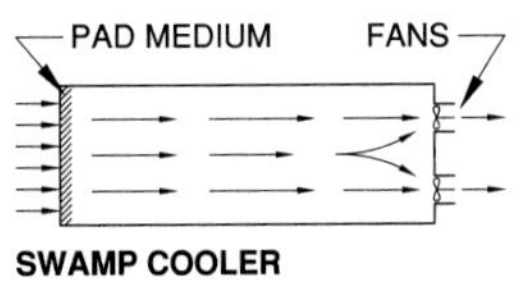

SWAMP COOLER

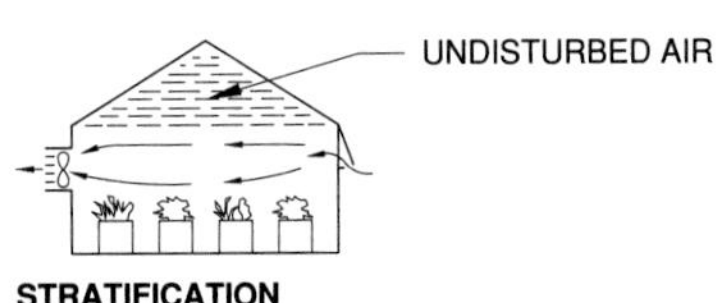

STRATIFICATION

NOTE

Fan and pad water pump are hooked up to the same thermostat.

COOLING SYSTEMS

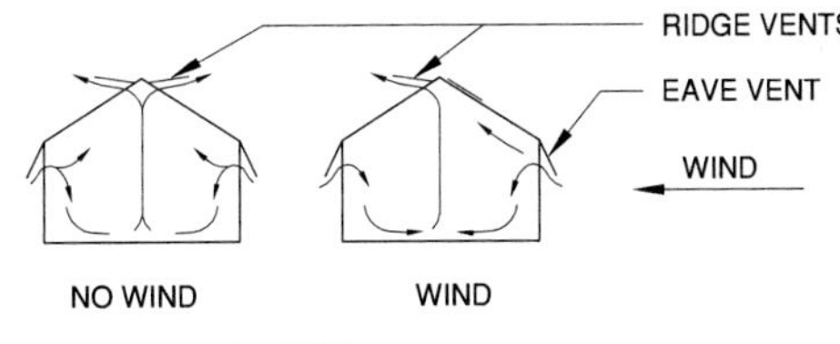

NATURAL VENTILATION

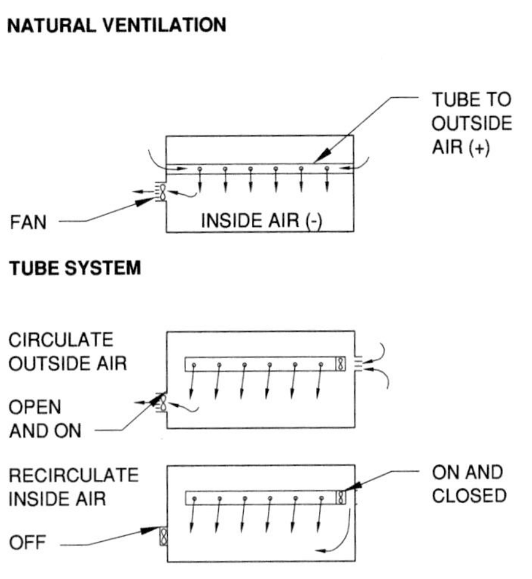

TUBE SYSTEM

FAN JET SYSTEM

VENTILATION SYSTEMS

Hot Air

Systems burn various fossil fuels and distribute the warmed air with fans.

GENERAL

Reduction of summer heat gain is achieved through shading systems, and natural and fan ventilation systems. Shading is most often achieved with the use of paint on the interior glass, lath rolled on the structure's exterior, or cloth of varying density on the structure's interior.

EVAPORATIVE COOLING

Mechanical refrigeration is generally cost prohibitive cooling with the exception of pad systems, or "swamp coolers," involving pulling air through a wet pad the length of the greenhouse wall with a fan mounted high on the opposite wall.

EXHAUST FANS

Fan placement depends on greenhouse orientation; optimal placement is the side opposite the normal wind direction. Fans from adjacent greenhouses should be placed opposite each other, spaced at not more than 25 ft. Stratification is desired in summer cooling, where only 15 to 60% of total air volume is moved mechanically.

Air exchange is necessary to moderate interior temperature and humidity. High humidity promotes plant disease and inhibits soil drying. The most common means of ventilation are natural venting, tube ventilation, and fan-jet ventilation.

Eric K. Beach; Rippeteau Architects, PC, Washington, D.C.

GEOTEXTILES

INTRODUCTION

A geotextile is a permeable textile material that is used with soil, rock, or other related geotechnical engineering-related material. Together with these other materials, it becomes an integral part of the structural system. Throughout history, natural fibers have been mixed with soils to stabilize soils and increase the longevity of travel routes that would otherwise become rutted or suffer erosion. Since the advent of synthetic fibers for geotextile fabrics, their use has steadily increased.

Today geotextiles are generally made from synthetic materials such as polypropylene, polyesters, nylon, or polyethylene. They do not decay and are rugged enough to stand up to the abuses of installation during the construction process. They are manufactured in a wide range of thicknesses, strengths, and textures, all contributing to varying functional attributes of a geotextile fabric. Geotextiles are produced either as a nonwoven or a woven fabric.

- The nonwoven fabric consists of fibers bonded together by chemical, thermal, or mechanical processes. The result is a feltlike material that will allow water to flow along the plane of the geotextile. It does, however, have a tendency to stretch more than the woven fabric.
- The woven fabric consists of perpendicular strands interlaced into a tight weave, much like clothing would be made. Many types of weave patterns affect porosity, strength, and elongation. By specifying the characteristics of the fabric needed, a manufacturer can recommend a particular weave and product to best suit the requirements.

Properly selected, one geotextile fabric can meet a number of functional criteria. Generally, a woven fabric is not as likely to stretch as a nonwoven fabric. A woven fabric does not allow water to pass through as freely as a nonwoven fabric.

GEOTEXTILE FUNCTIONS

Geotextiles provide four basic functions: separation; filtration; reinforcement; erosion control, and transmission. Not all geotextile fabrics are made the same, nor do they all provide the same level of performance for these functions, so selecting the proper product is critical.

Separation

Separation is accomplished by having the geotextile fabric separate two dissimilar soils. Using road construction as an example, this can be the geotextile fabric keeping the fines in the subgrade from mixing with the aggregate base course, causing a reduction in bearing capacity. The use of a geotextile fabric can increase the longevity of the pavement.

To accomplish the task of separation effectively, the fabric must allow water to pass through freely and at the same time retain the fine particles without becoming clogged. As the geotextile will be subjected to heavy traffic loads, a fabric should be selected that exhibits a high level of strength, both during the construction process and after it is in place.

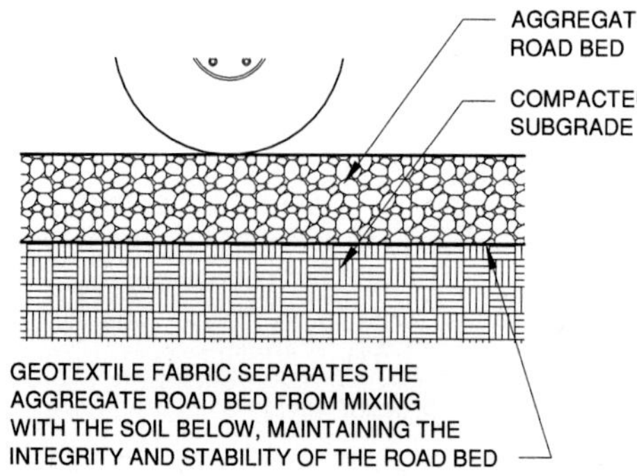

GEOTEXTILE USED TO PREVENT MIGRATION OF FINE-PARTICLE SOIL INTO AGGREGATE BASE COURSE

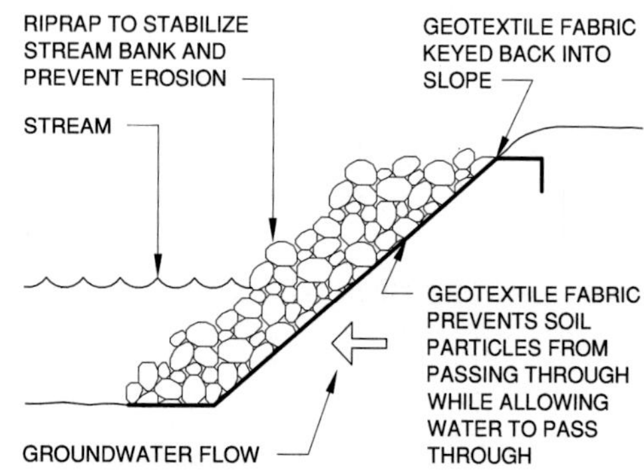

GEOTEXTILE IN COMBINATION WITH RIPRAP ON AN EMBANKMENT USED TO STEM EROSION

Filtration

Filtration requires the geotextile fabric to retain small particles of soil yet allow water to pass through freely. As the ability for water to pass through the fabric is a primary concern, a geotextile manufactured to address this characteristic would be a key feature to look for in the material selection process.

Filtration is one of the most common uses for geotextiles, and typical applications include separating gravel drainage trenches or pockets from surrounding soil; as a wrap for perforated pipe; as a weed control barrier for planted areas; and as silt barriers to prevent the washing away of soils during the construction process.

Reinforcement

A geotextile fabric can be used as reinforcement by adding tensile strength to soil and rock materials that are inherently better at withstanding compressive forces. Installed within the constructed layers of soil and aggregate, the geotextile increases the stability by helping to span over weak areas, preventing failure of the pavement.

Erosion Control

For erosion control, geotextiles can be used as follows:

- The geotextile laid flat on the ground helps dissipate the energy of precipitation and prevents the related displacement of soil that can take place.
- A geotextile with a layer of stone placed over the top can protect erodible soils beneath from washing away.
- In combination with riprap on embankments, geotextiles can prevent scouring around bridge piers and abutments.
- Geotextile grids or meshes can be used to help establish seeded areas, particularly on slopes where precipitation could cause erosion and a washing of the seed down the hill. In these circumstances, a geotextile manufactured from a natural material that will disintegrate as the planting becomes established is an excellent choice.

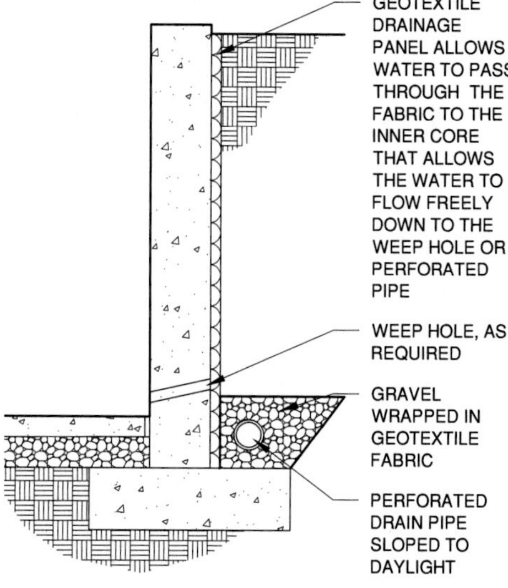

GEOTEXTILE USED TO PREVENT WATER BUILDUP AT A STRUCTURE

Transmission

In transmission, the geotextile allows liquids or gases to flow along the plane of the fabric (as opposed to through the fabric, as in filtration). Water is allowed to enter the fabric and then travels within the fabric to a desired location. Very often this is accomplished with a geotextile composite that is composed of a drainage core material bonded to a geotextile fabric on one or both sides. A typical example of this function would be to use geotextiles against foundation walls or retaining walls to prevent water buildup adjacent to the structure, and instead direct it away from the structure in conjunction with a perforated drainage pipe.

For a geotextile fabric to perform effectively, the material must be manufactured with the characteristics required for the specific function(s) it is expected to perform and the installation must be done properly, in accordance with the manufacturer's recommendation.

Leonard Hopper, RLA, FASLA

PAINTS AND COATINGS

GENERAL

Coatings are thin surface facings applied in liquid form which solidify to protect building components from harmful exposure. Appropriate coating selection depends upon performance, appearance, cost, and rate of deterioration of the substrate should the coating fail. Coatings are made up of the prepared substrate, prime costs or undercoats, and finish or topcoats, all of which should be compatible for adhesion and resistance to deterioration.

Design Considerations

Environmental and ambient conditions affect coating performance. Resistance to sun, moisture, pollution, chemicals, extremes of temperature, soiling, and abrasion will determine a set of coatings, from which a selection is made based on remaining criteria. Design considerations should also include:

- Flow, or ease of application.
- Leveling or smoothing after application.
- Drying time, of which two factors are important: (a) set-to-touch or surface drying, when surface resists contaminants, and (b) through-dry, when all layers are dry and ready to recoat.
- Permeability: moisture migration through coating.
- Wetting: penetration of coating to a lower level. Lower wetting ability requires greater surface preparation.
- Film thickness: amount of protection provided by coating.
- Adhesion between layers.
- Flexibility: accommodation to changes in moisture and temperature.
- Abrasion, impact, and stain resistance and ease of cleaning.

Types

Coatings are classified by appearance—clear, semitransparent, or opaque, and are water-based or organic solvent-based. Coatings are composed of a vehicle—alone when clear, or with pigments when semitransparent or opaque. The vehicle is in turn composed of binder and solvent. The binder is the nonvolatile part of the vehicle which forms the film of the coating and which bonds pigments when they are used. Additives for special properties, such as driers, stabilizers, plasticizers, and thinners, are included in the binder. The solvent is the volatile part of the vehicle which dissolves the binder to adjust viscosity, and which evaporates as the coating changes from liquid to solid state. Pigment adds opacity and/or color to the vehicle.

Clear coatings only slightly obscure the surface of the substrate. They are used when it is important to preserve appearance, such as the grain of wood or the color of an exposed concrete aggregate. Clear coatings are composed of a vehicle only, solvent and binder, with no pigment added. Sealers, waterproofing, and varnishes are typical examples of clear coatings.

Semitransparent coatings partially obscure the substrate surface. They can modify the appearance of the substrate by changing the color of wood without hiding its grain. Semitransparant coatings are composed of solvent, binder, and limited pigment. Stains are exemplary of this group.

Opaque coatings completely obscure the surface of the substrate. The color and/or texture of the substrate are changed; the original appearance unimportant or undesirable. Opaque coatings are made up of pigment, solvent, and binder. Paints are opaque coatings.

Coating properties are determined by the binder, which forms the surface film and bonds to the substrate. A combination of binders will alter the properties displayed by a coating, as will additives that modify the formation of the coating. Binders composed of small molecules (e.g., drying oils) penetrate rough surfaces and adhere well but dry slowly and are not chemically resistant. Binders composed of large molecules, built-up or polymerized of smaller molecules, yield strong, chemically resistant films but are susceptible to dissolution in the same solvent when formulated for solvent evaporation only. Large molecules may be formed by reaction between small molecules as in linseed oil; they may be made before application and dissolved in solvent to lower viscosity, or they may be formed by a combination of these two methods.

Pigments hide the substrate by adding opacity and color, but may also increase durability and protective characteristics by screening UV radiation, controlling transmission of moisture and gases, and inhibiting degradation or corrosion of the substrate. Colored pigments absorb some light rays while reflecting others, and white pigments absorb little light, so their hiding efficacy depends on the ability to scatter and reflect incident light. Scattering and reflecting ability in turn depends upon the size, distribution, and refractive index of the pigment particles. Pigment also determines the gloss of the coating finish through its relative proportion to binder and solvent in the vehicle.

Environmental exposure concurrent with or following application of the coating may affect the coating or the substrate. Some types of exposure to consider are atmospheric contamination, such as sulfurous or marine air which may discolor coatings and accelerate chalking and deterioration; mildew in humid environments; and sudden drops or rises in temperature at the time of application, which may flatten or blister a freshly applied coating.

External Factors

A number of external factors affect the stability of a coating.

Solar radiation/UV radiation: Sunlight exposure can fade colored pigments, cause chemical reaction in some binders or solvents, and degrade the substrate if the coating is not UV opaque. It may be necessary for the coating to reflect scatter, or absorb visible light to avoid this problem.

Temperature: Solar radiation raises the temperature of the coating, causing expansion and accelerating solvent evaporation. Exposure to heat through convection of hot air or other gases, or by conduction through the substrate (as through accidental exposure to fire) may also affect coating performance. Freezing temperatures hinder proper curing of some vehicles.

Rain: A heated coating can undergo thermal shock when exposed to rain. Rainwater can also be absorbed and cause swelling of the coating or leach pigments from the coating. Rain may also penetrate through cracks or checks and freeze, causing damage to the coating and the substrate.

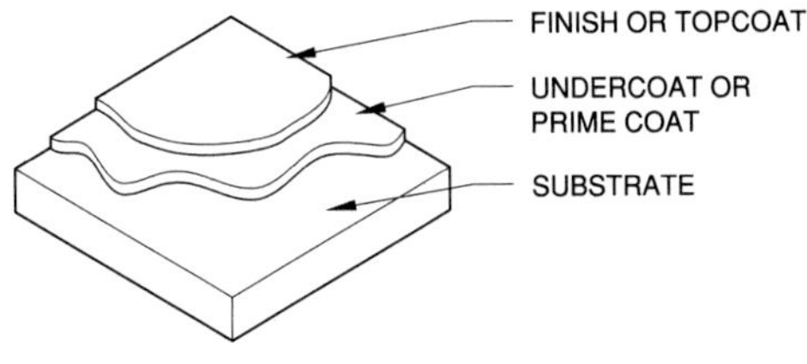

COMPOSITION OF COATINGS

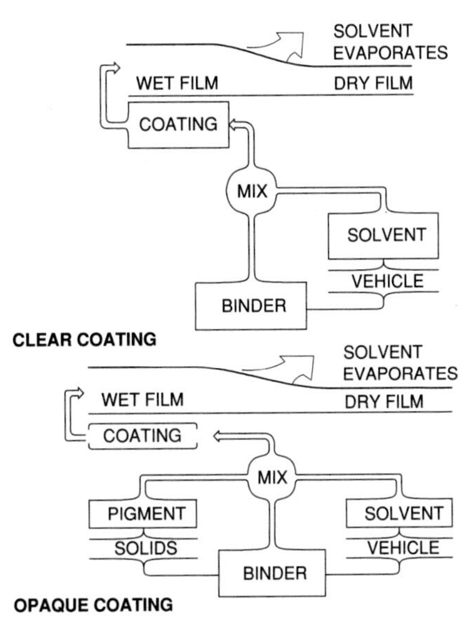

TYPES OF COATINGS

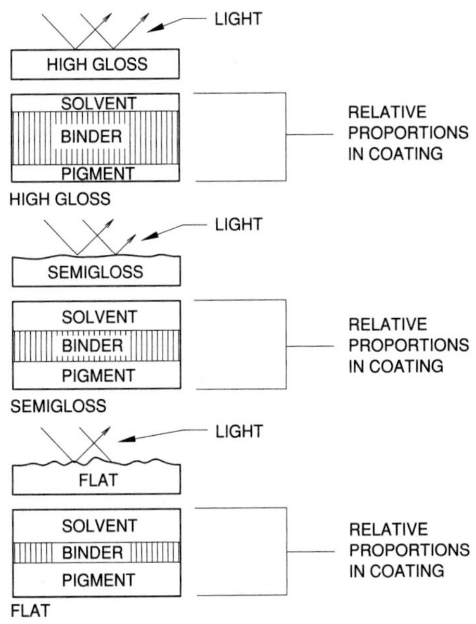

EFFECT OF PIGMENT CONTENT ON GLOSS OF COATING

James W. Laffey, Washington, D.C.

Water vapor: Vapor may be required to properly cure some coatings. Under some conditions water vapor should be allowed to permeate the coating to prevent condensation, while at other times permeation must be prevented to protect the substrate.

Chemical fumes: Generated by chemical processes or by burning fossil fuels, chemical fumes can leave deposits on the coating, by reacting directly with it or by entering solution with rainwater or condensation.

Dust, dirt: Dust penetrates porous coatings, collects airborne pollutants, and can stain and degrade the coating in reaction with rainwater. Marring of the coating may also be intentional, as with graffiti.

Abrasion, impact: Coatings can be abraded by high-velocity flow of gaseous or liquid substances, by traffic, vandalism, or airborne dust. Impact may be through natural causes such as hailstones, may be accidental, or may be intentional, as with vandalism.

Surface water: External fresh or sea water can rise and fall, exposing normally submerged portions of the surface to solar radiation and oxygen and subjecting the coating and substrate to differential thermal expansion between the exposed and submerged portions of the surface.

Chemical solutions: Coatings may be submerged in chemical solutions such as sea water, sewage, oils, lubricants, or solvents and some of these may react with specific constituent parts of the coating, degrading or dissolving it.

Selection Considerations

Coating selection should be based on external or environmental factors (see above), type, and degree of exposure to these factors, including an estimate of speed of substrate deterioration should the coating fail. Conditions met by the coating may vary over time, across a surface, or within the substrate, and contingencies should be planned. The possibility of an alkaline substrate such as concrete becoming moist through penetration or condensation should be considered before a non-alkaline-resistant coating is applied. Differential wear on walking or other surfaces should be considered, as well as applications of higher performance coatings.

The in-place cost of a coating accounts for surface preparation and application as well as the coating itself. Failure may result in permanent damage to the substrate, or may require complete removal and preparation for a new coating. The properties of the principal binder should determine the selection of a coating, with modifications and additions to the formulation made for specific job requirements.

Safety and Health Considerations

Hazards associated with coating application and surface preparation include toxic fumes from strong solvents; toxic dust from sandblasting, grinding, or fire; and toxicity of coating solvents when absorbed through skin or inhaled. In addition, use of photochemically reactive solvents may be limited or restricted by air-polution controlling ordinances.

James W. Laffey, Washington, D.C.

PAINTS AND COATINGS: PROPERTIES

TYPE	PRINCIPAL BINDER	BASE/ CURE	TYPICAL USES	COMPARATIVE COST RANGE	IN-SERVICE LIFE RANGE IN YEARS	GLOSS RETENTION	STAIN RESISTANCE	WEATHER RESISTANCE	ABRASION IMPACT RESISTANCE	FLEXIBILITY
Clear	Acrylic, methyl methacrylate copolymer	solvent; water	Waterproofing and surface sealer against dirt retention, graffiti; for vertical surfaces of concrete, masonry, stucco; may be pigmented.	moderate to high	5 to 10	excellent to good	fair	excellent to good	good	good
	Alkyd, spar varnish	solvent	For interior and protected exterior wood surfaces. Also as vehicle for aluminum pigmented coatings.	moderate	up to 1 exterior	fair to good	poor	poor	fair	good
	Phenolic, spar varnish	solvent	Exterior wood surfaces subject to moisture. May be used in marine environments. Also vehicle for aluminum pigment.	moderate to high	up to 2 exterior	fair to good	fair	good	good	good
	Silicone	solvent	Waterproofing and surface sealer against dirt retention for vertical surfaces of concrete, masonry, stucco.	moderate	5 to 7	flat	fair	good	penetrating coating	
	Urethane, one-part	moist cure[1]	Surfaces subject to chemical attack; abrasion, graffiti, heavy or concentrated traffic, such as gymnasium floors.	moderate to high	up to 15	excellent to good	good to excellent	good to excellent	good to excellent	excellent
Stain	Acrylic	solvent; water	Pigmented translucent or semi-opaque exterior surface sealers; solvent based for masonry, concrete; water based for wood.	moderate to low	3 to 5	flat finish	not a factor	good to fair	penetrating coatings—resistance same as for substrate	
	Alkyd	solvent; water	Pigmented exterior or interior surface sealer for wood surfaces such as shingles, does not impart sheen to surface.	moderate	3 to 5	flat finish		fair		
	Oil	solvent	Pigmented exterior or interior surface sealer for wood such as shingles, trim, opaque or semitransparent.	moderate	3 to 5	fair		fair		
Opaque	Acrylic	water	For exterior/interior vertical surfaces of wood, masonry, plaster, gypsum board, metals. Good color retention. Permeable to vapor.	moderate to low	5 to 8	good to fair	fair	good	good to fair	good to excellent
	Acrylic, apoxy modified, two-part	water	High performance coating for interior vertical surfaces subject to graffiti, stains, heavy scrubbing. May be used in food preparation areas.	high	10 to 15	good	good	good to excellent	good to excellent	good to excellent
	Alkyd	solvent; water	For exterior/interior vertical and horizontal surfaces, such as wood, metals, masonry. Poor permeability to vapor.	moderate	5 to 8	good to excellent	fair	fair to good	fair to good	fair to good
	Chlorinated rubber	solvent	Swimming pool coatings. Corrosion protection; isolating dissimilar metals.	high to very high	up to 10	fair	fair	good	fair to good	good
	Chlorosulfonated polyethylene	solvent	Protective coating for tanks, piping, valves, elastomeric roofing membranes.	very high	up to 15	not applicable	fair	excellent	fair to good	excellent
	Epoxy, two-part; epoxy ester, one part	solvent cure; solvent	Moisture/alkali resistant. Two-part for nondecorative interior uses highly resistant to chemicals. Esters in wide choice of colors.	high to very high	15 to 20; up to 10	poor to good	excellent for two-part	good to excellent	excellent	good to excellent
	Phenolic	solvent	Chemical- and moisture-resistant coatings. May be used over alkaline surfaces.	moderate to high	up to 10	fair	fair	good to excellent	good to excellent	good
	Polychloroprene	solvent[2]	Marketed as "Neoprene"; resistant to chemicals, moisture, ultraviolet radiation. Also used as roofing membrane; generally covered with Hypalon.	very high	up to 25	not applicable	good	excellent	excellent	good
	Polyester	solvent	Limited application in field: over cementitious surfaces, metal, plywood for exterior exposures.	high	up to 15	good to excellent	good to excellent	good to excellent	good	good to excellent
	Silicone	solvent	Surfaces with temperatures up to 1200 F. Often with aluminum pigments. Corrosion and solvent resistant.	very high	varies	not applicable, special purpose coating			good	good
	Silicone; modified acrylic, alkyd, epoxy	solvent	High-performance exterior coatings. Industrial siding, curtain walls, when shop-applied baked-on.	high to very high	15 to 20	good to excellent	good	good to excellent	good to excellent	good
	Styrene, butadiene	water	Interior coating for gypsum board, plaster, masonry. Limited exterior use over cementitious substrate, as filler over rough porous surfaces.	moderate to low	4 to 6	poor to fair	fair	poor	fair	good
	Urethane, one or two part	moist or chemical cure[3]	Heavy-duty wall and floor coatings. Resistance to stains, chemicals, graffiti, scrubbing, solvents, impact, abrasion.	high to very high	15 to 20	excellent	good to excellent	good to excellent	good to excellent	excellent
	Vinyl, polyvinyl chloride-acetate	solvent	Residential metal siding and trim, gutters, leaders, baseboard heating covers, when shop-applied, baked-on.	high	up to 15	good	fair	good	good	good to excellent
	Vinyl, polyvinylidene chloride	water	Metal and concrete surfaces in contact with dry and wet food, potable water, wastewater, jet and diesel fuels.	high	up to 10	good	fair	good	good	good
	Vinyl, polyvinyl acetate	water	Exterior and interior vertical surfaces, such as masonry, concrete, wood, plaster, gypsum board, metals. Permeable to vapor.	moderate to low	5 to 8	good to fair	fair	good	good to fair	good
	Bituminous, coal tar pitch, asphalt: emulsions, cut-backs	solvent	Waterproofing of metals, concrete, masonry, portland cement plaster, piping when below grade or immersed.	low	10 to 15 protected	not a factor		good	poor	fair
	Cement	water	Leveling coat over porous masonry or concrete not subject to abrasion or scrubbing. Cement and oil used as primers for metal surfaces.	low	varies	flat finish	poor	poor for color	good	poor

[1] Solvent-based, oil-modified urethane is also available; for use on interior/exterior vertical and horizontal wood surfaces. Cost is moderate.
[2] May be obtained as water-reducible coating; use as field-applied coating very limited; generally used as tank linings.
[3] Solvent base, oil-modified urethane is also available; for use on vertical and horizontal surfaces. Cost is moderate, but durability is lower than for other types.

Notes

Solvent-based acrylic is impermeable to water vapor, high gloss.
Water-based acrylic is semigloss, water vapor permeable.
Phenolic varnish has a dark tint; will darken with age; may be topcoated with clear alkyd.
Clear varnishes are not recommended for exterior wood because of limited durability.
Urethane may be formulated to yield hard, glossy surface so that graffiti can be removed with strong solvents.
Fillers may be required when using clear coatings over hardwood, such as oak; abraded wood may limit choice; consult manufacturer's literature.
Stains may be used as surface sealers to change color of wood and then be topcoated with clear coatings.
Stains over exterior wood surfaces generally will provide better protection than clear coatings, but usually will not last as long as opaque coatings.
Alkyd may be modified with silicone for better color retention.
Epoxy-esters have intermediate properties between two-part epoxies and alkyds and phenolics.
Bitumen-epoxy formulations are available for use as heavy-duty waterproofing of underground piping, structural members.
Phenolic may chalk upon exterior exposure; high degree of resistance to acids, alkalis, and solvents; some formulations available for surface temperatures of up to 300-350 F.
Polyesters available glass fiber reinforced; also used widely for baked-on factory applied finishes for formed metal wall panels.
Silicone for high temperature applications generally with aluminum pigment.
Polyvinyl chloride film is used for factory-applied finishes for formed metal wall panels.
Cement paint will absorb rainwater and will darken until water evaporates; requires moist curing after application; if not properly cured will tend to dust and rub off.
For high performance coatings under severe conditions, life expectancy may be less.

James W. Laffey, Washington, D.C.

ALUATING THE ENVIRONMENTAL AND HUMAN HEALTH IMPACTS OF MATERIALS

LIFE-CYCLE PHASES OF A MATERIAL OR PRODUCT

All phases in the life cycle of a material/product impact the environment, as inputs and outputs are generated from "cradle to grave." Therefore, any approach to decision making based on environmental impacts must consider the full spectrum of upstream and downstream impacts. Additionally, human health impacts can occur during any phase of a material's or product's life cycle.

RAW MATERIALS ACQUISITION

Raw materials acquisition includes all processes and activities required to obtain the raw materials and associated energies. These processes can include drilling, mining, dredging, logging, processing, refining, and transportation.

MANUFACTURING/PROCESSING

Manufacturing activities include conversion of natural resources, fabrication, assembly, packaging, and distribution. Manufacturing uses energy and water, produces waste by-products, and can contribute harmful pollutants to air, water, and soil. These pollutants can also affect the health of people in and around the manufacturing facility. Levels of processing vary widely by material/product. Some materials such as stone are minimally processed and have low embodied energy, while others such as aluminum are extensively processed using large amounts of energy and producing waste products.

Some manufacturers take steps toward minimizing the environmental and human health impacts of their materials/products by incorporating recycled materials and by-products into their products; minimizing energy and water use in manufacturing processes; burning waste as fuel; using alternative energy sources and containing toxic releases.

TRANSPORT

Transport of building materials/products in all phases uses energy and natural resources, and releases pollutants that negatively affect the environment and human health. Materials/products are transported from the extraction point to the manufacturer, then to the distributor and site, and after use, to the disposal point. Transport fuel uses nonrenewable resources and releases by-products (VOCs, CO2, carbon monoxide, and sulfur and nitrogen compounds) from internal combustion engines, which contribute to air pollution and global warming.

Transport may be one of the most important considerations for landscape architects because materials/products used in the landscape are heavy and bulky. Energy used in transport, especially by less efficient trucks and airplanes, can be greater than energy used in production if the manufacturer is located far from the site. Use of local materials can significantly reduce resource and pollution from transportation.

INSTALLATION, USE, AND MAINTENANCE

Installation, use, and maintenance can be the most important phases when considering the environmental and human health impacts of building materials/products, as they tend to be in use for very long periods of time. Durability of the product is, therefore, one of the most important concerns because the longer the installation lasts, the less need for replacements that use more resources. Therefore, it is important to match the expected life of the product with the expected life of the landscape.

An ideal building product or assembly will improve and support, or at least not damage, the ecological functions of the project site. For example, paving can have a negative effect on the site, in that it is usually an impermeable surface that speeds stormwater and pollutant runoff, causes erosion, and damages the soil underneath. In contrast, permeable paving would allow for some infiltration of water and air to the soil below.

Maintenance and repair of materials and products can have environmental and human health impacts as well. Adhesives, finishes, sealants, and maintenance products can contain hazardous chemicals, including volatile organic compounds (VOCs). Steps should be taken to specify materials and products that require few chemicals to maintain; or low-VOC and nontoxic cleaners and sealers should be used.

DISPOSAL, RECYCLING, AND REUSE

The end of the use phase sometimes results in disposal and release to the environment, but it can also include reuse, reprocessing, or recycling. Building materials can outlast the life of a landscape, so planning for their reuse is an important consideration. "Deconstruction" is the term used to refer to the disassembly and salvage of materials from a building or site, as opposed to "demolition," whereby everything is destroyed and hauled to a landfill.

Although deconstruction takes more time and incurs higher labor costs than demolition, it may ultimately be less expensive than paying landfill costs. Resale of the materials, either whole or ground, can generate additional income. Where the demolition contractor is also responsible for new construction, materials can be stockpiled for reuse on-site.

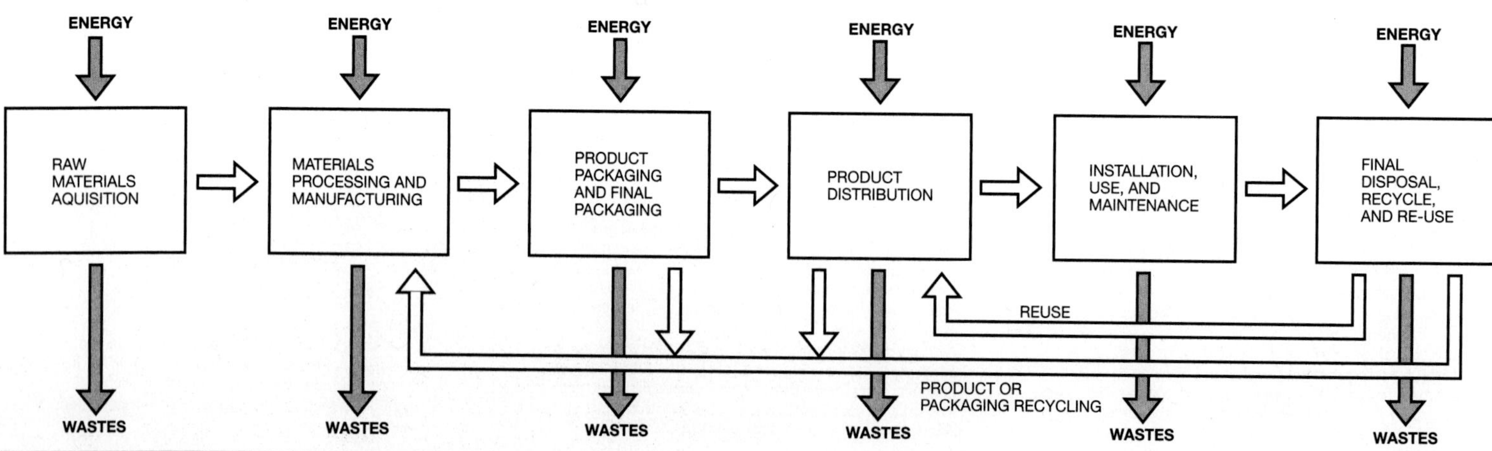

LIFE-CYCLE CHART

Source: Charles George Ramsey, Architectural Graphic Standards (New York, John Wiley & Sons, Inc.), 2000.

Meg Calkins, Ball State University, "Environmental and Health Considerations"

INPUTS AND OUTPUTS ASSOCIATED WITH BUILDING MATERIALS/PRODUCTS

RESOURCES

The mining of geologic materials alters habitats, causes increased runoff and soil erosion, and disrupts the ecological processes of the land where the mining occurs. Reduced forest cover from mining may negatively affect the planet's ability to process CO_2. Every time raw materials are extracted and harvested, the earth is affected and changed. With the exception of timber, plant, and fiber products, most materials are nonrenewable. Some materials are unlimited, but others are being depleted.

Using salvaged, reprocessed, or recycled-content materials eliminates some extraction of resources and associated energy use. It also keeps material out of the wastestream. However, it is important to remember that trucking salvaged materials to a location several hundred miles may negate the environmental benefits of using them. Many regions have local materials exchanges where basic materials such as bricks and concrete can be obtained, often at cost savings over those made from virgin resources. Some materials such as concrete and asphalt can be made from materials recycled on-site.

ENERGY

Energy expended in raw material extraction, processing, manufacture, fabrication, installation, and transport uses resources and contributes to global warming and acid deposition, as well as impacting respiratory and cardiovascular health in some people.

The energy used during all stages of a material's life is known as "embodied energy." This is the total amount of energy input used to produce and install the material for all phases of its life. If the product is complex (made from more than one material, such as a steel and wood bench), then the embodied energy of the bench includes all of the energy inputs from both the wood and steel components plus the energy inputs to assemble them. It is impossible to quantify all the energy used to manufacture a product, but one can get a good idea of relative energy use from the embodied energy information for common landscape materials (see the "Embodied Energy of Common Landscape Building Materials/Products" tables). The figures in the tables include estimated energy expended in raw material extraction, transport, and manufacturing.

WATER

Water is used and affected at many stages of a material's/product's life. Raw material extraction can affect water quality through habitat alteration, which increases runoff, contributing sediment and pollutants to streams, rivers, lakes, and wetlands. Processing and manufacturing of materials/products use water and create wastewater, which can pollute water bodies. Installation of materials and products can affect water quality around the site (e.g., on-site cleanup from concrete or mortar), and disposal of materials/products can affect groundwater and surface water quality.

Meg Calkins, Ball State University, "Environmental and Health Considerations"

EMBODIED ENERGY OF SELECTED LANDSCAPE MATERIALS BY VOLUME

MATERIALS BY VOLUME	CSI	AVG EST (BTU/CU.FT.)	LOW	HIGH	SD%	NUMBER
Concrete, ready cf	3.1	96,100				
Concrete, ready cy	3.1	2,590,000				
Lumber, hardwood	6.0	9,820				
Lumber, softwood	6.0	8,555			15	3
Lumber, glue-lam beams	6.1	15,611			10	3
Lumber, plywood	6.1	14,883				
Lumber, rough-sawn	6.1	495				
Waterproofing, asphalt	7.1	8,639			22	2
Insulation, rigid polystyrene	7.2	15,300				
Paint, exterior oil-based	9.9	488,264			0	2
Paint, exterior water-based	9.9	489,032			0	2
Stains and varnishes	9.9	503,668				

EMBODIED ENERGY OF SELECTED LANDSCAPE MATERIALS BY AREA

MATERIALS BY AREA	CSI	AVG EST (BTU/SQ.FT.)	LOW	HIGH	SD%	NUMBER
Paving brick 2.25 in. thick	2.7	133,000				
Paving, 4-in. concrete, wire reinforced	2.7	44,000				
Paving, 6-in. concrete, wire reinforced	2.7	60,000				
Paving, bitum, 1.5 in. (wearing surface only)	2.7	54,600				
Reinforced wire, welded 4x4 10/10	3.2	7,500				
Reinforced wire, welded 6x6 10/10	3.2	5,080				
Brick, common: wall 2 bricks thick, including mortar	4.2	281,000				
Metal expanded lath	5.7	52,100				
Lumber, ½ in. exterior plywood	6.1	Range	2,450	7,710	n/a	3
Lumber, ¾ in. exterior plywood	6.1	11,600				
Lumber, ⅜ in. exterior plywood	6.1	5,790				
Shingles, asphalt	7.3	26,787			8	3
Shingles, cedar	7.3	7,320				
Roofing, aluminum 0.032 in.	7.4	720,000				
Roofing, copper 20 oz.	7.4	97,700				
Roofing, plastic corrugated	7.4	50,000				
Roofing, steel 20 gauge	7.4	54,750				
Roofing, stainless steel 32 gauge	7.4	46,900				
Paint, external oil-based	9.9	1,390				
Paint, external water-based	9.9	1,400				

EMBODIED ENERGY OF SELECTED LANDSCAPE MATERIALS BY LENGTH

MATERIALS BY LINEAR MEASURE	CSI	AVG EST (BTU/LINEAR FT.)	LOW	HIGH	SD%	NUMBER
Rebar #2	3.2	2,620				
Rebar #3	3.2	5,900				
Rebar #4	3.2	10,500				
Rebar #5	3.2	16,400				
Rebar #6	3.2	23,600				
Masonry reinforced, 4 in. (truss or ladder)	4.0	3,670				
Pipe, ABS 2 in.	15.1	20,459			14	2
Pipe, cast iron 2 in.	15.1	86,368				
Pipe, copper 2 in.	15.1	32,107				
Pipe, PVC 2 in.	15.1	22,984				
Wire, copper insulated #10	16.1	1,740				
Wire, copper insulated #12	16.1	1,090				
Wire, copper insulated #14	16.1	688				
Wire, copper insulated #16	16.1	427				

EMBODIED ENERGY OF SELECTED LANDSCAPE MATERIALS BY EACH

MATERIALS BY EACH	CSI	AVG EST (BTU/EACH)	LOW	HIGH	SD%	NUMBER
Brick, common	4.2	14,300				
Brick, paving	4.2	25,600				
Concrete block 12x8x16 in.	4.2	49,400				
Concrete block 4x4x16 in.	4.2	9,330				
Concrete block 8x8x16 in.	4.2	27,401			16	3
Tile, structural facing, 6x12x4 in.	4.2	117,000				

Source: J. William Thompson and Kim Sorvig, Sustainable Landscape Construction: A Guide to Green Building Outdoors, *(Washington, DC: Island Press), 2000.*

TOXINS AND POLLUTANTS

Toxins and pollutants can be a concern at all phases of the life cycle of a material, and because the effects are not always visible, they are often overlooked. Some mine tailings left from extraction of raw materials can pollute habitats and watersheds. Harmful chemicals can be released into water used in processing and manufacture, and VOCs and other pollutants can be released into the air during processing of some materials. Some manufacturing processes can pose a risk to worker health. During use, materials such as hot asphalt and CCA-treated lumber pose toxin risks to people in contact with the materials. Commonly used adhesives, finishes, sealants, and maintenance products can contain hazardous chemicals and VOCs. During landfill disposal, some materials can threaten water and soil health, while incineration of some materials such as PVC can release hazardous chemicals and persistent bioaccumulative toxins (PBTs). Material Safety Data Sheets (MSDS) are mandated by the Occupational Safety and Health Administration's (OSHA's) hazard communication standard; they are available for all materials/products that may pose risks to human health. (See the References at the end of this article for sources of information on chemicals and toxins that may pose risks to human and environmental health.)

WASTE

Waste is generated at all phases of a material's/product's life cycle.

- *Extraction* of raw materials for a product is the first phase that can produce waste. Mining for metals such as iron, aluminum, and copper generates mineral waste on-site. Timber harvesting also produces waste in the form of slash.
- *Product manufacture* is another step at which wastes are generated, including potentially toxic substances that are a by-product of refining and manufacturing.
- *Construction* can produce waste in several ways. First, demolition of existing built elements on the site can produce waste materials such as masonry, lumber, and concrete or asphalt paving. Second, land clearing and earthwork can result in waste vegetation and soil. And, finally, building material waste can result during construction if the design overestimates actual project needs.

Waste can be reduced by salvage of job-site materials for reuse or recycling. Use of products and materials characterized by high durability or low maintenance can also lower waste by extending the time before a product may need to be replaced. Moreover, use of products with high recycled content reduces the wastestream.

ENVIRONMENTAL AND HUMAN HEALTH IMPACTS OF BUILDING MATERIALS/PRODUCTS

ENVIRONMENTAL IMPACT	DEFINITION AND STRESSORS
Global warming	Global warming occurs when energy from the Earth is reradiated as heat and is absorbed and trapped by greenhouse gases in the atmosphere (water vapor, carbon dioxide, methane, chlorofluorocarbons, and ozone). This greenhouse effect reduces heat loss to space, resulting in warmer temperatures on Earth. Increased emissions generated by humans and industrial processes (primarily carbon dioxide emissions from fossil fuel combustion, which provides electricity and powers equipment used in manufacture, transportation, construction, and maintenance) are thought to increase the greenhouse effect. The increased temperature can alter atmospheric and oceanic temperatures, with subsequent effects on global circulation and weather. In addition, thermal expansion of the oceans and melting of polar ice are expected to contribute to sea level rise.
Acidification	Acidifying gases, primarily sulfur and nitrogen compounds, may either dissolve in water or adhere to solid particles. These compounds reach ecosystems primarily as rainfall. Fossil fuel, used to produce electricity and to power equipment used in manufacture, transportation, construction, and maintenance, is the main human source of acidification. Sulfur dioxide interferes with photosynthesis, and nitrogen oxides affect animals (including humans) through respiratory irritation. Oxides of both sulfur and nitrogen contribute to acid precipitation, which stresses plants and fish. In addition, interaction of these compounds with other atmospheric pollutants can have toxic effects on animals and plants, through formation of photochemical smog.
Eutrophication	Eutrophication is the addition of nutrients, such as nitrogen and phosphorous, to soil or water, and is increased with input of untreated sewage and nutrient-containing runoff. Eutrophication can alter species composition and reduce ecological diversity in ecosystems. In water, it promotes growth of algae and plants, resulting in oxygen depletion and sometimes death of fish. Eutrophication impacts affect humans by affecting the taste of water (even after treatment) and by negative impacts on swimming, boating, and fishing. Nitrogen and phosphorous are major components of synthetic fertilizers used in landscape maintenance and agriculture. Unchecked nutrients from nonpoint source pollution in stormwater runoff are also a cause of eutrophication.
Fossil fuel depletion	Fossil fuels are being extracted at a faster rate than the time it takes for them to form. As these fuel reserves decrease, it is expected that extraction and refinement costs will increase. Humans use fossil fuels to power vehicles (used in transportation, construction, and maintenance) and electricity plants and as raw material for production of plastics and other synthetic polymers (e.g., fibers). Besides the impacts associated with extraction and combustion of fossil fuels, there are no direct environmental impacts of depletion, per se.
Habitat alteration	Habitats are altered when human activity results in a change in the species composition of plant and animal communities. This can occur through practices that change environmental conditions and reduce habitat, as well as through differential removal or introduction of species. Some of these practices include conversion of naturally occurring communities to other uses that support the human economy, such as housing, agriculture, transportation, and utility corridors, landfills, and commercial and industrial centers. Habitat alteration also can occur when human activity changes certain environmental conditions, such as water quality and quantity, in naturally occurring communities. Effects of habitat alteration include changes in ecosystem function and possible loss of rare species.
Water resource depletion	Human activities and land uses can deplete water resources, through use rates that exceed groundwater reserves, and through practices that prevent aquifer recharge. Product manufacturing activities use water, and irrigation of vegetation and turf depletes water supplies. In addition, the use of impervious surfaces (such as concrete and asphalt) seriously reduces groundwater recharge, as do stormwater management strategies that convey runoff away from the site. Water resource depletion has serious consequences, by disrupting hydrological cycles, reducing the water available to dilute pollutants, and decreasing water for human consumption and for plant and animal communities that require more abundant and constant water supplies.
Air pollution	Air pollutants are airborne solid and liquid particles; gases such as carbon monoxide (released by incomplete combustion of fossil fuels) also pollute the air. They result from many activities including production of electricity; operation of equipment used in manufacture, transport, construction, and maintenance; and mining and crushing of materials. These pollutants can worsen illnesses such as asthma, and fine particles can promote more serious respiratory problems.
Human health	Negative human health effects can result from exposure to toxic materials, either human-made or naturally occurring. Many of these substances are related to manufacturing industrial plastics and to processes using metals like mercury and cadmium. In addition, pesticide use in the landscape impacts human health. The effects of these substances vary, from momentary irritation to prolonged illness and disease (such as cancers) to death.
Smog	Smog is a type of air pollution, resulting when industrial and fuel emissions become trapped at ground level and are transformed after reacting with sunlight. For example, ozone is one component of smog, and occurs when volatile organic compounds (VOCs) react with oxides of nitrogen (NOx). Equipment used in landscape construction and maintenance contributes to smog-producing emissions. Like air pollutants and acidification compounds, smog has negative effects on the health of people and other biotic communities.
Ozone depletion	The naturally occurring ozone layer of the stratosphere is a critical barrier that prevents harmful shortwave ultraviolet radiation from reaching the Earth. Human-caused emissions of ozone-depleting substances, such as CFCs (used as a propellant in manufacturing), can cause a thinning of the ozone layer, resulting in more shortwave radiation on Earth. This has a number of potentially negative consequences, such as impacts on agriculture and increases in cancer and cataracts in people. Moreover, there may be effects on both climate and the functioning of different ecosystems, although the nature of these effects is not clear.
Ecological toxicity	Toxic materials can be released into ecosystems, as a by-product of manufacturing processes and from direct environmental application of toxic pesticides. Like substances that have negative effects on human health, these can also harm other animals and plants, with potential impacts on ecosystem function.

Sources: Barbara C. Lippiatt, 2002; U.S. Environmental Protection Agency, 2004; U.S. EPA Office of Research and Development, 2002; and M. Goedkoop, and R. Spriensma, 2000.

GREEN BUILDING MATERIALS DEFINED

Green building materials or products are those that:

- Reduce resource use, energy input, and waste.
- Reuse or recycle material.
- Are nontoxic and durable and have potential for reuse.
- Are made from renewable or sustainably harvested materials.
- Are locally produced.

Categories of green materials are discussed below, followed by a discussion of tools for evaluating the environmental and human health impacts of materials and products.

SALVAGED AND REUSED MATERIALS AND STRUCTURES

Materials with the least environmental impact are those that have been previously used, because no new raw materials are used and the energy that might have gone into raw material extraction and manufacturing is conserved. The only major impacts of reused materials are energy consumption in transport, reworking and refinishing, and installation. If materials are salvaged and reused on-site, transport energy can be further minimized, as can demolition waste. Whole structures such as paving slabs or retaining walls can be reused in place on-site; or structures can be removed, disassembled, and replaced elsewhere on-site. Reuse of materials on-site can offer economic advantage due to reduction in costs for transportation of demolition waste and new material import. Construction costs may be lower as well; however, deconstruction of structures with the intent to reuse parts will cost more than demolition of structures. This cost may be offset with savings on lower landfill fees.

Reuse of existing structures on-site can enhance the design of the site by referencing the identity of the previous intervention. Therefore, at the start of a project, designers should:

1. Evaluate project sites and old buildings for materials to reuse, including known subgrade structures.
2. Hire demolition contractors that have experience in deconstruction and salvage.
3. Require contractors to provide a plan for construction and demolition salvage and recycling.

Salvaged materials can be obtained from numerous sources beyond the project site. Materials exchanges are increasing in areas of the country with higher landfill fees, and many municipalities will list recycling and salvage facilities in the region. There also are many materials exchange Web sites on the Internet. Materials should be obtained from local sources, as energy use for transport can be considerable for heavy landscape materials.

Because a salvaged material is available in a limited quantity, type, and size, they should be located before the design development phase, as their unique character will influence the detailing of the structure in which they are used. Designs should remain flexible until salvaged materials are located. If the budget permits, more of the salvaged material than needed should be purchased, as the material will most likely not be available on a return trip to the source for more material. Appearance and environmental performance standards should be included in the specifications, and the contractor should be on board with using salvage early in the process.

RECYCLED CONTENT MATERIALS

Products with recycled content contain less virgin material and divert waste from landfills. Recycled content is defined by ISO 14021: Environmental Labels and Declarations—Self-Declared Environmental Claims (Type II Environmental Labeling).

- *Postconsumer recycled content* is defined as material generated by households or commercial, institutional, or industrial facilities as end users of a product that can no longer be used for its intended purpose.
- *Preconsumer material* is defined as material that is diverted from the wastestream during the manufacturing process. Material that is excluded from this is regrind, rework, scrap, and other material that could be reused within the same process.

Postconsumer recycled content is considered preferable to preconsumer waste material because it is more likely to otherwise end up in a landfill. Preconsumer recycled content is more likely to be reused by industry rather than find its way to a landfill. Products claiming recycled content should contain a minimum of 25 percent postconsumer or 40 percent preconsumer content.

MATERIALS WITH REUSE POTENTIAL

Planning for reuse of materials after their useful life in a landscape can extend the life of a material/product and reduce resource use and waste. Materials installed so that they can be easily removed at the end of the life of the landscape and reused elsewhere may not be "green" themselves, but the way they are assembled can be. For example, masonry installations in which no mortar is used, such as sand-set brick, stone, or concrete pavers, and interlocking retaining wall units, allow for easy disassembly and reuse of the materials. Also, use of metal fasteners, rather than welding, where applicable, facilitates removal of reusable parts.

RENEWABLE MATERIALS

A number of products are made from renewable resources. Wood is the most common building material that is renewable; it is considered to be a "long-cycle" renewable material. Rapidly renewable materials are primarily plants that are harvested in cycles shorter than 10 years. Coir and jute are used for geotextiles; succulents are used as stabilizers for loose aggregate paving; and plant oils are used in form release agents. Bamboo and willow can be used in landscape structures, and fiber from processed crops is used in engineered wood products.

CERTIFIED MATERIALS

Wood can be considered a green material if it comes from well-managed forests and is harvested sustainably. Environmentally responsible forest management comprises practices that protect the functional integrity and diversity of tree stands, minimize clear-cutting, protect old-growth forests, and minimize wasteful harvesting and milling techniques (Forest Stewardship Council).

The Forest Stewardship Council (FSC) has developed standards for third-party certification of sustainably harvested wood. Certification of lumber should be made by an FSC-certified independent party. The Sustainable Forestry Initiative is another organization that certifies lumber companies with sustainable harvesting practices.

LOW EMBODIED ENERGY MATERIALS

Embodied energy is the total energy required to produce and install a material or product during all stages of the life cycle. Life-cycle stages include: raw material extraction, processing, manufacture, fabrication, transport, installation, use and maintenance, and recycling or disposal. If the product is complex (made from more than one material, such as a steel and wood bench), the embodied energy of the bench would include the energy inputs from both the wood and steel components, plus the energy input to assemble them.

Products that are minimally processed, such as stone and wood, usually have lower embodied energy than highly processed materials such as plastics and metals. Evaluating the embodied energy of materials can be a useful baseline for comparing two different materials; however, this type of analysis does not take into account other factors of production such as pollutants produced, toxins released, resources used, or habitats disturbed.

LOCAL MATERIALS

Transport of building materials, especially heavy or bulky ones, not only requires a tremendous amount of fuel energy but contributes to air and water pollution. Using regionally extracted and manufactured materials can help lessen the environmental impact of a material, by reducing environmental impacts of transport. Transportation costs may also be reduced, at the same time the local economy is supported.

Availability of regionally manufactured materials depends on the project location. Ideally, most materials and products should be obtained within 500 miles of the project site. Heavy materials such as aggregate, concrete, and brick should be procured from even closer locations. Distances between raw material extraction locations and manufacturing/processing facilities should also be considered.

Researching regionally available materials and products during the schematic design phase can facilitate use of local materials. Creating databases of regional materials and products can save time on future projects in the region.

Meg Calkins, Ball State University, "Environmental and Health Considerations"

MATERIALS PRODUCED WITH NONTOXIC EXTRACTION AND MANUFACTURING PROCESSES

In some raw material extraction and manufacturing processes for building materials, waste by-products are produced that contribute harmful pollutants and particulates to air, water, and soil. A number of manufacturers today are taking steps to eliminate or mitigate air, water, and soil pollution from their processes, and to protect or remediate negative effects on extraction or manufacturing sites and regions.

LOW-EMITTING MATERIALS AND PRODUCTS

Materials, adhesives, sealers, preservatives, and coatings can contain volatile organic compounds (VOCs) and other harmful chemical ingredients. Construction workers and end users exposed to these chemicals can be adversely affected in many ways. And during manufacture of materials, hazardous by-products can be generated. Products with associated synthetic chemicals should be carefully examined for harmful effects. Many synthetic chemicals are not biodegradable or easily broken down. Furthermore, the Environmental Protection Agency (EPA), National Research Council, estimates that more than 65,000 synthetic chemicals in use have not been tested on humans (EPA, 1998).

For sustainable design, the rule of thumb is: If a material or product contains a chemical whose effects are unknown, avoid it. Material Safety Data Sheets (MSDS) can be obtained from the manufacturer for any material or product that has adverse human health effects. Many nontoxic, low-VOC, organic, and natural alternative products are being developed for adhesives, coatings, and sealers. Good sources for these products are Internet building supply stores.

NONTOXIC MATERIALS

Materials that contain or emit known toxins, particularly persistent bioaccumulative toxins (PBTs), should be avoided. PBTs are toxins that don't break down and accumulate in the fatty tissue of organisms moving up the food chain. For example, dioxin, a known carcinogen, is released during the manufacture and incineration disposal of polyvinylchloride (PVC) products such as rigid pipe, plastic fencing and railings, drip irrigation tubing, garden hoses, and lawn edging.

The EPA's Toxic Release Inventory maintains data on self-reported manufacturer data on toxic releases, along with a list of toxic chemicals and persistent bioaccumulative toxins. More EPA programs are listed in the References.

Meg Calkins, Ball State University, "Environmental and Health Considerations"

EVALUATION TOOLS

Environmental impacts associated with building material/product use can be minimized with careful attention to environmental costs throughout the life cycle. Life-cycle assessment (LCA), sustainability assessment (SA), and embodied energy analysis (EEA) are three techniques for evaluating and comparing the environmental impacts of building materials/products.

LIFE-CYCLE ASSESSMENT (LCA) OF BUILDING MATERIALS/PRODUCTS

LCA is a qualitative tool for the evaluation of environmental impacts of building materials/products, services, and processes. Evaluation activities consider all stages of a material's/product's life cycle, including raw materials acquisition, manufacturing, transportation, installation, use, maintenance, deconstruction, and disposal. Global, regional, and local impacts are identified.

An LCA comprises four phases (ASTM Standard E1991-05, 2005; ISO, 1996):

- *Goal and scope definition.* During this phase, the purpose of the LCA is defined, to include questions to be answered, the level of detail to be achieved, and priorities regarding the varying environmental impacts possible throughout the life cycle.
- *Inventory analysis.* This phase involves data collection on environmental inputs and outputs of the material/product under study at all phases of its life cycle. Inputs may include resources, water, and energy. Outputs consist of releases to water, air, and land. The depth of information gathered will be consistent with the goal and scope of the study.
- *Impact assessment.* This phase is an evaluation of the environmental impacts of the inputs and outputs identified in the inventory analysis phase.
- *Interpretation.* This phase is an analysis of the impacts in relation to the goals and intended use of the LCA.

It is a nearly impossible task to gather information on all of the environmental inputs and outputs and impacts of a given material/product, as new information is constantly emerging, and techniques of LCA are evolving. And some impacts, such as energy consumption and global warming, are more easily measured than others, such as habitat destruction or eutrophication.

LCA is a complex and time-consuming activity, and may be outside the time and skill constraints of many designers; thus, it is often performed by professionals dedicated to the task. The complexity and level of detail gathered for an LCA will vary greatly depending on the skills of the researcher, priorities of project, intended use of information, material/product being studied, and resources available to complete the study. LCA outcomes can vary or be skewed depending on the weight given to each type of impact. For example, a product might have relatively low embodied energy yet produce by-products that are persistent bioaccumulative toxins. If the LCA is not weighted, the product may still appear a viable alternative.

SUSTAINABILITY ASSESSMENT OF BUILDING MATERIALS/PRODUCTS

It is possible to identify major environmental and human health impacts of building materials/products without performing a full LCA. The sustainability assessment (SA) method involves a set of questions/instructions for the collection of pertinent data on environmental and human health impacts of a building material/product from cradle to grave. This method has also been called "life-cycle thinking." Information is gathered in categories of raw material acquisition; manufacturing process; packaging and distribution; installation; use and performance; resource recovery; and corporate policy. The compiled information is then evaluated based on the priorities and goals of the particular project. (ASTM E 2129-05, 2005)

The "Sustainability Assessment Questions" table lists common questions to consider when performing an SA of a building material/product. The questions are not intended to produce one right answer as to which product is best—that is nearly impossible given the potential complexity of information gathered. Also, different projects and clients will have differing priorities. Rather, the questions are designed to bring the major environmental impacts, hazards, and opportunities to light, to assist with material/product selection. Information can be obtained from a variety of sources, including: manufacturers and distributors; government programs and resources; Material Safety Data Sheets (MSDS); resources listed below; and an ever-evolving list of print and Web-based resources. Not all of the questions will be applicable to all materials/products, and some may require additional questions not listed.

Life-cycle assessment (LCA) and sustainability assessment (SA) differ from life-cycle costing (LCC) in that an LCA and SA deal with environmental costs over the life of a material and LCC deals with the economic costs. They all consider the length of time that the product will be in use and the maintenance it will need during that time. While LCA is of primary importance to sustainable design, performing an LCC may also be helpful as it could demonstrate that higher first costs of a material will be recovered over the material's life.

EMBODIED ENERGY ANALYSIS

Embodied energy refers to all energy consumed in raw material acquisition, manufacture, transport, and disposal of a building material/product. Minimally processed materials have a lower embodied energy than those with extensive manufacturing processes. An embodied energy calculation is one method of evaluating the environmental impacts of a building material/product. Because embodied energy is quantifiable, alternative materials/products can be easily compared where data are available.

Unlike life-cycle assessment (LCA), this method does not directly consider the health or ecological impacts of a building material/product. It also does not differentiate between sources of energy. Existing data are limited and can vary based on distances of raw materials acquisition and manufacture to point of use. The embodied energy of common landscape building materials is given in the four tables shown previously: "Embodied Energy of Selected Landscape Materials by Volume/Area/Length/Each," respectively.

TERMINOLOGY

ASTM International (Formerly American Society for Testing and Materials): An organization that develops characteristic and performance standards for materials, products, processes, systems, and services.

Carcinogen: A chemical, viral, or physical agent identified as causing cancer. Carcinogens are classified as known, probable, presumed, or suspected.

Deconstruction: The disassembly, sorting, and salvage of materials from a building or site with the intent to recycle or reuse.

Downcycling: Result of recycling a product into a new one with less value and greater disposability than the original.

Embodied energy: Refers to all energy consumed in raw materials acquisition, manufacture, transport, and disposal of a building material/product.

Fossil fuel: Hydrocarbon deposits from plant remnants, which include: coal, peat, tar sands, shale oil, petroleum, natural gas. Fossil fuels are considered to be nonrenewable resources.

Industrial waste: Liquid, sludge, or solid material remaining from industrial processes.

Life-cycle assessment (LCA): A qualitative tool for the evaluation of environmental impacts of building materials/products, services, and processes. Evaluation activities consider all stages of a material's/product's life cycle, including raw materials acquisition, manufacturing, transportation, installation, use, maintenance, deconstruction, and disposal. Global, regional, and local impacts are identified. Typcially, an LCA contains four phases: goal definition and scoping, inventory analysis, impact assessment, and interpretation.

Life-cycle cost (LCC) method: Factors in all internal and external costs, including capital, installation, operating, maintenance, and disposal, over the life of a material, product, or process. This definition could include environmental costs, but typically does not.

Material Safety Data Sheets (MSDS): Documents that provide information about safety and health hazards associated with chemicals or products containing the chemical. An MSDS typically includes guidelines for proper storage, handling, and disposal, as well as emergency procedures to take with exposure to the hazardous chemical. MSDS are mandated by the Occupational Safety and Health Administration's (OHSA's) hazard communication standard.

Nonrenewable resources: Resources that, once extracted, cannot be replaced in the environment.

Persistent bioaccumulative toxins (PBTs): Toxins that do not easily break down and that accumulate in fatty tissues moving up the food chain.

Meg Calkins, Ball State University, "Environmental and Health Considerations"

SUSTAINABILITY ASSESSMENT QUESTIONS

SUSTAINABILITY ASSESSMENT QUESTION	CONSIDERATIONS FOR EVALUATION
Raw Materials Acquisition	
What are the significant environmental impacts of raw material extraction or acquisition?	How does acquisition impact the local ecosystem? Does the manufacturer take any steps to minimize the impact of extraction on the surrounding environment? Acquisition of materials should not involve clear-cutting, strip mining, or dredging.
Do the raw materials or acquisition processes pose health hazards to humans, wildlife, or aquatic species?	Are there MSDS for the raw material? Has the EPA targeted any raw materials for reduction?
Are any raw materials highly energy-intensive?	Virgin aluminum, made from mined bauxite, is highly energy-intensive. Recycled aluminum should be used. Portland cement is energy-intensive, so industrial by-products should be substituted for some of the cement in concrete. Plastic can be energy-intensive.
Are any raw materials from rare or endangered resources or from areas with endangered species?	Threatened and endangered species information can be obtained from the U.S. Fish and Wildlife Service.
Are any raw materials from renewable sources or certified sustainable sources?	Hemp and bamboo are renewable resources. Wood can also be considered a renewable resource if it is sustainably harvested. The Forest Stewardship Council lists third-party certifiers of lumber companies that have sustainable harvesting practices.
Are any raw materials from agricultural or industrial by-products?	Using agricultural or industrial by-products keeps materials out of the wastestream and saves virgin resources. Fly ash, slag, and silica fume are common industrial by-products used in concrete.
Is the product or material from a salvaged source?	Materials reused in whole form save virgin resources and energy that would have been used to process the resources.
Does the product contain either postconsumer or preconsumer recycled content?	Products with recycled content should have minimum 25% postconsumer and 40% postindustrial recycled content.
Manufacturing Process	
Is the manufacturing facility near the raw materials extraction location?	Manufacturing facilities should be near raw materials extraction locations to reduce energy used in transport.
What steps does the manufacturing plant take to minimize impacts on the surrounding environment?	Manufacturers should be aware of and take steps to minimize the impacts of their processes on air, soil, water, and wildlife around their manufacturing facilities.
Is the manufacturing process energy-intensive?	Manufacturer should be able to provide energy use information. What is the total embodied energy of the product?
Is the manufacturing plant energy-efficient, or does it use alternative or renewable resources?	Does the manufacturer make any attempt to conserve energy, burn wastes, or use alternative energy sources such as wind, solar, or hydroelectric?
Is the manufacturing process water-intensive?	Does the manufacturing plant conserve or reuse water? Water should be filtered and reused on-site in a closed-loop system; or water-reduction strategies should be employed.
How much waste (solid, liquid, gaseous) is generated during manufacture?	Does the manufacturer reuse or recycle waste?
Are significant toxic or hazardous by-products generated during the manufacturing process?	Is any ingredient a hazard for workers during the manufacturing process?
Have toxic emissions, effluents, or ozone-depleting materials been eliminated from the production process?	These include chemicals that have ozone-depleting potential, greenhouse gases, or chemicals that contribute to acid rain or eutrophication.
Packaging and Distribution	
Are manufacturing and distribution facilities near the job site?	Manufacturing and distribution facilities should be within 500 miles of the job site, or even closer for heavy materials such as aggregate, concrete, and brick.
Is packaging for the material/product minimized?	Items should be bundled rather than packaged individually.
Is packaging reusable or recyclable?	Is packaging accepted by the manufacturer for reuse? Do local facilities exist for recycling of packaging?
Is packaging made from recycled materials?	One hundred percent postconsumer recycled content is ideal.
Are materials/products transported using energy-efficient methods?	Train and shipping methods are more energy-efficient than trucks and airplanes. Full loads and direct delivery methods are more fuel-efficient.
Installation	
Is the material/product an installation hazard for workers?	Are there Material Safety Data Sheets (MSDS) for any of the materials? Products that hold even the slightest risk for handling during use, installation, or manufacture are required by law to have MSDS for anyone who buys or works with the product.
Does installation of the material/product involve any materials such as adhesives, finishes, or sealants that are toxic or emit VOCs?	Are there nontoxic or zero-VOC alternatives? Do any products contain materials targeted for reduction by the EPA?
Does installation result in large amounts of waste material?	Assembly should be designed to minimize waste with awareness of standard board lengths, sheet sizes, and unit sizes.
Can construction waste be recycled locally?	Is construction waste accepted for recycling by the manufacturer or at local facilities? Is recycling of construction waste written into project specifications?
Use and Performance	
Is the material/product durable?	Does the expected life match the expected duration of the built landscape? Does the product have a warranty? Are there data on product testing and performance?
Can parts of the installation be replaced without removal of the entire installation?	Products such as sand-set bricks or unit pavers can easily be replaced, whereas use of mortar or monolithic paving is difficult to repair. Structures with bolted connections are easier to repair than those with welded connections.
What environmental impacts will the material/product have on the project site?	Does the material/product support the project's sustainable strategies?
Does the material/product require maintenance products that are toxic or contain VOCs?	Are there nontoxic or low-VOC alternatives? Do any products contain chemicals targeted for reduction by the EPA?
Resource Recovery/Disposal	
Can the material/product be salvaged and reused?	Can the product or material be easily separated from the installation and reused? Products such as sand-set bricks or unit pavers can easily be recovered, whereas use of mortar or monolithic paving makes salvage difficult. Structures with bolted connections are easier to recover than those with welded connections.
Is the material/product recyclable?	Is the product recyclable into another product without downcycling? Does the manufacturer provide a takeback option for the material/product? Are there hazards in recycling the material?
Is the material/product biodegradable?	Will the product break down into benign, organic components?
Is the material/product hazardous to dispose of?	Do Material Safety Data Sheets indicate hazards in disposal? If landfilled, will chemicals from the material/product affect soil or groundwater? If incinerated, will harmful chemicals or particulates be released? Has the EPA targeted any chemicals released during disposal for reduction?

Sources: ASTM, 2003; McGowan and Kruse, 2003; Mendler et al., 2006; Thompson and Sorvig, 2000.

Meg Calkins, Ball State University, "Environmental and Health Considerations"

Postconsumer recycled content: Waste material generated by end users such as households, or commerrcial, institutional, or industrial facilities, used in new materials or products. This category includes materials returned from the distribution chain such as packaging.

Preconsumer recycled content: Industrial waste material diverted from the wastestream during the manufacturing process for use in new materials/products. Material that is capable of reuse in the same manufacturing process is excluded from this category (ISO 14021).

Ozone-depleting potential (ODP): A relative measure of the potential of a chemical to break down the stratospheric ozone layer.

Risk assessment (RA): Qualitative and quantitative evaluation of the risk posed to human health or the environment by the actual or potential presence or use of specific pollutants (EPA, 1998).

Sustainability assessment (SA): A method of evaluating the environmental impacts of a material or product using a set of questions/instructions for the collection of pertinent data on environmental and human health impacts of a building material/product from cradle to grave.

Toxicity: The degree to which an agent has the potential to cause adverse health effects on humans or living organisms. Toxicity is usually expressed in exposure limits.

Volatile organic compound (VOC): A group of chemical compounds containing carbon and with varying degrees of toxicity. VOCs partially vaporize from material surfaces at normal room temperatures. This process is also called "off-gassing." Adhesives, solvents, sealers, paints, and cleaners are some products that contain VOCs.

REFERENCES

Publications

American Society for Testing and Materials (ASTM). ASTM Standard E1991-05: Standard Guide for Environmental Life-Cycle Assessment of Building Materials/Products. West Conshohocken, PA: ASTM International.

———. ASTM Standard E 2129-05 Standard Practice for Data Collection for Sustainability Assessment of Building Products. West Conshohocken, PA: ASTM International.

———. ASTM E 2114-06 Standard Terminology for Sustainability Relative to the Performance of Buildings. West Conshohocken, PA: ASTM International.

Demkin, Joseph, (ed.). 1996. *AIA Environmental Resource Guide.* New York: John Wiley & Sons.

EPA Office of Pollution Prevention and Toxics. 1998. "Chemical Hazard Data Availability Study: What do we really know about the safety of high production volume chemicals?" Washington, DC: U.S. EPA.

Goedkoop, M., and R. Spriensma. 2000. The Eco-indicator '99: *A Damage-Oriented Method for Life-Cycle Impact Assessment.* Amersfoort, Netherlands: PRe Consultants.

International Standards Organization (ISO). 1996. Environmental Management—Life-Cycle Assessment: Principles and Framework. Draft International Standard 14040. Geneva, Switzerland: International Standards Organization.

Lippiatt, Barbara C. 2002. BEES 3.0: *Building for Environmental and Economic Sustainability Technical Manual and User Guide* (NISTIR 6916). Gaithersburg, MD: National Institute of Standards and Technology. www.bfrl.nist.gov/oae/publications/nistirs/6916.pdf; accessed September 6, 2004.

McGowan, Mary Rose, and Kelsey Kruse. 2003. *Interior Graphic Standards.* Hoboken, NJ: John Wiley & Sons, Inc.

Mendler, Sandra, William Odell, and Mary Ann Lazarus. 2006. *The HOK Guidebook to Sustainable Design.* Hoboken, NJ: John Wiley & Sons, Inc.

Thompson, J. William, and Kim Sorvig. 2000. *Sustainable Landscape Construction: A Guide to Green Building Outdoors.* Washington, DC: Island Press.

U.S. Environmental Protection Agency. August 2002. Tool for the Reduction and Assessment of Chemical and Other Environmental Impacts (TRACI): *User's Guide and System Documentation.* EPA/600/R-02/052. Cincinnati, OH: U.S. EPA Office of Research and Development. www.epa.gov/ord/NRMRL/Pubs/600R02052/600R02052.pdf; accessed September, 6, 2004.

Organizations and Web Resources

American Forest and Paper Association's Sustainable Forestry Initiative: www.afandpa.org/Content/NavigationMenu/Environment_and_Recycling/SFI/SFI.htm

Athena Sustainable Materials Institute: www.athenasmi.ca/tools/software/index.html

Beyond Pesticides: National Coalition Against the Misuse of Pesticides: www.beyondpesticides.org

BuildingGreen: GreenSpec Database and Directory and Environmental Building News: www.buildinggreen.com

California Integrated Waste Management Board Recycled-Content Product Directory: www.ciwmb.ca.gov/RCP

Construction Materials Recycling Association: www.cdrecycling.org

Ecospecifier: www.ecospecifier.org

Environmental Council of Concrete Organizations: www.ecco.org

Environmental Yellow Pages: www.enviroyellowpages.com

Forest Stewardship Council: www.fscus.org

Healthy Building Network: www.healthybuilding.net

Green-e Renewable Electricity Certification Program: www.green-e.org

Greenguard: www.greenguard.org/DesktopDefault.aspx

Green Seal: www.greenseal.org

Heat Island Group, Lawrence Berkeley National Laboratory: http://eetd.lbl.gov/HeatIsland

Leadership in Energy and Environmental Design (LEED) Green Building Rating System: www.usgbc.org/leed/leed_main.asp

National Recycling Coalition: www.nrc-recycle.org

Oikos Green Product Information: http://oikos.com/products/index.lasso

Rocky Mountain Institute: www.rmi.org

Steel Recycling Institute: www.recycle-steel.org

Used Building Materials Exchange: http://build.recycle.net/exchange/

U.S. Green Building Council: www.usgbc.org

Wastespec: Model Specifications for Construction Waste Reduction, Reuse and Recycling: www.tjcog.dst.nc.us/cdwaste.htm

Whole Building Design Guide: www.wbdg.org

U.S. Government and EPA Programs

BEES Building for Environmental and Economic Sustainability: www.bfrl.nist.gov/oae/software/bees.html

Department of Energy Alternative Fuels Data Center: www.afdc.doe.gov

Department of Energy, Energy Star program: www.energystar.gov

Threatened and Endangered Species information from the U.S. Fish and Wildlife Service: http://endangered.fws.gov/wildlife.html

TRACI Users Guide: www.epa.gov/ord/NRMRL/Pubs/600R02052/600R02052.pdf

U.S. EPA Comprehensive Procurement Guidelines for Recycled Content Guidelines and Products: www.epa.gov/cpg

U.S. EPA Ground Water and Drinking Water, Drinking water contaminants: www.epa.gov/safewater/hfacts.html

U.S. EPA Heat Island: www.epa.gov/heatisland

U.S. EPA Municipal Solid Waste: www.epa.gov/msw

U.S. EPA National Center for Environmental Assessment http://cfpub.epa.gov/ncea

U.S. EPA National Pesticide Information Center: www.epa.gov/pesticides/factsheets/npic.htm

U.S. EPA National Toxicology Program (for listings of toxins): http://ntpserver.niehs.nih.gov/index.cfm?objectid=72016262-BDB7-CEBA-FA60E922B18C2540

U.S. EPA Technology Transfer Network, National Air Toxics Assessment: www.epa.gov/ttn/atw/nata/natsafaq.html#A1

U.S. EPA Toxics Release Inventory (TRI) Program: www.epa.gov/tri

U.S. EPA TRI Persistent Bioaccumulative and Toxic Chemical Program: www.epa.gov/tri/chemical.htm

U.S. EPA Volatile Organic Compounds: www.epa.gov/ebtpages/pollchemicvolatileorganiccompoundsvo.html

U.S. EPA WasteWise Program: www.epa.gov/wastewise

STANDARDS/ORGANIZATIONS

ASTM Standards

ASTM E 1991-05 Standard Guide for Environmental Life-Cycle Assessment of Building Materials/Products

ASTM E 2114-06 Standard Terminology for Sustainability Relative to the Performance of Buildings

ASTM E 2129-05 Standard Practice for Data Collection for Sustainability Assessment of Building Products

ISO Standards

Environmental Management—Life-Cycle Assessment: Principles and Guidelines (ISO 14040 Draft International Standard, 1996)

Environmental Management—Life-Cycle Assessment: Inventory Analysis (ISO 14041 Draft International Standard, 1997)

INDEX

T